W9-DJI-549

Goodheart-Willcox

Automotive Encyclopedia

Fundamental Principles, Operation, Construction, Service, and Repair

William K. Toboldt
Larry Johnson
W. Scott Gauthier

South Holland, Illinois
The Goodheart-Willcox Company, Inc.
Publishers

About the Authors

William K. Toboldt
Member, Society of Automotive Engineers
Associate Member, Automotive Engine Rebuilders Association
Associate Member, Association of Diesel Specialists

Larry Johnson
Certified Automobile Technician, National Institute for Automotive Service Excellence
Affiliate Member, Society of Automotive Engineers

W. Scott Gauthier
Technical Editor
Automotive Writer

1995 Edition

Previous editions 1989, 1983, 1981, 1979, 1977, 1972, 1970, 1968

ISSN 1080-627X
International Standard Book Number 1-56637-150-3

1 2 3 4 5 6 7 8 9 10 95 99 98 97 96 95

INTRODUCTION

recent years, there have been significant changes in the design and construction of automobiles. Although these changes have increased dependability, improved fuel economy, reduced emissions, and enhanced safety, they have made it more difficult to troubleshoot and repair late-model vehicles. Therefore, a thorough knowledge of the fundamentals of vehicle construction, operation, and service is now more important than ever.

Automotive Encyclopedia is a book of fundamentals. It explores the many sciences involved in vehicle operation: electricity and electronics, computers, hydraulics, pneumatics, internal combustion, power transmission, and steering and suspension geometry. **Automotive Encyclopedia** also covers vehicle design, operation, troubleshooting, service, and repair. This information establishes the foundation on which a thorough knowledge of automotive technology is based. Once these fundamentals are mastered, knowledge gained through experience will enable you to troubleshoot and service late-model vehicles.

Each chapter of **Automotive Encyclopedia** opens with a list of learning objectives. These objectives identify the skills that you should be able to master after completing the chapter. Important terms, which are printed in ***bold italics,*** are defined when introduced. Additionally, safety is stressed in the appropriate sections. Review questions are provided at the end of each chapter to help you evaluate your understanding of important concepts.

The 1995 edition of **Automotive Encyclopedia** has been updated to reflect the most-recent changes in the automotive field. It includes information on the latest developments in automotive technology, such as anti-lock brakes, air bags, computer control, R-134A refrigerant, refrigerant recovery, and automotive waste disposal. A new chapter on computer systems has been added to help you troubleshoot and service these complex networks. This edition of **Automotive Encyclopedia** also contains many full-color photographs.

Automotive Encyclopedia is designed to be used by students who are interested in entering the field of automotive technology. It can also be used by technicians who are preparing for ASE certification or who need to brush up on certain topics.

William K. Toboldt
Larry Johnson
W. Scott Gauthier

IMPORTANT SAFETY NOTICE

Proper service and repair is important to the safe, reliable operation of motor vehicles. Procedures recommended and described in this book are effective methods of performing service operations. Some require the use of tools specially designed for the purpose and should be used as recommended. Note that this book also contains various safety procedures and cautions which should be carefully followed to minimize the risk of personal injury or the posibility that improper service methods may damage the engine or render the vehicle unsafe. It is also important to understand that these notices and cautions are not exhaustive. Those performing a given service procedure or using a particular tool must first satisfy themselves that neither their safety nor engine or vehicle safety will be jeopardized by the service method selected.

This book contains the most complete and accurate information that could be obtained from various authoritative sources at the time of publication. Goodheart-Willcox cannot assume responsibility for any changes, errors, or omissions.

Table of Contents

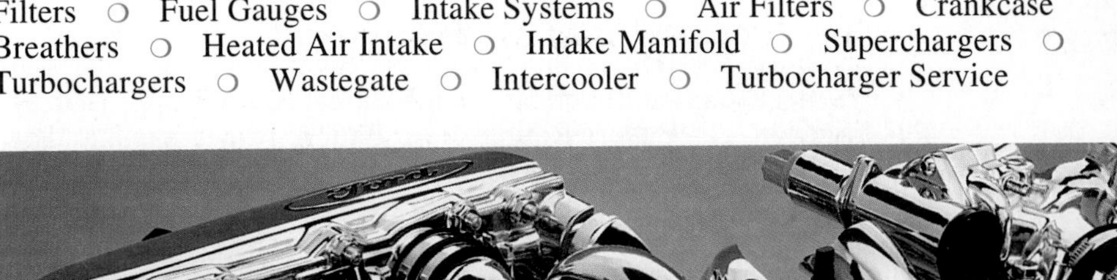
SHO
24 VALVE DOHC
ENGINE OIL
CHECK ENGINE OIL

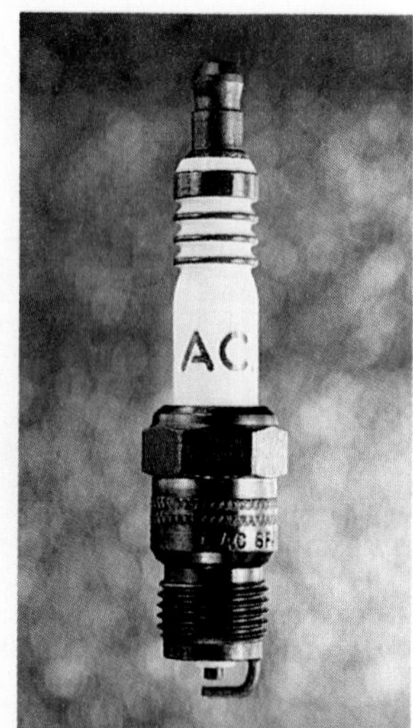
AC

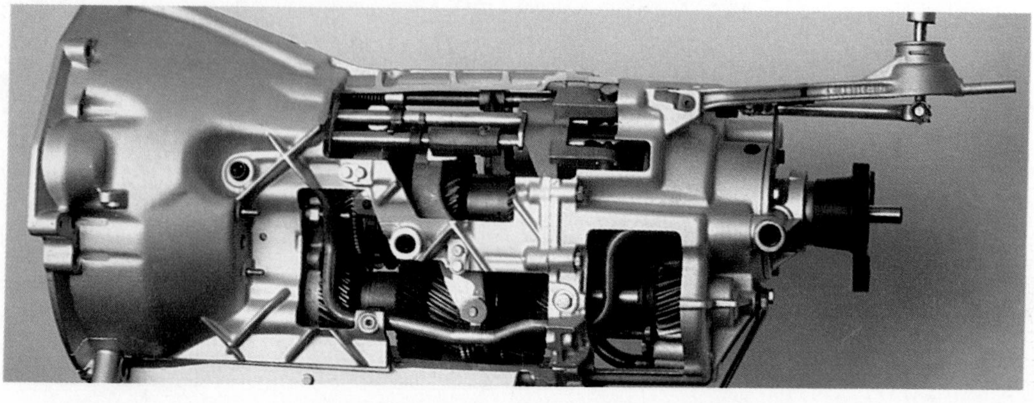

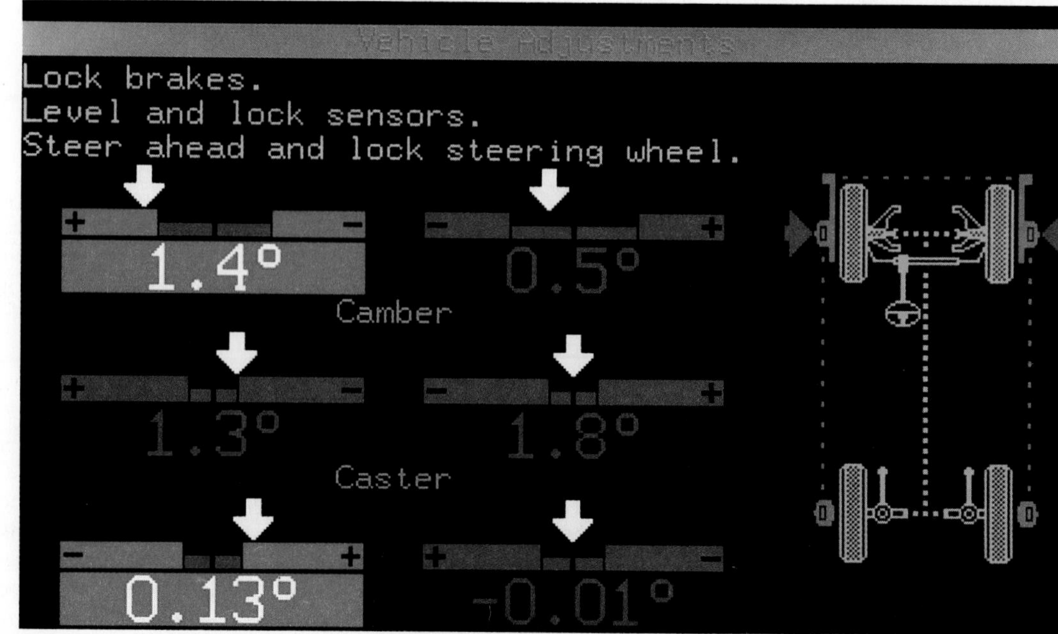

Vehicle Adjustments
Lock brakes.
Level and lock sensors.
Steer ahead and lock steering wheel.
1.4°
0.5°
Camber
1.3°
1.8°
Caster
0.13°
-0.01°

Amy

Acknowledgments

The publication of a book of this nature would not be possible without the assistance of many segments of the automotive industry. The authors and the publisher would like to thank the following companies, organizations, and agencies for their contributions to **Automotive Encyclopedia.**

AC-Rochester
Accurate Instruments
AC-Delco
Alfred Teves Corp.
Allen Test Products Div., Allen Group
Ammco Tools, Inc.
Audi of America, Inc.
Auto-Test
Battery Council International
BMW
Brake Systems, Inc.
Buick
Cadillac
Carter
Central Foundry Div., General Motors Corp.
Central Tools
Century Mfg. Co.
Champion Spark Plug Co.
Chevrolet
Chilton's Motor/Age
Christie Electric Corp.
Chrysler Corp.
C-R Industries
Curtis-Wright
Dayco Corp.
Deere & Co.
Delco-Remy Div., General Motors Corp.
Detroit Diesel Corp.
DeVilbiss
Dodge
ESB Incorporated
Everco
Federal Mogul
Fel-Pro, Inc.
Firestone Tire & Rubber Co.
Fisher Body Div., General Motors Corp.
Ford Motor Co.
Gates Rubber Co.
General Electric Corp.
General Motors Corp.*
Hein-Werner
Hercules Motor
Hofmann Corp.
Honda
Hunter Engineering Co.
Huth Mfg. Co.
Jeep
Kwik-Way
Lexus
Lincoln Div. of McNeil Corp.
Linde Div. of Union Carbide
Lisle Co.
LORS Machinery, Inc.
L.S. Starrett Co.
Marson Corp.
Mazda
Nilfisk of America, Inc.
Nissan
Oatey Co.
Oldsmobile
OTC Tools and Equipment
Peerless Instrument Co.
Perfect Circle
Peugeot, Inc.
Pontiac
Porsche
PPG Industries, Inc.
Robert Bosch Corporation
Robinair Div., SPX Corp.
Rochester
Rubber Manufacturers Association
Safety-Kleen
Sealed Power
Sioux
S-K Tools
Snap-on Tools Corp.
Star Machine and Tool Co.
Sun Electric Corp.
Sunnen Co.
Tecumseh Products Co.
3M Co.
Toyota Motor Sales, U.S.A. Inc.
Triad
U.S. Sales Co.
VICA
Volkswagen of America, Inc.
Winona Van Norman

* Portions of the materials contained in this text have been reprinted with the permission of General Motors Corporation, Service Technology Group.

Automotive technicians must always take proper safety precautions. Note that this technician is wearing safety goggles to protect his eyes from flying debris. (Hunter Engineering Co.)

Chapter 1
Automotive Safety

After studying this chapter, you will be able to:

- ❍ Describe what a clean shop should look like and why.
- ❍ State what type of eye protection should be worn for a specific job.
- ❍ Cite fire preventive measures that should be followed when working in an automotive shop.
- ❍ List the precautions when raising a car off the floor.
- ❍ List the safety measures that should be followed when using welding equipment.
- ❍ Demonstrate how to dress safely when in the shop.

Safety

Although automotive service and repair can be very rewarding, it can also be very dangerous. Figure 1-1. Therefore, you must be aware of the potential hazards encountered in the automotive repair shop and know how to minimize these hazards.

Safety is the responsibility of each person working in the automotive repair shop. Therefore, it is important to:

- Study all pertinent safety regulations.
- Learn to set up a safe shop.
- Establish safe working conditions.
- Make safety a part of every service procedure.

Even the U.S. government is in the act with far-reaching safety regulations for the business and industry. To be specific, the ***Occupational Safety and Health Administration*** (OSHA), which is a branch of the Department of Labor, was formed to establish and enforce guidelines for all types of businesses to ensure they are operated under conditions of maximum safety and health. Now, every auto repair shop and service station is under the watchful eyes of OSHA to ensure that the facility is operated under specific safe working conditions prescribed by the government.

Most of the safety regulations set forth by the Occupational Safety and Health Administration Act have already been put into practice by the careful shop owner. However, under the conditions of the act, which went into effect in April, 1971, inspections will be made to be sure that its rules are being followed.

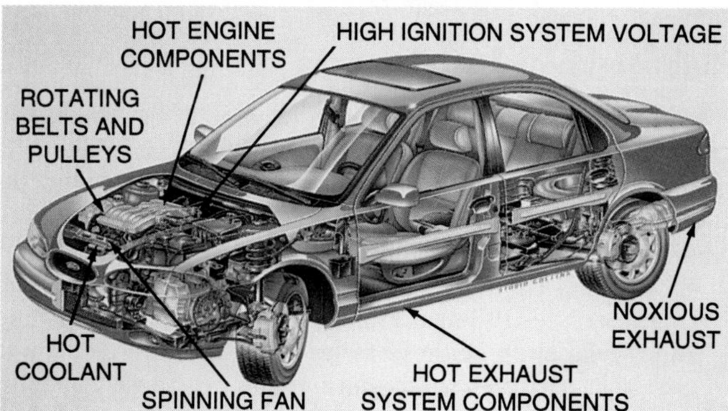

Figure 1-1. Automobile service and repair can be dangerous. A few of the most common hazards are identified above. (Ford)

Before discussing any of the provisions of the act, it is important to know that any employee (or representative thereof) who believes that a violation of job safety or health standards exists may request an inspection by sending a signed statement to the Department of Labor. While the employer may receive a copy of the complaint, the names of the persons making the complaint will not be furnished.

The safety inspectors may enter any establishment covered by the act to inspect the premises and to question privately any employer, owner, operator, agent, or employee.

When an investigation reveals a violation, the employer is issued a written citation describing the nature of the violation. All citations shall fix a reasonable time for correction of the violation.

Willful or repeated violations of the act's requirements by employers may incur very substantial fines for each particular violation. Citations issued for serious violations incur mandatory penalties. Any employer who fails to correct a violation for which a citation has been issued within the prescribed time period may be penalized by a substantial fine for each day that the violation persists.

A willful violation by an employer that results in the death of an employee is punishable by a large fine or up to six months imprisonment. A second conviction doubles these penalties.

Every employer must keep occupational injury and illness records of employees in the establishment where the employees usually report for work. The records must be kept up-to-date and available to governmental representatives. Also, the employer must post a summary of all occupational injuries and illnesses at the conclusion of the calendar year.

Some of the safety and health items set forth in the OSHA act include basic points, such as keeping floors free of grease, oil, and dirt. See Figure 1-2. Additionally, washrooms must be kept clean and sanitary; paint spray booths must be properly ventilated; and buildings must be designed with a sufficient number of exits.

Personal protective equipment for eyes, face, head, and extremities as well as protective respiratory devices, shields, and barriers must be provided, Figure 1-3. It is

Figure 1-2. A clean shop allows the technician to work in an efficient manner. A shop should look like this before, during, and after working hours.

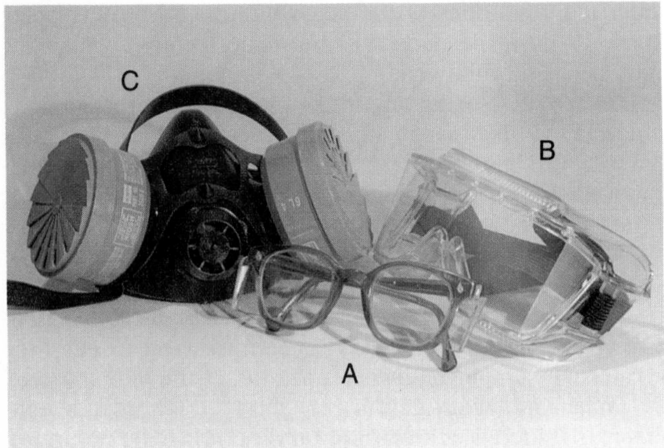

Figure 1-3. Typical personal protective equipment. A–Safety glasses. B–Safety goggles. C–Respirator.

important to note that brake and clutch linings may contain asbestos. The dust from these items is a carcinogen, which means it causes cancer. Always wear an approved ***respirator*** when working on brake and clutch linings. Additionally, never use compressed air to clean brake or clutch components. Compressed air will cause the asbestos dust to become airborne, endangering all technicians working nearby.

The employer is responsible for employee-owned and shop-owned equipment. Equipment must be in good condition and provided with ***safety guards,*** Figure 1-4, and safety devices that may be necessary. Management is also responsible for the safe operation of welding and cutting equipment. Electric wiring and equipment must meet underwriters' specifications and be in good condition, Figure 1-5. No smoking signs must be prominently displayed throughout the shop, Figure 1-6. Combustible liquids must be kept in specified containers and limited as to the quantity that is permissible within the building, Figure 1-7.

These are some of the major points set forth in the OSHA act. However, shop operators should not limit their safety and health program to the regulations of the OSHA act . There are many conditions not covered by the act that should be followed and enforced by every owner.

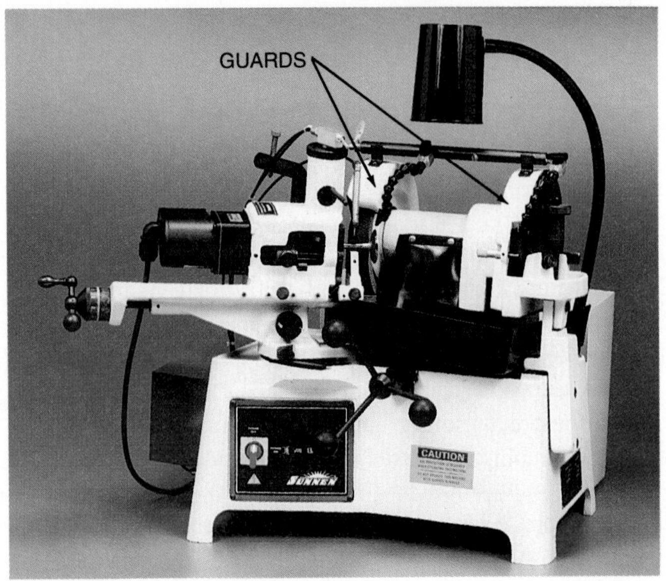

Figure 1-4. Guards must be in place when using grinding equipment, such as this valve grinder. (Sunnen)

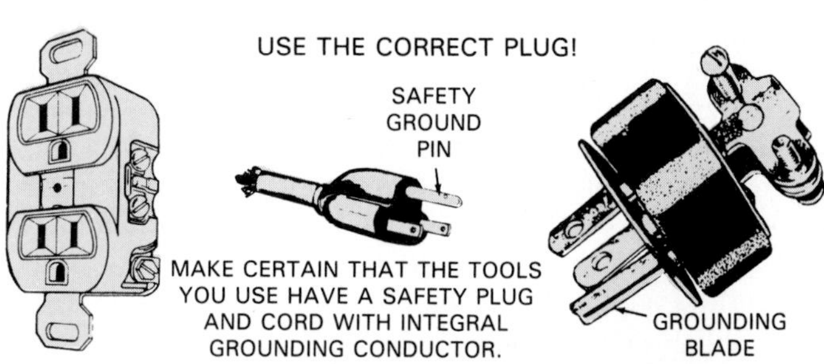

Figure 1-5. Electrical connections must be properly grounded.

Figure 1-6. No smoking signs must be prominently displayed in the automotive shop.

Right-to-know Laws

Automotive employees are protected by ***Right-to-know Laws.*** These laws require employers to provide their employees with a safe working environment. The Right-to-know law holds the employer responsible for the following:

- The employer must provide the employee with training about their rights under the Right-to-know Laws, the characteristics of hazardous materials in the workplace, and the labeling of these materials. The employer must also post ***material safety data sheets*** for the hazardous materials used in the shop. Material safety data sheets are available from the manufacturers of hazardous materials and chemicals. These sheets contain information on the handling of hazardous wastes, the use of protective

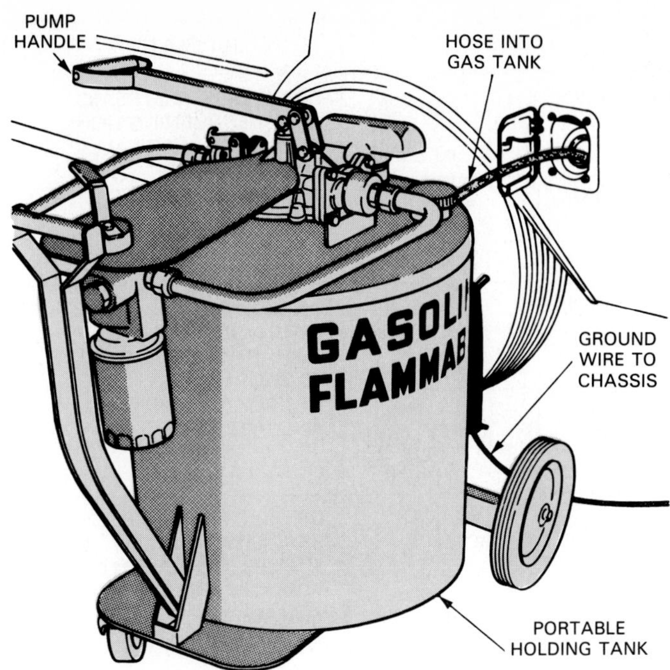

Figure 1-7. When gasoline is removed from a vehicle, it must be stored properly. (Chrysler)

equipment, and the procedures to follow in case of an accident. Each material safety data sheet contains the following sections:

- Product Information.
- Ingredients.
- Physical/chemical Characteristics.
- Fire and Explosion Hazard Data.
- Reactivity Data.
- Spill or Leak Procedures.
- Health Hazard Data.
- First Aid Procedures.
- Protection Information.

- The employer must label all hazardous materials with health, fire, and reactivity data. The labels should also contain information on the proper use of the material and the protective equipment required when handling the material.
- The employer must maintain proper documentation on the hazardous material used in the shop, proof of employee training, and accurate records of hazardous chemical accidents.

All employees should occasionally review material safety data sheets for the materials used in automotive service.

Proper Disposal of Automotive Wastes

There are many ***hazardous wastes*** generated during automotive maintenance and service procedures. Automotive wastes are considered hazardous if they are on the EPA's list of hazardous materials or if they have one or more of the following characteristics:

- Ignitability (has a liquid flash point below 140°F or can spontaneously ignite).
- Reactivity (reacts violently with water or other materials; releases dangerous gases when exposed to low pH acid solutions; or produces toxic vapors, fumes, or flammable gases.
- Corrosivity (dissolves metals or burns skin).
- EP Toxicity (leaches one or more of eight heavy metals in concentrations greater than 100 times the concentration found in standard drinking water).

The disposal of hazardous wastes is regulated by the ***Resource Conservation and Recovery Act.*** This federal act covers businesses that generate, transport, or manage hazardous wastes. Typical hazardous wastes generated from automotive service and repair include:

- Used motor oil and other discarded lubricants (contain toxic chemicals).
- Used oil filters (contain used motor oil and accumulated contaminants).
- Cleaning solvents (combustible and toxic).
- Batteries (contain lead and acid/alkaline wastes).
- Antifreeze (contains heavy metals and chlorinated solvents).
- Refrigerant (contain chemicals that deplete the earth's ozone layer).

It is interesting to note that used oil and used batteries are not considered hazardous wastes if they are sent off for recycling. Similarly, used oil filters are not considered hazardous if they are recycled. Nevertheless, oil filters should be drained of oil before they are transported.

Your state may have various regulations that pertain to transporting and disposing of hazardous wastes. Contact your Regional EPA Office for additional information. Information on handling specific hazardous materials and wastes will be presented in the appropriate chapters.

Fire Prevention

Because there are many ***combustibles,*** such as gasoline and solvents, used in automobile repair shops, special precautions are needed to prevent fire. Fuel, thinners, and other combustibles should always be kept in closed containers that are designed for this purpose.

Unshielded flames should never be permitted. All shops should be provided with an ample number of appropriate ***fire extinguishers,*** Figure 1-8. Everyone should be familiar with the location and use of the extinguishers, Figure 1-9.

As a further protection against fire, rags that are soaked with fuel, oil, or solvents should be kept in an ***oily waste container,*** Figure 1-10. Care must be exercised so that spontaneous combustion does not occur. Flame and sparks should be kept away from batteries. The fumes produced by a battery are highly explosive.

Ventilation

One of the most important safety precautions to be followed in an auto shop is to ensure proper ***ventilation.*** If it is necessary to operate an engine, the car should be driven outside. Exhaust fumes contain ***carbon monoxide,*** which is a deadly poison. In small quantities, it produces drowsiness and headaches. In large quantities, it will cause death.

FIRES	TYPE	USE	OPERATION
A CLASS A FIRES ORDINARY COMBUSTIBLE MATERIALS SUCH AS WOOD, PAPER, TEXTILES, AND SO FORTH. REQUIRES... COOLING–QUENCHING	**FOAM** SOLUTION OF ALUMINUM SULPHATE AND BICARBONATE OF SODA	OK FOR A B NOT FOR C	FOAM: DIRECT STREAM INTO THE BURNING LIQUID. ALLOW FOAM TO FALL LIGHTLY ON FIRE
B CLASS B FIRES FLAMMABLE LIQUIDS, GREASES, GASOLINE, OILS, PAINTS, AND SO FORTH. REQUIRES... BLANKETING OR SMOTHERING	**CARBON DIOXIDE** CARBON DIOXIDE GAS UNDER PRESSURE	NOT FOR A OK FOR B C	CARBON DIOXIDE: DIRECT DISCHARGE AS CLOSE TO FIRE AS POSSIBLE. FIRST AT EDGE OF FLAMES AND GRADUALLY FORWARD AND UPWARD
	DRY CHEMICAL	MULTI-PURPOSE TYPE: OK FOR A B C ORDINARY BC TYPE: NOT FOR A; OK FOR B C	DRY CHEMICAL: DIRECT STREAM AT BASE OF FLAMES, USE RAPID LEFT-TO-RIGHT MOTION TOWARD FLAMES
C CLASS C FIRES ELECTRICAL EQUIPMENT, MOTORS, SWITCHES, AND SO FORTH. REQUIRES... A NONCONDUCTING AGENT	**SODA–ACID** BICARBONATE OF SODA SOLUTION AND SULPHURIC ACID	OK FOR A NOT FOR B C	SODA–ACID: DIRECT STREAM AT BASE OF FLAME

Figure 1-8. This chart illustrates the various fire classifications and fire extinguisher types. Always use an extinguisher designed for electrical and chemical fires (types B and C) in the automotive repair shop.

Figure 1-9. Make sure fire extinguishers are displayed prominently. This particular extinguisher can be used for type A, B, or C fires.

Figure 1-10. Always place oily rags in an appropriate container.

Many shops use special conduits that are connected to the tailpipe of the automobile, Figure 1-11. These conduits conduct the exhaust gases outdoors, eliminating the danger from carbon monoxide poisoning.

Jacks and Lifts

Whenever placing a car on the lift, refer to the service manual for positioning the car on the lift, Figure 1-12. If the car is not positioned on the lift correctly, it could fall. Always raise the car a few inches off the ground. Then, shake the car to make sure it is squarely on the lift before fully raising the car.

If lifts are not available and it is necessary to keep the car raised, the car should be placed on jack stands, Figure 1-13. This will eliminate the chance of the car falling as the result of a faulty jack. In addition, this practice frees the jack for work on other vehicles.

Tool Safety

There are many safety precautions related to the use of tools. Files should never be used without a handle, since

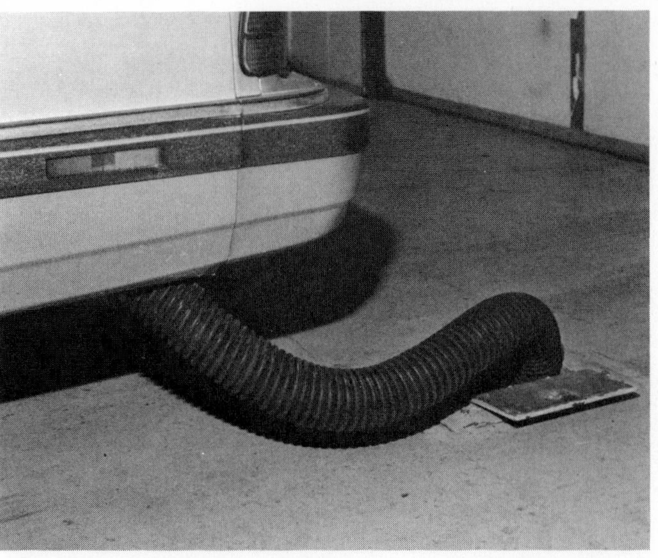

Figure 1-11. When an engine is left running during testing, the doors to the shop must remain open. If weather does not permit the doors to be opened, a ventilation system must be hooked to the car's exhaust system.

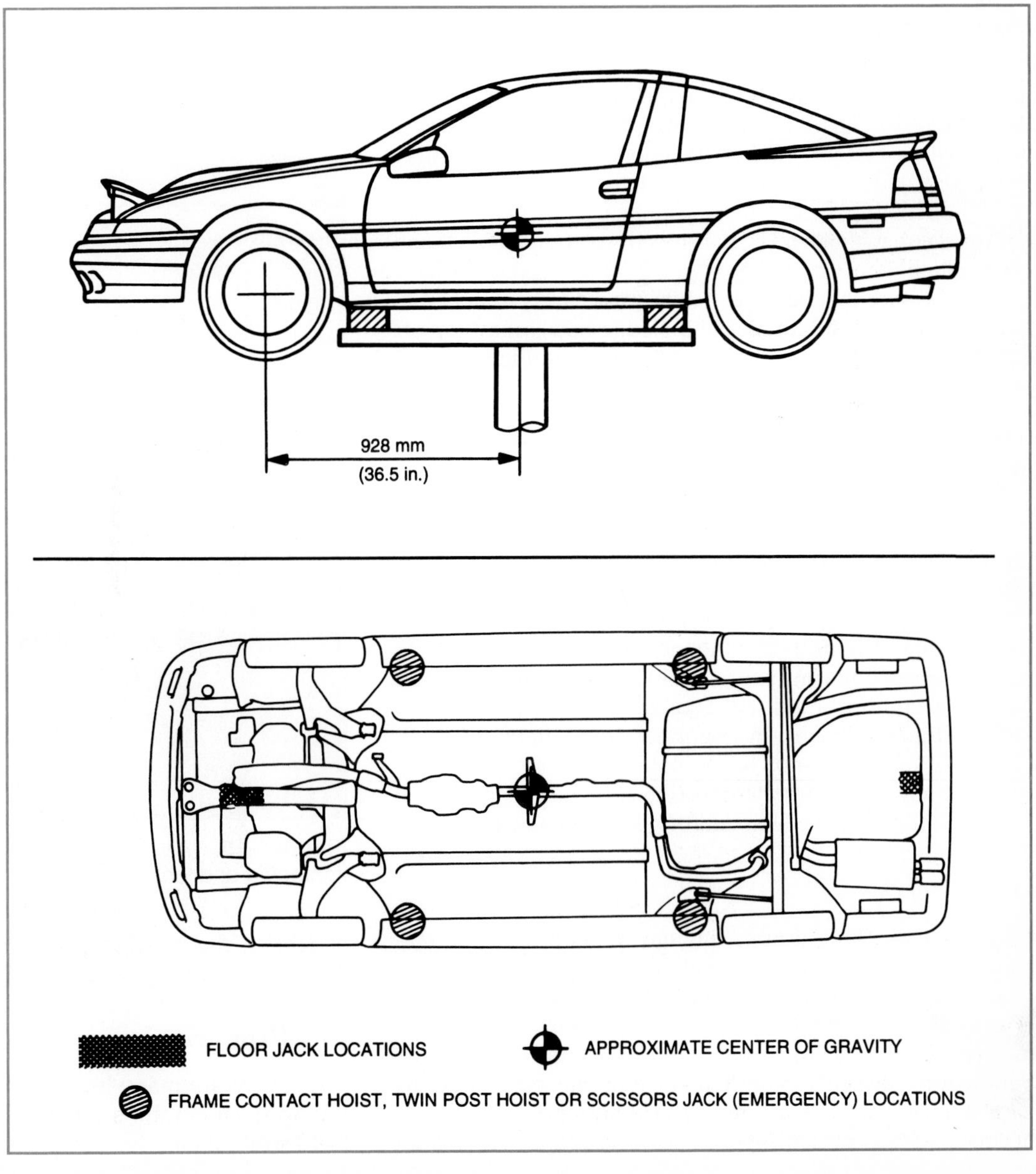

928 mm
(36.5 in.)
FLOOR JACK LOCATIONS
APPROXIMATE CENTER OF GRAVITY
FRAME CONTACT HOIST, TWIN POST HOIST OR SCISSORS JACK (EMERGENCY) LOCATIONS

Figure 1-12. Typical points that should be supported when working on a car. (Chrysler)

Figure 1-13. Make sure that the car is properly supported by a jack stand before working under it. The seals on a hydraulic floor jack can give out at any time without warning.

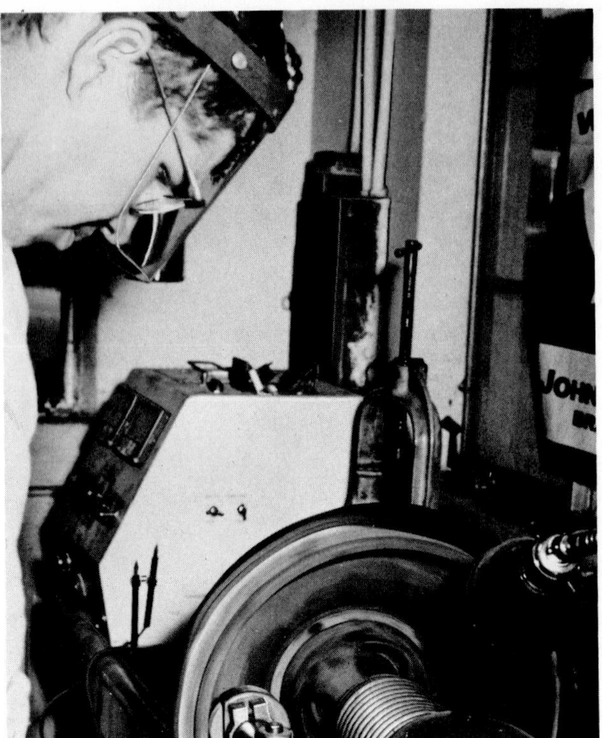

Figure 1-14. This type of shield not only protects the eyes, but it protects the entire face.

there is always the danger of running the pointed tang into the palm of the hand. Files are quite brittle and must never be hit with a hammer. When hammered, small pieces may fly off and cause severe wounds or loss of eyesight.

Hardened surfaces, such as the face of an anvil, should not be struck with a hammer, as bits of steel may fly off and cause damage.

Make sure that hammer heads are securely attached to the handles. Loose hammer and sledge heads may fly off when the tools are used. Anyone standing in the way will be struck and severely injured.

When the head of a chisel becomes mushroomed, it should be ground to remove the mushroomed edges. This will prevent bits of steel from flying off and causing damage.

Whenever grinding, the technician should wear a ***face shield*** to protect the face and eyes, Figure 1-14. The grinding wheel should always be provided with a guard to protect the technician from flying objects.

When using a wrench, pull on the handle rather than pushing on it, Figure 1-15. If the wrench slips, there will be less danger of injuring your knuckles. When the jaws of a wrench become worn, discard the wrench.

Compressed air is an important "tool" in every shop. The air gun should not be pointed at anyone. The high pressure can blow dirt particles at such high speeds that they will puncture the skin and/or get into the eyes.

Figure 1-15. Always pull on the wrench handle when tightening and loosening nuts and bolts.

Dress Safely

When working around engines or other rotating machinery, there is a chance that hair, jewelry, and loose clothing will be caught in rotating parts. For this reason, it is advisable to remove jewelry when working in the automotive shop. If long sleeves are worn, they should be buttoned at the cuff or rolled up past the elbows. Caps without brims are considered safer than those with brims, because of the possibility of the protruding brim being caught in the rotating parts. Also, wear a sturdy pair of shoes or boots to protect your feet from dropped objects.

Lift Properly

There are many heavy objects encountered when servicing an automobile. When lifting these objects, keep your back straight and lift with your legs, Figure 1-16. This will

Figure 1-16. When lifting heavy objects, keep your back straight and use your legs to lift the weight. A–Incorrect lifting procedure. B–Correct lifting procedure.

help to prevent back strain. When lifting extremely heavy objects, ask for assistance. If necessary, use a crane or dolly to move heavy objects.

Welding Safety

There are many hazards encountered when using welding equipment. Always wear the appropriate gear to protect your eyes, skin, and respiratory system.

Welding techniques produce sparks, splatters, and ultraviolet radiation–all of which can cause serious burns. Therefore, a welding helmet, long sleeve shirt, long pants, and gloves should be worn to help prevent injury.

Never weld around fuel, solvents, or other combustibles. Always protect the fuel tank, fuel lines, brake lines, etc., from the heat produced during the welding process.

There are many points to observe when working with oxygen and acetylene. Never allow oil or grease to contact oxygen under pressure. Do not lubricate welding and cutting apparatus. Never use oxygen as a substitute for compressed air, as a source of pressure, or for ventilation.

Be sure to keep a clear space between the cylinders and the work, because you may find it necessary to reach and adjust the regulators quickly. Do not risk hand burns by lighting the torch with a match. Use a friction-type lighter, Figure 1-17; it is safer and easier. Never use acetylene pressure higher than 15 psi. Never release acetylene where it might cause a fire or an explosion.

When using electric welders, be sure that cables, cords, and clamps are in good condition to prevent electrocution. Always check cables for loose connections and cracks in the insulation. Also, make sure that the welding equipment is grounded properly.

Grinding Precautions

Grinding operations are an important part of an automotive technician's job, and several safety precautions must be followed when using grinders of any type. Before mounting a grinding wheel, make sure it is the type recommended for that particular operation. Also check the soundness of the wheel by tapping it with the handle of a screwdriver or a similar tool (wheel not rotating). A ringing sound should be heard when the wheel is tapped in this manner. If not, the wheel is defective and should not be used.

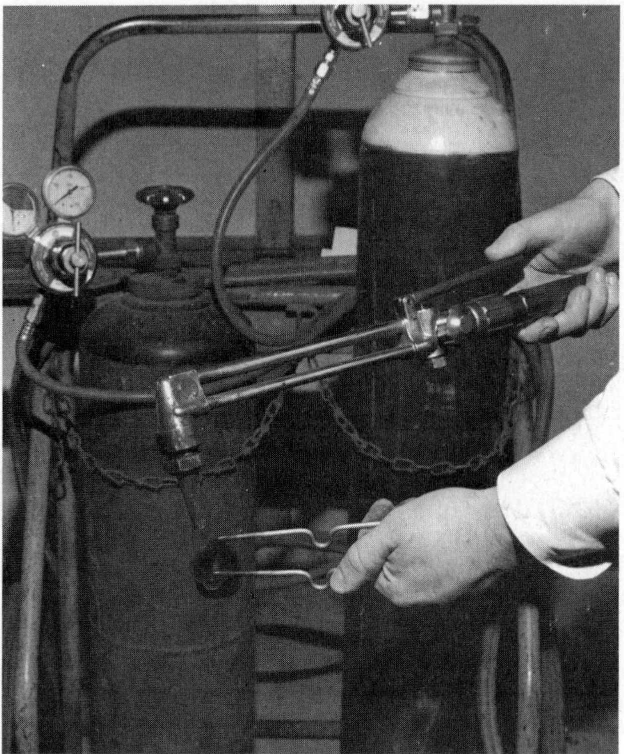

Figure 1-17. Never use a match or a lighter to ignite a welding torch. Use only a friction-type igniter, or striker.

The grinding wheel should fit the spindle snugly, and the compressible washers (known as blotters) should be large enough to extend beyond the wheel flanges. After mounting, bring the grinding wheel up to speed slowly if possible. Do not stand in the rotational plane of the wheel. In case of failure, the flying parts may cause severe injury. Always be sure that the wheel is provided with a proper guard.

After completing a grinding operation during which a coolant was used, let the wheel rotate for several minutes to throw off excess coolant. If this is not done, coolant will remain in the lower portion of the wheel. This could cause a severe unbalanced condition and, consequently, increase the danger of the wheel bursting during operation.

Remember:

- Always wear appropriate eye protection when grinding, Figure 1-14.
- Keep the part being ground as close to the grinding wheel as possible.
- When doing precision grinding, use a light feed.
- Do not strike a grinding wheel while it is rotating.

Chapter 1–Review Questions

Write all answers on a separate sheet of paper. Do not write in this book.

1. Why is it important to study OSHA (Occupational Safety and Health Administration) safety regulations?
   (A) Regulations affect all businesses.
   (B) Regulations give employee a voice in maintaining safe working conditions.
   (C) All of the above.
   (D) None of the above.

2. Used batteries and used oil are not considered hazardous wastes if they are sent off to be recycled. True or False?
3. Why are practical jokes and running prohibited in shops?
4. Why should special precautions be taken when working on clutch or brake linings?
5. Batteries produce a flammable gas when charging and discharging. True or False?
6. What happens when a file is used as a pry bar?
   (A) It bends.
   (B) It breaks.
   (C) It becomes soft.
   (D) None of the above.
7. Which of the following is correct?
   (A) Carbon monoxide is used in welding.
   (B) Carbon monoxide is a deadly poison.
   (C) Carbon monoxide is used to inflate tires on race cars.
   (D) Carbon monoxide is extremely flammable.
8. Why is it dangerous to stand in the plane of a rotating part, such as a grinding wheel?
9. Oxygen fittings on welding equipment should be well lubricated with mineral oil. True or False?
10. When grinding, position the component to be ground at least 1″ from the grinding wheel. True or False?

Hazardous wastes generated in the automotive shop must be disposed of properly. (Safety-Kleen Corp.)

Chapter 2
Owner's Manuals, Service Manuals, and Repair Manuals

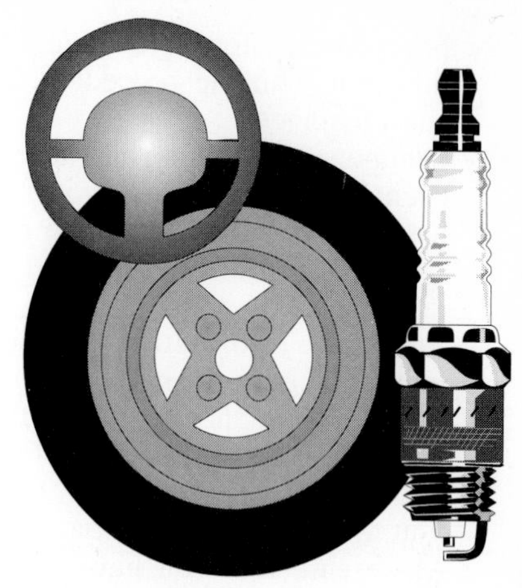

After studying this chapter, you will be able to:

- ❍ List what type of information can be found in the owner's manual.
- ❍ Explain what type of information can be found in service manuals and repair manuals.
- ❍ Determine the difference between a service manual and a repair manual.
- ❍ Demonstrate how to use a flat rate manual.

Introduction

There are many books and manuals that can be used to obtain information about a vehicle. Some of these publications contain general information about vehicle care and operation, while others contain detailed service and repair procedures.

Owner's Manuals

The ***owner's manual*** is normally kept in the vehicle's glove box. It contains nontechnical information about the proper operation of the car. It also contains data on when maintenance tasks should be performed, Figure 2-1.

Also, specifications on the types and levels of various fluids that are to be used are described. Other topics covered include:

1. Starting–explains how to start the engine under different conditions. Starting an engine with electronic fuel injection (EFI) is different than starting a carbureted engine. Also, starting a flooded engine calls for a different procedure than starting it if it were not flooded.
2. Towing–specifies the maximum weight limit that a specific car can tow behind it. Also, information on how the car should be towed if it is disabled. The

GENERAL MAINTENANCE SERVICE FOR PROPER VEHICLE PERFORMANCE

General Maintenance		Service Intervals	Kilometers in Thousands	24	48	72	80	96
			Mileage in Thousands	15	30	45	50	60
Timing Belt (Including the Balancer Belt)		Replace	at					X
Drive Belt (for Water Pump and Alternator)		Replace	at		X			X
Engine Oil	Non-Turbo	Change Every Year	or	Every 12,000 km (7,500 miles)				
	Turbo	Change Every 6 Months		Every 8,000 km (5,000 miles)				
Engine Oil Filter	Non-Turbo	Change Every Year	or	X	X	X		X
	Turbo	Change Every Year		Every 16,000 km (10,000 miles)				
Manual Transaxle Oil		Inspect Oil Level	at		X			X
Automatic Transaxle Fluid		Inspect Fluid Level Every Year	or	X	X	X		X
		Change Fluid	at		X			X
Engine Coolant		Replace Every 2 Years	or		X			X
Disc Brake Pads		Inspect for Wear Every Year	or	X	X	X		X
Brake Hoses		Check for Deterioration or Leaks Every Year	or	X	X	X		X
Ball Joint and Steering Linkage Seals		Inspect for Grease Leaks and Damage Every 2 Years	or		X			X
Drive Shaft Boots		Inspect for Grease Leaks and Damage Every Year	or	X	X	X		X
Exhaust System (Connection Portion of Muffler, Pipings and Converter Heat Shields)		Check and Service as Required Every 2 Years	or		X			X

Figure 2-1. Information on the inspection and/or replacement of maintenance items at prescribed intervals can be found in the owner's manual. (Chrysler)

procedure for towing a vehicle a long distance may be different than the procedure for towing a vehicle a short distance.

3. Components, gauges, and accessories–describes what each of the dash gauges is for and where they are located. Also, how to set the radio, clock, cruise control, air conditioning, and other accessories is discussed.
4. Warranty information–describes the terms of the manufacturer's warranty.
5. Service assistance–provides the addresses and telephone numbers for the manufacturer's zone offices. If you are having problems in getting your car repaired, you may wish to contact a zone office for assistance. Make sure that you have the following information when calling a zone office:
   a. Vehicle Identification Number (VIN), which is located on the car, Figure 2-2, and the warranty papers, which should be in the glove box.
   b. In-service date (when the car was bought), which is entered on the warranty papers.
   c. Current mileage.

Keep a copy of all warranty repair orders after the work has been done. If there is a recurring problem and the car goes out of warranty, the car maker will more than likely take care of the problem at no expense to you if it is documented with the warranty repair order. Also, if the problem is intermittent, make sure to have this documented. If the problem reoccurs after the warranty expires and it is documented, the car maker may take care of the problem at no cost to you.

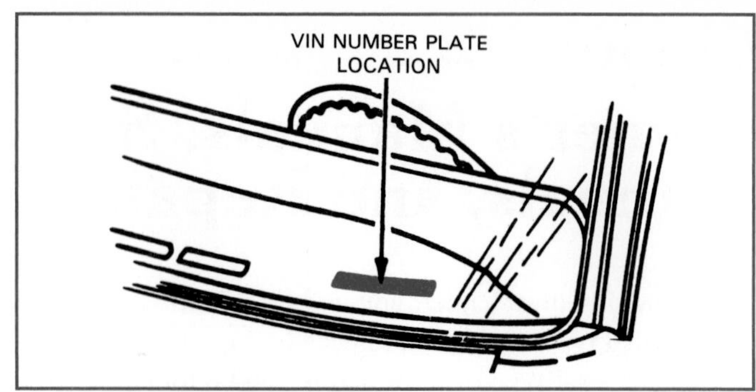

Figure 2-2. The VIN has 17 digits and is generally located at the upper left-hand corner of the dash. It can be seen through the windshield. (Cadillac)

Service Manuals and Repair Manuals

Service manuals and repair manuals contain very specific technical information about a vehicle. These manuals are needed by the technician to make the proper repairs. A ***service manual*** is published by the vehicle manufacturer for each different model every year.

A ***repair manual*** is published by a company other than the car maker. It contains a limited amount of technical information. Some repair manuals cover all domestic models for a seven year period. However, some are more detailed and contain data on all domestic models for one model year only.

Service manuals contain detailed procedures for disassembly, inspection, repair, and reassembly of the many parts of the car, Figure 2-3. Various specifications are also

TABLE OF CONTENTS	SECTION NUMBER
GENERAL INFOR. AND LUBE	
General Information	0A
Maintenance and Lubrication	0B
HEATING AND AIR CONDITIONING	
Heating and Ventilation (Non-A/C)	1A
Air Conditioning System	1B
V-5 A/C Compressor Overhaul	1D3
BUMPERS AND FRONT BODY PANELS	
Bumpers (See 10-4)	
Front End Body Panels (See 10-5)	
STEERING, SUSPENSION, TIRES AND WHEELS	
Diagnosis	3
Wheel Alignment	3A
Power Steering Gear & Pump	3B1
Front Suspension	3C
Rear Suspension	3D
Tires and Wheels	3E
Steering Column - Std.	3F1
Steering Column - Tilt	3F2
DRIVE AXLES	
Drive Axles	4D
BRAKES	
General Information - Diagnosis and On-car Service	5
Compact Master Cylinder	5A1
Disc Brake Caliper	5B2
Drum Brake - Anchor Plate	5C2
Power Brake Booster Assembly	5D2
ENGINES	
General Information	6
2.5 Liter L-4 VIN U	6A3
2.3 Liter L-4 VIN A & D	6A7
Cooling System	6B
Fuel Systems	6C
Engine Electrical - General	6D
Battery	6D1
Cranking System	6D2
Charging System	6D3
Ignition System	6D4
Engine Wiring	6D5
Driveability and Emissions - General	6E
Driveability and Emissions - TBI	6E2
Driveability and Emissions - PFI	6E3
Exhaust System	6F
TRANSAXLE	
Auto. Transaxle On-Car Service	7A
Auto. Trans. - Hydraulic Diagnosis	3T40-HD
Auto. Trans. - Unit Repair	3T40
Man. Trans. On-Car Service	7B
5-Sp. 5TM40 Man. Trans. Unit Repair	7B1
5-Sp. Isuzu Man. Trans. Unit Repair	7B2
Clutch	7C
CHASSIS ELECTRICAL, INSTRUMENT PANEL & WIPER/WASHER	
Electrical Diagnosis	8A
Lighting & Horns	8B
Instrument Panel & Console	8C
Windshield Wiper/Washer	8E2
ACCESSORIES	
Radio and Antenna	9A
Cruise Control	9B
Engine Block Heater	9E
Luggage Carrier	9F
Driver Information Center	9H
BODY SERVICE	
General Body Service	10-1
Stationary Glass	10-2
Underbody	10-3
Bumpers	10-4
Body Front End	10-5
Doors	10-6
Rear Quarters	10-7
Body Rear End	10-8
Roof	10-9
Seats	10-10
Safety Belts	10-11
Body Wiring	10-12
Unibody Collision Repair	11-1
Welded Panel Replacement	11-2
INDEX	
Alphabetical Index	

Figure 2-3A. Service manuals can be used for troubleshooting. Trouble codes for this car are found in Chapter 6, section E under Driveability and Emissions. (Pontiac)

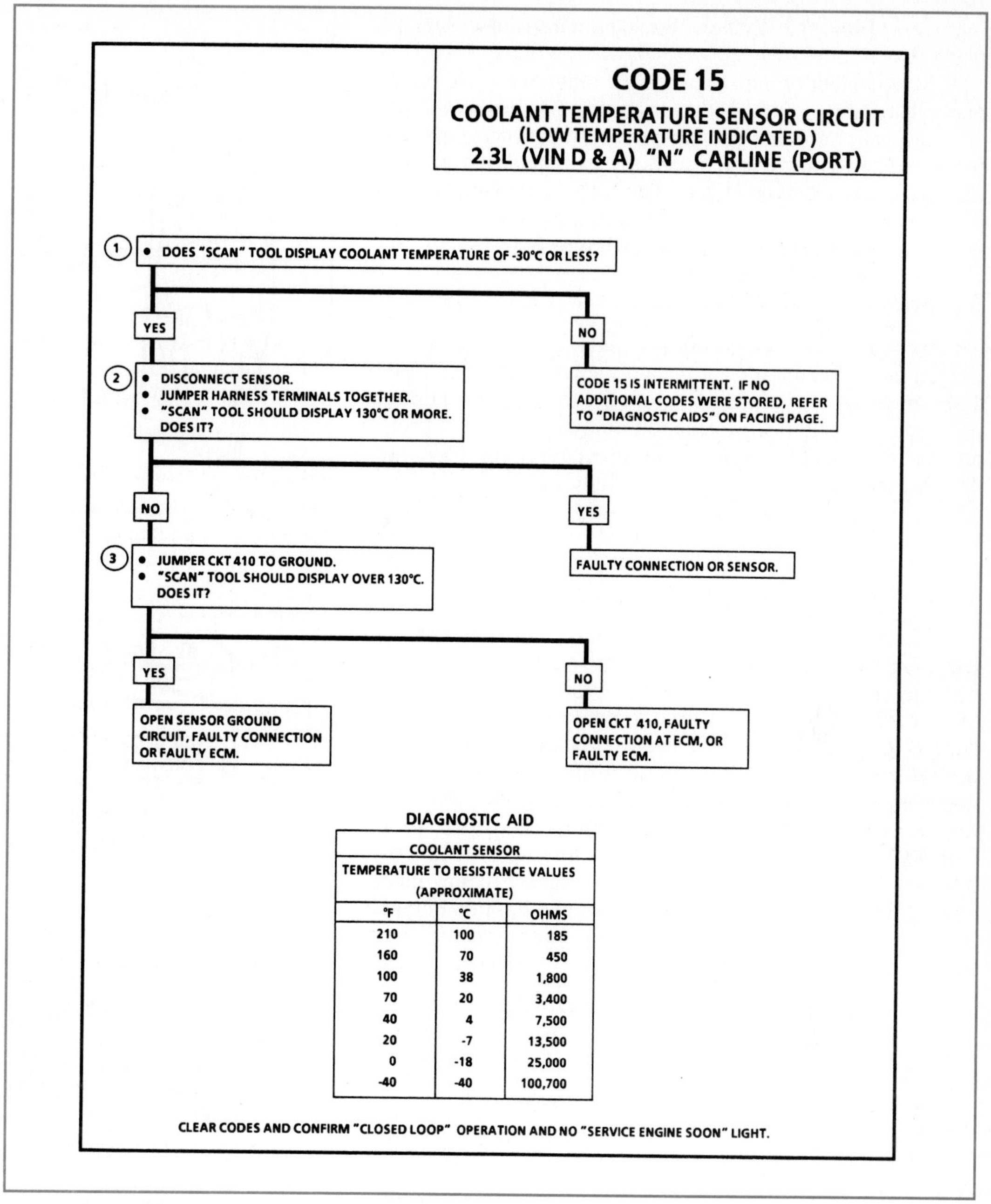

CODE 15

COOLANT TEMPERATURE SENSOR CIRCUIT
(LOW TEMPERATURE INDICATED)
2.3L (VIN D & A) "N" CARLINE (PORT)

(1) • DOES "SCAN" TOOL DISPLAY COOLANT TEMPERATURE OF -30°C OR LESS?

- NO → CODE 15 IS INTERMITTENT. IF NO ADDITIONAL CODES WERE STORED, REFER TO "DIAGNOSTIC AIDS" ON FACING PAGE.
- YES →

(2)
- DISCONNECT SENSOR.
- JUMPER HARNESS TERMINALS TOGETHER.
- "SCAN" TOOL SHOULD DISPLAY 130°C OR MORE. DOES IT?

- YES → FAULTY CONNECTION OR SENSOR.
- NO →

(3)
- JUMPER CKT 410 TO GROUND.
- "SCAN" TOOL SHOULD DISPLAY OVER 130°C. DOES IT?

- YES → OPEN SENSOR GROUND CIRCUIT, FAULTY CONNECTION OR FAULTY ECM.
- NO → OPEN CKT 410, FAULTY CONNECTION AT ECM, OR FAULTY ECM.

DIAGNOSTIC AID

COOLANT SENSOR
TEMPERATURE TO RESISTANCE VALUES (APPROXIMATE)

°F	°C	OHMS
210	100	185
160	70	450
100	38	1,800
70	20	3,400
40	4	7,500
20	-7	13,500
0	-18	25,000
-40	-40	100,700

CLEAR CODES AND CONFIRM "CLOSED LOOP" OPERATION AND NO "SERVICE ENGINE SOON" LIGHT.

Figure 2-3B. Trouble code 15 logic tree. (Pontiac)

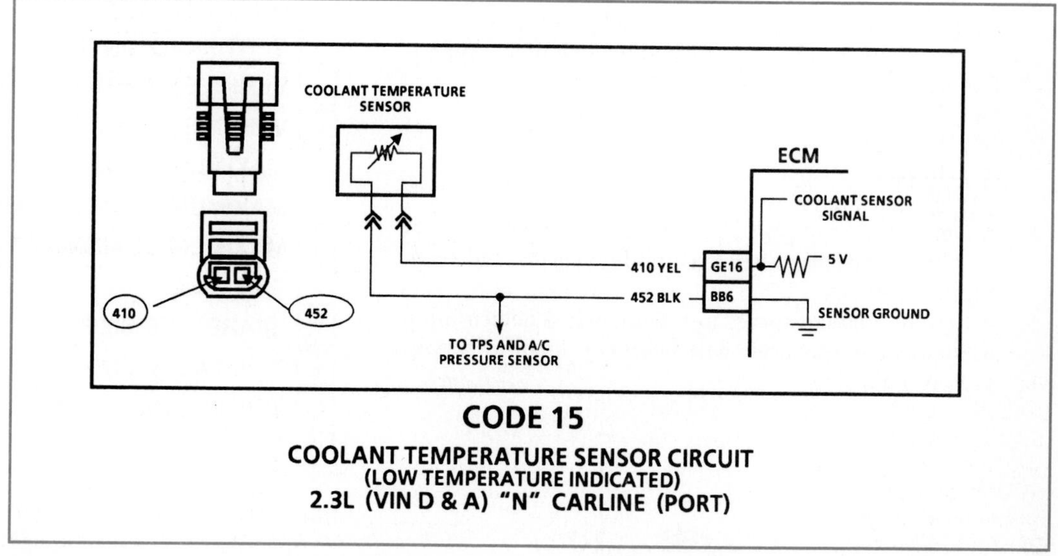

Figure 2-3C. Trouble code 15 electrical circuit. (Pontiac)

included, Figure 2-4. New car dealerships use service manuals.

Independent repair shops, on the other hand, use repair manuals because of the wide variety of cars they service.

To make sure that you have the correct service manual for the vehicle that you are working on, check the ***vehicle identification number*** (VIN). The VIN is a 17-digit code number that contains specific information about the vehicle, such as model year and origin, Figure 2-5.

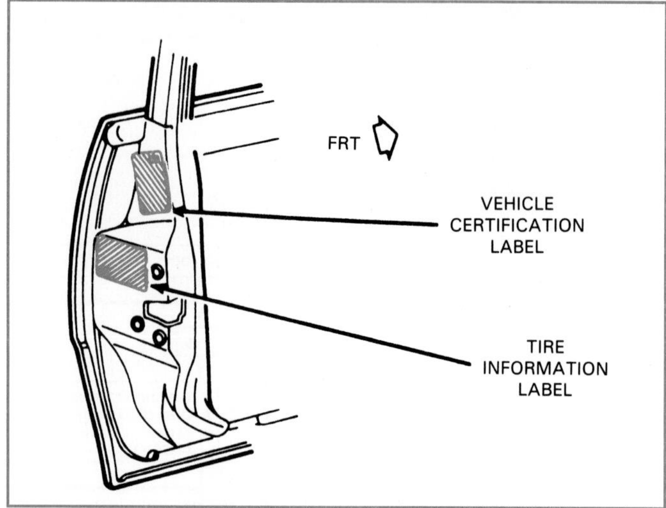

Figure 2-4A. Specifications can be found in the service manual. Service manual shows location of decal is on driver's door. (Cadillac)

Technical Service Bulletins

Technical service bulletins (TSBs) are another source of technical information for the automotive technician. The TSB makes it easy for the technician to diagnose certain problems. It contains information on symptoms of a problem and outlines the needed repair procedure. The TSBs are distributed to new car dealership technicians by the factory. This is because most TSBs cover only new car models. However, the TSB can be requested by anybody through the local zone office of the car maker. At the end of each new car model year, all TSBs are compiled into book form and are made available for purchase.

Flat Rate Manual

A ***flat rate manual*** is used to determine how much to charge the customer for the needed repairs. For example, the flat rate manual may list that a tune-up will take 1.8 hours on a 1993 Ford V-6 engine. The 1.8 is multiplied by the hourly rate charged by the shop. If this rate is $40.00/hr., then the labor for the tune-up would cost $72.00. The cost for parts has to be added to the labor charge. The amount of time specified in the flat rate manual is charged whether the technician takes one hour or three hours to complete the job.

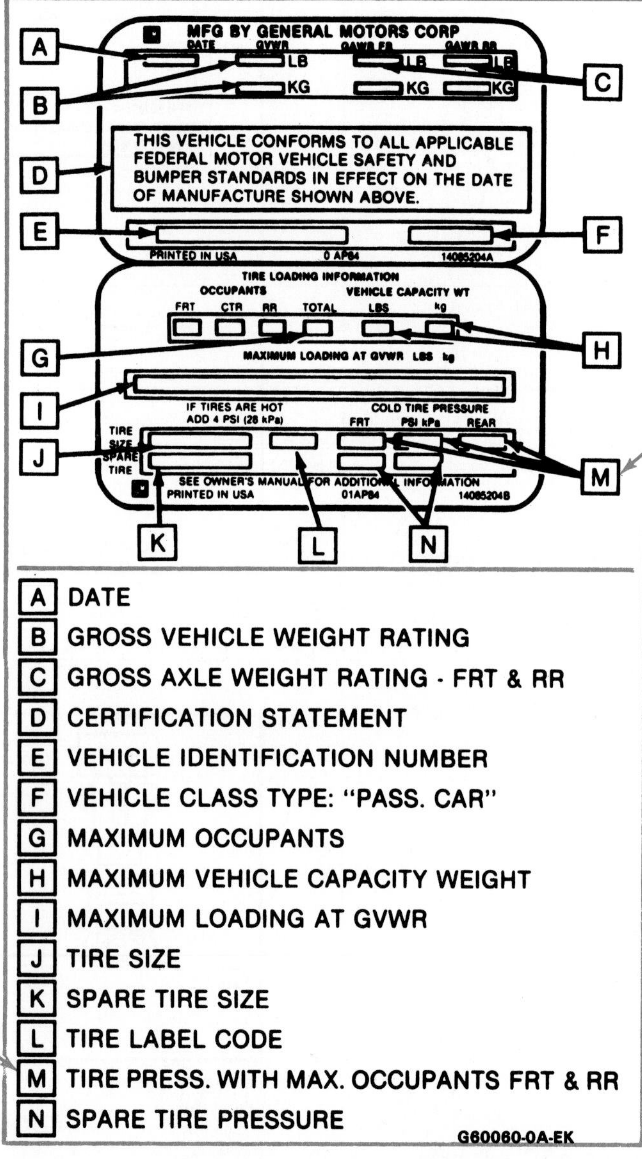

Figure 2-4B. This decal contains information about the recommended tire pressure. (Cadillac)

Review Questions–Chapter 2

1. The owner's manual contains information on:
   (A) how to start a cold engine.
   (B) when to change the oil.
   (C) how to use the radio.
   (D) All of the above.
2. A service manual contains technical information about one specific vehicle. True or False?
3. _____ manuals are not published by a vehicle's manufacturer.
   (A) Owner's
   (B) Service
   (C) Repair
   (D) None of the above.
4. A vehicle's _____ is a code number that contains specific information, such as model year, model type, engine size, etc.
5. A flat rate manual serves as a guide when determining what the labor charge will be for a specific repair. True or False?

Cylinder Block

Bore Diameter .... 96.5 mm (3.800")
Bore Out-of-Round-Max. .... .0381 mm (.0015")
Bore Taper-Max. .... .0381 mm (.0015")
Runout-Rear Face of Block to Crankshaft Centerline .... .203 mm (.008")

Piston

Clearance in Bore .... .019 - .044 mm (.00075" - .00175")
Piston Diameter (Nominal Outside) .... 96.5 mm (3.800")
Weight Less Pin & Rings (All) .... (596g ± 2g)
Skirt Taper (Larger at Bottom) .... .076 - .0431 mm (.003" - .0017")
Piston Pin Offset to Thrust Side .... 1.397 - 1.657 mm (.055" - .065")
Ring Grove Width-Both compression .... 2.052 - 2.029 mm (.0808" - .0798")
Ring Grove Width-Oil .... 4.803 - 4.777 mm (.1891" - .1881")

Piston Rings

Compression Ring Width (2) .... 1.9812 - 1.9558 mm (.0780" - .0770")
Compression Ring Gap Both .... .2286 - .4826 mm (.009" - .019")
Compression Ring Side Clearance in Grove .... .0457 - .0965 (.0018" - .0038")
Oil Ring Width .... .5969 - .640 mm (.0235" - .0252")
Oil Ring Gap .... .381 - 1.397 mm (.015" - .055")
Oil Ring Side Clearance in Grove .... .03 - .13 mm (.001" - .005")

Piston Pin

Diameter .... 24.90 - 24.906 mm (.98035" - .98055")
Pin Clearance, Check @ 21°C (70°F)
  Pin to Piston .... .0076 - .0127 mm (.0003" - .0005")
  Pin to Rod .... .0038 - .024 mm (.00015" - .00095")

Crankshaft and Connecting Rod

Main Bearing Journal
  Diameter
    (2, 3, 4 & 5) .... 63.4619 - 63.4873 mm - (2.4985" - 2.4995")
    (1) .... 63.4695 - 63.4949 mm (2.4988" - 2.4998")
  Width – Main, Thrust Bearing Journal (No. 3)
    Including Fillets .... 30.441 - 30.518 mm (1.1985 - 1.2015")
Out-of-Round-Max. .... .013 mm (.0005")

Figure 2-4C. Specifications for engine rebuilding are at the end of Chapter 6 in this specific service manual. (Cadillac)

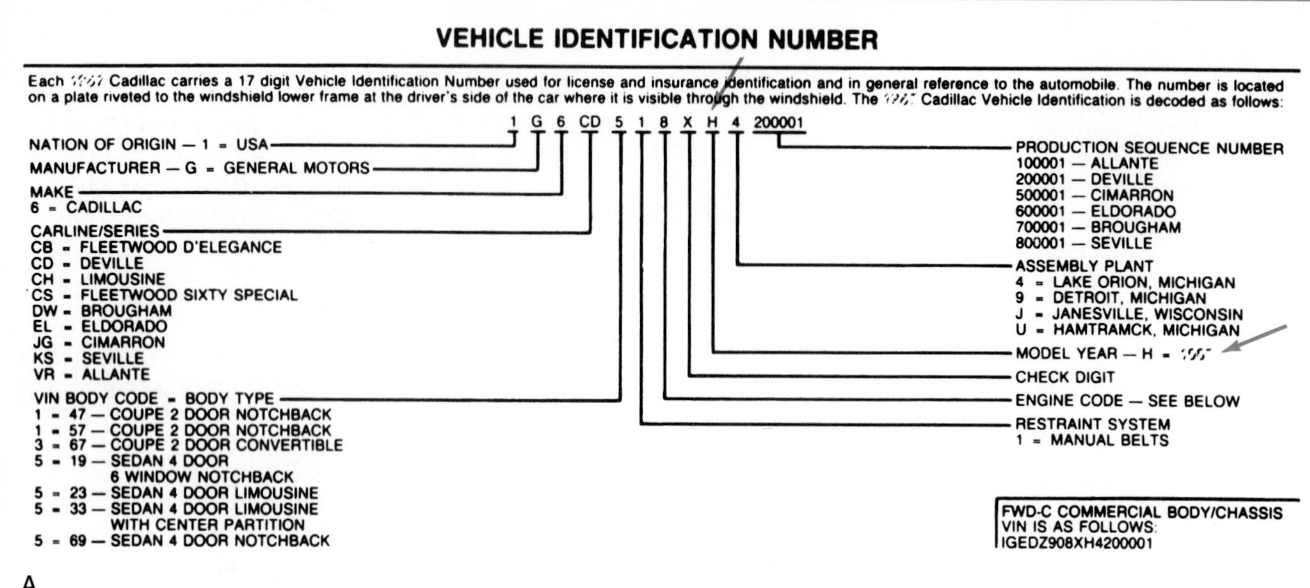

Figure 2-5. Interpreting the digits of the VIN. A–The position of the "H" indicates the model year. B–Instructions for interpreting the VIN is found in the service manual. (Cadillac)

Chapter 3
Automotive Tools

After studying this chapter, you will be able to:
- ❍ Identify the various tools used to service automobiles.
- ❍ Describe the purpose of each tool used in the shop.
- ❍ Use tools safely.
- ❍ Select the right tool for the job.

Tools

Tools play an important part in any automotive service operation. Almost every repair job requires the use of at least one tool to remove, disassemble, adjust, or replace parts.

Consequently, anyone studying to be an automotive technician should be thoroughly familiar with the tools that will be used on the job. In addition, the beginning mechanic must learn the correct methods of using tools, not only to perform the work as quickly as possible, but also to complete the job with maximum accuracy and safety.

Vehicles have become increasingly complex, and a greater variety of tools is needed to service them. Without an extensive collection of tools, an auto technician may not be able to find employment. Tools represent a large investment, but experienced technicians realize that quality tools help them turn out precision jobs quickly and safely. When a technician's tool kit is complete, it will include the right tool for virtually every job, Figure 3-1.

Tool care is important, too. Apprentice technicians soon learn that time will be saved if they take good care of their hand tools. This includes cleaning the tools after use and returning the tools to their proper storage place to prevent loss or damage.

Wrenches

Wrenches are used to loosen or tighten nuts and bolts. A wrench's size is determined by the width of its opening, and both U.S. customary and metric sizes are available. A standard set of wrenches in the English system usually ranges from 3/8″ to 1″, increasing by 1/16″ steps. Typical metric wrenches range in size from 7 millimeters to 10 millimeters. Larger and smaller sizes are available in both U.S. customary and metric wrenches, but are usually not part of a standard set.

One of the most important tools in a technician's tool box is the *open-end wrench,* Figure 3-2. This type of wrench has two flat sides that grip the fastener. To permit the open-end wrench to turn a nut in a restricted space, the opening of the wrench is designed at an angle to the centerline of the handle. Usually, this angle is 15°. By first placing one side of the wrench up, then the other, it is possible to turn the nut a few degrees at a time in each position until it is loose. Wrenches are also made with opening angles of 22 1/2°, 30°, 60°, and 90° to the handle.

Box wrenches, Figure 3-3, completely surround the nut or bolt being tightened or loosened, reducing the possibility of the wrench slipping from the fastener. Usually, the box has 12 grooves, which engage the corners of the nut

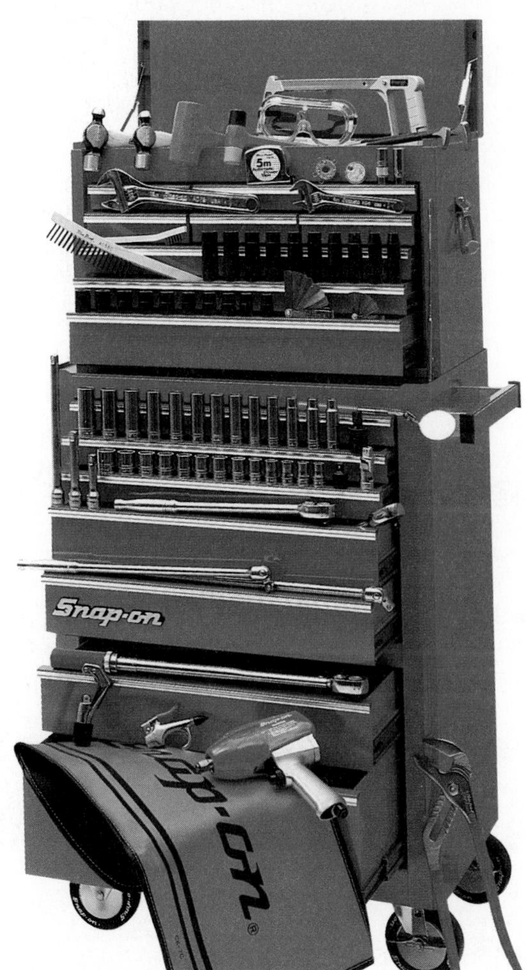

Figure 3-1. Successful technicians have a large investment in tools. (Snap-on Tools Corp.)

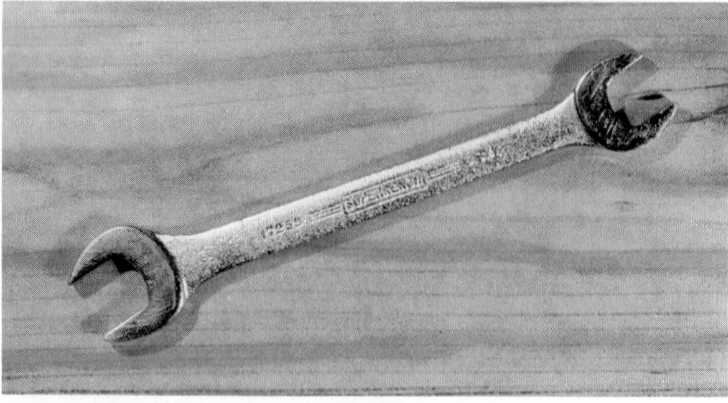

Figure 3-2. An open-end wrench is one of the most useful tools found in the automotive shop.

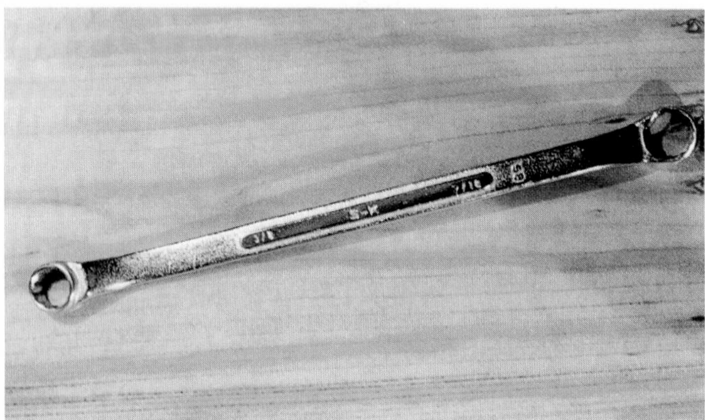

Figure 3-3. The head of this box wrench is offset 15°. The offset provides clearance for the technician's knuckles.

and permit moving the wrench through an arc of as little as 30° before repositioning. Also, the walls of the box are relatively thin, so less space surrounding the nut is required.

A box wrench cannot be used on tubing fittings. Therefore, a *tubing wrench* is available for this purpose, Figure 3-4. A crowfoot wrench can also be used on tubing fittings, Figure 3-5.

Figure 3-4. A tubing wrench is designed for use on line fittings.

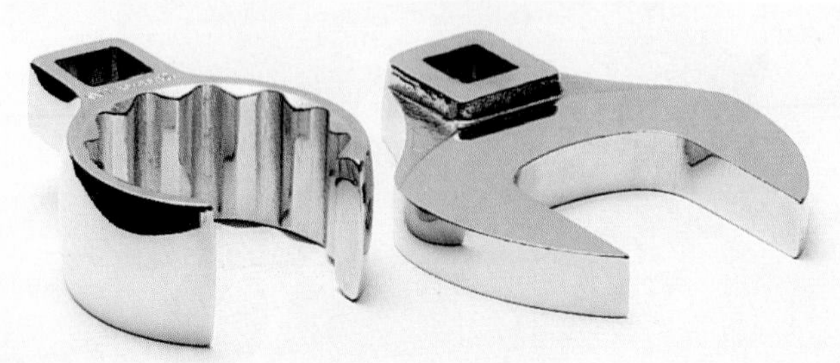

Figure 3-5. The crowfoot wrench must be used with an extension. (Snap-on Tools Corp.)

A *combination wrench* has a box on one end and is open on the other end, Figure 3-6. Both ends of this type of wrench are designed to fit the same size nut. Combination wrenches are general-purpose wrenches and are preferred by many technicians.

Sockets and Ratchets

Like the box wrench, ***sockets*** completely surround the nut or bolt to be tightened or loosened, Figure 3-7. Therefore, there is little chance of the socket slipping from the fastener. Used with a ratchet handle, sockets greatly reduce the time necessary to remove nuts and bolts.

Usually, the sockets used in automotive work usually have either 12 or 6 grooves that engage the corners of the nut. Sockets manufactured with six grooves give added protection against slippage.

The ***drive opening*** of the socket (opening in which ratchet handle is placed) is 1/4″, 3/8″, 1/2″, or 3/4″ square. Technicians usually have a set of 1/4″, 3/8″, and 1/2″ drive sockets in their tool kits. The 1/4″ square drive socket set usually includes sockets ranging in size from 3/16″ to 9/16″. The 3/8″ square drive socket set has sockets from 1/4″ to 1″. The 1/2″ square drive socket set is designed for use on nuts ranging in size from 3/8″ to 1 1/2″.

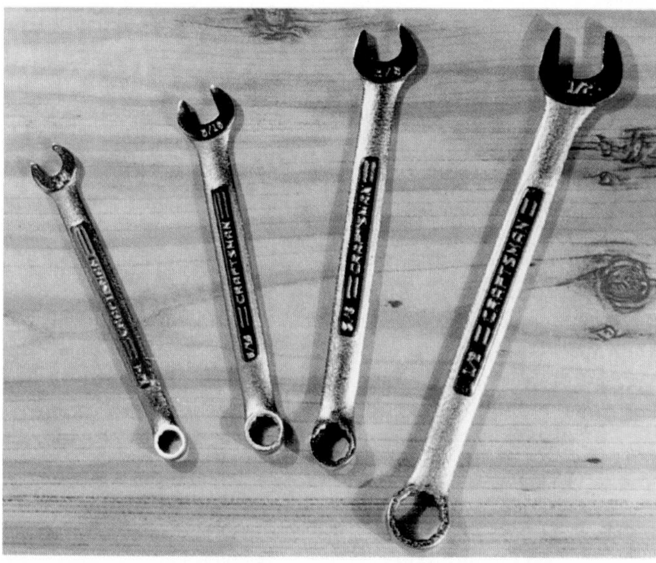

Figure 3-6. A combination wrench has a box wrench at one end and an open-end wrench at the other.

Figure 3-7. A variety of sockets is needed in the automotive shop. A–Conventional length sockets. B–Deep-well sockets are used for removing spark plugs.

In addition to standard sockets, ***deep-well sockets*** are available. Deep-well sockets are used primarily for removing spark plugs, sending units, etc., Figure 3-7.

A variety of ***ratchet handles*** are available for various purposes. See Figure 3-8. Some handles are designed to give increased leverage, others to facilitate reaching areas that are normally obstructed, Figure 3-9. Some ratchet handles are designed to speed the removal and installation of fasteners.

Inside the head of the ratchet handle is a pawl, which fits into one of the ratchet's teeth. When the handle is pulled in one direction, the pawl holds and the socket turns. When the handle is moved in the opposite direction, the pawl ratchets over the teeth, permitting the handle to be backed up without turning the socket.

Figure 3-10 illustrates a speed wrench, which is commonly called a speeder. As the name implies, a speed wrench is designed to loosen and tighten fasteners rapidly.

Various accessory handles are shown in Figure 3-11. A flex handle provides a great deal of leverage, which is often necessary when removing stubborn fasteners. Also, the angle of the handle in relation to the fastener can be changed as necessary. A sliding T-handle makes it possible to move the handle back and forth without detaching the tool from the fastener.

Extensions are available in a variety of sizes. Extensions permit sockets to be used in restricted areas. Socket drivers are often used with sockets to facilitate fastener removal. Both extensions and socket drivers are available with flexible shafts.

If it is not possible to get a direct pull when removing a fastener, a ***universal joint*** is available for use between the ratchet handle and the socket. Sockets complete with universal joints are also available. See Figure 3-12. Note that these are six point sockets. Universal sockets also come in eight point and 12 point sets.

Specialty Wrenches

Many ***specialty wrenches*** are designed to do one specific job. Figure 3-13 illustrates wrenches used when servicing automotive brake systems.

Allen Wrenches

The ***Allen wrench***, or hex wrench, Figure 3-14, is a hex-shaped wrench and is available in a wide variety of sizes. The speed hex wrench, Figure 3-15, has a ball at one end. The ball allows the wrench to swivel as the fastener is loosened or tightened, expediting removal or installation.

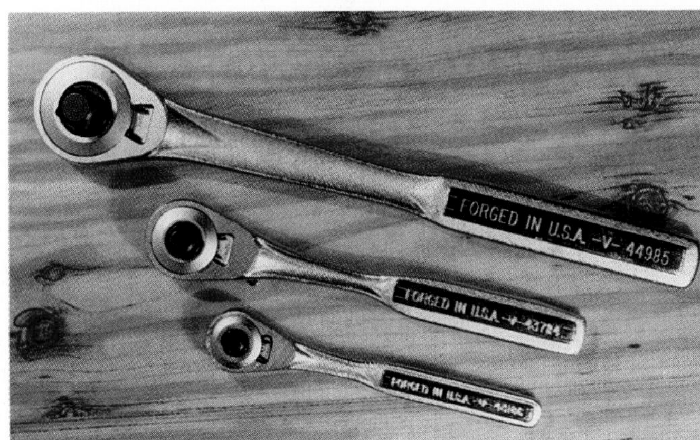

Figure 3-8. Ratchet handles are available in a variety of sizes.

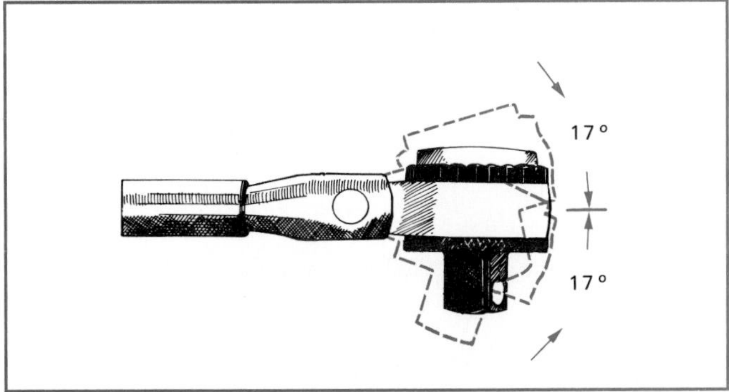

Figure 3-9. Some ratchets have a flex-head. This allows the ratchet to reach spots that a normal ratchet cannot. (Central Tools)

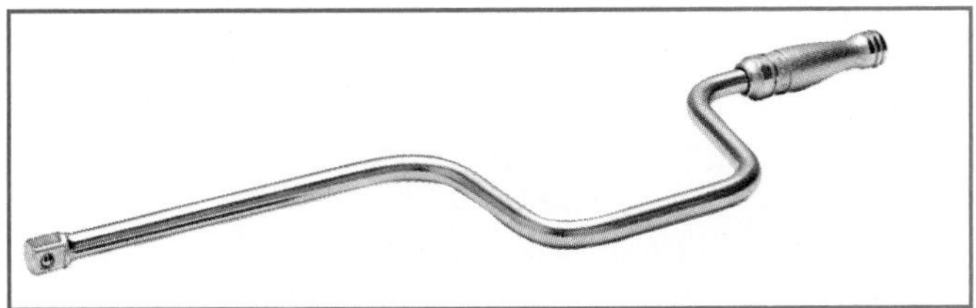

Figure 3-10. A speed wrench is used to remove fasteners quickly. (Snap-on Tools Corp.)

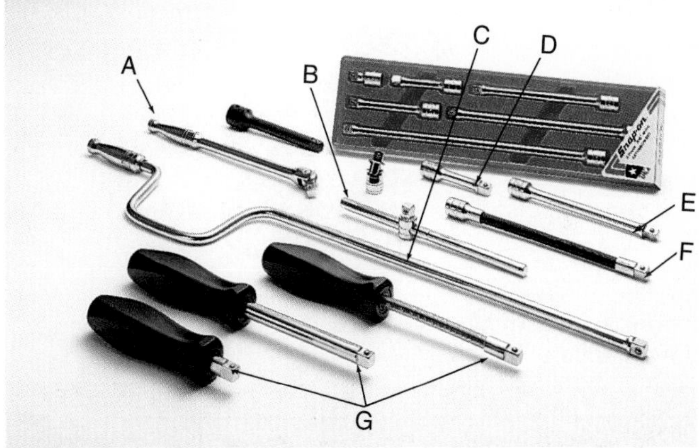

Figure 3-11. Various accessory handles. A–Flex handle. B–Sliding T-handle. C–Speed wrench. D–Short extension. E–Long extension. F–Flexible extension. G–Socket drivers. (Snap-on Tools Corp.)

Figure 3-12. A set of swivel sockets is useful when removing bolts in hard-to-reach places. (Snap-on Tools Corp.)

Torque Wrenches

Often, a fastener must be tightened to a specified torque. Torque is a measured amount of turning force. If a fastener is overtightened, mating parts may be distorted and leakage (oil, coolant, compression, etc.) may occur. Cylinder head bolts and engine bearing nuts and bolts must be "torqued" accurately. When tightening these fasteners, a ***torque wrench*** must be used. See Figure 3-16.

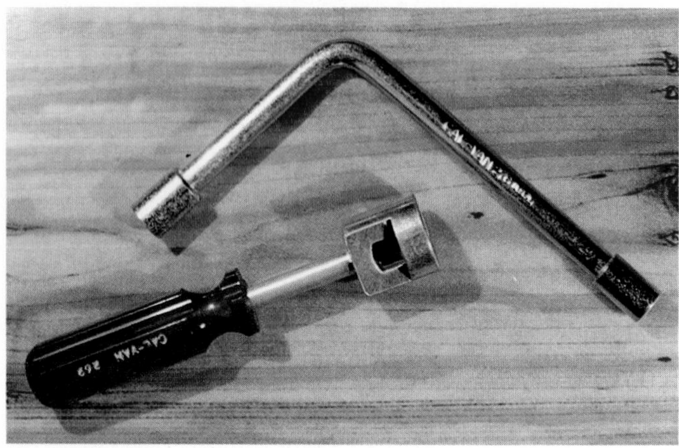

Figure 3-13. These specialty wrenches are designed for use when working on brake systems.

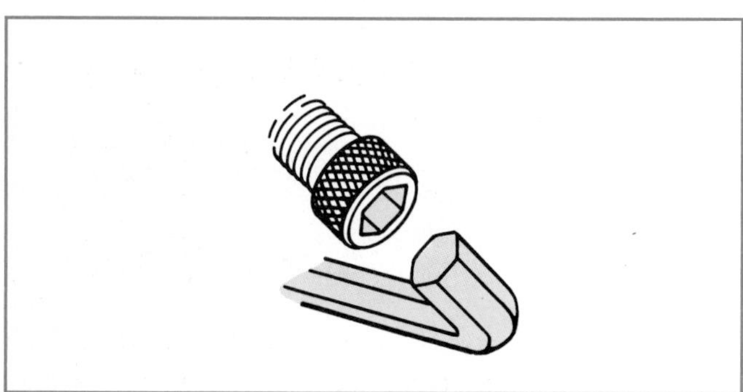

Figure 3-14. An Allen wrench is used on hex socket heads. (Deere & Co.)

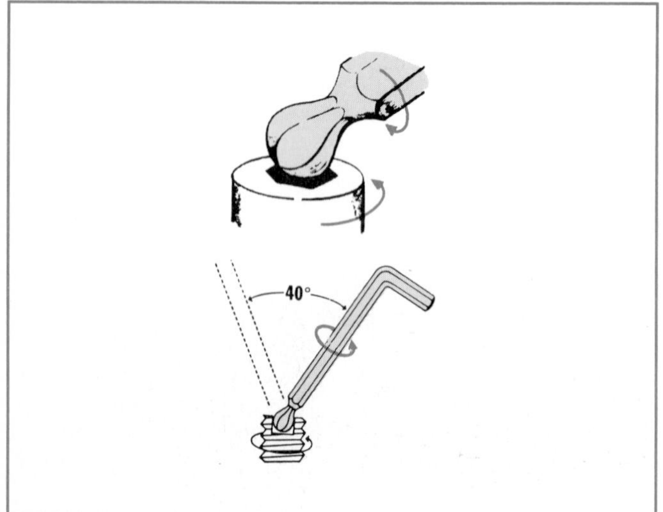

Figure 3-15. A speed hex wrench can swivel in tight spots. (Lisle Co.)

Torque wrenches indicate torque in foot pounds, inch pounds, or newton meters. To covert foot pounds to newton meters, multiply by 1.355. When using a torque wrench, clean and oil the threads of the fastener so that no additional friction will be present.

Pliers

There are many different types of ***pliers*** used in automotive work. It is important to note that pliers are used to grip various objects and should never be used as a substitute for wrenches. One of the most common types of pliers found in the automotive shop is the *combination slip-joint pliers,* Figure 3-17. The slip-joint permits the jaws of the pliers to be opened wider at the hinge for gripping large-diameter components.

Diagonal cutting pliers, Figure 3-18, are needed not only for cutting wire, but they are also used for removing cotter pins.

Long nose pliers, Figure 3-19, are frequently needed to recover washers or nuts that have dropped into an inaccessible place. These pliers are also used to aid in positioning small parts.

Like slip-joint pliers, *interlocking joint pliers,* Figure 3-20, are adjustable. The opening of the pliers can be adjusted to several different sizes. This permits the jaws of the

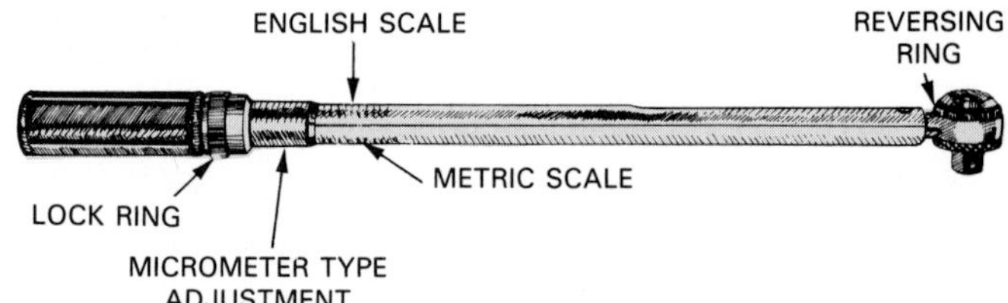

Figure 3-16. A click-type torque wrench can be used to tighten fasteners to a specified torque. An audible "click" is heard when the preset torque has been reached. Note that one side of the wrench has a metric scale, while the other side has a U.S. customary scale. (Central Tools)

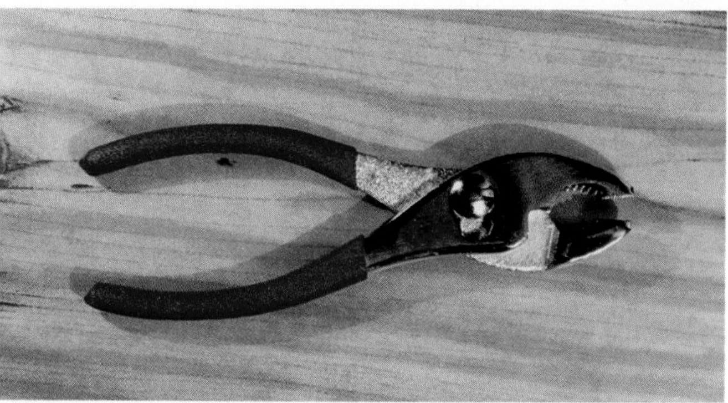

Figure 3-17. Slip-joint pliers are used to grip various components when servicing an automobile.

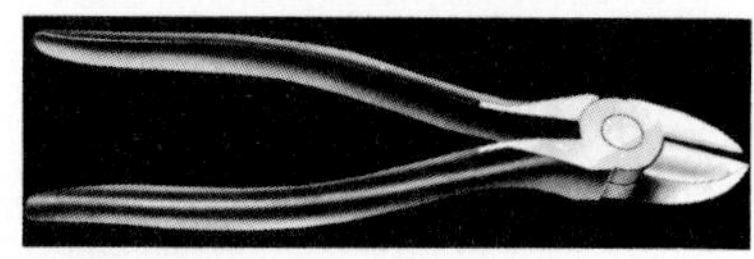

Figure 3-18. Diagonal cutting pliers are used to cut wire and to pull cotter pins.

pliers to remain approximately parallel, regardless of the size of the opening.

One of the most versatile tools in the technician's kit is the *locking pliers,* Figure 3-21. When locked in position on a part, these pliers will grip firmly, even when the area contacted by the jaws of the pliers is extremely small. Locking pliers have an infinite number of uses, ranging from holding two parts together to gripping the end of a broken stud and turning it out of its threaded hole.

Snap ring pliers, Figure 3-22, are important tools in every repair kit. They are used to remove snap rings from various parts, such as hydraulic valve lifters, transmission shafts, and bearings.

Special pliers that are designed to assist in the removal and installation of brake shoes and brake shoe springs are also available. See Figure 3-23.

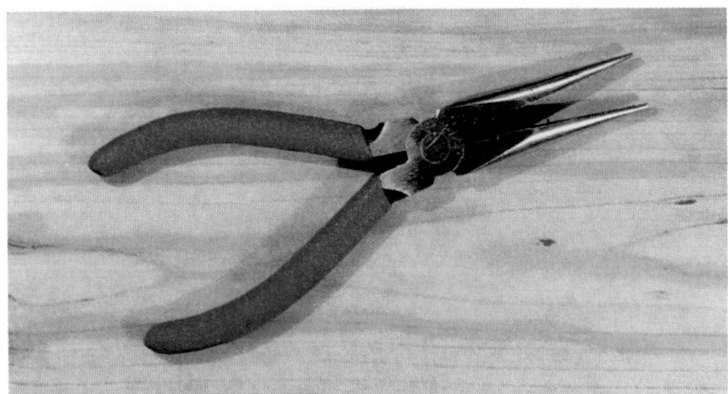

Figure 3-19. Long nose pliers are handy for gripping small objects.

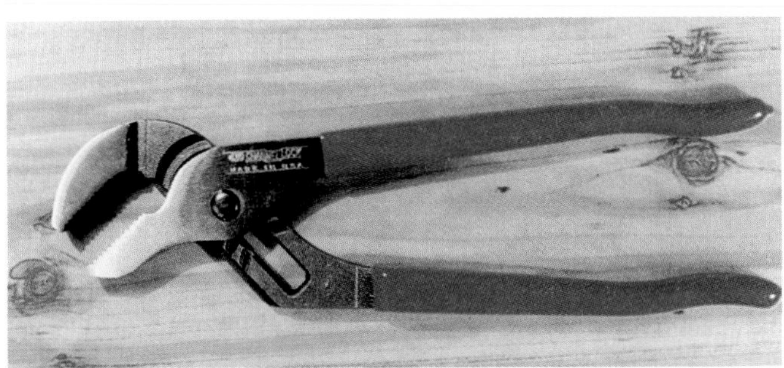

Figure 3-20. Interlocking adjustable joint pliers.

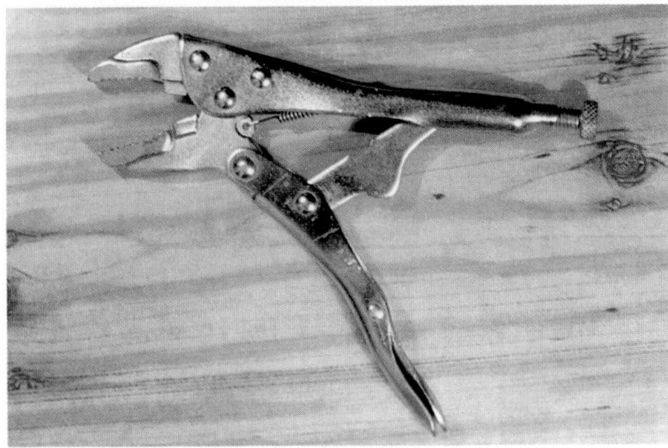

Figure 3-21. Locking pliers are used to hold parts together and to remove broken studs.

Stud Removers

When it becomes necessary to remove a stud, the preferred method is to use a *stud remover,* Figure 3-24. This particular tool is designed to be turned by hand. However, some stud removers are designed with either a 3/8″ or 1/2″ drive, so they can be used with a ratchet wrench.

Screwdrivers

There are many different types and sizes of ***screwdrivers*** used in the automotive shop. See Figure 3-25. The size

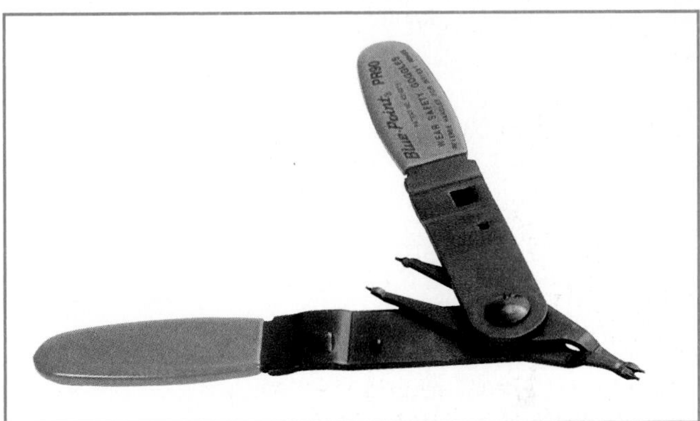

Figure 3-22. Snap ring pliers. (Snap-on Tools Corp.)

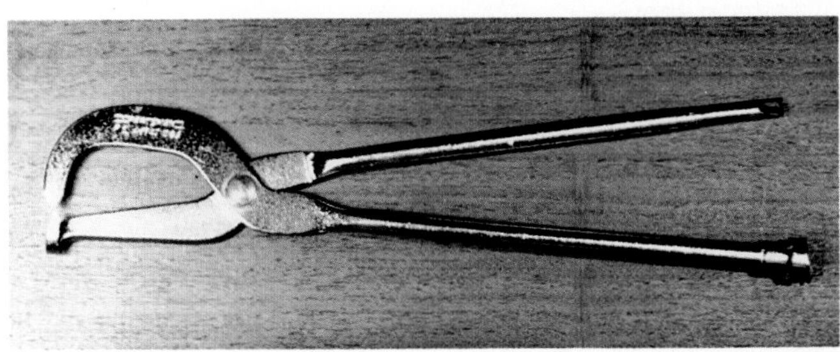

Figure 3-23. Brake pliers are necessary when performing a brake job.

Figure 3-24. This stud remover can be turned by hand.

of a screwdriver is determined by the size of its tip (bit). The size of a *standard screwdriver,* Figure 3-26, is determined by the width and thickness of the blade. The *Phillips screwdriver,* Figure 3-27, is pointed and has four grooves. Phillips screwdrivers come in sizes #0 (the smallest), #1, #2, #3, and #4 (the largest). The *Pozidriv® screwdriver,* Figure 3-28, is similar to the Phillips screwdriver, but provides a tighter, more-positive fit. This prevents the head of the screw from being rounded. The *clutch driver,* Figure 3-29, is sometimes referred to as a figure eight driver or a butterfly driver.

The *Torx® screwdriver,* Figure 3-30, is used to remove Torx-type fasteners that are common on late-model vehicles. The Torx driver comes in sizes T15 (the smallest), T20, T25, and T27 (the largest).

The *magnetic screwdriver,* Figure 3-31, is extremely useful when working on the dash of the car or in other restricted areas.

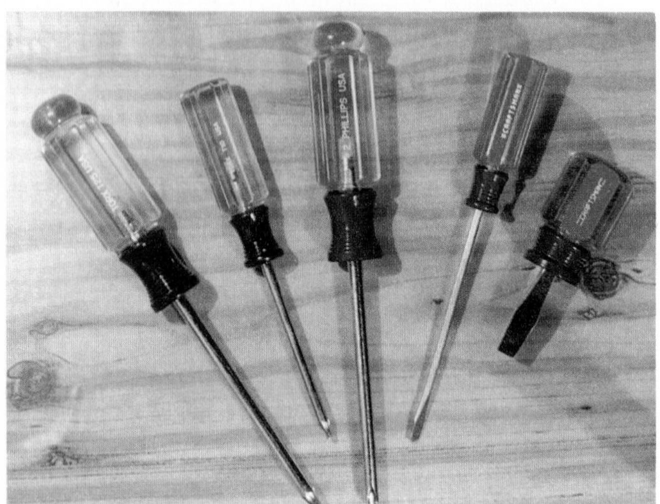

Figure 3-25. A variety of screwdrivers is used in the automotive shop.

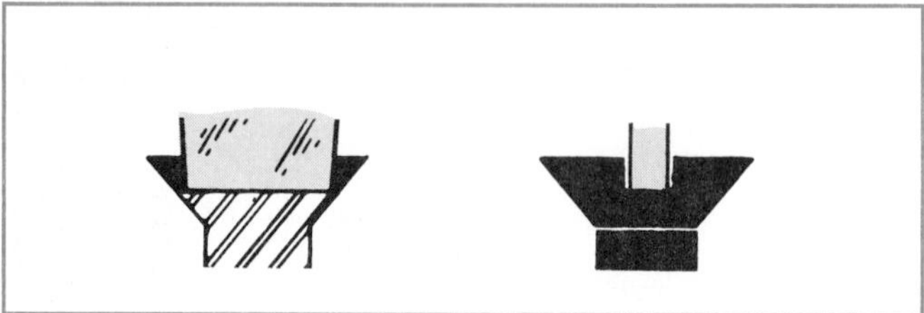

Figure 3-26. A blade type screwdriver must fit the slot.

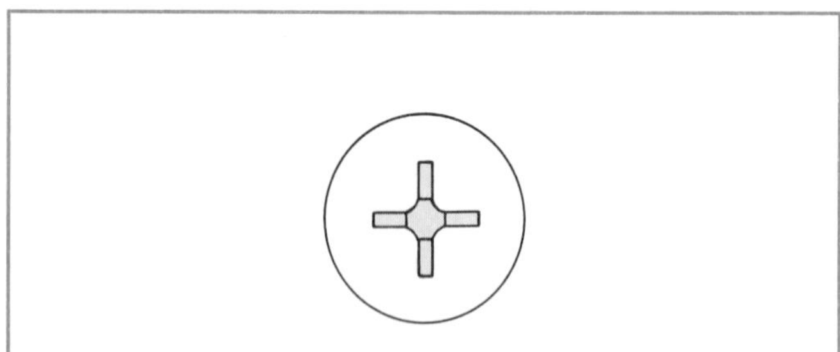

Figure 3-27. Tip configuration of a Phillips screwdriver.

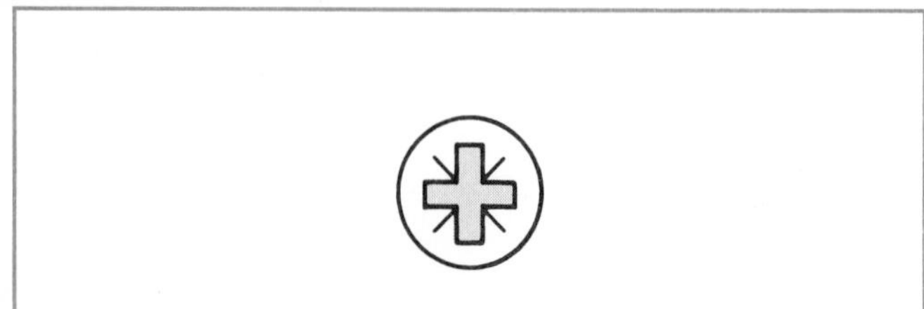

Figure 3-28. A Pozidriv screwdriver provides a positive grip.

Hammers

Automotive technicians require ***hammers*** of various types and sizes. The most important is the *ball peen hammer,* Figure 3-32. The flat portion of the head used for most hammering is called the face. The other end is the peen. When the peen is ball-shaped, it is known as a ball peen.

A ball peen hammer is usually classified according to the weight of its head without the handle. A good hammer set for automotive work would include 4 oz., 1 lb. and 3 lb. hammers. A small hammer is very handy for light work.

If there is any danger of damaging the surface of a component, *soft-faced hammers,* Figure 3-33, should be used. These special hammers have faces of rawhide, plastic, brass, or lead.

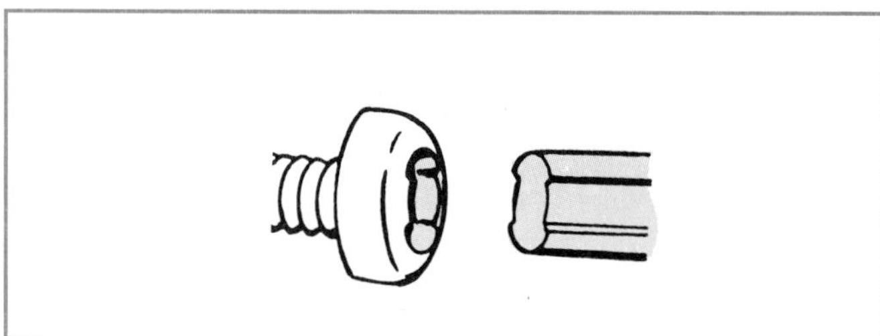

Figure 3-29. A clutch screwdriver.

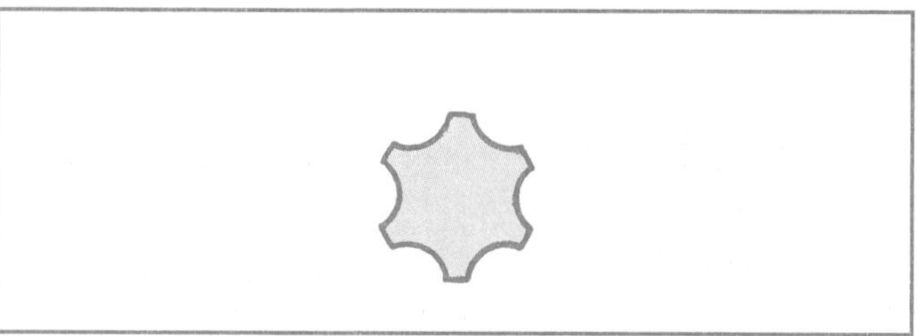

Figure 3-30. Tip configuration of a Torx screwdriver.

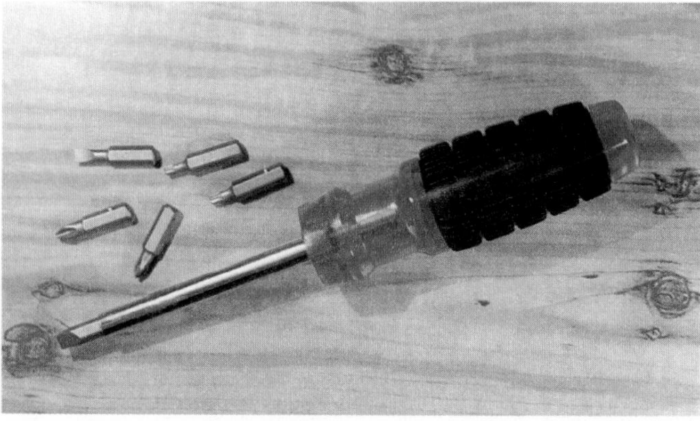

Figure 3-31. This magnetic screwdriver has interchangeable bits. Each bit is magnetized. (S-K Tools)

The hammer should be gripped close to the end of the handle, Figure 3-34. In this way, a heavier blow can be struck with minimal effort. Be careful not to strike the work with the edge of the hammer face, Figure 3-35. The full face of the hammer should contact the workpiece.

The end of the hammer handle should not be used for bumping purposes, as this will quickly ruin the handle. Additionally, hammer handles should never be used as levers.

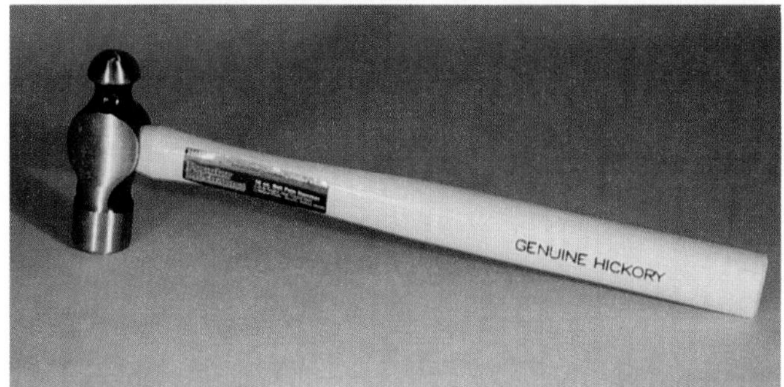

Figure 3-32. A ball peen hammer is commonly used in automotive repair work.

Figure 3-33. A soft-faced hammer prevents marring the work surface.

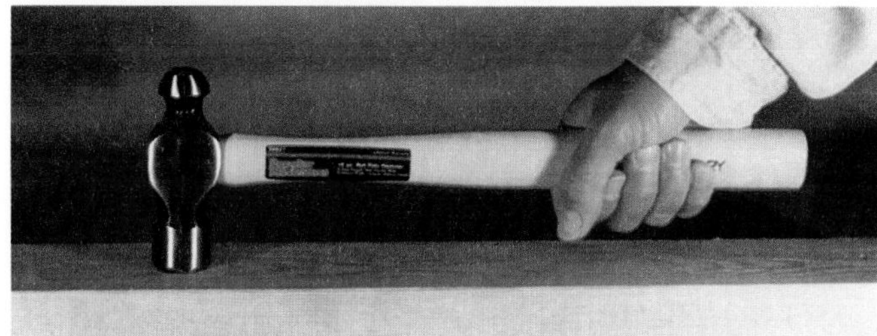

Figure 3-34. The hammer should be gripped near the end of its handle.

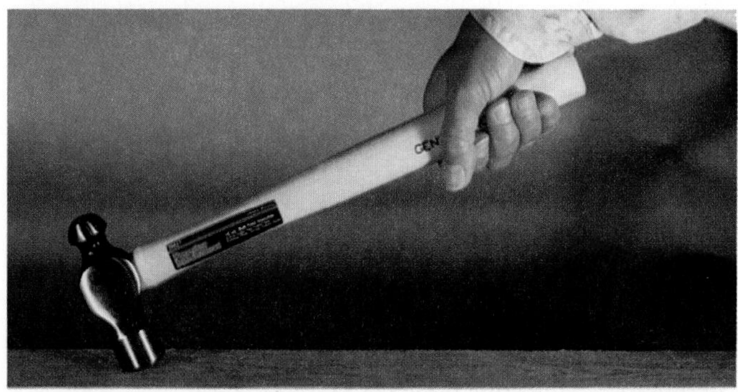

Figure 3-35. Never strike the work with the edge of the hammer.

Warning! The hammer handle must fit tightly in the head. Never use a hammer with a loose head, as the head may fly off and cause an injury.

Chisels

A variety of ***chisels*** are used in the automotive shop. Cold chisels, Figure 3-36, are used for cutting metal, removing the heads from rivets, chipping metal, and splitting rusted nuts.

The *cape chisel,* Figure 3-36, has a narrow cutting edge. It is used primarily for cutting keyways and narrow grooves.

In most cases, automotive technicians will use the cold chisel, or flat chisel. The sizes most frequently used are 3/8″, 1/2″, and 3/4″.

A *rivet buster,* Figure 3-37, is a special form of chisel designed specifically for cutting the heads from rivets. It

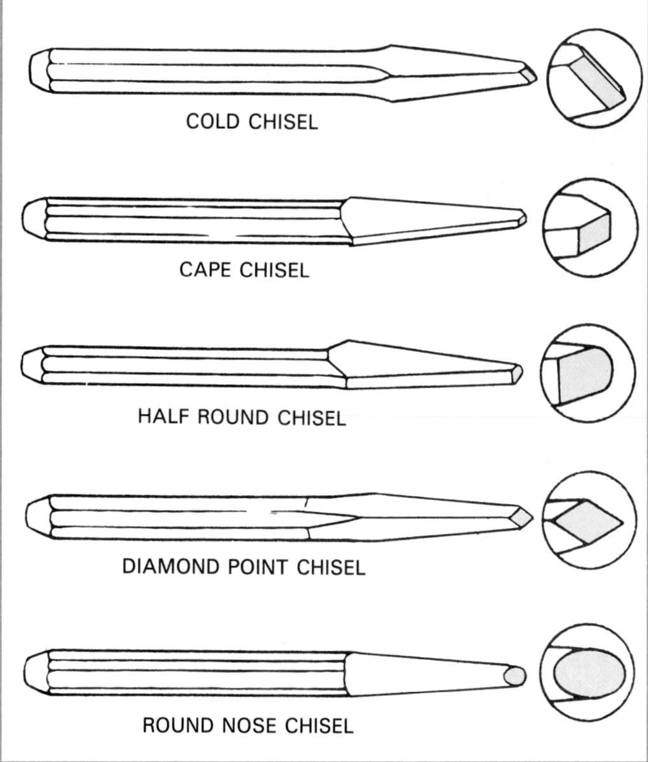

Figure 3-36. Cold chisels may have a variety of cutting edges.

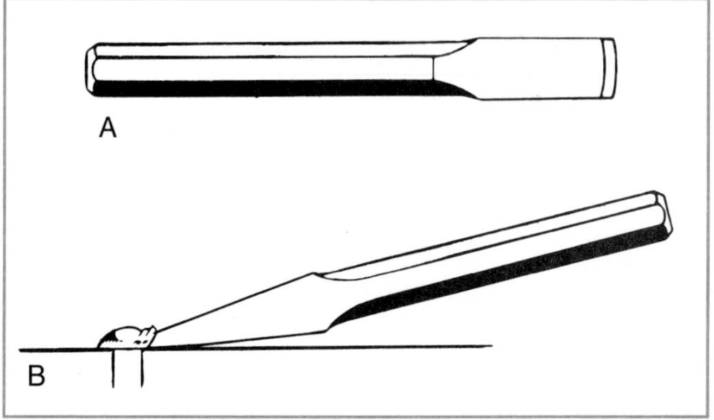

Figure 3-37. A rivet buster is used to shear the heads from rivets.

differs from the conventional cold chisel in that only one side of the cutting edge is ground.

The chisel should be held rather loosely, with fingers curled around the chisel about one inch from the head of the chisel. A special tool can also be used to help hold the chisel during use.

When chipping metal, the depth of the cut is controlled by the angle of the chisel, Figure 3-38. Deeper cuts are taken as the angle of the chisel approaches the vertical position. When chipping, the technician should watch the cutting edge, not the head of the chisel.

Goggles must be worn when chipping. Take precautions so that chips do not strike bystanders. Never use a chisel with a mushroomed end, Figure 3-39. When struck with a hammer, portions of the mushroomed head may fly off and cause severe injuries. If necessary, the mushroomed end of the chisel should be ground smooth, Figure 3-40.

When sharpening a cold chisel, Figure 3-41, the two ground surfaces should form an angle of 60°. Rivet busters are ground on one surface only at an angle of approximately 30°.

Punches

Many different types of ***punches,*** Figure 3-42, are required in automotive work. The *starting punch* is designed to punch out rivets after the heads have been cut off. These punches are also used to start driving out straight or tapered pins, Figure 3-43. After the pin has been driven partly from the hole, the starting punch can no longer be used because of its taper. A *pin punch* is then used to complete the job of punching out the pin. Pin punches should not be used to start such work because a hard blow on a punch could bend the slender shank.

An *aligning punch* has a long taper. It is used to shift parts to bring corresponding holes into alignment.

The *center punch,* is ground to a fine point. It is used to mark the locations of holes that are to be drilled. Without

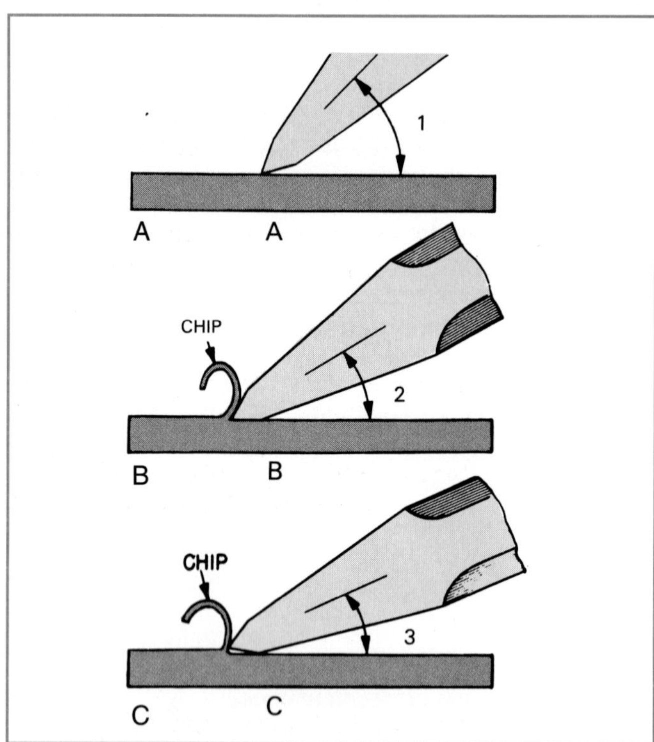

Figure 3-38. The depth of a cut is controlled by angle of chisel.

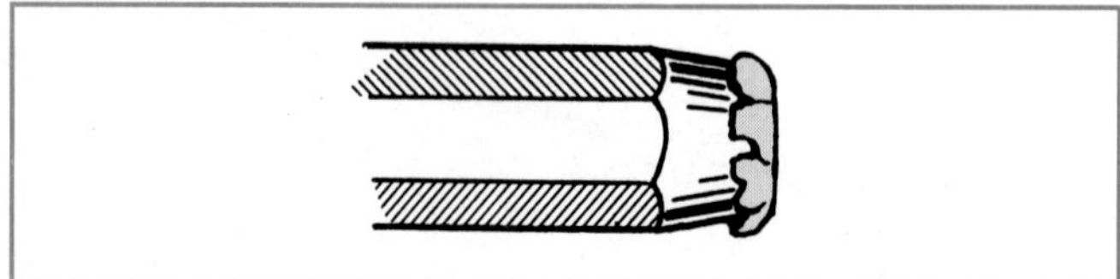

Figure 3-39. After striking the end of a chisel repeatedly, the end become mushroomed.

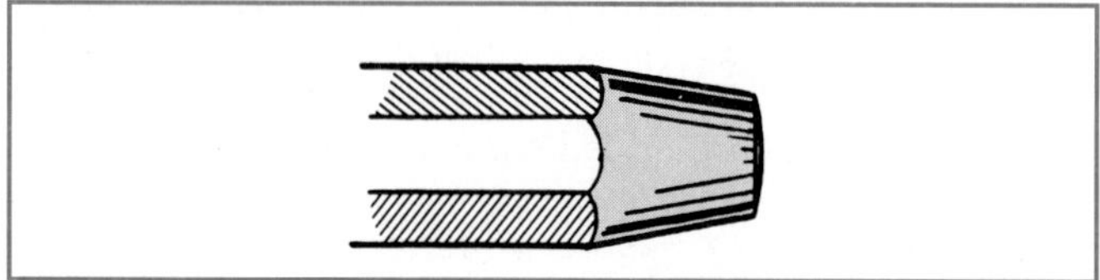

Figure 3-40. The mushroomed end of a chisel should be ground to prevent tiny pieces of metal from flying off when it is struck with a hammer.

Figure 3-41. The cutting edge of a chisel can be sharpened on an electric grinder.

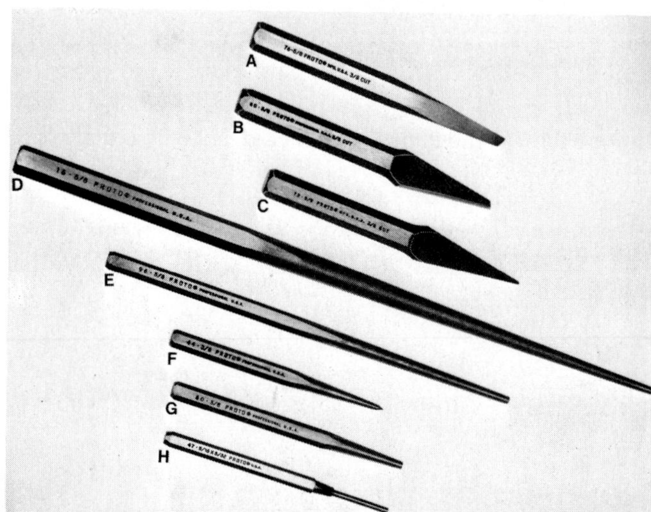

Figure 3-42. A–Diamond point chisel. B–Cape chisel. C–Round nose chisel. D–Aligning punch. E–Short aligning punch. F–Center punch. G–Starting punch. H–Pin punch.

such a mark, the drill may wander over the surface and start the hole at the wrong position.

Metal Shears

Metal shears, Figure 3-44, are needed for cutting sheet metal. The straight blade shear is the type most frequently used; however, the curved blade shear and the scroll pivoter snips are also convenient to have available. The curved blade shears are used for making curved cuts, and the scroll pivoter snips follow an irregular line easily.

Electric Drills

Electric drills, Figure 3-45, come in several sizes. They are a must in every technician's tool kit. Many technicians have both a 1/4″ drill and a 1/2″ drill.

Most drills are provided with variable speed controls. This feature is of value because some materials are more easily drilled at slow speeds, while others require a faster speed. For example, soft metals require a faster speed than extremely hard metals. Also, some drills are reversible, allowing the drill bit to be backed out if necessary.

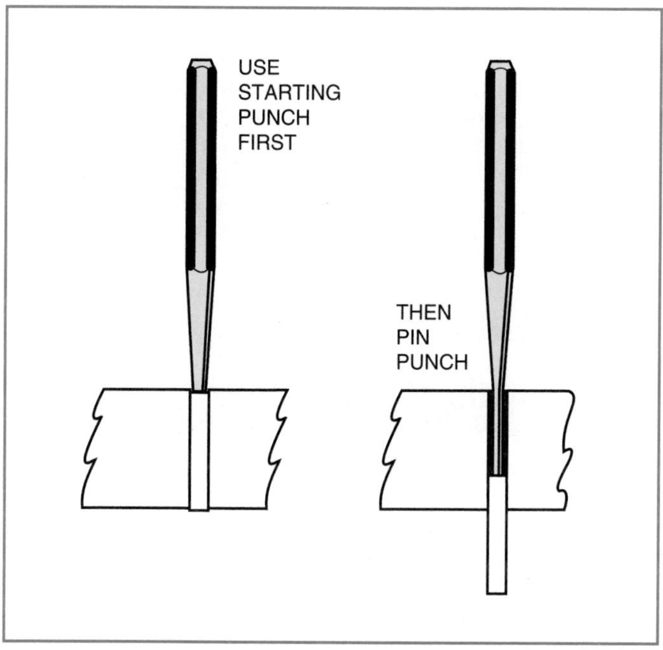

Figure 3-43. To remove a pin, begin with a starting punch and then knock the pin out with a pin punch.

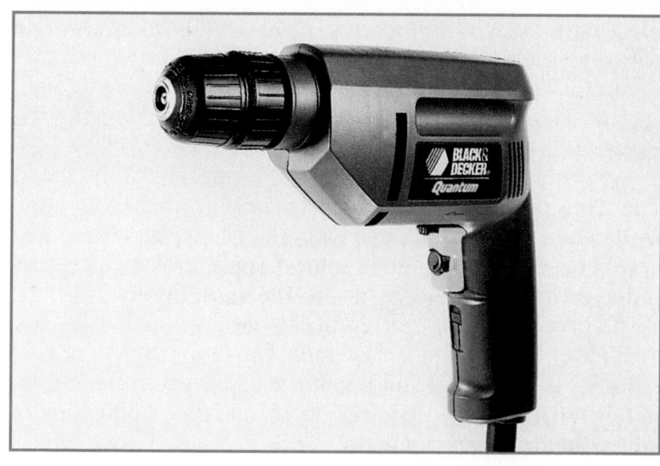

Figure 3-45. An electric drill is an indispensable tool.

The tool used with the electric drill to do the actual cutting is known as the ***drill bit,*** Figure 3-46. The drill bit has two cutting edges and is made of either carbon steel or high-speed steel. However, the former quickly becomes dull and, if heated excessively, will lose its hardness. High-speed steel will retain its temper when red hot, so drill bits of this material are preferred. The straight shank drill is generally used in the automotive shop.

Impact Wrenches

Impact wrenches (often called impact tools), Figure 3-47, are designed for loosening and tightening nuts and bolts quickly. Their use results in considerable time savings and a noticeable reduction in fatigue on the part of the technician. Designed for use with heavy-duty sockets, both electrical and pneumatic impact wrenches are available.

Files

Files are hardened steel hand tools designed to remove metal. They are also used to smooth and polish metal surfaces.

The cutting edges of a file consist of diagonal rows of parallel teeth. There are more than 20 different types of

Figure 3-44. Different types of shears.

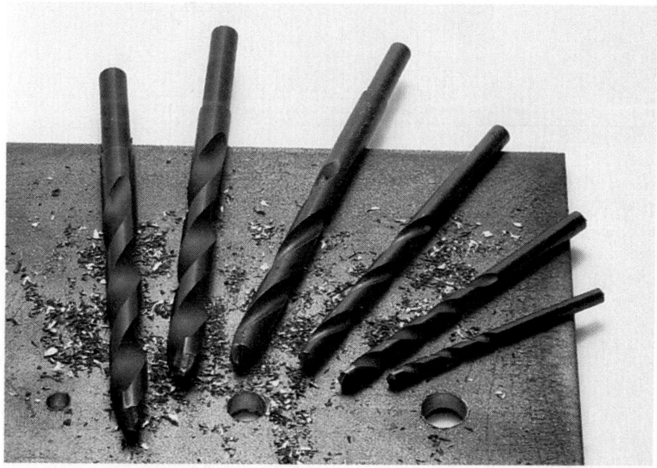

Figure 3-46. Drill bits are available in a variety of sizes.

files, with sizes ranging from 3″ to 18″ in length. A file with a single row of parallel teeth is called a *single-cut file,* Figure 3-48. Files that have a row of teeth crossing another row in a crisscross pattern are known as *double-cut files,* Figure 3-48.

Files are graded according to the spacing of the teeth. The terms used to indicate the coarseness or fineness of a file are bastard, second-cut, and smooth. The terms coarse and dead-smooth are also used in some classifications. The names of the different parts of a file are shown in Figure 3-49.

There are many different shapes in which files are available, Figure 3-50. The *mill file* is a single-cut file, tapering in thickness and width for one-third of its length. It is used primarily for fine work and is available with either square or round edges.

A double-cut file that tapers in thickness and width is known as a *flat file.* It is used when a fast cut is desired. The *hand file* is single-cut and is similar in shape to a flat file, with parallel sides and a slight taper in thickness. It has square edges, one of which is a safe edge. For rough filing, the *bastard file* is used.

The *round file* is tapered and usually single-cut. In larger sizes, it is also available in a double-cut configuration. For enlarging large holes, a round 12″ bastard file is usually used. If the hole is of small diameter, a round 6″ file, usually known as a *rat-tail file* is used. Untapered round files are also available. The principal use of round files is to enlarge circular openings and to file concave surfaces.

The *half-round file* is a double-cut file. It tapers in thickness and width, with one flat side and one oval side. It is used mainly for rough filing on concave surfaces.

The triangular file is useful for filing small notches and square or cornered holes. In addition, it can be used for recutting damaged threads on bolts.

As previously mentioned, files with coarse teeth are used when it is desired to remove a lot of metal as quickly as possible. Files with fine teeth remove less metal, but produce a smoother surface. In addition, the type of metal must be considered when selecting a file.

Figure 3-47. A pneumatic impact tool is a valuable time-saving device. (Snap-on Tools Corp.)

When filing cast iron, first use a bastard file, then use a second-cut file for finishing. On soft steel, a second-cut file is used first, and a smooth-cut file is used for finishing. On hard steel, start with a smooth-cut file and finish with a dead-smooth file.

On soft metals, such as brass or bronze, use a bastard-cut file first and then use a second-cut file. On aluminum, babbitt or lead, a Vixen-cut file, Figure 3-51, similar to those used by automotive body repairmen, is preferred. If that type file is not available, a bastard file may be used.

Never use a file without a handle, since the pointed tang may be driven into the palm of your hand, inflicting a wound. Whenever possible, clamp the work in the jaws of a vise. If the work is soft metal, cover the jaws of the vise with *soft caps* so that the work will not be marked or otherwise damaged, Figure 3-52.

Never hammer on files or use them as levers. Files are brittle and will quickly break if used in these ways.

File teeth are designed to cut only when the tool is pushed forward. Therefore, the preferred method of filing is to raise the file from the work before drawing it back to start the next stroke.

Apply only enough pressure to the file to keep it cutting. Excessive pressure only results in increased effort being required to move the file forward. The correct way to hold a file is shown in Figure 3-53.

If you are right-handed, grasp the file handle in your right hand. Hold the other end of the file in your left hand with your fingers curled over the end. Your feet should be

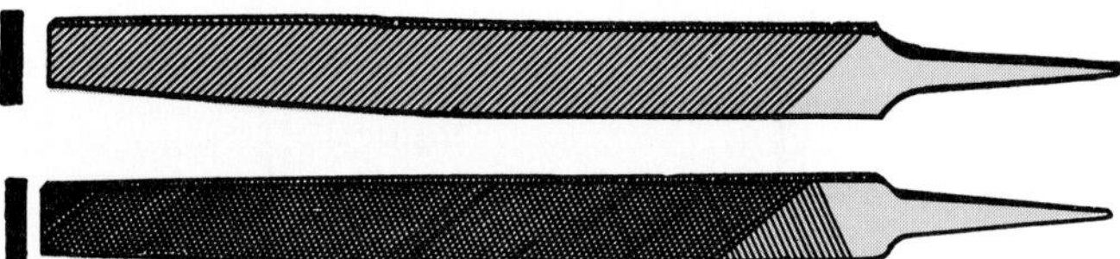

Figure 3-48. A–Single-cut file, or mill file. B–Double-cut file.

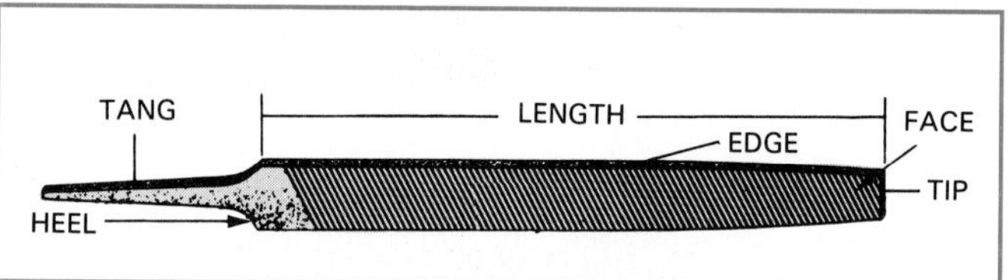

Figure 3-49. The different parts of a file.

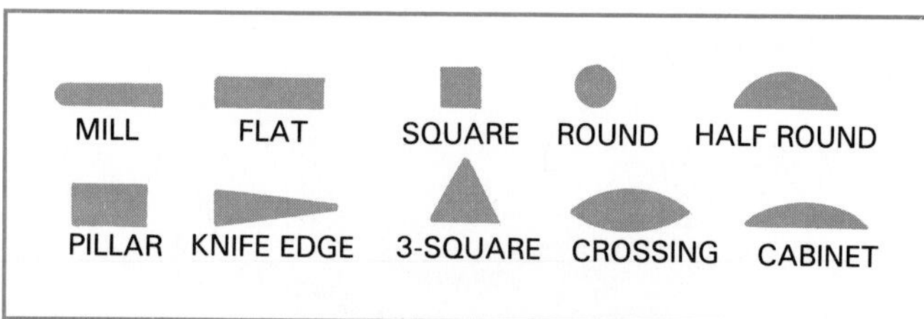

Figure 3-50. Sectional view of different files.

Figure 3-51. A Vixen-cut file is used to shape soft metals and body filler.

spread apart and your body should lean slightly forward so that your left shoulder is over the work. In order to file a flat surface, the forward movement of the file must be perfectly horizontal. Any rocking of the file will result in a convex surface. However, when filing a round surface, the file should be rocked as shown in Figure 3-54.

File teeth tend to become clogged, particularly when soft metals are being filed. As a result, material between the file teeth will tend to scratch the surface being filed. This can be overcome to a degree by rubbing chalk on the file before use. To clean the teeth of a file, brush them with a file card or other wire-bristled brush.

Files should be hung on a rack when not in use. Placing files in a drawer with other tools will quickly dull their teeth.

Figure 3-52. Soft caps can be easily added to a vise. The caps prevent marring of soft materials.

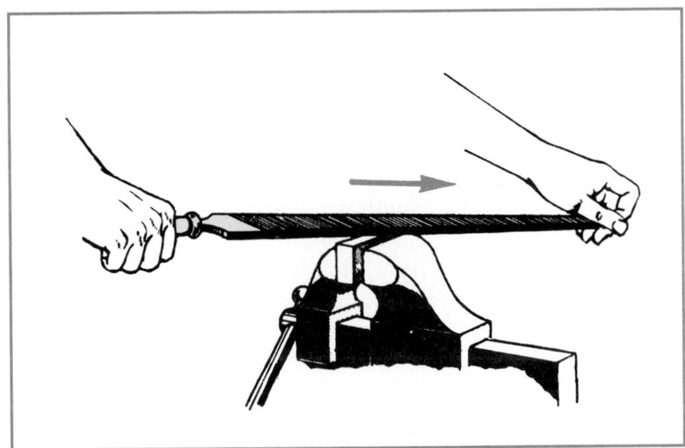

Figure 3-53. The correct method of using a file.

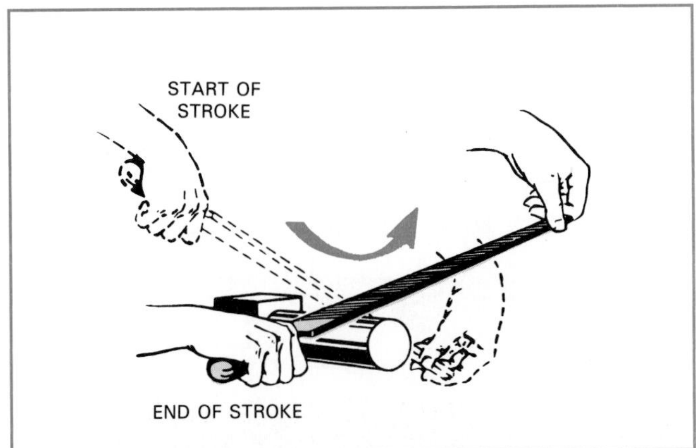

Figure 3-54. When filing round objects, the file should be rocked.

Retrieving Tools

Special ***retrieving tools*** have been designed to retrieve objects that have been dropped and are in places that are difficult to reach. A magnetic retrieving tool is shown in Figure 3-55. The magnet is attached to a handle by means of a universal joint, making the tool more flexible. Gripper-type retrieving tools are designed to grip the object to be retrieved.

Soldering Tools

Soldering guns and ***soldering irons*** are used to melt solder when joining two metals together. See Figure 3-56. In automotive body repair work, solder is sometimes used to fill areas to form a smooth surface. In electrical work, solder is used to connect wires together or to fasten wires to various components.

Solder is an alloy of lead and tin. Rosin core solder is used for electrical repairs. Acid core solder is used for non-electrical repairs.

Hacksaws

Hacksaws are used to cut metal. As shown in Figure 3-57, a hacksaw consists of a metal frame and a detachable cutting blade. Different length frames are available, and some frames are made adjustable, allowing various size blades to be used. Hacksaw blades are available in 8″, 10″, and 12″ lengths. The 10″ and 12″ lengths are most frequently used in automotive work.

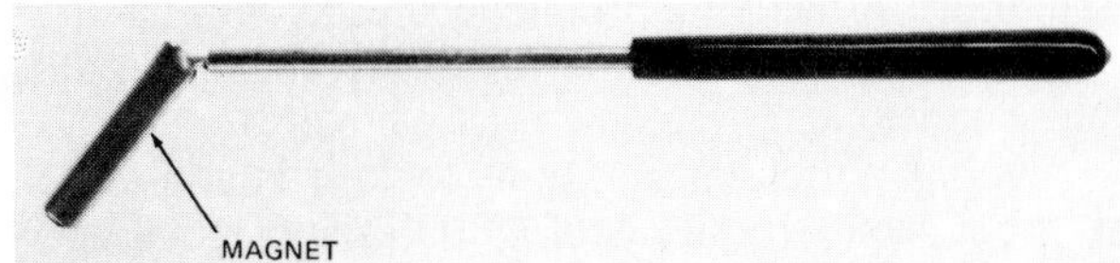

Figure 3-55. A magnetic retrieving tool can be used to remove items from restricted areas.

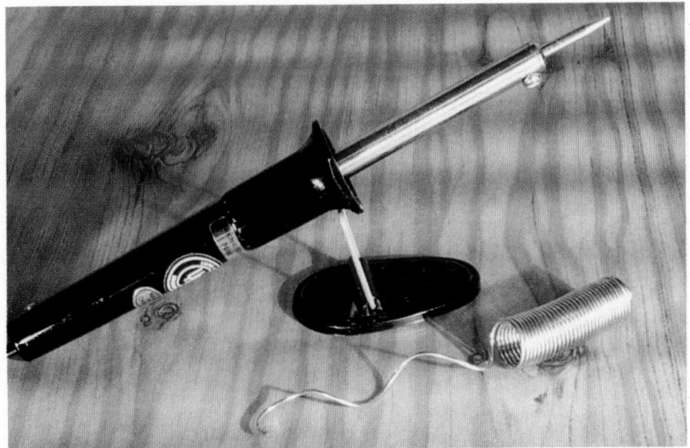

Figure 3-56. A typical electric soldering iron.

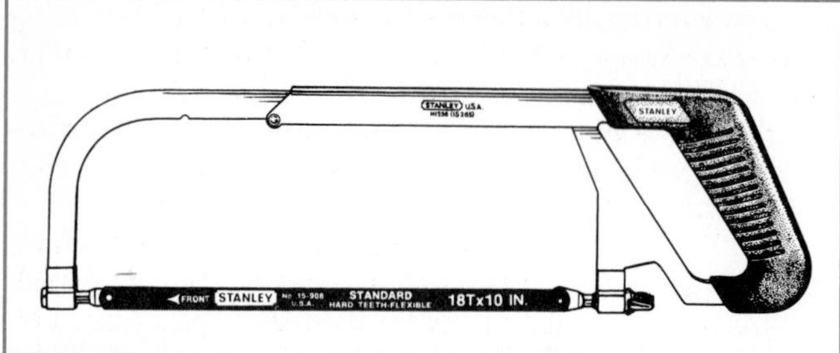

Figure 3-57. A typical hacksaw consists of a metal frame and a blade.

Hacksaw blades are made of high-grade tool steel, which is hardened and tempered. There are two types of blades: the all-hard blade and the flexible blade. All-hard blades are hardened throughout, while only the teeth of flexible blades are hardened.

The blades are provided with holes at both ends for installation on the pins on the frame. To adjust the tension of the blade and secure it tightly in the frame, the position of one of the pins is adjustable. This adjustment is made by either turning a wing nut or by turning the frame's handle.

The "set" of a saw refers to the amount the teeth extend out in opposite directions from the sides of the blade. The teeth of all hacksaw blades are "set" to provide clearance for the blade.

Blades for hand-operated hacksaws are available with 14, 18, 24, and 32 teeth per inch. It is important that the number of teeth per inch be considered when selecting a hacksaw blade for a particular job, Figure 3-58. Also, thought must be given to whether the all-hard or flexible blade is more suitable for a particular job.

In general, an all-hard blade is considered best for sawing brass, cast iron, steel, and other heavy stock. For cutting hollow shapes and metals of light section, such as channel iron, tubing tin, copper, aluminum, or babbitt, a flexible blade is preferable.

The most effective cutting speed is about one stroke per second. When the material is nearly cut through, the pressure on the blade should be reduced to prevent the teeth from catching. When cutting thin stock, it is advisable to clamp it between two pieces of wood or soft metal and to saw through all three pieces. This will prevent the saw from sticking and will prevent damage to the workpiece.

Hacksaw blade manufacturers recommend that 14-tooth saws be used for cutting soft steel, brass, cast iron, and stock of heavy cross section. For cutting drill rod, light angles, high-speed steel, tool steel, and small solids, 18-tooth blades are recommended. Use 24-tooth blades for cutting brass tubing, heavy BX cable, iron pipe, metal conduit, and drill rod. For cutting thin tubing, sheet metal, light BX cable, channels, etc., 32-tooth blades are suggested.

After selecting the correct blade for the material being cut, place it on the pins of the hacksaw frame with the teeth pointing *toward* the front of the frame. Then stretch the blade tightly in the frame.

If an accurate cut is to be made, it is advisable to mark the stock with a scribe and nick the work with a file. The nick will make it easier for the saw to start cutting and also ensure accuracy. Make sure the work is held securely in a vise, with the line to be cut as close to the vise jaws as possible. Use sufficient pressure on the saw when starting

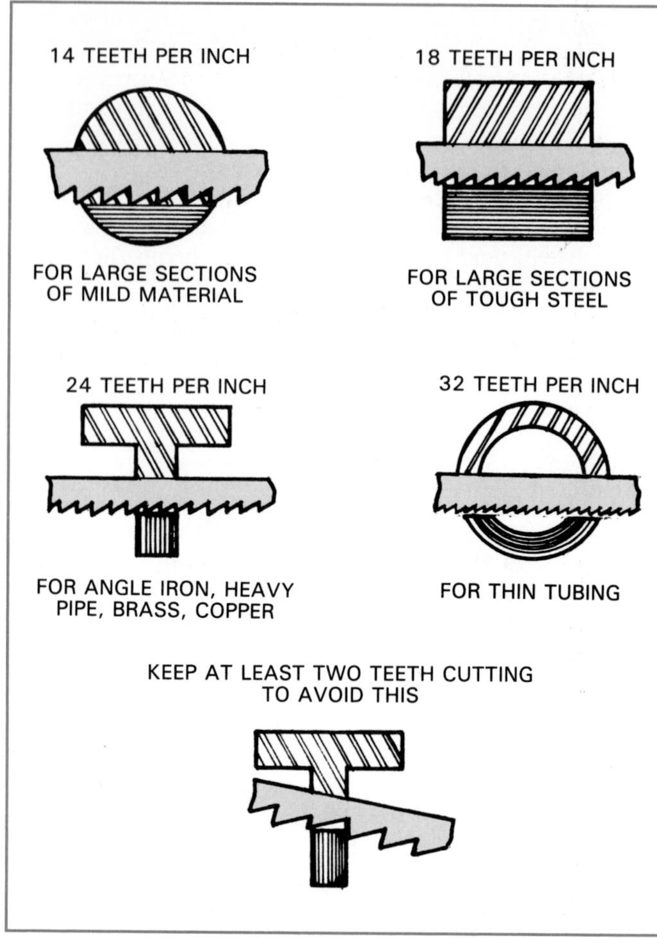

Figure 3-58. The type of metal to be cut determines the type of hacksaw blade.

the cut, so that the saw teeth immediately begin to bite into the metal. The hacksaw blade should be held vertically and moved forward with a light, steady stroke. At the end of the stroke, relieve the pressure and draw the saw straight back. See Figure 3-59.

Reamers

Reamers are used to enlarge or smooth holes. They create a much smoother finish than a drill. Figure 3-60

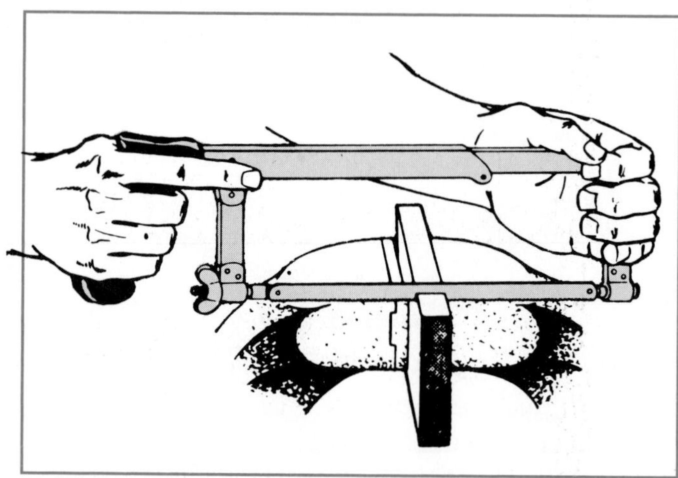

Figure 3-59. The correct method of using a hacksaw.

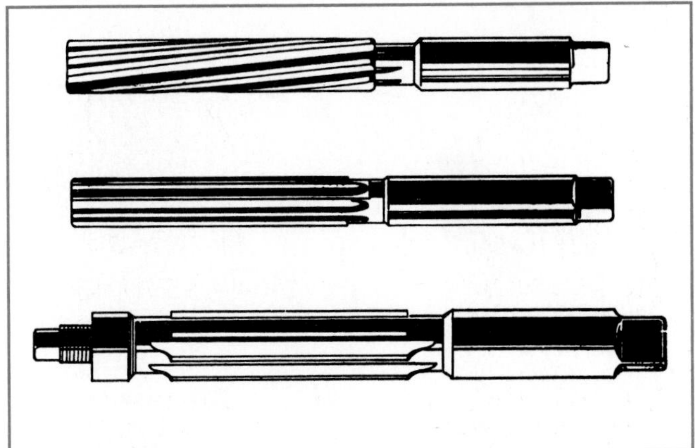

Figure 3-60. A–Spiral flute reamer. B–Straight flute reamer. C–Adjustable reamer.

shows two solid reamers–a straight flute reamer and a spiral flute reamer–and an adjustable reamer. The spiral flute reamer is more expensive than the straight flute reamer. Its advantage is that it has less of a tendency to chatter.

Solid reamers are available in standard sizes and also can be obtained in size variations of .001″ for special work. Adjustable reamers give more flexibility, but care must be taken when adjusting the size of the reamer to be sure it is correctly set. A micrometer should be used for this purpose.

Adjustable reamers are usually available in standard sizes from 1/4″ to 1″ in 1/32″ increments. They are designed to allow the blades to expand by 1/32″. For example, a 1/4″ adjustable reamer will cover hole sizes ranging from 1/4″ to 9/32″.

Taps and Dies

Taps, Figure 3-61, and dies, Figure 3-62, are thread-cutting tools. A ***tap*** is used to cut internal threads in holes, while a ***die*** is used to cut external threads on bolts, studs, or rods.

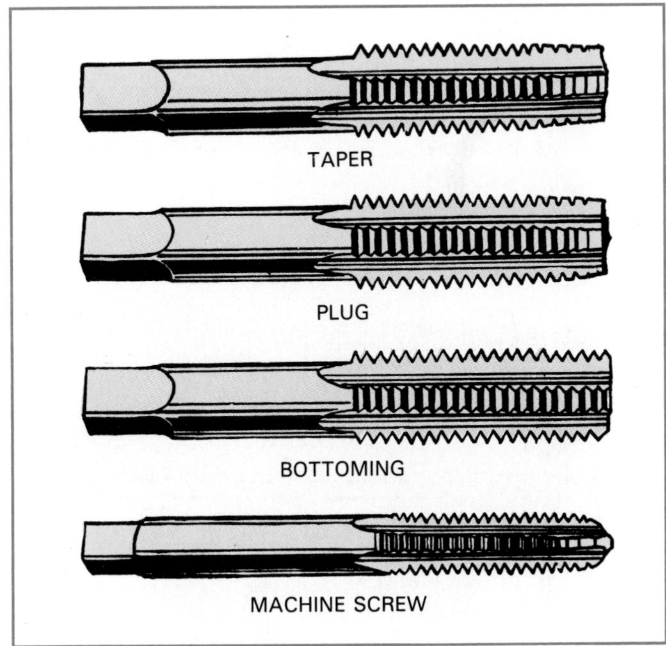

Figure 3-61. Various sizes of taps are used when repairing automobiles.

There is special terminology used when discussing threads, bolts, and nuts, Figure 3-63. To avoid confusion, it is essential that technicians know these terms.

The *major diameter*, also known as the outside diameter, is the largest diameter of the thread. The *minor diameter* is the diameter taken at the base of the thread.

The *pitch* of the thread is the distance from a point on one screw thread to a corresponding point on the next thread, measured parallel to the axis of the fastener, Figure 3-63. You can calculate the pitch (fine threads are hard to measure) by dividing one inch by the number of threads per inch.

If you want to drill and tap a hole, you have to drill the hole to the correct diameter for the particular tap. The drill used for this purpose is called a *tap drill.* Thread size, thread series, and tap drill required for a variety of threaded holes are given in Figure 3-64.

If you want to drill a hole through which a bolt is to be inserted, the drill is known as a *clearance drill,* or *body drill.*

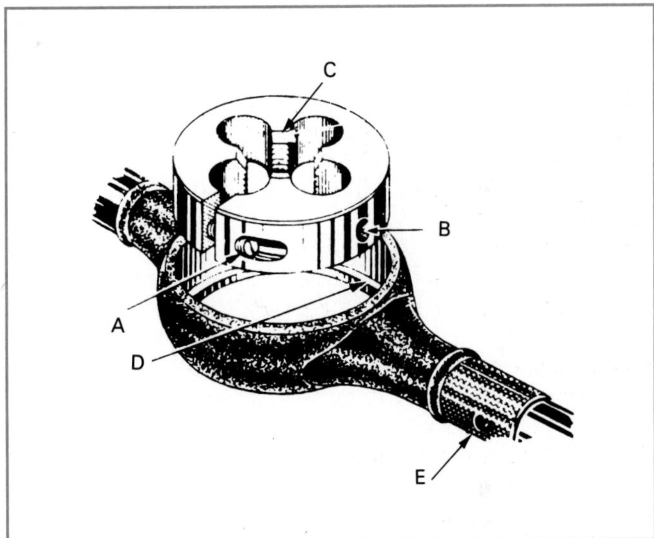

Figure 3-62. A die is used for cutting external threads. A–Adjusting screw. B–Drive hole. C–Cutting edge. D–Shoulder. E–Handle.

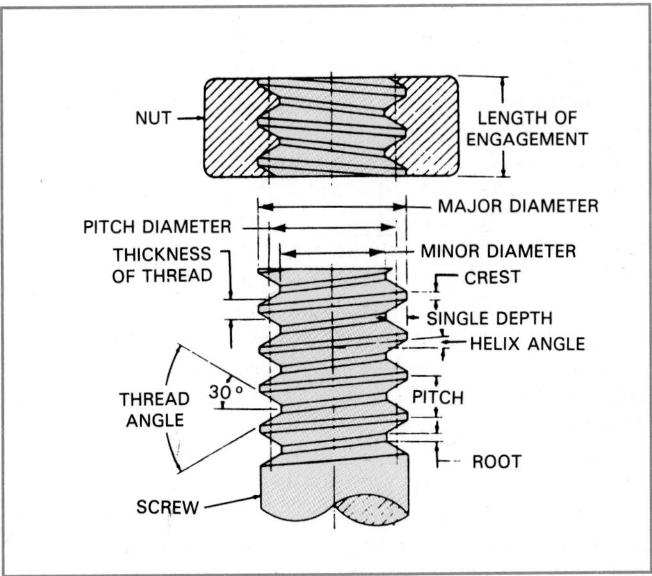

Figure 3-63. Nomenclature of screw threads.

Nominal size	Thr'd series	Major diameter, inches	Root diameter, inches	Tap drill to produce approx. 75% full thread	Decimal equivalent of tap drill
0–80	N. F.	.0600	.0438	3/64	.0469
1–64	N. C.	.0730	.0527	53	.0595
72	N. F.	.0730	.0550	53	.0595
2–56	N. C.	.0860	.0628	50	.0700
64	N. F.	.0860	.0657	50	.0700
3–48	N. C.	.0990	.0719	47	.0785
56	N. F.	.0990	.0758	45	.0820
4–40	N. C.	.1120	.0795	43	.0890
48	N. F.	.1120	.0849	42	.0935
5–40	N. C.	.1250	.0925	38	.1015
44	N. F.	.1250	.0955	37	.1040
6–32	N. C.	.1380	.0974	36	.1065
40	N. F.	.1380	.1055	33	.1130
8–32	N. C.	.1640	.1234	29	.1360
36	N. F.	.1640	.1279	29	.1360
10–24	N. C.	.1900	.1359	25	.1495
32	N. F.	.1900	.1494	21	.1590
12–24	N. C.	.2160	.1619	16	.1770
28	N. F.	.2160	.1696	14	.1820
1/4–20	N. C.	.2500	.1850	7	.2010
28	N. F.	.2500	.2036	3	.2130
5/16–18	N. C.	.3125	.2403	F	.2570
24	N. F.	.3125	.2584	I	.2720
3/8–16	N. C.	.3750	.2938	5/16	.3125
24	N. F.	.3750	.3209	Q	.3320
7/16–14	N. C.	.4375	.3447	U	.3680
20	N. F.	.4375	.3726	25/64	.3906
1/2–13	N. C.	.5000	.4001	27/64	.4219
20	N. F.	.5000	.4351	29/64	.4531
9/16–12	N. C.	.5625	.4542	31/64	.4844
18	N. F.	.5625	.4903	33/64	.5156
5/8–11	N. C.	.6250	.5069	17/32	.5312
18	N. F.	.6250	.5528	37/64	.5781
3/4–10	N. C.	.7500	.6201	21/32	.6562
16	N. F.	.7500	.6688	11/16	.6875
7/8–9	N. C.	.8750	.7307	49/64	.7656
14	N. F.	.8750	.7822	13/16	.8125
1–8	N. C.	1.0000	8376	7/8	.8750
14	N. F.	1.0000	9072	15/16	.9375

Figure 3-64. Tap chart shows the size hole needed for a specific tap size.

Taps and dies are marked according to the type and diameter thread they will cut. For example, an 8-32 is designed to cut 32 threads per inch on No. 8 stock.

When tapping a hole with a tap or cutting a thread with a die, considerable care is required. When using a tap or die, reverse the direction the tool is turned periodically to free the tool of chips and also recut the threads. Forcing the tool will result in tool breakage, ruined parts, and poor threads.

When threading steel parts, a lubricant such as lard oil should be used. Kerosene is preferred for use with aluminum. No lubricant is required for threading brass or cast iron.

Cleaning Equipment

Cleaning parts is a basic requirement of all automotive service work. Having clean parts not only speeds the work, but also aids greatly in locating flaws and wear. A number of essential ***cleaning tools*** are illustrated in Figures 3-65 and 3-66.

Cleaning tools such as scrapers and putty knives are hand tools, while certain brushes are designed for hand use and others are power driven. When using power driven wire brushes, goggles should be worn for safety's sake.

After excess dirt has been removed with wire brushes and scrapers, a *parts washer* can be used to clean remaining oil and grease from components. See Figure 3-67.

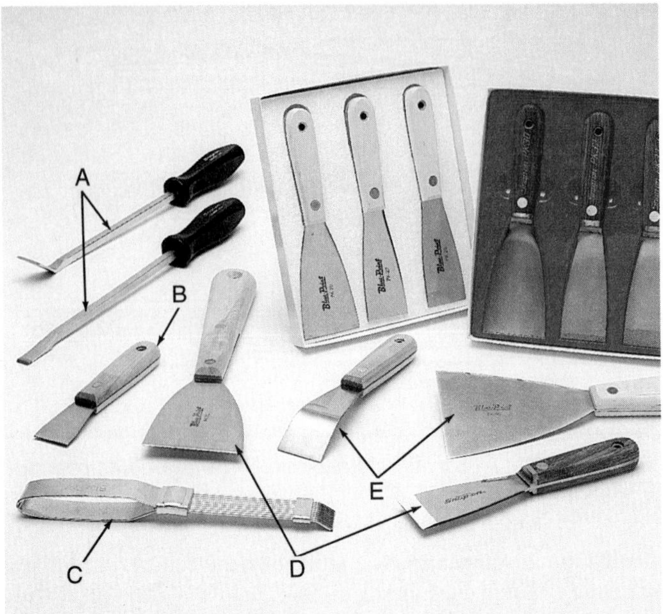

Figure 3-65. Various cleaning tools. A–Rigid carbon scrapers. B–Gasket scraper. C–Flexible carbon scraper. D–General-purpose scrapers. E–Putty knives. (Snap-on Tools Corp.)

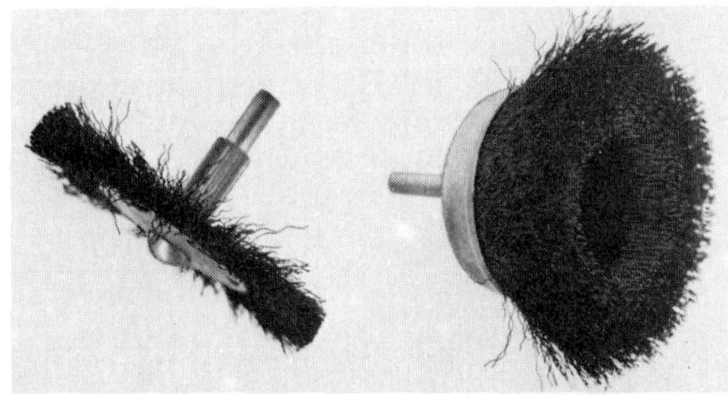

Figure 3-66. These wire brushes are designed to be used with an electric drill.

Figure 3-67. This parts cleaner can be used to remove grease and oil buildup from automotive components. (Snap-on Tools Corp.)

Chapter 3–Review Questions

Write answers on a separate sheet of paper. Do not write in this book.

1. The size of open-end wrenches increases in:
   (A) 1/16″ steps.
   (B) 1/32″ steps.
   (C) 1/8″ steps.
   (D) 1/4″ steps.
2. What is the main reason for using a box wrench?
3. List the three standard size drives for socket wrenches.
4. Why are torque wrenches needed?
5. A Torx screwdriver is similar to a Phillips screwdriver. True or False?
6. Interlocking joint pliers are designed to:
   (A) lock channels.
   (B) have adjustable openings of different sizes and, at the same time, allow the jaws remain parallel.
7. The end of a Phillips-type screwdriver is a:
   (A) flat blade.
   (B) pointed end with four grooves.
   (C) fluted end.
8. An Allen wrench has:
   (A) four sides.
   (B) six sides.
   (C) eight sides.
9. The rounded end of a machinist's hammer is known as the _____.
10. A cape chisel is used to cut:
   (A) narrow grooves.
   (B) rivet heads.
   (C) tool steel.
11. When using a chisel, it should be held:
   (A) tightly in the hand.
   (B) with a pair of slip-joint pliers.
   (C) loosely in the hand.
12. A magnetic screwdriver has interchangeable bits. True or False?
13. A file with one row of teeth that cross another row of teeth is called a:
   (A) crisscross file.
   (B) double-cut file.
   (C) Vixen-cut file.
14. A file with a single row of parallel teeth is called a _____.
15. When filing soft steel, which type file should be used first?
   (A) A bastard file.
   (B) A smooth-cut file.
   (C) A second-cut file.
16. Solder is an alloy of:
   (A) lead and tin.
   (B) lead and zinc.
   (C) tin and zinc.
   (D) lead and cadmium.
17. Hacksaw blades are made of:
   (A) high grade tool steel.
   (B) chilled cast iron.
   (C) carbaloy.
18. List the usual lengths of blades used in hacksaws.
19. Which saw blade is recommended to cut soft steel and cast iron?
   (A) 16 tooth.
   (B) 32 tooth.
   (C) 24 tooth.
   (D) 14 tooth.
20. A tap is used to cut external threads. True or False?

A tool storage unit, such as the one shown above, should be used to help keep tools secure and organized. (Snap-on Tools Corp.)

A variety of fasteners, seals, and gaskets is used in the manufacture of late-model vehicles. (Chrysler)

Chapter 4
Fasteners, Seals, and Gaskets

After studying this chapter, you will be able to:

- ❍ List the various types of fasteners used in the automobile.
- ❍ Determine which fastener is appropriate for a specific job.
- ❍ Explain how to select and measure a bolt.
- ❍ Describe the different methods of repairing threads.
- ❍ Select the appropriate seal for a specific job.
- ❍ Describe the various lubricants and sealers used in an automobile and list their applications.
- ❍ Demonstrate the steps in preparing a new gasket for installation.

Fasteners

There are many different devices used to fasten parts together in the modern automobile. These devices range from simple bolts and nuts to high-tech adhesives. You should be able to identify the various types of fastening devices and know when they are used.

Threaded Fasteners

There are several factors involved in describing bolts, cap screws, machine screws, sheet metal screws, and other ***threaded fasteners*** Figure 4-1. You need to know the length of the fastener, the type of head, the number of threads per unit length, and whether measurements are in inches or millimeters when ordering replacement parts.

Basically, ***bolts*** and ***screws*** are externally threaded fasteners, Figure 4-2. A *cap screw* is usually tightened with a wrench, Figure 4-3, while a *machine screw* is torqued with a screwdriver. The machine screw is smaller in diameter than the cap screw.

The diameter of a cap screw usually is measured in fractions of an inch, while the diameter of a machine screw is given in nominal size, which is represented by number (such as No. 8, No. 10, etc.) or by a fraction or decimal equivalent. Common types of machine screw heads are shown in Figure 4-1.

A ***stud,*** Figure 4-4A, is threaded on both ends. One end is screwed into a threaded hole. A part to be assembled is placed in position on the stud, and then a nut is placed on the exposed end of the stud. When tightened, the parts are held together, Figure 4-4B.

A popular fastening device is the familiar *sheet metal screw,* or *self-tapping screw,* Figure 4-5. Because of its fluted or tapered point, it cuts its own threads as it is screwed into sheet metal. Sheet metal screws are used extensively for holding two metal parts together, Figure 4-6.

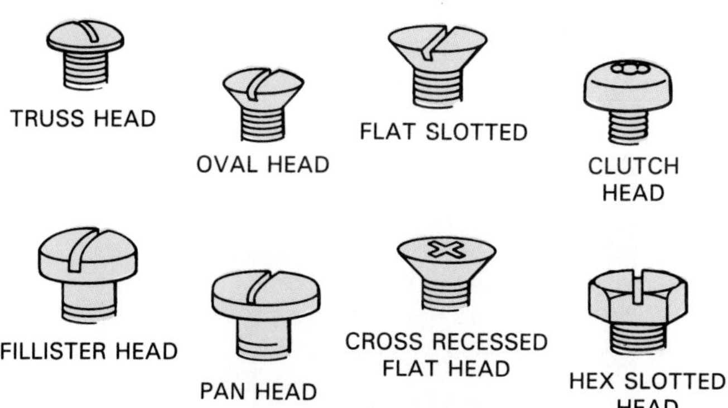

Figure 4-1. Various types of machine screw heads.

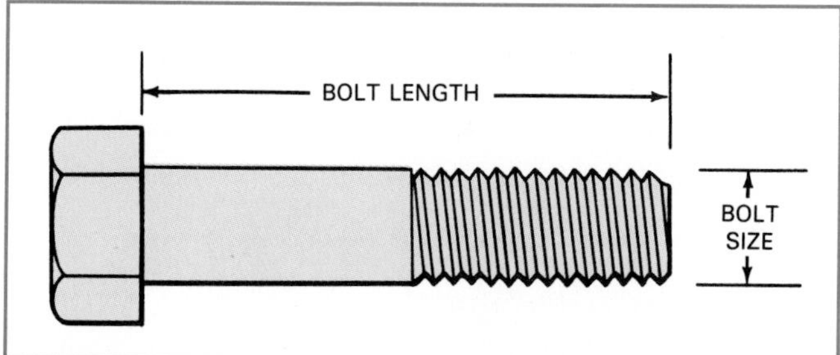

Figure 4-2. A bolt has a hex head and external threads. (Deere & Co.)

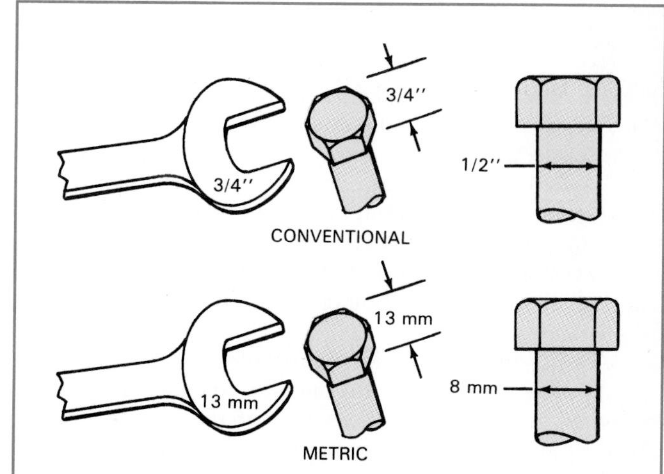

Figure 4-3. The bolt diameters are 1/2″ and 8 mm respectively. However, the size of the hex, or wrench size, is 3/4″ and 13 mm respectively.

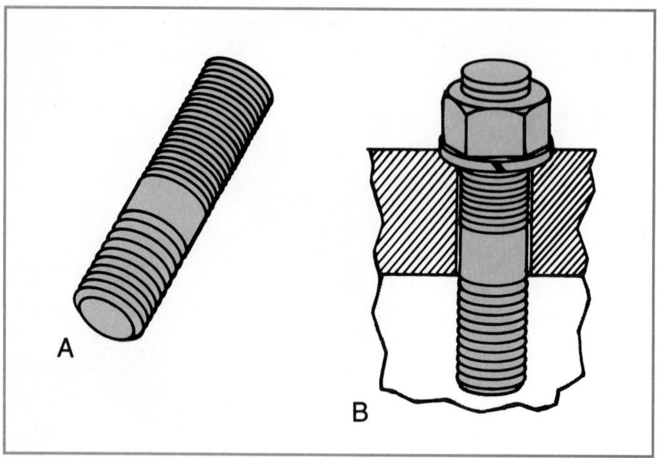

Figure 4-4. A stud has threads at each end and has no head. (Deere & Co.)

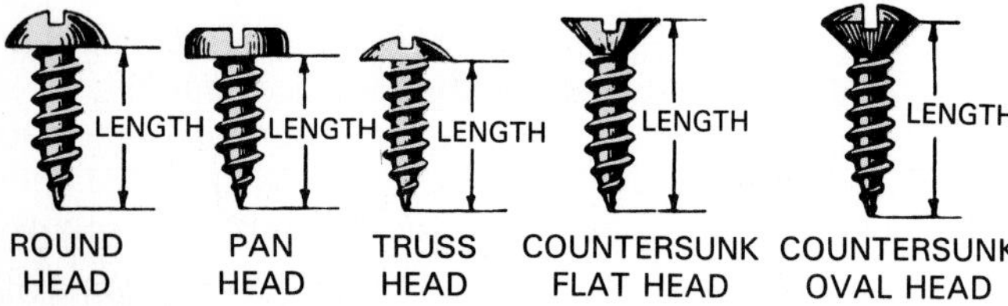

Figure 4-5. Types of sheet metal screws.

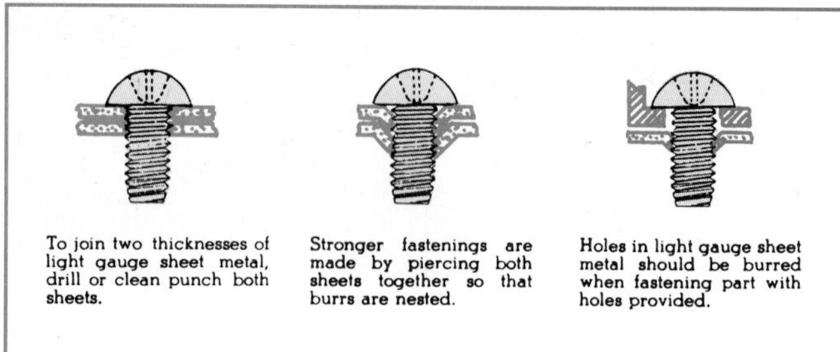

Figure 4-6. Different methods of using sheet metal screws.

A hole is simply punched or drilled into the sheet metal, and then the screw is turned into the hole.

Setscrews are designed to lock and position parts in position. Setscrews are hardened and have different types of heads and ends.

Setscrews are frequently used to secure a pulley to a shaft. In order to prevent the pulley from slipping, the shaft is usually spotted or slightly counterbored to take the point of the setscrew.

Various types of ***nuts*** are illustrated in Figure 4-7. *Hexagonal nuts* are generally used in the automotive field. The *castellated nut* is tightened on a bolt or threaded shaft. Then a cotter key is inserted through the castles of the nut and through a hole in the bolt or shaft. This prevents the nut from loosening.

A *wing nut,* Figure 4-7, is installed finger tight. It is used in places where the nut must be removed frequently and where torque is not necessary. *Cap nuts* are decorative nuts used in such places where conventional nuts would be unsightly.

There are several types of *self-locking nuts.* As the name implies, self-locking nuts are designed to resist loosening caused by vibration. The self-locking nut shown in Figure 4-8 has a composition plug which, when forced against the threads, prevents the nut from turning.

The *palnut* is a locking device, Figure 4-9, that is stamped from thin sheet steel and designed to bind against the threads of the bolts when installed. The palnut is turned down to make firm contact with the regular nut, then it is given an additional half turn. The regular nut must be torqued to the specified amount before the palnut is installed.

Lock washers are also designed to prevent nuts from coming loose. These washers are available in several different forms, Figure 4-10. A conventional flat washer, also shown in Figure 4-10, is used under the nut to prevent galling of the surface contacted.

Measuring Threads

The Unified National Thread Series is now the basic American standard for screw threads. The most commonly used types are Unified National Coarse (UNC) and Unified National Fine (UNF).

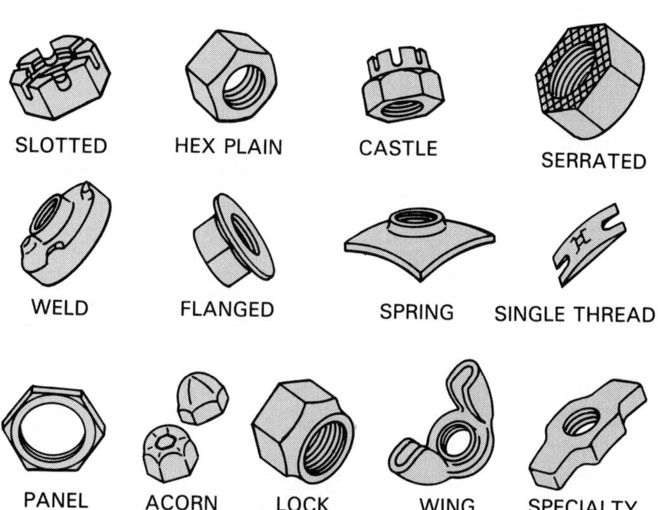

Figure 4-7. Different types of nuts.

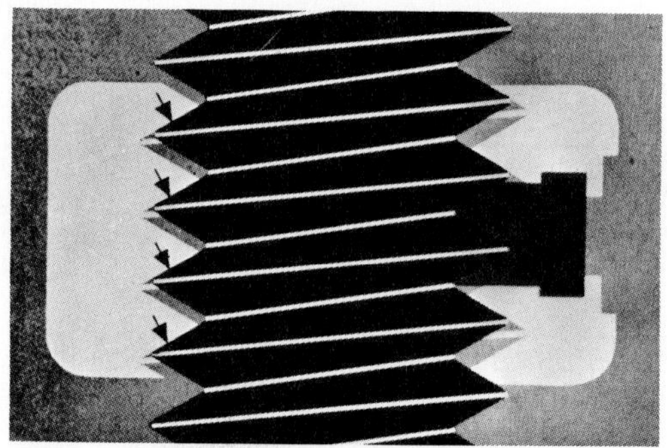

Figure 4-8. A self-locking nut has a composition plug, which is forced against the threads to prevent the nut from turning. (Deere & Co.)

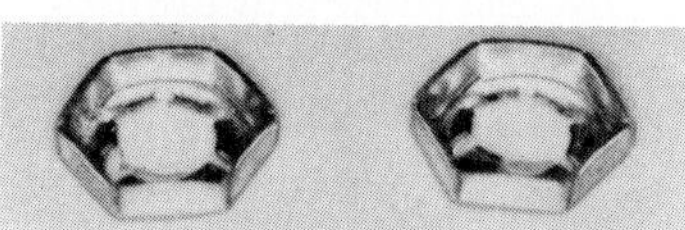

Figure 4-9. Palnuts are made of sheet metal and have an inner prong that engages the threads of a bolt to prevent the nut from turning.

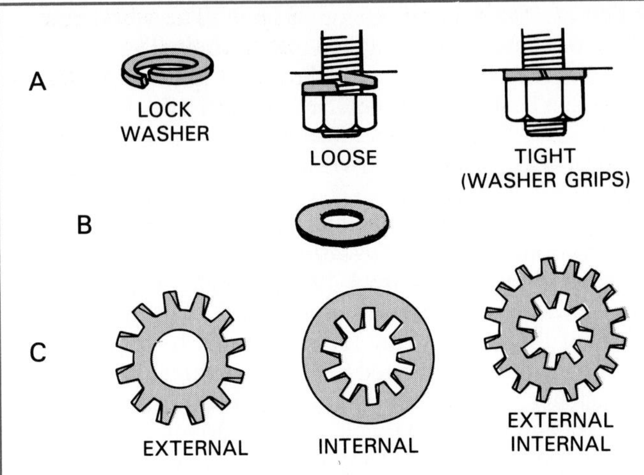

Figure 4-10. Various types of washers. A–A spring or lock washer. B–A typical flat washer. C–Tooth-type lock washers grip the metal. (Deere & Co.)

Details and terminology of threads were discussed in Chapter 3. In order to measure the number of threads per inch, or pitch if metric, a special gauge should be used, Figure 4-11.

Repairing Threads

When internal or external threads are stripped, often they can be repaired with a tap or die, Figure 4-12A. If the threads are severely damaged, other repair techniques can be used. One method is to drill out the thread and tap the hole to a larger size.

However, in some cases, this presents a problem. If a cylinder head bolt hole in the block was stripped, it would necessitate drilling out the head to accommodate the larger stud. In some cases, this could result in breaking into the water jacket.

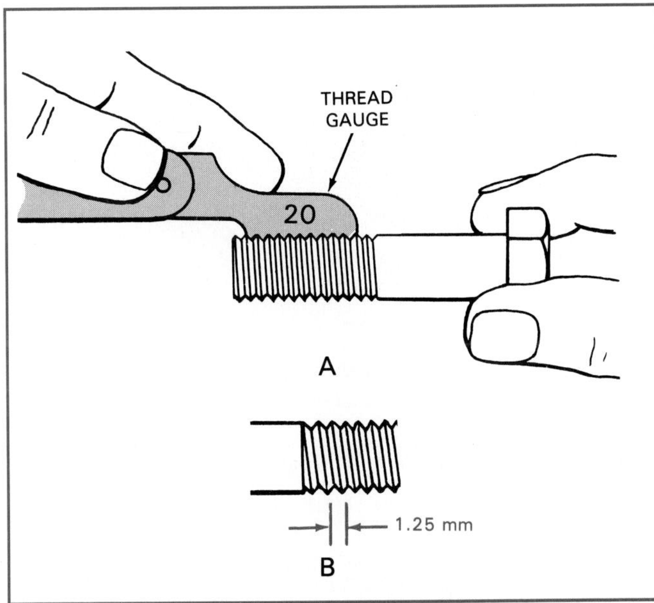

Figure 4-11. Using a thread gauge. A–When the thread gauge seats squarely on the threads, look at the number stamped on the gauge. This number indicates the number of teeth per inch. B–Pitch is the distance between the two crests. (Deere & Co.)

One method of thread repair provides a patented coil of wire that forms new threads. First, the stripped threads are drilled out of the hole, Figure 4-12B. Next, the hole is tapped, Figure 4-12C. Then, the coil is inserted, Figures 4-12D and 4-12E, restoring the threaded hole to its original condition, Figure 4-13.

Replacing Bolts and Nuts

Frequently, it is necessary to replace bolts and nuts when servicing an automobile. Be sure the new fasteners are equal in strength to the fasteners they are replacing.

The accompanying charts, Figures 4-14 to 4-17, show markings on bolt heads and nuts that indicate strength and bolt torque. The charts also show how to read the dimensions of a bolt.

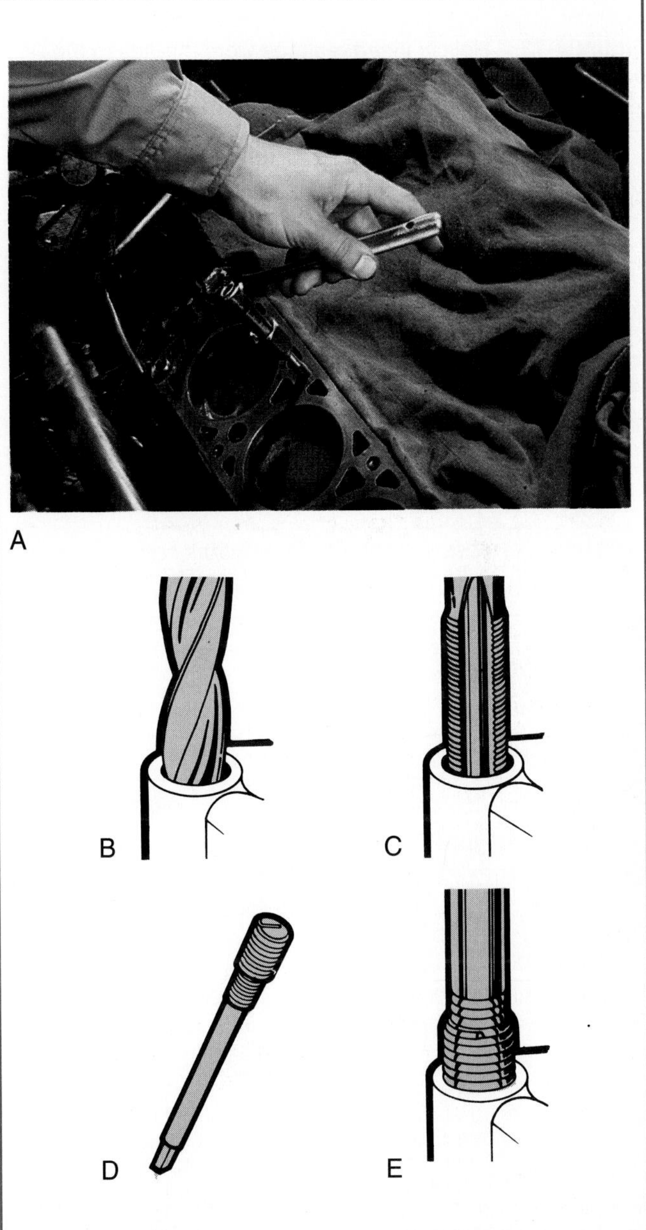

Figure 4-12. Different methods of thread repairs. A–Using a tap to repair threads in the engine block. (Fel-Pro, Inc.) B–Drill out the hole. C–Tap hole. D–Install insert on mandrel. E–Screw insert into tapped hole. (Oldsmobile)

Removing Broken Bolts

Every so often, a bolt will break off during removal or installation. When this happens, the broken portion remaining in the hole must be removed. This is usually accomplished with a screw extractor. The extractor, which has many spirals, is tapped into the broken bolt after a hole has been drilled at the top center of the broken fastener. This hole should be drilled at 1/2 the diameter of the bolt. The spirals on the extractor cause it to be wedged into the bolt. Then a wrench or socket is then applied to the hex head of the extractor and the broken bolt is backed out. See Figure 4-18.

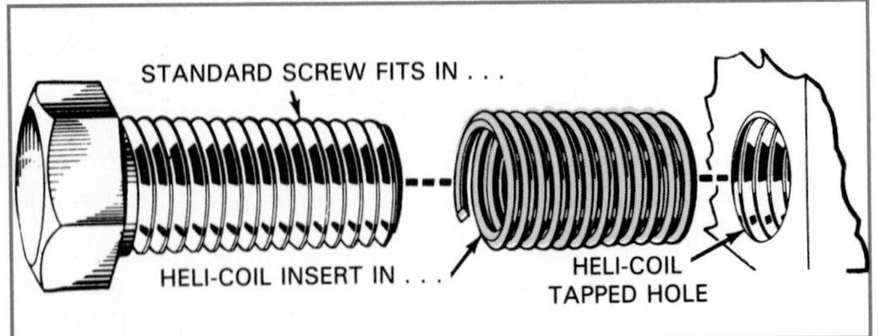

Figure 4-13. Helical insert restores worn threads to the original diameter.

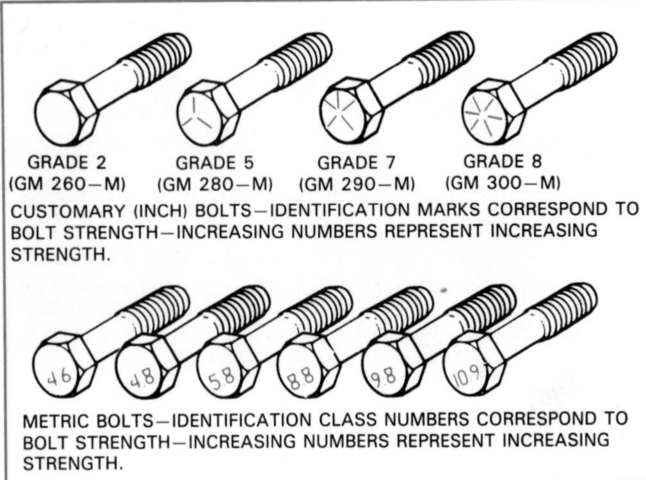

Figure 4-14. The strength of bolts is indicated on the top of the hex. (Cadillac)

BOLT TORQUE

Size	GRADE 5 In. Lbs. Ft. Lbs.	GRADE 5 Newton meters	GRADE 8 In. Lbs. Ft. Lbs.	GRADE 8 Newton meters
1/4-20	95 In. Lbs.	11	125 In. Lbs.	14
1/4-28	95 In. Lbs.	11	150 In. Lbs.	17
5/16-17	200 In. Lbs.	23	270 In. Lbs.	31
5/16-24	20 Ft. Lbs.	27	25 Ft. Lbs.	34
3/8-16	30 Ft. Lbs.	41	40 Ft. Lbs.	54
3/8-24	35 Ft. Lbs.	48	45 Ft. Lbs.	61
7/16-14	50 Ft. Lbs.	68	65 Ft. Lbs.	88
7/16-20	55 Ft. Lbs.	75	70 Ft. Lbs.	95
1/2-13	75 Ft. Lbs.	102	100 Ft. Lbs.	136
1/2-20	85 Ft. Lbs.	115	110 Ft. Lbs.	149
9/16-12	105 Ft. Lbs.	142	135 Ft. Lbs.	183
9/16-18	150 Ft. Lbs.	156	150 Ft. Lbs.	203
5/8-11	115 Ft. Lbs.	203	195 Ft. Lbs.	264
5/8-18	160 Ft. Lbs.	217	210 Ft. Lbs.	285
3/4-16	175 Ft. Lbs.	237	225 Ft. Lbs.	305

Figure 4-15. The greater the grade, the diameter of the bolt, and the number of teeth per inch, the greater the torque that can be applied to the bolt. (Chrysler)

Liquid Threadlock

To prevent nuts, bolts, and screws from loosening due to vibration, a ***liquid threadlock*** can be applied to the threaded fasteners, Figure 4-19. Although this prevents the threaded fastener from vibrating loose, it allows easy removal of the fastener should disassembly be required. The liquid threadlock is applied to the entire threaded portion of the fastener. The fastener is then torqued to specifications. A socket and ratchet, wrench, or screwdriver can be used to remove the fastener after any length of time.

Anti-seize Lubricant

Bolts and any connected metal components that are exposed to continuous heat can be "cold welded" together. To prevent this, an ***anti-seize lubricant*** should be applied to the bolt threads or the connecting metal, Figure 4-20. This is especially true of the threads on an oxygen sensor. If anti-seize lubricant is not placed on the threads, removal

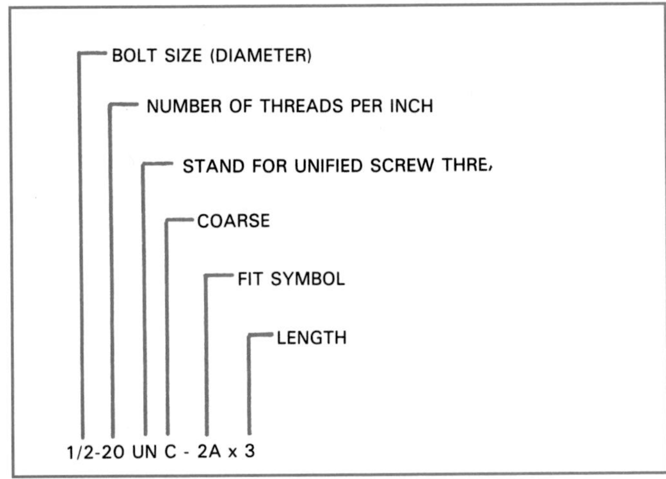

Figure 4-16. Deciphering the markings for an SAE bolt. (Deere & Co.)

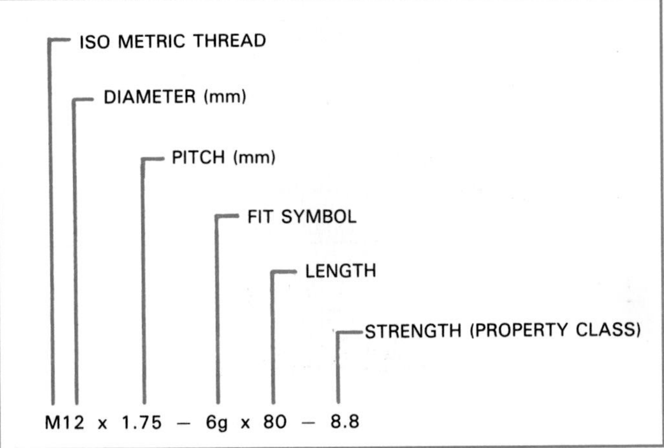

Figure 4-17. Deciphering the markings for a metric bolt. (Deere & Co.)

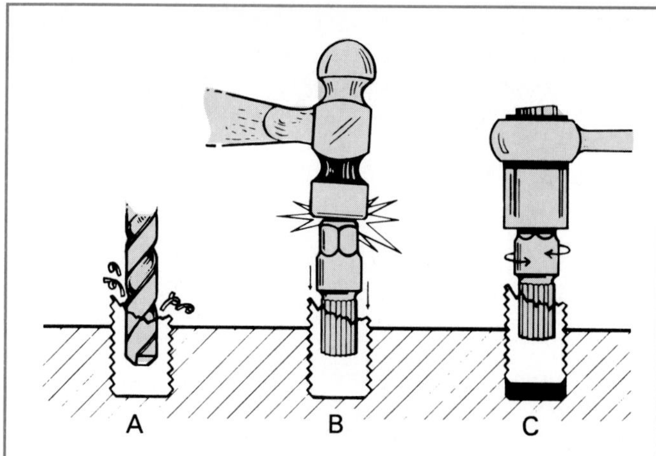

Figure 4-18. Removing a broken bolt. A–Drill a hole in the center of broken bolt. Drill size should be approximately 1/2 the diameter of broken bolt. B–Using a hammer, tap in the extractor in previously drilled hole of broken bolt. C–Using a wrench or ratchet, twist the extractor. This will bring the broken bolt out along with the screw extractor. (Lisle Co.)

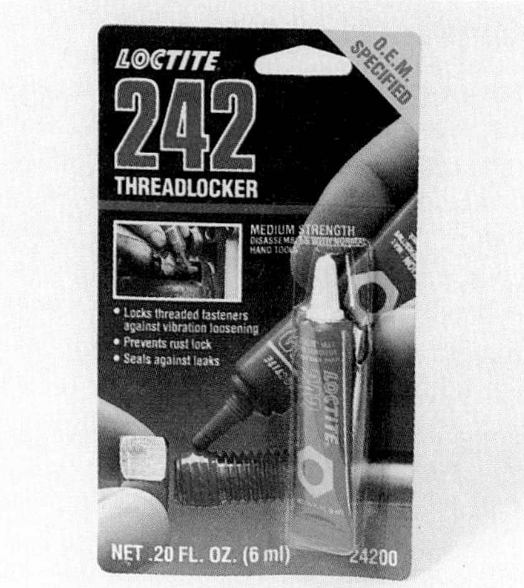

Figure 4-19. Liquid threadlock prevents threaded fasteners from vibrating loose.

Figure 4-20. Anti-seize lubricant is applied to the threads of fasteners, as well as to the connections of metal pipes that are exposed to continuous heat.

will be impossible after a period of driving time. Anti-seize lubricant can also be used on exhaust manifold bolts and other exhaust pipe connections. Remember, anti-seize compound is a lubricant, not a sealer.

Keys and Pins

Keys and ***pins*** are often used to prevent bolts, gears, and pulleys from spinning on their shafts. Keys used in automotive design include the Woodruff key, square key, and gib-head key, Figure 4-21. The key fits into a slot, or keyway, which is cut into both the shaft and the mating part, Figure 4-21. By design, the key extends into both the shaft and the mating part. This causes the parts to rotate as a unit.

The *cotter key,* also known as a *cotter pin,* Figure 4-22, is used with a castellated nut to prevent it from becoming loose. The cotter key is inserted through the castle of the nut and a hole in the bolt. The ends of the key are then bent back, and surplus ends are cut off. In addition to preventing nuts from coming loose, cotter keys are used with clevis pins and in the ends of control rods, such as those used to connect the accelerator pedal to the throttle lever.

Dowel pins and *taper pins,* Figure 4-23, are used to secure one part to another. A hole is drilled through the two parts, and the dowel or taper pin is driven into place.

Snap Rings

Snap rings, Figure 4-24, are employed to prevent endwise movement of cylindrical parts and shafts. There are both internal and external snap rings. An *internal snap ring* is used in a groove cut in a housing. An *external snap*

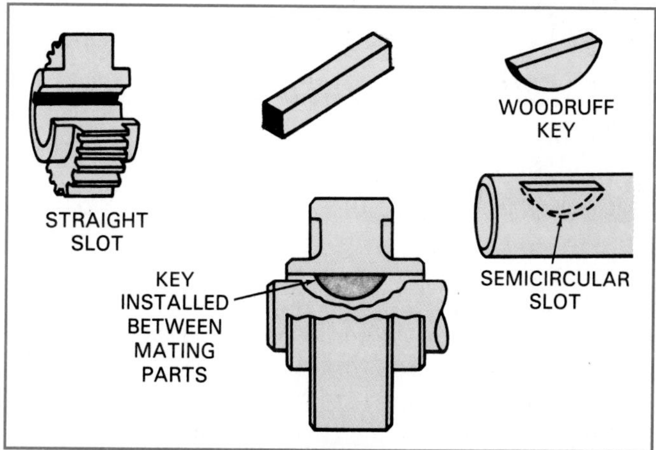

Figure 4-21. Woodruff key is placed in a semicircular slot. The slot on the inner diameter of the gear slides over the key and mates the two together. (Deere & Co.)

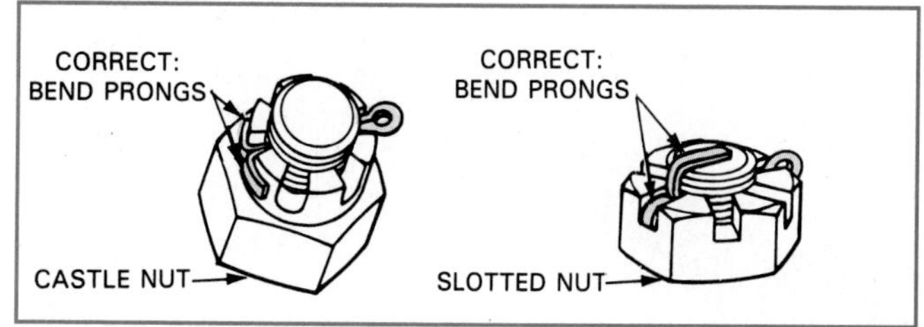

Figure 4-22. The cotter key prevents the nut from coming loose.

ring is designed to fit in a groove cut on the outside of a cylindrical shape, such as a shaft. Snap rings are used extensively in transmissions and transaxles.

Rivets

A ***rivet*** is a metal pin with a head at one end. It is designed to fasten two parts together. A *pop riveter* is a tool designed to install rivets when only one side of the parts to be joined can be reached, Figure 4-25. Rivets used in a hand-operated blind riveter are shown in Figure 4-26.

To install a blind rivet, drill a hole through the parts to be joined. Place the long stem of the rivet in the head of the tool and insert the short end in the hole in the parts. Squeeze the handle repeatedly to set the rivet and snap off its end.

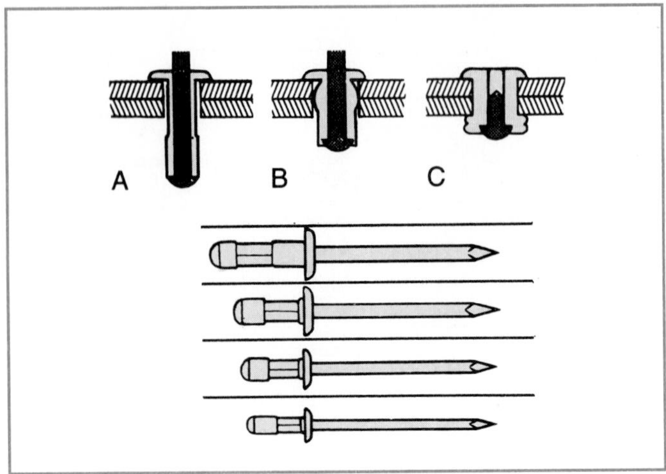

Figure 4-26. A–Rivet is placed into hole. B–Handle of riveter is squeezed and rivet starts to compress. C–Rivet is compressed and holds the two pieces of material together.

Adhesives

Adhesives are used in many areas of late-model vehicles. They are used to secure external moldings and emblems, hold weather strippings in place, and attach interior trim pieces. The properties of automotive adhesives vary, depending on the application. Some adhesives dry hard, while others remain pliable when dry.

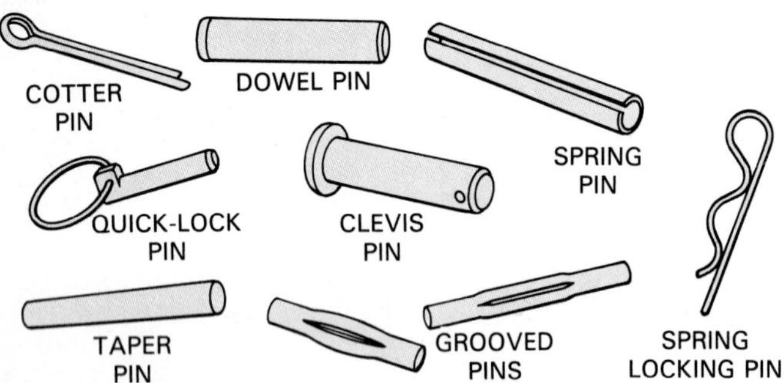

Figure 4-23. Pins come in different shapes and sizes. (Deere & Co.)

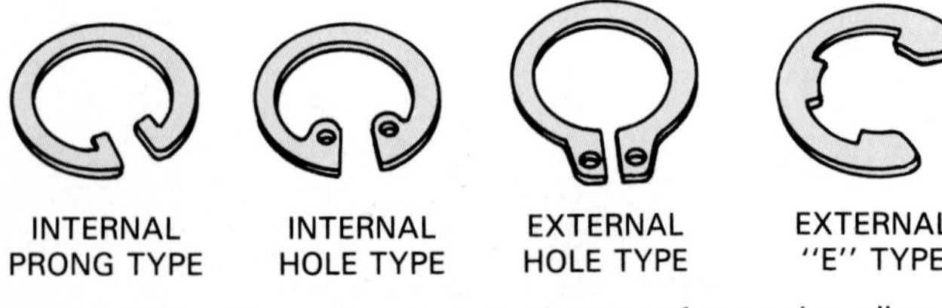

Figure 4-24. Snap rings require the use of snap ring pliers.

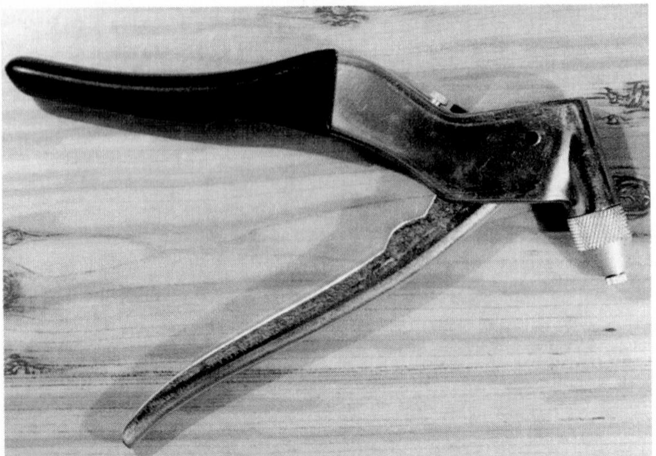

Figure 4-25. A pop riveter installs blind rivets.

Formed-in-place Sealants

Formed-in-place sealants can be used in place of some preformed gaskets, Figure 4-27. *Room temperature vulcanizing sealant (RTV)* is a formed-in-place sealant that is sometimes referred to as silicone sealer, Figure 4-28. It is clear in its pure form. However, a dye is sometimes added to make the sealer black, red, orange, blue, or copper colored. RTV is either an acid or an amine base. When RTV that is of the acidic formula is heated, it forms vapors that can interfere with the operation of the oxygen sensor. RTV can be used in place of paper, cork, or rubber gaskets. However, RTV *cannot* be used:

- In place of an intake manifold gasket.
- In place of a head gasket.
- On carburetors.
- On automatic transmissions.

To prevent oil leaks, a dab of RTV should be placed on the rear main bearing cap, Figure 4-29A. It can also be used where two gaskets or a gasket and a seal meet, Figure 4-29B.

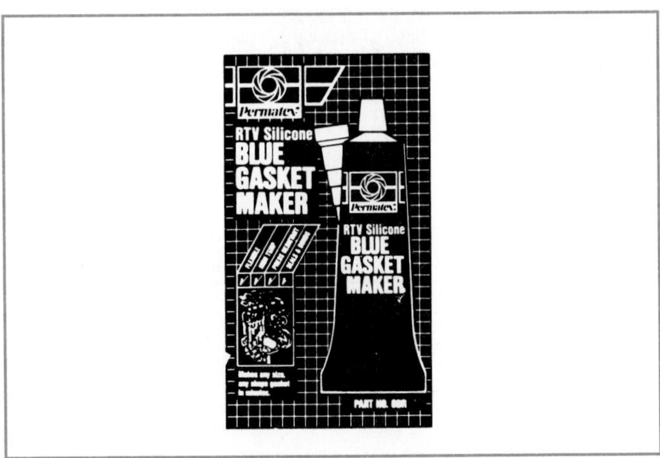

Figure 4-27. Silicone sealer can be used in place of conventional preformed gaskets for many areas that require a paper, rubber, or cork gasket.

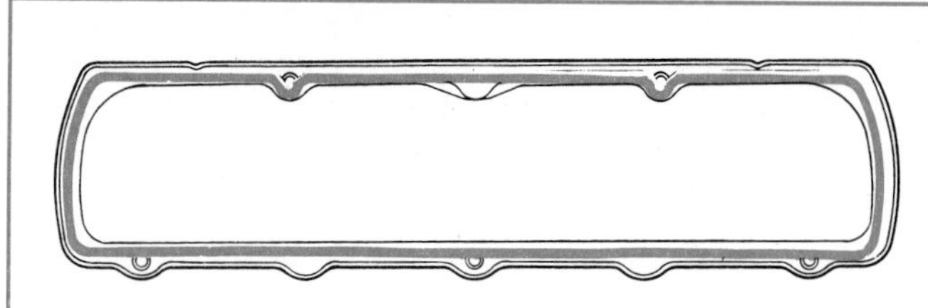

Figure 4-28. A typical RTV bead pattern used as a valve cover gasket. Bead diameter should be approximately 1/4". (Oldsmobile)

Some cylinder head bolts extend through a water jacket. The threads of these bolts must be coated with RTV or a suitable sealer, Figure 4-29C. If this is not done, coolant will seep past the threads and into the crankcase.

Anaerobic sealer is similar to RTV, but it can cure in the absence of air. This type of sealer can be used as a thread locking compounding or a retaining compound. It can also be used between the machined surfaces of rigid metal castings. However, it will not work on flexible flanges.

Seals

The purpose of any ***seal*** is to prevent a liquid from flowing into areas where it is not wanted. A rear axle shaft seal prevents rear axle oil from contaminating the brake linings. Valve seals prevent oil from entering the combustion chambers through the valve guides. There are several reasons for seal leaks. The seal may be installed backwards, it may be forced out of position, or it may simply be old and brittle. In some cases, a bushing or bearing may be so badly worn that it cannot control the oil flow. Consequently, the seal cannot handle the additional flow of oil. An example is when the rear axle bearing is worn, which may or may not be making noises, and the flow of oil to the seal is increased. The seal cannot handle this flood of oil, and some of the oil gets past the seal, even if the seal is good. Seals can be made of synthetic rubber, nylon, Teflon®, or steel.

O-rings

O-rings are doughnut-shaped seals that have a round cross section. They are generally made of neoprene. 0-rings are fitted into a groove between mating parts. The groove holds the O-rings in place. 0-rings are used where there is no rotational or axial movement of any kind, Figure 4-30. The 0-ring is usually used where a connection is made with a hose or tube fitting.

Square-cut Seals

Square-cut seals are doughnut-shaped seals that have a square cross section, Figure 4-31. The square-cut seal is made of neoprene and is used where there is slight axial movement and no rotational movement. The square-cut seal is used in the clutch packs of automatic transmissions and in disc brake calipers.

Sealing Rings

Like square-cut seals, ***sealing rings*** are doughnut shaped and have a square cross section. However, sealing rings are either made of Teflon or steel. The Teflon sealing

A

B

C

Figure 4-29. Other uses for silicone sealer. A–Applying silicone sealer to rear main bearing cap to prevent oil leakage. B–Whenever two gasket ends meet, a dab of silicone sealer should be added at this point to prevent oil leakage. C–Always apply a sealer to threads of a cylinder head bolt that extends into a water jacket, or coolant will seep past threads. (Fel-Pro, Inc.)

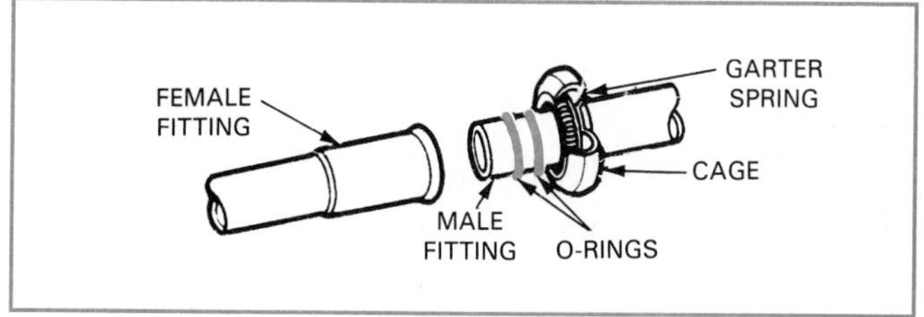

Figure 4-30. 0-rings are used where there is no axial or rotational movement. (Ford)

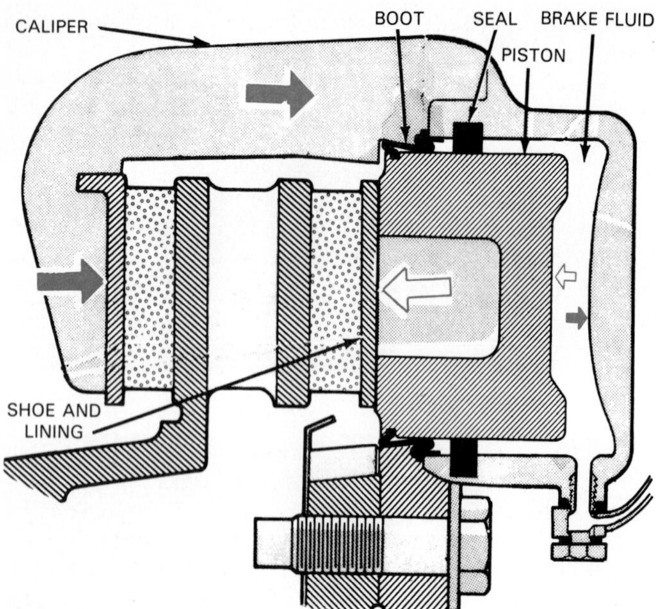

Figure 4-31. A square-cut seal is used where there is only axial movement, like a disc brake caliper. (Chrysler)

ring, Figure 4-32A, is distinguished by an angle cut. While the Teflon seal can conform to irregularities, the disadvantage is that metal particles can become embedded in the sealing surface, reducing its effectiveness. The steel sealing ring is distinguished by the ends that are hooked together, Figure 4-32B. Sealing rings are used where there is axial and rotational movement.

Shaft Seals

Shaft seals, or ***lip seals,*** Figure 4-33A, are usually made of Neoprene. Shaft seals are used against a shaft that rotates, Figure 4-33B. The shaft seal prevents the oil or lubricant from leaking out while the shaft turns. It also prevents dirt from reaching the lubricant. When the seal is doing its job, the seal can actually cut a groove into the shaft, as there is no lubrication at this point, Figure 4-34. This will only happen on high-mileage vehicles. When this occurs, the shaft must be reconditioned or replaced, as the oil will work its way under the seal at the groove.

Valve Seals

Valve seals are usually made of synthetic rubber, such as nitrile, polyacrylate, or viton. These seals are a synthetic rubber. Unfortunately, nitrile can only resist temperatures up to 250°F. The viton seal, however, can withstand temperatures up to 450°F. Since four-cylinder engines run hotter, the viton material must be used. Other seals will become brittle and crack, Figure 4-35.

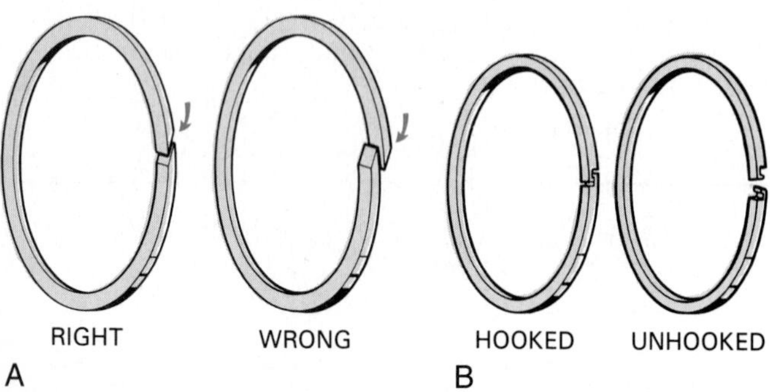

Figure 4-32. Different types of sealing rings. A–Teflon sealing rings have an angle cut. B–Metal sealing rings have an interlocking feature. (Oldsmobile)

Gaskets

A ***gasket*** compensates for small irregularities between two flat metal surfaces, preventing oil and coolant from leaking. In the case of a cylinder head gasket, combustion pressures are kept in the cylinder. Gaskets also dampen

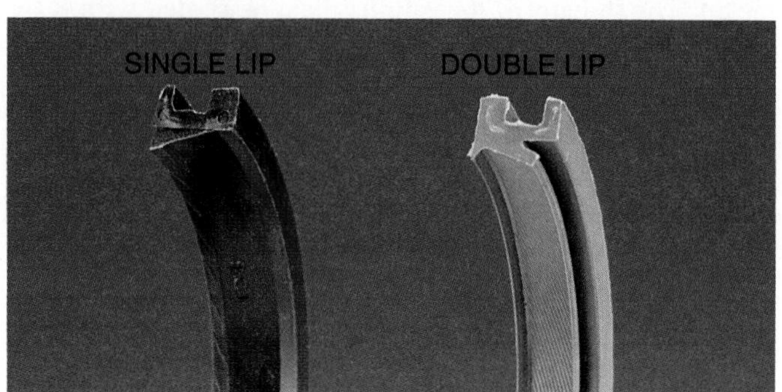

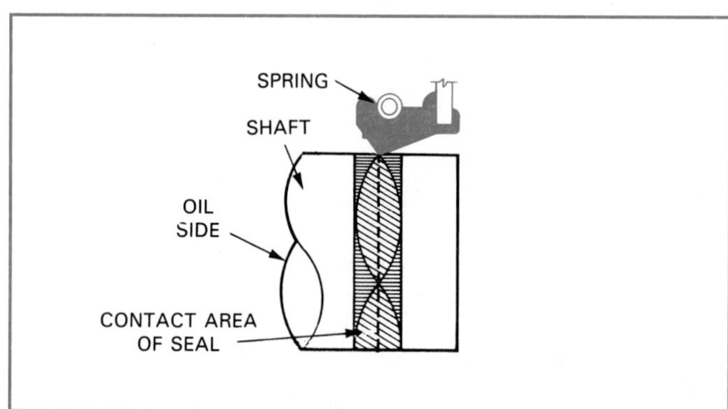

Figure 4-33. Shaft seals. A–Single and double lip seals. Double lip seal prevents dirt from tearing inner seal. B–Lip seal is used where there is rotational movement. (Fel-Pro, Inc., C-R Industries)

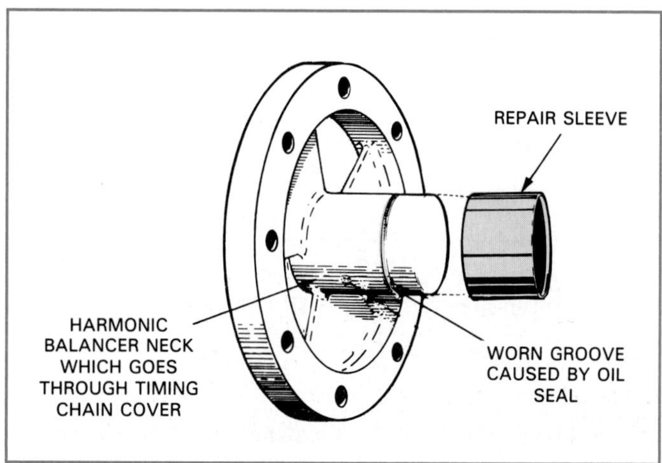

Figure 4-34. Groove caused by seal must be reconditioned.

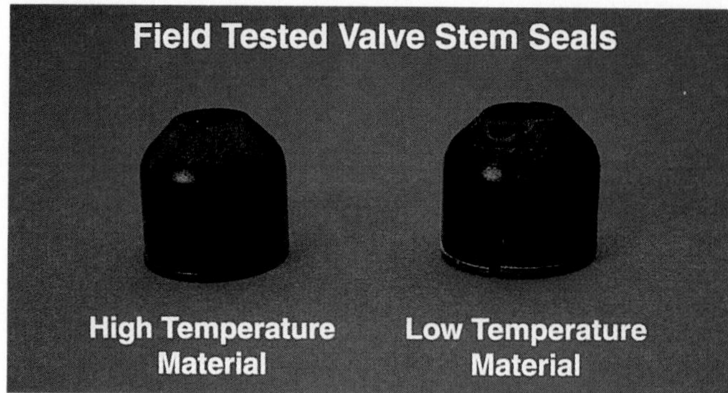

Figure 4-35. Most all valve stem seals look the same when they are new. If high quality is not selected, early failure will result. (Fel-Pro, Inc.)

vibration, act as spacers, and function as wear insulators. Gaskets can be made of steel, copper, pressed fiber, cork, rubber, silicon, graphite, etc. New gasket designs have been developed for use in bimetal engines that experience more movement between the block and the head.

The most common cause for gasket failure is overtightening of the bolts that hold the gasket between the metal surfaces, Figure 4-36. To prevent overtightening of the gaskets, some manufacturers incorporate metal washers in the bolt holes of the gasket. These metal washers limit the amount of torque that can be applied. Some auto manufacturers dimple the flange of the sheet metal that is bolted in place, Figure 4-37. This has the same effect as a washer placed in the bolt hole of the gasket. Some gaskets must be installed in a specific manner, Figure 4-38, while other gaskets do not.

Note: Never reuse a gasket. A used gasket will not form a proper seal when reinstalled.

Molded rubber gaskets prevent even minor oil leaks. Some rubber valve cover gaskets are slightly smaller than the surfaces they are designed to seal, which means that they must be stretched to fit the valve cover flanges. Molded rubber gaskets are one-piece units, which minimize the chance of leakage, Figure 4-39. However, molded rubber gaskets can only be used with flanges designed to accommodate them.

Figure 4-36. Overtightening of this valve cover gasket caused the gasket to bulge out. Look up torque specifications and use a torque wrench. (Fel-Pro, Inc.)

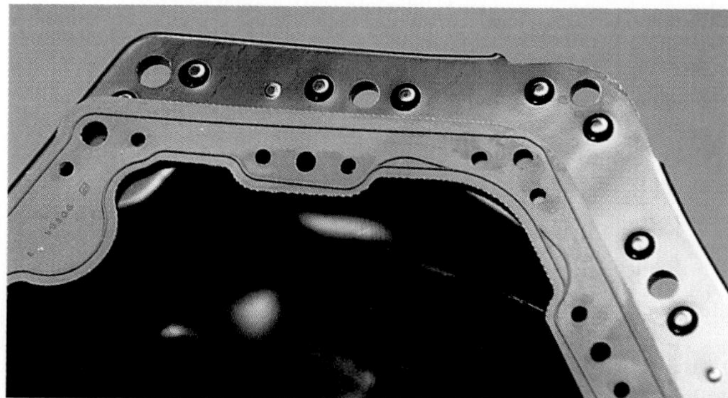

Figure 4-37. Dimples on this oil pan flange prevent the gasket from being overtightened. (Fel-Pro, Inc.)

Preparation for Gasket Installation

Before installing a gasket, clean both mating surfaces to the bare metal. All old gasket material must be removed, Figure 4-40. Check the mating surfaces for warpage, Figure 4-41. If the surface of the cylinder head is warped more than .006″, the head must be machined to obtain a flat surface. If more than .030″ must be removed from a head, the opposite head and the intake manifold on a V-type engine will have to be resurfaced. If this is not done, the bolt holes and passages will not align, Figure 4-42. If the oil pan or valve cover gasket flanges are bent, they must be straightened before installing the gasket, Figure 4-43. A gasket can only compensate for small irregularities between the flat mating surfaces.

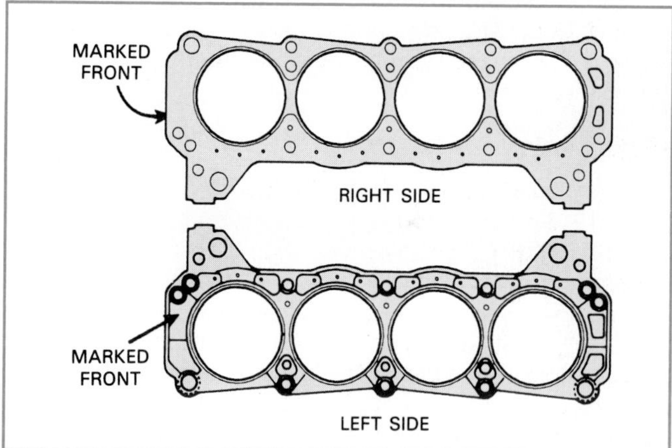

Figure 4-38. Some gaskets must be installed in a specific manner.

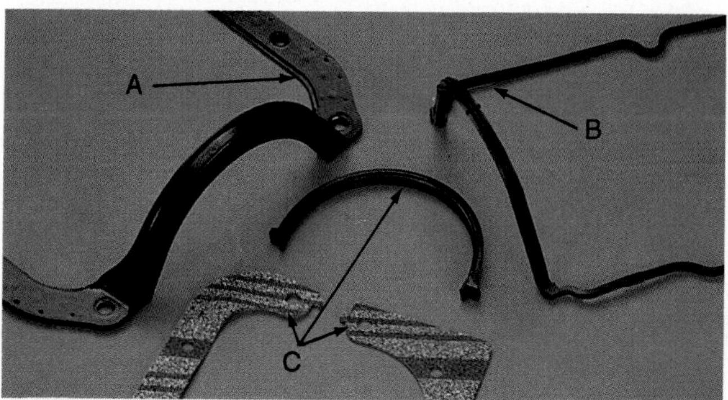

Figure 4-39. A–A one-piece molded rubber oil pan gasket prevents oil leakage. B–Conventional oil pan gasket has many places where oil can leak past. Silicone sealer must be used with this type of gasket. C–Molded rubber valve cover gasket. (Fel-Pro, Inc.)

A B

Figure 4-40. Before installing a new gasket, the mating surfaces must be cleaned of all old gasket material. A–Applying chemical gasket remover. B–Removing gasket material with a wire brush. (Fel-Pro, Inc.)

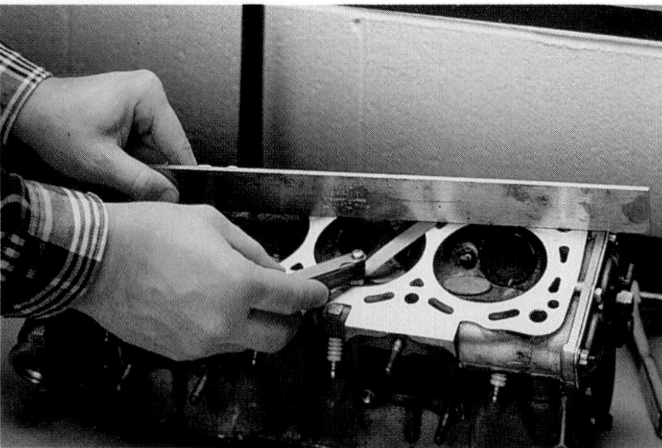

Figure 4-41. After cleaning the mating surfaces to bare metal, the surface must be checked for warpage. Place a feeler gauge between head and straightedge. (Fel-Pro, Inc.)

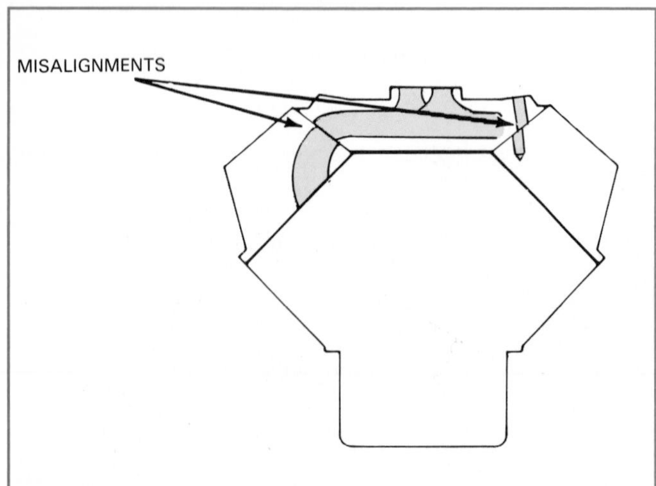

Figure 4-42. If more than .030 of an inch must be removed from a cylinder head, the remaining cylinder head on a V-type engine and intake manifold must also be resurfaced. If this is not done, the bolt holes and intake passages will not align. (Fel-Pro, Inc.)

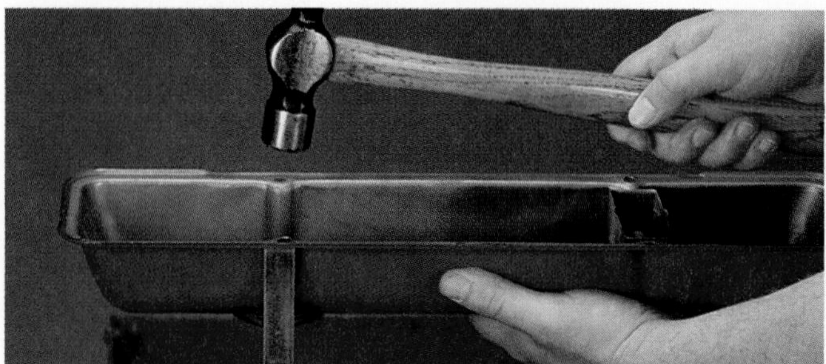

Figure 4-43. If valve cover or oil pan flanges are not flat, they must also be trued.

Chapter 4–Review Questions

Write your answers on a separate sheet of paper. Do not write in this book.

1. What is the major difference between a machine screw and a bolt?
2. A stud has threads on one end. True or False?
3. The largest diameter on a screw is known as the:
   (A) pitch diameter.
   (B) major diameter.
   (C) minor diameter.
   (D) None of the above.
4. Most bolts have a:
   (A) square head.
   (B) octagonal head.
   (C) hexagonal head.
   (D) round head.
5. What type of nut is used with a cotter key?
6. Name two methods used to keep nuts from working loose on a bolt.
7. Which can take more torque, a 7/16″ diameter, Grade 5 bolt, with 14 teeth per inch, or a 3/8″ diameter, Grade 8 bolt, with 24 teeth per inch?
8. A _____ is screwed down on another nut to keep it from getting loose.
9. Before using a sheet metal screw, it is necessary to tap the hole. True or False?
10. Silicone sealer can be used in place of a head gasket. True or False?
11. Stripped threads can:
    (A) not be repaired.
    (B) be repaired with tap or die.
    (C) be repaired with a helical insert.
    (D) Either B or C.
12. A square-cut seal is used where there is:
    (A) no axial or rotational movement.
    (B) axial movement only.
    (C) rotational movement only.
    (D) both rotational and axial movement.
13. Anti-seize lubricant should be used on the threads of an oxygen sensor. True or False?
14. RTV should be applied to the threads of cylinder head bolts that extend into the water jacket. True or False?
15. Before installing a new gasket, the mating surfaces must be:
    (A) cleaned of all old gasket material.
    (B) checked for warpage.
    (C) straightened or surfaced if warped.
    (D) All of the above.

Chapter 5
Measuring Instruments

After studying this chapter, you will be able to:

- ❍ List the different types of measuring instruments used when servicing automobiles.
- ❍ Explain how to read a micrometer.
- ❍ State the purpose of telescoping gauges.
- ❍ Demonstrate how to read a Vernier caliper.

Measuring Instruments

The size of many engine components is extremely critical. Installing a part that is too large or too small can cause engine failure. Therefore, it is extremely important to be able to use ***measuring instruments*** properly.

Micrometers

A ***micrometer*** is an instrument used to take linear measurements with accuracy of .001″ or better. Micrometers are available to measure in either the metric or U.S. customary system. An inside micrometer, Figure 5-1, is used for measuring the distance between two parallel surfaces. It can also be used for measuring the inside diameter of a cylinder.

The ***outside micrometer,*** Figures 5-2 and 5-3, is designed to measure the outside diameter of cylindrical forms and the thickness of materials. Its spindle is attached to the thimble on the inside, at the point of adjustment. Often, a friction stop is provided. The part of the spindle concealed within the sleeve and thimble is threaded to fit a nut in the frame. The frame is stationary.

When the micrometer thimble is revolved by the thumb and finger, the spindle revolves with it and moves through the nut in the frame, moving toward or away from the anvil. The distance or measurement of the opening

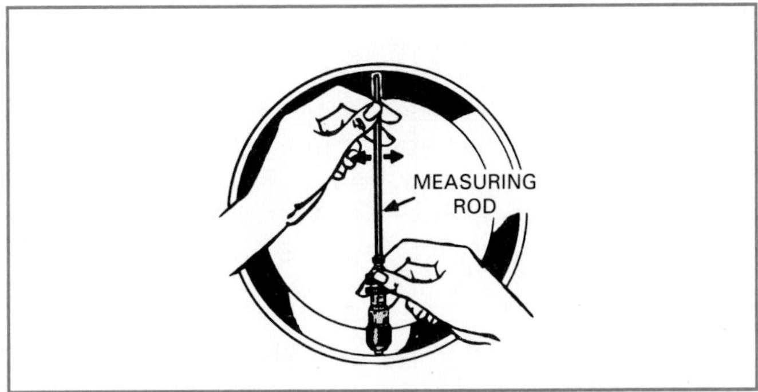

Figure 5-1. Measuring the inner diameter with an inside micrometer.

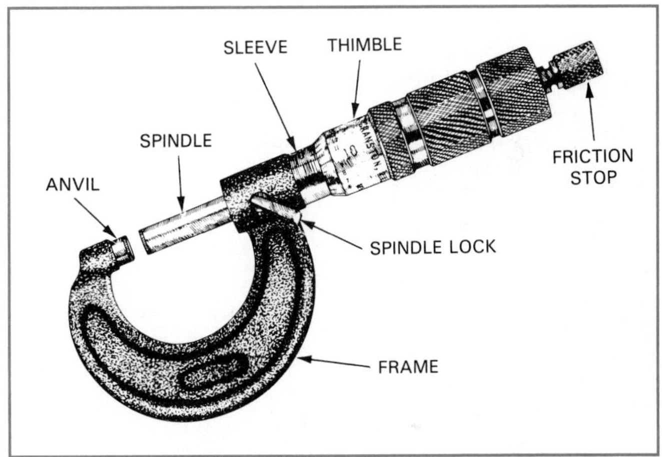

Figure 5-2. Nomenclature of a conventional micrometer. (Central Tools)

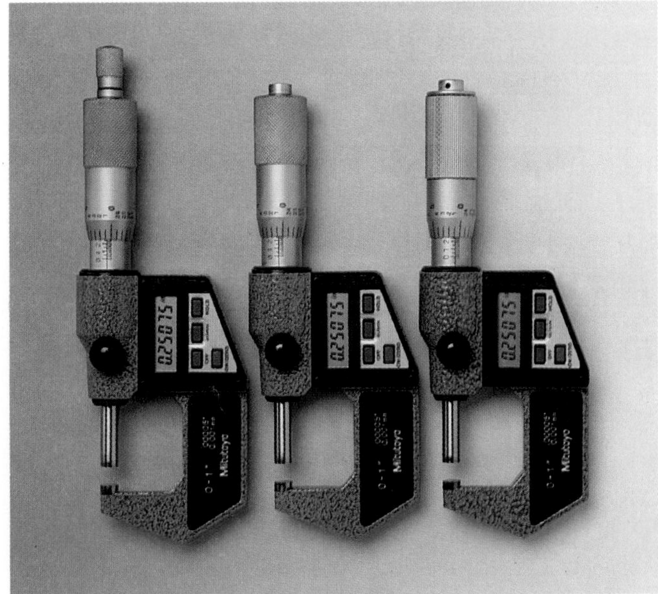

Figure 5-3. Digital micrometers directly read the measurement; no math is involved to obtain measurement. (Mitutoyo)

between the anvil and the spindle is indicated by the line and figures on the sleeve and the thimble. See Figure 5-4.

Reading a Micrometer

When the micrometer is closed, the beveled end of the thimble is aligned with the 0 mark on the sleeve and the 0 mark on the thimble is aligned with the horizontal line on the sleeve.

Opening the micrometer by revolving the thimble one full revolution will make the 0 line of the thimble align with the horizontal line of the sleeve. The distance between the anvil and spindle is now .025″.

The beveled edge of the thimble is marked in 25 divisions. Rotating the thimble from one of these divisions to the next moves the spindle .001″.

To read the micrometer, multiply the number of vertical divisions that are visible on the sleeve by 25. Then add the number of divisions on the bevel of the thimble from 0 mark to the line that aligns with the horizontal line on the sleeve. The closeup view of a micrometer's sleeve and thimble, Figure 5-4, shows a reading of .550″.

Figure 5-5 shows the correct method of holding a micrometer. The thimble is turned until the spindle and anvil just touch the object being measured.

When using a micrometer, take care not to turn the thimble too tight. This will distort the frame and result in inaccurate readings. Only gentle pressure is needed.

Metric Micrometers

Metric micrometers are used in the same manner as the standard type previously described. However, the graduations are in metric units. Readings are obtained as follows:

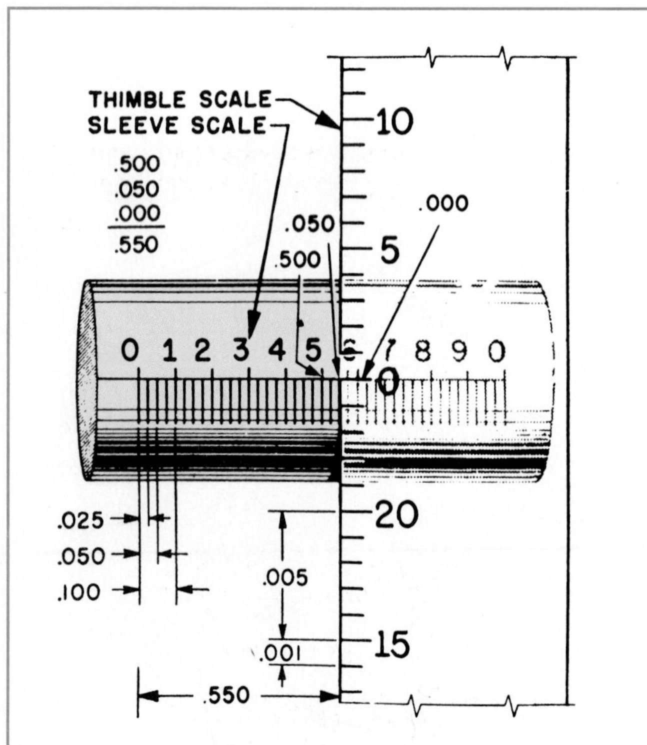

Figure 5-4. Micrometer readings on a conventional micrometer. The reading is 0.550″.

The pitch of the spindle screw in metric micrometers is 0.5 millimeters (mm). Therefore, one complete revolution of the thimble advances the spindle toward or away from the anvil by exactly 0.5 mm.

The longitudinal line on the sleeve is graduated from 0 to 25 mm, and each millimeter is subdivided in 0.5 mm increments. Therefore, it requires two revolutions of the thimble to advance the spindle a distance equal to 1 mm.

The beveled edge of the thimble is graduated in 50 divisions, with every fifth line being numbered from 0 to 50. Since a complete revolution of the thimble advances the spindle 0.5 mm, each graduation on the thimble is equal to 1/50 of 0.5 mm, or 0.01 mm. Two graduations equal 0.02 mm, etc.

To read a metric micrometer, add the total reading in millimeters visible on the sleeve to the reading in hundredths of a millimeter indicated by the graduation on the thimble, which aligns with the longitudinal line on the sleeve.

Example: Refer to Figure 5-6.

The 5 mm graduation is visible, representing	5	mm
There is one additional 0.5 mm line visible, representing	0.5	mm
Line "28" on the thimble aligns with the longitudinal line on the sleeve, each line representing .01 mm. .28 x .01 mm = ...	0.28	mm
The metric micrometer reading is	5.78	mm

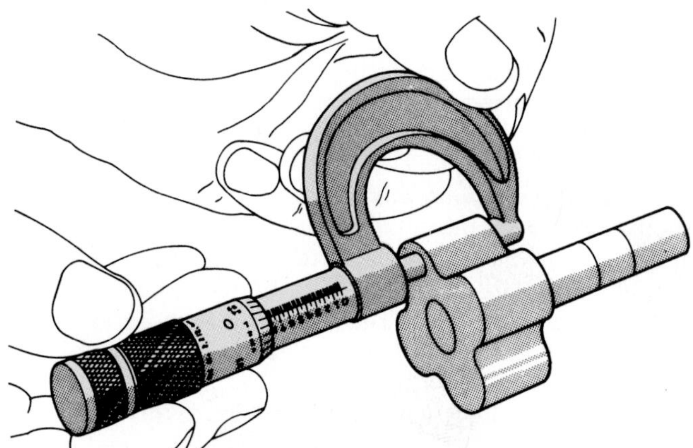

Figure 5-5. Measuring with a micrometer.

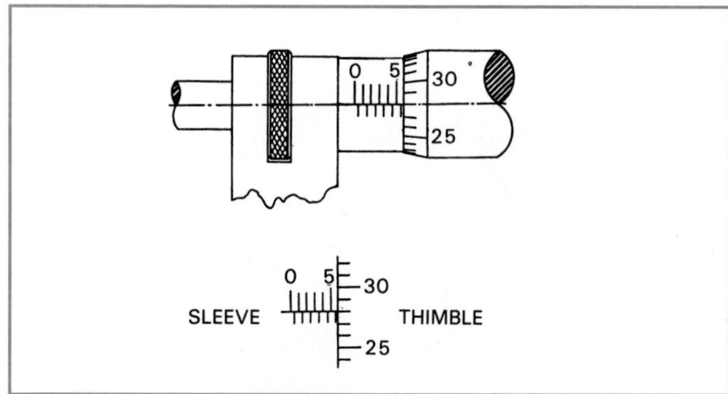

Figure 5-6. A metric micrometer scale. Reading is 5.78 mm. (L.S. Starret Co.)

Telescoping Gauges and Small Hole Gauges

Telescoping gauges, Figure 5-7, are available for measuring the diameter of small holes. After adjusting the gauge in the hole so that it fits snugly, the gauge is removed and measured with a micrometer.

The ***small hole gauge*** shown in Figure 5-8 is used in the automotive machine shop for measuring the diameter of valve guide bores. The small hole gauge is inserted in the bore and expanded until it fills the diameter. Then it is withdrawn, and its width is measured with a micrometer.

Vernier Calipers

The ***Vernier caliper*** is a measuring device capable of measuring to within one-thousandth of an inch (.001″). It can measure both internal and external diameters. Some Vernier calipers are provided with both metric and U.S. customary scales. Figure 5-9 shows a Vernier caliper.

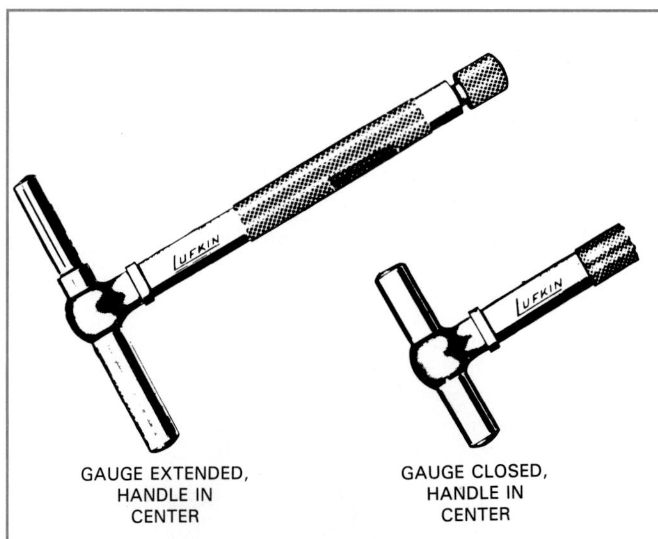

Figure 5-7. Telescoping gauges are used to duplicate inner dimensions. A micrometer is then used to measure the gauge.

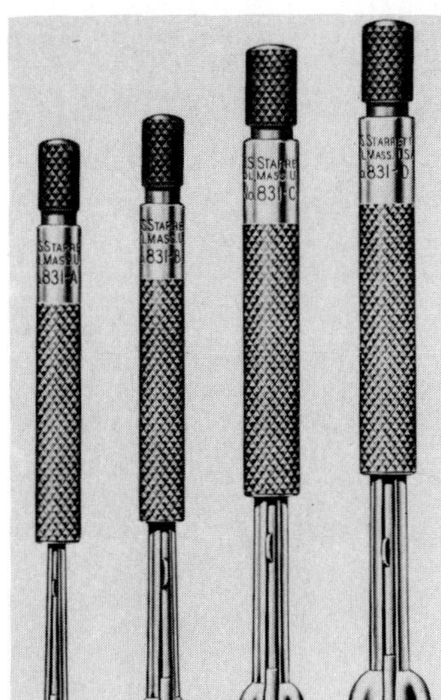

Figure 5-8. Small hole gauges duplicate the size of the hole. A micrometer then measures the gauge.

The main bar of a Vernier caliper is graduated in increments of .025″. Every fourth division, which represents one-tenth of an inch, is numbered, Figure 5-10. The Vernier plate has a space divided into twenty-five divisions. Every fifth division is numbered (0, 5, 10, 15, 20, and 25). The twenty-five divisions on the Vernier plate occupy the same space as the twenty-four divisions on the bar. The difference between the width of one of the twenty-five spaces on the Vernier and one of the twenty-four spaces on the bar is 1/1000″.

If the caliper is set so that 0 line on Vernier aligns with 0 line on bar, the line to the right of 0 on Vernier will differ from line to the right of 0 on bar by .001″; the second line by .002″, etc. The difference will continue to increase by .001″ for each division until line 25 on Vernier aligns with line 24 on bar.

To read this tool, note how many inches, .100″ and .025″ from the 0 mark on the bar. Then note the number of divisions on the Vernier from the 0 to a line that aligns exactly with a line on the bar. In Figure 5-10, the Vernier has moved to the right one and four-tenths and one-fortieth inches (1.425), as shown on the bar. Also, the eleventh line on the Vernier aligns with a line indicated by the star on the bar. Eleven-thousandths of an inch are added to the reading on the bar, and the total reading is 1.436″.

Dial Gauges

Dial gauges, Figure 5-11, are used extensively for measuring the backlash of gears and the end play of shafts, Figure 5-12. In addition, dial gauges can be used to determine out-of-roundness of a bore. Movement of the needle of the gauge will show the variation in measurement. Dial gauges are calibrated to read in .001″ increments.

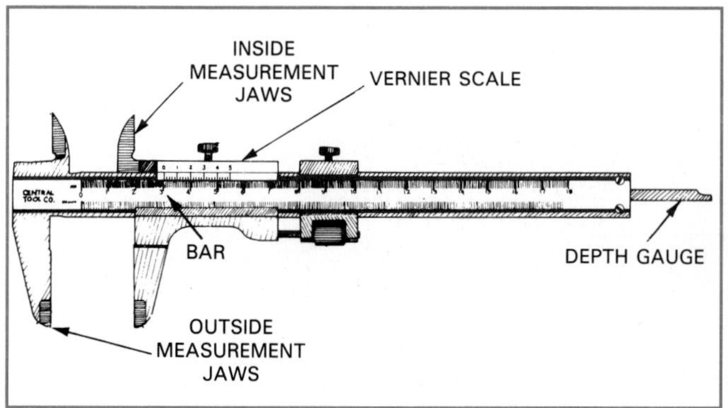

Figure 5-9. Nomenclature of a Vernier caliper. (Central Tools)

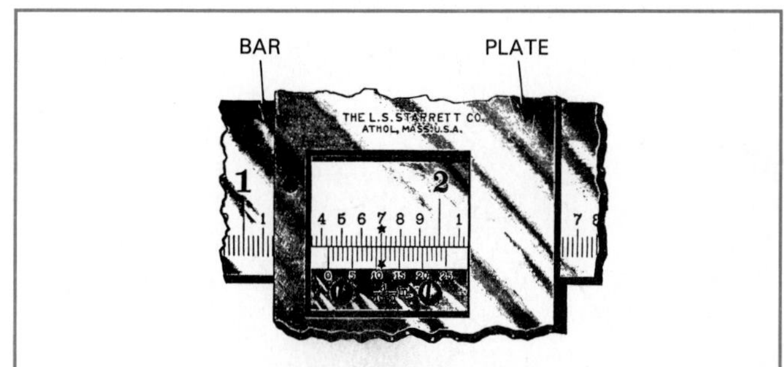

Figure 5-10. Reading on Vernier caliper is 1.436″.

Feeler Gauge

The ***feeler gauge,*** or ***thickness gauge,*** is used for measuring the distance between two surfaces that are only a few thousandths of an inch apart. A feeler gauge consists of an assortment of steel strips of graduated thickness.

Because of the increasing number of cars in the U.S. with service specifications given in millimeters, feeler gauges are now available with each blade marked in fractions of an inch and fractions of a millimeter, Figure 5-13. This eliminates any unnecessary conversions.

Using A Feeler Gauge

To use a feeler gauge, insert a blade in the space to be measured. If the gauge blade fits snugly, that space is equal to the blade thickness in thousandths of an inch or in millimeters. Feeler gauges are used extensively when measuring valve clearance and spark plug gap.

When a feeler gauge is used to measure the clearance between a piston and cylinder wall, the force required to withdraw it is measured by a spring balance. See Figure 5-14.

In addition to flat blade feeler gauges, thickness gauges having different diameter wire "feelers" are available, Figure 5-15. Wire gauges are generally preferred for measuring plug gaps.

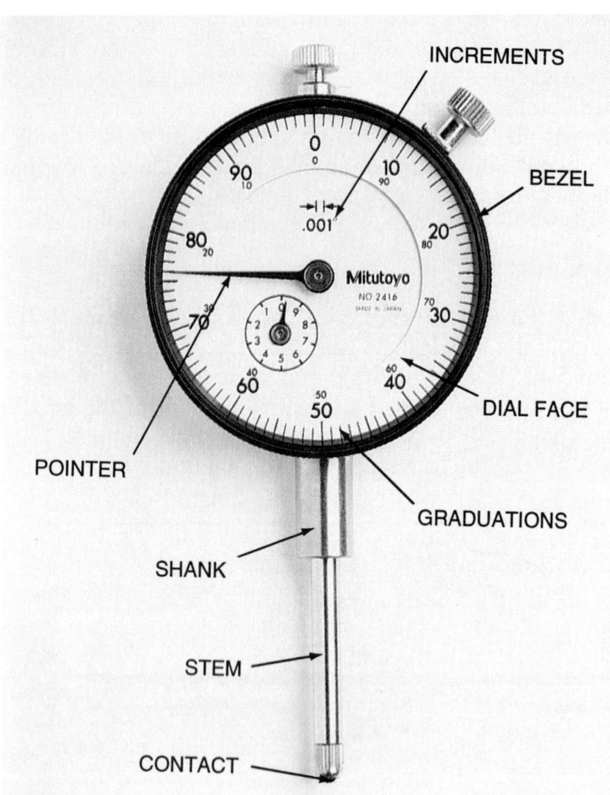

Figure 5-11. Nomenclature of a dial gauge. (Mitutoyo)

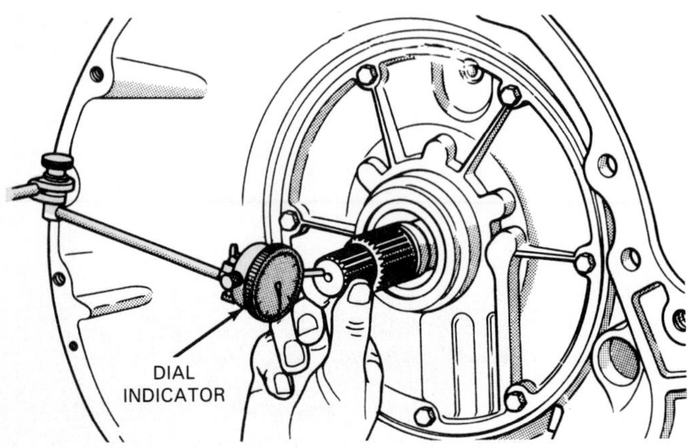

Figure 5-12. Checking end play with a dial indicator. (Chrysler)

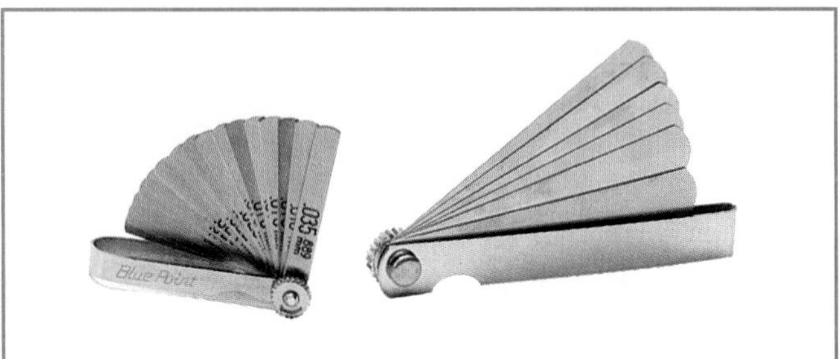

Figure 5-13. Typical feeler gauges. Note that the thickness dimensions on the gauge on the left are given in thousandths of an inch and in millimeters. (Snap-on Tools Corp.)

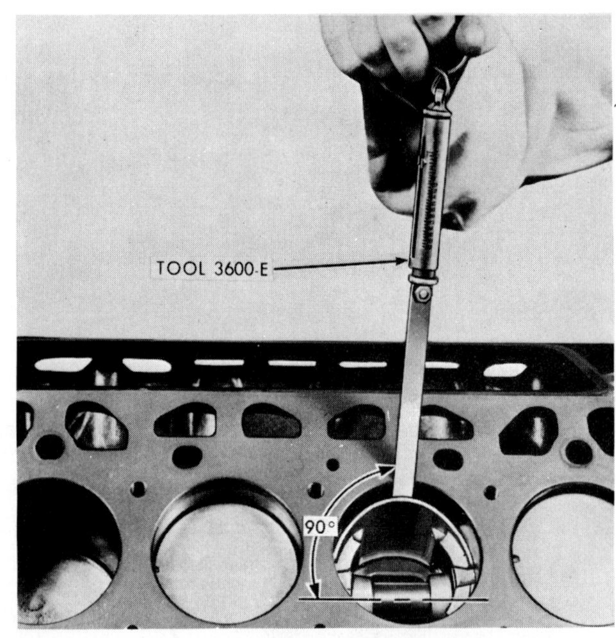

Figure 5-14. The feeler gauge is attached to a spring scale to check the clearance between a piston and a cylinder.

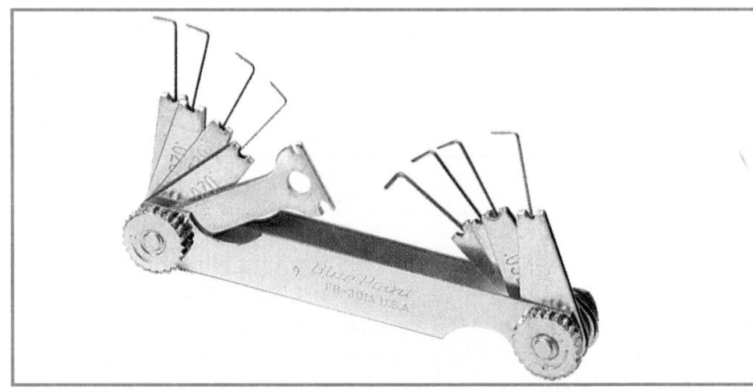

Figure 5-15. Wire-type feeler gauge is used for measuring gap on spark plugs. (Snap-on Tools Corp.)

Chapter 5–Review Questions

Write your answers on a separate sheet of paper. Do not write in this book.

1. For what purpose are inside micrometers frequently used in automotive service work?
2. When the thimble of a standard micrometer is turned one division as indicated by the lines on the beveled edge of the thimble, how far has the spindle moved?
   (A) .025″. (C) .001″.
   (B) .0025″. (D) .005″.
3. When the thimble of a metric micrometer is turned one division as indicated by the lines on the beveled edge of the thimble, how far has the spindle moved?
   (A) 5.0 mm. (C) .05 mm. (E) .1 mm.
   (B) .5 mm. (D) .25 mm. (F) .01 mm.
4. For what two purposes is a dial gauge frequently used in automotive service work?
5. A thickness gauge is used to measure:
   (A) the thickness of sheet metal.
   (B) the diameter of car engine cylinders.
   (C) the space between two surfaces.
   (D) None of the above.
6. A telescoping gauge is used to:
   (A) duplicate outside dimensions.
   (B) duplicate the thickness of an object.
   (C) duplicate inner dimensions.
   (D) duplicate itself.
7. What is the small hole gauge used for in the automotive machine shop?
8. A Vernier caliper can measure inside diameters only. True or False?

Late-model engines are built to exacting tolerances. Therefore, the proper use of measuring instruments during service and repair procedures is extremely important. (Honda)

This technician is using a sophisticated engine analyzer to determine the cause of a driveability problem. (Sun)

Chapter 6
Meters, Testers, and Analyzers

After studying this chapter, you will be able to:

- List the basic instruments used for electrical systems testing.
- Describe the D'Arsonval meter movement.
- Explain how voltmeter and ammeter leads must be hooked up to an electrical circuit.
- State tests that are possible with a battery fast charger/tester.
- Name and describe a broad range of engine analyzers.

Automotive Meters, Testers, and Analyzers

There is one particular demonstration of automotive knowledge that makes an engine service technician stand out as an expert. It is the ability to systematically test, evaluate, and correct performance problems in all five major engine systems: starting, charging, fuel distribution, compression, and ignition.

The professional technician, however, performs as an expert with the help of a full range of reliably accurate meters, testers, and analyzers. For electrical systems testing, basic instruments include the ***ammeter*** for measuring the current in amperes, the ***voltmeter*** for measuring the voltage, and the ***ohmmeter*** for measuring resistance.

The technician also makes regular use of a battery-starter tester, an alternator-regulator tester, a battery charger, a multimeter, an infrared exhaust analyzer, and an engine systems analyzer. For internal engine troubleshooting, support comes from a compression tester, vacuum gauge, and cylinder leakage tester.

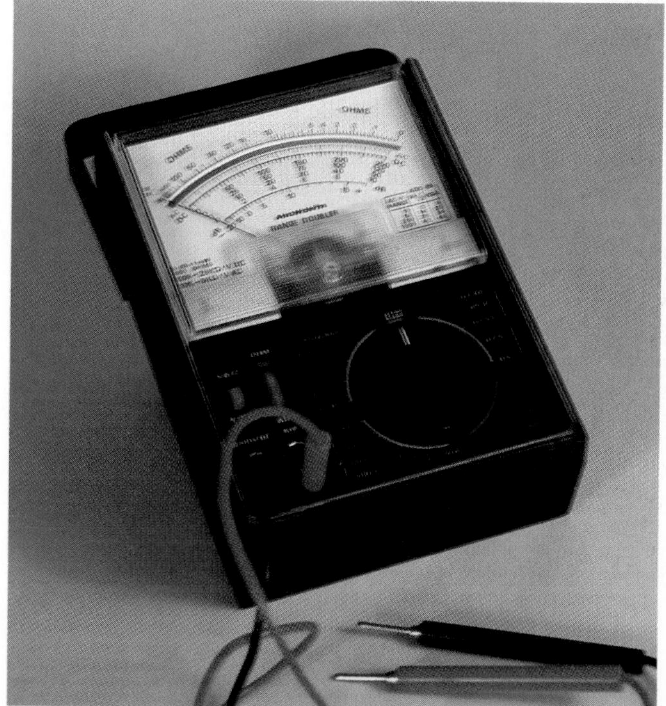

Figure 6-1. An analog meter uses a pointer to indicate values.

D'Arsonval Meter Design

Basically, two types of meters are used in automotive service work: analog meters and digital meters. These sensitive instruments are designed to measure and indicate electrical values.

An ***analog meter*** has a calibrated dial (face with marked values) and a pointer that indicates the value of the electrical unit under test, Figure 6-1. ***Digital meters*** "spell" the value of the unit under test, Figure 6-2. This type of meter is especially well suited for use in computerized engine systems analyzers, on-board computer testers, and exhaust emissions analyzers.

Most analog meters (ammeters, voltmeters, and ohmmeters) used in the automotive service field are of the moving coil type. See Figures 6-3 and 6-4. These instruments consist of a horseshoe-shaped or hoop-shaped permanent magnet and a movable coil. In addition, a damping spring (similar to hairspring of a watch) is attached to the pointer of the meter. The damping spring is used to prevent

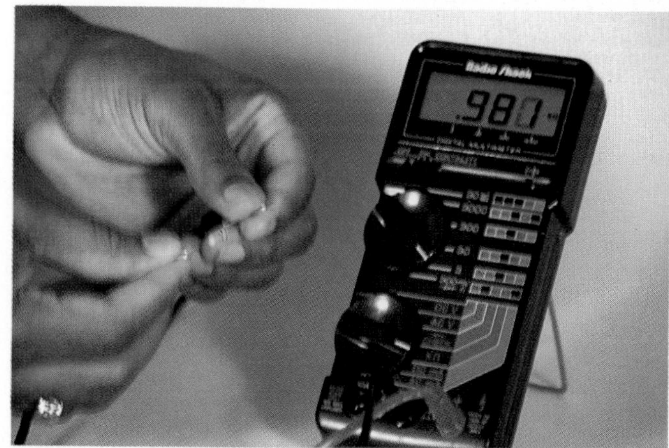

Figure 6-2. Digital meters have alpha-numeric displays.

the pointer from going full scale too quickly when current is applied and removed.

This long established meter design is known as the ***D'Arsonval movement.*** Usually, the D'Arsonval movement is "jeweled" to cut down on friction to ensure the accuracy of its readings. Therefore, a D'Arsonval meter is reliably accurate and sensitive. For this reason, it must be handled carefully. Any shock to the meter can damage the movement and ruin the meter.

When using any analog meter with multiple ranges, always start by adjusting the range selector switch to the highest range. Then reduce the switch setting until the meter is able to "read" the electrical value. Otherwise, a low range setting could result in "pegging the meter," which happens when the pointer strikes hard against the high end of the meter scale.

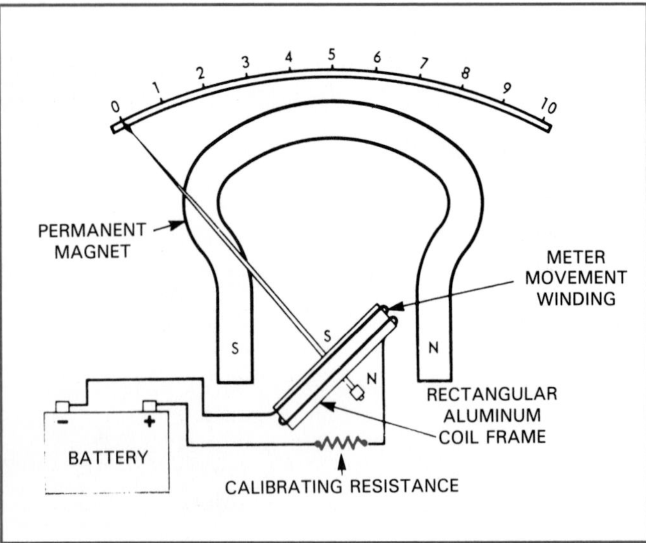

Figure 6-3. Schematic drawing of the makeup of a typical voltmeter. Note calibrating resistance in series with moving coil.

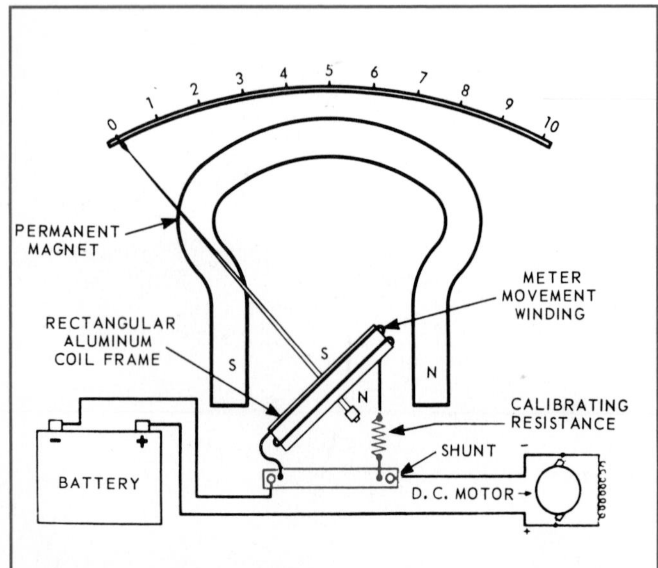

Figure 6-4. Note that the ammeter has a heavy resistance (shunt) connected across the moving coil and another resistance connected in series with the moving coil.

Ammeter/Voltmeter Operation

The basic design of an ammeter and a voltmeter is the same. However, as shown in Figure 6-4, the ammeter is provided with a heavy *shunt* (alternate path for current) of low resistance connected across the movable coil. Another resistance element is connected in series with one end of the shunt and the coil. This resistance is used for calibrating the instrument.

The voltmeter does not have a resistance shunted across the coil, but it does have the calibrating resistance in series with the movable coil. See Figure 6-3. When hooking up voltmeter leads, always connect them in parallel to the terminals of the device or circuit, Figure 6-5. On the other hand, always connect ammeter leads in series with the circuit, Figure 6-6.

When the circuit to be tested is closed, current flowing through the movable coil of the ammeter or voltmeter reacts with the magnetic field, causing the coil to rotate against the tension of the damping spring. Relative movement of the coil is directly proportional to the current flowing through it. A pointer attached to the coil moves across a calibrated scale on the meter face to indicate the amount of current or voltage flowing through the coil.

A single voltmeter can be designed to cover different ranges of voltage (0-2, 0-20, etc.). This is done by varying the resistance in series with the movable coil. A separate

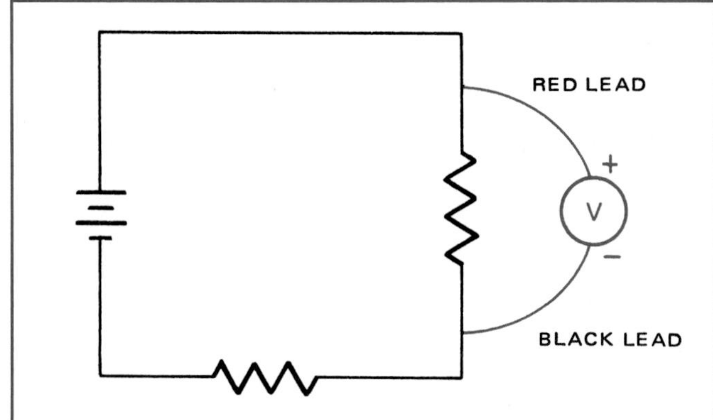

Figure 6-5. This schematic shows how to hook up a voltmeter across a circuit. Always connect the test leads so that the meter is in parallel to the circuit.

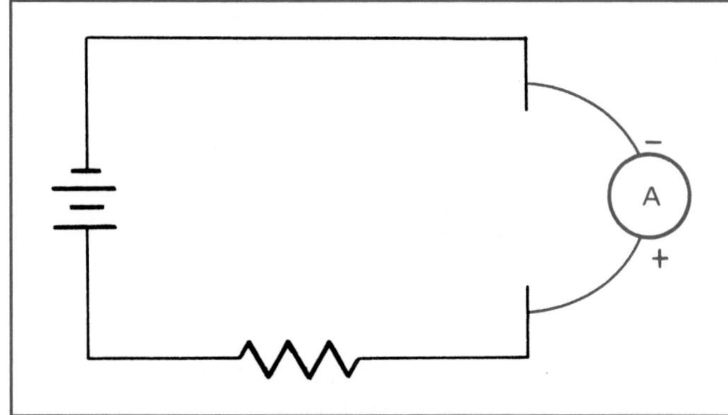

Figure 6-6. Schematic shows how to hook up an ammeter in series with circuit: open circuit; connect meter test leads; read meter.

resistance is provided for each range of the instrument. The resistance value–as well as the voltage range–is changed by means of a switch located on the instrument.

Ammeters also can be designed to cover different ranges of current (0-10, 0-100, etc.) by providing different shunts. When working with an ammeter, be sure to use the leads provided by the meter manufacturer. Leads having a different resistance will seriously affect the accuracy of the instrument.

In general, ammeters and voltmeters used for automotive service work should have an accuracy of one percent of full scale deflection. In addition, these instruments should be compensated for changes in temperature.

Ohmmeter Operation

The ohmmeter is designed to measure resistance of an electric circuit or unit in ohms. A typical automotive application of an ohmmeter is testing the resistance of high tension wiring. Another use is testing continuity (unbroken path for current flow).

Generally, the ohmmeter utilizes a D'Arsonval movement. In addition, it has a calibrated resistance, a variable resistance, and a self-contained dry cell. See Figure 6-7. All ohmmeters need dry cells to serve as the voltage supply needed to force current through the circuit or unit being tested. The power must be *off* in the circuit being tested.

The leads used to connect the ohmmeter to the circuit are made of a special low-resistance wire. Since they are used for calibrating the instrument, these same leads must be used when taking measurements. To calibrate the ohmmeter, it is necessary to "zero the meter." This is done by joining the two leads together to establish zero resistance. Then, the variable resistance is adjusted to bring the pointer to the zero mark on the calibrated dial.

To measure resistance, simply connect the leads from the ohmmeter (or contact the probes) to the terminals of the unit to be tested. Then read the resistance in ohms on the dial

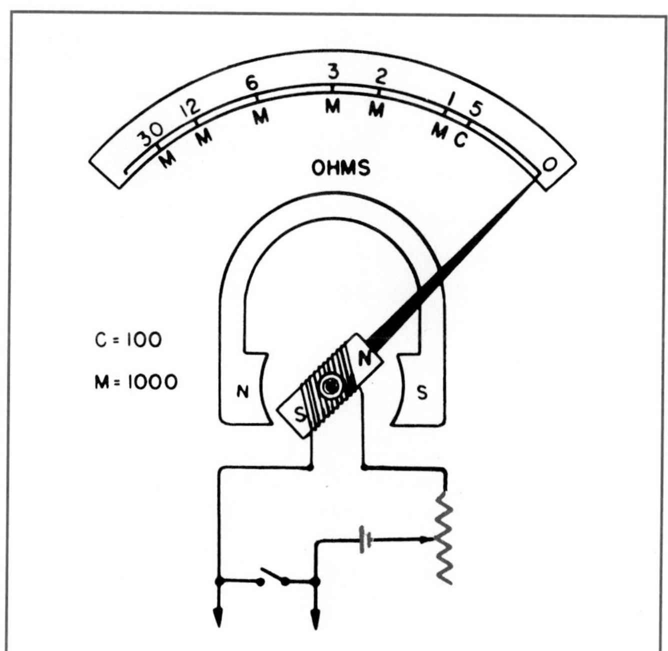

Figure 6-7. Schematic of a typical ohmmeter. Note the dry cell and the adjustable resistance.

of the meter. Most ohmmeters used in automotive service work have two ranges: 0-500 ohms and 0-50,000 ohms.

Multimeters

Compact digital ***multimeters*** are available that combine a voltmeter, an ohmmeter, and a milliammeter in one instrument. The multimeter shown in Figure 6-8 features a push-button switch that permits either manual or automatic ranging. A digital display provides a readout of test results. A continuity buzzer and diode function test are also featured.

Tachometers

The ***tachometer*** is designed to indicate the speed of a rotating part in revolutions per minute (rpm). For automotive use, the tachometer is "made" for measuring the speed of the engine.

Modern tachometers usually consist of a jeweled D'Arsonval movement, zero adjuster, and solid state circuitry. Low and high ranges are generally provided. The low range, for example, could be 0-1200 rpm. The high range could be 0-6000 rpm.

To test engine speed, connect one lead of the tachometer to the primary terminal of the distributor. Connect the other lead to ground. Set the control for low range to test curb idle and fast idle. Set the control for high range to make tests at speeds above 1200 rpm.

Dwell Meters

Often, a dwell meter is contained in the same case as a tachometer. Usually, these are hand-held units called "tach-dwell meters." The ***dwell meter*** is used mainly for measuring the angle through which the ignition distributor shaft turns while the breaker points are closed. This is known as point dwell, or cam angle.

The vehicle manufacturer specifies what the cam angle should be for different engine applications. Since the cam angle relates to opening and closing of the breaker points, adjusting the point gap also adjusts the cam angle. After making the point gap setting, it can be checked for

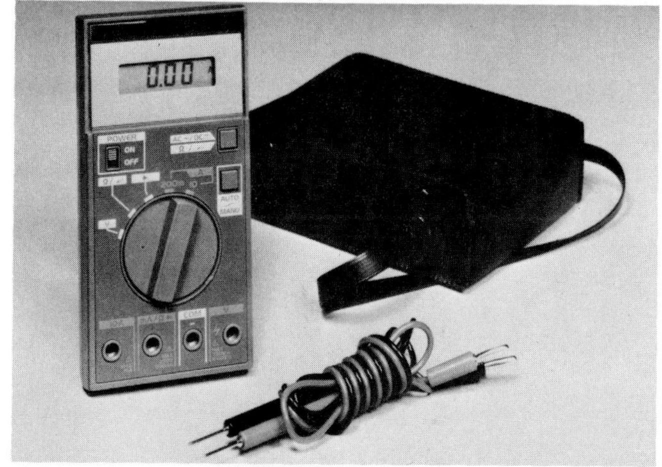

Figure 6-8. This digital multimeter has five voltage ranges, starting at 0-0.2 volts. Current ranges are from 0-200 milliamps and from 0-10 amps ac and dc. Five resistance ranges start at 0-200 ohms and climb to 20 megohms. (Accurate Instruments)

accuracy (and readjusted if necessary) by hooking up the dwell meter and measuring the cam angle.

Battery/Starter Testers

Battery testing equipment includes the hydrometer, the voltmeter, and the multi-purpose testing unit, which combines voltmeter, ammeter, and load control. See Figures 6-9 and 6-10. Housed in a single portable cabinet, some of these combination units can be used to test batteries, starters, alternators, voltage regulators, and related circuitry.

The tester shown in Figure 6-9 has a 0-750 amp current range, zero amps control, and LED (light emitting diode) displays. It also has a "ripple" indicator that analyzes the quality of an alternator's dc output. Tests that can be performed by this combination unit include: battery load, starter current load, cranking voltage, engine cranking speed, diode-stator condition, alternator current output, and voltage regulator operation.

The tester shown in Figure 6-10 is designed to test all recognized battery ratings, including cold cranking performance and ampere hours. It has a compensation adjustment for battery temperatures from 0-125 °F (–18-52 °C). A color-coded scale shows condition of battery, cables, alternator, and regulator.

Figure 6-9. Starting and charging systems tester shows amps and volts in digital display. It has an automatic return load control knob and a ripple indicator that reveals alternator defects. (Snap-on Tools Corp.)

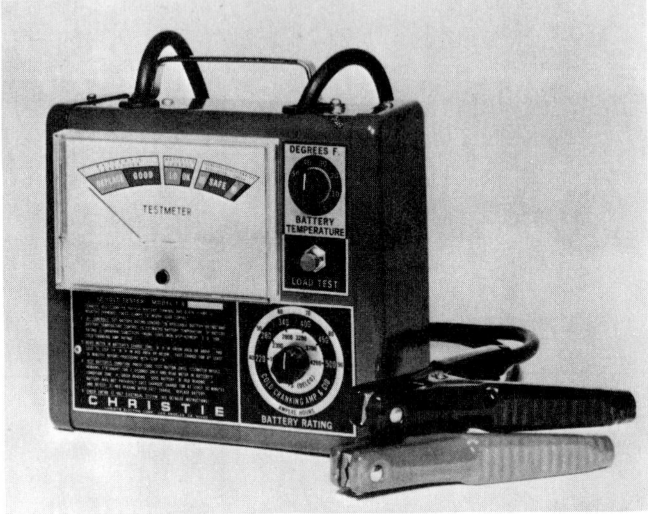

Figure 6-10. Portable battery tester also checks condition of alternator, regulator, and primary circuit cables. Tester has a built-in discharge load comparable to car's starter current draw. (Christie Electric Corp.)

Battery Fast Chargers

Battery fast chargers have become more automatic and foolproof. Most have alternator protection to guard against reverse hookup. One type of fast charger uses an LED indicator that shows "green" for a correct connection or "red" for a reverse connection.

Charging rate output selection is provided on fast chargers. Some also have an electric timer with 120 minute "hold" position for slow charging. Maximum charging rates are in the 60-100 amp range; cranking power is in the 200-300 amp range. See Figure 6-11.

One step up from the fast charger is the fast charger/tester. In addition to alternator protection and slow charge timer, the charger/tester provides a "start charge" for completely discharged batteries. It also has a thermal overload device and battery type selector (conventional or maintenance-free). A battery rating control compensates for capacity of the battery in cold cranking amps or ampere hours.

As a tester, the battery fast charger/tester can analyze the condition, state of charge, and operating performance of the battery. It can also test the charging system, starter, and cables. Additionally, it will reveal short circuits in the electrical system.

Exhaust Gas Analyzers

With so much emphasis on exhaust emission control, service technicians need suitable test equipment to verify (through various modes of engine operation) whether or

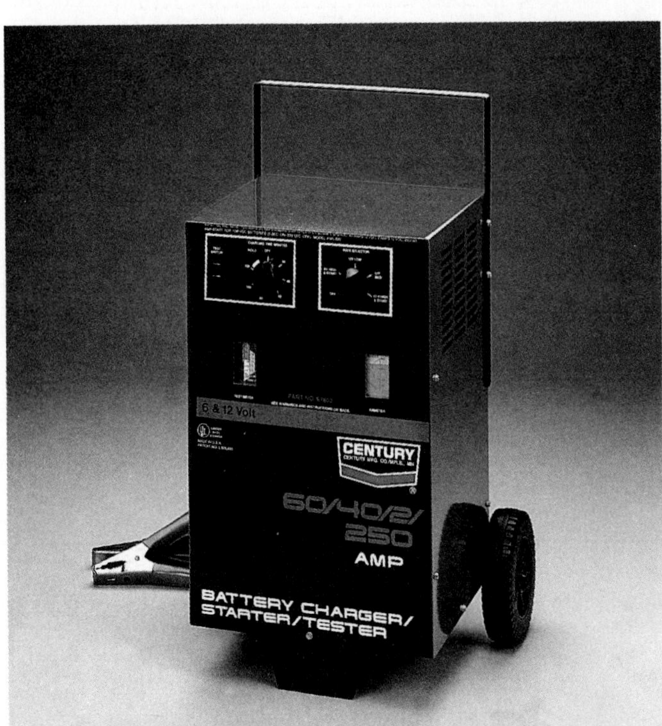

Figure 6-11. Battery fast charger offers low, medium, and high charging rates. (Century Mfg. Co.)

not the engine is emitting excessive amounts of air pollutants. ***Infrared exhaust gas analyzers*** are most commonly used to detect the amounts of hydrocarbons (HC) and carbon monoxide (CO) in the exhaust gas. See Figure 6-12.

Infrared exhaust gas analyzers measure HC and CO by determining how much infrared energy is absorbed by a sample of the vehicle's exhaust gas. In the infrared block diagram shown in Figure 6-13, infrared energy generated by an electrically heated element is projected through a sample tube (cell) that has the vehicle's exhaust gas flowing through it. Infrared radiation not absorbed by the exhaust gases hits an infrared detector and is converted to an electronic signal that causes the digital display of the test result to change. With this infrared exhaust gas analyzer, digital readouts have a 0-1999 ppm (parts per million) HC range, and a 0-9.99 percent CO range.

A four-gas analyzer is an advanced type of exhaust gas analyzer. This unit can test for HC, CO, CO_2 (carbon dioxide), and O_2 (oxygen). Some four-gas analyzers use emissions analysis to determine whether the cause of an engine performance problem is in the fuel system or in the ignition system, Figure 6-14.

Some equipment manufacturers couple the four-gas analyzer module with an engine analyzer said to provide "all systems" engine diagnosis. This computer test center is capable of identifying a variety of problems, such as rich, lean, or unbalanced air-fuel mixtures; closed loop system malfunctions; air pump or catalytic converter malfunction; fuel injection system malfunction; intake manifold leaks; EGR valve leaks; blown head gaskets; excessive misfire; excessive spark advance; and leaks or restrictions in exhaust systems.

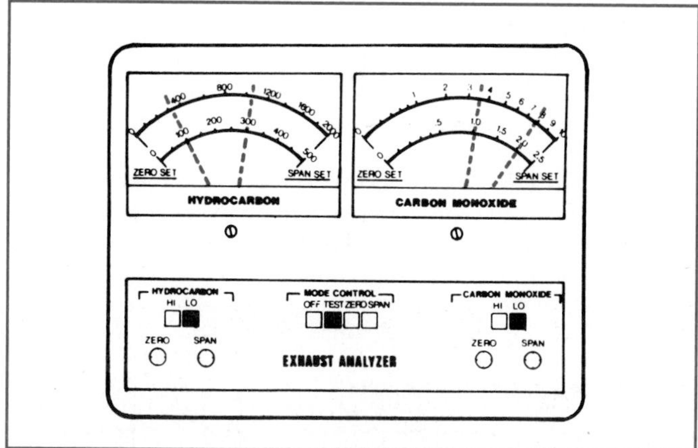

Figure 6-12. Diagram of a typical infrared exhaust analyzer. Dashed lines show normal range of readings on low scale of HC and CO meters.

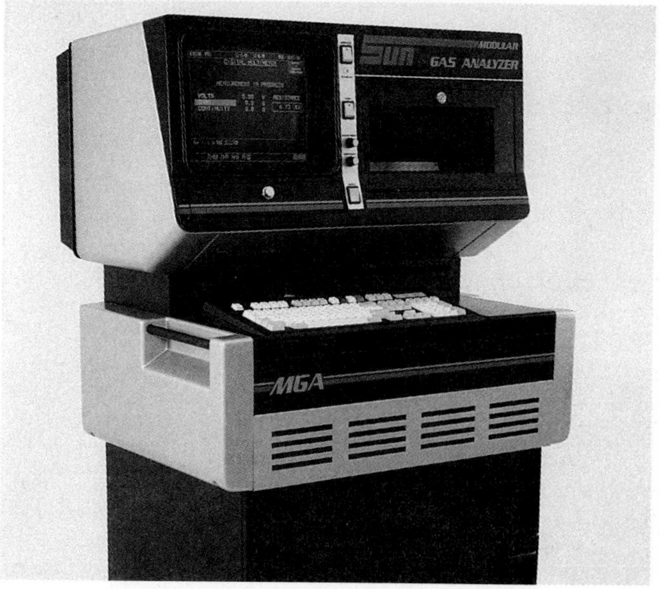

Figure 6-14. To meet challenge of diagnosing computer controlled engine systems, one test equipment manufacturer couples a four-gas analyzer with an engine analyzer. Note the video monitor and the printout. (Sun)

Other equipment manufacturers produce a digital performance gas analyzer that combines digital display with computer electronics. The unit is microcomputer controlled with an automatically timed warmup period and an automatically timed gas calibration. The digital display reads 0-2000 ppm HC in 10 ppm increments, and 0-10 percent CO in .05 percent increments.

Oscilloscopes

The ***oscilloscope,*** Figure 6-15, is an electronic device that allows technicians to visually observe and measure the instantaneous voltage in an electrical circuit. Basically, the oscilloscope consists of a cathode ray tube (CRT) and

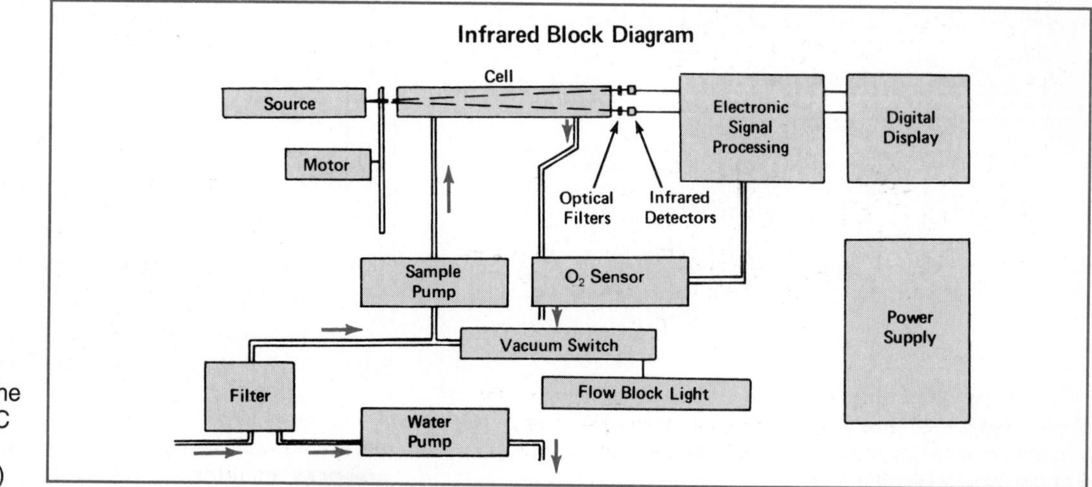

Figure 6-13. Infrared exhaust analyzer block diagram traces flow of exhaust gas sample through the cell. The sample absorbs infrared energy from the source. The digital display reads in HC and CO values. (Peerless Instrument Co.)

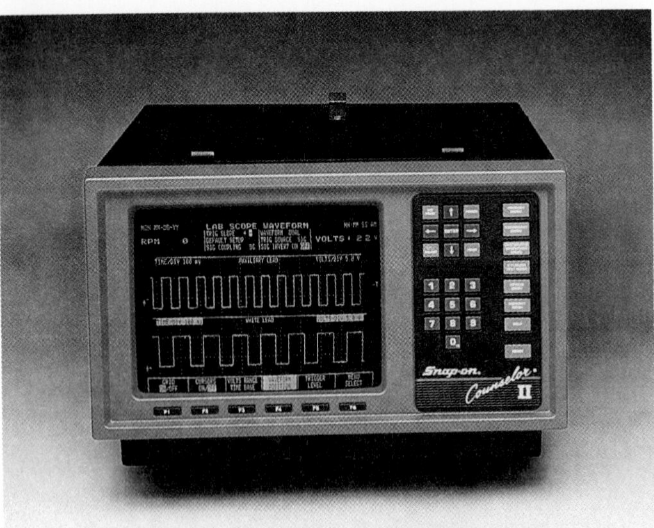

Figure 6-15. This digital oscilloscope can be used as a module in a console or as a stand-alone unit (Snap-on Tools Corp.)

operational circuitry. It operates in much the same manner as a television set.

The "scope" produces a graph-like picture showing voltage values with respect to time. The picture generally is referred to as the pattern or waveform. This pattern on the scope face or screen provides a visual means for comparing the performance of a vehicle's ignition system or charging system to a normal pattern for the system being tested, Figure 6-16.

Technically, the pattern is produced by the cathode ray, or electron beam, striking a phosphor coating on the inside of the CRT screen. When the electrons strike this material, it gives off a brilliant glow, making it possible to see the path of the beam as it moves across the screen.

The electron beam is moved or deflected by voltage applied to metal plates within the tube. Horizontal deflection, or sweep, moves the beam from left to right. Vertical deflection, or sweep, moves the beam up and down on the screen of the CRT. The screen, then, shows "time" on the horizontal axis and "voltage" on the vertical axis. The horizontal axis is called the "X-axis." The vertical axis is called the "Y-axis."

In addition to being able to measure voltage in an electrical circuit, the scope can be used to determine the polarity of the voltage. Polarity is indicated by the vertical movement of the electron beam. When the scope leads are properly connected to the secondary circuit of the ignition system, the voltage (normally negative) will appear above the zero reference line. See Figure 6-17.

The scope pattern is controlled by the voltage in the electrical system to which it is connected. Scopes can also be connected to non-electrical components by means of special pickups known as ***transducers***. These devices, which convert other forms of energy to electrical impulses, are used to observe engine compression and valve action, and to locate noises and vibrations.

Scope Controls and Operation

Today's basic oscilloscope can be used to test conventional and electronic ignition systems, alternator diode condition, and cylinder balance. Scopes can be used to test ignition coil performance, distributor component condition, and spark plug circuit firing voltages.

In operating the scope shown in Figure 6-15, many test patterns can be displayed. Function buttons provide the following pattern selections: 25 kV and 50 kV secondary patterns; secondary superimposed; secondary raster; primary parade; and alternator test.

Engine Analyzers

Engine analyzer is a generic term used to describe a host of testers, ranging from a hand-held, ten-function tune-up analyzer to a massive console of equipment modules that includes a large screen oscilloscope, an automatic computer analyzer, and banks of large scale test meters, Figure 6-18. In between, a popular group of compact digital engine analyzers are available for tying in with on-board computer systems, Figure 6-19. These special testers interpret the signals that indicate malfunctions in various engine systems. Data is entered into the tester and specific tests are requested. Trouble codes are digitally displayed.

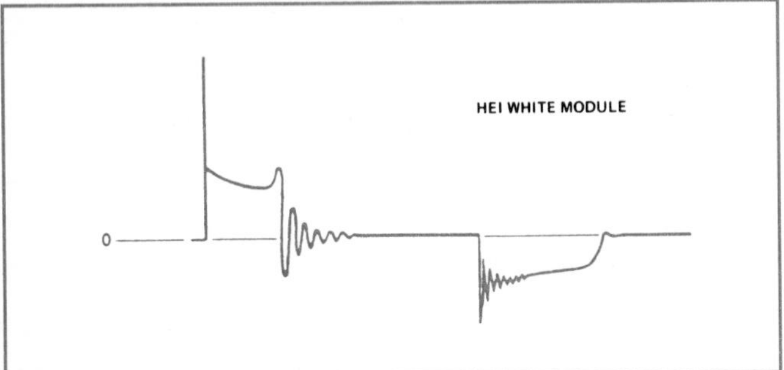

Figure 6-16. On this particular scope, the pattern, or waveform, is normal for a single cylinder in a GM High Energy Ignition system (HEI). (Peerless Instrument Co.)

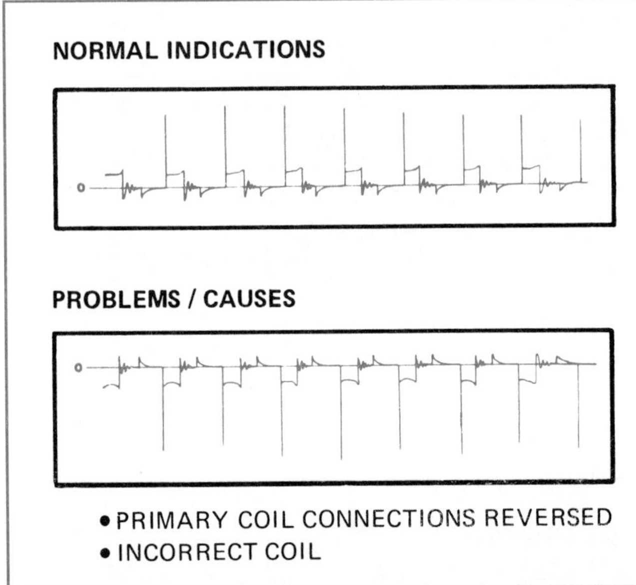

Figure 6-17. When testing spark polarity on a scope, the normal pattern is above the zero reference line (top). Reversed polarity (bottom) means the incorrect coil has been installed or the coil connections have been reversed. (Peerless Instrument Co.)

Figure 6-18. This modular analyzer can be expanded as necessary. (Sun)

Figure 6-19. This type of compact analyzer is often called a scan tool. (OTC Div. of SPX Corp.)

Console-type engine analyzers come in many packages. Some can be built up by adding modules to a basic test stand to suit individual needs. Others are unitized and put on wheels to provide mobility. Still others are suspended from an overhead track and travel from service bay to service bay. Some consoles are used in conjunction with a dynamometer to simulate road testing.

Probably the most sophisticated of modern engine analyzers is the automatic computer analyzer. Factory approved specifications are programmed into the computer. Data is then collected, based on the vehicle's actual operating characteristics. The computer analyzes this information and deduces which components are faulty in any of the major engine systems–starting, charging, fuel distribution, compression, timing, and ignition.

Test results are displayed automatically on the computer terminal. In addition, a hard-copy printout is provided by a multi-copy printer. The printout contains both "specified" and "actual" readings for each test for the technician's and customer's verification.

Chapter 6–Review Questions

Write your answers on a separate sheet of paper. Do not write in this book.

1. An ohmmeter is used to test:
   (A) current.
   (B) voltage.
   (C) resistance.
   (D) engine speed.
2. Basically, two "types" of meters are used in automotive service work. What are they?
3. When hooking up voltmeter leads to an electrical circuit, they are always connected in _____.
4. When hooking up ammeter leads to an electrical circuit, they are always connected in _____.
5. Usually, the D'Arsonval movement is _____ to cut down on friction and ensure the accuracy of its readings.
   (A) jeweled
   (B) calibrated
   (C) sensitized
   (D) micro-finished.
6. Why must you use the ammeter leads provided by the meter manufacturer?
7. What is meant by "pegging the meter"?
   (A) Having line of sight directly in front of meter pointer to ensure an accurate reading.
   (B) Allowing pointer to swing hard against high end of meter scale.
   (C) Calibrating the pointer exactly on zero.
   (D) Making incorrect meter lead hookups and reversing polarity.
8. When testing with an ohmmeter, why must the power be OFF in the circuit being tested?
9. Four-gas analyzers test exhaust gas for HC, CO, CO_2, and _____.
10. The oscilloscope screen shows time on the horizontal axis and _____ on the vertical axis.
11. The oscilloscope pattern is controlled by the voltage in the electrical system to which it is connected. True or False?

Match the question number for each of the following instruments with the letter designated for each correct associated term.

12. _____ Voltmeter.
13. _____ Ammeter.
14. _____ Ohmmeter.
15. _____ Tachometer.
16. _____ Dwell meter.
17. _____ Battery fast charger/tester.
18. _____ Exhaust gas analyzer.
19. _____ Oscilloscope.
20. _____ Engine analyzer.

(A) Engine rpm.
(B) Cold cranking amps.
(C) Waveform.
(D) Vacuum in in. Hg.
(E) Series hookup in circuit.
(F) Breaker point gap.
(G) On-board computer.
(H) Parallel hookup in circuit.
(I) Resistance in circuit.
(J) Cylinder leakage.
(K) Infrared.

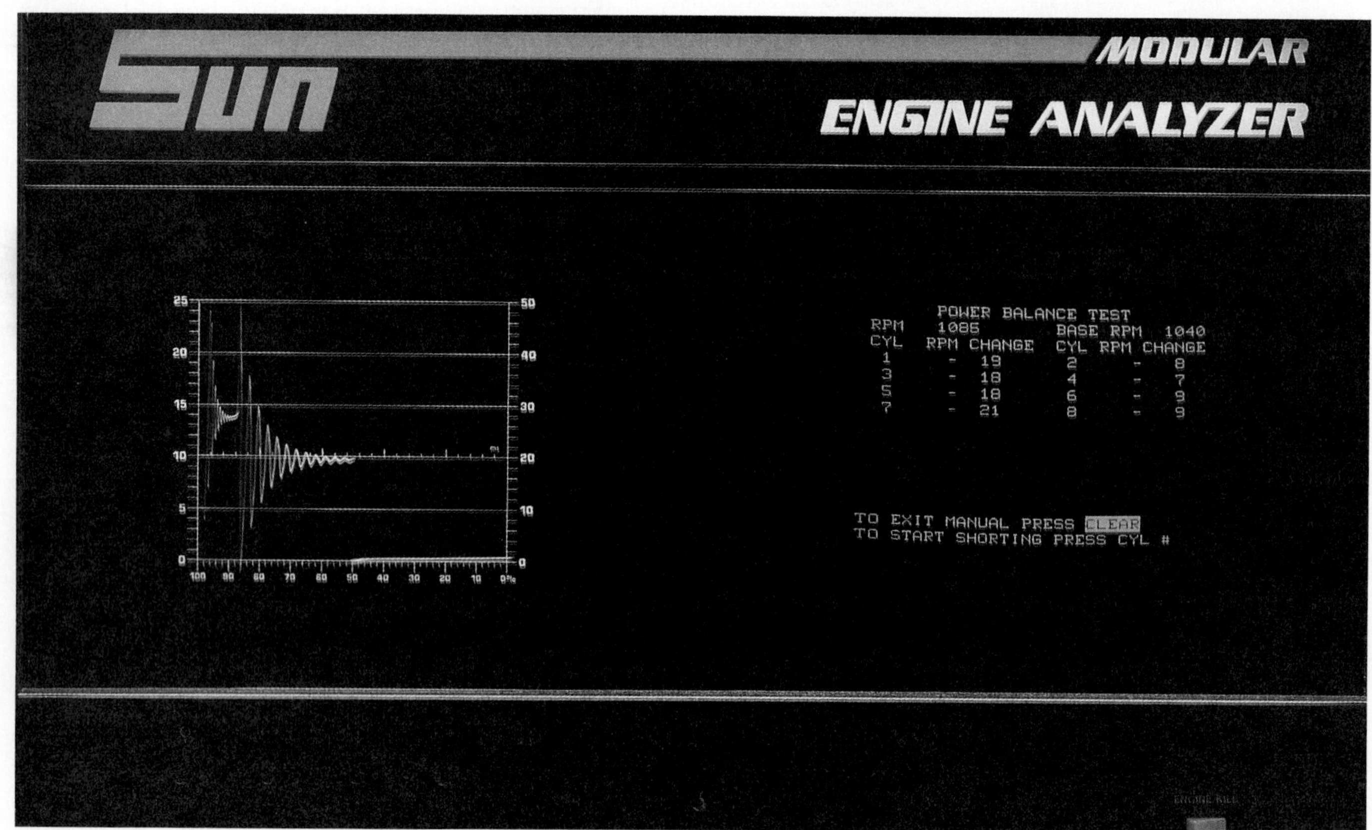

Typical engine analyzer display. On this particular analyzer, the oscilloscope is on the left and the digital display screen is on the right. (Sun)

Chapter 7
Engine Fundamentals

After studying this chapter, you will be able to:
❍ Differentiate between various engine types.
❍ Describe the construction and operation of the major engine components.
❍ List the sequence of events in two- and four-cycle engine operation.

Engine Fundamentals

Automobiles have been operated successfully by electric motors, steam engines, and internal combustion engines. The ***internal combustion engine*** burns fuel within its cylinders and converts the expanding force of the burning fuel, or combustion, into a rotary force used to propel the vehicle.

There are several types of internal combustion engines: two- and four-cycle reciprocating piston engines, gas turbine engines, free piston engines, and rotary combustion engines. However, four-cycle reciprocating engines have been refined to such a degree that they have almost complete dominance of the automotive field. Engines of other types are described in Chapter 18, Diesel and Other Engines.

Many things are demanded of an engine used to propel an automobile. Some of the requirements are:

- Ease of starting.
- Reliability.
- Power.
- Responsiveness.
- Economy in fuel, oil, and repairs.
- Ease of handling.
- Quiet operation.

Some of these factors conflict. For example, a great amount of power can be had from an engine of sufficient size, but a super-size engine is not economical to operate. Therefore, all automobile engines are a compromise in order to obtain the desirable combination of performance and economy.

Engine Fuels

Internal combustion engines can be made to operate on almost anything that can be converted into a combustible gas, such as wood, coal, alcohol, vegetable oils, mineral oils, etc. However, because of convenience, a variety of petroleum products are commonly used as fuel: gasoline, kerosene, fuel oil, liquefied petroleum gas (LP-Gas), etc. When kerosene, fuel oil, or LP-Gas is used, it is necessary to alter the design of the engine to achieve efficient operation.

Engine Design

Gasoline engines used in automotive vehicles are of two basic types: ***four-cycle engines*** and ***two-cycle engines.*** Either type may be water-cooled, Figure 7-1, or air-cooled, Figure 7-2. Four-, six-, and eight-cylinder engines are common. However, three-, five-, ten-, and twelve-cylinder engines are available.

Almost all automobile engines have more than one cylinder. These cylinders can be arranged in an inline, opposed, or V-type configuration, Figure 7-3. Engines for other purposes, such as aviation, are arranged as radial, inverted inline, inverted V, and X-shaped configurations.

Reciprocating Engines

In the typical automobile engine, a piston reciprocates (moves back and forth) within each cylinder. Each piston is connected to the crankshaft by means of a link known as a connecting rod. See Figure 7-4.

Other types of reciprocating engines substitute an eccentric, an inclined plate, or a cam mechanism for the crankshaft. The free piston engine has no crankshaft or connecting rods.

Engine Components

The typical automotive engine is made up of several essential components. These components are designed to provide efficient and reliable engine operation. The basic components in a four-cycle automotive engine include the following:

- Cylinder block.
- Crankshaft.
- Pistons.
- Piston rings.
- Connecting rods.
- Piston pin.
- Cylinder head.
- Valve train (includes valves and valve operating mechanism).

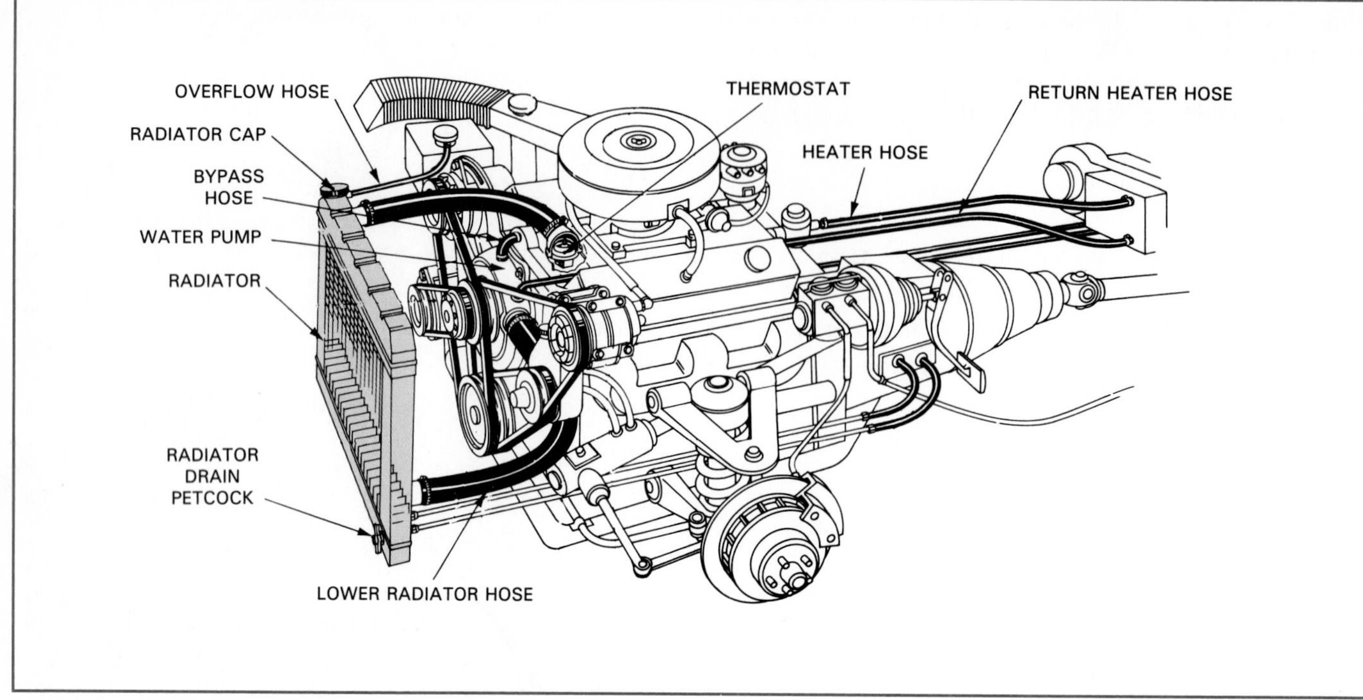

Figure 7-1. A water-cooled engine has a radiator. (Gates Rubber Co.)

Cylinder Block

Ordinarily, the ***cylinder block*** is the largest and most intricate single piece of metal in the automobile. Practically all of the engine parts are directly or indirectly attached to the block. See Figures 7-5 and 7-6. The cylinder block contains the pistons, which are attached to the crankshaft by the connecting rods, Figure 7-4.

While the metal used for these castings is ordinarily termed cast iron or aluminum, the terminology is rather loose because these metals are usually alloys. In the case of cast iron, small amounts of chromium, molybdenum, or other

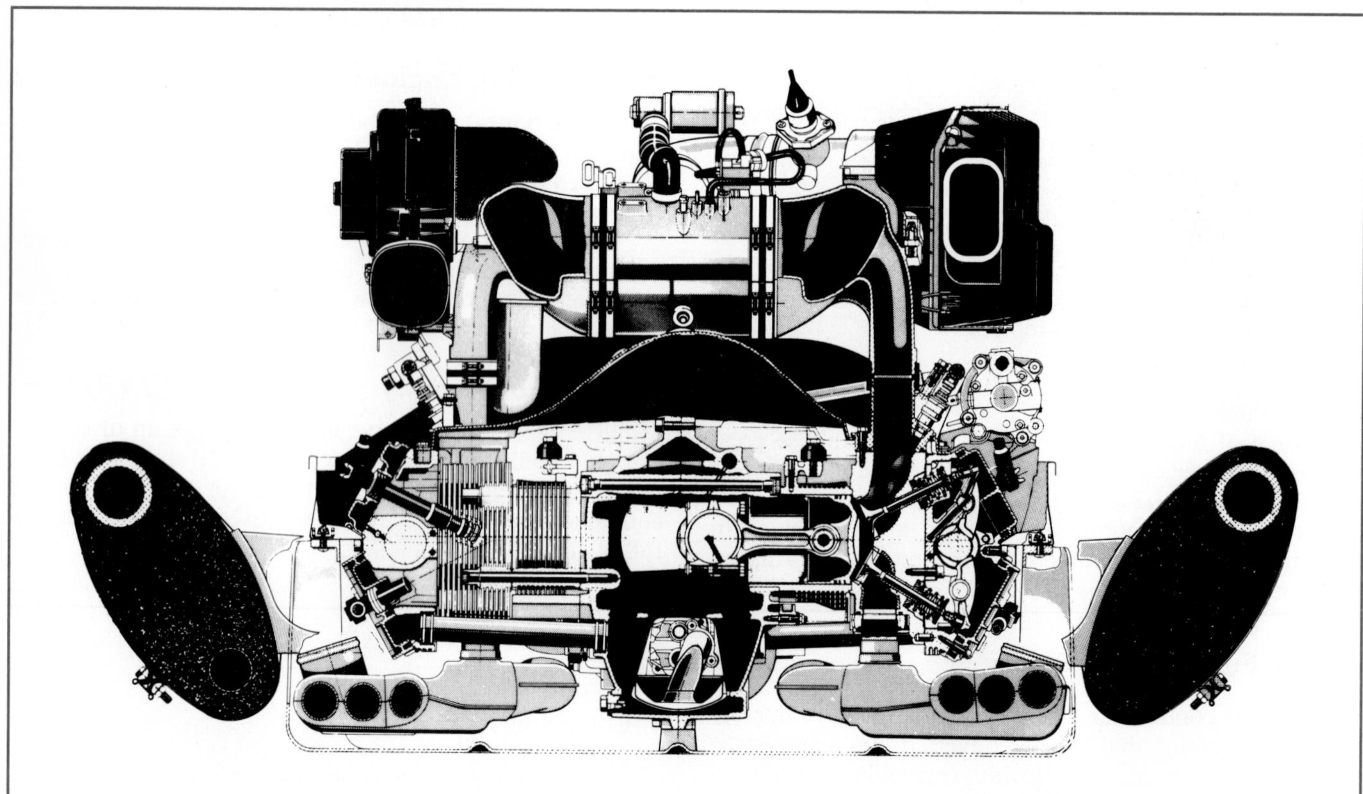

Figure 7-2. An air-cooled engine has no radiator. However, the engine has cooling fins. The cooling fins are exposed to the air, and heat from the engine is dissipated through the fins. (Porsche)

metals may be added. In the case of aluminum castings, it is customary to add other materials to create an alloy. This practice, along with heat and chemical treatment, increases the strength and wear resisting ability of the metal.

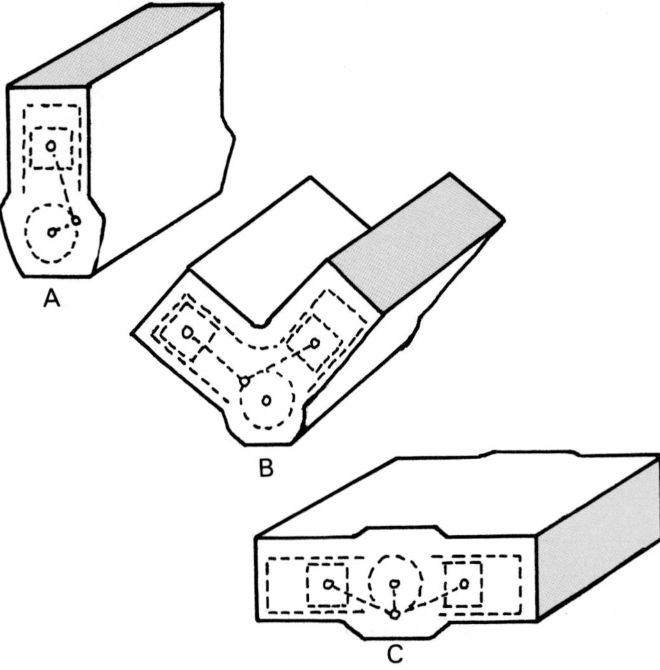

Figure 7-3. Arrangement of engine cylinders. A–Inline engine. B–V-type engine. C–Opposed engine.

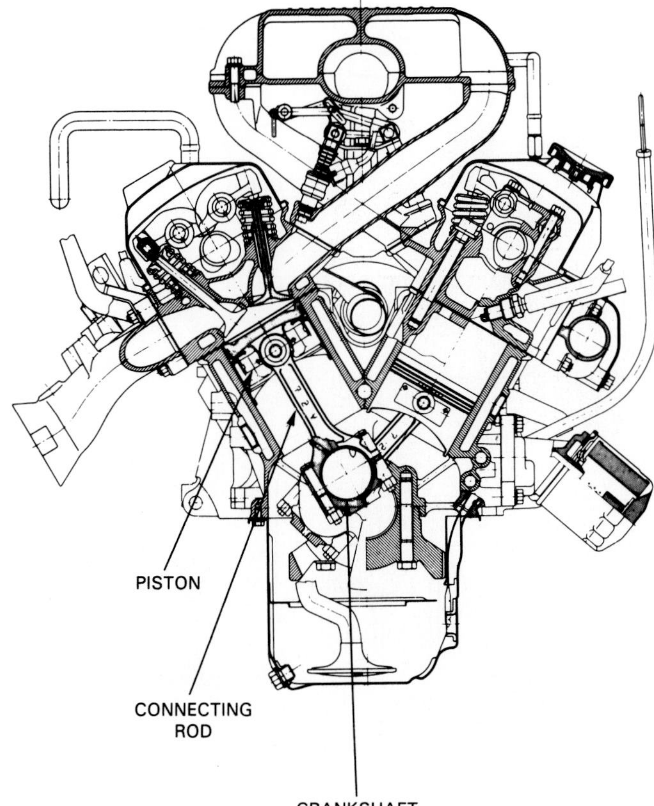

Figure 7-4. Note the position and arrangement of the various engine parts. (Chrysler)

In many aluminum engines, a steel sleeve is placed in the cylinder for the rings to move against. These sleeves are of two types: the dry sleeve and the wet sleeve. The dry type is simply a sleeve or barrel that is pressed into an oversize bore in the cylinder block. The wet type is a cylinder sleeve that replaces the cylinder wall. With a wet sleeve, the coolant circulates in contact with the outside surface of the sleeve. In this case, seals are required at both ends of the sleeve. See Figure 7-7.

The ***crankcase*** is cast as an integral part of the engine block. It houses the crankshaft and, in some cases, the

Figure 7-5. A four-cylinder engine block and crankshaft. (Ford)

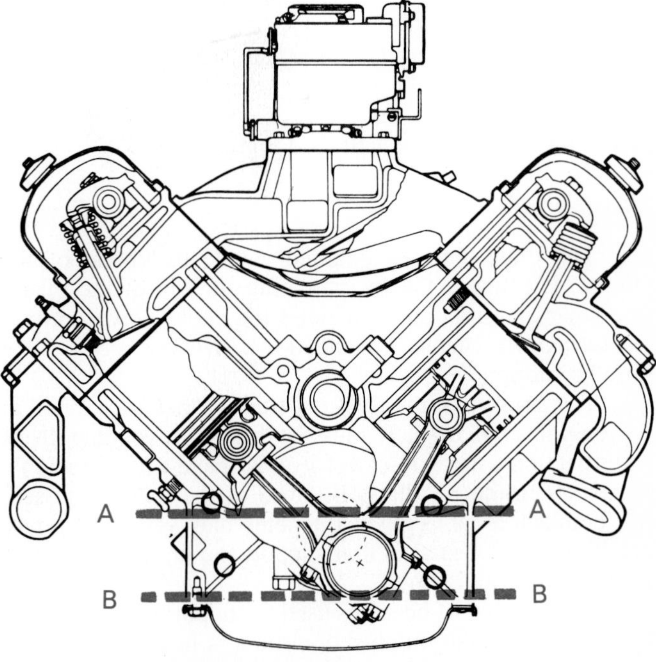

Figure 7-6. Line A is the center of the crankshaft. The crankshaft extends down to line B. Circles indicate the points of reinforcement on the engine block.

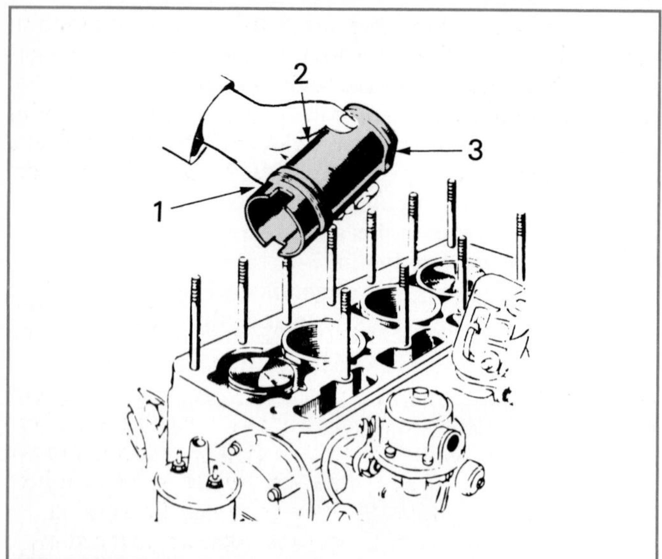

Figure 7-7. A wet-type cylinder sleeve. 1–Sleeve. 2–Sealing ring. 3–Sealing surface.

camshaft. With the oil pan, which mounts on the lower surface of the crankcase, the block forms an oil-tight housing in which the rotating and reciprocating parts operate.

The cylinder block is an intricate casting that varies in thickness and does not always cool uniformly. Internal stresses are created that sometimes cause warpage. However, much has been done in the way of design to minimize the effects of warpage of the cylinder bores.

Engine block distortion may occur from incorrect placing of the metal masses around the cylinders, from expansion and contraction due to the heat of operation, or from excessive mechanical stresses (unequal or extreme tightening of bolts, etc.). Distortion can occur in several directions. The cylinder head surface can warp or twist. The cylinder bore may warp longitudinally or become out-of-round. The crankshaft or camshaft bearing bores may be warped out of line, etc.

To stiffen and strengthen engine blocks, ***webs,*** or ***ribs,*** are often added to the castings at the points of greatest stress. In some cases, the crankcase is extended below the center line of the crankshaft. See Figure 7-6.

Crankshaft

The crankshaft is regarded as the backbone of the engine. It changes the reciprocating motion of the piston into rotary motion, and it handles the entire power output. ***Reciprocating*** means up and down. ***Rotary*** means in a circular motion.

The crankshaft revolves in ***bearings*** that are located in the engine crankcase. It must be free to revolve with as little friction as possible, yet it must have no appreciable looseness in the bearings. Because of the loads imposed, the crankshaft is large in diameter and very accurately machined. The bearings that support the crankshaft are of generous size and length.

The number of bearings used to support the crankshaft will depend on the number of cylinders in the engine and the design of the engine. The crankshaft is designed with a specific number of throws, which serve as points for attaching the connecting rods, Figure 7-8. By locating a main bearing journal between throws of the crankshaft, it is possible to use a lighter crankshaft than if two throws are placed between main bearing journals.

Engine crankshafts vary according to the design of the engine. The throws on a crankshaft in a multiple-cylinder engine are positioned so that one piston is always on its power stroke. A single cylinder engine will have one throw on the crankshaft, Figure 7-8. A crankshaft for a two-cylinder engine will have two throws that are spaced 180° apart. A crankshaft for a three-cylinder engine will have three throws that are spaced 120° apart. A crankshaft for a four-cylinder engine will normally have the throws for cylinders 1 and 4 on one side and the throws for cylinders 2 and 3 on the other side, 180° apart, Figure 7-9.

Inline Six-cylinder Crankshafts. An inline six-cylinder engine may have a left-hand crankshaft or a right-hand crankshaft, depending on the firing order of the cylinders (to be covered later). The crank throws are spaced 120° apart in either case, Figure 7-10. Cylinders 1 and 6 are on one throw, cylinders 2 and 5 are on the second throw, and cylinders 3 and 4 are on the third throw.

V-6 Crankshafts. If a 90° V-6 engine has a crankshaft with three throws spaced 120° apart (common crankpin for

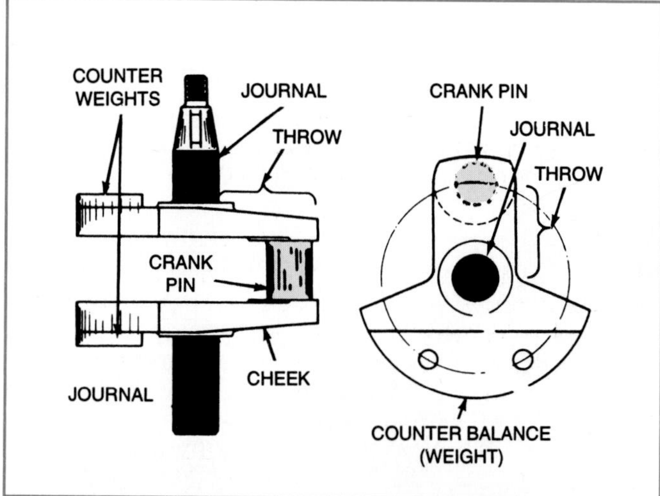

Figure 7-8. Main bearing journals are shown in black. Crankpin is in color.

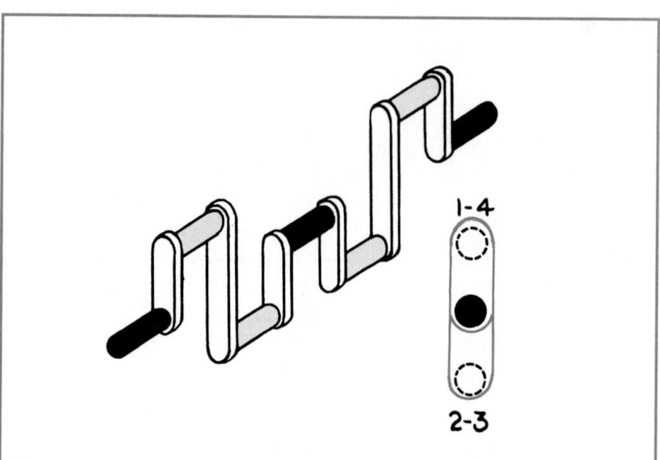

Figure 7-9. A crankshaft for an inline four-cylinder engine normally has throws that are 180° apart.

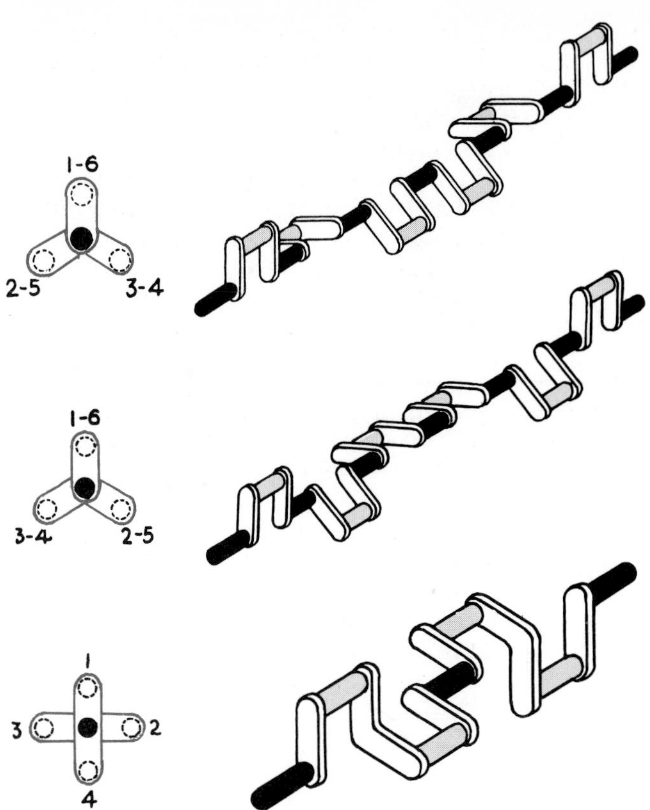

Figure 7-10. A–A right-hand crankshaft has the 3-4 throw to the right of the 1-6 throw. B–A left-hand crankshaft has the 2-3 throw to the left of the 1-6 arrow. C–The crankshaft for a V-8 engine is similar to the crankshaft for a four cylinder engine.

two connecting rods), it will have uneven firing intervals between cylinders. As a result, there will be varying torque impulses, which will cause vibration.

To overcome this problem, one manufacturer splits each crankpin on its V-6 crankshaft by an included angle of 30°. This advances the throws of the crankpins for cylinders 2, 4, and 6 by 15° on the right bank and delays the throws of the crankpins for cylinders 1, 3, and 5 by a similar amount on the left bank. The firing order of the V-6 engine that uses this crankshaft is 1-6-5-4-3-2. The firing interval is 120° for all cylinders.

Another manufacturer splits the crankpins on its V-6 engine by an included angle of 18°. This crankshaft design results in a firing interval of 132°-108°-132°-108°-132°-108°. The firing order is 1-6-5-4-3-2.

V-8 Crankshafts. A V-8 engine normally has a four-throw crankshaft with two cylinders attached to each throw. However, the location of the crankpins will vary. In one case, all four throws may be in the same plane (two on each side of the crankshaft). In another design, the throws may be in two planes that are 90° apart, Figure 7-10.

Crankshaft Balance Weights. Without special ***balance weights,*** or ***counterweights,*** on the crankshaft, severe vibration would result from the following:

- Weight of reciprocating parts.
- Weight of rotating parts.
- Inertial force of reciprocating parts.
- Combustion pressures.
- Variations in torque.

To reduce or eliminate such vibration, the crankshaft must be balanced. That is, it must be provided with counterweights that extend radially from the crankshaft centerline in the opposite direction of the crank throws, Figure 7-8. In this way, the forces acting on the crankshaft are balanced and vibration is reduced. In addition, bearing life is increased.

Pistons

The ***pistons*** move up and down in the engine cylinders. The piston head, or crown, Figure 7-11, is the top surface against which the explosive force of combustion is exerted. The head may be flat, concave, convex, or any one of a great variety of shapes to promote turbulence or help control combustion. In some applications, a narrow groove is cut into the piston above the top ring to serve as a heat dam, reducing the amount of heat reaching the top ring.

The main section of the piston is known as the ***skirt.*** It forms a bearing area that contacts the cylinder wall and takes the thrust caused by the crankshaft.

Some thrust is created on both sides of the piston. Major thrust is to the side opposite the crank throw as the piston is driven down on the power stroke. Minor thrust is the side opposite the crank throw as the piston moves up on the compression stroke. Pistons are internally braced to make them as strong as possible. See Figure 7-12.

In some designs, the piston skirt is extended downward on the thrust sides of the piston to form what is known as a slipper piston. This design feature increases the area of piston contact with the cylinder walls at the thrust faces.

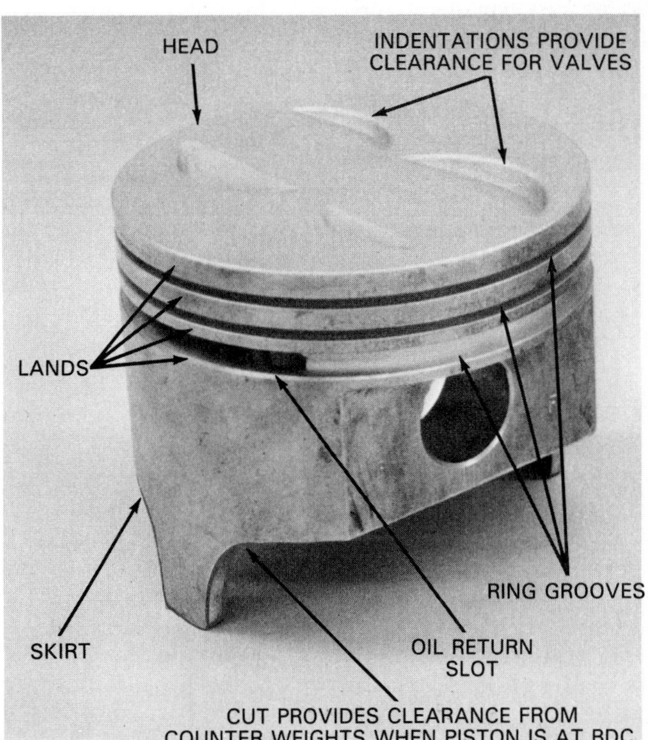

Figure 7-11. A typical slipper skirt piston derives its name from a portion of skirt that is cut away to provide clearance for counterweights. The lands are areas between the grooves that the rings ride against. Note that the piston pin hole is recessed, which prevents pin from coming in contact with the cylinder wall. (Ford)

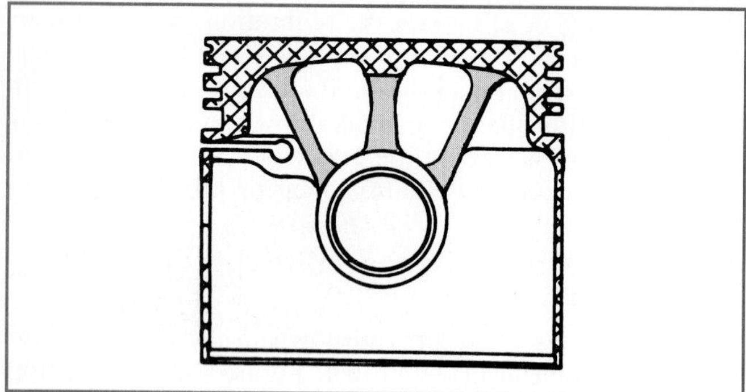

Figure 7-12. Ribs reinforce this piston head.

Piston Design. Cast iron pistons may have the skirts slotted in a variety of ways, Figure 7-13. These slots are placed on the thrust sides to provide flexibility in the piston skirt. By this means, the piston can be fitted more closely when cold, and it can expand when hot without damage.

Some pistons are of the strut type shown in Figure 7-14. In this case, an alloy steel insert is cast into the aluminum piston to control the expansion of the aluminum and maintain more constant clearance. Pistons are usually of the skeleton type and do not contact the cylinder walls around the piston pin holes.

Most aluminum pistons are ***cam-ground,*** or purposely machined with the skirts oval, Figure 7-15. While the skirts will be out-of-round when cold, they will become more nearly round when the piston expands at operating temperature.

Pistons are also slightly tapered in design, Figure 7-16. The top of the piston runs much hotter than the skirt, so the top is smaller in diameter. This is particularly true in the area above the top ring.

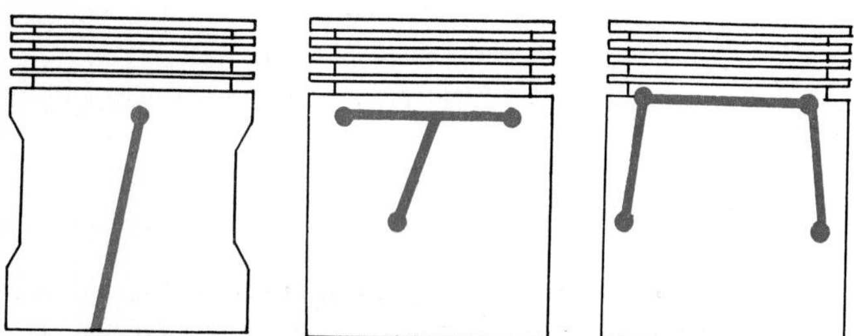

Figure 7-13. Some pistons may have a slot cut through the skirt on the minor thrust side of piston.

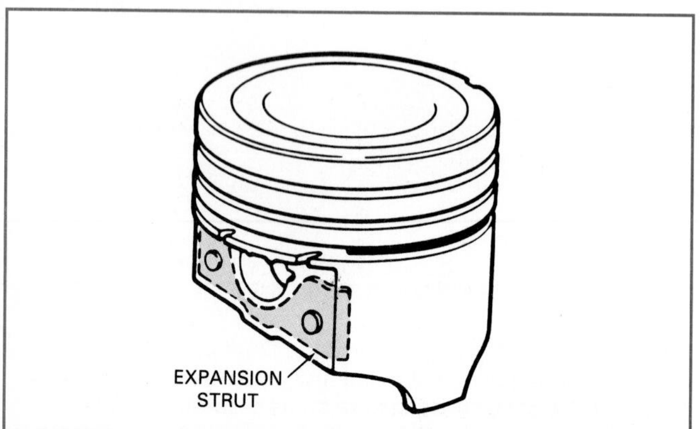

Figure 7-14. Strut helps control the rate and direction of expansion. (Chevrolet)

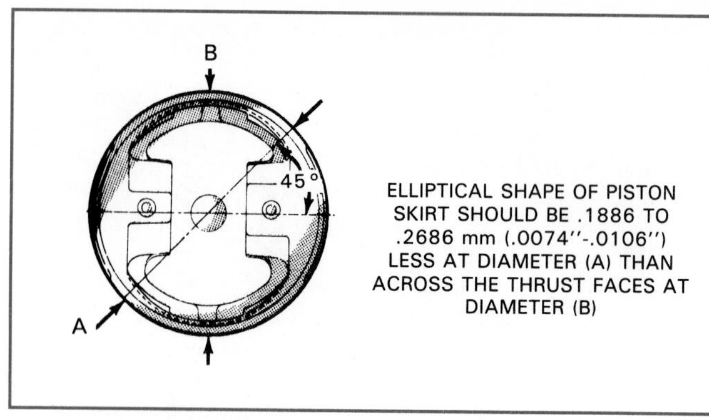

Figure 7-15. A cam-ground piston is slightly egg shaped when cold and becomes rounded as the engine reaches operating temperature. (Chrysler)

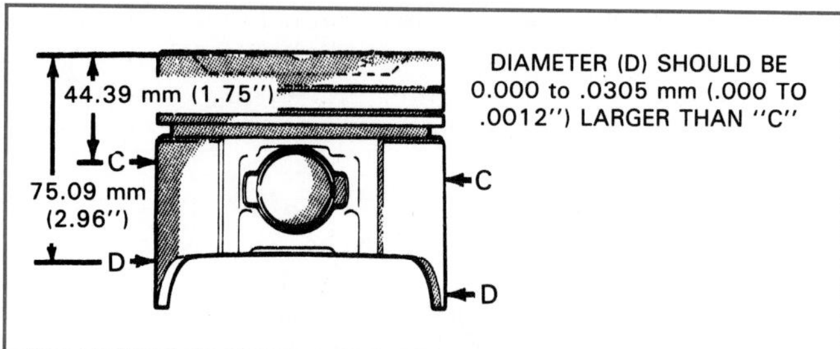

Figure 7-16. Piston is slightly tapered when cold. As operating temperature of the engine increases, the amount of taper is reduced. (Chrysler)

Piston Materials. Cast iron has been used extensively as a piston material. It is strong enough to withstand stresses imposed; has a melting point above the cylinder operating temperature; expands at the same rate as cast iron cylinders; and does not generate excessive friction when properly lubricated. The principal objection to iron is excessive weight, a design factor that becomes more important as engine speeds increase.

Aluminum alloy is now preferred as a material for pistons. Materials alloyed with the aluminum include copper, magnesium, nickel, and silicon. Aluminum alloy is lighter than cast iron, is readily cast and machined, and does not generate excessive friction in the cylinder, Figure 7-17.

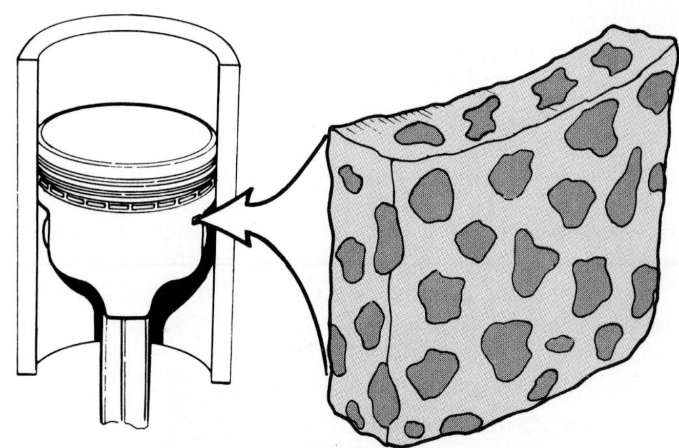

Figure 7-17. Some piston skirts are impregnated with silicon, which reduces friction and makes the piston more durable. (Chevrolet)

Aluminum alloy pistons can also be strengthened by a special heat treatment.

Aluminum alloy expands more rapidly than cast iron when subjected to the heat of operation, and it also has a much lower melting point. In material and design, the aluminum piston has been developed to a point where its advantages outweigh its disadvantages. Because of this, it is used in almost all automobile engines.

Lighter weight means less inertia for the reciprocating parts and higher speed for the engine, which lead to more responsive acceleration. Less inertia also decreases bearing loads at high speeds and reduces side thrust on the cylinder walls. The piston head runs cooler because of the greater heat transfer of aluminum, and it is possible to use higher compression ratios.

Early aluminum pistons were noisy because they had to be fitted in the cylinder with considerably more clearance than cast iron pistons. This resulted in piston slap and rattle when the engine was cold. The difficulty has been largely overcome by designing the piston skirt so it is flexible, by using special alloys, and by incorporating steel struts, Figure 7-14.

Aluminum pistons possess the desirable characteristic of transferring the heat away from the combustion chamber more rapidly than cast iron. However, if the rings are stuck in the groove, the top edge of the piston or the lands between the rings may soften and melt or be blown away by the hot gas, Figure 7-18. The aluminum may become soft when overheated, allowing the ring grooves to deform. Similarly, severe and continued detonation (rapid burning or explosion of air-fuel mixture in combustion chamber) can cause broken piston heads.

Piston Rings

Piston rings carried in the ring grooves are of two basic types: ***compression rings*** and ***oil control rings.*** Both types are made in a wide variety of designs.

The upper ring or rings prevent compression leakage; the lower ring or rings control the amount of oil being deposited on the cylinder wall. The lower groove or grooves often have holes or slots to permit oil drainage from behind the rings.

The piston ring lands are the parts of the piston between the ring grooves. The lands provide a seating surface for the sides of the piston rings.

Connecting Rods

The ***connecting rods*** link the pistons to the crankshaft, Figure 7-19. Each connecting rod is constructed with a large end and a small end. The large end is connected to the

Figure 7-18. Piston damage occurs when the piston is overheated.

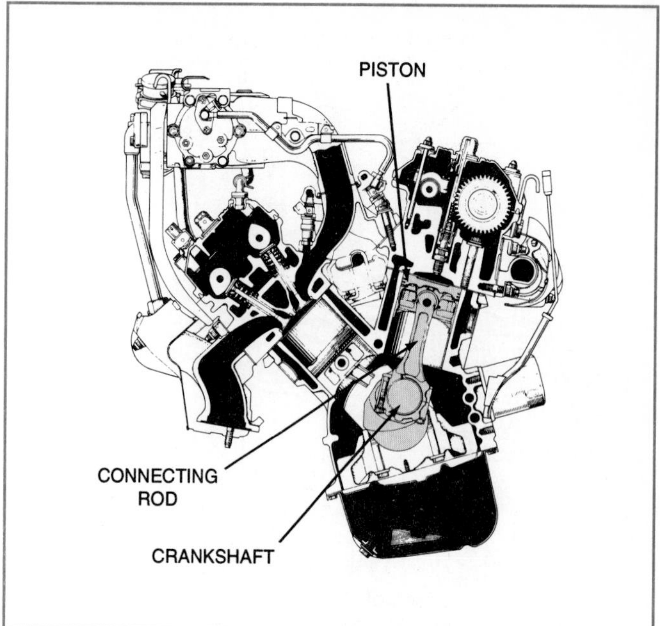

Figure 7-19. The connecting rod links the piston to the crankshaft. (Toyota)

crankshaft journal. The piston pin passes through the piston and the small end of the connecting rod. The large end of the rod is split to permit installation and removal. Insert-type bearings are generally installed between the crankshaft journals and the large end of the connecting rod.

Piston Pins

The ***piston pin,*** or ***wrist pin,*** is used to connect the piston to the connecting rod. The piston pin (wrist pin) hole in the piston also serves as a bearing for the piston pin, and is not located exactly in the middle of the piston. It is placed as much as 1/16″ from the center of the piston, Figure 7-20.

Cylinder Head

The ***cylinder head*** is mounted on top of the cylinder block and forms the top sections of the combustion chambers, Figure 7-21. The head contains intake and exhaust ports. These ports lead from the combustion chamber to the

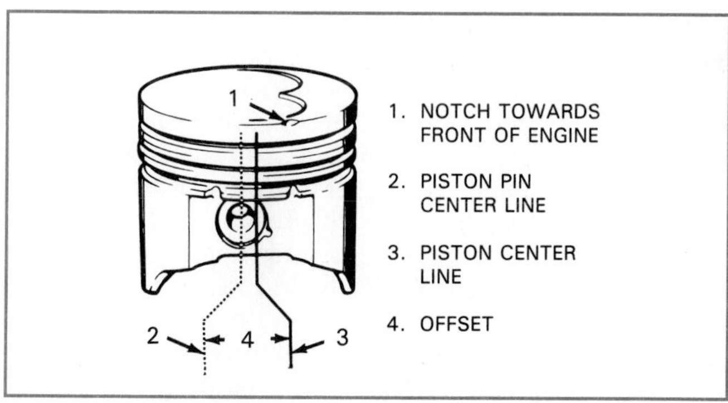

Figure 7-20. The piston pin is offset 1/16 in. from the centerline of the piston. This prevents the piston from slapping the cylinder wall as thrust changes from major to minor thrust face of the piston. (Oldsmobile)

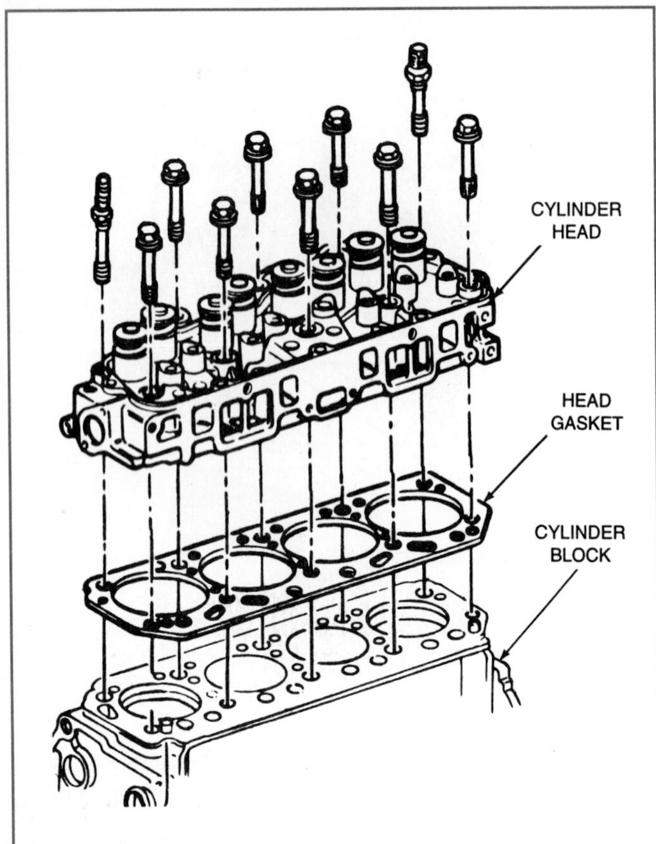

Figure 7-21. The cylinder head is mounted on top of the cylinder block. The head gasket seals the mating surfaces of the head and the block. (General Motors)

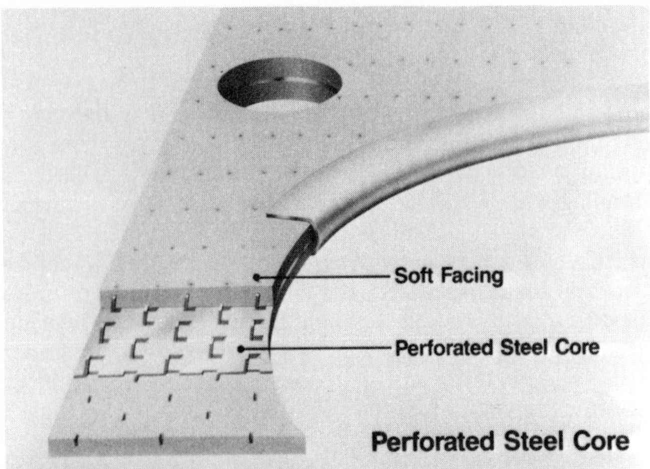

Figure 7-22. This cylinder head gasket design makes it necessary to retorque, but compensates for irregularities between the mating surfaces. (Fel-Pro, Inc.)

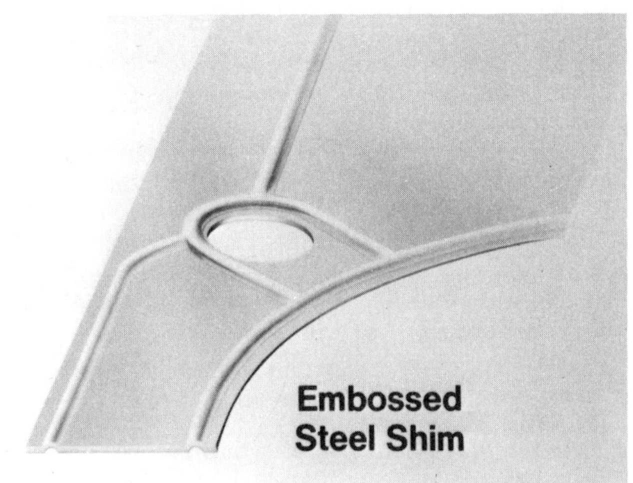

Figure 7-23. This cylinder head gasket design does not have to be retorqued, but does not do the best job of compensating for irregularities between the mating surfaces. Note that the critical sealing areas are raised. (Fel-Pro, Inc.)

intake and exhaust manifolds. The ends of these ports that enter the combustion chambers contain a valve seat. Additionally, valve guides, which help align the valves by supporting the valve stems, are machined into the cylinder head.

In addition to the intake and exhaust ports, the cylinder head also contains oil galleries, which provide lubricant to the components mounted in the head, and water jackets, which carry coolant through the head.

Cylinder head gaskets are by far the most important gaskets on the engine. These gaskets provide a seal between the cylinder block and the cylinder head. If the gasket is not sealing properly, engine performance will suffer. In addition, coolant may leak into the combustion chambers. There are several different types of cylinder head gaskets available on the aftermarket.

The perforated steel core cylinder head gasket, Figure 7-22, has a very thin perforated metal core that is sandwiched between soft material. This soft material does an excellent job of compensating for the irregularities between the mating surfaces. However, this feature makes it necessary to retorque the head bolts after approximately 500 miles of driving. This is due to the soft material relaxing.

The embossed steel shim cylinder head gasket, Figure 7-23, is usually used by the manufacturer and can also be purchased in the aftermarket. This type of cylinder head gasket does not require retorquing of the head bolts after any period of driving time. This is due to the steel's resilience. The steel does not relax after a period of time. However, the steel shim cylinder head gasket does not compensate for irregularities between the mating surfaces as well as the perforated cylinder head gasket. This is not a concern on new engines, as the mating surfaces are completely flat.

Because of its solid steel core, the multilayered cylinder head gasket, Figure 7-24, does not have to be retorqued after any period of driving time. The Teflon serves a dual purpose. First, when the cylinder head is torqued to specifications, the Teflon works its way into the irregularities between the mating surfaces for an effective seal. An aluminum cylinder head expands at a faster rate than the cast iron block on which it seats. The Teflon provides a slippery surface for the aluminum cylinder head to slide on as it expands and contracts.

Valve Train

The ***valve train*** consists of the valves and the valve-operating mechanism. The typical valve train consists of the camshaft, lifters, valves, and valve springs. Many valve trains also contain rocker arms and push rods.

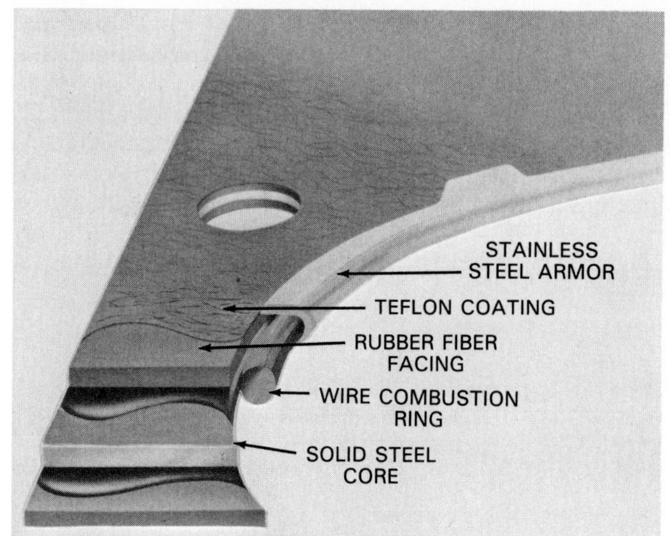

Figure 7-24. This cylinder head gasket design does not need to be retorqued, and the Teflon provides a very effective seal between the irregularities of the mating surfaces. The Teflon also allows aluminum cylinder heads to slide as they expand and contract. (Fel-Pro, Inc.)

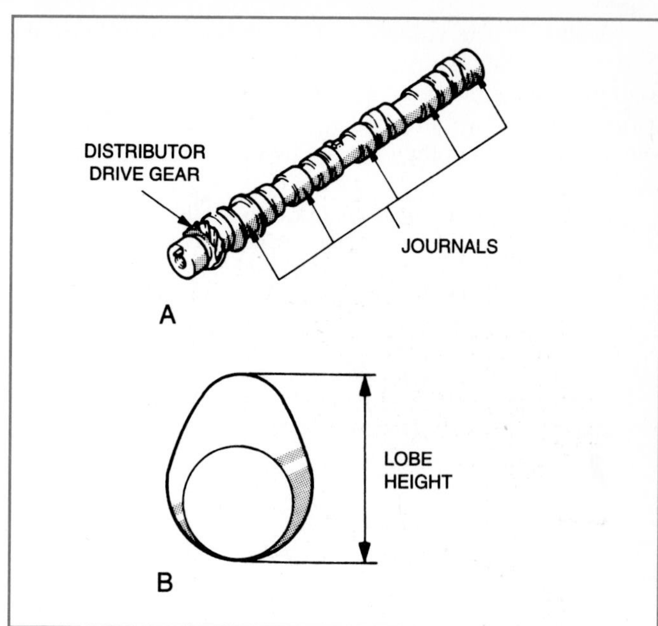

Figure 7-25. The camshaft lobes open the valves at the proper time. A–Typical camshaft. B–Camshaft lobe.

Camshaft. The ***camshaft*** opens the valves at the appropriate times in the combustion cycle. The camshaft is simply a shaft that contains a cam-shaped lobe for each engine valve. See Figure 7-25. Camshaft rotation causes the lobes to open the valves. Since the valves of the engine need to be opened at different times, the noses, or high points, of the cams are offset from one another. Most camshafts have twice as many cams as there are cylinders. The reason for this is that there is one cam for each exhaust valve and one cam for each intake valve. However, some overhead camshaft engines are provided with two camshafts for each bank of cylinders–one camshaft for the intake valves and the other for the exhaust valves.

The camshaft is driven by the crankshaft. In order to open the valves at the correct time, camshaft rotation is timed to crankshaft rotation. This is accomplished by using gears, a timing belt, or a timing chain, Figure 7-26. In a four-cycle engine, the camshaft turns at one-half crankshaft speed.

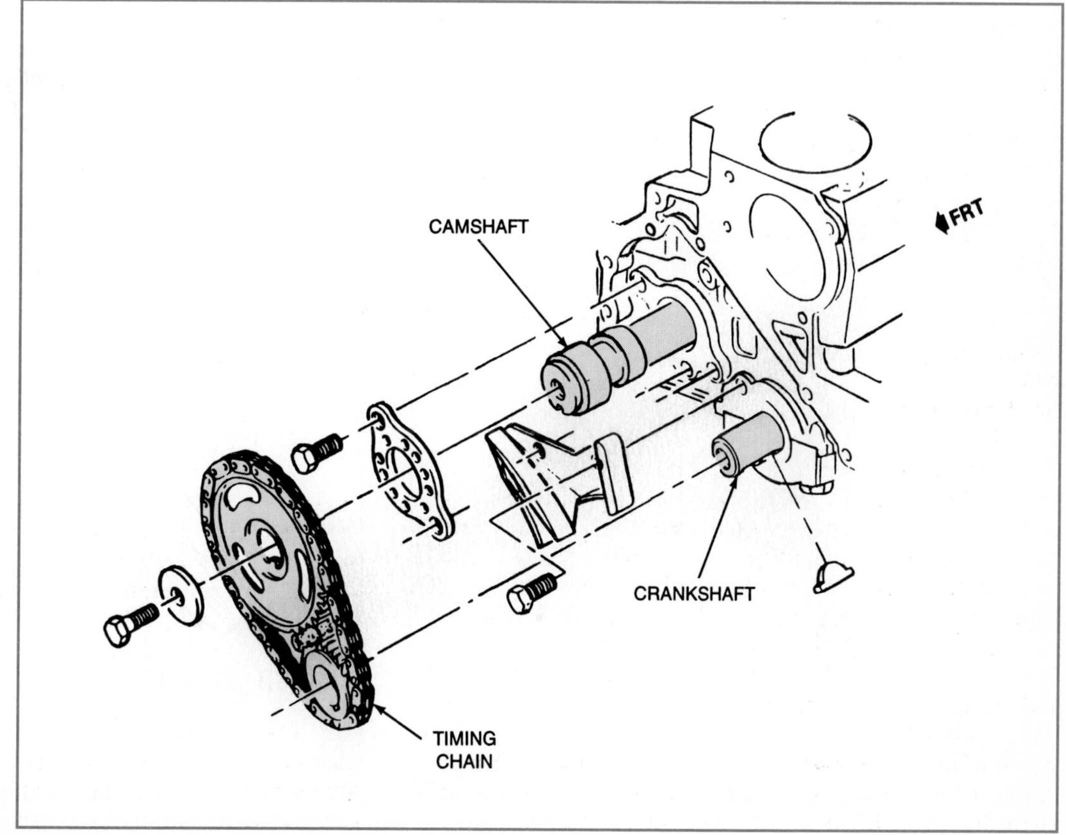

Figure 7-26. In this engine, a chain is used to connect the camshaft to the crankshaft. (General Motors)

Valves. The ***valves*** used in automobile engines are commonly called poppet valves. See Figure 7-27. They are used to regulate the flow of intake and exhaust gases. Valve springs, which are attached to the valve stems, force the valves closed when they are not being pushed open by the cam lobes.

The location of the valves in four-cycle engines is one of the basic elements of engine design. As mentioned, the valves are located in the cylinder head in late-model engines, Figure 7-28. In older designs, however, the valves were located in the engine block or in both the block and the head. See Figure 7-29 and 7-30.

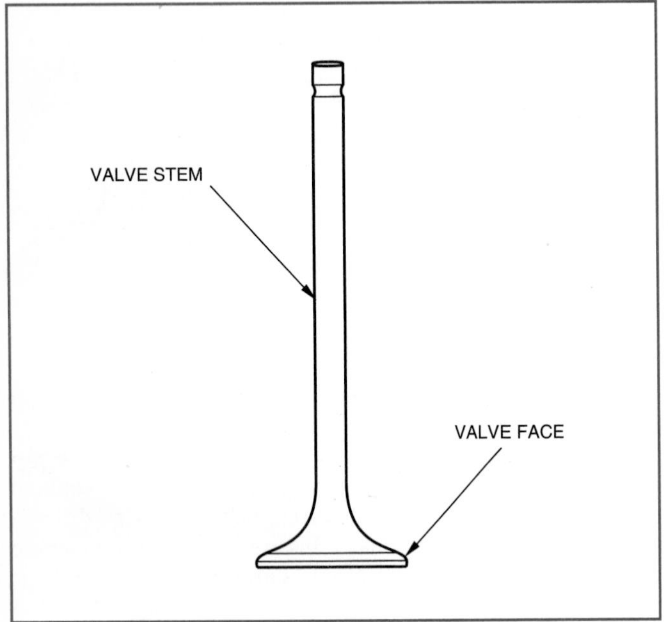

Figure 7-27. Typical poppet valve.

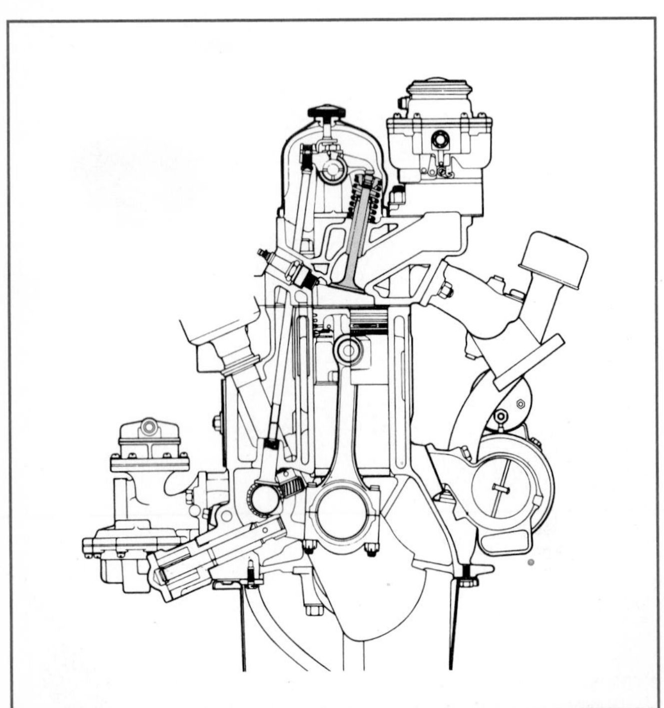

Figure 7-28. In an I-head engine, both valves are located above the piston.

Push Rods and Rocker Arms. ***Push rods*** and ***rocker arms*** are used on engines in which the camshaft is located in the cylinder block. These components help transmit the motion of the cam lobes to the valves, Figure 7-31. Rocker arms are sometimes used in overhead cam engines.

Lifters. The valve stems or the push rods do not ride directly on the camshaft. Instead, ***lifters*** are used between

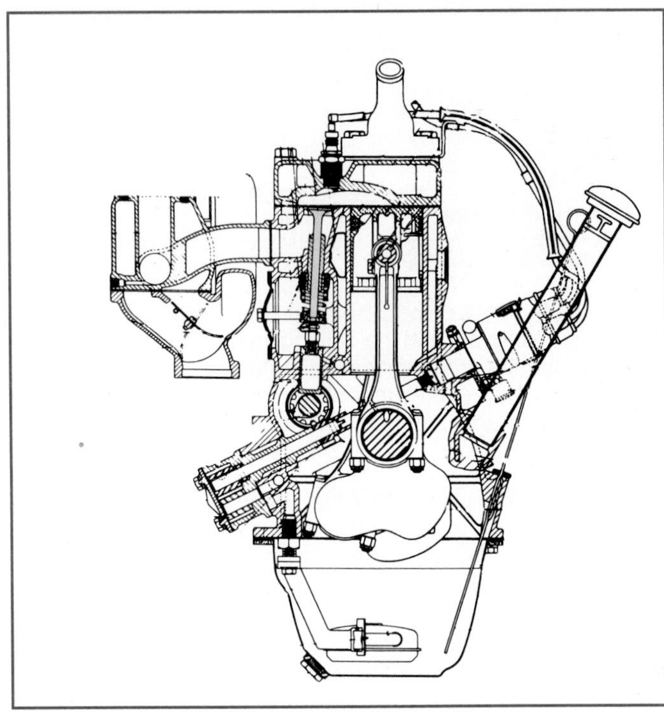

Figure 7-29. Cross section of an L-head engine. Both valves are located to the side of the piston.

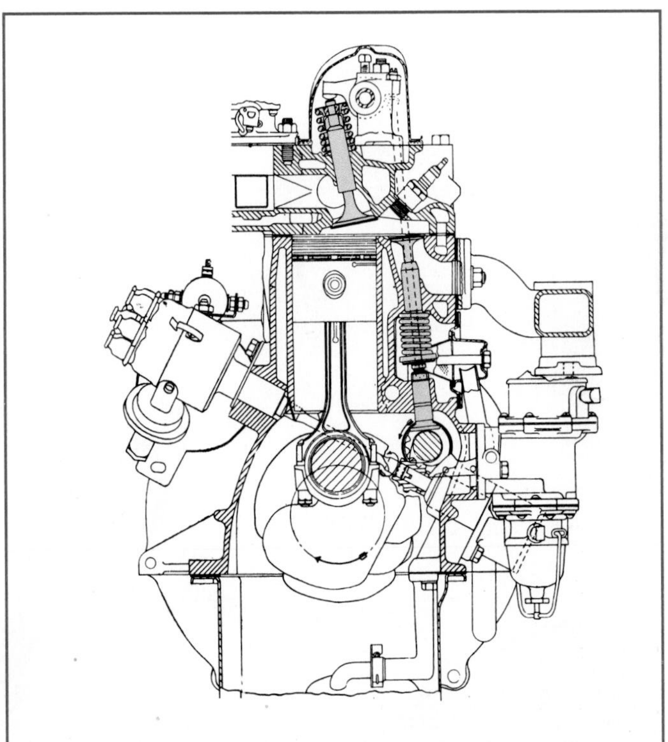

Figure 7-30. F-head engine. One valve is located above the piston, and the other valve is located to the side of the piston.

these components. See Figure 7-32. The lifter transmits the action of the cam to the valve or the push rod. There are two types of valve lifters: mechanical lifters and hydraulic lifters.

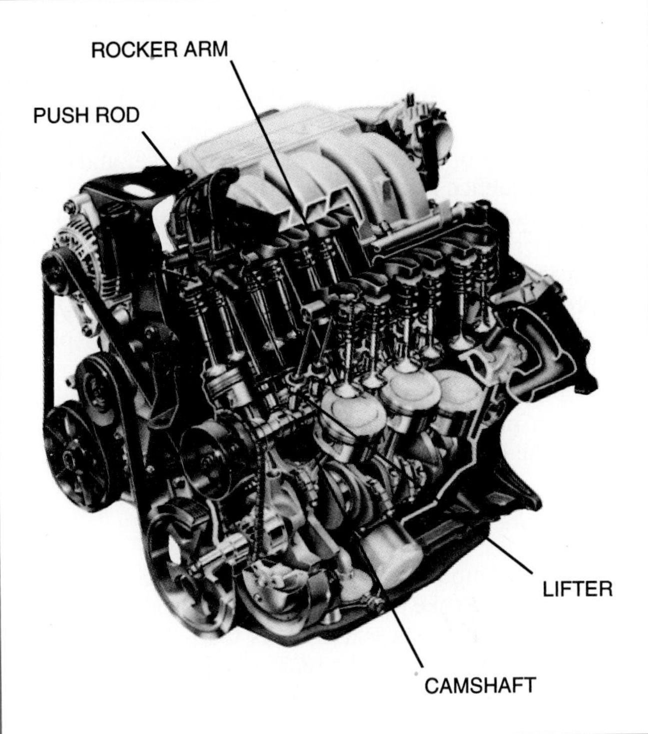

Figure 7-31. The rocker arms and push rods transmit motion from the cam lobes to the valves. (Chrysler)

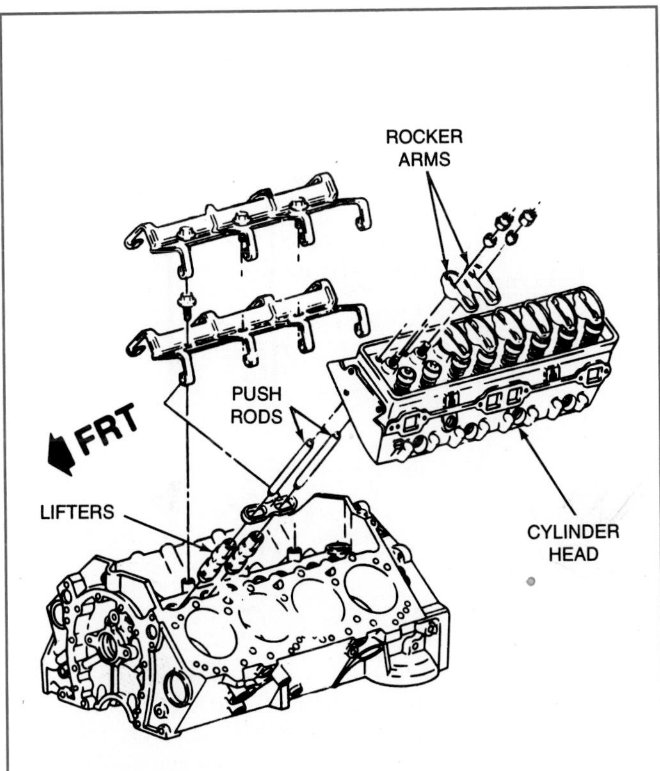

Figure 7-32. Lifters are located between the camshaft and the push rods in this engine. (General Motors)

Combustion Chamber Design

The ***combustion chamber*** is the space within the cylinder above the piston where the burning of the air/fuel mixture occurs. Improvements have been made, but research continues on the design characteristics of the combustion chamber. Combustion chamber design focuses on the creation and control of turbulence (movement of air and fuel within cylinder to create a more uniform mixture), Figure 7-33.

As fuel improved and higher compression ratios were sought, the L-head engine was largely superseded by the overhead valve (OHV) engine. OHV design permits larger engine valves and increased compression ratios, permitting more power by an engine of a given size.

The shape of the combustion chamber of the overhead valve engine has gone through many changes. It has ranged from the plain cylindrical form to the wedge type and hemispherical type shown in Figure 7-34.

The wedge-shaped combustion chamber is an efficient design used in most engines. It is noted for the turbulence produced in the air/fuel charge as the piston

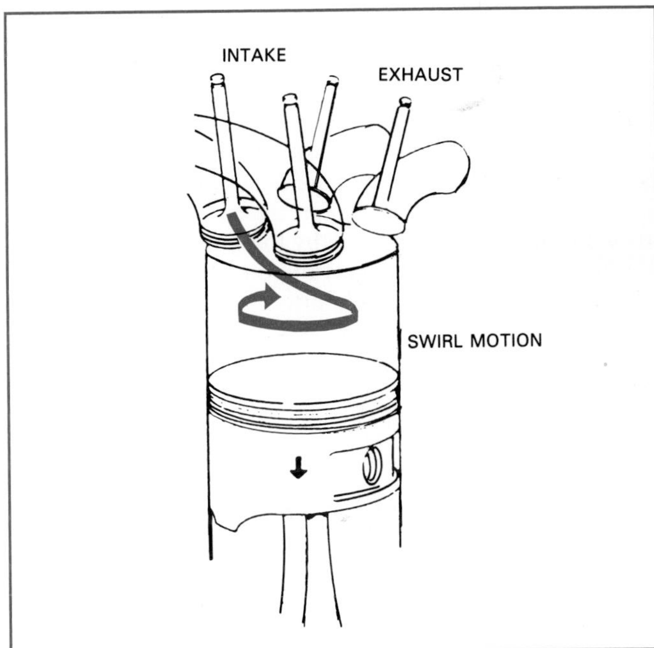

Figure 7-33. Swirling motion, or turbulence, improves the combustion characteristics of the air/fuel mixture.

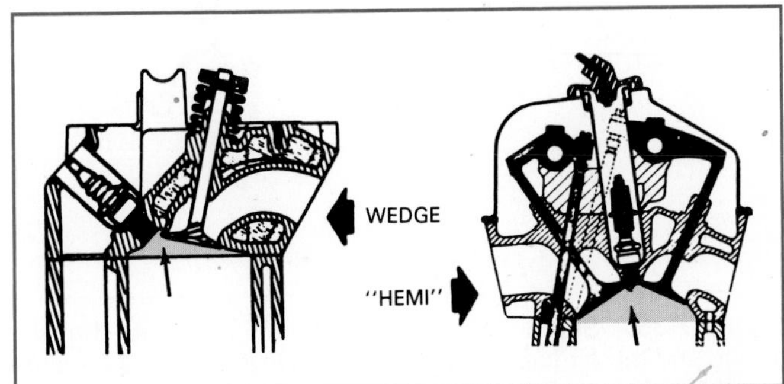

Figure 7-34. Modern engine combustion chamber shapes. Left–Wedge-shaped combustion chamber. Right–Hemi or hemispherical-shaped combustion chamber.

moves up on the compression stroke. This results in increased efficiency.

The hemispherical design, or "hemi," provides room for larger valves in a given bore. In addition, the "hemi" design permits a centrally located spark plug, which contributes to more efficient combustion, better heat dissipation, and higher thermal efficiency.

With increased emphasis being placed on cleaner exhaust, it is important to note that the unburned hydrocarbons are proportional to the surface area of the combustion chamber. As this area is reduced, the unburned hydrocarbons are also reduced. The combustion chamber surface area is at a minimum with a hemispherical combustion chamber. Both "wedge" and "hemi" designs feature a reduced tendency toward detonation.

Some engines use a double overhead camshaft to provide a hemispherical combustion chamber. This design permits the use of larger valves than in the same size engine with a single overhead camshaft. This results in an increase of power.

Further in this connection, when the cylinder heads and combustion chambers are made of aluminum, the valves operate approximately 212°F (100°C) cooler than in comparable cylinder heads of cast iron. In addition, the compression ratio can be increased approximately 1.0 over the cast iron head (11.0:1 over 10.0:1, for example).

The material from which the combustion chamber is made and the efficiency of the cooling system also have a distinct bearing on the compression ratio of a given engine. For example, aluminum cylinder heads and aluminum pistons can operate at higher compression ratios than cast iron or steel. This is made possible by the superior heat transfer ability of aluminum. The heat of combustion is dissipated more rapidly to the coolant or air.

Engine Operating Sequence

In internal combustion engines, there is a definite sequence of events that must occur:

1. The cylinder must be filled with an explosive mixture.
2. This mixture must be compressed into a smaller space and then ignited.
3. The explosive or expansive force of the burning fuel must be used for power production.
4. The burned mixture must be removed from the cylinder.

This series of events must be repeated over and over in the same sequence if the engine is to run.

The first need is to fill the cylinder with an explosive mixture. If gasoline is used as fuel, it must be mixed with the proper proportion of air (14.7 parts air to 1 part fuel). This proportion is maintained by the fuel injection system (or carburetor). In a gasoline engine, an electrical spark is used to ignite the fuel.

In a diesel engine, fuel oil is injected into the cylinder under high pressure. The heat generated by compressing the air in the cylinder ignites the fuel.

Four-Stroke Cycle

Most automobile engines operate on the ***four-stroke cycle.*** The four-stroke engine is sometimes called the "Otto engine," after its inventor, Nikolaus Otto. The power production cycle in a four-stroke reciprocating engine consists of four strokes of the piston. See Figure 7-35. The first stroke draws the combustible mixture into the cylinder through the valve in the cylinder head. The second stroke compresses the mixture in the cylinder. The combustible mixture is ignited at the end of this stroke. The third stroke

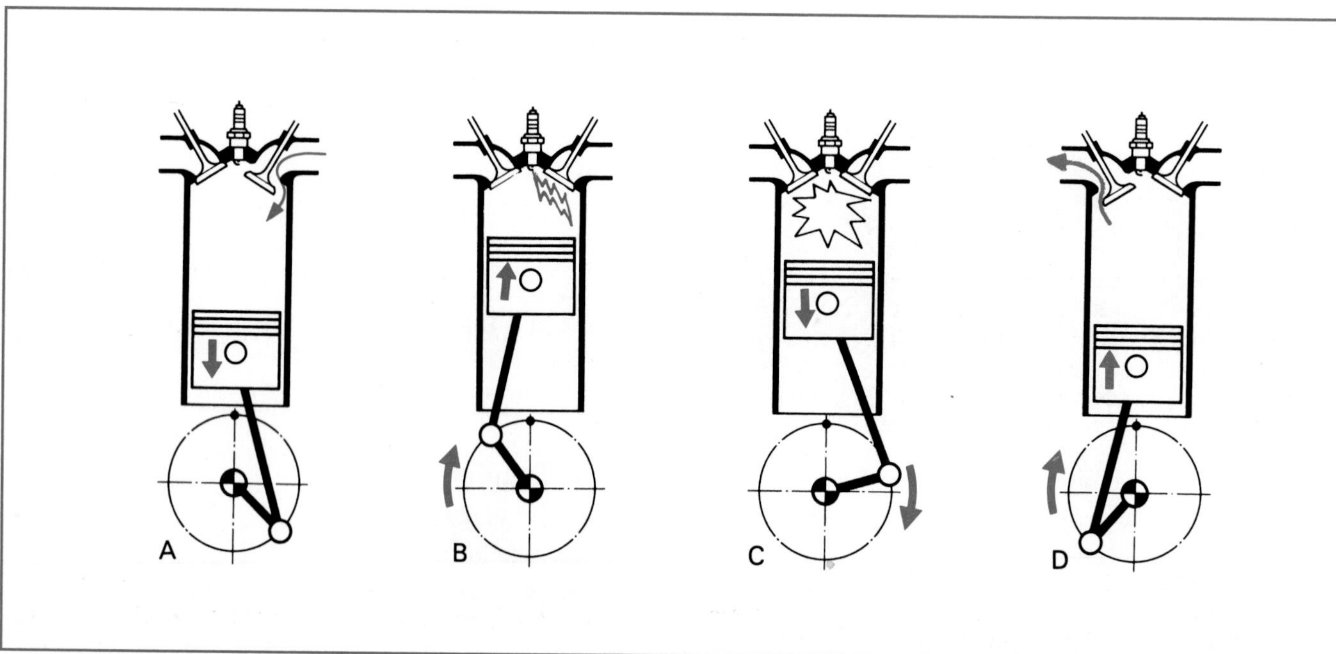

Figure 7-35. Sequence of a four-cycle engine. A–As the piston moves downward, a vacuum is created. The intake valve opens and the air/fuel mixture enters the cylinder. B–The air/fuel mixture is compressed as the piston moves upwards. The spark plug is fired to ignite the air/fuel mixture before the piston reaches top dead center. Note that both valves are closed. C–The air/fuel mixture explodes, forcing the piston downward. Note that both valves are closed. D–As the piston starts to move upward, the exhaust valve is opened. As the piston continues to move up, the exhaust gases are forced out of the cylinder. (Robert Bosch)

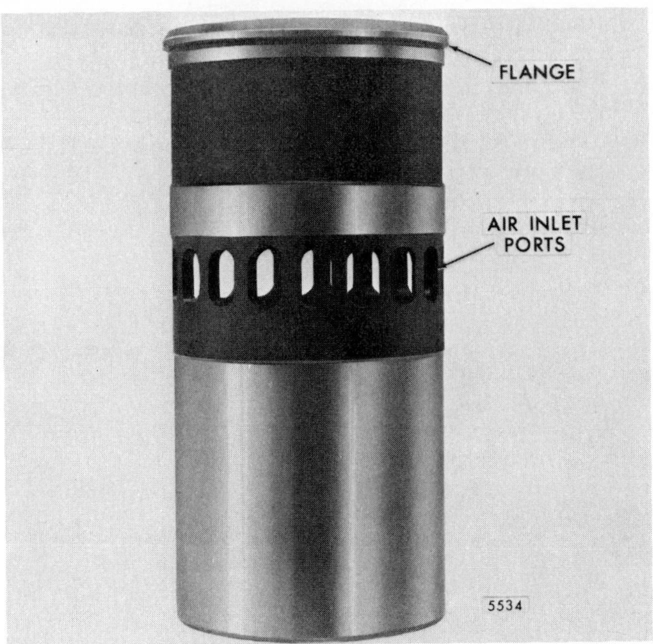

Figure 7-36. The ports in this cylinder allow the air to enter the cylinder when the piston is at bottom dead center (BDC). The ports are closed off as piston moves upward. (Detroit Diesel Corp.)

is the power stroke. During this stroke, the piston is forced downward by the burning mixture. (Note that the valves are closed in the second and third strokes.) The final stroke forces burned gases out of the cylinder through the exhaust valve in the cylinder head.

Two-Stroke Cycle

In the ***two-stroke engine,*** the piston takes over some of the valve function in order to obtain a power stroke during each revolution of the crankshaft. Two-cycle operation involves the use of ports in the cylinders, Figure 7-36. These ports are covered and uncovered as the piston moves. The piston acts like a valve in controlling the filling and emptying of the cylinder.

Alternate phases of vacuum and compression in the crankcase can be avoided by using a blower, or supercharger, to push air into the cylinder, Figure 7-37. In this particular design, a row of ports around the bottom of the cylinder serves as the inlet, Figure 7-36. The piston acts as an intake valve, and cam-operated exhaust valves are placed in the cylinder head. The blower pumps air into the cylinder and diesel fuel is injected under high pressure.

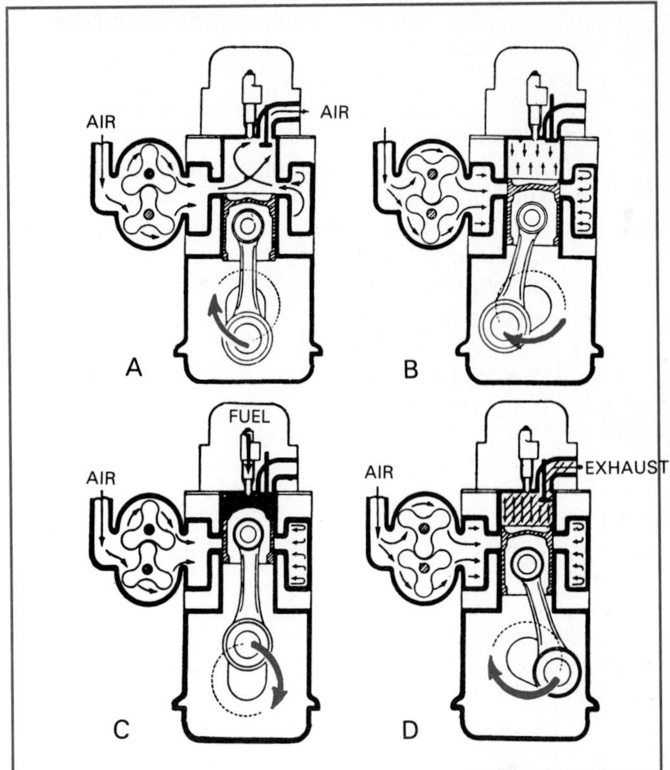

Figure 7-37. Two-cycle diesel engine operation. A–Piston at BDC. The intake ports are uncovered and the blower forces air into the cylinder. B–As the piston moves upward, the ports are closed. The air is compressed, causing the temperature of the air to increase. C–Fuel is injected into the cylinder. The temperature of the compressed air ignites the fuel mixture (there is no spark plug). D-Explosion forces the piston down. The exhaust valve starts to open and the exhaust gases escape.

Chapter 7–Review Questions

Write your answers on a separate sheet of paper. Do not write in this book.

1. Automobiles have been powered successfully by:
   (A) electric motors.
   (B) internal combustion engines.
   (C) steam engines.
   (D) All of the above.
2. The two-cycle reciprocating engine is used exclusively in late-model automobiles. True or False?
3. In a typical automotive engine, a _____ moves back and forth within each cylinder.
4. The largest single metal component in an engine is the:
   (A) crankshaft.
   (B) camshaft.
   (C) cylinder block.
   (D) piston.
5. The crankshaft changes the _____ motion of the piston into _____ motion.
6. A V-8 crankshaft normally has eight throws. True or False?
7. The force of combustion is exerted on the piston _____.
8. The skirt of a cam-ground piston is _____.
9. The pistons in most late-model engines are:
   (A) steel.
   (B) magnesium.
   (C) aluminum alloy.
   (D) None of the above.
10. When exposed to heat, aluminum expands more rapidly than cast iron. True or False?
11. The top rings on a piston are:
    (A) oil control rings.
    (B) compression rings.
    (C) pressure rings.
    (D) None of the above.

12. The _____ _____ link the pistons to the crankshaft.
13. The cylinder head forms the top section of the combustion chamber. True or False?
14. The _____ opens the valves at the proper time in the combustion cycle.
15. In a four-cycle engine, the camshaft turns at one-half ____ speed.
16. In late-model internal combustion engines, the valves are located in:
    (A) the cylinder head.
    (B) the cylinder block.
    (C) the crankcase.
    (D) None of the above.
17. Rocker arms are sometimes found in overhead cam engines. True or False?
18. The _____ _____ is the space above the piston where the burning of the air/fuel mixture occurs.
19. The first stroke in the four-stroke engine cycle is the:
    (A) power stroke.
    (B) intake stroke.
    (C) compression stroke.
    (D) exhaust stroke.
20. The power stroke in a two-stroke engine takes place during each revolution of the crankshaft. True or False?

Cutaway of a late-model four-cylinder engine. How many components can you identify? (Saturn)

Chapter 8
Measuring Engine Performance

After studying this chapter, you will be able to:
- ❍ Define work, inertia, energy, torque, and friction.
- ❍ Explain the different types of measurable horsepower.
- ❍ Determine the compression ratio of an engine.

Engine Performance

The study of ***engine performance*** deals with the ways in which engines are measured dimensionally and the power developed. Many factors enter into this study: the basics of inertia, work, power, torque, and friction; the effect of barometric pressure, temperature, and humidity of the ambient atmosphere; and the engineering decisions that determine engine bore, stroke, displacement, compression ratio, volumetric efficiency, thermal efficiency, and mechanical efficiency.

Inertia

Inertia is the force that causes an object to remain stationary unless it is acted on by an external force. A car remains at rest unless an external force acts on the car. This external force is produced by starting the engine and shifting the transmission into gear, Figure 8-1. Once an object is in motion, inertia is the force that causes it to remain in motion unless it is acted on by an external force. In an automobile, the external force that counteracts inertia is the brakes being applied, Figure 8-2, or the transmission being shifted into a lower gear. When the transmission is downshifted, the engine speed is reduced, thereby reducing the speed of the vehicle. This is known as engine braking. With a manual transmission, the driver downshifts to second gear. With an automatic transmission, downshifting occurs automatically.

Work

When an object is moved from one position to another, ***work*** is performed. Work is measured in units of foot pounds (ft./lb.). For example, if a 3 lb. weight is lifted 2 ft., Figure 8-3, the work performed would be 3 lbs. × 2 ft. = 6 ft./lb. In other words, work equals the force (in pounds) required to move the object multiplied by the distance it is moved (in feet). Work is performed when weights are lifted, springs are compressed, and shafts are rotated.

The ability or capacity to do work is known as energy. A lump of coal or a quart of gasoline has energy stored in it, which when released, will perform work.

Figure 8-1. For a car to move, it must overcome inertia. (Lexus)

Figure 8-2. For a car to stop, it must overcome inertia. (Lexus)

Power

Power is defined as the rate or speed at which work is performed. One ***horsepower*** is defined as performing 33,000 ft./lb. of work in one minute. This unit of measurement was originated by an engineer by the name of Watt, who found that a strong horse could hoist 366 lbs. of coal up a mine shaft at the rate of one foot per second. In one minute, the horse would have raised the 366 lbs. 60 feet. This would be equivalent to raising 21,960 lbs. a distance of 1 ft. in one minute. Arbitrarily, Mr. Watt raised this figure to raising 33,000 lbs. a distance of 1 ft. in one minute.

Expressed as a formula:

$$HP = \frac{\text{ft./lb. per min.}}{33{,}000} = \frac{DW}{33{,}000\ t}$$

Where: D = Distance the weight is moved.
W = Force in pounds required to move the weight through the distance.
t = Time in minutes required to move the weight through the distance.

Using this formula, determine how many horsepower would be required to raise a weight of 5000 lb. a distance of 60 ft. in three minutes.

$$HP = \frac{DW}{33{,}000\ t} = \frac{60 \times 5000}{33{,}000 \times 3} = 3.03\ \text{hp}$$

Energy

Energy is the capacity to do work. There are two different kinds of energy. The first type is potential energy. The second type is kinetic energy.

Potential Energy

Potential energy is energy in an object at rest. An example of potential energy is a piston at TDC, Figure 8-4. The formula for potential energy is as follows:

$$PE = \text{mass of an object} \times \text{acceleration of gravity } (32.2\ \text{ft./sec.}^2) \times \text{height}$$

Kinetic Energy

Kinetic energy is the energy in a moving object at its present velocity until that velocity is terminated. An example of kinetic energy is the downward motion of a piston from TDC until it reaches BDC, Figure 8-5. The formula for kinetic energy is:

$$KE = 1/2 \text{ the mass of an object} \times \text{velocity}^2$$

Torque

Torque is the turning or twisting force exerted on an object. While torque is measured in ft./lb., it differs from work or power because torque does not necessarily produce motion. For example, if a 50 lb. force was applied at the end of a 3 ft. lever, there would be 150 ft./lb. of torque.

In the case of the automotive engine, torque is low at low engine speeds and increases rapidly with the speed. Automotive engineers make every effort to increase the torque at low speeds. Note the relationship between torque and horsepower, as shown in Figure 8-6.

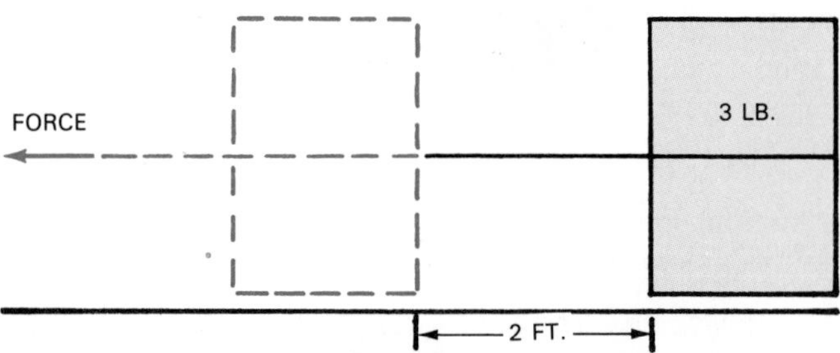

Figure 8-3. Work is done when an object is moved. The object in the illustration weighs 3 lb. This same object is moved 2 ft. The weight is multiplied by the distance moved. The answer is given in foot-pounds, which, in this case, is 6 ft./lb.

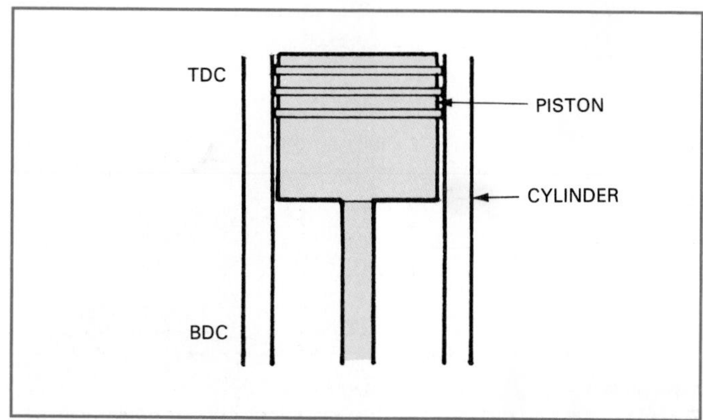

Figure 8-4. A piston at TDC is an example of potential energy.

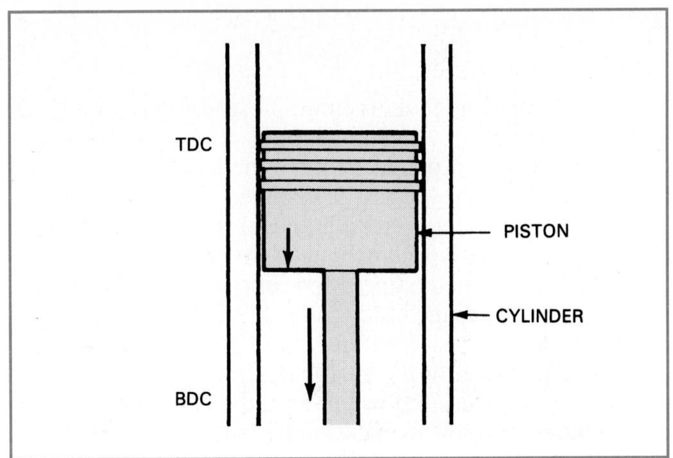

Figure 8-5. The downward motion of a piston from TDC to BDC is an example of kinetic energy.

Friction

Friction is the resistance between two bodies that contact each other or that are separated only by a lubricant.

Friction varies with different materials. It also varies with the surface condition of the materials. Friction was originally attributed to the interlocking of projections and depressions on the surfaces, but present day theory is that molecular attraction is the explanation.

The amount of friction between two surfaces that contact each other is proportional to the pressure between the surfaces and is independent of the area of the surfaces in contact, Figure 8-7. Friction also depends on the relative velocity of the moving surfaces.

In the case of viscous friction, such as that which occurs when solids move through liquids or gases (an automobile moving through air for example), the force of friction varies directly with the relative velocity and rises rapidly when the velocity becomes very great.

The friction of lubricated surfaces is much less than that of dry surfaces. Friction is also greatly reduced when rolling friction (ball and roller bearings) is substituted for sliding friction.

Experiments show that the quotient of dividing the force required to slide one object over another at a constant speed by the pressure holding them together is a constant, which is known as the coefficient of friction. The coefficient of friction is always the same for the given materials and surfaces, Figure 8-7.

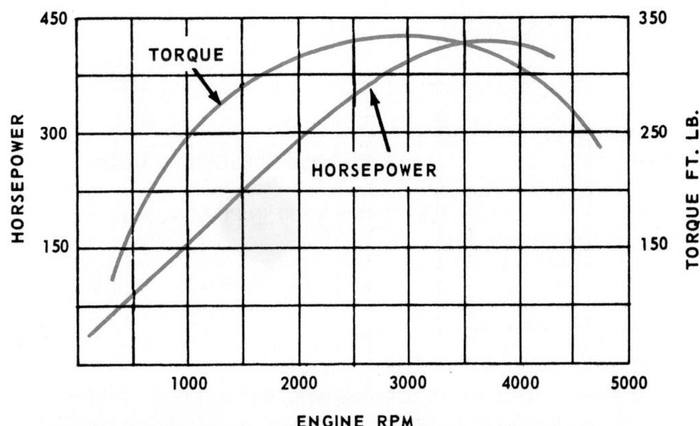

Figure 8-6. Note the variation in torque and horsepower as the engine speed changes.

For example, if a force of 60 lb. is required to keep a weight of 120 lb. sliding over a surface at a constant speed, the coefficient of sliding friction would be:

$$\frac{60}{120} = 0.5$$

It must be emphasized that more force is required to produce initial movement than to keep the object moving. Sliding friction is, therefore, measured after motion has started.

A lubricant is a substance placed or injected between two surfaces to reduce friction. The thin layer of lubricant adhering to the two surfaces is then sheared by the movement of the surfaces. Since the friction within the lubricant is less than that between the two surfaces, less force is required to produce movement.

A simple experiment to determine the coefficient of friction can be easily performed using a flat board and a weight. Place the weight on one end of the board. Raise the end of the board that contains the weight until the weight starts to slide. At this point, measure the height of the end of the board and the base of the triangle formed by the tilted board. Divide the height by the base to determine the coefficient of friction, Figure 8-8.

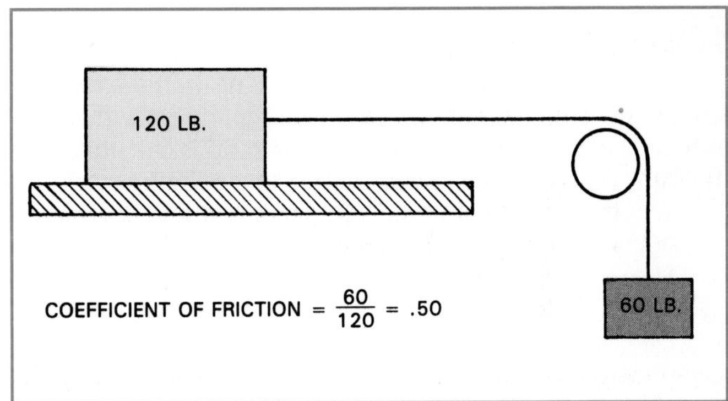

Figure 8-7. A method for determining the coefficient of friction.

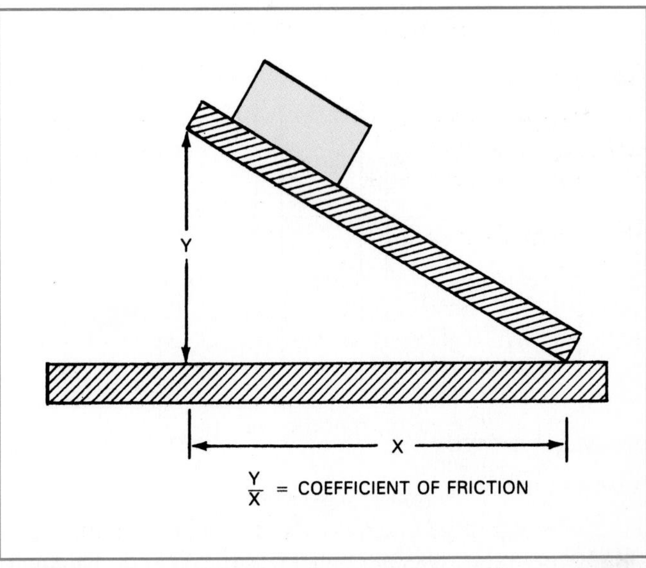

Figure 8-8. The coefficient of friction equals $\frac{Y}{X}$.

Bore, Stroke, Displacement

The diameter of an engine cylinder is referred to as the ***bore.*** The distance the piston moves from bottom dead center to top dead center is called the ***stroke.***

Displacement of an engine is a measurement of its size. In a one cylinder engine, it is equal to the number of cubic inches the piston displaces as it moves from bottom dead center to top dead center. In other words, it is equal to the area of the piston multiplied by the stroke. In the case of a multi-cylinder engine, it is also necessary to multiply the displacement of a single cylinder by the number of cylinders to determine engine displacement.

$$\text{Displacement} = A \times S \times N$$

"A" is the area of the piston in square inches, "S" is the length of stroke in inches, and "N" the number of cylinders. Assuming you have a six-cylinder engine with a 4″ bore and a 4 1/4″ stroke, the first step in determining engine displacement is to calculate the piston area:

$$\text{Area} = 4 \times 4 \times .7854 = 12.56 \text{ sq. in.}$$

The displacement equals:

$$12.56 \times 4.25 \times 6 = 320.28 \text{ cu. in.}$$

Compression Ratio

The ***compression ratio*** of an engine is the extent to which the combustible gases are compressed within the cylinder, Figure 8-9. The compression ratio is calculated by dividing the volume existing within the cylinder with the piston at BDC by the volume in the cylinder with the piston at TDC. For example, if the volume with the piston at BDC is 45 cu. in. and the volume at TDC is 5 cu. in., the compression ratio is:

$$\frac{45}{5} = 9 \text{ to } 1$$

Therefore, the gases are compressed to one-ninth the original volume.

Up to a certain point, the more the fuel charge is compressed, the more power will be obtained. Experiments made by General Motors engineers indicate that a 17 to 1 compression ratio offers peak efficiency in gasoline engines.

In the field, the compression ratio of an engine can be increased by shaving the cylinder head, installing higher compression pistons, installing thinner head gaskets, increasing the stroke, or increasing the bore.

In case it is desired to increase the compression ratio of an engine, the following formula may be used to determine the necessary combustion chamber volume:

$$\frac{B}{C - 1} = A$$

"A" equals the volume of the combustion chamber, "B" is the displacement of the cylinder, and "C" is the desired compression ratio. For example, if the displacement is 36 cu. in. and the desired compression ratio is 10 to 1, then:

$$\frac{36}{10 - 1} = 4 \text{ cu. in}$$

In that particular engine, the combustion chamber would have to have a volume of 4 cu. in. to obtain a compression ratio of 10 to 1.

Engine Efficiency

Engine efficiency is the ratio of power obtained to power supplied. There are many energy losses in gasoline engines. Therefore, in relation to the inherent power in the fuel, only about 15 percent appears as useful power, Figure 8-10. The

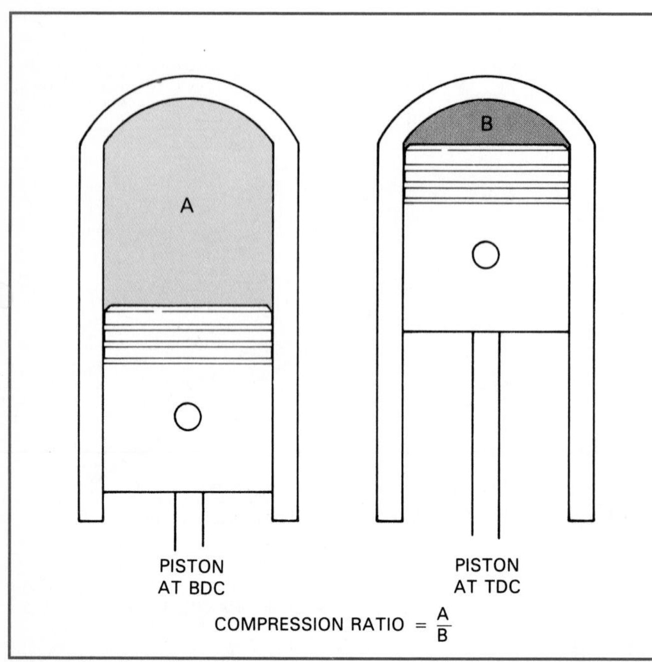

Figure 8-9. The compression ratio is equal to the volume of A divided by volume of B.

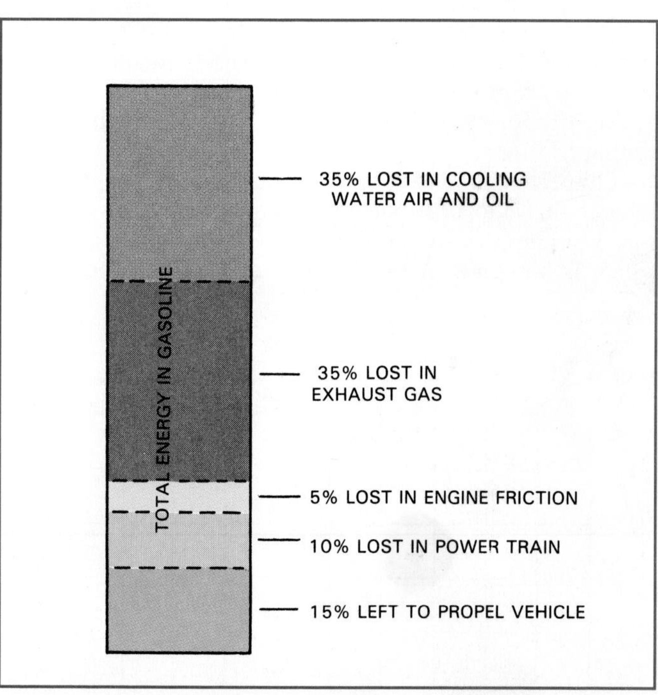

Figure 8-10. This graph shows where the power goes on a normally aspirated engine. If the engine is turbocharged, less power will be lost in the exhaust, which means more power is used to propel the car.

rest is lost to friction and to the cooling system and exhaust system.

The ***mechanical efficiency*** of an engine is equal to the relationship between brake horsepower and indicated horsepower.

$$\text{Mechanical Efficiency} = \frac{\text{BHP}}{\text{IHP}}$$

In most cases, mechanical efficiency is approximately 85 percent.

Volumetric Efficiency

No engine is 100% efficient. One of the factors affecting the efficiency of a gasoline engine is the difficulty of getting a full charge of combustible mixture into the cylinder. Because of restrictions of the intake manifold, atmospheric temperature, valve timing, and similar factors, a full charge does not reach the cylinder. The ratio of the amount of charge actually taken in per cycle to a complete charge is known as the ***volumetric efficiency.***

After a certain engine speed is reached, the volumetric efficiency drops rapidly. In general, maximum volumetric efficiency is reached at approximately the same point where maximum torque is reached. For example, one engine had a maximum volumetric efficiency of 82% at 1500 rpm, but at 2500 rpm, it had dropped to 65%.

One method of increasing volumetric efficiency is to use a turbocharger or a supercharger. See Chapter 20.

As atmospheric pressure drops with an increase in altitude, volumetric efficiency will also decrease as it is the difference in pressure between the pressure outside the cylinder and the pressure inside the cylinder that determines the amount of mixture that will enter the cylinder.

Thermal Efficiency

The performance of various engines is often compared on the basis of their thermal efficiencies. The ***thermal efficiency*** is the ratio of the heat equivalent of work done in an engine to the total heat supplied.

Brake Horsepower

Brake horsepower may be defined as the power that is available for propelling the vehicle. It is the power developed within the cylinder (indicated horsepower) less the power that remains after the effects of friction and the power that is required to drive the fan, water pump, oil pump, alternator, etc.

The term brake horsepower is derived from the equipment first used to determine the power developed by an engine, which is known as the Prony brake, Figure 8-11.

The ***Prony brake*** consists of a large drum and a band-type brake that operates on the outer surface of the drum. Attached to the brake is a lever. The free end of the lever rests on a weighing scale.

The drum is directly connected to the crankshaft of the engine to be tested. As the drum is rotated, the brake is tightened, imposing a load on the engine. This, in turn, causes the lever to be pressed against the scale.

When making a Prony brake test, the throttle is first set to operate the engine at some specific speed. The brake is then tightened until the speed drops off, and the weight on the scale is noted. This procedure is repeated several times, increasing engine speed by 100 rpm increments each time. Then, using 1 hp = 33,000 ft./lb. per min., the brake horsepower developed at each speed is calculated based on the following formula:

$$\text{BHP} = \frac{2\,\pi\,\text{LRW}}{33{,}000} = \frac{\text{LRW}}{5252}$$

Where: L = Length of lever arm in feet.
R = Engine speed in rpm.
W = Load in pounds on scale.

The data produced can then be plotted to scale, as shown in Figure 8-12.

Brake horsepower can also be measured on a dynamometer. Such equipment consists of a resistance creating device, such as an electric generator or a paddle wheel revolving in a fluid, that is arranged to absorb and dissipate the power produced by the engine. Suitable gauges are provided to indicate the amount of power absorbed.

In automotive manufacturers' testing laboratories, the engines are usually directly connected to the shaft of the

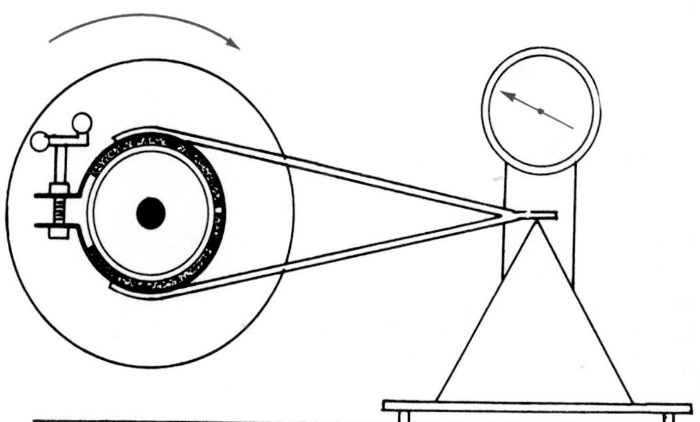

Figure 8-11. A Prony brake is used in measuring brake horsepower.

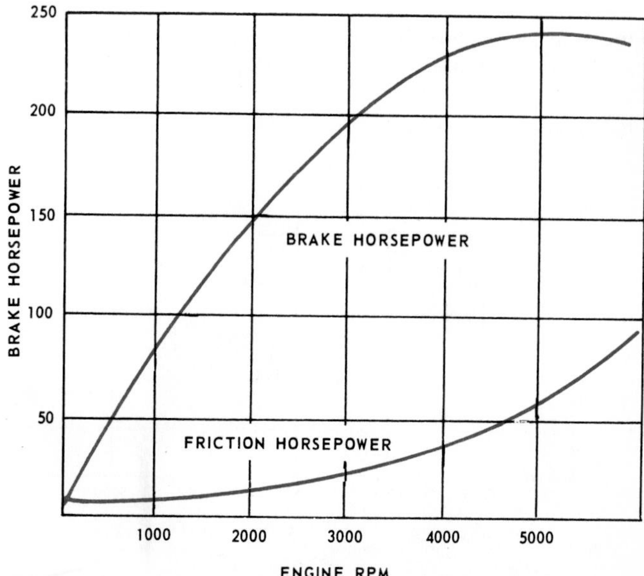

Figure 8-12. Brake horsepower determined by a Prony brake. Friction horsepower determined by a dynamometer.

dynamometer. When used in service facilities, the dynamometer is provided with rollers that are driven by the wheels of the vehicle, Figure 8-13. The drive-on type of dynamometer is now used extensively to supply factual information about the performance of a specific vehicle.

Engine Torque

As previously described, torque is turning effort. In the case of an automotive engine, the pressure on the pistons provides torque. As shown in Figure 8-14, the torque at idle speed is relatively low, but increases rapidly as the engine speed rises. The torque maintains a high level, but it decreases as higher speeds are reached.

In designing the engine, engineers try to have the engine maintain as high a torque as possible throughout the speed range of the engine. However, as engine speed increases, there is less time for the fuel mixture to fill the cylinders due to the inertia of the mixture, the resistance to its movement offered by the induction system, and the valve timing. As a result, volumetric efficiency and torque are reduced.

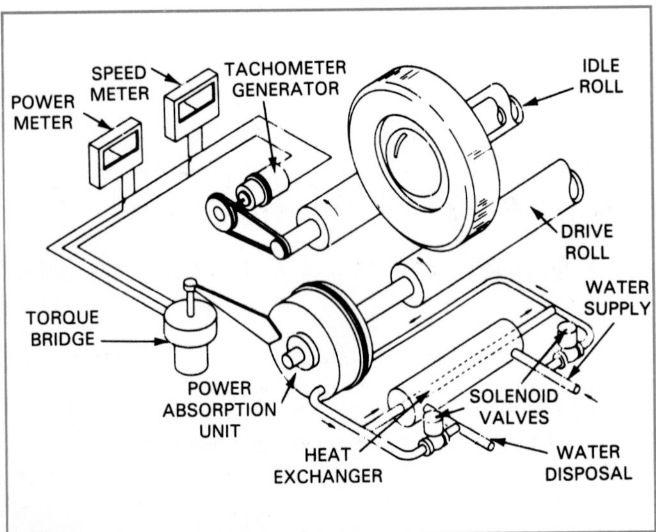

Figure 8-13. The parts of a chassis dynamometer. Vehicle's drive wheels drive the rollers.

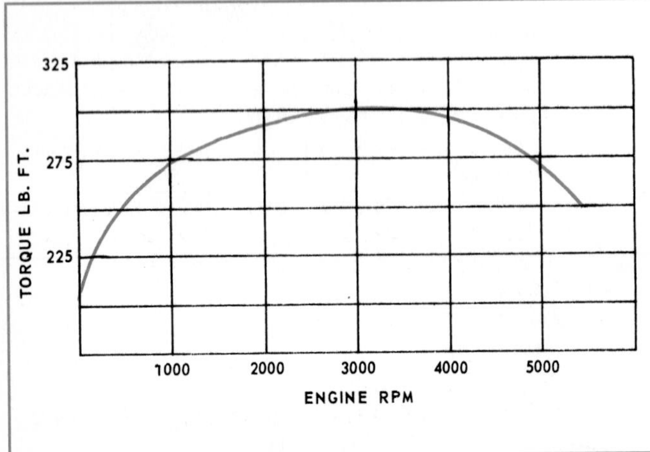

Figure 8-14. Torque curve of an automotive engine. Note that torque drops off at higher engine speed.

Rated Horsepower

The ***rated horsepower*** of an engine is based on a formula developed in the early days of the industry. It is also based on the assumption of a brake mean effective pressure of 67.2 psi and a piston speed of 1000 rpm.

Today's engines operate at much higher speeds and pressures. Consequently, the formula no longer gives any indication of the power output of an engine.

This rating is still used for purposes of licensing automotive vehicles. The formula is as follows:

$$\text{Rated Horsepower} = \frac{NB^2}{2.5}$$

"N" is the number of cylinders and "B" is the diameter of the engine bore in inches. For example; consider a six-cylinder engine with a bore of 4″. Then:

$$\text{Rated Horsepower} = \frac{6 \times 4 \times 4}{2.5} = 38.4$$

Indicated Horsepower

Another method of rating an engine is by the ***indicated horsepower.*** Indicated horsepower is based on the actual power developed in the engine from an indicator diagram, Figure 8-15. As the indicated horsepower is the power produced within the engine, it includes the power required to overcome the friction within the engine. Subtracting the friction horsepower from the indicated horsepower gives the brake horsepower:

$$BHP = IHP - FHP$$

The indicator diagram is obtained by means of an oscilloscope or a special instrument that makes an actual drawing of the events that are occurring in the cylinder. It records the pressure existing at each instant of a complete cycle of the engine from the time that the combustible mixture is first drawn into the cylinder until the end of the exhaust stroke. Therefore, the area of the diagram is proportional to the power developed and represents the indicated horsepower.

When calculating the indicated horsepower, it is first necessary to determine the mean effective pressure. The ***mean effective pressure*** is equal to the average pressure during the power stroke minus the average pressure during the other three strokes of the cycle. The indicated horsepower is then found by the formula:

$$IHP = \frac{PLANK}{33{,}000}$$

Where: P = Mean effective pressure in psi.
L = Stroke in feet.
A = Area of cylinder in sq. in.
N = Number of power strokes per minute.
K = Number of cylinders.

Friction Horsepower

Friction horsepower is the power required to overcome the friction within the engine. The friction results from the pressure of the piston and rings against the cylinder walls, the friction of the crankshaft and camshaft

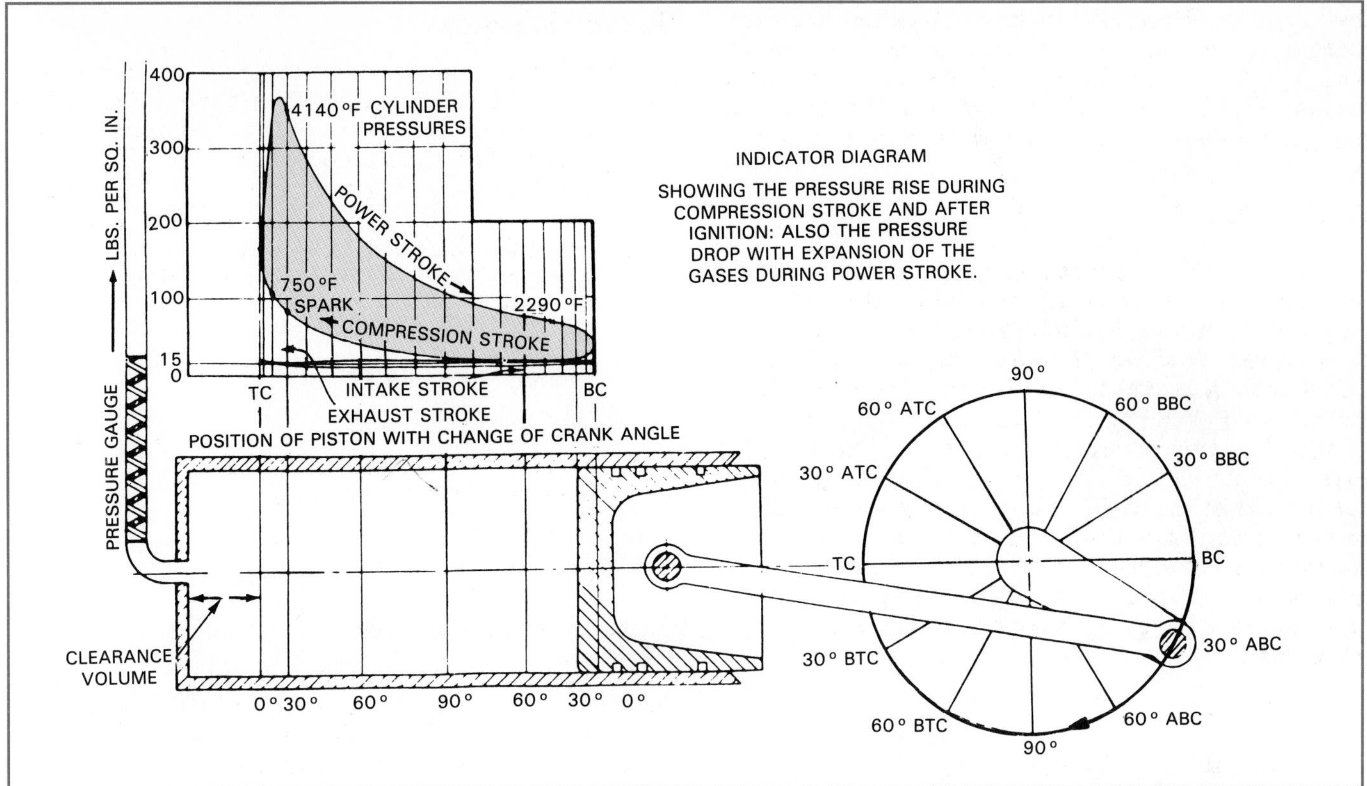

Figure 8-15. Curve of indicated horsepower for an automotive engine.

rotating in their bearings, and the friction of other moving parts such as the oil pump, fuel pump, engine valves, timing gear, etc.

Friction horsepower increases with the speed of the engine. It also increases as the size of the engine increases. A typical friction horsepower curve is shown in Figure 8-12.

Current Horsepower Ratings

Engine horsepower ratings have dropped since 1972. Some of this decrease results directly from the extra "plumbing" that has been installed to reduce the exhaust emissions of hydrocarbons, carbon monoxide, and oxides of nitrogen. But a major reason for the decrease results from quoting net horsepower ratings instead of gross horsepower ratings.

Net horsepower is the horsepower produced by the engine with all accessory items (alternator, air conditioning compressor, power steering pump, etc.) installed. ***Gross horsepower,*** on the other hand, is the horsepower produced by the engine without these accessories.

Increasing Horsepower

Horsepower of an engine can be increased by raising the compression ratio; reducing back pressure from the exhaust system; increasing the size or number of the valves; modifying the intake manifold; increasing cam lift or duration; and using superchargers or turbochargers. Currently, there is strong interest in turbochargers. These devices utilize the force of exhaust gases to drive more air-fuel mixture into the cylinders (see Chapter 20).

Chapter 8–Review Questions

Write your answers on a separate sheet of paper. Do not write in this book.

1. Define inertia.
2. Brake horsepower is a reliable measure of the power developed by an engine. True or False?
3. How is the displacement of an engine determined?
4. Torque is the same as power. True or False?
5. Friction is dependent on the area in contact. True or False?
6. Indicated horsepower does not take the friction losses within the engine into consideration. True or False?
7. Mean effective pressure is another name for _____.
8. Explain the difference between power and torque.
9. Why does torque decrease above a certain speed?
10. A gas is best measured by _____.
11. Given the bore of the cylinder and the volume of the combustion chamber, it is possible to determine the compression ratio. True or False?
12. Rated horsepower is the same as brake horsepower. True or False?
13. The volume within the cylinder of a certain engine is 50 cu. in. and the volume of the combustion chamber is 5 cu. in. What is the compression ratio?
    (A) 10 to 1.
    (B) 6 to 1.
    (C) One tenth.
    (D) None of the above.
14. Current horsepower ratings are net figures. True or False?
15. The use of a supercharger will increase volumetric efficiency. True or False?

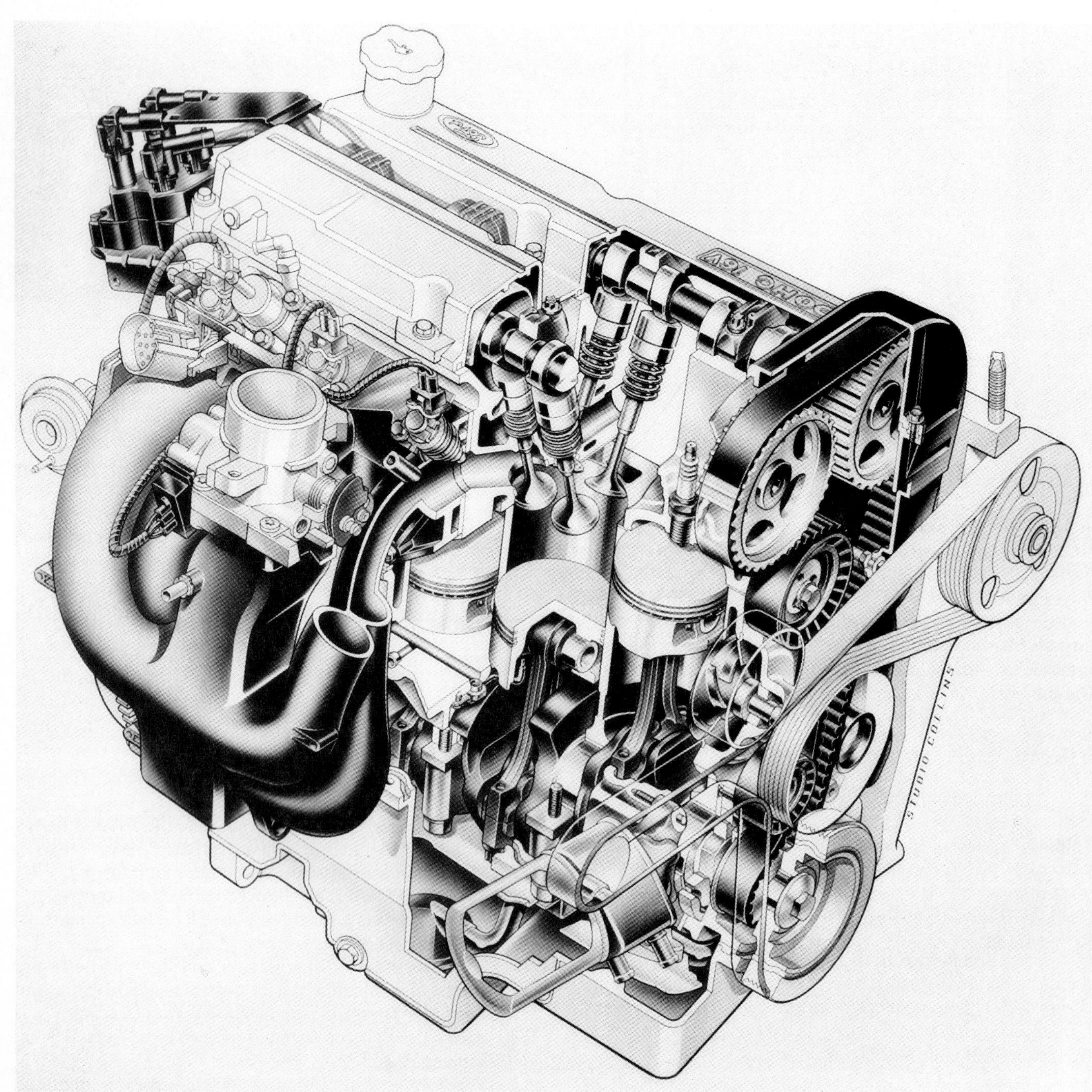

This four-cylinder engine is equipped with dual overhead camshafts and four valves per cylinder. Can you identify the piston rings and the piston pins? (Ford)

Chapter 9
Piston Rings and Pins

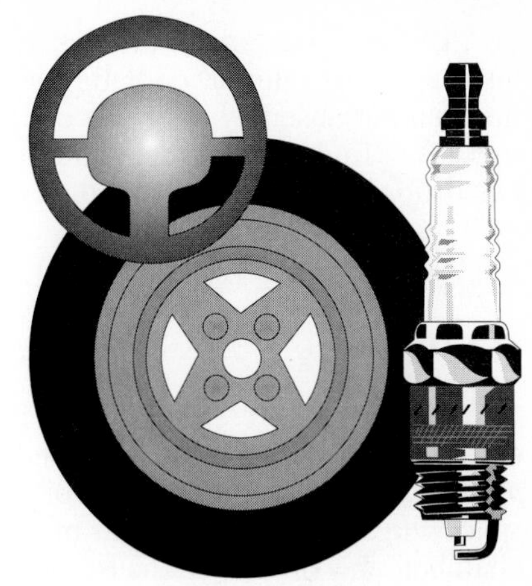

After studying this chapter, you will be able to:
❍ Identify the different types of rings.
❍ Explain the different design characteristics of piston rings.
❍ List the materials used to make piston rings.
❍ Describe how modern pistons are attached to the connecting rods.

Piston Rings

Piston rings have been designed in a multitude of variations. Originally, they were a simple split ring made of cast iron. Since engine power output has constantly increased and lubrication requirements have become more complicated, more efficiency and durability has been demanded of piston rings.

Modern piston rings are made of steel or cast iron. These rings are heat treated in various ways and plated with other metals. Today's piston rings, however, still fall into two distinct classifications: ***compression rings*** and ***oil control rings.*** A typical ring installation is shown in Figure 9-1.

Latest developments in the design of piston rings tend to reduce emissions, reduce oil consumption, and improve engine durability. Improvements in hydrocarbon emissions may be obtained by mounting the top compression ring near the top of the piston. Also, reducing ring friction reduces nitrogen oxide emissions because lower throttle settings are needed for a given load output.

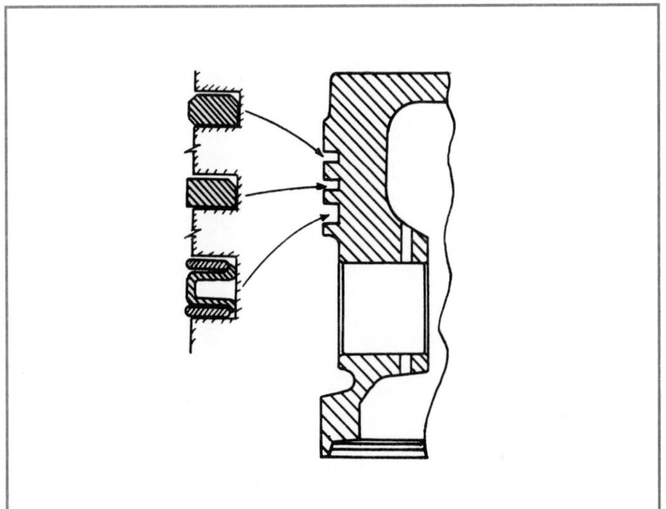

Figure 9-1. The upper two rings are compression rings, while the bottom ring is an oil control ring. Oil control rings often have multiple sections and are quite complicated in design.

Piston Ring Blowby

Piston rings would be less of a problem if cylinders and pistons did not expand, distort, and warp at operating temperatures. The rings must be capable of adapting to these changing conditions. If the cylinder is worn tapered, the rings will expand and contract as they move up and down in a bore that is larger at one end than the other. If the cylinder is out-of-round in spots, the rings will move in and out of the grooves as they try to follow the cylinder wall.

Furthermore, the rings are exposed to the high temperatures of combustion and to alternating pressure and vacuum. Rings are expected to prevent the ***blowby*** of pressure in one direction and to control the flow of oil in the other direction.

Compression pressure and explosion pressure can get by the rings in several ways. Blowby can go through the ring gaps, which change in width according to the expansion and contraction of the cylinder and rings. If the rings were fitted so precisely that ring ends touched to seal the gap, the cylinder walls would be scored when the rings expand.

Blowby also can occur if it gets behind the compression rings, as shown in Figure 9-2. If the rings were too tight in the grooves to avoid possible leakage, there would be danger of sticking when the piston and rings expand.

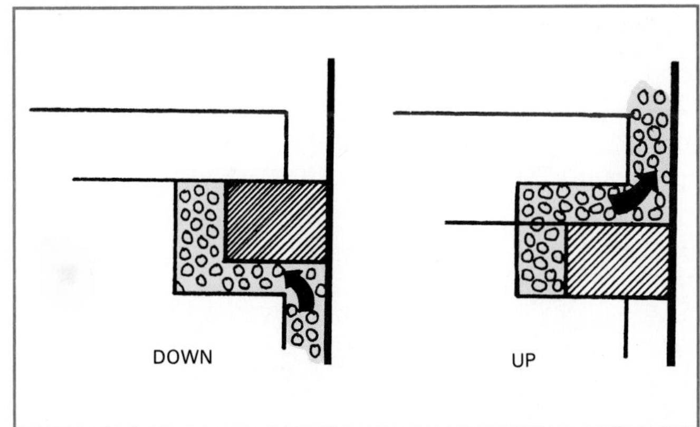

Figure 9-2. Oil can work its way past the ring. Combustion gases also work their way past the ring and into the crankcase.

Blowby is a serious problem when the cylinder walls distort out-of-round at operating temperature. This condition can be caused by improper cooling or unequal tightening of cylinder head bolts adjacent to the cylinders. Distortion may occur in more than one spot on the cylinder wall, and the different spots are often different sizes and shapes. See Figure 9-3.

Oil Pumping

Just as compression can leak down past the rings, oil can also pass upward into the cylinder. This is known as ***oil pumping.*** Oil pumping causes oil burning, fouling of the spark plugs, excessive deposits of carbon in the combustion chamber, and smoking exhaust.

It is easier for oil to pass upward, in some cases, than it is for compression to leak down past the rings. Therefore, it is possible to have an engine with good compression and power that is also an oil pumper. The oil may seal excessive side clearance in the ring grooves and prevent leakage of compression. Yet, alternating vacuum and pressure in the cylinder may cause the rings to act as a pump. See Figure 9-4.

This condition is aggravated if the walls of the ring grooves and the sides of the rings are not flat and true. The volume of oil leakage past the back of the ring can be much greater than through the tiny ring gaps.

From these explanations of blowby and oil pumping, you can see that great care is required in reconditioning cylinders to make sure they are round and true when new rings are installed. Equal care is required in selecting the new rings and fitting them to the pistons and cylinders.

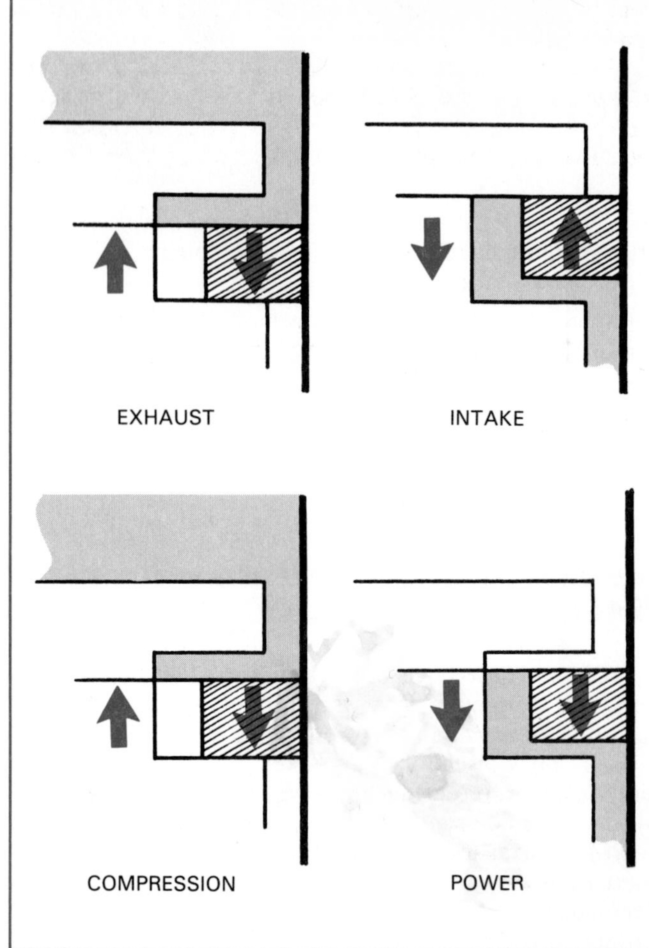

Figure 9-4. There must be some clearance between the ring and the groove to allow for ring movement. However, the ring can then act as a pump, drawing oil up into the combustion chamber and allowing combustion gases down into the crankcase. On the exhaust stroke, the piston moves upward, but the ring moves downward due to the exhaust gases. On the intake stroke, engine vacuum holds the ring against the top of the groove as the piston moves downward. On the compression stroke, the pressure forces the ring against the bottom of the groove as the piston moves upward. On the power stroke, the expanding gases push both the piston and the ring downward. This causes the ring to float in the groove.

Compression Rings

The top compression ring has a rectangular cross section. It may have a bevel cut on the inner top corner, Figure 9-5. Often, the ring is chrome plated, Figure 9-6, or is molybdenum-filled (moly) cast iron to provide better wearing qualities. The second compression ring is often a coated cast iron ring. Some compression rings have a tapered face, and they may or may not have an inside bevel.

The bevel on the inside upper corner of the ring is to help provide a better seal. The bevel causes the ring to twist in the groove so that the outside lower edge presses on the

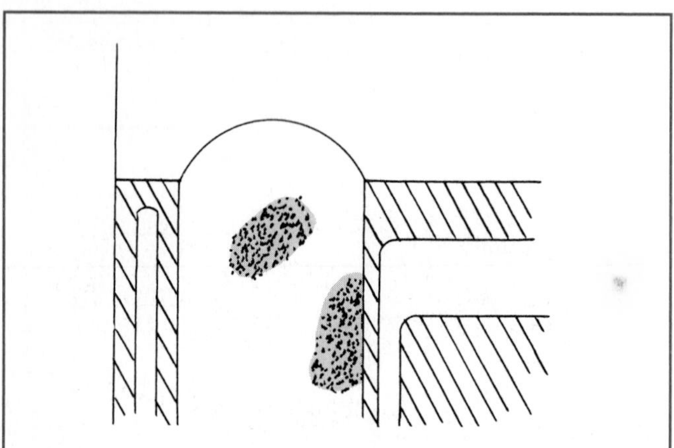

Figure 9-3. Distortion of cylinder walls can cause the cylinder to be out-of-round in spots.

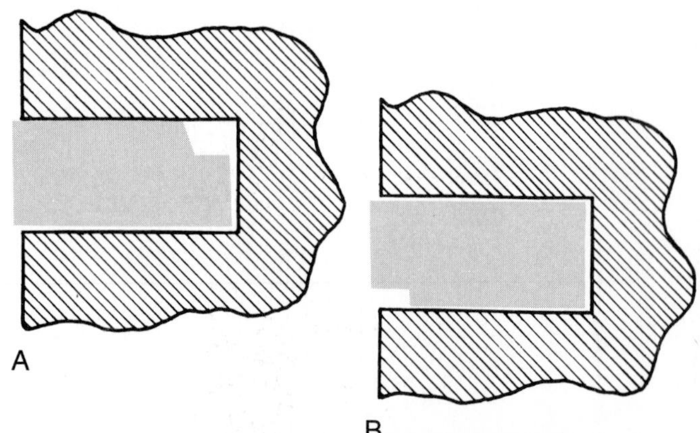

Figure 9-5. Two groove or bevel locations on a piston ring. A–A groove may be cut on the top inside of the ring. B–The groove may be cut on the bottom outside of the ring. (Perfect Circle)

cylinder wall more tightly than the rest of the ring face, Figure 9-7.

The compression ring with a tapered outer face does the same thing, Figure 9-8. In both cases, the limited area in contact with the cylinder wall offers a higher pressure at that point for better sealing. Beveled and/or tapered rings must be installed right side up and are usually stamped "TOP" on that side of the ring.

The second ring is also a compression ring, but it may be slightly different in design to help in oil control. This difference might be a bevel cut on the inner or outer corner, Figure 9-5, which might be combined with a taper on either the inside or outside. The second rings are also known as scraper rings, because one or more edges are designed to aid in scraping the oil from the cylinder walls.

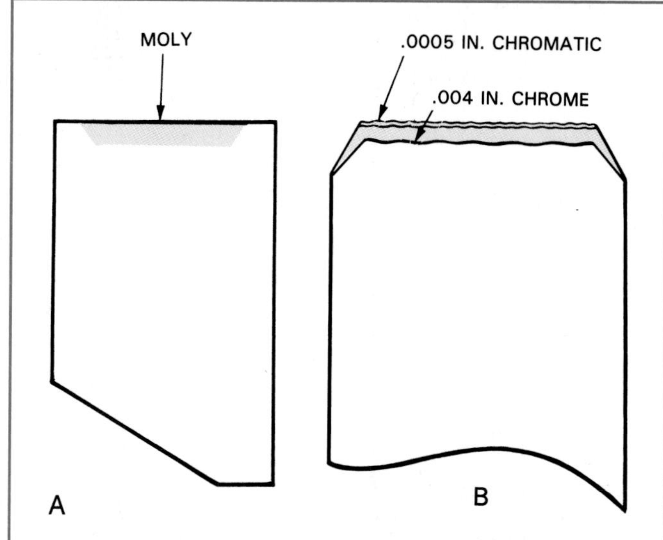

Figure 9-6. Molybdenum and chrome rings. A–The face of the ring is cut out and molybdenum is added. B–The face of the ring is coated with chrome. (Perfect Circle)

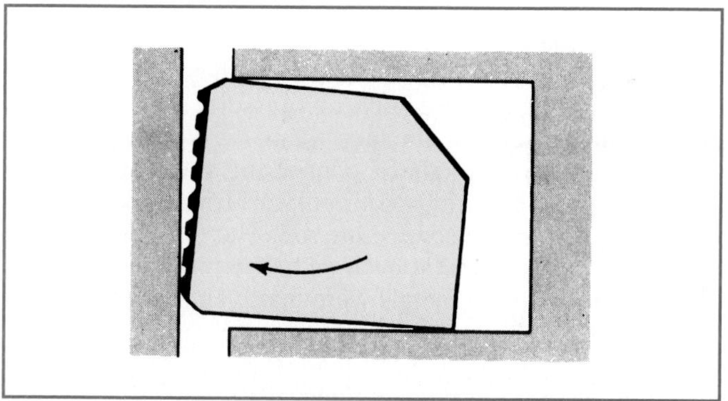

Figure 9-7. The bevel causes the ring to twist in the groove.

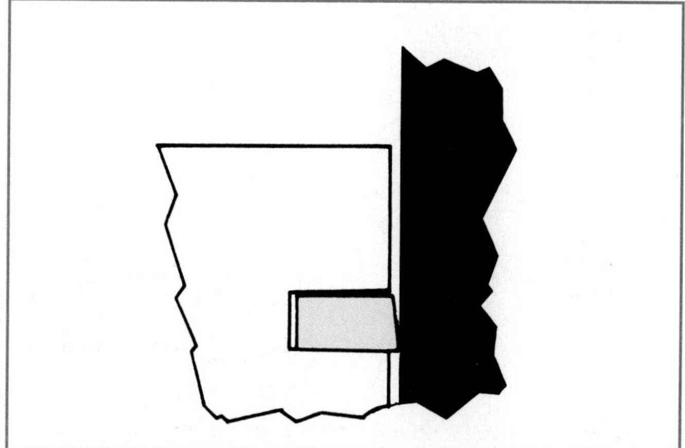

Figure 9-8. A tapered face ring ensures lower face contact with the cylinder wall for a positive seal. (Perfect Circle)

Oil Control Rings

The third ring from the top (and the fourth if four rings are used) is an oil-control ring, Figure 9-9. Oil-control ring designs vary from simple to extremely complicated.

Remember that oil scraped from the cylinder wall by the oil-control ring must have a free passage to the inside of the piston. For this reason, holes or slots are cut in the lower ring grooves. When an inner ring or expander is used, these openings must be kept open if the oil ring is to function as intended. See Figures 9-10 and 9-11.

Another type of oil control ring is shown in Figure 9-12. This ring is a cast iron ring with a self-expanding

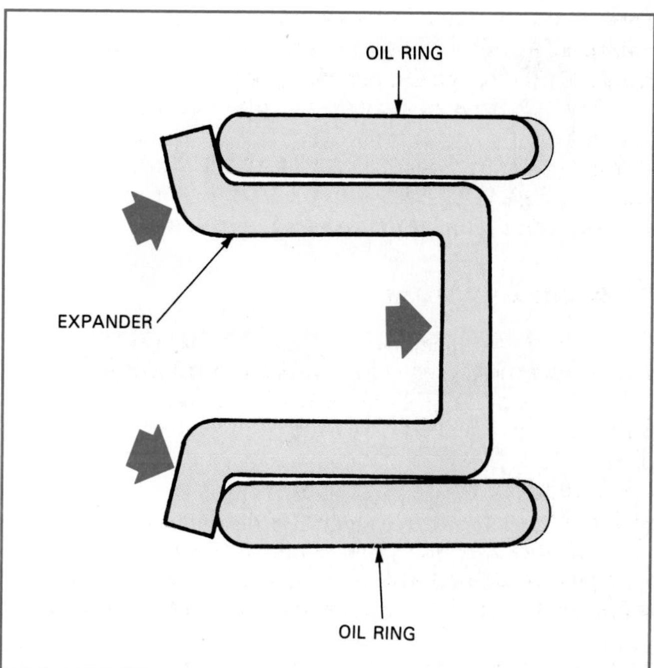

Figure 9-9. An expander is placed behind the oil control rings. This forces the rings against the cylinder wall. (Perfect Circle)

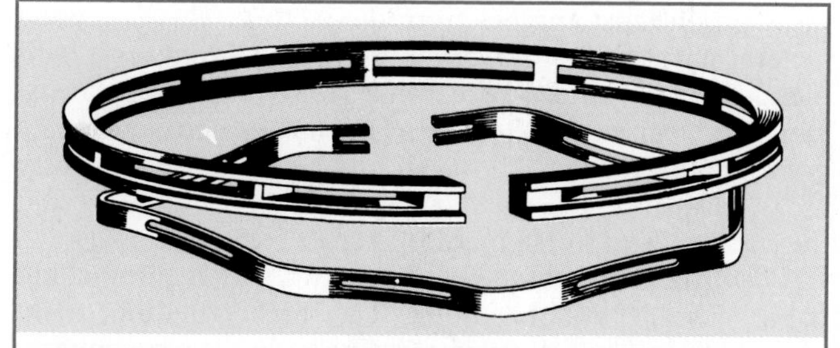

Figure 9-10. Oil passes through the slots in oil control ring to oil return holes in the piston groove.

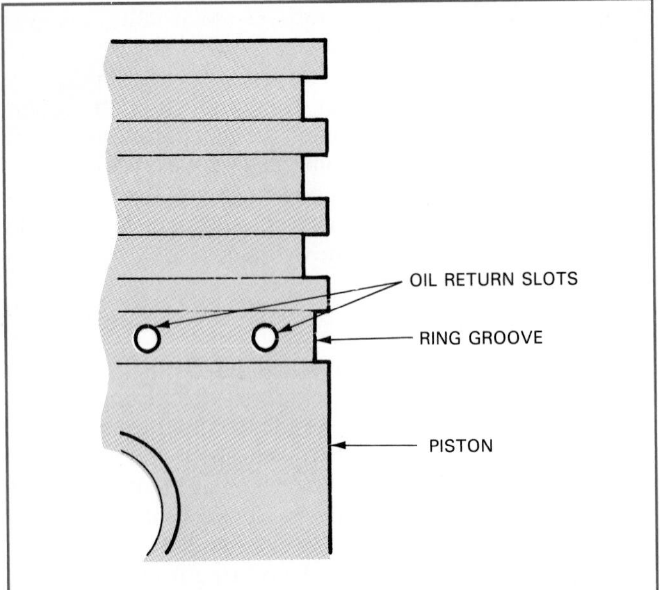

Figure 9-11. After the oil passes through the slots of the oil control ring, it passes through the slots in the groove of the piston and flows back to the crankcase.

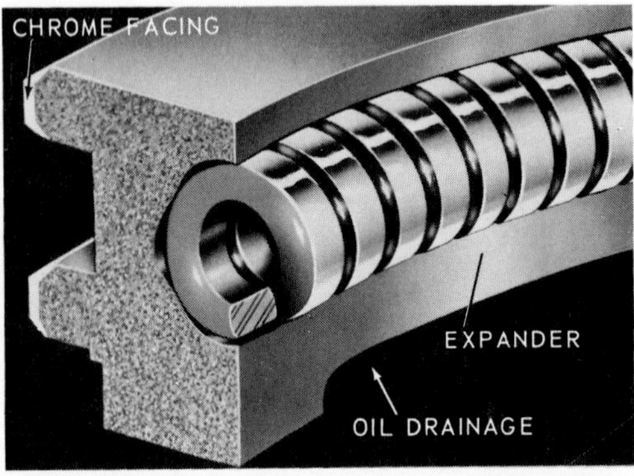

Figure 9-12. Chrome-faced oil control ring with stainless steel coiled spring expander.

stainless steel spring expander. It is designed specifically to prevent oil clogging in heavy-duty service. Note that the expander is located above the drainage slots, so oil flow will not be restricted. In addition, drainage slots at the bottom of the ring are curved to eliminate sharp corners. The ring is faced with chrome to reduce wear.

Selecting Piston Rings

The piston ring with a ***chrome*** face, Figure 9-6, comes installed on most engines from the factory. This is a good general purpose ring for passenger cars. Chrome is a hard metal. The advantage of chrome rings is that they resist abrasive wear extremely well. This makes chrome rings a good choice for installation in engines operated in dusty areas. However, the disadvantage of chrome rings is that they can take up to 1000 miles to seat.

Molybdenum is a metal that is softer than chrome, but it has a higher melting point. This higher melting point reduces the chance of "ring scuffing" (ring is momentarily welded to the cylinder wall), which is caused by an excessive amount of heat in the combustion chamber. Since molybdenum is a softer metal, rings made of this metal can seat within 5-10 minutes after the engine is first started. This type of ring should not be used in areas that are extremely dusty.

Breaking in New Rings

To aid in seating new rings, especially chrome faced rings, the car should be driven as follows: Accelerate the car rapidly to the maximum speed limit on the highway. As soon as the speed limit is reached, let off of the accelerator and coast to a speed of about 35 mph. Then accelerate rapidly to the maximum speed limit again. Repeat this cycle about 24-36 times. During the rapid acceleration, the rings are forced out against the cylinder wall. During deceleration, a high vacuum is formed in the combustion chamber drawing oil up around the face of the piston rings. These combined actions aid in seating the rings against the cylinder wall. If the rings do not seat, oil will get past the face of the rings. Oil consumption will be excessive, as it will be burned in the combustion chamber.

Piston Pins

Piston pins (wrist pins) connect the upper end of the connecting rod to the piston, Figure 9-13.

The proper size for a piston pin presents a design problem. If the pin is large enough in diameter to provide a long wearing bearing surface, the reciprocating weight will be greater and the bearing loads correspondingly increased. If it is as small as permissible to hold down bearing loads, it will be smaller in diameter and have less bearing surface to carry the load.

Piston pins are case hardened, as they are subject to 2000 pounds per square inch of pressure. Also, they are chrome plated to resist abrasive wear.

One of the methods of connecting the piston to the connecting rod, Figure 9-14, involves bronze bushings inside of the piston and connecting rod. The piston pin is held in place by a snap ring at each end. The problem with this is that three different metals were involved (aluminum pistons, bronze bushings, and steel piston pins). Each expands at a different rate. Also, if the snap ring were to fall out, the piston pin would score the cylinder wall.

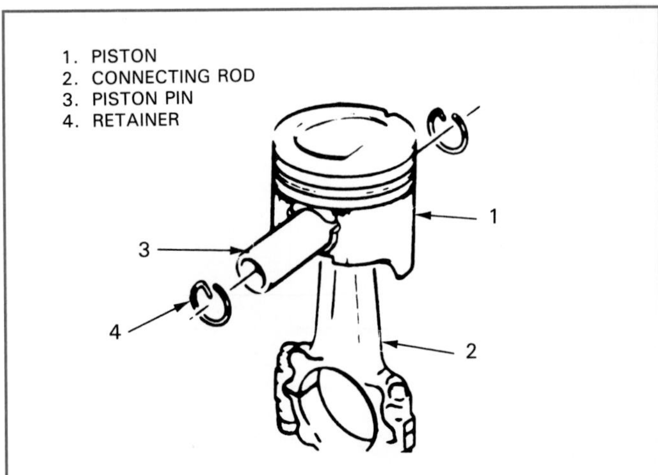

Figure 9-13. The piston pin joins the piston to the connecting rod. (Cadillac)

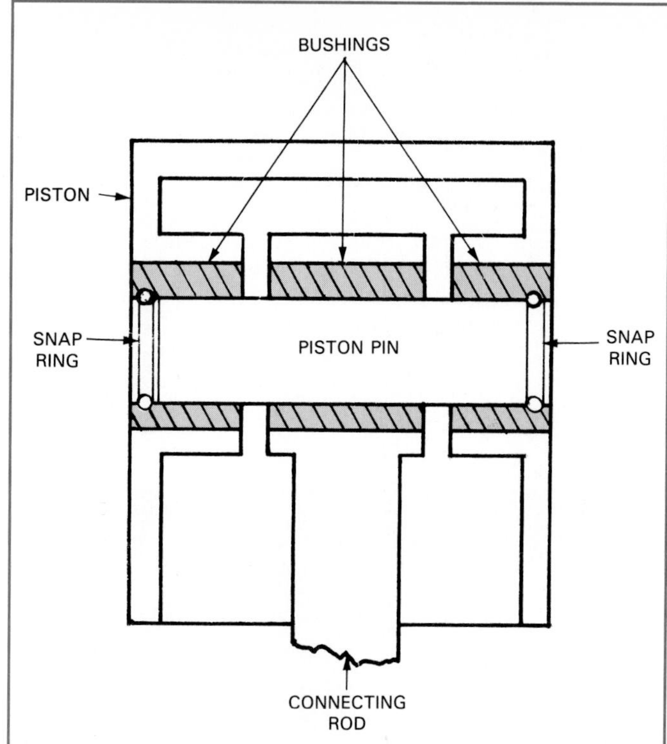

Figure 9-14. The bushings used in a piston and connecting rod assembly are an older method of retaining piston pins. If snap rings fall out, the cylinder wall will become scored.

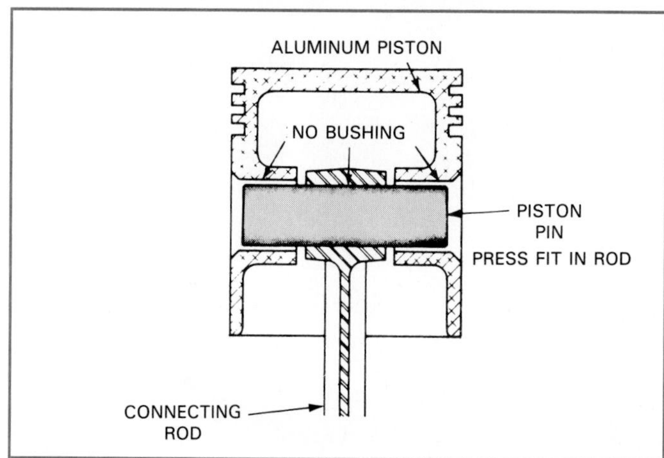

Figure 9-15. Notice that an aluminum piston has no bushings when the piston pin is pressed into the piston. This provides better heat transfer from the piston. (Sunnen Co.)

The modern method of connecting the piston to the connecting rod involves what is known as an ***interference fit***. This means that the bore in the connecting rod is slightly smaller in diameter than the piston pin, Figure 9-15. Since there is a difference in diameter, the piston pin must be pressed into the connecting rod.

In any case, the piston pin is exposed to a great amount of heat. This heat increases wear on the piston pin bore. If the wear becomes excessive, the clearance between the piston pin and the piston pin bore will increase to such an extent that the pin becomes noisy. This noise is a double knock.

Chapter 9–Review Questions

Write your answers on a separate sheet of paper. Do not write in this book.

1. Name two results of oil pumping.
2. Blowby may be a serious problem after the engine reaches normal operating temperatures. True or False?
3. Piston rings move up and down in their grooves. True or False?
4. Why must piston rings be flexible?
5. A piston ring may act as a pump. True or False?
6. Give two reasons for cylinder wall distortion.
7. Piston rings move in and out in their grooves. True or False?
8. If an engine has good compression, it will not pump oil. True or False?
9. Chrome rings are used when:
   (A) excessive oil is consumed.
   (B) an engine runs hot.
   (C) Both a and b.
   (D) Neither a nor b.
10. Describe an "interference fit."
11. Modern piston pins are held in place by:
    (A) snap rings.
    (B) press fit.
    (C) Both a and b.
    (D) Neither a nor b.
12. Molybdenum-faced rings are installed at the factory. True or False?
13. A hardened steel pin can be used in an aluminum piston without any bushings. True or False?
14. Aluminum and bronze have about the same rate of heat expansion. True or False?
15. Piston pins are not _____ for wear.

Precision insert bearings, such as the one shown above, help prevent wear of critical engine parts.
(Photo courtesy of AE Clevite Engine Parts)

Chapter 10
Engine Crankshafts and Bearings

After studying this chapter, you will be able to:
❍ Define the purpose of engine bearings.
❍ Describe the construction of a bearing.
❍ Explain the purpose of a vibration damper/balance shaft.

Engine Bearings

The purpose of any ***engine bearing*** is to provide a surface of dissimilar metal for the moving parts to rotate on, reducing friction. Dissimilar metal means that the bearing is made of a different metal than the crankshaft or camshaft. When dissimilar metals are used, there is less wear and friction than if two metals of the same type were to rotate against each other. There is even less wear and friction when oil is added between the dissimilar metals. Alloys of copper, tin, and lead do the best job of supporting a cast iron or steel crankshaft or camshaft. Modern engine bearings can be readily replaced.

Two types of antifriction bearings have been used in automobile engines. One is known as the ***poured, cast-in,*** or ***integral-type bearing.*** It is now virtually obsolete. The other type is known as the ***precision insert bearing,*** or slip-in bearing. The bearing surface is, in all cases, a soft metal with good heat conducting qualities. This surface will possess a low coefficient of friction in contact with the steel crankshaft journal. The bearing surface metal must be soft enough to allow any abrasive material to become embedded in the bearing rather than remain between bearing and journal surfaces, which would damage the journal.

Precision Insert Bearings

The precision insert bearing has become increasingly popular since engine speeds and loads have been increased so much that a material stronger than babbitt has become necessary. It is now used in all automobile engines for both main and connecting rod bearings. See Figure 10-1. The bearing material is an alloy of several metals and may include lead, tin, copper, silver, cadmium, etc. The proportion of the various metals varies considerably, and the development is the result of experience and experimentation.

The bearing insert consists of a hard shell of steel or bronze with additional metal linings, or laminations. A thin lining of anti-friction metal or bearing alloy forms the inner surface, Figure 10-2. Bearing inserts are manufactured to extremely close dimensions and must be handled carefully to avoid damage. When properly installed they are very durable. When they do wear from continued use, they are discarded and replaced with new inserts.

Precision-type bearing inserts must be used under closely controlled conditions. Fitting and installing them properly involves measurement in thousandths of an inch. Careless workmanship in installation cannot be tolerated.

Connecting rod bearings fit between the large end of the connecting rods and the crankshaft rod journals. ***Crankshaft main bearings*** support the crankshaft in the engine block. A one- or two-cylinder engine block usually has two main bearings: one at the front and one at the rear adjacent to the flywheel. A four-cylinder engine normally has three main bearings, Figure 10-3: one at the front, one between cylinders No. 2 and No. 3, and one at the rear. However, some four-cylinder engines have five main bearings: one at the front, one at the rear, and one between each crankshaft throw. An inline, six-cylinder engine has either three or five main bearings. A V-6 engine has four main bearings. A V-8 engine may have three main bearings, but it usually has five main bearings.

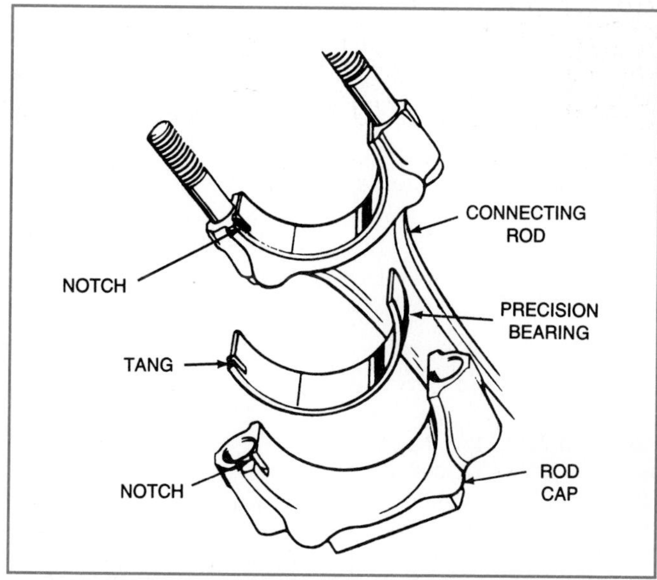

Figure 10-1. Precision insert bearing. Tang in bearing corresponds to notch in rod bearing cap and rod. This notch prevents misalignment of bearing halves. (Oldsmobile)

In a previous chapter, reference was made to cylinder block distortion. This can be serious if the crankcase distorts enough to throw the engine main bearings out of alignment with each other. An example of this is shown in Figure 10-4.

On engines having fewer than eight cylinders, it is customary to provide a journal on the crankshaft for each cylinder. On V-type engines, however, the rods are usually placed side by side, two on each journal.

Camshaft bearings are usually made of bronze and are bushings rather than split bearings. See Figure 10-5. Camshaft bearings are not adjustable and must be replaced

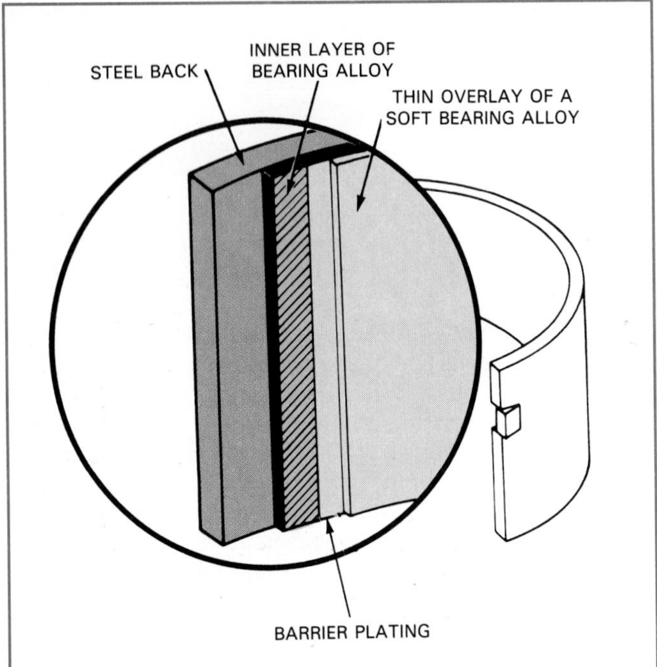

Figure 10-2. Construction of an engine bearing. On quality undersize bearings, the steel back thickness is increased. On inferior undersize bearings, the bearing alloy material is increased in thickness. (Federal Mogul)

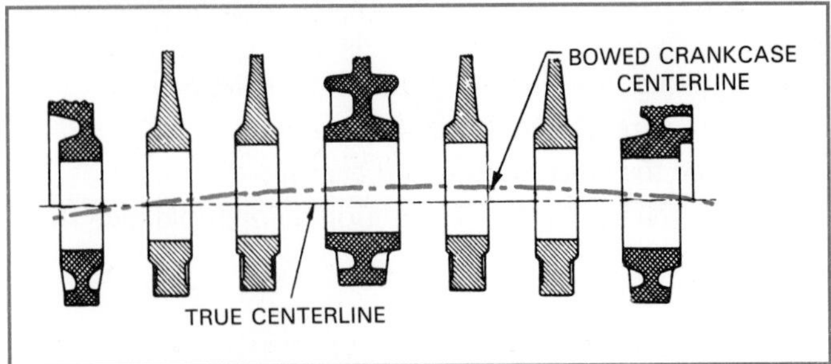

Figure 10-4. Main bearing bores in crankcase can warp out of alignment. If warpage is severe, the crankshaft will bind.

Figure 10-5. Holes in camshaft bushings provide lubrication to the camshaft and other parts of the engine. (Photo courtesy of AE Clevite Engine Parts)

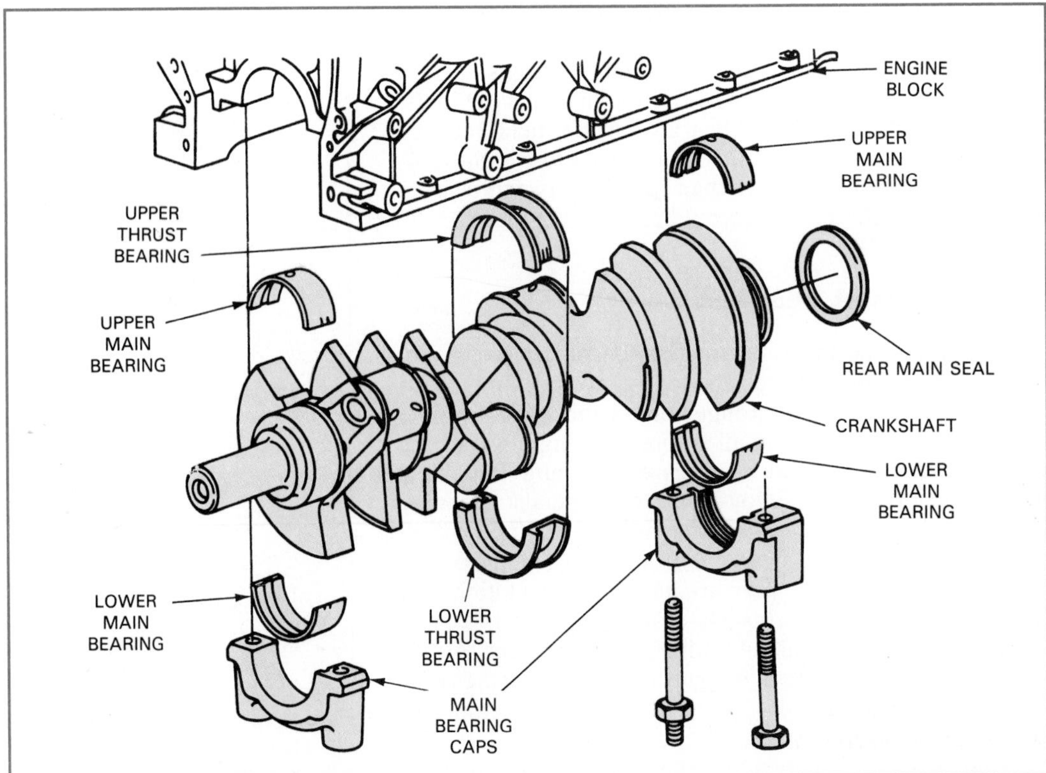

Figure 10-3. Crankshaft, bearings, bearing caps, and rear seal. The upper and lower thrust bearing is a main bearing with a flange on each side to control the fore-and-aft movement of the crankshaft. (General Motors)

when worn. The degree of wear dictating replacement is generally determined by the oil clearance between the camshaft journal and the bearing.

Main Bearing Caps and Seals

An exploded view of a typical crankshaft together with its bearings, caps, and seals is shown in Figure 10-6. Note that there are two bolts for each cap. In larger engines, four bolts are often used for each cap. The center main bearing in Figure 10-3 is designed to limit the end thrust as indicated by the flanges on the side. To prevent oil leakage, the rear main bearing is provided with a seal. Seals are either of the wick type or are made of neoprene. See Figure 10-7.

In most cases, the upper seal can be removed without removing the crankshaft. First, loosen the main bearing cap bolts and lower the crankshaft slightly. Then remove the rear bearing cap and push the upper seal around the shaft until one end protrudes. Then, grip the end of the seal with pliers and pull it the rest of the way out.

In the case of high-performance engines, the main bearing caps are provided with cross bolts in addition to the usual vertical bolts, Figure 10-8.

Engine Crankshafts

Automobile engine ***crankshafts*** are forged out of steel, Figure 10-9, or they are made out of cast steel by a special process.

The bearing journals are finished in precise alignment with each other. Also, great care is exercised to see that the journals are absolutely round and not tapered longitudinally. A high degree of accuracy is necessary in any work that is done with an engine crankshaft or with any of the bearings.

In automobile engines, a gear or sprocket is installed on the end of the crankshaft (opposite the flywheel end) to drive the camshaft by means of a timing chain, a timing

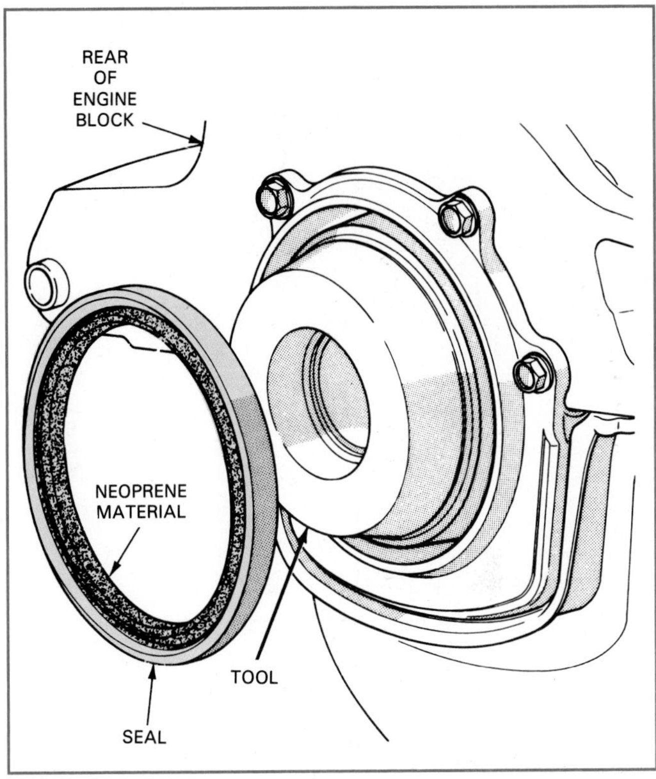

Figure 10-7. A neoprene rear main seal. This type of rear main seal is the most commonly used in modern engines. (Chrysler)

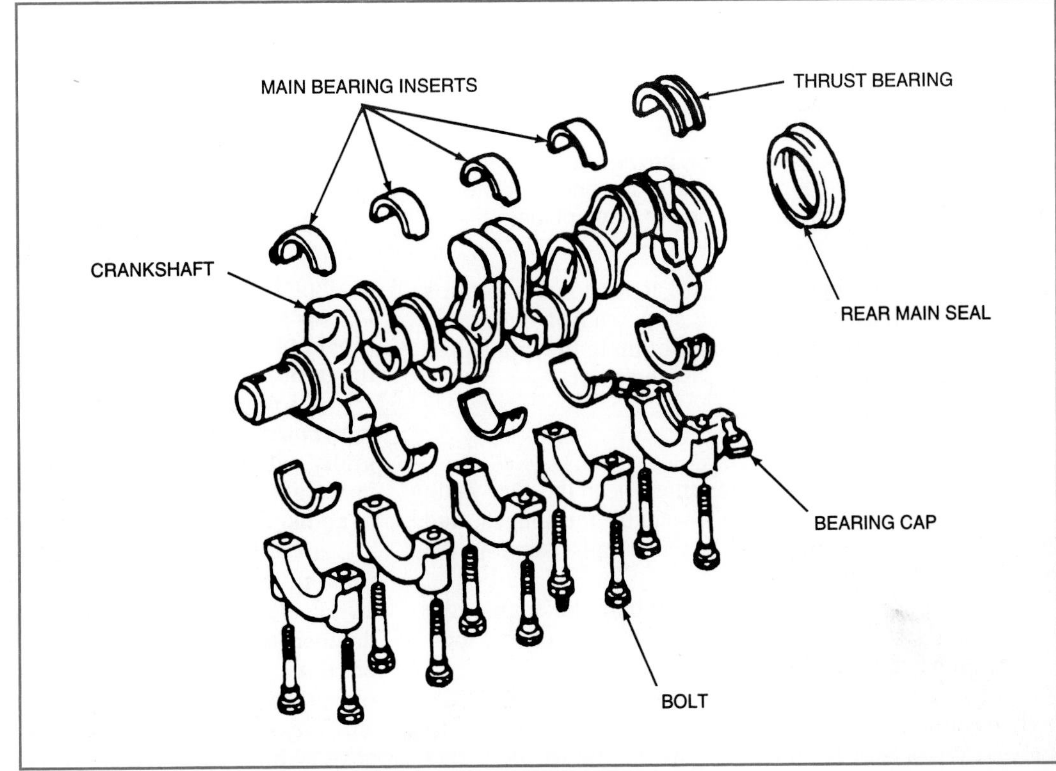

Figure 10-6. Detailed view shows an engine crankshaft.

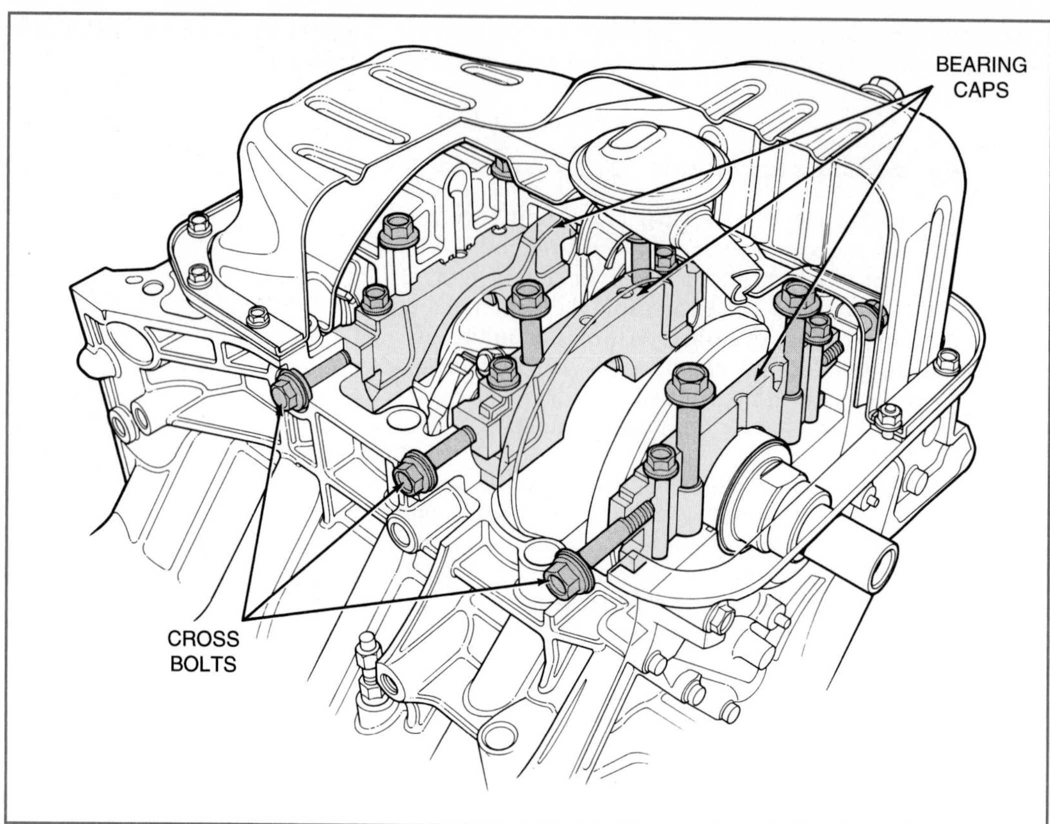

Figure 10-8. Cross bolts add strength to bearing caps on this engine. (Honda)

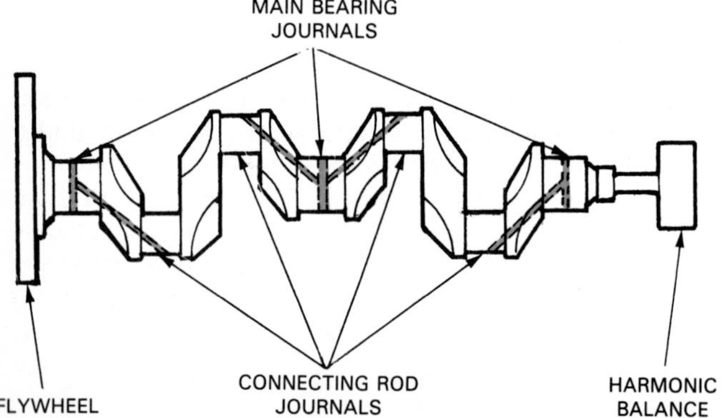

Figure 10-9. Oil passages, in color, provide lubrication to the engine bearings and to other parts of the engine. Note that the main bearing journals are on the same plane.

belt, or a gear arrangement. Also, a torsional vibration damper is usually attached to the same end of the crankshaft to help smooth out vibrations set up in the crankshaft by power impulses that tend to twist the shaft.

Engine Flywheels

A ***flywheel*** ordinarily is mounted near the rear main bearing. The rear main bearing is usually the longest and heaviest of the main bearings, since it must support the weight of the flywheel.

The purpose of the flywheel is to help the engine idle smoothly by carrying the pistons through parts of the operating cycle when power is not being produced.

The heavier the engine flywheel, the smoother the engine will idle. However, because of its inertia, an excessively heavy flywheel will cause the engine to accelerate and decelerate slowly. For this reason, heavy-duty or truck engines have large and heavy flywheels, while racing engines or high performance engines have light flywheels.

The rear surface of the flywheel is usually machined flat. This surface is used to mate with one surface of the clutch. With automatic transmissions, part of the torque converter is attached to the flywheel.

Crankshaft Balance

Because of the forces acting on the crankshaft and the speed at which it revolves, the crankshaft must be balanced with great care. The assembly is first balanced statically, then dynamically. ***Static balance*** of the crankshaft is obtained when the weight is distributed equally in all directions from the center of the crankshaft while it is at rest.

Dynamic balance is achieved while the crankshaft is turning. It is attained when the centrifugal forces of rotation are equal in all directions at any point. The dynamic balancing operation requires special machinery and involves removal of metal at the heavy points or addition of metal at the light points.

To obtain rotating balance, crankshafts are equipped with ***counterweights,*** which are usually forged or cast integrally with the crankshaft, Figures 10-10 and 10-11. Counterweights are located opposite the connecting rod journals to counterbalance the weight of the rods and pistons.

In addition to balancing the crankshaft itself, the entire rotating assembly must be balanced dynamically, Figure 10-12. This assembly includes the fan pulley, vibration damper, timing gears, crankshaft, flywheel, and the clutch or converter parts attached to it. In addition, the connecting rod assemblies, including piston pins, pistons, bearings, etc., are all carefully balanced so that the rotating mass will have as little vibration as possible.

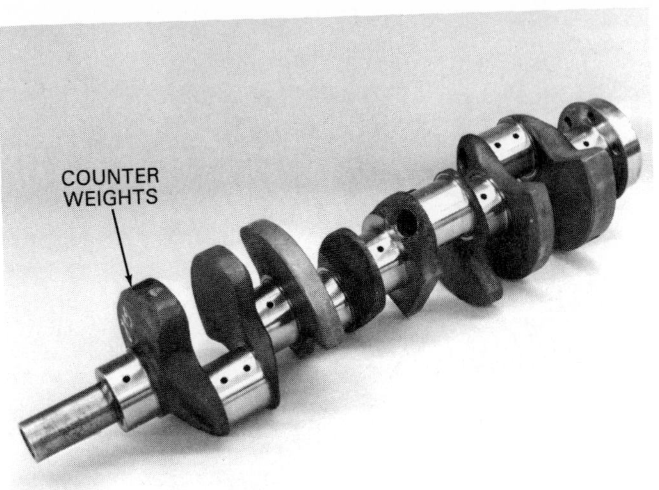

Figure 10-10. Counterweights offset the weight of piston and rod. (Ford)

For a further discussion on crankshaft balancing and the methods used to correct unbalance, see Chapter 14.

Torsional Vibration

The explosive forces acting on the pistons and the inertia forces of the reciprocating parts vary in intensity as the pistons move up and down in the cylinders. This variation in force, or torque, causes the crankshaft to twist, or transmit ***torsional vibration.*** Torsional vibration is more noticeable at certain speeds than others. The vibration is more intense on long shafts than on short ones.

When the No. 1 cylinder fires, it tends to turn the front end of the crankshaft instantly. This force is transmitted through the length of the crankshaft to the flywheel, which has considerable inertia. At this point, the crankshaft momentarily "winds up," or twists lengthwise (to a small degree, but enough to create vibration). Any piece of steel, no matter how heavy, can be twisted slightly when enough torque is applied to it.

Twisting of the crankshaft depends on the forces operating in the engine, so it is more severe at some speeds than others. Vibration dampers are used to help control crankshaft twist, Figures 10-12 and 10-14.

Figure 10-12. Special equipment is used to check the dynamic balance of an engine while crankshaft, piston, and connecting rods are in place.

Vibration Dampers

Regardless of the type of ***vibration damper*** used, they all accomplish the same purpose. They add mass to the end of the crankshaft opposite the flywheel to minimize crankshaft twist. The simplest vibration dampening device would be a flywheel at each end of the crankshaft. In this case, the weight of both flywheels would be about the same as the weight of a single normal flywheel.

A better way is to use a smaller flywheel on the front end of the crankshaft and mount it so that it floats. In one type, Figure 10-13, rubber is used between the small flywheel and its hub. This permits limited circumferential movement between the crankshaft and small flywheel.

Balance Shafts

The ***balance shaft*** does the same thing as a vibration damper. Balance shafts are used on large four cylinder engines and some small V-6 engines. On the smaller four-cylinder engines neither a vibration damper nor balance shaft is used, as the vibrations are so slight that neither is needed. Some manufacturers locate the balance shaft above the crankshaft, Figure 10-14A. Other manufacturers locate the balance shaft below the crankshaft, Figure 10-14B. Also, while some manufacturers use only one balance shaft, others use two, Figure 10-14C.

Critical Speeds

No matter how carefully the crankshaft and the parts attached to it are balanced, there will be certain speeds at

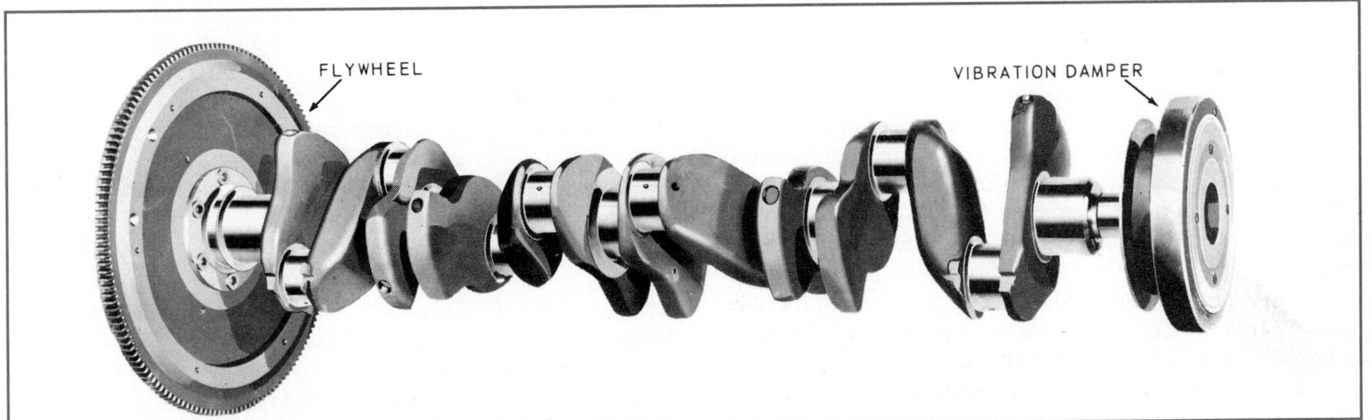

Figure 10-11. A crankshaft with vibration damper and flywheel.

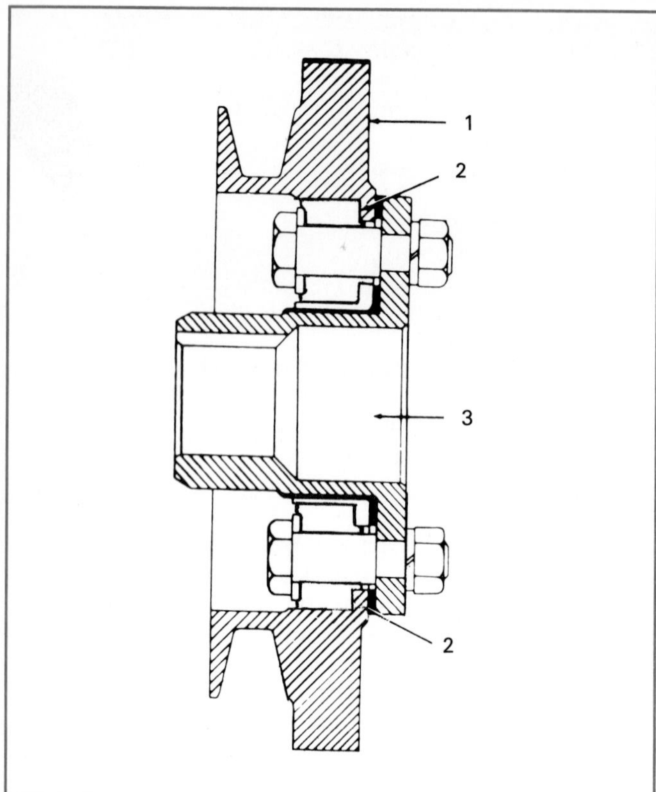

Figure 10-13. Construction of a vibration damper: 1–Pulley. 2–Rubber insert. 3–Pulley hub.

which some vibration will occur. These are known as ***critical speeds.*** By careful design and balancing, these critical periods occur at speeds outside the ordinary working speeds of the engine.

It is not too difficult to balance rotating parts. However, when reciprocating parts are attached, the problem becomes much more complicated. Consider that each heavy connecting rod and piston assembly must be started, speeded up, slowed down, and stopped twice during each revolution.

Other Causes of Vibration

Other factors enter into this matter of unbalance and vibration. The piston does not accelerate and decelerate uniformly during each quarter revolution. During the first quarter revolution from top dead center (TDC), the connecting rod moves down (length of crank throw) and away from the center of the cylinder. Both the downward and outward motions of the rod cause the piston to travel downward.

During the second quarter of a revolution, there is continued downward motion. However, the end of the connecting rod is now moving back toward the centerline of the cylinder. During the last portion of this movement, the piston is not moving downward. As a result, actual movement of the piston during the second quarter revolution is less than during the first quarter, Figure 10-15.

When you consider all of these forces acting on the crankshaft, it is easy to see why a fraction of an ounce cannot be added to or subtracted from any of these parts during a repair operation. Furthermore, the crankshaft, bearings, bearing journals, etc., must be in excellent mechanical condition at all times.

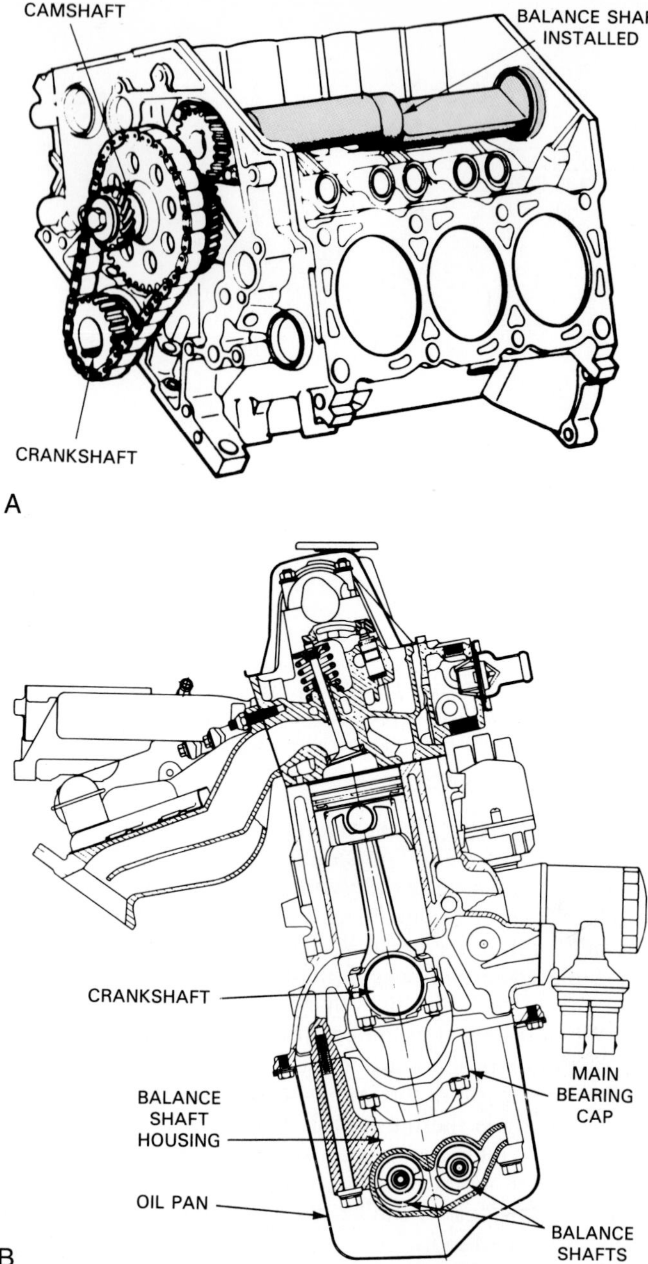

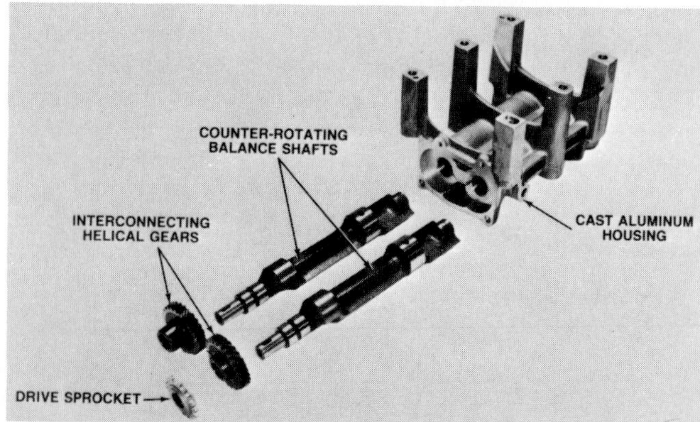

Figure 10-14. A–The balance shaft on this V-6 engine is located above the crankshaft and camshaft. Only one balance shaft is used. B–The balance shafts on this engine are located below the crankshaft. C–The balance shaft is driven by a chain, which is driven by the crankshaft. (Chrysler and Ford)

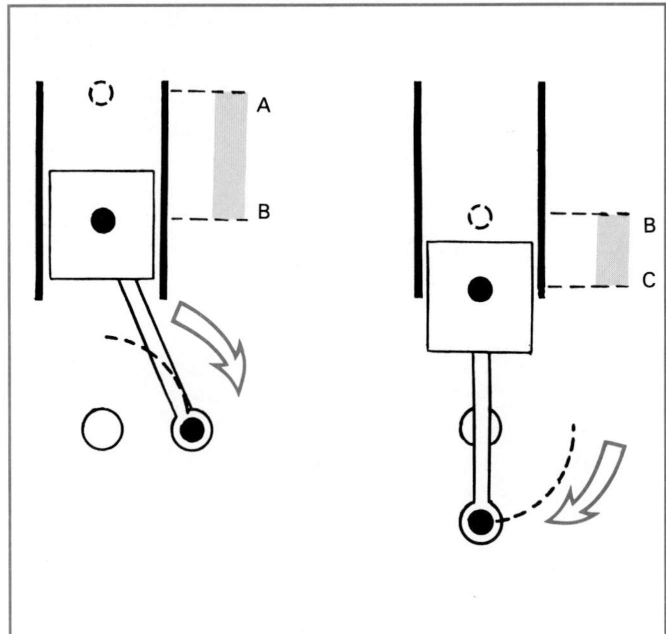

Figure 10-15. During the first quarter revolution of crankshaft, the piston moves the distance from A to B. During second quarter revolution, the piston moves from B to C. Crankshaft moves the same amount, but piston movement is less from B to C.

Chapter 10-Review Questions

Write your answers on a separate sheet of paper. Do not write in this book.

1. Bearings are made of the same type of metal as the crankshaft. True or False?
2. An integral bearing is the same thing as a precision bearing. True or False?
3. Why is bearing metal comparatively soft?
4. Bushings are always used on all camshaft journals. True or False?
5. Slip-in bearings are not adjustable for wear. True or False?
6. Name four metals used in bearing metal alloys.
7. What is the purpose of a flywheel?
8. What is the difference between static and dynamic balance?
9. Describe a vibration damper.
10. Small four cylinder engines:
    (A) use a vibration damper.
    (B) use a balance shaft.
    (C) Either A or B.
    (D) None of the above.
11. When the crankshaft rotational speed is constant, the distance traveled by the piston during each quarter revolution is the same. True or False?

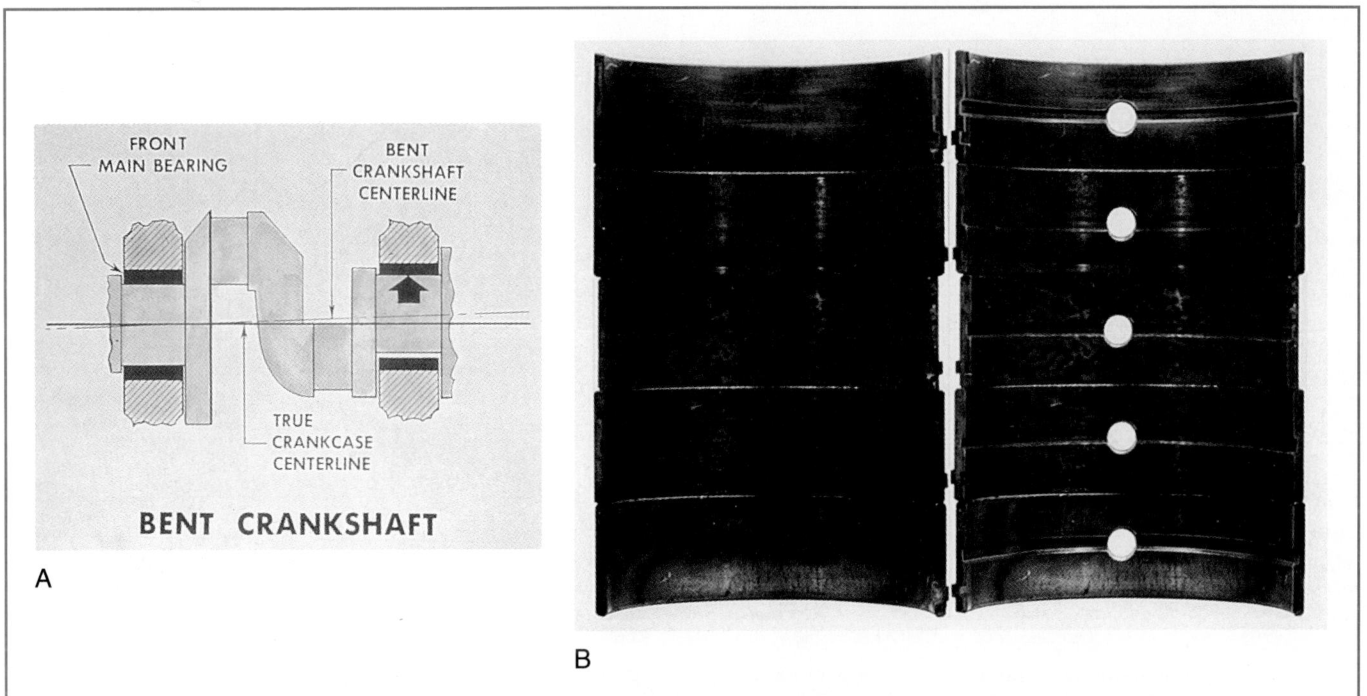

A bent crankshaft can cause severe bearing damage. A–This illustration shows how a bent crankshaft can place an excessive load (represented by the large arrow) on the bearings. B–These bearings were damaged by a bent crankshaft. (Photo courtesy of AE Clevite Engine Parts)

The condition of the camshaft, cam bushings, and lifters is critical to proper engine operation.
(Photo courtesy of AE Clevite Engine Parts)

Chapter 11
Engine Camshafts and Valves

After studying this chapter, you will be able to:

❍ Explain the purpose of the camshaft.
❍ State how a camshaft operates.
❍ Name the parts of a valve and the valve train.
❍ Explain how the valves are cooled.
❍ Define the relationship of the camshaft to the crankshaft.
❍ Determine the difference between an overhead camshaft design and an overhead valve design.
❍ List the parts of a hydraulic lifter.
❍ Explain how a hydraulic lifter operates.

Cams

A ***cam*** is a piece of metal that is somewhat egg shaped, Figure 11-1. As a cam rotates in an eccentric motion, it can open and close items that it comes in contact with. On a car's engine, the cams open and close the valves of the engine as they rotate, Figure 11-2.

These cams appear to have a simple shape, but actually the exact shape of the cam is a meticulous job of design. The design is worked out after a detailed program of mathematical calculation and checked by lengthy experimentation. If the shape of the cams is altered by wear, the efficiency of the engine deteriorates fast. There is much more to the matter than just opening and closing a valve.

Cam Functions

The cam is designed to open the valve at precisely the correct instant in relation to piston travel and hold it open long enough to obtain the most efficient filling and emptying of the cylinder. It exerts considerable control over the ***volumetric efficiency*** of the engine.

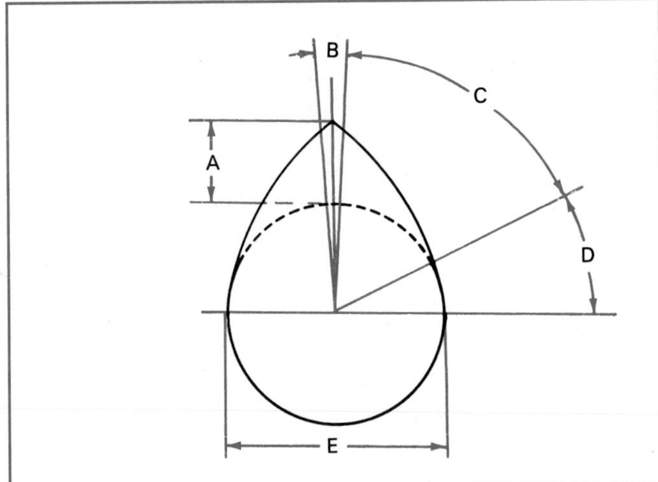

Figure 11-1. Nomenclature of a cam. A–Height of lift. B–Nose. C–Flank. D–Ramp. E–Diameter of cam.

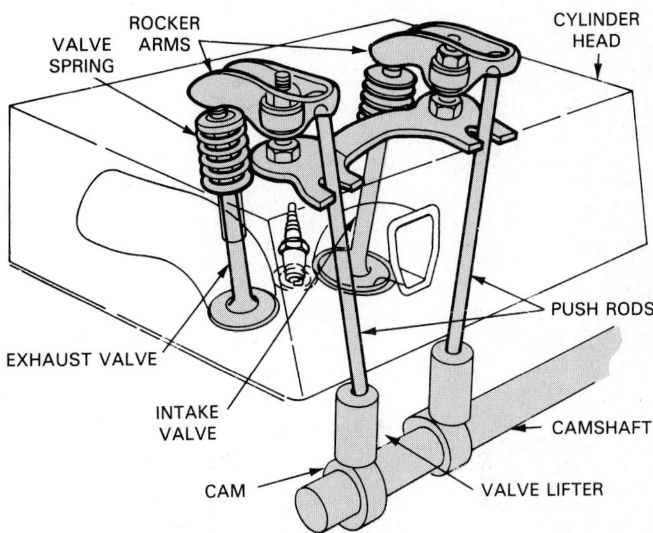

Figure 11-2. A typical valve train. When the nose of the cam pushes against the lifter, the lifter pushes up on the push rod to the rocker arm. The rocker arm acts as a lever and transmits this motion downward on the valve. Note that there is a separate cam for each valve. (Oldsmobile)

In a passenger car engine, ramps on the cams are designed to open the valves smoothly and gradually. This prevents shock to the valves, valve springs, etc., and provides for quiet operation. The final design is usually a compromise between efficiency and quietness of operation.

On racing engines, where noise is not important and utmost efficiency is desired, the cams are often shaped with more abrupt ramps, higher lift, a flatter flank, and a wider nose. The cam is intended to "bat" the valve open quickly, open it wider, hold it open longer, and close it rapidly. Such engines are noisy, idle roughly, and wear more quickly.

Camshafts

A ***camshaft*** is simply a shaft that has cams. Since the valves of the engine need to be opened at different times, the noses, or high points, of the cams are offset from one another. Most camshafts have twice as many cams as there are cylinders. The reason for this is that there is one cam for each exhaust valve and one cam for each intake valve. However, some overhead camshaft engines are provided with two camshafts for each bank of cylinders: one camshaft for the intake valves and the other for the exhaust valves. See Figure 11-3.

The camshaft is made of steel, and only the surface of each cam is hardened to avoid rapid wear. If the entire camshaft were hardened, it would snap apart, as it would not be able to absorb the twisting motion.

In a four-cycle engine, each valve is opened once for two revolutions of the crankshaft. Therefore, the camshaft turns at one-half the speed of the crankshaft, Figure 11-4. Since the camshaft runs at a slower speed than the crankshaft, it is not subject to as much wear as the crankshaft.

Camshaft Location

In the past, the camshaft was located in the engine block in most I-head engine designs (valves above the piston), Figure 11-4. However, to avoid the use of extensive linkage (which wastes power), the camshaft is placed in the cylinder head in most late-model engines, Figure 11-5. With this setup, the camshaft can be driven by a cog belt, Figure 11-6, or it may be chain driven or gear driven.

Race engines have their overhead camshaft driven either by a shaft or by a series of gears. The cog belt is made of neoprene reinforced with fiberglass. Among the advantages claimed for this construction are heat and oil resistance and the ability to absorb shock and constant flexing. In addition, it is inherently quiet and needs no lubrication.

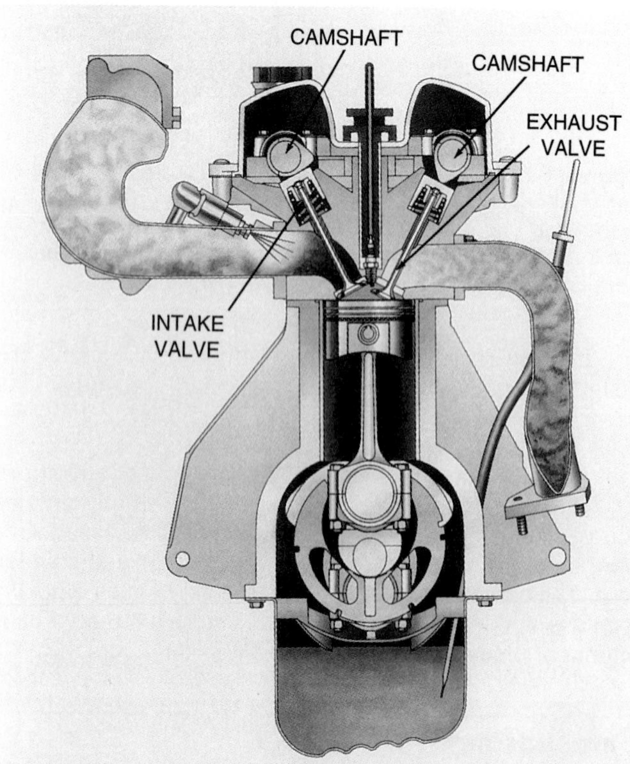

Figure 11-3. A dual overhead camshaft (DOHC) engine. One camshaft opens only the intake valves, and the other camshaft opens only the exhaust valves. (Saturn)

The ***overhead camshaft*** is efficient. It eliminates push rods and permits excellent valve action at high speeds since there is little inertia of moving parts.

It is necessary that the camshaft journals be round and true, and the camshaft be straight and true. There should be no measurable wear on the cam surfaces. Also, there must be no appreciable looseness in the bearings, since any radial movement or vibration of the cams would affect the operation of the valves.

If the camshaft is chain or belt driven, it rotates in the same direction as the crankshaft (clockwise from the front of the engine). If the camshaft is driven by a gear that is meshed with a mating gear on the crankshaft, the camshaft rotation is counterclockwise, or opposite from the crankshaft.

As the valves must be precisely opened and closed in relation to piston travel, any wear in the camshaft timing

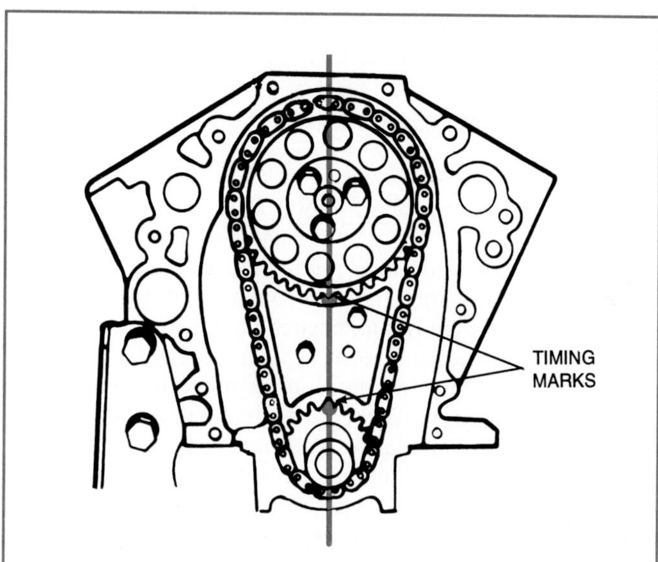

Figure 11-4. Camshaft is located in the engine block. Note that the size of the camshaft sprocket is twice the diameter of the crankshaft sprocket, which provides a reduction in camshaft speed. Also, timing marks on camshaft and crankshaft sprockets must align when first installed. (General Motors)

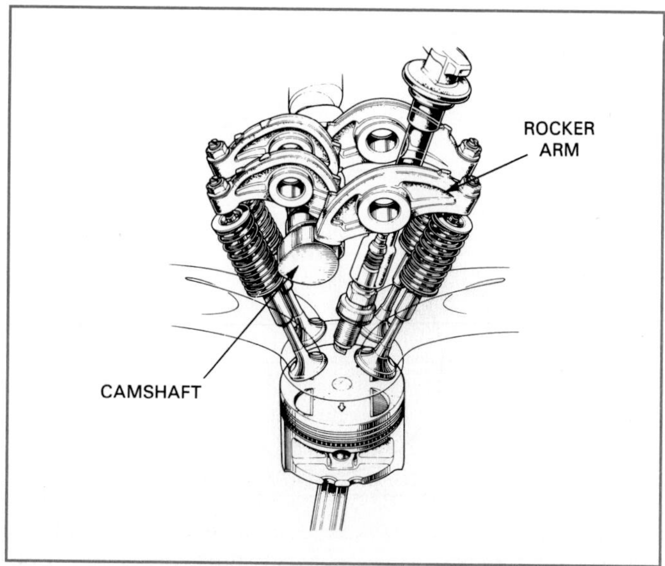

Figure 11-5. Overhead camshaft (OHC). (Honda)

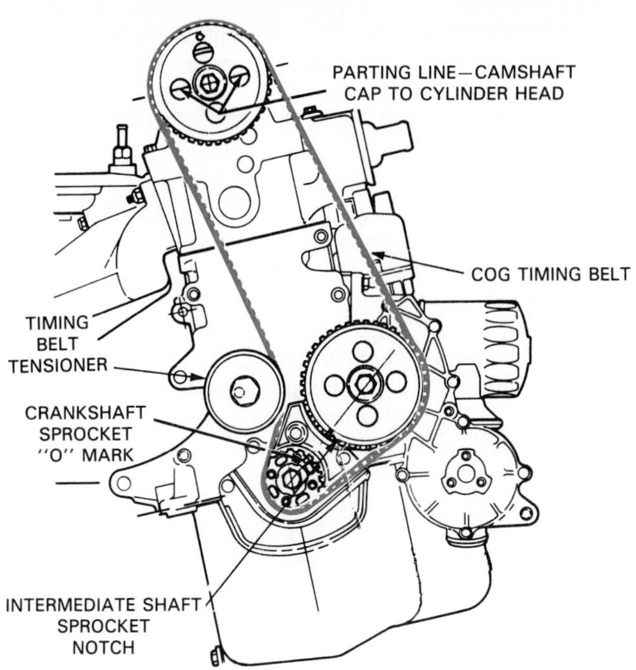

Figure 11-6. A cogged timing belt drives this overhead camshaft. Belt tensioner provides constant tension on the timing belt. (Chrysler)

chain or belt will result in the valve not being opened and closed at the exact instant desired and a loss in engine efficiency will be incurred.

Timing Chain Wear

In some cases, a device is provided to adjustment timing chains, such as an eccentric mounting for an accessory shaft, an automatic slack adjuster, etc. In most cases, however, it is necessary to install a new chain when the old one becomes worn and stretched. In general, a deflection of 1/2″ is permitted for timing chains when the chain is depressed.

The car manufacturers set up specifications as to the amount of wear permissible in the chain or between the gear teeth. They also mark the gears or chains to facilitate correct timing.

Timing Gear Wear

In a gear-driven camshaft, the crankshaft gear is usually made of steel. However, the camshaft gear is often made of ***nonmetallic composition.*** This nonmetallic substance is quite durable and also makes for quieter operation. These gears are not adjustable and must be replaced when worn.

Timing Belt Wear

The ***timing belt*** should be checked periodically for wear. See Figure 11-7A. The timing belt should be replaced during a valve job or major engine overhaul. Some premature wear can be attributed to wear of the teeth on the timing belt sprocket. See Figure 11-7B. It is important to service the timing belt at the recommended intervals. If the timing belt breaks, damage to the pistons, valves, and connecting rods may occur. The same is true for timing chains.

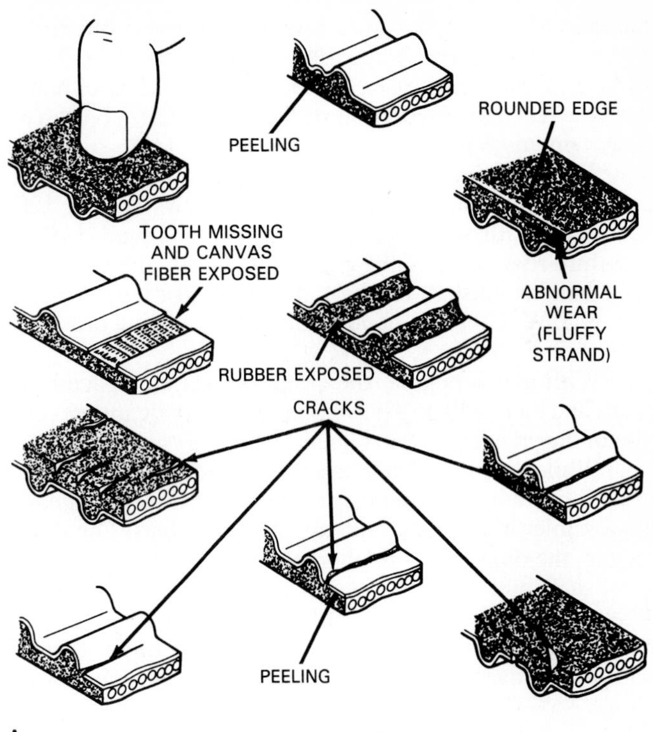

Figure 11-7. Timing belt wear. A–Inspecting the timing belt for various types of wear. B–Using a straight edge to determine if there is a gap on teeth of timing belt sprocket, as indicated by arrow. This sprocket must be replaced or the timing belt will wear prematurely. (Gates Rubber Co. and Chrysler)

Firing Order

The location of the cams around the camshaft and the design of the crankshaft determine the ***firing order*** of the engine. A one-cylinder, two-cycle engine fires once each revolution. A one-cylinder, four-cycle engine fires once every other revolution. A two-cylinder, two-cycle engine fires twice each revolution. A two-cylinder, four-cycle engine fires once every revolution.

In a four-cylinder, four-cycle engine, the No. 1 piston moves downward on the power stroke, while No. 4 moves down on the intake stroke. As No. 1 and No. 4 are going down, No. 2 and No. 3 are, of course, going up. One is on the exhaust stroke; the other is on the compression stroke. There are, therefore, two possible firing orders: 1, 2, 4, 3 or 1, 3, 4, 2. In either case, one power impulse is obtained during every half revolution of the crankshaft, giving two power impulses per revolution. See Figure 11-8.

The six-cylinder, four-cycle engine (and a three-cylinder, two-cycle engine) has the crank throws spaced 120° apart, rather than 180°, and gets a power impulse every one-third revolution of the crankshaft. The firing order of a right-hand crankshaft can be 1, 5, 3, 6, 2, 4 or it can be 1, 2, 4, 6, 5, 3. With the left-hand crankshaft, the firing order can be 1, 4, 2, 6, 3, 5 or 1, 3, 5, 6, 4, 2.

With a V-8 engine, the crank throws are spaced 90° apart, and there will be a power impulse every quarter revolution of the crankshaft. See Figure 11-8.

While different firing orders are used, the general idea of an inline engine firing order is to fire cylinders as nearly as possible at alternate ends of the crankshaft. On a V-8 engine, the objective is to alternate between the ends of the crankshaft and between the left and right cylinder banks. This tends to distribute the forces throughout the engine and avoid concentrating consecutive power impulses near one point of the crankshaft. This reduces vibration and results in a smoother running engine. A popular cylinder arrangement and typical firing order are shown in Figure 11-9.

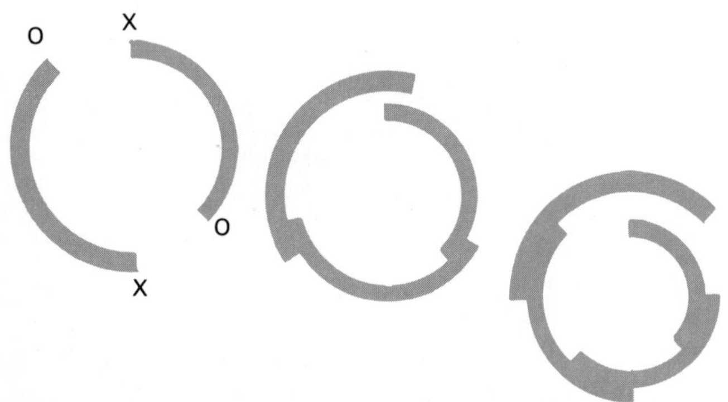

Figure 11-8. Distribution of forces around the crankshaft of a four-cycle engine. Left–Power impulses of a four-cylinder engine occur twice during each revolution. Space between O and X indicates the time the exhaust valve is open during power stroke; no power is obtained. Center–A six-cylinder engine has three power impulses per revolution. Right–An eight-cylinder engine has four power impulses per revolution. The constant flow of power provides a smoother running engine.

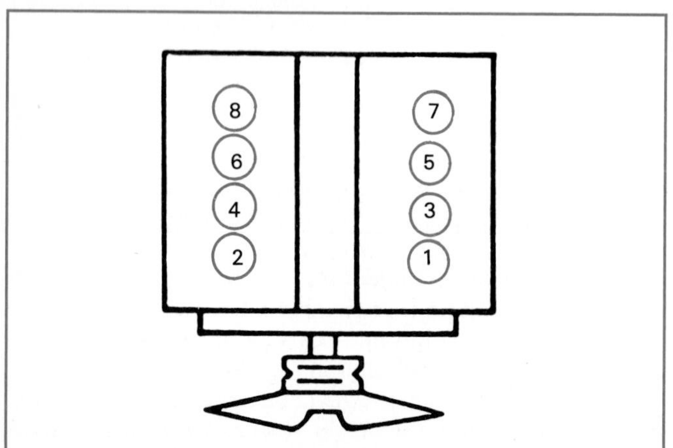

Figure 11-9. A popular V-8 firing order is 1-8-4-3-6-5-7-2.

Valves

Internal combustion engine ***valves,*** Figure 11-10, have a tremendous task to perform. Even under the very best conditions, they are not all that could be desired. The conditions under which the valves operate would seem to impose an impossible task upon them, but they have been developed to a point where they are fairly efficient. A great amount of ingenuity has been expended upon sleeve valves, rotary valves, slide valves, and poppet valves. The ***poppet valve***, despite its shortcomings, is used almost universally.

Poppet valves are noisy and are difficult to cool, but they are simple and they provide an effective seal under operating conditions. These operating conditions are brutal. The valves in the combustion chamber are exposed to the burning gases. They are not surrounded by coolant or oil. The explosion temperature within an engine combustion chamber may momentarily approach 5000° F (2700° C), and then the exhaust valve must open and permit these hot gases to flow by the valve head at high velocity.

The exhaust valve head may attain a temperature of 1000°F (540°C) or more under these conditions, Figure 11-11. The only cooling comes from contact with the valve guides and with the cylinder head during the short time it is in contact with the valve seat.

If an engine is operating at 3000 rpm, each cylinder will fire 1500 times per minute. Every time the cylinder fires, the ***exhaust valve*** must open to let the burned gases out. In spite of the fact that the valve is lifted off its seat 1500 times each minute, a large portion of the heat passes from the valve head, through the valve seat, and into the water jacket.

Valve Temperatures

It is not difficult to understand why exhaust valves are prone to cause trouble. In normal operation, the valve head around the seating surface will operate at a temperature of 1000-1200°F (540-645°C). The central portion of the valve head will run somewhat hotter, 1200-1400°F (645-760°C), and the stem adjacent to the head is 800-1000°F (425-540°C).

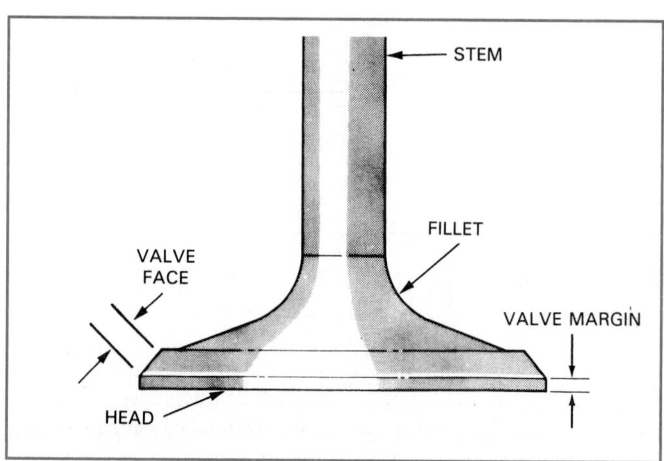

Figure 11-10. Nomenclature of a valve. (Chrysler)

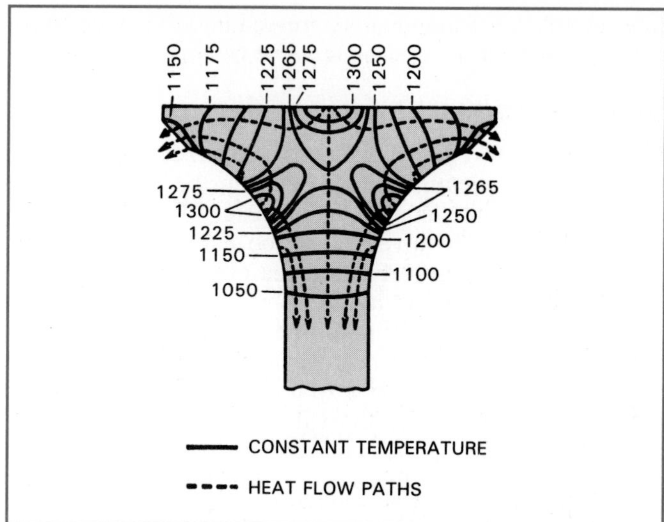

Figure 11-11. Various temperatures on an exhaust valve. The hottest location is the valve head.

Running red hot under normal conditions, the steel valve may melt under abnormal conditions.

The ***intake valve*** has a somewhat easier task, as it is not exposed to the burning gases while it is off its seat. The intake valve is also cooled by the incoming gas mixture, which is below atmospheric temperature.

Valve and Seat Materials

Exhaust valves are usually made of heat-resistant alloy steel. Quite often, they are partially filled with sodium to help transfer the heat. See Figure 11-12. The ***valve seat*** is often also made of heat resistant alloy in the form of an insert, which is set into the cylinder head. See the alloy inserts in Figure 11-13. These inserts are used in cast iron heads and aluminum heads. The particular construction shown in Figure 11-14 shows how heat is transferred to the water jacket.

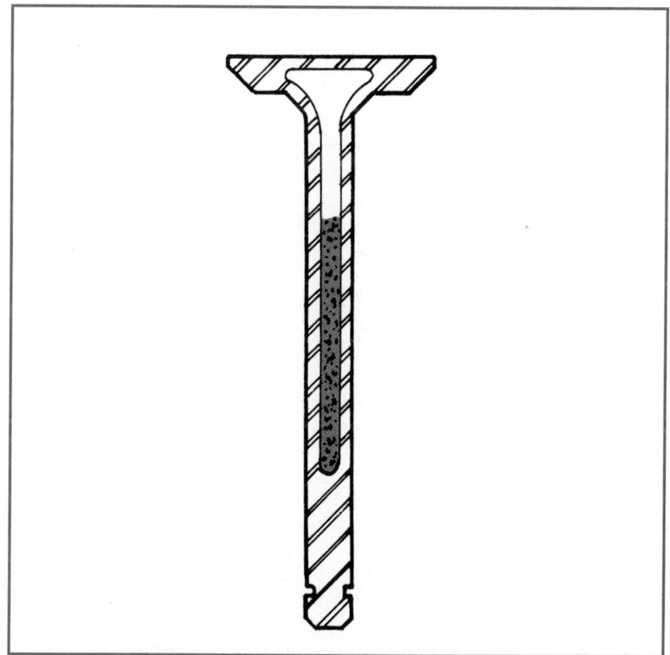

Figure 11-12. A portion of this hollow valve stem is filled with sodium. When the sodium melts, the liquid bounces between the valve head and the tip of the valve, transferring the heat of the valve. This aids in the heat transfer process. This type of valve is usually only found on diesel engines and high performance engines.

Induction Hardened Seats

One of the results of lead-free fuel is higher valve temperatures, which can cause valve and seat burning.

In the past, the lead in the fuel acted as a lubricant between the valve face and its seat. When there is no lead in the fuel, the cast iron seats become oxidized by the hot exhaust gases. These oxides abrade the valve face and seat, so there is metal transfer from the seat to the valve. Valve seat wear increases rapidly as valve lash becomes greater. When lash increases from 0.001″ to 0.040″, the impact loads increase up to 30 times. This increases valve and seat wear.

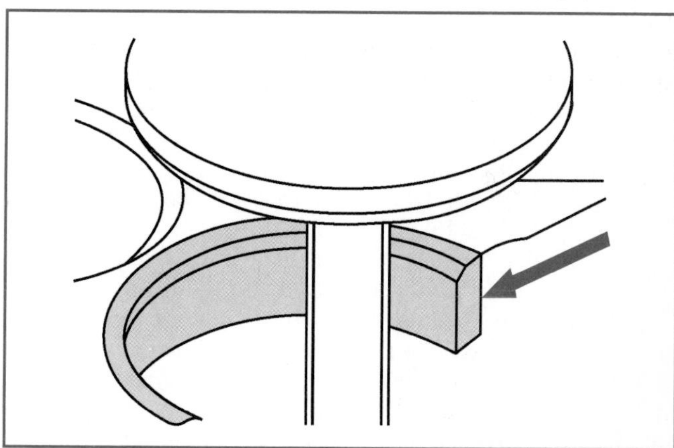

Figure 11-13. The valve seat insert can be shrunk by exposing it to extreme cold before placing it in the cylinder head.

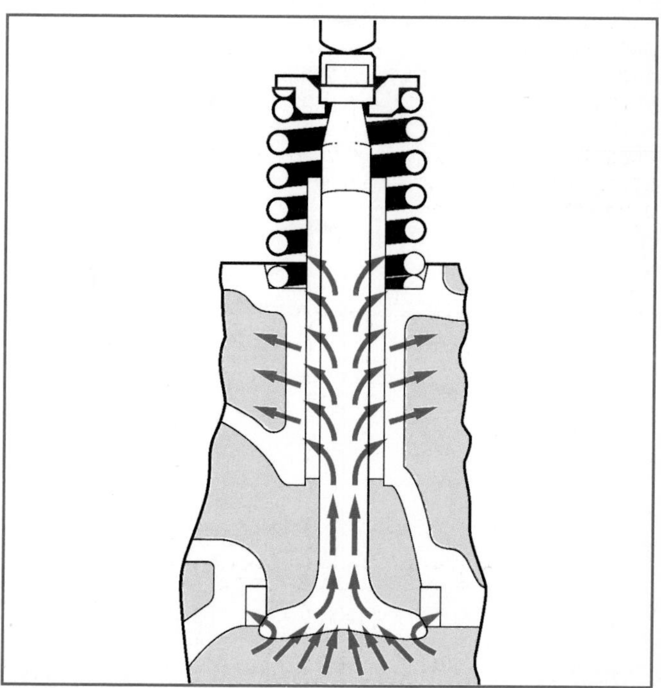

Figure 11-14. Heat transfer path from valve head and face to the seat. Heat also is transferred through the valve guide.

To overcome this situation, several methods are available. One method is to use alloys for the valve seats or hard, noncorrosive inserts. Instead of ethyl lead in the fuel, boron oxide or iron phosphate can be used, but these materials have an adverse effect on catalytic converters. Another method is to aluminize the valve face or chrome plate the valve head. Valve stems are also being chrome plated in order to reduce wear.

Internally cooled valves, such as shown in Figure 11-12, are also being used and extensive research on water-filled valve stems is promising, showing temperature reductions up to 600°F (315°C). To further aid in the dissipation of heat, valve stem diameter is sometimes increased.

Induction hardening of valve seats extends the life of the seat, Figure 11-15. This process heats the valve seats to 1700 °F (927°C) and hardens them to a depth of 0.05″ to 0.08″. This gives the seats approximately the same durability as is obtained with leaded fuel.

Valve Cooling

The heat of combustion flows from the valve head, through the valve seat, and into the coolant. Tests show that the popular conception that solid exhaust valves are cooled primarily by conduction down the stem is not true.

Most of the heat leaves the valve at the face. In fact, over half of the total heat absorbed by the valve leaves through the face.

It will also be noted that the heat flows from the valve stem to the valve guide and from the guide to the head, Figure 11-14. As heat will flow more readily through one piece of metal than from one piece to another, the ***removable valve guide*** on most passenger car engines has been discontinued. Instead, the cylinder head is reamed to form an ***integral valve guide.*** When it becomes necessary to recondition the valve guide, replacement valves are provided with oversize stems and the guides are then reamed to the desired size. The valve guide can also be knurled if wear is less than .006″. Also, the guide can be reamed oversize and a bushing can be pressed into the guide. With the last two methods, the same valve is used.

Valve Seat Contact Area

From the foregoing, it should be realized that anything that reduces the ***contact area*** between the valve and the cylinder head will hamper the transfer of heat from the valve. Thus, if the valve seat is too narrow or the valve guide is worn excessively, the area of contact will be reduced and the valve will overheat.

The area of contact could be increased by widening the valve seat, but it has been found that a wider seat also encourages flakes of carbon to adhere and hold the valve off its seat. This causes the valve face to burn. Another method of increasing the contact area would be to increase the diameter of the valve head and/or the valve stem by installing oversize valves, oversize stems, or longer guides.

There are, of course, mechanical limitations to the amount of increase in these dimensions. Of more importance, however, would be the increase of weight in the valve. The valve is required to move endwise with such speed that it must be as light as possible. Any excess weight would add to the inertia and slow down the valve action. Therefore, a compromise must be made and a reasonable limitation in size imposed. However, the major factor limiting the size of the valve is the diameter of the cylinder bore and shape of the combustion chamber.

Valve Heat Dissipation

The matter of valve ***heat dissipation*** must be thoroughly understood if automobile engines are to be serviced properly. There are several things to be considered in this area. Some of them are similar to problems previously discussed in connection with pistons and rings.

For example, the heat of operation causes distortion of cylinder heads, blocks, etc. The same conditions cause distortion of the valve and its seat. Any hot spots in the cylinder head or block near the valves or any unequal tightening of the

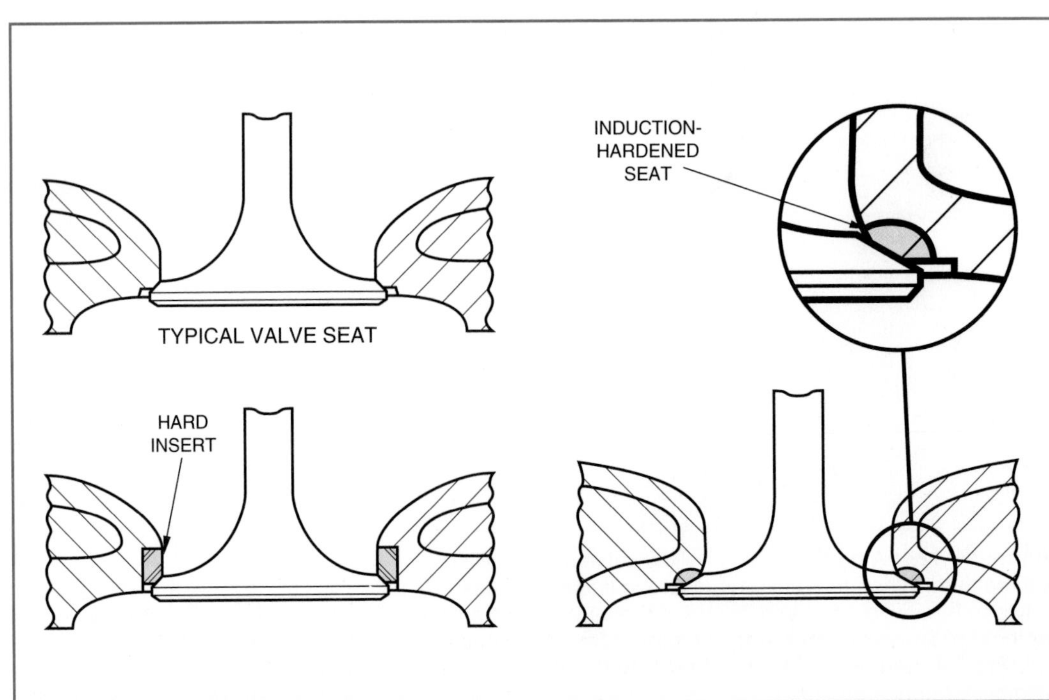

Figure 11-15. Induction-hardened seat is at right.

cylinder head bolts will aggravate distortion and cause valve difficulties. The valve and its seat may be round and true when the engine is cold, but may not be round and true when the engine reaches operating temperature.

The valve head is liable to warp due to the different temperatures at different points. This warpage will be aggravated if the ***margin*** of the valve is thin or uneven. See Figure 11-16. Furthermore, the temperature may vary around the margin of the valve. This is due to the difference in volume and velocity of the gas going between the valve and seat as determined by combustion chamber design and valve port shape.

In addition to changes in valve and valve seat shape, the diameter of both may change. The valve head runs hotter than the valve seat because the seat is closer to the circulating coolant. Therefore, the valve head may expand more than the seat, and as a result, the valve may rise on the seat as shown in Figure 11-17. This action results in a change in the valve seat area location.

It will be apparent that the dimension between the valve seat and the valve lifter will be lengthened by such expansion. The length of the valve between the seat surface and the end of the stem will be altered by lengthwise expansion of the valve and valve stem.

One of the most important factors affecting valve temperatures is that of ***valve lash,*** or ***tappet clearance.*** Insufficient clearance will result in the valves contacting the seats for a shorter time, and consequently, they will operate at higher temperatures. Excessive clearance will result in noisy operation and loss of power. Great accuracy should be used when adjusting the valve lash.

Valve Timing

Anything that occurs to change the time that the valve opens, the duration of the time it is held open, the size of the opening, or the time that it closes, will have a decided affect on engine performance. This fact is seldom fully realized. Many engines run constantly below par because of incorrect valve tappet clearance adjustment.

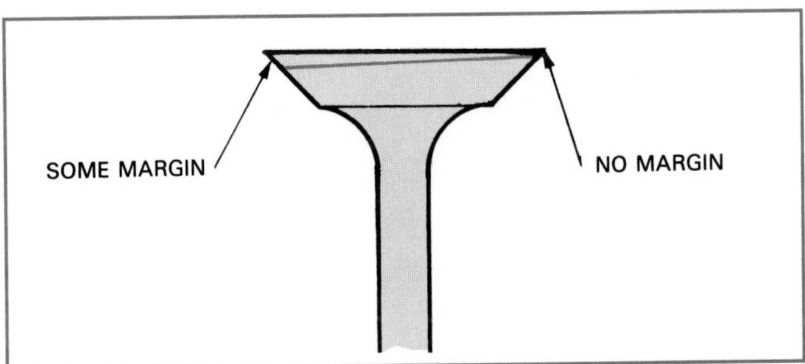

Figure 11-16. If there is no margin on the valve, the thin edges will become excessively hot and could cause preignition.

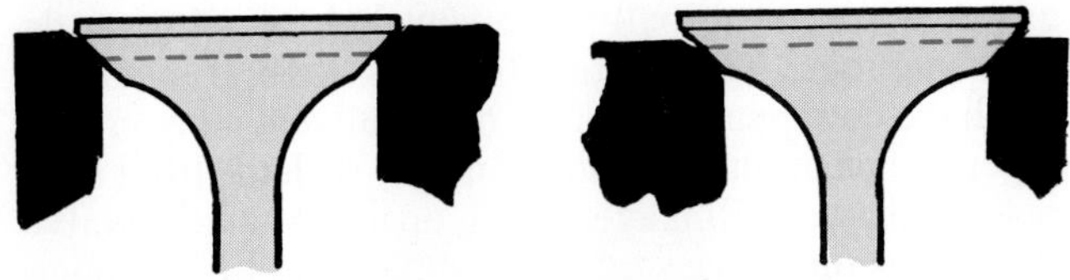

Figure 11-17. Left. Exhaust valve may seat properly when cold. Right. When exhaust valve is hot, the valve will move off its seat.

A full realization of the need for accurate adjustment can come only from a study of valve action and requirements. This study starts with the relationship between the crankshaft and camshaft. Due to the difference in the diameter of the circles described by the crank throw and the cam nose, and the difference in the comparative speed of rotation, the crank throw may travel many times faster than the cam nose. While the cam nose is moving 1/4″, the crank throw moves 1 1/2″. If the cam is a few thousandths late in opening the valve, the crank throw and the piston attached to it will move a considerable distance farther than it should before the valve begins to open.

In this manner, the motion of the piston is partially lost and the power output suffers. A worn timing chain or belt should be replaced as soon as the wear exceeds the specifications. They should not be allowed to run until they become noisy or break, which is all too often the case.

The extreme accuracy with which the valves must open and close may be better understood when thought is given to the speed at which the valve parts operate. Timing becomes more important as engine speeds are increased. This is the reason for what is known as ***valve overlap.*** Valve overlap means that the intake and exhaust valves are open at the same time to compensate for the time required by the air or gas to flow through the manifolds.

Many things have to be considered when designing the timing of an engine. In order that the engine may operate satisfactorily at high speeds, the exhaust valve must open before the end of the power stroke and close after the completion of the exhaust stroke. Also, the intake valve must open before the end of the exhaust stroke and close after the completion of the intake stroke. This involves an overlapping of the exhaust and intake periods, which is made necessary by the inertia of the gases. Also, the slow opening and closing motions of the valves is made necessary by the demand for quiet operation. See Figure 11-18.

Valve Springs

Valve springs, Figure 11-19, are required to close the valves after they have been opened by the action of the cam. Valve springs are of the coil type and are made of

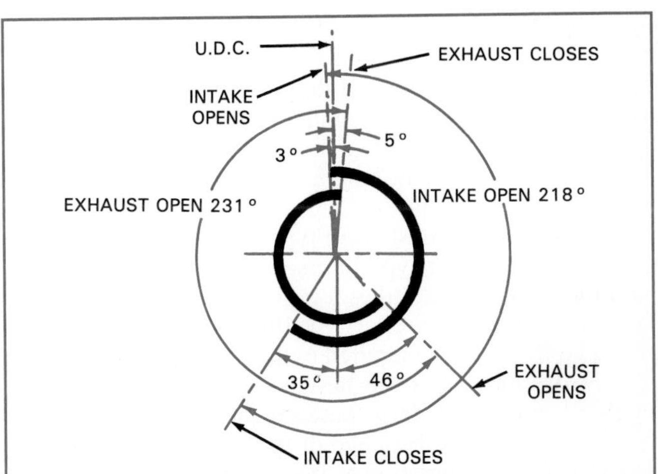

Figure 11-18. Diagram illustrates valve overlap. Valve overlap is the period when the exhaust valve and intake valve are both open. This is necessary at high speeds to compensate for inertia of the gases moving in and out of the cylinder.

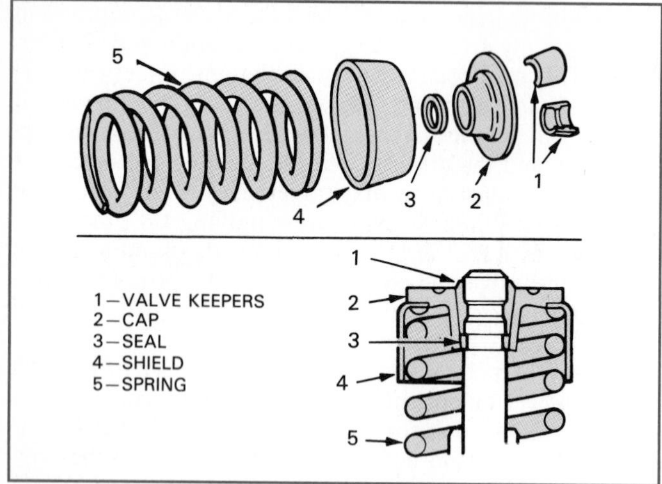

Figure 11-19. A valve spring and related parts. (Oldsmobile)

special high-grade steel that is designed to withstand the high rate of stress applications and the extreme temperatures. They also keep the valves from bouncing on their seats.

On some engines a single valve spring is used for each valve. On many high performance engines, two valve springs, one within the other, are required in order to obtain the desired pressure characteristics. Usually the end turns of the springs are closer together than the other turns in order to reduce vibrations. Valve springs are also provided with ***dampers,*** which help to reduce vibrations.

Valve spring pressure varies with the type of engine. Stronger springs are required on high speed engines and also on engines with heavier push rods, valves, rocker arms, etc.

Valve Lifters

The ***valve lifter*** is a device in the valve system that transmits the action of the cam to the valve or the push rod. There are two types of valve lifters: mechanical lifters and hydraulic lifters.

The ***mechanical lifter***, or ***solid lifter,*** is usually of the mushroom type and is provided with an adjusting screw. The adjusting screw is used to set the clearance, or lash, between the valve stem and the lifter. Clearance is necessary because engine heat will expand and lengthen the valve stems to such a degree that the valves would not close. Consequently, the combustible charge in the cylinder would not be compressed.

Instead of the mushroom-type lifter, some engines are equipped with roller-type lifters, Figure 11-20. In this design the engine cam strikes a roller mounted on the lower face of the lifter. The roller-type lifter has the advantage of reducing friction as compared to the mushroom-type lifter.

Hydraulic lifters are designed to automatically take up the clearance that exists between the valve and the lifter, Figure 11-21. The advantage of this type of valve lifter is that it is quiet in operation as it has zero valve lash.

Oil enters each lifter through grooves and oil holes in the lifter body and plunger and flows down into the chamber below the plunger, through the feed hole, and around the check ball, Figure 11-22. At the start of the cycle, the plunger spring holds all lash clearances out of the valve linkage. As the engine cam starts raising the valve lifter body, oil in the lower chamber and the check ball spring firmly seat the check ball to prevent loss of oil from the lower chamber. The lifting force is then transmitted through the entrapped oil to the check ball and plunger. The plunger and push rod seat move upward with the lifter body to operate the valve linkage, which opens the engine valve.

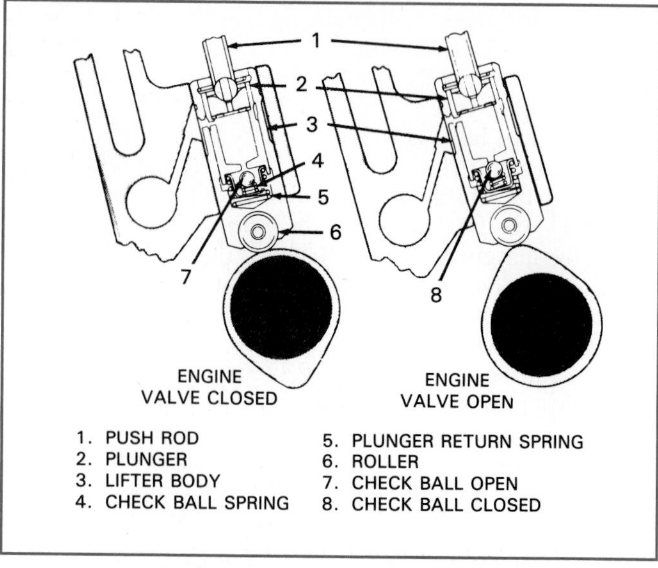

Figure 11-20. Operation of a hydraulic roller-type valve lifter. The roller reduces friction between the lifter and the camshaft. This type of lifter does not spin in its bore. Note that when engine valve is open, the check ball is seated, making the lifter solid. (Oldsmobile)

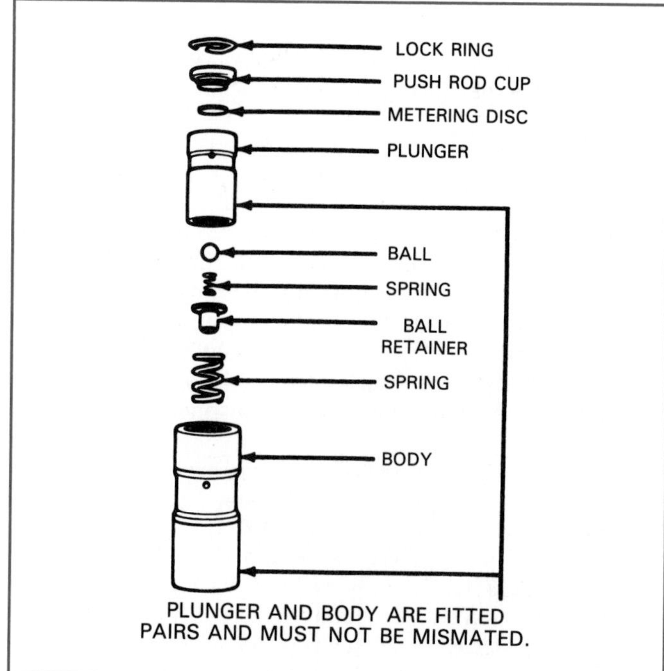

Figure 11-21. Parts of a hydraulic valve lifter. (Oldsmobile)

Then as the valve seats, the linkage and lifter plunger stop. The plunger spring forces the body of the lifter to follow the cam downward until it again rests on the cam base circle. Oil pressure against the check ball from the

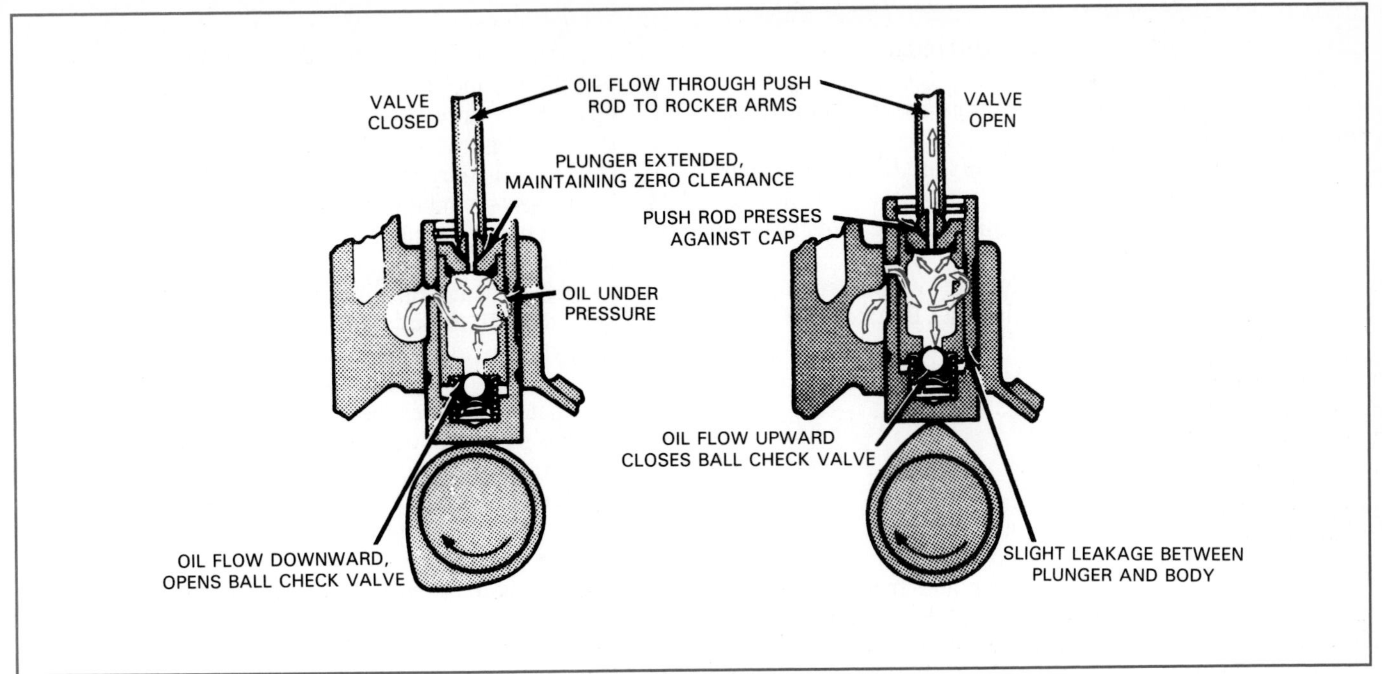

Figure 11-22. When the engine valve is closed, the check ball is unseated, allowing oil to flow through entire lifter. As the engine valve begins to open, the check ball is seated, making the hydraulic lifter solid. (Oldsmobile)

lower chamber ceases when the plunger movement stops. This allows passage of oil past the check ball into the lower chamber to replace the slight amount of oil lost through "leak down," which is the oil that escapes through the clearance between the plunger and the body.

When the valve linkage expands due to increased engine temperature, the plunger must move to a slightly lower position in the lifter body to ensure full closing of the engine valve. Similarly, when engine temperature drops, the plunger must move to a slightly higher position. In either case, the capacity of the lower chamber changes, and the volume of oil present is automatically controlled by passage of oil through the plunger feed hole.

Hydraulic Lifter Problems

While hydraulic valve lifters do provide ideal valve operation, they are subject to certain difficulties and require some attention. Clearances between the moving parts must be controlled closely. This has caused some difficulty because the dirt and varnish cause the lifters to stick.

The plunger and cylinder are held to dimensional tolerances of one ten-thousandth of an inch or less in manufacture. Different plungers are tried in different cylinders until a pair is found that fits closely without being too tight. For this reason, lifters should not be mixed up when they are removed for service. Each plunger should be kept with the cylinder in which it operates.

With clearances so small, the tiniest fleck of carbon, a fine thread of lint from a wiping cloth, a speck of dust, or any foreign matter could wedge between the plunger and cylinder, and cause them to stick. Anything as large as an eyelash or hair will put it completely out of order.

For this reason, it is necessary to keep the engine oil clean when hydraulic lifters are used. The very best grade of oil must be used in the engine, and the oil must be changed frequently. Also, oil filters must be replaced regularly.

Another reason for using the best possible engine oil and changing it frequently comes about from an increase in driving speeds for long continued periods. Highways and cars are so constructed that car owners do not hesitate to drive at high speeds for hours at a time. This type of operation generates heat, and the inside of the engine and the engine oil reach temperatures that are destructive to the oil.

The engine oil often becomes hot enough to "crack" some of the petroleum fractions (just as in an oil refinery). In decomposing, these elements form a ***varnish,*** which collects on the plunger and in the cylinder, and causes sticking. In many cases this varnish is so thin that it is invisible to the naked eye.

These deposits can be removed mechanically by brushing, but there is a danger of harming the surface of the plunger or cylinder. The safest method of removal appears to be the use of chemical solvents. After cleaning, the units should be dried by air and kept covered to avoid dust until they are installed in the engine. They should not be wiped with a cloth for fear that a thread of lint will adhere to them.

Of course, these parts must be handled with extreme care when they are out of the engine. If dropped, a nick or scratch could result that would cause them to stick. When clean and dry, the plunger should fall into or drop out of the lifter body of its own weight.

When reinstalled, the clearance should be checked to make sure it is adequate. The tappet clearance dimension is much greater than with mechanical linkage, and it varies considerably among the different makes. The manufacturers' recommendations should be followed.

As in the case of any other valve tappet adjustment, the lifter must be on the base circle of the cam when measured. The usual procedure is to turn the engine until the ignition distributor rotor is in the firing position for the cylinder to be checked. This assures that the piston is at TDC and that both valves are completely closed.

Chapter 11–Review Questions

Write your answers on a separate sheet of paper. Do not write in this book.

1. How many possible firing orders are there for a four-cylinder, four-cycle engine?
2. A six-cylinder, four-cycle, inline engine camshaft has how many lobes?
3. Technician A states that there are two valves per cylinder in many engines. Technician B states that there are two cams per cylinder in most engines. Who is right?
   (A) Technician A.
   (B) Technician B.
   (C) Both A & B.
   (D) Neither A nor B.
4. The timing gears must be aligned properly when installed. True or False?
5. What is the difference between an I-head engine and an overhead camshaft engine?
6. Name one advantage and one disadvantage of overhead camshaft engines.
7. How many power impulses per revolution occur in an eight-cylinder, four-cycle engine?
8. How many power impulses per revolution occur in a three-cylinder, two-cycle engine?
9. Why is the firing order of V-type engines arranged differently than on inline engines?
10. What is the advantage of the overhead camshaft engine as compared to having the camshaft in the crankcase?
    (A) Fewer moving parts.
    (B) Quieter operation.
    (C) Increase height of engine.
    (D) Permits larger valves.
11. Valve seats can be too wide. True or False?
12. Valves are sometimes hollow to make them lighter in weight. True or False?
13. Excessive heat gets out of valve by flowing to _____.
14. Why are valves not made larger?
15. An exhaust valve may reach a temperature of _____.
16. Valve length is not constant. True or False?
17. At what speed does the camshaft operate?
18. What is the objection to a long chain in a camshaft drive?
19. The cam nose on the camshaft travels faster than the crank throw on the crankshaft. True or False?
20. Are timing chains adjustable for wear?
21. What is valve overlap?
22. Are stronger or weaker valve springs used on high performance engines?
23. How many types of valve lifters are there?
24. What is the great advantage of a hydraulic valve lifter?
    (A) Better valve action.
    (B) Closes the valves faster.
    (C) Quieter valve action.
    (D) More accurate valve timing.
25. Lead-free fuels increase valve seat temperatures. True or False?

Cutaway of a four-cylinder, dual overhead cam engine. Note the position of the camshafts and the number of valves per cylinder. (Saturn)

Chapter 12
Engine Reconditioning

After studying this chapter, you will be able to:

- ❍ Describe the steps in cleaning, measuring, and examining engine parts.
- ❍ List which items of the engine need to be checked for wear.
- ❍ Explain how to recondition a cylinder.
- ❍ Give examples of a statically and dynamically balanced engine, and explain why balance is important.

Reconditioning Procedure

The first step in any job of reconditioning is to clean the assembly. There are many different methods of cleaning, and the one selected depends on the part and the type of dirt that is to be removed.

When overhauling an engine, many shops will remove the engine from the chassis, and then steam clean the entire unit with a steam and detergent solution. ***Steam cleaning*** can be done with a gun-type cleaner or in a tank-type cleaner.

Cleaning the engine before it is disassembled will make for an easier disassembly. In addition, cleaning will reveal defects and conditions that will help in diagnosing the cause of the trouble and aid in preventing its reoccurrence.

After removing the outer dirt and oil, the oil pan, valve cover(s), and cylinder head(s) are removed. To remove accumulations of sludge, carbon, dirt, and grease, these parts can be cleaned by a gun or one of the other cleaning methods: tank, jet, or ultrasonic.

Cleaning

In addition to steam cleaning, there are several methods used to clean disassembled components. A process used extensively for cleaning automotive parts is called the ***hot tank method.*** Briefly, this method utilizes a tank filled with a detergent solution, which is agitated to hasten the cleaning process. The temperature of the solution varies with the type of detergent used and particular metal to be cleaned. Parts made of aluminum are cleaned with special detergents at a lower temperature than is used for steel and iron.

Another efficient parts cleaning technique is called the ***jet method.*** The cleaning unit has two compartments: the lower chamber holds the solution; the upper chamber provides a revolving platform for the work. A series of jets spray detergent on the slowly revolving part in the upper compartment. Each jet delivers detergent at an extremely high velocity. The spray reaches the work from all sides. Each jet delivers approximately three gallons of hot detergent solution per minute.

Blasting with glass beads is another method used for cleaning automotive parts, Figure 12-1. Compressed air is the propellant that blasts the beads against the part. Both wet and dry blast machines are available.

Glass beads clean the part down to bare metal, leaving no film of detergent. The beads are round in shape and are not abrasive. They do not embed themselves in the surface being cleaned. Being round, the beads leave a uniform indented surface, imparting strength by compressing the metal being cleaned. This method is used when cleaning pistons, valves, and connecting rods.

Ultrasonic cleaning is a more recent advance. Ultrasonic sound differs from normal sound in that its pitch is above the human hearing range. When high-frequency vibrations are introduced into a liquid, cavitation (extreme agitation) occurs.

Cavitation causes thousands of bubbles to form in the liquid. These bubbles range in size from visible to submicroscopic. Under continued cavitation, the bubbles grow and then collapse. They are said to explode inwardly, at which time pressures up to 15,000 psi and temperatures up to 700°F (371°C) are created.

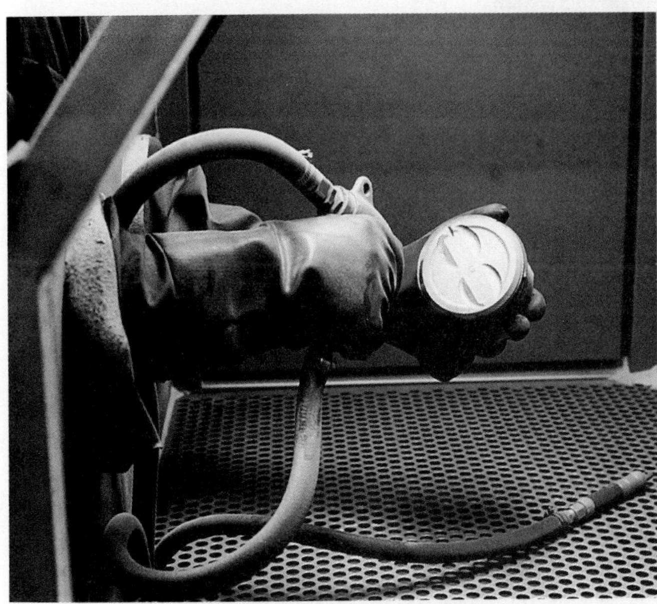

Figure 12-1. Cleaning a piston with a bead blaster. (Winona Van Norman)

The ultrasonic cleaner consists basically of three parts:

1. A generator, which is used to convert the line current into high frequency electrical energy.
2. A transducer, which converts this electrical energy into mechanical energy of the same frequency.
3. A tank, which contains a liquid through which the ultrasonic energy is passed. The liquid produces the cavitation that blasts away any dirt on parts placed in the solution.

Ultrasonic cleaners are used in production engine rebuilding shops servicing diesel engine injectors and pumps, and in large jobber machine shops.

Many small auto repair shops use a simple tank with a ***power sprayer,*** Figure 12-2, to clean parts that have been removed from the vehicle. Cleaning parts with a brush and a pan of gasoline is a fire hazard and, therefore, should never be attempted. Instead, use a solvent designed for the cleaning job at hand.

Before cleaning a cylinder block or a cylinder head, remove the core hole plugs. This will permit the cleaning solution to flush out any accumulation of rust and lime deposits.

Examination and Measurement

After cleaning, it is possible to carefully examine and accurately measure the individual parts to spot defects, determine the extent and type of wear, and pinpoint what caused the worn condition.

The starting point for actual engine reconditioning is the cylinder block, because practically all other parts are fitted to it. If the block is damaged in any way, it must be repaired or replaced. There are many things to be inspected and checked when reconditioning a cylinder block.

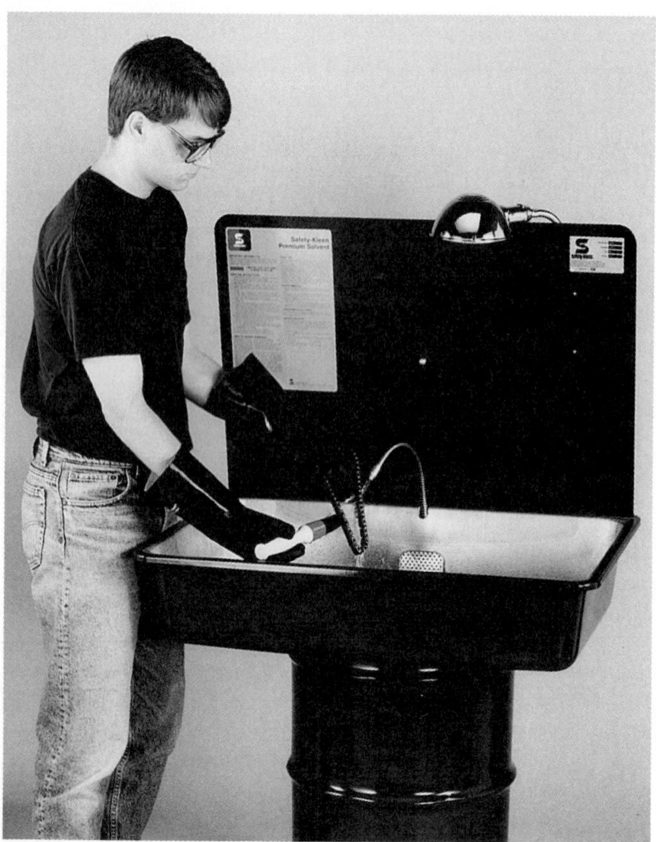

Figure 12-2. Cleaning parts in a modern parts cleaner. (Safety-Kleen)

The cylinder block (or a cylinder head) may be cracked, warped, worn, or otherwise damaged. The damage may affect the operation of the crankshaft, pistons, rings, bearings, camshaft, cooling system, lubrication system, etc. The extent of the damage will determine whether or not the block is repairable.

Metal Parts Restoration

There are many methods of changing the condition or dimensions of metal parts. In some cases, these methods can be used to restore an engine to good condition. However, engine parts are usually replaced if they are damaged or excessively worn.

If you want to increase the size of a part, you can add metal by ***soldering, brazing, welding, plating,*** or ***spraying.*** In some cases, you can expand it with heat and pressure. When adding metal, you have a wide choice of materials, each of which possesses certain characteristics that may be desired for a particular purpose. If you want a soft surface, use tin or bronze. If you want a hard surface, add steel of any desired degree of hardness by welding. Another method of adding a hard surface is by the electroplating process, such as the chrome surface on a piston ring.

In engine repair work, there is a way to add material to, or increase the size of, one part without disturbing the mating part. An example of this is to spray molten metal on a worn crankshaft journal to avoid installation of undersize bearings.

If you want to reduce the size of a part, you can ***cut, grind,*** or ***etch*** the metal away. In some cases, you can shrink the metal by freezing it. In other cases, removing metal from one part and installing an oversize mating part is the best solution. For example, a cylinder can be rebored and an oversize piston can be installed in the enlarged cylinder.

In still other cases, metal is removed for the sole purpose of obtaining better surface fit of two mating parts. An example of this is the correction of a warped cylinder head by ***surface grinding*** to restore a flat and true surface.

For all of these operations, special tools and equipment are available. These tools will do the job if they are properly handled. It will be essential to measure, adjust, and operate in accordance with the manufacturer's instructions. If the instructions are not followed, technicians may cause injury to themselves and their coworkers.

External Cracks

When the cylinder block and head are clean, make a visual inspection for ***external cracks*** or serious damage. Include a close look at the condition of the freeze plugs, Figure 12-3. If signs of leakage or corrosion are found, replace the plugs.

If the block was cracked by water freezing in the water jacket, the crack can usually be closed satisfactorily by copper welding, brazing, iron welding, or by one of the patented processes, such as the Seal Lock process. Many technicians prefer electric welding to gas welding, as lower temperatures in the area of repair are not likely to produce warpage of the cylinder block.

In the case of the ***Seal Lock process,*** the sides of the crack are tied together by driving special keys or locking

Figure 12-3. Leaking freeze plugs must be punched out and new freeze plugs installed. Always install new freeze plugs after cleaning a cylinder head or engine block in either a hot or cold tank solution.

pins into previously drilled holes. Then the surface is carefully peened and further sealed.

In cases where a panel or section of the water jacket is broken out, it is sometimes possible to shape a metal plate into a patch that corresponds to, and is slightly larger than, the opening. The patch is then attached to the block with screws. Holes are drilled and tapped in the block for the screws.

In the case of small cracks, ***iron cement*** can be used for a quick repair, Figure 12-4. Never repair an area with cement in or by the cylinder or cylinder head.

The choice of the repair method will depend upon the size of the damaged area, the location of the crack, the cost of a new block, and the value of the automobile.

Internal Cracks

At times, the cylinder wall or cylinder head will crack, Figure 12-5. Usually, a cracked cylinder head is replaced, rather than repaired.

Cracks in cylinder heads and blocks are often so fine that they are difficult to see with the naked eye. One procedure

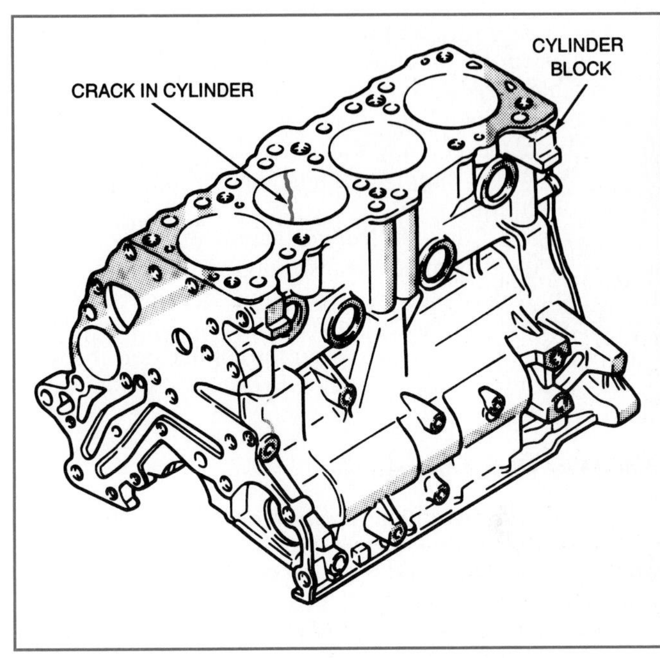

Figure 12-5. A crack in the cylinder makes this engine block useless. (Chrysler)

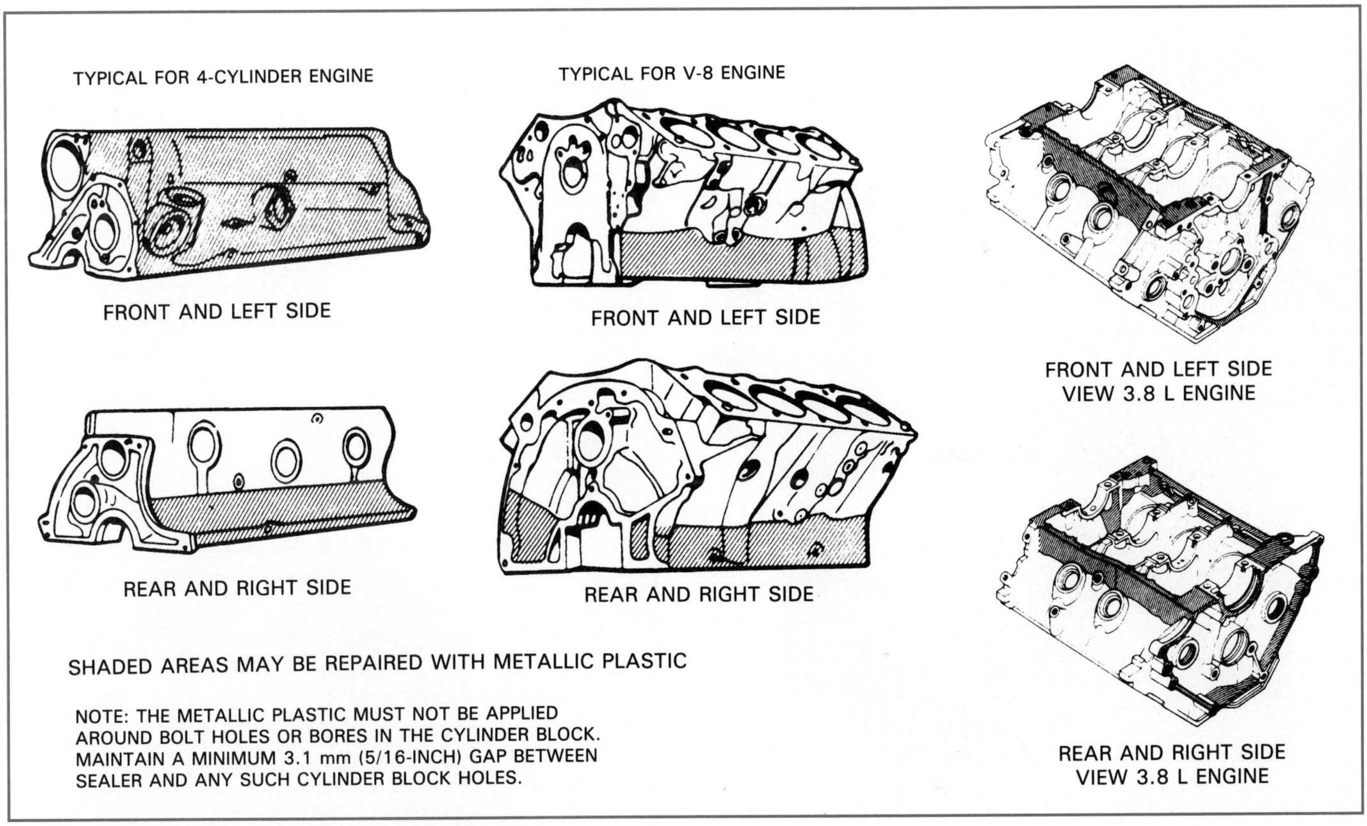

TYPICAL FOR 4-CYLINDER ENGINE

FRONT AND LEFT SIDE

REAR AND RIGHT SIDE

TYPICAL FOR V-8 ENGINE

FRONT AND LEFT SIDE

REAR AND RIGHT SIDE

FRONT AND LEFT SIDE
VIEW 3.8 L ENGINE

REAR AND RIGHT SIDE
VIEW 3.8 L ENGINE

SHADED AREAS MAY BE REPAIRED WITH METALLIC PLASTIC

NOTE: THE METALLIC PLASTIC MUST NOT BE APPLIED AROUND BOLT HOLES OR BORES IN THE CYLINDER BLOCK. MAINTAIN A MINIMUM 3.1 mm (5/16-INCH) GAP BETWEEN SEALER AND ANY SUCH CYLINDER BLOCK HOLES.

Figure 12-4. Cylinder block can be repaired with a metallic plastic in shaded areas only. Note that the area around the cylinders cannot be repaired. (Ford)

for finding these cracks is to use special dyes or chemicals that, when painted on the surface of the metal, will quickly make the cracks visible. This procedure is used on aluminum parts. Magnetic and electrical methods are specifically designed to reveal the location of cracks on ferrous metal components. See Figure 12-6.

Corrosion

In the case of aluminum engine blocks or heads, the visual inspection should be particularly thorough to detect any possible ***corrosion*** of the metal. Sometimes, corrosion of the metal around the water jackets will occur from chemicals in the cooling water, particularly in localities where the water supply contains more than the usual amount of chloride.

Corrosion from ***electrolytic*** action may also occur, because of the dissimilar metals found in the engine cooling system. If corrosion is serious enough, it may interfere with the seal of the gasket between the head and the block. This would permit coolant to enter the combustion chamber or allow compression pressure to escape to the water jacket.

Cylinder Head Warpage

Cylinder heads often become ***warped.*** Sometimes the cylinder block mating surface also warps. These surfaces should be true within .003″ in any 6″ span or within .006″ overall. Measurement is made by means of a steel straightedge and a feeler gauge, Figures 12-7 and 12-8. If the surfaces are warped or otherwise damaged, they can be reconditioned on special equipment, Figure 12-9. If .030″ is removed from a head on a V-type engine, the other head and intake manifold must also be shaved true. If not, the bolt holes connecting the intake manifold to the heads will not align properly.

Cylinder Wear

The greatest amount of wear in a cylinder occurs at the top of the cylinder. This is due to the lack of lubrication at the top of the cylinder and the side thrust of the piston. The wear at the top of the cylinder is referred to as ***out-of-round,*** Figure 12-10. The difference between the amount of wear at the top of the cylinder and the bottom of the cylinder is referred to as ***taper,*** Figure 12-10.

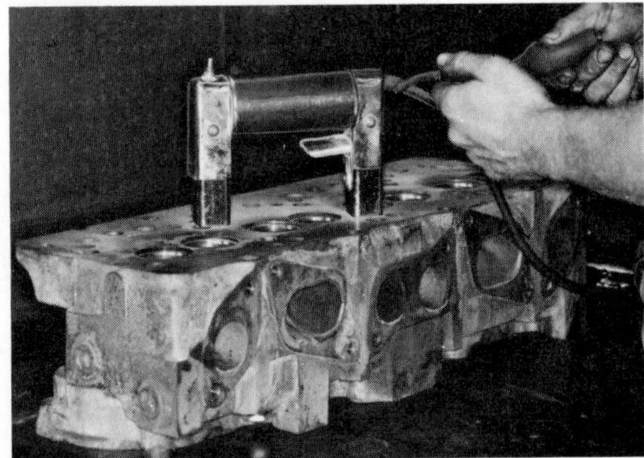

Figure 12-6. A magnetic field is created in this cast-iron cylinder head. Metal filings are dusted on and outline the crack. If the cylinder head is aluminum, a dye must be used to detect cracks in the head, as aluminum is a nonferrous metal.

Figure 12-7. Checking a cylinder head for warpage. If a .006″ feeler gauge can be placed between the straightedge and cylinder head, the head is warped and must be machined. (Fel-Pro Inc.)

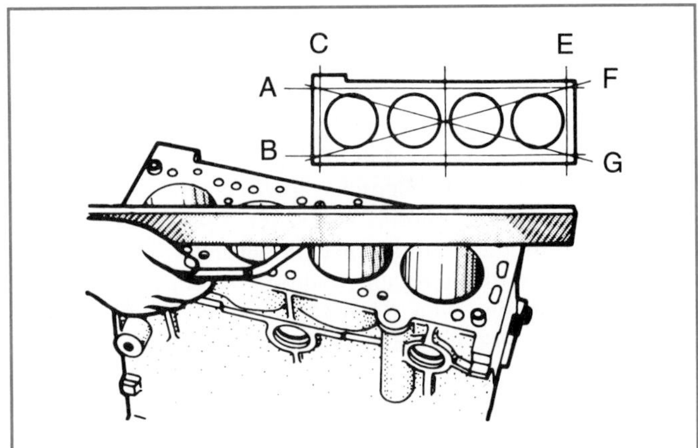

Figure 12-8. The engine block is checked for warpage in the same manner as the head. (Chrysler)

Figure 12-9. Equipment used to machine engine blocks.

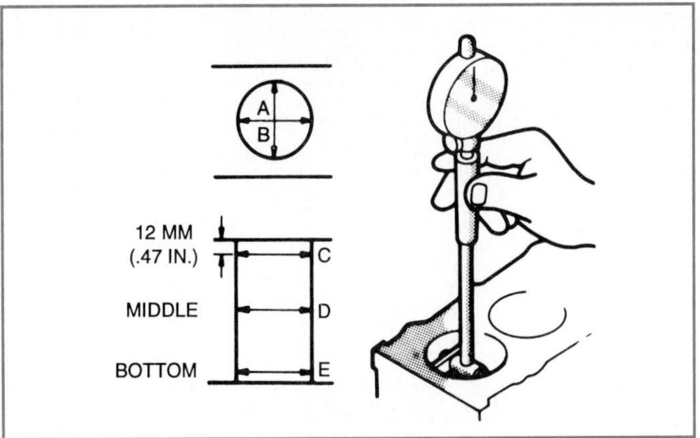

Figure 12-10. The difference in measurement between line A and line B is the amount the cylinder is out-of-round. This measurement must be taken at the top of the cylinder. The difference in measurement between line C and line D is the amount of taper in the cylinder. Line E will be the original diameter of the cylinder, as the piston rings do not travel that far down. (Chrysler)

Cylinder Reconditioning

Cylinder wall wear and the reasons for it were described previously in this text. They wear in tapered form and also wear out-of-round. When wear exceeds specifications, the cylinders must be machined to restore the wall surface. Common maximum wear limitations are .005″ out-of-round and .010″ taper.

Either ***boring bars,*** Figure 12-11, or ***hones,*** Figure 12-12, may be used to recondition the cylinder walls. In many shops, the preferred method is to first use a boring bar and then finish with a hone. Another method is to first use a hone with coarse stones and then finish with fine stones. Make sure the stones are clean and sharp.

Figure 12-11. Machine used to rebore cylinders.

Before any cylinder is refinished, all main bearing caps must be in place and tightened to the specified torque. Otherwise, the crankshaft bearing bores may become distorted during the refinishing operation.

Precautions must be taken to ensure that the cylinders be refinished parallel to each other and at right angles to the crankshaft. Special care must be taken when setting up the reconditioning equipment, particularly when the top of the cylinder block is not at right angles to the cylinder bore, Figure 12-13. When the cylinder block is formed with an angular surface, special adapters must be used with the cylinder boring bar so that the cylinder will be reconditioned parallel to its original centerline.

Regardless of the method used in reconditioning the cylinders, the block must be thoroughly cleaned after boring or honing to remove all cuttings and abrasives. Machinists advise scrubbing the block with soap and water. The cylinders should be oiled thoroughly after they are dry.

The job of cleaning a cylinder block after reconditioning is not easy. Many jobs that were mechanically correct have been ruined because abrasives and dirt remained in the cylinders. All oil holes in the block must be cleaned.

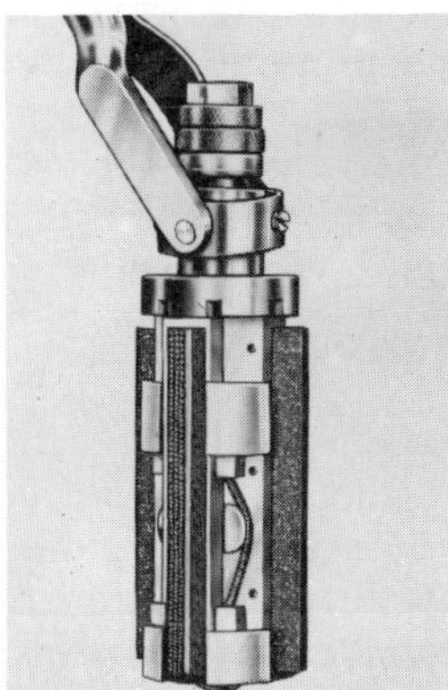

Figure 12-12. Cylinder hone.

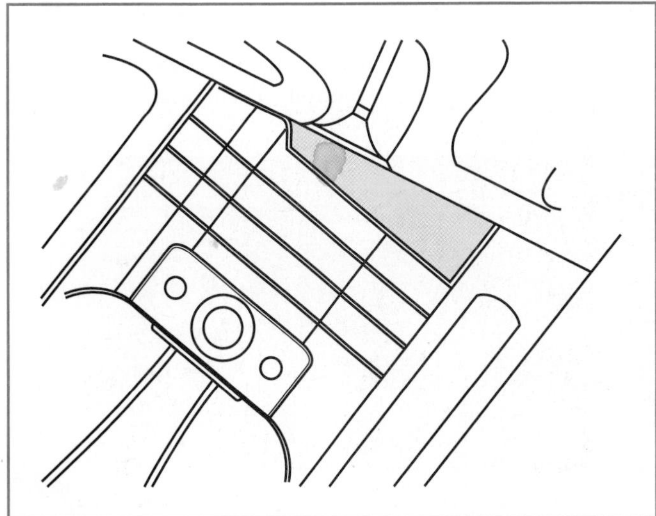

Figure 12-13. Note the angle of cylinder block at the cylinder head.

Core plugs should be removed so the water jacket can be flushed. The final cleaning is usually done with specialized cleaning equipment, Figure 12-14.

When reconditioning cylinders, it is best to find out what sizes are available in ***oversize pistons*** before starting the operation. Otherwise, the cylinders may be bored to a size for which stock pistons are not available.

Dry-type Cylinder Sleeves

If damage is so deep that reboring to fit the largest oversize piston is not sufficient to remove the score marks, it is still possible to recondition the cylinder by installing a ***cylinder sleeve.***

The ***dry-type cylinder sleeve*** does not come in contact with the coolant. The cylinder is bored out to an oversize dimension. The sleeve is then installed into the cylinder. An oversize piston is not needed, and the standard size piston can be used provided that it is in good shape. However, the transfer of heat is not as efficient as with a wet-type sleeve or a cylinder that is bored directly into the block.

Before installing a dry-type sleeve, the cylinder is bored or honed until the score marks are removed. Then, a sleeve is selected with an outside diameter .0001″ larger than the diameter of the rebored cylinder and an inside diameter slightly smaller than required for the available piston. The sleeve is shrunk in dry ice to reduce its diameter. Then, it is pressed into the cylinder with a hydraulic press. Finally, the cylinder is finish honed to remove any wrinkles that may have developed when the sleeve was pressed in position.

Cylinder Wall Surface

When new rings are installed in cylinders that have not been reconditioned, the hone should be run through the cylinder a few times to remove the glaze that formed on the cylinder wall during normal operation.

The desired cylinder wall finish is not a mirror surface. This type of surface does not produce the best lubricating conditions for the piston rings. The proper finish should have a pattern of diagonal ***crosshatch scratches,*** but no longitudinal scratches, Figure 12-15. This pattern can be obtained with a hone by pulling it up and down in the bore while it is rotating. After honing the cylinder, wash it with a warm soap and water solution. Then, rinse thoroughly with clear water. Dry each cylinder and then oil the cylinders to prevent rust.

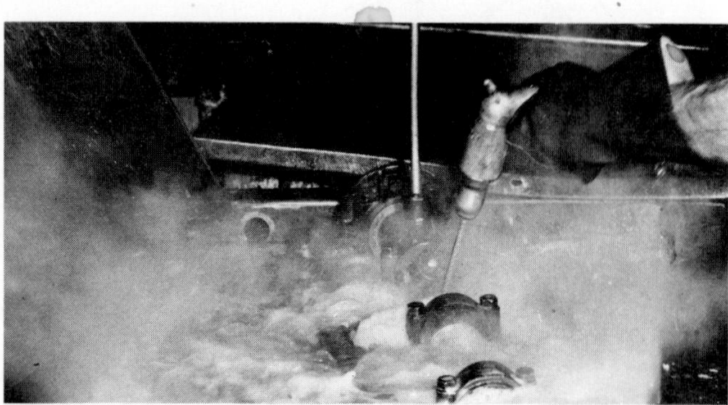

Figure 12-14. A cast-iron engine block being cleaned in a hot tank solution. Aluminum engine parts must be cleaned in a cold tank or in carburetor-type cleaner.

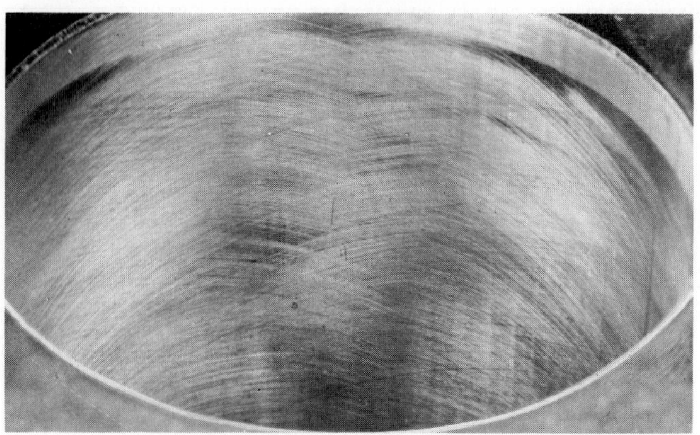

Figure 12-15. Cylinder walls must look like this after honing. This pattern is called "crosshatch."

Fine scratches in the cylinder wall surfaces permit rapid seating of rings. The fine scratches retain a film of oil to provide lubrication for the ring face and prevent scoring of the cylinder.

Wet-type Cylinder Sleeves

Passenger car engines built in the U.S.A. usually have the cylinders bored directly in the engine block. Some truck, tractor, and industrial engines use ***wet-type cylinder sleeves.*** A wet sleeve is essentially a barrel or sleeve that is inserted in the block in contact with the cooling water. Several European passenger car engines have wet sleeves, Figure 12-16.

In a wet sleeve construction, each cylinder barrel is a separate sleeve inserted in the block. Each sleeve is sealed at the bottom of the water compartment by a copper or rubber gasket, Figure 12-17. The cylinder head gasket, of course, provides a seal at the top end of the sleeve. Engine coolant circulates directly around the sleeve. Since the

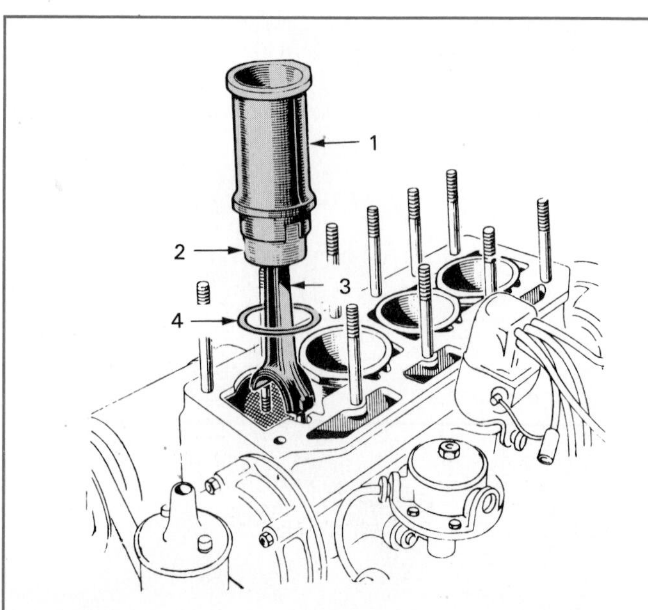

Figure 12-16. Wet-type sleeve. 1–Sleeve. 2–Piston. 3–Connecting rod. 4–Copper sealing ring.

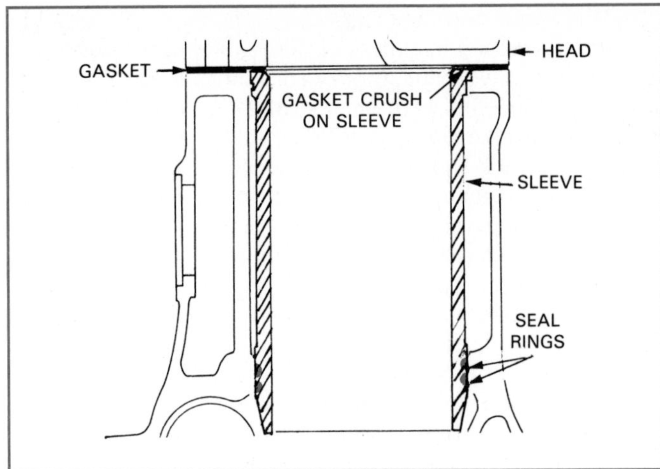

Figure 12-17. Rubber seals are used at the bottom of the sleeve in this Oliver engine.

thickness of the sleeve or cylinder wall is uniform, cylinder wall distortion is minimized.

Another advantage of cylinder sleeves is the ease and comparatively low cost of replacing a damaged cylinder sleeve. These sleeves quickly pull out, Figure 12-18, and a new sleeve is simply slipped in place.

Piston Clearance

There is no set amount of clearance to be provided between the piston and cylinder. Much depends upon the design of the engine cylinders and the cooling system, the piston design and material, and the conditions under which the engine operates.

For example, if a passenger car engine will be driven mostly at slow speeds in city traffic, the pistons can be fitted with a minimum of clearance. If the engine is in a race car, it may be required to run at full power for hours at a time. Such service would generate a great amount of heat in the cylinders and cause the pistons to expand considerably. Therefore, the internal engine parts would be fitted with maximum clearances.

In general, it is customary to fit solid-skirt cast-iron pistons with about .00075″ to .001″ of clearance per inch of piston diameter. Therefore, a 4″ piston would be .003″ to .004″ smaller than the cylinder. Some aluminum pistons can be fitted more closely. Instructions given by the manufacturer should be followed.

Surface treatment will also have an effect on the piston clearance. Some pistons are tin plated, others have an oxide coating, or some other surface treatment. Sometimes the surface is serrated or interrupted to provide minute scratches for the retention of oil. These treatments are intended to lessen the tendency of the piston to stick or score, particularly during the time it is seating to the wall.

Clearance Measurement

In most cases, the clearance between cylinder and piston is measured with a spring scale and a feeler gauge. The feeler gauge is inserted between the piston and the cylinder. See Figure 12-19. The strip of feeler gauge should be about 1/2″ wide and long enough to extend the full length of the cylinder. This strip, which should have a thickness equal to the desired clearance, should be placed on the thrust side of the skirt. Four to five pounds of force (as measured on the spring scale) should be required to remove the feeler gauge.

The clearance can also be measured by subtracting the maximum diameter of the piston from the minimum diameter of the cylinder, as measured with inside and outside micrometers. In this case, measurement must be made at several points in the cylinder and on the piston. All piston clearance recommendations are made for use with the temperature at approximately 70°F.

As pistons wear (or if they are overheated), the skirt has a tendency to collapse or to become smaller in diameter. When this happens the piston will ***slap*** in the cylinder. Also, it will allow an excessive amount of oil to reach the rings. This, of course, places an undue load on the oil control rings and may result in oil pumping.

Piston Resizing

Although worn pistons are usually replaced, there are several ways to expand or resize the pistons. One method

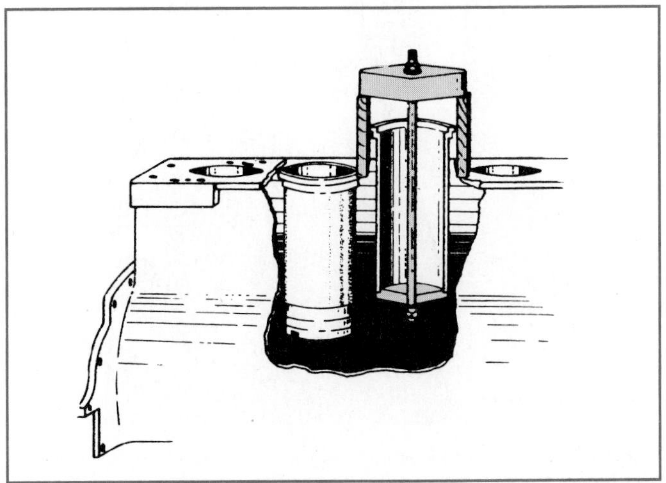

Figure 12-18. Method of removing wet-type sleeves.

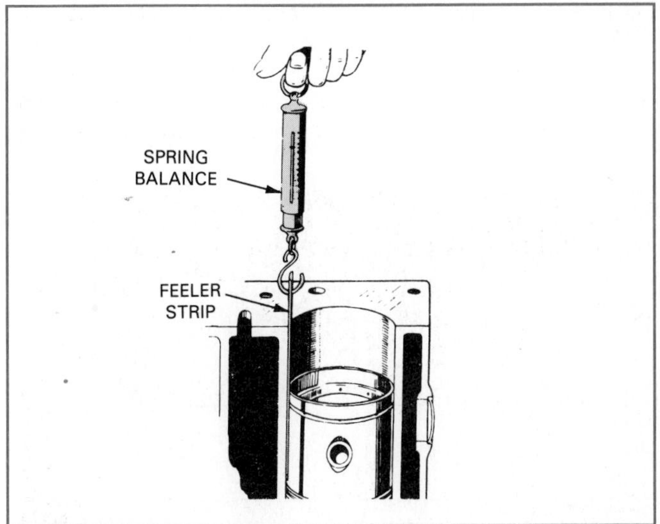

Figure 12-19. Checking piston clearance with feeler gauge attached to spring scale. The amount of pull required should be 4-5 lb.

consists of heating the piston and expanding it with special equipment made for the purpose. Another method requires special equipment for ***peening*** the inside of the piston with steel shot. This procedure compacts the metal on the inside of the piston and causes it to expand on the outside. Electric and pneumatic peening hammers are made for the purpose.

Various tools are available for ***knurling*** the piston skirt. This method raises the surface of the metal in ridges or patterns along the path of the knurling tool, increasing the diameter of the piston. An additional claim made for this method is that it creates "pockets" on the piston surface. These pockets gather and retain a film of oil to assist in sealing and lubricating.

Head Bolt Torque

All threads on the cylinder head bolts and in the engine block must be clean and undamaged. The cylinder head bolts must spin on easily. A thread compound should be used, particularly on aluminum heads and cylinder blocks. This will prevent leakage in locations where the bolt holes enter the water jacket.

Be sure to install the specified bolt in the correct hole, as bolt holes frequently vary in depth. A torque wrench should be used to tighten bolts to specified torque. The bolts should be tightened in the correct sequence to prevent distortion, Figure 12-20.

The usual procedure is to tighten the bolts in three successive steps. For example, first tighten the bolts to 25 ft. lb., then to 50 ft. lb., and finally to 95 ft. lb.

Balancing Engines

With the increase in engine speeds, it becomes increasingly important that all rotating and reciprocating parts of the engine are ***precision balanced.*** Unless this is done, wear is accelerated and engine life reduced. In addition, operating costs increase.

Unbalance causes increased bearing loads and greater vibration, both of which absorb power and cause wear and fatigue of parts. In addition, the vibration will cause alternator brackets and other accessory brackets to crack. Driver fatigue also increases.

With precision balancing of engine parts, bearing life has been increased in excess of 200%, and horsepower and acceleration have been improved nearly 15%. While increased top speed is what interests the speed enthusiast, it is the longer engine life and reduced maintenance costs that interest the truck and fleet operator.

Manufacturers producing parts for their engines specify certain tolerances for the various parts. For example, the weight specification for a piston may be given as 25 oz. plus or minus 1/4 oz. (1/4 oz. is equal to 7.09 grams). Connecting rods may have a similar weight specification and, in addition, the center-to-center length of the rod is held to a close tolerance.

It is, therefore, possible to have a V-8 engine with eight pistons of different weights, but all within the specified tolerance of 1/4 oz. In an extreme case, one of the pistons may weigh 25 1/4 oz. and another piston may weigh 24 3/4 oz.

A set of pistons of varied weights will result in considerable vibration and place higher loads on the bearings. If similar variations are found in the connecting rods, a very rough running engine will result. As pointed out, not only will top speed be affected, but extreme part wear will also result.

Precision balancing will help to eliminate the possibility of wear due to vibration. It also will step up performance and boost economy of operation. With modern balancing equipment, Figure 12-21, the weight of rotating and reciprocating parts can be brought within 1/2 gram of each other.

In order to achieve the highest engine output, greatest fuel economy, longest part life, and smoothest operation, the following parts must be precision balanced:

- Pistons.
- Piston rings.
- Piston pins.
- Connecting rods.
- Connecting rod bearings.
- Crankshaft.
- Front pulley or vibration damper.
- Clutch and disc.

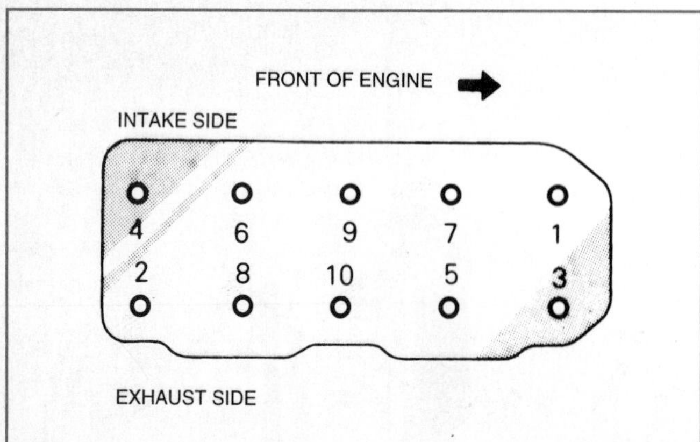

Figure 12-20. Tightening sequence of a cylinder head. Start from the center and work toward each end. This will prevent the cylinder bores from distorting and the head gasket from leaking coolant and oil. (Ford)

Figure 12-21. Preparing to balance the crankshaft. This machine can also be used to polish the journals of the crankshaft.

Unbalance

Unbalance is simply the uneven distribution of weight. When a part is rotated, the unbalance becomes a vibration that wastes power output. Even a small amount of unbalance is harmful. Just 1 oz. placed 1″ away from the center of rotation will be multiplied 40 times at a speed of 1200 rpm. At 5000 rpm, the force will reach 45 lb. 10 oz., Figure 12-22.

Static Balance

When a rotor has an absolutely even distribution of weight mass around its axis, it will be in ***static balance.*** That is, there will be no tendency toward rotation about its axis.

View A in Figure 12-23 shows a rotor and a shaft on two knife edges. A heavy area, indicated by a dot, will turn the rotor until it reaches its lowest point. In view B, this weight is 8 oz. located 2″ from the center.

To make the rotor in Figure 12-23 stop in any position, it will be necessary to add a counterweight directly opposite the heavy area, as shown in view C. This will put the rotor in static balance if the two weights provided the same torque (weight times distance from axis of rotation). Therefore, if the first weight is 8 oz. at a distance of 2″ from the center, the other weight could be 4 oz. at a distance of 4″ from the center. Both weights provide the same turning effort of 16 oz./in.

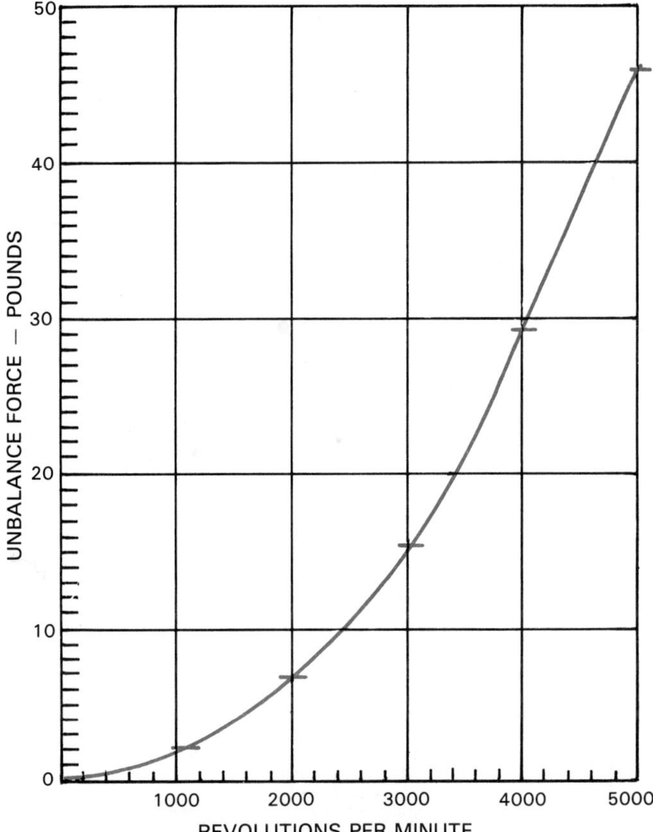

Figure 12-22. Note that as rpm increases, so does the unbalance.

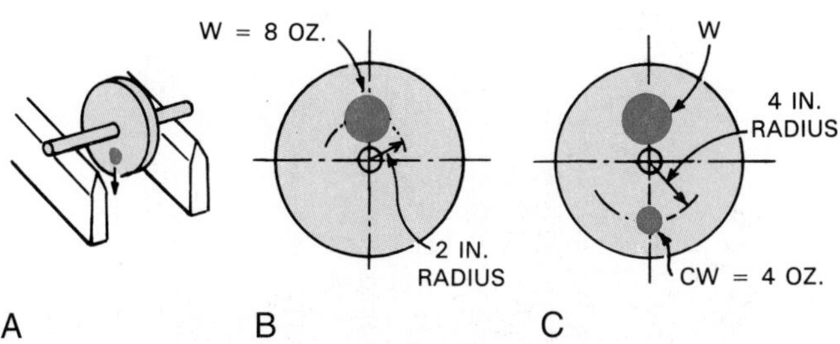

Figure 12-23. To test balance: A–Place the rotor on pointed blocks. B–Unbalance totals 8 oz., 2″ from center. C–Counterbalancing with a 4 oz. weight that is 4″ from center corrects the unbalance.

Dynamic Balance

A shaft or rotor may be in perfect static balance but, when rotated, will vibrate considerably because it is not in ***dynamic balance.*** When the centerline of the weight mass of a revolving rotor is in the same plane as the centerline of the rotor, it is in dynamic balance.

If there is excess weight on one side of the shaft at one end, which is balanced statically by an equivalent weight on the other side but at the opposite end, the shaft would not be balanced dynamically, Figure 12-24. When the shaft with this condition is rotated, a centrifugal couple is formed, resulting in an unbalanced condition with vibration.

In Figure 12-25, a heavy section W, weighing 9 oz., is located 2″ from the axis of the cylinder. A counterweight of 6 oz. is located 3″ from the axis, but at the other end of the cylinder. Both are equal to 18 oz./in., so the cylinder is in static balance. However, because the weights are at opposite ends of the cylinder, a centrifugal couple, or twisting action, is formed and a dynamic unbalanced condition exists. By adding compensating weights of 3 oz. and 6 oz., as indicated in Figure 12-25, the cylinder is in static balance and dynamic balance.

Balancing Inline and V-type Engines

In V-8 and V-12 engines, the crankshaft basically is in an unbalanced condition. To balance a V-type engine, it is

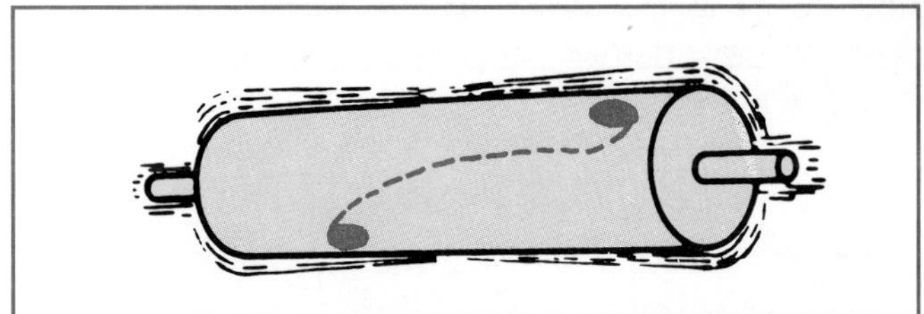

Figure 12-24. Weights at opposite ends of rotor cause a twisting motion. Rotor is balanced statically, but not dynamically.

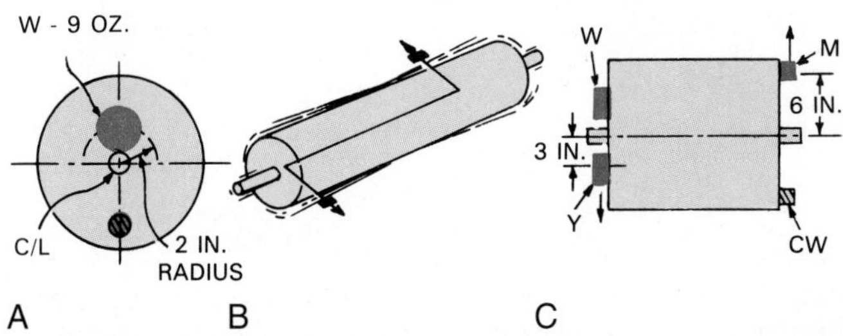

Figure 12-25. A–Cylinder is balanced statically. B–Cylinder vibrates. C–Additional weights correct unbalance.

necessary to attach weights to each of the crank throws as a substitute for the weights of the connecting rods and piston assemblies. Such weights are known as ***bob weights,*** Figure 12-26.

When balancing inline engines, bob weights are not needed because the crankshaft throws are symmetrically arranged.

In the case of two-cycle engines, the GMC series 71 diesel requires special consideration. These engines are counterbalanced by a combination of balance weights on the camshafts (on inline engine, one camshaft and a balance shaft are used), Figure 12-27. Connected to the crankshaft through a small gear are a pair of shafts driven by gears the same size as that on the crankshaft. On inline engines, the first shaft is the camshaft, the second is the balance shaft.

On V-type engines, both shafts are camshafts, with counterweighted gears. Also, on the far end of each shaft, a counterweight is located diametrically opposed to the counterweight on the gear. The amount of counterweight on one end should counterbalance the counterweight on the other end.

Theoretically, all four ends, gears, and balance weights should have identical oz./in. amounts of unbalance. Because these parts (gears and balance weights) are diametrically opposed, the shaft when assembled should have no force (kinetic) unbalance, but a desired high couple (dynamic) unbalance.

Therefore, in order to properly balance a GMC 71 series engine, bob weights must be used on the crankshaft, and the counterweighted gears and the counterbalance weights must be balanced on a special fixture.

Figure 12-26. Bob weights attached to crankshaft for balancing purposes.

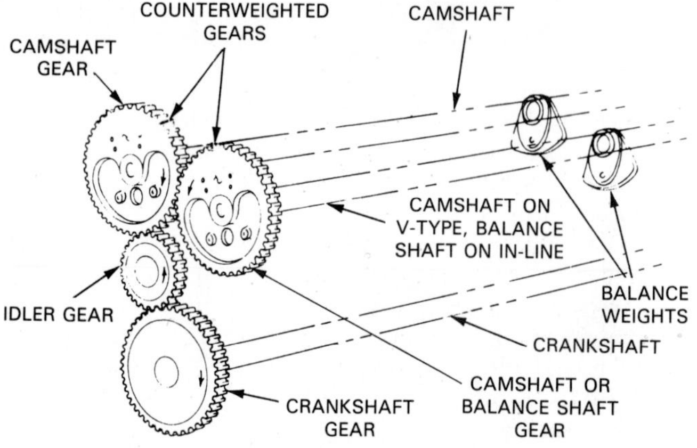

Figure 12-27. Balancing two cycle GMC 71 series diesel engine involves counterweighted gears. Balance weights at opposite ends of the shaft counter the weight of the gears.

Balancing Single-cylinder Engines

Single-cylinder engines and other inherently unbalanced engines, such as outboard, motorcycle, go-cart, etc., require special balancing procedures because of their relatively high speeds. These small engines will not be as vibrationless as multi-cylinder engines, but they are precision balanced for the smoothest operation possible.

When determining the bob weight for a single cylinder engine, use 100% of the rotating weight (same as for a V-8 engine), but use a higher percentage of the reciprocating weight. V-8 engines usually use 50% of the reciprocating weight.

For the single cylinder engine, the reciprocating weight should range from 55% to 65%, depending on engine speed.

Crankshaft Balancing Procedure

The degree of unbalance of the crankshaft is determined by placing the shaft (V-8 with bob weights or inline shaft without bob weights) in the balancing machine. As the shaft is rotated, the degree of unbalance and its location will be indicated.

In general, the unbalanced condition can be corrected by removing metal from the counterweights. In cases where the throws are too light, it is necessary to tack-weld thin steel sheets to the sides of the counterweights.

Normal weight removal is accomplished by using a 1/2″ drill. Special fixtures allow the drilling to be performed with the shaft in balancer. If too much metal is removed, the 1/2″ drilled hole can be plugged with 1/2″ rod and then redrilled the desired amount.

Bob Weights

As previously pointed out, bob weights are temporarily attached to the crankshaft before it is balanced to compensate for the weights of the pistons and connecting rod, assemblies.

Part of the piston and connecting rod assembly is a rotating weight and part of the assembly is a reciprocating weight. The weight of the piston with its pin and rings, along with a portion of the upper end of the connecting rod,

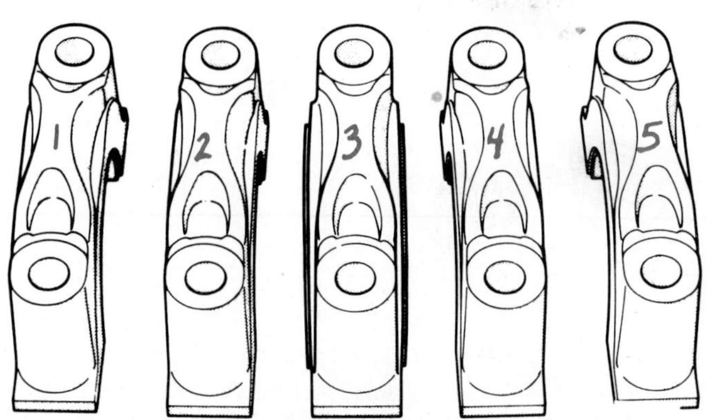

Figure 12-28. Number the main bearing caps prior to removal. If caps are mixed up, the engine will seize. (Chrysler)

is considered a reciprocating weight. The weight of the big end of the connecting rods is considered as rotating weight.

To obtain the actual weight of these parts, weigh all of the pistons with their rings and pins. Then, using the weight of the lightest piston assembly, reduce the weight of the other pistons to conform to the weight of the lightest one.

To reduce the weight of a piston, chuck it in a lathe and remove metal from the inside of the piston skirt. In some piston designs, pads have been provided on the inner surface of the skirt from which the necessary metal can be removed. Take care not to weaken the piston. To ensure that the exterior of the piston is not scored by the jaws of the lathe chuck, first cover the piston with thin sheet-steel or copper.

Special weighing scales are used to measure the weights of the pistons. These scales must be accurate to less than 1/2 gram. Special weighing scales are also used to weigh the connecting rods. While one end of the rod rests on the scales, the other end is supported. When the weight of the crank ends of the connecting rods is found, the heavier crank ends should be balanced by removing metal so they are equal in weight to the rod with the lightest crank end. Similarly, the weights of the pin ends of the rods must be made to conform to the weight of the rod with the lightest pin end. A grinder or belt sander is usually used to remove metal from the connecting rods. Note: The weight of the individual rods and pistons should be carefully recorded.

On V-type engines that carry two rod-and-piston assemblies on each crank throw, the bob weight for each throw will include:

1. The weight of the crank end of one rod with bearing inserts, lock nuts, and oil in crank throw.
2. The weight of one piston, pin, pin lock, one set of rings, and one piston end of rod.
3. The total of weights in 1 and 2 will be the weight of the bob weight to be attached to each crank throw when balancing the crankshaft.

On V-type engines that carry one rod and piston assembly on each throw, the bob weight for each throw will include:

1. The weight of the crank end of one rod (with its bearing inserts and lock nuts) and the weight of the oil in the crank throw. This is the rotating weight.
2. The reciprocating weight to be included in the bob weight includes 50% of the pin end of the rod, piston, piston pin, pin locks, and a set of rings.
3. The sum of the rotating and the reciprocating weights in 1 and 2 is the bob weight that must be attached to each crankpin when balancing the crankshaft.

As pointed out, inline four- and six-cylinder crankshafts do not require bob weights when they are being balanced. However, the weights of the piston and rod assemblies must be made equal within a tolerance of 1/2 oz.

By the Numbers

Before disassembling the engine, the technician should number the main bearing caps, Figure 12-28, and the pistons, Figure 12-29. Once each piston is removed, the rod and cap of each piston should be marked, Figure 12-30. This step will make reassembly easier. If the piston is installed in the wrong cylinder or the wrong rod cap installed on a connecting rod, the engine could seize. The same thing can happen if a main bearing cap is installed in the wrong position. Always turn the engine one complete revolution by hand after torquing the main bearing caps. Also, rotate the crankshaft by hand after installing and torquing each rod cap. This will determine if the rod and main caps are in the right position. If they are not, the crankshaft will not be able to make a complete revolution.

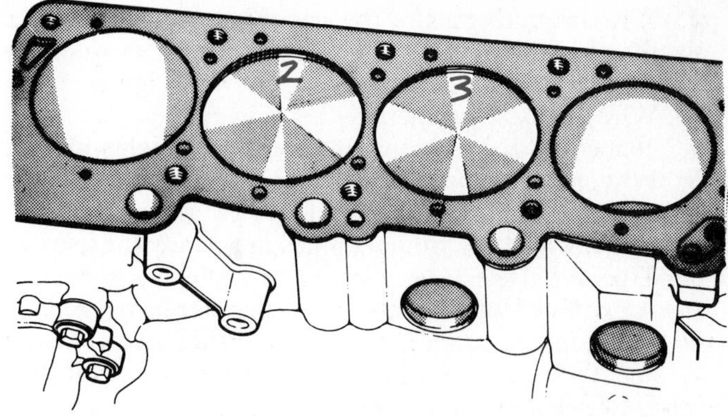

Figure 12-29. Number the pistons prior to removal. (Chrysler)

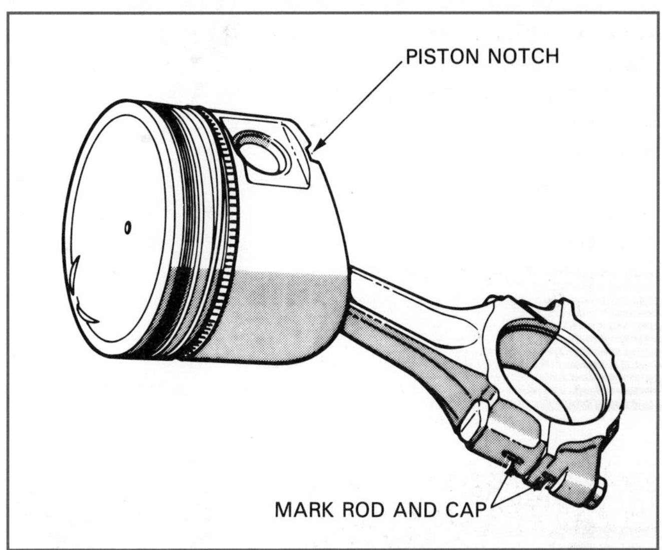

Figure 12-30. Mark the connecting rod and rod cap where indicated prior to removal. If caps are mixed up, the engine may seize. (Chrysler)

Chapter 12–Review Questions

Write your answers on a separate piece of paper. Do not write in this book.

1. Name five ways of increasing the size of a metal part.
2. An oversize bearing is required on a reground crankshaft journal. True or False?
3. Name five ways of repairing a cracked water jacket.
4. How much warpage can usually be tolerated in a cylinder head?
   (A) .001″.
   (B) .003″.
   (C) .006″.
   (D) None of the above.

5. When installing a new dry sleeve in a cylinder, should the sleeve be smaller or larger in diameter than the cylinder?
6. Why do pistons sometimes seize in cylinders?
7. Name two ways of repairing badly scored cylinders.
8. Why must dry cylinder sleeves fit tightly in the block?
9. If a newly installed dry sleeve is round, straight, smooth, and free from wrinkles, it is ready for service. True or False?
10. A cylinder sleeve should be _____ after installation.
11. The limitation for cylinder wear is .010″ out-of-round and .005″ taper. True or False?
12. Describe a proper cylinder wall finish.
13. Name three ways of expanding pistons.
14. In general, how much clearance per inch of diameter should cast iron pistons have in cylinders?
    (A) .0075″ to .01″.
    (B) .00075″ to .001″.
    (C) .00005″ to .00015″.
    (D) None of the above.
15. Aluminum cylinder heads can be cleaned with a:
    (A) bead blaster.
    (B) cold tank solution.
    (C) hot tank solution.
    (D) Either A or B.
16. The greatest amount of wear in the cylinder takes place at the _____ of the travel of the piston.
17. What is the maximum amount of taper specified for cylinder wear in passenger car engines?
    (A) .010″.
    (B) .005″.
    (C) .075″.
    (D) None of the above.
18. Only static balance of engine parts is required. True or False?
19. Unbalance of engine parts _____ bearing loads.
20. The effect of engine unbalance increases with engine speed. True or False?
21. Aluminum heads can be checked for cracks by:
    (A) using an electromagnet.
    (B) using a dye.
    (C) Either A or B.
    (D) Neither A nor B.

This cylinder-reconditioning machine can be used to resize and hone cylinder bores. (Sunnen)

Chapter 13
Piston Ring and Pin Fitting

After studying this chapter, you will be able to:

❍ Determine if the piston ring groove needs to be reconditioned.

❍ Explain why and how a piston ring groove wears.

❍ Tell how to measure the piston ring gap and explain why it is important.

❍ State how to properly install piston rings.

Piston Ring Service

Piston ring design and purpose was covered in a previous chapter. It included a reference to the fact that a ***ridge*** is formed at the top of the cylinder wall as the cylinder wears. To avoid damage to pistons and rings, this ridge must be cut away before any attempt is made to remove the pistons through the top of the cylinders. Special tools called ***ridge reamers*** are made for this purpose, Figure 13-1.

Cylinder wall reconditioning and piston fitting have also been discussed. Now, some consideration should be given to properly fitting the rings to the piston and the cylinder, and also to fitting piston pins in the pistons.

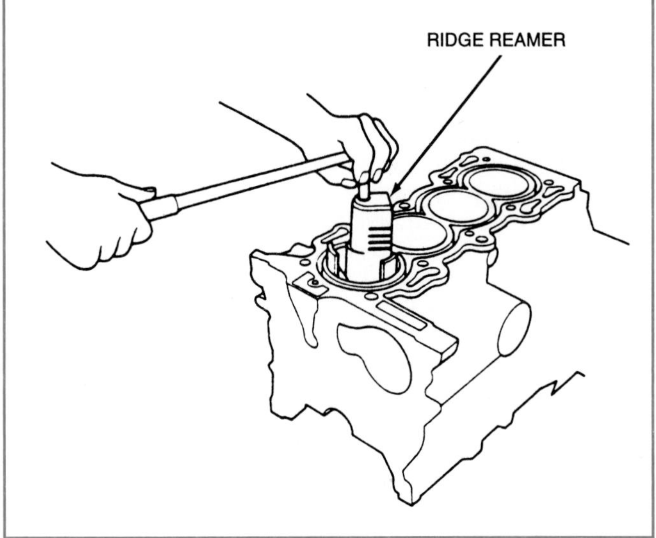

Figure 13-1. A ridge reamer is used to remove the ridge at the top of the cylinder. (Honda)

Piston Ring Gap

It is obvious that the top piston ring runs hotter than the lower rings. Therefore, the top ring will expand the most. This means that the top ring will need more gap clearance at the ends and more sideways clearance in the piston grooves than the other rings. The piston ring manufacturer specifies the amount of clearance needed. The manufacturer's instructions should be followed.

Piston ring gap clearance is measured as shown in Figure 13-2. The ring is pushed into the cylinder. An inverted piston without rings is used to push the ring in place since this method locates the ring squarely in the bore. Piston rings of the correct size for the application should be purchased. If necessary, minor increases in gap clearance can be made by filing the ends of the ring. However, if the ring side clearance is not within specifications, do not file the width of the ring. New rings are needed.

In case clearance dimensions are not available, it is customary to allow .004″ gap clearance per inch of piston diameter for the top ring and .003″ per inch of piston diameter for the other rings. For example, a 3″ diameter piston would require .012″ gap in the top ring and .009″ in the other rings. The exception to this rule is the "U" type oil ring, which is extremely flexible. These rings require no gap clearance.

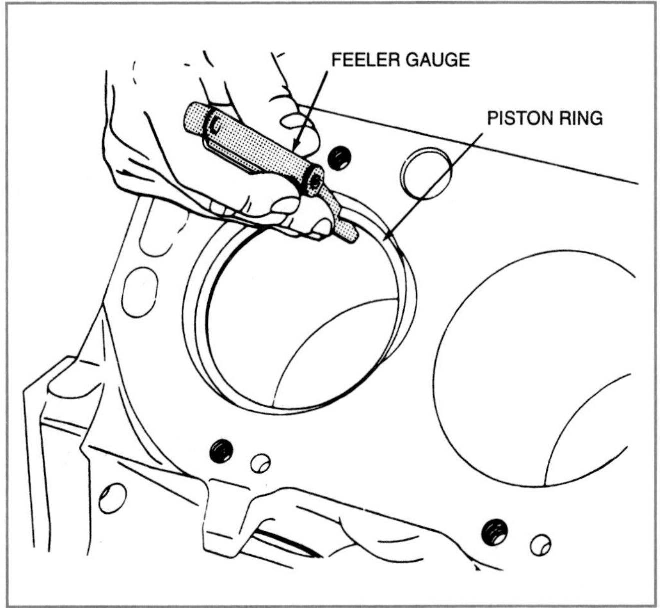

Figure 13-2. Measuring piston ring gap. (General Motors)

Ring Groove Clearance

The sideways clearance of the ring in the groove is measured using a feeler (thickness) gauge. See Figure 13-3.

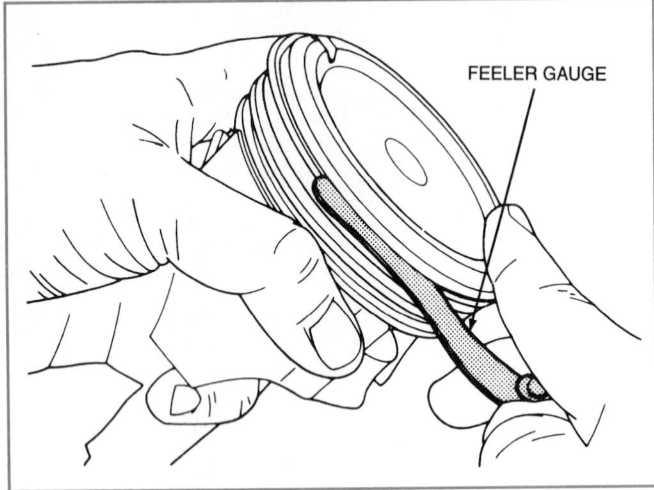

Figure 13-3. Measuring ring side clearance with a new ring installed. If clearance is excessive, the ring will twist more than usual and may break. (General Motors)

In the absence of instructions, it is customary to allow at least .003″ side clearance on the top ring and at least .002″ on the other rings. More than .005″ side clearance on any ring calls for the grooves in the piston to be reconditioned or the piston to be replaced.

New rings should never be installed in worn ring grooves. This practice results in poor oil economy and increased blowby, Figure 13-4. In addition, ring life will be shortened. No matter how accurately a piston ring is made, it cannot form an effective oil and blowby seal against the sides of a worn or uneven ring groove. The importance of checking ring grooves for wear cannot be overemphasized. New rings can be purchased in any standard size, oversize, or overwidth desired. Overwidth rings may be used if the sides of the ring grooves are flat, smooth, and square.

If the grooves are worn excessively, Figure 13-5, or in tapered fashion, Figure 13-6, they can be repaired in two ways. One way is to machine the grooves wider and install overwidth rings. The other way is to install spacers with standard width rings, as shown in Figure 13-7. In either case, the ring grooves in the piston will need to be trued up. Special equipment is available for this purpose, Figure 13-8.

The depth of the ring groove must also be checked when replacing rings. Sometimes, shallow grooves are

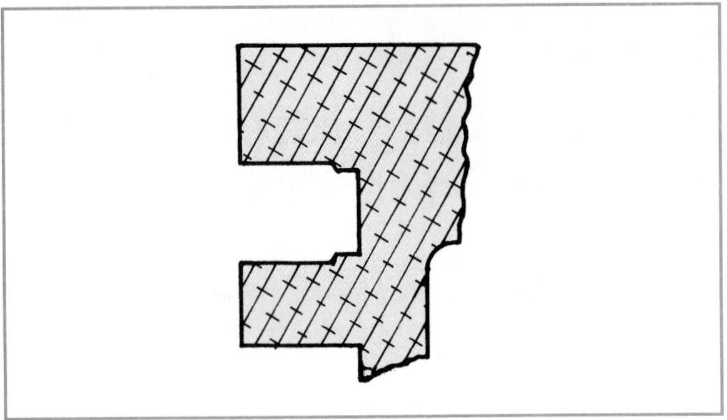

Figure 13-5. The shoulder in the groove may not leave enough clearance for new rings.

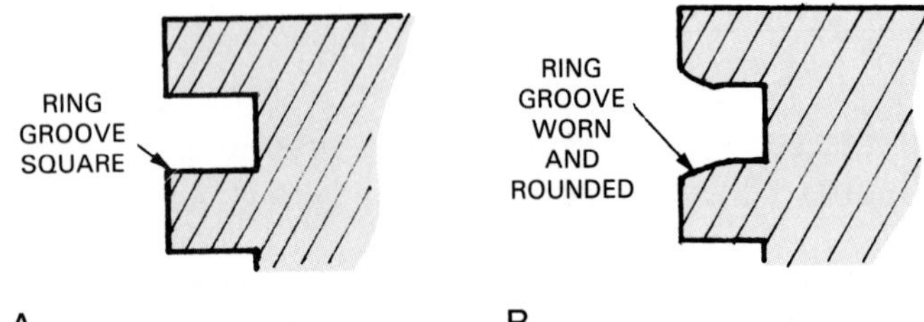

Figure 13-6. Piston ring grooves: A–New groove is perfectly square. B–Ring grooves wear in a bellmouth shape. This is due to the ring twisting in the groove as the piston moves up and down.

Figure 13-7. Standard rings may be used with a spacer installed above the ring in remachined grooves.

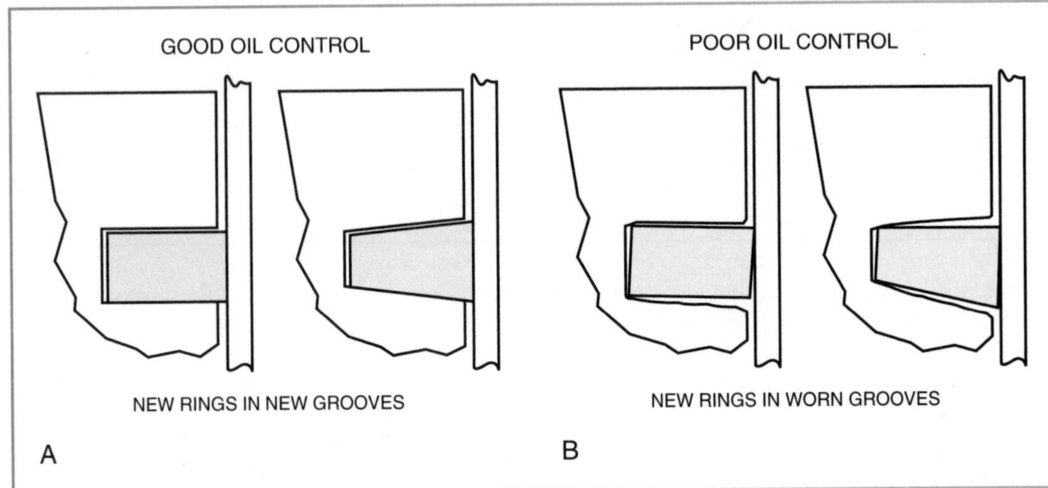

Figure 13-4. A–New rings in new grooves provide good oil control. B–New rings in worn grooves increase oil consumption and blowby.

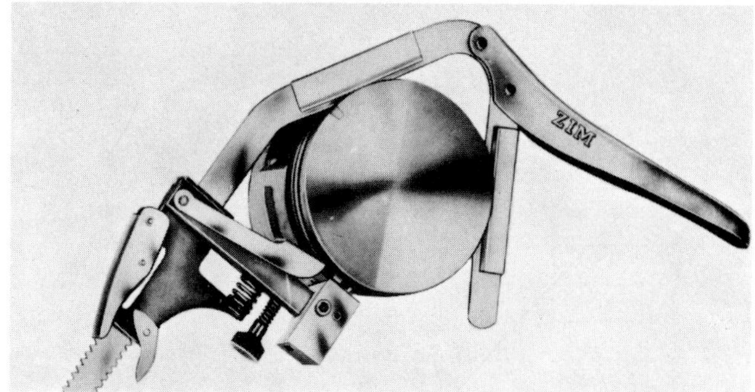

Figure 13-8. Widening grooves on a piston. Similar equipment is used as a ring groove cleaner.

used with thin rings, and a replacement with normal thickness rings will cause them to "bottom" in the groove. The groove must be deep enough to allow the ring to enter the groove below the surface of the ring land. If the grooves are too shallow, they can be machined deeper.

When installing rings, space the gaps around the pistons to avoid any possibility that the gaps will align with each other, increasing blowby, Figure 13-9. The manufacturers' instructions should always be followed when installing new rings. They know how their products should be fitted, and they have studied the peculiarities of various engines, Figure 13-10.

Piston ring grooves must be thoroughly cleaned before installing new rings. Special tools are available for scraping the carbon from the grooves. A broken segment of a piston ring may also be used for this purpose.

Piston rings are fragile and must be handled carefully. They should be placed in the piston ring grooves with the aid of a ***ring expander,*** Figure 13-11. The rings must never be stretched over the piston by hand. Even if they do not break, they may become distorted by careless handling. It is

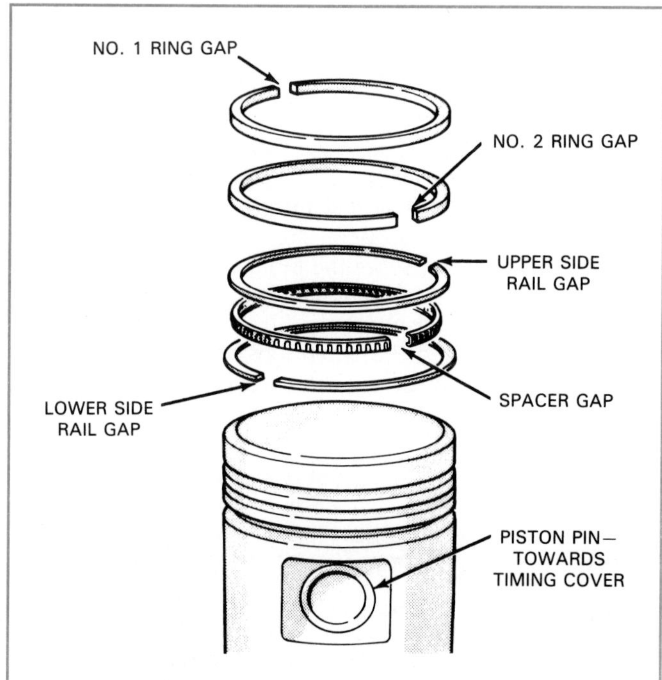

Figure 13-9. Ring gaps must be staggered when installed on the piston, or blowby will be excessive. (Chrysler)

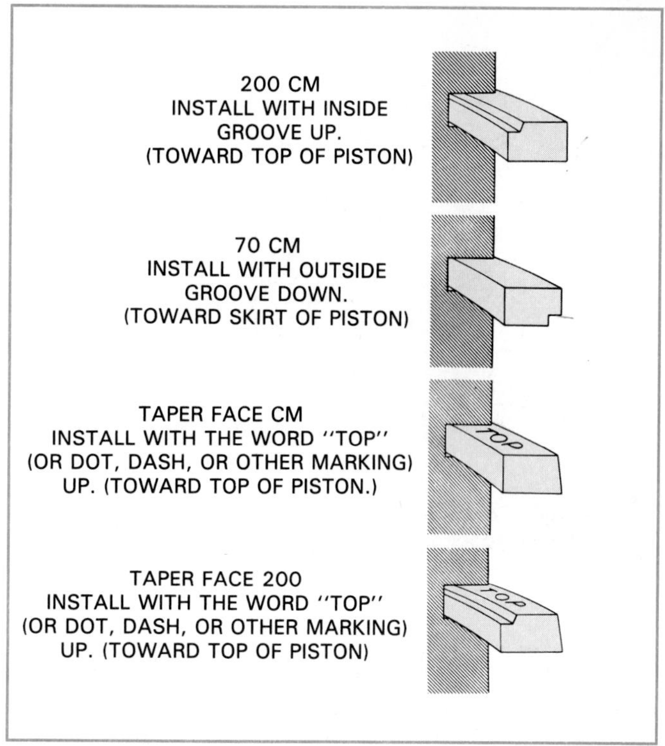

Figure 13-10. If rings are installed upside down, they will scrape oil into the combustion chamber. (Perfect Circle)

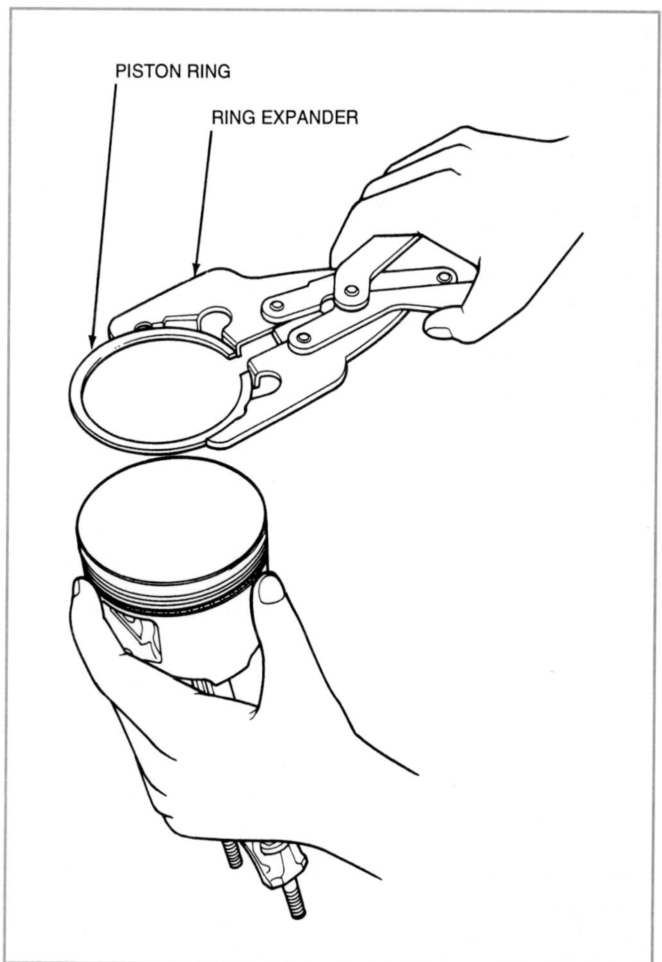

Figure 13-11. A ring expander must be used to place rings on the piston so that they do not break. (Honda)

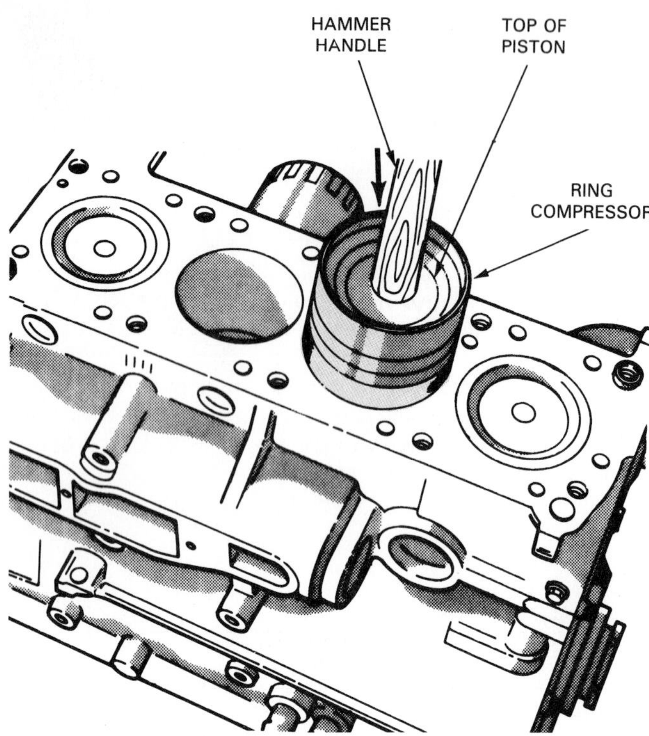

Figure 13-12. A ring compressor must be used to compress rings so that the piston can be inserted into cylinder. After the ring compressor is tightened around rings and piston, the wooden end of a hammer is used to tap piston into the cylinder. (Chrysler)

also important to use a ***ring compressor*** when inserting the piston with rings into the cylinder. Otherwise, the sharp edge of the rings may be deformed, and the rings will be rendered useless. See Figure 13-12.

If the bearings are worn in a pressure-lubricated engine, excess oil will be thrown upon the cylinder walls. The engine will pump oil, regardless of how good the rings are or how well they are fitted. The oil is supplied in such large quantities that it is beyond the ability of any ring to control it.

Piston Pins

Today, piston pins have an ***interference fit*** in the upper end of the rod. That is, the diameter of the piston pin is slightly larger than the diameter in the upper end of the connecting rod. Special equipment, Figure 13-13, is needed to remove and install the pins in the piston and rod assembly. In addition to a hydraulic press, equipment needed includes special anvils on which the piston assembly is mounted, pilots, and in some cases, a spring for the anvil. This equipment differs for each piston design.

The pressing procedure is to mount the piston assembly on the anvil. Then, the pin is pressed from the assembly with a pilot and hydraulic press or an electro-hydraulic pin press. A similar procedure is followed when assembling the piston pin to the rod and piston.

Oversize Piston Pins

In the full-floating piston pin arrangement, the installation of new ***oversize pins*** will require reaming or honing of the piston bushings or bosses and the rod.

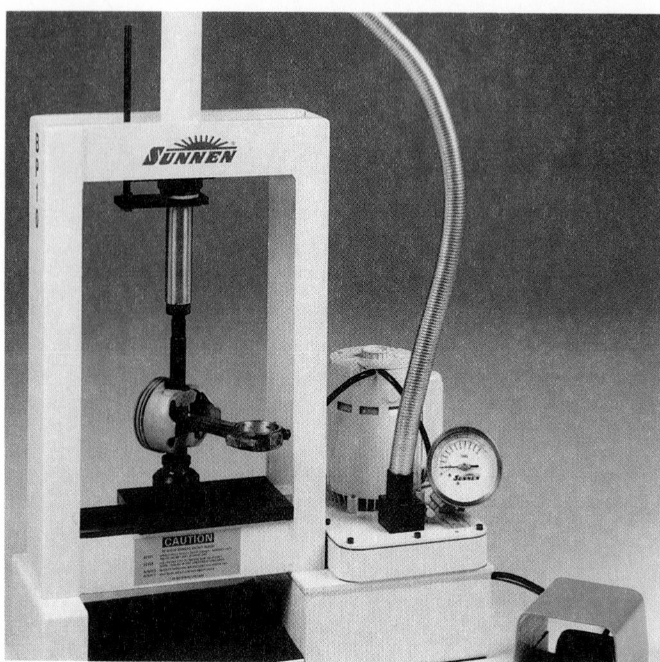

Figure 13-13. A hydraulic press can be used to remove and insert piston pins. (Sunnen)

In every case where reaming or honing is done on either the piston or the connecting rod, it is very important to have the finished hole at precisely 90° to the connecting rod. Also, both piston boss bearings must be in precise alignment. The hole must be straight through both bosses. Equipment used for reconditioning piston pin holes is shown in Figures 13-14 and 13-15.

Piston Pin Fitting

Fitting piston pins is one of the most delicate operations encountered in automobile repair work. Suitable equipment for fitting piston pins properly is available. Furthermore, you are dealing with steel, bronze, and aluminum–each of which has a different rate of heat expansion. The piston pins are fitted at room temperature (assumed to be 70°F [21°C]); then they are put in an engine that quickly attains a temperature of at least 140°F (60°C). This temperature expands the piston.

There must be room for a film of oil around the piston pin. Otherwise, metal-to-metal contact will occur and the friction generated will score the pin and/or the bushing.

Standards of manufacture have improved, and most piston pins are round and straight within one ten-thousandth of an inch. To the naked eye, a pin looks perfect and appears to be glass smooth. When the surface is magnified 100 times

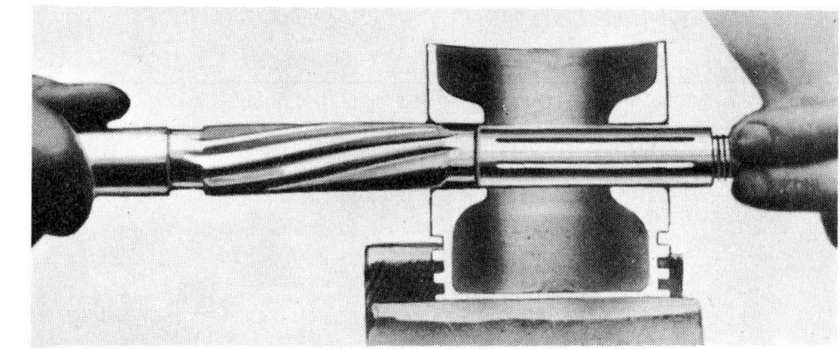

Figure 13-14. A reamer is used to make sure that holes for piston pin align.

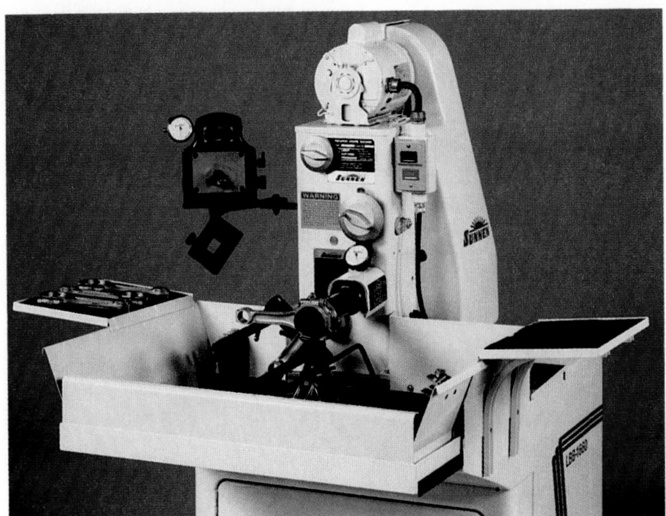

Figure 13-15. A honing machine can be used to recondition the piston pin bore and, as shown, the large bore of a connecting rod. (Sunnen)

it does not look as smooth. When magnified 1000 times, it actually looks rough. See Figure 13-16.

Reaming, grinding, and honing equipment is now available that will produce a hole which appears to be dead smooth. Like the pins, the hole must be accurate to one ten-thousandth of an inch. When magnified, however, it looks much like the bearing surface of the pins.

With the use of good equipment, it is possible to produce a hole that enables a good working fit to be made.

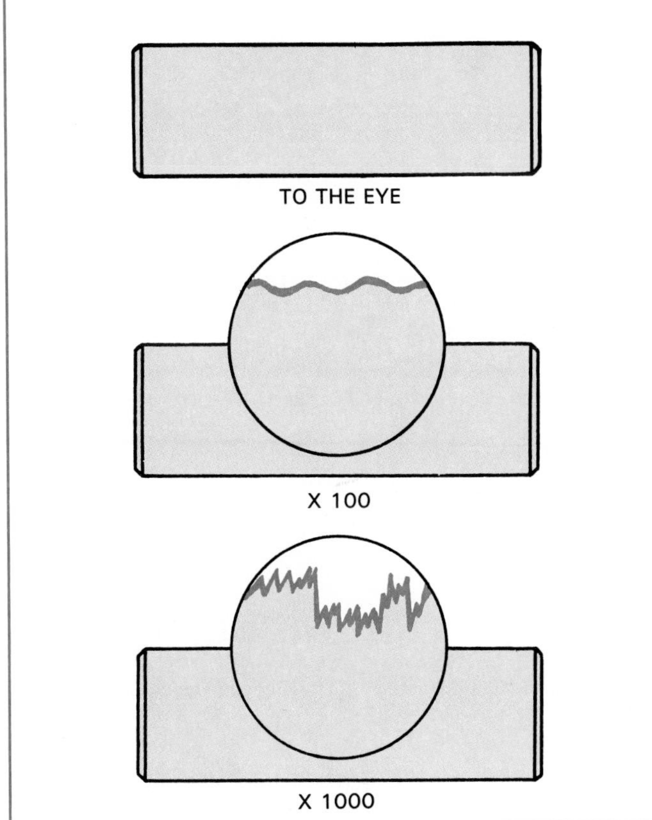

Figure 13-16. A piston pin may be smooth to the naked eye, but when magnified, the surface of the pin is rough.

When working with such close dimensions, the clearance will be determined by the surface finish.

Unless the hole finish is practically perfect, the "peaks" will be sheared off when the pin is forced into the hole, Figure 13-17. The result of such a condition is rapid wear of the peak base, and the pin and bushing will wear out before they wear in to a working fit.

Piston pins must never be too tight. If the hole is finished to the correct size, there will be room for a film of oil to prevent metal-to-metal contact. When such a fit is obtained, the pin will enter the hole readily. It will have sufficient bearing surface to wear satisfactorily. This precision fit can be obtained by a skillful operator using modern equipment in accordance with the manufacturers' instructions. Figure 13-18 pictures a connecting rod heater that is used in press-fit rod work.

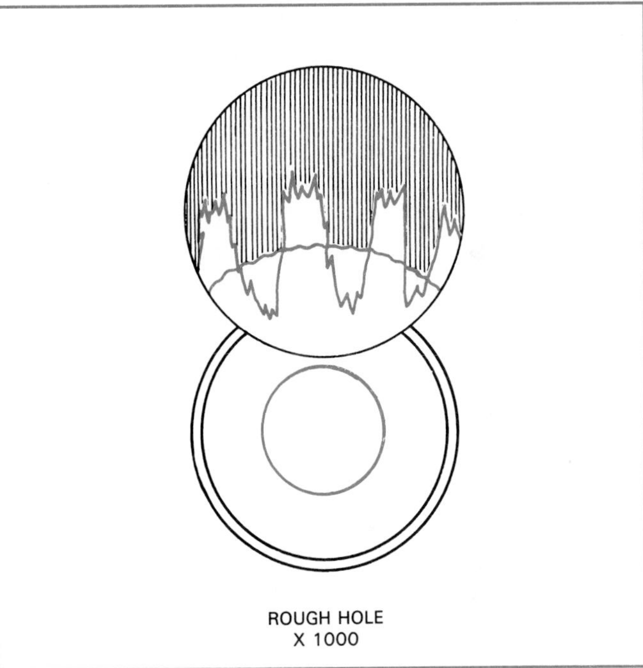

Figure 13-17. Forcing a smooth piston pin through a rough hole will cause the high points to be sheared off, which will result in metal-to-metal contact.

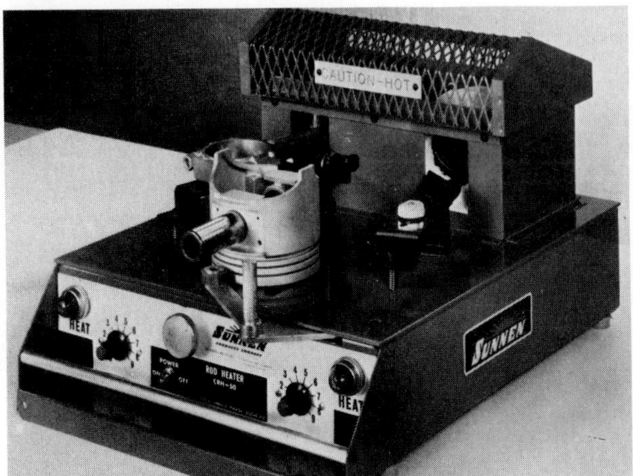

Figure 13-18. An electric heater expands the connecting rod eye so that the piston pin can be pushed in by hand. (Sunnen)

Chapter 13–Review Questions

Write your answers on a separate sheet of paper. Do not write in this book.

1. How much end gap should the top ring have in a four-inch diameter cylinder?
   (A) .009″.
   (B) .012″.
   (C) .016″.
   (D) None of the above.
2. How much gap should the oil ring have in a cylinder 3 1/2″ in diameter?
   (A) .009″.
   (B) .012″.
   (C) .015″.
   (D) None of the above.
3. The top ring should have at least .005″ side clearance in the ring groove. True or False?
4. How deep should the ring groove be?
5. Piston pins are case-hardened, so they do not wear. True or False?
6. Can oversize pins be installed when the pin floats in both piston and connecting rod?
7. New piston pins can be expected to be round within:
   (A) .002″.
   (B) .0001″.
   (C) .00005″.
   (D) .00001″.
8. Technician A states that the ring groove wears in a bellmouth shape. Technician B states that if a .006″ feeler gauge can be inserted between a new piston ring and the ring groove, the grooves must be reconditioned or the piston replaced.
   Who is right?
   (A) A only.
   (B) B only.
   (C) Both A & B.
   (D) Neither A nor B.
9. Explain how a ring groove wears and why?
10. Ring gaps on a piston should:
   (A) align with one another.
   (B) be about 90° from any other ring gap.

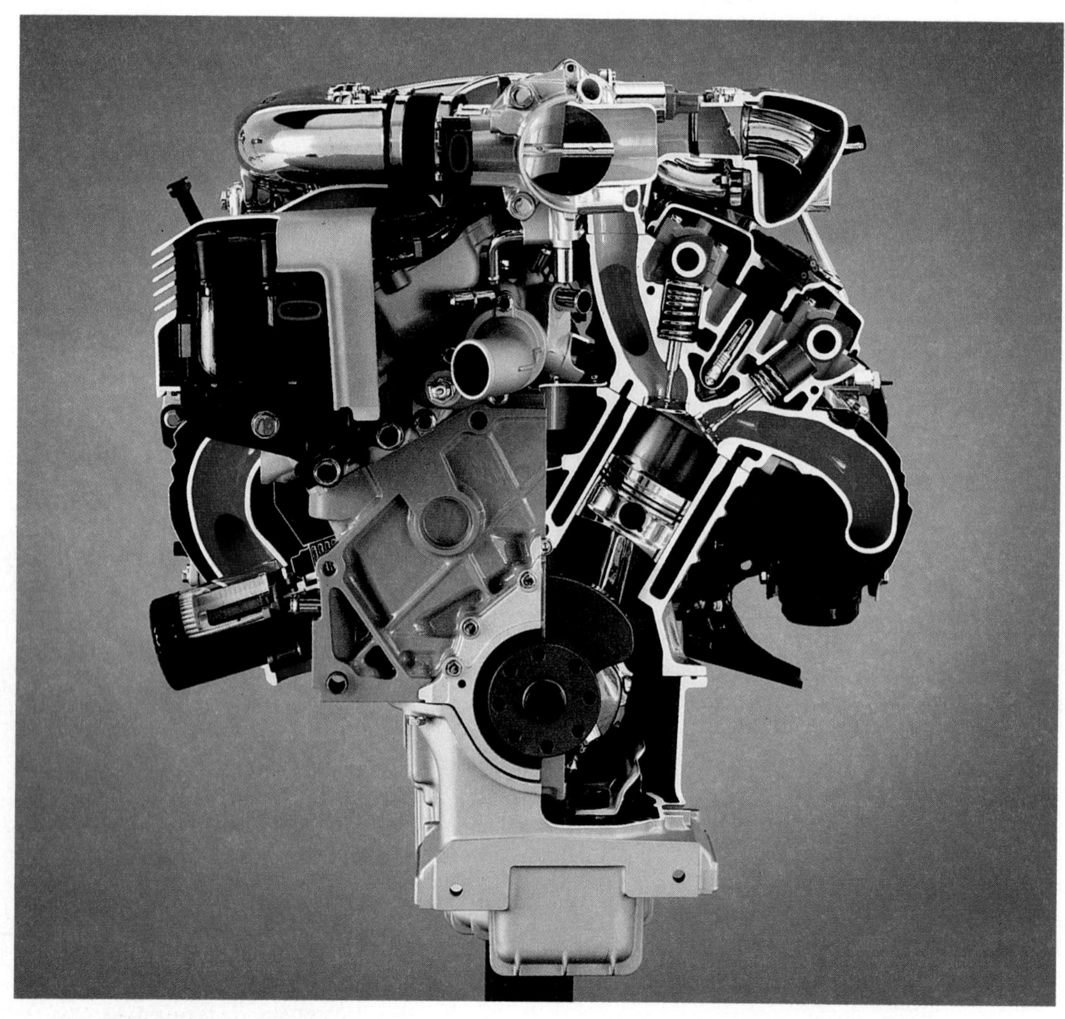

Cutaway of a late-model V-6 engine. Piston pins and rings must fit precisely for proper engine operation. (Ford)

Chapter 14
Crankshaft and Connecting Rod Service

After studying this chapter, you will be able to:
- Determine when a crankshaft needs reconditioning.
- Discriminate between a good and bad connecting rod.
- List the characteristics and types of engine bearings.
- State when an engine bearing needs replacement.
- Explain why an engine block needs to be align bored.

Crankshaft Service

In studying the forces applied to a journal of the ***crankshaft,*** it will be found that the load is much heavier at some points of rotation than others. For example, the force of the power stroke is several times stronger than the force of the compression stroke. Also, the power stroke always applies the force at the same spot on the journal.

Finally, an additional load is imposed by the action of centrifugal force resulting from the rotation of the crankshaft with its connecting rods and pistons. This results in out-of-round crankshaft journals and crankpins.

If a ***connecting rod*** is bent or is out of alignment, it will tend to wear the crankpin journal in a tapered fashion. In other words, it will wear more at one end of the bearing surface than the other end. Also any twisting of the engine crankcase or any excessive vibration of the crankshaft will cause the main crankshaft journals to wear in a tapered form.

Furthermore, if ***abrasive material*** gets into the engine oil, wear may be unequal. It may cause more wear at one bearing or on one spot of the bearing, depending on where the abrasive enters in greatest quantity.

Bearings seldom wear equally. One bearing may operate with a smaller volume of oil than another. Likewise, one bearing, because of its location in the engine, may operate at a higher temperature than the others. All of these things contribute to unequal wear on the crankshaft journals.

If a connecting rod journal has taper or a flat spot, it simply cannot be used. Either condition would ordinarily cause such an increase in oil consumption that it would be essential to replace the crankshaft or recondition the crank journal.

Because of close clearances in the bearings, a sprung crankshaft cannot be tolerated. The main bearings must fit the crankshaft journals all around the circumference with only enough clearance for a film of lubricating oil. If the bearing journal is scored or is out-of-round, it must be reconditioned or replaced.

Damaged Crankshafts

Engine crankshafts usually are large and expensive parts, so it may be desirable to repair damage rather than replace the shaft. Before any extensive work is started, however, it is well to have the shaft checked by a specialist with proper special magnetic or chemical equipment to make sure there are no cracks in it. See Figure 14-1 .

If damage has occurred to one or more crankpin journals, it is possible to recondition the crankpin with the aid of special equipment made for this purpose. See Figure 14-2.

An engine crankshaft is subjected to terrific vibration and stress. It may develop tiny cracks, particularly at or near the ends of the connecting rod throws or at the ends of the main bearing journals. Occasionally, a crack may develop near the oil feed holes in the shaft.

If the crankshaft is sound, journals worn slightly tapered or out-of-round can be reground and ***undersize bearings*** can be fitted. See Figure 14-3. Here again, it is desirable to check out the available sizes of bearing inserts, then have the shaft journals ground to an undersize that corresponds to these inserts.

Figure 14-1. A magnetic particle inspector is used to detect cracks that cannot be seen by the naked eye. (Kwik-Way)

Figure 14-2. Special machinery is needed to recondition crankshaft journals.

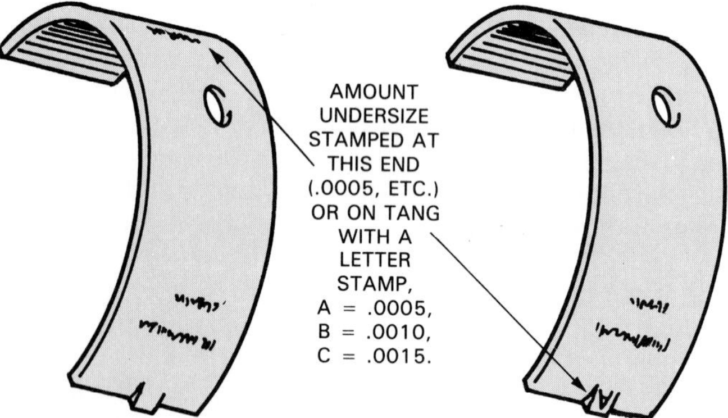

Figure 14-3. When a crankshaft journal is undersized, the bearings are oversized. However, the bearings, like the journal, are also referred to as undersized. (Oldsmobile)

A crankshaft journal can be checked for scoring by running a fingernail over the journal. If your fingernail detects the slightest ridge or scoring, the journal must be reconditioned. Your fingernail should glide over the entire journal surface.

If the shaft is badly damaged, it is generally replaced. However, it may be possible to restore the journal by spraying metal on it. The shaft is built up oversize, and then reground to the desired size. This type of work usually is done by specialists.

Bearing Clearances

A previous study of engine lubrication revealed that oil is pumped under pressure to the various bearings in the engine. However, to get this oil into the bearing and lubricate it, clearance for an ***oil film*** must exist.

The most important thing to keep in mind in this connection is that the steel crankshaft journal must be separated from the bearing metal when the engine is running or the bearing will melt. The heat generated by friction when steel moves rapidly on soft, dry metal will melt the soft metal. Therefore, an automobile engine uses a film of oil between the journal and the bearing.

The oil film holds the two metals apart and also circulates to carry away the heat generated by friction. The oil clearance is not great (measured in thousandths of an inch), but it is extremely important. See Figure 14-4.

The ***oil clearance*** will vary with the design of the engine and the type of lubrication system used. In general, a splash lubrication system is less critical of oil clearances than a pressure lubrication system. In the splash system, the oil is churned up by the internal parts of the engine into a combination of liquid and mist that is sprayed over the entire interior of the engine.

In the pressure lubricated engine, the oil is pumped under pressure to the bearings, Figure 14-5. In this case, the flow of oil must be controlled by maintaining limited clearance

Figure 14-4. A–The oil film holds the crankshaft journal away from the bearing. Improper clearance may lead to oil starvation. B–Oil starvation caused this bearing to melt. (Photo courtesy of AE Clevite Engine Parts)

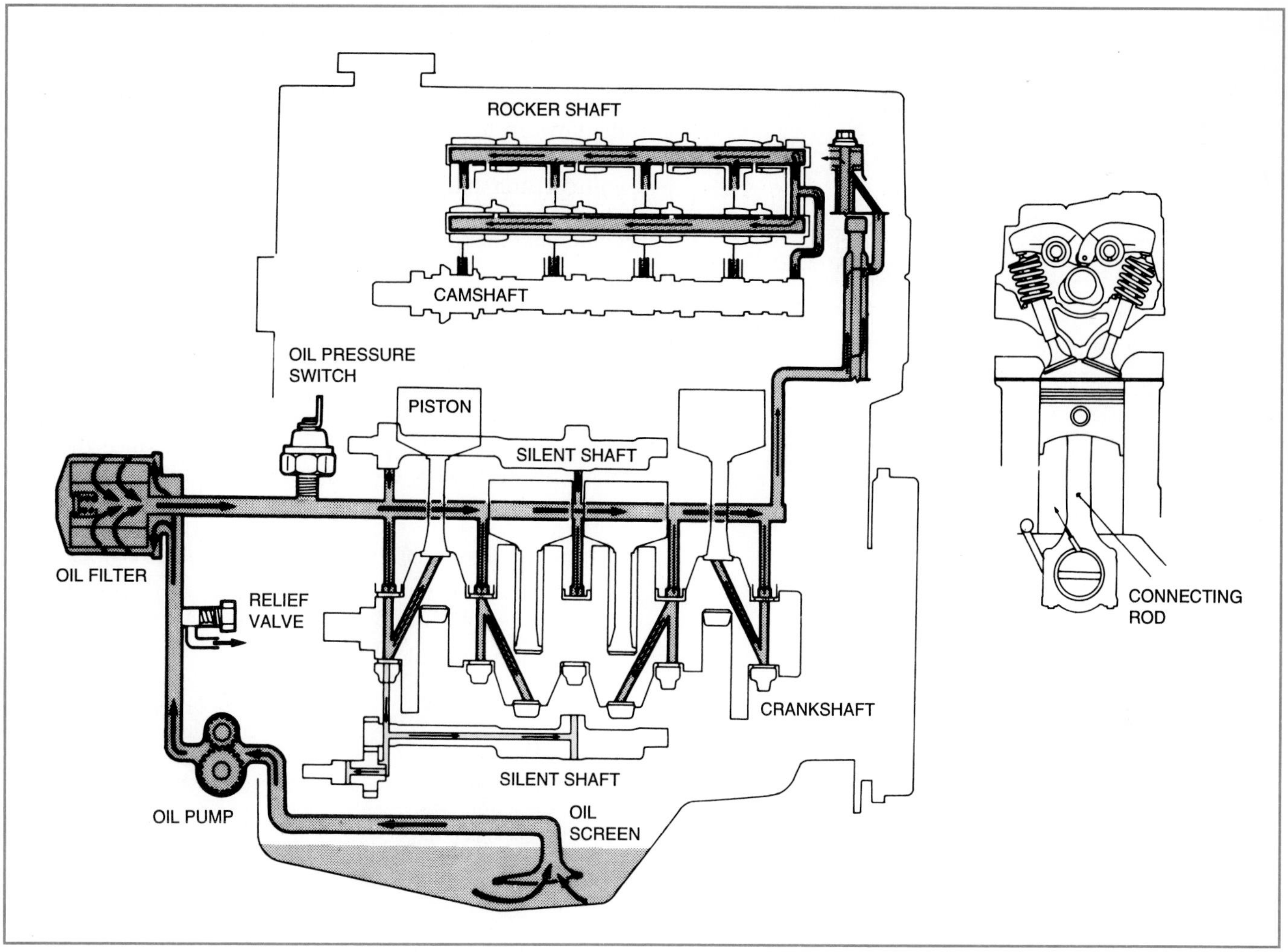

Figure 14-5. A pressurized lubrication system distributes oil to all parts of the engine. (Chrysler)

all the way around a round bearing and a round shaft. If there are unequal clearances in the circulation system, too much oil will collect in one place and not enough will travel to other places. This is because oil under pressure will go through the largest clearance space in the greatest quantity.

Clearance Measurement

The diameter of the shaft is measured at several points around the circumference to determine the size and to check for roundness. See Figure 14-6. Measuring each end of the journal will determine the amount of taper, if any.

The inside of the bearing bore, minus the bearing, is measured with the cap bolted in place. Use a telescoping gauge or an inside micrometer, Figure 14-7. The difference in these two measurements represents the amount that the bore is out of round.

The use of a plastic material called ***Plastigage,*** which flattens between the journal and bearing when the cap is drawn down to proper tightness, determines the oil clearance. The amount of increase in the width of the plastic material as it flattens out is measured with a furnished gauge to determine the clearance between journal and bearing. See Figure 14-8.

The amount of diametral clearance on crankshaft bearings is specified by the car manufacturer. In the absence of specifications, use a minimum of .0005-.001″ (0.0127 to 0.0154 mm) for small shafts and up to .0015-.002″ (0.381 to 0.0508 mm) for large shafts. Clearance in excess of .005″ (0.1270 mm) on either main bearings or rod bearings usually calls for the installation of new undersize bearings.

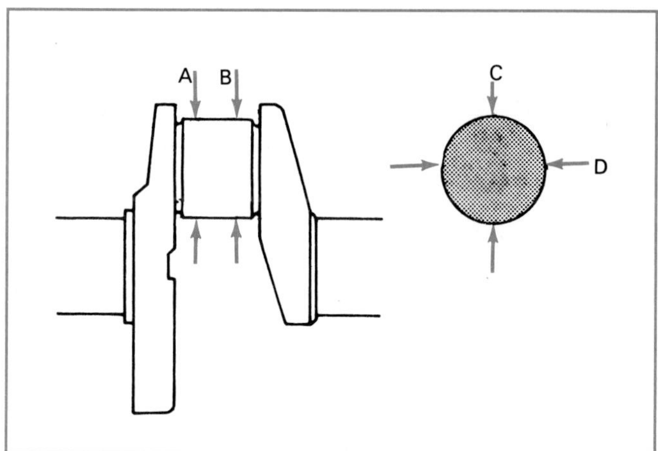

Figure 14-6. In addition to checking each journal for scoring, taper and out-of-round must also be checked. The difference between A and B is the amount of taper. The difference between C and D is the amount of out-of-round. (Nissan)

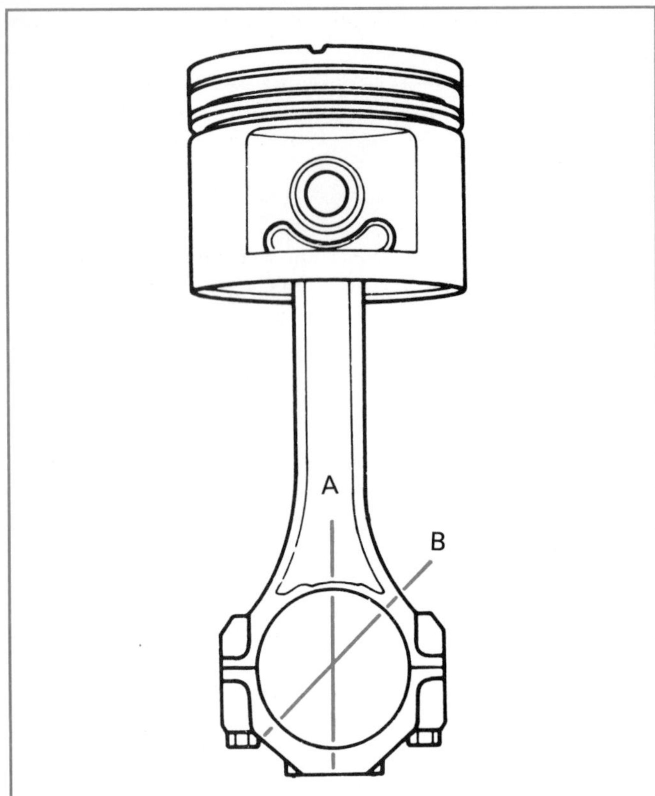

Figure 14-7. Distance at line A will be the greatest due to wear. The difference between line A and line B is the amount of out-of-round. If a rod is out-of-round more than .001″, a new one must be used. Use a dial indicator or a telescoping gauge and a micrometer. (Oldsmobile)

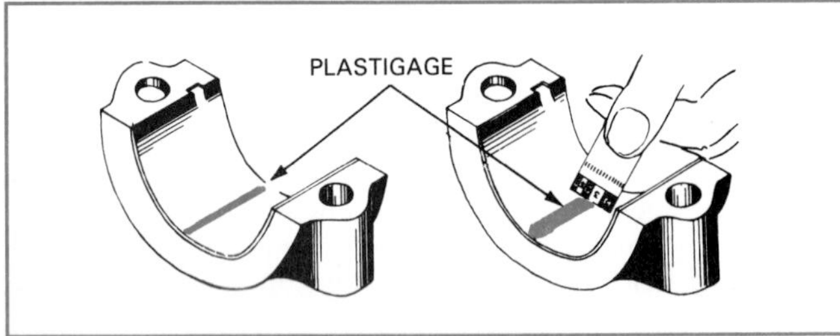

Figure 14-8. Using a Plastigage to check oil clearance.

Endwise Clearance

The crankshaft must not have excessive ***endwise movement.*** Therefore, one of the main bearings usually is provided with flanges that bear against a machined flange on the crankshaft. See Figure 14-9. There is always some end thrust on the crankshaft. This may originate from the clutch pushing against the end of the shaft or from the thrust of acceleration or deceleration of the engine.

Just as in the case of diametral clearance, there must be some clearance on the thrust faces. Otherwise, expansion of the shaft and bearings from the normal heat of operation will cause metal-to-metal contact and burning of the ***thrust bearing.*** Here again, the car manufacturers' instructions should be followed. It is customary to provide a minimum clearance of .004″ and a maximum clearance of .008″ clearance. End thrust can be measured with a feeler gauge, as shown in Figure 14-10.

Bearing Removal

The first step in bearing removal is to remove the piston from the cylinder. A ridge reamer is used to remove the unworn portion of the cylinder wall above piston ring travel, Figure 14-11. Then, the rod cap is removed, and the entire piston and rod assembly is pushed up and out of the cylinder. Rods and their respective caps must be kept together and marked for cylinder location, Figure 14-12.

Replacement of Inserts

With the ***insert bearing,*** or ***shell-type bearing,*** it is possible to replace all main and connecting rod bearings without removing the crankshaft. See Figure 14-13. These bearing inserts require no fitting by hand, since they are made to extremely close limits of accuracy. It is only

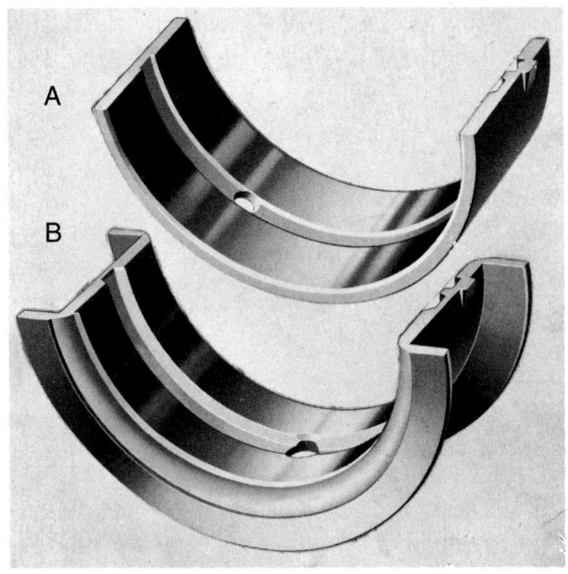

Figure 14-9. A–Precision insert bearing. B–Precision insert thrust bearing. Note that the thrust bearing has flanges.

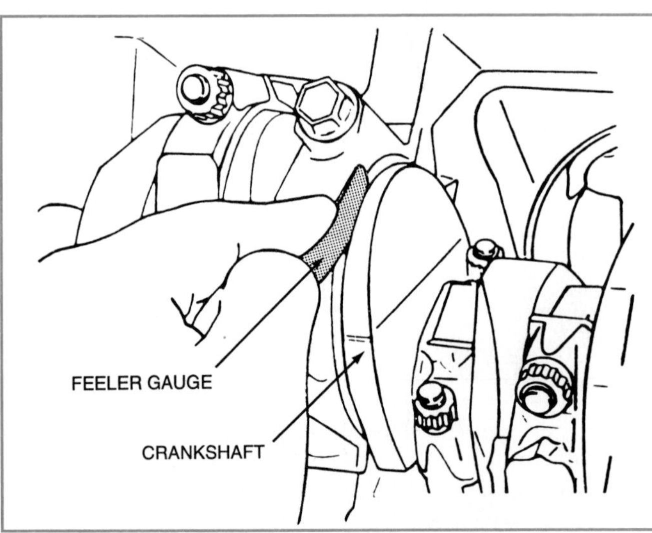

Figure 14-10. A feeler gauge is used to check end clearance of the crankshaft. End clearance is controlled by the thrust bearing. A screwdriver is used as a lever to move the crankshaft back and forth to obtain readings. (Oldsmobile)

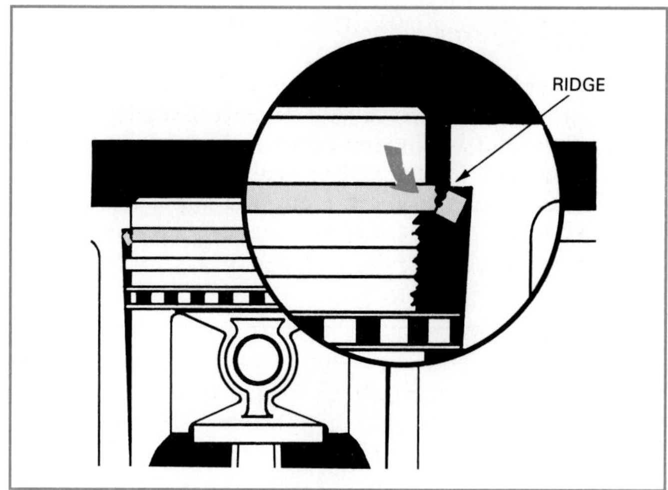

Figure 14-11. If the ridge is not removed before pushing piston upwards, the rings and the piston lands will be broken. (Sealed Power)

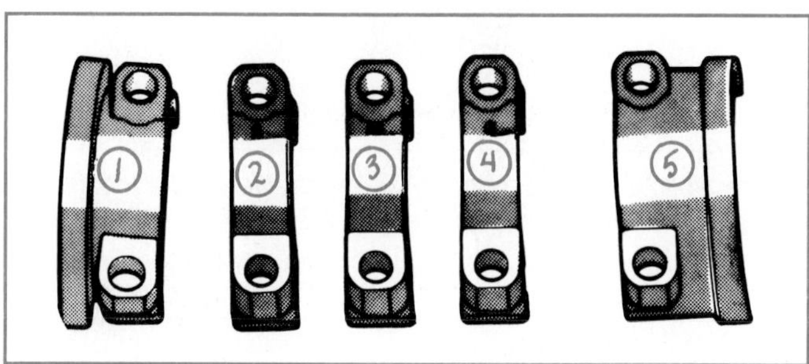

Figure 14-12. Number the main and rod caps prior to removing. (Chrysler)

necessary to obtain and install the correct size for the given application.

Even in the case of ***bushings,*** or ***sleeve-type bearings,*** used in old engines, Figure 14-14, replacement bearings are available in an assortment of sizes to meet almost any requirement.

If the crankshaft journal has been reduced in diameter so much that a standard insert will not fit and the crankshaft has not been damaged, the journal can be reconditioned to an undersize dimension and an undersize insert can be used.

If the crankshaft journal has been reduced in diameter so much that a standard undersize insert will not fit, inserts are available with excess bearing metal that can be bored out to the size desired, Figure 14-15.

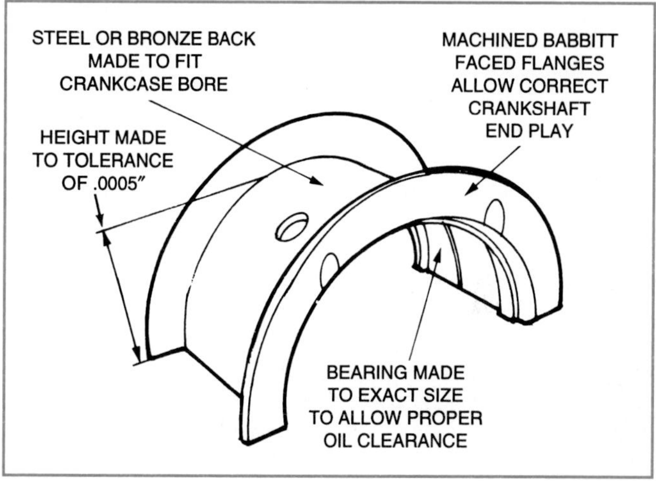

Figure 14-13. A typical thrust bearing.

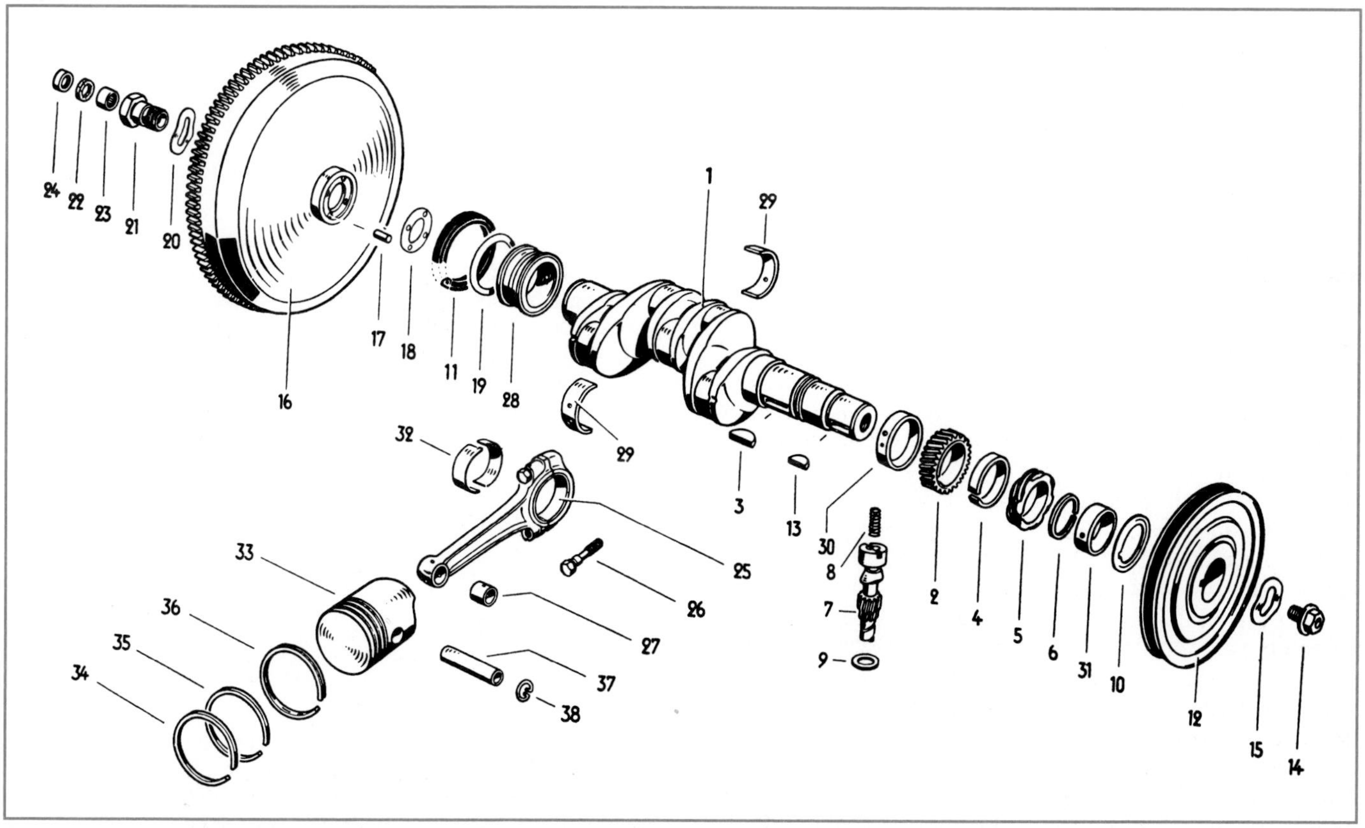

Figure 14-14. Main bearings, No. 28, 30, and 31, are sleeve type. Center bearing, No. 29, is a split type. (VW)

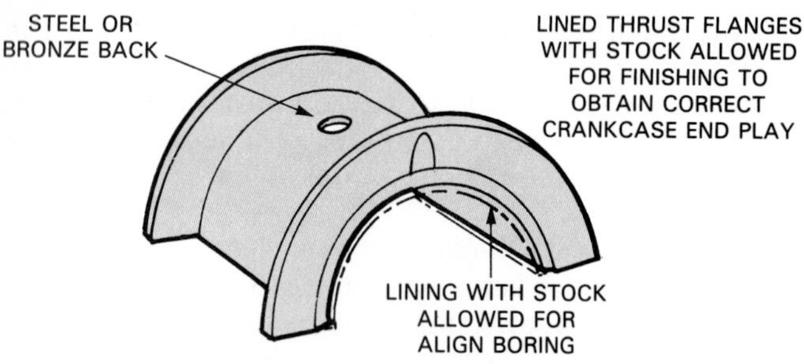

Figure 14-15. Reborable bearings permit any undersize desired. (Federal Mogul)

If the bearing bore and journal are round, new inserts require no fitting or adjustment. If the journal is out-of-round more than .0015″, it should be machined until it is round. The same applies to the bearing bore in which the insert seats. Any errors in the bore will distort the bearing shell when the nuts are drawn down to the proper specification. In general, when a connecting rod bearing has worn sufficiently to require replacement, the bore of the connecting rod will have worn to such an extent that replacement is also required.

Bearing Insert Seating

The bearing seat and bearing insert must be round and true, as there must be contact between the bearing seat bore and the back of the bearing insert. If contact does not exist, the heat will not flow from the insert to the crankcase or connecting rod and the bearing may melt. Note that no shims of any sort are used between the insert and seat in an effort to correct for wear or distortion.

The matter of heat dissipation is one reason for ***bearing crush.*** Crush means that the two halves of the bearing shell extend a few thousandths or an inch beyond the bearing seat bore, as shown in exaggerated form in Figure 14-16. When the bearing cap nuts are drawn down to specified tightness, the insert is forced to seat in its bore.

Another reason for crush is to make sure the bearing remains round. If the bearing insert is not held tightly against the bore, it may curl inward and touch the journal.

Still another reason for crush is to avoid any possible movement of the insert in the seat, Figure 14-17. If the shell should become slightly loose, it might oscillate in the seat and wear the bearing back. This would interfere with both oil control and heat transfer. Any dirt between the shell and the bore will have the same effect. See Figure 14-18.

Bearing crush must always exist, so the edges of the insert should not be dressed down flush with the bearing seats. Of course, the amount of crush must not be excessive. If excessive crush is present, the insert will be distorted when the cap is drawn down and the bearing would be deformed, Figure 14-19.

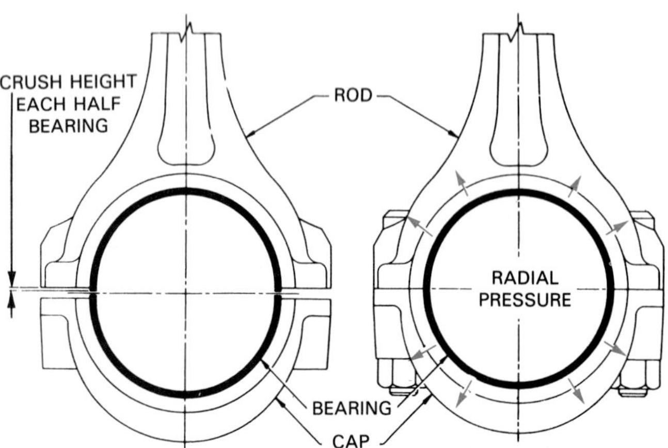

Figure 14-16. Bearing crush means that the bearing sits slightly higher than each half of the bore.

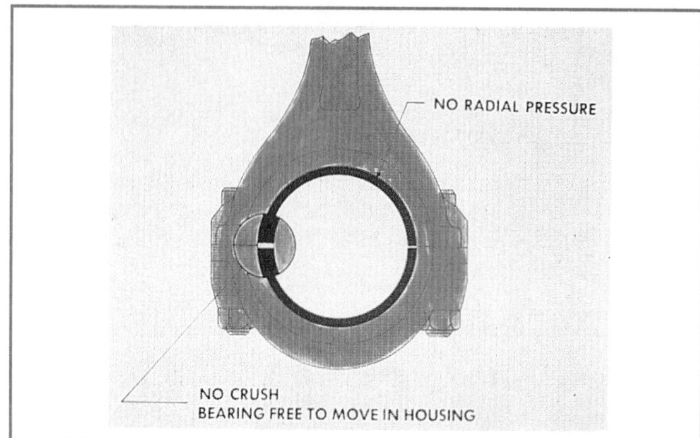

Figure 14-17. Lack of bearing crush may permit the inserts to move in the bore. (Photo courtesy of AE Clevite Engine Parts)

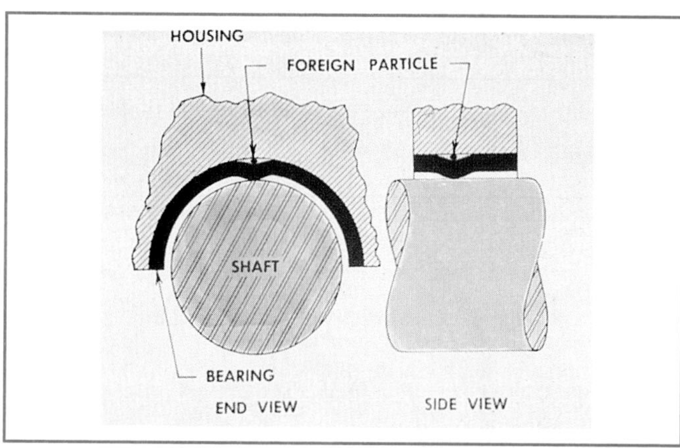

Figure 14-18. Dirt between the insert and bore creates a high spot on the bearing surface. This prevents an effective transfer of heat from the connecting rod and could cause the bearing to melt. (Photo courtesy of AE Clevite Engine Parts)

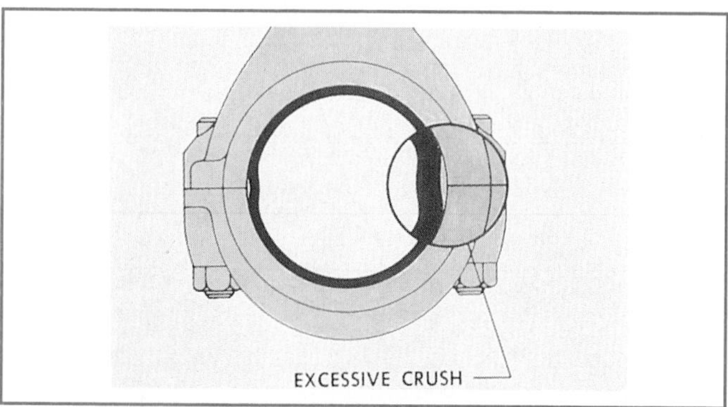

Figure 14-19. Excessive bearing crush will cause the bearing to distort when the cap is tightened. (Photo courtesy of AE Clevite Engine Parts)

The amount of crush is only .001″ or .002″. These inserts are extremely accurate and must be handled with care. They should be purchased to the precise size required and inserted with no alteration.

Bearing Spread

The diameter of the bearing is slightly wider than the bore. This is known as ***bearing spread,*** Figure 14-20. Bearing spread allows the bearing to remain in its seat during assembly, while the bearing or engine is inverted.

Lubrication Grooves

Lubrication grooves, Figure 14-21, are sometimes added to the bearing design to help distribute oil over a wider area of the journals. Annular grooves route oil to other oil passages in the engine block. The thumbnail grooves allow the oil to be distributed evenly over the flange of the thrust bearing.

Installation of Inserts

When all bearings are installed properly and the caps drawn up tight, there should be little resistance to rotation of the shaft. If there is resistance: one or more bearings are fitted too tightly; there is insufficient end clearance on the thrust bearing; the crankshaft is sprung; the bearings are not in correct alignment; or the bearing caps have been mixed-up.

If the engine is too tight after installing new bearings, it should not be started until the cause of the interference is located and eliminated.

The connecting rod must have some ***side clearance*** at the crankpin. If it has too much clearance, the bearing may move sideways and cause a knock. The clearance is measured by inserting a feeler gauge between the side of the cap and cheek of the crankshaft throw, as shown in Figure 14-22. Manufacturers' specifications vary somewhat, but the usual side clearance is .005″ to .010″. Since there is no adjustment of the side clearance, excessive clearance requires replacement of the bearing inserts.

The replacement of ***main bearings*** of the insert type presents a problem only when the cylinder block has become warped, Figure 14-23, and/or when the crankshaft is scored or badly worn. If the cylinder block is not warped and the shaft is in good condition, all that is necessary is to remove the old bearing inserts and slip in new ones of the correct size.

Main bearing inserts are replaced one at a time. The procedure is to remove the bearing cap and slip out the

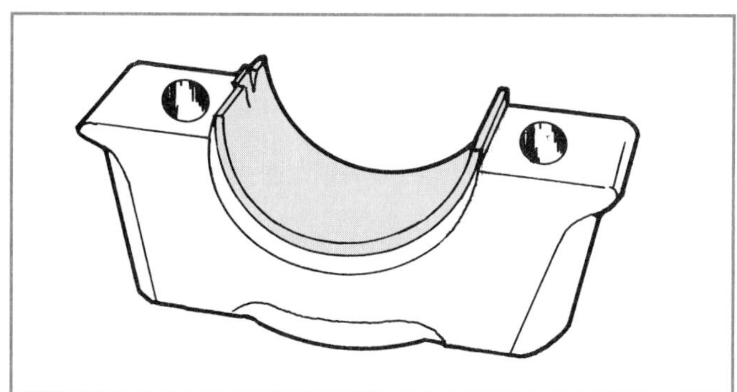

Figure 14-20. Bearing spread permits the bearing to be snapped into place.

Figure 14-21. The oil groove routes the oil through the hole in the bearing, which then flows to other areas in the engine. (Ford)

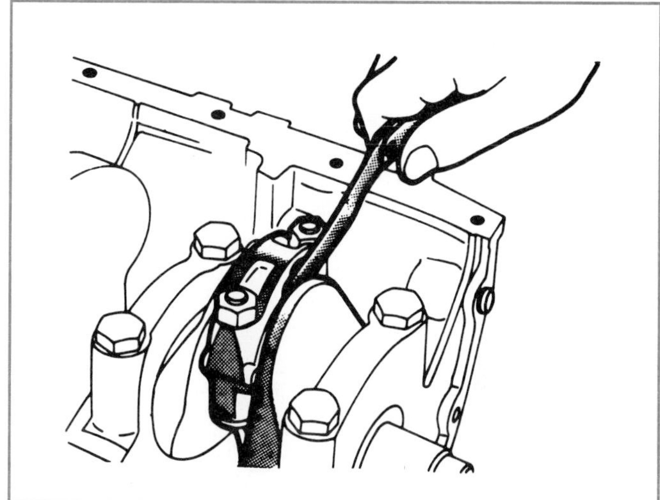

Figure 14-22. A feeler gauge is used to check side clearance.

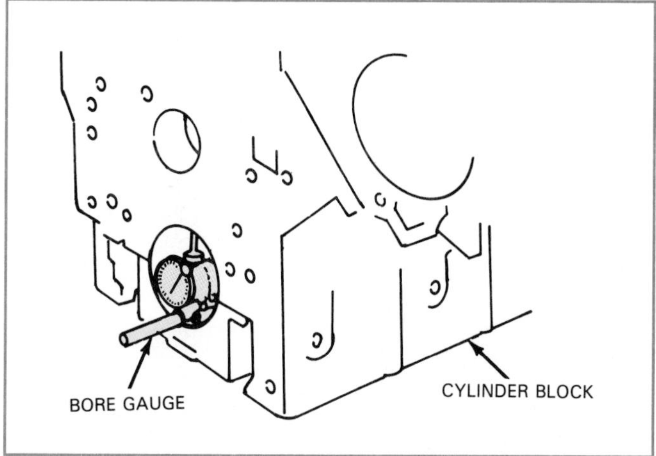

Figure 14-23. Using a dial indicator to measure out-of-round of main bearing bores. If any one bore exceeds .001″, the block must be align bored. (Chrysler)

bearing insert. To remove the upper half of the bearing insert, a "roll-out" pin is inserted into the oil hole of the crankshaft. The end of this pin protrudes slightly above the surface of the crankpin. When the crankshaft is rotated, the pin will force out the upper insert. A tool for this purpose can be fashioned from a cotter pin. See Figure 14-24.

The new bearing insert is slipped into position by hand. In some cases it may be necessary to use the "roll-out" pin to complete the installation. After installing the insert and bearing cap, the same procedure is followed with the other bearings.

Bearing caps are not tightened completely until all the bearing inserts are in position. Then the nuts are tightened to the specified torque. If the crankcase is not warped, the crankshaft is reground to a standard undersize for which bearing inserts are available.

If the crankshaft is scored and the crankcase warped, the engine must be removed and a complete reconditioning job must be performed. This includes regrinding the crankshaft, Figure 14-2, and ***align boring*** the bearing bores, Figure 14-25.

If the crankcase is warped, semifinished bearings can be installed in the crankcase. The bearings are align bored and then the crankshaft is reground to size to fit the bearings.

Before align boring the semifinished bearings, make sure caps are properly assembled and nuts tightened to the specified torque. Also, all oil passages should be plugged with substantial pieces of clean cloth to prevent chips from getting into the lubrication system.

When locating the ***boring bar***, great care must be exercised to ensure that the centerline of the finished bearings will be the correct distance from the top of the cylinder block, parallel with it, and at right angles to the cylinder bores.

In an engine built with a gear to drive the camshaft, the distance between the centerline of the camshaft and the bore of the main bearings must be very accurately maintained. Otherwise, the crankshaft and the camshaft gears will not mesh properly. More tolerance is permitted if the camshaft is driven by a chain or a belt.

After all boring operations are completed, all plugs must be removed from the oil passages and all chips cleaned from the interior of the crankcase. All inside edges of each bored surface should be hand chamfered with a scraper to about 1/64″.

In all bearing work, extreme accuracy and cleanliness are required. Particular attention must be paid to the areas contacting the backs of the bearing inserts, the bearing surfaces, and the interior of all oil lines and oil passages.

In case of a leaking rear main bearing, it is often possible to replace the bearing seal and bearing without removing the crankshaft. To do this, loosen all the main bearing caps slightly to lower the crankshaft. Then, remove the rear main bearing cap. With a small pin punch, start to drive out the seal. Grasp it with a pair of pliers and pull it out. To replace the upper part of the seal, first lubricate it with engine oil. Start it into the groove by hand and have the crankshaft turned until the seal slides in place.

The upper insert can be removed by first inserting a special tool or a bent cotter pin into the oil hole of the crankshaft. Then, as the crankshaft is turned, the pin will push out the bearing half. Start removing the seal with a punch, Figure 14-26, then pull it out with a pair of pliers.

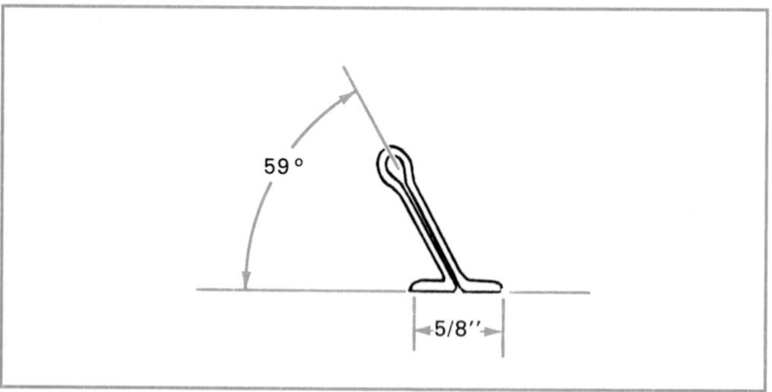

Figure 14-24. Bending a cotter pin so that it can be used to remove the upper main bearing inserts.

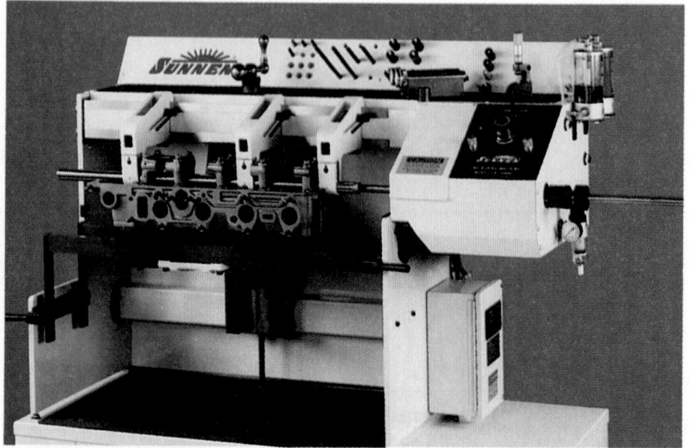

Figure 14-25. Align-boring machine. (Sunnen)

Connecting Rod Service

In addition to the proper fit of the large end of the connecting rod on the crankshaft and the proper condition of the piston pin at the other end of the rod, the alignment of the rod itself and the condition of the bearing bore in the big end of the rod must be checked.

Most V-type and opposed-cylinder engines have the cylinders slightly offset from each other to facilitate placement of the rod bearings on the crankshaft. It is also customary to offset the connecting rods, Figure 14-27, to place the power load as close to the main bearings as possible. This tends to reduce vibration of the crankshaft. On most engines, the connecting rods are marked on the same side.

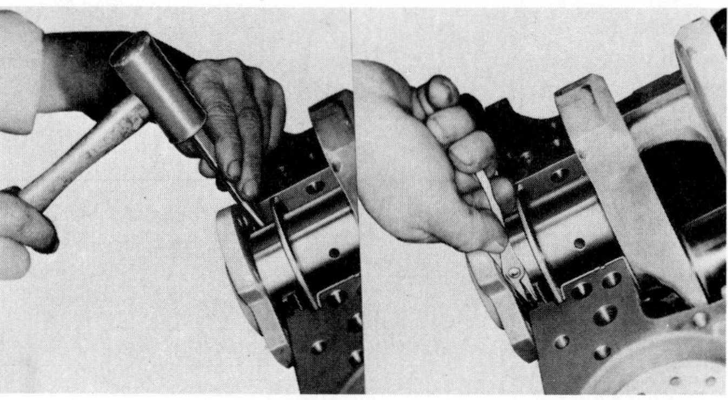

Figure 14-26. Removing rear main bearing seal while the crankshaft is in the engine.

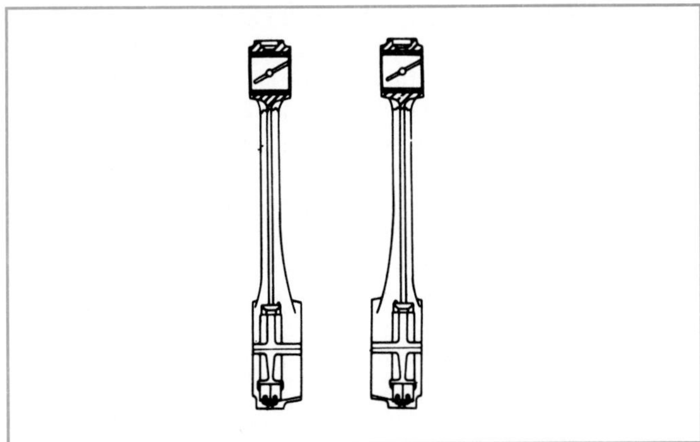

Figure 14-27. Connecting rods are offset. The short side is closest to the main bearing.

This should be watched during engine assembly. If unmarked, align prick-punch marks on the same side of each rod end and cap using one mark for cylinder No. 1, two marks for cylinder No. 2, etc.

The piston pin and crankshaft journal must be precisely parallel. If the piston pin is not parallel with the crankshaft, every force on the piston will cause it to try to slide endwise on the piston pin. This will cause ***piston slap*** in the cylinder, which is a knock created by the piston. The large end of the connecting rod will also have a tendency to knock.

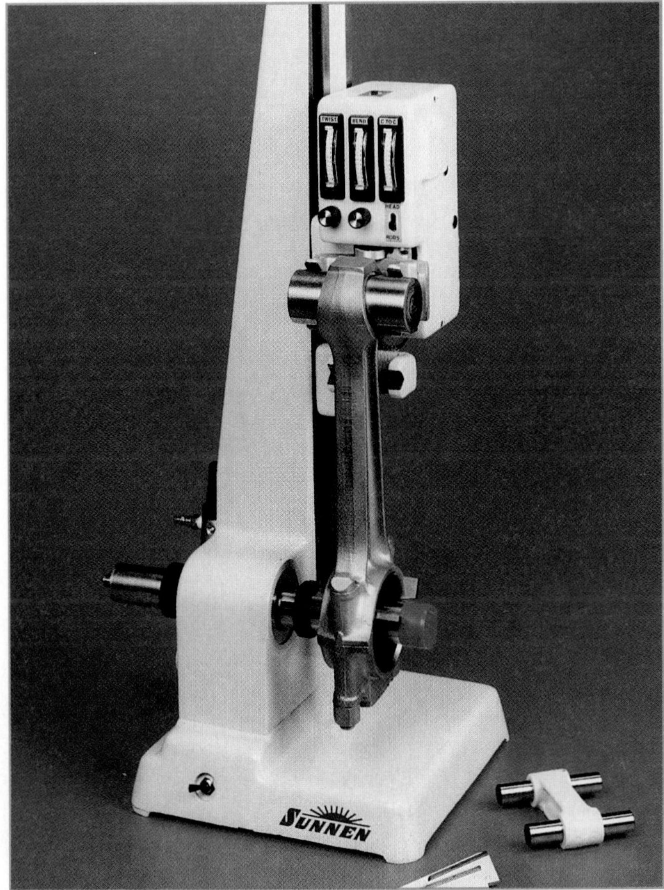

Figure 14-28. Checking the alignment of the connecting rod. If the connecting rod is twisted, it must be replaced. Never attempt to straighten a connecting rod. (Sunnen)

Special equipment is available for checking the connecting rods, Figure 14-28. This type of equipment checks the rods for twists and bends. Each connecting rod should be checked for proper alignment before it is installed in the engine. Many hard-to-locate noises in an engine originate from the misalignment of the connecting rods.

Each rod should be checked again for location after it is installed in the engine. The rod might have a double bend in it, which would not be noticed on the alignment tester. Such a double bend might leave the piston pin parallel with the crankshaft, yet the upper end of the rod might be close enough to one of the piston bosses to cause a knock.

Chapter 14–Review Questions

Write your answers on a separate sheet of paper. Do not write in this book.

1. Give three reasons for crankshaft wear.
2. Cracks in steel parts may be found with:
   (A) chemical equipment.
   (B) magnetic equipment.
   (C) hydraulic equipment.
   (D) All of the above.
3. An undersize crankshaft journal can be altered to become oversize. True or False?
4. Clearance between the crankshaft and the bearing in a splash-lubricated engine may be _____ than in a pressure-lubricated engine.
5. What happens if oil clearances are unequal in a pressure-oiling system?
6. Name two ways of measuring bearing clearance.
7. In general, the diametral clearance in a small engine main bearing should be:
   (A) .0005″ to .001″.
   (B) .001″ to .0015″.
   (C) .0015″ to .002″.
   (D) None of the above.
8. In general, endwise clearance for crankshafts should not exceed:
   (A) .004″.
   (B) .006″.
   (C) .008″.
   (D) None of the above.
9. A bearing bore should be trued up if it is out-of-round more than:
   (A) .0015″.
   (B) .0025″.
   (C) .005″.
   (D) None of the above.
10. Name two reasons for bearing crush.
11. The short side of the offset on the No. 1 connecting rod should be toward the _____ of the engine.
12. A piston pin can be properly fitted and parallel with the crankshaft and still cause a knock. True or False?
13. Bearing spread means:
    (A) The diameter of the bearing is wider than the bore.
    (B) The height of the bearing is higher than the cap.
    (C) Both A & B.
    (D) Neither A nor B.
14. Why must the piston pins be parallel with the crankshaft journals?

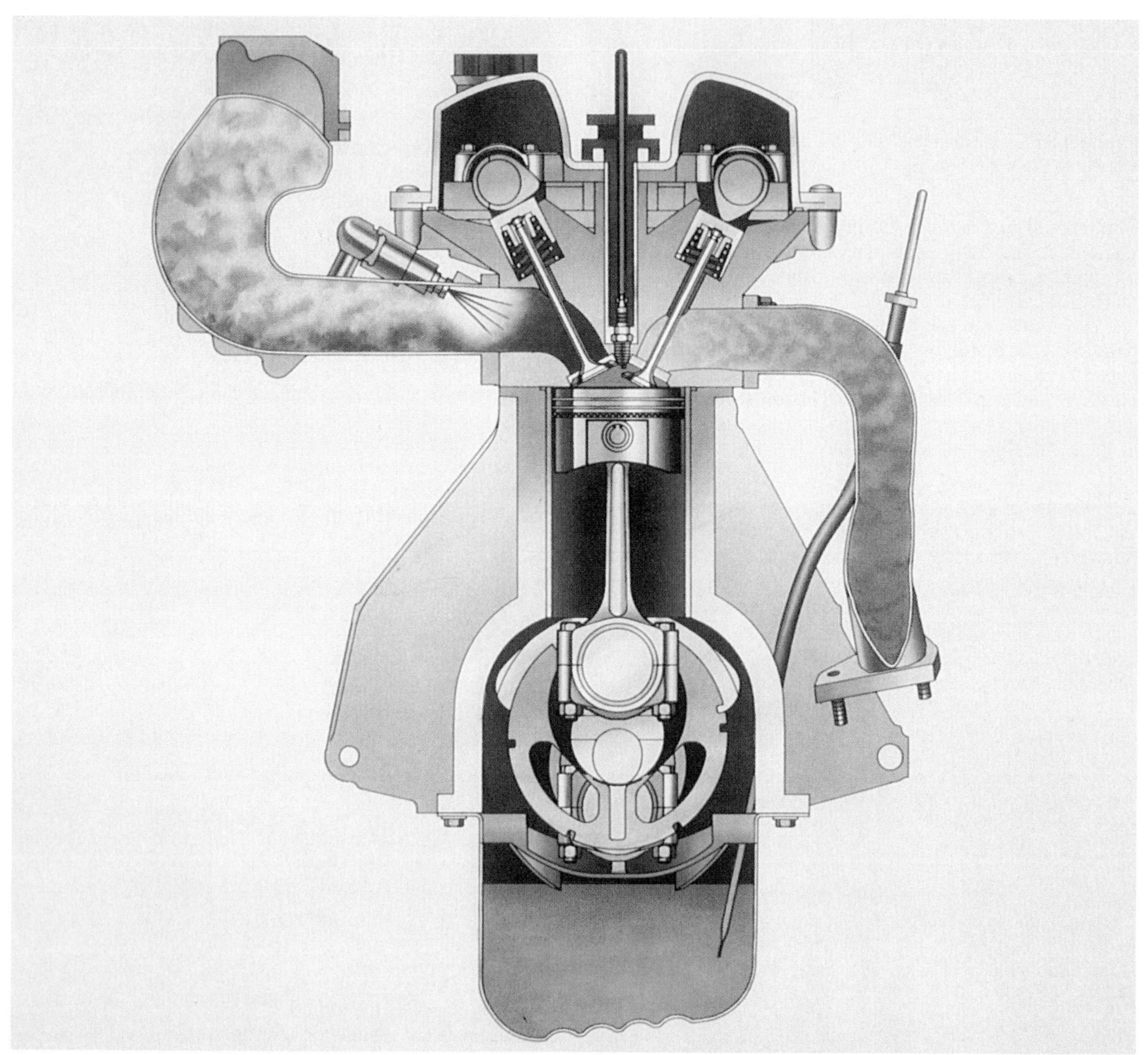

Cutaway of a dual overhead cam engine. Note the location of the camshafts and the valves. (Saturn)

Chapter 15
Valve Service

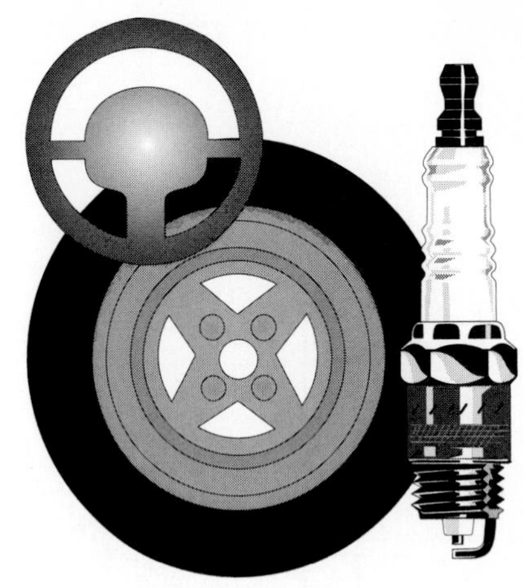

After studying this chapter, you will be able to:

- ❍ List the steps involved in a valve job.
- ❍ State the purpose of valve seals and list types of seals available.
- ❍ Explain why valve guides wear in a bellmouth shape and what can be done to correct this.
- ❍ Describe how, why, and when a valve rotator is used.
- ❍ Tell what check should be made on valve springs.

Valve Service

The condition of the valves has much to do with engine efficiency. ***Poppet valves*** lead a hard life, so it is not surprising that valve service is a frequently performed operation in automotive service shops.

Valve service was once a hand lapping procedure using an abrasive paste between the valve face and valve seat. This procedure was assumed to provide a gas-tight valve. Little attention or thought was given to valve seat width, heat dissipation, the concentricity of the valve with the seat, strength of valve springs, wear in valve guides, and all the other things that require attention on the modern high-speed engine.

Modern ***valve grinding*** is a true grinding process. Every part of the operation is governed by careful measurement with accurate test equipment. The first step after a valve has been removed and cleaned is to determine whether the valve can be reconditioned or whether it must be replaced. If the ***valve stem*** is scored, pitted, bent, or worn more than .002″, the valve should be discarded.

A dial gauge and V-blocks can be used to check the stem for straightness, Figure 15-1. For other visual checkpoints, see Figures 15-2 and 15-3. The stem diameter can be checked for wear with a micrometer, Figure 15-4.

Visual inspection, for example, may disclose a seriously warped ***valve head,*** a cracked ***valve face,*** or lack of ***margin.*** If the face is burned, badly warped, or worn to a thin margin, the valve is discarded. See Figure 15-3. If the valve appears to be in good condition, it is placed in a special grinding machine known as a valve ***refacer,*** and a new surface is ground on the face at the proper angle. See Figure 15-5.

Most valve faces are cut at an angle of 45° to the stem. An angle of 30° is also used. In either case, a ***slight interference angle,*** about 1/2° to 1°, may be cut on either the valve face or valve seat to improve the seating ability, Figure 15-6. However, it is invariably cut on the valve face as valve refacers can be adjusted to any desired angle.

Figure 15-1. Using a dial indicator to check valve stem straightness. If dial deviates .002″ while rolling the stem, the valve must be replaced.

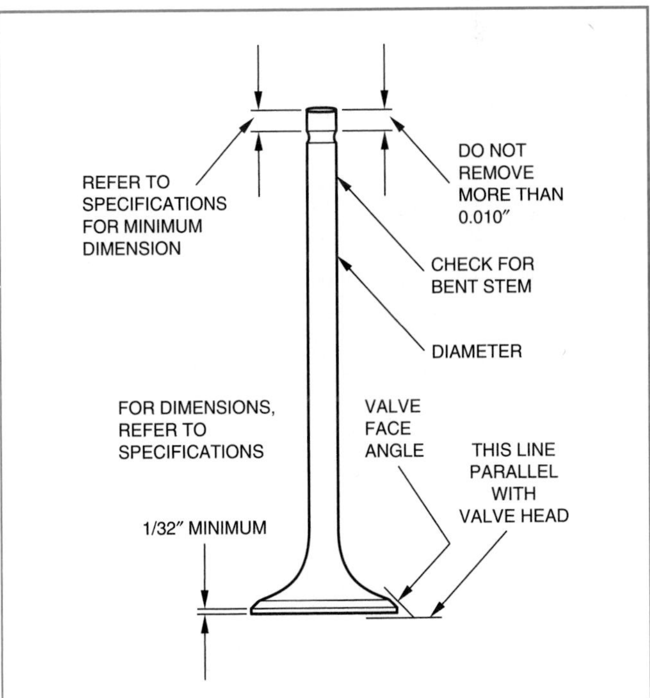

Figure 15-2. Points to check on a valve for wear. If the valve stem has even the slightest ridge or groove, the valve must be replaced.

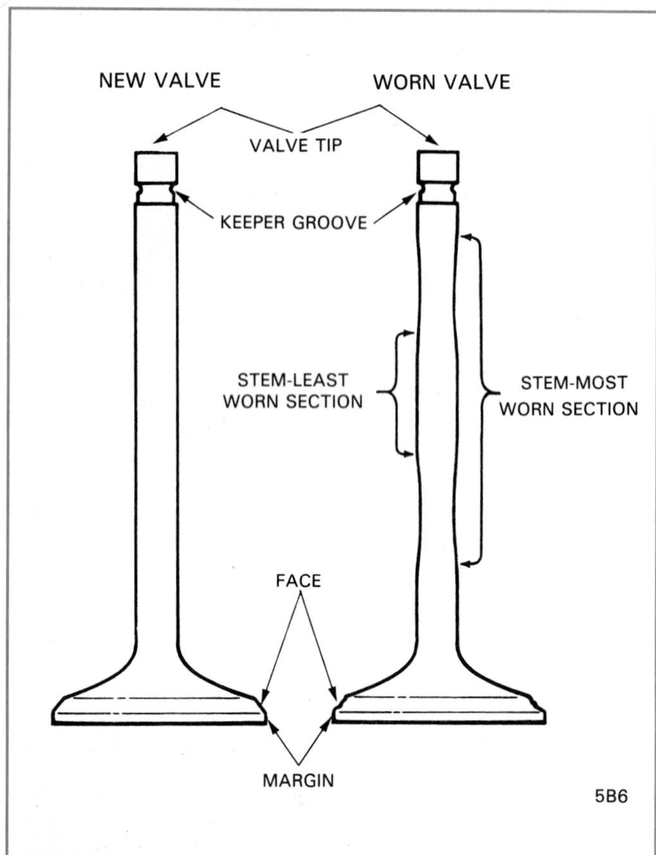

Figure 15-3. Examples of a good valve and a worn valve. (Oldsmobile)

Figure 15-4. The valve stem must be measured in several different locations to determine wear. If wear at any one point is .002″ or greater, the valve must be discarded.

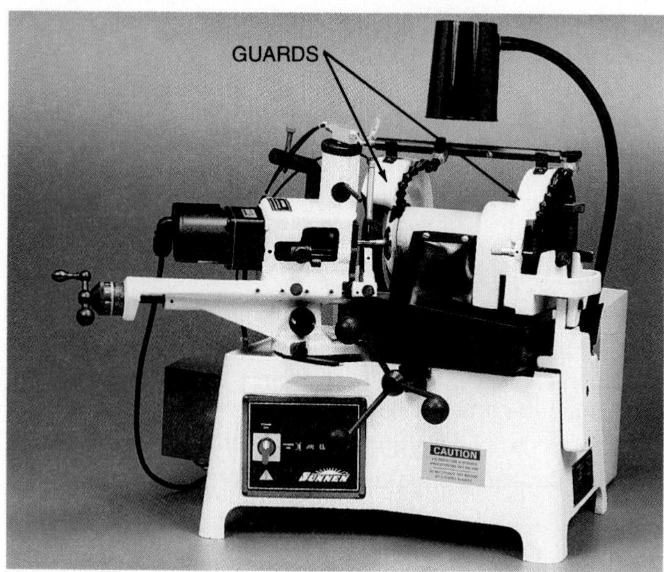

Figure 15-5. If the valve is in good shape, the face of the valve can be resurfaced. (Sunnen)

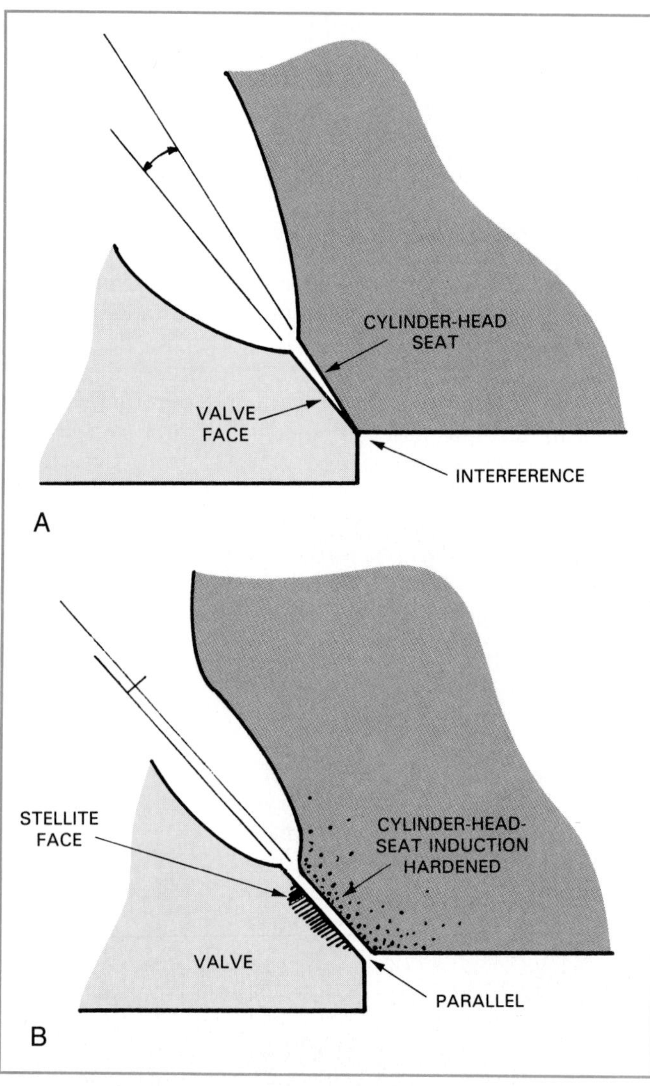

Figure 15-6. A–Interference angle is used when engines burn leaded fuels. This chips the deposits off of the valve face. B–With engines that burn unleaded fuels, an interference angle is not needed or wanted. This is because the unleaded fuels burn hotter and cleaner. (Oldsmobile)

Valve Seat Reconditioning

The ***valve seat*** in the block or head can be resurfaced with the aid of special grinders. First of all, it is necessary to position the tool so it will be located to cut the seat concentric with the valve stem guide, Figure 15-7. This is difficult to do if the guide is worn. Guides should be replaced or reconditioned if worn bellmouthed.

After reconditioning the valve guides, the valve seat surface is cut or ground to the proper angle, Figure 15-8. This cutting or grinding must produce a smooth, true surface if the valve is to seal properly. It cannot be true if the seat is not concentric with the valve stem. A method of testing this with a dial gauge is shown in Figure 15-9. The seat should be concentric within .001″ of the guide.

Valve seats that are too narrow will not dissipate the heat properly. If too wide, they will encourage carbon to adhere to them. In the absence of factory specifications, a seat 1/16″ wide is usually satisfactory. If the seat is wider than this, the first operation will be to narrow it by cutting an acute angle under the seat and an obtuse angle above the seat, Figure 15-10. This is done with special grinders made for the purpose.

To check the valve seat contact area, coat the face of the valve with ***Prussian blue.*** Insert the valve into the seat and rotate it with light pressure. Remove the valve and examine the face. A ring of bare metal should be left showing on the valve face. This ring should be approximately 1/16″ from the margin, as this is the point at which the valve face meets the seat. If measurement is other than 1/16″, the seat will have to be recut.

Valve Seat Inserts

Hardened ***valve seat inserts*** are ordinarily used in air-cooled automobile engines having aluminum cylinder heads. Induction-hardened valve seats are also used in many late-model engines having cast iron heads, Figure 15-6. If the insert is badly worn or burned, it may be easier to replace it than to recondition it. These seats are made of hard, heat-resisting metal and are refaced by grinding with special grinders.

If the seat is the old screw-in type, it is a simple matter to unscrew the old seat and screw in the new one. The seating surface is ground after the insert is in place. The pressed-in, or shrunk-in, insert is usually held tightly in place by rolling or peening the metal around the edge of the insert after it is in place.

Since it is sometimes difficult to clean up the peening enough to allow inserts to be pulled, they are usually broken for removal. Whether the old insert is pulled or broken out, it is essential that the hole for the insert be round and

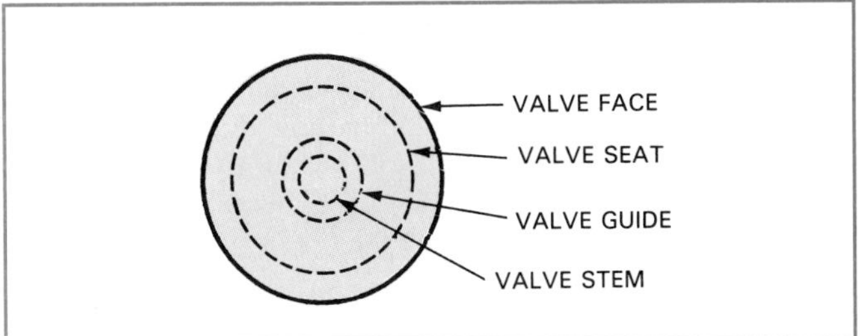

Figure 15-7. The valve guide must be perfectly round so that valve face can close squarely on the seat. (Sioux)

Figure 15-8. Grinding the valve seats is the last step in a valve grinding operation. (Sunnen)

Figure 15-9. Checking valve seat concentricity. A dial gauge is used to check that the seat is centered to the valve guide after grinding the seats.

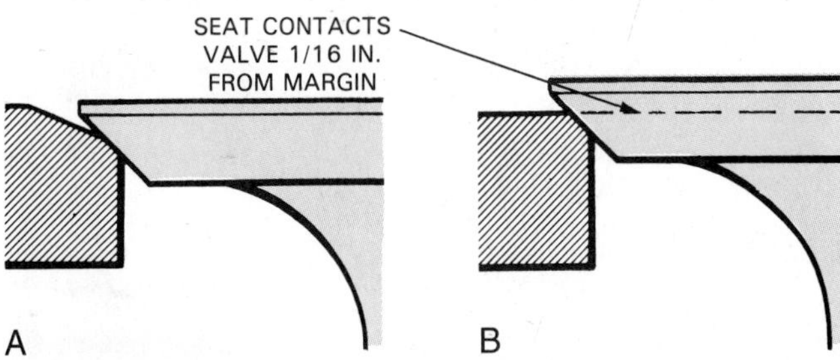

Figure 15-10. Valve seat contact. A–The valve is sitting too far into the head. The seat must be narrowed using either a 15° or 20° stone, or carbon will collect on the seat. B–The valve face should contact seat 1/16″ from the valve margin. (Sioux)

true. If the insert does not fully bottom in the hole, or if it does not fit tightly all around the hole, there will be poor heat transfer from the insert to the head or block. Then, of course, the insert will run hotter than it should.

For this reason, the inserts are usually sized to provide an interference fit. That is, the insert is one or two thousandths of an inch larger in diameter than the hole into which it is installed. To avoid the stresses imposed in pressing them in place, the inserts are often shrunk for insertion.

For service installation, the inserts may be placed in a deep freeze for a few hours or packed in dry ice for a few minutes. Either of these procedures will shrink them sufficiently for easy insertion. When frozen, the inserts must be handled carefully and quickly, since they are quite brittle and will crack or split easily. After insertion, the metal around the insert may be lightly rolled or peened over the top outside edge of the insert to help hold it firmly in place. The final step is to grind the valve seat true with the valve guide.

Valve Stem Guide Service

Older engines have ***pressed-in valve guides.*** Now, engines are built with the valve stem in direct contact with a hole bored in the cylinder head. Heat dissipation is better where pressed-in guides are not used. Wear in the ***integral guides*** means honing the holes out larger and then using valves with oversize stems. Pressed-in guides are made of cast iron. Bronze is also used because of the superior wearing characteristics and more rapid heat dissipating ability.

Press-in guides are often identical for the exhaust and intake valves. In other cases, the exhaust and intake guides are not the same. See Figure 15-11. In still another case, the guides are identical, but the intake guides are installed upside down from the exhaust guides. Some exhaust guides are cut off shorter in the port opening, and others are counterbored in the port end to reduce the tendency for carbon to accumulate in the guide.

Carbon does accumulate in the guide bore and on the stem of exhaust valves. This causes the valves to stick partly open or to slow down in action. The tendency for carbon to accumulate increases as the exhaust valve stem and guide wear, because more hot gas blows by between the worn components. Wear on the intake stem and guide is equally undesirable, because it permits air to be drawn in through the clearance to dilute the air and gasoline mixture. Under such conditions, it is impossible to obtain a satisfactory fuel mixture.

Also, oil from the valve chamber may be sucked in between valve and guide to increase oil consumption and carbon-up the engine. This oil leakage is sometimes pronounced on overhead valve engines, as oil is pumped up on the rocker arms. To discourage this tendency, a special cutter is available to cut a bevel on the end of untapered valve guides.

It is customary to place seals either on the valve stem or in the guide on overhead valve engines to exclude excess oil. Several types are shown in Figures 15-12 through 15-14.

Another undesirable result of excessive valve guide wear is that it may permit the valve to wobble enough to cause it to ride to one side of the seat, Figure 15-15. Quite naturally, this interferes with proper seating and sealing of the valve and promotes wear. It is customary to replace the valve guides and/or valves whenever more than .005″ clearance for a small valve or more than .006″ clearance for a large valve exists between valve stem and the guide. One method of measuring clearance is shown in Figure 15-16.

Before any measurement is made, the valve stem must be cleaned and polished. Additionally, the valve stem guide must be thoroughly cleaned of carbon deposits. Special tools are made for cleaning carbon out of valve guides, Figure 15-17. The measurement for clearance should be made with the valve slightly off the seat as shown in Figure

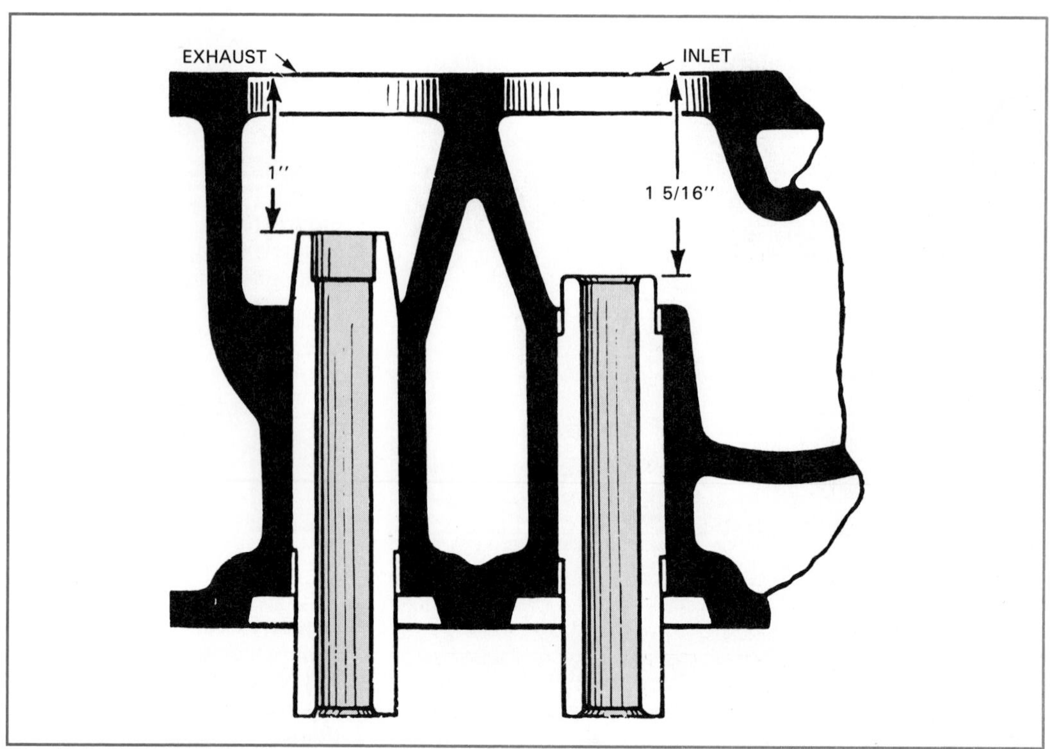

Figure 15-11. The exhaust valve guide extends farther into the port than the intake valve guide.

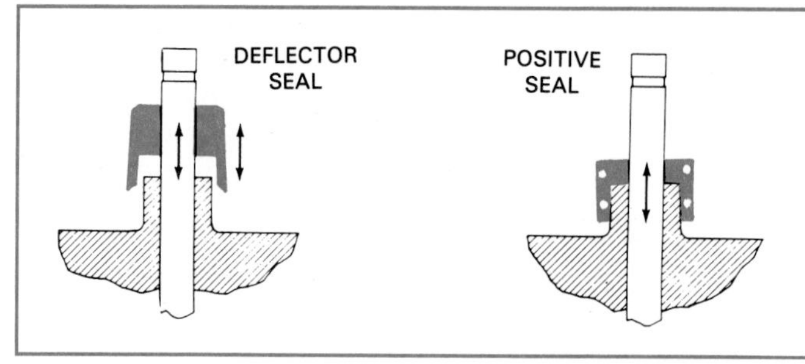

A

B

C

Figure 15-12. Valve seals. A–The deflector, or umbrella, valve seal grasps the valve stem and moves up and down with the valve stem. A positive valve seal remains fixed to the valve guide boss. As valve stem moves up and down, the seal wipes excess oil from the stem. B–Umbrella valve seals derive their name from their shape. C–Positive valve seals have two wire rings around the circumference of the seal. Note that a sleeve is temporarily installed on the valve stem. This sleeve aids in the installation of the seal and prevents the seal from being torn during installation. Once the seal is installed, the sleeve is removed from the valve stem. (Fel-Pro Inc.)

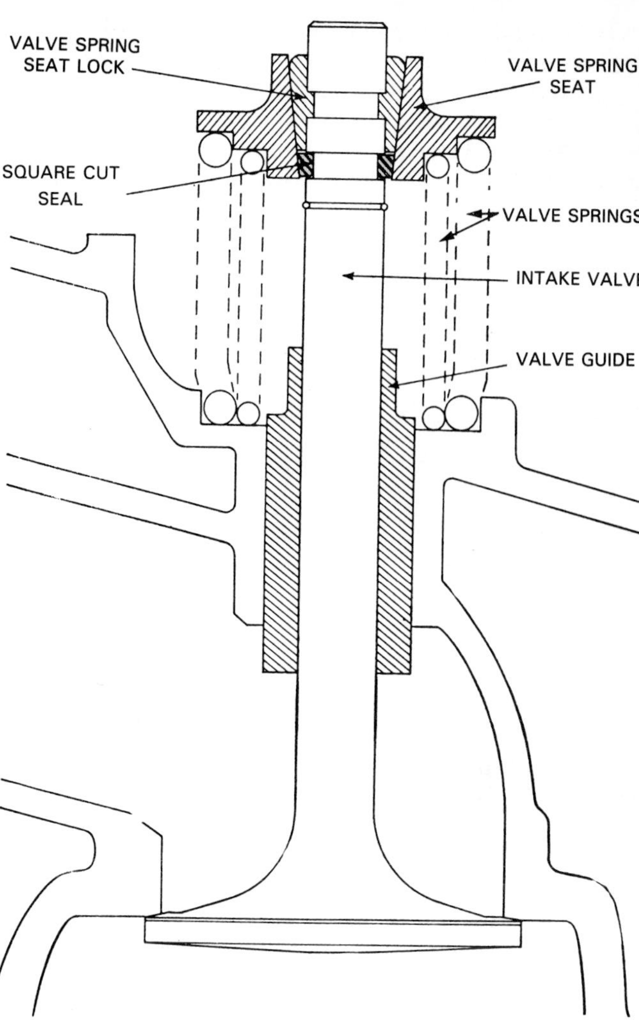

Figure 15-13. Some valve stems have a groove machined below the keeper grooves. A square cut seal is then placed in this groove and acts as a valve guide seal.

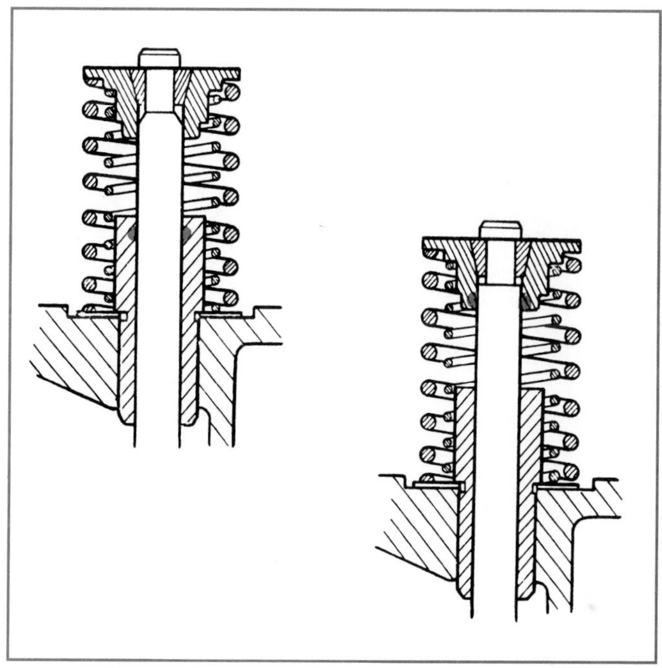

Figure 15-14. Some older engines use an 0-ring as a valve guide seal.

15-16. The valve spring must also be removed before making the measurement.

One repair method for valve guide troubles that does not involve replacement of the guides is to displace the metal inside the valve guide bore by rolling a spiral groove through it. See Figure 15-18. This decreases the inside diameter slightly and, at the same time, forms a continuous groove for oil to gather and act as a seal. A special tool is made for this purpose. The guide is then reamed to the desired diameter.

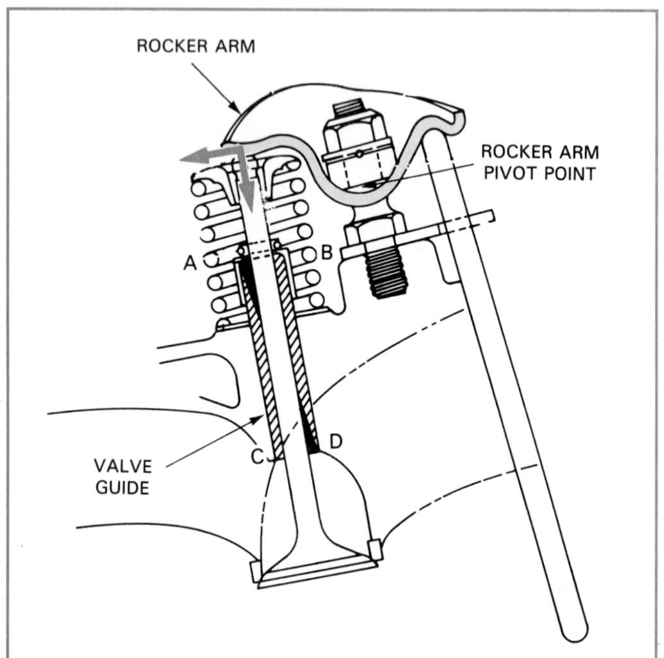

Figure 15-15. As the rocker arm moves downward, it opens the valve while forcing the stem sideways. This causes the valve stem to be pushed against the guide at points A and D. It also prevents oil from lubricating these areas, which causes the guide to wear at points A and D. Rocker arm action causes bellmouth wear of the guides. Note that at points B and C, the valve stem is forced away from the guide. The valve guides must be reconditioned before grinding the valve seats. (Oldsmobile)

Figure 15-16. Checking valve guide wear. If the valve guide is worn excessively, it will allow too much oil into the combustion chamber. (Chrysler)

When valve guides of the press-in type are replaced, it is important to position them properly in the block or head. See Figure 15-19. The car manufacturer specifies the proper position with regard to some accessible surface from which measurement can be made. An example of this is shown in Figure 15-20.

After the guides are pressed in place, it is usually necessary to ream them to the proper size and provide clearance for heat expansion of the valve stem. Special reamers are made for this purpose, Figure 15-21. This operation must be performed carefully so that the hole will be straight and true with a good surface. Exhaust valve stems require more clearance in the guides than intake valve stems. Fit intake valves with .001″-.003″ clearance and exhaust valves with .002″-.004″ clearance, depending on the size of the stem. To reduce reconditioning time, special equipment has been designed to recondition valve guides and seats.

Valve Spring Service

Valve springs seldom receive the attention they deserve. They are an important part of the engine and have much to do with the engine performance. They are seldom replaced unless they are broken. However, they should be replaced when not up to specifications. They are subjected to millions of cycles of high-speed operation under shock conditions.

The valves are opened with lightning-like speed by the action of the cam, and the springs close the valves just as fast as they are opened. If the spring is weak and does not hold the lifter in contact with the cam, noise will be created and the valve, spring, lifter, and cam will be subjected to hammer-like blows that cause metal fatigue. Many broken

Figure 15-17. Prior to checking the valve guides for wear, clean them so that an accurate reading can be obtained.

Figure 15-18. Knurling can recondition the guide if wear is less than .006″.

valves result from shock caused by sticking stems, weak valve springs, or excessive tappet clearance.

The car manufacturer provides specifications on the free length of the spring, and the pressure (in pounds) that the spring should exert when it is compressed to a measured length, Figure 15-22. Special tools are available for measuring the length and strength of the valve spring. Valve springs are simple coil wire springs. They should not be expected to last forever.

Valve springs should be square on each end. Otherwise, they will have a tendency to pull the valve stem to one side and cause undue wear on the valve stem and guide. Springs can be checked for squareness and free length as shown in Figure 15-23. When the coils of the spring are wound closer together at one end than at the other, the close coils are to be placed next to the engine block or head. See Figure 15-24. This uneven coiling is done to lessen the tendency of the spring to vibrate at high speeds.

Another method of reducing vibration is to install dampers. Still another method is to taper the spring or to use two lighter springs, one within the other, instead of one heavy spring. See Figure 15-24. The two springs are usually wound in opposite directions. Another method to control

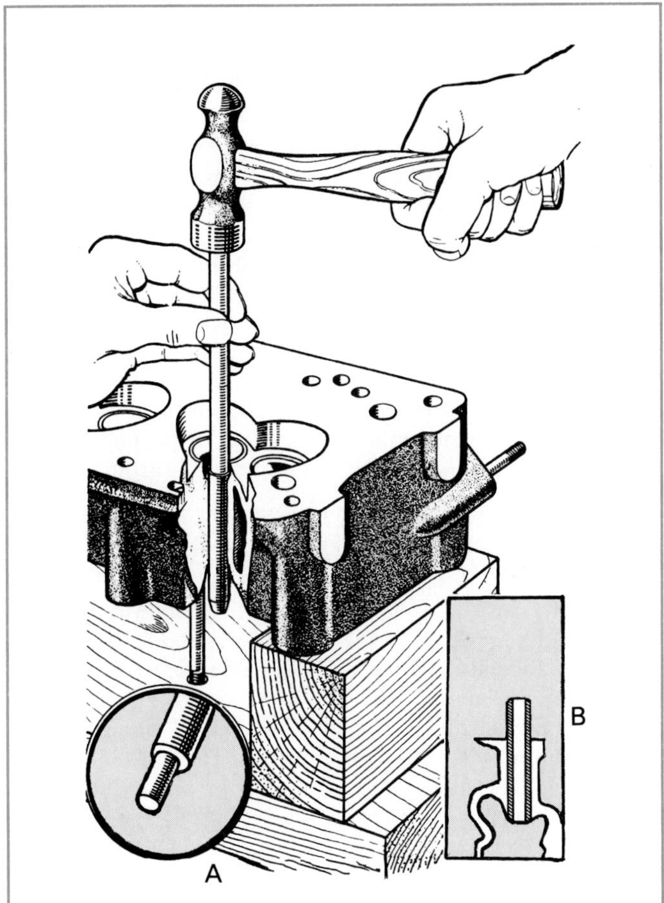

Figure 15-19. Removing valve guide inserts. A–Pilot end of driver. B–Dimension that guide must be installed above the head.

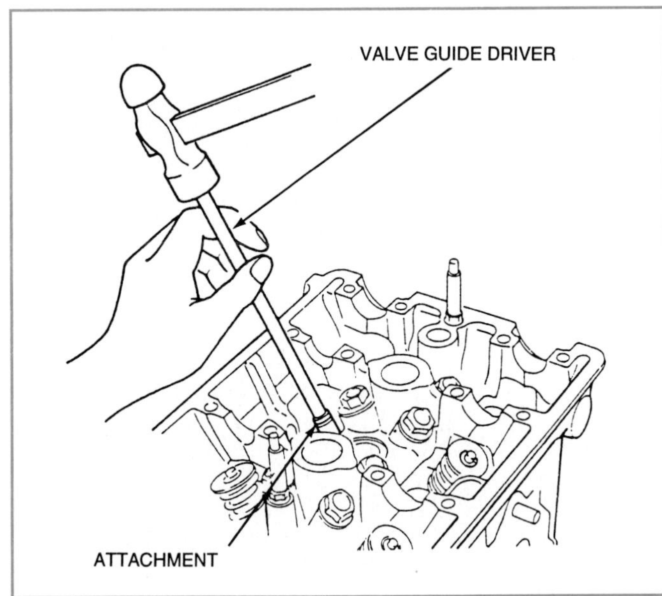

Figure 15-20. Valve guide inserts must be positioned accurately. (Honda)

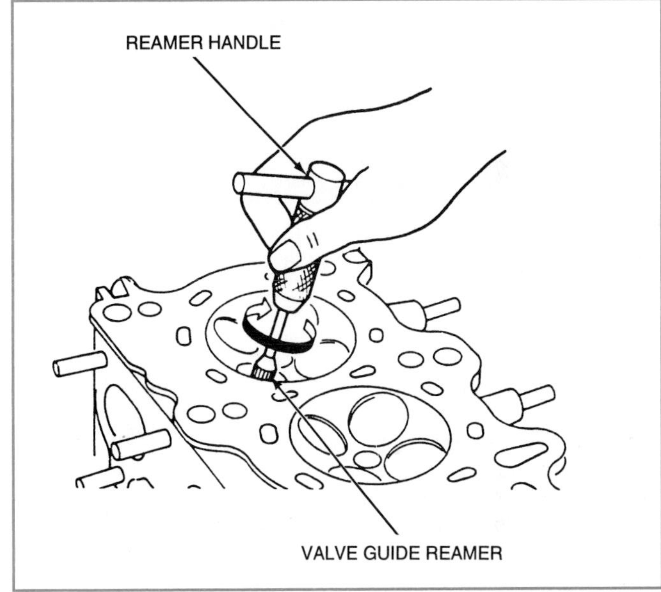

Figure 15-21. Reaming to a larger size is another method of reconditioning valve guides. New valves with oversize valve stems must then be used. (Honda)

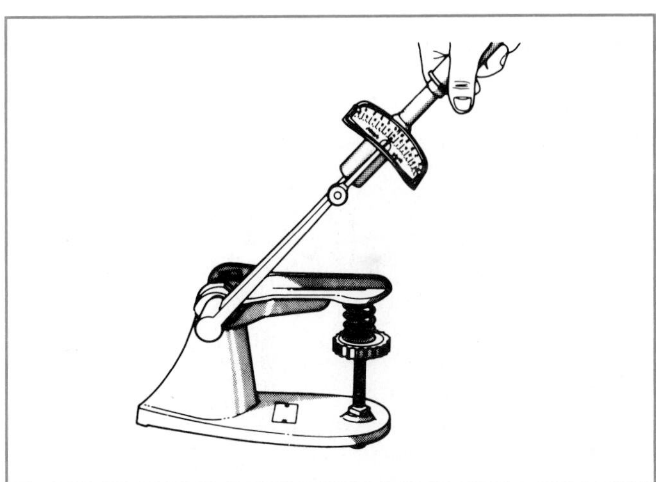

Figure 15-22. Testing the tension of the valve spring. If the valve springs are too weak, the valves will float at high rpm's. (Chrysler)

vibrations of the valve spring is to use a stiffer spring. Whatever construction is used, it is important to check the springs whenever they are out and to replace them when they are not up to specifications.

Periodic replacement is also recommended to prevent unexpected failure. Valve springs often become ***etched*** when the valve chamber is subject to corrosive vapors. Some valve chambers are not well ventilated and steam- or moisture-containing acids formed from combustion will collect and cause flecks of rust to form on the valve springs. This etching is likely to cause the spring to break, Figure 15-25.

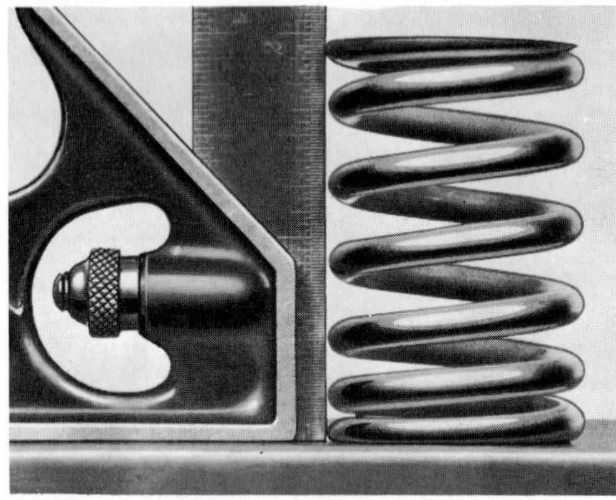

Figure 15-23. Valve springs must be square, or the pressure will be directed to one area of the valve face.

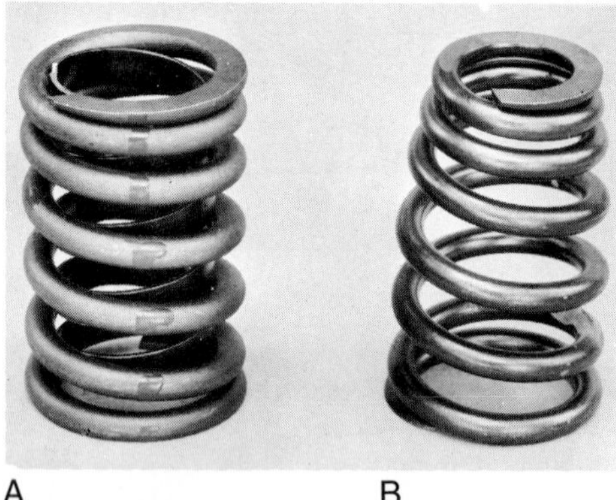

Figure 15-24. A–Valve spring has internal coil spring to dampen harmonic vibrations. B–Tapered valve spring also dampens harmonic vibrations.

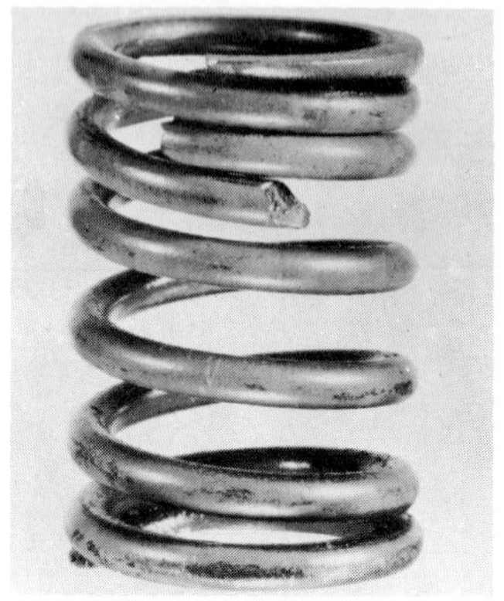

Figure 15-25. This broken valve spring was caused by acid vapor that was not venting from the crankcase.

This corrosive action is similar to the corrosion that causes pits and rust to eat into valve stems. On the valve stems, it leads to wear. A broken valve spring on an overhead valve engine may permit the valve to drop into the cylinder, damaging a piston or cylinder head.

Valve Spring Retainers

Valve spring keepers, or locks, are usually of the split-cone, horseshoe, or flat rectangular key type. They fit into an appropriate slot in the end of the valve stem. Figure 15-26 shows the split-cone type in position. A washer called the ***spring retainer*** fits over these keepers, and the tension of the spring bearing on the retainer holds the keepers in place.

Removal is accomplished by holding the valve stationary while the spring is compressed enough to allow the retainer to be raised from the keepers. See Figures 15-27 to 15-29. The keepers are then removed and the valve spring released. This allows the spring and retainer to be removed. Valves should never be mixed up when removed unless it is known that new valves or guides are to be installed. A valve should always be replaced in the guide from which it was removed.

Valve Spring Installed Height

As the result of valve and seat reconditioning, the valve will be recessed farther into the cylinder head. Consequently, the valve spring will not be compressed as much as it normally would be. In other words, the ***installed height*** of the spring would be increased. This causes the same symptoms as weak valve springs. The installed height is measured from the surface of the spring pad to the undersize of the spring retainer, Figure 15-30. If the height is

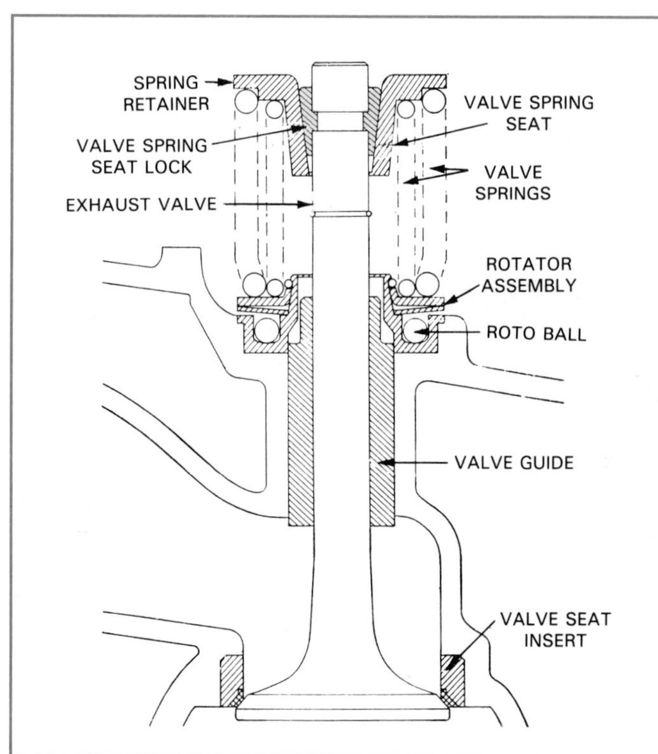

Figure 15-26. A tapered valve keeper, or lock, fits into the machined groove in the valve stem.

Figure 15-27. A valve spring compressor must be used to overcome valve spring pressure. Once the valve spring is compressed, the valve keepers can be removed or installed. (Fel-Pro Inc.)

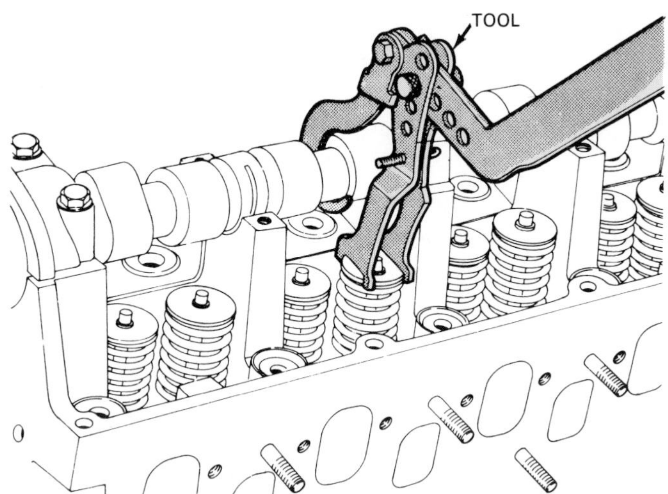

Figure 15-28. Compressing valve springs on an overhead camshaft engine. (Chrysler)

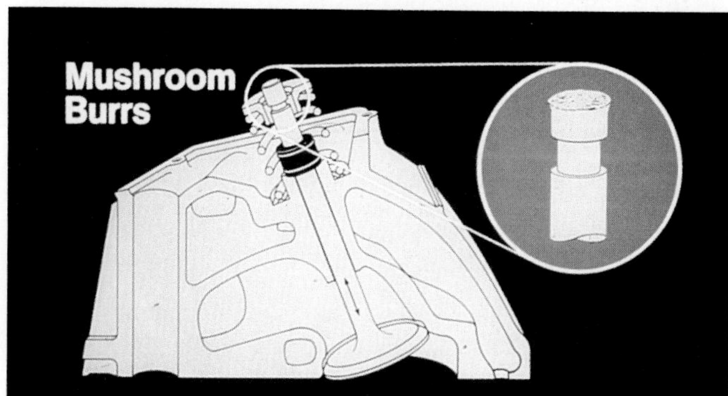

Figure 15-29. After removing the valve springs, the valve tip must be dressed with a file to remove the mushroomed burr. After this is done, the valve can be removed from the head. If the tip is not dressed and the valve is forced through the guide, the guide will break. The mushroomed tip is caused by rocker arm action. (Fel-Pro Inc.)

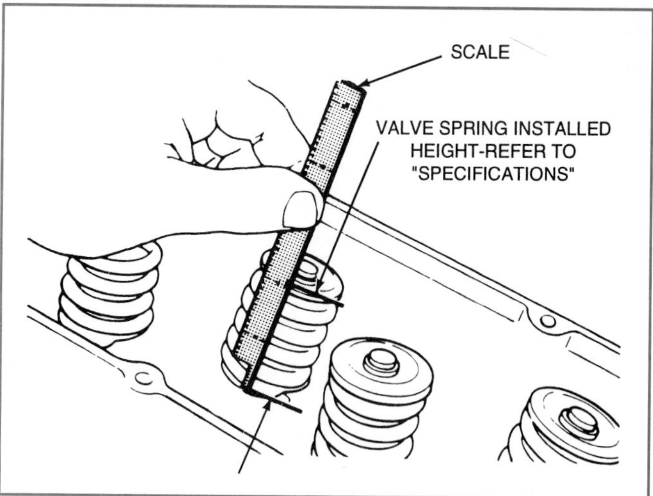

Figure 15-30. Measuring valve spring installed height should be the last measurement made in a valve job. If the height is greater than the specification, shims must be installed under the valve spring to reduce the height.

greater than specifications, shims will have to be installed under the valve spring.

Valve Rotators

Some retainers are more complicated and are intended to permit or encourage the valve to rotate slightly with regard to the seat. The purpose is to provide a longer lasting seal between the valve and the valve seat. Rotation of the valve will discourage the formation of carbon deposits and help prevent valve warpage.

Some of these devices release the valve from the valve spring tension at one point in the cycle of operation so that it is free to rotate slightly. With this type of device, it is important to maintain the clearances between the stem and the cup and between the cup and the retainer within specified limits. See Figure 15-31. If the clearance between stem end and cap is too little, the end of the valve stem is ground

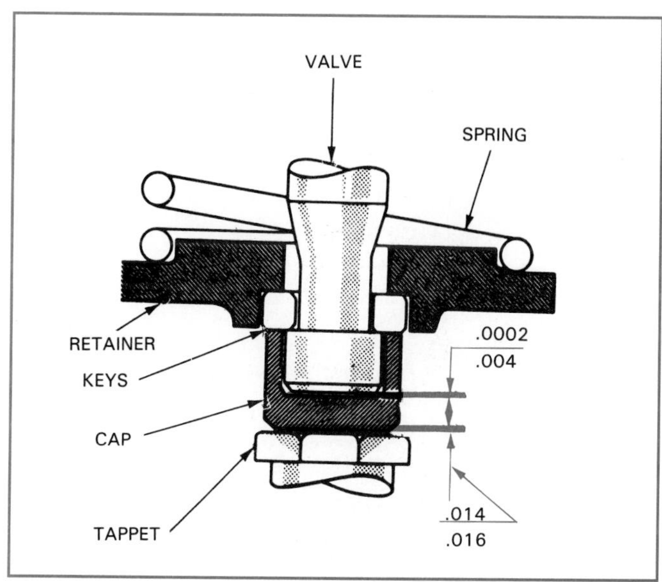

Figure 15-31. With this type of valve rotator, clearance must be maintained between the valve and the cap.

off as needed. If the clearance is too great, the skirt of the cap is ground off as required. A special tool is available for measuring the clearance accurately. See Figure 15-32.

Valve rotators impart a positive rotational effort to the valve once during each cycle of operation. One such device is illustrated in Figure 15-33.

Valve rotators keep the seat and valve face clean and, therefore, help maintain emission control. Valve rotators also minimize sticking and wear between the guide and the stem.

The valve rotators can easily be checked to see if they are functioning properly. To check rotator operation, examine the valve tip, Figure 15-34 (where the rocker arm contacts the valve). If the rotator is working properly, there will be no indentations on the valve tip. Late-model engines are not equipped with valve rotators. If rotators were used on an engine that burned unleaded fuel (or LP gas), valve face wear would be accelerated.

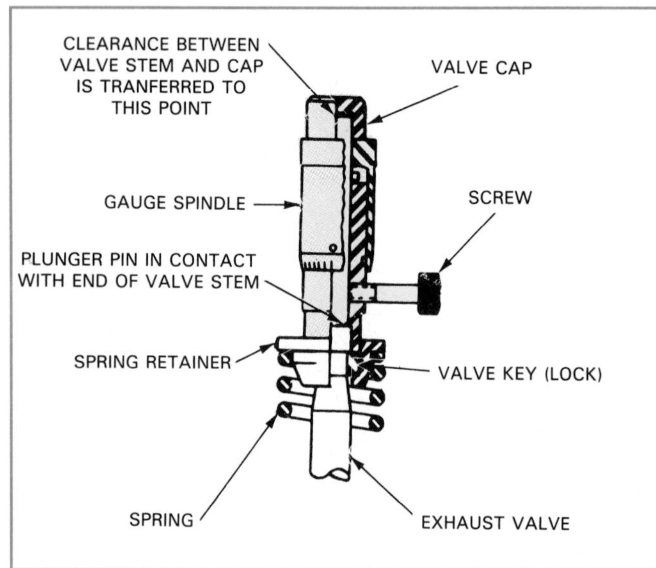

Figure 15-32. A special gauge is used to measure clearance.

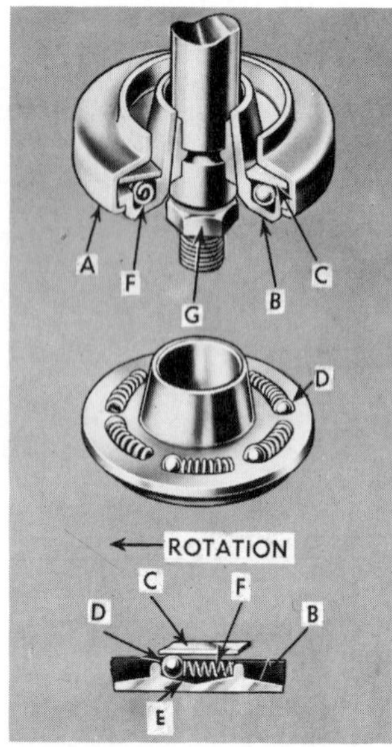

Figure 15-33. A positive-type valve rotator causes rotation of the valve when the ball moves to the valley of the ramp. A–Housing. B–Retainer. C–Cupped washer. D–Ball. E–Ram. F–Spring. G–Valve lifter.

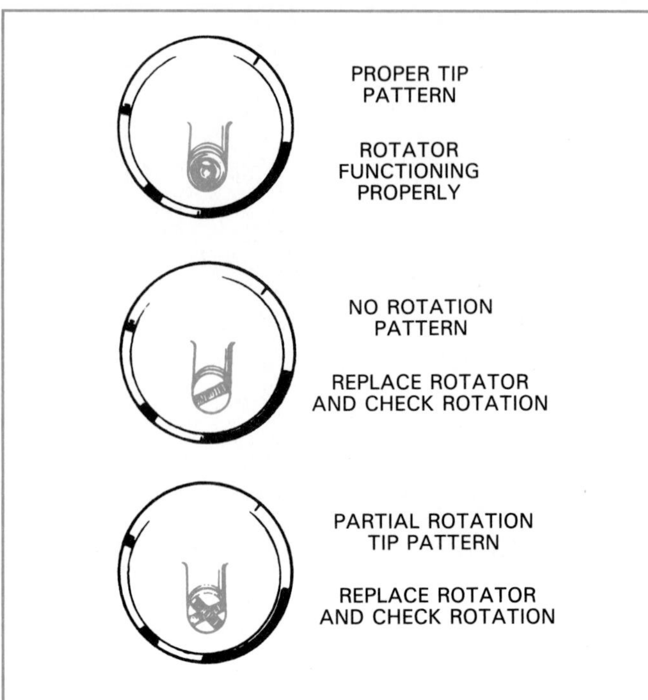

Figure 15-34. Wear patterns on the valve tip indicate whether or not the rotator is working. (Cadillac)

Valve Operating Mechanisms

It was customary in older engines to mesh the camshaft drive gear directly with the crankshaft gear or, in the case of chain drive, to locate the sprockets close to each other. See Figures 15-35 and 15-36.

The cog belt used on an overhead camshaft, Figures 15-37 to 15-39, is made of reinforced fiberglass. While this is a relatively long drive, no difficulties have resulted from stretching. The material of which the belt is made is heat resistant and oil resistant. It is inherently silent in operation, requires no lubrication, and absorbs the shock of opening and closing the valves.

Where long chains are used to operate camshafts, the problem of slack, Figure 15-40, or lost motion, presents

Figure 15-35. Timing gear installation.

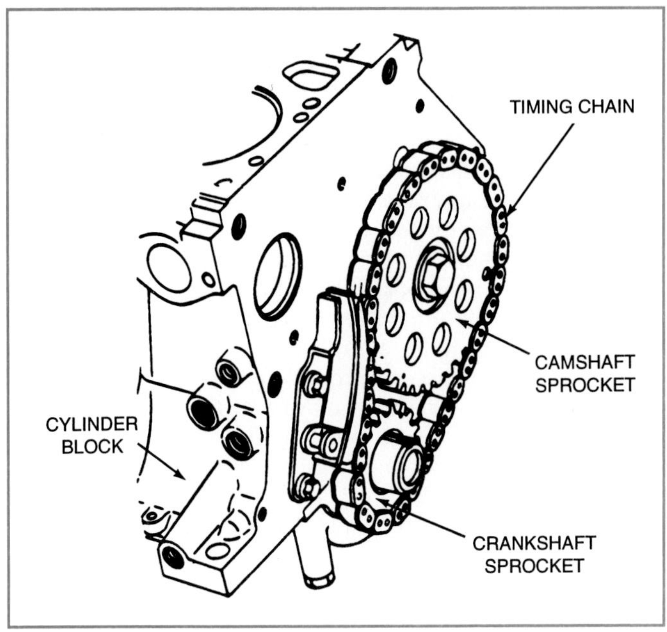

Figure 15-36. Timing chain on an inline engine. (Ford)

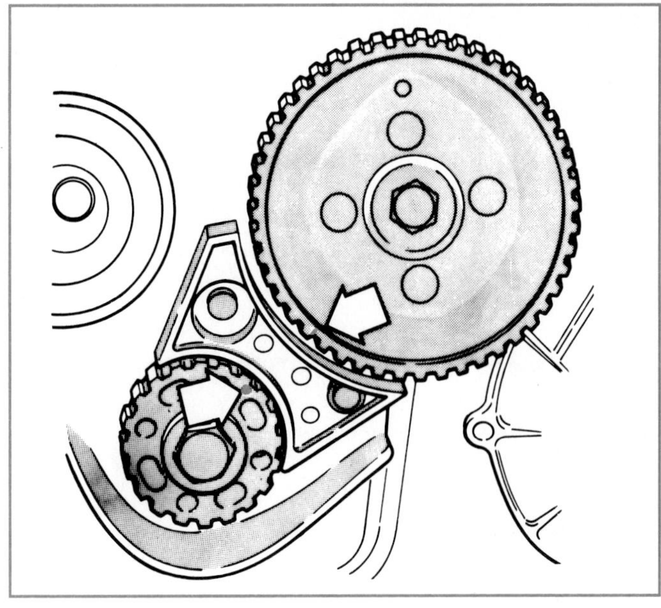

Figure 15-38. The intermediate and crankshaft sprockets must first be aligned properly.

Figure 15-37. A timing belt on a dual overhead camshaft engine. (Ford)

Figure 15-39. After aligning the intermediate and crankshaft sprockets, the camshaft sprocket must be positioned properly before installing the timing belt.

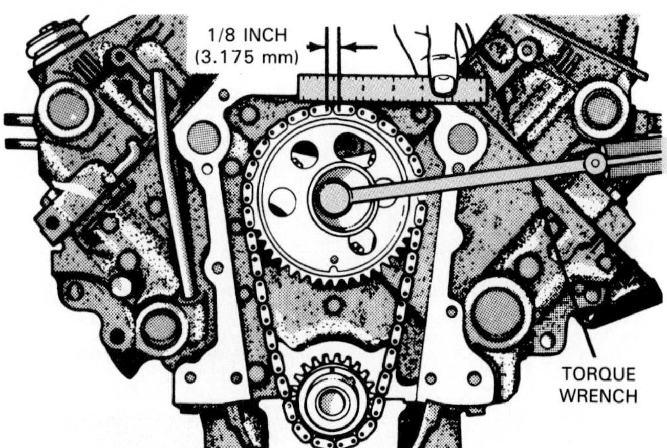

Figure 15-40. Using a torque wrench, apply 15 ft./lb. if the heads are removed or 30 ft./lb. if the heads are bolted to the engine. If the timing chain moves more than indicated, replace the chain.

itself. Valve timing must be precise. Sloppy motion cannot be tolerated. Several devices, such as automatic tensioners, have been used to control slack.

The camshaft and camshaft drive are only part of the mechanism used to operate the valves. To continue the study of valve action and timing, consider the operation of parts such as lifters, push rods, rocker arms, etc. Each has something to do with valve timing. Consider, too, that a little wear at many points in the valve train may be equal, in effect, to considerable wear at one point.

For example, suppose there is .005″ excess wear between the gear teeth. This will allow the valves to open late and close early. Add to this another .005″ excess wear in the camshaft bearings. This will reduce valve lift. It will also increase late opening and early closing of the valves. Add another .005″ worn from the cam contour, which also changes the valve lift and/or timing.

On an overhead valve engine, additional wearing parts include both ends of the push rod, the rocker arm, rocker arm bushing, and shaft. See Figure 15-41. On top of all this, add another .005″ excess wear between the lifter and the guide. This results in the lifter moving sideways in the guide before it starts to lift the valve. All of this cumulative wear will interfere with efficient operation of the engine.

On engines having solid valve lifters, such conditions are often further aggravated by careless adjustment of the valve tappets. Many technicians who do not understand valve action, adjust the lifters with too much clearance to make sure there is no possibility of the valve holding open. They do not realize that they are restricting the ability of the engine to draw in a full charge of mixture, and to dispose of the exhaust gas properly.

If excess wear exists at all of the points mentioned, it becomes a serious matter indeed. For these reasons, the valve tappet clearance on overhead valve engines must be more carefully adjusted.

It should be evident that accurate adjustment is impossible if the various contacting surfaces are worn to untrue dimensions. See Figure 15-41. If such parts are not too seriously worn, they can be restored by grinding with

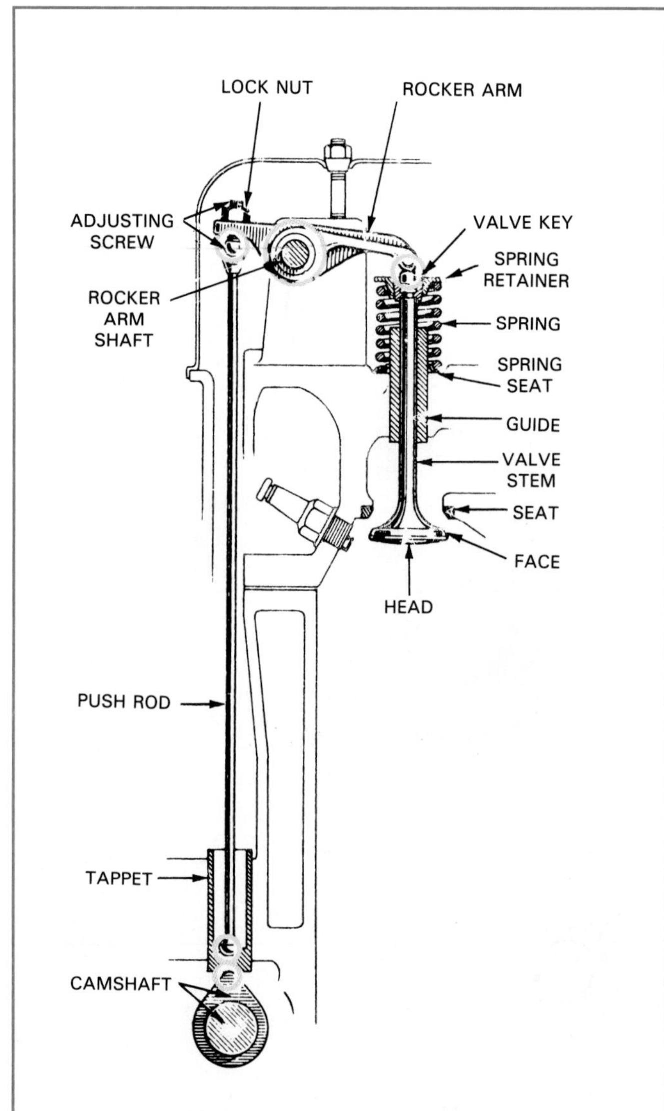

Figure 15-41. Many points in the valve train are prone to wear. A little wear at each point can add up to a significant overall amount in the entire valve train.

equipment made for the purpose. If they are worn enough to be through the case-hardened shell, they should be discarded and replaced with new parts.

When checking valve lifters, the surface contacted by the cam must be examined for wear, Figure 15-42. Figure 15-43 shows a lifter with normal wear and others with varying degrees of wear. One method of checking the cam for wear is stated in Figure 15-42.

Push Rods

The ***push rods*** on an overhead valve engine are a critical link between the lifters and the rocker arms. If a push rod should become warped or bent, the corresponding valve will not open sufficiently. This will cause a loss of power or performance.

To check for warping, place the push rod in a holding fixture. While watching the dial indicator, rotate the push rod, Figure 15-44. If the dial indicator moves more than .001″, the push rod must be replaced. Make sure to check all push rods. Another method for checking push rods is to roll them on a piece of glass. The technician will be able to visibly detect any distortion as the push rods roll.

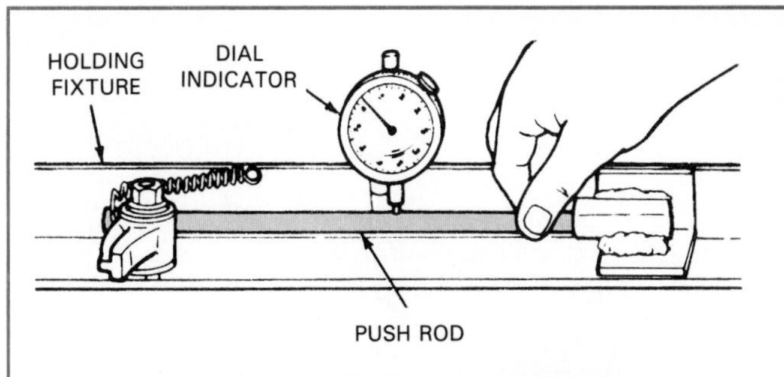

Figure 15-44. If push rods are bent or warped, the individual push rods must be replaced. Never attempt to straighten a push rod. (Ford)

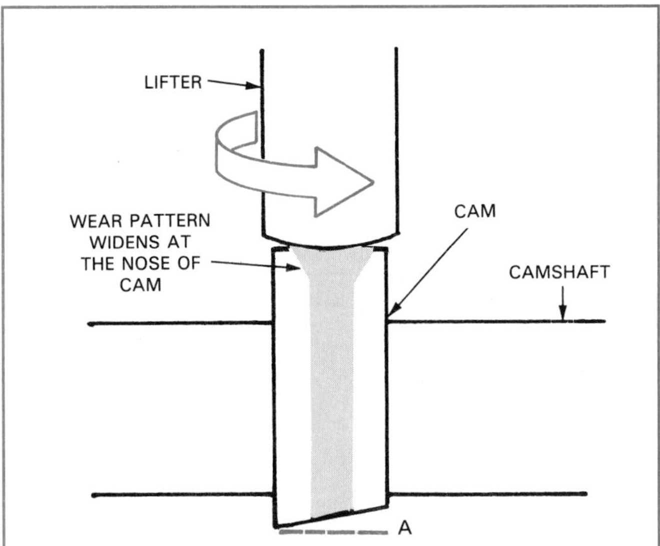

Figure 15-42. Note that the face of the cam is slightly tapered from true horizontal, which is indicated by line A. This taper, combined with a crowned lifter bottom, causes the lifter to spin in its bore. This prevents the lifter from premature wear. The spinning action of the lifter is transmitted to the push rod. If the push rod is not spinning extremely fast, a new camshaft and new lifters may be required.

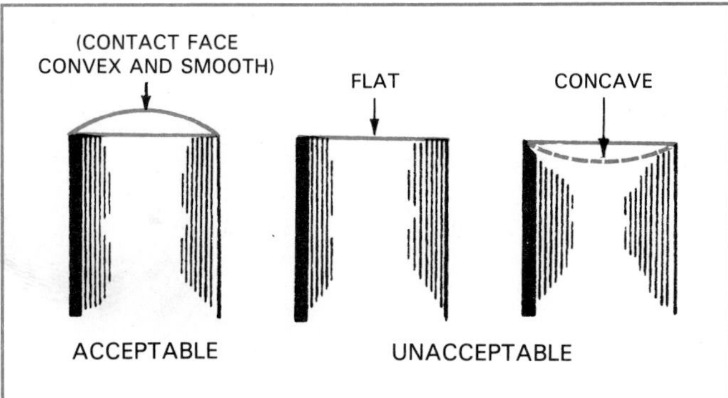

Figure 15-43. If the bottom of any lifter is not convex, a new set of lifters and a camshaft are required. (Ford)

Valve Tappet Adjustment

Adjustment of the ***tappet clearance*** is made with a feeler gauge, Figure 15-45, or with the aid of a special dial gauge, Figure 15-46. In these cases, the adjustment is readily accessible on an overhead valve engine. The adjustments should be made after the engine has reached operating temperatures. The valves must be adjusted properly, as the adjustment compensates for slightly worn valve train parts.

Camshaft Service

Some wear does occur on ***camshafts,*** as on any other engine part. Since the camshaft operates at slower speed than the crankshaft, wear usually is less pronounced. The

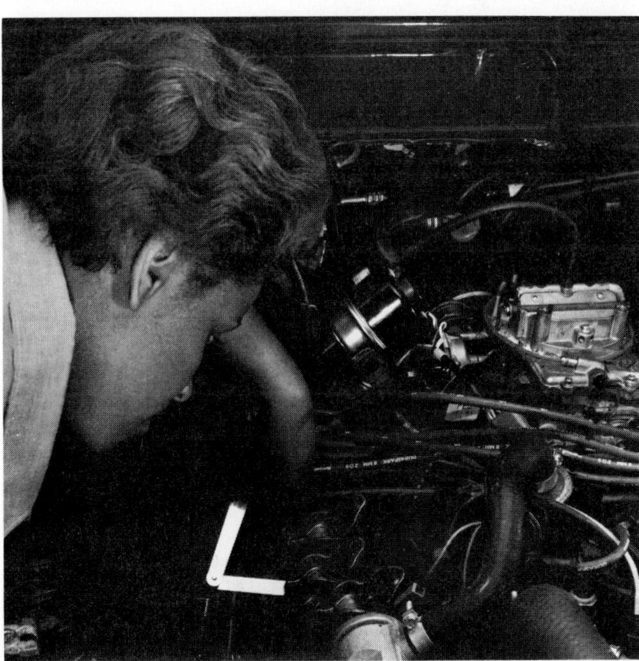

Figure 15-45. Using a feeler gauge to adjust mechanical valve lifters. Hydraulic valve lifters do not need adjusting. If hydraulic valve lifters become noisy, they may need to be replaced.

Figure 15-46. By loosening the locknut, the adjusting screw can be tightened to quiet noisy valves. Adjustment compensates for wear in the valve train. Make sure engine is hot when making the adjustment, or there will be no clearance between rocker arm and valve tip when the engine reaches operating temperature. Make sure to tighten the locknut after the adjustment is made.

cams and journals are hardened, so wear ordinarily occurs in the bushings rather than on the shaft journals.

The ***lift*** of the cam is the difference between measurements AA and BB, Figure 15-47. The amount of wear is then obtained by comparison with specified lift. Cam lift also can be measured by mounting a dial gauge on the cylinder head with its button contacting the upper end of the valve push rod. Then, as the engine is slowly cranked, the distance from the lowest point to the highest will be the lift of the cam, Figure 15-48.

Since the cams do not all wear at the same rate, it is important to measure the lift of all cams in the engine to determine if any are worn.

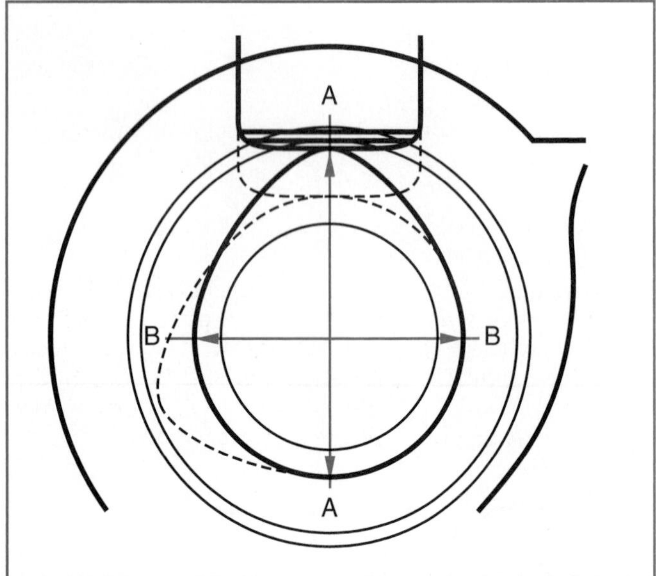

Figure 15-47. The difference between line A and line B is the amount of lift.

Worn cams, which are often overlooked in troubleshooting, are occasionally the cause of lost power or misfiring. If a check on valve lift shows that it is less than it should be, the cams can be reground on special machinery. In most cases, however, the camshaft is replaced, Figure 15-49.

Camshaft Bearings

Some camshafts ride directly in the metal of the crankcase, but most run in ***camshaft bearings*** in the form of bushings or inserts. These bushings and inserts are not adjustable for wear and must be replaced when worn. The degree of wear dictating replacement is generally determined by oil clearance rather than a tendency toward noise. However, if seriously worn, the bushings or bearings may create noise and vibration in the timing gears and valve train.

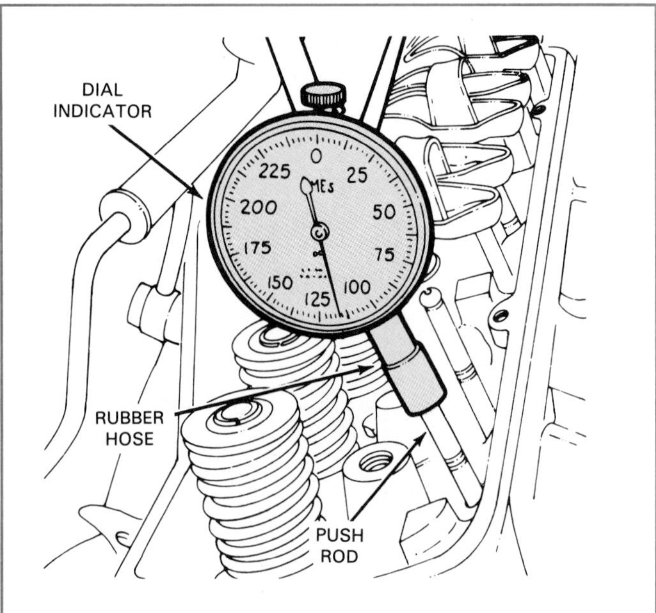

Figure 15-48. Using a dial gauge to measure cam lift.

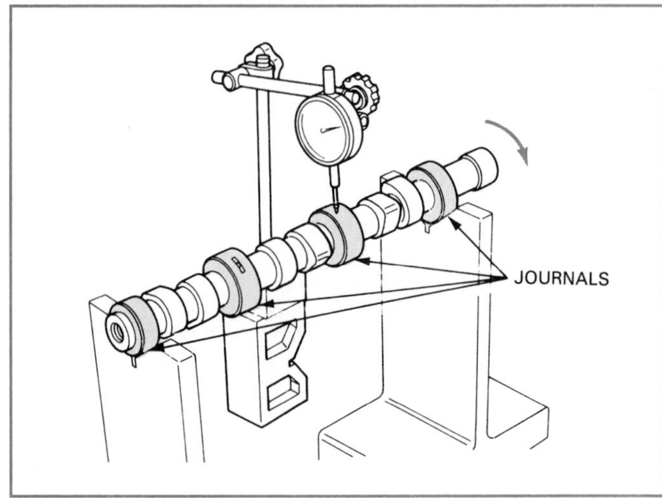

Figure 15-49. Each journal of the camshaft should also be checked for runout. If runout exceeds .0015″ on any journal, replace the camshaft. (Nissan)

The camshaft must be removed to replace the camshaft bearings. This involves removal of the valve operating mechanism. It is seldom necessary to replace a camshaft bearing or bearings until the engine is dismantled for other work.

After the camshaft is removed, the bushings are pressed out of their bores with a special tool made for the purpose. This special tool will also be needed for inserting the new bushings, Figure 15-50.

New bushings are available in the proper outside diameter and standard, as well as undersize, inside diameter. If the camshaft has been undersized by regrinding worn journals, the bushings can be align-bored to any size desired by use of the proper equipment, Figure 15-51.

It is essential to start the bushing squarely in the bore and apply pressure steadily and evenly. If the bushing cocks in the bore, it will be distorted and the inside diameter decreased. The bushings should be pushed fully into the bore. It is good policy to check the installation after the valve operating parts are installed to make sure there is sufficient clearance for the lifters. Also, endplay of the camshaft should be checked and corrected if it exceeds the manufacturers' specifications (usually about the same as for crankshafts).

When precision bearing inserts are used to support the camshaft, they are serviced in the same manner as crankshaft bearings.

Usually the camshaft is provided with a ***thrust plate.*** This holds the camshaft against a flange to eliminate excessive endwise movement. The thrust plate must be replaced if endplay is excessive.

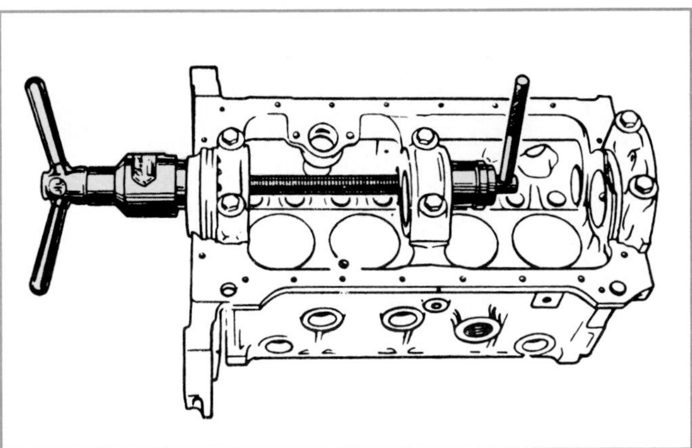

Figure 15-50. A special tool is needed to remove and install camshaft bushings.

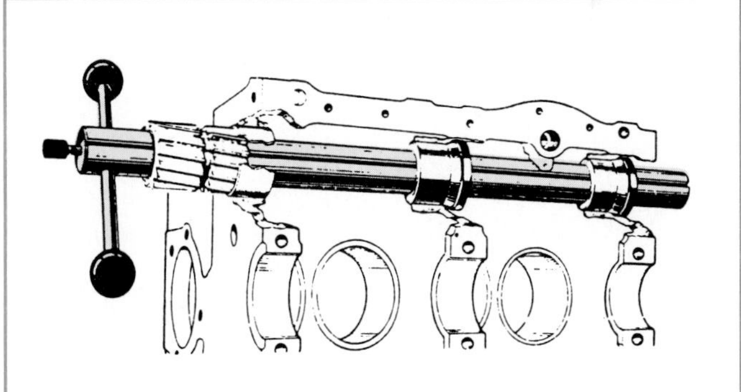

Figure 15-51. A special tool is used to align-bore the camshaft bushings.

Chapter 15–Review Questions

Write your answers on a separate piece of paper. Do not write in this book.

1. A valve should be discarded if the stem is bent more than:
   (A) .002″.
   (B) .004″.
   (C) .006″.
   (D) None of the above.
2. A valve interference angle should be cut on the:
   (A) combustion chamber side.
   (B) port side.
   (C) both sides.
   (D) None of the above.
3. A narrow valve seat will dissipate the heat better than a wide one. True or False?
4. The valve seat should be concentric with the guide within:
   (A) .001″.
   (B) .002″.
   (C) .003″.
   (D) None of the above.
5. Valve seat inserts are not used in cast iron cylinder blocks or heads. True or False?
6. Describe an interference fit for a valve seat insert.
7. Name two ways of shrinking inserts.
8. Heat dissipation is greater when valve guides are not used. True or False?
9. Leaking intake valve guides:
   (A) cause excessive oil consumption.
   (B) upset fuel mixture.
   (C) Both A & B.
   (D) Neither A nor B.
10. Valve stem seals are placed:
    (A) in the valve stem.
    (B) in the valve guide.
    (C) Both A & B.
    (D) Neither A nor B.
11. Valve stem to guide clearance should not exceed:
    (A) .003″-.004″.
    (B) .004″-.005″.
    (C) .005″-.006″.
    (D) .006″-.007″.
12. Why must valve springs be square on each end?
13. What causes valve stem and valve spring etching?
14. Technician A states that the purpose of an interference valve angle is to chip carbon off of the valve face. Technician B states that the purpose of a valve rotator is to lengthen valve life. Who is right?
    (A) A only.
    (B) B only.
    (C) Both A & B.
    (D) Neither A nor B.
15. Worn camshaft bearings will cause a valve to open early. True or False?

16. Technician A states that valve rotators are used on all valves. Technician B states that valve rotators are used only on engines that burn unleaded fuel. Who is right?
    (A) A only.
    (B) B only.
    (C) Both A & B.
    (D) Neither A nor B.

17. Technician A states that the rocker arm action causes valve guides to wear in a bellmouth shape. Technician B states that the positive valve seal remains stationary as the valve moves up and down. Who is right?
    (A) A only.
    (B) B only.
    (C) Both A & B.
    (D) Neither A nor B.

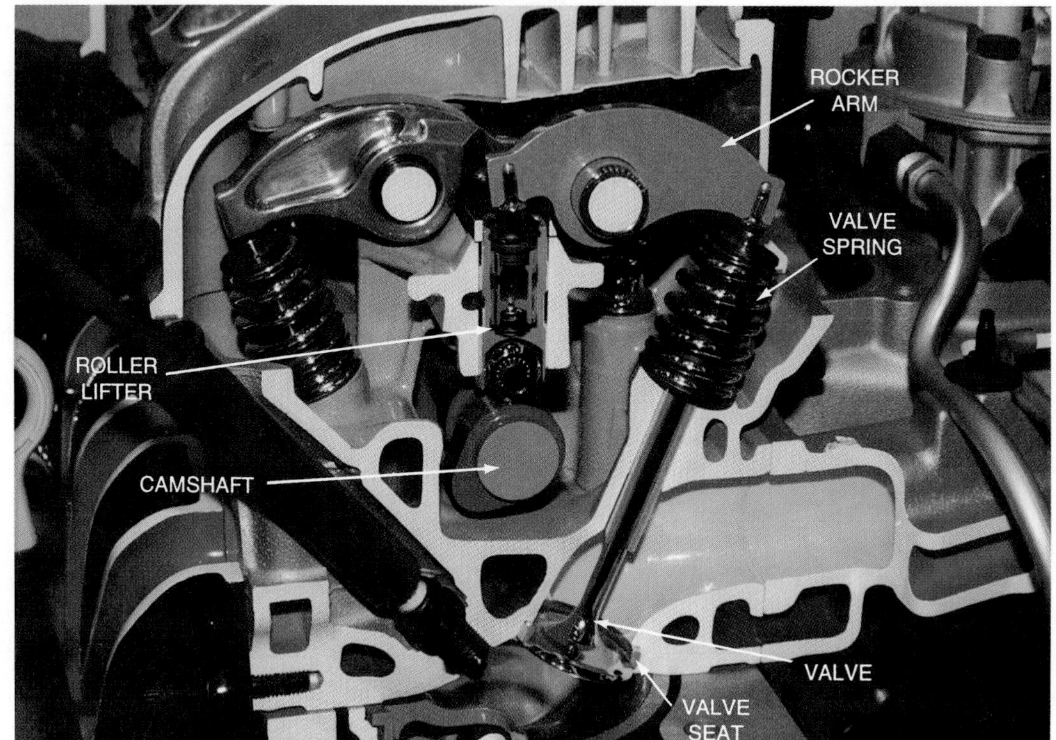

The proper operation of the valves and the valve operating mechanism is essential for efficient engine operation.

Chapter 16
Engine Lubrication

After studying this chapter, you will be able to:
- Explain how a lubricating system operates.
- State the purpose of lubrication.
- List the properties of engine oil.
- Select the proper engine oil for a specific engine.

Oil

Without the aid of ***friction,*** an automobile could not move itself. Excessive friction in the engine, however, would cause rapid destruction. We cannot eliminate internal friction, but we can reduce it to a controllable degree by using ***friction-reducing lubricants,*** Figure 16-1.

These lubricants are usually made from the same type of crude oil as gasoline. The petroleum oils are compounded with animal fats, vegetable oils, and other ingredients to produce satisfactory oils and greases for automotive use. Lubricating oils and greases are also manufactured from silicones and other materials and have no petroleum products in them.

Lubricating oil in an automobile engine has several tasks to perform:
- Lubricates the moving parts.
- Seals between the piston rings and the cylinder wall.
- Carries heat away from engine parts.
- Carries contamination away from moving parts.

Furthermore, the engine oil must function adequately whether the temperature is below 0°F (-18°C) or above 200°F (93°C). This is contrary to the nature of petroleum products, since they tend to thicken at low temperatures and thin out at high temperatures. The oil must go through many processes during manufacture to reduce this tendency to change viscosity with changes in temperature.

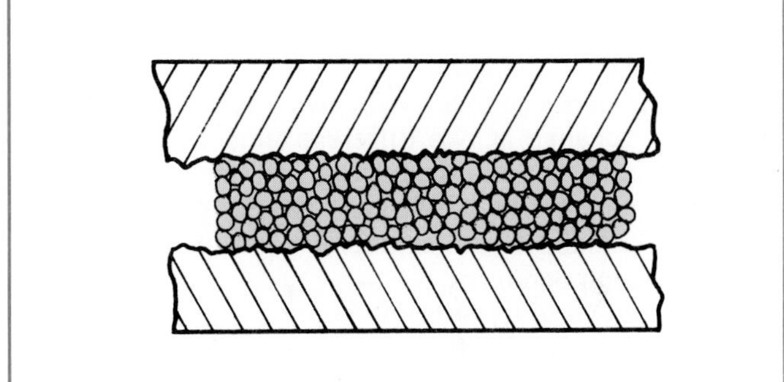

Figure 16-1. Oil molecules roll over one another to reduce friction. This action is similar to ball bearings.

Properties of Engine Oil

Engine oil is available in different viscosities. ***Viscosity*** is considered to be the internal friction of a fluid. An oil of low viscosity will flow more easily than an oil of high viscosity. Sometimes a low viscosity oil is referred to as a light oil and a high viscosity oil is referred to as a heavy oil.

Oils of different viscosities have been assigned numbers by the Society of Automotive Engineers. The lower the viscosity, the lower the assigned number. SAE 10 engine oil, for example, is recommended for cold weather operation and SAE 30 for warm weather. The SAE number of an oil has nothing to do with its quality.

Selecting Viscosities

There are single-viscosity and multi-viscosity oils. The ***single-viscosity oils*** are commonly referred to as straight-weight oils. Straight-weight oils are used in areas where the temperature is consistent. ***Multi-viscosity oils,*** or multi-weight oils, are used in areas where there are seasonal changes or extreme temperature differences between the morning and the evening. See Figure 16-2. Examples of a single-viscosity oil include SAE 10, SAE 20, SAE 30. Examples of a variable- or multi-viscosity oil include 5W-20,

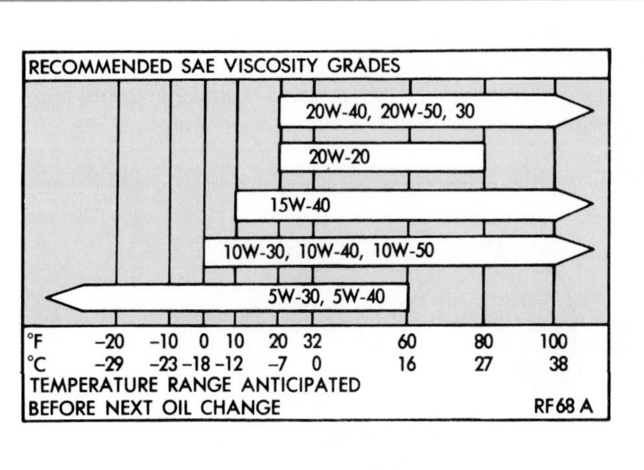

Figure 16-2. The atmospheric temperature determines the viscosity of the oil selected. (Chrysler)

10W-30, 10W-40, 20W-50. A low numerical viscosity is needed in cold weather, or the engine will have difficulty turning over due to the resistance of the thick oil. A high numerical viscosity oil is needed in hot weather, or the oil will thin out and will not provide enough protection for the engine components.

In oil grades, a "W" stands for winter grade and means that the viscosity test was performed at a temperature of 0°F (-18°C). The "W" in a 10W-40 oil, for example, means that a viscosity of 10 was obtained when the oil was tested at 0°F (-18°C). The absence of the "W" after the 40 designates that a viscosity of 40 was obtained when tested at 210°F (99°C).

Selecting Quality

Oil containers carry a logo, Figure 16-3. This logo provides the consumer or technician with the proper data of the type of oil in the container. With this information the right type of oil can be obtained for the type of weather and the specific engine application. Oil containers also contain a seal that ensures the purchaser that the oil meets the most current quality ratings.

Several groups are responsible for testing the quality of oil. One is the American Society for Testing Materials (ASTM). The American Petroleum Institute (API) and the Society of Automotive Engineers (SAE) also test oils. However, the API is the only group listed for testing the quality, and the SAE is the only group listed for testing the viscosity. Together, these groups have established the ratings for the quality of oil. They are as follows:

Gasoline Engines:

SA– For engines operating under mild conditions. No special protection capabilities (mineral oil).

SB– For light-duty engine operation. Has anti-scuff capabilities, resists oil oxidation, retards bearing corrosion.

SC– Minimum requirements for all 1964 to 1967 passenger cars and light trucks. Controls high- and low-temperature deposits. Retards rust and corrosion in gasoline engines.

SD– For 1968 and later engine warranty service. Better high- and low-temperature deposit control than SC. Also rust/corrosion resistant.

SE– For 1972 and later gasoline engine warranty maintenance service. It provides maximum protection against rust, corrosion, wear, oil oxidation, and high-temperature deposits that can cause oil thickening.

SF– For gasoline engines in passenger cars and some trucks beginning with 1980 models operating under engine manufacturers' recommended maintenance procedures.

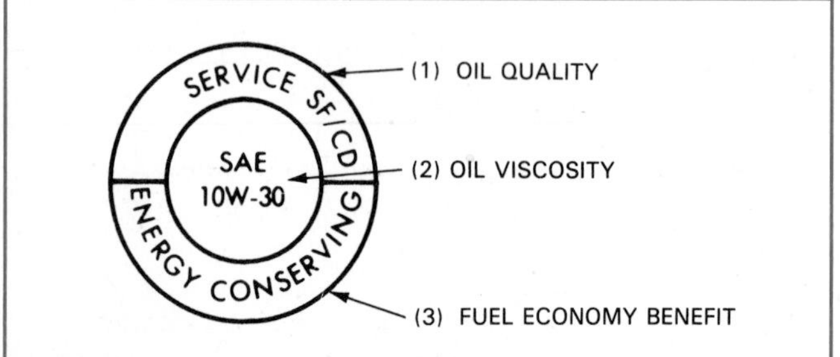

Figure 16-3. Information on the quality and viscosity of an oil is placed on the oil container. (Chrysler)

SG– This designation is for 1987 and newer car models.

SH– This designation is for 1994 and newer car models.

Diesel Engines:

CA– For light-duty normally aspirated diesel engines. Provides protection against high-temperature deposits and bearing corrosion.

CB– For moderate-duty, normally aspirated diesel engines operating on high-sulfur fuel. Protects against bearing corrosion and high-temperature deposits.

CC– For moderate-duty, lightly supercharged diesel engines and certain heavy-duty gasoline engines. Protects against rust, corrosion, and high- and low-temperature deposits.

CD– For severe-duty supercharged diesel engines using fuels of a wide quality range. Provides highly effective control of corrosion and deposits.

CE– For supercharged, heavy-duty diesel engines made since 1983.

If the proper quality of oil is not selected, the owner will experience premature engine failure.

Additives

The requirements of today's automobile engine lubricants are far beyond the range of straight mineral oils. All automobile manufacturers now recommend oils that have been improved by ***additives.*** The need for improved oil results from higher engine compression; increased speeds; and greater sensitivity to deposit formation, corrosion, and rusting.

There are many different additives used today. Probably the first one to be used was a ***pour point depressant.*** At low temperatures, the wax in the oil would crystallize and then form a sort of "honeycomb," which would block the flow of oil to the oil pump. Pour point depressants prevent this.

Detergent-dispersant additives are used to prevent sludge and varnish deposits, which would otherwise restrict the free flow of oil and cause the valves and lifters to stick.

Foam inhibitors are designed to prevent oil foaming, which would result from the "egg beater" action of the rotating engine parts. Unless the foaming is stopped, bearings and other parts would receive only foam instead of oil and would soon fail.

Oxidation inhibitors are used to reduce the possibility of the oil being oxidized. Oxidation usually occurs at the higher operating temperatures attained during sustained high-speed, full throttle operation. Series oxidation of the oil will result in deposit formation.

Viscosity index improvers, as the name implies, improve the viscosity index. The viscosity index is a measure of the rate of change or variation in the viscosity of a liquid with changing temperature.

A high viscosity index indicates a relatively low rate of viscosity change at two different temperatures. A low index indicates a high rate of viscosity change. Oils designed for automotive engine use have a relatively high viscosity index and are suitable for use in both high and low atmospheric temperatures.

Corrosion and rust inhibitors are designed to help the detergent-dispersant additives in the prevention of rust and corrosion.

Antiwear additives, one of the most important additives used, have the ability to coat metal surfaces with a strong and slippery film that prevents direct metal-to-metal contact. All modern, top-quality oils contain this additive.

All of these additives combine to produce an oil that will not only withstand heavier loads, reduce corrosion, stop foaming, maintain viscosity, and stop sludge and varnish formation, but will also keep the interior of the engine cleaner and increase its useful life.

Many of the additives in the engine oil lose their effectiveness over time due to the heat from the engine. Unless the oil is changed, wear is accelerated.

Oil Changes

The proper interval for oil changes is difficult to determine. Much depends on the conditions under which the vehicle is being operated. Most manufacturers have two recommendations. One is for normal driving and the other for severe conditions.

Severe conditions are described as short trip driving during which the engine does not reach operating temperature for an appreciable time; towing another vehicle; excessive idling; or driving in dusty areas. Since most cars are operated in cities or towns with a population of 25,000 or greater, it is evident that the cars are used mostly for short trips with much time spent idling. Therefore, most cars are operated under "severe" conditions.

Cars that fall into the ***normal driving*** category can be described as vehicles that are driven on individual trips of 10 miles or more. Also, they do not pull a trailer, and they operate in an atmosphere that is relatively free of dust.

Car manufacturers' oil change recommendations show a big difference for vehicles used for normal driving and for those being operated under severe conditions. One manufacturer, for example, recommends that the oil and oil filter should be changed every 3000 miles or three months under severe conditions and every 7500 miles or once a year under normal driving conditions. However, the oil in turbocharged engines should be changed every 3000 miles under all conditions. Oil change intervals are subject to frequent change, so always consult manufacturers' specifications.

While protecting the engine from wear and corrosion, oil in the crankcase becomes loaded with acids, dirt, and abrasives. Not all of these contaminants can be trapped by filters. Therefore, the only way to remove all of these wear-producing contaminants is to change the oil. Nondetergent oils and low-quality oils are not recommended. Use SH oil and make the prescribed oil filter changes.

Oil Filters

Oil filters are placed in the engine lubricating system to remove dirt and abrasives from the oil. Dilutents, such as gasoline and acids, are not removed. However, by removing the solid materials, the possibility of acids forming is reduced and the rate of engine part wear is greatly reduced.

Oil filters installed on modern passenger car engines are the ***full-flow type.*** In this type of filter, all oil passes through the filter before it reaches the bearings. However, in the event the filter becomes clogged or obstructed, a ***bypass valve*** is provided so that oil will continue to reach the bearings. The filters in use today are of the "throw-away" type. See Figures 16-4 through 16-7.

Figure 16-4. Cartridge-type, full-flow oil filter. The filter is thrown away and a new one installed at prescribed intervals.

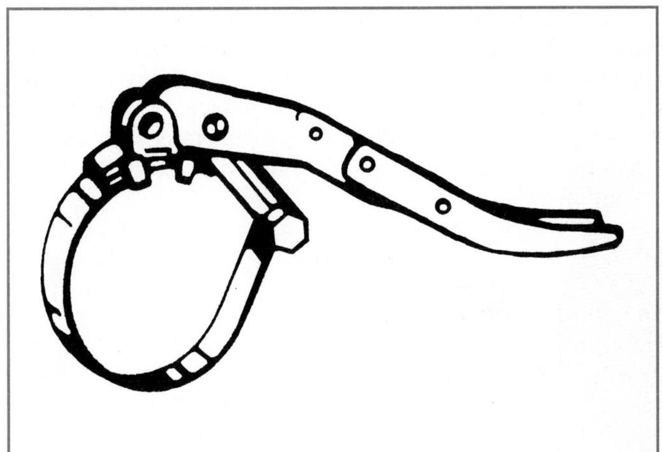

Figure 16-5. An oil filter wrench is needed to remove the oil filter.

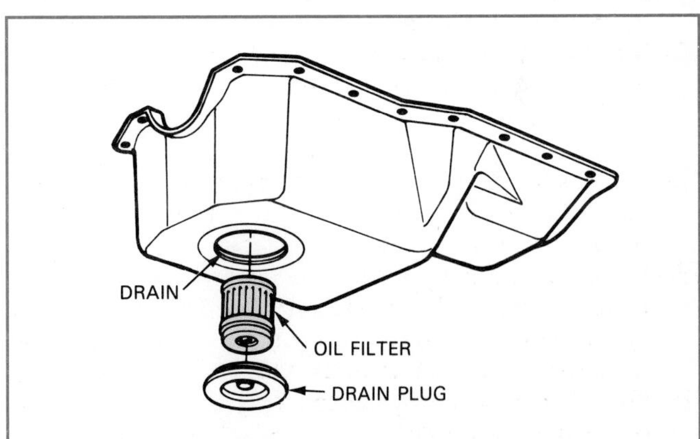

Figure 16-6. The oil filter on some engines is located inside the oil pan.

Lubricating Methods

Oil is supplied to moving parts of the engine by pump pressure, splashing, or a combination of both. Splashed oil usually becomes a mist for lubricating parts such as cylinder walls and pistons.

Oil is fed to the majority of engine parts under pressure, especially to main bearings and connecting rod bearings. Leakage or "throw-off" from the rod bearings splashes on the other moving parts inside the engine. A

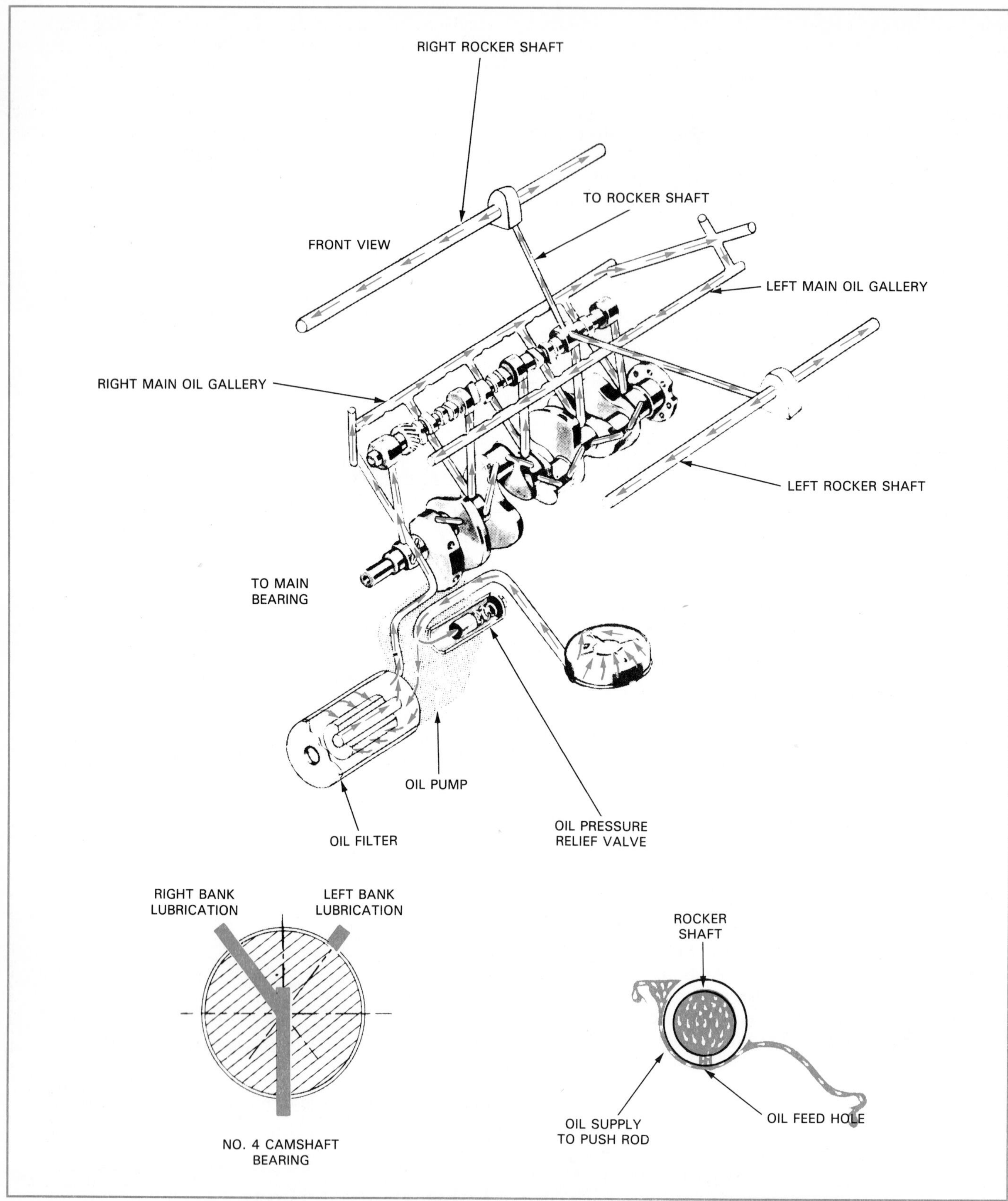

Figure 16-7. Oil is filtered before it is delivered through the various passages.

typical pressure lubrication system is shown in Figures 16-8 and 16-9.

Pressure Systems

Figures 16-8 and 16-9 show the oil pump located in the sump of the oil pan. The oil enters the pump through a screen. Quite often the intake screen is mounted so that it stays on top of or is submerged in the oil in the sump, Figure 16-8. The idea is to keep the pump intake away from any dirt that might settle in the bottom of the sump.

Figures 16-8 and 16-9 show the path of the oil from the pump to the oil gallery in the crankcase. The oil is

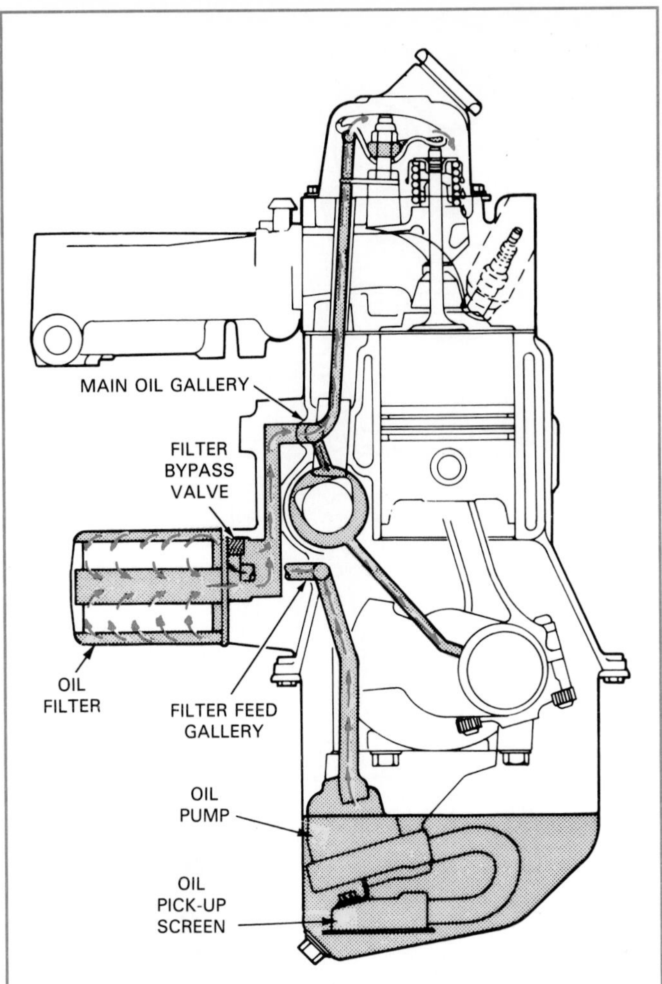

Figure 16-8. After oil is filtered, it enters the main oil gallery. (Oldsmobile)

conducted to the main bearings through drilled passages in the crankcase. Passages are also drilled in the crankshaft to carry oil from the main bearings to the connecting rod journals. The path of the oil to the overhead valve rocker shaft is shown in Figures 16-8 and 16-9. Some connecting rods have oil passages drilled lengthwise to carry oil to the piston pins, Figure 16-10. The connecting rods in some

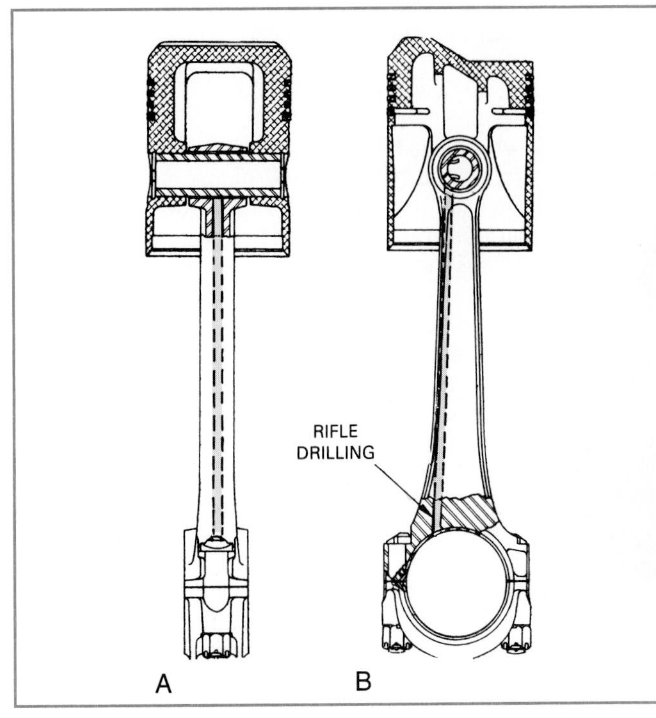

Figure 16-10. A–An oil passage is drilled lengthwise through the connecting rod. B–This oil passage provides lubrication to the piston pin.

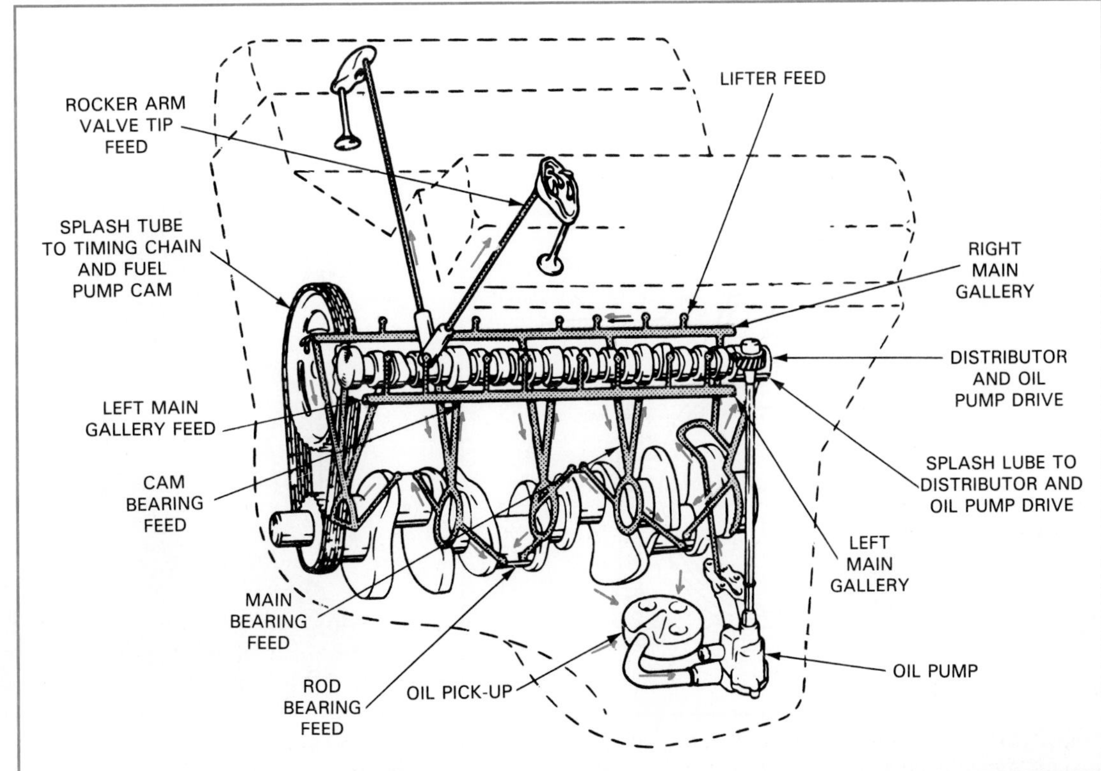

Figure 16-9. Oil is directed through passages that have been drilled in the crankshaft. (Oldsmobile)

engines also have a spurt hole drilled in them on one side. A squirt of oil shoots out on the cylinder wall when the hole aligns with the oil passage in the crankshaft. See Figure 16-11 .

Some manufacturers cool the pistons by shooting a stream of oil upward into a collecting hole that carries the lubricating oil into a cooling gallery. See Figure 16-12. Valves in the jets are provided to shut off the oil spray when the engine is idling in order to maintain oil pressure when piston cooling is not needed.

Oil Pumps

The ***oil pumps*** used to circulate the oil are of the positive displacement type. Vanes, plungers, rotors, and gears can all be used to build up the necessary pressure. A rotor and a gear pump are illustrated in Figure 16-13. These pumps are always positively driven–usually with gears from the camshaft.

Since these pumps handle oil, they are well lubricated at all times and do not suffer from excessive wear. They do, in time, develop excess clearance and require replacement. The gear teeth, or vane contours, as well as the gear ends and housings, may wear. When excessive wear does occur, the oil pressure will drop.

Oil Pressure

Most cases of lost ***oil pressure*** are due to excessive clearance in the bearings of the engine rather than worn oil pumps. If the oil pump is in good condition, the pressure relief valve will regulate the pressure of the oil within limits. However, it will not increase the capacity of the oil pump. The regulator is a simple spring-loaded valve that RELIEVES EXCESS PRESSURE in the circulating system by bypassing the excess oil back to the sump. See Figure 16-14.

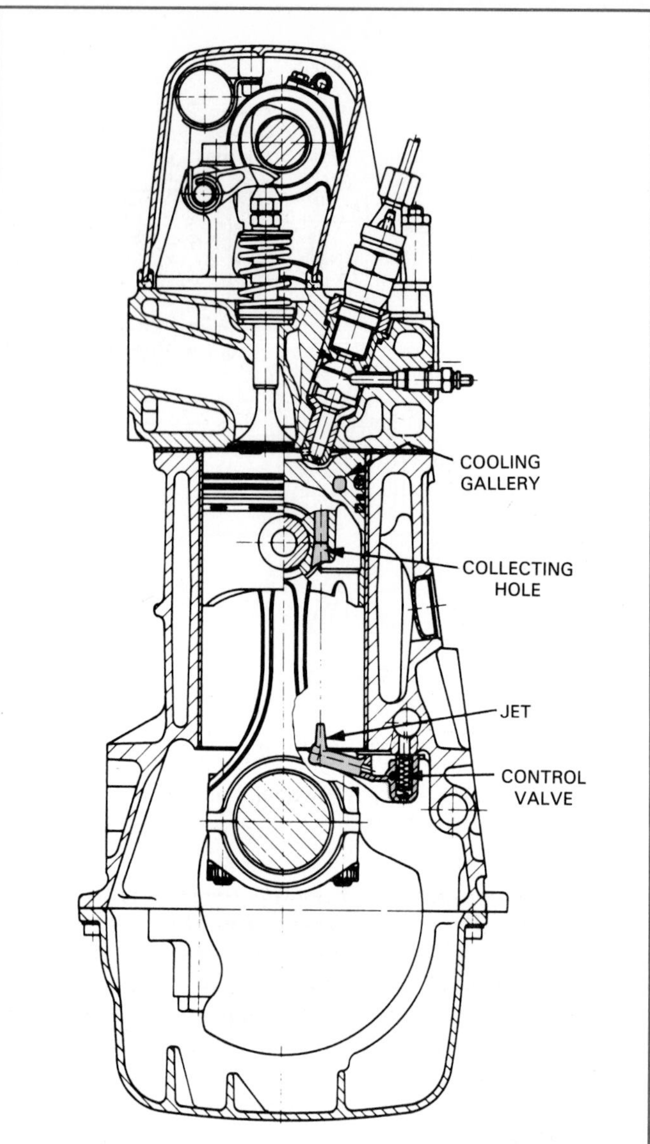

Figure 16-12. Oil is directed upward to cool the piston in this diesel engine.

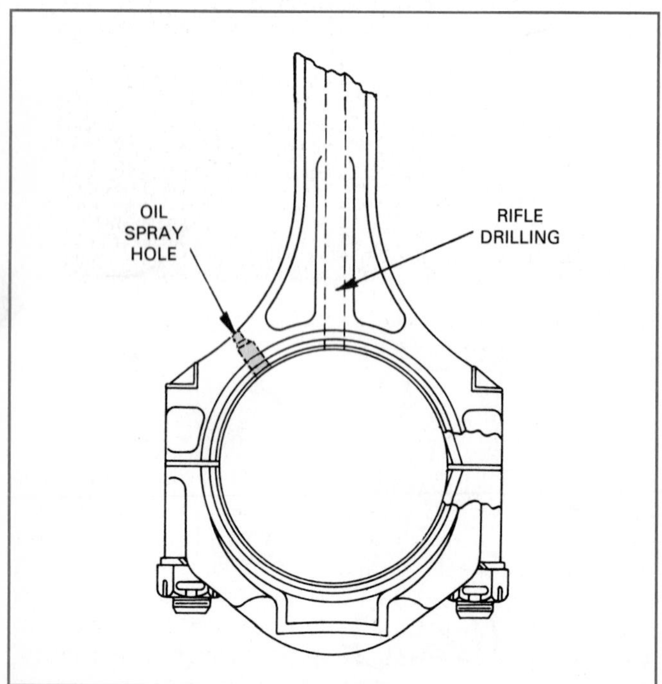

Figure 16-11. The oil spray hole directs a squirt of oil to the cylinder walls.

Figure 16-13. Oil pumps are of the rotor- or gear-type design.

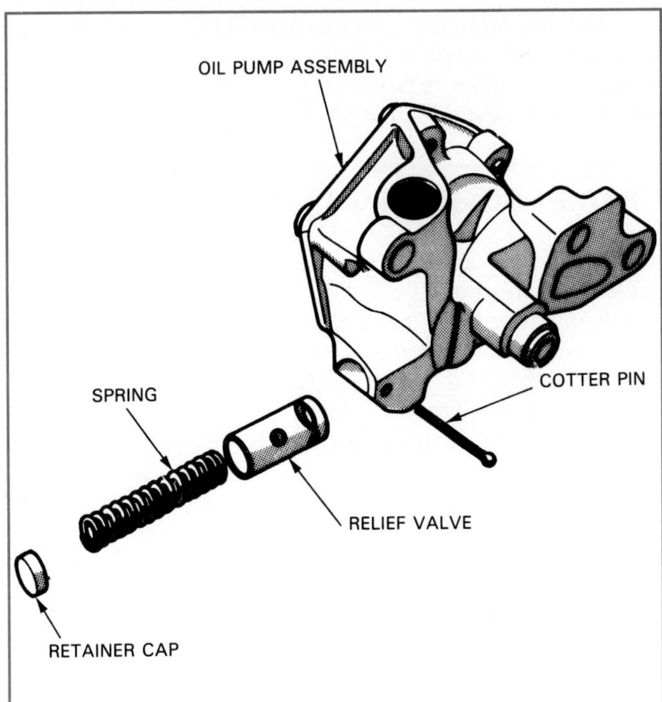

Figure 16-14. Oil pressure relief valve. If the relief valve sticks in the closed position, the oil filter will burst. If the pressure relief valve sticks in the open position, oil pressure will never develop. (Chrysler)

Another reason for lack of oil pressure is a blockage in the oil pump supply line or screen. This prevents oil reaching the pump in sufficient volume to maintain pressure. A typical case of "sludge" accumulation in a screen is shown in Figure 16-15. This sludge blocks the oil passages, resulting in a bearing that may "starve" for oil and friction that will melt the metal.

Oil Sludge

Sludge is a mayonnaise-like mixture of water, oil, and other products of combustion. It is most likely to form in an engine that seldom reaches a satisfactory operating temperature, such as a light truck used for postal delivery service in cold weather. Such a vehicle ordinarily runs a short distance at a slow speed, stops, and then runs another short distance at a slow speed.

Slow speed, stop-and-go operation means that the engine rarely gets hot enough to cause the water in the crankcase to evaporate. The water condenses on the cold walls of the crankcase. In some cases, moisture gets into the crankcase through leaking cylinder head gaskets. This water emulsifies with the oil, carbon, dirt, etc., to form sludge. See Figure 16-16.

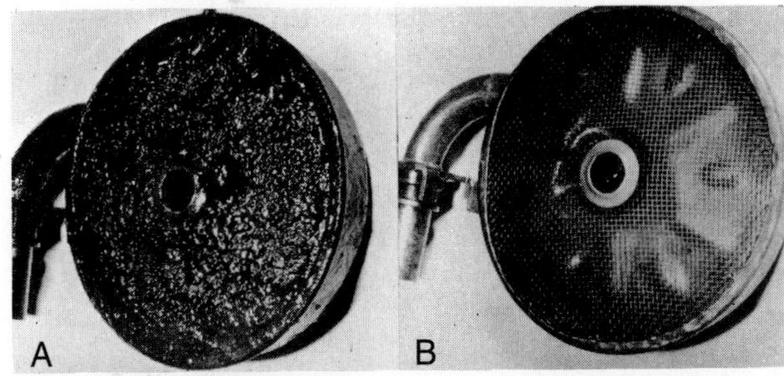

Figure 16-15. A–An accumulation of sludge on this oil pickup screen will stop the flow of oil. This will cause the engine to seize. B–An oil pick-up screen in good condition.

Sludge formation can be held to a minimum by using the correct cooling system thermostat to maintain a high engine operating temperature. High-detergent engine oils and frequent oil and filter changes are necessary. Adequate crankcase ventilation is also important.

Researchers have found that when the cooling system thermostat was removed from the engine water jacket outlet, temperatures barely exceeded 100°F (38°C) when the ambient temperature was 60°–70°F (16°–21°C). The engine operated at approximately 30°F (-1°C) above the ambient temperature, resulting in sludge buildup.

Water jacket outlet temperature usually corresponds to the setting of the cooling system thermostat. It must be emphasized that oil dilution and sludge formation decrease with 195°F (91°C) thermostat as compared to thermostats having a lower opening temperature. Not only is sludge reduced, but production of hydrocarbons and carbon monoxide in the exhaust are also reduced.

Equally important to keeping sludge formation to a minimum is proper crankcase ventilation. Adequate crankcase oil temperature must be maintained to assist in evaporation and purging of volatile blowby contaminants. Oil temperatures are usually only a problem under conditions involving excessive idling or operation in severely cold weather.

Fuel is a major factor in the formation of sludge. Modern oils help control sludge by keeping foreign materials in suspension.

Figure 16-16. An accumulation of sludge on the cylinder head and the valve covers.

Positive Crankcase Ventilation (PCV)

Since venting "blowby" gases into the atmosphere has been illegal since 1968, another method of crankcase venting has been implemented. This method is called ***positive crankcase ventilation,*** which is commonly referred to as the PCV system, Figure 16-17. Blowby is the exhaust gas that works its way past the piston rings and into the crankcase. Blowby mixed with the oil in the crankcase contributes to the formation of sludge. In the PCV system, blowby gases are forced out of the crankcase, Figure 16-17, and into the combustion chamber where they are reburned. This

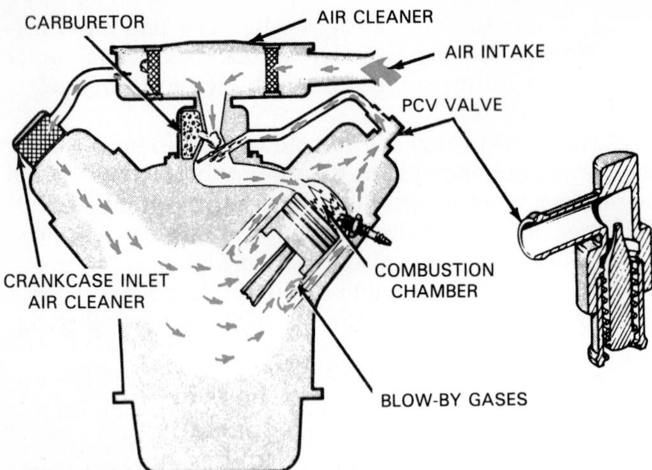

Figure 16-17. The PCV system forces fresh air into the crankcase. Blowby is then forced into the intake manifold. The PCV valve regulates the amount of blowby that enters the intake manifold in relation to engine load. (Chrysler)

prevents sludge from forming in the engine and reduces emissions.

Engine Varnish

Another type of engine deposit is known as ***varnish.*** Varnish is formed when an engine is worked hard enough to run hot for extended periods of time. The heat causes the oil to break down. Some of the elements separate out and deposit a varnish-like substance on the metal parts inside the engine.

To avoid such deposits, it is necessary to use the best oil obtainable and to change the oil regularly. It is also essential to make sure that the cooling system is functioning efficiently.

The importance of regular and frequent oil changes has been emphasized. It is more economical to throw away a quart of oil than it is to take a chance of damaging an engine worth several hundred dollars or more.

Chapter 16–Review Questions

Write your answers on a separate sheet of paper. Do not write in this book.

1. Name four tasks that the lubricating oil in an engine is expected to perform.
2. An SAE 10 oil can be used anywhere that SAE 10-W can be used. True or False?
3. A light oil is always better than a heavy oil? True or False?
4. What is meant by "oil throw-off"?
5. Oil passages are drilled in the:
   (A) engine block.
   (B) crankshaft.
   (C) connecting rods.
   (D) all of the above.
6. Oil pumps are sometimes belt driven. True or False?
7. What is the most frequent cause of low oil pressure?
8. Name three things found in oil sludge.
9. Sludge and varnish are not the same thing. True or False?
10. All engine oils recommended by automobile manufacturers have been improved by additives. Name three.
11. Slow-speed driving is always desirable in order to maintain the best engine lubrication. True or False?
12. How does engine oil become diluted?
13. Oil classification SA is recommended for use in late-model gasoline engines. True or False?
14. Oil classification _____ is for severe-duty supercharged diesel engines.

Chapter 17
Engine Cooling Systems

After studying this chapter, you will be able to:
- ❍ List components of the cooling system.
- ❍ Explain how the cooling system operates.
- ❍ Describe how the components of the cooling system operate.

Cooling Systems

A ***cooling system*** of some kind is necessary in any internal combustion engine. If no cooling system were provided, parts would melt from the heat of the burning fuel and pistons would expand so much they would seize (could not move in the cylinders).

The ***pressurized cooling system*** of a water-cooled engine, Figures 17-1 and 17-2, consists of the engine water jacket, thermostat, water pump, radiator, radiator cap, fan, fan drive belt (if necessary), and necessary hoses. It must be designed to operate at temperatures that reach the boiling point of the coolant under pressure, which, in the case of ethylene glycol antifreeze, may exceed 250°F (121°C).

As fuel is burned in the engine, about one-third of the heat energy in the fuel is converted into power. Another third goes out the exhaust pipe unused, and the remaining third must be handled by the cooling system. This third is often under-estimated and even more often misunderstood.

Perhaps it will be helpful to describe it in readily understood terms rather than by reference to Btu's (British thermal units). The heat removed by the cooling system of an automobile operating at normal speed is sufficient to keep a six-room house warm in 0°F (-18°C) weather.

This means that several thousand gallons of water must be circulated in the cooling system every hour to absorb the heat and carry it to the radiator for disposal. It also means that many thousands of cubic feet of air must flow through the radiator every hour to dissipate the heat to the air.

Considering these cooling factors, it is important to distinguish between ***heat transfer*** and ***heat dissipation.*** The heat generated by the mixture burned in the engine must be transferred from the iron or aluminum cylinder to the water in the water jacket. The outside of the water jacket dissipates some of the heat to the air surrounding it, but most of the heat is carried by the cooling water to the radiator for dissipation to the surrounding air. See Figure 17-1.

Heat Transfer

In an automotive engine, heat flows, or is transferred, from the iron or aluminum cylinder to the coolant and from the coolant to the copper or aluminum radiator. Iron,

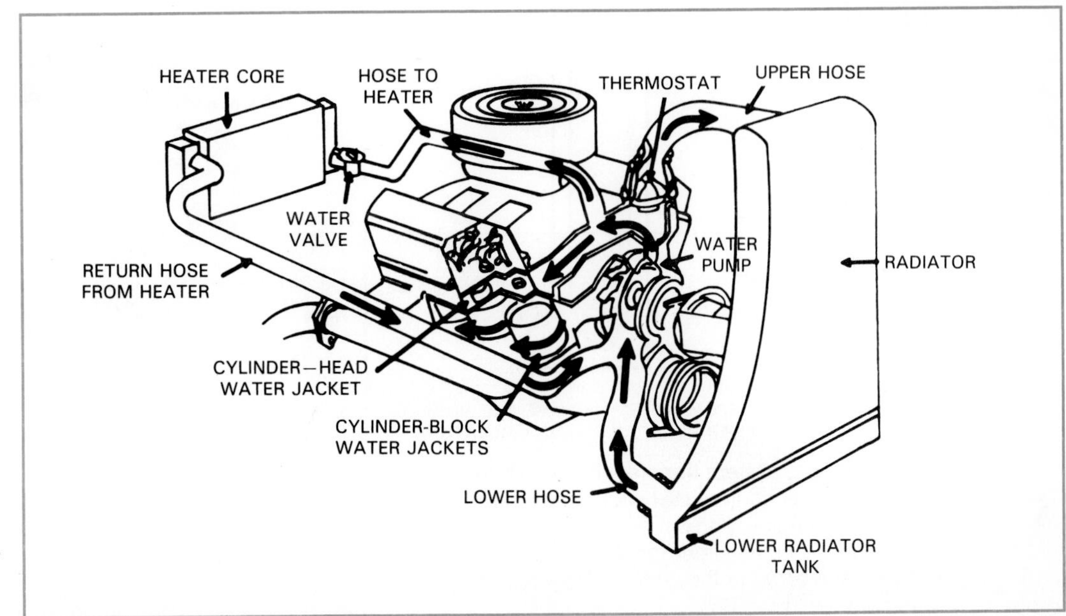

Figure 17-1. The coolant leaves the radiator through the lower radiator hose. After circulating through the engine, the hot coolant enters the radiator through the upper radiator hose. The heat that is picked up is dissipated to the air flowing through the radiator fins. This cycle continually repeats. (Everco)

aluminum, copper, and water are all good conductors of heat. If they are in contact with one another, the heat will flow readily from one to another.

If, however, there is a coating of lime or rust between the water and the metal, the flow of heat will be retarded since lime and rust are poor heat conductors. There is a great amount of surface within the water circulation system on which this lime and rust can accumulate. ***Lime*** is a white deposit formed by the heating of the water. As the water heats up, the lime separates from the water. When the water cools down, the white, powdery lime deposit is left on the metal surfaces of the water jackets and the radiator, Figure 17-2.

An engine is liable to have rust in the cooling system at any time. ***Rust*** is a combination of iron, water, and oxygen. We have iron in the engine, water in the engine, and some oxygen in the water. Additional oxygen enters through the air that finds its way into the cooling system.

This accumulation of rust and lime combines with a small amount of grease or oil, which often acts as a binder, and soon a coat of insulation forms on the inside surfaces of the water jacket. Grease or oil gets into the cooling system from the water pump lubricant, leaking cylinder head gaskets, etc.

Scale deposits also collect in corners or pockets of the water jacket where the water circulation is sluggish. This often causes ***hot spots,*** which can distort cylinders and valve seats. This type of overheating can occur without any indication of overheating on the temperature gauge. The gauge may be located at one spot in the water jacket, and the overheating condition may be localized in another spot.

The scale that collects in corners and narrow passages is also a deposit point for bits of rubber from the inside of hoses and other foreign matter that finds it way into the cooling system. The result is a mass of insulating sludge and scale that does considerable harm to the engine. These accumulations can be avoided by proper maintenance of the cooling system, the year-round use of ethylene glycol solutions, and the periodic flushing of the cooling system.

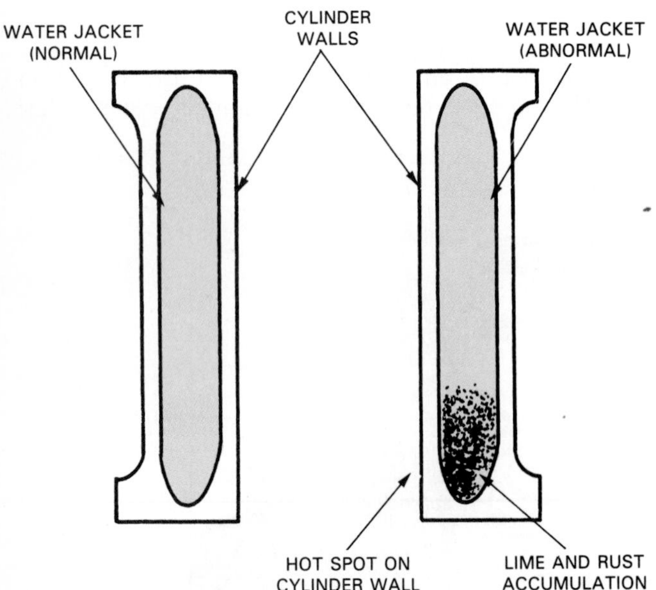

Figure 17-2. The cooling system transfers heat from the combustion chamber to the coolant that circulates through the water jackets in the engine block. If an accumulation of rust and/or lime develops in the water jackets, heat from the cylinder cannot be transferred to the coolant. This creates a "hot spot" within the cylinder. (Perfect Circle)

Water Pumps

Automobile engine ***water pumps*** are of many designs, but most are the centrifugal type. They consist of a rotating impeller. Sometimes the fan is installed on the water pump shaft, Figure 17-3.

An exploded view of a typical water pump assembly with all parts in proper relation to each other is shown in Figure 17-4. The vanes should not touch the housing, but at the same time, they should not have excessive clearance. For this reason, excessive endwise motion (end play) of the shaft to which the vane is attached is not permissible.

Impeller-type water pumps must turn rapidly to be efficient. Worn or loose belts will permit slippage, Figure 17-5, which is not readily detected. It is particularly difficult to detect a worn V-belt fan pulley. If a worn pulley is suspected, the groove can be compared with the groove of a new pulley. Also, alignment of the pulley should be checked.

Many water pumps have a spring-loaded seal to prevent leakage of water around the pump shaft. Modern pumps are fitted with prepacked ball bearings, which are sealed at each end to eliminate the need for periodic lubrication.

While most pumps run on sealed ball bearings and the shaft is sealed from the housing, they do occasionally require attention. Sand and grit in the water will wear the impeller blades and pump housing. Also, the sealing surfaces may be scored enough to leak air, if not water.

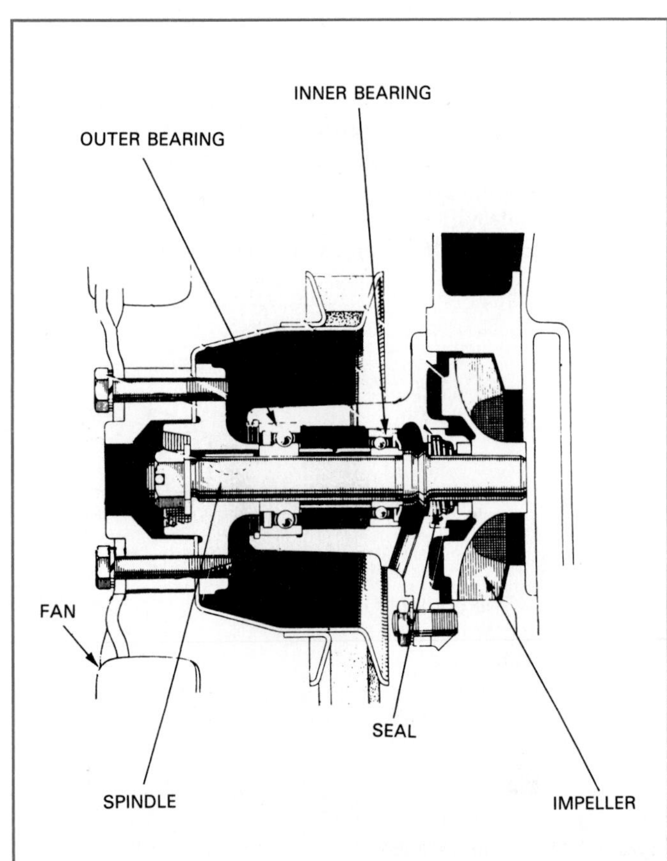

Figure 17-3. Nomenclature of a water pump.

Belts

The ***V-belt*** drives various engine accessories by a wedging action in the pulley groove. There are two different types of V-belt designs, Figure 17-6. The banded design is older and shows wear as it ages. The newer bandless design does not show wear as it ages, so it is extremely

Figure 17-4. The impellers of the water pump force the coolant through the engine block. (Everco)

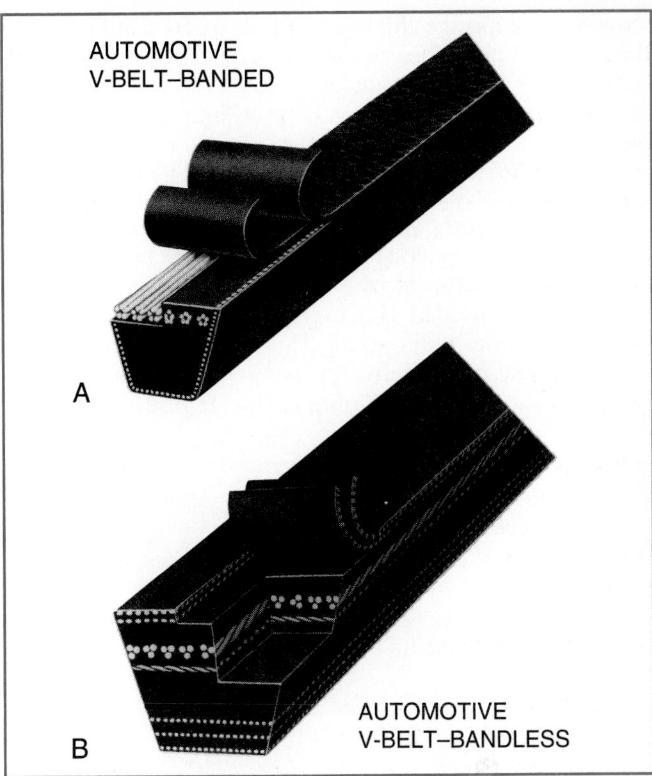

Figure 17-6. A–Older belts have a rubber covering on sidewalls to serve as a wear indicator. B–Modern belts are bandless, so there is no wear indicator. (Gates Rubber)

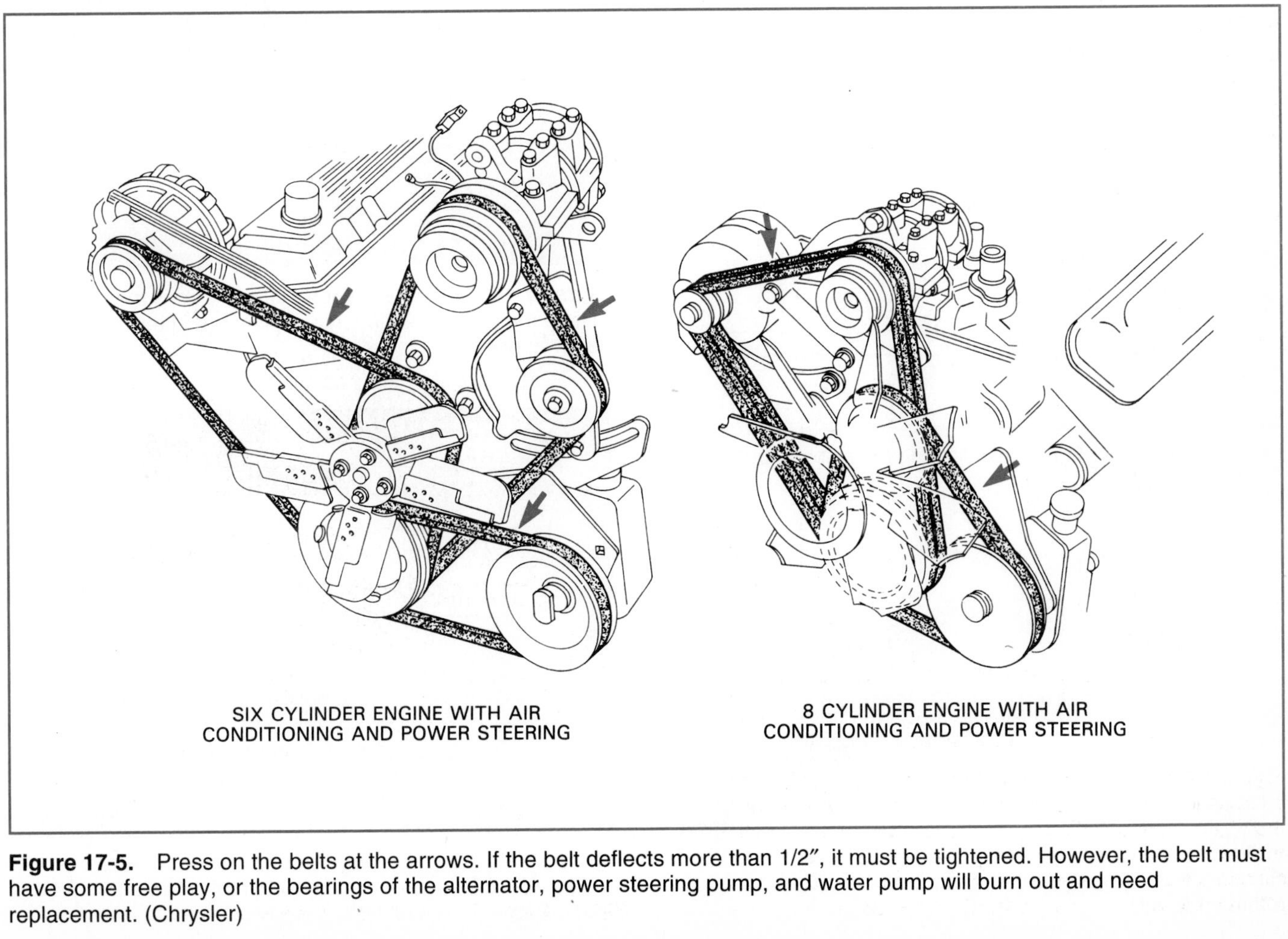

SIX CYLINDER ENGINE WITH AIR CONDITIONING AND POWER STEERING

8 CYLINDER ENGINE WITH AIR CONDITIONING AND POWER STEERING

Figure 17-5. Press on the belts at the arrows. If the belt deflects more than 1/2″, it must be tightened. However, the belt must have some free play, or the bearings of the alternator, power steering pump, and water pump will burn out and need replacement. (Chrysler)

important to change this type of belt periodically, even if the belt does not appear worn.

Serpentine Belts

The ***serpentine drive belt*** is a combination of a V-ribbed belt and a flat-back belt, Figure 17-7. The serpentine belt must be installed properly on the pulley grooves, Figure 17-8. The purpose of the serpentine belt is to eliminate the number of belts needed to drive the accessories. With the serpentine belt only one belt is needed. However, if this one belt breaks, none of the accessories will operate. This is why it is important to check for wear periodically, Figure 17-9. Most manufacturers install an ***automatic tensioning device***, Figure 17-10, when they use a serpentine belt. This device eliminates periodic adjustment of the serpentine belt. When the serpentine belt is used, a diagram indicating the routing of the belt is placed in the engine compartment, Figure 17-11.

Hoses and Clamps

Radiator hoses connect the radiator and engine. These hoses are fastened with ***hose clamps,*** Figure 17-12. The hoses should be inspected at every oil change to prevent problems from arising while traveling. Check the entire length of all coolant carrying hoses for either soft spots or hard, brittle spots, Figure 17-13. If either condition is found, the hose must be replaced.

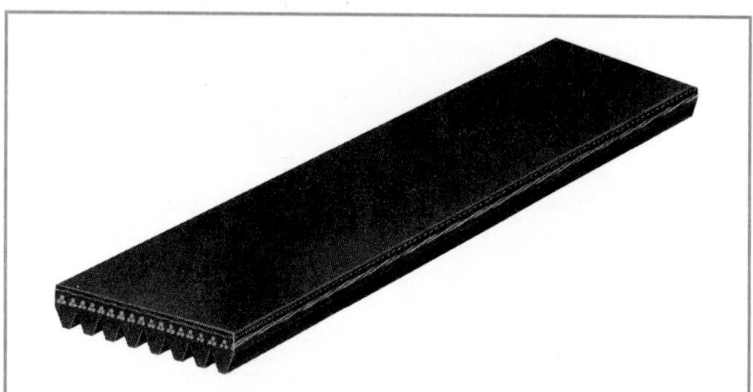

Figure 17-7. The serpentine drive belt is a V-ribbed belt. This combines the traditional V-belt, which drives by a wedging action, and a flat-back belt, which uses friction to drive the various components. Both sides transmit power on a serpentine drive. (Gates Rubber)

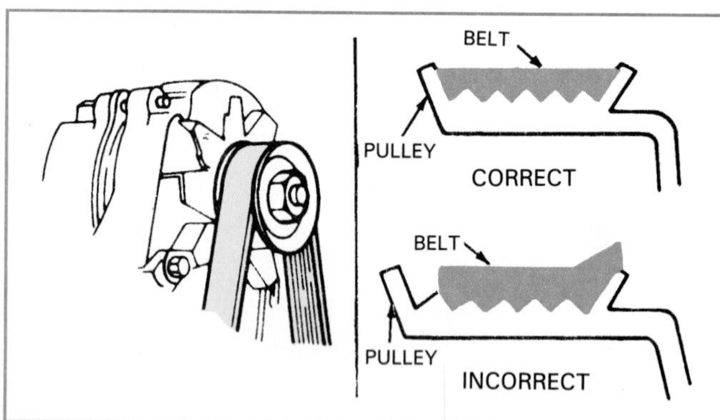

Figure 17-8. The correct installation of a V-ribbed belt is shown at the top. (Ford)

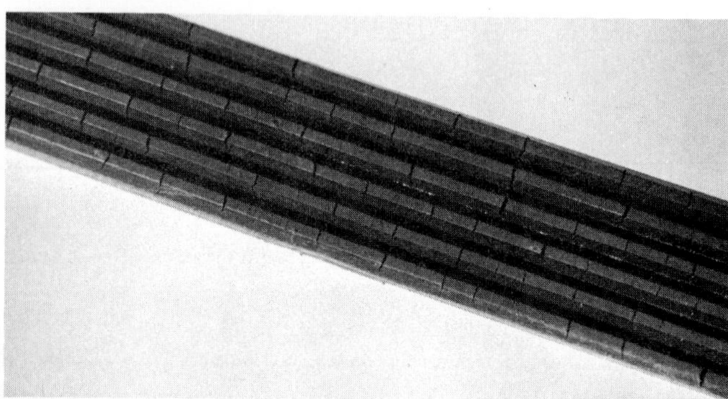

Figure 17-9. Cracks indicating wear on a V-ribbed belt. (Gates Rubber)

Figure 17-10. Automatic spring idler provides the proper tension and eliminates periodic adjustment of the belt. (Gates Rubber)

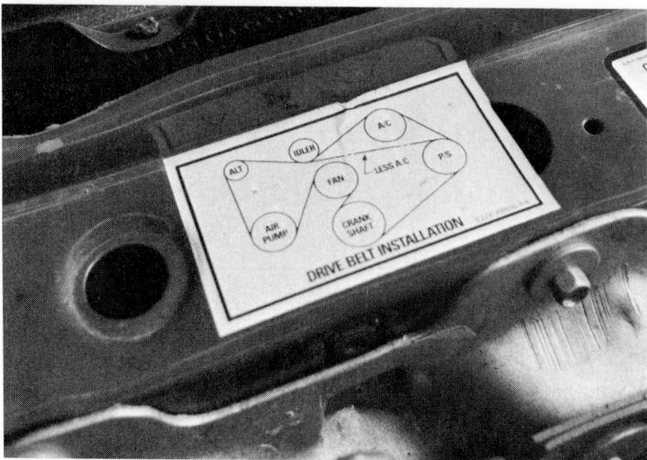

Figure 17-11. Decal in engine compartment provides routing instructions for the replacement of a serpentine belt. (Gates Rubber)

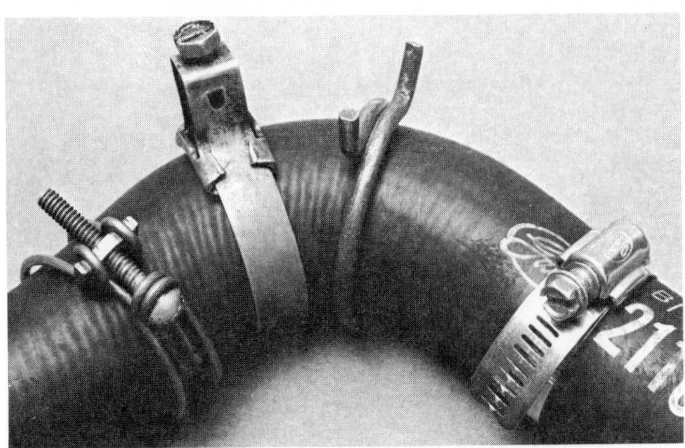

Figure 17-12. Various types of hose clamps. From left: twin wire; screw tower; spring or corbin clamp; worm drive clamp. (Gates Rubber)

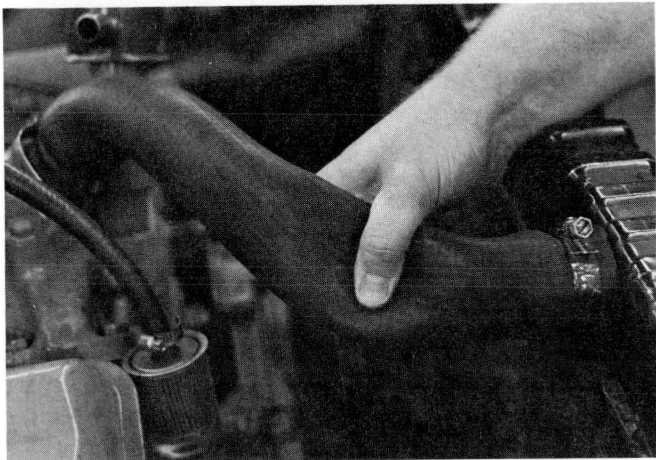

Figure 17-13. Check the entire length of each hose. If there are soft spots or hard, brittle spots, the hose will have to be replaced (Gates Rubber)

Sometimes, the simple removal of a radiator hose becomes difficult. Do not attempt to remove the hose by twisting it off with a pair of water pump pliers, as this will destroy the outlet. Instead, use a sharp knife and make an incision on the hose, Figure 17-14.

Lower Radiator Hose

The lower radiator hose connects the water pump to the radiator. As the pump turns, it creates a suction. The atmospheric pressure on the coolant forces it to the low pressure area at the water pump. To prevent the lower hose from collapsing due to this suction, a spring is generally placed inside the hose.

Radiators

The ***radiator*** is a device designed to dissipate the heat that the coolant absorbs from the engine. It is constructed to hold a large amount of water in tubes or passages that provide a large area in contact with the atmosphere.

The radiator usually consists of the ***radiator core*** (water-carrying tubes), the ***receiving tank,*** and the ***dispensing tank.*** In one design, the core is connected to the receiving tank at the top and to the dispensing tank at the bottom, Figure 17-15. In another design, the tanks are located on each side of the core.

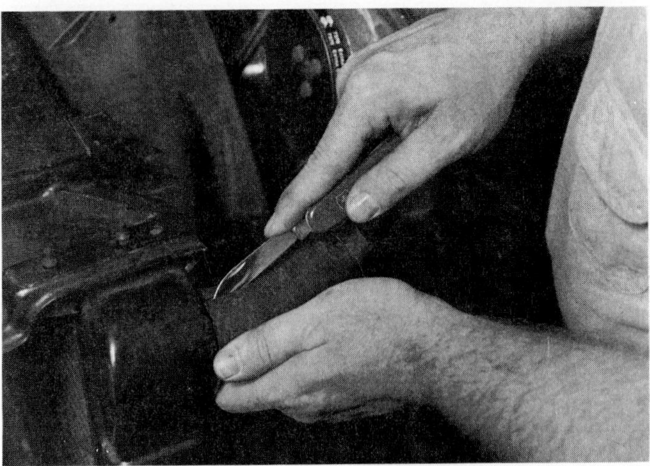

Figure 17-14. A sharp knife should be used to cut the radiator hose off if the hose is stuck on the outlet. (Gates Rubber)

Radiator cores are of two basic types, the fin-and-tube core, Figure 17-15A, and the ribbon-cellular, or honeycomb, core, Figure 17-15B. The popular fin-and-tube radiator core has the advantage of fewer soldered joints and is, therefore, a stronger construction. It consists of a series of parallel tubes extending from the upper tank to the lower tank. Fins are placed around the tubes to increase the area for radiating the heat.

The honeycomb core consists of a large number of narrow water passages that are made by soldering pairs of thin metal ribbons together along their edges. These tubes are crimped, and the soldered edges form the front and rear of the vertical tubes. These tubes are separated by fins of metal ribbon that help dissipate the heat.

In operation, water is pumped from the engine to the top (receiving) tank, where it spreads over the tops of the tubes. As the water passes down through the tubes, it loses its heat to the airstream that passes around the outside of the tubes.

To help spread the heated water over the top of all the tubes, a baffle plate is often placed in the upper tank, directly under the inlet hose from the engine.

While the usual construction of a radiator is to have the water circulate from the top to the bottom, crossflow radiators are designed to have the coolant flow from one side to the other, Figure 17-16. Additionally, some radiators are designed so that the coolant flows from the bottom to the top.

The core capacity of modern radiators is much smaller than the core capacity used in the past for a given engine. This is possible because systems now operate at pressures up to 17 psi. Pressurization makes the engine more efficient in terms of heat rejection to the coolant per horsepower developed. Smaller radiators also are the result of improved heat transfer efficiency of the radiator core.

Automatic Transmission Fluid Cooler

On cars that have automatic transmissions, a ***transmission fluid cooler*** is incorporated into the design of the

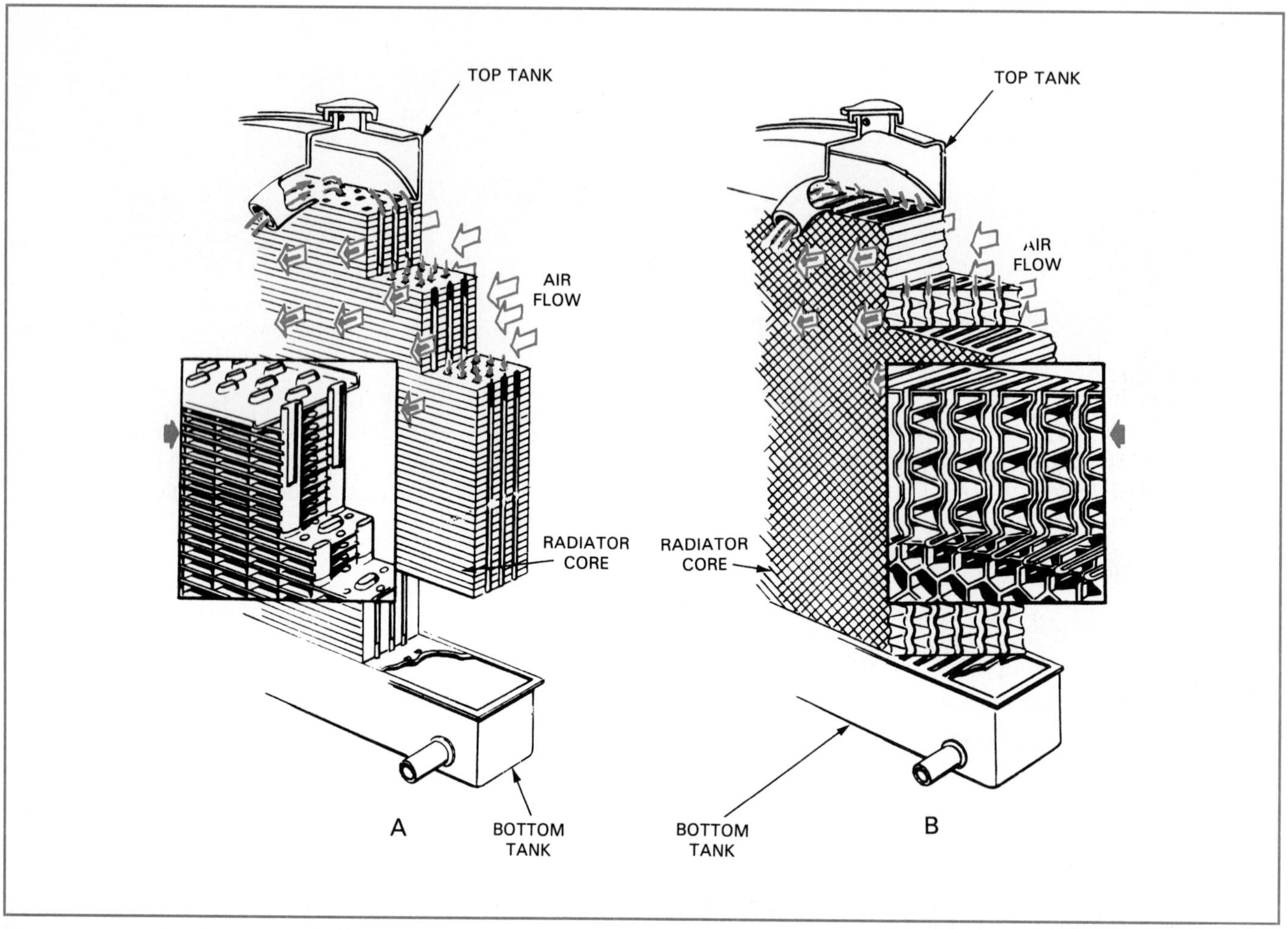

Figure 17-15. Radiator construction. A–Typical tube-type radiator. B–Cellular-type radiator.

radiator, Figure 17-17. This keeps the automatic transmission fluid at a low temperature, which prevents oxidation of the transmission fluid. This not only increases the life of the transmission fluid, but the transmission components as well. If the seams of the oil cooler should leak transmission fluid into the radiator, both the coolant and the automatic transmission fluid will turn into a thick, pink mixture. If this situation occurs, the radiator will have to be removed and the oil cooler repaired. In addition, the cooling system, the automatic transmission, the torque converter, and the oil cooler lines must be flushed out.

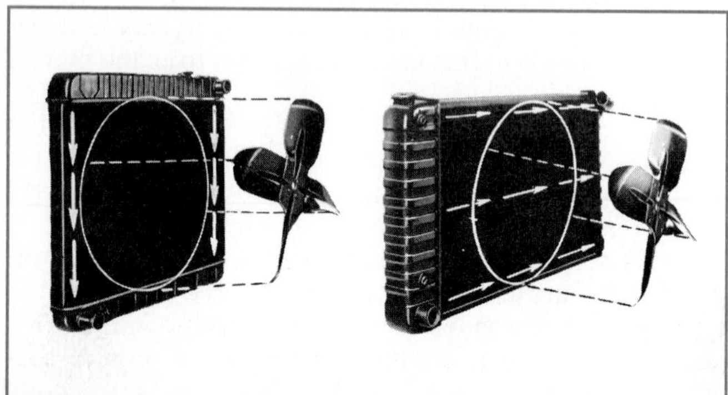

Figure 17-16. Flow of coolant can be from top to bottom or from side to side. The side-flow radiator allows a lower hood line for better aerodynamic styling.

Closed Cooling Systems

Most cooling systems today are ***closed systems.*** In these systems, a plastic tank is connected to the radiator by a rubber tube, Figure 17-18. As the coolant becomes hot and expands, the coolant flows out of the radiator and into the plastic tank, or reservoir. This prevents coolant from spilling out on the ground. Then, as the radiator tank cools, a vacuum is created forcing the coolant from the plastic reservoir back into the radiator, if needed. This brings the radiator to a specified level. Coolant should be added to this plastic tank when necessary.

Radiator Caps

Originally, the ***radiator cap*** served only to prevent the coolant from splashing out the filler opening. Today's radiator cap, Figure 17-19, is designed to seal the system so that it operates under 14 to 17 psi. This improves cooling efficiency and prevents evaporation of the coolant. Losses due to surging are also eliminated.

Since evaporation is reduced or eliminated, it is not necessary to add coolant as often. Consequently, the introduction of rust-forming materials is greatly reduced. Also, by operating at higher temperatures, the engine operates more efficiently.

The higher temperatures result from the higher pressure. Each psi placed on the coolant increases the boiling

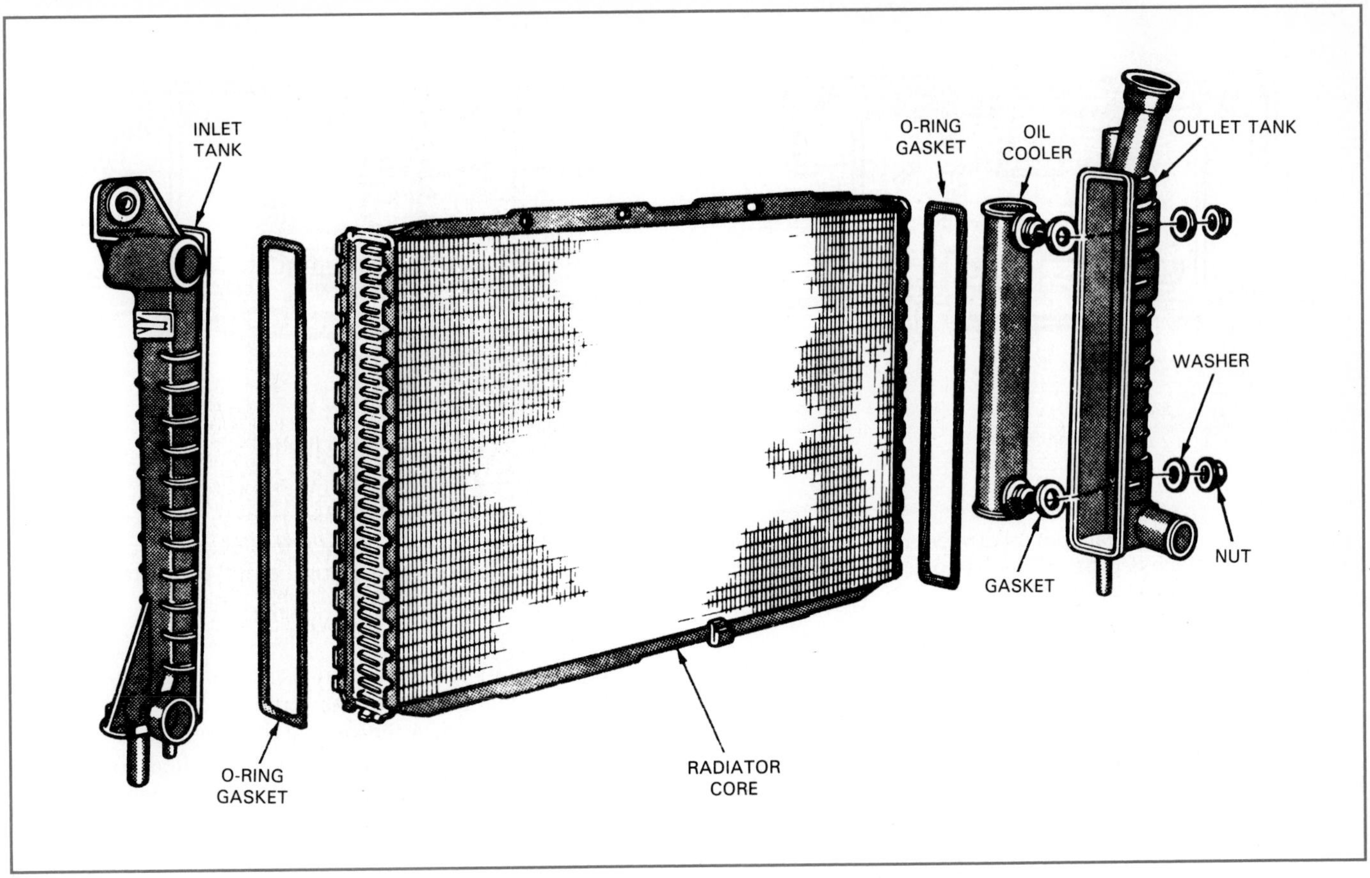

Figure 17-17. The automatic transmission oil cooler is located in the radiator outlet tank. (Ford)

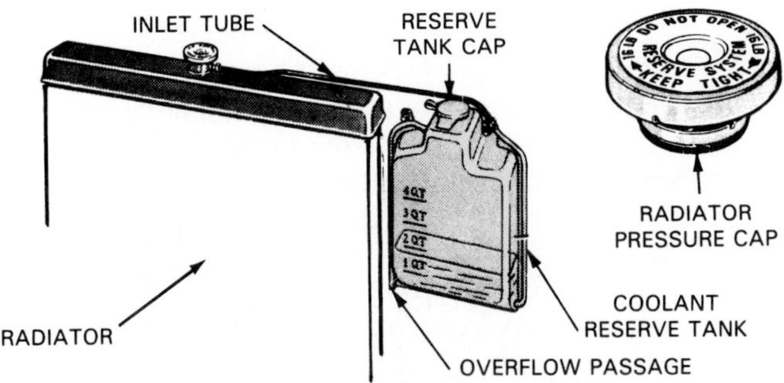

Figure 17-18. If the radiator level is low, coolant is siphoned from the reserve tank as the radiator cools.

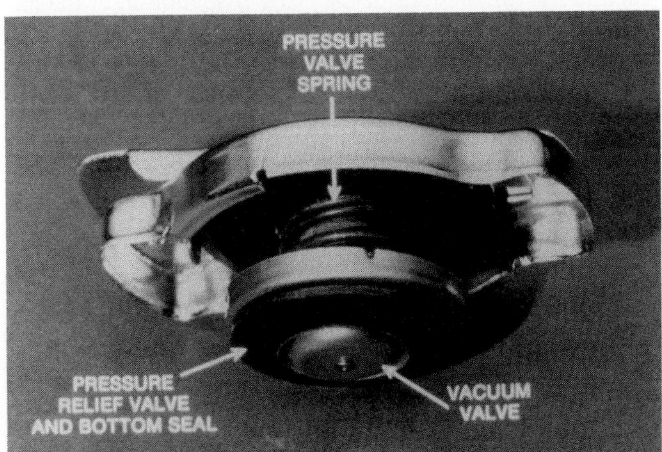

Figure 17-19. Nomenclature of a modern radiator pressure cap. (Everco)

point about 3.25°F. Since current radiator caps maintain a pressure of about 15 psi, the boiling point would be raised to 272°F (133°C).

The radiator cap fits over the radiator filler opening and seals it tightly. Two spring-loaded valves are provided. The larger valve is designed to relieve pressure at a predetermined value. The smaller valve opens to relieve the vacuum that forms when the steam in the system condenses after the engine is stopped, Figure 17-20. Otherwise, atmospheric pressure (14.7 psi) on the large, flat surface of the upper tank would cause it to buckle and open at the seams.

Warning: Never remove the radiator cap when the coolant is hot. Temperatures rise rapidly during the first few minutes after the engine is stopped, causing coolant to boil. Pressurized coolant may shoot from the radiator if the cap is removed, causing severe burns.

Cooling Fans

The ***cooling fan*** is designed to draw cooling air through the radiator core, Figure 17-1. This is necessary at slow speeds or when the engine is idling, since there is not enough air motion under these conditions to provide adequate cooling.

So that none of the force of the fan is dissipated, shrouding is often provided. In this way, the full force of the fan is used to draw air through the radiator core.

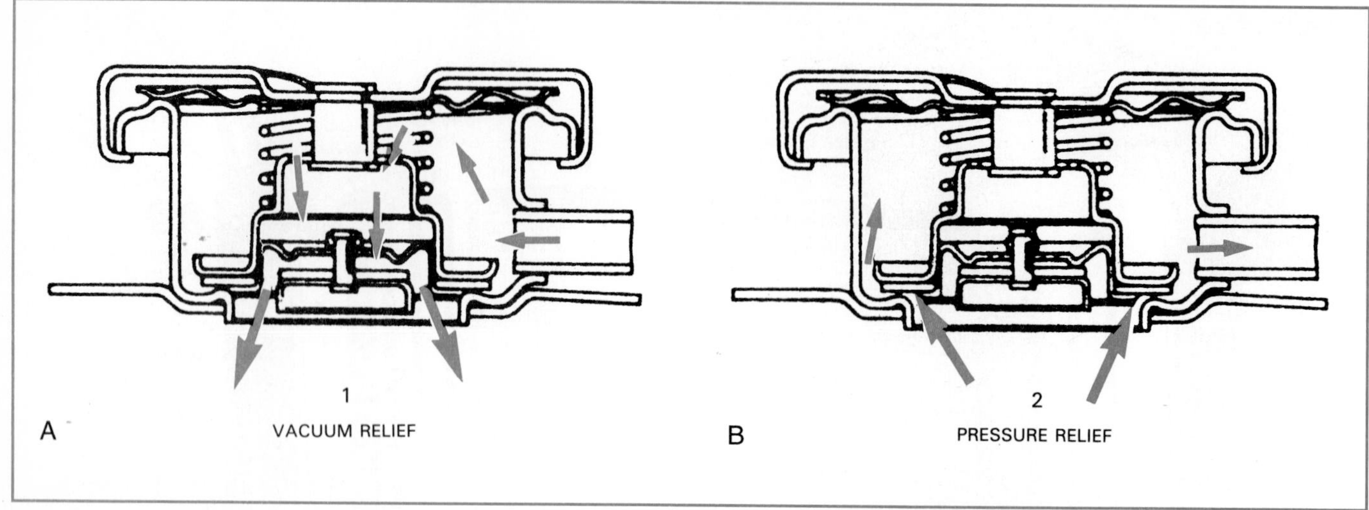

Figure 17-20. A–The vacuum relief valve is lowered allowing atmospheric pressure into the radiator to prevent the collapse of the radiator. B–Excess pressure in the cooling system is vented to the atmosphere or the reserve tank as the pressure relief valve is raised off its seat. (Oldsmobile)

The fan is sometimes mounted on an extension of the water pump shaft, Figure 17-3, and is driven by a V-belt from a pulley mounted on the front end of the crankshaft. Other fans are driven by an electric motor, Figure 17-21. Front wheel drive cars use an electric fan motor. It is mounted to a frame, which is connected to the radiator.

In order to reduce the noise made by the rotating fan, the fan blades are often placed asymmetrically, with the tips bent and rounded, Figure 17-22.

At 3000 rpm, an 18″ fan will consume over 2 hp, and power requirements increase very rapidly with the speed. Since the fan is required primarily at idle and at low vehicle speeds, couplings have been devised to disconnect or reduce the speed of the fan above certain engine speeds.

The ***fan drive clutch*** is a fluid coupling containing silicone oil. The more silicone oil in the coupling, the greater the fan speed. In one construction, Figures 17-23 and 17-24, a bimetallic coil on the front of the fluid coupling regulates the amount of silicone oil entering the coupling. This allows a valve to regulate the flow of oil to and from the reservoir.

Thermostats

Automotive internal combustion engines operate more efficiently when a high temperature is maintained within narrow limits. To accomplish this, a ***thermostat*** is inserted in the cooling system. In operation, the thermostat is designed to close off the flow of coolant from the engine to radiator until the engine has reached the desired operating temperature.

The thermostat is operated by a wax pellet, Figure 17-25, which expands and contracts with changes in engine temperature to open and close the valve.

When the water is cold, the thermostat closes the valve and stops the flow of water to the radiator. Then, as the water becomes hotter, the wax pellet expands to open the valve and allow the water to reach the radiator, Figure 17-26.

The opening and closing of the thermostat continues as more or less heat is developed by the engine. Consequently, the engine's operating temperature is maintained within narrow limits.

Thermostats are calibrated at the time of manufacture, and they are stamped with the temperature at which they are designed to open. A thermostat designed for use with an alcohol-type antifreeze usually is calibrated to open at 155°-160°F (68.3°-71.1°C), and be fully open at 180°F (82.2°C). Most modern cooling systems are designed to use permanent type antifreeze. The thermostats in these systems are calibrated to open between 188° and 195°F (86.7° and 90.6°C), and be fully open between 210° and 212°F (98.9° and 100°C).

Heater Core

The basic ***heater core*** used in automobiles is constructed in the same manner as the radiator. In operation, hot coolant from the cooling system is circulated through the heater core. The heater fan drives air past the hot heater core tubes and through ducts to the passenger compartment, Figure 17-27. Therefore, it is important to keep the heater water passages free from rust accumulations. When flushing the system, make sure any valves in the line going to the heater core are open.

The air that passes through the heater core is usually supplied from outside the vehicle through openings provided in the top or sides of the cowl. The motion of the car and the action of the fan force fresh air through the heater. Vent air valves control the amount of air passing through the heater and into the passenger compartment. Warm air from the heater is also directed to clear the inside of the windshield.

Antifreeze Solutions

When water freezes, it expands approximately nine percent in volume. Because of this great rate of expansion, it will break or seriously distort the vessel in which it is contained. Because of this characteristic, it is necessary to use a nonfreezing solution, or ***antifreeze solution,*** in the cooling system of water-cooled engines that are operated in climates where the temperature is below the freezing point of water.

The first type of antifreeze used was alcohol. However, when summer rolled around, the alcohol was flushed

A

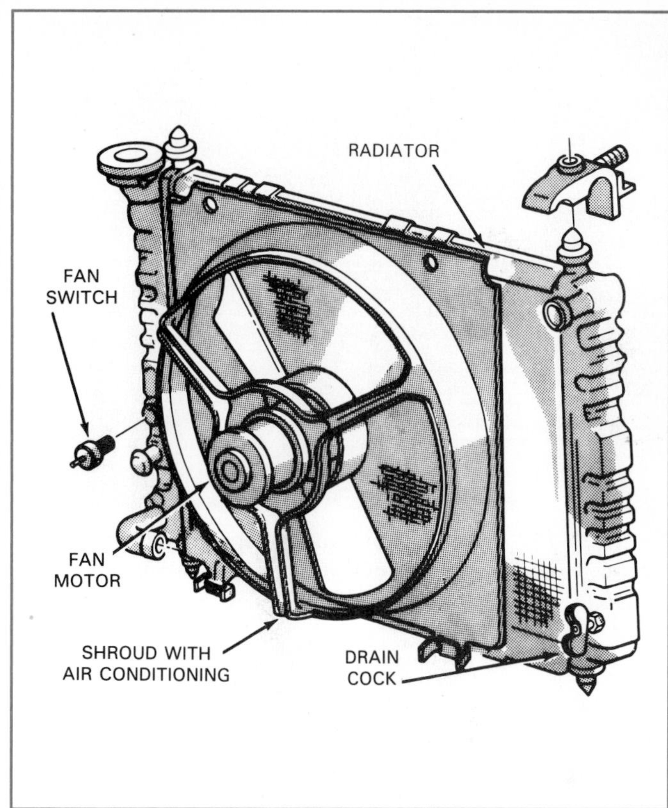

B

JUMPER
WIRE
FAN
SWITCH
ELECTRICAL
CONNECTOR

C

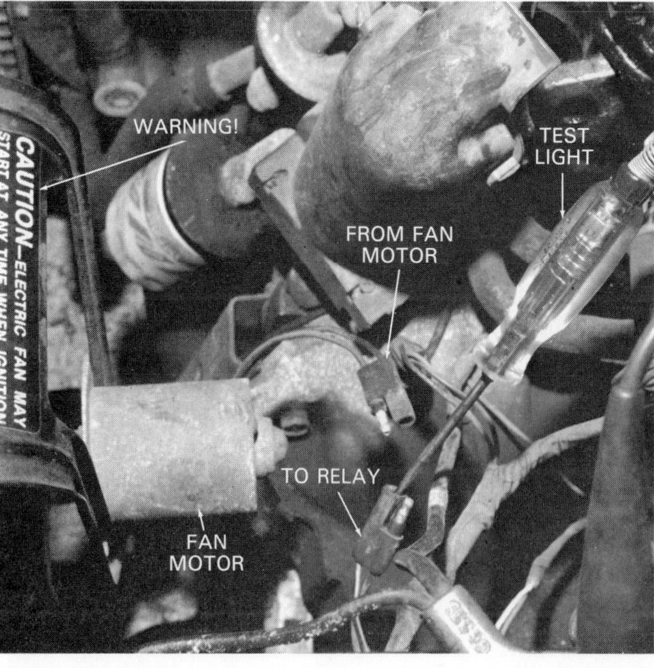

D

Figure 17-21. Transversely mounted engine. A–It is impossible for the engine to drive a fan on a front-wheel drive car. B–The fan switch on the radiator allows current to flow to the computer or fan relay after the coolant has reached operating temperature. The relay or computer then energizes the fan motor. C–If the fan fails to operate after the engine has reached operating temperature, remove the electrical connection from the fan switch. Then, jump the connections from the electrical connector and turn the ignition to the "on" position. If fan now operates, the fan switch on the radiator is defective. D–If the fan still fails to operate, disconnect the fan motor electrical connection and insert a test light as shown. If test light fails to glow, the wiring, relay, or computer is defective. However, if test light glows, the fan motor is defective. (Chrysler)

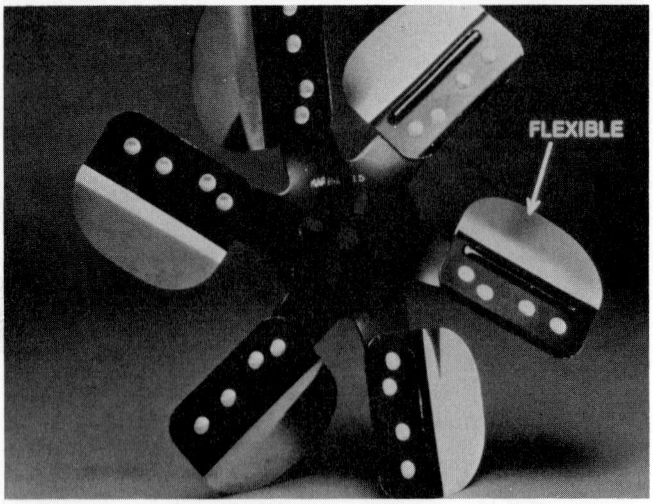

Figure 17-22. A flexible fan blade flattens out as rpms increase. This reduces the amount of drag on the engine, as the fan is not needed at high rpms to draw air through the radiator. (Everco)

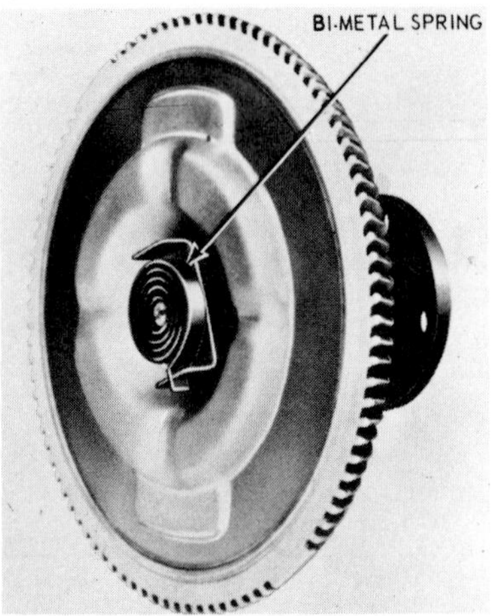

Figure 17-23. The bimetal spring is sensitive to heat and controls the flow of silicone oil to the fluid coupling.

Figure 17-24. A fluid coupling mounted to a fan. (Everco)

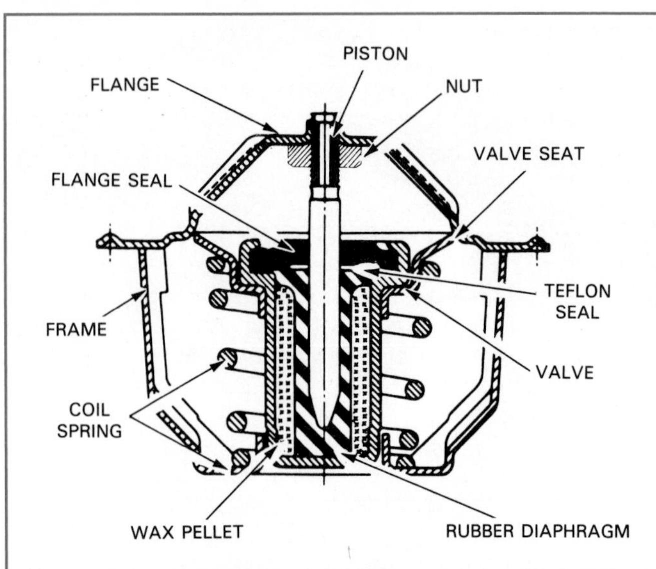

Figure 17-25. Nomenclature of a modern engine thermostat. (Cadillac)

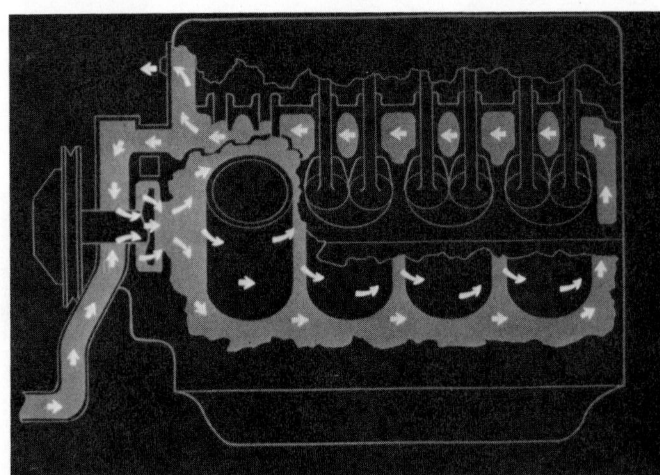

Figure 17-26. When the engine is cold, the coolant circulates through the engine block only. When the engine temperature rises, the thermostat opens and the coolant flows through the upper radiator hose to the radiator. (Everco)

Figure 17-27. A heater core is basically a mini-radiator located within the passenger compartment. (Everco)

from the system. It was replaced with water. This is because of the fast evaporation rate of alcohol when exposed to the heat that is incurred during summer. Pure water also has a higher boiling point than alcohol. When fall came again, the water was flushed from the cooling system and replaced with alcohol.

Today, antifreeze is of the permanent type. This means that the solution of antifreeze and water that makes up engine coolant does not have to be changed at the end of each season. However, engine coolant must be changed at least every two years. This is because the heat from the engine destroys the additives found in the antifreeze. These additives must be replenished, or rust will develop in the cooling system.

Since copper, iron, aluminum, brass, solder, etc., are used in parts of the engine in contact with the coolant, it is important that the antifreeze does not corrode any of these metals. Also, the material should not be harmful to the various types of rubber used in the hoses. The most suitable antifreeze is ***ethylene glycol.***

Freezing Protection

The mixing of an antifreeze with water forms a solution that has a lower freezing point than water. The temperature at which an antifreeze will freeze depends on the strength of the solution, Figure 17-28. This varies with each antifreeze, Figure 17-29. Pure ethyl alcohol freezes at -174.6°F (-114.8°C) and methyl alcohol freezes at -144.2°F (-97.9°C). A 68% solution of ethylene glycol freezes at -92°F (-68.9°C). Increased concentrations would not further reduce the freezing point of the solution.

Expansion of Antifreeze

Antifreeze solutions will expand slightly more than water when heated, Figure 17-30. When water is heated from 40°F to 180°F (4°C to 82°C), it will expand approximately 1/4 pint per gallon. For the same range of temperature, ethylene glycol will expand 1/3 pint per gallon, methyl alcohol 2/5 pint per gallon, and ethyl alcohol 1/2 pint per gallon.

To avoid loss of antifreeze due to expansion, the cooling system must not be completely filled. In the case

Figure 17-28. Checking the engine coolant with hydrometer. Coolant should test to at least -20°F (-29°C). (Everco)

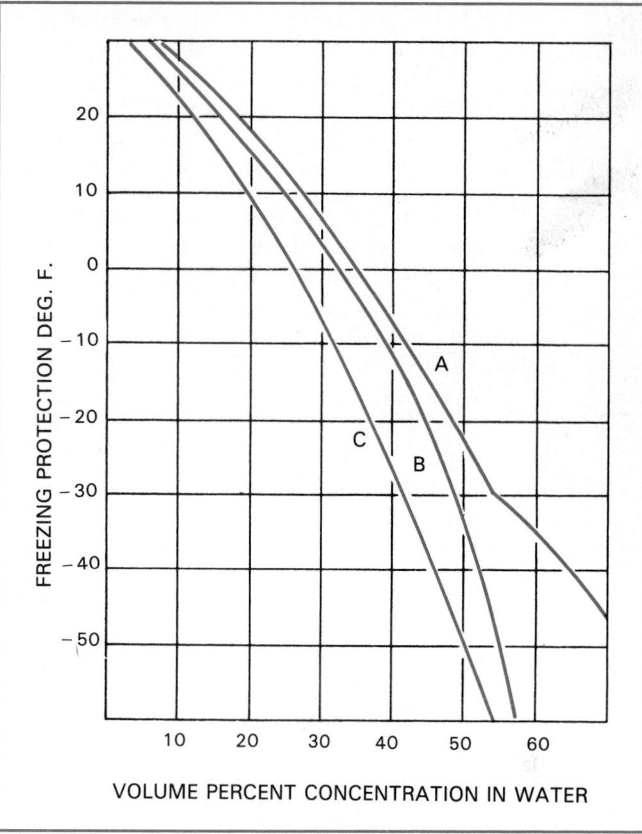

Figure 17-29. Freezing protection provided by different concentrations of antifreeze solutions. A–Ethyl alcohol. B–Ethylene glycol. C–Methyl alcohol.

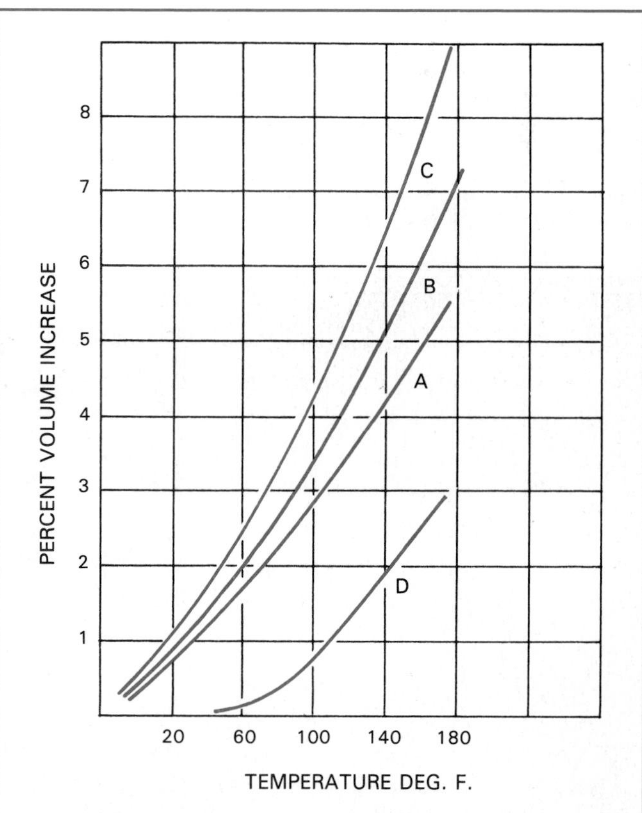

Figure 17-30. Expansion of antifreeze solutions from -20°F to 180°F (-29°C to 82°C). A–Ethylene glycol. B–Methyl alcohol. C–Ethyl alcohol. D–Water.

of a 20-quart capacity cooling system that was completely filled at -20°F (-29°C), there would be a loss of 2 1/3 pints of ethylene glycol; 2 7/8 pints of methyl alcohol; or 3 2/3 pints of ethyl alcohol when the temperature reaches 180°F (82°C).

Boiling Point

When ethylene glycol is added to water, the ***boiling point*** of the solution is raised. When either methyl alcohol or ethyl alcohol is added to water, the boiling point of the solution is lowered. For example, methyl and ethyl alcohol solutions affording protection to -20°F will have boiling points of about 180°F. A solution of ethylene glycol that protects to -20°F has a boiling point of 223°F (106°C). As the pressure that is placed on the coolant is increased, the temperature at which the solution boils is increased, Figure 17-31.

The normal boiling point of a coolant solution is important, and so is the change in boiling point brought about by placing the solution under pressure. With pressurized cooling systems used today, a coolant with a higher boiling point than water is necessary. Ethylene glycol fills these requirements and is installed in all vehicles built in the United States.

The higher boiling point of ethylene glycol makes it a highly satisfactory coolant for use in both warm and cold weather. In addition to its higher boiling point, ethylene glycol is provided with a rust inhibitor.

Car manufacturers advise against the use of water as a coolant. If it is used, boiling can result–particularly in hot weather, when towing another vehicle, or when the air conditioner is in use.

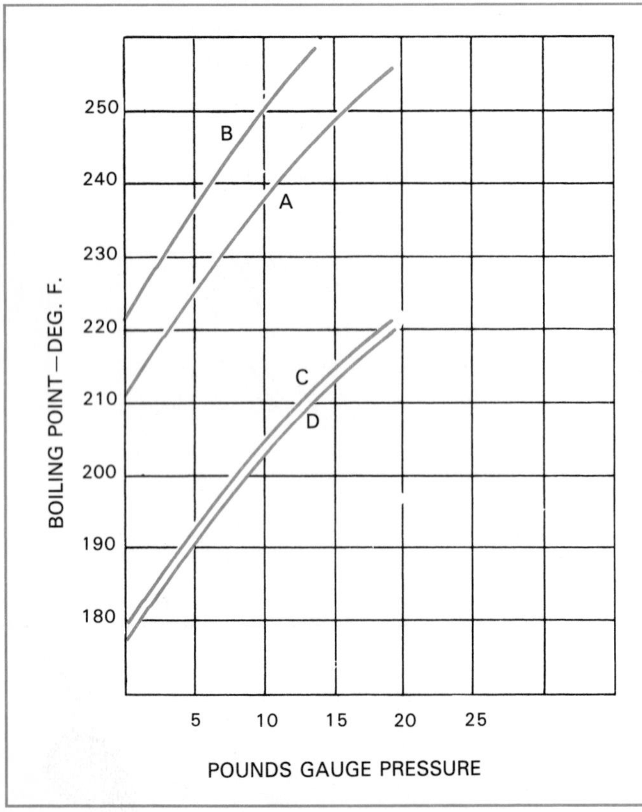

Figure 17-31. Chart shows effects of pressure on boiling points of various antifreeze solutions. A–Water. B–Ethylene glycol. C–Ethyl alcohol. D–Methyl alcohol.

Evaporation

There is virtually no loss of ethylene glycol solution due to ***evaporation.*** Any loss of coolant solution that does occur is practically all water. This evaporation loss is greatest under prolonged high speed driving conditions or extended idling periods. Alcohol-based antifreeze solutions have a greater rate of evaporation, so they are seldom used.

Rust Inhibitors

In order to reduce the formation of rust, commercial antifreeze contains a ***rust inhibitor*** designed to prevent corrosion. Some products also contain ***antifoaming agents.***

The prevention of rust is essential if the cooling system is to be maintained at maximum efficiency. After the cooling system is drained, a rust inhibitor should be added if water is used as a coolant. Year-round use of antifreeze is a more practical answer.

Air-Cooled Engines

Air-cooled engines were used successfully in the early days of the automobile. Air cooling of a reciprocating piston engine requires constant circulation of a lot of air. Forced air circulation is provided by a fan of generous capacity, which is usually driven from the engine crankshaft by a belt, or by fan blades formed in the flywheel, Figure 17-32.

Radiation fins are provided on the cylinders and cylinder heads, Figure 17-33. In some applications, the crankcase also is "finned," Figure 17-34.

Air-cooled engines are often surrounded by a metal housing and ***baffle plates*** to direct cooling air where desired. When the engine is running, forced air is directed over the fins to dissipate the heat. In order to regulate the

Figure 17-32. Tecumseh air cooled engine. The fan blades are built into the flywheel.

engine temperature by controlling the volume of cooling air, a thermostat is installed inside the metal housing that encloses the engine. The thermostat unit is connected to ***control flaps,*** or an ***air control ring.*** As the engine becomes hotter, the control ring opens wider to admit more air. When the engine is cold, the control ring closes. See Figures 17-35 and 17-36.

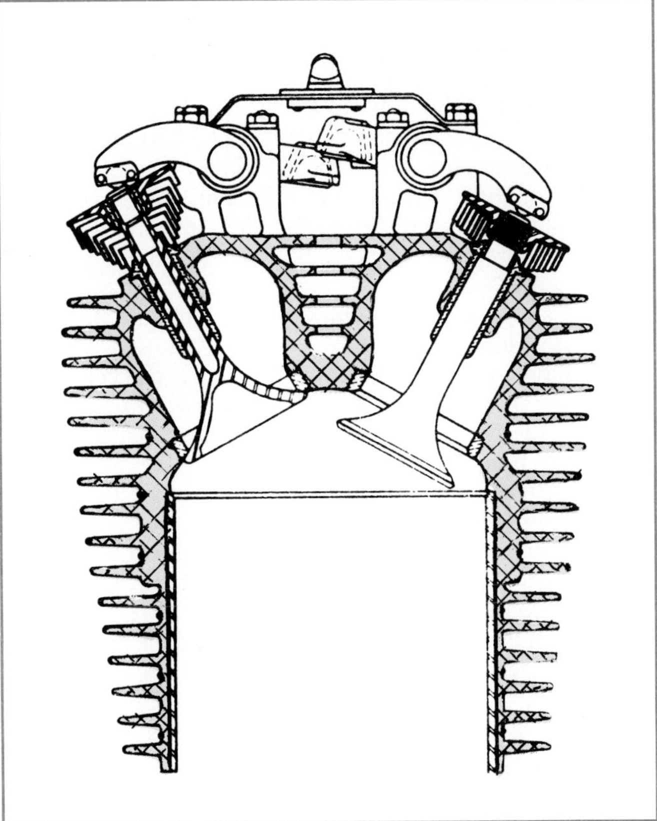

Figure 17-33. Cooling fins on the cylinder head are larger in diameter and heavier than those around the cylinder.

Figure 17-34. This Teledyne Wisconsin engine is completely finned.

With the ring closed, air circulation is restricted and a cold engine warms up more rapidly. Rapid warm-up is characteristic of air-cooled engines, since they do not have to heat the coolant in the water jackets and the radiator. This rapid warm-up is helpful in avoiding sludge and crankcase dilution.

Air-cooled engines normally operate at somewhat higher temperatures than water-cooled engines, but they do not overheat if the cooling system is maintained reasonably well.

However, air-cooled engines should never be "lugged." If the engine is pulling hard at slow speed, more heat than usual will be generated at a time when less cooling air is supplied. In this case, there is no reservoir of water to absorb excess heat (as on a water-cooled engine).

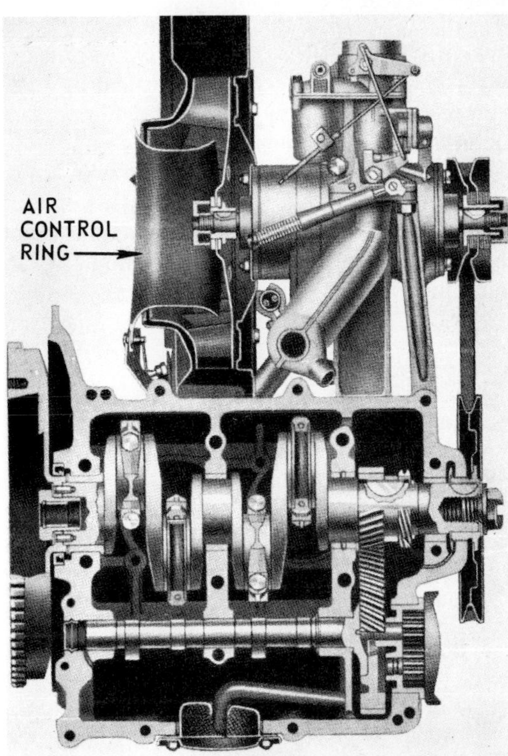

Figure 17-35. An air control ring moves in and out to control the volume of air supplied to the fan. (Volkswagen)

Figure 17-36. The air control ring is regulated by the cross shaft.

Therefore, engine speed should be maintained by shifting to a lower gear.

Higher engine operating temperatures mean higher engine efficiency, but this characteristic is also accused of causing noise. One reason given for air-cooled engines being noisier than water-cooled engines is that there is no silencing provided by water jackets. Another reason is the greater clearances sometimes provided between operating parts. This relates to the fact that higher temperatures require more room for expansion of the metals.

Regardless of the advantages and disadvantages of air cooling, it has been used successfully in automobiles, trucks, tractors, airplanes, and boats.

Oil Cooling

While it is unusual for passenger car engines to provide special cooling for the engine lubricating oil, many race car engines have cooling fins on the oil pan to reduce the temperature of the engine oil.

Figure 17-37 shows a sectional view of an Offenhauser race engine provided with cooling fins on the lower outside of the oil pan and on the sides of the crankcase. While this is a water-cooled engine, cooling fins are also provided on the exterior of the water jacket.

Cooling System Testing

The most frequent cooling system complaints are leakage of coolant and overheating. Generally, the best troubleshooting approach is to test and inspect, followed by the service or parts replacement required.

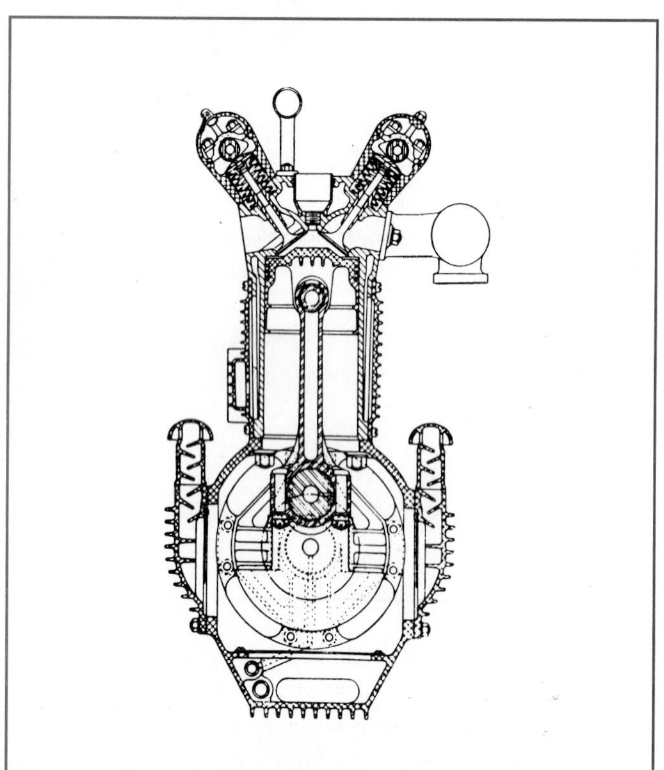

Figure 17-37. This Offenhauser race engine has cooling fins on the oil pan, around the water jackets, and around the crankcase.

Since the system is pressurized, it is logical to test the radiator pressure cap for pressure-holding ability and to pressure-test the entire cooling system for coolant leakage. First, make sure the correct cap for the vehicle is installed on the radiator. The cap must seat properly on the filler neck of the radiator and seal the system so that it operates under 14-17 psi.

Next, remove the radiator pressure cap and clean it thoroughly. Check the valves and seating surfaces for damage. Wet the rubber seals with water and install the cap on a ***pressure tester*** designed for this purpose.

Operate the tester pump and observe the highest pressure gauge reading, Figure 17-38. The release pressure should be within the manufacturer's specified limits (12 to 15 psi, for example). Allow the maximum pressure reading to remain on the gauge and watch for a pressure drop. If the cap holds this pressure for 30 seconds or more, the cap is good. If the pressure drops quickly, a new radiator pressure cap is needed.

Pressure-test the cooling system with the engine at normal operating temperature:

1. Carefully remove radiator pressure cap and check coolant level (should be 1 to 1 1/2″ below base of filler neck).
2. Test the protection level of the coolant, using an antifreeze hydrometer.
3. Wipe the inside of the filler neck and inspect the inside sealing seat for damage.
4. Inspect the overflow tube for dents, kinks, or obstructions.
5. Inspect the cams on the outside of the filler neck. Reform the cams if they are bent.
6. Attach the pressure tester to the filler neck and operate the tester pump to apply a specified pressure to the system.
7. Observe the pressure gauge reading, Figure 17-39. If the system holds this pressure for two minutes, no coolant leakage is indicated. If the pressure drops quickly, examine the entire cooling system for external coolant leakage. If the pressure drops slowly, tighten the hose clamp connections and then retest the cooling system. If no leakage is apparent, check for internal coolant leakage.

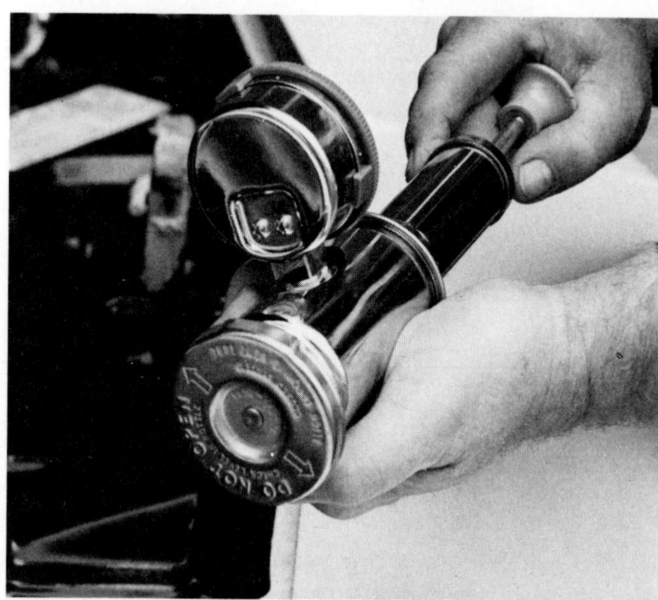

Figure 17-38. Testing a radiator pressure cap. (AC-Delco)

Figure 17-39. Pressure testing the cooling system. Make sure the engine is fully warmed up before testing. Pressure should hold for at least two minutes. (AC-Delco)

Testing for Leaks

If frequent additions of coolant are required to maintain the proper level in the system, check all units and connections for leakage. Make the inspection when the system is hot and operating. Grayish white areas, rust stains, or antifreeze dye stains are sure signs of coolant leakage.

Exhaust gas or air trapped in the cooling system may cause the level of the coolant in the system to rise. Air may be drawn into the system through leakage at the seal in the water pump. Exhaust gas may be forced into the system as the result of a defective cylinder head gasket or a damaged head. Extreme overheating can occur.

A piece of rubber tubing and a bottle of clear water can be used to check for air or gas leakage into the cooling system as follows:

1. With cooling system cold, add coolant to the proper level.
2. Install a non-pressurized radiator cap. Attach a length of rubber tubing to overflow pipe.
3. Operate engine at a high speed until it reaches operating temperature.
4. Maintain this speed and insert free end of the rubber tubing into the bottle of water. A continuous flow of bubbles indicates that air is being drawn into the system from the water pump seal or is being forced into system from a blown cylinder head gasket.
5. To determine whether defect is in the pump or head gasket, run a small amount of engine oil through carburetor throat or fuel injector throttle body. This will cause smoky bubbles to appear in the bottle if the head gasket is defective.

Removing Ethylene Gylcol from Crankcase

If ethylene glycol leaks into the engine oil (milky substance on the oil dipstick), it will clog the oil lines, cause the pistons to seize, severely damaging the engine.

When it has been determined that ethylene glycol is in the lubricating system, the first step is to locate the cause of the coolant leak (a blown gasket, cracked head, or cracked block), and then make the necessary repairs. Next, drain the engine oil and remove the engine oil filter. Then, fill the crankcase to the full mark on the dipstick with a mixture of 3 quarts SAE 10W engine oil and 2 quarts Butyl Cellusolve (can be obtained from a chemical supply house).

Run the engine at idling speed for about 30 minutes, paying particular attention to the oil pressure. Then, drain the engine and flush it with 3 quarts of SAE 10W oil and 2 quarts of kerosene. Idle the engine with this flushing oil for about 10 minutes. Finally, drain the flushing oil, install an new oil filter, and refill crankcase with the correct engine oil.

Cooling System Troubleshooting

Common cooling system problems and probable causes are outlined below.

Leakage of Coolant

- Faulty radiator pressure cap.
- Defective radiator.
- Bad thermostat housing gasket.
- Cracked or deteriorated radiator hose.
- Cracked or deteriorated heater hose.
- Defective heater core.
- Faulty heater water control valve.
- Defective water pump seal or gasket.
- Rusted out core hole plugs.
- Damaged coolant reserve tank.
- Bad cylinder head gasket.
- Cracked cylinder head, manifold, or block.

Overheating

- Faulty radiator pressure cap.
- Defective thermostat.
- Loose, slipping, or broken fan belt.
- Worn pulleys.
- Damaged fan.
- Faulty fan drive clutch.
- Collapsed lower radiator hose.
- Obstructed front grille.
- Clogged radiator fins.
- Clogged A/C condenser fins.
- Clogged radiator tubes. (See Figure 17-40.)
- Incorrect cooling system components.
- Defective water pump.
- Low coolant level.
- Low coolant protection (low boiling point).
- Water used as coolant (low boiling point).
- Cooling system capacity inadequate for load.
- Air trapped in cooling system.
- Clogged coolant passage in engine block.
- Excessive use of A/C while vehicle is parked or while operated in stop-and-go traffic.

Figure 17-40. To check if a radiator is plugged, remove the radiator cap after engine has reached operating temperature. Squeeze the upper radiator hose after the engine is placed on a fast idle. If coolant spills out of radiator, the radiator is plugged and must be rodded out. (Everco)

- Retarded ignition timing.
- Sticking manifold heat control valve.
- Clogged exhaust system.
- Low engine oil level.
- Excessive engine friction.
- Dragging brakes.

Low Operating Temperature

- Wrong cooling fan.
- Wrong radiator.
- Wrong thermostat.
- Defective thermostat.
- Fan pulley too small.

No Coolant Flow Through Heater Core

- Clogged water pump return pipe.
- Collapsed or clogged heater hose.
- Clogged heater core.
- Plugged outlet in thermostat housing.
- Obstructed heater bypass hole in cylinder head.

Inoperative Coolant Recovery System

- Faulty radiator pressure cap.
- Coolant level below add mark.
- Clogged or leaking overflow tube.
- Plugged vent in recovery reservoir.
- Pinched or kinked reservoir hose.

Noise

- Fan contacting shroud.
- Loose water pump impeller.
- Dry fan belt.
- Loose fan belt.

Figure 17-41. To see if the water pump bearings are worn, grip the fan blades 180° apart. Exert an up-and-down force on the fan blades. If there is any up-and-down movement of the fan blades, the water pump bearings are defective and the water pump must be replaced.

- Rough drive pulley.
- Worn water pump bearing. (See Figure 17-41.)

Cooling System Flush

There are several methods for removing the old coolant from the cooling system. The method requiring no special tools is to remove the cylinder block drain plug(s), Figure 17-42, and let water circulate through the engine while it is running. Make sure that a garden hose is placed in the radiator while the coolant is circulating and draining.

Another method that is used by most repair facilities is called ***fast flushing.*** This method involves the use of a flushing "T," placed in line of the heater hose, Figure 17-43. A special coupling is then used to connect a hose to the "T" and clear water is forced through the entire cooling system while the engine is running, Figure 17-43. Once clear water is flowing out of the radiator neck (radiator cap removed), the flush is complete.

If accumulations of lime and rust must be removed from the system, the engine and the radiator must be ***reversed flushed,*** Figure 17-44. This involves using a flushing gun that forces water through the radiator at high pressures. Compressed air is used to pressurize the water. In rare instances when the reverse flushing fails to clean the deposits from the radiator, the radiator must be removed and rodded out by a radiator repair shop.

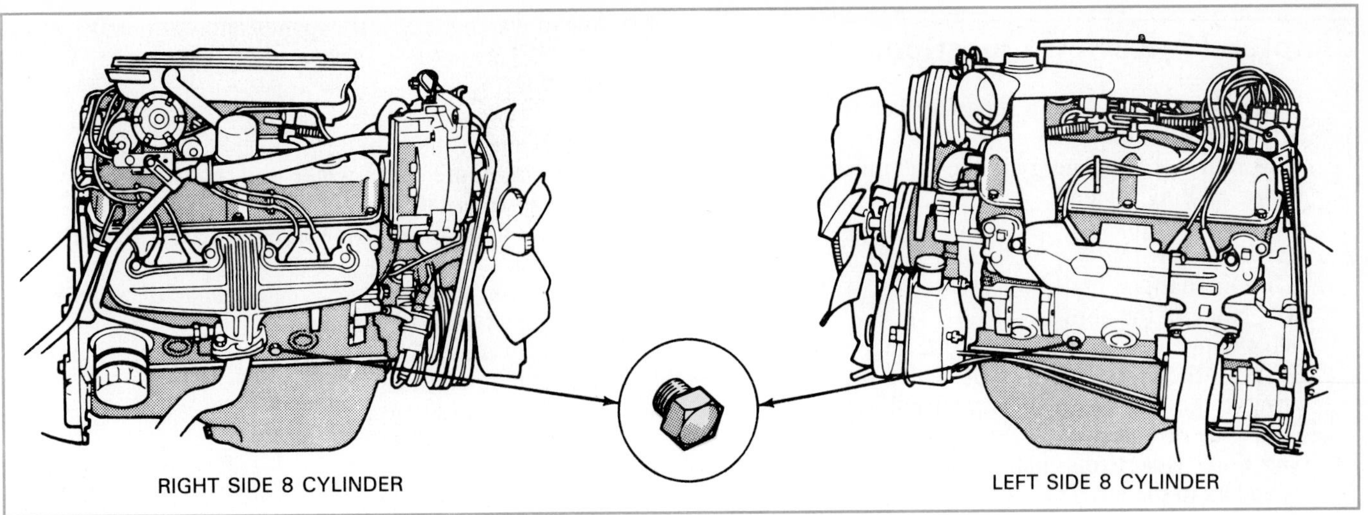

Figure 17-42. The cylinder block drain plug is located near the lowest point of the block. (Chrysler)

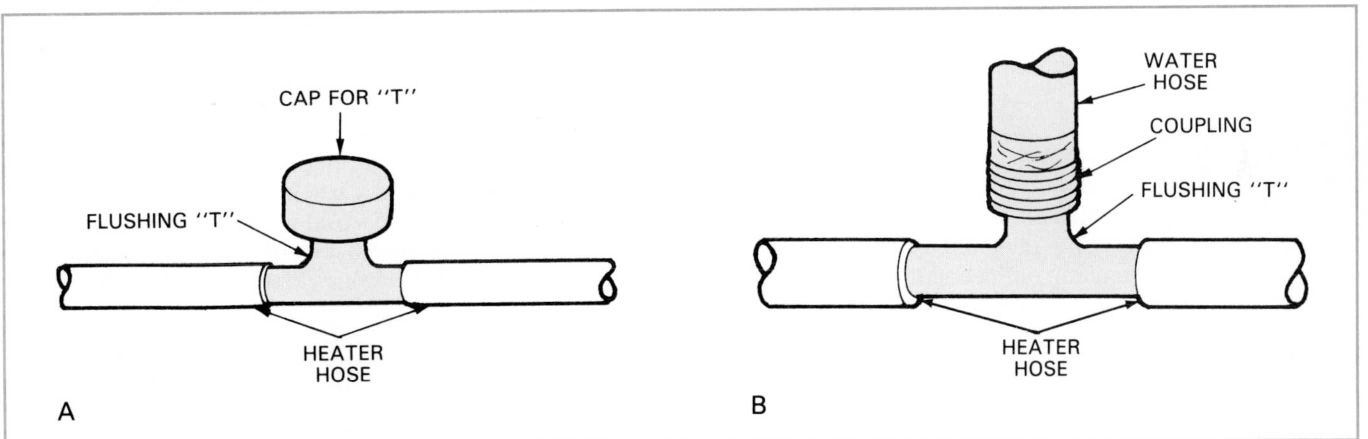

Figure 17-43. Fast flush. A–The flushing "T" is inserted in the heater hose. B–After removing the cap, a special coupling is screwed to the flushing "T." A water hose is then screwed into the coupling, and water is forced through the cooling system.

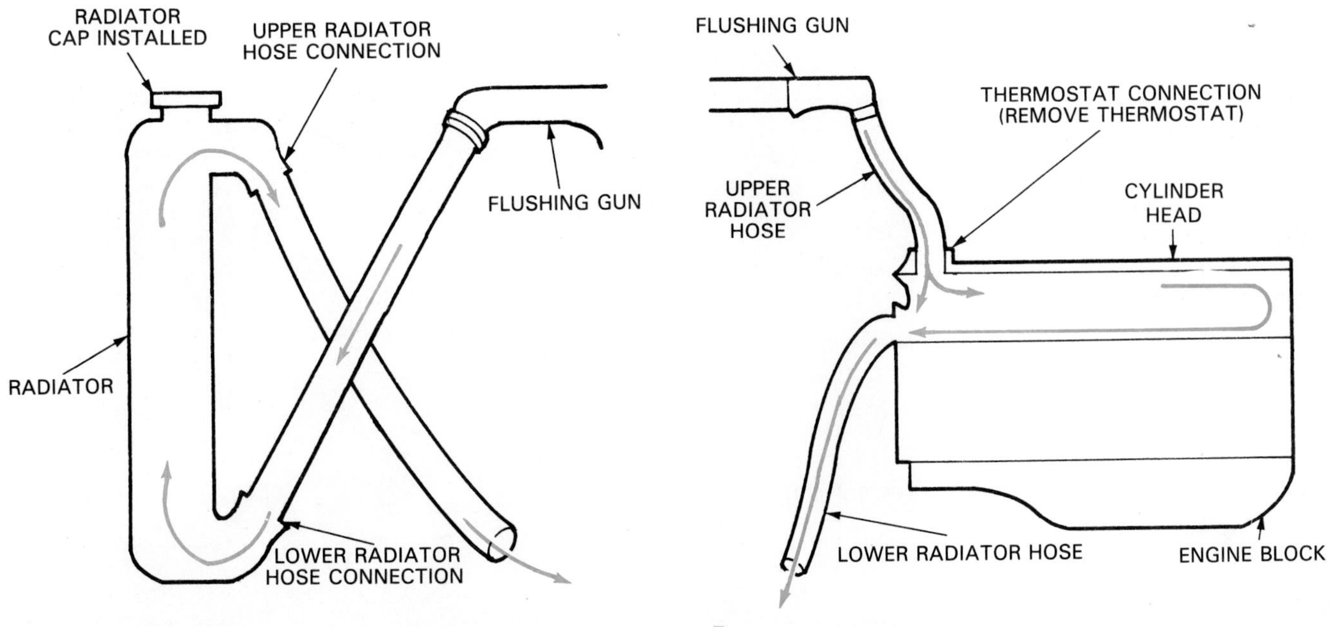

Figure 17-44. Reverse flushing. A–The flushing gun uses water under high pressure to remove rust and lime accumulation from the radiator. B–The flushing gun forces rust and lime accumulation from the engine block.

Chapter 17–Review Questions

Write your answers on a separate sheet of paper. Do not write in this book.

1. How much of heat energy in the fuel must be handled by the cooling system?
   (A) One-fourth.
   (B) One-third.
   (C) One-half.
   (D) None of the above.
2. What happens to the balance of the heat energy?
3. Several thousand gallons of water are circulated through the cooling system every half-hour of operation. True or False?
4. The water jackets dissipate most of the heat from the cylinders to the air. True or False?
5. What is rust?
6. Name two causes of engine hot spots.
7. Automobile engine water pumps are usually of the positive displacement type. True or False?
8. Antifreeze must be mixed with water. True or False?
9. A water pump seal may leak:
   (A) air.
   (B) water.
   (C) Both A & B.
   (D) None of the above.
10. Thermostats are installed:
    (A) between the pump inlet and the radiator.
    (B) between the pump outlet and the water jacket.
    (C) between the water jacket outlet and the radiator.
    (D) All of the above.
11. Where does the water from the engine usually enter the radiator?
    (A) Top.
    (B) Bottom.
    (C) Side.
    (D) None of the above.
12. When water freezes, it expands approximately:
    (A) 4%.
    (B) 6%.
    (C) 9%.
    (D) None of the above.
13. Under pressure, does water boil at a higher temperature or a lower temperature?
14. Why is a vacuum valve needed in a radiator pressure cap?
15. In addition to providing greater capacity, what is the purpose of an auxiliary tank?
16. Which of the following protects against freezing to the lowest temperature?
    (A) Ethylene glycol.
    (B) Methyl alcohol.
    (C) Ethyl alcohol.
    (D) None of the above.
17. An ethylene glycol solution will boil at a lower temperature than water. True or False?
18. In an air-cooled engine, how much of the total volume of cooling air is directed to the cylinder heads?
    (A) 40%.
    (B) 60%.
    (C) 80%.
    (D) None of the above.
19. How can an air-cooled engine with the cooling system in good working order become overheated?
20. What can be done to avoid such overheating?
21. Name two possible reasons why an air-cooled engine might make more noise than a comparable water-cooled engine?
22. Note one distinct advantage of an air-cooled engine.
23. A milky substance on the dipstick indicates:
    (A) a normal condition.
    (B) engine overheating.
    (C) coolant has entered the crankcase.
    (D) a loose water pump bearing.
    (E) None of the above.

A serpentine drive belt drives all engine accessories. (Pontiac)

Chapter 18
Diesel and Other Engines

After studying this chapter, you will be able to:
❍ List the different types of engines.
❍ Explain how a diesel engine works.
❍ Describe how the rotary engine operates.

Diesel Engines

Diesel engines are similar to gasoline engines, Figure 18-1. They are built in both two-cycle and four-cycle designs. They may be water cooled or air cooled. They are heavier in structure than gasoline engines to withstand the higher pressures resulting from the high compression ratios used. In a full diesel engine, the compression ratio may be as high as 22 to 1. A "semi-diesel" engine usually employs a somewhat lower compression ratio and may use spark plugs for ignition.

Previously, it was established that compressing a gas, such as air, generates heat. In the diesel engine, air is compressed so much that it becomes hot enough (1000°-1200°F [538°–649°C]) to ignite the fuel. The fuel, in this case, is a petroleum product that is lighter than crude oil but heavier than gasoline. Gasoline cannot be used in a diesel because it would start to burn from the heat generated by the high compression long before the piston reached the top of the stroke.

The diesel engine has no carburetor. The air is compressed in the cylinder and, at the proper time, fuel that is under pressure is sprayed into the heated air. The air/fuel mixture then ignites and burns to produce power. The entry of the fuel must be "timed," just as the spark is timed in a gasoline engine.

Two-cycle Diesels

Because two-cycle engines are not efficient as air pumps, it is necessary to force air into the cylinder and to force out burned gases out of the cylinder. One way to do this is to use a ***supercharger,*** or ***blower.*** The GM two-cycle diesel, Figure 18-2, uses a positive-displacement supercharger, Figure 18-3. There are two exhaust valves in each cylinder, and no intake valves. The fuel injection nozzle is located between the exhaust valves. It is operated by a camshaft, push rod, and rocker arm.

Figure 18-1. This 6.2 liter diesel engine is found on some passenger cars and light trucks. (Detroit Diesel Corp.)

Air enters the cylinder through holes in the cylinder liner as shown in Figure 18-3. The blower forces fresh air into the cylinder through these holes during the time the holes are uncovered when the piston is at the bottom of its stroke. At the same time, the blower forces the exhaust out through the exhaust valves.

Fuel Vaporization

Because diesel fuel is more like oil than gasoline, it does not vaporize as readily. This means that it must be broken up into fine particles and sprayed into the cylinder in the form of a mist. This is accomplished by forcing the fuel through a nozzle or a series of very fine holes. As it enters the cylinder, the fuel combines more thoroughly with the air in the cylinder to form a combustible mixture.

Diesel Combustion Chambers

A major difference in the design of the various diesel engines is the type of combustion chamber used. There are four general types of combustion chambers:

- Open combustion chambers.
- Precombustion chambers.
- Turbulence chambers.
- Energy cell combustion chambers.

Each type has certain advantages.

Open Combustion Chambers

Probably the most common type of diesel combustion chamber is the ***open combustion chamber,*** Figure 18-4. It is also known as the ***direct injection chamber.*** In addition to the form illustrated (known as the Mexican Hat type), there are many variations in the shape of the piston crown and cylinder head. Such variations range from the flat-topped piston head to the cylindrical forms made by a ridge around the edge of the piston.

However, the basic characteristic of the open combustion chamber is that the fuel is sprayed directly into the combustion chamber. The form of the combustion chamber, the manner in which the air enters the chamber, and the direction of the fuel spray are designed to give maximum turbulence and improved combustion. The turbulence is of maximum importance if complete combustion of fuel is to be obtained.

An important variation of the open combustion chamber is the M system, which has a special combustion chamber formed in the piston head, Figure 18-5. The fuel is directed to the upper portion of the spherical chamber. High turbulence is created by means of the directional intake port, the shape of the chamber, and the direction of the injected fuel.

Advantages claimed for the open combustion chamber include a high degree of efficiency, low manufacturing costs, and high turbulence. A special advantage of the M system is the ability to operate on a wide variety of fuels from gasoline to diesel fuel.

Precombustion Chambers

In the ***precombustion chamber,*** a portion of the combustion chamber is contained in the space above the piston and is connected with a small passage. See Figure 18-6.

Figure 18-2. A two-cycle diesel engine.

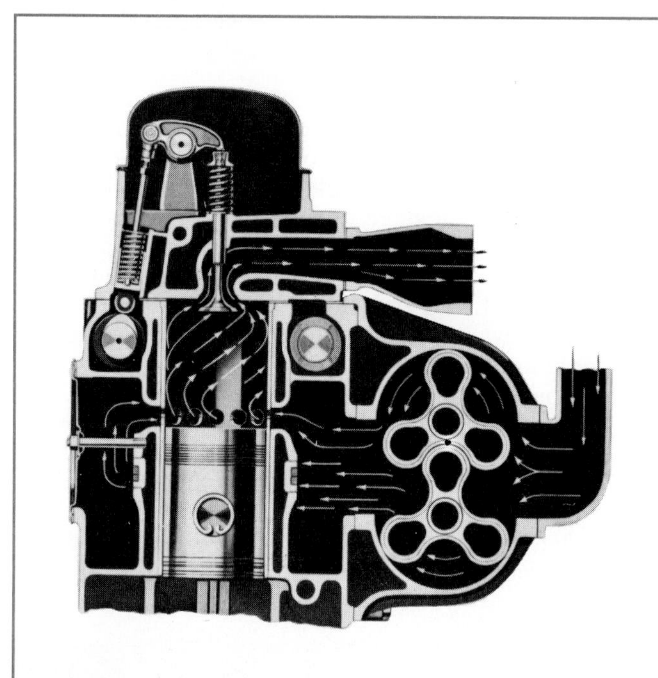

Figure 18-3. A supercharger, or blower, forces air into the cylinders.

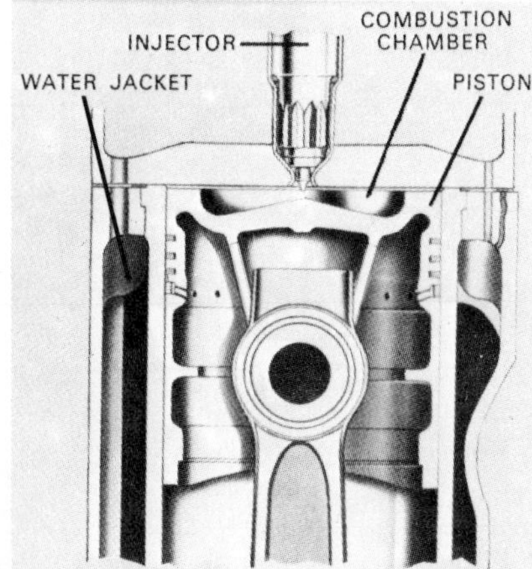

Figure 18-4. Direct fuel injection is used in this open combustion chamber.

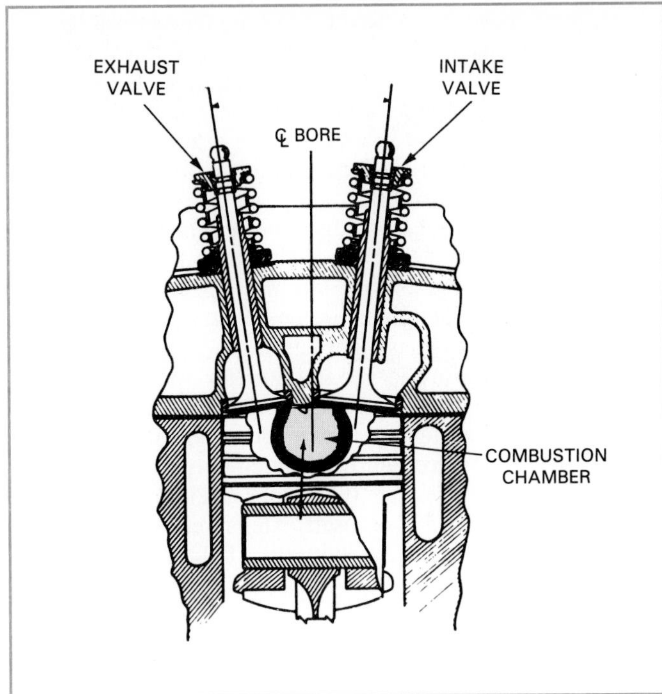

Figure 18-5. M-type combustion chamber.

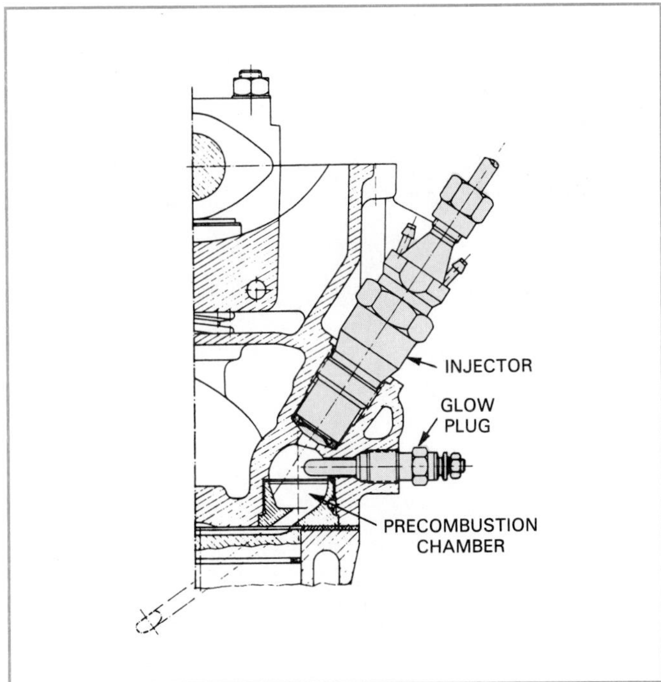

Figure 18-6. This illustration of a diesel engine shows the location of the injector and glow plug.

Thermal efficiency of the precombustion chamber engine is slightly lower than the open chamber type due to the greater heat loss from the larger combustion chamber area. The precombustion chamber contains approximately 30% of the total cylinder volume. However, cylinder pressure is lower and combustion is smoother. This is particularly important when the engine is used in an automobile. Another important advantage is that the precombustion chamber engine is not as sensitive to the type of fuel used. Additionally, it is not necessary to provide such fine atomization.

Turbulence Combustion Chamber

In the ***turbulence combustion chamber,*** up to 80% of the clearance volume is contained in the chamber, Figure 18-7. The passage to the space over the piston is relatively large, and a high degree of turbulence is developed to provide a good mixture of air and fuel. Like the precombustion chamber engine, the turbulence chamber engine is sensitive to the type of fuel provided. Cold weather starting without a glow plug is difficult in this system.

Energy Cell Combustion Chamber

The ***energy cell combustion chamber*** has the main combustion chamber located in the cylinder head and an anti-chamber located on the side of the combustion chamber opposite the injection nozzle, Figure 18-8. This design is used primarily in high-speed diesel engines with a cylinder bore of less than 5″.

Performance compares to that of the open chamber diesel. High peak pressure and rough operation are controlled as the result of the controlled combustion.

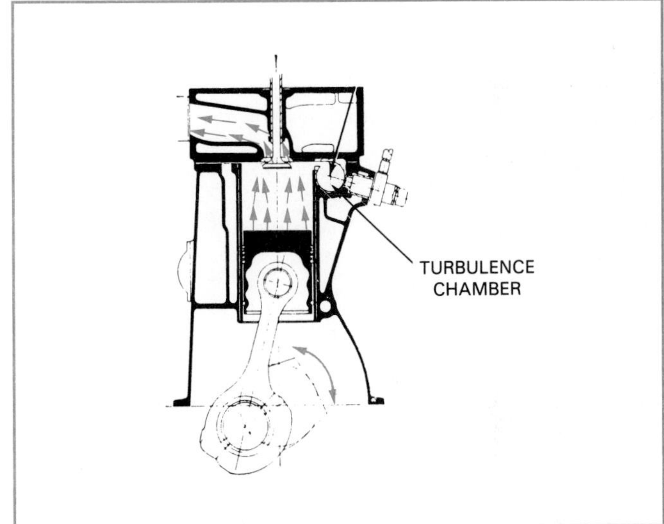

Figure 18-7. Turbulence combustion chamber. (Hercules Motor)

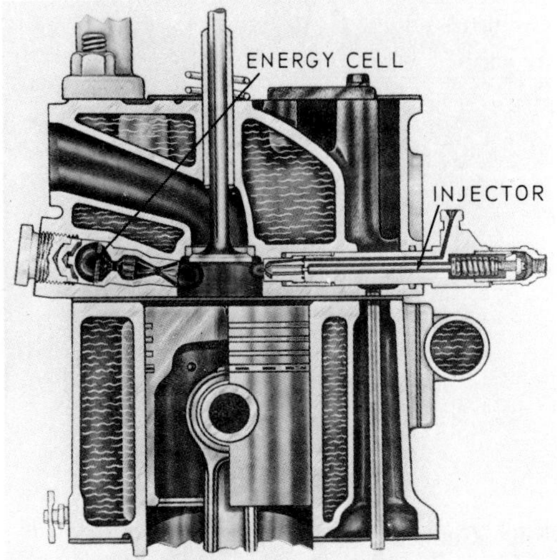

Figure 18-8. Energy cell combustion chamber.

Truck Engines

Truck engines used in light-duty applications are very similar to automobile engines. There are some differences in design and operating conditions, but they are minor in nature. Actually, many light trucks use passenger car engines without any change whatever. Heavy-duty trucks usually have special engines.

Any changes that are made in a passenger car engine to adapt it for truck use are intended to compensate for the difference in operating conditions. For example, the engine in a truck will be required to move a heavier load, so the axle gearing will be such that the engine can run at higher speeds for the same vehicle speed. The result may be that the truck will have a wide-open throttle at 60 mph. Therefore, the truck engine will be operating at full power more often.

Under these conditions, the exhaust valves will run hotter. Therefore, they need to be made of heat-resisting steel. The valve seat inserts must also be made from special steel. The pistons and rings need greater clearance for heat expansion. The cooling system may require a larger water pump, larger radiator, or some increase in capacity. A different bearing material is used on the crankshaft to withstand the higher bearing loads, and an oil pan of larger capacity is usually installed.

Heavy-duty trucks usually have engines that are designed and built for truck use. They may be of either the two-cycle or four-cycle type and may operate on gasoline or diesel fuel. Such engines are customarily much heavier in construction than passenger car engines. See Figure 18-9. The crankshafts are larger in diameter and the bearings are wider. The crankcases are heavier and braced with webs at points of strain. The piston displacement is increased and the engine speed decreased for a given amount of power.

The GMC Series 71 two-cycle engine is shown in Figure 18-10. The "71" is used extensively in trucks. To reduce vibration, it is provided with a balance shaft that is driven by the camshaft.

1. Exhaust valve rotator.
2. Carburetor.
3. Intake manifold.
4. Crankcase ventilation valve.
5. Intake valve rotator.
6. Exhaust manifold.
7. Camshaft.
8. Crankshaft.
9. Connecting rod and piston assembly.
10. Oil filter assembly.
11. Oil pump and governor valve assembly.
12. Oil inlet tube and screen assembly.
13. Starter assembly.
14. Valve lifters.
15. Spark plug.
16. Piston.

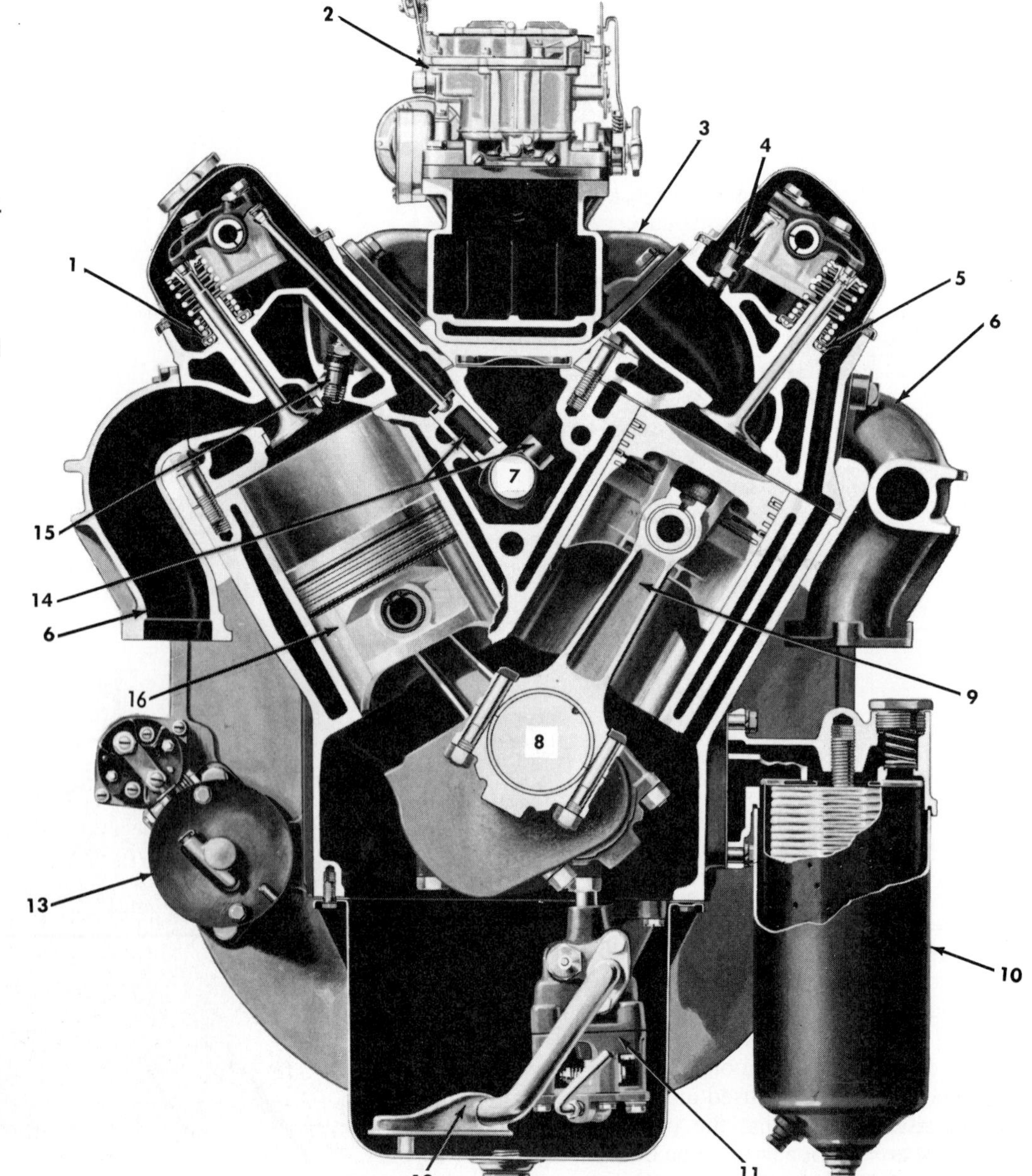

Figure 18-9. Sectional view of a GMC V-6 gasoline engine.

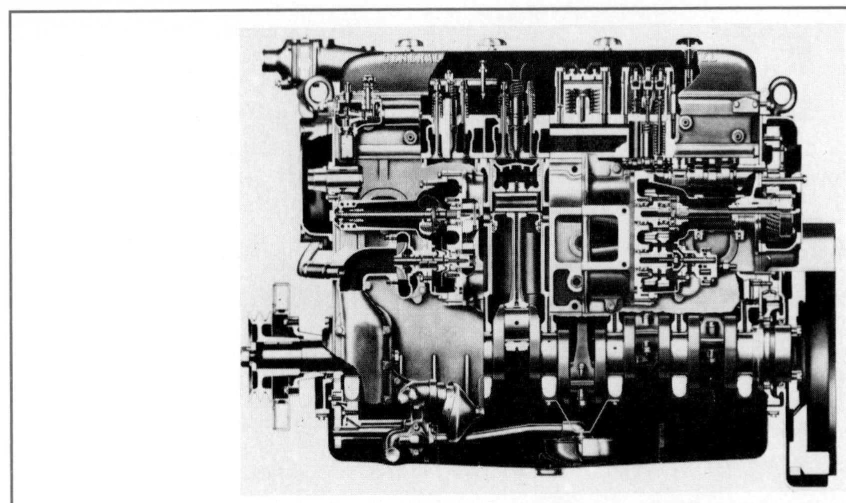

Figure 18-10. The two-cycle GMC Series 71 diesel engine has a balance shaft that is driven by the camshaft.

Racing Engines

The most successful ***racing engines*** are designed specifically for racing and are made of special materials. Passenger car engines can be adapted for racing purposes, but considerable alteration is usually required. When used for racing, the engine is designed or altered to get the utmost in power and rotational speed, regardless of anything else. See Figure 18-11.

Since noise is a minor consideration, the average race car engine roars and clatters. The clearances are very carefully measured on each working part. Some of this clatter comes from the valve mechanism, which is designed to open and close the valves quickly. Large valves with a high lift will expedite the flow of the gases in and out of the cylinders.

The opening and closing time of the valves and the duration of the valve opening are designed solely for efficiency at high speed. As a result, racing engines seldom idle smoothly. Other reasons for rough idling are lightweight flywheels, which allow acceleration and the extremely high compression ratios.

In addition to the greater clearances between all moving parts, each rotating part in the engine is balanced to extremely close tolerances. This is done to increase the speed of the engine and to reduce destructive vibration. Every part of the engine is made of the finest material available to ensure reliability.

The race car engine shown in Figure 18-12 is the Ford-Westlake engine that develops 455 hp @ 10,000 rpm. It is a 60° V-12 engine with an aluminum cylinder block. Displacement is 182.6 cu. in. (3 liters). Double overhead camshafts operate four valves per cylinder.

Turbines

Gas turbines can be used to propel automobiles, trucks, boats, and airplanes. They can also be designed to serve as stationary power plants. The fundamental principle of a turbine consists of an inclined plane that is mounted on a rotating shaft and located in the path of fluid force, Figure 18-13.

A gas turbine is a heat engine that transforms energy created by the expansion of the burning fuel and air in the combustion chamber to either thrust or shaft power. This power can be utilized directly to push a vehicle, or it can be turned into shaft power to drive an automobile.

Figure 18-11. Ford racing engine. Note that there are two camshafts for each bank of cylinders.

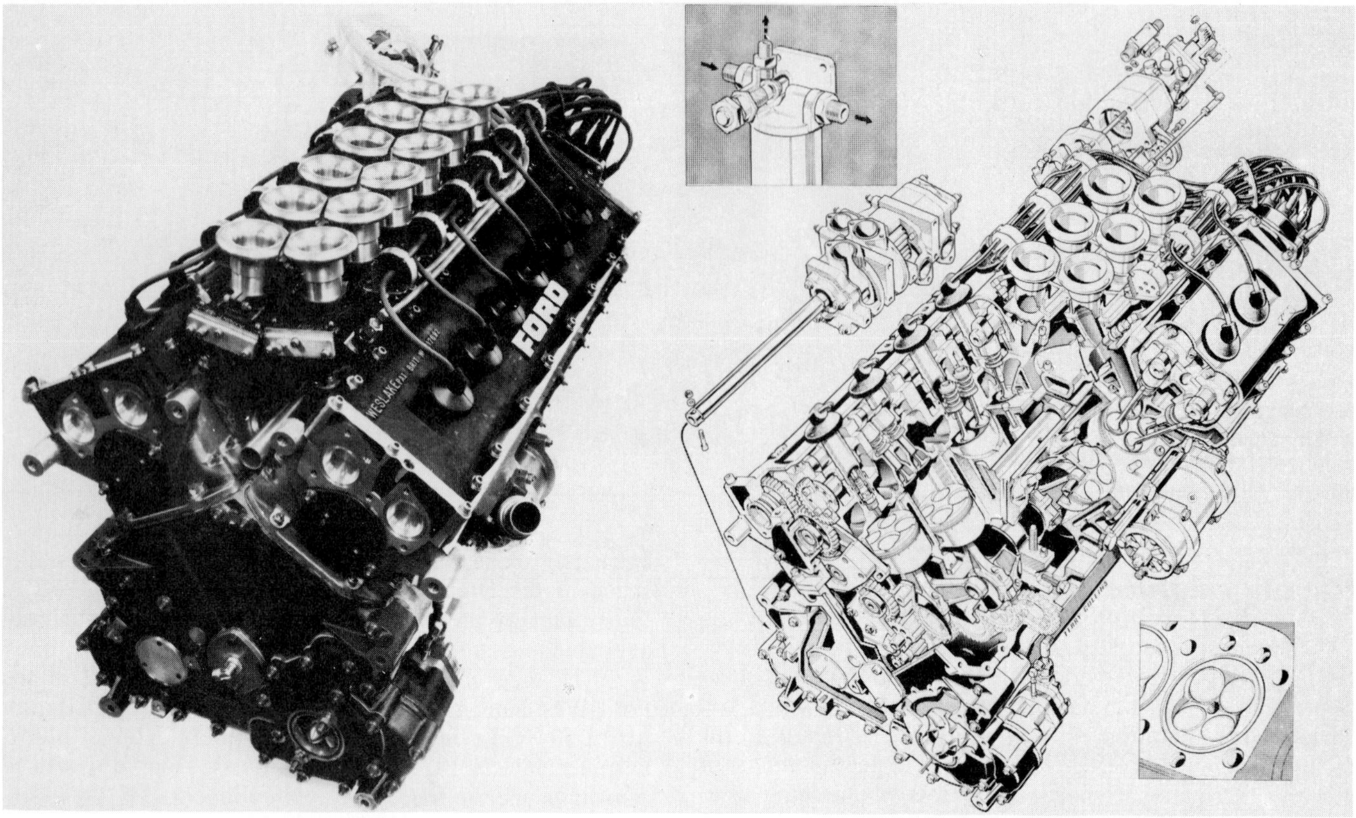

Figure 18-12. This 12-cylinder Ford Westlake engine develops 455 hp @ 10,000 rpm.

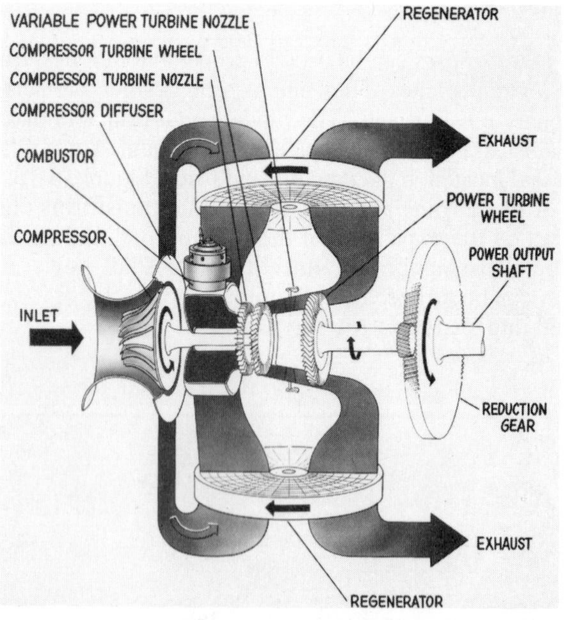

Figure 18-13. This drawing shows airflow path of a turbine. (Ford)

The ***thrust force*** developed by a turbine can be shown using a balloon for a demonstration. Inflate the balloon with air, and then release it. As the air rushes out through the neck of the balloon, the balloon will shoot away in the direction opposite the airflow. The force for propulsion is applied against the inside of the balloon, rather than being supplied by a jet of compressed air pushing against free air. This is the same principle of operation employed in a rocket or jet engine.

The same thrust force can be exerted against a turbine wheel to produce rotary motion, Figure 18-14. The first stage, or gasifier section, produces the thrust. If shaft power is wanted, the section to the right (power section) is added as a second stage. In this particular turbine, the first turbine wheel drives only the compressor. Fuel is sprayed into the two burners receiving compressed air from the compressor. Only a portion of the air is burned in the burners, and the compressor requires only a portion of the energy in the hot gas. The remainder of air and hot gas is used as a thrust force.

If shaft power is wanted instead of thrust, air and hot gas are directed to the second turbine. Basically, a gas turbine provides rotary power from the expansion of burning gas without the use of reciprocating pistons, connecting rods, or a crankshaft.

Rotary Engines

The ***Wankel rotary engine*** does not have reciprocating parts. Rotary engines of the Wankel type are being used in virtually all fields, including automotive (Mazda), aircraft, farm equipment, marine vehicles, motorcycles, and small electric generators.

The Wankel-type rotary engine, Figure 18-15, is a compact power plant requiring less space than a piston engine of the same horsepower. It is an exceptionally quiet engine with very little vibration.

There are approximately 630 parts in a Wankel engine, compared to about 1050 parts in a piston engine. Ports are used instead of valves, eliminating the need for the complicated valve train of the piston engine.

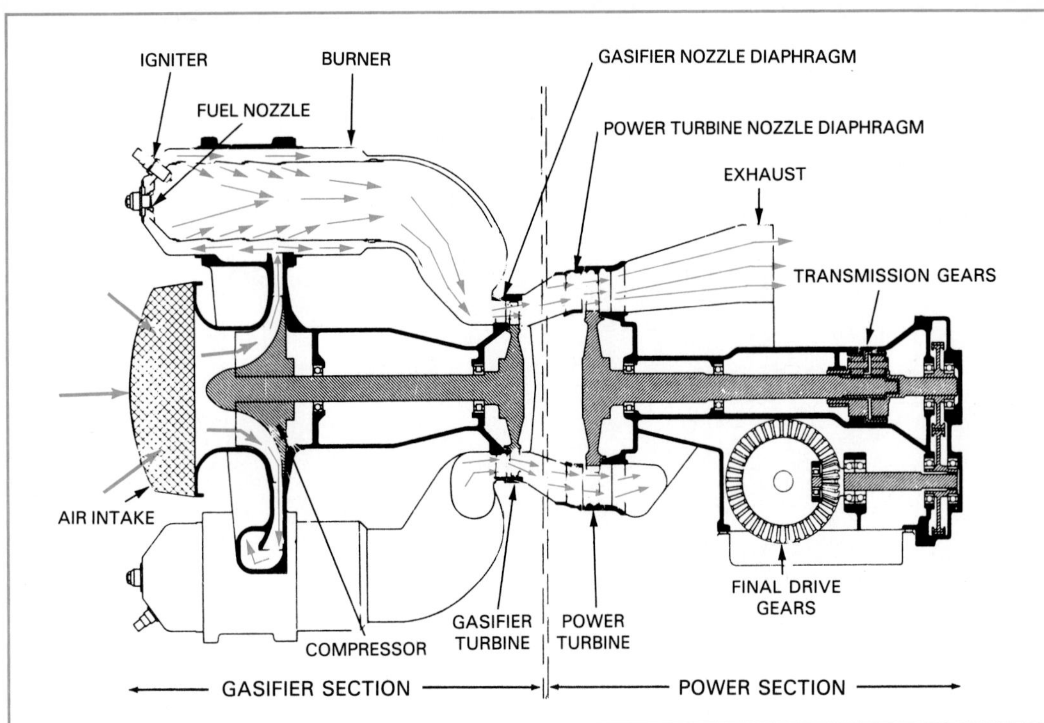

Figure 18-14. GM turbine arrangement.

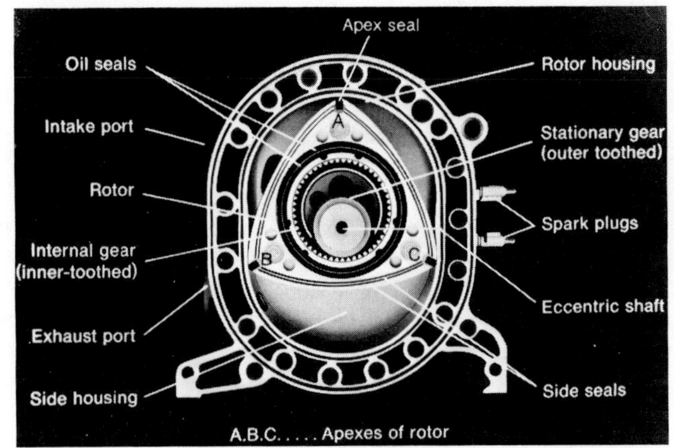

Figure 18-15. A reciprocating engine has almost twice as many parts as a rotary engine. (Mazda)

A Wankel engine weighing 237 lbs. will produce approximately the same power as a conventional V-8 weighing over 600 lbs. The Wankel occupies approximately 5.1 cu. ft. of engine compartment space, while the V-8 requires 23.2 cu. ft. of space. Fuel distribution to the rotor chambers is better than the distribution to the combustion chambers in the piston engine. Consequently, volumetric efficiency is higher.

Most of the Wankel-type rotary engines in production have two rotors. Figure 18-16, for example, shows the engine that powers the Mazda. Some rotary engines have three rotors, and four-rotor engines have been built. Wankel-type engines can be built as small as 18.5 cu. in. per working chamber up to 1920 cu. in. per working chamber.

Figure 18-17 shows heat balance chart of a typical Wankel rotary engine. The percentages compare favorably with the average piston engine.

Rotary Engine Fundamentals

The Wankel ***rotor*** is triangular in shape with slightly curved sides. It orbits eccentrically on a fixed gear in a housing that is shaped like a figure eight, Figure 18-15. That is, the rotor rotates around its own axis while orbiting around the ***mainshaft.*** However, the mainshaft makes three turns per rotor revolution. As a result, one operating cycle takes place per mainshaft revolution.

As the rotor swings around the fixed gear, the internal gear (rotor gear) transmits the rotary motion to the mainshaft. The mainshaft is an eccentric shaft, and the rotation is such that the tips of the ***apexes*** of the rotor, Figure 18-15, are always in contact with the side surface of the ***rotor housing.*** These tips are provided with seals shown at A, B, and C.

All four cycles (intake, compression, power, and exhaust) take place in one revolution of the rotor. Since there are three lobes to the rotor, there is a continuous performance of these cycles on every lobe. The mainshaft turns three times for every revolution of the rotor. With one power impulse for each of the rotor sides, there will be three power impulses per rotor revolution, or one power impulse per mainshaft revolution.

The sequence of the cycles is shown in Figure 18-18. In position A, intake is starting between lobes 1 and 3, compression is occurring between 1 and 2, power is being produced between 2 and 3, and exhaust is finishing between 3 and 1.

When the rotor has moved to position B, intake continues between 1 and 3, compression continues between 1 and 2, and power is finishing between 2 and 3.

In position C, intake is finishing between 1 and 3, spark has ignited the compressed charge between 1 and 2, and exhaust is occurring between 2 and 3.

In position D, intake of the charge is completed between 1 and 3, power is produced between 1 and 2, and exhaust is continuing between 2 and 3.

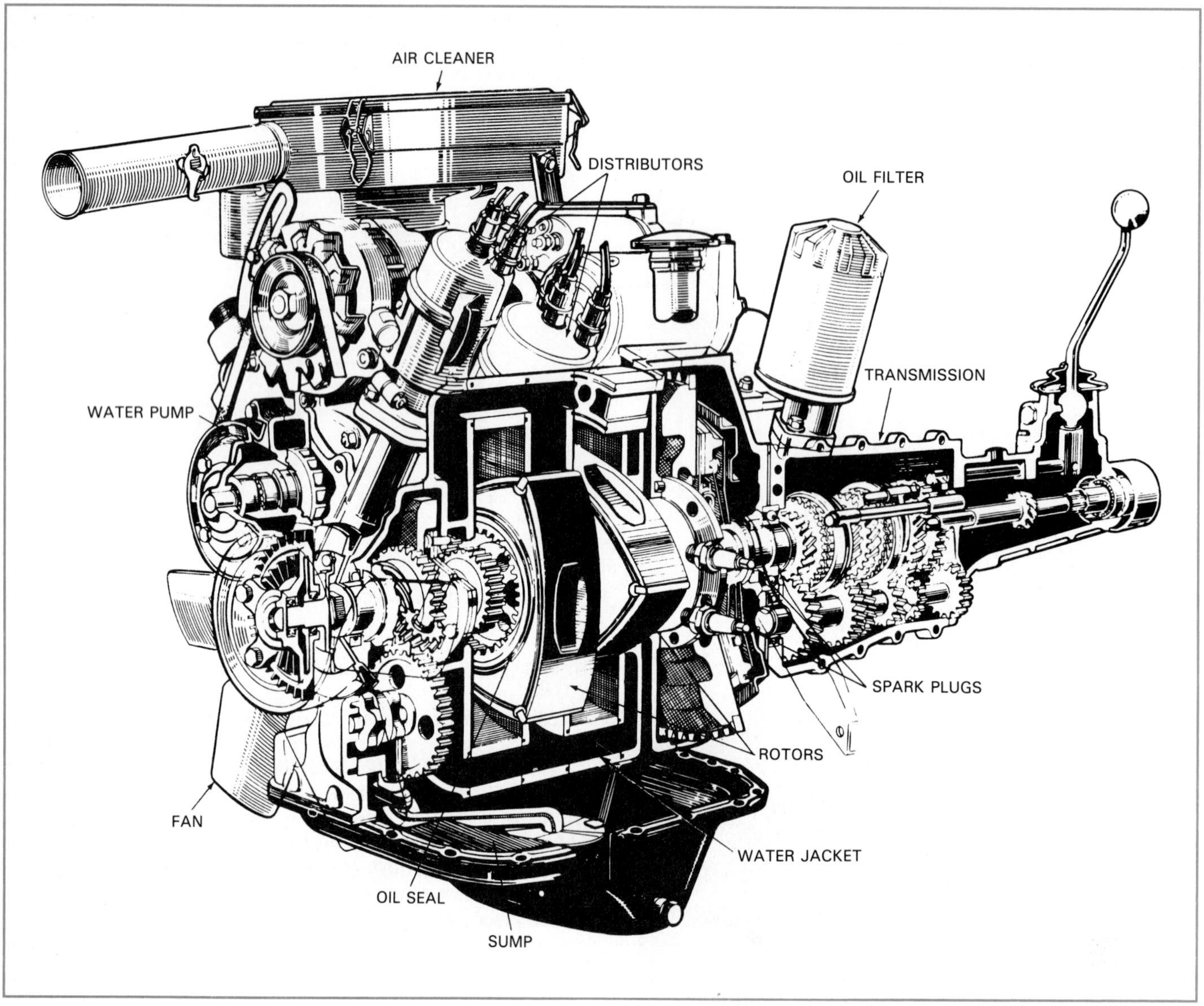

Figure 18-16. This Wankel engine uses only two rotors. (Mazda)

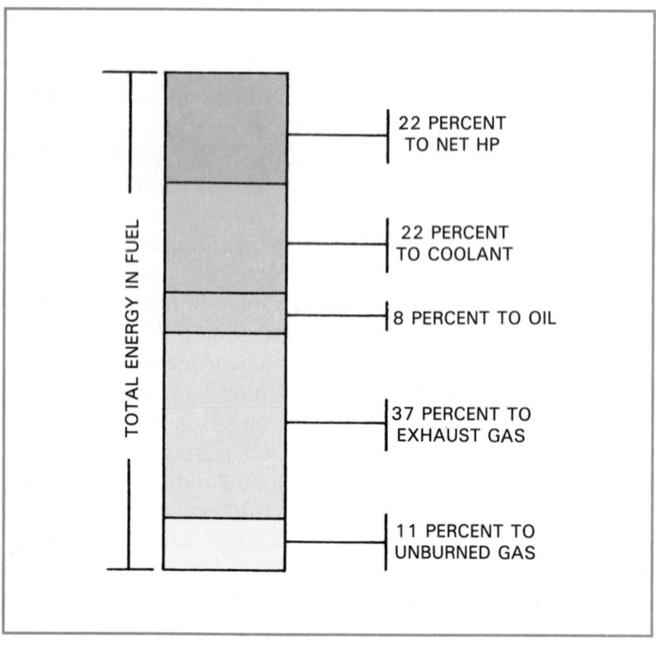

Figure 18-17. Power distribution in a Wankel engine.

From this operational description, it can be seen that when gas pressure on one face turns the rotor, it brings another face into position to produce power.

Displacement of the Rotary Engine

There has been considerable discussion as to the method of calculating the displacement of the Wankel engine. The currently accepted method is twice the combustion volume multiplied by the number of rotors.

Power Developed in a Rotary Engine

As is the case with the conventional piston engine, horsepower developed by different makes of the Wankel rotary engine varies considerably.

The Audi-NSU model R080 is a 60.7 cu. in. rotary engine that develops 130 hp @ 5500 rpm. The compression ratio is 9 to 1. The Mazda R100 engine has a displacement of 60 cu. in. and develops 100 hp @ 7000 rpm. The compression ratio for this engine is 9.4 to 1.

In a rotary engine, the compression ratio is limited by the rotor radius and the eccentricity. When these two di-

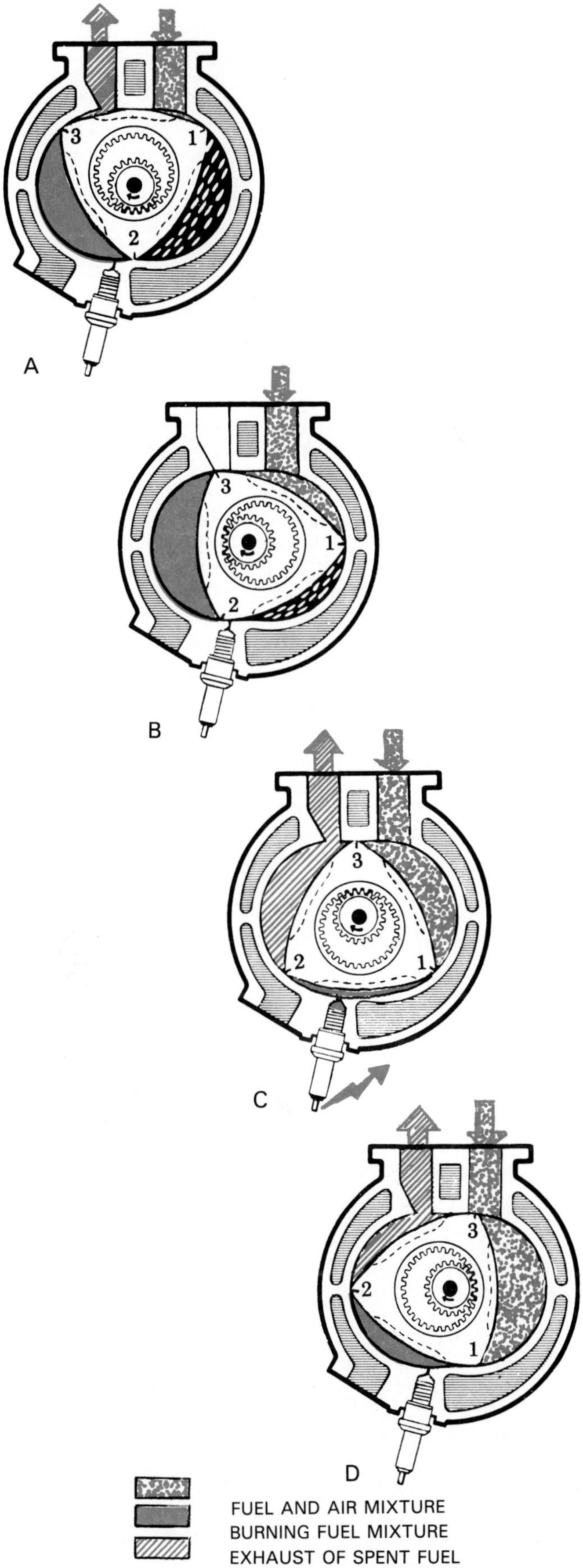

A

B

C

D

FUEL AND AIR MIXTURE
BURNING FUEL MIXTURE
EXHAUST OF SPENT FUEL

Figure 18-18. Sequence of events in a Wankel engine. Unlike a reciprocating engine, fuel is always entering a rotary engine.

mensions have been selected, the maximum compression ratio is determined. The compression ratio is equal to the radius to eccentricity ratio, or R/e, Figure 18-19.

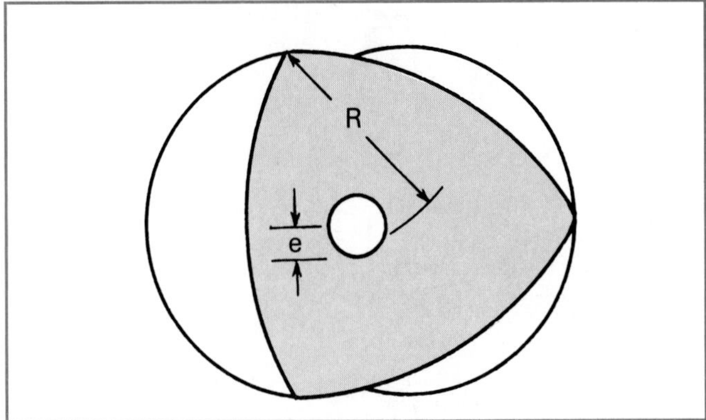

Figure 18-19. Compression ratio of a Wankel engine is determined by R/e.

Rotary Engine Performance

The locations of intake and exhaust ports are factors in performance and fuel economy. NSU and Mercedes-Benz are advocates of peripheral ports. Toyo Kogyo, manufacturer of the Mazda, prefers a side location for the ports, claiming better idling, low-speed performance, and light-load scavenging. In general, the peripheral ports, Figure 18-20, provide high speed and power, while the side ports, Figure 18-16, provide performance over a wide range.

The fuel used in the Wankel rotary engine is the same kind used in a conventional piston engine. Normal fuel ranges from 87 to 91 octane. Satisfactory operation has also been obtained on some rotary engines with diesel fuels.

Fuel flow to the Wankel engine is constant. There is no problem of uneven distribution, such as encountered in piston engines where some cylinders may receive a greater quantity of air/fuel mixture than others.

Rotary Engine Ignition

Two spark plugs per chamber are used in the Wankel engine. Note the location of the spark plugs in the Mazda rotary engine shown in Figure 18-16.

Spark plugs differ greatly from those used in the piston engine. Note the side electrodes shown in Figure 18-21. The location of the spark plugs is as important in rotary engines as it is in piston engines. Research has shown that by using two spark plugs in each chamber, exhaust emissions are reduced, power is increased, combustion is more complete, and duration of combustion is minimized.

Two distributors, Figure 18-16, are usually provided. Researchers have found that a spark advance of approximately five degrees usually is required. This corresponds to an advance of approximately 28° on a piston engine.

In piston engines, the spark plugs receive the benefit of the cooling effects of the incoming fuel charge. This is not the case in a rotary combustion engine. Consequently, spark plug temperatures are higher. Spark plugs used in these engines are extremely cold plugs.

Timing of the ignition on the rotary engine is in relation to the angle of the shaft. Top dead center is the same as

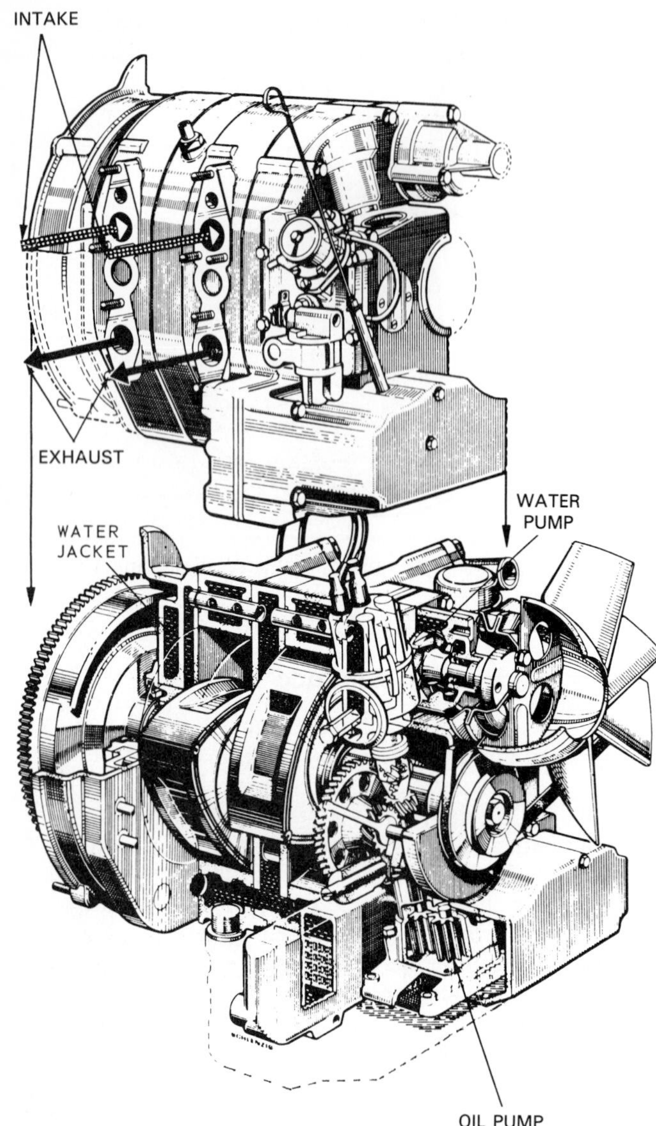

Figure 18-20. Peripheral intake and exhaust ports provide a higher speed and more power than side ports.

top dead center on a piston engine, but the angle of the shaft is greater than the corresponding angle of the piston engine crankshaft.

Rotary Engine Emissions

Currently, many rotary engines have met Federal requirements for low levels of exhaust emissions. Intense combustion chamber turbulence produced by the Wankel engine contributes largely to improved exhaust emissions. In addition, the Wankel engine can give satisfactory operation on relatively lean mixtures, which also contributes to improved exhaust emissions.

However, the hydrocarbon emission level of the Wankel rotary engine is higher than that of a piston-type engine of the same general size. The carbon monoxide and nitrous oxide levels are lower than that of a reciprocating piston engine.

As is the case of the piston engine, the exact emission quantity and composition of the Wankel exhaust depends on throttle opening and engine speed. With a rich or lean mixture, there is the possibility of incomplete combustion. The problem is worse under light-load conditions. However, the Wankel rotary engine operates well under a lean mixture and has an advantage over the piston engine in that respect.

Figure 18-21. A special spark plug must be used on a rotary engine. Note the two side electrodes.

Thermal reactors have been shown to produce a reduction in hydrocarbon emission from the Wankel engine. Tests have shown reductions up to 90% when a thermal reactor has been used, Figure 18-22.

Rotary Engine Cooling

While air-cooled Wankel engines have been produced, the water-cooled type is used most extensively. The coolant is primarily for cooling the housing, and oil is used to cool the rotor. Typical water-cooled rotary engines are shown in Figures 18-16 and 18-20.

Cooling the Wankel engine is required primarily in the area where combustion and expansion take place (area around the spark plugs). The concentration of heat in such a small area tends to cause distortion, which makes sealing the oil and the fuel mixture difficult. Unless adequate cool-

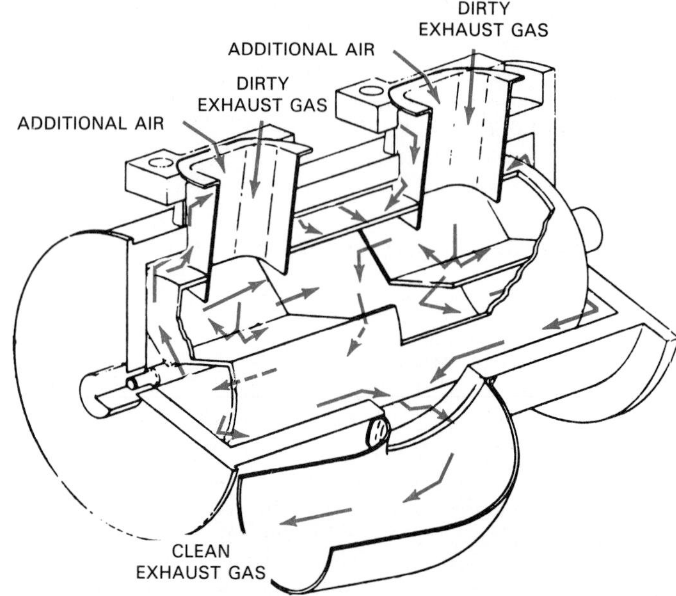

Figure 18-22. A thermal gas reactor reduces the level of hydrocarbon emissions in a rotary engine. (Curtis-Wright)

ing is provided, thermal fatigue or shock cracks may form in the spark plug hole area.

The cooling of the rotor presents a special problem. It is completely enclosed within the housing and does not have the benefit of the cooling provided by the crankcase in a reciprocating engine. In addition, the rotor turns at one third of the mainshaft speed.

While aluminum is lighter than cast iron and also has excellent heat conductivity, most manufacturers prefer cast iron for rotors. For actual cooling, lubricating oil is circulated from the sump, Figure 18-16, and then through the rotor. After cooling the rotor, the oil passes through a filter and heat exchanger, through the hub of the rotor, and returns to the sump. The inside of the rotor must be carefully designed, since it affects not only the cooling of the rotor but also engine balance. Excessive rotor temperatures will result in carbon formation on the interior of the rotor. This could cause an unbalanced condition and lead to a further increase in engine temperature.

The oil seals on the rotor bearings permit a measured amount of oil leakage to provide lubrication for the sides of the rotor.

Rotary Engine Seals

Adequate sealing for the various areas of a rotary engine proved to be one of the most difficult problems in the early stages of development. Apex seals and side seals, Figure 18-15, must be provided to prevent leakage from the working chambers.

The problem of designing effective seals for the apex of the rotor is complicated by the different forces that act on the seal. Forces include positive and negative centrifugal force, gas pressure, and friction against the working surfaces. In addition, the position of the apex seal varies. When at the major and minor axis, it is perpendicular to the working surface. At other positions of the rotor, the seal is at an angle other than 90° to the surface.

Apex seals are straight and are inserted in radius slots at each rotor apex. Side seals are curved to conform to the curvature of the rotor and are placed in grooves in the rotor sides. These seals are provided with interlocking ends to reduce leakage.

Various materials have been used for seals. Mazda, for example, originally used carbon for their apex seals because of its lubricating qualities. Later, a sintered material impregnated with aluminum was adapted. Ceramic seals have also been used.

Rotary Engine Lubrication

Since the lubricating oil in a rotary engine is not subject to blowby and consequent contamination, periodic oil changes have been eliminated in most rotary engine service recommendations. However, additional oil occasionally is needed to replace that metered for lubricating the rotor seals and housing. With high-speed driving, use of a quart of oil every 1000 miles has been experienced.

Bearings of the mainshaft are lubricated with oil from the sump in the normal manner; the oil is supplied under pressure from a gear-type pump, Figure 18-20. The oil supplied to the rotor seals keeps them from sticking. Originally, engine oil was mixed with the fuel, much in the same manner as oil and fuel are mixed for use in two-cycle outboard engines. Subsequently, automatic metering of the lubricating oil from the rotor side was adapted. A third method of lubricating the rotor seals consisted of introducing oil into the intake ports in accordance with engine operating conditions.

Servicing Rotary Engines

While the Wankel-type rotary engine is relatively rare, servicing should not present any major problem. First of all, there are no valves to stick or burn. There are no piston rings, but there are seals on the rotor. These, however, should present no problem when replacement is necessary. It can be expected that the life of the seals should equal that of piston rings.

The fuel injection (carburetion), and ignition systems are readily accessible, which greatly simplifies tune-up work. Ignition units also follow conventional design.

Ceramic Engines

Currently, ***ceramic engine blocks*** are being implemented in some diesel applications as an alternative to cast iron or aluminum. The ceramic engine is referred to as an ***adiabatic engine.*** An adiabatic engine does not gain or lose heat.

There are several advantages of a ceramic engine. First, it is lighter than even an aluminum engine block. But like the aluminum engine block, a steel sleeve must be inserted into the cylinder. Second, it is not necessary to have an engine cooling system. Finally, main bearings are not needed. Similarly, an oiling system to the main journals is not needed. This is because the ceramic surface becomes quite slippery when hot.

While most engines today are cast iron, aluminum, or a combination of the two, ceramics can be used for select components of these engines. Some of the components being tested include valves, pistons, and turbocharger blades. The disadvantage of ceramics is that they can fail suddenly and unexpectedly, which would be catastrophic.

Chapter 18–Review Questions

Write your answers on a separate sheet of paper. Do not write in this book.

1. Carburetors are used on diesel engines. True or False?
2. Diesel fuel pumps are usually driven by double or triple V belts. True or False?
3. Name two purposes of a supercharger on a two-cycle diesel engine.
4. How many general types of combustion chambers are used in diesel engines?
   (A) Four.
   (B) Five.
   (C) Two.
   (D) Six.
5. In the M system, the combustion chamber is formed in what part of the engine?
   (A) Cylinder head.
   (B) Piston.
   (C) Cylinder bore.
   (D) None of the above.

6. Name five alterations that are often made to passenger car engines to adapt them for use in light trucks.
7. Small industrial engines are usually air cooled. True or False?
8. Give three reasons for poor idling of racing engines.
9. The thrust developed by a turbine is similar to the thrust produced by a balloon. True or False?
10. A turbine:
    (A) converts reciprocating power into rotary.
    (B) uses only reciprocating power.
    (C) uses only rotary power.
    (D) All of the above.
11. Technician A states that a rotary engine usually has two spark plugs per chamber. Technician B states that the spark plugs used in rotary engines usually have two side electrodes. Who is right?
    (A) A only.
    (B) B only.
    (C) Both A & B.
    (D) Neither A nor B.
12. The Wankel engine must use special spark plugs. True or False?
13. The Wankel engine is a:
    (A) reciprocating engine.
    (B) rotary engine.
    (C) free piston engine.
    (D) None of the above.
14. Is special fuel required for the rotary combustion engine used in the Mazda car?
15. The Wankel engine requires more space than a piston engine of the same power. True or False?
16. The Wankel engine is limited to two rotors. True or False?
17. What is the shape of the rotor used in the Wankel engine?
    (A) Round.
    (B) Triangular.
    (C) Square.
    (D) Elliptical.
18. There are _____ power impulses in a rotary combustion engine for each revolution of the rotor.
19. Fuel injection cannot be used in a Wankel rotary engine. True or False?
20. In general, the hydrocarbon emission level of the Wankel engine is higher than a piston engine of the same general size. True or False?
21. A ceramic engine block must have:
    (A) aluminum sleeves in the cylinders.
    (B) steel sleeves in the cylinders.
    (C) Both A & B.
    (D) Neither A nor B.
22. Define an adiabatic engine.
23. What are the advantages of a ceramic engine?
    (A) Lighter than aluminum.
    (B) Needs no cooling system.
    (C) Engine main bearings are not needed.
    (D) All of the above.

This late-model passenger car is equipped with a 3.0-liter, 24-valve, six-cylinder diesel engine. The vehicle features extremely clean exhaust and a cruising range of 750 miles between fill-ups. (Mercedes-Benz of North America, Inc.)

Chapter 19
Fundamentals of Electricity, Magnetism, and Electronics

After studying this chapter, you will be able to:

- ❍ Explain the makeup of matter in terms of the molecular theory.
- ❍ State the basics of the electron theory of electricity.
- ❍ Employ Ohm's law in troubleshooting electrical circuits.
- ❍ Describe the characteristics of series, parallel, and series-parallel circuits.
- ❍ Give the theory of permanent magnets and electromagnets.
- ❍ Explain the construction and operation of diodes, transistors, and silicon controlled rectifiers.
- ❍ Recognize the tremendous effect of electronics on automotive advances.

Electricity

Electricity and electronics play a vital role in the safe and reliable operation of modern automotive vehicles. Demands range from a simple door switch or courtesy lamp to an engine electrical system so complex that a 40-way bulkhead disconnect may be required between the instrument panel and the engine compartment.

It logically follows that anyone who expects to successfully maintain, troubleshoot, and repair today's vehicles must have a thorough knowledge of the fundamentals of electricity and electronics.

Static Electricity

The word ***electric*** is derived from a Greek word meaning amber. The ancient Greeks found that by rubbing a piece of amber with a piece of silk, bits of paper, straw, and dry leaves were attracted to it. Later experiments showed that the same effect can be produced by rubbing a rod of glass or hard rubber with a handkerchief. In fact, many other nonmetallic materials are found to have this property, which is called ***static electricity.***

For example, if you rub a rod of hard rubber with a piece of fur, and then hold it close to a pith ball suspended on a thread, the pith ball will be attracted to the rod. But if you allow the rod to touch the ball, the ball will bounce away. You can get the same effect by rubbing a glass rod with a piece of silk.

Attraction and Repulsion

Further experiments show that all electrified materials behave either as glass or rubber. Glass is said to have a ***positive charge;*** hard rubber has a ***negative charge.*** If you electrify two strips of hard rubber by rubbing them with fur, they will repel each other. Two glass rods will behave in a similar manner. However, if you electrify a rubber rod and suspend it near an electrified glass rod, they will attract each other.

This simple experiment demonstrates one of the most important laws of electricity: *Bodies with similar charges repel each other, and bodies with opposite charges attract each other.* This law also applies to magnets (to be covered later).

Electron Theory of Electricity

People have experimented with and controlled the use of electricity for years, yet no one can explain just what electricity is. Many different theories have been advanced regarding the nature of electricity. Today, the ***electron theory*** is generally accepted.

In essence, the electron theory proposes that all matter (the earth, rocks, minerals, chemicals, elements, etc.) consists of tiny particles called ***molecules.*** These molecules, in turn, are made of two or more smaller particles called ATOMS. Atoms are further divided into even smaller particles called protons, neutrons, and electrons.

Protons, neutrons, and electrons are the same in all matter, whether a gas, a liquid, or a solid. The different properties, or characteristics, of the matter take form according to the arrangement and number of protons, neutrons, and electrons that make up the atoms.

The ***proton*** has a natural positive charge of electricity. The ***electron*** has a negative charge. The ***neutron*** has no charge at all, but adds weight to the matter.

Central Core of Atom

Protons and neutrons form the nucleus (central core) of the atoms. The electrons revolve around the nucleus, Figure 19-1. Electrons carry small negative charges of electricity, which neutralize the positive charges of the protons.

The simplest atom of all is the hydrogen atom. It consists of one positively charged proton and one negatively charged electron, Figure 19-2. Other atoms, such as

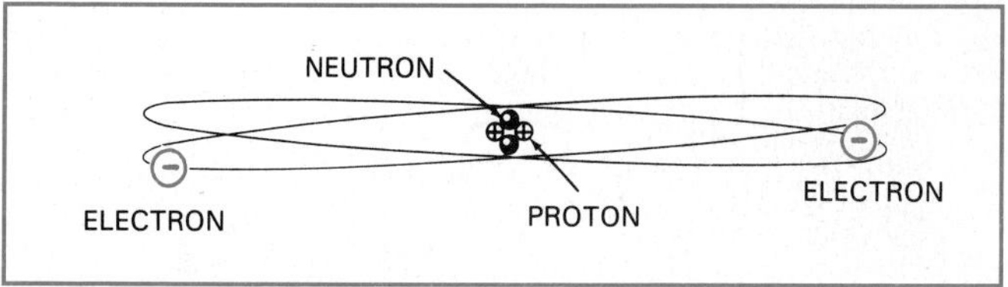

Figure 19-1. Electrons revolve about the central core of atoms.

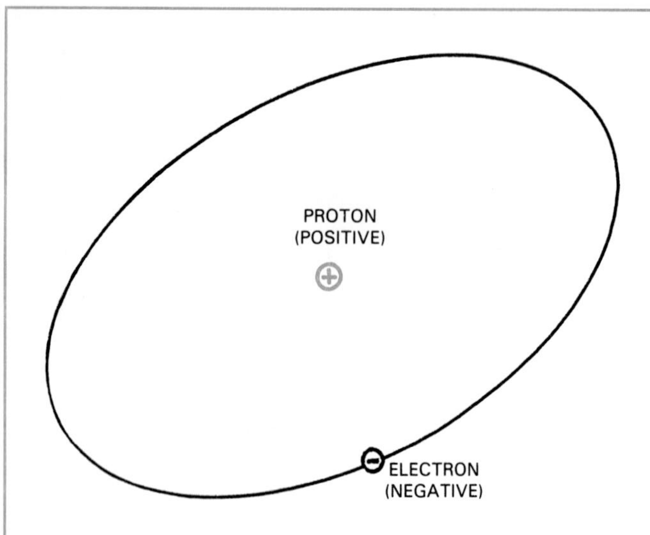

Figure 19-2. A simple hydrogen atom consists of one positively charged proton and one negatively charged electron.

those forming copper, iron, or silicon, are much more complicated. A copper atom, for example, has 29 electrons circling about its nucleus in four different orbits, Figure 19-3.

Size of Atom

It is difficult to conceive the size of the atom. Research by physicists has established that the mass of one electron is about .000,000,000,000,000,000,000,000,000,911 gram. If you assume that the size of a proton in a hydrogen atom is the size of a baseball and is located in Kansas City, its orbit would reach from the Atlantic coast to the Pacific.

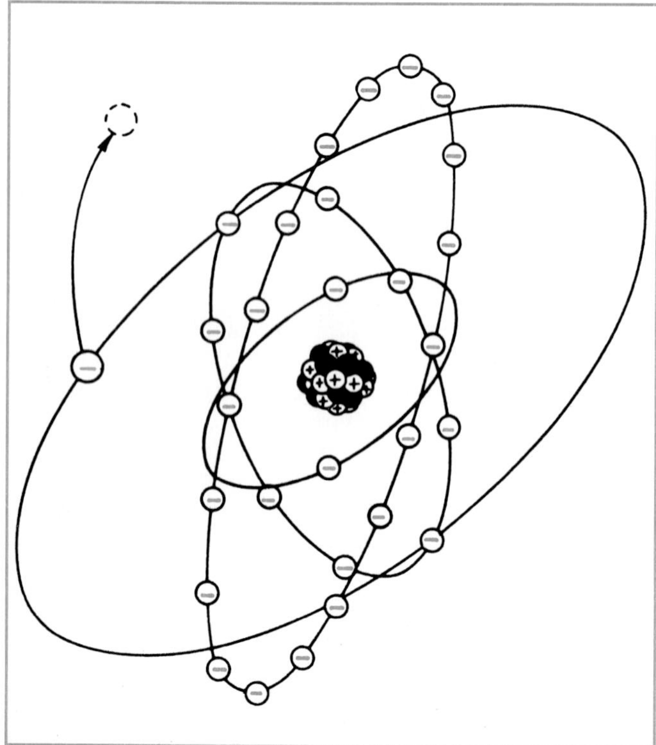

Figure 19-3. A copper atom consists of 29 electrons circling about its nucleus in four different orbits.

So, along with the extremely small size of electrons and protons, they are separated by relatively vast distances. An appreciation of the distance between the proton and electron is necessary to understand the electron flow.

Insulators

In most elements, the nucleus is surrounded by closely held electrons that never leave the atom. These are called ***bound electrons.*** When bound electrons are in the majority in an element or compounded material, the material is called an ***insulator,*** or a ***nonconductor*** of electricity.

Conductors

In other types of material, the nucleus is surrounded by another group of electrons that can be freed to move from one atom to another when electricity is applied, Figure 19-3. Electrons of this kind are known as ***free electrons,*** and the materials made up of these atom are called ***conductors*** of electricity.

Speed of Electricity

The speed of electricity is 186,000 miles per second. However, the electrons do not travel at this tremendous speed. Free electrons, which are available because electron orbits overlap in conducting materials, are pulled from one atom to another. As they move, the free electrons temporarily rotate about each new center. Since an electron carries a negative charge of electricity, electron flow (current flow) is assumed to be from negative to positive.

Electron Drift

The rate at which the free electrons drift from atom to atom determines the amount of ***current.*** In order to create a drift of electrons through a circuit, it is necessary to have an electrical pressure, or ***voltage.***

Electric current, then, is the flow of electrons. The more electrons in motion, the stronger the current. In terms of automotive applications, the greater the concentration of electrons at a battery or generator terminal, the higher the pressure between the electrons. The greater this pressure (voltage) is, the greater the flow of electrons.

Volts, Amperes, Ohms

The pressure between the electrons is measured in ***volts.*** The flow of electrons (current) is measured in ***amperes.*** Opposing the flow of electrons is the ***resistance*** of the conductors, which is measured in ***ohms.***

Some materials offer greater resistance to electron flow than others. Iron offers more resistance than copper, but copper offers more resistance than silver. The length of the connecting wiring also contributes to the amount of resistance in a circuit. Finally, the size of the wiring is also a resistance factor. A conductor of small diameter will offer greater resistance to the flow of electrons than will a conductor of large diameter.

Ohm's Law

Ohm's law is the mathematical relationship between voltage, resistance, and current in an electrical circuit. Each affects the other, and the relationship is stated as follows:

$$E = IR$$

E is the voltage in volts, I is the current in amperes, and R is the resistance in ohms. Also, by transposing the factors:

$$R = E \div I \text{ or } I = E \div R$$

As a memory aid in learning to make good use of Ohm's law, try writing the basic equation as follows:

$$\frac{E}{IR}$$

Using this arrangement, you can use Ohm's law to calculate an unknown voltage, current, or resistance value if the other two values are known. Simply cover the unknown factor with a fingertip, and you will have the formula you need to get your answer. For example:

If you cover the E, the formula is I × R.
If you cover the I, the formula is E ÷ R.
If you cover the R, the formula is E ÷ I.

Ohm's law is used extensively in checking and troubleshooting electrical circuits and parts in automobiles. For example: the current flowing through the coils of a 12V alternator is 3.0 amperes. What is the resistance of the coils?

R = E ÷ I
R = 12 volts ÷ 3.0 amperes
R = 4 ohms

Studying Ohm's law reveals exactly how a change in one factor affects the others. If the resistance of a circuit increases and the voltage remains constant, current will decrease.

If the connections of a starting battery are loose or corroded, for example, a high resistance will be caused. The result will be insufficient current reaching the starting motor, lights, or other units to provide for proper operation.

Types of Electrical Circuits

There are three general types of electrical circuits:

- Series circuits, Figure 19-4.
- Parallel circuits, Figure 19-5.
- Series-parallel circuits, Figure 19-6.

All circuits, regardless of type, consist of a source of electricity (battery or alternator), pieces of electrical equipment or devices, and electrical conductors that connect the equipment or devices to the source.

In a ***series circuit,*** Figure 19-4, the current passes from the power source (battery, in these examples) to each device in turn, and then flows back to the other terminal of the battery. The current has only one path. The amount of current (amperage) will be the same in all parts of the circuit.

In ***parallel circuits,*** Figure 19-5, there is more than one path for the current to flow. In this type of circuit, one terminal of each device is connected to a common conductor, which leads to one terminal of the battery. The remaining terminals of each device are connected to another common conductor, which, in turn, is connected to the other terminal of the battery.

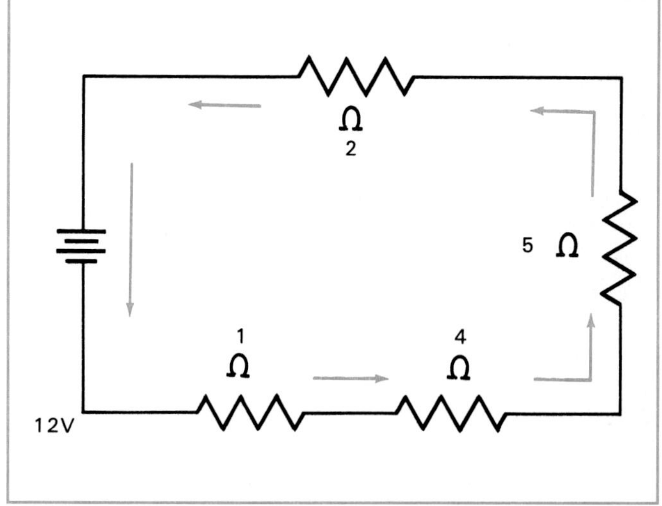

Figure 19-4. In a series circuit, total resistance is the sum of individual resistances, which are shown by Greek letter Omega.

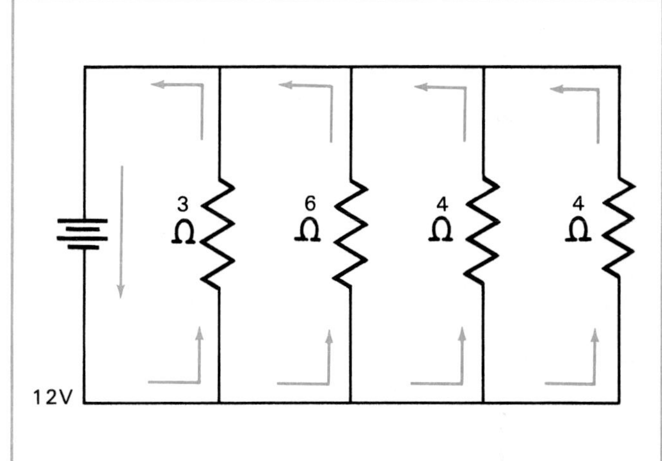

Figure 19-5. Note how current divides through different branches of this parallel circuit.

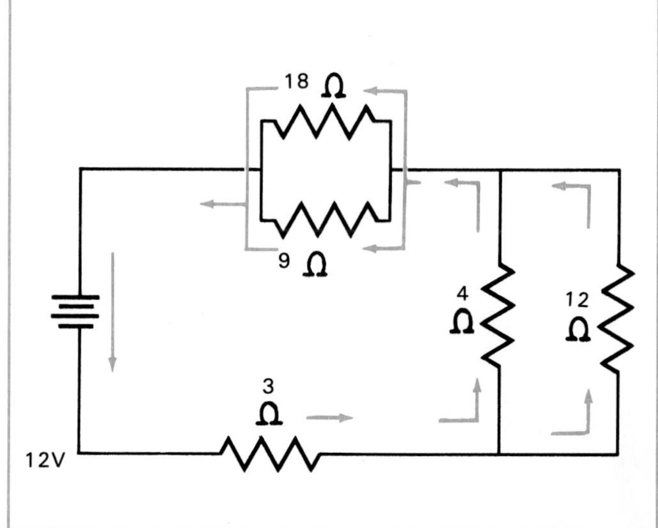

Figure 19-6. A series-parallel circuit has some electrical devices connected in series, and others are connected in parallel.

Series-parallel circuits, Figure 19-6, are those that have some electrical devices connected in series and others in parallel.

Measuring Resistance

To find the total resistance (R_T) of a series circuit, add the resistance of each device. In Figure 19-4, this would be:

$$R_T = R_1 + R_2 + R_3 + R_4$$
$$R_T = 2 \text{ ohms} + 5 \text{ ohms} + 4 \text{ ohms} + 1 \text{ ohm}$$
$$R_T = 12 \text{ ohms}$$

The current flowing in this series circuit can be found by applying Ohm's law as follows:

$$I = E \div R$$
$$I = 12 \text{ volts} \div 12 \text{ ohms}$$
$$I = 1 \text{ ampere}$$

In a parallel electrical circuit, there is more than one "path" for the current to take. Therefore, the total resistance of all the devices will be less than the resistance of any single device.

There are several ways to compute total resistance in a parallel circuit. Probably the simplest way is to utilize the conductance formula. ***Conductance*** is the reciprocal (opposite) of resistance. It is the current-carrying ability of any wire or electrical component. Resistance, as mentioned, is the ability of any wire or electrical component to oppose the flow of current.

To find total resistance, then, use this conductance formula and invert the answer:

$$\frac{1}{R_T} = \frac{1}{R_1} + \frac{1}{R_2} + \frac{1}{R_3} + \frac{1}{R_4}$$

To solve total resistance of the parallel circuit shown in Figure 19-5, substitute the resistance values for R factors in the equation given:

$$\frac{1}{R_T} = \frac{1}{3} + \frac{1}{6} + \frac{1}{4} + \frac{1}{4}$$
$$\frac{1}{R_T} = \frac{4}{12} + \frac{2}{12} + \frac{3}{12} + \frac{3}{12} = \frac{12}{12}$$

Invert both sides of the equation (equal factors):

$$R_T = \frac{12}{12} = 1 \text{ ohm}$$

The total current flowing through the circuit will be:

$$I_T = E \div R_T$$
$$I_T = 12 \text{ volts} \div 1 \text{ ohms}$$
$$I_T = 12 \text{ amperes}$$

The current flowing through any single branch of a parallel circuit is found by dividing the voltage by the resistance of that particular path or branch. In Figure 19-5, the current flowing in each branch would be as follows:

First:	12 volts ÷ 3 ohms = 4 amperes
Second:	12 volts ÷ 6 ohms = 2 amperes
Third:	12 volts ÷ 4 ohms = 3 amperes
Fourth:	12 volts ÷ 4 ohms = 3 amperes

Adding these values gives 12 amperes, which checks with the value found for the total circuit.

To make the R_T calculations for a series-parallel circuit, treat each portion separately. Then, having calculated the resistance of each parallel branch, add these resistances as you would in a simple series circuit.

In Figure 19-6, the resistance of the upper parallel circuit is 3 ohms. The parallel circuit on the left side of the diagram is 6 ohms. Adding these values to 3 ohms of the series circuit at the right makes a total of 12 ohms.

Voltage Drop

The decrease in voltage as current passes through a resistance is known as ***voltage drop.*** The sum of the individual "drops" is equal to the total voltage impressed on the circuit.

Ohm's law can be used to calculate voltage drop in different parts of the circuit. In Figure 19-4, assume that 1 ampere of current is flowing:

Voltage drop E = IR
First part = 1 ampere × 2 ohms = 2
Second part = 1 ampere × 5 ohms = 5
Third part = 1 ampere × 4 ohms = 4
Fourth part = 1 ampere × 1 ohm = 1

If you add these drops in voltage, you will have 2 + 5 + 4 + 1 = 12 volts, which checks with the voltage impressed on the circuit.

Electrical Work and Power

The electrical unit for measuring work is called the ***joule.*** One joule is equal to one ampere flowing for one second under the pressure of one volt.

First bear in mind that ***work*** is done when energy is expended. Work is the product of force multiplied by the distance through which it acts in overcoming resistance.

An electrical force may exist without work being done. This is the condition that exists between the terminals of a battery when no equipment is connected to them. When a piece of equipment is connected to the terminals of the battery, current will flow and work will be done.

Power is the rate of doing work:

$$\text{Power} = \frac{\text{work}}{\text{time}}$$
$$\text{Electrical power} = \frac{\text{electrical work}}{\text{time}}$$

The ***watt*** is the electrical unit of power and is equal to one joule of electrical work per second.

$$\text{Watt} = \frac{\text{Joules}}{\text{Seconds}} = \frac{\text{Volts} \times \text{Amperes} \times \text{Seconds}}{\text{Seconds}}$$
$$\text{Watts} = \text{Volts} \times \text{Amperes}$$

In an automotive lighting circuit, the current may be 8 amperes and the voltage may be 12 volts. The number of watts is 8 amperes × 12 volts = 96 watts.

The unit for measuring mechanical power is ***horsepower*** (hp). Experimentally, it has been found that one horsepower is equal to 746 watts.

Magnetism

Magnetism, like electricity, is still a mystery. We know many laws governing its behavior and have applied it in the automotive field to starting motors, alternators, ignition coils, voltage regulators, etc. However, no one knows just what magnetism is.

The effects of magnetism were first discovered when it was found that pieces of iron ore from certain parts of the world would attract each other and also other pieces of iron. In addition, it was found that when suspended in the air, fragments of this ore would always point toward the North Star. The end of the ore that pointed toward the north was called the "north pole;" the other end was called the "south pole."

Magnetic Fields

All magnets have a magnetic field, which is evidenced by ***lines of force,*** or ***magnetic flux,*** around the magnet, Figure 19-7. The strength of the magnetic field varies. It is strongest close to the magnet and gets progressively weaker as it moves away from the magnet.

The area or extent of the magnetic field can be determined by means of a compass, which also shows the direction of the lines of force. In Figure 19-7, note how the lines of force leave the north pole of a magnet (and coil) and reenter at the south pole. Also note that the lines of force exerted by the horseshoe magnet are more concentrated between the two poles of the magnet.

Theory of Permanent Magnets

The effects, direction, and extent of magnetic fields can be studied. However, there is no actual knowledge as to why certain materials have magnetic properties and others do not. The ***domain theory*** generally is accepted as the best explanation of magnetism.

According to this theory, an electron moving in a fixed circular orbit around the proton creates a magnetic field with the north pole on one side of the orbit and the south pole on the other side, Figure 19-8. It is assumed that the orbiting electron carries a negative charge of electricity, which is the same as electrical current flowing through a conductor. Current flow, then, is from negative to positive.

When a number of magnetized orbiting electrons exist in a material, they interact with each other and form "domains," or groups of atoms having the same magnetic polarity. However, these domains are scattered in random patterns throughout a material, and the material is, in effect, unmagnetized. See Figure 19-9.

Under the influence of a strong external magnetic field, these domains become aligned and the total material

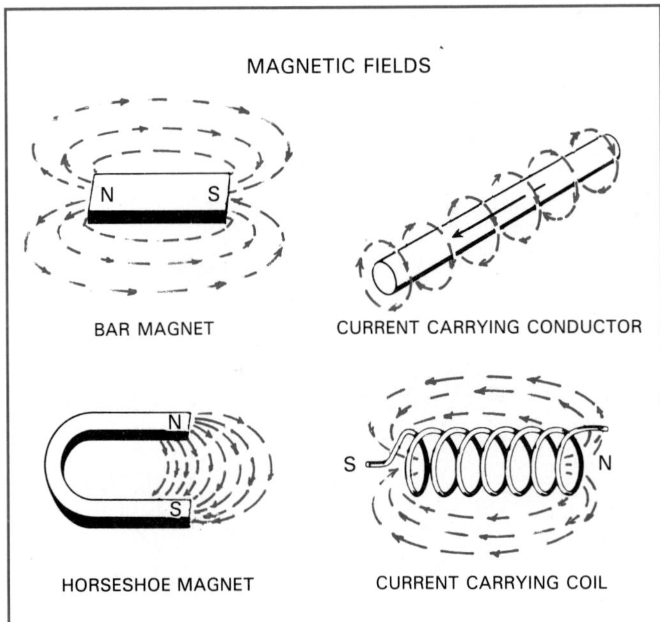

Figure 19-7. Note that lines of force leave a magnet or loop of wire at north pole and re-enter at the south pole.

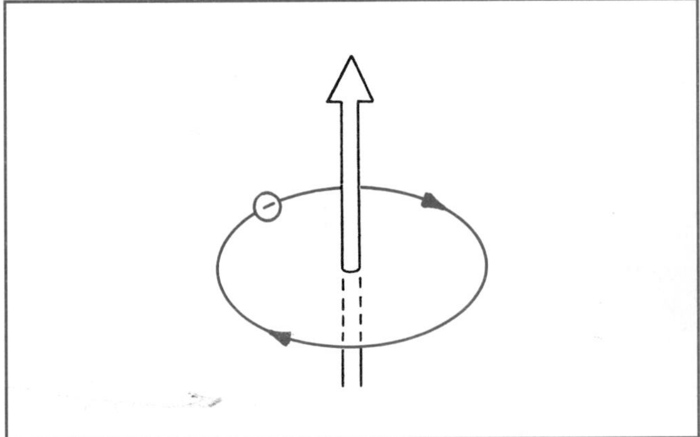

Figure 19-8. An electron, moving in a fixed circular orbit, creates a magnetic field.

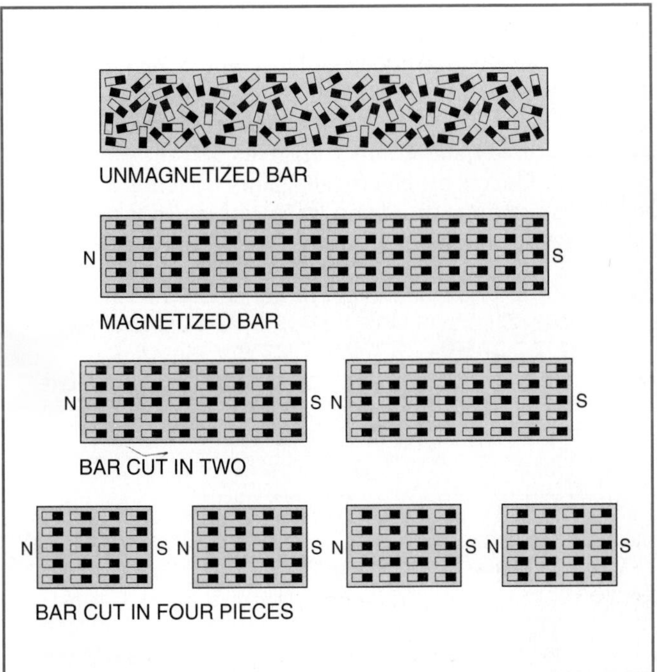

Figure 19-9. In magnetic substances, domains align themselves in parallel planes and in same direction when placed in a magnetic field.

is magnetized, Figure 19-9. The strength of its magnetic field depends on the number of domains that are aligned.

In magnetic substances (iron, cobalt, and nickel), the domains align themselves in parallel planes and in the same direction when placed in a magnetic field, Figure 19-9. This arrangement of the electron-created magnets produces a strong magnetic effect.

It is also interesting to note that soft iron will lose virtually all of its magnetic effect as soon as it is removed from the magnetic field. Hard steel will retain its magnetic characteristics for an indefinite period. Special alloys of tungsten, chromium, and cobalt produce magnetic fields of considerably greater strength than other materials. They also retain their magnetism for a longer period. These alloys are used to form the magnets used in specialized electrical equipment, where a strong magnetic field is required.

Magnetic lines of force seem to penetrate all substances. They are deflected only by magnetic materials or by another magnetic field. There is no insulator for magnetism or lines of force.

Another interesting property of magnets is illustrated by the following experiment. Cut a magnet in two and check the individual pieces for north and south poles. You will find that each piece has north and south poles that are situated as in the original magnet. See Figure 19-9.

Magnetic Attraction and Repulsion

When two permanent magnets are placed so that the north pole of one is close to the south pole of the other, the magnets attract each other. Also, if the magnets are placed with similar poles close together, they repel each other, Figure 19-10. This attraction and repulsion of magnets forms a fundamental law of magnetism: *Like poles of magnets repel each other; unlike poles attract each other.*

Producing Magnets, Magnetic Fields

If you stroke a piece of hardened steel with a natural magnet, the piece of steel will become a magnet. (Steel railroad tracks laid in a north-to-south direction become magnetized because they lie parallel to the magnetic lines of the earth.) Much stronger magnets and magnetic fields can be produced by electrical means. Placing a piece of steel in any strong magnetic field will cause it to become magnetized.

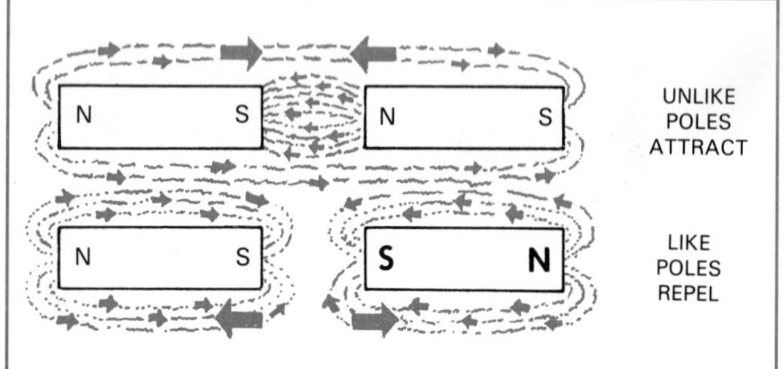

Figure 19-10. Lines of force leaving the north pole of one magnet will enter the south pole of an adjacent magnet, since all lines of force are in same direction. Lines leaving similar poles are repelled since they are in opposite directions.

A magnetic field surrounds any conductor carrying an electrical current. The discovery of this fact resulted in the development of much of our electrical equipment. The field of force is always at right angles to the conductor. This can be shown by placing a magnetic compass close to a conductor of electricity, Figure 19-11.

Since a magnetic force is the only force known to attract a compass needle, it is obvious that a flow of electric current produces a magnetic field similar to that produced by a permanent magnet. When making this experiment, pass direct current through the conductor. Alternating current will cause the magnetic field to change with each alternation of the current.

Not only is the field of force at right angles to the conductor, but the field of force also forms concentric circles about the conductor, Figure 19-12. Also, when the current in the conductor increases, the field of force is increased. Doubling the current will double the strength of the field of force.

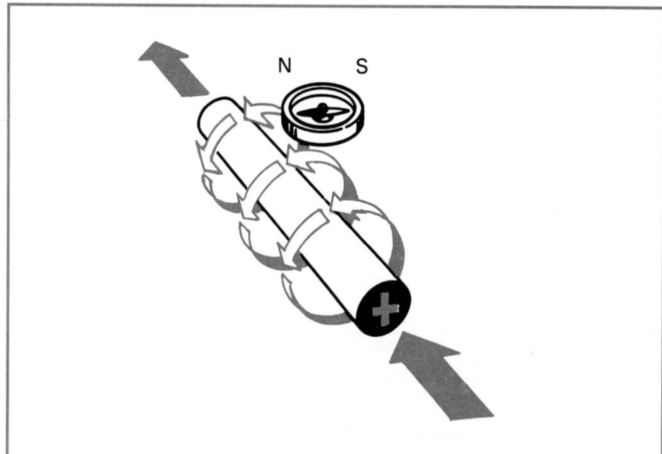

Figure 19-11. A magnetic field surrounds any conductor carrying an electric current. The magnetic field is at right angles to the conductor.

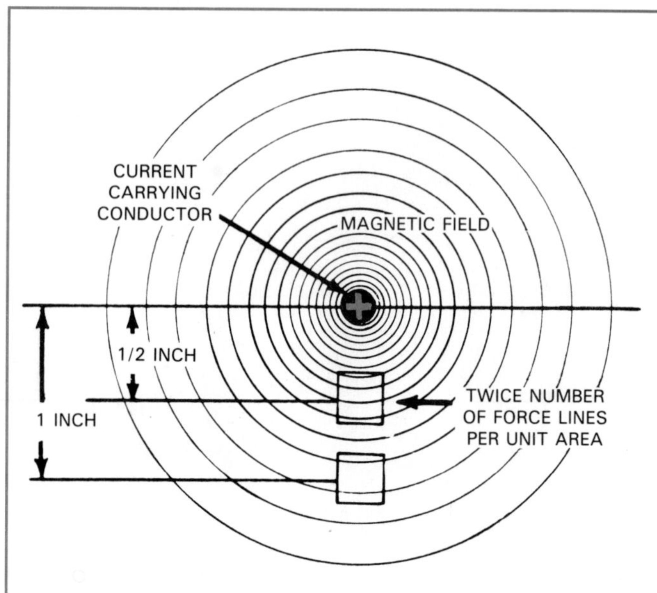

Figure 19-12. A magnetic field forms concentric circles around a conductor carrying an electric current.

Left-hand Rule

In many cases, it is helpful to know the direction of the lines of force that surround a conductor. Their direction is dependent on the direction the current is traveling in the conductor. Use the ***left-hand rule*** to make this determination.

To determine the direction of the lines of force, grasp the conductor with the left hand with the thumb extended in the direction the current is flowing. The fingers will then indicate the direction in which the lines of force surround the conductor, Figure 19-13. This left-hand rule can be used to determine the direction the current is flowing after having first determined the direction of the magnetic field by means of a compass.

Strengthening Magnetic Fields

As mentioned, the magnetic field surrounds a conductor that is carrying an electric current. If this conductor is formed into a loop, Figure 19-14, the lines of force on the outside of the loops spread out into space; lines on the inside of the loop are confined and crowded together. This increases the ***density*** of lines of force in that area. A much greater magnetic effect is produced with the same amount of current flowing.

In this setup, one side of the loop will be a north pole and the other side will be a south pole. By increasing the number of loops, the magnetic field will be greatly increased. By winding the loops or coils on a core of soft iron, the field is further intensified.

Combining Magnetic Fields

Another interesting experiment with magnetism is combining magnetic fields. Figs. 19-7 and 19-10 show the fields of horseshoe magnets and the fields resulting from similar and unlike poles. Figure 19-15 shows magnetic fields surrounding adjacent conductors. In accompanying drawings, the + mark on the end of the conductor simulates the butt end of an arrow. It indicates that the current is moving away from you. The dot on the other end is the point of the arrow. It indicates that current is coming toward you.

Current flowing in the same direction and in opposite directions in two adjacent and parallel conductors is shown in Figure 19-15. A field of force surrounds each conductor, and the direction of the field can be determined by applying the left-hand rule. The field will be clockwise around one

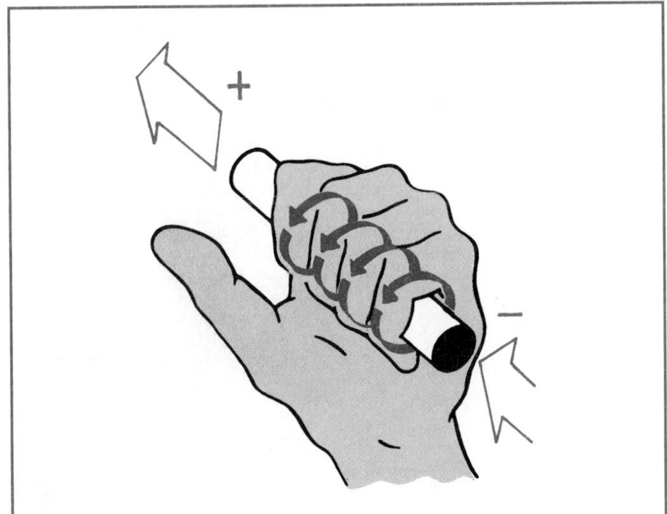

Figure 19-13. Fingers of the left hand around the conductor show the direction of the lines of force, and the extended thumb shows the direction of current in the conductor.

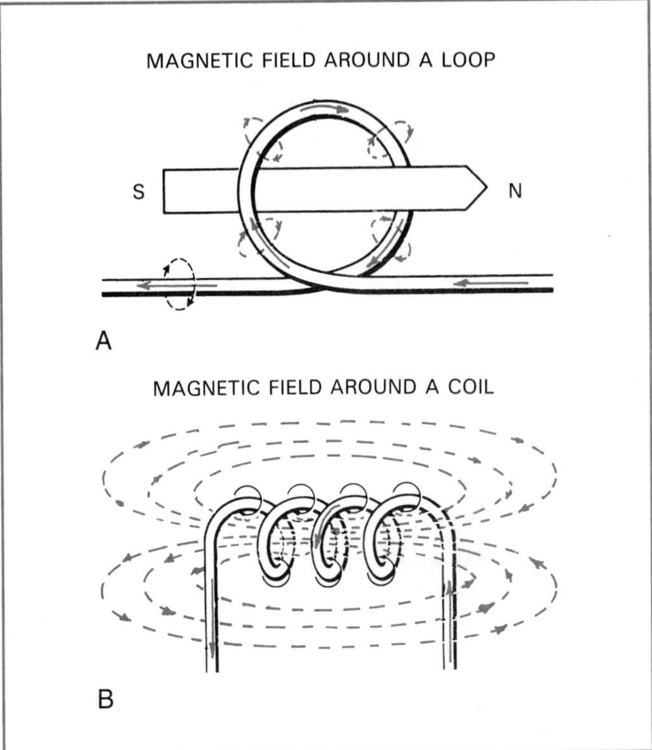

Figure 19-14. A–Magnetic field surrounding a single loop carrying current. B–Magnetic field surrounding a coil of wire.

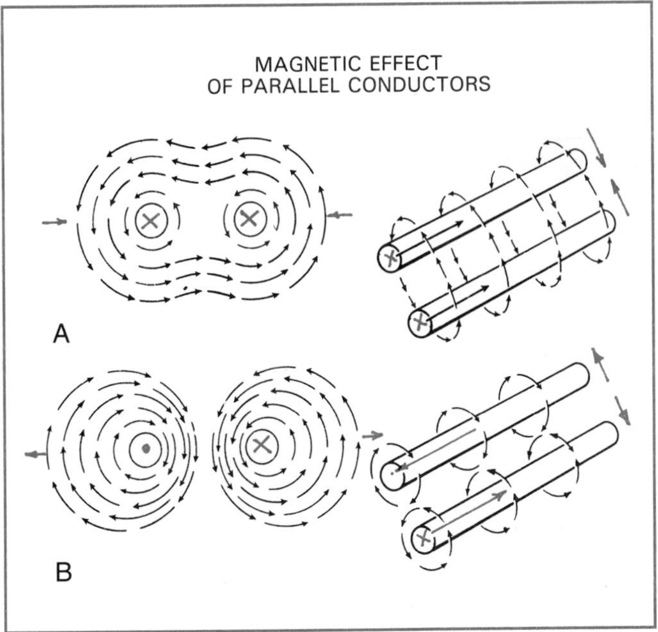

Figure 19-15. A–With current flowing in the same direction in adjacent conductors, the magnetic field tends to draw conductors together. B–If current is flowing in the opposite direction, the magnetic field will force the conductors apart.

conductor and counterclockwise around the other. However, in the area between conductors, the lines of force move in the same direction.

Since the amount of current is the same in both conductors, the number of lines of force between the conductors is the same as the number of lines outside the conductors. Also, since the distance between the conductors is limited, the lines of force will be more dense in that area than beyond the conductors. This condition is known as ***unbalanced density,*** which will cause forces to act on the conductors.

When current is moving in the same direction in two parallel conductors, the unbalanced density will tend to draw the conductors together, Figure 19-15A. If the current is moving in opposite directions in two parallel conductors, the unbalanced density will tend to force the conductors apart, as shown in Figure 19-15B.

As illustrated in Figure 19-15A, two parallel conductors carrying current in the same direction will tend to move closer together. The two conductors act basically like a single conductor carrying a current equal to the sum of the two currents. As a result, twice as many lines of force are created than would be produced by either conductor with its original current. When several more current-carrying conductors are placed side by side, Figure 19-16, the lines of force join and surround all of the conductors. This kind of magnetic pattern is obtained in coils of an alternator, starter solenoid, or ignition coil.

The strength of the magnetic field surrounding the coil of wire is directly proportional to the number of turns of wire in the coil and the strength of the current. To calculate the magnetizing force created, multiply the amperes flowing by the number of turns of wire. This force is known as ***ampere-turns***.

Determining Polarity

To determine the ***magnetic polarity*** of any coil or electromagnet when the direction of current flow is known, use the left-hand rule for coils. Grasp the coil with your left hand so that your fingers extend in the direction the coil is wound and in the direction of current flow, Figure 19-17. The thumb will then point toward the north pole created by the current flow through the coil. Remember that both the direction of current flow and the direction of coil winding determine the polarity of a coil.

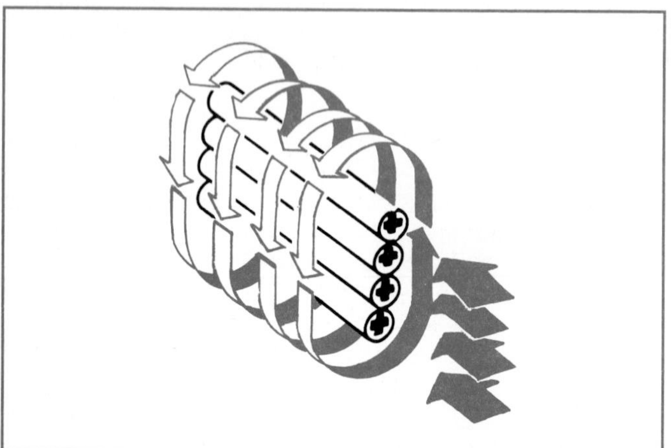

Figure 19-16. When several current-carrying conductors are placed side by side, magnetic lines of force join and surround all conductors.

Magnetic Conductivity

The conductivity of air for lines of force has been adopted as a standard, so air is rated as having a permeability of one. "Permeability of a substance," as defined by Kelvin, "is the ease with which lines of force may be established in any medium as compared with a vacuum." Basically, ***permeability*** is the magnetic conductivity of a substance.

When a soft iron core is inserted in a coil to form a true electromagnet, Figure 19-18, the lines of force, or ***magnetic flux,*** will be increased several hundred times. By means of the better conductor (iron core), more lines of force are created. Field coils in starters, regulator windings on iron cores, and ignition coils all use this same principle.

Solenoids

A ***solenoid*** is a tubular coil of wire with an air core. It is designed to produce a magnetic field. In most cases, the solenoid also includes an iron core that is free to move in and out of the tubular coil, Figure 19-19. The movement of the iron core is used to operate some mechanism or switch. One major application of the solenoid in the automotive field is to shift a starting motor drive into engagement with the flywheel ring gear. When a solenoid is used to close the

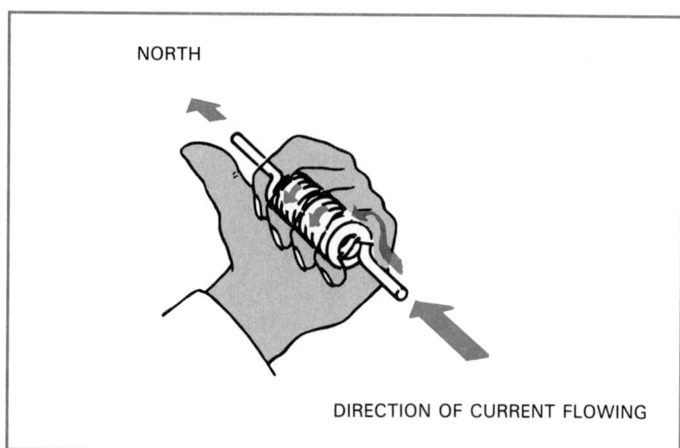

Figure 19-17. Left-hand rule for coils may be used to determine the polarity of a current-carrying coil.

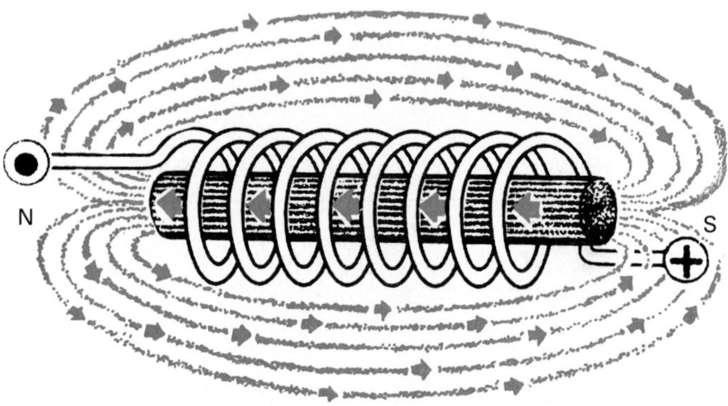

Figure 19-18. The magnetic field of a coil can be strengthened by winding a coil on a core of soft iron to form an electromagnet.

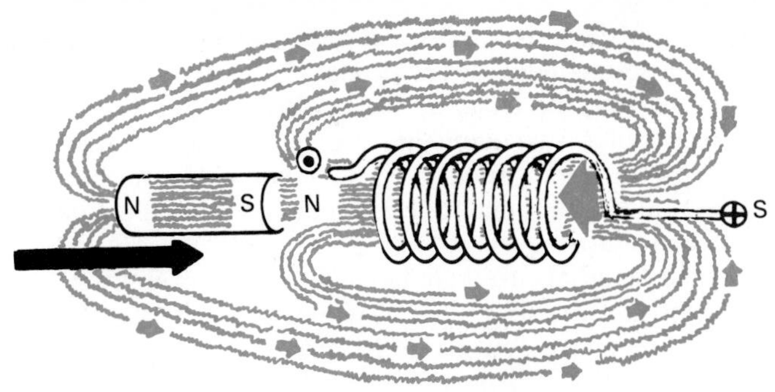

Figure 19-19. A solenoid usually consists of a tubular coil of wire and an iron core.

contacts of an electrical switch, it is called a magnetic switch.

In Figure 19-19, note that the south pole of the iron core is adjacent to the north pole of the coil. The polarity of the movable iron core is induced by the lines of force from the coil. Because the adjacent poles of the coil and the core are of opposite polarity, there is an attraction that draws the movable core into the center of the coil whenever current flows through the coil.

Electronics

Electronics refers to any electrical component, assembly, circuit, or system that uses solid state devices. ***Solid state*** means that these devices have no moving parts, other than electrons. Examples of solid state devices include semiconductor diodes, transistors, and SCRs (silicon controlled rectifiers). These and many other solid state devices have broad application in automotive electronics.

Semiconductors Devices

In the electrical portion of this chapter, you learned that conductors are materials that will pass an electric current. You also learned that nonconductors, or insulators, are materials through which it is difficult to pass an electric current.

In electronics, you will study semiconductors. ***Semiconductors*** are made from material somewhere between the range of conductors and nonconductors. Semiconductor devices are designed to do one of three things:

- Stop flow of electrons.
- Start flow of electrons.
- Control amount of electron flow.

Semiconductor Diodes

A ***semiconductor diode*** is a two-element solid state electronic device. It contains what is termed a P-type material that is connected to a piece of N-type material. See Figure 19-20. The union of the P and N materials forms a PN junction with two connections. The ***anode*** is connected to the P material, and the ***cathode*** is connected to the N material, Figure 19-21.

A diode is, in effect, a one-way valve. It will conduct current in one direction and remain nonconductive in the reverse direction. When current flows through the diode, the diode is said to be ***forward biased.*** See Figure 19-22.

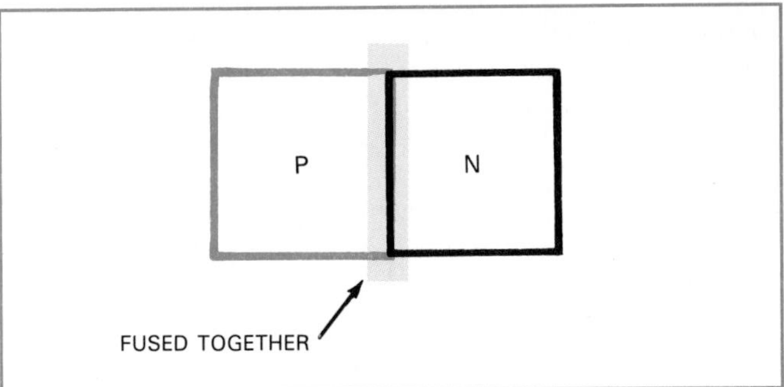

Figure 19-20. Positive and negative semiconductor materials must be fused together to form a diode.

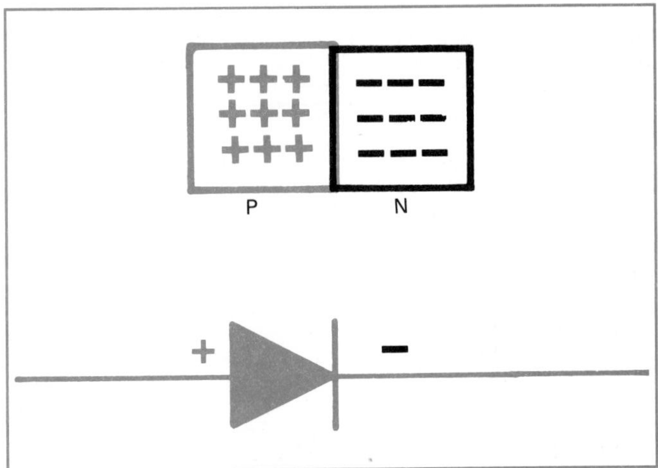

Figure 19-21. A–With P and N materials joined at the PN junction, the diode is ready to pass current in one direction only. B–Diode symbol.

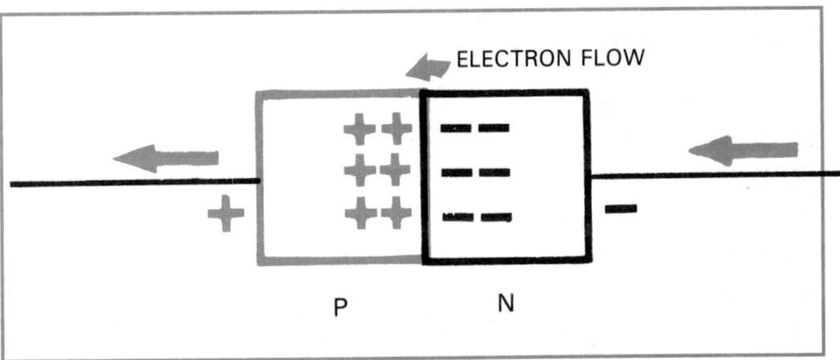

Figure 19-22. With current flow from - to +, electrons in N material are repelled toward the PN junction to meet hole flow. Current will flow through the diode.

When current flow is blocked by the diode, the diode is ***reverse biased,*** as shown in Figure 19-23.

NOTE: When a diode is reverse biased, there is an extremely minute current flow. In practice, however, reverse bias current flow is said to be "negligible."

With the P and N materials fused together to form a diode, it can be placed in a circuit. The P material is connected to the positive side of the battery and the N material is connected to the negative side of the battery. See Figure 19-24. Connected in this manner, current will flow. If connections are reversed, current will not flow.

Diode Polarity. Because of the "one way" characteristic of a semiconductor diode, it is obvious that it must be placed in the circuit with correct polarity. Otherwise, it

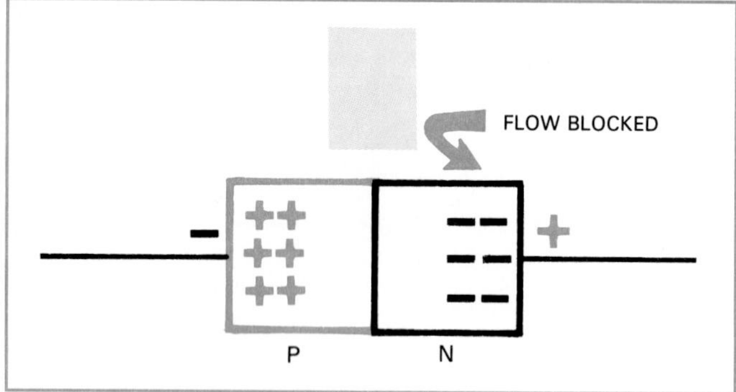

Figure 19-23. With current flow from + to -, electron flow will be away from PN junction. Current will not flow through the diode.

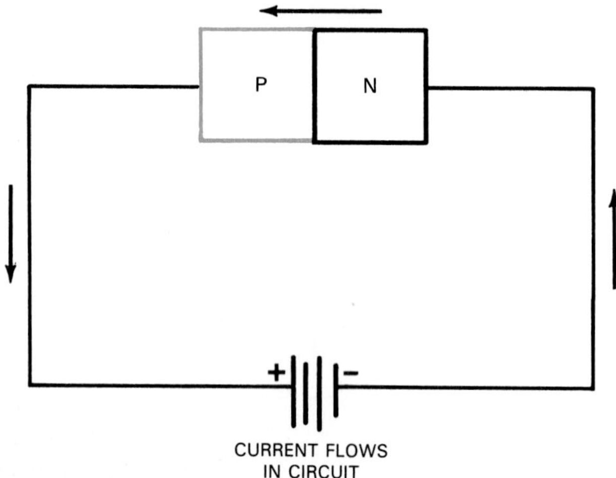

Figure 19-24. When a battery is connected to a diode with the positive side to the P material and the negative side to the N material, current will flow.

will block current flow or even be damaged by a surge of voltage above peak inverse voltage. ***Peak inverse voltage*** (PIV) is the amount of voltage a diode can take in the reverse direction (reverse bias) without being damaged.

Generally, diodes are labeled plus (+) and minus (-). Those that are not labeled can be tested with an ohmmeter and properly labeled before being placed in the circuit. Simply hook the positive lead from the ohmmeter to one end of the diode and the negative lead to the other end. See Figure 19-25. If you get a low resistance reading, you are forward biasing the diode. Mark a minus sign on the end of the diode hooked to the negative lead from the ohmmeter. Mark a plus sign on other end of diode.

If the ohmmeter reads high resistance, Figure 19-26, you are reverse biasing the diode. Polarity is incorrect. Just reverse the leads and retest, then mark the ends of the diode for correct polarity.

Transistors

A ***transistor*** is a solid state device used to switch and/or amplify the flow of electrons in a circuit. A typical automotive switching application would be an ignition system in which a transistor switches the primary system off and on. An amplifying application could be a stereo system where a radio signal needed strengthening.

A transistor is a three-element device made of two types of semiconductor materials The three elements are called ***emitter,*** the ***base,*** and the ***collector.*** See Figure 19-27. The outer two elements (collector and emitter) are made of the same material. The other element (base) is made of a different material. Each element has a conductor attached to it.

The materials used are labeled for their properties. P is for positive, meaning a lack of electrons. It has "holes" ready to receive electrons. N is for negative, which means the material has a surplus of electrons.

The hole theory is based on the assumption that the movement of a free electron from one atom to another leaves a hole in the atom that it left. This hole is quickly filled by another free electron. As this electron movement is transmitted throughout the conductor, an electric current is created from negative to positive.

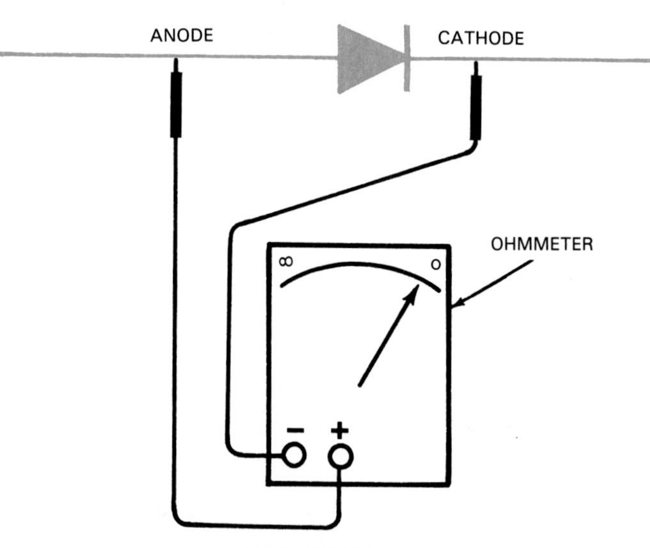

Figure 19-25. To test diode polarity, connect ohmmeter leads as shown. Low resistance indicates that diode is forward biased.

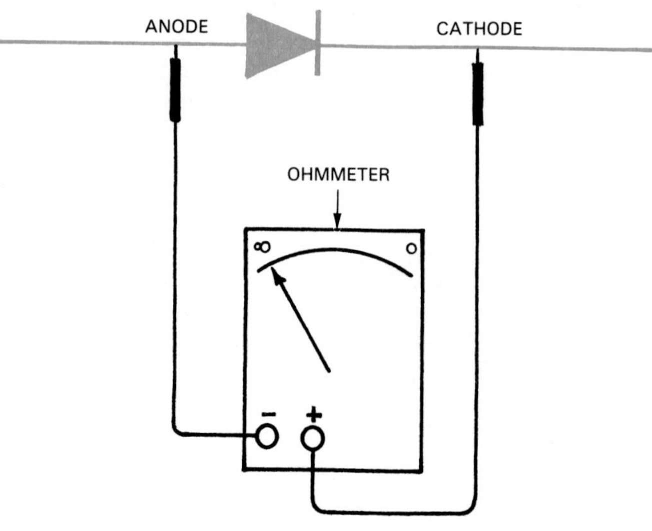

Figure 19-26. If the ohmmeter test for diode polarity results in resistance, the diode is reverse biased.

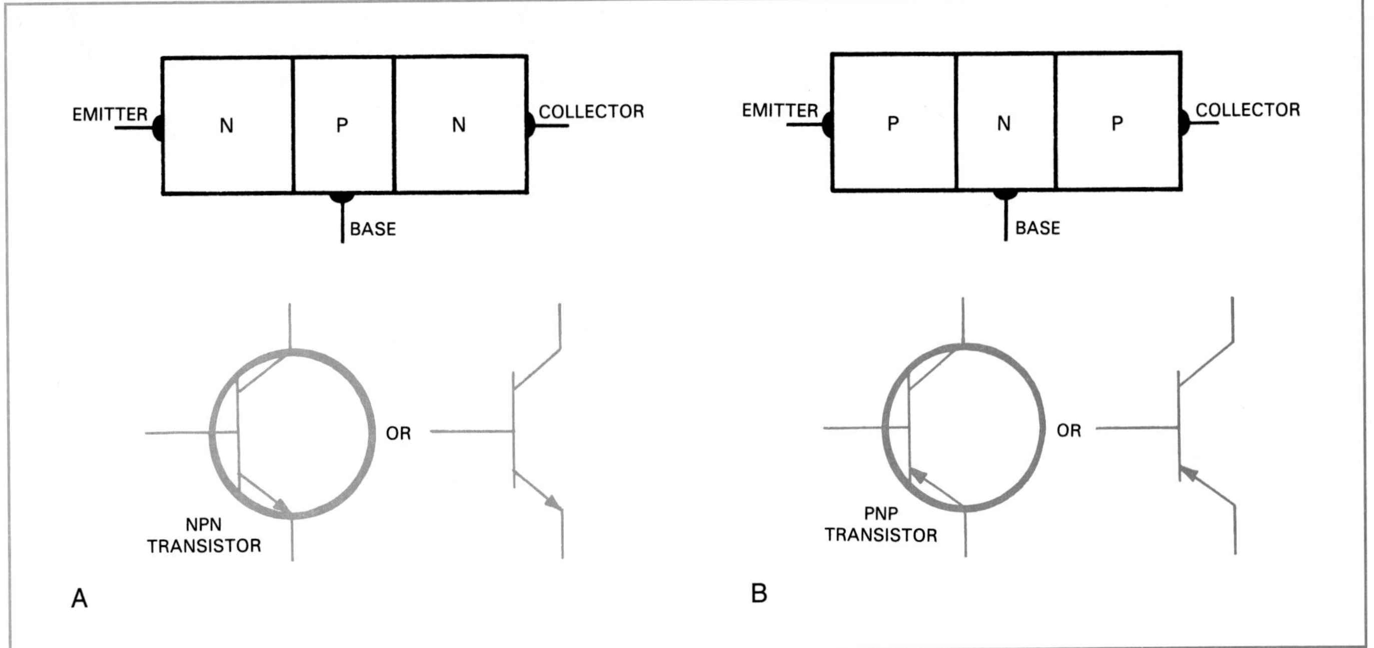

Figure 19-27. Transistors are manufactured in two basic types. A–PNP transistor. B–NPN transistor. Symbols are shown below.

At the same time, the "hole" has been moved backward in the conductor as one free electron after another takes its place in sort of a chain reaction. "Hole flow" is from positive to negative. Current flow in a transistor, then, may be either electron movement or hole flow, depending on the type of material.

Transistor Types. Transistor types are either PNP or NPN, and their operation is basically the same. The differences are in the current carriers (electrons or holes) and direction of current flow. In either case, the polarity of the source voltage must be reversed to make a transistor operate. Symbols for PNP and NPN transistors are illustrated in Figure 19-27.

Transistor Leads. The transistor leads (wires) are known as the emitter lead, the base lead, and collector lead. The PNP transistor will have its leads labeled as shown in Figure 19-28. Note that the emitter lead in the symbol always has an arrow. In order to identify the PNP symbol, think of the PNP as "pointing in" with reference to the arrow.

The NPN transistor leads will be labeled as shown in Figure 19-29. To identify the NPN transistor symbol, think of NPN as "not pointing in." Using these catchwords will be a help when working with transistors and transistorized circuit drawings.

When transistors are placed in a circuit, the emitter-base (E-B) junction is forward biased. Forward biasing of the E-B junction will cause current to flow in the normally reverse-biased base-collector (B-C) junction.

In order to turn on a PNP transistor in a lamp circuit, Figure 19-30, a negative signal must be placed on the base. When this happens, the flow of electrons is from the collector to the emitter. Note that the flow of electrons is against the direction indicated by the arrow on the emitter, Figure 19-31.

With an NPN transistor, a positive signal must be placed on the base to make it conduct. This will let the electrons flow from emitter to collector, Figure 19-31. Again, the flow of electrons is against the direction indicated by the arrow on the emitter.

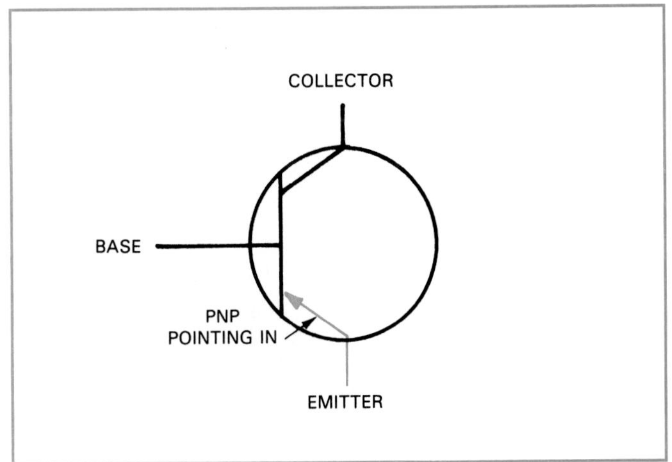

Figure 19-28. On the PNP transistor symbol, the arrow is "pointing in."

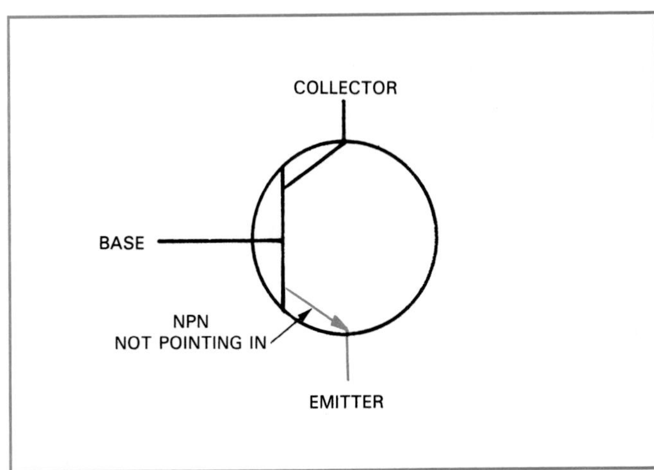

Figure 19-29. On the NPN transistor symbol, the arrow is "not pointing in."

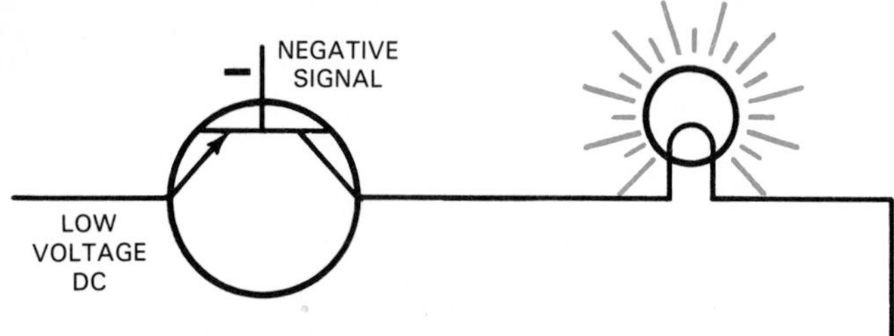

Figure 19-30. In a low-voltage dc circuit with a PNP transistor and a lamp, putting a negative signal on base of transistor will turn on the transistor and light the lamp.

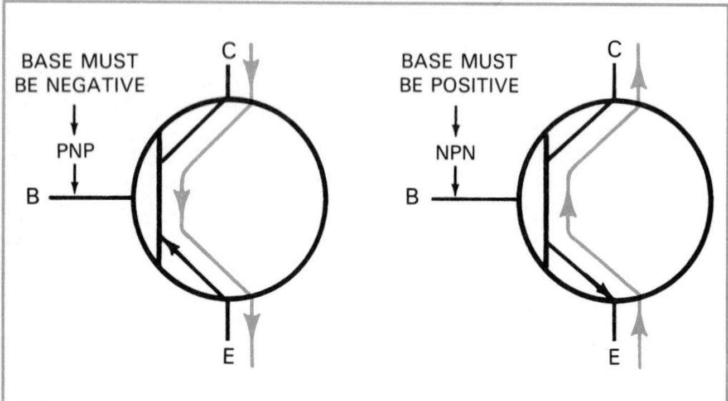

Figure 19-31. When transistor is forward biased, flow of electrons is against direction indicated by arrow on emitter.

Silicon Controlled Rectifiers

A ***silicon controlled rectifier*** combines two diodes so that their junctions appear as shown in Figure 19-32. With this arrangement, junction 1 is forward biased, junction 2 is reverse biased, and junction 3 is forward biased.

The anode is positive in Figure 19-32 and the cathode is negative, but the SCR will not conduct because one of the junctions will be reverse biased. A third connection made to the SCR is called the GATE. If dc is applied to the gate, it will trigger the SCR into conduction.

After initiating the induction, the gate will lose control until the anode-cathode path to the source is broken momentarily. Then the gate is again in control for the next triggering action. The triggering capability of the SCR makes it suitable for use in electronic ignition systems and in battery chargers.

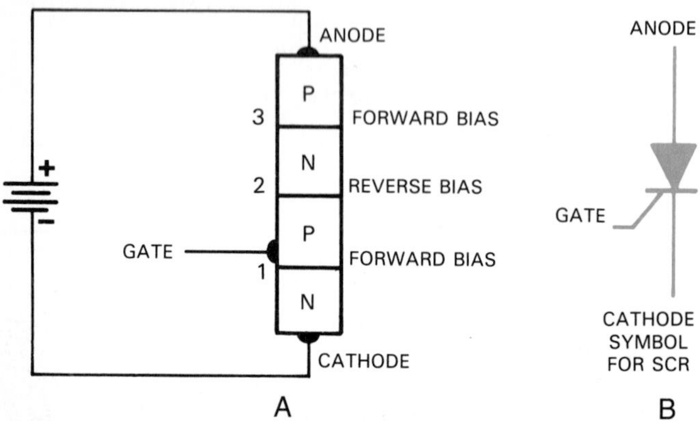

Figure 19-32. A–Schematic of silicon controlled rectifier construction and placement in a simple dc circuit. B–Symbol for SCR.

Sensors

Many electronic circuits use sensors to trigger a control signal. A ***sensor*** is a solid state semiconductor that controls electron flow as its temperature or pressure changes.

A typical automatic temperature control system uses three sensors:

- A sensor to monitor outside (ambient) temperature.
- A sensor to monitor in-car temperature.
- A sensor to monitor air discharge duct temperature.

Electronics Advances

In the automotive field, electronics have touched on almost all operating systems. Common applications of electronics in the automotive field include:

- Electronic ignition with sensors that read engine speed, load, and temperature and feed these signals to a microcomputer. The microcomputer adjusts spark timing once per crankshaft revolution to match engine operation requirements.
- Electronic fuel injection (EFI) systems that are under the precise control of key sensing units and an electronic control unit (ECU).
- An electronic data processing center for the engine that combines digital control of individual systems, such as fuel injection and ignition, in a single unit. Sensors deliver data on engine rotational speed crankshaft position, and ambient air temperature to determine ideal spark advance and fuel quantity.
- Electronically controlled diesel fuel injection that uses an electronic control unit to process inputs from various sensors into electrical outputs. These outputs, in turn, are translated into mechanical actions that regulate the fuel injection pump by means of a transducer.
- Electronic control for automatic transmission. Input sensors sense engine and transmission rotational speeds and engine loads. The selector lever position, kickdown switch, and program switch are taken into account. Based on this information, the transmission's electronic program selects the best gear for operating conditions. It also smooths shifts, cuts fuel consumption, and protects the engine and transmission from driver mistakes.
- An electronically controlled anti-lock braking system that utilizes rotational speed sensors, an electronic control unit, and a hydraulic modulator to control braking. Magnetic valves in the modulator can lower line pressure, hold it steady, or increase it because of electronic signal processing. With this type of system, no wheel actually skids. The vehicle retains its directional stability.
- Electronic trigger unit for passive restraint systems that measures vehicle deceleration. Its signal is compared electronically with preprogrammed values. If these values are exceeded (in an accident), the trigger's electronic control signals the air bag(s) to inflate. Or, in the case of an automatic shoulder/lap belt tensioner, the ECU triggers the tensioning.
- Electronic thermostatic control (ETC) for auto heating and air conditioning systems. The desired interior temperature is set and the ETC system maintains it, inde-

pendently of vehicle speed, engine temperature, or ambient conditions.

- Trip computers that deliver information on fuel consumption; average speed; estimated distance to the next fuel stop; exact trip time; time of day; and outside temperature.

With engine operation, fuel economy, emission control, and safety systems under electronic control, it appears that the next breakthrough will be in the area of total information systems for the automobile. The total system would integrate all driver-information functions into a single display unit, eventually leading to replacement of today's instruments.

For situations that could endanger the driver or vehicle, a multi-purpose display would signal the threat. If more than one threat is imminent, the system would decide which threat has priority.

Whatever direction future automotive advances take, you can be sure that electronics will be deeply involved.

Chapter 19–Review Questions

Write your answers on a separate sheet of paper. Do not write in this book.

1. How will an electrified piece of rubber react when placed close to an electrified piece of glass?
2. Similarly charged electrified bodies attract each other. True or False?
3. What tiny particles form an atom?
4. Electrons have a ____ (positive or negative) charge.
5. The nucleus of atoms consists of:
   (A) protons and electrons.
   (B) protons and neutrons.
   (C) neutrons and electrons.
   (D) electrons.
6. Electrons in a conductor are ______ (bound or free).
7. Electron flow is from ____ to ____.
8. Electric current is the ____.
9. The pressure between the electrons is measured in:
   (A) amperes.
   (B) ohms.
   (C) volts.
   (D) watts.
10. State Ohm's law.
11. Write the Ohm's law formula for finding voltage (E).
12. Write the Ohm's law formula for finding current in amperes (I).
13. Write the Ohm's law formula for finding resistance (R).
14. What is the total resistance in a series circuit having four individual resistances of 4 ohms, 8 ohms, 6 ohms, and 2 ohms?
15. When you place the fingers of your left hand around a current-carrying conductor with your thumb showing the direction of current, your fingers will indicate the direction in which ____ surround the conductor.
16. In an automotive circuit, how many watts are there if the current is 4 amperes and the voltage is 12 volts?
    (A) 3 watts.
    (B) 16 watts.
    (C) 48 watts.
    (D) 72 watts.
17. How many watts are there in an electrical horsepower?
    (A) 764.
    (B) 464.
    (C) 746.
    (D) 674.
18. The area surrounding a magnet is called the ____.
19. Which of the following metals are magnetic substances?
    (A) Iron.
    (B) Brass.
    (C) Nickel.
    (D) Lead.
20. The magnetic field of force surrounding any conductor carrying electrical current is always____ (parallel or at right angles) to the conductor.
21. Basically, ______ is the magnetic conductivity of a substance.
22. If you insert an iron core in a coil of wire carrying electrical current, the magnetic field is ____.
23. When using the left-hand rule as applied to a current-carrying coil, what does the direction of the thumb indicate?
    (A) Direction of current flow.
    (B) Direction of electron flow.
    (C) North pole.
    (D) South pole.
24. A solenoid is a tubular coil of wire with an ____ or _____core.
25. Electronics refers to any electrical component, assembly, circuit, or system that uses ____ devices.
26. Semiconductors are made from materials with characteristics somewhere between those of ____ and ____.
27. Semiconductors are designed to:
    (A) stop flow of electrons.
    (B) start flow of electrons.
    (C) control amount of electron flow.
    (D) All of the above.
28. A semiconductor diode is a(n) ____-element solid state electronic device.
    (A) one
    (B) two
    (C) three
    (D) four
29. A semiconductor diode contains P material and N material. The ____ is connected to the P material; the ____ is connected to the N material.
30. When current flows in a diode, the diode is said to be ____-biased.
31. What is peak inverse voltage?
32. What instrument is used to test the polarity of a diode?
    (A) Ohmmeter.
    (B) Ammeter.
    (C) Voltmeter.
    (D) None of the above.
33. A transistor is a solid state device used to ____ and/or ____ the flow of electrons in a circuit.
34. A transistor is an electronic device made of ____ types of semiconductor materials.
35. Transistor types are either ____ or ____.
36. Many electronic circuits use ____ to trigger a control signal.
37. The polarity of the source voltage must be reversed to make a transistor operate. True or False?

38. Transistor ____ are known as emitter lead, base lead, and collector lead.
39. A silicon controlled rectifier combines ____ diodes.
40. On an SCR, the anode is positive and the cathode is negative. A third connection made to the SCR is called the:
    (A) emitter.
    (B) base.
    (C) collector.
    (D) gate.

Electric vehicles, such as this General Motors prototype, may become more common as manufacturers strive to meet increasingly stringent emissions standards. (General Motors)

Chapter 20
Automotive Fuels

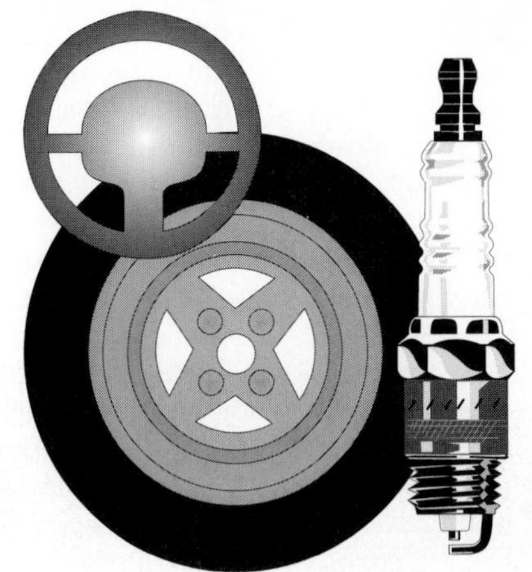

After studying this chapter, you will be able to:

❍ Describe detonation and preignition.
❍ List and explain the characteristics of various fuels.
❍ Compare various fuels, including alcohol, diesel fuel, and LP-Gas.

Automotive Fuels

The fuel used in most automobiles and internal combustion engines is gasoline. Other fuels include methanol, benzol, alcohol, alcohol-gasoline blends, and liquid petroleum gas (LP-Gas).

Gasoline is a colorless liquid obtained from crude petroleum as a result of a complicated distillation and cracking process. Two important characteristics of gasoline used for fuel in automotive engines are volatility and antiknock characteristics.

Volatility

The ***volatility*** of any liquid is its vaporizing ability. In the case of a simple substance, volatility is usually determined by its boiling point. For example, the boiling point of water is 212°F (100°C). Gasoline is a mixture of ***hydrocarbon compounds,*** each having its own boiling point. Gasoline used for fuel in automobiles has a range of boiling points from approximately 100°F (38°C) up to 400°F (204°C), Figure 20-1.

The fuel must remain a liquid until it enters the air stream in the carburetor, the fuel injection throttle body, or the fuel injection intake plenum. At this time, it must quickly vaporize and mix uniformly in the correct proportions with the intake air.

The volatility of gasoline affects ease of starting, length of warm-up period, and engine performance during normal operation. For easy starting with a cold engine, the fuel must be highly volatile. In other words, it must vaporize easily. Therefore, when cold weather approaches, fuel refiners increase the percentage of highly volatile fuel contained in gasoline to ensure easier starting under the cold weather operating conditions.

A portion of the fuel must be sufficiently volatile to ensure proper vaporization during periods of acceleration. If fuel injected during heavy acceleration does not vaporize readily, it could result in a lean mixture that would exist only for a moment. This produces a ***flat spot,*** which is a hesitation on acceleration.

If the volatility of fuel is too low, the engine will never start. This is best illustrated by a vehicle that is placed in storage for a long time. When the vehicle is removed from storage, the engine turns over but does not start. The troubleshooting process shows that both spark and fuel are present. However, the fuel in the tank has lost its volatility and cannot be ignited in the combustion chamber. Fuel should always be removed from a vehicle prior to long term storage.

If the volatility of the fuel is too high, it will contribute to a vapor lock condition. In vapor lock, the liquid fuel vaporizes at any point before the metering process of the carburetor or fuel injector. This prevents fuel from reaching the carburetor or fuel injector as a liquid.

Vapor Lock

Just as water turns to steam when it is heated, gasoline turns to vapor when sufficient heat is applied. Early ***vaporization*** of the fuel can cause complete or partial interruption

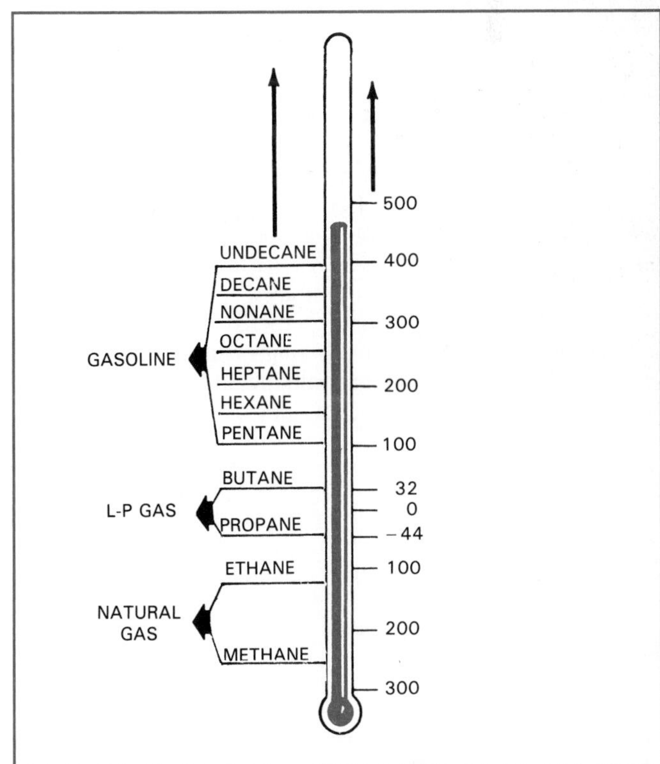

Figure 20-1. Range of boiling points for various hydrocarbons.

of fuel flow. Since the fuel vapor occupies a greater volume than the liquid fuel, the amount of fuel flow will be reduced. Loss of power and missing will occur. Under extreme conditions, the engine will stop or will not start. This condition, which is known as ***vapor lock,*** may occur anywhere in the fuel line.

Whether or not vapor is likely to form depends on ***vapor pressure,*** or the ease with which the fuel will vaporize. The standardized method of measuring vapor pressure in the laboratory is known as the Reid Method. U.S. Government specifications for motor gasoline require that the Reid vapor pressure at 100°F (38°C) should not exceed 12 psi.

Carburetors are vented to a charcoal canister as part of the evaporative emission control system. This also aids in relieving the problem of vapor blocking the flow of liquid fuel.

In another design technique, a molded phenolic-resin fuel bowl keeps the fuel about 20°F cooler than in an all-metal fuel bowl. Also, some manufacturers place a gasket approximately 1/2″ thick between the carburetor and manifold. This reduces the transmission of heat to the carburetor.

Fuel pumps are placed where they will be cooled by air blasts and shielded from the heat of the exhaust manifold. Additionally, fuel lines are routed away from the exhaust pipe, catalytic converter, and muffler to reduce the chances of vapor lock.

Low pressure on the fuel will also promote vaporization. An electric fuel pump located in or near the fuel tank would help prevent the vapor lock problem that conventional, mechanical-type fuel pumps have.

Vaporization is also controlled by gasoline refineries by changing the vapor pressure of the fuel. During winter months, a fuel that is easily vaporized is supplied to facilitate starting. During summer months, a fuel that is not so easily vaporized is provided. However, during unseasonably warm weather in the spring and before refineries have supplied their summer-grade fuel, it is not unusual to encounter vapor lock in vehicles with mechanical fuel pumps.

Boiling Range

The ***boiling temperature*** of fuel is also the temperature at which it is completely vaporized. Furthermore, fuel can be completely burned in an engine only in vaporized form. Because of this, the boiling range of fuel should be low enough to permit complete vaporization with the existing engine temperature.

For engines operating at reduced speed and load or in cold weather, lower boiling point fuels will give more satisfactory performance. Fuels that cannot be completely vaporized and burned will accumulate and form sludge and other harmful deposits in the engine.

Sulfur Content

Sulfur content in fuel oil should be as low as possible in order to keep the amount of corrosion and deposit formation at a minimum. Tests have shown that increasing sulfur content from .25% to 1.25% increases deposits and wear by 135%.

Heat Value

The power obtained from any fuel is determined by its ***heat value,*** which is measured by burning a unit amount of fuel in an excess of air or oxygen. Heat value is measured in British thermal units per pound of fuel. One British thermal unit (Btu) is the amount of heat required to raise one pound of water 1°F. One Btu is equal to 778.6 foot-pounds.

Some of the higher heat values of the hydrocarbons found in gasoline are as follows:

- Hexane 20700
- Heptane 20600
- Octane 20500
- Nonane 20450
- Decane 20420
- Undecane 20375
- Dodecane 20350

Combustion of Gasoline

Rapidly combining fuel with oxygen produces heat. This is known as ***combustion.*** In the case of gasoline, combustion is the rapid oxidation of the carbon and the hydrogen constituting the fuel. The heat produced is the result of the chemical change.

The chemical equation of combustion for octane is:

$$C_8H_{18} + 12.5\ O_2 = 8\ CO_2 + 9\ H_2O$$

In this equation, C_8H_{18} represents the chemical formula for gasoline. The 12.5 O_2 is the oxygen required to burn one part of gasoline. This produces eight parts of carbon dioxide (CO_2) and nine parts of water (H_2O).

However, air is used in actual operation of an engine instead of pure oxygen. Air consists of a mixture of 1/5 oxygen and 4/5 nitrogen by volume. From the standpoint of weight, it consists of one part oxygen and 3 1/2 parts nitrogen, or more exactly, 23 parts oxygen and 77 parts nitrogen.

The atomic weights for the different elements entering into the combustion of octane and air are as follows:

- Carbon = 12
- Nitrogen = 14
- Oxygen = 16
- Hydrogen = 1

On a weight basis, the chemical formula of combustion is:

$$114\ C_8H_{18} + 400\ O_2 = 352\ CO_2 + 162\ H_2O$$

Since air is a mixture of oxygen and nitrogen in a ratio of 23 to 77, the nitrogen must also be considered when writing the combustion equation for octane and air. The amount of nitrogen present with 400 weight units of oxygen is:

$$400 \times \frac{77}{23} = 1339$$

This nitrogen is present in the combustible mixture and also in the products of combustion. So, it must be added to both sides of the equation:

$$114\ C_8H_{18} + 400\ O_2 + 1339\ N_2 = 352\ CO_2 + 162\ H_2O + 1339\ N_2$$

For one pound of octane, the formula becomes:

$$3.09\text{ lb. } CO_2 + 1.42\text{ lb. } H_2O + 11.76\text{ lb. } N_2 = 16.27\text{ lb. of exhaust gas}$$

or

$$1\text{ lb. of fuel} + 15.27\text{ lb. air} = 16.27\text{ lb. of exhaust gas.}$$

The amount of power developed in an internal combustion engine is dependent on the heat that can be obtained from burning the fuel. This, in the case of gasoline or any of the hydrocarbons, is equal to the total heat produced by the combustion of the carbon and hydrogen *minus* the heat required to break up the hydrocarbon molecules.

When carbon becomes carbon dioxide due to combustion, 14,542 Btu are liberated for each pound of carbon burned. In the combustion of hydrogen to steam, 62,032 Btu are liberated for each pound of hydrogen. To break up the octane into carbon and hydrogen, 1523 Btu are required for each pound of octane.

In octane (C_8H_{18}), the carbon is 84.2%, while the hydrogen is 15.8%. The heat produced by combustion is:

84.2% of 14,542 Btu = 12,244 Btu
15.8% of 62,032 Btu = 9,801 Btu

This makes a total of 22,045 Btu. From this, subtract the 1523 Btu required to break up the fuel into carbon and hydrogen. The difference, 20,522 Btu, is the total heat from burning one pound of octane.

Combustion Chamber Temperature

During combustion, temperatures vary through a relatively wide range. ***Combustion temperatures*** are affected by the compression ratio, combustion chamber contour, cooling system effectiveness, air/fuel mixture, and amount of burned gases remaining in the cylinder from the previous cycle.

At the end of the compression stroke (but before ignition), temperatures of approximately 985°F (529°C) may be considered average for an engine with a compression ratio of 9 to 1. Immediately after ignition, the temperature increases very rapidly and will reach a value of approximately 5500°F (3038°C).

Normal Combustion

The ***normal combustion*** process in the combustion chamber, Figure 20-2, goes through three stages termed formation (nucleus of flame), hatching out, and propagation.

As soon as the ignition spark jumps the gap of the spark plug, a small ball of blue flame develops in the gap. This ball is the first stage, or ***nucleus,*** of the flame. It enlarges relatively slowly, and during its growth, there is no measurable pressure created by the heat.

As the nucleus enlarges, it develops into the ***hatching-out stage.*** The nucleus is torn apart, so that it sends fingers of flame into the mixture in the combustion chamber. This causes enough heat to provide a slight rise in temperature and pressure in the entire air/fuel mixture. Consequently, a lag still exists in the attempt to raise pressure in the entire cylinder.

It is during the third stage, or ***propagation,*** that the effective burning of the fuel takes place. The flame burns in a front that sweeps across the combustion chamber, burning rapidly and causing great heat with an accompanying rise in pressure. It is this pressure that causes the piston to move downward.

During normal combustion, the burning is progressive. It increases gradually during the first two stages. But, during the third stage, the flame is extremely strong as it sweeps through the combustion chamber. However, there is no violent or explosive action, such as detonation (ordinarily responsible for pinging or knocking).

Detonation

If ***detonation*** takes place, it occurs during the third stage of combustion, Figure 20-3. In the propagation stage, the flame sweeps from the area around the spark plug toward the walls of the combustion chamber. The parts of the chamber the flame has passed may contain inert, nonburnable gases. The section not yet touched by flame contains highly compressed, heated, combustible gases.

As the flame races through the combustion chamber, the unburned gases ahead of it are further compressed and are heated to higher temperatures. Under certain conditions, the extreme heating of the unburned part of the mixture may cause it to ignite spontaneously and explode.

It is this rapid, uncontrolled burning in the final stage of combustion that is called detonation. It is caused by the rapidly burning flame front compressing the unburned part of the mixture to the point of self-ignition. This secondary wave front collides with the normal flame and makes an audible knock or pinging sound.

Detonation harms an engine and hinders its performance in several ways. In extreme cases, pistons may shatter, cylinders burst, or cylinder heads crack. At times, tempera-

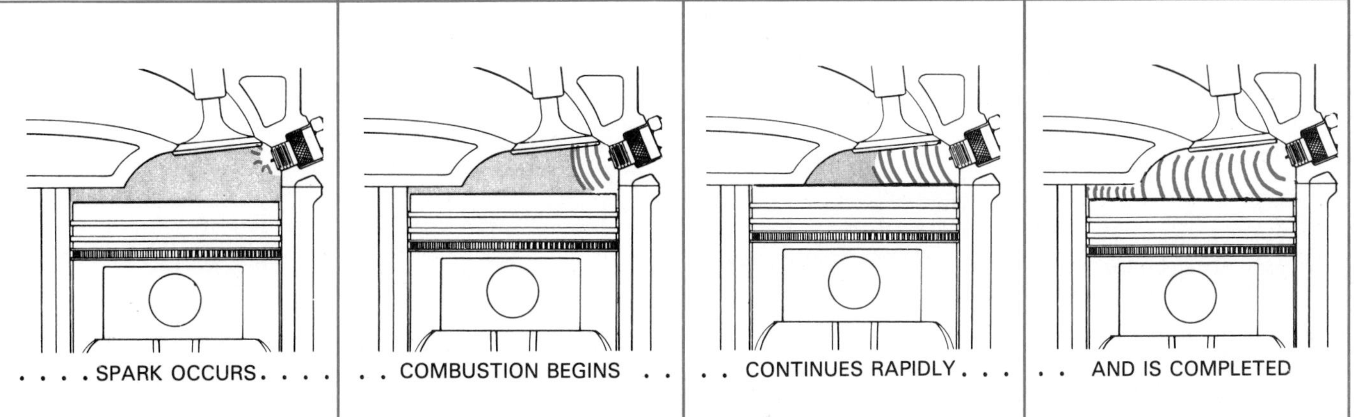

Figure 20-2. During normal combustion, the air/fuel mixture does not burn all at once. The flame front moves rapidly, but it moves in a controlled manner. (Perfect Circle)

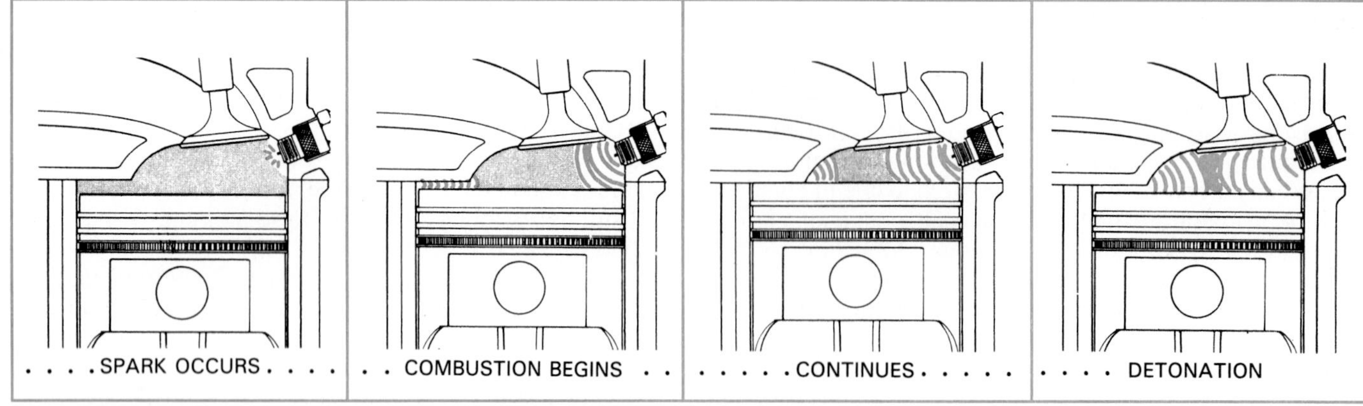

Figure 20-3. Detonation is the rapid and uncontrolled burning of fuel within the combustion chamber that creates a secondary flame front. The two flame fronts collide and cause a knock or pinging.

tures resulting from detonation may reach the point where the piston actually melts. Other effects of detonation may be overheating of the engine, broken spark plugs, overloaded bearings, high fuel consumption, and loss of power. The causes of detonation include:

- Lean air/fuel mixtures (vacuum leaks).
- Low octane fuel.
- Ignition timing over-advanced.
- Lugging the engine (gear is too high for the speed of the engine).
- Excessive carbon accumulations in the combustion chamber.

Preignition

Preignition is the igniting of the fuel charge before the regular ignition spark. If the premature combustion is completed before the occurrence of the regular spark, there may be no identifying noise. However, if the regular ignition spark follows shortly after the preignition occurs, there will be a pinging noise when the two flame fronts collide, Figure 20-4. Also, preignition can lead to detonation. These two types of abnormal combustion are closely linked, and it is often difficult to distinguish between them. The main causes of preignition include:

- Carbon deposits that remain incandescent.
- Valves operating at higher-than-normal temperature.
- Hot spots caused by defects in the cooling system.
- Spark plugs that run too hot.
- Sharp edges in the combustion chamber.
- Detonation.

Antiknock Qualities

One of the most important qualities of modern fuel is the ability to burn without causing knocking. The tendency toward knocking is overcome by adding certain compounds, such as tetraethyl lead or butane, to the fuel. In addition, refining processes also aid in producing knock-free gasoline.

To understand what is meant by ***antiknock quality,*** consider the process of combustion. When a substance burns, it is actually uniting with oxygen (one constituent of air) in a rapid chemical reaction. During the burning process, the molecules of the substance and oxygen are set into very rapid motion and heat is produced.

In the combustion chamber of an engine cylinder, the gasoline vapor and oxygen in the air are united and burned. They combine, and the molecules begin to move about very rapidly as the high temperatures of combustion are reached. The molecules bombard the combustion chamber walls and the head of the piston. It is this bombardment that causes the heavy push on the piston, forcing it downward on the power stroke.

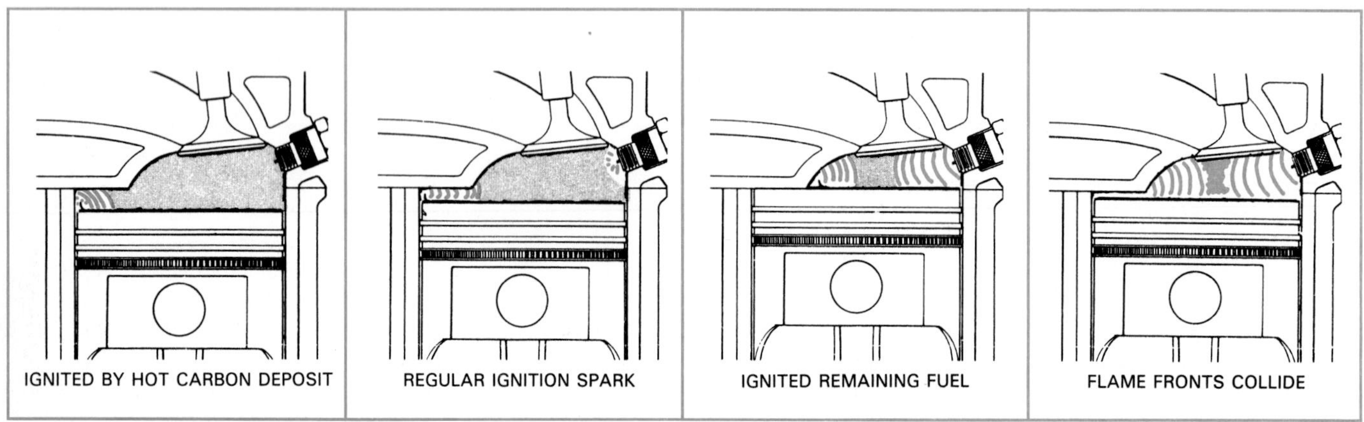

Figure 20-4. Preignition occurs when a flame front, which is caused by a localized hot spot, ignites the air/fuel mixture prior to the spark plug. When the two flame fronts meet, a knock or pinging sound can be heard. (Perfect Circle)

Octane Rating

The ability of a fuel to resist knocking is measured by its ***octane rating.*** The octane rating of a fuel is determined by matching it against mixtures of normal heptane and iso-octane in a test engine under specified test conditions. The test continues until a mixture of these pure hydrocarbons is found that gives the same degree of knocking in the engine as the gasoline being tested.

The octane number of the fuel, then, is the percent of the iso-octane in the matching iso-octane/normal-heptane mixture. For example, a gasoline rating of 90 octane is equivalent in its knocking characteristics to a mixture of 90% iso-octane and 10% normal heptane.

The tendency of a fuel to knock varies in different engines. It even varies in the same engine under different operating conditions. The shape of the combustion chamber is important, but most important of all is the compression ratio.

It should be emphasized that octane number of a fuel has nothing to do with its starting qualities, power, volatility, or other major characteristics. If an engine operates satisfactorily with a fuel of a certain octane rating, its performance will not be improved by using fuel with a higher octane rating.

Cetane Rating

The delay between the time the fuel is injected into the cylinder and ignition is expressed as a ***cetane number.*** Usually, this number is generally between 30 and 60. Fuels that ignite rapidly have high cetane ratings, while slow-to-ignite fuels have low cetane ratings.

A fuel with better ignition quality would assist combustion more than a lower cetane fuel during starting and idling conditions when compression temperatures are cooler. Ether with a very high cetane rating of 85-96 is often used for starting diesel engines in cold weather. The lower the temperature of the surrounding air, the greater the need for fuel that will ignite rapidly.

When the cetane number of the fuel is too low, it may result in difficult starting, engine knock, and puffs of white exhaust smoke, particularly during engine warmup and light-load operation. If these conditions continue, harmful engine deposits will accumulate in the combustion chamber.

Fuel Additives

Tetraethyl lead was used in some gasoline to reduce or prevent knocking. However, in 1975 it became illegal to use a leaded gasoline except for cars built prior to this date. Also, with the addition of a catalytic converter, it is undesirable to burn leaded fuel. Leaded fuel will clog the converter, increasing the backpressure of the exhaust. This, in turn, reduces the amount of power that the engine can produce. ***Methyl Tertiary Butyl Ether*** (MTBE) is used in unleaded fuel to increase the octane.

Detergents

Gasoline exposed to heat and air oxidizes and leaves a gummy film. ***Detergents*** are currently added to gasoline to prevent this. The detergents keep the carburetor passages and fuel injectors free from deposits, Figure 20-5. These deposits can cause hard starting and driveability problems.

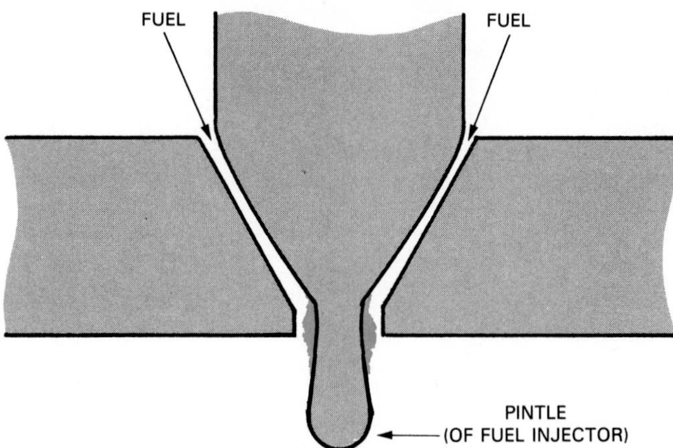

Figure 20-5. Detergents prevent fuel deposits from accumulating on the pintle of fuel injector. These deposits can restrict the flow of fuel and cause a rough idle, a lack of power, hesitation on acceleration, surging, and stalling.

Lead-free Gasoline

Lead-free gasoline is motor fuel without tetraethyl lead. Formerly, lead was added to gasoline to improve its octane rating. Now, lead-free gasoline is required because leaded fuel would quickly destroy the catalytic converter. Catalytic converters are designed to reduce the amount of carbon monoxide and hydrocarbons in the exhaust. Methyl Tertiary Butyl Ether (MTBE) is usually added to lead-free gasoline to increase the octane rating.

Both leaded and lead-free gasolines have certain advantages. In addition to the higher octane rating, leaded gasoline had a good effect on valves and valve seats. With lead in the fuel, valve and valve seat life was lengthened, particularly at high speeds. The lead in the fuel was deposited on the valve seats, where it acted as a lubricant.

Valve seat wear has been shown to result from the adhesion of hard abrasive oxide particles from the valve seat onto the valve face. This is followed by the failure of the valve and seat. Tests show a 10 to 20 times greater valve recession rate when lead-free gasoline is used. However, engine manufacturers have improved the valve seats in their engines to better withstand the effect of lead-free gasoline.

Alcohol as a Fuel

The increasing cost of gasoline and its effect on the environment have turned the attention of automotive designers and the motoring public to various substitutes. Chief among the alternate fuels is ***alcohol.***

Considerable research has been done using alcohol in spark ignition engines. During World War II, alcohol fuels were used extensively in Germany. Currently, alcohol blends are used in many vehicles.

Methanol and ethanol are two forms of alcohol receiving the most attention. Both are made from nonpetroleum products. ***Methanol*** can be produced from coal. ***Ethanol*** can be made from farm products such as sugar cane, corn, and potatoes. Characteristics of these alcohols are compared in Figure 20-6.

Both alcohols have a higher octane number than gasoline. The high heat of vaporization indicates that the use of alcohol could give hard starting problems. The calorific heat values of the alcohols are higher than those of gaso-

PROPERTY	METHANOL	ETHANOL	GASOLINE
Heat of vaporization	265	216	70-100
Calorific heat value	4200	6400	10,500
Air required	6.4	9.0	14.9
Air/fuel ratio	2.15 to 15.5	3.5 to 17.0	6.0 to 22.0
Self-ignition Temperature	478 °F (248°C)	420 °F (216°C)	300°-450 °F (149°-232°C)
Research octane number	110	100	92-98
Motor octane	92	89	84-88

Figure 20-6. Characteristics of methanol, ethanol, and gasoline.

line, which translates into the need for a larger fuel tank and larger injectors or carburetor jets. However, the alcohols require less air for combustion, which compensates for the high calorific values. Proportionately, this could result in practically the same air/fuel ratio for all three fuels. In fact, experimental tests have shown that alcohol-fueled spark ignition engines can produce as much or slightly more power than gasoline-fueled engines.

Alcohol fuels have a higher self-ignition temperature than gasoline, which rates them better from a safety standpoint. However, this same quality bars them from use in a diesel engine, which depends on the heat of compression to ignite the fuel.

Currently, only ethanol can be blended in small concentrations (10%) with gasoline. Because of the high octane rating, alcohols can be used in engines with relatively high compression ratios ranging from 8:4:1 to 11:1. Experiments also indicate that emissions from alcohol-fueled engines would not require the use of exhaust gas recirculation controls.

Alcohol as an Additive

Alcohol is frequently used as an additive to commercial gasoline. It will absorb any condensed moisture that may collect in the fuel system.

Water will not pass through the filters in the fuel line. Consequently, when water collects, it will prevent the free passage of fuel. In addition, water will tend to attack, or corrode, the zinc die castings of which many carburetors and fuel pumps are made. This corrosion will not only destroy parts, but also clog the system and prevent the flow of fuel.

Diesel Fuels

The type of fuel available for use in diesel engines varies from highly volatile jet fuels and kerosene to the heavier furnace oil. Automotive diesel engines are capable of burning a wide range of fuel between these two extremes. How well a diesel engine can operate with different types of fuel is dependent upon engine operating conditions and fuel characteristics.

A large variety of ***diesel fuels*** (fuel oils) are marketed by the petroleum industry for diesel engine use. Their properties depend on the refining practices employed and the nature of the crude oil from which they are produced. Fuel oils, for example, may be produced within the boiling range of 300°-750°F (149°-399°C) and have many possible combinations of other properties.

The classification of commercially available fuel oils that has been set up by the American Society for Testing Materials is shown in Figure 20-7. Grade 1–D fuels range from kerosene to what are called intermediate distillates. Grades 2–D and 4–D each have progressively higher boiling points and contain more impurities.

The fuels commonly known as high-grade fuels (kerosene, and 1–D fuels) contribute a minimum amount to the formation of harmful engine deposits and corrosion. There are fewer impurities present in those fuels. Therefore, the tendency to form deposits is kept to a minimum.

While refining removes the impurities, it also lowers the heat value of the fuel. As a result, the higher grade fuels develop slightly less power than the same quantity of low-grade fuel. Often, however, this is more than offset by the maintenance advantages.

Liquefied Petroleum Gas (LPG)

A mixture of gaseous petroleum compounds–principally butane and propane with small quantities of similar gases–is known as ***liquefied petroleum gas*** (LP-Gas). LP-Gas is used as fuel for internal combustion engines, principally in the truck and farm tractor fields.

ASTM DIESEL FUEL CLASSIFICATION DO75-49T

GRADE OF DIESEL FUEL OIL	CETANE NUMBER (MIN.)	SULFUR % BY WT. (MAX.)	DISTILLATION TEMPERATURES		VISCOSITY AT 100°F (38°C) KINEMATIC CENTISTOKES (OR SUS)	
			90% BOILING POINT (MAX.)	100% BOILING POINT (MAX.)	(MIN.)	(MAX.)
No. 1-D	40	0.50		625°F (329°C)	1.4 1.8	 5.8
No. 2-D	40	1.0	675°F (357° C)		(32.0)	(45)
No. 4-D	30	2.0			5.8 (45)	26.4 (125)

Figure 20-7. Grade No. 1 diesel fuel must be used in the winter. If Grades No. 2 and 4 are used during winter, the fuel will gel and will cut off the flow of fuel to the injectors. Grade No. 4 diesel fuel must be used in hot weather to provide adequate protection.

Chemically, LP-Gas is similar to gasoline since it consists of a mixture of compounds of hydrogen and carbon. However, it is a great deal more volatile. At usual atmospheric temperatures, it is a vapor. For this reason, a special type of fuel system is required when LP-Gas is used for fuel in an internal combustion engine.

For storing and transporting LP-Gas, it is compressed and cooled so that it is a liquid. Depending upon conditions, it takes approximately 250 gallons of LP-Gas to make one gallon of compressed liquid. Because of the pressure it is under, it must be stored in strong tanks.

The boiling point of propane is approximately 44°F (7°C) below zero. At temperatures below their boiling points, butane and propane exert no pressure. But as the temperature increases, the pressure increases rapidly. At 40°F (4°C), liquid propane will have a pressure of 65 lbs., while butane will have a pressure of about 3 lbs. At 65°F (18°C), the pressure of propane will have increased to 100 lbs. and butane to 15 lbs.

LP-Gas is made of surplus material in the oil fields. It is becoming more widely distributed as an increasing number of trucks and tractors are being fitted with the equipment required to make use of it. In addition to its low cost, LP-Gas has the advantage of having a high octane value. Pure butane has a rating of 93 octane, while propane is approximately 100. The octane rating of LP-Gas will range between these two values, depending upon the proportion of each gas used.

Since it is a dry gas, LP-Gas does not create carbon in an engine and does not cause dilution of the engine oil. As a result, maintenance and internal parts replacement on engines is reduced. In addition, oil changes for the engine can be made at less frequent intervals because LP-Gas is a cleaner burning fuel. Other advantages claimed for LP-Gas are easy cold-weather starting, lack of objectionable exhaust odor, and elimination of evaporation.

Chapter 20–Review Questions

Write your answers on a separate sheet of paper. Do not write in this book.

1. Name three different fuels used in internal combustion engines.
2. The volatility of gasoline is equivalent to its:
   (A) octane rating.
   (B) boiling point.
   (C) cetane rating.
   (D) distillation.
3. What characteristic of fuel affects easy starting?
4. Name the three stages of normal fuel combustion in an internal combustion engine.
5. Describe detonation.
6. Describe preignition.
7. Iso-octane and what other material are used to determine the octane rating of a fuel?
   (A) Cetane.
   (B) Propane.
   (C) Heptane.
   (D) Benzol.
8. Alcohol is added to gasoline primarily to:
   (A) provide easier starting.
   (B) absorb any moisture that may be present.
   (C) increase the volatility of the fuel.
   (D) None of the above.
9. Automobile diesel engines are capable of burning a wide range of fuels. True or False?
10. The cetane number of a diesel fuel is a measure of:
    (A) volatility.
    (B) viscosity.
    (C) time between fuel injection and ignition.
    (D) None of the above.
11. Sulfur content of a fuel should be as:
    (A) high as possible.
    (B) low as possible.
    (C) Does not matter.
12. LP-Gas is a mixture of:
    (A) benzol and heptane.
    (B) butane and propane.
    (C) butane and heptane.
    (D) heptane and cetane.
13. The power of any fuel is determined by its:
    (A) molecular weight.
    (B) heat value.
    (C) octane rating.
    (D) None of the above.
14. Immediately after ignition, combustion chamber temperatures may reach a value of:
    (A) 1500°F.
    (B) 2500°F.
    (C) 5500°F.
    (D) 7500°F.
15. Carbon deposits in the combustion chamber are responsible for increased levels of hydrocarbon emissions. True or False?
16. Lead-free gasoline promotes longer valve and valve seat life. True or False?

Top view of a supercharged V-6 engine. (Buick)

Chapter 21
Fuel Supply Systems, Intake Systems, Superchargers, and Turbochargers

After studying this chapter, you will be able to:

- List the different types of fuel pumps and gauges.
- Explain how mechanical and electrical fuel pumps operate.
- Explain the purpose of an intake system.
- Explain how to service an air cleaner.
- Describe various intake manifold designs.
- Describe turbocharger and wastegate operation.

Fuel Pumps

On small gas engines and many industrial engines, fuel is gravity fed. On automobiles, either mechanical or electric fuel pumps are used.

Mechanical fuel pumps are operated by means of a cam or an eccentric on the camshaft of the engine. Service is limited to replacement.

Electric fuel pumps are energized by a built-in electric motor. Some are designed to be submerged in the fuel in the tank. Others are installed in the fuel line between the tank and carburetor or fuel injection system. Service is also limited to replacement.

Mechanical Fuel Pump

Mechanical fuel pumps are often used on carbureted engines. A typical, single-action, "sealed" mechanical fuel pump is shown in Figure 21-1. Working parts include the rocker arm, diaphragm, spring, inlet valve, and outlet valve.

In operation, the eccentric presses down on the pump rocker arm, lifting the pull rod and diaphragm against the tension of the main spring of the pump. This creates a vacuum in the valve housing, opening the intake valve and drawing fuel into the valve housing chamber, Figure 21-2.

On the return stroke, the main spring forces the diaphragm down. This closes the inlet valve, and fuel from the chamber is pumped through the outlet valve to the fuel filter. Each revolution of the camshaft repeats this cycle.

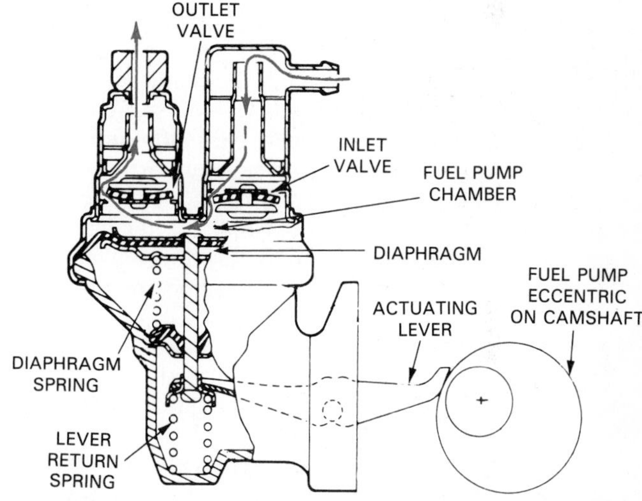

Figure 21-2. The rocker arm of the fuel pump is depressed by an eccentric on the camshaft. This action causes the diaphragm to be pulled downward against spring pressure. As the diaphragm moves downward, a suction is created. (Chrysler)

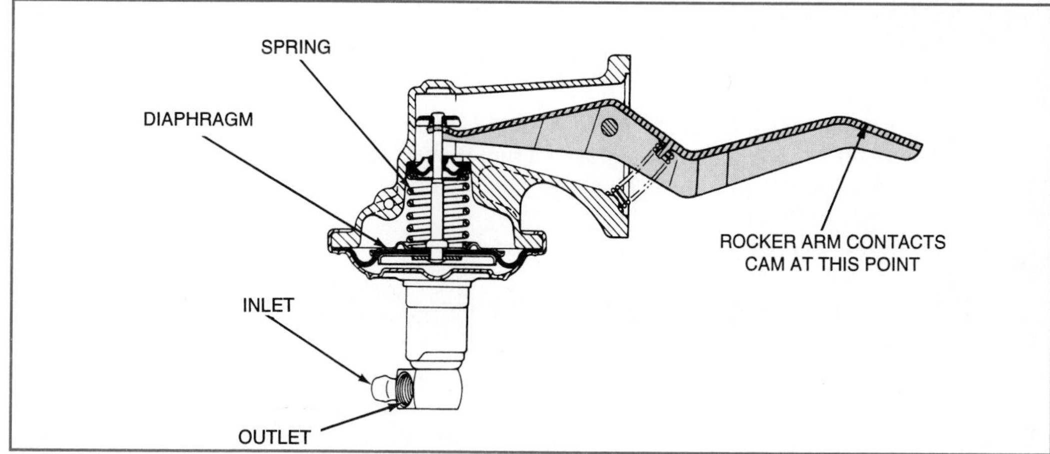

Figure 21-1. If any part of a mechanical fuel pump is found defective, the entire pump must be replaced. (Chrysler)

Most mechanical fuel pumps are designed to prevent an oversupply of fuel when the carburetor float rises and fuel flow is shut off by the needle and seat assembly. At this point, the fuel pump diaphragm spring is held in a compressed position and the rocker arm "idles" on the camshaft eccentric. Diaphragm action is reduced to a slight movement, just enough to provide a reduced flow of fuel to replace fuel which enters the carburetor between pump strokes.

In effect, this idling action produces a constant pressure on the fuel in the line to the carburetor. This pressure is proportional to the force exerted by the diaphragm spring.

Mechanical Fuel Pump Troubles

Modern fuel pumps give many thousands of miles of trouble-free service without the need for maintenance. When a pump no longer supplies fuel in sufficient volume, it should be replaced with a new unit.

To determine if the fuel pump is at fault, first make sure the supply tank has a sufficient quantity of fuel and that the tank is properly vented. If satisfactory, disconnect the fuel supply line at the carburetor and direct the fuel line into a small container. Then, with the distributor primary wire to the ignition coil grounded, crank the engine with the starter. If the fuel pump is in good condition, fuel will spurt from the supply line.

If little or no fuel is pumped, the pump is probably defective and should be replaced. Of course, it must be verified that the fuel line between the pump and supply tank is not clogged and does not have an air leak. Also, check the condition of the fuel filter and the flexible fuel line connecting the pump with the rigid fuel line leading to the supply tank. These flexible lines may develop air leaks, or the interior of the lines may swell and obstruct the flow of fuel.

An infrequent trouble is when the fuel pump supplies too much fuel. Excessive pressures result in flooding of the carburetor. Fuel pump pressure may be tested with a suitable pressure gauge.

To make the test, connect the gauge to the outlet side of the pump. When the engine is cranked by the starter, the gauge should register 4-6 lbs. of pressure. The length of the hose connecting the gauge to the fuel pump should not exceed 6″, otherwise inaccurate readings may result.

Another fuel pump test can be made by directing fuel flow from the pump into a pint or quart container. With the engine operating at idling speed, a pint of fuel should be pumped in approximately 45 seconds. The fuel in the float bowl will keep the engine operating long enough to make the test.

It has been established that there are four points where wear or damage will affect the performance of a fuel pump. These points are worn linkage, worn valves or seats, a worn pull rod, and a punctured diaphragm.

While a carbureted engine usually uses a mechanical fuel pump, a fuel injected engine uses an electric fuel pump. An electric fuel pump reduces the chances of vapor lock.

Electric Fuel Pumps

Electric fuel pumps are of two basic types: suction-type pumps and pusher-type pumps. ***Suction-type pumps*** draw fuel from the tank in a manner similar to mechanically operated pumps. ***Pusher-type pumps*** are placed in the bottom of the fuel supply tank and "push" fuel to the injectors or the carburetor.

An in-tank, pusher-type fuel pump is illustrated in Figure 21-3, and a Bendix electric fuel pump is shown in Figure 21-4. An advantage of the externally mounted electric pump is that several pumps can be installed and larger quantities of fuel can be supplied. If one pump should fail, the others would continue to supply fuel.

An important advantage of an electric fuel pump is that there is a considerable reduction in vapor lock problems. The reason for this is that the vacuum created to "pull" the fuel from the tank reduces the boiling point. The mechanical pump, on the other hand, is driven by the engine camshaft and must be installed in a location where it will operate at a higher temperature. Another advantage of the electric pump is that as soon as the ignition is turned on, it will supply fuel.

There are no valves between the electric pump and the throttle body. Therefore, the fuel drains back into the tank when the engine is stopped. This eliminates pressure

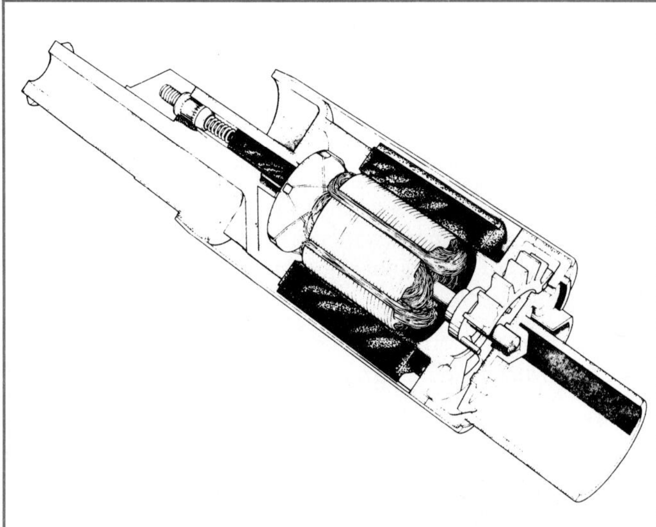

Figure 21-3. Some electric fuel pumps are mounted inside the gas tank. (AC Spark Plug)

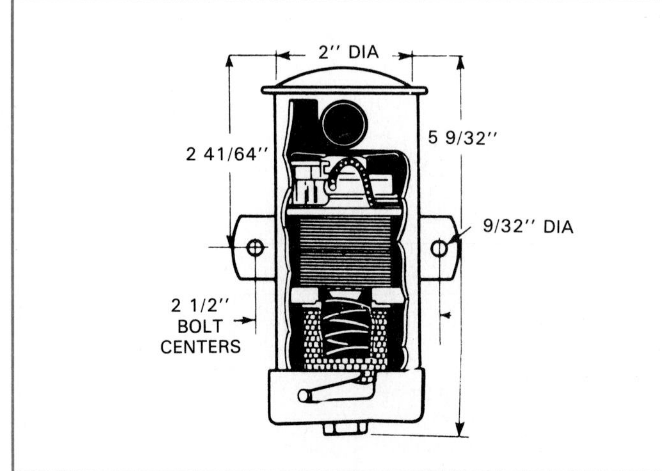

Figure 21-4. A Bendix electric fuel pump.

buildup and consequent hard starting of a hot engine. The delivery of the fuel is steady and non-pulsating.

In-tank Electric Fuel Pumps

The electric fuel pump in Figure 21-5 is located in the fuel tank and is part of the fuel pump and fuel gauge tank assembly. The assembly is installed through the fuel tank access hole in the trunk floor. Electrical connections are made with two wires to the fuel pump terminals, an outside ground wire, and a two-way connector.

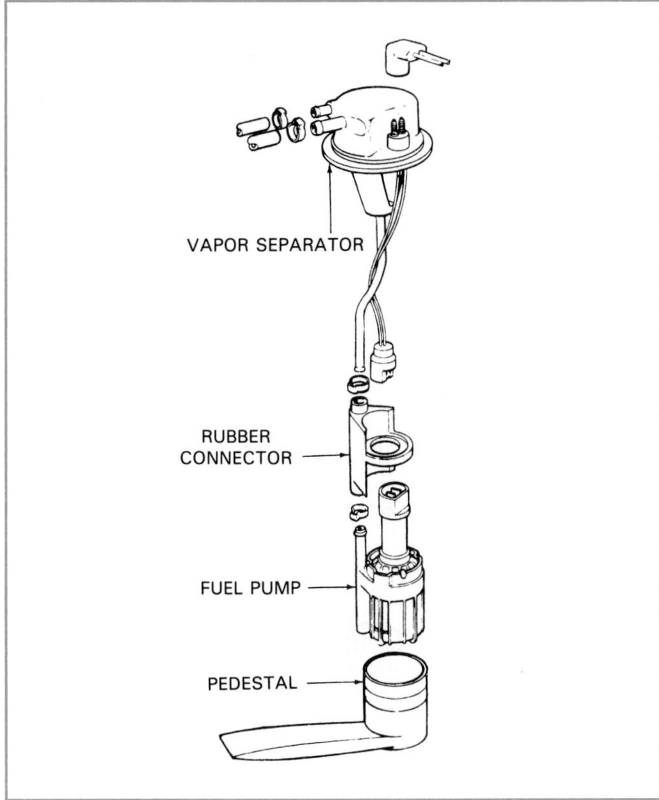

Figure 21-5. Components of an electric fuel pump. (Carter)

The pump is a turbine-type hydraulic unit that is directly coupled to a permanent-magnet motor, Figure 21-5. Fuel is drawn into the pump through a woven plastic filter, and is then "pushed" through the fuel line.

A ***fuel pump control switch*** located near the oil filter is connected to the engine oil system, so that oil pressure actuates the diaphragm of the switch. If oil pressure drops below 3 psi during engine operation, the pump will be de-energized and the engine will stop running. When the engine is being cranked, current is delivered through a special bypass circuit. Current passes through the oil pressure switch to the pump, delivering the full 12 V. When the engine starts, the current will pass through a resistor, cutting voltage to 8 1/2-10 V. Electric fuel pumps are serviced as an assembly.

The electric fuel pump in Figure 21-6 is a ***roller-type pump.*** As the roller assembly spins, Figure 21-7, a low-pressure area is created on the left side of the pump. Atmospheric pressure pushes fuel from the tank to the low-pressure area created within the pump. As the roller continues to spin, the fuel is pushed into an increasingly smaller area within the pump. As this happens, the fuel is pressurized and forced out the pump discharge outlet and into the fuel lines.

A fuel pump relay is mounted on the fuse box. The relay acts as a safety device. In the event the car is in an accident, the relay breaks the electrical circuit to the fuel pump, and prevents fuel from being pumped. This reduces the chance of a fire. Electric fuel pump diagnosis is covered in Chapter 22, Fuel Injection Systems.

Fuel Filters

Clean fuel is essential because of the many small orifices in the fuel injectors or jets and passages in the carburetor. To ensure this cleanliness, ***fuel filters*** are installed in the fuel line between the fuel pump and the injectors or the carburetor.

Fuel filters of various types and construction are used. All are designed to filter out foreign matter. Some filters remove water that may be present in the fuel.

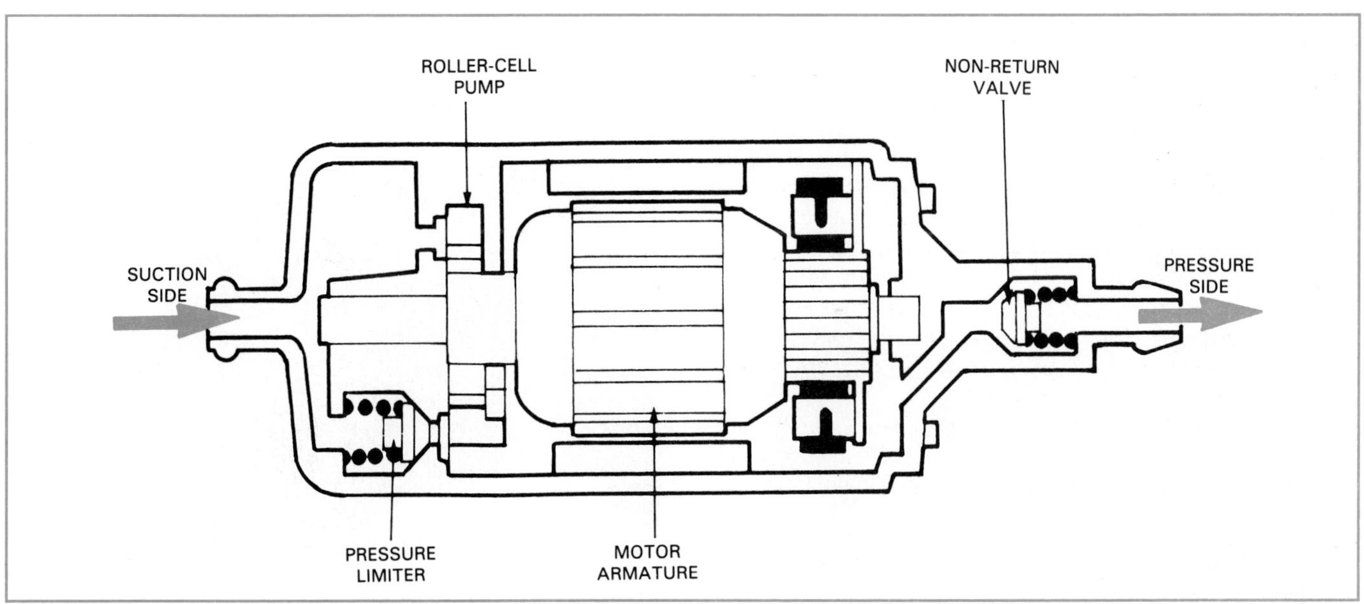

Figure 21-6. Construction of an electric roller-type fuel pump. (Robert Bosch)

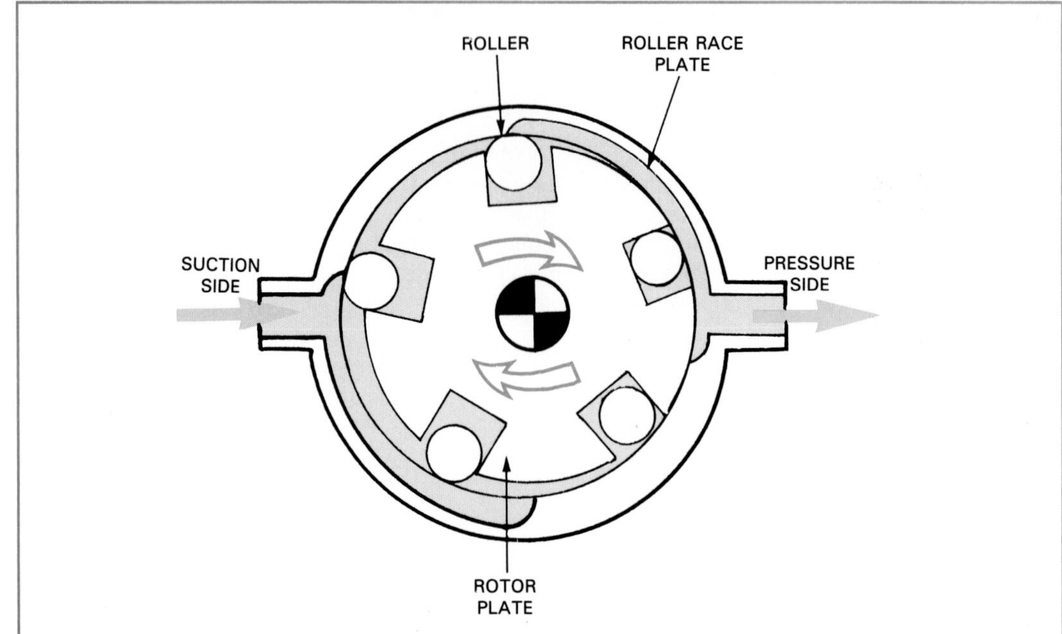

Figure 21-7. Operation of an electric roller-type fuel pump. A low-pressure area is created within the pump, and fuel is forced to it. The fuel is then forced to an increasingly smaller area and is pressurized. (Robert Bosch)

In many cases, the filter is built into the carburetor. A ceramic-type filter is shown in Figure 21-8, and a paper element filter is shown in Figure 21-9.

Since accumulations of dirt and water in the filter tend to restrict the flow of fuel, it is essential that the unit is replaced periodically. Usually, this is done once a year. A disposable cartridge-type fuel filter is also used, Figures 21-10 and 21-11. This type of fuel filter is placed in the fuel line.

Fuel Gauges

There are two basic types of fuel gauges in use: the thermostatic gauge and the balancing coil gauge.

Thermostatic Gauge

The ***thermostatic fuel gauge*** consists of a sending unit located in the fuel tank, Figure 21-12, and a gauge (registering unit) located on the instrument panel. In addition, there is a voltage regulator unit, which is designed to maintain an average value of 5.0 volts at the gauge terminals. It is compensated for temperature variations and is provided with an adjustment that controls the rate at which the contacts make and break. It controls the voltage supplied to the gauge system.

The gauge pointer is controlled by a bimetallic arm and a heating coil, Figure 21-13. The sending unit in the

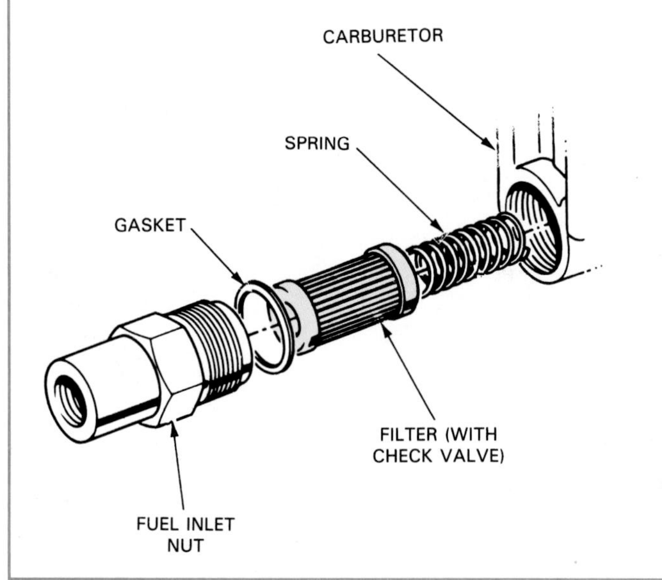

Figure 21-9. A paper-type fuel filter must be replaced with a new fuel filter. (Oldsmobile)

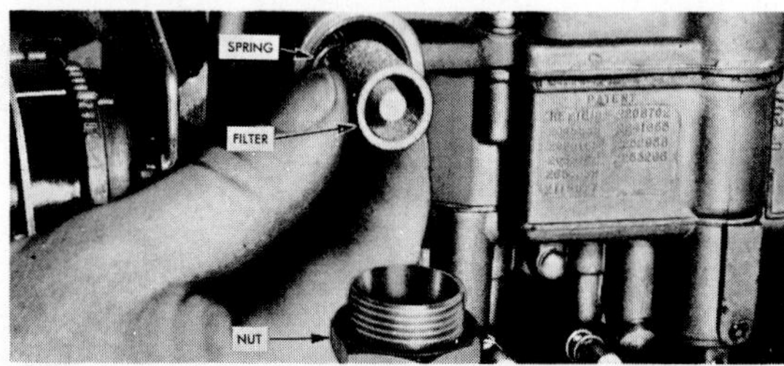

Figure 21-8. A ceramic fuel filter can be cleaned and reinstalled.

Figure 21-10. An inline fuel filter must also be replaced with a new filter.

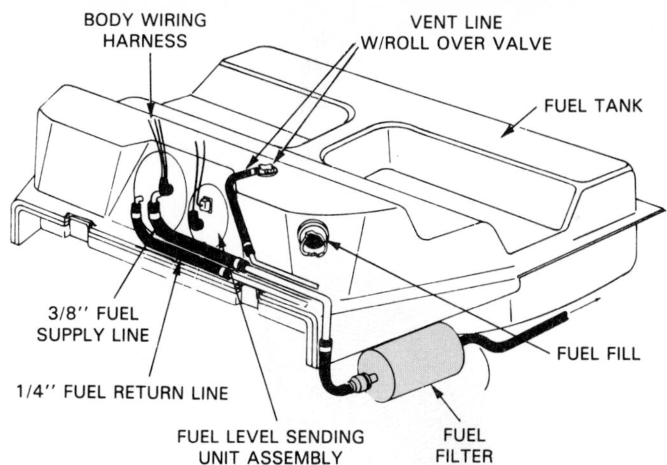

Figure 21-11. The filter for fuel injected engines can be located in the engine compartment or, as shown here, near the fuel tank. (Chrysler)

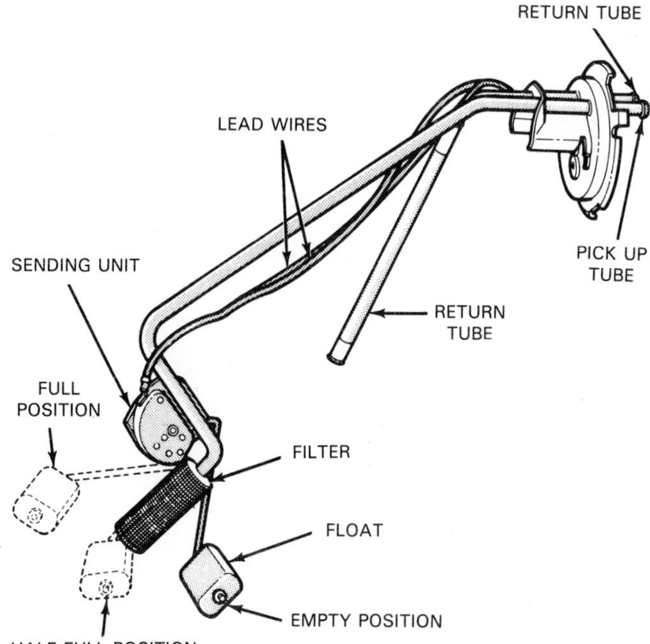

Figure 21-12. The sending unit is located in the fuel tank. Note that there is an in-tank filter located on the suction side. (Chrysler)

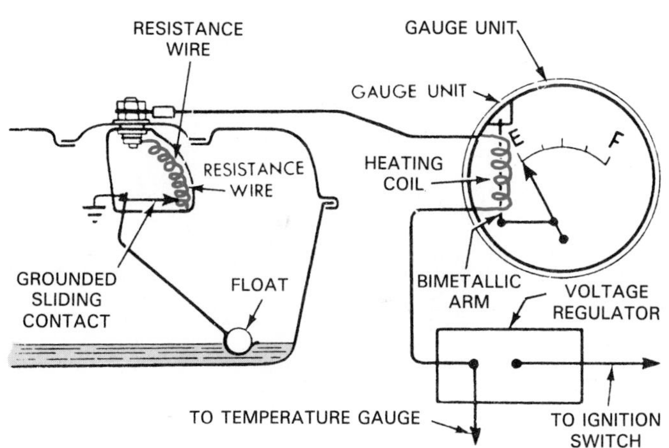

Figure 21-13. Thermostatic fuel gauge.

fuel tank has a rheostat that varies its resistance depending on the amount of fuel in the tank.

When the fuel tank is empty, the grounding sliding contact, Figure 21-13, is at the end of the resistance wire of the rheostat. With all of the resistance in the circuit, only a small amount of current will flow through the heating coil of the gauge unit and the gauge will register zero.

When the tank is full, the float rises with the fuel and moves the grounded contact toward the beginning of the resistance coil. More current will flow through the heating coil, and the bimetallic arm of the gauge will deflect the pointer to the "Full" position.

Balanced Coil Fuel Gauge

The fuel gauge used in some cars and trucks is an electrically operated ***balanced coil gauge.*** It consists of a dash unit and a tank unit, Figure 21-14.

The dash unit is made of two coils placed at 90° to each other. An armature and pointer assembly is mounted at the intersection of the centerlines of the two coils. To prevent vibration of the pointer, the armature is provided with a dampening device.

The tank unit consists of a rheostat with a movable contact arm. The position of the contact arm is controlled by a float that rests on the surface of the fuel. To prevent splashing of the fuel from affecting the movement of the float, a torque washer and spring are used.

The tank unit is grounded out of the gauge circuit when the fuel tank is empty, and the float is in its lowest position. Then, current passes through the coil on the empty side of the dash unit ("full coil" is of higher resistance), and the pointer is pulled to indicate zero.

As fuel is added to the supply tank, there is a corresponding rise of the float. Movement of the rheostat arm places resistance in the circuit, and current will flow through the "full" coil. As a result, the pointer will be attracted to indicate the quantity of fuel in the tank.

Since an increase or decrease of battery voltage will affect both coils equally, the accuracy of the gauge will not be affected. Compensation for temperature variation is also provided.

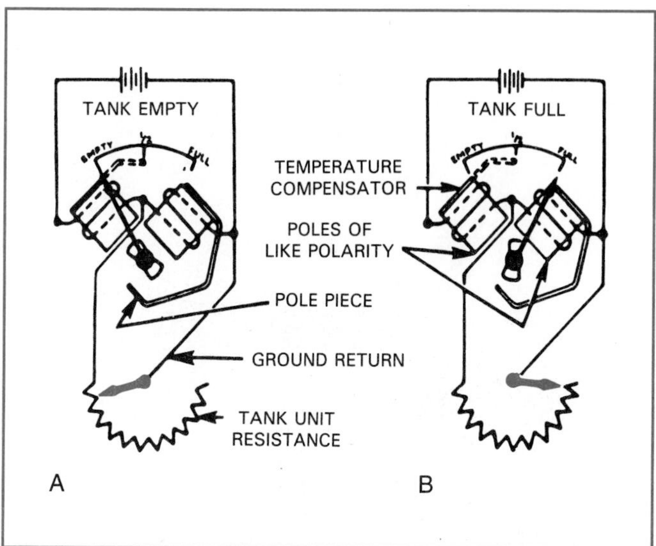

Figure 21-14. Balanced coil fuel gauge. A–Conditions for an empty tank. B–Conditions for a full tank. (AC Spark Plug)

Intake Systems

The main function of the ***intake system,*** or induction system, is to deliver air and fuel to the cylinders. The air must be free from dirt and dust. Additionally, the air and fuel must be distributed evenly to the cylinders.

Air Filters

Air that is drawn into the cylinders must be clean. If dust or other foreign matter enters the engine, it acts to grind away machined parts to a rough finish. Under extreme conditions, it results in the need for complete engine reconditioning.

To reduce the amount of dust entering the engine, an ***air cleaner*** is installed at the air intake. The air cleaner houses a ***filter element*** that filters all incoming air. Several types of filter elements have been used over the years, including:

- Oil wetted mesh filter elements.
- Oil bath filter elements.
- Polyurethane filter elements.
- Paper filter elements.

Today, car engines are fitted with paper filter elements, Figure 21-15. The pleated paper element was found to be more efficient than any other type, and it is compatible with emission control devices.

Paper Element

The ***paper element,*** or dry-type element, is the most efficient air filter element. To service this type of filter element, replacement is all that is needed. However, the filter can be cleaned by tapping it against a hard, flat surface to shake loose the dirt. Then, direct compressed air at the filter to blow off any remaining dirt. Make sure that the nozzle of the compressed air remains at least 2" from the filter, Figure 21-16. Never dip the filter element in a solvent to clean it.

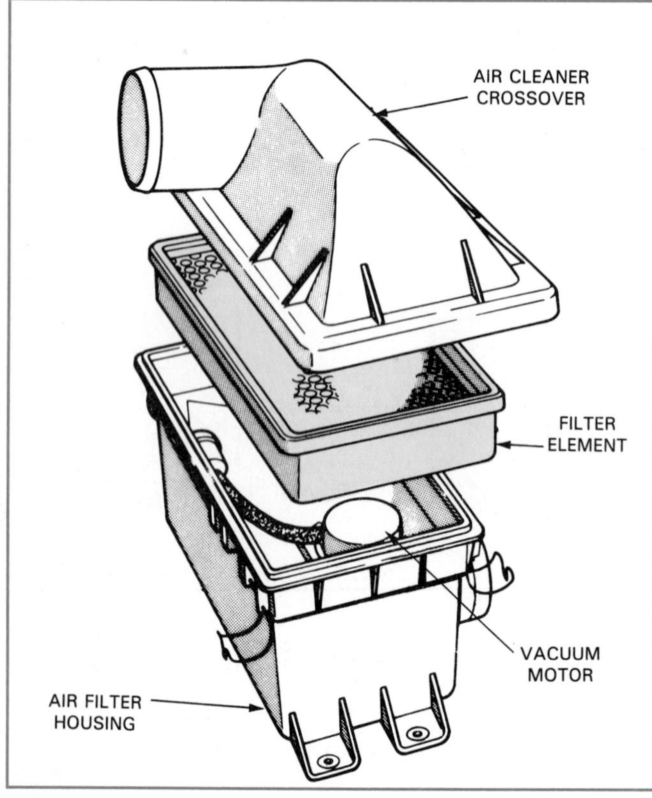

Figure 21-15. Paper air filter element for a late-model vehicle. (Chrysler)

Crankcase Breathers

The positive crankcase ventilation system directs atmospheric pressure to the crankcase. The atmospheric pressure then pushes the blowby gases to a low pressure area, which is at the PCV valve. The air that is directed into the crankcase must first be filtered, Figures 21-17 and 21-18. If it is not, the airborne particles will destroy the engine parts. Also, when blowby is excessive, it is routed back through the ***crankcase breather element,*** Figure 21-19. It then

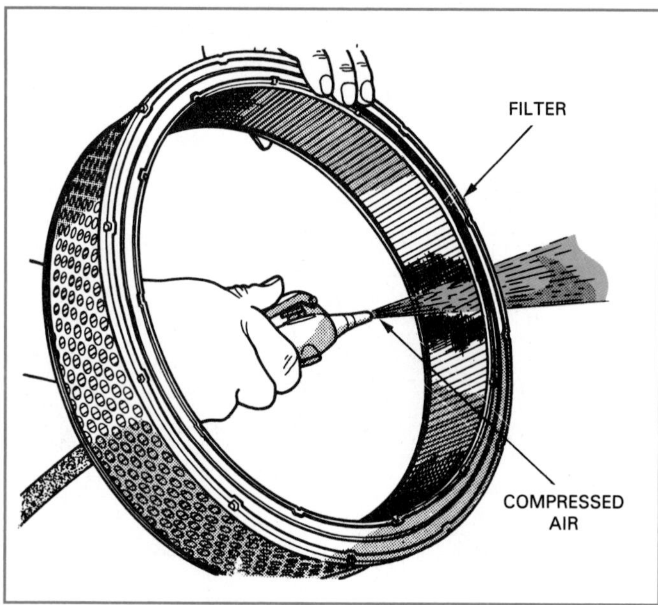

Figure 21-16. Compressed air can be used to clean a paper filter element. (Chrysler)

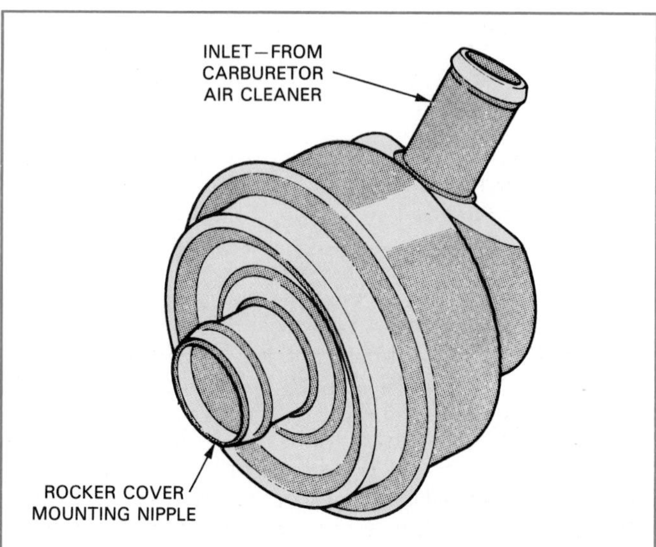

Figure 21-17. Air is filtered by the crankcase breather before it enters the crankcase. (Chrysler)

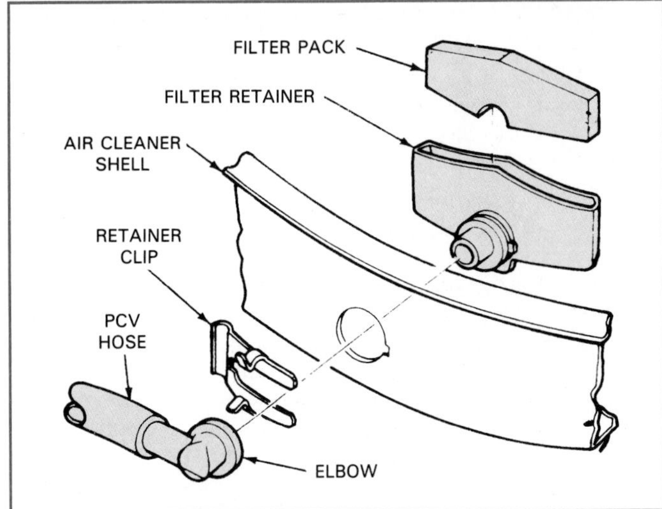

Figure 21-18. The crankcase breather element helps prevent frequent replacement of the regular air filter. (Ford)

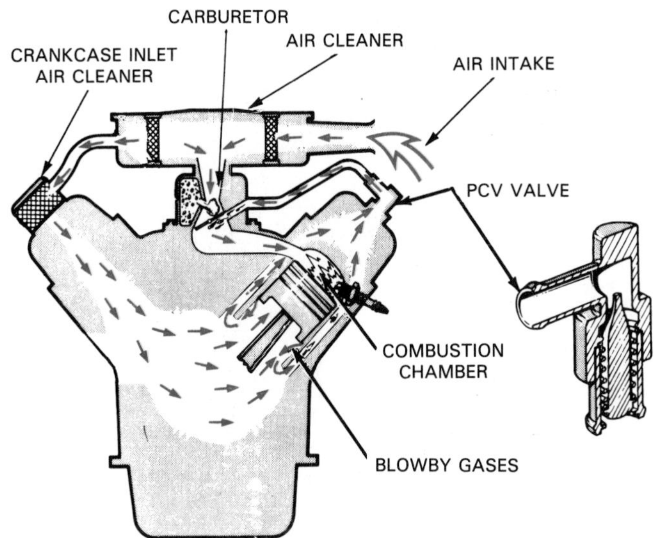

Figure 21-19. During high vacuum conditions, fresh air is directed through the crankcase breather to the crankcase. During periods of low vacuum, blowby gases are forced from the crankcase through the crankcase breather element instead of through the PCV valve. The blowby gases then enter the throttle body or carburetor along with the incoming air. (Chrysler)

enters the carburetor or throttle body with the incoming fresh air to be burned in the cylinders. In addition, the breather helps keep the regular air filter clean for a longer period of time, as blowby contains oil vapor from the crankcase.

Heated Air Intake

The ***heated air intake system*** forms part of the air cleaner, Figures 21-20 and 21-21. It is an essential part of the exhaust emission control system.

A ***temperature sensor*** is attached to the air cleaner. It controls the temperature of air that enters the air cleaner. The assembly takes the heated air from a shroud around the exhaust manifold. The heated air is then passed through the air cleaner.

The temperature sensor, Figures 21-20 and 21-21, in the air duct is exposed to the heated air. This action of the

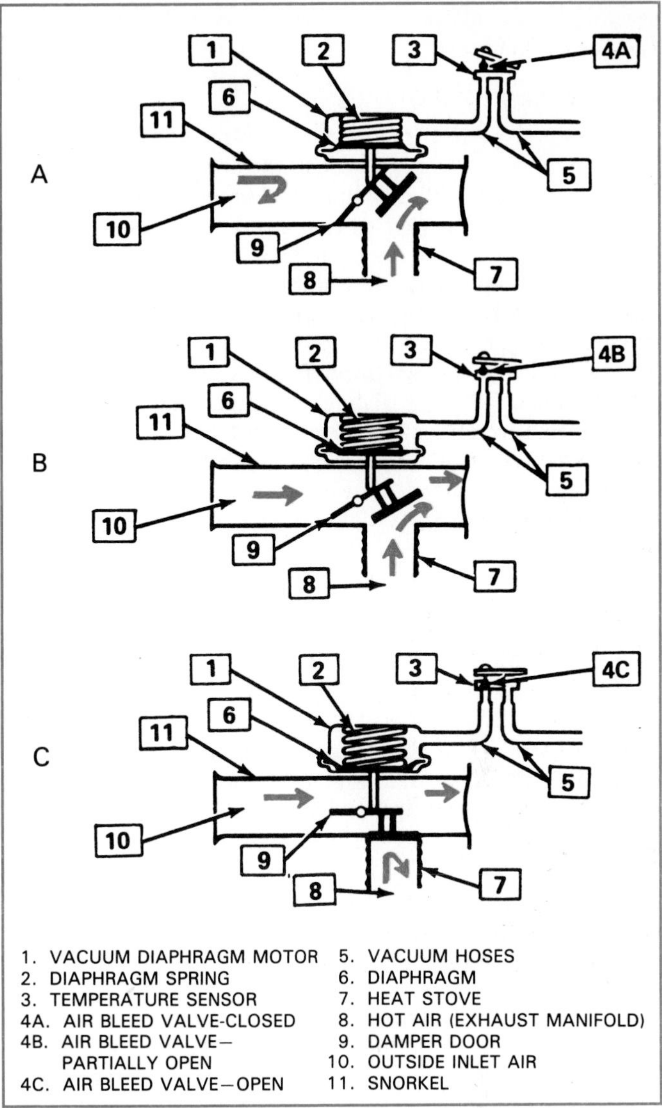

Figure 21-20. Operation of the heated air intake valve. A–Hot air delivery. B–Modulating hot and cold air. C–Valve is closed to block off hot air, which could cause detonation. (Oldsmobile)

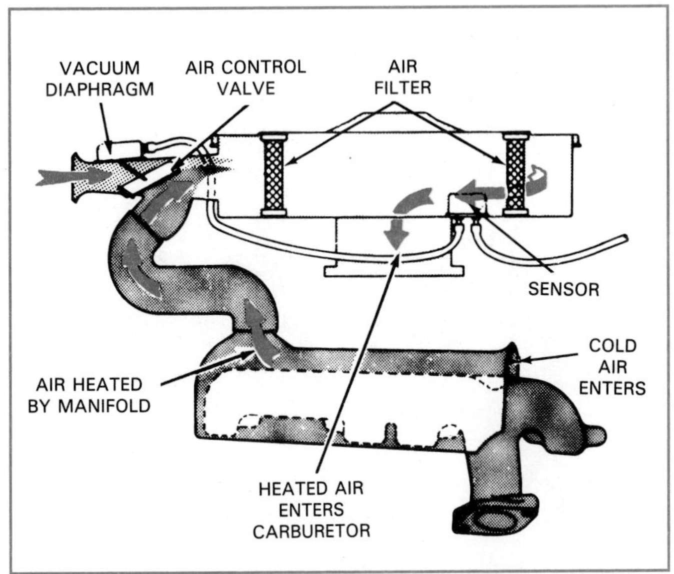

Figure 21-21. Air is heated by the exhaust manifold. Hot air is then directed to the snorkel of the air cleaner. (Chrysler)

sensor controls the position of the valve so that the hot and cold air are blended to maintain 100°F (38°C).

When the temperature in the engine compartment is less than 100°F (38°C), the duct valve should be in the "heat on" position. If the engine is cold and the duct valve does not close during idle, check for disconnected or leaking vacuum lines to the vacuum motor and bimetal switch.

The ***bimetal switch*** can be checked for operation by subjecting the switch to heated air or by removing and immersing the switch in water heated to 80°F (27°C). Only slight movement of the bimetal switch will unseat the bleed valve.

Vacuum at the ***vacuum motor*** should be 15 in. To check the vacuum motor, connect it to a vacuum source of 15 in., Figure 21-22. The motor should move the motor rod 1/2″. If not, the motor should be replaced.

Intake Manifold

The ***intake manifold*** distributes air and fuel to the cylinders. In the past, intake manifolds were of simple design. Today, however, manifold design is quite complicated. The problem in designing intake manifolds lies in providing each cylinder with the same quality and quantity of air and fuel, Figure 21-23.

One factor that affects fuel distribution is the fact that the larger particles of the fuel mixture have greater inertia than the lighter particles. As a result, the heavier particles tend to move past some of the intake runners in the manifold, Figure 21-24. Therefore, some of the cylinders receive fewer heavy particles than others.

There are large variations in the air/fuel mixture delivered to the cylinders of an engine equipped with a carburetor or a throttle body fuel injection system. This may cause poor gas mileage and high exhaust emissions.

To help eliminate the problem of unequal fuel distribution, manufacturers are installing multi-point fuel injection systems in most new vehicles. In these systems, there is one injector for each cylinder and fuel is injected as close to the intake valve as possible. The manifolds used with port fuel injection systems are often called ***tuned intake manifolds.*** These manifolds are designed to deliver equal amounts of air to each engine cylinder. See Figure 21-25.

Manifolds for passenger car engines are usually made of cast iron or aluminum. The number of manifold outlets depends on the number of cylinders and valves in the engine. Some manifolds contain coolant passages that are

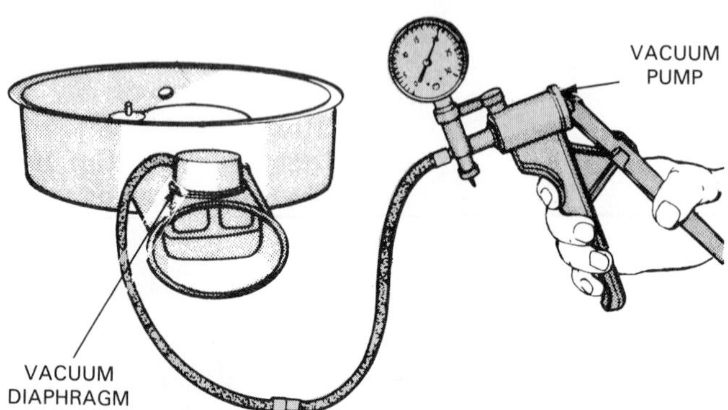

Figure 21-22. Testing a vacuum motor diaphragm with a vacuum pump. If the motor fails to hold a vacuum, it is defective and must be replaced. (Chrysler)

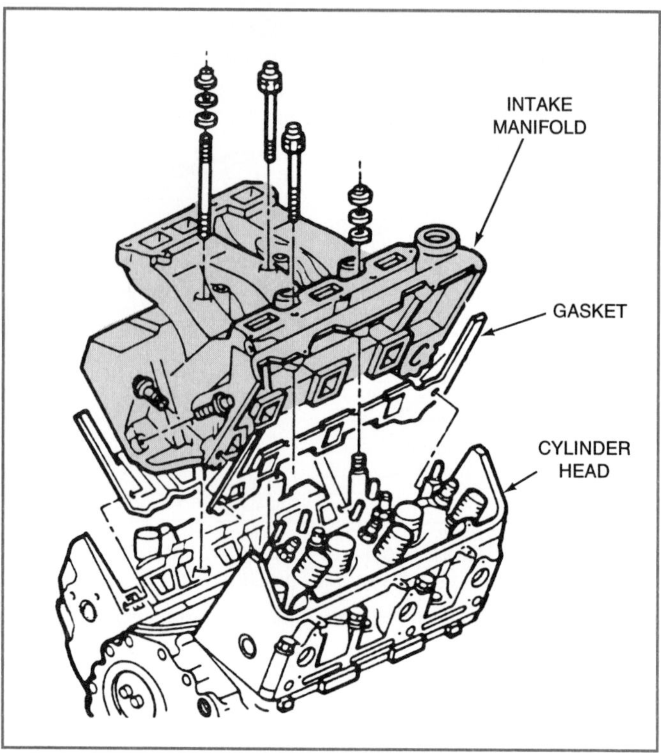

Figure 21-23. Typical intake manifold.

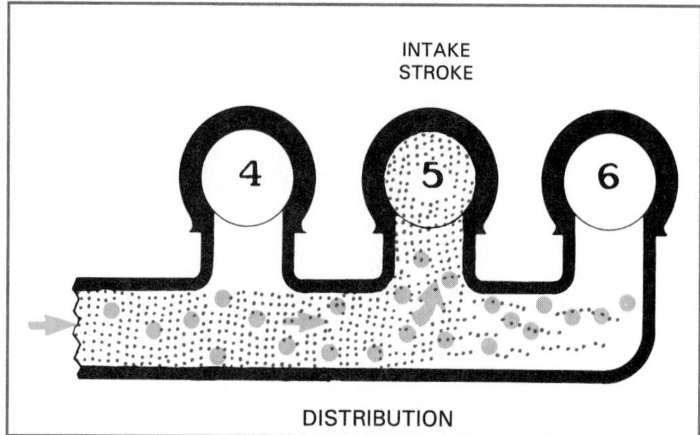

Figure 21-24. Heavy particles of the air/fuel mixture move to the end of the manifold instead of entering an intake runner.

Figure 21-25. Tuned intake manifold on an engine equipped with port fuel injection. Note the long runner, which increases inertia of the air. (Pontiac)

connected to passages in the cylinder heads. In V-type engines, the thermostat is housed in the intake manifold.

Some intake manifolds are designed with an ***exhaust crossover passage.*** Exhaust gases are directed through this passage to warm the air/fuel mixture until the engine reaches its normal operating temperature. This improves fuel vaporization, which leads to more equal fuel distribution. See Figure 21-26.

The flow of exhaust gases through the crossover passage must be controlled. If heat is applied to the air/fuel mixture after the engine has reached its normal operating temperature, exhaust valves will burn and detonation will result.

Many vehicles are equipped with a ***manifold heat control valve*** to control exhaust gas flow, Figure 21-27. This valve is commonly actuated by a thermostatic control spring. In some systems, however, a vacuum-operating servo motor is used instead of a thermostatic spring to control the valve. See Figure 21-28.

Often, the valve shaft is mounted on stainless steel bushings. This is important because the high temperatures and acids in the exhaust gases can cause the valves to seize.

To ensure free operation of the heat control valve, special oils should be applied to the ends of the valve shaft and the bushings at regular intervals. To free a stuck valve, penetrating oil should be applied when the manifold is cold. After allowing the oil to penetrate, tap the valve with a light hammer.

Superchargers

The power developed by an internal combustion engine is largely dependent on the amount of combustible mixture reaching the cylinders. The design of the manifolds, carburetors, and fuel injectors and the size of valves and valve ports are important factors in determining the amount of this mixture. Therefore, to overcome friction losses in the intake system and to aid in scavenging the cylinders of burnt gases, ***superchargers*** can be used to blow the combustible mixture into the cylinders of spark ignition engines, Figure 21-29.

Superchargers were first developed for racing cars and other high-performance engines. Later, they found wide

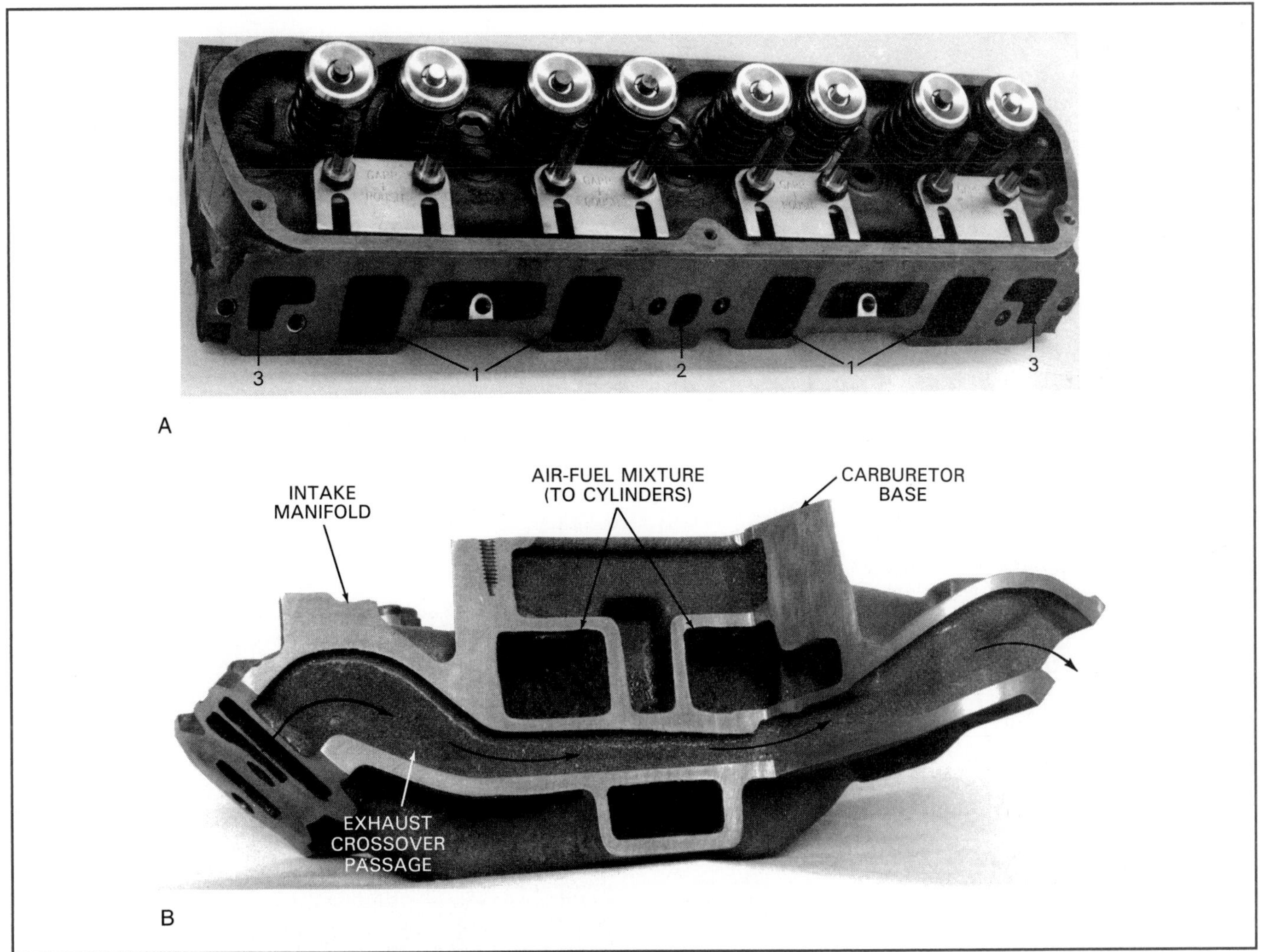

Figure 21-26. Exhaust gas passages. A–No. 1 indicates the intake ports of the cylinder head that align with the intake manifold. No. 2 indicates where the exhaust gases exit the cylinder head when the heat control valve is closed. Exhaust gases then enter the crossover passage of the intake manifold. No. 3 indicates coolant passages. B–Exhaust gases flow through a separate passage under the throttle body or the carburetor to heat the incoming air/fuel mixture. Exhaust gases then exit through a port in the remaining cylinder head on a V-type engine. (Ford)

application on aircraft. In this application, the power of an engine falls rapidly as the airplane attains higher altitudes. As air density decreases, smaller amounts of air will be drawn into the cylinders. Finally, at an altitude of 18,000 feet, only one-half the normal charge will reach the cylinder and only one-half the power will be developed. Superchargers are used on aircraft to help maintain power at high altitudes.

A supercharger is a compressor. Therefore, a supercharged engine will have higher overall compression than a non-supercharged engine having the same combustion chamber volume and piston displacement.

However, this higher overall compression will increase the tendency toward detonation of spark ignition engines. So, when a supercharger is used, fuel of higher-than-standard octane rating is required to prevent detonation. However, when a supercharger is installed on a diesel engine, only air is blown into the cylinders and the tendency toward detonation is reduced.

Superchargers are designed to develop from 4-20 lb. of pressure. The greater the pressure developed, the more air/fuel mixture or air will be carried to the cylinders. The power required to drive the supercharger increases rapidly.

A supercharged engine will burn more fuel than one that is not supercharged. However, the increase in power is not proportional to the increase in fuel consumed.

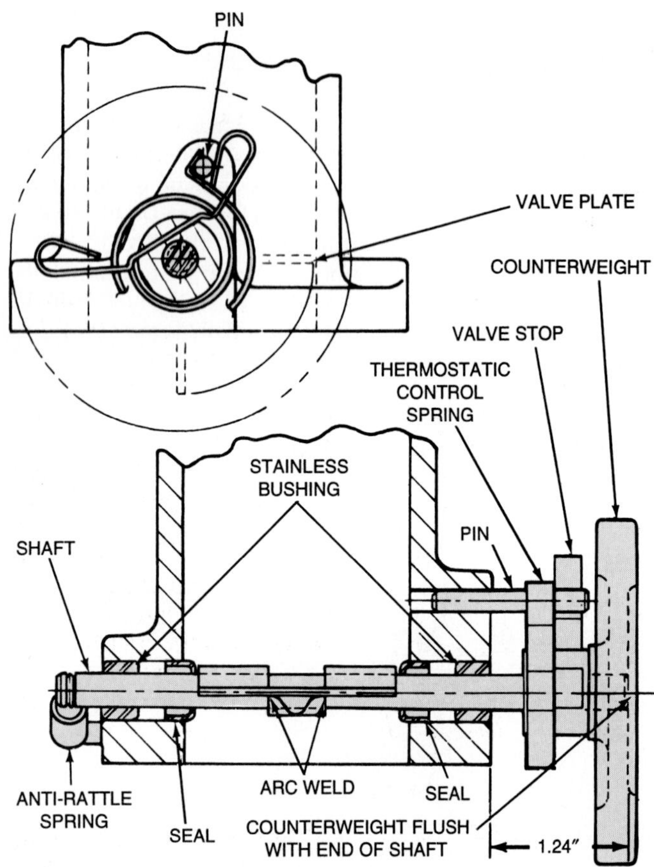

Figure 21-27. The manifold heat control valve is installed in the exhaust manifold.

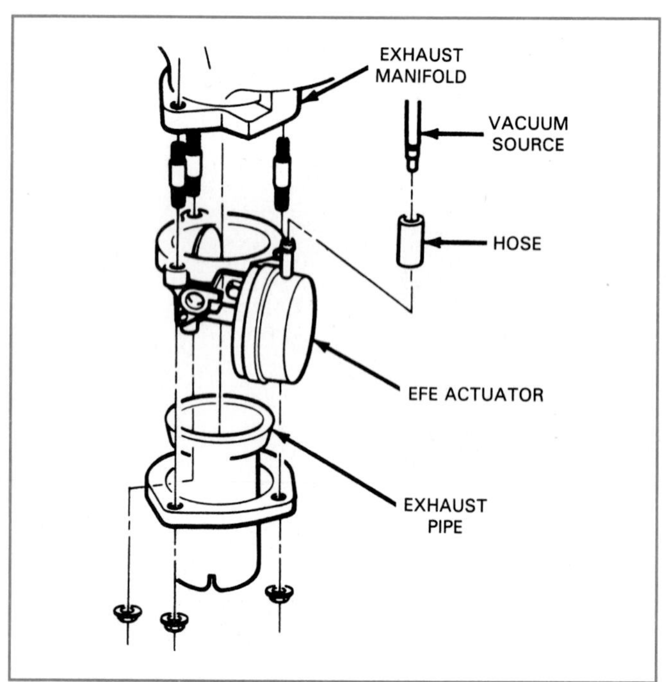

Figure 21-28. On some vehicles, a vacuum-operated servo motor is used to control the heat control valve.

Types of Superchargers

There are two general types of superchargers: the Rootes-type supercharger and the centrifugal-type supercharger. The Rootes-type supercharger, "blower," has two rotors, Figure 21-30. The centrifugal supercharger utilizes an impeller that rotates at high speeds inside a housing.

In most ***Rootes superchargers,*** each rotor has two lobes. However, some Rootes units are fitted with rotors that have three or more lobes, Figure 21-30. The shafts of the two Rootes rotors are connected through gearing and operate at the same speed, with action similar to that of the

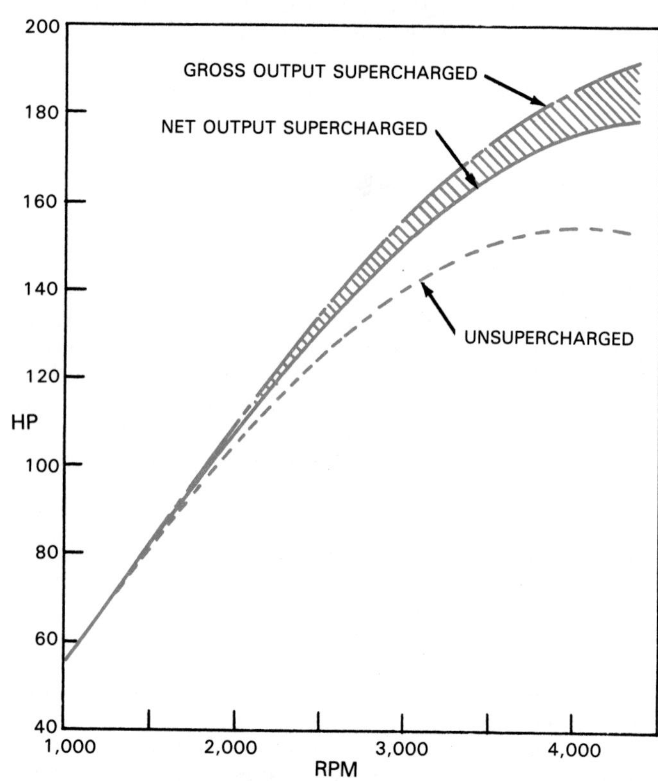

Figure 21-29. Comparing power output of a non-supercharged engine and a supercharged engine.

Figure 21-30. A Rootes-type supercharger.

gear-type oil pump. The rotors do not quite touch each other. There is also a slight clearance between the rotors and the surrounding housing.

In operation, air enters the housing by the action of the rotors. It passes between the lobes of the rotors and the housing, and then is forced through the outlet of the unit.

With the Rootes blower, the rate of delivery varies slightly faster than the speed of rotation, because the leakage decreases as the speed increases. Above a certain minimum speed, the amount of supercharging is almost constant. Rootes blowers are driven at speeds from one to two times engine speed.

The ***centrifugal-type supercharger*** consists of an impeller rotating at a high speed inside a housing. Clearance between the blades and the housing must be kept to a minimum. Since the speed of rotation is approximately five times greater than engine speed, the impeller can easily attain a speed of 25,000 rpm.

Therefore, it is essential that the rotor is accurately balanced. Furthermore, the rotor blades must be made strong enough so that the centrifugal force at high speeds will not cause them to stretch and strike the housing.

On racing car installations, the air from the impeller first passes through a diffuser, where the force of the moving air is converted to static energy. The diffuser consists of a ring-shaped housing that contains blades or vanes.

Coolers are used in conjunction with centrifugal superchargers to reduce the temperature of the air. This is important because the act of compressing the air will increase its temperature. The warm air entering would reduce the efficiency of the engine. The coolers consist of several lengths of finned tubing.

The rate of delivery of the centrifugal supercharger increases as the square of the speed of rotation. As a result, very little supercharging is obtained at lower speeds and the variation between different speeds is large.

Location of Superchargers

Superchargers can be placed between the throttle body of the carburetor or fuel injection system and the manifold or at the air inlet before the throttle body. Racing cars usually have the supercharger between the throttle body and the manifold.

The throttle body/manifold design has the advantage that the fuel can be supplied through the throttle body without modification to any part of the system. If the supercharger is placed in front of the throttle body, fuel must be supplied under sufficient pressure to overcome the added air pressure created by the supercharger. The advantage of a supercharger over a turbocharger is that there is no lag time of boost. The moment the accelerator pedal is depressed, the boost is increased.

Turbochargers

While turbochargers and superchargers perform the same function, the ***turbocharger*** is driven by exhaust gases and the supercharger is driven by belts or gears. However, a turbocharger requires less power to be driven than a supercharger. A turbocharger consists of a turbine and a compressor, Figure 21-31. The pressure of the hot exhaust gases causes the turbine to spin. Since the turbine is mounted on the same shaft as the compressor, the compressor is forced to spin at the same time, Figure 21-32. When the compressor spins, 50 percent more air is drawn into the cylinders than without a turbocharger. This creates more power when the air/fuel mixture explodes.

A turbocharged engine's compression ratio must be lowered. This is usually accomplished by using a lower compression piston. If the compression is not lowered, an excessive amount of pressure will be placed on the piston, connecting rods, and crankshaft. Excessive pressure will cause detonation, which can destroy an engine. The connecting rods, crankshaft, and the gears in the transmission must all be strengthened on a turbocharged engine. If this is not done, the engine and transmission will be torn apart by the increased horsepower.

Wastegate

The ***wastegate,*** Figure 21-33, controls the amount of ***boost*** that the turbocharger can put out. Boost is a pressure

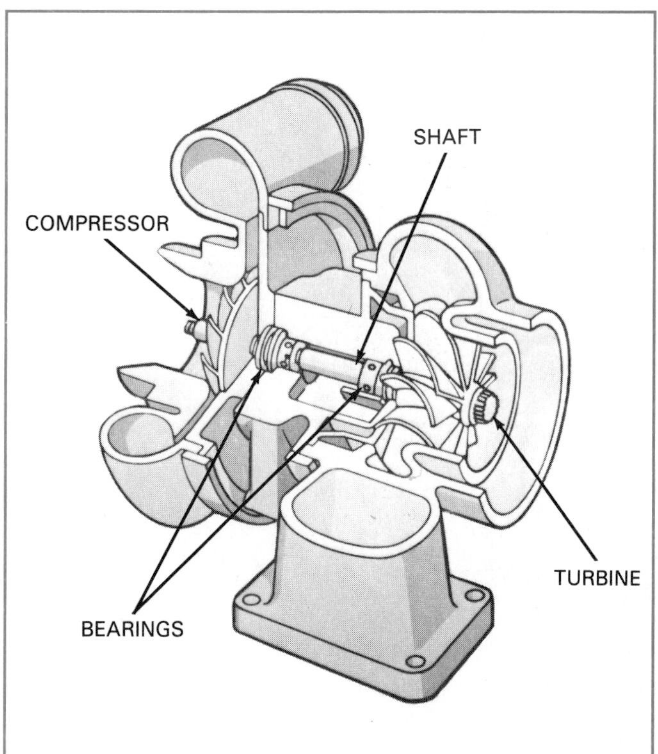

Figure 21-31. Parts of a typical turbocharger. (Chrysler)

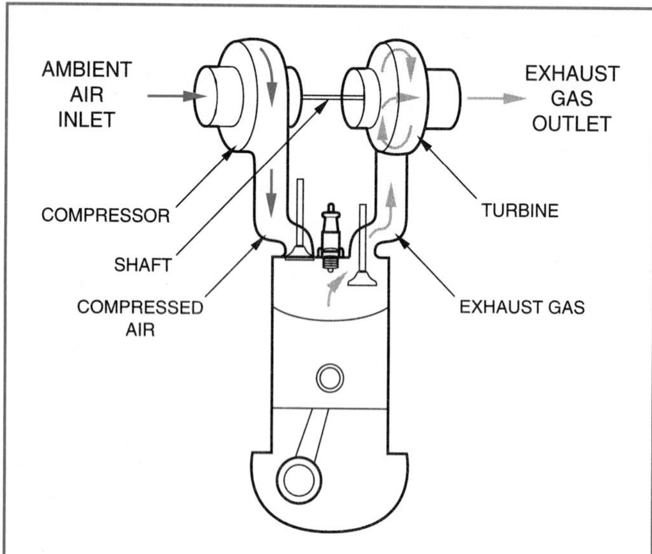

Figure 21-32. As the exhaust gases leave the cylinder, they must pass through the turbine. This causes the turbine to spin. Since the shaft is connected to the compressor, the compressor also spins. As the compressor spins, air is forced into the cylinder. (Chrysler)

greater than atmospheric pressure. When the boost pressure reaches a predetermined value, the wastegate opens and bypasses some of the exhaust gases directly into the exhaust manifold. This causes the turbine to reduce its speed, thereby reducing the speed of the compressor. This limits the amount of boost. As pressure is reduced, the wastegate begins to close again. If the boost is not controlled, the turbocharger will explode. In addition, engine components will be damaged from the excessive pressure.

On some computerized engines the wastegate is controlled by a solenoid, which is activated by the computer.

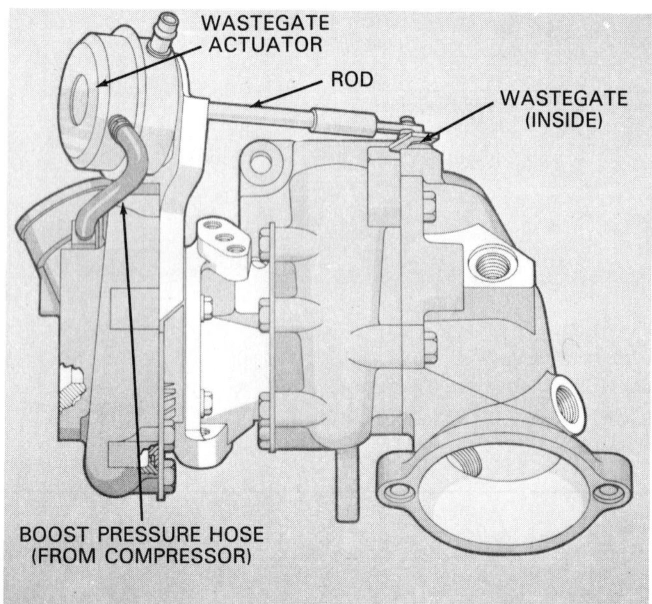

Figure 21-33. The wastegate is located in the turbo housing. On some computerized engines, the wastegate actuator is a solenoid that sits directly on top of the wastegate. The wastegate limits the amount of boost to approximately 5-10 psi on street cars and 50 psi on race cars. (Chrysler)

This eliminates the pressure-operated wastegate actuator, the rod that connects the actuator to the wastegate, and the rubber hose that connects from the compressor side of the turbocharger to the actuator. On these engines, the boost is monitored through the MAP sensor.

Wastegate Operation

The wastegate is held closed by spring pressure, Figure 21-34. The compressed air from the compressor is routed to the cylinders and the wastegate actuator. As pressure increases, the wastegate begins to open. This occurs anywhere from 5 to 10 psi on street engines and 50 psi on race engines.

To verify that the wastegate is operating properly, install a vacuum/pressure gauge to a manifold vacuum source. Consult the individual manual for the specified

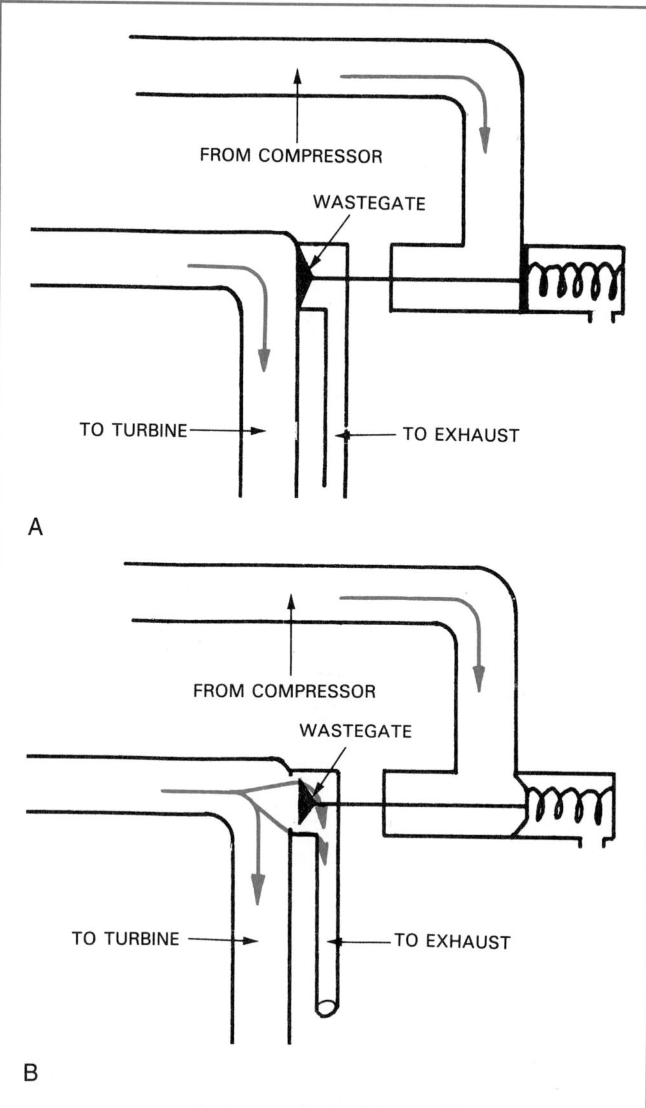

Figure 21-34. Wastegate operation. A–The compressor is connected to the wastegate actuator by a rubber hose. When boost is low, the wastegate remains closed and allows boost to increase. B–When boost reaches the specified limit, the boost pressure overrides the spring pressure in the wastegate actuator. This forces the wastegate to open. Some of the exhaust gases are then diverted past the turbine, reducing the turbine's speed and limiting the amount of boost.

amount of boost. While driving under all different conditions, note the readings. If the specified boost is never obtained, the wastegate is stuck in the open position. If the specified pressure is exceeded, the wastegate actuator is defective or the wastegate is stuck in the closed position.

As stated earlier, some computerized engines replace the wastegate actuator with a solenoid. So, if the correct pressures are not obtained, the solenoid, MAP sensor, or computer may be defective. However, the wastegate may also be stuck in either the closed or open position.

Intercooler

While the compressor of the turbocharger is forcing air into the cylinders, the air is pressurized. Pressure is directly related to heat. The greater the pressure, the greater the heat. The air, after being compressed, is extremely hot. Hot air expands and is less dense than cooler air. Therefore, it is desirable to cool down the compressed air before it enters the intake manifold. This is done by an ***intercooler,*** Figure 21-35. The cool compressed air is packed tighter in the cylinder than if it had not been cooled. Since the air/fuel mixture is packed tighter, more power is created when this air/fuel mixture explodes. Not all turbocharged engines have an intercooler, as this is an added expense.

Figure 21-35. The intercooler is basically a radiator for heated air from the turbocharger. (Ford)

Turbocharger Service

To provide the proper maintenance for a turbocharged engine, the engine oil must be changed more frequently than in a non-turbocharged engine. This is due to the excessive amount of heat generated by the turbocharger. The heat reduces the effectiveness of the oil. Also, the slightest contamination can destroy the bearings in the turbocharger, as the turbo rotates at speeds in excess of 100,000 rpm. The engine oil used must be recommended for turbocharged engines. Follow the manufacturer's recommendations and specifications carefully.

Turbocharger Problems

The most common problems associated with a turbocharger is the wastegate or its actuator. If the wastegate remains in the closed position, fuel consumption will be increased and detonation will result. If the wastegate sticks in the open position, there will be a lack of power on acceleration. This is due to a lack of boost. Other problems are:

- Vibration due to excessive axial play caused by bearing wear in turbo. Nicks or dents on the compressor or turbine wheel can also cause a vibration.
- Turbo housing becomes cherry red due to an excessively lean air/fuel mixture (vacuum leak) and/or advanced timing.
- Oil consumption due to a carbon seal defect in the turbo housing. To correct this problem, the entire turbocharger must be replaced. However, do not consider a small amount of oil inside the turbo housing a problem; this is normal. Since the turbo is increasing the amount of air in the cylinders, there will be an increase of blowby. Blowby carries oil vapors from the crankcase into the turbo housing, where they condense. Suspect the carbon seal only when there is an excessive amount of oil in the turbo housing and no other defects are found for excessive oil consumption.

Chapter 21–Review Questions

Write your answers on a separate sheet of paper. Do not write in this book.

1. On small gas engines, how is fuel usually supplied to the carburetor?
2. On modern passenger cars, what two methods are used to drive the fuel pumps?
3. How much pressure should the mechanical-type fuel pump develop?
   (A) 5 lb.
   (B) 10 lb.
   (C) 15 lb.
   (D) 20 lb.
4. In 45 seconds, how much fuel should be pumped by the average mechanical-type fuel pump?
   (A) 1 pint.
   (B) 2 pints.
   (C) 3 pints.
   (D) 32 ounces.
5. Technician A states that a fuel filter for a fuel injected engine is usually located in the engine compartment. Technician B states that a fuel filter for a fuel injected engine is located near the fuel tank. Who is right?
   (A) A only.
   (B) B only.
   (C) Both A & B.
   (D) Neither A nor B.
6. What is a major advantage of using an externally mounted electric fuel pump?
7. Name two main types of mechanically driven superchargers.
8. Which type of internal combustion engine will tend to detonate more?
   (A) Supercharged.
   (B) Non-supercharged.

9. What is a major advantage of the turbocharger over the supercharger?
10. Name the two general types of fuel gauges.
11. Name two types of materials used in fuel filters.
12. How should a paper air filter element be cleaned?
    (A) It should be washed in cleaning solvent.
    (B) It cannot be cleaned. It must be replaced.
    (C) It should be tapped against a hard flat surface.
    (D) None of the above.
13. What is the purpose of the intake manifold?
14. What is the purpose of the manifold heat control valve?
15. _____ intake manifolds are used on many late-model vehicles that are equipped with port fuel injection.
16. Technician A states that the wastegate limits the amount of boost. Technician B states that a wastegate cools the compressed air. Who is right?
    (A) A only.
    (B) B only.
    (C) Both A & B.
    (D) Neither A nor B.
17. The purpose of the intercooler is to:
    (A) limit the amount of boost.
    (B) limit fuel pressure.
    (C) cool the compressed air.
    (D) None of the above.
18. What else must be done to the engine when it is turbocharged?
    (A) Lower the compression ratio.
    (B) Strengthen the drive train parts.
    (C) Both A & B.
    (D) None of the above.
19. Fuel moves from a low-pressure area to a high-pressure area. True or False?
20. What drives the turbocharger?
    (A) The camshaft.
    (B) The crankshaft.
    (C) Incoming air.
    (D) Exhaust gas.

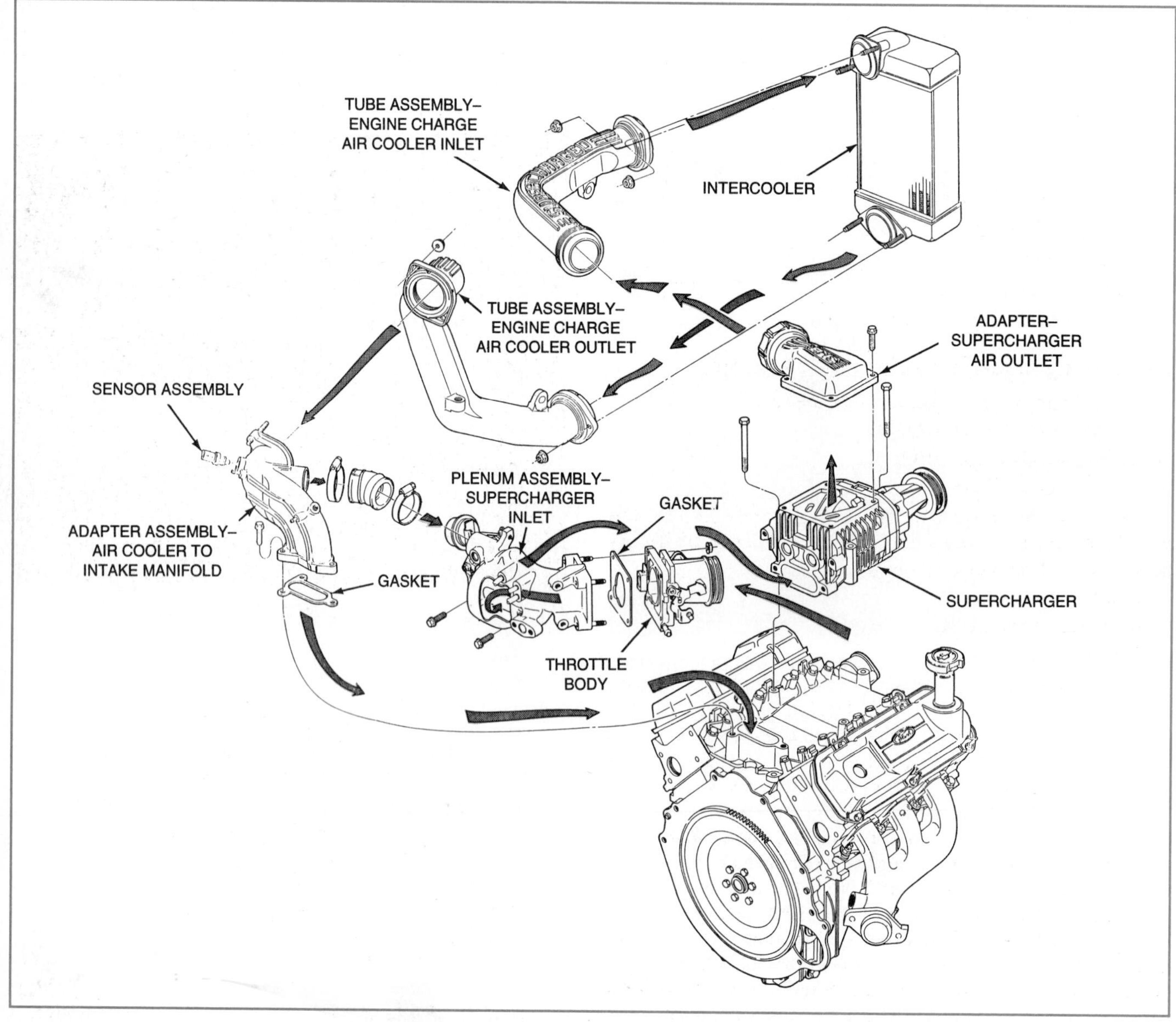

Exploded view showing airflow through a supercharger and an intercooler. (Ford)

Chapter 22
Fuel Injection Systems

After studying this chapter, you will be able to:
- ❍ List the various types of fuel injection systems.
- ❍ Describe the three sub-groups of an EFI system.
- ❍ Explain how the pressure regulator and fuel injector operate.
- ❍ Troubleshoot the fuel injection system.
- ❍ Tell why fuel pressure must be released and explain how it is released.

Gasoline Injection

A ***fuel injection system*** meters fuel much more precisely than a carburetor. Also, there are fewer parts in a fuel injection system than a carbureted system, which makes it easier to troubleshoot.

Other advantages of fuel injection include:
- Increased power.
- Higher torque.
- Improved fuel economy.
- Quicker cold weather starting.
- Faster warmup.
- No need for manifold heat.
- Lower intake temperatures.

Classifying Gasoline Injection Systems

The types of fuel injection systems are:
- Single-point injection systems.
- Multi-point injection systems.
- Direct injection systems.

Fuel injection systems can also be classified by the way in which they inject fuel into the combustion chambers. These classifications include:
- Continuous injection.
- Intermittent injection.
- Sequential injection.

In a ***continuous injection system,*** fuel is sprayed continuously from the injectors. Fuel quantity to the injection chambers is controlled by changing the pressure at which the fuel is forced through the injectors. When pressure is increased, a greater amount of fuel is injected into the combustion chambers.

The injectors in an ***intermittent injection system*** pulse on and off to control the amount of fuel entering the combustion chambers. When fuel needs increase, the injector "on" time is increased to supply additional fuel.

In the ***sequential injection system,*** there is generally one injector for each cylinder of the engine. The injectors fire independent of each other and in relation to the position of intake valves. Multi-point injection systems are commonly of the sequential injection type.

Single-point Fuel Injection

Single-point injection is also referred to as throttle body injection (TBI). Single point refers to a centrally located fuel injector. One or two fuel injectors are located in the throttle body, Figures 22-1 and 22-2. Fuel is sprayed into an intake manifold and then delivered to the cylinders.

Figure 22-1. Single-point, or throttle body, injection.

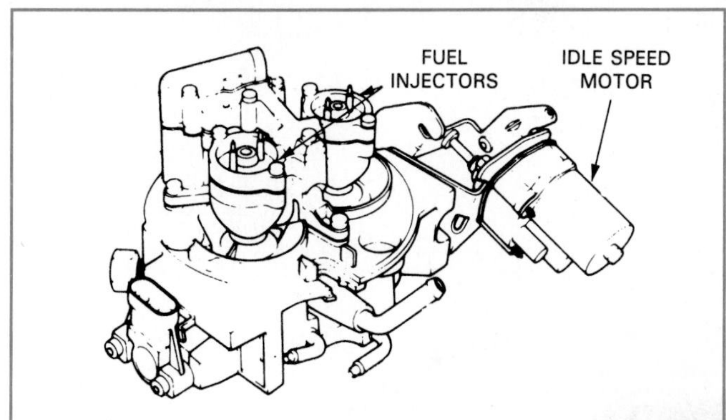

Figure 22-2. Some single-point systems have two injectors. Both injectors are pulsed on and off at the same time. (Cadillac)

The injector is pulsed on and off so fast that it sprays a steady stream of fuel into the manifold. Single-point injection, whether one or two injectors are used, is pulsed on for each intake stroke. This means there are two pulses per crankshaft revolution on a four cylinder engine, or 26 pulses per second at idle.

Multi-point Fuel Injection

In ***multi-point injection systems***, there are generally as many injectors as there are cylinders. On this type of system, the fuel injectors are attached to a fuel rail, Figure 22-3.

Most multi-point systems are intermittent. This means that the injectors are not energized at the same time. There are different types of intermittent injection. The injectors can be turned on and off in pairs or in a specific sequence that is related to valve timing.

Most multi-point systems are ported. Ported injection means that the fuel is sprayed directly into an intake runner, Figures 22-4 and 22-5. This eliminates the problems associated with intake manifolds. This contrasts to fuel being sprayed in the intake manifold as in the single-point injection system.

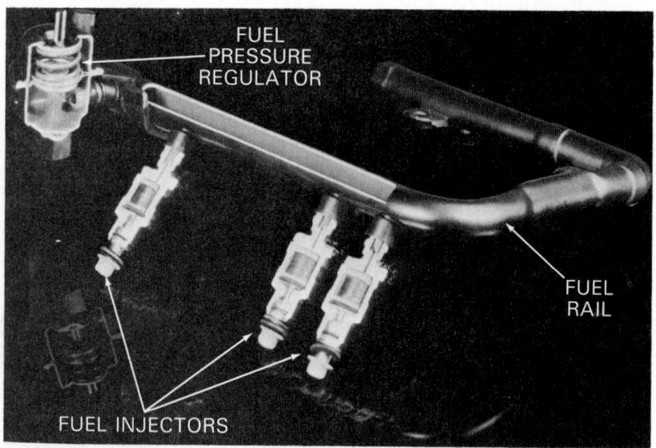

Figure 22-3. Multi-point system has fuel injectors attached to a fuel rail. Fuel flows through the rail to all of the injectors. (Buick)

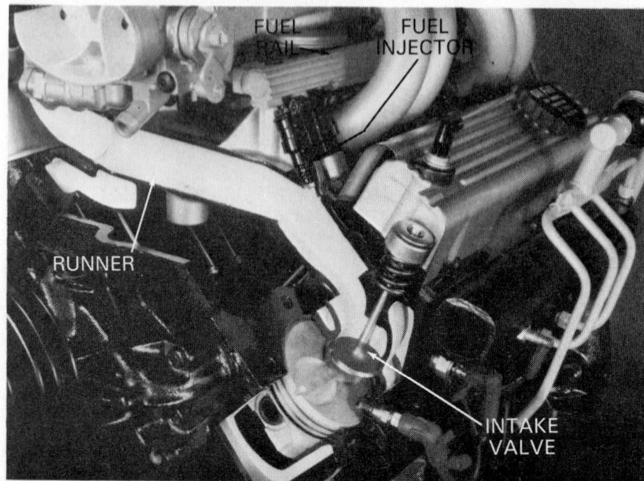

Figure 22-4. With a ported fuel injection system, fuel is sprayed directly into the individual intake runners. There are as many intake runners as cylinders. (Pontiac)

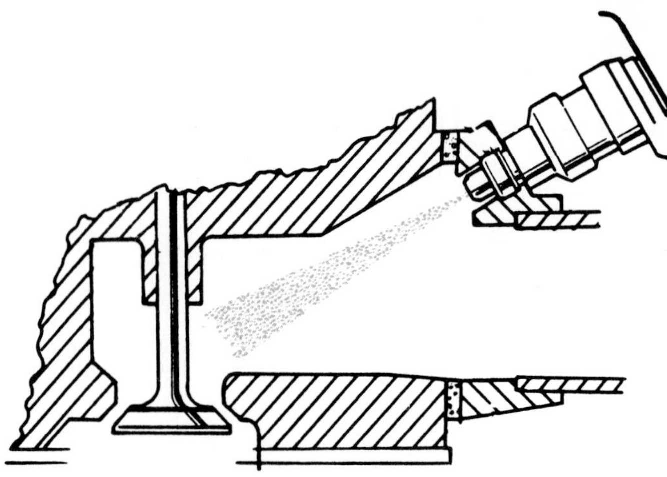

Figure 22-5. Ported injection sprays fuel into the intake port. (Oldsmobile)

Direct Fuel Injection

Direct fuel injection means that the fuel is sprayed directly into the combustion chamber. The fuel injector nozzle is located in the combustion chamber. This system is used by diesel engines.

Classifying the Control Systems

There are three methods for controlling the delivery of fuel to the injectors. ***Mechanical fuel injection*** is the oldest of the fuel injection systems. This system uses throttle linkage and a governor. ***Hydraulic fuel injection*** has been used by a few manufacturers. Hydraulic pressure is applied to a fuel distributor. The fuel distributor is used as a switching device to route fuel to a specific injector. Currently, the most common method used on gas engines is ***electronic fuel injection*** (EFI). This system is divided into three subgroups. They are:

- Air Induction.
- Fuel Injection.
- Electronic Controls.

Air Induction

The incoming air is regulated by the throttle valve, which is located in the throttle body, Figure 22-6. The throttle valve is connected by linkage to the accelerator pedal. As the accelerator pedal is depressed, the valve is opened, allowing air to enter the intake. Fuel is added to the incoming air.

Fuel Injection

The fuel from the tank is carried under pressure to the fuel injector(s). This is done by an electric fuel pump, which is located in or near the fuel tank. The excess fuel is returned to the fuel tank, Figure 22-7. A relay for the electric fuel pump, Figure 22-8, is used to complete the circuit to the fuel pump. The relay cuts off the current to the fuel pump in the event of an accident.

Regulator. The fuel pressure ***regulator,*** Figure 22-9, keeps the fuel pressure at the injectors constant under all driving conditions. A diaphragm inside of the regulator is

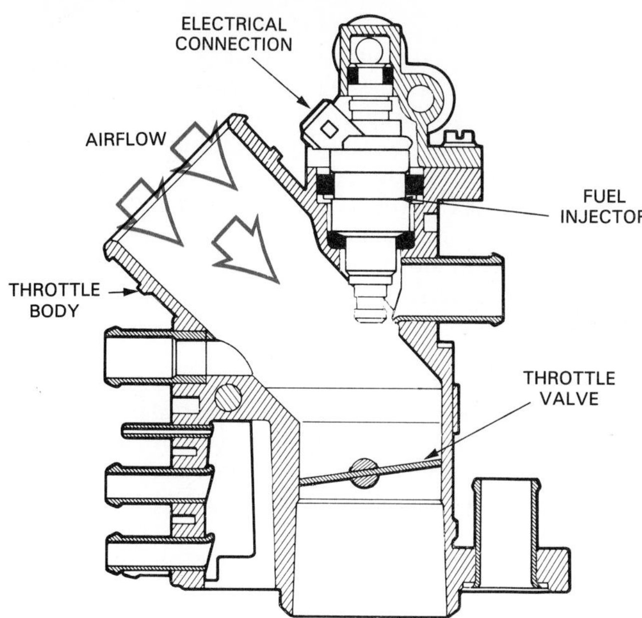

Figure 22-6. The throttle valve regulates the airflow. A multi-point fuel injection system uses a throttle body (without injectors) to control airflow. (Chrysler)

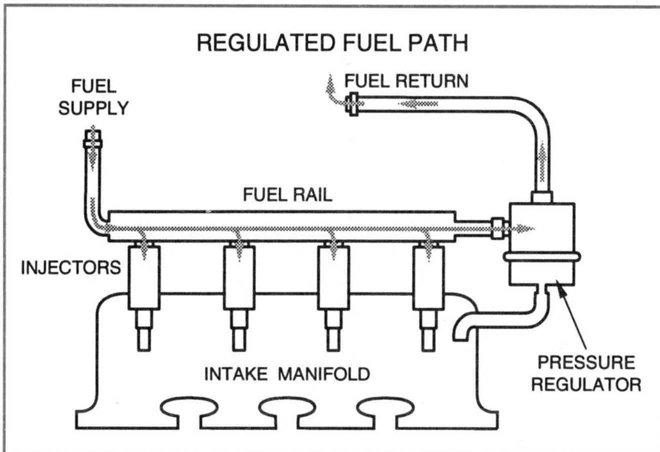

Figure 22-7. Path showing flow of fuel. Unused fuel is returned to the tank through the fuel pressure regulator. Note that this multi-point system still uses an intake manifold. (Chrysler)

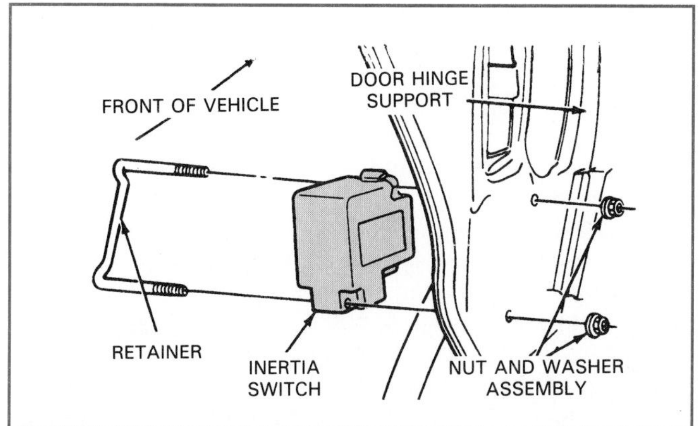

Figure 22-8. Some fuel systems use an inertia switch in addition to a fuel pump relay. The inertia switch stops the electrical current to the fuel pump in the event of an accident. The inertia switch can be reset. (Ford)

held in place by spring pressure. Vacuum from the engine is applied to the spring side of the diaphragm. When vacuum is high, (idle and low load conditions), it overcomes the spring pressure and lifts the diaphragm from the return port. The unused fuel is returned to the tank. During periods of low engine vacuum, such as during wide open throttle operation (WOT), the engine needs all of the fuel it can get. In these cases, spring pressure is greater than the vacuum, and the spring forces the diaphragm against the return port. This prevents the fuel from returning to the tank, as all of the fuel is needed by the engine. The diaphragm is constantly opening and closing to maintain the desired fuel pressure.

Injector. The ***fuel injector,*** Figure 22-10, is an electromechanical device that sprays and atomizes the fuel. The fuel injector is nothing more than a solenoid through which gasoline is metered. When electric current is applied to the injector coil, a magnetic field is created. This causes the armature to move upward. This action pulls a spring-loaded ball or pintle valve off its seat. Then, fuel (under pressure) can flow out of the injector nozzle. The contour of the ball or pintle valve causes the fuel to be sprayed in a cone-shaped pattern. When the injector is de-energized, the spring pushes the ball or pintle valve onto its seat, stopping the flow of fuel.

Controlling the Fuel Injectors. A lean air/fuel mixture produces a high level of nitrous oxides (NOx) in the exhaust. A rich air/fuel mixture produces a high level of hydrocarbons (HC) and carbon monoxide (CO) in the exhaust. However, the byproducts of perfect combustion produce water (H_2O) and carbon dioxide (CO_2) in the exhaust,

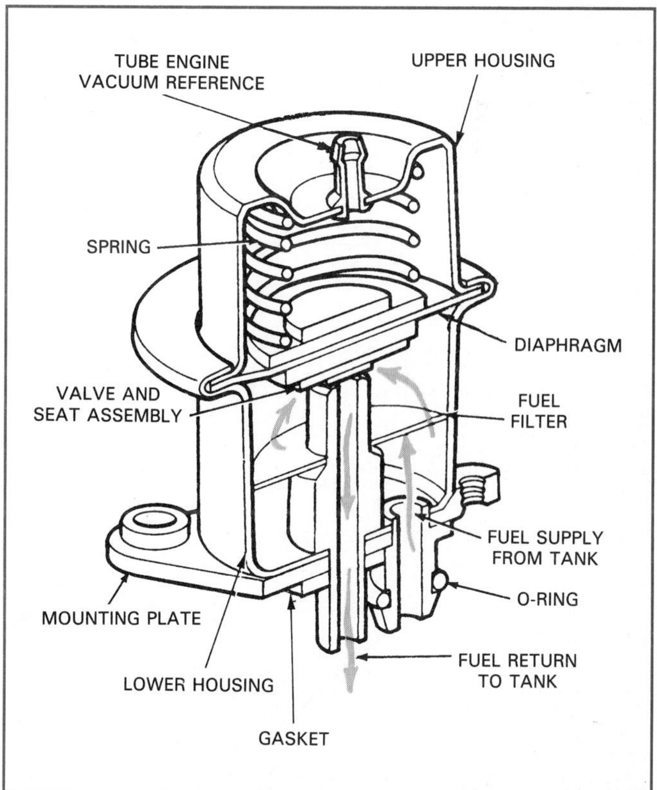

Figure 22-9. When engine vacuum is high, the fuel return port is uncovered, allowing unused fuel to return to the tank. The pressure regulator is always located downstream of fuel injectors. (Ford)

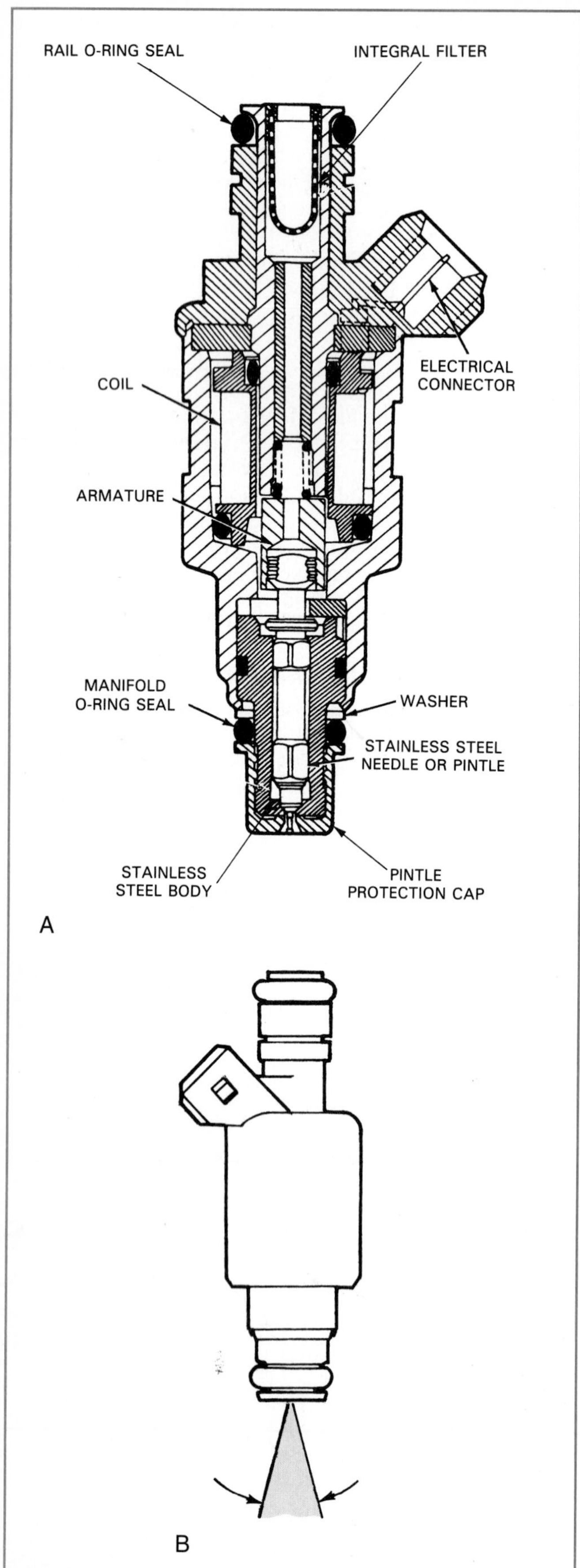

Figure 22-10. Fuel injectors. A–When energized, fuel flows through the injector. B–Fuel spray pattern should always be cone shaped. (Ford and Delco-Rochester)

provided that the engine is 100% efficient. Unfortunately, even the best designed engine is not 100% efficient.

A ***stoichiometric*** air/fuel mixture comes closest to providing the byproducts of perfect combustion. A stoichiometric air/fuel mixture is neither too rich nor too lean. It is 14.7 parts air to 1 part fuel. However, even with this desired air/fuel mixture, hydrocarbons, carbon monoxide, and nitrous oxides remain in small percentages.

To achieve the stoichiometric mixture, the combustion process and other engine variables must be measured. The variables determine the length of time that the injectors are turned ON to provide the desired mixture.

Sensors/Actuators. Most sensors are supplied a reference voltage. A ***sensor*** is a device that measures. The measurement is then converted into an electrical signal. This signal is then compared, by the computer, to the reference voltage. This determines the amount of time that an actuator is energized. An ***actuator*** is a device that is controlled by the computer. The idle speed motor, ignition coil, and fuel injectors are examples of actuators.

Electronic Controls

The ***computer,*** or microprocessor, receives information from the various sensors, Figure 22-11, and then adjusts the actuators accordingly. The fuel injector is one of the actuators that the computer controls. The longer the fuel injector is energized, the richer the fuel mixture becomes. The injector pulse width, Figure 22-12, is the length of ON time. The pulse width is determined by signals from the:

- Crankshaft position sensor. This sensor determines when the injector is energized. Most crankshaft position sensors double as an engine speed sensor. The higher the rpm, the more times the injector(s) is energized.
- Manifold Absolute Pressure (MAP) sensor. This senses the engine load. The greater the load, (low vacuum), the longer the injector is energized.
- Throttle position sensor. This determines the angle of the throttle blades. The greater the angle, the longer the fuel injector is energized.
- Coolant temperature sensor. This senses the temperature of the engine. A cold engine needs the injector(s) to be energized longer. Other systems provide a cold start valve to richen the fuel mixture on a cold engine, Figure 22-13.
- Manifold air temperature sensor. This senses the temperature of the incoming air. Colder air is denser. To compensate for the denser air, the injector ON time must be increased.
- Oxygen sensor. This senses the amount of oxygen in the exhaust. When there is an excess of oxygen in the exhaust (lean mixture), and the "on" time of the injector is increased. When there is a lack of oxygen (rich mixture) in the exhaust, the "on" time is reduced. When the computer uses the signal from the oxygen sensor, it is referred to as operating in CLOSED LOOP. When the exhaust gases are below 600°F, the oxygen sensor does not provide the computer with a signal. The computer operates from predetermined values. This is referred to as OPEN LOOP. Also, when the throttle is wide open (WOT), the signal from the sensor is ignored, regardless of the temperature.

Automatic Idle Adjustment. On computerized systems, the idle speed is controlled by an ***idle speed motor,***

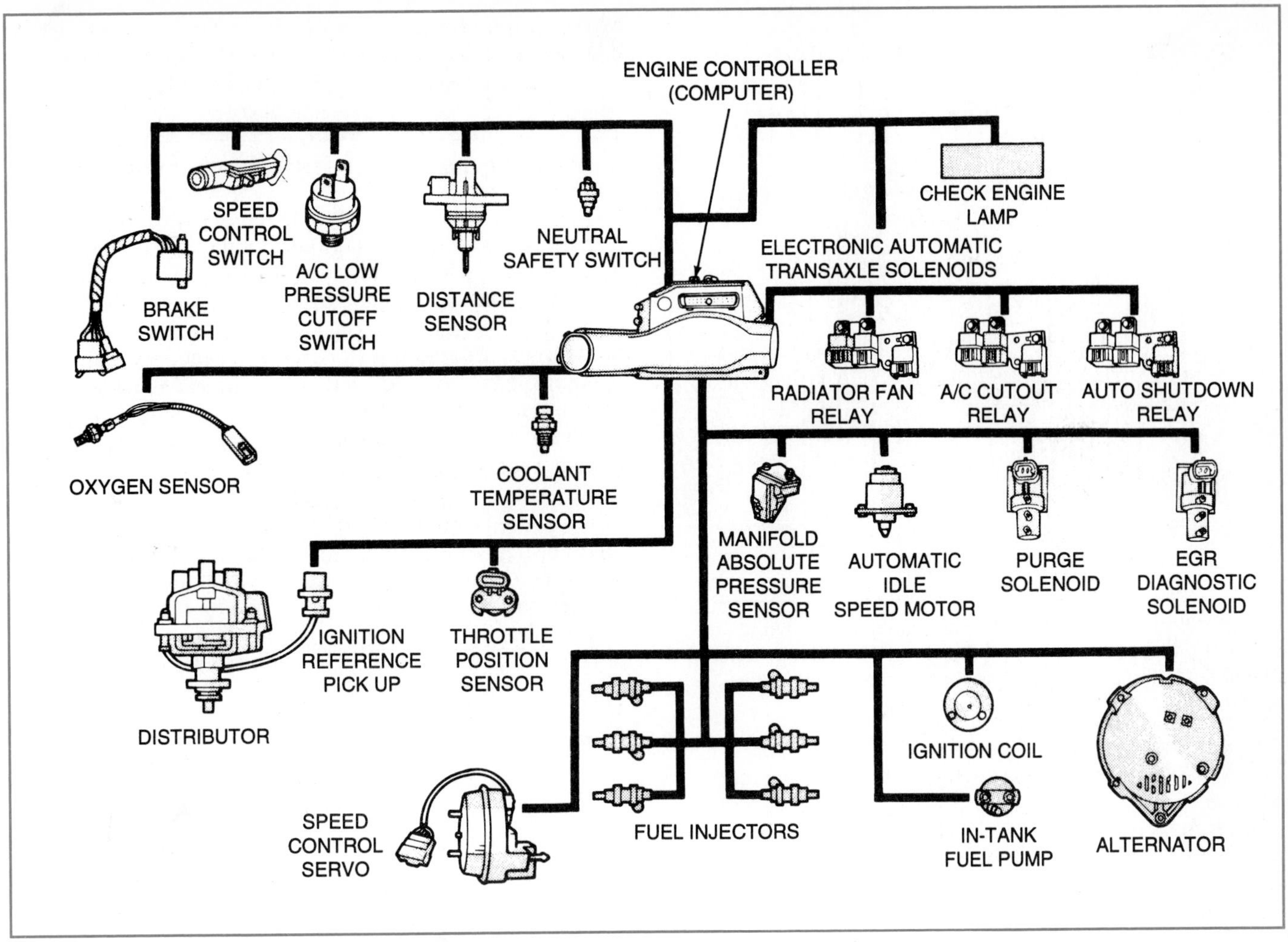

ENGINE CONTROLLER (COMPUTER)
SPEED CONTROL SWITCH
BRAKE SWITCH
A/C LOW PRESSURE CUTOFF SWITCH
DISTANCE SENSOR
NEUTRAL SAFETY SWITCH
CHECK ENGINE LAMP
ELECTRONIC AUTOMATIC TRANSAXLE SOLENOIDS
RADIATOR FAN RELAY
A/C CUTOUT RELAY
AUTO SHUTDOWN RELAY
OXYGEN SENSOR
COOLANT TEMPERATURE SENSOR
MANIFOLD ABSOLUTE PRESSURE SENSOR
AUTOMATIC IDLE SPEED MOTOR
PURGE SOLENOID
EGR DIAGNOSTIC SOLENOID
IGNITION REFERENCE PICK UP
THROTTLE POSITION SENSOR
DISTRIBUTOR
IGNITION COIL
FUEL INJECTORS
SPEED CONTROL SERVO
IN-TANK FUEL PUMP
ALTERNATOR

Figure 22-11. The computer processes many input signals before adjusting the fuel injector pulse width and other output devices. (Chrysler)

FUEL INJECTOR PULSE WIDTH
CRUISE CONDITION
CYL 1
CYL 3
CYL 4
CYL 2
INJECTOR ON
INJECTOR OFF
2MS
30MS
180 DEG. CRANK
1000 RPM
INJECTOR ON
INJECTOR OFF
2MS
15MS
180 DEG. CRANK
2000 RPM
LOAD CONDITION
INJECTOR ON
INJECTOR OFF
4MS
30MS
180 DEG. CRANK
1000 RPM
INJECTOR ON
INJECTOR OFF
4MS
15MS
180 DEG. CRANK
2000 RPM

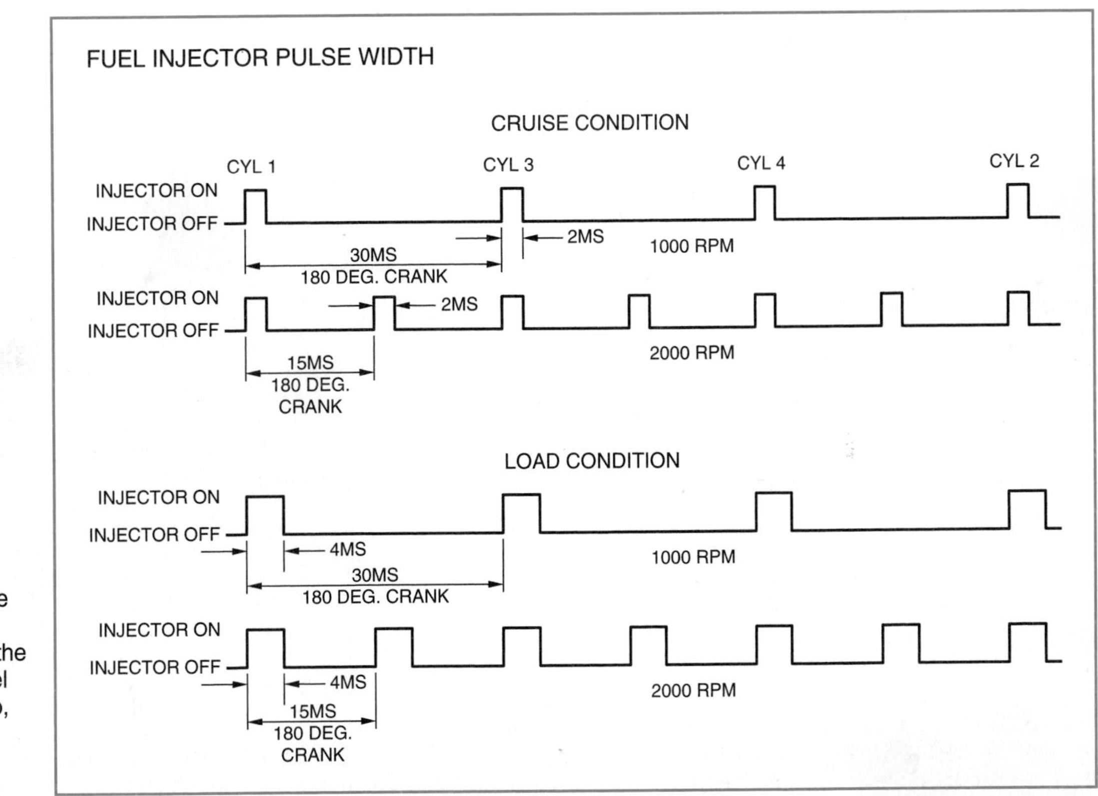

Figure 22-12. The "on" time, or pulse width, of the injector is measured in milliseconds. The higher the rpm, the more times a fuel injector is energized. Also, the greater the load, the longer the fuel injector is energized. (Chrysler)

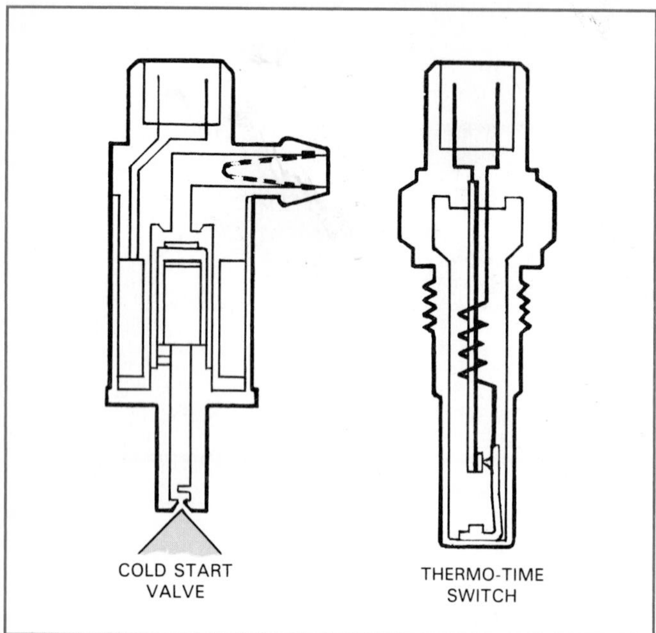

Figure 22-13. Some systems use a cold start valve to richen the fuel mixture on a cold engine. The thermo-time switch limits the amount of time that the cold start valve is energized. (Robert Bosch)

Figure 22-14. The motor is another actuator. The computer decides to increase or decrease the idle rpm after receiving input signals from the sensors. This keeps the idle speed at a constant rpm, regardless of the load placed on the engine while idling.

The technician should never attempt to adjust the idle speed. If there is a problem with the idle speed, the motor, sensors, or the computer is defective. A mechanical defect could also interfere with the idle speed. This could be due to a large vacuum leak. The computer will compensate for a small vacuum leak by adjusting the idle speed.

On-Board Diagnostics

When a light on the dash informs the driver to "check engine," a problem has been detected by the computer. Any of the components of the system could be at fault. For detailed information on diagnosing the cause, see Chapter 29, Computer System Fundamentals and Service.

Servicing the Fuel Injection System

A fuel injector has only one moving part, but if defective it can create more than one symptom. The most common problem with a fuel injector is that the orifices in the nozzle become dirty and restrict the flow of fuel. This can cause stalling, hesitation on acceleration, and hard starting. Sometimes, the fuel injector can be cleaned by adding fuel injector cleaner to a full gas tank. The car must be driven until the tank is nearly empty. If this does not correct the problem, the injector should be cleaned with a cleaning system recommended by the manufacturer. When using many of these systems, the injectors can be cleaned when installed on the engine. In other cases, the injectors must be removed for cleaning. Make sure to follow the manufacturer's recommendations when cleaning injectors. If cleaning fails to solve the problem, the injector must be replaced. Another common problem is a leaky fuel injector. A leaky injector will flood the engine and may cause the engine to run on after the key has been turned to the "off" position.

Low Fuel Pressure

Low fuel pressure creates a lean air/fuel mixture. This can cause a surging while driving at a steady speed. Causes for low fuel pressure include:

- A plugged fuel filter.
- A defective fuel pump.
- A leaking fuel pump hose coupling (inside gas tank).
- A defective fuel pressure regulator (stuck open).
- A defective fuel pump check valve or accumulator.
- A leaking fuel line.

Testing Fuel Pressure

To test fuel pressure, connect a fuel pressure gauge to the test port, Figure 22-15. Fuel pressure should register as soon as the ignition is turned ON (engine not running).

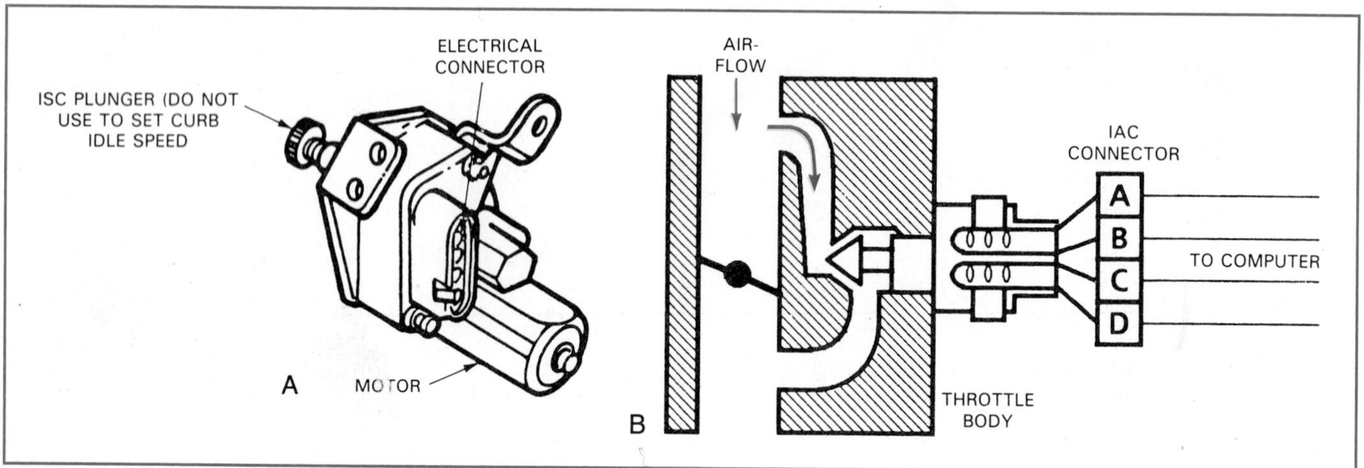

Figure 22-14. Automatic idle speed adjustment. A–Some systems use a motor that retracts or extends a plunger to control idle speed. When the plunger is extended, idle speed is increased. B–Other systems use a motor that retracts or extends a valve, regulating airflow past the throttle blades. When the valve is retracted, airflow is increased past the throttle blades, increasing the idle speed. No attempt should be made to adjust the idle speed on either system. (Cadillac)

Figure 22-15. Testing fuel pressure. A–Remove dust cap to access the Schrader valve. B–Screw the threaded adapter to the Schrader valve. The lever is then lowered to allow pressurized fuel to the gauge. C–If fuel pressure is at the specified level, no further testing is needed. Note the drain valve and drain tube. To relieve fuel pressure, open the drain valve with the ignition in the "off" position. (Rochester)

Note the pressure and compare it to specifications. If pressure is good, start the engine and note the operating pressure. Fuel pressure should drop about 5 to 10 psi after engine has started and is idling. If fuel pressure does not drop, remove the vacuum hose from the pressure regulator. Make sure that a suction can be felt at the end of the vacuum hose. If not, locate and repair the leak. If a suction is felt, reconnect the vacuum hose to the pressure regulator. Fuel pressure should drop about 3 to 6 psi after reconnecting the vacuum hose. If pressure does not drop, the pressure regulator is bad.

If the fuel pressure starts to fall shortly after connecting the gauge with the ignition on and the engine not running, the fuel pump check valve or accumulator is bad, the fuel pump coupling hose is leaking, or the fuel injector is leaking.

To determine which is at fault, energize the fuel pump, Figure 22-16. Then, pinch shut the fuel return line or flex hose located in the fuel return line, Figure 22-17. Fuel pressure should be around 75 to 100 psi with the pump energized and the fuel return line pinched. If not, the fuel pump or filter is bad. However, if fuel pressure is good and now fails to fall, the fuel pump check valve or accumulator is bad or the pump coupling hose is leaking. On the other hand, if fuel pressure continues to fall, one or more of the injectors are leaking.

Sometimes, a leaky fuel injector can be detected by removing all the spark plugs from the engine. Note the condition of the porcelain insulators. If any are wet, the injector for that cylinder is leaking. In some cases, however, an injector balance test may be needed to detect a leaky injector.

High Fuel Pressure

If fuel pressure is above specifications, the fuel return line is restricted or the pressure regulator is defective. If there are no restrictions in the return line, replace the regulator.

NOTE: Always consult the individual service manual for test procedures and specifications. If fuel is found in the vacuum hose connection of the pressure regulator, the regulator is bad.

Checking Multi-point Injectors

Checking the fuel injectors on a multi-point system requires more time and special tools for testing. A defective fuel injector on a multi-point system may cause an engine miss, dieseling, and flooding. An ***oscilloscope*** can detect an injector that is only partially defective, Figure 22-18. An injector balance test is another method for detecting bad fuel injectors, Figure 22-19.

Hard Starting

Sometimes, a hard-start condition will be experienced on fuel injected engines. This can be caused by many things. If a fuel injector is leaking, it will flood the engine. A fuel pump check valve that is bad will allow fuel to drain back into the tank. Other systems may have a fuel ***pressure accumulator*** that prevents fuel from draining back into the tank. If the accumulator or check valve is bad, it will take time for the fuel to pressurize in the lines.

To determine if a fuel injector or check valve is causing a hard start, connect a fuel pressure gauge and start the engine. As soon as maximum pressure is reached, turn the engine off. Watch the gauge pressure. If pressure maintains for at least 15 minutes, all is fine. However, if pressure drops during that time, the injector, check valve, or accu-

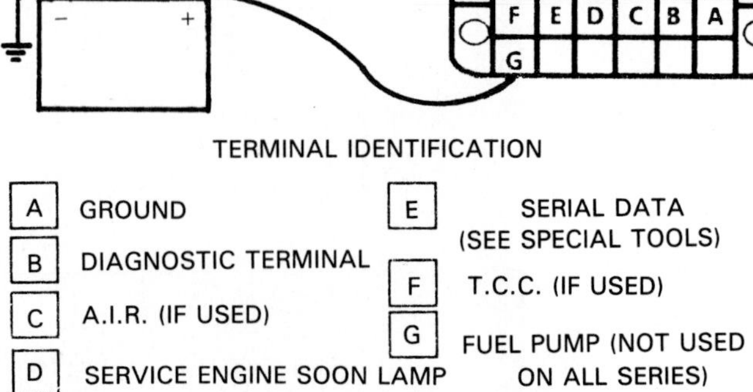

Figure 22-16. To energize the pump on some computerized GM engines, connect a jumper wire from a hot source to terminal G of the diagnostic connector. (Cadillac)

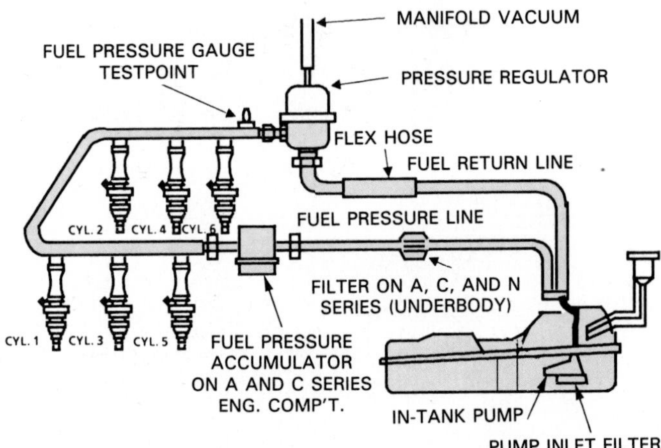

Figure 22-17. Pinch the flex hose or return line closed. With pump energized, fuel pressure should be at least 75 psi. Note the fuel pressure accumulator. (Oldsmobile)

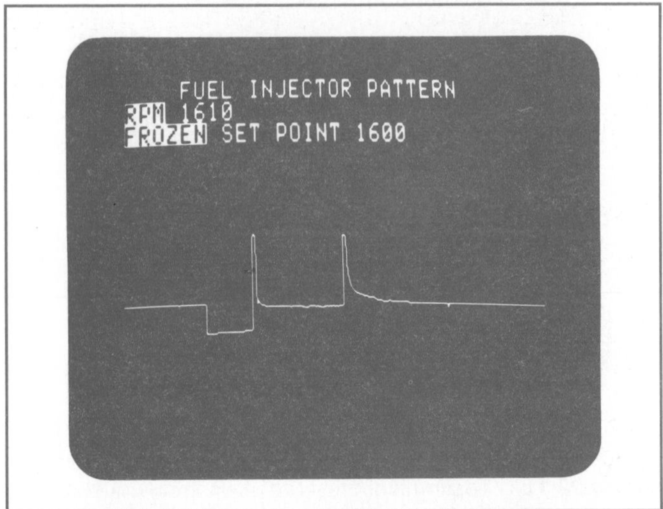

Figure 22-18. An oscilloscope can be used to detect a sticking fuel injector. (Snap-On)

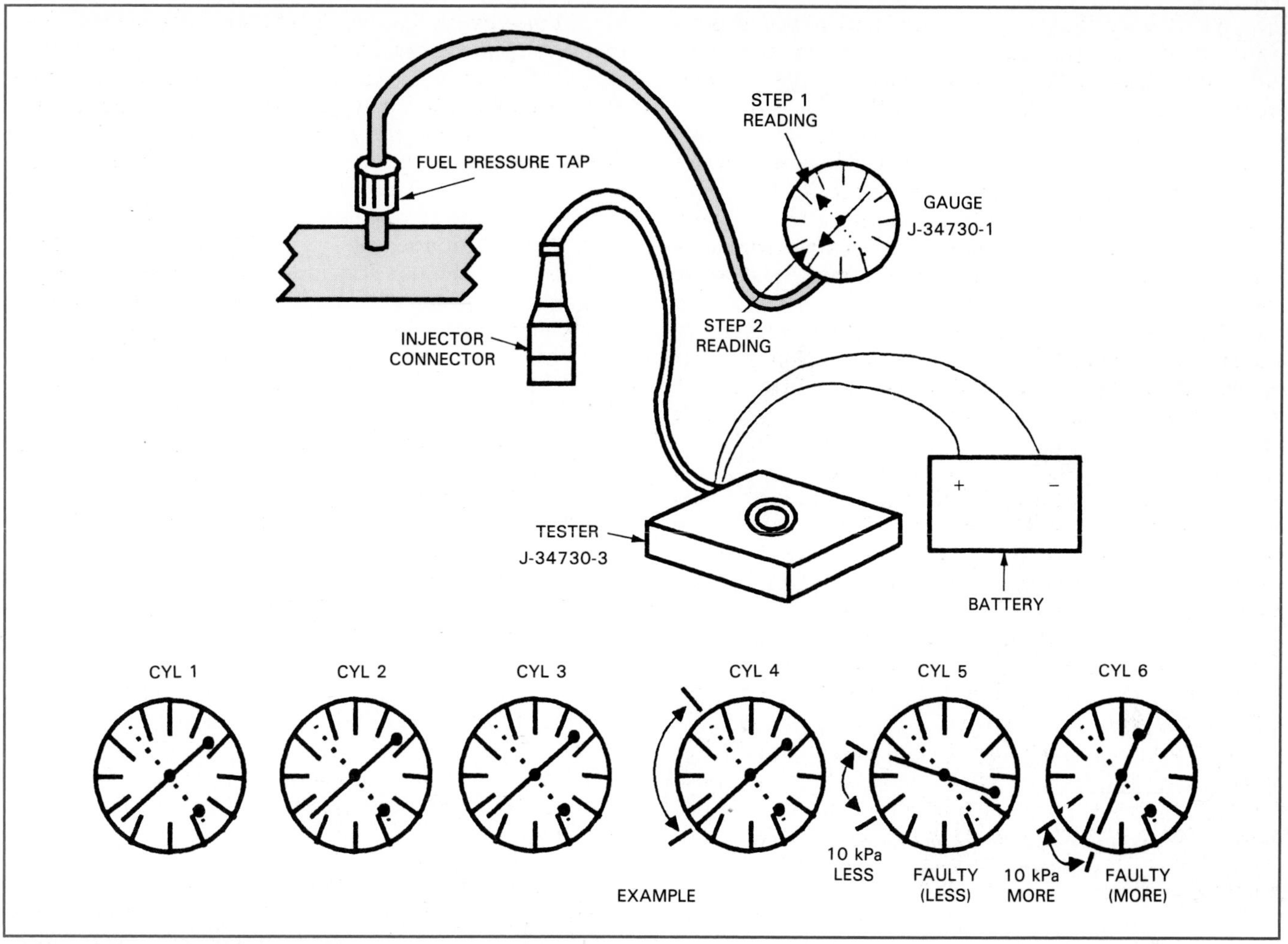

Figure 22-19. With gauge and tester installed, note the drop in pressure after energizing the injector with the tester. Before moving the tester to the electrical connection at the next injector, turn the ignition to the "off" position. Once the tester has been connected, the ignition is again turned to the "on" position. After testing all injectors, compare the readings. If any reading is more or less than 10 kPa, the corresponding injector is defective. (Oldsmobile)

mulator is defective. A leaky fuel injector will show up in an injector balance test as shown in Figure 22-19. A defective pressure regulator may also cause a hard-start condition. The test for this was covered earlier in the chapter.

A defective fuel pump relay may also cause hard starting. The fuel pump is wired in parallel with the oil pressure switch. This acts as a back-up for the relay. If the relay is defective, it will take a lot of cranking for the engine to build up enough oil pressure to close the switch. The closed switch then allows current to the fuel pump motor.

Releasing Fuel Pressure

⚠ The high fuel pressure in the lines of a fuel injection system can cause serious harm if opened without first releasing pressure. When releasing the pressure in a fuel injection system, follow the manufacturer's recommendations carefully.

Most fuel injection systems have a port to test and relieve fuel pressure, Figure 22-20. A gauge is connected to

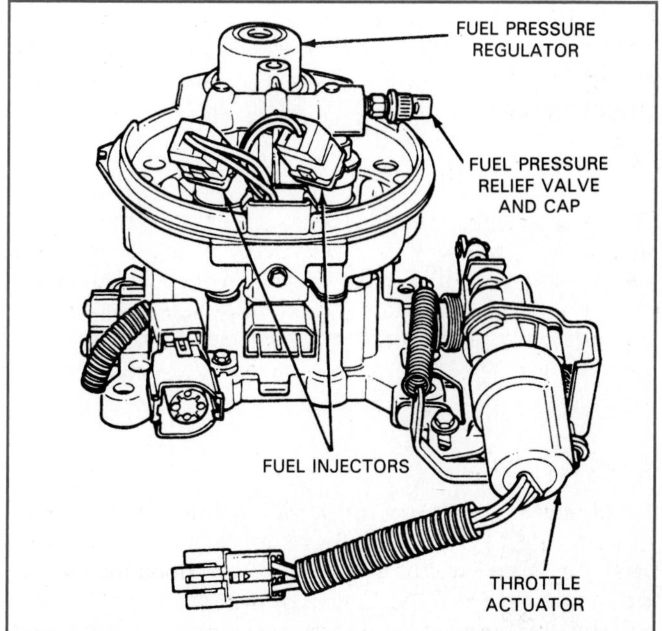

Figure 22-20. With a fuel pressure relief valve, a gauge can be easily connected to this point. Fuel is then discharged through the gauge. (Ford)

the port, Figure 22-15. Fuel is discharged through drain tube after opening the drain valve. Make sure that the pump is not energized and that the ignition is at the "off" position when relieving pressure.

On systems that do not have a port to relieve fuel pressure (Chrysler), the electrical connection at the injector must be removed, Figure 22-21. Attach two jumper wires to the electrical connections of the injector, Figure 22-22. Attach the other end of one jumper wire to a good ground. Touch the other end of the remaining jumper wire to the battery positive post for no longer than 10 seconds to avoid shorting out the injector, Figure 22-23. The energized injector will discharge the fuel through the injector. The system will then be safe to open and service. To test fuel pressure on this system, a "T" must be inserted in the fuel return line.

Fuel Injection Hoses/Clamps

The fuel hose on fuel injection systems is of a special type. Use only a fuel hose that is marked "EFM/EFI." Regular fuel hose cannot be used on a fuel injection system. Also, use only fuel hose clamps that have a "rolled edge." If regular worm-type clamps are used, the sharp edges can cut into the fuel hose. The fuel in a fuel injection system is under greater pressure than the fuel in a carbureted system. A small nick or cut in the fuel line will have a serious effect in a fuel injection system.

Starting an EFI Engine

On carbureted engines, the driver has to depress the accelerator once or twice before turning the ignition switch to start the engine. This action sets the choke and squirts a shot of fuel into the manifold.

On EFI systems, the accelerator pedal is *never* depressed before or during the start of the engine; there is no choke to set. When the engine is not being cranked, the driver can depress the accelerator pedal all day and fuel will NOT come out of the injector. The fuel injector is energized by the computer when it sees a signal from the crankshaft position sensor.

If the accelerator is held to the floor while cranking the engine, the computer interprets this as a flooded engine. The computer then shuts off the supply of fuel. Therefore, no fuel is supplied during cranking and the engine will not start. If the engine does not start by simply turning the key, there is something wrong with the system. It is also possible for a maladjusted or binding throttle position sensor to cause a no-start condition.

Diesel Injection

A diesel engine compresses air in the combustion chamber. At the point of maximum compression, fuel is injected into the chamber. Ignition takes place as a result of the high temperature in the combustion chamber.

The fuel is forced into the combustion chamber of a diesel engine by means of a pump and an injector. Since high pressures exist in the combustion chamber at the time of injection, the injection system must develop pressures in excess of combustion chamber pressure.

Figure 22-21. On systems that do not provide a port to test or relieve pressure, disconnect the electrical connection at the injector.

Figure 22-22. Connect one end of each jumper wire to the fuel injector electrical connection.

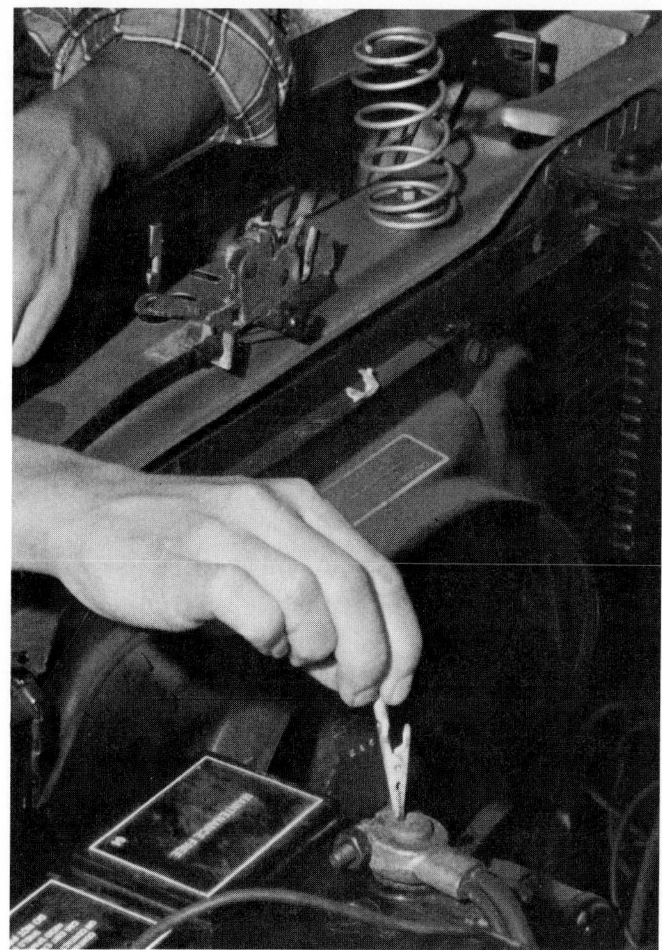

Figure 22-23. Connect the free end of one jumper wire to a good ground. With the remaining jumper wire end, touch it to the battery positive post. Fuel will be discharged through injector into the intake manifold.

In delivering the fuel to the combustion chamber, a diesel fuel injection system must fulfill several requirements:

- Meter or measure correct quantity of fuel injected.
- Time of fuel injection.
- Control rate of fuel injection.
- Atomize fuel into fine particles.
- Properly distribute fuel in combustion chamber.

Methods of Diesel Injection

There are two different methods of diesel fuel injection: air injection and mechanical injection.

In the ***air injection system,*** a blast of air from an external source forces a measured amount of fuel into the cylinder.

In the ***mechanical injection system,*** fuel is forced into the cylinder by hydraulic pressure on the fuel. This is the most common type of diesel injection system.

There are four types of mechanical diesel fuel injection systems:

- Common rail system.
- Pump controlled (or jerk pump) system.
- Unit injection system.
- Distributor system.

Common Rail System. The ***common rail system*** consists of a high-pressure pump that distributes fuel to a common rail or header to which each injector is connected by tubing, Figure 22-24.

Pump-controlled System. The ***pump-controlled system*** is also known as the jerk pump system. It consists of a single pump for each injector. The pump is mounted separately. It is driven by an accessory shaft. Connection to the injectors is made by suitable tubing.

Unit Injector System. The ***unit injector system*** combines the pump and the injector into a single unit. High-pressure fuel lines are not needed. The unit injector is operated by push rods and rocker arms.

Distributor System. There are several types of ***distributor systems.*** One type provides a high-pressure metering pump with a distributor. Another design provides low-pressure metering and distribution. High pressure needed for injection is met by the injection nozzles, which are cam operated.

Mechanical Injection Pumps

The ***mechanical fuel injection pump*** performs many functions. It times, meters, and forces the fuel at high pressure through the spray nozzle.

Most designs are of the plunger type and are cam operated, but there is variation in the method used to control the quantity of fuel delivered. Among the methods of controlling the amount of fuel are the:

- Variable-stroke method.
- Throttle inlet method.
- Throttle bypass method.
- Timed-bypass method.
- Port control method.

Current design favors the port opening method of control.

Variable-stroke Method. In the ***variable-stroke method,*** the stroke is changed by sliding a cam plate in or out of its slot in the hollow camshaft. Axial movement of the camshaft is governor controlled, which, in turn, creates radial displacement of the cam plate.

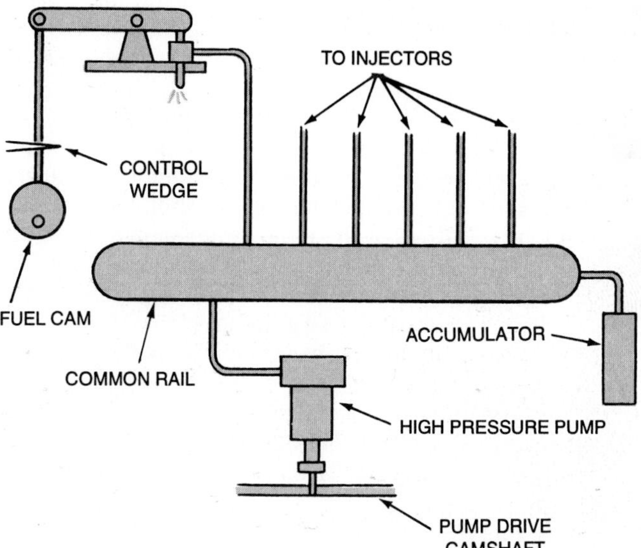

Figure 22-24. Simple drawing of a common rail system for mechanical fuel injection.

Throttle Inlet Method. In the ***throttle inlet method,*** the flow of fuel into the pumping cylinder is throttled. This is done by rotation of a metering valve, which varies the port opening into the plunger bore.

Throttle Bypass Method. In the ***throttle bypass method***, metered fuel in the plunger chamber is discharged to the nozzle. At the same time, it is bypassed through a throttle valve back to the inlet. The size of the bypass port opening is varied by governor action controlling a needle valve.

Timed-bypass Method. In the ***timed-bypass method,*** fuel is controlled by spilling the excess to a mechanically operated bypass valve. The amount of fuel discharged is controlled by the rotation of an eccentric shaft on which a rocking lever pivots. Fuel delivery starts on the upstroke of the plunger and stops when the bypass valve is lifted by contact with the rocking lever.

Port Control Method. In the ***port control method,*** a portion of the plunger functions as a valve to cover and uncover ports in the plunger barrel. A groove on the plunger is designed to rotate so that the plunger stroke can be varied, thus controlling the amount of fuel delivered on each stroke.

American Bosch Diesel Systems

The American Bosch Corporation produces fuel injection pumps for single and multi-cylinder engines. The pumps for single cylinder engines are of the constant-stroke, lapped-plunger, port-controlled type. For multi-cylinder engines, American Bosch produces the constant-stroke type and the single-plunger distributor-type pump.

Typical of the port-controlled type are the APE and the APF series. An APE series pump is shown in Figure 22-25. Each pump element is so accurately fitted in the barrel that it provides a seal without any packing, even at high pressures and low speeds. The plunger jacket is milled out along a helical line to provide for the control helix on the plunger. The plunger has two opposing radial holes through which the fuel oil reaches the delivery chamber of the barrel. See Figure 22-26.

The pump plunger is actuated by a cam on the compression stroke and by the plunger spring on the suction stroke. The valve is closed by a spring-loaded delivery valve that is connected with the delivery pipe to the respective nozzles in the engine cylinder.

To vary pump output, the pump valve has a control sleeve with a toothed quadrant clamped on the upper end. A control rod meshes with the toothed quadrant so that the pump plunger can be rotated during operation.

Various positions of the plunger are shown in Figure 22-27. In its upward movement, the plunger closes the intake port, shown at 2 in Figure 22-27. This forces the fuel through the delivery valve to the delivery pipe. Fuel delivery stops as soon as the helix and the inlet port align. The delivery chamber of the barrel is (from that moment) connected to the suction chamber through the longitudinal and annular grooves. The fuel is forced back into the suction chamber. If the plunger is turned far enough for the longitudinal groove and inlet port to meet, as at 6 in Figure 22-27, the fuel in the delivery chamber is not subjected to pressure and no fuel will be delivered.

The injection nozzle used in the diesel system made by American Bosch is designed to control the mixture in the combustion chamber. American Bosch nozzles are of the pintle type or hole type, Figures 22-28 and 22-29.

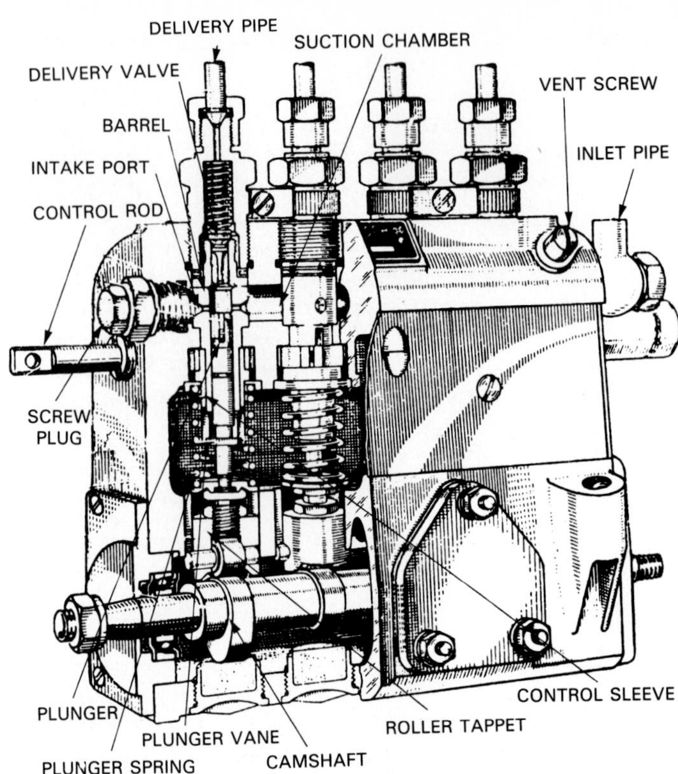

Figure 22-25. Bosch APE series diesel injection pump.

In the case of the pintle type, the nozzle valve carries an extension on the lower end in the form of a pin called a ***pintle.*** The pintle protrudes through the closely fitting hole in the nozzle bottom. This requires the injected fuel to pass through a ring-shaped orifice to produce a hollow cone-shaped spray. The projection of the pintle through the nozzle

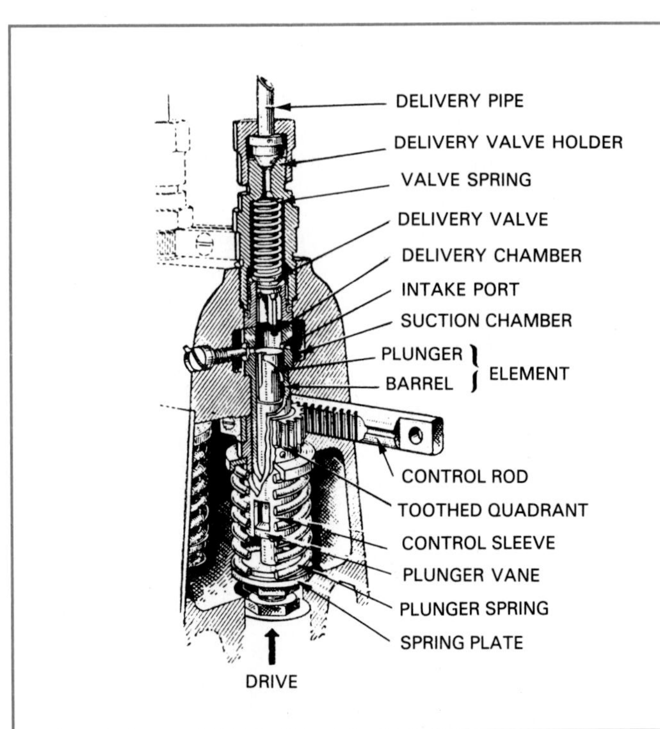

Figure 22-26. Cross section of a Bosch pump element.

creates a self cleaning effect. This reduces the amount of carbon build-up at that point.

The hole-type nozzle has no pintle, but is similar to the pintle type. The hole-type nozzle has one or more spray orifices, which are straight round holes through the tip of the nozzle body beneath the valve seat, Figure 22-29. Spray from each individual orifice is relatively dense and compact. The spray pattern is determined by the number and arrangement of the holes. As many as 18 holes can be provided in the larger nozzles. The diameter of the individual orifices may be as small as .006″. The spray pattern may or may not be symmetrical (regular in shape), depending on the contours of the combustion chamber and fuel distribution needs.

Nozzle Operation

The operation of the nozzle is controlled by the fuel pressure. As soon as pressure is exerted during the delivery stroke, the injection pump exceeds the tension of the pressure spring in the nozzle holder. Pressure acting on the taper of the nozzle needle causes the needle to be lifted off its seat. Fuel is then injected into the combustion chamber.

Nozzle opening pressure (which is adjustable) is determined by the tension of the pressure spring in the nozzle holder, Figure 22-28. The needle stroke is limited by the plane surface of the nozzle holder.

When injected, fuel flows through the delivery pipe, connector, and pressure passage of the nozzle holder, Figure 22-28. It then flows through the groove and passage of the nozzle, out the injection hole or holes of the nozzle, and into the combustion chamber.

Delivering clean fuel to the nozzles cannot be stressed enough. Because of the closely fitted parts, even microscopic foreign matter can cause problems and wear of the parts. Because of this, two or more filters are installed, Figure 22-30. The first, or primary, filter is designed to remove the larger and heavier particles. The final filter should be capable of removing particles down to 3 to 5 microns (0.00012-0.00020″).

American Bosch Distributor-type Pumps

There are two American Bosch distributor-type pumps: the PS series and the series 100. These pumps utilize a single hardened steel plunger that moves back and

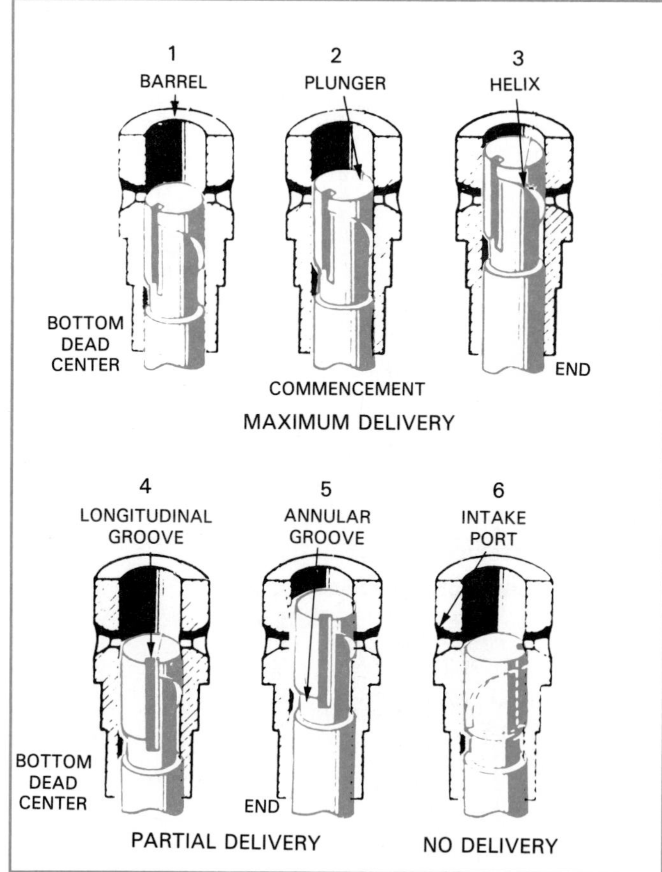

Figure 22-27. Rotation of the plunger controls the quantity of fuel delivered.

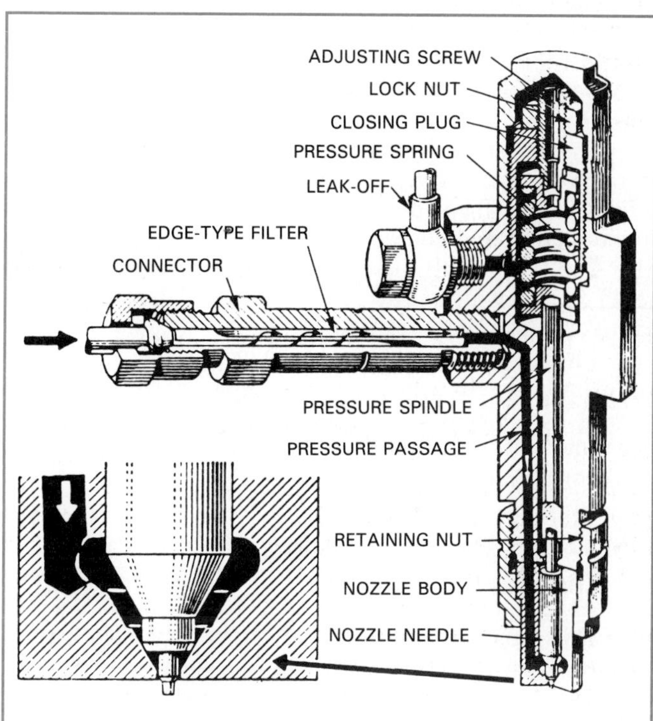

Figure 22-28. Bosch pintle-type nozzle.

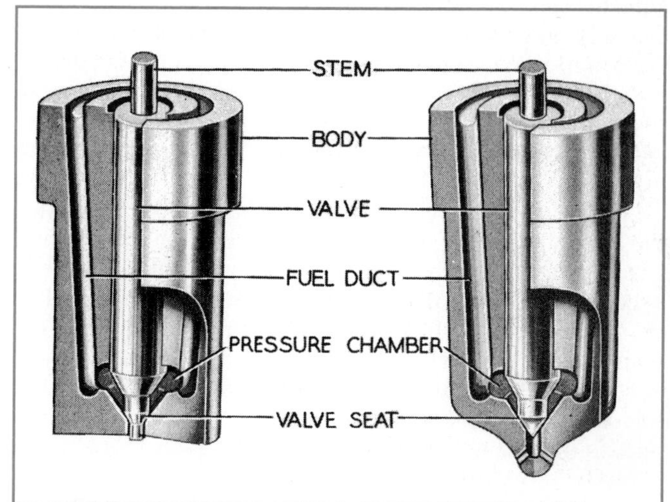

Figure 22-29. Pintle- and hole-type fuel injectors.

forth for pumping action. It also rotates for constant distribution of the fuel to the discharge outlets and from the discharge outlets to the engine.

The model 100 is a flange-mounted, high-speed (up to 3200 rpm), variable-timing, governor-controlled, high-pressure, single-plunger, distributor-type injection pump. It is designed for off-highway vehicles and for marine and industrial use.

The replaceable hydraulic head contains a delivery valve and a plunger, which, in addition to being actuated by a multi-lobe cam, is continuously rotated to serve as a fuel distributor.

Fuel distribution does not need to be adjusted. Therefore, the only adjustments are for average fuel deliveries. Changes in fuel delivery are controlled by the vertical movement of the plunger metering sleeve. This sleeve is actuated by the control unit which, in turn, is operated by the control rod.

A centrifugal, mechanical-type governor actuates the control rod. The governor controls idle speed, maximum no-load speed, and fuel delivery throughout the speed range for any given throttle position.

The fuel supply pump draws fuel from the supply tank through a primary filter and then supplies the fuel through a final filter to the hydraulic head sump area. Fuel pressure in the sump area is controlled by the overflow valve assembly. The fuel supply pump contains an integral pressure relief valve, which prevents fuel system damage in the event of downstream restriction.

An internal timing device, which is known as the Intravance®, automatically advances or retards the beginning of fuel injection as engine speed changes. Also, there is an internal starting device that provides increased fuel at cranking speeds.

GM Diesel Injection System for Commercial Vehicles

This General Motors diesel engine operates on the two-cycle principle and has a unit injector fuel system. In this system, a single unit measures the amount of fuel to be injected under varying conditions of speed and load. Next, it builds up the high pressure needed to inject the fuel into the combustion chamber, which is filled with air at a pressure of 1000 lbs. per sq. in. Then, it atomizes the fuel. There is no central metering or pressure pump and, therefore, high-pressure fuel distributing lines are not needed.

In the GM unit-injection system, high pressures exist only at the tip of the injector. Each injector is complete. After repair work, or having run dry, it is not necessary to prime the GM injector.

The complete fuel system, Figure 22-31, consists of the fuel supply tank, fuel line, fuel filters, fuel pump, fuel line manifold, and the fuel injector. A separate injector is needed for each cylinder. From the supply tank, fuel is drawn through the first fuel strainer or filter by the fuel pump. Then, the fuel is forced through the second filter to the fuel intake manifold that supplies fuel to each of the injectors. The unused fuel is returned through the outlet manifold to the supply tank.

The cross-sectional view of the engine, Figure 22-32, shows the injector mounted in the cylinder head. Figure 22-33 shows details of the injector.

In the GM unit injector, Figure 22-33, fuel is supplied to the injector at about 20 psi and enters the body through the filter cap. The fuel passes through the filter and fills the chamber between the bushing and the spill deflector. The plunger moves up and down by means of the engine camshaft, push rods, and rocker arms. It operates in a bushing

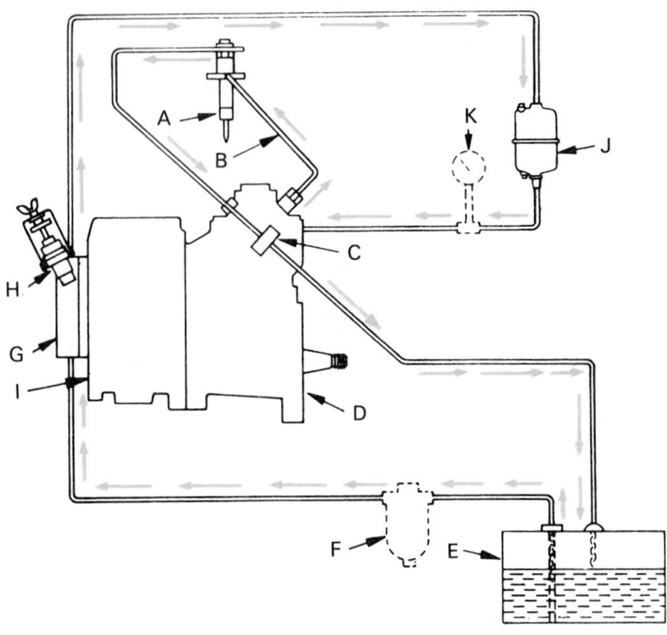

Figure 22-30. American Bosch PSJ system. A–Injector. B–High-pressure fuel. C–Overflow valve. D–Injection pump. E–Tank. F–Primary filter. G–Supply pump. H–Priming pump. I–Governor housing. J–Final filter. K–Fuel pressure gauge, if used.

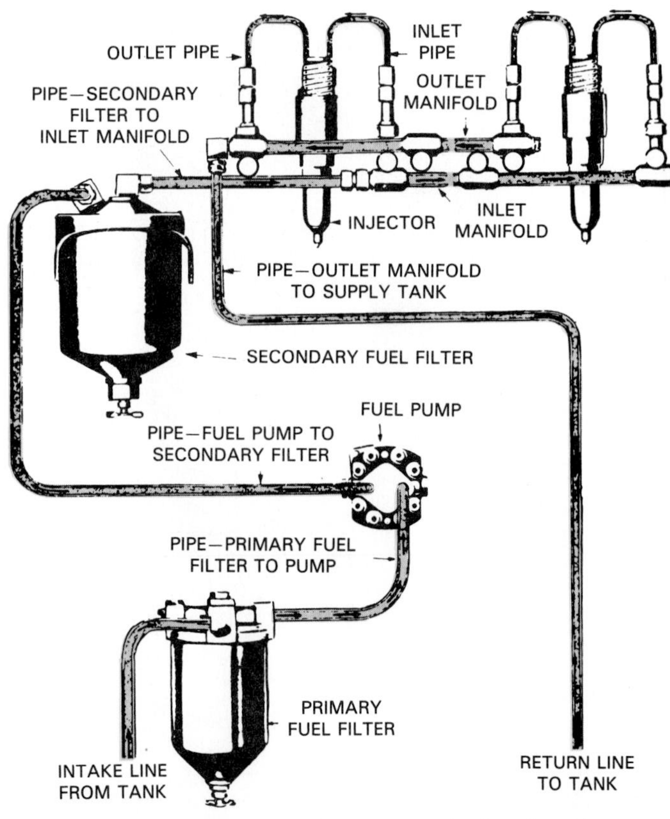

Figure 22-31. Fuel system for a two-cycle diesel engine.

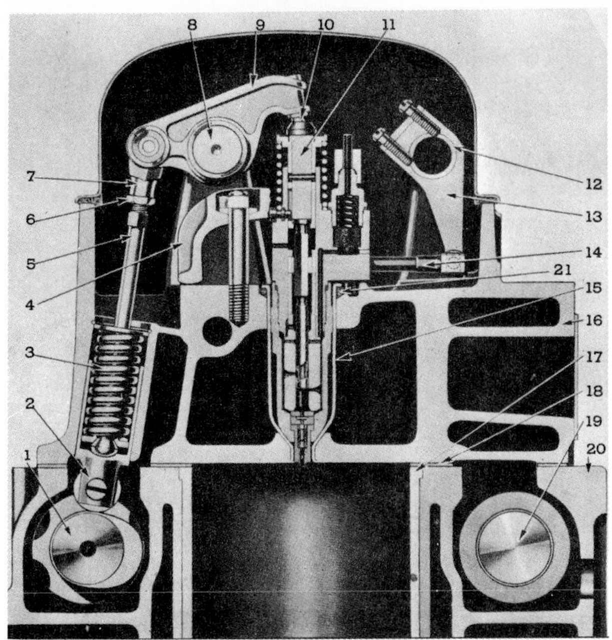

Figure 22-32. Cross section of a GM diesel cylinder head and injector.

connected by means of ports to the fuel supply in the annular chamber.

The motion of the injector rocker arm is relayed to the plunger by the follower that bears against the return spring. By means of the gear and rack, the plunger can be rotated. An upper helix and a lower helix are machined into the lower end of the plunger for the purpose of metering fuel. As the plunger is rotated, the relation of the two helixes with the plunger ports is changed.

As the plunger moves downward, fuel in the injector high-pressure cylinder is displaced through two ports. It flows back into the supply chamber until the lower edge of the plunger closes the ports. The remainder of the oil is then forced upward through the central passage in the plunger and into the recess between the two helixes. From there, it can still flow back into the supply chamber of the injector until the upper helix closes the upper port.

At this point, both upper and lower ports are closed. The fuel remaining under the plunger is then forced through the spray tip and into the combustion chamber of the engine. Changing the position of the helixes by rotating the plunger retards or advances the closing of the ports. It also signals the beginning and ending of the injection and

1. FOLLOWER.
2. FOLLOWER GUIDE.
3. PLUNGER SPRING.
4. FOLLOWER PIN.
5. STOP PIN.
6. GEAR.
7. RACK.
8. SEAL RING.
9. GEAR RETAINER.
10. UPPER HELIX.
11. METERING RECESS.
12. UPPER PORT.
13. BUSHING.
14. SPILL DEFLECTOR.
15. SPACER.
16. CHECK VALVE.
17. VALVE SEAT.
18. VALVE.
19. VALVE SPRING.
20. VALVE STOP.
21. FILTER CAP.
21A. GASKET-FILTER CAP.
22. FILTER SPRING.
23. FILTER ASSEMBLY.
24. INJECTOR BODY.
25. INJECTOR NUT.
26. INJECTOR PLUNGER.
27. FUEL CHAMBER.
28. LOWER HELIX.
29. LOWER PORT.
30. SPRAY TIP.

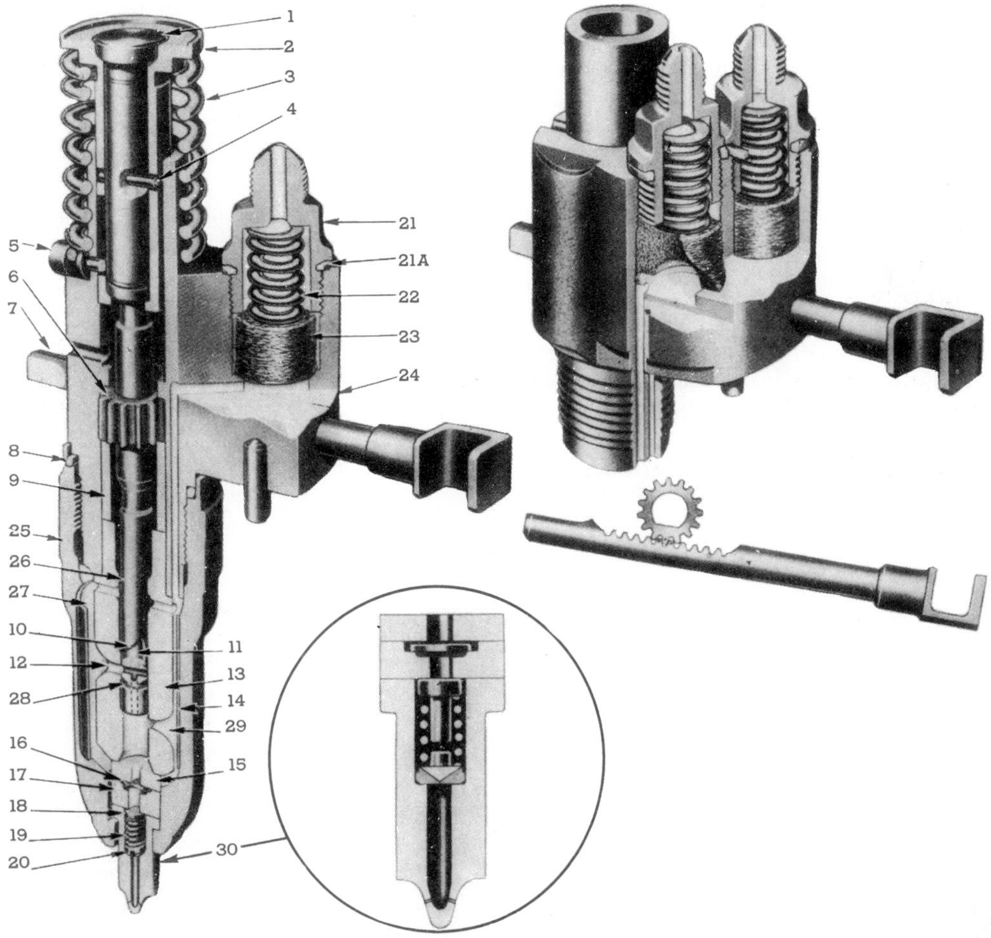

Figure 22-33. A GM injector.

controls the desired amount of fuel that remains under the plunger for injection into the combustion chamber.

The positions of the plunger from no injection to full injection are shown in Figure 22-34. Full injection is obtained with the control rack pushed in. In this position, the upper port is closed shortly after the lower port has been covered. In this way, a full effective stroke and maximum injection is produced. When the control rack is pulled out completely, the upper port is not closed by the helix until after the lower port is uncovered. As a result, all of the fuel charge is forced back into the supply chamber and no injection of fuel occurs.

The four positions for the downward travel of the plunger are shown in Figure 22-35. On downward travel, the plunger forces the metered amount of fuel through the valve assembly, through the check valve, Figure 22-33, and against the spray tip valve.

When enough pressure has been built up on the fuel, the spray tip valve is lifted from its seat and fuel is forced through the small orifices in the spray tip and into the combustion chamber. The check valve prevents air leakage from the engine combustion chamber into the injector. If the valve is held open by carbon or dirt, the check valve permits the injector to operate until the foreign matter works through the valve.

On the upward return movement of the plunger, the high-pressure cylinder is again filled with fuel through the ports. The constant circulation of fresh fuel oil in the fuel supply chamber helps maintain even operating temperatures. Also, all traces of air are done away with.

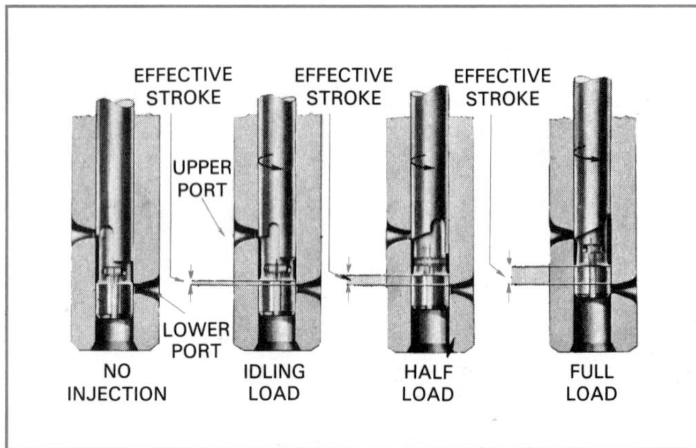

Figure 22-34. Four positions of a GM injector.

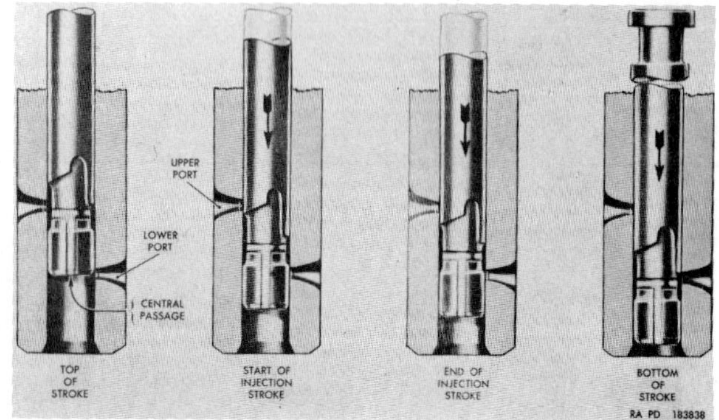

Figure 22-35. Four positions of downward travel of a GM injector.

Each injector control rack is operated by a lever on a common control shaft. This shaft, in turn, is linked to the governor and the throttle. These levers can be rotated independently on the control shaft by the adjustment of two screws, and permit an even setting of the injector racks.

Cummins Pressure-time System

The Cummins pressure-time system for diesel engines operates on the pressure-time principle. This principle is based on the fact that by changing the pressure of a liquid flowing through a pipe, the amount of liquid coming out the open end is changed. Raising the pressure increases the amount of liquid delivered. This system consists of the fuel pump (with governor), the supply and drain lines, and the injectors, Figure 22-36.

The fuel pump, Figure 22-37, is made of three units:

- Gear pump–Draws fuel from the supply tank and delivers it under pressure through pump and supply lines to each injector.
- Pressure regulator–Limits pressure of fuel to injectors.
- Governor and throttle–Act independently of pressure regulator to control fuel pressure to regulators. Fuel pump is driven at crankshaft speed.

The gear pump is located at the rear of the fuel pump, Figure 22-37. It consists of one set of gears that pick up and deliver fuel throughout the system, Figure 22-36.

The pressure regulator is a bypass valve to regulate the fuel under pressure to the injectors. Fuel for the engine flows past the pressure regulator to throttle shaft, Figure 22-38. The fuel passes around the shaft to the idle jet in the governor. For operation above idle, fuel passes through the throttling hole in the shaft and enters the governor through the primary jets.

Mechanical governor action is met by a system of springs and weights, Figure 22-38. The governor maintains enough fuel for idling and cuts it off above the rated rpm. Governors vary according to engine needs.

Cummins Injectors

The injector used with the Cummins PT system is shown in Figure 22-39. Fuel constantly circulates through the injector, except during a short period following injection into the combustion chamber. From the inlet connection, fuel flows down the inlet passage of the injector, around the injector plunger, between the body end and cup, out the drain passage to the drain connections and manifold, and back to the supply tank.

As the plunger comes up, the injector feed passage is opened and fuel flows through the metering orifice and into the cup. At the same time, fuel flows past the cup and out the drain orifice. The amount of fuel entering the cup is controlled by the fuel pressure against the metering orifice. Fuel pressure is controlled by the fuel pump.

During injection, Figure 22-40, the plunger comes down until the orifice is closed. The fuel in the cup is injected into the cylinder. When the plunger is seated in the cup, all fuel flow in the injector is stopped. The flow diagram for this system is shown in Figure 22-41.

Cummins Metering Pump Injection System

Another Cummins system, the metering pump injection system, employs a metering pump to measure each

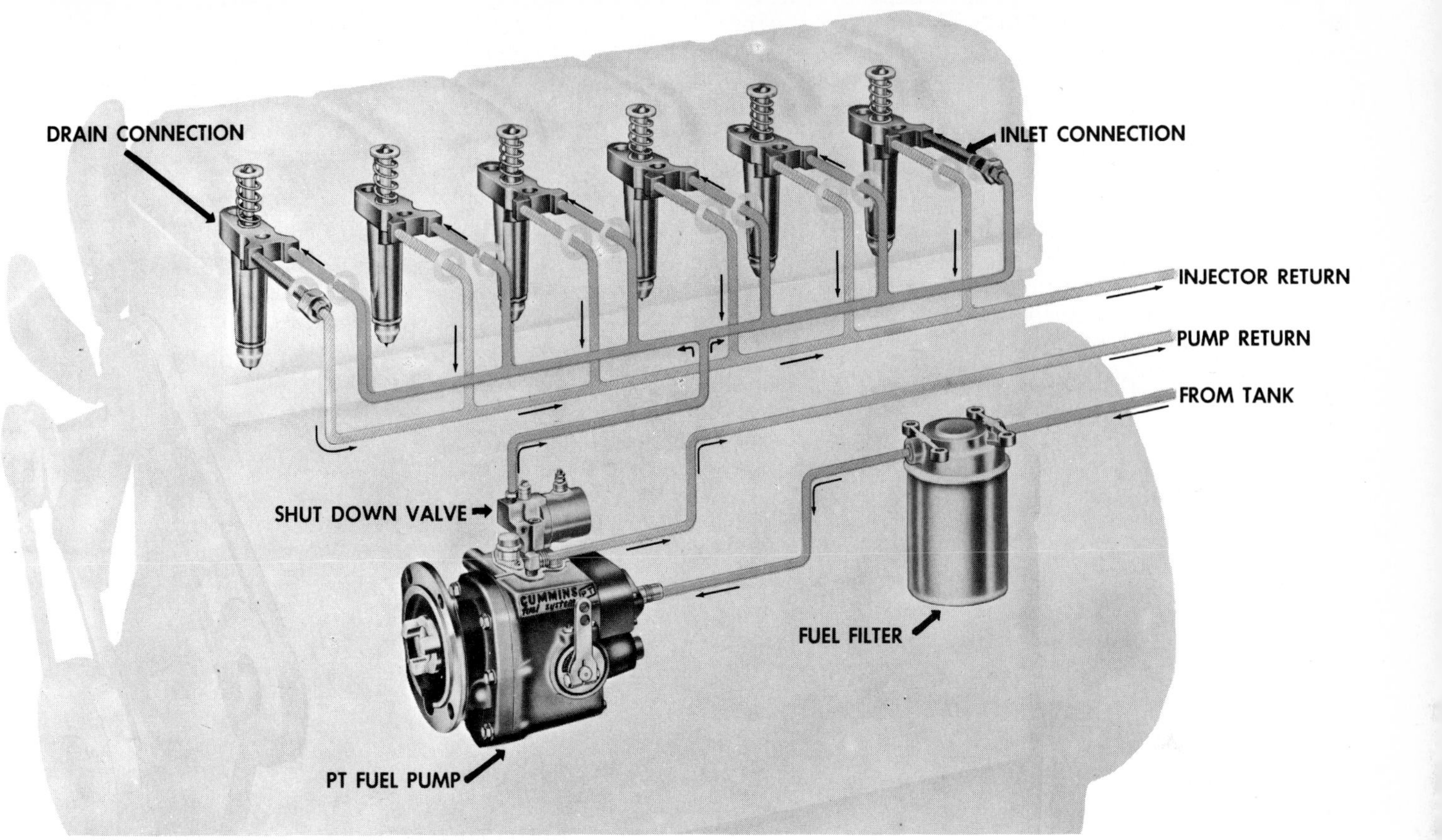

Figure 22-36. Fuel flow of a Cummins PT system.

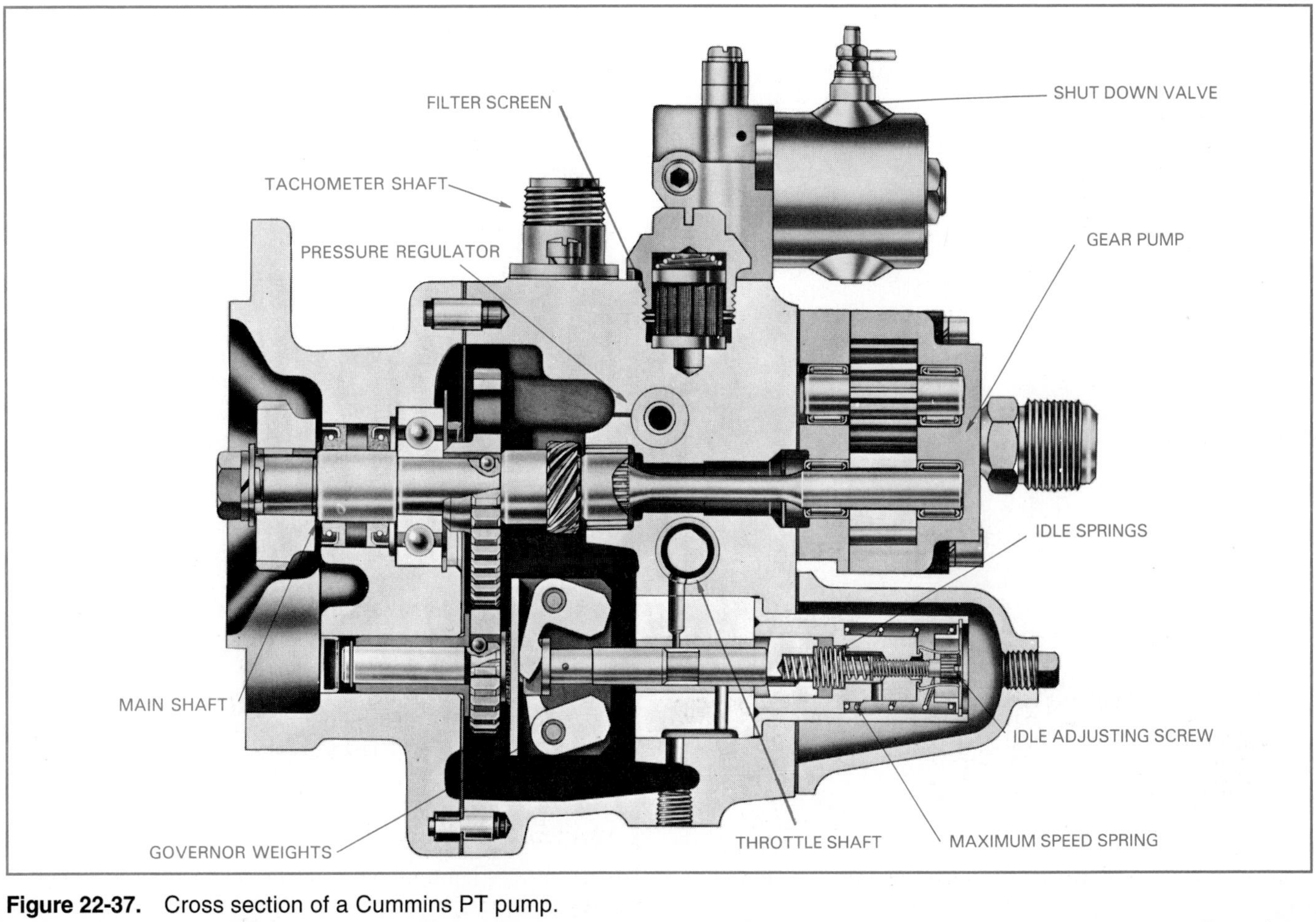

Figure 22-37. Cross section of a Cummins PT pump.

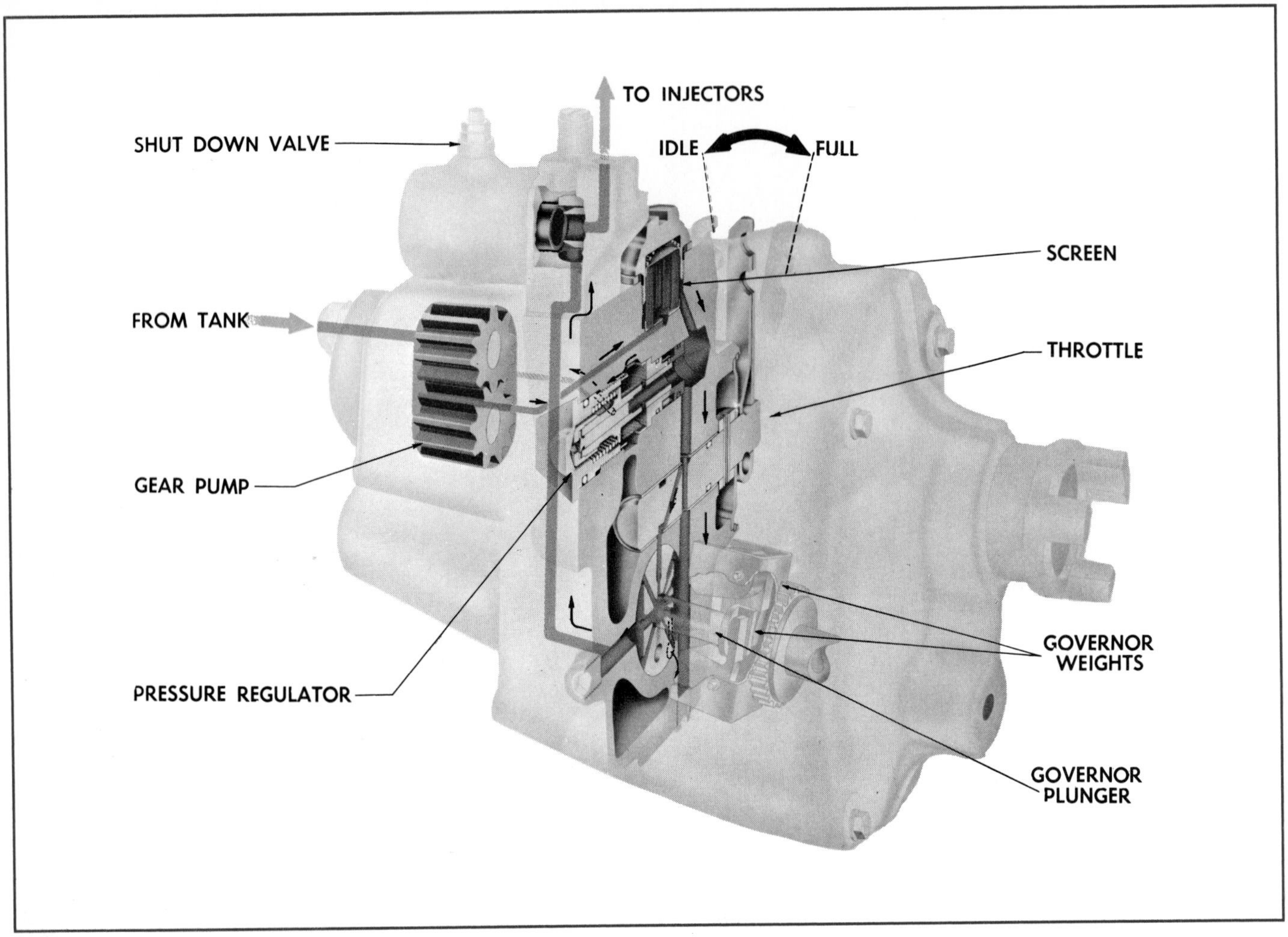

Figure 22-38. Fuel flow through the pump.

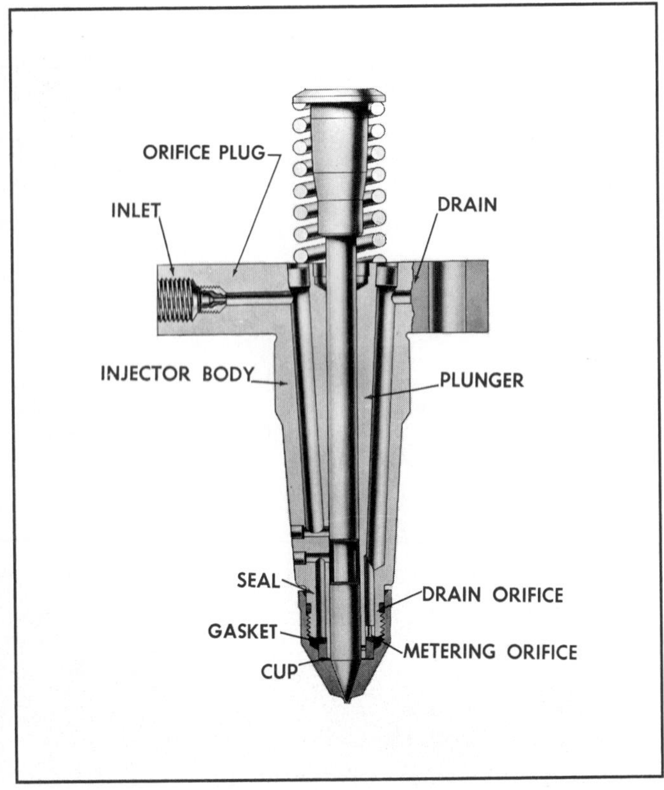

Figure 22-39. Cross section of a Cummins injector.

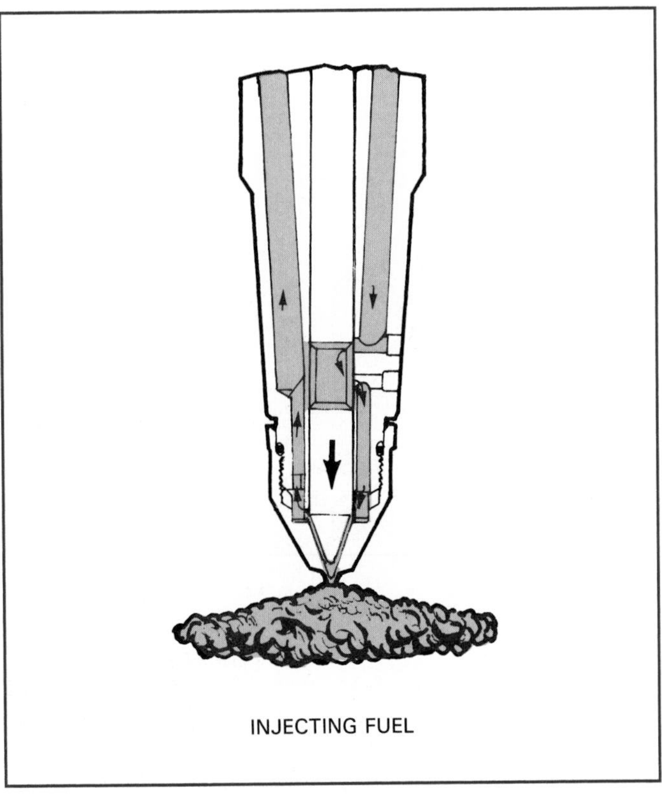

Figure 22-40. Fuel flow through the injector.

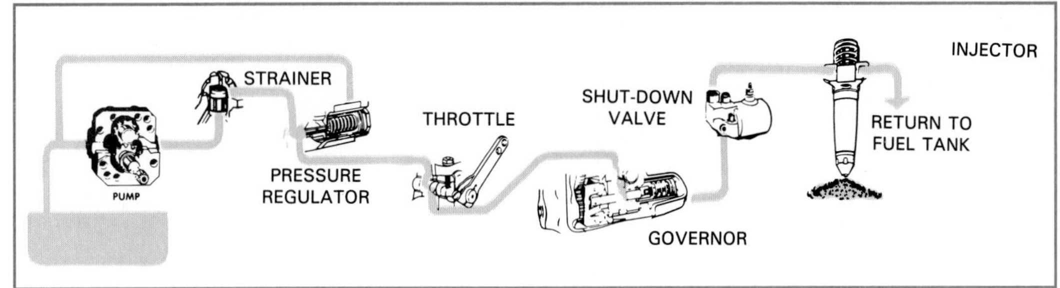

Figure 22-41. Fuel flow through a Cummins PT system.

charge of fuel delivered at low pressure to the injectors. The injectors build up the pressure of the fuel and inject it into the combustion chamber.

The Cummins diesel fuel pump performs four functions:

- Draws fuel from supply tank.
- Meters fuel in equal charges for each cylinder.
- Distributes and delivers metered fuel at the correct instant to each injector.
- Provides a governor for control of idling and maximum engine speeds.

Robert Bosch Injection System

The diesel fuel injection pump installed on many engines is a Bosch PE series pump, Figures 22-42, 22-43, and 22-44. The PE pump contains one pump element, consisting of a cylinder and plunger for each engine cylinder. The plunger is lapped in the cylinder and has a clearance of two to three thousandths of a millimeter. This small clearance serves to stress the importance of extreme cleanliness when working on injectors.

Plungers and cylinders are interchangeable only in complete sets. An injection timing device is built into the drive assembly of the pump, so fuel injection is timed to engine speed. The control rod, 11 in Figure 22-44, is geared to the pinion, 12. The pump plunger, 9, can be turned with the control rod, and the discharge rate of the pump can be varied from zero to maximum.

During the pressure stroke, the plunger is lifted by the cam. During the suction stroke, the plunger is forced down again by the plunger spring, 15 in Figure 22-44. The stroke of the pump plunger cannot be varied. The suction space, 8, is constantly filled with fuel and is kept under pressure by the feed pump. If the pump plunger is at bottom dead center, the control port, 7, is opened and the pressure space, 5, is filled with fuel.

During the upward motion, the plunger closes the control port and pushes fuel through the pressure valve, 4 in Figure 22-44, and into the pressure line, 1. The delivery ends as soon as the upper control edge has reached the

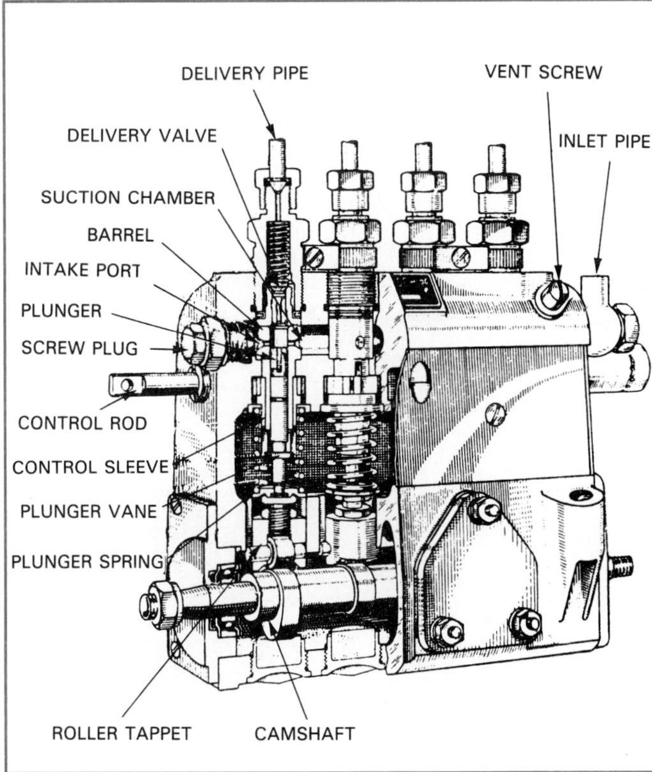

Figure 22-42. Bosch model PE diesel injection pump.

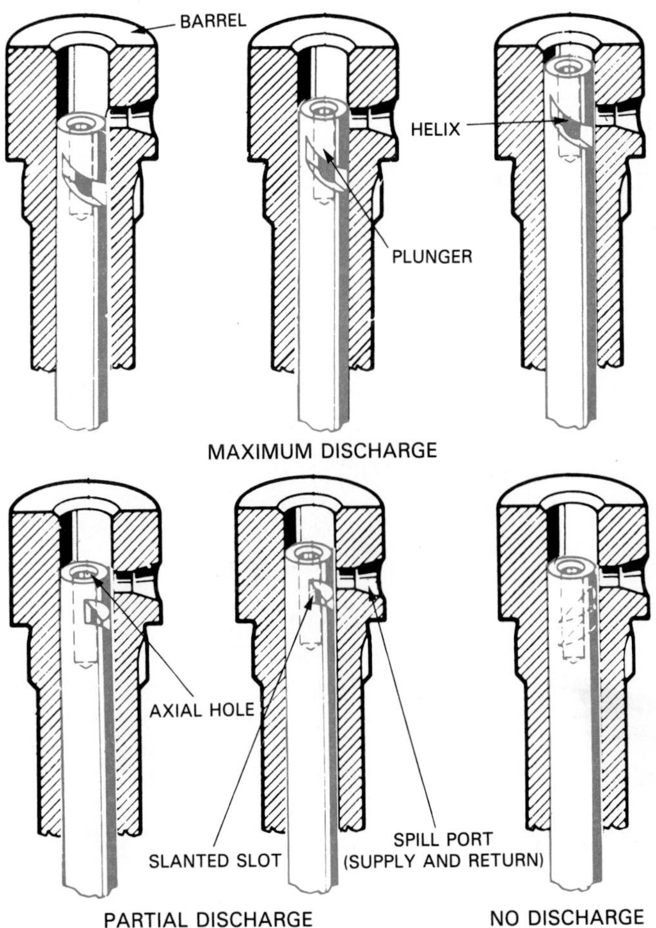

Figure 22-43. Sequence of plunger positions in a Bosch diesel injection pump.

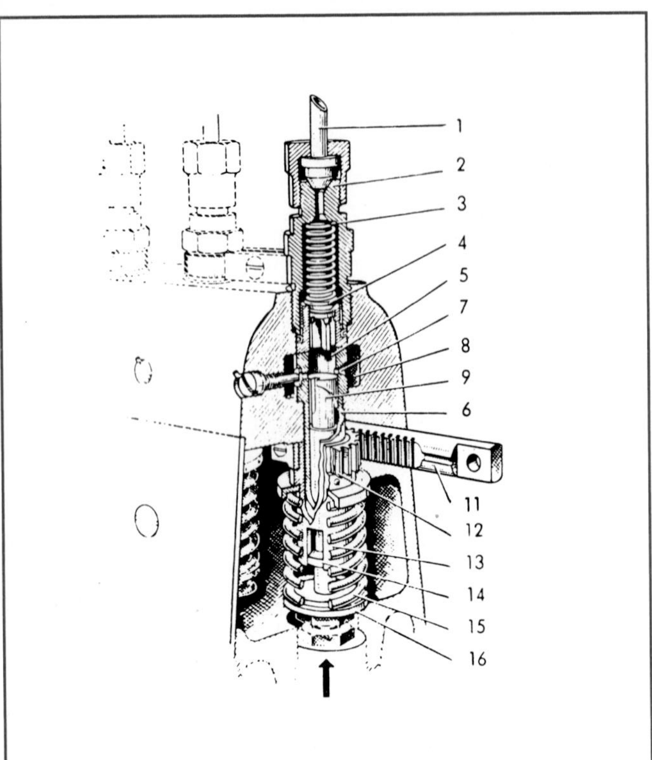

Figure 22-44. Drive mechanisms of a Bosch PE fuel injection pump. 1–Pressure line. 2–Connection. 3–Valve spring. 4–Pressure valve. 5–Pressure space. 6–Pump cylinder. 7–Control port. 8–Suction space. 9–Plunger. 11–Control rod. 12–Pinion. 13–Control rod. 14–Plunger. 15–Plunge spring. 16–Spring retainer.

control port, since the pressure space is connected with the suction space by the compensating hole in the plunger. The discharge rate is varied by turning the plunger, Figure 22-44. The plunger opens the control port sooner or later, depending on the amount the plunger is rotated.

Stanadyne Fuel Injection Pump

The Stanadyne fuel injection pump is a single-cylinder, opposed-plunger, inlet-metering, distributor-type unit, Figure 22-45. It is used largely in high-speed diesel engines. The main components are the drive shaft, distributor rotor, transfer pump, pumping plunger, internal cam ring, hydraulic ring, end plate, and governor.

The Stanadyne fuel injection pump is self-lubricated by the filtered fuel it pumps. There are no spring-loaded lapped surfaces, no ball bearings, and no gears. The rotating members revolve on a common axis. The rotating members include the drive shaft, distributor rotor (containing plungers and mounting governor), and transfer pump.

Fuel is drawn from the supply pump into the inlet strainer, Figure 22-45, by the vane-type transfer pump. Excess fuel is bypassed through the regulating valve back to the inlet side. The amount of flow bypassed increases in proportion to the speed, and the regulating valve is designed so that transfer pressure also increases with speed.

Fuel, which is under transfer pump pressure, is forced through an axial passage to the head and into an annular groove milled around the rotor shank. The fuel flows around the groove and through the metering valve in an amount determined by engine demands.

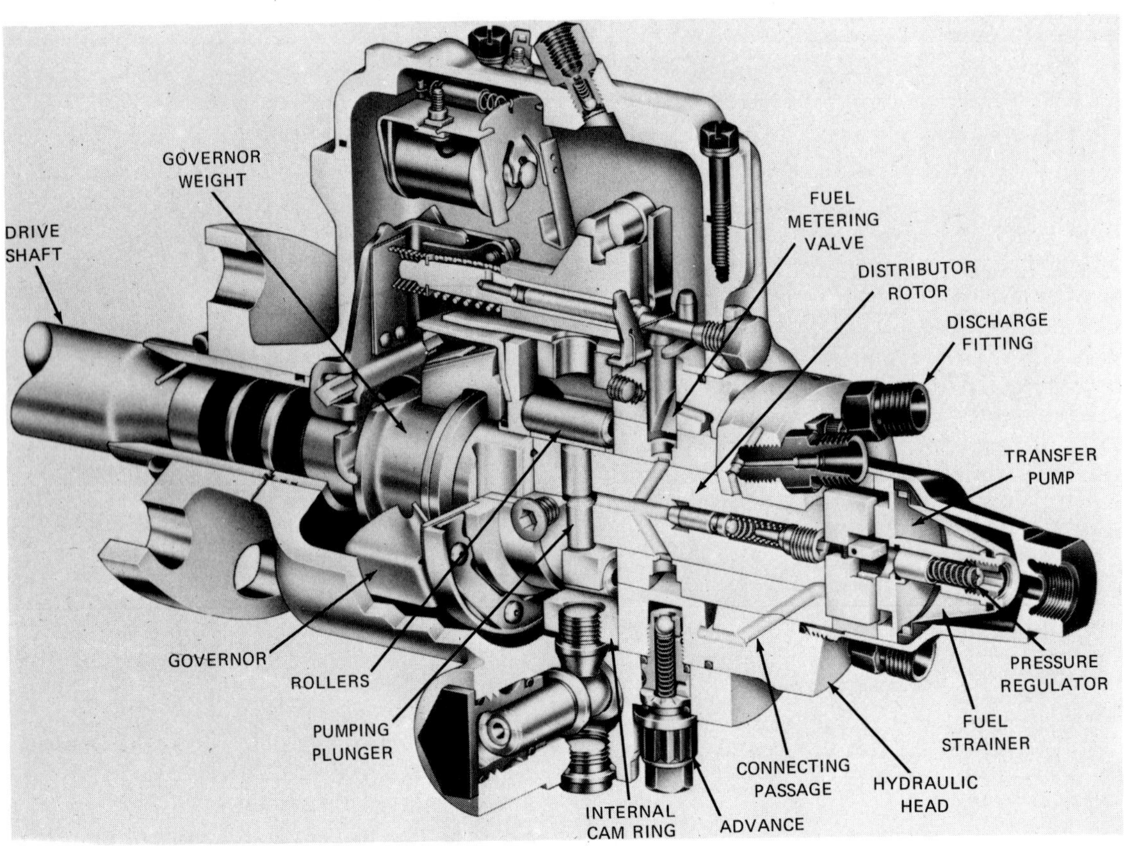

Figure 22-45. Cross section of a Stanadyne pump.

As the rotor revolves, one of its charging ports aligns with a passage, permitting the fuel to enter the axial passage. Inflowing fuel forces the plungers outward for a distance that is equal to the amount of fuel to be injected on the following stroke.

If only a small amount of fuel is admitted into the pumping cylinder, as at idling, the plungers move out very little. As extra fuel is admitted, the plunger stroke increases to the maximum amount allowed by a leaf spring arrangement. See Figure 22-45.

At this point of the cycle, the rollers are in the "valley" of the cam. The fuel is trapped in the cylinder for a short period of time after charging is complete. During this time, the charging port is no longer aligned with the passage and the rotor discharge port has not yet aligned with an outlet port in the hydraulic head. Once it is aligned, fuel is injected into the line.

Chapter 22–Review Questions

Write your answers on a separate sheet of paper. Do not write in this book.

1. When the fuel injector is located in the throttle body, the system is referred to as:
   (A) multi-point injection.
   (B) single-point injection.
   (C) ported injection.
   (D) direct injection.
2. Sequential fuel injection is associated with:
   (A) multi-point injection.
   (B) single-point injection.
   (C) Both A & B.
   (D) Neither A nor B.
3. When the injector sprays fuel directly into a runner instead of an intake manifold, the system is called a _____ system.
   (A) multi-point
   (B) single-point
   (C) ported
   (D) direct
4. Electronic fuel injection includes:
   (A) air induction.
   (B) fuel injection.
   (C) electronic controls.
   (D) All of the above.
   (E) None of the above.
5. Technician A states that the MAP sensor measures the load placed on the engine. Technician B states that the airflow meter measures the load placed on the engine. Who is right?
   (A) A only.
   (B) B only.
   (C) Both A & B.
   (D) Neither A nor B.
6. Hot air is denser than cold air. True or False?
7. Cold air needs a richer fuel mixture. True or False?
8. A stoichiometric air/fuel ratio in an engine that is 100 percent efficient produces:
   (A) water.
   (B) carbon dioxide.
   (C) Both A & B.
   (D) Neither A nor B.
9. A lean air/fuel mixture produces:
   (A) carbon monoxide (CO).
   (B) carbon dioxide (CO_2).
   (C) hydrocarbons (HC).
   (D) None of the above.
10. A rich air/fuel mixture produces:
    (A) carbon monoxide (CO).
    (B) carbon dioxide (CO_2).
    (C) hydrocarbons. (HC).
    (D) None of the above.
11. Define closed loop.
12. Define open loop.
13. Low fuel pressure can be caused by a:
    (A) pressure regulator valve that is stuck open.
    (B) defective fuel pump.
    (C) Both A & B.
    (D) Neither A nor B.
14. Before replacing a fuel filter, the pressure in the fuel system must be released. True or False?
15. Any type of fuel hose and clamps can be used on a fuel injection system. True or False?
16. Technician A states that low fuel pressure can cause a surging condition. Technician B states that low fuel pressure can be caused by a bad fuel pump or a bad pressure regulator. Who is right?
    (A) A only.
    (B) B only.
    (C) Both A & B.
    (D) Neither A nor B.
17. Technician A states that removing the vacuum hose from the pressure regulator should cause a drop in fuel pressure. Technician B states that removing the vacuum hose from the pressure regulator should cause fuel pressure to increase. Who is right?
    (A) A only.
    (B) B only.
    (C) Both A & B.
    (D) Neither A nor B.
18. Technician A states that a leaking injector may cause hard starting or dieseling. Technician B states that a defective fuel pump relay can cause hard starting. Who is right?
    (A) A only.
    (B) B only.
    (C) Both A & B.
    (D) Neither A nor B.
19. Technician A states that the accelerator pedal must be pumped several times prior to and during the starting of an EFI engine. Technician B states that only the key has to be turned to start an EFI engine. Who is right?
    (A) A only.
    (B) B only.
    (C) Both A & B.
    (D) Neither A nor B.
20. On the compression stroke, what does a diesel engine compress?
    (A) Air.
    (B) Air/fuel mixture.
    (C) Diesel fuel.
    (D) None of the above.
21. What are the four basic types of diesel fuel injection used?

22. What five requirements must a diesel fuel injection system fulfill?
23. In the Bosch system, what does the rotation of the pump plunger control?
    (A) The quantity of fuel delivered.
    (B) Timing of injection.
    (C) Compression.
    (D) None of the above.
24. After repair work, is it necessary to prime a General Motors injector?
25. Describe the Cummins PT diesel system.

Cutaway of a fuel-injected V-6 engine. Note the location of the injectors. (General Motors)

Chapter 23
Carburetor Fundamentals and Service

After studying this chapter, you will be able to:
- State the purpose of the carburetor.
- List the circuits of the carburetor.
- Explain Bernoulli's Principle.
- Describe how each circuit of the carburetor works.
- Define what is meant by closed and open loop.
- Diagnose carburetor-related problems.
- Describe the procedure for adjusting carburetor idle speed and air/fuel mixture.

Carburetors

The purpose of the ***carburetor*** is to supply and meter the mixture of fuel vapor and air in relation to the load and speed of the engine. Because of engine temperature, speed, and load, perfect carburetion is difficult to obtain. When a cold engine is first started, a richer than normal air/fuel mixture is needed. When the engine reaches operating temperature, the fuel is easily vaporized and the rich fuel mixture is not needed or wanted. The engine will not run as well with a rich fuel mixture after the engine has warmed up.

Another problem must be overcome by the carburetor. When the engine is at idle or at low speeds, a richer mixture is needed than when it is at medium speeds. However, when maximum power is needed, the air/fuel mixture must be as rich as possible. The problem in designing carburetors is the fact that the airflow rate through the carburetor changes considerably. This is a result of changes in engine speed. At low speeds, the airflow through the carburetor is at a minimum. At maximum engine speed, it will be 100 times greater.

Fuels also present problems in carburetor design. Gasoline is a blend of fractions of crude oil. As a result, some fractions contained in gasoline will boil at 100°F (38°C). Others have boiling points that reach 400°F (204°C). Depending on the temperature of the intake manifold, some cylinders will receive a mixture that is fully vaporized, while others may receive the mixture in a liquid form. Also, some cylinders receive fuel having greater antiknock qualities than others. When the intake manifold is cold, the problem is greater.

Air/fuel Ratio

The best economy is obtained by a mixture of 1 part gasoline to between 16 to 17 parts of air. For quick acceleration and maximum power, a richer mixture of about 1 part gasoline to 12 to 13 parts of air is needed. For idling, a richer mixture is also needed. When starting a cold engine, an extremely rich mixture is needed.

Carburetion Principles

To cause a liquid to flow, there must be a high pressure area, which, in this case, is atmospheric pressure, and a low pressure area. See Figure 23-1. The low pressure is less than atmospheric pressure. The average person refers to a low pressure area as a vacuum. Since atmospheric pressure is already present, a low pressure area can be created by air or a liquid flowing through a venturi, Figure 23-2. The downward motion of the piston also creates a low pressure area.

Likewise, air and gasoline are drawn through a carburetor and into the engine by suction created as the piston moves downward. As the piston moves down, a partial vacuum is created in the cylinder. The difference between this low pressure within the cylinder and atmospheric pressure outside of the carburetor causes air and fuel to flow into the cylinder from the carburetor.

Bernoulli's Principles

The effect of ***Bernoulli's Principle*** is summarized as follows:

A ***venturi*** is a specially designed section of pipe, line, or tube. The area of the tube at the center is reduced in diameter. The same volume of air or fluid flows through all sections of the tube. Therefore, the speed, or velocity, of

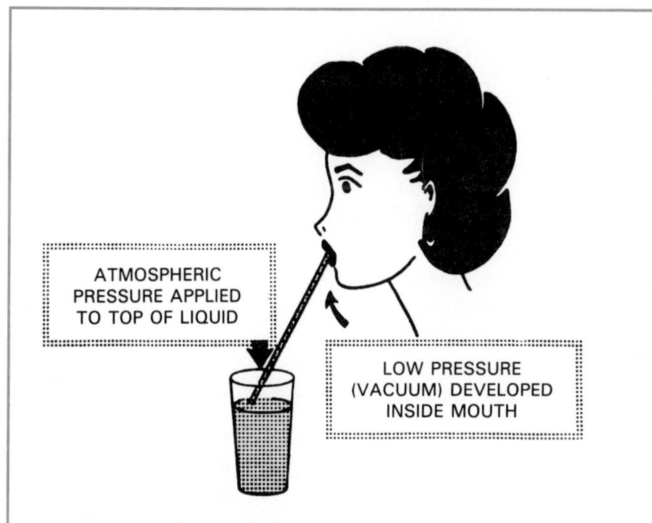

Figure 23-1. Liquid moves from a high-pressure area to a low-pressure area. (Rochester)

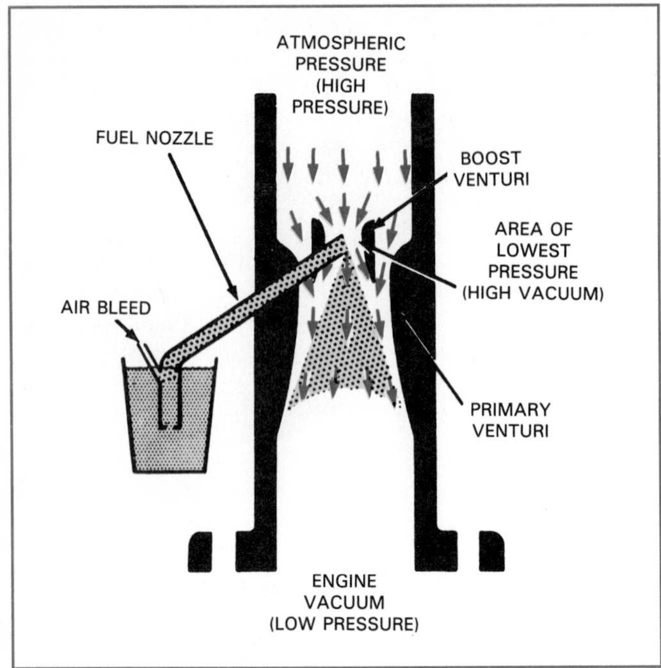

Figure 23-2. As airflow increases, a low pressure area is created within the venturi. (Rochester)

the air or fluid must increase as it passes through the reduced diameter.

The venturi not only increases the velocity of the flow of air that passes through it, but it also produces a low pressure at its point of reduced diameter, Figure 23-2. The outlet of a fuel jet is placed at that point. Fuel is drawn from the jet and mixes with the passing air. This mixing of the fuel with air is known as vaporization, and it closely resembles the action of a spray gun, Figure 23-3.

Some carburetors have as many as three venturis. This design permits a more precise metering of the flow of air and fuel for different conditions. It improves combustion, which has become increasingly important in reducing exhaust emissions.

The difference between the pressure at the venturi and atmospheric pressure on the fuel in the float bowl, Figure 23-2, causes the fuel to flow.

Change of State

All substances, whether solid, liquid, or gas, are made of molecules. In solids such as steel and copper, the particles are so close together they seem to have no motion. In liquids, the molecules are not held together so tightly. As a result, liquids flow. In gases, such as air, the molecules move quite freely.

When molecules of a liquid move from the liquid into the air, the liquid is said to evaporate. As this continues, the liquid disappears from its container and forms vapor in the air. Evaporation varies with a number of factors. These factors include temperature, the pressure above the liquid, the amount of liquid that has already evaporated into the air, and the volatility of the liquid. The term volatility refers to the ease with which a liquid vaporizes. For example, alcohol and benzene are more volatile than water because they evaporate more easily. A highly volatile liquid evaporates rapidly. A liquid of low volatility evaporates slowly.

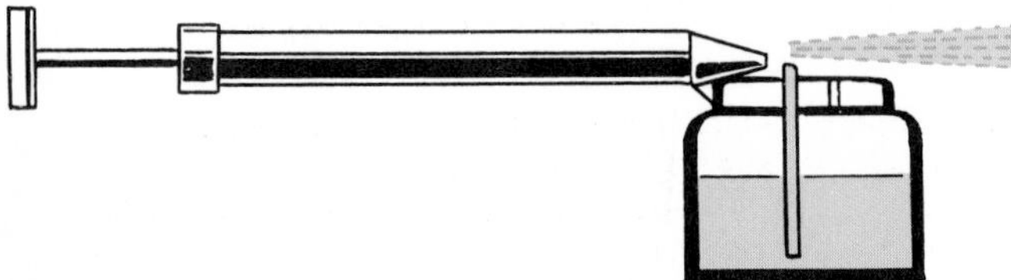

Figure 23-3. A carburetor operates on the same principle as a spray gun.

At higher temperatures, molecules move faster. As a result, the rate of vaporization is increased. When there is little pressure above the liquid, the molecules can escape from the liquid easily. If evaporation takes place in a closed chamber, the evaporation of the liquid will soon stop because the limited space above the liquid becomes filled with vaporized molecules of the liquid. When this occurs, the space above the liquid is said to be saturated.

If a liquid is broken up into tiny particles, it will vaporize more easily. Breaking a liquid into tiny particles is known as ***atomization.*** Spray guns of the type used for spraying insecticides or paint will atomize a liquid. If gasoline is placed in an ordinary spray gun, Figure 23-3, the fuel will be broken into a fine mist that will change into vapor almost instantly.

It is impossible for liquid gasoline to burn until it is changed into a vapor. Therefore, it is only the vapors of gasoline that burn. In order for gasoline to be of any use in a modern engine, the liquid gasoline is changed into a vapor. Whenever atmospheric pressure is reduced on the gasoline, it undergoes a change of state from a liquid to a vapor.

Carburetor Circuits

In order to supply an air/fuel mixture suitable for all conditions–from low speeds to high speeds and from light loads to full loads–a carburetor must be equipped with many circuits and controls. These circuits include the choke circuit, float circuit, idle circuit, transfer circuit, main metering circuit, acceleration circuit, and power circuit. The controls used on the carburetor include the choke unloader, anti-icing, hot idle compensator, and anti-stall dashpot.

Choke Circuit

The purpose of the ***choke circuit*** is to provide a richer-than-normal fuel mixture for a cold engine. A richer mixture is needed because some of the fuel is condensed on the walls of the cold carburetor. Therefore, a rich fuel mixture compensates for the lack of vaporized fuel.

The choke coil forces the ***choke valve*** closed and adjusts the linkage to increase the idle speed, Figure 23-4. The choke plate reduces the amount of cold air that enters the carburetor. This action assists in the evaporation of the fuel in cold weather. The increased idle speed provides the extra fuel needed to compensate for the fuel that is condensed on the walls of the carburetor.

If both actions were not taken, the engine would stall and be hard to start until it had reached operating temperature. Once the engine reaches its normal operating temperature, the choke plate is fully opened and the idle speed is reduced. This is caused by the choke coil relaxing due to the engine heat.

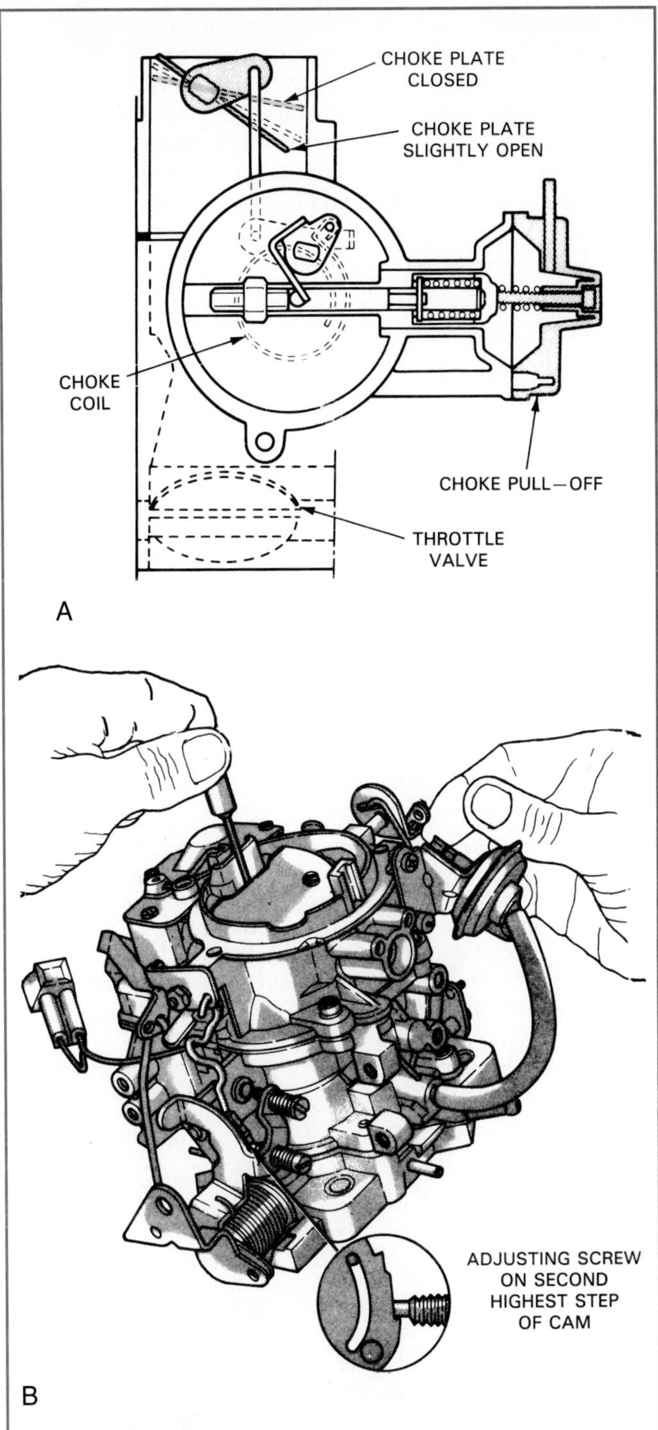

Figure 23-4. When cold, the choke coil sets the choke plate and fast idle speed. A–The choke plate reduces the amount of cold air that enters the carburetor until the engine reaches operating temperature. B–The fast idle speed is obtained by a wedge-shaped cam. Fast idle allows more fuel to flow. (Chrysler)

To start a cold engine, a rich fuel mixture is needed. This is because not all of the fuel will vaporize when the engine is cold. The rich fuel mixture compensates for the fuel that condenses in the throat of the carburetor.

When the choke coil is cold, and after the accelerator is depressed, the coil forces the choke plate closed and, at the same time, positions the fast idle cam. When the choke plate is closed it blocks out the cold air. With the cold air blocked, it is easier for the fuel to vaporize. However, once the engine is started, the choke plate opens slightly. The choke plate is placed slightly off-center in relation to the shaft, Figure 23-5. This helps open the choke plate. The amount that the choke plate opens is controlled by the choke pull-off, Figure 23-6. After the fast idle cam has been positioned, fuel flows out of all ports, Figure 23-5. This provides the needed rich fuel mixture. As the engine warms up, the choke plate opens and the fast idle speed is reduced.

Choke Controls. The opening and closing of the ***choke valve*** can be controlled manually or automatically. When it is manually controlled, a push-pull cable is used. The cable extends from the choke on the carburetor to the instrument panel. The driver closes the choke when starting

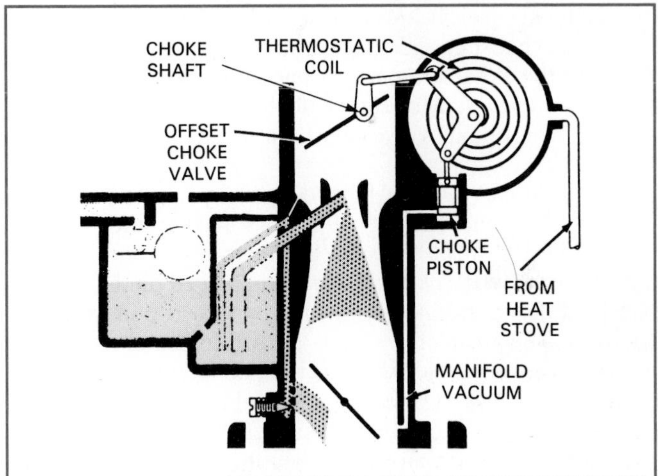

Figure 23-5. The thermostatic coil closes the choke valve, or choke plate. Note that the shaft is not centered on the valve. Also, the fuel is discharged at all ports to provide the needed rich fuel mixture. (Rochester)

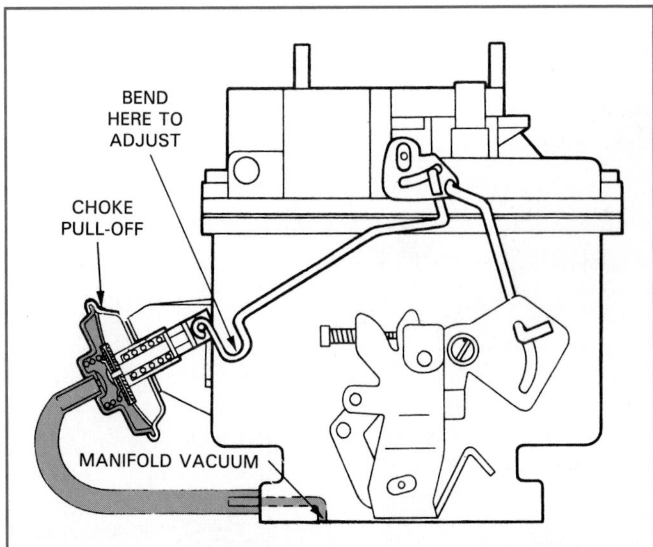

Figure 23-6. The choke pull-off assists in opening the choke plate a fraction of an inch. The "U-shaped" bend in the link determines how far the choke valve is opened. To increase the choke valve opening, decrease the width of the "U." To decrease the choke valve opening, increase the width of the "U." Make sure a vacuum source is applied to the choke pull-off before making adjustments. (Chrysler)

the engine and then opens it gradually as the engine reaches operating temperature.

The problem with a manual choke is that the driver is likely to forget to open the choke fully. A rich mixture will result, and cause carbon to form in the combustion chambers and on the spark plugs.

To eliminate this problem, the automatic choke was developed. Some automatic chokes depend on exhaust manifold heat for their operation; others combine manifold heat with intake manifold vacuum, and the velocity of air acting on the offset choke valve for their operation.

Automatic Choke Operation. The automatic choke depends on the unwinding of a ***thermostatic coil spring*** as heat is supplied. As the spring unwinds, it causes the choke valve in the carburetor air horn to open. This permits more air to pass through the carburetor.

In most cases, heat for the thermostatic coil is obtained from the exhaust gases. The thermostatic coil is mounted in a well in the exhaust crossover passage of the intake manifold, Figure 23-7. Movement of the bimetal spring is relayed to the choke valve shaft by means of linkage and levers.

The choke valve is helped open by a vacuum break unit, or choke pull-off, Figure 23-6. Some carburetors have two choke pull-offs. This vacuum-controlled unit adjusts the choke valve in relation to the load placed on the engine. The load on the engine is reflected by the drop in manifold vacuum. The rush of air past the off-center choke valve provides the extra needed force to open the choke valve.

As the engine warms up, manifold heat is transmitted to the choke housing. The heat causes the bimetal spring to relax. In some cases, an electric heating coil in the automatic choke shortens the length of time that the choke valve is closed, Figures 23-8 and 23-9. This reduces the emissions in the exhaust and is part of the emission controls.

Choke Unloader. Should the engine become flooded during the starting period, the choke valve can be opened by pushing the accelerator pedal to the floor. This is accomplished by means of the ***choke unloader,*** Figure 23-10, which rotates the fast idle cam and opens the choke valve.

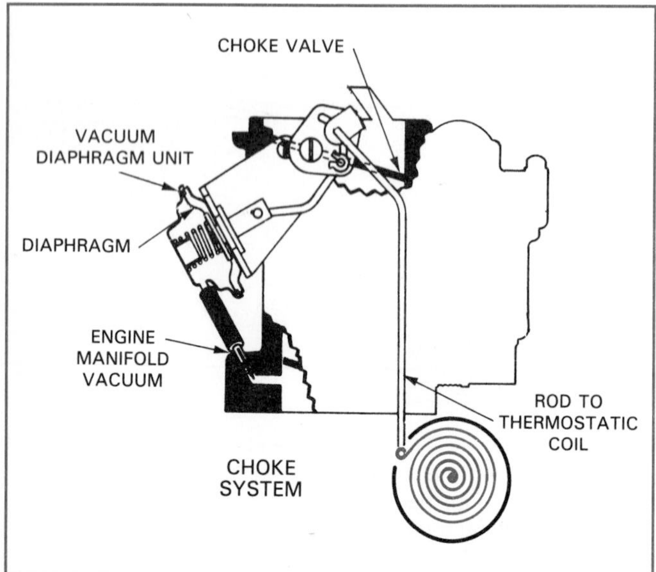

Figure 23-7. Heat relaxes the tension of the thermostatic coil spring. This allows the choke valve to fully open.

Secondary Lockout. On four barrel carburetors, it is necessary to prevent the secondaries from opening while the engine is cold. If the secondary side were permitted to open on a cold engine, there would be a severe hesitation and stumble on acceleration until the engine warmed up. The secondary side is prevented from opening by a ***secondary lockout lever,*** Figure 23-11.

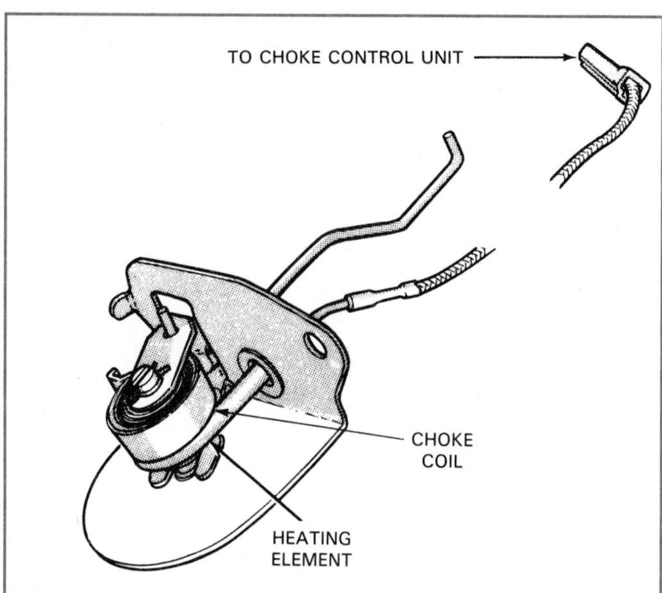

Figure 23-8. One type of electrically heated choke coil. The problem with some electric choke coils is that with the ignition on and the engine not running, the coil will heat up. Then, if the engine is cold and is started, the choke plate will be open when it should be closed. This will cause hard starting and stalling until the engine has warmed up. (Chrysler)

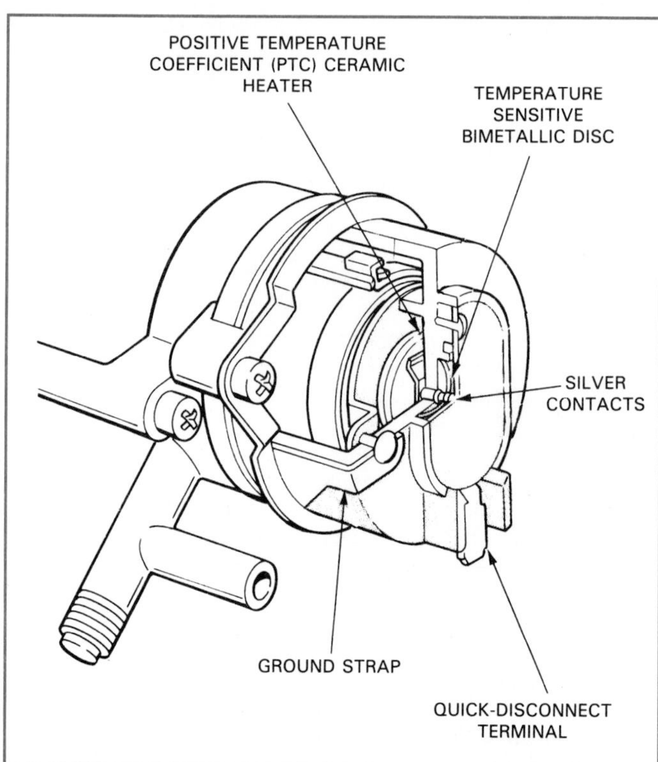

Figure 23-9. This type of choke coil receives current from the alternator. (Ford)

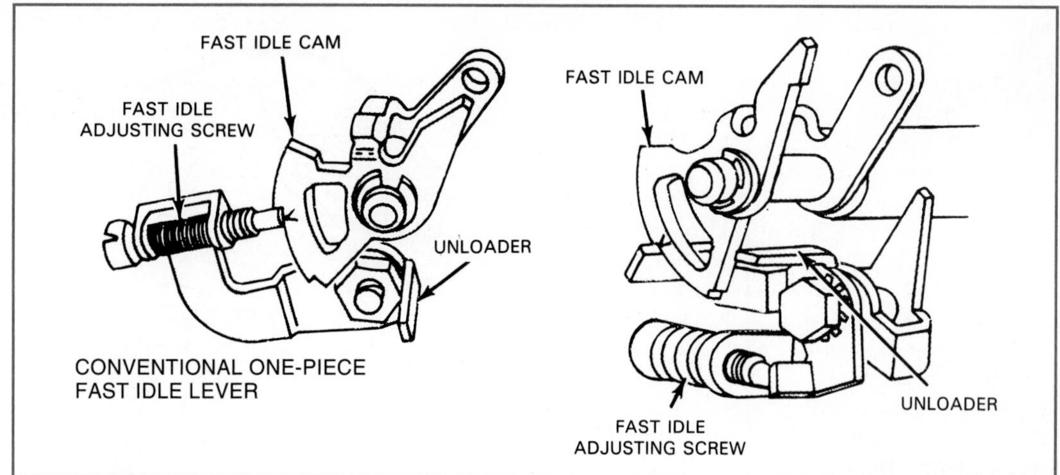

Figure 23-10. The choke unloader causes the choke valve to open when the accelerator is pressed to the floor.

Exhaust-heated Chokes. The crossover-type automatic choke is thermostatically controlled. The thermostatic coil, Figure 23-12, is mounted in a well in the exhaust crossover passage in the intake manifold on V-type engines. The choke valve is controlled by the thermostatic spring.

As the thermostatic coil gains heat, it unwinds and allows the choke valve to open. At the same time, the choke pull-off, which is connected by a rod to the valve, keeps a constant pull on the valve against the tension of the spring. This continues as long as the engine is running, so the choke valve opens slowly. Also, the offset choke valve assists in opening the valve.

When the thermostatic coil is mounted on the side of the carburetor, Figure 23-13, heat is conducted from the exhaust manifold to the choke housing and coil. This is done by passing a tube through the exhaust manifold.

Air drawn through the choke tube is heated by exhaust gases passing around the tube. In this way, the tube serves to supply heated air to the choke housing and the thermostatic coil.

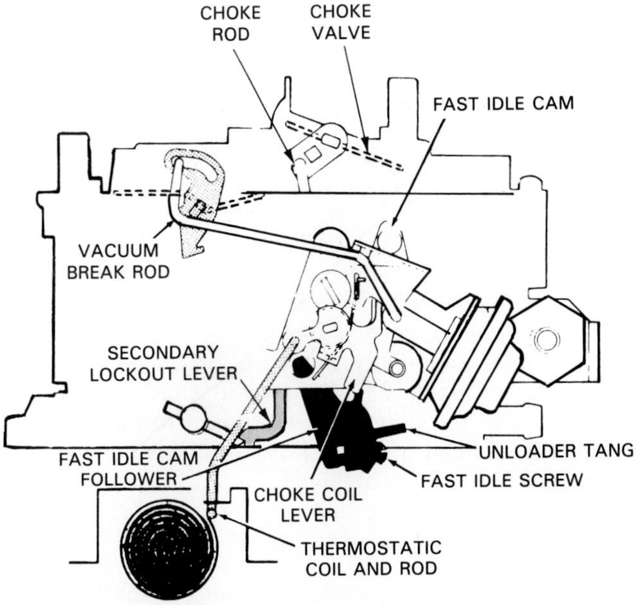

Figure 23-11. The secondary lockout lever prevents the secondary side of a four barrel carburetor from engaging while the engine is cold. (Rochester)

Water-heated Choke. Instead of using exhaust heat to control the automatic choke, some engines use coolant from the engine water jacket. By this design, the choke will remain open as long as the water in the water jacket re-

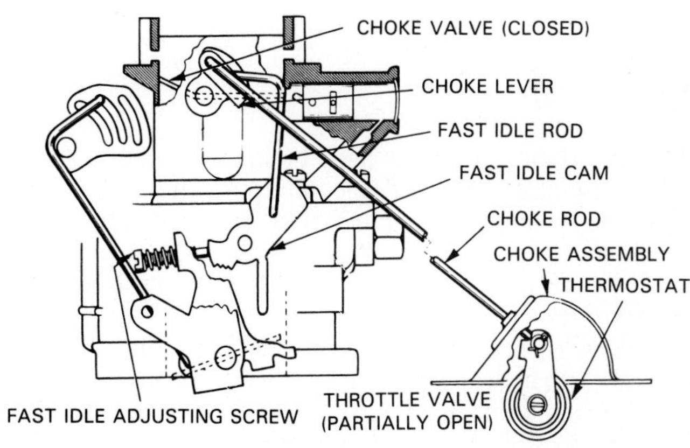

Figure 23-12. A crossover-type choke has a thermostatic coil placed in a well on the intake manifold. This well sits directly above the exhaust crossover passage.

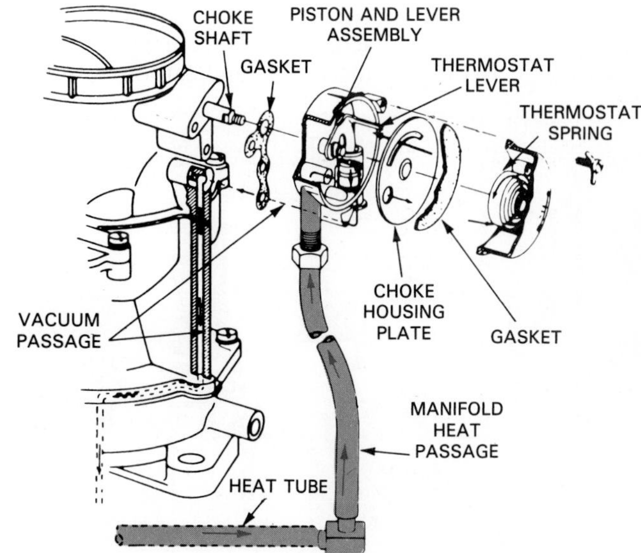

Figure 23-13. Heat for the thermostatic coil that is mounted on the side of the carburetor is directed through a tube from the exhaust manifold.

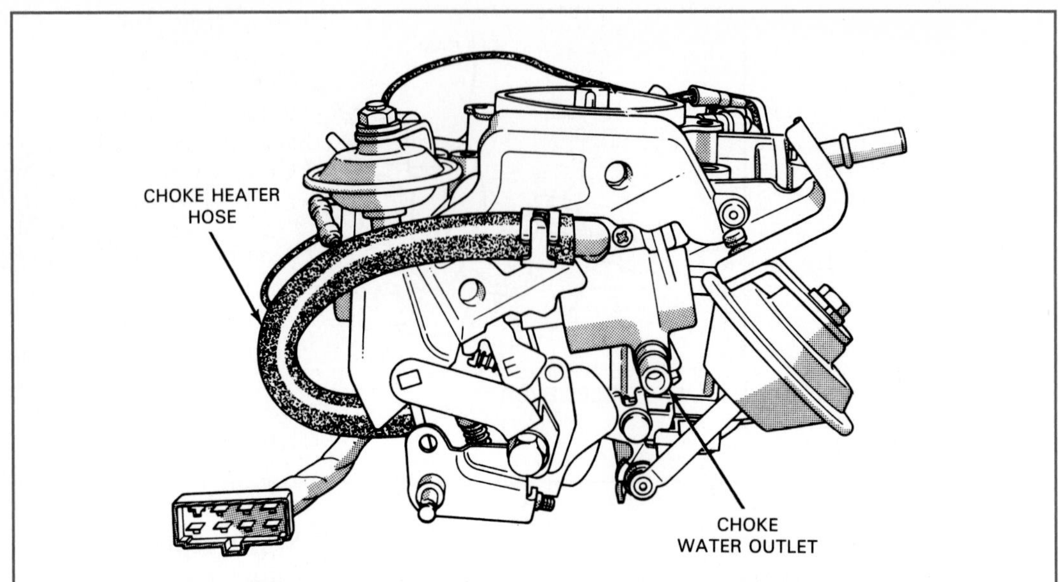

Figure 23-14. Heat for this thermostatic coil is supplied by the hot coolant carried through the heater hoses. (Chrysler)

mains hot, Figure 23-14. Coolant, in some ways, is better than heated air. This is because water retains heat longer than air. This prevents overchoking.

Float Circuit

Fuel in the carburetor must be maintained at a specified level under all operating conditions. This is the function of the ***float circuit,*** Figure 23-15. The needed fuel level is maintained by the float. When its attached lever forces the needle valve closed, the flow of fuel from the pump is stopped.

Then, as soon as fuel is discharged from the float bowl, the float drops. The needle valve opens, and fuel again flows into the bowl. In this way, the fuel is level with the opening of the main discharge nozzle.

The float level must be set with a high degree of accuracy. If the level is too low, not enough fuel will be supplied to the system and the engine will stall on turns. On the other hand, if the level is too high, too much fuel will flow from the nozzle.

Under conditions of a high fuel level in the float bowl, excessive fuel consumption results and carbon will accumulate in the combustion chambers. The float and needle valve maintain a position that permits the fuel coming into the float bowl to balance the fuel passing through the carburetor jets.

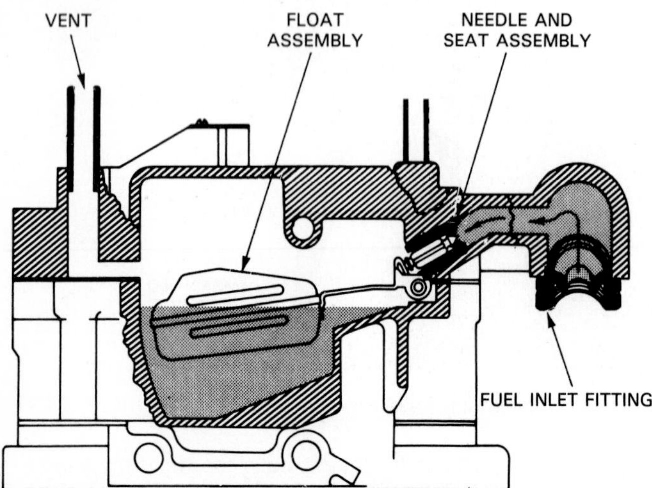

Figure 23-15. Typical float circuit. (Chrysler)

Idle Circuit

The ***idle circuit,*** Figure 23-16, is designed to supply the proper amount of mixture for the engine at idle and low speeds. It operates from idle speed to approximately 25 mph. Above that speed, the idle system is phased out and fuel is supplied by the main metering system.

When the throttle valve is almost closed, there will be very little air passing through the venturi. There will be very little vacuum to draw fuel from the fuel nozzle.

However, on the intake manifold side of the throttle valve, the vacuum will be at a maximum as long as the throttle is in the closed position. Fuel is then discharged at this port below the throttle valve. An idle mixture needle is used to adjust the amount of fuel that flows to the discharge port.

Transfer Circuit

When the throttle is opened a little, the flow of air is too limited for the venturi to discharge fuel from the main nozzle, Figure 23-16. However, with the increased movement of air through the carburetor, more fuel must be supplied in order to maintain the correct air/fuel mixture. This is accomplished by the ***transfer circuit.***

To supply the needed fuel during this stage, another port is positioned slightly above the closed position of the throttle valve, Figure 23-16. As soon as the valve opens a small amount, the port will be exposed to manifold vacuum. This will cause fuel to flow from this port also, and the needed fuel will be obtained.

Main Metering Circuit

As the throttle is opened, vacuum at the venturi increases. Therefore, fuel starts to flow from the ***main metering circuit.*** The main circuit consists of the main nozzle, which is centered in the venturi, Figure 23-17. Fuel is

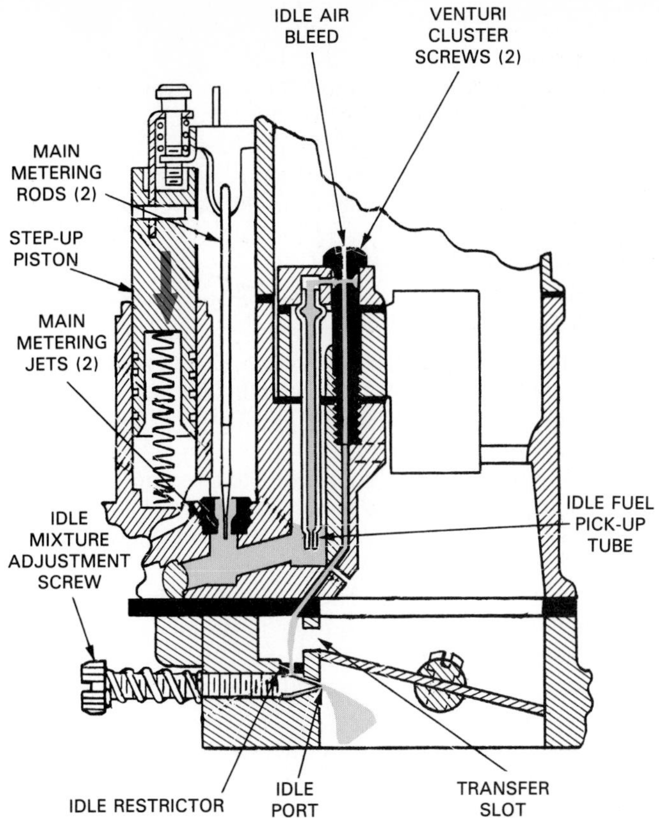

Figure 23-16. When manifold vacuum is high, the step-up piston is pulled downward. Since the metering rod is attached to the step-up piston, the metering rod is pulled into the jet. This limits the flow of fuel to the idle port. A low-pressure area is created by the downward motion of piston, as velocity of air is not great enough to cause a low-pressure area with the venturi. As the throttle blade opens slightly, fuel begins to flow out of the transfer slot. (Chrysler)

discharged from the nozzle during part-throttle through full-throttle positions.

As the airflow through the carburetor increases, the flow of fuel also increases at a faster rate. This is because the density of the fuel does not change, while that of the air does. Consequently, the mixture in a simple carburetor will be too rich under wide open throttle (WOT).

Since the correct air/fuel mixture on a simple carburetor would be supplied at only one position of the throttle valve, steps must be taken to provide the correct mixture of all positions of the throttle valve.

Metering Rod. A ***metering rod*** varies the size of the carburetor jet opening. In this design, Figure 23-18, fuel from the float bowl is metered through the jet and the metering rod within it. The fuel is forced from the jet to the nozzle extending into the venturi.

As the throttle valve is opened, its linkage raises the metering rod from the jet. The rod has several steps, or tapers, on the lower end. As it is raised in the jet, it makes the opening of the jet greater in size. This allows more fuel to flow through the jet to the discharge nozzle. The metering rod must keep pace with the slightest change in the throttle valve position so that the correct air/fuel mixture is obtained through all engine speeds.

Power Circuit

The ***power circuit*** consists of a step-up piston fastened to metering rods, Figure 23-19. When high vacuum develops in the intake manifold (part throttle operation), atmospheric pressure holds the step-up piston down against spring pressure. This, in turn, holds the metering rods down in the main metering jet, closing the jet.

When no vacuum is in the intake manifold (wide-open throttle), the difference in pressure above and below the piston is the same. The piston is then moved up by spring

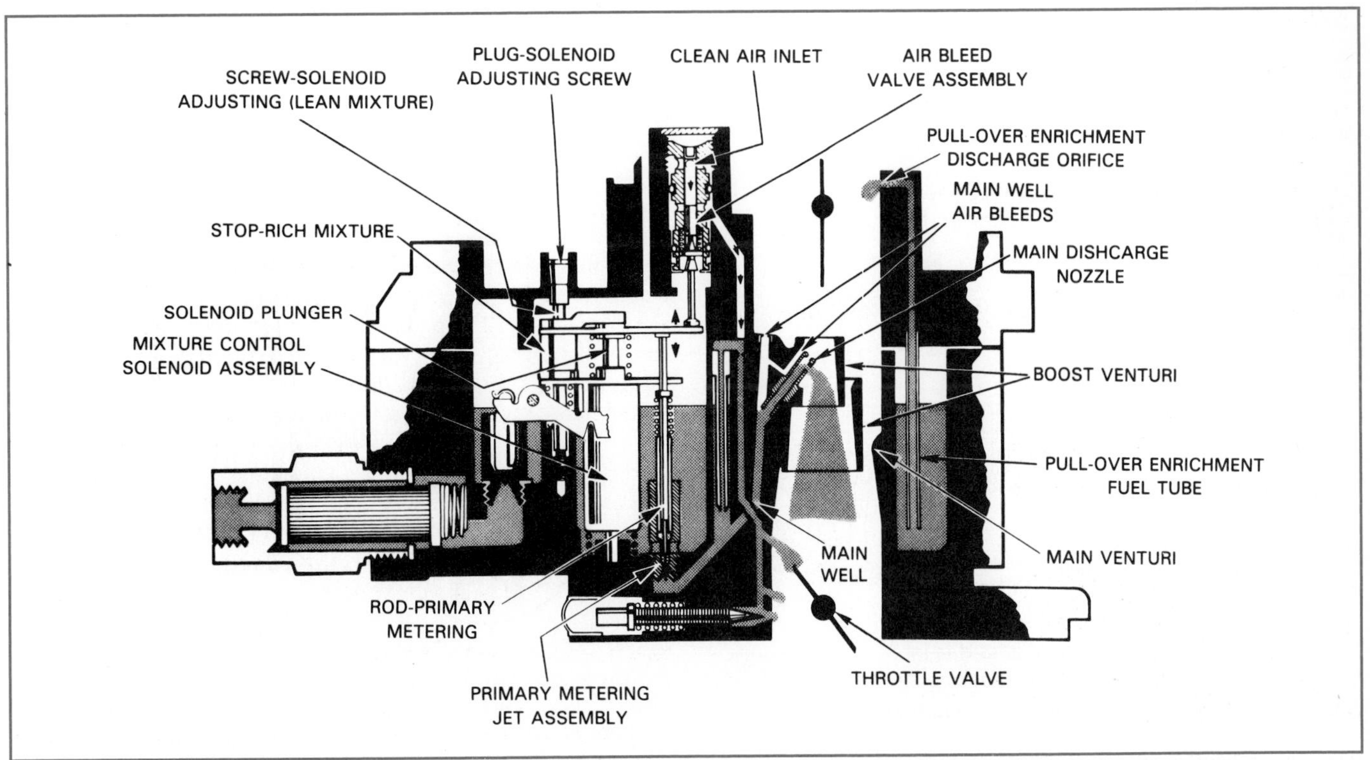

Figure 23-17. The main metering system provides just enough fuel to maintain a constant cruising speed. (Rochester)

pressure and the rod is raised out of its jet. In this way, additional fuel is allowed to flow through the jet for maximum power.

Power Valve. Some power circuits use a ***power valve*** instead of metering rods attached to a step-up piston. The concept is the same, which allows the increased flow of fuel to provide the necessary power. The power valve, Figure 23-20, is held closed during normal operation. As vacuum drops due to the increased load placed on the engine, the piston located above the power valve is pushed downward. This piston pushes on the power valve, opening the valve and allowing more fuel to flow. When vacuum increases again, the piston is forced up off the power valve. This shuts off the flow of fuel from the power valve.

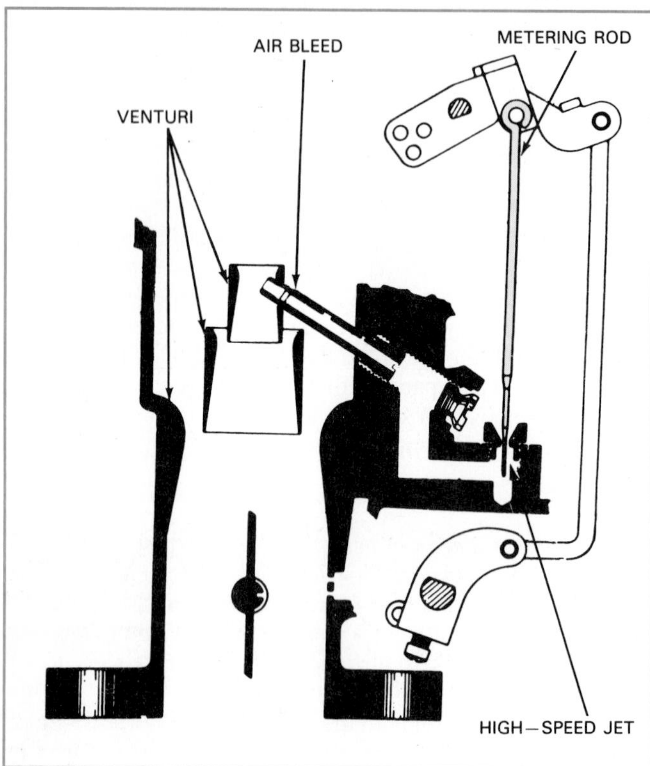

Figure 23-18. The metering rod varies the amount of fuel flowing through the jet. As speed increases, the metering rod is lifted out of the jet, allowing more fuel to flow.

Accelerator Pump Circuit

When a throttle valve is opened quickly to produce rapid acceleration, the carburetor fuel mixture tends to become too lean and a hesitation occurs. This results from the fact that the fuel is of greater weight than air. When the accelerator is opened suddenly, the flow of fuel will lag behind the flow of the air.

To supply the extra fuel needed to overcome this situation, an ***accelerator pump*** is part of the carburetor design, Figure 23-21. This pump is operated by the throttle linkage. In some designs, the stroke of the pump can be adjusted to any one of three positions. The longest stroke provides the most fuel. Therefore, this setting is usually used during cold weather.

The accelerating pump circuit generally consists of the following:

- A pump well.
- A plunger, which is mechanically actuated by a lever connected to the throttle shaft.
- An intake check ball located in bottom of pump well to control passage of fuel from bowl to pump cylinder.
- A discharge check ball located in the discharge passage to prevent fuel in the accelerator pump well from being siphoned into the air stream.
- A discharge nozzle (pump jets) located in the throat of the carburetor.

As the throttle is opened, the pump plunger moves downward. The downward travel of the plunger forces fuel

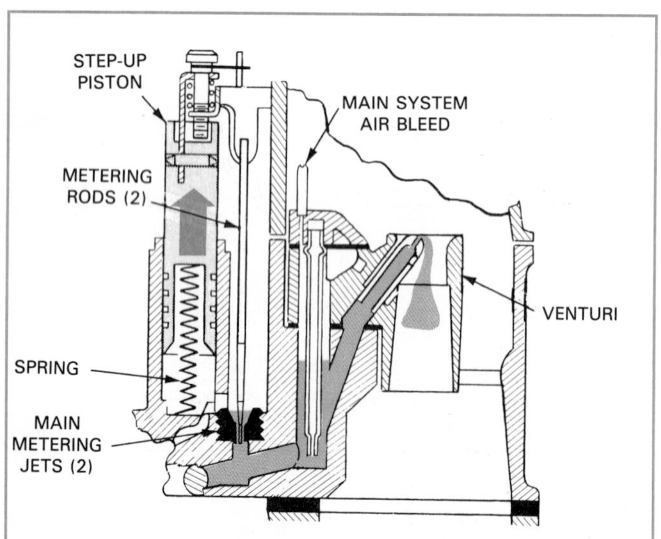

Figure 23-19. Power circuit. As speed is increased, vacuum drops and the spring pushes the step-up piston upward. This brings the metering rod out of the jet, which allows the needed fuel to provide the necessary power. The velocity of air is now great enough to create a pressure drop within the venturi. (Chrysler)

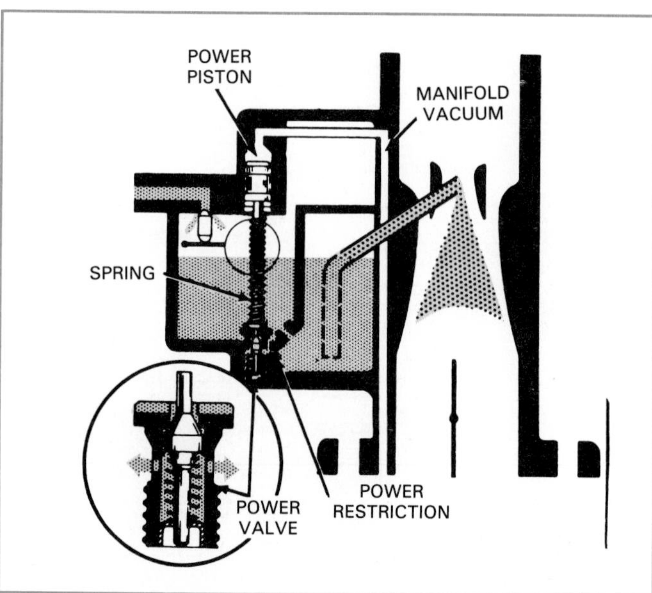

Figure 23-20. When the manifold vacuum is reduced, the piston is forced down against the power valve. The power valve is opened and the flow of fuel is increased. When manifold vacuum increases, the piston is pulled off the power valve. This reduces the flow of fuel. (Rochester)

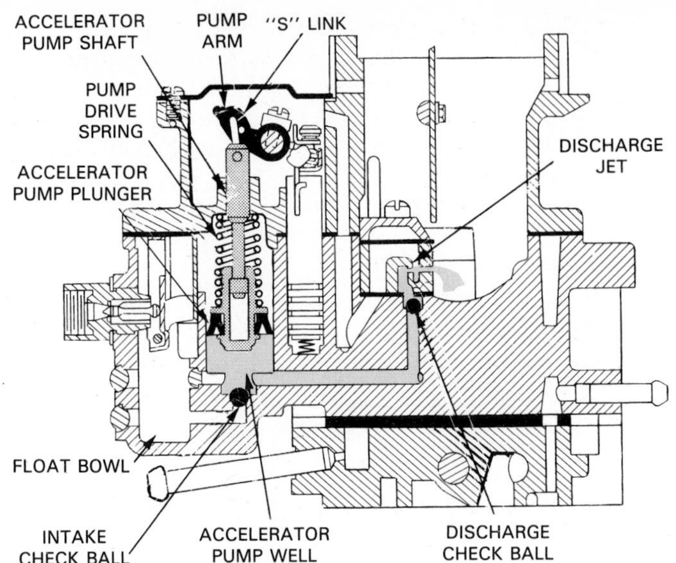

Figure 23-21. Accelerator pump circuit. When the accelerator pump moves upward, the intake check ball is unseated, allowing fuel from float bowl to fill the accelerator pump well. When the accelerator pump moves downward, the intake check ball is seated and the discharge check ball is unseated, allowing a squirt of fuel into the airstream. The discharge check ball prevents fuel siphoning from accelerator pump well, which would deplete the needed fuel for smooth acceleration. (Chrysler)

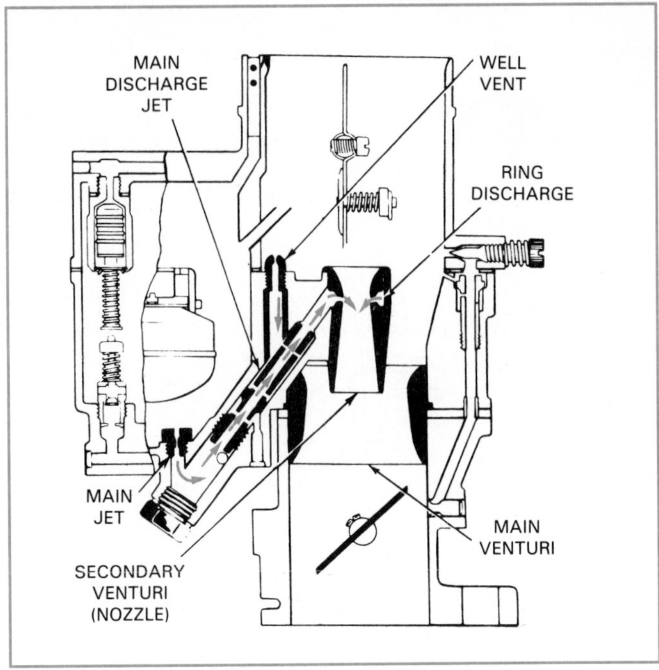

Figure 23-22. The well vent acts as an air bleed on this carburetor.

past the discharge check ball. Fuel is then supplied to the pump cylinder through the intake check ball at the bottom of the well. This check ball permits a supply of fuel to reach the cylinder, but closes on the down stroke of the plunger to prevent fuel in the well from being pushed back into the float bowl.

Air Bleed Principle. The use of ***air bleeds*** is a method to compensate for the increased richness of the mixture caused by increased air velocity through the carburetor. Figure 23-22 shows the air bleed system used on a carburetor.

Air at this point reduces the surface tension of the fuel and helps fuel flow at low pressures. This bleed also prevents fuel flow through the main jets under high vacuum conditions. These two factors control the air/fuel mixture. The increased richness of a mixture occurs when a plain nozzle is exposed to increased air velocity.

Balanced Pressure. A tube connects the top of the float bowl chamber to the upper section of the air horn, Figure 23-23. This tube vents the vapors from the fuel bowl into the airstream through the air horn. These vapors are also burned with the fuel that is discharged at the various ports within the carburetor. Venting the carburetor in this manner relieves any pressure in the float bowl. Also, the

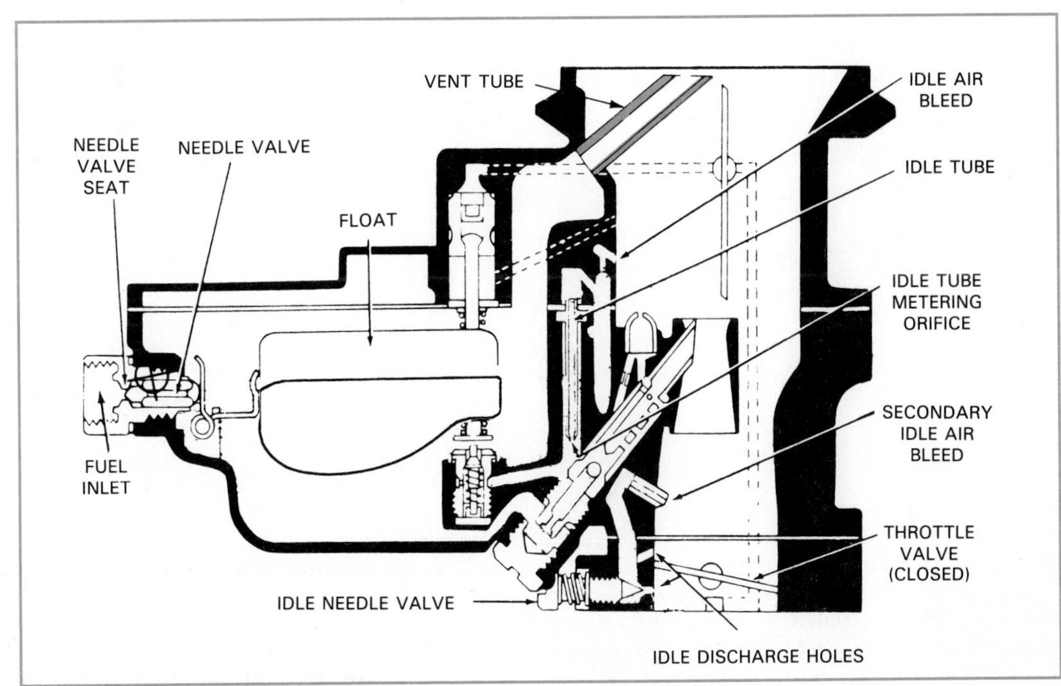

Figure 23-23. The vent tube directs atmospheric pressure to the float bowl after the air has been filtered. This equalizes the effects of a partially clogged air filter and prevents an overly rich fuel mixture.

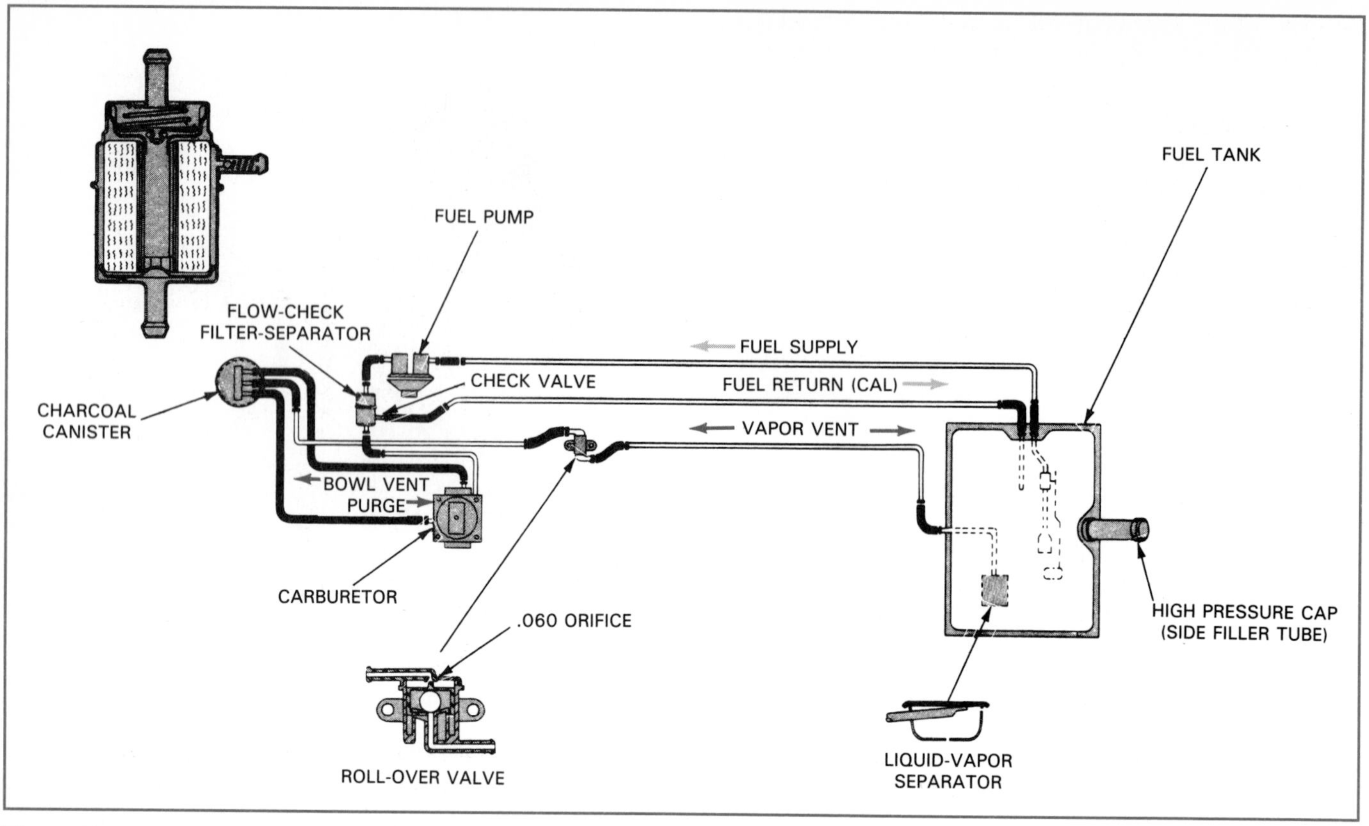

Figure 23-24. Due to federal regulations, the fuel tank and carburetor can no longer be vented to the atmosphere. All fuel vapors are routed to a charcoal canister and then later purged through the carburetor. (Chrysler)

atmospheric pressure directed to the float bowl through the balance or vent tube will equalize the pressure in the float bowl if the air filter is too dirty.

A dirty air filter will cause a greater pressure difference at the venturi. This is because the airflow through a dirty air filter will be reduced. This causes a drop in pressure on the inner side of the filter. However, atmospheric pressure in the fuel bowl will remain the same. The greater pressure difference will cause more fuel to flow than needed. Therefore, a balance tube routes the pressure from the inner side of the air filter to the fuel bowl. This prevents a richer fuel mixture. The balance tube compensates for a partially restricted air filter.

Today, fuel vapors from the float bowl are externally vented to a charcoal canister, Figures 23-24 and 23-25. At

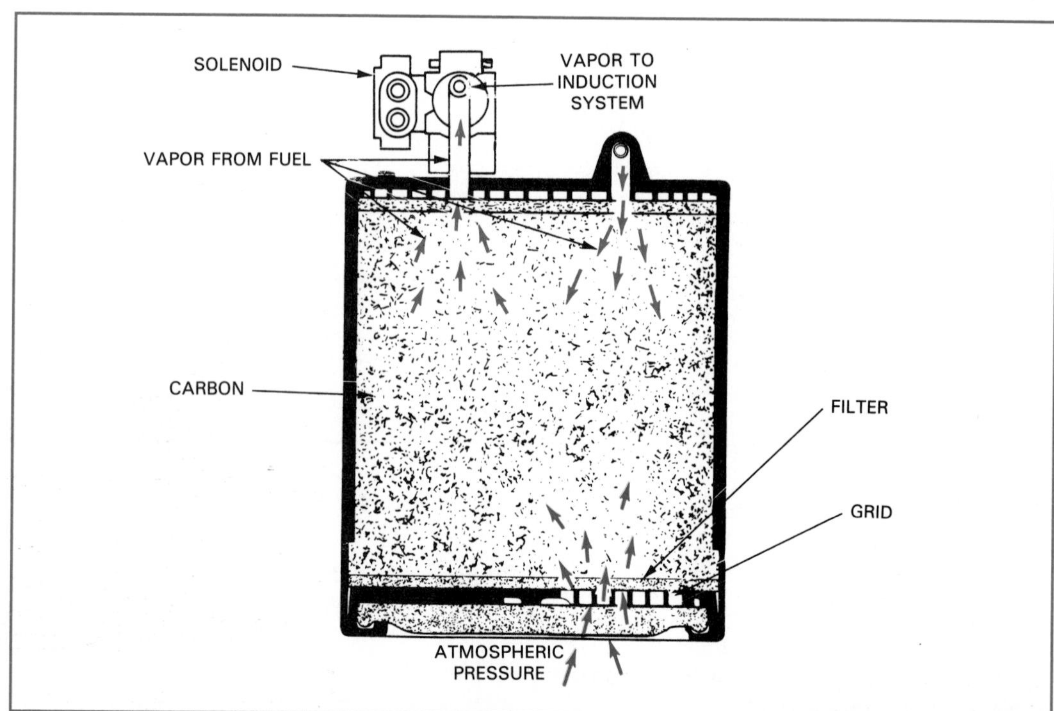

Figure 23-25. A typical charcoal canister. (Oldsmobile)

the proper time, the vapors are purged through the carburetor. However, the internal vent or balance tube remains.

Choke Unloader

When an engine does not start immediately, prolonged cranking will result in a flooded condition. The air/fuel mixture in the engine is so rich that it is no longer a vapor. The spark plugs cannot ignite liquid gasoline. To overcome this, linkage is provided on the carburetor that will hold the choke valve open when the accelerator is pushed to the floor, Figure 23-10. Then, as the engine is cranked again, air will enter the cylinders to clear excessive gasoline from the system.

Anti-icing Passages

As fuel evaporates, the temperature is decreased and it absorbs heat from the air and metal parts. When the humidity of the air is high and temperatures are at the freezing point, the evaporation of fuel in the carburetor often causes "icing." The ice forms around the closed position of the throttle plate. The idle port becomes closed with ice. This, in turn, will cause the engine to stall at low speeds.

To overcome this icing condition, some carburetors are provided with ***anti-icing passages*** that carry hot exhaust gases around the carburetor, heating the area around the throttle plate, Figure 23-26.

Hot Idle Compensator

During long periods of idling with an extremely hot engine, the fuel in the carburetor bowl becomes hot enough to form vapors. These vapors enter the carburetor bores by way of the inside bowl vents or the balance tube. When these vapors mix with the idle air, an extremely rich mixture is created. This will result in loss of engine rpm and stalling. To overcome this condition, a ***hot idle compensator*** valve is placed in some of the carburetors. This permits extra air to enter the manifold below the throttle valve, Figure 23-27, where it mixes with the fuel vapors to provide a leaner fuel mixture.

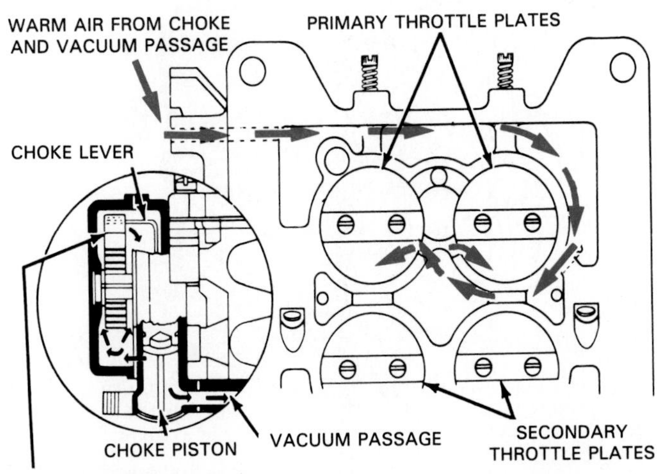

Figure 23-26. The path of hot air is directed around throttle valves to prevent ice formation.

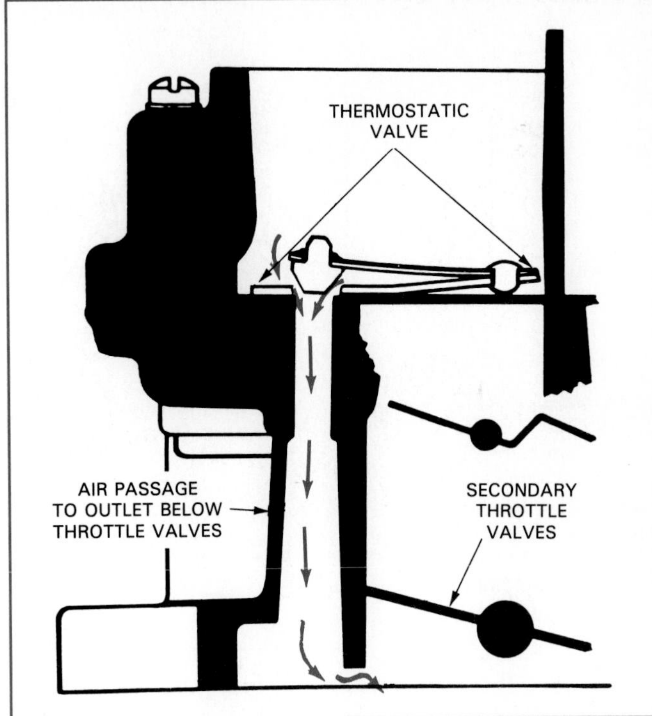

Figure 23-27. The hot idle compensator permits additional air to enter the carburetor under extremely hot conditions.

Anti-stall Dashpot

Most older cars with automatic transmissions have an ***anti-stall dashpot*** connected to the carburetor linkage, Figure 23-28. The purpose of this dashpot is to prevent the throttle valve from closing too fast. Rapid closing often causes the engine to stall. The dashpot prevents the throttle from being closed too quickly, thereby avoiding stalls.

This condition would not occur with a manual transmission since the momentum of the vehicle would continue to drive the engine through the stall period.

Single-barrel Carburetor

A carburetor is classified by the number of throats, or barrels. A ***single-barrel carburetor,*** Figure 23-29, has one outlet to the intake manifold. This outlet is designed to take care of all the needs of the engine under all conditions. A single-barrel carburetor is used on engines having a maximum of six cylinders.

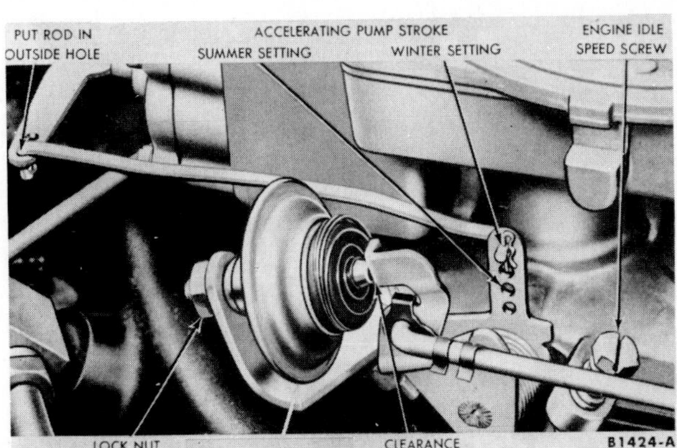

Figure 23-28. A typical anti-stall dashpot. (Ford)

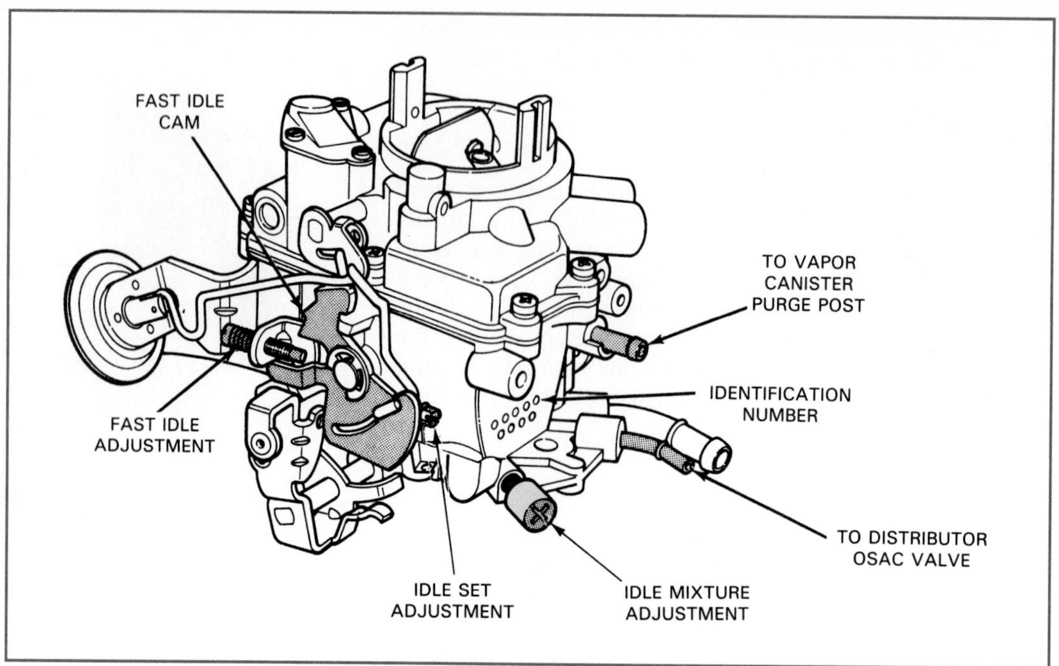

Figure 23-29. A single-barrel carburetor. Note that a single-barrel carburetor has only one idle mixture adjustment screw. (Chrysler)

Two-barrel Carburetor

Carburetors with two outlets to the intake manifold are known as ***two-barrel carburetors,*** Figure 23-30. These units are two single-barrel carburetors in one, with two complete idling circuits, two high-speed circuits, two power circuits, two accelerator discharge passages, and two throttle valves. However, they have only one float system.

With a two-barrel carburetor, each barrel supplies alternate cylinders in the firing order. In a six-cylinder engine, one barrel supplies cylinders 1, 3, and 2. The other barrel supplies cylinders 5, 6, and 4.

Four-barrel Carburetor

In the ***four-barrel carburetor,*** there are four openings to the intake manifold. Some systems, such as the float system, may be common to all four barrels. In four-barrel designs, half of the carburetor operates as a two-barrel unit during light loads and cruising speeds. The other half of the carburetor is supplemental for top speed and full-throttle. The two barrels that supply fuel for light loads are known as the primary side. The supplementary two barrels are known as the secondary side, Figure 23-31.

In this design, the secondary throttle plates remain closed at lower engine speeds. As engine speed increases, the throttle plates of the secondary barrels are opened.

In some designs, the secondary throttle plates are operated mechanically through linkage. On other models, the secondary throttle plates are controlled by a vacuum-operated diaphragm. The secondary throttle plates will start to open when the primary plates are open 50°.

Manifolding for both two-barrel and four-barrel carburetors is designed as follows: One-half of the carburetor supplies fuel to the end cylinders on one side of the engine and two center cylinders on the other side. The other half of the carburetor supplies fuel to the remaining cylinders.

In a four-barrel carburetor on a V-8 engine, the primary and secondary barrels supply cylinders 1-7-4-6. The other primary and secondary barrels supply fuel to

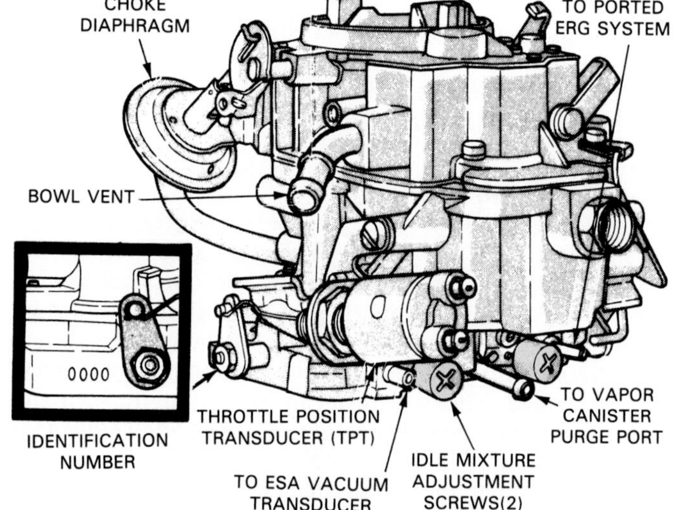

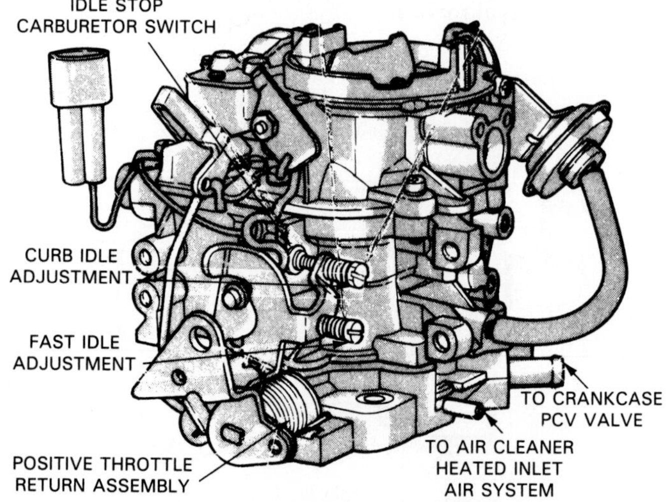

Figure 23-30. A two-barrel carburetor. Note that a two-barrel carburetor has two idle mixture adjustment screws. However, a four-barrel carburetor also has only two idle mixture adjustment screws, which are located on the primary side. (Chrysler)

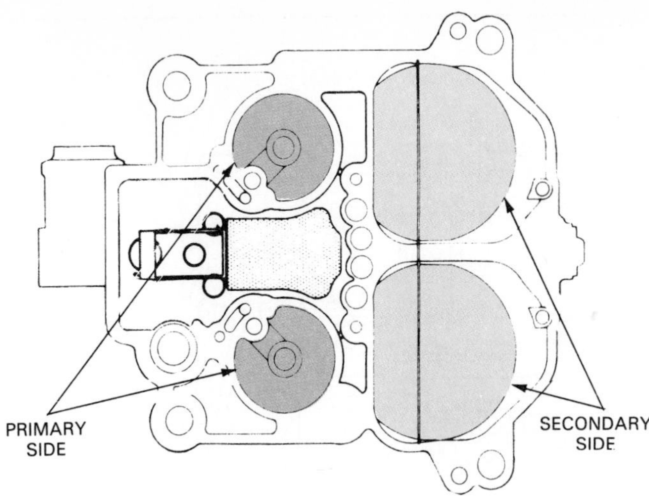

Figure 23-31. A typical four-barrel carburetor. Note that the primary side bores are smaller than the secondary bores. (Rochester)

cylinders 3-5-2-8. However, this applies only to an engine having a firing order of 1-8-4-3-6-5-7-2.

Variable-venturi Carburetor

A ***variable-venturi carburetor,*** Figures 23-32 and 23-33, varies the area of the venturi as a function of speed and load. Most carburetors have venturis that are fixed. In this design, changing the size of the venturi maintains enough air velocity and pressure drop to the main metering system. This is accomplished by means of tapered metering rods attached to the venturi valve, which change the area of the venturi.

There is one rod and one jet for each bore of the carburetor. The rod moves back and forth in the jet when the air valve moves. When the venturi valve is closed, the largest diameter of the rod is in the jet. When the valve is wide open, the smallest diameter of the rod is in the jet. In this way, metering of the fuel is controlled by the position of the rod, Figure 23-33.

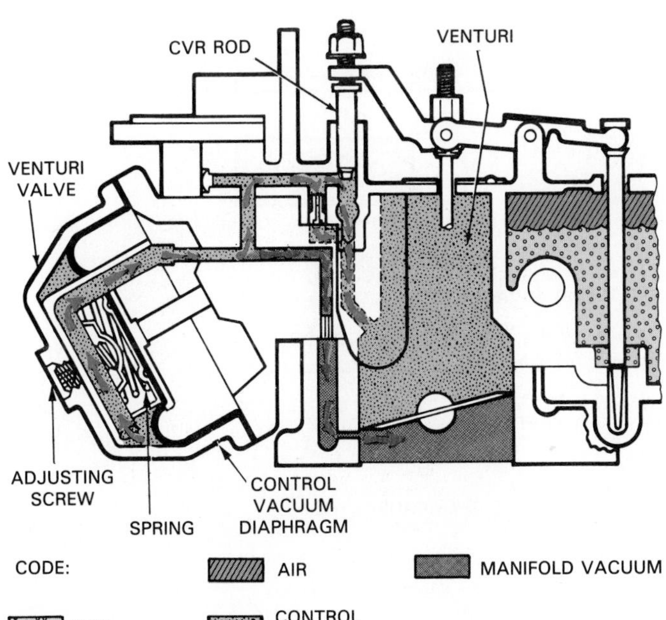

Figure 23-32. Variable venturi carburetor. Spring pressure tends to close the venturi valve and control vacuum opens it. (Ford)

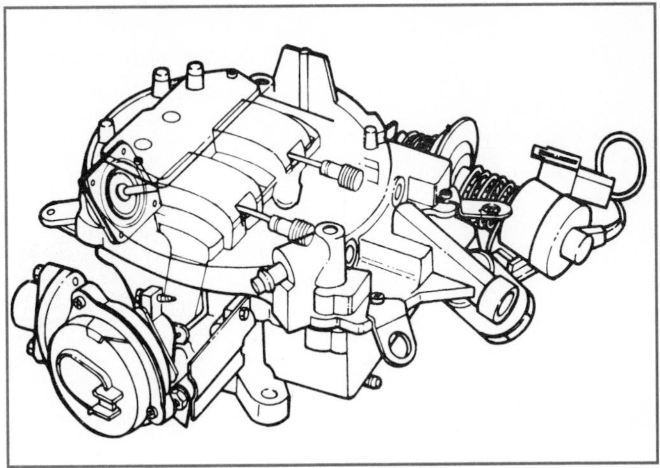

Figure 23-33. Variable-venturi carburetor.

Air/fuel Mixture

Carburetors have been modified to provide leaner air/fuel mixtures to conform to federal regulations that concern exhaust emissions.

These leaner mixtures result from better control of the idle mixture. In some cases, the idle mixture screws have a finer pitch, making for more accurate control of the air/fuel ratio.

On 1980 and newer car models, the air/fuel mixture adjustment screws have been sealed, Figure 23-34. This prevents tampering with the air/fuel mixture adjustment, as this will affect emissions.

Stoichiometric Mixture

A lean air/fuel mixture produces a high level of nitrous oxides (NO_X) in the exhaust. A rich air/fuel mixture produces a high level of hydrocarbons (HC) and carbon monoxide (CO) in the exhaust. However, the byproducts of perfect combustion are water (H_20) and carbon dioxide (CO_2). This is provided that the engine is 100% efficient. Unfortunately, not even the best designed engine is 100% efficient.

A ***stoichiometric*** air/fuel mixture is as close as you can get in obtaining the byproducts of perfect combustion. A stoichiometric air/fuel mixture is neither too rich nor too lean. It is 14.7 parts air to 1 part fuel. However, even with this desired air/fuel mixture, hydrocarbon, carbon monoxide, and nitrous oxides remain, but only in small percentages. To achieve this, the combustion process and other engine variables must be monitored.

Computerized Systems

The only practical method for monitoring all of the engine variables at once is with the use of an ***onboard computer.*** The onboard computer receives information signals from the various sensors located near or on the engine, Figure 23-35. Once the computer processes the input signals, it adjusts the fuel mixture, timing, and other actuators. This process is continuous, as long as the engine is running.

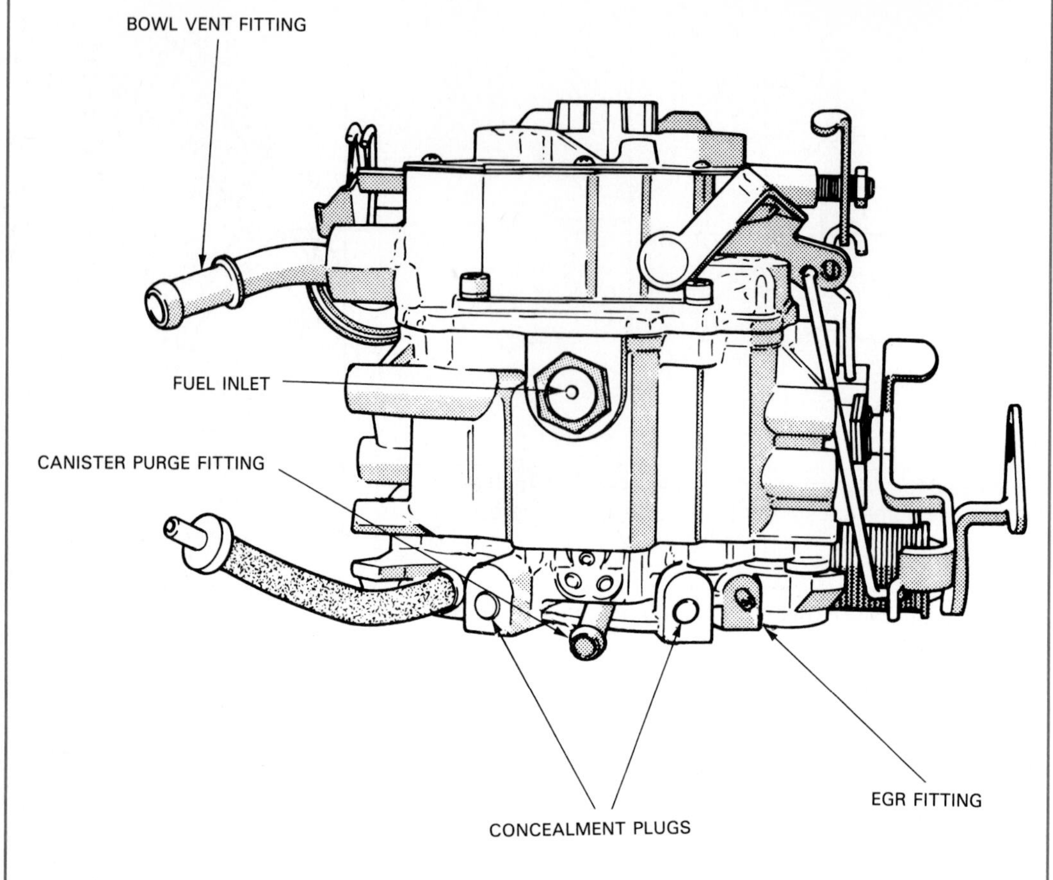

Figure 23-34. The air/fuel mixture screws are located behind concealment plugs. The plugs must be drilled out in order to gain access to the fuel mixture screws. This usually involves removing the carburetor from the engine. (Chrysler)

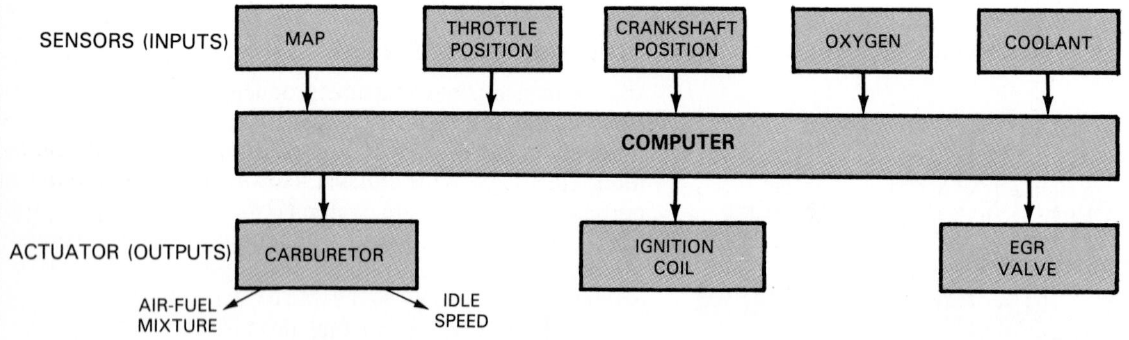

SENSORS (INPUTS): MAP | THROTTLE POSITION | CRANKSHAFT POSITION | OXYGEN | COOLANT

COMPUTER

ACTUATOR (OUTPUTS): CARBURETOR | IGNITION COIL | EGR VALVE

AIR-FUEL MIXTURE
IDLE SPEED

MAP SENSOR: SENSES ENGINE VACUUM. AS THE LOAD IS INCREASED (LOW VACUUM), THE FUEL MIXTURE IS RICHENED AND THE TIMING ADVANCED.

THROTTLE POSITION SENSOR: SENSES THE ANGLE OF THROTTLE BLADES. AS THE ANGLE INCREASES, SO DOES THE TIMING. ALSO, THE FUEL MIXTURE IS RICHENED.

CRANKSHAFT POSITION SENSOR: SENSES THE ANGLE OF THE CRANKSHAFT TO DETERMINE WHEN THE IGNITION COIL FIRES.

OXYGEN SENSOR: SENSES THE AMOUNT OF OXYGEN IN EXHAUST, AND THEN CAUSES THE FUEL MIXTURE TO BE ADJUSTED ACCORDINGLY.

COOLANT SENSOR: SENSES ENGINE TEMPERATURE AND DETERMINES IF COMPUTER OPERATES FROM PREDETERMINED VALUES OR NOT: ALSO CONTROLS WHEN THE EGR VALVE IS OPERATED.

Figure 23-35. The computer receives information from the various sensors and then adjusts the actuators.

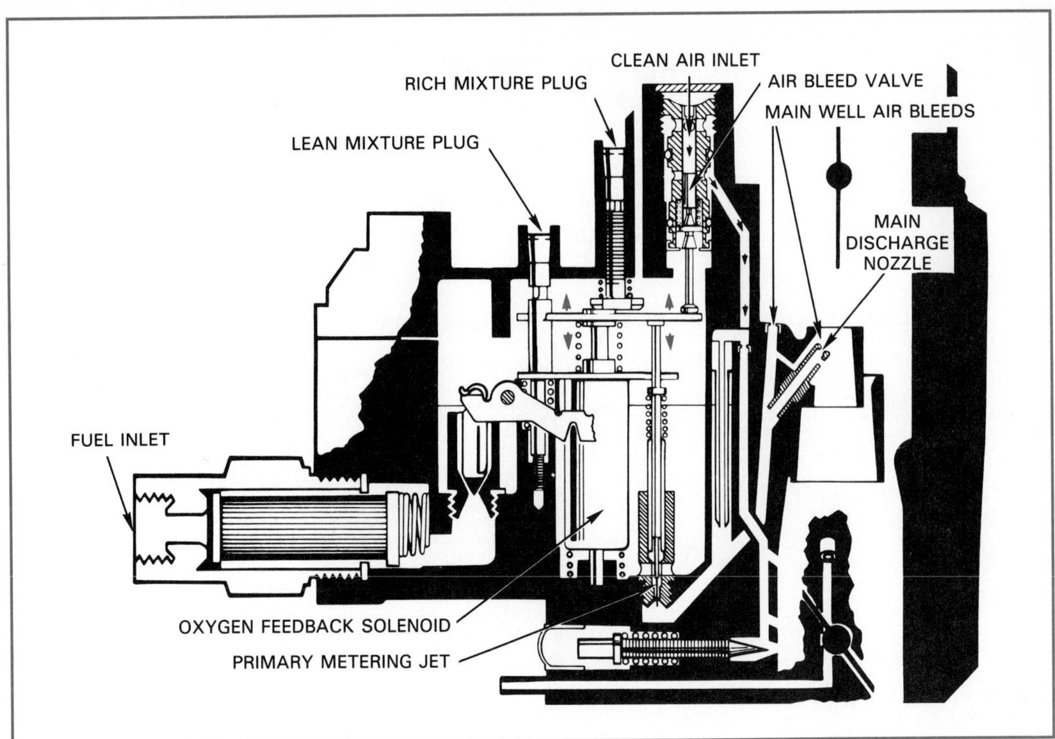

Figure 23-36. When the oxygen feedback solenoid is energized, the metering rod is pushed into the jet, reducing the flow of fuel. (Rochester)

Electro-mechanical Carburetors

The ***electro-mechanical carburetor*** is controlled by the computer. The fuel mixture is controlled by an ***oxygen feedback (mixture control) solenoid*** located within the carburetor, Figures 23-36 and 23-37. The idle speed is maintained by an electric motor that automatically adjusts the idle speed, Figure 23-38. When the engine is cold, the computer operates from predetermined values and the fuel mixture is fixed at full rich. When operating temperatures have been reached, the fuel mixture varies, Figure 23-39.

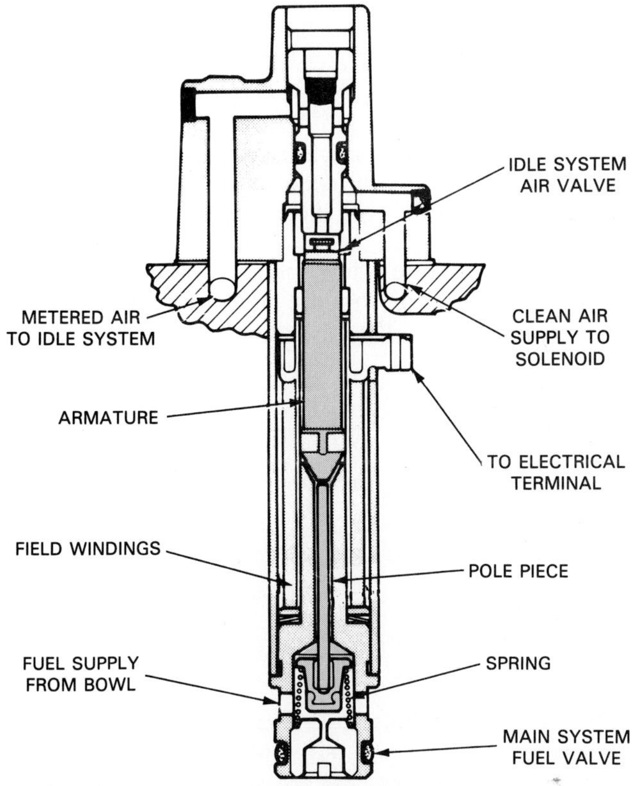

Figure 23-37. When de-energized, the pole piece is pushed upward by spring pressure, allowing more fuel to flow through the jet. (Chrysler)

Open Loop

When the temperature of the exhaust gases is below 600°F (316°C), the computer operates from predetermined values and ignores signals for the oxygen sensor. Similarly, if the driver depresses the accelerator to the floor (wide open throttle) after the exhaust gases have reached the specified temperature, the signal from the oxygen sensor is ignored by the computer. When the oxygen sensor signal is ignored by the computer, it is referred to as being in ***open loop.***

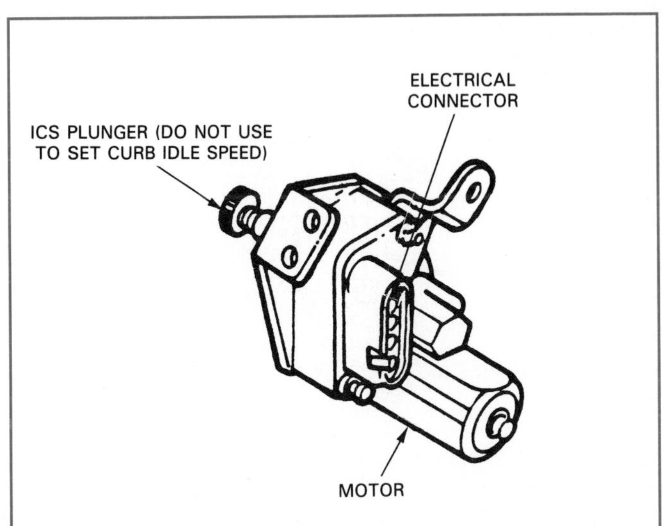

Figure 23-38. The idle speed motor is controlled by the computer and automatically adjusts the idle. (Oldsmobile)

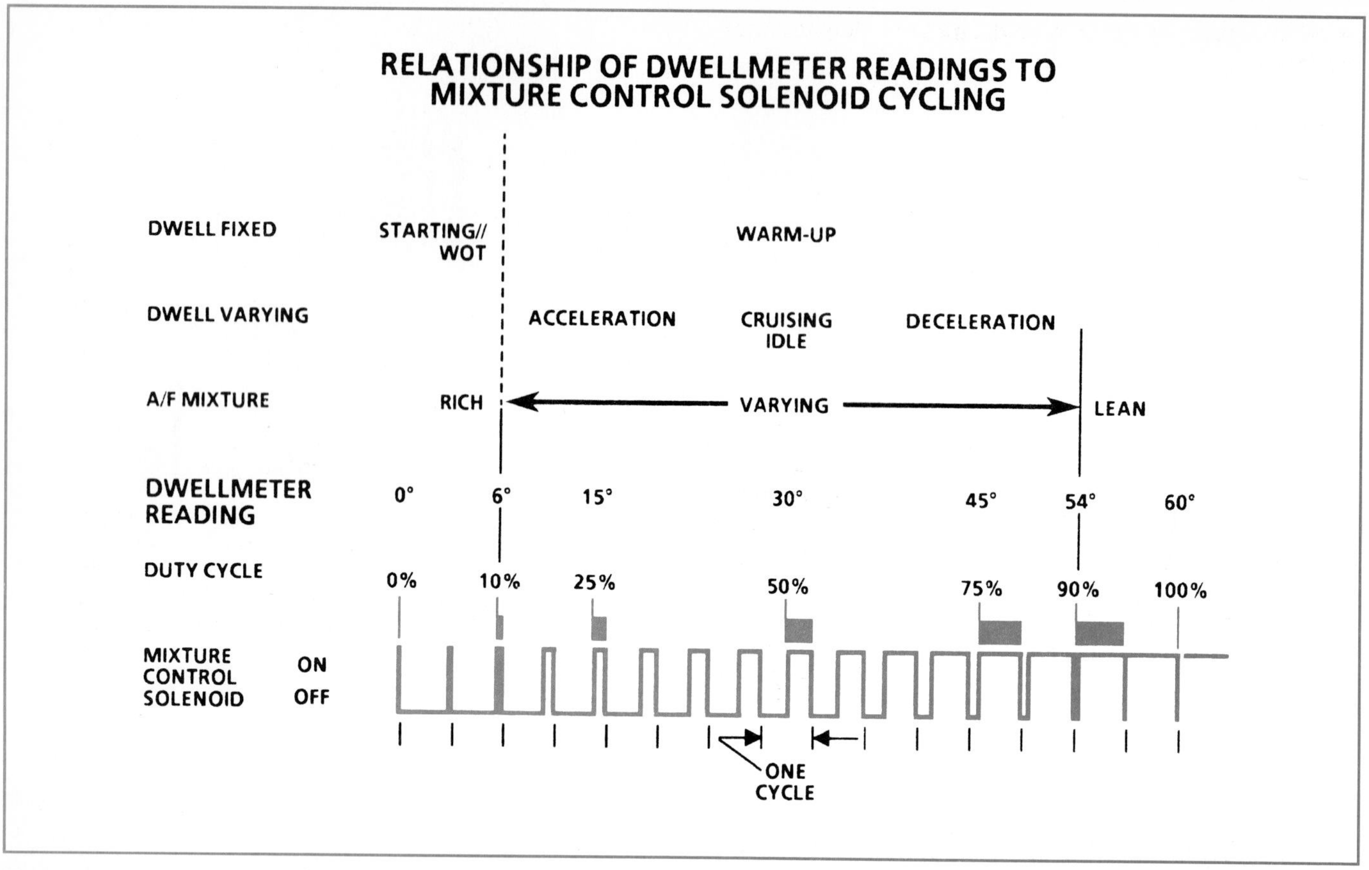

RELATIONSHIP OF DWELLMETER READINGS TO MIXTURE CONTROL SOLENOID CYCLING

DWELL FIXED	STARTING// WOT		WARM-UP				
DWELL VARYING		ACCELERATION	CRUISING IDLE	DECELERATION			
A/F MIXTURE	RICH ←		VARYING	→	LEAN		
DWELLMETER READING	0°	6°	15°	30°	45°	54°	60°
DUTY CYCLE	0%	10%	25%	50%	75%	90%	100%

MIXTURE CONTROL SOLENOID ON OFF

ONE CYCLE

Figure 23-39. When the engine is cold, the air/fuel mixture is set to full rich. The mixture control solenoid, or oxygen feedback solenoid, is energized only 10% of the time. When the engine reaches operating temperature, the fuel mixture will vary. (Cadillac)

Closed Loop

After the exhaust gases have reached a temperature of 600°F (316°C), the computer energizes and de-energizes the oxygen feedback solenoid within the carburetor at the rate of 10 times per second. The computer decides what to do after receiving the signal from the oxygen sensor, Figure 23-40. When the computer uses this signal to decide if the fuel mixture should be leaned out or richened, the system is referred to as being in ***closed loop,*** Figure 23-41.

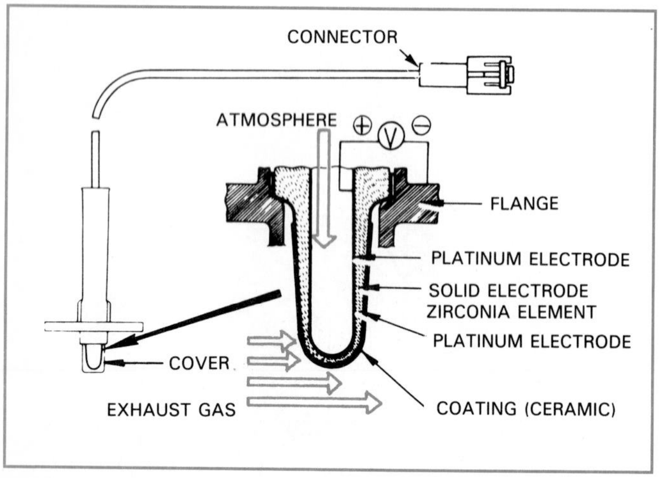

CONNECTOR
ATMOSPHERE
FLANGE
PLATINUM ELECTRODE
SOLID ELECTRODE ZIRCONIA ELEMENT
PLATINUM ELECTRODE
COVER
EXHAUST GAS
COATING (CERAMIC)

Figure 23-40. The oxygen sensor compares oxygen in the atmosphere to the amount of oxygen in the exhaust. The sensor provides a 1 volt signal to the computer when there is a lack of oxygen in the exhaust. No voltage signal is sent to the computer when there is an excess of oxygen in the exhaust. (Toyota)

Oxygen Sensor Operation

If the fuel mixture is too rich (a lack of oxygen in the exhaust), the sensor produces a 1 volt signal. The computer then energizes the oxygen feedback solenoid. This causes the fuel flowing through the metering jets to be reduced or leaned out.

If the fuel mixture is too lean (an excess of oxygen in the exhaust), the sensor does not produce any voltage. The computer de-energizes the oxygen feedback solenoid. This

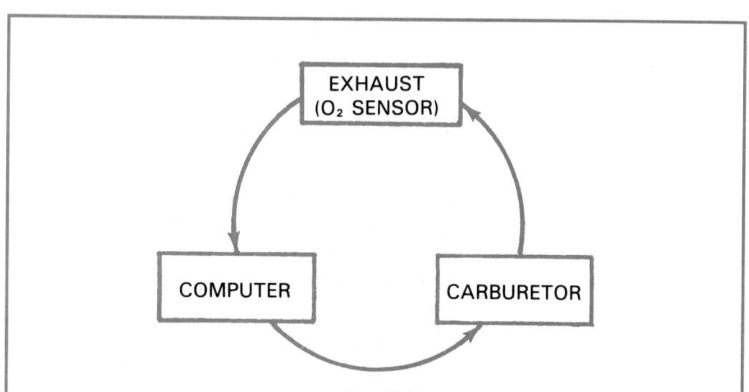

Figure 23-41. Closed-loop operation. The oxygen sensor monitors the combustion process and relays this information to the computer. The computer then adjusts the fuel mixture in the carburetor. This cycle is continuous after the engine reaches its operating temperature, except during wide open throttle.

causes more fuel to flow through the metering jets to richen the mixture.

Carburetor Service

Modern carburetors are designed to work with a specific engine. In the past, carburetors required a great amount of time and skill to adjust. After these adjustments were made, prolonged road testing under all speeds and conditions was needed. Today, the adjustments are few and can be done in a short amount of time by a qualified technician.

Adjustments

Before making carburetor adjustments, make sure that the ignition system is in good shape and that compression is within 10% of specifications for all cylinders. There must be no leaks in the intake manifold. The carburetor float level must be within specifications. The engine must be at operating temperature so that the idle speed can be set. Then, connect a tachometer according to the manufacturer's recommendations. With manual transmission cars in "neutral" and automatic transmission cars in "drive," the idle speed can be checked and adjusted (if necessary), Figures 23-42 to 23-44.

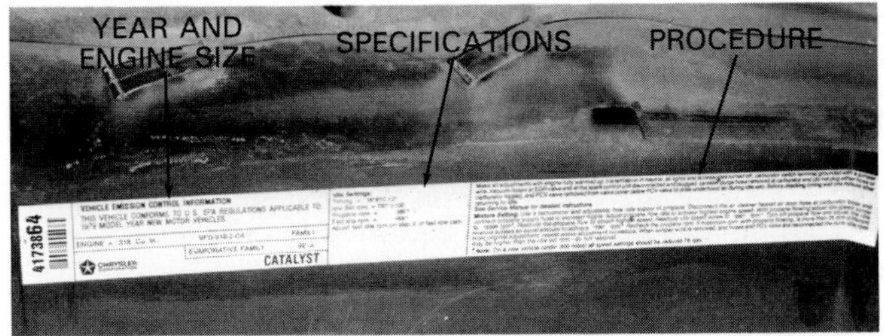

Figure 23-42. A decal placed in the engine compartment provides the necessary information for timing, idle speed, and fuel mixture.

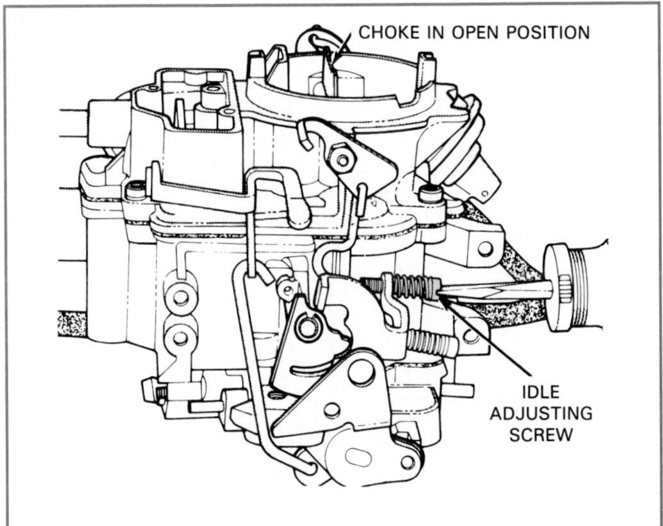

Figure 23-43. Make sure that the engine has reached its normal operating temperature and the choke plate is wide open before adjusting the idle. Turn the screw clockwise to increase idle speed and counterclockwise to decrease idle speed. (Chrysler)

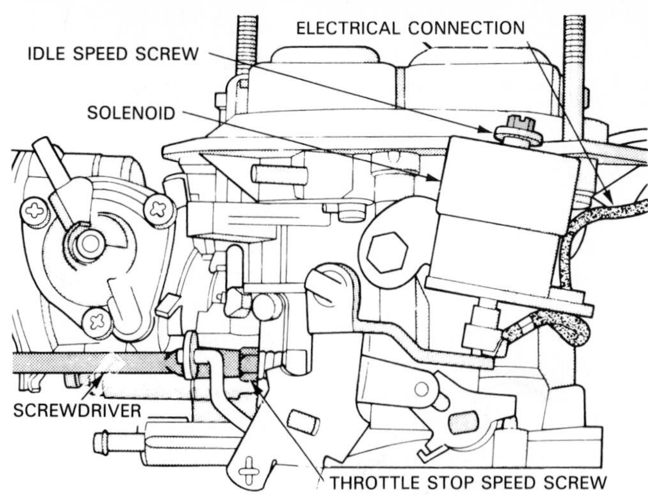

Figure 23-44. Some idle speed adjustments are two-step processes. First, the idle speed screw on the solenoid is adjusted. Then, the solenoid is de-energized by removing the electrical connection. The final adjustment is made by turning the throttle stop speed screw to the specified speed. The electrical connection at the solenoid is then reconnected. (Chrysler)

The choke spring coil forces the choke valve closed when it is cold, after depressing the accelerator pedal. At the same time, the fast idle cam is positioned by linkage connected to the choke valve shaft, Figure 23-45. Therefore, the fast idle screw is adjusted after it touches the fast idle cam with the engine running. When the choke valve is wide open, the fast idle screw will not touch the fast idle cam. The engine will then be at a "curb" idle speed.

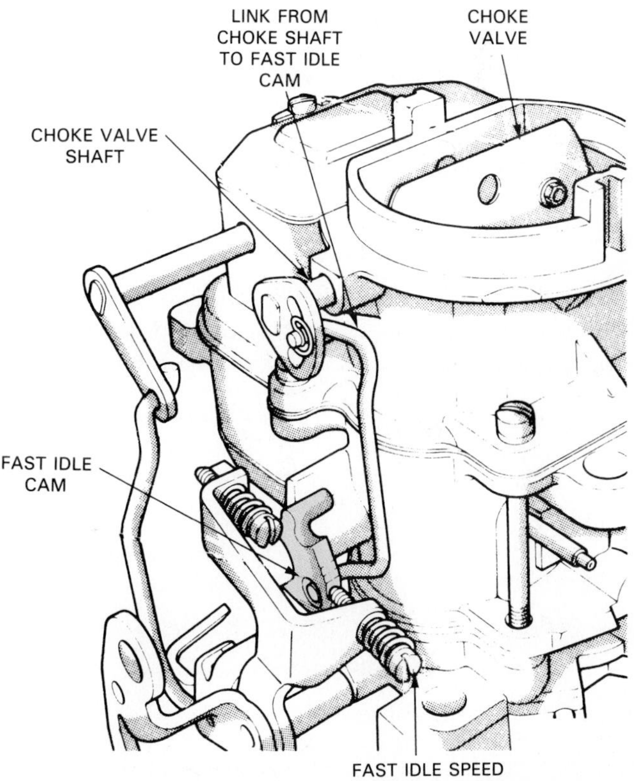

Figure 23-45. To set the fast idle speed, the fast idle cam must be placed under the fast idle screw. (Chrysler)

NOTE: On some computerized engines, the computer controls the idle and fast idle speed. No attempt should be made to adjust the idle or fast idle speed on these engines. Consult the individual service manual.

Idle Mixture Check

An infrared exhaust gas analyzer is used to check the ***idle mixture.*** Always consult the individual service manual for specifications. The following procedure is an example:

1. Set parking brake and place transmission or transaxle in neutral. Turn off all lights and accessories. Connect a tachometer. Start and run the engine until the normal operating temperature is reached.
2. On feedback-equipped cars, turn engine off and then disconnect negative battery cable for 10 seconds before reconnecting cable. Disconnect oxygen sensor electrical connection. Restart the engine and run at 2500 rpm for 10 seconds before returning to curb idle.
3. Disconnect the electrical connection at the radiator fan, if so equipped. Allow engine to idle for two minutes.
4. Insert probe from exhaust gas analyzer into tailpipe, Figure 23-46.
5. Adjust the idle speed (if possible) to specified idle rpm.
6. Check reading of carbon monoxide at the exhaust gas analyzer. The reading should be between 0.1 to 0.3%. If it is not, the idle mixture may need adjustment. It is possible that a high float level, dirty air filter, etc., may also cause a high percentage of carbon monoxide in the exhaust.
7. If the reading is within the specified range, turn the engine off and reconnect the fan motor and the oxygen sensor wire. Finally, disconnect tachometer.

NOTE: If an infrared machine is not available, an alternate (but not as accurate) method adds propane to the carburetor to temporarily enrich the fuel mixture.

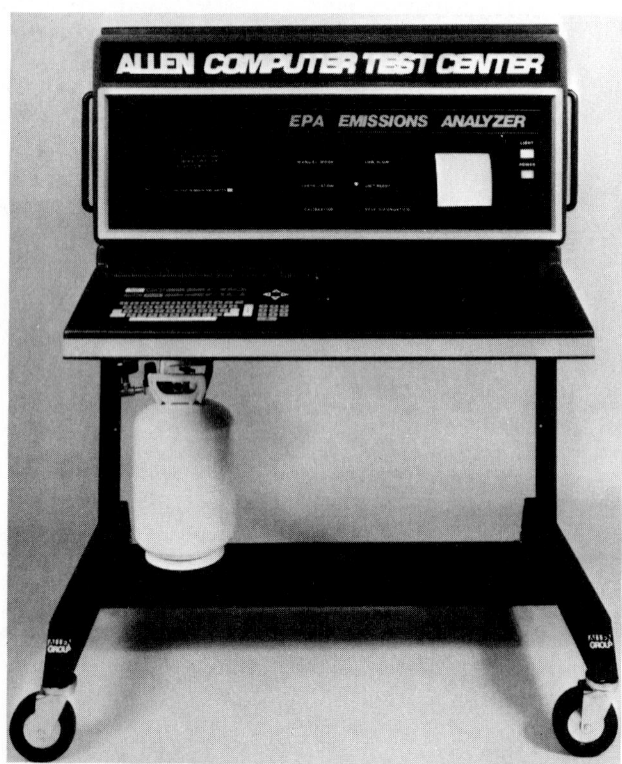

Figure 23-46. Special equipment is needed to analyze exhaust gases.

Idle Mixture Adjustment

If the carbon monoxide reading is not within specifications, the fuel mixture may have to be adjusted. Prior to adjustment, the concealment plugs must be removed to gain access to the mixture screws, Figures 23-47 and 23-48. This requires removing the carburetor from the intake manifold. After the plugs have been removed, the carburetor must be reinstalled on the engine. With the engine running and test equipment hooked up, the fuel mixture screws can be adjusted.

To lean the fuel mixture, turn the mixture screws clockwise. To enrich the fuel mixture, turn the mixture screws counterclockwise. The mixture screws should be turned only 1/16 of a turn at a time. This allows for precise adjustment.

On two- and four-barrel carburetors, both fuel mixture screws must be turned the same amount and in the same direction. Alternate between fuel mixture screws after each adjustment. For example, if you turn one fuel mixture screw clockwise 1/16 of a turn, turn the other screw 1/16 of a turn in the same direction. When you do this, the engine will run smoothly at idle.

Caution! Idle mixture screws are sealed for a purpose. Federal laws prohibit the tampering with these screws unless an infrared machine is used while adjusting the fuel mixture. If caught, a technician can expect stiff fines and a possible jail sentence.

Carburetor Cleaning

Cleaning the carburetor is the first step in rebuilding it. Carburetor cleaning solutions dissolve the gum that accumulates on the inside and outside of carburetors. This gum is formed by heat acting on the fuel.

Carburetors are disassembled, and then individual parts are washed in special carburetor cleaner. This also

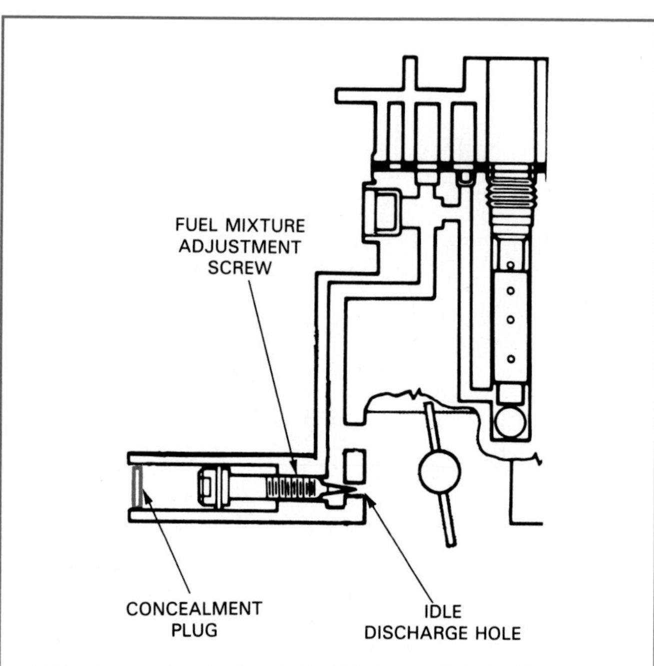

Figure 23-47. The fuel mixture screws are located behind concealment plugs. (Chrysler)

provides the opportunity for inspection and replacement of worn parts, Figure 23-49.

Some carburetors can be damaged by immersion in a "dunk-type" carburetor cleaner. This is because of a thermo-wax element at the end of drilled passage. The dunk-type carburetor cleaning solution will dissolve the thermo-wax element. This will cause the carburetor to malfunction. If you are not sure that a carburetor has a thermo-wax element, use a spray-type carburetor cleaner.

Wash all parts except the accelerator pump diaphragm or plunger, power valve diaphragm, and anti-stall dashpot assembly. Do not wash parts made of fabric or rubber. They could be injured by the cleaning solution.

After cleaning, wash all traces of the cleaning solution with hot water. Then, blow the parts dry with compressed air. Force compressed air through all passages of the carburetor to be sure they are clean and dry. Do not use a wire brush. Do not run a fine wire through any of the jets. This may damage the ports. Once this is complete, the carburetor is ready to be rebuilt.

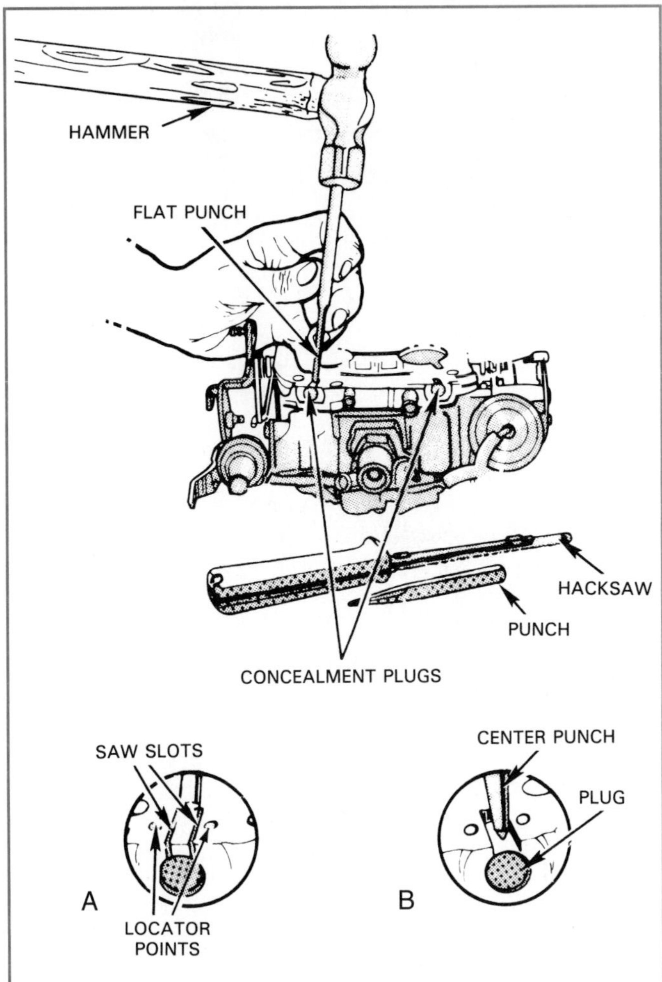

Figure 23-48. Gaining access to the fuel mixture screws. A–Turn the carburetor upside down and cut where indicated. B–Using a punch, drive the plug out. The carburetor is then ready to reinstall and adjust. (Rochester)

Carburetor Overhaul

After cleaning and inspecting the parts of a carburetor, it is time to reassemble it. Also, all adjustments are made during this time. A carburetor ***rebuild kit,*** Figure 23-50, is used in the process. This kit contains new gaskets, accelerator pump, needle and seat, check balls, and instructions that include specifications for all of the adjustments.

Carburetor floats are either mounted in the fuel bowl, Figure 23-51, or attached to the air horn assembly, Figure 23-52. The float assembly should also be replaced during a rebuild. This is inexpensive insurance, since the floats can absorb gasoline as they age. This makes the float heavier. Consequently, it rides lower in the fuel bowl and allows more fuel into the bowl than specified. This causes an overly rich fuel mixture. A new fuel and air filter completes the carburetor rebuild.

Questions Before Testing

Prior to testing and making a diagnosis of the problems, a good technician will act as a detective. Asking the driver questions will eliminate guessing when deciding where to start the testing procedure. This reduces diagnostic time and helps eliminate the needless replacement parts. Some of the questions the technician should ask include:

- Is the engine hot or cold when the problem occurs? How long and how far do you drive before experiencing problems?

Figure 23-49. Check the throttle body for warpage using a straightedge.

Figure 23-50. A carburetor rebuild kit is primarily made up of gaskets.

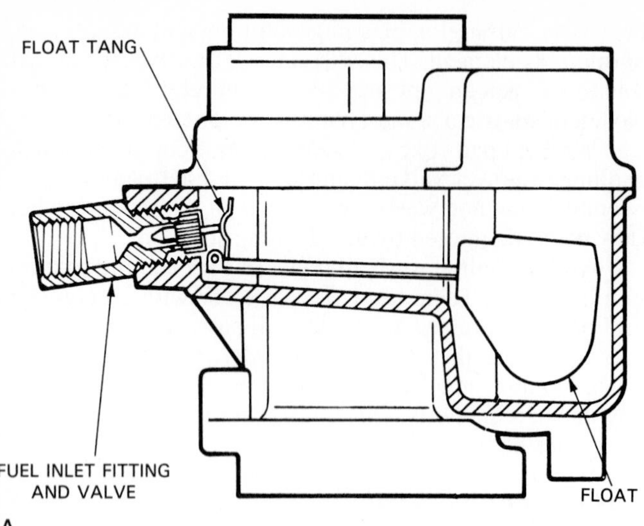

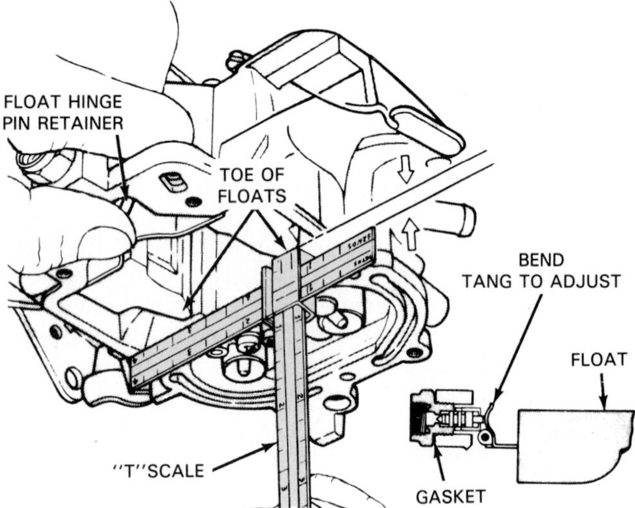

Figure 23-51. Float mountings. A–Float is mounted in the fuel bowl. B–When a float is mounted in the fuel bowl, the bowl and the float must be inverted to take the float measurement. Place the carburetor upright and then bend the tang to adjust the float level. (Chrysler)

- When does the problem occur?
  - At idle?
  - Acceleration-full or part throttle?
  - At a constant low speed?
  - At a constant high speed?
  - During deceleration (foot off gas pedal)?
  - When making a left or right turn?
  - When hauling cargo?
- Are atmospheric conditions a factor?
  - Is it raining, snowing, or is high humidity present when the problem occurs?
  - What is the ambient temperature when the problem occurs? (hot or cold)
  - Is there a strong head wind?
- Where does the problem occur?
  - Going up a gradual or steep grade?

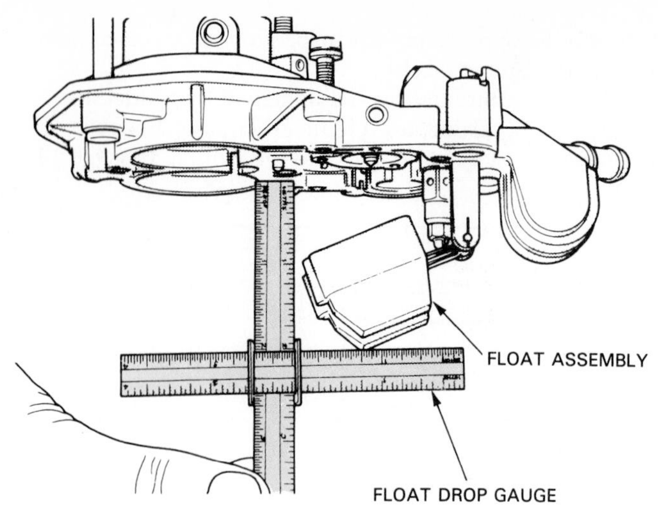

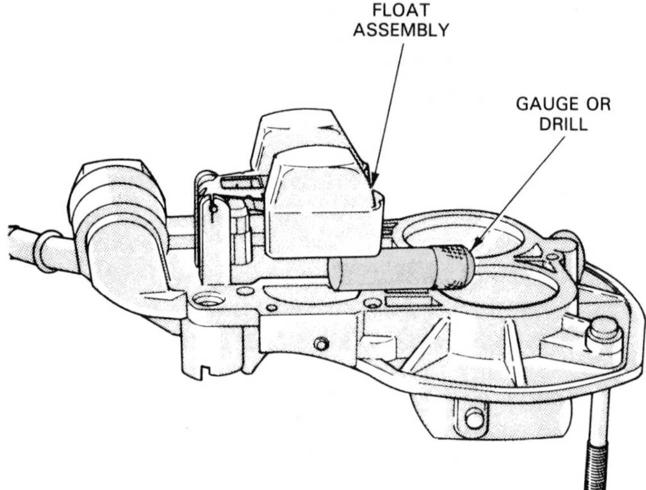

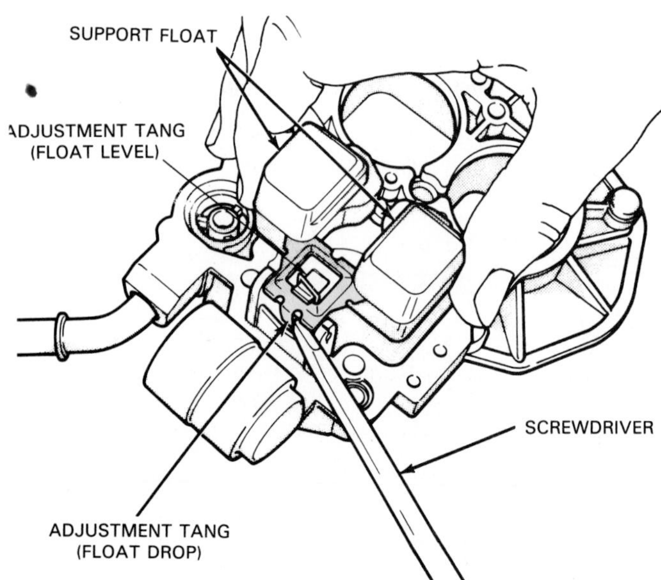

Figure 23-52. Float mountings. A–Floats mounted to the air horn must have the float drop measured. B–Measuring float level. C–Adjustment points for float drop and float level. (Chrysler)

  - On a level grade?
  - At high altitudes?
  - Near high power lines?
- What is the fuel tank level when the problem occurs?
- What type of gas did you last purchase? Where was it purchased?
- Other factors:
  - Were any recent repairs made? (Were they done correctly with quality parts?)
  - Has there been any modifications to the fuel or ignition system?
  - Is the problem intermittent?
- Verify that the problem exists. Some drivers mistake a surging condition for:
  - The air conditioning clutch cycling on and off.
  - The torque converter clutch (TCC) locking and unlocking. If this is severe, a problem may exist with the TCC system.

Troubleshooting Carburetors

A defective or poorly adjusted carburetor will affect the fuel economy and performance of the car. Failure of the engine to perform is seldom in the carburetor. Therefore, when the engine fails to start or perform, check the ignition, compression, choke, and fuel supply before disassembling the carburetor.

If the above mentioned inspections fail to pinpoint a problem, the following procedure should be used. Operate the throttle lever by hand while looking in the carburetor. Fuel should squirt from the accelerator pump jets. If no fuel is seen squirting from the accelerator pump jets, there is no fuel in the carburetor float bowl. This could mean that the fuel pump is bad, the fuel filter is clogged, a fuel line is clogged or leaking, or there is no atmospheric pressure in the tank pushing on the fuel. Disconnect the fuel line at the carburetor and direct the line into a small bottle. Fuel should flow in heavy spurts when the engine is cranked (if the engine is equipped with a mechanical fuel pump). Also, check the fuel line by blowing air back to the fuel tank. A gurgling sound should be heard back at the tank or the fuel line is clogged.

Dwell Readings

On some carbureted engines that are computerized, a ***dwell meter*** can be used in the troubleshooting process, Figure 23-53. If the engine is cold and/or has just been started, the dwell should be fixed at 6° for about two minutes. After this time dwell will be around 30° at idle and will vary as the engine is accelerated or decelerated.

The technician should be able to hear the mixture control solenoid "click" after starting the engine. If not, the mixture control solenoid may be defective. After the engine has reached operating temperature, remove a vacuum hose. The dwell should decrease. Then, reconnect the vacuum hose and choke the engine. The dwell should increase. If not, consult the individual service manual for test and repair procedures.

Trouble Codes

A light may appear on the dash that informs the driver to "Check Engine" or "Service Engine Soon," Figure 23-54. This same light is used by the technician to pull ***trouble codes*** from the computer by flashing out numbers. Look in the service manual to find what the Trouble Code means. Not all computerized systems have trouble codes. For more information on trouble codes, see Chapter 29, Computer Systems.

Carburetor Problems

While the basic causes of carburetor trouble will vary with different makes and designs, the usual problems and their causes are outlined below.

Poor Engine Performance

- Air leak at carburetor or manifold.
- Air leak in fuel line.
- Clogged or dirty carburetor air filter.
- Clogged fuel lines or fuel filter.
- Defective fuel pump.
- Incorrect fuel level in fuel bowl.
- Automatic choke incorrectly set.
- Dirt in carburetor jets and passages.
- Worn or inoperative accelerator pump.
- Wrong or incorrectly set metering rod.
- Inoperative power valve, economizer, or jet.
- Damaged or wrong main metering jet.
- Worn idle needle valve and seat.
- Loose jets.
- Defective gaskets.
- Worn throttle valve shaft.
- Clogged exhaust system.
- Defective manifold heat control valve.
- Leaking vacuum lines.
- Defective sensors.
- Defective computer.

Poor Idling

- Incorrect adjustment of idle needle valve.
- Incorrect float level.
- Sticking float needle valve.
- Defective gasket between carburetor and manifold.
- Defective gaskets in carburetor.
- Loose carburetor-to-manifold nuts.
- Loose intake manifold attaching bolts.
- Idle discharge holes partly clogged.
- Defective automatic choke.
- Loose jets in carburetor.
- Leaking vacuum lines to accessory equipment.
- Vacuum leaks that are partly compensated for by a rich idle adjustment.
- Worn main metering jet.
- Restricted or clogged air cleaner.
- High float level.
- Defective sensors.
- Defective computer.
- Defective O_2 feedback solenoid.

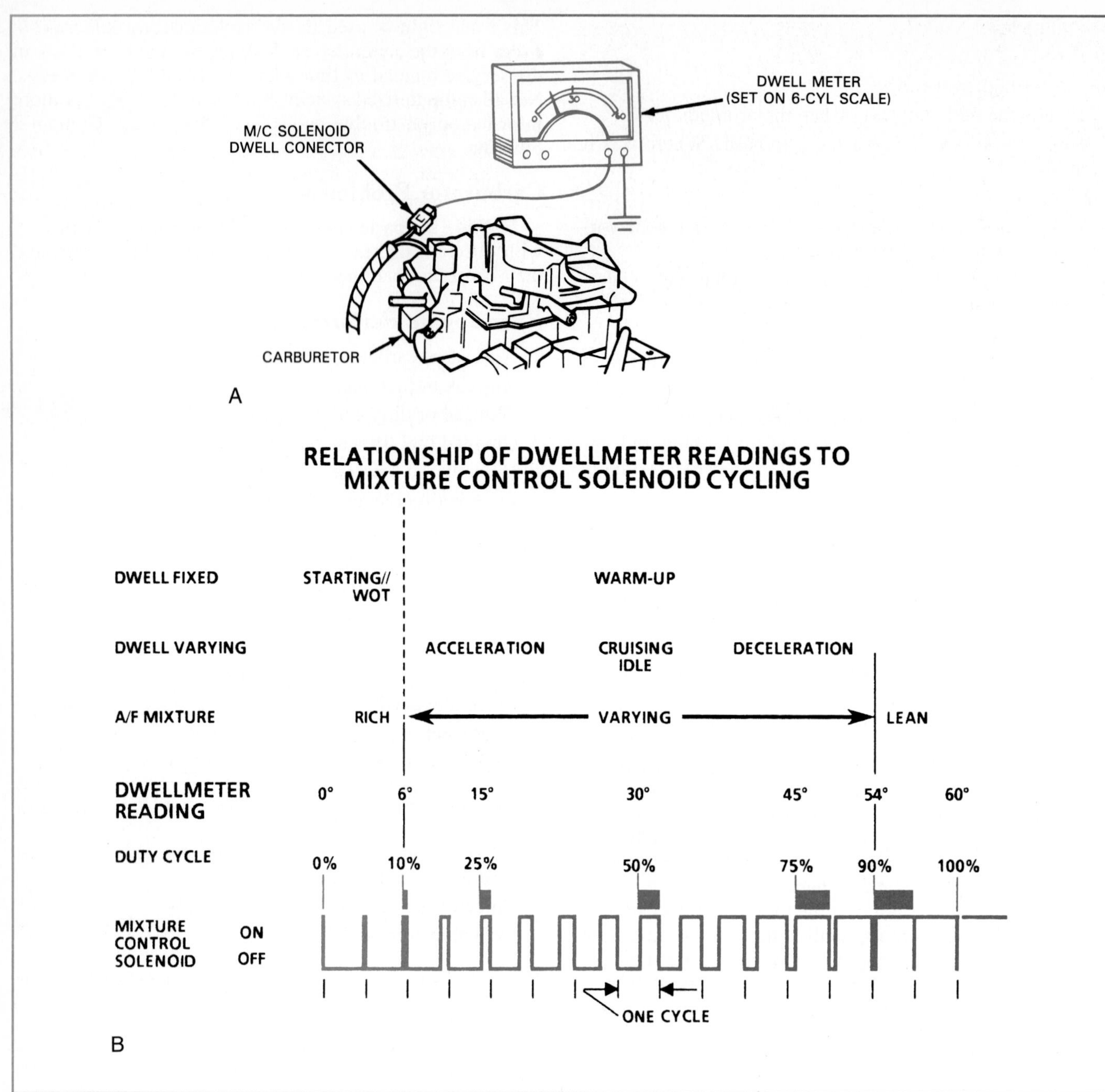

Figure 23-53. A–A dwell meter is used to determine the fuel mixture. This meter must be set on the six cylinder scale, regardless of the number of cylinders. B–A dwell reading of 6° indicates a rich fuel mixture–the solenoid is energized 10% of the time. A dwell reading of 54° indicates a lean mixture–the solenoid is energized 90% of the time. (Cadillac and Oldsmobile)

Hard Starting

- Incorrect choke adjustment.
- Defective choke.
- Incorrect float level.
- Incorrect fuel pump pressure.
- Sticking fuel inlet needle.
- Improper starting procedure.

Poor Acceleration

- Accelerator pump incorrectly adjusted.
- Accelerator pump inoperative.
- Corroded or bad seat on accelerator bypass jet.
- Accelerator pump leather hard or worn.
- Clogged accelerator jets or passages.
- Defective ball checks in accelerator system.
- Incorrect fuel level.
- Misadjusted throttle position sensor.

Carburetor Floods

- Float level too high.
- Stuck float needle valve.
- Defective gaskets in carburetor.

Figure 23-54. The "Check Engine" or "Service Engine Soon" light indicates a problem. The technician uses these lights to pull trouble codes from the computer.

- Cracked carburetor body.
- Excessive fuel pump pressure.

Excessive Fuel Consumption

There are many causes of excessive fuel consumption other than defective carburetion. Consider poor engine compression, excessive engine friction, dragging brakes, misaligned wheels, clogged muffler, defective ignition, quick starts, and high-speed driving.

- Adjustment of idle mixture.
- Fuel leaks in carburetor or lines.
- Dirty air cleaner.
- High float level.
- Defective fuel economizer.
- Defective manifold heat control valve.
- Dirty carburetor.
- Turbo wastegate stuck closed.
- Excessive fuel pressure.
- Sticking fuel inlet needle.

Choke Troubleshooting

The basic check for choke operation is to make sure the choke valve is closed when the engine is cold. When the engine is hot, the choke valve should be open.

Choke troubles may be the cause of:

- Hard or no starting cold. This could be caused by the choke valve remaining in the open position. If the temperature is mild, the engine may start but will stall as soon as it is started. If the temperature is extremely cold, the engine may not even start if the choke valve remains open. This may be due to a defective choke coil spring.
- No starting cold. This could be caused by the choke valve remaining closed, which would not allow air to enter the carburetor. This may be caused by the choke coil spring being set too tight. When the choke coil is set too tight, the spring coil exerts excessive pressure on the choke valve, keeping it closed. To determine if this is the cause, wedge the choke valve open with the shank of a screwdriver. The car will start if this is the cause and the engine is not flooded.

Chapter 23–Review Questions

Write your answers on a separate sheet of paper. Do not write in this book.

1. The rate of flow through a carburetor is the same under all operating conditions. True or False?
2. When starting an internal combustion engine, the fuel mixture should be:
   (A) rich.
   (B) lean.
   (C) average.
   (D) None of the above.
3. Which speed requires a richer mixture?
   (A) Idling.
   (B) 30 mph.
4. Will all cylinders of a multi-cylinder engine receive an air/fuel mixture having the same octane rating?
5. For normal operating conditions, what air/fuel ratio will give the best economy?
   (A) 16 to 1.
   (B) 20 to 1.
   (C) 25 to 1.
6. For quick acceleration, what is the best air/fuel ratio?
   (A) 5 to 1.
   (B) 10 to 1.
   (C) 12 to 1.
   (D) 20 to 1.
7. Are the molecules forming a gas held more tightly together than those forming a metal?
8. Name two factors affecting evaporation.
9. What causes the air/fuel mixture to be drawn into the combustion chamber of an internal combustion engine?
10. The purpose of a venturi in a carburetor is to:
    (A) increase speed of air passing through carburetor.
    (B) maintain correct air/fuel ratio.
    (C) provide extra fuel for acceleration.
11. There are five main circuits in a modern carburetor. Name four of them.
12. In a carburetor venturi, which point has the highest vacuum?
    (A) Entrance to the venturi.
    (B) Narrowest point of the venturi.
    (C) Point one inch beyond the venturi.
    (D) None of the above.
13. The idle system of a carburetor supplies fuel at which speeds?
    (A) Idle speed only.
    (B) Speeds up to 40 mph.
    (C) Speeds up to 25 mph.
    (D) None of the above.
14. How many fuel discharge ports does the conventional idle system have?
    (A) One.
    (B) Two.
    (C) Three.
    (D) Four.
15. When the idle system is no longer supplying fuel to the engine, which system then supplies fuel?
    (A) Air bleed system.
    (B) Main system.
    (C) Vaporizing system.
    (D) None of the above.

16. The purpose of a power valve is to supply _____ (more or less) fuel.
17. The metering rod is designed to vary the size of:
    (A) the float.
    (B) the venturi.
    (C) the accelerator pump.
    (D) the carburetor jets.
18. Under what conditions is ice most likely to form in a carburetor?
    (A) -20°F and high humidity.
    (B) -32°F and high humidity.
    (C) 0°F and low humidity.
    (D) None of the above.
19. On what type of car are you most likely to find an anti-stall dashpot?
    (A) Cars with automatic transmission.
    (B) Cars with conventional transmission.
    (C) Cars fitted with one-barrel carburetors.
    (D) Cars fitted with four-barrel carburetors.
20. What is the purpose of an oxygen sensor?
21. Explain what is meant by closed loop.
22. In your own words, define what is meant by a stoichiometric air/fuel ratio.
23. Which should be adjusted first?
    (A) Ignition system.
    (B) Carburetor.
24. Briefly describe the procedure for adjusting a single-barrel carburetor.
25. Describe the procedure for adjusting a two-barrel carburetor.
26. What is the advantage of analyzing the exhaust gas?
27. On engines with emission controls, adjustment of _____ and _____ is important.
28. Which of the following parts should not be washed in carburetor-cleaning solution?
    (A) Carburetor float.
    (B) Anti-stall dashpot.
    (C) Idle needle valve.
    (D) Accelerator pump diaphragm.
    (E) Accelerator pump plunger.
    (F) Main jets.
    (G) Throttle valve.
29. List three causes for carburetor flooding.
30. List three causes for hard starting that start in the fuel system.
31. List five causes of excessive fuel consumption that start in the fuel system.
32. A dwell meter is used to determine if a problem exists in the computer, carburetor, or oxygen sensor. True or False?
33. Technician A states that the "Check Engine" light informs the driver of a problem. Technician B states that the "Check Engine" light is used by the technician to pull trouble codes from the computer.
    Who is right?
    (A) A only.
    (B) B only.
    (C) Both A & B.
    (D) Neither A nor B.

Chapter 24
Ignition System Fundamentals and Service

After studying this chapter, you will be able to:
- ❍ Distinguish between the primary and secondary side of the ignition system.
- ❍ Describe how battery voltage is transformed into 20,000 volts or more.
- ❍ Explain how the different types of ignition systems operate.

Ignition

The first section of this chapter is on the components in the secondary side of the ***ignition system.*** The ***secondary side*** of the ignition is the same on most ignition systems. Although the primary side of the ignition is discussed to an extent, it will be covered in detail in the second section.

The ***primary side*** of the ignition system carries battery voltage. The primary side controls the secondary side of the ignition. The design of the primary side can vary from manufacturer to manufacturer. The secondary side of the ignition system is where battery voltage is transformed into 20,000 or more volts.

Ignition Coils

The ***ignition coil,*** Figure 24-1, is a transformer designed to increase primary voltage (received from battery) of 12 V to at least 20,000 V. It is composed of a primary winding, a secondary winding, and a core of soft iron.

The ***primary winding*** is made up of 200 turns of heavy wire (No. 18 gauge). The ***secondary winding*** may have as many as 22,000 turns of fine wire, (No. 38 gauge). The coil is constructed so that the secondary winding is wound around the soft iron core and the primary winding surrounds the secondary winding. The purpose of the core is to concentrate the magnetic field.

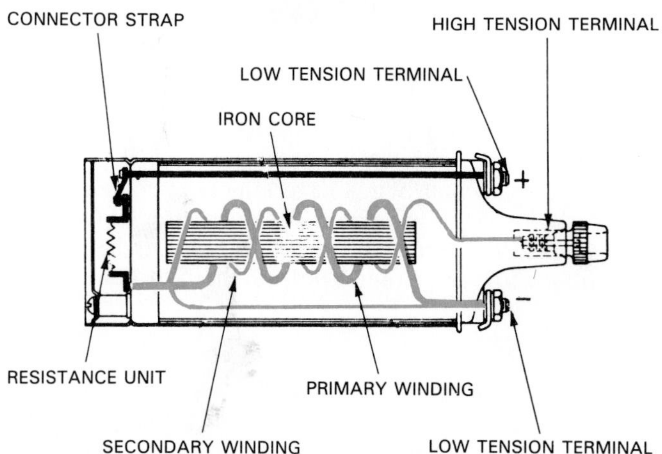

Figure 24-1. The ignition coil is constructed of primary and secondary windings that are wound around a soft iron core.

This coil assembly is housed in a steel case with a cap of molded insulating materials that carries the terminals. Some ignition coils have their windings immersed in oil or paraffin-like material. This is done to improve insulation and reduce the effects of moisture. Oil-filled coils can better withstand corona (faint glow) and heat. Oil has the advantage of healing itself if any breakdown in insulation occurs.

To prevent coils from absorbing moisture, they are hermetically sealed. Heavy-duty coils are built with larger cores and provided with greater insulation. Although the life of the coil is lengthened, the higher inductance of these coils limits top speed performance.

The current flowing through the primary winding of the ignition coil produces a magnetic field in the coil. When the primary circuit is interrupted to the coil, the magnetic field collapses. The movement of the collapsing magnetic field induces current in the secondary winding of the coil. Since there are many more turns of wire in the secondary winding than there are in the primary winding, the battery voltage is increased to 20,000 volts or more.

Negative Polarity

Most manufacturers consider ***negative polarity*** of the high tension outlet of the ignition coil as a means of saving electrical energy. This is because the center electrode is the hottest part of the spark plug.

When the center electrode is connected to the negative high tension voltage, the spark gap becomes ionized more readily and forms a lower resistance path for the spark. Therefore, a lower voltage is needed to fire the same plug gap.

A simple means of testing coil polarity on a car can be made with a voltmeter. The positive lead is connected to a good ground and the negative lead is connected to the spark plug terminal of No. 1 cylinder. With this connection, the voltmeter is connected across the coil high tension windings. Run the engine at idle. If the voltmeter indicates "up" scale, the coil has a negative polarity.

Distributor Cap

The ***distributor cap*** should be checked to see that sparks have not been arcing from point to point within the cap. The inside of the cap must be clean. The firing points should not be eroded, Figure 24-2, and the inside of the towers must be clean and free from corrosion.

If needed, the inside of the distributor cap towers can be cleaned by means of a round wire brush. When cleaning distributor caps, never use any cleaning solution that would injure the cap.

There are two methods of holding the distributor cap in place on the distributor housing. One is by means of clips or cap springs, and the other is by means of a latch. The clips can be pulled back, permitting the cap to be lifted from the distributor housing. To release the latch, a screwdriver is inserted in upper slotted end of cap retainer. It is then pressed down and turned until the latch is disengaged.

Rotor

A distributor ***rotor*** is designed to rotate and distribute the high tension current to the towers of the distributor cap. The firing end of the rotor, Figure 24-3, from which the high-tension spark jumps to each of the cap terminals, should not be worn. Any wear will result in excessive resistance to the high-tension spark.

Rotors are mounted on the upper end of the distributor shaft, Figure 24-4. In this connection, the rotor must have a snug fit on the end of the shaft. On another design, two screws are used to attach the rotor to a plate on the top of the distributor shaft. Built-in locators on the rotor and holes in the plate ensure correct reassembly. One locator is round, and the other is square. One method used to hold the rotor in place is shown in Figure 24-5.

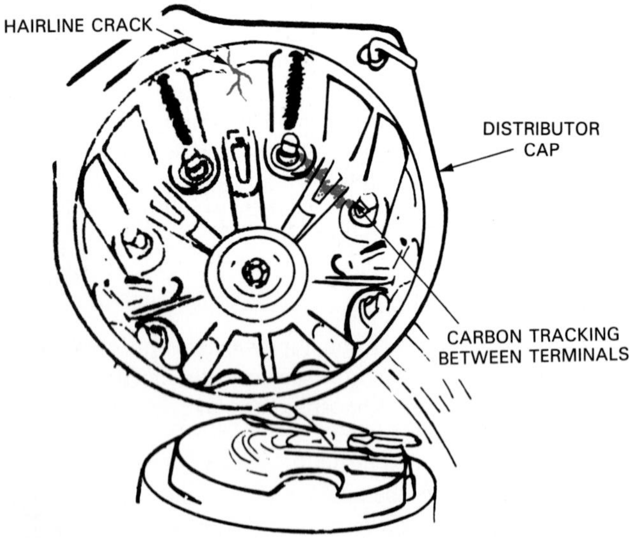

Figure 24-2. Check the inside of the distributor cap for carbon tracking and hairline cracks.

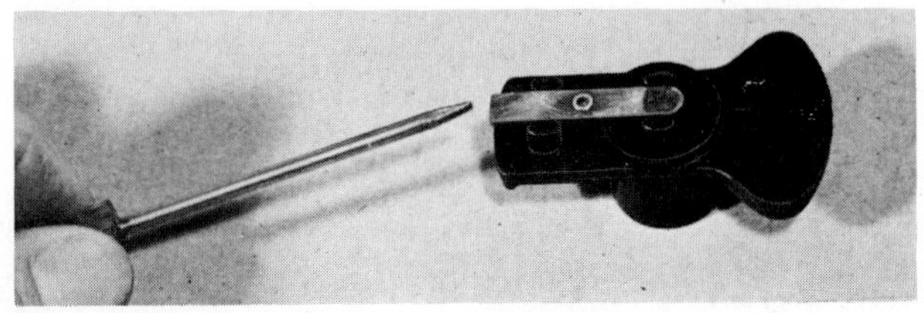

Figure 24-3. The firing end of the rotor must not be worn or it will have to be replaced.

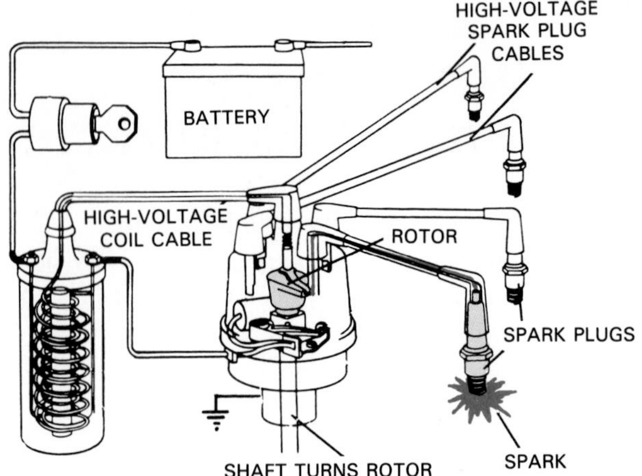

Figure 24-4. As the rotor rotates inside the distributor cap, it delivers the high voltage from the ignition coil to each spark plug.

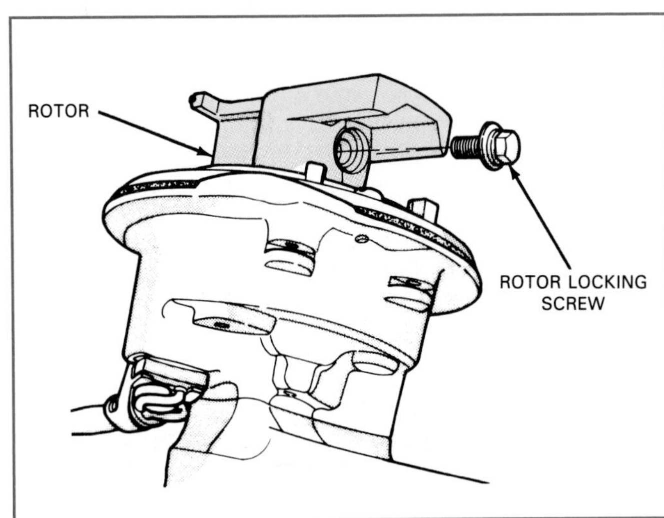

Figure 24-5. This rotor is held in place by a screw in this system. (Chrysler)

Spark Plug Wires

The ***spark plug wire*** carries 20,000 or more volts from the distributor cap to the spark plug. Spark plug wires, Figure 24-6, are made of various layers of materials. The fiber core inside the spark plug wire carries the high voltage. The older design of spark plug wires used a metallic wire to carry the high voltage. This caused an electrical interference with radio and TV reception.

Some spark plug wires have a locking connection at the distributor cap, Figure 24-7. The distributor cap must be removed and the terminals squeezed together before the spark plug wire can be removed from the distributor cap.

Spark Plugs

The ***spark plug*** in a spark ignition engine provides the gap across which the high tension voltage jumps, creating the spark that ignites the compressed air/fuel mixture.

The spark plug, Figure 24-8, contains a ***center electrode,*** which is connected to the ignition coil secondary

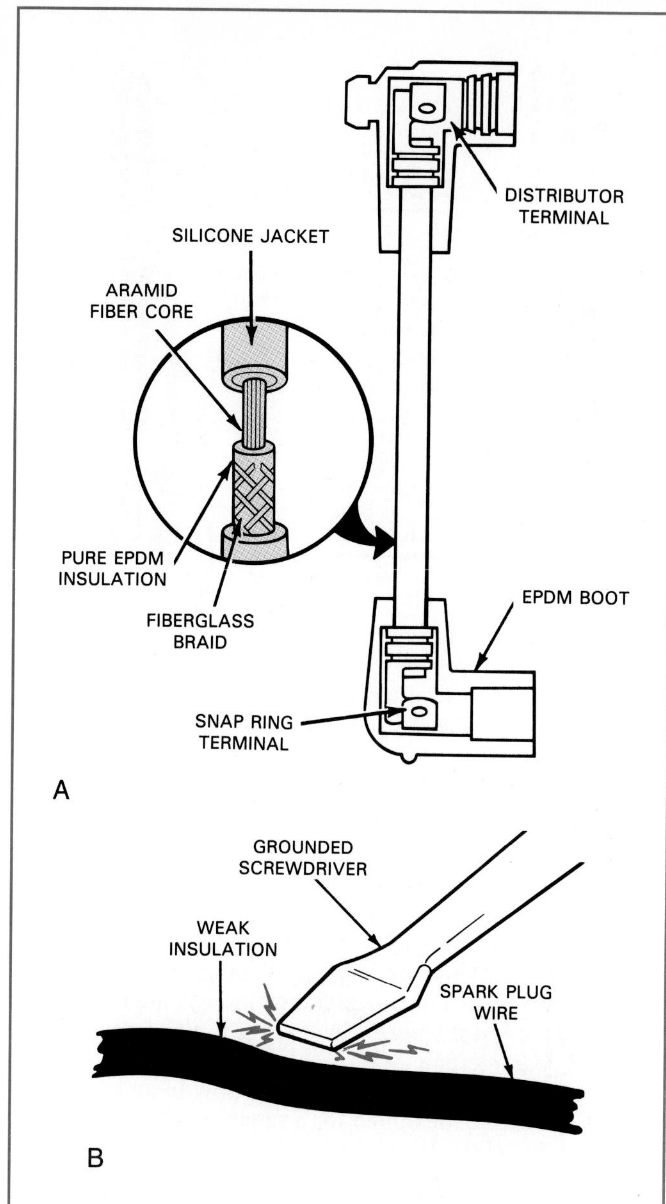

Figure 24-6. Spark plug wires. A–A fiber core carries the high voltage to the spark plug. B–To check the insulation around the fiber core, ground the shank of a screwdriver with a jumper wire and run the screwdriver along the length of each spark plug wire. If the pattern on the oscilloscope changes, the spark plug wire insulation is bad and may be the cause of a driveability problem. (Champion Spark Plug Co.)

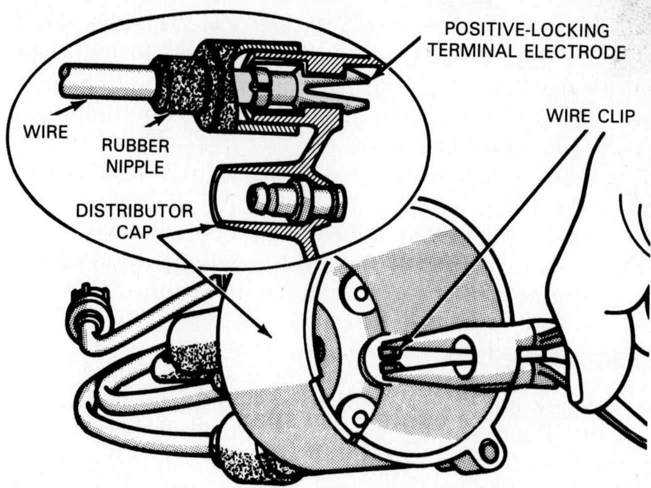

Figure 24-7. This type of distributor cap is found on four-cylinder Chrysler products. After removing the cap from the distributor, squeeze the locking terminal together before removing the spark plug wire from the cap. (Chrysler)

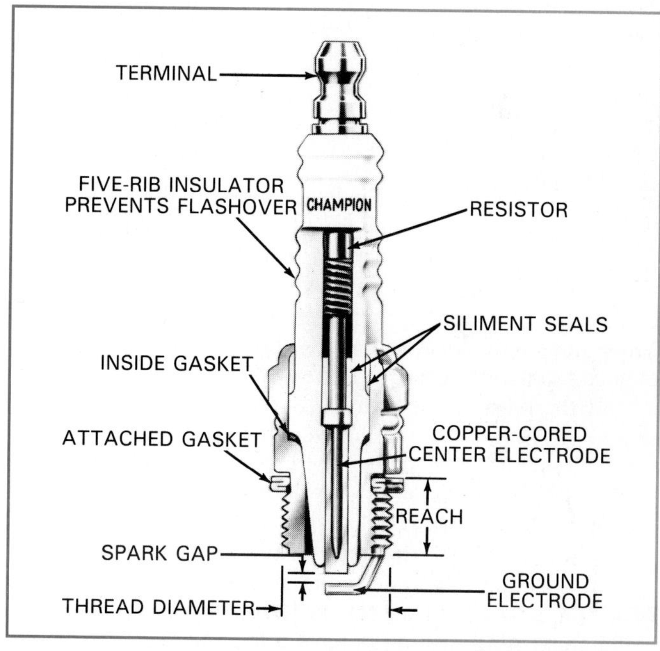

Figure 24-8. Construction of a typical spark plug. (Champion)

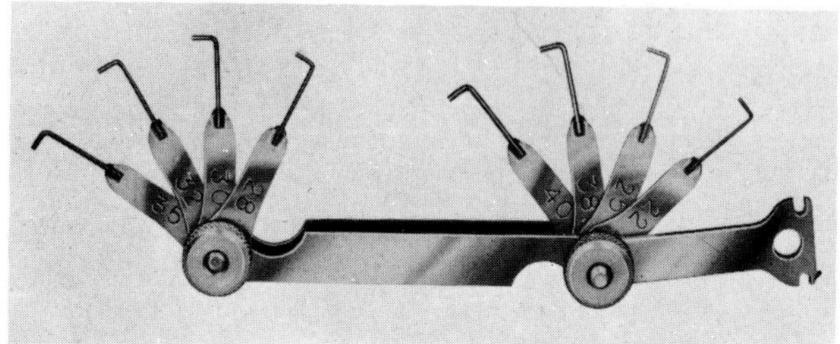

Figure 24-9. A wire-type spark plug gauge is more accurate than other gauges. The gap adjuster is at the right end of the gauge. The gap is adjusted by bending the side electrode.

through the distributor. The center electrode is insulated from the spark plug shell by a porcelain insulator. The ***side electrode*** protrudes from the bottom edge of the spark plug shell. It is positioned so that there is a gap between it and the center electrode.

The spark plug gap is adjusted by bending the side electrode. Figure 24-9 shows a combination spark plug gauge and gap adjusting tool. Spark plug gaps range from .020-.080 in. (0.501-2.032 mm). The gap must be set to the manufacturer's specifications. The size of the gap depends on the compression ratio of the engine and the design of the combustion chamber and ignition system.

Today, manufacturers specify gaps of .030, .035, .060, and .080 in. (0.762, 0.890, 1.52, and 2.03 mm). A wider gap includes more air/fuel mixture than a narrow gap, so there is more to ignite.

The ***shell*** of the spark plug is threaded, so it can be installed and removed with ease. All spark plugs except tapered-seat plugs require a gasket. The following thread sizes are used: 10 mm, 14 mm, and 18 mm. The spark plug must extend the proper distance into the combustion chamber . The distance that the plug extends into the combustion chamber is called the ***reach.***

Using plugs with a longer reach may result in the valves or piston striking the spark plug. If a plug with a short reach is installed, the electrodes become partly sheltered by the spark plug hole in the cylinder head. In this case, engine roughness and missing may result.

Heat Range

Spark plugs must be designed so the temperature of the firing end of the plug is high enough to burn off any carbon or other deposits. However, the plug must not get too hot or it will cause preignition, which will lead to deterioration of the insulator and the electrodes. This is difficult since the temperature of the spark plug tip varies with different engines and conditions. The center electrode temperatures range from a low of 392°F (200°C) at 10 mph to a high of 1472°F (800°C) at 80 mph.

The temperature of the spark plug insulator depends on the design of the spark plug and on the burning fuel in the combustion chamber. The temperature of the burning fuel will, of course, vary with the design of the engine, compression ratio, cooling system, and air/fuel ratio.

As the tip of the spark plug absorbs heat from the burning air/fuel mixture, the heat travels up the insulator to the spark plug shell. It then travels to the cylinder head and to the water jacket. The path that the heat travels is shown in Figure 24-10. The heat absorbed by the insulator increases as the temperature in the combustion chamber rises. More heat will be absorbed as the area of the insulator exposed to the hot gases is increased.

If the path the heat must follow to reach the cooling system is short, the tip will have a low temperature. Therefore, plugs with short paths for the heat to travel are known as ***cold plugs.*** Plugs with long paths for the heat to travel are known as ***hot plugs.***

The length of the path traversed by the heat in reaching the cooling system, the insulator material, and the insulator shape will affect its temperature. As a result, some spark plug insulators have a narrow neck just above the tip. Another design will have recessed tip sections that more readily follow temperature changes in the combustion chamber.

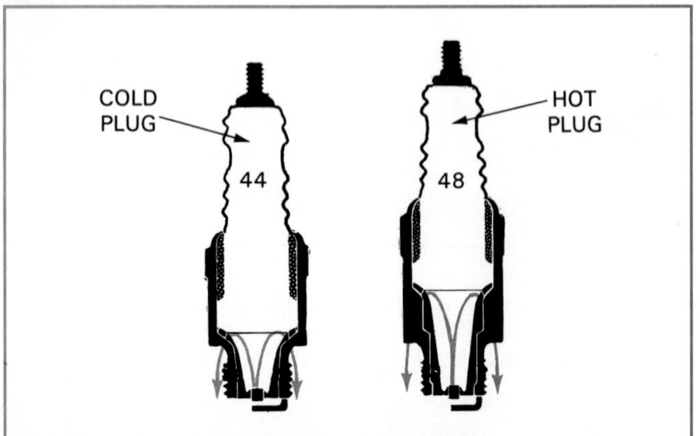

Figure 24-10. On a cold plug, heat does not have far to travel before dissipating. The higher the number on the spark plug, the hotter the plug. (Champion)

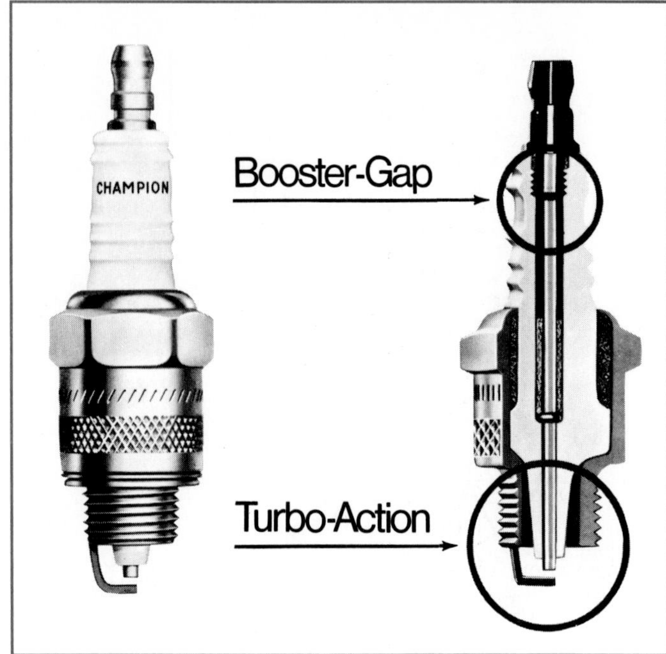

Figure 24-11. A special spark plug with a booster gap provides protection against fouling at low temperatures.

Other designs provide increased volume between the shell and the insulator to permit more cooling, Figure 24-11. Still other designs have the tip of the insulator protruding beyond the end of the shell for improved heat characteristics.

The ***heat range*** of any spark plug is its ability to transfer heat from the firing end to the cylinder head and water jacket. A spark plug's heat range is also known as the "thermal characteristic."

Figure 24-12 shows typical heat flow in an auto spark plug. A spark plug designed for a rotary engine is shown in Figure 24-13. Note the dual firing points.

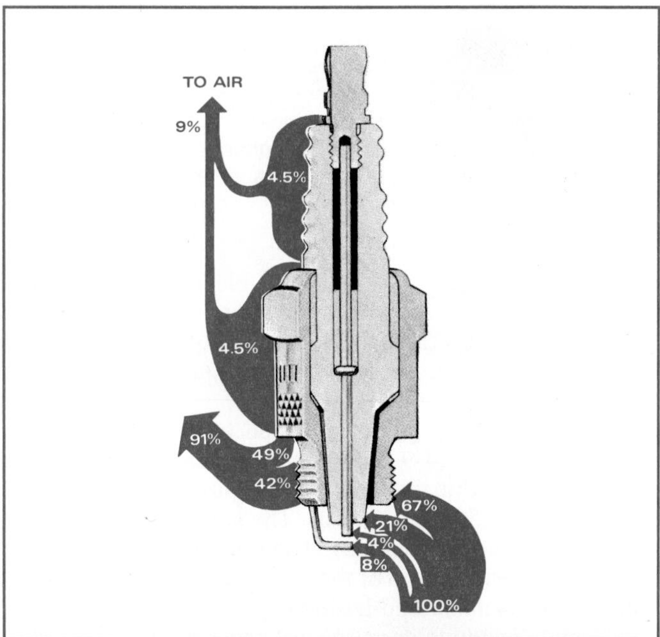

Figure 24-12. Heat flow from a spark plug.

Figure 24-13. The spark plug for a rotary engine has two ground electrodes.

Engine designers select spark plugs that will give good performance for average driving conditions. However, if the engine is run for a long time under full-load conditions, the standard plug will run too hot and preignition will result. Therefore, a colder plug is needed to carry off the heat faster.

On the other hand, if the engine is run for a long time at part throttle opening, the standard plug will tend to foul. The insulator tip will become covered with carbon and other products of combustion. As a result, high tension voltage will leak across the carbon (because of its lower resistance) rather than jump the gap at the electrodes. In this case, a hotter plug (with a longer heat path) should be used.

Spark Plug Fouling

As mentioned, products of combustion accumulate on the portion of the insulator of the spark plug within the combustion chamber. The two most common types of ***spark plug fouling*** are carbon fouling and oil fouling.

Carbon fouling, Figure 24-14, results from extended low-speed operation and from an excessively rich fuel mixture. Carbon fouling causes missing or roughness and creates soft black soot that is easy to remove from the plug.

Oil fouling, Figure 24-14, is found on engines that are so badly worn that excess oil reaches the combustion chamber.

Required Voltage

There are many factors that will affect the voltage needed to jump a certain gap. These factors include the shape of the electrodes forming the gap; the conductivity of the gases in the gap; and the temperature, pressure, and air/fuel ratio existing within the gap.

When fuel mixtures are lean, voltage needed to jump the gap may be as much as 40% higher than normal. The highest voltage needs exist at low engine speeds under very light acceleration. Missing under such conditions indicates that there is not enough voltage to fire the plug.

In Figure 24-15, note that voltage required to jump a gap increases rapidly until 12,000 volts are needed to jump a gap of .060 in. The measurements were made in an auto engine at road load.

The current delivered to the plugs depends on the current flowing in the primary winding of the coil. The amount of current decreases as the engine speed increases. The voltage at the plug also depends on the cleanliness of the spark plug electrode. For example, an ignition system that can deliver 20,000 volts to a clean plug may only deliver one half that amount to a plug that is partly fouled.

The reason plug fouling cuts down on peak voltage is because it takes time for the voltage to build up to a value where it can jump the plug gap. This high voltage is not reached instantaneously. It is built up to a maximum and then drops to zero, which, electrically speaking, takes a relatively long time (about 1/20,000 second).

The secondary voltage increases until it reaches a value that is capable of jumping the gap at the spark plug. However, if the plug is partly fouled, some current will flow across the coating on the insulator, which acts as a shunt across the gap. This loss of current reduces peak voltage to the point that it will not jump the gap of a badly fouled plug, Figure 24-16.

The faster the high tension voltage is built up, the less effect fouling will have. One method of attaining fast electrical buildup is by means of high-frequency ignition systems. Another method is by means of a series gap.

Spark Plug Gaps

Spark plug gaps (space between the electrodes) do not remain constant. Instead, they increase in size. The amount of increase is dependent on mileage, chemical characteristics of the fuel, combustion chamber temperatures, and the action of the electrical spark, which tears off portions of the electrode.

The electrical characteristics of the ignition system also affect the rate of wear of the spark plug electrodes. The electrical capacity of the ignition coil and the wiring is an important factor. Systems with high capacity will cause more rapid gap wear than systems with low capacity. Inserting a resistor in or near the spark plugs will tend to counteract this condition. Resistors reduce the peak current that passes through the electrodes when the capacity of the system is being discharged.

Some engines operate better with wider spark plug gaps than others. Many engineers agree that the explanation for this is in the characteristics of the air/fuel mixture in the vicinity of the plug gap. The mixture varies in different parts of the combustion chamber. This is due to the design of the combustion chamber, the turbulence of the mixture, and the amount of burned gases that remain in the combustion chamber from the last cycle.

Spark Plug Life

Under good conditions, the life of a spark plug ranges from 15,000 to 30,000 miles. Beyond that, they lose efficiency and should be replaced. Plug condition is important in the maintenance of low emission levels. Higher engine temperatures, added emission controls, and greater loads have made the conditions under which the spark plug operates severe.

Higher voltages are needed to fire a spark plug with worn electrodes. As shown in Figure 24-17, higher voltage is

GAP BRIDGED

IDENTIFIED BY DEPOSIT BUILD-UP CLOSING GAP BETWEEN ELECTRODES.

CAUSED BY OIL OR CARBON FOULING, REPLACE PLUG, OR IF DEPOSITS ARE NOT EXCESSIVE. THE PLUG CAN BE CLEANED.

OIL FOULED

IDENTIFIED BY WET BLACK DEPOSITS ON THE INSULATOR SHELL BORE ELECTRODES.

CAUSED BY EXCESSIVE OIL ENTERING COMBUSTION CHAMBER THROUGH WORN RINGS AND PISTONS, EXCESSIVE CLEARANCE BETWEEN VALVE GUIDES AND STEMS, OR WORN OR LOOSE BEARINGS. REPLACE THE PLUG.

CARBON FOULED

IDENTIFIED BY BLACK, DRY FLUFFY CARBON DEPOSITS ON INSULATOR TIPS, EXPOSED SHELL SURFACES AND ELECTRODES.

CAUSED BY TOO COLD A PLUG, WEAK IGNITION, DIRTY AIR CLEANER, DEFECTIVE FUEL PUMP, TOO RICH A FUEL MIXTURE, IMPROPERLY OPERATING HEAT RISER ON EXCESSIVE IDLING. CAN BE CLEANED.

NORMAL

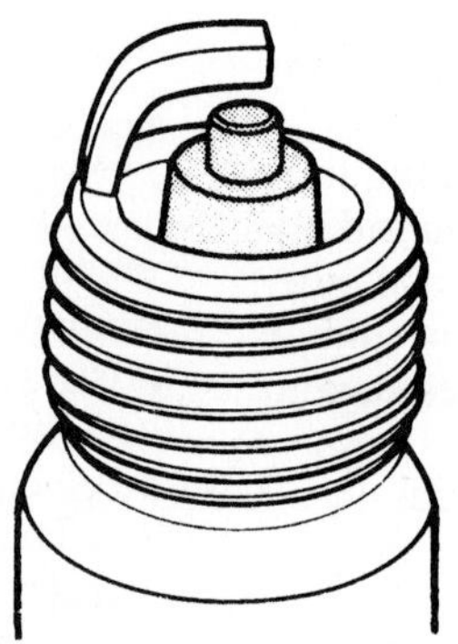

IDENTIFIED BY LIGHT TAN OR GRAY DEPOSITS ON THE FIRING TIP.

PRE-IGNITION

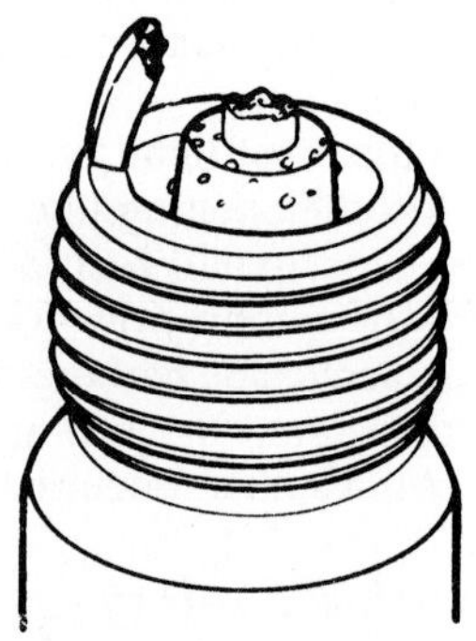

IDENTIFIED BY MELTED ELECTRODES AND POSSIBLY BLISTERED INSULATOR METALLIC DEPOSITS ON INSULATOR INDICATE ENGINE DAMAGE.
CAUSED BY WRONG TYPE OF FUEL, INCORRECT IGNITION TIMING OR ADVANCE, TOO HOT A PLUG, BURNT VALVES OR ENGINE OVERHEATING. REPLACE THE PLUG.

OVERHEATING

IDENTIFIED BY A WHITE OR LIGHT GRAY INSULATOR WITH SMALL BLACK OR GRAY BROWN SPOTS AND WITH BLUISH-BURNT APPEARANCE OF ELECTRODES.

CAUSED BY ENGINE OVER-HEATING, WRONG TYPE OF FUEL, LOOSE SPARK PLUGS, TOO HOT A PLUG, LOW FUEL PUMP PRESSURE OR INCORRECT IGNITION TIMING. REPLACE THE PLUG.

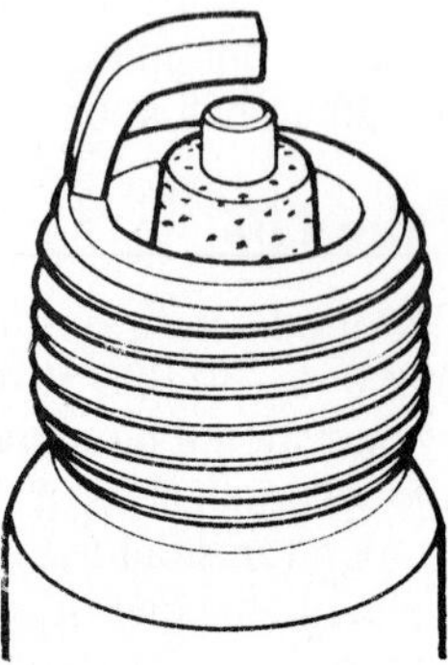

FUSED SPOT DEPOSIT

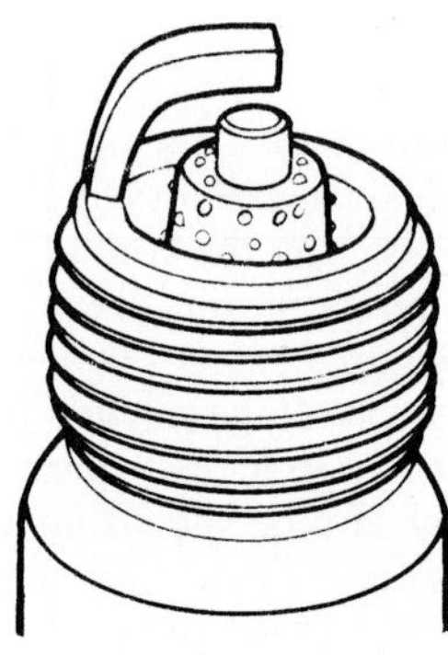

IDENTIFIED BY MELTED OR SPOTTY DEPOSITS RESEMBLING BUBBLES OR BLISTERS.

CAUSED BY SUDDEN ACCELERATION. CAN BE CLEANED IF NOT EXCESSIVE, OTHERWISE REPLACE PLUG.

Figure 24-14. Examples of spark plug fouling. (Ford)

.060
.040
.020
.010
GAP INCHES
4
6
8
10
SPARKING VOLTAGE - KILOVOLTS

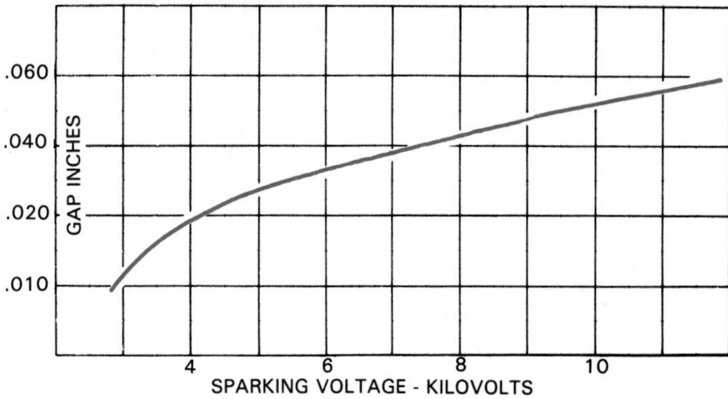

Figure 24-15. Voltage needed to jump different spark plug gaps.

A
B
14
12
10
8
6
4
2
REQUIRED VOLTAGE
USED SPARK PLUGS
REQUIRED VOLTAGE
NEW SPARK PLUGS
A
B
VOLTAGE (KILOVOLTS)
0
10
20
30
40
50
60
70
80
SPEED M.P.H.

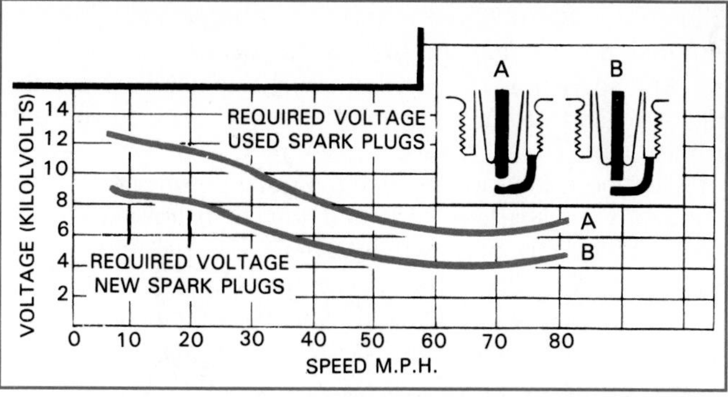

Figure 24-17. Voltage needed to fire new and old spark plugs.

needed to fire a used spark plug than a new plug. This is true at low speeds, where the difference may be as much as 4000 V.

Secondary Circuit Check

In the event of a "no start" condition, the ignition system will have to be checked in the following manner (provided the ignition coil is externally mounted). Remove the coil wire from the distributor cap. Hold the coil wire about 1/4″ from a good ground and crank the engine, Figure 24-18. If there is no spark, a check of the primary side of the ignition system is needed. Start by checking voltage at the positive terminal of the ignition coil with the ignition switch to the "on" position, Figure 24-19. Repeat the process at the negative terminal. Battery voltage should be observed at each terminal. If battery voltage is not obtained at the positive terminal, this wire will have to be traced to the point at which the circuit is open. If battery voltage is

IGNITION
COIL
A GOOD
ENGINE
GROUND
CHECK HERE
FOR SPARK

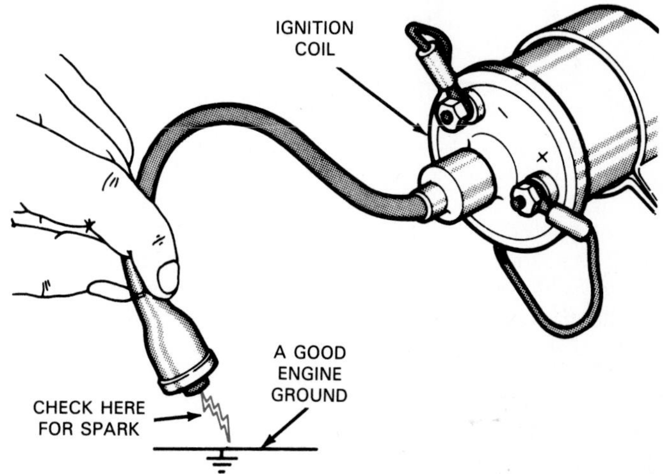

Figure 24-18. Hold the coil wire about 1/4″ from a good ground while cranking the engine. (Chrysler)

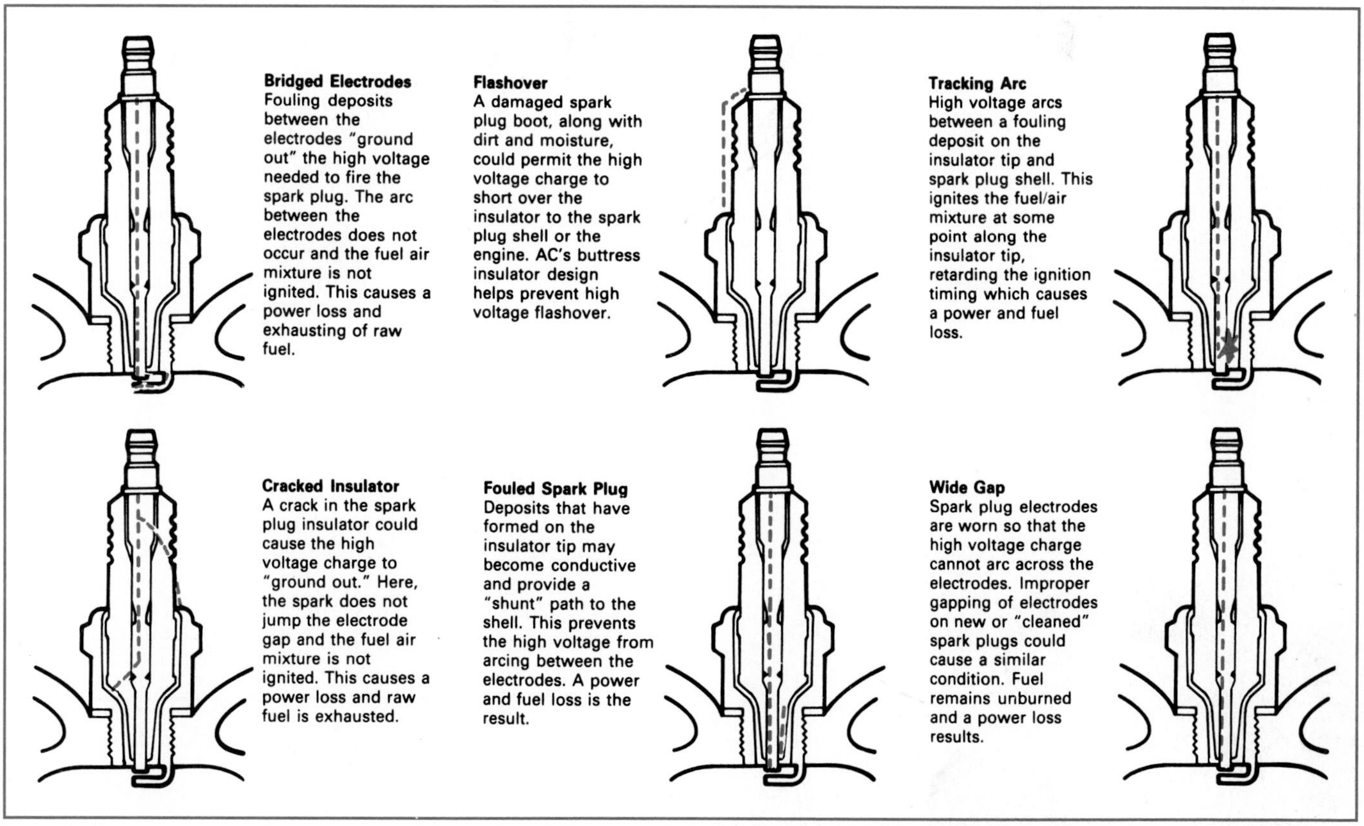

Bridged Electrodes
Fouling deposits between the electrodes "ground out" the high voltage needed to fire the spark plug. The arc between the electrodes does not occur and the fuel air mixture is not ignited. This causes a power loss and exhausting of raw fuel.
Flashover
A damaged spark plug boot, along with dirt and moisture, could permit the high voltage charge to short over the insulator to the spark plug shell or the engine. AC's buttress insulator design helps prevent high voltage flashover.
Tracking Arc
High voltage arcs between a fouling deposit on the insulator tip and spark plug shell. This ignites the fuel/air mixture at some point along the insulator tip, retarding the ignition timing which causes a power and fuel loss.
Cracked Insulator
A crack in the spark plug insulator could cause the high voltage charge to "ground out." Here, the spark does not jump the electrode gap and the fuel air mixture is not ignited. This causes a power loss and raw fuel is exhausted.
Fouled Spark Plug
Deposits that have formed on the insulator tip may become conductive and provide a "shunt" path to the shell. This prevents the high voltage from arcing between the electrodes. A power and fuel loss is the result.
Wide Gap
Spark plug electrodes are worn so that the high voltage charge cannot arc across the electrodes. Improper gapping of electrodes on new or "cleaned" spark plugs could cause a similar condition. Fuel remains unburned and a power loss results.

Figure 24-16. Abnormal voltage paths at the spark plug cause problems. (Cadillac)

obtained at the positive terminal but not at the negative terminal, the ignition coil must be replaced.

If a spark was observed jumping this gap between the coil wire and ground, reconnect the coil wire to the distributor cap. Then, remove a spark plug wire from a spark plug and hold it about 1/4″ from a good ground. Crank the engine. If no spark is observed, the distributor cap, the rotor, or the spark plug wire is at fault. Use an ohmmeter to test the spark plug wire for continuity. If a spark was observed, remove and examine the spark plug. If the plug appears normal, a check of the fuel system is needed.

Warning! Spark tests should not be used when testing distributorless or direct ignition systems. These systems produce extremely high voltages, which can cause electrocution.

Firing Order

In order to reduce engine vibration and secure an even flow of power, the cylinders of an engine must fire in the correct sequence. The sequence of spark plug firing is known as the ***firing order.*** On inline engines, the No. 1 cylinder is behind the timing gears. On GM and Chrysler V-8 engines, the front cylinder on the left bank is No. 1. The front cylinder on the right bank would be No. 2.

The firing order of inline six-cylinder engines manufactured in the United States is 1-5-3-6-2-4, Figure 24-20. The most popular firing order of a V-8 is 1-8-4-3-6-5-7-2. Other firing orders used on V-8 engines are 1-5-6-3-4-2-7-8, 1-5-4-2-6-3-7-8, and 1-3-7-2-6-5-4-8. The firing order of four-cylinder inline engines can be either 1-3-4-2 or 1-2-4-3.

Ignition Timing

The ignition system must be timed so that the spark occurs in the combustion chamber at the correct instant. Incorrect ***ignition timing*** results in loss of efficiency and power. If the spark "fires" too early, preignition and "pinging" will occur. If continued, the engine will be damaged. If the spark "fires" too late, both fuel economy and power will be reduced.

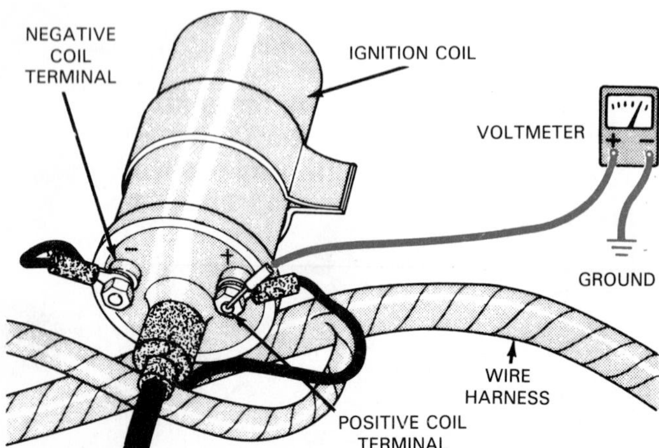

Figure 24-19. If a spark is not observed while cranking the engine, check the voltage at the positive terminal and then at the negative terminal. (Chrysler)

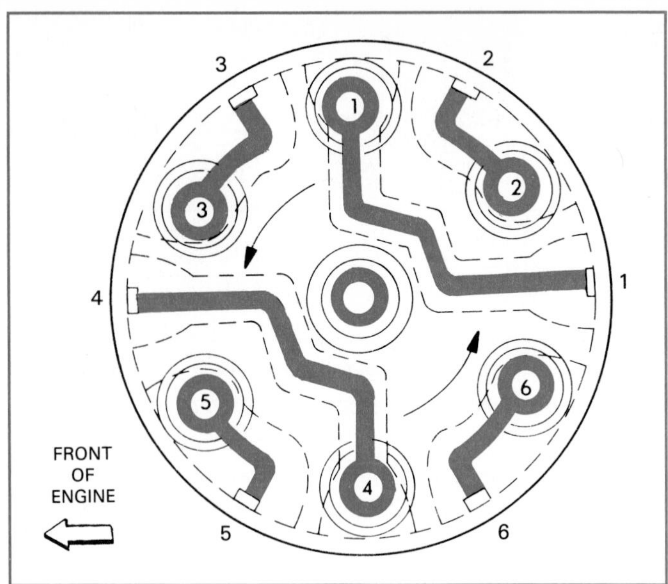

Figure 24-20. Note that the electrodes inside of this distributor cap are offset from the outside terminals. (Chrysler)

Timing of the spark varies in engines. For this reason, specifications must be observed. The spark is timed in relation to the position of the No. 1 piston in most engines. Timing is specified as a number of degrees before top dead center (BTDC). Top dead center occurs when the piston reaches the end of its compression stroke. ***Timing marks*** are placed on the flywheel or the vibration damper at the front of the crankshaft. A timing mark setup is shown in Figure 24-21.

To time the ignition of an engine, a ***timing light*** must be used, Figure 24-22. The timing light is connected to the battery and to the No. 1 spark plug wire. The beam of the timing light is then directed to the timing marks on the engine. With the engine running, the light will flash each time the spark occurs. The timing marks will appear to stand still, so that the time the spark occurs is easily noted.

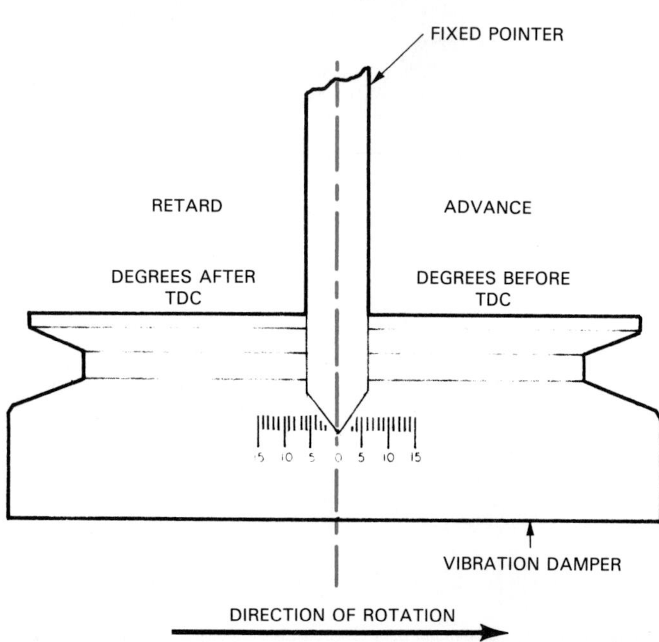

Figure 24-21. Timing marks on a vibration damper.

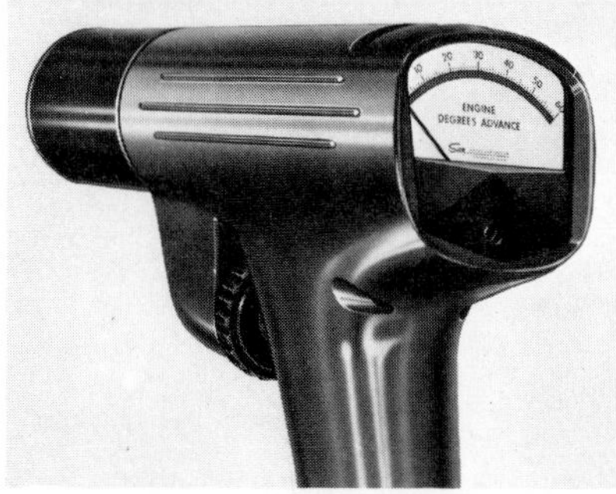

Figure 24-22. Timing light with an advance control and a meter. The meter indicates the amount of advance.

The timing mark should align with the index mark. If it does not, the clamp screw of the distributor is loosened and the distributor is rotated to the correct position. Moving the distributor housing against shaft rotation advances the timing. Moving it with shaft rotation retards the timing.

Special timing setups exist. For example, the notch shown in Figures 24-23 and 24-24 is designed to receive a magnetic probe when timing the engine. With the aid of this device, precision timing is assured for the lowest emission levels.

Spark Advance

When the engine is idling, the spark is timed to occur just before the piston reaches the top of the compression stroke. When the engine is idling or operating at a sustained speed under part-throttle conditions, cylinders take in only part of the full charge. As a result, compression pressures are low and combustion is slow. To obtain maximum efficiency under such conditions, the spark has to be advanced. Also, at higher engine speeds, there is a shorter interval of time for the mixture to ignite. Therefore, in order to obtain maximum power at higher speeds, the spark must occur slightly earlier in the cycle.

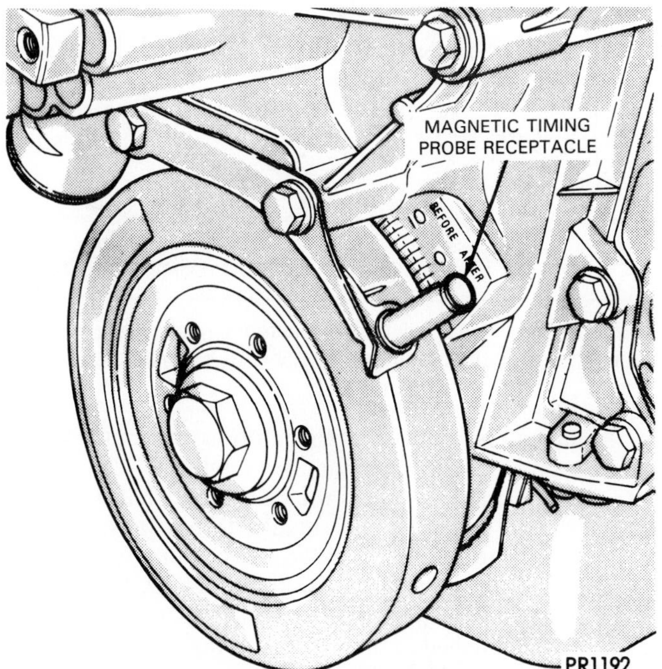

Figure 24-23. When using a magnetic timing device, an offset angle must be entered into the diagnostic machine. (Chrysler)

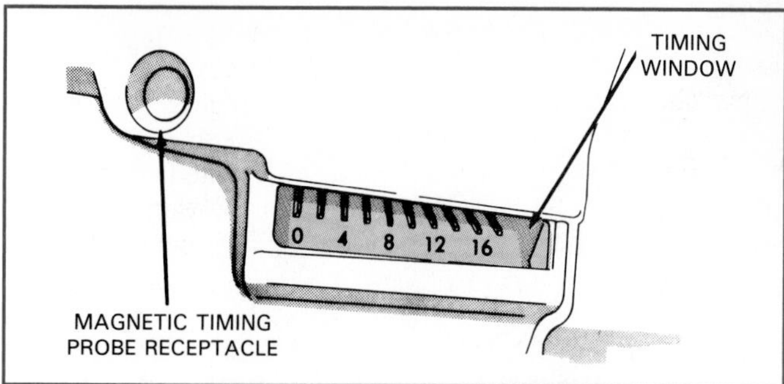

Figure 24-24. These timing marks are located at the flywheel end of a transversely mounted engine. (Chrysler)

Factors Governing Spark Advance

Many variables affect spark advance, Figure 24-25, in an engine and ignition system. Consider these factors:

- Manifold pressure.
  - High vacuum (low manifold pressure): combustion is slower and more spark advance is needed.
  - Low vacuum (high manifold pressure): combustion is faster and less spark advance is needed.
- Engine speed.
  - Low speed and load: combustion is slower and more spark advance is needed.
  - Low speed and full load: combustion is faster and less spark advance is needed.
  - High speed and full load: combustion is slower and more spark advance is needed.
- Engine temperature.
  - Cold engine: combustion is slower and more spark advance is needed.
  - Hot engine: combustion is faster and less spark advance is needed.
- Cylinder bore.
  - Larger bore: combustion is slower and more spark advance is needed.
  - Smaller bore: combustion is faster and less spark advance is needed.
- Compression ratio.
  - Low compression ratio: combustion is slower and more spark advance is needed.
  - High compression ratio: combustion is faster and less spark advance is needed.
- Character of fuel.
  - Low volatility: combustion is slower and more spark advance is needed.
  - High volatility: combustion is faster and less spark advance is needed.
- Throttle angle.
  - Small angle: combustion is faster and less spark advance is needed.
  - Large angle: combustion is slower and more spark advance is needed.

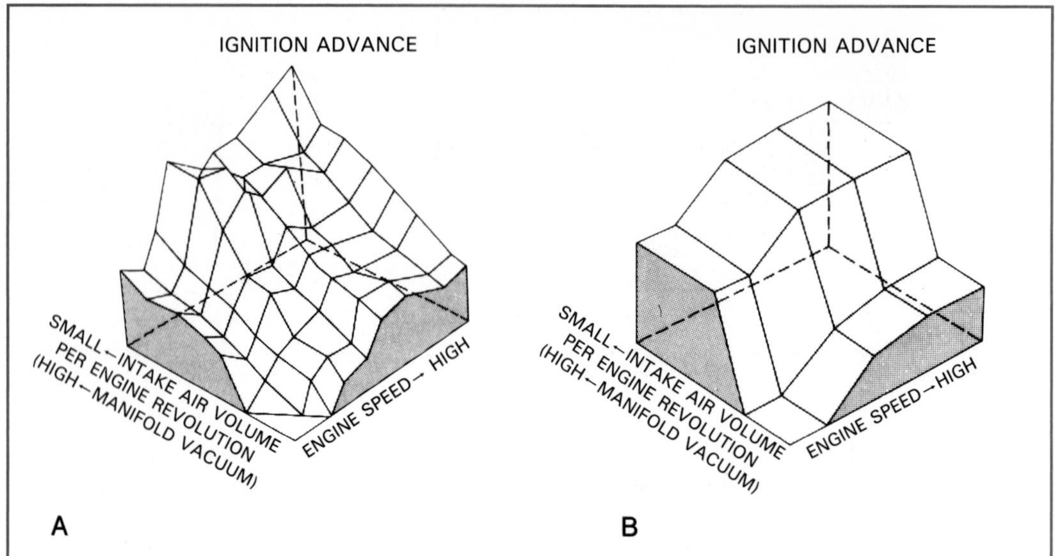

Figure 24-25. A–Computerized ignition systems calculate many variables before advancing the spark. This creates more horsepower and reduces emissions. B–Conventional and electronic ignition systems calculate spark advance for load and speed only.(Toyota)

- Octane rating.
  - High octane fuel: combustion is slower and more spark advance is needed.
  - Low octane fuel: combustion is faster and less spark advance is needed.

In addition to the above factors that affect spark timing, others include:

- The shape of the combustion chamber.
- The location of the spark plug, Figure 24-26.
- The amount of carbon in the combustion chamber.
- The fuel distribution to each cylinder.

Spark Advance Controls

On breaker point and electronic ignitions, the spark advance is controlled by the centrifugal advance and vacuum advance systems. The amount of centrifugal advance is determined by engine rpm. Vacuum advance is supplied in addition to centrifugal advance. However, the amount of vacuum advance is determined by engine load or manifold pressure.

On computerized ignition systems, the amount of advance is determined by the throttle angle, manifold pressure, engine rpm, coolant temperature, and atmospheric temperature and pressure. The computer processes this information from the sensors. The computer then advances the timing accordingly.

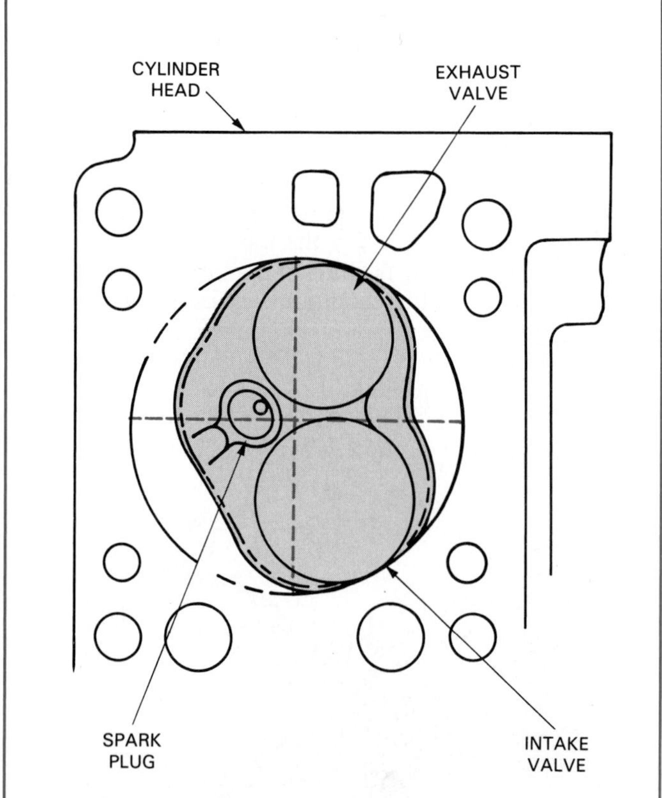

Figure 24-26. The spark plug is located almost in the center of a wedge-shaped combustion chamber. (Oldsmobile)

Specific Ignition Systems

This section of the chapter will discuss breaker point, electronic, and computerized ignition systems. The most common system types are included.

Breaker Point Ignition

In a ***breaker point system,*** the ignition distributor, Figure 24-27, makes and breaks the primary ignition circuit. It also distributes high-tension current to the proper spark plug at the correct time. The distributor is driven at one-half crankshaft speed on four-cycle engines. It is driven by the camshaft.

Detailed construction of the ignition distributor varies from manufacturer to manufacturer, Figure 24-28. It consists of a housing into which the distributor shaft and centrifugal weight assembly are fitted with bearings. In most cases, these bearings are of the bronze bushing type.

In the distributor shown in Figure 24-29, the contact set is attached to the movable breaker plate. A vacuum advance unit attached to the distributor housing is mounted under the breaker plate. The rotor covers the centrifugal advance mechanism, which consists of a cam that is actuated by two centrifugal weights, Figure 24-28.

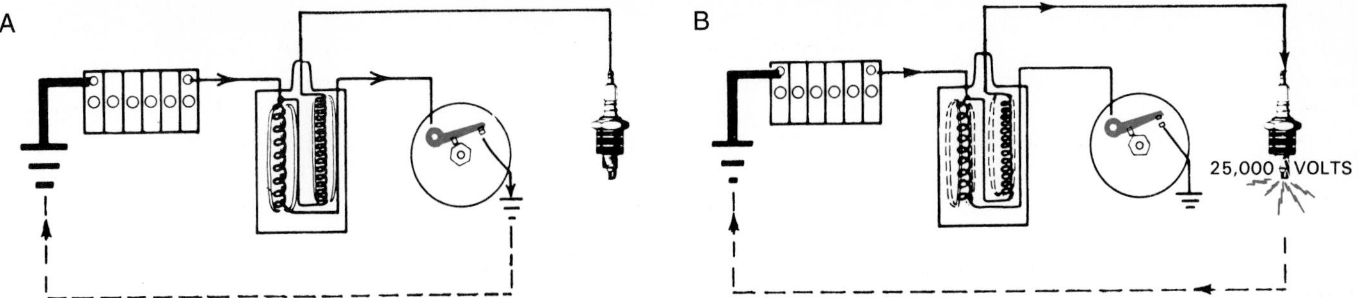

Figure 24-27. A–The breaker points are closed, allowing current to flow through the primary windings and creating a magnetic field. B–As points begin to open, the magnetic field collapses and induces a high voltage in the secondary circuit.

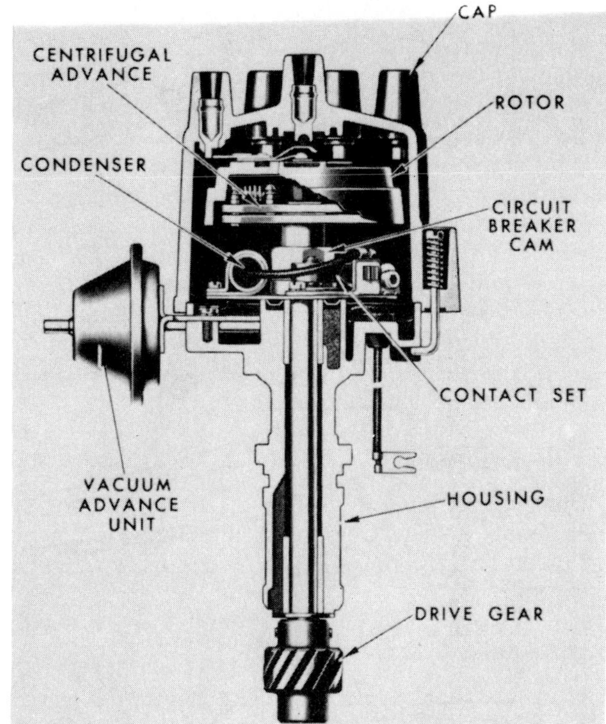

Figure 24-28. A Delco-Remy distributor.

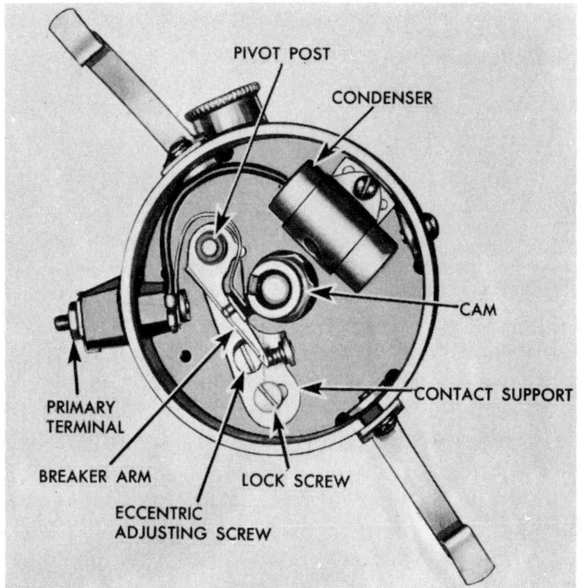

Figure 24-29. An eccentric adjustment is used to control point gap.

As the breaker cam rotates, each lobe passes under the rubbing block, causing the breaker points to open. Since the points are in series with the primary winding of the ignition coil, current will pass through that circuit when the points close. The period of time that the points are closed is referred to as ***dwell.*** When the points open, the magnetic field in the coil collapses and a high tension voltage is induced in the secondary windings of the coil by the movement of the magnetic field through the secondary windings, Figure 24-27.

The design provides one lobe on the breaker cam for each cylinder of the engine. A six-cylinder engine will have a six-lobe cam in the distributor, and a V-8 will have an eight-lobe cam. As a result, every revolution of the breaker cam will produce one spark for each cylinder of the engine.

On a four-cycle engine, each cylinder fires every other revolution. Therefore, the distributor shaft must revolve at one-half crankshaft speed.

After the high-tension surge is produced in the ignition coil by the opening of the breaker points, the current passes from the coil to the center terminal of the distributor cap. From that point, it passes down to the rotor, which is mounted on the distributor shaft and revolves with it. The current passes along the rotor and then jumps the minute gap to the cap electrode under which the rotor is positioned at that instant. This cap electrode is connected by high-tension wiring to the spark plug. As the rotor continues to rotate, it distributes current to each of the cap terminals in turn.

Condenser

Primary current produces a magnetic field around the coil windings. However, this does not occur instantly. It takes time for the current and the magnetic field to reach maximum value.

This time element is determined by the resistance of the coil winding or the length of time the distributor contacts are closed. The current does not reach the maximum because the contacts remain closed for such a short time.

When the breaker points begin to open, the primary current will continue to flow. This condition in a winding is increased by means of the iron core. Without an ***ignition condenser,*** the induced voltage causing this flow of current would create an arc across the contact points and the magnetic energy would be consumed in this arc. As a result, the contact points would be burned and ignition would not occur.

The condenser prevents this arc by making a place for the current to flow. As a result of condenser action, the magnetic field produced and continued by the current flow will quickly collapse. It is this rapid cutting out of the magnetic field that induces high voltage in the secondary windings. So, if the condenser should go bad, the high voltage needed to jump the gap at the spark plugs will not be possible. This could cause a no-start condition or a driveablity problem.

Resistors

In most 12-volt systems, a ***resistor*** is connected in series with the primary circuit of the ignition coil. However, during the cranking period, the resistor is cut out of the circuit so that full voltage is applied to the coil. This ensures a strong spark during cranking.

Contacts on the cranking motor solenoid are used to cut the resistor out of the primary circuit during the cranking period. The ignition coil and its windings are designed to operate at a voltage that is lower than full battery voltage. Therefore, when full battery voltage is applied, a hotter than normal spark is provided. During cranking, the excessive load applied on the battery will reduce the voltage reaching the ignition coil. On some systems, the resistor is of the block type. Other systems, Figure 24-30, use a wire that is sensitive to heat. As the temperature of the wire increases, so does its resistance. As a result, when the engine reaches operating temperature, its resistance allows only six volts to be applied to the coil. However, the starting circuit is designed so that as long as the starting motor is in use, full battery voltage is applied to the coil. When the starter is not cranking the engine, the resistance wire is cut into the circuit to reduce the voltage applied to the coil.

If the engine starts when the ignition switch is turned on but stops when the switch is released to the run position, it can indicate that the resistor is bad and should be replaced. At no time should the resistor be bypassed out of the circuit, as this would supply constant battery voltage to the coil, causing it to burn out.

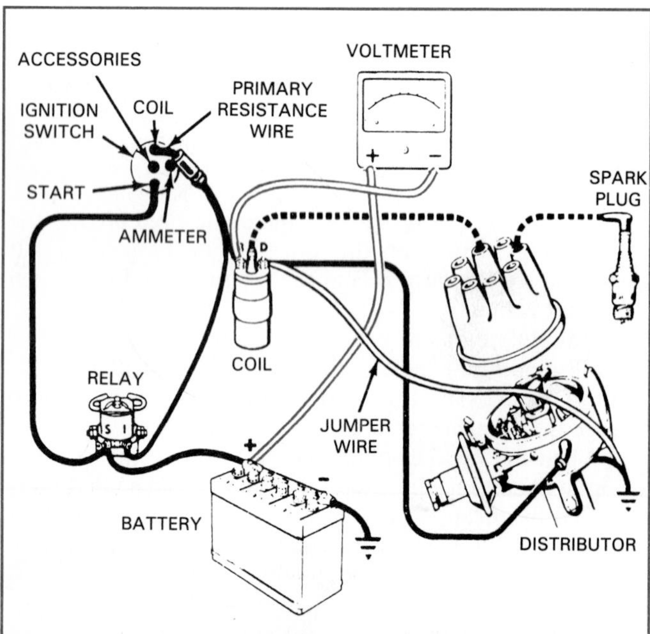

Figure 24-30. This diagram shows the voltage drop at the ignition coil being checked. If the voltage drop is excessive, a loose connection, ignition switch, or resistance wire is at fault. (Ford)

Resistors and resistor wires should be checked whenever the breaker points are burned or when the ignition coil is bad. With the ignition switch turned on, the voltage reading from the resistor side of the coil to the ground should be about 5 to 7 V, unless other specifications are available. Resistance of a resistor used on 12 V systems is about 1.5 ohms.

Electronic Ignition

The short-lived ***electronic ignition system*** was a transition from the breaker point system to the computerized ignition system. It came into widespread use in the mid-1970s and was overshadowed by the computerized ignition system by the late 1970s. However, there are still many vehicles on the road that use electronic ignition systems.

Many of the components in an electronic ignition system are identical to those used in a conventional breaker point system. However, the breaker points have been replaced by an ignition module and a pickup coil assembly in an electronic ignition system. Like breaker point systems, electronic ignition systems depend on centrifugal and vacuum advance systems to adjust spark timing. Electronic ignition systems are more dependable than breaker point systems. Additionally, they are capable of providing higher secondary voltages, which allow the use of leaner air/fuel mixtures. These leaner mixtures help to improve fuel economy and reduce exhaust emissions.

Ignition Module

The ***ignition module*** used in electronic ignition systems is simply a switching device. It contains a transistor that is used to control the voltage to the primary side of the ignition coil.

Pickup Assemblies

There are many types of ***pickup assemblies*** used in electronic ignition systems. However, they all produce voltage pulses to trigger the ignition module, so that the spark plugs can be fired at the proper time, Figure 24-31. The pickup assemblies described below often double as crankshaft position sensors in computerized ignition systems.

Magnetic Pickup Assembly. The ***magnetic pickup assembly,*** Figure 24-32, produces an alternating current, Figure 24-33. This is the most common type of pickup assembly. Each of the metal tabs corresponds to a cylinder at TDC of the compression stroke. This particular assembly would be used on an eight-cylinder engine.

Optical Pickup Assembly. An ***optical pickup,*** Figure 24-34, can be mounted in the distributor or at the back end of the crankshaft. The light from the LED is carried through fiber optics. The beam of light is interrupted by a steel disk, except when a hole in the disk aligns with the two fiber optic light pipes. When this occurs, the beam of light is directed to the base of a phototransistor. Current is then allowed to flow through the phototransistor to the primary windings of the ignition coil. When the steel disk again interrupts the beam of light, the current flowing to the primary windings is interrupted and a spark plug is fired. Each hole in the disk represents TDC of a compression stroke. The problem with fiber optics is that they must be protected from dirt and/or oil so that they can perform their job. If dirt collects at one end of a light pipe, the beam of light will never reach the phototransistor and the coil will not be able to fire the spark plugs.

Hall Effect Pickup Assembly. In most cases, the ***Hall Effect pickup assembly*** does not measure the position of the crankshaft directly. However, it does measure the position of the camshaft, which rotates at half the speed of the crankshaft. This sensor is mounted in the distributor, Figure 24-35. It contains a thin slab of semiconductor material that has voltage supplied to it constantly. When the metal tab passes between the magnet and the sensor, the magnetic field is interrupted and the voltage at the sensor, which is sent to a transistor in the switching device, is lowered. See Figures 24-36 and 24-37. Each metal tab corresponds to TDC of a compression stroke. So, a spark plug is fired when a metal tab is between the magnet and the sensor.

NOTE: The reverse is true on some Hall Effect sensors. The magnetic field in the ignition coil is built up when the metal tab is between the magnet and the sensor. Therefore, a spark plug is fired when the metal tab has passed between the magnet and sensor.

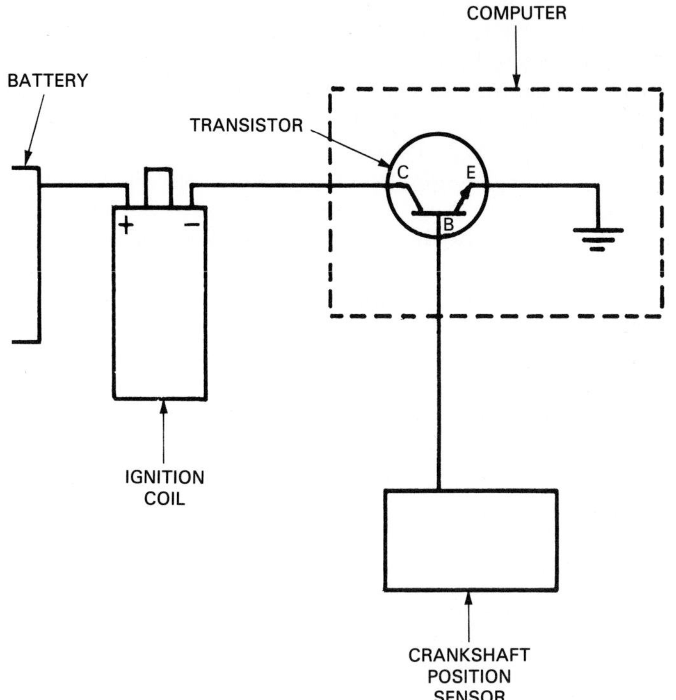

Figure 24-31. A simplified sketch of how a crankshaft position sensor is connected to the base of a transistor in the computer. The transistor increases battery voltage to the coil primary windings. It also breaks the flow of current to the coil much faster than a set of points. These two facts produce a higher secondary voltage than a breaker point ignition system.

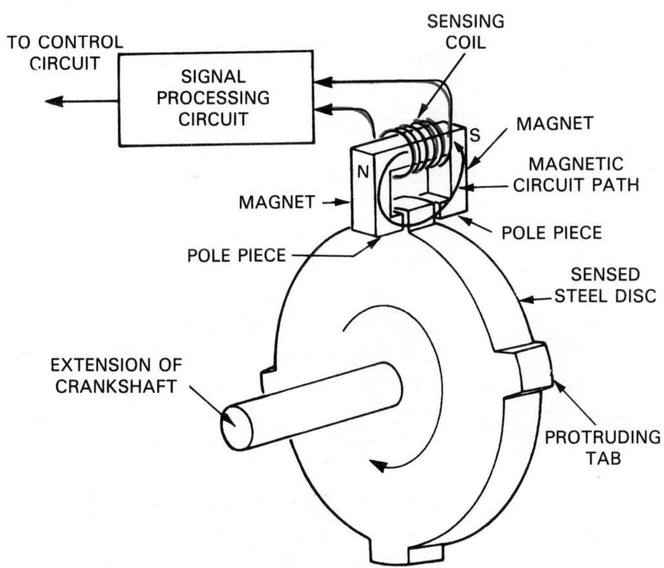

Figure 24-32. A magnetic reluctance crankshaft position sensor. The voltage signal is sent to the computer through windings around the magnet.

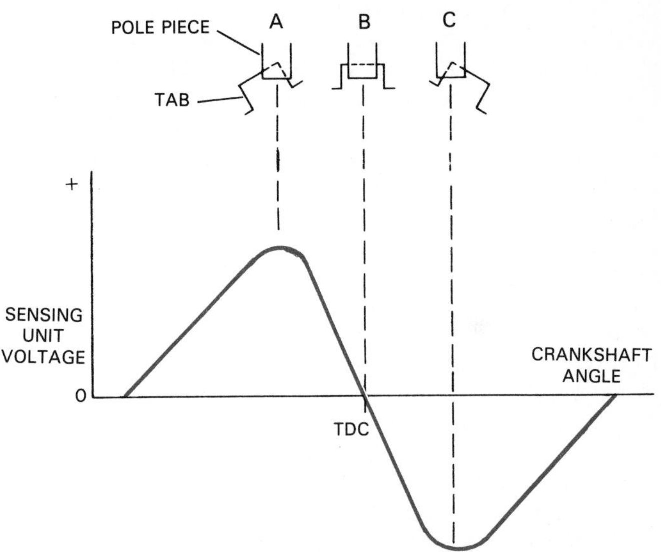

Figure 24-33. An alternating current is produced by this crankshaft position sensor. A–Voltage peaks just before the metal tab aligns with the magnet. If the transistor is the NPN type, the voltage is applied to the base of the transistor. This turns the transistor on and allows current to flow through it to the primary windings of the coil. B–The metal tab aligns with magnet and voltage drops to zero. The lack of voltage at the transistor base turns the transistor off and interrupts current to the coil primary windings. The coil then fires 20,000 volts or more to the spark plug. C–As the metal tab begins to leave the magnetic field, the polarity is reversed. This portion of the signal is irrelevant unless the transistor is the PNP type.

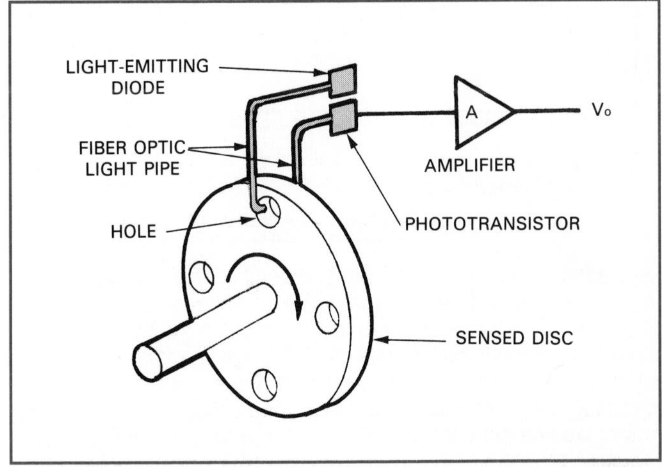

Figure 24-34. This crankshaft position sensor uses fiber optics.

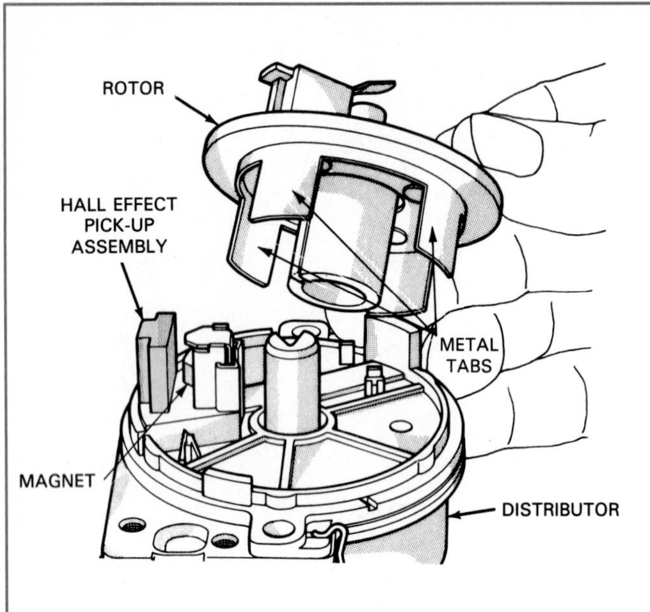

Figure 24-35. A typical Hall Effect sensor. The disadvantage of locating the sensor in the distributor is that it cannot compensate for wear in the timing chain or belt. (Chrysler)

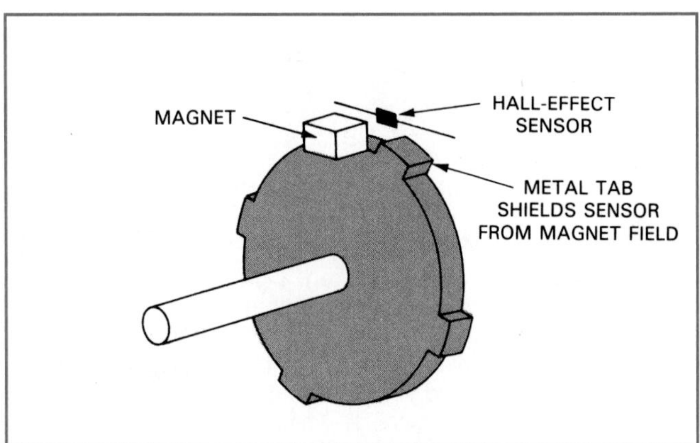

Figure 24-36. The metal tabs interrupt the magnetic field to the sensor.

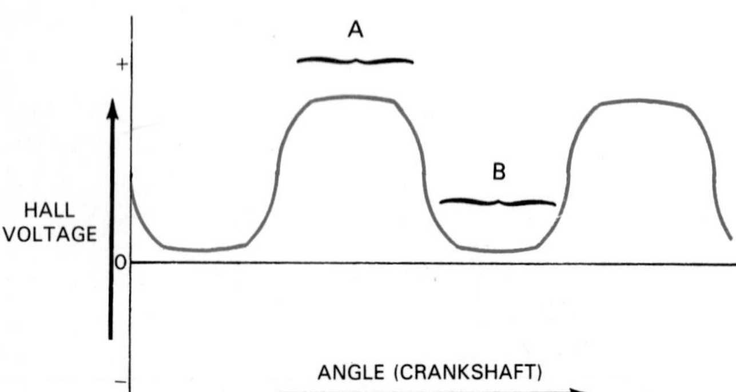

Figure 24-37. Hall voltage. A–The metal tab has passed between the sensor and the magnet. This voltage turns the transistor on and allows current to flow through the transistor to primary windings in coil. B-The metal tab aligns with the magnet and the sensor. Voltage is decreased at the sensor. The lower voltage is not great enough to turn the transistor on, and the current flowing through transistor is interrupted. The ignition coil then fires 20,000 or more volts. Note that the voltage never reaches zero.

Electronic Ignition System Operation

The basic circuits of one particular electronic ignition system are shown in Figure 24-38. The primary circuit consists of the battery, the ignition switch, the compensating side of the dual ballast resistor, the primary winding of the ignition coil, the power switching transistor of the control unit, and the car's frame, which acts as a ground. The secondary circuit consists of the ignition coil secondary winding, the distributor cap, rotor, and the spark plugs.

The resistor serves the same purpose as in the contact ignition system. It maintains constant primary current with variation in engine speed. During starting, this resistance is bypassed, applying full battery voltage to the ignition coil. The compensating resistance is in series with both the control unit feed and the auxiliary ballast circuits, Figures 24-39 and 24-40.

In addition to the two basic circuits, there are the auxiliary ballast circuits, the pickup circuit, and the control unit feed circuit. Two circuits are used to operate the circuit of the control unit. These are the auxiliary ballast circuit (which uses 5 ohm section of dual ballast resistor) and the control unit feed circuit.

The pick-up circuit is used to sense the proper timing for the control unit switching transistor, Figures 24-40 and 24-41. The reluctor, rotating with the distributor shaft, produces a voltage pulse in the magnetic pickup each time a spark plug is to be fired. This pulse is transmitted from the pickup coil to the power switching transistor in the control unit, causing the transistor to interrupt current flow through the primary circuit. This break in the primary circuit induces high voltage in the secondary coil and fires a spark plug.

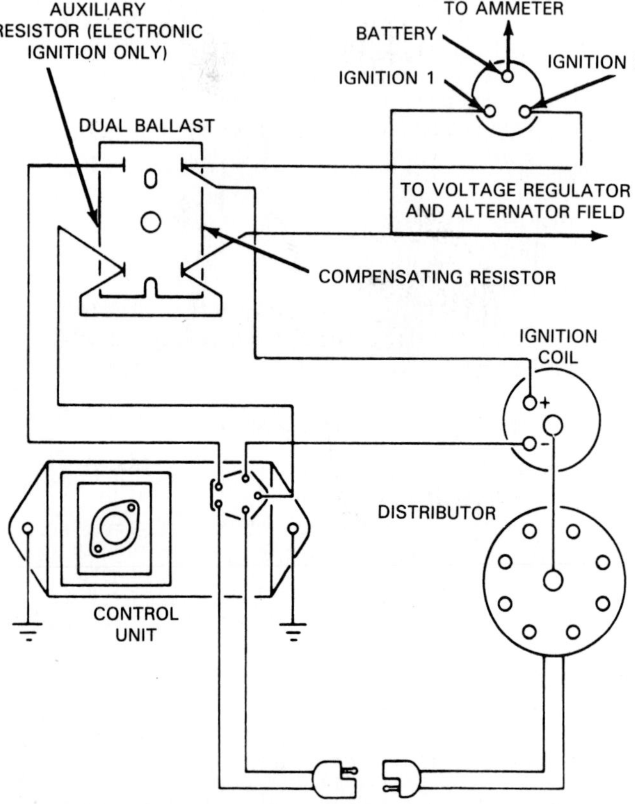

Figure 24-38. Diagram of an electronic ignition system.

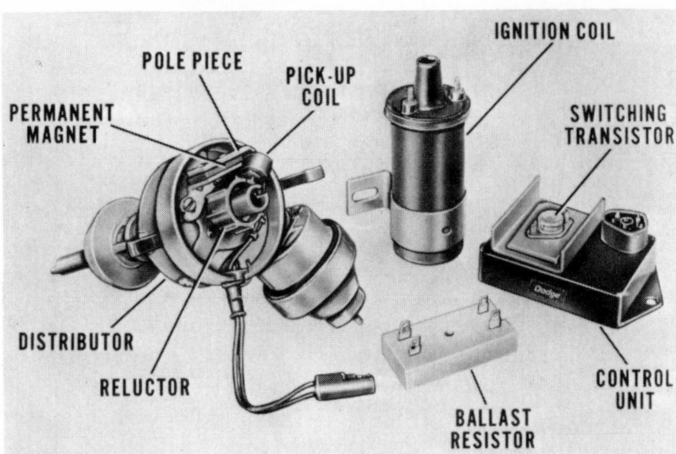

Figure 24-39. The Chrysler electronic ignition system.

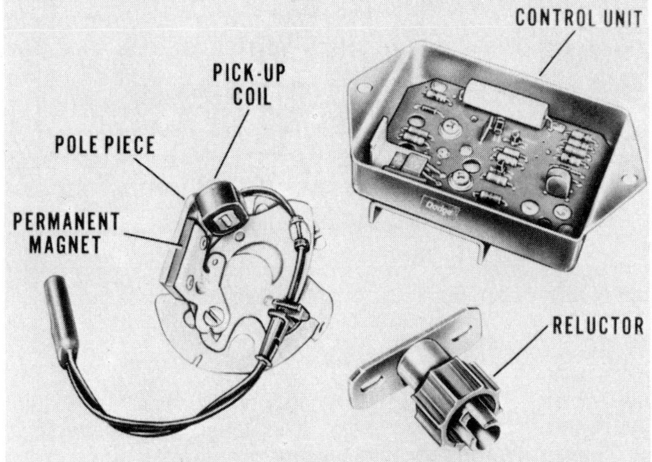

Figure 24-40. The pickup coil and reluctor create a voltage signal, which is sent to the control unit. The control unit interrupts the primary current at the ignition coil. (Chrysler)

The length of time that the switching transistor blocks the flow of current to the primary circuit is determined by the electronic circuitry in the control unit. Even though dwell may be read with a dwell meter, there is no means provided to change it.

The magnetic pick-up and the control unit have replaced the function of the breaker points and, unlike the breaker points, show no signs of wear, as there is an air gap between the two.

Electronic Ignition System Service

Many of the components used in an electronic ignition system are serviced in the same manner as those found in breaker point systems. However, the pickup assembly and the ignition module must be tested according to the manufacturer's recommendations. In many cases, the resistance of the components is measured and compared to the manufacturer's specifications. Additionally, dedicated electronic ignition system testers are available to quickly verify proper system operation.

Computerized Ignition Systems

In addition to controlling spark plug firing, ***computerized ignition systems*** use a computer and several sensors to control spark timing. Therefore, vacuum and centrifugal advance systems are eliminated. The computer uses signals from the sensors to make decisions about spark timing and triggers the ignition module to fire the spark plugs accordingly. See Figure 24-42.

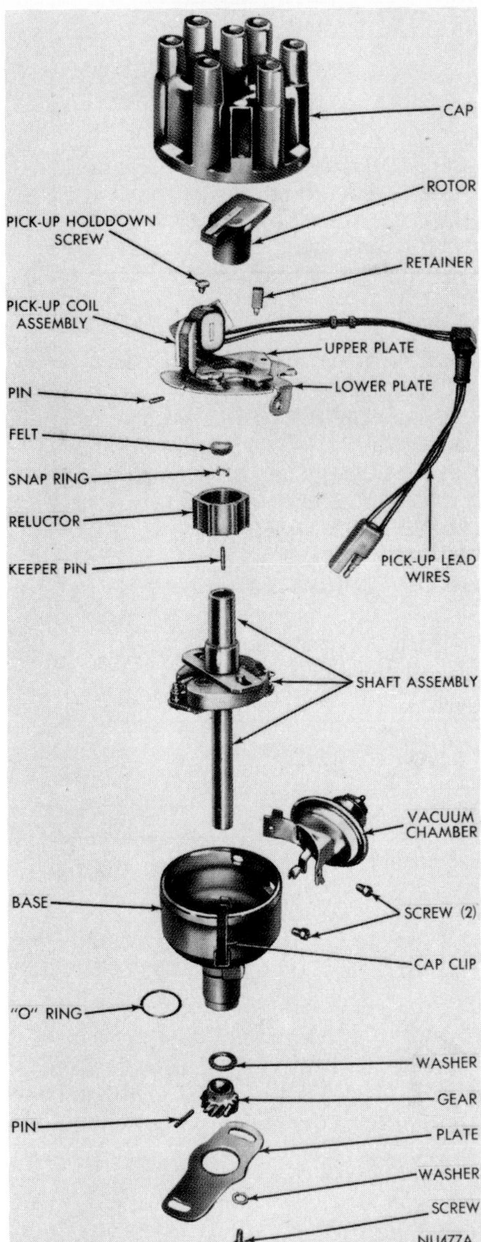

Figure 24-41. Electronic ignition distributor.

The sensors commonly used in a computerized ignition system include:

- Crankshaft position sensor.
- Detonation sensor.
- Coolant temperature sensor.
- Throttle position sensor.
- Manifold pressure sensor.
- Airflow sensor.

The construction, service, and troubleshooting of the computer and sensors used in a computerized ignition system are covered in Chapter 29, Computer Systems.

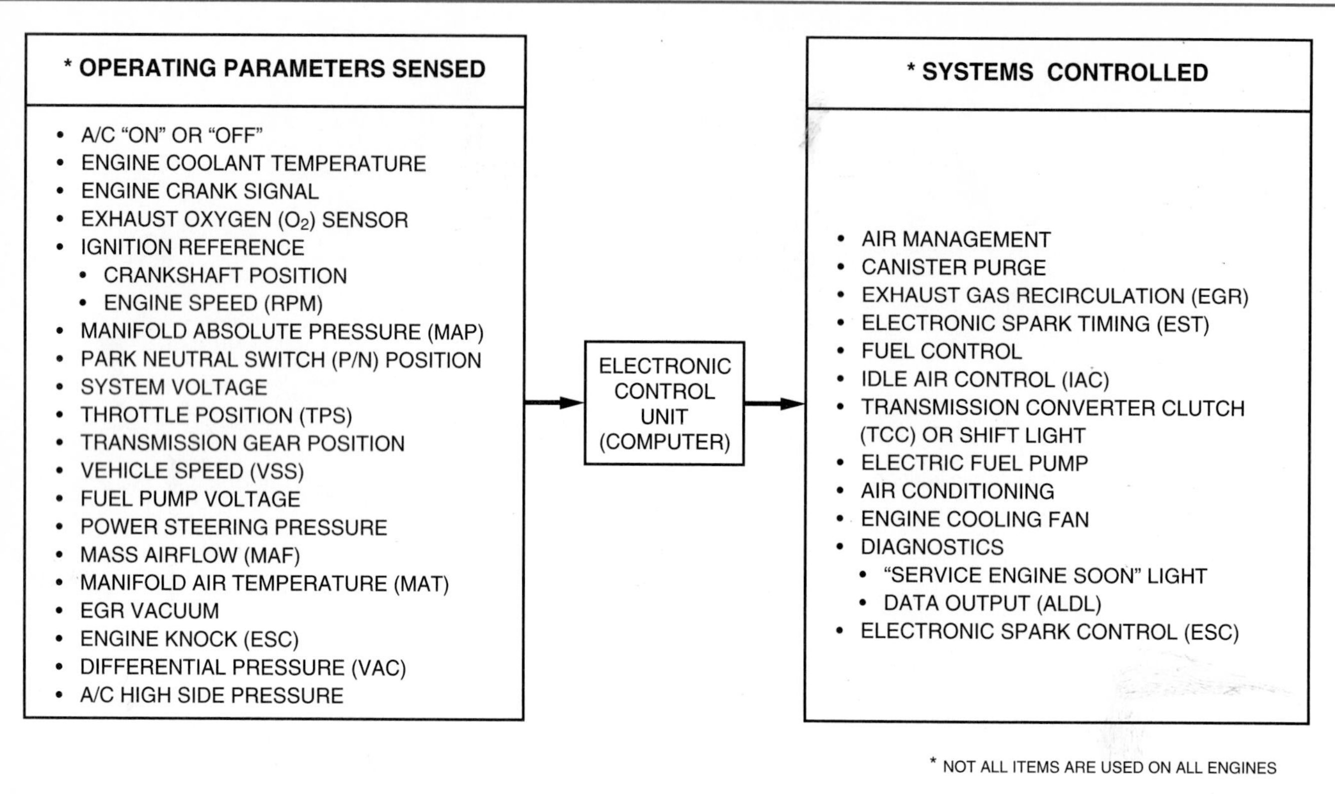

Figure 24-42. Computerized ignition systems rely on the electronic control unit, or computer, to control spark timing. Note that the computer also controls other systems in the vehicle. (General Motors)

Checking Timing in a Computerized Ignition System

Before checking the timing on computerized ignition systems, a diagnostic terminal must often be grounded after the engine is started, Figure 24-43. This activates base timing. ***Base timing*** is the spark timing without the influence of the computer control system. After checking the timing and making any needed adjustments, remove the jumper wire grounding the diagnostic terminal. If the diagnostic terminal remains grounded, it may be the cause of hard starting and other driveability problems.

Figure 24-43. Before checking and adjusting the timing in a computerized ignition system, the diagnostic terminal must be jumped to the ground terminal. (Cadillac)

Distributorless Ignition

The ***distributorless ignition system*** is characterized by the absence of a distributor, Figure 24-44. The advantage of this system is that there are no moving parts to wear out and replace.

The distributorless ignition system carries the high voltage from the ignition coils to the spark plugs through spark plug wires, Figure 24-45. The four-cylinder engine uses two ignition coils, while a six-cylinder engine uses three ignition coils, Figure 24-46. The ignition module is located under the ignition coils, Figure 24-47.

The ignition module receives a voltage signal from the crankshaft position sensor. Sometimes a camshaft position sensor is also used. The ignition module then sends voltage signals to the ECM. The ECM processes these signals and transmits a voltage signal back to the ignition module.

Distributorless Ignition System Operation

On engines that have a firing order of 1-3-4-2, one of the ignition coils fires the spark plugs at cylinders 1 and 4 at the same time. This means that the spark plug at cylinder 1 is fired near the end of the compression stroke, while the spark plug at cylinder 4 is fired at the end of the exhaust stroke. On the next cycle, the same ignition coil will fire the spark plug at cylinder 4 near the end of the compression stroke, while firing the spark plug at cylinder 1 at the end of

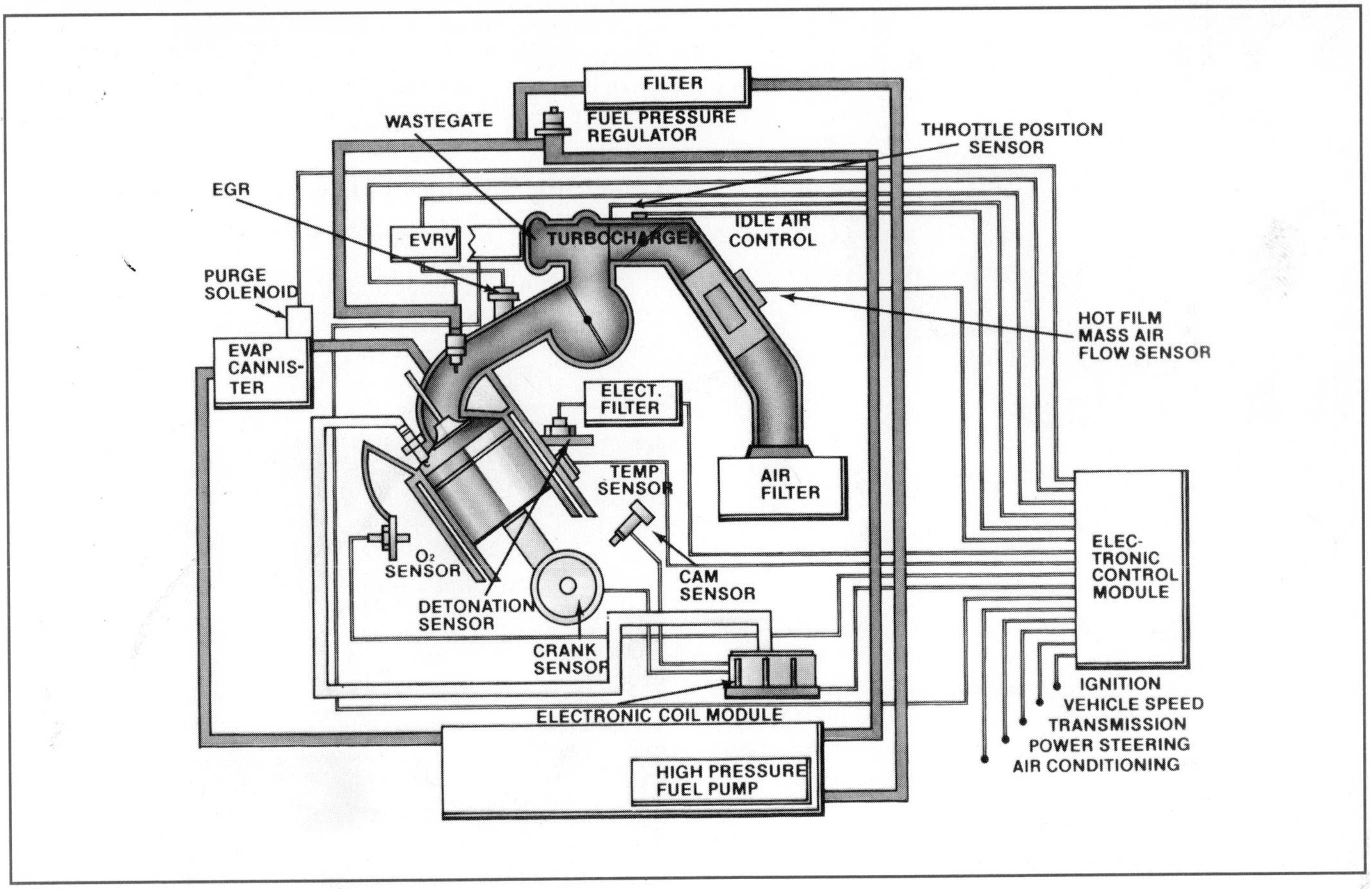

Figure 24-44. Typical distributorless ignition system. In this particular system, a crankshaft position sensor and a camshaft sensor send signals to the electronic control module. The control module uses these signals, as well as signals from other sensors, to calculate spark timing. (Buick)

the exhaust stroke. The other ignition coil fires cylinders 2 and 3 in the same manner. Since very little voltage is needed to fire a spark plug during the exhaust stroke, most of the available voltage is directed to the spark plug firing on the compression stroke. The ECM controls the timing during normal operating conditions.

Warning! A distributorless ignition system can produce 100 watts, which is far more than a conventional ignition system. This amount is enough to kill you!

Figure 24-45. This ignition system has three ignition coils. Each coil services two cylinders. (Buick)

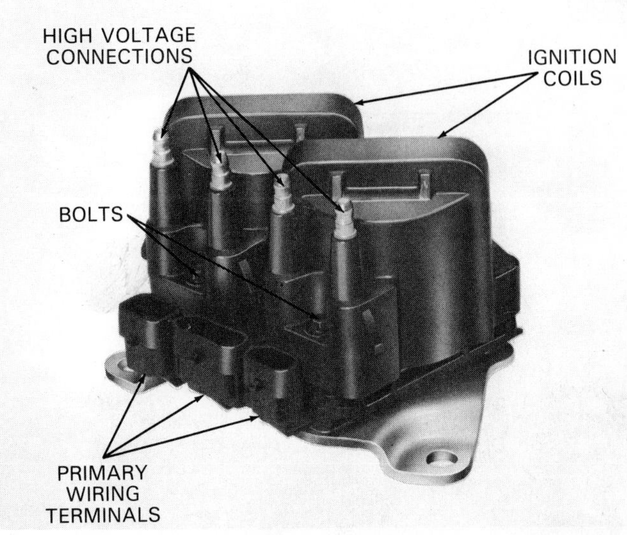

Figure 24-46. This ignition system has only two ignition coils, which means the engine has four cylinders. (Delco-Remy)

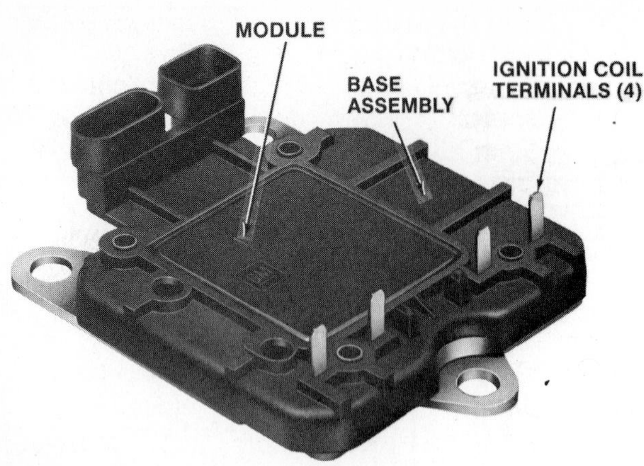

Figure 24-47. The module is located under the ignition coils and interacts with the ECM. (Delco-Remy)

Direct Ignition

The ***direct ignition system*** operates in the same manner as the distributorless ignition, except that there are no spark plug wires and that there is a coil for each spark plug, Figure 24-48. The spark plugs, ignition module, ignition coils, and secondary conductors are all located under the cover, Figure 24-49. The high voltage from the coils is carried to the spark plugs through the secondary conductors, Figure 24-50.

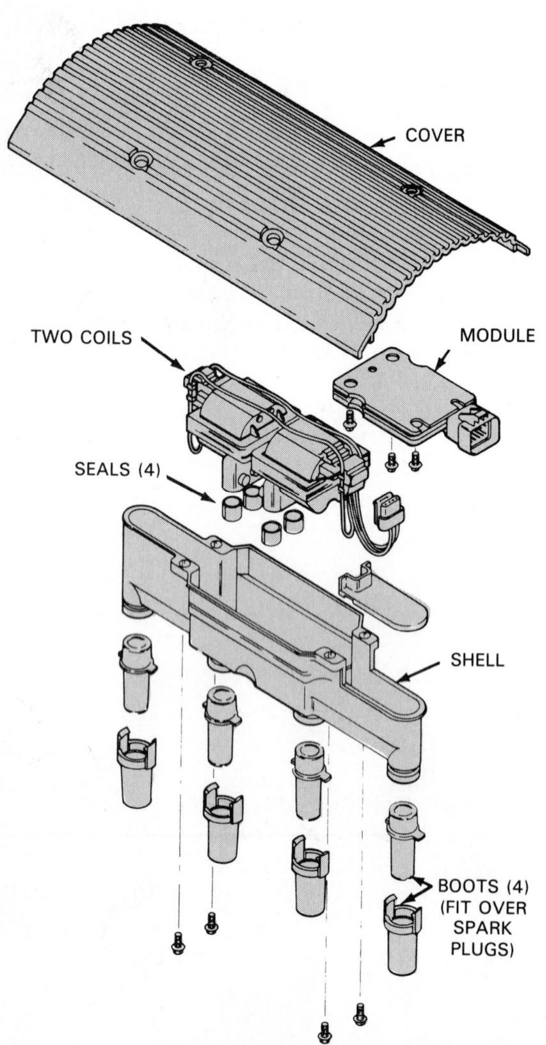

Figure 24-48. The direct ignition system. (Delco-Remy)

Checking Timing in Distributorless and Direct Ignition Systems

The timing cannot be adjusted in direct ignition systems, as there is nothing to adjust. However, when the camshaft position sensor is used in this system, it is often

Figure 24-49. All the ignition components are located under the cover in this direct ignition system. Note that the spark plugs are not visible. (Pontiac)

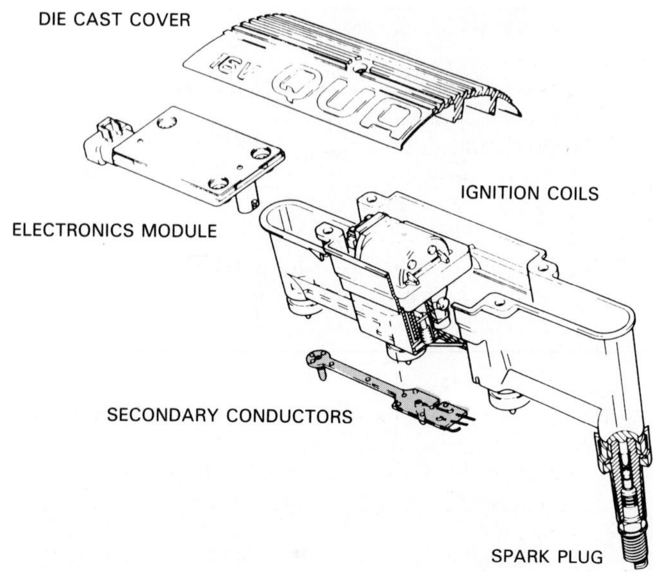

Figure 24-50. The secondary conductor carries the high voltage from the ignition coils to the spark plugs. (Pontiac)

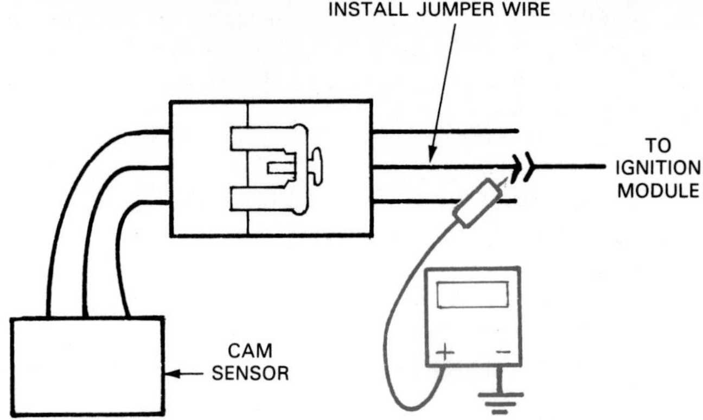

Figure 24-51. Rotate the crankshaft so that No. 1 cylinder is at TDC of the compression stroke. Mark the harmonic balance, and then rotate the crankshaft to 25° ATDC. Using a digital voltmeter, rotate the camshaft sensor counterclockwise until a reading of 2 to 0 V is obtained. This should only be checked if there is a driveability problem. (General Motors)

adjustable, Figure 24-51. If the sensor is maladjusted, engine performance will be affected.

Chapter 24–Review Questions

Write your answers on a separate sheet of paper. Do not write in this book.

1. Which are components of the secondary side of the ignition?
   (A) Distributor cap, rotor, ignition coil, and the spark plugs.
   (B) Points and condenser.
   (C) Computer.
   (D) Battery.
   (E) All of the above.
2. The ignition coil is a transformer designed to increase secondary voltage. True or False?
3. The high tension outlet of the ignition coil has:
   (A) positive polarity.
   (B) negative polarity.
   (C) neutral polarity.
   (D) None of the above.
4. The rotor:
   (A) is located under the distributor cap.
   (B) moves at camshaft speed.
   (C) distributes high voltage at the proper time.
   (D) All of the above.
   (E) None of the above.
5. The spark plug wires on late-model vehicles use a _____ _____ to carry the high voltage.
   (A) copper wire
   (B) metallic core
   (C) fiber core
   (D) None of the above.
6. Briefly explain how battery voltage is transformed into 20,000 volts in the ignition system.
7. The center electrode of the spark plug is connected to the ignition coil _____ through the distributor.
   (A) primary
   (B) ground
   (C) secondary
   (D) None of the above.
8. The size of the spark plug gap depends on the compression ratio of the engine. True or False?
9. The heat range of a spark plug is an indication of its ability to transfer heat from the plug's firing end to the:
   (A) cylinder head.
   (B) water jacket.
   (C) Both A & B.
   (D) Neither A nor B.
10. If the spark plugs are fouled, the technician should first diagnose the cause before replacing the plugs. True or False?
11. Spark plugs can be expected to last between _____ and _____ miles under good conditions.
12. The sequence of spark plug firing is known as:
    (A) ignition sequence.
    (B) ignition order.
    (C) firing order.
    (D) None of the above.
13. The timing marks are located only on the harmonic balancer. True or False?
14. When using a timing light, it should generally be connected to the:
    (A) coil.
    (B) No. 1 spark plug wire.
    (C) center terminal of the distributor cap.
    (D) None of the above.
15. Hot engines require additional spark advance. True or False?
16. In a breaker point ignition system, the _____ makes and brakes the primary circuit.
    (A) coil
    (B) distributor
    (C) spark plugs
    (D) None of the above.
17. The pickup assembly tells the ignition module:
    (A) that the piston is at TDC of a compression stroke.
    (B) that the piston is at BDC of a compression stroke.
    (C) Both A & B.
    (D) Neither A nor B.
18. In most cases, the Hall Effect device is located in the distributor and measures the position of the crankshaft indirectly. True or False?
19. How many different types of pickup assemblies are described in this chapter?
    (A) 1.
    (B) 2.
    (C) 3.
    (D) 4.
    (E) 5.
20. On a computerized ignition system, the spark is advanced proportionately in relation to many factors. True or False?
21. Before checking timing in a computerized ignition system, _____ timing must be activated.
22. A distributor is not used in a _____ ignition system.
23. A four-cylinder engine with distributorless ignition uses _____ ignition coils.
    (A) 4
    (B) 3
    (C) 2
    (D) None of the above.
24. Conventional spark plug wires are used in a direct ignition system. True or False?

25. To adjust timing in a distributorless ignition system, a _____ _____ must be used.
    (A) timing light
    (B) scan tool
    (C) engine analyzer
    (D) None of the above.

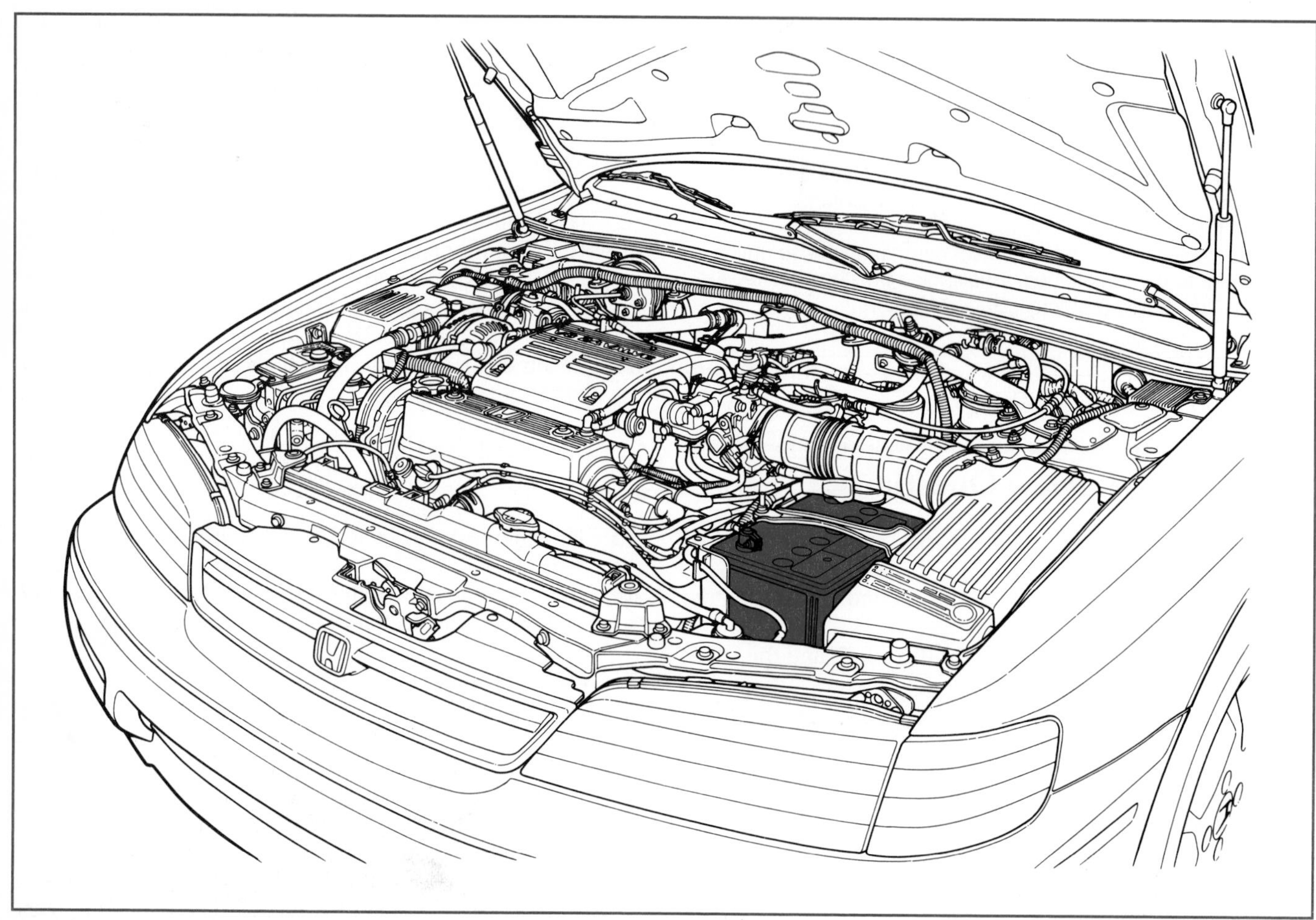

In most cases, the battery is located in the front of the engine compartment to facilitate service and replacement. (Honda)

Chapter 25
Batteries and Battery Service

After studying this chapter, you will be able to:
❍ State three functions of an automotive battery.
❍ List basic parts of a typical automotive battery.
❍ Give two methods of rating battery performance.
❍ Explain three methods of testing an automotive battery.
❍ List safe battery servicing practices.
❍ Identify four methods of charging a battery.
❍ State the sequence of steps for jump starting an engine.

Batteries

The ***lead-acid storage battery*** used in automobiles and other vehicles is an electrochemical device that converts chemical energy into electrical energy. When the battery is connected to an external load, such as a starting motor, the energy conversion takes place and electricity flows through the circuit.

Battery Functions

The lead-acid automotive battery, Figures 25-1 and 25-2, has three main functions:

- It serves as a source of power for the starting motor and ignition system when cranking and starting an internal combustion engine.
- It acts as a stabilizer of voltage for the entire automotive electrical system.
- It furnishes current for a limited time when electrical demands exceed alternator output.

Sizes and Types

Storage batteries used in automobiles vary in size, capacity, and cranking power. In addition, there are ***conventional batteries*** (wet, moist, or dry charged) and ***maintenance-free batteries*** (low water loss). Nevertheless, their basic construction is very similar.

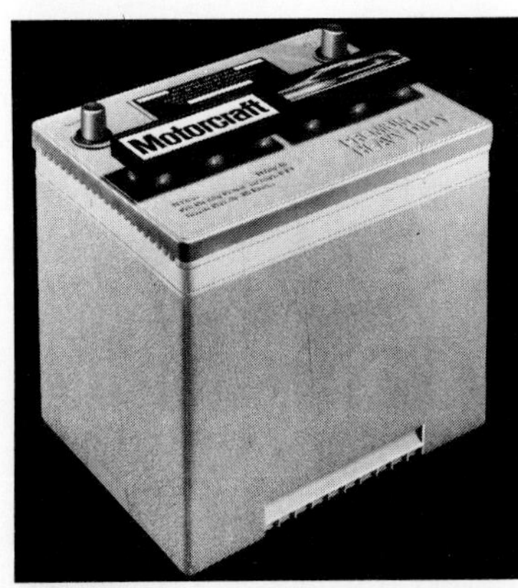

Figure 25-1. Typical conventional battery for use in cranking, starting, and lighting passenger cars.

Battery Construction

A typical 12-volt, lead-acid automotive battery is made up of six CELLS connected in series, Figure 25-3, and filled with ***electrolyte*** (sulfuric acid diluted with water). Each cell will produce approximately two volts.

Cells

Each battery cell contains ***plates*** composed of special active materials contained in cast grids. The ***plate grids*** usually are rectangular, flat, lattice-like castings with a

Figure 25-2. This battery has a sealed-in lifetime supply of electrolyte. The test indicator shows state of charge.

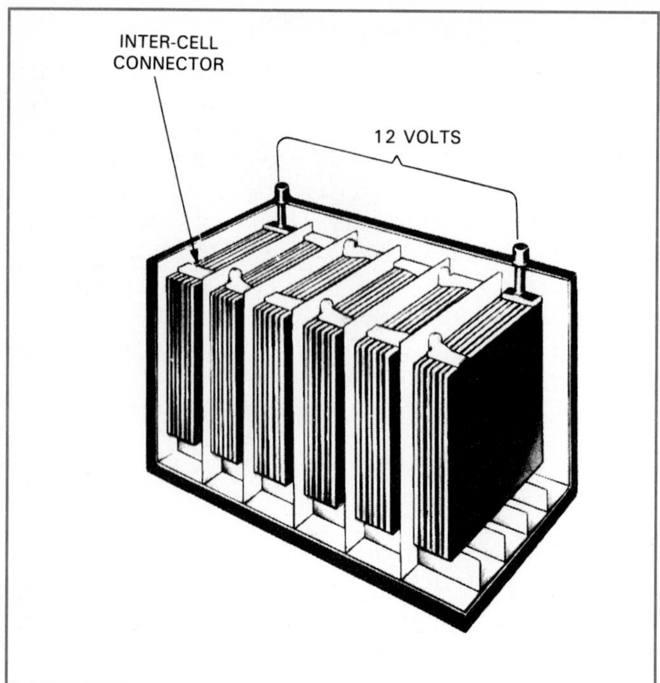

Figure 25-3. Typical arrangement of cells and straight-through cell connectors in a 12 volt battery.

relatively heavy framework around a hexagonal, diagonal, or vertical and horizontal mesh. See Figure 25-4. The ***positive plates*** generally contain lead dioxide (PbO_2), which is brown. The ***negative plates*** contain sponge lead (Pb), which is gray.

Plates and Plate Groups

Each cell of a storage battery is made up of alternate positive and negative plates. A ***plate group*** is made by welding a number of plates of the same polarity to a ***post strap.*** During assembly, plate groups of opposite polarity are interlaced, Figure 25-4.

Usually, negative plate groups contain one more plate than the positive plate groups within the same cell to help equalize the chemical activity.

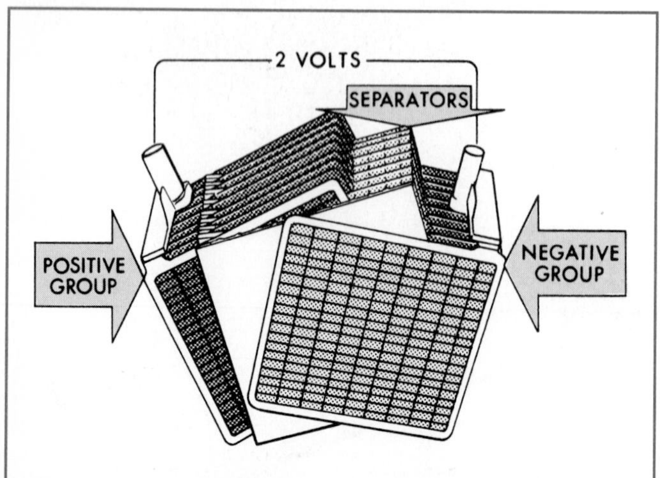

Figure 25-4. One element of a battery consists of a group of positive plates, a group of negative plates, and the necessary separators.

Separators

To ensure that adjacent plates do not touch each other, ***separators*** are placed between them. See Figure 25-4. The assembly of positive and negative plates and separators is called an ***element.*** There is one element per cell.

Separators are made of sheets of porous, nonconducting material, such as resin impregnated cellulose fibers, various plastic materials, rubber, or fiberglass. Battery separators must be chemically resistant to sulfuric acid. They must be strong, yet porous enough to permit free passage of the electrolyte. The separators prevent the active chemicals in the plates from touching each other through expansion.

Some maintenance-free batteries use ***envelope separators*** rather than sheets. See Figure 25-5. Each plate is contained in an envelope that is closed on three sides. The envelopes extend to the bottom of the battery case, eliminating the need for sediment chambers.

Elements and Case

The elements of positive and negative plates and separators are placed in each cell of the outside case, or shell, of the battery. Generally, the case is molded polypropylene (impact and acid-resistant) or hard rubber.

The lower edge of each element of conventional batteries is supported on element rests, or "bridges," at the bottom of the case. The element rests run the full length of each cell. See Figure 25-3. The plates are positioned at right angles to the element rests. The spaces between the rests are sediment chambers designed to collect active material shed from the plates.

Most battery cases are formed with hold-down ramps on two sides at the bottom. See Figures 25-1 and 25-2. Many cases are designed for top or bottom hold-down mounting.

Intercell Connectors

With the elements in place in the battery case, ***intercell connectors*** (element terminal posts) are inserted either through holes in the case partitions or over the partitions. This design provides a short, low-resistance path through the battery. See Figure 25-6.

In conventional batteries, the intercell connectors are placed on the top of the plates on the side opposite the posts

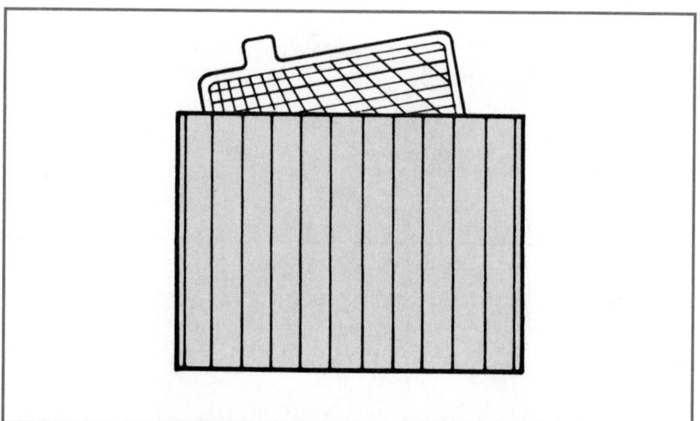

Figure 25-5. Envelope separators are used in many maintenance-free batteries instead of "sheet" separators. (ESB Incorporated)

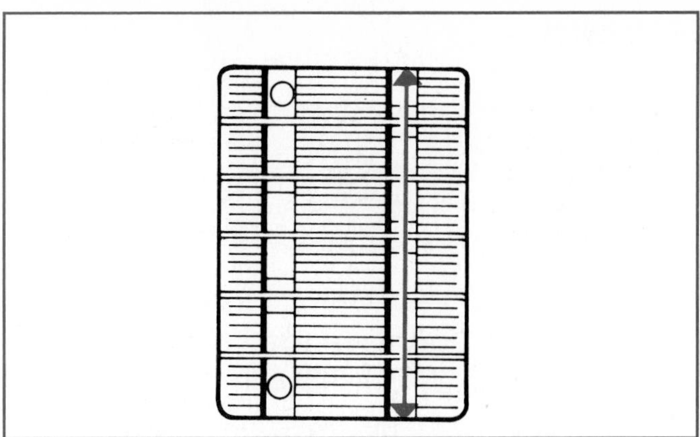

Figure 25-6. Intercell connectors provide a direct, low-resistance path through or over the battery case partitions. (ESB Incorporated)

and post straps. In some maintenance-free batteries, the through-the-partition intercell connectors are centered for increased vibration protection.

Electrolyte

The battery is ***activated*** by the addition of electrolyte. ***Electrolyte*** is a mixture of sulfuric acid and water. This solution causes the chemical actions to take place between the lead dioxide of the positive plate and the sponge lead of the negative plate. The electrolyte is also the carrier that moves electric current between the positive and negative plates through the separators.

Lead-acid storage batteries use a fairly concentrated solution of sulfuric acid and water, which has a "fully charged" specific gravity of 1.265 corrected to 80°F (26.7°C). ***Specific gravity*** is the weight of a given volume of a liquid divided by the weight of an equal volume of water. Water has arbitrarily been assigned a value of 1.000. Therefore, electrolyte with a specific gravity of 1.265 means it is 1.265 times heavier than an equal volume of pure water when both liquids are at the same temperature.

Forming Charge

Batteries may be produced as charged and wet, charged and moist, or dry charged. When a battery is charged and wet, it has been given a ***forming charge*** at the factory, and it is shipped filled with electrolyte of 1.265 specific gravity.

When a battery is charged and moist, it has been given the forming charge, but then practically all of the electrolyte was removed. After draining, the cells were sealed and the battery was shipped. Upon being placed in service, it must be "activated" with electrolyte of 1.265 specific gravity.

When a battery is dry charged, it received the forming charge, and then the plates or elements were washed and dried before the battery was sealed. Dry charged batteries must be filled with electrolyte and ***boost charged*** (light finishing charge of 5 to 15 amps.) before being placed in service.

Some maintenance-free batteries are dry charged. These batteries feature an access vent on the cover that can be opened for activation, testing, or the replacement of water if overcharging has occurred.

Covers and Terminals

Cell covers usually are made of plastic material or hard rubber, Figures 25-1 and 25-2. The one-piece cover is bonded (usually heat-sealed) to the case, and the ***battery terminals*** are sealed at the cover. There are three major types of terminals:

- Tapered posts. The positive post is slightly larger in diameter at the top than the negative post to help guard against installing the battery in reverse.
- Side terminals. Internally threaded terminals are molded into the side wall of the battery near the top edge. Each battery cable is attached to the proper terminal by means of a bolt that threads into the terminal.
- "L" terminals. L-shaped metal terminals are mounted on top of the battery. The upright portion of the "L" has a hole. The battery cable is attached to the terminal by means of a bolt and a wing nut.

Vent Plugs and Vents

Vent plugs of various designs are used. Usually, the vent plugs are baffled so gas can escape but electrolyte splashed into the vent will drain into the cell. The plugs may be screw type or push-in type. The push-in type may be a single plug or a gang vent plug (three-plug-manifold).

Most maintenance-free batteries do not use vent plugs, Figure 25-7. Instead, the gas is vented through baffled passages and small vent holes in the cover. Most conventional batteries have flame arrester vent plugs, Figure 25-8. In maintenance-free batteries, the flame arresters are located at the exits of the baffled passages.

Maintenance-free Batteries

While the internal construction of maintenance-free batteries appears to be similar to conventional batteries, differences may include the use of envelope separators, Figures 25-5 and 25-9, and expanded plate grids containing calcium, cadmium, or strontium to reduce gassing and self-discharge. Also, activation and booster charging are eliminated.

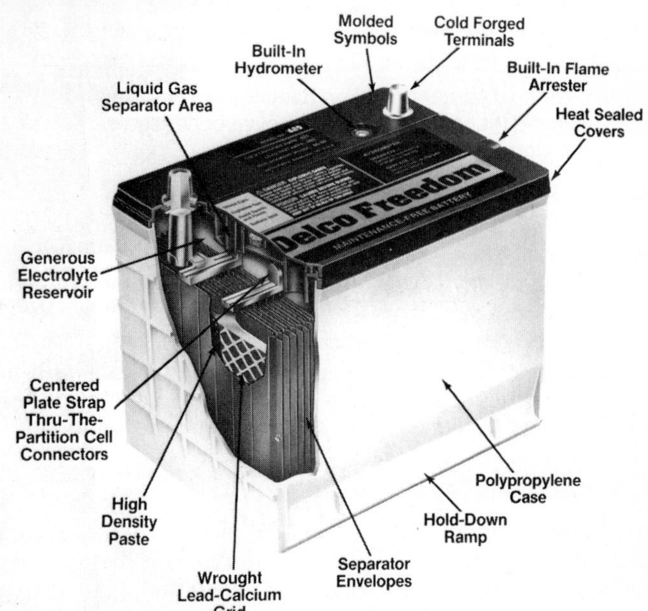

Figure 25-7. Maintenance-free batteries generally are vented through baffled passages and vent holes in the cover.

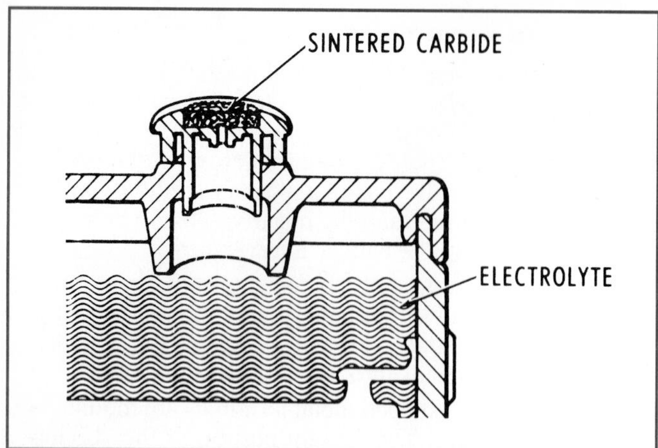

Figure 25-8. This vent cap has a flame arrestor of sintered carbide that disperses fumes and protects the battery from flame entry.

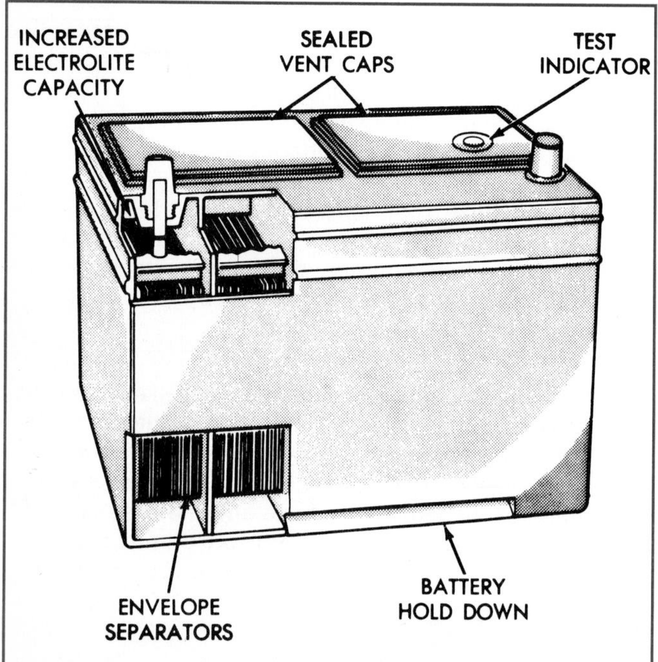

Figure 25-9. Maintenance-free batteries provide many advantages over conventional automotive batteries. (Chrysler Corp.)

Maintenance-free batteries also have a greater electrolyte reserve above the plates, better overcharge resistance, and less tendency toward terminal corrosion than conventional batteries.

With maintenance-free batteries, no electrolyte level checks or additions are necessary. Most have a built-in hydrometer or a visual test indicator in the cover. See Figure 25-10.

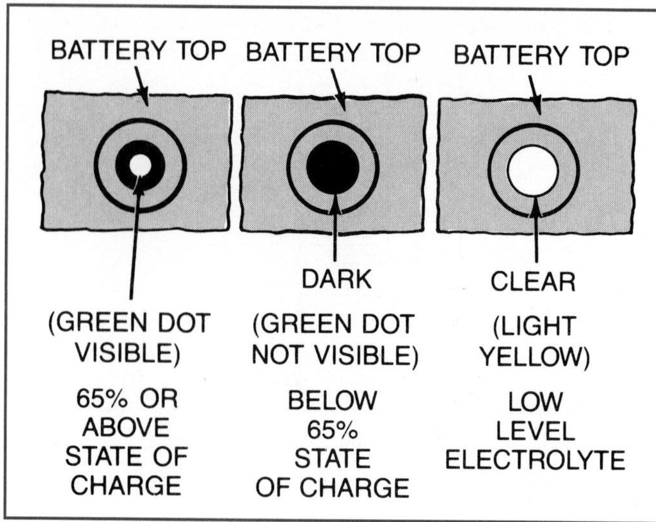

Figure 25-10. Maintenance-free batteries usually have a temperature-compensated hydrometer built into the top of the battery. (Cadillac)

Chemical Actions

The ***chemical actions*** that take place during charging and discharging of a lead-acid automotive battery are shown in Figure 25-11. In a charged condition, the positive plate material is essentially pure lead dioxide (PbO_2). The active material of the negative plates is spongy lead (Pb). The electrolyte is a solution of sulfuric acid (H_2SO_4) and water. The voltage of the cell depends on the chemical difference between the active materials. The concentration of the electrolyte also has an affect on voltage.

Discharge Cycle

The ***discharge cycle*** occurs when an electric load is connected to the battery and current flows. The current is produced by the chemical reactions between the active materials of the two kinds of battery plates and the sulfuric acid. As shown in Figure 25-11, the oxygen in the PbO_2 combines with the hydrogen (H_2) from the sulfuric acid to form water (H_2O). At the same time, the lead in the lead dioxide combines with the SO_4 portion of the sulfuric acid to form lead sulfate, $PbSO_4$.

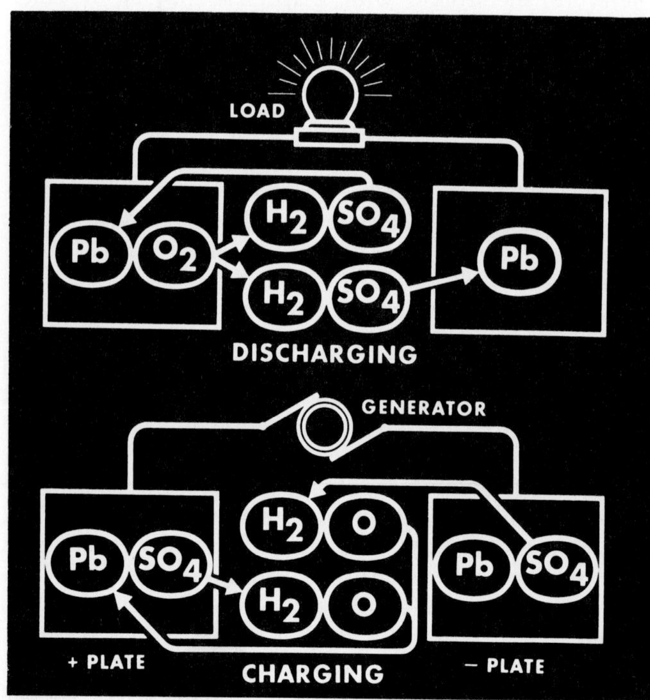

Figure 25-11. Chemical reactions within a lead-acid automotive battery are graphically shown.

A similar action takes place at the negative plate, where the lead of the negative active material combines with the SO_4 of the sulfuric acid to form $PbSO_4$, lead sulfate. As the discharge continues, the plates are becoming more alike and the electrolyte is getter weaker. Therefore, the voltage is becoming lower, since it depends on the difference between the two plate materials and the concentration of the electrolyte.

While there is an electric load on the battery, lead sulfate is formed on both positive and negative plates and the electrolyte becomes diluted with water. As the discharge continues, the accumulation of lead sulfate on the plates and the dilution of the electrolyte lower the specific gravity. When the chemical action can no longer take place, the battery is said to be discharged.

Charge Cycle

The lead-acid storage battery is chemically reversible. A discharged battery can be charged by passing current through the plates in a direction opposite to the direction of discharge. See Figure 25-11. Its active chemicals will be restored to a charged condition.

During the ***charge cycle,*** the chemical reactions are basically the reverse of those that occur during discharge. The $PbSO_4$ (lead sulfate) on both plates is split into Pb and SO_4, while the water (H_2O) is split into hydrogen (H_2) and oxygen (O). The passage of the charging current, which is in the reverse direction of the discharging current, forces the SO_4 from the plates. The SO_4 combines with the H_2 to form H_2SO_4, or sulfuric acid. At the same time, the oxygen combines with the lead at the positive plate to form PbO_2.

The specific gravity of the electrolyte decreases during discharge for two reasons. Not only is the sulfuric acid used up, but new water is formed. Since the water is formed at the positive plates and diffuses slowly through the electrolyte, the positive plates are more likely to be damaged during freezing weather. When the battery is fully charged, the specific gravity of the solution increases, sulfuric acid is formed, and the water is used up. As a result, there is little danger of a fully charged battery freezing.

Battery Voltage and Capacity

The ***open circuit voltage*** (no load voltage) of a fully charged automotive battery is 12.6 volts or more for electrolyte of approximately 1.265 specific gravity. This is true regardless of the number of plates per cell or the area of the plates. The voltage is determined only by the character of the chemicals in the plates and the specific gravity of the electrolyte.

The ***capacity*** of a battery is the amount of current it will deliver. Capacity depends on the number and area of plates in the cells and also on the amount of electrolyte present. Cells having a large number of plates will deliver more current than cells having a smaller number. Automotive lead-acid batteries are built with large, porous, low-density plates, so the electrolyte will have quick access to as much active plate surface area as possible.

Battery capacity drops rapidly as the temperature drops. This "drop" occurs because the battery is an electrochemical device and, like virtually all chemical actions, it is aided by heat. For example, if the capacity of cranking power of a battery at 80°F (26.7 °C) is given as 100 percent, the capacity will be only 65 percent at 32°F (0°C). At 0°F (- 17.8°C), it will be only 40 percent. See Figure 25-12.

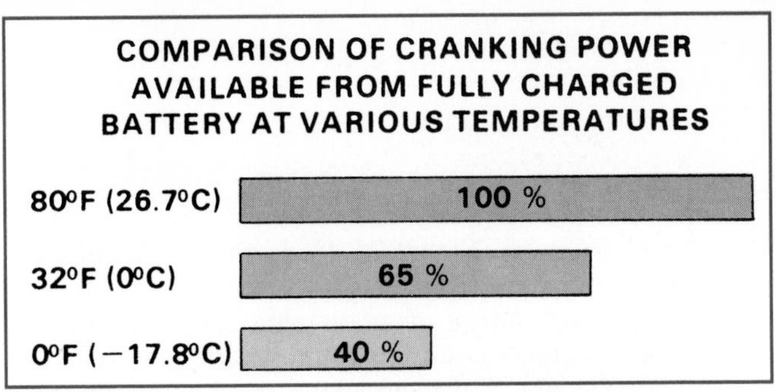

Figure 25-12. The capacity of cranking power falls off sharply with a drop in temperature. (Battery Council International)

Battery Ratings

Two methods of rating the performance of lead-acid batteries have been established by the Battery Council International (BCI). These standards are designed to indicate a battery's power-delivering capability:

- Cold cranking rating.
- Reserve capacity rating.

The ***cold cranking rating*** determines the amount of current (amps.) a battery can deliver for 30 seconds at 0°F (- 17.8°C) and still maintain a terminal voltage of 7.2 volts, or 1.2 volts per cell. The rating is given as amps at 0°F (- 17.8°C). The cold cranking rating provides a means of determining whether a battery will crank a given engine (based on amperage draw of starter) over a wide range of ambient temperatures.

The ***reserve capacity rating*** is the time required to reduce a fully charged battery's terminal voltage below 10.2 volts, or 1.7 volts per cell, at a continuous discharge rate of 25 amps at approximately 80°F (26.7°C). The test is a straight draw on the battery, without any charging system input.

The reserve capacity rating appears on the battery as a time interval. For example, a rating of 100 minutes means that once the indicating lamp comes on, the driver has one hour and 40 minutes of driving time under minimum electrical load to get to a service facility.

Battery Inspection

The first test of the condition of any used battery is a visual inspection, backed by a manual check for loose cable connections and loose battery posts. Look carefully for defective cables, eroded cable clamps, accumulated corrosion deposits, cracks in the battery cover or case, and loose or broken hold-down devices. Clean, repair, or replace parts as required.

The next consideration–when servicing conventional batteries–is an electrolyte level check. If necessary, add distilled water or a clean tap water (not mineral water). Refill to the electrolyte level indicator or to 1/2″ (13 mm) above the top of the separators. Do not overfill.

Battery Testing

There are several methods used to test the state of charge and condition of an automotive battery. In general, these methods include:

- Hydrometer test.
- Heavy-load test.
- Open-circuit voltage test.

Hydrometer Test

The ***hydrometer,*** Figure 25-13, is an instrument used to test state of charge of a battery.

The ***state of charge*** of a conventional lead-acid battery can be determined by testing the specific gravity of the electrolyte. Do not, however, make the hydrometer test immediately after water has been added to the electrolyte. Measurement should be made before the water is added in order to obtain a representative sample. If the level is too low to obtain a sample, water should be added as needed. Then, after the battery has been in use long enough to thoroughly mix the water with the electrolyte, the sample may be taken with the hydrometer.

See Figure 25-13 for instructions on how to read the hydrometer. To make the hydrometer test, check the specific gravity of each cell. The generally accepted full-charge reading is 1.265. Compare the lowest and highest readings. If there is more than .050 difference in the readings, replace the battery. If the readings are about the same, they can be checked against the chart in Figure 25-13 to determine percent of full charge, or in effect, the state of charge.

Note that hydrometer readings should not be taken while the battery is gassing. This condition would affect the accuracy of the reading.

Remember, too, when checking the specific gravity of a battery cell, you must check the temperature of the electrolyte and make the necessary correction. Fill, empty, and refill the hydrometer tube with samples of electrolyte to get a sample of the proper temperature. See Figure 25-14.

As mentioned earlier, most maintenance-free batteries have a built-in hydrometer or a visual test indicator in the cover. When making a visual test, for example, a green, black, clear or yellow color code is used on General Motors Freedom batteries. Green signals a state of charge of 65 percent or above. Black indicates a state of charge of less than 65 percent. Clear means a low electrolyte level. See Figure 25-10.

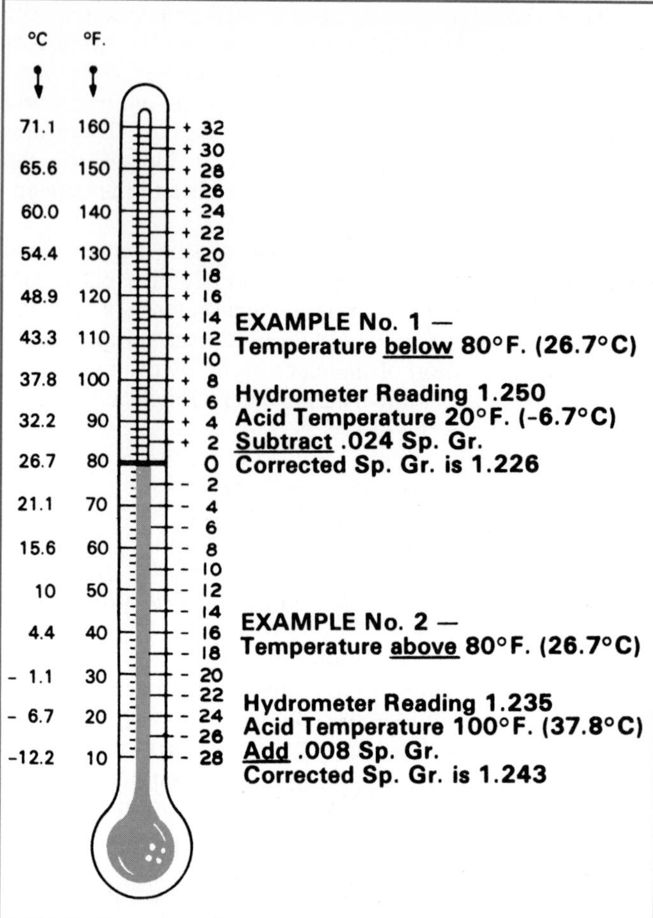

Figure 25-14. Temperature correction of a hydrometer reading involves changing the reading by .004 points of specific gravity for each 10°F (5.5°C) that the electrolyte temperature is above or below 80°F (26.7°C).

On late-model Chrysler products, the visual test indicator uses a green, black, red, and yellow color code. Green indicates a state of charge of 75 percent or above. Black means a state of charge between 50 and 75 percent. Red signals a state of charge below 50 percent. Yellow indicates a low electrolyte level.

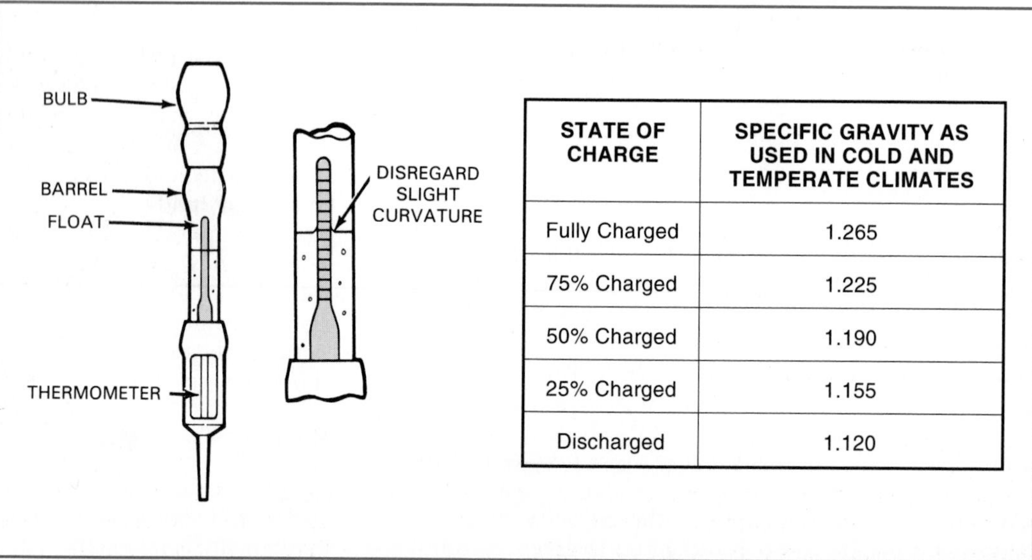

STATE OF CHARGE	SPECIFIC GRAVITY AS USED IN COLD AND TEMPERATE CLIMATES
Fully Charged	1.265
75% Charged	1.225
50% Charged	1.190
25% Charged	1.155
Discharged	1.120

Figure 25-13. To read a hydrometer, squeeze the bulb to draw enough electrolyte from the cell to raise the float. The float should not touch the barrel of the hydrometer. Release the pressure on the bulb and observe the specific gravity reading on the float. Check the thermometer and compute the temperature-corrected specific gravity of the electrolyte.

These readings merely reveal "state of charge," not battery condition. Various tests must be made to establish whether recharging or replacement is required.

Heavy-load Test

The ***heavy-load test*** (also called "high-rate discharge" or "capacity" test) is a good test of the battery's ability to perform under load. In this test, a good battery will produce current equal to 50 percent of its cold cranking rating (or equal to three times its ampere/hour rating) for 15 seconds and still provide minimum voltage to start the engine.

To make the heavy-load test:

1. Charge battery, if necessary, until all cells are at least 1.225 specific gravity. Remove vent caps, if so equipped, and install a thermometer in electrolyte.
2. Connect a battery load tester, Figure 25-15 and 25-16, or a battery starter tester directly to the battery posts: positive to positive and negative to negative.
3. Turn the carbon pile knob to apply a load equal to 50% of the cold cranking rating of the battery being tested.
4. Read the voltmeter while the load is being applied for 15 seconds. Turn the carbon pile knob to the "off" position. Record the voltage.
5. Read the thermometer, record the temperature, and check the temperature and voltage against the chart in Figure 25-15.
6. Replace the battery if the minimum voltage is below specifications.
7. If the reading is the same or greater than the voltage shown on the chart, clean and fully charge the battery. The battery should remain in service.

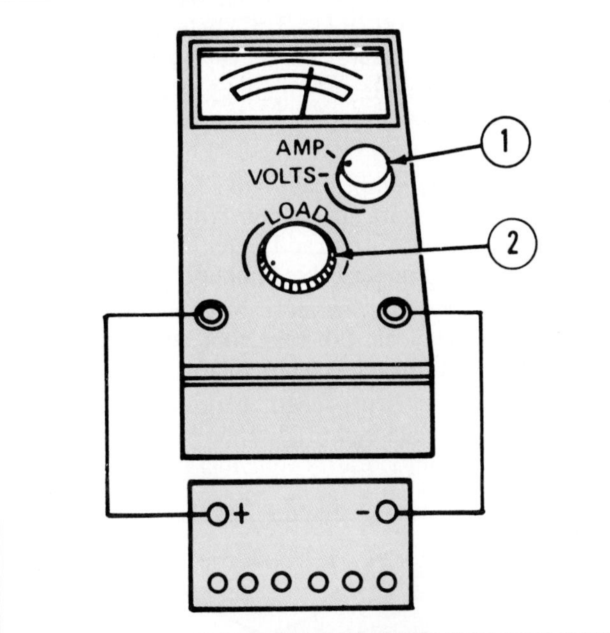

MINIMUM VOLTAGE	TEMPERATURE	
	F°	C°
9.6	70 and above	21 and above
9.5	60	16
9.4	50	10
9.3	40	4
9.1	30	-1
8.9	20	-7
8.7	10	-12
8.5	0	-18

Figure 25-15. A battery load tester has a carbon pile to impose a heavy load of three times the ampere/hour rating of the battery. The voltage reading after 15 seconds under load determines the battery condition. See the minimum voltage values at temperatures shown in chart. (Chrysler)

Open-circuit Voltage Test

If the battery fails the heavy load test, check its state of charge by making a stabilized ***open-circuit voltage test.*** Allow at least 10 minutes after the load test for the battery voltage to stabilize, then measure and record open circuit voltage.

There are many types of test equipment available for making the open-circuit voltage test. In general, a voltmeter is used by connecting its positive lead to the positive post of the battery and its negative lead to the negative post of the battery. See Figure 25-17.

To analyze the open circuit voltage test result, consider that a battery at a temperature of 60°-100°F (16°-38°C) in good condition should show approximately 12.4 volts on the voltmeter. See Figure 25-17. If the state of charge is 75 percent or more, the battery is considered "charged."

However, if the state of charge is under 75 percent, the battery should be recharged and load tested again. If it fails the load test the second time, the battery should be replaced. If it passes, the battery should remain in service.

Battery Safety Precautions

Working with batteries poses several safety problems. Spilled electrolyte can "eat" holes in clothing and burn the skin. Electrolyte splashed into the eyes is sight-threatening. Also, explosive gases are generated within the battery cells. Always wear safety goggles or a face shield and observe all safe servicing practices when working on or near batteries.

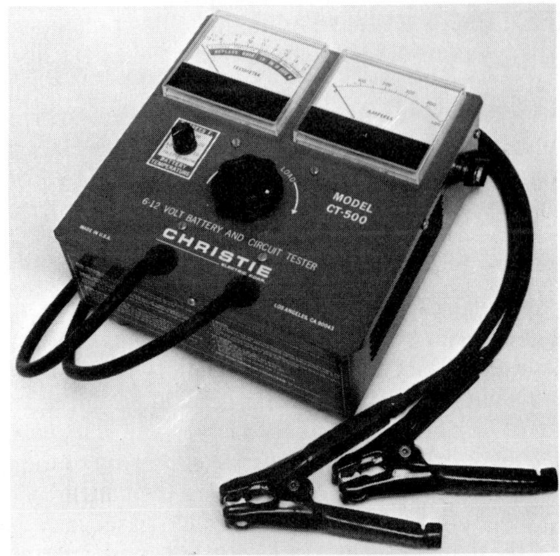

Figure 25-16. Heavy-load tester has an adjustable load control up to 500 amps, battery temperature compensation, and state of charge reading. (Christie Electric Corp.)

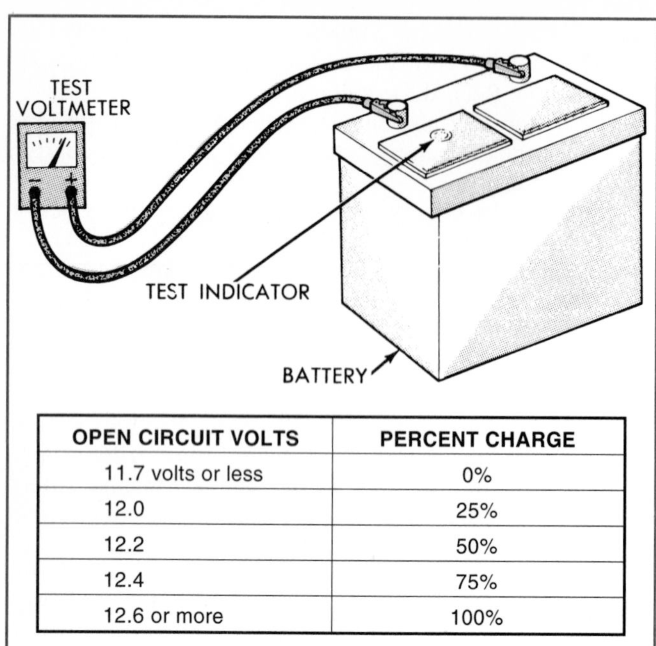

OPEN CIRCUIT VOLTS	PERCENT CHARGE
11.7 volts or less	0%
12.0	25%
12.2	50%
12.4	75%
12.6 or more	100%

Figure 25-17. An open-circuit voltage test is made by connecting the voltmeter leads across the battery terminals. The voltage reading indicates percent charge as shown in the chart. (Chrysler Corp.)

Handling Electrolyte

Avoid contact with the battery electrolyte, if possible. If electrolyte does get on your clothing, your body, or the finish of the car being serviced, neutralize it immediately with a solution of baking soda and water. Then, rinse with clean water.

If electrolyte is splashed into your eyes, flood them with cool, clean water for about five minutes and get medical help as quickly as possible. If electrolyte is accidentally swallowed, drink large quantities of water or milk, followed by milk of magnesia or vegetable oil. Call a doctor immediately.

If you are mixing sulfuric acid and water to make up an electrolyte solution of a certain specific gravity:

1. Use a lead, lead-lined, or nonmetallic container.
2. Always pour acid slowly into the water. Do not pour water into the acid.
3. Add small amounts of acid at a time while stirring the solution.
4. Repeatedly test specific gravity with a hydrometer until the solution reaches the desired gravity reading.

Danger of Explosion

Chemical reactions within the battery create explosive mixtures of hydrogen and oxygen. These gases are generated within the cells during normal battery operation. Even a battery standing idle self-discharges and produces a small amount of hydrogen. There is always the danger of an external spark or flame setting off an explosion of the gases within the cells and possibly shattering the battery.

Another danger is that the generated gases may escape through the battery vents and form an explosive atmosphere around the battery. In these situations, a match being struck, a lighted cigarette, or any spark or flame could ignite the gases and cause an explosion.

Most vent plugs on conventional batteries have flame arresters designed to prevent the ignition of gases within the battery by external sparks or flames. See Figure 25-8. Maintenance-free batteries have flame arresters at exits of the baffled passages in the cover. See Figure 25-7. In spite of these preventive measures, an external spark may ignite the gases within the battery and result in an explosion.

Safe Servicing Practices

With these dangers of a battery explosion in mind, always observe the following safe battery servicing practices:

- Never lean over a battery when charging, testing, or jump-starting an engine. Wear goggles or a face shield.
- Do not "break" live circuits. For example, do not disconnect positive cable first when working on a battery. Always disconnect negative cable first and reconnect it last, Figure 25-18.
- Avoid accidental "grounds" and resulting sparks caused by dropped tools or metal parts bridging a live circuit and any grounded part.
- Charge batteries only in a well ventilated area.
- Never attempt to charge a frozen battery. Allow the battery to warm to 60 °F (15.5 °C) before charging.
- When preparing to charge a battery, see that charger ac (alternating current) lead is unplugged or the switch is turned off before attaching, adjusting, or removing charger clamps.
- Never connect the jumper cables to a frozen battery in an attempt to jump start an engine. Allow the battery to warm to 40 °F (4.4 °C) and add water if necessary before proceeding with jumper cable hookup.
- See that the battery charger cable clamps or jumper cable clamps are clean and make good connections. Poor connections can cause an electrical arc.
- If violent gassing occurs when charging a battery, or if the battery case feels hot (125 °F or 52 °C), reduce the charging rate or temporarily stop charging.

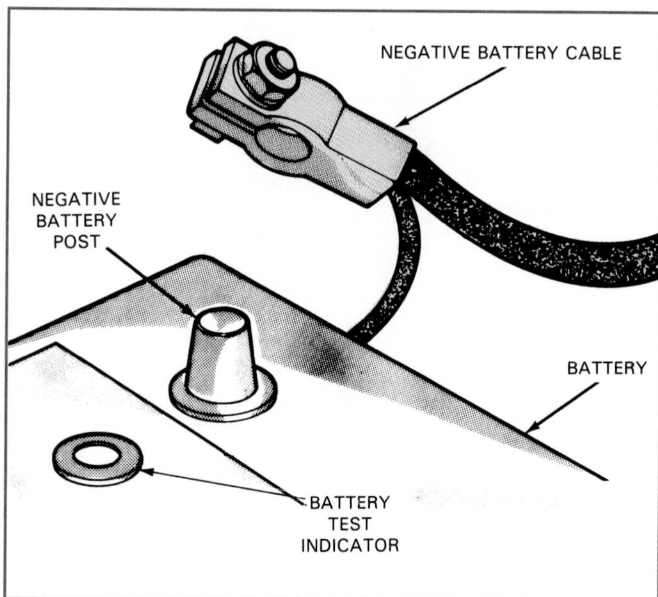

Figure 25-18. When it becomes necessary to disconnect the battery cables, always disconnect the negative cable first and reconnect it last. (Chrysler Corp.)

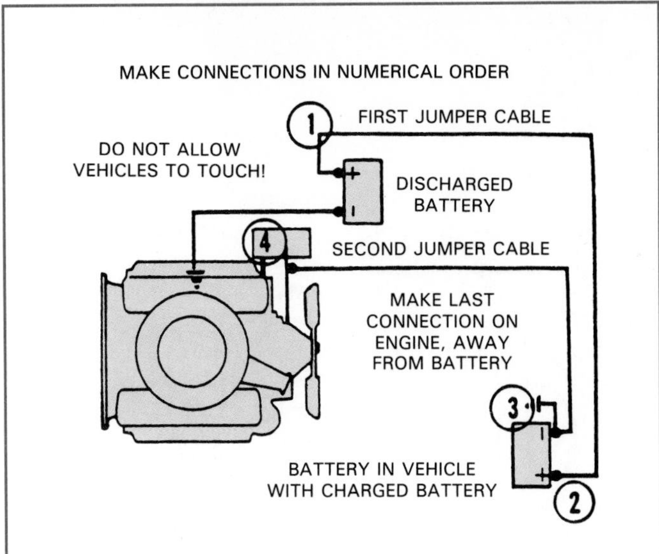

Figure 25-19. Proper jumper cable hookup stresses the need to connect a second jumper cable from the negative terminal of the booster battery to the engine, away from the discharged battery.

- Strictly observe directions for jumper cable hookup sequence. See Figure 25-19. An improper hookup could result in an explosion of one of the batteries.

Battery Service Tips

Observe all safety suggestions given earlier and use proper tools when performing battery service. Proper tools include the correct size open-end wrenches, a cable clamp puller, a cable clamp spreader, a tapered post and cable clamp cleaning brush, a scraper, and a wire brush. A "filling" device (either self-leveling type or syringe type water dispenser), a battery carrier, and jumper cables are also necessary.

When servicing batteries:

- Use a fender cover.
- Inspect and/or test the cables, hold-down, and battery.
- Repair or replace parts as required.
- Remove the cables from the battery (ground cable first) using an open end wrench and a cable clamp puller.
- Spread the clamps with a cable clamp spreader.
- Clean the tapered posts and the mating surfaces of the cable clamps with a special cleaning brush, Figure 25-20. Use a baking soda and water solution to clean the side terminals or the "L" terminals.
- Clean the battery cover with a scraper and a wire brush.
- If necessary, remove the battery and clean corrosion and rust from the hold-down and battery tray.
- Reinstall the battery, tighten the hold-down (do not overtighten), and finish cleaning with a baking soda and water solution. See Figure 25-21.
- Connect the cables to the battery posts or terminals (ground cable last), tighten them securely, and coat them with high-temperature grease.
- Use an open-end wrench to tighten nuts at the starter relay or solenoid switch and at the ground cable connection at the engine block.

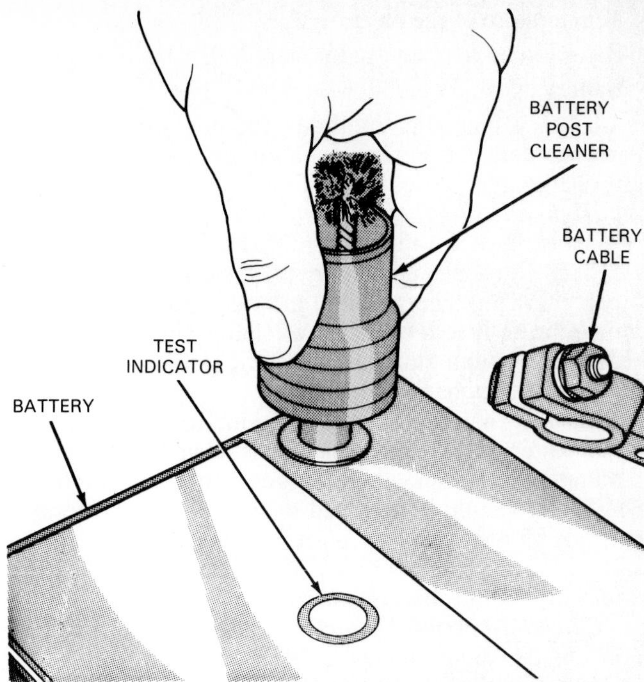

Figure 25-20. Use a suitable battery post cleaning tool to remove dirt and corrosion from the posts and mating surfaces of the cable clamps. (Chrysler Corp.)

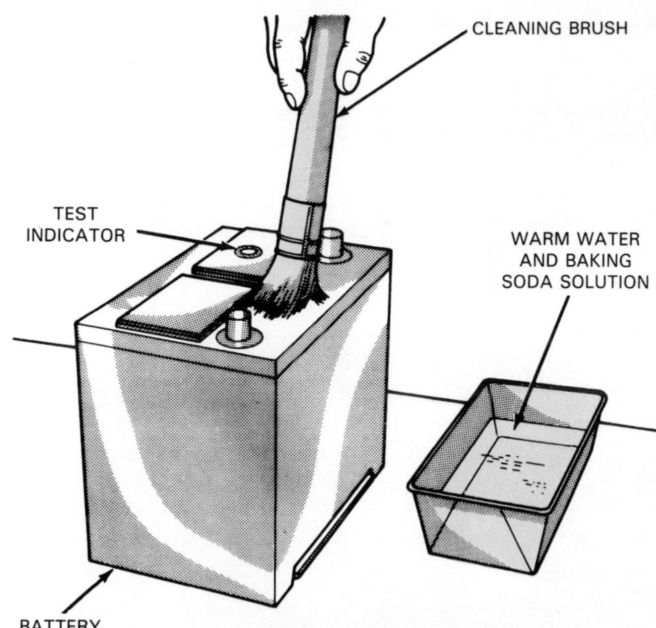

Figure 25-21. Finish battery maintenance by cleaning the cover with a stiff bristle brush and a solution of baking soda and warm water. (Chrysler Corp.)

- Check the level of electrolyte in the cells of conventional batteries. Refill to the level indicator or to 1/2″ (13 mm) above tops of separators with distilled water or tap water.

Battery Charging Methods

Battery charging methods vary, based on several considerations:

- Electrical capacity of the battery being serviced.

- Temperature of the electrolyte.
- Battery state of charge at the start of the charging period.
- Battery age and condition.

Battery charging methods include high-rate fast charging, constant-potential charging, constant current slow charging, and trickle charging.

High-rate fast charging provides a high charging rate for a short time. See Figure 25-22. Usually, the intent of a fast charge is to give the battery the "boost" it needs (70 to 90 percent of full charge) until the vehicle's charging system can bring it to a full state of charge. In keeping with this, a battery with electrolyte specific gravity of 1.225 or above should not be fast charged.

The fast charging rate should be limited to 60 amps for 12 volt batteries. Generally, the rate is set at 40-60 amps for 30 minutes. To completely recharge a battery, the high-rate fast charger should be adjusted to slow charge, preferably at a rate of one amp per positive plate per cell. If, for example, the battery has nine plates per cell (four positive, five negative), the charging rate would be four amps.

Constant-potential charging, as the name implies, maintains the same voltage on the battery throughout the period of the charge. As a result, the current is automatically reduced as the battery approaches full charge. This feature reduces the amount of overcharge the battery can receive. Therefore, batteries in good condition will not be damaged by this method of charging. However, if the battery is badly sulfated, the temperature may rise soon after it is placed on charge. These batteries should be placed on slow charge.

Constant-current slow charging uses a low charging rate for a relatively long time, Figure 25-23. Charging rates of three to five amps or one percent of cold cranking rating are typical. Another acceptable charging rate for slow charging is one amp per positive plate per cell.

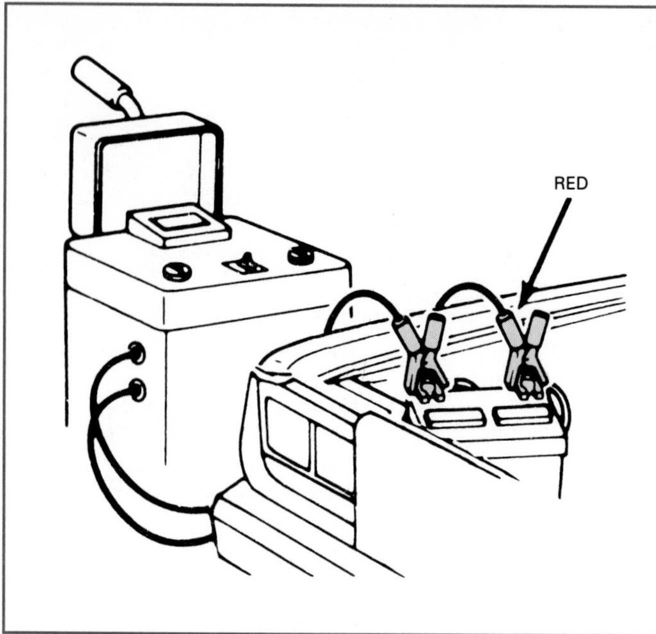

Figure 25-23. Battery charging hookup is as follows: charger red cable to positive post of battery; charger black cable to negative post of battery. (Chrysler Corp.)

Constant-current slow charging periods as long as 24 hours may be needed to bring the battery to full charge. To check the progress of the charge, hydrometer readings should be taken every hour. The battery is fully charged when the cells are gassing freely, and there is no increase in the hydrometer reading for three successive hourly tests.

Trickle charging, Figure 25-24, is designed to charge batteries at a rate of approximately one amp. Trickle

Figure 25-22. High rate fast chargers provide the convenience of an in-car "boost charge" of the battery to get the vehicle back on the road. (Christie Electric Corp.)

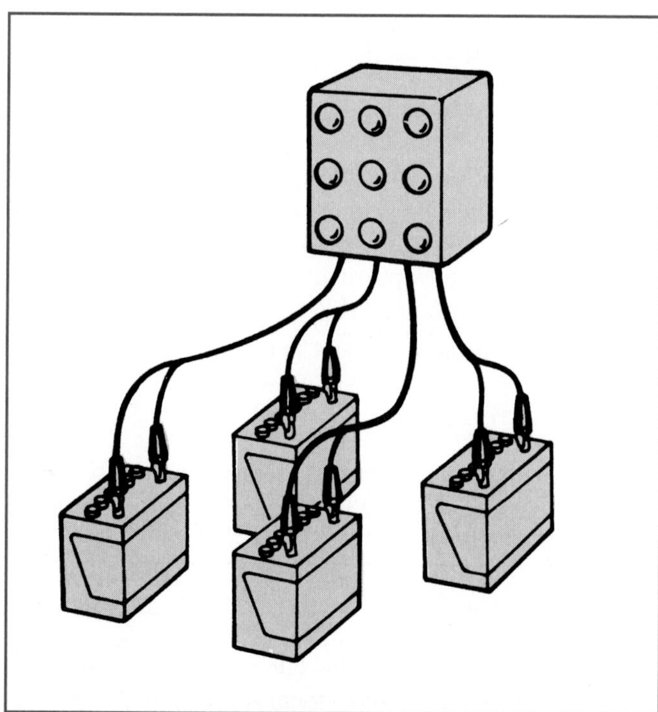

Figure 25-24. While trickle chargers have a low charging rate, continuous overcharging can cause the grids of the positive plates to disintegrate. Follow the battery charger manufacturer's instructions. (Battery Council International)

charges are used primarily for maintaining displays and stocks of batteries in fully charged condition.

While the trickle charging rate is extremely low, batteries can be damaged if left on trickle charge for long periods. Common practice is to leave the batteries on a trickle charge during the day and take them off charge during the night. In that way, the danger of severe overcharging is lessened.

When preparing to charge a battery, be aware of all of the safety precautions you should observe during the charging operation. Familiarize yourself with the manufacturer's battery charger guide and follow the step-by-step instructions in the sequence given.

Ideally, use an automatic battery charger that senses battery voltage and automatically shuts off–or almost shuts off–when the battery reaches or approaches the fully charged state. These chargers sense temperature and, usually, sense polarity to help prevent sparks if the charger clamps are connected in reverse.

Activating Dry Charged Batteries

A dry charged automotive battery contains no electrolyte until it is placed in service. The cell elements are given an initial charge on special equipment at the factory. Then they are thoroughly washed, dried, and assembled into battery cases. The batteries are shipped in the dry state.

A dry charged battery will retain its full charge indefinitely if moisture does not enter the cells. When ready for service, the battery is filled with electrolyte and, generally, is given a boost charge.

When filling a dry charged battery with electrolyte, the manufacturers advise that protective glasses be worn. The procedure for filling the battery is as follows:

1. Remove the vent plugs and discard the restrictors.
2. Open the container of electrolyte.
3. Using a glass or an acid-proof funnel, fill each cell with electrolyte, Figure 25-25, to top of separators.
4. Boost charge the battery at 15 amps until the specific gravity of electrolyte is 1.250 or higher and the temperature is at least 60°F (15.5°C).
5. After the boost charge, check the level of electrolyte in all cells. Add electrolyte to bring the level to the level indicator or 1/2″ (13 mm) above the top of the separators.
6. After the battery has been put in service, add only distilled water or a good grade of drinking water. Do not add electrolyte.

Jump Starting an Engine

Jump starting an engine is a common procedure whereby jumper cables are used to transfer power from a good (booster) battery, Figure 25-26, to a discharged battery.

The key to safe and effective jump starting is the correct hookup of the jumper cables. See Figure 25-19. The following steps must be performed in sequence:

1. Position the vehicle with the booster battery next to the vehicle with the discharged battery so that the jumper cables can reach the batteries in both vehicles. The vehicles must not touch each other.
2. Turn off all electrical loads; set the parking brake; and place the automatic transmission in park or the manual transmission in neutral.
3. See that the vent plugs are tight and place a damp cloth over the plugs of each battery.
4. Connect the positive jumper cable to the positive post or terminal of the discharged battery, Figure 25-19.
5. Connect the other end of the positive jumper cable to the positive post of the booster battery.
6. Connect the negative jumper cable to the negative post or terminal of the booster battery.
7. Connect the other end of the negative jumper cable–away from discharged battery–to the engine block, car frame, or other good metallic ground.

Figure 25-25. To activate a dry charged battery: fill the cells with electrolyte to the top of the separators. Then, boost charge the battery and fill the cells with electrolyte to 1/2″ (13 mm) above the top of the separators.

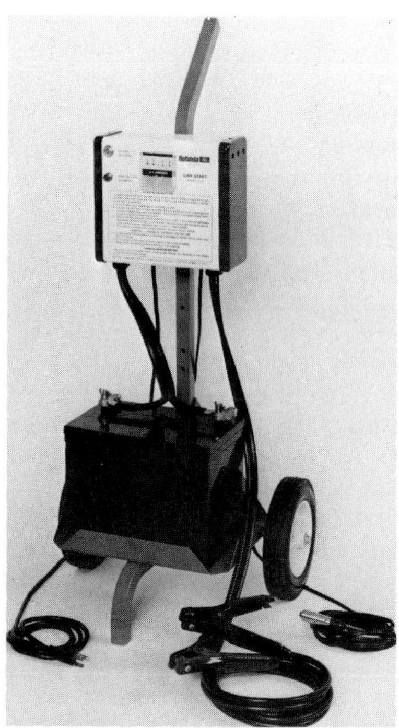

Figure 25-26. Mobile car starting equipment is available. This setup includes a two-wheel cart, a high-capacity booster battery, jumper cables, and a battery charger. (Ford Motor Co.)

8. See that the cables are clear of fan blades and other moving parts of both engines. Then, start the engine of the vehicle with the booster battery.
9. Allow a few minutes of engine operation, and then try to start the engine of the vehicle with the discharged battery.
10. After starting, allow the engine to return to idle speed and remove the negative jumper cable at the engine block or other ground connection.
11. Remove the other end of the negative jumper cable from the booster battery.
12. Remove the positive jumper cable from the discharged battery.
13. Remove the other end of the positive jumper cable from the booster battery.
14. Discard the damp cloths that were placed over the vent plugs of both batteries.

NOTE: If the engine in the vehicle with the discharged battery fails to start after cranking for 30 seconds, stop the jump starting procedure. A second problem, in addition to the discharged battery, must be solved.

Chapter 10–Review Questions

Write your answers on a separate sheet of paper. Do not write in this book.

1. Define the lead-acid storage battery.
2. The sole function of an automotive battery is to serve as a source of power for the starting motor and ignition system during cranking and starting of an internal combustion engine. True or False?
3. A typical 12-volt automotive battery is made up of _____ cells connected in series and filled with _____.
4. A(n) _____ is an assembly of positive and negative plates and separators.
5. The _____ of a battery is the amount of current it will deliver.
6. Name two methods of rating the performance of lead-acid batteries.
7. A hydrometer is an instrument used to test which of the following:
   (A) Open-circuit voltage.
   (B) Closed-circuit voltage.
   (C) Specific gravity of electrolyte.
   (D) Level of electrolyte in cells.
8. When checking a color-coded, built-in hydrometer in the cover of a maintenance-free battery, which color indicates 3/4 to full charge?
   (A) Yellow or clear.
   (B) Green.
   (C) Red.
   (D) Black.
9. When mixing sulfuric acid with water to make up an electrolyte solution of a certain specific gravity, should you pour the acid into the water or the water into the acid?
10. When testing the specific gravity of a battery electrolyte, what is the generally accepted full-charge reading?
    (A) 1.265.
    (B) 1.275.
    (C) 1.285.
    (D) 1.295.
11. The specific gravity readings merely reveal _____, not battery condition.
12. When comparing the lowest and highest specific gravity readings, the battery should be replaced if there is more than _____ difference in the readings.
    (A) .025.
    (B) .050.
    (C) .075.
    (D) .100.
13. When making a heavy-load test, what is the maximum length of time the test load should be applied?
    (A) 5 seconds.
    (B) 10 seconds.
    (C) 15 seconds.
    (D) 20 seconds.
14. When making a stabilized open-circuit voltage test, a battery is considered to be in good condition if the voltmeter reading is:
    (A) 12 volts.
    (B) 12.2 volts.
    (C) 12.4 volts.
    (D) 12.6 volts.
15. When disconnecting battery cables, do not "break" live circuits. Always disconnect the _____ (positive/negative) cable first and reconnect it last.
16. What is the correct level of the electrolyte in the battery cells in relation to the tops of the separators?
17. Battery charging methods include: _____-constant potential charging, constant-current slow charging, and trickle charging.
18. The battery is fully slow charged when the cells are _____ and there is no increase in the hydrometer reading for _____ successive hourly tests.
19. When filling a dry charged battery with electrolyte, the manufacturers recommend that protective _____ be worn.
20. The key to safe and effective jump starting is the _____ use of the jumper cables.

Match the question number for each of the following descriptive phrases with the letter designated for each correct term.

21. _____	Sulfuric acid diluted with water.	(A) Specific gravity.
22. _____	Assembly of positive plates, negative plates, and separators in connectors.	(B) Intercell.
		(C) Electrolyte.
		(D) Separators.
		(E) Element.
23. _____	"Bridges" at bottom of case.	(F) Element rests.
		(G) Plate group.
24. _____	Lead dioxide.	(H) Positive.
25. _____	Active materials contained in cast grids.	(I) Plates.
		(J) Discharge.
26. _____	Spongy lead.	(K) Charge.
27. _____	Element terminal posts.	(L) Negative.
28. _____	When specific gravity of the electrolyte increases.	
29. _____	Nonconducting material between plates.	
30. _____	When specific gravity of the electrolyte decreases.	

Chapter 26
Starting System Fundamentals and Service

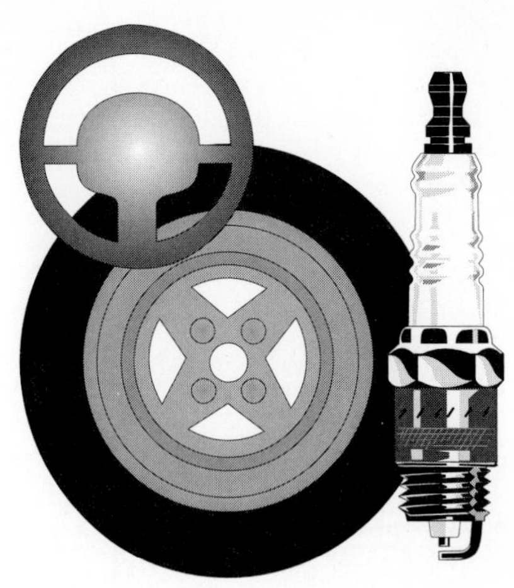

After studying this chapter, you will be able to:
- ❍ Describe how the starting system works.
- ❍ Explain the principles of electric motor operation.
- ❍ Cite the function of an overrunning clutch.
- ❍ Give examples of possible causes of starting system problems.
- ❍ List the various steps of starter maintenance.
- ❍ Describe ways of testing a starting motor to determine its operating condition.

Starting System Fundamentals

The purpose of the ***starting system*** is to use electricity from the battery and an electric motor to turn over the engine during starting. The starting system consists of the battery, a starting motor, a solenoid or relay, an ignition switch, a neutral safety switch, and related electrical wiring. See Figure 26-1. When the ignition switch is placed in the "start" position, the solenoid windings are energized and the resulting shift lever movement causes the the drive pinion gear to engage the flywheel ring gear, Figure 26-1. This causes the flywheel to rotate, cranking the engine.

When the engine starts, an overrunning clutch (part of the drive assembly) protects the armature from excessive speed until the switch is opened. At this point, a return spring causes the pinion gear to disengage from the flywheel.

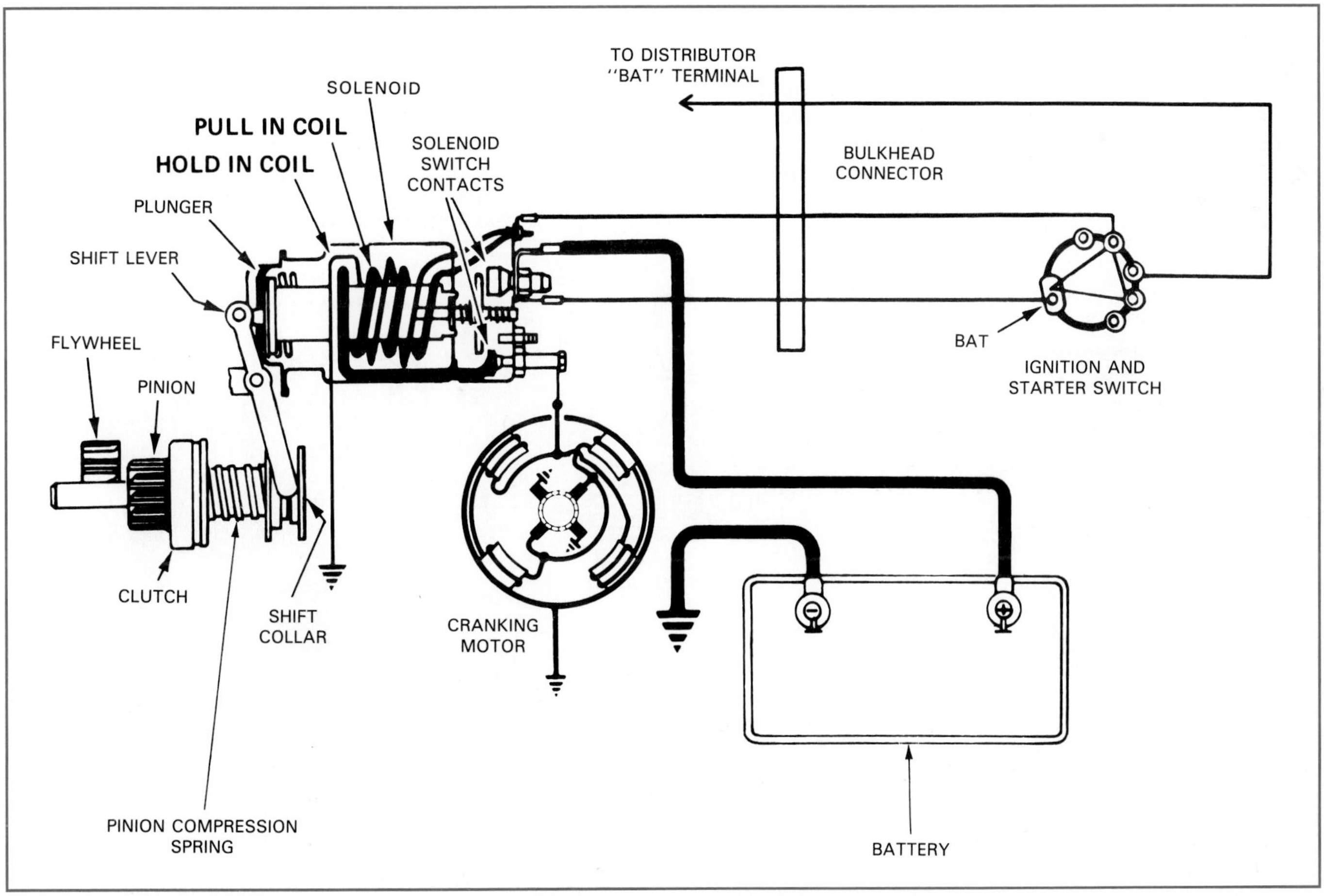

Figure 26-1. Trace the starting circuit from the battery to the ignition switch, to the solenoid windings and solenoid switch contacts, and to the starting motor. Also note the shift lever and the starter drive mechanism at left. (Chevrolet)

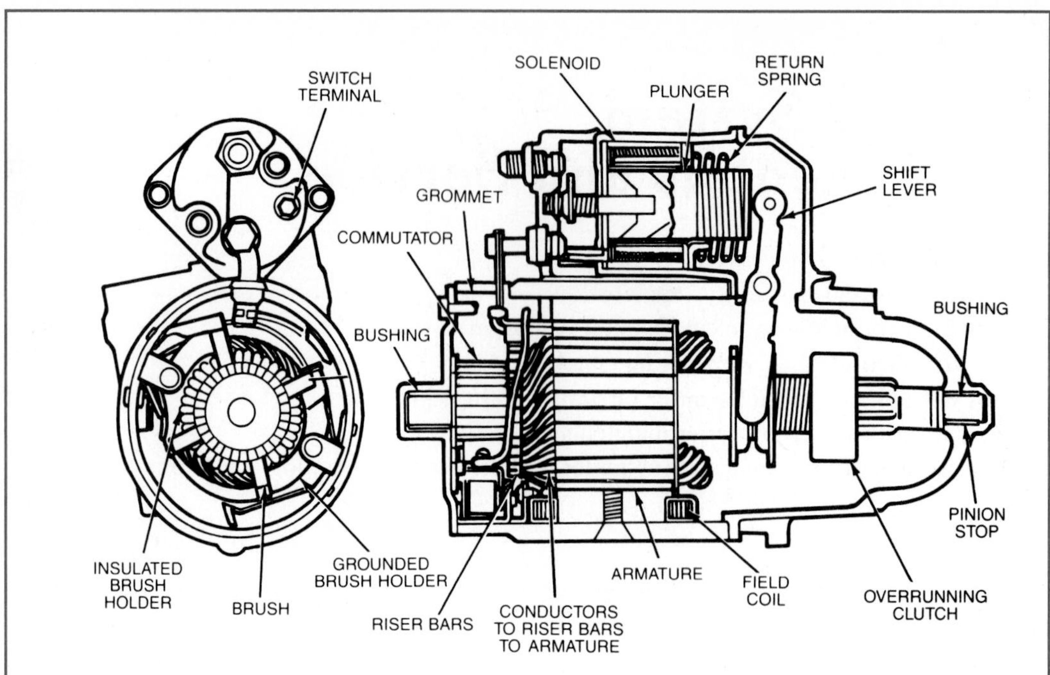

Figure 26-2. Cross-sectional views reveal internal parts of a typical, positive engagement starting motor. (Chevrolet)

The ***automotive starting motor,*** Figure 26-2, is an electromagnetic device that converts electrical energy into mechanical energy. It is designed specifically for cranking internal combustion engines at speeds that will permit starting.

A typical starting motor, Figure 26-3, is made up of a frame and field assembly, an armature, a drive mechanism, a drive end housing, a brush and holder assembly, and a relay and/or solenoid switch. The starting motor mounts on the flywheel housing or on a flange at the rear of the engine. See Figure 26-4. The solenoid operates a starter drive mechanism that has a small pinion gear (having about eight teeth), which can be meshed with a large flywheel ring gear (having about 100 teeth) to crank the engine. See Figure 26-1.

Starting Motor Operating Principles

Electric motors of the type used in "starters" operate on the principle that a current-carrying conductor will tend to move from a strong magnetic field to a weak magnetic field. If a single current-carrying conductor is placed in a magnetic field created by a permanent magnet, as in Figure 26-5, the flow of current in the conductor will cause a

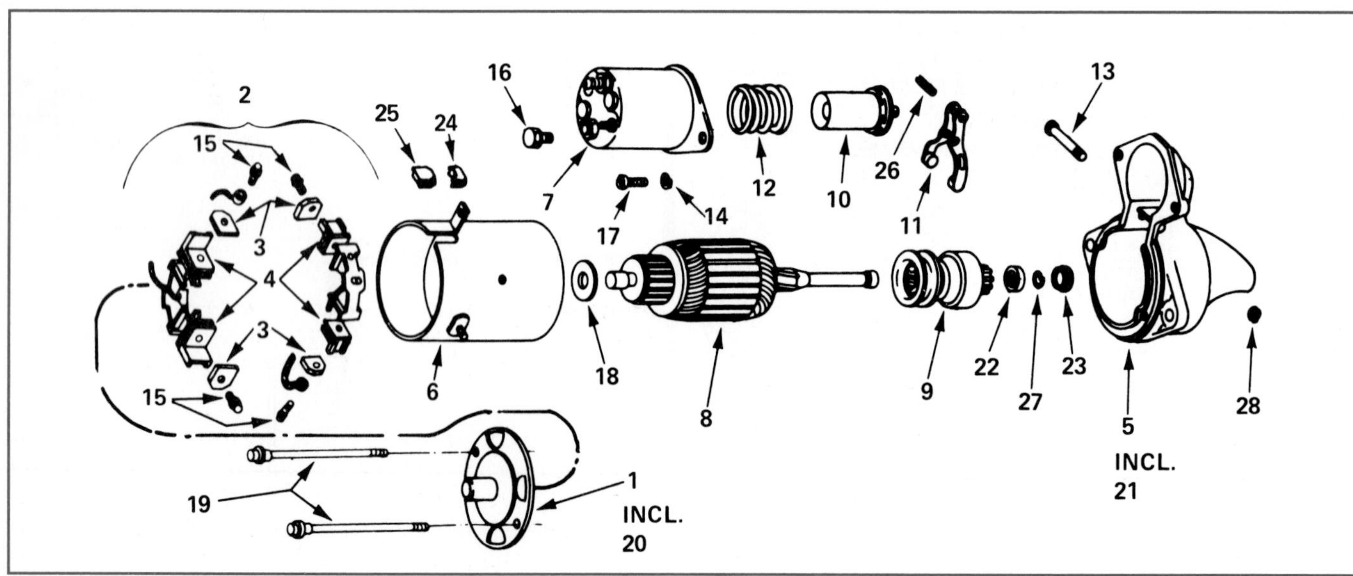

Figure 26-3. Parts of disassembled starting motor include: 1–Commutator end frame. 2–Brush and holder package. 3–Brush. 4–Brush holder. 5–Drive end housing. 6–Frame and field assembly. 7–Solenoid switch. 8–Armature. 9–Drive assembly. 10–Plunger. 11–Shift lever. 12–Plunger return spring. 13–Shift lever shaft. 14–Lock washer. 15–Brush attaching screw. 16–Field lead to switch screw. 17–Switch attaching screw. 18–Washer. 19–Through bolt. 20–Commutator end bushing. 21–Drive end bushing. 22–Pinion stop collar. 23–Thrust collar. 24–Grommet. 25–Grommet. 26–Plunger pin. 27–Pinion stop retaining ring. 28–Lever shaft retaining ring. (Cadillac)

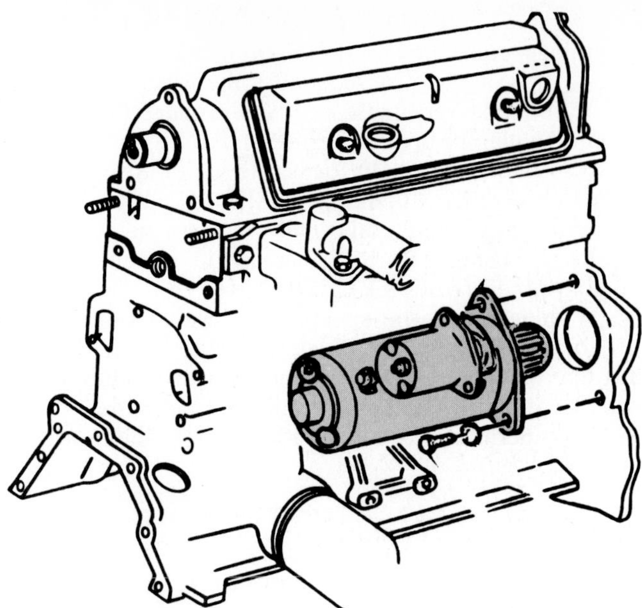

Figure 26-4. A starter assembly is installed in the opening in the flywheel housing or in a flange at the rear of the engine. (Chevrolet)

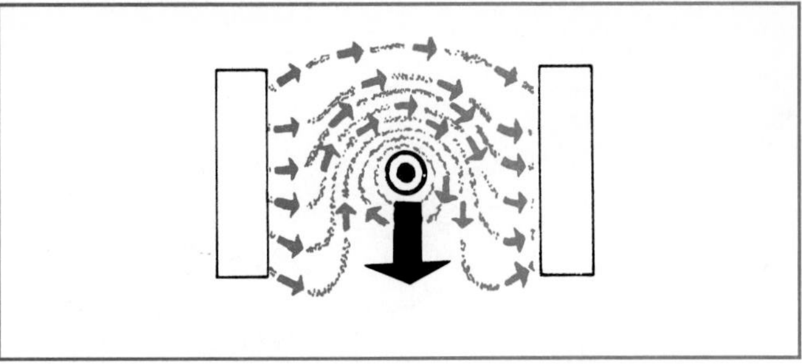

Figure 26-5. When a current-carrying conductor is placed in a magnetic field, the conductor will tend to move in direction indicated.

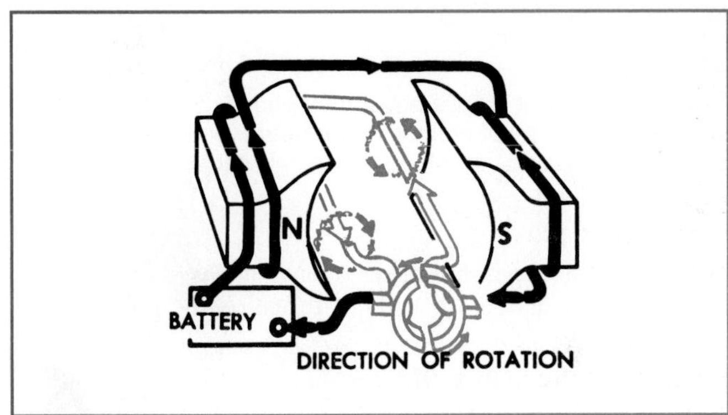

Figure 26-6. This drawing depicts a simple electric motor using a single loop of wire for an armature. Note the direction of current flow (outlined arrows) and the field around the conductor (solid arrows).

magnetic field to encircle the conductor in a clockwise direction. This circular magnetic field will tend to cancel out and weaken the lines of force between the poles of the permanent magnet below the conductor. At the same time, both fields will combine above the conductor to create a strong magnetic field. In effect, there is more magnetism above the conductor and less below it. Then, as the distorted lines of force tend to straighten out, they exert a downward thrust on the conductor.

Rotary Motion

In a starting motor, the downward thrust is converted into ***rotary motion.*** Assume that the conductor in Figure 26-5 is bent into a loop, as shown in Figure 26-6. This will be the rotating part, which is known as the ***armature.*** The ends of the armature are connected to two semicircular brass bars called the ***commutator.*** The magnetic field of the two magnetic poles (marked N and S) is created by two electromagnets. Current for the electromagnets called–***field coils*** in this setup–is provided by a battery.

The current flowing through the field coils, Figure 26-6, produces a strong magnetic field that flows from the north pole (N) to the south pole (S). At the same time, current flowing through the armature coil produces a circular magnetic field that surrounds the armature, as shown by the arrows in Figure 26-6. This circular magnetic field is in a clockwise direction on the left-hand conductor of the armature and a counterclockwise direction around the right conductor. Note that the current in the left-hand side of the armature coil is flowing toward the commutator, which is the same direction shown in Figure 26-5. This results in a downward thrust on the armature. Since the current is flowing in the opposite direction in the right-hand side of the armature coil, the thrust will be in the opposite direction, or upward, Figure 26-7.

The combination of the two thrusts causes the armature to rotate. This rotation will continue because each time

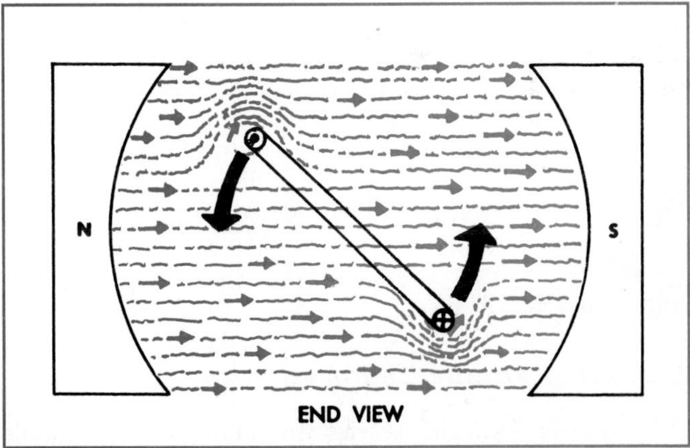

Figure 26-7. Lines of force react to distortion of the magnetic field to create a downward thrust at left and an upward thrust at right, causing armature coil to rotate.

the armature coil passes the vertical position, the commutator (which rotates with the armature) will automatically connect the armature coil so the current will continue to flow away from the commutator in the right-hand coil and toward the commutator in the left-hand coil.

The tendency for a current-carrying coil to move when placed in a magnetic field can be easily demonstrated by means of a permanent magnet, a battery, and some wire. See Figure 26-8. First, connect the battery to points A and B. Then, reverse the connections, and the wire, which is bent in the form of a yoke, will swing in the opposite direction.

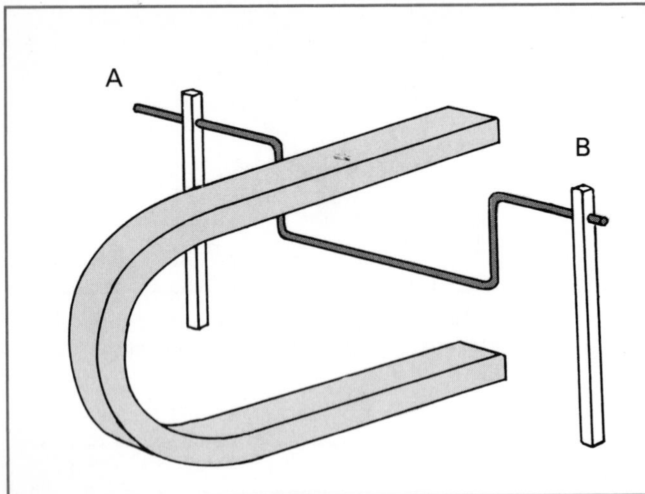

Figure 26-8. The simple equipment shown will demonstrate the basic principles of electric motor operation. Connecting a battery to the ends of a loop of wire will cause the loop to swing.

Turning the horseshoe magnet over from its original position will also change direction of thrust on the yoke.

Effect of Counter EMF

As pointed out in Chapter 19, Fundamentals of Electricity, Magnetism, and Electronics, when any conductor is moved through a magnetic field, a voltage will be induced in the conductor. This condition also occurs in a motor when the conductor is being supplied with current. However, the voltage induced in the conductor (by cutting magnetic lines of force) will be in the opposite direction to voltage being supplied to the motor. Such voltage is known as a ***back voltage,*** or ***counter electromotive force*** (CEMF).

The CEMF limits the current in the armature. When the speed of the armature increases, the CEMF also increases. Since CEMF is opposed to the voltage applied to the motor, it has the effect of decreasing the effective voltage. As a result, the voltage that is forcing current through the armature is the difference between the applied voltage and the CEMF.

Speed and Torque Characteristics

A reason for using a series-wound motor for cranking internal combustion engines is that it has extremely high torque. Torque varies with the strength of the magnetic field and the current in the armature. With the armature and field coils in series, any increase in current will produce an increase in the strength of the field. As the load on the motor increases, the current through the fields and armature will also increase. As a result, the torque will keep increasing as the load increases. See Figure 26-9.

The speed of a series-wound motor will vary with the load. For any particular load that a given series motor is driving, there will be a certain definite speed. With heavy loads, series-wound motors will operate at a relatively slow speed. With a light load, these motors will operate at very high speeds. This is because any armature always tends to operate at a speed where the voltage used in overcoming its resistance, plus the CEMF, will be equal to the voltage being applied to the motor. At heavy loads, the current–and the voltage consumed in overcoming the internal resistance–will be large. Consequently, the armature will not have to rotate at very high speeds to produce the required CEMF to equal the applied voltage.

However, under light loads, the motor speeds up, inducing a higher CEMF and decreasing the current through the field and armature coils. This weakens the strength of the field, causing a further increase in armature speed, which again decreases the CEMF.

With no load, the speed of a series-wound motor will continue to increase to such an extent that centrifugal force will destroy the armature. Series-wound motors used for cranking internal combustion engines should never be operated without a load except under controlled conditions.

Starting Motor Types

Starting motors basically operate on the same principle: first using a light current to energize the relay and/or solenoid, and then using a heavy current to power the starting motor. The solenoid serves to actuate the drive mechanism, causing a pinion gear to engage with the flywheel ring gear and crank the engine.

To accomplish this, various types of starting motors are currently in use. Conventional field motor designs feature current-carrying, wire-wound field coils. Newer designs utilize permanent magnets and gear reduction.

Figures 26-2 and 26-10 illustrate ***positive engagement starting motors***. These motors incorporate a shift fork or lever connected by linkage to the solenoid plunger. When the ignition switch is turned to the "start" position, the solenoid windings are energized. Electromagnetic action moves the solenoid plunger and shift fork, causing the pinion gear on the drive mechanism to engage the flywheel. At the same time, the main contacts close in the solenoid switch, and heavy current cranks the engine.

Figure 26-11 presents an exploded view of a ***movable pole shoe*** type of starting motor. With this arrangement, the pole shoe is attached to the starter drive yoke. When heavy

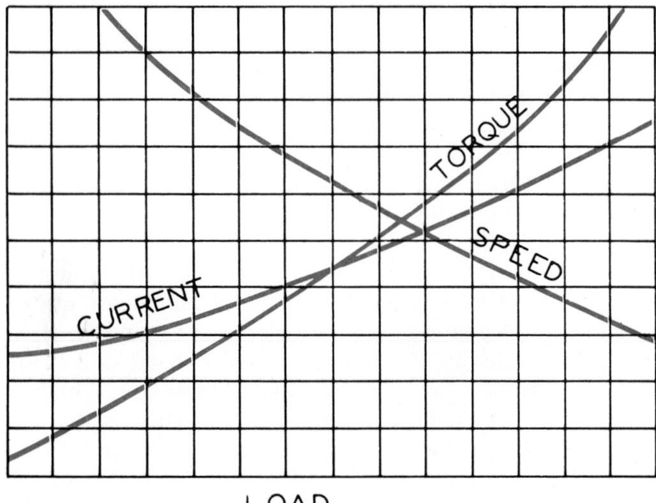

Figure 26-9. Chart curves illustrate the fact that increased load on a series motor will cause its speed to drop, while current and torque will rise.

current passes through a grounded field coil, the pole shoe moves and the yoke pushes the starter drive pinion gear into mesh with the flywheel ring gear.

Figure 26-12 shows a starting motor equipped with a 3.5 to 1 reduction gearset. The ***gear reduction mechanism*** adds to starter size and weight because one gear goes above the other. However, the gear reduction principle boosts cranking speed, a plus for cold weather starts. Again, a solenoid assembly and shift fork are used to actuate the drive mechanism.

Figure 26-13 pictures a ***permanent magnet starting motor.*** The permanent magnets, which replace the conventional wound fields, reportedly increase starter performance by 16%. In addition, a ***planetary gearset*** is used to transmit power between the motor and the output shaft. The use of six permanent magnets reduces starter current draw. The planetary reduction gearing permits compact, lightweight design and increases cranking speed.

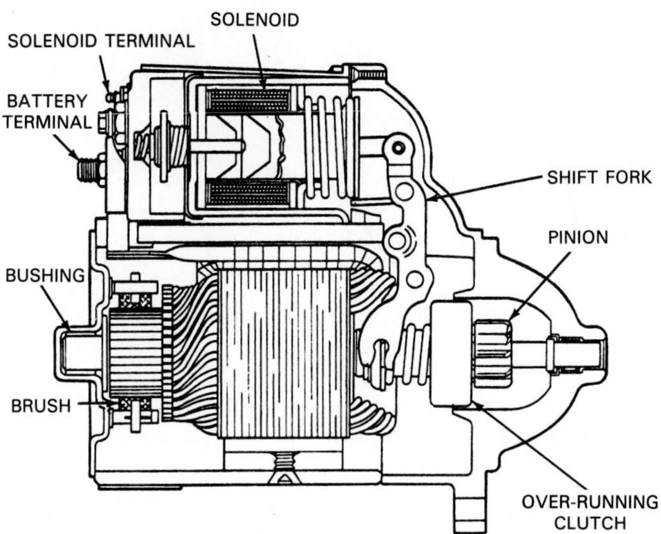

Figure 26-10. Sectional view of a typical positive engagement starting motor gives details of solenoid and solenoid-actuated shift fork, starter drive, and overrunning clutch.

Starting Motor Internal Circuits

While the basic characteristics of the conventional, series-wound motor is used in many starting motors, there are some modifications of the method of connecting the field coils to each other and to the armature. Some variations in the internal circuits of starting motors are shown in Figures 26-14, 26-15, and 26-16.

Figure 26-14A shows a four-pole, two-field coil design used on many motors. The two windings are connected in parallel to each other and in series with the armature, permitting the high current to divide in equal amounts and pass through each field winding. All of the current then passes through the armature, with the result that high cranking torque is produced. The two poles which have no windings serve to complete the magnetic circuits.

The starting motor in Figure 26-14B has four field coils on four poles. With this setup, one-half of the current flows through one pair of windings to one of the insulated brushes. The other half flows through another pair of windings to the other insulated brush. The current then combines at the commutator and goes through the armature. Four field coil windings of low resistance create stronger magnetic fields and produce starting motors with greater torque and cranking ability.

A variation of this principle of dividing the current is found in starting motors having six poles and six field windings paired off three ways, Figure 26-14C. In this motor, one-third of the current flows through each of three pairs of field windings to one of three insulated brushes. Increasing the number of circuits through the starting motor keeps resistance low, so that high horsepower can be developed for use in heavy-duty service.

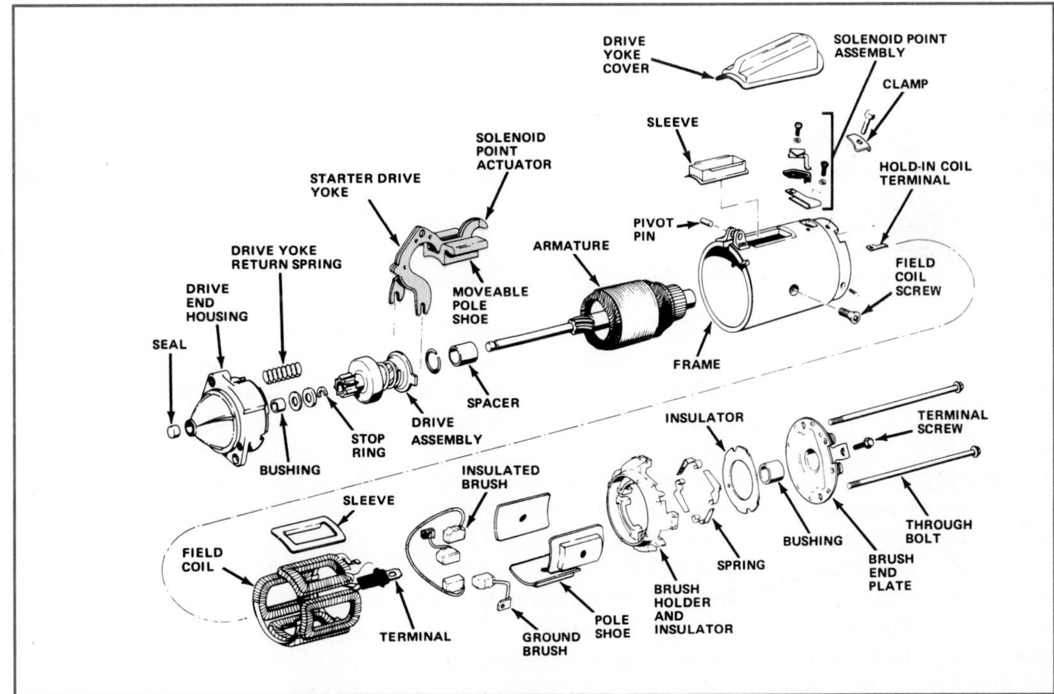

Figure 26-11. This starter has a movable pole shoe attached to the starter drive yoke. When heavy current passes through a grounded field coil, the pole shoe moves and the yoke pushes starter drive into mesh with flywheel.

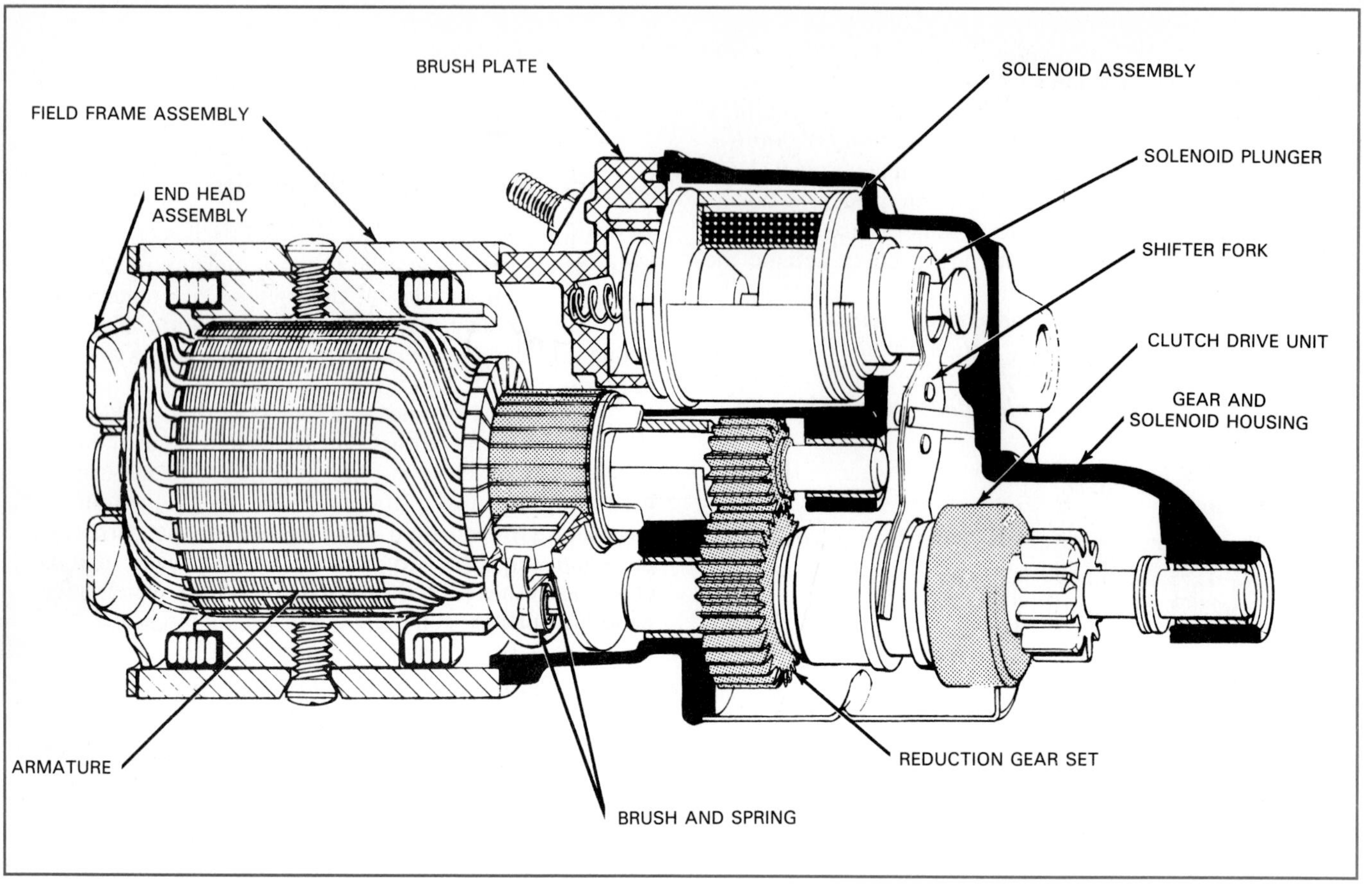

BRUSH PLATE
SOLENOID ASSEMBLY
FIELD FRAME ASSEMBLY
SOLENOID PLUNGER
END HEAD
ASSEMBLY
SHIFTER FORK
CLUTCH DRIVE UNIT
GEAR AND
SOLENOID HOUSING
ARMATURE
REDUCTION GEAR SET
BRUSH AND SPRING

Figure 26-12. Some starters are reduction gear type, using either a 2.0 to 1 or a 3.5 to 1 reduction gearset.

PLANET GEARS
OUTPUT SHAFT
ARMATURE WITH WINDING
BRUSH-HOLDER
AND BRUSHES
RING GEAR
ARMATURE SHAFT
WITH SUN GEAR
COMMUTATOR

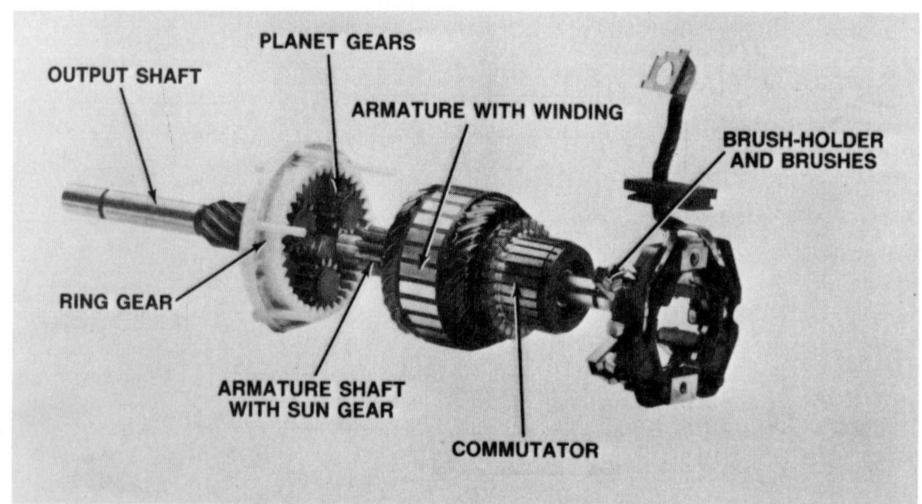

Figure 26-13. Permanent magnets are used in place of wound field coils in certain late-model applications. Also featured is reduction-type planetary gearing. (Chrysler)

As mentioned earlier, a starting motor with all field coils connected in series, Figure 26-15A, would crank up to an extremely high top speed if not controlled. With this in mind, shunt connections are used on many 12-volt starting systems, Figures 26-15B and 26-15C. Two or three heavy field coils are connected in series and carry current to the armature. The remaining field coil, or coils, are shunt coils connected between the starting motor terminal and ground. The shunt coil assists the series coils to build up and maintain a high magnetic field, and prevents excessive motor speed and noise when the armature is not subjected to cranking load.

When the motor is cranking the engine, heavy current flows through the series windings to form the magnetic field. The turns in the shunt field provide additional strength under this condition. When the engine starts, the load on the starter immediately drops. Less current flows through the armature and series field, which makes this field weaker. This would result in high rotational speed if the shunt field was not used. The shunt field continues to produce its maximum field strength so that the motor is held to a safe speed.

One manufacturer produces a variation of the internal circuit with four field coils in series between the terminal

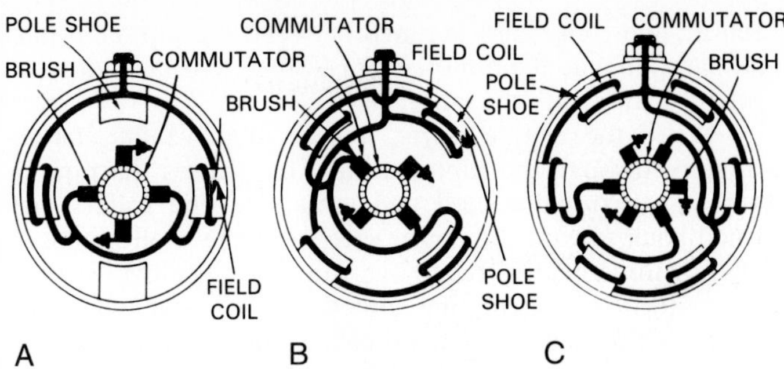

Figure 26-14. Three typical starting motor circuits. A–Four-pole, two-field coil design. B–Four-pole, four-field coil design. C–Six-pole, six-field coil design.

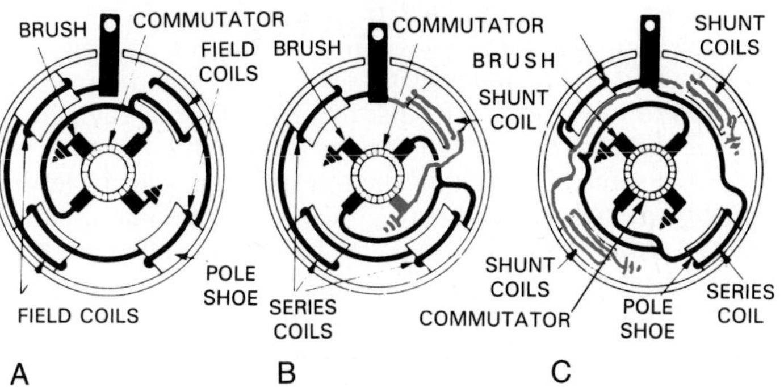

Figure 26-15. Four-pole starting motor circuits. A–Four field coils all in series. B–Three series-wound field coils and one shunt field coil. C–Two series-wound field coils and two shunt field coils.

and armature. Note in Figure 26-16 that, in addition to windings connecting the four poles of the motor, a separate lead connects the insulated brush leads. Therefore, this winding is not a straight series circuit, and it is not a straight shunt hookup. It is called a "series compound winding."

Control Mechanisms and Circuits

The starting motor armature must revolve at a fairly high speed to produce sufficient torque (turning effort) to rotate the engine. As soon as the engine starts, its speed is much greater than cranking speed. If the starter drive pinion gear remained engaged with the flywheel, the starter rpm would be excessive and ruin the armature.

To prevent this problem, various mechanisms have been developed that permit the gears to mesh during the cranking period and to demesh as soon as the engine is started. Most modern starters use a ***positive engagement*** or pre-engagement drive mechanism, Figure 26-10, a moving pole shoe, Figure 26-11, or a reduction mechanism, Figures 26-12 and 26-13.

Electrically, most starting motor control circuits use a relay and/or solenoid switch connected in series with the ignition switch. When the ignition switch is turned to the "start" position, the solenoid operates and the circuit between the battery and starter is completed.

The solenoid switch also shifts the starter pinion gear into engagement with the flywheel ring gear. This is accomplished by means of linkage between the solenoid plunger and the shift lever on the starter. When the circuit

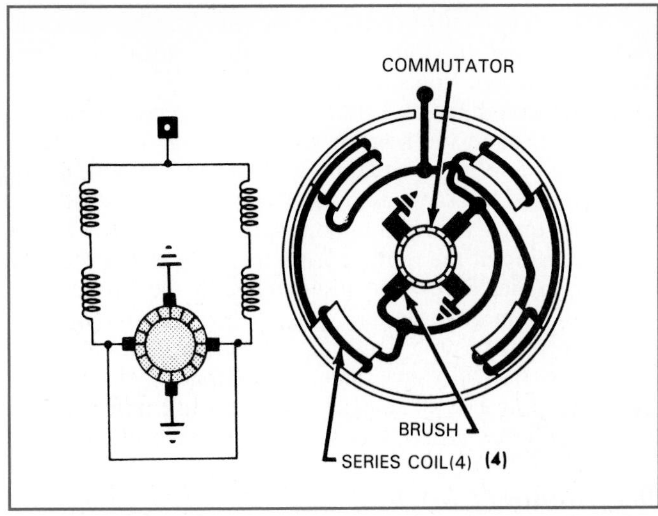

Figure 26-16. A starting motor with four field coils is used on certain engines. Wiring arrangement is termed a "series compound winding." Note separate lead between insulated brushes.

is completed to the solenoid, current from the battery passes through two separate windings, known as the ***pull-in*** and ***hold-in*** windings. The combined magnetic field of these windings pulls in the plunger, the drive pinion gear is shifted into mesh, and the main contacts of the solenoid switch are closed. See Figure 26-17.

The heavy pull-in winding is used to complete the plunger movement, but when the air gap is decreased, the hold-in winding is sufficient to retain the plunger. The closing of the main contacts closes the circuit between the battery and the starter and, at the same time, shorts out the pull-in winding.

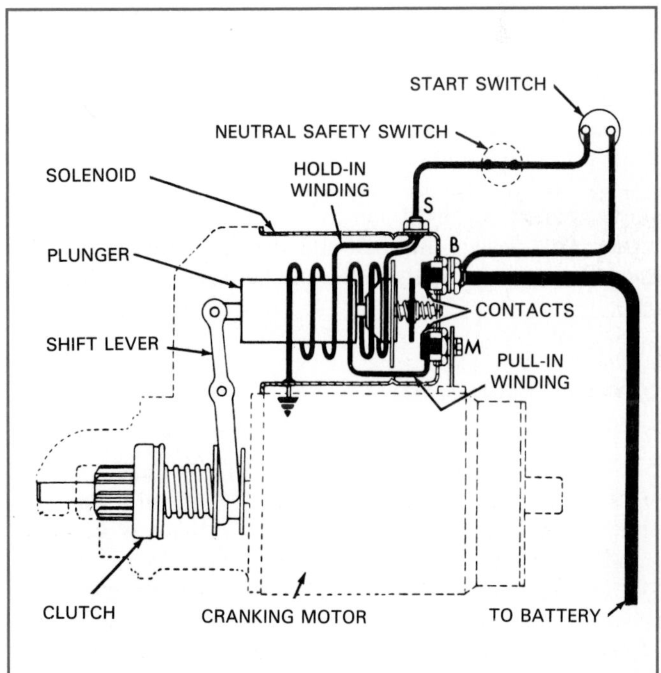

Figure 26-17. Schematic of a positive engagement starting motor shows the windings of the solenoid circuit and details of the shift lever and overrunning clutch starter drive mechanism.

When the control circuit is opened after the engine is started, current no longer reaches the hold-in winding. However, current flows from the battery, through the main contacts, through the pull-in winding (in reverse direction), and then through the hold-in winding to the ground. See Figure 26-17. With an equal number of turns of winding in both coils and the same amount of current in each coil, the magnetic forces are equal but opposed and counteract each other. Tension of the return spring then causes the plunger to return to the "at rest" position and break the circuit.

Reduction gear starters, Figure 26-12, differ in construction from positive engagement starters, but electrical circuitry is basically the same. Two separate circuits are used: a supply circuit to power the starting motor and a light-duty circuit to energize the solenoid control circuit.

Overrunning Clutch

Positive engagement starters use an ***overrunning clutch,*** Figure 26-18, to provide positive meshing and demeshing of the starter drive pinion gear and flywheel ring gear. The overrunning clutch transmits cranking torque from the starter to the flywheel gear, but permits the pinion gear to run faster than, or overrun, the armature once the engine has started. This protects the armature from excessive speed during the brief period that the starter drive pinion gear remains meshed and the engine has started.

The overrunning clutch consists of a shell-and-sleeve assembly that is splined internally to match the splines on the armature shaft. Both the shell-and-sleeve assembly and the armature shaft turn together. A pinion gear and collar assembly fits loosely into the shell, and the collar is in contact with four hardened steel rollers that are assembled into notches cut in the inner face of the shell. The notches taper inward slightly and are spring loaded Figure 26-18.

When the shift lever is operated, the clutch assembly is moved along the armature shaft until the pinion gear meshes with the flywheel ring gear. If the teeth should butt against each other instead of meshing, the clutch spring compresses so that the pinion gear is spring loaded against the ring gear teeth. Then, as the armature starts to rotate, the gears are forced into engagement.

As movement of the shift lever is completed, the starter switch is closed and the starter armature begins to rotate. This rotates the shell and sleeve assembly, causing the rollers to jam tightly in the smaller sections of the shell rotator. The rollers are jammed between the pinion collar and the shell, and the pinion gear is forced to rotate with the armature and crank the engine.

When the engine starts, it tries to drive the starter armature through the pinion gear. This causes the pinion gear to overrun the shell and armature. The rollers are turned back toward the larger section of the shell notches, and the pinion gear is free to overrun. The shift lever spring then pulls the overrunning clutch out of mesh with the flywheel ring gear. Movement of the shift lever also opens the starting motor main switch.

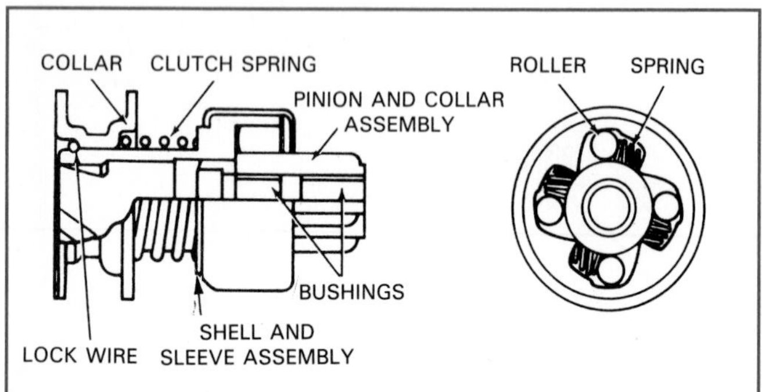

Figure 26-18. Sectional view of an overrunning clutch reveals the details of construction and the location of the rollers and the spring in the clutch shell-and-sleeve assembly. (Pontiac)

Neutral Safety Switch

All cars equipped with an automatic transmission are provided with a ***neutral safety switch,*** Figure 26-19. This switch eliminates the possibility of starting the engine when the transmission selector lever is in gear to drive the car. Note in Figure 26-19 that the neutral safety switch is connected between the ignition switch and the solenoid.

On some applications, the transmission selector lever may be placed either in park or neutral position before the circuit to the starter is completed. In other installations, the lever must be placed in PARK position. In vehicles with manual transmissions, the clutch pedal must be depressed before the electrical circuit to the starter is completed.

Troubleshooting The Starting System

A few simple tests can be used to help determine the source of starting system trouble. If the starter does not crank properly, turn on the headlights and have a helper attempt to start the engine. If the starter will not crank the engine and the headlights do not light, the battery may be dead or the electrical connections to the starter may be faulty. If the lights become dim when the starter motor is cranking, the starter may be shorted out, the battery may be weak, or the engine may be dragging due to mechanical problems. If the starter does not crank properly but the

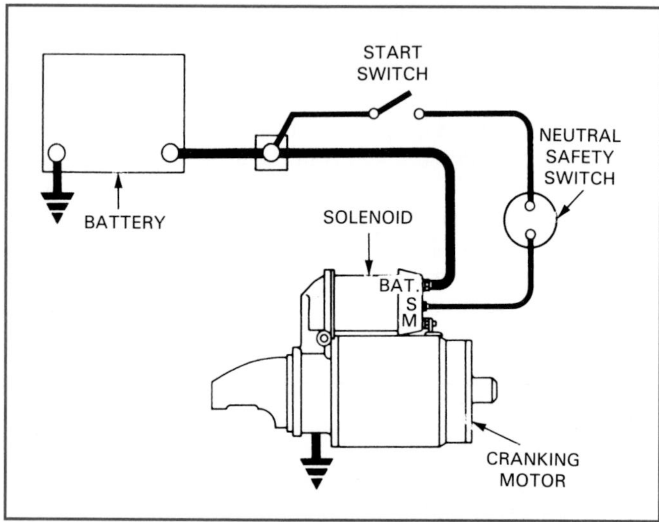

Figure 26-19. Diagram of a simplified starting system circuitry includes the location of the neutral safety switch and labels the solenoid connections. (Delco Remy Div., General Motors Corp.)

headlights remain bright, there may be excessive resistance or a short in the starting system.

It is also important to listen to the starting motor operate when a problem exists. If the starter will not crank but a single clicking sound is heard, the battery may be weak, the starter may be faulty, or the engine may be dragging due to mechanical problems. If the starter will not crank the engine but a consistent clicking or buzzing sound is heard, low current to the starter is the probable cause. Check the battery voltage and the connections between the battery and the starter. A grinding noise during starter operation is generally a sign of worn or broken flywheel gear teeth or starter pinion gear teeth.

There are many causes of starting system problems. Common problems and their causes are listed below:

Inoperative Starter

- Loose or corroded battery terminals.
- Discharged battery.
- Dead battery.
- Open cranking circuit.
- Inoperative solenoid or relay.
- Faulty ignition switch.
- Defective starter.
- Inoperative neutral safety switch.

Inoperative Starter and Headlights Dim

- Weak battery or dead cell.
- Loose or corroded battery connections.
- Internal ground in starting motor windings.
- Grounded starting motor field.
- Armature rubbing on pole shoes.

Starter Turns but Drive Does Not Engage

- Broken teeth in flywheel ring gear.
- Rusted starter drive shaft.
- Defective starter drive.
- Slipping overrunning clutch.

Slow Cranking Speed

- Discharged battery or defective cell.
- Excessive resistance in the starter.
- Excessive resistance in the starting circuit.
- Engine oil too heavy for conditions.
- Excessive engine friction.
- Burned solenoid contacts.
- Bent armature.
- Loose pole shoe screws.
- Worn bearings.

Starter Does Not Disengage

- Faulty ignition switch.
- Short circuit in solenoid.
- Stuck solenoid contact switch plunger.
- Broken solenoid plunger spring.
- Faulty starter relay.
- Loose starter mounting bolts.
- Worn drive end bushing.
- Broken drive yoke return spring.
- Defective overrunning clutch.

Starter Maintenance

Periodically checking the condition of the starting motor and cranking system helps reduce the possibility of failures on the road. The frequency of inspection is dependent on the type of operation. However, a visual inspection of the cranking system, an operational test of starting motor performance, and a test of neutral safety switch operation should be done annually and as part of an engine tune-up.

Modern starters do not permit thorough inspection unless disassembled. A visual inspection for clean, tight electrical connections, Figure 26-19, and secure mounting at the flywheel housing is about the extent of a maintenance check. Then, operate the starter and note speed of rotation and steadiness of operation. To prevent the starting motor from overheating, do not operate the starter for more than 15 seconds at a time.

If necessary, remove the starter for cleaning and careful inspection. Steps for removal generally include:

1. Disconnect the cable from the battery negative terminal.
2. Remove the wires from the solenoid.
3. Remove the starter upper mounting bolt.
4. Raise and support the vehicle.
5. Remove the brackets or shields that may interfere with starter removal.
6. Remove the starter.

NOTE: On some transaxle applications, disconnect the speedometer cable at the transaxle and remove the transaxle rear strut.

Disassemble the starter, Figure 26-20, and examine the commutator and brushes. If the commutator is dirty, clean it with a strip of #00 sandpaper. If the commutator is rough, pitted, or out of round, or if the mica (insulation between commutator bars) is high, chuck the armature in a lathe and recondition the commutator. Also, undercut the mica 1/32″.

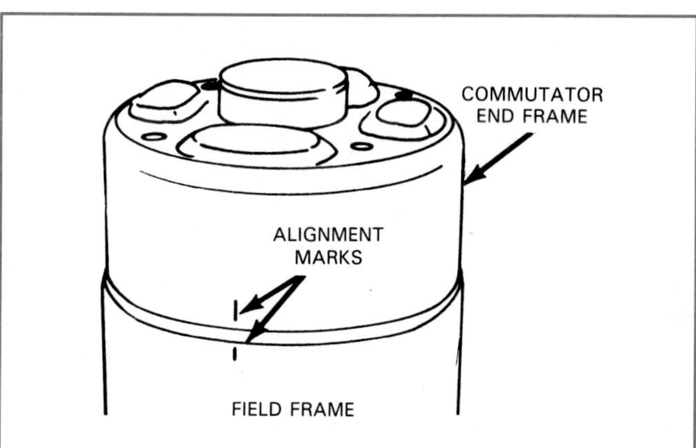

Figure 26-20. Before disassembly of a starting motor, scratch alignment marks on the field frame and the end frame to ease reassembly. (Oldsmobile)

Brushes should be at least half of full length. If not, replace them. The brushes should have free movement in the brush holders. They should have the specified spring tension and make full contact with the commutator.

Do not use a grease-dissolving solution or a high-temperature cleaning solution on the commutator and field windings. It could damage the insulation. The same caution goes for the overrunning clutch drive units.

Test the operation of the drive pinion gear on the overrunning clutch drive unit. It should turn freely in the overrunning direction, and it should not slip in the driving direction.

When reassembling the starter, use a special lubricant to coat the armature shaft, drive end bushing, and commutator end bushing. Make sure the brushes are fully seated. Align the housing and end frame, Figure 26-20, and securely install the through bolts. Reinstall the starter in the opening in the flywheel housing and tighten the mounting bolts to specified torque tightness. Connect the cables and wire leads firmly to clean terminals. See Figure 26-19.

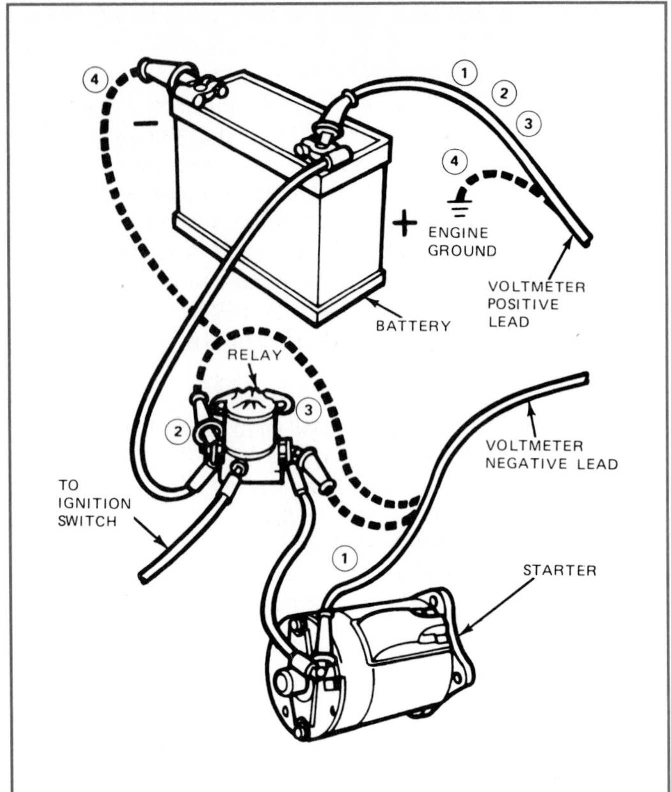

Figure 26-21. To test for high resistance in cranking system, use an expanded scale voltmeter (0.1 volt calibrations) to test voltage drop between four sets of points indicated by numbers. (Ford)

Starting Motor Tests

There are many ways of testing a starting motor to determine its operating condition. Begin by making on-car tests, follow up with a no-load test, then pinpoint the cause of the problem with bench tests.

On-car Starting Motor Tests

The following tests will reveal ***excessive resistance*** in the cranking circuit. Use an expanded-scale voltmeter to test the voltage drop across the various points shown in Figure 26-21. Remove the primary lead from the ignition coil and crank the engine.

Maximum allowable voltage drop, typically, is as follows:

1. With the voltmeter leads connected to the positive post of the battery and to the starter terminal–0.5 volt.
2. With the voltmeter connected to the positive post of the battery and to the battery terminal of the starter relay–0.1 volt.
3. With the voltmeter connected to the positive post of the battery and to the starter terminal of the starter relay–0.3 volt.
4. With the voltmeter connected to the negative terminal of the battery and to ground–0.3 volt.

The following test of the starting motor on the car under load gives a result in ***amperage draw.*** The engine must be at normal operating temperature.

1. Disconnect and ground ignition coil secondary wire.
2. Connect a remote control switch between the battery positive terminal and S terminal on the starter solenoid.
3. Connect the load tester as shown in Figure 26-22 and place the tester load control knob in the full-counterclockwise position (decrease).
4. Close the remote control switch and observe the voltage indicated on the voltmeter after the starter has reached maximum rpm.
5. Do not crank engine more than 15 seconds, then open the remote control switch.

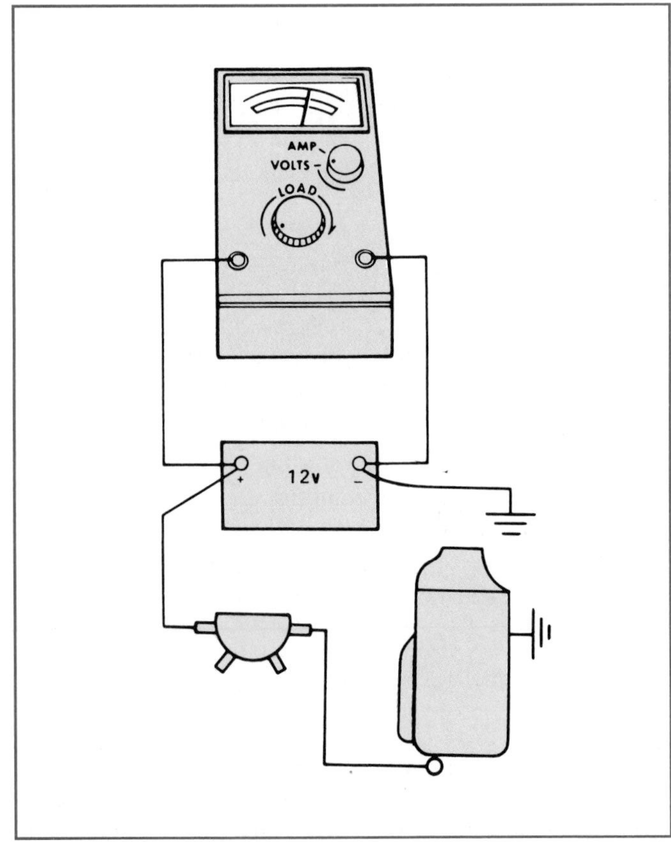

Figure 26-22. Hookup of test equipment is shown for making an amperage draw test.

6. Turn the tester load control knob clockwise (increase) until the voltmeter indicates the same voltage as obtained when the starter cranked the engine.
7. Read the amperage draw on the ammeter scale and compare it with the manufacturer's specification–typically 150-250 amps.

No-load Test. The ***no-load test*** will determine how fast the armature will revolve and the amount of current draw at a specified voltage. To make the test, connect test equipment leads as shown in Figure 26-23, using a tachometer attached to the end of the armature shaft.

1. Adjust the variable resistance control to obtain a given voltage value.
2. The starter will run at no-load speed.
3. Read the amperage and the rpm values and compare these readings with specifications–typically 50-75 amps and 6000-11,500 rpm (reduction gear starters: 3700 minimum rpm) at 10 volts.

Analyzing No-load Test Results. If under no-load conditions, the starter rotates at normal rpm at specified voltage and amperage draw, the starting motor is in good condition. However, if trouble is indicated, consider the following:

1. If starter fails to rotate under no-load tests and shows high amperage draw, there may be a direct ground in the armature or field windings or "frozen" armature shaft bearings.
2. Low no-load speed and a high amperage draw indicate a dragging armature, worn bearings, or tight and dirty bearings.
3. Low no-load speed and a low current draw point to high resistance in the starting motor. One of the field windings may be "open." Other causes could be broken brush springs, badly worn brushes, high insulation between the commutator bars, or an extremely dirty or oily commutator.
4. High no-load speed and high current draw are signs of "shorted" field windings.

Bench Tests

When your analysis of no-load test results indicate that trouble exists in the starting motor, perform the following ***bench tests*** to pinpoint the cause.

Armature and Field Open Circuit Tests. An open circuit armature may be detected by examining the commutator for evidence of burning. The spot burned on the commutator is caused by an arc formed every time the commutator segment connected to the open circuit winding passes under a brush.

An open circuit test of the field can be made with a 120-volt test lamp, Figure 26-24, or by connecting a jumper lead from the positive post of a battery to the starter terminal, the voltmeter negative lead to the negative post of the battery, and the voltmeter positive lead to each field brush in turn. If the lamp fails to light or if no reading is obtained on the voltmeter, the field winding is open.

Armature and Field Grounded Circuit Tests. If the armature or field coil insulation has failed, it would permit a conductor to touch the starter frame or armature core. This test can be made with a 120-volt test lamp or by using a voltmeter.

To test the armature with a test lamp, touch one test prod to the armature shaft and touch the other prod to each commutator bar in turn. If the lamp lights, the armature winding is grounded.

To make the test with a voltmeter, connect a jumper lead from the positive post of a battery to the armature shaft. Connect the voltmeter leads to the negative post of the battery and to each commutator bar in turn. If any voltage is indicated, the winding is grounded.

To test for grounded field circuit windings, connect a jumper lead from one terminal of the starter to one post of the battery. Contact the other post of the battery with a test

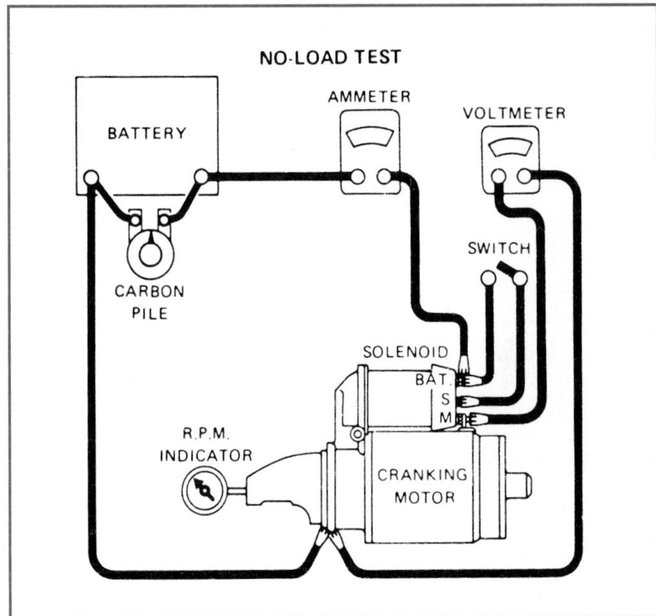

Figure 26-23. Schematic shows ammeter and voltmeter lead connections and the attachment of the tachometer for making a no-load test.

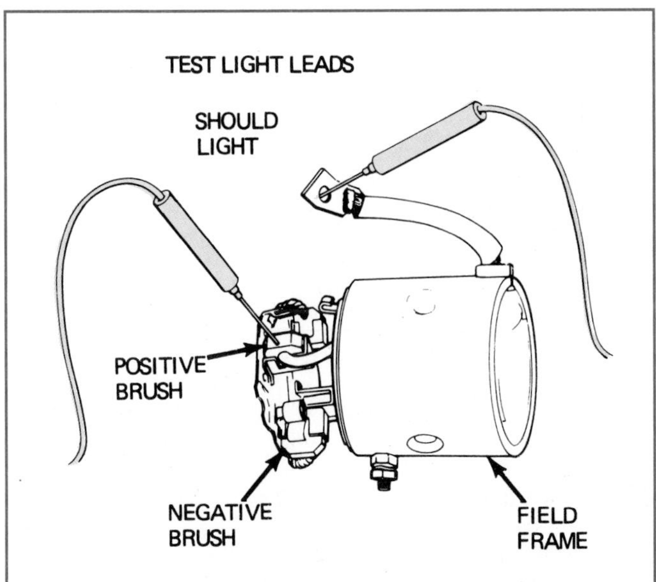

Figure 26-24. Bench tests of starting motor circuitry include testing the field windings for an open circuit by means of a 120 volt test lamp. If lamp fails to light, the field winding is open. (Oldsmobile)

prod while keeping the brushes away from the frame of the starter. Then touch the other test prod to the field frame of the starter. If the lamp lights or if any voltage is indicated on the meter, the field windings are grounded.

Chapter 26–Review Questions

Write your answers on a separate sheet of paper. Do not write in this book.

1. In which direction does a current-carrying conductor tend to move when placed in a magnetic field?
   (A) From a strong magnetic field to a weak one.
   (B) From a weak magnetic field to a strong one.
2. The rotating part of an electric motor is known as a(n) _____.
3. To what are the ends of an armature coil connected?
4. In an electric motor, the rotating coils are cutting magnetic lines of force, thereby generating voltage. Relative to applied voltage, in which direction does the induced voltage cause the current to flow?
   (A) In the same direction as applied voltage.
   (B) In the direction opposed to the applied voltage.
5. Why is a series-wound starting motor used for cranking an internal combustion engine?
   (A) High speed.
   (B) High torque.
   (C) Low speed.
   (D) Low torque.
6. The speed of a series-wound motor will vary with the load. True or False?
7. What is the purpose of the overrunning clutch in a positive engagement starter drive mechanism?
8. What is the purpose of the neutral safety switch on cars equipped with an automatic transmission?
9. Give three starting motor and cranking system maintenance procedures that should be done annually or as part of an engine tune-up.
10. When attempting to start an engine or when testing starting motor performance, do not operate the starter for more than _____ seconds at a time.
    (A) 15
    (B) 20
    (C) 25
    (D) 30
11. If the commutator is dirty, it can be cleaned with a strip of No. _____ sandpaper.
12. When checking internal parts of a starting motor, brushes should be at least half of full length. True or False?
13. Test the operation of the drive pinion gear on the overrunning clutch unit. It should turn freely in the _____ direction, and it should not slip in the _____ direction.
14. A car brought in for service was tested and mechanics found that the starter turned but the starter drive did not engage. Technician A said it could be caused by broken teeth in the flywheel ring gear. Technician B said it could be caused by a slipping overrunning clutch. Who is right?
    (A) A only.
    (B) B only.
    (C) Both A & B.
    (D) Neither A nor B.
15. A customer complained that the starter did not disengage when the engine started. Technician A said it could be caused by a faulty ignition switch. Technician B said it could be caused by loose starting motor mounting bolts. Who is right?
    (A) A only.
    (B) B only.
    (C) Both A & B.
    (D) Neither A nor B.
16. In testing a stalled vehicle, it was found that the starter would not crank the engine and the headlights dimmed when the ignition switch was turned to "start" position. Technician A said it could be caused by a defective starter drive mechanism. Technician B said it could be caused by a grounded starting motor field. Who is right?
    (A) A only.
    (B) B only.
    (C) Both A & B.
    (D) Neither A nor B.
17. The no-load starting motor test will determine how fast the _____ will revolve.
18. The no-load starting motor test also will determine the amount of _____ at a specified _____.
19. An open circuit armature may be detected by examining the _____ for evidence of burning.
20. Using a 120-volt test lamp, how would you test for a grounded armature? Describe the process.

Chapter 27
Charging System Fundamentals

After studying this chapter, you will be able to:

- ❍ Explain the principle of electromagnetic induction.
- ❍ Describe how alternators differ from dc generators.
- ❍ Name the major components of an alternator.
- ❍ Tell how an alternator produces alternating current and then converts it to direct current at the output terminal.
- ❍ Give some examples of alternator design and construction differences.
- ❍ Tell why voltage regulation is necessary in a charging system.
- ❍ Discuss the three basic phases of voltage regulator development.
- ❍ Describe the operating principles of an electromagnetic voltage regulator.
- ❍ Describe the operating principles of an electronic voltage regulator.
- ❍ Explain how an electronic control unit can control alternator voltage output.

Charging Systems

The purpose of the ***charging system*** is to recharge the battery after it cranks the engine and to provide all electrical power to the vehicle after the engine has started. The typical automotive charging system consists of the alternator (generator), voltage regulator, alternator drive belt, battery, and related wiring.

An ***automotive generator,*** Figure 27-1, is an electromagnetic device that converts the mechanical energy supplied by the engine into electrical energy. In operation, the generator maintains the storage battery in fully charged condition and supplies electrical power for the ignition system and accessory equipment.

The various automotive generator manufacturers have different names for their products. However, "alternator" is the most common terminology.

Electromagnetic Induction

The operation of the automotive ***alternator*** is based on the principle of electromagnetic induction. That is, when a coil of wire is moved through a magnetic field, a voltage will be induced, or generated, in the coil.

Actually, voltage can be induced in either of two ways:

- By moving a coil of wire through a magnetic field.
- By keeping the coil stationary and moving the magnetic field.

The old dc (direct current) generator operated on the first principle. The ***dc generator*** induced voltage in coils of wire as the assembly (armature) rotated in a stationary magnetic field. See Figure 27-2.

The ac (alternating current) generator operates on the second principle. The magnetic field, or ***rotor,*** is rotated and voltage is generated in the stationary coils, or ***stator.*** See Figure 27-1.

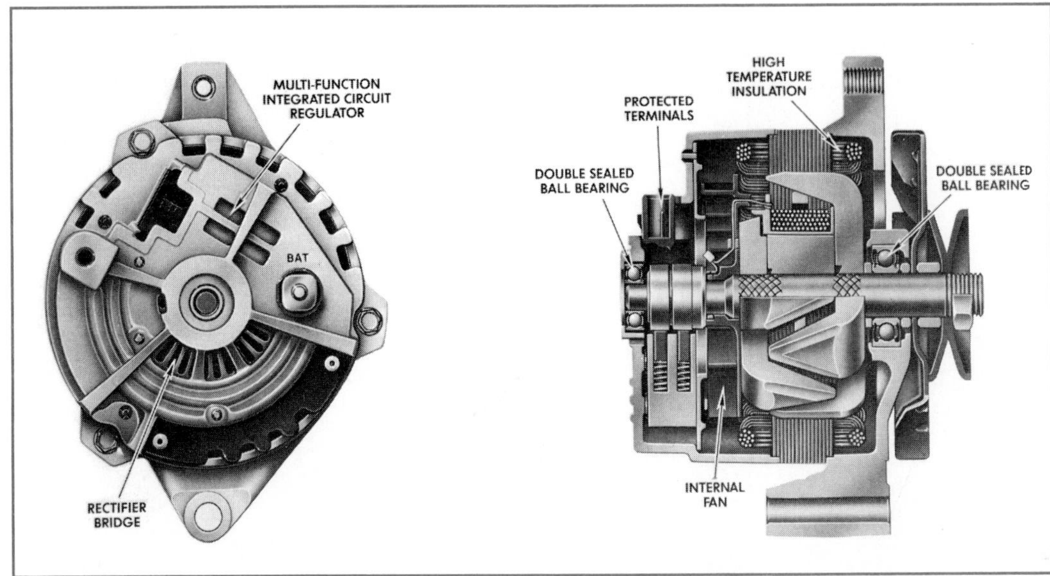

Figure 27-1. This late-model alternator features an integrated circuit voltage regulator and capacitor, a "chip-type" bridge rectifier (diode assembly), dynamically balanced rotor, and internal and external fans. (Delco-Remy)

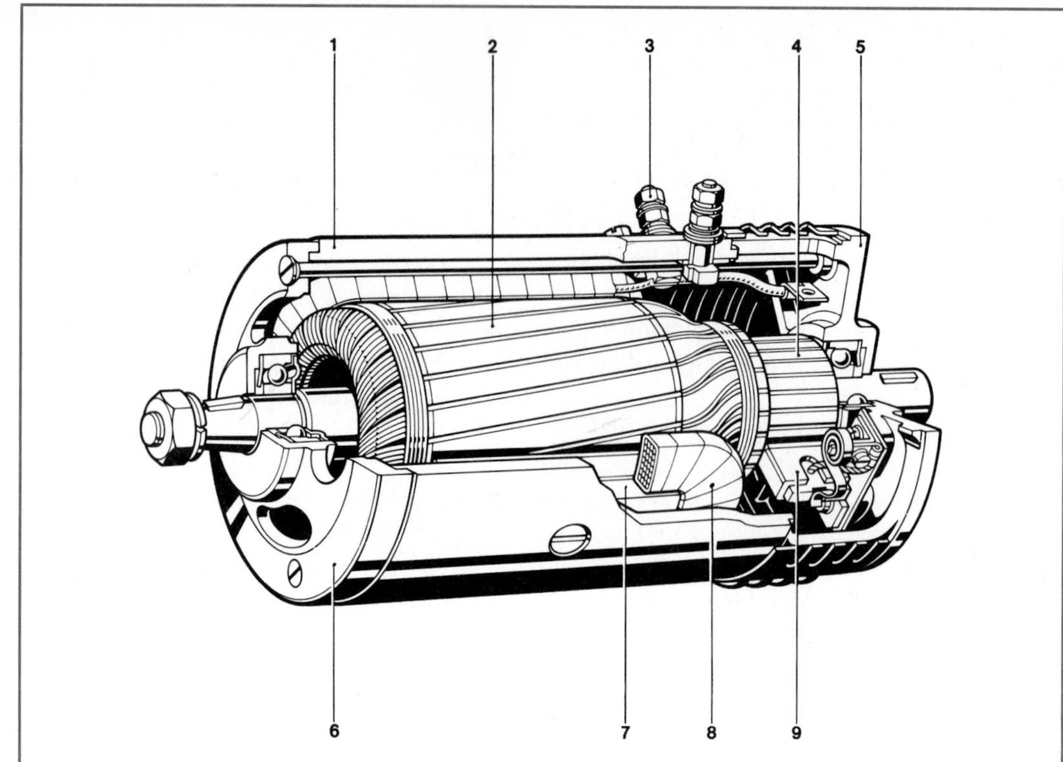

Figure 27-2. Construction of a dc generator: 1–Stator frame. 2–Armature. 3–Terminal. 4–Commutator. 5–Commutator end shield. 6–Drive end shield. 7–Pole shoe. 8–Excitation winding. 9–Brush holder and carbon brush. (Robert Bosch Corporation)

In general, then, voltage is induced in a coil whenever there is a change in the lines of force passing through the coil. Figure 27-3 illustrates what happens when lines of force are cut by a rotating coil.

When the coil is in the vertical position, as shown at A in Figure 27-3, the lines of force surrounding the conductor are balanced. For that instant, no lines of force are being cut. Therefore, no voltage will be induced in the coil.

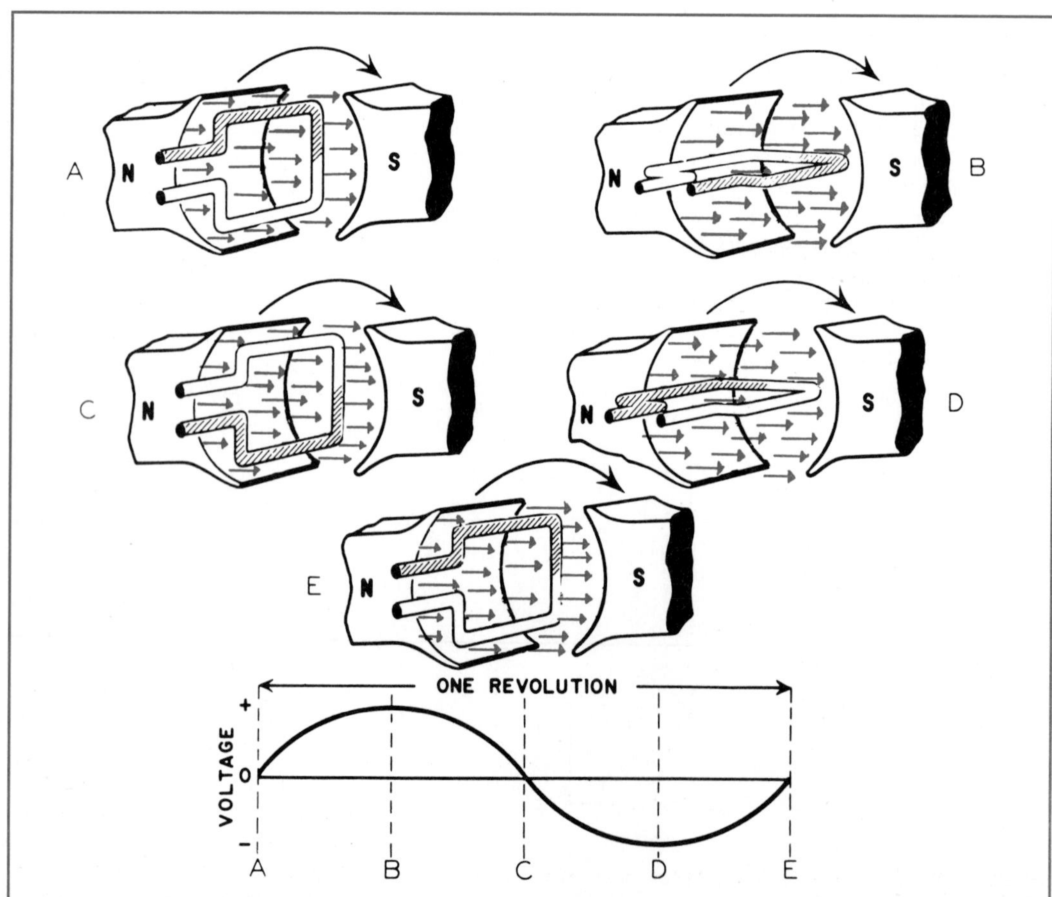

Figure 27-3. Illustrating how voltage is induced in a coil that is revolved in a magnetic field. The curve at the bottom shows the variation in voltage for each position of the revolving coil.

As the coil approaches position B, an increasing number of lines of force will be cut. The generated voltage will continue to increase until it reaches a maximum at position B.

After passing position B, the voltage will start to decrease as fewer lines of force are being cut. It will become zero when position C is reached. As rotation continues, another maximum will be reached at position D. However, the lines of force are now being cut in the opposite direction to that of position B. Therefore, the current generated will flow in the opposite direction.

Because the current keeps changing its direction as the loop of wire is rotated, it is called an ***alternating current.*** The variations in the value and direction of the generated voltage are shown in the lower portion of Figure 27-3.

To make use of the electrical energy that is being generated, each end of the coil is connected to a ring that rotates with the coil of wire. Contact with these rotating ***slip rings*** is made by ***brushes*** that bear against the rings.

Alternating Current Generator

All automotive generators produce alternating current that, in turn, must be rectified (converted) to direct current to satisfy the needs of the storage battery and the various electrical systems and accessories.

In an ac generator, or alternator, Figure 27-4, the magnetic field is rotated and voltage is generated in the stationary coils. Rectifiers, or diodes, are built into the alternator to limit current flow to one direction only to provide direct current at the output terminal.

Direct Current Generator

A dc generator, Figure 27-2, operates basically the same as an alternator in that it produces alternating current. However, the dc generator works on the principle that voltage is generated in a coil of wire (armature) as it is rotated in a stationary magnetic field. Instead of using a rectifier to convert the ac to dc, a mechanical switch (brushes and a commutator) is provided.

In operation, the armature rotates between pole shoes wound with field coils. The spinning armature builds voltage in the field coils, and the field coils, in turn, produce more voltage and current in the armature.

The commutator is attached to the armature shaft and rotates with it. Coils of the armature are connected to bars, or segments, of the commutator. Each segment is insulated from the other, and spring-loaded brushes ride on the commutator and transmit the voltage and current to the generator terminals. It then flows to the battery and other electrical accessories.

A shortcoming of dc generators is that low-speed output is limited. As a result, the battery does not receive a charge at idling and low-speed operation. In addition, there is insufficient current for the operation of other electrical equipment. These are the main reasons why the dc generator was replaced by the alternator.

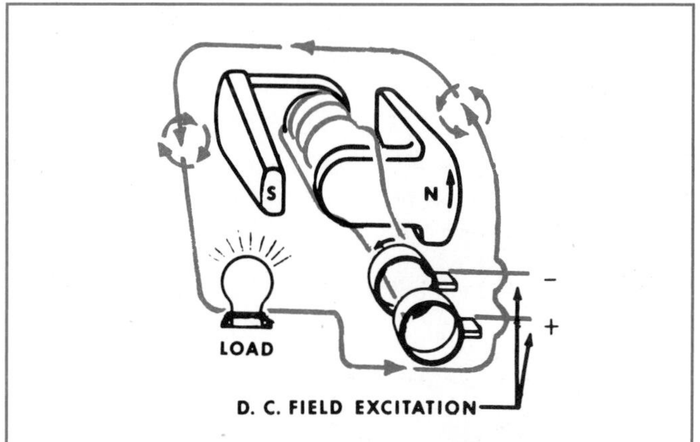

Figure 27-4. Current for field excitation of an alternator is supplied by the battery through brushes and slip rings.

Alternator Construction

An alternator, Figure 27-5, consists of three major units:

- A ***rotor,*** which provides the magnetic field.
- A ***stator***, in which voltage and current are produced.
- A ***diode assembly,*** or ***rectifier,*** which changes ac to dc.

The rotor assembly incorporates an iron core on a shaft with a wire coil wound around it. The coil is enclosed between two iron pole pieces with interspaced fingers or claws. The ends of the coil are connected to two slip rings.

Small brushes ride on the slip rings. One brush is grounded. The other brush is insulated and connects to the alternator field terminal. This terminal, in turn, is connected through the alternator regulator and ignition switch to the battery.

The stator has three sets of windings that are assembled around the inside circumference of a laminated core, Fig, 27-5. This core forms part of the exterior frame in most alternators, and it provides a path for the flow of magnetic flux between two adjacent poles of the rotor.

Each winding of the stator generates a separate voltage, Figure 27-6. One end of each winding is connected to a positive diode and a negative diode. The other ends of the stator windings are connected to form a "Y" arrangement. See Figure 27-7. On heavy-duty applications, the windings are connected to form a triangle (delta-connected stator). See Figure 27-8.

The diode assembly basically consists of six diodes mounted at the slip ring end of the alternator housing, Figure 27-9. The three negative diodes are mounted in the end frame or in a heat sink that is bolted to the end frame. The three positive diodes are mounted in a heat sink insulated from the end frame. Some alternators use ***diode trio*** assemblies.

The ***diodes*** are connected to the stator leads and serve as one-way valves that permit current to flow through in one direction only. Each phase of the three-phase output of the alternator ranges from positive to negative and back to positive again. The diodes convert this alternating current to direct current at the alternator output terminal.

Note in Figure 27-10 that while the voltage of each phase ranges from zero to maximum, the effective voltage of all phases maintains a reasonably even current output.

The front and rear housings, or frames, of the alternator generally are held together by "through bolts." A fan mounted on the front of the rotor shaft draws air through the housing for cooling. The housings support the bearings–usually a sealed thrust ball bearing at the front housing and an axial roller bearing at the rear housing.

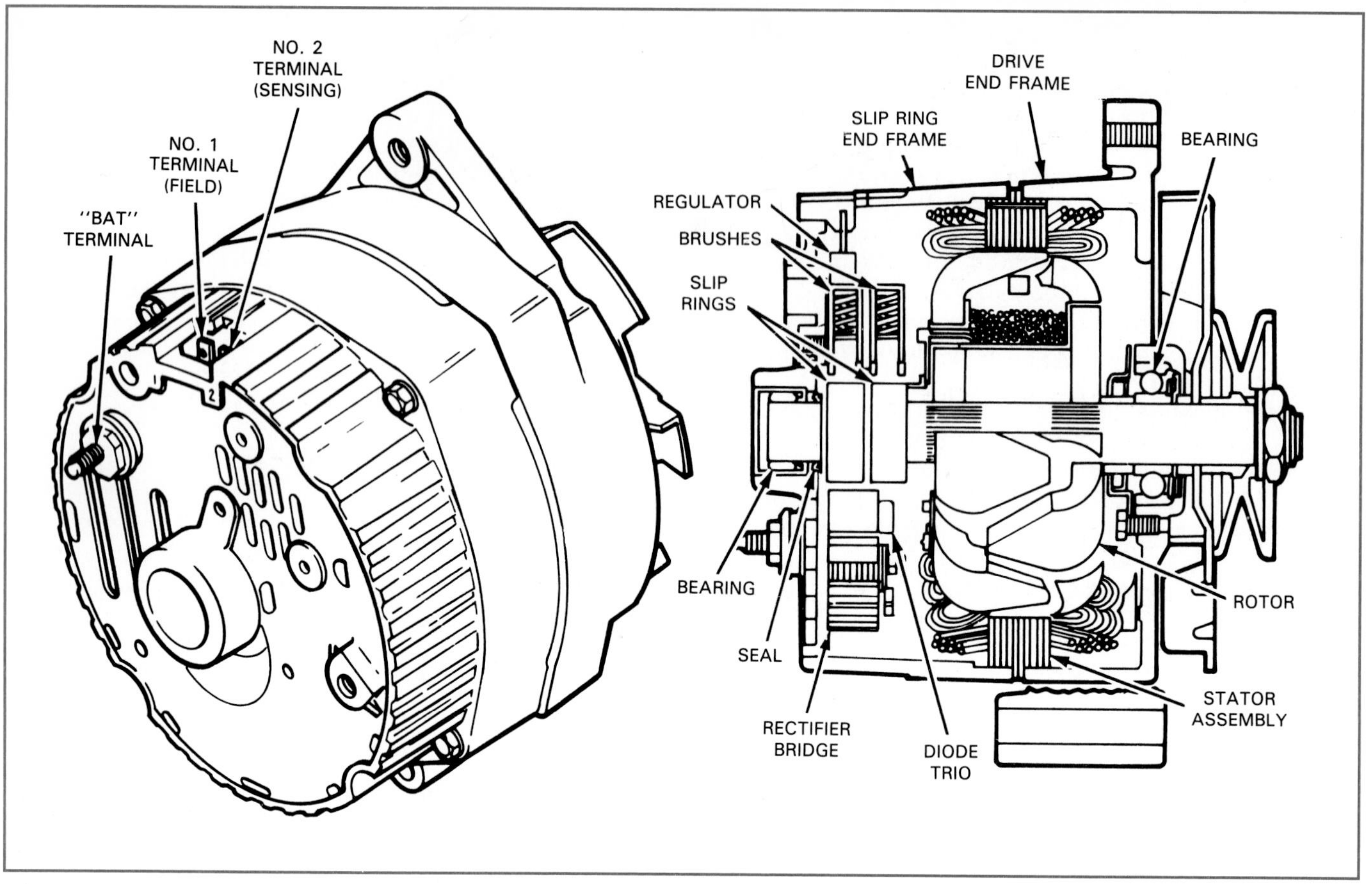

Figure 27-5. A rear view and a sectional side view of a typical alternator reveal all major components. (Chevrolet)

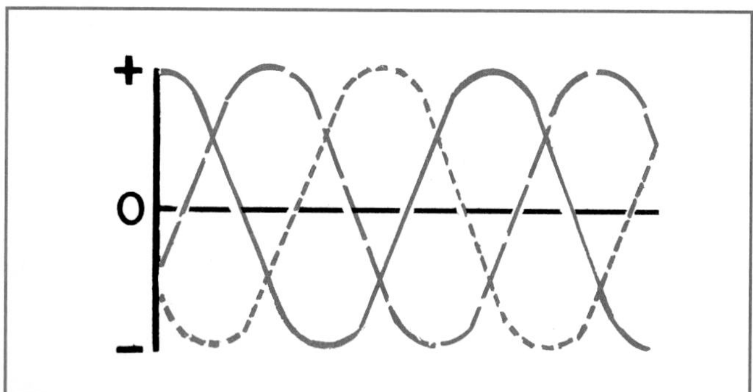

Figure 27-6. Each winding of the stator generates a separate voltage, making alternator a three-phase unit.

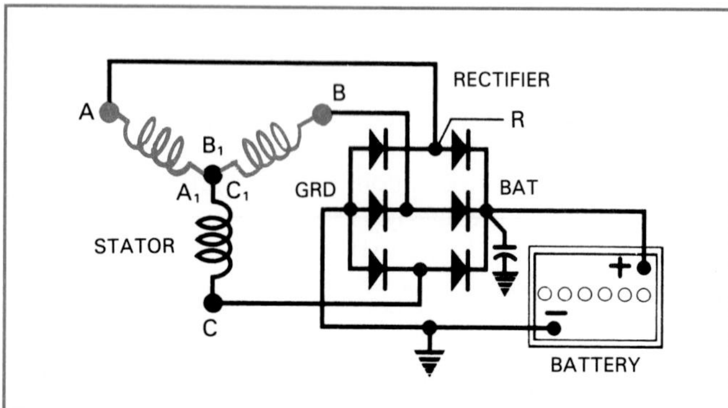

Figure 27-7. When the stator leads A, B, and C are connected together at A_1, B_1, and C_1, a three-phase "Y" circuit stator is formed.

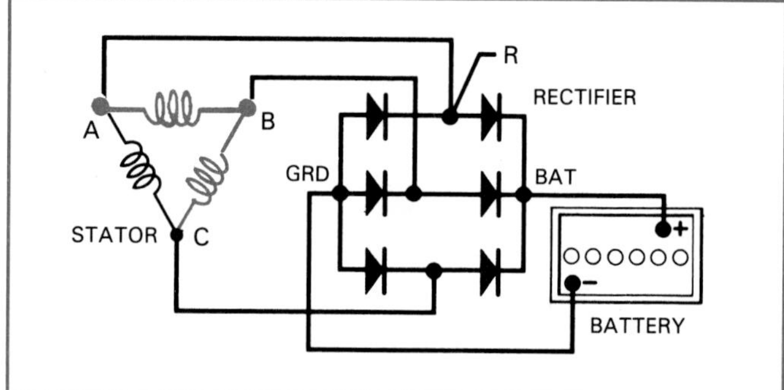

Figure 27-8. When stator lead A is connected to B, B to C, and C to A, a triangular, three-phase "delta-connected" stator is formed.

Alternator Operation

Basically, an alternator produces alternating current and then converts it to direct current at the output terminal. But before an alternator will begin to charge, direct current must flow through the rotor field coil to magnetize the pole pieces, Figure 27-4. That is, the rotor (alternator field) must be externally excited before it will deliver voltage and current.

To help provide field excitation, some alternators utilize an ***isolation diode*** and a ***charge indicator lamp*** hooked up in parallel. This extra diode acts as an automatic switch between the battery and alternator to block current flow back to the alternator and regulator when the alternator is not operating.

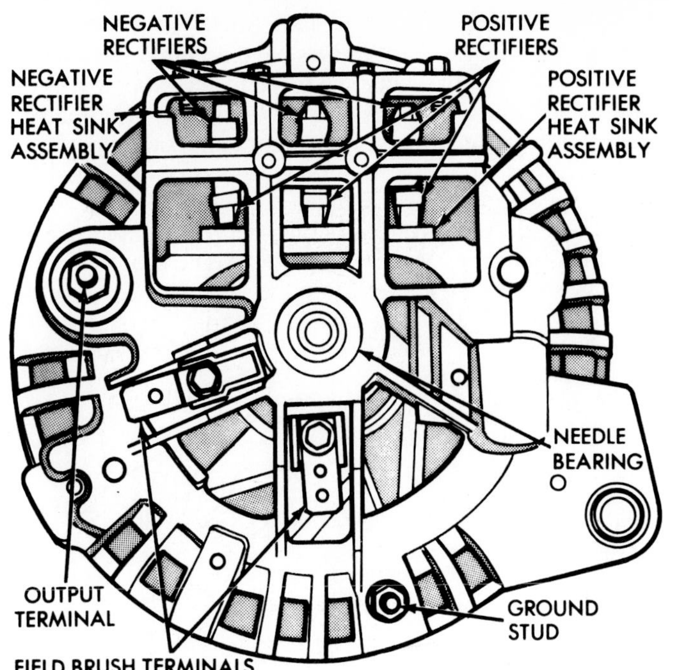

Figure 27-9. Rear view of an alternator rectifier (diode assembly) end shield shows the location of positive and negative rectifiers and heat sink assemblies. (Chrysler)

When the ignition switch is turned ON, voltage is supplied to one side of the indicator lamp on the dash. This causes a small amount of current to pass through the regulator to the insulated brush. It flows through the slip ring, the field coil, the other slip ring, and the other brush to ground. This direct current passing through the coil creates

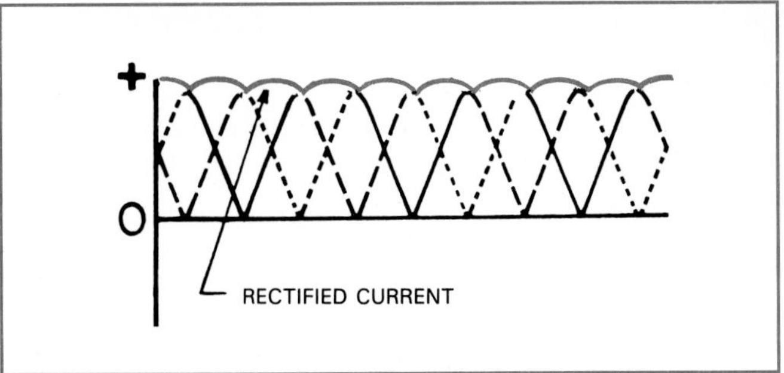

Figure 27-10. A rectifier (diode assembly) permits current to pass through in one direction only. Rectified three-phase current is shown.

a magnetic field in each section of the rotor and lights the charge indicator lamp.

Then, as the rotor turns, its magnetic field induces voltage in the stator windings. Because the rotor sections have alternate north and south poles, and because current direction is reversed each half revolution of the rotor, alternating current is produced. See Figure 27-6.

The stator sends this three-phase alternating current to the diode assembly, which permits current to pass through in one direction only to provide direct current at the alternator output terminal. See Figure 27-10.

Figure 27-11 shows the circuitry of an alternator application with a charge indicator light and an electronic voltage regulator. When the ignition switch is turned ON, the warning lamp control circuit passes current to the warning lamp. When the voltage at terminal S rises to a preset value, current is cut off to the warning lamp. With input voltage present at terminal S, a switching circuit energizes

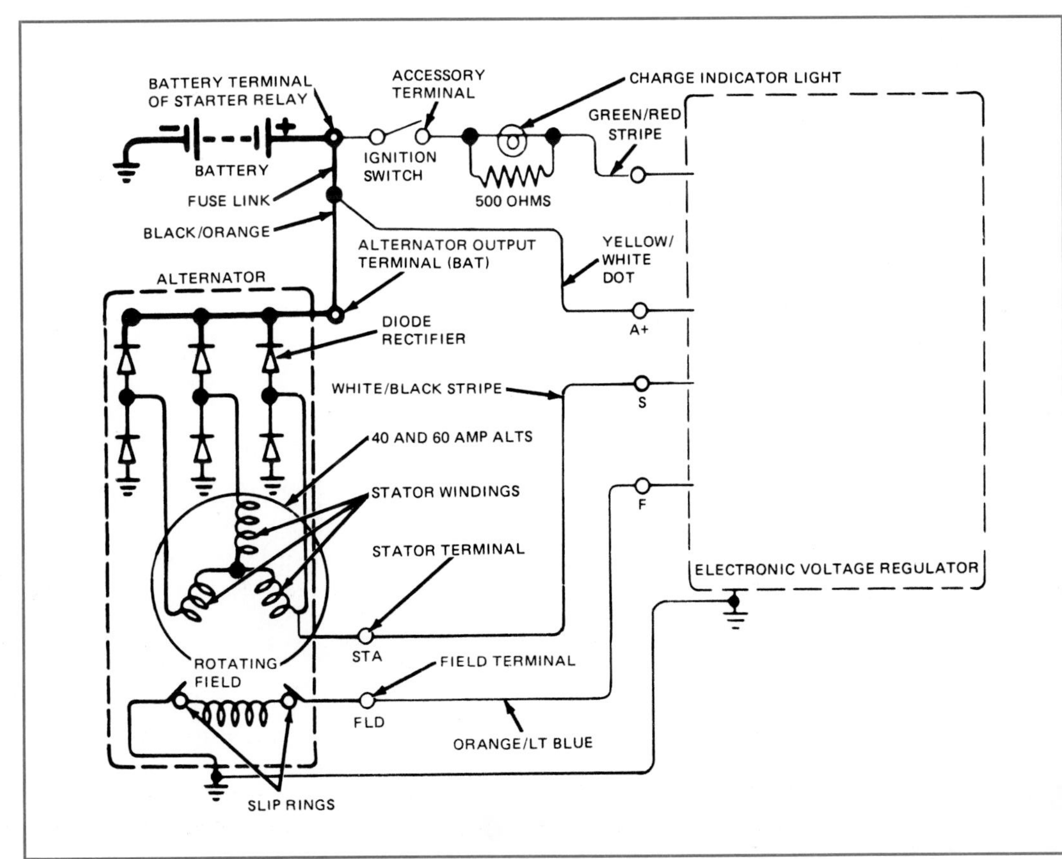

Figure 27-11. Wiring diagram of a typical alternator charging system that includes a charging indicator light circuit and an electronic voltage regulator. (Ford)

the voltage control circuit, which in turn, controls the output circuit.

In this charging system application, current is supplied from the alternator-regulator system to the rotating field of the alternator through two brushes and two slip rings. The alternating current is rectified to direct current by six diodes. Typically, this particular alternator is self-current limiting. Note in Figure 27-11 that the charging system contains a ***fuse link*** at the starter relay battery terminal. The fuse link also helps to prevent damage to the wiring harness and alternator if the wiring harness becomes grounded or if booster battery cables are connected to the charging system with the wrong polarity.

Alternator Design Differences

Alternator design and construction varies according to vehicular application and the electrical demands of the vehicle. Passenger car alternators range in rated output from 40 to 85 amps. Some special applications, such as fleet operations or police cars, have alternators that put out from 90 to 120 amps. Heavy-duty truck alternators are generally 105 to 160 amps.

In addition to higher output, design differences affect internal makeup, size, shape, and mounting configuration of the alternator. For example, open frame (vented) alternators are generally used in passenger cars, Figure 27-12. Closed units are used in marine and off-road applications. Some models feature enclosed brushes and slip rings for use where explosive mixtures may be present. Oil cooled, enclosed units with stationary conductors are available for use on motor coaches.

Some alternators have 12 claw-pole rotors; others have 14 or 16 claw poles. The rotors may be riveted or welded. Voltage regulators may be built in or mounted away from the alternator. Drive-end and rectifier-end bearings may be ball type or roller type. Diodes may be pressed in, screwed in, or come as a "trio" assembly. Heavy-duty alternators may have dual internal fans or an internal fan and an external fan. Some alternators have rear terminals; others have side terminals. See Figure 27-13.

Some alternators have dual brush sets; others are brushless. ***Brushless alternators*** have no moving electrical connections. Both the stator and the field are stationary, eliminating shorts or grounds from rotor windings. The rectifier bridge, integrated voltage regulator, and other parts are located under a removable service access cover. The location of special features is indicated in Figure 27-14.

These design differences only serve to emphasize the fact that whatever the alternator design, diodes change

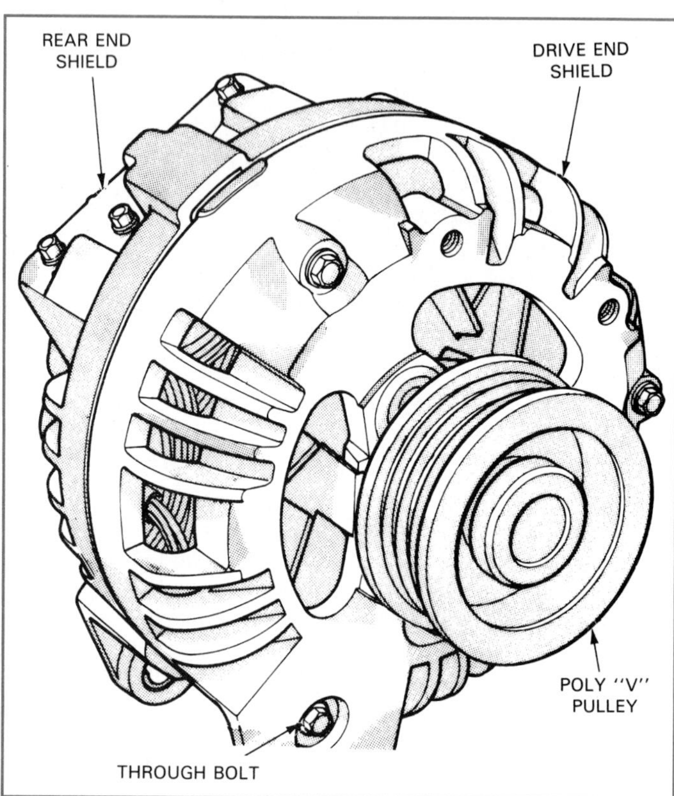

Figure 27-12. External view of an alternator assembly calls attention to the finned, "open-frame" design of passenger car alternators. (Chrysler)

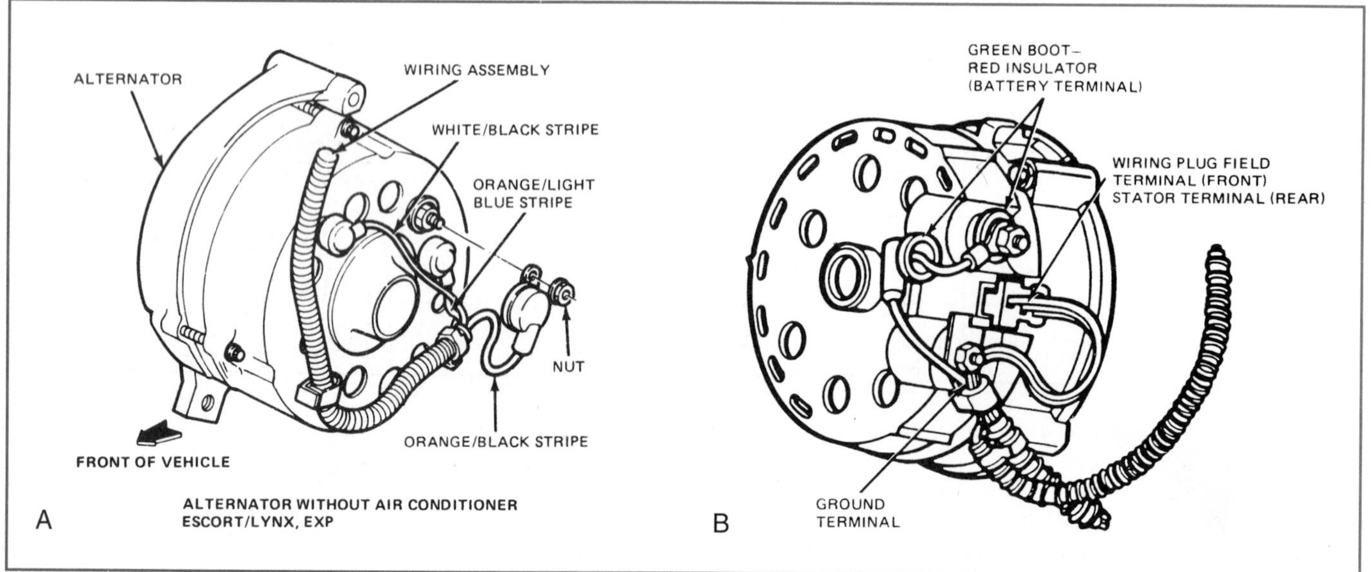

Figure 27-13. Alternators have either rear terminals, A, or side terminals, B, as influenced by the internal design or for compatibility with the location at the front of the engine. (Ford)

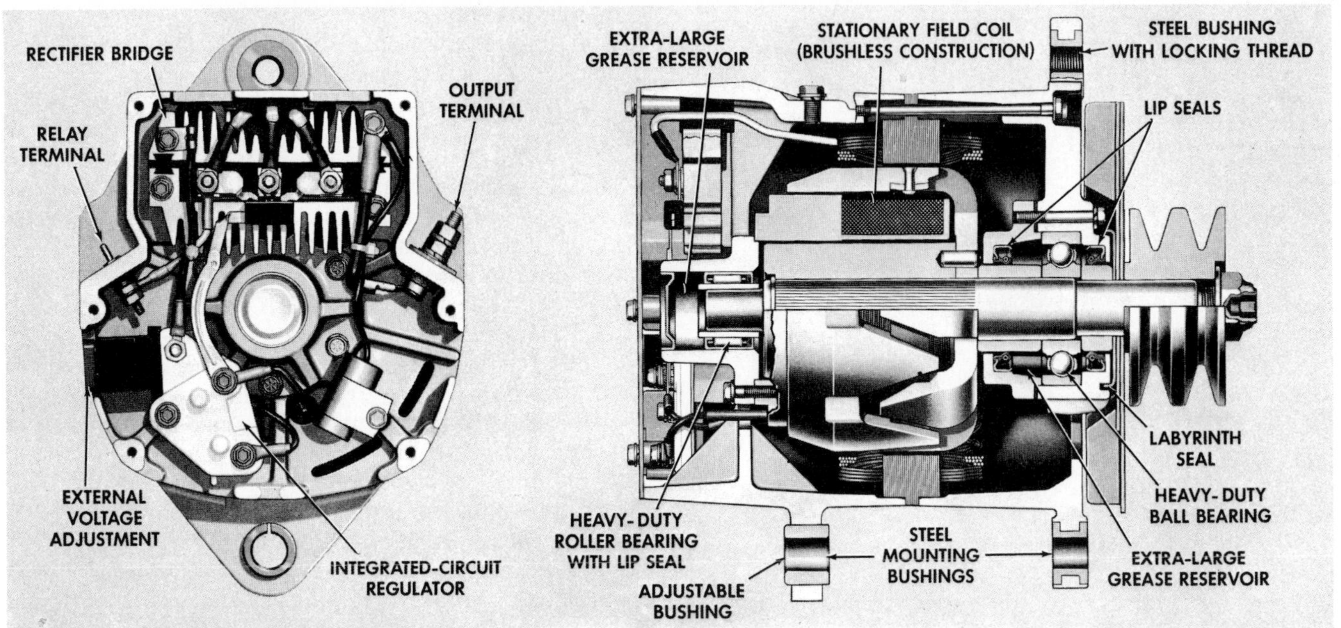

Figure 27-14. Both the stator and the field coil in this brushless alternator are stationary, eliminating shorts and grounds that are more likely to occur when the field winding must rotate. (Delco-Remy)

alternating current from the stator windings to a flow of direct current at the output terminal of the alternator. The rotor (magnetic field), stator (conductors), and diodes (rectifiers) act as a team to produce direct current electricity to keep the battery fully charged and to supply electrical energy to the vehicle's current-consuming devices.

Voltage Regulators

As previously mentioned, the automotive alternator produces the electricity needed to charge the battery and to operate electrical equipment. By design, however, its output continues to rise as its speed increases. Therefore, the charging system is provided with a voltage regulator.

Basically, the ***alternator voltage regulator*** is an automatic switch that controls charging system output so that voltage and current will not exceed predetermined values. If regulation is not provided, excessively high current will damage the battery, alternator, or other elements of the charging system.

The task of the voltage regulator, then, is to sense the amount of voltage present, determine when the battery needs to be charged, and control alternator output accordingly.

Voltage Regulator Types

Voltage regulators are in their third phase of development. First, there were ***electromagnetic voltage regulators.*** These regulators were used in both dc generator and alternator charging systems. See Figures 27-15 and 27-16.

Then, ***electronic voltage regulators*** were introduced. These solid state devices, Figure 27-17, did away with wire-wound coils, contact points, and bimetallic hinges. The electronic units are more reliable, more durable, and less affected by temperature changes.

In many late-model applications, the voltage regulator function has become part of the ***engine computer control system.*** Chrysler, for example, controls the alternator

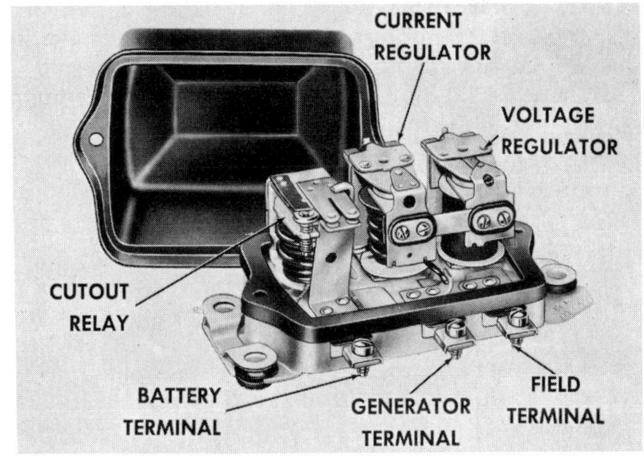

Figure 27-15. The three-unit regulator assembly shown is typical of electromagnetic units used on many dc charging systems. (Delco-Remy)

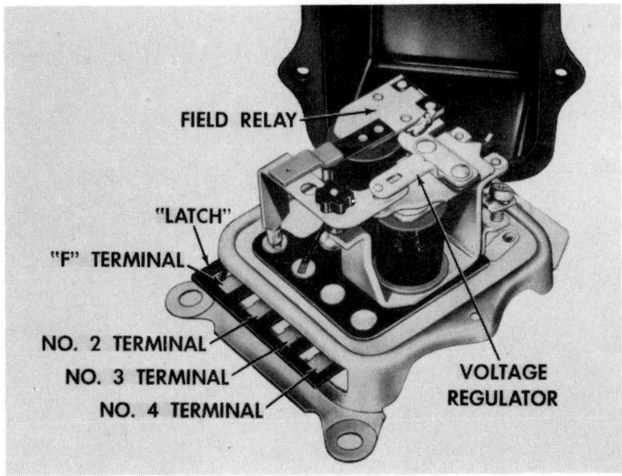

Figure 27-16. Older General Motors charging systems utilized an electromagnetic, two-unit, double-contact voltage regulator and a Delcotron generator. (Delco-Remy)

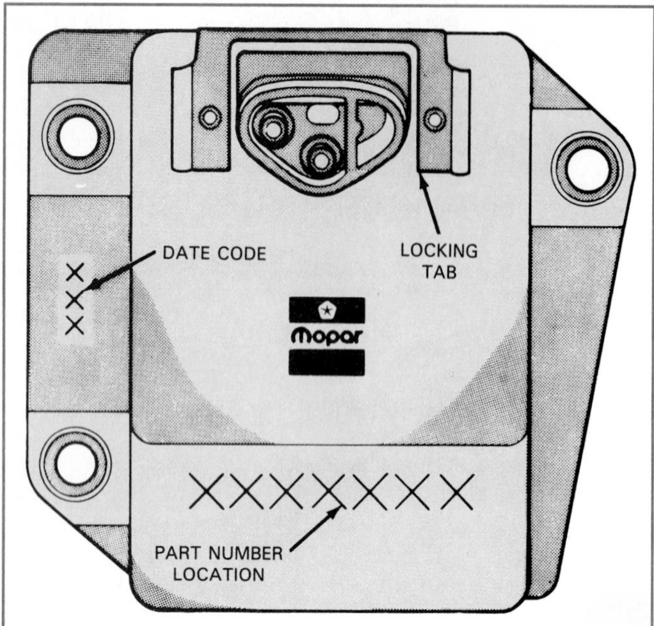

Figure 27-17. Electronic voltage regulators generally contain sealed-in transistors, diodes, resistors, and capacitors. (Chrysler)

output voltage by means of two computer modules. See Figure 27-18.

Regardless of type, however, the voltage regulator controls voltage and current output of the alternator by automatically cutting resistance in or out of the field circuit. Varying the resistance alters the amount of current passing through the field. This changes the strength of the magnetic field, and alternator output is regulated.

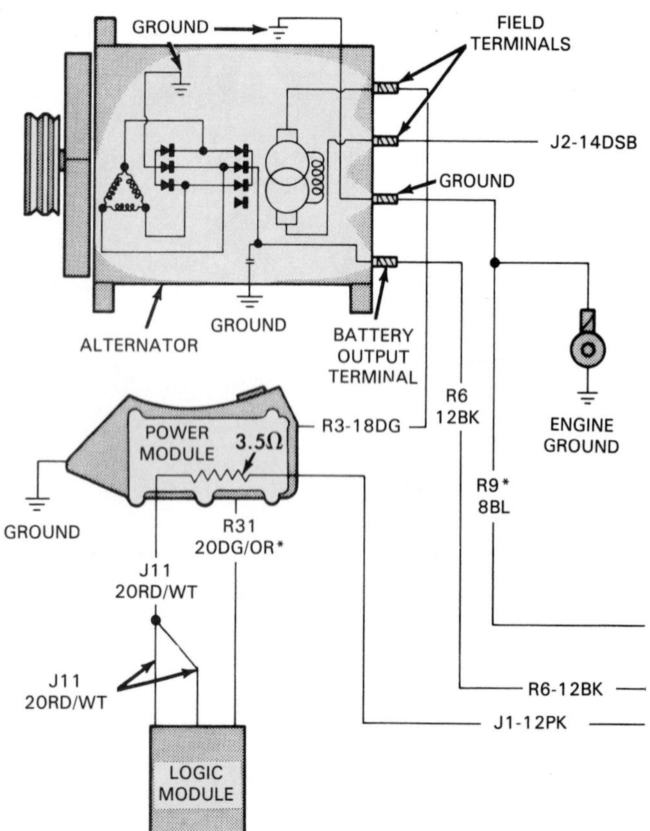

Figure 27-18. Voltage regulator units in some applications have been replaced by engine computer modules. (Chrysler)

DC Generator Regulator Operation

Electromagnetic regulators used on many dc generator charging systems consist of three elements: a cutout relay, a current regulator, and a voltage regulator, Figure 27-15. Others utilize a cutout relay and a step-voltage control unit. Still others use a cutout relay with a vibrating voltage regulator or a cutout relay with a combined current-voltage unit.

The purpose of the ***cutout relay*** is to prevent the battery from discharging through the generator when the engine is stopped or turning over at slow speed.

The ***current regulator*** is a magnetic switch in the charging circuit designed to protect the dc generator from overload by limiting current output to a safe value.

The ***voltage regulator*** controls charging circuit voltage from exceeding a safe value. When the battery needs charging, the voltage regulator cuts resistance out of the field circuit. This increases the flow of current and boosts generator output. When the battery becomes fully charged, the resistance is cut into the field circuit and the charging rate is decreased.

Because of increased electrical loads, many dc charging system regulators are provided with voltage regulator units of the double-contact type. These units are equipped with two sets of contact points to accommodate the high field currents in the generator.

Regulators for Alternators

Regulators used with alternators include the electromagnetic, transistorized, electronic types (including integral type). Additionally, computer-controlled regulation is found in many late-model vehicles. Carbon pile regulators are also used, but mainly in heavy-duty, high-output applications. In electromagnetic regulators, Figure 27-16, the voltage regulator unit limits voltage output by controlling the amount of current applied to the rotating field (alternator rotor). The field relay, on regulators so equipped, connects the alternator field windings and voltage regulator windings directly to the battery. In some cases, it also serves as an indicator lamp relay.

The conventional cutout relay unit is eliminated by the diodes in the alternator. The current limiter (regulator) is eliminated by the current-limiting characteristic of alternator design.

Transistorized and electronic regulators, Figure 27-17, have no moving parts. Consequently, they have a long life. These regulators usually consist of transistors, diodes, resistors, and capacitors, all working together to regulate alternator field current–thereby limiting alternator output voltage to a safe value.

Integral regulators, as the name implies, are built into the alternator. In most applications, the integral regulator is small, flat, transistorized, and attached to the inside of the slip ring end frame.

Electromagnetic Alternator Regulators

Electromagnetic regulators used on earlier alternator charging systems also utilized a voltage regulator unit to limit voltage output to a predetermined value. This unit is incorporated in single-, two-, or three-unit regulators in many standard equipment applications. The single-unit regulator is used only in circuits with an ammeter. The two-unit, double contact regulator is suitable for use in circuits containing either an ammeter or indicator lamp. The three-unit, double contact regulator contains a voltage regulator, field relay, and indicator lamp relay.

Regulator terminals usually are slip-connection type. Slots in the regulator base are keyed to mating surfaces of a connector on the wiring harness to ensure correct connections.

The two-unit regulator consists of a double contact voltage regulator unit and a field relay. If an indicator lamp is used in the charging circuit, Figure 27-19, it lights when the ignition switch is turned ON and goes out when the alternator begins to produce charging voltage.

A voltage regulator actually has many stages of operation. A typical General Motors two-unit, double contact regulator, Figure 27-19, operates as follows:

1. The field relay points close when the engine starts and the alternator stator windings put out voltage. As soon as the points close, the field current is supplied directly from the battery instead of through the ignition switch and resistance wire.
2. When engine speed is low and the battery or accessories need a lot of current, the lower contacts of the voltage regulator unit remain closed to allow full field current (about 2 amps) to flow.
3. As engine speed increases or the load lessens, the lower contacts vibrate between the open and closed position to reduce the field current to between 2 amps and 3/4 amp.
4. When the speed and load requirements reach a point where exactly 3/4 amp field current provides the needed output, the voltage regulator armature will "float" between the upper and lower contacts. In this situation, the entire field current passes through a resistor that limits current to 3/4 amp.
5. When engine speed is high and load is low, increased voltage in the charging circuit will cause the voltage regulator armature to be drawn down, closing the upper set of contacts to ground circuit. Consequently, no field current will flow.
6. As engine speed is reduced and the load again calls for a small charge, the upper contacts will vibrate and field current will flow at 0 to 3/4 amp, depending on the rate of vibration.

Ford Motor Company electromagnetic two-unit alternator regulators consist of a field relay and a double contact voltage limiter (regulator), Figure 27-20. As is generally the case with alternator-equipped charging systems, a cutout relay and a current regulator are not needed.

The field relay connects the battery and alternator output to the field circuit when the engine is running. The double contact voltage limiter controls the amount of current supplied to the rotating field.

At low engine speed and with a load applied, the upper contacts of the voltage limiter are closed, full system voltage is applied to the field, and maximum field current will flow. At high engine speed and with little or no load, the lower contacts are closed and no current flows to the field. A resistor is connected from the field terminal to ground to absorb electrical surges when the voltage limiter armature vibrates on the contacts or floats between them.

On Ford cars with charge indicator light on the dash, battery current flows through the indicator light and a parallel resistor. It then flows through the voltage limiter contacts to the field coil. When the ignition switch is turned on, this small current permits the alternator to start charging. On cars with ammeters, closing of the field relay contact connects battery and alternator output to the field through the voltage limiter contacts.

Chrysler electromagnetic regulators generally are single-unit, double contact voltage regulators. See Figure 27-21 for construction features. Underneath, these regulators have three resistance units, two of which are connected in series with the field circuit.

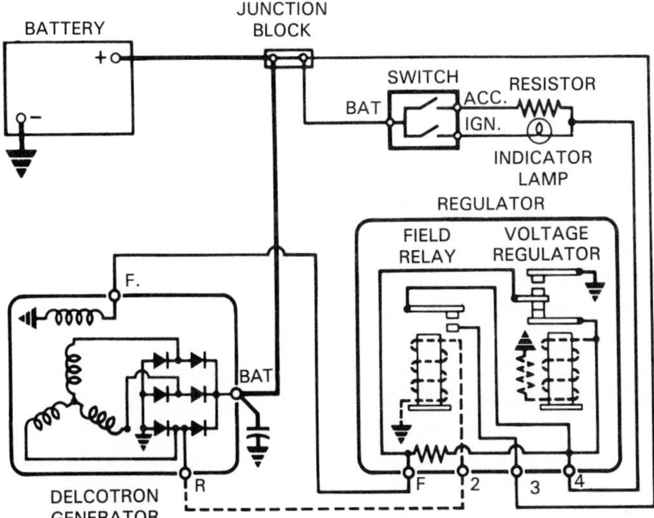

Figure 27-19. This schematic details the charging system circuitry of the Delcotron generator and double-contact regulator shown in Figure 27-16. (Delco-Remy)

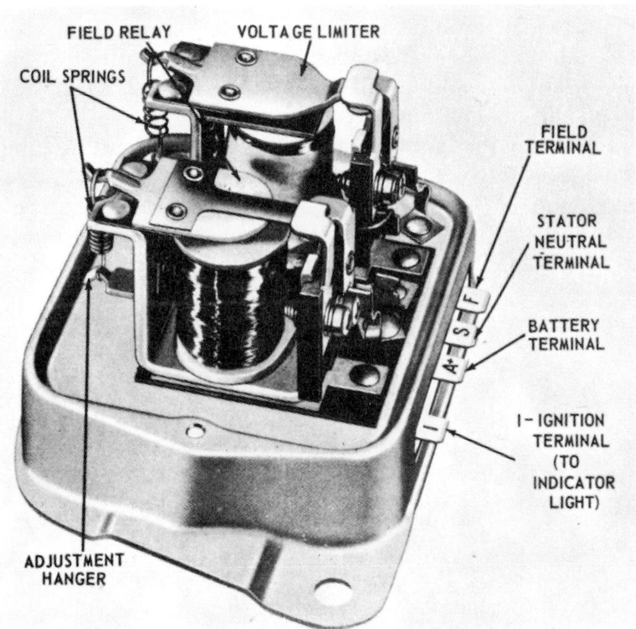

Figure 27-20. Some Ford electromagnetic alternator regulators have two control units and four slip-on terminals.

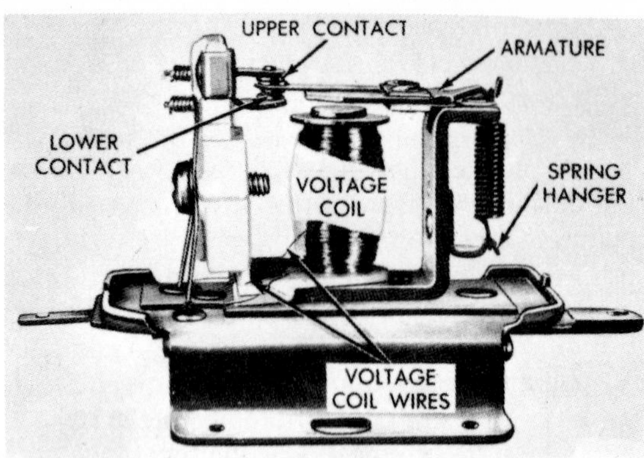

Figure 27-21. Some Chrysler cars are equipped with electromagnetic, single-unit, double-contact voltage regulators with resistance units mounted underneath.

Transistorized/Electronic Regulators

Each of the various models of General Motors transistorized regulators is matched to the alternator field circuit it must control and to the vehicle application. See Figure 27-22. Internal construction is similar, but the various models are not interchangeable.

Basically, the transistor is "switched" on and off to control alternator field current. The frequency of switching depends on alternator speed and accessory load, with the possibility that the "on-off cycle" may be repeated as often as 7000 times per second.

Ford transistorized and electronic voltage regulators operate on the principle of controlling alternator voltage output by regulating the alternator field current. The transistorized units have a voltage limiter and adjustment. The electronic units are factory calibrated, sealed, and nonadjustable.

Ford's transistorized voltage regulators, Figure 27-23, control alternator voltage output electronically by the use of transistors and diodes. The voltage sensing element is a zener diode that changes its resistance to suit voltage requirements.

Ford electronic regulators consist of transistors, diodes, and resistors. These parts are arranged in four different circuits, or stages: output, voltage control, solid state relay, and field current overprotection.

Closing the ignition switch turns on the warning lamp and output stage. See Figure 27-24. The alternator receives maximum field current, and output terminal voltage increases from zero to a level determined by the voltage control stage. The stator terminal voltage is one-half of

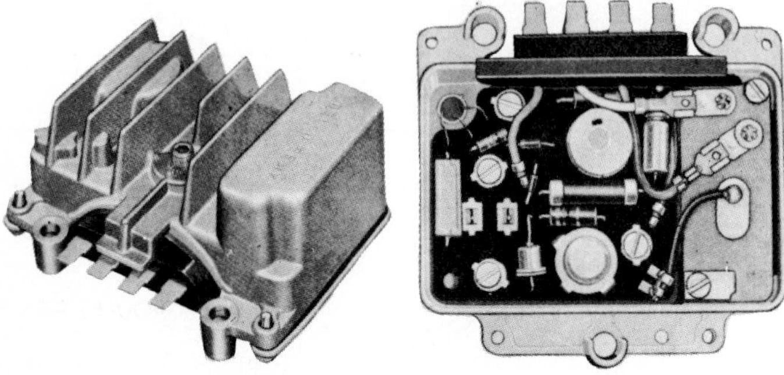

Figure 27-22. Delco-Remy transistorized regulators are similar in appearance, but internal construction may differ.

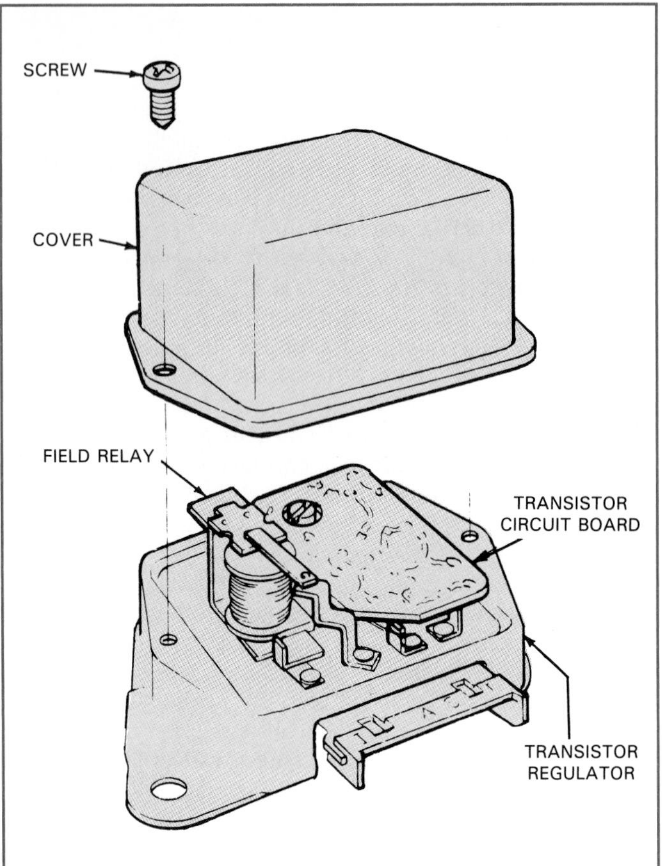

Figure 27-23. Ford uses an adjustable transistorized regulator charging system for certain engine applications.

output voltage and turns off the indicator lamp by way of the solid-state relay circuit.

When the ignition switch is switched off, the solid-state relay circuit turns off the output stage, thus turning off all current flow through the regulator. With that, there is no current drain on the battery.

The field current overprotection stage protects the regulator against damage that could be caused by a "short" in the field circuit.

Chrysler Corporation engines have a variety of alternators and electronic voltage regulators in their charging systems. See Figure 27-25. As with earlier systems, the electronic units limit alternator output voltage by controlling the amount of current passing through the alternator field winding.

Chrysler electronic voltage regulators are made up of several solid-state components, including a large transistor placed in series with the alternator field winding. These regulator units function as a voltage sensitive switch. A control circuit in the regulator turns the transistor on and off as required by speed and load conditions. In addition, the control circuit is designed to vary regulated voltage up or down with temperature changes.

A Bosch alternator used in some Chrysler high-output charging systems has 16 built-in rectifiers. A compact electronic voltage regulator, Figure 27-26, is built into the rear housing of the alternator.

A Mitsubishi alternator installed on certain other Chrysler applications has 15 built-in rectifiers. An internal electronic voltage regulator unit, Figure 27-27, is used.

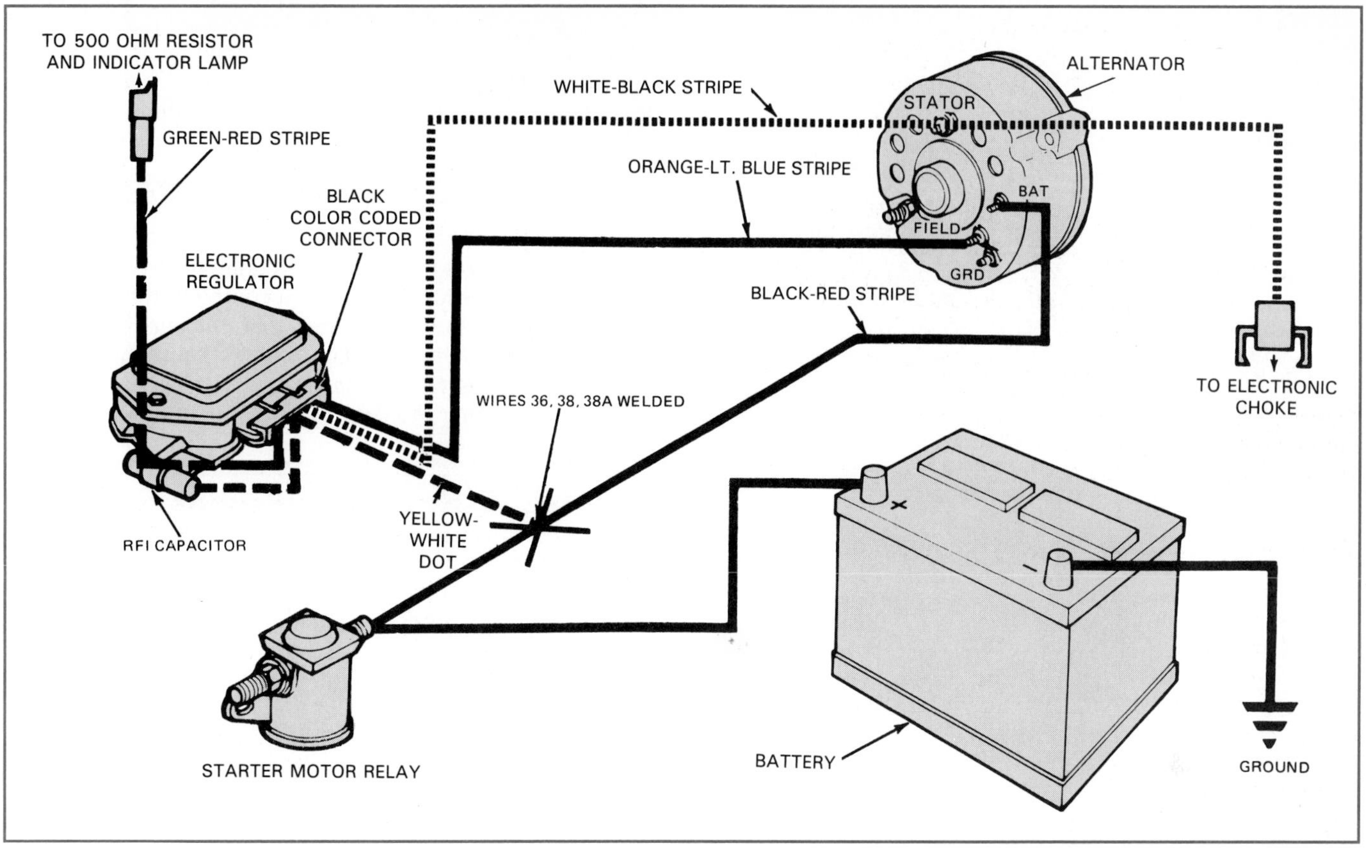

Figure 27-24. Wiring diagram shows color-coded wiring of a Ford alternator charging system equipped with an electronic voltage regulator and an indicator lamp.

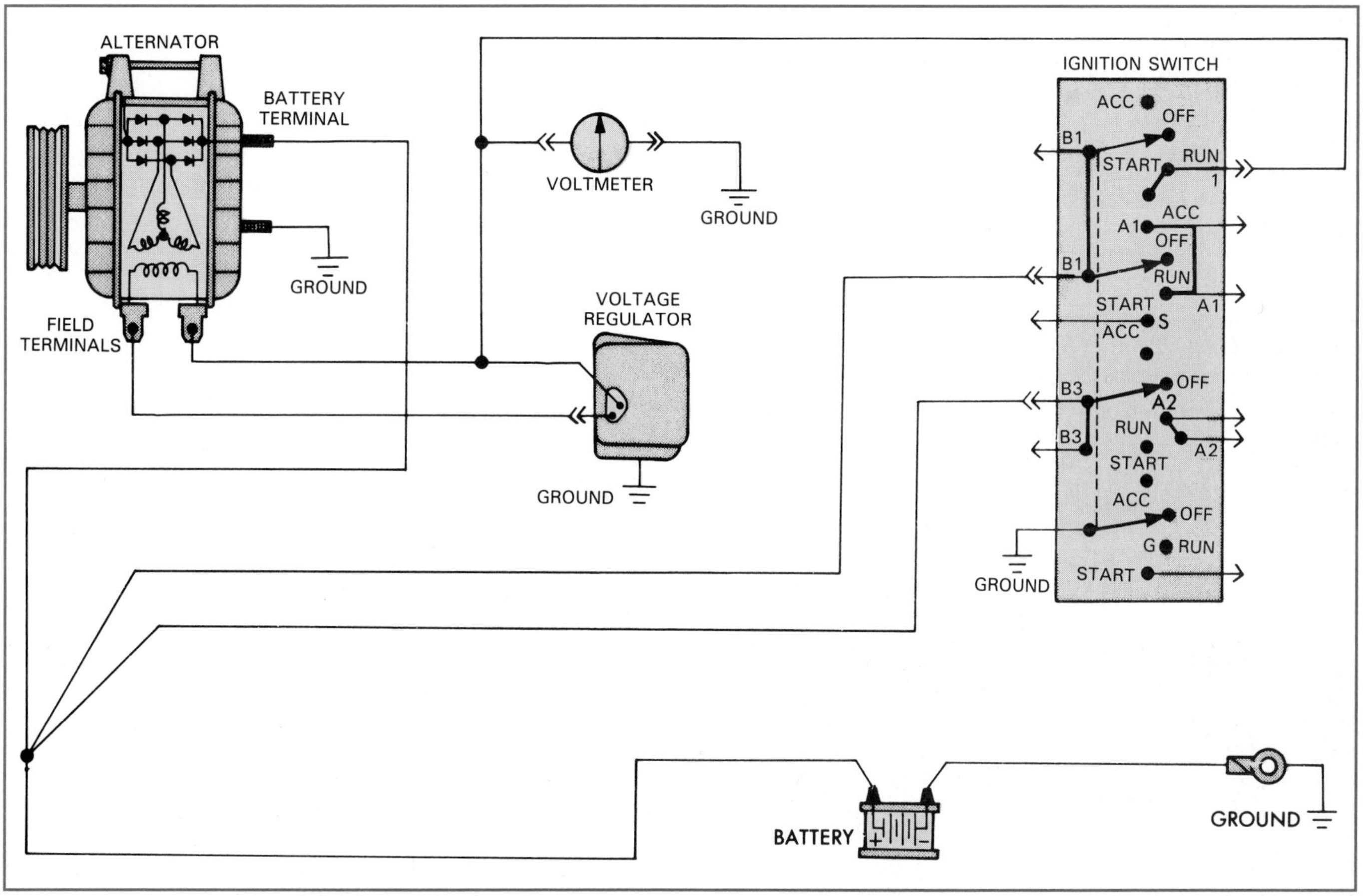

Figure 27-25. This Chrysler charging system features a six-diode alternator and an electronic voltage regulator.

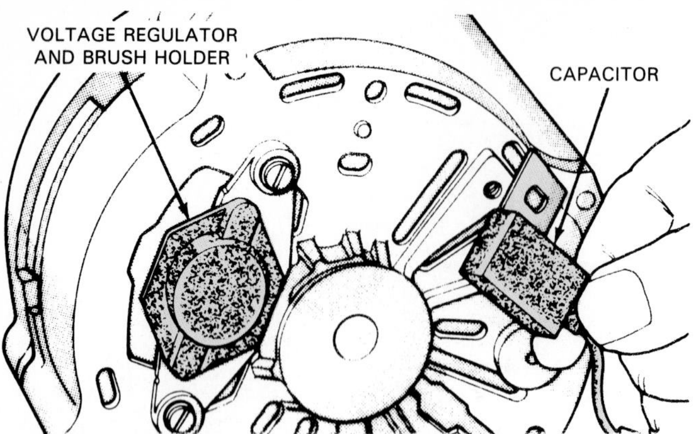

Figure 27-26. Chrysler also uses a Bosch 16-rectifier alternator, which has an electronic voltage regulator and capacitor attached to its rear end shield.

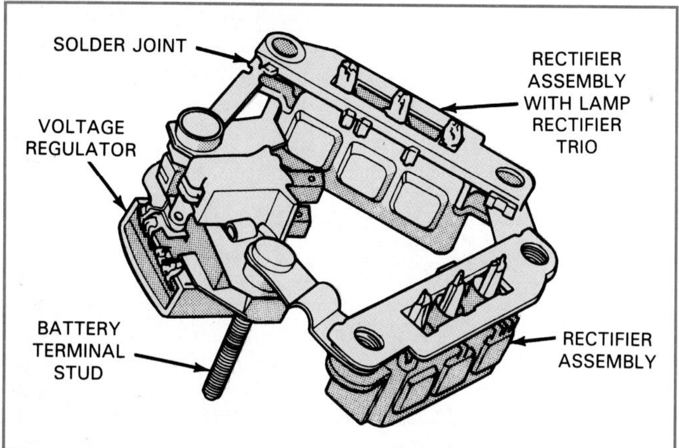

Figure 27-27. Chrysler also uses a Mitsubishi 15-rectifier, high-output alternator with an internal electronic voltage regulator.

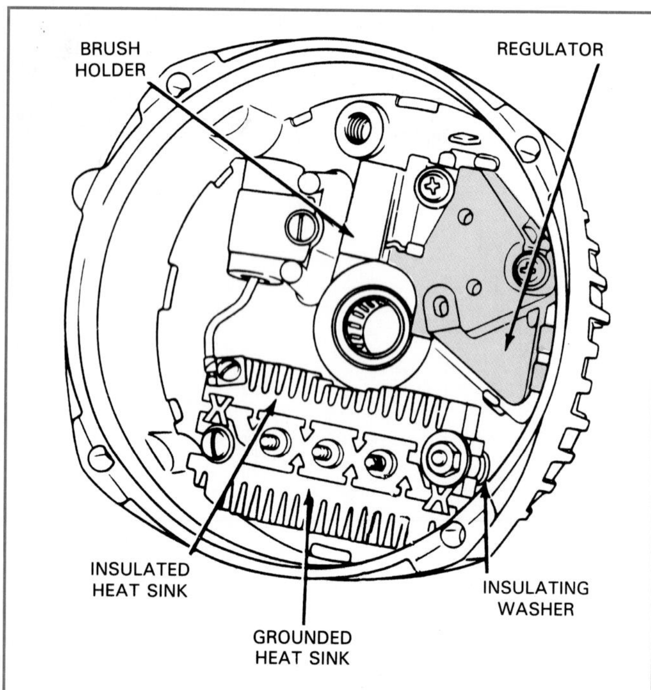

Figure 27-28. General Motors cars use a variety of Delco Remy alternators. An integrated circuit electronic voltage regulator is mounted inside generator rear housing. (Chevrolet)

General Motors electronic voltage regulators utilize solid-state circuitry to regulate current applied to the generator field. These nonadjustable electronic units and the brush holder assembly are attached inside the rear housing of the generator. See Figure 27-28.

Computer-controlled Voltage Regulation

In many late-model vehicles, the ***engine computer*** controls the alternator output, eliminating the need for a conventional voltage regulator. To accomplish this, the computer varies the amount of time that current is fed to the alternator's field winding. This time is known as the ***duty cycle*** and is expressed as a percentage. The higher the electrical load, the greater the duty cycle to the field windings.

Chapter 27-Review Questions

Write your answers on a separate sheet of paper. Do not write in this book.

1. What is an automotive generator?
2. What is the purpose of an automotive generator?
3. When rotating a coil of wire through a horizontal magnetic field, maximum voltage will be produced in the _____ (horizontal/vertical) position of the coil.
4. Voltage can also be produced by keeping the coil stationary and moving the magnetic field. True or False?
5. Name the three major units of an alternator.
6. The _____ has three sets of windings around the inner circumference of a laminated core.
   (A) armature
   (B) rotor
   (C) field coil
   (D) stator
7. In most alternators, which part is the rotating magnetic field?
   (A) Armature.
   (B) Rotor.
   (C) Field coil.
   (D) Stator.
8. In an alternator, which part changes the current from alternating to direct?
   (A) Commutator.
   (B) Converter.
   (C) Regulator.
   (D) Diode.
9. Name the two types of generators.
10. What is the purpose of the voltage regulator?
11. What is the function of the voltage regulator unit when the battery is low in charge?
    (A) To maintain a constant charging rate.
    (B) To prevent the battery from discharging through the alternator.
    (C) To cut resistance out of the field circuit.
    (D) To cut resistance into the field circuit.
12. Why are two sets of contact points used on some electromagnetic voltage regulators?
13. Name the two major basic types of voltage regulators.
    (A) Single and double contact.
    (B) Two-unit and three-unit.
    (C) Integral and externally mounted.
    (D) Electromagnetic and electronic.

14. In many late-model vehicles, the voltage regulator function has become part of the _____.
    (A) electronic ignition system
    (B) engine computer control system
    (C) emission control system
    (D) electronic fuel injection system
15. Transistorized and electronic voltage regulators have no moving parts. True or False?
16. Computer-controlled regulation systems vary the _____ _____ to the alternator's field windings to control alternator output.

Late-model vehicles are equipped with sophisticated electronic systems. Therefore, the proper operation of the charging system is extremely important. (Ford)

The high-mounted alternator on this engine helps simplify charging system service procedures. (Buick)

Chapter 28
Charging System Service

After studying this chapter, you will be able to:
❍ State precautions concerning charging system testing and servicing.
❍ Give quick checks for solving charging system problems.
❍ Explain need for follow-up current output and circuit resistance tests.
❍ Recognize importance of service manual information.
❍ Describe bench testing of charging system components.
❍ Interpret charging system test results.

Charging System Testing and Service

Alternator ***charging systems*** require regular inspection and maintenance. The frequency of inspection depends on operating conditions. High-speed operation, high temperatures, dust, and dirt all tend to increase wear on alternator components.

Charging System Inspection

Inspect the charging system alternator at recommended intervals. Also test the battery's state of charge and check the condition of starting and charging system cables, wires, and connections. It pays to check the condition of the battery and starting system before performing charging system electrical tests.

Check for tightness of starter, alternator, and regulator mounting bolts to ensure good ground circuits. Look over the alternator drive belt for signs of wear or slippage. See that the tension adjustment is correct. The belt should deflect 1/4" in the center of a long span. Belt tension testers generally show color-coded *good* and *bad* ranges, Figure 28-1. If not, check the tester tension reading against manufacturer's specifications.

Figure 28-1. Alternator drive belt condition and tension are two primary considerations in alternator maintenance.

Charging System Precautions and Tests

Alternator testing and servicing call for special precautions since the alternator output terminal is connected to the battery at all times.

- Use care to avoid reverse polarity when performing battery service of any kind. A surge of current in opposite direction could burn out alternator diodes (rectifiers) and damage vehicle wiring.
- Do not purposely or accidentally "short" or "ground" the system when disconnecting wires or connecting test leads to the terminals of the alternator or regulator. For example, grounding of field terminal at either the alternator or regulator will damage the regulator. Grounding of alternator output terminal will damage the alternator and/or the charging circuit.
- Never operate an alternator on an open circuit. With no battery or electric load in circuit, alternators are capable of building high voltage (50 to over 110 volts), which may damage diodes and could be dangerous to anyone who might touch the alternator output terminal.
- Do not try to polarize an alternator. Polarity of an alternator system cannot be lost or damaged, so attempts to polarize the system serve no purpose and may cause damage to diodes, wiring harness, or other components.

Maintenance is minimized by the use of prelubricated rotor bearings and long brushes in most modern alternators. If a problem exists, such as low output or overcharging, check for a complete field circuit (rotor) by placing a large screwdriver on the alternator rear bearing surface. If the field circuit is complete, there will be a strong magnetic pull on the blade of the screwdriver. This indicates that the field windings are energized. If there is no field circuit, an alternator will not charge because the field windings must be "excited" by battery voltage.

Quick Checks

Generally, certain other ***quick checks*** for possible sources of charging system problems can be made before getting into extensive electrical tests.

If the charging system has a fuse (fusible) link, Figure 28-2, check it for appearance and continuity. The link is designed to "blow" if heavy current flows in the circuit. If

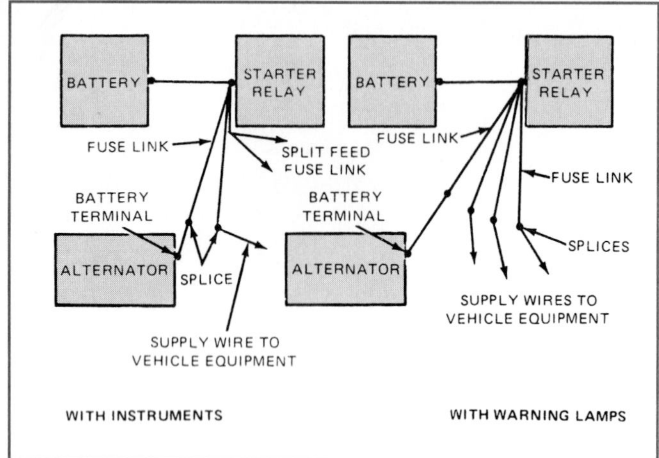

Figure 28-2. Note the fuse link between the starter relay terminal and the alternator battery terminal. An open circuit usually means that the fuse link has "blown." (Ford)

the link is blackened or "open" (no continuity), replace it with a "matching" link. Do not bypass it or replace it with a wire.

Also check the charge indicator lamp on the dash. The only time the lamp should light is when the ignition switch is in the "run" position and the engine is off. Once the engine starts and the alternator begins to produce voltage, the indicator lamp should turn off. If it stays on, there is a malfunction in the charging system. If the lamp fails to light in any ignition key position, the indicator lamp bulb is probably at fault.

On alternators with an integral voltage regulator, make the following checks on charging systems having an indicator lamp outage. Unplug No. 1-2 connector and ground the No. 1 wire. If the lamp fails to light, check for an "open" in the No. 1 wire. If the lamp lights, reconnect the No. 1-2 connector and "ground" the tab in the alternator end frame access hole. See Figure 28-3. If the light stays on, replace the regulator. If the light turns off when the tab is "grounded," check the rotor, brushes, and slip rings for an "open."

If the problem is "undercharging," a good way to begin electrical tests of the charging system is to bypass the voltage regulator (called "full fielding" because the alternator field winding is receiving full current input). ***Full fielding*** can be accomplished by using a plastic "full fielder," a piece of "jumper" wire, or a screwdriver. See Figure 28-3.

If full fielding allows the alternator to produce at least a normal charging voltage (13.8-14.9 volts), the voltage regulator is at fault. If the alternator is still "undercharging," there is a problem in the alternator or wiring.

Before condemning any particular component or assembly in the charging system, make further tests of current output and circuit resistance.

A current output test measures the alternator's ability to produce its rated current output at specified speed and voltage at normal operating temperatures. It is usually performed by connecting an ammeter in series between the alternator output terminal and the positive terminal of the battery, and connecting a variable pile rheostat across the battery terminals. As the engine is operated at specified speeds, the rheostat is adjusted to obtain the maximum alternator current output. The maximum output is then

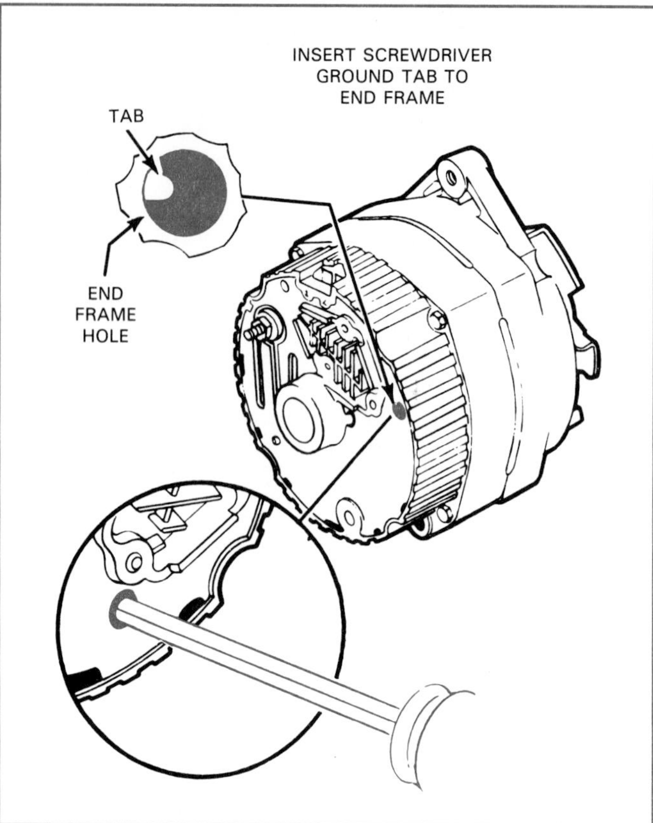

Figure 28-3. Some alternators have a test hole that provides a point of access for using a screwdriver to ground the field winding. (Chevrolet)

compared with specifications. If the current output test indicates that a problem exists in the charging circuit, a circuit resistance test should be performed. This test will tell whether the problem lies in the insulated circuit, the ground circuit, or the alternator. The ground circuit resistance test is performed by connecting one voltmeter lead to the negative battery terminal and the other lead to the alternator's housing. If the voltage reading does not fall within the manufacturer's specifications, the ground circuit contains excessive resistance. The insulated circuit resistance test is performed by connecting the voltmeter across each insulated circuit connection. The charging system must be under load when this test is performed. If the voltage across the insulated circuit connections exceeds the manufacturer's specifications, the connection contains excessive resistance. The exact procedures for these tests vary from one manufacturer to another. Refer to the appropriate service manuals for specific test instructions.

Importance of Service Manuals

When making tests or performing service operations, consult the manufacturer's ***service manuals*** for step-by-step instructions and acceptable values or ranges for a comparison with test results. See Figure 28-4.

The alternator rated amp output and current output minimum values given in the preceding test results are condensed from information contained in one particular Chrysler service manual. The fact that the various alternators listed are available in different vehicle applications during the same model year emphasizes the need for consulting

CHRYSLER 40/90 AMP ALTERNATOR WITH VOLTAGE REGULATOR IN ELECTRONICS	
Output	40/90
Rotation	Clockwise (as viewed from pulley end)
Voltage	12 Volt System
Current Output	Design Controlled
Voltage Output	Limited by Voltage Regulator in Electronics
Brushes (Field)	2
Condenser Capacity	0.5 Microfarad plus or minus 20%
Field Current Draw (Bench Test) Rotating by Hand	2.5 to 5.0 Amperes @ 12V
Current Rating	**Current Output**
40/90 Amp	96 Amp Minimum
Current output is measured at 1250 engine rpm and 15 volts at the alternator. Voltage is controlled by variable load (carbon pile) across the battery.	

Figure 28-4. This service manual specification chart gives alternator identification details, test requirements, and performance specifications. (Chrysler)

service manuals for complete and authoritative service information and specifications.

Alternator Removal

If the charging system fails to meet current output specifications, and "full fielding" (bypassing voltage regulator or computer modules) shows that the alternator is at fault, remove the alternator for disassembly and bench tests. See Figure 28-5.

1. Place the ignition switch in the "off" position.
2. Remove the ground cable from the negative post of the battery.
3. Disconnect the leads from the alternator output terminal (BAT) and from the two field terminals. (FLD).
4. Disconnect the ground lead from the alternator.
5. Remove the wiring retainer nut and disengage the retainer from the alternator.
6. Unscrew the mounting bolts and the adjusting arm bolts.
7. Slip off the drive belt, or belts, and remove the alternator from the engine.

Figure 28-5. Exploded view of a typical alternator installation shows arrangement of brackets, mounting bracket, adjusting bracket, bolts, and nuts. (Chrysler)

Alternator Disassembly

To disassemble the alternator:

1. Scribe marks on the front and rear housings or end shields and the stator frame to aid reassembly.
2. Remove the dust cover, Figure 28-6.
3. Remove the brush holder mounting screws and the brush holder assembly, Figure 28-7.
4. Remove the three stator-to-rectifier attaching screws.
5. Remove the two rectifier assembly mounting screws.
6. Remove the rectifier insulator.
7. Remove the condenser (capacitor) mounting screw and remove the rectifier assembly.
8. Remove the through bolts, then separate the end shields by using two screwdrivers to pry gently between the drive end shield and the stator. See Figure 28-8. The stator should remain with the rear end shield.
9. Remove the pulley nut, pulley washer, pulley, and fan.
10. Remove the bearing spacer and press the rotor out of the drive end shield, Figure 28-9.
11. Remove the stator from the rear end shield, Figure 28-10.

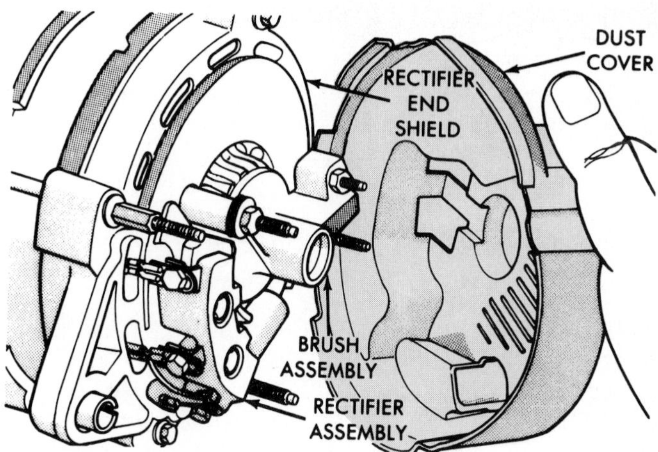

Figure 28-6. Disassembly of Chrysler alternator with voltage regulated by electronics begins with the removal of the dust cover.

Bench Tests

With all major parts disassembled, they may be tested by making various ***bench tests.***

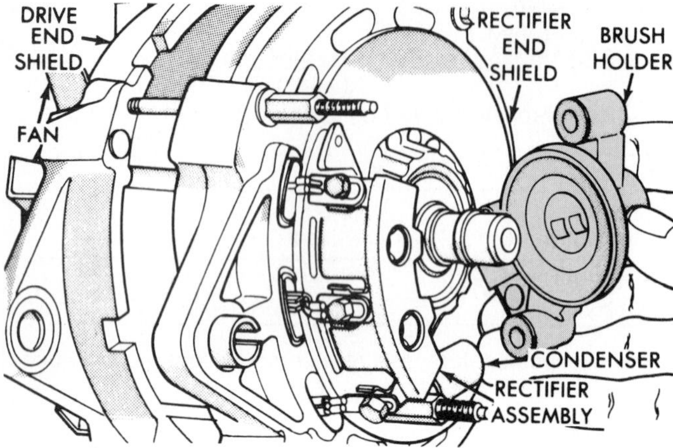

Figure 28-7. Removal of the brush holder assembly permits access to the rectifier assembly and the condenser. (Chrysler)

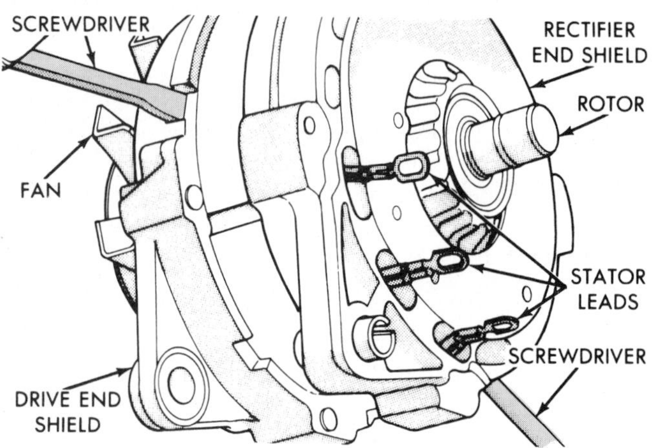

Figure 28-8. To separate end shields, use two screwdrivers to pry between the stator and the drive end shield. (Chrysler)

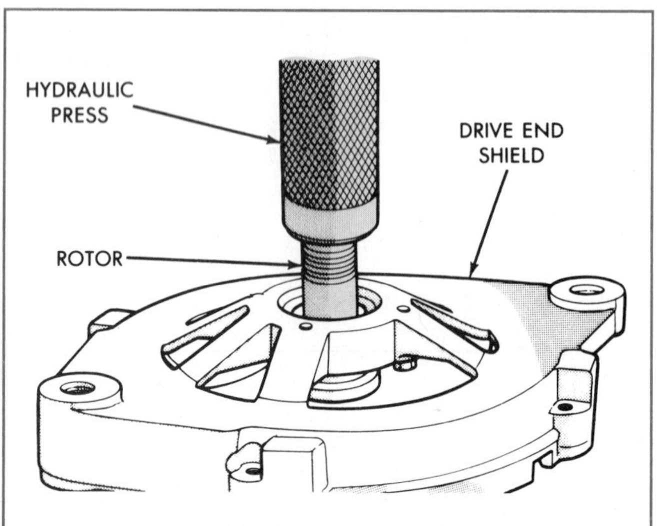

Figure 28-9. If rotor removal is necessary, support the drive end shield on the bed of a hydraulic press and press out the rotor. (Chrysler)

Rotor Tests

To test the rotor for an ***open circuit,*** connect the test lamp leads to each slip ring. If the lamp fails to light, the circuit is incomplete or "open."

To test for a ***short circuit,*** connect one test lamp lead to the rotor shaft. Connect the other lead to one slip ring, Figure 28-11. If the lamp lights, there is a "short to ground" between the windings or slip rings and the rotor shaft. If the rotor fails either test, replace it.

Stator Tests

To test the stator for a ***grounded circuit,*** connect one test lamp lead to the stator core (remove varnish first). With other test lead, prod each of three stator leads. If the test lamp lights, the stator lead is "grounded."

To test stator windings for an ***open circuit,*** use a test lamp to contact each of the three stator leads in turn, two at a time. See Figure 28-12. If the lamp fails to light, there is an "open" in the stator coil. If the stator fails either test, replace it.

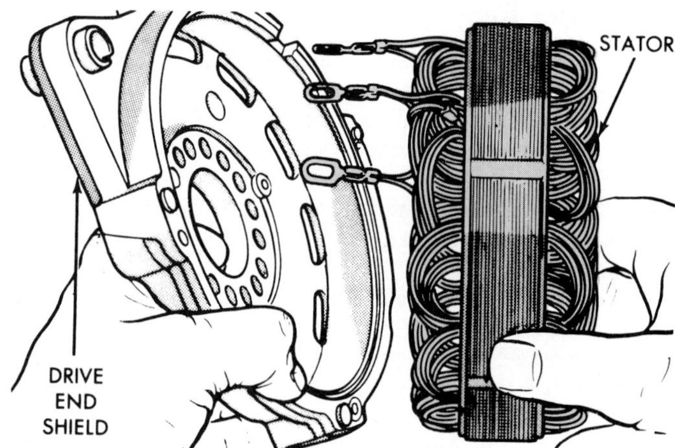

Figure 28-10. Remove the stator from the rectifier end shield for making bench tests. (Chrysler)

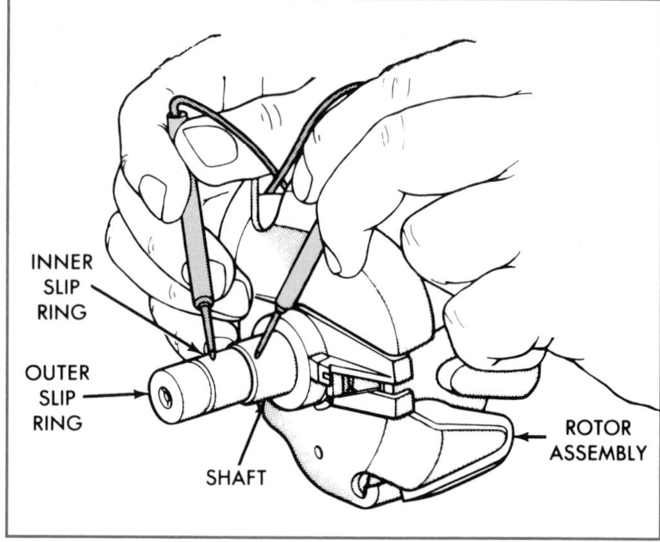

Figure 28-11. To test for a "short to ground," touch the test lamp probes to the rotor shaft and slip ring. If the lamp lights, the rotor is grounded. (Chrysler)

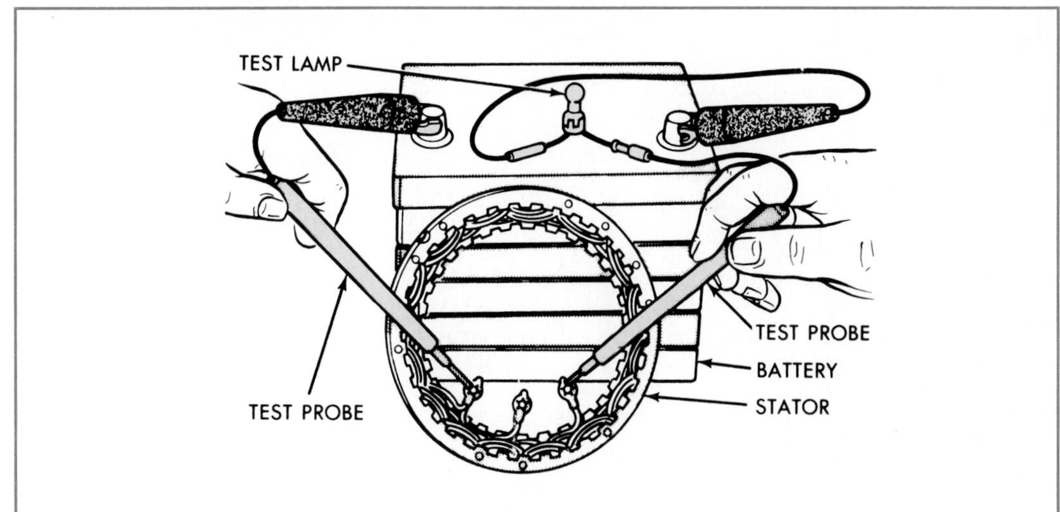

Figure 28-12. To test the stator for "open," touch the test lamp probes to two stator leads at a time. If the lamp does not light, the stator has an open circuit. (Chrysler)

Diode Tests

Several testers on the market permit diode testing without removing the stator leads; others require that the leads be disconnected.

To make a positive diode test, clip one test lead to the output (BAT) terminal of the alternator. Clip the other test lead to the metal strap or pin of each positive diode in turn. See Figure 28-13. Meter readings should fall in the *good* band and in relatively close range of each other.

To test negative diodes, move the test lead from the output terminal of the alternator to the rectifier end shield. Touch the other test lead to each negative diode in turn. Again, meter readings should be in the *good* zone and relatively close to each other.

To test individual diodes, connect one test lamp clip to the diode base and the other lead to the diode lead. Note whether or not the lamp lights. Then reverse the connections. The lamp should light only once, and in the same direction for each diode. If the lamp lights both times, the diode is "shorted." If the lamp does not light at all, the diode is "open."

Repairs/Replacement

Slip rings that need cleaning may be polished with #00 sandpaper or a #400 polishing cloth. Scored or worn slip rings usually necessitate the replacement of the rotor assembly.

Diode replacement generally requires the removal of the four screws holding the positive and/or negative diode and heat sink assemblies to the alternator end shield. Reverse the procedure to install new diode assemblies.

Diode Replacement

On some older alternators, diode replacement can be handled by disconnecting, cutting, or unsoldering the diode lead, and then pressing out the defective unit. Special diode removing tools are available, and the end housing must be supported during the pressing operation to avoid distortion.

Alternator Reassembly

After all bench tests have been completed, defective parts have been replaced, and the diodes have been connected to the stator leads, the parts can be reassembled in the reverse order of disassembly. See Figure 28-14.

Alternator Reinstallation

To install an alternator, position the assembly on the engine and install the pivot bolt and nut and the outer mounting bracket bolts, Figure 28-5. Install the alternator drive belt and the adjusting bracket bolt. Adjust the alternator drive belt to the specified tension, Figure 28-1, but do not pry against the stator section of the alternator.

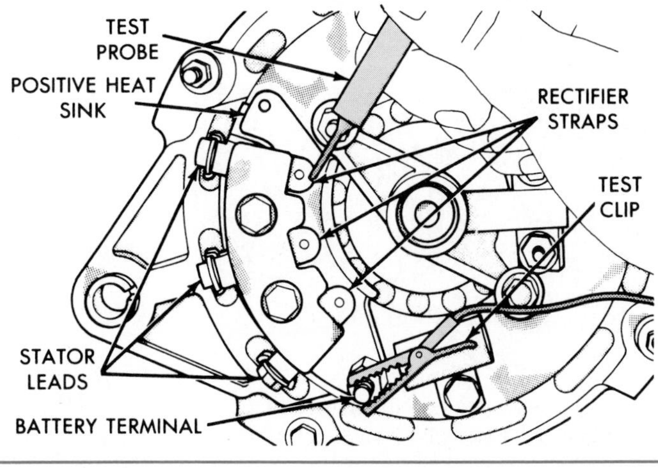

Figure 28-13. To test positive rectifier (diode) condition, clip one test meter lead to the alternator battery terminal. Touch the other lead to each rectifier strap in turn. The meter readings should be in the *good* range and relatively close. (Chrysler)

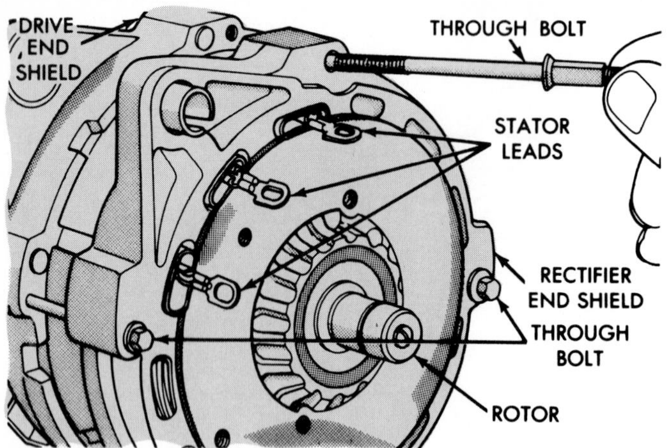

Figure 28-14. Reassemble the alternator in the reverse order of disassembly. Manually compress the stator and the end shields, and install the through bolts. Make sure the rotor turns freely and the fan does not hit the stator winding leads. (Chrysler)

Then, tighten all alternator mounting bolts and nuts. Connect the lead wires to the alternator field (FLD) terminals, the output (BAT) terminal, and the ground terminal, Figure 28-15. Reconnect the ground cable to the negative post of battery. The alternator will be polarized when the ignition switch is turned "on."

Start and operate engine. Check alternator operation. Test the current output and compare the test result with the manufacturer's specification.

Troubleshooting Charging Systems

Common charging system problems and their causes are as follows:

Charge Indicator Light Flickers

- Loose or worn alternator belt.
- Loose or corroded wiring connections.
- Faulty alternator.
- Defective voltage regulator.
- Corroded or loose battery cable clamps or terminals.
- Loose alternator ground wire or strap.
- Poor ground at voltage regulator.

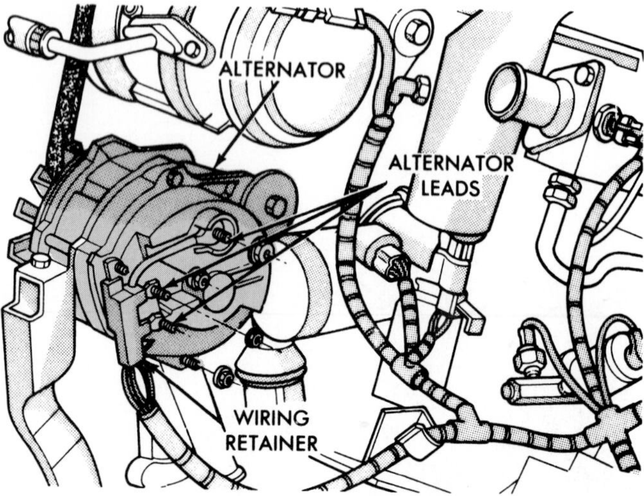

Figure 28-15. With the alternator securely mounted and the drive belt adjusted, connect the leads to the alternator battery terminal, field terminals, and round terminal. (Chrysler)

Charge Indicator Light Stays On

- Loose, worn, or broken alternator belt.
- Open or grounded wiring from battery to alternator.
- Faulty alternator (rotor, stator, diodes, or brushes).
- Defective voltage regulator.
- Corroded or loose battery cable clamps or terminals.
- Grounded field circuit.
- Malfunction in other electrical systems.

Unsteady or Low Charging

- Excessive charging circuit resistance.
- Corroded or shorted cables.
- High resistance across fusible link.
- Defective alternator diodes.
- Open stator winding.
- Excessive carbon on slip rings.

Excessive Charging

- Defective voltage regulator.
- Grounded alternator field wire, field terminal, or connections.
- Internally grounded alternator field.

Lights and/or Fuses Burn Out

- Too high alternator output.
- Defective charging circuit wiring.
- Faulty voltage regulator.
- Grounded alternator field wire, field terminal, or connections.
- Internally grounded alternator field.

Noisy Alternator

- Loose or worn alternator belt.
- Bent pulley flanges.
- Loose alternator mounting.
- Interference between rotor fan and stator leads.
- Worn or defective alternator bearings.
- Open or shorted diodes.
- Open or shorted wiring in stator.

Testing and Servicing

Charging system testing entails checking battery state of charge; performing visual and manual inspections of charging system components; doing quick checks and current output and circuit resistance tests to aid in problem diagnosis; and making bench tests of electrical parts.

Charging system servicing includes cleaning and tightening battery, starter, alternator, and voltage regulator terminals and connections; removing the alternator, disassembling the alternator, replacing faulty alternator parts; reassembling the alternator and reinstalling alternator.

When servicing computer controlled charging systems, always refer to the appropriate service manual for specific troubleshooting and service procedures. See Chapter 29 for more information on automotive computer systems.

Chapter 28 – Review Questions

Write your answers on a separate sheet of paper. Do not write in this book.

1. Alternator charging systems require regular _____ and _____.
2. Dust and dirt tend to increase wear on alternator components. Give two operating conditions that also contribute to component wear.
3. When checking alternator drive belt tension, how much should the belt deflect in the middle of a long span?
   (A) Zero deflection.
   (B) 1/4 inch.
   (C) 1/2 inch.
   (D) 1 inch.
4. If there is no field circuit, an alternator will not charge because the field windings must be _____ by battery voltage.
   (A) charged
   (B) regulated
   (C) controlled
   (D) excited
5. If the charging system has a fusible link, check it for appearance and _____.
   (A) amperage draw
   (B) voltage
   (C) continuity
   (D) resistance
6. If a fusible link has "blown," replace it with a _____ link.
7. What on/off warning device is used in the charging system?
8. What term is used to describe a charging system circuit that is "incomplete?"
   (A) Open.
   (B) Closed.
   (C) Shorted.
   (D) Grounded.
9. What is normal charging voltage?
   (A) 12.2-12.6 volts.
   (B) 12.5-13.0 volts.
   (C) 13.0-13.8 volts.
   (D) 13.8-14.9 volts.
10. The charge indicator lamp should light when the ignition switch is in the "run" position and the engine is off. True or False?
11. If a current output test indicates that a problem exists in the charging circuit, what follow-up test will reveal whether the problem lies in the insulated circuit, ground circuit, or alternator?
12. What is the term used for bypassing the voltage regulator or computer modules in order to test unregulated alternator voltage output?
13. Which one of the following component "condition" tests usually is NOT a bench test?
    (A) Voltage regulator test.
    (B) Rotor test.
    (C) Diode or rectifier test.
    (D) Stator test.
14. As the final step of alternator reinstallation, reconnect the _____ cable to the _____ post of battery.
15. A car in for service has a charge indicator light that flickers. Technician A says is could be caused by a loose or worn alternator drive belt. Technician B says it could be caused by open or grounded wiring from battery to alternator.
    Who is right?
    (A) A only.
    (B) B only.
    (C) Both A & B.
    (D) Neither A nor B.
16. Tests show that a vehicle's charging system has an excessive charging rate. Technician A says it could be caused by a defective voltage regulator. Technician B says it could be caused by a grounded alternator field.
    Who is right?
    (A) A only.
    (B) B only.
    (C) Both A & B.
    (D) Neither A nor B.

Cutaway of a late-model automobile. Computers are used to monitor and control many of the operating systems in this vehicle. (Cadillac)

Chapter 29
Computer System Fundamentals and Service

After studying this chapter, you will be able to:

❍ Explain the stages of computer control system operation.
❍ Explain the function and operation of various sensors and actuators.
❍ Troubleshoot and service sensors, actuators, and electronic control units.

Computer Control Systems

The computer control systems used in late-model vehicles consist of complicated networks of electronic components. The most important tool for troubleshooting and servicing computer control systems is a thorough understanding of how they operate. The untrained technician cannot service vehicles equipped with these systems based on mechanical aptitude alone.

This chapter will provide you with the general theory necessary to tackle computer control system problems. It covers the operation, diagnosis, and service of the most common computer control system components. See Figure 29-1.

As mentioned in previous chapters, computer systems are used to monitor and control the fuel system, the ignition

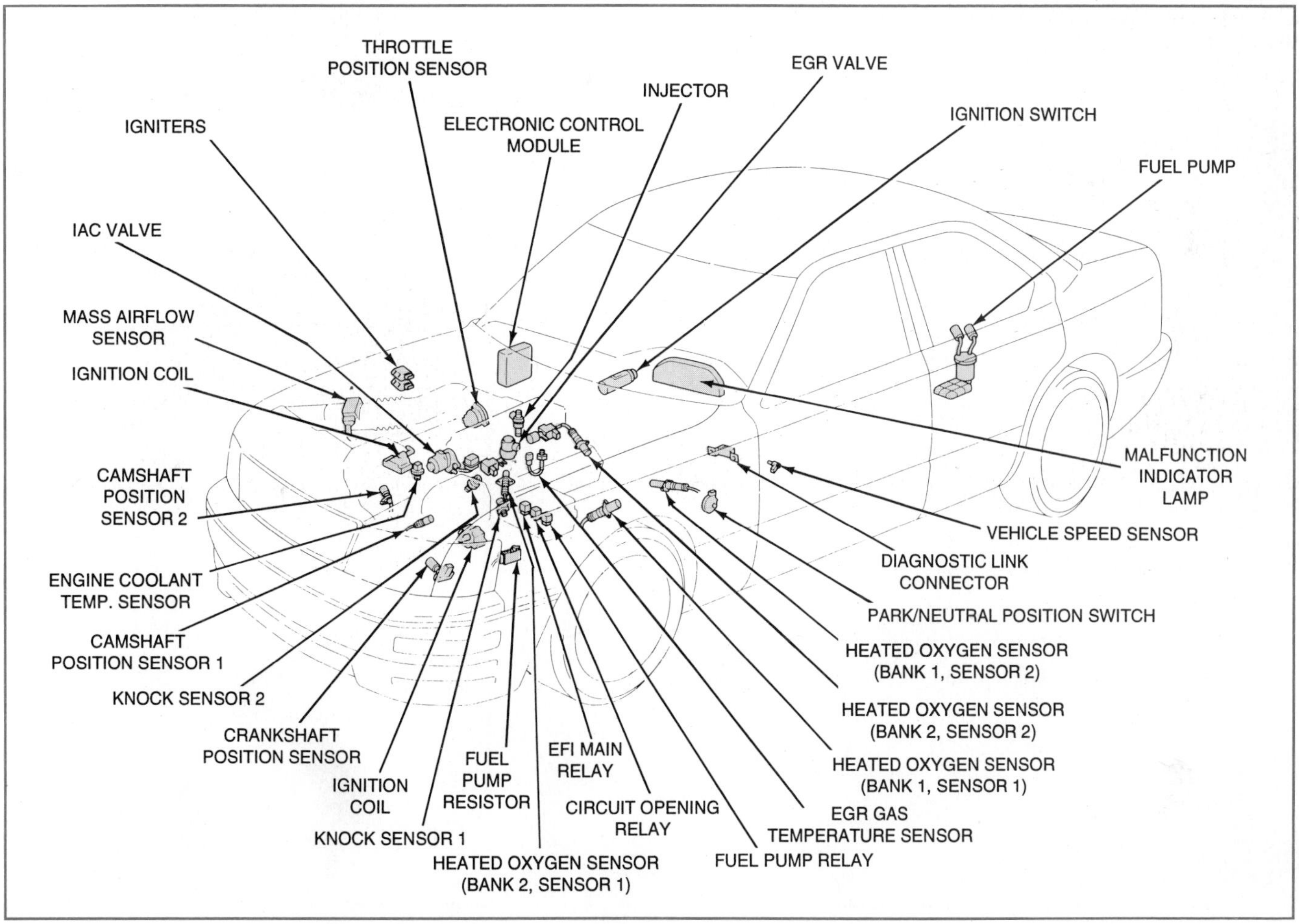

Figure 29-1. Various computer control system components. Note that this highly advanced system contains two ignition coils, two camshaft position sensors, two knock sensors, and four oxygen sensors. In most systems, one of each component is used. (Lexus)

system, and several other engine operating systems. The use of computers in the automotive industry was prompted by governmental regulations that required manufacturers to build vehicles that were more fuel efficient and produced fewer exhaust emissions. Computer control systems offered accurate and instant control over the ignition, fuel, and emission systems. These systems provided better gas mileage, lower exhaust emissions, and smoother operation than their mechanical predecessors. Most components in a computer control system are not subject to physical wear and, therefore, do not require periodic replacement or adjustment.

To accurately control engine operating conditions, the computer control system must be able to monitor and alter these conditions, Figure 29-2. To accomplish this, most systems use the following components:

- Sensors (convert physical conditions to electrical input signals).
- Electronic control unit (processes input signals and supplies output data based on these inputs).
- Actuators (convert output signals from the computer into physical actions).

WARNING! It is very important to keep the charging system in top shape, as its voltage affects the operation of the computer system. If the voltage falls below 12 V, the computer will malfunction. If voltage exceeds 15 V, the computer may be destroyed.

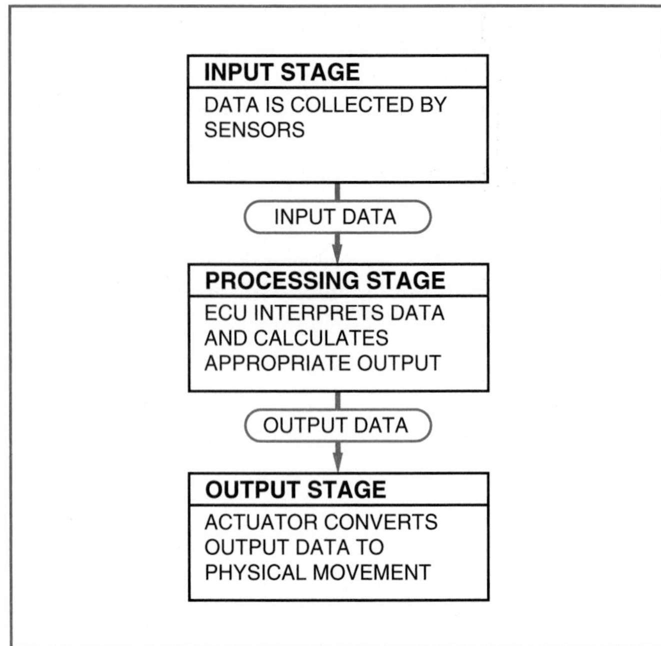

Figure 29-3. There are three stages of computer control system operation: the input stage, the processing stage, and the output stage. These stages are repeated continuously during control system operation.

Computer Control System Stages of Operation

The operation of the computer control systems can be broken down into three stages: the input stage, the processing stage, and the output stage. See Figure 29-3. These stages are repeated thousands of times each second during computer control system operation.

The first stage in the computer control process is the ***input stage.*** During the input stage, the sensors monitor various operating conditions and send electrical signals, which represent these conditions, to the electronic control unit (ECU).

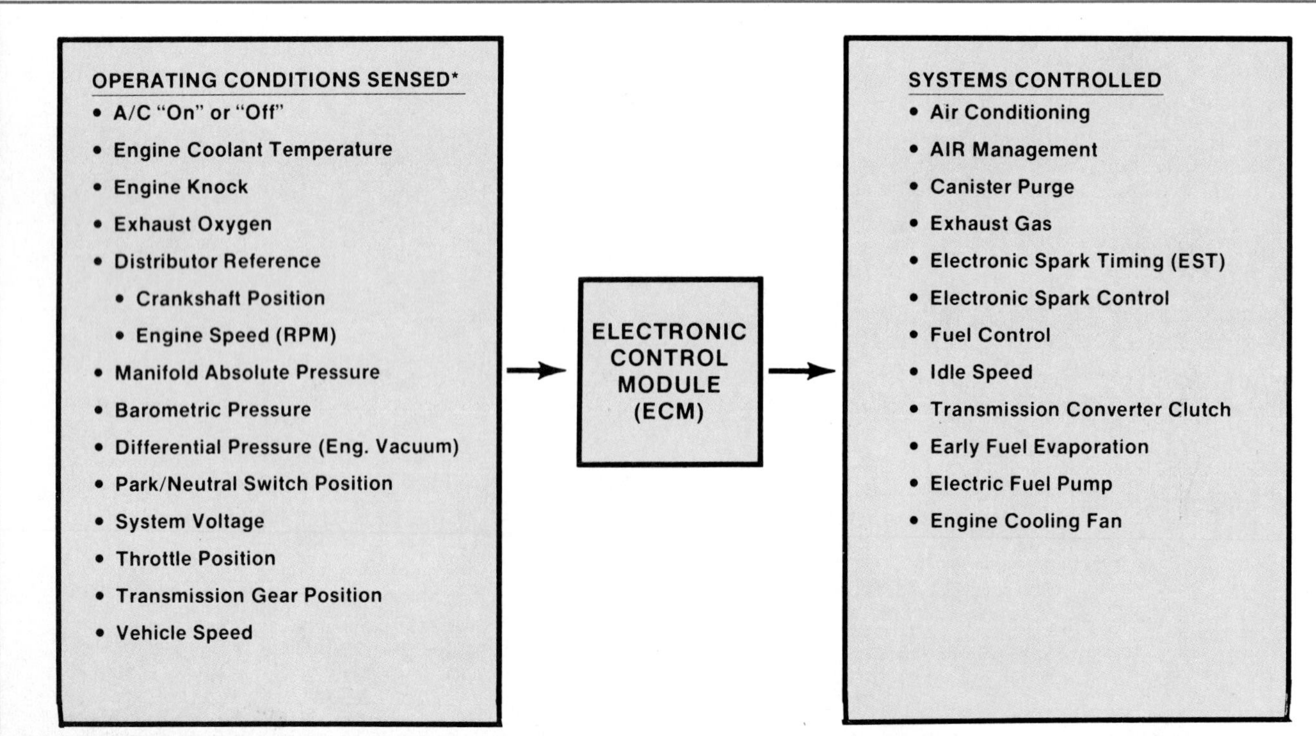

Figure 29-2. The computer must monitor, or sense, many conditions and make the necessary adjustments. (Delco-Remy)

During the ***processing stage,*** the input signals from the sensors are analyzed by the electronic control unit. The electronic control unit uses this input information to decide if an adjustment should be made in the monitored operating system. If an adjustment is required, the decision of how it will be made takes place during the processing stage.

During the ***output stage*** of computer control system operation, the computer carries out the decisions made during the processing stage. Electrical signals that represent these decisions are sent to output devices called actuators. Actuators make physical adjustments to change engine operating conditions.

Components of a Computer Control System

Sensors, actuators, and electronic control units are used to govern many systems in a vehicle. For clarity, however, the following sections on the operation, troubleshooting, and service of computer system components will emphasize the actuators, sensors, and control units that affect engine operating conditions.

Sensors

As mentioned previously, ***sensors*** monitor various operating conditions throughout the automobile. Sensors convert physical conditions into electrical signals. The electronic control unit uses sensor signals to analyze operating conditions. There are two general types of sensors used in an automotive computer control system:

- Active Sensors.
- Passive Sensors.

Active Sensors

Active sensors generate a voltage signal in response to specific operating conditions, Figure 29-4. This signal is sent to the electronic control unit for processing. Typical active sensors include:

- Oxygen sensors.
- Speed sensors.
- Detonation sensors.

Oxygen Sensors

The ***oxygen*** (O_2) sensor is one of the most important sensors on today's automobile. It is usually located in the exhaust manifold or near the catalytic converter and monitors the amount of oxygen in the exhaust gases. See Figure 29-5.

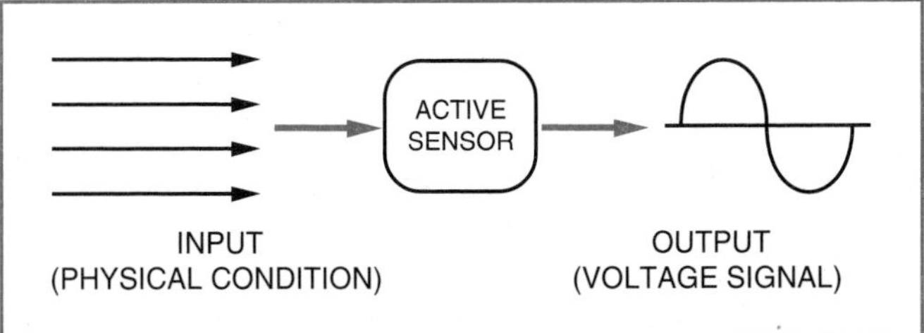

Figure 29-4. Active sensors generate a small voltage signal that varies as operating conditions change.

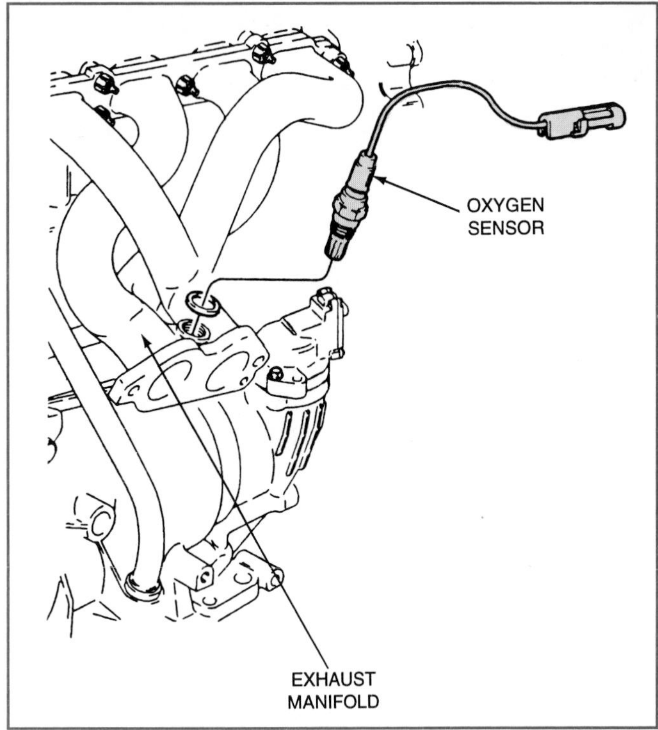

Figure 29-5. The oxygen sensor monitors the amount of oxygen in the exhaust gases.

The common ***zirconia oxygen sensor*** operates like a small battery. Differences in the oxygen content between the sensor's inner and outer surfaces cause it to generate a small voltage. As the oxygen content of the exhaust gas changes, the oxygen sensor's voltage signal also changes. The electronic control unit uses the signals from the oxygen sensor to monitor the engine's air/fuel ratio. A faulty oxygen sensor can cause an excessively rich or lean fuel mixture.

It is important to note that some manufacturers use a ***titania oxygen sensor.*** Unlike the zirconia oxygen sensor, the titania sensor varies its resistance in response to changes in the oxygen content of the exhaust gases.

Loop Operation. When the computer control system is receiving inputs from the sensors, processing these inputs, and sending output signals, it is said to be operating in a ***closed loop*** state, Figure 29-6A. If this cycle is broken, the system goes into an ***open loop*** state. When in open loop, the computer does not control operating conditions within a vehicle, Figure 29-6B.

Most computer control systems rely on the oxygen sensor to govern loop operation. If the sensor's temperature is below 600°F (315°C), it will not send a signal to the computer and the system will remain in an open loop state. When the sensor reaches the correct operating temperature, it will send a signal to the ECU and the control system will begin closed loop operation.

Engine Speed Sensors

The ***engine speed sensor*** sends information about engine speed (rpm) and piston position to the electronic control unit. The ECU uses this information to calculate fuel injection timing and ignition timing. Engine speed sensors may monitor crankshaft motion or distributor shaft

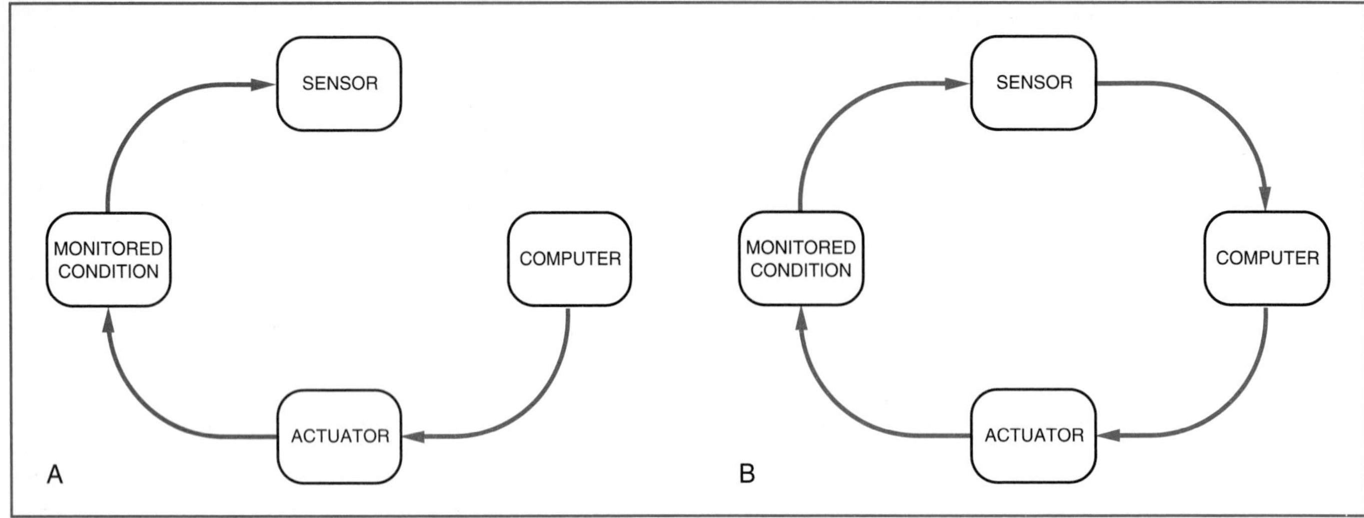

Figure 29-6. Loop operation. A–When the computer control system is operating in the open loop state, the computer does not receive a signal from the sensor. B–In the closed loop state, the sensor sends a signal to the computer.

rotation, Figure 29-7 and Figure 29-8. A magnetic field produced by the rotation of the crankshaft (or distributor shaft) creates a small voltage in the sensor. The strength of this voltage varies in relation to the speed of shaft rotation. An engine speed sensor that monitors crankshaft motion is commonly called a ***crankshaft position sensor.*** A camshaft position sensor works on the same principles as the crankshaft sensor, but it monitors camshaft rotation.

Vehicle Speed Sensor

This sensor tells the computer how fast the car is traveling. The ***vehicle speed sensor*** is driven by the speedometer cable, Figure 29-9. The speedometer cable drives a pulse generator in the speedometer pinion housing. Some cars have the speedometer pinion drive the pulse generator. As the pulse generator makes one revolution, a certain

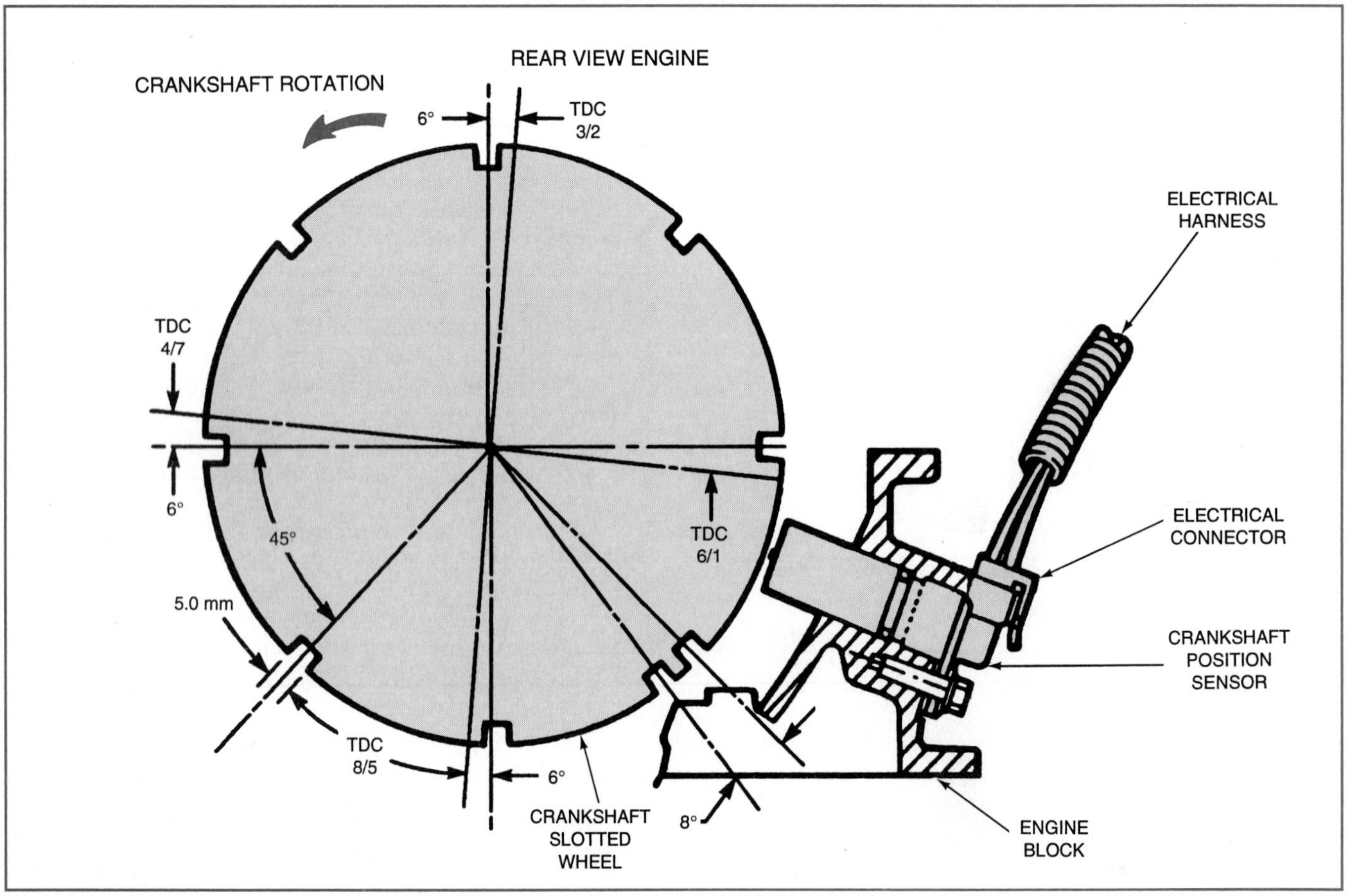

Figure 29-7. This engine speed sensor monitors crankshaft motion. The slotted wheel rotates with the crankshaft. The sensor is mounted in the engine block. (General Motors)

number of pulses or voltage signals are sent to the computer. The computer must be programmed to "know" how many pulses equal one revolution of the speedometer cable. This information is also used for a digital dash and trip computer, if the vehicle is so equipped.

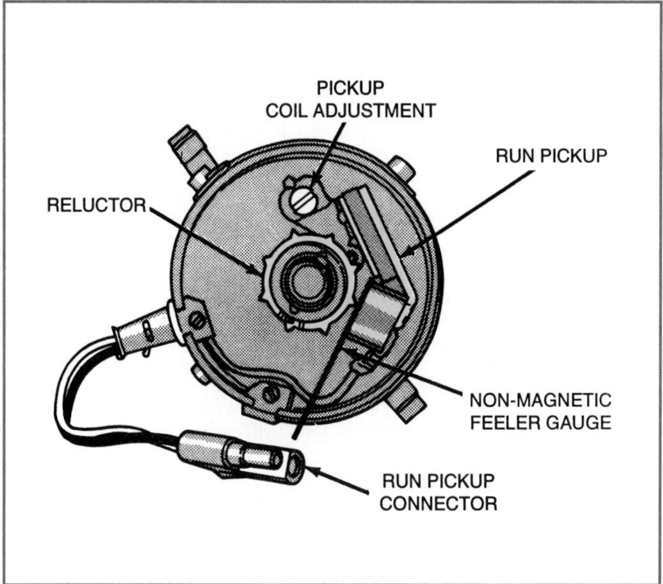

Figure 29-8. This engine speed sensor monitors the rotation of the distributor shaft.

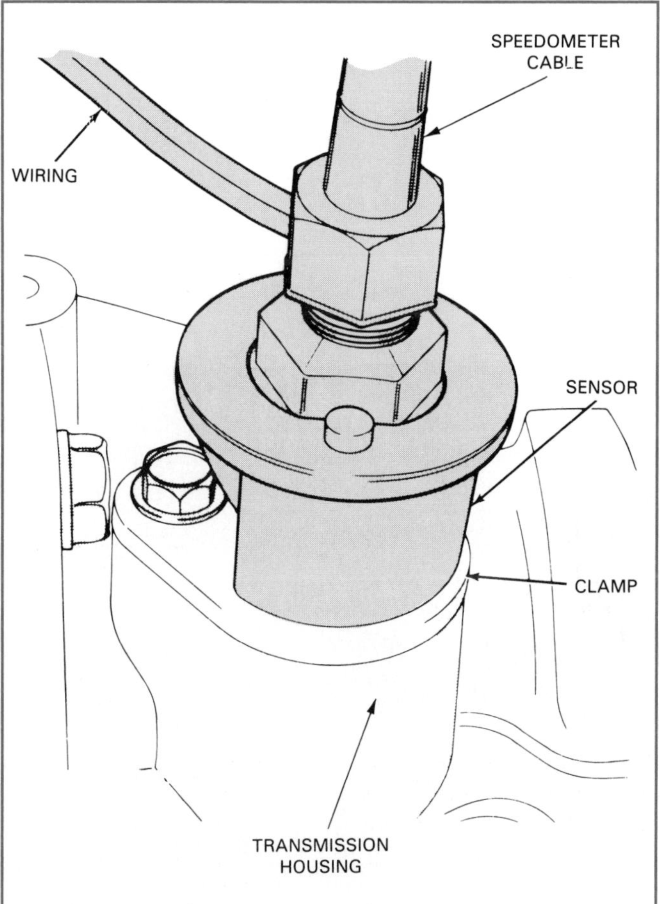

Figure 29-9. This vehicle speed sensor is mounted in the transmission housing and monitors vehicle speed. (Chrysler)

Knock Sensors

A ***knock sensor,*** or ***detonation sensor*** converts abnormal engine vibrations, such as knocking and pinging, into electrical signals. Upon receiving these signals from the knock sensor, the electronic control unit can retard the ignition timing to correct the condition. A knock sensor is shown in Figure 29-10.

Passive Sensors

Passive sensors do not have the ability to produce a voltage signal and must rely on a ***reference voltage*** supplied by the electronic control unit. The reference voltage, which is usually 5 volts, is modified by the sensor and sent back to the ECU, Figure 29-11. The ECU analyzes the changes in reference voltage and makes adjustments accordingly. Most passive sensors alter the reference voltage by varying their resistance in response to changes in operating conditions. As the resistance of the sensor changes,

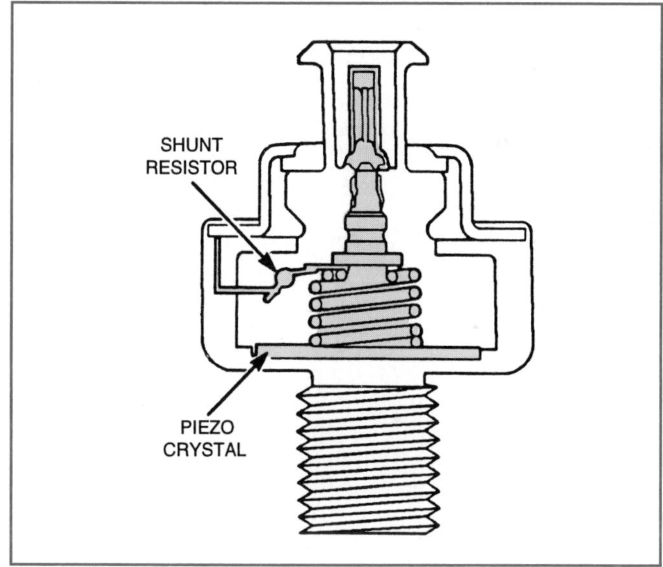

Figure 29-10. Cutaway view of a knock sensor. This sensor monitors engine knocking and pinging.

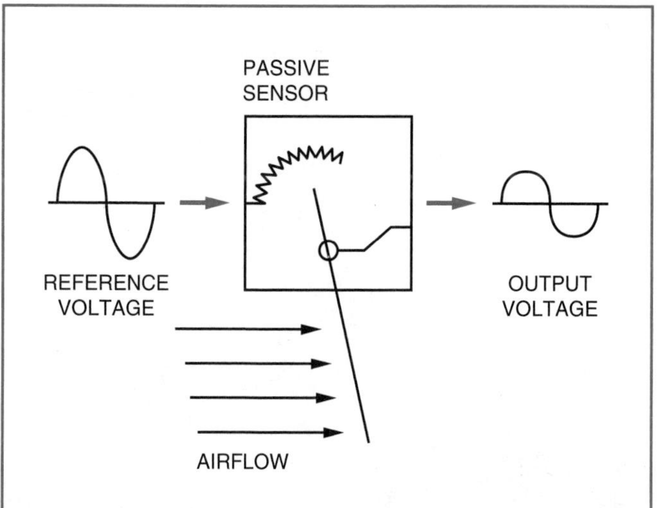

Figure 29-11. Typical passive sensor. This particular passive sensor varies its resistance as airflow changes.

the voltage returned to the ECU also changes. Common passive sensors include:

- Manifold air temperature sensors.
- Coolant temperature sensors.
- Airflow sensors.
- Manifold absolute pressure sensors.
- Barometric pressure sensors.
- Throttle position sensors.
- Switching sensors.

Manifold Air Temperature Sensors

The ***manifold air temperature (MAT) sensor*** monitors the temperature of the air entering the intake manifold, Figure 29-12. As the temperature of the intake air changes, the internal resistance of the MAT sensor changes. This change in resistance varies the voltage signal that returns to the electronic control unit. The ECU uses the output signal from the MAT sensor circuit to help determine the optimal air/fuel mixture. As intake air becomes warmer, less fuel is needed to operate the engine efficiently.

Coolant Temperature Sensors

The ***coolant temperature sensor*** monitors the temperature of the engine coolant. The tip of this sensor is exposed to the coolant. The coolant temperature sensor varies its internal resistance as the coolant temperature changes. The electronic control unit uses the signal from the coolant temperature sensor circuit to calculate the appropriate air/fuel mixture for cold or warm engine operating conditions. See Figure 29-13.

Airflow Sensors

Airflow sensors monitor the amount of air entering a vehicle's throttle body or carburetor. The ***flap airflow sensor*** contains a pivoting flap that is connected to a variable resistor, Figure 29-14. As the amount of air flowing through the sensor varies, the flap moves and the sensor's resistance changes. This change in resistance alters the reference voltage. The output from the flap airflow sensor circuit is used to help calculate the proper air/fuel mixture.

Like the flap airflow sensor, the ***mass airflow sensor*** is used to measure the volume of air entering the engine, Figure 29-15. The mass airflow sensor, however, can compensate for

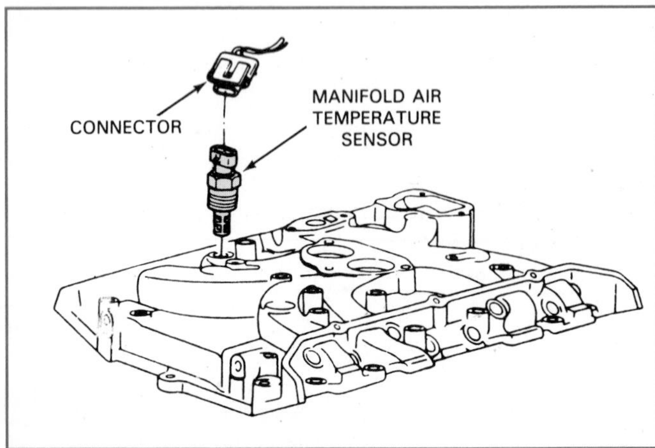

Figure 29-12. This manifold air temperature sensor is located on the intake manifold. (Cadillac)

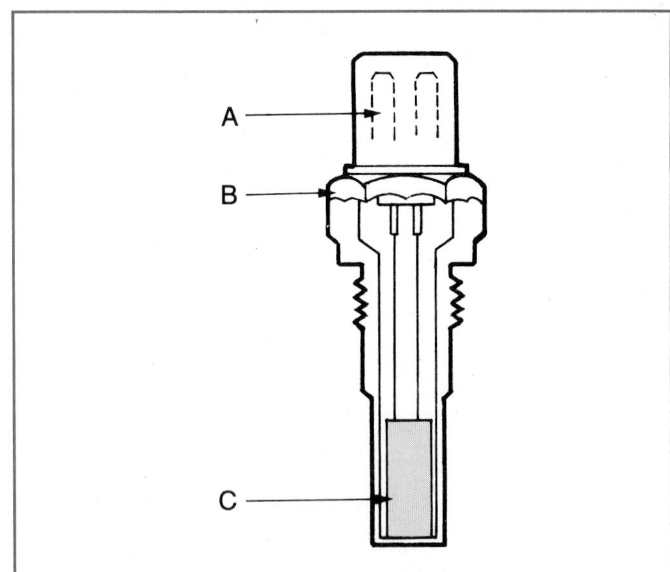

Figure 29-13. A typical coolant temperature sensor. A–Electrical connector. B–Case. C–Thermistor. (Robert Bosch)

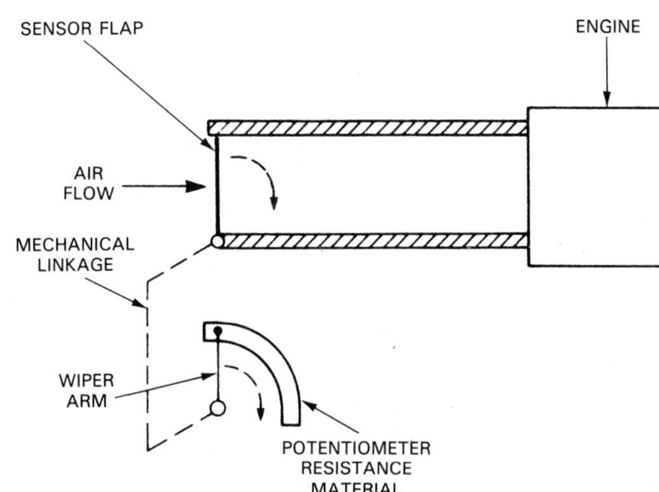

Figure 29-14. Schematic of a simplified flap airflow sensor.

Figure 29-15. The mass airflow sensor measures the temperature and mass of incoming air. This helps the computer determine the correct air/fuel mixture. (Buick)

changes in air temperature and atmospheric pressure. Therefore, an air temperature sensor and a barometric pressure sensor are not used in systems containing a mass airflow sensor.

A mass airflow sensor uses a wire screen located in the airflow path to monitor the amount of air entering the intake manifold. The screen is heated by a reference voltage supplied by the electronic control unit. As air flows through the screen, its temperature is reduced. As the temperature drops, the ECU increases the reference voltage to maintain a constant temperature at the screen. The ECU analyzes reference voltage changes and calculates the airflow rate. The ECU can then adjust the air/fuel ratio to compensate for changes in the airflow rate.

Manifold Absolute Pressure Sensors

The ***manifold absolute pressure (MAP) sensor*** monitors the engine's intake manifold pressure, Figure 29-16. As the manifold pressure changes, the MAP sensor's internal resistance varies. The ECU uses the output signal from the MAP sensor circuit to help determine how much fuel should be entering the engine.

Barometric Pressure Sensors

The ***barometric pressure sensor*** measures atmospheric pressure, Figure 29-17. When barometric pressure drops due to weather or altitude, the timing must be advanced and the fuel mixture leaned. This sensor can be similar in design to any MAP sensor.

Throttle Position Sensors

The ***throttle position sensor*** (TPS) monitors the position of the throttle valve and varies its resistance in relation to the position of the throttle shaft. See Figure 29-18. The output signal from the TPS circuit is low when the throttle valve is closed. The TPS circuit output voltage rises proportionally as the throttle is opened. The electronic control unit uses the signals from the TPS circuit to control ignition timing, fuel delivery, and EGR valve position. It is interesting to note that the TPS is one of the only computer control system components that is mechanical in nature.

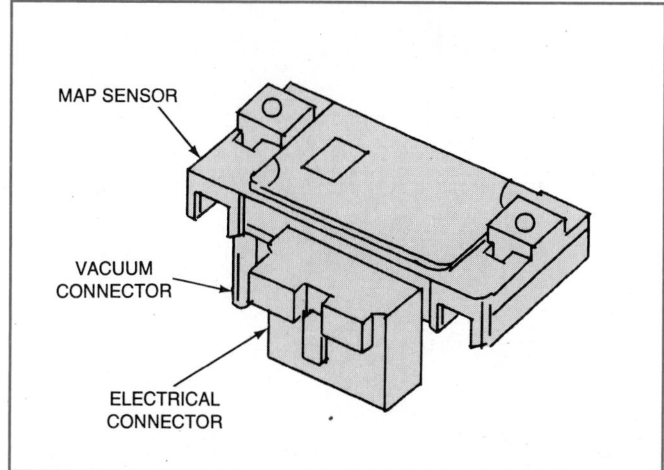

Figure 29-16. The manifold absolute pressure sensor varies its resistance as intake manifold pressure changes. (General Motors)

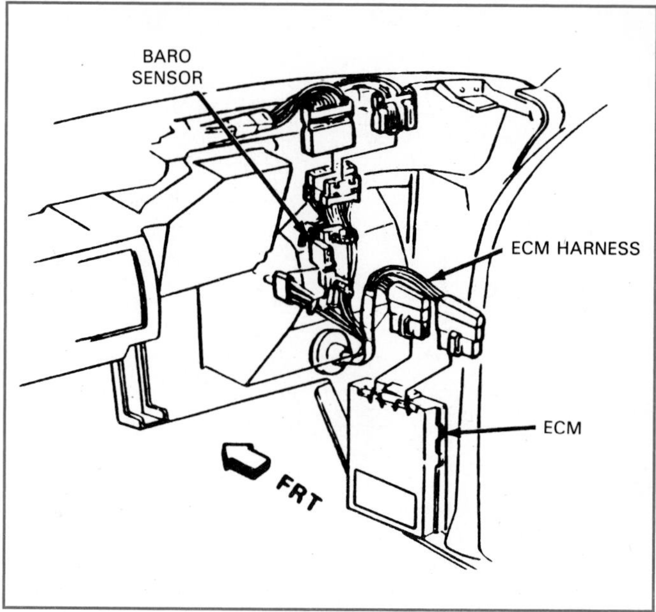

Figure 29-17. Location of the barometric pressure sensor on one particular vehicle. (Cadillac)

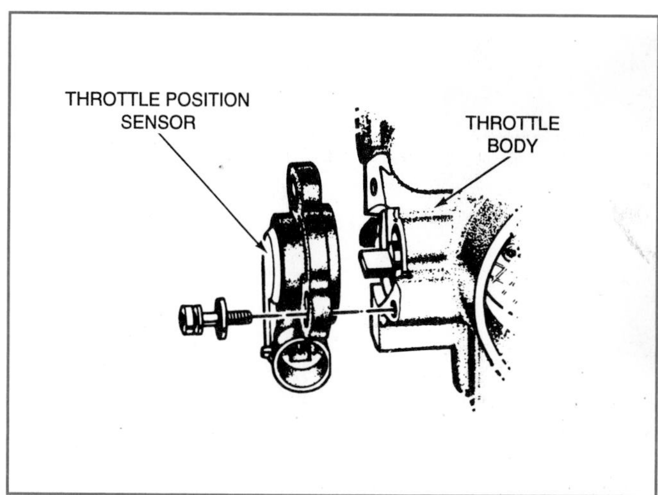

Figure 29-18. The throttle position sensor is mounted on the throttle body and monitors throttle valve movement. (General Motors)

Switching Sensors

A number of ***switching sensors*** monitor certain engine operating conditions. These sensors turn on and off in response to specific conditions. Some switching sensors use an internal pressure-sensing element to monitor these conditions, Figure 29-19. Many switching sensors are switched on and off by moving parts in the monitored circuit. Switching sensors are considered passive sensors because they receive a reference voltage from the electronic control unit.

Sensor Multiplexing

With recent technical advances, it has become possible to connect all of the engine-monitoring sensors to the computer with one wire, Figure 29-20. This practice is referred to as ***multiplexing*** (MUX). Multiplexing reduces

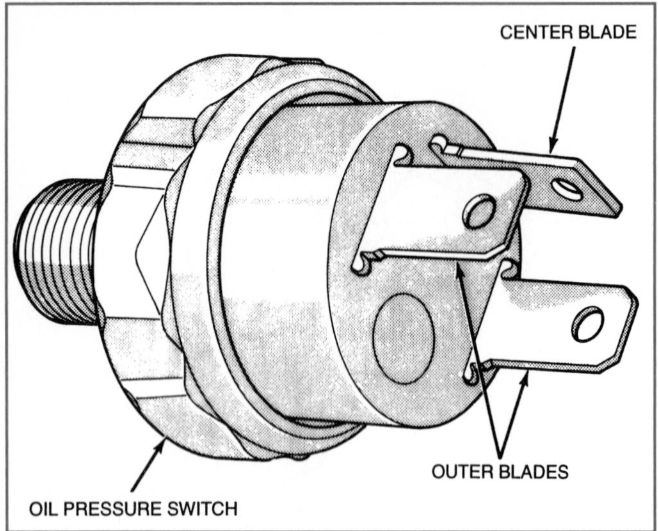

Figure 29-19. A switching sensor is used to monitor oil pressure on many vehicles. This oil pressure switch alerts the ECU when pressure drops below a certain level. (Chrysler)

the amount of wiring that is needed in the vehicle. The single wire is called a ***data bus,*** and all sensors transmit a signal to it. This data bus can even be composed of fiber optics. The use of fiber optics is even more desirable than copper wiring, as there will be no interference of the signal by other electrical devices.

Each sensor receives a signal at a separate and predetermined time. Only one sensor is sending and receiving signals at a time, Figure 29-20. The concept of multiplexing can be used not only for sensors, but throughout the entire car.

Electronic Control Unit Operation

The ***electronic control unit*** (ECU) is a very complex device. It is constructed from a number of integrated circuits, printed circuit boards, and other miscellaneous electronic components.

Although it is not necessary to know how the internal components of the ECU work, it is helpful to understand the basic operation of the unit in order to effectively troubleshoot a computer control system.

The electronic control unit can be divided into five basic sections. Each section performs a specific function within the unit, Figure 29-21:

- The ***input section*** (converts sensor signals to a form that the computer can use).
- The ***memory section*** (stores data until it is needed for processing operations).
- The ***arithmetic logic section*** (analyzes input information and calculates output data).

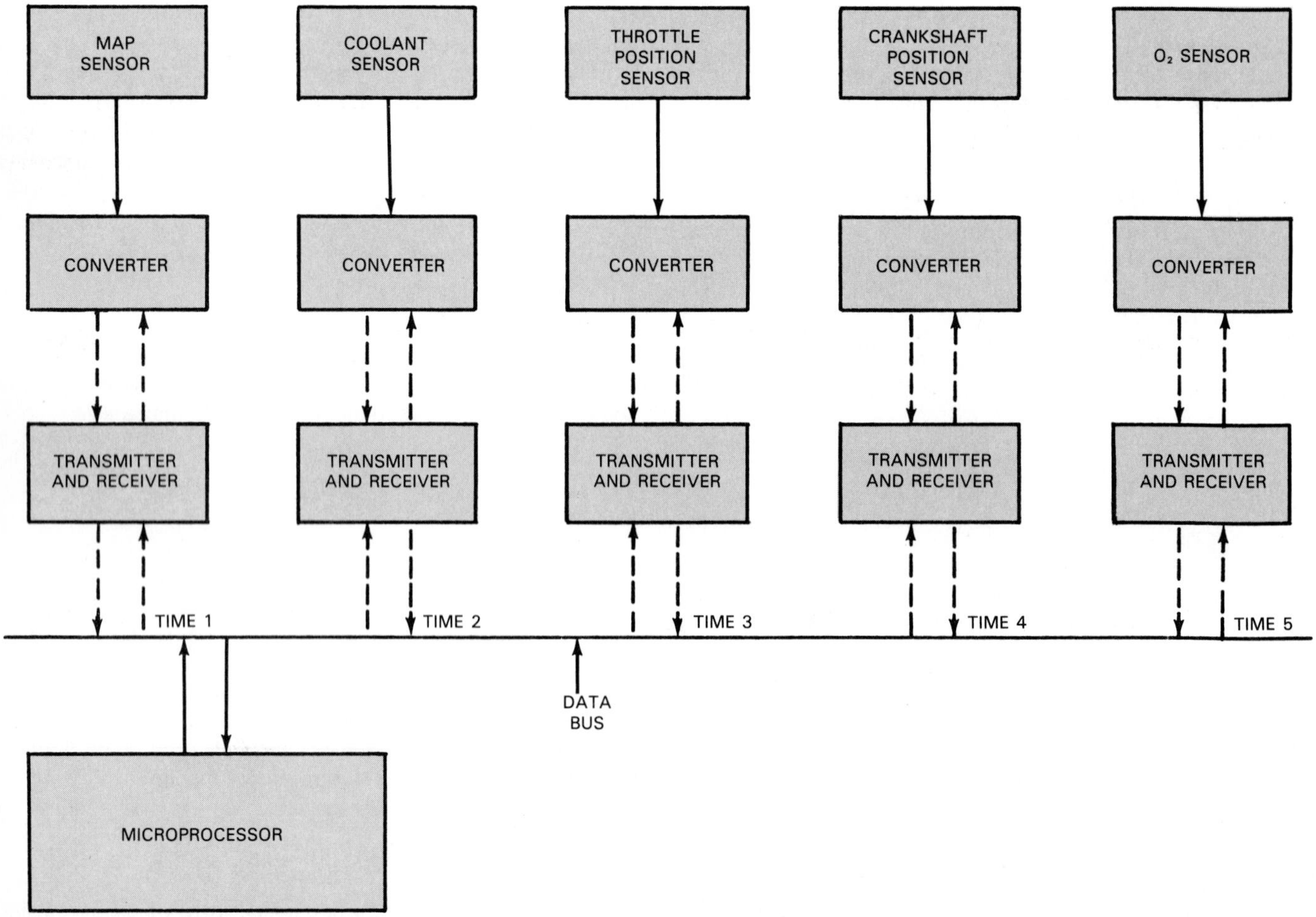

MAP SENSOR
COOLANT SENSOR
THROTTLE POSITION SENSOR
CRANKSHAFT POSITION SENSOR
O_2 SENSOR
CONVERTER
CONVERTER
CONVERTER
CONVERTER
CONVERTER
TRANSMITTER AND RECEIVER
TRANSMITTER AND RECEIVER
TRANSMITTER AND RECEIVER
TRANSMITTER AND RECEIVER
TRANSMITTER AND RECEIVER
TIME 1
TIME 2
TIME 3
TIME 4
TIME 5
DATA BUS
MICROPROCESSOR

Figure 29-20. Sensor multiplexing. When the computer needs information from a specific sensor, a signal is sent on the data bus to the appropriate transmitter/receiver. Only one sensor signal interacts with the computer at a time. Each sensor has a designated time to interact with the computer.

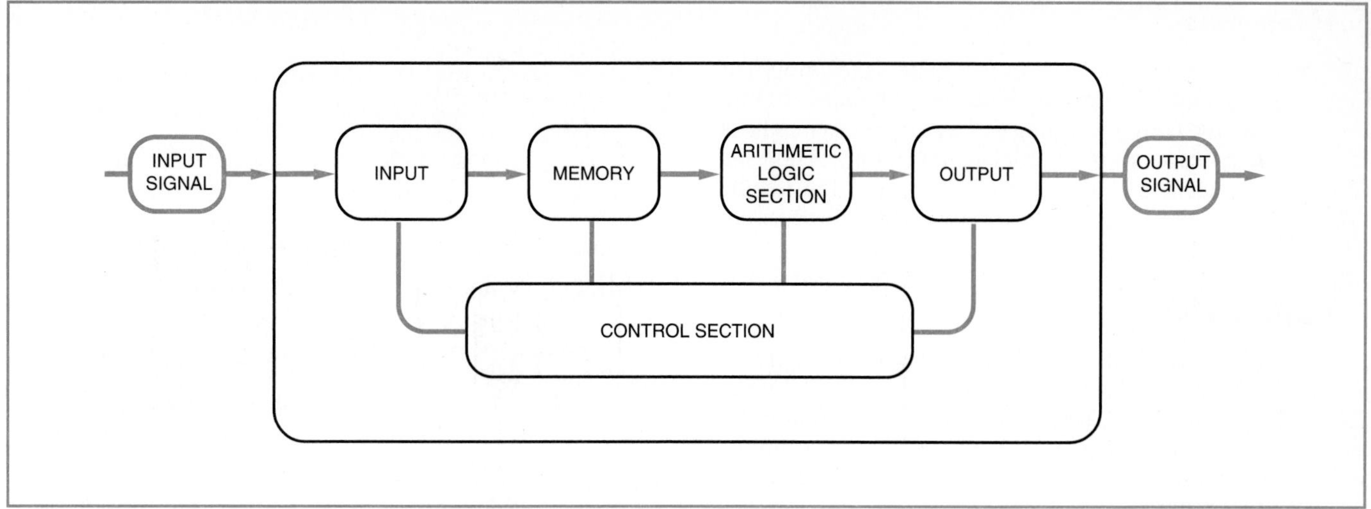

Figure 29-21. The electronic control unit can be divided into five sections. Each section performs a specific function within the computer.

- The ***control section*** (governs all of the other sections in the computer).
- The ***output section*** (converts the computer's output signal to a form that an output device can use to produce an appropriate control function).

Computer Memory

As mentioned, the memory section of the electronic control unit stores data until it is needed for processing operations. The three types of memory commonly used in automotive ECUs include ROM, RAM, and PROM. Each memory type performs a specific function in the computer's memory system.

ROM (read only memory) contains the computer's operating instructions (programs). It also stores general information that tells the computer how various components should perform under specific operating conditions. As its name implies, data in ROM can only be read. The information in ROM can never be modified. If power to the computer is disconnected, the data in ROM will not be lost. The data stored in ROM is universal. Therefore, a manufacturer can use the same ROM memory for an entire product line. The electronic control unit compares information from the sensors to the data stored in ROM. If the result of the comparison is not acceptable, the ECU will take action to change operating conditions.

RAM (random access memory) is used as a temporary storage place for data from the sensors. The electronic control unit uses the information stored in RAM to analyze operating conditions. RAM also stores trouble codes when abnormal operating conditions occur. Trouble codes will be covered in detail later in this chapter. RAM is a volatile memory, which means that its contents will be lost if battery voltage is disconnected from the computer.

PROM, like ROM, contains permanent information about how components should perform under various operating conditions. The information in PROM, however, is much more specific than the data stored in ROM. The information in PROM depends on a vehicle's options. For example, a vehicle with an automatic transmission would have a different PROM than an identical vehicle with a standard transmission. The PROM is the only part of the electronic control unit that can be replaced in the field.

On some late-model vehicles, an ***erasable PROM,*** or ***flash memory,*** is used instead of a PROM. This type of memory can be reprogrammed in the field to correct operating variables such as injector pulse width, idle speed, and ignition timing.

Actuators

Actuators convert the output signals sent by the electronic control unit into physical movements, Figure 29-22. The ECU uses actuators to make physical adjustments that change operating conditions. Commonly used actuators include:

- Fuel injectors.
- Idle speed motors.
- Mixture control solenoids.
- Electric fan relays.
- EGR valves.

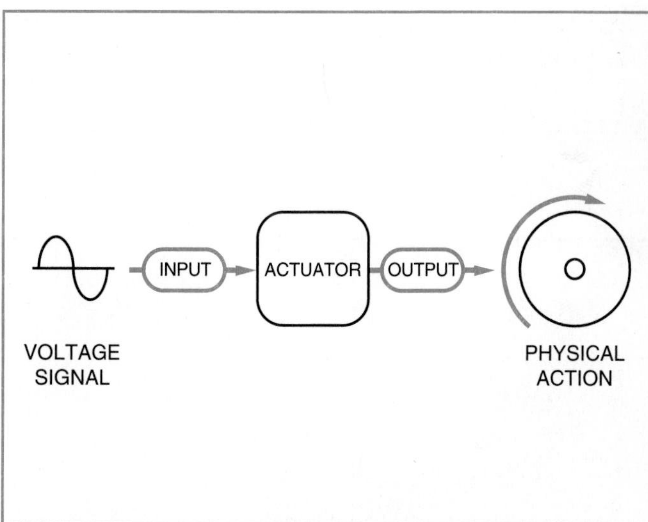

Figure 29-22. Actuators convert output signals from the computer into physical actions. Most actuators are motors, solenoids, or relays.

Fuel Injectors

A ***fuel injector*** is an actuator that meters the amount of fuel injected into the throttle body or cylinders, Figure 29-23. When the computer energizes an injector, a needle is lifted from its seat, allowing fuel to spray out. When the computer signal stops, spring pressure forces the needle valve closed. Fuel injector operation was explained in detail in Chapter 22.

Idle Speed Motor

The computer uses the ***idle speed motor*** to increase idle speed when the engine is under a heavy load, Figure 29-24. This actuator increases idle speed by moving the throttle lever. A load, such as an air conditioning compressor, can cause the engine to stall if the idle speed motor is not working properly.

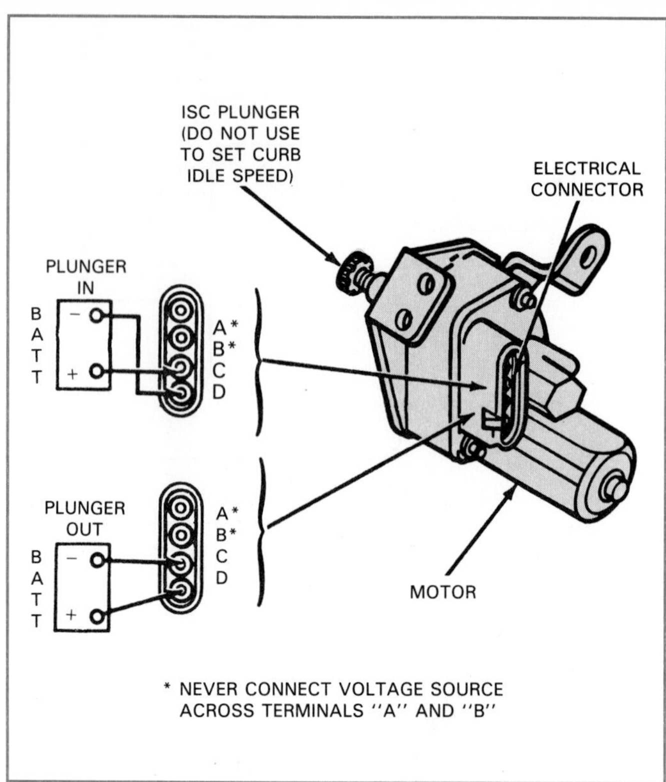

Figure 29-24. The plunger of the idle speed motor is extended or retracted automatically. The plunger position is determined by the load on the engine while idling. (Oldsmobile)

Mixture Control Solenoid

The ***mixture control solenoid*** is only used on engines equipped with carburetors. See Figure 29-25. When this actuator is energized, the solenoid moves the carburetor's metering rod in and out of the metering jet. The mixture control solenoid is typically cycled on and off several times a second.

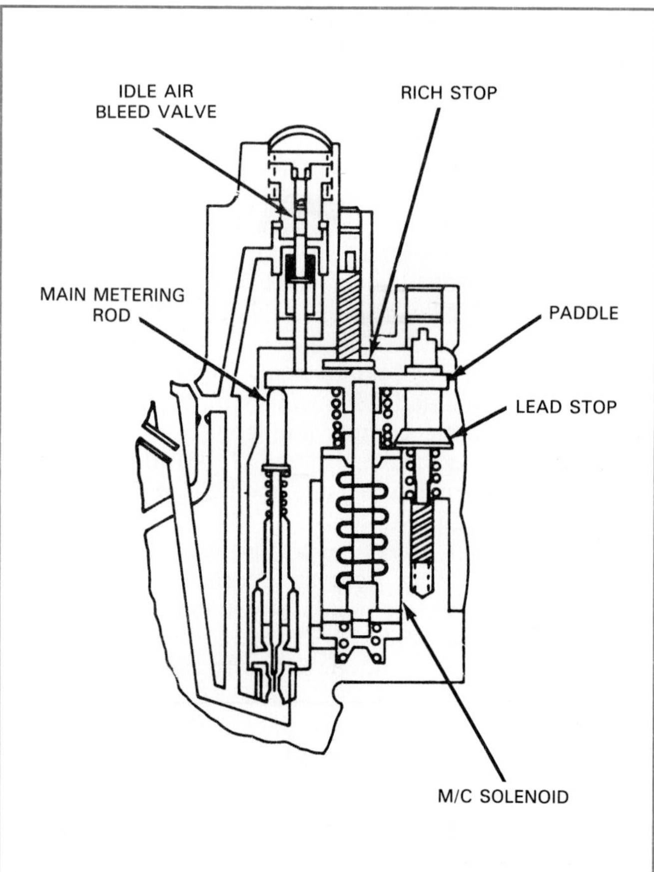

Figure 29-25. The mixture control solenoid is an actuator on carbureted engines. The mixture control solenoid is opened and closed at a rate of 10 times per second. (Cadillac)

Electric Fan Relay

When engine coolant reaches approximately 226°F (108°C), the ECU energizes the ***electric fan relay.*** This relay activates the electric fan motor. In some cases, fan relays are automatically activated each time the air conditioner is switched on.

EGR Valve

In many cases, the ECU controls a solenoid that switches vacuum to the EGR valve on and off. See Figure 29-26. In other systems, the ***EGR valve*** itself is controlled by the electronic control unit. The EGR valve illustrated in Figure 29-27 contains three solenoids that are controlled by

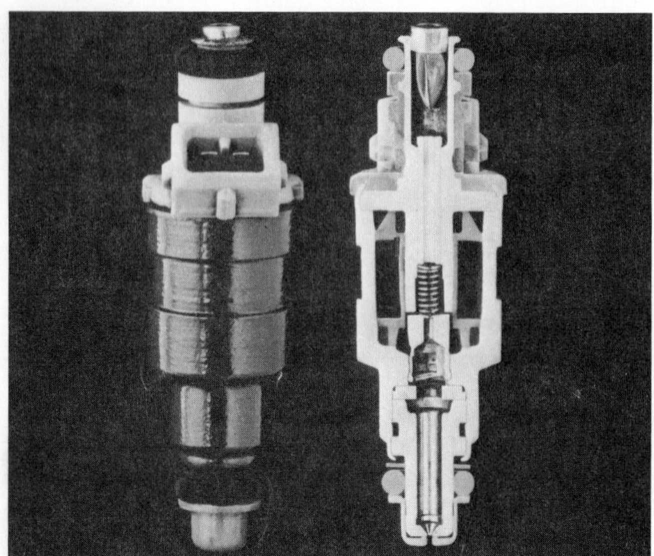

Figure 29-23. The fuel injector is considered an actuator. (Buick)

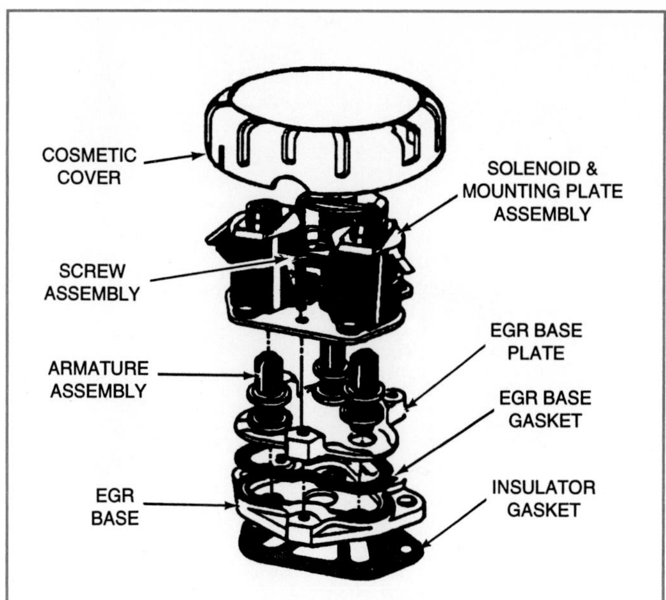

Figure 29-26. This EGR solenoid is an actuator. It is energized and de-energized by the ECU to control vacuum flow to the EGR valve. (General Motors)

the ECU to allow exhaust gases to flow into the intake manifold. This type of EGR valve operates independent of intake manifold vacuum.

Computer Control System Troubleshooting

Note: The balance of this chapter is designed to be used as a supplement to the manufacturer's service manual when troubleshooting and servicing automotive computer systems. It is not intended to replace the service manual. Computer control systems vary from manufacturer to manufacturer. Always consult the appropriate manual before attempting to service a computer system. Incorrect testing procedures can destroy delicate computer system components.

To effectively troubleshoot computer control systems, you must have a thorough understanding of basic computer control system operation. A logical approach must be taken when attempting to locate a problem. There are many sophisticated procedures involved in testing computer control systems. Consequently, it is not within the scope of this text to explain every possible testing method. Therefore, a general overview of the most common testing procedures is presented in the following sections. They are designed to provide you with the background information necessary to effectively use the diagnostic resources available when servicing computer control systems.

Even experienced technicians cannot expect to learn enough about computer control systems to solve problems on their own. Today's automotive technicians must rely on the information found in manuals, diagnostic charts, and other service publications when troubleshooting computer control systems.

Self-diagnostic Systems

To help the technician troubleshoot computer control systems, manufacturers have designed ***self-diagnostic systems*** into their products. These systems continuously monitor the operation of the sensors, the actuators, and the ECU. If an abnormal condition is detected, a trouble code is stored in the electronic control unit's memory.

Trouble Codes

When the electronic control unit's self-diagnostic system detects an abnormal operating condition, it places a ***trouble code*** in the unit's memory. Whenever a trouble code is stored in memory, a warning light is activated on the vehicle's dashboard, Figure 29-28. The "Service Engine Soon" or "Check Engine" light is often used for this purpose. The warning light alerts the driver to the fact that a problem exists and the vehicle requires service.

Activating Self-diagnostic Systems

If the warning light remains on when the engine is running, the technician can assume that there is at least one trouble code stored in the electronic control unit's memory.

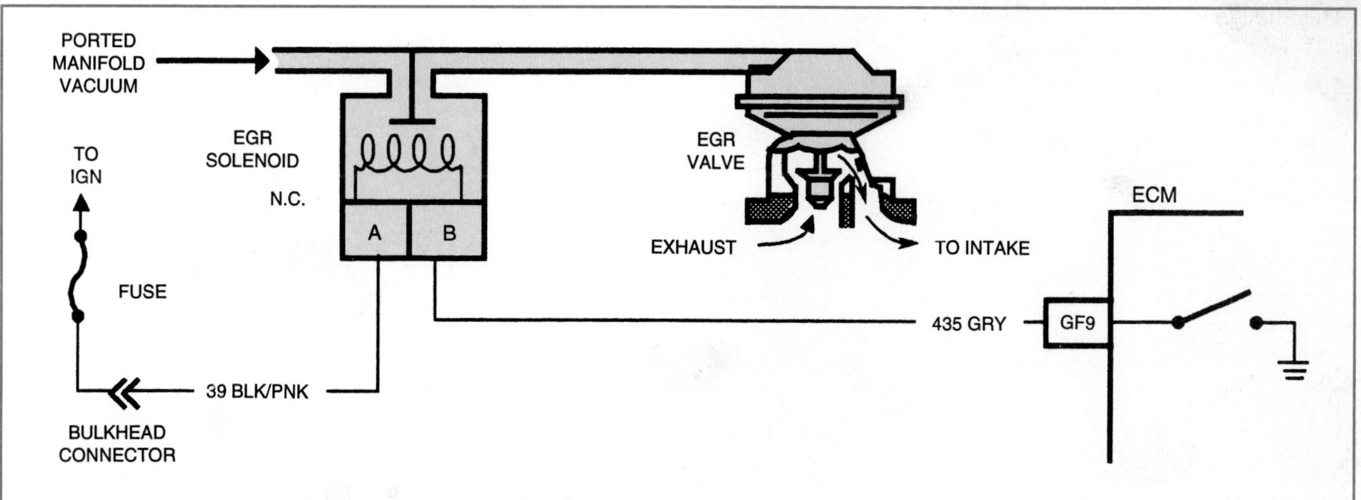

Figure 29-27. This EGR valve is an actuator. The computer decides when to energize the solenoids in the valve. The solenoids control exhaust gas flow through the orifices in the valve. (General Motors)

Figure 29-28. The "Check Engine" light or the "Service Engine Soon" light informs the driver that there is a problem in the computer control system.

In order to retrieve stored trouble codes, the technician must prompt the ECU's self-diagnostic system to release them from memory. Methods for extracting trouble codes vary. Some systems simply require connecting test leads across individual pins of a diagnostic link, Figure 29-29. Others require the use of special testing equipment. The most common methods of retrieving trouble codes from the computer's memory include the following:

- Switching a control mode selector on the side of the electronic control unit.
- Turning the ignition switch on and off several times in a specified period of time. See Figure 29-30
- Connecting a voltmeter to one or more terminals of the diagnostic test link.
- Grounding one of the terminals on the diagnostic test link.
- Connecting two specific diagnostic test link terminals.

Always consult an appropriate service manual to determine which method is correct for the vehicle at hand.

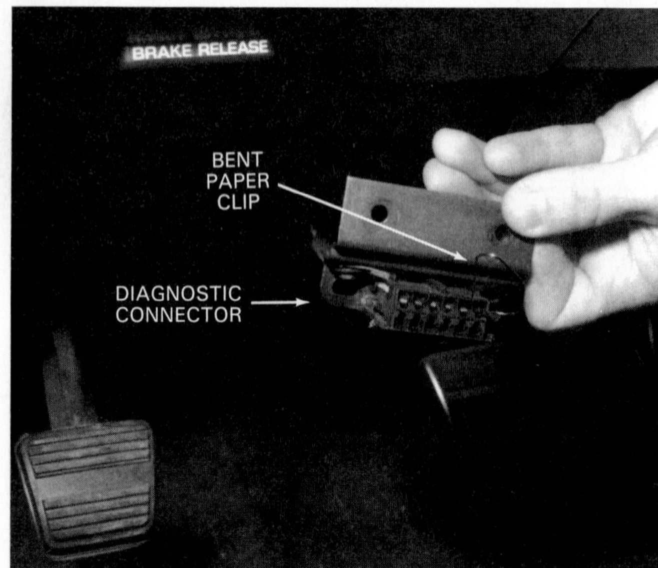

Figure 29-29. The pins in this diagnostic link can be jumped using a paper clip. Always refer to the manufacturer's service manual for specific instructions.

Figure 29-30. To trigger the computer to release trouble codes, the ignition switch on this vehicle must be cycled on and off a specified number of times in less than five seconds.

The wrong test hookup or grounding the incorrect terminals can destroy delicate computer system components.

Most vehicles are equipped with a ***diagnostic link*** that is used to check the computer control system at the factory. These multi-pin terminals also serve as connecting points for test equipment in the field. The diagnostic link can be located in various sections of the automobile, Figure 29-31. Some manufacturers refer to the diagnostic link as an assembly line diagnostic link (ALDL) or as a self-test connector.

Reading Trouble Codes

Once the self-diagnostic system has been activated, the computer will release the stored trouble codes. The codes can be displayed in several ways. Always refer to the service manual for information on how to read trouble codes for the system at hand. Some typical ways that these codes are displayed include:

- Counting the flashes of a warning light.
- Counting meter needle sweeps.
- Observing digital dash readout.

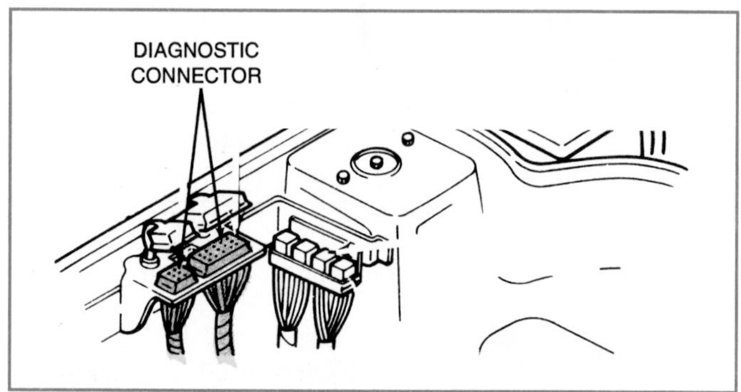

Figure 29-31. This diagnostic link is located in the vehicle's engine compartment. Note that there are two diagnostic connectors. (Chrysler)

Flashing Warning Light

A flashing warning light is one of the most common methods used to display trouble codes. After triggering the computer to release the trouble codes, the technician counts the flashes produced by a warning light (check engine or service engine soon) in the vehicle's dashboard. The number of flashes represents the trouble code stored in memory. For example, if the trouble code is 4, the light will flash four consecutive times. If there is more than one code in memory, there will be a 2 1/2 second pause before the second code is displayed. Some systems are set up to display two-digit trouble codes. In these systems, the light flashes the first digit, pauses for 1 1/2 seconds, and then flashes the second digit. Again, when more than one code is stored in memory, there will be a 2 1/2 second pause between codes. A two-digit trouble code is illustrated in Figure 29-32.

Analog Meter Sweeps

Some systems require the use of an analog voltmeter to retrieve trouble codes. The meter's needle "sweeps" for each digit of the trouble code. The code is counted in a manner similar to the flashing warning light. For example, if the trouble code is seven, the needle would sweep seven consecutive times. If the code is 14, the needle would sweep once, pause for approximately 1 1/2 seconds, and sweep four more times. See Figure 29-33.

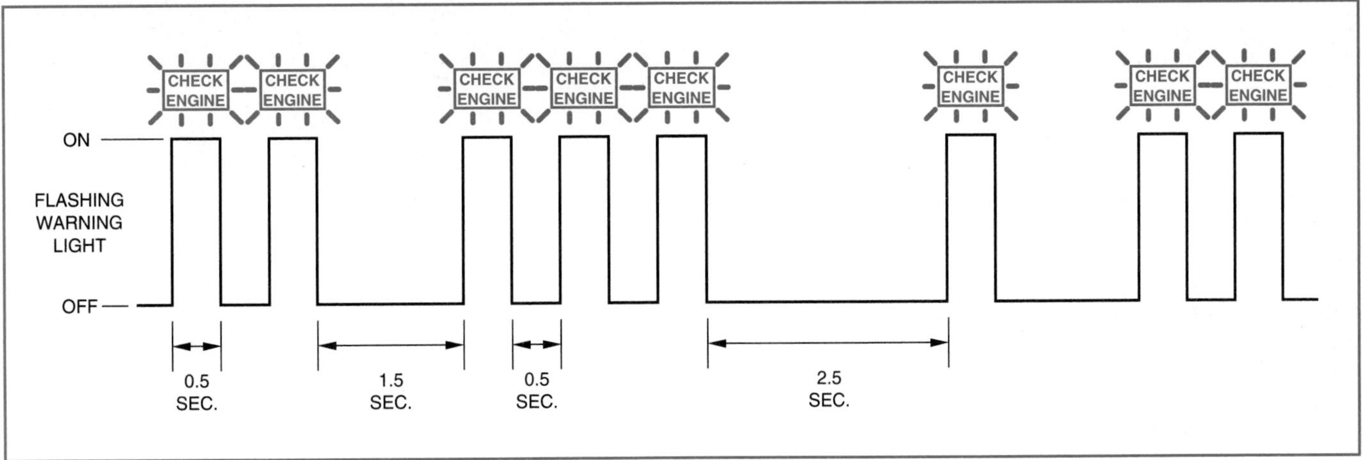

Figure 29-32. Trouble codes are often displayed with flashing warning lights. Note the 1.5 second pause between the digits of two-digit codes and the 2.5 second pause between each code. Trouble codes 23 and 12 are represented here.

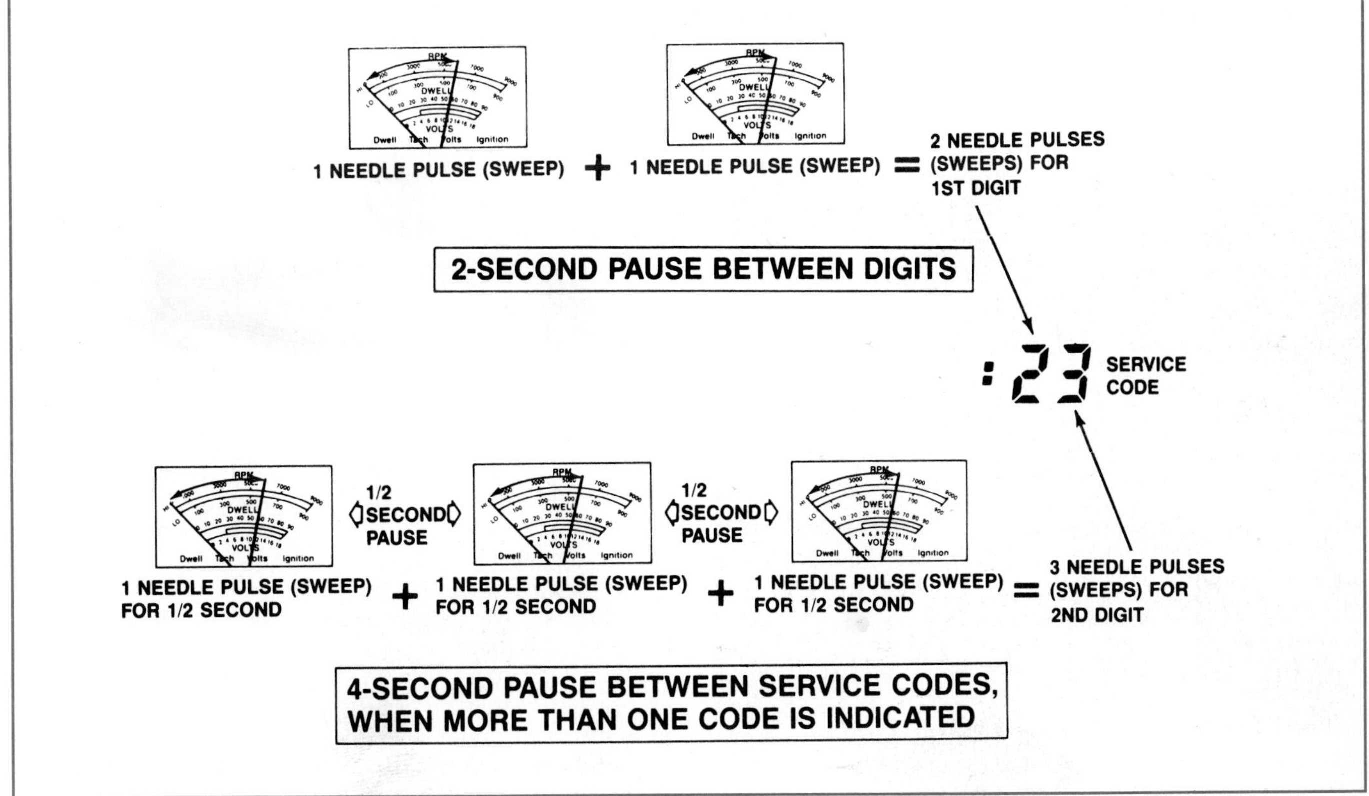

Figure 29-33. Reading trouble codes on an analog voltmeter. (Ford)

Digital Dash Readout

Some self-diagnostic systems display trouble codes directly onto a CRT screen in the vehicle's instrument panel. This method eliminates the possibility of error from misinterpreting flashing codes or analog meter sweeps. Most digital display systems are activated by simply pressing designated instrument controls simultaneously until an audible signal is detected.

Trouble Code Charts

Once the trouble codes have been obtained, you must compare the code numbers to a ***trouble code chart.*** The trouble code chart contains information about the meaning of each trouble code. This information can be used as a starting point in the troubleshooting process. Most trouble codes simply identify the circuit in which a problem has been detected. See Figure 29-34.

Scan Tools

A diagnostic ***scan tool*** is often used to retrieve trouble codes, Figure 29-35. Most scan tools convert the codes directly into a digital display. Scan tools do not have the ability to pinpoint problems within a circuit. However, many scan tools have the capability to record the signal values that the electronic control unit receives from the sensors. This eliminates the need to check each sensor individually.

FAULT CODE	DESCRIPTION OF FAULT CODE
11	No ignition reference signal detected during engine cranking.
13	No variation in MAP sensor signal is detected. No difference is recognized between the engine MAP reading and the barometric pressure reading at start up.
14	MAP sensor input below minimum acceptable voltage. MAP sensor input above maximum acceptable voltage.
15	No distance sensor signal detected during road load conditions.
17	Engine coolant temperature remains below normal operating temperature during vehicle travel (thermostat).
21	Neither rich nor lean condition is detected from the oxygen sensor input. Oxygen sensor input voltage maintained above normal operating range.
22	Coolant temperature sensor input above the maximum acceptable voltage. Coolant temperature sensor input below the minimum acceptable voltage.

Figure 29-34. Typical trouble code chart.

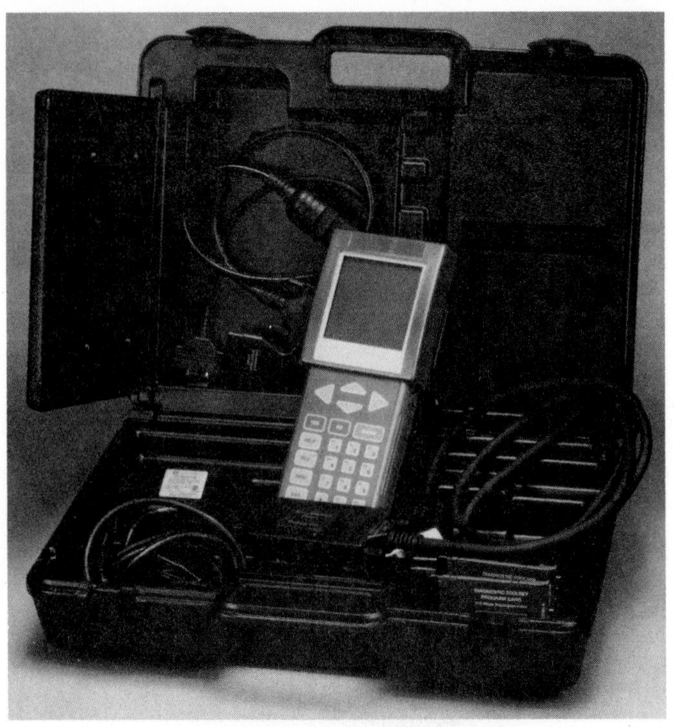

Figure 29-35. This hand-held scan tool can be used to retrieve trouble codes from a vehicle's computer system. (Toyota)

Diagnostic Analyzers

Modern ***diagnostic analyzers*** can be used to troubleshoot computer control systems. Most analyzers connect directly to the vehicle's diagnostic link. The analyzer uses information from the sensors and the electronic control unit to determine if the system is operating properly. Many analyzers have the ability to supply the technician with troubleshooting and repair instructions based on these values. Some systems are so sophisticated that they can communicate with a mainframe computer at a remote location. One type of diagnostic analyzer is illustrated in Figure 29-36.

OBD II Standards

Although most vehicles were equipped with self-diagnostic systems by the early 1980s, the California Air Resources Board (CARB) passed a law that required all vehicles sold in California to have on-board diagnostic systems by 1988. This law is known as ***OBD I.***

Currently, automakers are working to equip their vehicles with diagnostic systems that conform to ***OBD II*** standards. OBD II systems, which will be required by CARB and endorsed by the EPA, must be used in all new North American vehicles by the 1996 model year.

OBD II systems are designed to ensure that a vehicle's emission controls will operate properly for the life of the vehicle. Therefore, these systems will monitor all components that can measurably affect emissions. When a problem is detected, the system will trigger a malfunction indicator lamp (MIL) on the vehicle's instrument panel and place a diagnostic trouble code (DTC) in the electronic control unit's memory. The system will also record

Figure 29-36. In addition to retrieving trouble codes, this diagnostic analyzer can perform sophisticated computer system tests.

the various engine operating conditions present when the problem occurs.

All manufacturers will be required to use a common OBD II data link connector (DLC). Additionally, the same test modes and DTCs must be used by all manufacturers. Therefore, a generic scan tool can be used to read OBD II diagnostic trouble codes on any vehicle. The OBD II DTCs will be five digit codes instead of the two digit codes currently used in OBD I systems.

Using Diagnostic Information

Trouble codes indicate the circuit or area that is operating improperly. The trouble could be a shorted wire; a loose connection; or a faulty sensor, actuator, or control unit. Once a trouble code has been obtained, it is often necessary for the technician to perform a series of specialized tests to locate the faulty component(s) within a circuit. These tests are often referred to as pinpoint tests.

Although some systems require specialized testing equipment, many components can be checked using the following traditional test instruments:

- High impedance multimeter.
- Tachometer.
- Vacuum pump and gauge.
- Timing light.

The most common methods for testing computer control system components will be covered in the following sections. Always consult an appropriate service manual before attempting to troubleshoot any computer system component.

Visual Inspection

The first step in pinpointing a computer control system problem is to visually inspect the questionable circuits and all related components. Most computer system problems are caused by loose connections, leaking vacuum hoses, or physical damage. Check electrical connections for signs of oxidation and misalignment. Wiggling a connector may help locate an open circuit or an area of high resistance. Wiring problems should always be suspected when an open circuit or a faulty sensor is indicated by trouble codes. Examine all vacuum hoses for cracks and restrictions. Also, check hoses for proper connections. Improper hose routing can upset the operation of a computer control system.

Testing Wiring

Computer control circuit wiring can be checked with a standard ohmmeter. To test a wire, disconnect it at both ends of the circuit and measure its resistance with the meter. If the ends of the wire are far apart, the measurement can be taken by attaching one end of the wire to ground. Attach one meter lead to the ungrounded end of the wire and the other lead to a common ground. If the resistance measured in either of these tests is greater than 5 ohms, the wiring must be repaired, Figure 29-37.

An ohmmeter can also be used to check for a short circuit. Connect the ohmmeter to one end of the wire in question and the other lead to a good ground. If the resistance is less than several hundred thousand ohms, the wire may be shorted to ground.

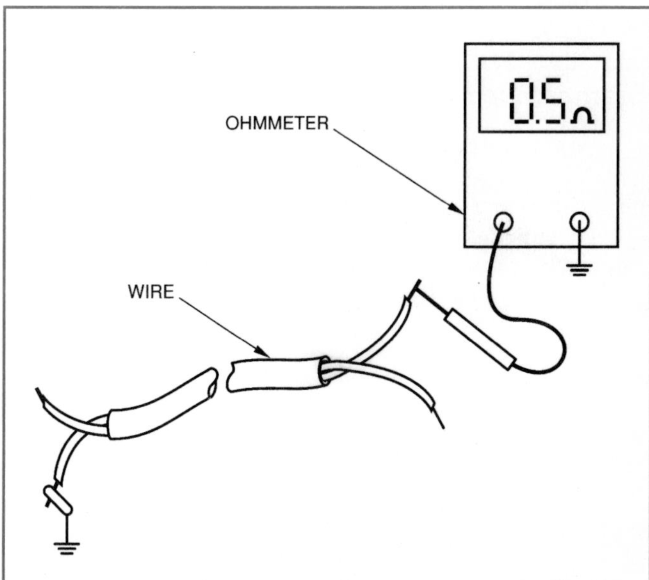

Figure 29-37. Wire condition can be checked with an ohmmeter. Make sure the wire is disconnected from the power source before connecting the meter.

Sensor Service

In most cases, sensor service consists of testing the questionable components and replacing them if they are faulty. An ohmmeter is often required to verify the internal resistance of passive sensors. A voltmeter is usually used to test the output of active sensors. All measured values should be compared with the manufacturer's specifications. Some systems require the use of a special scan tool, which extracts voltage and resistance values from the sensors. Never conduct tests on electronic and computerized components without consulting the appropriate service manual. Improper testing methods can destroy a sensor.

Oxygen Sensor Service

As previously mentioned, most oxygen sensors produce a small voltage signal, which is used by the electronic control unit to determine the oxygen content in the exhaust gas. When there is a high oxygen content in the exhaust gas (lean mixture), the sensor generates a low signal of approximately 0.10 volt. When the oxygen content is low (rich mixture), the sensor generates approximately 1.0 volt. Many manufacturers require a scan tool to measure oxygen sensor output. Some oxygen sensors can be checked using a digital voltmeter.

There are two common causes of oxygen sensor failure. The first is age. Under normal operating conditions, an oxygen sensor can be expected to last approximately 70,000 miles. The second and most common cause of oxygen sensor failure is contamination. Carbon, lead, silica, and oil can all contaminate an oxygen sensor. The buildup of these substances will eventually cause sensor failure.

If a vehicle experiences multiple oxygen sensor failures, check for sensor contamination, Figure 29-38. Carbon leaves a black, fluffy coating. ***Silica contamination*** appears in the form of a white powder. Engine oil usually leaves a brown residue on the oxygen sensor. The cause of the contamination should be eliminated before replacing sensor.

NOTE: The oxygen sensor is a very delicate device and should never be tested with an ohmmeter.

Engine Speed Sensor Service

When operating properly, the engine speed sensor generates a small voltage signal, which is proportional to the speed of the engine. If the sensor is faulty, the correct voltage will not be produced. A defective engine speed sensor can cause problems with the ignition system and prevent the engine from running, Figure 29-39. A voltage check is commonly recommended for the engine speed sensor. As the engine is cranked, a small voltage should be produced in the sensor. If the voltage is not within the manufacturer's specifications, the sensor must be replaced. Many manufacturers recommend checking the resistance of the sensor coil. The resistance should be within the recommended range.

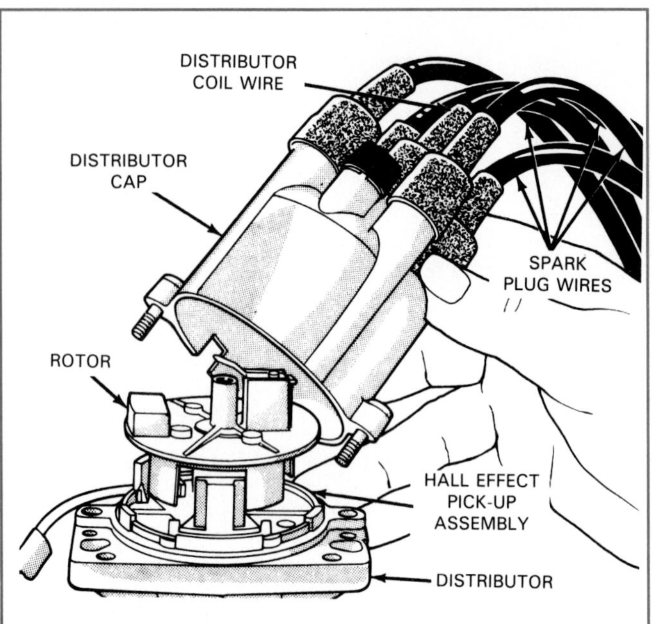

Figure 29-39. Make sure that the engine speed sensor is in good condition before checking resistance.

Knock Sensor Service

The knock sensor converts abnormal engine vibrations into electrical signals. A faulty knock sensor can adversely affect engine performance and fuel economy. If a trouble code indicates a problem in the knock sensor circuit, the sensor can be easily checked with a variable timing light. Connect the timing light as recommended and run the engine at a fast idle. Lightly tap the intake manifold or the engine block near the sensor and watch the ignition timing, Figure 29-40. If the sensor is working correctly, it should retard the timing to compensate for the knock. The amount of change in timing should be proportional to the strength of the tapping. The maximum amount of timing change should be approximately 10 degrees. As an alternate method, some manufacturers recommend the use of a voltmeter or an ohmmeter to check the sensor. If the sensor does not produce the required readings, it must be replaced.

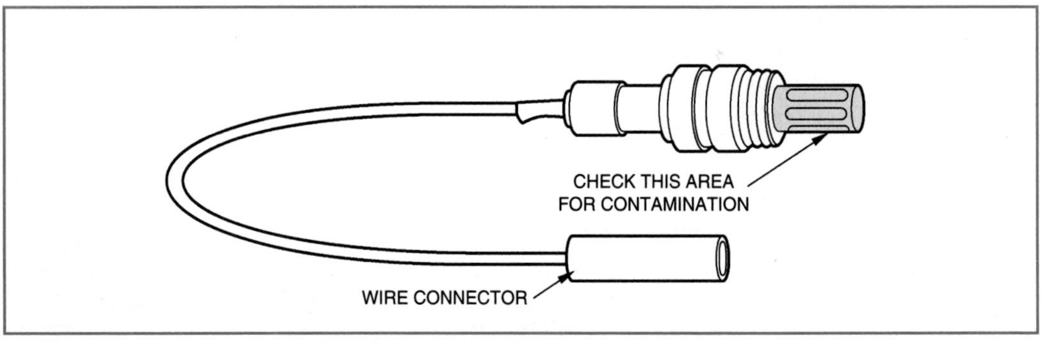

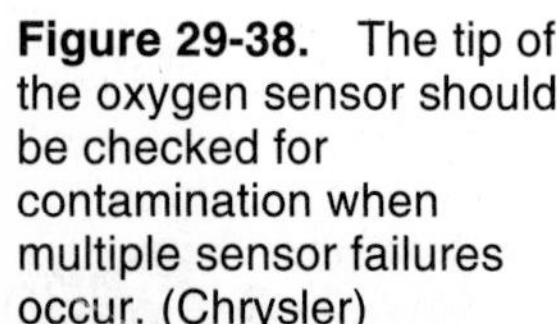

Figure 29-38. The tip of the oxygen sensor should be checked for contamination when multiple sensor failures occur. (Chrysler)

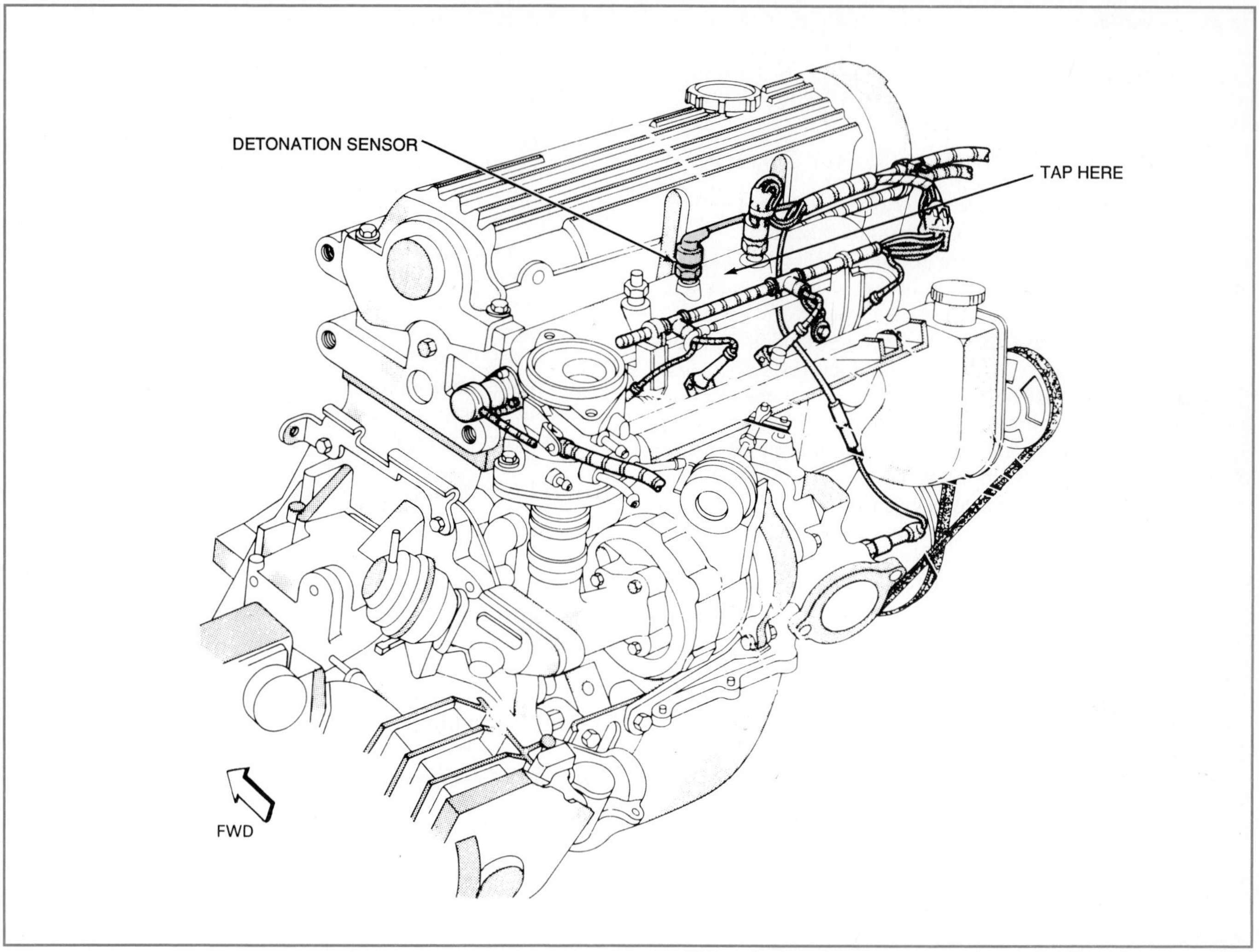

DETONATION SENSOR
TAP HERE
FWD

Figure 29-40. Knock sensor operation can be verified by tapping lightly on the engine block while observing ignition timing. The change in ignition timing should be proportional to the strength of the tapping. (Chrysler)

Coolant Temperature Sensor Service

The coolant temperature sensor varies its internal resistance as the operating temperature of the engine changes. The resistance is usually low when the engine is hot, and it climbs as the temperature decreases. Most manufacturers recommend checking the resistance of the sensor at different engine operating temperatures. If the resistance does not change or is not within recommended specifications, check the wiring for shorts or open circuits before condemning the sensor, Figure 29-41.

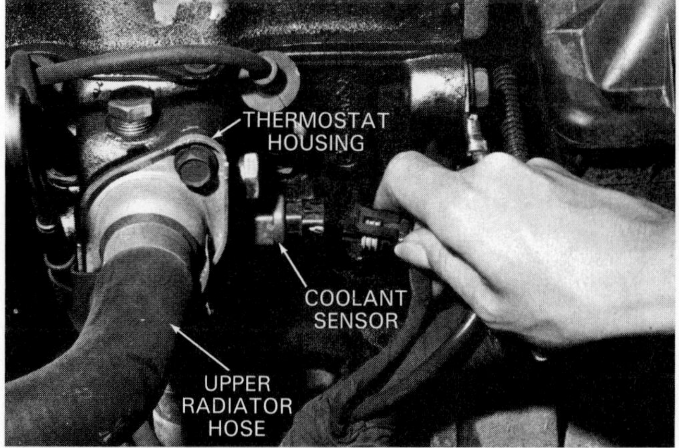

Figure 29-41. Disconnect the electrical connection at the coolant temperature sensor to check the sensor's resistance.

Manifold Air Temperature Sensor Service

The manifold air temperature sensor is similar to the coolant temperature sensor. Usually, the resistance of the sensor is checked with a scan tool or an ohmmeter. Always follow manufacturer's instructions when testing. A faulty air temperature can cause an excessively lean or rich fuel mixture.

Throttle Position Sensor Service

The throttle position sensor (TPS) changes its output signal in relation to the position of the throttle valve. The signal can range from 0.5 volts at idle to approximately 5 volts at wide open throttle. Many manufacturers recommend checking the TPS with a scan tool. Many of these tools are capable of displaying the signal voltage and the percentage of throttle opening. A voltmeter or an ohmmeter is sometimes recommended to check the operation of the TPS. A common test performed on a TPS involves slowly opening the throttle while monitoring changes in the output voltage. The voltage should rise smoothly and continuously in relation to the rate of throttle movement. If the voltage readout is erratic, the TPS must be replaced, Figure 29-42.

Manifold Absolute Pressure Sensor Service

The manifold absolute pressure sensor (MAP) responds to changes in manifold pressure (vacuum). An external vacuum source is often required when checking a MAP sensor. The sensor circuit's output voltage is usually checked while applying a specified amount of vacuum to the sensor. If the voltage at the recommended vacuum reading does not agree with the manufacturer's specifications, the sensor must be replaced. Always check vacuum hose connections when a faulty MAP sensor is suspected, Figure 29-43. Some manufacturers recommend taking resistance readings while applying vacuum to the sensor. A scan tool can also be used to check the manifold absolute pressure sensor. Using the scan tool usually eliminates the need for an external vacuum source. Always follow manufacturer's recommendations when using a scan tool.

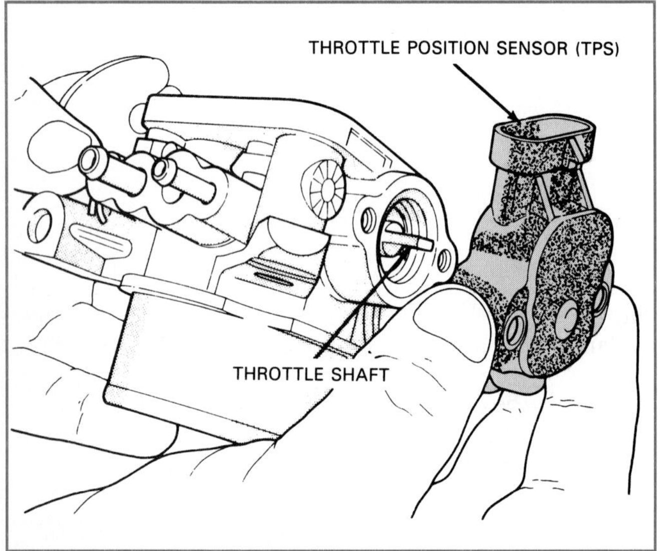

Figure 29-42. The throttle position sensor fits over one end of the throttle shaft and is easily replaced.

Airflow Sensor Service

Most airflow sensors vary their resistance in relation to the amount of air entering the engine. The resistance of some units can be checked with an ohmmeter and compared to the manufacturer's specifications. Some manufacturers recommend checking the sensor circuit output voltage using a digital voltmeter. Always check areas around the sensor for possible air leaks. An air leak around the sensor can cause false readings. Some airflow sensors must be tested with a scan tool. If a flap airflow sensor is used, make sure that the flap is pivoting freely. When checking a mass airflow sensor, make sure that the wire screen is free from obstructions that could restrict airflow.

Switching Sensor Service

Switching sensors are usually checked with an ohmmeter. If a switching sensor can be manually operated, it should be opened and closed while checking the component's resistance. These sensors should have high resistance when open and no resistance when closed. Switching sensors that use pressure sensitive elements are usually tested by checking resistance readings under specified operating conditions.

Checking Reference Voltage

Passive sensors will not operate properly if they are not receiving an acceptable reference voltage from the electronic control unit. When testing signal-modifying sensors, some manufacturers recommend that the reference voltage be verified.

To check reference voltage, connect a voltmeter to the sensor's input lead, Figure 29-44. The voltage reading should equal the value recommended by the manufacturer. A low voltage reading can be caused by an area of high resistance, such as an open circuit or a corroded connector. If wiring proves to be adequate, a faulty ECU could be the problem. Always consult the service manual for recommended procedures before attempting to measure the reference voltage.

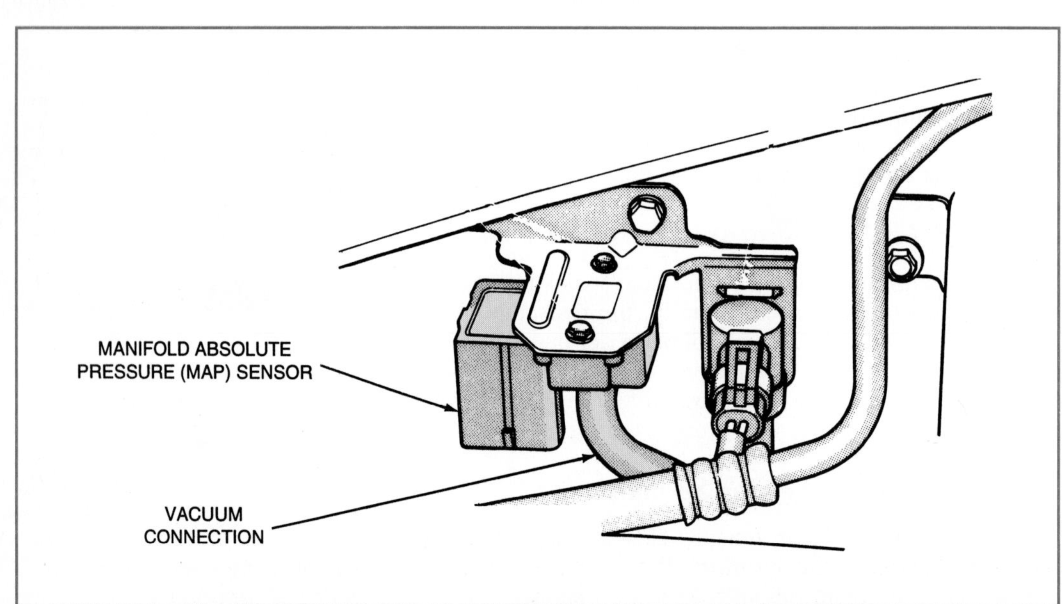

Figure 29-43. When a faulty MAP sensor is suspected, always check the vacuum connections before condemning the sensor.

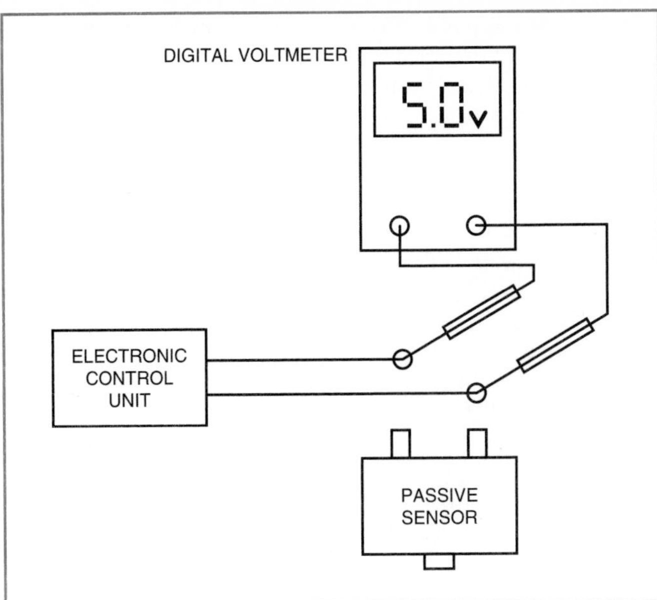

Figure 29-44. The reference voltage can be checked with a voltmeter. Make sure the sensor wiring is in good condition.

Actuator Service

Actuators can also cause problems in a computer control system. If an actuator is not operating correctly, the computer cannot control the system properly. Therefore, when a trouble code points to a specific circuit, it is important to verify the operation of the actuators in the circuit. Because actuators are either relays, motors, or solenoids, most actuator tests are fairly standard.

Output Cycling Tests

Some systems with self-diagnostic capabilities have the ability to cycle the computer's output signals on and off. These signals trigger the actuators. Because actuators convert electrical signals into physical movements, most can be seen or heard when cycled on and off.

Standard Actuator Tests

In many systems, individual actuator tests must be performed to verify proper operation. Most units can be checked by measuring their internal resistance with an ohmmeter. If the value measured does not fall within the range specified by the manufacturer, the actuator must be replaced.

Some manufacturers recommend using jumper wires to apply an external voltage source (often battery voltage) to the actuator. If the component functions, you can assume that it is working properly.

NOTE: Always follow manufacturer's recommendations when testing actuators. Improper testing methods or excessive voltage can severely damage these units. Always disconnect the actuator from the ECU prior to performing any testing procedures.

Electronic Control Unit Troubleshooting

The electronic control unit is one of the most trouble-free components on today's automobile. Therefore, all other potential trouble spots should be tested before condemning the ECU. Always check the sensors and actuators before attempting to troubleshoot the electronic control unit. Check the wiring to the control unit for shorts and opens. To check for proper connections, unplug and reconnect all connectors going into the ECU.

Most manufacturers require the use of special testing equipment to verify ECU operation. Some units, however, can be tested with ordinary voltmeters and ohmmeters. Some self-diagnostic systems have the ability to locate ECU problems and to place appropriate trouble codes in memory.

Many technicians still depend on the process of elimination when servicing computer control systems. If all other system components are working properly, they are forced to assume that the electronic control module is causing the problem. This method is not recommended and should only be used as a last resort.

The electronic control module is a very delicate and expensive component. Always follow manufacturer's recommendations when testing and servicing these units.

NOTE: Most electronic control units are sensitive to electrostatic discharge. The static electricity generated by sliding across a seat can destroy an ECU or a PROM chip. To reduce the risk of damage due to static electricity, always touch a good ground before handling the ECU or related electronic components, Figure 29-45. A grounding strap can also be worn to protect sensitive electronic parts.

Servicing the ECU

The electronic control unit, like most sensors, is not serviceable as a unit. When an ECU is found to be defective, it must be replaced. The computer's programmable read only memory chip (PROM), however, is removable and is usually reused when a new electronic control unit is installed. When removing the ECU from a vehicle, always turn the ignition key off. As an added precaution, the battery should be disconnected. The computer can be removed from a vehicle by simply disconnecting all wires from the unit and unbolting it from its mounting brackets.

When changing an ECU, always replace it with an identical unit. Manufacturers produce many different types of electronic control units. Always record the faulty unit's identification number. The year and model of the vehicle you are working on may not provide the information required to obtain an exact replacement.

Figure 29-45. Always touch a good ground or put on an approved grounding strap before handling components that are sensitive to static electricity. Some components are labeled with a warning similar to the one shown above. (General Motors)

Changing a PROM

When replacing an electronic control unit, the original PROM chip is often installed in the new unit. This is because the information stored in PROM is very specific to the vehicle being repaired.

A special tool should always be used when handling a PROM chip. Never touch a PROM chip directly. Oil from hands and fingers can have an adverse effect on the operation of the chip. Before removing the chip, note its position. Many manufacturers mark the PROM to insure proper installation. Gently pull the PROM chip from its socket.

Before installing a PROM into a new unit, make sure it is positioned correctly. If the PROM is installed incorrectly, it will be destroyed, Figure 29-46.

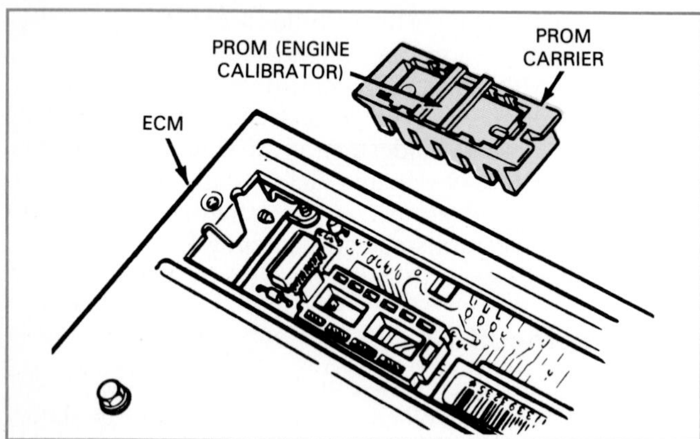

Figure 29-46. When replacing a PROM, make sure it is installed correctly. If the PROM is installed backwards, it will be destroyed.

To install a PROM, simply press it into the correct socket in the ECU. A blunt, non-metallic object should be used to avoid touching the chip with your fingers. Gently press on the corners of the PROM to make sure it is seated properly.

Reprogramming a Flash Memory

As mentioned previously, a flash memory, or erasable PROM, is used in some late-model vehicles. If necessary, this type of memory can be reprogrammed to correct engine operating variables. In most cases, a special service tool and a computer must be used to reprogram the flash memory. However, the flash memory should never be reprogrammed unless changes are recommended by the manufacturer. Tampering with the flash memory may have a negative effect on exhaust emission levels and fuel efficiency. Additionally, unauthorized changes may void the manufacturer's warranty.

Chapter 29–Review Questions

1. Automotive computers are used to control the:
   (A) ignition system.
   (B) fuel system.
   (C) exhaust emissions.
   (D) All of the above.
2. Sensors convert physical actions into electrical signals. True or False?
3. _____ convert output signals from the computer into physical actions.
4. The three stages of computer control system operation include the ______ stage, the ______ stage, and the ______ stage.
5. Active sensors convert physical conditions into electrical signals. True or False?
6. The oxygen sensor monitors the amount of oxygen in the _____ gases.
7. When a computer is receiving inputs from the sensors, processing these inputs, and sending output signals to the actuators, the system is said to be operating in:
   (A) the processing mode.
   (B) closed loop.
   (C) open loop.
   (D) None of the above.
8. A(n) _____ sensor converts engine knocking and pinging into an electrical signal.
9. Passive sensors rely on a _____ voltage that is supplied by the ECU.
10. The throttle position sensor monitors the position of the _____ _____.
11. The electronic control unit uses signals from the throttle position sensor to control:
    (A) ignition timing.
    (B) fuel delivery.
    (C) EGR valve position.
    (D) None of the above.
12. The basic sections of the electronic control unit include the:
    (A) arithmetic/logic section.
    (B) input section.
    (C) memory section.
    (D) All of the above.
13. Name the three types of memory commonly used in automotive computers.
14. Self-diagnostic systems continuously monitor the operation of the sensors, the actuators, and the electronic control unit.
15. Name three ways that trouble codes can be displayed.
16. The first step in pinpointing a computer control system problem is to test wiring with a digital ohmmeter. True or False?
17. Name two common causes of oxygen sensor contamination.
18. Most actuators can be tested by measuring their:
    (A) voltage.
    (B) current.
    (C) resistance.
    (D) capacitance.
19. Special test equipment is often needed to verify proper control unit operation. True or False?
20. The only part of the electronic control unit that can be serviced in the field is the:
    (A) power supply.
    (B) PROM.
    (C) RAM.
    (D) output section.

Chapter 30
Exhaust Systems

After studying this chapter, you will be able to:

❍ List the components of the exhaust system.
❍ Explain the purpose of each component of the exhaust system.
❍ Describe what backpressure is and how it affects the operation of the engine.

Exhaust Systems

The ***exhaust system*** of an engine, Figures 30-1 and 30-2, is designed to conduct the burned gases (exhaust) to the rear of the car and into the air. This system also serves to silence the sounds of combustion.

Major parts of the exhaust system include the exhaust manifold, exhaust pipe, catalytic converters, muffler, and tailpipe (tail spout). Also, V-type engines have a crossover pipe and an intermediate pipe (connecting the crossover pipe to the muffler). Sometimes a resonator, a secondary silencing device, is installed. If the exhaust valve were closed during the entire combustion process, there would not be a need for the muffler and resonator.

Catalytic converters have been used in the exhaust systems of most cars since 1975. They are emission control devices that contain chemically treated substances that convert harmful emissions into harmless carbon dioxide and water vapor.

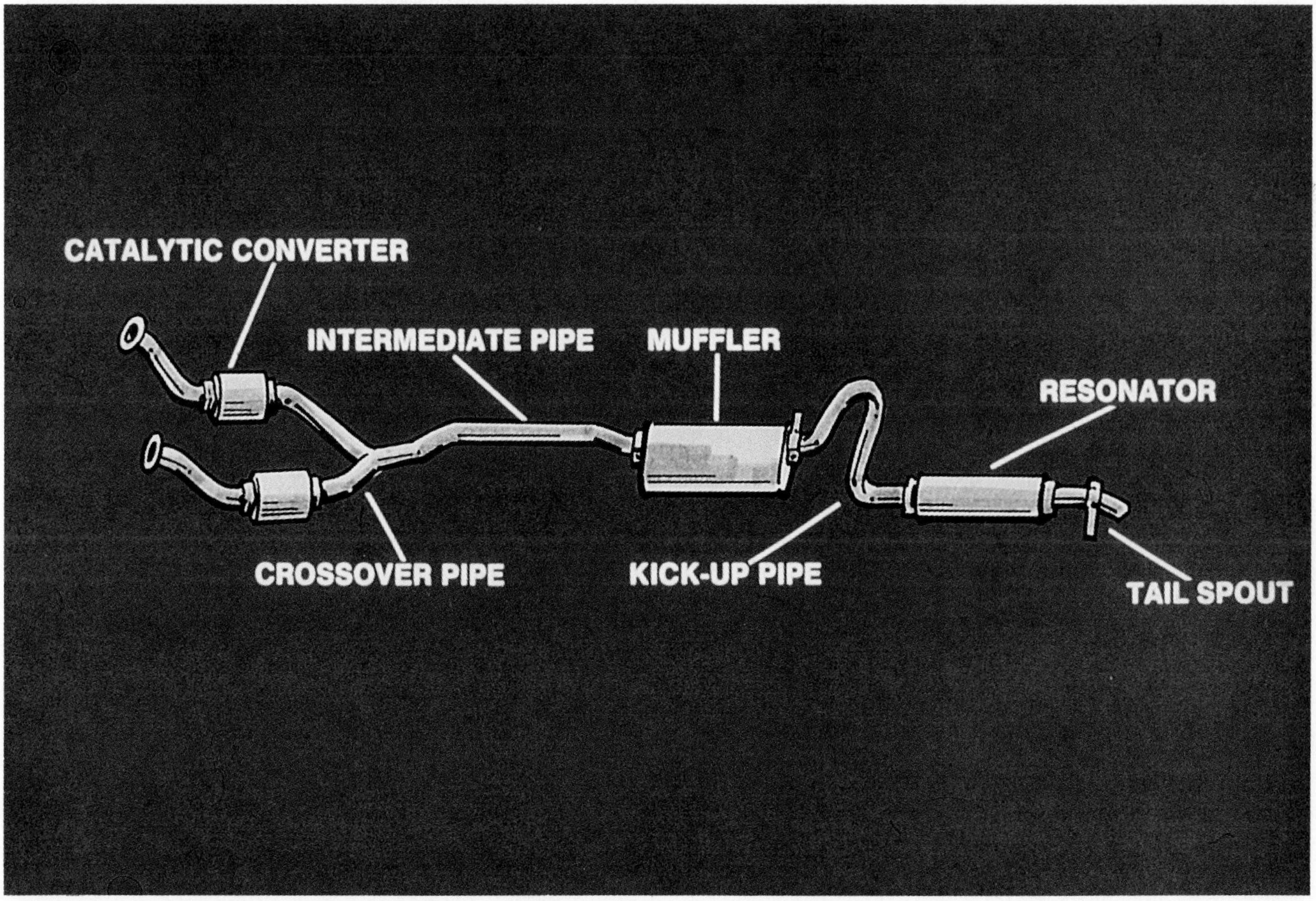

Figure 30-1. Illustration shows the location of common exhaust system components. (Walker)

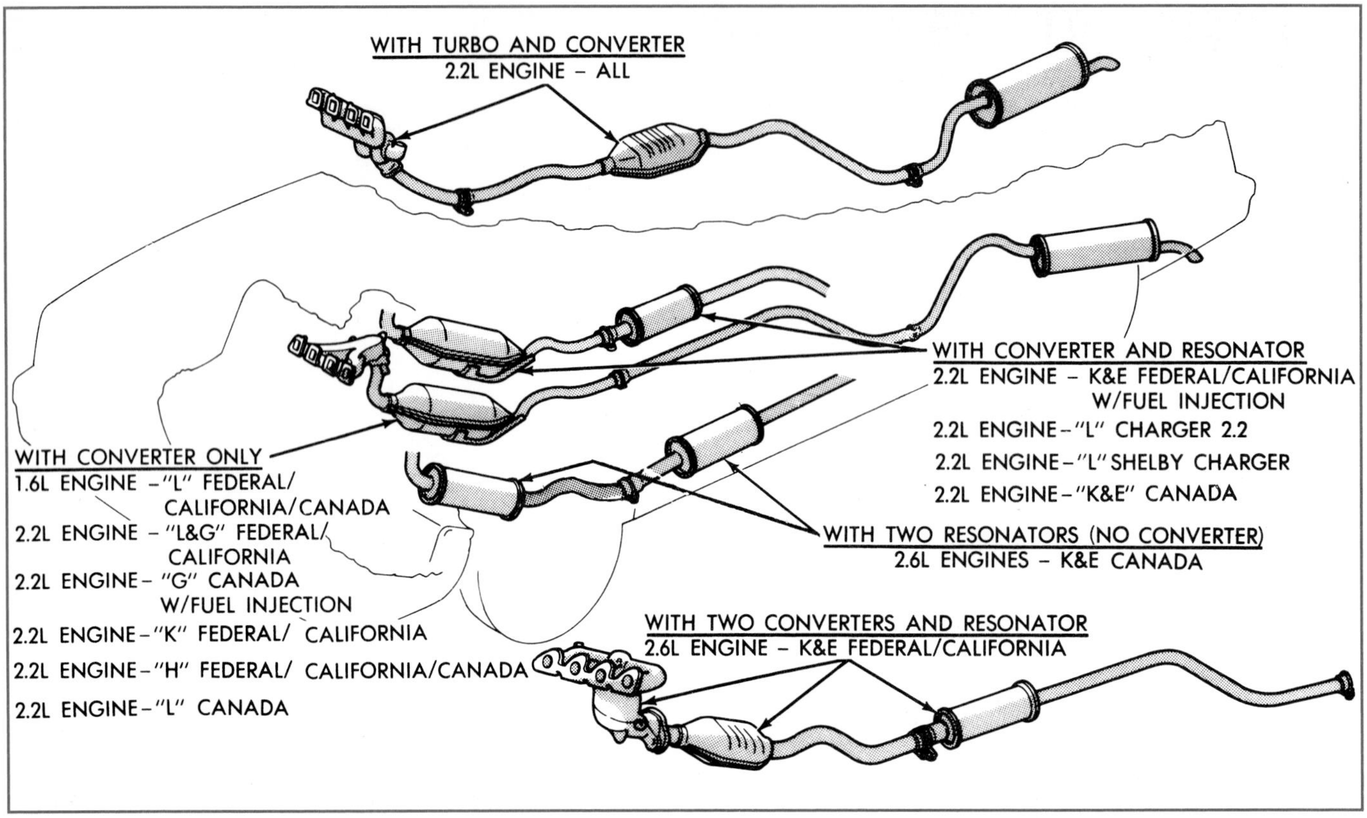

Figure 30-2. The type of exhaust system depends on the engine size, if it is normally aspirated or turbocharged, and where the car will be sold. (Chrysler)

Exhaust Manifold

Exhaust manifolds are of many types. On an inline engine, the manifold is bolted to the side of the engine. On V-type engines, separate manifolds are used for each side of the "V," Figures 30-3 and 30-4. In V-type applications, a separate exhaust system may be provided for each side of the engine, or the two sides may be joined together by means of a ***crossover pipe.***

Regardless of the design, the passages forming the manifold are made as large in size as practical. This reduces the resistance to the flow of the burned gases. Included in the design of the exhaust manifold on some engines is the ***manifold heat valve.*** This, together with special passages,

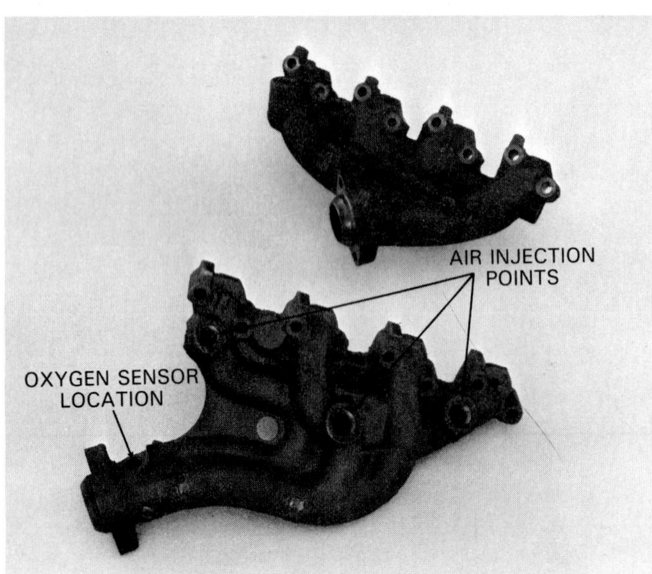

Figure 30-3. Exhaust manifolds of a V-type engine. Air is injected into the exhaust manifold on some engines. This dilutes the exhaust gases and provides the needed air for catalytic converter operation. (Ford)

Figure 30-4. Cutaway view of an exhaust port and manifold. (Ford)

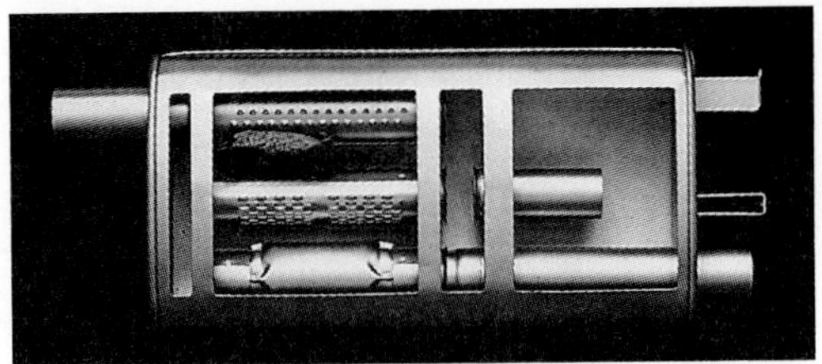

Figure 30-5. Cutaway view of a muffler. Note that pipes are not connected to one another. (Walker)

conducts heat to the intake manifold to improve the vaporization of the fuel.

Mufflers

In order to reduce the noise of the combustion of an engine, exhaust gases from the engine are passed through a ***muffler,*** Figure 30-5. The muffler is designed so that the gases expand slowly.

Muffler design must be such that there is the least amount of backpressure developed. ***Backpressure*** prevents free flow of the exhaust gases from the engine. As a result, not all of the burned gases will be forced from the cylinders. Remaining exhaust gases dilute the incoming air/fuel mixture and engine power is reduced. The exhaust of a car passes into the exhaust manifold, Figures 30-3 and 30-4. Then, the gas passes through the exhaust pipe into the muffler. From the muffler, it passes into the tailpipe and from there into the atmosphere. Also, some cars use resonators in the system, Figure 30-2.

A certain amount of room for expansion and cooling of the exhaust gas is designed into the exhaust manifold and exhaust pipe. They provide from two to four times the exhaust volume of a single cylinder of the engine. Additional expansion is provided for in the muffler.

Catalytic Converters

The ***catalytic converter*** is installed to reduce hydrocarbons (HC), carbon monoxide (CO), and nitrous oxides (NO_X). The catalytic converter does this by operating at temperatures in excess of 1500°F (815.5°C). The high temperature burns the unwanted byproducts of combustion. This is the reason heat shields are installed at various points around the car, Figure 30-6. Some catalysts are honeycomb shaped, Figure 30-7. Other catalysts use beads, Figure 30-8. If leaded fuel is used, it will clog the catalyst. This will create an excessive amount of backpressure in the exhaust system. A ***restrictor*** is placed in the fuel filler tube, Figure 30-9, that prevents a larger diameter fuel nozzle (leaded gasoline) from being inserted.

Muffler Design

The design of the muffler varies from one manufacturer to another. One is the straight-through type. See Figure 30-10A. In this design, a straight path for the gases extends from the front to the rear of the unit. With the straight through muffler, a centrally located pipe with holes is provided. Surrounding this pipe is a sheet metal shell three times the diameter of the pipe. In some cases, the space between the outer shell and inner pipe is open. In other cases, it is filled with steel wool or some other heat-resistant sound-deadening material.

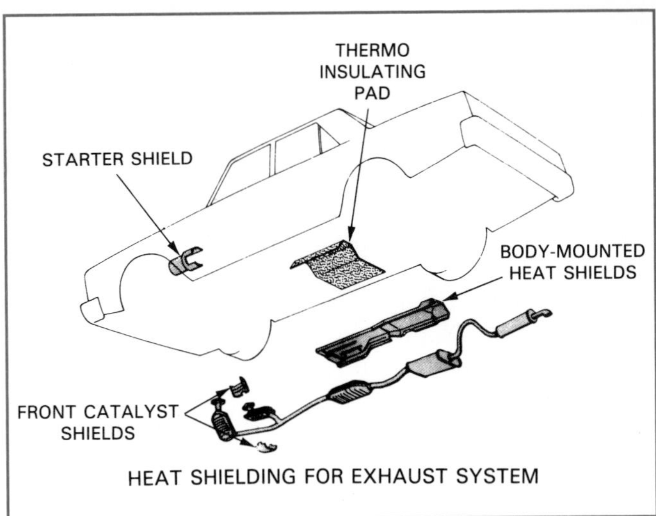

Figure 30-6. Heat shields prevent higher-than-normal temperatures, which are created by the catalytic converter, from being transferred into the passenger compartment. Undercoating material should never be applied to heat shields. (Chrysler)

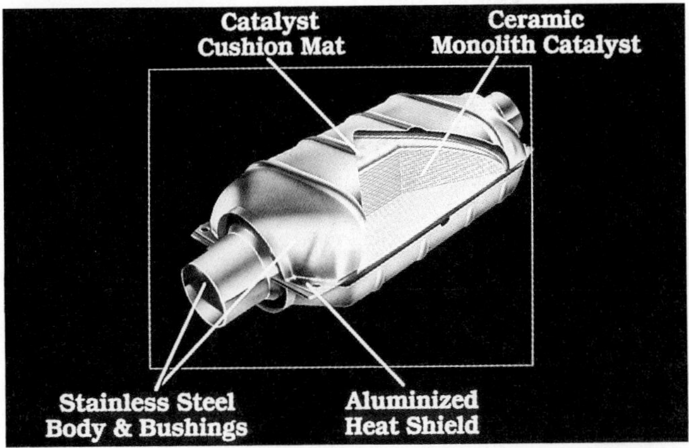

Figure 30-7. A honeycomb monolith catalytic converter. If leaded fuel is used, passages will become plugged. (Walker)

Figure 30-8. Some catalysts use beads or pellets instead of a honeycomb. (Universal Oil Products)

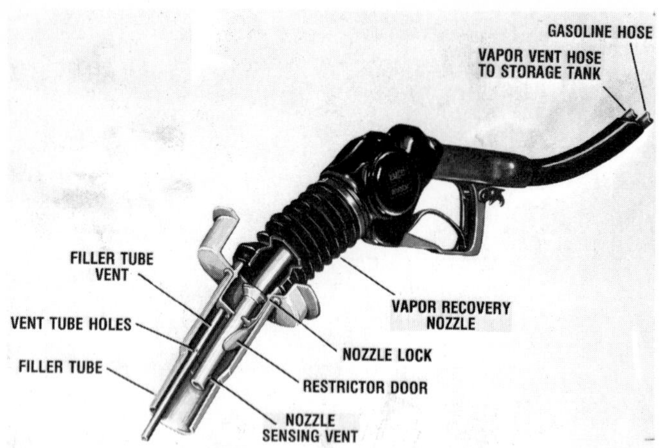

Figure 30-9. Catalytic-equipped cars have a restrictor in the fuel filler tube. This prevents the accidental use of leaded fuels, which have a larger diameter fuel nozzle.

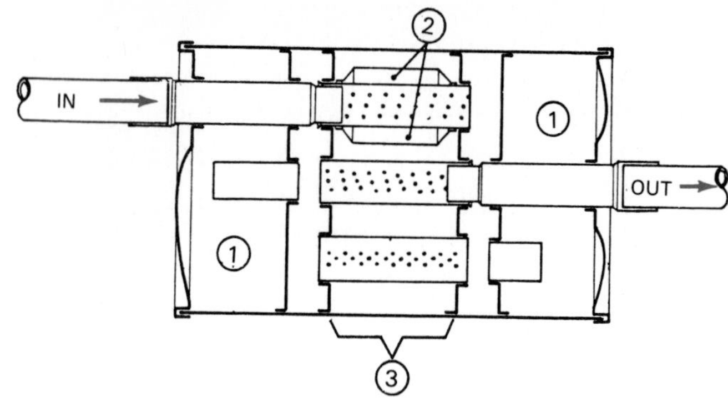

Figure 30-11. Reverse-flow muffler. 1–Helmholtz tuning chambers. 2–High frequency tuning chamber. 3–Reversing crossover passages. (Maremont)

Another type of muffler reverses the flow of the exhaust gases, Figure 30-10B, and has the advantage of saving space. The double shell and two shell designs are other forms of modern mufflers.

In order to reduce the noise of the exhaust below that attained by a single muffler, many systems are equipped with two mufflers in each line, Figure 30-2. This design is needed on cars with a long wheelbase and a high output engine. The extra unit is called a resonator.

The design of a muffler is precise. The size and shape of the different chambers will affect the noise level and backpressure. In Figure 30-11, chambers marked 1 are known as ***Helmholtz tuning chambers.*** These areas within the muffler are precisely tuned. Chamber volume, tuning tube size, and temperature of the gases in the chamber are taken into account.

If the exhaust pipe is the right length and diameter, the frequency of the explosions can cause a resonance in that pipe. This is the same as blowing across the neck of a bottle. The Helmholtz tuning chambers can be designed to absorb resonance and reduce the noise level of the exhaust system.

The high-frequency tuning chamber, marked 2 in Figure 30-11, reduces the sound level of the high frequencies present in the exhaust system. (Helmholtz chambers primarily affect low-frequency sounds.) The high frequencies can be generated by exhaust flow past a sharp edge in the exhaust system, venturi noise in the carburetor, and friction between the forceful exhaust flow and the pipes. High frequencies show up as a whistling noise. Therefore, each hole in the inner tube of the high-frequency tuning chamber acts as a small tuning tube.

The reversing unit crossover shown at 3 in Figure 30-11 is most effective in removing or reducing the mid-range frequencies missed by the high- and low-frequency chambers. The amount of crossover is determined by the size and number of holes in the adjacent tubes.

Backpressure

In Figure 30-12, the loss in engine power due to ***backpressure*** from the exhaust system is charted. Note that as the speed of the car increases, backpressure increases. For a given car speed, the loss in power increases very fast with the increase in backpressure. For example, with 2 lb. backpressure at 70 mph, the power loss is 4 hp. When the backpressure is 4 lb., power loss has increased by 8 hp.

Also, fuel consumption is increased as backpressure increases. This is shown in Figure 30-13.

Care must be used so that there are no kinks or flattened areas in the exhaust system that would obstruct the

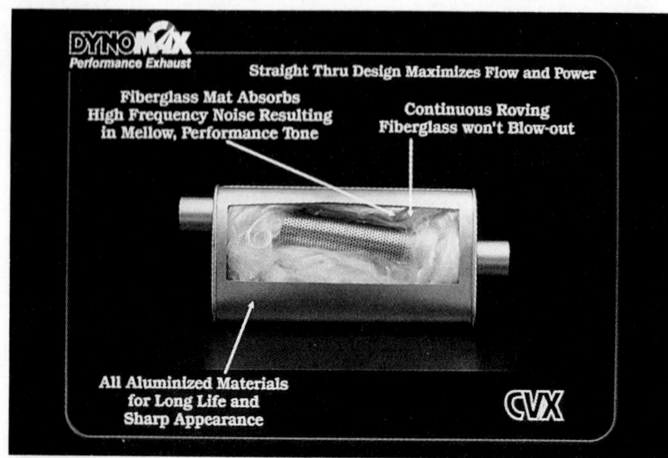

A

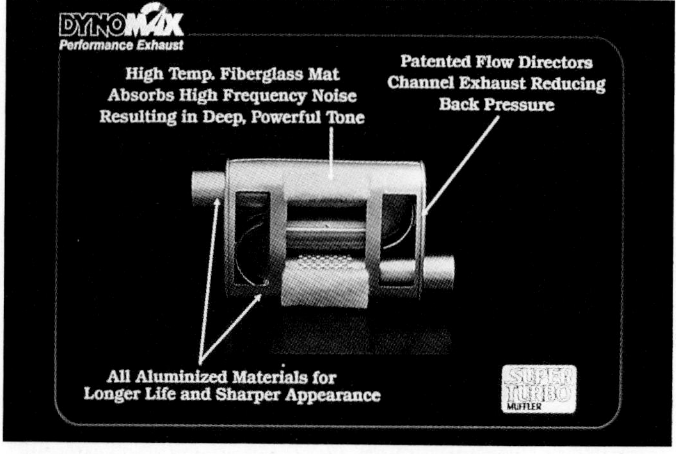

B

Figure 30-10. A–Although straight-through mufflers reduce backpressure, they are the noisiest of all muffler designs. B–Reverse-flow mufflers are quieter than straight-through mufflers and require less space for installation. (Walker)

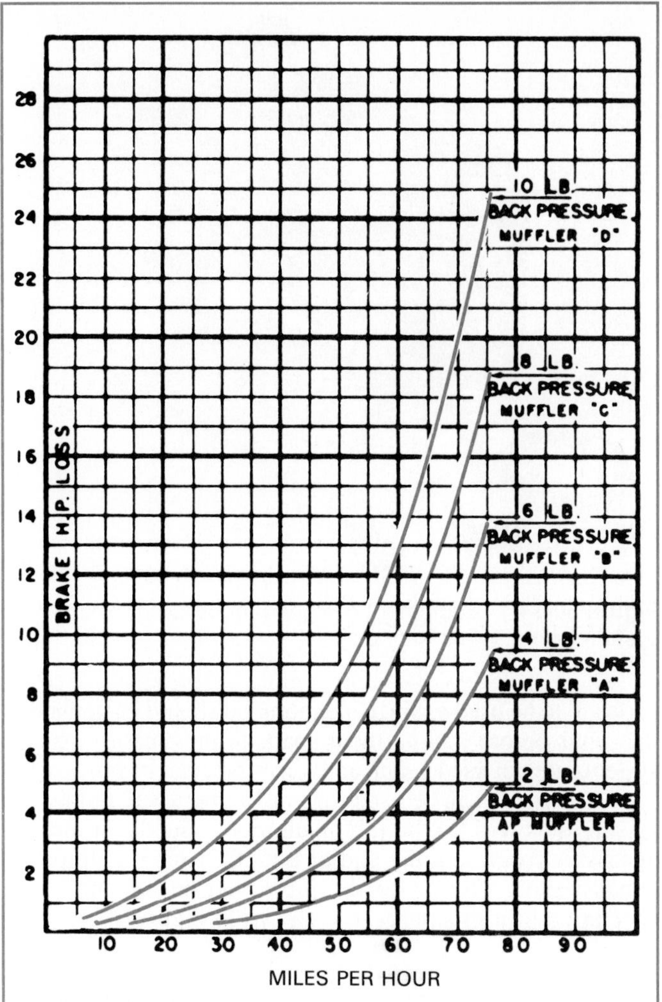

Figure 30-12. Loss in horsepower due to backpressure.

free flow of the exhaust gases. Any obstruction caused by internal blockage will reduce power and fuel economy. This could be caused by:

- A defective EGR valve/system.
- A clogged catalytic converter.
- A collapsed muffler.
- Frozen heat control valve.
- Kinks in exhaust pipes.

Exhaust System Corrosion

Mufflers, tailpipes, and exhaust pipes wear out due to ***corrosion.*** External rusting is due to rain, snow, and humidity. In some northern states, this external rusting is speeded up by the use of salt on icy roads.

The greatest amount of corrosion occurs inside the exhaust system, mostly in the muffler. This is because a gallon of water is formed for every gallon of fuel burned. Acids are also formed in the combustion process. The acids and water combine to quickly rust the inside of the exhaust system.

Until the exhaust system has reached operating temperature, much of the moisture will condense on the cool surfaces and collect in the muffler. Then as the muffler becomes hot, the moisture will evaporate. On short drives, the muffler will not get hot enough and corrosion will occur.

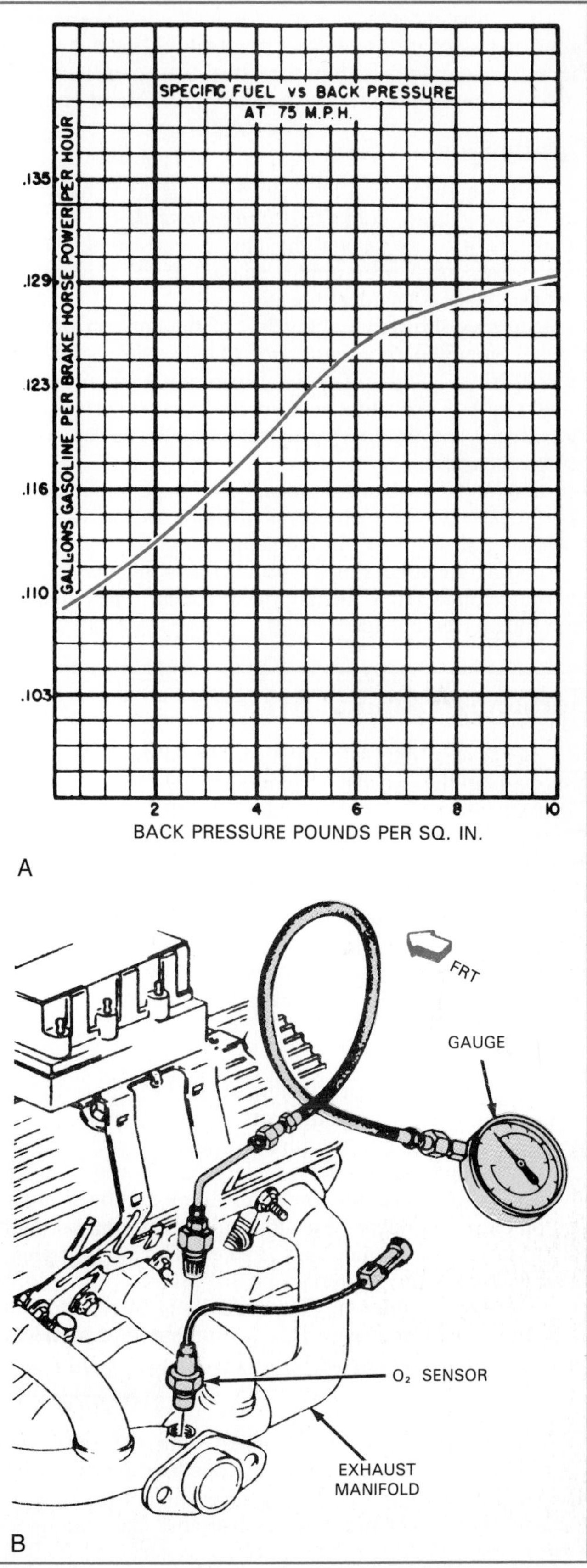

Figure 30-13. Backpressure. A–Fuel consumption increases as backpressure increases. B–Remove the oxygen sensor and install a pressure gauge in its place. Operate the engine at 2500 rpm. If the pressure exceeds specifications, backpressure is a problem. A vacuum gauge can also be used to detect backpressure. (Oldsmobile)

To reduce corrosion, most manufacturers are using rust-resisting coatings and/or special alloys in the design of the mufflers and pipes. Stainless steel is used or a ceramic coating is applied to the inside of the muffler and pipes.

Deadly Exhaust Gas

It is important that no leaks occur in the exhaust system. Exhaust gases contain ***carbon monoxide*** (CO). When CO finds its way inside the car, it causes headaches, drowsiness, and nausea. As the amount of CO is increased, unconsciousness and death result.

Surveys show that about 5% of the cars on the road contain enough carbon monoxide to cause drowsiness and impair driver judgment and reflexes if the windows are rolled up. Any leaks that occur in the exhaust system, from the exhaust manifold to the tailpipe, should be repaired as soon as possible.

Not only is exhaust gas deadly to the people inside the car, but also to the technicians working in the shop. Engines should never run in the shop unless there is enough ventilation. In large shops, special ducts are used. These ducts are connected to the tailpipe of the car. The exhaust is then transferred outside.

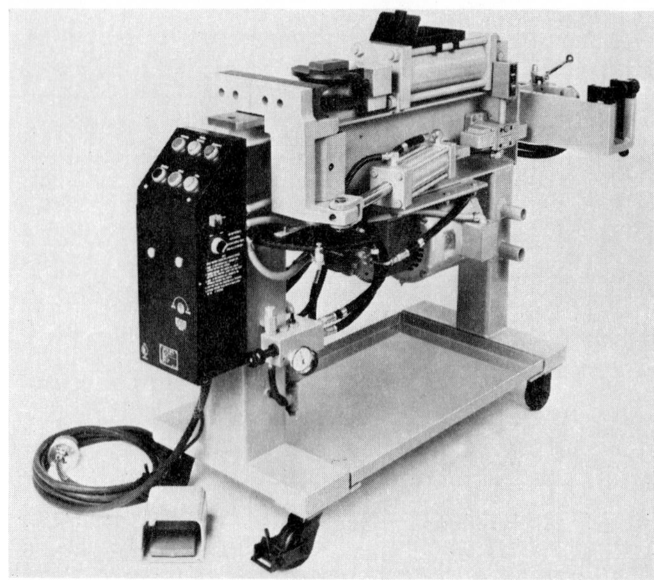

Figure 30-14. Equipment designed for bending exhaust system tubing. (Huth Mfg. Co.)

Servicing Exhaust Systems

Because of the rusting that occurs in the exhaust system, parts in the exhaust system often need to be replaced. The parts most often replaced are the muffler and tailpipe. Their life depends on the type of service in which the car is used. If it is used for short trips, it is not uncommon for the muffler and tailpipe to be replaced by 20,000 miles.

The joint between the manifold and exhaust pipe is of the flange-and-gasket type. Brass nuts are used to hold the flanges together. Brass nuts are used as they will not rust to the stud, which makes removal easy.

Parts Replacement

Exhaust system parts can be obtained from a supplier or by keeping a supply of parts in the shop. However, stocking enough exhaust pipes, mufflers, and tailpipes takes much space and involves a large amount of money.

To help overcome these problems, tube bending equipment is available. With this equipment, only straight tubing in various diameters is stocked. The straight pieces are then bent to the desired shape.

The ***tube bender*** in Figure 30-14 is fully automatic with foot pedal controls. This equipment is designed to produce bends through 3" outside diameter tubing. A heavy-duty expander is used on the ends of the cut to form slip connections.

The exhaust pipe is designed with the lower end slightly larger in diameter than the opening in the muffler. The muffler opening can then be slipped into the end of the exhaust pipe. A clamp is placed around the end of the exhaust pipe. When tightened, the two parts are held together. Metal or metal-and-fabric straps are used to hold the muffler and pipes in proper alignment.

To replace a muffler and tailpipe, remove the clamps and straps holding the tailpipe in place. Next, remove the tailpipe from the muffler. The tailpipe rusts to the muffler, which makes it hard to separate at the joint. If any of the parts are to be used again, penetrating oil should be applied to the joints before pulling them apart. In most cases, exhaust systems are not used again, and, therefore, can be cut apart.

Hacksaws can be used for muffler removal, but power driven tools will do the job much more quickly. It may be necessary to expand the end of a muffler pipe, tailpipe, or exhaust pipe. This is so the pipes can be assembled. A special tool for this purpose is shown in Figure 30-15.

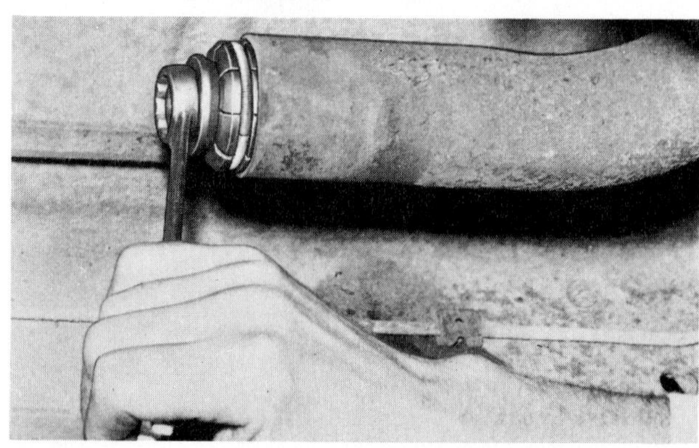

Figure 30-15. An expander is used to slightly increase the diameter of exhaust pipes for muffler installation.

Chapter 30-Review Questions

Write your answers on a separate sheet of paper. Do not write in this book.

1. What four parts form the exhaust system on a car?
2. On an inline engine, where is the exhaust manifold attached?
3. What effect does backpressure have on the operation of an engine?
   (A) Reduces power.
   (B) Increases power.
   (C) Increases the amount of carbon monoxide.

4. What effect does backpressure have on fuel economy?
   (A) None.
   (B) Reduces it.
   (C) Increases it.
5. What is a major factor in the rusting of a muffler?
   (A) Short distance driving.
   (B) Long distance driving.
   (C) High speed.
   (D) Idling for extended periods.
6. What material is used in making the nuts used to bolt the manifold to the cylinder head?
   (A) Cast iron.
   (B) Steel.
   (C) Castellated.
   (D) Brass.
7. Technician A states that the catalytic converter is a secondary silencing device. Technician B states that the catalytic converter burns the unwanted byproducts of combustion. Who is right?
   (A) A only.
   (B) B only.
   (C) Both A & B.
   (D) Neither A nor B.

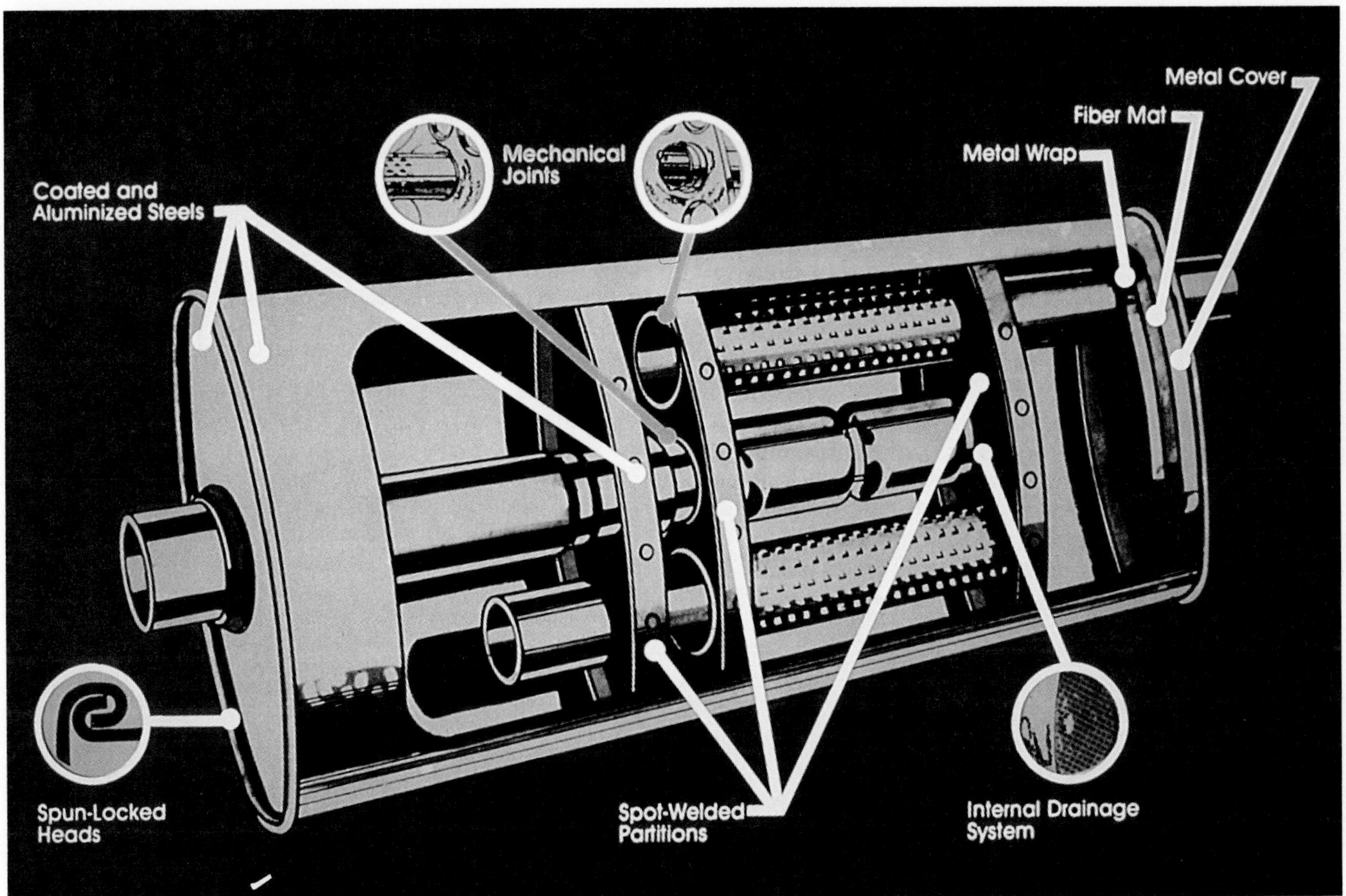

Cutaway of a reverse-flow muffler. (Walker)

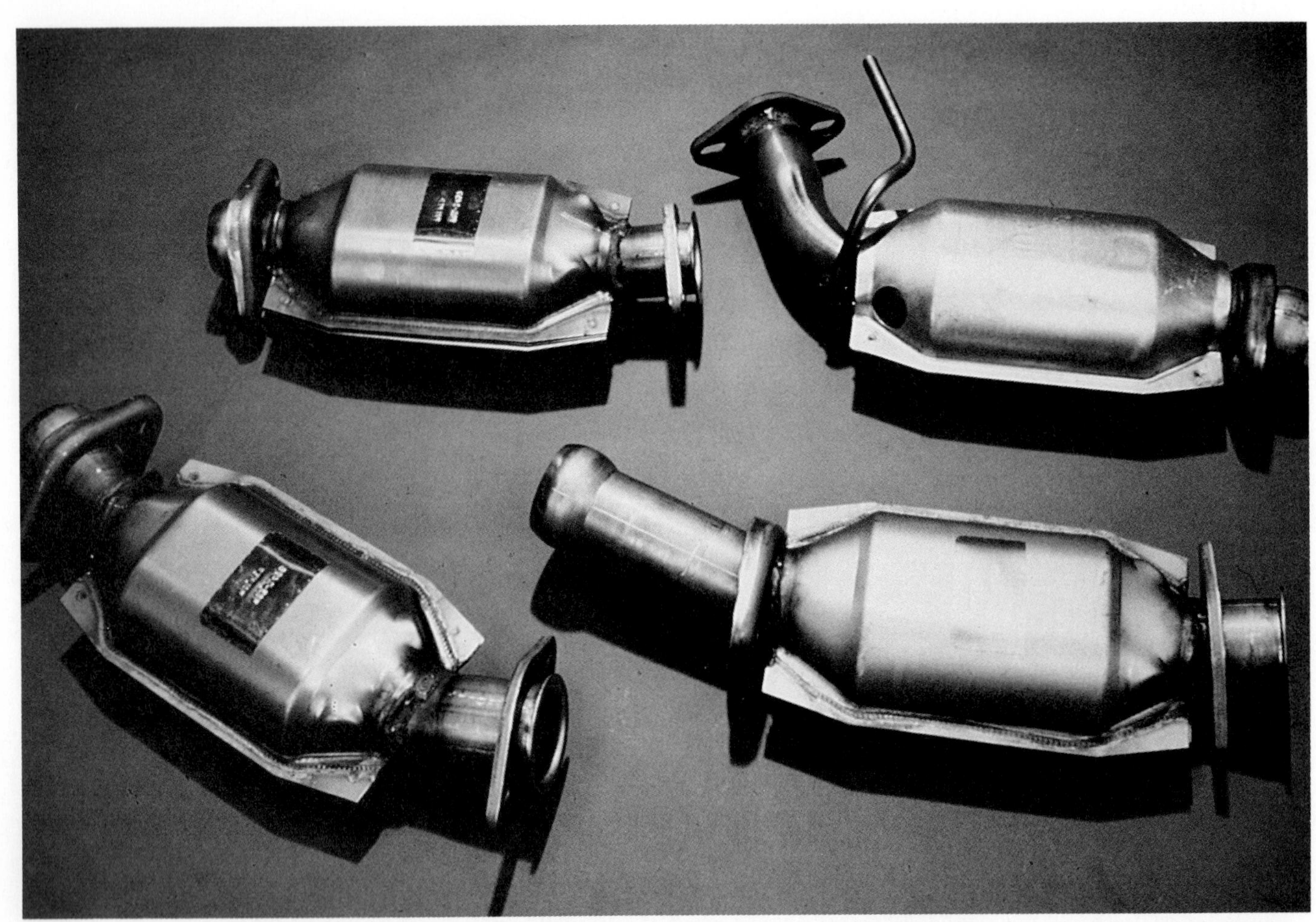

Catalytic converters, such as those shown above, convert the noxious by-products of combustion into harmless gases. (Walker)

Chapter 31
Emission Controls

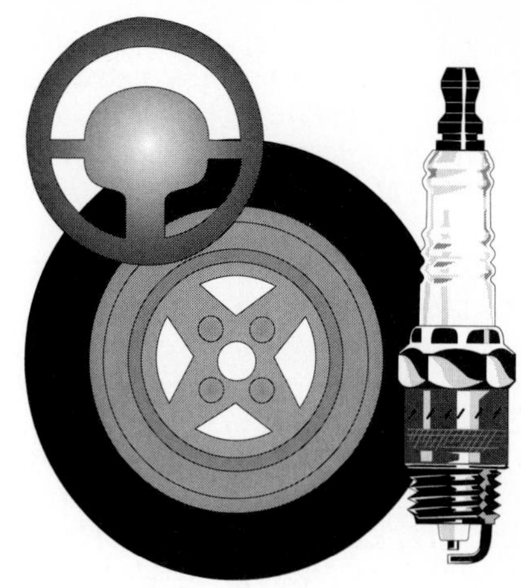

After studying this chapter, you will be able to:

- ❍ Name the noxious automotive emissions that created the need for car manufacturers to install emission controls.
- ❍ Explain the function of the positive crankcase ventilation system.
- ❍ Cite the various engine design modifications made to combat emissions.
- ❍ Classify precombustion and post-combustion emission control systems.
- ❍ Give examples of emission control failures and services required.

Introduction

Many factors, natural and otherwise, contribute to the pollution of the air we breathe. Our atmosphere is being polluted daily by the growing and decaying processes of nature; by emissions from motor vehicles; and by smoke from factories, power plants, homes, commercial buildings, industrial plants, and institutions.

Industry contributes the largest share of air contaminants, mostly in the form of sulfur compounds and particulates (solid matter). Motor vehicle emissions, on the other hand, are ***carbon monoxide*** (CO), ***hydrocarbons*** (HC), and ***oxides of nitrogen*** (NO_X). These are ***noxious.*** This means they are harmful to the body. They can cause damage to the lungs, as well as skin irritation and other problems.

Automotive Emission Standards

In 1970, the U.S. government moved to combat the steadily increasing level of air pollutants. The ***Federal Clean Air Act*** was passed. This act was the first in a series of legislative steps aimed at ridding the atmosphere of harmful automotive emissions. In addition, the ***U.S. Environmental Protection Agency*** (EPA) was assigned to implement the Clean Air Act.

Automotive emission standards (limits) were set and, through the ensuing years, regularly revised downward. The car manufacturers responded with great strides in engine engineering and in the development of emission control systems and devices. Today's stringent (tight) emission standards are being met and motor vehicle emissions are on the decline.

Positive Crankcase Ventilation

The first of the emission controls adopted by the automotive industry was the crankcase ventilation system. This system routes blowby gases, condensation vapors, and crankcase fumes to the combustion chambers of the engine. See Figure 31-1.

Called the ***positive crankcase ventilation (PCV) system,*** the early version is classified as the open-type PCV system because it uses an oil filler cap that is open to the atmosphere. Fresh air enters the oil filler cap and filler pipe. It passes through the crankcase, picks up blowby gases, enters the cylinder head cover chamber, flows through the PCV valve and hose, and travels into the intake manifold. The incoming mixture of fresh air and crankcase gases blends with the air/fuel charge, and the mixture is distributed to the cylinder combustion chambers and burned.

Figure 31-1. The positive crankcase ventilation system controls the flow of gases and vapors from the crankcase into the engine combustion chambers. 1–PCV valve. 2–Air cleaner. 3–Crankcase vent hose. 4–PCV valve hose. (Chevrolet)

The open type of PCV system was satisfactory–to a point. As long as the PCV valve was working and the hoses and intake manifold port were open, blowby gases were recycled to the combustion chambers. However, a sticking valve or clogged hoses would cause pressure to build in the crankcase. With no other place to go, the blowby gases would be forced through the "open" oil filler cap, polluting the atmosphere.

Recognizing the problem, the emission control engineers came up with the ***closed-type PCV system,*** Figure 31-1. In the closed system, incoming air passes through the carburetor air cleaner before entering the cylinder head cover. A separate air filter is incorporated in the air cleaner for this system. See Figure 31-2. The fresh incoming air circulates in the crankcase, picking up blowby gases and vapor. This mixture is drawn through the PCV valve and hose to the intake manifold.

The PCV valve, Figure 31-3, meters the flow in the system at a rate that depends on manifold vacuum. The function of the PCV valve is to restrict the flow of crankcase emissions when vacuum is high to preserve satisfactory engine idle. If excessive blowby occurs, it back flows through the vent hose to the air cleaner to be consumed by normal combustion.

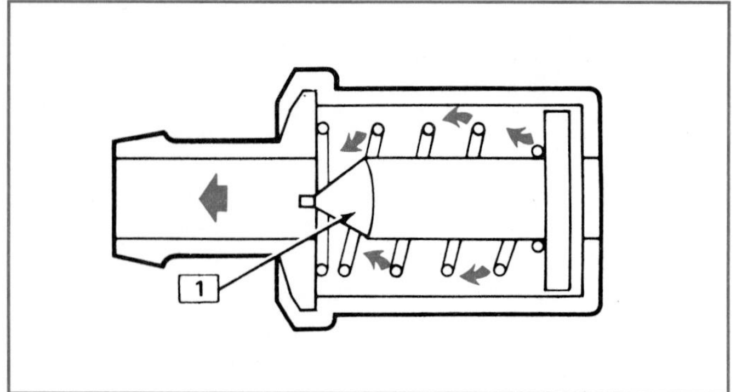

Figure 31-3. The PCV valve (1) meters the flow of the mixture of crankcase gases and fresh air into the intake manifold, based on the strength of the vacuum. (Chevrolet)

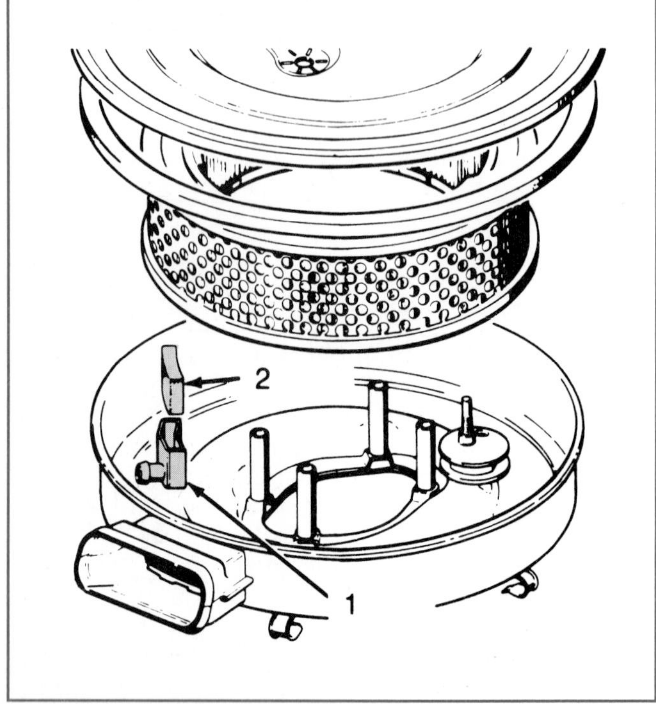

Figure 31-2. Fresh air is supplied from the air cleaner to the crankcase through a special PCV air filter: 1–Retainer. 2–Filter. (Chrysler)

Several different PCV systems are shown and described in Figures 31-4, 31-5, and 31-6. The setups differ but all function to recycle blowby gases to the combustion chambers.

PCV System Service

If the PCV valve is sticking or hoses are plugged, the engine will have a rough idle, idle too slow, or stall. Also, check for oil in the air cleaner and sludge (black, mushy deposits of oil, dirt, and water whipped together by moving parts) in the engine. If the PCV valve or hose leaks, the engine will have a rough idle, idle too fast, or stall.

To diagnose PCV system operation:

1. Lift the PCV valve from the valve cover with the hose intact.
2. Run the engine at idle.
3. Place your thumb over the end of the PCV valve to check for vacuum. See Figure 31-7. If no vacuum is present, check for a plugged hose or intake manifold port. Replace defective hoses and/or clean the port.
4. Remove the PCV valve from the hose and shake the valve vigorously back and forth.
5. Listen for a rattle of the check needle inside the valve. If the valve does not rattle, replace it.
6. Check and clean or replace the PCV filter in the air cleaner.

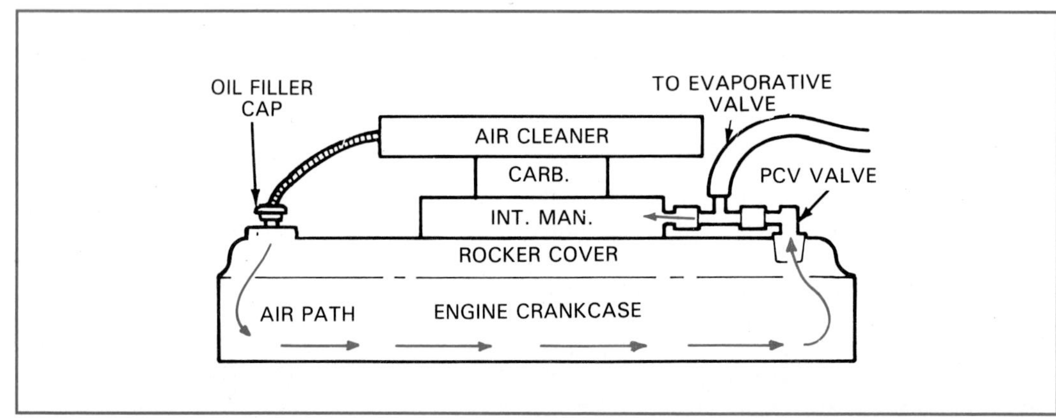

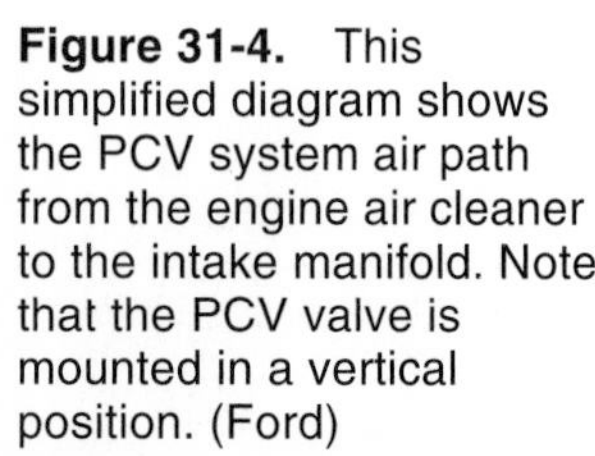

Figure 31-4. This simplified diagram shows the PCV system air path from the engine air cleaner to the intake manifold. Note that the PCV valve is mounted in a vertical position. (Ford)

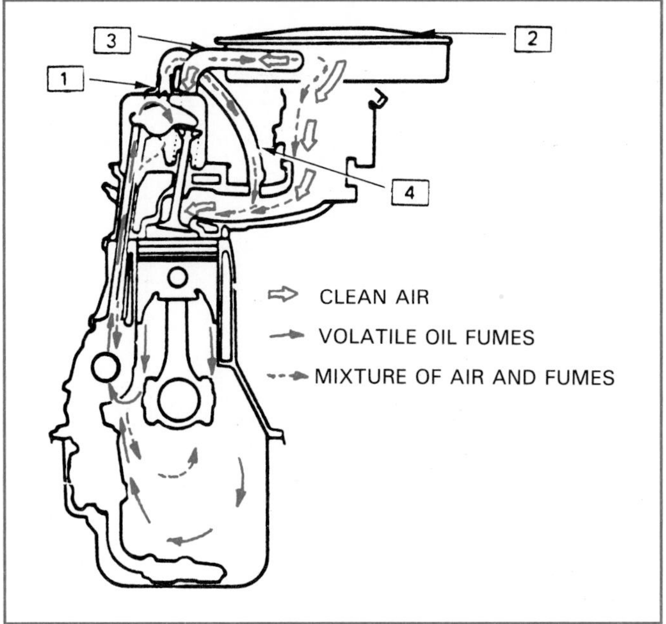

Figure 31-5. End view of a four-cylinder engine illustrates the PCV system flow as clean air picks up oil fumes from the crankcase. 1–PCV valve. 2–Air cleaner. 3–Crankcase vent hose. 4–PCV valve hose. (Cadillac)

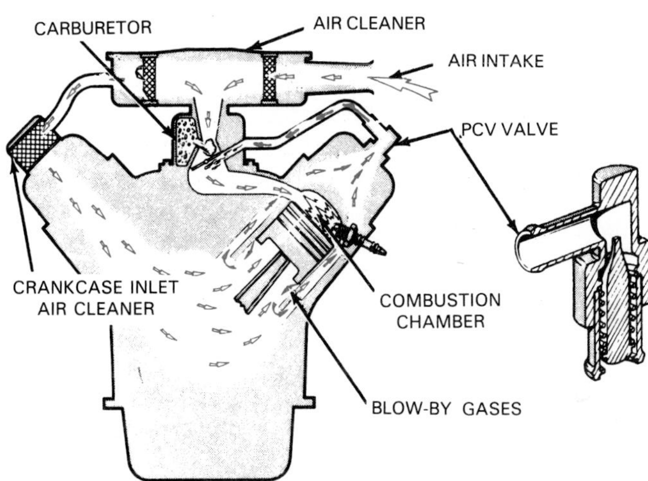

Figure 31-6. End view of a V-8 engine shows the cross flow of fresh air and blowby gases. Note the filter at the engine oil crankcase inlet. (Chrysler)

Exhaust Emission Controls

With crankcase emissions eliminated by positive crankcase ventilation, engine engineers concentrated their efforts on the control of exhaust emissions from the vehicle tailpipe and on the gasoline vapors being emitted from the fuel tank and carburetor. This vapor loss problem has been solved by ***evaporative emission controls,*** but the struggle to reach near-zero exhaust emissions goes on.

Since 1970, a substantial improvement in exhaust emission levels has been accomplished through changes and modifications in internal engine design. Interim standards for emission levels were met through the use of a wide array of emission control systems and devices. Then, the emission standards became so low that meeting them required the installation of catalytic converters in the exhaust

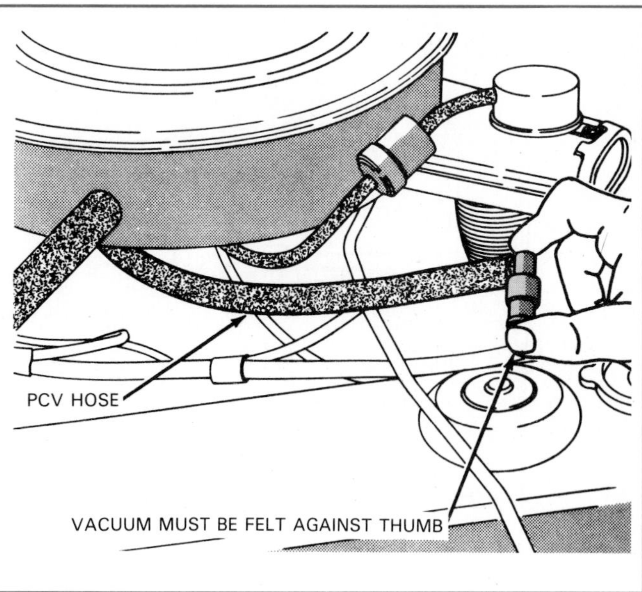

Figure 31-7. Test the PCV system vacuum by idling the engine, removing the PCV and hose assembly from the valve cover, and placing your thumb over the valve inlet. A strong vacuum should be felt. (Chrysler)

system. ***Catalytic converters*** chemically transform noxious emissions into harmless carbon dioxide and water.

Systems and Devices

There are several different methods of precombustion control of exhaust emissions. Attempts have been made to eliminate the emissions problem at its source by modification of engine design, carburetion, and ignition.

To comply with federal regulations for the control of exhaust emissions, the car manufacturers and their suppliers developed and installed many different systems and devices. Eventually, they were led to switch to some form of electronic fuel injection, electronic ignition, and engine computer control systems. See Figure 31-8.

In their original design, these "controls" can be grouped into two broad classes:

- ***precombustion controls*** (designed to reduce or eliminate the formation of harmful pollutants in the engine).
- ***post-combustion controls*** (designed to destroy or otherwise alter the pollutants after they have been formed).

Precombustion Controls

The difficulties to overcome in solving the emissions problem can be appreciated by considering the many different conditions that help produce the pollutants:

- Combustion chamber design.
- Displacement of cylinders.
- Coolant temperature.
- Engine temperature.
- Inlet air temperature.
- Air/fuel charge temperature.
- Air/fuel ratio.
- Engine speeds.
- Manifold vacuum.

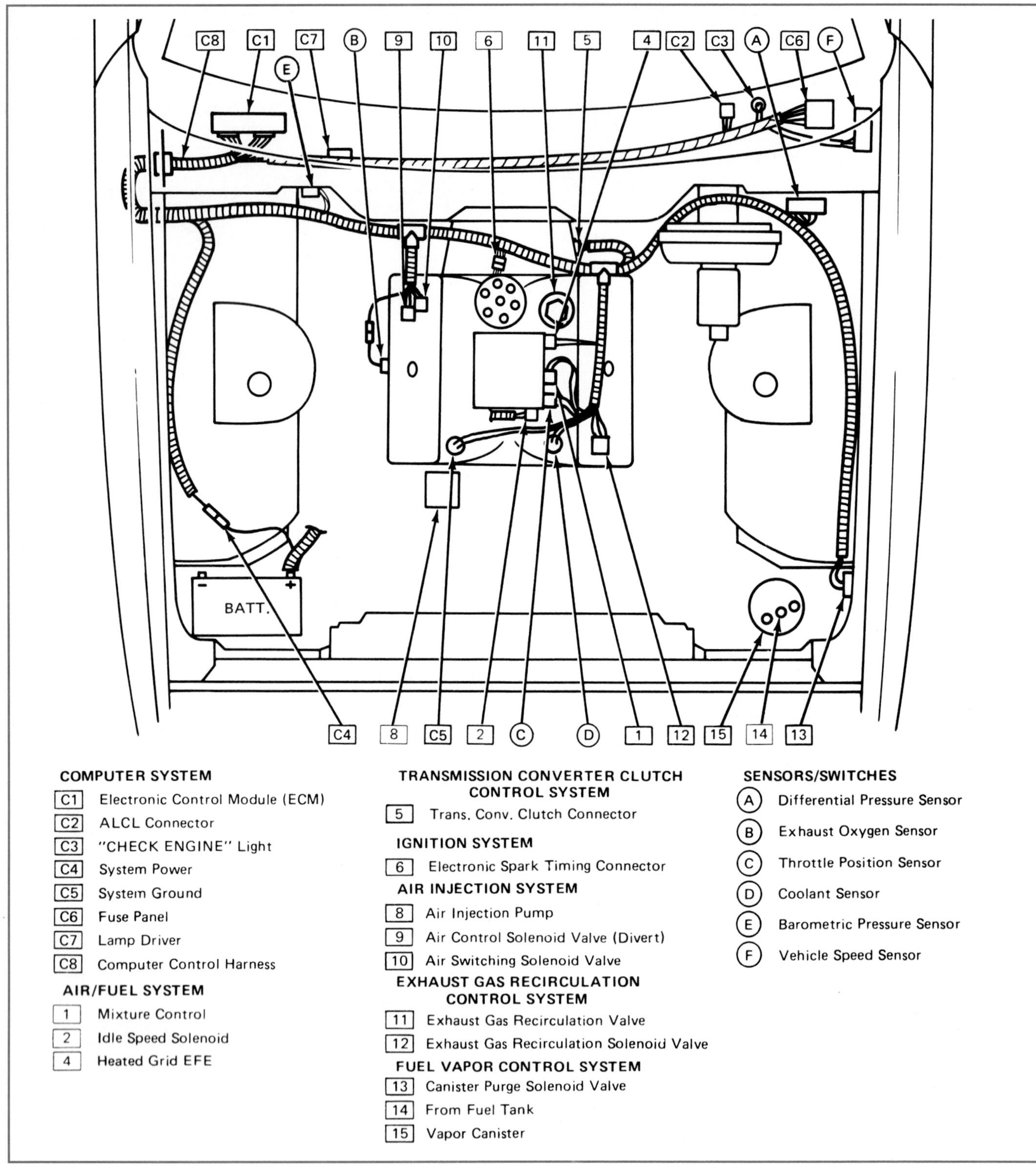

Figure 31-8. Underhood component locations are broken down by systems and sensors. Trace the circuits from the electronic control module to various emissions control systems. (Pontiac)

- Spark timing.
- Valve timing.
- Exhaust back pressure.
- Type of transmission.
- Lack of maintenance.

Engine modifications, a primary means of precombustion control, have brought about many new advances in internal engine design. The areas affected include the following:

- Compression ratios lowered for compatibility with no-lead gasoline.
- Combustion chamber configuration redesigned for better surface-to-volume ratio (area of combustion chamber surface compared to its volume with piston at top dead center).

- Combustion chamber modifications made for more efficient flow rate and burning time of the air/fuel charge, such as "swirl" chambers. See Figure 31-9.
- Pistons redesigned in crown contour and with smaller upper ring lands, moving top piston ring closer to top of piston.
- Intake manifolds redesigned for better air/fuel flow and balanced distribution of charge to each combustion chamber.

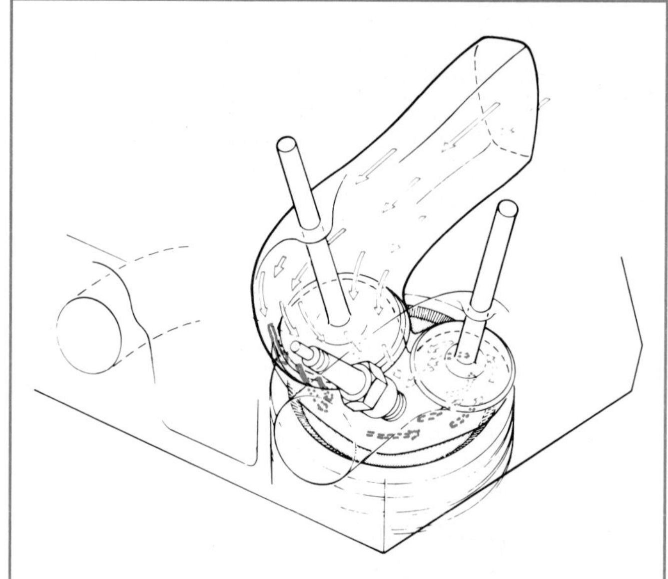

Figure 31-9. Cylinder head design with cyclonic port induction increases the air/fuel mixture velocity. Fast-burn mixture and centrally located spark plug speed the combustion process and lower the exhaust emission levels. (Chevrolet)

- Exhaust gas recirculation incorporated in manifolds to provide a metered amount of exhaust gas for recirculation with air/fuel mixture to slow combustion and reduce combustion chamber temperatures.
- Camshafts redesigned to modify valve timing and to increase valve overlap periods.
- Valve ports given soft curves and smooth surfaces.
- Cylinder heads modified to permit air injection near each exhaust valve.
- Cylinder head gaskets engineered for correct construction and designed for each engine with improved "fit" and no-retorque.
- Spark plug port location changed to suit combustion chamber design. See Figure 31-9.

Also incorporated in most late-model engines are the following conditions, modes of operation, or "controls" designed to provide more complete combustion and/or fewer emissions:

- Higher engine operating temperatures.
- Ignition distributor recalibrations, modified ignition advance, and better correlation with speed and load.
- Leaner carburetor recalibrations with higher curb idle speeds, idle stop solenoids, and limiter caps on idle mixture screws.
- Electric assist automatic chokes with more sensitive action and faster release.
- Fuel evaporation control systems.
- Thermostatically controlled air cleaners.
- Electronic engine control systems which precisely control fuel metering and ignition spark timing based on signals from key sensing elements.
- Electronic fuel injection systems for more efficient combustion control, Figure 31-10.

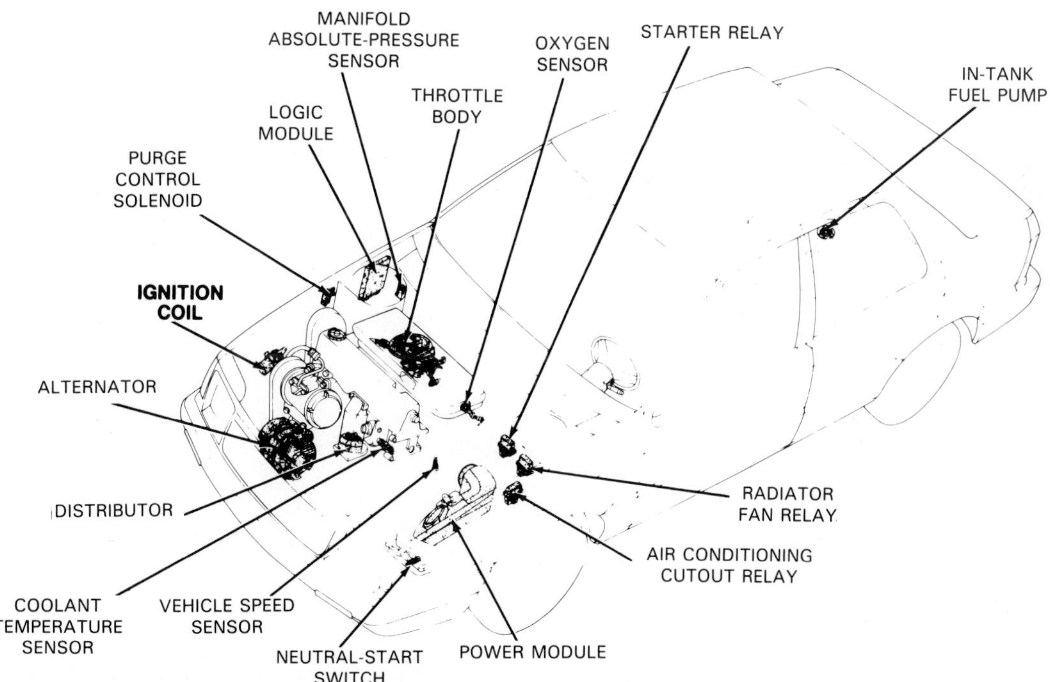

Figure 31-10. The adoption of a low-pressure, single-point, electronic fuel injection system on this engine improves combustion efficiency and reduces emissions. (Chrysler)

Thermostatically Controlled Air Cleaners

All domestic emission control engines are equipped with ***thermostatically controlled air cleaners.*** By controlling the temperature of the air entering the carburetor or fuel injection system, air/fuel mixtures can be made leaner and hydrocarbon emissions will be reduced.

The various thermostatically controlled air cleaners in use differ in makeup but provide the same effect–a uniform inlet air temperature. The names differ, too. General Motors calls theirs Thermac. Ford uses inlet air temperature system. Chrysler has heated inlet air systems.

A common GM Thermac system includes:

- A heat stove or shroud built around the exhaust manifold.
- Ducting from the heat stove to the air cleaner snorkel.
- Ducting from the outside air vent to the air cleaner snorkel.
- A damper door in the snorkel and a vacuum diaphragm motor to control movement of the damper door, Figure 31-11.
- A temperature sensor in the air cleaner.
- Vacuum hoses from the intake manifold to the sensor and from the sensor to the vacuum motor.
- An air bleed valve.

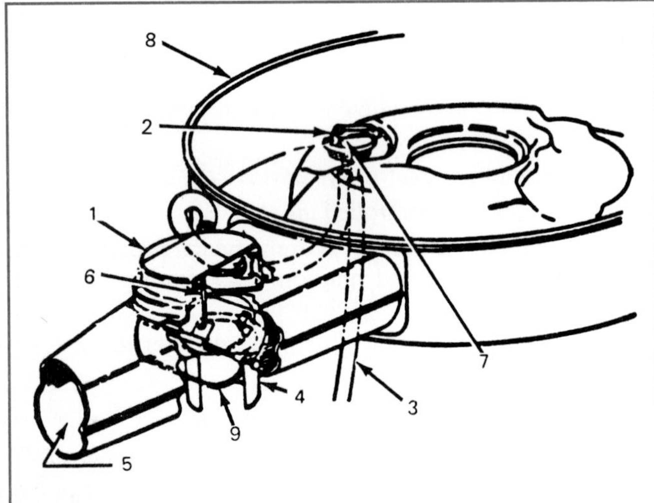

Figure 31-11. Key elements of a thermostatically controlled air cleaner are: 1–Vacuum diaphragm motor. 2–Temperature sensor. 3–Vacuum hose to intake manifold vacuum. 4–Heat stove duct. 5–Snorkel. 6–Linkage. 7–Air bleed valve. 8–Air cleaner assembly. 9–Damper door. (Cadillac)

Thermac Operation

When the temperature is below 86°F (30°C), the sensor allows vacuum to the vacuum motor. The motor raises the damper door, Figure 31-12A, cutting off outside airflow and passing only heated air from the heat stove into the air cleaner.

When the temperature is between 86°F (30°C) and 131°F (55°C), the damper door is partially open to both the outside air and heated air, Figure 31-12B.

When the temperature is above 131°F (55°C), the damper door drops down, cutting off heated airflow and passing only outside air into the air cleaner. See Figure 31-12C.

Thermac Service

To check the operation of GM's Thermac system:

1. Inspect the system for kinked, plugged, or deteriorated hoses.
2. Check the connections of all hoses and ducting.
3. Check the condition of the air cleaner to the TBI (throttle body injection) seal.
4. Check the air cleaner cover seal.
5. Check for a loose cover or a loose air cleaner.
6. With the air cleaner in place, the damper door should be open to outside air.
7. Start the engine. The damper door should move and close off outside air.
8. As the air cleaner warms up, the damper door should gradually open to outside air.
9. If the system fails to operate in this manner, test vacuum motor operation.
   a. Shut off the engine. Disconnect the hose at the vacuum diaphragm motor.
   b. Use a vacuum pump to apply at least 7 in. Hg. (23.8 kPa) of vacuum to the motor.
   c. The damper door should close to outside air.
   d. If not, check the linkage hookup and the inside of the snorkel for corrosion.

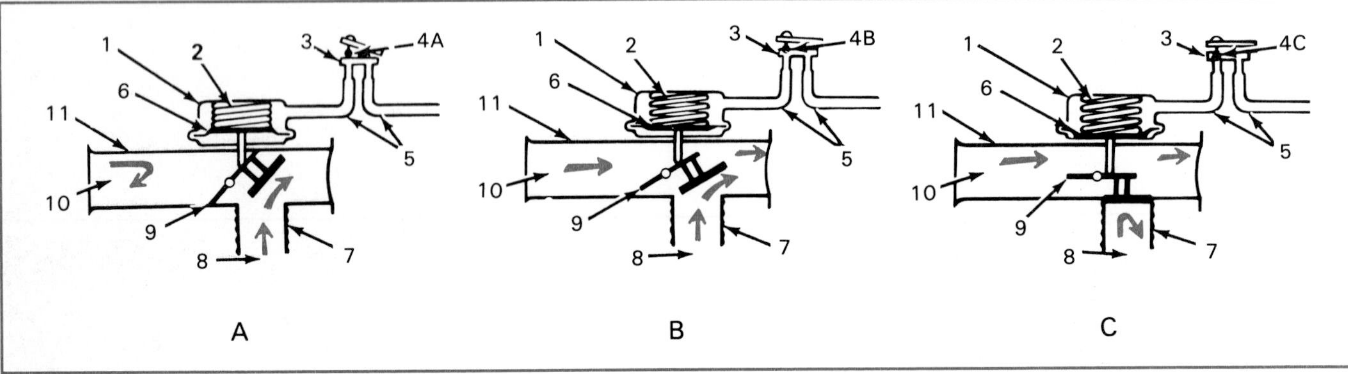

Figure 31-12. Thermac components related to operational description in text: 1–Vacuum diaphragm motor. 2–Diaphragm spring. 3–Temperature sensor. 4A–Air bleed valve–closed. 4B–Air bleed valve–partially open. 4C–Air bleed valve–open. 5–Vacuum hoses. 6–Diaphragm. 7–Heat stove. 8–Hot air from exhaust manifold. 9–Damper door. 10–Outside inlet air. 11–Snorkel. (Chevrolet)

   e. With vacuum applied, bend the hose to trap vacuum in the motor. The damper door should remain closed.
   f. If not, replace the vacuum diaphragm motor assembly.
10. If a driveability problem is experienced during warm-up, make a temperature sensor check:
   a. Allow the air cleaner temperature to fall below 86 °F (30 °C). Place a thermometer close to the sensor.
   b. Reinstall the air cleaner cover.
   c. Start the engine. The damper door should close to outside air, then gradually open as the engine warms up.
   d. Remove the air cleaner cover and check the thermometer reading. It should be about 131°F (55°C).
   e. If not, replace the temperature sensor.

Two other thermostatically controlled air cleaner systems are shown and described in Figures 31-13 and 31-14. The system valves, sensors, and vacuum controls differ, but all systems function to maintain a uniform inlet air temperature.

Early Fuel Evaporation System

Some carbureted engines are equipped with an ***early fuel evaporation system*** (EFE) as an aid to engine warmup and cold driveaway. The system consists of an EFE heater under the primary base of the carburetor, Figure 31-15, and a temperature switch located at the rear of the intake manifold. When engine temperature is below a calibrated

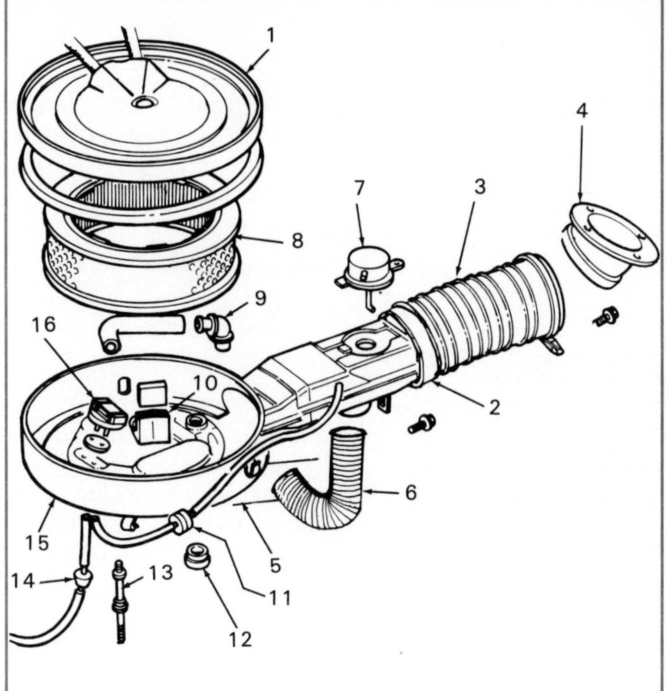

Figure 31-13. Typical AMC thermostatic air cleaner: 1–Cover. 2–Air duct adapter. 3–Flexible duct. 4–Adapter. 5–Heat stove. 6–Heated air tube. 7–Vacuum motor. 8–Filter element. 9–Elbow. 10–PCV filter retainer. 11–Reverse delay valve. 12–Grommet. 13–Stud. 14–Check valve. 15–Air cleaner body. 16–Thermal switch. (Chrysler)

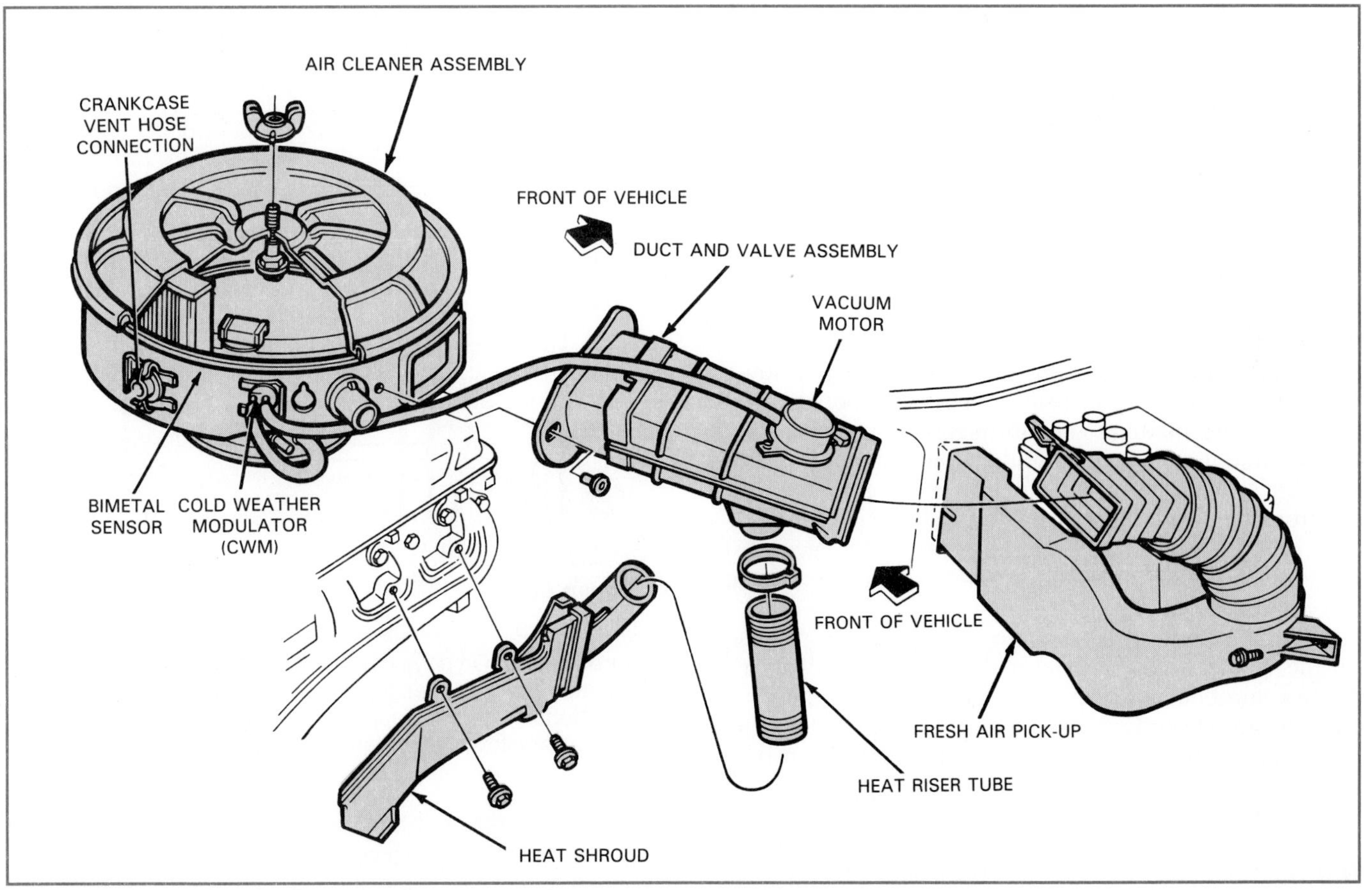

Figure 31-14. Exploded view of a typical Ford inlet air temperature system shows the major assemblies in detail: air cleaner; duct, valve, and motor; heat shroud and riser tube; fresh air pickup. (Ford)

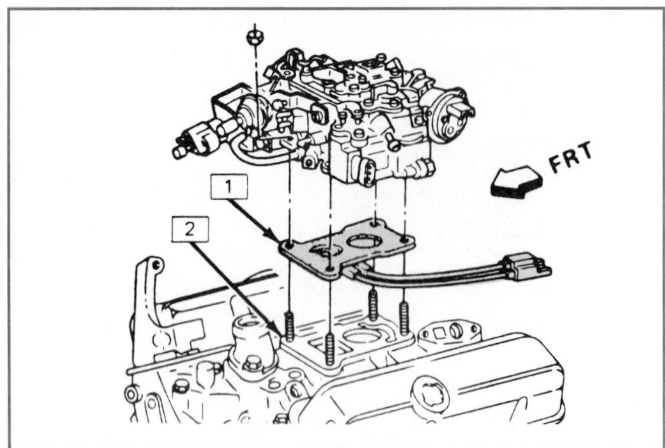

Figure 31-15. An early fuel evaporation system involves the use of an electrically heated grid between the intake manifold and the carburetor to help vaporize fuel when the engine is cold. 1–EFE heater. 2–Intake manifold. (Pontiac)

number of degrees, electrical current is supplied to the heater and quick fuel evaporation is provided.

Since the EFE system reduces the length of time that carburetor choking is required, it helps to reduce exhaust emissions.

Manifold Heat Control Valve

Some carbureted six-cylinder and V-8 engines are equipped with a ***manifold heat control valve.*** This unit is sandwiched between the exhaust manifold outlet and exhaust pipe. Its thermostatically controlled damper valve circulates heated exhaust gases in a heat chamber of the intake manifold under the carburetor.

The hot gases help vaporize the air/fuel mixture during engine warmup. After warmup, the damper valve redirects the exhaust gases into the exhaust pipe.

Evaporative Emission Control Systems

Evaporative emission controls (EEC) prevent the escape of gasoline vapors from the fuel tank and carburetor or throttle body, whether or not the engine is running. Late-model engines use an activated charcoal canister to trap the vapors when the engine is shut off. On restarting, a flow of filtered air through the canister purges the vapors from the charcoal. The mixture goes through one or more tubes feeding into the intake manifold, carburetor, and/or carburetor air cleaner, and it is burned in the engine. On many electronic-controlled, module-equipped engines, an ECM-controlled solenoid valve permits manifold vacuum to purge evaporative emissions from the charcoal canister. See Figure 31-16.

Certain engines also use a secondary damping canister on the intake manifold side of the primary canister as a purge control device. See Figure 31-17. The damping canister cushions the effect of the sudden charge of fuel vapors when the control valve releases them from the primary canister. The vapors are momentarily held, then gradually phased into the intake manifold.

Ignition Timing and Fuel Mixture Controls

Over the years, car manufacturers have concentrated their emission control efforts in two areas: ignition timing

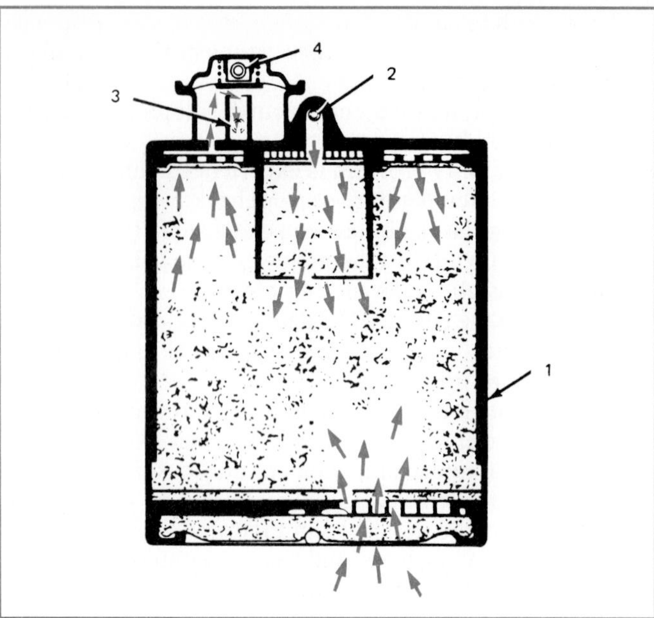

Figure 31-16. On GM engines with an electronic control module, the ECM actuates the solenoid valve to purge or prevent purging of fuel vapor from the evaporative emission control canister. 1–Charcoal canister. 2–To fuel tank. 3–Purge valve to ported vacuum. 4–Control valve to manifold vacuum. (Cadillac)

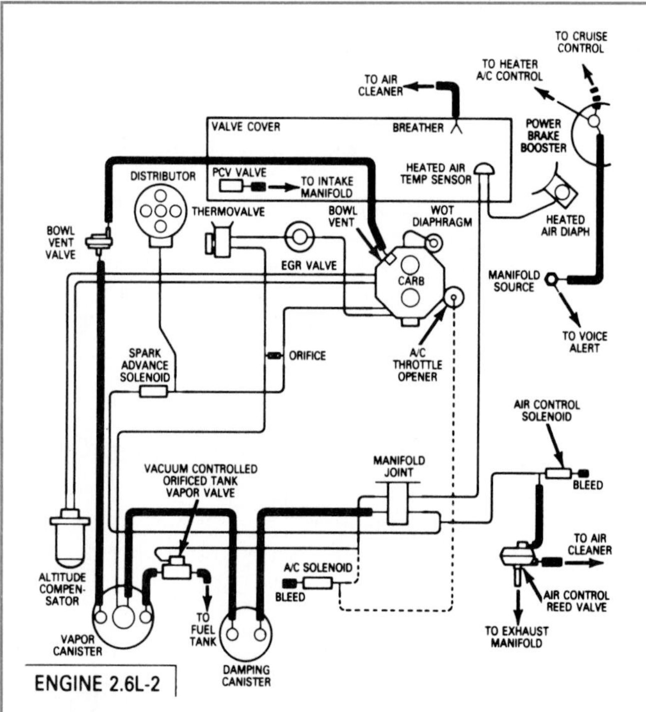

Figure 31-17. On a typical Chrysler vacuum hose routing diagram, the heavy lines represent hoses and hose connections. Note the vapor canister and the connecting damping canister at lower left. (Chrysler)

(and timing advance) and air/fuel mixture control to suit operating conditions. Since ignition timing and air/fuel ratio in all modes of engine operation have a strong influence on combustion efficiency, a wide variety of control devices have been introduced and regularly improved upon.

Most of the timing and fuel mixture control systems and devices proved to be interim answers to the emission control problem. As the emission control standards became more stringent, the car manufacturers' engineers solved the problem by developing electronic ignition systems, electronic fuel injection systems, engine computer control modules, and tie-ins with various sensors, switches, actuators, and vacuum controls. See Figures 31-8 and 31-10. The computer monitors the input signals, evaluates them, and provides output signals to control ignition timing and air/fuel ratio to match changing operating conditions.

The entire monitoring process takes split seconds, and it is constant. For further details on these various engine computer controls, see Chapter 29.

Post-combustion Controls

Emission controls designed to reduce carbon monoxide, hydrocarbons, and oxides of nitrogen after the combustion process can be termed ***post-combustion controls.*** These controls include:

- Exhaust gas recirculation.
- Air injection.
- Catalytic converters.

Exhaust Gas Recirculation Systems

The ***exhaust gas recirculation (EGR) system*** is specially designed to lower NO_X (oxides of nitrogen) emission levels caused by high combustion temperatures. The system uses an EGR valve operated by intake manifold or ported vacuum to feed exhaust gas back into the combustion chambers. See Figure 31-18. This recirculation of exhaust gas into the air/fuel mixture tends to slow down the combustion process and absorb heat, thereby reducing NO_X.

Only a small amount of exhaust gas is allowed to pass through the EGR valve and only when the engine is warm and operating above idle speed. Otherwise, the entry of the exhaust gas would halt combustion. Various supplemental controls, valves, or switches are used to limit EGR valve actuation to proper operating conditions.

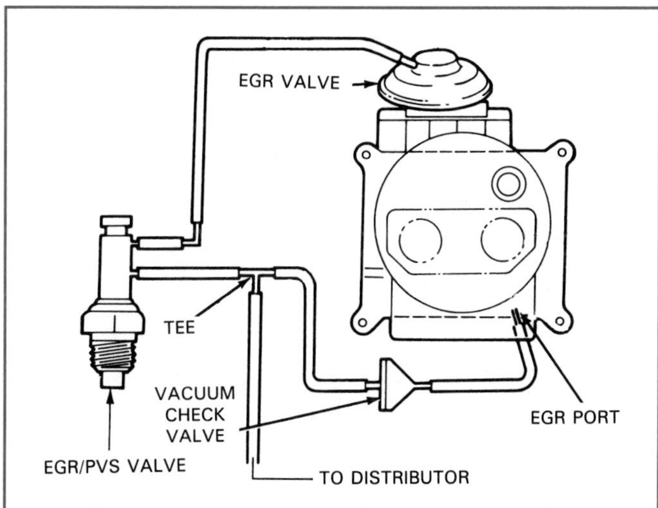

Figure 31-18. Drawing of a typical exhaust gas recirculating valve installation illustrates how the EGR system is vacuum actuated. The EGR/PVS (ported vacuum switch) unit controls vacuum based on coolant temperature. (Ford)

Exhaust gas recirculation valves vary in construction and operation. The ***ported EGR valve,*** Figure 31-19, uses ported vacuum taken from above the carburetor throttle valve to overcome the pressure of a large, single spring. Movement of the diaphragm opens the valve in the exhaust gas port and allows exhaust gas to be drawn into the intake manifold and engine cylinders.

General Motors engines also use a ***positive backpressure EGR valve***, Figure 31-20, or a ***negative backpressure EGR***

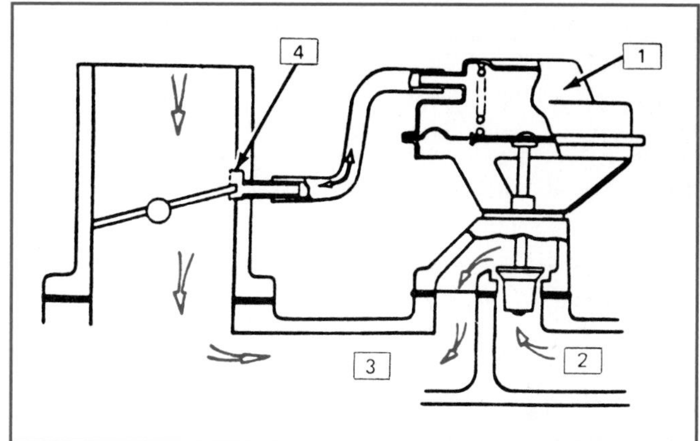

Figure 31-19. Ported EGR valves operate on ported vacuum taken from above the throttle valve: 1–EGR valve. 2–Exhaust gas. 3–Intake manifold. 4–Calibrated carburetor port or throttle body injection port. (Chevrolet)

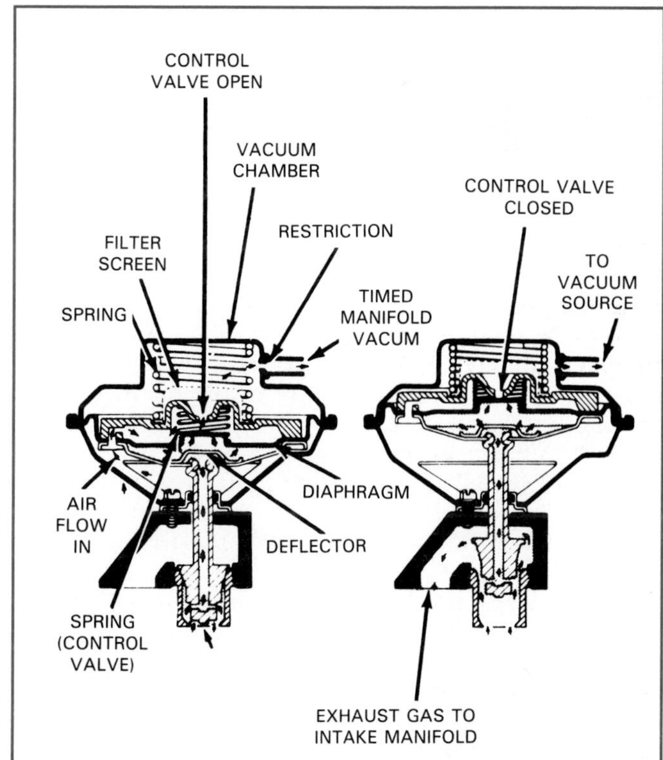

Figure 31-20. A positive backpressure EGR valve uses exhaust backpressure fed through a hollow shaft to actuate the spring-loaded control valve. When the backpressure increases, the valve bleed closes, and vacuum applied to the diaphragm opens the EGR valve. (Cadillac)

valve to meter the flow of exhaust gas. An air bleed inside the EGR valve acts as a vacuum regulator by bleeding vacuum to the atmosphere when the valve is open. When the EGR valve receives a prescribed amount of exhaust backpressure (through a hollow shaft), it closes the bleed. Then, maximum available vacuum is applied to the diaphragm and the EGR valve opens.

In this way, the air bleed controls the amount of vacuum in the vacuum chamber. If the vacuum chamber has little or no vacuum–such as at idle or wide-open throttle–or if there is little or no backpressure in the exhaust manifold, the EGR valve will not open.

The negative backpressure EGR valve is similar to the positive backpressure valve in construction. The difference is in the location of the bleed valve spring. It is above the diaphragm on the positive backpressure valve, Figure 31-20, and below the diaphragm on the negative backpressure valve.

Chrysler uses two types of EGR valves, a ported vacuum unit and a ***dual EGR control valve,*** Figure 31-21. The "dual" EGR valve has primary and secondary valves controlled by different carburetor vacuums. The primary valve controls EGR flow over a narrow range of lower speeds. The secondary valve takes effect at higher speeds. EGR flow is suspended at idle and wide-open throttle operation. A ***sub EGR control valve*** is directly opened and closed in response to throttle valve opening to further modulate EGR flow controlled by the EGR valve.

Vacuum applied to the dual EGR valve is controlled by a thermo valve. This valve prevents EGR flow until engine temperature reaches a prescribed level.

American Motors uses a double-diaphragm, ported vacuum EGR valve mounted on the side of the intake manifold. A coolant temperature override (CTO) switch in the EGR system cuts off recirculation of exhaust gases until a prescribed coolant temperature level is reached.

Ford uses four basic types of EGR valves:

- Ported valve.
- Integral backpressure valve.
- Valve and transducer assembly.
- Electronic valve.

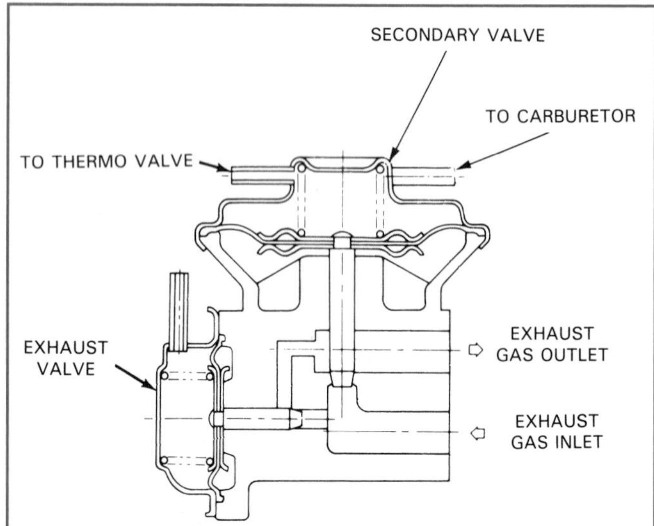

Figure 31-21. The dual EGR control valve has primary and secondary valves actuated by two different vacuum sources to improve driveability and reduce NO_x. (Chrysler)

The ***electronic EGR valve*** assembly, Figure 31-22, is used in EEC (Electronic Engine Control) systems where EGR flow is controlled according to computer demands. The computer controls an EGR Valve Position (EVP) sensor attached to the valve. The EGR valve is operated by a vacuum signal from dual EGR solenoid valves.

The ***valve and transducer assembly*** consists of a ported EGR valve and a remote transducer, Figure 31-23. This EGR valve operates the same as Ford's integral

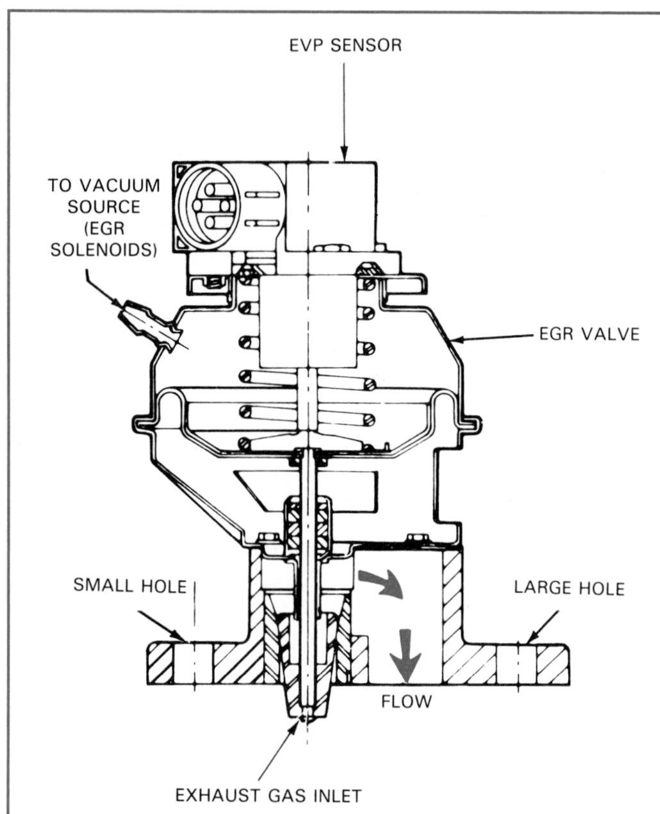

Figure 31-22. An electronic EGR valve assembly is operated by computer-controlled solenoid valves. Exhaust gas flow is through an opening in the base of this base entry type EGR valve. (Ford)

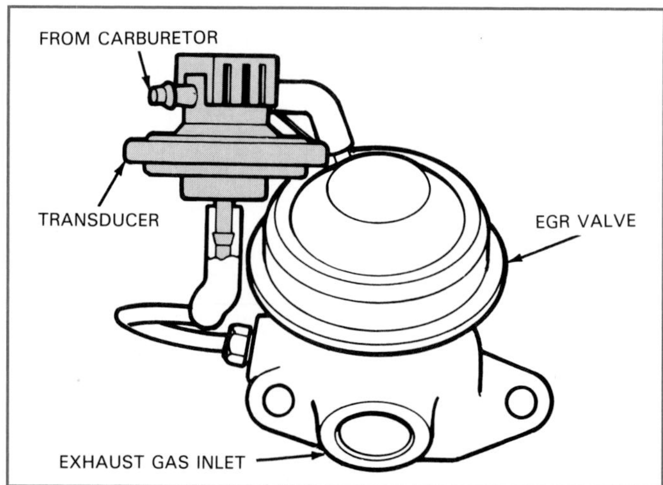

Figure 31-23. Valve and Transducer EGR assembly requires vertical positioning of the transducer. The nipple of the transducer must point straight down after installation. (Ford)

backpressure valve, controlling EGR flow by means of ported vacuum and exhaust backpressure.

Ford also uses a ***backpressure variable transducer (BVT) system,*** Figure 31-24. It consists of a vacuum regulator, EGR valve, and a flow control orifice. The regulator, Figure 31-24, modulates EGR vacuum by using two backpressure inputs.

Electronic Vacuum Regulator Valve

An ***electronic vacuum regulator valve (EVRV)*** is designed to modulate the strength of the vacuum that reaches the EGR valve. These valve actions, in turn, regulate the amount of exhaust gas to be recirculated to the intake manifold.

In operation, the Electronic Control Module (ECM) computes the required amount of exhaust gas flow, based on signals concerning rpm, load, torque converter clutch engagement, and engine temperature. These signals are evaluated by the ECM and sent to a constant current electronic circuit (part of EVRV system). The CCEC interprets the ECM data and converts it to signals that are transmitted to the vacuum regulator.

The regulator body has vacuum inlet and outlet ports and a vented port at one end and an electromagnetic diaphragm at the other end. A steel disk is spring loaded against a brass seat that surrounds the vented port. Vacuum at the inlet port tends to pull the disc away from the seat. Vacuum is then precisely modulated to the EGR valve as the stator (plunger) attracts the disc toward the vented port at a rate of 128 cycles per second.

EGR System Service

To check an EGR system for faulty operation:

1. Check the routing of all vacuum hoses and lines (see vacuum hose diagram on emissions and tune-up decal in the engine compartment).
2. Check the vacuum hoses for condition and secure connections.
3. Disconnect the hose at the vacuum port of the EGR valve. There should be no vacuum when the engine is cold or at warm curb idle.
4. There should be vacuum to the EGR valve at higher rpm (generally 2000-3000) at normal operating temperature. See the manufacturer's specifications.
5. If there is no vacuum, check back through the vacuum hose from the EGR valve to the vacuum source and correct as required.

To check operation of a ported vacuum EGR valve, Figure 31-19:

1. Start the engine and warm it up to its normal operating temperature.
2. Allow the engine to idle in neutral for one minute; then abruptly accelerate the engine to about 2000-3000 rpm (check the manufacturer's specifications). The EGR valve stem should move (use a mirror, if necessary).
3. If not, remove the EGR valve and clean the inlet and outlet ports with a wire brush. Do not wash the assembly in solvents. Also clean the mounting surfaces of the EGR valve and manifold.

To check operation of exhaust backpressure EGR valve, Figure 31-20:

1. Temporarily plug the tailpipe of the vehicle with a socket wrench that is slightly smaller in diameter than the inside of the tailpipe.
2. Start and warm the engine to its normal operating temperature.
3. With the engine idling, disconnect the vacuum hose from the EGR valve port and plug the hose.
4. Use a hand-operated vacuum pump to apply vacuum to the EGR valve port.
5. The EGR valve stem should move, and engine idle should become rough.

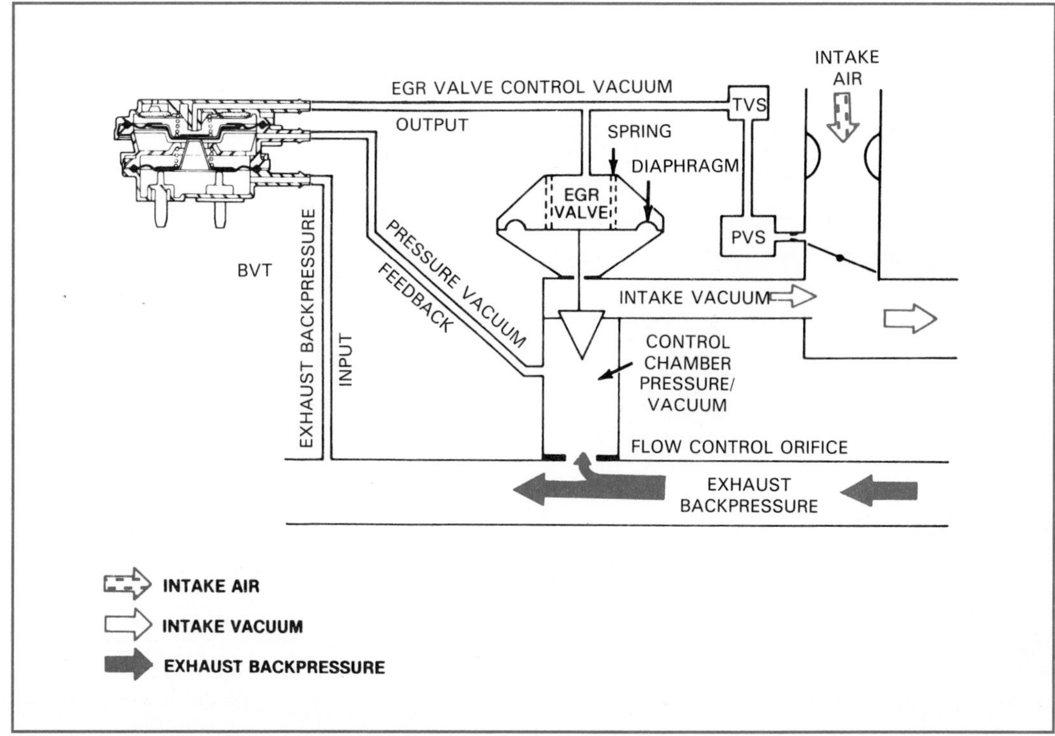

Figure 31-24. This backpressure variable transducer schematic shows the relationship of a ported EGR valve to the vacuum regulator at the top left. Vacuum tests are made at the top, center, and bottom ports of the regulator. (Ford)

To check operation of dual EGR valve, Figure 31-21:

1. Cold start the engine and run it at idle speed.
2. Abruptly accelerate the engine to 2500 rpm. The secondary valve (at top of EGR valve) should not operate. If it does, replace the thermo control valve.
3. Warm the engine to its normal operating temperature.
4. Abruptly accelerate the engine to 2500 rpm. The secondary valve should operate.
5. Disconnect the hose from the secondary valve port to the carburetor at the carburetor.
6. Connect a hand-operated vacuum pump to the disconnected hose.
7. Pull open the sub EGR valve and apply above 6 in. Hg. (20.4 kPa) of vacuum to the secondary valve hose. Idle speed should become rough.
8. If not, replace the EGR valve or the thermo control valve.
9. Disconnect the vacuum pump and reconnect the hose to the carburetor.
10. Disconnect the hose from the primary valve port to the carburetor at the carburetor.
11. Repeat steps 6, 7, and 8.

To check operation of solenoid vacuum control EGR systems, Figure 31-25:

1. With the ignition on and the engine stopped, the solenoid should not be energized and vacuum should not pass to the EGR valve.
2. Ground the diagnostic terminal. The solenoid should be energized and allow vacuum to pass.

To check the operation of a backpressure variable transducer EGR system, Figure 31-24:

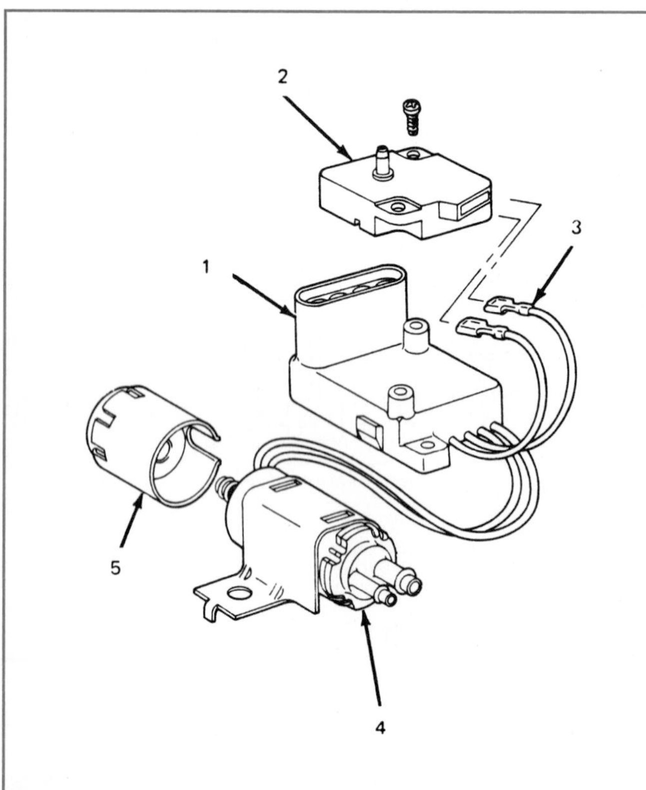

Figure 31-25. Exploded view of a typical EGR solenoid vacuum control assembly: 1–Base. 2–EGR vacuum diagnostic switch. 3–Diagnostic switch connectors. 4–EGR solenoid. 5–Filter. (Cadillac)

1. Disconnect one hose at a time from the vacuum regulator ports and use a hand-operated vacuum pump to apply at least 5 in. Hg. (17.0 kPa) of vacuum to each of the three ports in turn.
2. The top port in Figure 31-24 should not hold vacuum.
3. The center and bottom ports should hold vacuum.
4. If the test at top, center, or bottom port fails, replace BVT assembly.

Air Injection Systems

Air injection systems are a form of postcombustion emission control devised to reduce HC and CO emissions by injecting fresh air into the hot gases in the exhaust manifold. Basically, either one of two air injection systems is used:

- ***Air pump injection*** (supplies air to exhaust manifold by means of a belt-driven air pump and air distribution system. See Figure 31-26).
- ***Pulse air*** (uses natural pulses present in exhaust system to pull air into exhaust manifold through pulse air valves. See Ford system in Figure 31-27).

Earlier single-purpose air injection systems perform the job of reducing the amount of HC and CO in the exhaust gases by injecting air directly into the exhaust port of each cylinder. The air, added to the hot gases, causes further oxidation (burning) of the gases before they enter the exhaust pipe.

The equipment commonly used in this type of air injection system includes a belt-driven pump, air hoses, a metal tubing air manifold, injection tubes (or internal passages to the rear of each exhaust valve), a diverter valve, a check valve, a pressure relief valve, and a silencer.

The ***diverter valve*** prevents backfire by sensing an increase in manifold vacuum on deceleration. It opens to divert air under pressure to pass through the valve and ***silencer*** to the atmosphere. The ***check valve*** prevents hot exhaust gases from backing up into the hose and pump. The ***pressure relief valve*** controls pressure in the system by releasing excessive pump output to the atmosphere at higher engine speeds.

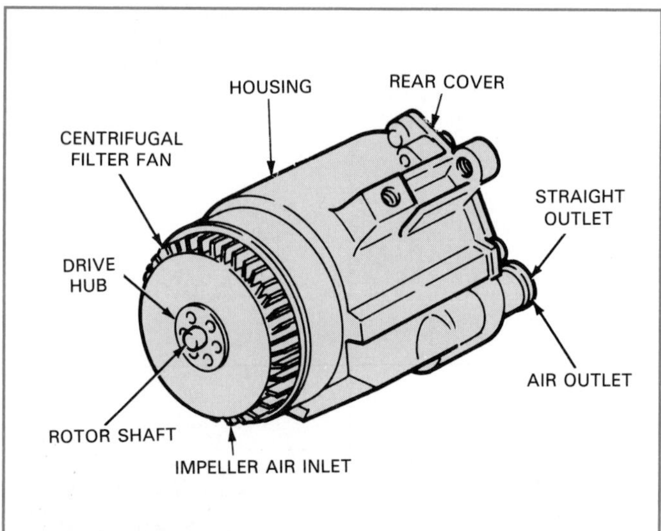

Figure 31-26. Typical thermactor air supply pump uses an impeller-type air filter fan to separate contaminants from the intake air by centrifugal force. (Ford)

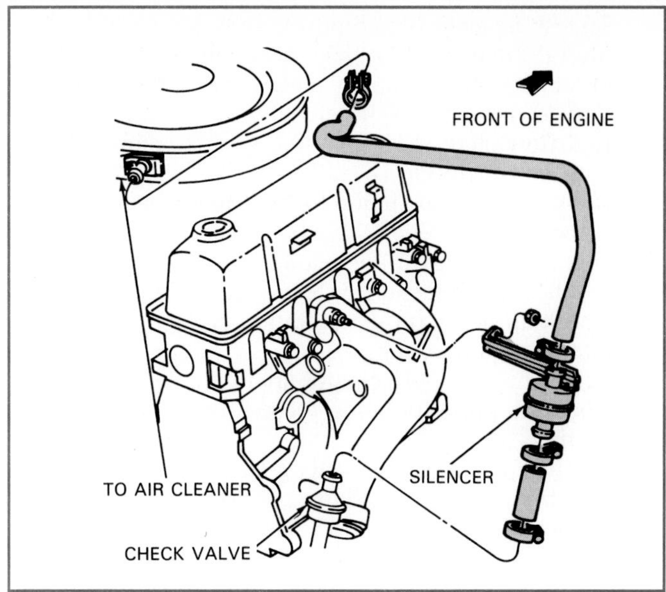

Figure 31-27. A pulse air system does not use an air supply pump. It is a setup of hoses and pulse air valves that uses "pulses" in the exhaust system to draw fresh air from the air cleaner into the exhaust manifold for injection into the hot gases to reduce HC and CO. (Ford)

Most later air injection systems work in conjunction with engine computer control units and ***three-way catalyst*** catalytic converters.

Ford's managed air thermactor system is used to divert air under pressure to either the exhaust manifolds or to the dual catalyst in the catalytic converter. See Figure 31-28. The system also has an ***air bypass valve*** to divert air to the atmosphere during certain operating modes.

Ford also uses a combined bypass/control valve in electronically controlled air injection systems. As indicated by its name, this combination air bypass and air control valve is installed in line with the air pump. Air under pressure and vacuum (controlled electronically by two solenoids) operate the combination valve. Air under pressure, then, is diverted either to the intake manifolds or to dual catalytic converters.

The General Motors Air Injection Reaction System (A.I.R.) is shown in Figure 31-29. The A.I.R. system uses a vacuum-operated, ECM-controlled electric divert/electric air switching valve that combines "divert" and "switching" functions in a single housing. See Figure 31-30. The divert valve diverts air to the air cleaner for converter protection or passes air to the switching valve. The switching valve directs air to exhaust ports during cold engine operation or to a pipe between the two catalyst beds in the converter to heat up the catalysts quickly on engine start-up.

Some GM engines also use a deceleration valve to help prevent backfiring during high vacuum conditions. Attached to the air cleaner, this valve opens under high vacuum, allowing air from the air cleaner to flow into the intake manifold and "lean" the air/fuel mixture.

Air Injection System Service

The air injection system requires little maintenance. The air pump, Figure 31-26, is permanently lubricated. It

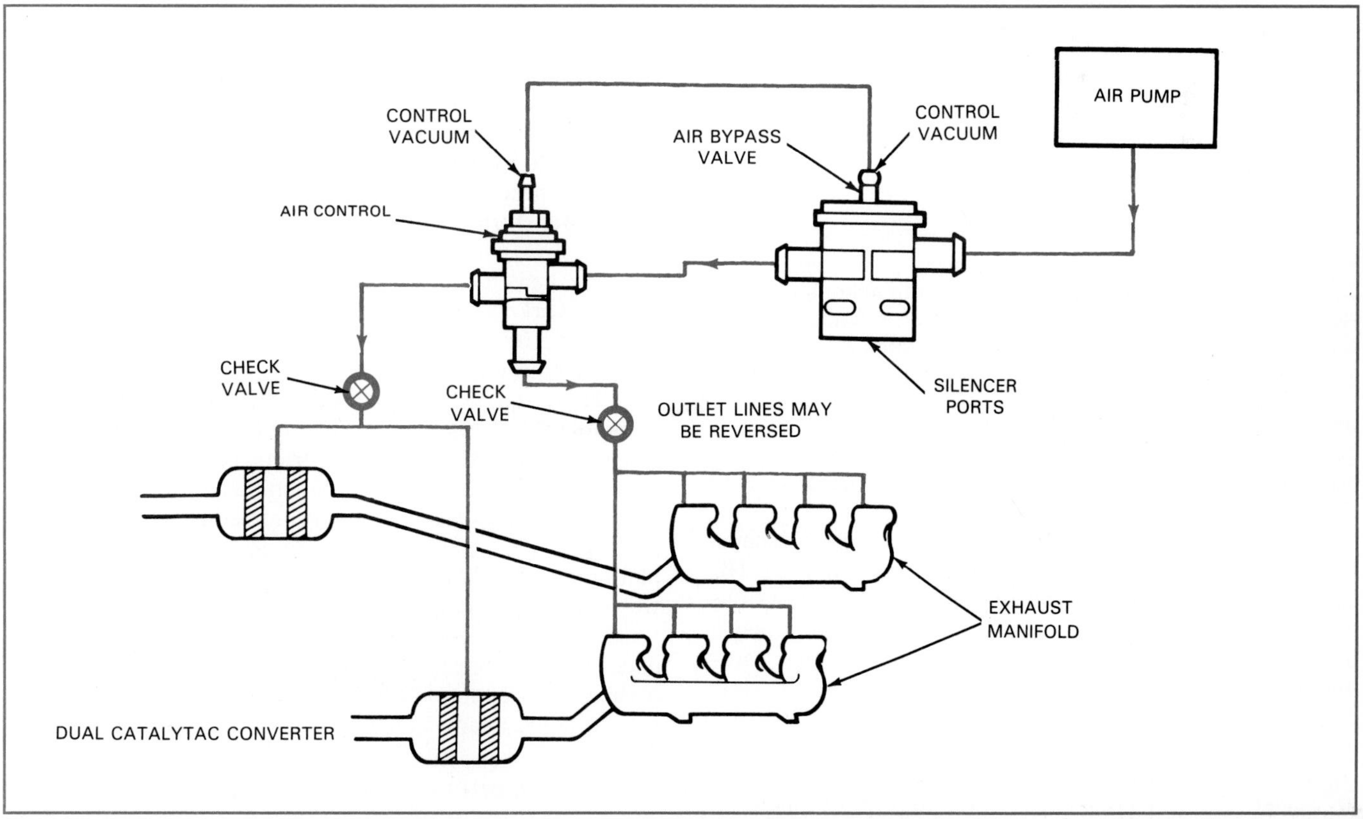

Figure 31-28. A managed air thermactor system uses an air control valve to direct the thermactor air either upstream to the exhaust manifold or downstream to the dual catalytic converter. During certain operating modes, the air bypass valve dumps air to the atmosphere. (Ford)

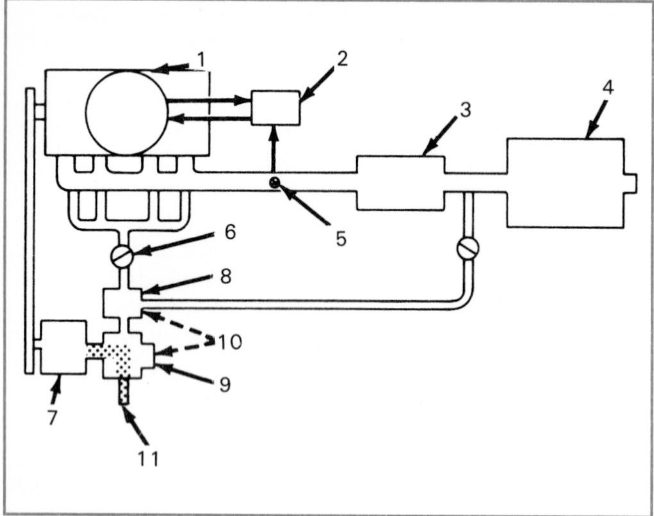

Figure 31-29. Typical air injection reaction system. 1–Closed loop fuel control. 2–ECM. 3–Reducing catalyst. 4–Oxidizing catalyst. 5–O_2 sensor. 6–Check valve. 7–Air pump. 8–Air switching valve. 9–Air divert valve. 10–Electrical signals from ECM. 11–Bypass air to air cleaner. (Pontiac)

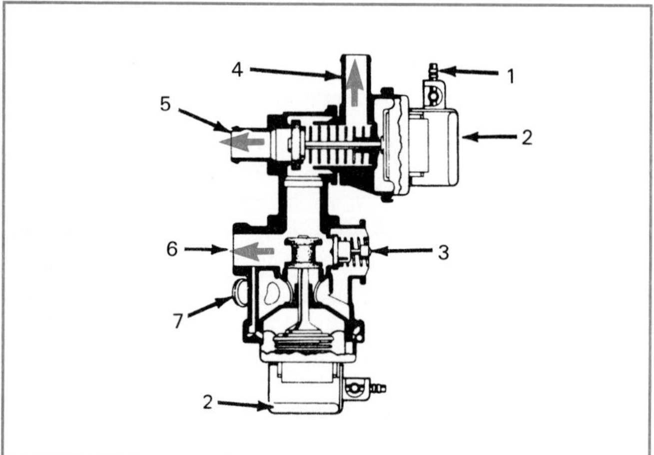

Figure 31-30. The electric divert/electric air switching valve diverts air to the air cleaner or switches air to either the exhaust ports or the dual catalytic converter. 1–Vacuum signal. 2–Solenoid. 3–Relief valve. 4–Converter air. 5–Port air. 6–Air from pump. 7–Divert air. (Pontiac)

cannot be disassembled and serviced. If the pump fails to provide sufficient air for satisfactory system operation, it should be replaced.

If airflow from the pump does not enter the exhaust stream at the exhaust ports or at the catalytic converter, HC and CO emissions levels will read high on the emissions tester. If airflow from the pump is constant to the exhaust ports, the ECM unit will command a richer mixture, causing increased temperature of the converter and possible damage.

Noise complaints may be checked out by operating the engine with the air pump drive belt removed. If the noise disappears, inspect for a seized air pump. Also check all hoses and tubes for improper routing. Inspect all connections for leaks. Check the air pump for improper mounting and incorrect bolt torque.

To test the air pump output:

1. Start the engine and accelerate to about 1500 rpm.
2. Disconnect the pump air outlet hose and observe airflow as the engine is accelerated.
3. If airflow increases with rising rpm, the pump is operating satisfactorily.
4. If not, listen to the pump for air leaking.
5. If the pressure relief valve is not leaking, shut off the engine and check drive belt tension.

To check air injection system components:

1. Check all hoses for deterioration or wear at points of interference in routing.
2. See that all the hose clamps are tight.
3. Check all pipes for holes, loose fittings, and improper routing.
4. If a leak is suspected on the pressure side of the system, run the engine and use a soap and water solution to check for bubbles at the connections.
5. To test a check valve, blow through the valve toward the cylinder head and then suck back through the valve. Flow should only be in one direction (toward head). If not, replace the check valve.
6. To test other valves in the air injection system (switching, divert, deceleration, pressure relief, air bypass valves), see the manufacturers' service manuals for procedures.

Catalytic Converters

Major air pollutants contained in exhaust gas are hydrocarbons (HC), carbon monoxide (CO), and oxides of nitrogen (NO_X). To help reduce the volume of these pollutants during the post-combustion stage, the car manufacturers use ***catalytic converters.***

Basically, a catalytic converter is a container of chemically treated pellets or honeycomb element that is incorporated in the exhaust system. Earlier converters utilized pellets coated with platinum or with platinum and palladium to reduce HC and CO. Operating at about 1500°F (815°C), these catalysts provided a heated chemical reaction to transform noxious emissions into harmless carbon dioxide (CO_2) and water vapor (H_2O).

The heated chemical reaction of the platinum and palladium worked well in reducing HC and CO, but had the opposite effect on NO_X emissions. High heat serves to increase NO_X emissions.

Then, as NO_X limits were drastically reduced, the manufacturers' engineers turned to ***dual catalytic converters,*** Figure 31-31. Dual converters contain two catalyst elements. The "upstream" element is termed ***three-way catalyst*** because it is chemically treated to reduce all three pollutants–HC, CO, and NO_X. In addition to platinum or platinum and palladium to decrease HC and CO, the three-way catalyst is treated with rhodium to reduce NO_X.

With all three major pollutants (HC, CO, and NO_X) reduced by the upstream catalyst, HC and CO are further reduced (oxidized) by the introduction of air (from air injection system) into the downstream oxidizing catalyst. See Figure 31-32.

Catalytic Converter Maintenance

Catalytic converters require little attention as long as unleaded gasoline is used (to avoid "lead poisoning" of catalysts). Also important to converter life is the positioning

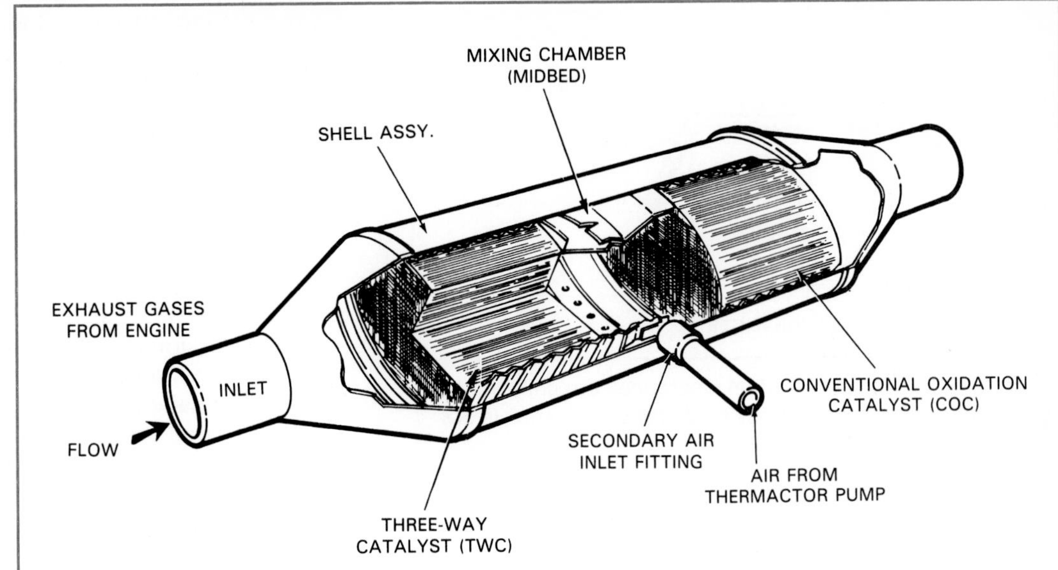

Figure 31-31. This widely accepted dual catalytic converter uses an upstream three-way catalyst to reduce HC, CO, and NO_X. The downstream catalyst and air provided by the air injection system further reduce HC and CO emissions. (Ford)

of the converter in relation to underbody heat shields and surrounding underbody parts. See Figure 31-33. If clearances are too small, overheating of the converter could result. In addition, excessive floor pan temperature could damage passenger compartment carpets.

Anytime a car is hoisted for service, it pays to check the general condition of the catalytic converter, along with other exhaust system components. If exhaust system work is performed on GM cars, a special sealer should be used at all slip joint connections except at the catalytic converter. The sealer cannot withstand converter temperatures.

Occasionally, because of age, high mileage, or contamination of catalysts in the catalytic converter, engine performance may be sluggish due to backpressure in the exhaust system. If the catalyst elements are damaged or become heavily coated with contaminants, the resulting restriction of exhaust gas flow could cause loss of power and, finally, engine stalling and failure to restart.

A primary cause of catalyst damage or contamination is an overly rich air/fuel mixture. As mentioned, failure of the air injection system to supply air under pressure to the catalytic converter could cause the ECM unit to command a richer air/fuel mixture. Also, a "missing" engine will allow unburned gases to travel to the catalytic converter and damage the catalysts. Likewise, do not "fast idle" engine for more than five minutes. If there is a diagnostic need to "short" out a spark plug, do not allow the engine to run more than one minute while "missing."

If the existing catalytic converter is damaged or contaminated, replace it with an original equipment converter or the equivalent. While the external appearance may be similar, there may be internal differences in some replacement converters. Also be sure to observe the clearance specifications between the converter and the heat shields, Figure 31-33. Connect the air line securely to the air injection port on a dual catalytic converter.

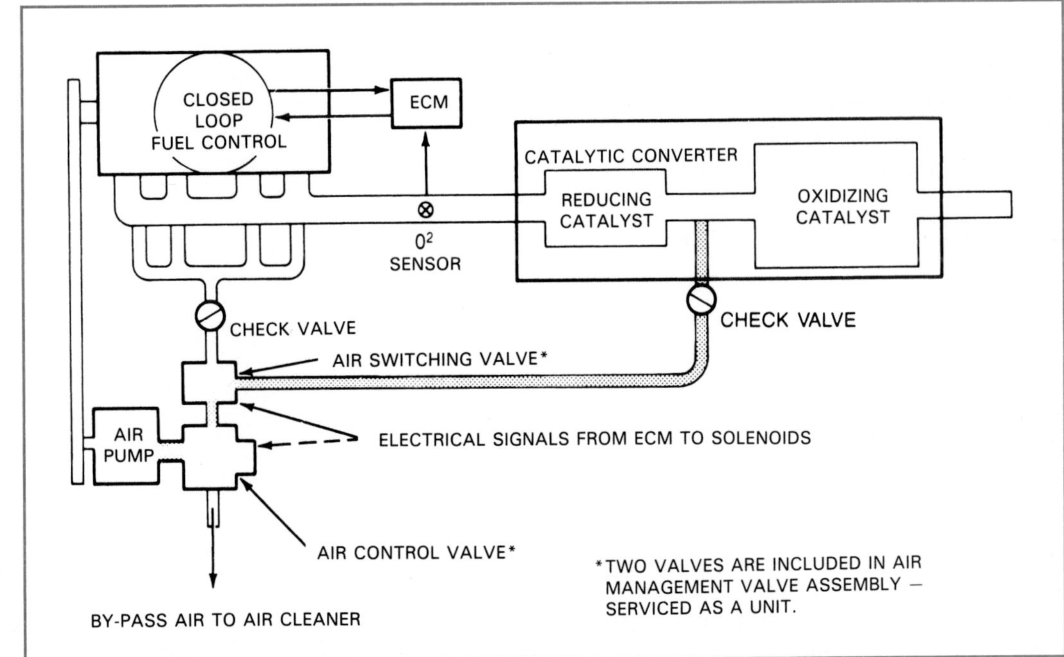

Figure 31-32. This diagram illustrates how the air switching valve switches airflow from the exhaust manifold to the downstream oxidizing catalyst of catalytic converter. "Switches" are signalled by the ECM. (Cadillac)

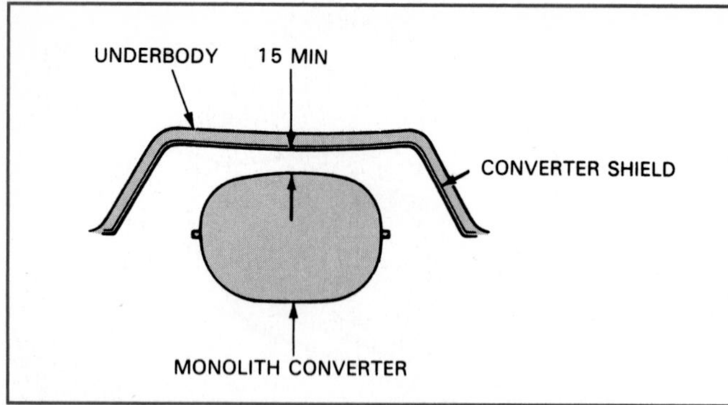

Figure 31-33. Exhaust system clearances are critical. Typical converter-to-underbody heat shield clearance is 5/8″ (15 mm). (Cadillac)

Chapter 31–Review Questions

Write your answers on a separate sheet of paper. Do not write in this book.

1. Name three noxious automotive emissions.
2. The _____ type of positive crankcase ventilation system has eliminated the emission of crankcase fumes, blowby gases, and vapors.
   (A) open
   (B) closed
   (C) pressure
   (D) bypass
3. What is the purpose of the PCV valve?
4. To test a PCV valve, remove the hose and valve assembly from the valve cover and shake the valve vigorously. If it rattles, the valve is defective. True or False?
5. _____ emission controls solve the problem of fuel vapors being emitted from the fuel tank and carburetor or throttle body.
6. Catalytic converters _____ transform noxious emissions into harmless carbon dioxide and water.
   (A) chemically
   (B) statically
   (C) electromagnetically
   (D) electronically
7. What are precombustion emission controls?
8. _____ controls are designed to destroy or otherwise alter the pollutants after they have been formed.
9. What is the objective of a thermostatically controlled air cleaner?
10. What is the "effect" of a thermostatically controlled air cleaner?
11. Some carbureted engines are equipped with an _____ system as an aid to engine warmup and cold driveaway.
12. Evaporative emission controls prevent the escape of fuel vapors even when the engine is not running. True or False?
13. Over the years, car manufacturers have concentrated their emission control efforts in two areas: _____ and air/fuel mixture control.
    (A) internal engine modifications
    (B) ignition timing
    (C) exhaust gas recirculation
    (D) catalytic converters
14. For what purpose does the exhaust gas recirculating system feed exhaust gas back into the combustion chambers of the engine?
15. The ported EGR valve uses ported vacuum taken from _____ (above, below) the throttle valve.
16. An engine has a rough idle and is sluggish when cold. The EGR system appears to be at fault. Technician A says the EGR valve is stuck in the open position. Technician B says the vacuum hose from the EGR valve to the vacuum source may be clogged or deteriorated. Who is right?
    (A) A only.
    (B) B only.
    (C) Both A & B.
    (D) Neither A nor B.
17. Name two types of air injection systems.
18. Air injection systems are designed to reduce HC and CO emissions by injecting air into the _____ in the _____.
19. Dual catalytic converters contain two catalyst elements–one "upstream" and the other "downstream." Why is the "upstream" element called a three-way catalyst?
20. The "downstream" catalyst element in a dual catalytic converter and air provided by the air injection system further reduce:
    (A) NO_x.
    (B) HC.
    (C) CO.
    (D) HC and CO.

Chapter 32
Engine Troubleshooting

After studying this chapter, you will be able to:
- ❍ Explain the process of engine troubleshooting.
- ❍ Tell why modern engine analyzers should be used to supplement visual inspection and manual checks.
- ❍ Describe the function of "plug-in" diagnosis.
- ❍ Give an example of "self diagnosis."
- ❍ List various engine troubles and identify possible causes.
- ❍ Elaborate on more common causes of engine overheating, excessive oil consumption, and engine noises.

Engine Troubleshooting

Engine troubleshooting is a process of studying the symptoms of the existing trouble and reasoning possible causes and corrections. This process is supported throughout by analysis, deduction, and elimination.

Since a defect in one part or a maladjustment in one system may have a definite relationship to trouble in another area, you must keep the functions of the entire automobile in mind at all times. This aspect of troubleshooting requires mental alertness as well as specific knowledge.

Test Equipment

Troubleshooting in its most basic form consists of "shorting out" spark plugs to locate a misfiring cylinder. In its most advanced form, it involves the use of an elaborate diagnostic computer engine analyzer. See Figure 32-1. In addition, many late model vehicles feature a plug-in diagnostic connection so that a special tester can be plugged into the circuit to quickly locate existing trouble.

In some situations, trouble areas can be located by visual inspection and manual checks. However, this method of attempted problem solving should be supplemented by tests made with modern ***engine testing equipment.*** Then, the "hidden" sources of trouble can be pinpointed more quickly and with greater accuracy.

Typical modern ***engine analyzers*** are shown in Figures 32-1, 32-2, and 32-3. With this equipment, it is possible to test everything from condition of the spark plugs to 4-gas emissions (carbon monoxide, carbon dioxide, oxygen, and hydrocarbons).

In some cases, the tester is actually a ***diagnostic computer*** that provides visual and/or "voice" instructions,

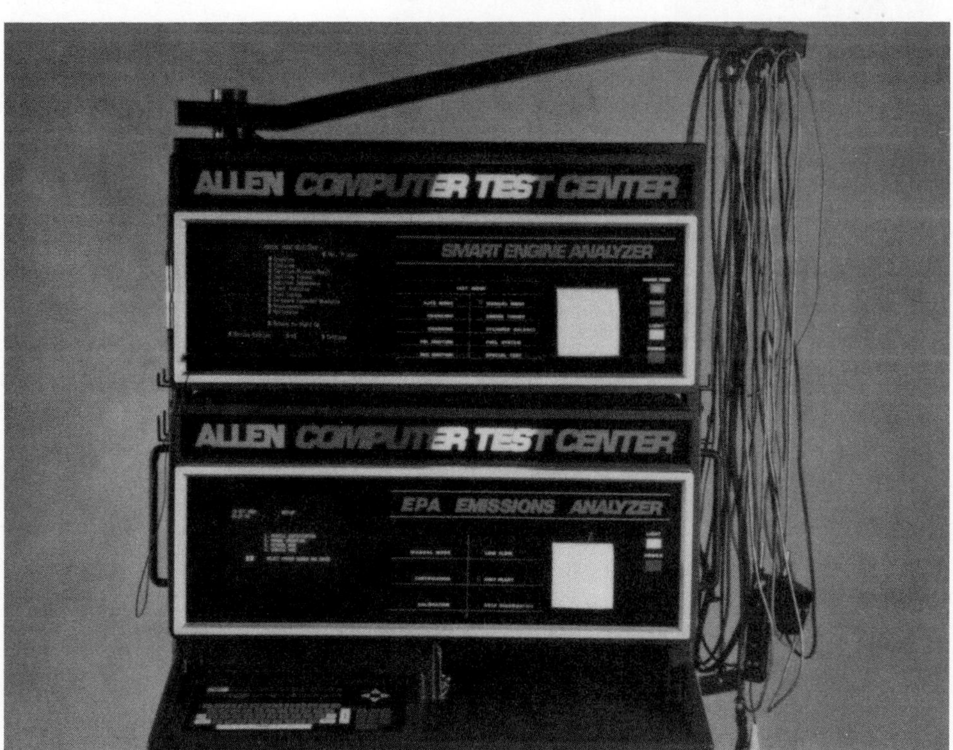

Figure 32-1. The latest computerized engine and emissions analyzers provide the diagnostic help needed to pinpoint causes for engine performance complaints and for excess emissions. The operator can "freeze" data on screen, display readouts of test results, and obtain emissions printouts. (Allen Test Products Div., Allen Group)

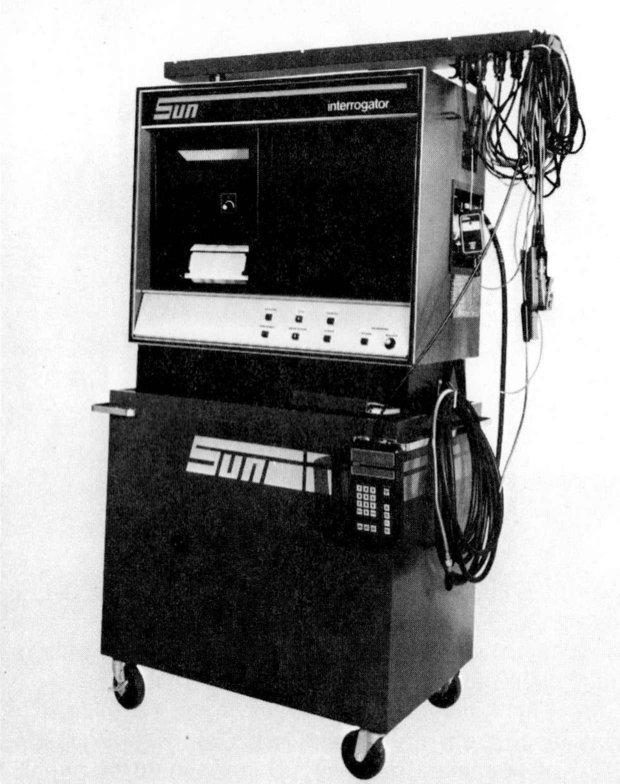

Figure 32-2. This diagnostic computer will analyze six major engine systems. Test instructions are visual and oral. A remote-control keypad permits the operator to work in the car or under the hood. The computer identifies problems, possible causes, and logical solutions. (Sun Electric Corp.)

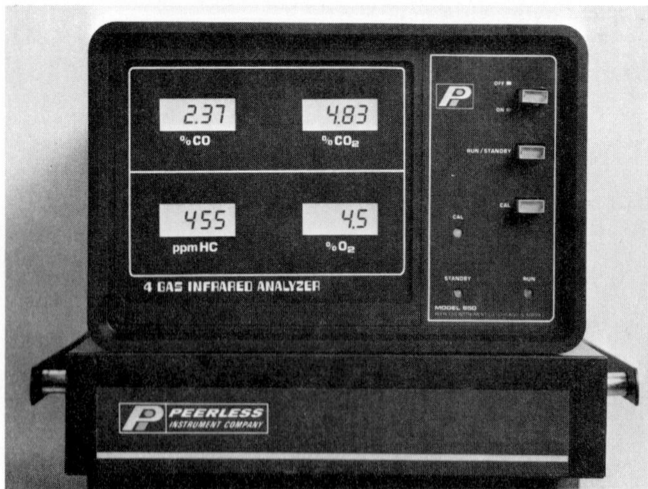

Figure 32-3. A four-gas infrared analyzer uses emissions analysis to determine whether the cause of engine performance problem is in the fuel system or in the ignition system. (Peerless Instrument Co.)

Figure 32-2. The computer is preprogrammed with test specifications. In operation, it displays the vehicle's actual performance readings on a screen. A printout of these readings is also furnished for the technician and for the car owner to substantiate the need for repairs. This specialized equipment is covered in detail in Chapter 5, Meters, Testers, and Analyzers.

Effect of Emission Controls

Troubleshooting has become more difficult since numerous emission control systems were added or incorporated into the various engine systems. Limits for the emission of carbon monoxide, nitrogen oxides, and hydrocarbons have been set by the government. Therefore, modern engines must be tuned and adjusted to conform to these stringent limits. Therefore, latest test equipment includes necessary instruments for checking chemical content of the exhaust gases. See Chapter 31, Emission Controls, and Chapter 33, Driveability and Tune-up.

Plug-In Diagnosis

Early diagnostic systems used special test equipment that plugged into a diagnostic connector on the vehicle. In this way, a series of programmed tests could be made to check the condition of various units and systems on the car.

One of the pioneers of this method of engine diagnosis was Volkswagen. The original setup consisted of a computer, a card reader, a hand control unit, an umbilical cord for connecting the test equipment to the vehicle's diagnostic connection, a tachometer, and a timing light.

A more sophisticated diagnostic arrangement was used on many U.S. cars. Some Chrysler products, for example, utilized an electronic spark advance computer that had been programmed to monitor several different systems. If a problem was detected in a monitored circuit, its fault code was stored for display on a diagnostic readout tool, Figure 32-4.

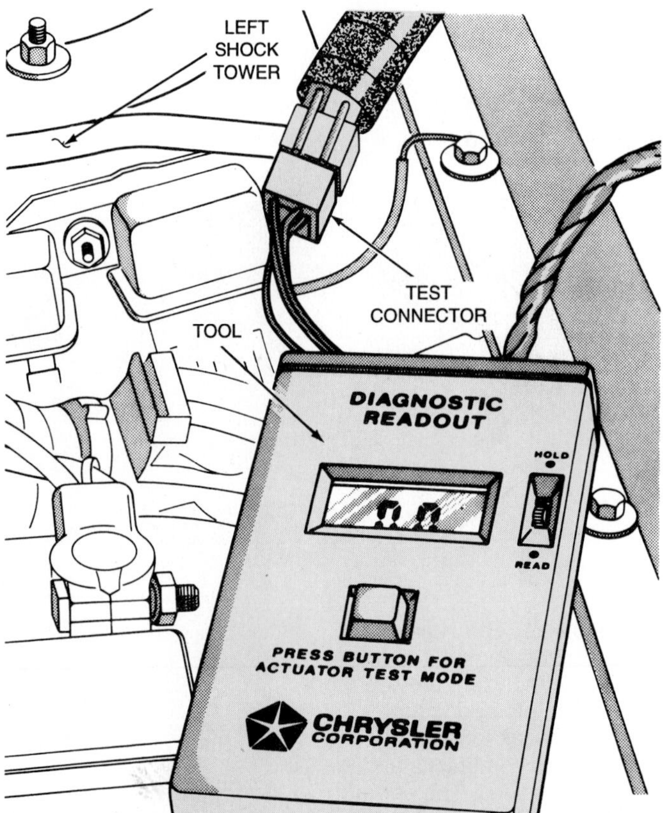

Figure 32-4. Chrysler's plug-in diagnosis requires use of a diagnostic readout tool attached to a vehicle's test connector. Trouble code numbers that appear on the screen of the tool indicate where problems exist. (Chrysler)

To make a series of tests, the readout tool was attached to a test connector located under the hood at the left shock tower. The readout tool was used to check out three different modes:

- Diagnostic test mode, which was used to retrieve fault codes stored in the computer.
- Circuit actuation test mode, which was used to check out specific system components.
- Switch test mode, which was used to check certain switch circuits.

As code numbers appeared on the readout tool, they were recorded for later reference to a listing of problem areas related to those particular code numbers. When the problem area was corrected, the electronic spark advance computer would cancel the fault codes. Also see Figure 32-5.

Self Diagnosis

The next step up from plug-in diagnosis is ***self diagnosis.*** On vehicles so equipped, the ECU monitors operating conditions for possible malfunctions. It compares system conditions against standard limits. A two-digit numerical trouble code is stored in the computer memory.

When a malfunction is detected by the self-diagnostic system, the trouble codes can be retrieved by the service technician. The technician then consults trouble code diagnostic charts to determine what service is required to correct the problem found by the system.

Troubleshooting Charts

Troubleshooting charts have been a traditional means of relating specific symptoms of trouble to possible causes. A series of engine problems are covered in this manner in the following troubleshooting charts.

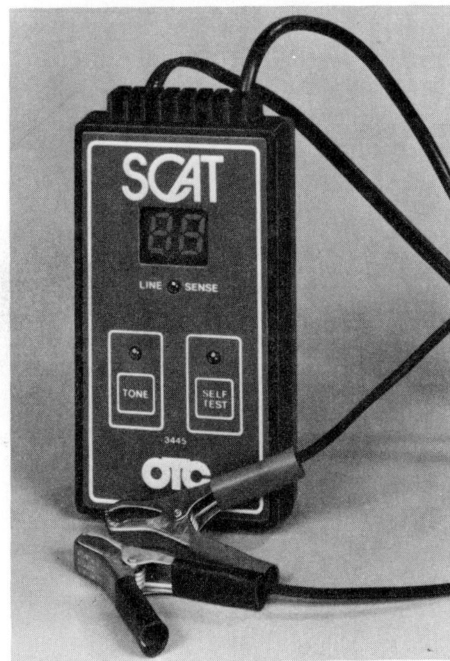

Figure 32-5. Various diagnostic testers are available that provide access to the trouble codes stored in onboard computers. (OTC Tools and Equipment)

Engine Diagnosis

Engine Will Not Start

- Weak battery.
- Corroded or loose battery connections.
- Loose engine and/or battery ground connection.
- Defective ignition switch.
- Faulty starter or solenoid.
- Faulty ignition coil.
- Moisture on high tension wiring and distributor cap.
- Faulty ignition distributor.
- Faulty high tension wiring.
- Incorrect spark plug gap.
- Incorrect ignition timing.
- Dirt, water, or ice in fuel line or carburetor.
- Faulty fuel pump.
- Obstructed air filter.
- Flooded carburetor.
- Sticking choke.
- Maladjusted choke.
- Incorrect carburetor float setting.
- Empty fuel tank.
- Defective neutral starting switch.
- Faulty emission control unit.
- Faulty engine computer control system.

Engine Starts But Will Not Run

- Back pressure in exhaust system.
- Obstructed air filter.
- Restricted or inadequate fuel supply to fuel pump.
- Weak fuel pump pressure or volume.
- Clogged fuel filter.
- Misaligned distributor rotor.

Hard Starting

- Maladjusted choke.
- Faulty fuel pump.
- Clogged fuel filter.
- Maladjusted or faulty carburetor.
- Clogged electronic fuel injection system injectors.
- Air leak into intake manifold or vacuum hoses.
- Obstructed air filter.
- Defective exhaust gas recirculation (EGR) valve.
- Sticking positive crankcase ventilation (PCV) valve.
- Faulty ignition coil.
- Faulty spark plugs or incorrect gap.
- Incorrect ignition timing.
- Moisture on high tension wiring and distributor cap.
- Incorrect valve timing.

Rough Idle

- Maladjusted carburetor.
- Obstructed air filter.
- Faulty evaporative emission control (EEC) system.

- Improper feedback system operation.
- Air leak into intake manifold or vacuum hoses.
- Backpressure in exhaust system.
- Faulty EGR valve.
- Faulty PCV system operation.
- Faulty ignition coil.
- Defective distributor rotor or cap.
- Leaking engine valves.
- Incorrect valve timing.

Engine Stalls

- Low idle speed.
- Incorrect choke adjustment.
- Too lean or too rich idle mixture setting.
- Low carburetor float level.
- Inoperative carburetor float needle valve.
- Air leak into intake manifold or vacuum hoses.
- Loose engine and/or battery ground connection.
- Faulty ignition coil.
- Worn distributor rotor.
- Moisture on high tension wiring and spark plugs.
- Incorrect valve lash (solid lifters).

Engine Stalls on Quick Stops

- Low idle speed.
- Incorrect choke adjustment.
- Incorrect carburetor float level.
- Faulty carburetor accelerator pump.
- Corroded or loose EEC connections.
- Clogged electronic fuel injection system injectors.
- Defective EGR valve.
- Incorrect ignition timing.

Loss of Power

- Dirt or water in fuel line.
- Faulty fuel pump.
- Obstructed air filter.
- Low carburetor float level.
- Lean air/fuel mixture.
- Improper feedback system operation.
- Defective or maladjusted emission control system.
- Faulty ignition coil.
- Worn distributor shaft.
- Loose trigger wheel (reluctor) in distributor.
- Worn or burned distributor rotor.
- Fouled or incorrectly gapped spark plugs.
- Leaking engine valves.
- Incorrect valve lash (solid lifters).
- Weak valve springs.
- Incorrect valve timing.
- Blown cylinder head gasket.
- Backpressure in exhaust system.

Engine Hesitates on Acceleration

- Restricted fuel line.
- Improper thermostatic air cleaner operation.
- Clogged fuel filter.
- Maladjusted choke.
- Faulty carburetor accelerator pump operation.
- Improper feedback system operation.
- Faulty ignition coil.
- Faulty spark plugs.
- Incorrect ignition timing.
- Leaking engine valves.

Engine Misses on Acceleration

- Lean air/fuel mixture.
- Dirt in carburetor.
- Defective carburetor accelerator pump.
- Faulty ignition coil.
- Fouled or incorrectly gapped spark plugs.
- Incorrect ignition timing.
- Weak valve springs.
- Sticking engine valves.
- Leaking engine valves.

Engine Misses Under Load

- Low fuel pump pressure or volume.
- Improper feedback system operation.
- Air leak into intake manifold or vacuum hoses.
- Faulty ignition coil.
- Worn or burned distributor rotor.
- Faulty distributor cap or moisture on cap.
- Defective high tension wiring.
- Fouled or incorrectly gapped spark plugs.
- Worn camshaft lobes.
- Sticking hydraulic lifters.
- Bent push rod.
- Weak valve springs.
- Blown cylinder head gasket.

Engine Misses at High Speed

- Dirt in fuel line.
- Clogged carburetor jets.
- Faulty ignition coil.
- Worn or burned distributor rotor.
- Worn distributor shaft.
- Fouled or incorrectly gapped spark plugs.
- Incorrect ignition timing.
- Worn camshaft lobes.
- Worn valve lifters.
- Sticking engine valves.
- Leaking engine valves.
- Incorrect valve lash (solid lifters).

Engine Backfires

- Air leaks into intake manifold or vacuum hoses.
- Incorrect ignition timing.
- Incorrect valve timing.
- Low compression pressure.

Engine Speed Surges

- Low fuel pump pressure or volume.
- Clogged fuel filter.
- Obstructed air filter.
- Improper thermostatic air cleaner operation.
- Sticking carburetor linkage.
- Incorrect carburetor float level.
- Malfunctioning carburetor.
- Air leak into intake manifold or vacuum hoses.
- Faulty ignition timing advance and retard.
- Faulty PCV system.
- Defective EGR valve.

Excessive Fuel Consumption

- Obstructed air filter.
- Improper thermostatic air cleaner operation.
- Maladjusted or sticking choke.
- High carburetor float level.
- Faulty carburetor accelerator pump.
- Maladjusted carburetor.
- Fouled or faulty spark plugs.
- Incorrect ignition timing.
- Backpressure in exhaust system.
- Incorrect vacuum hose connection.
- Owner's driving habits.

Engine Vibration

- Loose or collapsed engine mounts.
- Defective vibration damper.
- Loose mounting of belt-driven accessories.
- Out-of-balance cooling fan.

Engine Runs Cold

- Defective cooling system thermostat.
- Defective temperature gauge or warning light circuit.

Engine Overheats

- Low coolant level.
- Faulty temperature gauge or sending unit.
- Air in cooling system.
- Too much antifreeze in coolant.
- Collapsed radiator hose.
- Blocked radiator airflow.
- Faulty radiator cap.
- Defective cooling fan or fan clutch.
- Inoperative electric fan.
- Slipping fan belt.
- Faulty water pump.
- Loose water pump belt.
- Defective cooling system thermostat.
- Incorrect ignition timing.
- Excessive engine friction.

Excessive Oil Consumption

- High oil level.
- Plugged drainback in cylinder head.
- Excessive bearing clearance.
- Worn crankshaft journals.
- Excessive oil throw-off from engine bearings.
- Worn piston rings.
- Clogged drain holes in rings.
- Incorrect ring gap.
- Ring gaps incorrectly spaced.
- Compression rings installed upside down.
- Too little piston ring side clearance.
- Wrong size rings installed.
- Worn pistons and cylinder walls.
- Damaged or missing valve seals.
- Worn valve stems and guides.
- Sticking PCV valve.
- Overheated engine.

External Oil Leakage

- Defective fuel pump gasket.
- Defective cylinder head cover gasket.
- Defective oil filter gasket.
- Defective oil pan gasket or end seal.
- Defective timing chain (or gear) cover gasket.
- Worn timing chain (or gear) cover oil seal.
- Worn rear main bearing oil seal.
- Loose oil gallery plug.
- Improperly seated engine oil pan drain plug.
- Improperly seated camshaft rear plug.

Low Oil Pressure

- Low oil level.
- Diluted oil or excessive oil temperature.
- Faulty oil pressure sending unit.
- Clogged oil filter.
- Worn oil pump.
- Excessive bearing clearance.
- Sticking oil pump relief valve.
- Loose, bent, or cracked oil pump suction tube.

Ping or Spark Knock

- Low octane fuel or poor fuel quality.
- Low compression pressure.
- High compression pressure.
- Excessive combustion chamber deposits.
- Sharp edges in combustion chamber.
- Air leak into intake manifold.
- Incorrect ignition timing.

- Malfunctioning ignition distributor advance.
- Wrong spark plugs for application.
- Faulty EGR valve.

Engine Knocks

- Noisy connecting rods or bearings.
- Noisy pistons, piston pins, or piston rings.
- Noisy main bearings.
- Detonation.
- Preignition.

Noisy Connecting Rods or Bearings

- Insufficient oil in crankcase.
- Defective oil pump.
- Low oil pressure.
- Thin or diluted oil.
- Excessive connecting rod bearing clearance.
- Bent connecting rods.
- Out-of-round connecting rod bearing journals.

Noisy Pistons, Pins, or Rings

- Excessive piston-to-cylinder wall clearance.
- Collapsed piston skirt.
- Loose piston strut.
- Incorrectly fitted piston pin.
- Misaligned connecting rods.
- Excessive carbon deposits on pistons.
- Piston rings striking ridge at top of cylinder wall.
- Broken ring.
- Incorrect ring gap.
- Excessive ring-to-groove side clearance.

Noisy Main Bearings

- Insufficient oil supply.
- Low oil pressure.
- Worn main bearings.
- Out-of-round crankshaft journals.
- Excessive end play of crankshaft.
- Loose flywheel.
- Loose or damaged vibration damper.

Noisy Valves

- High or low oil level in crankcase.
- Thin or diluted oil.
- Low oil pressure.
- Dirt in hydraulic lifters.
- Excessive hydraulic lifter leakdown.
- Worn valve lifters.
- Excessive valve lash (solid lifters).
- Bent push rods.
- Excessive runout of valves or seats.
- Worn rocker arms and/or pivots or shafts.
- Broken or cocked valve spring.
- Bent valve.

Burned Valves and Seats

- Lean air/fuel mixture.
- Insufficient valve lash (solid lifters).
- Excessively thin valve head margin.
- Excessively narrow valve seat.
- Loose valve seat insert.
- Warped valve head.
- Worn valve stems and guides.

Dieseling

- High engine idle speed.
- Poor quality fuel.
- Excessive carbon in combustion chamber.
- Wrong type spark plugs for application.
- Defective exhaust emission control system.

Diesel Engine Diagnosis

Hard Starting

- Air in fuel system.
- Clogged fuel filter.
- Blocked fuel supply line.
- Blocked injection lines.
- Defective injection pump.
- Blocked injection pump.
- Incorrect injection timing.
- Defective preheating device.
- Low engine compression.

Engine Surges While Idling

- Incorrectly adjusted governor.
- Defective fuel injection pump.

Loss of Power

- Clogged fuel filter.
- Blocked or leaking injection lines.
- Defective injection pump.
- Incorrect injection timing.
- Defective timing device.
- Obstructed air filter.
- Maladjusted low idle.

Engine Misses Under Load

- Air in fuel system.
- Clogged fuel filter.
- Blocked fuel supply line.
- Blocked injection lines.
- Defective fuel injector.
- Incorrect injection timing.
- Defective overflow valve.

Excessive Fuel Consumption

- Leaking fuel lines.
- Defective injection pump.
- Incorrect injection timing.

- Defective timing device.
- Defective injection nozzle.
- Obstructed air filter.
- Uneven engine compression.

Engine Cannot Be Shut Off

- Defective shutoff device.
- Defective injection pump.
- Incorrect governor setting.

Black Smoke and Poor Performance

- Air in fuel system.
- Defective injection pump.
- Defective governor.

White or Blue Smoke

- Blocked fuel tank vent.
- Air in fuel supply line.
- Clogged fuel filter.
- Blocked injection lines.
- Defective injector or injection nozzle.
- Obstructed air filter.
- Defective governor.
- Uneven engine compression.

Exhaust System Backpressure

Certain troubles and possible causes listed in the Engine Diagnosis charts deserve further explanation. ***Exhaust system backpressure,*** for example, appears as a possible cause for many different engine problems.

If the exhaust pipe, muffler, catalytic converter, or tailpipe is partially restricted, the hot exhaust gases will be unable to escape readily and a backpressure will be created in the exhaust system. As a result, the combustible charge will be severely diluted and full engine power will not be developed. In extreme cases, the exhaust valves will burn.

Engine Overheats

There may be many "conditions" that result in ***engine overheating.*** In some vehicles, the degree of overheating is indicated by the temperature gauge on the instrument panel. In other vehicles, a signal lamp on the panel lights as a warning when a prescribed high temperature is reached. Certain conditions will cause only a slight change in recorded temperature. Other conditions will result in a rapid rise in temperature and violent boiling of the coolant.

When troubleshooting the cause for engine overheating, the first step is to make a careful visual inspection to see if there is any evidence of external leakage of coolant. Check all surfaces of the radiator and its hose connections. Leaks generally cause corrosion, which is easily seen. Also check the heater, heater hoses, and hose connections.

The engine also needs careful inspection. Pay particular attention to the core hole plugs and edges of the cylinder head gasket. Check the cooling fan, water pump, and drive belts. The belts must be in good condition and adjusted to proper tension. Test the radiator cap, Figure 32-6. Test the operation of the thermostat, Figure 32-7. A thermostat "frozen" in the closed position will also cause extreme overheating.

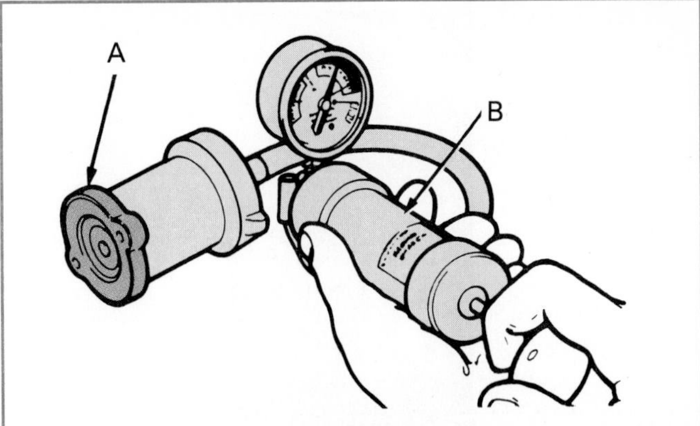

Figure 32-6. To test the condition of a radiator cap (A), attach it to a low-range pump-type pressure gauge (B). Test the cap for pressure hold (at least 30 seconds) and for pressure release point. These are usually marked on the cap. (Chrysler)

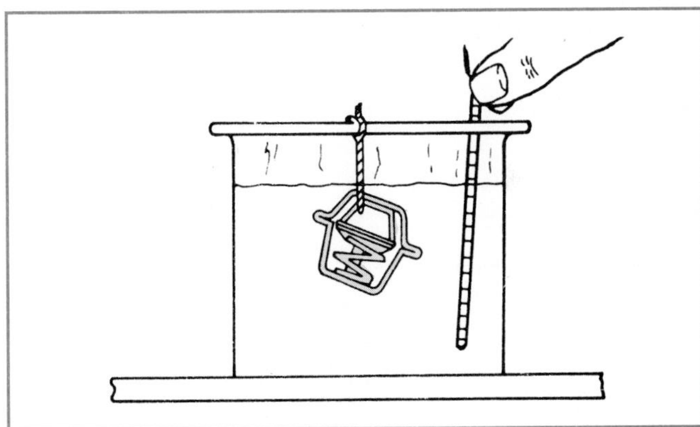

Figure 32-7. To test the operation of a thermostat, suspend it in a boiling 50/50 solution of antifreeze and water. Record the opening and closing temperatures and compare these readings with the manufacturer's specifications. (Ford)

To test for restrictions in the radiator, first bring the system up to operating temperature. Then shut off the engine and feel the front surface of the radiator. On crossflow radiators, the radiator should feel hot along the left side and warm along the right side with an even temperature rise from right to left and bottom to top. On vertical flow radiators, the radiator should feel warmer at the top than at the bottom. Any cold spots would indicate clogged sections.

Water pump operation can be checked by running the engine while squeezing the radiator upper hose. A pressure surge should be felt. Also check for a plugged vent hole in the pump housing.

Not all coolant leakage is external. Severe cases of overheating and coolant loss can result from leaks into the combustion chamber. When the cylinder head is cracked, or there is a blown cylinder head gasket, the hot gases of combustion can enter the cooling system. Coolant temperature rises rapidly and boiling takes place.

To test for an internal coolant leak, use a combustion leakage tester, Figure 32-8. This is a chemical test. The tester is applied to the filler neck of the radiator. Then, with the engine running, any gas from the combustion chamber

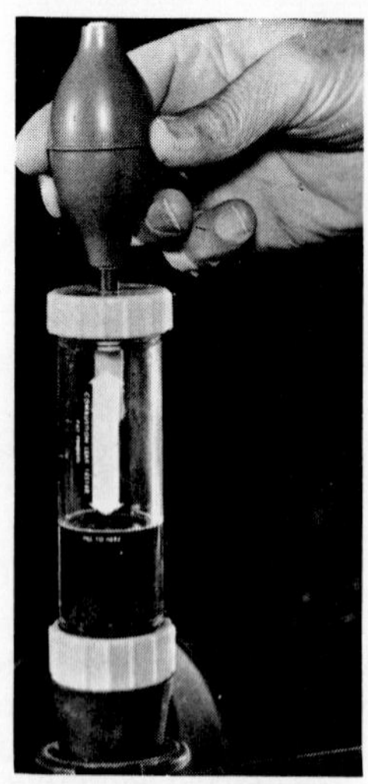

Figure 32-8. To test for combustion leakage, use a special tester that attaches to the radiator filler opening. Combustion gases in the sample of coolant will cause the color of the chemical in the tester to change.

that enters the coolant will be drawn into the tester and cause the chemical to change its color.

Making a compression test of the engine cylinders will also be helpful in checking for internal coolant leaks, particularly in the case of a blown head gasket. (Low readings on adjacent cylinders indicate blown gasket.)

Excessive Oil Consumption

Excessive oil consumption can result from external leakage of oil or as the result of oil passing through the engine. It will be necessary to determine the exact source of the oil loss or whether the oil is passing through the combustion chambers of the engine.

External Loss of Oil. If there is an external loss of oil, the exterior of the engine will be coated with oil, particularly in the area of the source of the leakage. The usual procedure for locating the source of the oil leak is to first carefully clean the exterior of the engine. Then, take the vehicle for a short drive. Stop the vehicle over a clean area and examine the engine for evidence of oil leakage. See Figure 32-9. Also see if oil has dripped on the pavement.

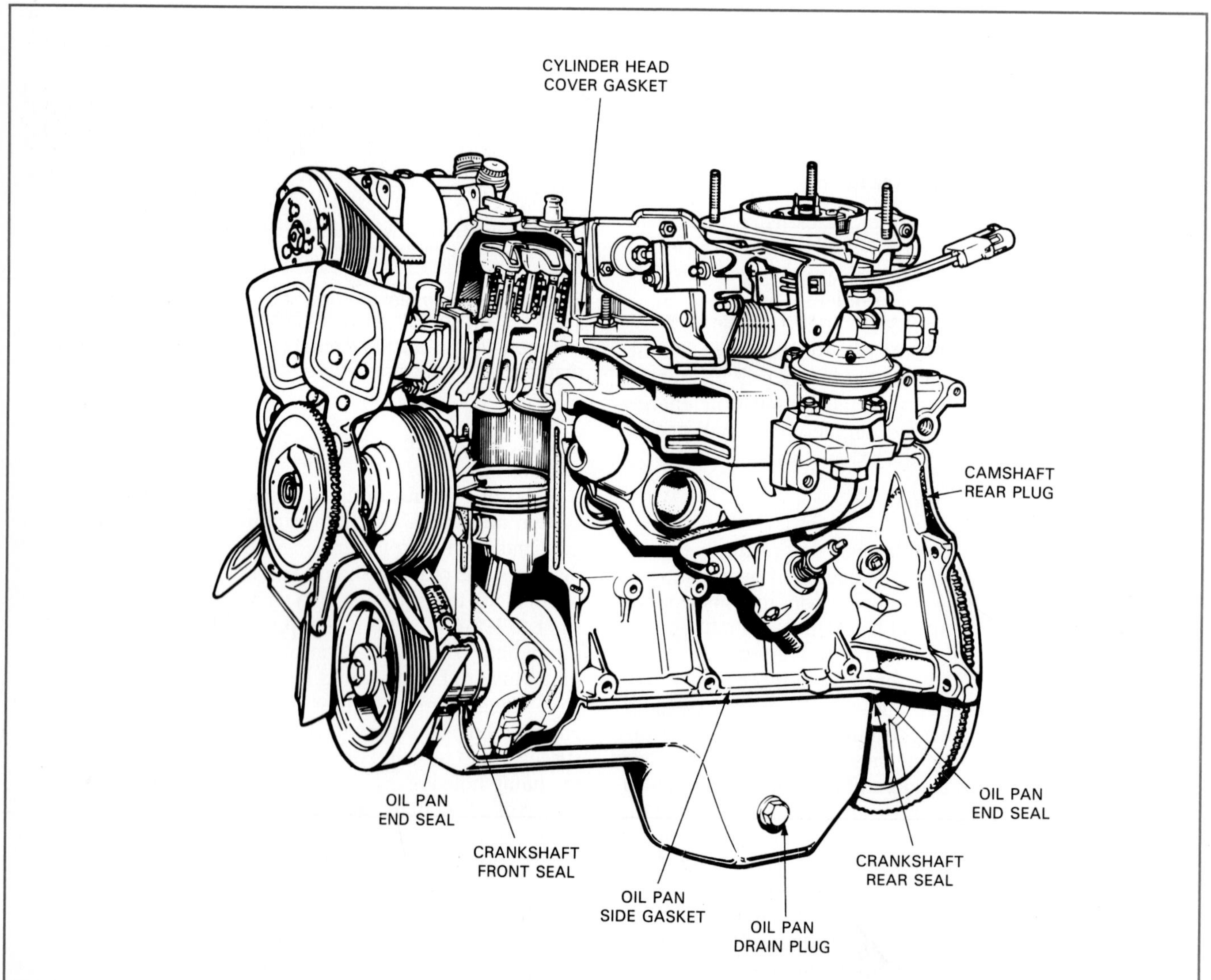

CYLINDER HEAD COVER GASKET
CAMSHAFT REAR PLUG
OIL PAN END SEAL
CRANKSHAFT FRONT SEAL
OIL PAN SIDE GASKET
OIL PAN DRAIN PLUG
CRANKSHAFT REAR SEAL
OIL PAN END SEAL

Figure 32-9. Various points of possible external leakage of engine oil are shown in this drawing of a typical fuel-injected four-cylinder engine. (Chrysler)

This will aid in locating the source of the leakage, front or rear, left or right.

It is not unusual to confuse an oil leak at the rear main bearing seal with oil leakage from some other point. To determine the exact source of the leakage, plug the oil filler pipe. With the engine idling, blow compressed air into the dipstick tube or hole in the block. Watch for oil leakage and trace it to its source.

Internal Consumption of Oil. When oil is being consumed by passing through the engine, it usually will cause heavy blue smoke to come from the tailpipe, particularly after the engine has idled for several minutes. After the idling period, the engine should be raced briefly and blue smoke should appear.

While worn piston rings and tapered cylinder walls can cause excessive oil consumption, there are a great number of other problem areas that could be at fault, either singly or in combination. In most cases of internal consumption of oil, the oil is leaking out of one or more of the pressure lubricated engine bearings (connecting rod, main, or camshaft bearings). The oil is being splashed or thrown up into the cylinders under the pistons in such large quantities that no piston ring can control the excess.

Related Troubles

It is obvious that many engine defects are common to both engine overheating and excessive oil consumption. There is a definite relationship between the two engine problems. Searching for the cause of either trouble will often disclose the need for correction in either or both the engine oil circulation system and coolant circulation system.

Compression Test

A ***compression test*** of each cylinder while the engine is warm and cranking is a well-accepted method of checking the condition of internal components of the engine. The compression pressure of each cylinder is taken and recorded, then the readings are compared with compression values supplied by the engine manufacturer. See Figure 32-10. Compression loss in excess of stipulated values usually means that the engine valves need service or the engine requires an overhaul.

A typical compression testing gauge kit for gasoline-fueled engines is shown in Figure 32-11. Since the compression ratio of a diesel engine may be as high as 23 to 1, a gauge which will check pressures up to and exceeding 650 psi (4500 kPa) is needed.

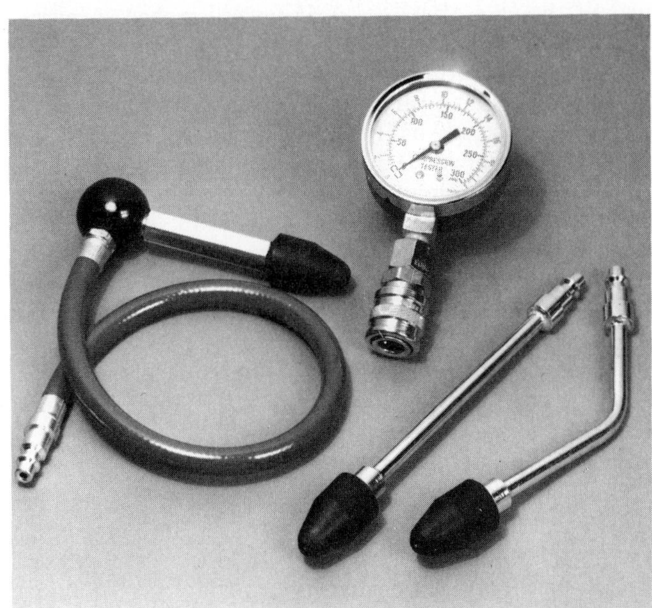

Figure 32-11. This compression tester is designed for testing the compression pressure of gasoline-fueled engines. Quick connect-disconnect attachments will adapt the tester to most engine applications. (Accurate Instruments)

COMPRESSION PRESSURE LIMIT CHART

Maximum PSI	Minimum PSI	Maximum PSI	Minimum PSI	Maximum PSI	Minimum PSI	Maximum PSI	Minimum PSI
134	101	164	123	194	145	224	168
136	102	166	124	196	147	226	169
138	104	168	126	198	148	228	171
140	105	170	127	200	150	230	172
142	107	172	129	202	151	232	174
144	108	174	131	204	153	234	175
146	110	176	132	206	154	236	177
148	111	178	133	208	156	238	178
150	113	180	135	210	157	240	180
152	114	182	136	212	158	242	181
154	115	184	138	214	160	244	183
156	117	186	140	216	162	246	184
158	118	188	141	218	163	248	186
160	120	190	142	220	165	250	187
162	121	192	144	222	166		

Figure 32-10. A typical compression pressure limit chart is calculated so that the lowest reading on the compression tester is 75% of the highest reading. (Ford)

Vacuum Gauge Test

The use of a ***vacuum gauge*** is another basic method of determining the operating condition of an engine. The test is made with the engine running at normal operating temperature and with the vacuum gauge attached to the intake manifold. If the gauge needle is steady at 15 to 20 in. Hg and drops sharply when the throttle is opened quickly, the engine is in good condition.

If the vacuum gauge reading does not drop on sudden acceleration, then recover, the piston rings may be worn. If the reading occasionally drops 1 to 5 in. Hg, an engine valve is sticking or a spark plug is not firing. If the gauge reading shows a steady drop of several inches, a burned valve is indicated.

A steady but low vacuum gauge reading in the 12 to 15 in. Hg range is a signal that the spark may be retarded. If the reading is steady but below 12 in. Hg, the engine valve timing may be incorrect or there is an intake manifold leak. If, while holding engine speed at 2500 rpm, the gauge reading drops slowly but steadily downward, there could be back pressure in the exhaust system. A large variation in readings at different engine speeds is a sign that the valve springs may be weak. Wide sweeping readings while holding the engine speed constant could mean that the cylinder head gasket is leaking.

Engine Noise

One of the most difficult of all troubleshooting jobs is to locate the source of noise or "knocks" in an engine. Actually, every rotating or reciprocating part in the engine is a potential source of noise. In many cases, however, certain noises possess characteristics which help identify their origin.

These characteristics vary somewhat between different engines. In most cases, it will be helpful to utilize an instrument of the stethoscope type to localize the noise at some definite section of the engine. See Figure 32-12. These instruments magnify the intensity of the noise, and the sound becomes louder as the tip of the instrument nears the origin of the noise.

Connecting Rod Bearing Knock. The conditions of operation under which the connecting rod bearing noise is heard and the "timing" of the noise are also useful in determining the source. Some noises are louder as the engine speed is increased, or while the engine is under load. For example, a connecting rod bearing that is slightly "loose" will usually knock loudest around an engine speed of 40 mph and, of greatest intensity, just as the engine goes from a pull to a coast (as driver releases accelerator).

A pronounced rod knock will be heard at all speeds and under both idle and load conditions. One rod will make a distinct noise. If all rods are loose, the noise becomes a rattle or clatter. In many cases, rod bearing knocks are confused with piston slap or loose piston pins. This is particularly true when all rods are loose, and experience will be helpful in deciding which part is at fault. It is not of too much importance to decide definitely, because the remedy for either fault involves removal of the piston and rod assemblies in practically all cases. Measurement and inspection of the parts will then disclose where the trouble lies.

Piston Pin Noise. Using a stethoscope is sometimes helpful, since piston or pin may sound loudest when the instrument prod is placed on the cylinder head or block. The rod knock is often loudest with the prod on the crankcase. Shorting out the spark plug on one cylinder may change the intensity of the knock, but it will not always eliminate it. Shorting will help locate which cylinder or rod is at fault in cases where a single knock exists.

Loose piston pins usually, but not always, produce a double rap each revolution of the crankshaft. They rap once at the top of the stroke and again at the bottom. On most engines, the knock is loudest at idling speed, and it will become even louder if the spark is advanced. Often, the knock will be louder if the spark plug is shorted out in cases where not all pins are loose.

Piston Slap. There is much confusion between the noise caused by a piston with excessive clearance in the cylinder and a loose piston pin. Either defect produces a click which is quite distinct. If noisy in all cylinders, it becomes a rattle. One indication of piston slap is a decrease in the noise as the engine warms up. A piston slap is always louder when the engine is cold.

Piston Ring Noise. New piston rings will cause a knock if the ridge at the top of the cylinder bore is not removed before the new rings are installed. Somewhat similar is the condition where the cylinders have been rebored oversize, and the standard cylinder head gasket extends into the combustion chamber. The piston strikes the gasket and makes a distinct knock.

Piston rings that are loose in the grooves will not ordinarily make any noise, since the oil tends to cushion them. If they are excessively loose, particularly the top rings, they may cause a clicking noise similar to a worn valve lifter. There is a difference in the timing of the click. The piston rings will click twice each revolution of the

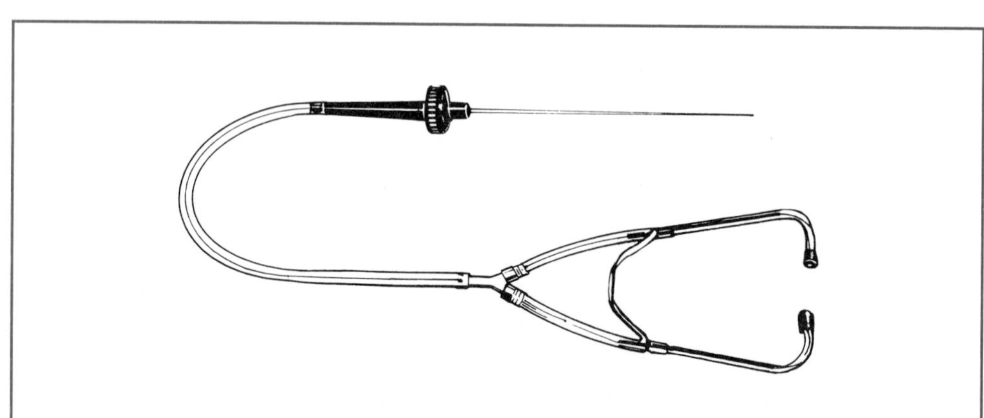

Figure 32-12. A stethoscope-type tool can be used when checking for the approximate location of engine noises. The stethoscope generally has a built-in diaphragm to amplify sounds.

crankshaft, while the valve click will be heard once every other revolution.

Main Bearing Knock. A main bearing knock is more of a bump than a knock. It can be located by shorting out the plugs near it. The noise is loudest when the engine is "lugging" (pulling hard at slow speed). The sound is heavier and more dull than a connecting rod knock.

Crankshaft End Play. Excessive end play in the crankshaft will produce an intermittent rap or knock that is sharper than a main bearing knock. The noise usually will be affected by applying or releasing the clutch. If the car is equipped with an automatic transmission, the noise is more difficult to diagnose. It will rap once, loudly, on sudden acceleration.

Loose Flywheel. If the flywheel is loose on the crankshaft flange, the noise will be similar to a main bearing knock. Ordinarily, it will not change when the plugs are shorted out. Furthermore, the noise may come and go rather than being constant. One sure test is to turn off the ignition, then turn it on again just as the engine is about to stop. The sudden twist applied to the crankshaft will produce a definite knock.

Noisy Engine Mountings. If the rubber engine mountings are drawn down too tight, or, if the rubber had deteriorated enough to allow the metal parts of the mounting to contact each other, a knock may occur. This particular knock appears under high torque conditions during rapid acceleration.

Valve Noises. Valves are a common source of noise for two reasons. There are several points in each unit of the valve train that can create noise. Usually, it is easy to determine which valve (or valves) are causing the noise by inserting a feeler gauge of suitable thickness between the end of the valve and the rocker arm pad with the engine running.

Clicking caused by wear between the valve lifter and lifter guide, or by damage on the end of the lifter next to the camshaft, is not readily located. Here, the timing of the click is helpful, as well as the use of a stethoscope.

Hydraulic valve lifters often will be noisy when the engine is first started, because oil has leaked from the unit. The noise should disappear after a few minutes operation, during which the lifter will be filled with oil. If the noise does not disappear, the defective lifter can be located by means of a stethoscope.

Diesel Engine Diagnosis

Since the diesel engine does not have an ignition distributor or a carburetor, the troubleshooting procedure is simplified. Basically, it includes checking compression pressure and fuel injector performance.

Checking compression requires the removal of the injectors and testing compression pressure at each cylinder with a compression gauge. Special equipment is necessary to check the injectors and the pattern of spray.

Troubleshooting Electronic Systems

For details concerning electronic ignition and fuel injection, see Chapter 22 , Fuel Injection Systems; Chapter 24, Ignition System Fundamentals and Service; and Chapter 29, Computer System Fundamentals and Service.

Test equipment manufacturers continually upgrade their products to keep pace with automotive advances. Latest models provide complete on-board computer testing, make diagnostic circuit checks, and display and define car manufacturers' trouble codes. In effect, each tester is designed to simplify engine troubleshooting.

Chapter 32 – Review Questions

Write your answers on a separate sheet of paper. Do not write in this book.

1. What is engine troubleshooting?
2. What advantage does a diagnostic computer engine analyzer have over visual inspection and manual checks?
   (A) Pinpoints "hidden" sources of trouble more quickly and with greater accuracy.
   (B) Displays performance readings on a screen.
   (C) Furnishes a printout of performance readings.
   (D) All of the above.
3. Name the four gases that a four-gas emissions tester will analyze.
4. Chrysler's "plug-in" diagnostic setup utilizes a computer programmed to monitor several different engine systems. To make the tests, a _____ is attached to a test connector located under the hood.
   (A) Diagnostic readout tool.
   (B) Diagnostic pick-up meter.
   (C) Diagnostic printout unit.
   (D) Diagnostic computer module.
5. In _____ _____ systems, the ECU monitors operating conditions for possible malfunctions.
6. An engine starts but will not run. Technician A says it could be caused by backpressure in the exhaust system. Technician B says it could be caused by an obstructed air filter. Who is right?
   (A) A only.
   (B) B only.
   (C) Both A & B.
   (D) Neither A nor B.
7. An engine hesitates on acceleration. Technician A says it could be caused by a faulty PCV system. Technician B says it could be caused by a faulty carburetor accelerator pump. Who is right?
   (A) A only.
   (B) B only.
   (C) Both A & B.
   (D) Neither A nor B.
8. The first step in troubleshooting the cause of engine overheating is to make a careful _____ to see if there is any evidence of external coolant leakage.
9. Not all coolant leakage is external. Severe cases of overheating and coolant loss can result from leaks into the _____.
10. Testing the _____ of each cylinder while the engine is warm and cranking is a well-accepted method of checking the condition of internal components of the engine.
    (A) vacuum
    (B) compression pressure
    (C) combustion leakage
    (D) coolant leakage

A computerized engine analyzer, such as the one shown, can be used to determine the cause of a driveability problem. (Sun)

Chapter 33
Driveability and Tune-up

After studying this chapter, you will be able to:

- ❍ Define engine tune-up.
- ❍ Explain the close relationship of engine tune-up and emission control.
- ❍ Describe test equipment needed to tune up late-model engines.
- ❍ State necessary preliminary tests and inspections required to determine whether or not an engine is "tunable."
- ❍ List the steps of a logically sequenced engine tune-up test procedure.
- ❍ Assess the value of compression pressure tests and the use of a vacuum gauge to diagnose engine problems.

Driveability and Tune-up

An ***engine tune-up*** is a service operation designed to restore the engine's best level of performance while maintaining good fuel economy and minimum exhaust emissions. A tune-up consists of a series of tests, checks, and corrections made according to a prescribed tune-up test procedure.

In the past, peak engine performance was the only goal sought by the tune-up technician. Today, the technician must try to meet two new objectives:

- ❍ Fulfill the obligation to tune the engine to meet federal and state emissions standards.
- ❍ Satisfy the car owner's demand for economy of operation.

As a result, car maintenance services, including engine tune-ups, are more complex and costly. See Figure 33-1. In some applications, even spark plug replacement has become a tune-up specialist's chore. On the positive side, the more difficult-to-service emission control engines have taken tune-up from the hands of the do-it-yourselfer and given it back to the trained automotive service technician.

Today's auto technician must be able to test and correct problems that exist in compression, ignition, and carburetion or fuel injection; see that the various emission control systems are operable (working as designed); and maintain all related systems (induction, exhaust, temperature control, electronic engine controls, etc.) in good working order. An auto technician must constantly read to keep up with these changes.

Engine Tune-up and Air Pollution

Automobile exhaust emissions are said to be one of the main sources of air pollution in the United States. Combustion of the air/fuel mixture gives off hydrocarbons (HC), carbon monoxide (CO), oxides of nitrogen (NO_X), and other unburned gases that pollute the atmosphere. See Chapter 31, Emission Controls.

Even a well-tuned, clean-burning engine emits some pollutants. If the engine operates inefficiently because of

Figure 33-1. In spite of maintenance-free systems and extended service intervals, today's engine tune-ups are more complex. Elaborate equipment is needed to perform the required tests and components are less accessible.

maladjustments (incorrect settings) or malfunctions (improper operation), it will discharge excessive exhaust emissions. According to the results of research conducted by a spark plug manufacturer, a tuned engine, on the average, produces 57% less carbon monoxide at idle and 48% fewer hydrocarbons than an untuned engine.

In the past, engine tune-up data and specifications charts provided enough information to help the tune-up technician get maximum performance from a vehicle. However, with today's governmental regulations covering emissions limits, more detailed tests and finer adjustments are necessary–along with regional recommendations for vehicles in different climates and altitudes.

Today's engine tune-up specifications vary from car to car–even for the same make and model–based on the type of fuel system, ignition system, and accessory equipment installed on the vehicle. As a result, the engine tune-up specifications and emissions control information for each particular vehicle are provided on a label (decal) placed conveniently under the hood. See Figure 33-2.

The tune-up and emissions label contains up-to-date emissions specifications and setting procedures along with a vacuum hose schematic with emission components identified. In order to tune-up a late model engine, the ***specifications label*** must be duly noted and diligently followed.

Tune-up Equipment

An engine tune-up requires the use of certain types of gauges, testers, and test equipment. Figure 33-3. With this instrumentation, you can perform tests that will reveal weak or defective components that should be replaced. On the other hand, test results will also verify the satisfactory condition of good used units that need not be replaced.

In still another valuable application, you can connect these testers to a given system or circuit to see if a particular setting is as specified. If it is not, the reading on the tester will serve as a means of guiding you in making adjustments to obtain the correct setting.

Tune-up test equipment in the list that follows will permit you to perform all of the checks and tests described

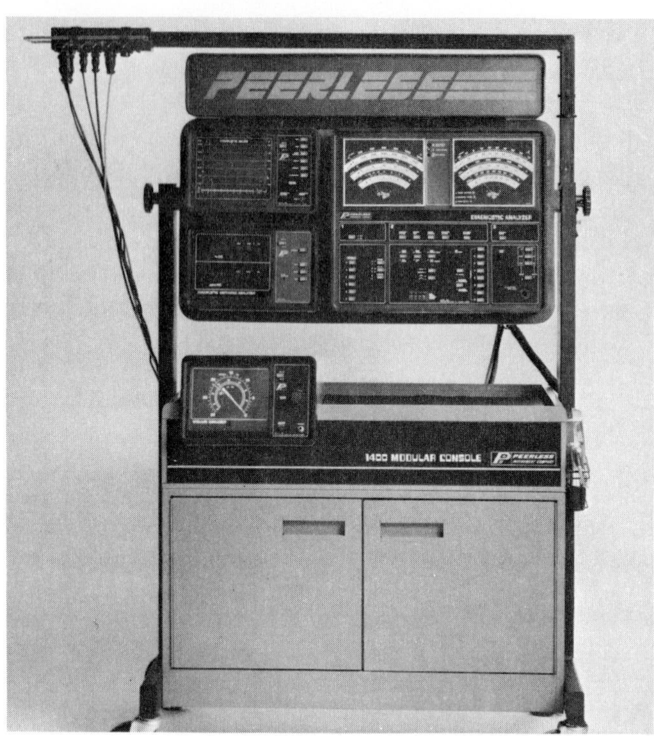

Figure 33-3. To meet today's need for engine tune-up test instrumentation, this modular console contains an ignition systems analyzer, an infrared gas analyzer, a vacuum systems analyzer, fuel system tester, and gimbal (overhead track) mount. (Peerless Instrument Co.)

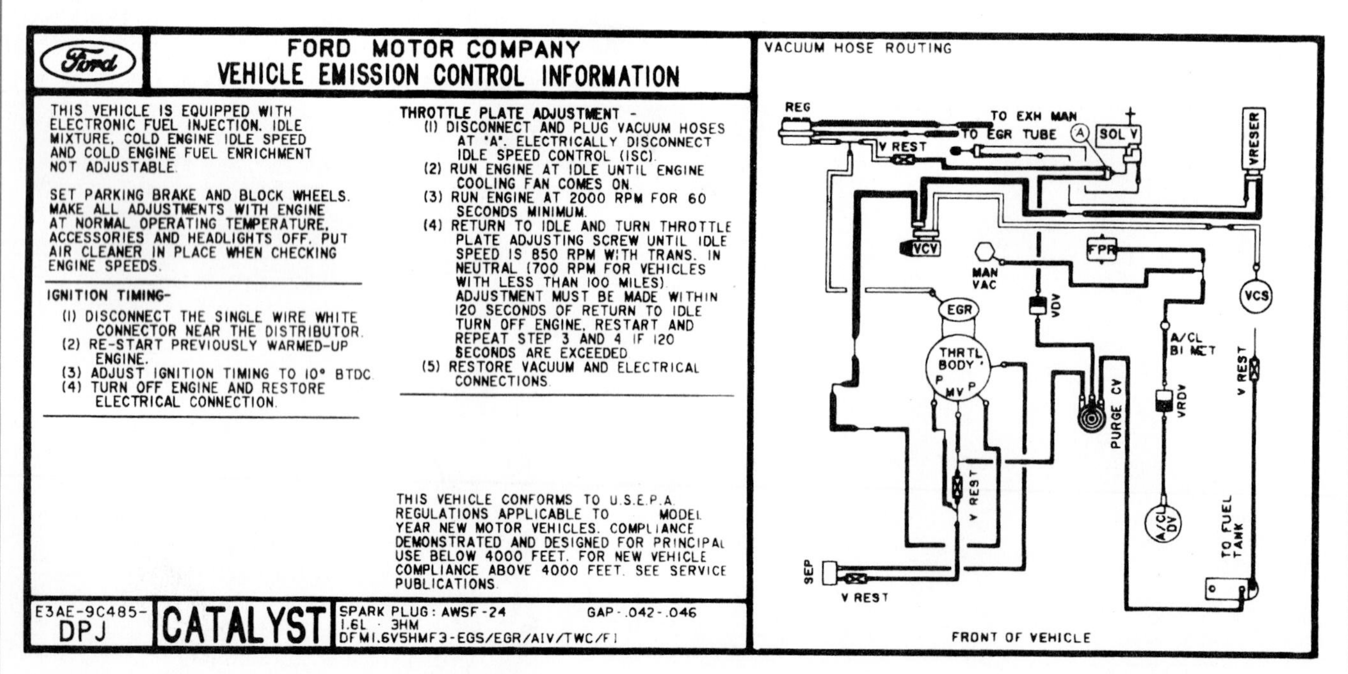

Ford

FORD MOTOR COMPANY
VEHICLE EMISSION CONTROL INFORMATION

THIS VEHICLE IS EQUIPPED WITH ELECTRONIC FUEL INJECTION. IDLE MIXTURE, COLD ENGINE IDLE SPEED AND COLD ENGINE FUEL ENRICHMENT NOT ADJUSTABLE.

SET PARKING BRAKE AND BLOCK WHEELS. MAKE ALL ADJUSTMENTS WITH ENGINE AT NORMAL OPERATING TEMPERATURE, ACCESSORIES AND HEADLIGHTS OFF. PUT AIR CLEANER IN PLACE WHEN CHECKING ENGINE SPEEDS.

IGNITION TIMING-
(1) DISCONNECT THE SINGLE WIRE WHITE CONNECTOR NEAR THE DISTRIBUTOR.
(2) RE-START PREVIOUSLY WARMED-UP ENGINE.
(3) ADJUST IGNITION TIMING TO 10° BTDC.
(4) TURN OFF ENGINE AND RESTORE ELECTRICAL CONNECTION.

THROTTLE PLATE ADJUSTMENT -
(1) DISCONNECT AND PLUG VACUUM HOSES AT "A". ELECTRICALLY DISCONNECT IDLE SPEED CONTROL (ISC).
(2) RUN ENGINE AT IDLE UNTIL ENGINE COOLING FAN COMES ON.
(3) RUN ENGINE AT 2000 RPM FOR 60 SECONDS MINIMUM.
(4) RETURN TO IDLE AND TURN THROTTLE PLATE ADJUSTING SCREW UNTIL IDLE SPEED IS 850 RPM WITH TRANS. IN NEUTRAL (700 RPM FOR VEHICLES WITH LESS THAN 100 MILES). ADJUSTMENT MUST BE MADE WITHIN 120 SECONDS OF RETURN TO IDLE TURN OFF ENGINE, RESTART AND REPEAT STEP 3 AND 4 IF 120 SECONDS ARE EXCEEDED.
(5) RESTORE VACUUM AND ELECTRICAL CONNECTIONS.

THIS VEHICLE CONFORMS TO U.S.E.P.A. REGULATIONS APPLICABLE TO MODEL YEAR NEW MOTOR VEHICLES. COMPLIANCE DEMONSTRATED AND DESIGNED FOR PRINCIPAL USE BELOW 4000 FEET. FOR NEW VEHICLE COMPLIANCE ABOVE 4000 FEET. SEE SERVICE PUBLICATIONS.

E3AE-9C485-
DPJ

CATALYST

SPARK PLUG: AWSF-24 GAP-.042-.046
1.6L · 3HM
DFM1.6V5HMF3-EGS/EGR/AIV/TWC/FI

Figure 33-2. All modern cars have an engine tune-up and emissions control information label in engine compartment. Each label contains specifications for that particular engine application. (Ford)

later in the ***tune-up test procedure.*** They will assist you in making precise settings to manufacturer's specifications.

- Compression tester.
- Vacuum gauge or hand-operated vacuum pump.
- Fuel pressure gauge.
- Voltmeter (or volt-amp tester).
- Ammeter.
- Ohmmeter.
- Digital volt-ohmmeter.
- Tachometer (or tach-dwell meter).
- Dwell meter (see above).
- Battery-starter tester.
- Alternator-regulator tester.
- Emissions tester (infrared exhaust gas analyzer or 4-gas analyzer).
- Engine analyzer or diagnostic computer.
- Electronic engine controls tester.
- Distributor tester.
- Stroboscopic timing light.
- Hydrometer.
- PCV (positive crankcase ventilation) system tester.
- Cooling system pressure tester.
- Fuel injection pressure gauge.
- Cylinder leakage tester.
- Solid state circuit testers.
- Belt tension gauge.
- Unpowered test lamp.
- Jumper wires.

In addition, more sophisticated instrumentation is available, Figure 33-4, that will speed the process and, in some cases, provide more precise readings of a unit's capacity, output, range or level of performance.

Figure 33-4. The diagnostic equipment automatically analyzes information from vehicle's engine computer control and tells service technician where problems exist. (Buick)

Tune-up Test Procedure

Most of the work involved in an engine tune-up job is concerned with tests of the engine electrical systems, fuel system, electronic engine controls, and emission controls. Each is a complete subject in itself, and each is covered in detail in separate chapters of this text.

To illustrate the broad scope of an engine tune-up, the procedure that follows gives brief descriptions of the key steps, arranged in the most logical sequence for doing an efficient and effective job. Tests requiring a more in-depth explanation are spelled out in detail after the basic steps have been covered.

Preliminary Tests and Inspections

1. Check the engine oil, coolant, and automatic transmission fluid levels.
2. Note where the vacuum hoses attach to the carburetor or throttle body. Use color-coded tags, if necessary. Disconnect the vacuum hoses and air intake ducting, and remove the air cleaner assembly.
3. Make a general visual inspection of the engine and accessories, including battery condition and the possible need for carburetor or fuel injection system service. If any fluid levels are low, look for evidence of oil, fuel, or coolant leaks.
4. Use an oscilloscope, ignition system analyzer, or diagnostic computer engine analyzer to make area checks of ignition system operation. See Chapter 24, Ignition System Fundamentals and Service, and Chapter 32, Engine Troubleshooting.
5. Observe the "Check Engine" light on vehicles so equipped. If the lamp lights when the engine is running, the self-diagnostic system has detected a problem. Follow through with the attachment of a diagnostic tester and use the manufacturer's diagnostic charts to find the problem.

Check Internal Engine Condition

1. Use a voltmeter to test battery voltage while cranking the engine. (Should be 9 volts or more.) Also listen to the sound of the cranking engine. (Should be strong and steady.) Remove the spark plugs. Use a compression gauge and a remote starter switch to test the compression pressure of the individual cylinders (with choke and throttle valves wide open). If remote cranking will damage the ignition switch in the "lock" or "off" positions, turn the key "on."
2. Use a cylinder leakage tester to test for leakage of air under pressure into the intake or exhaust manifold, crankcase, or cooling system.
3. Use a vacuum gauge to check for vacuum leaks, Figure 33-5. Perform a manifold vacuum test with the throttle valve closed and the vacuum gauge connected directly to the intake manifold (should hold steady reading). Then check vacuum to the emission control units. See Chapter 31, Emission Controls.

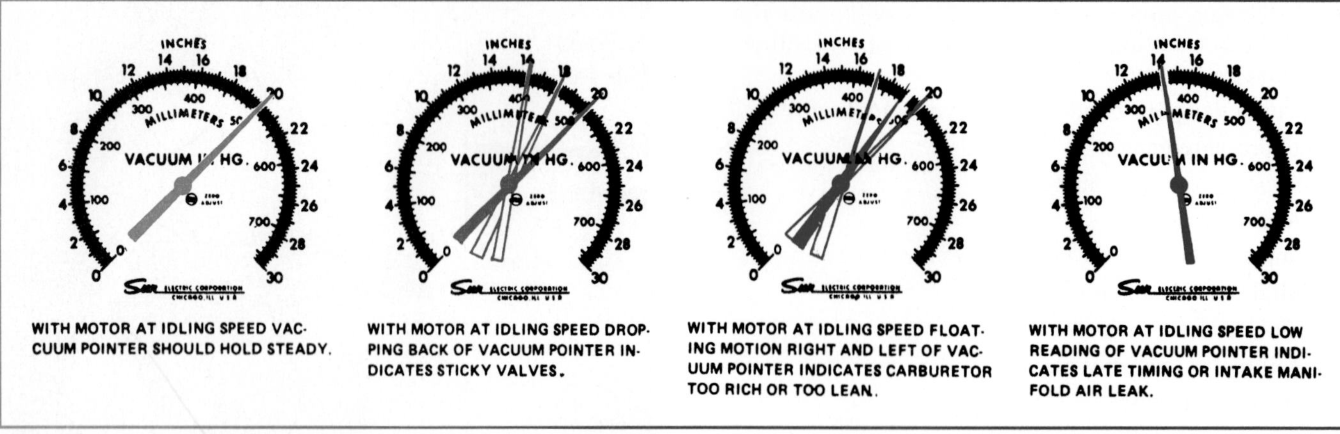

Figure 33-5. Diagrams show typical action of vacuum gauge needle when various conditions exist in the engine under test. (Sun Electric Corp.)

Test and Service the Battery

1. Clean the posts, the cable clamps, and the top of the battery.
2. Check the level of electrolyte in the cells, if possible, and use a hydrometer to check the specific gravity of each cell. (Should be at least 1.250, corrected to 80°F [27°C] with no more than 25 points of gravity difference between high and low cells.)
3. Load test the battery at a load equal to 50% of the cold cranking rating, noting the voltmeter reading after 15 seconds of discharge. (Should be 9.5 volts or more.) Make an open circuit voltage test to verify the battery's state of charge.
4. Recharge the battery if it is weak. Replace the battery if it is defective.

Check the Starting System

1. Inspect the condition of the cables and wires. Check the components for proper mounting.
2. Test for voltage drop in the battery cables, connections, switch, solenoid, and starting motor. See Figure 33-6.
3. Test for amperage draw of the starting motor. Remove the high tension coil wire from the distributor cap tower. Ground the coil wire to a metal part of the engine. Connect the leads of the battery-starter tester to the battery terminals. Crank the engine for 15 seconds and note the voltmeter reading. Stop cranking and adjust the resistance unit on the tester to obtain the voltage previously noted, then read the amperage draw on the ammeter. (Check the reading against the manufacturer's specifications.)

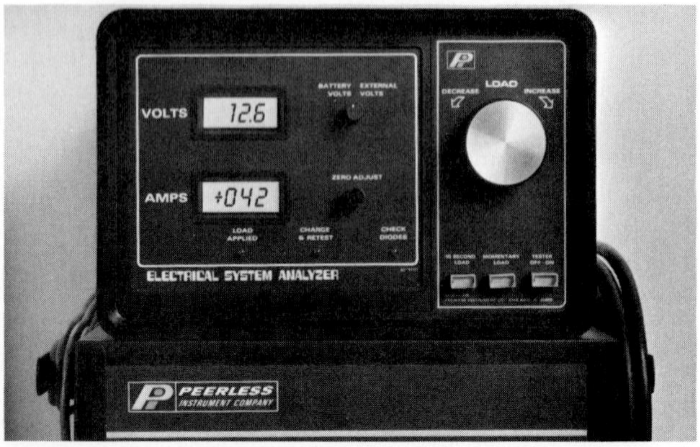

Figure 33-6. Digital electrical systems analyzer checks batteries, starting motors, starter switches, and cables. It has a carbon pile and an automatic 15-second load switch. The analyzer simulates a discharged battery when testing the charging system. (Peerless Instrument Co.)

Test the Ignition Coil

1. With the ignition switch OFF, use an ohmmeter to test the coil primary resistance between the positive and negative terminals. Test the secondary resistance between the center tower and the positive terminal. Check the readings against the manufacturer's specifications. If an oscilloscope or a special coil tester is available, check the maximum and required high tension voltages. Also, the high tension polarity should be negative.
2. Test the resistance of the high tension cables with an ohmmeter. (Typically, the readings should be at least 3000 ohms/ft. and no more than 5000 to 7200 ohms/ft., depending on the application. Check the manufacturer's specifications.)

Check the Ignition Distributor (electronic type)

1. Remove the distributor cap.
2. Check the condition of the distributor cap (inside and outside). Look for cracks, burned contacts, broken carbon button, carbon tracking, and corroded tower contacts. Clean or replace the cap.
3. Remove the rotor and check it for cracks, carbon tracking, or burns on the tip. Clean or replace the rotor.
4. Wiggle the distributor shaft to check for bushing wear.
5. Check the distributor pickup for signs of damage. Study the pickup wires for wear.
6. Test the pickup as recommended by the manufacturer. Most manufacturers recommend checking the resistance of the pickup. If the test results are not within specifications, the pickup must be replaced. After performing the pickup tests, reconnect all wiring.

7. Check the condition of the ignition module. Make sure that wiring to the module is in good condition. If necessary, replace the module.
8. Check operation of mechanical and vacuum advance units. Free or replace inoperative units. (In late-model vehicles, the spark advance is controlled by the computer. These sytems do not have mechanical and vacuum advance mechanisms.)
9. Reinstall the distributor cap and rotor.
10. Check the routing of the spark plug wires from the distributor towers to the spark plugs. See Figure 33-7.

Service the Ignition Distributor (breaker point type)

1. Check the condition of the distributor cap (inside and out) and the rotor.
2. Note the position of the rotor and remove the distributor.
3. Clean the distributor and check the condition of the lead wires, plate, cam, bushings, and advance mechanisms.
4. Replace the breaker points and condenser, Figure 33-8. Align the points, if necessary, and adjust the gap to the manufacturer's recommended setting.
5. Test the breaker arm spring tension.
6. Lubricate the wick in the center of the cam assembly with two drops of engine oil. Lubricate the cam lobes with a light coating of high-melting-point grease or replace the cam lubricator.
7. Check the operation of mechanical and vacuum advance units. Free or replace inoperative units. Check the emission controls that affect timing advance. See Chapter 35.
8. Use a dwell meter to test the distributor point dwell (cam angle) and readjust the point gap, if necessary. Test dwell variation. (Generally, variation should not exceed 3 deg. from 250 rpm to 2000 rpm.)
9. Install the distributor in the engine with the rotor in the original position.
10. Leave the spark advance vacuum line(s) disconnected, but plug the open end(s).

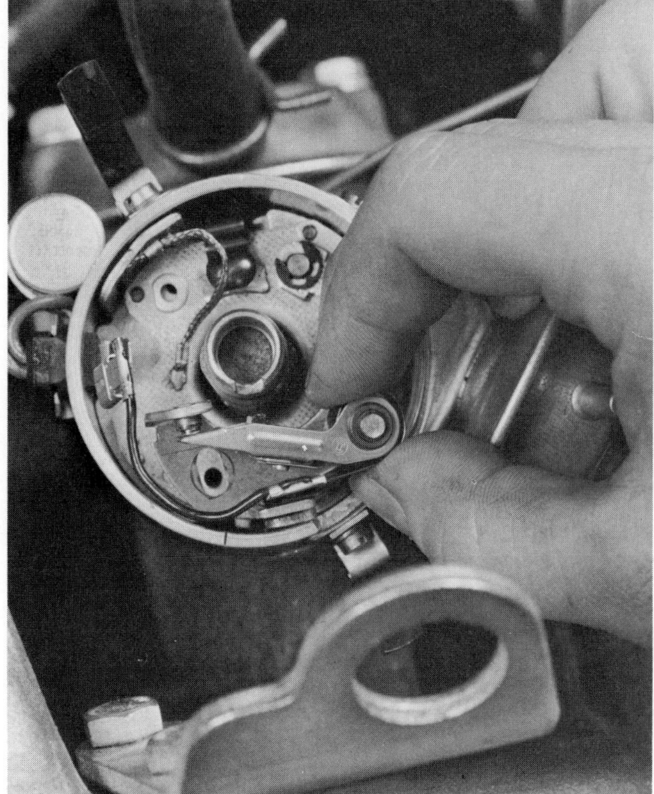

Figure 33-8. Generally, replace the breaker points and the condenser when performing an engine tune-up on any vehicle having this type of ignition system.

Inspect Spark Plugs

1. Examine all spark plug electrodes for wear. Check insulators for breakage.
2. Analyze deposits to pinpoint source of problem.
3. Clean the electrodes, then file and regap good used plugs. See Figure 33-9. Replace defective plugs with a new set of specified type and proper heat range. (Use new gaskets unless plugs have a tapered seat.)

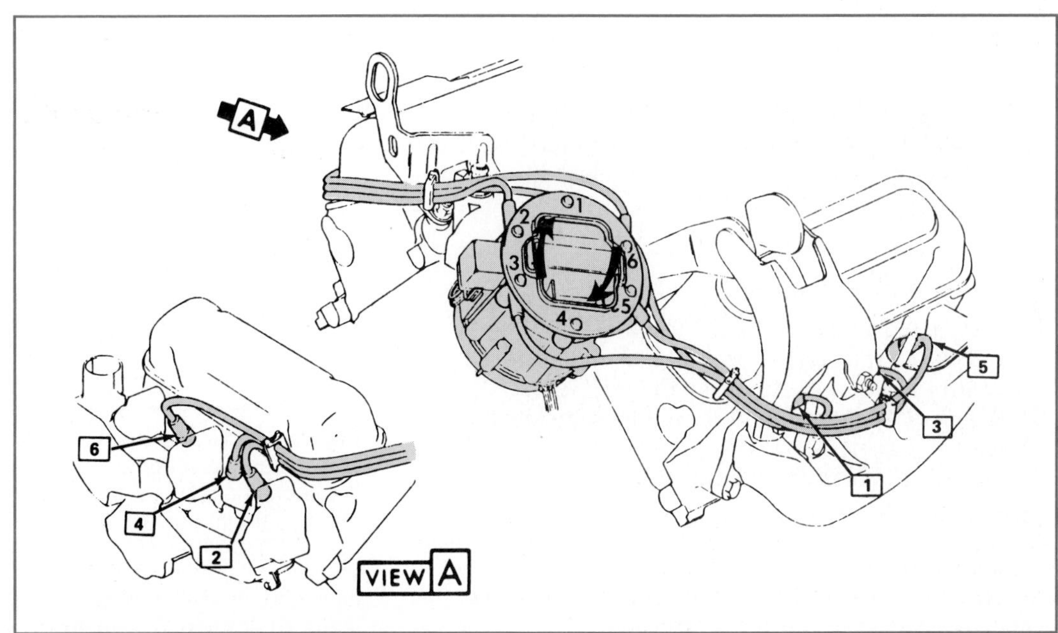

Figure 33-7. This simplified diagram gives the routing of the high tension wiring from the distributor to the spark plugs on a 3.0 liter or 3.8 liter V-6 engine. (Oldsmobile)

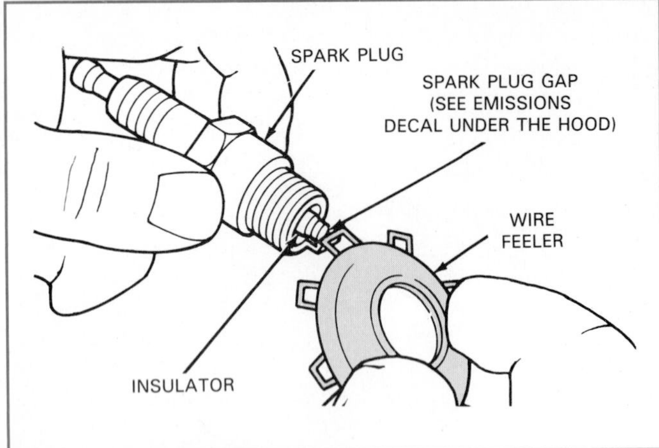

Figure 33-9. Always check the spark plug gap with a round wire feeler gauge. Adjust the gap measurement by bending the side electrode. (Ford)

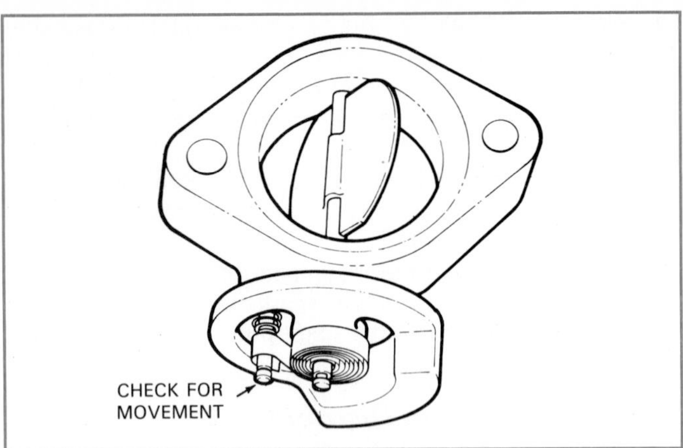

Figure 33-10. The exhaust manifold heat control valve provides quick warmup of the induction system. If the valve counterweight does not move freely, use penetrating oil and tap the counterweight lightly with a hammer. (Chrysler)

4. Install the spark plugs to the correct torque tightness. Typical torque values for various types and sizes are:
   a. Gasketed:
      18 mm – 25-30 ft. lb. (33-38 N.m)
      14 mm – 22-26 ft. lb. (30-35 N.m)
      10 mm – 10-12 ft. lb. (14-18 N.m)
   b. Tapered seat:
      18 mm – 15-20 ft. lb. (20-27 N.m)
      14 mm – 7-15 ft. lb. (10-20 N.m)
      10 mm – 5-11 ft. lb. (8-16 N.m)
5. Apply silicone dielectric compound to the inside of spark plug boots, if recommended. Connect the spark plug cable terminals securely to the plugs in the correct firing order. Make sure the boots fit firmly over the plug porcelains.

Check Cooling System

1. Inspect the condition of the radiator, hoses, and clamps, including transmission oil cooler lines and fittings.
2. Test the radiator cap for pressure release point and pressure-hold.
3. Check the level of the coolant in the radiator or in the coolant reserve tank and check the degree of anti-freeze protection.
4. Use a pressure tester to test the cooling system for leaks. Pressurize the system to the pressure release point of the cap and observe the reading for at least two minutes. (Drop in pressure indicates leak in system.)
5. Check the condition and tension of the V-belts. See Chapter 17, Engine Cooling Systems.

Inspect the Fuel System

1. Torque the intake manifold attaching bolts.
2. Check the freedom of operation of the manifold heat control valve, if so equipped, Figure 33-10.
3. Check the components of the thermostatically controlled air cleaner.
4. Service all air filters and fuel filters. Clean or replace the elements as required.
5. Tighten the carburetor or fuel injection system attaching nuts or bolts and cover screws.
6. Clean the automatic choke mechanism and check the choke valve and linkage for freedom.
7. Check the adjustment of the choke, unloader, and kickdown. See Figure 33-11. Tighten the heat tube fittings, if so equipped. Test continuity (current flow) of the circuit on electric choke applications.
8. Check the components of the throttle body injection (TBI) system or the individual port injection system, including various sensors and sensor circuitry to the electronic control system.
9. Inspect the fuel lines, hoses, and connections for fuel leaks, kinks, restrictions, or deterioration.
10. Check the operation of accelerator linkage. Clean, lubricate, and adjust as required.
11. Check the fuel tank for fuel leaks. Check the condition of the fuel tank filler cap.
12. Check the evaporative emissions control system hoses, canister, and filter. See Chapter 31, Emission Controls.

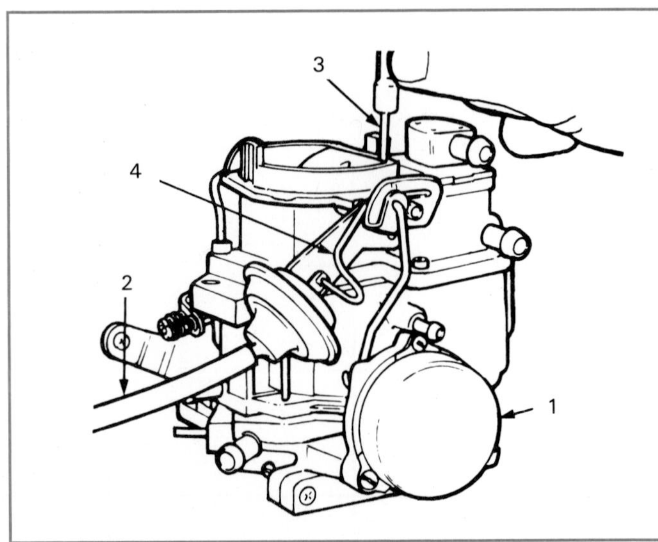

Figure 33-11. To check choke valve clearance, place the fast idle speed screw on the high step of the cam and turn the choke housing (1) to 1/4 turn rich. Apply vacuum to force the diaphragm against the stop (2). Insert the specified plug gauge (3) as shown. Adjust the clearance between the choke valve and the air horn wall by bending the vacuum diaphragm connector link (4). Readjust the cover index to the specified lean/rich position. (Chrysler)

13. Test the fuel pump pressure, capacity (volume), and vacuum.
14. Service the positive crankcase ventilation (PCV) system. Replace the PCV valve if defective or if required by manufacturer's service interval.
15. Check the condition of all emission control systems, Figure 33-12.

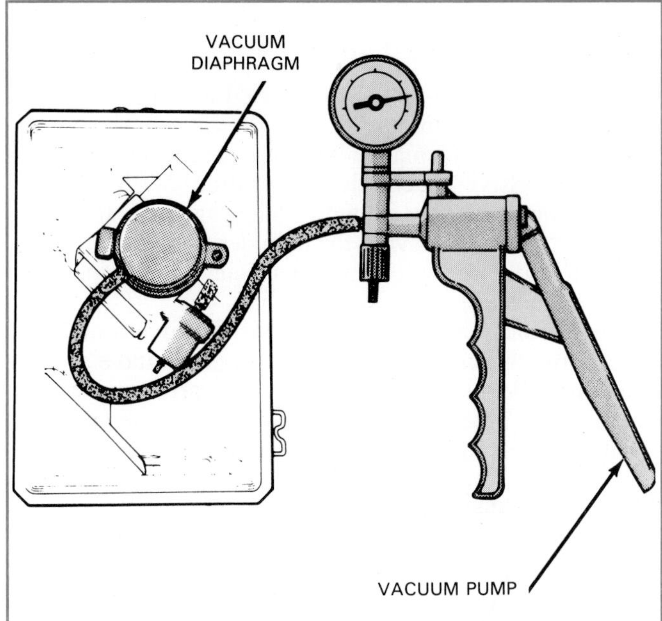

Figure 33-12. In one of many tests of emission controls during an engine tune-up, use a hand-operated vacuum pump to test the operation of the vacuum diaphragm on a thermostatically controlled air cleaner. (Chrysler)

Start the Engine and Make Preliminary Adjustments

1. Run the engine. Check the choking action and fast idle operation.
2. Connect a timing light, Figure 33-13, or other pickup equipment to the ignition system and check initial (base) timing. Reconnect the vacuum line, if disconnected, and recheck the advance with the timing light. Note: Many late-model engines have computer controlled spark timing.
3. Examine the entire exhaust system for leaks.
4. Run the engine to normal operating temperature and check the cooling system thermostat operation.
5. Install a tachometer and vacuum gauge. Adjust the air/fuel mixture and engine idle speed. Adjust the throttle stop solenoid and/or vacuum break on carburetors so equipped.
6. Connect an emissions tester (infrared exhaust gas analyzer, four-gas analyzer, etc.) to the engine and tailpipe of the car. Test HC and CO emission levels at the various speeds recommended by the equipment manufacturer. Check the results against specifications.
7. Adjust valve lash if engine has solid lifters.

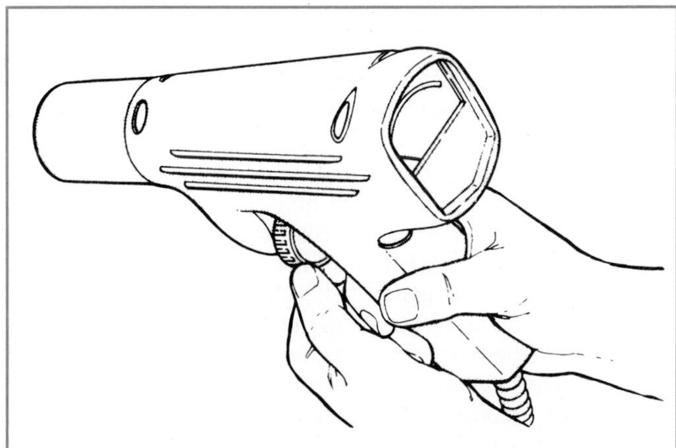

Figure 33-13. To check ignition timing, connect the stroboscopic timing light leads to ground and to an adapter placed between the No. 1 spark plug and the No. 1 spark plug wire. (Chrysler)

Test the Charging System

1. Use an alternator tester to test the voltage and current output of the alternator. See Figure 33-6.
2. Check the operation of the voltage regulator.

Road Test the Car

1. Check the starting and idle. Warm the engine to normal operating temperature and test engine performance at all speeds.
2. Check the automatic transmission shift points and kickdown operation.
3. Make final adjustments to obtain the best possible engine performance, fewest emissions, and most fuel mileage.

Checking Compression Pressure

Never attempt to tune-up an engine having worn piston rings, faulty valves, incorrect valve timing, worn camshaft lobes, or an internal coolant leak. If internal parts are not sound (not in good working order), poor engine performance usually results. This performance problem, however, is beyond the corrective powers of an engine tune-up.

Most internal engine problems can be detected by making a compression pressure test, which is one of the first and most important steps of an engine tune-up. Manufacturers provide minimum/maximum compression pressure charts. See Chapter 32, Engine Troubleshooting. Most specify that the lowest compression reading must be 70% or 75% of the highest.

To use the chart, first record compression pressures for each engine cylinder. Use a special compression gauge to make the test. The engine should be at normal operating temperature. The engine oil should be of the proper grade and not seriously diluted.

Make the test with all spark plugs removed and with choke and throttle valves of the carburetor wide open. Use a remote starter switch to crank over the engine while holding the tip of the compression gauge in each spark plug port in turn. Crank the engine for at least four revolutions, recording the highest reading on the gauge for each cylinder. Compare the high and low figures on your list with the satisfactory ranges shown on the manufacturer's specification chart, Figure 32-10. If one or more cylinders is "out-of-specification," there is no use tuning up the engine until the cause has been determined and corrected.

Using a Vacuum Gauge

In the hands of an experienced operator, a vacuum gauge can provide considerable useful information about the condition of the internal parts of an engine. However, it is easy to misinterpret the readings of the instrument and reach false conclusions. In using the gauge on an engine, it is much more important to note the action of the needle (floating or vibrating, for example) rather than the numbers on the dial.

When properly used and understood, a vacuum gauge will indicate incorrect carburetor adjustment, ignition timing errors, ignition defects, improper valve action, exhaust system restrictions, cylinder leakage, and intake system leakage.

If an engine is in good internal condition and operating properly, the vacuum gauge needle will hold steady at a reading between 15 and 20 at idling speed. See Figure 33-5. There will be some variation with changes in altitude and atmospheric conditions. For example, each 1000 ft. (304.8 m) above sea level will lower the reading about one point (or one inch of mercury). Vacuum gauges are manufactured with dials marked in inches of mercury (in. Hg) to correspond to "U" tube laboratory instruments that serve as a standard.

Interpreting the Readings

With the engine warmed up to operating temperature and running slightly higher than at low idling speed, attach a vacuum gauge to the intake manifold. Attach it directly to the manifold, in order to avoid any air leaks that might exist in vacuum-operated systems or connections. Then make the following analysis of the various readings.

Normal: Needle will be steady between 15 and 20 in. Hg. while idling. When the throttle is suddenly opened and closed, the needle will drop to below 5, then bounce up to around 25.

Leaking rings: Needle may be fairly steady, but will read 3 to 4 points lower than normal. When throttle is suddenly opened and closed, needle may not drop.

Late timing: If compression is good and needle reads low, ignition timing may be late, Figure 33-5. If reading is considerably lower than it should be, valve timing may be late. If adjusting carburetor will not increase vacuum to normal, make a check to see if either or both, ignition or valve timing, should be advanced.

Leaking intake: If needle is steady but from 3 to 9 points low, throttle valve is not closing or an air leak exists in carburetor or intake manifold.

Leaking cylinder head gasket: If needle floats regularly between a low and a high reading, the cylinder head gasket probably is "blown" between two adjacent cylinders.

Carburetor out of adjustment: Needle floats slowly over a range of 4 to 5 points.

Spark plug gaps: If needle floats slowly over a narrower range, perhaps 2 points, the spark plug gaps may be spaced too close.

Restricted exhaust: If needle reads in normal range when engine is first started, sinks to zero, then rises slowly to below normal, the muffler may be clogged or the tailpipe kinked or plugged.

Defective valve action: Experience will help you to distinguish between valve troubles such as leaking, burned, sticking valves, weak valve springs, or worn valve guides. Action of the needle and range of motion are indications of which is at fault, Figure 33-5. Since the valve must be removed in most cases to remedy the defect, correctness of diagnosis can be determined.

Engine mechanical condition: If vacuum gauge indicates loss of compression or improper valve action, do not proceed with tune-up until all faults are corrected. If, however, tests indicate timing errors, intake leaks, carburetor out of adjustment, or a restricted exhaust system, correct these defects as the next step.

High-performance Tuning

An engine tune-up can be carried to extremes if you want to get maximum speed and power from a given engine. A high-performance tune-up procedure often involves extensive mechanical alteration of the engine. Typical modifications include enlarging the valves and seats; porting and relieving the cylinder heads; altering the bore and stroke of the engine; increasing the compression ratio; and installing a custom camshaft.

Additional changes include revising valve timing and ignition timing; enlarging and streamlining intake and exhaust manifolds; and installing multiple carburetors or fuel injection. High-performance tuning is a separate and complicated subject that is not within the scope of this text.

Tuning Emission Controls

Great care, methodical checks, and precise adjustments are required when tuning emission controlled engines. Failure to follow factory instructions and specifications may result in rough idle, surging, loss of power, increased emissions, and dieseling (run-on after ignition key is turned off).

The emission control devices must be in good working order and properly adjusted to function as designed. It is also worth noting that government regulations forbid removing, disconnecting, disengaging, or otherwise rendering emission controls inoperative. Set them up as specified by the manufacturer to maintain the controls at maximum operating efficiency to help fight air pollution. These are federal regulations and must be followed.

Chapter 33–Review Questions

Write your answers on a separate sheet of paper. Do not write in this book.

1. What is an engine tune-up?
2. Combustion of the air/fuel mixture gives off _____, _____ _____ and other unburned gases that pollute the atmosphere.
3. Engine tune-up specifications and emission control information are provided on a tune-up and emissions _____ placed in a convenient location under the hood.
4. Most of the work involved in an engine tune-up job is concerned with tests of the engine electrical system, fuel system, electronic engine controls, and _____.
5. If the "Check Engine" display lights when the engine is running, what is indicated?
6. What is maximum engine cranking time when making an amperage draw test?
   (A) 5 seconds.
   (B) 10 seconds.
   (C) 15 seconds.
   (D) 30 seconds.

7. Use an ohmmeter to test ignition coil primary resistance by connecting leads between:
   (A) the center tower and the positive terminal.
   (B) the center tower and the negative terminal.
   (C) the center tower and ground.
   (D) the positive and negative terminals.
8. What check is required on a manifold heat control valve?
   (A) Valve lash measurement.
   (B) Torque tightness.
   (C) Freedom of operation.
   (D) Opening temperature.
9. If an engine is in good condition and operating properly, the vacuum gauge needle will hold a _____ in. Hg.
   (A) 5 to 10
   (B) 10 to 15
   (C) 15 to 20
   (D) 20 to 25

Match the question number for each of the following engine tune-up tests with the letter designated for each piece of test equipment required to perform the test.

10. _____ Specific gravity of each battery cell.		(A) Ohmmeter.
11. _____ Amperage draw of starting motor.		(B) Tachometer.
12. _____ Air leak at intake manifold.		(C) Alternator-regulator tester.
13. _____ Ignition system performance		(D) Dwell meter.
14. _____ Charging system output.		(E) Hydrometer.
15. _____ Emission levels.		(F) Vacuum gauge.
16. _____ Resistance of high tension cables.		(G) Oscilloscope.
17. _____ Breaker point cam angle.		(H) Exhaust gas analyzer.
18. _____ Engine speed.		(I) Battery-starter tester.

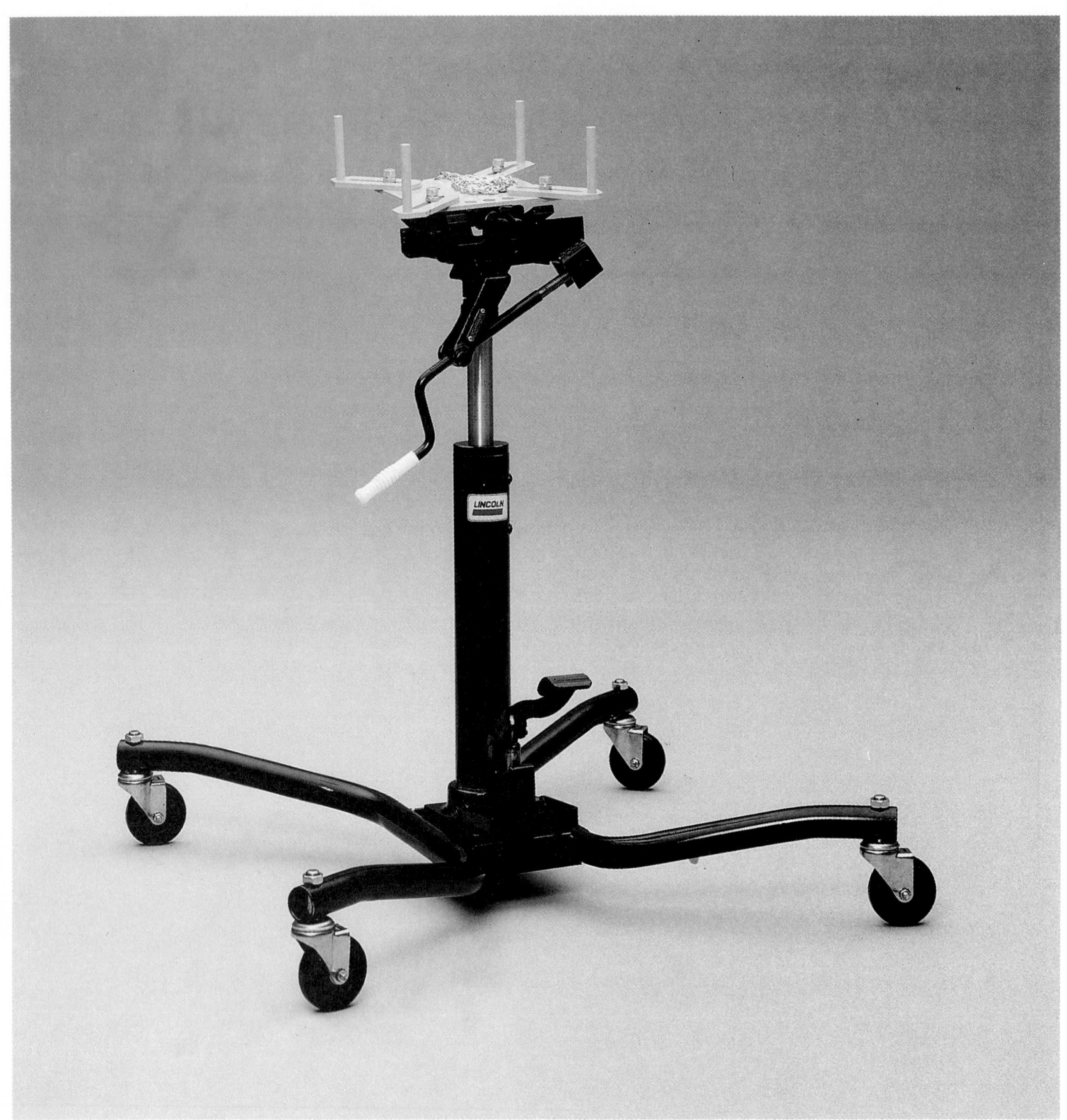

A high-lift transmission jack, such as the one shown above, can be used when removing and installing a transaxle or transmission during clutch repair procedures. This type of transmission jack is used when the car is raised on a lift. (Lincoln)

Chapter 34
Clutches

After studying this chapter, you will be able to:
- ❍ Explain the purpose of an automotive clutch.
- ❍ Describe the operation of major components of a clutch assembly and its actuating parts.
- ❍ Give examples of various cable-operated clutch control mechanisms.
- ❍ List typical clutch service procedures and precautions.
- ❍ Recognize symptoms of pending clutch failure.

Purpose of the Clutch

A ***clutch*** is a friction device used to connect and disconnect a driving force from a driven member. In automotive applications, the clutch is designed to provide smooth and positive engagement and disengagement of the engine and manual transmission or manual transaxle. See Figures 34-1 and 34-2.

The clutch is needed because an internal combustion engine develops little power or torque at low rpm. It must gain speed before it will move the vehicle. At higher speeds, however, a violent engagement would occur if the rapidly rotating engine were suddenly connected to the driveline of a stationary vehicle.

Therefore, a gradual application of load and some slowing of engine speed are needed to provide reasonable and comfortable starts. In vehicles equipped with a manual transmission or manual transaxle, this is accomplished by means of a mechanical clutch.

Engagement of the engine and transmission provides the necessary linkup of engine and drivetrain that permits power transfer to the driving axles and wheels. Disengagement provides the necessary halt to power transfer that allows the engine to operate while the transmission does not.

Figure 34-1. Typical clutch-driven plate (dry disc) used in cars equipped with a manual transmission or transaxle. (Chrysler)

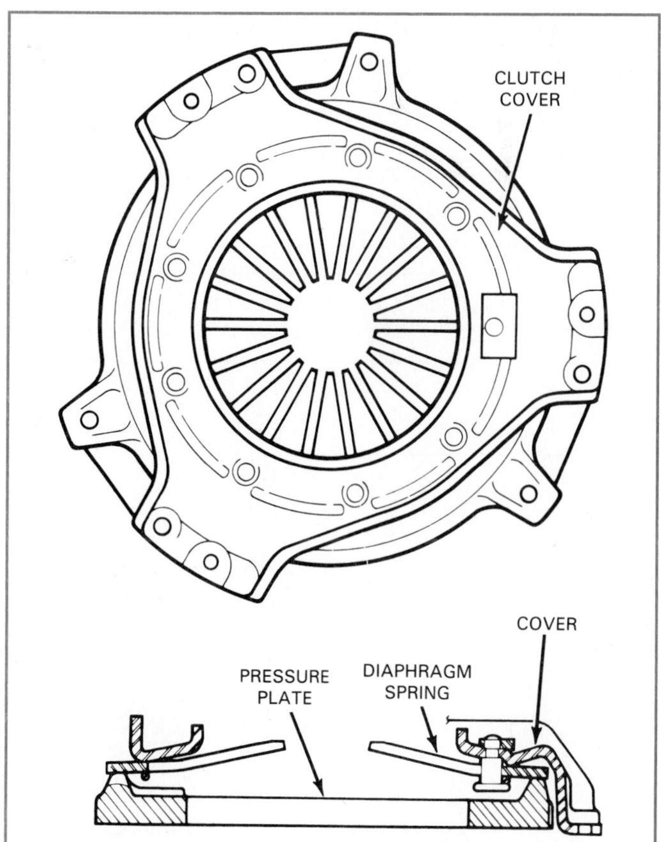

Figure 34-2. Typical diaphragm-type clutch pressure plate used in conjunction with the clutch-driven plate shown in Figure 34-1. (Chrysler)

Design and Construction

Most cars equipped with a manual transmission or manual transaxle use a single plate, dry clutch disc, a diaphragm type pressure plate and cover assembly, a clutch release bearing (throwout bearing), and a clutch release fork. See Figures 34-3 through 34-5.

Parts Location and Relationship

In its operating position in the engine/transmission or transaxle linkup, the clutch disc is sandwiched between the engine flywheel and the clutch pressure plate. The pressure plate is bolted to the engine flywheel, and a strong clamping force is developed between the heavy plate and cover.

Engagement and disengagement of the clutch assembly is controlled by a foot pedal and linkage (rods or cable) that must be properly adjusted and relatively easy to apply.

The machined surfaces of the flywheel and pressure plate (against which the clutch facings bear) must be flat, true, and free from cracks or score marks.

The transmission, pressure plate, flywheel housing, clutch disc, flywheel, and crankshaft must be properly aligned to prevent slippage, vibration, and noise.

Clutch Disc

The ***clutch disc,*** or ***driven plate,*** consists of a circular metal plate attached to a reinforced splined hub. Often the hub is mounted on coil springs to provide cushioned engagements. See Figure 34-1.

The splined hub is free to slide lengthwise along the splines of the transmission input shaft. See Figure 34-6. When engaged, the clutch disc drives the input shaft through these splines.

The outer half of the clutch disc has a friction material facing on each side. Generally, the facings are riveted or bonded to the clutch disc. The thickness of the disc assembly must be uniform and its friction facings must be smooth.

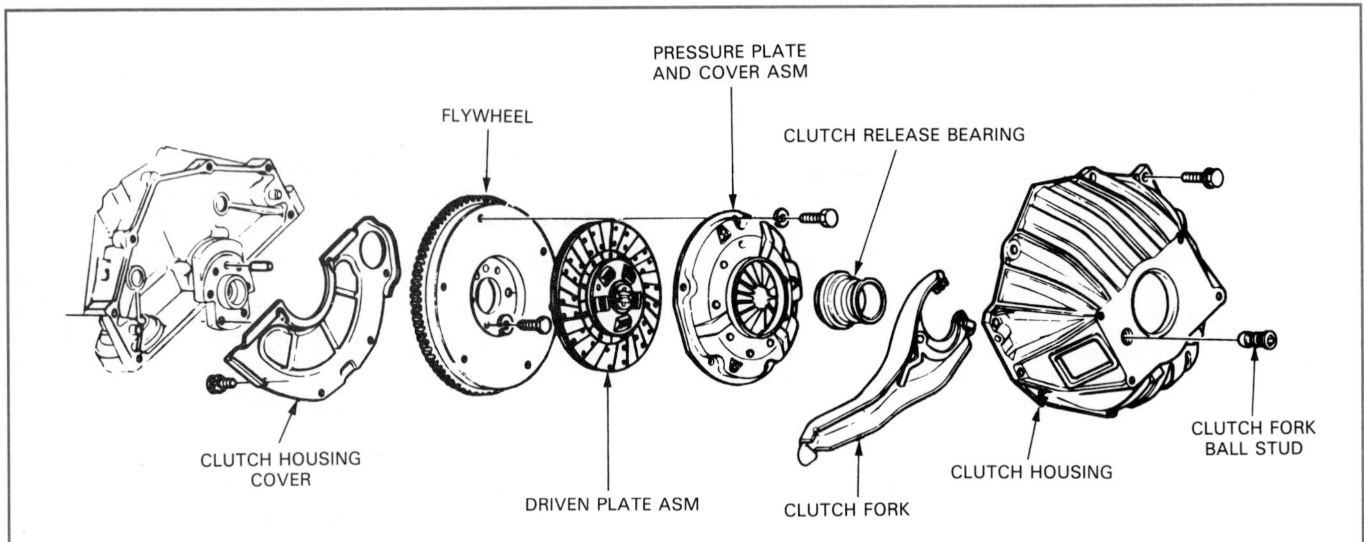

Figure 34-3. Exploded view of a mechanical clutch system used with a manual transmission. Operational components include the flywheel, driven plate, pressure plate, release bearing, and fork. (Chevrolet)

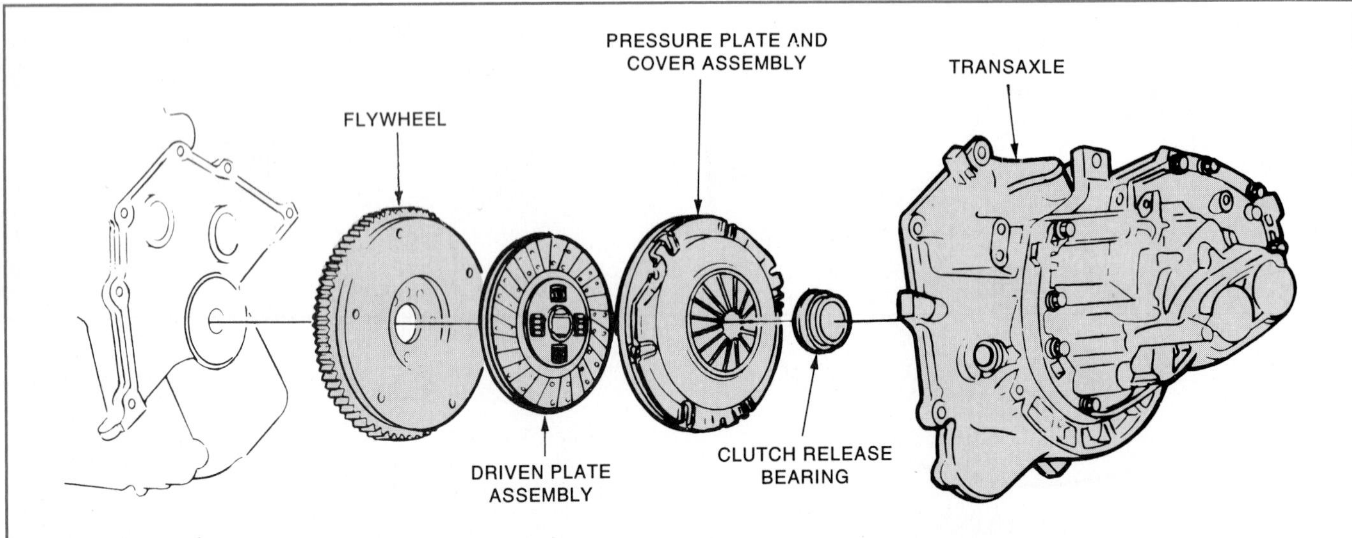

Figure 34-4. Exploded view of a mechanical clutch system used with a manual transaxle. (Oldsmobile)

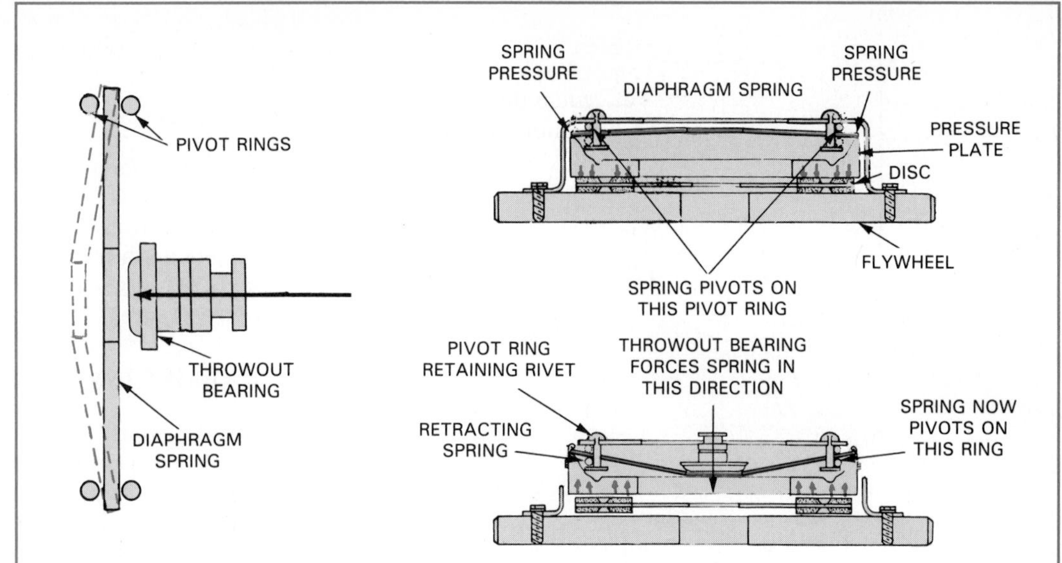

Figure 34-5. These three views illustrate how pivot rings give the diaphragm spring an over-center action when the clutch release bearing forces the spring toward the engine flywheel.

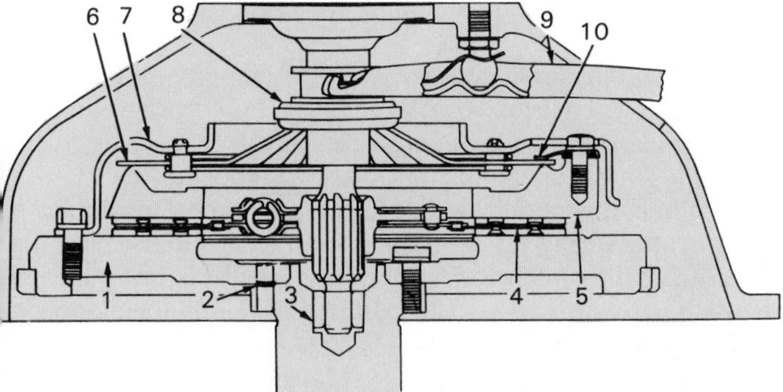

Figure 34-6. Cross section of a clutch assembly: 1–Flywheel. 2–Dowel hole. 3–Pilot bushing. 4–Driven plate. 5–Pressure plate. 6–Diaphragm spring. 7–Clutch cover. 8–Clutch release bearing. 9–Clutch fork. 10–Retracting spring. (Chevrolet)

Warning: The dust created when servicing clutch assemblies may contain asbestos fibers. Breathing this dust may cause serious bodily harm. Asbestos is a known carcinogen–a substance which tends to cause cancer. When working on clutches, wear a mask with a government-approved filter and flush clutch parts with water or use a vacuum source.

Pressure Plate

The clutch disc operates in conjunction with a ***pressure plate,*** or ***clutch cover,*** Figure 34-2. The pressure plate assembly usually consists of a heavy plate, a diaphragm spring with release fingers, and a cover. See Figure 34-5. The pressure plate diaphragm is shaped like a dished plate. It utilizes over-center action in applying and releasing pressure on the pressure plate and clutch disc.

The cover serves to contain the pressure plate assembly. Most covers are vented to allow heat to escape and cooling air to enter. Some are designed to provide a fan action for forced circulation of air to help cool them. Even proper use of the clutch generates some heat because of normal slippage while it is being engaged.

Clutch Release Bearing and Fork

The ***clutch release bearing,*** or ***throwout bearing,*** in most cases, is a ball bearing assembly with a machined face on one side that is designed to contact the pressure plate diaphragm release fingers during disengagement. See Figures 34-7 and 34-8. The release bearing is mounted on a sleeve that is designed to slide back and forth on the transmission input shaft bearing retainer whenever the clutch pedal is depressed or released.

The sleeve is grooved or has raised flat surfaces and retaining springs that hold the inner ends of the ***clutch fork*** in place. The fork and connecting linkage provide the means of converting the up-and-down movement of the clutch pedal to the back-and-forth movement of the clutch release bearing assembly. See Figure 34-5.

Transaxle clutch assemblies generally use a different arrangement of connecting the linkage to the clutch fork and the fork to the clutch release bearing. In transaxle applications, Figure 34-9, the release bearing is constantly engaged with the release fingers of the pressure plate diaphragm. A clutch fork and a release lever are utilized in

Figure 34-7. Various clutch release bearings are pictured, along with a ball bearing cage and ball bearing assembly.

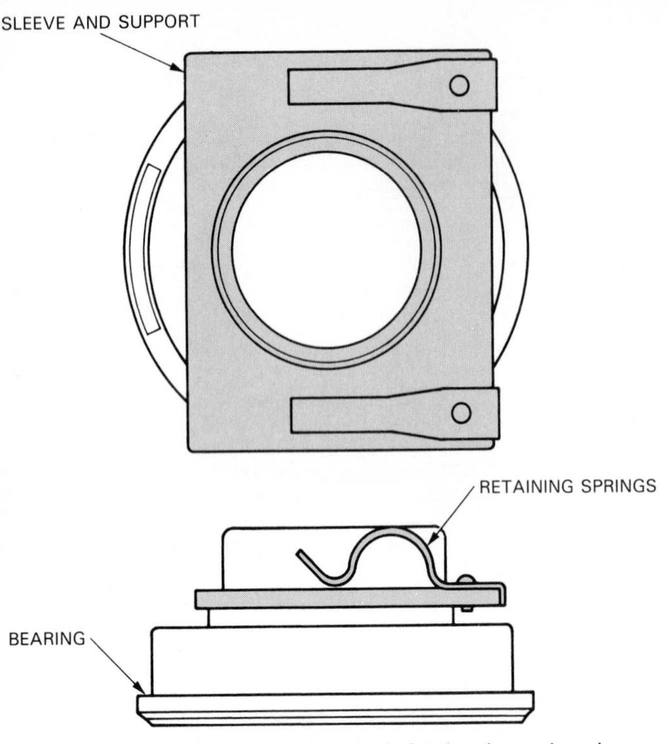

Figure 34-8. Side view of a typical clutch release bearing fitted to a sleeve and support assembly. (Chrysler)

conjunction with the clutch cable to depress the pressure plate diaphragm and release the clutch disc. See Figure 34-9.

Also note that this setup does not require a pilot bearing. In most cars, a clutch ***pilot bearing,*** or ***pilot bushing,*** is placed in the back end of the crankshaft or in the center of the flywheel. This bearing or bushing is used to support the outer end of the manual transmission input shaft.

Clutch Linkage

The ***clutch linkage*** connects the clutch pedal to the outer end of the clutch fork. Earlier model cars and some current models use a series of rods, shafts, levers, and springs to make up the linkage arrangement, Figures 34-10 and 34-11. Many domestic and import models use cable operation. See Figures 34-12 through 34-15.

Rod-and-shaft Clutch Control

A typical pedal rod and cross shaft (torque shaft) clutch control linkage setup is shown in Figure 34-10. It also incorporates a fork push rod, clutch and brake pedal bracket, and an over-center spring.

Basically, depressing the clutch pedal causes the pedal rod to move a lever attached to the cross shaft. The cross shaft starts to rotate, causing another lever on the shaft to move the fork push rod and, in turn, the clutch fork and release bearing.

When the clutch pedal reaches the end of its travel, the clutch fork will have moved the clutch release bearing enough to completely release the clutch disc. At this point, the driver is able to shift gears in the transmission without difficulty.

When the clutch pedal is released, the "tensioned" over-center spring returns the linkage to original position. With that, the clutch fork moves the release bearing away from the pressure plate and the clutch disc is again clamped into engagement. Figure 34-11 presents another rod-and-shaft clutch control system.

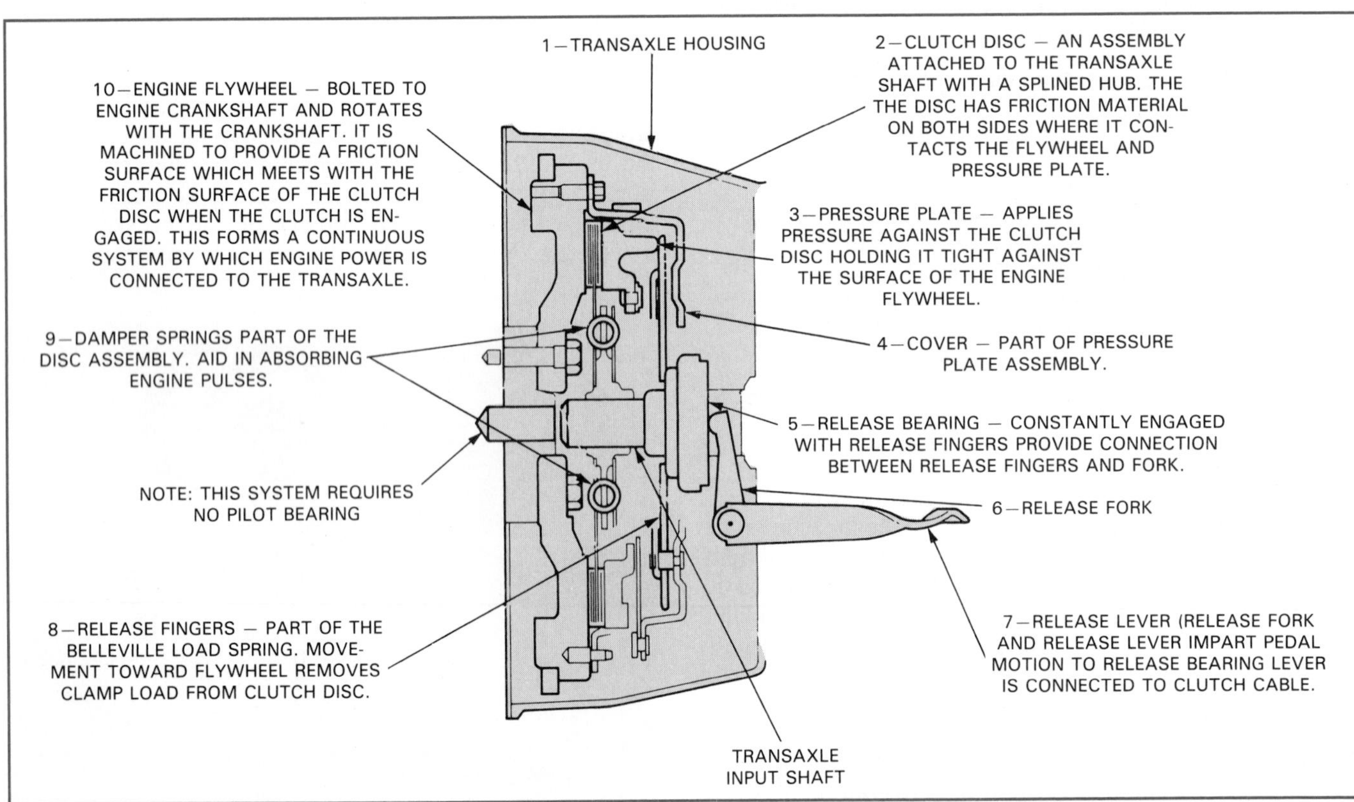

Figure 34-9. This top view shows the clutch components in a manual transaxle application. The notes provide complete operational information. (Ford)

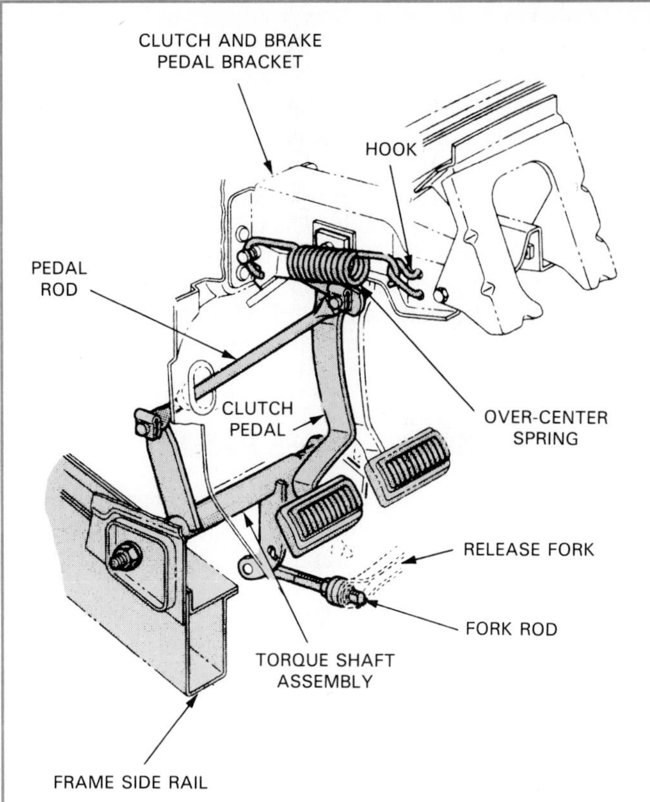

Figure 34-10. This rod-and-shaft clutch control linkage arrangement features clutch pedal, pedal rod, and over-center spring. Pedal free play adjustment is at end of fork rod. (Dodge)

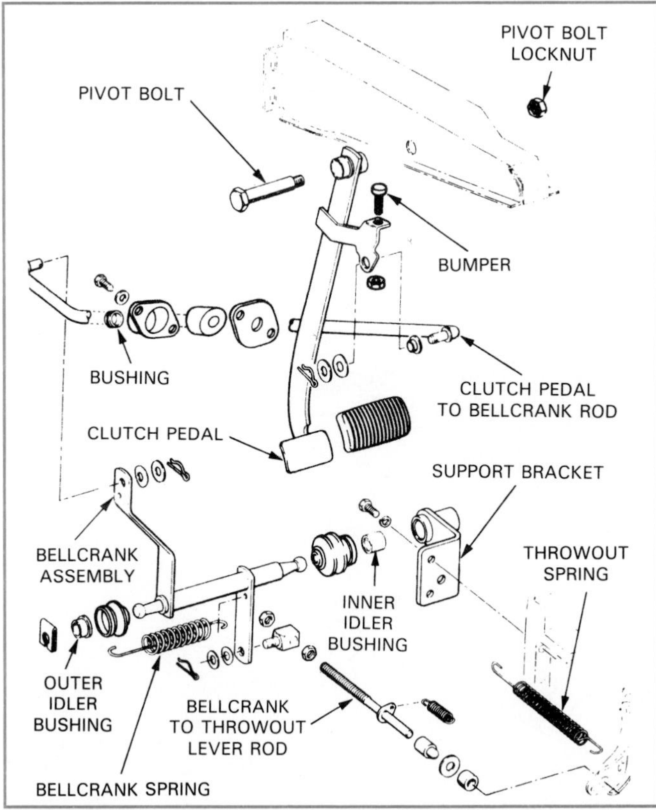

Figure 34-11. This clutch linkage works on same principle as the linkage shown in Figure 34-10. Both have a cross shaft with opposed bellcrank levers. (Chrysler)

Cable Clutch Control–Manual Transmission

Cable control of clutch operation is common in many manual transmission applications. A simple setup is shown in Figure 34-12. A circlip (1) holds the pedal in place on the shaft. The cable fork end (4) is attached to the top end of the pedal shank by a pin (3) that extends through the fork end and a hole in the pedal shank. A return spring (2) is attached to the pin by passing the spring hook through a hole in the pin. The cable is held firmly in place by a cable stop at the firewall.

The other end of the clutch control cable is connected to the outer end of the clutch release fork, Figure 34-13. This end is threaded and fitted with an adjusting nut and a locknut to provide a means of adjusting clutch pedal free play.

When the clutch pedal is depressed, the cable is drawn inward. This forces the end of the release fork to actuate the clutch release bearing, disengaging the clutch disc.

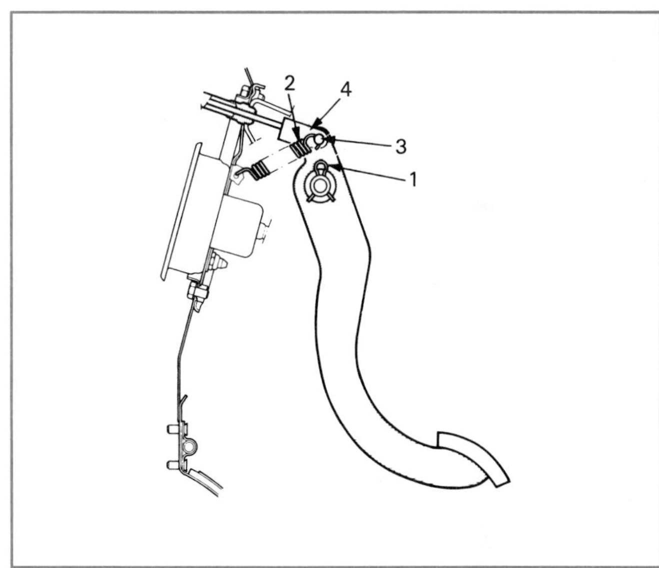

Figure 34-12. This cable-operated clutch control system simply connects the clutch pedal with the outer end of the clutch fork: 1–Circlip. 2–Return spring. 3–Pin. 4–Cable fork end.

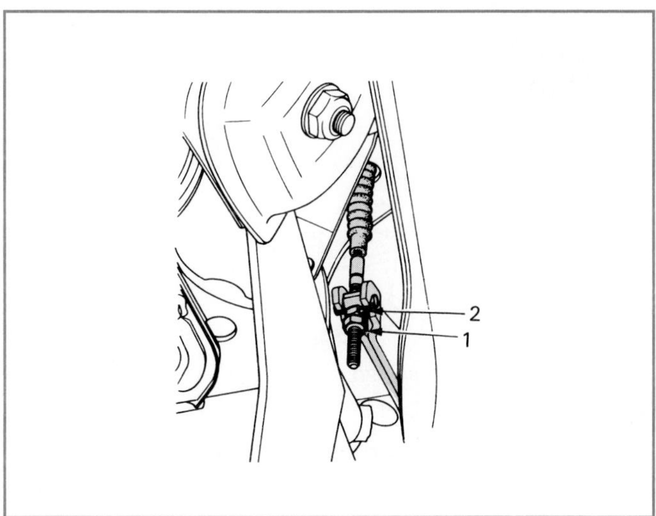

Figure 34-13. The lower end of clutch cable shown in Figure 34-12 provides a means of clutch pedal free play adjustment: 1–Locknut. 2–Adjusting screw.

Cable Clutch Control–Manual Transaxle

Various systems have been devised to provide self-adjustment of the clutch cable mechanism on manual transaxle applications. Since the clutch release bearing is a constant running bearing, the self-adjustment feature primarily affects the cable release mechanism.

Chrysler's Self-adjusting Clutch Release

Chrysler's manual transaxle clutch cable release mechanism is self-adjusting. It cannot be adjusted manually. A heavy-duty spring between the clutch pedal assembly and the positioner adjuster, Figure 34-14, holds the clutch cable in the proper position, regardless of clutch disc wear.

Key elements in the self-adjusting mechanism are the clutch pedal spring, the position adjuster, and the adjuster pivot, Figure 34-14. When the clutch pedal is depressed, the adjuster pivot meshes with and moves the positioner adjuster to hold the clutch release cable in place to effect complete clutch release.

General Motors' Clutch Self-adjusting Mechanism

General Motors cars equipped with a manual transaxle utilize a cable-operated system with a self-adjusting mechanism mounted on the clutch pedal and bracket assembly. See Figure 34-15.

When the clutch pedal is in the released position, a pawl is lifted free of the quadrant. Meanwhile, a spring in the hub of the quadrant causes the quadrant to rotate. This movement automatically adjusts cable length to balance the force being applied at the clutch release bearing. This system, too, employs a constant running clutch release bearing in the normal driving position.

When the clutch pedal is applied, the pawl moves downward to mesh its teeth in the quadrant, Figure 34-16. The quadrant pulls on the end of the cable, and the clutch fork forces the release bearing against the release fingers of the pressure plate. This disengages the clutch disc, and the transaxle is disengaged from the engine.

When the clutch pedal is released, the pedal and quadrant return to the "rest" mode. The pawl is again lifted free of the quadrant and the spring in the hub of the quadrant applies just enough tension on the cable to keep a constant light pressure against the clutch release bearing. The clutch disc is fully engaged and the engine is transferring power to the transaxle.

Ford's Self-adjusting Clutch Pedal

Ford's self-adjusting clutch control mechanism is very similar to the General Motors setup. It, too, is cable-actuated and fitted with a pawl-and-quadrant self-adjustment mechanism.

Study Figure 34-17 to familiarize yourself with the relationship of the parts of the mechanism. After proper installation of the cable, initial adjustment of the cable is made by pulling the clutch pedal all the way up. In this position, the pawl is disengaged from the quadrant. The quadrant position, then, is governed by the position of the clutch pressure plate release fingers.

As the clutch disc facings wear, the pressure plate release fingers gradually move away from the flywheel. This movement is transferred to the quadrant, which automatically adjusts itself to keep the clutch release bearing in constant contact with the pressure plate release fingers. This is the clutch control system employed with the clutch assembly shown in Figure 34-9.

Ford also incorporates a starter/clutch interlock switch in the clutch control system. This switch is designed to prevent

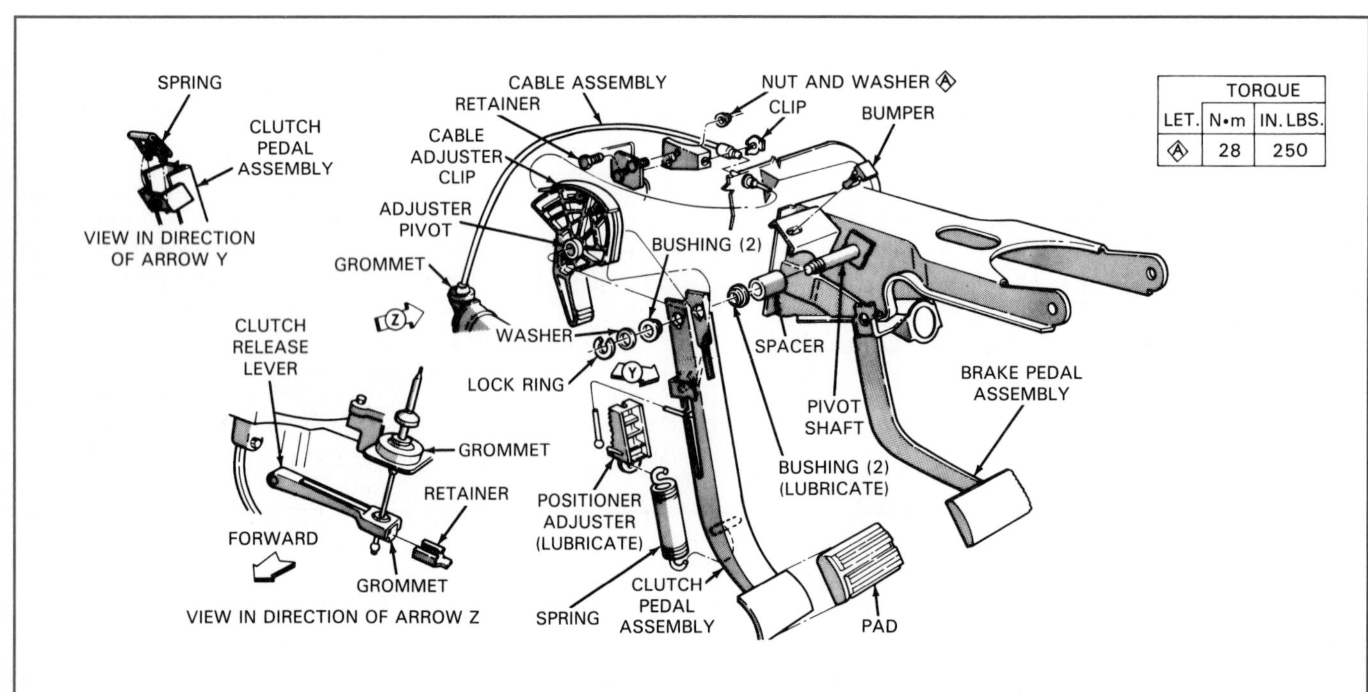

TORQUE		
LET.	N•m	IN. LBS.
A	28	250

Figure 34-14. This self-adjusting clutch release mechanism is used on certain Chrysler-Plymouth cars equipped with either four-speed or five-speed transaxles.

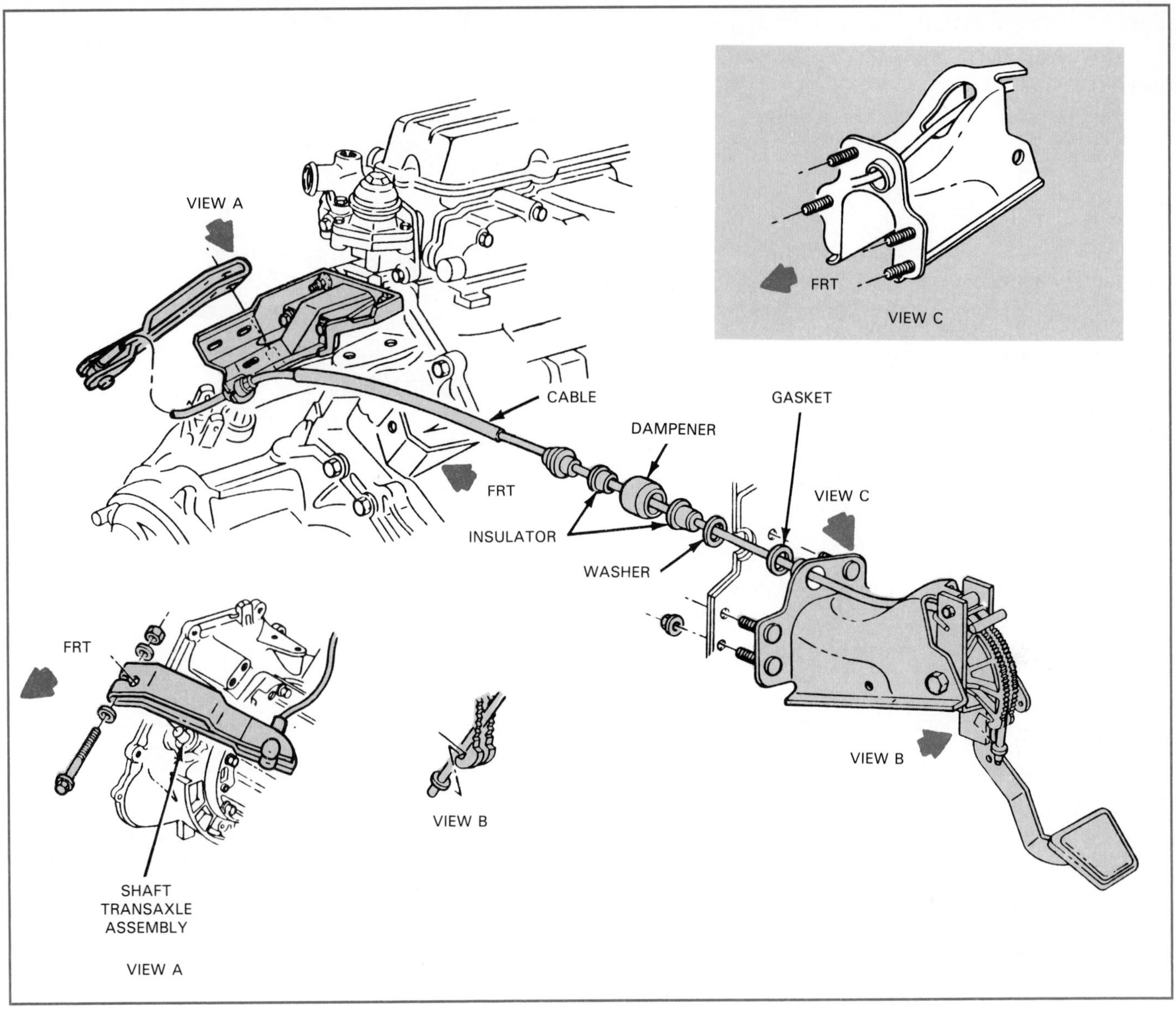

Figure 34-15. General Motors cars equipped with a manual transaxle also use a cable-operated, self-adjusting clutch mechanism. (Oldsmobile)

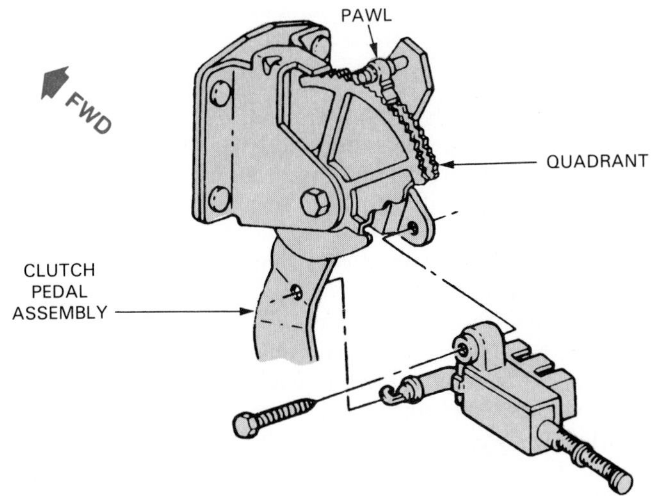

Figure 34-16. The key to operation of the GM self-adjusting clutch mechanism is a quadrant, spring, and pawl arrangement. (Oldsmobile)

starting the engine with the clutch engaged. The switch, Figure 34-18, is connected between the ignition switch and starter motor relay coil. It maintains an open circuit with the clutch pedal up (clutch engaged). The first time the clutch pedal is pressed to the floor, it automatically adjusts itself to close the starter circuit.

The starter/clutch interlock switch is located on a bracket alongside the clutch pedal stop bracket and pedal shank. Note the instructions in Figure 34-18 for installing the switch. If the self-adjusting clip is out of position, the switch will not operate properly. Once the clip is properly installed on the switch bar, the switch can be reset by pressing the clutch pedal to the floor.

American Motors' Hydraulic Clutch

Some American Motors cars equipped with a manual transmission use a hydraulic clutch operating mechanism. See Figure 34-19. The system uses a remote reservoir, a clutch cylinder, and a slave cylinder. The clutch cylinder is mounted on the dash panel, and it is operated directly off

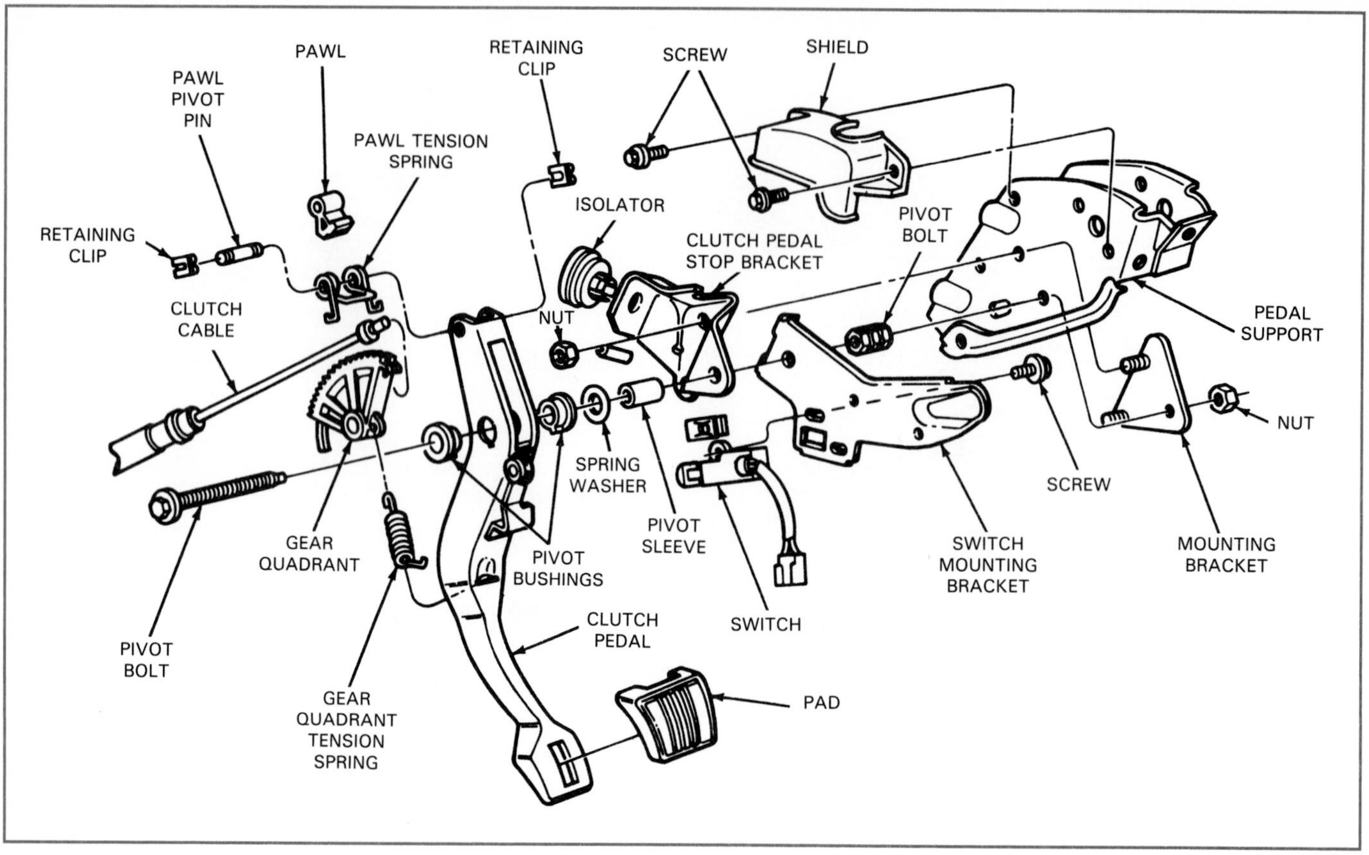

PAWL
RETAINING CLIP
SCREW
SHIELD
PAWL PIVOT PIN
PAWL TENSION SPRING
ISOLATOR
PIVOT BOLT
RETAINING CLIP
CLUTCH PEDAL STOP BRACKET
CLUTCH CABLE
NUT
PEDAL SUPPORT
NUT
SPRING WASHER
SCREW
PIVOT SLEEVE
GEAR QUADRANT
PIVOT BUSHINGS
SWITCH MOUNTING BRACKET
MOUNTING BRACKET
CLUTCH PEDAL
SWITCH
PIVOT BOLT
GEAR QUADRANT TENSION SPRING
PAD

Figure 34-17. Exploded view shows the relative locations of parts that make up a typical self-adjusting, cable-operated clutch control linkage arrangement for Ford manual transaxle applications.

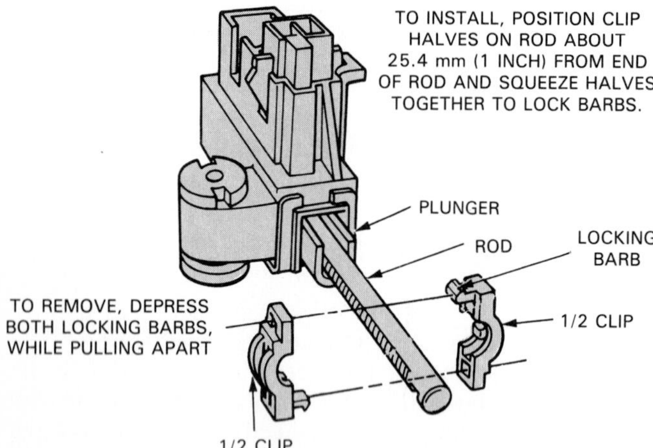

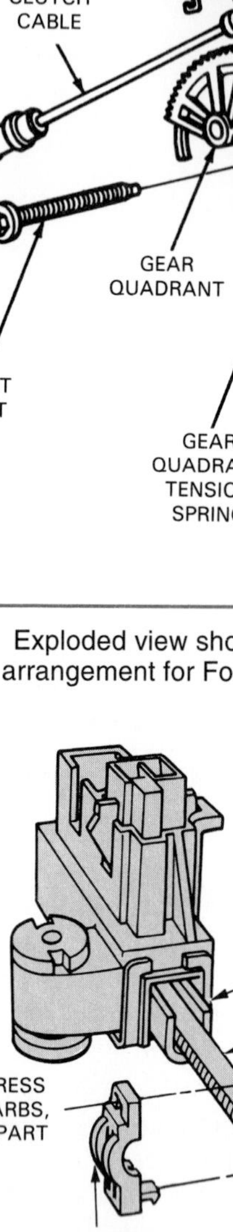

Figure 34-18. The self-adjusting clutch control mechanism shown in Figure 34-17 also includes a starter/clutch interlock switch. (Ford)

the clutch pedal. The slave cylinder is mounted on the clutch housing.

When the clutch pedal is depressed, hydraulic fluid under pressure created in the slave cylinder causes its push rod to extend. Since the outer end of the push rod is connected to the outer end of the clutch release fork, the fork pivots and forces the clutch release bearing to disengage the clutch.

The hydraulic clutch mechanism is self-adjusting. When the clutch pedal is released, hydraulic pressure falls off and the slave cylinder push rod retracts. A spring keeps the outer end of the clutch release fork in contact with the push rod, so the fork and release bearing are returned to their released positions.

Figure 34-20 shows the clutch hydraulic system used on various Chevrolet cars. Note that this system also uses a reservoir, master cylinder, and slave cylinder.

If the reservoir requires fluid, remove boots and check for leakage past the pistons. If excessive leakage is evident, replace the entire system. The Chevrolet clutch hydraulic system must be serviced as a complete unit.

Clutch Service

One of the most common causes of clutch trouble is misalignment. The transmission input shaft (which supports the clutch disc) should be in perfect alignment with the engine crankshaft and at right angles to the flywheel face. A worn transmission input shaft bearing or excessive wear in the pilot bearing or bushing will permit the input shaft to run untrue.

Another frequent cause of misalignment is a sprung input shaft or clutch disc. This problem usually is caused by carelessness in removing or replacing the transmission. If the transmission is unsupported while being removed or installed, the weight of the unit is liable to spring the shaft of disc. For this reason, a transmission lift or jack should always be used to aid in moving the transmission in or out of place. See Figure 34-21.

To check clutch housing alignment, use a dial indicator attached to a special tool installed in the pilot bearing or

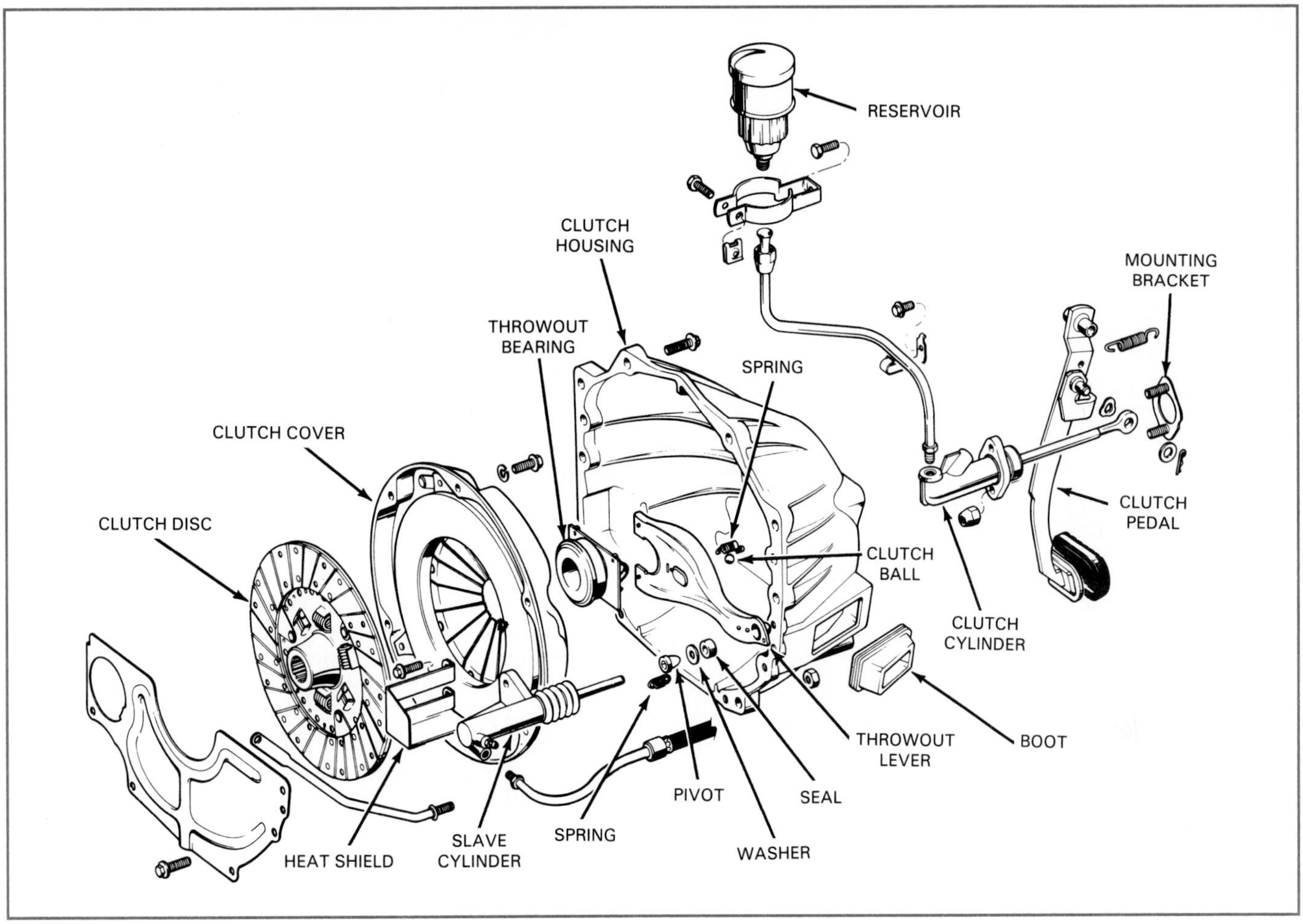

Figure 34-19. The hydraulic clutch mechanism used on American Motors cars is self-adjusting. Depressing the clutch pedal pressurizes the system; releasing the pedal relieves the pressure.

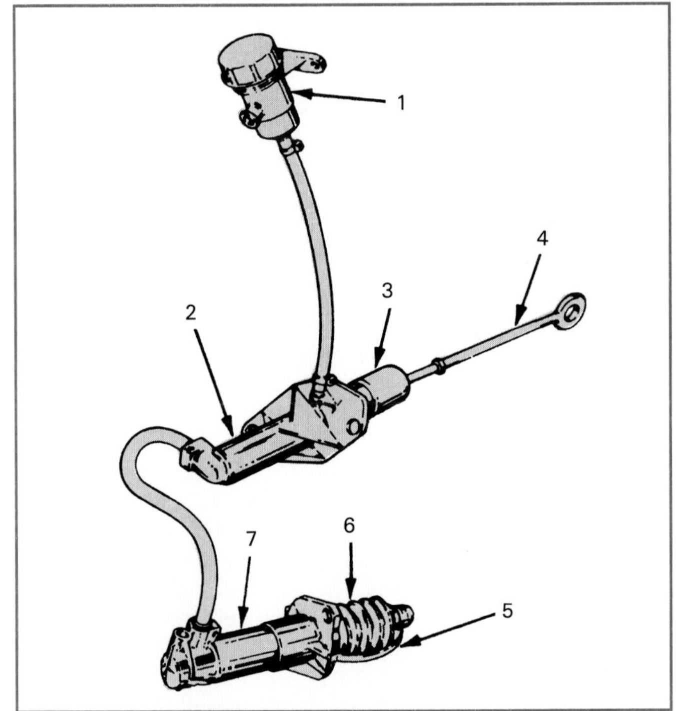

Figure 34-20. Clutch hydraulic system used on Chevrolet cars: 1–Fluid reservoir. 2–Clutch master cylinder. 3–Boot. 4–Push rod. 5–Shipping strap. 6–Boot. 7–Clutch slave cylinder.

Figure 34-21. This 1/2 ton hydraulic transmission jack safely cradles the transmission during removal and reinstallation. (Lincoln)

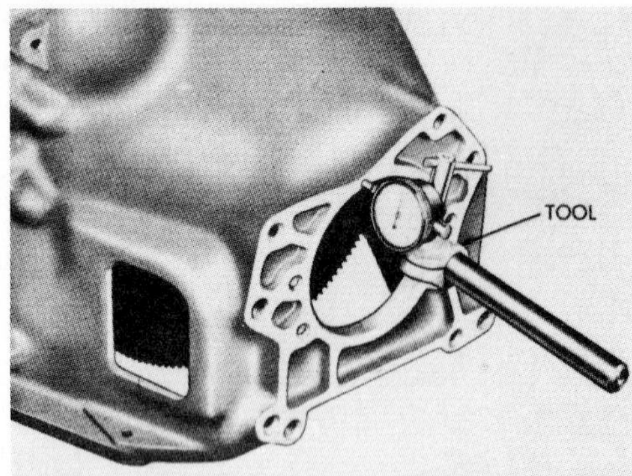

Figure 34-22. To check clutch housing face alignment, a dial indicator is mounted on a special tool installed in the pilot bushing; then the flywheel is turned one revolution.

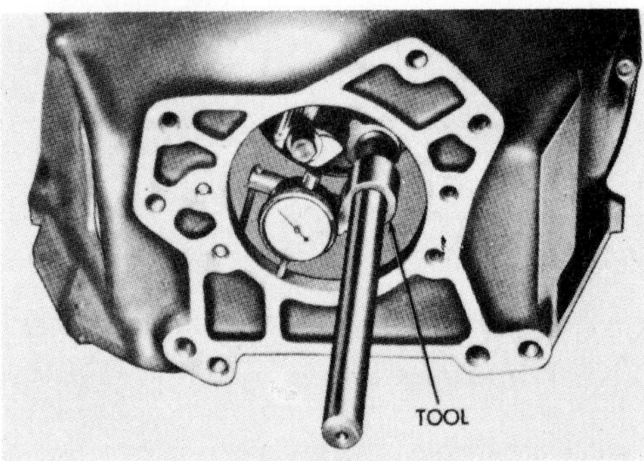

Figure 34-23. To check the housing bore for runout, use a dial indicator with a tool installed in the pilot bushing; then rotate the flywheel one revolution.

bushing. See Figures 34-22 and 34-23. Then check the flywheel for proper alignment by mounting the dial indicator on the clutch housing.

In most applications, the misalignment limit is .010″ (0.25 mm), although some manufacturers hold the limit to .005″ (0.1270 mm). Check the manufacturer's specification.

To correct misalignment of the face of the clutch housing, shims must be installed between the clutch housing and the rear of the engine block. Some engines have offset dowel pins on the rear face, permitting adjustment to compensate for runout of the clutch housing bore.

Distortion of the clutch cover will also cause misalignment. Such distortion or warpage is caused by carelessness in removing or installing the cover. The attaching bolts must be loosened or tightened evenly, or the cover may be sprung or distorted by spring pressure.

Also bear in mind that the engine usually is balanced by the manufacturer with the clutch installed. Before removing the clutch cover, punch mark the cover and flywheel, Figure 34-24, so you can reinstall the cover in the same relative position. Otherwise, the rotating balance of the engine assembly may be disturbed, and vibration will occur.

Clutch Adjustment

The principal cause of a damaged clutch release bearing in manual transmission applications is neglect of clutch adjustment to compensate for disc wear.

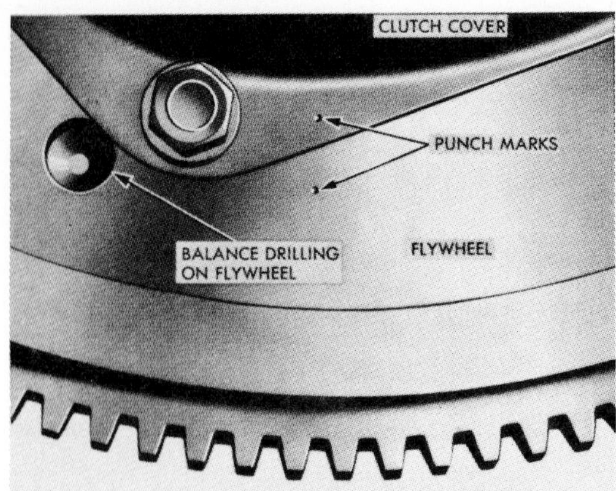

Figure 34-24. Before removing the pressure plate and clutch disc, punch the flywheel face and the clutch cover to maintain balance if the original pressure plate is to be reinstalled.

As the friction material gradually wears from the disc in normal use, the pressure plate moves closer to the flywheel and the clutch release fingers of the pressure plate move outward. This forces the clutch release bearing backward and the clutch pedal with it. If the pedal is forced against the pedal stop, the bearing will contact the release fingers and turn at all times. This continuous pressure on the clutch release bearing will tend to partially disengage the clutch disc, causing the friction facings to slip and wear rapidly.

Therefore, it pays to check clutch pedal free play regularly, and adjust the clearance when necessary. Clearance, or pedal free play, should be about 1 in. That is, when you depress the clutch pedal, it should travel approximately 1 in. before you feel the contact of the release bearing against the fingers of the clutch diaphragm.

The adjustment of clutch pedal free play usually can be made at the clutch fork push rod, Figures 34-10 through 34-12, or at the outer end of the clutch pedal rod.

Clutch Overhaul

Corrective clutch service usually consists of repair, adjustment, or replacement of the faulty part or assembly. To inspect and correct major troubles in clutch operation, proceed as follows:

1. Remove drive shaft(s) and the transmission or transaxle. See Figure 34-25.
2. Remove the flywheel cover or the clutch bell housing, if so equipped.
3. Locate the X marks on the flywheel and clutch cover, or put aligned prick-punch marks on these units to ensure proper reinstallation if existing clutch assembly is to be reused. See Figure 34-24.
4. Unhook the clutch return spring, back off the clutch adjustment, if necessary, and remove the clutch release bearing assembly.
5. Loosen the clutch cover-to-flywheel attaching bolts in alternate order, one turn at a time, until spring pressure has been released.
6. Remove the bolts and the clutch assembly.
7. Remove the pilot bushing wick, if so equipped. Soak a new wick in engine oil.
8. Clean the flywheel face and check it for runout.

9. Inspect the pilot bearing or bushing for wear or score marks. Replace the bearing or bushing if necessary. See Figure 34-26.
10. Pack the pilot bearing with lubricant, or coat the bushing with engine oil. Install a new pilot bushing wick.
11. Check the clutch housing bore and face alignment. Correct as required.
12. Check the fit of the new clutch disc on the transmission or transaxle input shaft spline.

Figure 34-25. This service technician is positioning a transmission on a 1/4 ton high-lift transmission jack. Adaptors permit the jack to handle all passenger car transmissions and transaxles. (Lincoln Div. of McNeil Corp.)

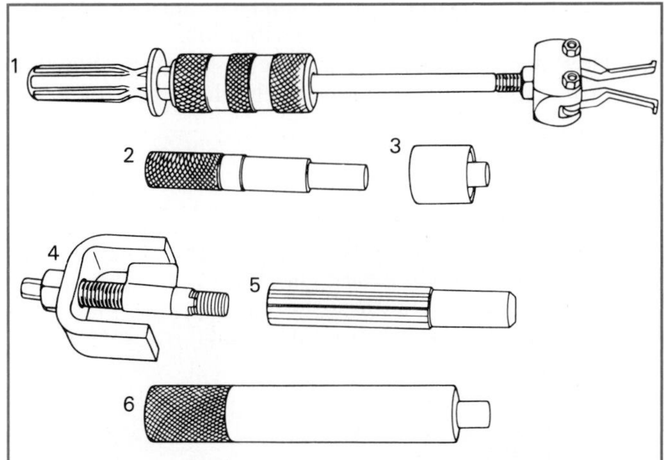

Figure 34-26. Clutch special tools: 1–Bearing puller. 2–Clutch disc aligner. 3–Pilot bearing installer. 4–Pilot bearing remover. 5–Clutch disc aligner. 6–Pilot bearing installer. (Oldsmobile)

13. Install the clutch disc and clutch cover, using an aligning tool, Figure 34-26, or an old transmission input shaft. Generally, install the clutch disc with the damper springs offset toward the transmission or transaxle. In some applications, stamped letters on the disc identify the "flywheel side."
14. Tighten the clutch cover-to-flywheel bolts evenly–one turn at a time–to correct torque tightness, then remove the aligning tool or input shaft.
15. Install a new clutch release bearing on the bearing sleeve, using care to ensure proper seating and to avoid damage to the bearing. Or, use a new sleeve and release bearing assembly. Check the sliding fit of the bearing assembly on the transmission input shaft bearing retainer. Wipe a film of lubricant on the retainer.
16. Wipe a light coating of lubricant on the face of the release bearing and pack lubricant in the inner recess of the sleeve. Use care to avoid getting lubricant on the clutch disc. Also, wipe a film of lubricant on the arms of the clutch release fork and lubricate clutch fork ball and socket.
17. Install the clutch bell housing if so equipped.
18. Install the transmission or transaxle and the drive shaft(s), torquing the bolts to the specified value. See Figure 34-25.
19. Adjust the clutch release fork push rod, or other point of the clutch pedal free play adjustment, Figures 34-10 through 34-12.
20. Install the flywheel cover if so equipped.
21. When servicing hydraulic clutches, check the fluid level in the reservoir. Refill to the level indicated with SAE-approved brake fluid.
22. Test clutch operation.

Clutch Troubleshooting

Slipping

- Worn clutch disc facing.
- Oil or grease on disc facing.
- Warped or distorted disc.
- Weak diaphragm spring in clutch cover.
- Warped pressure plate surface.
- Improper linkage adjustment.
- Clutch disc overheated.
- Binding, broken, bent, or worn clutch linkage.

Dragging

- Oil or grease on clutch disc facing.
- Warped or distorted disc.
- Broken disc facing.
- Splined disc hub sticking on splined transmission input shaft.
- Accumulation of dust in clutch assembly.
- Warped pressure plate surface.
- Excessive clutch pedal free play.
- Sticking pilot bearing or bushing.
- Sticking release bearing retainer.
- Misalignment of clutch housing or clutch assembly.

Chattering

- Oil or grease on clutch disc facing.
- Glazed or worn facing.
- Warped clutch disc.
- Binding, worn, bent, or broken clutch linkage.
- Worn or loose splines in disc hub or on transmission input shaft.
- Splined disc hub sticking on splined shaft.
- Warped pressure plate surface.
- Cracked or scored pressure plate or flywheel face.
- Broken or collapsed diaphragm spring.
- Bent transmission input shaft.
- Worn, loose, or spongy engine mounts.
- Worn or loose universal joint, differential, or torque rod mounting.
- Loose clutch housing-to-engine and/or clutch housing-to-transmission attaching bolts.
- Misalignment of clutch housing or clutch assembly.

Grabbing

- Oil or grease on clutch facing.
- Glazed or worn clutch disc facing.
- Splined disc hub sticking or binding on splined transmission input shaft.
- Sticking or binding clutch pedal linkage.
- Misalignment of clutch housing or clutch assembly.
- Loose engine mounts.
- Warped or distorted pressure plate.
- Clutch release fork and bearing improperly assembled.

Squeaks

- Dry clutch release bearing.
- Dry release bearing sleeve bore.
- Worn or dry pilot bearing.
- Misalignment of clutch housing or clutch assembly.
- Release fork shaft improperly installed.

Rattles

- Loose hub in clutch disc.
- Broken or loose coil springs in clutch disc.
- Worn splines in disc hub or in transmission input shaft.
- Worn release bearing.
- Loose release fork.
- Worn pilot bearing or bushing.
- Bent transmission input shaft.
- Worn transmission bearings.
- Wear in transmission or driveline.
- Misalignment of clutch housing or clutch assembly.

Failure

- Disc hub torn out.
- Friction facing torn off or worn off.
- Splined disc hub stuck on splined transmission input shaft.
- Broken springs in pressure plate.
- Insufficient clutch pedal free play.

Vibration or Pulsation

- Defective clutch disc.
- Dust in clutch assembly.
- Broken or collapsed pressure plate diaphragm spring.
- Improper installation of clutch assembly.
- Bent transmission input shaft.
- Misalignment of clutch housing or clutch assembly.
- Loose engine mountings.

Chapter 34 – Review Questions

Write your answers on a separate sheet of paper. Do not write in this book.

1. A clutch is a friction device used to _____ and _____ a driving force from a driven member.
2. The clutch disc is sandwiched between the engine _____ and the clutch _____.
3. The outer half of the clutch disc has a friction material facing on each side. True or False?
4. Most cars with a manual transmission or manual transaxle use a _____ type pressure plate.
5. The pressure plate is bolted to the engine _____.
   (A) crankshaft
   (B) flywheel
   (C) rear face
   (D) flex plate
6. The clutch _____ is designed to contact the pressure plate diaphragm release fingers during disengagement.
   (A) disc
   (B) release fork
   (C) release bearing
   (D) pilot bearing
7. The machined surfaces of the flywheel and pressure plate must be flat, true, and free from _____ or _____.
8. The transmission, pressure plate, flywheel housing, clutch disc, flywheel, and crankshaft must be properly _____ to prevent slippage or vibration.
9. How does a transaxle clutch release bearing function differ from a transmission clutch release bearing in the clutch engaged position?
10. Where is the clutch pedal free play adjustment usually located?
    (A) At the clutch cross shaft.
    (B) At the clutch pedal stop.
    (C) At the clutch release bearing.
    (D) At the clutch fork push rod.
11. Rule-of-thumb figure for clutch pedal free play is:
    (A) zero.
    (B) 1/2″.
    (C) 1″.
    (D) 1 1/2″.
12. What is the function of the clutch pilot bearing?
13. Various systems have been devised to provide self-adjustment of the clutch _____ mechanism on manual transaxle applications.

14. General Motors and Ford use a similar self-adjusting clutch control mechanism. It is fitted with a _____ self-adjustment mechanism.
    (A) pawl and quadrant
    (B) rod and shaft
    (C) lever and cross shaft
    (D) clutch pedal and bracket
15. One of the most common causes of clutch trouble is misalignment. True or False?
16. A transmission _____ should always be used to aid in moving the transmission in or out of place.
17. Where should a dial indicator be mounted to check runout of the flywheel?
    (A) Clutch housing.
    (B) Pilot bushing.
    (C) Rear face of engine.
    (D) Front face of transmission.
18. Where should the dial indicator be mounted to check alignment of the clutch housing?
    (A) Clutch housing.
    (B) Pilot bushing.
    (C) Rear face of engine.
    (D) Front face of transmission.
19. Generally, what is the maximum allowable runout on the machined face of the flywheel housing?
    (A) .003″.
    (B) .007″.
    (C) .010″.
    (D) .015″.
20. Why should you put aligned prick-punch marks on the flywheel and clutch cover if the existing clutch assembly is to be reinstalled?

A

B

This diaphragm spring turnover (DST) clutch features 12 turnover tabs to locate the diaphragm spring in the clutch cover, replacing the rivets, sleeves, and fulcrum ring support usually used in diaphragm-type clutches. A–Turnover tabs locate the spring and are pressed in place. B–The pressure plate is riveted to the drive straps. (Automotive Products Limited)

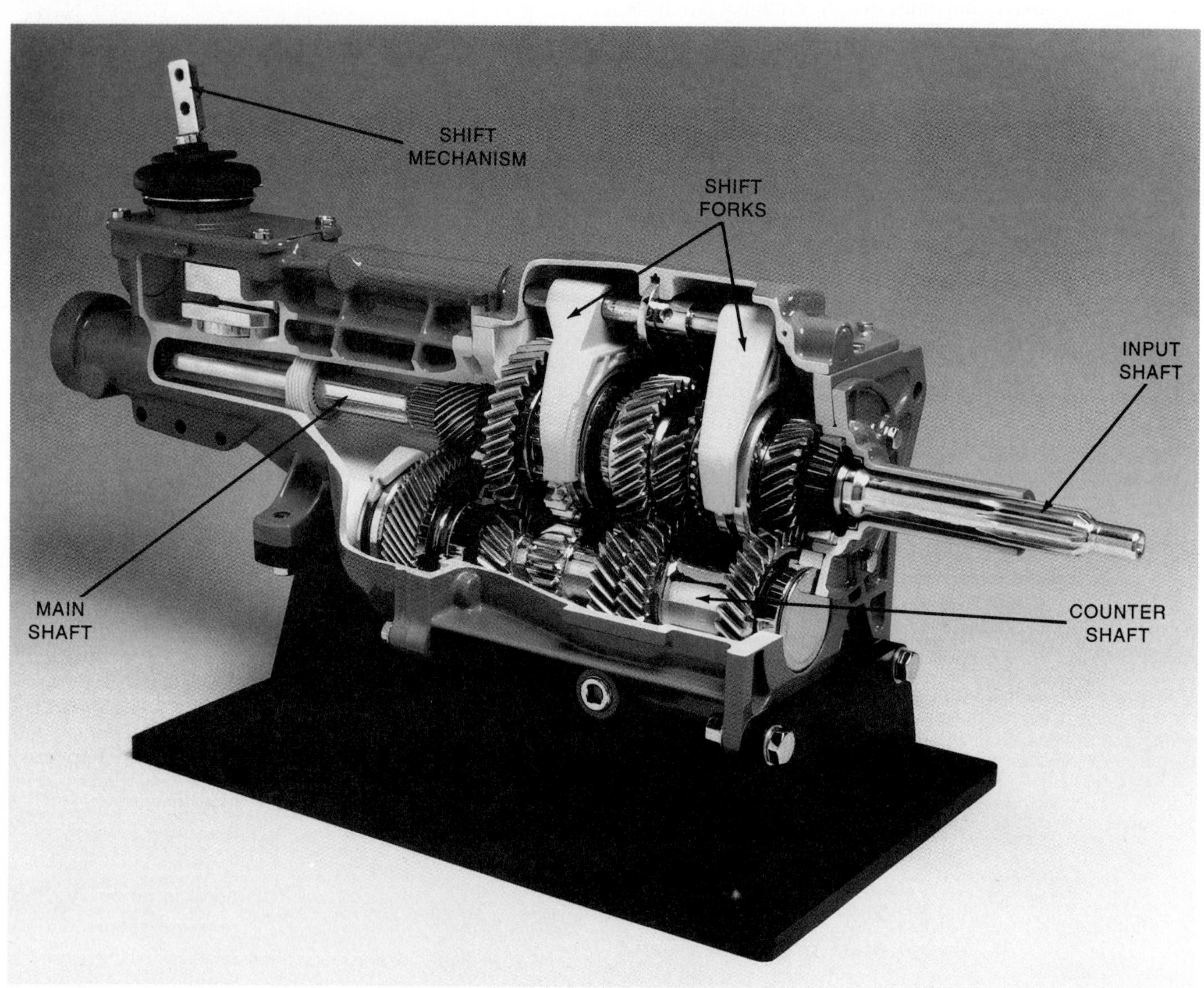

Cutaway of a late-model, five-speed manual transmission. Study the location of the major components. (Borg-Warner)

Chapter 35
Manual Transmission Fundamentals

After studying this chapter, you will be able to:

- ❍ Explain the function of a transmission in an automotive vehicle.
- ❍ Give examples of various gear combinations that provide different ratios to produce more power and less speed or more speed and less power at the output shaft of the transmission.
- ❍ Trace the power flow through each "gear" of three-speed and four-speed manual transmissions.
- ❍ Tell how the three basic elements of a planetary gearset work together to provide gear reduction or direct drive.
- ❍ Trace the power flow through each "gear" of a five-speed manual transmission, including fifth-gear overdrive.

Manual Transmissions

A ***transmission*** is a speed and power-changing device installed at some point between the engine and driving wheels of the vehicle. It provides a means for changing the ratio between engine rpm (revolutions per minute) and driving wheel rpm to best meet each particular driving situation.

Given a level road, an automobile without a transmission could be made to move by accelerating the engine and engaging the clutch. However, a start under these conditions would be slow, noisy, and uncomfortable. In addition, it would place a tremendous strain on the engine and driving parts of the automobile.

In order to get smooth starts and have power to pass and climb hills, a power ratio must be provided to multiply the torque (turning effort) of the engine. Also required is a speed ratio to avoid the need for extremely high engine rpm at high road speeds. The transmission is geared to perform these functions.

Application of Torque

Power is the rate or speed at which work is performed. ***Torque*** is turning or twisting effort.

Torque is derived from power. However, because of operating characteristics, a gasoline engine does not attain maximum torque at the peak of power output. The engine section of this text makes it clear that the amount of torque obtainable from a source of power is proportional to the distance from the center of rotation at which it is applied.

It follows, then, that if we have a shaft (engine crankshaft) rotating at any given speed, we can put gears of different sizes on the shaft and obtain different results. If we put a large gear on the shaft, we will get more speed and less power at the rim than with a small gear.

If we place another shaft parallel to our driving shaft and install gears or pulleys on it in line with those on the driving shaft, we can obtain almost any desired combination of speed or power within the limits of the engine's ability. That is exactly what an automobile transmission does by means of gears and devices.

Gear Usage

Gears are simply a means of applying leverage to rotating parts. An ordinary lever, for example, has more power as the fulcrum gets closer to the object of power application, Figure 35-1. The closer the fulcrum approaches the object, the longer the distance the lever end has to be moved. The same principle applies to gears and pulleys. The smaller the number of teeth on the driving gear, the slower the driven gear rotates, but with multiplied power.

A modern transmission provides both speed and power. The engineers who designed it selected the gear sizes that would give the best all-around performance. It is geared to a power ratio that puts the car in motion, then it shifts, or is shifted, to one or more speed ratios that keep it rolling.

A Frenchman named Levassor is generally credited with developing the first sliding gear transmission. It consisted of two shafts mounted parallel to each other and fitted with sliding spur gears of different sizes. The gears were arranged to mesh with each other to provide a change in the relative speed of the driving and driven shafts, Figure 35-2. Levassor's transmission had a first, second, and third gear, as well as reverse. It was an ingenious "first."

Gear Ratios

Gear ratios in transmissions are not standardized. Instead, they are engineered to fit changes in the engine, car weight, etc., in order to obtain maximum performance.

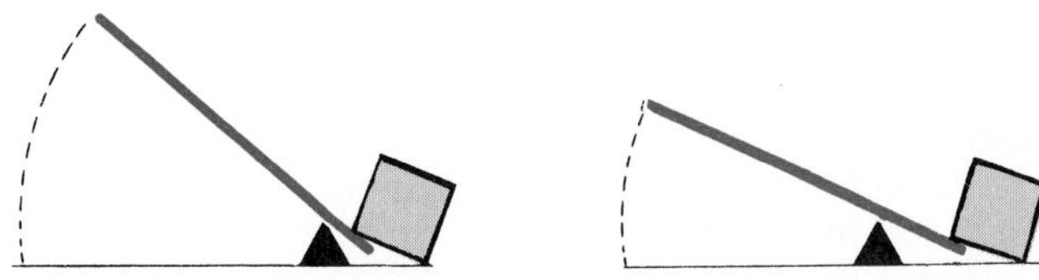

Figure 35-1. The principle of the lever and fulcrum can be compared to gear ratios. The distance between the fulcrum and the object is comparable to the distance between the center of a gear and its rim. Therefore, a small gear will drive a large gear slowly, but with great power.

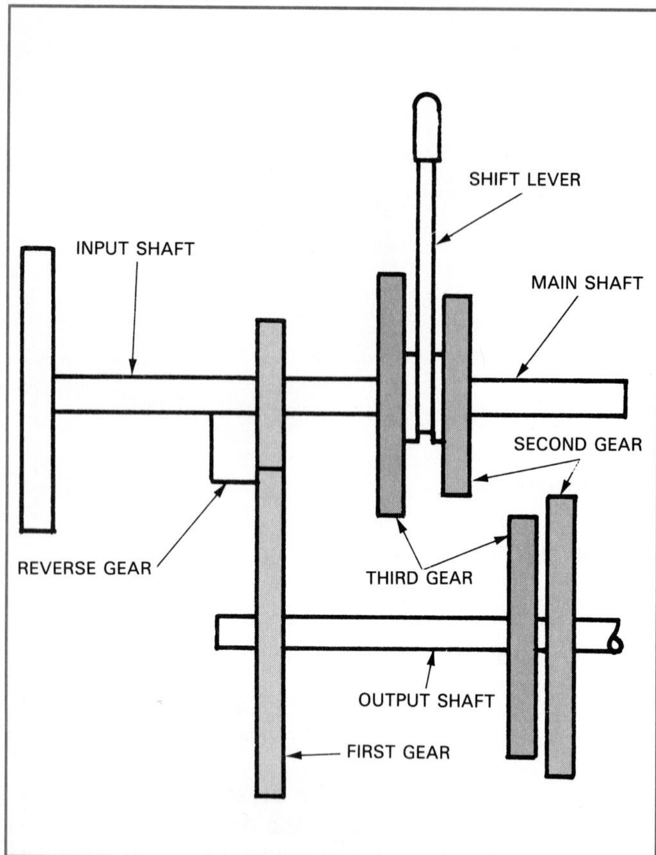

Figure 35-2. In diagrammatic form, a small gear on the main shaft is meshed with a large "low" gear for maximum power. Second gears are nearly the same size for more speed of drive shaft. The high-speed gear on the main shaft is larger than the high gear on the drive shaft, so higher speed on the driven shaft would result.

A typical automobile manual transmission has ratios as follows:

Reverse gear	3.8:1
First gear	2.8:1
Second gear	1.7:1
Third gear	1.0:1
Overdrive	0.7:1

Note that high-gear output is direct drive or a 1.0:1 ratio. To figure other ratios, compute each meshing of gears in a given speed as a separate ratio. Then, the overall transmission gear ratio for that speed would be a mathematical computation of all of these values.

The gear ratio can be determined by counting the teeth on a pair of gears. If the driving gear has 20 teeth and the driven gear 40 teeth, the ratio would be 2.0:1. If the driving gear had 40 teeth and driven gear 20 teeth, the ratio would be 1.0:2.

Transmission gear ratios should not be confused with the final drive ratio or car gear ratio which refers to the overall ratio between the engine revolutions and the driving axle revolutions. This, of course, includes the gear reduction in the differential.

In third gear, for example (1.0:1 ratio), the output shaft of the transmission turns at the same speed as the engine crankshaft. In overdrive, the output shaft turns faster. In all other gear combinations, the output shaft turns more slowly, but provides greater power.

Three-speed Manual Transmission

To illustrate gear arrangement, a simplified, spur gear, ***three-speed transmission*** is shown in Figure 35-2. The clutch attaches to the input shaft at the left; the drive shaft attaches to the output shaft at the right. The transmission gears are in the neutral position.

Neutral Position

In *neutral position*: The clutch turns the input shaft, which rotates the countershaft gear and the second-speed, first-speed, and reverse gears. The output shaft does not revolve. See Figure 35-3.

Reverse Gear

In order to engage *reverse gear:* First and reverse sliding gear A on the output shaft is moved backward to engage reverse gear B, which is driven by gear C on the countershaft. Interposing idler gear B between gears A and C reverses the rotation of the output shaft. See Figure 35-4.

First Gear

To engage *first gear:* The first and reverse sliding gear on the output shaft is moved forward into mesh with the first gear. With this move, the input shaft turns the countershaft gear, which turns the first and reverse gear. The first gear on the countershaft, being smaller than the mating gear on the output shaft, provides a gear reduction. Therefore, it turns the output shaft at slower speed with greater power. See Figure 35-5.

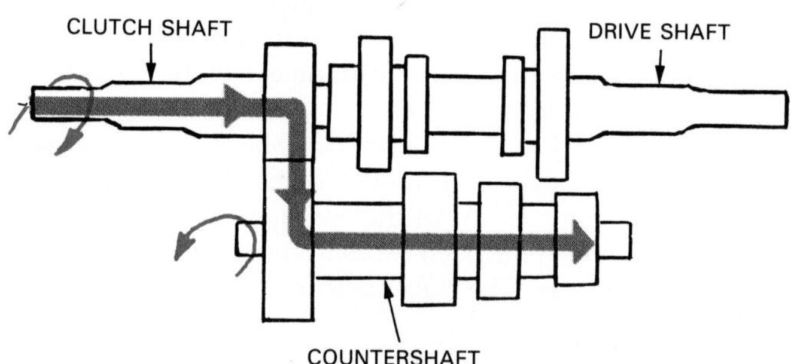

Figure 35-3. Neutral: With the engine running and the three-speed manual transmission in the neutral position, the input shaft turns the countershaft, but no power is applied to the output shaft.

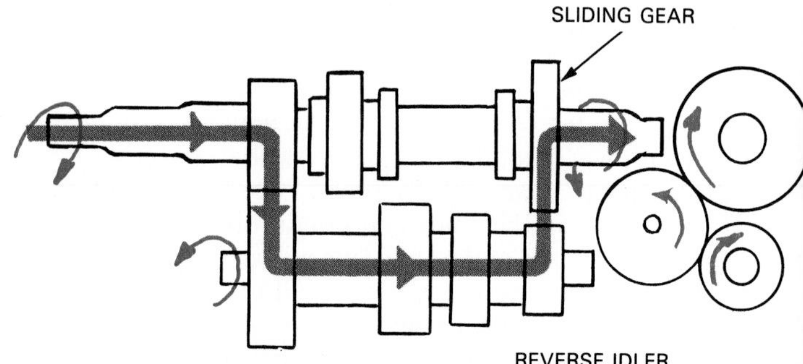

Figure 35-4. Reverse: When the shift lever is moved to the reverse position, an idler gear is interposed between the countershaft and the output shaft to reverse the direction of rotation of the output shaft.

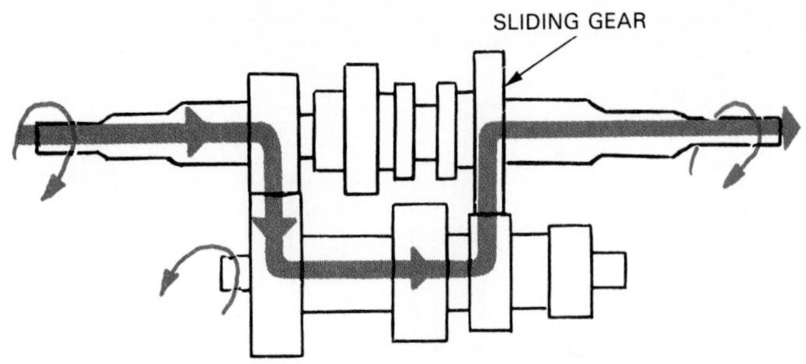

Figure 35-5. First gear: When the shift lever is placed in first gear, power is transmitted through the countershaft, through the first and reverse sliding gear, and to the output shaft.

Second Gear

To shift into *second gear:* The first and reverse sliding gear is returned to neutral, Figure 35-3, and the output shaft second-speed gear is moved backward into mesh with the second-speed gear on the countershaft. Since there is less difference in the size of these gears, the output shaft will turn at a higher rate of speed than in first gear. The principle gear reduction is now between the input shaft gear and the countershaft gear, Figure 35-6.

Third Gear

For *third gear:* The output shaft second-speed gear is disengaged from the second-speed gear on the countershaft and moved forward until projections on the rear face of the input shaft gear engage with matching indentations or notches in the forward face of the output shaft second-speed gear. This locks the input shaft and output shaft together, and they turn at the same speed. The gears on the countershaft continue to rotate, but they do not carry power since they are not coupled to any of the gears on the output shaft. See Figure 35-7.

All shift operations on the output shaft are controlled by collars or forks. The forks are attached to two parallel shafts, and the gear shift lever can be moved to the side, forward, or backward to engage either shifting shaft as desired. An interlocking device is placed between the shafts so that only one shaft can be moved at a time to avoid engaging more than one pair of gears at a time.

Helical Gears

Today's ***helical gear synchromesh transmissions,*** Figure 35-8, are somewhat similar to the spur gear type. The principal differences are:

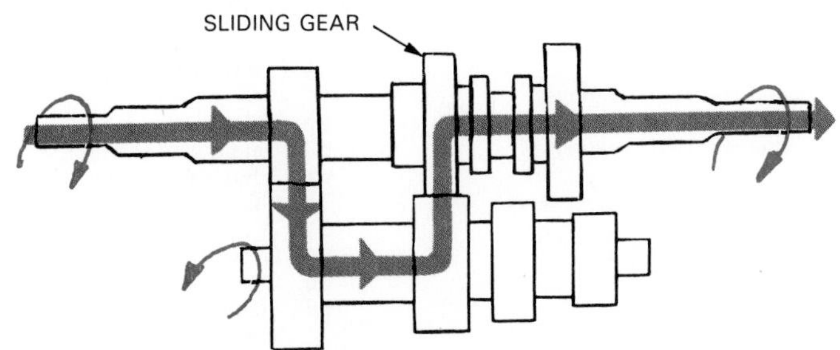

Figure 35-6. Second gear: With the shift lever in second gear, power flow is through the countershaft, through the second speed sliding gear, and to output shaft.

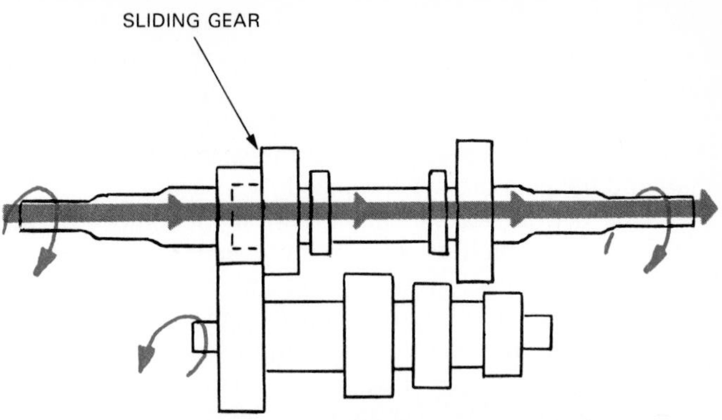

Figure 35-7. Third gear: In third gear, power does not go through the gears, but is transmitted directly from the input shaft to the output shaft.

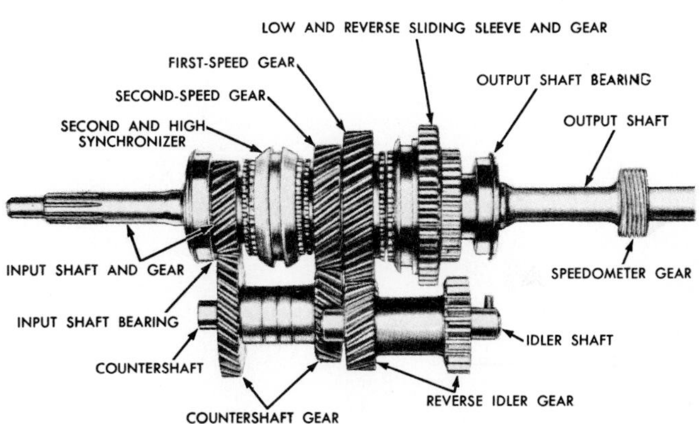

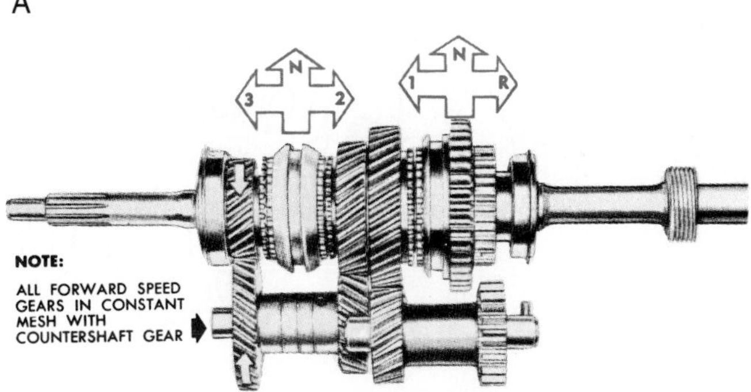

Figure 35-8. A–The gear setup in a typical, helical gear, synchromesh three-speed transmission features constant mesh gears with synchronized shifts. B–The position of the shift forks is indicated for neutral, first, second, third, and reverse.

- The shape of the gear teeth.
- The addition of synchronizing clutches to the second- and third-speed gears (first gear, too, in many cases).
- The fact that some of the output shaft gears are free to turn on bearings until engaged.

Synchronizing Clutch

The ***synchronizing clutch*** is a drum or sleeve that slides back and forth on the splined output shaft by means of the shifting fork. Generally, it has a bronze cone on each side that engages with a tapered mating cone on the second- and third-speed gears. When this drum is moved along the output shaft, the cones act as a clutch. Upon touching the gear which is to be engaged, the output shaft is speeded up or slowed down as required until the speeds of the output shaft and the gear are synchronized.

This action occurs during partial movement of the shift lever. Completion of lever movement then slides the drum and gear into complete engagement. This action can be readily understood by remembering that the hub of the drum slides on the splines of the output shaft to engage the cones, then the drum slides on the hub to engage the gears. See Figure 35-9. Figure 35-8 shows the synchronizers and all other parts in their assembled positions. Figure 35-10 shows an exploded view of a typical three-speed transmission.

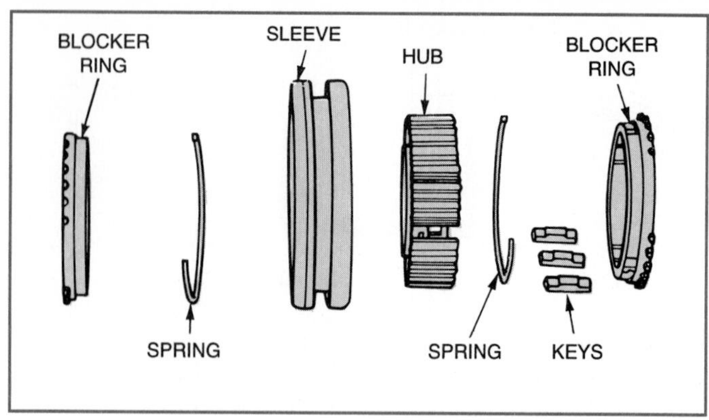

Figure 35-9. Exploded view of a synchronizer assembly shows the relative positions of the internal and external splined hub, sleeve keys, springs, sleeve, and blocker rings.

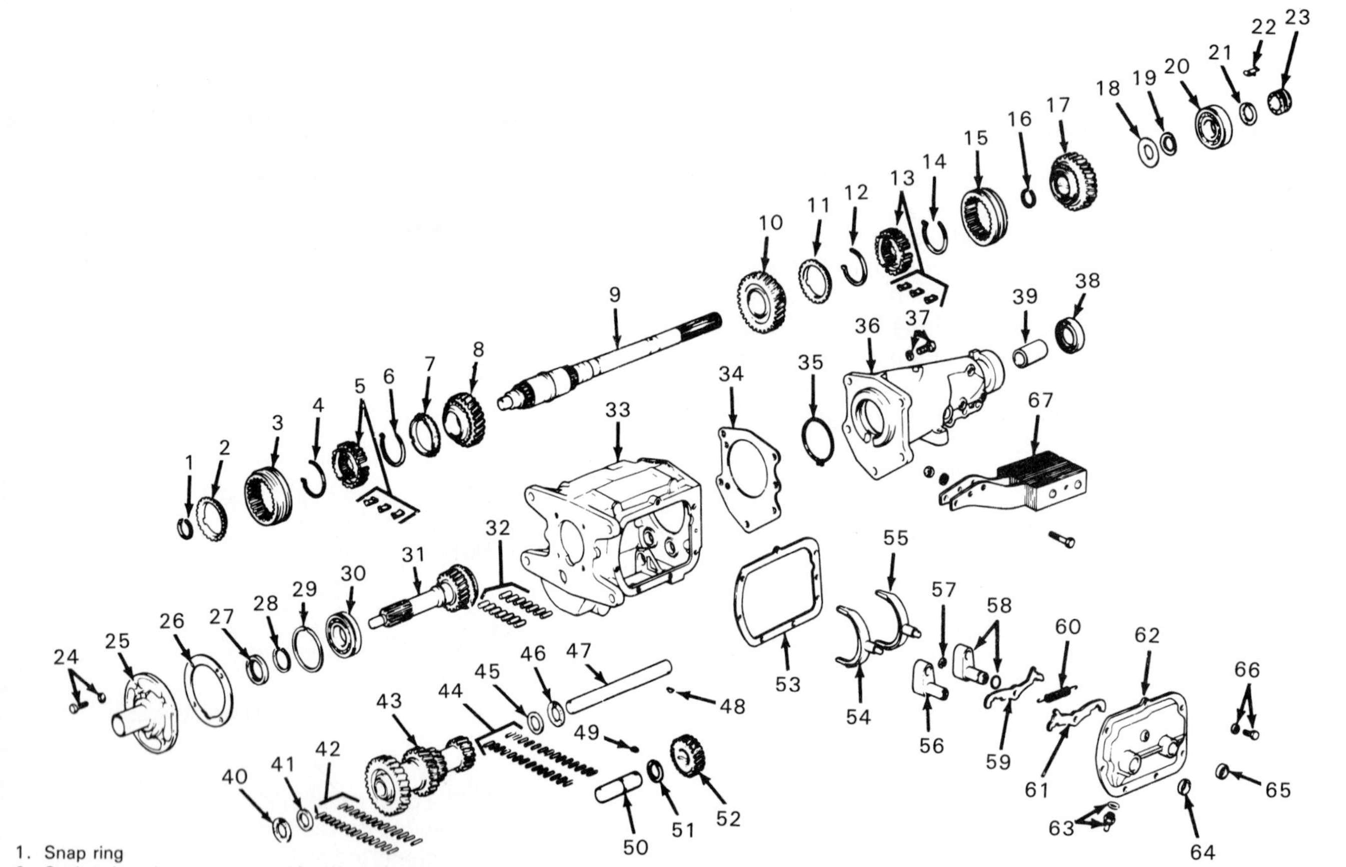

1. Snap ring
2. Sychronizer ring
3. 2-3 synchronizer sleeve
4. Synchrnoizer key spring
5. Synchronizer hub and keys
6. Synchronizer key spring
7. Synchronizer ring
8. Second gear
9. Main shaft
10. First gear
11. Synchronizer ring
12. Synchronizer key spring
13. Synchronizer hub and keys
14. Synchronizer key spring
15. 1-2 synchronizer sleeve
16. Snap ring
17. Reverse gear
18. Thrust washer
19. Waved washer
20. Rear bearing
21. Snap ring
22. Speedometer gear clip
23. Speedometer drive gear
24. Bearing retainer bolts and washers (4)
25. Front bearing retainer
26. Bearing retainer gasket
27. Bearing retainer oil seal
28. Snap ring
29. Bearing snap ring
30. Front bearing
31. Drive gear
32. Pilot bearings
33. Case
34. Extension to case gasket
35. Rear bearing to extension retaining ring
36. Rear extension
37. Extension to case retaining bolts and washers
38. Rear extension bushing
39. Rear seal
40. Thrust washer
41. Spacer
42. Countergear shaft bearings
43. Countergear
44. Countergear shaft bearings
45. Spacer
46. Thrust washer
47. Countergear shaft
48. Countergear shaft key
49. Idler shaft key
50. Reverse idler shaft
51. Snap ring
52. Reverse idler gear
53. Side cover gasket
54. 2-3 shift fork
55. 1-Rev shift fork
56. 2-3 shifter shaft
57. Retaining "E" ring
58. 1-Rev shifter shaft with "O" ring
59. 2-3 detent cam
60. Detent cam spring
61. 1-Rev detent cam
62. Shift cover
63. TCS switch and gasket
64. Shifter shaft seal
65. Shifter shaft seal
66. Shift cover bolts and washers
67. Damper assembly

Figure 35-10. This exploded view shows the assembly sequence of a typical three-speed manual transmission. (Pontiac)

Four-speed Manual Transmission

Four-speed manual transmissions and high performance engines are popular combinations. Generally, all four forward speeds are synchronized and engineered with closely spaced gear ratios to provide minimum loss of engine speed at shift points. All gears are in constant mesh with the exception of the reverse sliding gear, Figure 35-11. With four-speed transmissions, manual gear shifting is usually accomplished with a floor-type shift lever mounted on a console.

When a four-speed manual transmission is in neutral, with clutch engaged, the input shaft drives the countershaft. However, with all synchronizers neutrally positioned and the reverse sliding gear out of mesh, power does not flow to the output shaft. See Figure 35-11.

In all forward speeds, power is transmitted from the input shaft to the countershaft gear and to first gear, then to second-, third-, or fourth-speed gears, in turn, each locked with a synchronizer assembly to drive the output shaft. See Figure 35-12.

In reverse, the reverse sliding gear is moved into mesh with the reverse rear idler gear. Power is transmitted from the input shaft to the countershaft gear, then to the constant mesh reverse front idler gear and through splines and reverse gearing to the main shaft. Figure 35-12.

To illustrate all components of a four-speed manual transmission, an exploded view is shown in Figure 35-13. With the four-speed setup, we have the following typical gear ratios:

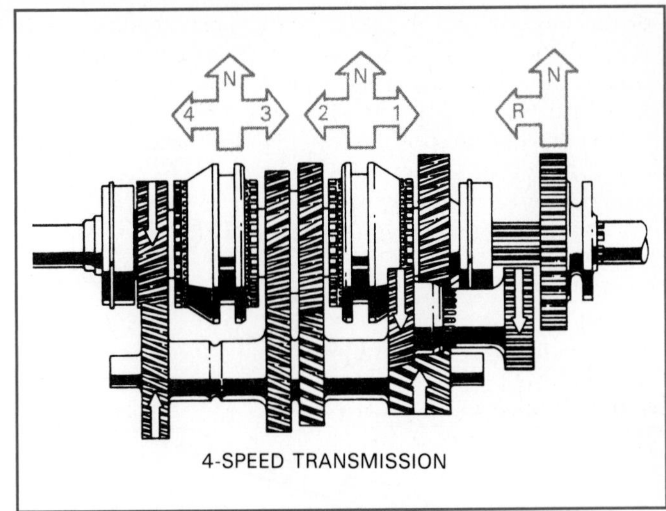

Figure 35-11. The four-speed manual transmission is a favorite of sports car enthusiasts. Because it is fully synchronized, all upshifts and downshifts can be made while the car is in motion.

Reverse gear	4.0:1
First gear	4.0:1
Second gear	2.14:1
Third gear	1.42:1
Fourth gear	1.0:1

All components of a four-speed manual transmission are shown in Figure 35-13.

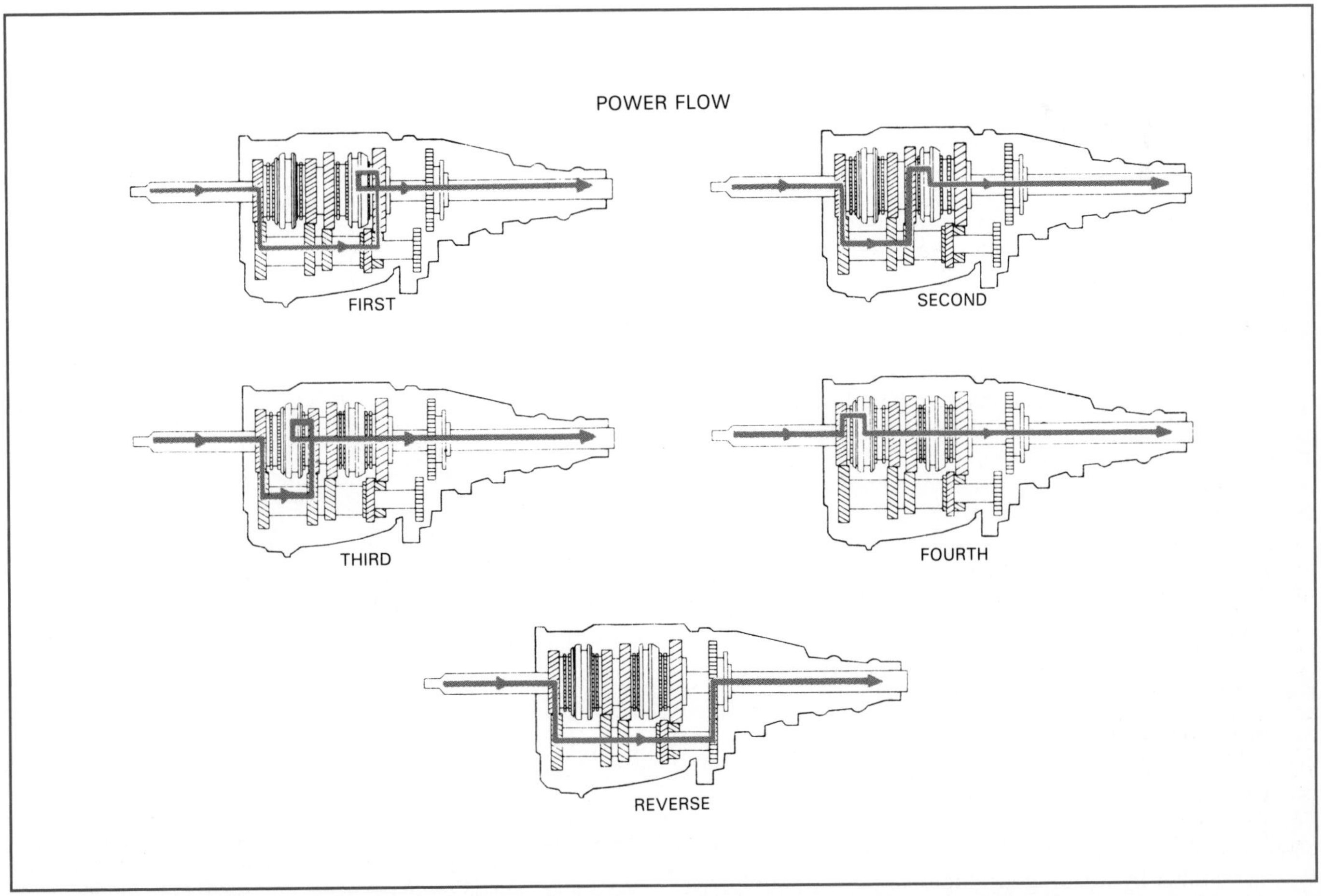

Figure 35-12. Power flow in four-speed manual transmission is illustrated in each forward position and in reverse.

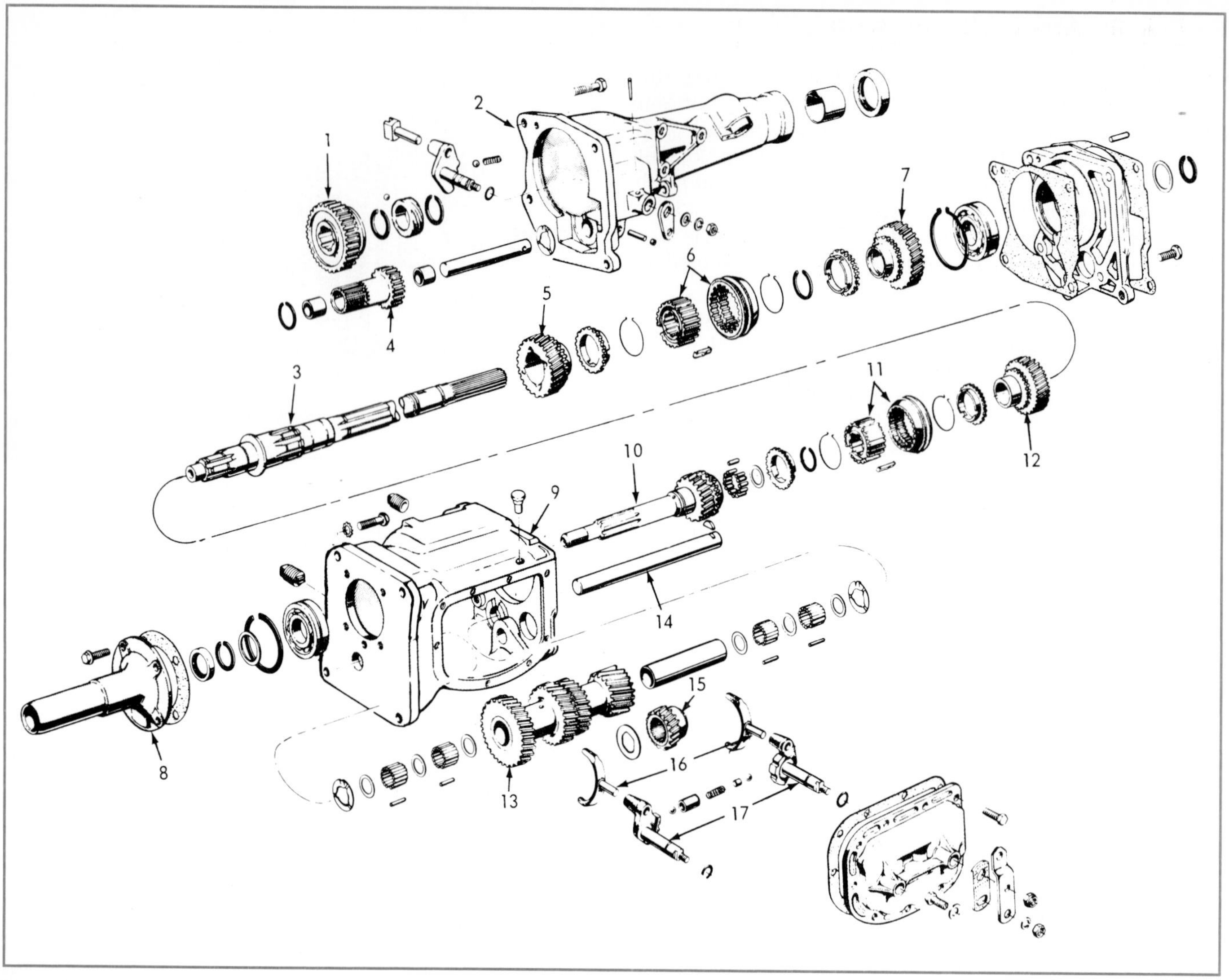

Figure 35-13. The major elements of a typical four-speed manual transmission. 1–Reverse gear. 2–Reverse gear housing. 3–Main shaft. 4–Reverse idler gear. 5–Second gear. 6–First-and-second clutch assembly. 7–First gear. 8–Front bearing retainer. 9–Case. 10–Pinion gear. 11–Third-and-fourth clutch assembly. 12–Third gear. 13–Countershaft gear. 14–Countershaft. 15–Reverse idler gear. 16–Shifter forks. 17–Shifter fork shafts.

Overdrive Revival

After a lengthy lull, overdrive units are popular again. Either the "planetary" type or those with built-in or built-on gears and synchronizers are available from almost all automobile manufacturers.

Overdrive is an arrangement of gearing which produces more revolutions of the driven shaft than the driving shaft. That is: the engine rpm will be reduced about 30 percent while the vehicle maintains the same road speed. As a result, fuel consumption will be reduced and engine life prolonged.

Planetary Gear Systems

Planetary gears are sometimes used in one form or another in overdrive transmissions. The name "planetary" is derived from this system's similarity to our solar system. The pinions or planet gears each turn on their own axis while rotating around the sun (central) gear. These gears are surrounded by a ring gear, Figure 35-14, to complete the gearset.

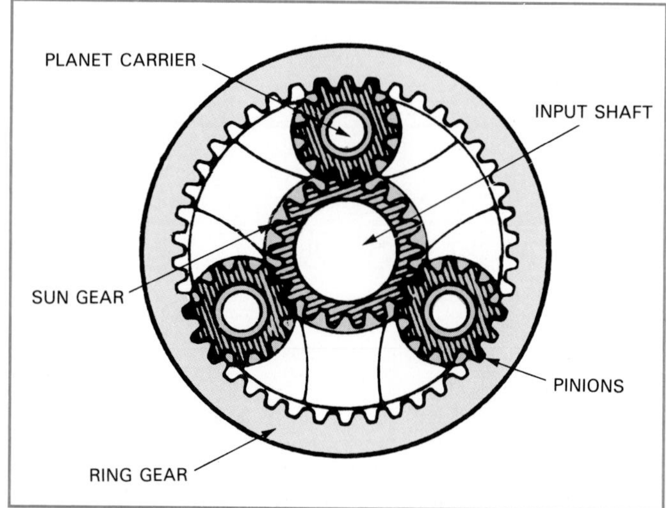

Figure 35-14. This end view of a planetary gearset shows a three-pinion arrangement. Note that the gears are in mesh at all times. As different elements are "held" from turning, different gear ratios are affected.

Basically, planetary gearsets are used as a reduction gear. They are used for reverse and are used in multiple sets where more than two forward speeds are desired.

When a planetary gearset is installed in an overdrive application, it is used as an overgear. That is, output rpm exceeds input rpm, or as stated earlier, the arrangement of gearing (planetary gearset) produces more revolutions of the driven shaft than the driving shaft.

Methods of Connecting Parts

In a planetary gearset, the gears are in mesh at all times and are never shifted in and out of engagement. The gears are attached to different drums which, in turn, are attached to other operating parts of the system. This enables the gears to function in different ways as the various drums are held from rotation by brake bands.

A simple form of planetary gearset, Figure 35-14, has three pinions mounted between, and meshed with, both the sun gear and ring gear at all times. The pinions revolve on pins or axles which are a part of the planet carrier drum. The pinions are held in spaced relationship with one another, yet can turn freely on their own pins and also can rotate around the sun gear and within the ring gear.

Basically, we have three units:

- Sun gear.
- Planet carrier, drum, and pinions.
- Ring gear and drum.

The gears can be arranged so that they will function as driving elements or driven elements to provide different results by connecting them in different ways. For example, if the engine is connected to the sun gear and the planet or pinion carrier is connected to the drive shaft, the entire assembly will rotate as a unit (pinions do not turn on their pins). In this case, there will be no gear reduction. The drive shaft will rotate at the same speed as the engine crankshaft.

If, however, a brake band is placed around the ring gear to hold it from turning, the pinions will be forced to travel around inside the ring gear, carrying the pinion carrier along at reduced speed. In this case, the pinion gears turn on their pins in the opposite direction of rotation of the sun gear, while the pinion carrier turns in the same direction as the sun gear but at reduced speed.

With these few gears and a band to hold the drum, we have a basic transmission of the planetary type with gear reduction for low gear and direct drive for high gear.

Transmission Overdrives

Utilizing the same fundamental gears used in planetary transmissions, we can change the hookup to get an overdrive. If we attach the engine to the planet carrier instead of the sun gear and attach the drive shaft (or driven shaft) to the ring gear instead of the planet carrier, we would change the entire operation.

By holding the sun gear, we can reverse the action of the gearing and get an increase in gear ratio instead of a reduction. This combination is light in weight, not too expensive to build, and it could be attached to the transmission where it would be carried by the car springs as part of the sprung weight. Furthermore, it could be controlled by the driver and could be made automatic in operation.

Arranging Overdrive

There are several ways of hooking up planetary gearing to accomplish different results. One method is to increase gear ratio by attaching the driven shaft to the ring gear, while holding the sun gear from rotating. However, when the sun gear is released, the pinions will simply chase around between the sun gear and ring gear in the opposite direction and no power will be transmitted.

This problem was solved by installing a free-wheel unit on the transmission output shaft. Then, when drive shaft speed exceeds engine speed (coasting), the rollers release. When accelerating the engine, the rollers are wedged on the cam and power is transmitted. See Figure 35-15.

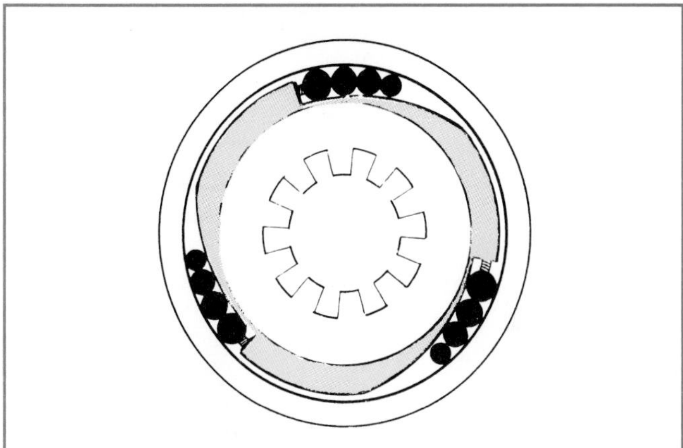

Figure 35-15. If the outer rim turns clockwise on an overrunning clutch, the rollers will roll up on the cams and the hub will turn at the same speed as the rim. If the rim turns counterclockwise, the rollers roll down the cams against the springs and the hub will "free wheel" (cease to rotate).

Methods of Control

Older overdrive assemblies were considered an auxiliary unit because they were attached to the rear of a three-speed manual transmission. Control of these overdrive transmissions is in the hands of the driver. A control handle is pushed in to engage overdrive. It is pulled out to "lock out" overdrive. The entire operation is controlled by a solenoid, a mechanical centrifugal governor, a kickdown switch, and a locking pawl and balk ring assembly. See Figure 35-16.

Other planetary type overdrive transmissions were introduced, but the trend in overdrives turned toward "built-in" gears and synchronizers. This trend, plus a strong move toward transaxle applications, has resulted in the development of four-speed and five-speed overdrive transmissions.

Five-speed Overdrive Transmission

A typical ***five-speed transmission*** is a fully synchronized unit with blocker ring synchronizers and a constant mesh reverse gear. It has the shift lever mounted on top of the extension housing.

In *neutral* with clutch engaged, Figure 35-17, the input shaft turns the countergear, which then turns the fifth, fourth, third, second, first, and reverse idler gears. However, since the clutch sleeves are neutrally positioned, power will not flow through the output shaft. See Figure 35-17.

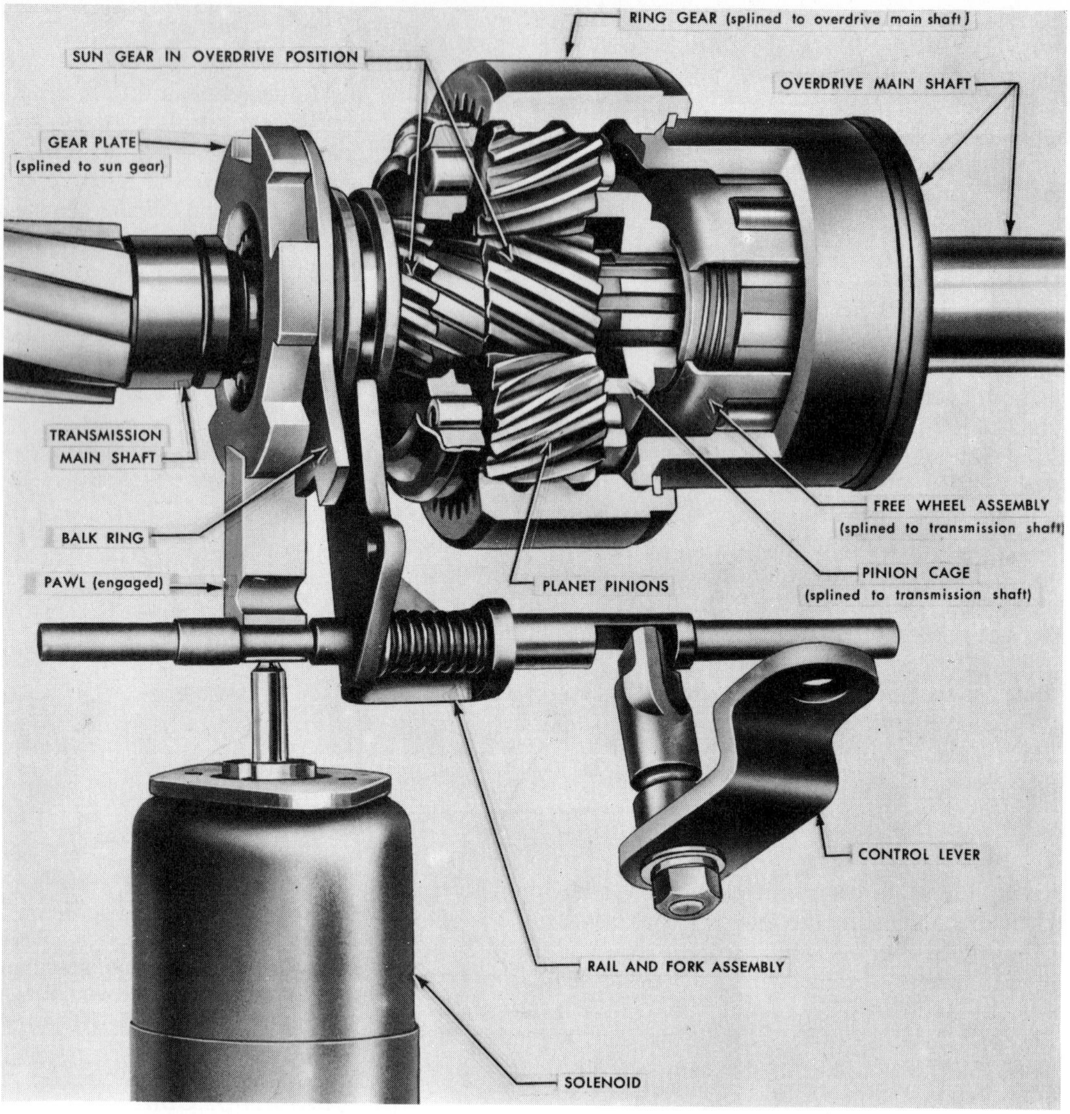

RING GEAR (splined to overdrive main shaft)
SUN GEAR IN OVERDRIVE POSITION
OVERDRIVE MAIN SHAFT
GEAR PLATE
(splined to sun gear)
TRANSMISSION
MAIN SHAFT
BALK RING
PAWL (engaged)
PLANET PINIONS
FREE WHEEL ASSEMBLY
(splined to transmission shaft)
PINION CAGE
(splined to transmission shaft)
CONTROL LEVER
RAIL AND FORK ASSEMBLY
SOLENOID

Figure 35-16. When a planetary overdrive transmission is in overdrive, the sun gear is locked in place by the pawl in the balk ring. The planet gears drive the internal ring gear. The ring gear drives the overdrive main shaft.

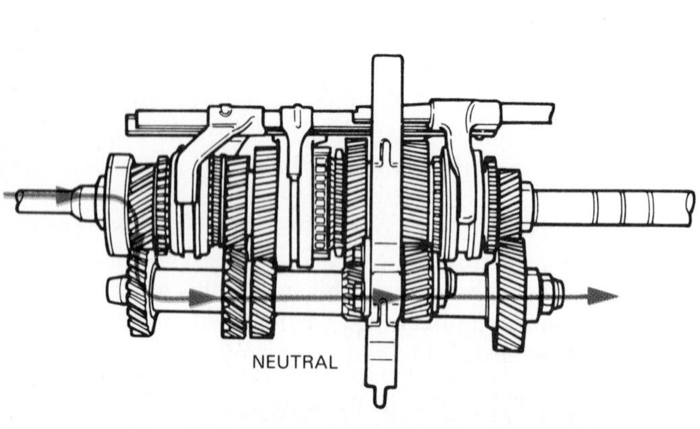

5 SPEED TRANSMISSION

NEUTRAL

Figure 35-17. Neutral: Although the input shaft at left drives the countergear and countershaft, no power flows to the output shaft because the clutch sleeves are neutrally positioned. (Chevrolet)

5 SPEED TRANSMISSION

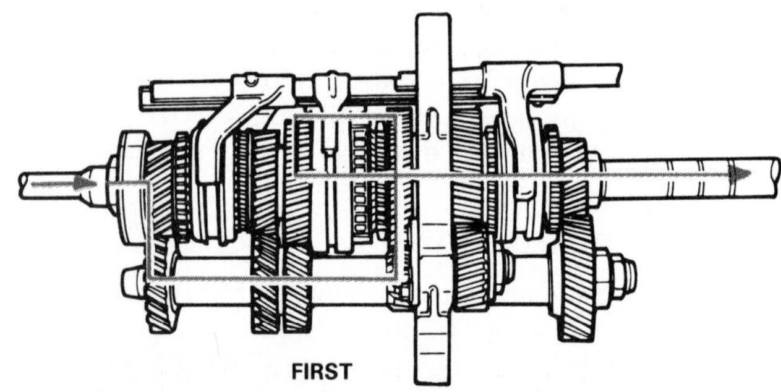

Figure 35-18. First gear: Follow power flow lines in color from the input shaft, to the countergear, to the first-speed gear, to the first-and-second-speed clutch sleeve, and to the output shaft. (Chevrolet)

In first speed, Figure 35-18, the first-and-second-speed clutch sleeve assembly is moved rearward to mesh with the first-speed gear (which is being turned by countergear). Since the first-and-second-speed clutch hub is splined to the output shaft, power flows from the first-speed gear through the clutch assembly to the output shaft. See Figure 35-18.

In *second speed,* Figure 35-19, the first-and-second-speed clutch sleeve assembly is moved forward to mesh with

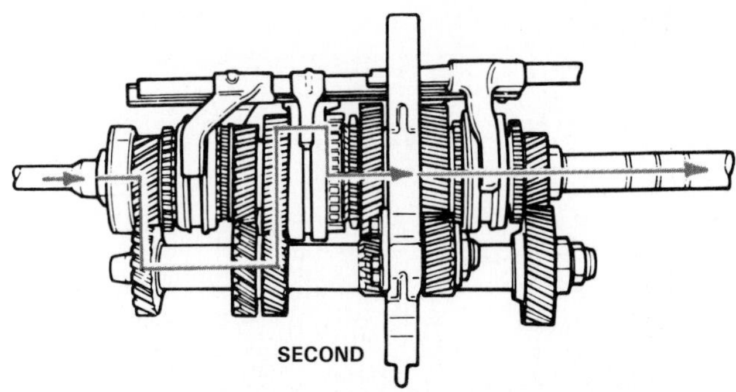

Figure 35-19. Second gear: Power flow as indicated is from the input shaft, to the countergear, to the second-speed gear, to the first-and-second-speed clutch sleeve, and to the output shaft. (Chevrolet)

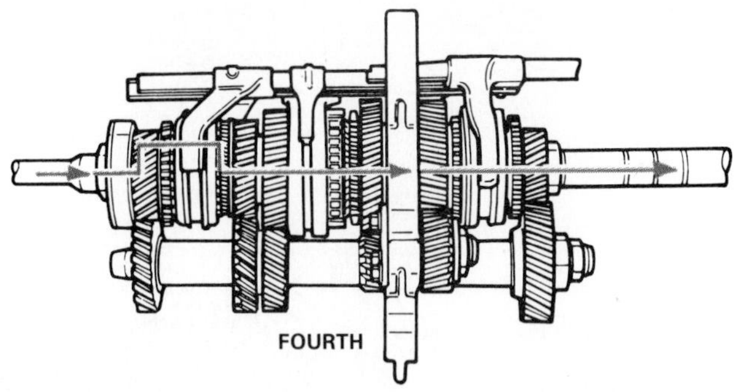

Figure 35-21. Fourth gear: Power flow is from the input shaft, to the third-and-fourth-speed clutch assembly, and to the output shaft. This is "direct drive," or a 1.0:1 ratio. (Chevrolet)

the second-speed gear (which is being turned by countergear). Since the first-and-second-speed clutch hub is splined to the output shaft, power flows from the second-speed gear through the clutch assembly to the output shaft. See Figure 35-19.

In *third speed,* Figure 35-20, the third-and-fourth-speed clutch assembly is moved rearward to mesh with the third-speed gear (which is being turned by countergear). Since the third-and-fourth-speed clutch hub is splined to the output shaft, power flows from the third-speed gear through the clutch assembly to the output shaft. See Figure 35-20.

In *fourth speed,* Figure 35-21, the third-and-fourth-speed clutch sleeve assembly is moved forward to mesh with the input shaft main drive gear. This engagement results in "direct drive" from input shaft to output shaft. See Figure 35-21.

In *fifth speed,* Figure 35-22, or overdrive, the reverse-and-fifth-speed clutch sleeve assembly is moved rearward to mesh with the fifth-speed gear. This engagement results in power flow from the fifth-speed gear through the reverse-and-fifth-speed clutch assembly to the output shaft. See Figure 35-22.

In *reverse gear,* Figure 35-23, the reverse-and-fifth-speed clutch sleeve assembly is moved forward to mesh with the reverse gear. This engagement results in power flow from the countershaft and reverse idler to the reverse gear and directly to the output shaft, Figure 35-23.

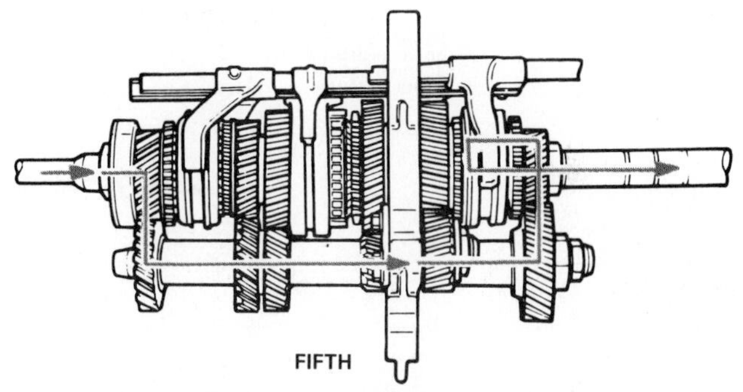

Figure 35-22. Fifth gear: Power flow is from the input shaft, to the countergear, to the fifth-speed gear, to the reverse-and-fifth-speed clutch assembly, and to the output shaft. This is "overdrive." (Chevrolet)

To illustrate all components of a five-speed manual transmission, an exploded view is shown in Figure 35-24. This transmission is designed for use in a four-wheel drive application. Therefore, it features an adapter housing (rather than an extension housing) to adapt the transmission to the transfer case. An exploded view of a four-speed overdrive transmission is shown in Figure 35-25.

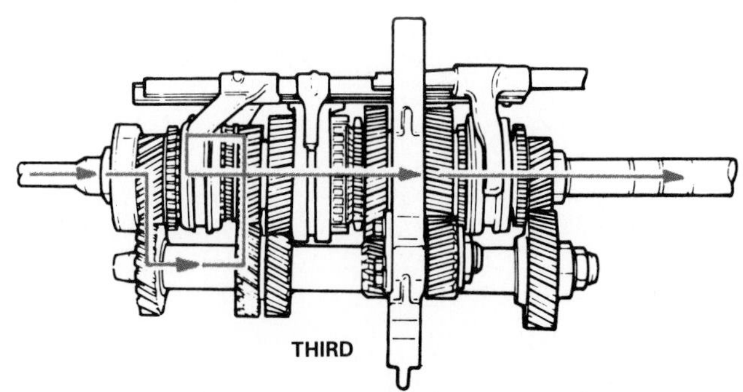

Figure 35-20. Third gear: Power flow is from the input shaft, to the countergear, to the third-speed gear, to the third-and-fourth-speed clutch sleeve, and to the output shaft. (Chevrolet)

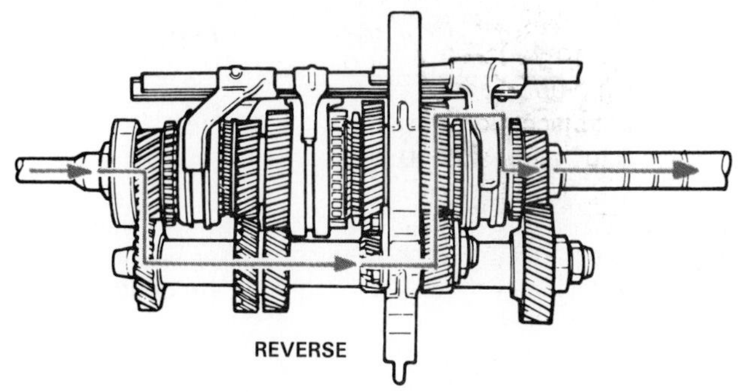

Figure 35-23. Reverse gear: Power flow is from the input shaft, to the countergear, to the reverse gear, to the reverse idler, to the reverse-and-fifth-speed clutch assembly, and to the output shaft. (Chevrolet)

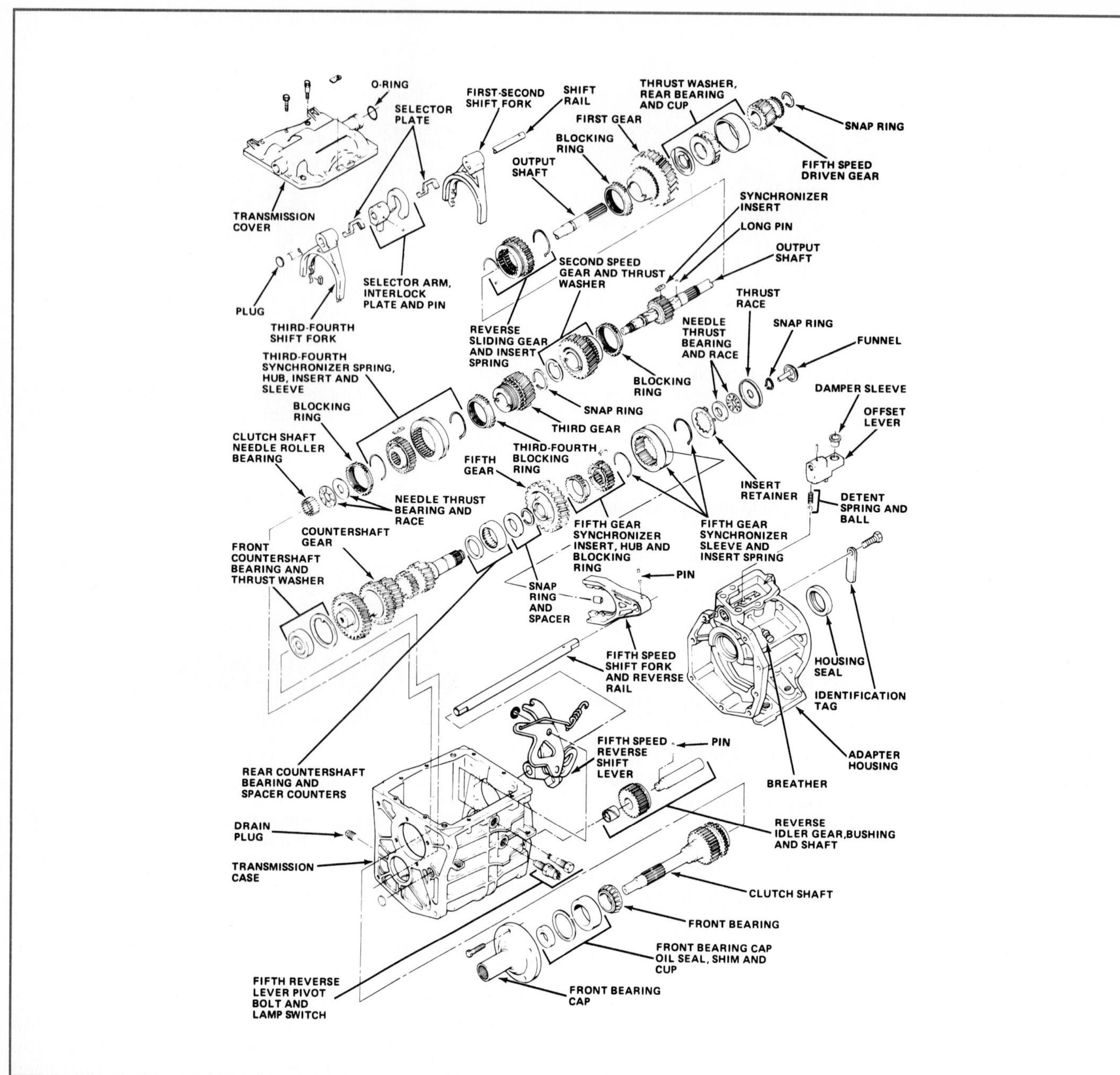

Figure 35-24. Exploded view shows the assembly sequence of a typical five-speed manual transmission with overdrive. (Chrysler)

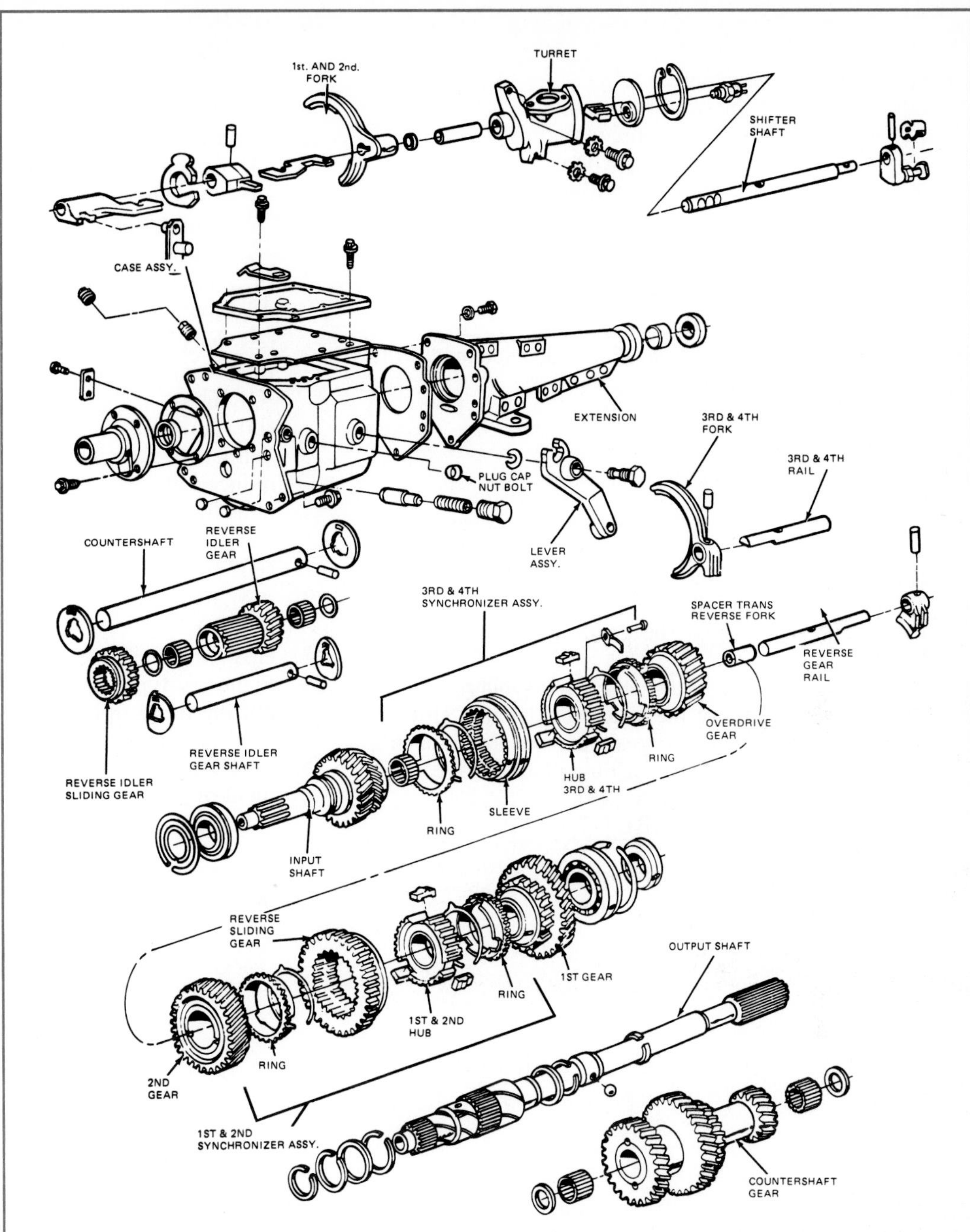

Figure 35-25. Exploded view of a four-speed overdrive transmission.

Chapter 35–Review Questions

Write your answers on a separate sheet of paper. Do not write in this book.

1. What function does a transmission perform?
2. What is "power"?
3. What is "torque"?
4. A larger gear on the driving shaft will increase the speed of rotation of the driven shaft. True or False?
5. How can the ratio of mating gears be determined?
6. What is the gear ratio of a setup where the driving gear has 20 teeth and the driven gear has 40 teeth?
   (A) 2.0:1.
   (B) 1:2.0.
   (C) 4:2.0.
   (D) 2.0:4.
7. Which two manual transmission shafts turn in neutral?
   (A) Input shaft and output shaft.
   (B) Input shaft and countershaft.
   (C) Output shaft and countershaft.
   (D) Countershaft and drive shaft.
8. When a manual transmission is shifted into reverse, what extra gear is interposed to reverse the direction of the output shaft?
   (A) Low and reverse sliding gear.
   (B) Reverse idler gear.
   (C) Reverse synchromesh ring.
   (D) Overrunning gear.
9. Name the three major units in a planetary gearset.
10. If the ring gear is held and the pinion carrier is driven by the sun gear and pinions in an overdrive planetary transmission, will the speed of the driveshaft increase or decrease?

11. What is the function of an overrunning clutch in an overdrive transmission?
    (A) Eliminates the clutch.
    (B) Disengages the overdrive unit.
    (C) Restricts drive to one direction only.
    (D) Permits drive in both directions.
12. Which control device on an auxiliary overdrive transmission operates the locking pawl?
    (A) Solenoid.
    (B) Governor.
    (C) Relay.
    (D) Kickdown unit.
13. Which control device connects and disconnects the overdrive unit?
    (A) Solenoid.
    (B) Governor.
    (C) Relay.
    (D) Balk ring.
14. What is the purpose of the balk ring in an overdrive?
15. When a planetary gearset is installed in an overdrive application, it is used as a(n) _____.
16. With overdrive, output rpm _____ input rpm.
17. In a planetary gearset, the gears are in mesh at all times. True or False?
18. What is the function of a blocker ring synchronizer?
19. Match the numbers of the following "gear positions" at the left with the typical gear ratios at the right in a three-speed manual transmission with overdrive.

1. Reverse.	(A) 1.0:1.	________
2. First gear.	(B) 0.7:1.	________
3. Second gear.	(C) 3.8:1.	________
4. Third gear.	(D) 2.8:1 .	________
5. Overdrive.	(E) 1.7:1.	________

20. Match the numbers of the following "gear positions" with the typical gear ratios at the right in a five-speed manual transmission.

1. Reverse.	(A) 0.68:1.	________
2. First gear.	(B) 1.0:1.	________
3. Second gear.	(C) 1.29:1.	________
4. Third gear.	(D) 1.93:1.	________
5. Fourth gear.	(E) 3.15:1.	________
6. Fifth gear.	(F) 3.35:1.	________

21. In a four-speed manual transmission without overdrive, which "gear" would have a 1.0 to 1 ratio?
    (A) First.
    (B) Second.
    (C) Third.
    (D) Fourth.
22. With fifth-speed overdrive, the engine rpm will be reduced about _____ percent while the vehicle maintains the same road speed.
    (A) 5
    (B) 10
    (C) 20
    (D) 30
23. How was the name "planetary" derived?
24. Planetary-type overdrive transmissions were popular, but the trend in overdrives has turned toward "built-in" _____ and _____.
25. This trend in overdrives has resulted in the development of _____ overdrive transmissions.

Chapter 36
Manual Transmission Service

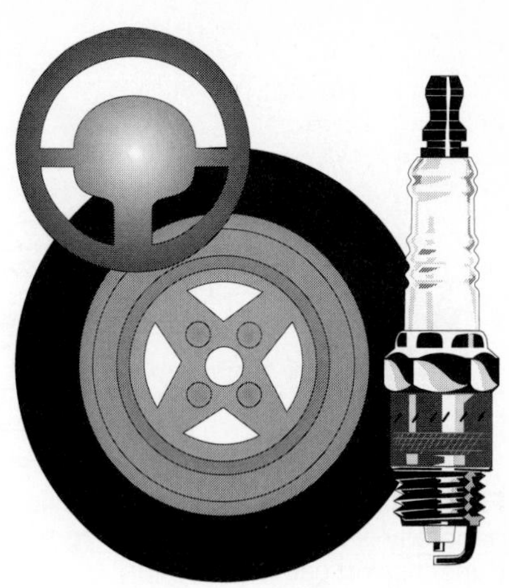

After studying this chapter, you will be able to:
- ❍ Name six manual transmission maintenance operations.
- ❍ List various manual transmission troubles and identify possible causes.
- ❍ Explain general procedure for manual transmission removal and reinstallation.
- ❍ Describe procedures for manual transmission disassembly and internal parts cleaning and inspection.
- ❍ Describe procedure for manual transmission reassembly.

Manual Transmission Maintenance

Manual Transmissions are durable, dependable, positive engagement power transfer mechanisms that require little maintenance. Modern "manuals" have helical-cut gears that are in constant mesh in all forward gear ranges. See Figure 36-1. This feature, plus synchromesh engagement, generally avoids clashing of gears and the resulting gear tooth wear or breakage.

Basically, manual transmission maintenance involves:
- ❍ Making periodic "fluid" level checks, Figure 36-2.
- ❍ Making an external inspection of the transmission for possible fluid leaks.
- ❍ Testing gearshift operation through all the gear ranges.
- ❍ Checking clutch pedal free play.
- ❍ Examining the condition of the transmission mount.
- ❍ Testing the torque tightness of the transmission-to-clutch housing attaching bolts.

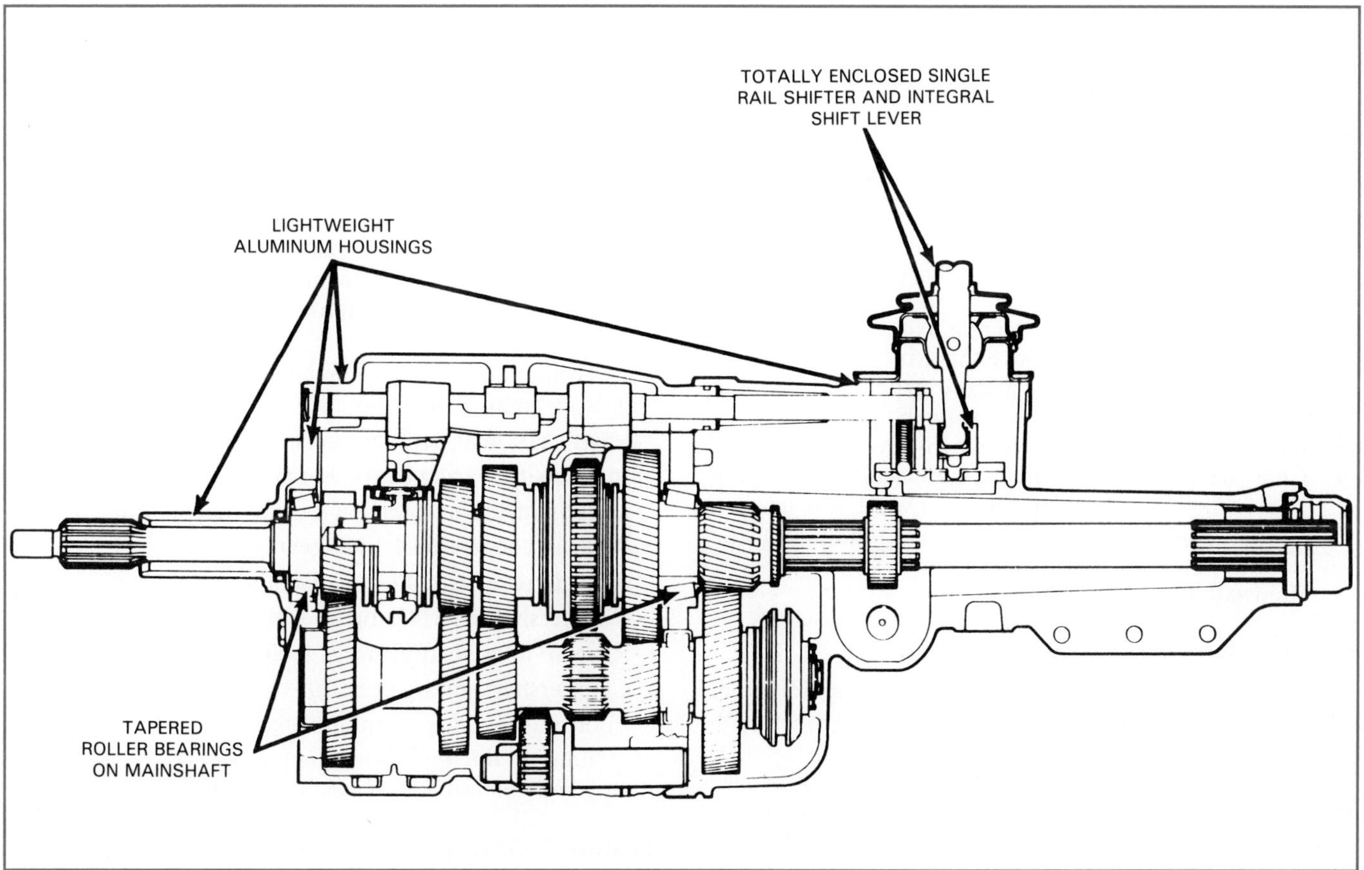

Figure 36-1. This five-speed manual transmission has an aluminum housing, a single rail enclosed shift mechanism, helical gears, and a 0.78:1 fifth gear overdrive. (Pontiac)

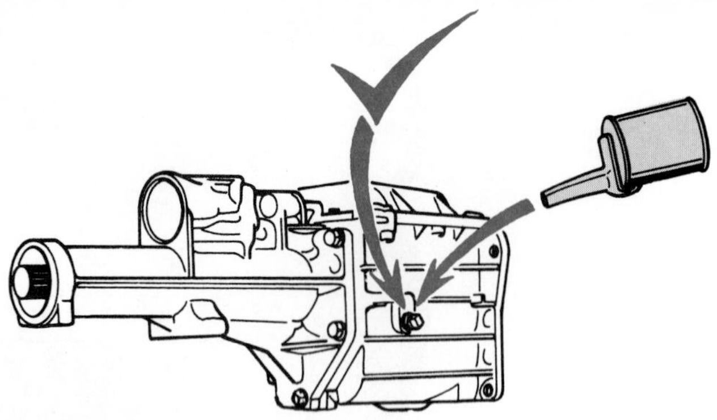

Figure 36-2. A manual transmission's check and refill point generally is located at the fill plug hole in the side of the transmission case. (Chrysler)

Check Fluid Level

To check fluid level in a manual transmission:

1. Raise the vehicle on a hoist.
2. Clean the area around fill plug, Figure 36-2, before removing it.
3. Remove the fill plug and insert your little finger in the fill hole. The fluid level should be even with or just below the lower edge of fill hole. Note: Some manual transmissions have specified levels 1/2 in. to 1 in. below the lower edge of the fill hole. Check the manufacturer's specification for fluid level and fluid change interval. Drain and refill if the fluid is contaminated.
4. If the fluid level is low, add the recommended type and grade of lubricant to bring the level up to the lower edge of the fill hole. Note: Lubricant recommendations vary. Generally, three-speed and four-speed transmissions call for 75W or 80W-90 gear oil; five-speed transmissions require 5W-30SF engine oil or automatic transmission fluid (ATF).
5. Reinstall and tighten the fill plug.
6. Lower the hoist.

Replace the Rear Seal

If the fluid is leaking from the transmission at the rear end of the extension housing:

1. Mark the drive shaft and the rear axle flange for reference on reassembly. Remove the drive shaft.
2. Pry out the oil seal or use a screw-type pulling tool to remove the seal from the extension housing.
3. Clean the counterbore of the extension housing.
4. Coat the outer diameter of a new seal with cement and–with the sealing lip facing inward and using a special installing tool–drive the seal into the housing until it bottoms in the counterbore.
5. Reinstall the drive shaft.

Test the Gearshift Operation

A methodical run-through of gearshift operation in all gear ranges should be part of any manual transmission maintenance routine. See Figure 36-3.

Test gearshifting effort and proper engagement in each forward position and in the reverse position. If binding is noted, or if shift lever fails to indicate a firm detent, place the lever in neutral and check for a smooth and free crossover. If necessary, make adjustments of floor-mounted gearshift or steering column-mounted shift linkage.

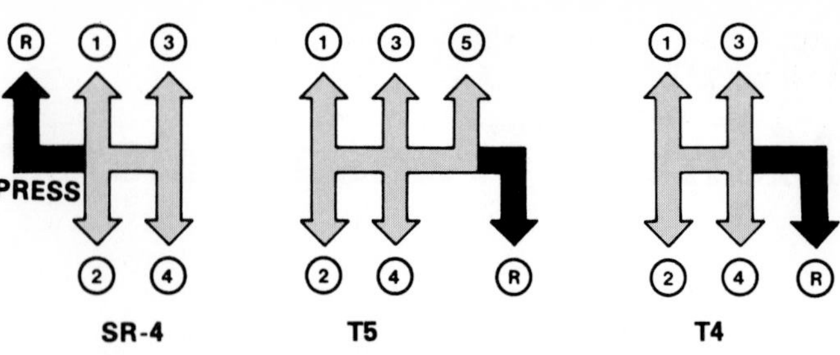

Figure 36-3. Gearshift patterns vary with make and model of vehicle. Three different four-speed and five-speed patterns are diagrammed. (Chrysler)

Note: Adjusting procedures vary. Check shop manual instructions for the specific make and model at hand.

Check Clutch Pedal Free Play

To check clutch pedal free play, depress the pedal slowly while noting at which point in its travel it first meets resistance. The resistance occurs when the clutch release bearing makes contact with the clutch pressure plate diaphragm.

The usual clutch pedal free play specification is 1 in. This play is necessary to insure that the clutch release bearing is not in constant contact with the pressure plate diaphragm and partially releasing the clutch disc.

If free play adjustment is necessary, adjust the length of the rod that engages the clutch release fork. Note: Occasionally, the adjustment is located elsewhere in the clutch control linkage setup. See Chapter 34, Clutches.

Manual Transmission Troubleshooting

Transmission Noisy in Neutral

A noise in neutral may be a growl or hum that can be stopped by depressing clutch pedal. In some cases a bump or thud also will be present, indicating a broken gear or bearing. Defects in output shaft (main shaft), other than pilot bearing, are not included in this group because output shaft does not rotate when transmission is in neutral.

- Low lubricant level.
- Abnormal end play in countershaft gears, reverse idler gear, or input shaft.
- Input shaft gear badly worn or broken.
- Input shaft bearing badly worn or broken.
- Misalignment between engine and transmission.
- Wear in countershaft drive gear.
- Wear in reverse and/or reverse idler gear.
- Countershaft bearings badly worn.
- Reverse idler shaft bearings badly worn.
- Countershaft sprung or bent.
- Pilot shaft bearing worn or broken.

Note: If the replacement of a gear is required, the mating gear should be replaced too.

Transmission Noisy in Gear

Most causes of noises in neutral will also appear when the transmission is in gear. Same parts are still in operation, plus the output shaft (main shaft), which adds the following:

- Output shaft rear bearing worn or broken.
- Gears badly worn or broken.
- Excessive end play of output shaft.
- Badly worn speedometer gears.

Transmission Noisy in Reverse

- Worn or damaged reverse idler gear or idler bushing.
- Worn or damaged reverse gear on main shaft.
- Damaged or worn reverse countergear.
- Damaged shift mechanism.

Transmission Slips Out of Gear

Principal cause is misalignment between transmission and engine. Front end of input shaft runs in a bearing in crankshaft, and rear end in transmission case. If this shaft is not in a straight line with engine crankshaft, it will create an angular contact. Less frequent causes are:

- Input shaft gear teeth worn or tapered.
- Input shaft gear bearing badly worn.
- Improper adjustment of shift linkage.
- Worn shift detent parts.
- Damaged output shaft pilot bearing.
- Pilot bearing loose in crankshaft.
- Transmission loose on clutch housing.
- Input shaft gear retainer broken or loose.
- Badly worn or broken gear.
- Badly worn transmission bearings.
- Excessive end play of output shaft or countershaft.
- Output shaft splines worn or distorted.

Transmission Difficult to Shift

- Engine clutch not releasing.
- Distorted or burred output shaft splines.
- Improper adjustment of shift linkage.
- Misalignment of column control levers.
- Incorrect clutch adjustment.
- Internal bind in transmission, caused by shift forks or synchronizer assemblies.
- Binding shift rail.
- Incorrect lubricant.

Transmission Leaks Oil

- Damaged oil seals.
- Damaged O-rings at speedometer driven gear.
- Damaged or missing gaskets.
- Case or cover bolts loose or missing.
- Case plugs loose or threads stripped.
- High lubricant level.
- Vent stopped up.
- Use of lubricant that foams excessively.
- Loose or broken input shaft bearing retainer.
- Worn shift lever seals.

Transmission Gears Clash When Shifting

- Incorrect clutch adjustment.
- Binding clutch cable or linkage.
- Worn or damaged synchronizer assemblies.
- Low lubricant level.
- Engine idle speed too high.
- Misaligned clutch housing.

Transmission Will Not Shift into One Gear

- Worn or damaged gearshift selector plates, interlock plate, or selector arm.
- Worn shift rail detent plunger or broken spring.
- Worn or damaged gearshift lever assembly.
- Worn or damaged synchronizer assembly.

Transmission Locked in One Gear

- Worn or broken shift rail.
- Bent shifter fork.
- Broken gear teeth.
- Worn or broken gearshift lever assembly.
- Broken shift mechanism in cover.

Manual Transmission Service

The need for major transmission service usually is signaled by noisy operation or gear clash. A transmission that jumps out of gear, will not shift gears, or is locked in one gear may also require major service.

Note that most of the corrections for these complaints call for transmission removal and disassembly. With this in mind, typical procedures are given for removing and reinstalling a manual transmission. In addition, general procedures and precautions are included for disassembling and reassembling a three-speed unit, four-speed unit, and five-speed overdrive unit.

Removal of Transmission From Car

Warning: Transmissions are extremely heavy. Be very careful when removing the transmission from a vehicle. Use a transmission jack if possible. If a transmission jack is not available, seek the help of another technician during removal.

1. Shift the transmission into neutral.
2. Remove the screws attaching the gearshift lever bezel and boot to the floor or console.
3. Slide the bezel and boot upward on the lever and remove the lever mounting cover screws.
4. Pull the gearshift lever up and out of the transmission case, Figure 36-4.
5. Raise the hood.
6. Raise the vehicle on a hoist.
7. On steering column shift transmissions, disconnect the shift rods from the shift levers.

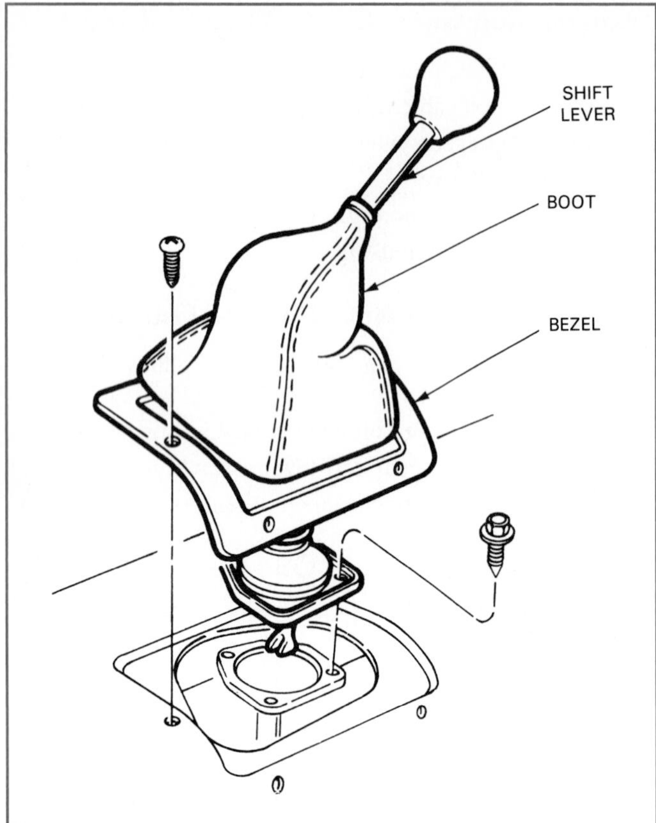

Figure 36-4. Often, the first step in the removal of a manual transmission is to unscrew the bezel screws and lift the gearshift lever from the transmission case. (Chrysler)

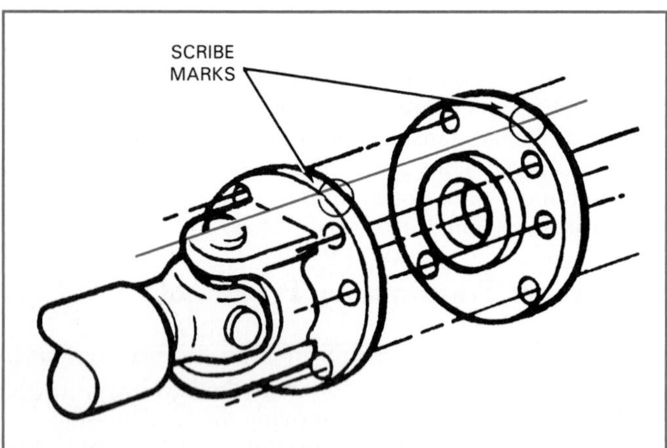

Figure 36-5. Before drive shaft removal, the end yoke and rear axle companion flange are marked to ensure proper positioning of the drive shaft on reassembly. (Ford)

8. Place alignment marks on the drive shaft and the rear axle yoke or flange, Figure 36-5, for reference on reassembly.
9. Remove the drive shaft.
10. Disconnect the speedometer cable from the extension housing, and remove the backup lamp switch wires.
11. Install a jack or support stand under the clutch housing to support the engine.
12. Remove the nuts and bolts attaching the rear crossmember to the frame. See Figure 36-6.

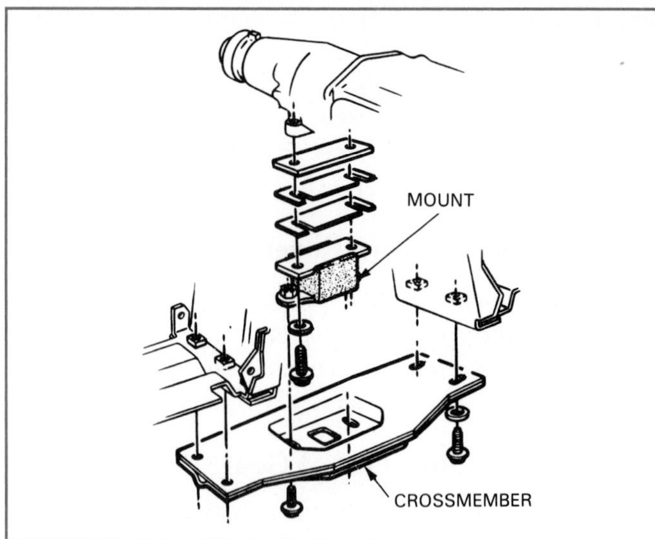

Figure 36-6. The rear cross member and transmission mount are removed. (Ford)

13. Remove the catalytic converter support bracket, and disconnect the exhaust pipe from the manifold.
14. Remove the nuts and bolts attaching the transmission mount to crossmember.
15. Remove the crossmember-to-frame attaching screws and drop the crossmember.
16. Remove the transmission-to-clutch housing attaching bolts, Figure 36-7.
17. Pull the transmission straight back, holding it level to avoid damaging the input shaft, pilot bushing, or clutch disc.
18. Remove the clutch release bearing and pilot bushing lubricating wick, if so equipped.
19. Soak the wick in engine oil.

Disassembly: Three-speed Manual Transmission

Study the exploded view in Figure 36-8.

1. Remove the case cover.

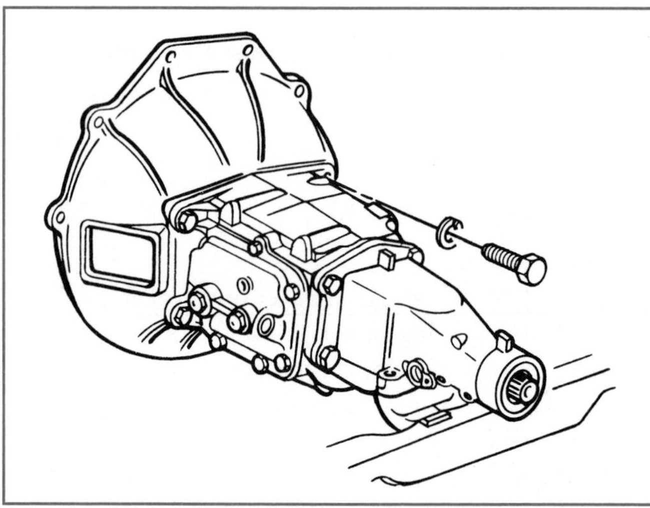

Figure 36-7. The final step is to unscrew the transmission-to-clutch housing attaching bolts and remove the transmission. (Chevrolet)

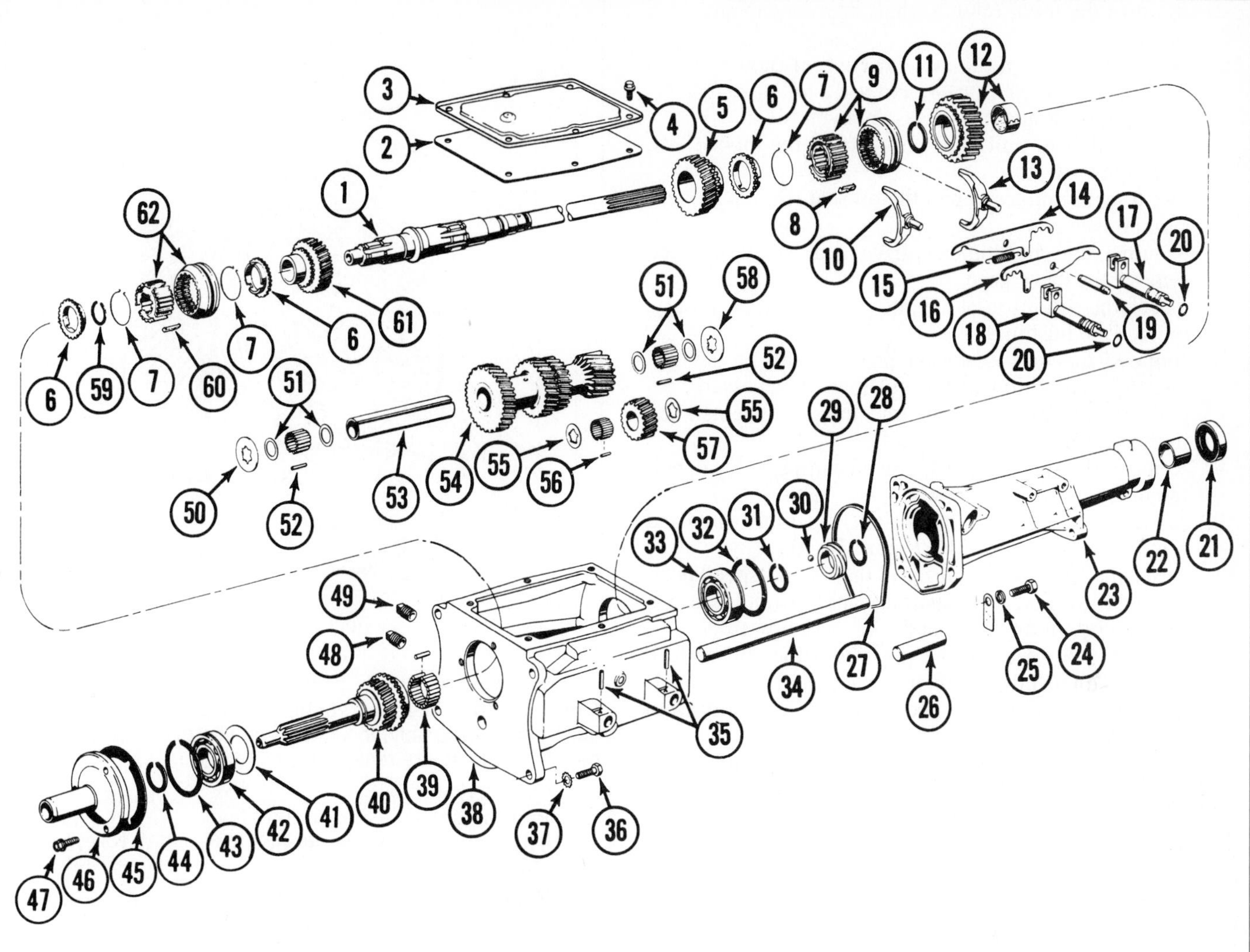

1. MAIN SHAFT
2. GASKET
3. CASE COVER
4. BOLT
5. FIRST GEAR
6. CLUTCH FRICTION RING SET
7. SHAFT PLATE RETAINING SPRING
8. CLUTCH SHAFT FIRST AND REVERSE SHIFT PLATE
9. FIRST AND REVERSE CLUTCH ASSEMBLY
10. SHIFTER SECOND AND HIGH FORK
11. CLUTCH FIRST AND REVERSE GEAR SNAP RING
12. REVERSE GEAR
13. SHIFTER FIRST AND REVERSE R FORK
14. SHIFTER INTERLOCK FIRST AND REVERSE LEVER
15. INTERLOCK POPPET SPRING
16. SHIFTER INTERLOCK SECOND AND THIRD LEVER
17. SHIFTER FORK FIRST AND REVERSE SHAFT
18. SHIFTER FORK SECOND AND THIRD SHAFT
19. SHIFTER FORK INTERLOCK LEVER PIVOT PIN
20. SHIFTER FORK SHAFT SEAL
21. OIL SEAL
22. BUSHING
23. EXTENSION HOUSING
24. BOLT
25. LOCK WASHER
26. IDLER GEAR SHAFT
27. GASKET
28. SPEEDOMETER DRIVE GEAR RING
29. SPEEDOMETER DRIVE GEAR
30. SPEEDOMETER DRIVE GEAR BALL
31. REAR BEARING LOCKRING
32. REAR BEARING LOCKRING
33. REAR BEARING
34. COUNTERSHAFT
35. SHIFTER FORK RETAINING PIN
36. BOLT
37. LOCK WASHER
38. CASE
39. SPLINE SHAFT PILOT BEARING ROLLER
40. CLUTCH SHAFT
41. FRONT BEARING WASHER
42. FRONT BEARING
43. FRONT BEARING LOCKRING
44. FRONT BEARING SNAP RING
45. GASKET
46. FRONT BEARING CAP
47. BOLT
48. DRAIN PLUG
49. FILLER PIPE PLUG
50. FRONT COUNTERSHAFT GEAR THRUST WASHER
51. COUNTERSHAFT GEAR BEARING ROLLER WASHER
52. COUNTERSHAFT GEAR BEARING ROLLER
53. COUNTERSHAFT GEAR ROLLER BEARING SPACER
54. COUNTERSHAFT GEAR
55. REVERSE IDLER GEAR BEARING ROLLER WASHER
56. REVERSE IDLER GEAR BEARING ROLLER
57. REVERSE IDLER GEAR
58. REAR COUNTERSHAFT THRUST
59. CLUTCH SECOND AND THIRD SNAP RING
60. CLUTCH SHAFT SECOND AND THIRD SHIFT PLATE
61. SECOND AND THIRD CLUTCH ASSEMBLY
62. SECOND GEAR

Figure 36-8. Exploded view of a three-speed manual transmission provides good reference information for disassembly and reassembly. (Chrysler)

2. Remove the input (clutch) shaft bearing cap and snap rings.
3. Align the notch in the input shaft gear (notch down) with the countershaft gear, and use a puller to remove the input shaft and bearing as an assembly.
4. Use a puller to pull the bearing from the input shaft. See Figure 36-9.
5. Use a seal remover to pull the oil seal from the extension housing.
6. Remove the speedometer drive gear snap ring and remove the drive gear.
7. Check the condition of the pilot bushing. If necessary, replace the bushing.
8. Remove the rear extension housing and gasket. Inspect the condition of the bushing. If necessary, replace the bushing when the transmission is reinstalled in the vehicle.
9. Remove the snap rings and use a bearing puller to pull the rear bearing.
10. Move the output shaft (main shaft) assembly aside and remove both shifter forks, Figure 36-10.
11. Move the front synchronizer to the second-speed position and lift the output shaft assembly from the transmission by tilting the front of the shaft upward.
12. Use a punch to drive the pins from the shifter fork shafts and push the shafts into the case, Figure 36-11. Then, remove the shafts and the detent assembly from the case.
13. Tap the reverse idler gear shaft and the countershaft toward the rear of the case to permit the removal of the shaft lock plate on the rear of the case.

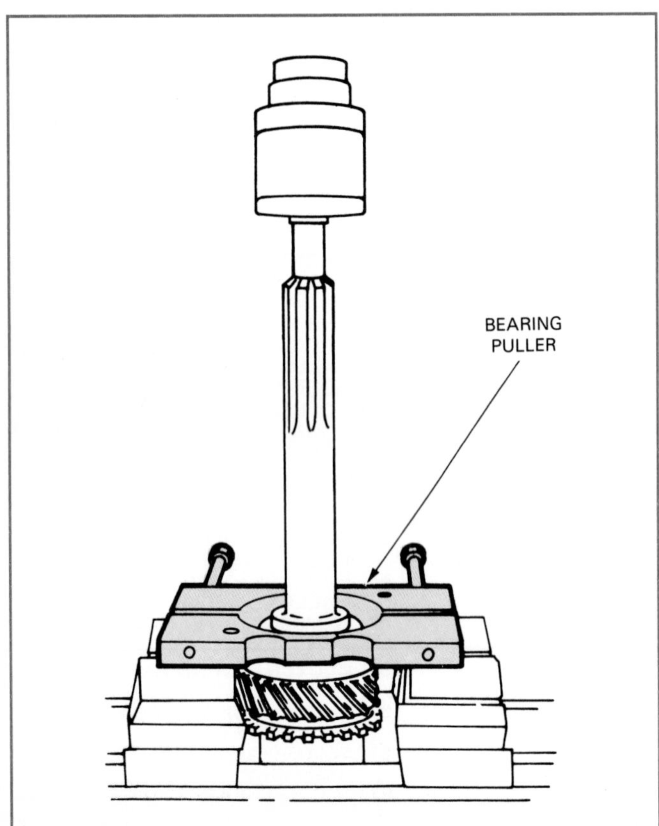

Figure 36-9. A special bearing puller is used in conjunction with a press to pull the front bearing from the input (clutch) shaft. (Chrysler)

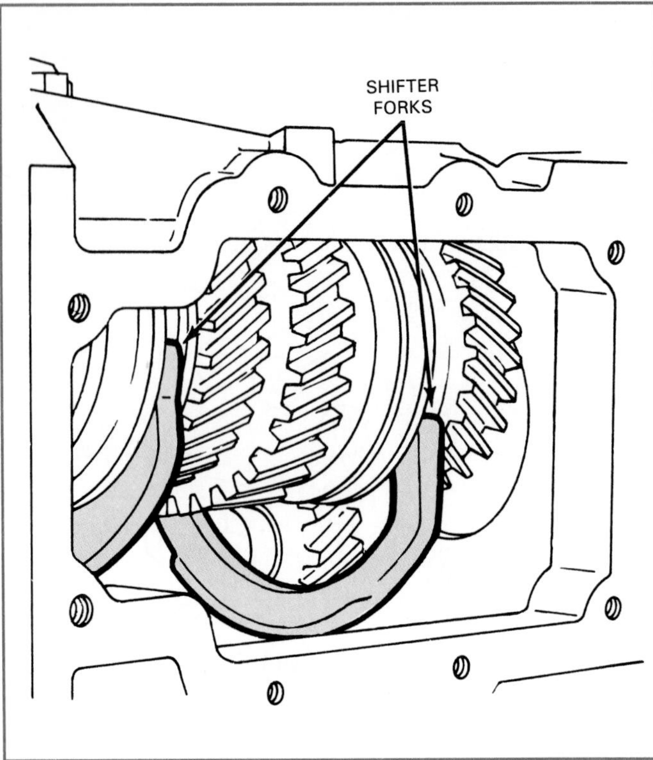

Figure 36-10. After the rear bearing is pulled from the output shaft assembly, the shaft is moved to one side and both shifter forks are removed.

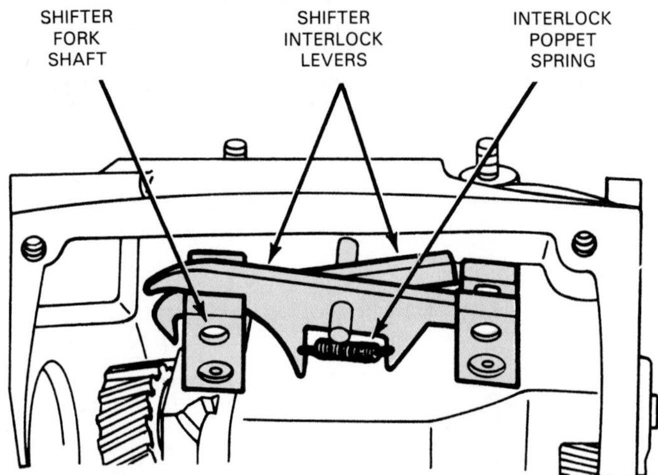

Figure 36-11. The roll pins are driven from the shifter shafts and the assembly is lifted from the case. (Chrysler)

14. Use a brass drift to drive the reverse idler gear shaft from the case, Figure 36-12.
15. Use a dummy shaft to drive the countershaft from the case and lift the countershaft gear with the dummy shaft from the case to retain the roller bearings in the proper position within the countershaft.
16. Remove the output shaft front snap ring, second-and-third-speed synchro-clutch assembly, and second gear from the shaft. See Figure 36-8.
17. Slide the reverse gear from the rear of the output shaft, and then remove the rear snap ring, the rear synchro-clutch assembly, and the first gear.

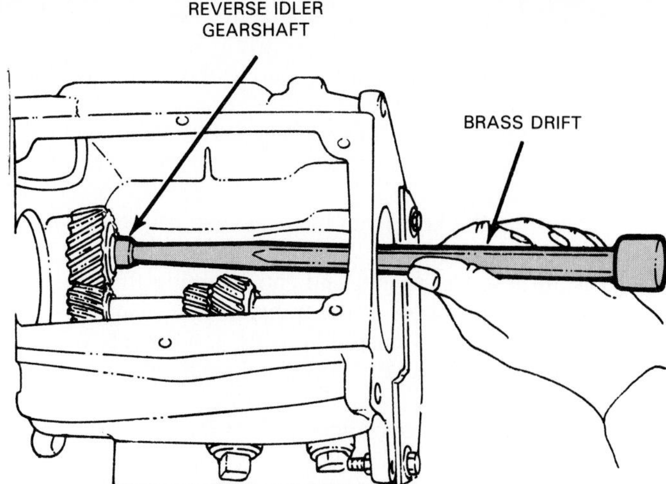

Figure 36-12. A long brass drift is used to tap the reverse idler gear shaft from the case. (Chrysler)

Clean and Check: Three-speed Manual Transmission

Wrap bearings in a clean cloth or paper until washed. Use a fresh solvent to clean transmission case and all parts. Examine case for cracks and all bearing surfaces on case and front face for nicks, wear, or scoring. Check cover for warpage or distortion. Smooth nicks with a fine stone (on cast iron) or a fine file (on aluminum), or replace parts.

Check all gears for worn, cracked, or chipped teeth. Replace defective gears; also replace mating gears. Test fit of gears on output shaft. Replace gears that are too loose. Slide synchro-clutch and blocker rings on cones of gears and on input shaft. See Figure 36-13 for typical minimum clearance between the face of the blocker ring and the clutch teeth on the gear. Replace worn or pitted parts.

Wash bearings in a fresh cleaning solution, rotating each bearing to flush away oil and dirt. Dry bearings with a clean lint-free cloth. Check condition of shift levers, forks, shift rails, and shafts. Check splines of output shaft and input shaft for wear, scoring, or distortion.

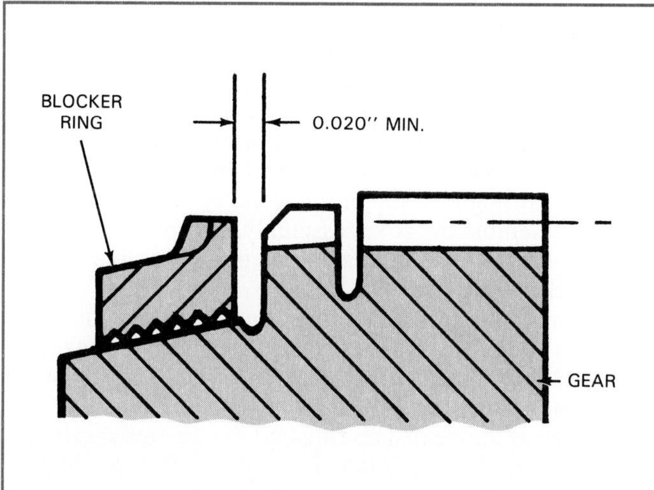

Figure 36-13. An important step in the clean and check procedure is inspecting the synchro-clutches and blocker rings for wear. (Ford)

Reassembly: Three-speed Manual Transmission

1. Install the first-speed gear and the friction ring on the main shaft. See Figure 36-8. The friction ring hub must face the rear of the output shaft. (Some installation procedures vary; consult manufacturer's service manual.)
2. Assemble the first-speed synchro-clutch, place it on the output shaft, and then install the thickest snap ring that will fit into the groove.
3. Place the second-speed gear and friction ring on the front of the output shaft.
4. Assemble the second-speed synchro-clutch, Figure 36-14, place it on the output shaft, and then install the thickest snap ring that will fit into the groove.
5. Install a dummy shaft in the countershaft gear. Coat the roller bearings with petroleum jelly and install spacer washers and roller bearings in the countershaft gear.
6. Place the countershaft gear in the transmission case, and then position the thrust washers at each end of the gear so that the tabs align with the slots in the transmission.
7. Use a plastic mallet to install the countershaft, driving out the dummy shaft.
8. Install the roller bearings in the reverse idler gear. Use petroleum jelly to hold the bearings in place.
9. Place the reverse idler gear in the case and position thrust washers at each end of the gear. Then install the reverse idler gear shaft. Install the lock plate.
10. Partially install the shifter fork shafts in the case, Figure 36-11. Then, position the shift levers so that the notches are located to the rear of the case stud.
11. Align the shift detent assembly with the shifter fork shafts and the transmission case stud. Then, push the detent assembly and the shifter fork shafts into place and install the roll pins.

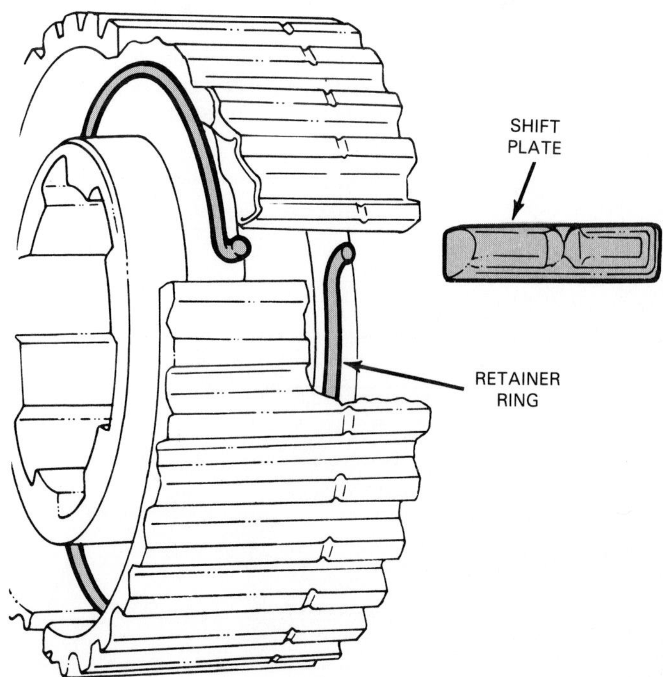

Figure 36-14. Assembly of synchro-clutch unit requires the installation of the retainer rings in the clockwise direction to ensure smooth shifts. (Chrysler)

12. Install the front synchronizer in the second-speed position and place the output shaft assembly in the case.
13. Move the output shaft assembly to one side and install the shift forks, Figure 36-10.
14. Move the output shaft assembly to the center of the case and install the pilot end support, Figure 36-15. Install the front bearing cap to hold the support in place.
15. Use a driving tool or a 1 1/4 in. pipe to the drive rear bearing on the output shaft. Install the thickest rear bearing snap ring that will fit into the groove.
16. Install the speedometer drive ball, drive gear, and snap ring.
17. Press the front bearing on the input shaft, Figure 36-16.

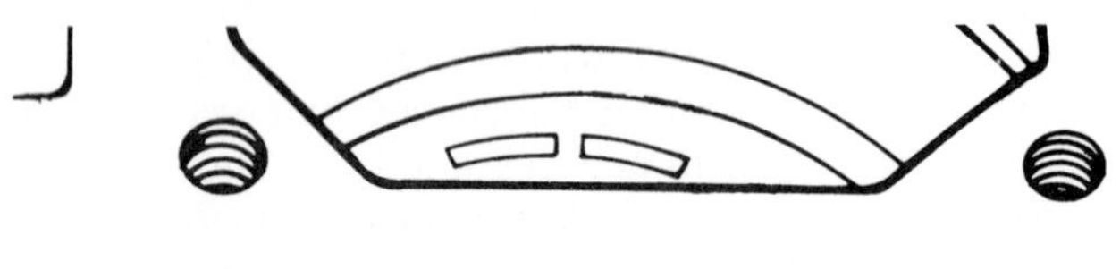

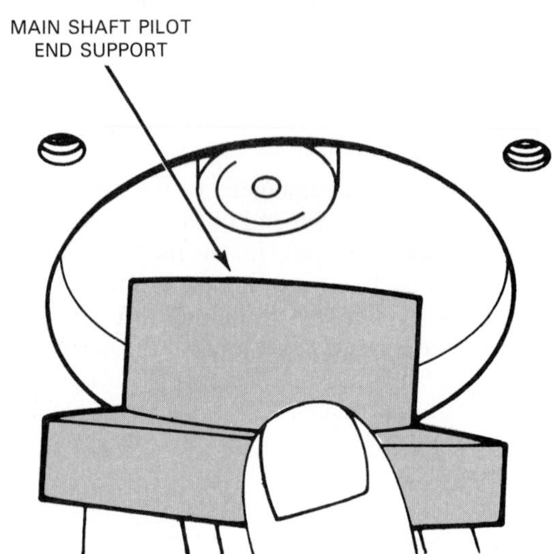

Figure 36-15. After the shift forks are installed, the output shaft is centered in the case and the pilot end support is installed over the pilot end of the shaft. (Chrysler)

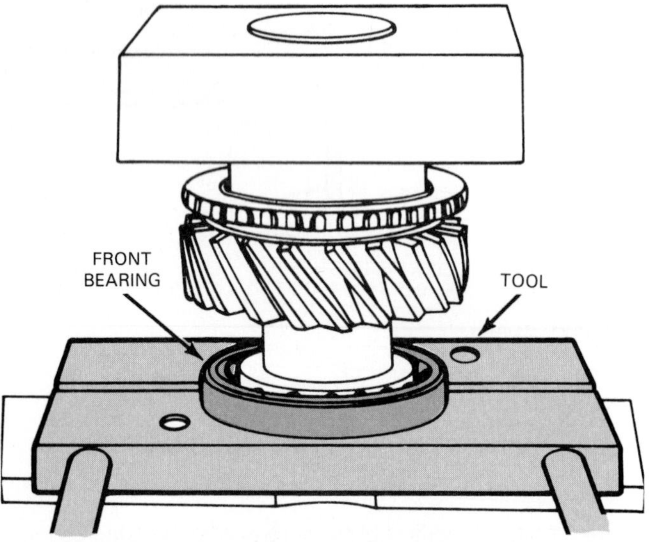

Figure 36-16. A special tool and a press are used to install the front bearing on the input shaft. (Chrysler)

18. Install the roller bearings in the input shaft cavity. Use petroleum jelly to hold the bearings in place.
19. Remove the front bearing cap and the output shaft pilot end support.
20. Install the friction ring on the output shaft and slide the input shaft into position through the front of the case.
21. Install the thickest front bearing snap ring that will fit into the groove.
22. Install new cap gasket and cap, aligning the cap with the lubrication hole in the transmission case.
23. Install the rear extension housing and the rear oil seal.
24. Install the shift levers and check transmission operation in all gears.
25. Install the case cover and gasket. Be sure the vent is open.

Disassembly: Four-speed Manual Transmission

1. Study the exploded view illustration of the transmission being serviced, Figure 36-17.
2. Drive the access plug from the extension housing, Figure 36-18, remove the nut from the offset lever assembly, and then remove the assembly.
3. Unscrew remaining extension housing bolts and remove the extension housing from the case.
4. Remove the cover, the shifter forks, and the shift rod assembly.
5. Remove the front bearing retainer.
6. Remove the spring clip retaining the reverse lever to the pivot bolt, unscrew the pivot bolt, and remove the bolt and the reverse lever.
7. Remove the snap rings from the input shaft and use a puller to pull the bearing from the input shaft.
8. Remove snap ring holding the speedometer gear to the output shaft and slide the gear and lock ball from the shaft.
9. Remove the snap rings from the output shaft and bearing. Use a puller to pull the output shaft bearing from the case.
10. Remove the input shaft from the front of the case.
11. Lift the output shaft and the gear train through the top of the case.
12. Slide the reverse idler gear shaft out the rear of the case and remove the reverse gear.
13. Insert a dummy countershaft through the front of the case to drive the countershaft out the rear of the case. Lift the countershaft gear, thrust washers, and dummy shaft through the top of the case.
14. Disassemble the cover assembly, Figure 36-19.
15. Scratch alignment marks on the synchronizer and blocker rings.
16. Remove the front snap ring from the output shaft and then slide the third-and-fourth-speed synchronizer assembly, blocker rings, and third-speed gear from the output shaft. See Figure 36-17.
17. Remove the next snap ring and the second-speed gear thrust washer from the shaft. Slide the second-speed gear and the blocker ring from the shaft.
18. Remove the first-speed gear thrust washer and the roll pin from the rear of the output shaft. Slide the first gear and the blocker ring from the shaft.

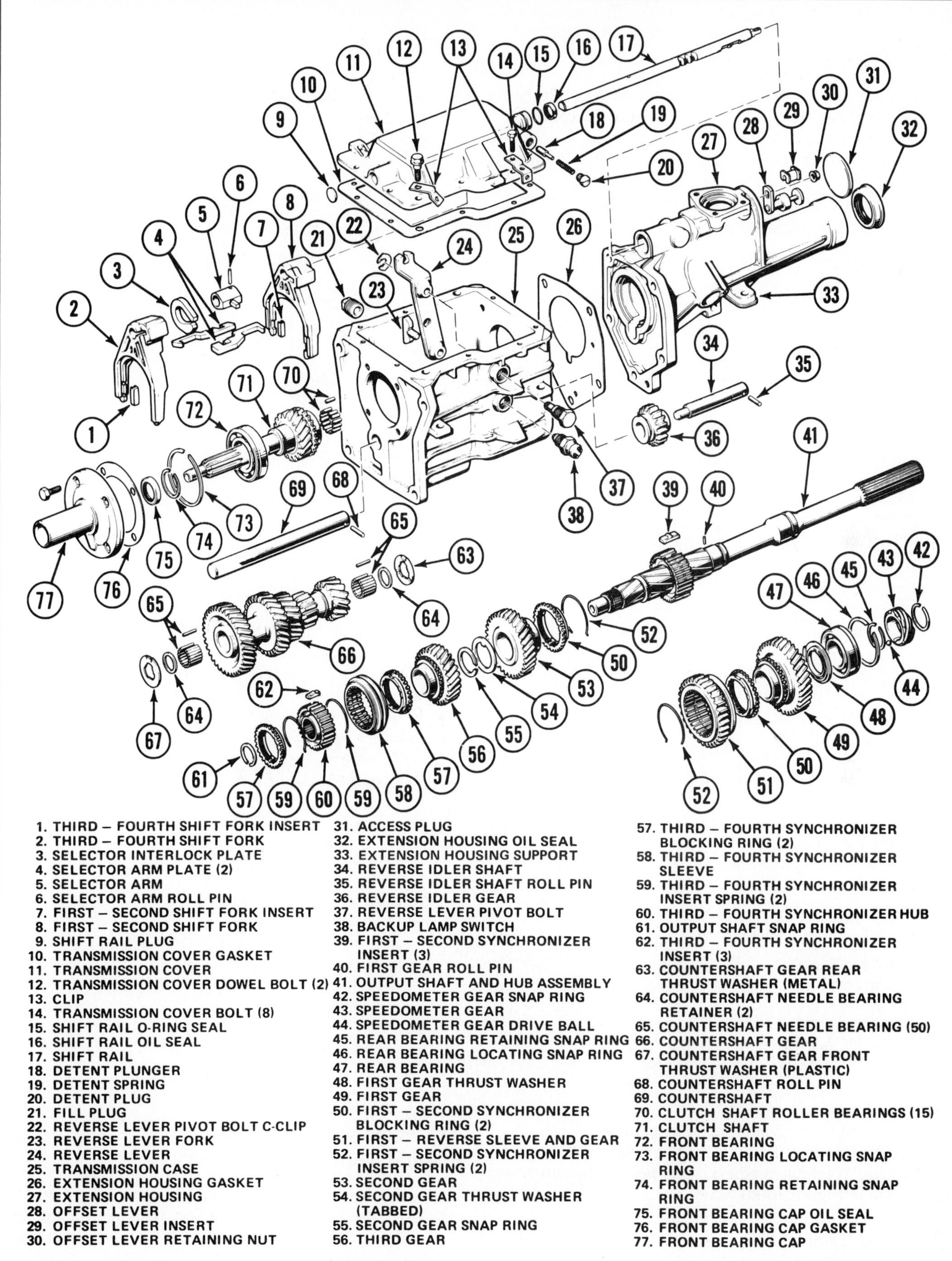

Figure 36-17. Exploded view of a four-speed manual transmission shows the relative positions of all internal parts. (Chrysler)

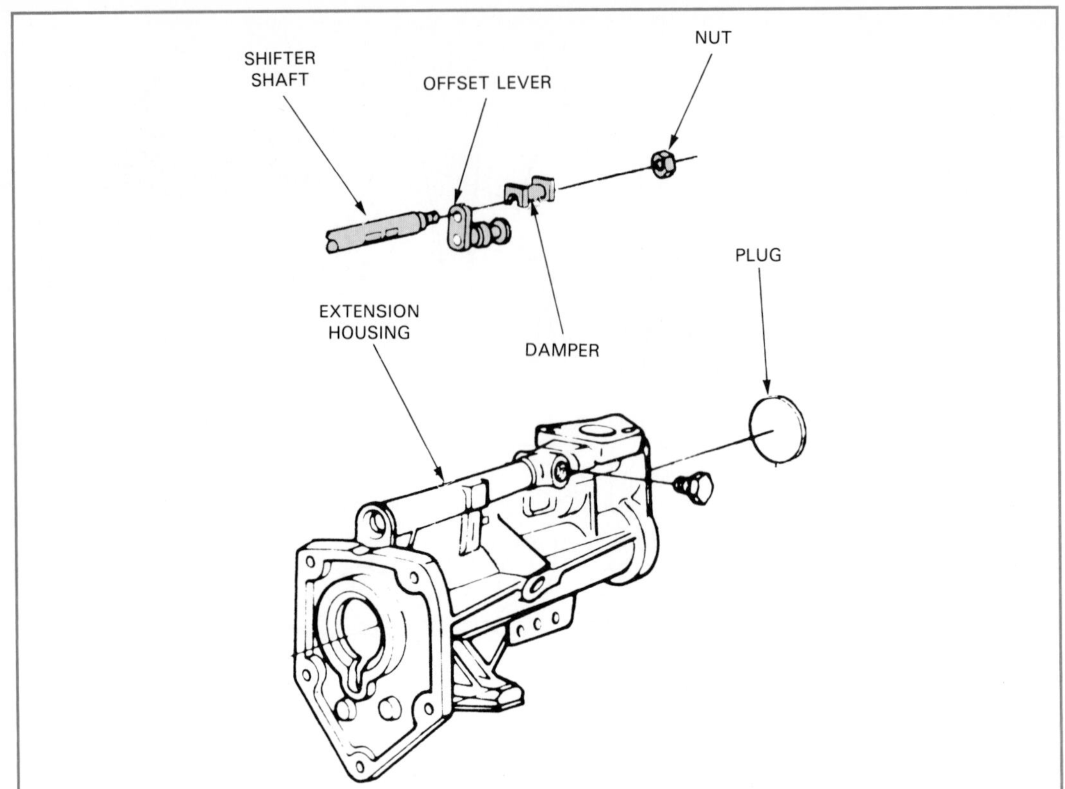

Figure 36-18. Locations of access plug at the rear of the extension housing, shifter shaft, and offset lever assembly are shown. (Ford)

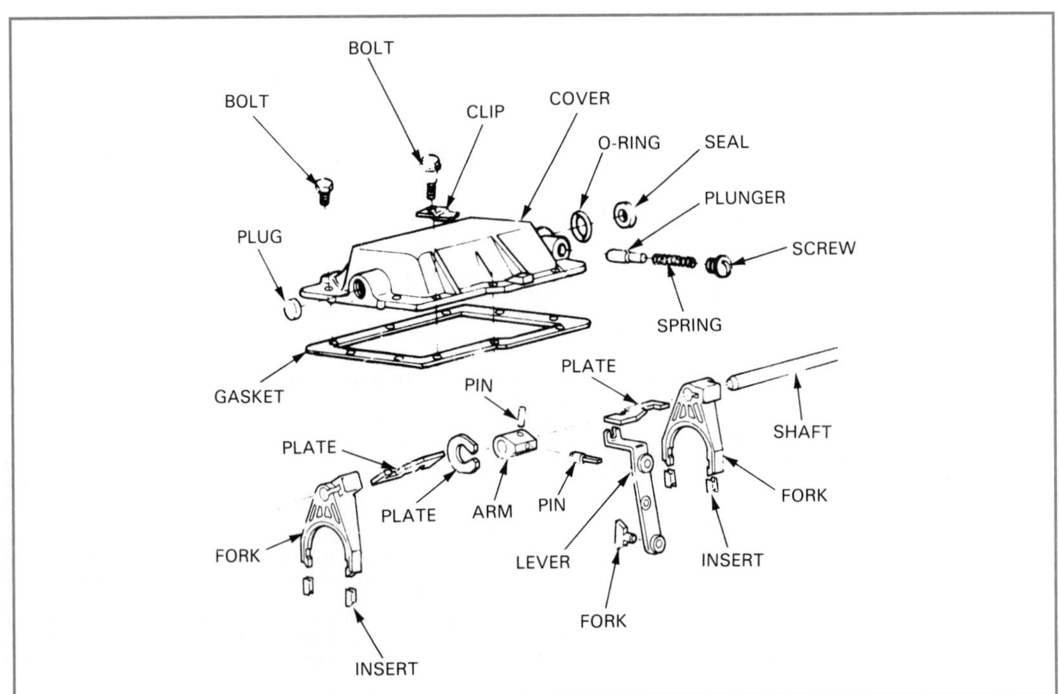

Figure 36-19. The transmission cover assembly primarily includes cover, shifter shaft, shifter forks, selector arm lever, and plates. (Ford)

19. Disassemble the synchronizer assemblies.
20. Remove the dummy shaft from the countershaft gear, bearing retainer washers, and needle bearings as shown in Figure 36-20.

Clean and Check: Four-speed Manual Transmission

1. See the instructions for Clean and Check: Three-speed Manual Transmission.

Reassembly: Four-speed Manual Transmission

1. Install the reverse idler gear and shaft, Figure 36-17.
2. Coat the countershaft washers with petroleum jelly and position them on the countershaft gear assembled on the dummy shaft.
3. Align the countershaft gear bore and the thrust washers with the bore in the case and install the countershaft from the rear of the case.

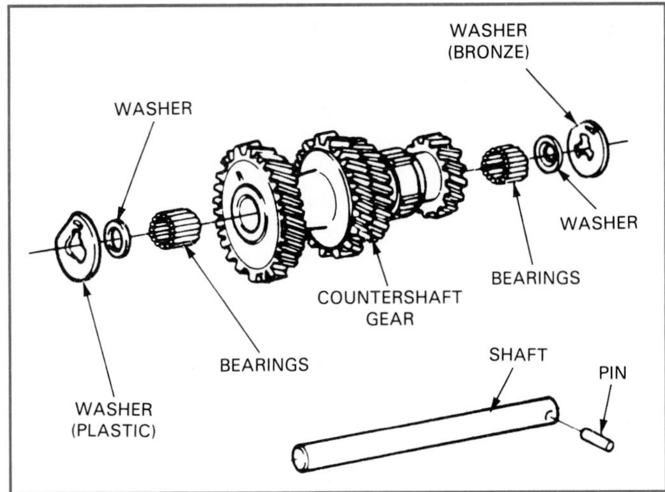

Figure 36-20. The countershaft assembly requires the use of a dummy shaft to hold the roller bearings in place during installation. (Ford)

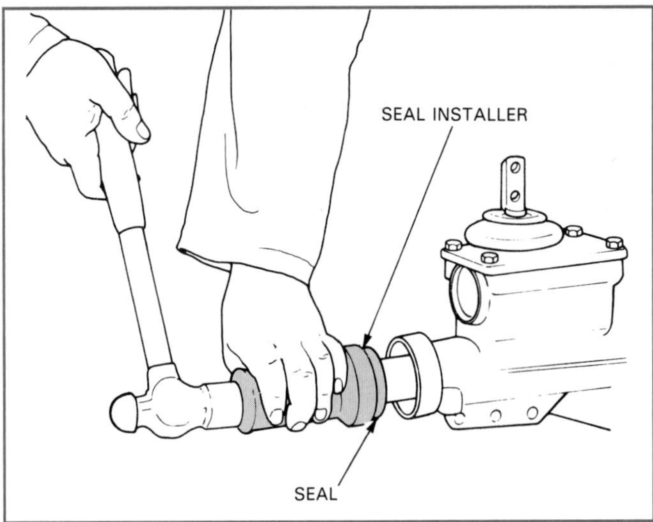

Figure 36-21. A special driving tool is used to install the seal in the transmission extension housing. (Ford)

4. Assemble the gears, thrust washers, synchronizers, and blocker rings on the output shaft. See Figure 36-17.
5. Position the output shaft assembly in the case through the cover opening. Then, slide a dummy bearing on the shaft to support the assembly in the case.
6. Assemble the input shaft and position the shaft and the fourth gear blocker ring through the front of the case.
7. Install the snap ring on the input shaft bearing and press the bearing into position on the shaft.
8. Install a new bearing retaining snap ring on the input shaft.
9. Install the front bearing retainer and a new gasket.
10. Remove the dummy output shaft bearing. Install a new snap ring on the output shaft bearing and press the bearing on the output shaft.
11. Install a new output shaft rear bearing retaining snap ring.
12. Install the reverse idler gear lever assembly.
13. Install the offset lever assembly, reverse lever, and retaining spring clip. See Figure 36-18.
14. Assemble the cover assembly with a new gasket, Figure 36-19, and install the cover.
15. Install the speedometer drive gear lock ball, drive gear, and snap ring.
16. Install the extension housing and a new gasket; drive the oil seal into place, Figure 36-21.
17. Install the offset lever assembly on the shift shaft and secure the assembly with the nut.
18. Insert the gearshift lever in position and check all gear positions.
19. Install the access plug into the rear of the extension housing, Figure 36-18.

Disassembly: Five-speed Manual Transmission

Study an exploded view of the transmission being serviced, Figure 36-22.

1. Punch out the roll pin attaching the offset lever to the shift rail.
2. Remove the extension housing and the offset lever as an assembly, Figure 36-23.
3. Remove the detent ball and spring from the offset lever and the roll pin from the extension housing.
4. Remove the plastic funnel, Figure 36-24, thrust bearing race, and thrust bearing from the rear of the countershaft.
5. Remove the cover assembly, Figure 36-25.
6. Drive the roll pin from the fifth gearshift fork.
7. Remove the fifth synchronizer gear snap ring, shift fork, fifth gear synchronizer sleeve, blocking ring, and fifth-speed gear from the rear of the countershaft. See Figure 36-22.
8. Remove the snap ring from the fifth-speed gear.
9. Punch mark the front bearing cap and the case for assembly reference.
10. Remove the bearing cap, bearing race, and end play shims.
11. Rotate the input (main drive) shaft until the flat surface faces the countershaft. Then, pull the input shaft from the case, Figure 36-26.
12. Remove the reverse lever C-clip and the pivot bolt. Then remove the output shaft rear bearing race, tilt the output shaft assembly upward, and remove the assembly from the case. See Figure 36-27.
13. Unhook the overcenter link spring from the front of the case.
14. Rotate the fifth gear reverse shift rail to disengage the rail from the reverse lever assembly. Then remove the rail from the rear of the case.
15. Remove the reverse lever and fork assembly from the case.
16. Drive the roll pin from the forward end of the reverse idler shaft, and then remove the shaft, O-ring, and gear from the case. See Figure 36-28.
17. Remove the rear countershaft snap ring and spacer. Then insert a brass drift through the front of the case and use an arbor press to remove the rear countershaft bearing.
18. Move the countershaft assembly toward the rear of the case, tilt the assembly upward, and remove it from the case. Also remove the countershaft front thrust washer and rear bearing spacer.
19. Use an arbor press to remove the front bearing from the case.
20. Disassemble the output shaft, Figure 36-22.

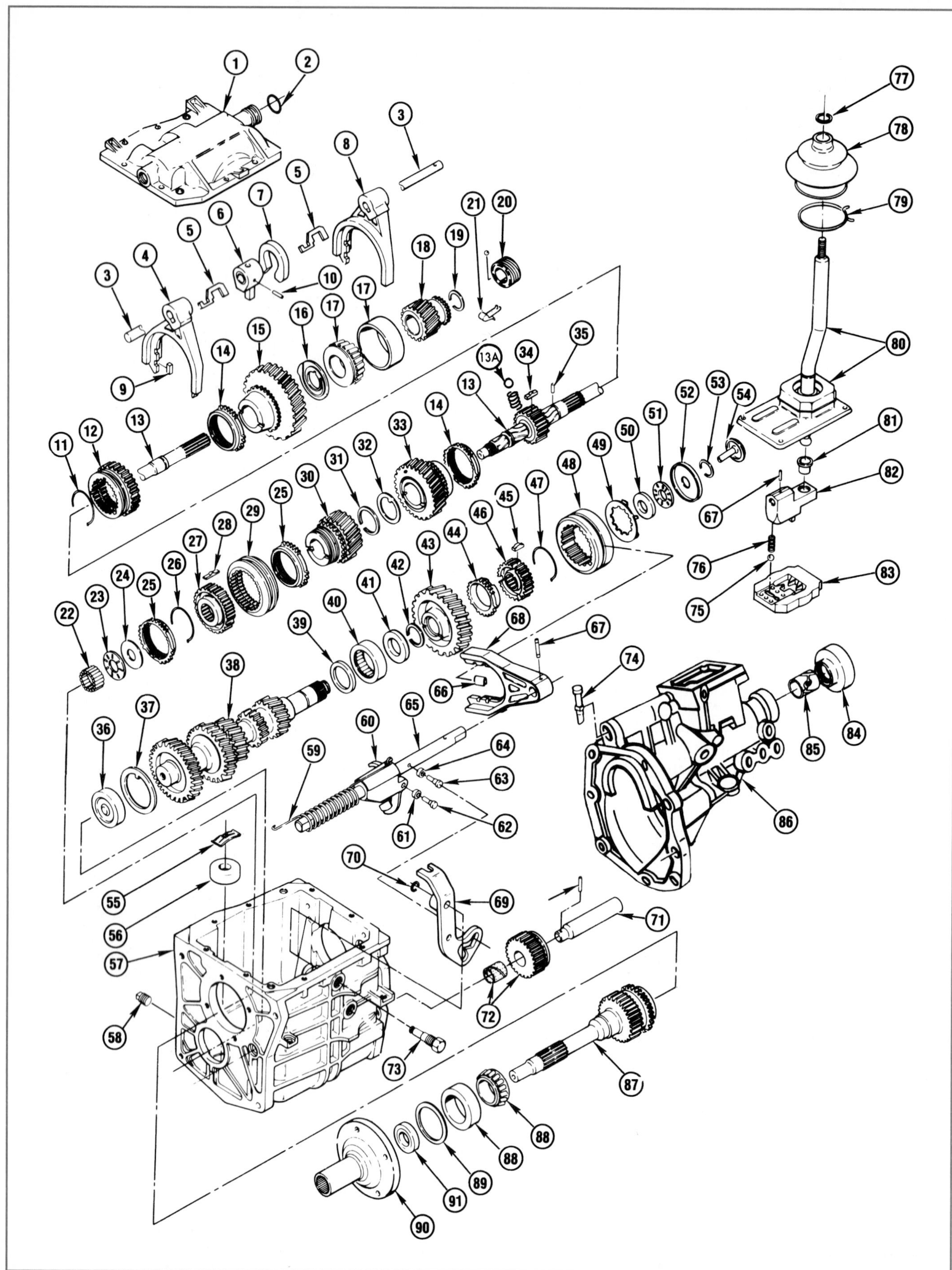

Figure 36-22A. Exploded view locates and identifies all components in a typical five-speed manual overdrive transmission. (Chevrolet)

1. COVER, Trans
2. SEAL, "O" Ring, Cvr to Ext.
3. SHAFT, Shift
4. FORK, 3rd & 4th Shift
5. PLATE, Shift Fork
6. ARM, Control Selector
7. PLATE, Gear Sel Intlk
8. FORK, 1st & 2nd Shift
9. INSERT, Shift Fork
10. PIN, Roll
11. SPRING, Syn
12. GEAR, Rev Sldg
13. SHAFT, Output, W/1 & 2 Syn
13A. SPRING/BALL, Anti-Rattle
14. RING, 1 & 2 Syn Blkg
15. GEAR, 1st Speed
16. WASHER, 1st Spd Gr Thrust
17. BEARING, Rear
18. GEAR, 5th Spd Drvn
19. RING, Snap
20. GEAR, Speedo Dr
21. CLIP, Speedo Dr Gr
22. BEARING, Main Shf Rir
23. BEARING, Main Dr Gr Thr Ndl
24. RACE, Main Dr Gr Ghr Brg
25. RING, 3 & 4 Syn
26. SPRING, 3 & 4 Syn
27. HUB, 3 & 4 Syn
28. KEY, 3 & 4 Syn
29. SLEEVE, 3 & 4 Syn
30. GEAR, 3rd Speed
31. RING, Snap
32. WASHER, 2nd Spd Gr Thr
33. GEAR, 2nd Speed
34. KEY, 1 & 2 Syn
35. PIN, 1st Spd Gr Thr Wa Ret
36. BEARING, Cntr Gr Frt
37. WASHER, Cntr Gr Frt Thr
38. GEAR, Counter
39. SPACER, Counter Gr Brg Frt
40. BEARING, Cntr Gr Rr
41. SPACER, Counter Gr Brg Rr
42. RING, Snap
43. GEAR, 5th Spd Drive
44. RING, 5th Syn
45. KEY, 5th Syn
46. HUB, 5th Syn
47. SPRING, 5th Syn
48. SLEEVE, 5th Syn
49. RETAINER, 5th Syn Key
50. RACE, 5th Syn Thr Brg Frt
51. BEARING, 5th Syn Ndl Thr
52. RACE, 5th Syn Thr Brg Rr
53. RING, Snap
54. FUNNEL, Trans Oiling
55. NUT, Magnet
56. MAGNET
57. CASE, Trans
58. PLUG, Fill & Drain
59. SPRING, Rev Lock
60. FORK, Rev Shift
61. ROLLER, Fork
62. PIN, Rev Fork
63. PIN, Shift Rail
64. ROLLER, Rail pin
65. RAIL, 5th & Rev Shft
66. INSERT, Shift Fork
67. PIN, Roll
68. FORK, 5th Shift
69. LEVER, 5th & Rev Relay
70. RING, Rev. Relay Lever Ret
71. SHAFT, Rev Idler Gr
72. GEAR, Rev Idler (Incl Bshg)
73. PIN, 5th Spd Shft Lvr Piv
74. VENTILATOR, Ext
75. BALL, Steel
76. SPRING, Detent
77. RETAINER, Cont Lvr Boot
78. BOOT, Cont Lvr
79. RETAINER, Cont Lvr Boot Lwr
80. CONTROL, Trans Lvr & Hsg
81. SLEEVE, Shft Lvr Dmpr
82. LEVER, Offset Shift
83. PLATE, Detent & Guide
84. SEAL, Ext Rr Oil
85. BUSHING, Extension Housing
86. HOUSING, Extension
87. GEAR, Main Drive
88. BEARING, Front
89. SHIM, Brg Adj
90. RETAINER, Drive Gr Brg
91. SEAL, Drive Gr Brg Oil

Figure 36-22B. Check the numbered components in Figure 36-22A with the numbers and component names in this list.

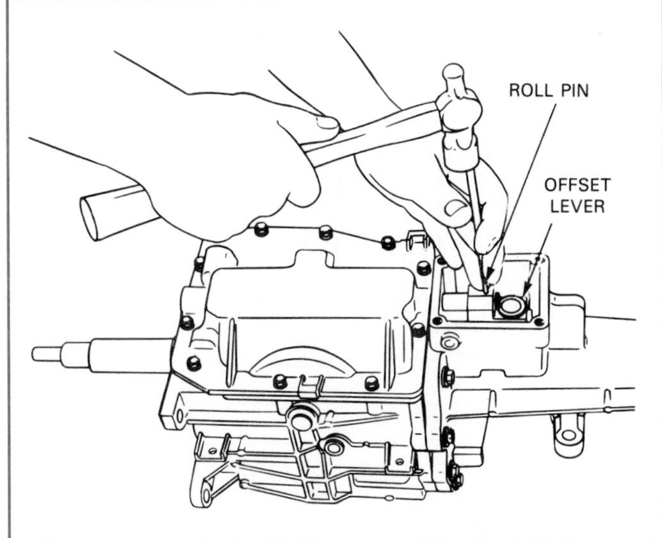

Figure 36-23. After punching out the roll pin holding the offset lever to the shift rail, the extension housing and the offset lever can be removed as a unit. (Chevrolet)

21. Remove the bearing race, thrust bearing, and roller bearings from the input shaft, and use the arbor press to remove the bearing from the input shaft.
22. Disassemble the cover. See Figure 36-22.

Clean and Check: Five-speed Manual Transmission

1. See instructions for Clean and Check: Three-speed Manual Transmission.

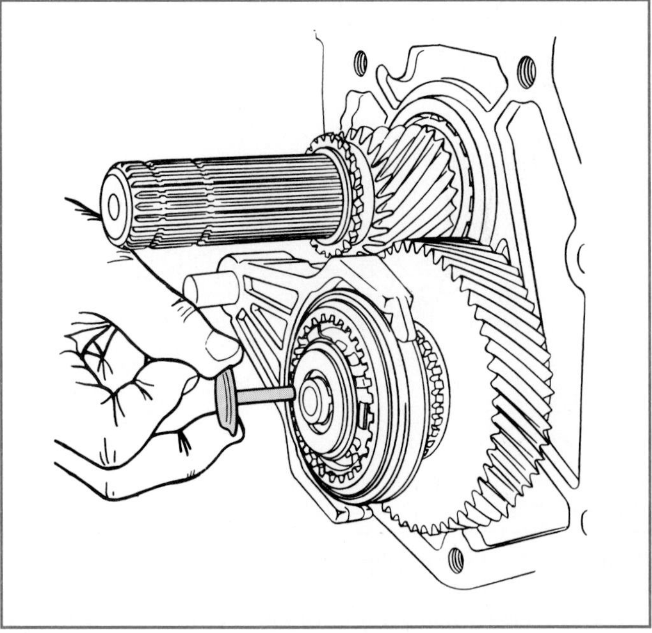

Figure 36-24. Plastic funnel, thrust bearing, and thrust bearing race slide off the back end of the countershaft. (Chevrolet)

Reassembly: Five-speed Manual Transmission

1. Assemble the transmission cover, Figure 36-22.
2. Assemble the input shaft, Figure 36-29.
3. Assemble the output shaft, Figure 36-22.
4. Use the arbor press to install the front countershaft bearing flush with the front facing of the case.

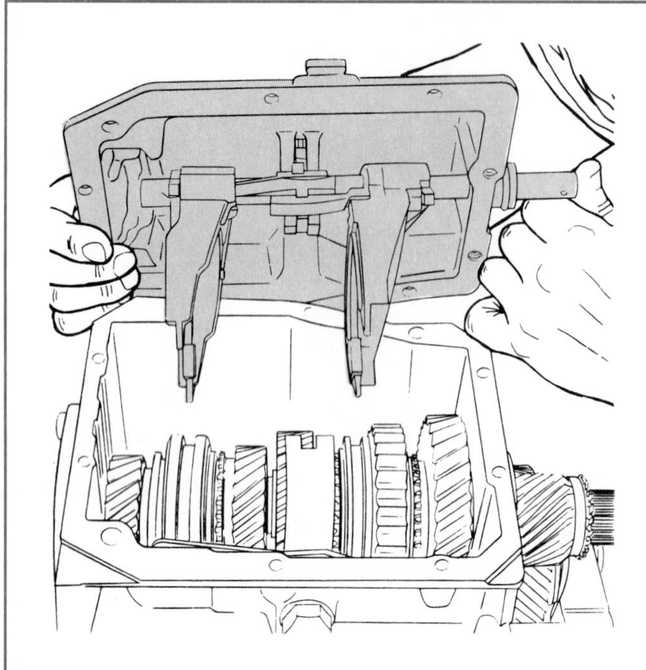

Figure 36-25. With the transmission cover attaching bolts removed, the cover and the shifter fork assembly may be lifted from the case. (Chevrolet)

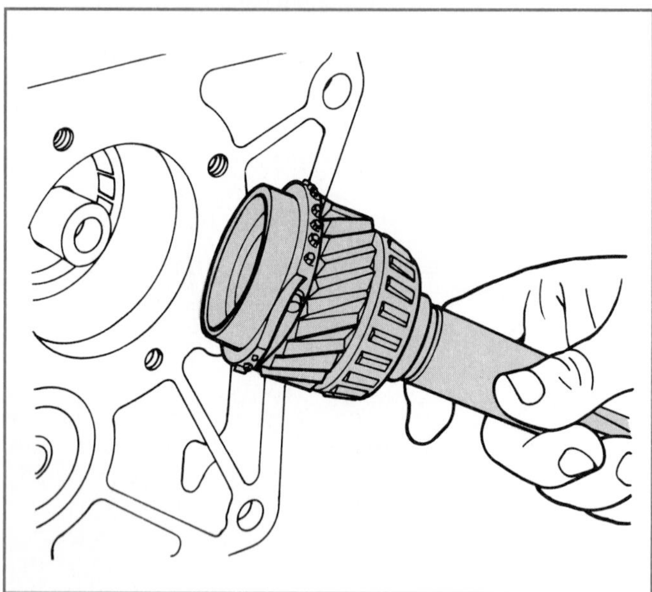

Figure 36-26. With the flat surface of the input shaft (main drive) gear facing the countershaft, the input shaft can be pulled from the front of the transmission case. (Chevrolet)

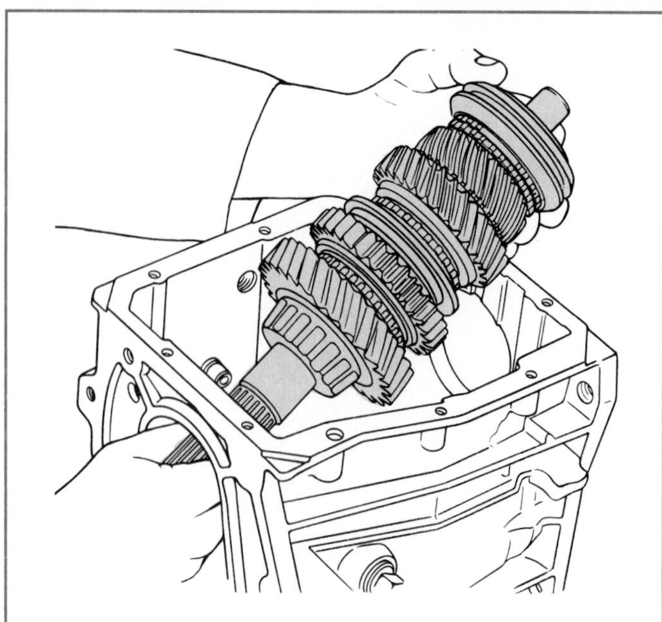

Figure 36-27. With the output shaft rear bearing race removed, the output shaft assembly can be tilted up and removed from the case. (Chevrolet)

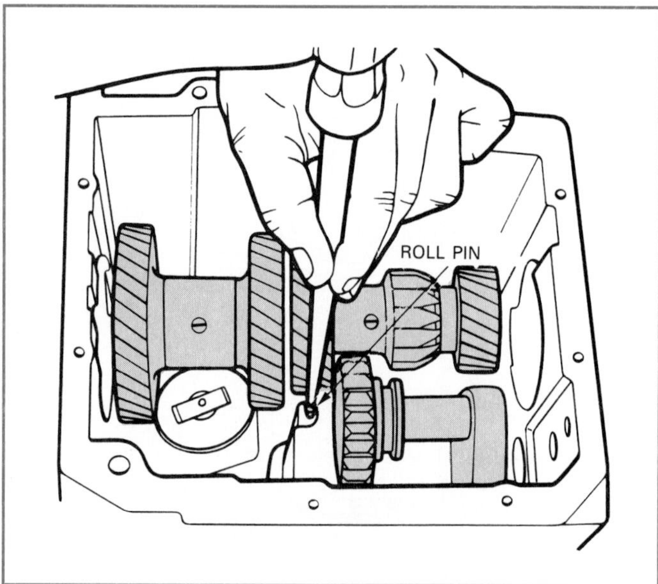

Figure 36-28. After punching out the roll pin from the reverse idler shaft, the shaft assembly can be lifted from the case.

5. Coat the countershaft thrust washer with petroleum jelly and install the washer so the tab engages the depression in the case.
6. Install the countershaft in the front bearing bore.
7. Install the countershaft rear bearing spacer. Coat the rear bearing with petroleum jelly and use a driving sleeve and tool to install the bearing.
8. Position the reverse idler in the case with the shift lever groove facing the rear and install the shaft from the rear of the case. Install the roll pin in the idler shaft, Figure 36-28.
9. Install the assembled output shaft, Figure 36-27, and install the rear output shaft bearing in the case.
10. Install the assembled input shaft in the case, Figure 36-26, and engage it in the third-fourth synchronizer sleeve and blocker ring.
11. Install the front bearing race in the front bearing cap (no shims).
12. Temporarily install the front bearing cap.
13. Install the fifth-speed/reverse lever, pivot bolt, and retaining clip, making sure that the reverse lever fork engages the reverse idler gear.
14. Install the countershaft rear bearing spacer and retaining snap ring.
15. Install the fifth-speed gear on countershaft.

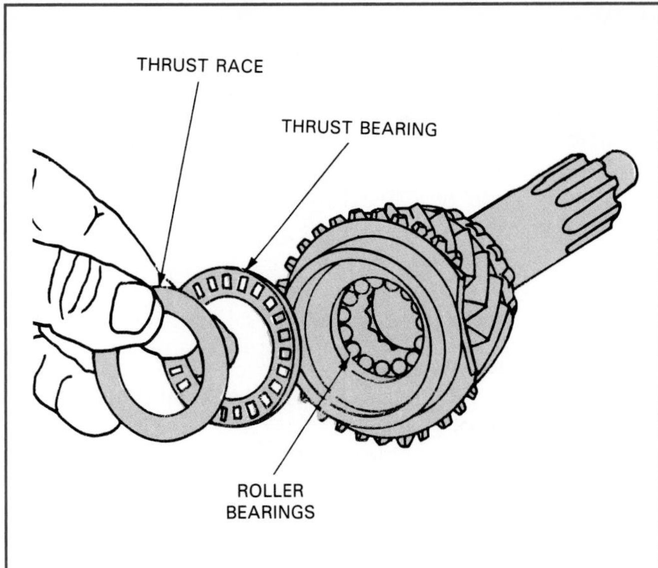

Figure 36-29. Input shaft reassembly requires the use of petroleum jelly to hold the roller bearings in the shaft cavity. The thrust bearing and the race are installed and the input shaft is pushed into place in the front of the case. (Chevrolet)

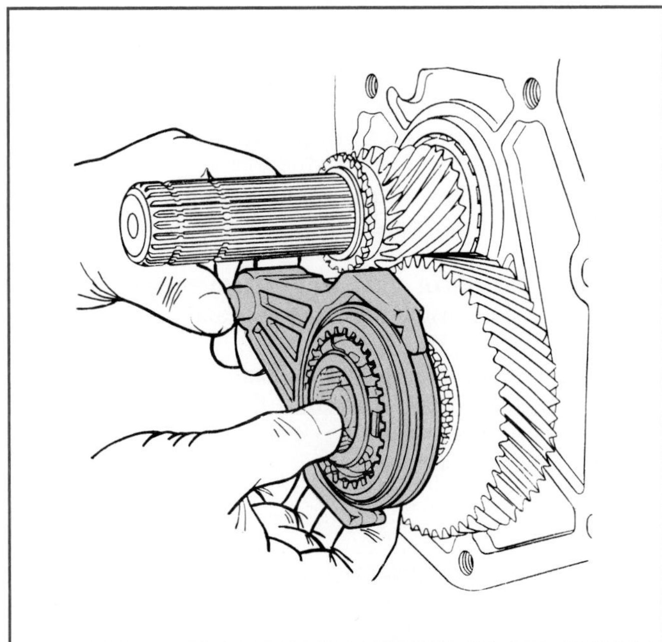

Figure 36-30. A fifth gear synchronizer assembly is placed on the shift fork, and then installed on the countershaft with the fork installed on the shift rail. (Chevrolet)

16. Install fifth-speed/reverse rail in the rear of the case. Rotate the rail while installing it in the fifth-speed/reverse lever. Connect the spring to the front of the case.
17. Position the fifth gear shift fork on the fifth gear synchronizer assembly. Install the synchronizer on the countershaft and place the shift fork on the shift rail, Figure 36-30. Align the roll pin holes in the fork and the rail, and then install the pin.
18. Install the thrust race against the fifth-speed synchronizer hub and install the snap ring. Install the thrust bearing against the race on the countershaft. Coat the bearing and race with petroleum jelly.

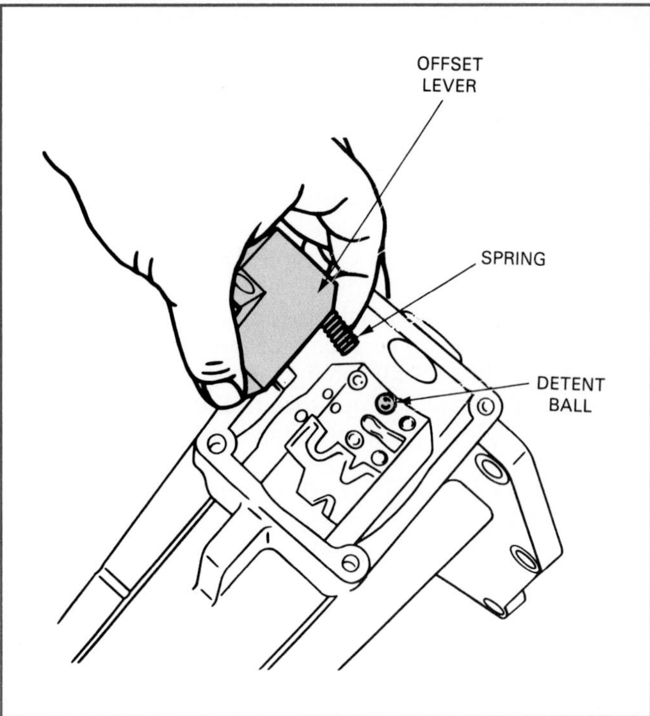

Figure 36-31. While holding the offset lever and the spring in position over the detent ball, the extension housing can be installed. (Chevrolet)

19. Install the lipped thrust race over the needle thrust bearing and insert the plastic funnel in the hole in the end of the countershaft gear, Figure 36-24.
20. Temporarily install the extension housing. Use a dial indicator to measure the output shaft end play. Install a shim pack to establish the correct output shaft bearing preload.
21. Remove the front bearing cap and the front bearing race. Install shims to obtain the desired bearing preload and reinstall the bearing race. Install the front bearing cap.
22. Remove the extension housing.
23. Move the shift forks on the assembled transmission cover and the synchronizer sleeves in the transmission to the neutral position. Install the cover, Figure 36-25.
24. Install the extension housing over the output shaft and shift rail to where it just enters the shift cover opening.
25. Install the detent spring into the offset lever and the steel ball in the neutral guide plate detent. Position the offset lever on the steel ball, Figure 36-31, apply pressure on the lever, and install the extension housing.
26. Align and install the roll pin in the offset lever and the shift rail.
27. Check transmission operation in all gears.

Reinstallation of the Transmission in the Car

1. Remove excess oil from the pilot bushing lubricating wick, and then install it in the bushing.
2. Install the clutch release bearing on the fork.
3. Place the transmission in gear. Lift and align the transmission with the hub hole in the clutch disc.
4. Slide the transmission forward while slowly rotating the output shaft to align the splines in the transmission input shaft with the splines in the clutch disc hub.

5. When the splines align, slide the transmission into place against the clutch housing.
6. Install the transmission-to-clutch housing attaching bolts and lock washers; tighten to manufacturer's torque specification.
7. Install the exhaust pipe to the manifold and the converter bracket to the transmission.
8. Connect the clutch cable and the adjust clutch, if necessary, to provide the correct pedal free play.
9. Position the rear crossmember to the frame and loosely install the attaching bolts.
10. Lower the jack to seat the transmission mount on the crossmember; install and tighten the attaching bolts or nuts to the correct torque specification.
11. Torque-tighten the crossmember-to-frame attaching bolts.
12. Install the speedometer cable in the transmission extension housing and connect the backup lamp switch.
13. Install the drive shaft, aligning the marks on the drive shaft and the rear axle yoke or flange to ensure proper reassembly. See Figure 36-5.
14. On steering column shift transmissions, connect the shift rods to the shift levers.
15. Refill the transmission with recommended lubricant, Figure 36-2.
16. Lower the vehicle to the floor.
17. On floor-mounted shift transmissions, install the gearshift lever. Make sure the fork is properly engaged in the grooves, and then bolt the gearshift lever assembly to the extension housing.
18. Install the gearshift lever bezel and boot; tighten the attaching screws.
19. Test the gearshift for smooth and free crossover in neutral and satisfactory operation through the complete range, Figure 36-3. Recheck the clutch pedal free play and make necessary final adjustments.
20. Road test the car and check transmission performance in all gears.

Chapter 36 – Review Questions

Write your answers on a separate sheet of paper. Do not write in this book.

Name six manual transmission maintenance routines:

1. Make periodic _____ checks.
2. Make an external inspection of the transmission for possible _____.
3. Test gearshift operation in all _____.
4. Check clutch pedal _____.
5. Examine the condition of transmission _____.
6. Test _____ of transmission-to-clutch housing attaching bolts.
7. Modern manual transmissions have _____ gears that are in constant mesh in all forward speeds.
   (A) worm
   (B) spur
   (C) helical
   (D) planetary
8. The fluid level should be even with or just below the lower edge of _____ in the side of the transmission case.
9. Why should you place alignment marks on the drive shaft and rear axle flange before removing the drive shaft?
10. A car equipped with a manual transmission is noisy in neutral. Technician A says the noise could be caused by a worn or broken input shaft gear. Technician B says it could be caused by a worn or broken output shaft bearing. Who is right?
    (A) A only.
    (B) B only.
    (C) Both A & B.
    (D) Neither A nor B.
11. What is the principal cause for a manual transmission slipping out of gear?
12. What is the probable cause if manual transmission gears clash when shifting?
13. When removing a manual transmission from a car, pull the transmission straight back to avoid damaging input shaft, pilot bushing, or _____.
14. If an aluminum transmission case has nicks on the front face, smooth out the nicks with a _____ (fine stone/fine file).
15. Why is a dummy countershaft used when removing or reinstalling the countershaft assembly?
16. When installing roller bearings in a reverse idler gear, use _____ to hold bearings in place.
17. With the input shaft and bearing in place in the front of a three-speed transmission case, you should install the thickest snap ring that will fit into the groove. True or False?
18. When reinstalling the cap (front bearing retainer) on the front face of the transmission, align the cap with _____ in case.
19. In the final step of reassembly of a three-speed manual transmission, install the case cover and gasket. Be sure the _____ is open.
20. In four-speed manual transmission disassembly, removing the access plug from the extension housing permits access to the:
    (A) offset lever assembly.
    (B) rear seal.
    (C) shifter lever.
    (D) reverse idler gear shaft.
21. Which gear assembly is reinstalled first in the reassembly of a four-speed manual transmission?
    (A) Input shaft main drive gear.
    (B) Fourth-speed gear.
    (C) Countergear.
    (D) Reverse idler gear.
22. When installing an output shaft assembly in a transmission case, a dummy bearing is installed on the output shaft to _____ assembly in the case.
23. A speedometer drive gear assembly includes the drive gear lock ball, drive gear, and:
    (A) roll pin.
    (B) nylon bushing.
    (C) snap ring.
    (D) lock nut.
24. When removing the front bearing cap from a five-speed transmission, also remove the bearing race and the _____ shims.

25. To remove the input shaft from the transmission case, rotate the shaft until the _____ faces the countershaft, then pull the shaft from the case.
    (A) notch
    (B) flat surface
    (C) cutaway
    (D) alignment mark
26. A dial indicator is used to measure output shaft end play. True or False?
27. When installing an assembled transmission cover, the shift forks should be placed in the _____ position.
    (A) neutral
    (B) first gear
    (C) fifth gear
    (D) reverse
28. When reinstalling a transmission in a vehicle, place the transmission in neutral, and lift and align it with the hub hole in the clutch disc. True or False?
29. After the transmission is installed and the gearshift lever assembly is bolted in place, test the gearshift for _____ crossover in neutral.
30. Also, check for satisfactory _____ throughout the complete range.

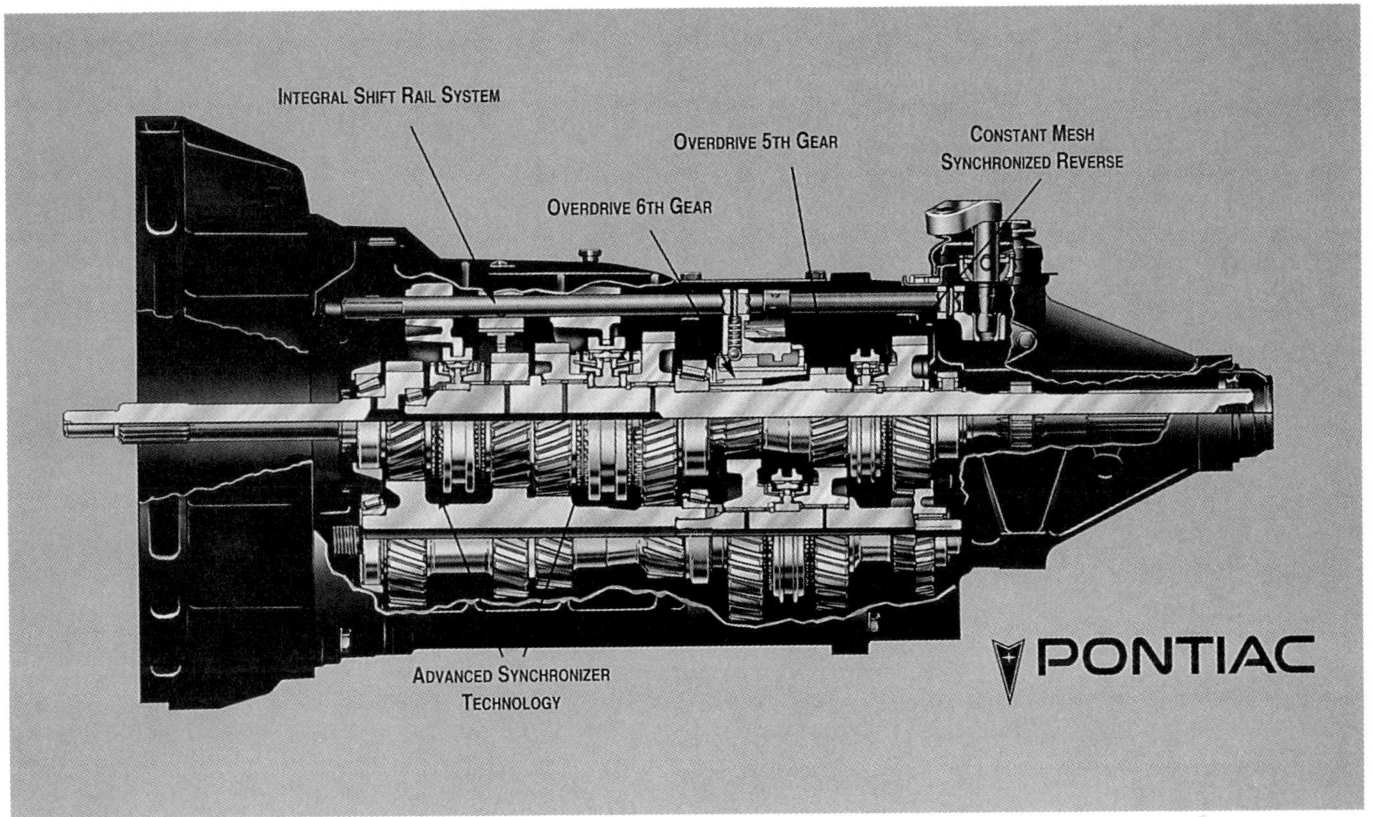

Cutaway of a six-speed manual transmission used on a late-model high-performance vehicle. (Pontiac)

Cutaway of a five-speed automatic transmission. The first gear in this transmission is "lower" than usual to boost low-speed performance. (BMW)

Chapter 37
Automatic Transmission Fundamentals

After studying this chapter, you will be able to:

- ❍ State the primary differences between a fluid coupling and a torque converter.
- ❍ Explain how a torque converter multiplies engine torque.
- ❍ Tell how a converter clutch locks the turbine to the impeller in direct drive.
- ❍ Discuss the function of clutches and bands in automatic transmission operation.
- ❍ Detail the principles of planetary gearset operation.
- ❍ Trace power flow in the various modes of operation in a three-speed automatic transmission.
- ❍ Point out the path of power flow in the overdrive mode of a four-speed automatic transmission.

Automatic Transmissions

Automatic transmissions are installed in over 85 percent of U.S. cars coming off the assembly lines. Car buyers want the comfort and convenience afforded by these labor-saving, automatically controlled, power transfer devices.

Fluid Couplings

Basic, two element fluid couplings were once widely used with semiautomatic and automatic transmissions. Today's torque converter is a direct descendent of the basic fluid coupling. Both transmit engine torque (turning or twisting force) to the gear train of the transmission. The difference is the ***torque converter*** multiplies that turning power; the ***fluid coupling*** does not.

A typical fluid coupling has two facing halves called "torus members." Each member is divided into many sections by designed arrangement of inner and outer shells and vanes. The torus members are splined to separate shafts and operate in a fluid-filled housing, Figure 37-1. The drive side of the fluid coupling is attached to the engine. The driven side connects to the drive shaft of the vehicle.

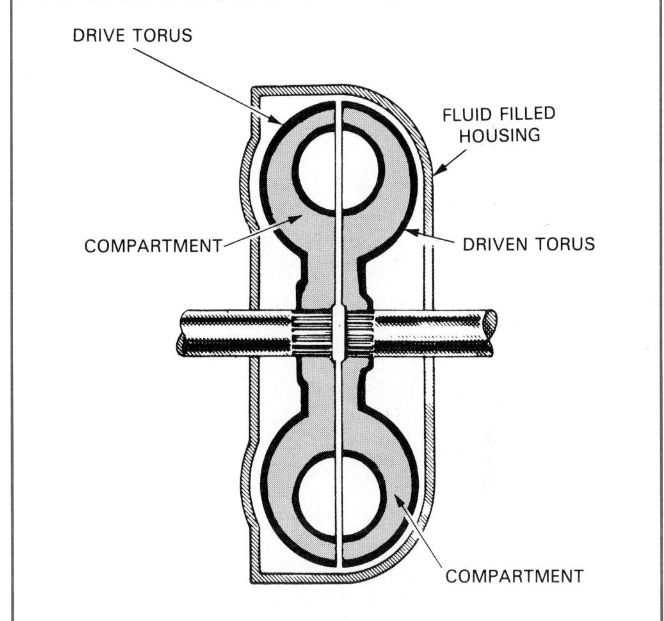

Figure 37-1. A typical fluid coupling has two torus members. The drive torus is connected to the engine crankshaft. The driven torus transmits engine torque to the transmission input shaft.

In operation, a fluid coupling acts like an automatic clutch. It "slips" at idle speed; "holds" to transmit power as engine speed is increased. Power is transmitted through the fluid. There is no mechanical connection between the engine and the drive shaft.

The automatic transmission fluid is circulated by pump pressure to the fluid coupling as well as to other parts of the automatic transmission. Rotation of the drive torus causes the fluid within it to be forced radially outward against vanes of the driven torus. See Figure 37-2. When the engine runs fast enough, the increased force of the fluid being thrown by the drive torus causes the driven torus to rotate in the same direction.

In addition to the use of fluid couplings in conjunction with automatic transmissions, a fluid coupling was used in the past with a semiautomatic sliding gear transmission. In this application, the fluid coupling served to reduce slippage and wear of the dry clutch disc and eased the shifting of gears.

Torque Converters

Typically, the conventional torque converter consists of a front cover (housing), impeller (pump), turbine, stator, and stator overrunning (one-way) clutch, Figure 37-3. The ***impeller*** is connected to the engine crankshaft through the front cover (which is welded to the impeller). The ***turbine*** is splined to the transmission input shaft.

The ***stator*** is splined to a reaction shaft or to the stationary hub shaft of the ***overrunning clutch.*** See Figures 37-3 and 37-4.

Operating Principles

Basically, all torque converters utilize the rotating elements in a fluid-filled housing to multiply engine torque.

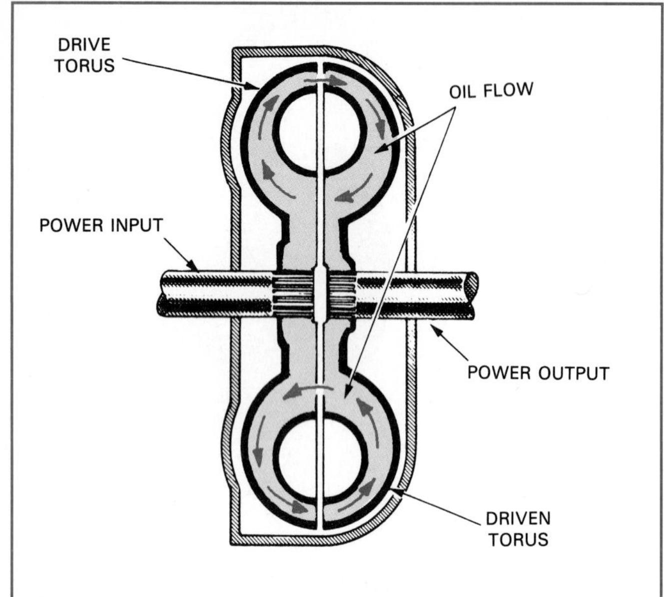

Figure 37-2. The rotation of the drive torus forces fluid against the vanes of the driven torus, which transmits engine torque to the transmission gear train.

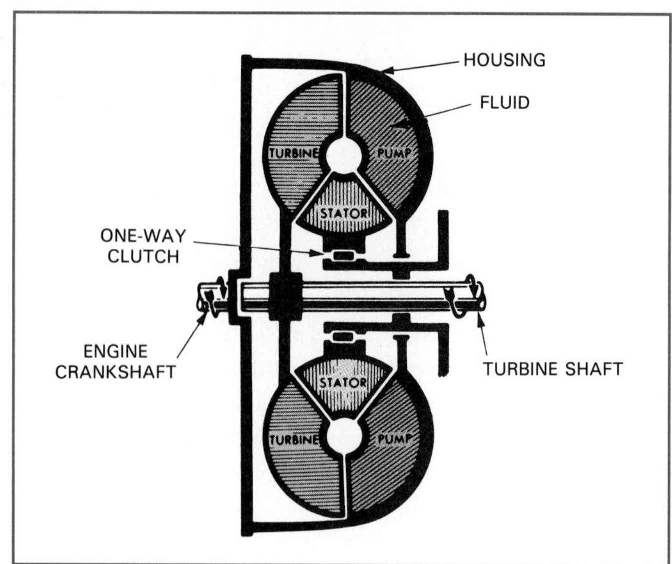

Figure 37-4. This graphic representation of a three-element torque converter depicts the arrangement of the elements. Note that the engine crankshaft turns the converter housing and pump (impeller). The stator is mounted on the overrunning clutch.

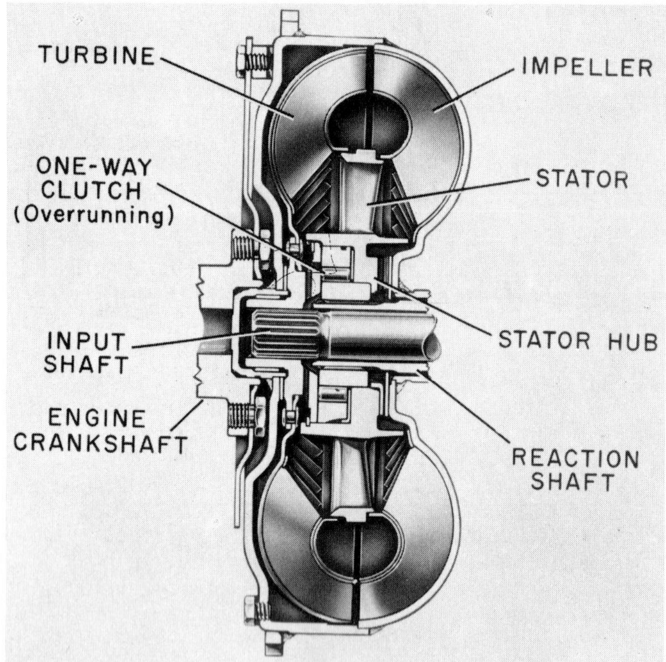

Figure 37-3. This cross-sectional view of a typical torque converter shows the attachment of the converter to the engine crankshaft and the relationship of the three major elements: impeller (pump), turbine, and stator.

All use the engine to drive the impeller which, in turn, impels the fluid against the vanes of the turbine. The turbine is connected through transmission gears to the drive shaft of the automobile. The third (middle) element–the stator–serves to redirect oil flow from the turbine against the impeller vanes to boost impeller action and multiply engine torque. See Figure 37-4.

This action of centrifugal force within the torque converter sets up a vortex flow of oil, while the angle of the vanes tends to set up a rotary flow, Figure 37-5. The combined flow results in a corkscrew action, which sets up a pattern something like a coil spring with the ends connected. See Figure 37-6.

This whirling ring of oil emerges from the twisting passages of the turbine in a direction opposite to impeller rotation. If directed into the impeller at this time, it would cause a loss of power. Instead, it is directed against the curved face of the stator blades, Figure 37-7. The impact of the oil flow creates reaction torque since the stator is held stationary by the overrunning clutch. This multiplies engine torque at variable ratios up to at least 2:1 when the turbine is in start-up stall (not rotating).

When enough torque is developed by the impeller, the turbine begins to rotate, along with the transmission input shaft. As turbine speed approaches impeller speed, torque multiplication lessens, since the angle of fluid flow against the face of the stator blades becomes less efficient. Then, just before turbine speed equals impeller speed, the fluid strikes the back face of the stator blades, which releases the overrunning clutch and permits the three elements to rotate together as a fluid coupling. See Figure 37-8 for details.

Variable Pitch Stator

In most torque converters, the stator blades are "fixed" at a predetermined angle. In special designs, a ***variable pitch stator*** assembly is used. For normal operation in the drive range, the stator blades are automatically set at a low angle. For increased acceleration, greater torque is obtained by setting the stator blades at a high angle.

The angle of the variable pitch stator blades usually is controlled by a switch mounted on the throttle linkage, a stator solenoid, and a stator valve. At engine idle speed, the switch activates the solenoid, which exhausts line pressure and the stator valve shifts the blade angle from low to high. At light or medium throttle, the solenoid is not activated and line pressure on the stator valve puts the blades at a low angle. At about 3/4 throttle opening or under heavy acceleration,

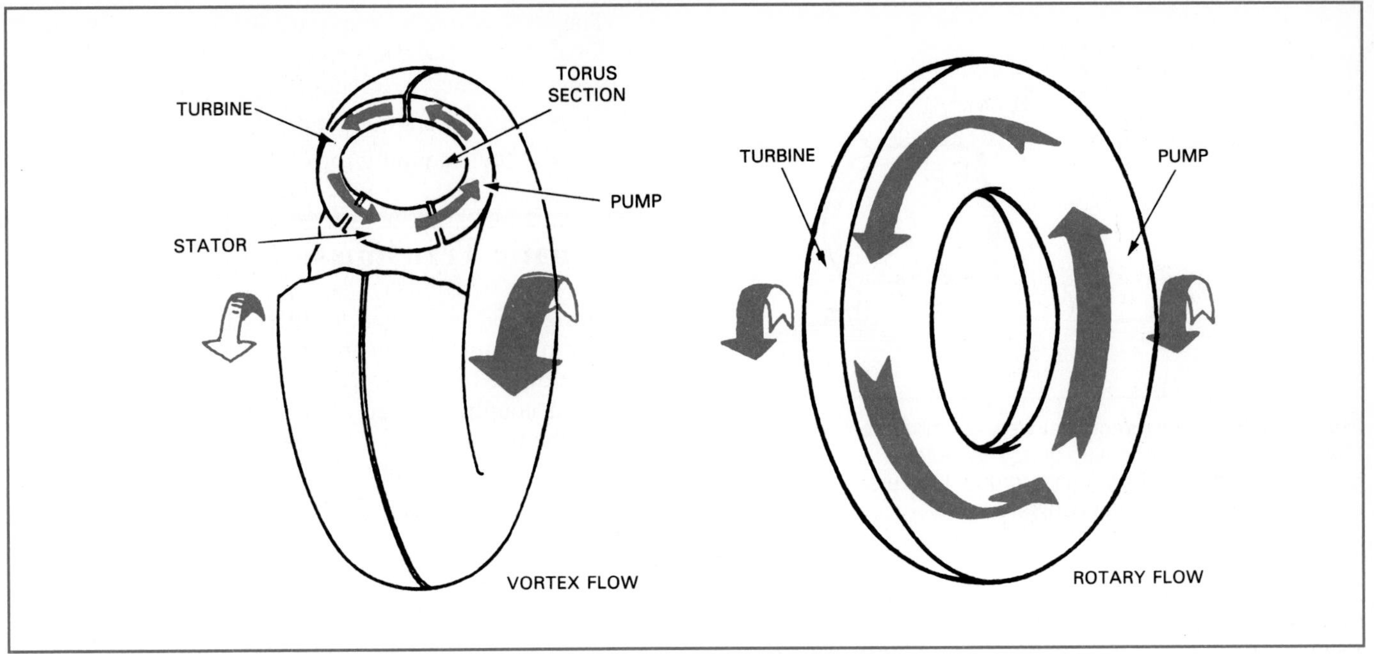

Figure 37-5. When the torque converter is in operation, there are two types of oil circulation within the unit: vortex flow and rotary flow.

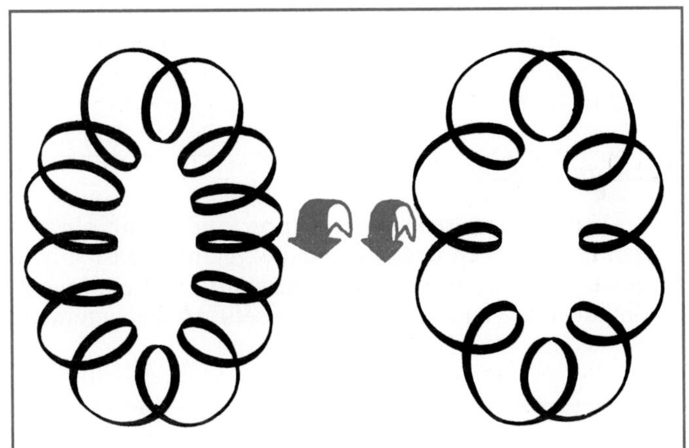

Figure 37-6. Vortex flow and rotary flow within a torque converter combine to produce a spiral action or "coil spring" effect.

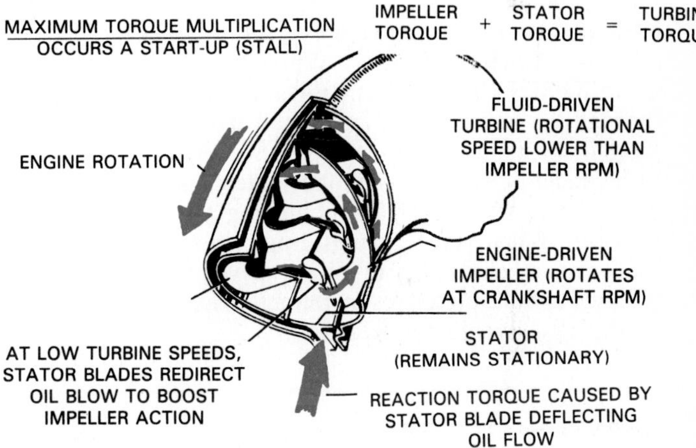

Figure 37-7. Torque converter cutaway shows the impeller, turbine, and stator in operation at the point of start-up stall. The stator is stationary and torque multiplication is at maximum.

the solenoid again exhausts line pressure and the stator valve moves the stator blades to the high angle for maximum performance.

Lockup Torque Converter

In a conventional torque converter, there is always some slippage between the impeller and turbine in direct drive. Since the impeller is connected to the engine crankshaft, it always rotates at engine speed. As engine speed increases, the turbine gradually builds up rotational speed as oil flow between the elements intensifies. However, the turbine only approaches impeller speed, Figure 37-8. It never quite catches up, so several percentage points of efficiency are lost to slippage.

To overcome this slippage, ***lockup torque converters*** were introduced. These converters are equipped with an internal locking mechanism called a "converter clutch" that locks the turbine to the impeller in direct drive. See Figure 37-9.

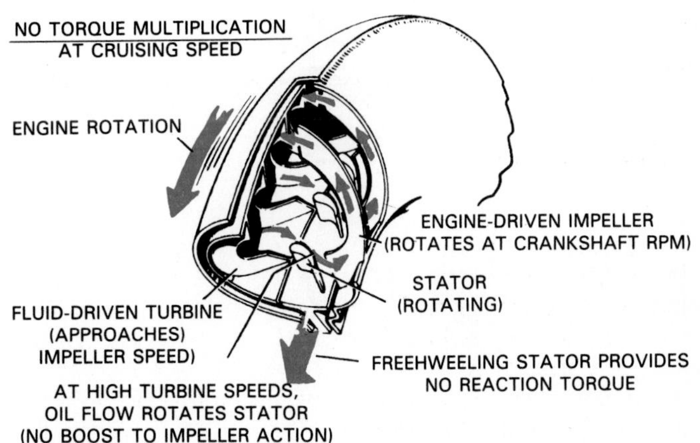

Figure 37-8. In this operation, the car is at cruising speed and the overrunning clutch permits the stator to free wheel and rotate with the impeller and turbine.

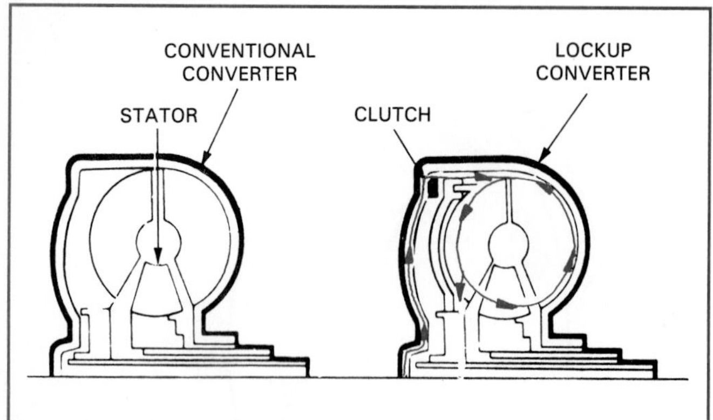

Figure 37-9. Cross-sectional views compare a conventional torque converter to a lockup unit. The clutch mechanism locks the turbine to the impeller in direct drive at a predetermined car speed. (Chrysler)

Various types of lockup mechanism are used. One application consists of a sliding clutch piston, torsion springs, and clutch friction material, Figure 37-10. The friction material is attached to the front cover of the converter. The clutch piston is mounted on the turbine. The torsion springs are located on the forward side of the turbine where they absorb engine power pulses and shock loads that occur during lockup.

How Lockup Occurs. When the vehicle reaches approximately 40 mph, transmission fluid is channeled through the transmission input shaft into the area between the clutch piston and the turbine. See Figure 37-10. This fluid under pressure forces the clutch piston against the front cover friction material, locking the turbine to the impeller. When vehicle speed drops below 40 mph or the transmission shifts out of direct drive, fluid pressure is released and the clutch piston retracts. The torque converter returns to conventional operation.

The lockup torque converter has several advantages over the conventional converter:

- Greater efficiency in direct drive.
- Reduced fluid operating temperatures.
- Improved fuel economy for vehicles so equipped.

Automatic Transmission Operation

Design and construction differs between makes, but all modern automatic transmissions–with rare exceptions–make use of the following key elements:

- A fluid coupling called a "torque converter" that connects the transmission to the engine and serves to multiply and transmit engine torque.
- An oil pump (or two) which develops fluid pressure for the operation and lubrication of the transmission parts and assemblies. See Figure 37-11.
- A system of hydraulic circuits and spool valves, Figure 37-12, that directs the flow of ATF to control the application of bands and clutches.
- A system of holding devices called "bands" and driving devices called "clutches" that are used selectively to control the operation of the planetary gearsets.
- One or more planetary gearsets which receive incoming torque from the torque converter and multiply it still further by means of gear reduction.

Actions of Key Elements

Torque converter construction and principles of operation have been described and explained. Basically, a torque converter multiplies and transmits engine torque to the input shaft and planetary gearsets of the automatic transmission.

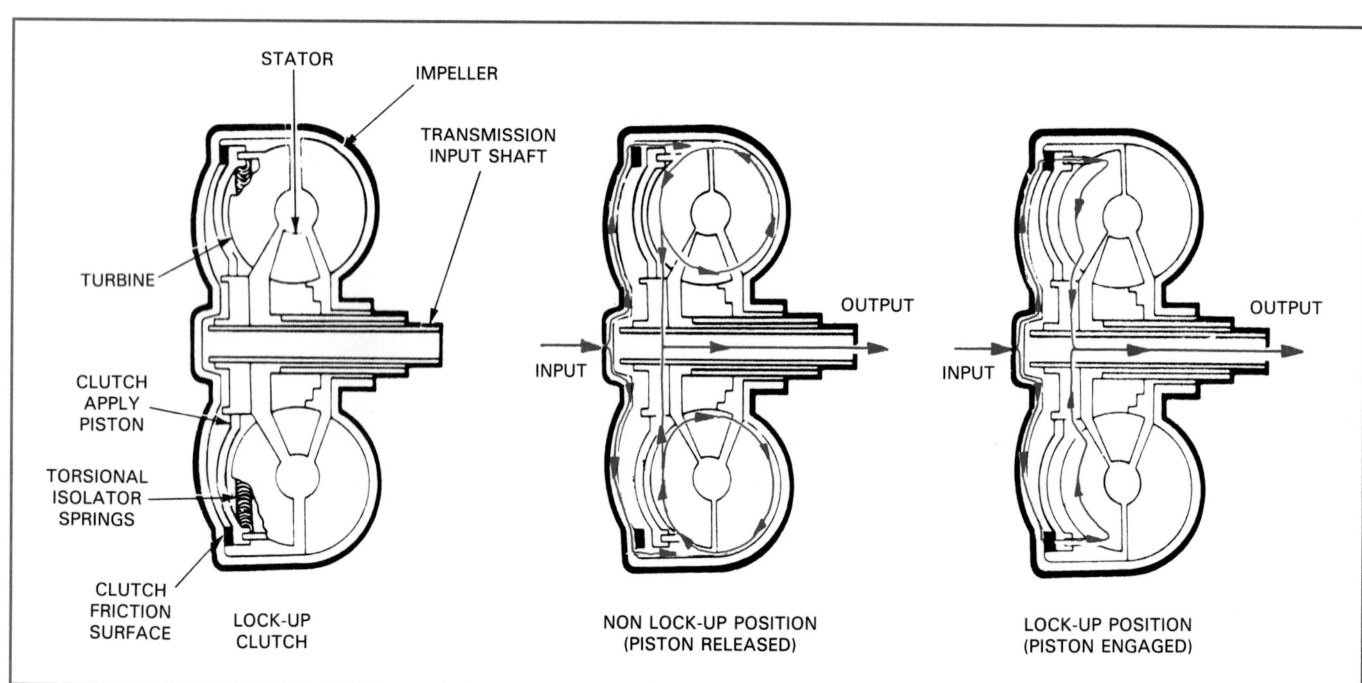

Figure 37-10. Lockup torque converter components: Left–Relationship of elements. Center–Non-lockup position (piston released). Right–Lockup position (piston engaged). Arrows denote the direction of power flow. (Chrysler)

OIL SEAL
REACTION SHAFT SUPPORT
BOLT AND WASHER (6)
NO. 1 THRUST WASHER
OUTER ROTOR
SEAL RINGS
OIL PUMP BODY
INNER ROTOR
GASKET
O-RING

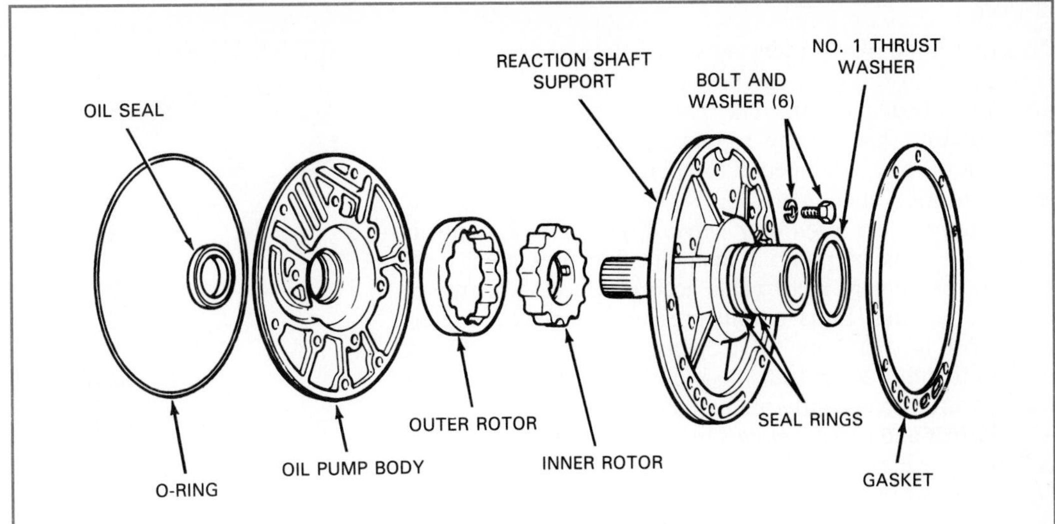

Figure 37-12. This exploded view of an automatic transmission rotor-type oil pump shows assembly/disassembly sequence. Gear-type and vane-type oil pumps are also used. (Chrysler)

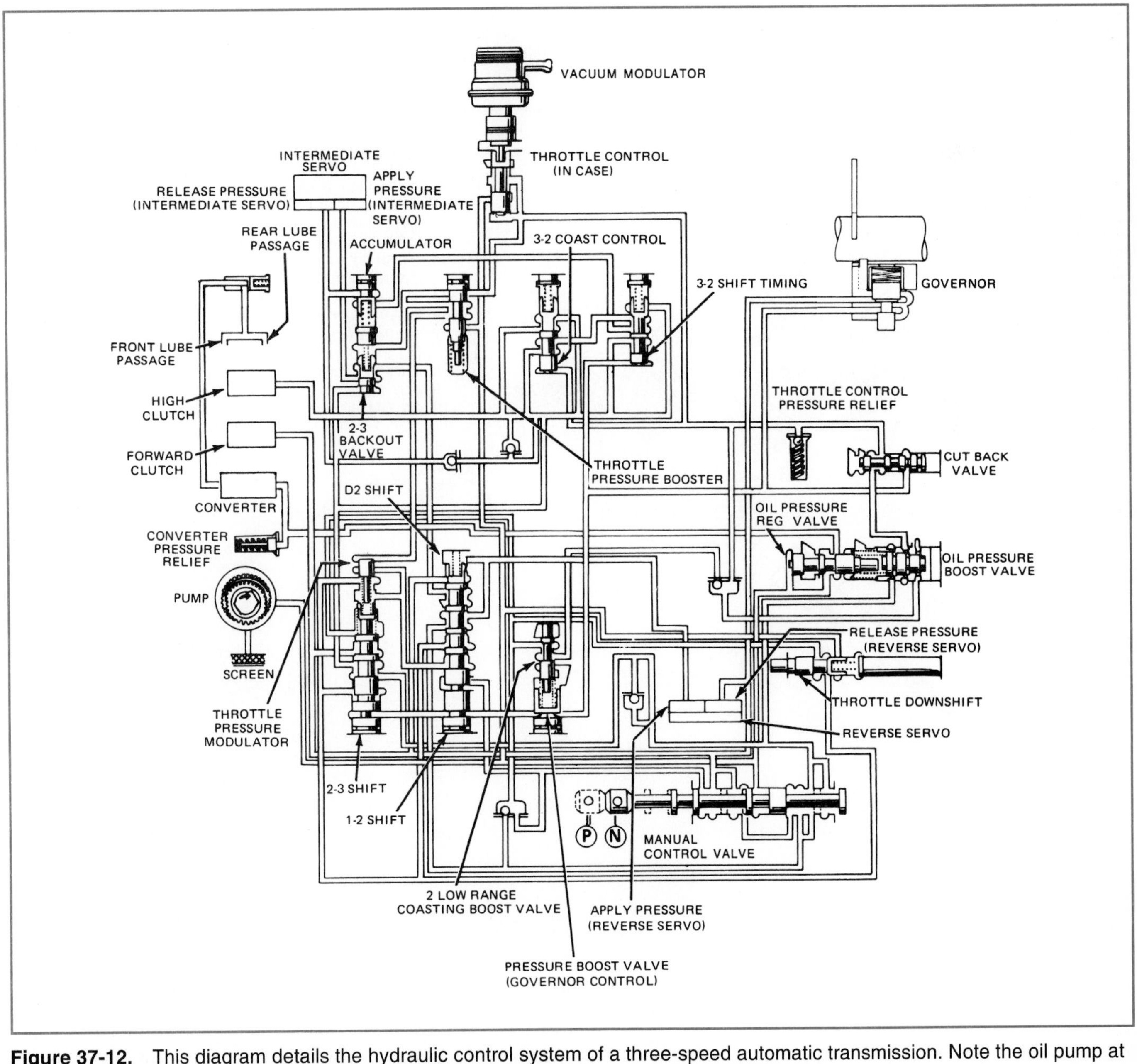

VACUUM MODULATOR
INTERMEDIATE SERVO
THROTTLE CONTROL (IN CASE)
APPLY PRESSURE (INTERMEDIATE SERVO)
RELEASE PRESSURE (INTERMEDIATE SERVO)
REAR LUBE PASSAGE
ACCUMULATOR
3-2 COAST CONTROL
3-2 SHIFT TIMING
GOVERNOR
FRONT LUBE PASSAGE
HIGH CLUTCH
THROTTLE CONTROL PRESSURE RELIEF
2-3 BACKOUT VALVE
FORWARD CLUTCH
THROTTLE PRESSURE BOOSTER
CUT BACK VALVE
CONVERTER
D2 SHIFT
OIL PRESSURE REG VALVE
CONVERTER PRESSURE RELIEF
OIL PRESSURE BOOST VALVE
PUMP
RELEASE PRESSURE (REVERSE SERVO)
SCREEN
THROTTLE DOWNSHIFT
THROTTLE PRESSURE MODULATOR
REVERSE SERVO
2-3 SHIFT
1-2 SHIFT
P
N
MANUAL CONTROL VALVE
2 LOW RANGE COASTING BOOST VALVE
APPLY PRESSURE (REVERSE SERVO)
PRESSURE BOOST VALVE (GOVERNOR CONTROL)

Figure 37-12. This diagram details the hydraulic control system of a three-speed automatic transmission. Note the oil pump at left; the oil pressure regulator at right; and the manual control valve at lower right. (Ford)

The ***oil pump,*** Figure 37-11, usually is located immediately behind the torque converter. It is driven by the converter and serves as the pressure supply system for the automatic transmission. The pump circulates automatic transmission fluid to the torque converter and provides working oil pressure needed to operate valves, valve controls, and friction elements.

The ***pressure regulator valve,*** Figure 37-12, controls the output of the oil pump. It maintains line pressure at a psi (pounds per square inch) value according to the degree of throttle opening. If its output pressure exceeds predetermined psi, the regulator valve opens, and bypasses oil back to the oil sump in the transmission. In that way, main line oil pressure is constantly maintained.

Valves and ***valve controls*** range from simple mechanical linkage, Figure 37-13, to a complicated control valve body assembly, Figure 37-14. The control valves are needed to direct the flow of ATF, to turn the flow off and on, and to regulate pressure. This built-in hydraulic control system provides a combination of balanced pressures predicated on car speed, engine speed, and the demands of the driver.

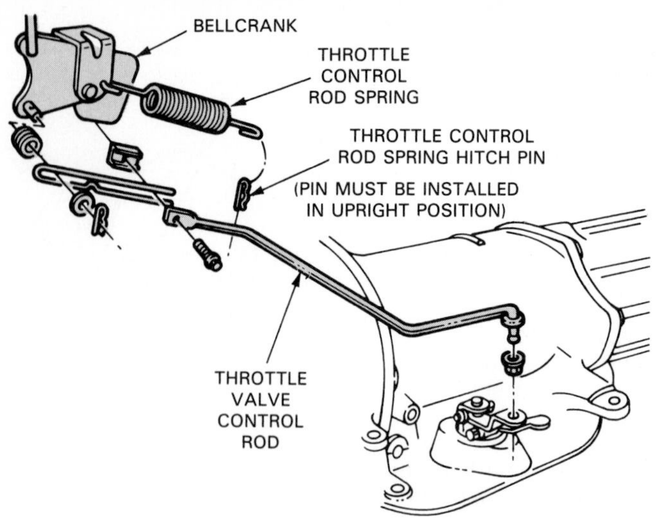

Figure 37-13. This drawing shows a typical throttle rod arrangement and the points of adjustment on a car equipped with a six-cylinder engine and an automatic transmission. (Chrysler)

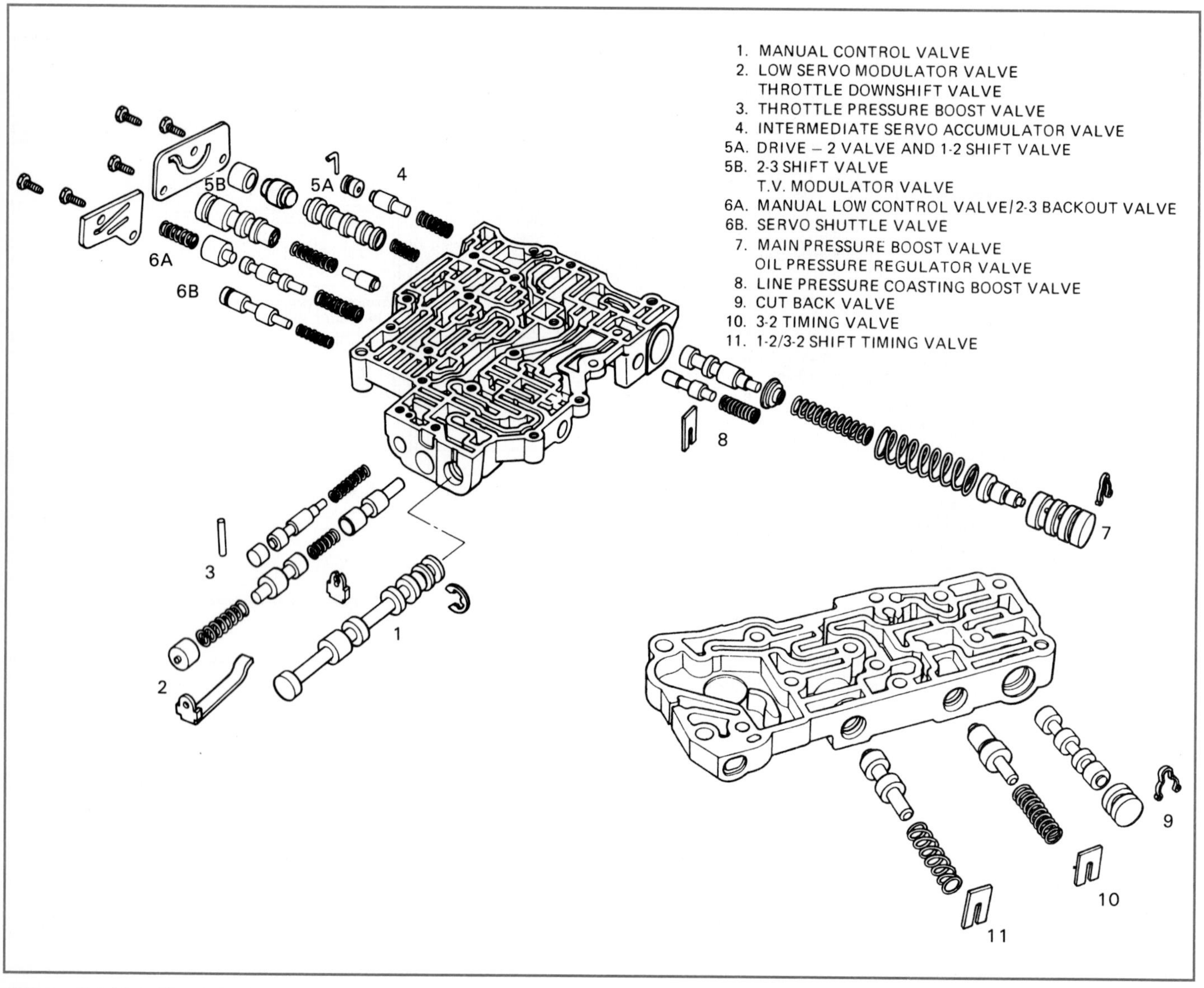

1. MANUAL CONTROL VALVE
2. LOW SERVO MODULATOR VALVE
   THROTTLE DOWNSHIFT VALVE
3. THROTTLE PRESSURE BOOST VALVE
4. INTERMEDIATE SERVO ACCUMULATOR VALVE

5A. DRIVE – 2 VALVE AND 1-2 SHIFT VALVE
5B. 2-3 SHIFT VALVE
T.V. MODULATOR VALVE
6A. MANUAL LOW CONTROL VALVE/2-3 BACKOUT VALVE
6B. SERVO SHUTTLE VALVE

7. MAIN PRESSURE BOOST VALVE
   OIL PRESSURE REGULATOR VALVE
8. LINE PRESSURE COASTING BOOST VALVE
9. CUT BACK VALVE
10. 3-2 TIMING VALVE
11. 1-2/3-2 SHIFT TIMING VALVE

Figure 37-14. The valve body on this automatic transmission contains fluid passages and valves that control the flow of fluid and regulate pressure. (Ford)

A ***manual control valve,*** Figures 37-12 and 37-14, establishes the particular range of transmission operation selected by the driver. For example, when the manual valve is opened, fluid pressure actuates the low band servo and the vehicle will move forward in low gear.

Shift valves automatically permit 1-2 or 2-1 shifts, 2-3 or 3-2 shifts, etc., depending on vehicle operation. See Figure 37-15.

The ***governor valve assembly*** is connected to the output shaft of the transmission and controls line pressure and shift speeds. Governor pressure is almost in direct proportion to vehicle speed.

At a predetermined speed, the governor valve will open and fluid under pressure will travel to the shift valve. At a certain level of pressure, the tension of the shift valve spring will be overcome, the shift valve will open, and fluid will flow to a multiple-disc clutch.

In any case, the various valves and valve controls in automatic transmissions operate independently or in combination to compensate for changes in car speed, load, and the demands of the driver.

The ***throttle valve*** usually is indirectly connected to the accelerator pedal through linkage (TV rod), so that pressure on the pedal will automatically operate the valve. Movement of the throttle valve, in turn, regulates pressure to the transmission to control upshift, downshift, and "lockup" speeds.

A ***vacuum modulator valve,*** rather than a TV rod, is used on some automatic transmissions to control the throttle valve, Figure 37-12. The vacuum modulator valve, Figure 37-16, usually is attached to the outside of the transmission case and is connected to the engine intake manifold. As the vacuum modulator diaphragm reacts to changes in engine vacuum, the modulator constantly alters throttle valve pressure to meet engine needs.

For example, the vacuum modulator increases TV pressure at full throttle or under heavy load (low vacuum)

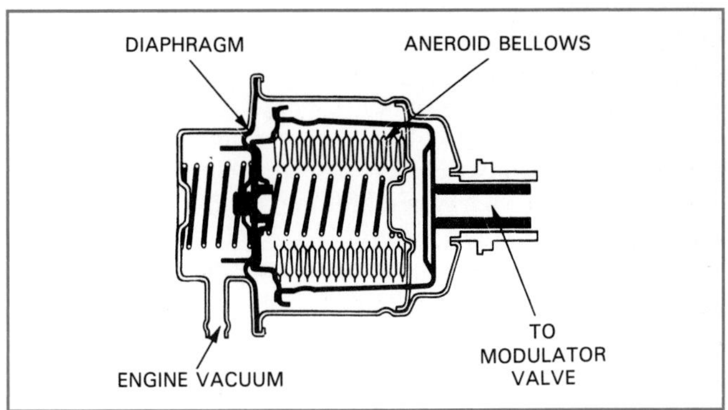

Figure 37-16. The vacuum modulator is a pressure-regulating device that is operated by engine vacuum and spring action. (Cadillac)

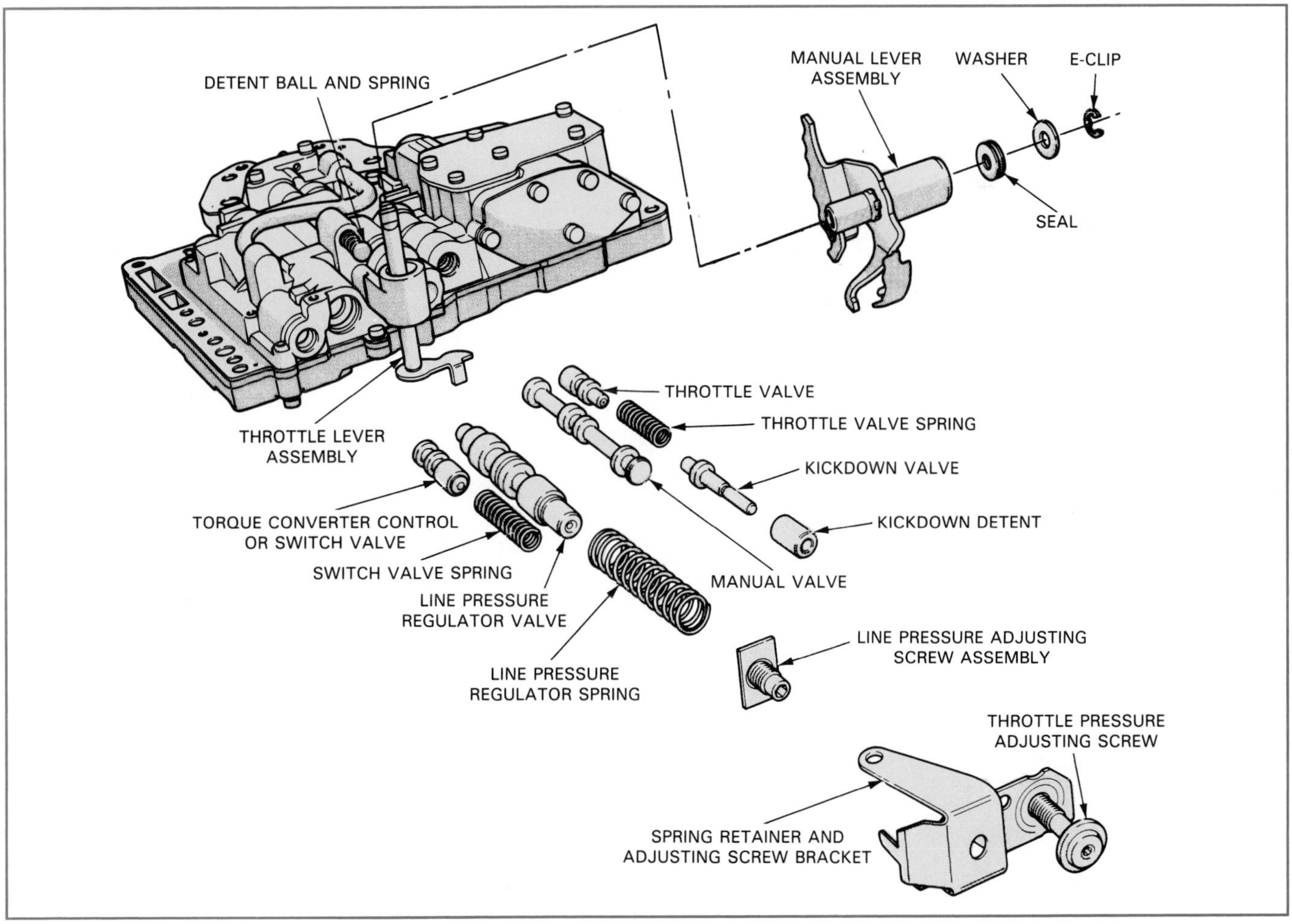

Figure 37-15. This exploded view of part of a control valve body reveals the shape, size, and location of the manual valve, throttle valve, kickdown valve, and line pressure regulator valve. (Chrysler)

to provide more "holding" power for the clutches. Under light load (high vacuum), the vacuum modulator reduces TV pressure to promote smooth shifts.

A ***detent valve*** or ***kickdown valve***–sometimes part of the throttle valve–allows a forced downshift from 3-2 or 2-1 (breakaway), depending on vehicle speed. The detent valve is actuated by pressing the accelerator to near wide open throttle.

The ***throttle pressure plug,*** Figure 37-15, on certain automatic transmissions, provides a 3-2 downshift at various vehicle speeds. It is used in conjunction with the limit valve, which determines the maximum speed at which a part throttle 3-2 kickdown can be made.

The ***shuttle valve*** provides for fast release of the kickdown band. It allows smooth clutch engagement when the driver lightly lifts his foot from the accelerator pedal to permit a 2-3 shift. The shuttle valve also regulates application of the kickdown servo and band for making 3-2 kickdowns.

The ***lockup valve,*** Figure 37-17, automatically applies the converter clutch if the vehicle speed is above a predetermined mph (30-40) in direct drive.

The ***fail-safe valve,*** restricts oil flow to the converter clutch if the front clutch pressure drops. The fail-safe valve permits lockup only in third gear and provides for a quick release of the converter clutch during kickdown. See Figure 37-17.

The ***switch valve*** is a multi-purpose control valve. It directs oil flow to apply the converter clutch in one position and releases it in the other position. It directs oil flow to the cooling and lubricating circuits within the transmission. It regulates the oil pressure to the torque converter and limits maximum oil pressure.

Servos, Figure 37-18, apply and release bands that control the operation of drive shells and planetary gearsets.

Multiple-disc clutches, Figures 37-19 and 37-20, are the "drive" members of the team. They are applied by hydraulic

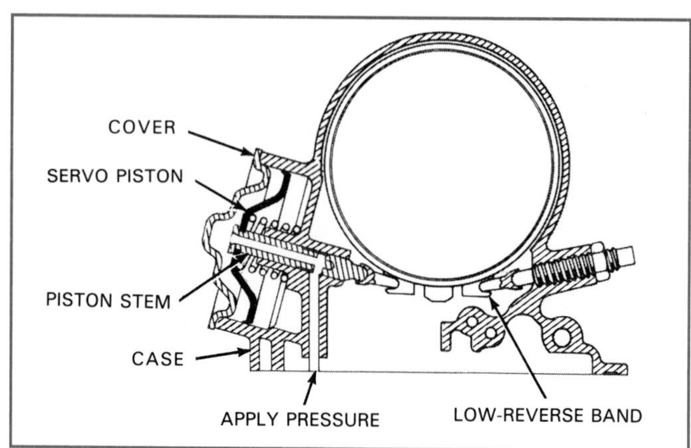

Figure 37-18. This cross-sectional view gives details of low–reverse band setup in an automatic transmission. Note the servo assembly at left and the band adjustment screw at right. (Ford)

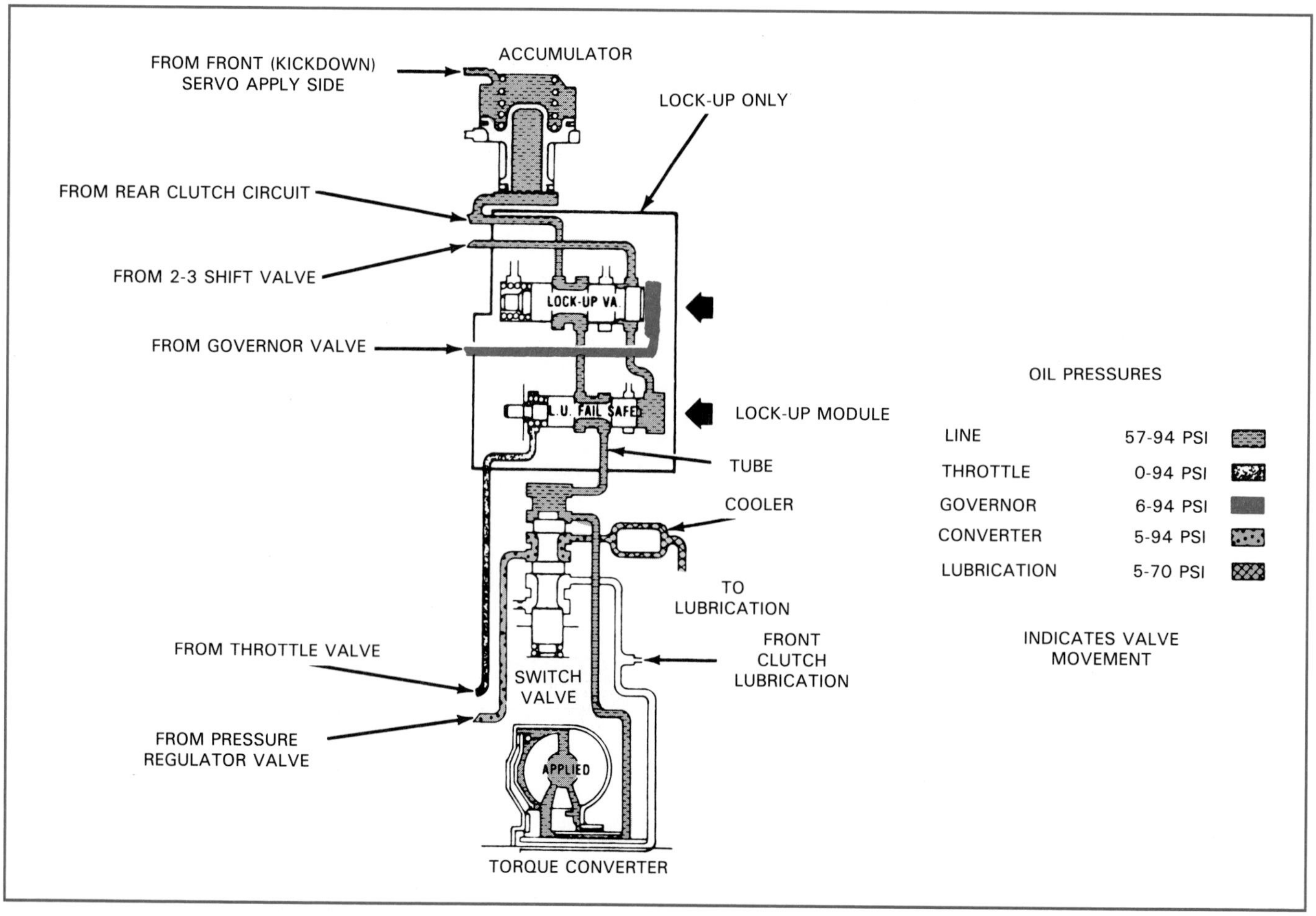

Figure 37-17. This schematic of a lockup torque converter control system shows the valves, lines, and oil pressure values in various circuits of the system. (Chrysler)

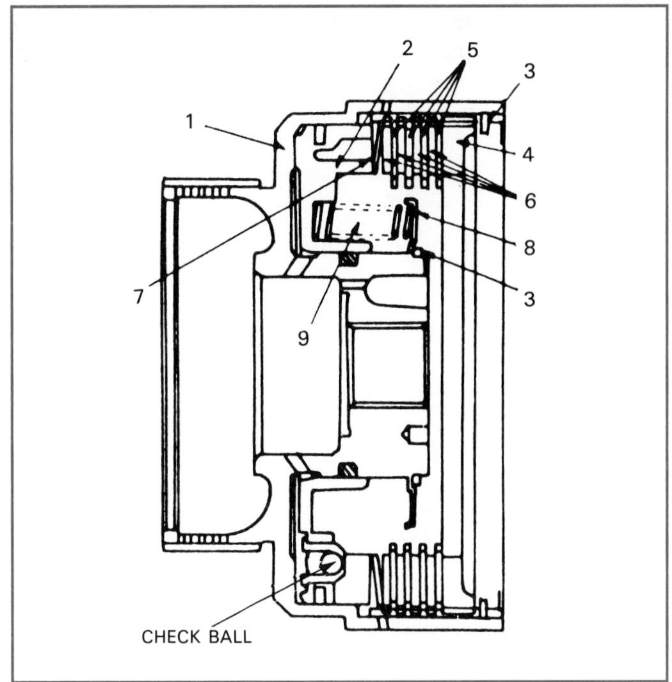

Figure 37-19. Sectional view of forward clutch assembly on typical three-speed automatic transmission: 1–Forward clutch drum. 2–Piston. 3–Snap ring. 4–Retaining plate. 5–Drive plate. 6–Driven plate. 7–Dish plate. 8–Coil spring retainer. 9–Coil spring.

pressure. Heavy springs release the clutch discs when hydraulic pressure drops.

The multiple-discs are arranged in alternate fashion. The driving discs are splined to the clutch hub. The driven discs are splined to the clutch drum. In operation, a piston in the clutch drum squeezes the clutch discs together when hydraulic pressure is applied. A heavy spring releases the discs when hydraulic pressure drops.

Planetary gearsets, Figure 37-21, operate by means of ***pinion gears*** turning on their own axis while rotating around a ***sun gear***–and with a ***ring gear*** (annulus gear) having internal teeth.

When planetary gearsets are used in combination with multiple-disc clutches, bands, valve controls, and valves, they automatically provide all of the forward and reverse

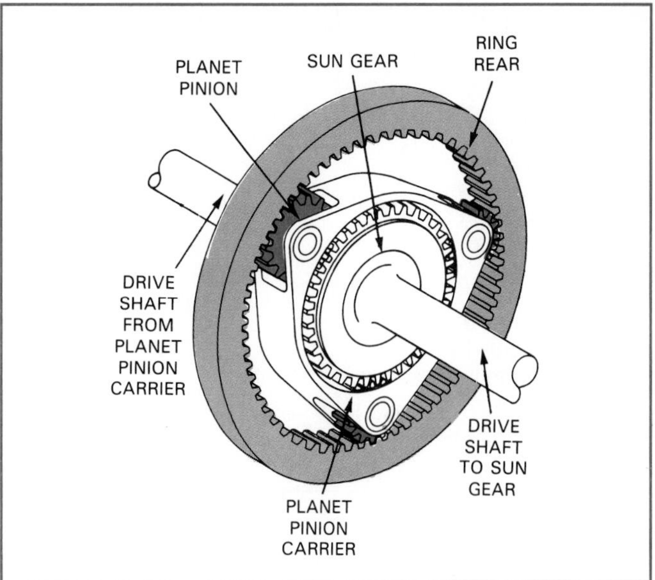

Figure 37-21. The key parts of a single planetary gearset are the sun gear, pinion carrier and planet pinions, and ring gear. All gears are in constant mesh.

gear ratios needed for efficient operation under normal driving conditions.

Overrunning clutches are used both in the torque converter, Figure 37-4, and in the planetary gearsets where they act as one-way driving elements. See Figure 37-22. One type of overrunning clutch, the ***sprag clutch,*** uses specially shaped sprag segments, Figure 37-22, to lock inner and outer races together in one direction only. The ***roller clutch,*** another popular type of overrunning clutch, utilizes rollers and ramps to provide lockup one way and freewheeling in the other direction.

Planetary Gearset Construction

Basically, a planetary gearset has three major elements:

- Sun gear.
- Planet carrier, drum, and pinions.
- Ring gear and drum.

The name "planetary gears" is derived from their similarity to our solar system, since the pinions (planet gears)

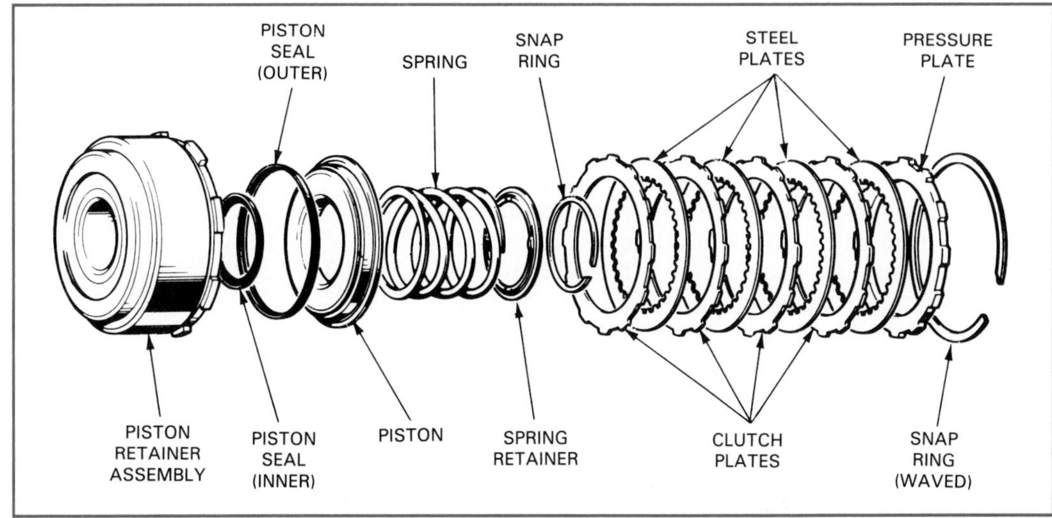

Figure 37-20. This exploded view shows the assembly sequence of a front clutch on an automatic transmission. Note the alternate arrangement of the clutch plates and steel plates. (Chrysler)

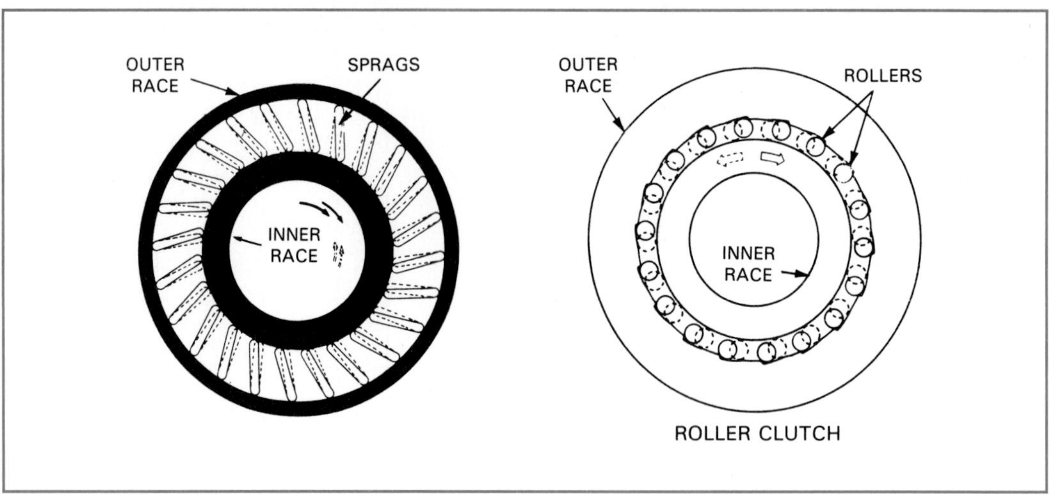

Figure 37-22. Overrunning clutches. Left–The principle of sprag clutch is illustrated by the tipping action of the sprag segments to lock the inner and outer races in one direction. Right–The principle of a roller clutch is shown by the rollers moving up ramps to lock the races together in one direction.

each turn on their own axis while rotating around the sun gear. These gears are surrounded by the ring gear. See Figure 37-21.

In a planetary gearset, the gears are in mesh at all times and are never shifted in or out of engagement. The gears are attached to different drums which, in turn, are attached to other operating parts of the system. This enables the gears to function in different ways as the various drums are held from rotation by "applied" bands.

A simple form of planetary gearset, Figure 37-21, has three pinions mounted between–and meshed with–both the sun gear and the ring gear at all times. The pinions revolve on pins or axles which are a part of the planet carrier drum. The pinions are held in spaced relationship with one another, yet can turn freely on their own pins and also rotate around the sun gear and within the ring gear.

The gears can be arranged so that they will function as driving elements or driven elements to provide different results by connecting them in different ways. In this manner, planetary gears for forward speeds are used in one form as a reduction gear and in another form as an overgear. In still another form, the planetary gears are used for reverse. Multiple planetary gearsets are needed where more than two forward speeds are wanted.

Planetary Gearset Operation

With a single planetary gearset, there are a number of possible gear combinations: direct drive, reduction, reverse, and neutral. Study Figures 37-23 and 37-24 and follow these planetary gear actions.

Direct drive is accomplished by locking together any two planetary gearset members. In Figure 37-23, assume that the engine is connected to the sun gear and the pinion carrier is splined to the output shaft of the transmission. Then, if the sun gear and the ring gear are locked together and driven through the gearset, the entire assembly will rotate as a unit. The output shaft will rotate at the same speed as the engine crankshaft (high gear ratio of 1.0:1).

Reduction means operating at a reduced gear ratio (low gear). Usually, in this forward position, an applied band holds the ring gear from turning. The pinions, in turn, are forced to rotate on their pins and travel around inside the ring gear. In this action, the pinions turn in the opposite direction of rotation of the sun gear, while the pinion carrier turns in the same direction as the sun gear, but at

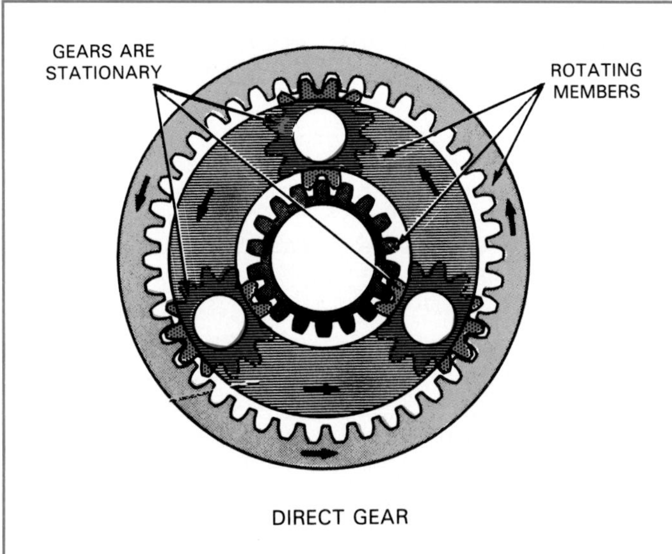

Figure 37-23. This planetary gearset is shown in direct drive. The entire gearset is locked together and rotates as a unit. (Chrysler)

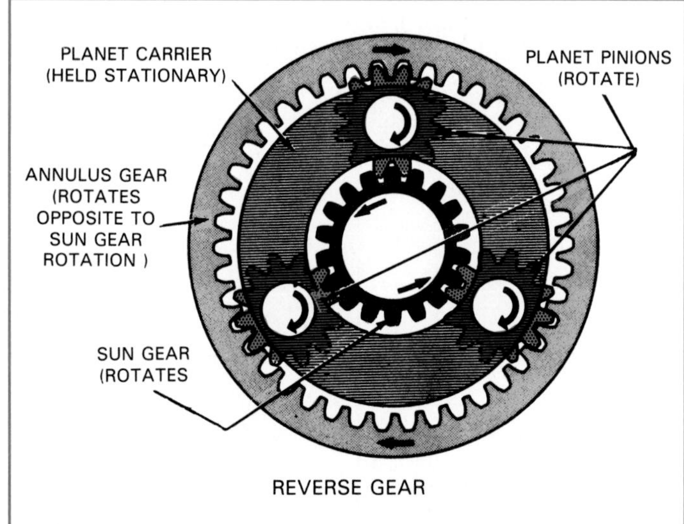

Figure 37-24. Planetary gearset is pictured in reverse. The planet carrier is stationary and the pinions rotate, driving the annulus gear in the opposite direction. (Chrysler)

reduced speed. Since the pinion carrier is connected to the output shaft of the transmission, the output shaft will turn more slowly than the engine crankshaft.

Reverse operation requires that the pinion carrier is held stationary. Then, when torque is applied to the sun gear, the pinions rotate on their pins, causing the ring gear to rotate in the opposite direction. See Figure 37-24. In ***neutral,*** no clutches or bands are applied.

Automatic Transmission Operation

An example of how a three-speed automatic transmission operates will be given in the following section. A careful reading of the descriptive copy and a follow-up study of the power flow arrows in the accompanying illustrations will provide you with a basic understanding of automatic transmission operation.

To understand automatic transmission operation, consider the operation of clutches, bands, and planetary gears in a typical three-speed automatic transmission, Figure 37-25. This transmission has two multiple-disc clutches, two bands and servos, an overrunning clutch, and two planetary gearsets. The sun gear is interconnected to the multiple-disc clutches through a driving shell that is splined to the sun gear and front clutch retainer. See Figure 37-25.

In *neutral* and *park* positions, with the engine running, power flow is from the input shaft to the front clutch hub and rear clutch retainer, Figure 37-26. Since none of the clutches or bands are applied, power flow stops at the rear clutch retainer. The rear clutch plates (splined to the rear clutch retainer) rotate with the retainer at engine speed. The rear clutch discs (splined to front annulus gear) and the output shaft remain stationary.

In *drive-first gear,* Figure 37-27, the rear clutch is applied and the overrunning clutch "holds" the rear planetary gear carrier (pinion carrier). When shifted into drive, the rear clutch retainer, front annulus gear, and front planetary gears rotate at engine speed.

Both front and rear planetary gears are in mesh with the sun gear. See Figure 37-27. The sun gear has a reverse helix that causes it to revolve opposite engine rotation when turned by the front planetary gears. However, the

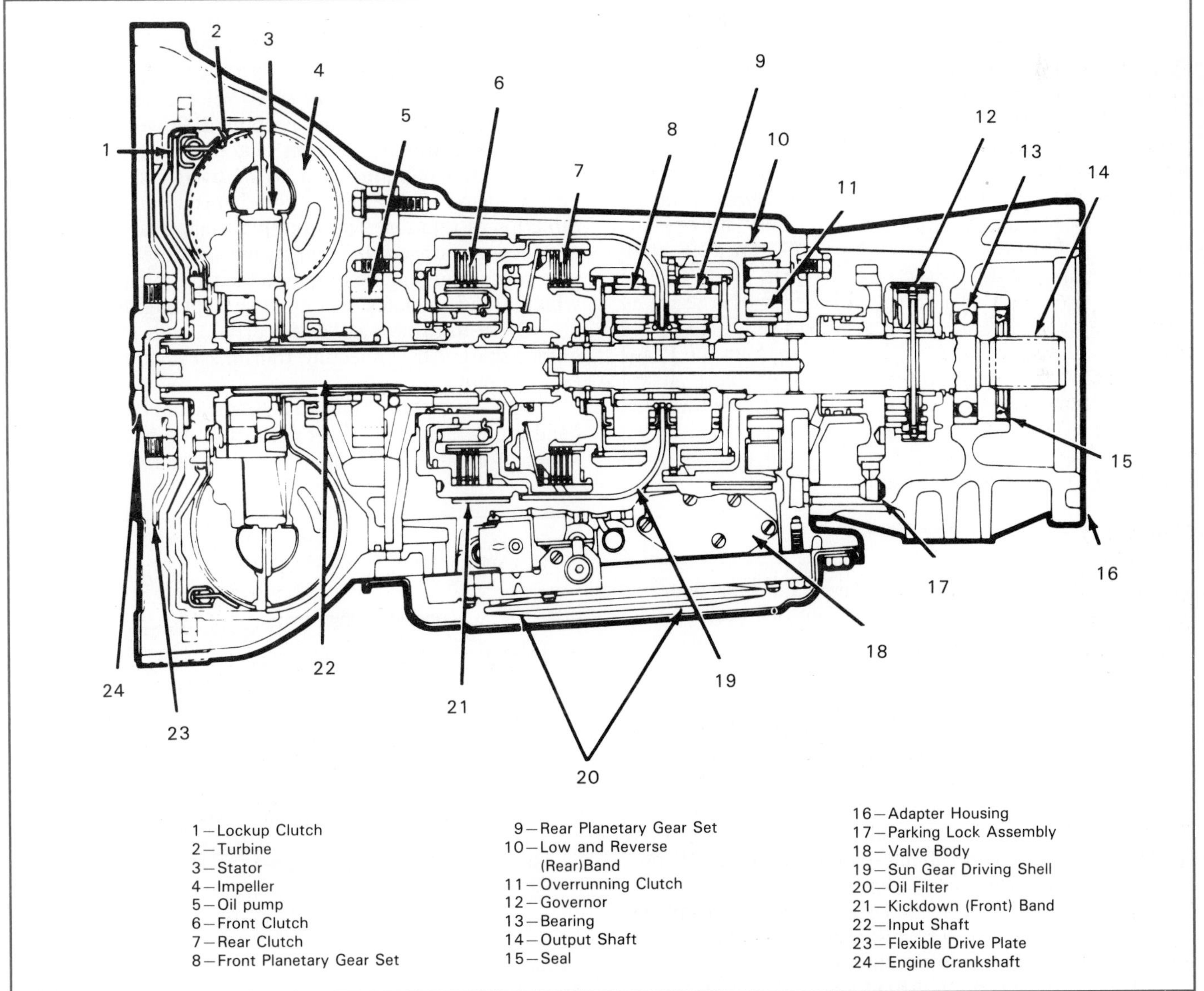

Figure 37-25. Major components and assemblies are called out in this sectional view of a typical three-speed automatic transmission. (Chrysler)

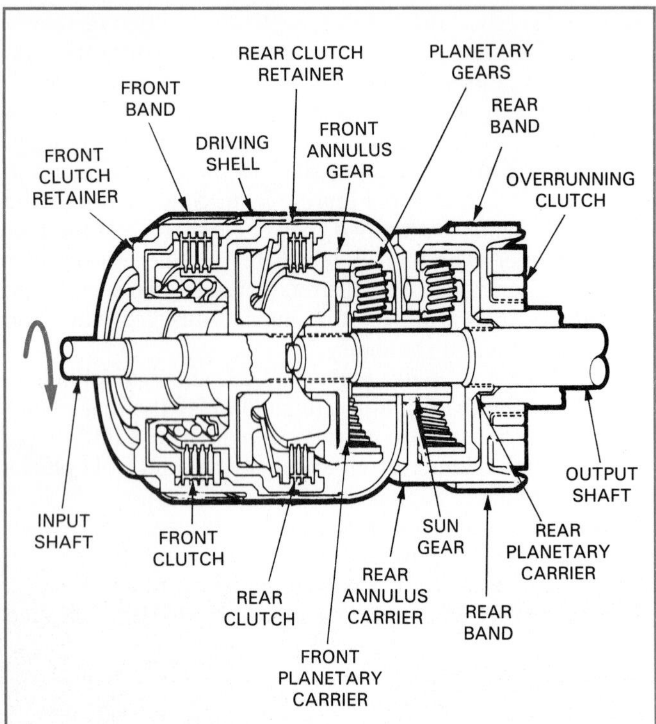

Figure 37-26. With the clutch, band, and gear system in neutral, the input shaft turns and the output shaft remains stationary. (Chrysler)

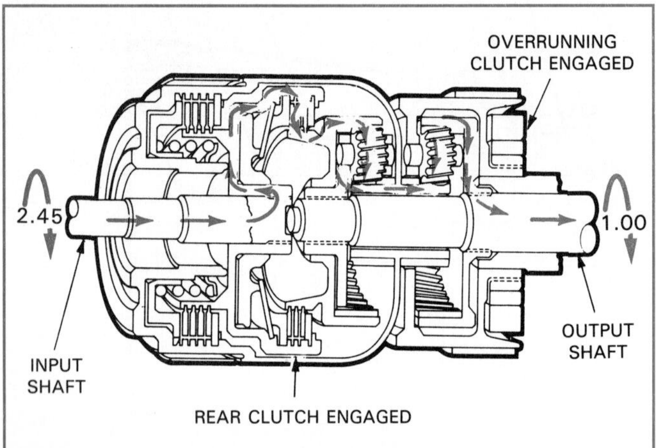

Figure 37-27. Arrows trace power flow in drive-first gear from the input shaft to the output shaft. Note the gear reduction of 2.45:1.0 through the rear planetary annulus gear to the output shaft. (Chrysler)

design of the helix also causes it to revolve the rear planetary gears in the same direction as engine rotation.

Power flow, then, is through the rear clutch and front annulus gear, into the front planetary gears, and to the rear planetary gears by way of the counter-rotating sun gear. At this point, the rear overrunning clutch locks up and prevents the rear planetary carrier and low/reverse drum from turning opposite to engine rotation. With the carrier and drum held stationary, power flow is transferred through the rear annulus gear to the output shaft of the transmission.

Power flow in *manual-first gear* is the same as in drive-first except that, in manual-first, the rear band is applied to provide for engine braking.

In *drive-second gear,* Figure 37-28, the rear clutch is still applied from drive-first and the overrunning clutch freewheels. The front servo applies the front band in response to increased speed and hydraulic pressure signals from the governor and throttle linkage. This completes the 1-2 upshift.

The applied front band keeps the front clutch retainer from turning, which prevents the driving shell and sun gear from turning. The applied rear clutch permits power flow through the rear clutch retainer to the front annulus gear, turning it at engine speed and in the same direction of rotation.

Since the sun gear is stationary, front annulus gear rotation causes the front planetary gears and carrier to turn in the direction of engine rotation, but at reduced speed. Power flow is then transferred directly to the output shaft of the transmission. See Figure 37-28.

In drive-second gear, the rear planetary gears are "idling" and the low/reverse drum is freewheeling with the overrunning clutch.

In *manual-second gear,* the transmission components are used in the same sequence and with the same response as in drive-second, except that there is no 2-3 shift. This transmission only performs a 1-2 shift.

In *drive-third gear,* Figure 37-29, the rear clutch is still applied from drive-second. When car speed reaches the 2-3 upshift range, the front servo releases the front band and the front clutch retainer is applied. Power flow is then transmitted through the front clutch retainer, rear clutch retainer, front annulus gear, rear driving shell, and sun gear, causing it to turn at engine speed and in the same direction of rotation. The front planetary gears are stationary (do not turn on their pins), but are forced by the sun gear to transmit engine torque to the front planetary carrier which, in turn, rotates the output shaft at engine speed.

Drive-third gear is "direct drive" from input shaft to output shaft. All connecting transmission components rotate as a unit.

In *reverse gear,* Figure 37-30, the front clutch and rear band are applied. Power flow is from the front clutch retainer to the driving shell, which is locked to the retainer

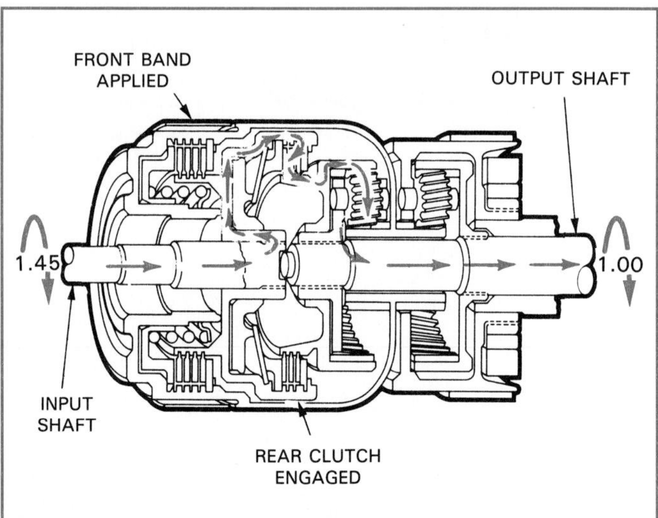

Figure 37-28. Power flow in drive-second results in 1.45:1.0 gear reduction through the front planetary pinions and the pinion carrier to the output shaft. (Chrysler)

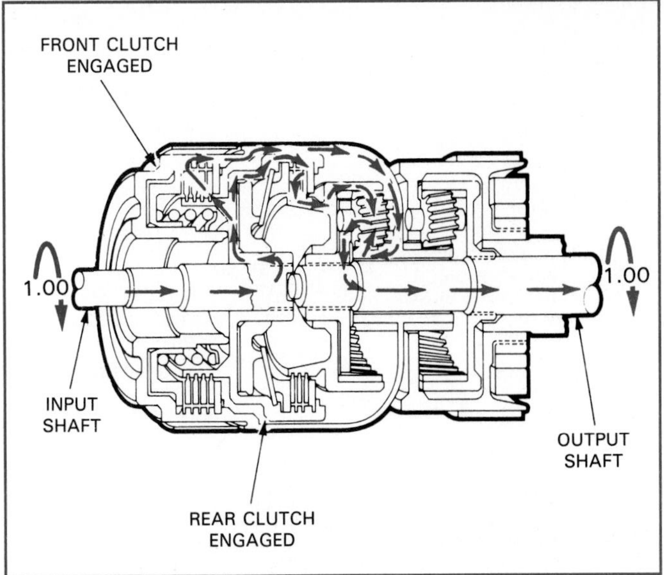

Figure 37-29. Power flow in drive-third is through the locked front planetary gearset to the rear output shaft to produce a direct drive or a 1:1 gear ratio. (Chrysler)

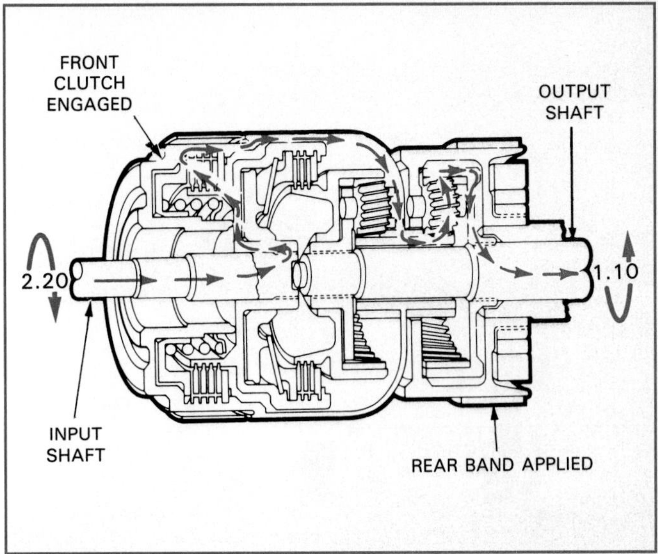

Figure 37-30. Power flow in reverse is through the rear planetary pinions and annulus gear to the output shaft in a direction opposite to engine rotation. Note the gear reduction of 2.2:1 . (Chrysler)

and turns the sun gear in the direction of engine rotation. The sun gear, in turn, rotates the planet pinions in a direction opposite to engine rotation.

The rear planetary pinion carrier is "held" by the rear band. This permits power flow from the sun gear through the rear planetary pinions to the rear annulus gear and to the output shaft of the transmission. The front planetary gears are "idling" during reverse operation.

Other Automatic Transmissions

Other three-speed and four-speed automatic transmissions are shown in Figures 37-31 to 37-35. Study the parts and assemblies that make up the units and try to visualize power flow to the output shaft. Note, too, that the numbers called out in Figures 37-34 and 37-35 are utilized in the Review Questions.

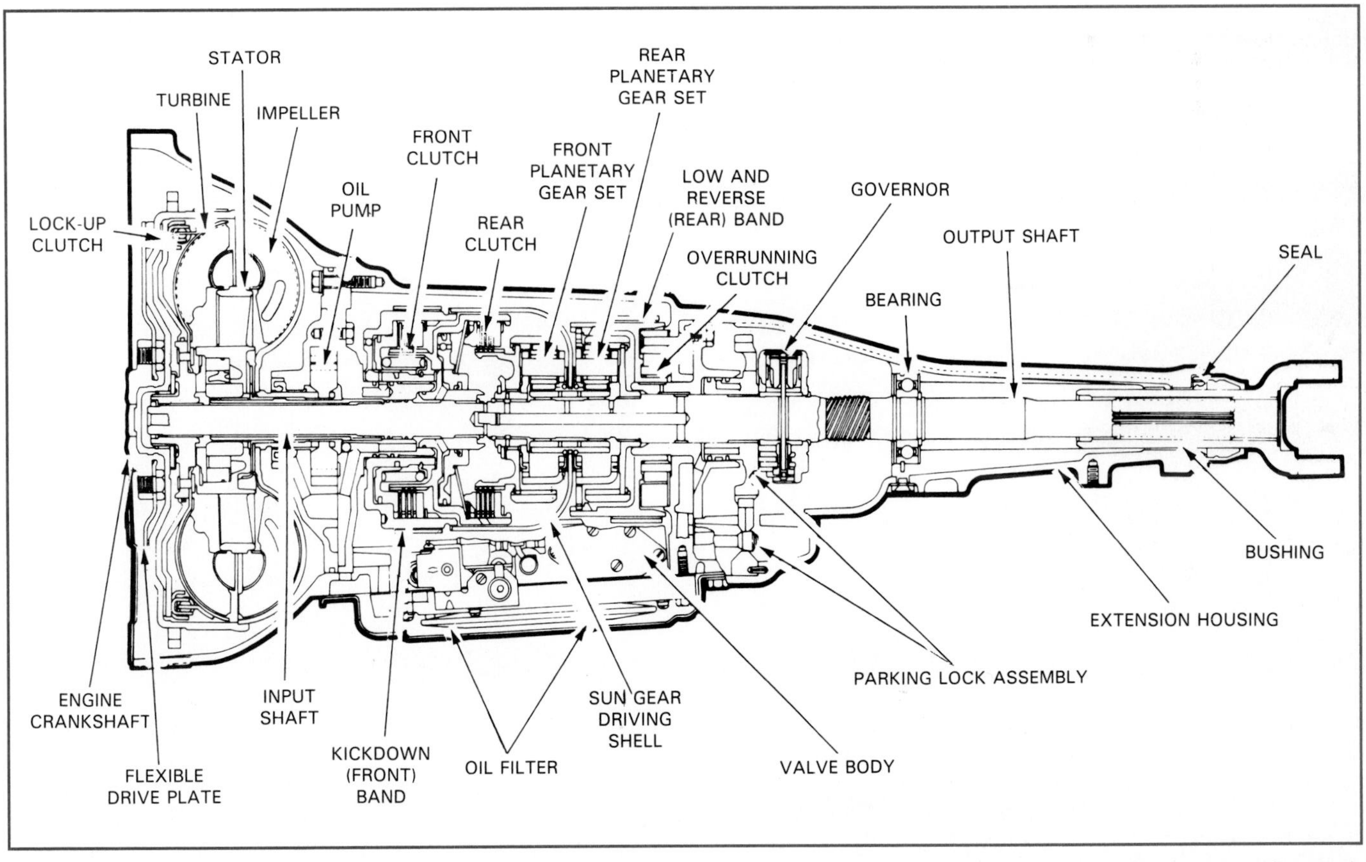

Figure 37-31. This three-speed automatic transmission is designed for use in vehicles equipped with four-cylinder engines. (Chrysler)

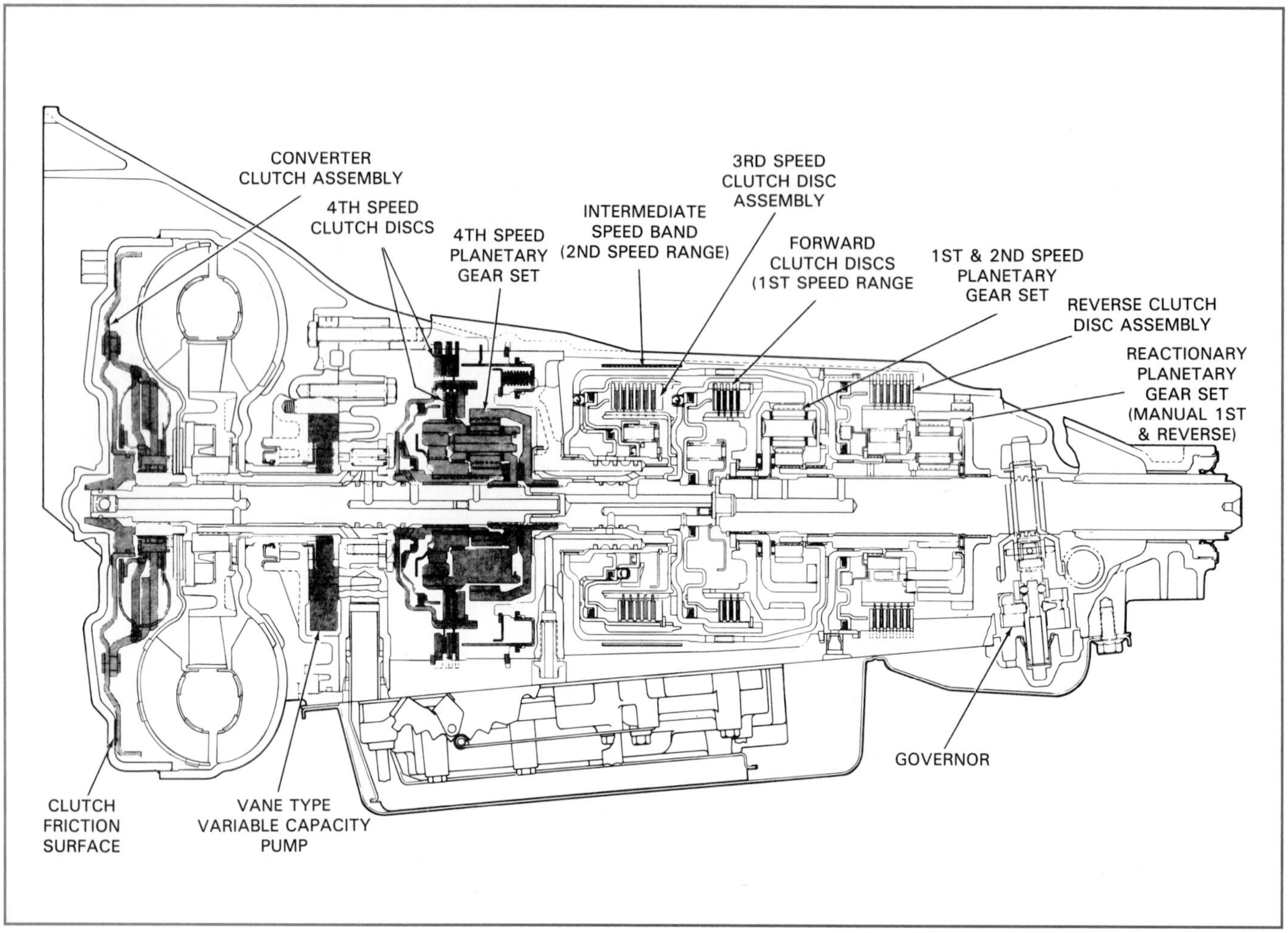

CONVERTER CLUTCH ASSEMBLY
4TH SPEED CLUTCH DISCS
4TH SPEED PLANETARY GEAR SET
INTERMEDIATE SPEED BAND (2ND SPEED RANGE)
3RD SPEED CLUTCH DISC ASSEMBLY
FORWARD CLUTCH DISCS (1ST SPEED RANGE
1ST & 2ND SPEED PLANETARY GEAR SET
REVERSE CLUTCH DISC ASSEMBLY
REACTIONARY PLANETARY GEAR SET (MANUAL 1ST & REVERSE)
GOVERNOR
CLUTCH FRICTION SURFACE
VANE TYPE VARIABLE CAPACITY PUMP

Figure 37-32. Fully automatic overdrive transmission with three-element torque converter and a computer controlled converter clutch. Note the fourth speed clutch and the planetary gearset in the shaded area. (Chevrolet)

Figure 37-33. This four-speed automatic overdrive transmission features an electronically controlled torque converter clutch. (Ford)

Figure 37-34. This four-speed automatic overdrive transmission is specifically designed to take advantage of 2.4 liter turbo diesel engine characteristics. It has a fourth gear ratio of 0.72:1. Can you identify the various clutch assemblies by the number? See Review Questions. (Ford)

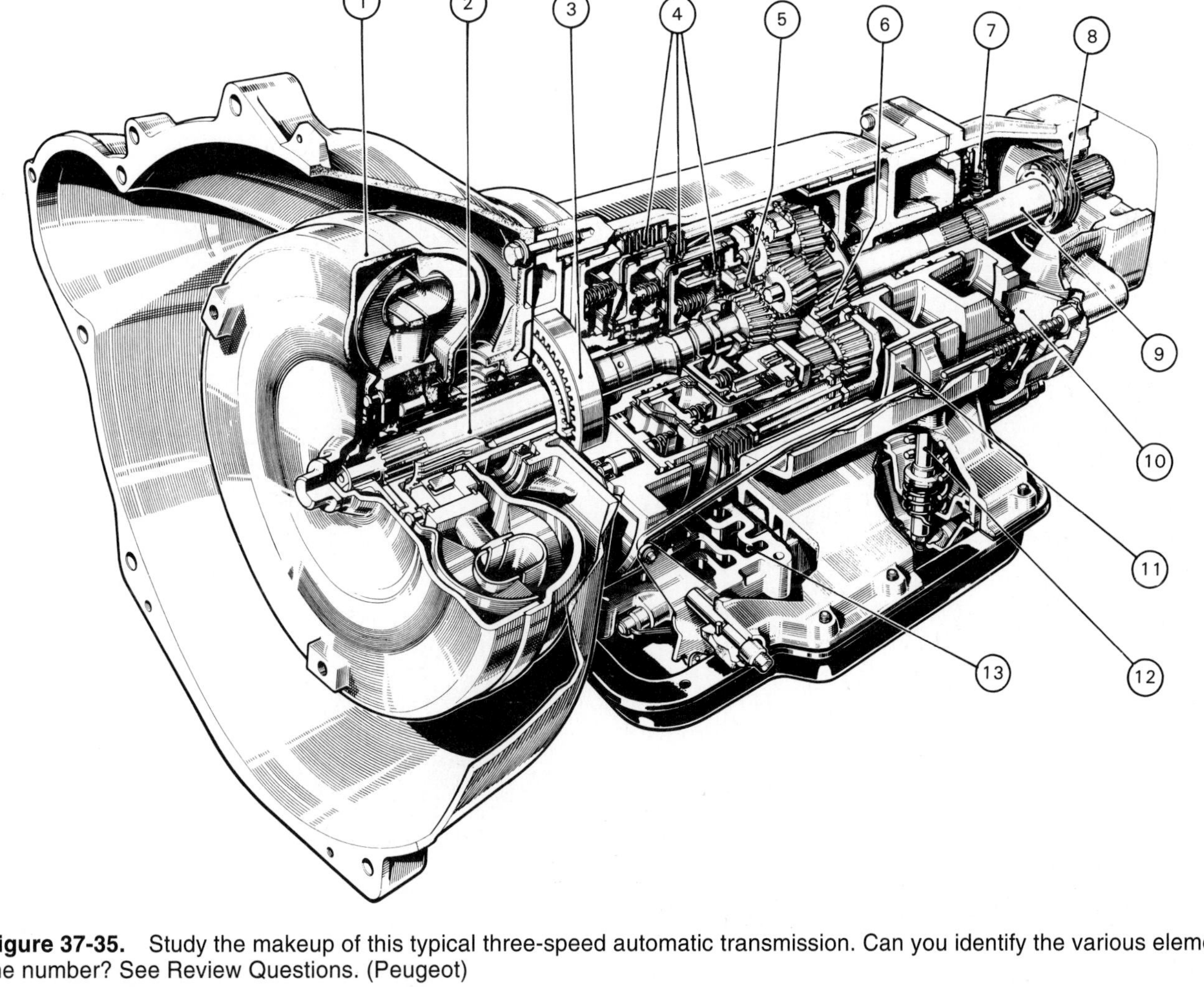

Figure 37-35. Study the makeup of this typical three-speed automatic transmission. Can you identify the various elements by the number? See Review Questions. (Peugeot)

Electronic Transmission Control

In many late-model cars, the transmission is controlled electronically. In ***electronically controlled transmissions,*** sensors, an electronic control unit (ECU), and solenoids are used to control torque convertor lockup and shift points, Figure 37-36. The sensors monitor various operating conditions, such as throttle position, engine load, and engine speed, and send signals representing these conditions to the ECU. The ECU processes these signals and then sends output signals to the solenoids. As the solenoids are turned on and off, they open and close fluid passages to control the transmission. Electronically controlled transmissions operate more efficiently than conventional transmissions, improving vehicle performance, smoothing shifts, and increasing fuel economy. See Figure 37-37.

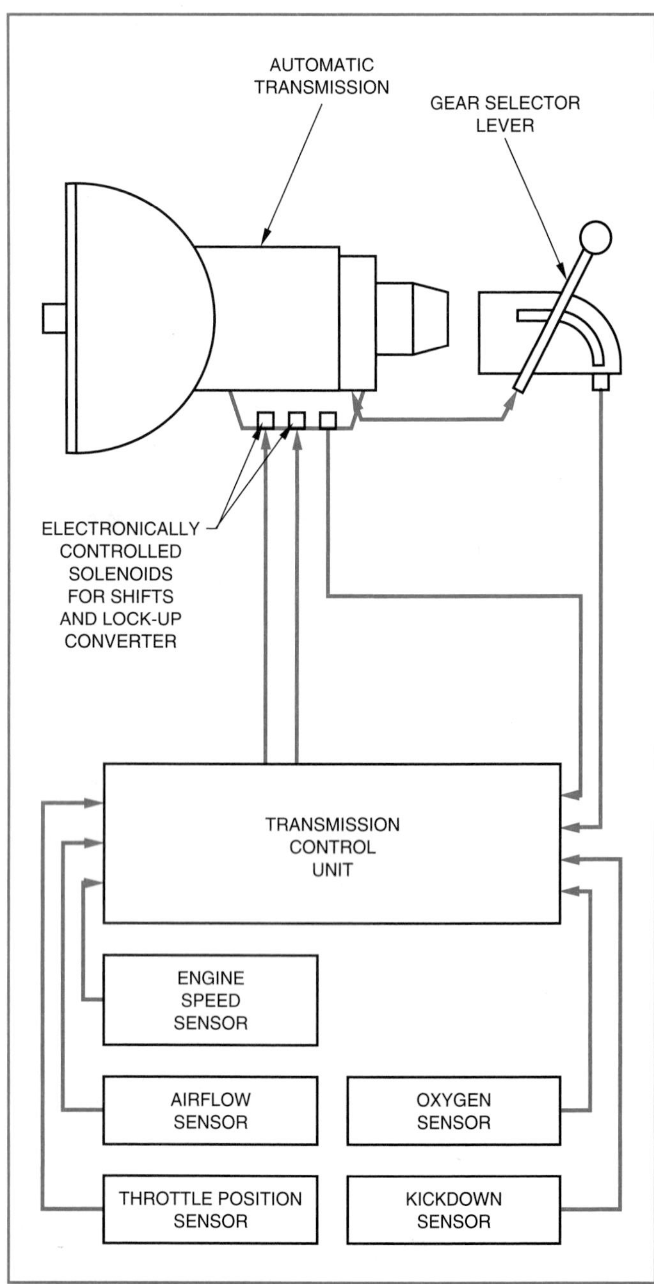

Figure 37-36. Schematic of an electronic transmission control system. Note the various sensors that send input signals to the transmission control unit.

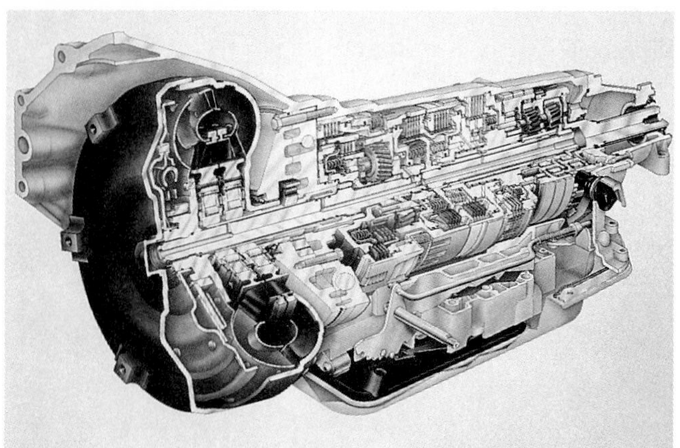

Figure 37-37. Cutaway of an electronically controlled four-speed transmission. (Oldsmobile)

Continuously Variable Transmissions

Continuously variable transmissions (CVT) have been under development for many years. Now these compact, "stepless" transmissions are being installed in motor scooters, Figure 37-38, commuter cars of up to one-liter engine displacement, Figure 37-39, and in a subcompact, front-wheel drive foreign car with transverse engine.

Industrial use of CVTs is broadening, too. The design problems of mechanical, adjustable-speed industrial drive systems are similar to those of the automotive CVTs. High-power/density rubber belts used in automotive CVT development are being adapted to industrial use. See Figure 37-40.

The CVT is called "stepless" because it allows almost unlimited ratio changes between engine and final drive. The advantage of a CVT is that it permits the engine to run at near-constant speed, within its most fuel-efficient rpm range, regardless of load or driver's demands.

Figure 37-38. With the motor scooter a on a test stand, its continuously variable transmission (CVT) is under evaluation for shifting characteristics and load-handling capability. (Dayco Corp.)

Figure 37-39. This CVT setup consists of a high-power/density rubber belt, a hydraulically operated driving sheave (upper right), and a mechanical torque-sensing driven sheave, with microprocessor control of sheave actuation based on driver demand, road load, and engine state. (Dayco Corp.)

Figure 37-40. An industrial CVT belt developed from automotive CVT belt technology is tested on a dynamometer. (Dayco Corp.)

In the subcompact, foreign car application mentioned earlier, two multiple-disc wet clutches take up engine torque and transmit it to a planetary gearset and transmission input shaft for forward and reverse operation. Key elements are a primary pulley, a steel drive belt, and an output pulley. A hydraulic unit controls all operations, including compression of the steel belt "blocks" in response to variations in drive torque and ratio.

The CVT transmission operates by varying the working diameters of two pulleys. See Figure 37-41. The pulleys

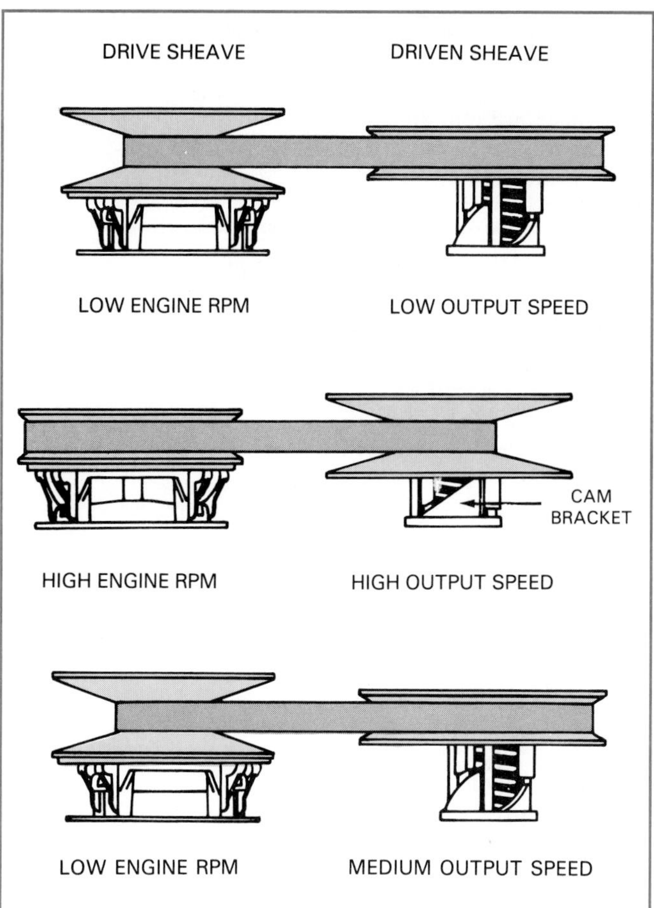

Figure 37-41. The principle of operation of a continuously variable transmission is shown in these four pulley sheave arrangements. Note that spacing of sheaves and working diameter of pulleys determines output ratio and speed.

have V-shaped grooves in which the steel belt rides. The continuous range of transmission ratio changes is effected by changing the belt position in the groove between the pulley sheaves. The input gearset drives the primary pulley, which is linked to the secondary pulley and output gear by the steel drive belt.

The pulleys each have a fixed cone and a movable cone, with a hydraulic cylinder built in. Actuation of the hydraulic cylinders causes the pulleys to move axially and change the space between the fixed and movable cones. This, in turn, creates a "pinching" action on the steel belt anywhere along the pulley grooves. Basically, the deeper the belt rides in the groove, the smaller the working diameter of the pulleys.

During startup, the primary pulley is automatically set for maximum spacing and minimum working diameter. Conversely, the secondary pulley is set for minimum spacing and maximum diameter, which gives the equivalent of a very low gear ratio. Spacing of the two pulleys changes in reverse proportion as the car speed increases, giving continuous shifts in ratio. Since the pulleys shift V-groove spacing in unison, the steel belt loop is always taut.

The variations in cone spacing–and the resulting variations in working diameters of the pulleys–is controlled automatically by a system of hydraulic valves. These valves are regulated by input signals that register throttle position, engine speed, and torque demand.

In operation, the CVT generally is slower to respond to engine torque than a conventional automatic transmission or transaxle. However, its makers claim that it has better acceleration than the conventional units after 25 mph, thanks to its smooth transition to the most suitable ratio for the given need.

Chapter 37–Review Questions

Write your answers on a separate sheet of paper. Do not write in this book.

1. What purpose does a fluid coupling accomplish in an automatic transmission?
   (A) Serves as hydraulic clutch.
   (B) Multiplies engine torque.
   (C) Builds up hydraulic pressure to operate valves.
   (D) Effects gear changes in transmission.
2. Which of these factors is used to control automatic transmission operation?
   (A) Ignition timing.
   (B) Engine speed.
   (C) Engine compression.
   (D) Engine temperature.
3. Which of these factors is *not* used to control automatic transmission operation?
   (A) Shift lever.
   (B) Throttle rod linkage.
   (C) Manifold vacuum.
   (D) Ignition timing.
4. What is the difference between a fluid coupling and a torque converter?
5. What are the three major rotating elements in most torque converters?
6. Torque multiplication in a torque converter is greater at what speed?
   (A) Start-up stall.
   (B) Low speed.
   (C) Cruising speed.
   (D) High speed.
7. Which element creates reaction torque in a torque converter?
   (A) Impeller.
   (B) Turbine.
   (C) Stator.
   (D) Converter clutch.
8. What is the purpose of a torque converter clutch?
9. What is the primary function of automatic transmission clutches and bands?
   (A) Smooth transmission shifts.
   (B) Transmit engine torque through planetary gears.
   (C) Provide various gear ratios selected by driver.
   (D) Engages and disengages torque converter from engine.
10. Name three principal elements of a planetary gearset.
11. What is the primary function of a planetary gearset in an automatic transmission?
   (A) Connects engine to automatic transmission.
   (B) Cushions the effect of gear changes in transmission.
   (C) Provides suitable gear ratios for efficient operation.
   (D) Engages and disengages the torque converter.
12. Servos apply and release bands that control the operation of the elements of a planetary gearset. True or False?
13. An accumulator permits smooth _____ and _____ engagements.
14. Can more than one multiple-disc clutch be used in an automatic transmission? Yes or No?
15. What is the purpose of a manual valve in an automatic transmission?
16. The output of the oil pump is controlled by a _____ valve.
17. In a planetary gearset, the gears are in mesh at all times. True or False?

In the following seven questions, name the various clutches pointed out in Figure 37-34.

18. 1. ________________________.
19. 2. ________________________.
20. 3. ________________________.
21. 4. ________________________.
22. 5. ________________________.
23. 6. ________________________.
24. 7. ________________________.

To answer the following 13 questions, match each numbered assembly in Figure 37-35 with identifying letter given alongside its correct name.

25.	1. _____.	(A) Multiple-disc clutches
26.	2. _____.	(B) Output shaft
27.	3. _____.	(C) Speedometer drive gear
28.	4. _____.	(D) Planetary gearset
29.	5. _____.	(E) Governor
30.	6. _____.	(F) Servo
31.	7. _____.	(G) Oil pump
32.	8. _____.	(H) Overrunning clutch
33.	9. _____.	(I) Input shaft
34.	10. _____.	(J) Band
35.	11. _____.	(K) Torque converter
36.	12. _____.	(L) Control valve body
37.	13. _____.	(M) Parking pawl

38. Electronically controlled transmissions use sensors, an electronic control unit (ECU), and solenoids to control _____ _____ and _____ _____ lockup.
39. Electronic transmission control helps:
   (A) improve performance.
   (B) improve fuel economy.
   (C) smooth shifts.
   (D) All of the above.
40. The CVT transmission changes the ratio between the engine and the final drive by _____ the working diameters of two pulleys.

Chapter 38
Automatic Transmission Service

After studying this chapter, you will be able to:

- ❍ Name maintenance checks, adjustments, and services that will keep automatic transmissions in satisfactory operating condition.
- ❍ Demonstrate how to check level and condition of the automatic transmission fluid (ATF).
- ❍ Determine by inspection where an automatic transmission is leaking ATF.
- ❍ Change ATF and replace the filter.
- ❍ Explain how to adjust automatic transmission bands.
- ❍ Describe throttle linkage and gearshift linkage adjustments.
- ❍ Explain road testing, hydraulic pressure and air pressure testing, and stall testing procedures.

Automatic Transmission Maintenance and Service

Automatic transmissions have been engineered into highly desirable, highly reliable mechanisms for transmitting engine torque to the driveshaft of rear-wheel drive vehicles. See Figure 38-1. They also have been very successfully incorporated into automatic transaxles for front-wheel drive vehicles, Figure 38-2. A ***transaxle*** is a power transmission device that combines the transmission and differential assemblies in a single housing.

That automatic transmissions are desirable is proven by the fact that over 85 percent of new car buyers choose "automatic" over "manual." That automatic transmissions are reliable is evidenced by the typical car owner's lack of

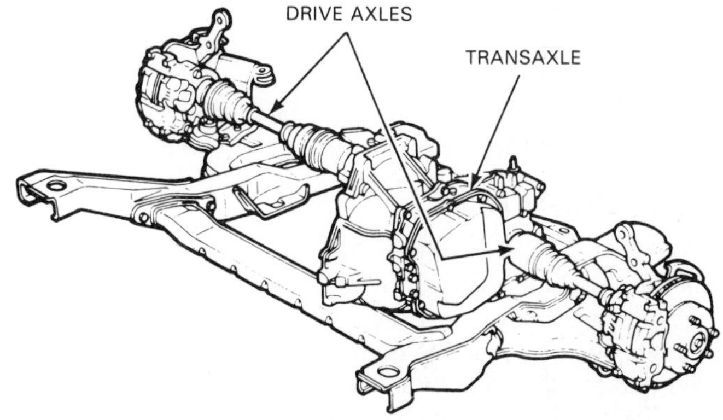

Figure 38-2. A front-wheel drive vehicle transmits engine power to front wheels by way of an automatic transaxle and two drive axles. (Buick)

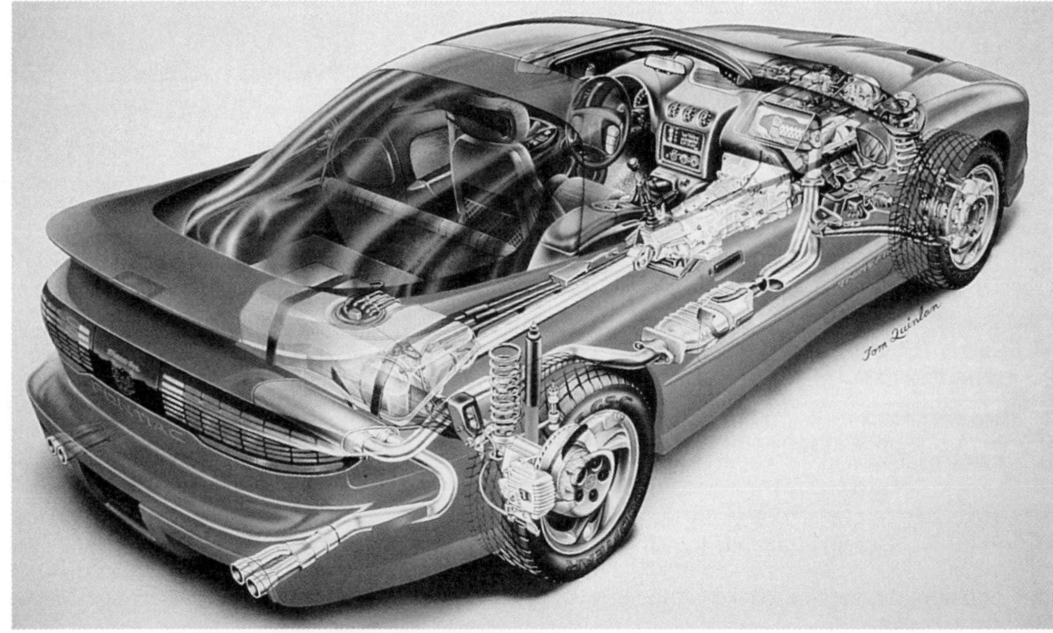

Figure 38-1. Phantom view of a rear-wheel drive vehicle reveals the automatic transmission at the front end of the drive train. (Chevrolet)

concern for transmission maintenance. It takes a very sizable oil slick on the garage floor or pronounced slippage in direct drive to cause the car owner to seek out a service technician for help. By then, it usually is too late for maintenance, and possibly too late for repair.

While an automatic transmission requires little maintenance, that "little" amount is vital to its continued trouble-free operation. Basically, the following checks, adjustments, and services will keep the automatic transmission in satisfactory operating condition, possibly for the life of the vehicle barring driver abuse:

1. Regularly check the automatic transmission fluid level. See Figure 38-3.
2. Check the condition of the ATF on the dipstick.
3. Inspect the transmission housings, oil pan, and cooler lines for fluid leakage.
4. Check the transmission mount for possible separation of rubber from the metal plate.
5. Make periodic ATF changes, Figure 38-4.
6. Check the residue in the bottom of the transmission oil pan.
7. Replace the filter or clean the fine mesh wire screen.
8. Adjust the bands on transmissions that require it.
9. Refill the transmission, using only the manufacturer's recommended ATF or the equivalent.
10. If necessary, adjust the engine curb idle speed to specified rpm.
11. Check the gearshift linkage adjustment.
12. Check the throttle or TV linkage or cable adjustment.

Check ATF Level

The car manufacturers recommend regular checks of the automatic transmission fluid level. A fairly common recommendation is to check the ATF level at each oil change. A good practice is to check the ATF level whenever making any underhood inspection.

To check the automatic transmission fluid level:

1. Drive the car or run the engine until the transmission fluid is at the normal operating temperature (about 175-200°F or 80-88°C).
2. Park the car on a level surface.
3. Shift the transmission into neutral and apply the parking brake.
4. Operate the engine at curb idle speed.
5. Move the transmission selector lever through all the gear ranges, pausing momentarily at each detent to allow complete circulation of the fluid through the valves and passages. Return the shift lever to neutral.
6. Wipe the dirt from the transmission fluid filler cap and tube, then remove the dipstick (usually located at extreme right rear or engine compartment).
7. Wipe the dipstick clean, and then reinsert it in the filler tube until fully seated.
8. Remove the dipstick and check the fluid level reading. Fluid level should be between the add mark and the full mark. See Figure 38-3.
9. If the fluid appears to be in good condition, but the level is low, add the manufacturer's specified ATF through the filler tube to bring the level to the full mark on the dipstick. Caution: Do not overfill. Overfilling can result in fluid loss, foaming, or erratic shifting.

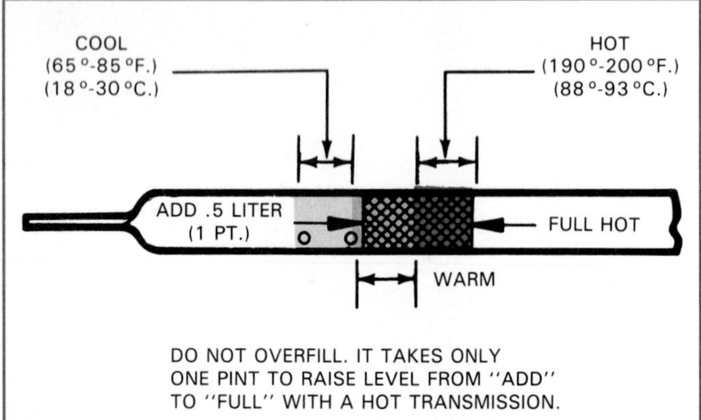

Figure 38-3. Typical automatic transmission dipstick markings include the add line and the full hot line. Note the difference hot temperature makes in the level of fluid on the dipstick. (Oldsmobile)

Check ATF Condition

When making the fluid level check, always inspect the fluid adhering to the dipstick for evidence of the condition of the fluid. Check the color of the fluid. It should be bright cherry red (transmissions using DEXRON-II) or dark red (transmissions using Type F fluid). Note: Some ATF contains a detergent which may have a darkening effect.

Fluid that is a deep reddish brown could be contaminated. Very dark brown or black fluid carrying a burnt odor indicates that the transmission has overheated because of slipping bands and clutches. Fluid that is milky pink is contaminated by engine coolant, usually caused by a leak between the radiator and transmission oil cooler.

Figure 38-4. If the car manufacturer recommends periodic ATF changes, the fluid must be drained when hot. This service technician prepares to empty fluid into a portable 15 gal. oil drain. Only specified ATF should be installed. (Lincoln)

Next, wipe the fluid sample from the dipstick with your thumb and index finger and "feel" the condition of the fluid. It should be smooth and slippery with no evidence of solid contaminants. Then, wipe the fluid from your fingers on a clean white cloth or tissue and inspect the oil stain for metal particles or friction material. If one or both of these conditions exist, the transmission may require an overhaul.

Finally, make a careful, closeup inspection of the lower end of the dipstick for signs of varnish buildup or gum deposits. Varnish or gum on the dipstick is a good indication that a similar condition exists within the control valve body. If, in fact, the internal working parts and passages of this assembly are coated with varnish, it could result in sticking valves and consequent erratic and/or delayed upshifts and downshifts. See Figure 38-5.

Gum deposits on internal parts of the transmission are caused by antifreeze contamination of the fluid. The varnish buildup results from high temperatures attacking the ATF and causing severe oxidation of the fluid. The high temperatures could result from underfilling or overfilling the transmission with ATF. Either of these conditions could cause foaming of the fluid which, in turn, could create the high temperatures and resulting varnish formation.

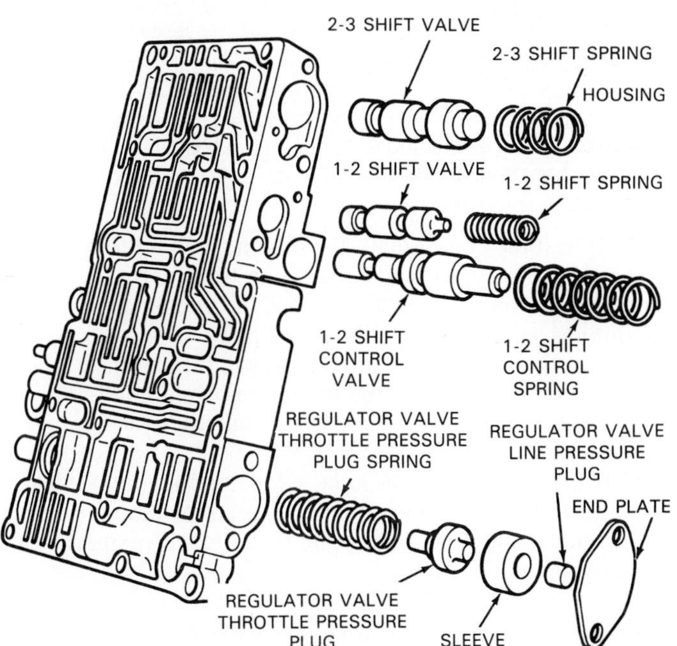

Figure 38-5. Old ATF or fluid that has been overheated will leave deposits of varnish or gum on the dipstick and on the valves in the control valve body. (Chrysler)

Inspect for ATF Leaks

When preparing to check for the source of an automatic transmission fluid leak, place the vehicle on a lift, and start by cleaning the underside of the transmission and torque converter housing cover. If the leak seems to be in the area of the converter, you need to use care in identifying the type of fluid it is. Although it probably is ATF, it could be engine oil leaking past the rear main bearing oil seal or down from the rocker arm cover; or power steering fluid blown back around the converter housing by road draft.

With this in mind, remove the torque converter housing cover. Then, clean the fluid from the top and bottom of the converter housing; from the front of the transmission case; from the rear face of the engine; and from the engine oil pan. Finally, spray some powder on the areas cleaned for inspection.

Then, proceed to carefully look for the source of the automatic transmission fluid leak as follows:

1. Check the transmission case breather vent for clogging. If clogged, clean the vent and recheck.
2. Check the ATF filler tube connection at the transmission case (on some applications). If a leak is evident, remove the tube, replace the O-ring, and reinstall the tube.
3. Examine the perimeter of the oil pan in the gasketed area. If it is leaking ATF, replace the gasket and torque-tighten the pan attaching screws.
4. Check for ATF leakage at the downshift control lever shaft and at the manual lever shaft. Replace the seals if necessary.
5. Check the connection between the transmission case and the extension housing. If a leak is evident, replace the gasket or seal. See Figure 38-6.
6. Inspect the pressure test port plugs for leakage, Figure 38-7. If leaking, remove the plug, coat the threads with sealant, and reinstall the plug.

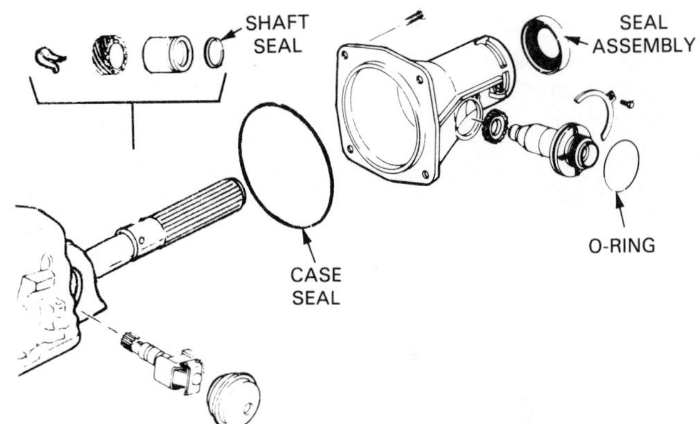

Figure 38-6. Exploded view of an extension housing of a typical automatic transmission helps pinpoint "sealed" areas where ATF leakage may occur.

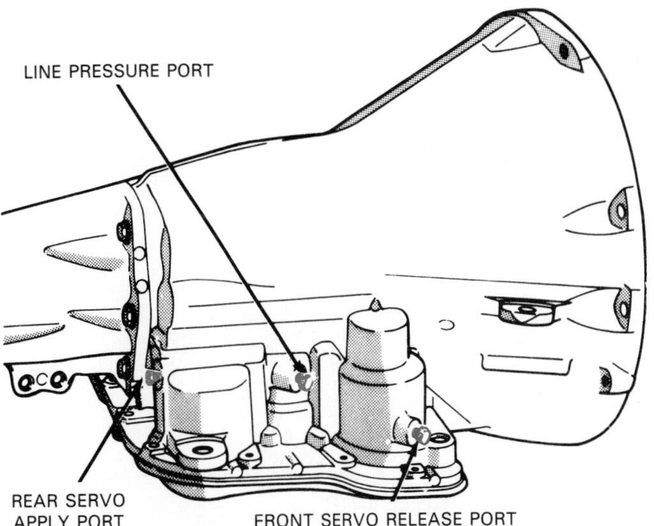

Figure 38-7. If ATF leakage is evident at the pressure test port of the transmission, remove the plug, install sealant on threads, and then reinstall the plug. (Chrysler)

7. Inspect the speedometer cable connection to the transmission. If ATF is leaking, replace the oil seal.
8. Check for an ATF leak at the transmission output shaft seal in the extension housing or adapter housing. Replace the oil seal if necessary.
9. Check the entire length of the ATF lines and the fittings between the transmission and the oil cooler in the radiator for looseness, wear, or damage. See Figure 38-8. Replace the line and/or fittings as required.
10. Operate the engine at 2000 rpm for two minutes, and then check for ATF leakage at the front of the transmission and around the torque converter housing. See Figure 38-9. If the source of leakage is at the oil pump seal, pump body, oil pump-to-case gasket, or oil pump-to-case bolt, repair requires the removal of the transmission.
11. Check the engine coolant in the radiator for contamination by ATF. If contaminated, the oil cooler in the radiator probably is leaking. Remove the radiator for repairs.

Test for Broken Transmission Mount

While the vehicle is on the lift, test the condition of the transmission mount, Figure 38-10. If it is broken or collapsed, replace the mount.

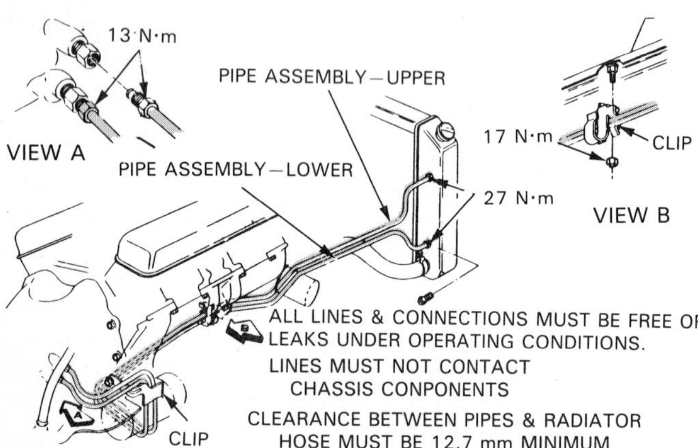

Figure 38-8. Inspect for ATF leakage along the entire length of each oil cooler line and at the fittings at the transmission and the radiator. (Oldsmobile)

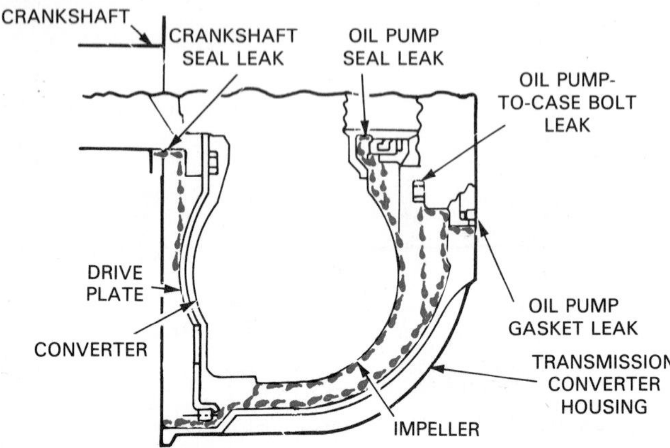

Figure 38-9. This diagram of a torque converter housing pinpoints possible areas where leakage of ATF or engine oil may occur. (Chrysler)

Figure 38-10. A service technician uses a high-lift transmission jack to aid in checking the condition of the transmission mount. Foot-pedal operation relieves the weight of transmission, permitting a closer inspection of the mount for breakage or collapse. (Lincoln)

To test the condition of the mount, push up (or pry up) and pull down on the tailshaft of the transmission. At the same time, observe whether or not the rubber part of the mount has separated from the metal plate.

Continue to push up and pull down. If the transmission moves up but not down, the mount has "bottomed out." It has lost its resiliency and collapsed. In either case, replace the mount.

If the mount appears to be whole and resilient during these tests, watch for movement between the metal plate of the mount and its attaching point (usually a crossmember). If there is any movement, tighten the screws or bolts attaching the mount to the transmission and to the crossmember. Torque specifications for this varies by make and model. Check the manufacturer's service manual for exact torque specifications for the vehicle being serviced.

Changing Automatic Transmission Fluid

Periodic ATF changes are generally recommended by the vehicle manufacturers. Once the pan has been removed and the fluid drained, always remove the filter for cleaning or replacement. Usually, screen type filters can be cleaned and reinstalled. Filters made of paper, fiber, and cloth should be replaced whenever the oil pan is removed. See Figure 38-11.

Warning: ATF can be extremely hot and can cause serious burns. Take necessary precautions when changing transmission fluid.

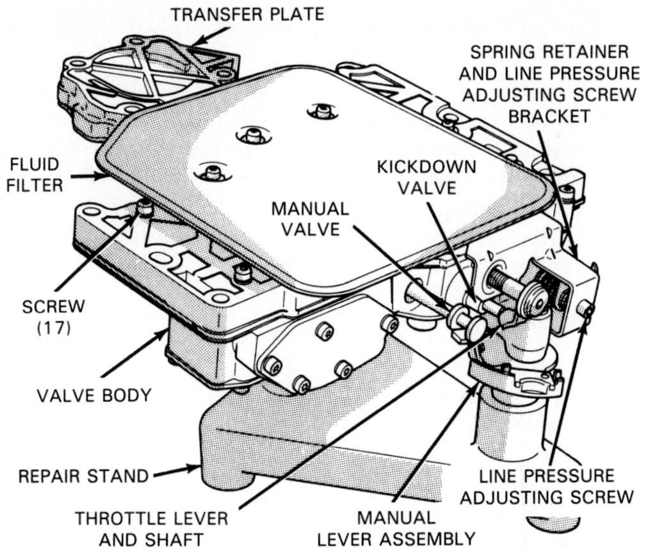

Figure 38-11. Install a new automatic transmission filter whenever the pan is removed. (Chrysler)

A general procedure for draining automatic transmission fluid is as follows:

1. Run the engine to bring the fluid to normal operating temperature of about 175-200°F (80-88°C).
2. Turn off the ignition key and raise the vehicle on a lift. See Figure 38-4.
3. Position the drain drum with a large funnel under the transmission oil pan.
4. Some transmissions can be drained by removing a drain plug or transmission dipstick filler tube, but most require pan removal.
5. Loosen the pan screws in a pattern that lets pan tilt at one corner and slowly drain the fluid.
6. When most of fluid has drained out, remove the screws completely (observing each for varying lengths).
7. Remove the pan and carefully inspect the inside surface and the remaining fluid for metal particles or bits of friction material that signal clutch and band wear.
8. Clean the pan thoroughly, especially gasket flanges. Also clean the mating surfaces on the transmission case.
9. Clean the fine mesh wire screen (if so equipped) in nonflammable solvent. Dry it with compressed air (wiping with a rag may leave lint on screen). If the screen has any holes, replace the screen.
10. Replace the filter (if so equipped), Figure 38-11.
11. Reinstall the pan, using a new gasket, without cement or sealer. Place the longer screws in holes from which they were removed. Torque the attaching screws in a crisscross pattern to the manufacturer's specification.
12. If the fluid was drained by removing a drain plug or dipstick filler tube, reinstall these parts and tighten to the manufacturer's torque specifications.
13. Fill the transmission with the proper type and quantity of ATF shown in the specifications. If you need to flush the transmission oil cooler, add one quart of fluid.
14. Disconnect the cooler return line at transmission. Start the engine and let it idle until about one quart of fluid has been pumped from the cooler return line into a drain pan. Shut off the engine and reconnect the cooler return line. (Note: A more involved back-flushing procedure using mineral spirits is required if considerable foreign matter was discovered in the transmission oil pan.)
15. Start the engine and let it idle. With your foot on the brake pedal, move the gear selector lever to each position, pausing momentarily to allow full circulation of ATF and purging of air from the hydraulic circuits.
16. Return the gear selector lever to the neutral or park position as specified by manufacturer, and add fluid to bring the level to the add mark on the dipstick.
17. Run the engine until the transmission reaches the normal operating temperature, and then adjust the fluid level to the full mark on the dipstick.
18. Inspect the underside of the transmission, torque converter housing, oil cooler lines, and fittings for leaks, as shown in Figure 38-8.

Adjust Bands

A general procedure for automatic transmission band adjustment involves tightening the band adjusting screw to a given torque tightness; backing off the adjusting screw a specific number of turns; and holding the adjusting screw from turning while torque-tightening the locknut.

Tightening the band adjusting screw, in effect, simulates correct band-apply pressure. The backing off operation represents the band servo travel during application. Study the following examples of specific band adjusting procedures.

Front (kickdown) Band–Chrysler

1. Raise the automobile.
2. Locate the front band adjusting screw on the left side of the transmission case above the manual valve and the throttle lever control levers, Figure 38-12.
3. Loosen the band adjusting screw locknut about four or five turns.
4. Check the adjusting screw for freedom of rotation.
5. Tighten the band adjusting screw to 72 in./lb. (8 N·m) torque using a 5/16 in. (8mm) square socket. See caution in Figure 38-13.
6. Back off the adjusting screw three turns. (Check the service manual for adjustment variations from model to model.)

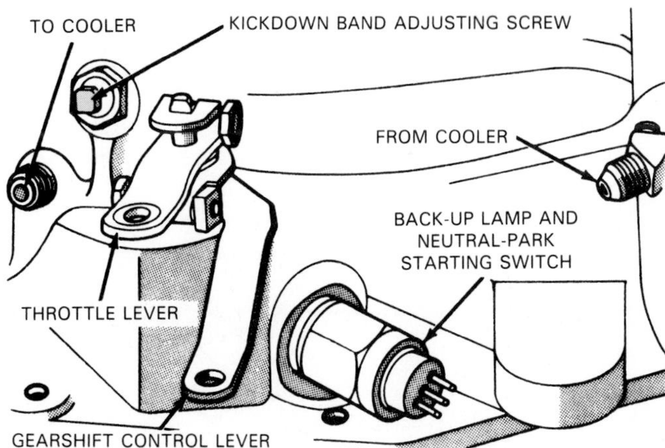

Figure 38-12. On Chrysler automatic transmissions, the kickdown band adjusting screw is located high on the left side of the transmission case. (Chrysler)

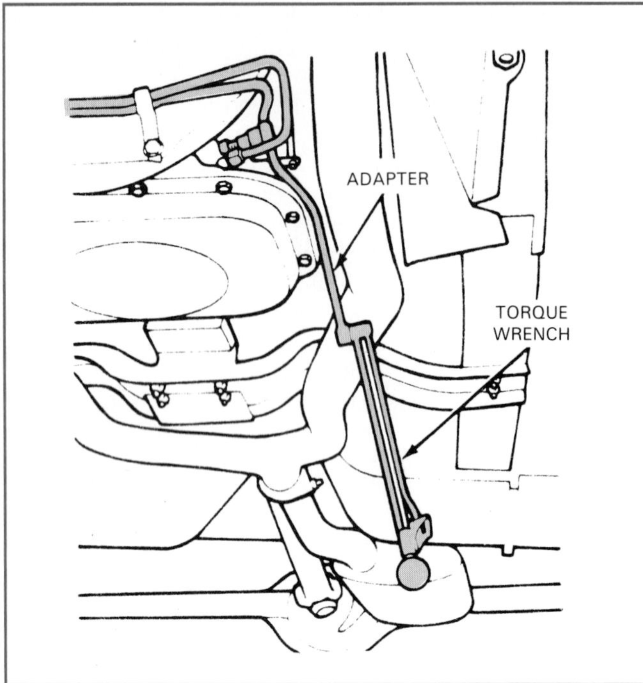

Figure 38-13. Adjusting kickdown band on Chrysler transmissions requires the use of an in./lb. torque wrench and adapter tool. If the adapter tool is not used, torque specification must be doubled. (Chrysler)

7. Hold the adjusting screw from turning and tighten the adjusting screw locknut to 35 ft./lb. (47 N·m).

Rear (low/reverse) Band–Chrysler

1. Loosen the transmission oil pan, drain the ATF, and remove the pan.
2. Remove the band adjusting screw locknut.
3. Tighten the band adjusting screw to 41 in./lb. (5 N·m), using a torque wrench and a 1/4 in. hex socket as shown in Figure 38-14.

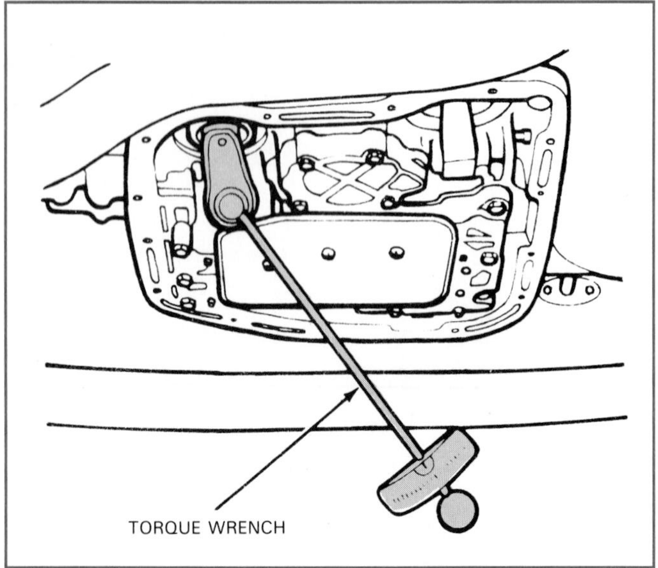

Figure 38-14. Adjusting the rear band on Chrysler transmissions calls for draining of ATF and pan removal for access to the adjusting screw. (Chrysler)

4. Back off the adjusting screw seven turns. (Check shop manual.)
5. Hold the adjusting screw from turning and then tighten locknut to 35 ft./lb. (47 N·m).
6. Install the oil pan and replace the pan gasket. Torque-tighten the attaching bolts to 150 in./lb. (17 N·m).
7. Lower the automobile.
8. Fill the transmission with recommended ATF. (See Changing ATF.)

Intermediate Band–Ford

1. Locate the intermediate band adjusting screw on the left side of the transmission case in front of shift levers.
2. Remove the locknut from the band adjusting screw and discard the locknut, which also serves to seal in fluid.
3. Install a new locknut loosely on the adjusting screw.
4. Tighten the band adjusting screw to 10 ft./lb. (13.5 N·m).
5. Back off the adjusting screw exactly 4 1/4 turns. (Check manufacturer's shop manual.)
6. Hold the adjusting screw from turning and tighten the locknut to 40 ft./lb. (54 N·m).

Low/Reverse Band–Ford

1. Locate the low/reverse band adjusting screw on the right side of the transmission case above the rear pan bolts.
2. Remove the locknut from the adjusting screw and discard the locknut.
3. Install a new locknut loosely on the band adjusting screw.
4. Tighten the adjusting screw to 10 ft./lb. (13.5 N·m).
5. Back off the band adjusting screw exactly three turns. (Check shop manual.)
6. Hold the adjusting screw from turning and tighten the locknut to 40 ft./lb. (54 N·m).

Intermediate Band–GM Turbo Hydra-Matic

Band adjustment on late model Turbo Hydra-Matic transmissions calls for the use of safety glasses and specialty tools. Checking band adjustment on certain GM 200/200 C/200 4R transmissions, for example, requires removal of the intermediate servo, disassembly of the servo, and testing of the length of the band apply pin by means of a dial indicator and a special pin gauge. If adjustment is necessary, a new band apply pin of the correct length is installed.

Adjust Engine Curb Idle Speed

On some engines, it is necessary to adjust the engine ***curb idle speed.*** There are so many different engine idle speed adjusting procedures, reference to specific manufacturer's service manuals is required. Some of the simpler engine curb idle speed adjustments are given in Chapter 23.

Warning: When the engine is operating during warmup and while making tests and adjustments of curb idle speed, do not stand in direct line with the fan. Do not put your hands near the pulleys, belts, or fan. Do not wear loose clothing.

Curb idle speed adjustment has become increasingly complex. Air conditioning, electric cooling fans, throttle modulators, throttle solenoid positioners, dashpots, and emission controls all contribute to the complexity.

To illustrate a typical Ford curb idle speed adjustment on a 4.2 liter engine equipped with a 2150-2 barrel carburetor, study Figure 38-15 as you follow along with this procedure:

1. Place the transmission selector lever in the neutral or park position.
2. Connect a tachometer to the coil negative terminal.
3. Run the engine to the normal operating temperature.
4. Place the A/C-Heat selector in the off position.
5. Place the transmission in the specified position (see manufacturer's service manual).
6. Check curb idle speed. If adjustment is required, adjust the saddle bracket adjusting screw.
7. Place the transmission in neutral or park. Accelerate the engine momentarily. Place the transmission in the specified position and recheck curb idle speed. Readjust if required.
8. Check/adjust the dashpot clearance (see manufacturer's service manual).
9. Remove the tachometer.

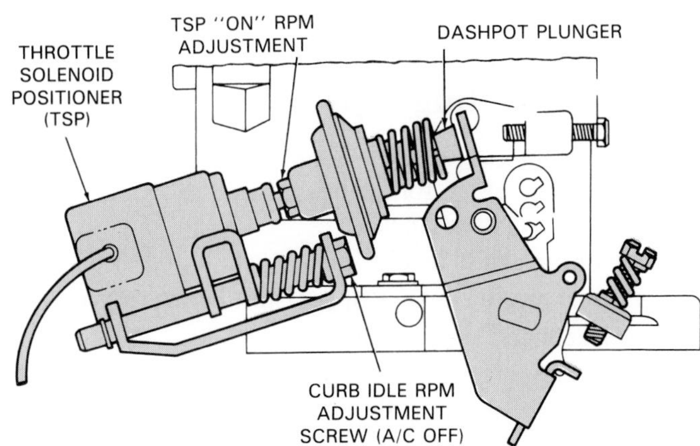

Figure 38-15. The idle speed setting is important to automatic transmission operation. In one of many Ford idle speed setting arrangements, adjustment is made at the saddle bracket adjusting screw. (Ford)

Throttle Linkage Adjustment

The ***throttle linkage adjustment*** is critical to proper operation of the automatic transmission. Correct adjustment of the linkage will position a valve that controls shift speed, shift quality, and part of throttle downshift control.

If the throttle linkage setting is too short, early shifts and slippage between shifts may occur. If the throttle linkage setting is too long, shifts may be late and the part throttle downshifts may be overly sensitive.

The general rule for adjusting throttle linkage is to remove all slack from the linkage. The particular adjusting procedure shown in Figures 38-16 and 38-17 requires the use of an extra spring to remove slack from the linkage:

1. Disconnect throttle control rod spring, which is shown at 1 in Figure 38-17.
2. Connect this spring so that it holds the adjusting link (2) forward against the nylon washer (3).
3. Block the choke valve open and set the throttle off the fast idle cam.
4. Raise the vehicle.

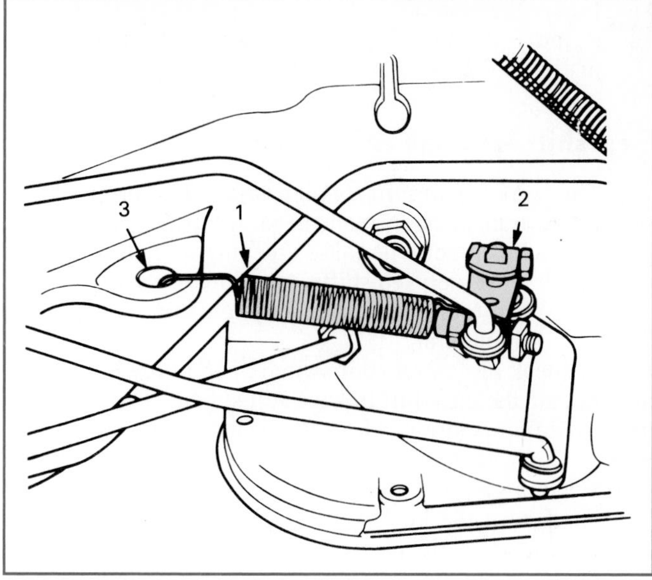

Figure 38-16. The rule of thumb for making throttle linkage adjustments is to remove all slack in the linkage before making the adjustment. In this step of procedure, a spare spring (1) holds the transmission throttle lever (2) forward against the stop. (Chrysler)

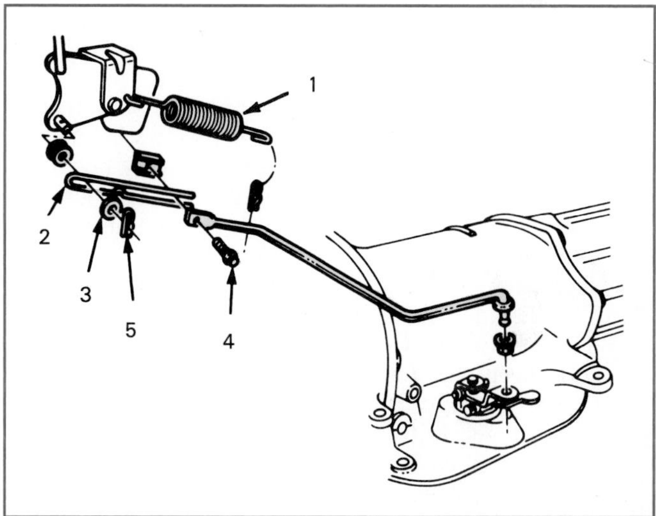

Figure 38-17. Step 2 in preparing for proper adjustment of the throttle linkage is to unhook the throttle control rod spring (1) and connect it to the adjusting link (2) to hold it forward against the nylon washer (3). (Chrysler)

5. Loosen both bolts (4) on the throttle control adjusting link. Note: Do not remove the spring clip (5) and nylon washer (3).
6. Connect a spare throttle return spring, shown in Figure 38-16, so that it holds the transmission throttle lever (2) forward against a stop.
7. Push on the end of the adjusting link, (2) in Figure 38-17, to eliminate lash and pull the clamp assembly so the bolt (4) bottoms in the rear of the slot in the rod.
8. Tighten the forward bolt to clamp the link in place.
9. Pull the throttle control rod to the rear so the bolt in the rod bottoms in the front of the slot. Tighten the rear retaining bolt.
10. Remove the spare return spring from the throttle lever.

11. Lower the vehicle.
12. Remove the throttle control rod spring from the adjusting link and install it on the control rod.

Gearshift Linkage Adjustment

The correct ***gearshift linkage adjustment*** properly positions the transmission manual valve in the valve body. Incorrect adjustment will cause creeping in neutral, excessive clutch wear, delayed shifts, or failure to start in neutral or park. When removing a transmission from a car, place the selector in neutral.

A check of neutral start switch operation will confirm or condemn the gearshift linkage adjustment. Turn the ignition key to on position. Move the gearshift lever slowly to park position. It should click into place in this detent in the shift selector gate.

Next, turn the key to the start position and start the engine. If it starts, the park position setting is correct.

Stop the engine and slowly move the gearshift lever into neutral position. It should click into place in this detent. If the engine starts, the neutral position is correct and the gearshift linkage setting is satisfactory.

However, if the starter failed to operate in park or neutral, or if the gearshift lever had to be moved back and forth to cause the starter to operate, a gearshift linkage adjustment is required.

Study Figure 38-18 as you follow along with this console gearshift linkage adjusting procedure:

1. Make sure the adjustable swivel block is free to turn on the shift rod. Clean or repair parts if necessary.
2. Place the console gearshift lever in the park position.
3. With all linkage assembled and the swivel block lock screw loose, move the shift lever on the transmission to the rear detent position (park).
4. Tighten the swivel block screw to 90 in./lb. (10 N·m).
5. Test the adjustment: Detent positions for neutral and drive should be within the limits of the console gearshift lever gate stops. Key start must occur only when the console lever is in park or neutral.

Another gearshift linkage adjusting procedure is illustrated and described in Figure 38-19. Late-models are generally equipped with a transmission control cable rather than mechanical linkage.

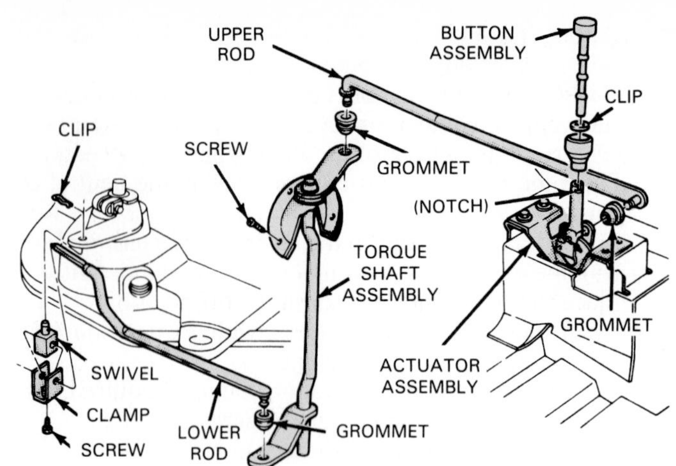

Figure 38-18. Chrysler uses a swivel block in the gearshift linkage. To adjust the linkage, loosen the lockscrew, move the shift lever on the transmission to the park position, and tighten the swivel block. (Chrysler)

Troubleshooting Tips

Automatic transmission problems usually are created by one or more of the following causes:

- Poor engine performance.
- Low or high fluid level.
- Incorrect throttle linkage or gearshift linkage adjustment.
- Incorrect band adjustment.
- Incorrect hydraulic control pressure adjustments.
- Malfunction of hydraulic system.
- Malfunction of mechanical parts.

Knowing the basics of automatic transmission operation and understanding the importance of correct fluid level and the various key adjustments helps greatly in diagnosing transmission problems. Road testing, then, is the next step after fluid level and adjustments have been checked and corrected.

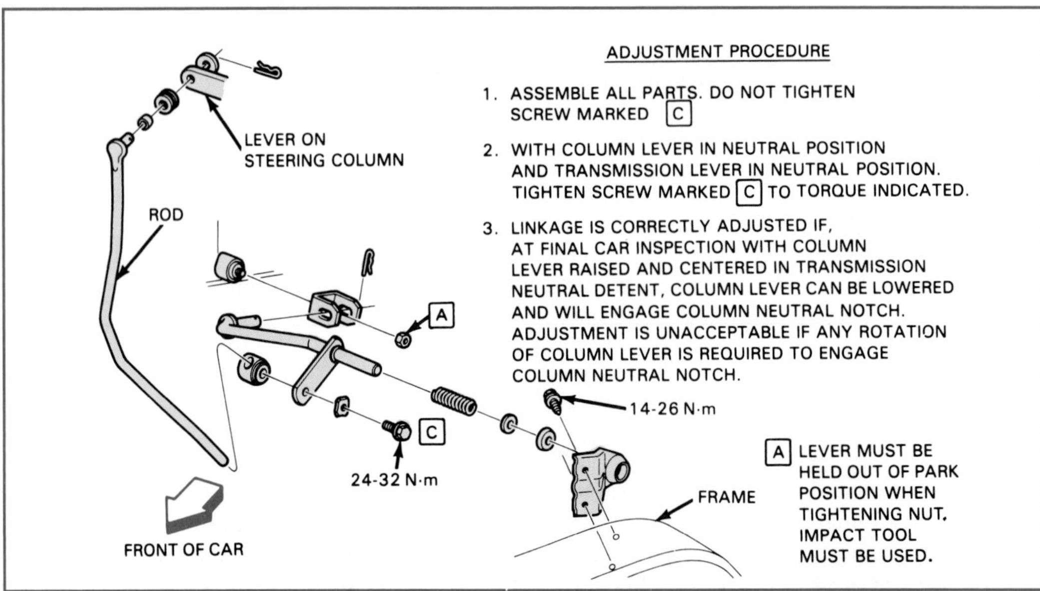

Figure 38-19. A column shift adjustment procedure is given. Note warning at A. (Cadillac)

Road Testing

Road testing is a quick way to begin diagnosis of an automatic transmission problem. Operate the transmission in each gear range and check for slippage, shift points, harsh or spongy shifts, and speeds at which upshifts and downshifts occur. Slippage or engine speed flare-up in any gear usually signals clutch, band, or overrunning clutch problems.

The key to diagnosing the source of a transmission problem during a road test is to know which elements of the transmission are in use in the various gear ranges. This information is available in ***clutch and band application charts*** contained in manufacturers' service manuals. A sample chart is shown in Figure 38-20.

To put the chart to use, note that both clutches are applied in drive, third gear only, Figure 38-20. Therefore, if the transmission slips in third gear, either the front or rear clutch is slipping. To determine which clutch is slipping, select another gear–such as reverse–which does not use one of these units. Then, if the transmission slips in reverse, the front clutch is slipping. See Figure 38-20. If the transmission does not slip in reverse, the rear clutch is slipping.

Road testing and use of the clutch and band application chart provide a means of diagnosis by the process of elimination. By this process, you can pinpoint the malfunctioning unit. However, hydraulic pressure tests must be performed to find the cause.

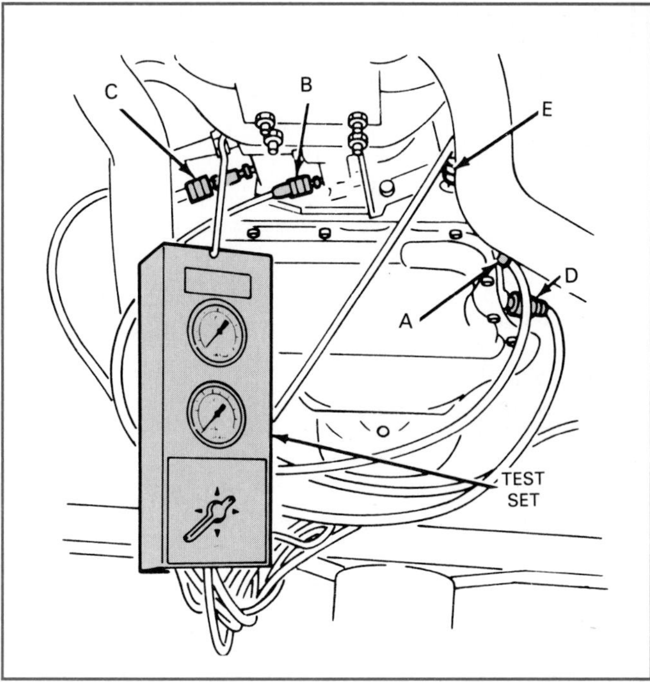

Figure 38-21. To make hydraulic pressure tests, the test set is connected to: A–Accumulator line pressure port. B–Governor pressure port. C–Lubrication pressure port. D–Front servo release pressure port. E–Rear servo apply pressure port. (Chrysler)

Hydraulic Pressure Testing

All automatic transmissions have ***hydraulic pressure testing*** ports, Figure 38-7, to which a pressure gauge may be attached, Figure 38-21. Then, with fluid level and fluid condition checked—and control linkage adjustments found to be correct—pressure test procedures are followed and diagnosis charts consulted to determine the cause of problems within the transmission. The car manufacturers' service manuals carry this information, along with full details on transmission disassembly, parts replacement, and reassembly.

Stall Testing

Stall testing provides a means of checking the holding ability of the converter-stator overrunning clutch and front and rear clutches of the transmission. It basically determines the maximum engine rpm available at full throttle with the rear wheels locked and the transmission in drive.

To make the stall test:

1. Connect a tachometer to the engine.
2. Check and adjust the transmission fluid level.
3. Run the engine until ATF reaches normal operating temperature.

ELEMENTS IN USE AT EACH POSITION OF THE SELECTOR LEVER										
LEVER POSITION	STANDARD RATIO	WIDE RATIO	START SAFETY	PARKING SPRAG	CLUTCHES				BANDS	
					FRONT	REAR	OVER-RUNNING	LOCK-UP	(KICKDOWN) FRONT	(LOW-REV.) REAR
P–PARK			X	X						
R–REVERSE	2.21	2.21			X					X
N–NEUTRAL			X							
D–DRIVE										
FIRST	2.45	2.74				X	X			
SECOND	1.45	1.54				X			X	
DIRECT	1.00	1.00			X	X		X		
2–SECOND										
FIRST	2.45	2.74				X	X			
SECOND	1.45	1.54				X			X	
1–LOW (FIRST)	2.45	2.74				X				X

Figure 38-20. Study this clutch and band application chart to learn which elements are in use in various gear ranges. This application chart is especially useful in conjunction with road test results. (Chrysler)

4. Block the front wheels.
5. Apply the parking brakes.
6. Apply the service brakes.

Warning: Do not allow anyone to stand in front of the vehicle under test.

7. Accelerate the engine to wide open throttle and note the maximum engine rpm on the tachometer.
   Note: Do not hold the throttle open longer for more than five seconds at a time. If more than one stall test is required, cool the transmission fluid between the tests by operating engine at 1000 rpm with the transmission in neutral for at least 20 seconds.
8. If the engine exceeds the rpm indicated on the stall speed chart for the vehicle under test, release the accelerator immediately; transmission clutch slippage is occurring.
9. Shift the transmission into neutral, operate the engine for 20 seconds at 1000 rpm.
10. Stop the engine, shift into park, and release the parking and service brakes.
11. Check the test results with the stall speed charts. (Example: Six-cylinder engine–three-speed automatic transmission–1850-2150 rpm.)

Air Pressure Testing

As a follow-up diagnostic "tool," ***air pressure testing*** before automatic transmission removal will confirm suspected improper clutch, band, and servo operation. Also, after repairs have been made, repeat air pressure testing to confirm proper operation of these units.

The air pressure testing procedure involves substituting air pressure for hydraulic pressure at appropriate transmission case passages after the control valve body has been removed. See Figure 38-22. Generally, pressures of 30 to 100 psi (210 to 690 kPa) are required to perform the air pressure tests.

Caution: Use dry, filtered compressed air only when performing air pressure tests.

Basically, the tests require the introduction of air pressure to specific passages while placing two fingers on the transmission case in the general area where movement of a piston being applied can be felt. An example of typical passage locations and identification is given in Figure 38-22.

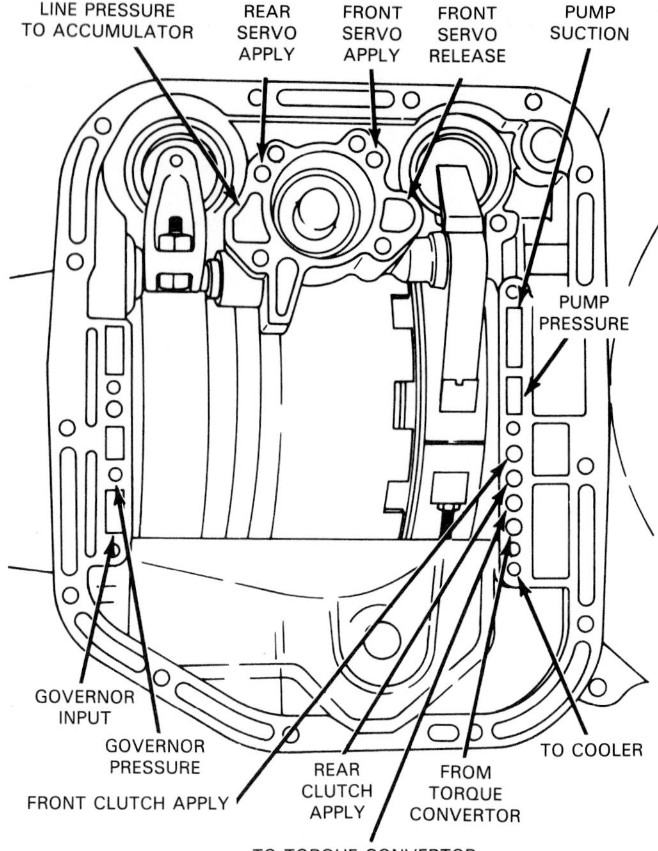

Figure 38-22. Air pressure tests substitute air pressure for hydraulic pressure in testing for proper or improper operation of the transmission control mechanism. (Chrysler)

Testing Electronically Controlled Transmissions

Note: Always consult an appropriate service manual before attempting to service an electronically controlled transmission. Improper testing and service procedures can damage electronic control system components.

When electronically controlled transmission problems are suspected, check the engine and the engine's computer control system for proper operation. If the engine is not operating properly, the electronically controlled transmission will not shift correctly.

Additionally, many of the sensors that send inputs to the engine control computer also provide inputs to the transmission control unit. Common inputs to the transmission control unit include the following:

- Vehicle speed sensor.
- Throttle position sensor.
- Coolant temperature sensor.
- Manifold absolute pressure sensor.
- Transmission speed sensor.
- Brake switch.
- Accelerator switch.
- Transmission fluid temperature sensor.
- Overdrive switch.
- Neutral safety switch.

It is important to note that in some vehicles, the engine and the transmission are controlled by the same computer.

If the engine and the engine's computer control system are operating correctly, check the power supply to the transmission control unit. Also check the ground to the control unit and inspect all connectors. A faulty ground or a corroded connection can cause a variety of shift problems.

Most electronically controlled transmissions have self-diagnostic capabilities. Trouble codes are produced by the transmission control unit when a system malfunction is detected. A scan tool is generally used to retrieve the trouble codes from the control unit.

In some cases, the transmission must be isolated from its control system to determine whether the problem is in the control system, the solenoids, or the transmission itself.

This is accomplished by using a scan tool or remote switches to control the solenoids. If the solenoids are working properly, they should produce a metallic click when triggered with the scan tool or the switches.

If the solenoids do not respond when activated with the scan tool or the remote switches, the connections to the solenoids should be inspected. Additionally, the resistance of each solenoid can usually be checked with an ohmmeter. Solenoids that do not meet the manufacturer's specifications must be replaced.

Some manufacturers recommend activating the solenoids manually while road testing the vehicle. If the transmission is working properly, it will shift into the desired gear when the appropriate solenoids are activated, Figure 38-23. If the solenoids operate properly but the transmission does not shift correctly, the transmission may need mechanical repairs. When performing this test, do not be alarmed if the shifts are a bit harsh. This is normal when the solenoids are activated manually.

If the transmission shifts properly when the solenoids are activated manually but does not shift correctly when governed by the control unit, the control system should be checked for malfunctions. Use a digital voltmeter to measure the control unit's inputs and outputs. If your measurements are not within specifications, refer to the service manual for appropriate repair procedures.

GEAR	SOLENOID 1	SOLENOID 2
FIRST	ON	ON
SECOND	OFF	ON
THIRD	OFF	OFF
FOURTH	ON	OFF

Figure 38-23. Solenoid operating combinations vary from manufacturer to manufacturer. This chart shows the solenoid operating combinations for one specific electronically controlled transmission.

Working with Service Manuals

Car manufacturers' ***service manuals*** provide quick reference troubleshooting charts for automatic transmission problem diagnosis. A step-by-step approach to solving automatic transmission problems is used.

In-automobile diagnostic procedures are given first, listing problem conditions that can be corrected with the transmission in the automobile. Out-of-automobile diagnostic procedures list problems that call for transmission removal and disassembly.

Familiarize yourself with both types of troubleshooting charts and the service procedures required to return the automatic transmission to normal operating efficiency.

Chapter 38–Review Questions

Write your answers on a separate sheet of paper. Do not write in this book.

1. Automatic transmissions transmit _____ to the drive shaft of rear-wheel drive vehicles.
2. A transaxle combines the _____ and _____ assemblies in a single housing.
3. When transmission trouble occurs, check _____ first.
4. What color is "normal" for automatic transmission fluid?
   (A) Dark brown.
   (B) Milky pink.
   (C) Cherry red.
   (D) Clear.
5. Technician A says that varnish buildup on the transmission dipstick is caused by high temperatures and severe oxidation of the ATF. Technician B says that varnish buildup on the transmission dipstick is caused by antifreeze contamination of the ATF. Who is right?
   (A) A only.
   (B) B only.
   (C) Both A & B.
   (D) Neither A nor B.
6. Technician A says that gum deposits on the transmission dipstick are caused by high temperatures and severe oxidation of the ATF. Technician B says that gum deposits on the transmission dipstick are caused by antifreeze contamination of the ATF. Who is right?
   (A) A only.
   (B) B only.
   (C) Both A & B.
   (D) Neither A nor B.
7. With the vehicle up on a lift, what is the first step in looking for an ATF leak?
   (A) Drain the fluid.
   (B) Check tightness of transmission drain plug.
   (C) Clean underside of engine oil pan, torque converter housing, and transmission case and extension housing.
   (D) Check oil cooler lines and fittings.
8. Technician A says that a low level of ATF can cause foaming of the fluid. Technician B says that overfilling the transmission with ATF can cause foaming. Who is right?
   (A) A only.
   (B) B only.
   (C) Both A & B.
   (D) Neither A nor B.
9. If the source of ATF leakage is at the oil pump seal, pump body, oil pump-to-case bolt, repair requires removal of the transmission. True or False?
10. When the vehicle is on the lift, check the condition of the engine mount. If it is _____ or _____, replace the mount.
11. Once the transmission oil pan has been removed, always remove the _____ for cleaning or replacement.
12. Most late-model automatic transmissions have a drain plug in the oil pan. True or False?
13. When service is completed, reinstall the oil pan using a new gasket without _____ or _____.
14. A general procedure for automatic transmission band adjustment is:
   (A) Tighten band adjusting screw to a specified torque tightness.
   (B) Tighten band adjusting screw to a specified torque tightness, then back it off a given number of turns.
   (C) Tighten band adjusting screw to the point where the torque wrench just begins to indicate no clearance and no torque tension.
   (D) Back off band adjusting screw two turns.

15. Transmission band adjusting screws are always externally accessible for adjustment. True or False?
16. When adjusting bands on certain Ford automatic transmissions, _____ and _____ the locknut from the band adjusting screw because it also serves to seal in fluid.
17. Name four reasons why engine idle speed adjustment generally has become increasingly complex.
18. The throttle linkage adjustment is critical to proper operation of the _____.
19. Technician A says that if the throttle linkage setting is too short, early shifts may occur. Technician B says that if the throttle linkage setting is too short, slippage between shifts may occur. Who is right?
    (A) A only.
    (B) B only.
    (C) Both A & B.
    (D) Neither A nor B.
20. The general rule for throttle linkage adjustment is to remove all _____ from the linkage.
21. The correct gearshift linkage adjustment properly positions the _____ in the valve body.
    (A) throttle valve
    (B) manual valve
    (C) governor valve
    (D) regulator valve
22. A check of _____ operation will confirm or condemn gearshift linkage adjustment.
23. Name four common causes of automatic transmission problems.
24. A(n) _____ is a quick way to begin diagnosis of an automatic transmission problem.
    (A) hydraulic pressure test
    (B) air pressure test
    (C) road test
    (D) stall test
25. _____ application charts show which elements of the transmission are in use in the various gear ranges.
26. _____ pressure tests require ATF drain and transmission oil pan removal.
27. _____ pressure tests do not require ATF drain and transmission oil pan removal.
28. The stall test basically determines the maximum _____ available at full throttle with the rear wheels locked and the transmission in drive.
29. During the stall test, do not hold the throttle open and longer than _____ at a time.
    (A) five seconds
    (B) ten seconds
    (C) twenty seconds
    (D) thirty seconds
30. Generally, air pressure of _____ psi is used to perform air pressure tests of clutch, band, and servo operation.
    (A) 10-50
    (B) 30-100
    (C) 50-150
    (D) 100-200

Chapter 39
Transaxles

After studying this chapter, you will be able to:

❍ Define transaxle and state its function.
❍ Explain how transaxle gear ratios are determined.
❍ Describe the makeup and operation of a typical manual transaxle.
❍ Describe the makeup and operation of a typical automatic transaxle.
❍ Tell how to perform common maintenance checks and adjustments.
❍ Discuss the many ways in which manufacturers' service manuals provide mechanics with helpful automotive service information.

Transaxles

A ***transaxle*** is an engine power transfer mechanism that combines a transmission assembly and a differential (final drive) assembly in a single unit. It receives power from the engine and transmits it to the drive axles at the gear ratio selected by the driver. The transaxle is used mainly in front-wheel drive applications, Figure 39-1. Some mid-engine cars and some with rear-wheel drive are also equipped with a transaxle.

Transaxle Construction

Like conventional transmissions, transaxles may be either manual or automatic. Generally, manual transaxles are either four-speed or five-speed units. Automatic transaxles are either three-speed or four-speed units. In front-wheel drive applications, the transaxle may be mounted transversely (crosswise) or longitudinally (lengthwise) in the engine compartment.

A typical four-speed manual transaxle, Figure 39-2, consists of an aluminum transaxle case, a gear selector lever, input cluster gear (shaft), main shaft with various gears and synchronizer assemblies, output gear (shaft), differential housing, and a differential assembly.

A typical five-speed manual transaxle is similar in design and function to a four-speed unit employed by the same manufacturer. The five-speed transaxle, however, has an additional fifth gear, a fifth gear and synchronizer assembly, and a shifter fork to provide the fifth gear drive range.

A typical three-speed automatic transaxle is made up of an aluminum transaxle case, a gear selector lever, a

Figure 39-1. This phantom view of a front-wheel drive sedan shows a typical application of a transverse-mounted engine and an automatic transaxle. (Ford)

1. MAINSHAFT
2. FOURTH SPEED GEARS
3. INPUT CLUSTER
4. THIRD SPEED GEARS
5. SECOND SPEED GEARS
6. REVERSE GEAR
7. REVERSE IDLER GEAR
8. FIRST SPEED GEARS
9. HALF SHAFTS
10. DIFFERENTIAL OIL SEALS
11. FINAL DRIVE RING GEAR
12. FIRST/SECOND SPEED SYNCHRONIZER BLOCKER RINGS
13. THIRD/FOURTH SPEED SYNCHRONIZER HUB
14. THIRD/FOURTH SPEED SYNCHRONIZER SLEEVE
15. PINION GEAR–PART OF MAIN SHAFT

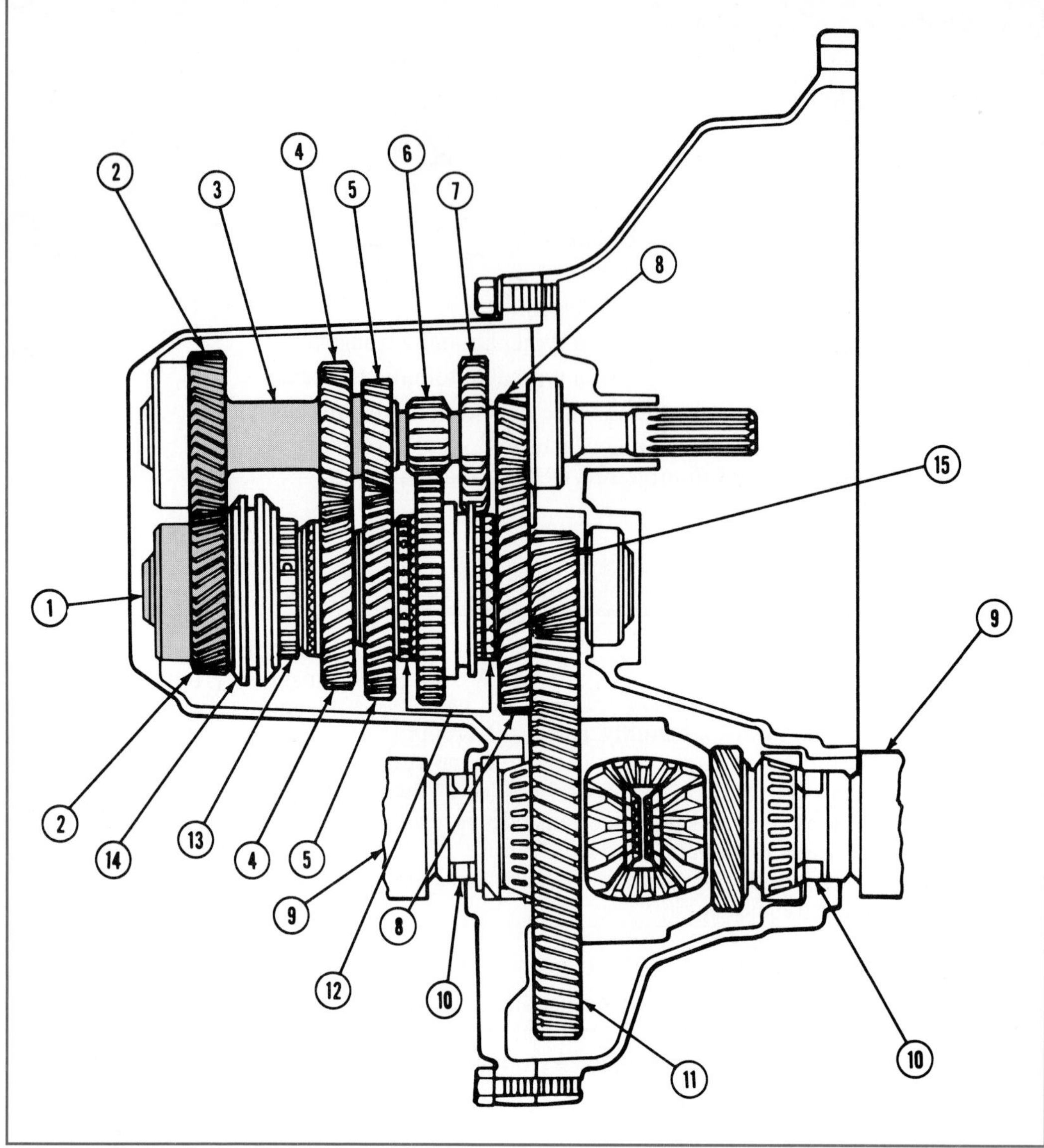

Figure 39-2. A typical four-speed manual transaxle assembly includes: 1–Main shaft. 2–Fourth speed gears. 3–Input cluster. (Ford)

torque converter, valve body, input shaft, output shaft, two multiple disc clutches, an overrunning clutch, front and rear planetary gearsets, drums, bands and servos, a transfer shaft, governor assembly, extension housing, and differential assembly.

Transaxle Gear Ratios

As with manual transmissions, transaxle gear ratios are determined by how many teeth are on the input cluster gear and how many teeth are on the matching gear on the main shaft. For example, assume that first gear in the input cluster has 13 teeth. Next, assume that the main shaft has 42 teeth. See Figure 39-2. Then, by dividing the number of teeth on the main shaft by the number of teeth on the input cluster (42 + 13), you would have a gear ratio of 3.23:1.

Looking at actual gear ratios in use, Ford's four-speed manual transaxle has the following gear ratios: first–3.23:1; second–1.92:1; third–1.23:1; fourth–0.8:1; reverse–3.46:1. Note that fourth speed is overdrive. The 0.81:1 ratio permits engine speed to be reduced by 20 percent over the conventional 1.0:1 direct drive of three and four-speed manual transmissions.

Oldsmobile's five-speed manual transaxle has the following gear ratios: first–3.91:1; second–2.15:1; third–1.45:1; fourth–1.03:1; fifth–0.74:1; reverse–3.50:1. Here, fifth speed is overdrive.

Chrysler's three-speed automatic transaxle has the following gear ratios: first–2.69:1; second–1.55:1; third–1.00:1; reverse–2.10:1. Here, there is no overdrive. Third speed is direct drive.

Transaxle Operation

A typical four-speed manual transaxle uses a cable to operate the clutch. It connects the clutch pedal to the clutch lever on the transaxle. See Chapter 38. When the driver depresses the clutch pedal, the cable moves the clutch lever which, in turn, moves the clutch release bearing to disengage the clutch. When the driver lets up on the clutch pedal, the cable relaxes the tension of the release bearing against the pressure plate fingers, and the clutch is re-engaged. However, in transaxle applications–unlike manual transmission applications–the release bearing remains in light contact with the pressure plate under normal driving conditions.

Four-speed Manual Transaxle

A typical Ford four-speed manual transaxle is shown in Figure-39-2. Study the list of parts of the assembly, identify those parts on the accompanying illustration, and follow this description of four-speed transaxle operation.

From the clutch, engine power is transmitted to the main shaft by way of the input cluster gear. Each gear on the input shaft is in constant mesh with a matching gear on the main shaft. These matching gearsets provide the four forward gear ratios as each is put into operation by shifting synchronizers into and out of engagement with the selected gear. See Figure 39-3.

When the engine is running, the input cluster shaft will turn, too. The main shaft gears, however, will freewheel unless locked to the main shaft by one of the synchronizers. In neutral, the main shaft gears will turn freely, and the engine torque will not be transmitted to the pinion gear on the end of the main shaft. See Figure 39-3.

If one of the synchronizers is shifted, the gear it controls will be locked to the main shaft. The main shaft will turn at a speed determined by engine speed and the gear ratio of the gear selected.

The pinion gear on the end of the main shaft is part of the shaft. It is also in constant mesh with the ring gear of the differential assembly. Therefore, both the pinion gear and ring gear will rotate when the main shaft is rotating. See Figure 39-2.

The power flow from the engine, then, is from the input cluster gear to the matching gear on the main shaft; from the main shaft and pinion gear to the differential ring gear; through the differential assembly to the half shafts to the driving wheels. The differential is a conventional final drive arrangement of gears that divides the torque between the drive axles and allows them to rotate at different speeds.

Five-speed Manual Transaxle

A typical Oldsmobile five-speed manual transaxle is shown in Figure 39-4. Study the lists of parts of the assembly, identify the parts by the number on the accompanying

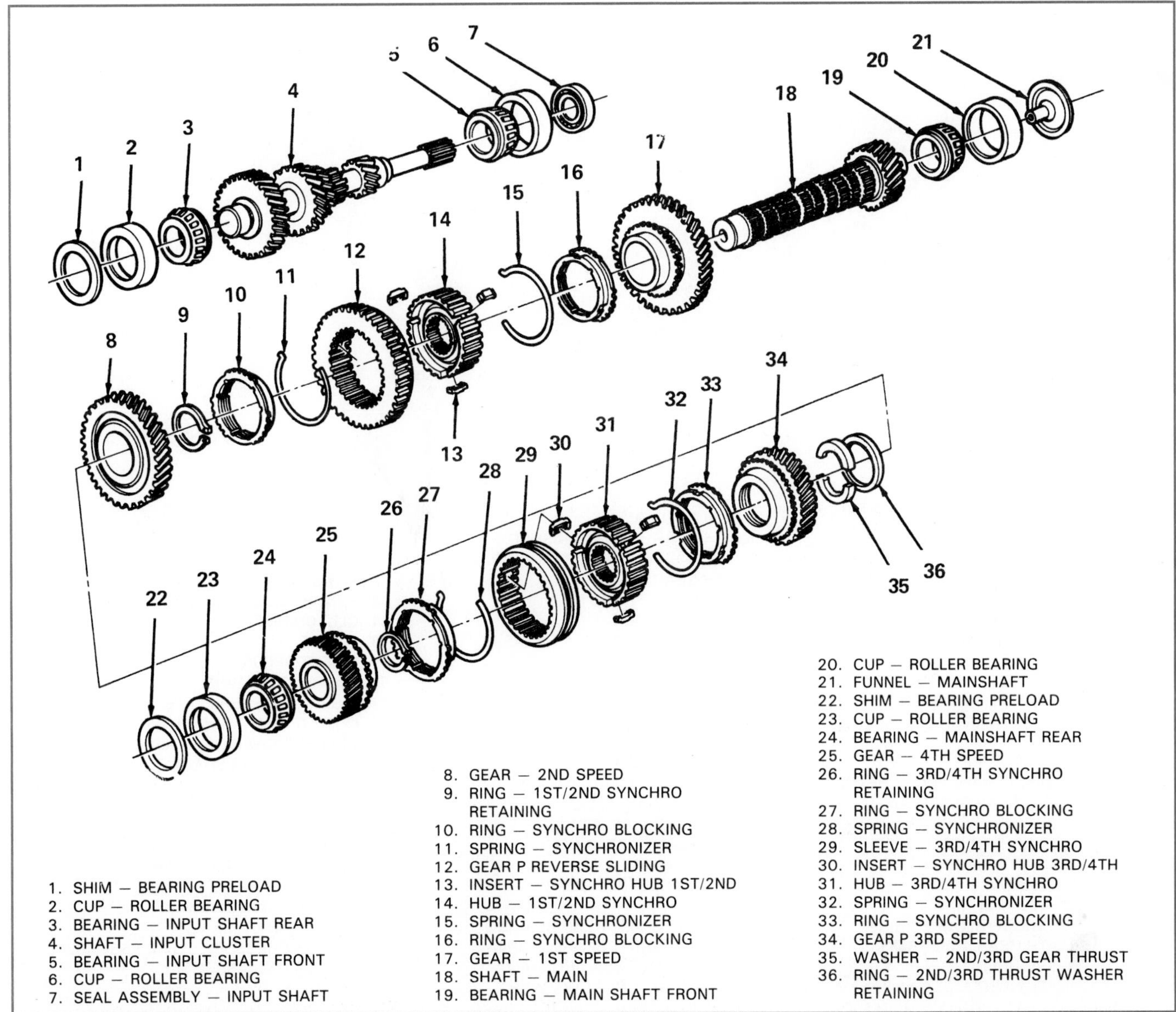

Figure 39-3. Exploded view details the components of a four-speed manual transaxle input and main shaft clusters. (Ford)

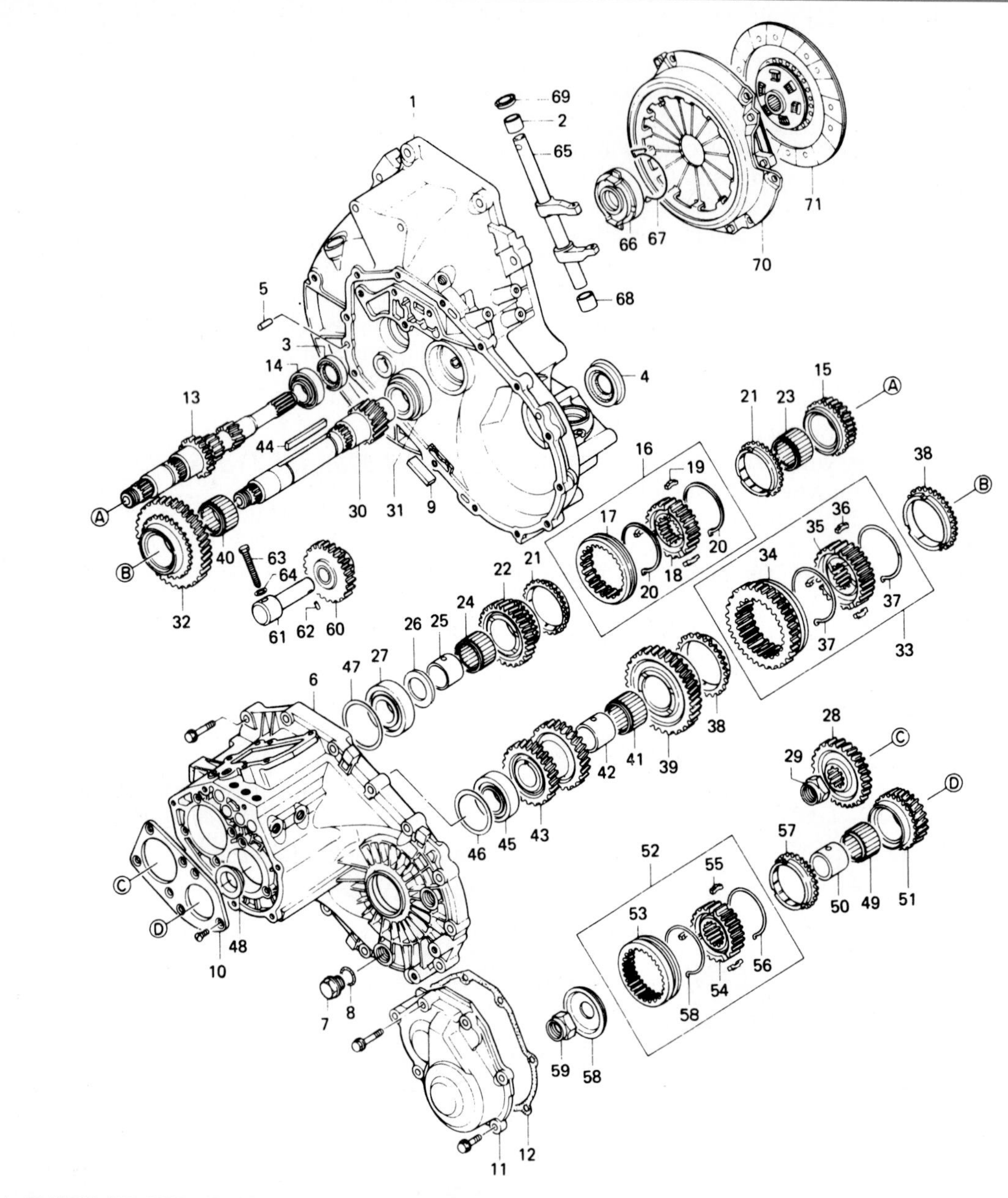

1. CLUTCH AND DIFF. HOUSING
2. CLUTCH SHAFT BUSHING
3. INPUT SHAFT OIL SEAL
4. DRIVE SHAFT OIL SEAL
5. STRAIGHT KNOCK PIN
6. TRANSAXLE CASE
7. DRAIN PLUG
8. GASKET
9. MAGNET
10. BEARING RETAINER
11. REAR COVER
12. GASKET
13. INPUT SHAFT
14. INPUT SHAFT FRONT BEARING
15. 3RD GEAR ASSEMBLY
16. 3RD/4TH SYNCHRONIZER ASM.
17. SYNCHRONIZER SLEEVE
18. CLUTCH HUB
19. INSERT
20. INSERT SPRING
21. 3RD/4TH BLOCKER RING
22. 4TH GEAR ASSEMBLY
23. 3RD NEEDLE BEARING
24. 4TH NEEDLE BEARING
25. 4TH COLLAR
26. 4TH GEAR THRUST WASHER
27. INPUT SHAFT REAR BEARING
28. 5TH GEAR
29. INPUT SHAFT END NUT
30. OUTPUT SHAFT
31. OUTPUT SHAFT FRONT BEARING
32. 1ST GEAR ASSEMBLY
33. 1ST/2ND SYNCHRONIZER ASSEMBLY
34. REVERSE GEAR
35. CLUTCH HUB
36. INSERT
37. INSERT SPRING
38. 1ST/2ND BLOCKER RING
39. 2ND GEAR ASSEMBLY
40. 1ST NEEDLE BEARING
41. 2ND NEEDLE BEARING
42. 2ND COLLAR
43. 3RD/4TH OUTPUT GEAR
44. KEY
45. OUTPUT SHAFT REAR BEARING
46. OUTPUT SHAFT BEARING SHIM
47. INPUT SHAFT BEARING SHIM
48. 5TH GEAR THRUST WASHER
49. 5TH NEEDLE BEARING
50. 5TH COLLAR
51. 5TH GEAR ASSEMBLY
52. 5TH SYNCHRONIZER ASSEMBLY
53. SYNCHRONIZER SLEEVE
54. CLUTCH HUB
55. INSERT
56. INSERT SPRING
57. 5TH BLOCKER RING
58. INSERT STOPPER PLATE
59. OUTPUT SHAFT END NUT
60. REVERSE IDLER GEAR ASSEMBLY
61. REVERSE IDLER SHAFT
62. STRAIGHT PIN
63. REVERSE IDLER SHAFT BOLT
64. GASKET
65. CLUTCH FORK SHAFT ASSEMBLY
66. CLUTCH RELEASE BEARING
67. RELEASE BEARING SPRING
68. CLUTCH SHAFT BUSHING
69. CLUTCH SHAFT SEAL
70. CLUTCH PRESSURE PLATE ASSEMBLY
71. CLUTCH DISK ASSEMBLY

Figure 39-4. This exploded view shows the relationship of parts in a typical five-speed manual transaxle. (Chevrolet)

illustration, and follow this description of five-speed transaxle operation.

As with the four-speed manual transaxle, engine power is transmitted from the clutch to the five-speed transaxle output shaft by shifting a synchronizer assembly into engagement with a selected gear on the input shaft. This causes the output shaft to turn at a speed determined by engine speed and the gear ratio selected.

The difference in five-speed transaxle makeup is the addition of a fifth speed gear at the rear end of the input shaft, which is in mesh with a fifth speed gear and synchronizer assembly at the rear end of the output shaft. See Figure 39-5.

Power flow, then, in fifth gear, would be from the clutch to the input shaft, to the fifth gear on the output shaft; from the integral pinion gear on the front end of the output shaft to the ring gear of the differential, Figure 39-6; through the differential assembly to the half shafts to the driving wheels.

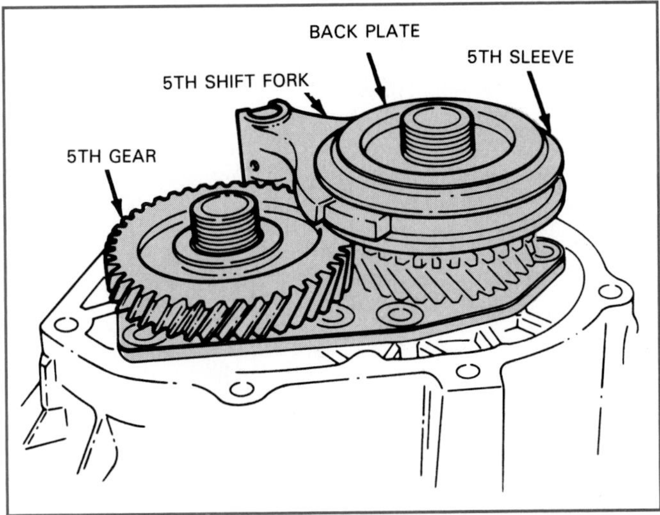

Figure 39-5. The design of this five-speed manual transaxle is similar to a four-speed unit, but it includes a fifth speed gear and a fifth speed gear and synchronizer assembly at the rear of the transaxle. (Oldsmobile)

Three-speed Automatic Transaxle

A Chrysler three-speed automatic transaxle is shown in Figure 39-7. Study the parts identified in this illustration, and follow the description of three-speed automatic transaxle operation.

Engine power is transmitted to the torque converter. From the converter, power flow is through the input shaft to the multiple disc clutches. Flow continues to the planetary gearsets based on which clutches are engaged and which bands are applied. See chart of "Elements in Use at Each Position of the Selector Lever" shown in Figure 39-8.

The common sun gear of the two planetary gearsets is connected to the front clutch by a driving shell, which is splined to the sun gear and the front clutch retainer. Consulting the chart in Figure 39-8, you can see that in first gear, the rear clutch is engaged and the rear band is applied. Also note that in reverse gear, the front clutch is engaged and the rear band is applied. Output direction and gear ratio are determined by which parts of the planetary gearsets are held and which parts are driven.

Output from the planetary gearsets is by way of the output shaft, Figure 39-7. The output shaft gear then drives the transfer shaft gear. An integral gear on the other end of the transfer shaft drives the ring gear of the differential. From here, the differential distributes power flow to the axle shafts as required by vehicle operation.

Four-speed Automatic Transaxle

A General Motors four-speed automatic transaxle of unusual design is shown in Figure 39-9. Study the parts identified in this illustration and note the "different" features of this unit.

1. RING GEAR
2. RING GEAR BOLT
3. DIFFERENTIAL CASE
4. DIFFERENTIAL PINION GEAR
5. DIFFERENTIAL SIDE GEAR
6. SIDE GEAR THRUST WASHER
7. PINION GEAR THRUST WASHER
8. CROSS PIN
9. LOCK PIN
10. SPEEDOMETER DRIVE GEAR
11. SIDE BEARING
12. SIDE BEARING SHIM

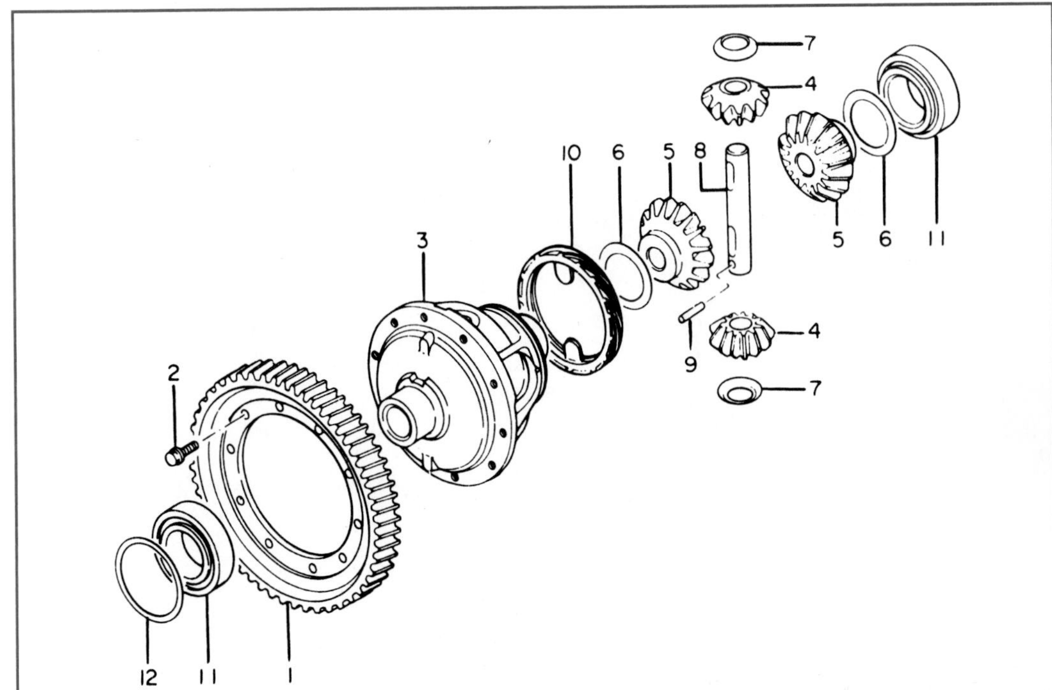

Figure 39-6. Parts of the differential assembly of a five-speed manual transaxle are pictured and identified. (Oldsmobile)

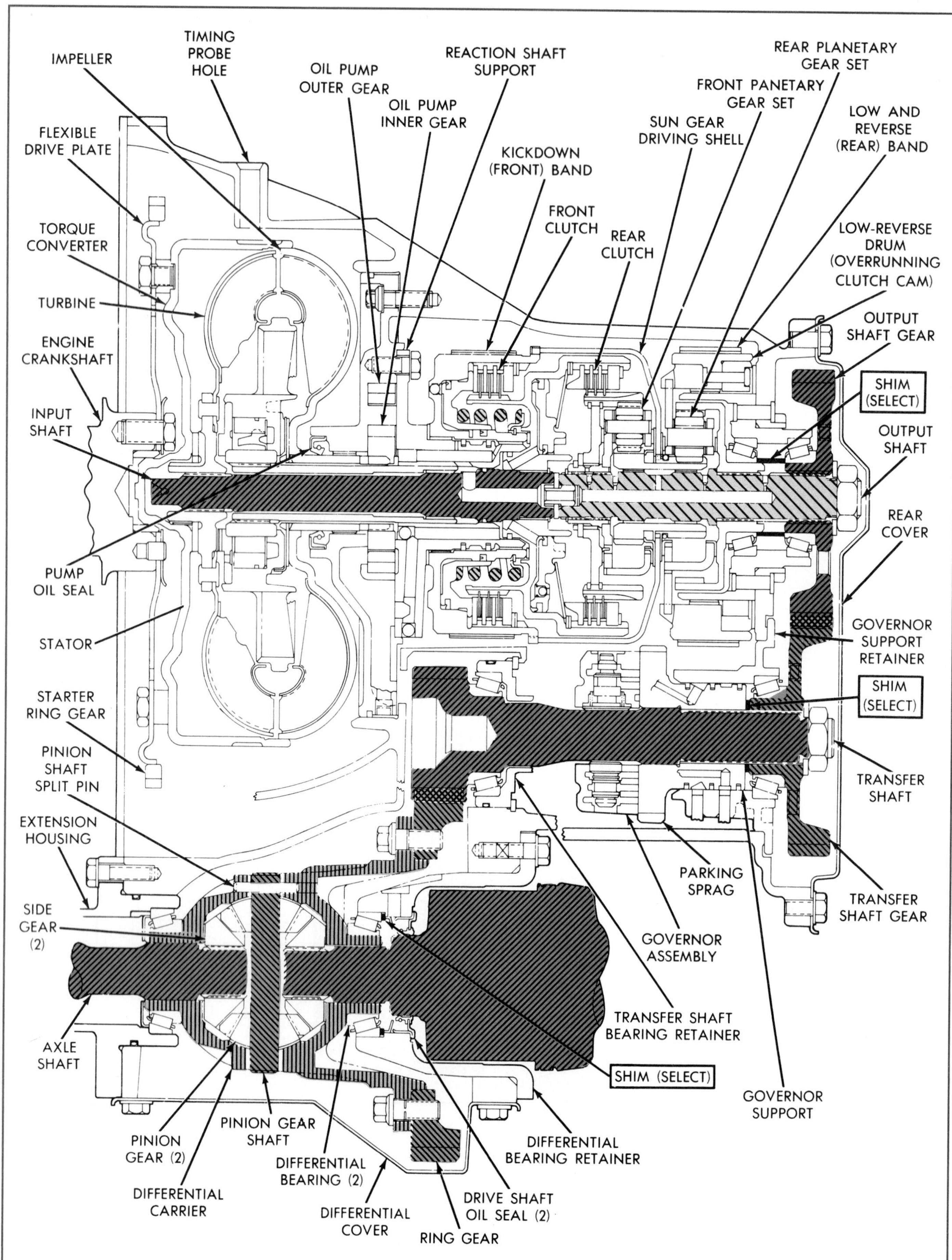

Figure 39-7. Crosshatched parts of this three-speed automatic transaxle indicate power flow. (Chrysler)

ELEMENTS IN USE AT EACH POSITION OF THE SELECTOR LEVER							
LEVER POSITION	START SAFETY	PARKING SPRAG	CLUTCHES			BANDS	
			FRONT	REAR	OVER-RUNNING	(KICKDOWN) FRONT	(LOW-REV.) REAR
P–PARK	X	X					
R–REVERSE			X				X
N–NEUTRAL	X						
D–DRIVE:							
FIRST				X	X		
SECOND				X		X	
DIRECT			X	X			
2–SECOND:							
FIRST				X	X		
SECOND				X		X	
1–LOW (FIRST)				X			X

Figure 39-8. This chart provides a means for a quick check to determine which elements of a three-speed manual transaxle are in use in each shift lever position. (Chrysler)

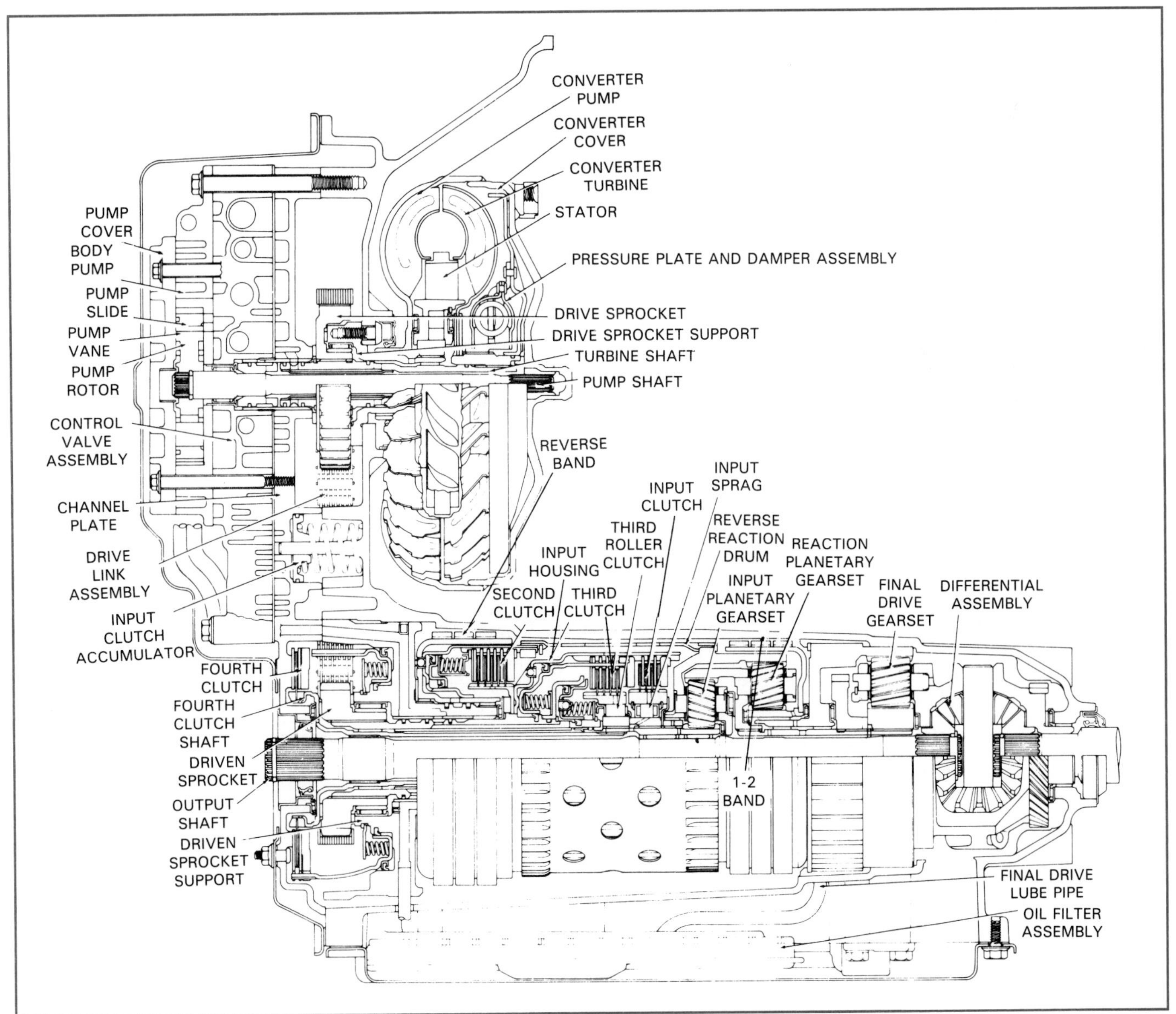

Figure 39-9. Unusual construction of this GM four-speed automatic transaxle includes a reverse reaction drum, input planetary gearset, reaction planetary gearset, and final drive planetary gearset. (Buick)

The GM four-speed, front-wheel drive, automatic overdrive transaxle uses only two planetary gearsets to perform all functions. Shifting is accomplished by the application and release of clutches that connect specific gearset components.

From input to output, Figure 39-9, the four-speed unit consists of the torque converter with converter clutch; sprocket and drive link assembly; 1-2 and reverse band assemblies; input, 3rd, 2nd, and 4th multiple disc clutches; input sprag and 3rd roller clutch, compound planetary and gearset; differential/final drive assembly.

When engine power is applied to this GM transaxle in first gear, high reduction is achieved through components in both planetary gearsets. Each gear in use helps step down the gear ratio to 2.92:1.

In first gear, the input sun gear drives the pinion carrier and internal gear of the input gearset. This assembly, in turn, drives the internal gear and pinion carrier of the reaction gearset. A servo applies the 1-2 band, locking the reaction sun gear, and power output is by way of the reaction gearset pinion carrier, Figure 39-10.

In second gear, the second clutch becomes the power input to the input gearset. Power flow takes place when the input clutch housing drives the second clutch housing by means of splined clutch plates. From here, power flow is transmitted to the reverse reaction drum. This drum drives the input gearset internal gear, which turns the reaction gear pinion carrier gearset as the final drive output.

In third gear, the third clutch is engaged and drives the input gearset sun gear at the same speed as the torque converter turbine. The input gearset is still driven by the second clutch. In this setup, Figure 39-9, the input sun gear and carrier pinion gears are rotating at the same speed. This forces the internal gear to turn with them, which results in direct drive. Output is by way of the internal gear of the reaction gearset at a 1:1 ratio.

In fourth gear, power flow is from the second clutch to the input gearset. The input sun gear is held stationary, causing the input carrier to drive the reaction gearset carrier. The reaction internal gear then becomes the output in overdrive. The large size internal gear drives the final drive sun gear to achieve an overdrive ratio of 0.7:1.

In reverse, the reverse band is applied to hold the input carrier assembly. With the carrier held stationary, the carrier pinion gears react as idler gears to drive the internal gear in the opposite direction.

The differential/final drive is also of unusual construction. It utilizes a planetary gearset (instead of conventional ring and pinion gears) to actuate the differential side gears and differential pinion gears. See Figure 39-11. The side gears are connected to the axle shafts. The pinion gears act as idlers to transfer power from the carrier to the side gears, while allowing unequal speeds of axle rotation when the vehicle is rounding a curve.

Automatic Transaxle Advances

Lockup torque converters in automatic transmissions were described in detail in Chapter 41. These converters are equipped with an internal locking mechanism called a "converter clutch" that locks the converter turbine to the impeller in direct drive. In effect, the converter clutch provides a direct, mechanical drive to eliminate hydraulic converter slippage for greater efficiency and economy.

Some transaxles, too, are equipped with converter clutches to provide these advantages. Ford Motor Company, for example, has a three-speed automatic transaxle with "CLC" (centrifugally linked converter). See Figure 39-12. This converter has a bypass clutch that is actuated when centrifugal force causes it to lock up.

Ford also developed a four-speed automatic overdrive transaxle with an electronically controlled torque converter bypass clutch. This converter clutch is controlled by the EEC-IV engine control system to provide direct, mechanical torque flow in third and fourth gear ranges under certain conditions.

Many manufacturer's are installing electronically controlled automatic transaxles in their vehicles. It utilizes a

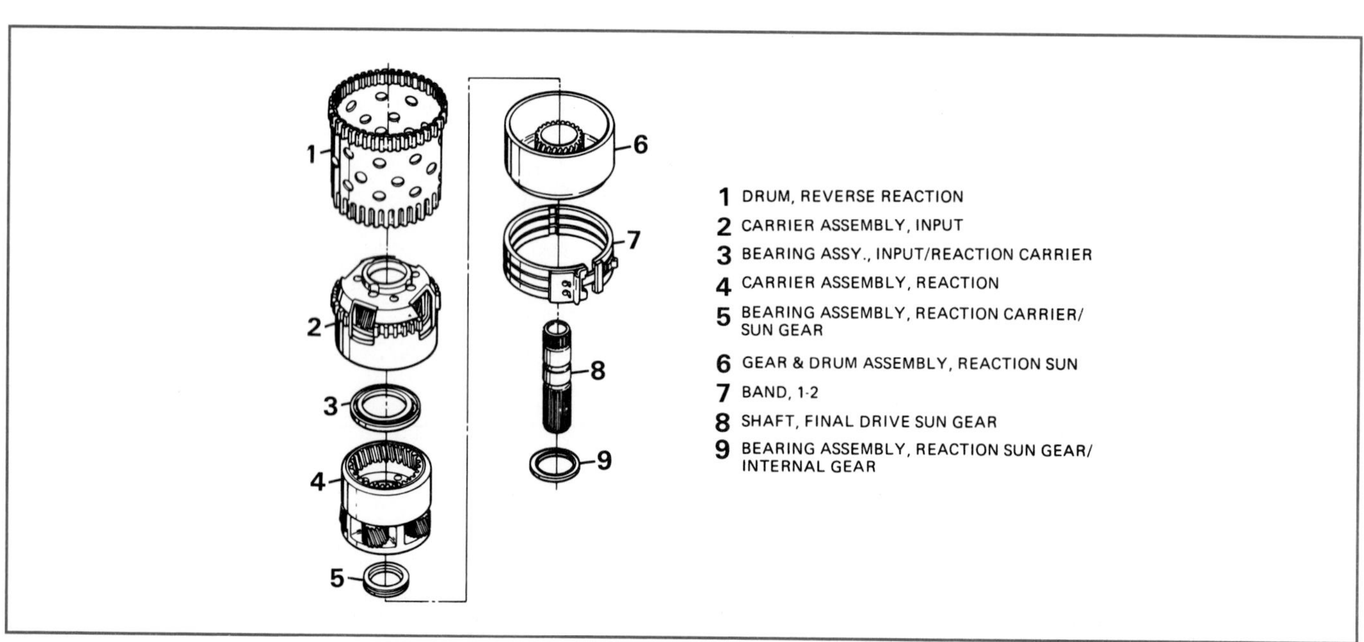

Figure 39-10. Exploded view shows the reverse reaction drum and reaction planetary gearset elements of a four-speed automatic transaxle. (Buick)

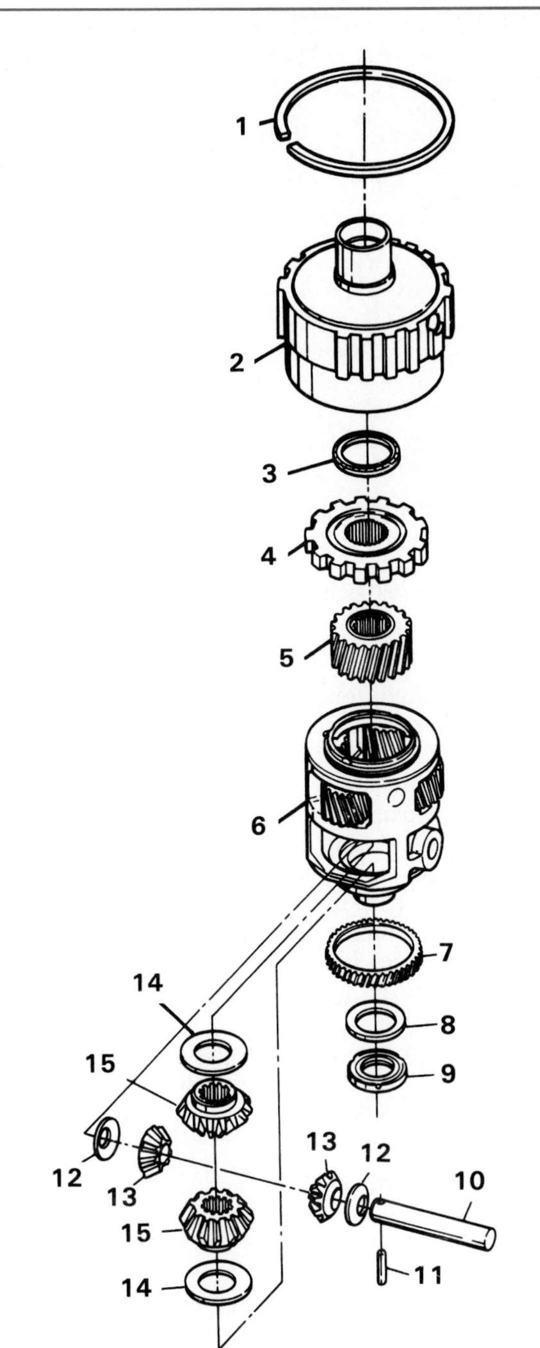

Figure 39-11. This exploded view reveals the individual parts arrangement of the final drive planetary gearset and final drive assembly of a GM four-speed automatic transaxle. (Buick)

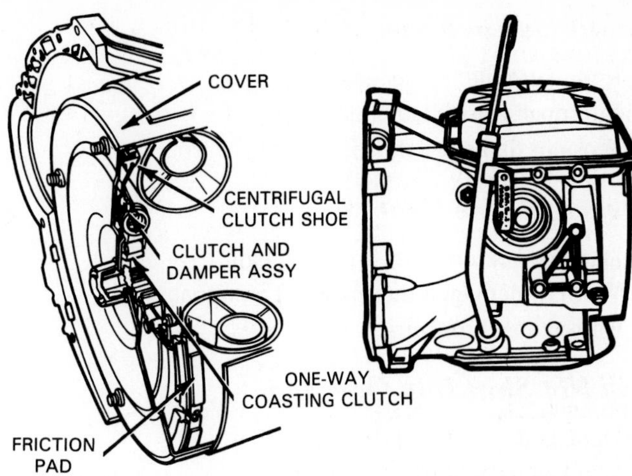

Figure 39-12. This three-speed automatic transaxle torque converter has a bypass clutch that "locks up" to provide a mechanical connection from the flywheel to the gear train. (Ford)

computer to actuate two electric solenoids that control shifts and torque converter lockup. A "shift schedule" stored in the computer's memory establishes which gear range is required for any given situation.

Manual Transaxle Troubleshooting

Noise in Neutral

- Neutral rollover rattle (normal).
- Damaged input gear bearings.
- Damaged clutch release bearing.

Noise in Forward Gears

- Low lubricant level.
- Binding external shift mechanism.
- Improperly installed clutch disc.
- Worn or damaged input/output bearings.
- Worn or damaged gear teeth.
- Worn or damaged synchronizer.
- Gear rattle.

Difficult to Shift

- Improper clutch disengagement.
- Binding external shift mechanism.
- Improperly installed clutch disc.
- Damaged synchronizers or shift mechanisms.
- Incorrect lubricant.
- Sticking blocker ring.

Slips Out of Gear

- Damaged or binding gearshift linkage.
- Stiff or blocked floor shift.
- Broken or loose engine mounts.
- Worn or damaged internal components.
- Transaxle loose on engine housing.

Gear Clash in Forward Speeds

- Improper clutch disengagement.
- Improperly installed clutch disc.
- Worn or damaged shift forks or synchronizers.

Locked in One Gear

- Damaged external shift mechanism.
- Worn or damaged internal shift components.
- Burred synchronizers.

Will Not Shift Into One Gear

- Damaged external shift mechanism.
- Blocked floor shift.
- Restricted travel of internal shift components.

Will Not Shift Into Reverse

- Damaged external shift mechanism.
- Worn or damaged internal components.

Leaks Lubricant

- Excessive lubricant in transaxle.
- Damaged drive axle seals.
- Damaged shift lever seal.
- Damaged input gear bearing retainer seals.

Manual Transaxle Maintenance

Maintenance checks and services on manual transaxles are quite simple. Basically, they include checking fluid level, inspecting for fluid leakage, draining and refilling the transaxle, torque tightening the transaxle-to-engine attaching bolts, and inspecting the condition of the transaxle mounts.

Check Fluid Level

The procedure for making fluid level checks varies with make and model of vehicle. Some manual transaxles have fill plugs located on the side of the case, much like manual transmissions. See Figure 39-13. Others have dipsticks similar to automatic transmissions.

To check fluid:

1. Locate the transaxle dipstick at the rear of the engine.
2. Remove the dipstick, wipe it clean, and reinstall it until fully seated.
3. Remove the dipstick and check the fluid level on the marked blade. It should be between the add mark and the full mark. If not, add the specified fluid to maintain the proper fluid level.
4. Or, remove the fill plug on the side of transaxle, Figure 39-13, and insert your little finger in the fill hole. The level should be at the lower edge of the hole or within 3/16″ of the lower edge. If not, add the specified fluid to maintain the proper fluid level.

Drain and Refill

Most manufacturers state that manual transaxle fluid need not be changed, unless the fluid has become contaminated by water or if the vehicle has been operated under severe service conditions (sustained high speed driving during hot weather, towing a trailer, etc.).

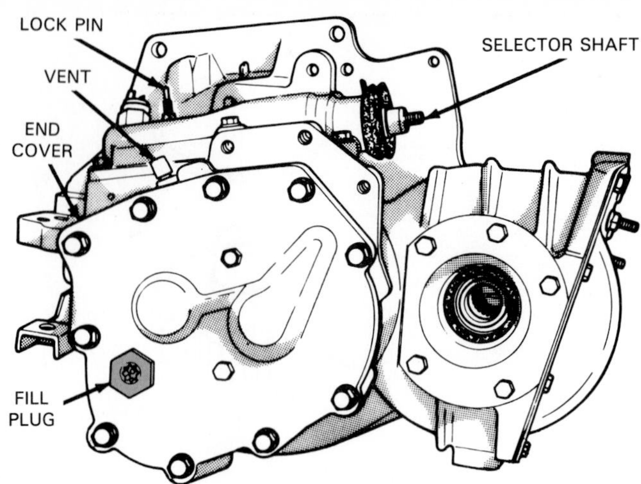

Figure 39-13. Some manual transaxles have a fill plug located on the side of the case. When the plug is removed, the threaded hole serves as an access point for checking the fluid level and as a "fill" hole. (Chrysler)

If drain and refill becomes necessary:

1. Raise the vehicle on a hoist.
2. Remove the pan from the side of the differential case and allow the fluid to drain completely.
3. Clean the pan and magnet, if so equipped.
4. Reinstall the pan, using a prescribed gasket or RTV (room temperature vulcanizing) sealer.
5. Tighten the attaching screws to the manufacturer's torque specification.
6. Lower the hoist.
7. Refill the transaxle to the proper level with the manufacturer's approved fluid, or refill with a fluid having equivalent properties.

Tighten Attaching Bolts

An important consideration in maintaining manual transaxles is checking the torque tightness of the transaxle-to-engine attaching bolts. Looseness could result in transaxle slipping out of gear. See Figure 39-14.

The transaxle-to-engine attaching bolts–correctly tightened–help ensure the integrity of the power train. They serve to preserve the proper alignment of engine and transaxle. Tighten the attaching bolts to manufacturer's torque specification.

Tighten Transaxle Mounts

Any maintenance procedure on manual transaxles requires a check of the condition of the mount (or mounts) and the torque tightness of the mount-to-transaxle case attaching screws or nuts. See Figure 39-15.

To check the condition of the transaxle mount:

1. Raise the car on a hoist.
2. Push up or pull down on the transaxle case while observing the mount.
3. If the rubber separates from the metal plate of the mount, replace the mount.

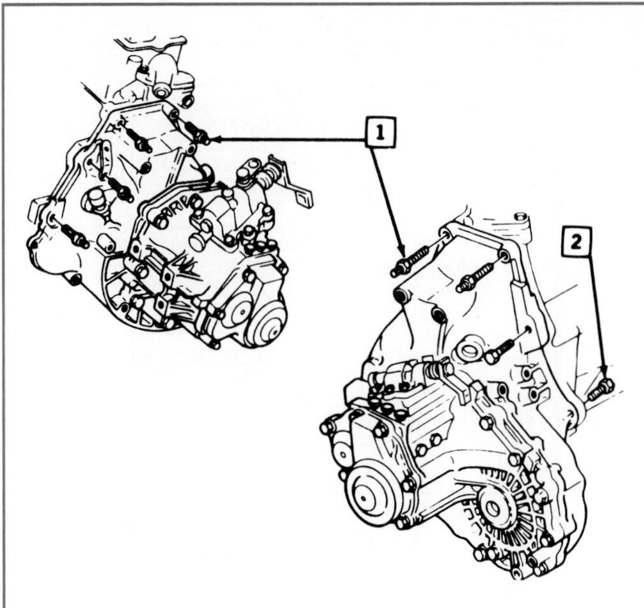

Figure 39-14. Correct torque tightness of the transaxle-to-engine attaching bolts is essential. Torque specification for this five-speed manual transaxle is 60 ft./lb. (75 N·m). (Oldsmobile)

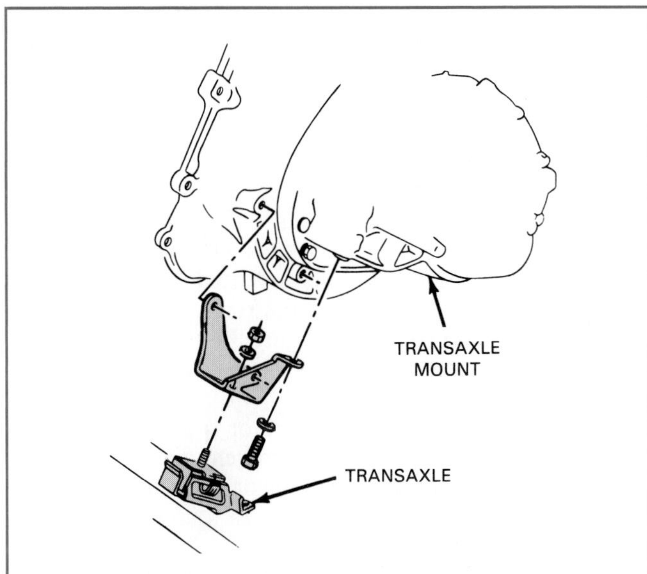

Figure 39-15. Transaxle mounts vary in design and location, but all support, position, and cradle the transaxle assembly in back of the engine. (Buick)

4. If the case moves up but not down, the mount has collapsed. Replace the mount.
5. If the mount appears to be intact, tighten the screws or nuts attaching the mount to the crossmember and to the transaxle case. Observe the manufacturer's torque specifications.

Automatic Transaxle Troubleshooting

No Drive Forward

- Hydraulic pressures too low.
- Low fluid level.
- Valve body malfunction or leakage.
- Worn or broken input shaft seal rings.
- Faulty overrunning clutch.
- Worn or faulty rear clutch.
- Broken or seized planetary gearset.

No Drive in Reverse

- Hydraulic pressures too low.
- Worn low-reverse band.
- Valve body malfunction or leakage.
- Low-reverse servo, band, or linkage malfunction.
- Incorrect gearshift control linkage setup or cable adjustment.
- Worn or faulty front clutch.

No Drive In Any Position

- Low hydraulic pressures.
- Malfunctioning valve body.
- Low fluid level.
- Clogged oil filter.
- Faulty oil pump.
- Broken or seized planetary gearsets.

Slips In All Positions

- Low hydraulic pressures.
- Malfunctioning valve body.
- Low fluid level.
- Clogged oil filter.
- Worn or broken input shaft seal rings.
- Aerated fluid.

Harsh Engagement

- Too high engine idle speed.
- Malfunctioning valve body.
- Too high hydraulic pressures.
- Worn or faulty rear clutch.
- Poor engine performance.

Erratic Shifts

- Low hydraulic pressures.
- Malfunctioning valve body.
- Low fluid level.
- Incorrect gearshift control linkage setup or cable adjustment.
- Clogged oil filter.
- Faulty oil pump.
- Aerated fluid.
- Incorrect throttle linkage adjustment.
- Worn or broken seal rings.
- Worn or faulty front clutch.

Drives In Neutral

- Malfunctioning valve body.
- Incorrect gearshift control linkage setup or cable adjustment.
- Insufficient clutch plate clearance.

- Worn or faulty rear clutch.
- Dragging rear clutch.

Grating, Scraping, or Growling Noise

- Worn low-reverse band.
- Maladjusted kickdown band.
- Damaged drive shaft bushings.
- Broken or seized planetary gearsets.
- Worn, broken, or seized overrunning clutch.

Buzzing Noise

- Malfunctioning valve body.
- Low fluid level.
- Too low engine idle speed.
- Damaged overrunning clutch.

Oil Blows Out Filler Hole

- Clogged oil filter.
- Aerated fluid.
- High fluid level.

Automatic Transaxle Maintenance

A quick review of these problems will reveal that certain causes repeatedly appear. Among common causes are: low fluid level, aerated fluid, clogged oil filter, and incorrect gearshift control linkage or cable adjustment.

It follows that regular checks of fluid level, fluid condition, and gearshift control linkage or cable adjustment–with corrective steps taken if necessary–will help avoid problems. See Figures 39-16 and 39-17.

Check Fluid Level

Always check fluid level at normal operating temperature (180-200°F or 83-93°C).

To check:

1. Park the car on a level surface.
2. Apply the parking brake.
3. Run the engine at slow idle.
4. Move the gear selector through all the gear positions.
5. Shift the selector to park and read the fluid level on the dipstick (wipe dipstick clean, reinsert until seated, then remove and read level).
6. If the fluid is hot, reading should be in the "cross-hatched" or "marked" area as shown in Figure 42-16.
7. Check the fluid for a burnt smell, indicating overheating of the transaxle.
8. Wipe some fluid from the dipstick with your thumb and index finger and feel for metal particles from worn internal parts.

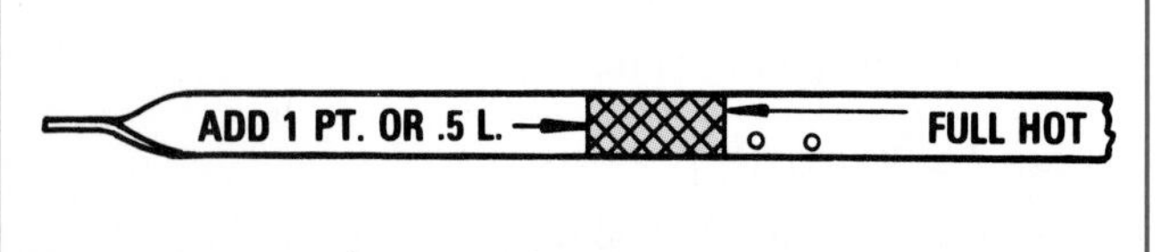

Figure 39-16. Transaxle dipsticks are marked to indicate a safe operating area immediately below the "full hot" level. Maintain the fluid level in this area. (Cadillac)

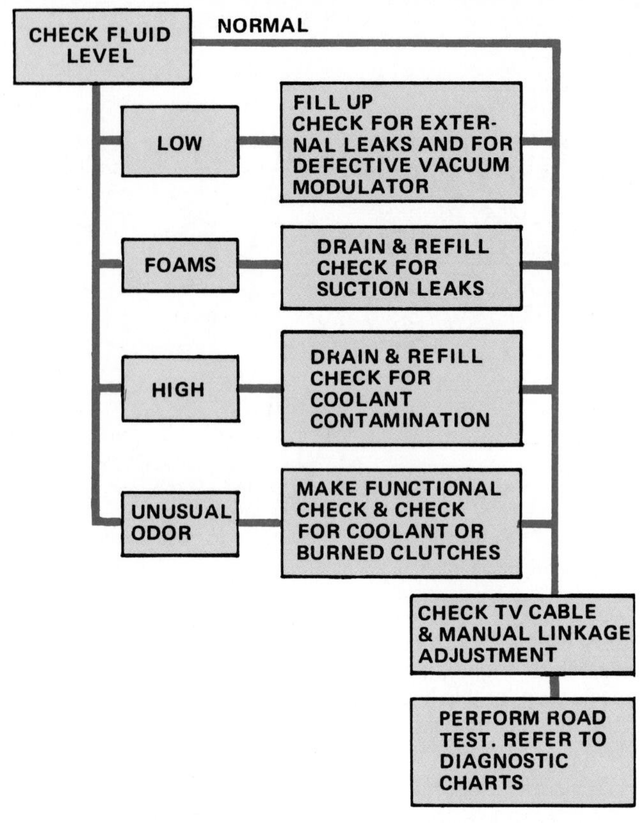

Figure 39-17. This chart lists the recommended steps for checking the automatic transaxle fluid level and condition. (Cadillac)

9. Wipe the remainder of the fluid on a clean, white cloth and check the stain for evidence of contaminants.
10. If the hot fluid passes these tests but the fluid level is low, add enough recommended fluid through the dipstick tube or filler hole to bring the level within "marks" on dipstick. See Figure 39-16.
11. Wait at least 60 seconds, and then recheck the fluid level. Do not overfill.
12. Install the dipstick in the tube or filler hole, making sure that it is fully seated to prevent dirt and/or water from entering the dipstick tube or filler hole.

Drain and Refill

If the fluid level is low, inspect the area all around the bottom of the transaxle for signs of fluid leakage. Leakage at the pan gasket, extension housing oil seal, or at the speedometer pinion adapter can be corrected without removing the transaxle from the vehicle.

Fluid coming from the transaxle vent usually indicates that the transaxle has been overfilled with fluid. When overfilled, the operation of the transaxle aerates the fluid, and foamy fluid is forced from the vent. When this occurs, the transaxle should be drained and refilled with the manufacturer's approved fluid or fluid with equivalent properties.

If the fluid needs to be changed:

1. Raise the vehicle on a hoist.
2. Place an oil drain barrel with large opening under the transaxle oil pan.
3. Loosen the pan bolts and tap the pan at one corner to break it loose from the gasketed surface and allow the fluid to drain into the barrel. Note: Certain transaxles

have a drain plug, Figure 39-18, simplifying the drain procedure.

4. Remove the oil pan and dump the remainder of the fluid into the barrel.
5. Remove and replace the filter with a new filter.
6. Clean and reinstall the pan, using the prescribed gasket or RTV (room temperature vulcanizing) sealer. Tighten the pan attaching screws to the manufacturer's in./lb. torque specification.
7. Lower the hoist.
8. Refill the transaxle with the manufacturer's approved fluid or fluid with equivalent properties.

Note: Some transaxles have separate sumps (fluid reservoirs) for transmission fluid and final drive fluid. In others, the final drive sump is integral with the transmission sump. Check the manufacturer's service manual for details.

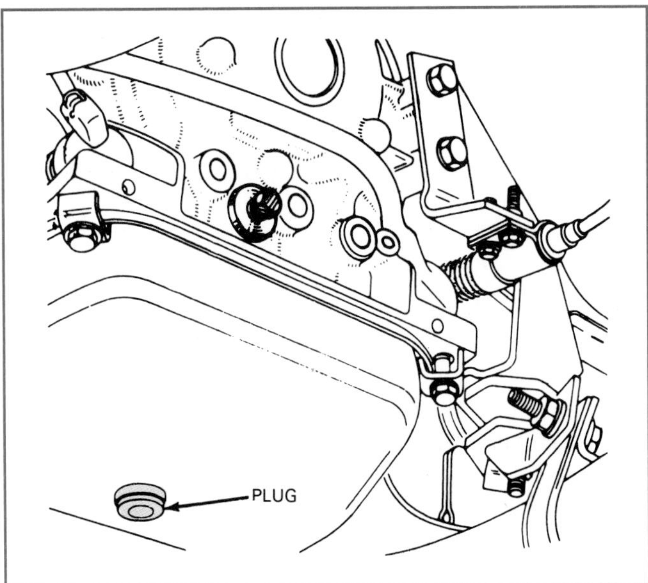

Figure 39-18. Automatic transaxle fluid drains usually require pan removal. This transaxle has a drain plug. Drain the fluid when it is hot to help remove as much old fluid as possible. (Chrysler)

Adjust Gearshift Control Linkage or Cable

Checking and adjusting the gearshift control linkage are key steps of automatic transaxle maintenance. Some setups only require a simple positional adjustment of the cable at the gearshift lever end, Figure 39-19. Others require a step-by-step procedure from securing body bolts to torque tightening the cable pin attaching nut.

Adjust TV Control Linkage

On certain Ford automatic transaxles, the key linkage adjustment is in the TV (throttle valve) control linkage. Correct positioning of the sliding trunnion block, Figure 39-20, will ensure proper actuation of the internal TV control mechanism that regulates TV control pressure.

To adjust typical TV control linkage for a Ford automatic transaxle:

1. Run the engine to the normal operating temperature with all accessories turned off.
2. Check to see that the hot engine curb idle speed is set to specifications.
3. Use care when working near a hot exhaust gas recirculation valve.
4. Loosen the bolt on the sliding trunnion block.
5. Remove the corrosion from the TV control rod so that the trunnion block slides freely.
6. With the engine idling in park, use one finger to rotate the TV control lever upward with light force to bring the lever against its internal idle stop.
7. Holding firm with light upward pressure on the lever, tighten the bolt on the trunnion block to 7-11 ft./lb. (9-14 N·m).

Consult Service Manuals

Refer to manufacturers' service manuals for major service operations. Detailed procedures are given for points of inspection, analysis of problems, parts replacements, fits and adjustments with the transaxle in car or out-of-car. Exploded views and step-by-step procedures are spelled out for transaxle removal from the vehicle, for disassembly and reassembly of internal parts, and for transaxle reinstallation.

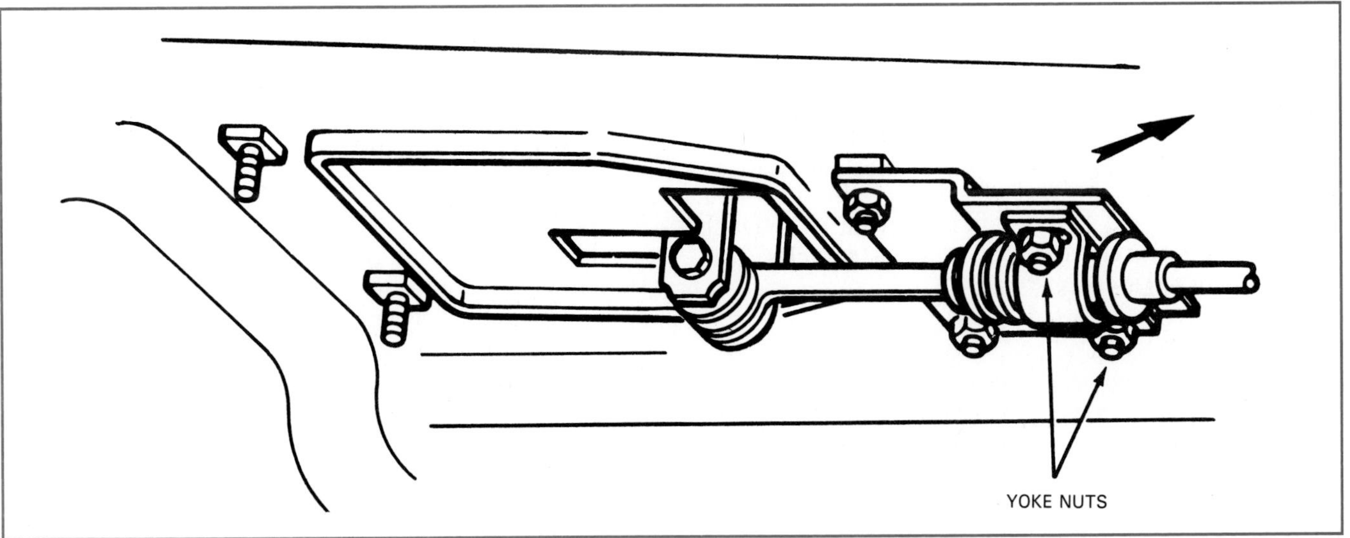

Figure 39-19. One simple automatic transaxle gear selector cable adjustment only requires that the yoke and cable be shifted forward to remove slack in cable. Yoke nuts secure the adjustment. (Chrysler)

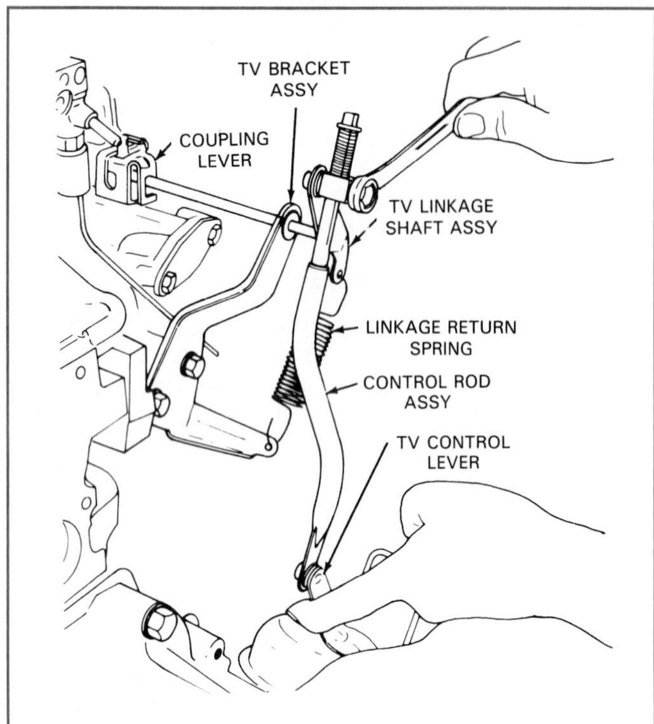

Figure 39-20. This diagram and the specific adjustment procedure given in text reference are typical of service and repair information contained in manufacturers' service manuals. (Ford)

Service manuals contain directions and specifications for air pressure checks, control pressure tests, shift point checks, and for torque tightening attaching nuts and bolts. Special service tools are listed. Fluid capacities are given. In-depth troubleshooting charts are furnished and road test diagnosis is described in detail.

Service manuals are generally recognized as the ultimate authority for service information for specific makes and models of vehicles.

Chapter 39–Review Questions

1. A transaxle is an engine power transfer mechanism that combines a _____ assembly and a _____ assembly in a single unit.
2. Transaxles may be either manual or automatic. True or False?
3. Transaxles may be used in which of the following applications?
   (A) Front-wheel drive cars.
   (B) Mid-engine cars.
   (C) Rear-wheel drive cars.
   (D) All of the above.
4. How are transaxle gear ratios determined?
5. Which of the following gear ratios is overdrive?
   (A) 0.81:1.
   (B) 1.23:1.
   (C) 1.92:1.
   (D) 3.2:1.
6. In transaxle applications, the _____ remains in light contact with the clutch pressure plate under normal driving conditions.
7. Trace power flow in a Ford four-speed manual transaxle from the engine to the driving wheels.
8. The differential (final drive) assembly divides the torque between the _____ and allows them to rotate at different speeds.
9. In transaxles, the differential is also called:
   (A) drive axle.
   (B) final drive.
   (C) torque divider.
   (D) torque converter.
10. Power flow to the planetary gearsets in a Chrysler three-speed automatic transaxle is based on which _____ are engaged and which _____ are applied.
11. A General Motors four-speed automatic transaxle of unusual design utilizes a _____ instead of conventional ring gear and pinion differential gears
    (A) sprocket and drive link assembly
    (B) synchronizer and blocker ring
    (C) planetary gearset
    (D) reaction gearset
12. A manual transaxle slips out of gear. Technician A says it could be caused by broken or loose engine mounts. Technician B says it could be caused if transaxle is loose on the engine housing. Who is right?
    (A) A only.
    (B) B only.
    (C) Both A & B.
    (D) Neither A nor B.
13. A manual transaxle has gear clash in forward speeds. Technician A says it could be caused by burred synchronizers. Technician B says it could be caused by an improperly installed clutch disc. Who is right?
    (A) A only.
    (B) B only.
    (C) Both A & B.
    (D) Neither A nor B.
14. Name three maintenance checks on manual transaxles.
15. Manual transaxle fluid should be changed if it has become contaminated by _____ or if the vehicle has been operated under _____.
16. Name two indications of faulty transaxle mounts.
17. An automatic transaxle has harsh engagement. Technician A says it could be caused by a high engine idle speed. Technician B says it could be caused by low fluid level. Who is right?
    (A) A only.
    (B) B only.
    (C) Both A & B.
    (D) Neither A nor B.
18. Automatic transaxle fluid coming from the transaxle vent usually indicates that the fluid level is _____.
19. Some transaxles have separate sumps for transmission fluid and final drive fluid. True or False?
20. Refer to manufacturers' service manuals for:
    (A) major service operations.
    (B) analysis of problems.
    (C) specifications for fits and adjustments, fluid capacities, and torque tightness values.
    (D) All of the above.

Chapter 40
Driveline, Universal Joints, Differentials, and Driving Axles

After studying this chapter, you will be able to:
- Trace the transfer of power in the drive train of a rear-wheel drive vehicle.
- Discuss the need for universal joints in the driveline.
- State the principles of operation of the differential.
- Distinguish between Hotchkiss drive, torque tube drive, and control arm drive.
- Explain the types and functions of various constant velocity joints.
- Give examples of several different front-wheel drive driving axle systems.

Drivelines

In basic passenger car design, the ***driveline*** connects the transmission with the driving axles. In effect, the driveline transmits engine power to the driving wheels. See Figure 40-1.

Rear-wheel Drive Driveline

In rear-wheel drive applications, the driveline consists of one or more universal joints, the drive shaft, and differential drive pinion gear. The ***drive train,*** on the other hand, includes the engine, transmission, driveline, differential assembly, and driving axles.

In rear-wheel drive cars, the engine and transmission are mounted on the frame or unit body crossmembers, and the driving wheels are free to move up and down in relation to the frame. This causes constant changes in the angularity of the line of drive. Therefore, flexibility is needed in the drive train, and it usually is provided by universal joints. See Figure 40-2.

Universal Joints

A ***universal joint,*** Figure 40-3, is a mechanical device that can transmit torque and/or rotational motion from one shaft to another at fixed or varying angles. Most cars utilize a universal joint at the front and rear of the drive shaft. See Figure 40-4. A third "U-joint" is used on applications having two drive shafts.

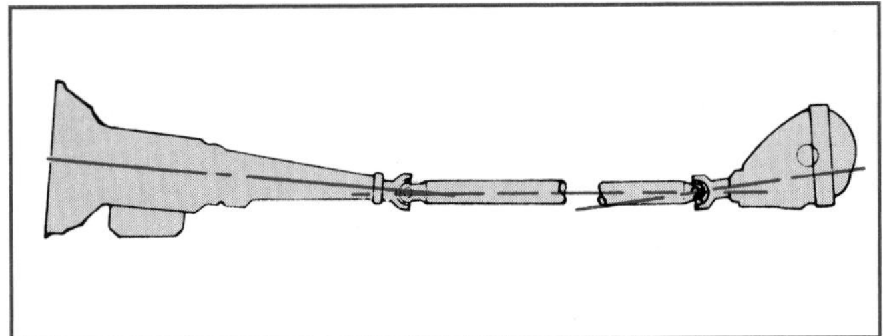

Figure 40-1. Driveline angle is the difference in alignment between the transmission output shaft, drive shaft, and drive pinion shaft centerlines. (Ford)

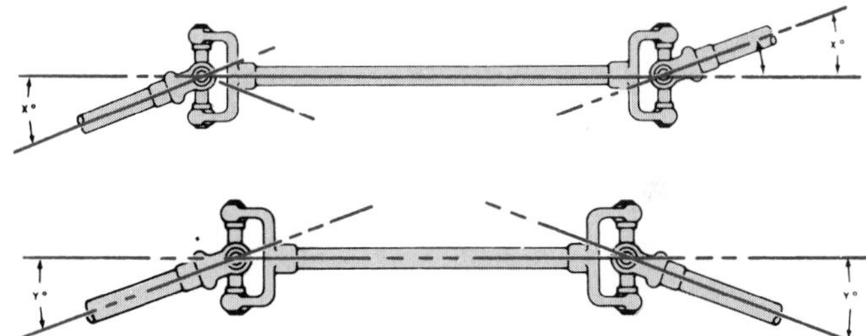

Figure 40-2. Universal joints at both ends of the drive shaft compensate for changes in the angularity of the driveline. Here X° = X° and Y° = Y°. (Chevrolet)

The front universal joint is connected to the transmission output shaft. The rear universal joint is connected by a yoke to the differential drive pinion gear shaft. This balanced arrangement of power transfer components serves to compensate for any changes in the line of drive.

Drive Shaft

The ***drive shaft*** or ***propeller shaft*** on rear-wheel drive vehicles usually is tubular steel with a yoke (slotted end that straddles another part) aligned and welded to each end. See Figures 40-4 and 40-5. Most drive shafts are of solid tube, one-piece construction. In certain rather rare applications, the drive shaft is made up of two concentric (having a common center) tubes separated by molded rubber rings to absorb vibrations.

Differential

The ***differential*** is a gear system that transfers power from the drive shaft to the driving axles. Since the driving axles are splined to the differential side gears at right angles to the line of drive, the differential assembly uses a drive pinion gear and ring gear to redirect the transfer of power to the driving axles. See Figure 40-6.

The differential assembly also permits one driving wheel to turn faster than the other to prevent skidding and scuffing of rear tires on turns. See explanation in Figures 40-7 and 40-8.

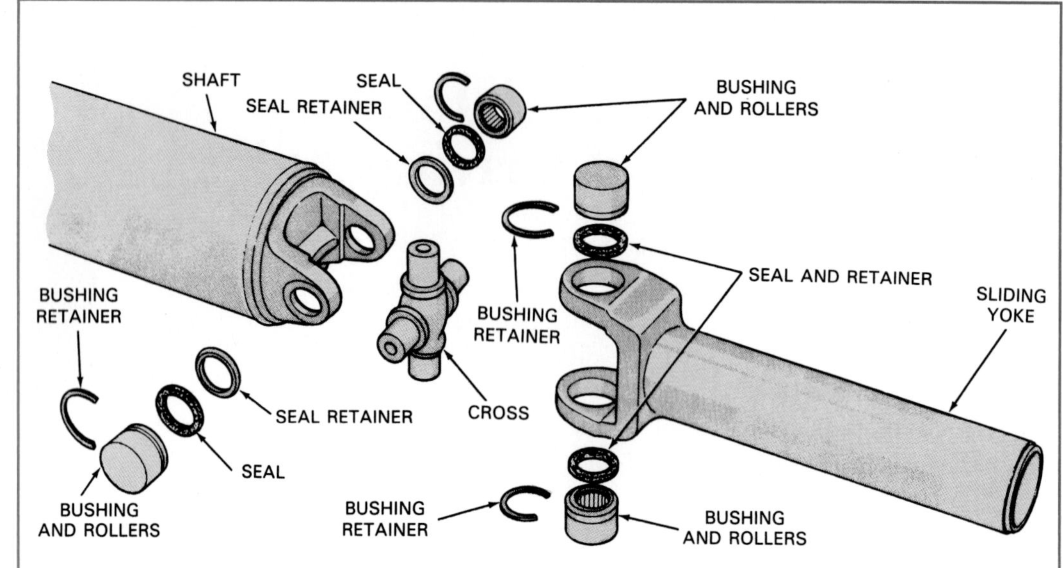

Figure 40-3. Exploded view shows a typical cross-and-roller universal joint that permits changes in angularity between the drive shaft yoke and the sliding or slip yoke that connects to the transmission output shaft. (Chrysler)

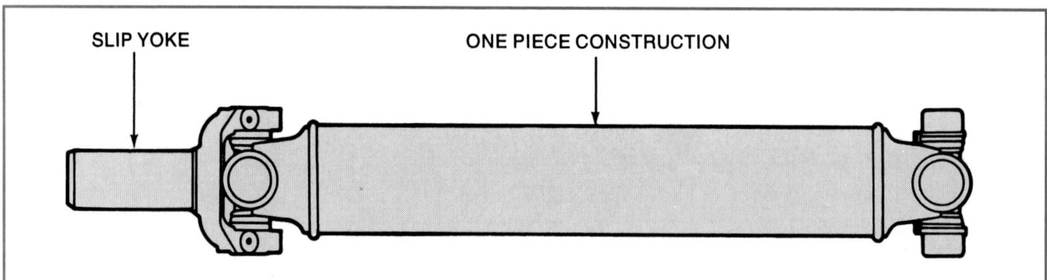

Figure 40-4. Usually, a one-piece drive shaft with front and rear universal joints is used on rear-wheel drive passenger cars. (Chevrolet)

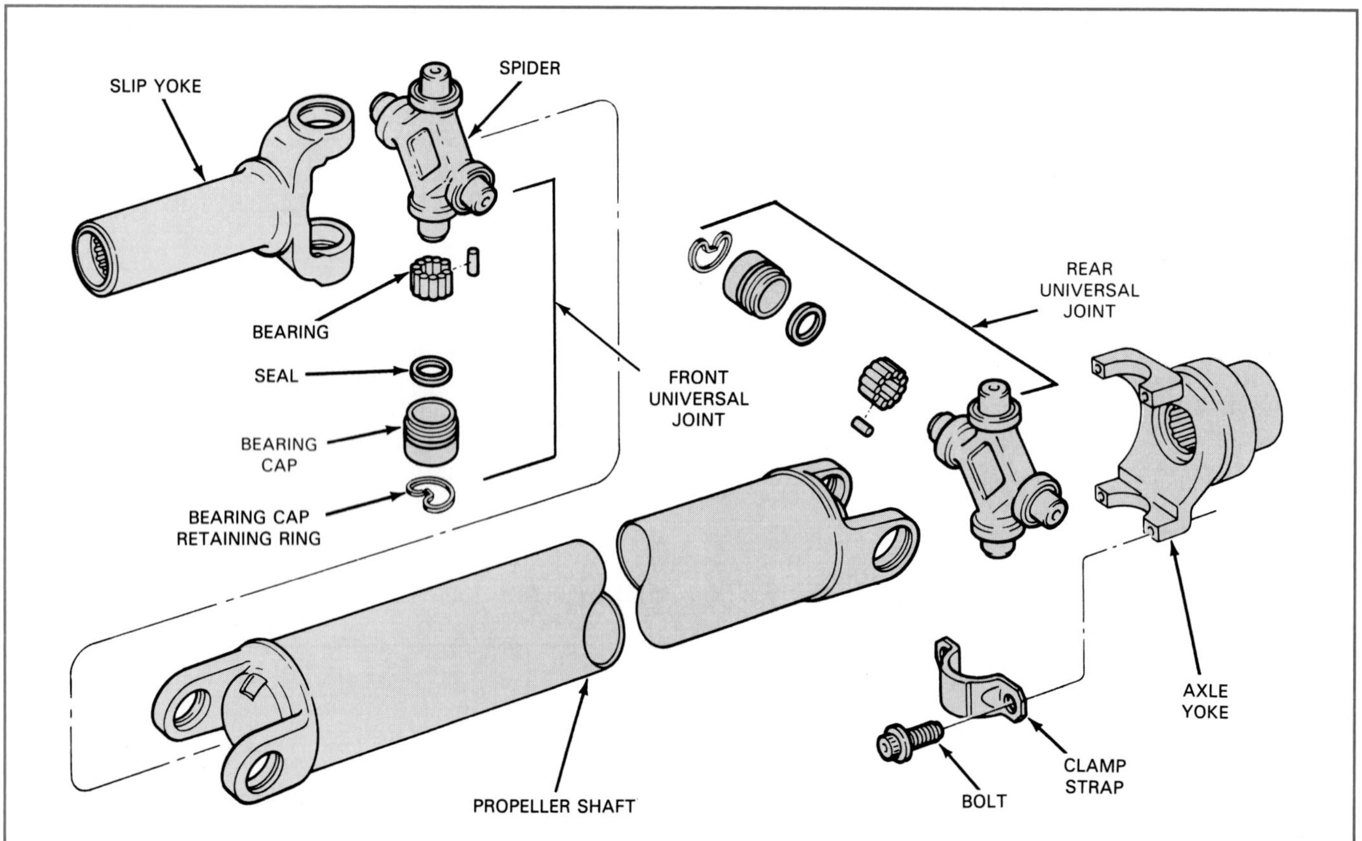

Figure 40-5. Exploded view of a complete drive shaft assembly includes shaft, universal joints, front slip yoke, and rear axle yoke that connects to the differential drive pinion shaft. (Chrysler)

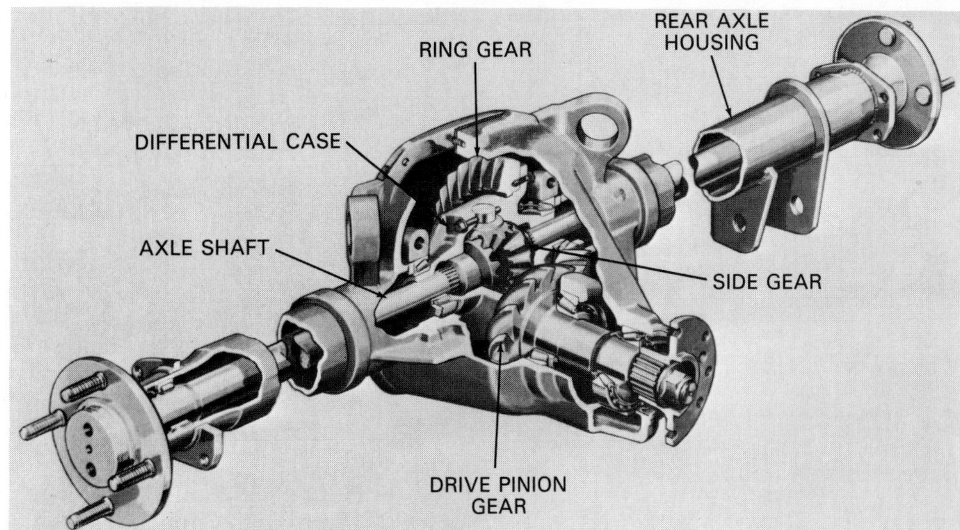

Figure 40-6. Cutaway view of a complete differential and rear axle assembly details the right angle drive of the drive pinion gear to the ring gear. Also note the "spline mesh" of the side gears and axle shafts. (Ford)

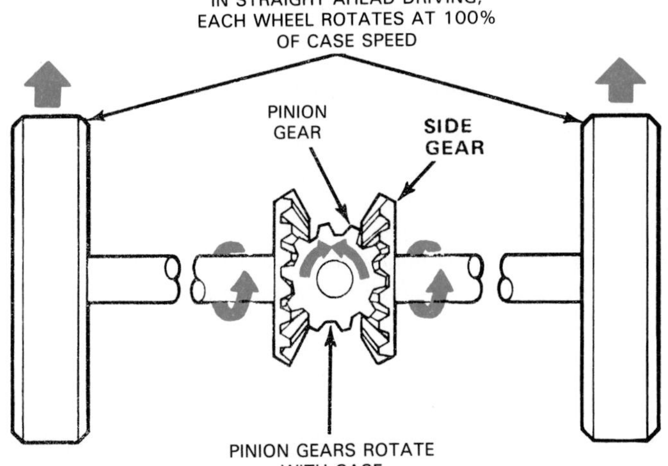

Figure 40-7. In straight ahead driving, the entire differential assembly rotates as a unit with the side gears and pinion gears locked together in the case. (Chrysler)

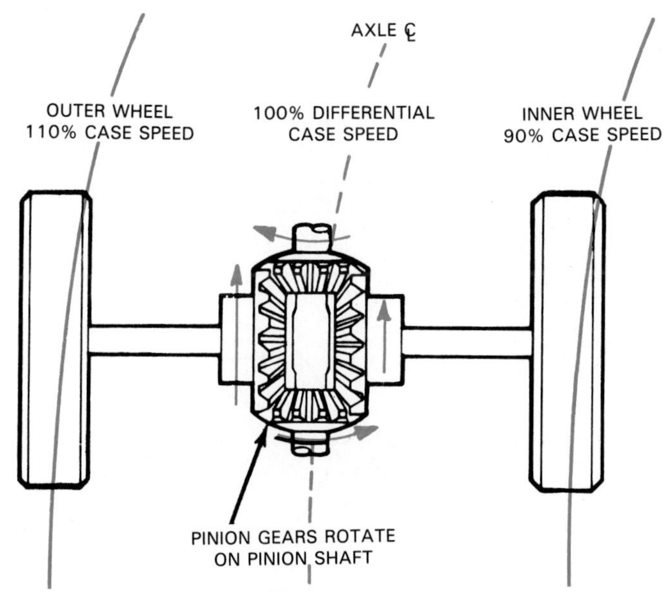

Figure 40-8. On turns, the pinion gears turn on their axes and roll around the side gears to permit the driving wheels to rotate at unequal speeds. (Chrysler)

Driving Axles

The ***driving axles*** of a rear-wheel drive passenger car are used to hold, align, and drive the rear wheels and support the weight of the vehicle. These ***semifloating axles*** generally are flanged on the outer end, Figure 40-9, and fitted with press-fit bolts for use with lug nuts for installing the brake drums and the wheels.

The rear axle shaft wheel bearings usually are the straight roller type, Figure 40-9, and roll directly on the

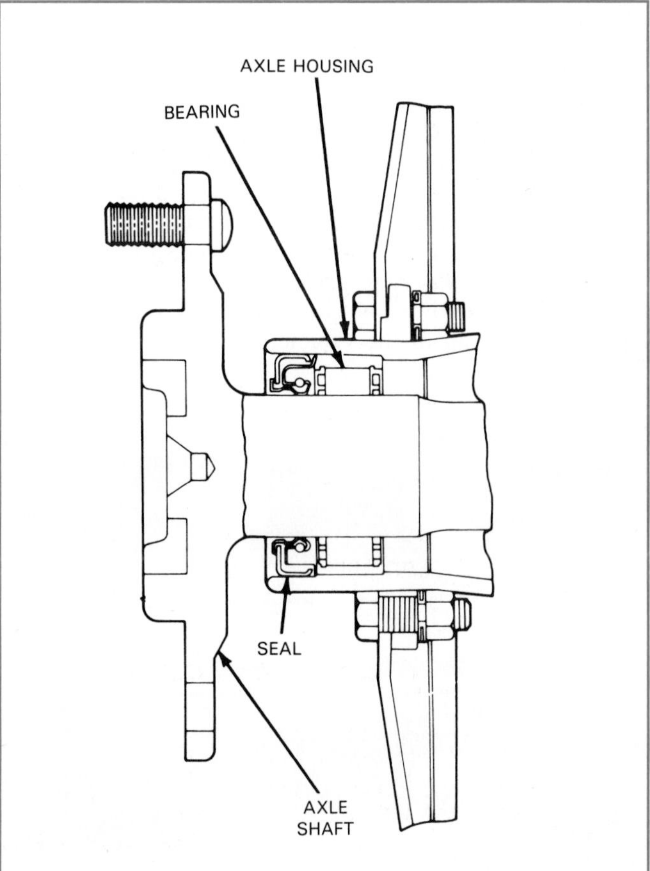

Figure 40-9. Rear axle shaft bearing and seal installed in the axle housing ride on the machined surface of the axle shaft. (Chevrolet)

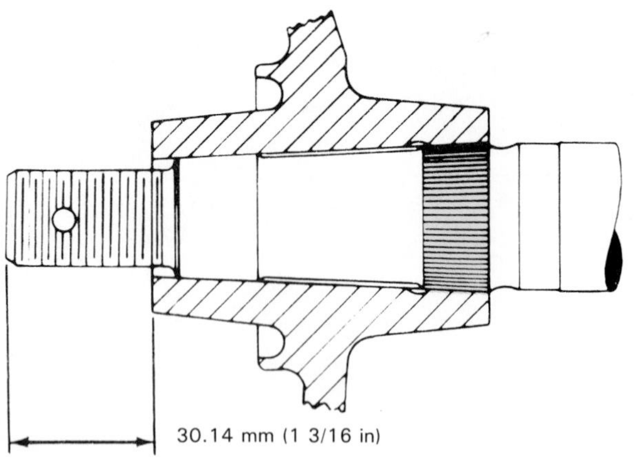

Figure 40-10. In this rear axle shaft design, the axle has external serrations and the hub has internal serrations. Note the specification given for how far the hub must be pressed on the axle shaft. (Chrysler)

axle shaft. The bearing assembly is held in position in the axle housing by the axle shaft seal.

The inner ends of the axle shafts are externally splined for meshing with the internally splined differential side gears that drive the axle shafts. See Figure 40-6.

In another design of semi-floating rear axle, the axle shaft is tapered at the outer end to fit into a tapered hub. The shaft is also keyed in place and secured by a nut on the threaded end of the axle shaft. To remove the hub from this type of axle, it is necessary to use a wheel puller.

In still another tapered axle and hub design, a key is also used to align the keyway in the hub with the keyway in the axle shaft. Also note in Figure 40-10 that the hub and axle shaft are serrated. In order to fully engage the hub serrations with the axle shaft serrations, the hub must be installed to a specified dimension from hub outer face to the end of the axle shaft.

A ***full-floating rear drive axle*** used primarily on trucks drives the wheel, but it does not hold the wheel or support the weight of the vehicle. See Figure 40-11. The axle housing is fitted with two roller bearings that carry the weight of the vehicle.

The axle shaft in full-floating applications is flanged on the outer end and bolted to the hub. A full-floating axle can be removed from the axle housing without disturbing the wheel.

Driveline to Driving Wheels

In tracing the driveline, differential, driving axles, and driving wheels, power is transferred:

1. From the transmission output shaft through the front universal joint to the drive shaft.
2. From the drive shaft through the rear universal joint to the differential drive pinion gear.
3. From the drive pinion gear to the ring gear.
4. From the ring gear to the attached differential case, pinion gears, and side gears.
5. From the side gears to the driving axles.
6. From the driving axles to the driving wheels.

Torque Effect on Driveline

As mentioned, the balanced arrangement of power transfer components (universal joints and drive shaft) serves to compensate for any changes in the line of drive. However, when engine power is applied to the drive train, torque is developed in the driving wheels. See Figure 40-12. This twisting action creates further changes in the angularity of the line of drive.

When power is transmitted by the drive shaft, the drive pinion gear tries to turn the ring gear. The ring gear must turn the axle shafts and the wheels, so it resists being moved. The pinion gear then attempts to "roll around" the ring gear. Since it cannot, the pinion gear transfers the torque to the axle housing. The obvious visible effect of this torque is the tendency of the back end of the car to dip when power is suddenly applied to the driving wheels.

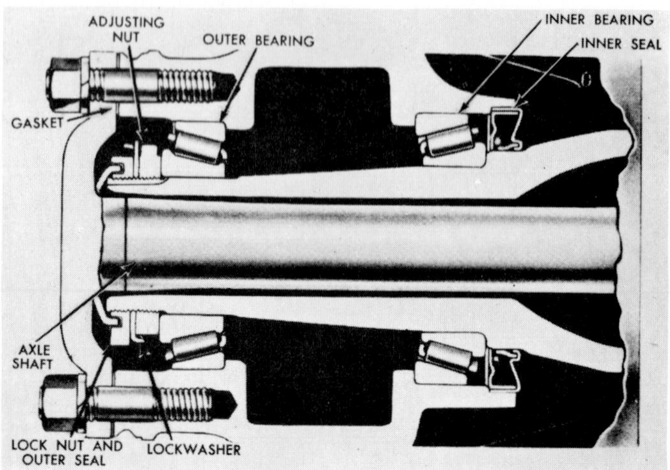

Figure 40-11. The full-floating rear axle and hub is used in truck applications. The weight of the vehicle rests on roller bearings mounted on the axle housing.

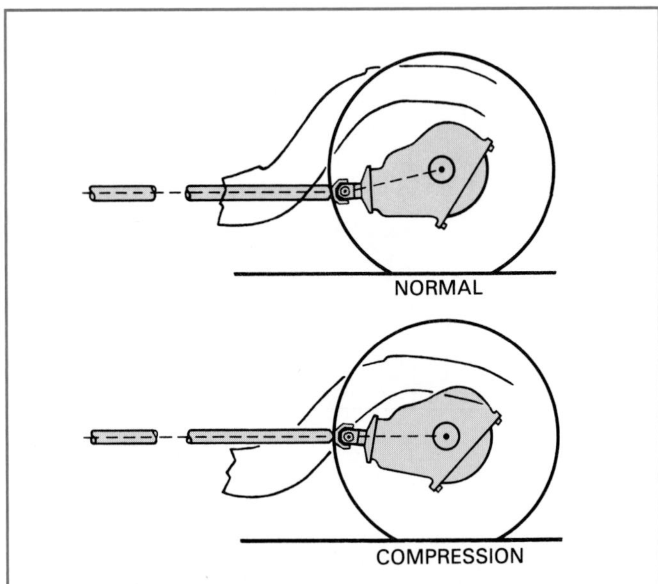

Figure 40-12. The differential housing will tilt upward when engine torque is relayed from the drive shaft to the drive pinion and rear axle housing.

Torque Transfer or Drive

When torque force from the engine is applied to the drive train, power to drive the vehicle is transferred from the drive pinion shaft to the rear axle housing and from the axle housing to either the springs, torque tube, or control arms, depending upon which type of "drive" is built into the vehicle.

Hotchkiss Drive

The ***Hotchkiss drive*** features leaf spring rear suspension and an open drive shaft with two universal joints to compensate for variations in road surfaces, load conditions, and power application (torque) that cause changes in alignment between the transmission output shaft and the drive pinion shaft. When the Hotchkiss drive is used, the driving wheel force is transmitted to the front end of the springs, which push against the vehicle's frame. See Figure 40-13.

Torque Tube Drive

In cars equipped with ***torque tube drive,*** the pushing action is at the front end of the torque tube. Only one universal joint is used in the driveline at the front end of the drive shaft. In this case, the drive shaft is within a long, large tube which is anchored to the axle housing. The torque tube does not permit the axle housing to twist when engine power is applied. Also, the springs do not absorb any torque and are required only to cushion the ride.

With the torque tube drive, the engine usually is mounted as low as possible in the frame or at an angle with the rear end lower than the front end. The object is to obtain a line of drive as straight as possible for power transmission.

Control Arm Drive

In ***control arm drive,*** driving and braking forces are transferred to the front end of heavy-duty control arms, Figure 40-14. The torque transfer effect is similar to a Hotchkiss drive, but coil springs are used at the rear rather than leaf-type springs. Some cars use three control arms, most use four.

Drive Shaft Length

In addition to line of drive problems caused by angularity of the drive shaft, the distance between the transmission output shaft and the drive pinion shaft is subject to change. This creates the need for some flexibility in the length of the drive shaft.

In referring to the Hotchkiss drive in Figure 40-15, the front end of the drive shaft is attached to the transmission shaft at B. The rear end is attached to the drive pinion shaft at C. As the wheels move up and down, the drive shaft swings up and down at arc A-A around pivot B. At the same time, the pinion shaft C–being attached to the rear axle–swings in an arc D-D around the pivot where the spring is anchored to the frame at E. Therefore, as the arcs A-A and D-D do not coincide, it will be necessary for the drive shaft to alternately lengthen and shorten as the wheels move up and down in relation to the frame.

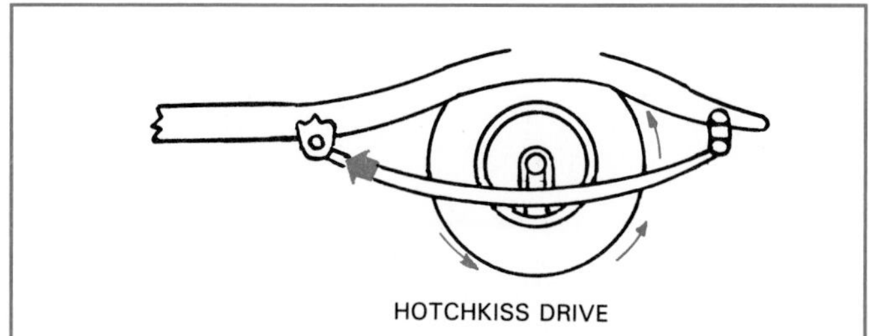

Figure 40-13. In a Hotchkiss drive setup, the driving force is transmitted from the rear wheels to the front of the rear springs.

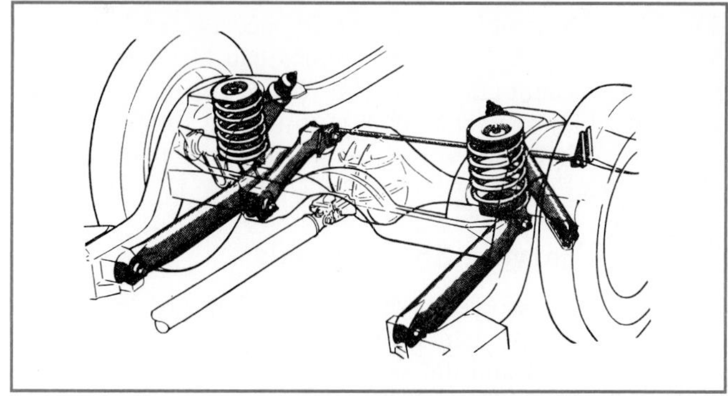

Figure 40-14. This Ford-Mercury rear suspension features a control arm drive. Two parallel lower arms extend forward to rubber-bushed anchors for transfer of driving force. (Ford)

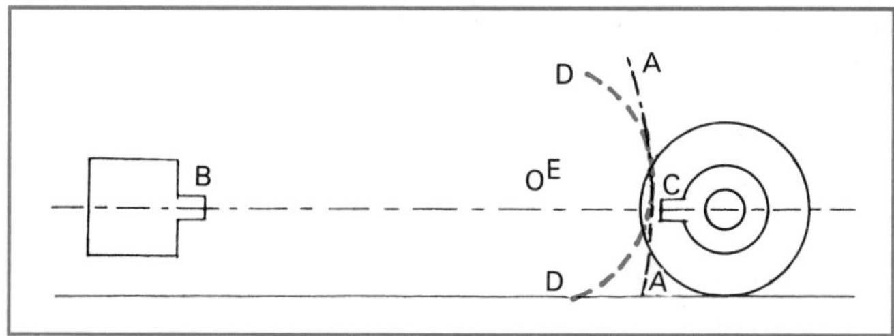

Figure 40-15. In a Hotchkiss drive, the length of the drive shaft varies because of changes in the wheelbase as the rear wheels move up and down with road surface irregularities.

Slip Joints

One method of lengthening or shortening the drive shaft is by means of a splined shaft coupling or ***slip joint.*** See Figure 40-16. When this type of slip joint is used, it is

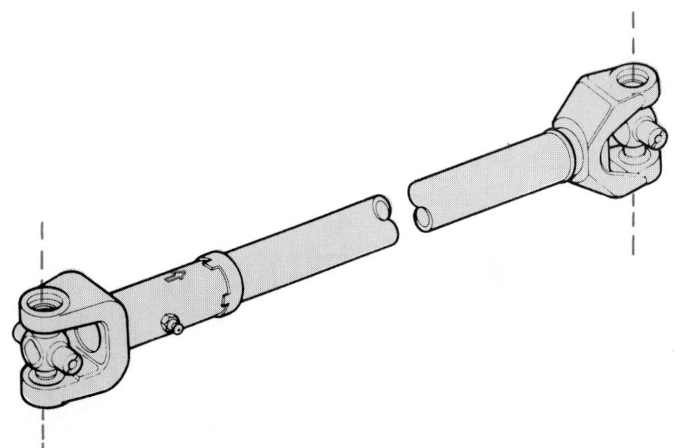

Figure 40-16. The front and rear drive shaft yokes must be "in phase." The shaft must be assembled into the front yoke so that the marks align and the yokes are in the same plane.

possible to assemble it incorrectly because of the many different ways in which the splines can be aligned. This results in an annoying vibration. These slip joints usually are marked for correct assembly. If not, the splines must be aligned so that both yokes are in the same plane, or "in phase." See Figure 40-16.

Effect of Varying Shaft Speeds

When the two yokes of the drive shaft are "in phase," the speed of the transmission output shaft and pinion shaft will be constant and the same if the line of drive of both shafts is uniform. The velocity of the drive shaft will not be constant, but this is unimportant as long as the velocity of the driving and driven shafts is uniform.

When the two yokes are "out of phase," the rotational speed of the shafts will be uniform only if the shafts are operated in a straight line. When operating at an angle with the yokes "out of phase," a conventional universal joint will cause the driven shaft to speed up and slow down each revolution. The number of turns per shaft will be the same, but the velocity of the driven shaft will fluctuate.

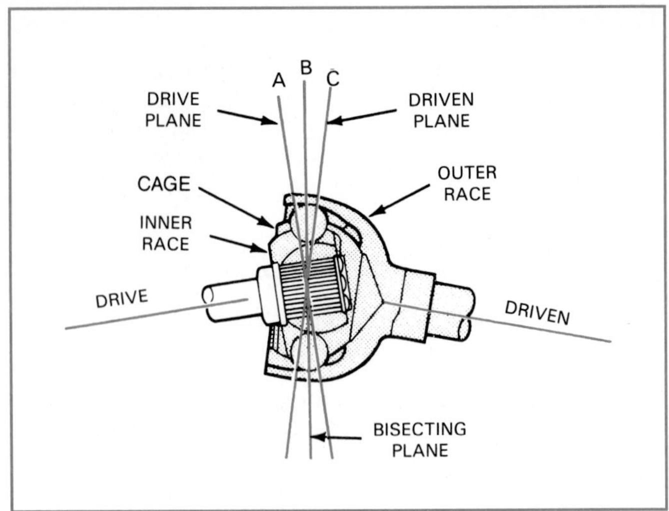

Figure 40-17. Rzeppa-type constant velocity joint used in front-wheel drive applications: A–Angle of driving axle shaft. B–Plane of driving contact. C–Angle of shaft that turns front wheel. (Ford)

Constant Velocity Joints

The fluctuation of speed of the driven shaft is further emphasized in the design of driving axles. In the case of front-wheel drive vehicles, the universal joints used in the driving axle assemblies must transfer driving power to the front wheels and, at the same time, compensate for steering action on turns.

To solve this fluctuation problem, special universal joints known as ***constant velocity joints*** were developed, Figure 40-17. In the example shown, rolling balls in curved grooves are utilized to obtain uniform motion. The balls, which are the driving contact, move laterally as the joint rotates. This permits the point of driving contact between the two halves of the coupling to remain in a plane which bisects the angle between the two shafts. See Figure 40-17. By this means, the fluctuation in speed of the driven shaft is avoided.

In a parallel development for use in rear-wheel drive shafts, Figures 40-18 and 40-19, two yoke-and-cross universal joints are placed adjacent and connected to form a constant velocity joint. A similar design of constant velocity joint is called a ***double cardan.*** A double cardan joint with lubrication fittings is shown in Figure 40-20.

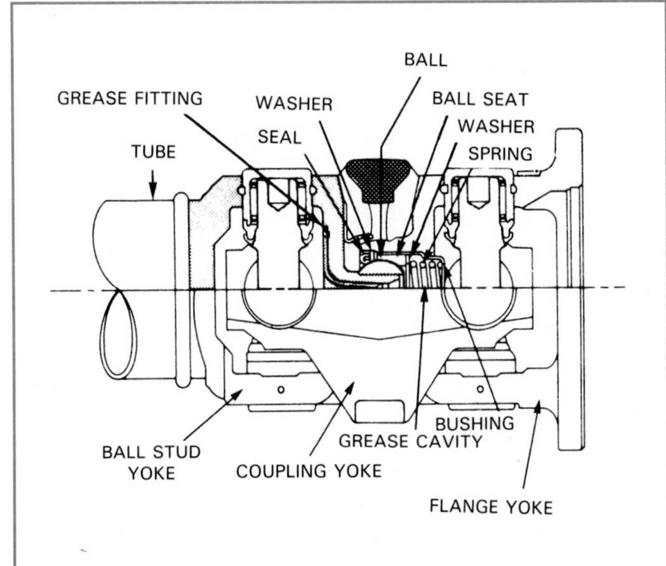

Figure 40-18. This rear-wheel drive constant velocity universal joint consists of two single joints connected by a link yoke and maintained in relative position by a center ball and socket.

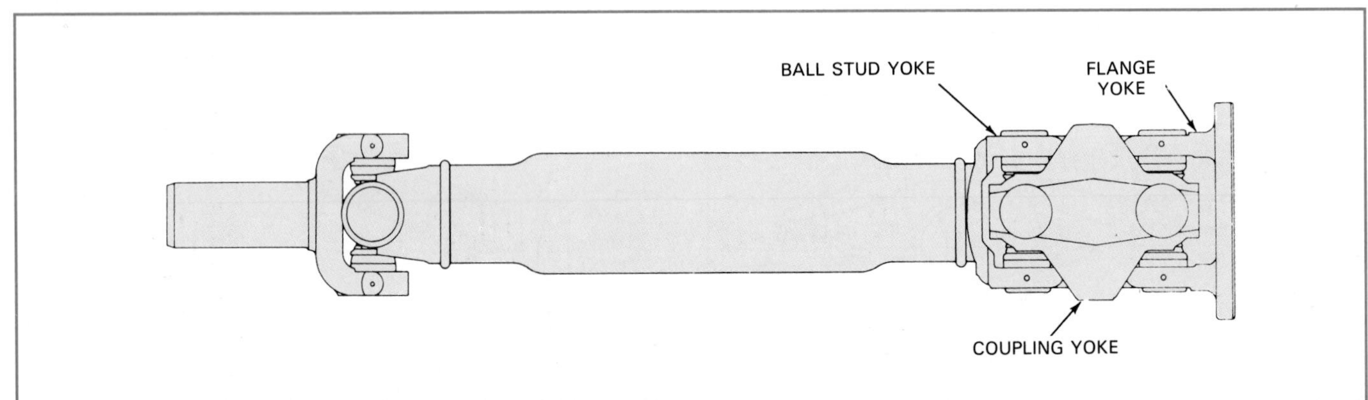

Figure 40-19. Constant velocity joint (at right) cancels out vibration that could occur from speed fluctuation with single universal joints at both ends of drive shaft.

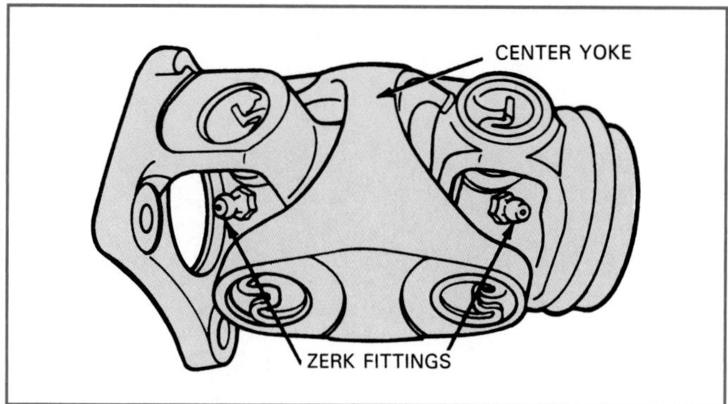

Figure 40-20. The double cardan constant velocity joint consists of two cross-and-roller universal joints (with ball studs and a centering spring in between) that are coupled by a center yoke. (Ford)

Transfer Cases

When a vehicle is driven by both front and rear wheels (four-wheel drive), it is equipped with a ***power takeoff*** to drive both axles. This auxiliary device is known as a ***transfer case,*** Figure 40-21. It is customary to provide a shifting device on these units so that the front drive can be disengaged if desired.

On four-wheel drive vehicles, the angularity of the drive shafts between front and rear wheels changes constantly. Therefore, the transfer case is positioned in the best possible compromise to serve both axles. Each drive shaft is fitted with a slip joint to accommodate changes in distance between axles and transfer case as the wheels move up and down.

Center Bearings

In some full-size passenger cars, the drive shaft is divided into two sections and a supporting ***center bearing*** is utilized. The center bearing serves to stabilize the shaft and reduces vibration and "whip." The whip comes from centrifugal force aided by any unbalance that may exist in the shaft. For this reason, all drive shafts are carefully balanced.

Differentials and Axles

Early automobiles were driven by means of belts or ropes around pulleys mounted on the driving wheels and engine shaft or transmission shaft. Because there always was some slippage of the belts, one wheel could rotate faster than the other when turning a corner.

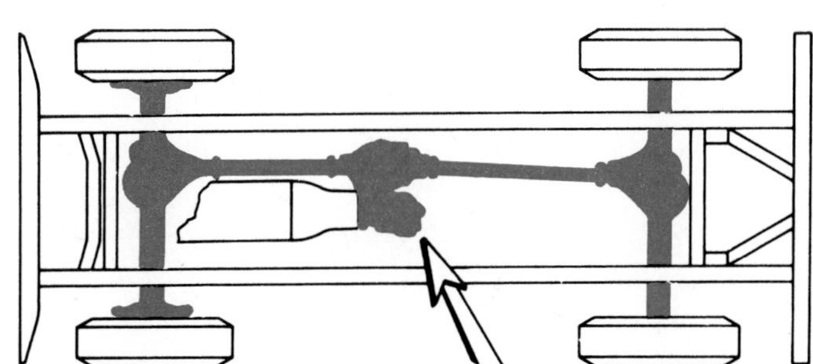

Figure 40-21. Engine torque goes from the transmission to the transfer case, where it is applied to the drive shafts extending to each driving axle. (Chrysler)

When belts and pulleys proved unsatisfactory, automobile builders borrowed an idea from bicycle design and applied sprockets and chains. This was a positive driving arrangement, so it was necessary to provide differential gearing to permit one driving wheel to turn faster than the other, Figures 40-8 and 40-22.

Differential Gears

In a typical differential gear arrangement, Figure 40-22, the ***drive pinion gear*** turns the ***ring gear*** and the ***differential case*** attached to it. The differential pinion gears mounted in the case mesh with the differential ***side gears*** that are splined to the rear axle shafts.

In straight ahead operation, the ring gear and differential case (with enclosed differential pinion gears and side gears) rotate as a unit. The differential pinion gears do not turn about their own axes, but apply equal effort to each of the differential side gears and axle shafts.

On turns, the resistance against the rotation of one axle increases as the wheels turn at different speeds. This causes the differential pinion gears to turn on their own axes and roll around the differential side gear on the reluctant one of the two axles.

This action allows the reluctant axle to slow down or stand still, causing a corresponding increase in the speed of rotation of the other axle. If one axle does not turn at all, the other axle will turn at almost twice the normal speed. It is possible for the drive wheels to turn at unequal speeds while the same amount of power is applied to both of them.

Bevel Gears. Pinion and ring gears have different tooth designs. The original type was known as a ***straight bevel.*** The teeth were straight, like a spur gear, Figure 40-23. Another type is known as a ***spiral bevel.*** In this case, the teeth are curved and operate quietly because the curved teeth make a sliding contact. The spiral bevel ring gear and pinion setup is stronger because more than one tooth is in contact at all times.

Hypoid Gears. Note that the pinion shaft in Figure 40-23 is in line with the center of the ring gear. Figure 40-24 shows a ***hypoid gear*** with the pinion shaft below the center of the ring gear. The advantage of this design is that it allows the drive shaft to be placed lower to permit reducing the hump in the floor.

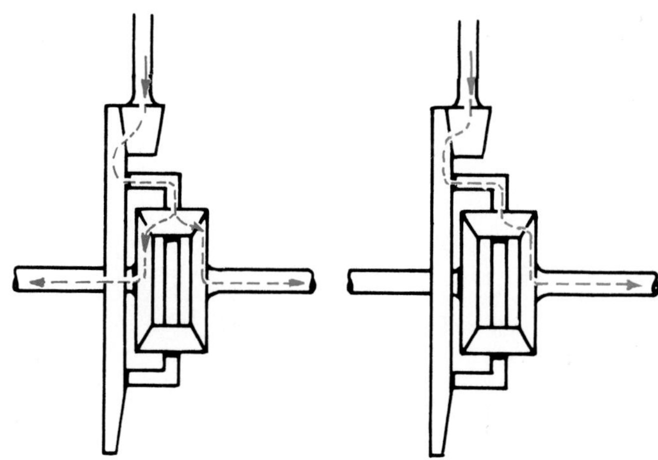

Figure 40-22. Differential gearing shown in the diagram indicates flow of power: Left–Straight ahead. Right–During left turn.

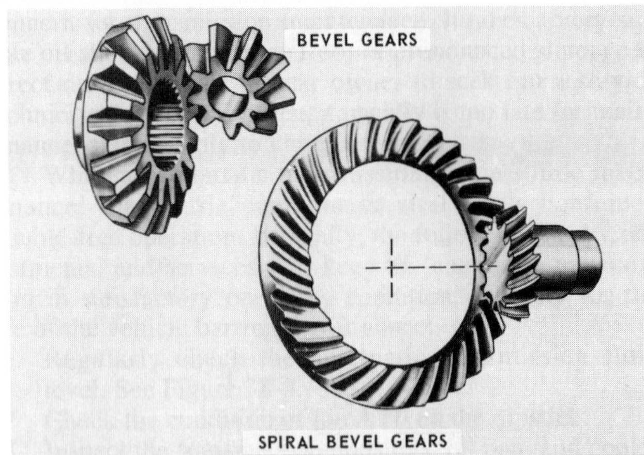

Figure 40-23. Left–A bevel gear has straight teeth and makes tooth-to-tooth contact. Right–A spiral bevel gear has curved teeth, which places more than one tooth in contact at all times.

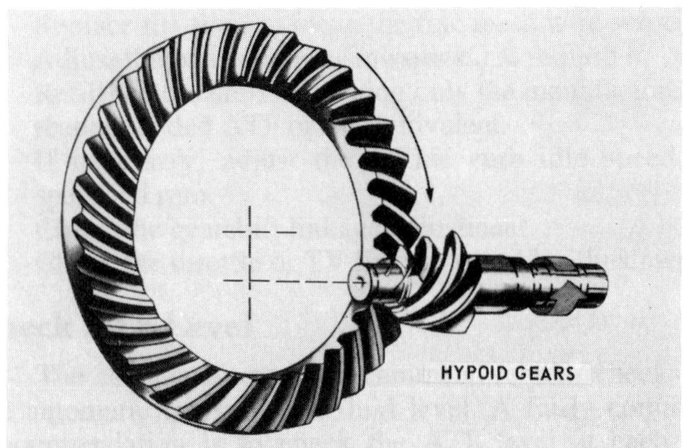

Figure 40-24. Hypoid gears are of the spiral bevel design, but the center of the pinion shaft is below the center of the ring gear.

Differential Mounting

Passenger car differentials ordinarily use two differential pinions on a straight shaft. The exploded illustration, Figure 40-25, shows the differential case and gears.

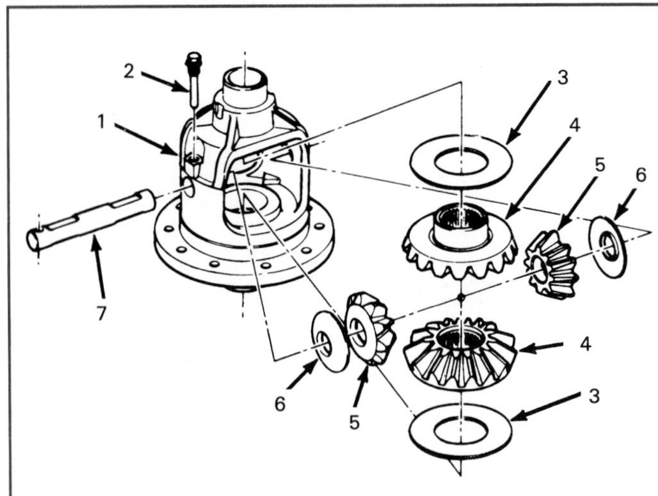

Figure 40-25. Typical differential case assembly: 1–Case. 2–Screw. 3–Side gear thrust washer. 4–Side gear. 5–Differential pinion gear. 6–Pinion gear thrust washer. 7–Shaft. (Pontiac)

The differential assembly is mounted either on a differential carrier, Figure 40-26, or directly in the rear axle housing, Figure 40-27. In all cases, there is a bearing and shim on each side of the assembly which provides a means of adjustment to move the ring gear toward or away from the drive pinion gear. See Figure 40-28.

When the setting is completed, the bearings are locked in place by heavy caps, Figures 40-26 and 40-28.

Drive Pinion Mounting

The drive pinion gear that meshes with the ring gear is also mounted on bearings in the pinion carrier or axle housing, Figure 40-29.

If the torque tube type of drive is used, the mounting is quite similar. Instead of using a pair of opposed tapered roller bearings, some constructions consist of a roller bearing and a ball bearing.

Whatever the construction, the bearings must prevent any endwise motion of the pinion shaft. In the case of the opposed angular roller bearings, the bearings themselves handle both radial and thrust loads. In the case of the ball

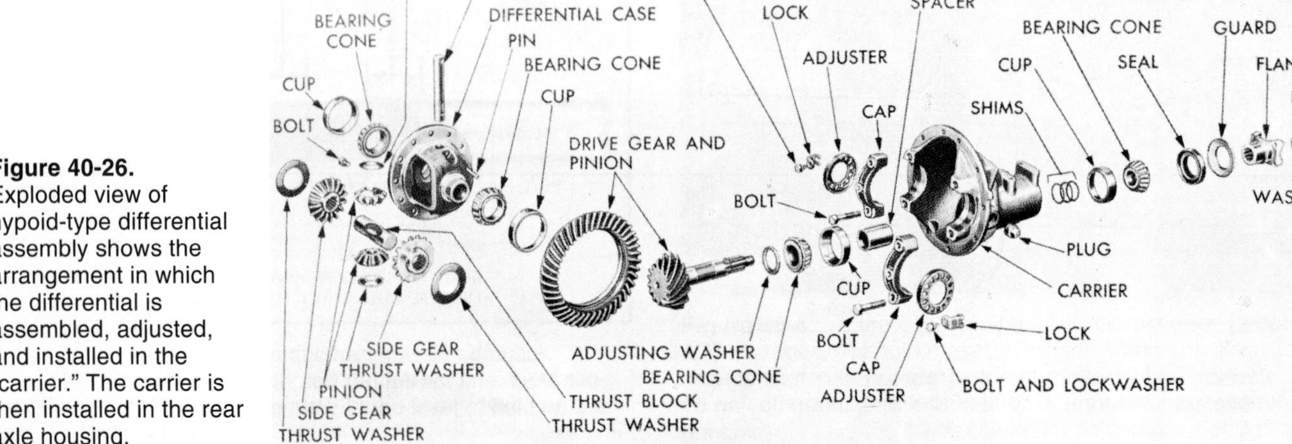

Figure 40-26. Exploded view of hypoid-type differential assembly shows the arrangement in which the differential is assembled, adjusted, and installed in the "carrier." The carrier is then installed in the rear axle housing.

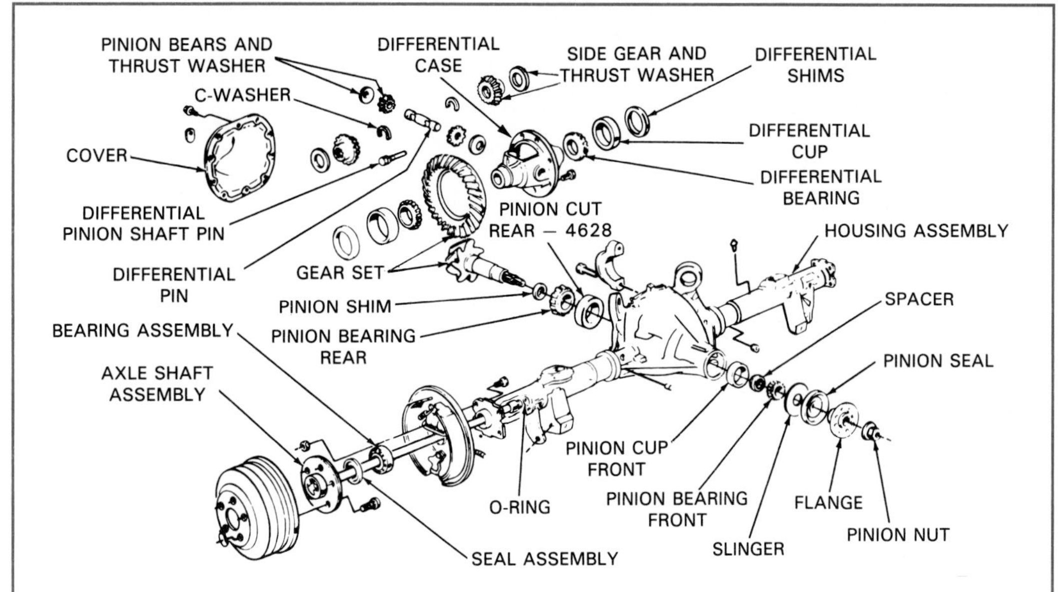

Figure 40-27. In this "integral carrier" rear axle setup, parts and subassemblies must be installed in the axle housing and then adjusted and torqued to specifications. (Ford)

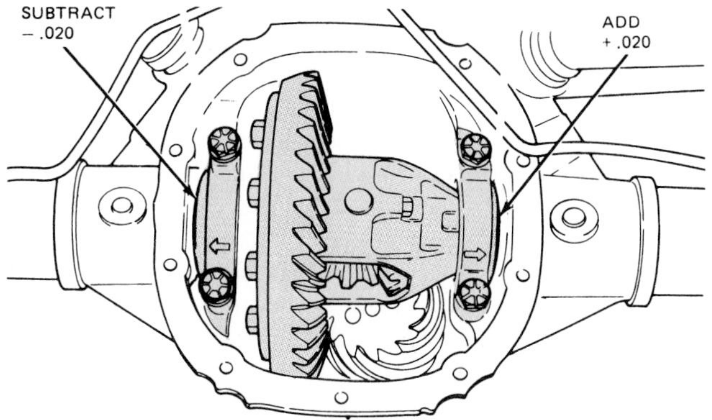

Figure 40-28. Generally, differential bearing preload and ring gear backlash are adjusted by shims located between the differential bearing cup/races and the carrier housing. Caps lock the bearings in place when adjustment is correct. (Ford)

Figure 40-29. Pinion shaft and bearing assembly is arranged in proper sequence of assembly. Note the special preload spacer at the center.

bearing-roller bearing setup, the ball bearing is a combination radial and thrust design.

Pinion Bearing Preload

Many car manufacturers specify ***preloading*** of drive pinion bearings. In some cases, this is done by the use of a special bearing spacer or sleeve. See Figure 40-29. The spacer between the two bearings is made with a weakened section. After installation, the bearings are pulled together by heavy torquing of the pinion shaft nut, causing the spacer to collapse, Figure 40-30. Equally important, there should be no radial movement of the pinion.

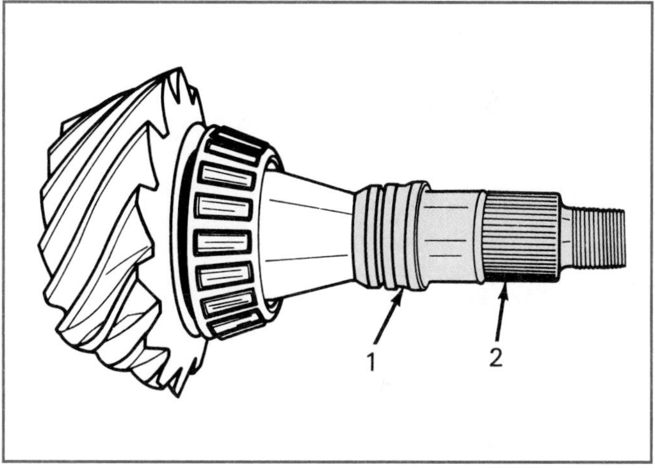

Figure 40-30. A collapsed bearing spacer (1) is shown on the drive pinion shaft (2). Obviously, a new spacer must be installed each time the assembly is taken apart and reassembled. (Pontiac)

Limited-slip Differentials

Limited-slip differentials are a popular option on a number of different makes of automobiles under a number of different names. Some use disc clutches to direct power flow to the axle of the wheel having the best traction. At the same time, less power is applied to the wheel that tends to slip, so better traction is obtained for both driving wheels. See Figures 40-31 and 40-32.

An earlier limited-slip design has beveled ends on the differential pinion shafts and corresponding "ramps" cut in the shaft openings of the differential case. With this construction, the differential pinions and pinion shafts float between the differential side gears and the case. When power is applied, the ramps tend to force the side gears apart and apply pressure to the clutch assembly having the best traction.

Another more popular limited-slip differential utilizes cone clutches that are preloaded with five springs. The frictional surface of the cones contain a coarse spiral thread

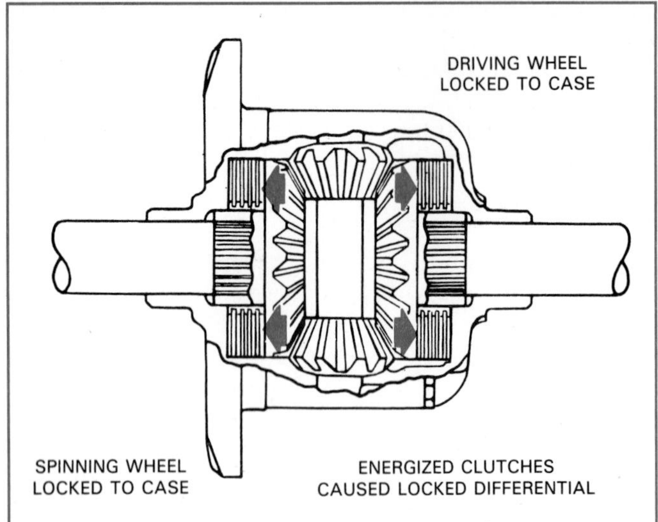

Figure 40-31. In wheel spinning situations with a disc clutch-type limited-slip differential, power is transmitted through the side gears and energized clutches to the driving wheel having the best traction.

that provides passages for the flow of lubricant, Figure 40-33. In straight ahead operation, the pressure of the springs and separating force created by the pinion gears pushes each clutch cone/side gear against the case. On turns, the axles are automatically unlocked by differential action, overcoming the spring load on the clutch cones and permitting them to overrun.

Another disc clutch type of limited-slip differential is shown in Figure 40-34. In this unit, a one-piece, S-shaped spring is used to apply initial force to the side gears and clutch packs. Additional force is provided by side gear thrust loads. When the vehicle is cornering, the clutches slip and allow normal differential action. When one rear wheel slips, friction between the clutch plates transfers torque to the wheel having the most traction.

Planetary Differentials

A ***planetary differential*** is used on certain front-wheel drive cars to provide an axle gear package of minimum width alongside the engine. Early models of the Oldsmobile Toronado, for example, coupled a spiral bevel ring gear with a spiral bevel drive pinion gear that is straddle mounted by two tapered roller bearings. During straight ahead driving, the ring gear, planet pinions, and sun gear rotate as a unit. On turns, the planet gears and sun gear rotate within the ring gear and allow the drive axles to rotate at different speeds.

Front-wheel Drive Driveline

A key element in the driveline–and drive train–of a front-wheel drive vehicle is a power transfer mechanism called a ***transaxle.*** The transaxle is attached to the rear of the engine which, in most cases, is mounted crosswise in the engine compartment. The transaxle combines transmission and differential (final drive) in a single unit. See Figure 40-35.

In front-wheel drive vehicles, the drive train is compacted into an engine/transaxle/driving axles (halfshafts) "package" that provides torque force to the front wheels.

The driveline probably is best described as extending from the mainshaft pinion gear to the final drive ring gear, and through the rotating differential case assembly (during

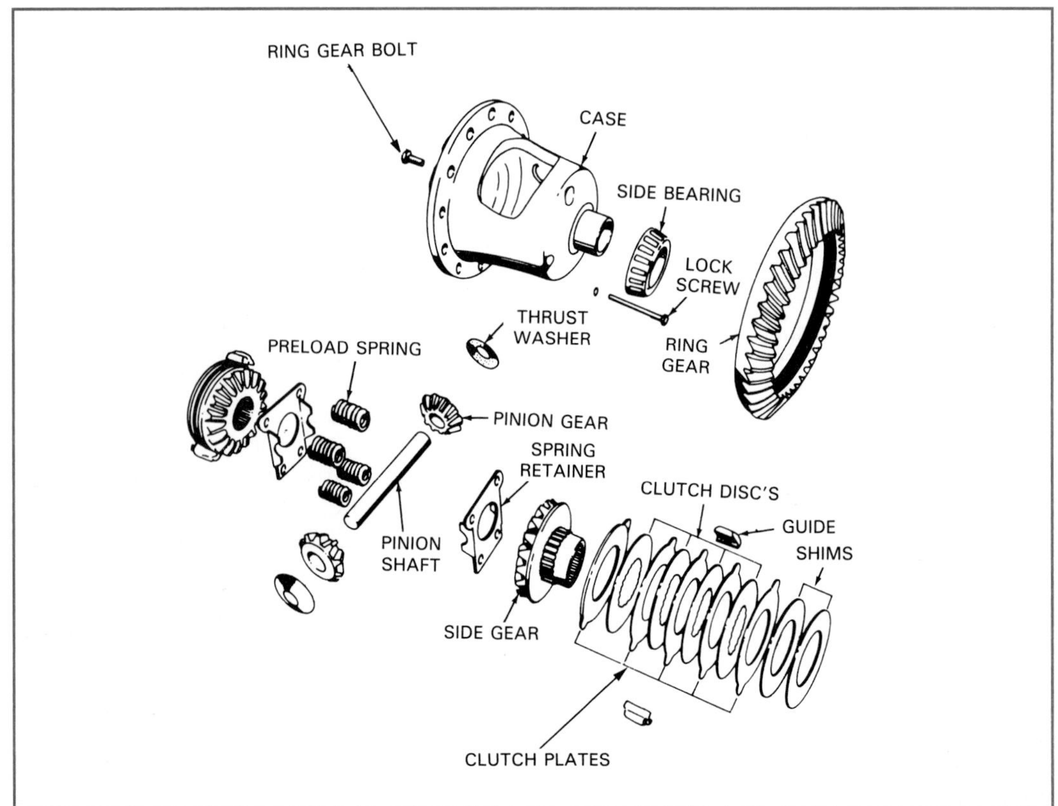

Figure 40-32. Exploded view shows the makeup of a disc clutch-type limited-slip differential. Note the preload springs and the alternate placement of the clutch plates and clutch discs. (Oldsmobile)

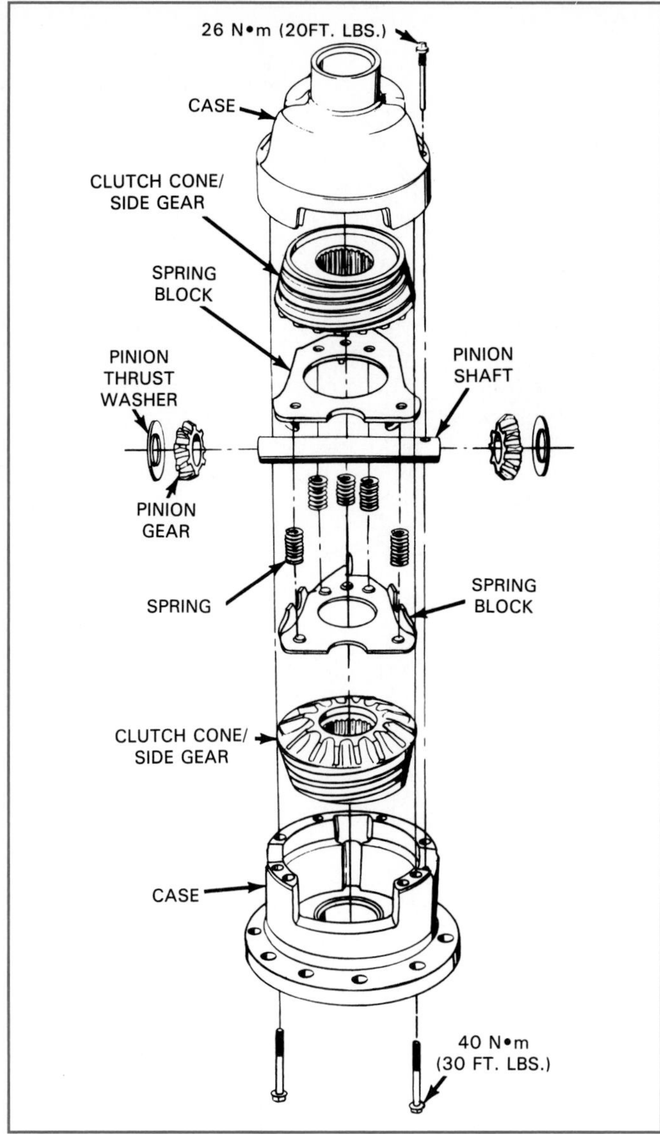

Figure 40-33. Exploded view details the sequence of components of a cone-type limited-slip differential. Note the clutch cone/side gear construction. (Oldsmobile)

straight ahead operation) to the driving axles. See Figures 40-35 and 40-36.

Emphasis in this chapter will be placed on front-wheel drive constant velocity joints and driving axles. For basic transaxle operation and service information, see Chapter 39, Transaxles.

Constant Velocity Joints

The main purpose of the driving axles is to transmit engine torque from the final drive unit to the front (driving) wheels. As part of the driving axle assembly, the ***constant velocity joints*** (CV joints) are designed to operate at varying angles, both vertically and to accommodate wheel turning angles. Some CV joints also permit shaft length changes caused by up-and-down movement of the front wheels and by engine movement due to torque reaction.

The front-wheel drive ***halfshaft*** (driving axle) shown in Figure 40-36 is a typical Ford application. The driving axle has constant velocity joints at both "inboard" and "outboard" ends. The ***Rzeppa CV joints*** shown are named for the inventor, Alfred Rzeppa, who patented this ball bearing joint over half a century ago.

The inboard CV joint, Figure 40-36, consists of an outer race and stub shaft, inner race, cage, six ball bearings, and a ball retainer. The outer race is called "plunge" type because it has elongated grooves which allow the bearing cage and bearings to slide in and out as the front wheels go up and down. The inboard CV joint stub shaft is splined to the differential side gear. See Figure 40-35.

The outboard CV joint, Figure 40-36, consists of an outer race, cage, inner race, and six ball bearings. The outboard CV joint is splined to the front-wheel end of the driving axle. The CV joint outer race stub shaft is also splined to accommodate a splined hub that is pressed on and held by a staked nut.

Another type of constant velocity joint used in many front-wheel drive driving axle assemblies is called a ***fixed tripod joint.*** See Figure 40-37. The tripod CV joint basically consists of a grooved housing and spider assembly. The spider assembly has three trunnions, needle rollers, and balls that ride in the grooves of the housing.

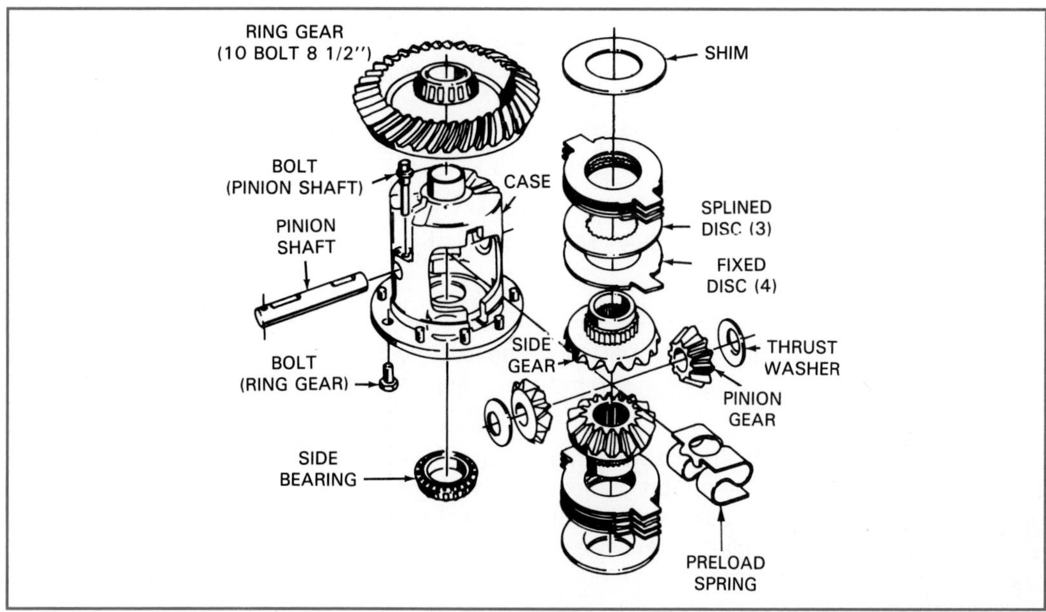

Figure 40-34. Exploded view gives disassembly/assembly order of the parts in a disc clutch-type limited-slip differential having an S-shaped preload spring. (Oldsmobile)

1. MAINSHAFT
2. 4TH SPEED GEARS
3. INPUT CLUSTER
4. 3RD SPEED GEARS
5. 2ND SPEED GEARS
6. REVERSE GEAR
7. REVERSE IDLER GEAR
8. 1ST SPEED GEARS
9. HALF SHAFTS
10. DIFFERENTIAL OIL SEALS
11. FINAL DRIVE RING GEAR
12. 1ST 2ND SPEED SYNCHRONIZER BLOCKER RINGS
13. 3RD 4TH SPEED SYNCHRONIZER HUB
14. 3RD 4TH SPEED SYNCHRONIZER SLEEVE
15. PINION GEAR PART OF MAINSHAFT

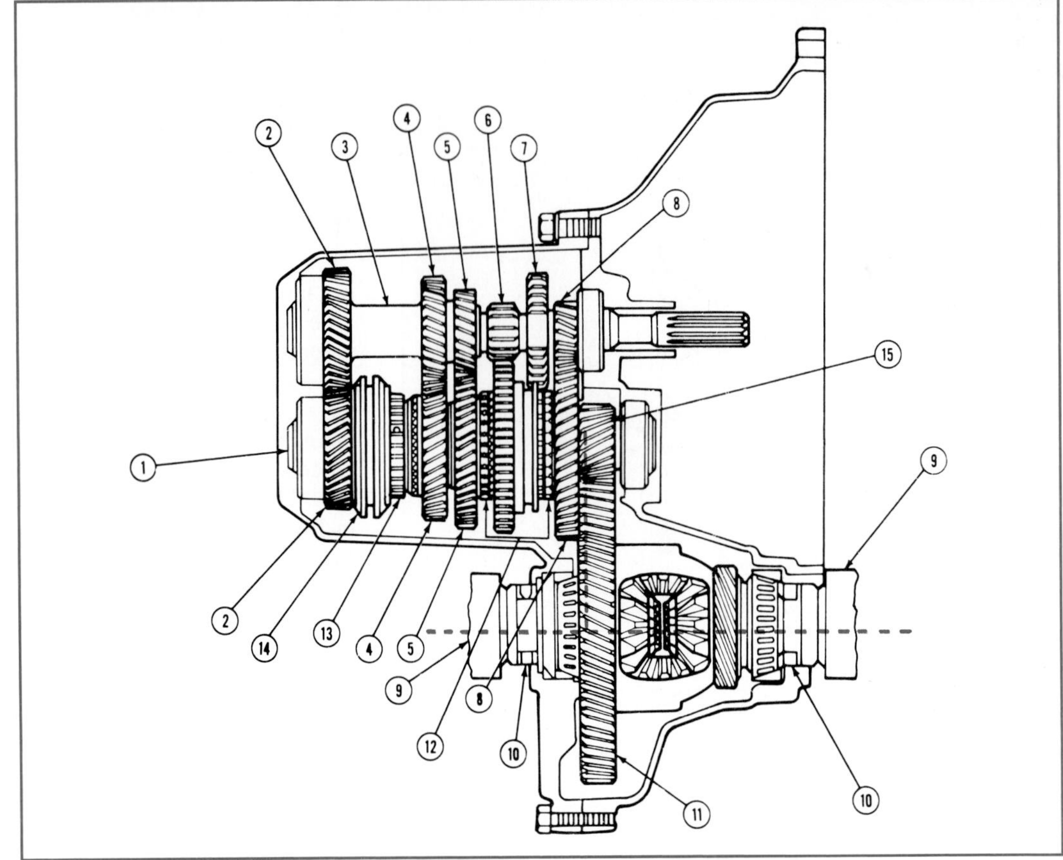

Figure 40-35. The dashed line indicates the driveline of a typical front-wheel drive system: From the transaxle mainshaft pinion gear (15); to the final drive ring gear (11); to the differential side gears, pinion gears, and case; and to the halfshaft assemblies (9). (Ford)

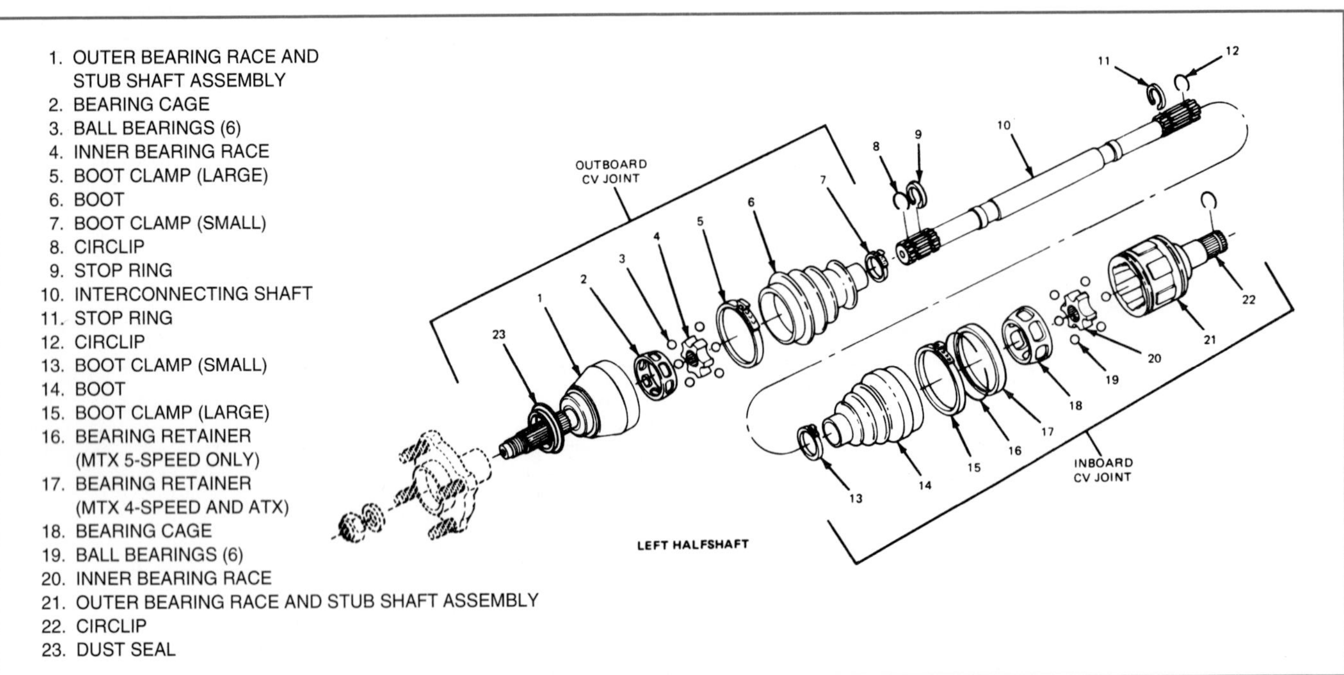

Figure 40-36. Exploded view of a typical left driving axle (halfshaft) of a front-wheel drive system. (Ford)

On some front-wheel drive applications, tripod CV joints are used at both inboard and outboard ends of the driving axles. In other cases, the tripod joint is used at the inboard end only with a "plunge" type race. A Rzeppa CV joint is used at the outboard end of the shafts in these driving axle assemblies. See Figure 40-37.

Chrysler uses three different types of constant velocity joints in their front-wheel drive "drive shaft systems." The constant velocity Rzeppa and tripod types of joints are used in all "systems." In addition, a single cardan universal joint is included in certain driving axle assemblies. See Figure 40-38.

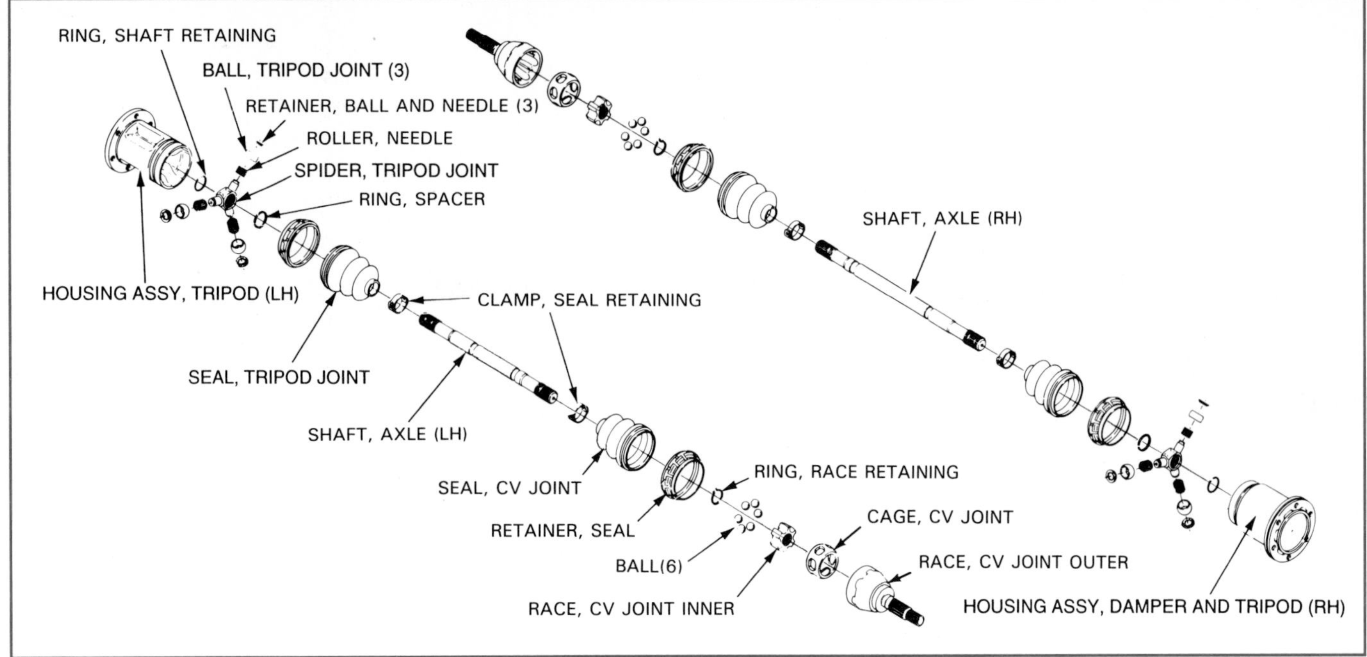

Figure 40-37. Exploded view of left (top) and right (bottom) driving axles shows details of constant velocity joint construction. Note that the Rzeppa CV joints are outboard and the tripod joints are inboard. (Oldsmobile)

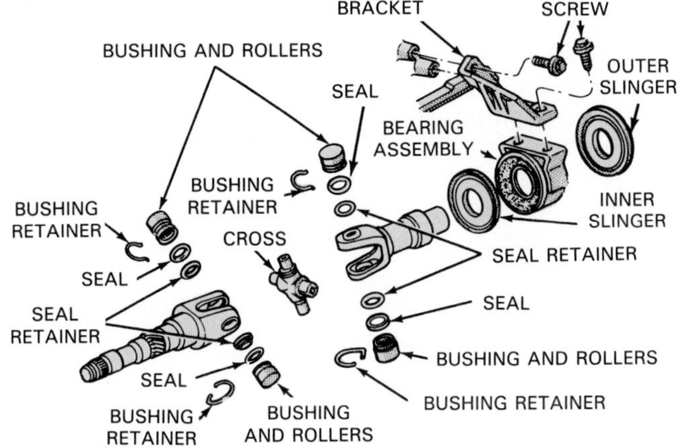

Figure 40-38. In certain Chrysler front-wheel drive cars, a single cardan universal joint is used. The stub shaft at left is splined to the transaxle side gear to transmit torque force to the driving axle. (Chrysler)

Driving Axles

Driving axles is a generic term for front-wheel drive shaft-and-joint assemblies that extend from inboard CV joints to outboard CV joints.

Chrysler uses two different driving axle systems on front-wheel drive vehicles. Because of design differences, one is called an ***equal-length system;*** the other is called an ***unequal-length system.***

The "equal-length system" shown in Figure 40-39 has short, solid interconnecting shafts of equal length in the left and right driving axle assemblies. The right axle also has a tubular intermediate shaft attached to a cardan universal joint with a stub shaft splined into the transaxle side gear. A tripod CV joint is splined to the other transaxle side gear. Another tripod joint is used between the intermediate shaft and right interconnecting shaft. Rzeppa CV joints are used at the wheel hubs.

The second driving axle system utilized by Chrysler is shown in Figure 40-40. Note that two "unequal length"

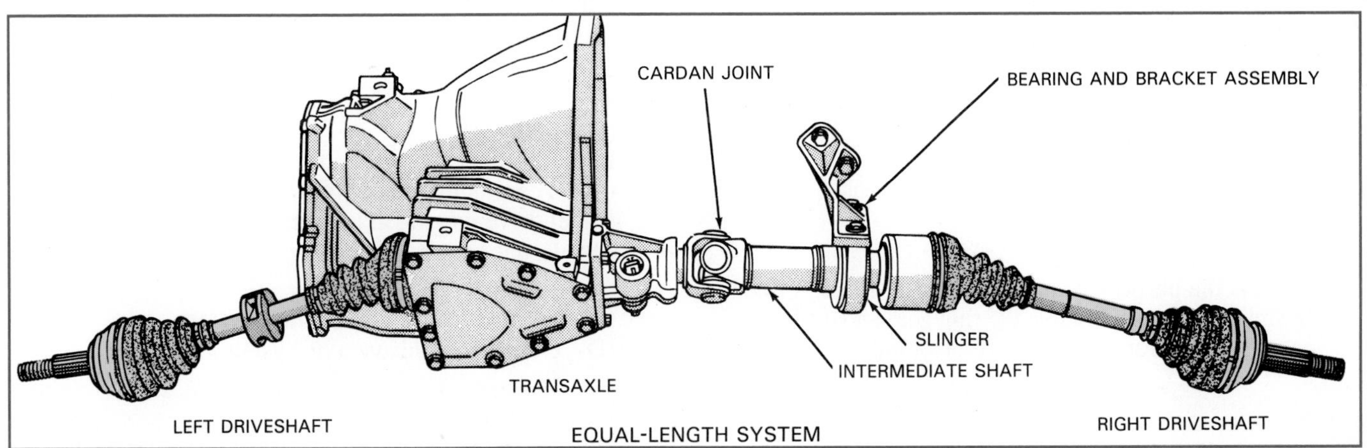

Figure 40-39. An equal-length drive shaft system includes a cardan universal joint in the right driving axle. The left and right drive shafts are of equal length. (Chrysler)

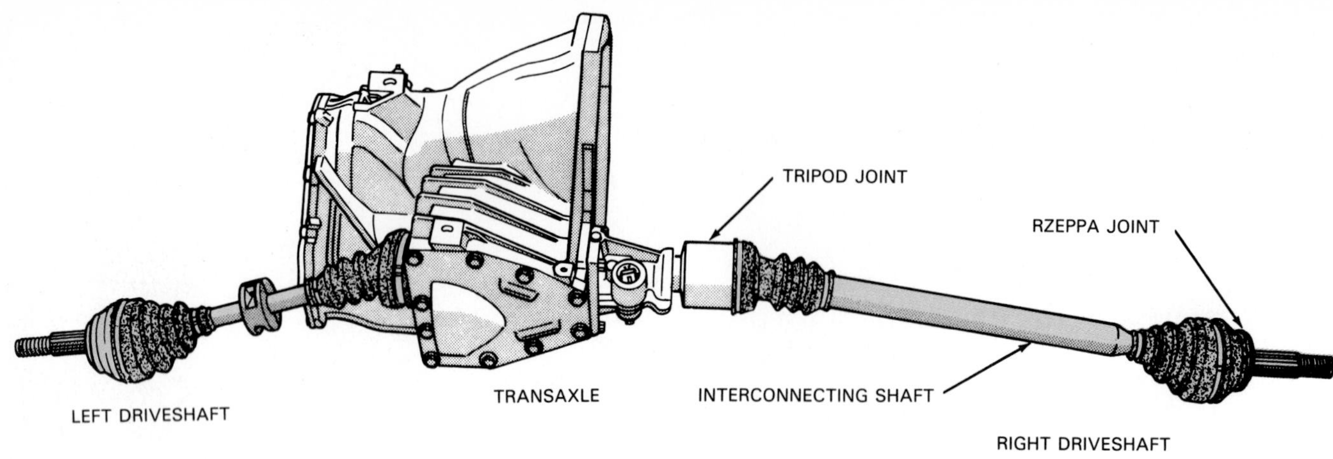

Figure 40-40. An unequal-length front-wheel drive shaft system does away with the intermediate shaft and cardan universal joint. Left and right drive shafts are of unequal length. (Chrysler)

interconnecting shafts are used along with tripod inboard CV joints and Rzeppa outboard CV joints.

Chapter 40–Review Questions

Write your answers on a separate sheet of paper. Do not write in this book.

1. In rear-wheel drive applications, the _____ (driveline or drive train) consists of one or more universal joints, the drive shaft, and the differential drive pinion gear.
2. Flexibility in the drive train usually is provided by _____.
3. The differential assembly uses a drive pinion gear and _____ _____ to redirect the transfer of power to the driving axles.
   (A) differential gear
   (B) differential pinion gear
   (C) ring gear
   (D) planetary gear
4. The differential assembly prevents one driving wheel from turning faster than the other to avoid skidding and scuffing of the rear tires on turns. True or False?
5. What type of driving axles are generally used in rear-wheel drive passenger cars?
6. On acceleration, engine torque will cause the differential housing to _____ _____ (tilt downward or tilt upward).
7. Driving force is transmitted to the front of the rear leaf springs on cars equipped with a:
   (A) Hotchkiss drive.
   (B) torque tube drive.
   (C) open drive shaft drive.
   (D) control arm drive.
8. What is the purpose of the slip joint in the driveline?
9. In straight ahead operation, the ring gear and differential case assembly rotate as a unit. True or False?
10. In the differential assembly, what is the purpose of the spacer or sleeve between the two drive pinion bearings?
11. Name two types of limited-slip differentials.
12. A key element of a front-wheel drive driveline is a power transfer mechanism called a _____.
    (A) transmission
    (B) differential
    (C) transaxle
    (D) final drive unit
13. The main purpose of the driving axles on front-wheel drive cars is to transmit engine torque from the _____ _____ _____ to the driving wheels.
14. Constant velocity joints are designed to operate at varying angles, both vertically and to accommodate _____ _____ angles.
15. Some CV joints also permit shaft length changes caused by up-and-down movement of the front wheels. True or False?
16. A _____ (Rzeppa or tripod) CV joint is a "ball bearing" joint.
17. A _____ (Rzeppa or tripod) CV joint is a "spider" assembly.
18. What is a "plunge-type" CV joint?
19. What type of splined shaft is used at outboard CV joints to accommodate the installation of splined wheel hubs?
    (A) Interconnecting.
    (B) Intermediate.
    (C) Output.
    (D) Stub.
20. In addition to Rzeppa and tripod CV joints, Chrysler uses a cardan universal joint in which one of its front-wheel drive driving axle assemblies?
    (A) Equal-length system.
    (B) Unequal-length system.
    (C) Interconnecting drive shaft system.
    (D) Output shaft/drive axle system.

Chapter 41
Driveline Service

After studying this chapter, you will be able to:

❍ Identify elements of rear-wheel drive and front-wheel drive drivelines.
❍ Describe differential pinion gear/ring gear adjusting procedures for obtaining correct tooth contact.
❍ Tell how to check angularity of drive shaft on rear-wheel drive vehicles.
❍ Cite driveline lubrication requirements.
❍ Explain driving axle services, both on rear-wheel drive and front-wheel drive systems.

Driveline Service

The ***driveline*** of a rear-wheel drive vehicle consists of one or more universal joints, the drive shaft, and differential drive pinion gear. Each of these elements must be maintained properly in order to provide a smooth running, relatively quiet, vibration-free power transfer system.

Drive Shaft

The ***drive shaft*** is a long, usually tubular steel member of the driveline that connects the transmission output shaft to the differential drive pinion shaft. The ***universal joints*** are considered to be part of the drive shaft assembly, Figure 41-1. This assembly rotates at fluctuating speeds and operates at constantly changing angles. Therefore, it is susceptible (subject) to vibration. Add to this any rotating imbalance and the result is a serious vibration that will shake the entire vehicle.

For example, a one ounce weight placed on a drive shaft 2″ from the center of rotation will exert a force of 50 lb. at 3750 rpm. At that speed, this force will be exerted in opposite directions 62 1/2 times per second, causing a heavy vibration.

From this example, it is easy to see why all drive shafts must be balanced, properly mounted assemblies with all working parts lubricated by a special, high melting point lubricant.

Also, on cross and roller universal joints, Figure 41-2, the cross must be centered within the bearing cups. Most bearing assemblies are held in place by snap rings,

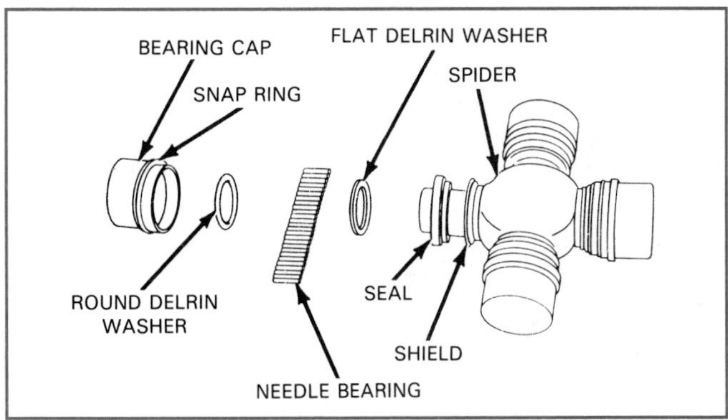

Figure 41-2. This exploded view shows the parts of a typical replacement cross-and-roller universal joint. (Chevrolet)

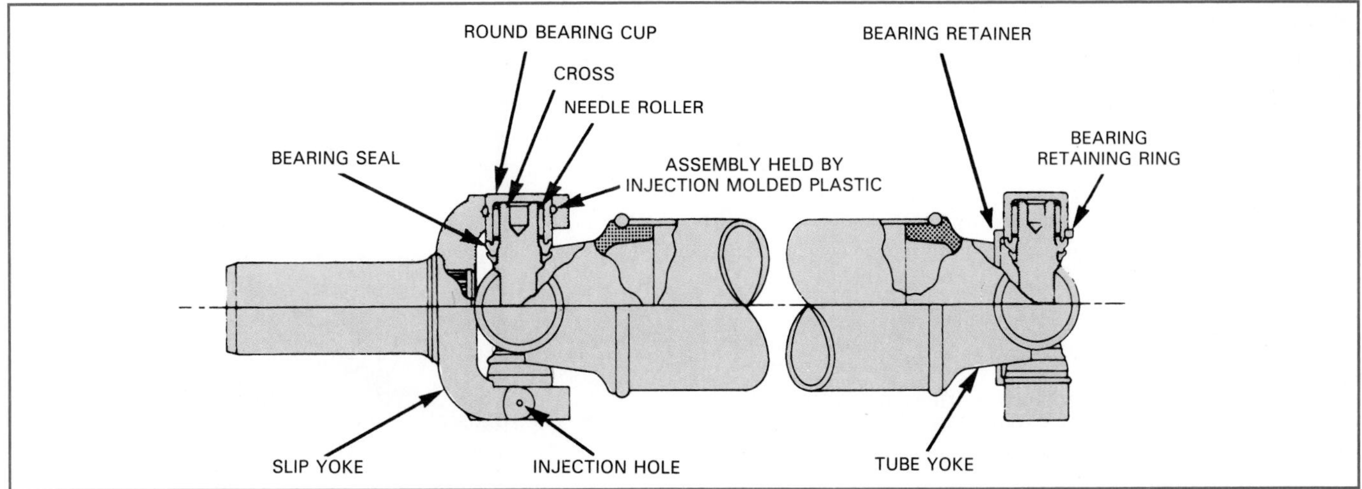

Figure 41-1. Cross-and-roller universal joints at both ends of a one-piece driveshaft provide the flexibility needed in the line of drive of a rear-wheel drive vehicle. (Pontiac)

others by trunnion straps or bearing plates. Some original equipment universal joints have trunnions retained by a plastic material injected into a groove in the yoke. See Figure 41-1.

In any case, all parts must be "opposed identical pairs" to help maintain drive shaft balance. In addition, all bolts, nuts, washers, seals, and retainers used to assemble the joints and flanges must be the same weight as the opposed pair.

It follows, then, that drive shafts must be:

- Carefully and accurately manufactured.
- Correctly assembled.
- Straight.
- Balanced.
- Properly mounted in the automobile.
- Frequently checked.

Even when all these things are done, the shaft still can get out of balance when in use. The drive shaft can bend, journal cross bearings can wear, splines can wear, bolts and keys can loosen, balance weights can fall off, and lubricant can leak out. Sometimes, a drive shaft is thrown out of balance by careless spraying of undercoating.

The drive shaft may have incorrect angularity. It may be dented. A weld may be cracked. The universal joints may bind or "clunk" on shifts into reverse. There may be burrs or nicks on support yokes or excessive looseness at slip yoke splines.

However, new developments in universal joint design and the use of constant velocity joints, Figure 41-3, have eliminated the need for regular maintenance service. The joints are prelubricated and sealed at the time of manufacture. Note: The manufacturers specify frequent inspections for universal joint wear or lubricant leakage.

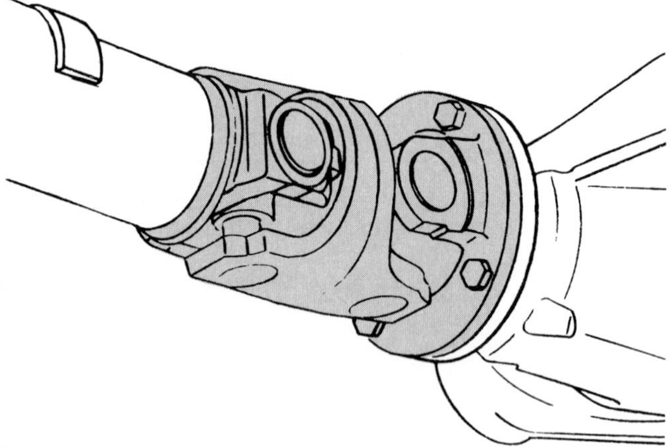

Figure 41-3. Constant velocity joints used in rear-wheel drive applications usually are double universal joints separated by a centering ball. (Chevrolet)

Universal Joint Service

If a universal joint becomes worn or noisy, a service kit may be installed. Replacement parts in the kit usually include a cross, bearing cup assemblies, seals, washers, and snap rings, Figure 41-2.

The drive shaft must be removed from the car to service or repair the universal joints. Mark the relationship of the yoke or companion flange to the drive shaft. Disconnect the rear universal joint by removing bearing straps or unscrewing bolts from the companion flange, Figure 41-4. Then tape bearing caps, if necessary, and remove the drive shaft.

If a double drive shaft is used, handle it with care to avoid jamming the joints, and keep it in a relatively straight line. Clamp the drive shaft in a vise by the universal joint yoke.

Disassemble the universal joints by means of a special tool set or press, Figure 41-5. Constant velocity joints, in particular, require special service equipment to do the job right. Inspect the bearing cups for wear, roughness, pitting, or brinelling (rippled effect). If wear or damage is evident, install a complete service kit.

Reassemble the drive shaft carefully to maintain balance. See that the newly installed joints operate freely in all directions. Tap the yoke with a hammer, if necessary, to seat parts. Reinstall the drive shaft, align the scribe marks, Figure 41-4, and tighten the attaching bolts to the proper torque value.

Then, check the angularity of the drive shaft and universal joints against manufacturer's specifications. See Figure 41-6. Angularity can be checked with a protractor or an inclinometer, Figure 41-7; then:

1. Rotate the drive shaft until the universal joint cups on the axle yoke and the transmission yoke are facing straight down.
2. Clean the cup surfaces and install the inclinometer magnet against the cup surface.

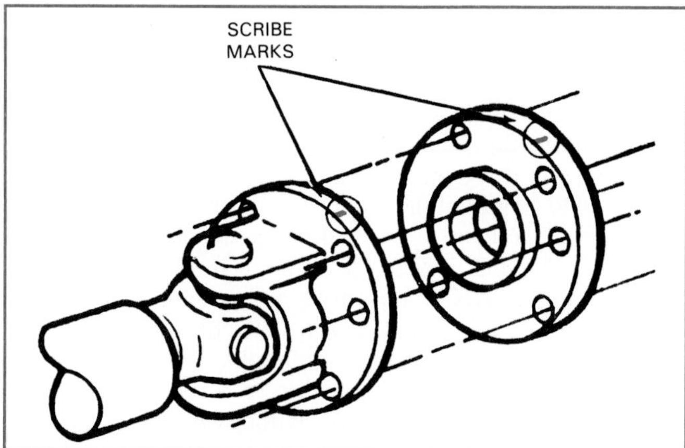

Figure 41-4. When removing a drive shaft, place scribe marks on the drive shaft and the companion flange to aid in reinstallation and to maintain balance. (Ford)

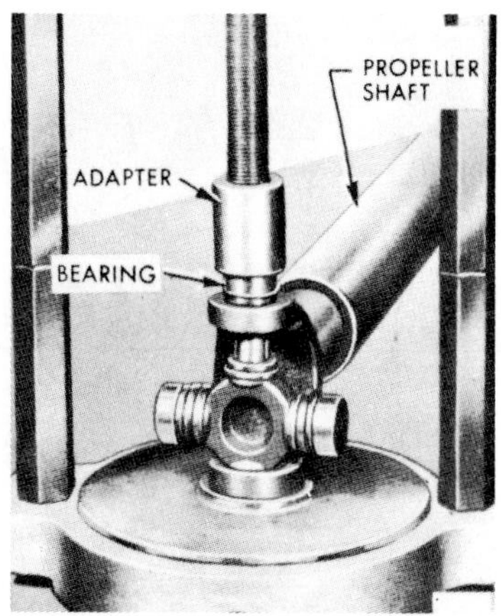

Figure 41-5. Special tools or a press and adapters are needed to disassemble and assemble cross-and-roller universal joints.

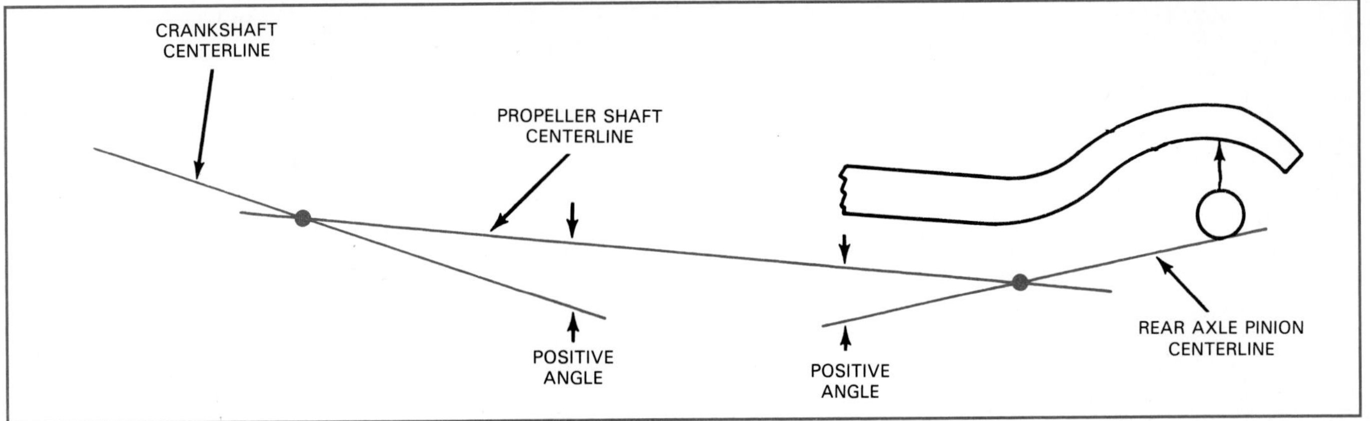

Figure 41-6. This diagram depicts the angles formed by the crankshaft, propeller shaft, and drive pinion centerlines. Positive angles of the front and rear universal joints are shown. (Chrysler)

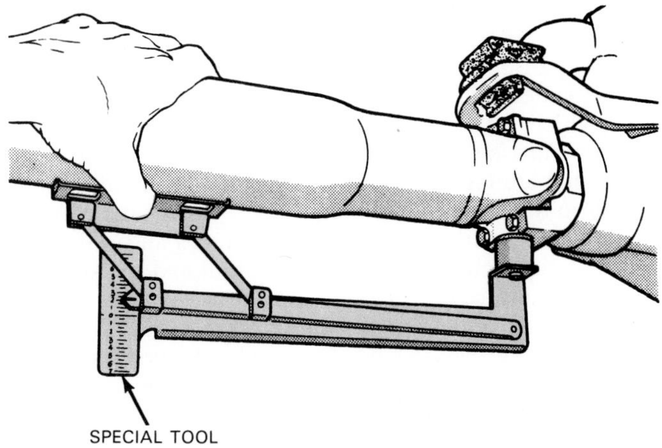

Figure 41-7. A special tool (inclinometer) is used to measure the universal joint angle at the rear axle. (Chrysler)

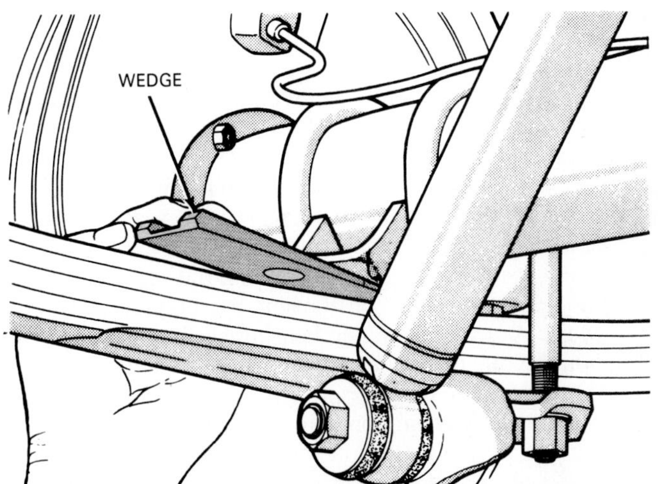

Figure 41-8. Placing a tapered wedge between the leaf spring and the rear axle housing spring seat is one method of correcting rear universal joint angle. (Chrysler)

3. Work the inclinometer contact shoe firmly against the drive shaft until both tabs contact the bottom of the shaft.
4. Read the indicated angle.

If front universal joint angle is incorrect, place shims between the transmission extension housing and the engine rear mount. If the rear universal joint angle is incorrect, place a tapered wedge between rear leaf spring and rear axle housing spring seat. See Figure 41-8.

Center Bearing Service

The ***center bearing*** is usually attached to a crossmember mounted between the left and right side rails of the frame. Center bearings on older models and some double cardan constant velocity joints are equipped with lubrication fittings. Most late models have prepacked bearings that do not require maintenance. If service is required, the center support can be disassembled by use of a special puller.

Differentials

Differentials are heavy-duty, precision-produced, mated-gear assemblies, Figure 41-9, that generally do not require maintenance other than occasional lubrication. Because of the tremendous power transmitted through the differential assembly, the pressures involved are exceptionally high. The pressures are so high that some distortion of the heavy and, in most cases, hardened parts may occur. Because of the high standards of quietness demanded, adjustments must be made to extremely close dimensions.

The differential case is attached to the ring gear, and the entire propelling force is transmitted through the drive pinion gear and the ***differential case assembly.*** This assembly also includes side gears, pinion gears, pinion shaft, and pinion shaft lock bolt. To ensure a tight union of parts, a series of 8 to 12 special bolts extend through precisely machined holes in the case and screw into threaded holes in the ring gear. Torque tightness is in the area of 70 to 85 ft./lb. (95 to 115 N·m)

Troubles and Remedies

Service problems with differentials usually are limited to lubricant leakage at the drive pinion oil seal or noisy operation of the differential.

To replace the drive pinion oil seal:

1. Mark the relationship of the yoke or flange to the drive shaft.
2. Disconnect the rear universal joint.
3. Tape the bearing caps, if necessary, and remove the drive shaft.

Figure 41-9. The drive pinion gear and the ring gear comprise a mated-gear assembly. They are manufactured and installed as a matched set. Nodular iron hypoid gears are shown. (Central Foundry Div., General Motors Corp.)

4. Remove the drive pinion shaft nut, washer, and yoke or flange.
5. Use a special puller to remove the drive pinion oil seal.

Reassemble in reverse order, but observe the following precautions:

1. Install the oil seal with the sealing lip facing the lubricant.
2. Coat the OD (outside diameter) of the seal with non-hardening sealing compound.
3. Use a special driving tool to bottom the seal against the shoulder in the rear axle housing. See Figure 41-10.
4. Make sure the machined bearing surface of the drive pinion yoke or flange is not worn, scored, or nicked in the area where it rotates against the seal.
5. Tighten the drive pinion shaft nut to its original position, plus 1/8 turn to preload the pinion bearings (typical).
6. Refill the rear axle housing to the correct level with recommended lubricant.

Noisy operation of a differential unit is usually caused by worn or damaged gears or bearings. However, a thorough test should be made to pinpoint where the noise is coming from: rear axle assembly; rough road surface; underinflated tires, or tires with unevenly worn tread; front or rear wheel bearings; engine or transmission. Noises telegraph to other parts of the car, so establishing the source of the noise is of first importance.

If the differential assembly is noisy, check for: low level of lubricant in rear axle housing (howl and whine); excessive backlash between teeth of drive pinion gear and ring gear (chuck); looseness of drive pinion bearings (howl and whine); worn differential side and pinion gears (howl and whine on turns). Removal and complete disassembly of the differential probably is required.

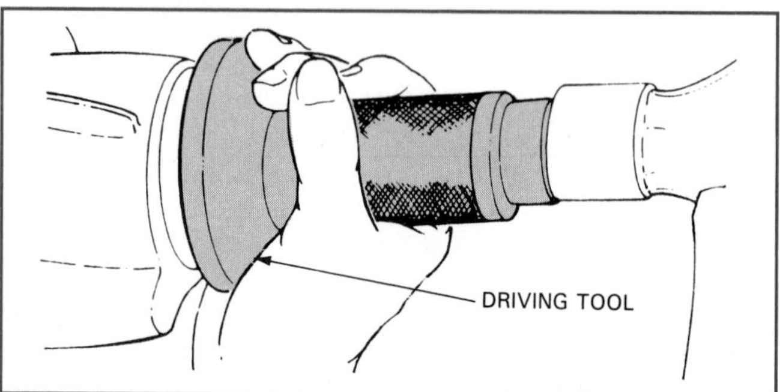

Figure 41-10. Drive pinion oil seal replacement calls for the use of a special puller and a special driving tool as shown. (Ford)

Disassembly and Inspection

When disassembling the differential, Figures 41-11 and 41-12, be sure to mark mating parts so that they can be reassembled on the correct side and in the proper position. For example, carrier bearing caps are marked L and R to prevent a mix-up. Since gears and bearings are a press fit in many cases, avoid the use of hammers and drifts. Use a suitable press or puller to prevent chipping and distortion of parts, Figure 41-13.

After the parts have been disassembled and thoroughly cleaned, carefully inspect them for scuffed surfaces, cracks, warpage, or any other visible defects. If the surfaces of the gear teeth are scratched or scuffed, the gears must be replaced. If there are any cracks visible in the differential case, the case should be replaced. If the differential pinion bushings or shaft are worn or loose, new parts are required.

Pay particular attention to the pinion shaft and differential side bearings. Check the shaft or housings on which, or in which, the bearings seat. The inside cone of the bearings must be a tight fit on the shaft or housing upon which they are mounted. The outer race or cone must be a snug fit in the housing in which it seats. The bearings must not show any indication of wear. The races and rollers or balls and cups must be absolutely smooth and polished on the contact surfaces.

Hardened anti-friction bearings are used. No other type of bearing could stand the speeds and pressures and continue to maintain correct alignment of the gears.

Reassembly and Adjustment

When reassembling, use new shims, spacers, washers, gaskets, and oil seals. Thoroughly clean the inside of the housing of all grease and oil to make sure that no metal chips or abrasive material is left inside to be circulated by the lubricant.

The manufacturer's instructions concerning whether or not the bearings are to be preloaded, and how much, are needed for proper assembly. Also required is the method of adjusting gear contact by measurement with special gauges or micrometers. Necessary, too, are specifications on the amount of torque to be applied to all the bolts and nuts.

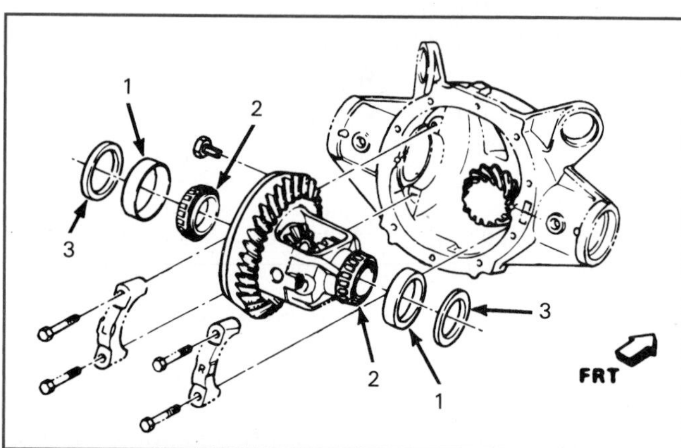

Figure 41-11. Exploded view of this standard differential case assembly is illustrated outside the carrier. Other related parts include: 1–Race. 2–Roller bearing. 3–Shim. (Oldsmobile)

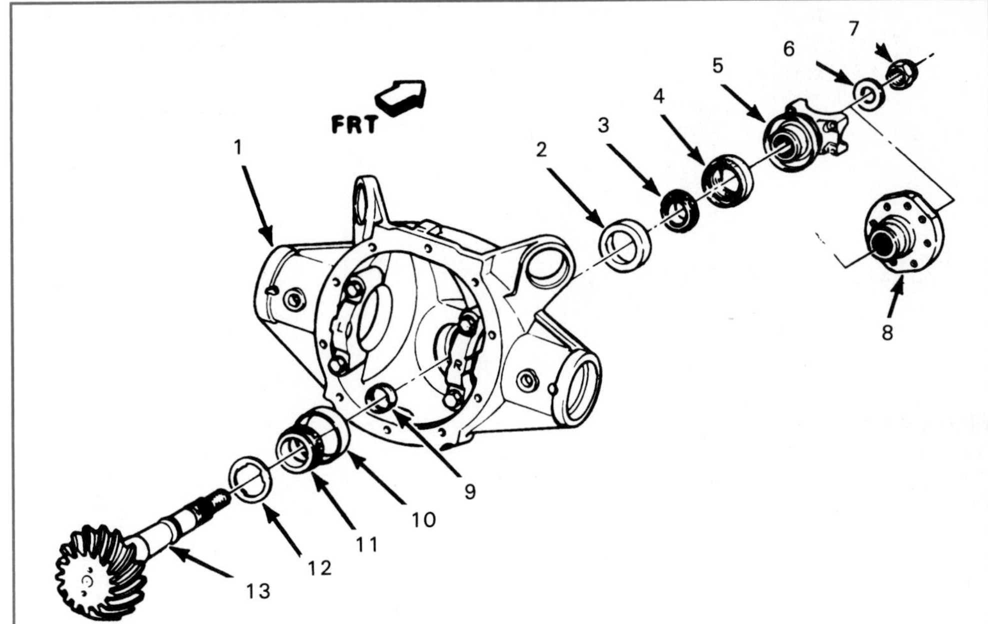

Figure 41-12. Exploded view of drive pinion gear and related parts. 1–Carrier. 2–Pinion front race. 3–Pinion front roller bearing. 4–Seal. 5–Flange. 6–Washer. 7–Nut. 8–Flange (some applications). 9–Spacer. 10–Pinion rear race. 11–Pinion rear roller bearing. 12–Shim (as required). 13–Drive pinion gear. (Oldsmobile)

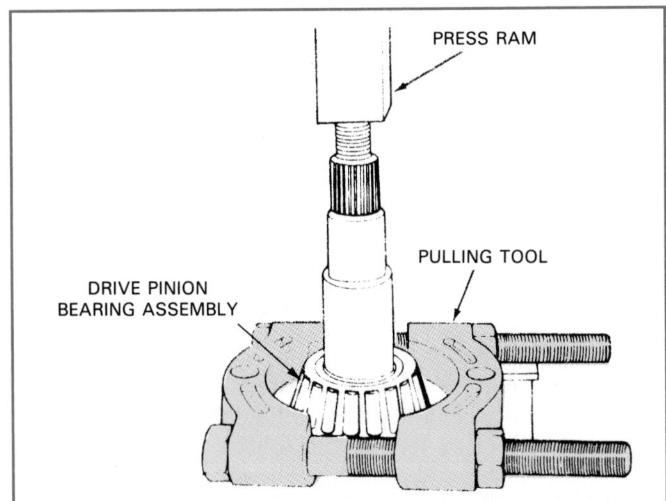

Figure 41-13. Differential disassembly requires the use of special pullers, drivers, and a press to remove and install bearings and certain gears. (Ford)

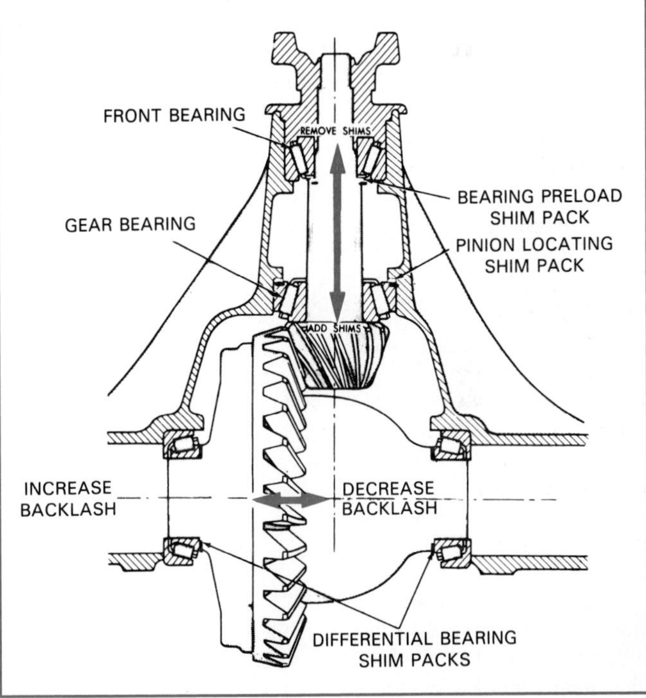

Figure 41-14. Some differential designs require placement of shims under the side bearings to adjust backlash between the drive pinion gear and the ring gear. (Ford)

Two adjustments can be made which will affect tooth contact pattern between the drive pinion gear and the ring gear: backlash and the position of the drive pinion gear in relation to the ring gear.

Backlash between mating teeth is adjusted by means of side bearing adjusters (on older models) or by bearing adjusting shims, Figures 41-14 and 41-15. Shims of varied thicknesses are used to move the entire case and ring gear assembly closer to, or farther from, the drive pinion gear.

To increase backlash in differential case assemblies where the shims are inboard of the side bearings (between bearing and case), remove shims from ring gear side and install them on pinion gear side, Figure 41-14. To decrease backlash, reverse this shim switching process.

In differential case assemblies where the shims are outboard of the side bearings, Figure 41-16, start by installing a shim of specified size against the left bearing. Then install progressively larger shims against the right bearing until a slight drag is felt. Next, install caps over bearings finger-tight and check backlash. Then, make balanced shim size adjustments until correct backlash is obtained. See Figure 41-17.

The position of the drive pinion is adjusted by increasing or decreasing shim thickness between the pinion head and the inner face of the rear drive pinion bearing, Figure 41-15. Adding shims will move it closer to the centerline of the ring gear; removing shims will move the pinion gear farther away.

Check the tooth contact with red lead and oil or with white marking compound. Move the ring gear experimentally (or follow manufacturer's depth gauge method) until

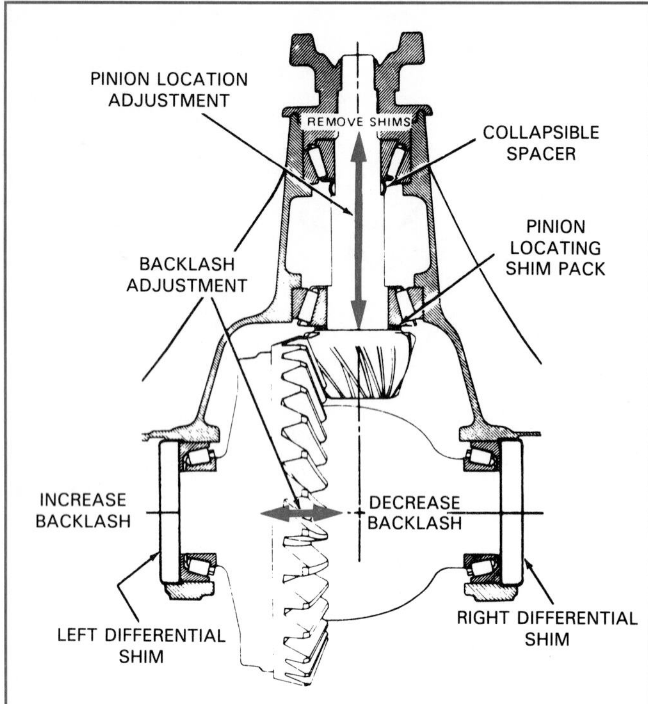

Figure 41-15. Later differential designs have shims outboard of the side bearings. Shim size changes determine the increase or decrease in backlash. (Ford)

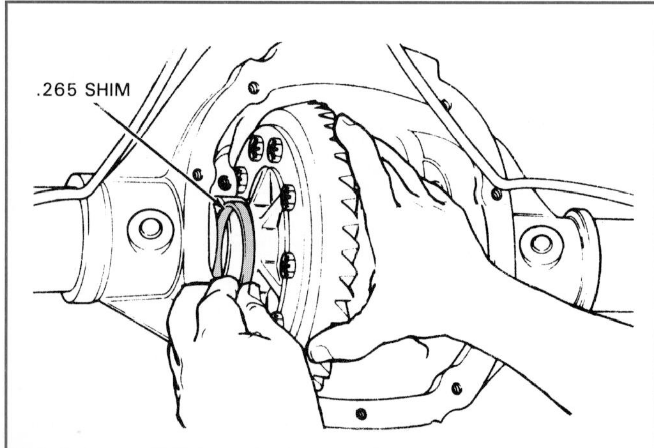

Figure 41-16. The first step of backlash adjustment is placement of a shim of specified size against the left side bearing. (Ford)

proper contact is obtained. See Figure 41-18. Tighten all bolts gradually and equally to specified torque tightness.

Correct adjustment of hypoid gears is of paramount importance because they will often wear excessively without making any noise. There is such a pronounced wiping action between the gear teeth, they can overheat and gall very quickly unless correctly adjusted and lubricated by a special hypoid lubricant.

Gear and Bearing Lubrication

Proper lubrication is of utmost importance. The straight bevel and spur gears were successfully lubricated with a heavy mineral gear oil. When spiral bevel gears were adopted, it was found necessary to add some ingredients to the oil to enable it to withstand the high pressure sliding or wiping action of the gear teeth.

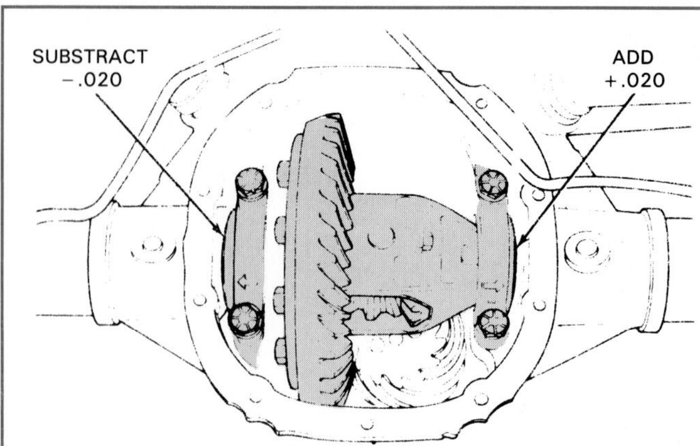

Figure 41-17. After shimming against the right side bearing, shim size adjustments (both left and right) are made until the backlash amount meets specifications. (Ford)

With the adoption of hypoid gears, the sliding action was greatly increased, and previously used straight gear oils and extreme pressure gear oils were found inadequate. Special hypoid lubricants were developed and must be used with these gears. The vehicle manufacturer furnishes specific recommendations for type of lubricant, proper level, and frequency of change.

The ring gear acts as a circulating pump to distribute the lubricant over the gear teeth and to the bearings. Since the oil is in constant circulation when the vehicle is in motion, any abrasive material or metal chips will be promptly carried to the working surfaces. If abrasive, undue wear of gear teeth and bearings will occur. If a metal chip goes through the gears, it probably will break gear teeth, spring parts out of alignment, or both. Care must be exercised to keep the oil clean before and during refilling.

In any case, clean the area around the fill plug before removing it. Remove the plug and check the level of lubricant in the differential housing. The proper level in most applications (check manufacturer's recommendation) is at the lower edge of the fill hole. When adding or changing lubricant, use the recommended type and grade. The type of lubricant is specified in the service manual. Reinstall and tighten the fill plug.

Transaxle Lubrication

In transaxles, the differential (final drive) unit is combined with either a manual or automatic transmission. While some types of gearing require an extreme pressure type of lubricant, this lubricant may be unsuitable for other types of gears.

When the transaxle is manual, the lubricant usually flows between the transmission and the final drive unit, with a single level check and fill plug provided. Automatic transaxles may have a separate housing for the final drive gears. Then, the two units may require different lubricants. Always refer to the manufacturer's specifications for the vehicle being serviced.

Wheel Bearing Lubrication

Rear wheel bearings on rear-wheel drive cars are automatically lubricated by oil creeping along the axle

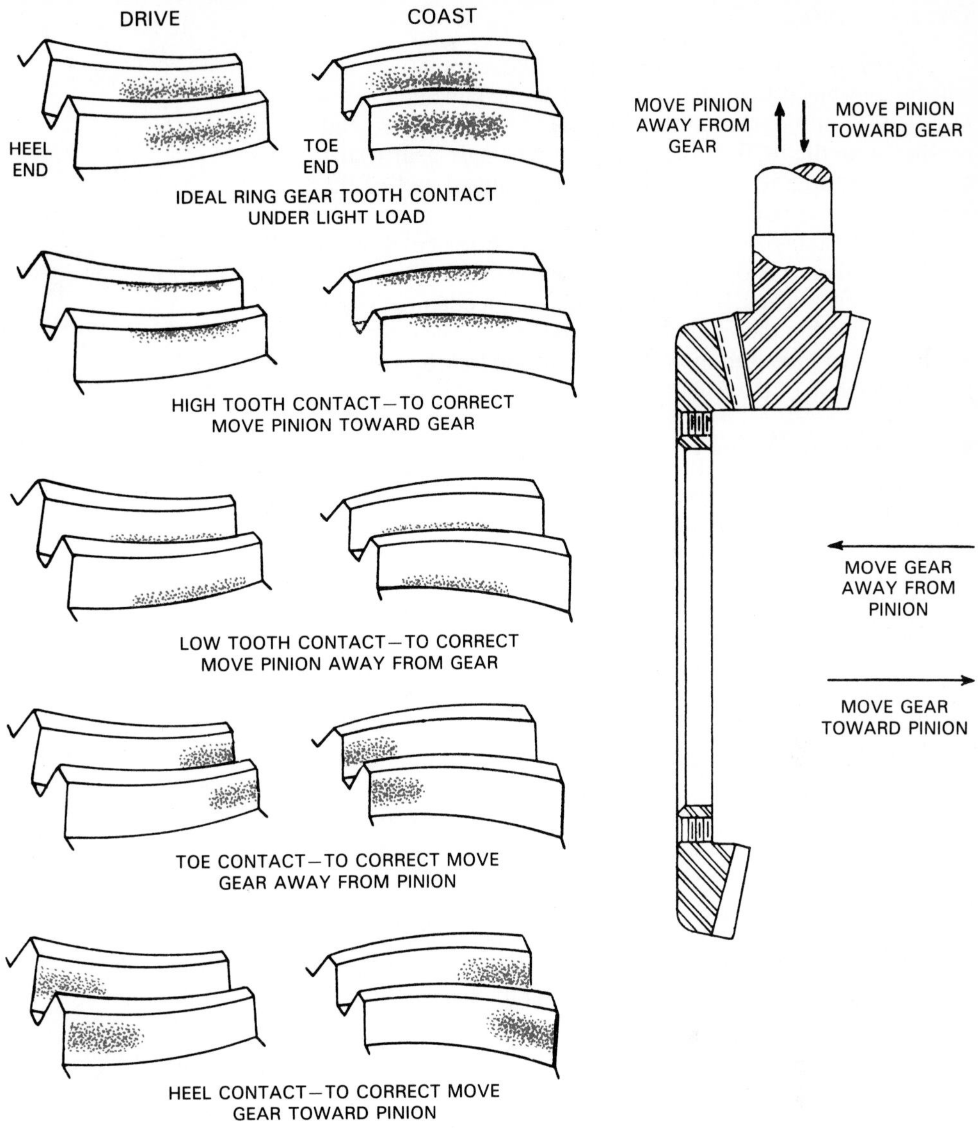

DRIVE COAST

HEEL END TOE END

IDEAL RING GEAR TOOTH CONTACT UNDER LIGHT LOAD

HIGH TOOTH CONTACT—TO CORRECT MOVE PINION TOWARD GEAR

LOW TOOTH CONTACT—TO CORRECT MOVE PINION AWAY FROM GEAR

TOE CONTACT—TO CORRECT MOVE GEAR AWAY FROM PINION

HEEL CONTACT—TO CORRECT MOVE GEAR TOWARD PINION

MOVE PINION AWAY FROM GEAR

MOVE PINION TOWARD GEAR

MOVE GEAR AWAY FROM PINION

MOVE GEAR TOWARD PINION

Figure 41-18. The pattern of a drive pinion gear to ring gear tooth contact is shown, along with the corrective steps required to improve contact.

shafts from the differential housing. Front wheel bearings call for repacking at regular intervals with a special wheel bearing grease having a high melting point. The high melting point is essential because the wheel hub and brake rotor surrounding the bearings get very hot. Not all this heat is applied to the wheel bearings, but a considerable amount is absorbed by the hub. If the grease melts, it may get by the oil seal and ruin the brake lining.

Front wheel bearings on rear-wheel drive cars may be "packed" by hand or, preferably, by the use of a bearing packer. After the wheel hub is thoroughly cleaned, a thin film of wheel bearing grease is placed in the hub and on the wheel spindle. The packed bearings are put in place and a new seal is installed. The wheel and tire assembly is reinstalled on the spindle and the bearings are seated by tightening the wheel nut, usually to a prescribed torque tightness. See Figure 41-19. Then the spindle nut is adjusted to provide zero preload or end play according to manufacturer's specifications.

Most front-wheel drive cars are equipped with permanently sealed front wheel bearings. No periodic lubrication is required. Rear wheel bearing lubrication on these models consists of bearing repacking, much like front wheel bearing lubrication on rear-wheel drive cars.

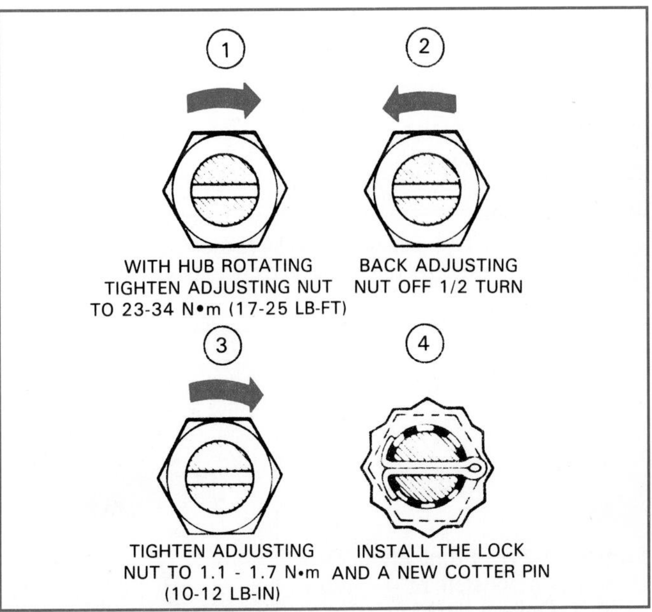

Figure 41-19. Wheel bearing adjusting procedure is given in views 1, 2, 3, and 4 for tightening the hub nut and locking it in place. (Ford)

Driving Axles

Driving axles on rear-wheel drive cars are long, sturdy, one-piece steel shafts, splined at one end and generally flanged at the other end, Figure 41-20. The splined end meshes with the differential side gear. The side gear transfers torque force to the axle shaft. The flanged end of the shaft rotates the rear driving wheel.

Driving axles on front-wheel drive cars consist of a shaft, or shafts, inboard and outboard constant velocity joints, and boots. See Figure 41-21 . The inboard CV joint outer race stub shaft is splined to the final drive unit side gear. The outboard CV joint outer race stub shaft is splined to and transfers torque force to the hub of the front driving wheel.

Rear Driving Axles

The ***rear-wheel drive driving axle*** is a durable, heavy-duty part that seldom requires service. Occasionally, a rear wheel seal will leak differential lubricant or a rear wheel bearing will fail. In rare circumstances, the axle shaft will break.

Axle shaft removal and installation are accomplished as follows:

1. Remove the wheel and tire assembly and the brake drum.
2. Drain the differential lubricant by removing the carrier cover.
3. Remove the differential pinion shaft lock bolt and the pinion shaft.
4. Push the flanged end of the axle shaft toward the center of the car and remove the clock from the inboard end of the axle shaft. See Figure 41-22.
5. Pull the axle shaft from the rear axle housing.
6. Use a special puller to remove the axle bearing and seal.
7. Lubricate the new bearing with differential lubricant and use a special driving tool to seat the bearing in the rear axle housing bore.

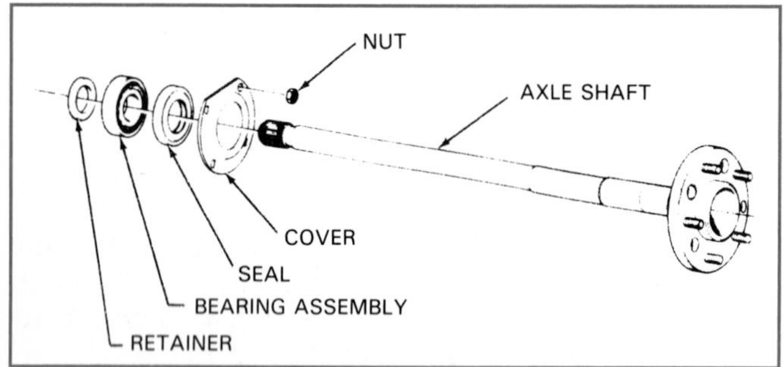

Figure 41-20. This axle shaft and its related outboard parts are typical of rear-wheel drive driving axle construction. (Cadillac)

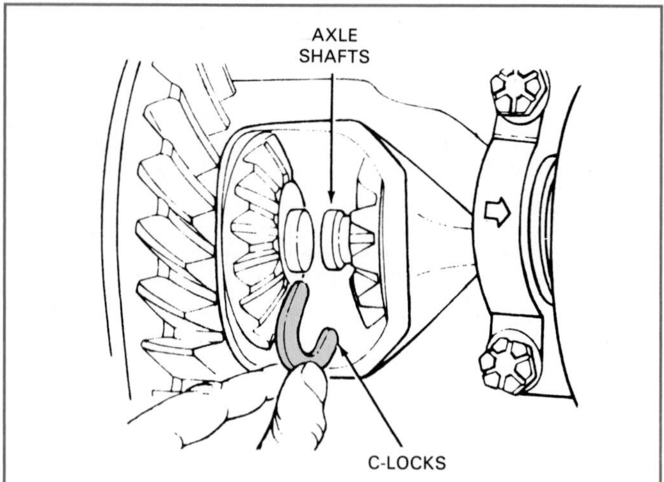

Figure 41-22. To "unlock" this rear-wheel drive driving axle, push the axle inward and remove the clock from the groove at the inboard end of the axle. (Ford)

8. Install a new axle shaft seal, using a special driving tool, and apply grease between the lips of the seal.
9. If called for, install an 0-ring on the spline end of the axle shaft.
10. Slide the axle shaft into the rear axle housing, taking care not to damage the seal or bearing.
11. Start the axle shaft splines into the side gear splines, then push the shaft into the differential case.
12. Install the clock on the end of axle shaft spline and push the shaft outboard until the clock seats in the counterbore (recess) in the differential side gear.
13. Install the pinion shaft and shaft lock bolt, Figure 41-23.
14. Apply sealant to the face of the clean carrier cover, install the cover, and tighten the bolts to the specified torque value.
15. Fill the differential housing to the proper level with prescribed hypoid gear lubricant.
16. Install the brake drum and the wheel and tire assembly.

Front Driving Axles

Front-wheel drive driving axles are of many different designs and arrangements of components. Service problems mainly stem from ruptured constant velocity joint boots, which permits loss of CV joint lubricant and entry of dirt and contaminants.

Service procedures for driving axle assemblies vary among the many different front wheel driving axle systems. This holds true to the extent that driving axle removal

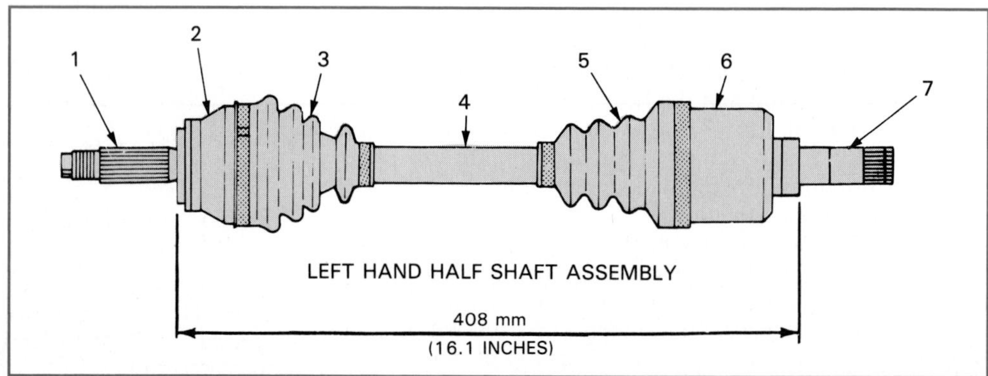

Figure 41-21. Front-wheel drive driving axle consists of: 1–Stub shaft. 2–Outboard CV joint outer race. 3–Boot. 4–Interconnecting shaft. 5–Boot. 6–Inboard CV joint outer race. 7–Stub shaft. (Ford)

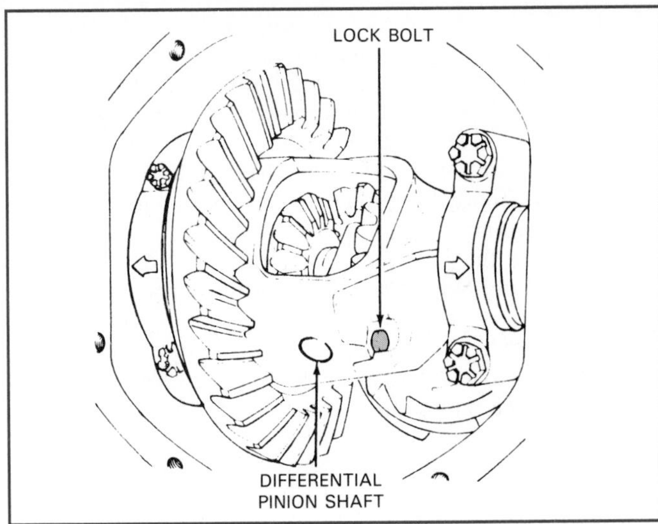

Figure 41-23. With the rear driving axle "locked" in place, install the differential pinion shaft and lock bolt. (Ford)

differs for a given manufacturer's manual and automatic transaxle applications. Therefore, the manufacturer's service manual should be consulted for detailed procedures and cautions for the driving axle system being serviced.

Driving Axle Handling Hints

Certain general recommendations are given for handling and servicing front-wheel drive driving axles:

1. During removal and installation, always support the free end, or ends, of the driving axle assemblies at the CV joint housings. See Figure 41-24.
2. Do not allow the CV joints to "over angle" beyond their capacity.
3. Do not pry against, press on, or cut into the CV joint boots.
4. Use care to see that the machined surfaces and splines are not nicked or damaged in any way.
5. Use special tools when removing and installing pressed-on components. Never use a metallic hammer.
6. CV joint components are matched. Do not interchange components with components from another CV joint. See Figure 41-25.
7. When replacing a boot, CV joint, shaft, or complete right or left driving axle assembly, know the vehicle's transaxle type, transaxle ratio, and engine size. Also, specify right or left side and inboard or outboard end when requesting replacement parts.
8. Do not drop the assembled driving axle, or bump it against adjacent parts during installation, Figure 41-26.
9. During installation, do not "over-plunge" outward on assembled inboard plunge-type CV joint.
10. When replacing a boot, thoroughly clean the CV joint and refill the housing and boot with special CV joint lubricant, Figure 41-27. Always use new boot clamps to seal-in lubricant and seal-out contaminants.

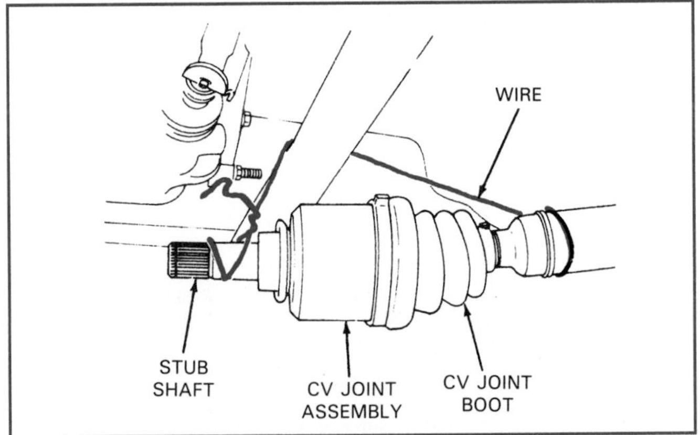

Figure 41-24. When removing a front-wheel drive driving axle from the final drive unit or wheel hub, always support the free end at the CV joint housing. (Ford)

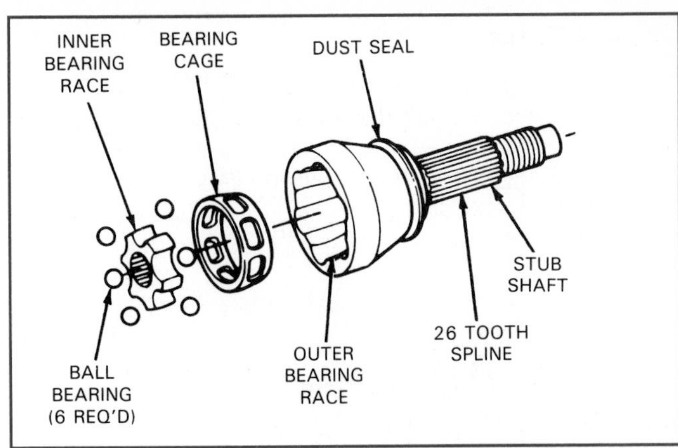

Figure 41-25. CV joints are "matched" assemblies. Components cannot be interchanged with components from another CV joint. (Ford)

Front Driving Axle Service

Front-wheel drive driving axle removal and installation procedures vary with make, model, and driving axle system. Very general procedures for removal, disassembly and reassembly, and reinstallation follow, with numerous "notes" calling out exceptions. See Figures 41-28 and 41-29.

Front driving axle removal:

1. Raise the vehicle.
2. Remove the wheel and tire assembly.
3. Remove the hub nut and washer. Discard the nut if torque prevailing type.
4. Remove the brake caliper (wire it to underbody component) and brake rotor, if required. Note: On some systems, remove the bolt attaching the brake hose routing clip to the suspension strut.

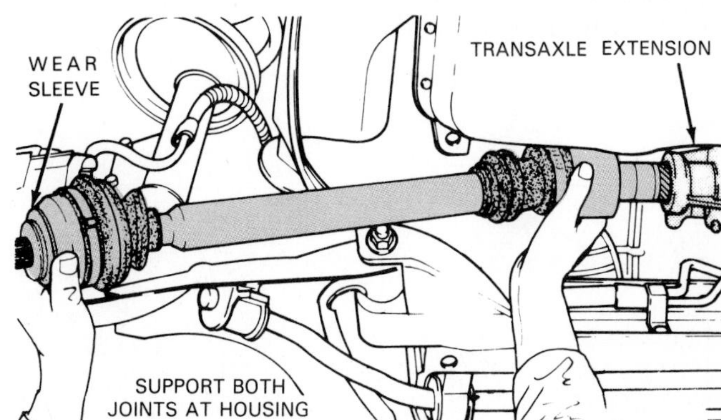

Figure 41-26. Handle front-wheel drive driving axles with care to avoid damage to boots, CV joints, or shafts. (Chrysler)

1. Flush grease from housing and repack housing with approx. half of grease furnished with new seal.
2. Put remainder of grease in seal.
3. Install parts as shown.

TRI-POT HOUSING
SHAFT RETAINING RING
SPIDER ASSEMBLY
SEAL RETAINER
TRI-POT JOINT SEAL
SPACER RING
COAT INSIDE SEAL LIP WITH GREASE
SEAL RETAINING CLAMP
AXLE
SEAL GROOVE

Figure 41-27. Exploded view of an inboard CV joint reveals a plunge-type tripod housing and matched internal parts. Note CV joint lubricant repacking instructions. (Oldsmobile)

5. Remove the nut from the ball joint-to-steering knuckle attaching bolt, Figure 41-30, and the drive bolt from the steering knuckle. Note: Discard the nut and bolt, if so specified.
6. Separate the ball joint from the steering knuckle. Note: Use a pry bar with care if prying is required.
7. Position a special tool, Figure 41-31, or pry bar, between the final drive unit housing and the inboard CV joint stub shaft and pry the driving axle assembly from the housing. Pry with care to avoid damaging the housing, oil seal, or CV joint.
8. Wire the inboard end of the driving axle assembly to the underbody component to maintain somewhat normal angularity.
9. Separate the outboard CV joint stub shaft from the wheel hub. Note: On some systems, a special puller is required.
10. Remove the driving axle assembly from vehicle.

Front driving axle disassembly and reassembly:

1. Clamp the interconnecting shaft of the driving axle in a soft jaw vise.
2. Use a cutting pliers to cut away the boot clamp, peel it away from the boot, and roll the boot back over the shaft.
3. Inspect the CV joint.
4. If CV joint replacement is required, use a hammer and brass drift to tap sharply on the inner bearing race to dislodge the internal circlip. Note: Some CV joints use a wire ring ball retainer, which can be pried out of the groove in the outer race.
5. Support the parts when the CV joint and shaft separate.
6. Remove the old boot and clamp from the shaft.
7. Remove and discard the old circlip and install a new circlip on the shaft.
8. Install a new small clamp and boot on shaft. Seat the boot in the groove in the shaft and tighten the clamp.
9. Disassemble and inspect the CV joint, Figure 41-32. Thoroughly clean all parts and reassemble the CV joint or replace the complete CV joint assembly.

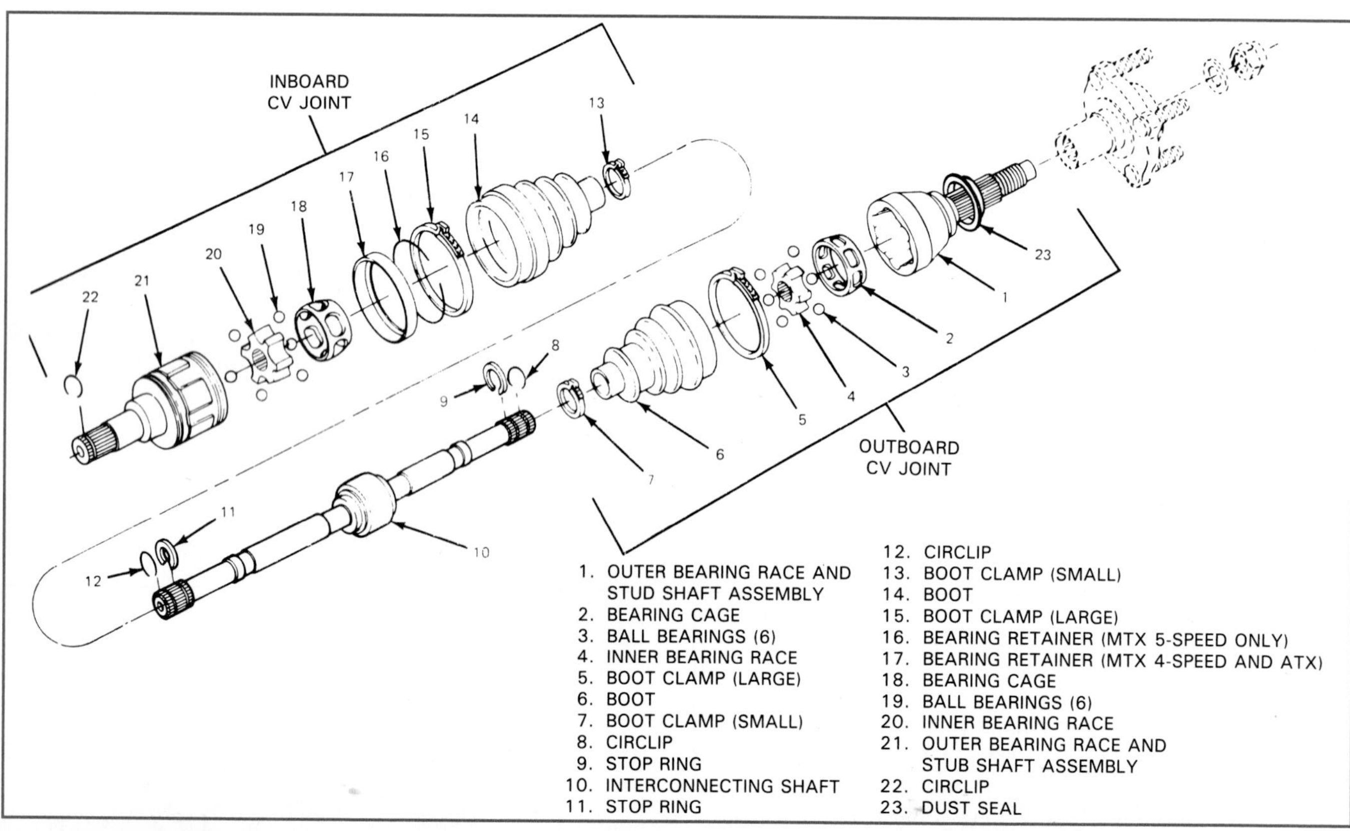

Figure 41-28. Exploded view of this right driving axle provides the sequence for component disassembly and assembly. (Ford)

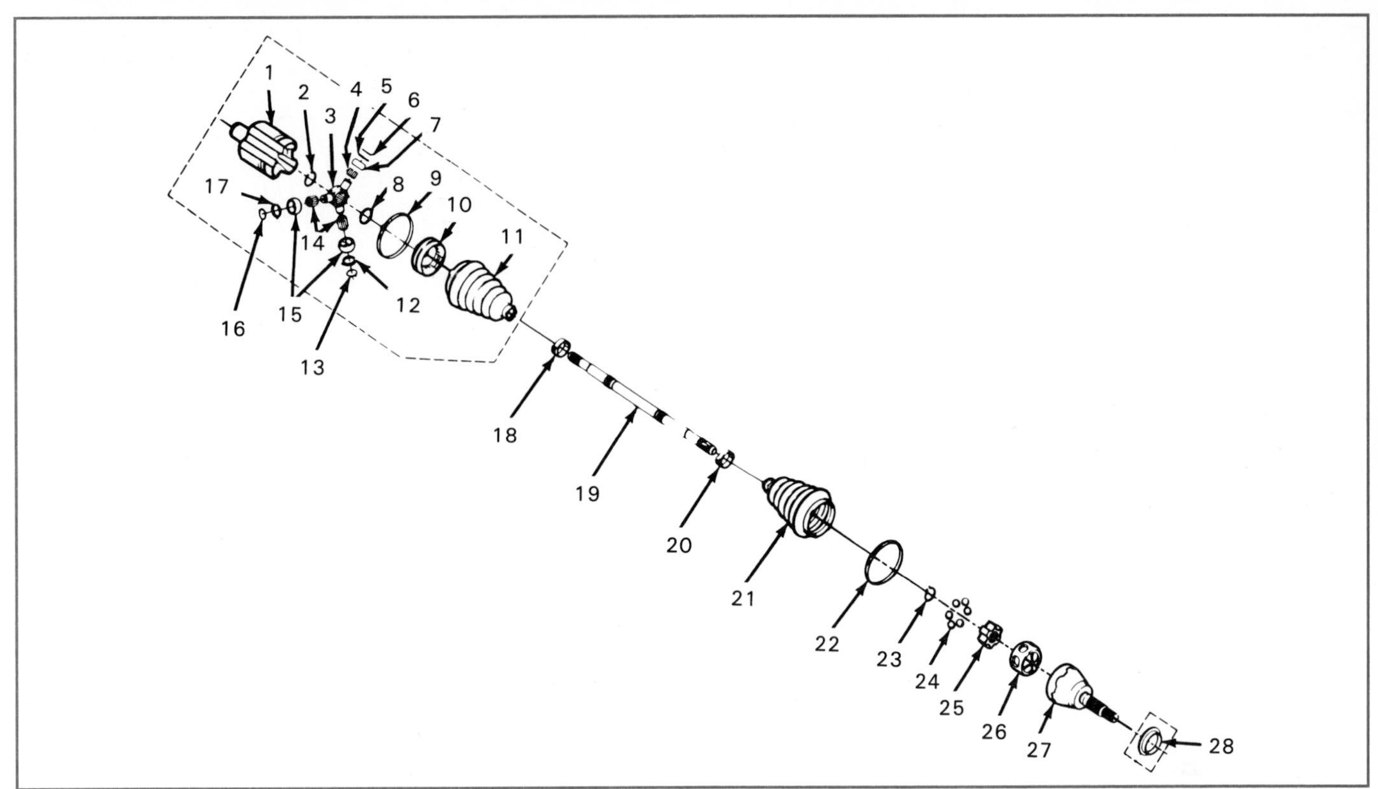

Figure 41-29. Exploded view of a typical right driving axle shows the following parts arrangement: 1–Tripod CV joint housing. 2–Retaining ring. 3–Spider. 4–Needle rollers. 5–Retainer. 6–Ring. 7–Ball. 8–Spacer ring. 9–Clamp. 10–Bushing. 11–Boot. 12–Retainer. 13–Ring. 14–Needle rollers. 15–Ball. 16–Ring. 17–Retainer. 18–Clamp. 19–Axle shaft. 20–Clamp. 21–Boot. 22–Clamp. 23–Ring. 24–Ball. 25–Rzeppa CV joint inner race. 26–Cage. 27–Outer race. 28–Deflector ring. (Cadillac)

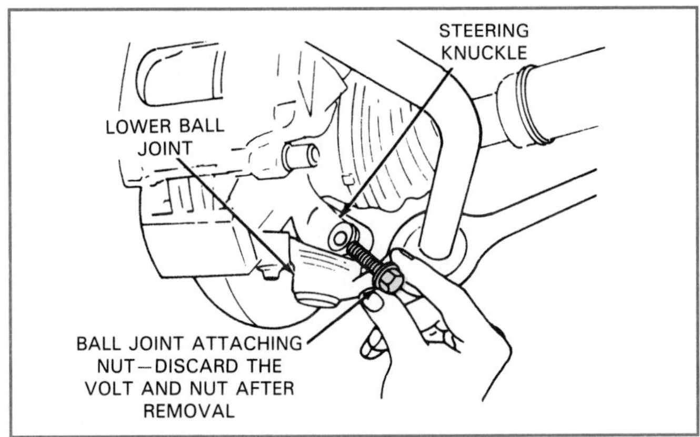

Figure 41-30. In preparing for driving axle removal, remove the nut and drive out the bolt holding the lower control arm ball joint to the steering knuckle. (Ford)

10. Pack the CV joint and boot with special CV joint lubricant.
11. Peel back the boot. Position the CV joint on the end of the shaft and use a plastic-tipped hammer to tap the CV joint into place, Figure 41-33. The circlip must seat in the groove of the CV joint inner bearing race. Note: On some CV joints, install a new wire ring ball retainer.
12. Remove excess lubricant and position the large end of the boot over the CV joint housing. Install and tighten the new large clamp.
13. Move the plunge-type CV joint in or out to adjust the driving axle to the length specified. See Figure 41-21.

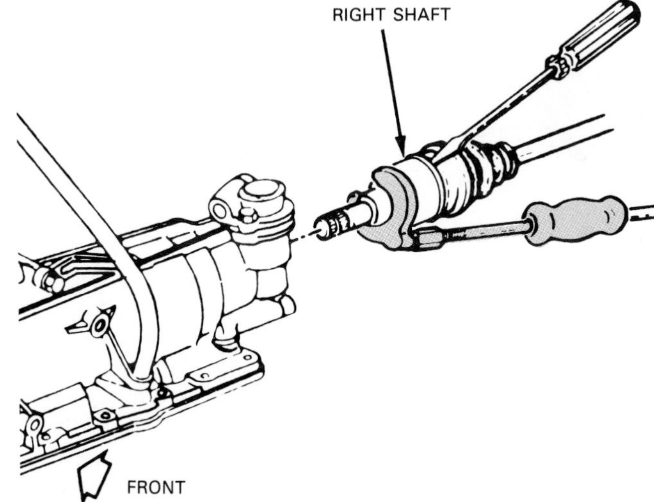

Figure 41-31. On many GM cars, a special tool is required to pull the inboard CV joint stub shaft from the final drive unit. (Cadillac)

14. Relieve any trapped air from the boot, and then install the boot clamp.

Front driving axle reinstallation:

1. Place a new circlip on the inboard CV joint stub shaft.
2. Carefully align the splines of the inboard CV joint stub shaft with the splines in the final drive unit side gear, Figure 41-34.
3. Push the CV joint into the final drive unit until the circlip seats in the side gear.

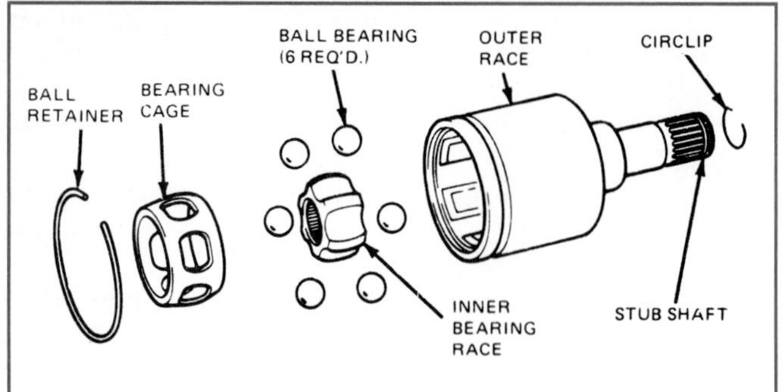

Figure 41-32. Disassembly of a constant velocity joint permits the careful inspection of matched components. (Ford)

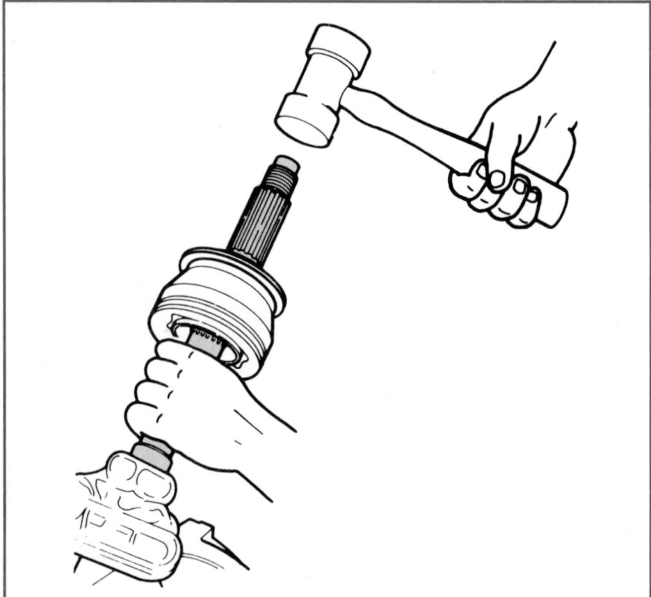

Figure 41-33. To install the CV joint on the shaft, peel back the boot, position the CV joint assembly on the end of the shaft, and tap it in place. (Ford)

4. Carefully align the splines of the outboard CV joint stub shaft with the splines in the wheel hub, Figure 41-35.
5. Push the shaft into the hub as far as possible. Note: On some systems, use a special puller and adapters to complete installation of the shaft in the hub.
6. Connect the control arm to the steering knuckle and install a new bolt and nut to the specified torque value.
7. Install the brake caliper and rotor. Note: On some systems, install the bolt attaching the brake hose routing clip to the suspension strut.
8. Install a washer and a new torque prevailing nut, fingertight, on the outboard CV joint stub shaft. Note: Some hub nuts have a nut lock and cotter pin.
9. Install the wheel and tire assembly.
10. Lower the vehicle and final-tighten the wheel nuts.
11. Tighten the hub nut to the specified torque value, and make sure that the locking tab on the nut aligns with the slot in the CV joint stub shaft. See Figure 41-36. Note: On some hub nuts, a nut lock and cotter pin must be installed after proper torque tightening.
12. Fill the transaxle to the correct level with the recommended transaxle lubricant.

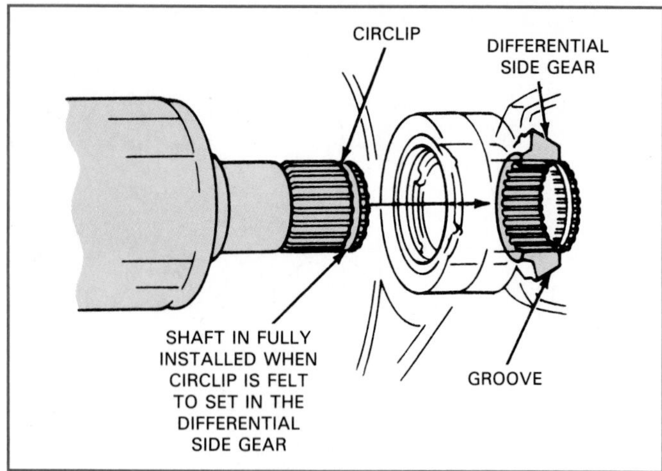

Figure 41-34. During installation of a driving axle assembly, the splines on the inboard CV joint stub shaft are aligned with, and are fully installed in, the splines of the final drive unit side gear. (Ford)

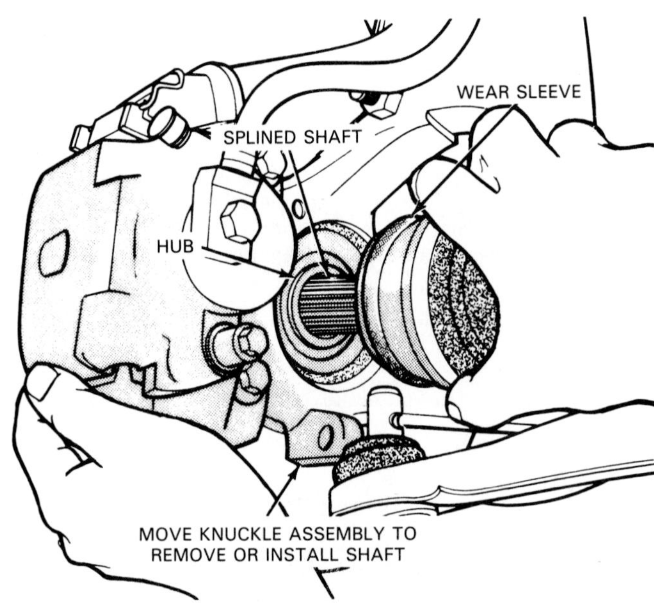

Figure 41-35. With the inboard CV joint locked in place, the outboard CV joint stub shaft splines are meshed with the wheel hub splines. (Chrysler)

Care in Servicing Drivelines

When servicing drivelines and driving axles, bear in mind that you are working with parts and assemblies designed, produced, and quality controlled to meet exacting standards of size, shape, and finish. Such high standards of manufacture deserve equally high standards of skill and care and attention to detail when performing services.

When working on these important elements of the drive train, you are dealing with low-to-high speed rotating parts, centrifugal force, and the effects of engine torque and power transfer. With shafts, you need to maintain proper angularity and balance to avoid vibration. With constant velocity joints, you are involved with matched parts, opposed identical pairs, and a special CV joint lubricant.

Likewise, you must provide special and specified lubricants for transaxles, transmissions, differentials, univer-

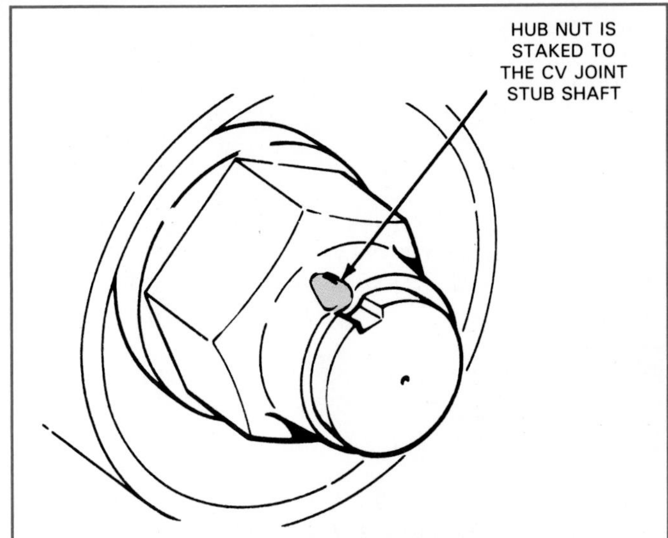

Figure 41-36. After a new torque prevailing nut is tightened to specified torque value, it must be "staked" to the outboard CV joint stub shaft. (Ford)

sal joints, and wheel bearings. In all areas, you must ensure freedom of operation of moving parts to help eliminate friction and wear, and to furnish maximum power transfer to the driving wheels.

Chapter 41–Review Questions

Write your answers on a separate sheet of paper. Do not write in this book.

1. The driveline of a rear-wheel drive vehicle consists of one or more universal joints, the drive shaft, and _____.
   (A) transmission output shaft.
   (B) transaxle side gears.
   (C) differential drive pinion gear.
   (D) driving axles and wheels.
2. The universal joints are considered to be part of the drive shaft assembly. True or False?
3. All drive shafts must be balanced, properly mounted assemblies with all working parts lubricated by a special _____ lubricant.
4. After installing new universal joints, why should you reassemble the drive shaft carefully?
5. What measuring device should you use to check the angularity of the drive shaft and universal joints?
6. The differential drive pinion gear and ring gear comprise a _____ assembly.
7. The differential case is attached to the _____.
   (A) drive pinion gear
   (B) ring gear
   (C) drive shaft
   (D) None of the above
8. Service problems with differentials usually are limited to lubricant leakage in what area?
9. What two adjustments can be made that will affect tooth contact between the drive pinion gear and the ring gear?
10. Front wheel bearings on front-wheel drive cars require periodic lubrication much like front wheel bearings on a rear-wheel drive car. True or False?
11. Driving axles on rear-wheel drive cars are splined at one end and are generally _____ (flanged or tapered) at the other end.
12. The splined end of the rear driving axle meshes with the:
    (A) differential side gear.
    (B) differential pinion gear.
    (C) ring gear.
    (D) drive pinion gear.
13. A car owner complained of a "clunk" at the rear of a rear-wheel drive car. Technician A says it could be caused by a faulty rear universal joint. Technician B says it could be caused by too much backlash between the differential drive pinion gear and ring gear. Who is right?
    (A) A only.
    (B) B only.
    (C) Both A & B.
    (D) Neither A nor B.
14. In most rear-wheel drive cars, the driving axles are retained in the differential by:
    (A) clocks.
    (B) circlips.
    (C) snap rings.
    (D) stop rings.
15. In many front-wheel drive systems, the driving axles are retained in the final drive unit by _____ (clocks or circlips).
16. Constant velocity joint components are matched. You _____ (may or may not) interchange components with components from another CV joint.
17. What type of nut or bolt should be discarded once it has been removed from a shaft or spindle?
18. After assembly of front-wheel drive driving axle, move the plunge-type CV joint in or out to adjust the driving axle to the specified length. True or False?
19. A car owner complained of vibration under a rear-wheel drive car. Technician A says it could be caused by an out-of-balance drive shaft. Technician B says it could be caused by over-angularity of the drive shaft and universal joints. Who is right?
    (A) A only.
    (B) B only.
    (C) Both A & B.
    (D) Neither A nor B.
20. In performing driveline service, you must ensure freedom of operation of moving parts to help eliminate friction and wear and to furnish maximum _____ to the driving wheels.

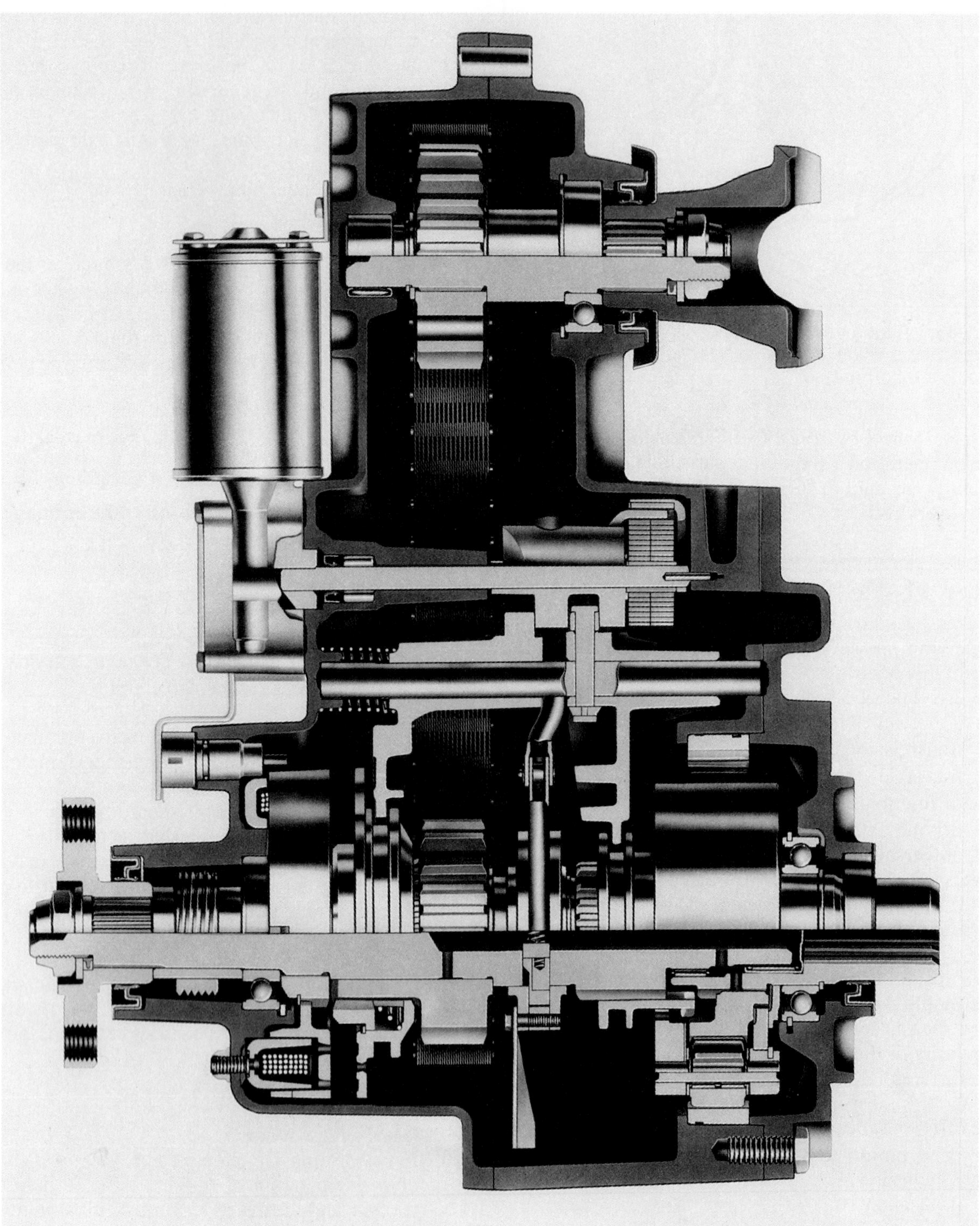

Cutaway of a typical transfer case used in a four-wheel drive system. (Borg-Warner)

Chapter 42
Four-wheel Drive Systems

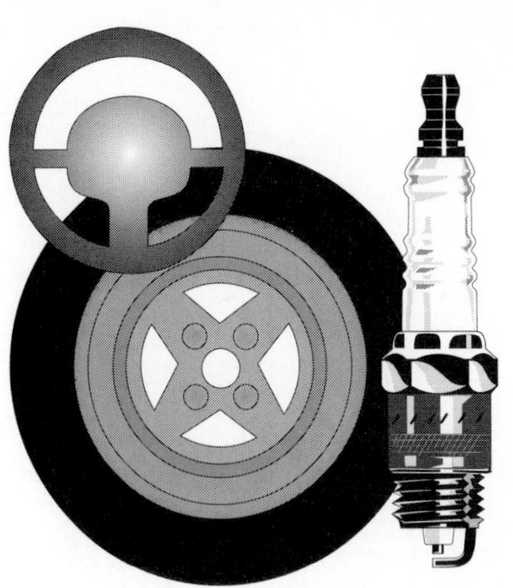

After studying this chapter, you will be able to:

- ❍ Define four-wheel drive.
- ❍ Explain how four-wheel drive and all-wheel drive differ.
- ❍ Tell how a viscous coupling in a four-wheel drive system builds internal resistance and provides "limited-slip" action.
- ❍ State why differential "locks" are used in four-wheel drive systems.
- ❍ Identify some typical four-wheel drive troubles and give possible causes.

Four-wheel Drive/All-wheel Drive

Four-wheel drive is a power transfer system that permits a vehicle to be driven by all four wheels. The principal advantages of four-wheel drive (4WD) are better traction and greater control of the vehicle in adverse conditions such as muddy roads, wet or oily highways, snow or ice-covered roads, loose surfaces, or hazardous off-road terrain.

Four-wheel drive has a long history. It was pioneered in 1910 with the introduction of the truck-like 4WD "Duplex" power car. In 1913, the Jeffrey Quad was produced as a 4WD commercial vehicle. Later, it was adapted for military use and became the Nash Quad, the most famous Army truck of World War I.

Then, the "go anywhere" World War II Jeep established the superior flexibility and capability of 4WD vehicles in adverse conditions. The Jeep, however, was created as a dual-purpose vehicle. It not only had a rigidly connected 4WD system, but was equipped with a transfer system that permitted the vehicle to be shifted into a two wheel drive mode for on-highway use.

Today, the dual-mode (2WD/4WD) system is used in a wide-range of large and compact pickup trucks, sport utility vehicles, vans, station wagons, and passenger cars. The versatility of 4WD and its added safety aspects of better traction and greater control have made it an ever-expanding part of the new vehicle market. See Figure 42-1.

Also contributing to 4WD popularity is a relatively recent development termed ***all-wheel drive*** (AWD). All-wheel drive systems automatically react to normal or adverse situations without the need for the driver to decide when or when not to shift into 4WD.

In all-wheel drive applications, then, the shifting is automatic. Most four-wheel drive vehicles, however, have a shifting device so that the front wheel drive or rear-wheel drive can be disengaged if desired and the vehicle becomes two-wheel drive. See Figure 42-2. In some cases, the vehicle must be stopped with the engine idling when the "shift" is made, either from 2WD to 4WD or from 4WD to 2WD. In other applications, the driver can "shift on the fly."

Figure 42-1. Four-wheel drive vehicles, such as this sport utility vehicle, are becoming increasingly popular. These vehicles offer superior traction and control in adverse driving conditions. (Honda)

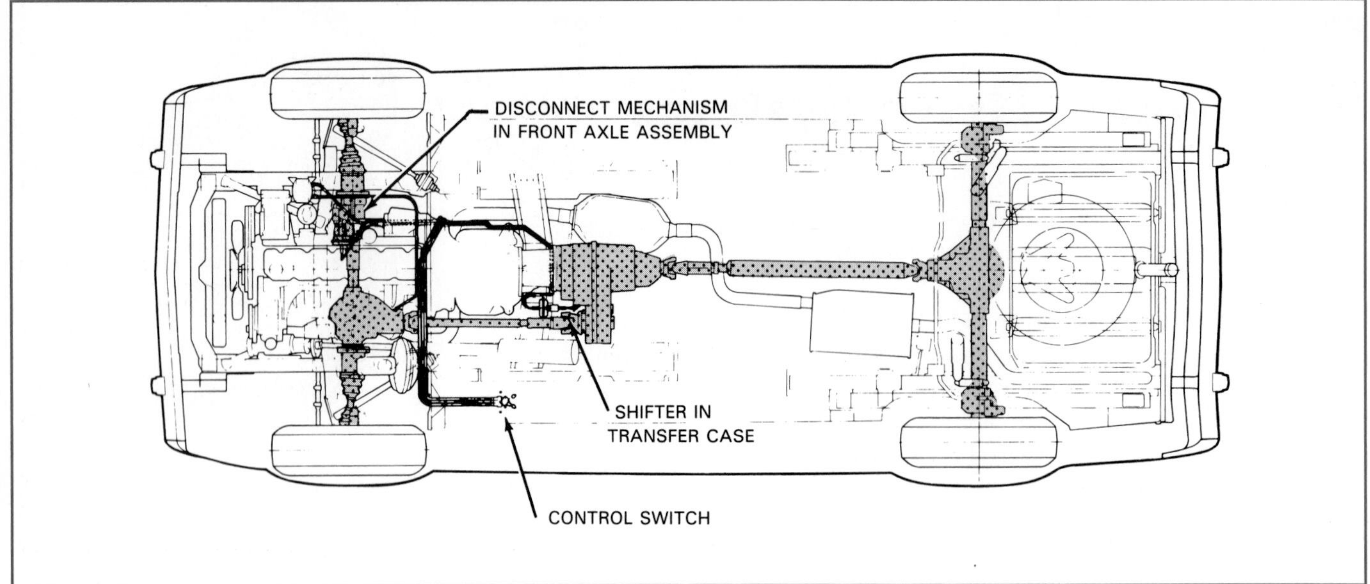

Figure 42-2. The AMC Eagle 4WD drive train is highlighted by the dot formation. This system has direct drive through the transfer case to the rear differential. The chain drive in the transfer case powers the front differential when the control switch and the front axle disconnect mechanism are in the 4WD mode. (Chrysler)

Four-wheel Drive Systems

A study of various 4WD systems as they evolved should provide a basic understanding of how these systems operate and why advanced 4WD and AWD designs have improved the "breed."

AMC/Jeep 4WD Systems

In 1973, the introduction of the Jeep Quadra-Trac system brought full-time four-wheel drive into an expanding market. The Quadra-Trac 4WD system uses an interdrive shaft differential that has unloading cone type limited-slip action. It restricts the difference in rotational speeds between the two drive shafts, thus delivering better traction.

Quadra-Trac II was introduced on American Motors Eagle 4WD vehicles. It, too, uses an inter-drive shaft differential with limited-slip action–but by way of a viscous coupling, Figure 42-3. The viscous coupling is part of a single-speed transfer case. The rear drive shaft is driven directly from the rear of the transfer case. The front drive shaft is offset to the left and is driven by a chain.

When the drive shafts operate at different rpm (when a wheel, or pair of wheels, tends to spin), the liquid silicone in the viscous coupling interacts with 43 closely spaced plates alternately attached to the housing and the hub of the coupling. This builds resistance and effectively "locks" the drive shafts together to prevent all of the power from going to the axle with the spinning wheel (or wheels).

Select Drive

American Motors went to a Select Drive system, Figure 42-4, on Eagle models with a dash-mounted switch that controls two vacuum motors to provide either 2WD or 4WD capability. For 2WD operation, one motor disengages the front axle drive chain in the transfer case, Figure 42-5. The other motor actuates a front axle disconnect mechanism. A "shift on the fly" feature on later models permits shifts while the vehicle is in motion.

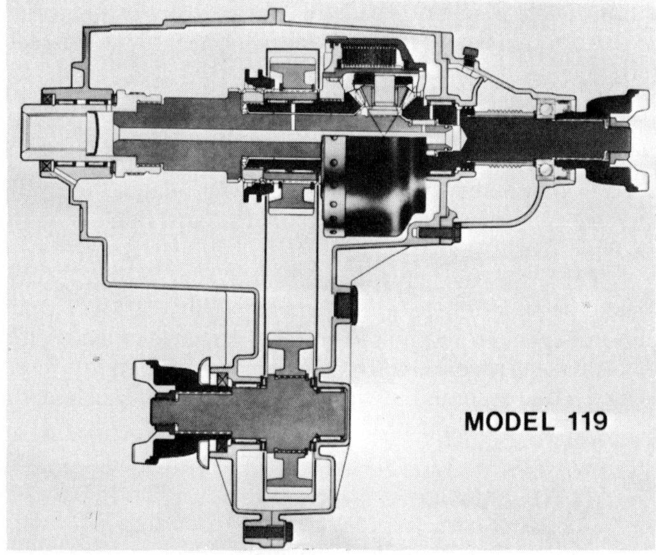

Figure 42-3. The Eagle transfer case has a viscous coupling in the case to provide "limited-slip" action to the drive shafts. (Chrysler)

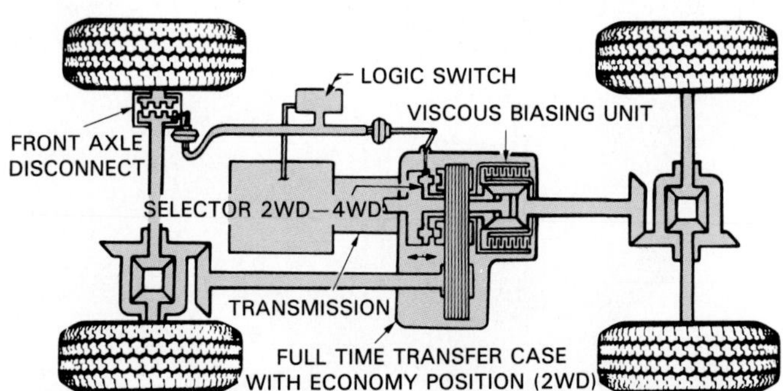

Figure 42-4. Layout of an Eagle Select Drive system is diagrammed in the 2WD mode. Note that the selector in the transfer case and the front axle disconnect device are in the "disconnect" position. (Chrysler)

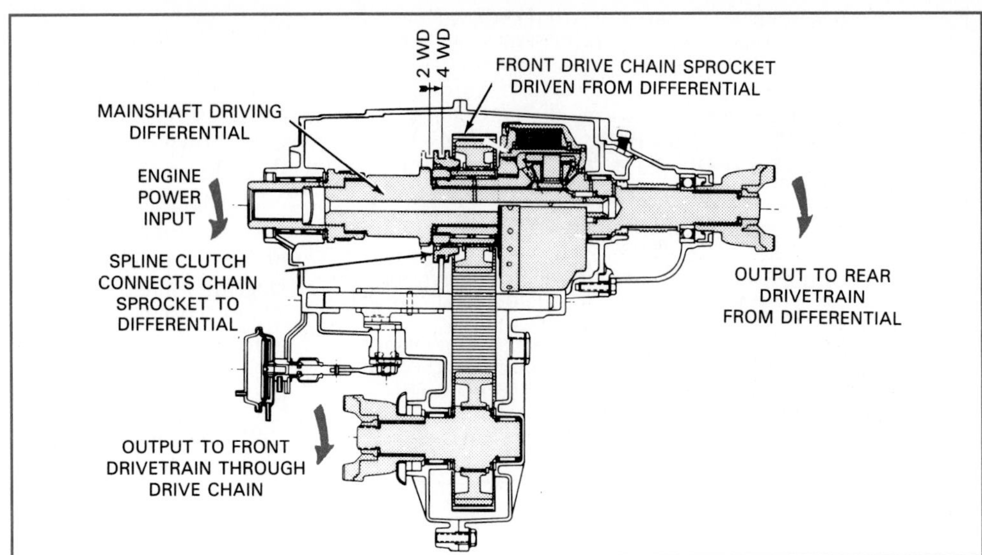

Figure 42-5. Sectional view gives particulars of the Select Drive transfer case operation in the 4WD mode. (Chrysler)

On later Eagle models, a switch was made in the transfer case to a four-pinion, open type differential instead of the viscous coupling. A vacuum control system, actuated by a selector switch on the dash panel, is used to change drive mode. The name, Select Drive, also applies to the later four-pinion gear system.

Command-Trac

Some Jeep models use a Command-Trac part-time, dual range, chain-driven, gear type 4WD system. Later models feature "shift on the fly." Shifting into or out of 4WD while the vehicle is moving is made possible by use of a synchronizer assembly in the sliding spline clutch that locks the front axle drive chain sprocket to the transfer case. See Figures 42-6 and 42-7. Also in later models, a front axle disconnect mechanism is employed for 2WD, which eliminates the need for locking hubs.

Some Jeep models adopted the viscous coupling setup in the Selec-Trac full-time 4WD/2WD system. This system is similar to Select-Drive, but it has a low range, or two-speed, capability in the transfer case when extra torque is needed.

The low range mode is activated by a floor-mounted lever, but only when the vehicle is in 4WD. Figures 42-8 and 42-9 reveal how the Selec-Trac system operates.

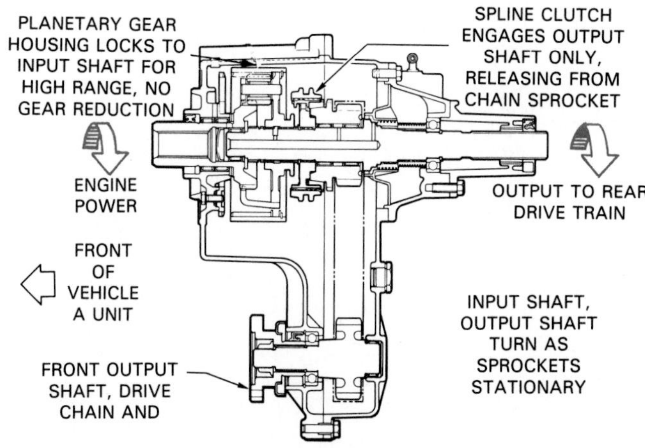

Figure 42-6. Diagram of the internal features of a Jeep Command-Trac transfer case shows the elements in the 2WD mode. (Jeep)

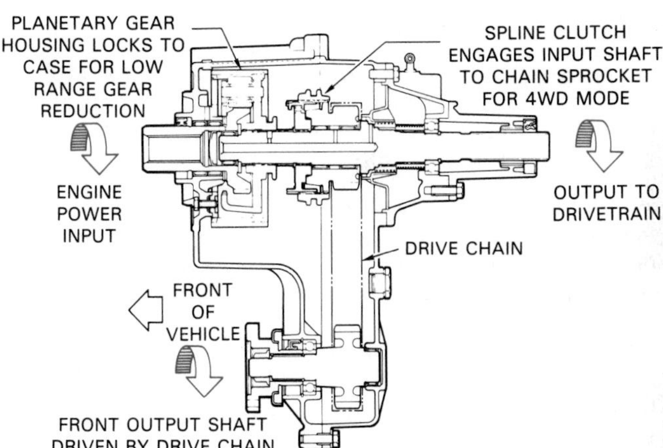

Figure 42-7. Command-Trac transfer case elements are pictured in the 4WD mode. Note in this mode that the spline clutch engages the input shaft to the chain sprocket. (Jeep)

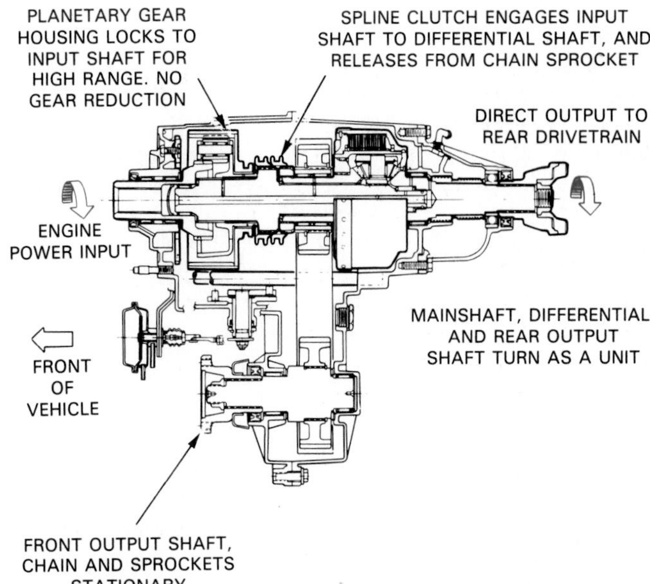

Figure 42-8. The Jeep Selec-Trac transfer case makeup is detailed. The transfer case elements are shown and described in the 2WD "high" mode. (Jeep)

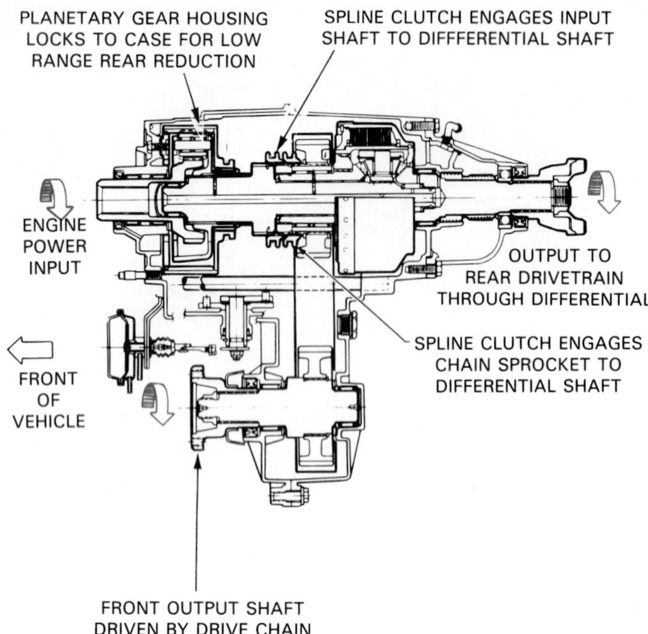

Figure 42-9. With a Selec-Trac transfer case in the 4WD mode, the arrows indicate output to the rear drive train and the front output shaft. (Jeep)

In later models, Jeeps are equipped with a redesigned transfer case within the Selec-Trac 4WD system. This transfer case affords the use of a five-position shift lever: 2WD, Hi Lock, 4WD, Neutral, and Lo Lock.

A planetary differential within the transfer case provides a constant torque split to the front and rear axles. The differential action can be overridden, or locked, in either high or low range.

Ford Four-wheel Drive

Ford 4WD systems are used on light-duty trucks and sport utility vehicles. One system uses the front driving axle shown in Figure 42-10 in conjunction with the transfer case shown in an exploded view in Figure 42-11.

The front driving axle assembly consists of two independent yoke and arm assemblies. The driving axle shafts utilize universal joints to give independent suspension. The steering knuckles are connected to the yokes by ball joints. These 4WD vehicles are equipped with either manual or automatic locking hubs.

The part-time, two-speed transfer case, Figure 42-11, has a two-piece aluminum housing. This exploded view shows the sequence of components, including parts of the planetary gear assembly, shift levers, front output shaft and yoke, and 4WD indicator switch.

The transfer case used on later light trucks has magnesium case halves. It includes a positive displacement oil pump for lubrication whenever the mainshaft is turning. A "touch drive" electrical shift selector system is available. See Figure 42-12. With this system, shifts between 2WD and high-range 4WD can be made at any speed or with the vehicle stopped. Shifts into or out of low-range 4WD require that the vehicle is stopped with the transmission in neutral. Obviously, the touch drive system uses automatic locking front wheel hubs.

Ford All-wheel Drive

Some Ford front-wheel drive passenger cars are equipped with an all-wheel drive system. See Figure 42-13. This system is intended to provide improved traction and can be "switched" into and out of all-wheel drive at any speed or when the vehicle is standing still.

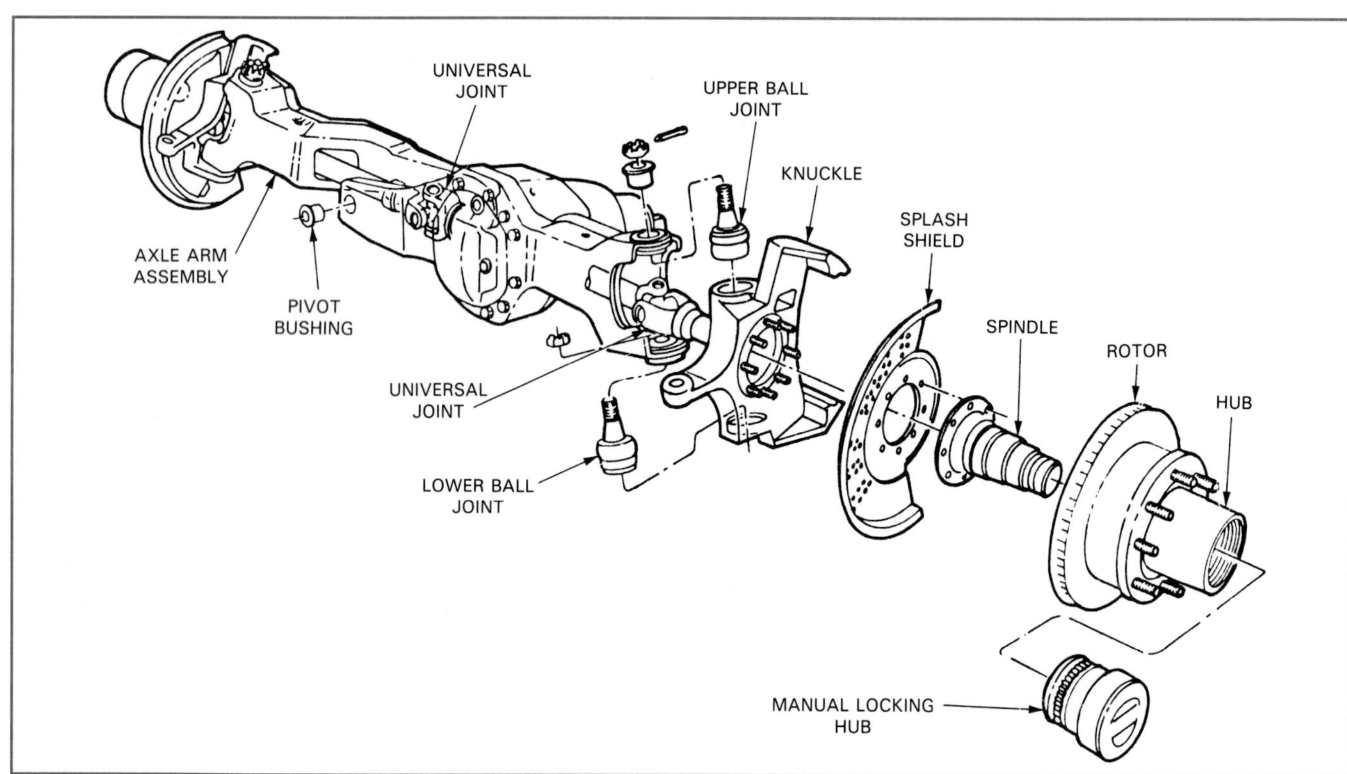

Figure 42-10. Three-quarter front view shows details of a Ford Bronco front driving axle, including the steering knuckle, wheel spindle, hub and rotor assembly, and locking hub. (Ford)

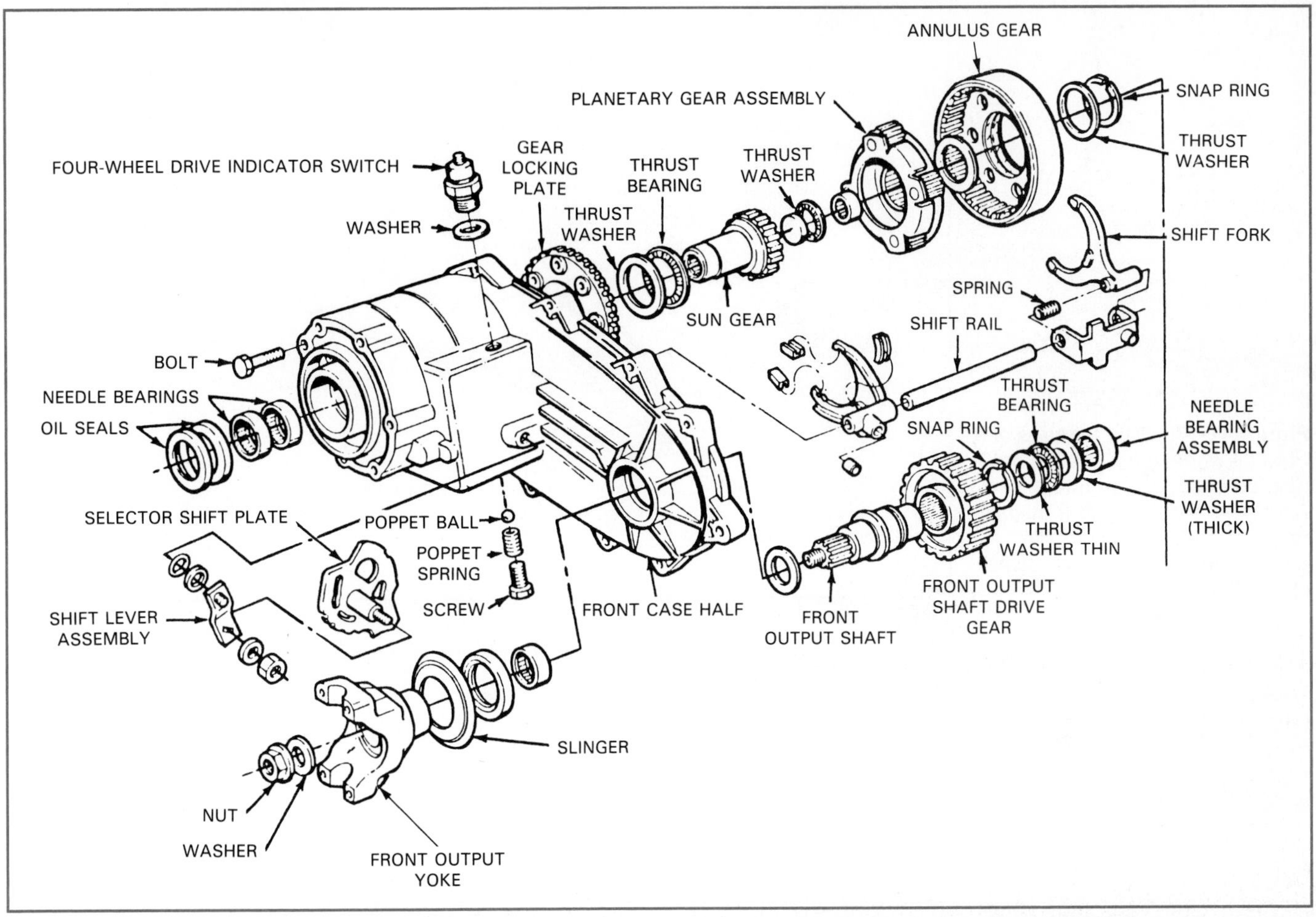

Figure 42-11. Exploded view gives the disassembly/assembly sequence of a Ford Bronco transfer case. (Ford)

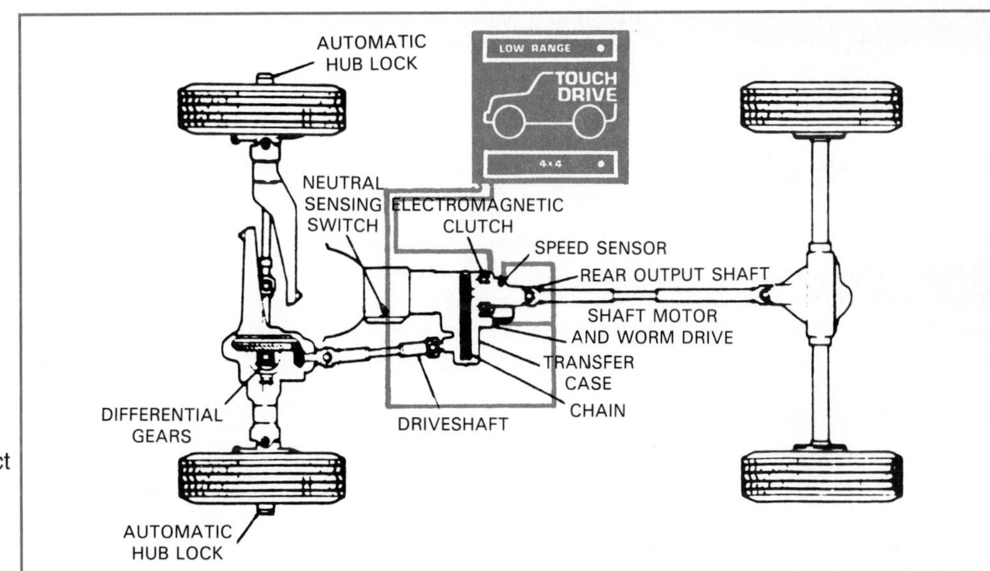

Figure 42-12. The Ford electric "touch drive" four-wheel drive control system is used on compact trucks and sport utility vehicles. The touch drive switch and the selection indicator display are in an overhead console. (Ford)

The heart of the all-wheel drive system is a single-speed, part-time transfer case mounted under the automatic transaxle. The gear that drives the transfer case mechanism is in constant mesh with the final drive ring gear of the transaxle.

For all-wheel drive operation, a sliding clutch collar links the driving gear with a two-piece, hollow tube drive shaft that transfers power to the rear limited-slip differential. The sliding clutch collar is engaged and disengaged by a shift fork. The fork is activated by a vacuum motor, which is actuated by solenoids when a two-position (2WD/AWD) electric switch is turned on or off.

Chevrolet Four-wheel Drive

Some Chevrolet vans, sport utility vehicles, and pickup trucks are equipped with four-wheel drive systems.

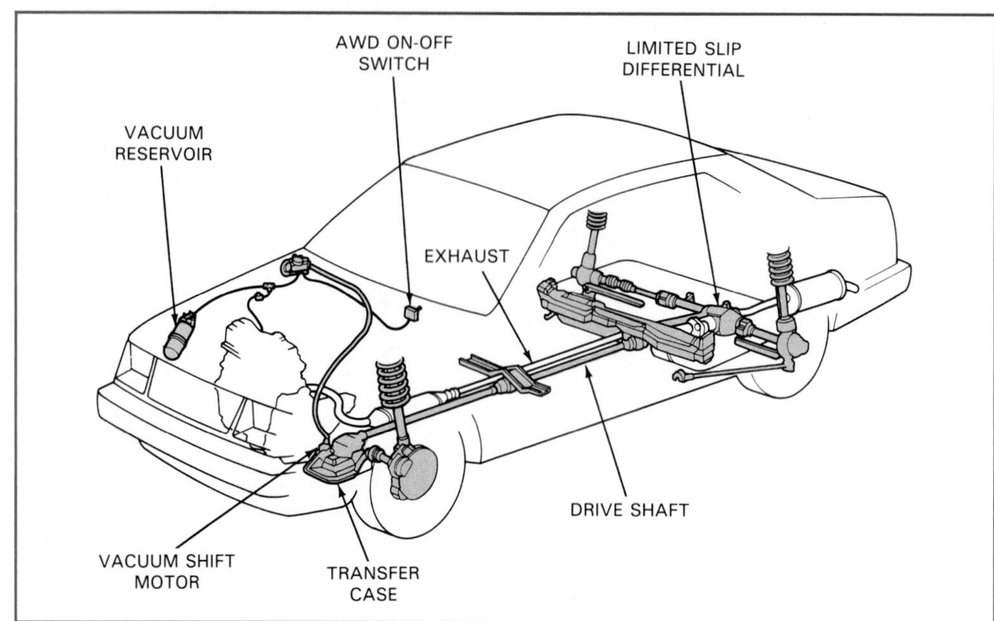

Figure 42-13. Key features of a Ford all-wheel drive system are pointed out in this phantom view. A two-piece drive shaft transmits power to the rear limited-slip differential when the AWD switch is on. (Ford)

These systems let the driver shift from 2WD to 4WD "high" and back again without stopping. This provides convenience for the driver.

The full-size Blazer has an automatic locking hub system that allows the driver to shift into or out of 4WD without leaving the cab.

Chrysler/Mitsubishi 4WD

The Colt Vista four-wheel drive wagon was imported by Chrysler for the Plymouth and Dodge lines. Figure 42-14 calls out all of the 2WD/4WD mechanisms. Trace the system in this schematic from select button to select control valve, actuator, transaxle, front differential, transfer case (for 2WD/4WD switching), bevel gear setup, propeller shaft, and rear differential.

Audi Four-wheel Drive

The Audi Quattro four-wheel drive system is permanently engaged, freeing the driver from reacting to rapidly changing road conditions. Power is transmitted through a five-speed manual transaxle to the front wheel drive driveline and front wheels. Power to the rear wheels is by way of a two-piece drive shaft, differential, and driving axles. The axles are supported by fully independent rear suspension members. See Figure 42-15.

For even greater traction, a differential lock control can be triggered by a rotating knob to lock the center differential. This locks or synchronizes the rotation of the front wheels to the rotation of the rear wheels. Under worst conditions, the rear differential also can be locked for maximum traction.

Volkswagen All-wheel Drive

Certain Volkswagen models are equipped with an automatically engaging, permanent all-wheel drive system. This system is based on the use of a viscous coupling, Figure 42-16, designed to enhance the positive traction already provided by the vehicle's rear engine, rear-wheel drive setup.

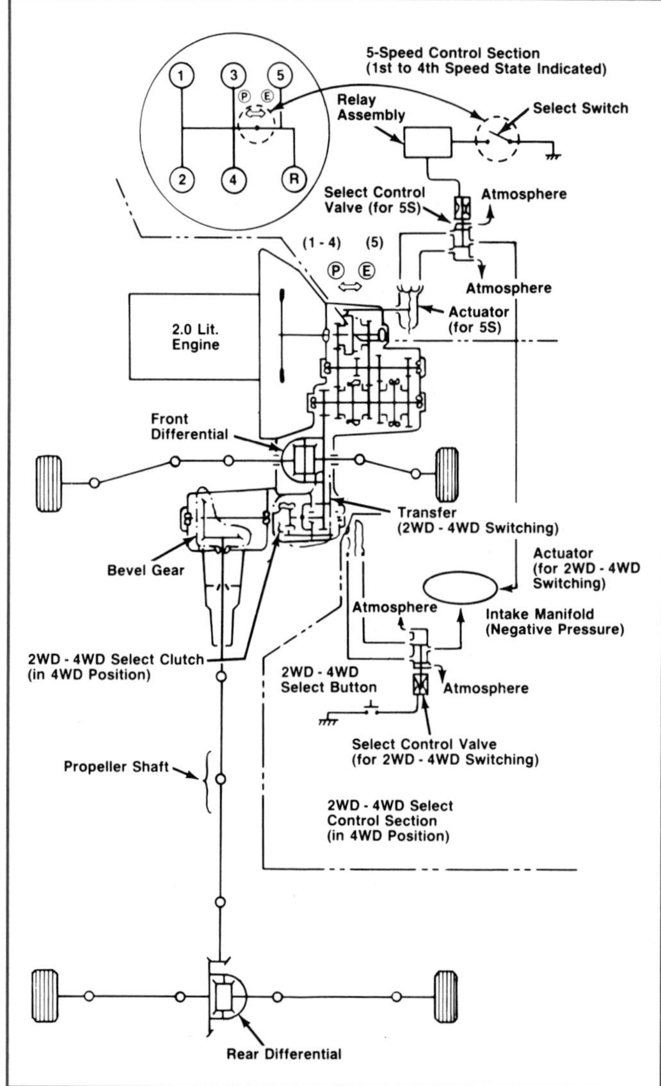

Figure 42-14. Schematic shows 2WD/4WD mechanisms on a Colt Vista wagon. The arrows point out features and functions of the 4WD system and related components. (Chrysler)

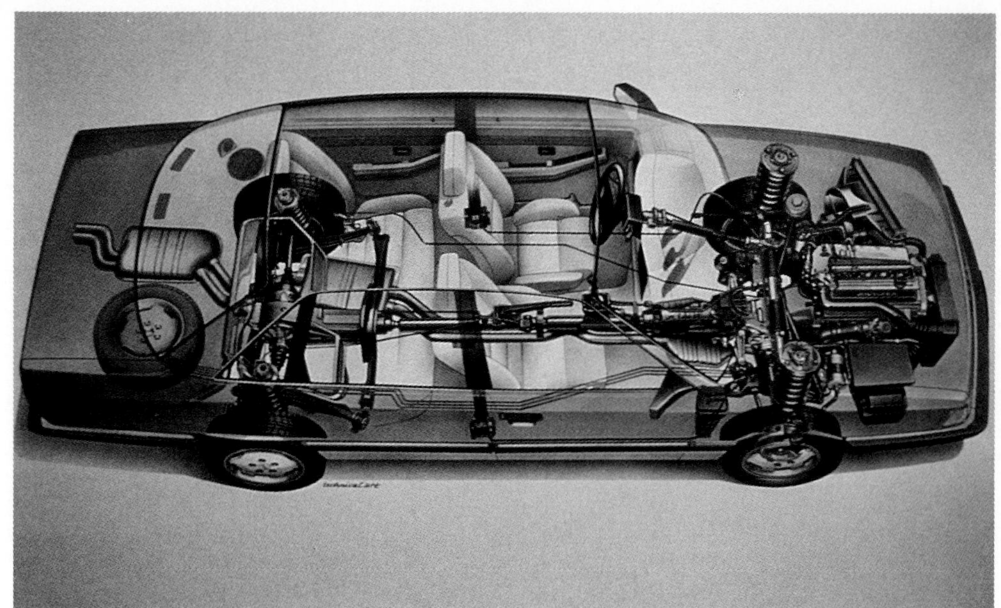

Figure 42-15. Audi has engineered a permanently engaged all-wheel drive system for its sports coupes and sedans. The AWD system utilizes a unique differential between the front and rear wheels that provides added traction when needed. (Audi)

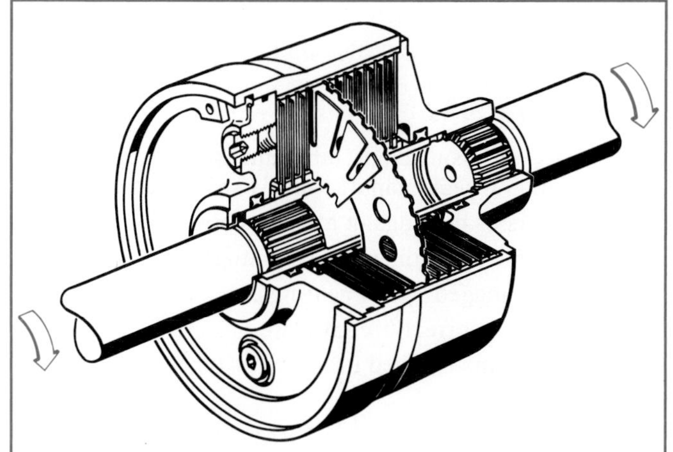

Figure 42-16. Volkswagen uses a sealed viscous coupling unit in the front differential of the four-wheel drive Vanagon models. When required by driving conditions, silicone fluid thickens and gives direct drive to the plates in the coupling, thus transmitting power to the front wheels. (Volkswagen)

The viscous coupling is mounted in the front final drive housing. It operates constantly and automatically to transmit power to the front differential as required by the need for greater traction.

The viscous coupling is filled with a patented silicone fluid. In operation, the coupling allows up to six percent speed difference between the drive shaft and front axle before the thick silicone fluid effects a rigid connection.

An optional rear differential lock is offered. It is designed for use at low speeds only when the vehicle is in danger of being stuck in the mud or snow. A shift valve on the dash panel controls the engagement and disengagement of a lock sleeve in the differential housing.

Certain Volkswagen Quantum models have all-wheel drive. This 4WD system has three differentials, one for each driving axle and one between the front and rear axles. The center differential is integrated into the transmission, where it provides the 4WD handling characteristics. The three differentials can be locked in different positions to suit difficult or hazardous driving conditions.

Subaru Four-wheel Drive

Some older Subaru models have on-demand, part-time four-wheel drive. One system setup uses an electric 4WD engagement switch in the manual transmission shift lever. Another setup has an auxiliary two-speed transfer case operated by a second shift lever. Moving the 4WD shift lever an extra notch gives the vehicle 42 percent more low speed pulling power.

Later models couple 4WD with a microprocessor controlled air spring suspension system. This system automatically raises the vehicle one inch when 4WD is engaged. It lowers the vehicle at a speed of 50 mph.

Subaru's newer, full-time 4WD system uses a mechanical center differential to transfer power to the front and rear driving axles. Under hazardous driving conditions, the center differential can be locked to provide power to each axle.

Honda Four-wheel Drive

Certain Honda models offer 4WD and improved traction by pressing a push-button switch. Also featured is a special low gear in a six-speed manual transmission.

The 4WD system uses a viscous coupling in the drive shaft to the rear axle. The coupling has interlaced plates and is filled with a silicone fluid. If the front wheels slip, the fluid heats up and expands, causing the coupling to lock and transfer power to the rear wheels.

Toyota Four-wheel Drive

Late-model Toyota Land Cruisers are available with an electronically controlled all-wheel drive system that incorporates on-demand front and rear locking differentials. See Figure 42-17. By locking the differential, wheels on the same axle are locked together and turn at the same speed. When both differentials are locked, all four wheels are

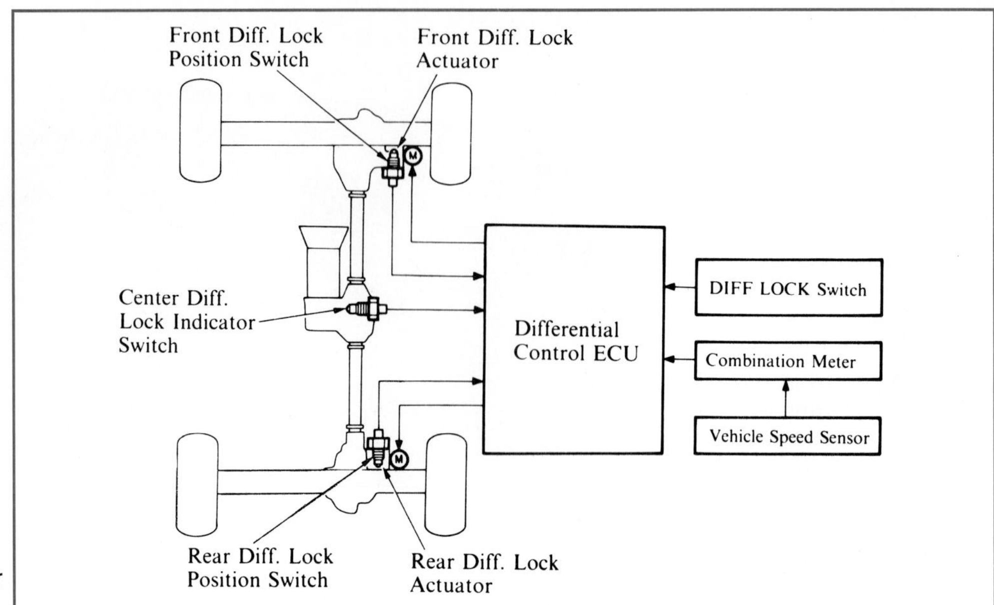

Figure 42-17. Toyota offers an all-wheel drive system that features on-demand front and rear locking differentials. (Toyota)

driven in unison. This provides true four-wheel drive, even in severe poor-traction situations.

Four-wheel Drive Service

Servicing four-wheel drive systems can be the end result of lengthy processes of elimination. Since all 4WD systems affect or are affected by at least two drivelines and all four driving axles, pinpointing a problem area is a wide-ranging, systematic search for the source of trouble.

Manufacturers warn that before attempting to repair a suspected transfer case malfunction, you should check all other driveline components. The actual cause of the problem may be related to the axles, hubs, propeller shafts, transmission or transaxle, wheels and tires.

Also consider the many 4WD types in present use. Some are designed around a front-mounted engine and rear-wheel drive. These require the use of a transfer case to send power forward to the front differential.

Other 4WD designs are based on a front-mounted engine and front-wheel drive. With this basic layout, the primary drive remains at the front axle and power goes back to the rear wheels by way of a "power takeoff," which can be connected or disconnected. Most are part-time, selector-engaged, or on-demand 4WD.

Some 4WD systems utilize three differentials with "lock-up" capabilities for improved traction. Others have manual or automatic locking hubs. Still others use a viscous coupling to provide "full-time" or "all-wheel drive."

With this in mind, always refer to the manufacturer's service manual for diagnostic information and step-by-step service procedures.

A listing of four-wheel drive troubles and possible causes follows. This list is general, touching on a variety of types of 4WD, but it could serve to sharpen your problem-solving ability.

Vehicle Tends to Wander

- Unequal or incorrect tire pressures. (Pressure should be within 1/2 to 1 psi (3.50 to 7.0 kpal wheel to wheel.)
- Unequal or mismatched tire sizes and types.
- Incorrect front wheel caster angle.

Noisy Operation

- Incorrect or insufficient lubricant in transfer case or differential. Check manufacturer's specifications.
- Worn gears or bearings in transfer case.
- Worn gears or bearings in differential.
- Worn or damaged wheel bearings.
- Unequal or incorrect tire pressure.
- Unequal or mismatched tire sizes or types.

Lubricant Leaks

- Overfill condition in transfer case.
- Vent closed or restricted.
- Yoke seals worn or damaged.
- Yoke seal-bearing surfaces rough or worn.
- Silicone fluid from viscous coupling. (Replace entire unit.)

System Will Not Shift Into 2WD

- No vacuum at mode selector harness.
- No vacuum at storage tank or vacuum hose from storage tank.
- No vacuum at intake manifold supply fitting.
- Defective select control valve or actuator.
- Inoperative transfer case vacuum motor.
- Malfunctioning transfer case shift linkage.
- Inoperative front axle shift vacuum motor.
- Automatic locking front hubs not unlocking.

System Will Not Shift Into 4WD

- No vacuum at mode selector harness.
- No vacuum at storage tank or vacuum hose from storage tank.
- No vacuum at intake manifold supply fitting.

- Defective select control valve or actuator.
- Inoperative transfer case vacuum motor.
- Malfunctioning transfer case shift linkage.
- Inoperative front axle shift motor.
- Automatic locking front hubs not locking.

Vibration or Shudder

- Defective or loose steering linkage.
- Defective steering damper.
- Faulty universal joints.
- Bent wheels.
- Low level of silicone fluid in viscous coupling. (Replace entire unit.)
- Runout or unbalance of propeller shaft.

Review Questions–Chapter 42

1. Define the term "four-wheel drive."
2. What are the principal advantages of four-wheel drive?
3. With "all-wheel drive" systems, the "shifts" from 2WD to 4WD and from 4WD to 2WD are:
   (A) manual, with vehicle stopped.
   (B) manual, and "on the fly."
   (C) semiautomatic.
   (D) automatic.
4. Key element of the Quadra-Trac 4WD system is:
   (A) viscous coupling.
   (B) two-speed transfer case.
   (C) front axle disconnect.
   (D) automatic locking front wheel hubs.
5. Jeeps equipped with a redesigned transfer case within the Selec-Trac 4WD system have a five position shift lever. True or False?
6. The Ford all-wheel drive system for passenger cars has a single-speed, part-time transfer case mounted under the _____.
   (A) manual transaxle
   (B) automatic transaxle
   (C) front differential
   (D) rear differential
7. The Audi Quattro has a _____ 4WD system.
   (A) real time
   (B) part-time
   (C) on-demand
   (D) permanently engaged
8. A driver complained that a four-wheel drive pickup truck with transfer case and automatic locking front hubs would not shift into two-wheel drive. Technician A says it could be caused by an inoperative transfer case vacuum motor. Technician B says it could be caused by the automatic locking hubs not locking. Who is right?
   (A) A only.
   (B) B only.
   (C) Both A & B.
   (D) Neither A nor B.
9. Manufacturers warn that before attempting to repair a suspected transfer case, all other _____ components should be checked.
10. Give two possible causes why a 4WD vehicle would tend to wander.

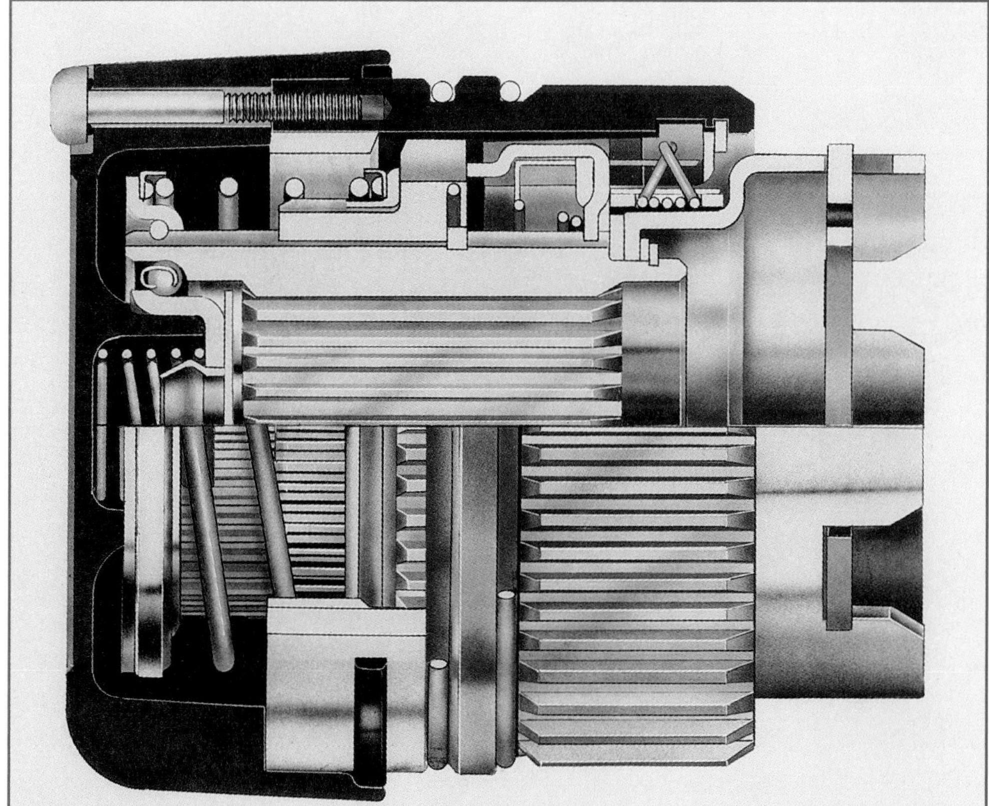

Cutaway of an automatic locking hub used in many part-time four-wheel drive systems. (Borg-Warner)

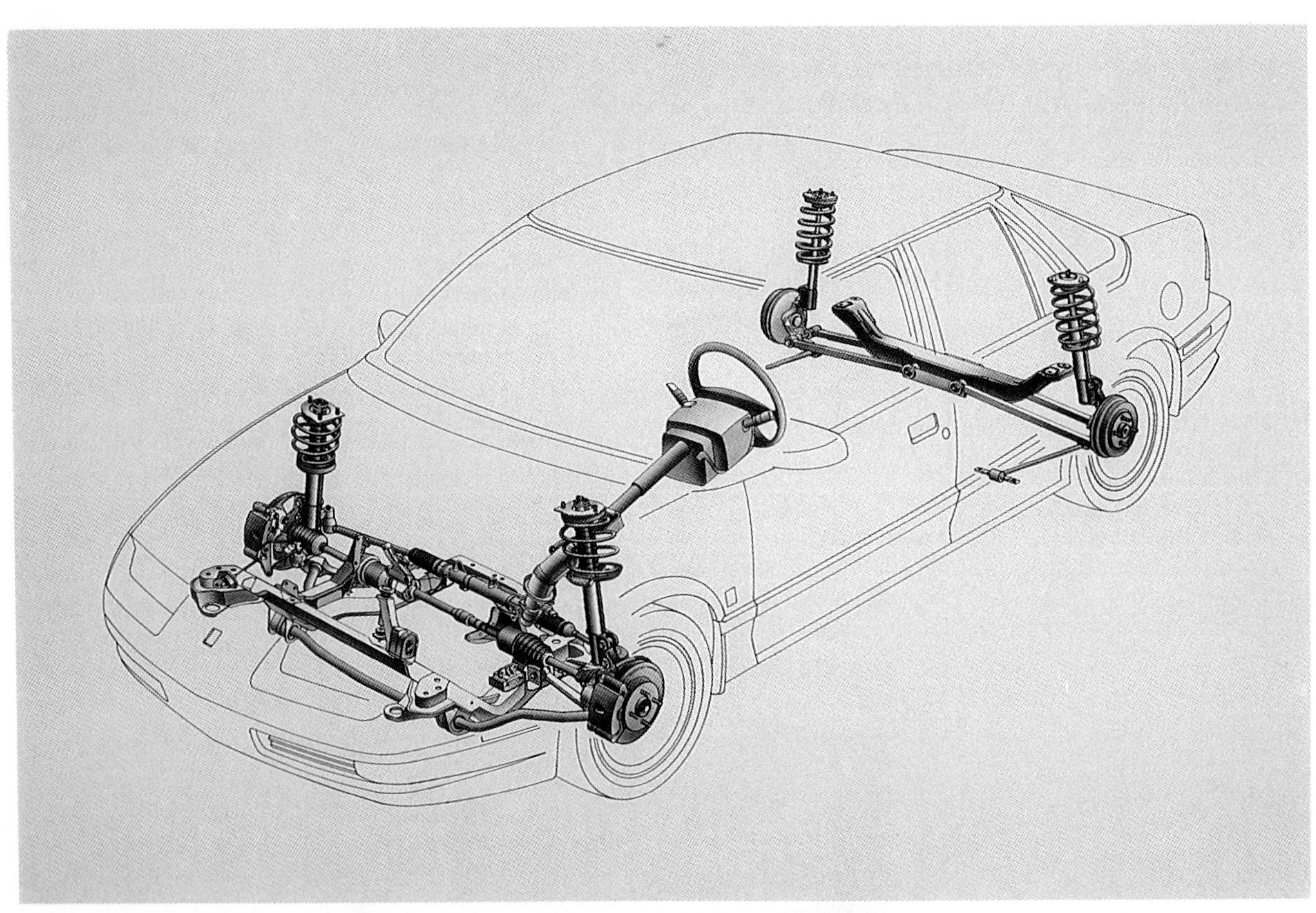

Supension and steering components for a late-model front-wheel drive vehicle. (Saturn)

Chapter 43
Suspension and Steering Systems

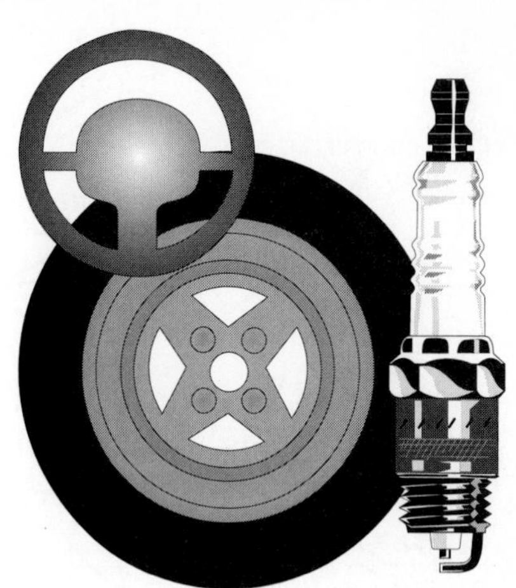

After studying this chapter, you will be able to:

- ❍ Explain the function of the various front and rear suspension components and assemblies.
- ❍ Name the three basic types of front and rear suspension systems.
- ❍ Tell how a typical "automatic level control system" works.
- ❍ Describe the makeup of manual rack-and-pinion and recirculating ball types of steering systems.
- ❍ State the operating principles of a power rack-and-pinion steering gear assembly and the integral power steering gear assembly.
- ❍ Identify some typical suspension and steering system troubles and give possible causes.

Suspension and Steering Systems

The modern automobile has come a long way since the days when "just being self-propelled" was enough to satisfy the car owner. Improvements in suspension, Figures 43-1 and 43-2, and steering, increased strength and durability of components, and advances in tire design and construction have made large contributions to riding comfort and driving safety.

Suspension Systems

Basically, ***suspension*** refers to the use of front and rear springs to suspend a vehicle's frame, body or unitized body, engine, and power train above the wheels. These relatively heavy assemblies constitute what is known as "sprung" weight. The "unsprung" weight, on the other hand, includes wheels and tires, brake assemblies, the rear axle assembly, and other structural members not supported by the springs.

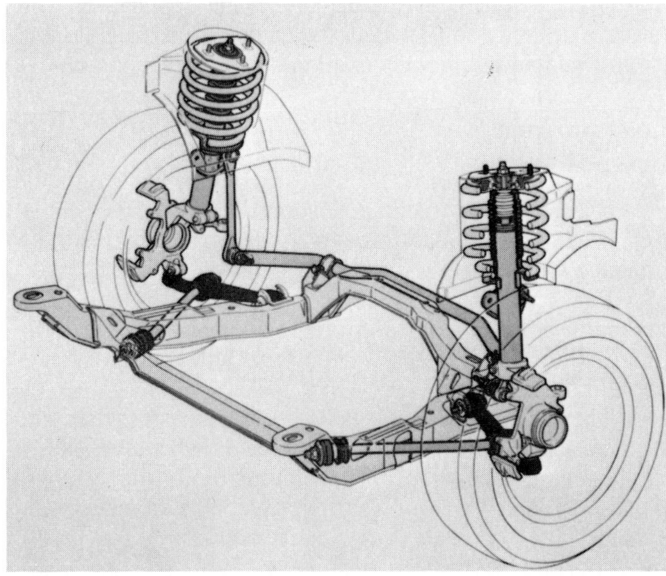

Figure 43-1. A typical MacPherson strut front suspension system features long shock absorber struts surrounded by coil springs. Lower control arms, wheel spindles, a stabilizer bar, and diagonal struts are part of the MacPherson design. (Ford)

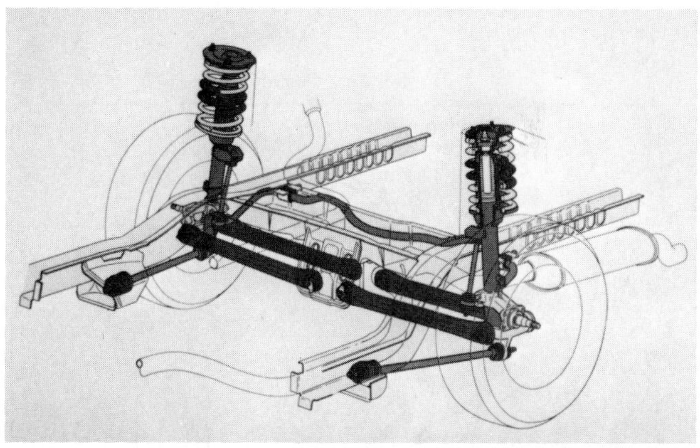

Figure 43-2. MacPherson strut suspension is also well suited for use at the rear of front-wheel drive vehicles. Here, four transverse, parallel control arms are used in conjunction with a stabilizer bar and tie rods that are attached to spindle and knuckle assemblies. (Ford)

The ***springs*** used on today's cars and trucks are engineered in a wide variety of types, shapes, sizes, rates, and capacities. Types include leaf springs, coil springs, air springs, and torsion bars. These are used in sets of four per vehicle, or they are paired off in various combinations and are attached to the vehicle by a number of different mounting techniques.

Coil Springs

Many front and rear suspension systems incorporate compression type ***coil springs.*** Some front coil springs are mounted between the lower control arm and spring housing or seat in the frame, Figures 43-3 and 43-4.

Other front suspension systems have the coil springs mounted above the upper control arms, compressed between

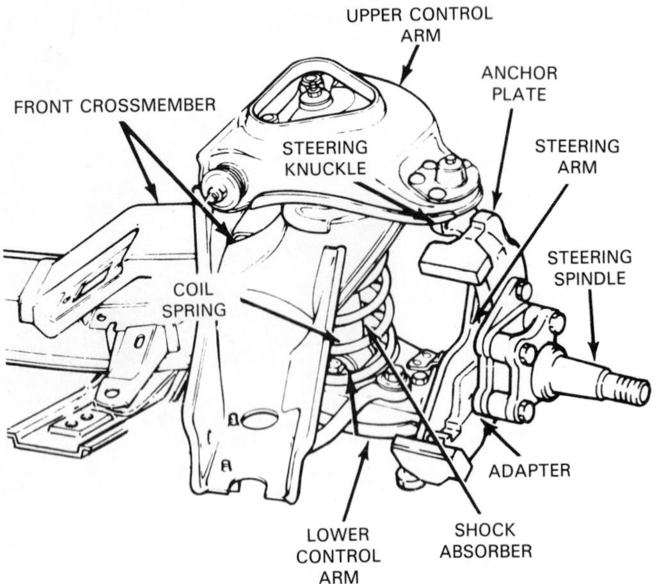

Figure 43-3. Independent front suspension with coil springs and control arms of short- and long-arm type is used on most rear-wheel drive passenger cars. (Chrysler)

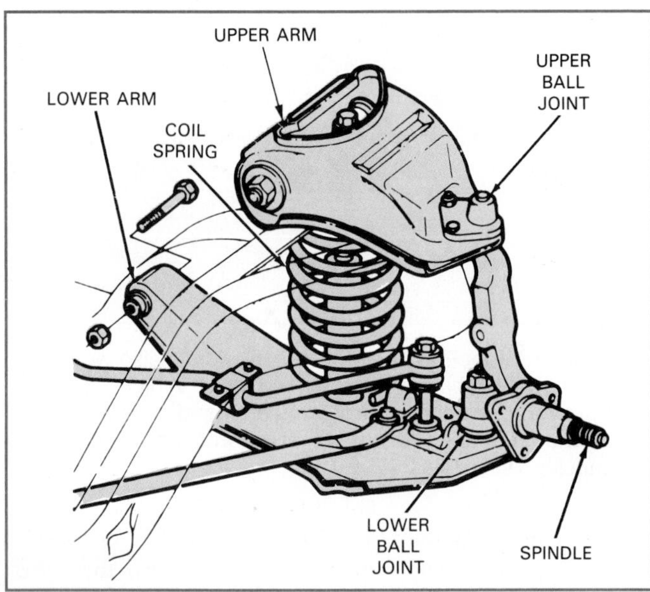

Figure 43-4. Short- and long-arm front suspension generally includes the ball (spherical) joints as "swivel points" for each front wheel. (Ford)

a pivoting spring seat bolted to the control arm and a spring tower formed in the front end sheet metal. See Figure 43-5.

When coil springs are used in both front and rear suspension, three or four control arms are placed between the rear axle housing and the frame to carry driving and braking torque. The lower control arms pivot in the frame members and sometimes support the rear coil springs to provide for up and down movement of the axle and wheel assembly.

In addition, a ***sway bar*** (track bar) is usually attached from the upper control arm to the frame side rail to hold the rear axle housing in proper alignment with the frame and to prevent side sway of the body. However, if the rear coil springs are mounted between the frame and a swinging half axle, the independently suspended rear wheels have a

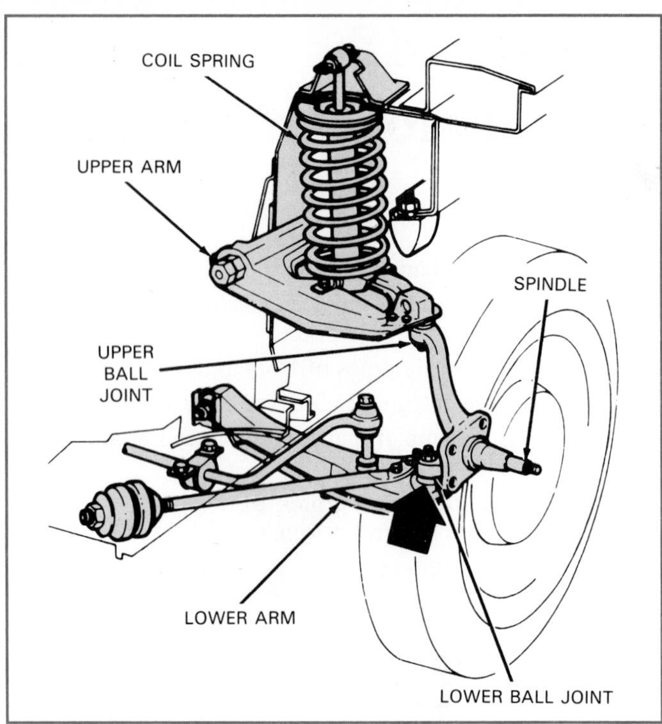

Figure 43-5. In front suspension systems of some subcompact and compact cars, the coil springs are mounted above the upper control arms. Note the use of a strut to support the lower control arm. (Ford)

sturdy axle housing attached to the differential housing which, in turn, is bolted to the frame.

Coil springs are also used in MacPherson strut suspension systems. The spring is installed between a spring seat insulator on the strut and the top mount of the strut assembly. See Figure 43-6.

Coil springs are made of steel or steel alloy. Some have evenly spaced coils, others have variable spacing. Each is manufactured to meet the prescribed Rated Suspension Spring Capacity for the particular vehicle application. This rating is designed to provide for adequate coil spring durability and vehicle stability under all intended load conditions.

Leaf Springs

Front ***leaf springs*** are used in conjunction with solid axle beams in most truck applications. Corvettes use single-leaf, filament-wound, glass/expoxy front and rear springs mounted transversely (crosswise to vehicle centerline).

Rear leaf springs are used on trucks and some passenger cars. Single leaf or multi-leaf springs are usually mounted longitudinally over the front axle beam or under the rear axle housing.

The spring center bolt fastens the leaves together, and its head locates the spring in the front axle beam or saddle on the rear axle housing. U-bolts clamp the spring firmly in place and keep it from shifting. Eyebolts, brackets, and shackles attach it to the frame at each end.

Torsion Bars

Torsion bar suspension is a method of utilizing the flexibility of a steel bar or tube twisting lengthwise to provide spring action. Instead of the flexing action of a leaf

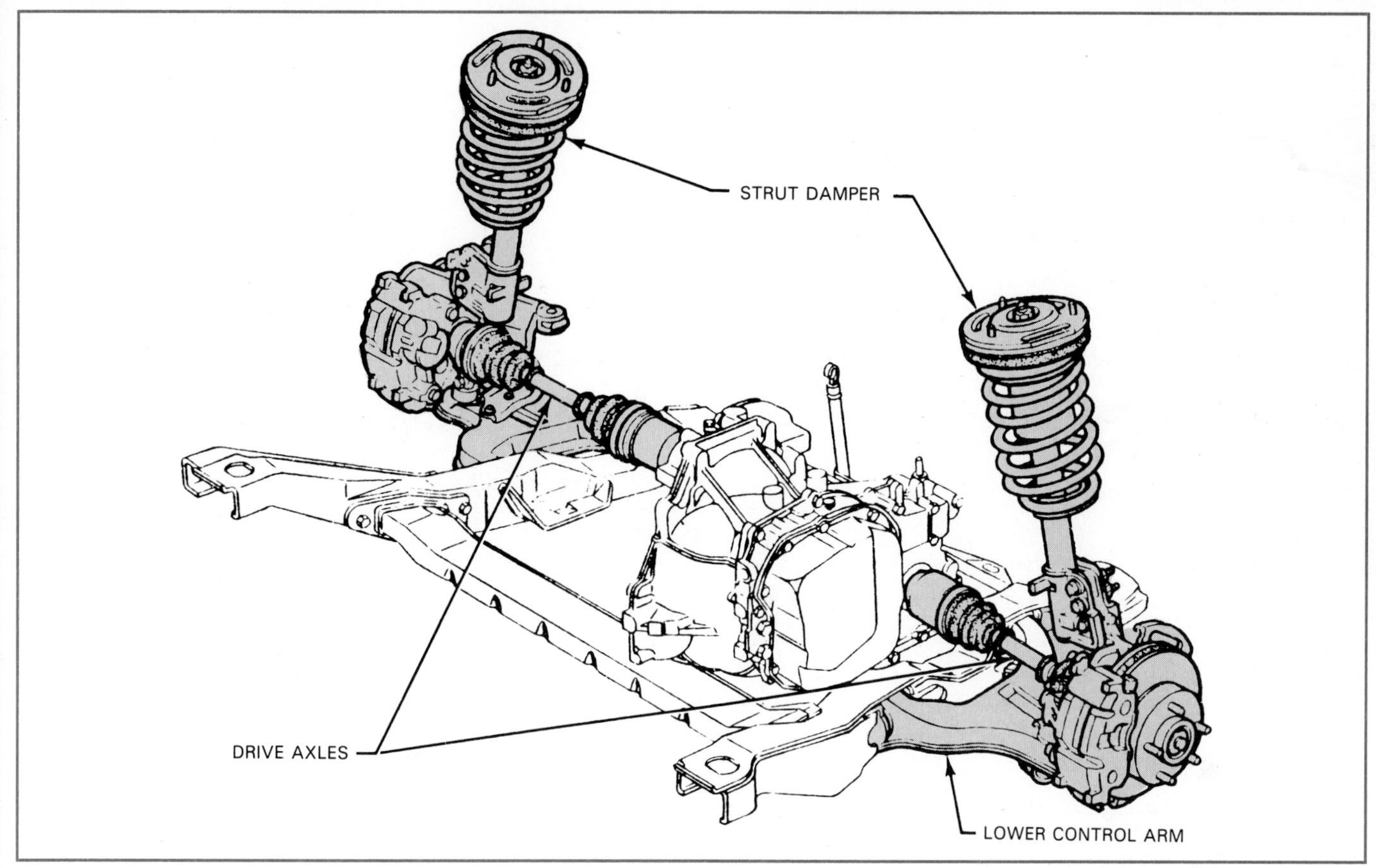

Figure 43-6. Coil springs are high-mounted on the strut in typical MacPherson strut fashion on this front-wheel drive application. Note the relative positioning of the transaxle and drive axles. (Pontiac)

spring, or the compressing-and-extending action of a coil spring, the torsion bar twists to exert resistance against up-and-down movement.

An independent front suspension system with torsion bars mounted lengthwise has one end of the bars anchored to the car frame and the other end attached to the lower control arms. With each rise and fall of a front wheel, the control arm pivots up and down, twisting the torsion bar along its length to absorb road shock and cushion the ride. See Figure 43-7.

Some independent front suspension systems on rear-wheel drive cars have transverse (crosswise) torsion bars. On Chrysler cars so equipped, two bars of modified L-shape are used. See Figure 43-8.

The straight end of each torsion bar is anchored in the front crossmember opposite the wheel its spring action affects. Each bar extends parallel to the transverse part of the crossmember and is supported by a pivot cushion bushing, Figure 43-8. Outboard of the bushing, each torsion bar bends backward to terminate in another bushing bolted to the lower control arm. This end of each bar serves as a lower control arm "strut."

Adjustment of the torsion bars controls the height of the front end of the vehicle. The adjusting bolts are located at the torsion bar anchors in the front crossmember. The right torsion bar is adjusted from the left side. The left torsion bar is adjusted from the right side. See Figure 43-8. The inner ends of the lower control arms are bolted to the crossmember and pivot through a bushing. When the control arm pivots up and down, the torsion bar twists and absorbs the road shock.

Shock Absorbers

In the past, a wide variety of direct and indirect shock absorbing devices has been used to control spring action of passenger cars. Today, direct, double-acting, "telescoping" hydraulic ***shock absorbers*** and ***shock absorber struts*** have almost universal application. See Figure 43-9.

The operating principle of direct-acting hydraulic shock absorbers consists of forcing fluid through restricting orifices in the valves. The restricted flow serves to slow down and control the rapid movement of the car springs as they react to road irregularities. Generally, fluid flow through the piston is controlled by spring-loaded valves.

The hydraulic shock absorber automatically adapts itself to the severity of the shock. If the axle moves slowly, resistance to the flow of fluid will be light. If the axle movement is rapid or forceful, the resistance is much stronger since more time is required to force fluid through the orifices.

By these hydraulic actions and reactions, the shock absorbers permit a soft ride over small bumps and provide firm control over spring action for cushioning large bumps. The double-acting units operate effectively in both directions. Spring rebound can be almost as violent as the original action that compressed the shock absorber.

At the front of a vehicle with short/long arm (S.L.A.) suspension, each shock absorber usually extends through the coil spring from the lower control arm to a bracket attached to the frame, Figure 43-9. On Chrysler cars with transverse torsion bar suspension, the front shock absorbers attach to the lower control arm and mount to a bracket on the frame crossmember.

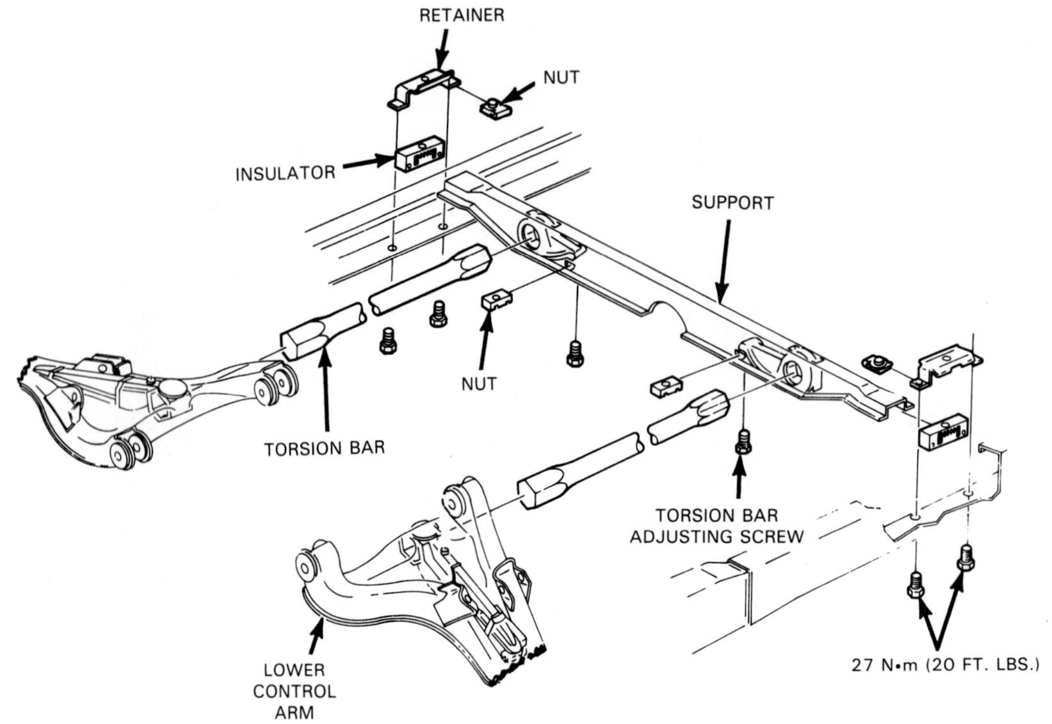

Figure 43-7. Exploded view of a Toronado front suspension shows torsion bars mounted between the lower control arms and the adjustable arms in the frame support member. (Oldsmobile)

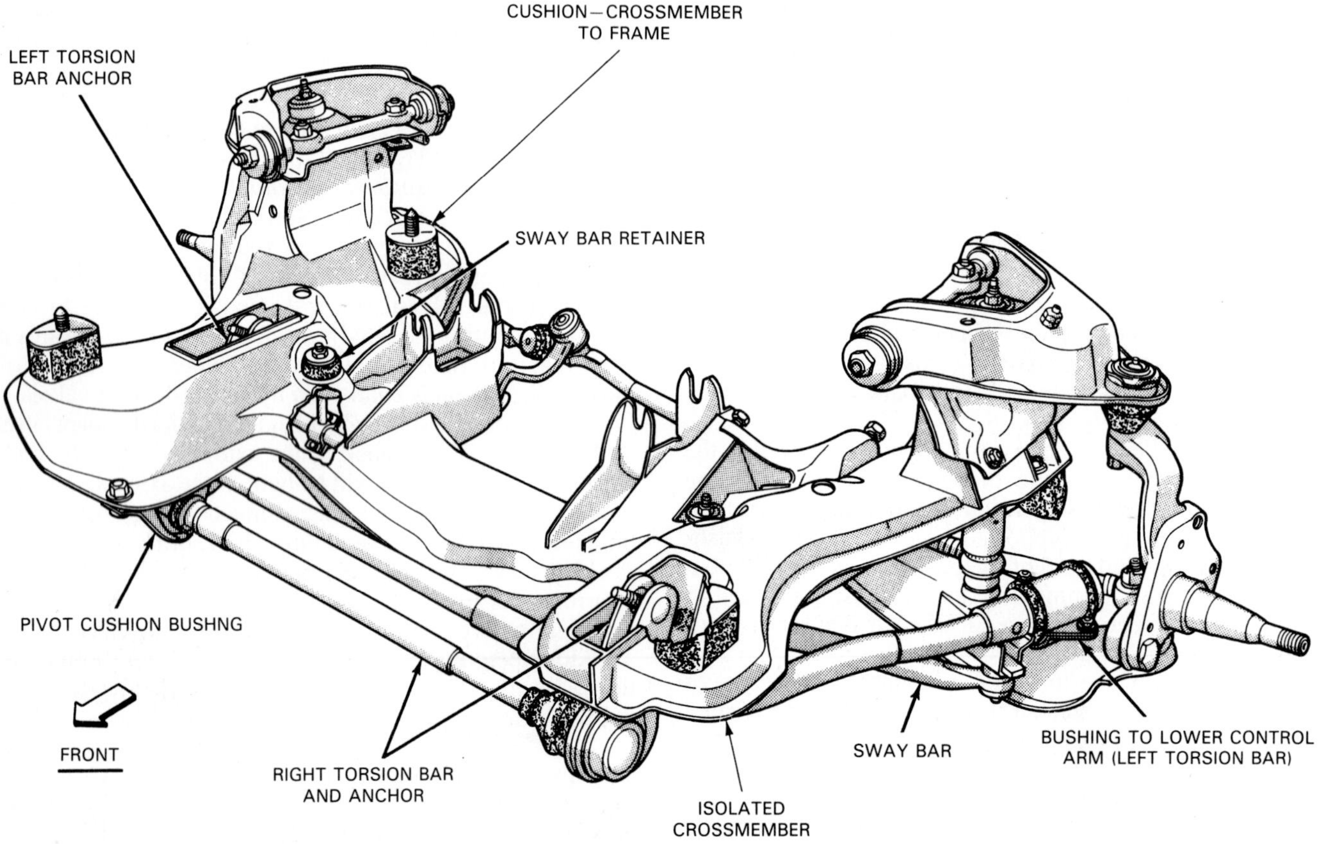

Figure 43-8. Some rear-wheel drive cars have transverse torsion bar front suspension. Each torsion bar provides a twisting reaction on the outboard end of the opposite lower control arm. (Chrysler)

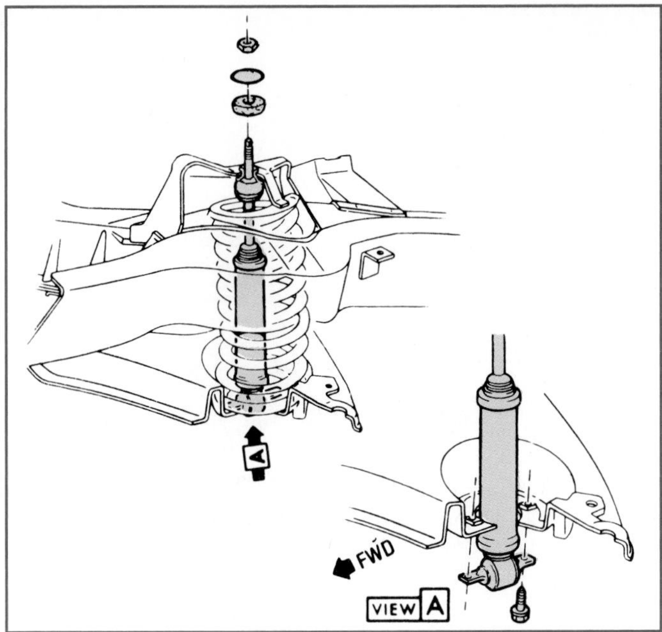

Figure 43-9. Hydraulic shock absorbers are commonly placed inside the front coil springs on cars with S.L.A. suspension systems. Typical upper and lower mountings are shown. (Chevrolet)

In the case of high-mounted coil springs, Figure 43-5, front shock absorbers extend from the upper control arm to a platform mounted in the spring tower or to a bracket on the wheel housing in the engine compartment.

At the rear, the lower end of the shock absorber usually is attached to a bracket welded to the axle housing. The upper end is fastened to the frame or coil spring upper seat, which is integral with the frame or body.

On cars with rear leaf springs, the rear shock absorbers generally extend from a stud attached to the spring U-bolt mounting bracket to the frame cross member. Quite often the rear shock absorbers are mounted at an angle to assist in restricting lateral movement as well as vertical movement.

Shock Absorber Struts

On typical ***MacPherson strut*** applications, the shock absorber is built into the strut. See Figure 43-10. Most of these shock absorber struts are hydraulic units.

Some MacPherson systems are equipped with low-pressure, gas-filled shock struts. They are nonadjustable and nonrefillable. Like the hydraulic shock struts, faulty units must be replaced as an assembly.

A similar front suspension system is termed "hydraulic shock strut" type. See Figure 43-11. Like the MacPherson type, this strut serves as a shock absorber and replaces the upper control arm. The coil spring, however, is located between the lower control arm and the body structure instead of being mounted directly on the strut.

Front Suspension Systems

There are three basic types of front suspension: independent systems; MacPherson strut systems; and solid-axle systems.

Independent Front Suspension

Independent front suspension systems, Figure 43-3, usually operate through coil springs or torsion bars, upper and lower control arms, and direct, double-acting shock absorbers. Most independent suspension systems also use

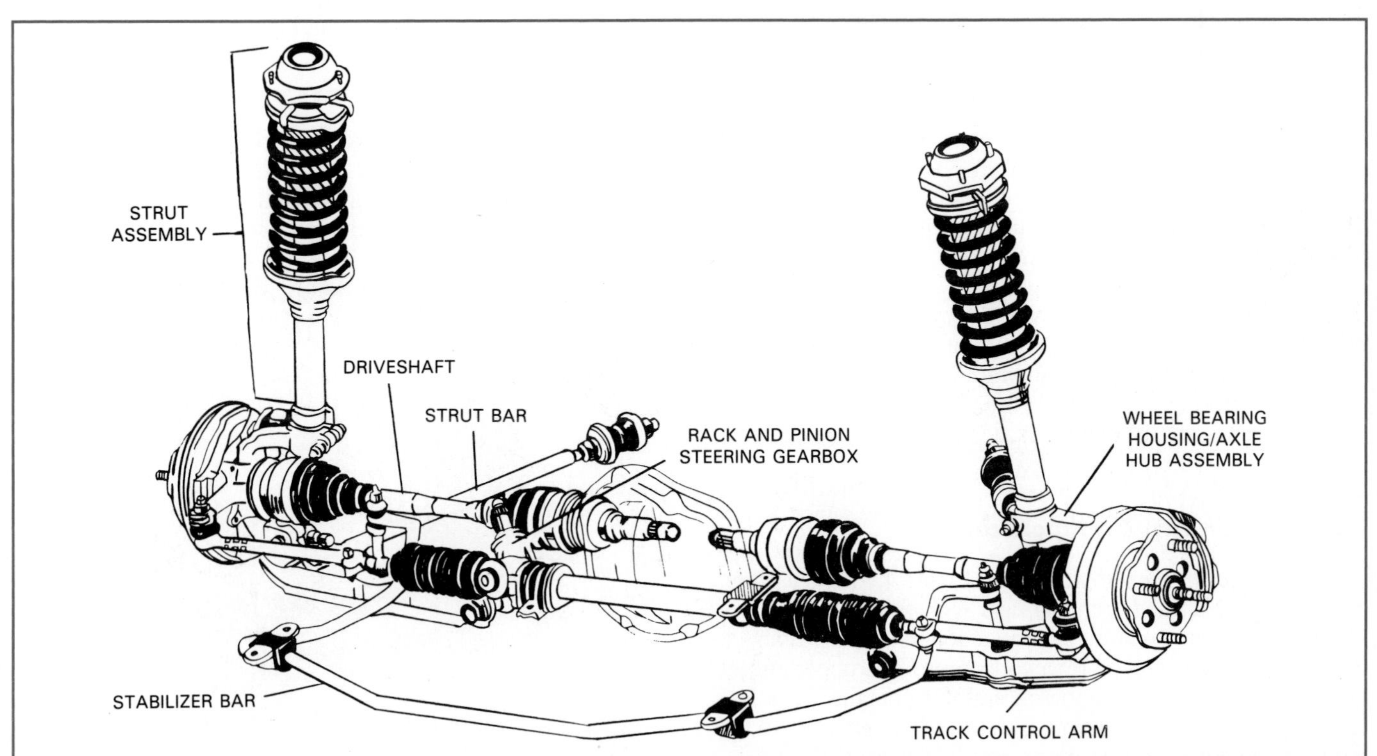

Figure 43-10. Front-wheel drive, rack-and-pinion steering, and MacPherson struts have been used on imported cars for many years. Also note the typical application of a stabilizer bar and strut bars. (Toyota)

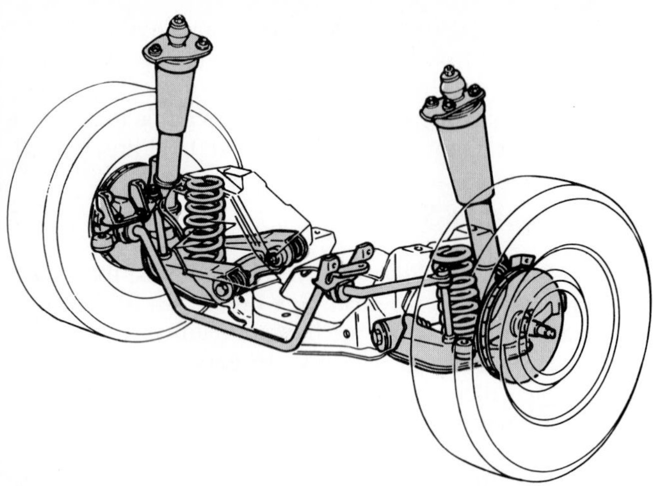

Figure 43-11. Ford's "shock strut" front suspension is a modified MacPherson strut suspension. The difference lies in the separate location of the coil springs and the shock strut setup. (Ford)

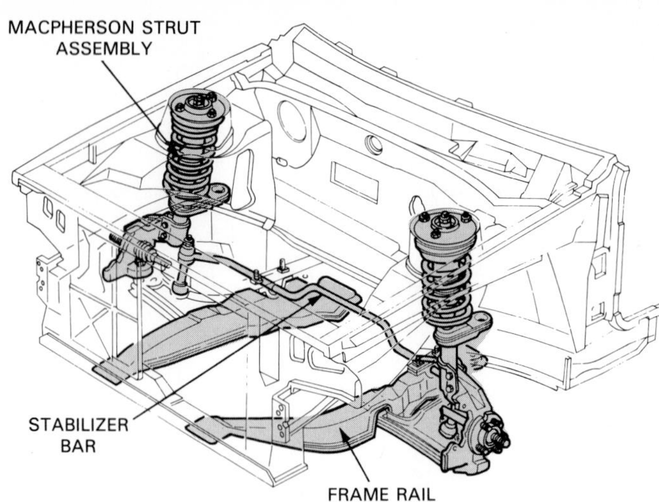

Figure 43-12. Typical General Motors MacPherson strut arrangement on compact cars is outlined against the phantom view of the vehicle's engine compartment. (Chevrolet)

diagonal struts and a ***stabilizer bar,*** especially those designed for heavy-duty applications.

Independent front suspension systems utilize ball joints, Figure 43-4, to provide pivot points for each front wheel. In operation, the swiveling action of the ball joints allows the wheel-and-spindle assemblies to be turned left or right and to move up and down with changes in the road surface.

Generally, the upper control arm pivots on a bushing and shaft assembly which is bolted to the frame. The lower arm pivots on a bushing and shaft assembly or on a bolt in the frame crossmember. When the lower control arm is not the A-frame type, it is supported by a strut which runs diagonally from the lower control arm to a bracket attached to the frame. See Figure 43-5. On some models, this strut serves as a support; on others, it provides a means of adjusting caster.

This general arrangement of control arms is called the S.L.A. (short/long arm) system of front suspension. The proportionate lengths of the upper and lower control arms (and their engineered placement) are designed to keep the rise and fall of each front wheel in a vertical plane. With this arrangement, changes in wheel angularity, weight balance, and tire-scuffing tendencies are negligible when compared with solid-axle suspension.

Stabilizers or sway bars are used in conjunction with front suspension on many cars to dampen road shocks and minimize road sway. These bars are bracketed to the frame front crossmember and extend from one lower control arm to the other.

Independent suspension is designed to provide anti-dive characteristics during braking.

MacPherson Strut Suspension

The ***MacPherson strut system,*** Figure 43-12, is used on most subcompact and compact cars with front-wheel drive. The MacPherson system features a long, telescopic shock absorber strut surrounded by a coil spring. The upper end of the strut is isolated by a rubber mount that contains an oilless ball bearing for wheel turning. The lower end attaches to the steering knuckle or lower control arm ball joint.

The lower control arm is attached to the underbody side apron or lower side rails and to the steering knuckle. A stabilizer bar usually is connected to both lower control arms and the front crossmember. See Figure 43-12. Some systems also include adjustable strut bars, Figure 43-10, connecting the control arms to the subframe.

Solid-axle Suspension

In ***solid-axle suspension systems,*** Figure 43-13, the axle beam and wheel assemblies are connected to the vehicle (usually a medium or heavy-duty truck) by leaf springs and direct or indirect-acting shock absorbers.

With the solid-axle setup, the steering knuckle and wheel spindle assemblies are connected to the axle beam by bronze-bushed king pins, or spindle bolts, which serve as pivot points for the steering knuckles.

Rear Suspension Systems

Rear suspension systems are engineered in many different designs. The primary design consideration is whether the vehicle is front-wheel drive or rear-wheel drive. Next, does the vehicle require a solid rear axle or independently suspended wheels? Should it have coil spring and control arm suspension, MacPherson struts, leaf springs, or transverse torsion bars?

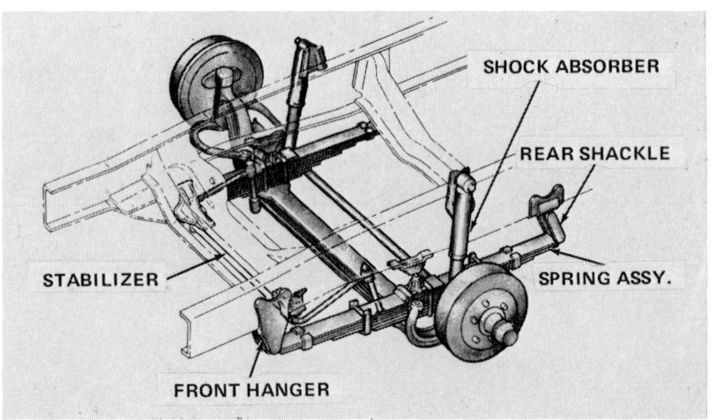

Figure 43-13. A solid front axle beam and leaf springs are used on most medium- and heavy-duty trucks.

Rear Suspension/Front-wheel Drive

Front-wheel drive vehicles generally are equipped with one of the following rear suspension arrangements:

- Coil springs and control arms or trailing arms with a solid axle and independently suspended wheels.
- MacPherson struts and independently suspended wheels.
- Transverse torsion bars and suspension arms.

Coil Spring/Control Arm Suspension. The front-wheel drive rear suspension arrangement shown in Figure 43-14 has coil springs mounted between the lower control arms and body crossmember/side rails. The shock strut is attached to the body panel by a rubber insulated top mount. The bottom end is bolted to the wheel spindle.

The lower control arms serve to stabilize the lateral (side-to-side) movement of the rear wheels. The tie rods control fore-and-aft wheel movement. The shock strut reacts to braking forces and provides necessary suspension damping.

MacPherson Strut Suspension. Some mid-size, front-wheel drive vehicles have ***MacPherson strut independent rear suspension,*** Figure 43-15. The struts are gas filled. Parallel, transverse lower control arms and longitudinal tie rods control the position of the wheel spindles at the bottom of the struts.

Figure 43-2 shows and describes this unusual rear suspension system.

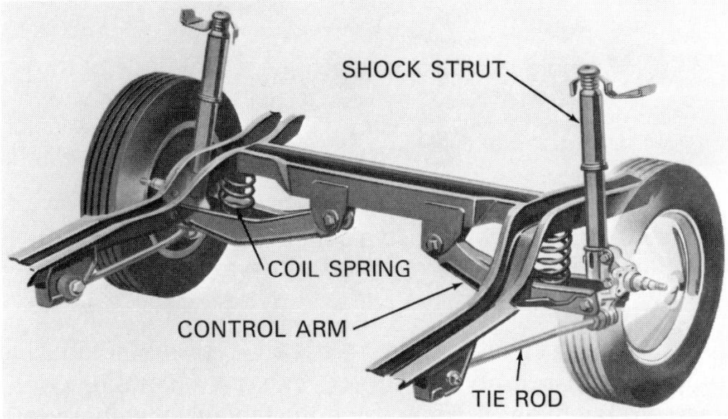

Figure 43-14. This independent rear suspension utilizes coil springs mounted on the lower control arms and attached to the underbody and to the forged spindles. The shock struts also bolt to the wheel spindles. (Ford)

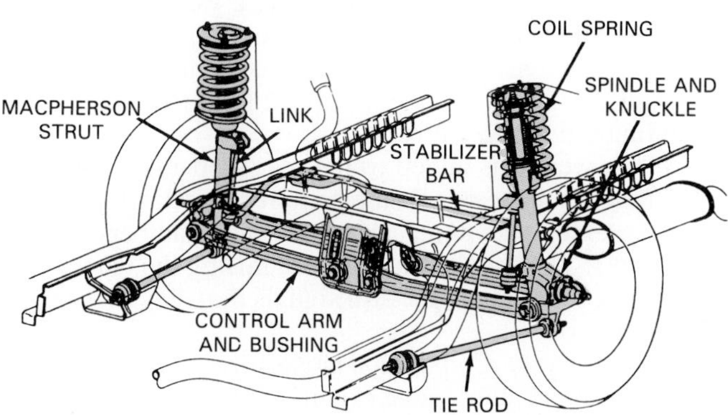

Figure 43-15. This MacPherson strut rear suspension used on certain front-wheel drive, mid-size models locates the struts by means of four parallel control arms and diagonal tie rods. (Ford)

Transverse Torsion Bar Suspension. ***Transverse torsion bars*** are used at the rear on some front-wheel drive subcompact cars. See Figure 43-16. The system shown utilizes trailing suspension arms attached to a crossmember at inner pivot points and to torsion bar ends at outer pivot points.

A stabilizer bar is mounted on the suspension arms in back of the torsion bars. The shock absorbers are attached to the body and suspension arms. The right and left non-interchangeable torsion bars are marked with symbols on each end to aid identification.

Rear Suspension/Rear-wheel Drive

Rear-wheel drive automobiles usually are produced with one of the following rear suspension setups:

- Coil spring and control arms with fixed rear axle housing.
- Longitudinal leaf springs with fixed rear axle housing.
- Transverse leaf spring with independently suspended rear wheels.

Coil Spring/Control Arm Suspension. Some rear-wheel drive cars have a rear suspension system that includes coil springs between upper seat brackets in the frame rails and integral seats in the lower suspension arms. See Figure 43-17.

The longitudinal lower suspension arms extend from brackets on the rear axle housing to brackets welded to the outboard side of the frame rails. The lower arms control front-to-rear movement. Diagonally mounted upper suspension arms control side-to-side movement.

The shock absorbers are mounted vertically from shock brackets welded to the axle housing and to shock towers on the floorpan.

Longitudinal Leaf Spring Suspension. Certain rear-wheel drive models are equipped with ***semi-elliptical leaf springs*** (one main leaf plus progressively shorter spring leaves) at the rear. The springs are attached to mounting brackets bolted to the body at the front and to spring shackles at the rear. See Figure 43-18.

Each spring center bolt seats in a hole in a bracket welded to the rear axle tube. U-bolts and a spring plate hold

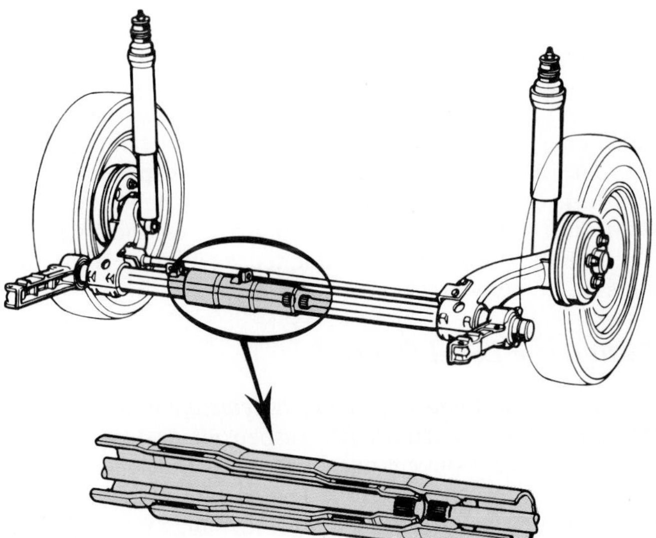

Figure 43-16. Certain vehicles use transverse torsion bar rear suspension. Note the detail of the splined bar inner ends. (Chrysler)

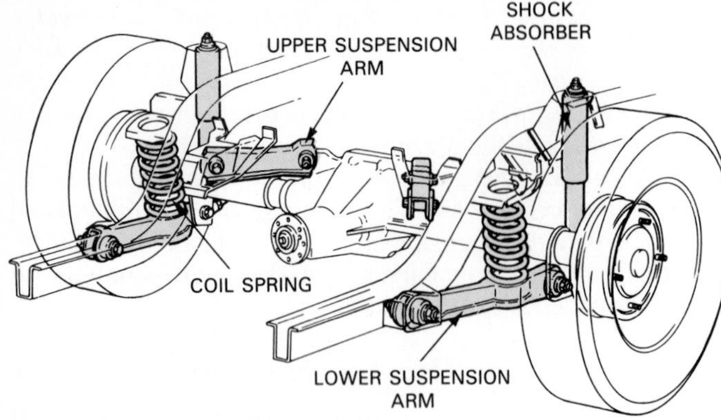

Figure 43-17. Some rear-wheel drive cars with coil spring rear suspension use four suspension arms to provide stability and coil spring support. Note the vertical mounting of the shock absorbers. (Ford)

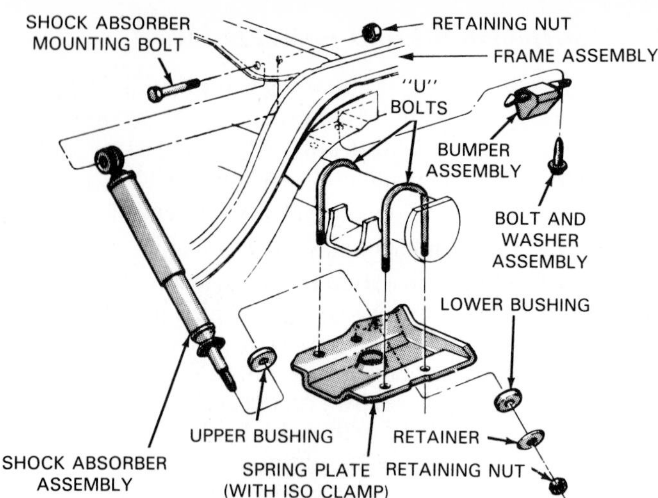

Figure 43-19. This exploded view reveals the position of the rear shock absorber and additional leaf spring hardware, including the U-bolts and the spring plate. (Chrysler)

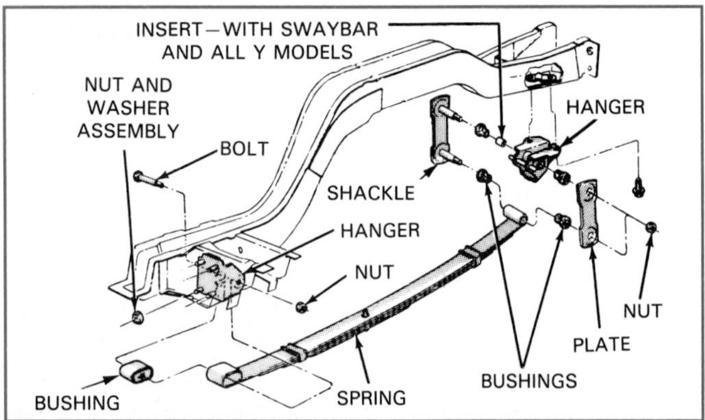

Figure 43-18. Some rear-wheel drive cars are equipped with rear leaf springs that suspend the vehicle body above the rear axle housing. Typical spring and mounting hardware and bushings are shown. (Chrysler)

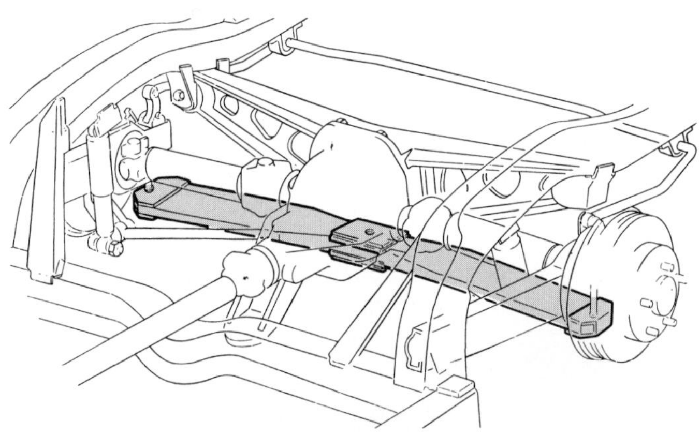

Figure 43-20. Corvettes use a composite, single-leaf rear spring that is transversely mounted. (Chevrolet)

the spring securely in place against the bracket. The shock absorbers are mounted between the spring plate and a frame crossmember. See Figure 43-19.

Transverse Leaf Spring Suspension. Chevrolet Corvettes are equipped with a ***transverse leaf spring rear suspension system.*** Earlier models use a multi-leaf steel spring; later models use a single-leaf, filament-wound, glass/epoxy spring. See Figure 43-20. The spring is mounted to a fixed differential carrier cover beam.

The rear wheels are independently suspended by a four-link or five-link setup composed of a wheel drive shaft, strut rod, upper and lower control arms, and a tie rod. The shock absorbers are mounted vertically from the knuckles to body brackets.

Automatic Level Control

Various ***automatic leveling systems*** are in use. Ford's microprocessor controlled Air Suspension system, for example, replaces conventional coil spring suspension with automatic front and rear load leveling by means of four rubber and plastic air springs. Most leveling systems, however, are designed to automatically extend or compress the rear shock absorbers or shock struts. This brings the rear of the car back to design level when the car is loaded with additional passengers and/or luggage.

GM's Electronic Level Control system includes a compressor assembly, air dryer, exhaust solenoid, compressor relay, height sensor, air adjustable shock absorbers or shock struts, Figure 43-21, wiring, air tubing, and pressure limiter valve.

The air adjustable shock strut is basically a conventional unit constructed with a sleeve attached to the dust tube and reservoir. This sleeve forms a flexible chamber that will extend the shock strut when air pressure in the chamber is increased. When the pressure is reduced, the weight of the car will cause the shock strut to compress to a "minimum pressure" level.

When weight is added to the rear suspension, an arm on the height sensor signals the compressor relay to turn on the compressor and pump air to the air chambers of the shock struts. The shock struts extend, raising the rear of the car. At the proper level, the arm signals the relay to turn off the compressor.

Some Chrysler Corporation models are equipped with an Electronic Automatic Load Leveling system, Figure 43-22. An electronic sensor linked to the rear suspension track bar detects changes in rear suspension height and directs the system to either add or exhaust air from rubber bladders on the rear shock absorbers. See inset in Figure 43-22. The

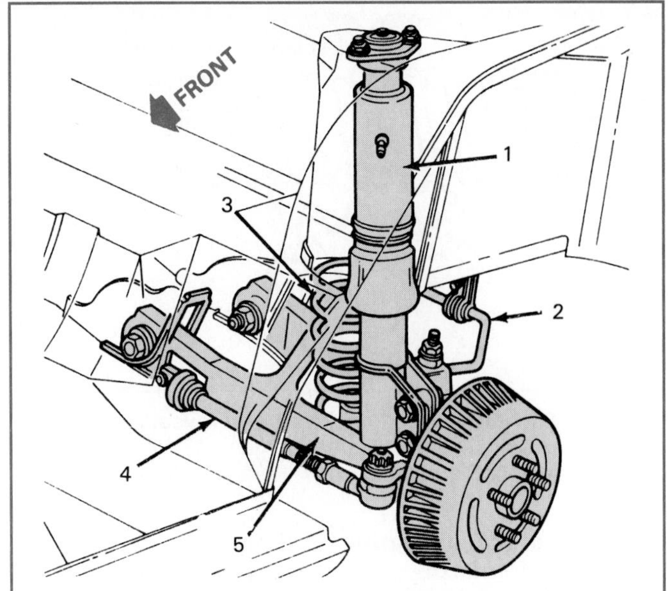

Figure 43-21. This electronic level control system features air adjustable shock struts. 1–Strut. 2–Stabilizer bar. 3–Coil spring. 4–Suspension adjustable link. 5–Lower control arm. (Buick)

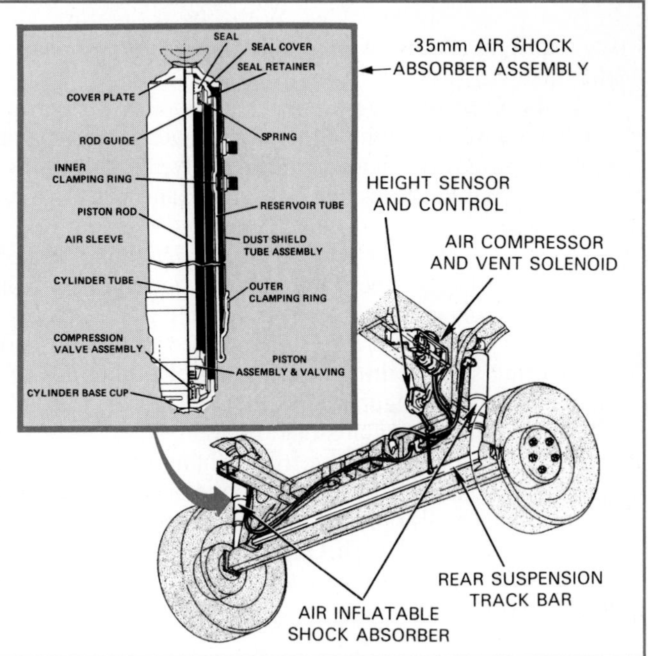

Figure 43-22. This electronic load leveling system uses air inflatable shock absorbers to automatically adjust the rear of the vehicle to a designated height. (Chrysler)

sensor also allows for normal ride motions to prevent unnecessary height adjustments.

Air for the shock absorbers is provided by a sealed air compressor driven by an electric motor. The combination compressor and motor is mounted behind the right rear wheel well. A flexible air hose connects the compressor with the special shock absorbers.

Automatic Ride Control

Certain vehicles are provided with an electronically operated ***automatic ride control system.*** It consists of a two-position mode selector switch, sensors (for speed, steering, brake application, and acceleration force input), shunt motor actuators (on top of each front shock strut and rear shock absorber), an electronic control module (ECM), and the wiring harness. See Figure 43-23.

The mode selector switch provides positions for "auto" or "firm" ride control. In the automatic mode, the system provides a "soft ride" until sensor input indicates the need for firm ride control. Then, the ECM simultaneously operates all four actuators to increase the shock struts' resistance to vehicle motion. A specific time lag for the return to "soft ride" is programmed into the ECM.

Steering Systems

There are two basic types of steering systems on passenger cars: manual and power. In the manual system, the driver's effort to turn the steering wheel is the primary force that causes the front wheels to swivel to the left or

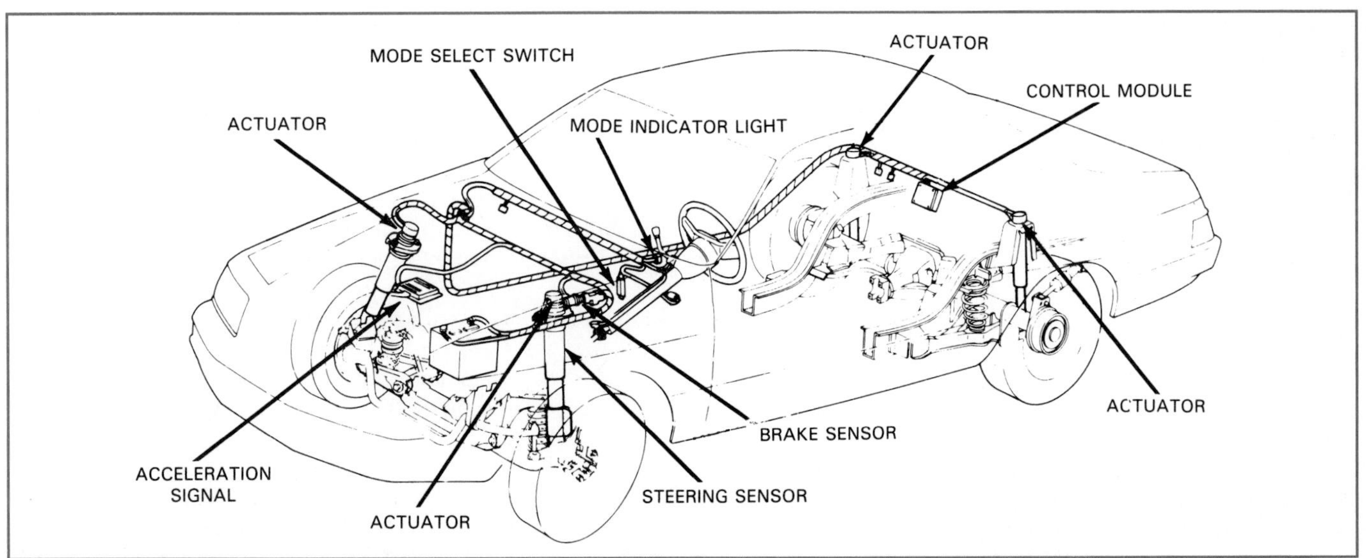

Figure 43-23. Phantom view highlights the major elements of Ford's automatic ride control system. A soft ride is provided until a firm ride is needed for good handling. (Ford)

right on the steering knuckles. With power steering, the driver's turning efforts are multiplied by a hydraulic or an electro-hydraulic assist.

The *manual steering system* incorporates a steering wheel; shaft and column; either a manual gearbox and pitman arm or a rack-and-pinion assembly, Figure 43-24; linkage; steering knuckles and ball joints; and wheel spindle assemblies.

The *power steering system* adds a hydraulic pump; fluid reservoir; hoses; lines; and either a power assist unit mounted on, or integral with, a power steering gear assembly.

Generally, steering wheels are splined to the top end of the steering shaft. Tilting steering wheel assemblies offer the advantage of angular adjustment to suit the individual driver and the particular situation.

For driver protection, all steering columns and shafts are designed and constructed to collapse and/or deform in the event of a frontal collision. Some collapsible steering columns are made of slotted steel mesh. Other columns, steering shafts, and shift shafts are two-piece, telescoping type, interconnected by plastic inserts or collars and shear pins.

Manual Steering Gears and Linkage

There are several different manual steering gears in current and recent use. The rack-and-pinion type is the current choice of most manufacturers. See Figure 43-24. The recirculating ball type is a past favorite because the balls act as a rolling thread between the wormshaft and the ball nut, Figure 43-25. Another manual steering gear once popular in imported cars is the worm and sector type. Other manual gears are the worm and tapered pin steering gear and the worm and roller steering gear.

Manual Rack-and-pinion Steering. A typical ***manual rack-and-pinion steering gear assembly*** consists of a pinion shaft and bearing assembly, rack gear, gear housing, two tie rod assemblies, an adjuster assembly, dust boots and boot clamps, and mounting grommets and bolts, Figure 43-26.

When the steering wheel is turned, this manual movement is relayed to the steering shaft and shaft joint, then to the pinion shaft. Since the pinion teeth mesh with the teeth on the rack gear, the rotary motion is changed to transverse movement of the rack gear. Then, the tie rods and tie rod ends transmit this movement to the steering knuckles and wheels.

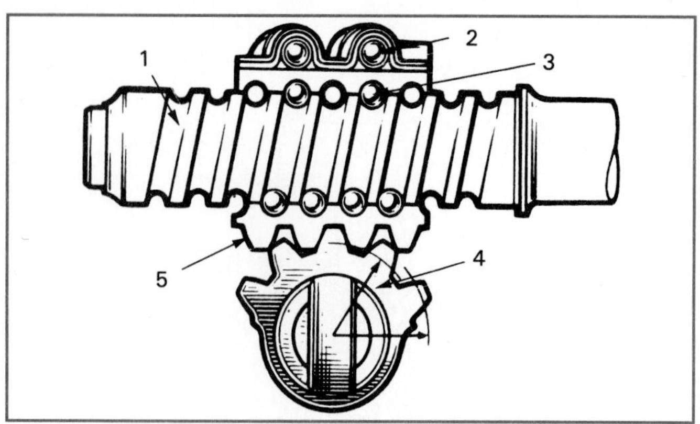

Figure 43-25. Cross section of a ball nut reveals the details of a manual recirculating ball steering gear. 1–Worm gear. 2–Return guides. 3–Ball bearing. 4–Sector gear. 5–Ball nut.

Manual Recirculating Ball Steering. A typical ***manual recirculating ball steering gear assembly*** is shown in Figure 43-27. With this steering gear, turning forces are transmitted through ball bearings from a worm gear on the steering shaft to a sector gear on the pitman arm shaft. A ball nut assembly is filled with ball bearings which "roll" along grooves between the worm teeth and grooves inside the ball nut.

When the steering wheel is turned, the worm gear on the end of the steering shaft rotates, and movement of the recirculating balls causes the ball nut to move up and down along the worm. Movement of the ball nut is carried to the sector gear by teeth on the side of the ball nut. The sector gear, in turn, moves with the ball nut to rotate the pitman arm shaft and activate the steering linkage. The balls recirculate from one end of the ball nut to the other through ball return guides, Figure 43-28.

Manual Worm and Sector Steering. The ***manual worm and sector steering gear assembly*** employs a steering shaft with a three-turn worm gear supported by, and straddled by, ball bearing assemblies. The worm meshes with a 14-tooth sector attached to the top end of the pitman arm shaft. See Figure 43-29.

In operation, a turn of the steering wheel causes the worm gear to rotate the sector–and the pitman arm shaft. This movement is transmitted to the pitman arm and throughout the steering train to the wheel spindles.

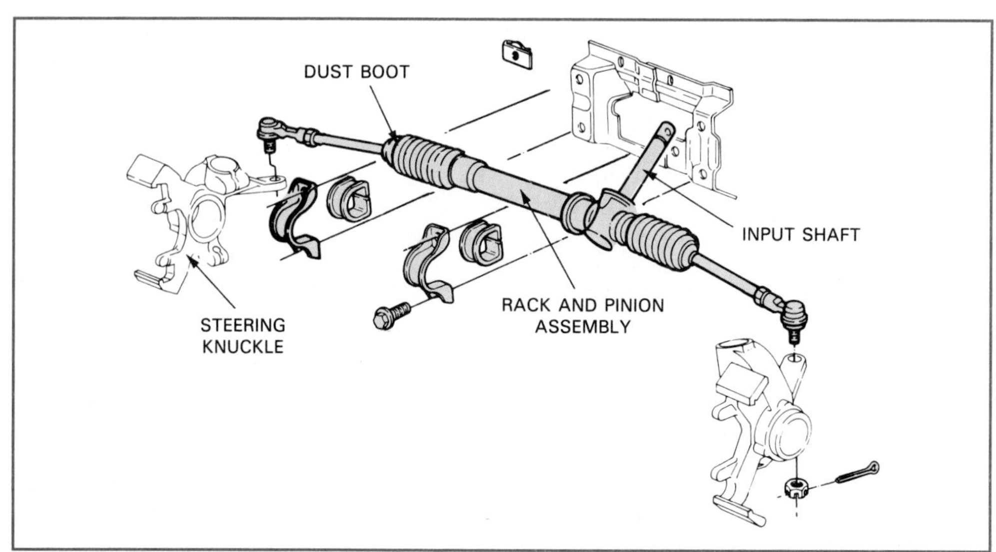

Figure 43-24. This simplified drawing shows a typical manual rack-and-pinion steering gear assembly, mounting insulators and brackets, and tie rod assemblies. (Ford)

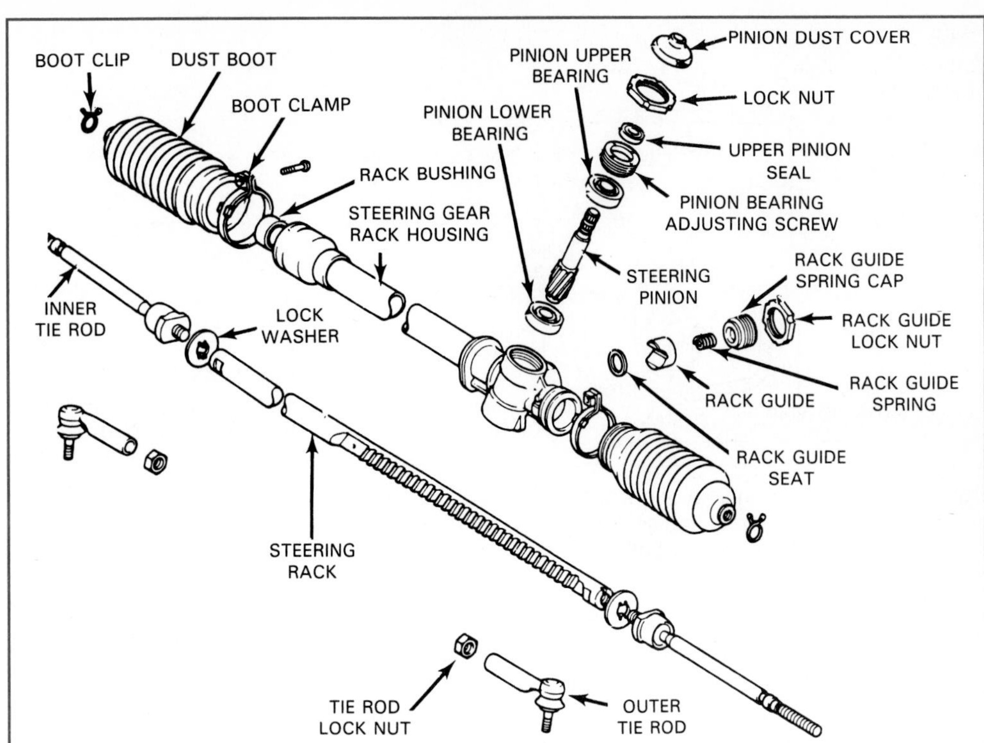

Figure 43-26. Exploded view gives the disassembly/assembly sequence for the components of a typical rack-and-pinion steering gear assembly. Study the relationship of the parts. (Chevrolet)

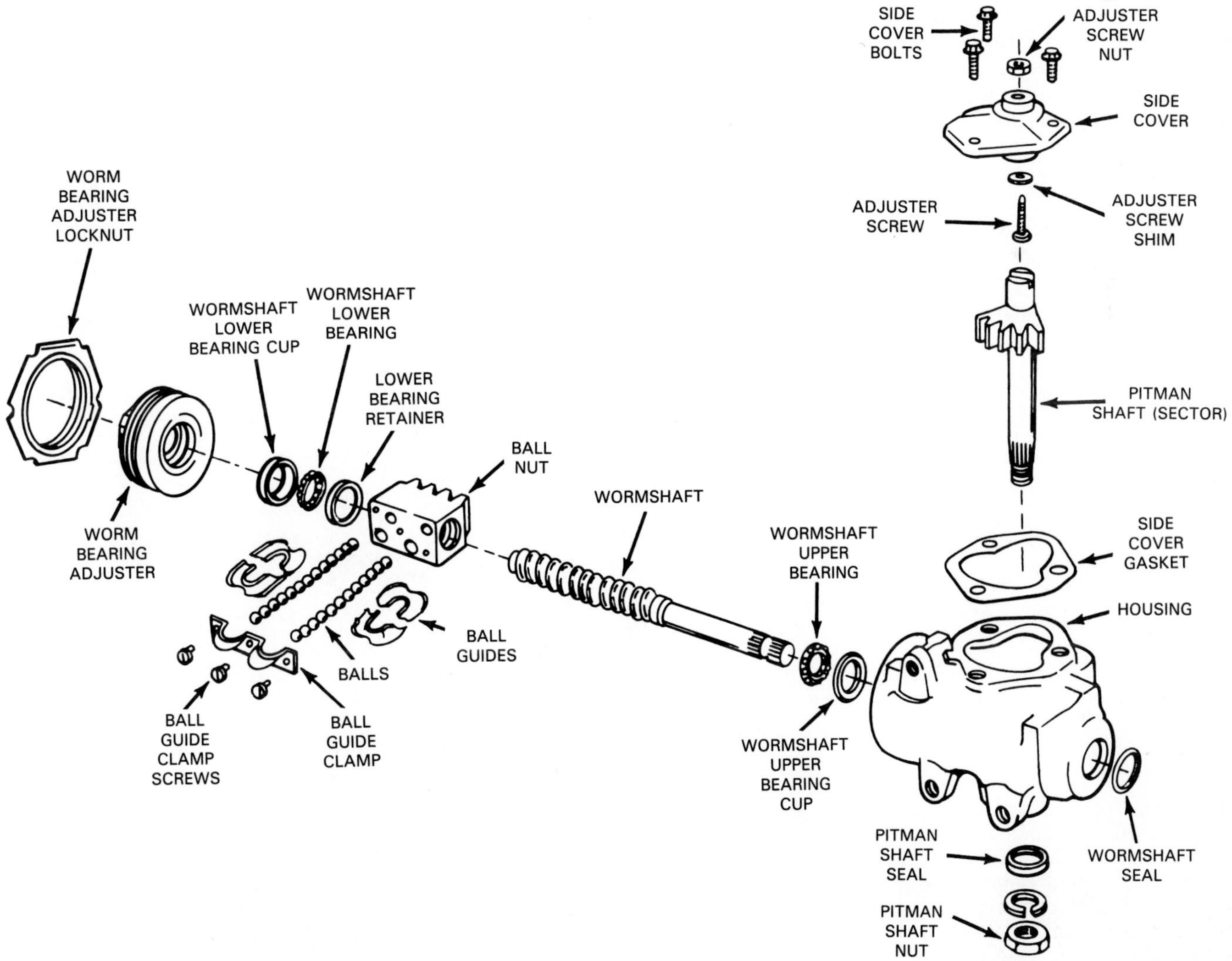

Figure 43-27. This exploded view shows the relative positions of parts that make up a recirculating ball manual steering gear, which is used mainly on rear-wheel drive cars. (Chrysler)

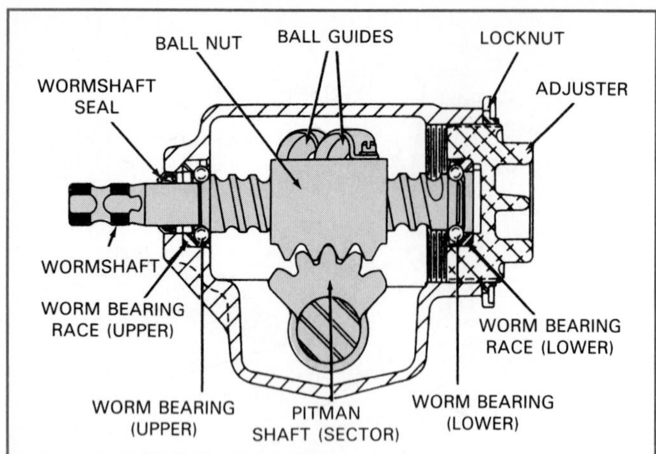

Figure 43-28. The principle of a worm and recirculating ball steering gear is revealed in this sectional view. Note the ball return guides, which permit the ball bearings to recirculate.

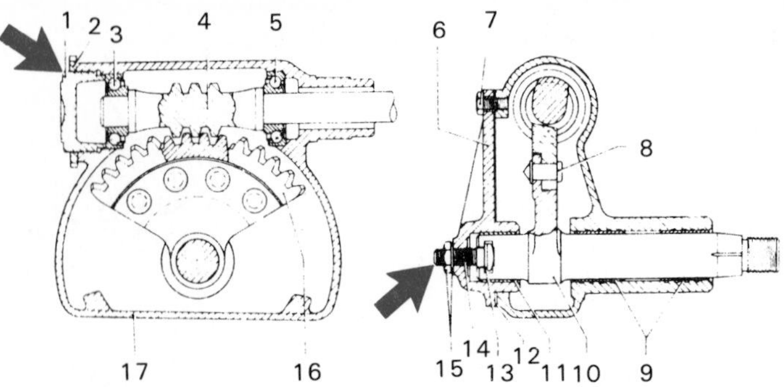

Figure 43-29. Cross sections of a manual worm and sector steering gear picture the assembled parts and points of adjustment (see arrows): 1–Worm bearings adjuster. 14-Gear mesh adjuster screw.

Worm and Tapered Peg Steering. The ***manual worm and tapered peg steering gear*** has a three-turn worm gear at the lower end of the steering shaft supported by ball bearing assemblies. The pitman shaft has a lever end with a tapered peg that rides in the worm grooves.

When the movement of the steering wheel revolves the worm gear, it causes the tapered peg to follow the worm gear grooves. Movement of the peg moves the lever on the pitman shaft and, in turn, the pitman arm, steering linkage, etc.

Worm and Roller Steering. The ***manual worm and roller steering gear*** is used by various Japanese manufacturers. This steering gear also has a three-turn worm gear at the lower end of the steering shaft. Instead of a sector or tapered peg on the pitman arm shaft, this gearbox has a roller assembly (usually two roller teeth) that engages the worm gear.

The roller assembly is mounted on anti-friction bearings. When the roller teeth follow the worm, the rotary motion is transmitted to the pitman arm shaft, pitman arm, etc.

Manual Steering Gearbox and Linkage

Except for the rack-and-pinion steering gear, a ***steering gearbox*** is used to house the manual steering gear assembly. The gearbox is securely attached to the frame side rail, and it is filled with a water-resistant, extreme pressure lubricant. The ***pitman arm shaft*** projects downward from the gearbox. It is splined to the ***pitman arm,*** which converts rotary motion of the shaft to lateral movement of the arm. See Figure 43-30.

The pitman arm, generally, is connected to a ***relay rod*** which reaches across to an ***idler arm*** attached to the frame side rail on the opposite side. The relay rod, in turn, is connected to two adjustable ***tie rods*** that transmit lateral movement of the relay rod to the ***steering arms,*** Figure 43-30.

The various rods and arms roughly form a parallelogram during a turn, so the arrangement is called ***parallelogram linkage.*** In some cars, the linkage is in front of the front wheel spindles. In others, the linkage is to the rear of the spindles.

Manual steering is considered to be entirely adequate for subcompact cars and for cars with the engine

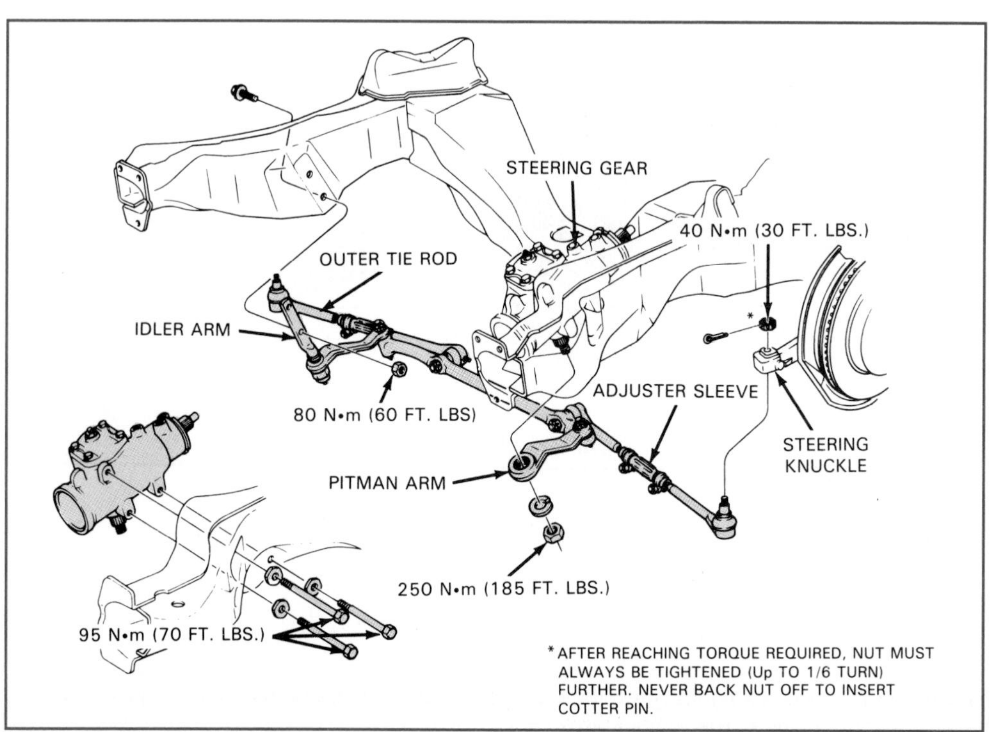

Figure 43-30. Components of a typical manual gearbox and steering linkage arrangement are identified. Particular emphasis is placed on torque values of fasteners. Also note gearbox mounting detail in inset at left. (Buick)

in the rear. It is light, fast, and accurate in maintaining steering control.

Power Steering Systems

Over the years, ***power steering*** has become a standard equipment item on many larger domestic models. With that, and the optional demand for this system, power steering is installed on over 90 percent of all domestic new car production.

Most late model passenger cars with power steering use either a power rack-and-pinion system, Figure 43-31, or an integral power steering gear assembly, Figure 43-32. Generally, the rack-and-pinion system is installed on front-wheel drive cars. The integral power steering gear is used on many rear-wheel drive cars.

All systems require a power steering pump attached to the engine and driven by a belt, a pressure hose assembly, and a return line. Also, a control valve is incorporated somewhere in the hydraulic circuit.

Automobile power steering is actually ***power-assisted steering.*** All systems are constructed so that the car can be steered manually when the engine is not running or if any failure occurs at the power source.

Power Rack-and-pinion Steering. A typical ***power rack-and-pinion steering assembly*** used on many cars is shown in Figure 43-31 and Figure 43-33. This rack-and-pinion assembly is a hydraulic-mechanical unit with an integral piston and rack assembly. An internal rotary valve directs power steering fluid flow and controls pressure to reduce steering effort. See Figure 43-33 for details of construction.

When the steering wheel is turned off, resistance created by the weight of the car and tires-to-road friction causes a torsion bar in the rotary valve to deflect. This changes the position of the valve spool and sleeve, thereby directing fluid under pressure to the proper end of the power cylinder. See Figure 43-34.

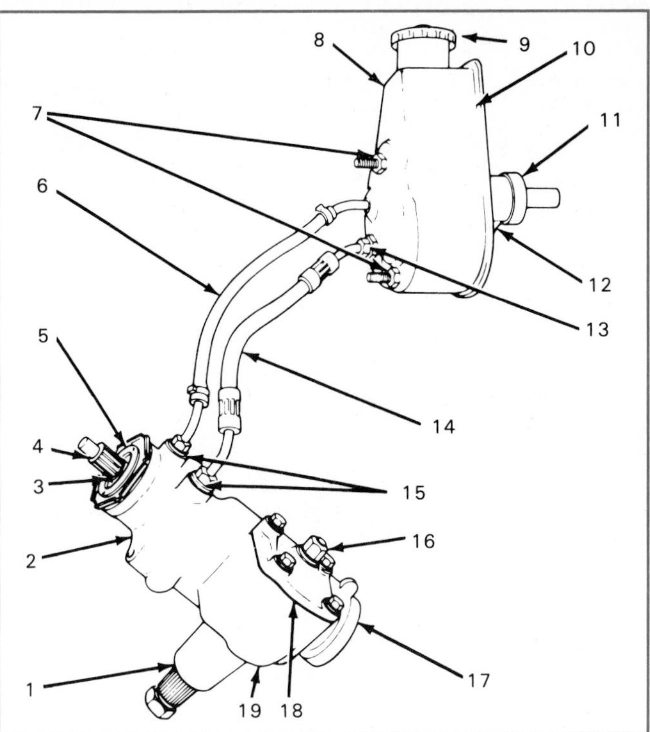

Figure 43-32. Parts of an integral power steering gear assembly and hydraulic system include: 1–Pitman shaft. 2–Gear housing ball plug. 3–Stub shaft. 4–Torsion bar. 5–Adjuster plug. 6–Return hose. 7–Stud bolts. 8–Reservoir. 9–Cap. 10–Reservoir O-ring. 11–Pump shaft seal. 12–Pump housing. 13–Pressure port. 14–Pressure hose. 15–Pressure and return ports. 16–Adjusting screw lock nut. 17–End cover. 18–Side cover. 19–Gear housing. (Chrysler)

The difference in pressure on either side of the piston (attached to rack) helps move the rack to reduce turning effort. The fluid in the opposite end of the power

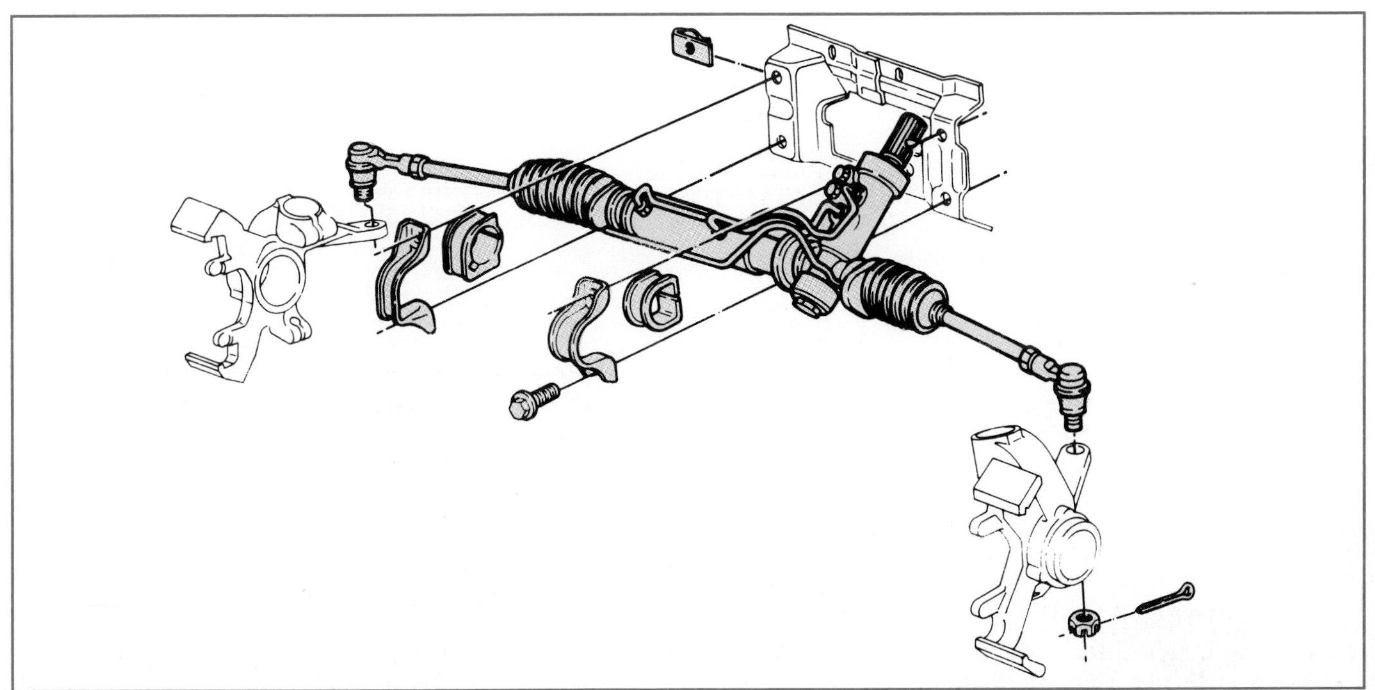

Figure 43-31. This simplified drawing of a typical power rack-and-pinion steering gear assembly is similar to the drawing of the manual assembly in Figure 43-24. (Ford)

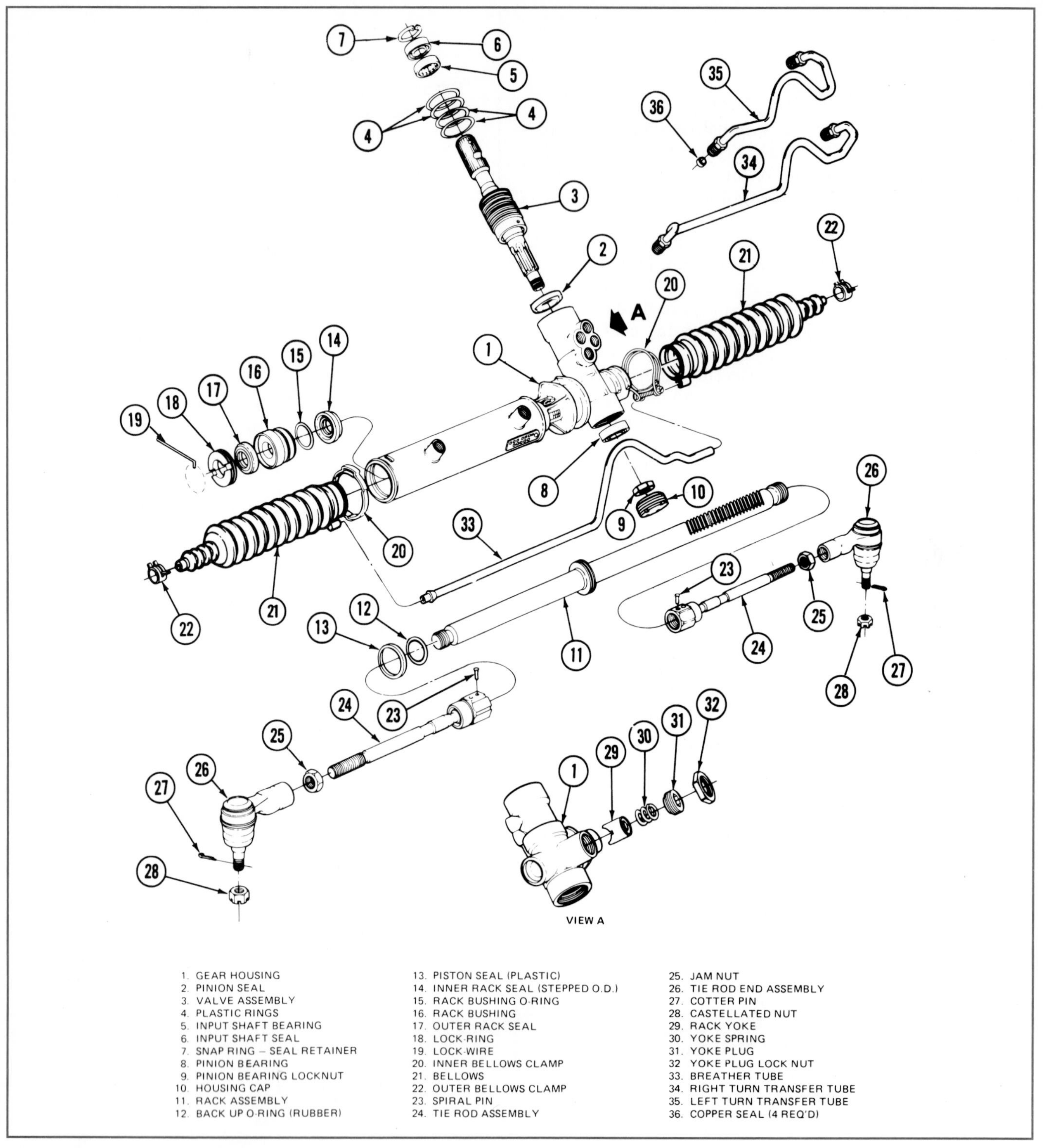

Figure 43-33. Exploded view gives the sequence of disassembly/assembly of a power rack-and-pinion steering gear. View A shows the detail of the rack yoke assembly. (Ford)

cylinder is forced to the control valve and back to the pump reservoir.

When the steering effort stops, the control valve is centered by the twisting force of the torsion bar, pressure is equalized on both sides of the piston, and the front wheels return to the straight ahead position.

Integral Power Steering Gears. A typical ***integral power steering gear*** is shown in an exploded view in Figure 43-35. This power steering gear utilizes a recirculating ball system wherein steel balls act as rolling threads between the steering worm shaft and the rack piston.

The key to the operation of the integral power steering gear is a rotary valve that directs power steering fluid under pressure to either side of the rack piston. The rack piston then converts hydraulic power to mechanical force.

The rack piston moves up inside the gear when the worm shaft turns right. It moves down when the worm shaft turns left. During these actions, the steel balls recirculate

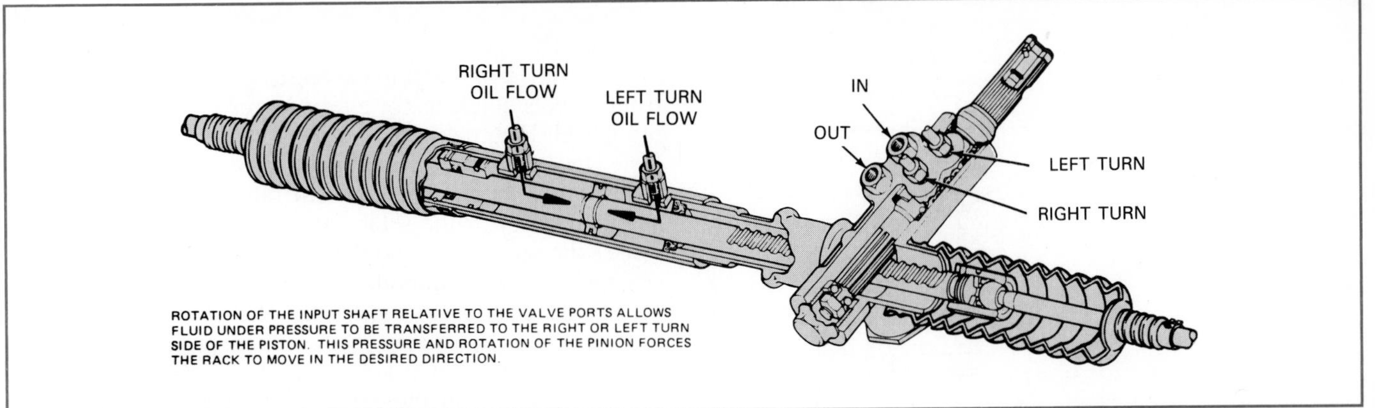

Figure 43-34. Cutaway view and explanation clarify the hydro-mechanical operation of the power rack-and-pinion steering gear assembly. Note the piston cutaway between the large arrowheads. (Ford)

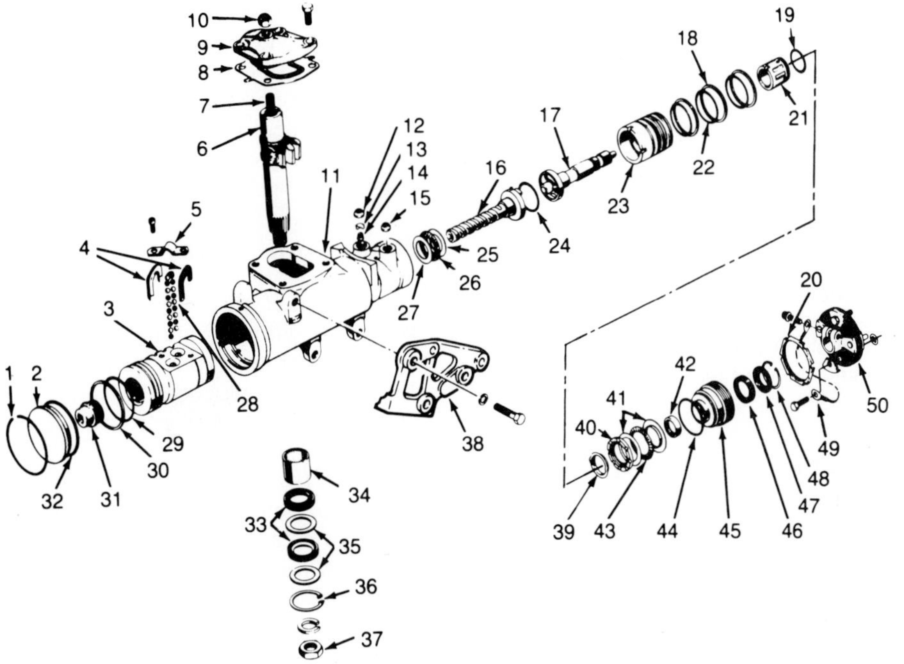

1. Retaining Ring
2. Housing End Plug
3. Rack-Piston
4. Ball Return Guide Halves
5. Clamp
6. Pitman Shaft
7. Adjusting Screw
8. Gasket
9. Side Cover
10. Lock Nut
11. Housing
12. Pressure Port Seat
13. Poppet Valve
14. Spring
15. Return Port Seat
16. Worm
17. Stub Shaft
18. Teflon Rings (3)
19. Damper O-Ring
20. Adjuster Plug Lock Nut
21. Valve Spool
22. Backup O-Rings (3)
23. Valve Body
24. O-Ring
25. Race
26. Thrust Bearing
27. Race
28. Ball Bearings (24)
29. Backup O-Ring
30. Piston Ring
31. Rack-Piston End Plug
32. O-Ring
33. Oil Seals
34. Needle Bearing
35. Washers
36. Retaining Ring
37. Pitman Arm Nut
38. Spacer
39. Bearing Retainer
40. Spacer
41. Races
42. Bearing
43. Thrust Bearing
44. O-Ring
45. Adjuster Plug
46. Oil Seal
47. Washer and Dust Seal
48. Retaining Ring
49. Ground Wire
50. Flexible Coupling

Figure 43-35. Parts of a typical recirculating ball and rack piston type integral power steering gear. (Chrysler)

within the rack piston, which is power assisted in movement by hydraulic pressure.

Force created by the movement of the rack piston is transmitted from the rack piston teeth to the sector teeth on the pitman shaft, through the shaft and pitman arm to the steering linkage.

In some cases, the power steering gear assembly used on rear-wheel drive cars is contained in a gear housing at the bottom of the steering column. The gear assembly includes a sector shaft with sector gear, Figure 43-36; a toothed power piston that is in constant mesh with the sector shaft teeth; and a worm shaft connecting the steering wheel to the power piston.

The worm shaft is geared to the power piston through recirculating balls. A steering valve body is mounted on top of the steering gear, Figure 43-37. This valve directs the flow of power steering fluid in the system.

In operation, movement of the steering wheel rotates the worm shaft, which actuates the power piston. Fluid supplied by the power steering pump is fed under pressure to the steering valve. The steering valve, in turn, directs

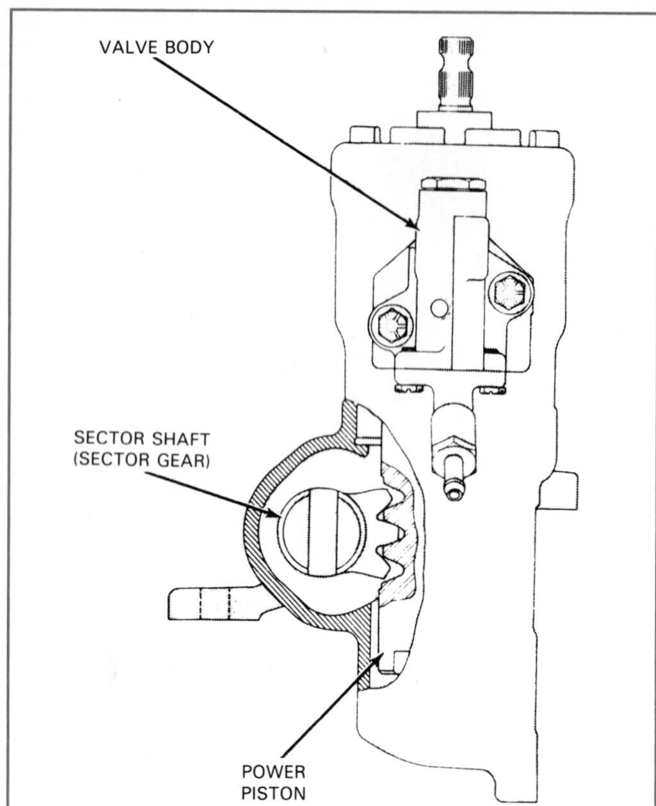

Figure 43-36. Cutaway view pictures the constant mesh of the toothed power piston and sector gear of one particular power steering gear assembly. A control valve in the valve body directs the flow of fluid to either side of the power piston. (Chrysler)

fluid flow to either side of the power piston to provide a hydraulic power assist on turns.

Variable-ratio Steering. A major step forward in steering gear design was accomplished with the introduction of variable-ratio steering. In conventional (constant ratio) steering, the degree of turn of the front wheels is always in direct proportion to the degree of turn of the steering wheel. In ***variable-ratio steering,*** the ratio remains constant for approximately the first 40° of steering wheel movement. Then the ratio decreases and the response of the front wheels quickens for every degree of turn of the steering wheel, Figure 43-38.

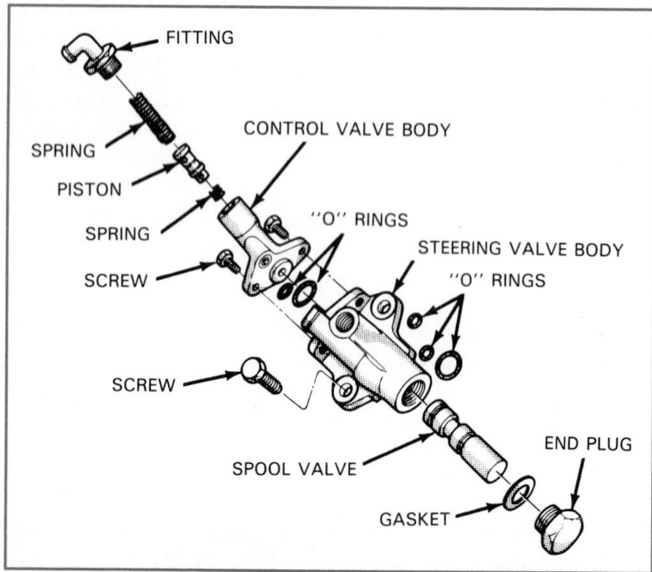

Figure 43-37. Parts of a power steering gear control valve are identified in this exploded view. (Chrysler)

The "variable" effect is made possible by the design of the steering gear. With constant ratio gears of the sector type, the teeth of the sector are all the same length. This causes the sector to swing the pitman arm the same number of degrees with each tooth of the sector.

With variable-ratio gears, the center tooth of the sector is longer than the other teeth, which produces a slower response of the pitman arm in shallow turn situations and faster response near the extremes of steering wheel travel for sharp turns. In some applications, Figure 43-25, a specially contoured worm gear alters the ratio.

Typically, a variable-ratio steering gear will provide a ratio of about 16:1 for straight ahead driving, and about 13:1 ratio in full turns. In relation to steering wheel movement with variable-ratio steering, the first quarter turn in either direction will produce a relatively "slow" response from the front wheels. Then the response "speeds up" as the steering wheel is turned from one half to a full turn. After that, the lowest ratio comes into effect when it is needed for parking or backing up.

Pumps and Hoses

Several types of power steering pumps are in use. The ***vane-type pump,*** Figure 43-39, incorporates a rotor with six to 10 vanes which rotate in an elliptical pump ring. Fluid trapped between the vanes is forced out under pressure as the vanes move from the long diameter of the pump ring to the short diameter.

A ***roller-type pump*** operates much like the vane type. Instead of vanes, six rollers on a toothed carrier unit rotate inside of a cam insert to build up fluid pressure.

A ***slipper-type pump*** produces hydraulic pressure by means of four to 10 spring-loaded slippers in a toothed rotor rotating inside of a cam insert within the pump body. See Figure 43-40.

Most modern power steering pumps contain a flow control valve, Figure 43-39, which limits fluid flow to the power cylinder to about two gallons per minute, and a relief valve which limits pressure according to system demands.

The power steering hoses serve as a means of transmitting the fluid under pressure from the pump to the

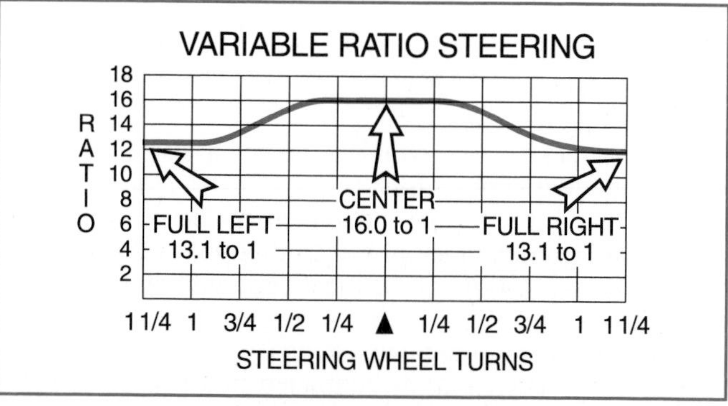

Figure 43-38. The advantage of variable-ratio steering is that the front wheels respond more quickly to steering wheel movement as the degree of the turn increases.

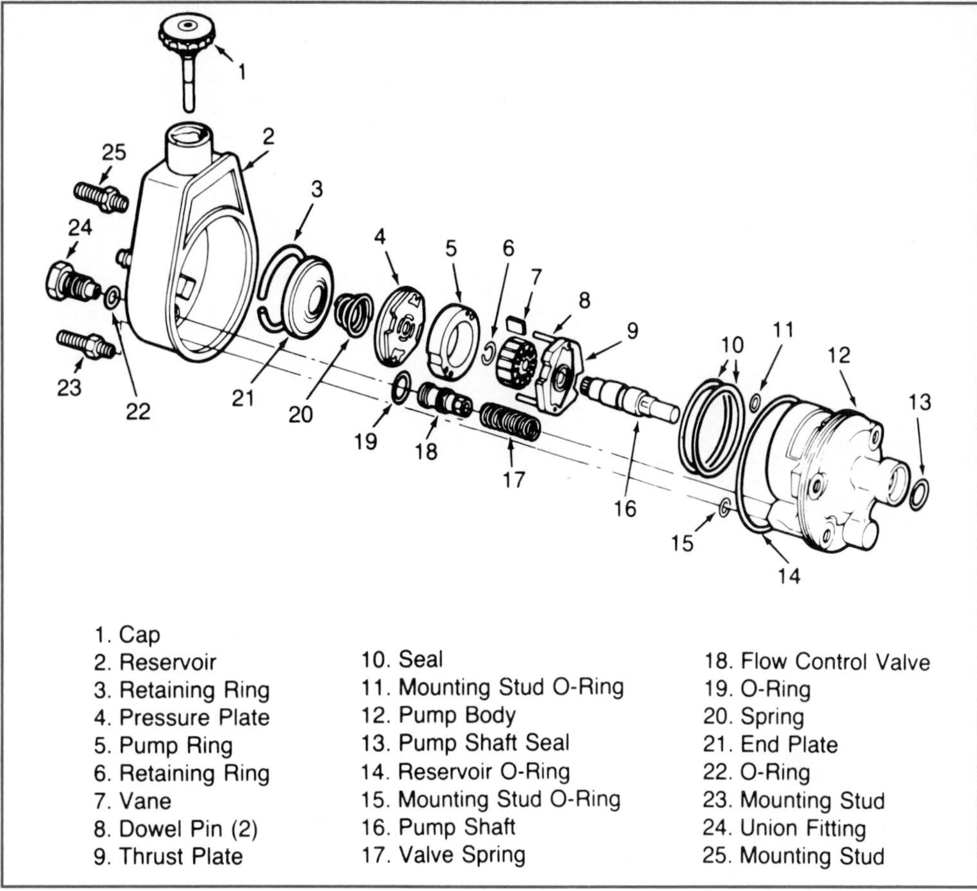

Figure 43-39. Typical vane-type power steering pump parts are pictured. (Chrysler)

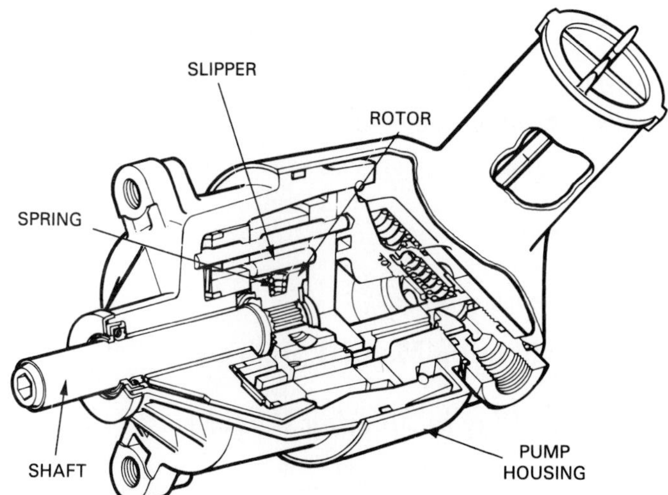

Figure 43-40. The key operating parts of Ford's slipper-type power steering pump are noted. Pumping motion of the slippers in the rotor grooves creates hydraulic pressure. (Ford)

power cylinder and return. See Figure 43-41. In addition, the hoses must provide the proper amount of expansion to absorb any shock surge and offer enough restriction to the fluid flow to keep the pump cavity full of fluid at all times.

Suspension and Steering Service

Basically, suspension and steering services begin with the use of recommended types of fluids and lubricants during inspections and when performing periodic maintenance services.

Always check simpler possible causes of trouble first, such as power steering fluid level, hose routing, pump drive belt condition and tension, tire condition and inflation pressures, etc. Use special equipment and tools designed for removal and installation of coil springs, struts, bearings, and seals.

When bearings and seals are removed, they should be discarded and replaced with new complete assemblies. When prevailing torque fasteners are loosened, tightened, or removed, they should be discarded and replaced with new fasteners.

Follow the vehicle manufacturers' directions and specifications for all suspension and steering adjustments. Always consult their torque tightness specifications for suspension system and steering system fasteners.

Troubleshooting Suspension

Front Wheel Shimmy

- Worn upper ball joints.
- Worn strut bushings.
- Worn shock absorbers.

Front End Noise

- Worn shock absorbers.
- Loose or worn shock absorber mountings.
- Worn shock struts or strut mountings.
- Loose or worn lower control arm.

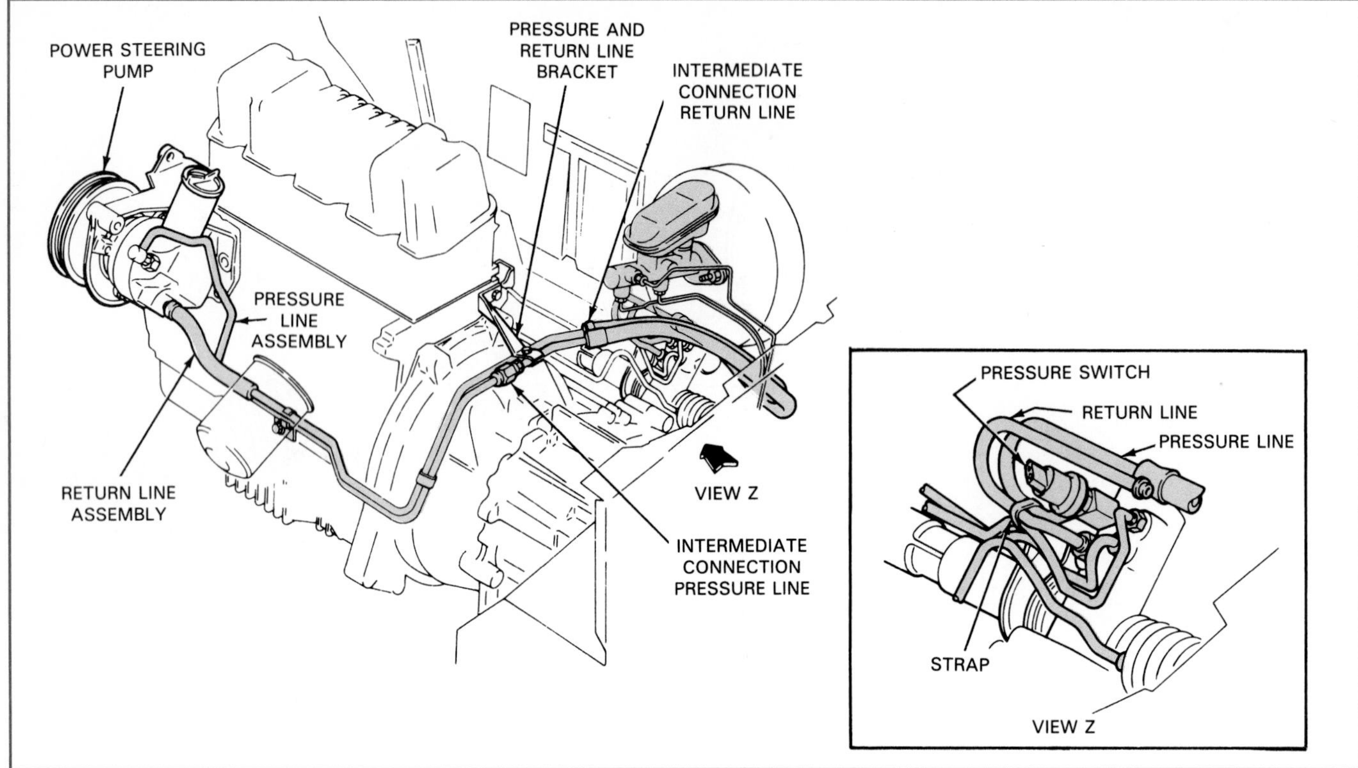

Figure 43-41. Checking the routing and bracketing of all power steering system hoses and lines is an important step during any power steering service operation. (Ford)

- Worn control arm bushings.
- Dry ball joints.

Spring Noises

- Loose U-bolts.
- Loose or worn spring bushings, brackets, or shackles.
- Worn or missing spring interliners.
- Broken spring.

Springs Bottom or Sag

- Weak or broken springs.
- Leaking or worn shock absorbers.

Shock Absorber Noise

- Loose mountings.
- Worn bushings.

Rear Wheels Do Not Track

- Broken leaf spring.
- Bent rear axle housing.
- Misaligned frame.

Car Leans on Corners

- Faulty shock absorbers.
- Loose or worn shock absorber mountings.
- Weak springs.
- Broken springs.

Car Pulls to One Side

- Mismatched or unevenly worn tires.
- Weak springs.
- Broken springs.
- Loose or worn strut bushings.

Excessive Tire Wear

- Weak springs.
- Broken springs.
- Faulty shock absorbers.

Troubleshooting Manual Steering

Excessive Play in Steering Wheel

- Loose or worn steering gear shaft.
- Steering arm loose on steering gear shaft.
- Loose or worn steering linkage.
- Loose steering gear housing bolts.
- Loose steering gear adjustment.
- Loose steering arms at knuckles.
- Loose rack-and-pinion mounting.
- Maladjusted rack-and-pinion.
- Loose tie rod end.
- Loose or worn wheel bearings.

Rattle in Rack-and-pinion

- Loose mounting bracket.
- Lack of lubricant.

- Incorrect lubricant.
- Loose steering gear mounting bolts.

Instability

- Low tire pressure.
- Uneven tire pressure.
- Loose or worn wheel bearings.
- Loose or worn idler arm bushing.
- Loose or worn strut bushings.
- Steering gear not centered.
- Incorrect front wheel alignment.

Car Pulls to One Side

- Uneven tire pressure.
- Mismatched front tires.
- Maladjusted wheel bearings.
- Incorrect wheel alignment.

Poor Return of Steering Wheel

- Dry ball joints or suspension joints.
- Binding in ball joints or linkage.
- Incorrect wheel alignment.
- Maladjusted steering gear.
- Low tire pressure.
- Tight steering shaft seal.

Troubleshooting Power Steering

Heavy Steering Effort

- Low on power steering fluid.
- Loose rack piston.
- Restricted fluid passages in gear assembly.
- Bent or damaged rack assembly.
- Internal fluid leakage in valve assembly.
- External fluid leakage at pump.
- Incorrect drive belt tension.
- External fluid leakage at hoses.
- Incorrect engine idle speed.
- Weak pump flow pressure.

Hissing Noise When Parking

- Internal leakage in steering gear.
- Steering wheel at end of travel (normal).
- When turning steering wheel at standstill (normal).

Growl in Steering Pump

- Excessive pressure in hoses.
- Worn cam ring in pump.
- Scored thrust plates or rotor in pump.
- Scored pressure plates.

Swish Noise in Pump

- Defective flow control valve.

Whine in Pump

- Air in power steering fluid.
- Low power steering fluid level.
- Pressure hose or line contacting other part.
- Misaligned hose and line brackets.
- Missing or damaged pump cover O-ring.

Rattle in Steering

- Pressure hose contacting another part.
- Loose pitman shaft.
- Loose pitman arm.
- Loose tie rod ends.
- Loose rack-and-pinion mounts.
- Loose steering gear housing bolts.
- Loose steering gear adjustments.

Car Wanders to One Side

- Incorrect front wheel alignment.
- Unbalanced steering gear valve.
- Loose tie rod ends.

Steering Wheel Surges or Jerks

- Low power steering fluid level.
- Loose pump drive belt.
- Weak pump pressure.
- Sticking flow control valve.

Excessive Play in Steering Wheel

- Air in hydraulic system.
- Incorrect steering gear adjustments.
- Loose steering gear coupling.
- Loose steering shaft universal joint.
- Faulty rotary valve.

Increased Steering Effort on Fast Turn

- Slipping pump drive belt.
- Internal pump leakage.
- Low power steering fluid level.
- Too low engine idle speed.
- Air in hydraulic system.
- Weak pump output.
- Malfunctioning steering gear.

Poor Return of Steering Wheel

- Maladjusted steering gear.
- Dry ball joints or linkage joints.
- Binding ball joints or linkage joints.
- Incorrect front wheel alignment.
- Maladjusted wheel bearings.
- Kinked return hoses.
- Internal pump leakage.
- Contaminated power steering fluid.
- Misaligned steering gear-to-steering column.

- Tight steering shaft bearings or bushings.
- Bent or damaged rack.
- Sticking or plugged spool valve.

Special Safety Precautions

All general safety measures should be taken when working on suspension systems or steering systems. See Chapter 1. In addition, be sure to observe the following caution stressed by car manufacturers in their service manuals:

"To help avoid personal injury when a car is on a hoist, provide additional support for the car at the opposite end from which components are being removed. This will reduce the possibility of the car falling off the hoist."

Chapter 43–Review Questions

Write your answers on a separate sheet of paper. Do not write in this book.

1. Coil springs are manufactured to meet the prescribed Rated Suspension Spring _____ for the particular vehicle application.
2. This rating is designed to provide for adequate coil spring durability and vehicle stability under all _____ conditions.
3. Give two functions of a leaf spring center bolt.
4. What type of suspension system utilizes the flexibility of a steel bar or tube twisting lengthwise to provide spring action?
5. Most MacPherson struts are _____ (hydraulic or gas-filled) units.
6. Name three basic types of front suspension.
7. Independent front suspension systems utilize _____ to provide pivot points for each front wheel.
   (A) steering arms
   (B) steering knuckles
   (C) ball joints
   (D) wheel spindles
8. In the S.L.A. (short/long arm) system of front suspension, the proportionate lengths of the upper and lower control arms are designed to keep the rise and fall of each front wheel in a horizontal plane. True or False?
9. The MacPherson strut system of front suspension is used on most subcompact and compact cars with _____ (front-wheel drive or rear-wheel drive).
10. Most car leveling systems are designed to automatically extend or compress the rear shock absorbers or shock struts. True or False?
11. Some collapsible steering columns are made of slotted steel mesh. Other columns are two-piece _____ type.
    (A) sleeved
    (B) shear
    (C) splined
    (D) telescoping
12. With manual rack-and-pinion steering, _____ (rotary or transverse) motion of the pinion is changed to _____ (rotary or transverse) movement of the rack.
13. With manual recirculating ball type steering, the balls act as a _____ between the worm shaft and the ball nut.
    (A) rolling thread
    (B) rolling spline
    (C) rolling sector
    (D) rolling pinion
14. With a manual steering gearbox, the pitman arm is splined to the pitman arm shaft. _____ motion of the shaft is converted to _____ movement of the arm.
15. All power steering systems are actually "power assisted steering." What does this mean?
16. Which of the following terms is NOT associated with power rack-and-pinion steering?
    (A) Pitman arm.
    (B) Torsion bar.
    (C) Rotary valve.
    (D) Power cylinder.
17. What steering gear design produces slower response of the pitman arm in shallow turn situations and faster response near the extremes of steering wheel travel on sharp turns?
18. There are three types of power steering pumps generally used in modern cars. Name two.
19. When checking out a suspension or steering complaint, always check the simpler possible causes first. Give three quick checks for power steering problems.
20. A driver of a car equipped with power steering complained that the steering wheel surges and jerks on turns. Technician A says the problem could be caused by weak power steering pump pressure. Technician B says it could be caused by a sticking flow control valve in the pump. Who is right?
    (A) A only.
    (B) B only.
    (C) Both A & B.
    (D) Neither A nor B.

Chapter 44
Tires, Tire Service

After studying this chapter, you will be able to:
- ❍ Compare basic tire types and tire structures.
- ❍ Interpret the meaning of tire sidewall markings.
- ❍ Describe excessive and uneven treadwear patterns and possible causes.
- ❍ Outline steps for checking wheel and tire radial and lateral runout.
- ❍ Demonstrate proper techniques for using a power operated tire changer to demount and mount tires on wheels.
- ❍ State several methods for making satisfactory permanent tire repairs.

Tires

By definition, an automobile ***tire*** is a tubular corded carcass covered with rubber or synthetic rubber, mounted on a wheel and inflated to provide traction for moving the vehicle and to assist the brakes in stopping it. Properly inflated, today's tires will absorb irregularities of the road surface, and give a safe and comfortable ride while providing a reassuring grip on the road at all speeds.

Tire Types and Basic Structure

There are two basic tire types: tubeless tires for passenger cars and light-duty trucks; and those requiring inner tubes for medium and heavy-duty trucks.

The tubeless tire is designed so that the air is sealed within the rim of the wheel and the tire casing, Figure 44-1. When an inner tube is used in the tire casing, the air is contained within the tube, while the casing serves mainly to protect the tube and provide traction.

A ***tubeless tire*** is composed of a carcass, sidewall, and tread. The ***carcass*** is the entire tire structure except sidewall and tread. The ***sidewall*** is that portion of the tire between the bead and tread. The ***tread*** is the portion of the tire that comes in contact with the road.

The carcass of a tire is made up of layers of cord materials such as rayon, nylon, polyester, fiberglass, or steel wire strands. The ***cords*** are laid parallel in layers and impregnated with rubber to form plies.

The ***plies*** are arranged at various angles and in different combinations of ***layers*** and ***belts*** (plies laid circumferentially around tire). See Figure 44-2. Then the sidewall and tread material is applied and vulcanized in place, Figure 44-3.

Cord Materials and Ply Layout

There are three general methods of arranging or laying down tire plies. They may be laid down "on the bias," or "on the bias and belted," or "radially." See Figure 44-4.

The ***bias ply tire*** was once used extensively as original equipment and for replacement. The term "bias" means that the plies are laid in criss-cross fashion from bead to bead, Figure 44-4, giving strength to the tire carcass. The bias ply

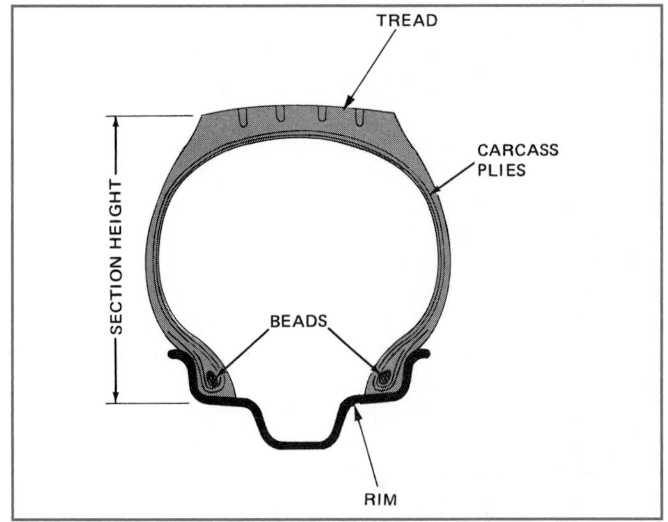

Figure 44-1. This cross section of a tubeless tire shows the basic structure and air tight fit of tire beads in the bead seats of a wheel.

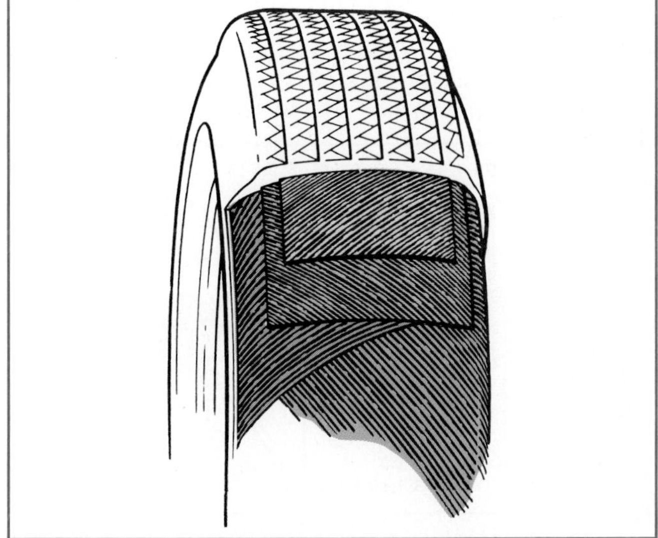

Figure 44-2. The carcass of a belted bias tire consists of plies that are laid diagonally and belts that are laid around the circumference of the tire.

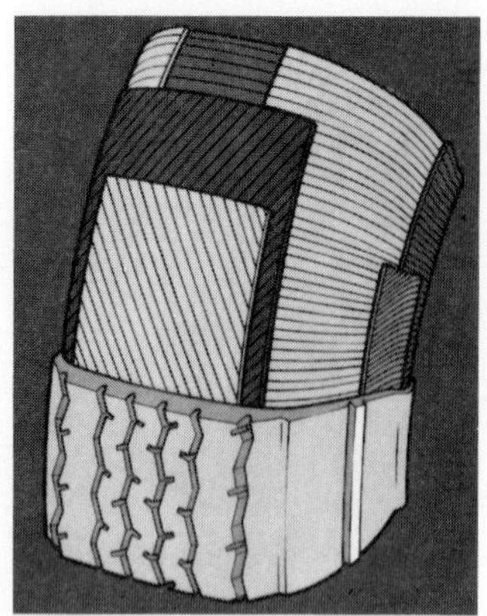

Figure 44-3. In radial construction, the carcass plies are laid radially and the steel belts circle the tire. The sidewall and tread material is vulcanized in place.

tire may have two, four, or more carcass plies that cross at an angle of approximately 35° with the centerline of the tire. Alternate plies extend in opposite directions.

The ***belted bias tire*** has a carcass construction similar to the bias ply tire, but it also has two or more belts of cord that circle the tire under the tread. See Figures 44-2 and 44-4. Often, the belts are made of a different cord material than the carcass plies. For example, the belt may be fiberglass or steel, while the carcass plies may be rayon or polyester.

Belted tires reportedly give longer mileage than bias ply tires, and the belts make the belted bias tire much more resistant to punctures, cuts, and bruises. The belts also serve to keep the tread of the tire more firmly on the road and virtually eliminate "tire squirm."

The ***radial tire*** has the carcass plies laid across the circumference of the tire from bead to bead, plus two or more "belts" are laid under the tread, Figures 44-3 and 44-4. This construction gives flexibility to the sidewall and greater strength to the tread.

Radial tires are said to give longer tread life, better handling, and a softer ride at medium and high speeds than either bias or belted bias tires. However, radial tires are more likely to give a firm, almost hard, ride at low speeds.

Ply Rating

The ***ply rating*** of a tire is its index of tire strength. The rating does not necessarily represent the actual number of plies in the tire. Rather, ply rating is used to relate a given size tire with its load and inflation limits.

In use, a passenger car tire marked "4-ply rating/2-ply" has the same load-carrying capacity as a 4-ply tire of the same size at the same inflation pressure. When the 2-ply tire was introduced, some objections were raised with regard to cutting the conventional number of plies in half. However, cord break strength for the two plies totaled 142 lb., while four plies totaled only 104 lb.

Load Range

The ply rating system has been phased out in favor of the load range system. The term ***load range*** is used in conjunction with a letter, such as B, C, D, etc., to identify a given tire size with its load and inflation limits when used in a specific type of service. As load range increases, letters progress in the alphabet.

Sometimes, both ply rating and load range designations may be found on tire sidewalls. See Figure 44-5. For example, load range B tires may be marked 4-ply rating/2-ply, or 4-ply. Load range C tires may be marked 6-ply rating/4-ply, or 6-ply. Load range D tires may be marked 8-ply rating/4-ply or 8-ply rating/6-ply or 8-ply.

A tire's load range and proper inflation pressure determine how much of a load the tire can safely carry. These important figures are marked on the sidewall of the tire, along with size designations, tire ply composition, manufacturer's name, and the letters DOT, which signify that the tire complies with Department of Transportation safety standards. In addition, tire sidewalls must be marked either "tubeless" or "tube-type" and, if a radial tire, the word "radial" must appear. See Figure 44-5.

"Proper inflation," according to the Rubber Manufacturers Association (RMA), "is the most important rule in tire safety and tire mileage." Correct tire inflation provides better traction and braking, easier steering, better cornering, and longer, safer tire life.

The U.S. Department of Transportation (DOT) has established ***uniform tire quality grading*** (UTQG) for passenger car tires. The grades are molded on the sidewall of the tire. All tires are graded in accordance with DOT test

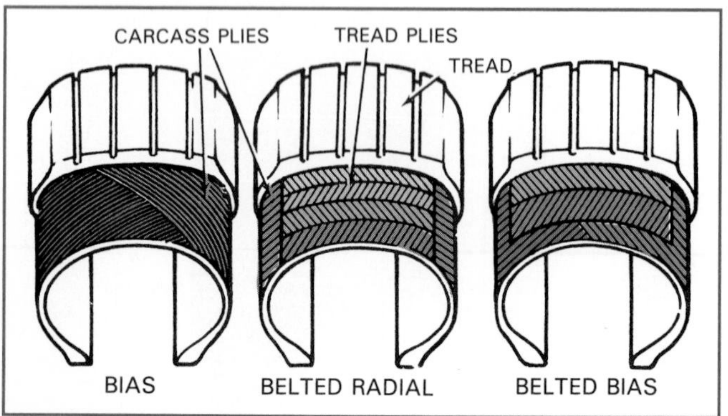

Figure 44-4. Three basic types of tire construction can be identified by the direction in which plies are laid to form the carcass of the tire. Bias and belted bias plies are diagonal; radial plies cross tire from bead to bead.

Figure 44-5. Tire sidewall markings are shown for an F78-14 tire, which replaced the old size designation 7.75-14. (Rubber Manufacturers Association)

procedures in the areas of tread wear, traction, and temperature resistance.

The ***tread wear grading system*** uses comparative ratings by the number (100, 110, 120, etc.) with regard to tests performed under controlled conditions. A tire graded 150, for example, can be expected to give 50% more tread life than a tire graded 100.

The ***traction grade*** uses the symbols A, B, C, with A being the top grade based on the tire's ability to stop on wet pavement in tests made on concrete and asphalt surfaces.

The ***temperature resistance grading system*** also rates tires as A, B, or C, with A the highest grade. Grade C corresponds to the level of Federal Motor Vehicle Standard No. 109.

Tread Patterns

Tire treads are grooved traction surfaces around the circumference of the tire. The grooves and ribs formed during the tire manufacturing process are carefully engineered to provide good traction on wet or dry roads, control when cornering, minimum distortion at high speeds, reduced rolling resistance, and increased wear resistance. The tread and tire are designed to place the full width of the tread on the road when the tire is properly inflated.

The variety of ***tread patterns*** is very broad. Consider the fact that one publisher has produced a tread pattern identification guide that illustrates over 3000 patterns. Apparently, the number of patterns is so great because of design improvements and the manufacturers' desire for distinctive patterns of their own. See Figure 44-6.

Tread Wear Indicators

Tread wear indicators molded into modern tires serve as visual proof that the tire tread is approaching worn-out condition. These 1/2″ (12.7 mm) wide indicators are located in several positions around the circumference of the tire.

As long as the tread grooves are at least 1/16″ (1.6 mm) deep, the grooves are unbroken. When tread depth reaches that point, the tread wear indicators will appear as solid strips across the tire, Figure 44-7. These strips interrupt tread continuity and are clearly visible on inspection. The tire should be replaced when this condition occurs.

Figure 44-6. Tread patterns are designed to improve traction, cornering, and handling. This technician is using a gauge to check tread depth. (Firestone Tire & Rubber Co.)

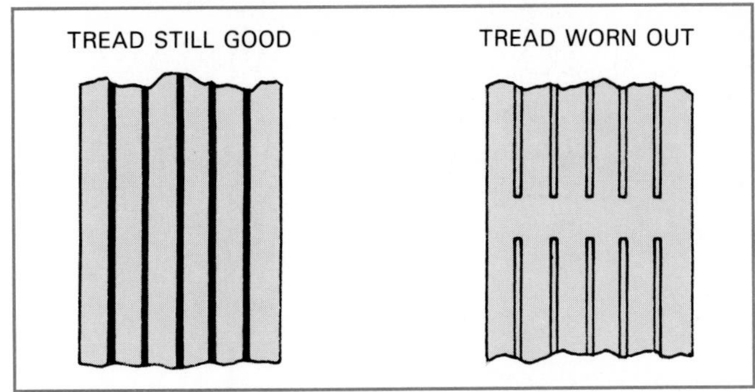

Figure 44-7. The tire tread wear indicator appears as solid strip in the tread when tread depth is reduced to 1/16" (1.6 mm).

Tire Sizes

In the past, ***tire sizes*** were designated only by section width and rim diameter. Then, research and development in the tire manufacturers' laboratories and at the proving grounds and test tracks triggered many major advances in tire design and construction.

When "wide oval" and "low profile" tires were introduced, the need for new tire size designations became clear. The simple, two-dimension system for specifying tire size was no longer valid because it did not take "section height" into consideration. See Figure 44-8.

Section height is the height of an inflated tire from the bottom of the bead to the top of the tread. It is an important size factor since modern tires generally are low profile in contrast to the almost round cross section of older tire designs. Section height also governs aspect ratio, and aspect ratio is a key area of identification of tires by size. See Figure 44-9.

Aspect Ratio

The ***aspect ratio*** of a tire is the ratio of tire section height to section width. It is height divided by width. A "78 series" tire, for example, has a section height that is 78% of the section width. See Figure 44-10.

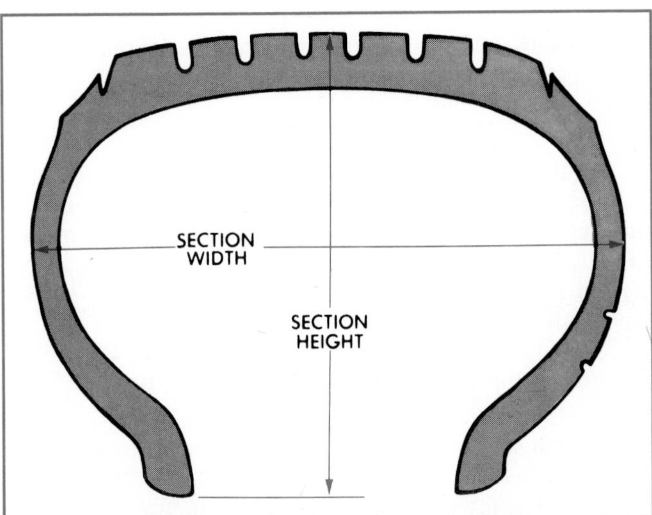

Figure 44-8. Section height became a factor in tire size designations when tire design changed from "round" to "oval." (Oldsmobile)

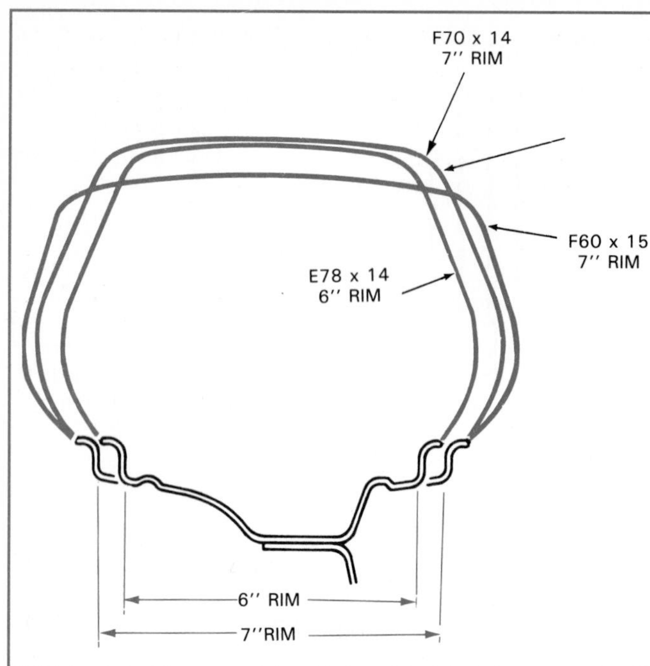

Figure 44-9. The profile of modern tires is low and wide, resulting in aspect ratios of 78, 75, 70, 60, and 50.

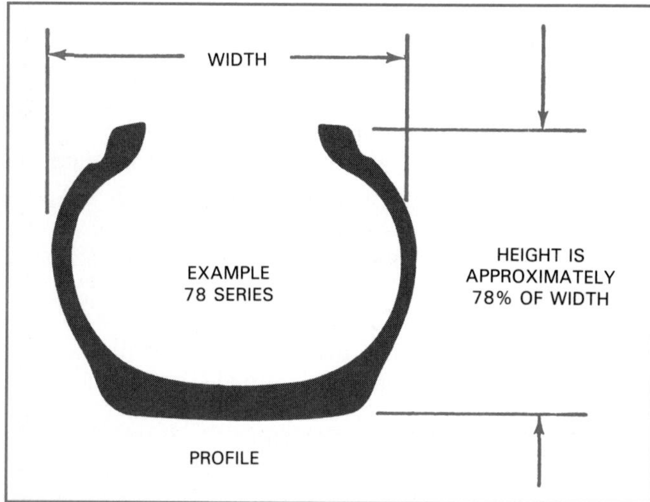

Figure 44-10. The aspect ratio, or profile, is figured by dividing section height by section width. In this example, the aspect ratio of the tire is 78.

Under the old tire size system, a tire bearing the size designation 8.25-14 will measure 8 1/4″ from outside sidewall to outside sidewall. The 14 stands for rim diameter. The new tire size designations provide all information previously contained in the size code, plus the aspect ratio.

Under the new tire size designation system, an F78-14 size, for example, tells three things about the tire:

- The first letter, F, is the load carrying capacity.
- The first set of numbers, 78, is the aspect ratio, meaning that the section height of the tire is 78% of the section width. The lower the ratio, the wider the tire.
- The second set of numbers, 14, is the rim diameter. Some car manufacturers refer to this designation as the inner diameter of the tire.

Obviously, the variety of aspect ratios available has broadened tire applications for any given vehicle. In addition, other elements of tire construction have affected tire designations and applications. The size comparison chart shown in Figure 44-11 indicates tire availability by size and type.

Metric Markings

Metric tires are available in two load ranges, standard load and extra load. Most metric tire sizes do not exactly match corresponding alpha-numeric tire sizes. See Figure 44-11. Therefore, if metric tires are replaced with other sizes, a tire dealer should be consulted to ensure the closest match to the metric size tires being replaced.

An example of a popular size tire in metric is P205/75R15, Figure 44-12, which replaces the former alpha-numeric size FR78-15. Each letter and number has a meaning:

P–Indicates passenger car tire.
205–Width of tire cross section in millimeters.
75–Means the tire cross section is 75% as high as it is wide (aspect ratio).
R–Denotes radial construction.
15–Rim diameter in inches.

If the tire is bias belted construction, the letter before the rim diameter would be "B." If the body construction is bias ply, the letter would be "D" (for diagonal). Many tires have both metric and the alpha-numeric size designations molded in the sidewalls.

Another marking on tires is tire ***inflation pressure,*** usually printed in both metric kilopascals (kPa) and pounds per square inch (psi). A typical inflation pressure would be 207 kPa (30 psi). Air pressure gauges that measure in kilopascals are available. To convert, multiply psi by 6.9 to get kilopascals.

Maximum load is also given in metric and English measures. Maximum load typically could be 790 kilograms or 1742 pounds. Still another, more recent tire marking is a T.P.C. Spec. No. (Tire Performance Criteria Specifications Number). Replacement tires with the same T.P.C. Spec. No. should be installed.

A ***speed rating symbol*** is an additional sidewall marking on performance tires. It is a requirement in Europe, but not in the U.S. The letter Z, V, H, T, or S is located between the aspect ratio and tire construction. For example, P205/60HR 15. The letters mean that the tire can sustain speeds of Z–above 149 mph; V–above 130 mph; H–up to 130 mph; T–up to 118 mph; S–up to 112 mph.

Tire Service

Excessive or uneven ***tread wear*** results from underinflation, rapid stops, fast acceleration, misalignment, and/or unbalanced conditions. Road surface condition also affects tire life. Gravel roads and rough finished concrete will wear tires quickly. Smooth concrete and asphalt surfaces aid in promoting maximum tire life.

Normal wear causes the tire tread to be reduced evenly and smoothly. Types of abnormal tread wear include:

- Spotty wear.
- Overinflation wear.
- Underinflation wear.
- Toe-in wear.

Size Comparison Chart

Interchangeability is **NOT** implied.

Interchangeability between corresponding sizes of different construction tires is not always possible due to differences in load ratings, tire dimensions, fender clearances and rim sizes, or vehicle manufacturers' recommendations.

DIAGONAL (BIAS) PLY	DIAGONAL (BIAS) AND BELTED BIAS PLY				RADIAL PLY				
	'78 Series'	'70 Series'	'60 Series'	'50 Series'	Metric	'78 Series'	'70 Series'	'60 Series'	'50 Series'
					155R13				
6.00-13					165R13				
	A78-13	A70-13	A60-13			AR78-13	AR70-13	AR60-13	
6.50-13	B78-13	B70-13	B60-13	B50-13	175R13	BR78-13	BR70-13	BR60-13	BR50-13
7.00-13	C78-13	C70-13	C60-13	C50-13	185R13	CR78-13	CR70-13		CR50-13
	D78-13	D70-13	D60-13	D50-13		DR78-13	DR70-13		
					195R13	ER78-13		ER60-13	
					155R14				
	A78-14					AR78-14		AR60-14	
6.45-14	B78-14		B60-14		165R14	BR78-14			
6.95-14	C78-14	C70-14	C60-14		175R14	CR78-14	CR70-14		
	D78-14	D70-14	D60-14			DR78-14	DR70-14		
7.35-14	E78-14	E70-14	E60-14		185R14	ER78-14	ER70-14	ER60-14	
7.75-14	F78-14	F70-14	F60-14	F50-14	195R14	FR78-14	FR70-14	FR60-14	
8.25-14	G78-14	G70-14	G60-14	G50-14	205R14	GR78-14	GR70-14	GR60-14	GR50-14
8.55-14	H78-14	H70-14	H60-14	H50-14	215R14	HR78-14	HR70-14	HR60-14	
8.85-14	J78-14	J70-14	J60-14		225R14	JR78-14	JR70-14	JR60-14	JR50-14
		L70-14	L60-14				LR70-14	LR60-14	
				M50-14					
				N50-14					
	A78-15	A70-15				AR78-15			
	B78-15		B60-15	B50-15	165R15	BR78-15	BR70-15		
6.85-15	C78-15	C70-15	C60-15		175R15	CR78-15	CR70-15		
	D78-15	D70-15				DR78-15	DR70-15		
7.35-15	E78-15	E70-15	E60-15	E50-15	185R15	ER78-15	ER70-15	ER60-15	
7.75-15	F78-15	F70-15	F60-15		195R15	FR78-15	FR70-15	FR60-15	
8.25-15	G78-15	G70-15	G60-15	G50-15	205R15	GR78-15	GR70-15	GR60-15	GR50-15
8.55-15	H78-15	H70-15	H60-15	H50-15	215R15	HR78-15	HR70-15	HR60-15	HR50-15
8.85-15	J78-15	J70-15	J60-15		225R15	JR78-15	JR70-15	JR60-15	JR50-15
9.00-15		K70-15				KR78-15	KR70-15		
9.15-15	L78-15	L70-15	L60-15	L50-15	235R15	LR78-15	LR70-15	LR60-15	LR50-15
	M78-15					MR78-15	MR70-15		
8.90-15	N78-15			N50-15		NR78-15			

Figure 44-11. This chart compares old and new tire size designations, but interchangeability is not implied. (Rubber Manufacturers Association)

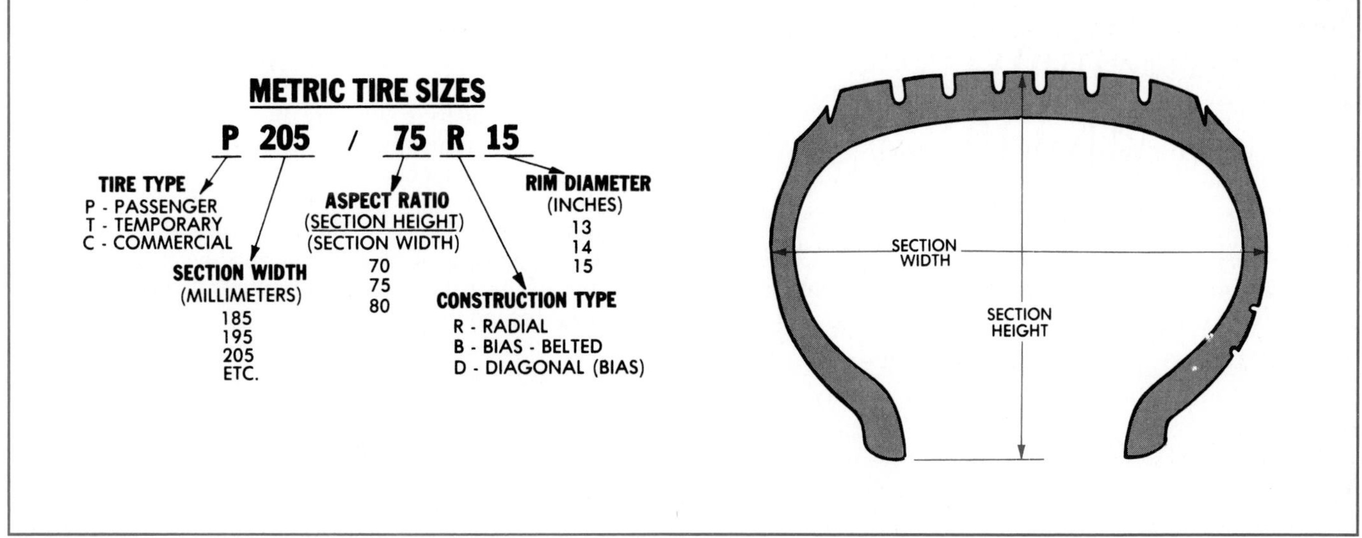

Figure 44-12. Passenger car tire size designations are stamped in metric markings. Note P 205/75RI5. Section width is 205 millimeters. (Oldsmobile)

- Toe-out wear.
- Camber wear.
- Cornering wear.

Figure 44-13 shows a condition of spotty wear. This wear pattern usually results from a combination of conditions, including the design of the particular tire tread. Underinflation and incorrect camber are the main factors, along with excessive toe-in or toe-out.

Overinflation causes tires to wear excessively at the center of the tread surface, Figure 44-14. In addition, there usually is a little wear on the outer edges of the tire. This causes early failure at the center ribs and breaks in the tire sidewall.

Wear due to ***underinflation*** is shown in Figure 44-15. This is characterized by excessive wear on the two tread ribs adjacent to the inner and outer shoulder ribs. In many cases, underinflation also causes spotty wear.

The amount of front wheel ***toe-in*** or ***toe-out*** is one of the most important factors governing tire wear. Unless toe-in is correct, the tires will have a scrubbing action on the road surface, and excessive wear will result. Figure 44-16 shows typical tread wear due to excessive toe-in. It produces a featheredge on the inner edges of the tread ribs, which can be felt by rubbing the hand across the face of the tire.

Wear resulting from toe-out is just the reverse. The featheredge is produced on the outer edges of the tread ribs. See Figure 44-17.

Excessive ***camber*** will produce wear on one side of the tire tread, as illustrated in Figure 44-18. If there is too much positive camber, the tread wear will be on the outer ribs. If camber is negative, the wear will occur on the inner side of the tire tread. If there is excessive wear on both inner and outer areas of the tread, it probably was caused by excessive skidding on turns.

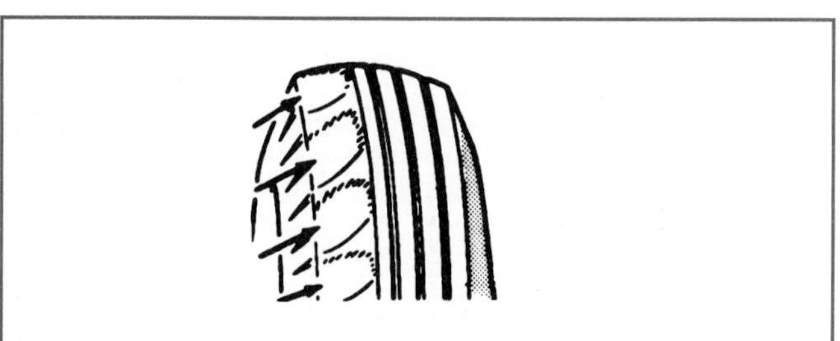

Figure 44-13. Spotty wear results from a combination of causes, including underinflation and misalignment. (Chrysler)

Figure 44-14. Overinflation causes wear in the center of the tire tread. (Chrysler)

Figure 44-15. Underinflation wear occurs at both shoulders of the tire tread. (Chrysler)

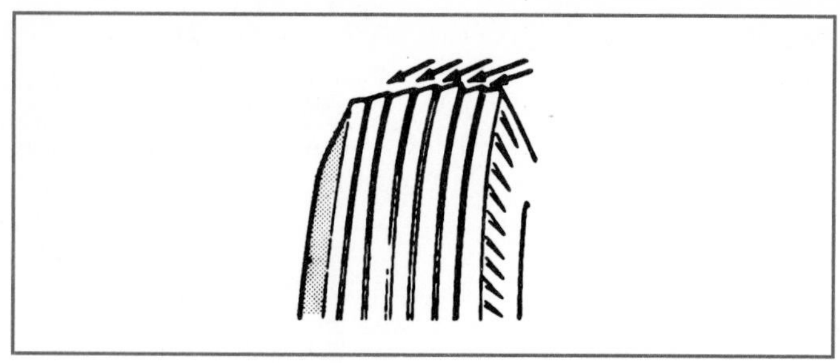

Figure 44-16. Excessive toe-in will cause featheredging of the inner edges of the tread ribs. Note that this is the left front tire as viewed from the front. (Chrysler)

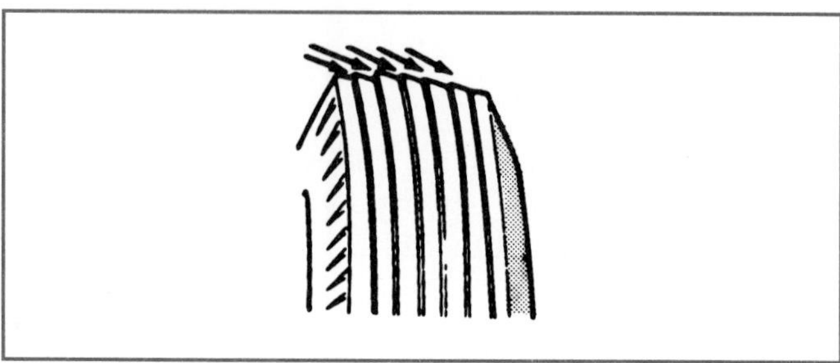

Figure 44-17. Excessive toe-out will cause featheredging of the outer edges of the tread ribs. Note that this is the left front tire as viewed from the front. (Chrysler)

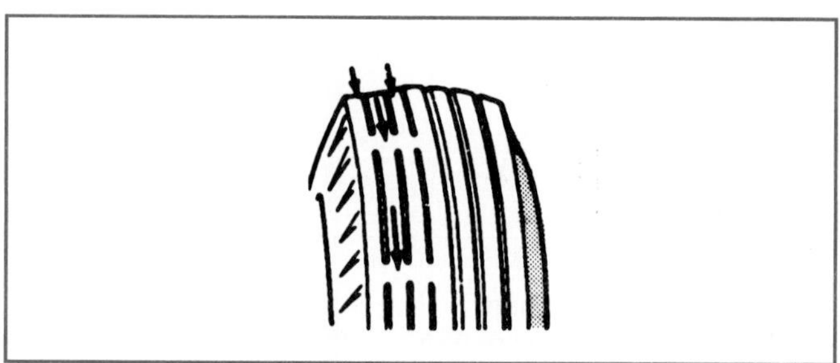

Figure 44-18. Excessive side-of-tread wear results from incorrect camber. (Chrysler)

When considering any tire tread wear condition and what caused it, remember that excessive or uneven wear usually results from a combination of conditions. Tires wear at a different rate on all four wheels due to driving conditions, weight of the vehicle, power on the driving wheels, crown of the road, alignment of wheels, overloading the vehicle, tire inflation, and probably most important of all, driving habits of the person behind the steering wheel.

Fast starts, quick stops, high speeds, and fast turns, all take their toll of tire life. Conservative driving habits promote maximum tire life and economy.

Tire Rotation

In order to equalize tire wear, some car manufacturers recommend that wheel and tire assemblies should be rotated from one position to another every 7500 miles (12,000 km). Other manufacturers recommend service as required or whenever uneven tire wear is noticed. While the generally accepted plan for rotating radial tires has been front to rear and rear to front, some manufacturers have approved the criss-cross plan, Figure 44-19.

Wheel and Tire Runout

Precision balanced wheel and tire assemblies are essential for a smooth, comfortable ride and for maximum tire life. See Chapter 45, Wheel Alignment. When checking wheel balance, remember that unbalance and out-of-round are two separate conditions. A perfectly round wheel and tire assembly can be out of balance, and an annoying thump or vibration will be evident when the car is driven. An out-of-round assembly can be in balance, yet a tire thump on a smooth road will be heard and felt.

One of the major difficulties in trying to obtain smooth, vibration-free rotation of the wheel and tire assemblies is eccentricity (deviation from a circular path). The wheel and tire assembly is out-of-round, so the first step is to determine whether the runout problem is in the wheel or tire. To make the check, the wheel bearings must be properly adjusted and the tires inflated to recommended pressure. An accurate dial indicator should be used.

The correct procedure is to first check radial runout of the entire assembly as it slowly rotates through one revolution. Place the tip of the stylus of a dial indicator against the tread, rotate the assembly and see if it is running true. If radial runout of the assembly exceeds .050″ (1.27 mm), the tire should be removed from the wheel, and the wheel checked separately for radial runout. See Figure 44-20. Likewise, if lateral runout (wobble or waddle) exceeds .050″, the wheel must be checked separately.

When checking a wheel for runout, it should be mounted on a hub that is free to rotate, but without end play that would give a false indicator reading. Often, a wheel balancing machine is used for this purpose, Figure 44-21. Generally, radial runout of a steel wheel should not exceed .035″ (0.89 mm). The lateral runout limit for a steel wheel is .045″ (1.14 mm). Radial runout of an aluminum wheel should not exceed .030″ (0.76 mm). The lateral runout for an aluminum wheel is also .030″.

If the wheel checks out satisfactorily, the tire can be reinstalled in a different position (180 deg.). Of course, dust and dirt must be removed from the bead seats of the wheel, and the seats must be free of nicks or burrs. The tire beads must be clean and lubricated with a light film of rubber lubricant before the tire is reinstalled on the wheel.

With the tire on the wheel, properly inflated, and the wheel carefully installed on the drum or axle flange, the wheel nuts are tightened in an alternating sequence with uniform snugness. See Figure 44-22. Then, using the same alternating sequence, the wheel nuts are tightened firmly, and runout of the wheel and tire assembly is rechecked.

If moving the tire to different positions on the wheel does not bring lateral runout within limits, a new tire must be installed. If radial runout is excessive, the tire tread can

ACCEPTABLE ROTATION PATTERNS FOR RADIAL TIRES

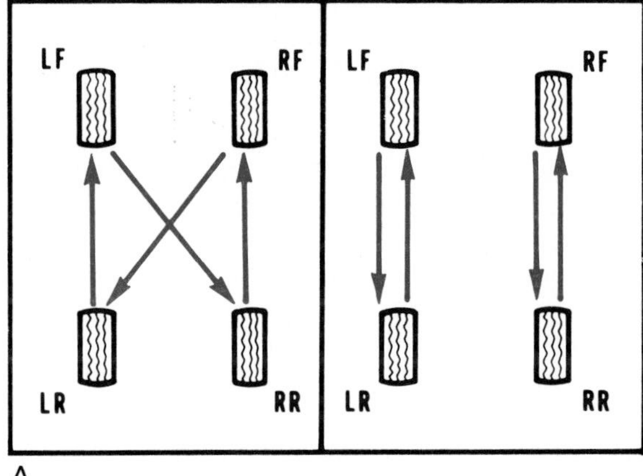

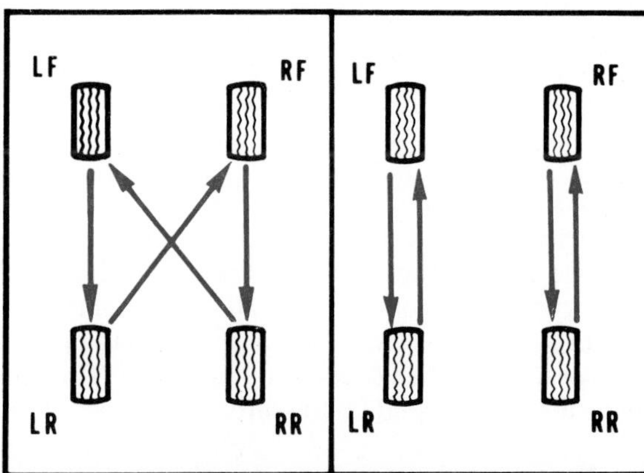

Figure 44-19. Radial tire rotation patterns. Top–Front-wheel drive models. Bottom–Rear-wheel drive models. (Oldsmobile)

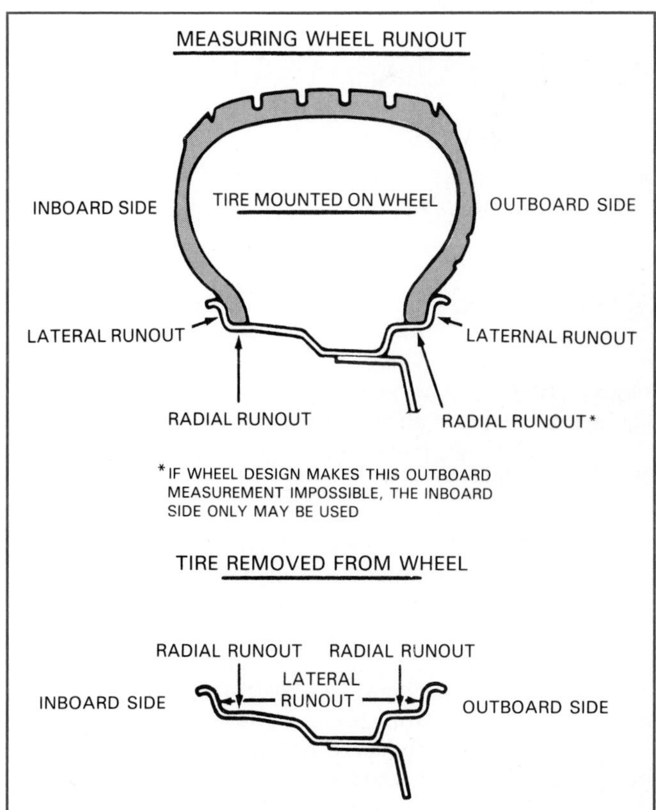

Figure 44-20. Wheel and tire runout guide shows locations for checking radial and lateral runout of the wheel and tire assembly and of the wheel alone. (Cadillac)

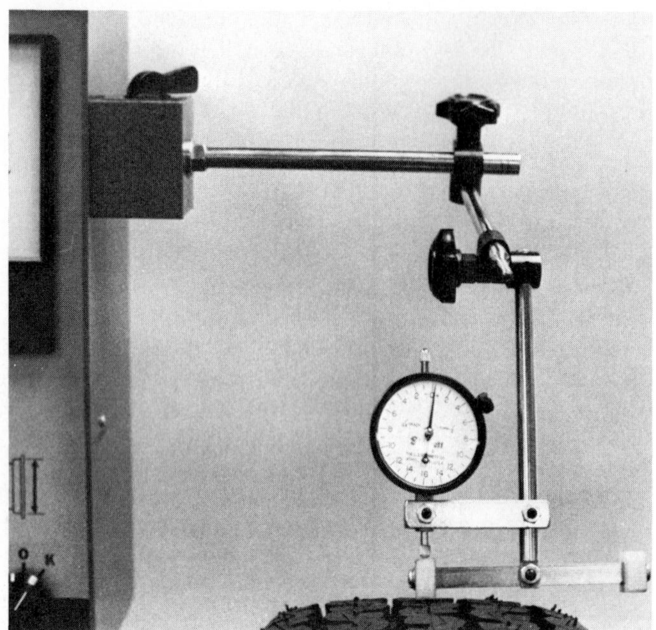

Figure 44-21. This indicator is set up to check radial runout of a wheel and tire assembly mounted on a wheel balancing machine.

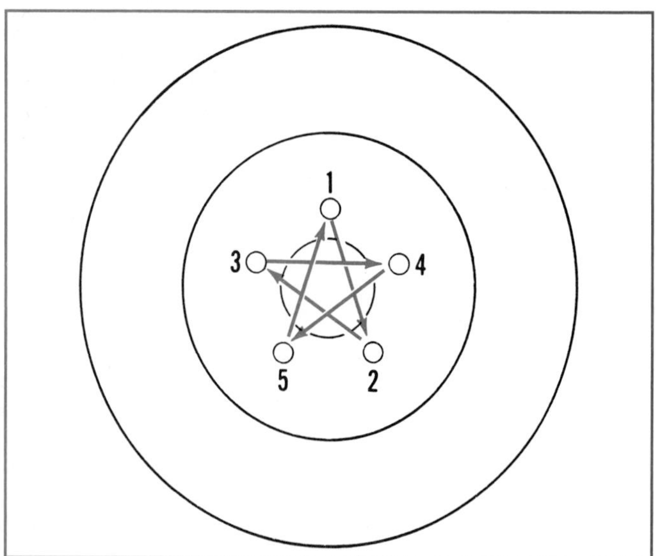

Figure 44-22. Correct wheel nut installation involves tightening the nuts in an alternating sequence to a uniform snugness. Final tightening should take place in the same sequence. (Cadillac)

be "trued" or "buffed." Removing rubber from the tire tread would seem to shorten the life of the tire. Actually, its life is extended since the tire will roll smoothly without thumping.

Tire trueing is done by placing the out-of-round tire in a machine that shaves off only the high spots, rounding the tire. Tire buffing is done in a machine that buffs small amounts of rubber from the outer two tread rows. These methods should be followed by checking wheel and tire balance on an off-car wheel balancer, Figure 44-23.

Manual Tire Demounting and Mounting

Originally, tires and wheels are match mounted. The radially stiffest part of the tire is matched to the smallest radius of the wheel. The high spot is marked with yellow paint. The low spot will be in line with the tire valve. If the paint mark is worn off, scribe a mark at the valve stem (before demounting tire) to ensure remounting in the same position.

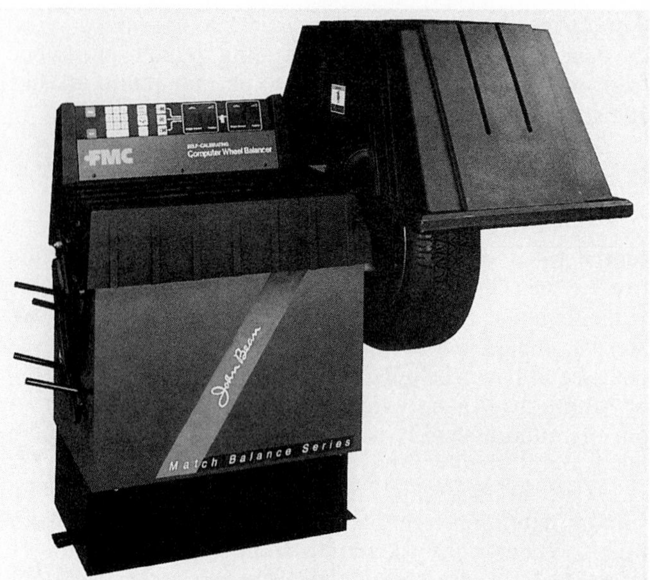

Figure 44-23. Wheel and tire assemblies that have been serviced should be checked for "balance." This computer wheel balancer panel lights up when the wheel is balanced. (Hofmann)

With today's low profile tires and safety wheel rims, manual demounting and mounting of tires is not recommended. In an emergency, the job can be done with smooth tire irons to avoid scoring the beads or nicking the bead seats. After breaking the bead loose from the bead seats, the tire is worked off of the wheel by taking "small bites" with the two tire irons while the beads on the opposite side are pressed into the wheel well.

To mount the tire on the wheel, a light film of rubber lubricant is applied to the beads and the tire bead is "started" on the wheel, then worked into place with the two tire irons. Again, care must be exercised to avoid damaging the beads or bead seats.

Once the tire is in place on the wheel, the tire is lifted to place the outer bead against the outer bead seat and a sudden rush of compressed air is introduced to seat the bead. Air pressure up to 40 psi (275 kPa) may be used to seat the bead, with the valve core removed. Once the beads are seated, the valve core is reinstalled and the tire is inflated to recommended pressure.

Before installing the assembly on the car, check the position of the tire in relation to the rim, making sure that it is concentric. To assist in this check, tires have a locating ring molded on the tire sidewall, Figure 44-24. The ring should be concentric with the edge of the wheel rim. If it is not concentric, the tire and wheel assembly can be jounced on the floor until the tire is correctly mounted. Then inflate the tire to the recommended pressure.

Power Tire Demounting and Mounting

The recommended means of demounting and mounting tires is by use of a power operated tire changer. See Figure 44-25. Many different tires changers are available,

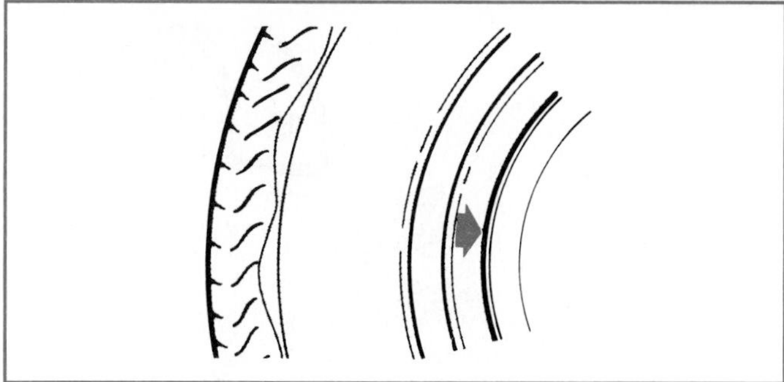

Figure 44-24. The locating ring on a tire should show equal spacing around the rim flange of the wheel when the tire is inflated and the beads are seated. (Oldsmobile)

Figure 44-25. This multi-purpose power tire changer handles bead-breaking and mount-demount actions on a wide range of car and light truck tires and wheels. (Ammco Tools, Inc.)

Figure 44-26, and each is designed to do the demounting and mounting quickly and without damage to the tire or wheel.

Generally, the wheel and tire is installed on the bed of the tire changer and locked in place. Shoes of the power bead breaker are dropped in place at the point where bead and rim meet, and pressure is applied. After loosening both beads from the rim flanges, the inside of the wheel and both beads are lubricated. A special tool is used manually, or with power assistance, to remove the beads from the rim of the wheel, using the center post of the tire changer as a fulcrum.

The procedure is reversed to mount the tire on the wheel. Again, a film of lubricant is applied. Remove the valve core when preparing to inflate the tire to seat the beads in the wheel bead seats. Do not bend over or stand over the tire when inflating. The bead may break when it snaps over the safety hump of the wheel. Also, do not exceed 40 psi (275 kPa) when inflating to seat the bead of any tire, including the compact spare tire. If the bead fails to seat at 40 psi, a bead expander can be installed around the circumference of the tire. Tightening it, or inflating it, will force the tread inward and the beads outward to aid the bead-seating process.

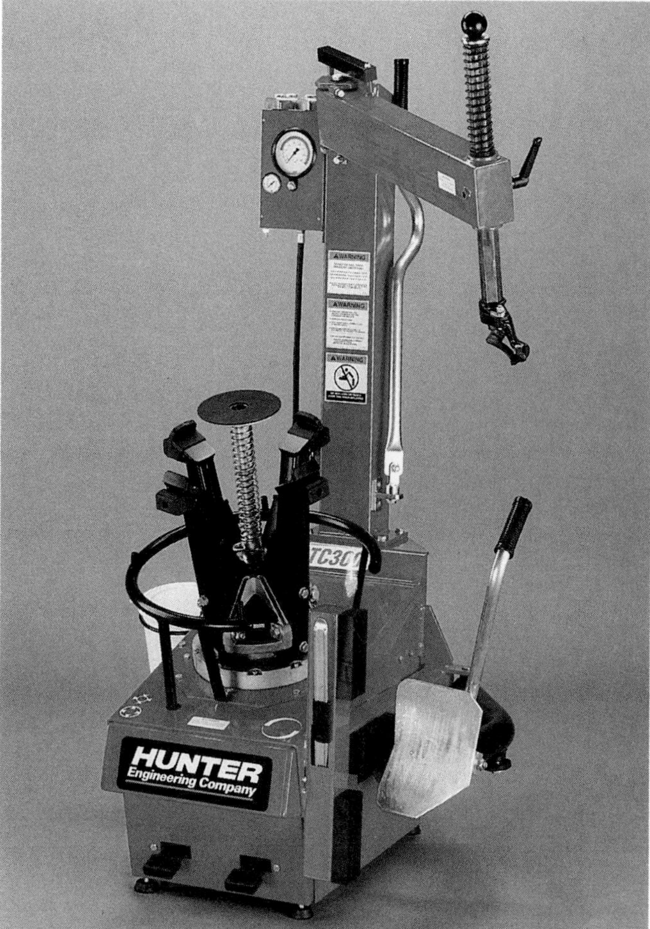

Figure 44-26. This specialty power tire changer is designed to handle standard tires and wheels as well as small import wheels with no center hole. (Ammco Tools, Inc.)

After the tire beads are seated, check for equal spacing of the tire locating ring around the rim flange. See Figure 44-24. Then install the valve core and inflate the tire to the specified inflation pressure. Inflate the compact spare tire to 60 psi (415 kPa).

Tire Repairs

Tire repairs can be made in many different ways. However, repairing a tire from the outside is no longer acceptable. Additionally, puncture holes in radial tires are repairable only in the tread area, as shown in Figure 44-27.

Permanent tire repair methods include chemical or heat curing repair units, one-piece patch/plug units, and a combination plug/patch repairs. A typical procedure for using a plug and a patch to repair a punctured tire is as follows:

1. Before demounting, locate the damaged area of the tire using a soap-and-water solution. Be sure to check the area around the valve. Mark the damaged area, deflate the tire, and carefully remove the tire from the wheel.
2. Study the damaged area from the inside of the tire to determine the full extent of the injury. Punctures that are larger than 1/4″ should not be repaired.
3. Clean the damaged area thoroughly with an approved solvent to remove dirt and lubricants.
4. Ream out the puncture with a drill bit to clean the inside of the injury.

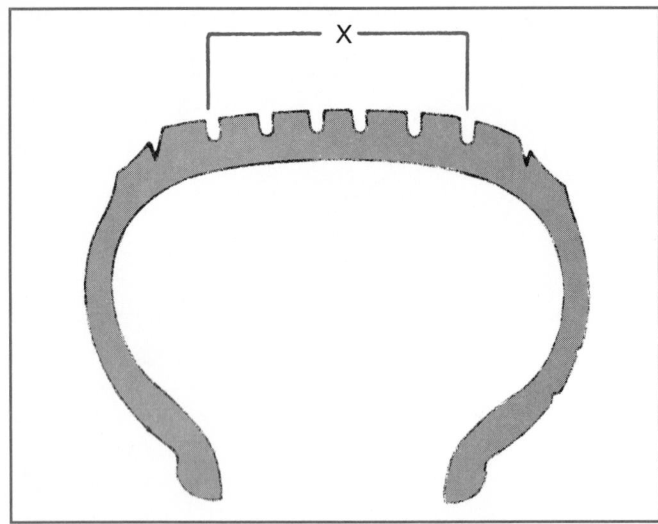

Figure 44-27. The general rule on radial tire puncture repair is to limit actual repairs to the tread area shown at X. (Chrysler)

5. Fill the puncture from the inside of the tire with an appropriate vulcanizing material or a rubber plug. If a plug is used, cut it off slightly above the inside surface of the tire after installation.
6. Buff the area around the puncture with an appropriate tool. See Figure 44-28. (The buffed area should be approximately twice the size of the patch that will be applied.) Be careful not to gouge the inside of the tire. Remove any dust from the repair area.
7. Apply the proper cement to the repair area and allow it to dry thoroughly. Install a patch over the damaged area and use a stitching tool to secure the patch. After the repair is complete, inspect it thoroughly before mounting the tire on the wheel.

Tire Valves

Basically, ***tire valves*** are air checks that open under air pressure and close when pressure is removed. Details of a tire valve used in a tubeless tire are shown in Figure 44-29. The inner valve or core acts as a check valve for the air. Positive sealing is provided by the valve cap, which contains a soft rubber washer or gasket. It is this gasket, pressed against the end of the valve stem, that seals the air in the tire. The careless practice of operating tires without the valve cap should not be followed. Without the valve cap in place, there usually is a slow seepage of air from the tire, with the result that the tire will be operated in an underinflated condition.

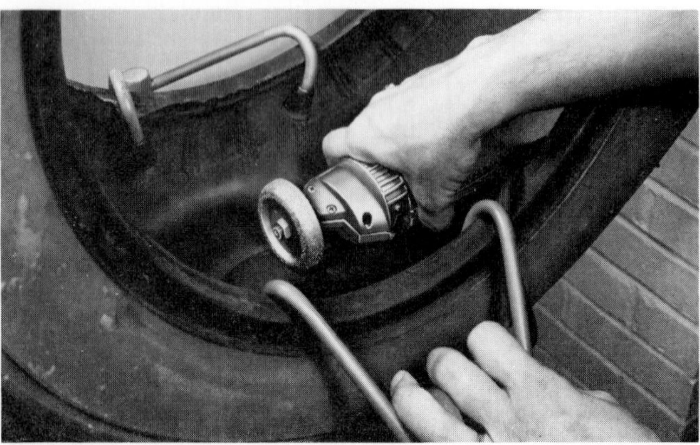

Figure 44-28. One recommended tire puncture repair is made by buffing the area around puncture, then installing a plug from the inside out and covering it with a cold patch or with a self-vulcanizing patch.

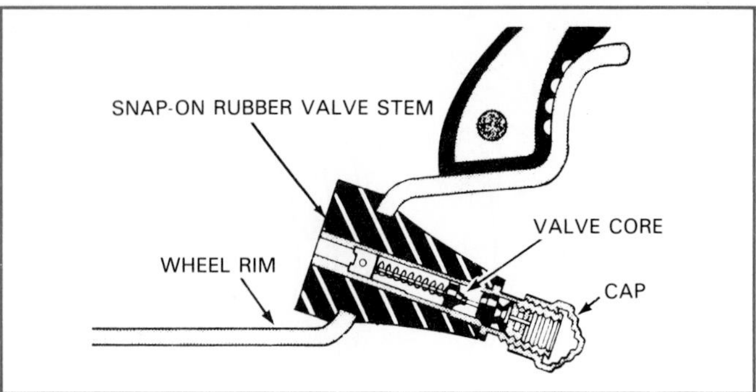

Figure 44-29. This cross section shows the details of a tire valve in the rim of a tubeless tire.

Should air leaks occur around the valve base, it is necessary to install a new tire valve assembly. This is easily accomplished by means of a special lever type tool shown in Figure 44-30.

Retreading and Recapping

The life of a tire can be materially extended by either recapping or retreading. ***Recapping*** means adding a top strip (called camelback) of synthetic or reclaimed rubber to the buffed and roughened surface of a worn tire. ***Retreading*** means adding full width new rubber to the worn tire. The terms are used rather loosely and interchangeably in the tire industry, but a retread is ordinarily a better and more thorough job since new rubber is bonded to the tire from one shoulder to the other.

The experience of truck fleet operators shows that by retreading, tire life is increased from 75 to 100%. In general, truck tires are in need of retreading after 35,000 to 70,000 miles of service, depending on road conditions, climate, and type of service. Radial tires are said to add 12% more mileage to these figures.

Figure 44-30. Lever-type tools are available for pushing or pulling a tire valve assembly into a wheel rim.

Tires with weak spots should not be retreaded. Most operators retread before the tread design is worn smooth.

Wheel and Tire Service Cautions

Certain wheel and tire assembly cautions need to be observed:

- Do not mix radial, bias ply, and belted bias tires on the same car except in emergencies.
- Normally, install new tires in pairs on the same axle. If replacing only one tire, pair it with the tire having the most tread.
- Always follow the car manufacturer's tire inflation pressure recommendations.
- Generally, rotate radial tires from front to rear and from rear to front. However, certain manufacturers give an optional diagonal rotation plan for radial tires. Check specifications. See Figure 44-19.
- Although tread designs may differ, tires built by different manufacturers with identical T.P.C. Spec. No. can be interchanged on the same car.
- To remove "tight" wheels, tighten all lug nuts and then loosen each nut two turns. Rock the car from side to side as hard as possible or start the engine and rock the car from drive to reverse, allowing car to move several feet each way before applying the brakes firmly. Never use heat to loosen tight wheels.
- Replace wheels if they are bent or dented, have excessive radial or lateral runout, leak air through welds, have elongated bolt holes, or are heavily rusted .
- Replace faulty wheels with new ones that are equivalent to original equipment wheels for load capacity, diameter, rim width, offset, and mounting configuration.
- Tighten wheel nuts in sequence, Figure 44-22. Make sure the nuts are tightened to the proper torque to avoid bending the wheel and the brake drum or rotor.
- Follow equipment manufacturer's instructions for checking wheel and tire assembly balance and alignment to ensure maximum tire life.

Improvements and Advances

Remarkable advances have been made in automobile tire design and construction over the past two decades. Tire manufacturers' research and development have led to the production of a wider range of tire sizes with much improved traction for starting, stopping, and cornering; greater durability; and less rolling resistance with the resulting reduction of tread wear and increased fuel economy.

According to a spokesperson for the Goodyear Tire & Rubber Company, proof of the impact of tire design on fuel mileage lies in the fact that tires have contributed 21% of the fuel economy improvement gained in automobiles since 1980.

Looking ahead, high technology computer techniques are creating the tire of the future. Computers are being used to design tread patterns and improve internal tire construction. Different tires for front and rear are being studied. Differences could be in size, width, construction, or tread patterns. A "thinking" or "sensor" tire is also being considered. It would receive data such as tire pressure, tread wear, spring rate, traction, and lateral friction coefficient, brake antiskid, leak and sealing rate, and tire alignment.

Chapter 44–Review Questions

1. Name the three major parts of a tubeless tire.
2. In tubeless tire construction, cord materials are laid _____ in layers.
3. The plies are arranged _____ in different combinations of layers and belts.
4. What are the three basic types of tire construction?
5. The ply rating of a tire is its index of tire _____.
6. Load range identifies a given tire size with its load and _____ when used in a specific type of service.
   (A) ply rating
   (B) inflation limits
   (C) tire construction
   (D) tire size
7. The U.S. Department of Transportation (DOT) has established Uniform Tire Quality Grading (UTQG) for passenger car tires. Tires are graded in all of the following areas except:
   (A) tread wear.
   (B) traction.
   (C) load range.
   (D) temperature resistance.
8. When tire tread groove depth is less than 1/16" (1.6 mm), the tread wear indicators will appear as solid strips across the tire. True or False?
9. What is "section height" of an inflated tire?
10. _____ is the ratio of tire section height to section width.
11. Most metric tire sizes exactly match corresponding alpha-numeric tire sizes. True or False?
12. Metric tires are available in two load ranges: standard load and _____ load.
    (A) extra
    (B) super
    (C) heavy
    (D) premium
13. A speed rating symbol is an additional sidewall marking on specially designed performance tires. The speed rating appears as the letter _____, _____, _____, _____, or _____.
14. A driver complained that front tires are wearing excessively at the center of the tread surface. Technician A says the wear problem is caused by underinflation. Technician B says the problem is caused by excessive camber. Who is right?
    (A) A only.
    (B) B only.
    (C) Both A & B.
    (D) Neither A nor B.
15. If the wheel and tire assembly is out-of-round, the first step is to determine whether the _____ problem is in the wheel or tire.
16. Generally, radial runout of a steel wheel should not exceed _____.
    (A) .030" (0.76 mm)
    (B) .035" (0.89 mm)
    (C) .040" (1.02 mm)
    (D) .045" (1.14 mm)

17. Radial and lateral runout limits of aluminum wheels are the same:
    (A) .030″ (0.76 mm).
    (B) .035″ (0.89 mm).
    (C) .040″ (1.02 mm).
    (D) .045″ (1.14 mm).
18. What is the purpose of the locating ring that is molded in the sidewall of the tire?
19. Are puncture holes in radial tires repairable?
20. Permanent tire repair includes all but one of the following methods. Which repair is an emergency only method?
    (A) Rubber rivet.
    (B) Cold patch.
    (C) Hot patch.
    (D) Head type plug.

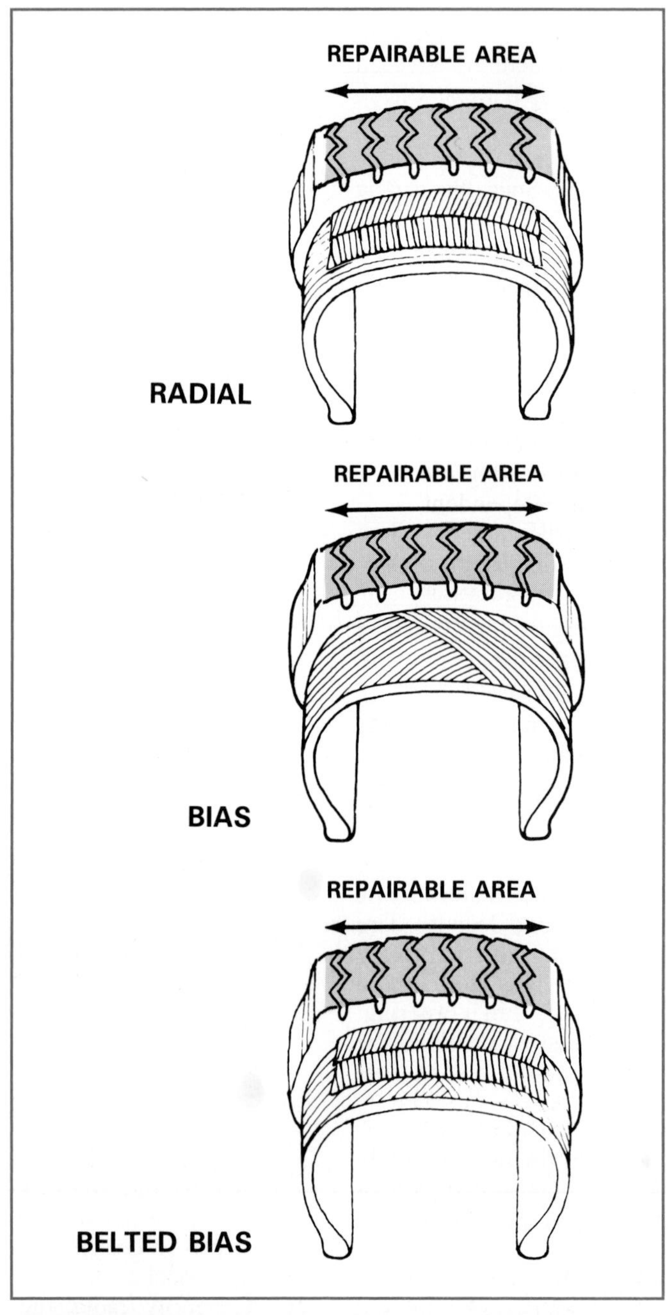

The Rubber Manufactures Association recommends that tubeless tire puncture repairs be made in the tread and shoulder areas only. Also, every tire must be removed from the wheel for inspection. All tread punctures, nail holes, or cuts up to 1/4″ must be repaired by industry-approved methods from inside the tire. (Rubber Manufactures Association)

Chapter 45
Wheel Alignment

After studying this chapter, you will be able to:

❍ Tell why four-wheel alignment is necessary.
❍ Explain how certain elements have an influence on tire-to-road contact.
❍ List preliminary steps required before wheel alignment angles are set.
❍ Identify and describe the angles involved in front wheel alignment.

Wheel Alignment

Aligning a vehicle's front wheels is the task of balancing the steering angles with the physical forces being exerted. The ***steering angles*** are caster, camber, toe-in, steering axis inclination, and toe-out on turns. The ***physical forces*** are gravity, momentum, friction, and centrifugal force.

Since so many factors are involved in front wheel alignment, it is also called front end alignment, steering alignment, steering balance, or steering geometry. Alignment, then, is more than adjusting the angularity of the front wheels. Today, with the steadily increasing production of front wheel drive vehicles with independent rear suspension, ***four-wheel alignment*** (quadralignment) usually is required. Therefore, in addition to aligning the front wheels, you also must consider and correct if necessary:

❍ Front and rear suspension, steering, and tire condition.
❍ Wheel bearing adjustment and wheel balance.
❍ Car weight balance.
❍ Wheelbase and tread width.
❍ Thrust line and rear-wheel track.
❍ Suspension height.
❍ Strut and shock absorber action.

Steering Balance

Steering control of a vehicle in motion is maintained by keeping the vehicle's tires in close contact with the road surface. ***Tire-to-road contact*** is influenced by the condition of the tire treads, tire inflation, wheel balance, weight on the wheels, shock absorber action, spring action, and wheel angularity. A balanced condition between these elements will establish a perfect pivot point from which the front wheels can rotate with the least friction. This point on the tread of each front tire is the target of all steering angle adjustments, Figure 45-1.

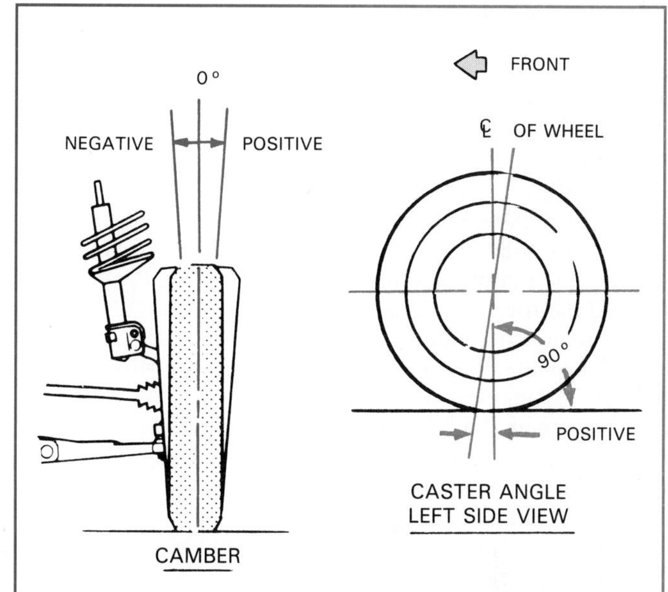

Figure 45-1. Exaggerated alignment angles show various settings of the front wheels that work together to provide smooth rolling, easy steering, and long tire life. (Buick)

The area of tire-to-road contact varies with tire inflation pressure and load, Figure 45-2. Underinflation or overinflation affects the rolling characteristics of the wheels by changing the degree of friction between the tires and the road surface. If one tire is underinflated, it will hold back, and the car will steer toward the side holding back. Anything that tends to increase the area of tire tread contact with the road will increase the rolling resistance, and the car will steer to that side.

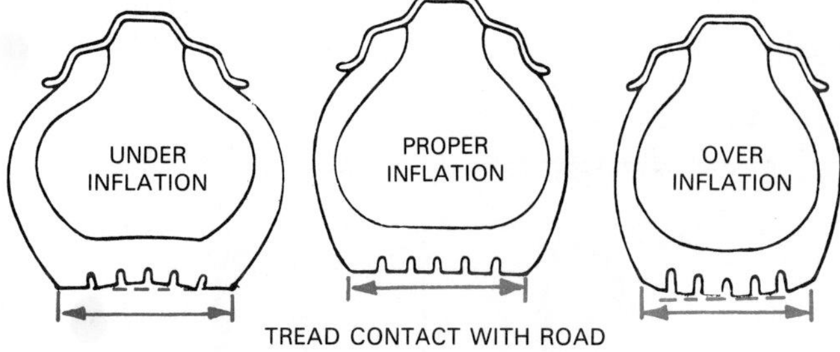

Figure 45-2. Tire wear is governed by tread contact with the road surface. Note the area of contact under the conditions of underinflation, proper inflation, and overinflation.

For satisfactory wheel alignment, certain conditions must be met. Ideally, both front tires will be the same brand, size, and type. Each will have the same degree of tread wear, and be inflated to the same pressure. Each will be carrying the same weight. Then, if each front wheel is properly and equally adjusted for angularity, each tire will maintain the same area of tread contact on a smooth road surface.

Obviously, though, it is impossible to maintain constant contact. The wheels bounce up and down at different times, at different rates of speed, and to varied heights. Here, the effects of momentum and inertia change the area of tread contact. Deflection of the car springs constantly changes the angles at which the steering system operates. Centrifugal force on the wheels emphasizes any lack of balance. Also, the extremely flexible characteristic of tires defeats the possibility of true and uniform steering geometry.

Wheel Balance and Unbalance

An important matter to be considered before alignment angles are set is checking to see that the wheel and tire assemblies are in ***balance.*** Basically, ***static balance*** is the equal distribution of weight around the wheel and tire assembly. ***Dynamic balance*** is the equal distribution of weight on each side of the vertical centerline of the wheel and tire assembly.

It follows, then, that ***unbalance*** (imbalance) exists when there is an unequal distribution of weight around the horizontal axis of the wheel and tire assembly. See Figure 45-3. The tires may be round and true when rotated slowly, yet give trouble on the road when they turn fast enough to get into the realm of centrifugal force. This unbalance can exist in the tire, wheel, brake drum or rotor, or hub. It may occur in any combination of these components.

When an unbalanced wheel revolves, centrifugal force acts on the heaviest portion and tends to lift the wheel off the road, then slam it down during each revolution. This results in flat spots on the tire tread and worn out ball joints, tie rod ends, steering gears, and shock absorbers.

If the unbalance lies in the plane of wheel rotation, it is known as static (or kinetic) unbalance, Figure 45-3. If it lies on either or both sides of the plane of rotation, it is dynamic unbalance. Either condition will cause the wheels to bounce. Dynamic unbalance in the front wheels will cause them to wobble as well. Rear wheels should be kept in balance to avoid a bouncing action, which could set up a heavy vibration in the chassis and affect steering balance.

Unbalance can be detected with the aid of special equipment, Figure 45-4, which usually indicates the proper location for wheel weights to restore balance. In spite of regular maintenance, however, uneven tire wear can result from drivers' habits as their modern automobiles accelerate faster, take curves at a higher rate of speed, and stop more quickly. To counteract uneven wear that leads to unbalance, the tire industry recommends that tires should be rotated every six to eight thousand miles. See Figure 45-5.

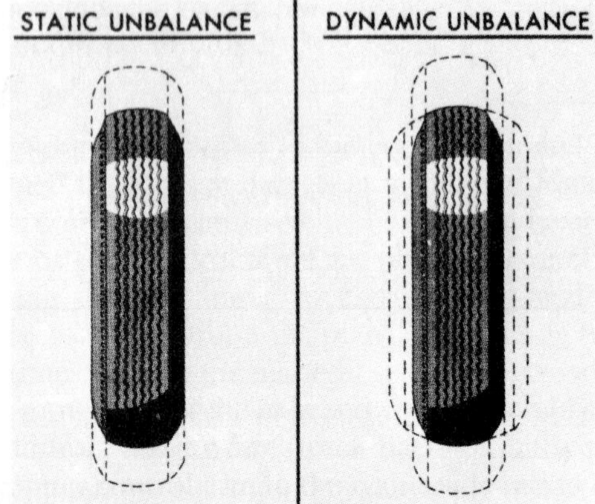

Figure 45-3. Static (kinetic) unbalance is the uneven distribution of weight in a tire assembly in the plane of rotation. Dynamic unbalance is the uneven distribution of weight to the right and left of the plane of rotation.

Figure 45-4. This computerized wheel balancer has a digital display that shows the amount of imbalance to 1/10th oz. (2.8 g) on the upper and lower planes. (Hunter Engineering Co.)

Car Weight Balance

Another preliminary step in balancing wheel alignment is to check the accuracy of attachment of the wheels

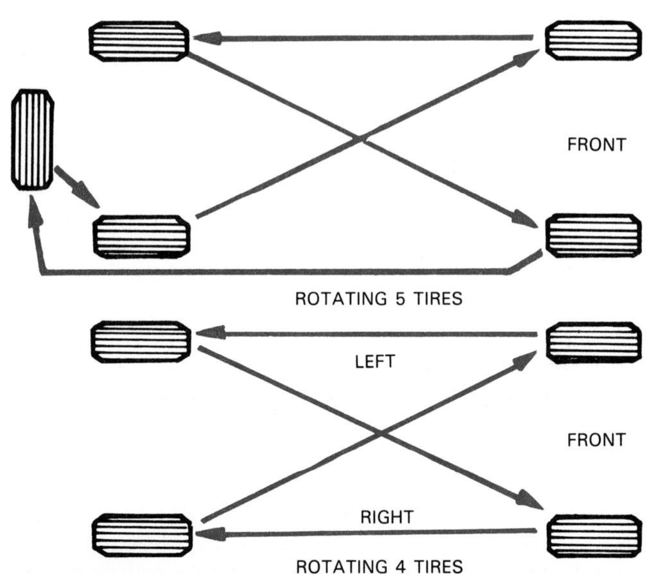

Figure 45-5. Planned tire rotation extends tire life. Tire industry approved patterns are shown for rotating bias, belted bias, and radial tires. (Chrysler)

to the vehicle. The frame or unitized body must be checked to see that it is square and level. The axles and wheels must be located properly in relation to the frame or body. This involves making a series of measurements to establish the parallel and right angle relationships between the frame and wheels.

The essential part of this car weight balance relationship is a straight, undistorted frame or unibody, Figure 45-6. First, an accurate centerline must be established. Then, if straight lines are drawn through the centers of both rear axles and both front spindle locations, they must be parallel to each other and form right angles with the centerline of the unibody or the frame, Figure 45-7.

Then, when the wheels are attached to the front spindles and rear axles, the rear wheels should be parallel to the centerline of the frame. Likewise, the front wheels in their straight ahead position should be parallel to this line (except for slight toe-in or toe-out). This is necessary so that each wheel will roll straight and true in relation to the frame centerline.

Wheelbase–Tread Width

Another point of importance when locating axles and spindles is the wheelbase measurement. ***Wheelbase*** is the distance between the center of the front wheel and center of the rear wheel, Figure 45-8. This distance (left front to left rear, right front to right rear with front wheels in "straight ahead" position) must be exactly the same on each side for proper weight balance. Correct wheelbase also contributes to the ability of the car's rear wheels to ***track*** (follow directly in line with front wheels).

Tread width is also a key measurement with respect to weight balance and rear-wheel track. ***Tread width*** is the distance between the center points of the left tire tread and right tire tread as they come in contact with the road. See Figure 45-9. While the front and rear wheels may have different tread widths, each front wheel must be the same distance from the centerline of the frame, and each rear wheel must be the same distance from this centerline.

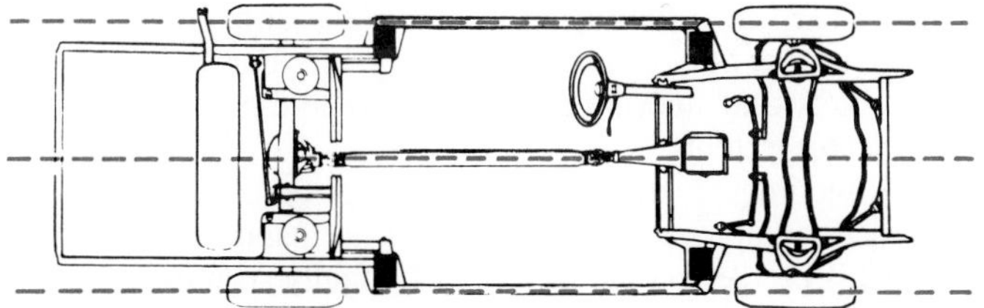

Figure 45-6. Before making alignment checks, see that the vehicle's frame is straight, square, and level. Side rails must be parallel to the centerline of the frame or unibody.

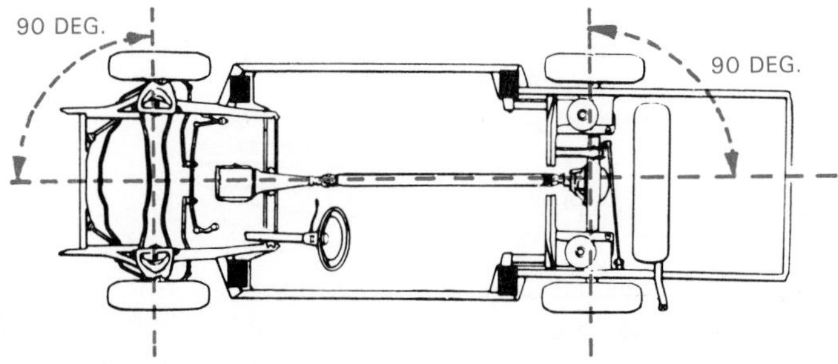

Figure 45-7. Straight lines drawn through the centers of the rear axle and the front spindle locations must be parallel and form right angles with the centerline of the frame or unibody.

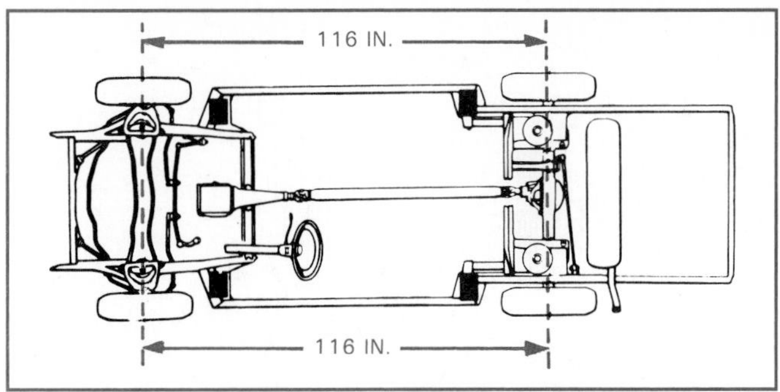

Figure 45-8. The wheelbase, or the distance between the centers of the front and rear wheels, must measure as specified by the manufacturer and be exactly equal on each side.

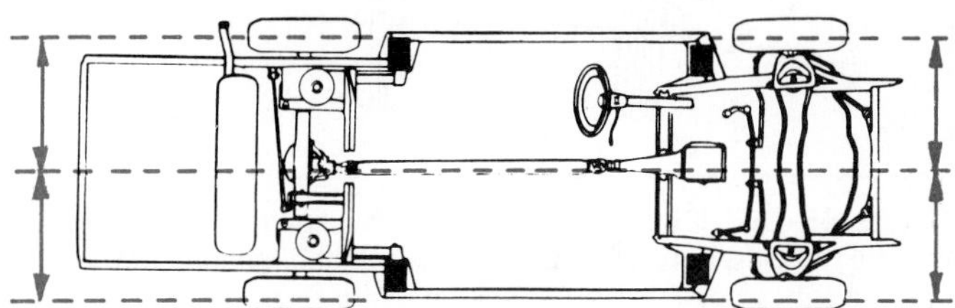

Figure 45-9. Tread width is the distance between the center points of the left tire tread and the right tire tread. Note that the measurements are the total taken from the frame centerline to the center of each tire to establish the correct frame-to-wheels relationship, left to right.

This parallel relationship between the frame centerline and wheels establishes a balance between front and rear, and between right and left. While this balance may not mean equal weight at these points, it does mean that a balanced distribution of weight and stress has been acquired for the proper setting of front wheel angles.

Rear-wheel Track

As previously pointed out, the growing popularity of front wheel drive and four-wheel drive vehicles has sharply increased the need for correct alignment of all four wheels. In fact, some designs require camber and toe-in adjustments on all four wheels.

The four-wheel alignment (quadralignment) procedure is required so that correct rear-wheel track is established. Remember, the front wheels steer the vehicle, but the rear wheels direct it. The rear wheels determine the ***thrust line,*** Figure 45-10, which in effect is the ***rear rolling direction.*** When the thrust line is made to agree with the vehicle frame's centerline (by aligning front and rear wheels and centering the steering wheel), correct rear-wheel track will be achieved. See Figure 45-11.

See Chapter 46 for details on making four-wheel alignment checks and adjustments on a variety of vehicle makes and models.

If the car has been damaged in an accident, the impact may have forced the frame into a diamond shape, changing the relationship between the thrust line and the frame centerline. An out-of-line condition not caused by an accident usually can be traced to a mechanical defect or sag due to

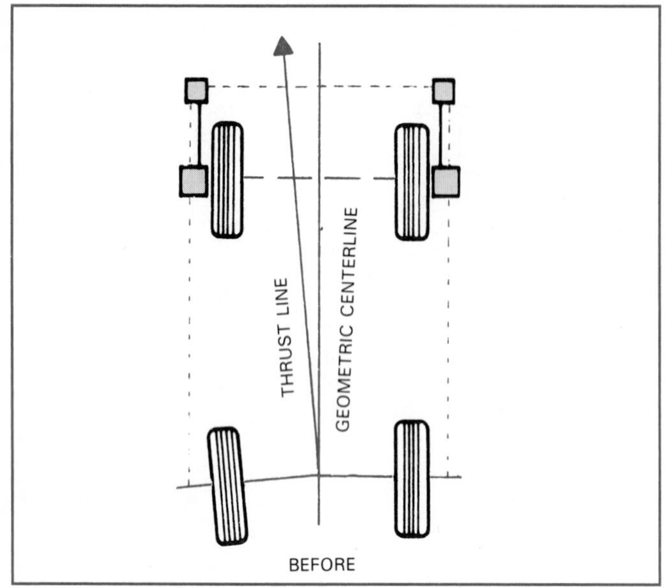

Figure 45-10. If the rear wheels are misaligned, the front wheels must be turned to maintain a straight direction of travel and the rear wheels will not "track." (Hunter Engineering Co.)

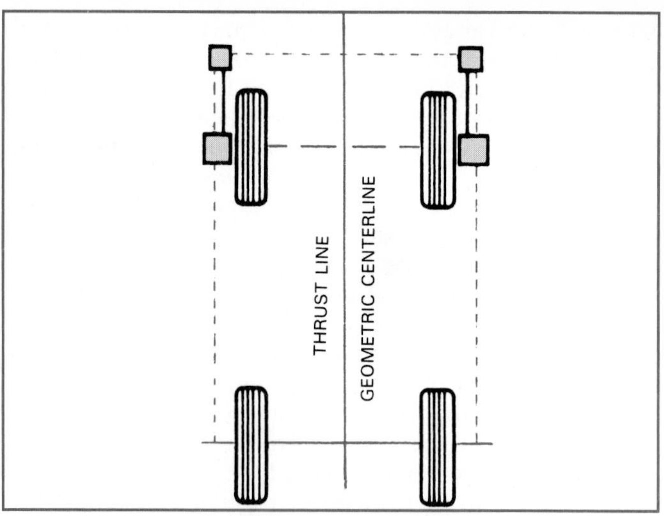

Figure 45-11. If the rear wheels are realigned so that the thrust line and the frame centerline agree, the rear wheels will "track" with the front wheels. (Hunter Engineering Co.)

stress in the middle or corner of the frame. In any case, a frame that is out of line must be straightened before it is possible to obtain correct steering alignment. The frame rails must be the same height from the floor on each side at the spring seats, along with the essential parallel and right angle relationships.

Springs

Also vital in this matter of weight balance is the condition of the car springs. They control the up-and-down motion of the car and, therefore, the heights of the car above the road. If one or more of the springs is collapsed or broken, it causes an unbalanced distribution of weight. This unbalance creates a lopsided appearance, puts an added strain on related parts, and changes the angularity of the front wheels.

This condition also may occur when the load is distributed unequally. In fact, anything that changes the ratio of weight on the springs will have a definite bearing on the alignment angles and on the area of tire-to-road contact.

Suspension Height

The heights of the car above the road must be checked (front and rear, right and left) before any steering angles are adjusted, Figure 45-12. Although the method of checking varies with type of suspension, the measurements should be made with the car parked on a level floor with the tires equally inflated, fuel tank full, no passenger load, and no excess weight on either side.

Shock Absorber Action

The shock absorbers are still another factor involved in controlling the up-and-down motion of a moving vehicle. Efficient shock absorber action aids wheel alignment by furnishing a dampening effect that protects the springs from sudden overloading or unloading action. If the shock absorbers are not operating properly, the car will bounce excessively and steering angles will change more often and to a greater extent.

Sometimes steering angles will check out correctly on the alignment equipment, yet the car will not handle well on the road. This problem could be caused by faulty springs or shock

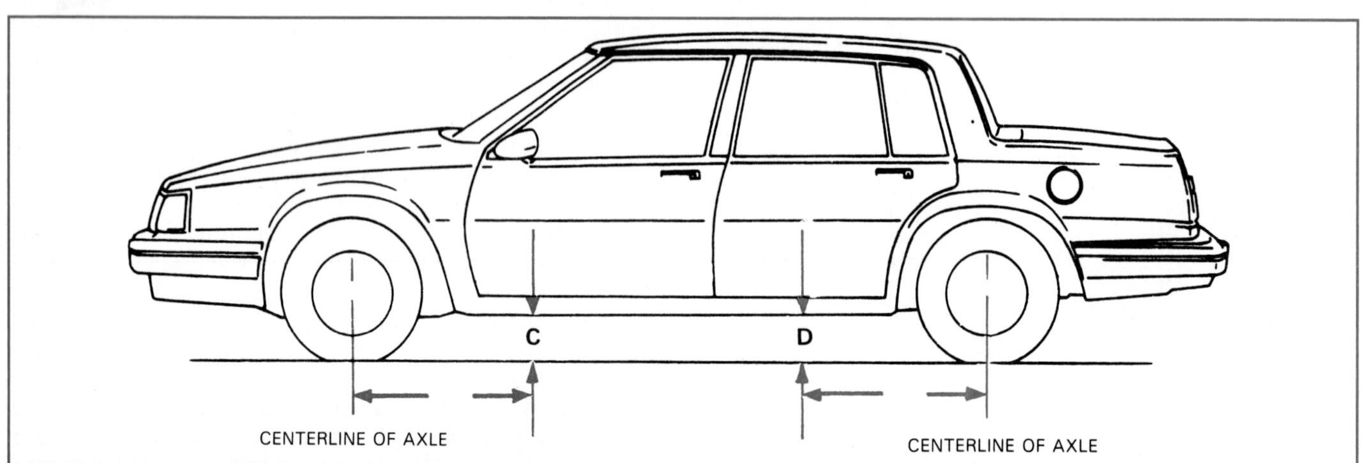

Figure 45-12. Frame height on this vehicle is determined by measuring the heights at C and D at specified distances A and B from the centerlines of the axles. (Buick)

absorbers, worn parts in the steering gear or front suspension system, driving conditions, or habits of the driver.

One other chassis control feature that merits consideration is the use of ***stabilizers*** or ***sway bars.*** See Figure 45-13. Some cars require stabilizers to steady the chassis against front end roll and sway on turns. Stabilizers are designed to control this centrifugal tendency that forces a rising action on the side toward the inside of the turn.

With all of these weight balance factors to be checked out and corrected, it is obvious that wheel alignment is more than just an adjustment of the steering angles. The whole theory of wheel alignment revolves around balanced weight distribution on the wheels and proper tire tread contact with the road surface while the vehicle is in motion.

Front-wheel Angularity

The angles involved in front wheel alignment are caster, camber, toe-in, steering axis inclination, and toe-out on turns. They refer to the tilt of the wheels and steering axis, Figures 45-14 through 45-19. These angles govern the way the front wheels behave while the vehicle is in motion.

Actually, the alignment angles are so closely related that changing one will often change the others. In order to check and adjust them properly, it is necessary to use special equipment capable of a high degree of accuracy. In many cases, caster and camber specifications are given in minutes (fractions of a degree).

Here again, balance enters the picture. The adjustment goal becomes a balanced relationship of the steering angles, with due regard for road and load factors involved in each individual case.

Caster

Caster is the steering angle that utilizes the weight and momentum of the car's chassis to lead the front wheels in a straight path. See Figures 45-1 and 45-14. ***Caster*** is the backward or forward tilt of the steering axis that tends to stabilize steering in a straight direction. It places the weight of the vehicle either ahead or behind the area of tire-to-road contact.

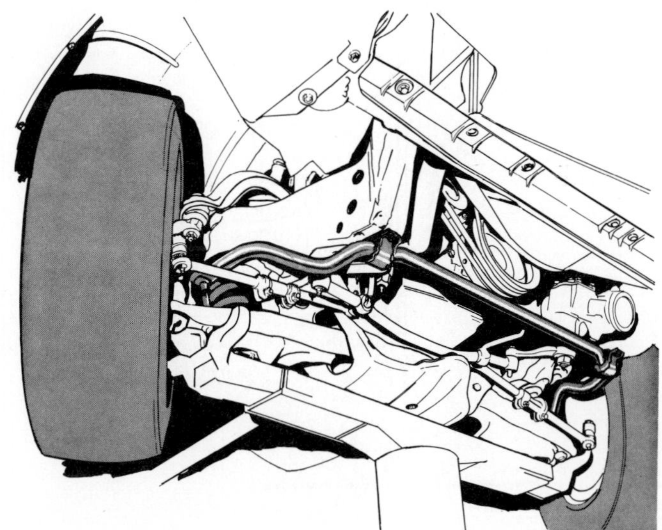

Figure 45-13. Stabilizers provide added support for the front suspension members. This 1 1/8" (28.6 mm) stabilizer is part of a "handling package" offered by one car manufacturer. (Pontiac)

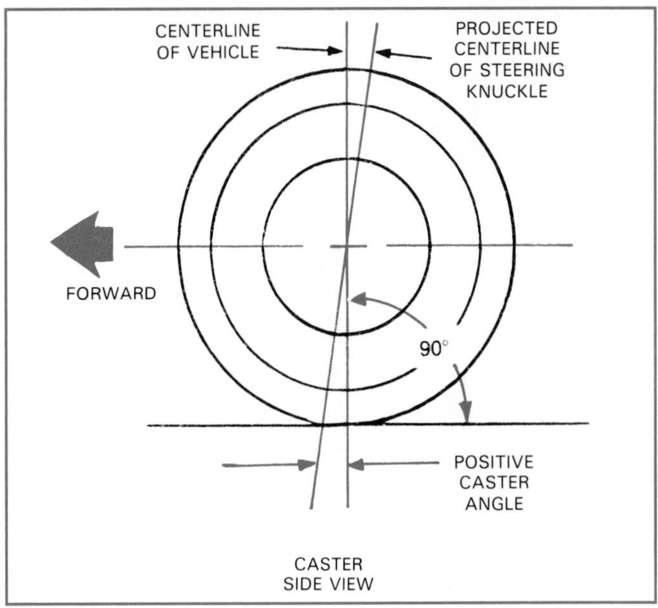

Figure 45-14. Caster is the degree of tilt of the steering axis forward or backward from the vertical centerline of the wheel. (Chrysler)

It would be easier to visualize the effect of the caster angle by projecting an imaginary line lengthwise through the center of the ball joints and downward to the road surface. This line, called the "steering axis," would be found to intersect the road at a point ahead of or in back of the center point of tire-to-road contact. Considering this, if the front wheels were given a generous amount of caster, they would be subjected to a leading or trailing action like a furniture caster that tends to line up and drag its wheel in the direction of movement.

Positive caster is the angular amount that the upper ball joint is farther back than the lower joint, Figure 45-14. ***Negative caster*** is the condition when the upper ball joint is farther ahead than the lower one. The ***caster angle,*** then, is the number of degrees (or fraction of one degree) that the steering axis is tilted backward or forward from the vertical axis of the front wheels.

Camber–Steering Axis Inclination

Camber is the inward or outward tilt of the wheel at the top, Figure 45-15. It is built into the wheel spindle by forming the spindle with a downward tilt to provide positive camber. ***Steering axis inclination*** is the inward tilt of the steering knuckle, Figure 45-16. It is so interrelated with camber that they share a common side (vertical axis of wheel). The combination of these two angles forms what is known as the ***included angle.***

The purpose of this two-angle team is to place the turning point of the wheel at the center of the tire tread contact area. Originally, the front wheels were pivoted to swing in a vertical position. This difference between the pivoting centerline and the wheel centerline caused the wheels to pull or scuff on rough roads. The car manufacturers solved this problem by tilting the pivoting centerline in at the top (steering axis inclination) and tilting the wheel out at the top (camber). This created an included angle that intersected close to the center of the tire tread contact and reduced the scuff area to a minimum.

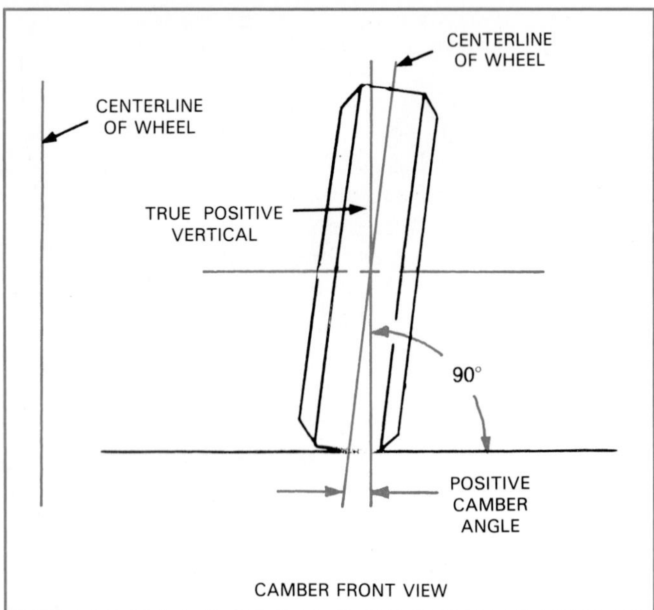

Figure 45-15. Camber is the amount that the top of a wheel is tilted in or out from its vertical centerline. (Chrysler)

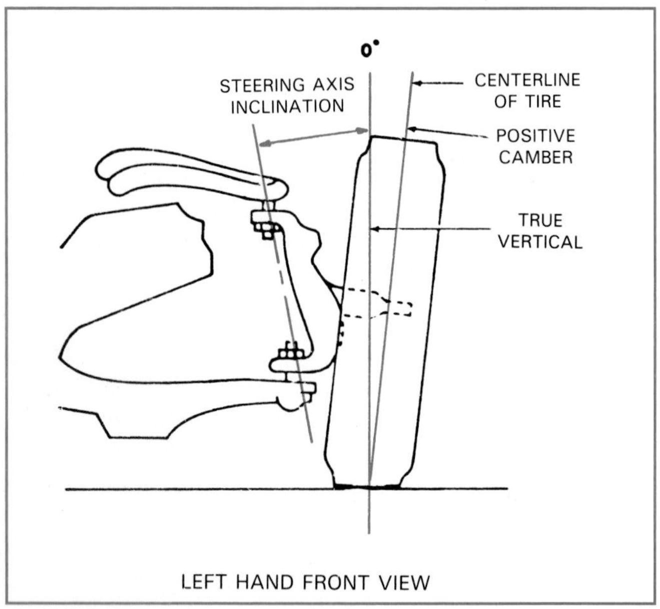

Figure 45-16. Steering axis inclination is the inward tilt of the steering knuckle from the vertical centerline of the wheel. (Oldsmobile)

When camber and steering axis inclination are correct, they contribute to steering ease and extended tire life. Also, by placing the tread contact area more nearly under the point of load, a "straightening up" tendency is provided.

With the steering axis tilted inward (steering axis inclination), the end of the spindle will describe an arc that is noticeably lower in the extreme turn position than in the center or straight ahead position. In normal operation, the weight of the car prevents the spindle from moving up and down. Therefore, the car is forced upward when the front wheels are turned, and the force of gravity tends to straighten the wheels.

In this way, the weight of the car helps to provide an automatic steering effect brought about by accurate adjustment of the steering angles. Additional alignment benefits become apparent when some of the troubles caused by misalignment are noted. These include hard steering, wander, pull to one side, and unequal or excessive tire wear.

Also in the area of steering axis inclination, car manufacturers have come up with negative kingpin offset, a modification of MacPherson strut design. ***Negative kingpin offset*** refers to the fact that the steering axis of each front wheel is offset so that an imaginary line drawn along the axis would strike the ground outside the centerline of the tire, Figure 45-17.

Most cars have a front end setup in which the steering axis is closer to vertical. In conventional design, a line drawn along the steering axis would strike the ground inside the centerline of the tire. Both designs, conventional and negative kingpin offset, provide easy steering.

However, the side benefit of negative kingpin offset is a self-centering effect. Under uneven braking or rough road conditions, or if one front tire goes flat, a car with conventional geometry would pull toward the side with more resistance. With negative kingpin offset, the wheel encountering more resistance automatically turns toward the straight ahead path.

Toe-in

Equally important with respect to steering ease is the correct setting of toe-in. ***Toe-in*** is the term used to specify

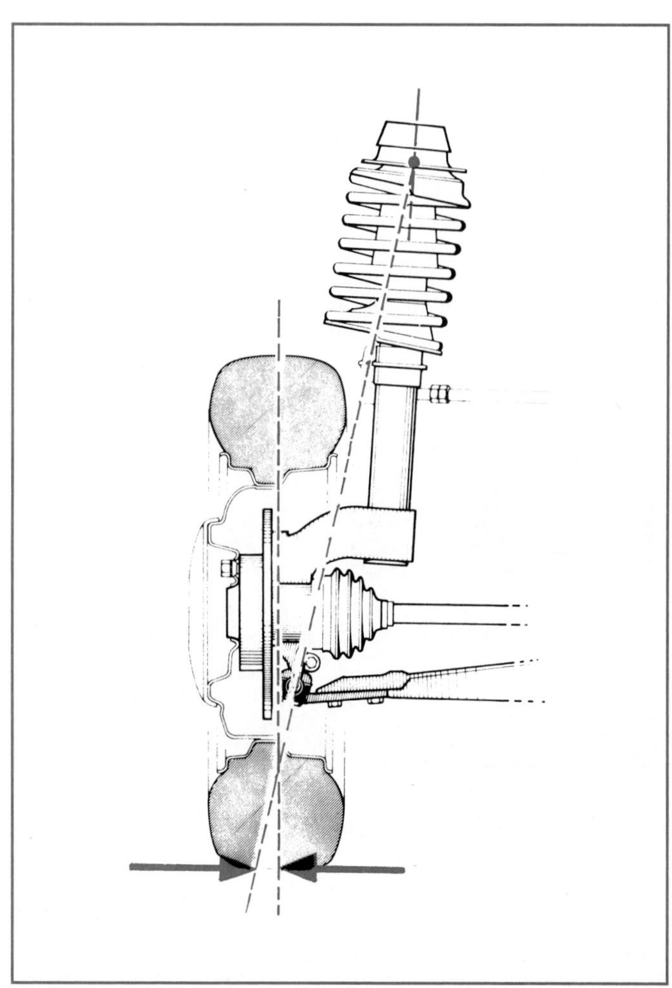

Figure 45-17. A negative kingpin offset gives small car steering a self-centering effect. (Volkswagen)

the amount (in fractions of an inch) the front wheels are closer together in front than at the rear, when measured at hub height, Figure 45-18. Here again, precision testing equipment and careful measurement and correction will prevent any slipping or scuffing action between the tires and road. See Figure 45-19.

Actually, the slight amount of toe-in specified serves to keep the front wheels running parallel on the road by offsetting other forces which tend to spread the wheels apart. The major force is the backward thrust of the road against the tire tread while the car is moving forward. Other factors include compensation for unavoidable play in the tie rod assembly, and allowance for angular changes caused by wheel bounce or variations in road conditions.

If toe-in is incorrect, the tires will be dragged along the road, scuffing and featheredging the tread ribs. Changes in road or load conditions will affect more than one steering angle, and uneven tread wear patterns will result. Also in this respect, toe-in will change when other angular adjustments are made. For this reason, front wheel toe-in should be measured first and corrected last on all wheel alignment jobs.

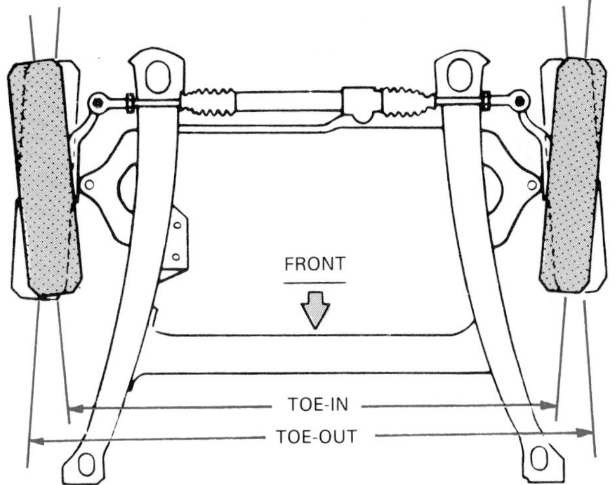

Figure 45-18. Toe-in is the amount that the front wheels are closer together in the front than at the rear at hub height. (Buick)

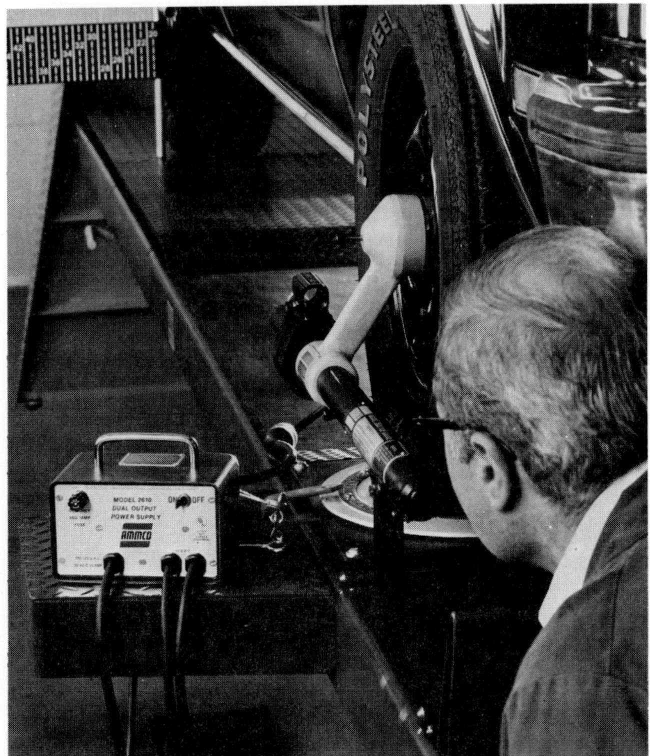

Figure 45-19. All four wheels must be centered and "tracking" before wheel alignment correction. This technician is sighting through the scope of a wheel tracking and toe gauge to check tracking. (Ammco Tools, Inc.)

Toe-out on Turns

It is obvious that driving conditions make it impossible to keep the front wheels parallel at all times. Regardless of how accurately the front wheels are positioned for straight ahead driving, they could be out of their correct relative positions on turns. From the mechanical standpoint, the parallel relationship between the front wheels is controlled by the tie rod (rods) and the angularity of the steering arms, Figure 45-20. Considering that the outside wheel is approximately five feet farther away from the point about which the car is turning, it must turn at a lesser angle and travel in a greater circle than the inside wheel. See Figure 45-21. This condition is called ***toe-out on turns,*** which means that each front wheel requires a separate turning radius to keep the inside tire from slipping and scuffing on turns.

Toe-out on turns, then, is the relationship between the front wheels which allows them to turn about a common center. To accomplish this, the steering arms are designed to angle several degrees inside of the parallel position, Figure 45-22. The exact amount depends on the tread and wheelbase of the car and on the arrangement of the steering control linkage.

The theory of this design is that an imaginary line drawn through each steering arm will intersect near the differential. In practice, this serves to speed the action of the steering arm on the inside of the turn as it moves toward the centerline of the wheel spindle. The effect on the outside steering arm is to slow it down as it moves away from the center of the wheel spindle. Therefore, the outside wheel turns at a lesser angle, and its turning circle is greater. True rolling contact is obtained.

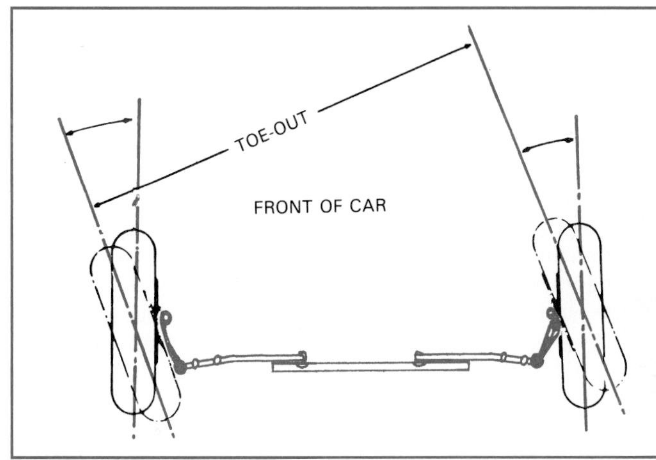

Figure 45-20. Tie rods and steering arms control the parallel relationship between the front wheels.

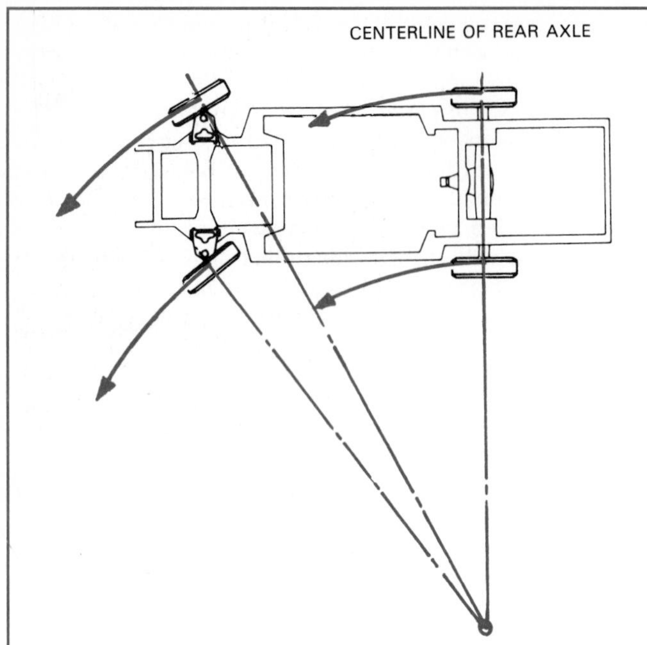

Figure 45-21. Toe-out on turns is the angular relationship between the front wheels when they are turned to the right or left. (Ford)

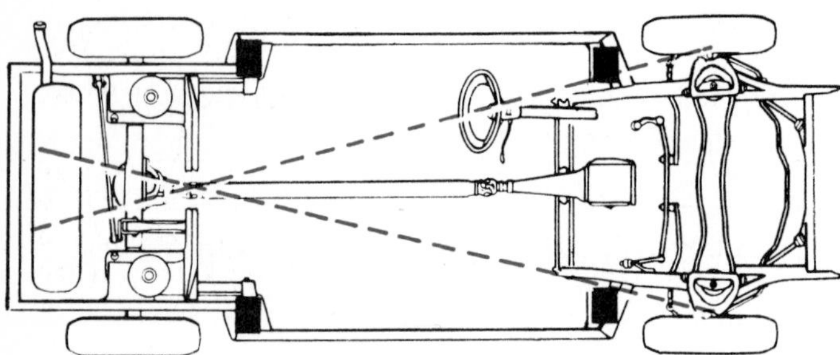

Figure 45-22. Steering arms are angled inward to provide a separate turning radius for each front wheel.

Chapter 45–Review Questions

Write your answers on a separate sheet of paper. Do not write in this book.

1. Name the five steering angles.
2. The physical forces being exerted on the front wheels when the vehicle is in motion are gravity, momentum, friction, and _____.
3. Name five things that influence tire tread contact with the road surface.
4. The area of tire-to-road contact varies with _____ and load.
5. The extremely flexible characteristics of modern tires defeats the possibility of true and uniform steering geometry. True or False?
6. What is static balance of a wheel and tire assembly?
7. What is dynamic balance of a wheel and tire assembly?
8. Unbalance can exist in all but one of the following components:
   (A) Wheel and tire assembly.
   (B) Brake drum or rotor.
   (C) Hub.
   (D) Spindle.
9. What is the correct terminology for the distance between the center of the front wheel and the center of the rear wheel?
   (A) Wheelbase.
   (B) Tread width.
   (C) Toe-in.
   (D) Steering axis inclination.
10. What is the correct terminology for the distance between the center points of the left tire tread and the right tire tread as they come in contact with the road?
    (A) Wheelbase.
    (B) Tread width.
    (C) Toe-in.
    (D) Steering axis inclination.
11. Four-wheel alignment is required so that correct _____ is established.
12. The rear wheels determine the _____, which in effect is the rear rolling direction.
13. _____ is the backward or forward tilt of the steering axis.
    (A) Caster
    (B) Camber
    (C) Toe-in
    (D) Steering axis inclination
14. If the upper ball joint is farther back than the lower ball joint, what angularity is the wheel said to have?
    (A) Positive caster.
    (B) Positive camber.
    (C) Positive steering axis inclination.
    (D) Negative steering axis inclination.
15. _____ is the inward or outward tilt of the wheel at the top.
    (A) Caster
    (B) Camber
    (C) Toe-in
    (D) Steering axis inclination
16. _____ is the inward tilt of the steering knuckle.
17. Which two steering angles make up the included angle?
    (A) Caster and camber.
    (B) Caster and steering axis inclination.
    (C) Camber and steering axis inclination.
    (D) Camber and toe-in.
18. What is the purpose of the included angle?
    (A) To reduce the tire scuff area to a minimum.
    (B) To contribute to steering ease and extend tire life.
    (C) To provide a "straightening up" tendency.
    (D) All of the above.
19. _____ of the front wheels should be measured first and corrected last on alignment jobs.
20. When a vehicle is turning, should the front wheels toe in or toe out?

Chapter 46
Wheel Alignment Correction

After studying this chapter, you will be able to:
- ❍ Define the six front wheel alignment angles and list the order in which they should be checked.
- ❍ List preliminary steps that are necessary before making measurements of caster, camber, and toe-in.
- ❍ Give examples of typical front wheel caster and camber adjustment methods on both rear-wheel drive and front-wheel drive cars.
- ❍ Describe how various front wheel toe-in adjustments are made.
- ❍ Explain the importance of "rear wheel tracking."
- ❍ Give examples of typical rear wheel camber and toe-in checks and adjustments.

Wheel Alignment Correction

Wheel alignment correction calls for a careful determination of whether or not the problem lies in misalignment, steering, suspension, or in the wheel and tire assemblies. A good alignment specialist must be able to visualize the behavior of a loaded vehicle going at high speed on the highway, while making corrective adjustments on an empty car standing on floating turntables on an alignment rack.

A thorough understanding of the principles involved and enough imagination to visualize actual operating conditions are absolutely essential in this specialized field. In addition, the service technician must have and know how to use equipment of outstanding accuracy.

As for the vehicles themselves, the need for frequent and regular wheel alignment checks has increased with technological advances. Power steering, softer springing, rubber-bushed suspension parts, more moving parts, and the use of low profile tires allow constant abuse of car suspension without forewarning the driver.

With this set of circumstances in mind, most manufacturers recommend wheel alignment checks at least once a year. Or, for another rule-of-thumb, wheel alignment should be checked at the first sign of uneven tread wear.

Rear-wheel Drive/Front-wheel Drive Alignment

In reality, front wheel alignment service procedures on the familiar engine-in-front/rear-wheel drive cars has changed very little over the years. The checking and adjusting methods have remained basically the same.

However, with today's engineering and production emphasis on front-wheel drive cars, front and rear wheel alignment procedures were found to be necessary. For example, some of these front-wheel drive cars are prone to problems in the area of "tracking." It is not unusual to find that the rear axle has shifted and the rear wheels do not track (follow directly in line with) the front wheels when the steering wheel is in the straight-ahead position.

Consider Interrelated Angles

Remember, front wheel alignment correction includes adjustment of all interrelated factors affecting the running and steering of the vehicle. Changing one angle will often change others, Figure 46-1, so it is necessary to recheck all angles when one is changed.

The method of wheel alignment inspection and detection varies with type of equipment but, generally, the angles should be checked in the following order:

1. Front suspension height.

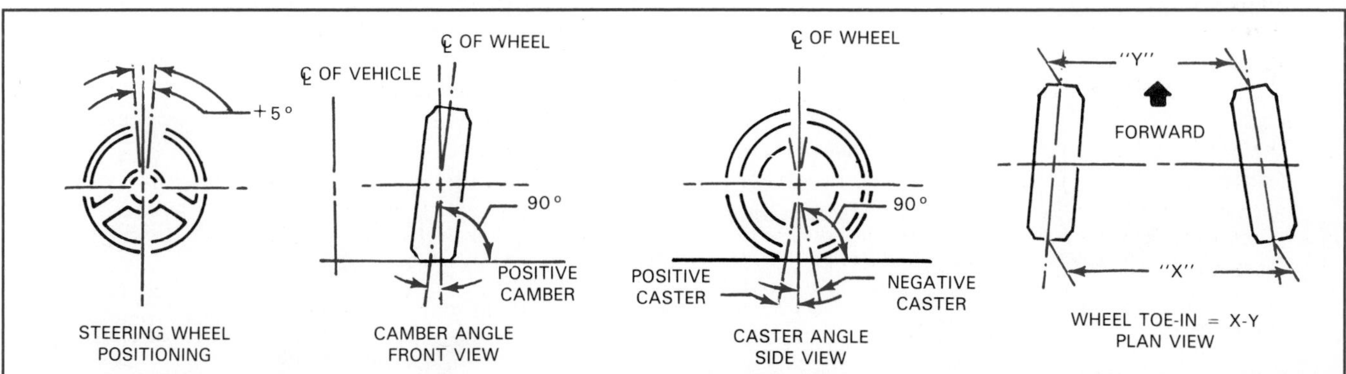

Figure 46-1. The interrelation of alignment angles is shown in these views of centered steering wheel and camber, caster, and toe-in angularity. (Chevrolet)

2. Caster.
3. Camber.
4. Toe-in.
5. Steering axis inclination.
6. Toe-out on turns.

Preliminary Checks

Regardless of design of the suspension systems and the wheel alignment geometry, car manufacturers state that certain preliminary steps are necessary before making any measurements of caster, camber, and toe-in.

Ordinarily, cars should be checked for alignment at "curb height" or "trim height" and "curb weight." (Certain manufacturers specify use of alignment spacers to ensure proper suspension heights.) Curb weight means the basic automobile, less passengers, with a full fuel tank and proper amounts of coolant and lubricants. The spare tire and wheel, jack and jack handle must be in design position, and the front seats should be in their rear-most position.

Then proceed as follows:

1. Place the car on an alignment rack or level floor.
2. Check the air pressure in all four tires. Inflate the tires to the manufacturer's specifications.
3. See that tire tread wear is approximately the same and not abnormal, Figure 46-2. Remove stones and caked mud from the wheels and tires.
4. Check the wheel lugs for looseness and/or improper installation.
5. Test the action and rebound of the shock absorbers by jouncing the car an equal number of times from the center of the bumpers. Jounce alternately at the rear, then the front, releasing at the bottom of the stroke. The car should rebound slowly and should not bounce.
6. Test the steering effort and steering wheel return from both directions. Check for inconsistent effort, harshness, noise, binding, or excessive free play. Check the steering gear for excessive backlash and for "high point," with reference to the steering wheel position and the straight ahead position of the front wheels. Adjust the steering gear, if required.
7. Raise the vehicle and test the front wheel bearings for looseness. Grasp the tire at the top and bottom and try to rock the assembly on its spindle. Adjust the bearings, if necessary, Figure 46-3.
8. Use a dial indicator to check each front wheel and tire assembly for runout, Figure 46-4, making sure that the wheel is not damaged and the tire beads are seated in the rim of the wheel. Mark the point of maximum runout on the tire sidewall, Figure 46-5, then spin each front wheel and balance as required.
9. Check the front end parts for looseness or wear. Inspect the control arm pivot shafts or bolts, suspension ball joints, struts, stabilizer, and all mounting bolts

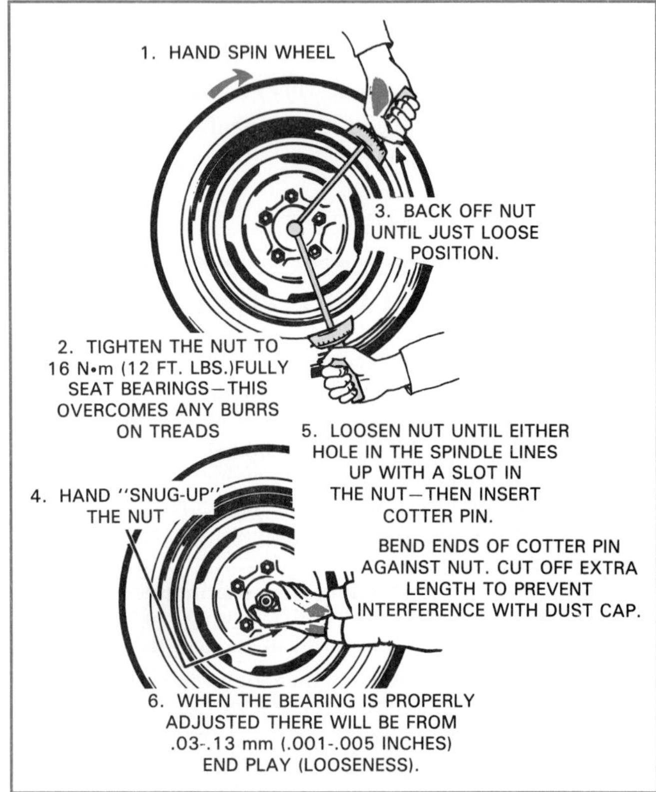

Figure 46-3. A typical front wheel bearing adjusting procedure is pictured and described. (Chevrolet)

	RAPID WEAR AT SHOULDERS	RAPID WEAR AT CENTER	CRACKED TREADS	WEAR ON ONE SIDE	FEATHERED EDGE	BALD SPOTS	SCALLOPED WEAR
CONDITION	1. 2.						
CAUSE	UNDERINFLATION OR LACK OF ROTATION	OVERINFLATION OR LACK OF ROTATION	UNDERINFLATION OR EXCESSIVE SPEED	EXCESSIVE CAMBER	INCORRECT TOE	UNBALANCED WHEEL OR TIRE DEFECT	LACK OF ROTATION OF TIRES OR WORN OR OUT-OF-ALIGNMENT SUSPENSION
CORRECTION	ADJUST PRESSURE TO SPECIFICATIONS WHEN TIRES ARE COOL ROTATE TIRES			ADJUST CAMBER TO SPECIFICATIONS	ADJUST TOE-IN TO SPECIFICATIONS	DYNAMIC OR STATIC BALANCE WHEELS	ROTATE TIRES AND CHECK ALIGNMENT

Figure 46-2. The condition, cause, and correction of various types of abnormal tire wear are pictured in this troubleshooting chart. (Chrysler)

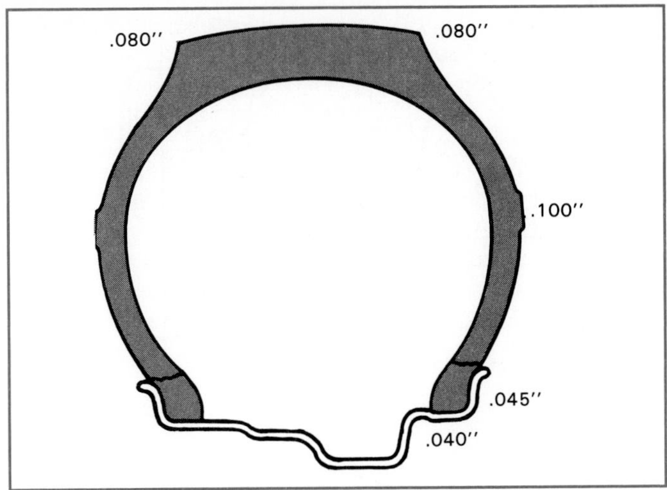

Figure 46-4. Steel wheel and radial tire runout specifications are shown. (Chevrolet)

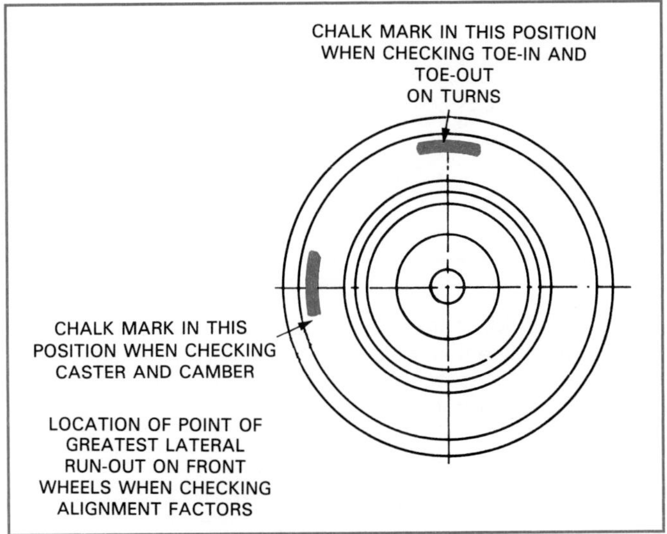

Figure 46-5. Mark the point of maximum lateral runout on the front tire sidewall. Place a mark to the front for caster/camber checks and at the top for toe-in and toe-out on turns. (Ford)

and nuts. Visually check the condition of the suspension ball joints and seals.

10. Inspect all springs for sagging or breakage. Check for looseness of the brake caliper attaching bolts.
11. Test for looseness of the steering gear attaching bolts at the frame. Manually check for looseness or wear at all steering pivot points: pitman arm, relay rod, tie rod ends, and idler arm. See Figure 46-6. Inspect for bent steering arms.

Setting Up the Car

Lower the car and drive it far enough in a straight line to establish the straight ahead position of the front wheels. Then, mark the steering wheel hub and steering column collar for use as a reference point during the alignment procedure, Figure 46-7.

At this time, rear wheel track can be checked by running the car in and out of a wet area and examining the tread marks left by the front and rear tires. Since front and rear tread widths are seldom the same, the marks may not coincide. However, there should be equal spacing between marks left by the left front and rear tires and the right front and rear tires. See Figure 46-8.

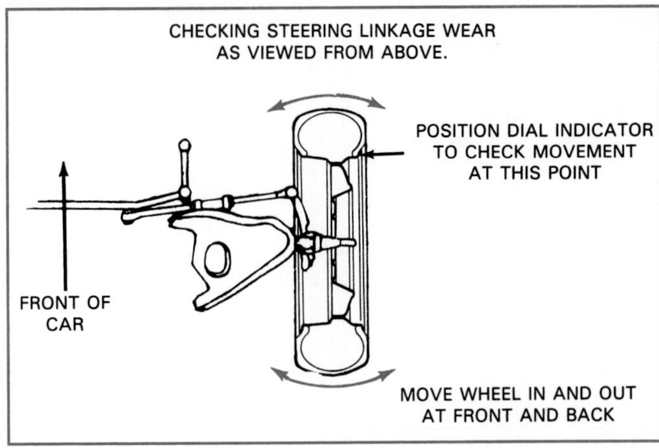

Figure 46-6. The points of greatest wear in this steering linkage setup include the tie rod ends, idler arm bushings, and relay rod to tie rod connections. (Oldsmobile)

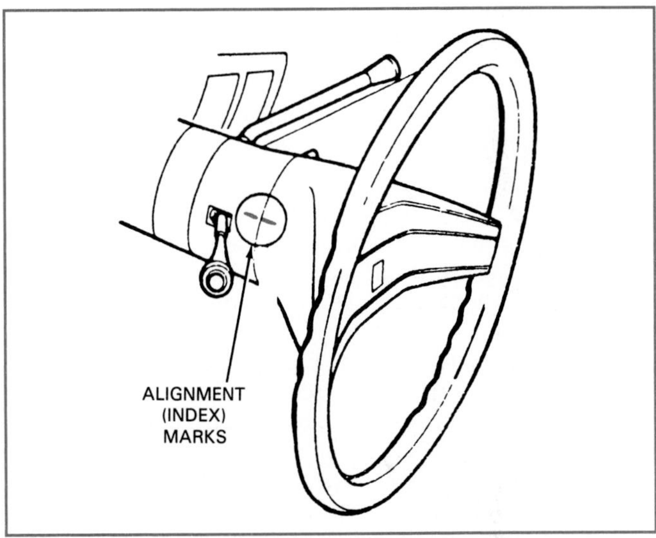

Figure 46-7. Mark the straight ahead position of the front wheels on the steering wheel hub and the steering column collar for future reference when making alignment checks.

Measuring Suspension Height

To prepare the car for a suspension height check, jounce it lightly front and rear until suspension parts equalize. If excessive friction in the suspension system is suspected, make two quick checks of bumper height and compare the difference. First lift the car manually by the bumper and let it settle slowly to normal standing height. Measure from the center of the bumper to the floor. Then push down on the bumper and release it slowly. Take this measurement and compare it with the first. If the two height measurements are not within one inch of each other, excessive suspension system friction exists.

If the above checks are within the limit, jounce the car lightly and measure front suspension height at the points specified by the car manufacturer. Then, compare the measurements with specifications. If the suspension height

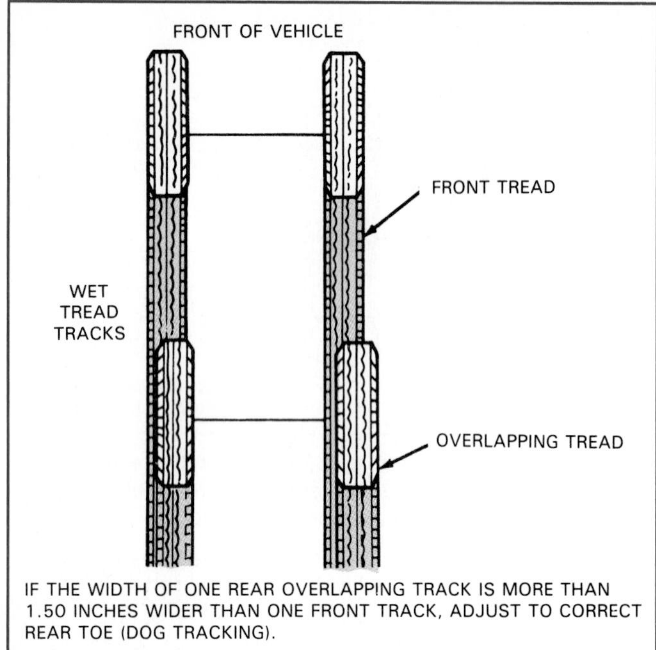

Figure 46-8. To check "rear wheel track," run the vehicle straight through a wet area, then examine the tread marks. (Ford)

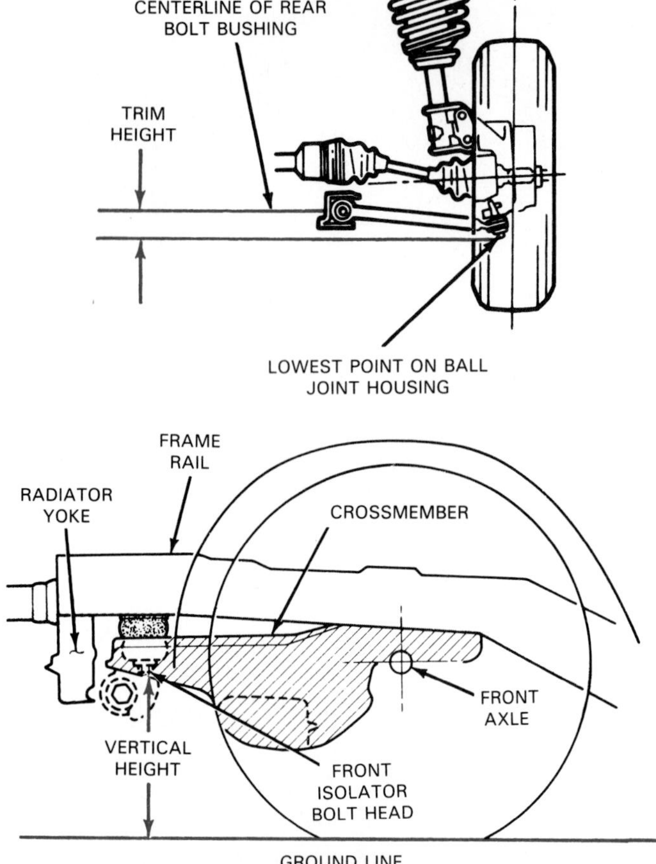

Figure 46-9. Measure and compare front suspension trim height, left and right, to help guarantee accuracy of the angular checks that follow. Top–Cadillac front-wheel drive. Bottom–Chrysler front-wheel drive.

is below minimum requirements on cars with coil springs, replace both springs. If one side is within specifications and the other side is not, replace the weak spring. In cars equipped with torsion bars, make the necessary adjustments to obtain correct front suspension height, Figure 46-9.

If alignment spacers are required for making certain angular checks: place car on floating turntables; raise car body and install spacers front and rear; lower car body. Generally, spacers in front are placed between suspension lower control arms and frame spring pockets. At rear, install spacers between the rear axle housing and frame.

Checking and Setting Caster

Caster is the angle measured between a true vertical line through the center of the wheel and the center-line through the upper and lower ball joints. See Figure 46-1. To increase positive caster, move the upper ball joint to the rear or the lower ball joint to the front.

Many cars are provided with shims under the upper control arm mounting bolts, Figure 46-10. In this design, transferring shims from under the rear bolt to the front bolt increases caster. Reversing this transfer of shims decreases caster. However, if the control arm pivot shaft is located inboard of the frame bracket, then the entire shimming procedure is reversed. See Figure 46-11.

Either of these caster adjustments affects camber, so caster and camber adjustments should be made simultaneously. Detailed charts in service manuals give exact shim changes for each misalignment situation.

Another popular caster adjustment design is the strut rod type. With this arrangement, adjustable strut rods run diagonally from the lower control arms to the frame front cross member, Figure 46-12. To make an adjustment, loosen the lock nuts at the forward end of the struts, then shorten the rod to increase caster (this moves lower ball joint forward). Lengthening the rod by lock nut adjustment decreases caster.

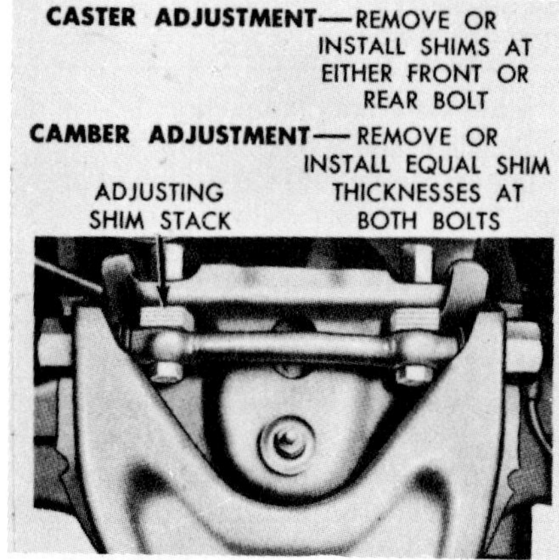

Figure 46-10. Shim adjustment of caster and camber provides a simple means of positioning the suspension control arms.

Some have used still another means of caster adjustment, Figure 46-13. Elongated bolt holes are provided in the chassis frame where the upper control arm pivot shaft attaches. To make an adjustment, loosen the attaching bolts and move the shaft in or out at the front or rear to tilt the steering axis forward or backward as required by the pre-

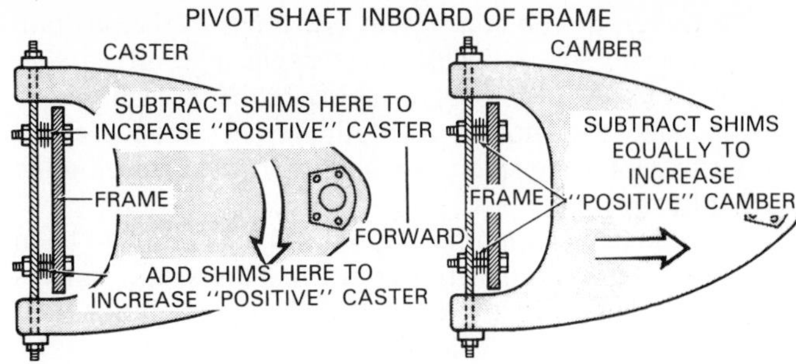

Figure 46-11. If the pivot shaft is inboard of the frame bracket, adding shims will move the pivot shaft farther inboard, which contrasts the outboard movement in Figure 46-10. (Buick)

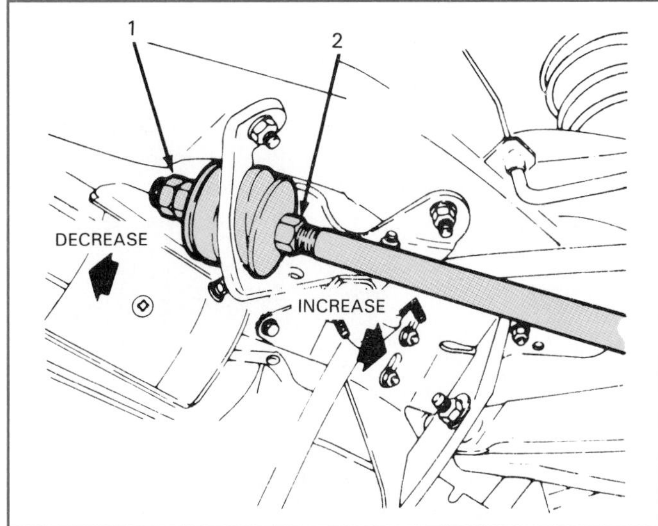

Figure 46-12. Some cars use diagonal strut rods as a means of caster adjustment. Loosen lock nut (1) and then turn the adjusting nuts (2) in or out to move the control arm forward or rearward. (Chrysler)

scribed caster setting. See Figure 46-13. Here again the same adjustment point is used for obtaining correct camber, so both angular adjustments should be made simultaneously.

Some cars have cam bolt adjustments located in the inner ends of the upper control arms, Figure 46-14, or at the lower control arms. After loosening the lock nut, turn each cam bolt to reposition the control arm and obtain correct caster and camber settings. For least effect on camber, the correct caster setting can be obtained by turning the cams an equal amount in opposite directions.

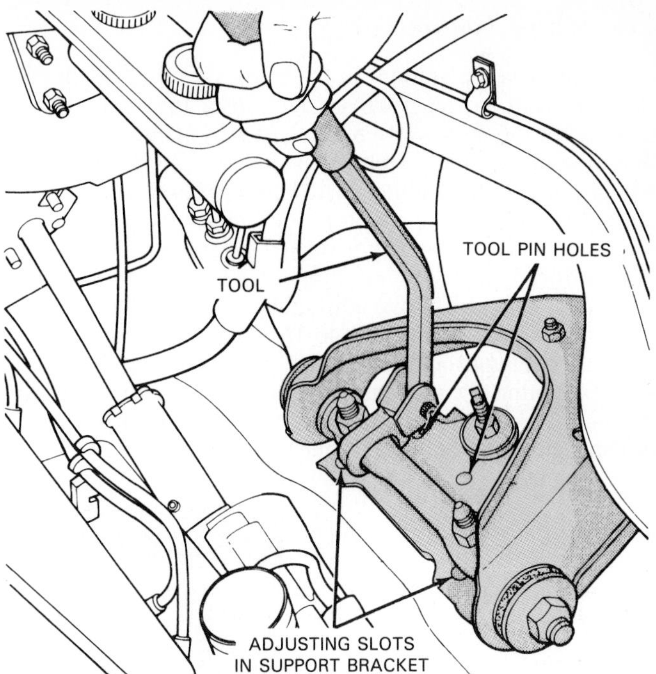

Figure 46-13. Caster and camber on some rear-wheel drive cars are adjusted by moving the pivot shaft of the upper control arm in or out by means of elongated bolt holes. Special tools aid in moving and holding the pivot shaft. (Chrysler)

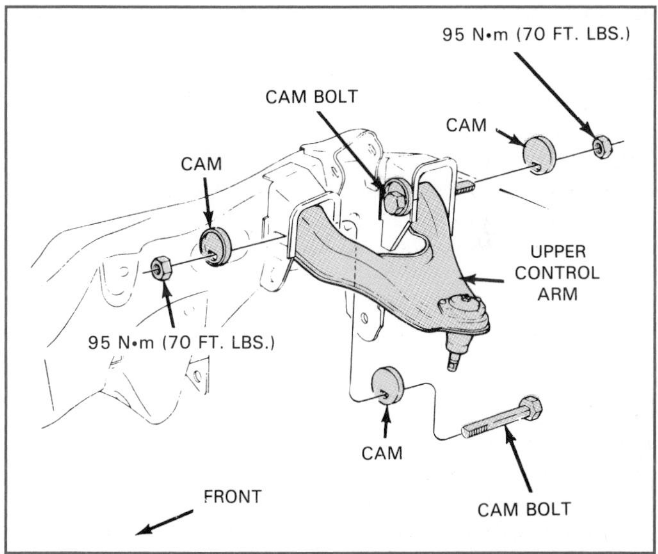

Figure 46-14. Cam bolt adjustment at the inner ends of the upper control arm offers a convenient way of positioning the control arm to set correct caster and camber. (Oldsmobile)

Adjusting Camber

Camber is the angle formed by the true vertical centerline and the vertical centerline of the tire. See Figure 46-1. Increase positive camber by moving the upper ball joint outward or lower ball joint inward. On cars with shims under the upper control arm pivot shaft bolts, add an equal number of shims under front and rear bolts to increase positive camber; remove an equal number of shims to decrease camber, Figures 46-10 and 46-11. This adjustment must be made in conjunction with the caster adjustment to relate the angles to each other.

If the control arm pivot shaft is located inboard of the frame bracket, reverse the shimming procedure. Naturally, if the shims are located under the lower control arm pivot shaft, the opposite effects are obtained, so opposite shimming procedure must be followed.

Other types of camber adjustments that are integrated with caster settings (elongated bolt holes in chassis frame and cam bolts) must be adjusted with both caster and camber settings in mind. This means many trial-and-error settings are necessary, although several car manufacturers and equipment manufacturers provide detailed charts giving the number of shims or amount of cam bolt rotation necessary to obtain a given degree of correction.

Correcting Toe-in

Toe-in is the amount in fractions of an inch or degree that the front (or rear) wheels are closer together in front than at the rear. It is often measured by means of a calibrated trammel bar extended at hub height between the wheel and tire assemblies with the wheels in the straight ahead position. More precise "toe" measurements can be made with the latest sophisticated alignment equipment, Figure 46-15.

Most cars utilize two adjustable tie rods to facilitate the "toe" adjustment. See Figure 46-16. To make the adjustment, loosen the clamp bolts on the tie rod sleeves and turn the sleeves to adjust tie rod length, Figure 46-17. A tie rod behind the front wheels must be lengthened to increase toe-in; a tie rod ahead of the front wheels must be shortened.

However, tie rod adjustment also controls the position of the steering wheel. Make the "centering" adjustment after correct toe-in has been established. Turn each tie rod adjusting sleeve to shorten or lengthen each tie rod an equal amount to center the steering wheel without disturbing the toe-in adjustment.

In some cases, alignment spacers are specified to be in place during the toe-in adjustment. In others, the spacers are removed and the car must be correct curb weight before the adjustment can be made.

Checking Steering Axis Inclination

Steering axis inclination is the angle formed by the true vertical centerline and the centerline of the upper and

Figure 46-15. Checks for toe-in and toe-out are an important part of wheel alignment troubleshooting. (Hunter Engineering Co.)

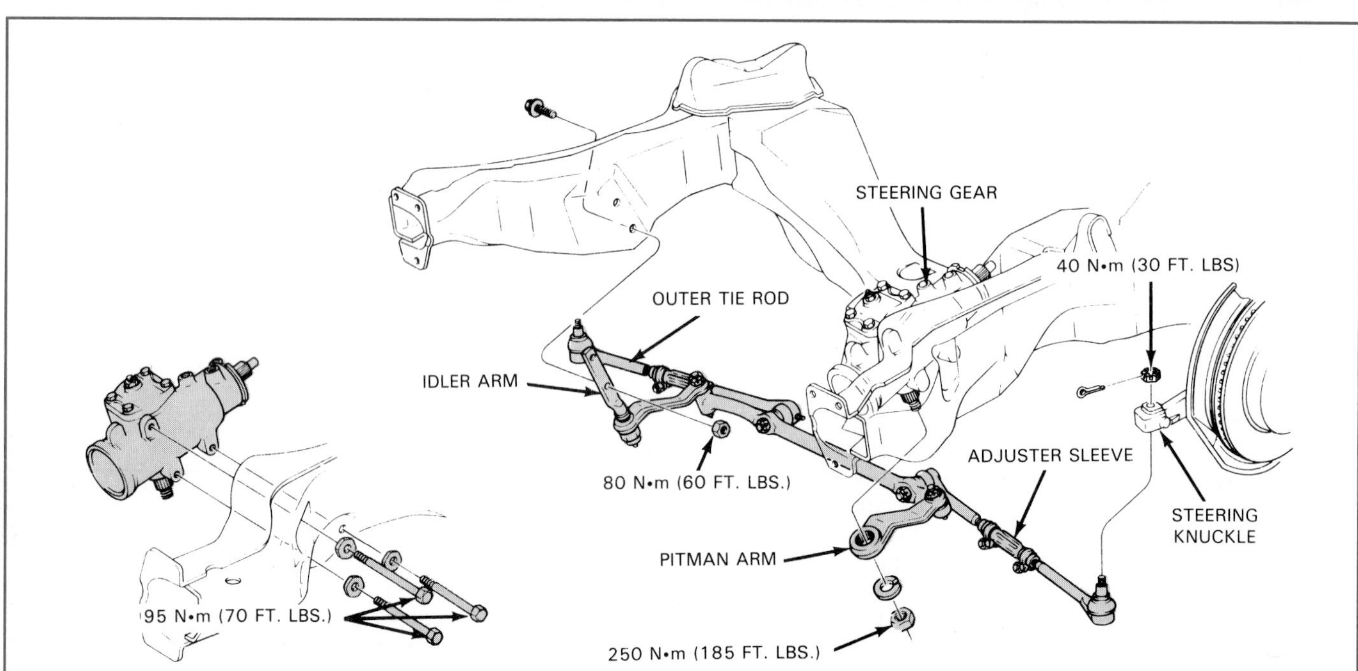

Figure 46-16. Most cars use tie rods and adjuster sleeves in the steering linkage to provide for toe-in adjustment and centering of the steering wheel. (Oldsmobile)

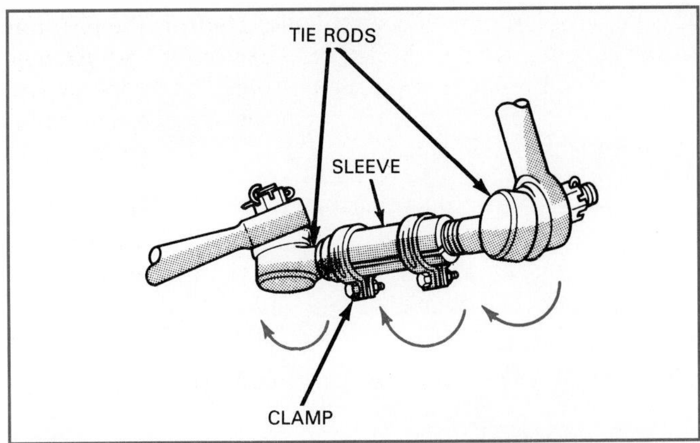

Figure 46-17. Tie rod sleeves permit adjustment of toe-in. After making the adjustment, place the clamp opening away from the sleeve slot and position the clamp bolt at or near the bottom to avoid interference. (Chrysler)

lower ball joints. It is created by the inward tilt of the steering knuckle and is not adjustable. If steering axis inclination is out of specifications, replace the steering knuckle and check all alignment factors.

Setting Toe-out on Turns

Toe-out on turns is the variation in the respective turning angles of the front wheels to avoid side slip on turns. It is built into the steering arms and is not adjustable. To get comparative readings, place the car on floating turntables, with weight of car on wheels. Set the inside wheel to a 20° turn, then check the reading of the outside wheel against specifications.

Repeat this check with the wheels turned in the opposite direction. If all other angles are correct and toe-out on turns is not, replace the steering arm on the side that is out of specifications.

Straightening or welding of parts should not be attempted. Bending of parts when cold may cause stresses and cracks. Straightening by heat will destroy the original heat treatment. Welding will change the grain structure of the metal.

Front-wheel Drive–Alignment

The design requirements for driving a vehicle by way of the engine, transaxle, and half shafts have resulted in certain changes in how front wheel alignment angles are adjusted. In some late model front-wheel drive (FWD) cars, caster and camber are not adjustable. In others, only camber and toe-in can be adjusted.

The procedure for adjusting camber and toe-in on a specific front-wheel drive vehicle follows. Refer to an appropriate service manual for adjustment procedures for a specific vehicle.

To adjust camber and toe-in:

1. Loosen the cam and through bolts (each side) at the strut lower housing. See Figure 46-18.
2. Rotate the cam bolt to move the top of the wheel in or out to obtain the specified amount of camber.
3. Tighten the cam and through bolts to the recommended torque value.
4. Recheck the camber setting.

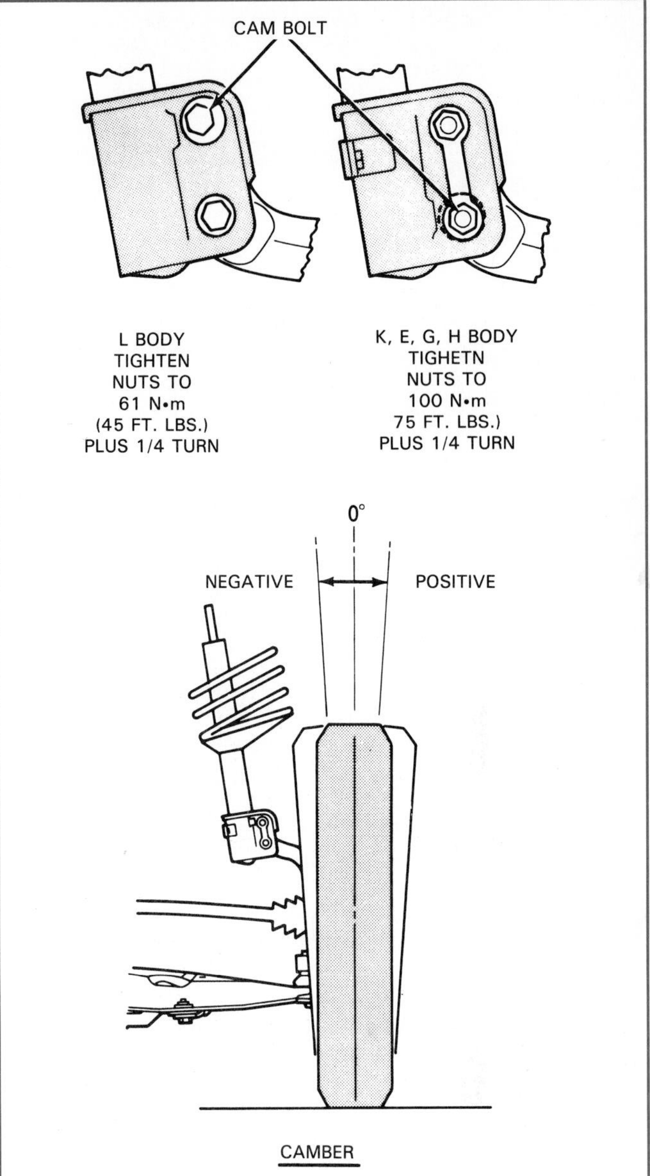

Figure 46-18. Camber on some front-wheel drive cars can be adjusted by means of a cam bolt at the base of the front suspension struts. Note the design differences between models in upper views.

5. Center the steering wheel and hold it in place with a steering wheel clamp.
6. Loosen the tie rod lock nuts, Figure 46-19, and rotate the rods to obtain the specified amount of toe-in.
7. Readjust the clamped end of the boots if twisted during adjustment.
8. Tighten the tie rod lock nuts to the specified torque value.
9. Remove the steering wheel clamp.

Rear Wheel Alignment

While a basic check of "rear wheel tracking" has always been a part of the steering alignment procedure, front-wheel drive and four wheel drive have put much greater emphasis on this phase of the procedure. Many car manufacturers furnish specifications for rear wheel camber and

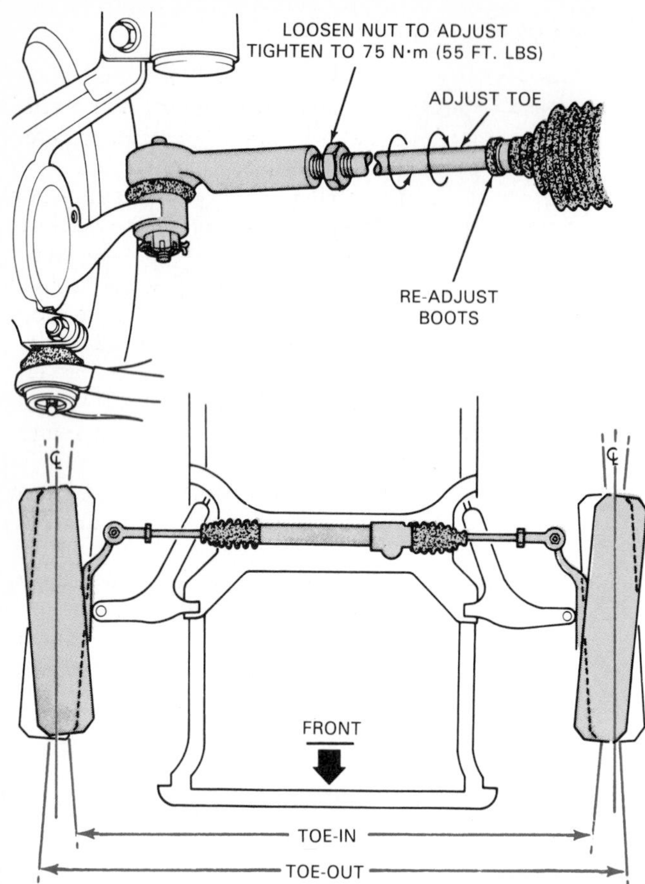

Figure 46-19. Toe-in on certain front-wheel drive cars can be adjusted by loosening the lock nuts and rotating tie rods.

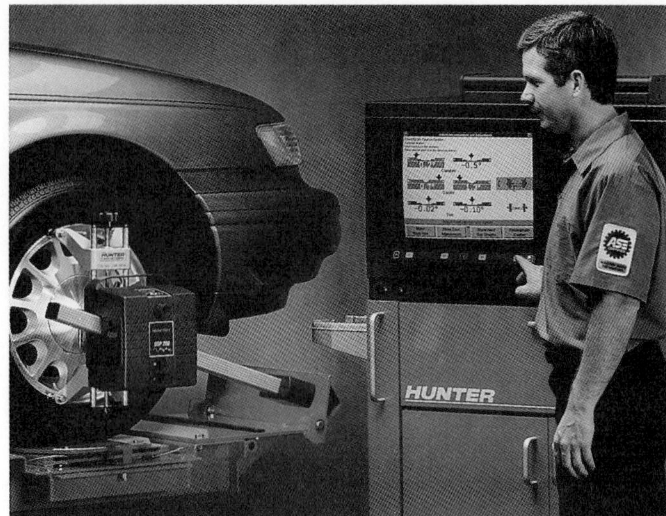

Figure 46-20. The latest alignment equipment aligns all four wheels to a common vehicle centerline. All wheels are referenced to each other. (Hunter Engineering Co.)

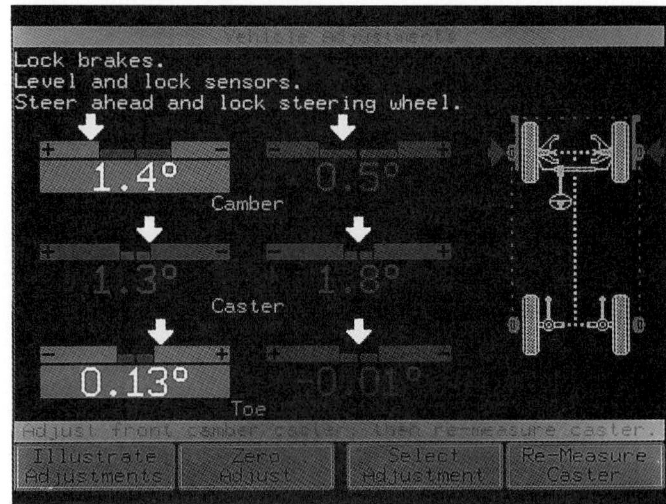

Figure 46-21. As adjustments are made to correct alignment, results are displayed on the alignment equipment's screen. Measurements in red are out of specification. Measurements in green are within specification. Measurements in blue have no specification. (Hunter Engineering Co.)

toe-in. In addition, and of key importance to four wheel alignment, the rear wheels must follow directly in line (track) with the front wheels.

Special equipment is available for checking the alignment of all four wheels. Usually, this type of test equipment uses front and rear wheel sensors to measure alignment angles of each wheel relative to the vehicle's thrust line, Figure 46-20. As adjustments are made, the alignment settings are displayed on the equipment's screen. See Figure 46-21.

The special four wheel alignment equipment actually is a diagnostic tool. For example, it will quickly reveal the cause for abnormal rear tire wear, whether the vehicle is front-wheel drive or rear-wheel drive.

The following procedure can be used to check some rear-wheel drive vehicles for a bent or shifted rear axle housing.

1. Raise both rear wheels off the floor using a frame contact hoist.
2. Place a 1″ long piece of masking tape at the center of each rear tire tread as a reference marker.
3. Position the tires with both reference marks pointing to the front of the vehicle, then measure the distance between the outside edges of tape.
4. Record this measurement as "front of tire reading" or (FTR).
5. Rotate the rear wheels so that the reference marks point to the rear of the vehicle.
6. Measure the distance between the outside edges of the two pieces of tape.
7. Record the measurements as "rear of tire reading" (RTR).
8. Subtract RTR from FTR to obtain the "toe" of axle being checked. Chrysler specification is 1/16″ (1.6 mm) toe-in to 3/16″ (4.8 mm) toe-out.
9. Rotate both rear wheels so that the reference marks are pointing down.
10. Measure the distance between the outside of the two pieces of tape.
11. Record this measurement as the "bottom of tire reading" (BTR).
12. Average the sum of FTR and RTR. From this average, subtract the BTR to obtain the existing camber reading. One manufacturer's specification is 1/16″ (1.6 mm) to 3/32″ (2.4 mm).
13. The equation is: $\frac{FTR + RTR}{Z} - BTR = \pm$ Camber

Note: If BTR is smaller than average figure, camber is positive (+); if BTR is larger than average figure, camber reading is negative (–).

14. Lower the hoist.

In some front-wheel drive vehicles, rear camber adjustment is performed at the rear strut and knuckle assemblies. The toe-in adjustment is made by shortening or lengthening the tie rods. Both rear camber and toe adjustments are shown in Figure 46-22.

To adjust rear wheel camber:

1. Normalize the suspension by jouncing the front and rear bumpers up and down several times.
2. Install the alignment equipment according to the equipment manufacturer's directions.
3. Loosen the strut-to-knuckle mounting nuts.
4. Install the camber adjusting tool, Figure 46-22.
5. Tighten or loosen the camber adjusting screw on the tool as required to set the camber to the manufacturer's specification.
6. With the camber set, tighten the strut-to-knuckle nuts to the correct torque tightness: typically 144 ft./lb. (195 N·m).
7. Remove the camber adjusting tool.
8. Install the tool on the other strut and knuckle assembly and repeat the camber adjusting steps 1 to 5.

To adjust rear wheel "toe:"

1. Loosen the lock nut at both rear tie rod ends, Figure 46-22.
   Note: Left and right side toe must be set separately "per wheel."
2. Adjust the "toe" by turning the inner tie rod.
   Note: Make sure the boot is not twisted.
3. Adjust the toe link to the full toe-out position, then adjust inward to obtain the correct setting.
4. Tighten the lock nut on both tie rod ends to 48 ft./ lb. (65 N·m).
5. Repeat the toe adjusting steps 1 to 4 on the other side.

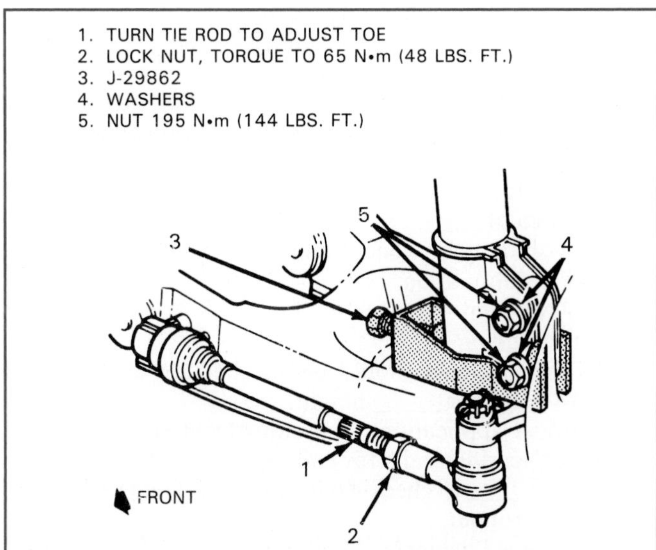

Figure 46-22. Rear camber and toe adjusting points on certain General Motors cars. 1–Turn the tie rod to adjust toe. 2–Tighten the lock nut. 3–Turn the camber tool adjusting screw to set camber. 4–Washers. 5–Torque tighten the strut-to-knuckle nuts.

Alignment Troubleshooting

Proper steering control depends on more than just the steering system. Suspension and wheel alignment contribute so much to steering that all three must be considered when troubleshooting car handling complaints.

Bear in mind that the car, load, and passengers must be balanced above the tires and springs while the vehicle is being subjected to many and varied driving conditions. This weight on the wheels moves up and down with road irregularities, tends to go sideways from the action of centrifugal force and wind pressures, and alternately shifts forward and backward under acceleration and braking. Or, there may be an unequal distribution of load because of engine torque reaction on the frame, uneven passenger loading, or uneven cargo loading.

Usually there is no quick easy remedy for a given handling problem. A series of causes and effects must be analyzed with due regard for the alignment theories involved. Often a combination of minor defects adds up to more serious trouble.

The following alignment troubleshooting checklist gives some of the more common causes of car handling problems.

Shimmy or Wheel Tramp

- Incorrect or unequal tire pressures.
- Cupped, eccentric, or bulged tires.
- Unbalanced wheels.
- Out-of-round wheel or brake drum.
- Weak or inoperative shock absorbers.
- Loose wheel bearing adjustment.
- Incorrect front wheel alignment, particularly caster.
- Loose or worn control arm bushings.
- Loose or worn suspension ball joints.
- Loose or worn steering linkage.
- Loose steering gear on frame.
- Loose steering gear adjustment.
- Inoperative stabilizer.
- Loose or worn strut bushings.

Hard or Rough Ride

- High air pressure in tires.
- Wrong type or size of tire.
- Tight steering gear adjustment.
- Incorrect wheel alignment, particularly caster.
- Inoperative shock absorbers.
- Overloaded or unevenly loaded vehicle.
- Sagging or broken spring.
- Lack of lubrication of front suspension or steering linkage.

Car Leads to One Side

- Unequal tire pressures.
- Varied tire sizes.
- Unevenly loaded vehicle.
- Dragging front brakes.
- Tight front wheel bearings.

- Bent spindle, spindle arm, or steering knuckle.
- Incorrect or uneven front wheel alignment.
- Loose strut bushings.
- Sagging or broken front spring.
- Inoperative shock absorber.
- Broken or off-center rear spring center bolt.
- Shifted rear axle housing.
- Out-of-line frame or underbody.
- Damaged rear suspension components.

Wander to Either Side

- Incorrect or uneven tire pressures.
- Varied tire sizes or excessive wear.
- Unmatched tire construction.
- Overloaded or unevenly loaded vehicle.
- Tight front wheel bearing adjustment.
- Bent spindle, spindle arm, or steering knuckle.
- Incorrect front wheel alignment.
- Tight suspension ball joints.
- Binding control arm shafts.
- Tight idler arm bushing.
- Loose, worn or damaged steering linkage.
- Loose steering gear on frame.
- Incorrect steering gear adjustment.
- Inoperative shock absorbers.
- Broken rear spring center bolt.

Rear Suspension Out of Line

- Broken or off-center rear spring canter bolt.
- Mislocated rear spring front hanger.
- Shifted rear axle housing.
- Bent lower control arm.
- Out-of-line frame or underbody.

Uneven Tire Tread Wear

- Incorrect tire pressures.
- Failure to rotate tires.
- Incorrect front wheel alignment, particularly camber and toe-in.
- Excessive wheel runout.
- Bent spindle, spindle arm, or steering knuckle.
- Grabbing brakes.
- Loose, worn or damaged suspension parts.
- Excessive speed on turns.

Tire Squeal on Turns

- Low air pressure in tires.
- Varied tire sizes.
- Bent spindle, spindle arm, or steering knuckle.
- Incorrect front wheel alignment, particularly toe-in.
- Loose or weak shock absorbers.

Tire Vibration

- Wheel and tire assembly imbalance.
- Wheel and tire assembly runout.
- Incorrectly adjusted front wheel bearings.
- Loose or worn suspension or steering components.
- Worn or defective tires.
- Rotor or brake drum runout.

Noise in System

- Loose front wheel bearing adjustment.
- Loose shock absorber mountings.
- Loose steering gear adjustment.
- Loose steering gear on frame.
- Worn steering linkage.
- Worn control arm bushings.
- Loose suspension strut bushings.
- Insufficient suspension ball joint lubrication.
- Worn idler arm bushings.
- Loose or worn spring shackles.
- Loose or worn stabilizer bushings.

Chapter 46–Review Questions

Write your answers on a separate sheet of paper. Do not write in this book.

1. The need for frequent and regular wheel alignment checks has _____ (increased/decreased) with technological advances.
2. Wheel alignment should be checked at the first sign of _____ tread wear.
3. Generally, the three key wheel alignment angles should be checked in the following order:
   (A) Camber, caster, and toe-in.
   (B) Caster, camber, and toe-in.
   (C) Toe-in, caster, and camber.
   (D) Toe-in, camber, and caster.
4. With today's emphasis on front-wheel drive cars, _____ and _____ wheel alignment procedures were found to be necessary.
5. Some front-wheel drive cars are prone to problems in the area of _____.
   (A) shimmy or wheel tramp
   (B) leading to one side
   (C) wander
   (D) tracking
6. Ordinarily, cars should be checked for alignment at curb height or _____ height.
7. In most applications, the adjustment of front wheel roller bearings calls for end play. True or False?
8. Use a _____ to check each front wheel and tire assembly for runout.
   (A) wheel balancer
   (B) dial indicator
   (C) straightedge
   (D) feeler gauge
9. Test action and rebound of _____ by jouncing car an equal number of times from center of bumpers.

10. Explain the "wet tread" test for rear wheel tracking.
11. Incorrect front suspension height can be corrected on Chrysler cars by:
    (A) installing new coil springs.
    (B) installing new shock absorbers.
    (C) adjusting torsion bars.
    (D) adjusting MacPherson struts.
12. Name two common caster adjusting points.
13. How is toe-in adjusted?
    (A) Shortening or lengthening tie rods.
    (B) Shimming control arms.
    (C) Shortening or lengthening strut rods.
    (D) Turning cam bolts.
14. A car was found to have shimmy or wheel tramp during a road test. Technician A said it could be caused by incorrect front wheel alignment, particularly caster. Technician B said it could be caused by unbalanced wheels. Who is right?
    (A) A only.
    (B) B only.
    (C) Both A & B.
    (D) Neither A nor B.
15. A car owner complained of a hard or rough ride. Technician A said it could be caused by inoperative shock absorbers. Technician B said it could be caused by excessive wheel runout. Who is right?
    (A) A only.
    (B) B only.
    (C) Both A & B.
    (D) Neither A nor B.

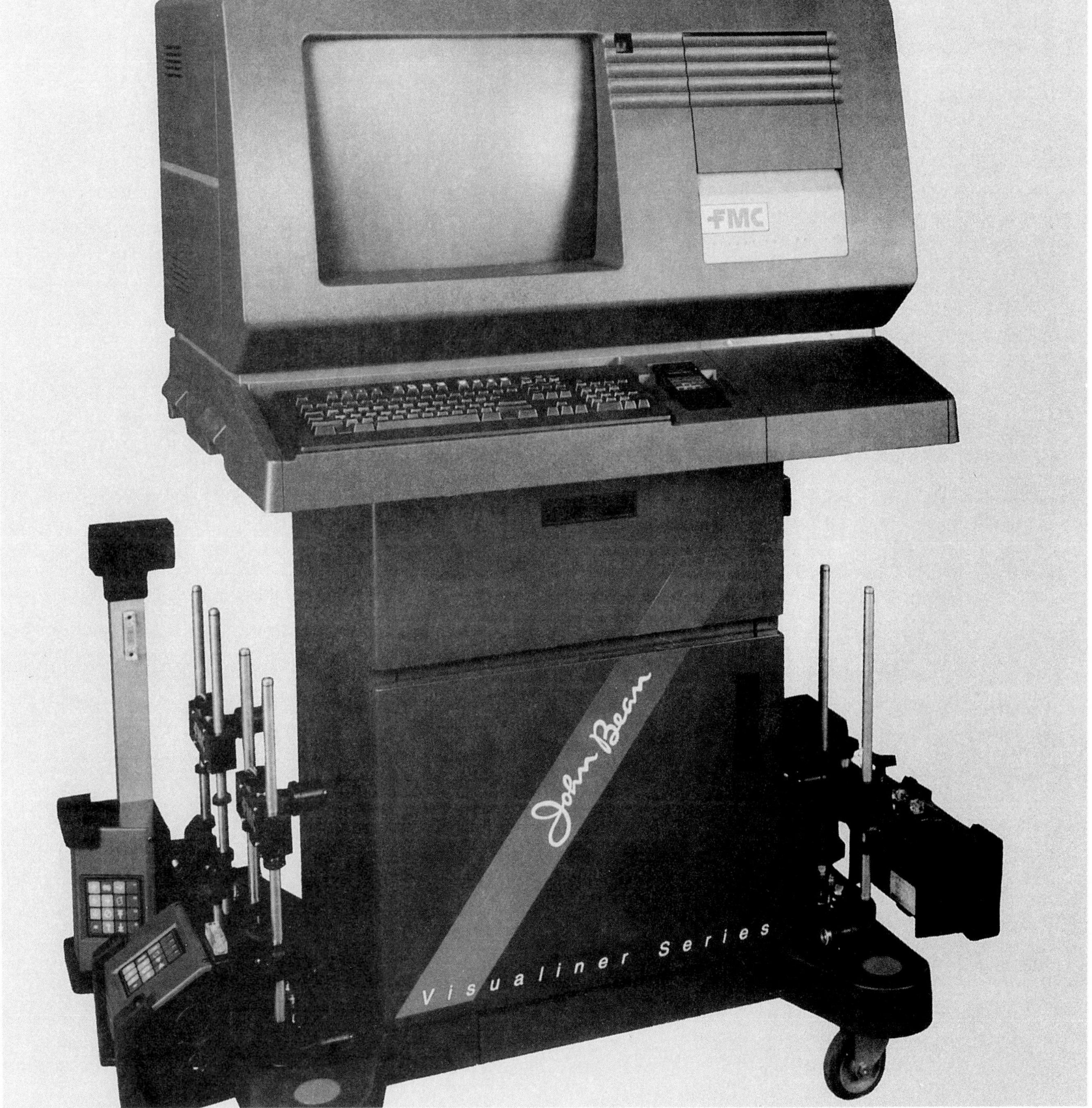

Precision equipment, such as the unit shown above, is needed to align late-model vehicles properly. (FMC Corporation)

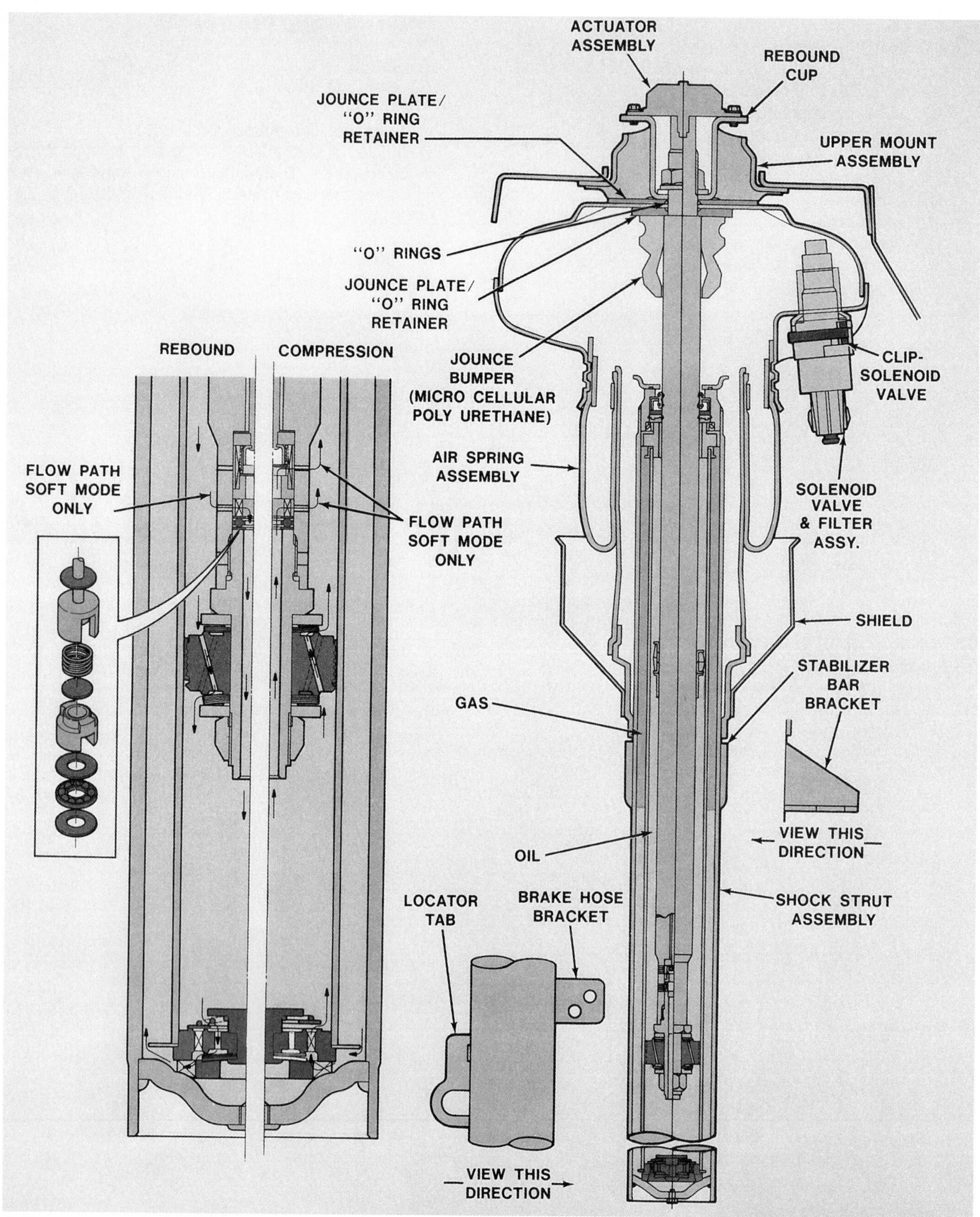

Principles of hydraulics and pneumatics are put to use in a four-wheel air suspension system. Air springs and MacPherson struts are utilized. Air pressure in the springs is monitored and adjusted by a microcomputer to keep the car level. Shock struts are filled with oil and gas. Valves control oil flow to provide the damping action. (Ford)

Chapter 47
Hydraulics and Pneumatics

After studying this chapter, you will be able to:
❍ Give examples of the principles of hydraulics.
❍ Cite the advantages of hydraulic systems.
❍ Define pressure and force.
❍ Describe various automotive applications of hydraulic principles.
❍ Define pneumatics.
❍ Name various automotive applications of pneumatic systems.
❍ State Boyle's law.
❍ State Charles' law.

Hydraulics

The study of ***hydraulics*** is important to the auto mechanic because so many parts of the automotive vehicle are operated by liquids under pressure, and in motion. For example, the conventional braking system used on passenger cars is of the hydraulic type, and the automatic transmission depends on hydraulics for its operation. Hydraulics also actuate the power steering system and shock absorbers.

In the automotive service field, hydraulic jacks, lifts, presses, and various body spreading and straightening devices are in daily use.

Technically, liquids and gases are considered as fluids. They do have many characteristics in common, but differ mainly in that liquids change but slightly when they are compressed. In addition, they have a free surface. Gases, however, are compressible and will fill all parts of the containing vessel.

The science of hydraulics includes:

- The manner in which liquids act in tanks and pipes.
- The laws of floating bodies, and the behavior of liquids on submerged surfaces.
- The flow of liquids under various conditions and methods of directing this flow to do useful work.

In this text, however, the study will be limited primarily to hydraulics as applied in the automotive field.

Advantages of Hydraulic Systems

Among the advantages of hydraulic systems are:

- The elimination of complicated systems of gears, cams, and rods.
- Motion can be transmitted without slack or lost motion.
- Liquids are not subjected to wear or breakage as is the case with mechanical parts.
- Hydraulic systems require no lubrication.
- Applied force can be greatly multiplied and transmitted considerable distances with negligible loss.

Physical Properties of Liquids

Liquids differ from solids in that they do not have a definite form of their own. They conform to the shape of the vessel in which they are contained. Because of their shapelessness, liquids can be carried in tubing by gravity or by applying force to them.

In general, liquids may be considered as being incompressible. In fact, a force of 15 lb. (66.7 N) on a cubic inch of water will compress it only 1/20,000, and it would take a force of 32 tons to reduce it 10 percent. When pressure is removed, the liquid immediately returns to its original volume.

Transmission of Forces

When force is applied to a confined liquid, it will be transmitted in all directions. This is one of the most important characteristics of liquids, and it is known as ***Pascal's law.***

To make this clear, consider that when a metal bar is struck on the end, the force will be transmitted the length of the bar, Figure 47-1. The more rigid the bar, the less force lost inside the bar or transmitted at right angles to the direction of the blow.

However, when a force is applied to the end of a confined liquid, Figure 47-1, it is transmitted straight through to the other end (same as metal bar). In addition, however, the force is transmitted equally and undiminished in every direction (forward, backward, sideward) so that the containing vessel is literally filled with pressure at right angles to the containing surfaces.

To illustrate another hydraulic principle, pressure of a liquid standing in an open vessel is dependent on the depth of the liquid. This is known as the ***hydraulic head.*** Pressure due to the hydraulic head is also dependent on the weight of the liquid, which is known as the density of the liquid. ***Density*** is the weight in pounds of a cubic inch or cubic foot of the liquid. Water weighs 62.36 lb. per cu. ft.–or .036 lb. per cu. in. Heavy petroleum oil weighs .032 lb. per cu. in. and light oil .029 lb. per cu. in.

In the example illustrated in Figure 47-2, the water would have to be 222″ deep to exert a pressure of 8 psi

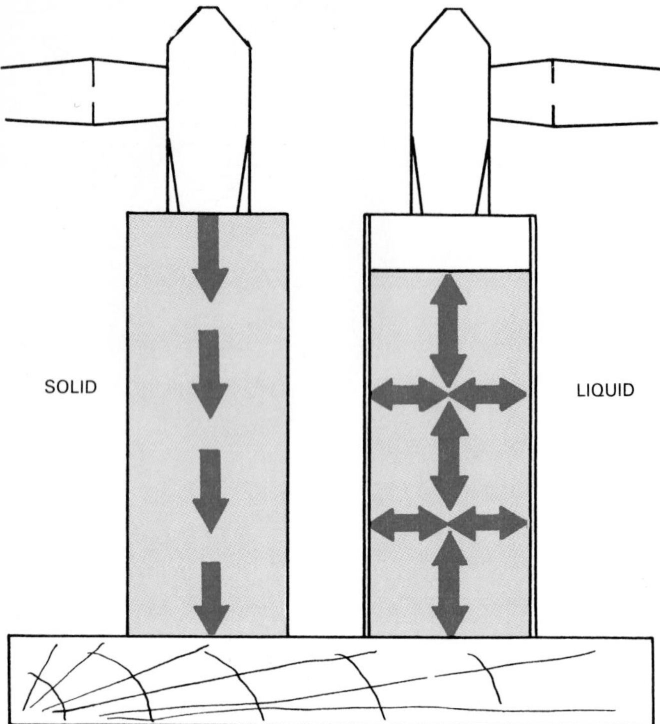

Figure 47-1. Arrows illustrate the difference in action of forces when a solid bar is struck and when a force is applied to the end of a confined liquid.

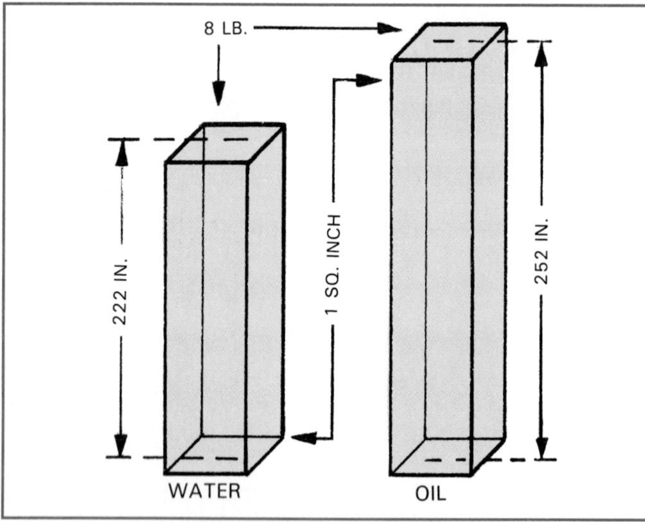

Figure 47-2. As an illustration of the effect of density on pressure, a 222 in. column of water and a 252 in. column of oil produce the same pressure.

(pounds per square inch). In the case of heavy oil, it would have to be 252″ deep.

Specific Gravity

Specific gravity (sp. gr.) is a common method of comparing liquids. It is the ratio of the weight of a unit volume of that substance (its density) to the weight of 1 cu. in. of water. Since the weight may vary with temperature changes, the measurement is always made at 39.1°F or 4°C.

Therefore, the specific gravity of water is 1.0. The 1.0 becomes the standard for specific gravity against which all other liquids are measured. For example, the weight of a cubic inch of water is .036 lb., while the weight of a typical hydraulic brake fluid used in an automobile is .0357 lb. per cu. in. The specific gravity of the fluid is obtained by dividing .0357 by .036, which equals 0.99 sp. gr.

In automotive service work, specific gravity is used in testing antifreeze solutions to determine at what temperature the solution in the cooling system will freeze. It is also used in measuring the state of charge in a starting battery.

Hydrometers

To measure the specific gravity of a solution, an instrument known as a ***hydrometer*** is used, Figure 47-3. The hydrometer consists of a glass tube that contains a calibrated float. The fluid to be measured is drawn into the glass tube by means of a rubber suction bulb. Then, the height of the float at the surface of the liquid is a measurement of its specific gravity. See inset in Figure 47-3.

Pressure and Force

According to Pascal's law, any force applied to a confined liquid is transmitted equally in all directions through the liquid regardless of the shape of the container. In Figure 47-4, when a force is applied to piston No. 1, pressure created throughout the entire system will act at right angles to all surfaces with equal strength.

Force is the strength or power exerted on an object. ***Pressure*** is defined as the force divided by the area over which it is distributed. In the case illustrated in Figure 47-4, the force applied at piston No. 1 is 100 lb. Since the area of the piston is 10 sq. in., then the pressure is 100 divided by 10 or 10 psi.

This pressure of 10 psi is exerted over the entire system; on the sides as well as on piston No. 2, which is at the greatest distance from piston No. 1. Since the vessel containing the fluid is of uniform cross section, and both pistons have the same area, the upward force on piston No. 2

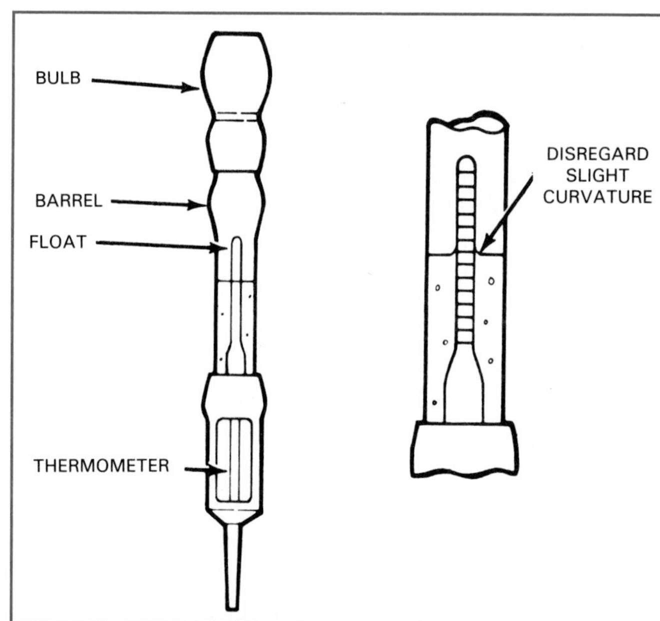

Figure 47-3. Example of a hydrometer used to measure the specific gravity of the electrolyte solution in a storage battery.

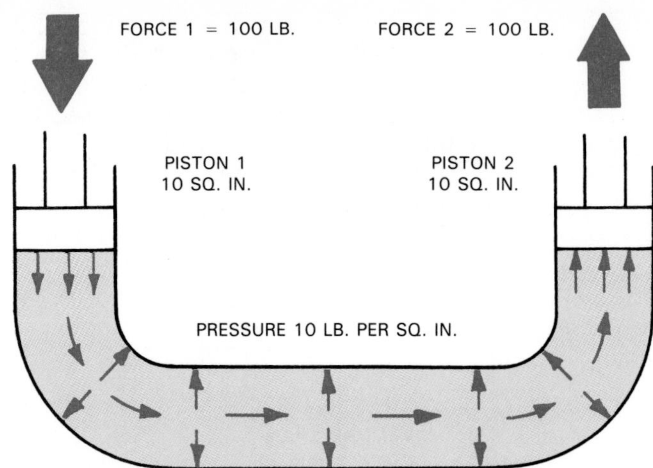

Figure 47-4. Force applied to a fluid in a confined system is transmitted equally in all directions throughout system, regardless of its shape.

is the same as the force applied to piston No. 1. What has been done is to change the direction of the force from downward at piston No. 1 to upward at piston No. 2.

Although the system shown in Figure 47-4 has a uniform cross section, this is not a necessary requirement if you want the same force available at the output side as applied at the input side. Because of Pascal's law, the connection between piston No. 1 and piston No. 2 can be any shape or size. This hydraulic principle is made clear in Figure 47-5, where the connection between the two pistons is a tube of smaller diameter than the pistons.

Multiplying the Force

In the examples shown so far, there has been no increase in force at the output piston because it has been the same size as the input piston. However, if the output piston is larger than the input piston, the force will be increased in the same proportion as the areas of the two pistons. For example, in Figure 47-6, piston No. 1 (input) has an area of 2 sq. in., while the area of piston No. 2 (output) is 20 sq. in.

If a force of 20 lb. is applied to piston No. 1, the pressure on the liquid will be 10 psi (20 lb. divided by 2 sq. in. equals 10 psi). Since this pressure acts equally throughout the system, there will be 10 psi acting on piston No. 2. Its area, however, is 20 sq. in., so the total force on that piston will be 200 lb. (20 sq. in. times 10 psi equals 200 lb.).

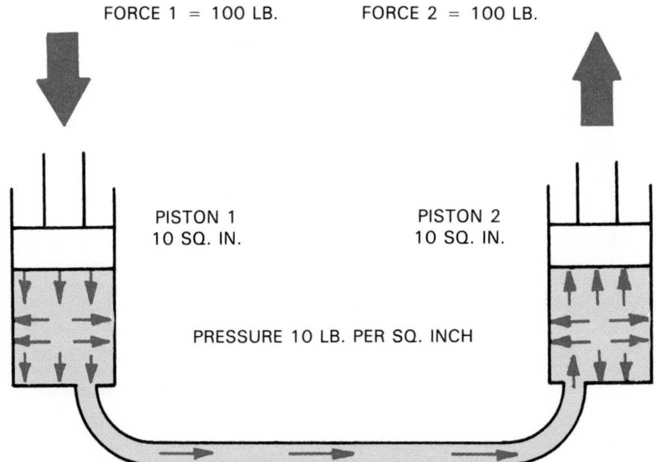

Figure 47-5. Shape and size of the connecting tube has no effect on the pressure in the cylinders.

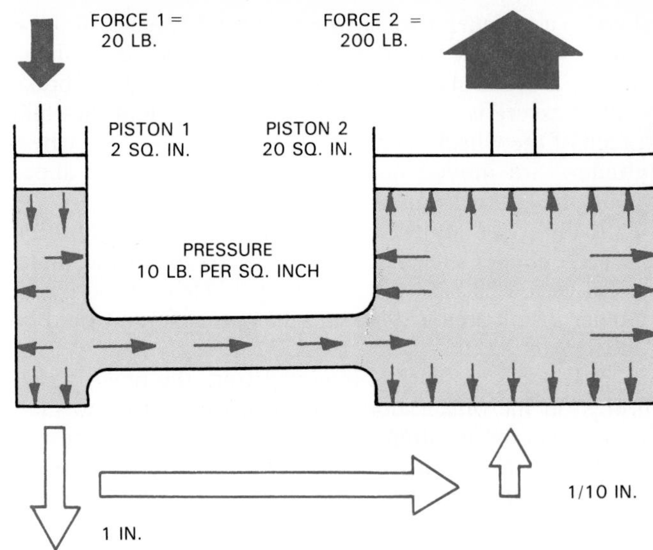

Figure 47-6. Forces can be multiplied if the output piston is larger than the input piston.

The system shown in Figure 47-6 could also be used in a reverse manner. It could be used to reduce force rather than increase it.

Movement of Liquid

In the examples given in Figures 47-4 and 47-5, the areas of the pistons are equal. Therefore, if one piston is moved down 1″, the other piston will move up a corresponding amount. Since liquid is virtually incompressible, the liquid displaced by the first piston must have some place to go, and it can move only by displacing the second piston an equal amount.

Applying this to the system shown in Figure 47-6, pushing piston No. 1 down 1″, will displace 2 cu. in. of liquid. To accommodate this volume of liquid, piston No. 2 will have to move 0.10″. The volume of fluid 2 cu. in. divided by the area of the piston 20 sq. in. equals 0.10″ movement of the piston.

Application of Hydraulic Principles

These principles of hydraulics have wide application in the automotive industry. By proper application of these principles, heavy vehicles can be stopped with ease, and jacks are designed so that a small child can raise a heavy truck. The special application of hydraulics to automatic transmissions is discussed in the transmission chapters of this text.

Hydraulic Brakes

The modern ***hydraulic brake system*** is an application of multiple outlet pistons (wheel cylinders or disc brake calipers), which distribute forces applied at the foot pedal and transmitted by the master input cylinder.

In four-wheel drum brake applications, the master cylinder in which the input piston moves is connected by tubing to a cylinder at each wheel. Generally, each of these cylinders contains two opposed pistons, and each piston operates a brake shoe. When force is applied at the brake pedal, pressure is transmitted equally throughout the fluid to each of the wheel cylinders. As a result, all of the wheel cylinders are moved outward, forcing the brake shoes against the brake drums.

If the force applied at the master cylinder is 800 lb., and the cylinder area is .8 sq. in., pressure in the brake system would be 800 × .8 or 1000 psi. Then, if the wheel cylinder piston area is .9 sq. in., the output force would be 1000 × .9 or 900 lb.

When the pressure is removed from the brake pedal, springs on the brake shoes force the shoes back to their normal released position. This movement of the shoes, in turn, forces the pistons inward, returning the fluid to the master cylinder reservoir.

This description covers the operation of a simple hydraulic brake with all wheel cylinders of the same diameter. In some instances, the wheel cylinders have stepped diameters with a large piston operating the forward shoe and a smaller piston operating the rear shoe of a single brake. This type of construction is discussed in the chapter on brakes.

The principle of operation of the floating or sliding caliper disc brake is to allow the fluid pressure to build up between the bottom of the piston and the bottom of the cylinder bore. Pressure on the piston forces the inboard shoe and lining against the inboard rotor surface. Pressure against the bottom of the bore causes the caliper to float or slide on mounting bolts or sleeves, Figure 47-7, forcing the outboard lining against the outboard rotor surface. Then, as line pressure continues to build up, the clamping action of the friction surfaces stops the rotor and the vehicle.

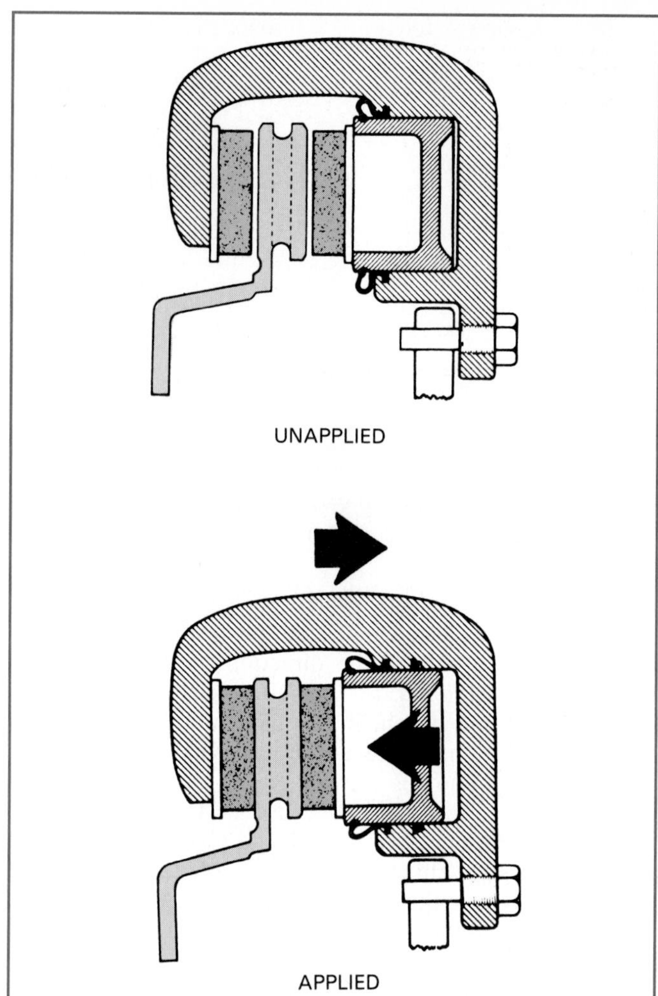

Figure 47-7. Key to floating brake caliper operation is when hydraulic pressure on the bottom of the cylinder bore causes the caliper to float sideways and apply the brake pads to the rotor surfaces.

Hydraulic Jacks

A schematic drawing of the principle used in the operation of ***hydraulic jacks*** is shown in Figure 47-8. In the illustration, the small piston (where force is applied) has an area of 5 sq. in. Its cylinder is connected to a large cylinder with a piston having an area of 250 sq. in. This large piston supports the platform used to raise the load.

If a force of 25 lb. is applied to the small piston, a pressure of 5 psi will be produced in the hydraulic fluid. This 5 psi will act over the entire area of the large piston with its 250 sq. in. surface. The resulting force will be 250 × 5 psi = 1250 lb. lifting force. The initial force of 25 lb. has been multiplied into a force capable of lifting more than one-half ton.

Remember, however, that while the original force has been multiplied 50 times, the distance traveled is just the opposite. The large piston will travel only 1/50 as much as the small piston.

By way of explanation: if the small piston is moved 5″, then 25 cu. in. of liquid will be displaced. Distributing this amount over 250 sq. in. of the larger piston, it will be raised 25 divided by 250, or 0.1″ (1/50 of 5″).

To prevent the weight of the load on the platform from forcing the fluid back through the system, and to provide a means of lowering the load, it is necessary to include various valves in the hydraulic system, Figure 47-9.

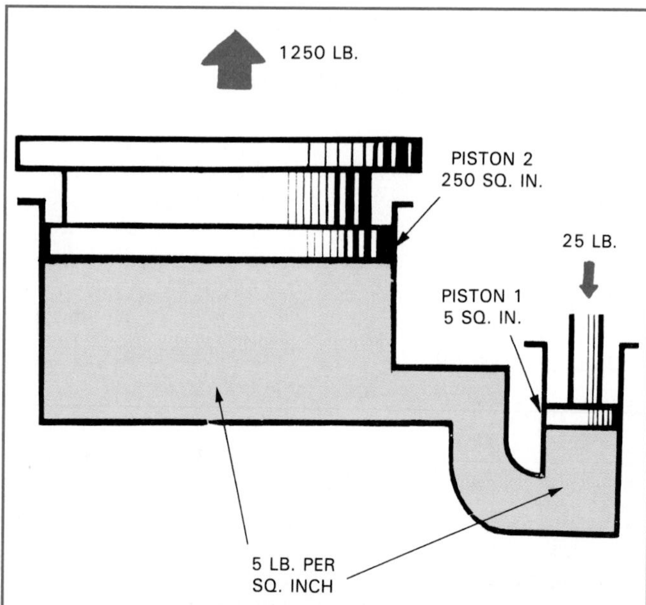

Figure 47-8. Principle of a hydraulic jack is based on the multiplication of force applied at the small piston.

Pneumatics

Pneumatics is the study of the mechanical properties of air and other gases. It has many automotive applications,

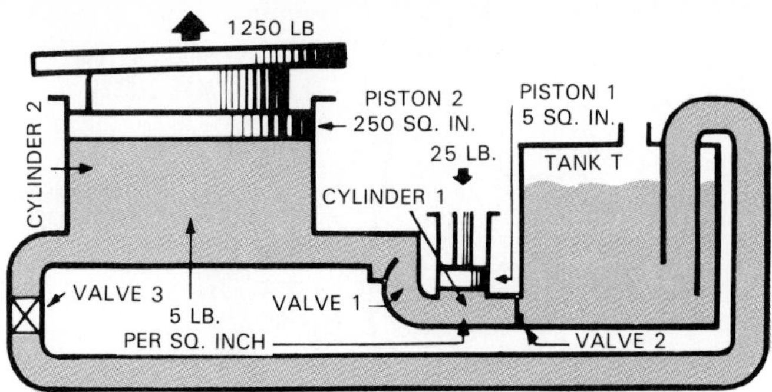

Figure 47-9. Schematic drawing of a hydraulic jack shows the valving necessary to maintain a load at a desired height and also to permit a load to be lowered when desired.

particularly in the study of fuel systems, tires, and vehicle leveling systems. Air brakes are a major consideration in the trucking field.

Technically, air and other gases are considered ***fluids.*** They have many of the same characteristics as liquids, but differ mainly in that they are highly compressible and completely fill any containing vessel. Gases are the same as liquids in two ways: they conform to the shape of their containers; and pressure in a gas acts equally in all directions.

Pressure of Air at Sea Level

Air, like any gas, has weight. Therefore, pressure is exerted by virtue of its head; that is, the depth from its upper surfaces to its lower surface. Although any small volume of any gas weighs very little, the pressure of air at sea level under normal conditions amounts to 14.7 psi. The pressure, or the head, is the weight of the air from the surface of the earth to many miles up in space.

Since air is compressed by its own weight, the same volume of air at sea level will weigh considerably more than on a mountain top. In other words, air becomes less dense as altitude, or distance from the earth, increases.

This natural factor is particularly important because of its affect on carburetion. As altitude increases, less air enters the carburetor. Consequently, the mixture of fuel and air becomes richer. Instruments designed to measure the pressure of the atmosphere are known as "barometers." In most applications, they are used for forecasting weather and in measuring altitudes.

As pointed out, gases are compressed by their own weight. In addition, gases expand as their temperature increases, making a volume of gas at high temperature weigh less than the same volume of gas at low temperature. This particular property of gases is why the efficiency of an automobile decreases as the temperature of the air entering the carburetor increases.

Effect of Atmospheric Pressure

Atmospheric pressures obey Pascal's law in the same manner as liquids, Figure 47-10. Atmospheric pressure acting on the surface of the gas is transmitted equally to the inner walls of the container, but it is balanced by the pressure on the outer walls.

In another example, the thinnest paper suspended in the atmosphere will not be torn, in spite of the fact that air pressure of 14.7 psi is pressing on it, Figure 47-11. It is not torn because atmospheric pressure is exerted on both sides of the sheet and the pressures are balanced.

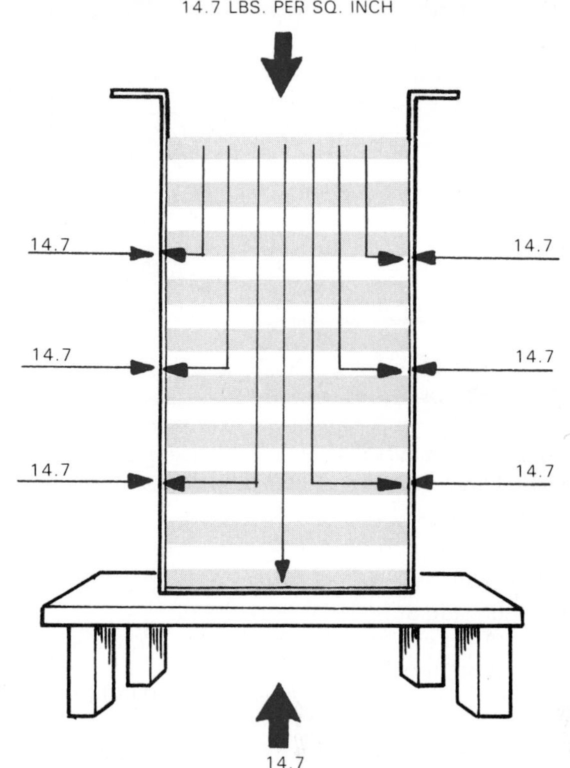

Figure 47-10. Atmospheric pressure acting on surface of gas or liquid is transmitted equally throughout.

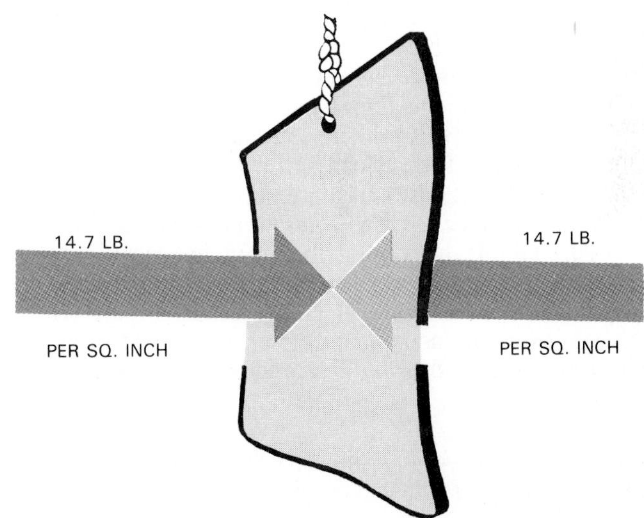

Figure 47-11. Thin paper suspended in the atmosphere will not be torn because a pressure of 14.7 psi is pressing on both sides.

In Figure 47-12, atmospheric pressure acting on one piston is balanced by the same pressure acting on the surface of the other piston. The fact that the two pistons are of different areas makes no difference since the unit pressure (pressure per square inch) is the same on both pistons.

Effect of Vacuum

With equal atmospheric pressure acting on the two surfaces, Figure 47-12, the liquid will be at the same height

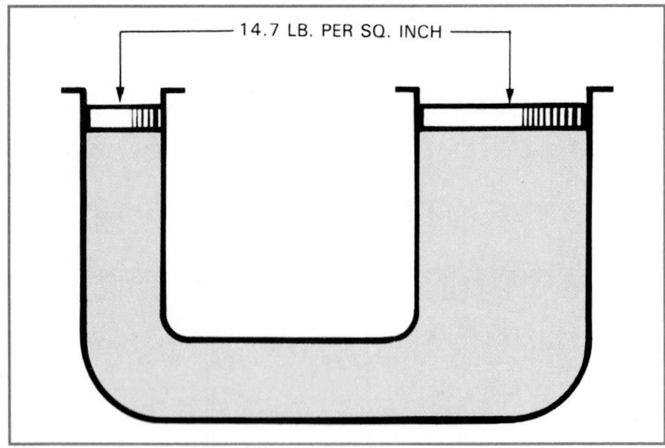

Figure 47-12. Atmospheric pressure acting on one piston is balanced by the same pressure acting on the other piston.

in both sides of the U-shaped tube. If the pressure on one side of the tube is reduced, there will be a movement of liquid to the side of reduced pressure.

This effect can be illustrated by the familiar situation of drinking liquid through a straw, Figure 47-13. Sucking on the straw disturbs the balance of pressures acting on the liquid. Pressure within the straw is reduced, as the result of suction, and atmospheric pressure (14.7 psi) acting on the surface of the liquid in the glass forces the liquid into the straw.

The liquid can be held at any desired level in the straw. This level will always be at a point where the pressure of the head of the liquid, Figure 47-13, equals the difference between the pressure in the straw and that on the surface of the liquid.

Sucking on the straw has produced a partial vacuum on the surface of the liquid within the straw. A ***partial vacuum*** is actually a pressure less than prevailing atmospheric pressure. Theoretically, the limit of this process would be a condition of zero pressure, or a complete vacuum. In actual practice, this condition is never attained.

This simple principle, illustrated by sucking liquid through a straw, is identical with that which is used in the operation of a conventional power brake, Figure 47-14. Vacuum from the intake manifold is connected to one side of a cylinder. Atmospheric pressure on the other side

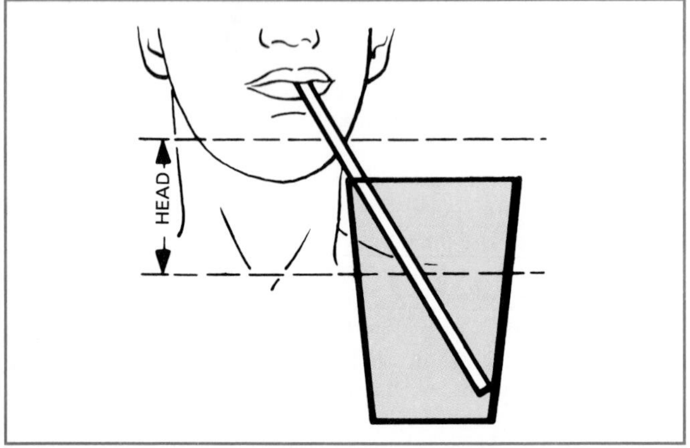

Figure 47-13. When air pressure within a straw falls below the pressure of the atmosphere, liquid is forced through the straw.

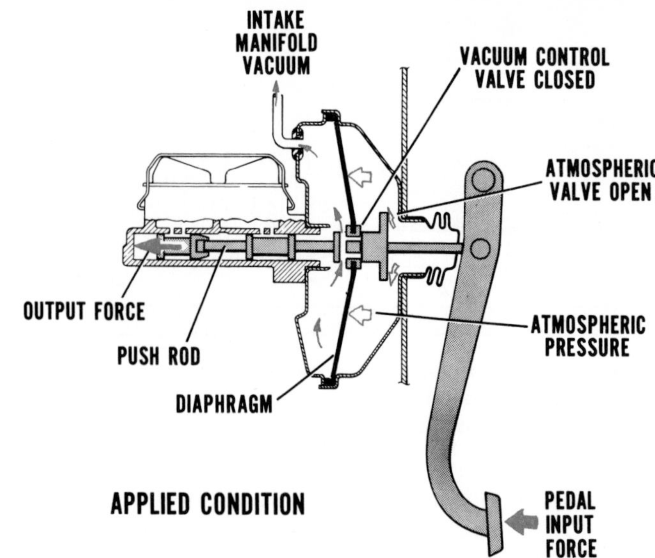

Figure 47-14. This single diaphragm power brake booster utilizes the difference in pressure between the manifold vacuum and atmospheric pressure to operate the master cylinder push rod and apply the brakes. (Chrysler)

causes a piston to move toward the vacuum side. This motion is used to apply the brakes.

Compressed Air

Compressed air is air that has been forced into a smaller space than which it would ordinarily occupy in its free or atmospheric state. In the automotive field, compressed air has many uses. In addition to inflating tires, it is used for such purposes as spraying paint, blowing dirt and other foreign matter from parts, operating brakes on heavy trucks, and in powering impact tools and wrenches.

As mentioned, normal air (due to the weight of air above it) has a pressure of 14.7 psi. However, when speaking of compressed air, its initial pressure of 14.7 psi is ignored, and the pressure of the compressed air is given as the amount of pressure above atmospheric. In other words, a gauge for measuring the pressure of compressed air registers zero when connected only to the atmosphere.

By providing suitable piping, compressed air will "flow" in much the same manner as liquids flow through connecting pipes. For example, if one reservoir contains air under pressure, and another one contains air at atmospheric pressure, air will flow from the reservoir of higher pressure to that of lower pressure. This flow will continue until both reservoirs are at the same pressure.

Air Brakes

The application of compressed air in the operation of automotive ***air brakes*** is relatively simple. In Figure 47-15, compressed air is admitted into a cylinder which encloses a piston. The force of the compressed air will cause the piston to move until it encounters a resistance equal to the force developed by the compressed air. For example, the piston in Figure 47-15 has an area of 10 sq. in., while the compressed air has a pressure of 10 psi. The total force developed will be 10×10 or 100 psi. This is similar to the effect of hydraulic power illustrated in Figures 47-4 and 47-6.

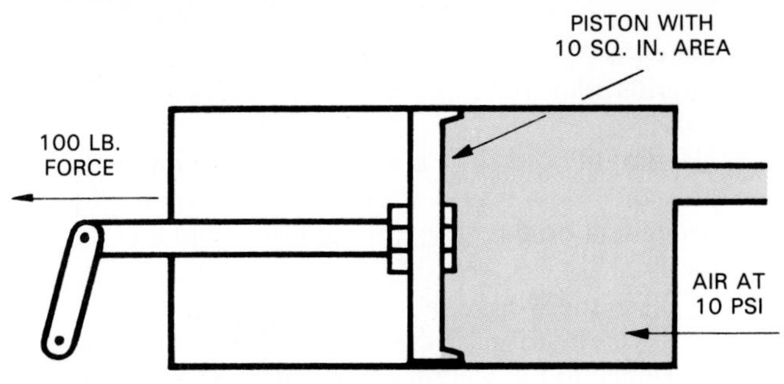

Figure 47-15. Principle of a simple air brake.

Remember that the quantity of air acting on the piston does not affect the force developed. The only factors involved are the air pressure and the area of the piston on which the air pressure is acting.

Principle of the Syphon

Normal air pressure (atmospheric pressure) is used to do many kinds of work. For example, a ***syphon*** drains tanks by means of atmospheric pressure. In a syphon, a tube or pipe is connected to two tanks, one higher than the other. See Figure 47-16. Once the connecting tube has been filled with liquid, it will continue to flow to the lower tank until the level of the liquid is the same in both tanks or until the upper tank is empty.

The force that causes the liquid to flow is the pressure of the atmosphere. This pressure forces the liquid up the short arm of the syphon, AB. (Theoretically, water can be raised a height of 34 ft.) At higher altitudes, where air pressure is less than at sea level, the liquid would be raised a shorter distance.

The action of the syphon is interesting. The force of the atmosphere tending to push the liquid up the short arm of the syphon is opposed by downward pressure of the weight of the liquid. See AB in Figure 47-16. Similarly, atmospheric pressure tends to drive the liquid up the long arm, CD. However, it is resisted by the weight of the liquid in CD, which is greater than in AB. Therefore, the atmospheric pressure meets greater resistance in pushing the liquid up CD than in pushing it in the opposite direction. The liquid will therefore flow up arm AB and continue until it reaches the lower reservoir.

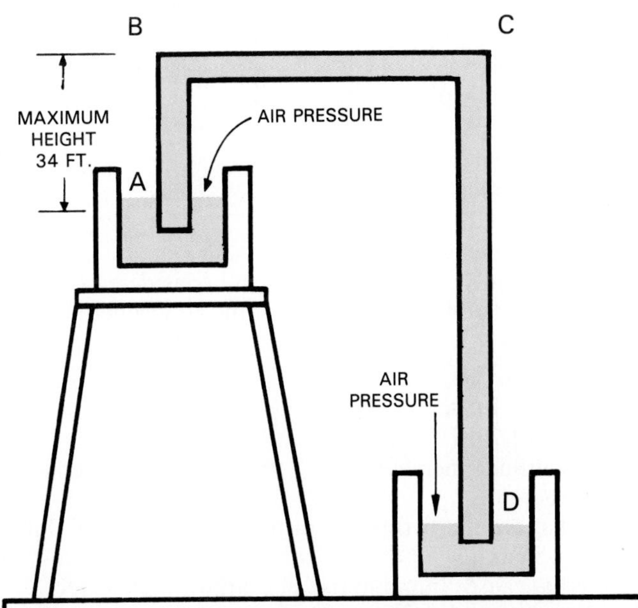

Figure 47-16. Atmospheric pressure causes liquid in a syphon to flow from the upper tank to the lower tank.

Venturi Tube

The ***venturi tube*** is important in carburetion. A venturi is a tube with a restricted section. See Figure 47-17. When a liquid or air is passed through a venturi tube, the speed of flow is increased at the area of restriction, and fluid pressure is decreased. The same amount or volume of air flows through all sections of the carburetor throat. Obviously, if the throat area decreases, the velocity must increase in order to maintain the same rate of flow. Then, when the area increases, the velocity will decrease.

This is clearly illustrated in Figure 47-17, which shows how venturi action vacuum varies in different sections of the carburetor. Vacuum is measured in inches of mercury and designated as inches Hg (initials used in chemical symbol representing mercury). Note that vacuum and velocity of airflow are at a maximum at the point of maximum restriction. Also worth noting, vacuum is zero at the air inlet to the carburetor where air pressure is normal.

Venturi action is used in carburetors to maintain the correct air/fuel ratio throughout the range of speeds and loads of the engine.

Boyle's Law

An important characteristic of air and other gases is explained in ***Boyle's law.*** It states that if the pressure on a gas in a confined space is doubled, the gas will be com-

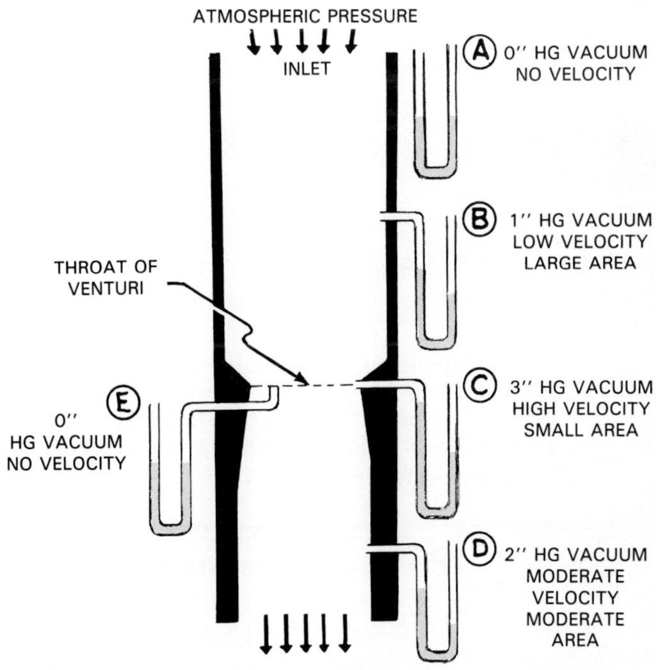

Figure 47-17. Air moving in the throat of a venturi will have greater velocity, and maximum vacuum will exist. If airflow is stopped, however, vacuum becomes zero.

pressed to half its original volume, provided the temperature remains the same.

Boyle's law is normally given as follows: If the temperature of a confined gas is kept constant, its volume will vary inversely with its pressure.

This may be expressed as follows:

$$P'V' = PV$$

P and V represent the pressure and volume of a gas before compression; P′ and V′ are the pressure and volume after compression.

EXAMPLE: The pressure of a quantity of gas is 50 psi, and it occupies 10 cu. ft. This air is compressed until it exerts a pressure of 75 psi while the temperature remains constant. What is the volume of the gas after compression?

$$\frac{V}{V'} = \frac{P'}{P}$$

$$\frac{75}{50} = \frac{10}{P}$$

$$75P = 500$$

$$P = 6.7 \text{ cu. ft.}$$

Charles' Law

Another important law relating to the behavior of gases under different conditions is known as ***Charles' law.*** It states that under constant pressure, the volume of a gas varies directly with its absolute temperature. The absolute temperature is the temperature in degrees Celsius plus 273. This law is expressed as follows:

$$\frac{V'}{V_2} = \frac{T'}{T_2}$$

V′ is the volume of a gas when its absolute temperature is T′ and V_2 is the volume of the same gas when its absolute temperature is T_2.

EXAMPLE: To what volume will 110 cu. ft. of gas at 15°C. expand if heated at a constant pressure to 55°C?

$$T' = 150 + 273 = 288° \text{ absolute}$$

$$T_2 = 550 + 273 = 328° \text{ absolute}$$

$$\frac{110}{V_2} = \frac{288}{328}$$

$$36080 = 288V_2$$

$$V_2 = 125.3 \text{ cu. ft.}$$

An understanding of the principles of pneumatics is more important than ever to auto technicians. Today's energy-absorbing bumpers, passenger restraint systems, air pumps, vacuum door locks, and temperature control systems utilize those principles.

Chapter 47–Review Questions

Write your answers on a separate sheet of paper. Do not write in this book.

1. Define hydraulics.
2. Give three examples of the use of hydraulics in automotive systems.
3. Name four major advantages of a hydraulic system.
4. State Pascal's law.
5. Liquids may be considered incompressible. True or False?
6. "Hydraulic head" is based on the principle that the pressure of a liquid standing in an open vessel is dependent on the _____ of the liquid and the _____ of the liquid.
7. _____ is the weight in pounds of a cubic inch
8. _____ is the ratio of the weight of a unit volume of a substance to the weight of one cubic inch of water.
   (A) Specific gravity
   (B) Hydraulic head
   (C) Hydraulic pressure
   (D) Hydraulic force
9. In vessels containing fluid, if the output piston is larger than the input piston, the force will be _____ (increased or decreased) in the same proportion as the areas of the two pistons.
10. Define pressure as applied to a hydraulic system.
11. What automotive "assembly" depends on specific gravity for its operation?
12. When force is applied at the brake pedal in hydraulic brake operation, pressure is transmitted _____ throughout the fluid to the wheel cylinders and caliper cylinders.
13. What is the weight of a cubic foot of water?
    (A) 31.18 lb.
    (B) 47.77 lb.
    (C) 54.57 lb.
    (D) 62.36 lb.
14. If a force of 50 lb. is applied to a piston in a hydraulic cylinder of 2 sq. in. in area, what is the pressure?
    (A) 25 psi.
    (B) 50 psi.
    (C) 100 psi.
    (D) 200 psi.
15. In hydraulic jack operation, the input piston is _____ (smaller or larger) than the output piston.
16. In a hydraulic jack, the input piston has an area of 3 sq. in. and the output piston has an area of 300 sq. in. If 30 lb. of force is applied to the input piston, what is the lifting force of the output piston?
    (A) 100 lb.
    (B) 300 lb.
    (C) 1000 lb.
    (D) 3000 lb.
17. Define pneumatics.
18. Technically, _____ and _____ are considered fluids.
19. What is the normal pressure of the atmosphere?
    (A) 0.0
    (B) 4.17 psi.
    (C) 7.14 psi.
    (D) 14.7 psi.
20. As altitude increases, _____ (more or less) air enters a carburetor.
21. What are the two major differences between a liquid and a gas?
22. What causes liquid to rise in a straw?
23. In a conventional power or booster brake on a passenger car, what power is used to assist the driver to apply the brakes?

24. What will a conventional gauge on a tank of compressed air register when the tank is open to the atmosphere?
    (A) 0.0
    (B) 4.17 psi.
    (C) 7.14 psi.
    (D) 14.7 psi.
25. Explain the principle of the syphon.
26. A venturi is a tube with a _____.
27. For what purpose is a venturi used in a carburetor?
28. In what area of the carburetor is airflow the fastest?
    (A) At top of carburetor throat.
    (B) At start of restricted section.
    (C) At point of maximum restriction.
    (D) At bottom of restricted section.
29. State Boyle's law.
30. Charles' law states that under constant pressure, the volume of a gas varies indirectly with _____.
31. Name three automotive applications of pneumatics.

An understanding of basic hydraulic and pneumatic principles will help the technician troubleshoot and repair many systems in late-model vehicles. (Honda)

This rotor reconditioning system allows the technician to machine disc brake rotors without removing them from the vehicle. (RTI Technologies, Inc.)

Chapter 48
Automotive Brakes

After studying this chapter, you will be able to:
- Explain the forces and factors involved when braking a vehicle.
- Describe brake system materials, hydraulic components, and mechanical parts.
- State how disc brakes and drum brakes operate.
- Describe how various power brake systems and anti-lock brake systems operate.
- Tell how to service brake hydraulic systems.
- Give steps of performing disc brake overhaul and drum brake overhaul.
- Solve brake troubleshooting problems.
- Give examples of power brake system and anti-lock brake system service operations.

Fundamentals of Automotive Brake Systems

An ***automotive brake mechanism*** is a friction device designed to change power into heat. When the brakes are applied, they convert the power of momentum of the moving vehicle (kinetic energy) into heat by means of friction. The ***brake system,*** then, is a balanced set of mechanical and hydraulic devices used to retard the motion of the vehicle by means of friction.

Friction

Friction is the resistance to relative motion between two bodies in contact. It is caused by the interlocking of projections and depressions of the two surfaces in contact. Therefore, there is less friction between polished surfaces than between rough surfaces.

Friction varies with different materials and with the condition of the materials. There is less friction between surfaces of different materials than between those of the same material. There is less friction when one surface (tire tread) rolls over the other (pavement) than when it slides.

Coefficient of Friction

The amount of friction created is proportional to the pressure between the two surfaces in contact. It is independent of the area of surface contact. The amount of friction developed by any two bodies in contact is said to be their *coefficient of friction* (C.O.F.).

The coefficient of friction is found by dividing the force required to slide the "weight" over the surface by the weight of the object. See example in Figure 48-1. If a 60 lb. pull is required to slide a 100 lb. weight, then the C.O.F. would be 60 divided by 100 or .60. If only 35 lb. is required to slide the 100 lb. weight, then the C.O.F. would be .35.

It has been established that the coefficient of friction will change with any variation of the condition of the surfaces. Any lubricant, of course, will greatly reduce the C.O.F., which is why it is so important to keep any grease, oil, or brake fluid from brake lining. Even an extremely damp day will cause some variation in C.O.F.

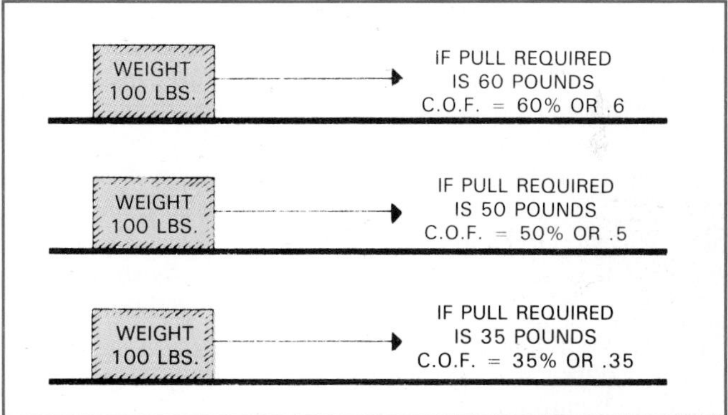

Figure 48-1. The coefficient of friction is equal to the force required to slide a body across a surface divided by the weight of the body.

Braking Forces

Tremendous forces are involved when braking a vehicle. The vehicle must be brought to a stop in a much shorter time than is required to bring it up to speed. To better visualize this, compare horsepower required to accelerate a vehicle and horsepower needed to stop it.

A compact vehicle with a 75 hp four cylinder engine requires about 15 sec. to accelerate to 60 mph. The same vehicle is expected to be able to stop from 60 mph in not more than six sec. That is: the brakes must do the same amount of work as the engine, but 2 1/2 times faster.

Effect of Weight and Speed

The effect of weight and speed of the vehicle on braking is a big factor in heat generation in both passenger cars and trucks. If the weight of the vehicle is doubled, the energy of motion to be changed into heat energy is doubled. Also, the amount of heat to be absorbed and dissipated will be doubled. The effect of higher speeds on braking is even more serious. If the vehicle speed is doubled, four times as much stopping power must be developed. Also, the brake mechanisms must absorb and dissipate four times as much heat.

It follows that if both weight and speed of a vehicle are doubled, the stopping power must be increased eight times, and the brakes must absorb and dissipate eight times as much heat.

Brake Temperatures

The amount of heat generated by brake applications usually is greater than the rate of heat absorption and dissipation by the brake mechanisms, and high brake temperatures result. Ordinarily, the time interval between brake applications avoids a heat buildup. If, however, repeated panic stops are made, temperatures may become high enough to damage the brake lining, Figure 48-2, brake drums or rotors, and brake fluid. In extreme cases, the tires have been set on fire.

Brake and Tire Friction

When brakes are applied on a vehicle, the brake shoes and friction pads are forced into contact with the brake drums and rotors to slow the rotation of the wheels. Then, the friction between the tires and the road surface slows the speed of the vehicle.

However, friction between the shoes and drums and between the pads and rotors does not remain constant. Rather, it tends to increase with temperature. From tests, the coefficient of friction of brake lining has been found to range from 0.35 to 0.50.

The coefficient of friction of the tire on the road is approximately .02. However, this varies with the road surface. Surface contact is the determining factor. The fastest stops are obtained with the wheels rotating. As soon as the wheels become locked, there is less friction and the car will not stop as quickly or as evenly. The ***anti-lock braking systems*** work on the principle of very rapid and repeated brake applications and releases to bring the vehicle to a stop without locking or skidding.

Stopping Distance

Average stopping distance is an important consideration directly related to vehicle speed. As charted in Figure 48-3, a vehicle that can be stopped in 45 ft. from 20 mph will require 125 ft. to stop from 40 mph. At 60 mph, the vehicle will require 272 ft. to stop; almost the length of a football field.

Note in reading the chart in Figure 48-3, you need to consider "reaction time" in addition to the time required to make a sudden stop. It is the time you need to react to a warning of danger, move your foot, and apply the brakes. For example, when the vehicle is going 20 mph, it will travel 22 ft. before the brakes are actually applied.

Braking System Operation

As covered in detail in Chapter 47, Hydraulics and Pneumatics, liquids are virtually incompressible, and pressure throughout a closed hydraulic system will be the same in all directions. These principles are used to operate hydraulic service brakes on all passenger cars.

A simplified drawing of an automotive hydraulic brake system is shown in Figure 48-4. Typically, the brake pedal is connected to a master cylinder by a push rod. The master cylinder is connected to the service brakes at each wheel by brake lines and hoses. The entire hydraulic system is filled with a special brake fluid, which is forced through the system by the movement of the master cylinder pistons.

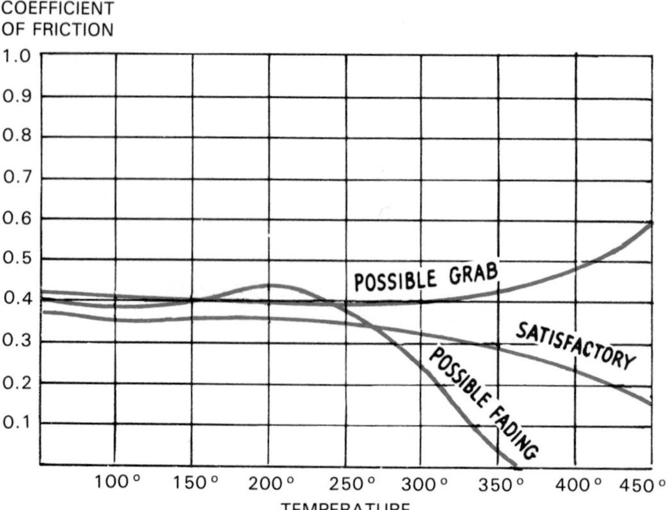

Figure 48-2. Note how temperature affected the coefficient of friction of three different brake linings.

MINIMUM STOPPING DISTANCES AT DIFFERENT SPEEDS			
MPH	REACTION TIME DISTANCE	BRAKING DISTANCE	TOTAL STOPPING DISTANCE
10	11 FEET	9 FEET	20 FEET
20	22	23	45
30	33	45	78
40	44	81	125
50	55	133	188
60	66	206	272
70	77	304	381

Based on tests made by the Bureau of Public Roads, F.H.A.

Figure 48-3. Chart compares the minimum stopping distances at different speeds on dry, level concrete surfaces.

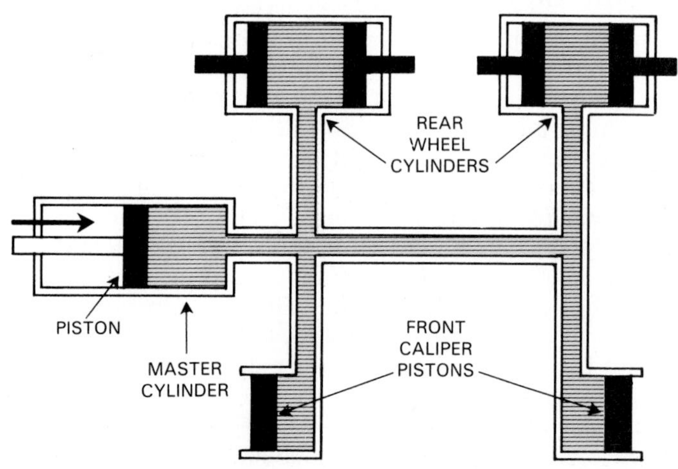

Figure 48-4. Simplified drawing depicts the major components of an automotive hydraulic brake system.

The front brakes are "disc" type, wherein friction pads in a brake caliper are forced against machined surfaces of a rotating disc (rotor) at each wheel to slow and stop the vehicle, Figure 48-5.

The rear brakes are "drum" type, wherein internal expanding brake shoe assemblies are forced against the machined surface of a rotating drum at each wheel to slow and stop the vehicle, Figure 48-6.

As the brake pedal is depressed, it moves pistons within the master cylinder, forcing hydraulic brake fluid throughout the brake system and into cylinders at each wheel. The fluid under pressure causes the cylinder pistons to move which, in turn, forces the brake shoes and/or friction pads against the brake drums and/or rotors to retard their movement and stop the vehicle.

Figure 48-7 shows how the force applied to the brake pedal is multiplied. In this instance, 800 lb. of force is applied to a master cylinder piston area of 0.8 sq. in., resulting in a pressure of 1000 psi (800 ÷ 0.8) in the hydraulic brake system.

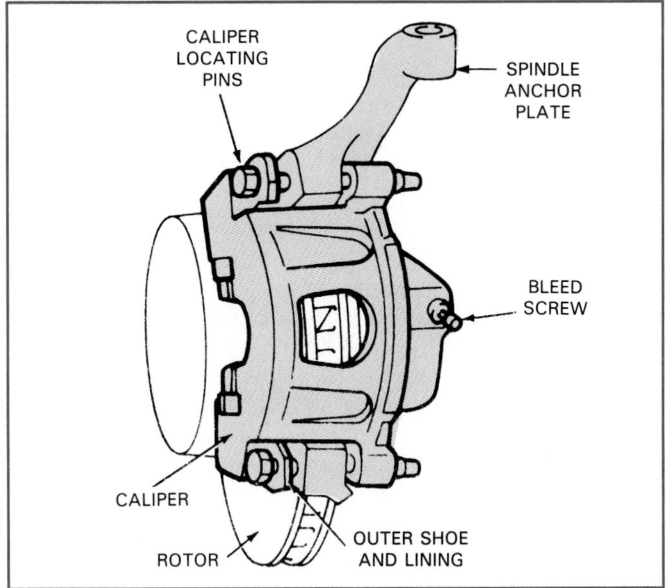

Figure 48-5. Typical disc brake assembly uses a hydraulic caliper to apply inboard and outboard brake shoes to a moving rotor. (Ford)

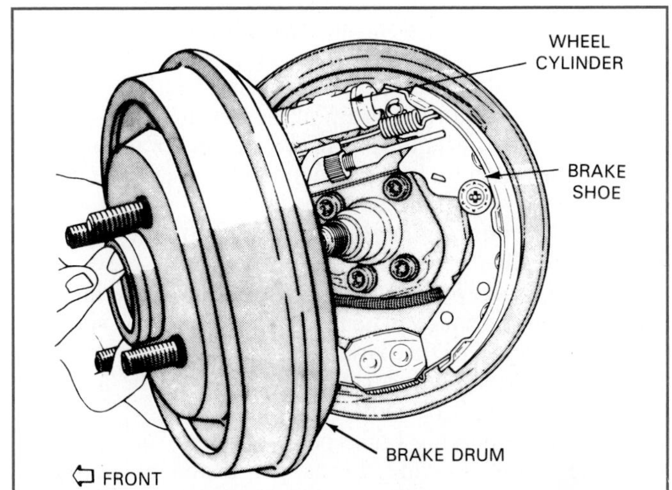

Figure 48-6. Typical drum brake assembly uses a hydraulic wheel cylinder to apply primary and secondary brake shoes to rotating drums.

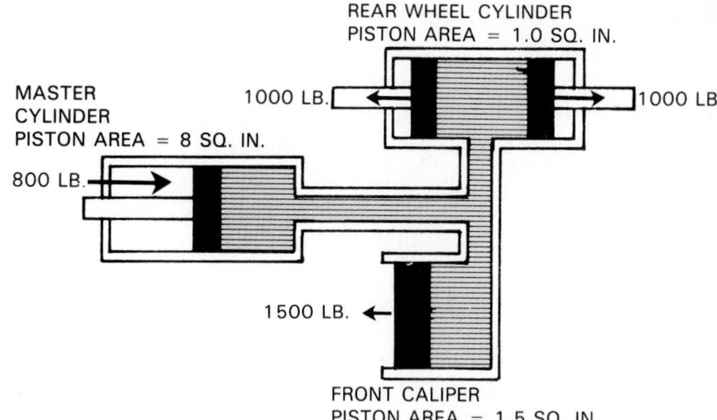

Figure 48-7. Diagram illustrates how force applied to the brake pedal is multiplied hydraulically at the wheel cylinders and calipers.

Each front brake caliper bore has a piston area of 1.5 sq. in. Since the caliper is single piston type, a force of 1500 lb. (1000 × 1.5) is applied to the brake friction pads. Each rear wheel cylinder has a piston area of 1.0 sq. in. Since each rear wheel cylinder has two pistons, a total force of 2000 lb. (1000 × 1.0 × 2) is produced.

Brake Lining Materials

There are three basic types of brake lining in current original equipment use: non-asbestos organic, metallic, and semi-metallic. In the past, asbestos was used almost exclusively in the manufacture of brake lining. Then it was discovered that breathing dust containing asbestos fibers can cause serious bodily harm.

Organic lining usually consists of a compound of non-asbestos friction materials, filler materials, and high temperature resins. These elements are thoroughly mixed, formed into shape, and placed under heat until a hard, slate-like board is formed. The material is cut and bent into individual segments and attached to drum brake shoes, or it is cut into individual "pads" and attached to disc brake shoes. See Figure 48-8.

Metallic brake lining is made of sintered metal. It is composed of finely powdered iron or copper, graphite, and lesser amounts of inorganic fillers and friction modifiers. After thorough mixing, a lubricating oil is usually added to prevent segregation of different materials. The mixture is

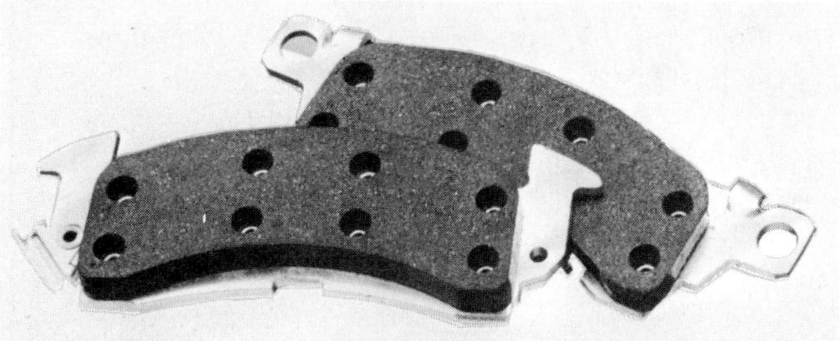

Figure 48-8. New formula disc brake friction pads are compounded from special resins, friction modifiers, and a blend of advanced non-asbestos fibers. (Brake Systems, Inc.)

then put through a briquetting process and compressed into desired form.

The non-asbestos organic type brake lining or semimetallic lining is used for conventional brake service. Under extreme braking conditions (police cars, ambulances, sports cars), the metallic type lining is used. Under severe usage, the frictional characteristics of the metallic lining are more constant than that of the organic lining.

Brake Rotor and Drum Materials

A ***disc brake rotor*** is defined as the parallel-faced circular rotational member of a disc brake assembly. Generally, rotors are made of cast iron with ventilating fins separating the two braking surfaces. See Figure 48-9. Venting makes the rotors run cooler and provides quicker cool-down after a brake application.

Disc brake rotor braking surfaces are precisely machined for quality of finish, thickness, parallelism, and absence of lateral runout. Some rotors have a groove machined in the braking surfaces to help reduce brake noise.

The use of cast iron for the braking surface of ***brake drums*** is almost universal. The drums are either solid cast iron or steel with an inner lining of cast iron. Some all steel drums were used in the past. However, cast iron has a higher coefficient of friction than steel so it generally is the first choice of the car manufacturers. The steel/cast iron brake drums are used on heavier vehicles because the assembly has the strength of steel and the frictional properties of cast iron.

Some brake drums are made of aluminum with a cast iron liner for the braking surface. Since aluminum has a higher conductivity of heat than cast iron, brake drums of the aluminum/cast iron construction will operate at much lower temperatures than solid cast iron drums. Regardless of the material used in brake drum construction, drums occasionally are provided with cooling fins.

Disc Brakes

Single piston, sliding or floating caliper disc brakes have been used on the front wheels of passenger cars for many years. See Figure 48-10. In the past, fixed calipers with four pistons per caliper actuated the friction pads to stop the rotors and the vehicle. The two caliper housings were "fixed" in place. There was no lateral movement as with the single piston caliper.

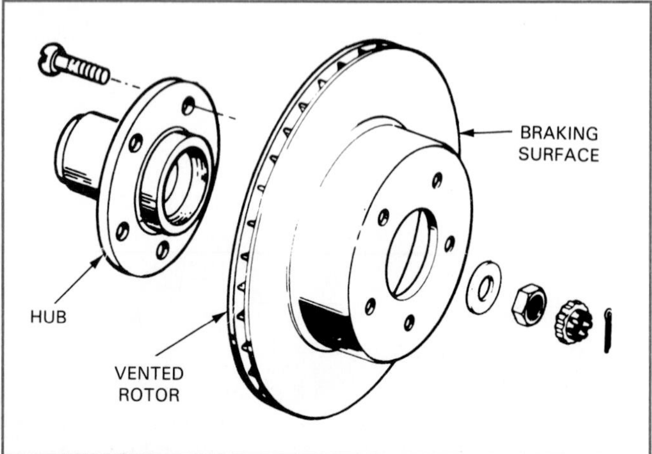

Figure 48-9. Vented rotors are commonly used on disc brakes because they run cooler than solid rotors. (Chrysler)

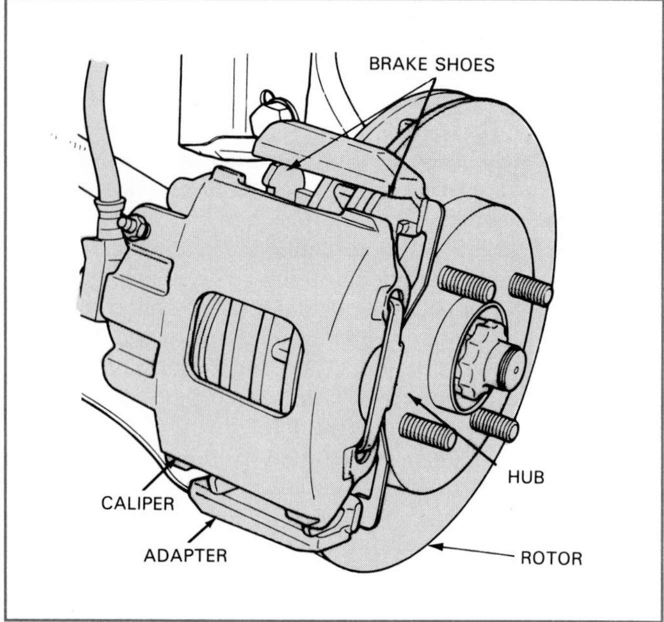

Figure 48-10. Typical disc brake assembly consists of a hydraulic caliper and brake shoes mounted on an adapter and straddling a machined rotor installed on a wheel hub. (Chrysler)

With ***single piston disc brake calipers,*** Figure 48-11, the caliper slides or floats on mounting bolts or on sleeves on mounting bolts or pins to apply friction pads to the machined surfaces of a rotating disc. Disc brakes are self adjusting. The caliper piston seals are designed to retract the piston enough to allow the friction pad to lightly contact the rotor without any drag.

Generally, when front-wheel drive moved into prominence, some modifications of the single piston caliper became necessary. Chrysler, for example, introduced an assembly featuring a sliding caliper and adapter setup utilizing pins, bushings, and sleeves. See Figure 48-12.

GM Rear Disc Brakes

Some General Motors cars have disc brakes front and rear. ***Rear disc brakes,*** like front disc brakes, operate by means of a single piston caliper applying friction pads to a rotating disc or rotor. In addition, however, each GM rear disc brake caliper is equipped with a parking brake actuator mechanism which, in turn, is operated by a series of cables connected to the parking brake pedal.

The GM ***parking brake mechanism*** on the rear caliper, Figure 48-13, consists of a lever and screw setup whereby the screw is threaded into a nut built into the caliper piston assembly. The lever is actuated by a series of cables connected to the parking brake pedal. The parking brake pedal assembly is a ratcheting mechanism that must be pumped (up to 3 1/2 strokes) to set.

When the parking brake pedal is depressed, the lever turns the screw, moving the caliper piston outward and causing the caliper to slide inward. The resulting clamping action of the friction pads on each rear rotor locks the brakes. This action causes the rotor to reduce its speed, and therefore the car speed is reduced.

1. BOLT BOOT
2. MOUNTING BOLT
3. BUSHING
4. SLEEVE
5. BLEEDER VALVE
6. CALIPER HOUSING
7. PISTON SEAL
8. PISTON
9. BOOT
10. INBOARD SHOE AND LINING
11. OUTBOARD SHOE AND LINING
12. WEAR SENSOR

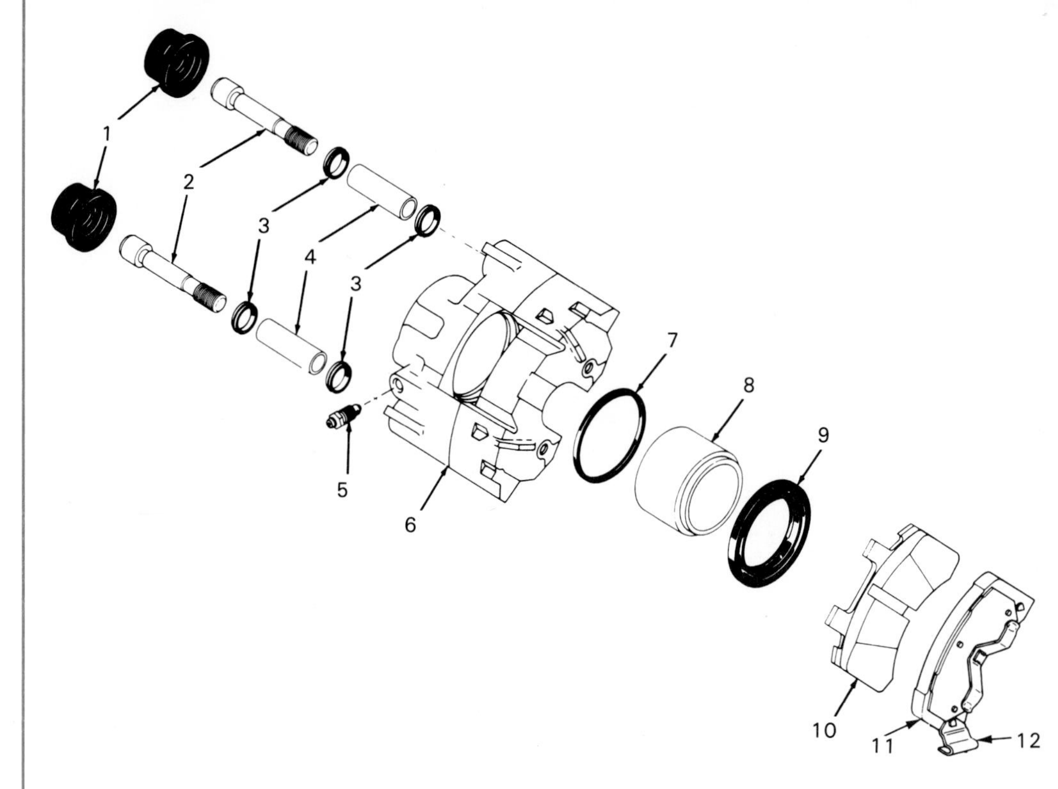

Figure 48-11. Exploded view of a disc brake caliper reveals the relative locations of parts. (Cadillac)

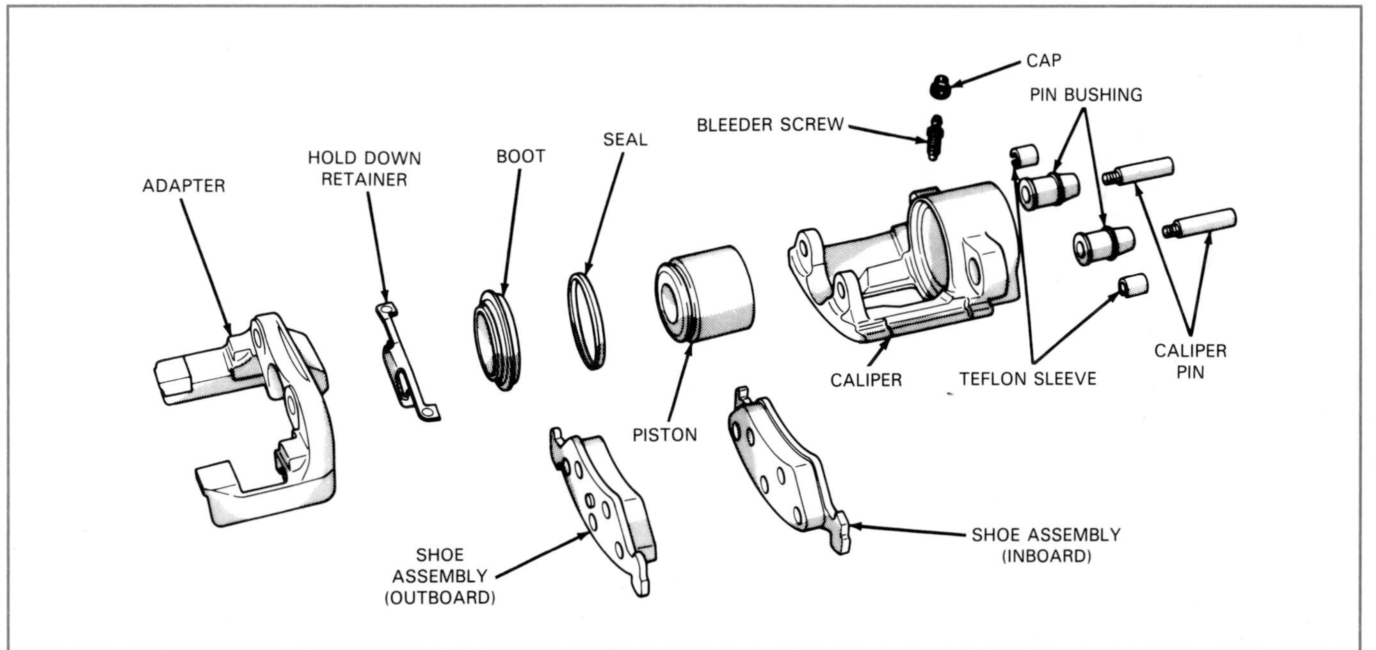

Figure 48-12. Various parts that make up a sliding disc brake assembly are identified. (Chrysler)

Typically, the GM parking brake will release automatically when the transmission selector lever is placed in reverse or any drive position with the ignition ON. The automatic release system utilizes a vacuum diaphragm on the parking brake pedal assembly, a vacuum switch on the transmission range selector, and connecting vacuum hoses.

The GM parking brake system uses four separate cables. The front cable joins the intermediate cable at the adjuster screw. From there, the intermediate cable extends to the rear of the car where right and left rear cables connect by means of an equalizer.

Ford Rear Disc Brakes

Ford's four wheel disc brake system uses a dual master cylinder, hydraulic brake booster, and a two-way pressure control valve to balance front and rear braking action.

The rear disc brake caliper assembly is similar to Ford's pin slider front brake caliper, except for the addition

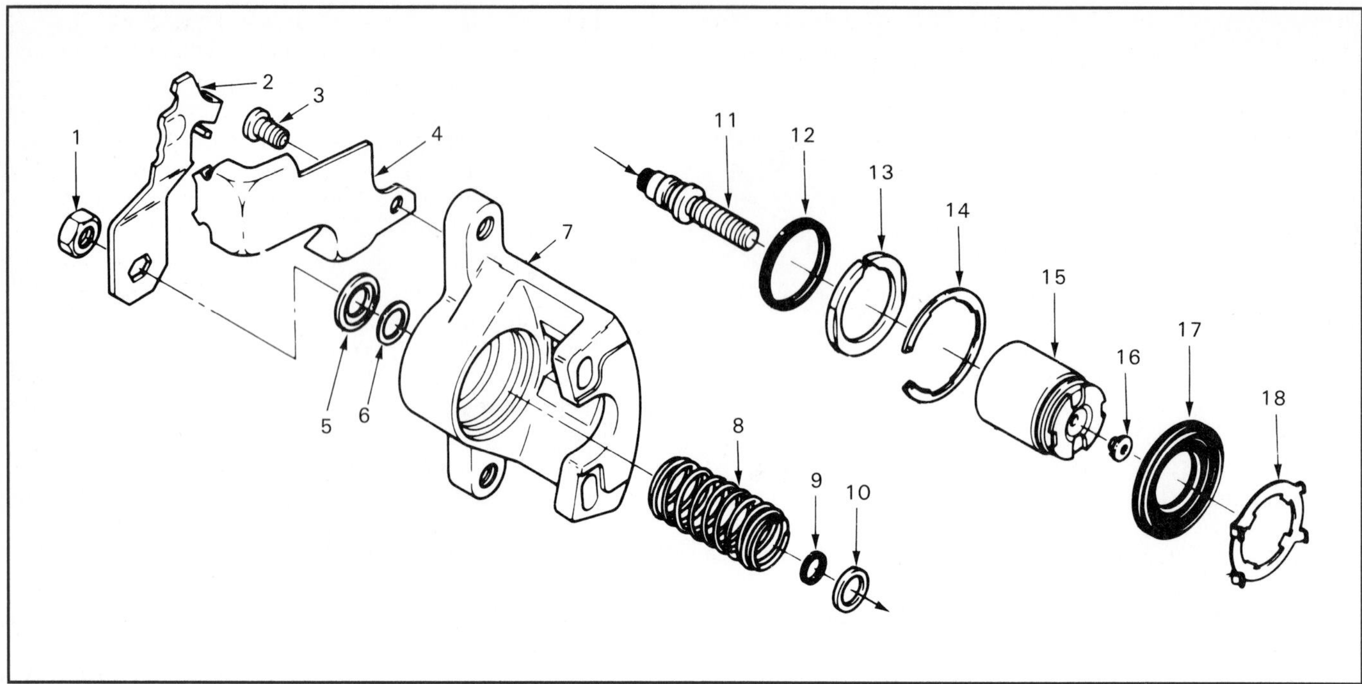

Figure 48-13. General Motor's rear disc brake assembly includes: 1–Nut. 2–Parking brake lever. 3–Bolt. 4–Bracket. 5–Seal. 6–Washer. 7–Caliper housing. 8–Balance spring and retainer. 9–Shaft seal. 10–Thrust washer. 11–Actuator screw. 12–Piston seal. 13–Piston locator. 14–Retainer. 15–Piston assembly. 16–Two-way check valve. 17–Caliper boot. 18–Shoe retainer. (Cadillac)

of a parking brake mechanism. The parking brake lever on the back of the caliper is cable operated by the parking brake pedal.

The caliper assembly consists of a housing, piston, parking brake mechanism, inboard and outboard friction pads, wear indicator, anti-rattle clip, and anchor plate. See Figure 48-14. The caliper assembly slides on two greased locating pins (attaching bolts) between the caliper and anchor plates. Rubber insulators keep the pins from direct contact with the caliper housing.

The parking brake lever is attached to the operating shaft. When the parking brake is applied, the cable rotates the lever and shaft. Three steel balls roll between ramps formed in pockets on the opposing heads of the operating

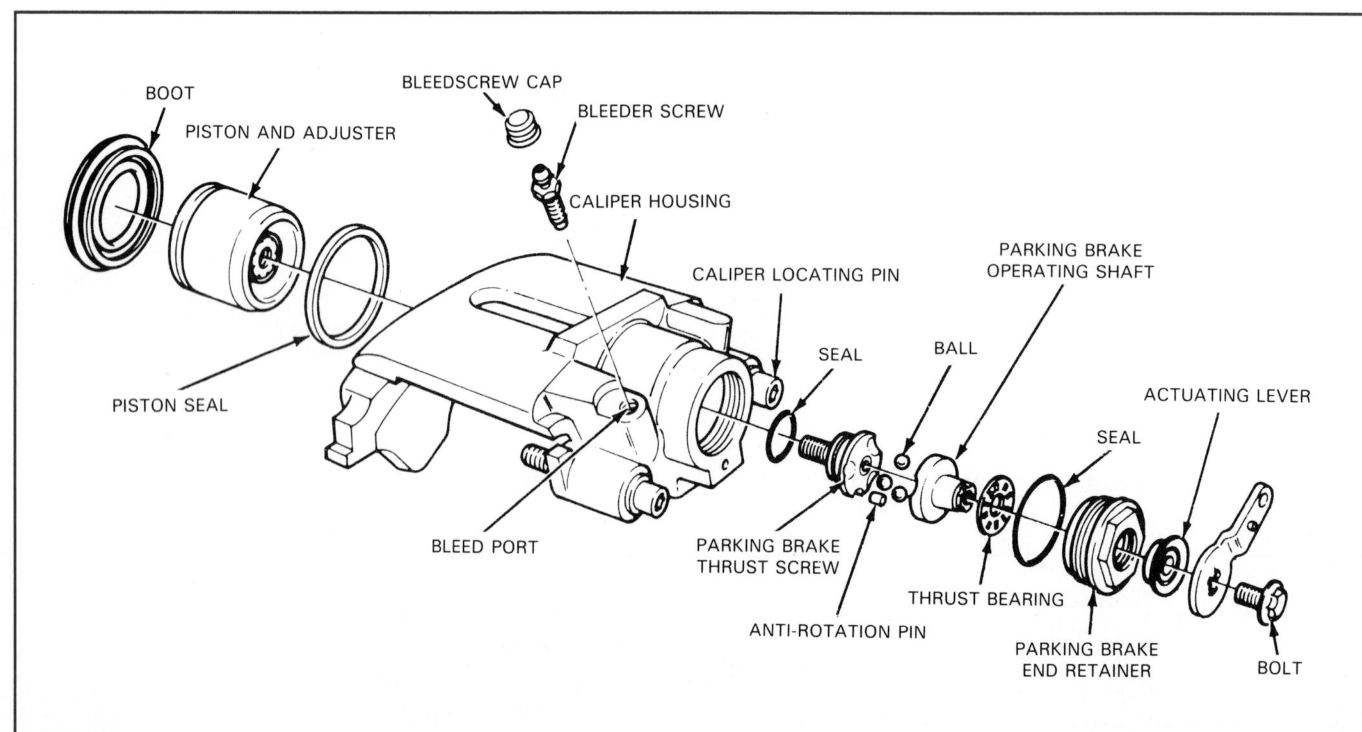

Figure 48-14 Exploded view of Ford rear disc brake assembly shows parts disassembly of screw-type parking brake mechanism. (Ford)

shaft and thrust screw. The steel balls force the thrust screw away from the operating shaft, forcing the friction pads against the rotor.

The parking brake is self adjusting. An automatic adjuster in the piston moves on the thrust screw to compensate for lining wear.

Drum Brakes

There are many factors that contribute to the effectiveness of ***drum brakes,*** including:

1. The radius of the brake drum.
2. The radius of the vehicle's wheel.
3. The area of the brake lining.
4. The amount of force applied to the brake shoes.
5. The coefficient of friction of the braking surfaces.
6. Self-energization.
7. Servo action.
8. The coefficient of friction between the tires and the road surface.

Factors 1 and 2 are simply a matter of leverage. It is obvious that a small brake drum on a large wheel will require more frictional surface, or higher pressure on the surface, than a large brake drum on a small wheel.

Factor 3 presents another obvious contribution to drum brake effectiveness. Certainly the greater the area of frictional material on the brake shoes, the more effective braking action will be.

Factor 4 is important because the pressure of the brake shoes against the drums starts with the force applied to the brake pedal. Then, that force is multiplied by leverage (and usually assisted by a power brake unit) and further increased hydraulically by the size of the master cylinder bore and bore of the wheel cylinders.

Factor 5 takes into consideration the coefficient of friction of the brake lining material, its area, and the material used in the casting of the brake drums.

Factor 6 greatly multiplies the force pressing the brake shoes against the drums. ***Self-energization*** is created by the tendency of the rotating drum to drag the brake lining and brake shoe along with it. The frictional force between the brake drum and lining tries to turn the brake shoe around the anchor pin. Since the drum itself prevents this, the brake shoe is "self-energized" or forced even more strongly against the drum, Figure 48-15.

Factor 7, ***servo action,*** is obtained by the "wedging" action of the brake shoe, which starts at the toe of the shoe and keeps increasing as the shoe tries to rotate with the brake drum.

Factor 8 involves tire-to-road surface contact, emphasizing braking to rapidly reduce wheel rotation before stopping the vehicle, rather than locking the brakes and going into a potentially dangerous skid.

Duo-servo Action

Self-energization and servo action are amplified by letting one brake shoe push the other in a move called ***duo-servo action.*** To accomplish this, the shoes are linked together at the bottom by means of an adjusting mechanism. See Figure 48-15.

When the brakes are applied, the toe of the primary shoe is pulled away from the anchor pin by the revolving brake drum. The heel of the primary shoe then pushes the adjusting mechanism against the heel of the secondary shoe. This forces the toe of the secondary shoe against the anchor pin and both brake shoes are applied against the brake drum with multiplied effect.

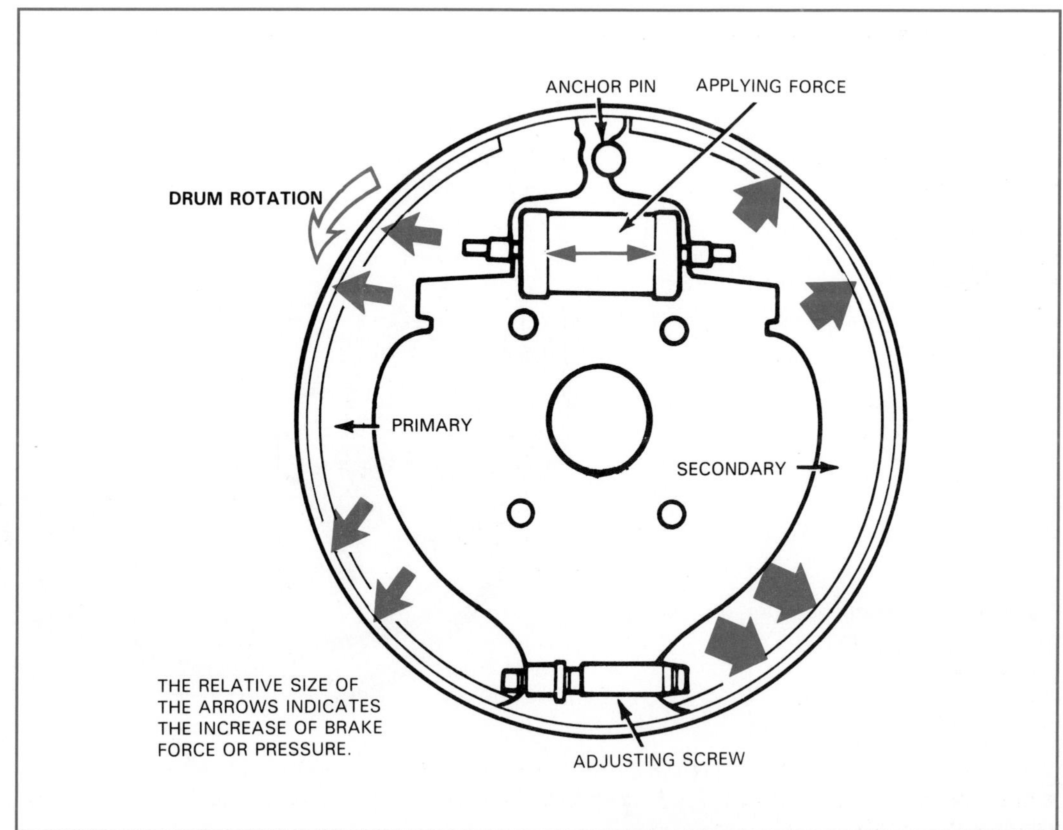

Figure 48-15. Drum braking action involves the self-energization of the primary shoe by drum rotation; servo wedging action of the primary shoe against the drum; duo-servo action as the primary shoe pushes the secondary shoe against the drum with increased force. (Ford)

Non-servo Action

Some front-wheel drive vehicles are equipped with ***non-servo rear wheel brake assemblies.*** See Figure 48-16. These non-servo systems utilize a ***leading-trailing shoe design*** in place of the popular duo-servo design.

The non-servo brake assembly has twin anchors at the lower end of the backing plate. Since the heel end of each brake shoe contacts the anchor, there is no duo-servo action created between the shoes. Instead, the leading shoe does most of the drum-stopping action during forward motion. The trailing shoe, in turn, does most of the work during rearward motion.

Drum Brake Mechanical Parts

Mechanical parts of a typical single anchor automatic adjuster rear wheel drum brake assembly include: backing plate, brake shoes, shoe retracting springs, hold-down spring assemblies, self-adjusting assembly, and parking brake parts. See Figure 48-17.

Drum Brakes–Rear-wheel Drive Cars

Most modern drum brake assemblies on rear-wheel drive cars are look-a-likes. See Figures 48-18 and 48-19. The brake shoes are placed on the backing plate with the star wheel adjuster in place between the heel ends of the shoes. The toe ends seat against the anchor pin, Figure 48-17. The primary shoe and the secondary shoe each slide on three separate raised sections of the backing plate. Each raised section is referred to as a "boss." So, there are a total of six bosses on any one backing plate.

Hold-down assemblies keep the shoes in place against lubricated bosses on the backing plate. The wheel cylinder is mounted below the anchor with the wheel cylinder links engaged in the web of each brake shoe. Hydraulic pressure at the wheel cylinder must be great enough to overcome spring pressure of the retracting springs. Once hydraulic pressure is greater than the retracting springs, the primary shoe and secondary shoe are each pushed out against the brake drum. Retracting springs hold and serve to retract the shoes after each brake application.

The ***self-adjusting brake assembly*** consists of an actuating lever; actuator link, Figure 48-18 or guide plate and adjuster cable, Figure 48-19; lever return spring; and adjusting screw assembly. The ***self-adjusting principle*** involves actuating the lever to rotate the adjusting screw by driving the vehicle in reverse and making repeated "hard" stops with one forward brake application between each reverse stop.

The ***parking brake*** parts include: a strut and strut spring; front and rear cables; and operating lever. The parking brake is actuated by means of a foot lever or hand lever in the passenger compartment, Figure 48-20.

When the parking brake pedal (or lever) is pushed (or pulled), the front cable moves forward and carries the rear cable (or cables) with it. Since the rear cable is attached to the parking brake lever in each wheel brake assembly, the levers pivot forward and actuate the struts. The struts, in turn, move forward and apply the brake shoes against the drums.

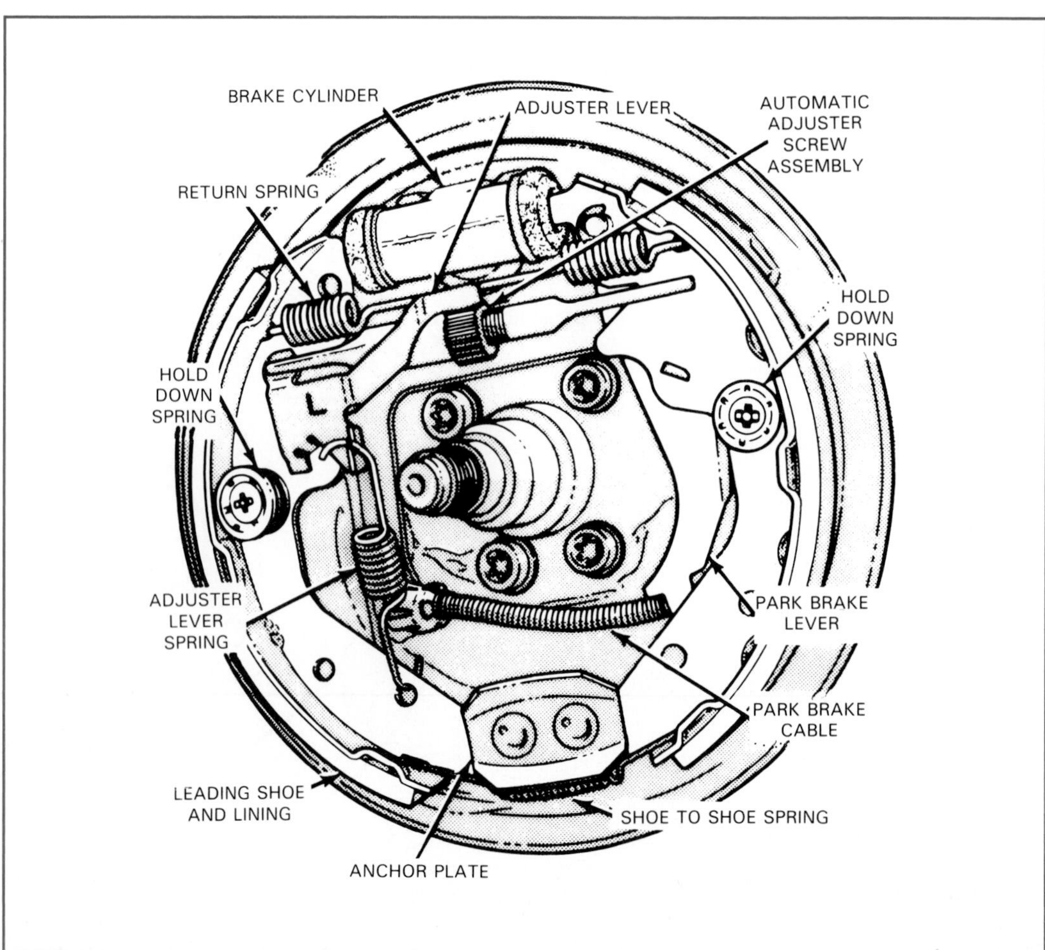

Figure 48-16. Parts of Chrysler's leading-trailing type of rear wheel drum brake assembly are pointed out and identified. This non-servo design has solid anchors between the heels of the brake shoes. (Chrysler)

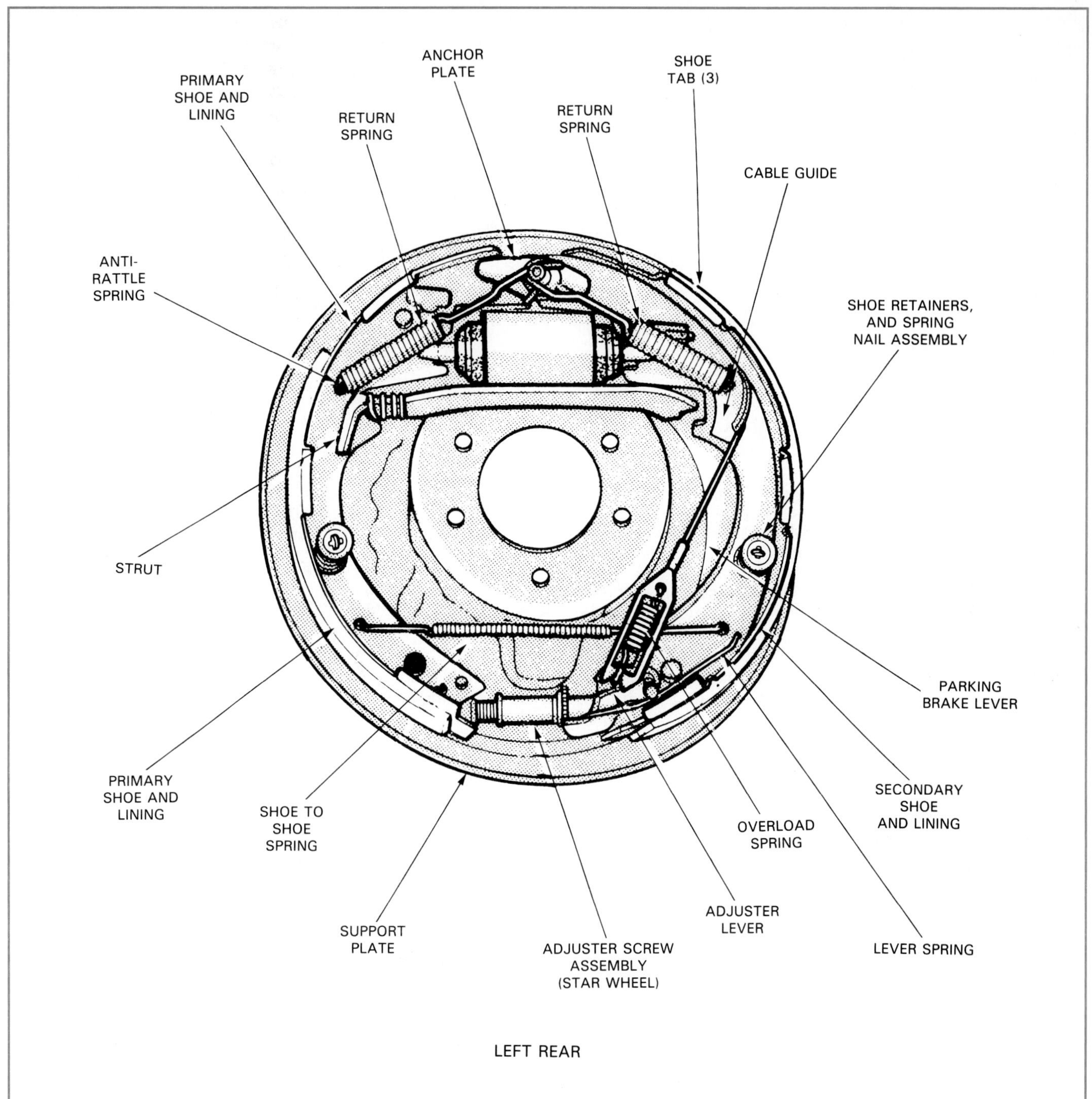

Figure 48-17 Parts of Chrysler's single anchor duo-servo rear wheel drum brake assembly are indicated. (Chrysler)

Drum Brakes–Front-wheel Drive Cars

On some front-wheel drive cars, the rear wheel drum brake has higher placement of the wheel cylinder and a different arrangement of the mechanical parts. See Figure 48-16. The wheel cylinder is located high on the backing plate and the toe ends of the brake shoes directly engage the wheel cylinder pistons. The star wheel adjuster assembly fits between the shoe webs just below the wheel cylinder. The heel ends of the brake shoes seat against twin anchors behind an anchor plate.

The self-adjusting brake assembly usually consists of an automatic adjuster lever, a lever spring, and an automatic adjuster screw assembly. See Figure 48-21.

The parking brake parts include: parking brake lever; rear cable and cable spring; front cable and operating lever in passenger compartment. See Figure 48-16.

Brake Hydraulic System

The basic ***brake hydraulic system*** usually consists of a dual reservoir master cylinder, a combination valve, front disc brake calipers, rear drum brake wheel cylinders, and the connecting brake lines, hoses, and fittings.

Hydraulic Brake Fluid

To provide positive braking action under all conditions, hydraulic brake fluid must meet a lot of special requirements.

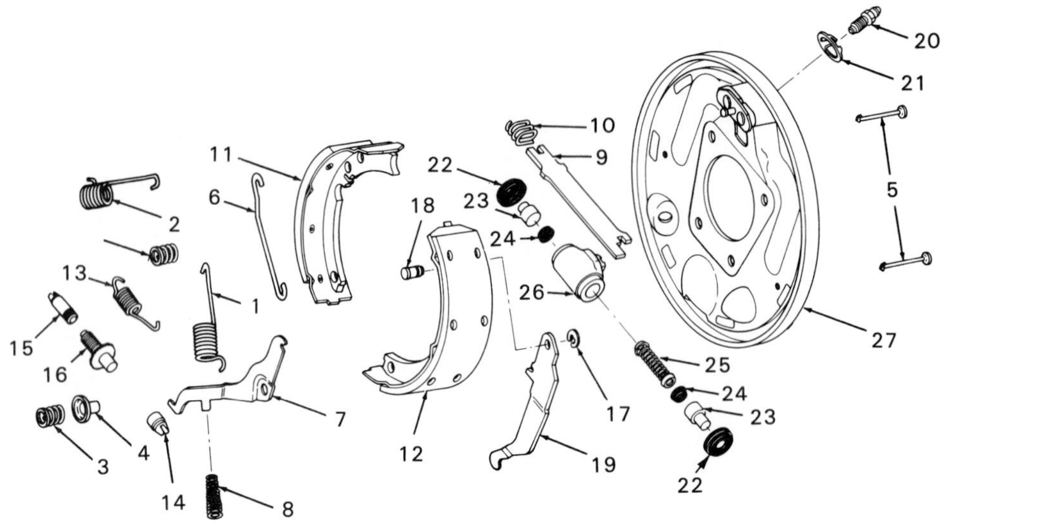

1. RETURN SPRING
2. RETURN SPRING
3. HOLD-DOWN SPRING
4. LEVER PIVOT
5. HOLD-DOWN PIN
6. ACTUATOR LINK
7. ACTUATOR LEVER
8. LEVER RETURN SPRING
9. PARKING BRAKE STRUT
10. STRUT SPRING
11. PRIMARY SHOE AND LINING
12. SECONDARY SHOE AND LINING
13. ADJUSTING SCREW SPRING
14. SOCKET
15. PIVOT NUT
16. ADJUSTING SCREW
17. RETAINING RING
18. PIN
19. PARKING BRAKE LEVER
20. BLEEDER VALVE
21. CYLINDER RETAINER
22. BOOT
23. PISTON
24. SEAL
25. SPRING ASSEMBLY
26. WHEEL CYLINDER
27. BACKING PLATE

Figure 48-18. Exploded view shows a typical automatic adjuster rear wheel drum brake. Note parts of self-adjusting mechanism at: 6–Actuator link. 7–Actuator lever. 8–Return spring. 13–Adjusting screw spring. 14, 15, 16–Adjusting screws. (Cadillac)

1. GUIDE PLATE AND ADJUSTER CABLE
2. WASHER AND U-CLIP
3. SHOE RETRACTING SPRINGS
4. SECONDARY BRAKE SHOE
5. PARKING BRAKE LEVER
6. ADJUSTER SCREW, SPRING, AND LEVER
7. HOLD-DOWN PIN AND RETAINERS
8. PARKING BRAKE LEVER STRUT AND SPRING
9. ANCHOR PIN

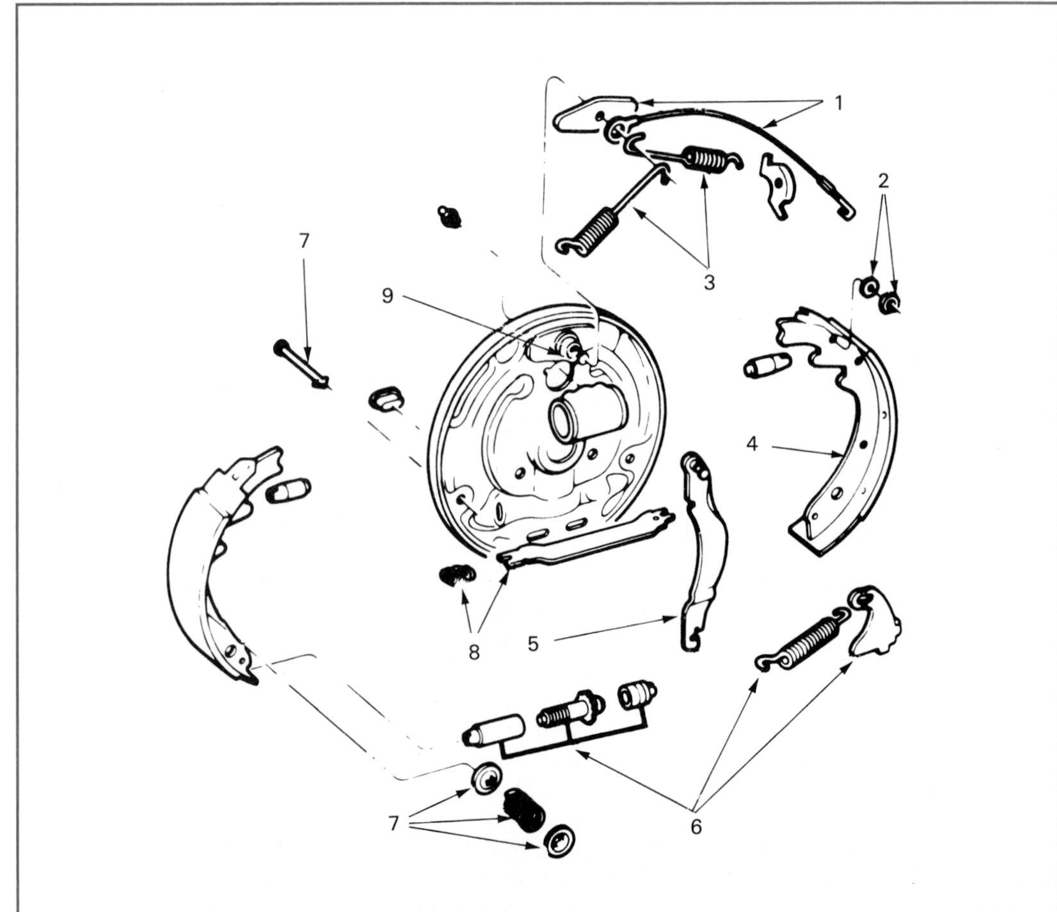

Figure 48-19. Exploded view presents another automatic adjuster rear wheel drum brake. (Chrysler)

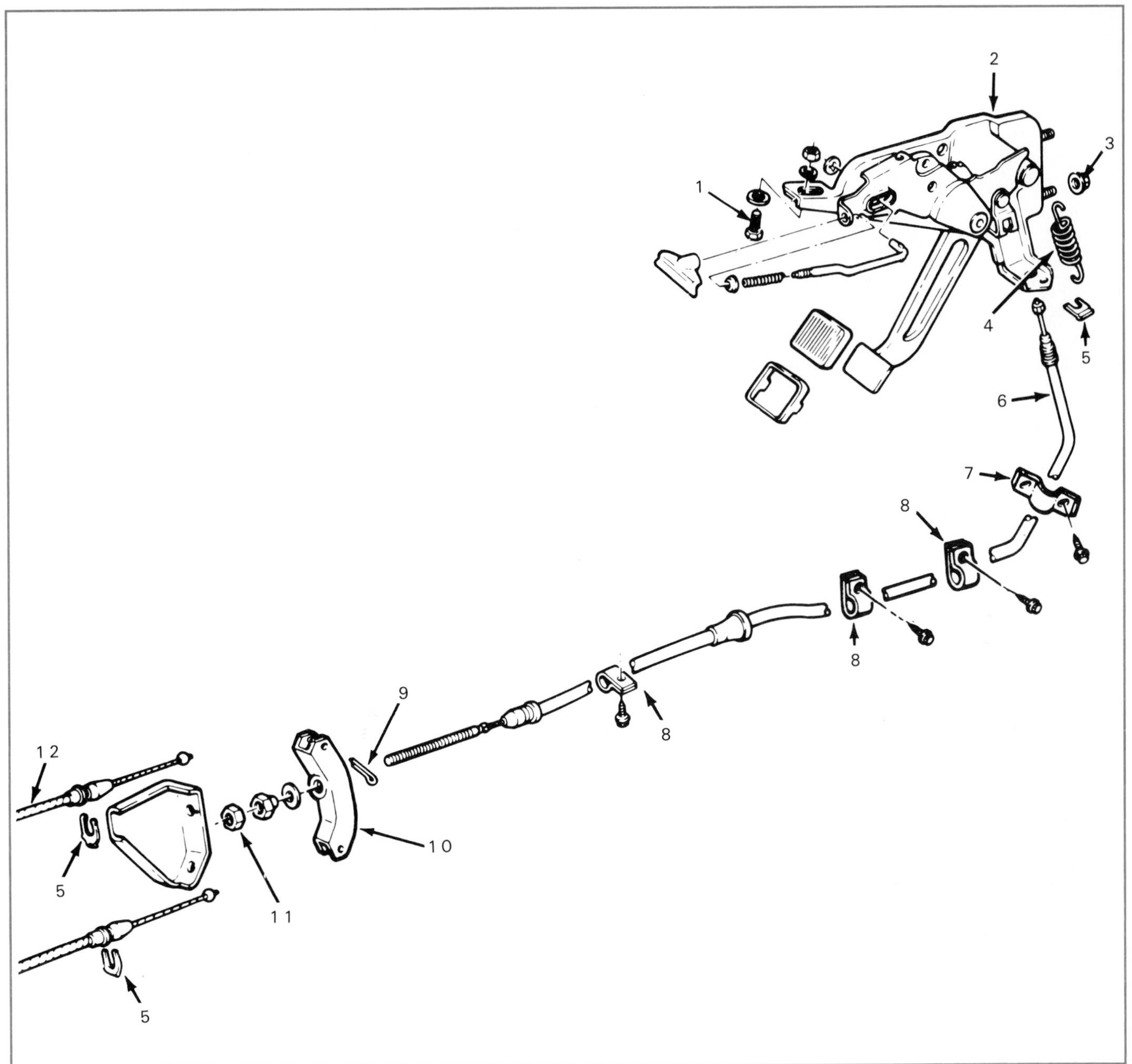

Figure 48-20. Parking brake lever assembly and cables. 1–Mounting bolt. 2–Lever assembly. 3–Mounting stud nut. 4–Return spring. 5–Cable retaining clips. 6–Front cable. 7–Retaining clip. 8–Mounting clips. 9–Cotter pin. 10–Equalizer. 11–Cable adjuster unit and lock nut. 12–Rear cable. (Chrysler)

The Society of Automotive Engineers has established these requirements and submitted them to the American National Standards Institute, and they are recognized as an American National Standard. With this in mind, use only brake fluids that are labeled as meeting SAE Specification J1703 (DOT-3 or DOT-4).

The SAE J1703 specification requires that brake fluids pass tests for boiling point (not less than 401°F or 205°C); viscosity; pH (acidity-alkalinity) value; fluid high temperature and chemical stability; corrosion resistance; fluidity and appearance at low temperatures; evaporation; water tolerance; compatibility; resistance to oxidation; effect on rubber.

Silicone Brake Fluid. ***Silicone brake fluid*** is used in some applications, especially in high performance and commercial vehicles. It is said to be chemically stable and nonhydroscopic (will not absorb water). The manufacturers claim that silicone brake fluid serves as a lubricant between rubber-metal and plastic-metal parts, and it will not attack painted surfaces.

The Society of Automotive Engineers has established a set of minimum performance standards for silicone and other low water tolerant type brake fluids. Silicone brake fluids meeting SAE Specification J1705 (DOT-5) are functionally compatible with existing motor vehicle brake fluids conforming to SAE Specification J1703 and with braking systems designed for such fluids.

Silicone brake fluids are said to perform uniformly over climate extremes. Brakes reportedly will not fail or fade due to fluid malfunction at temperatures as high as 550°F (288°C).

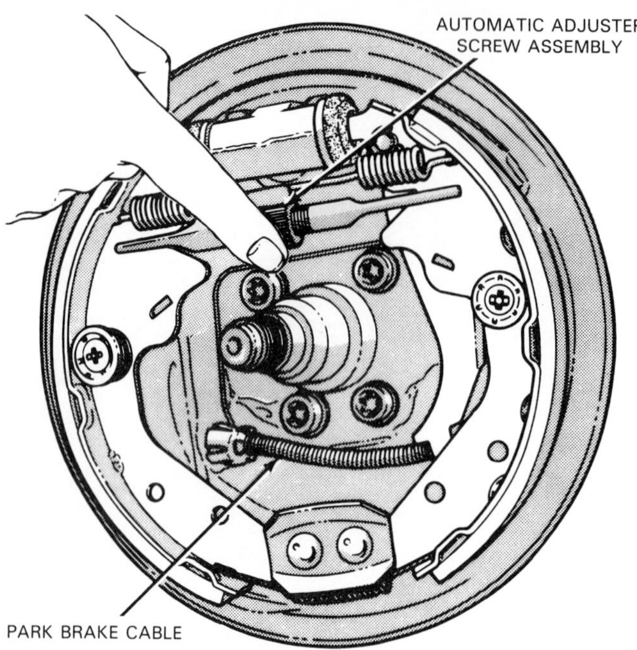

Figure 48-21. Chrysler's leading-trailing rear brake assembly utilizes an automatic adjuster screw assembly between the brake shoe webs near the toes of the shoes. (Chrysler)

Brake Fluid Vapor Lock. With friction and heat governing braking action, there is always a chance of brake fluid and brake mechanisms becoming overheated.

If the brake fluid in the hydraulic system becomes hot enough to vaporize, it emits gas. A drop of brake fluid changed into vapor forms a gas bubble many times the volume of the liquid drop. Small quantities of bubbles produce a problem called ***vapor lock*** that could cause partial loss of braking. If vapor lock occurs in the master cylinder, the brakes could fail without warning.

Mountain driving puts an increased work load on the brakes and brake fluid. With every 2000 ft. rise in altitude, the atmospheric pressure drops approximately one pound, and the boiling point of the brake fluid drops two to three degrees. This lowered boiling point naturally increases the tendency toward vapor lock.

Dual Master Cylinder

The ***dual master cylinder*** is designed to give the front and rear brakes separate hydraulic systems. Should a brake fluid leak occur in one system, the other system will still operate, making it possible to stop the car.

The dual master cylinder is provided with two separate reservoirs for storage of the brake fluid, one primary piston, and one secondary piston, Figure 48-22. The primary piston transfers pressure to the front brakes. The secondary piston transfers pressure to the rear brakes. This setup is a front-to-rear "split" system.

Most late model cars utilize a diagonal "split" brake hydraulic system. That is: the primary piston in the master cylinder transfers pressure to one front brake and one diagonally opposite rear brake. The secondary piston transfers pressure to the opposite front and rear brakes. See Figure 48-23.

Dual Master Cylinder Operation. When the brake pedal is depressed, the push rod of the ***dual master cylinder*** moves the primary piston forward in the cylinder. The hydraulic pressure created and the force of the primary piston spring move the secondary piston forward. When the forward movement of the pistons causes their primary cups to cover the bypass holes, hydraulic pressure is built up and it is transmitted to the front and rear brake assemblies.

When the brake pedal is released, hydraulic pressure in the dual master cylinder is reduced. This pressure relief allows the drum brake shoe retracting springs to retract the shoes from contact with the drums, forcing brake fluid out of the wheel cylinders and back into the master cylinder.

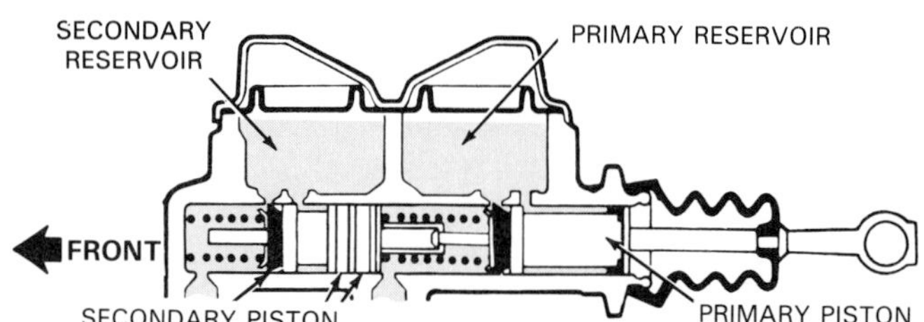

Figure 48-22. Dual master cylinder provides two separate hydraulic brake systems to guard against brake failure if a fluid leak occurs.

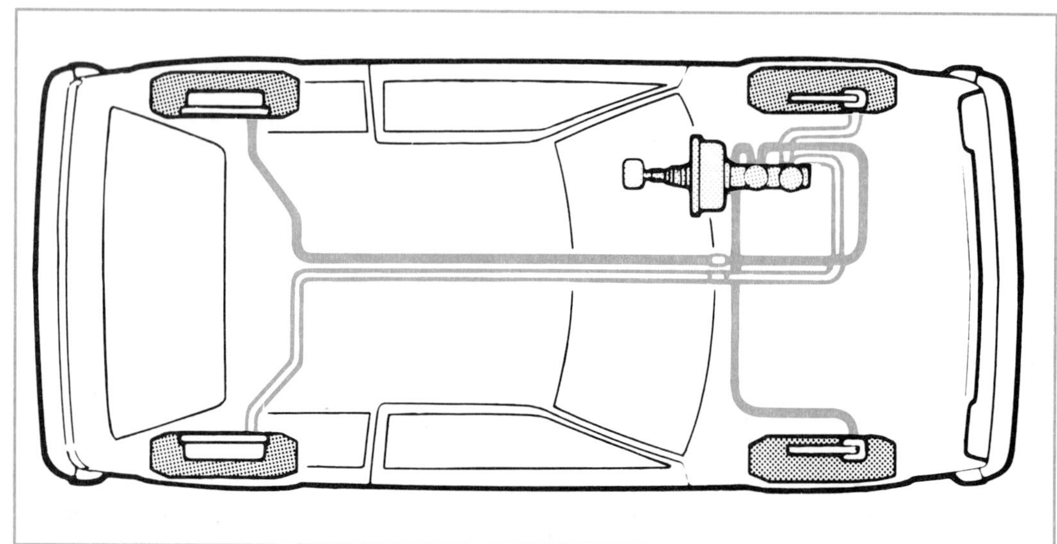

Figure 48-23. A typical dual diagonal braking system is pictured. The primary system of the master cylinder operates the right front and the left rear brakes. The secondary system operates the left front and right rear brakes. (Chrysler)

The reduction in hydraulic pressure also allows the caliper pistons to retract by action of the piston seals, Figure 48-24.

On fast release of the brake pedal, the retracting master cylinder pistons move faster than the returning fluid and a partial vacuum is created. Brake fluid enters the pressure chamber of the master cylinder via breather and bleeder holes in the piston heads. At the finish of release, the pistons return against retaining rings and fluid returns to the master cylinder reservoirs by way of compensating ports.

Master Cylinder Types

Earlier models and some cars having a diesel engine use a conventional ***cast iron master cylinder*** with integral reservoir. A removable metal top and bail wire completes the assembly. See Figure 48-25.

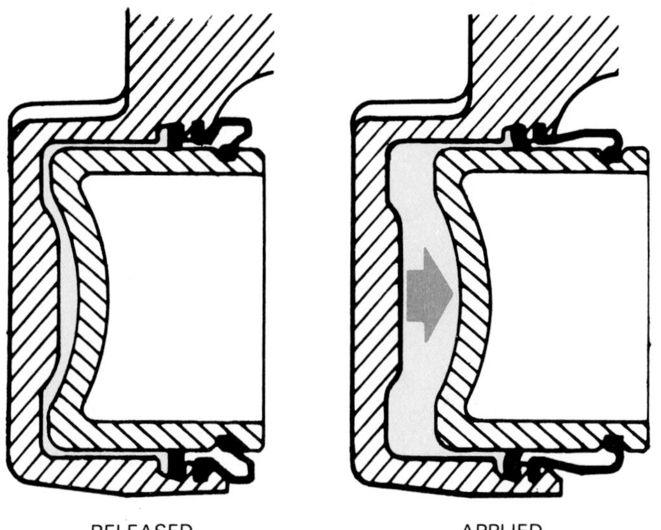

Figure 48-24. Disc brake caliper piston and seal movement is shown in brake-released and brake-applied positions. (Chrysler)

Currently, ***aluminum master cylinders*** are used in most applications, Figure 48-26. The aluminum body is topped by a translucent plastic reservoir. The reservoir carries minimum/maximum markings to permit visual inspection of the brake fluid level.

Also, in keeping with a trend toward "low drag" caliper pistons (deep-set piston seals to aid in piston retraction), a ***quick take-up master cylinder*** is employed. See Figure 48-27. The quick take-up valve is generally built into the master cylinder. It uses a spring loaded ball check to "hold" pressure in the large rear chamber. When the brakes are first applied, movement of the rear piston causes fluid to be displaced forward past the primary piston seal and into the primary chamber which feeds the front brakes.

When hydraulic pressure reaches a predetermined pressure, the check ball unseats and allows fluid to pass from the large rear chamber into the reservoir. Meanwhile, the primary and secondary chambers supply hydraulic pressure to the front and rear brakes in the conventional manner.

When the brake pedal is released, suction created in the large chamber draws fluid from the reservoir through a small bleed hole in the ball seat and around the quick take-up lip seal. In this way, the large rear chamber is quickly refilled with fluid in readiness for the next brake application.

Combination Valves

Most brake hydraulic systems with disc brakes in front and drum brakes at rear utilize a combination valve. See Figure 48-28. The ***combination valve*** usually combines a pressure differential valve, metering valve, and proportioning valve. Earlier models used similar valves, individually mounted, to accomplish specific braking effects.

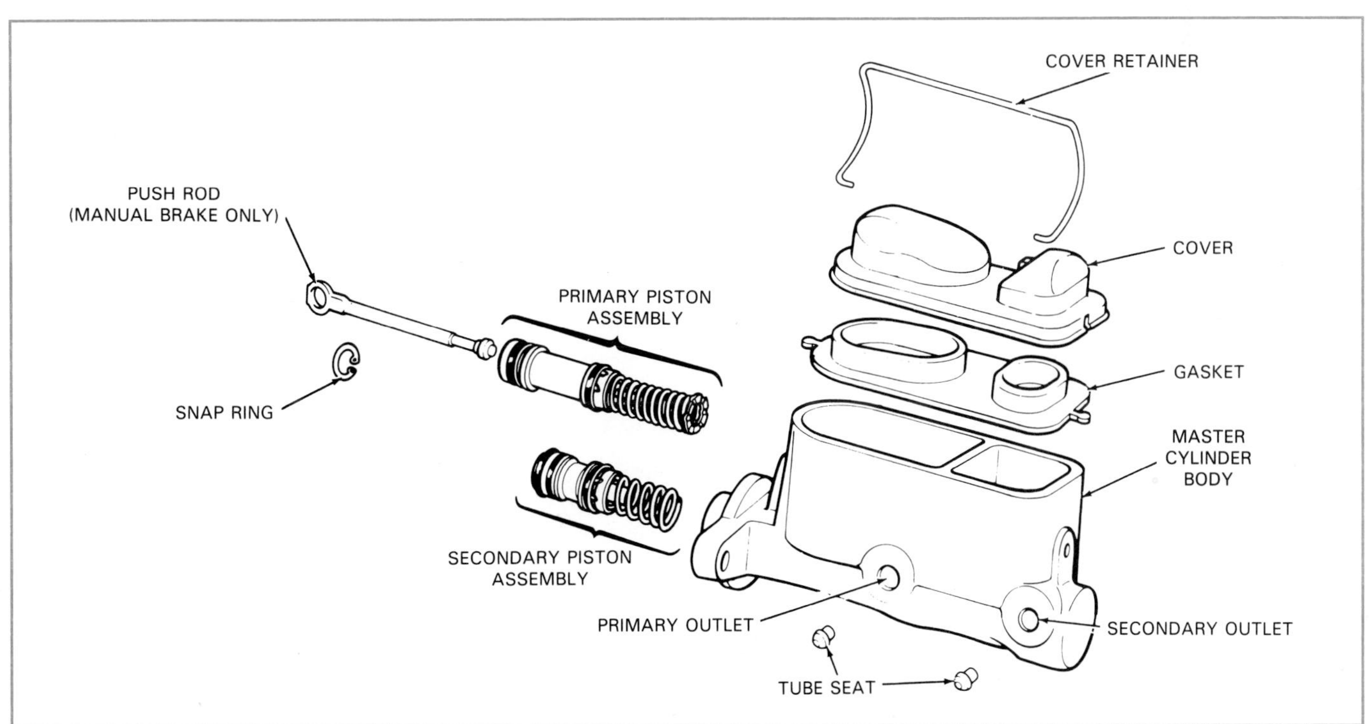

Figure 48-25. For many years, a cast iron dual master cylinder served most passenger car applications. Parts of a disassembled cast iron unit are identified. (Ford)

1. RESERVOIR COVER
2. RESERVOIR DIAPHRAGM
3. RESERVOIR
4. GROMMETS
5. CYLINDER BODY
6. SPRING RETAINER
7. SECONDARY SEAL
8. PRIMARY SEAL
9. SECONDARY PISTON
10. SECONDARY SEAL
11. PRIMARY PISTON ASSEMBLY
12. LOCK RING

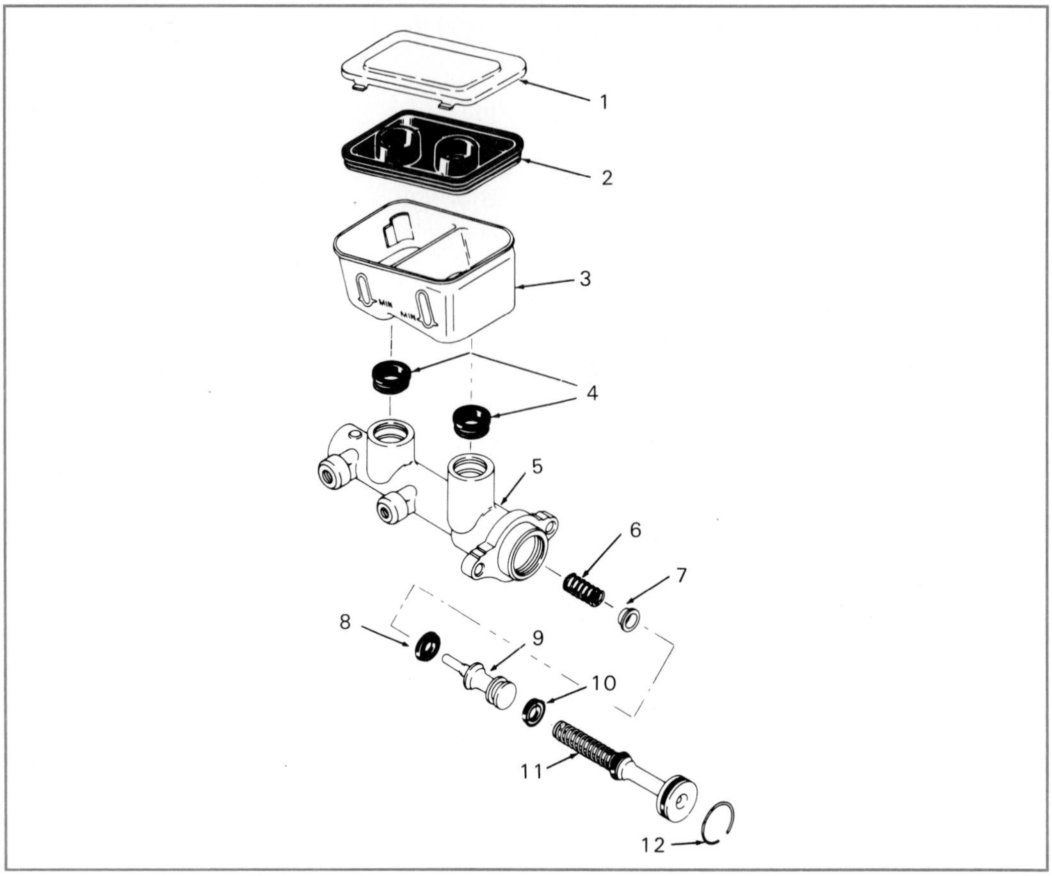

Figure 48-26. Late-model master cylinders have an aluminum body and a plastic reservoir. Note arrangement of internal parts. (Oldsmobile)

1. RESERVOIR COVER
2. DIAPHRAGM
3. RESERVOIR COVER
4. FLUID LEVEL SWITCH
5. O-RING
6. PROPORTIONER
7. PROPORTIONER
8. O-RING
9. GROMMETS
10. CYLINDER BODY
11. SPRING
12. SPRING RETAINER
13. PRIMARY SEAL
14. SECONDARY PISTON
15. SECONDARY SEAL
16. PRIMARY PISTON ASSEMBLY
17. LOCK RING

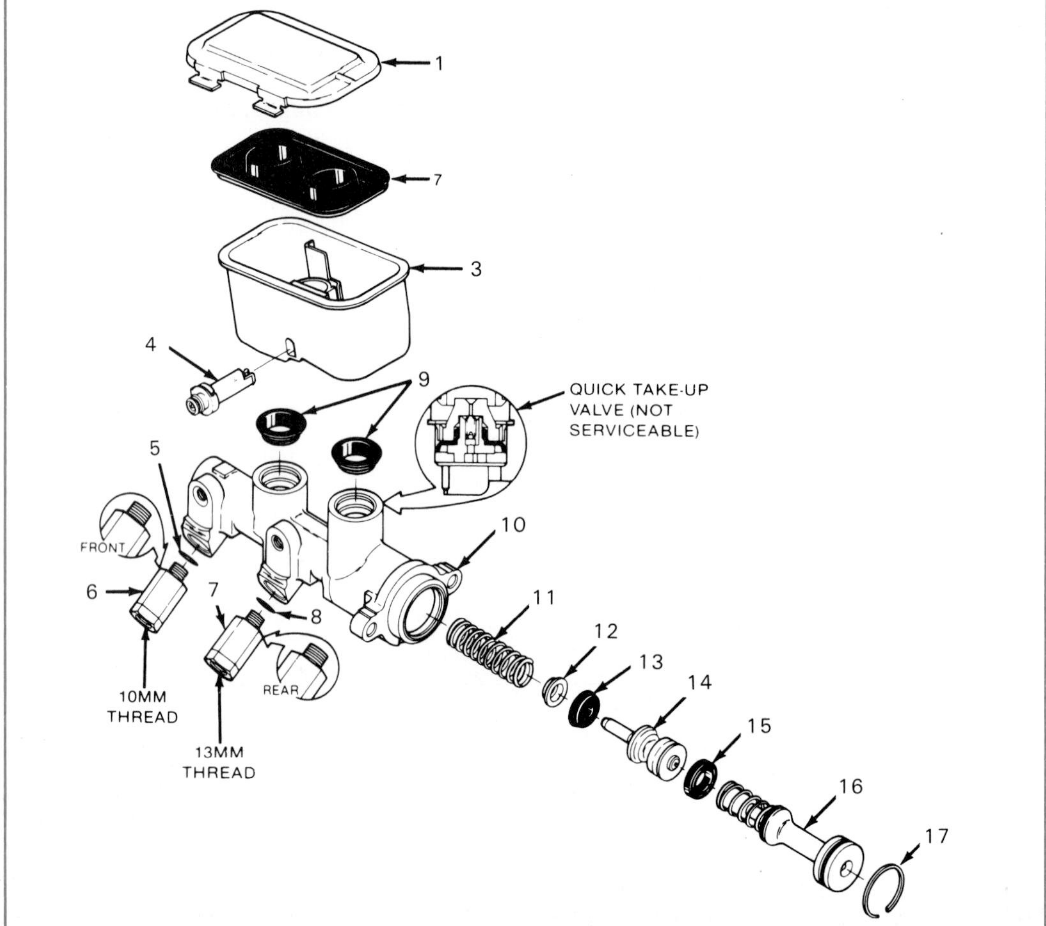

Figure 48-27. Quick take-up valve in the master cylinder provides quick recovery of fluid in the large rear chamber after each brake application. (Cadillac)

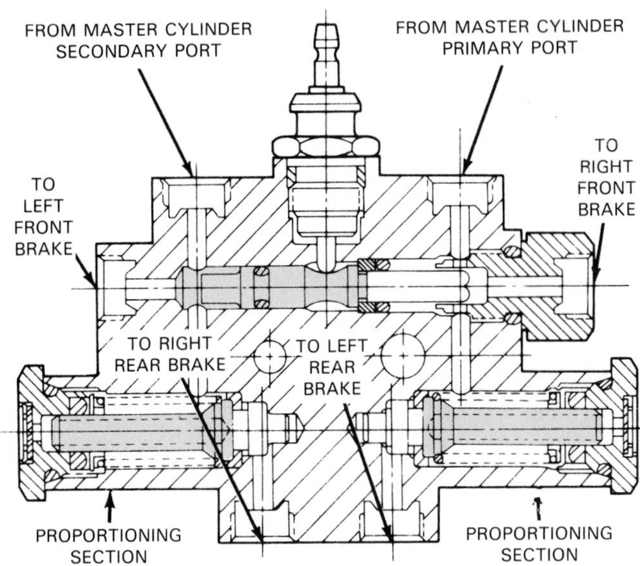

Figure 48-28. Combination valve in the brake hydraulic system utilizes three separate valves to balance pressures and braking action between front and rear brakes. (Chrysler)

The ***pressure differential valve*** section of the combination valve is designed to sense unbalanced hydraulic pressure between the two halves of the "split" system. If the pressures are unbalanced during a brake application, a brake warning lamp switch, Figure 48-29, will activate a red light on the instrument panel.

After the brake system is serviced to correct the unbalanced pressures, the red brake warning light will shut off when the system is properly bled and the brakes are applied to center the piston in the pressure differential valve.

The ***metering valve*** section of the combination valve, Figure 48-29, limits hydraulic pressure to the front disc brakes until a predetermined front input pressure is reached. This pressure approximates the pressure required to overcome the retracting force of the rear brake shoe retracting springs.

The ***proportioning valve section*** of the combination valve regulates outlet pressure to the rear brakes. See Figure 48-29. When the brake pedal is applied, the full brake fluid pressure is permitted to flow through the proportioning valve to the rear brakes. At a specific pressure point, the valve reduces the pressure to the rear brakes to create balanced braking between the front and rear wheels.

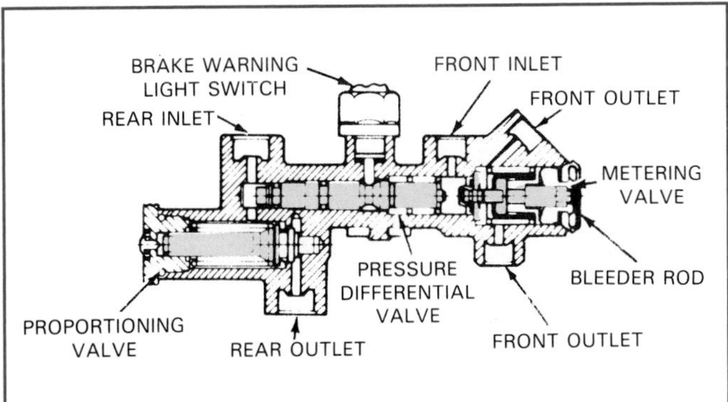

Figure 48-29. Combination valve on cars with front disc brakes and rear drum brakes contains a pressure differential valve, metering valve, and proportioning valve. (Ford)

Disc Brake Calipers

As mentioned earlier, braking with disc brakes is accomplished by forcing friction pads, Figure 48-30, against both sides of a rotating metal disc (rotor). The rotor turns with the wheel of the vehicle and is "straddled" by a housing called a ***caliper assembly.*** Modern disc brakes use the ***single piston caliper.*** However, at least one manufacturer is installing ***two piston calipers*** to go with thicker rotors and friction pads of greater area.

When the brake pedal is depressed, hydraulic fluid forces the caliper piston and the friction pads against the machined surfaces of the rotor. The "clamping" action of the friction pads, Figure 48-30, creates friction and heat to slow down and stop the vehicle.

The principle of operation of a single piston caliper involves the following steps:

1. Hydraulic pressure builds up and exerts equal pressure against bottom of piston and bottom of piston bore. See Figure 48-30 at right.
2. Pressure applied to piston is transmitted to inboard friction pad, forcing it against inboard rotor surface.
3. Pressure applied to bottom of piston bore causes caliper to "slide" or "float" inboard on mounting bolts.
4. Since caliper is one piece, its sliding action causes outboard section of caliper to apply pressure to outboard friction pad, forcing it against outboard surface of rotor.
5. As fluid pressure builds up, clamping action of friction pads stops rotor and vehicle.
6. When hydraulic pressure is released, friction pads and caliper piston move away from rotor, aided by retracting action of piston seal, Figure 48-30.

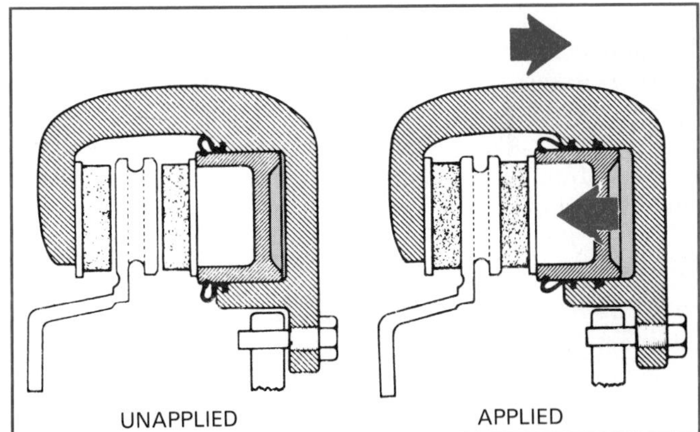

Figure 48-30. Key to floating or sliding caliper operation is when hydraulic pressure on the bottom of the cylinder bore causes the caliper to move sideways and apply friction pads to the machined surfaces of the rotor.

Wheel Cylinders

Wheel cylinders are used in drum brake systems to hydraulically actuate the brake shoes. A typical wheel cylinder is composed of: a single-bore cylinder casting; internal compression spring; two pistons; two rubber piston cups or seals; two rubber boots to prevent entry of dirt and water; and a bleeder screw (valve). See Figure 48-31. In addition, wheel cylinders are generally fitted with "links" that extend from the outboard side of each piston, through the rubber boots, where they bear against the toe end of each brake shoe.

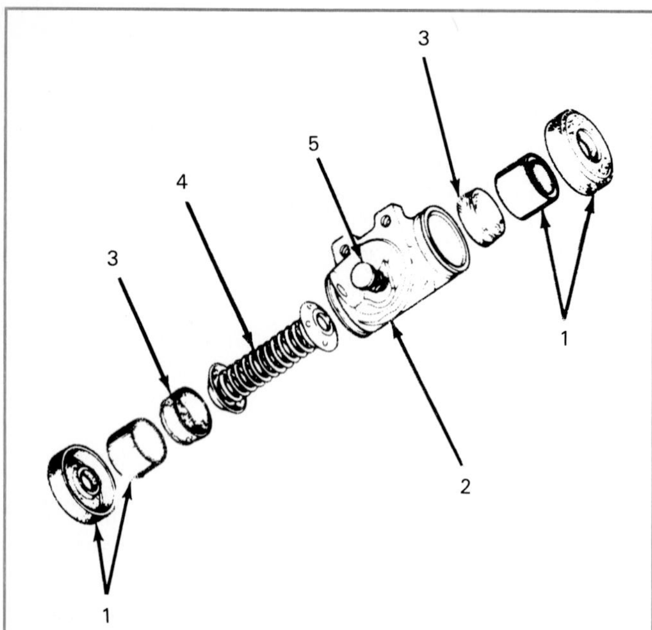

Figure 48-31. Typical drum brake wheel cylinder. 1–Boots and pistons. 2–Cylinder casting. 3–Rubber cups. 4–Spring and expanders. 5–Bleeder screw. (Chrysler)

When the brake pedal is depressed, hydraulic fluid pressure produced by the master cylinder forces the wheel cylinder pistons apart and outward in the cylinder. This movement, in turn, is transmitted to the toe ends of the brake shoes, causing the shoes to contact the revolving brake drum and stop the vehicle.

When the brake pedal is released, the shoe retracting springs force the wheel cylinder pistons and cups inward. This movement pushes brake fluid back to the master cylinder reservoir. Meanwhile, outward force created by the wheel cylinder spring keeps the two sets of pistons and cups apart. This provides space between the sealing cups for brake fluid to be retained for immediate response to the next brake application.

Brake Lines, Hoses, and Fittings

Double walled steel brake lines are used to safely transport the brake fluid from master cylinder to disc brake calipers and drum brake wheel cylinders. See Figure 48-32.

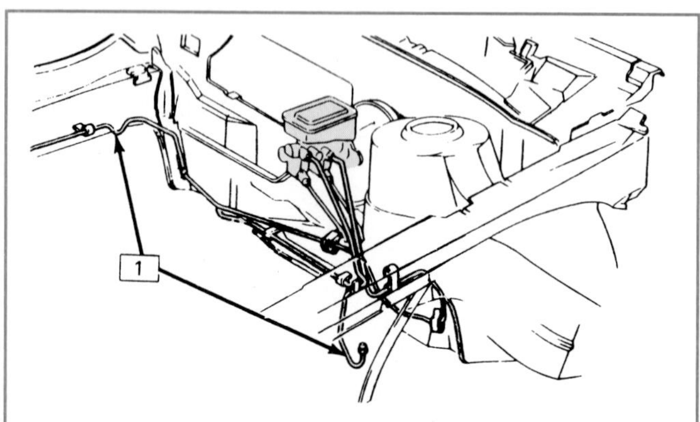

Figure 48-32. Steel brake lines are used to carry brake fluid from the master cylinder to the calipers and wheel cylinders: 1–Front brake line routing is shown. (Oldsmobile)

Never use copper tubing, which could crack or corrode and cause brake failure.

Some brake lines are "double flared" and some "bubble flared" to provide leakproof connections. During service, a flaring tool must be used when a new brake line is made, Figure 48-33. The new line must be an entire section of the same type, size, shape, and length as the line being replaced.

Flexible hydraulic brake hoses connect the steel brake lines on the rear axle housing or body to the rear wheel brake lines and to the front disc brake calipers. See Figure 48-34. This flexibility is needed to compensate for the up and down movement of the vehicle and the turning motion of the front wheel assemblies.

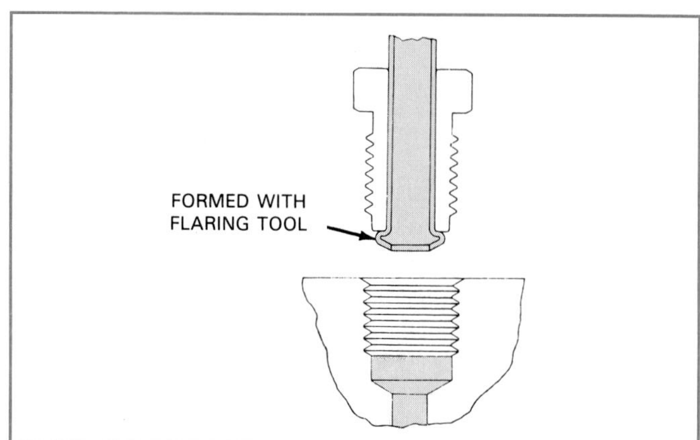

Figure 48-33. A special flaring tool is used to form a "bubble type" flare at the end of the brake line. This type flare cannot be used where a double-type flare is to be used.

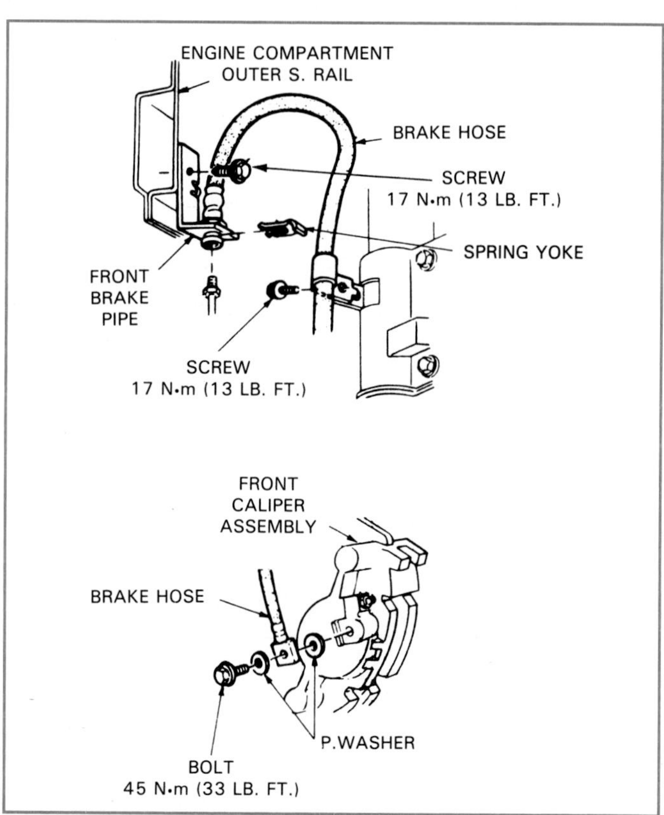

Figure 48-34. Flexible brake hoses connect the brake lines to the calipers and wheel cylinders to compensate for motion of the wheel assemblies. (Buick)

A replacement flexible brake hose should be positioned to avoid contact with other chassis parts. Some original equipment hoses and equivalent replacement hoses have a lengthwise white stripe which will reveal whether or not the hose was twisted when installed.

All fittings in the hydraulic brake system must be matched to the original equipment part for type and size, and tightened to the car manufacturer's torque specifications.

Power Brakes

Power brake units used on passenger cars are of four general types: vacuum suspended; air suspended; hydraulic booster; electro-hydraulic booster. Most power brake applications utilize vacuum suspended units.

Vacuum Suspended Operation

In the released position, both sides of the power piston and single diaphragm of a vacuum suspended power brake unit are open to intake manifold vacuum, Figure 48-35. As the brakes are applied, air is admitted to one side of the piston and diaphragm. Immediately, atmospheric pressure moves the diaphragm and power piston forward, causing the push rod to actuate the master cylinder pistons and apply the brakes.

Some larger vehicles are equipped with a tandem diaphragm, vacuum suspended power booster. Operation is similar to the single diaphragm unit with air being admitted to one side of each diaphragm to provide power assist.

A typical General Motors single diaphragm, vacuum suspended power booster is shown in Figure 48-36.

Air Suspended Operation

In the released position, both sides of the power piston are under atmospheric pressure. When the brakes are applied, manifold vacuum is admitted to one side of the piston. Immediately, atmospheric pressure on the other side causes the piston to move, forcing the push rod forward and actuating the master cylinder pistons to apply the brakes.

Hydraulic Booster Operation

General Motors and Ford use Hydro-Boost II, a hydraulically operated power brake booster, Figure 48-37. The power steering pump provides the hydraulic pressure

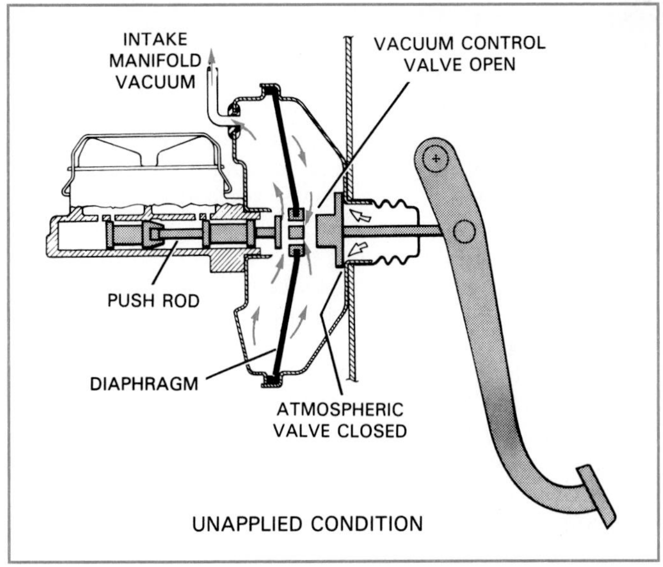

Figure 48-35. Simplified diagram illustrates the unapplied condition of a single diaphragm power brake unit. Both sides of the diaphragm are open to the intake manifold vacuum. In the applied condition, the atmosphere valve opens to permit atmospheric pressure to provide power assist to the master cylinder push rod. (Chrysler)

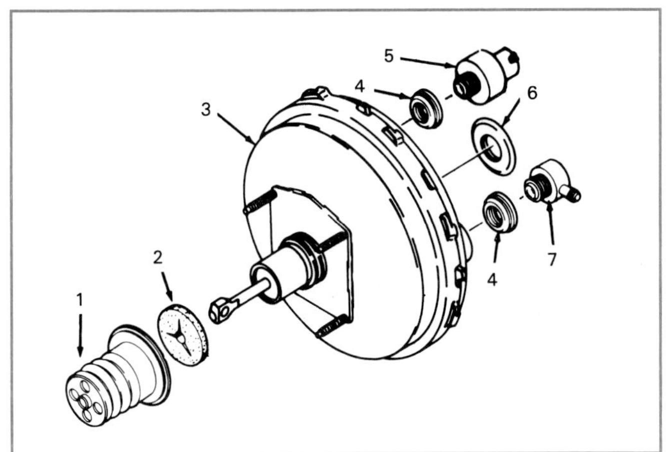

Figure 48-36. Drawing shows exterior components of a General Motors single diaphragm power brake unit. 1–Boot. 2–Silencer. 3–Booster. 4–Grommets. 5–Vacuum switch. 6–Front housing seal. 7–Vacuum check valve. (Buick)

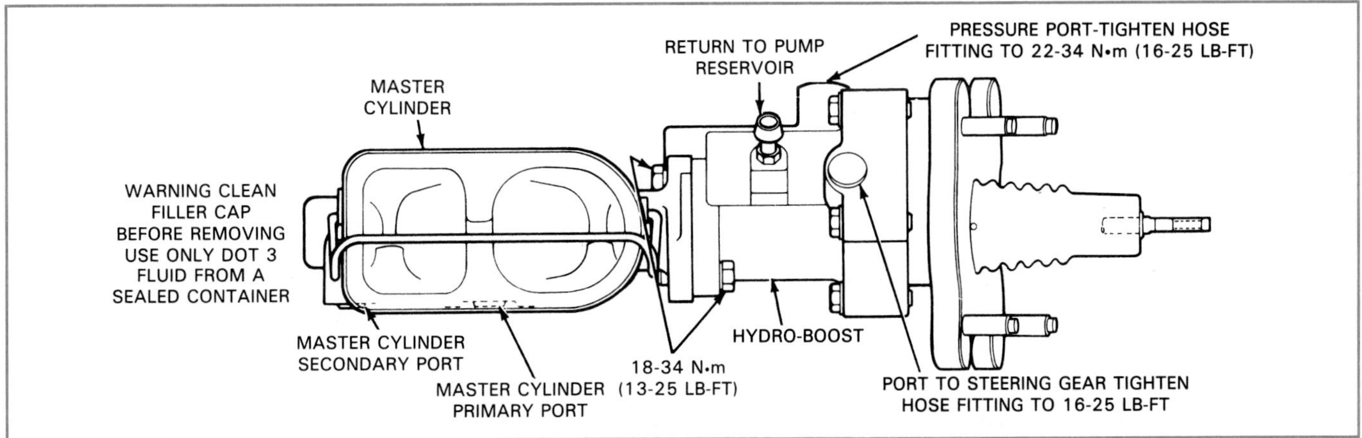

Figure 48-37. Top view provides a service technician's view of Hydro-Boost II and master cylinder. (Ford)

needed to operate the power brake booster and the power steering gear.

Hydro-Boost II combines an open center spool valve with a hydraulic cylinder in a single housing, Figure 48-38. This hydraulic brake booster also has a reserve system–an *accumulator*–that stores power steering fluid under pressure to provide one or two power assisted brake applications in case of a pressure drop.

In the released position, fluid flows from the power steering pump through the open center spool valve in the power booster, to the power steering gear, and back to the pump reservoir.

When the brakes are applied, the open center spool valve closes the fluid return port from the booster chamber to the pump and admits fluid into the booster chamber from the pressure port, Figure 48-38. The closing of the spool valve also restricts fluid flow to the steering gear, causing the pump to increase fluid pressure.

As hydraulic pressure in the booster chamber increases, it actuates the booster piston which, in turn, moves the master cylinder pistons forward to apply the brakes.

If there is a fluid pressure loss, foot pressure on the brake pedal causes an actuator on the spool valve to open the accumulator valve, Figure 48-38. Pump pressure then furnishes a reserve power supply of fluid to the booster. When the supply is depleted, the system reverts to manual operation. Manual operation occurs when there is a lack of power assist during brake application. This increases the effort needed to apply the brakes.

Electro-hydraulic Operation

General Motors Powermaster unit is a power brake supply system featuring an electro-hydraulic pump, fluid accumulator, dual-pressure switch, and hydraulic booster with an integral dual master cylinder, Figure 48-39.

The Powermaster pump operates between certain pressure switch limits to maintain satisfactory fluid pressure for power-boosted brake applications. When the brake pedal is depressed, fluid under pressure from the accumulator actuates the booster power piston to apply the master cylinder.

Anti-lock Brake Systems

Many late-model vehicles are equipped with ***anti-lock brake systems.*** See Figure 48-40. These systems use electronic and hydraulic components to help prevent wheel lockup during periods of hard braking. Anti-lock brake systems improve occupant safety by maintaining directional control while providing maximum braking efficiency.

Anti-lock System Components

Most anti-lock brake systems contain several common components, including:

- Wheel speed sensors.
- Toothed rotors.
- Hydraulic actuator.
- Control module.

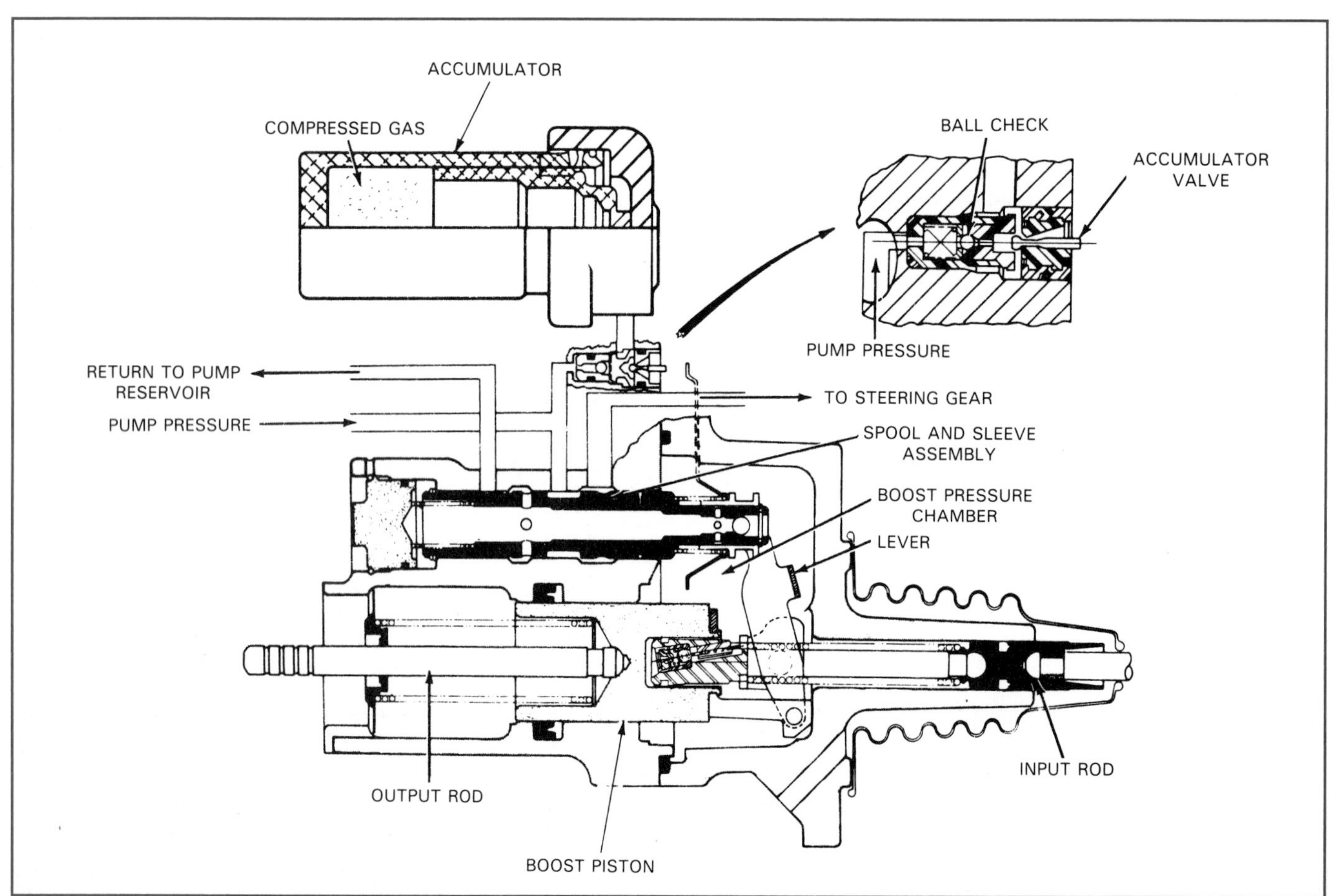

Figure 48-38. Sectional view of Hydro-Boost II power brake unit shows the internal parts and the direction of the flow of power steering fluid. (Ford)

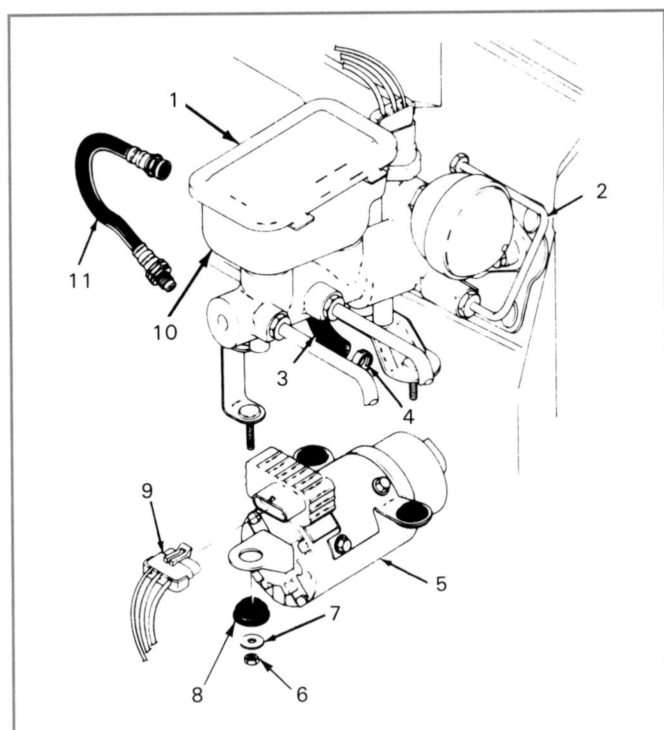

Figure 48-39. General Motors Powermaster system. 1–Reservoir cover and diaphragm. 2–Tube and nut assembly. 3–Sump hose. 4–Hose clamp. 5–Electro-hydraulic pump. 6–Nut. 7–Washer. 8–Grommet. 9–Electrical connector. 10–Master cylinder and reservoir. 11–Pressure hose assembly. (Cadillac)

Wheel speed sensors are used in the anti-lock brake system to determine the rate of wheel rotation. The tip of the sensor is located near a ***toothed rotor,*** which is generally attached to the vehicle's axle or steering knuckle and rotates at the same speed as the wheel assembly, Figure 48-41. As the rotor spins, a voltage is induced in the sensor. The strength and frequency of this voltage vary in relation to the speed of the wheel.

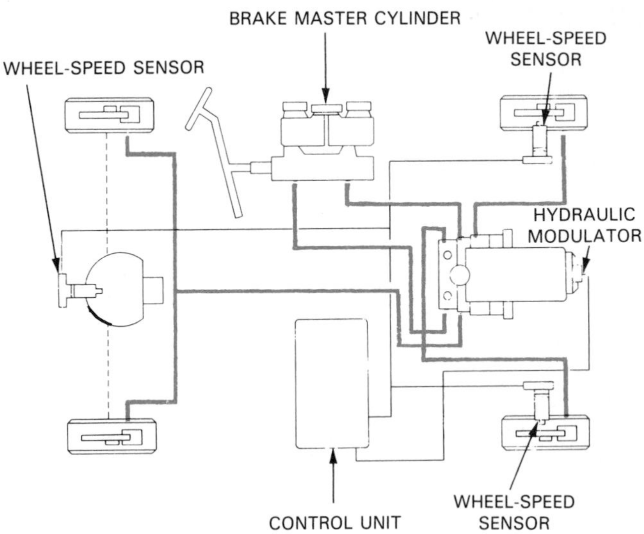

Figure 48-40. Setup of major elements of an anti-lock brake system is presented in diagrammatic form. (Robert Bosch Corp.)

In some anti-lock brake systems, a wheel speed sensor is mounted at each wheel. In other systems, speed sensors are mounted on the axle housing or in the transmission.

The ***hydraulic actuator*** is the unit that can increase brake pressure, decrease brake pressure, or hold brake pressure steady based on signals it receives from the control module. The hydraulic actuator typically consists of the following components:

- Pump/motor assembly (provides pressurized brake fluid to the accumulator.)
- Accumulator (holds high-pressure brake fluid.)
- Valve block assembly (contains hydraulic solenoid valves.)

In *integrated anti-lock brake systems,* the master cylinder/booster assembly is an integral part of the hydraulic unit, Figure 48-42. In these systems, power brake assist is provided by pressurized brake fluid that is supplied by the

Figure 48-41. Orientation of wheel speed sensor and toothed rotor on one vehicle. (General Motors)

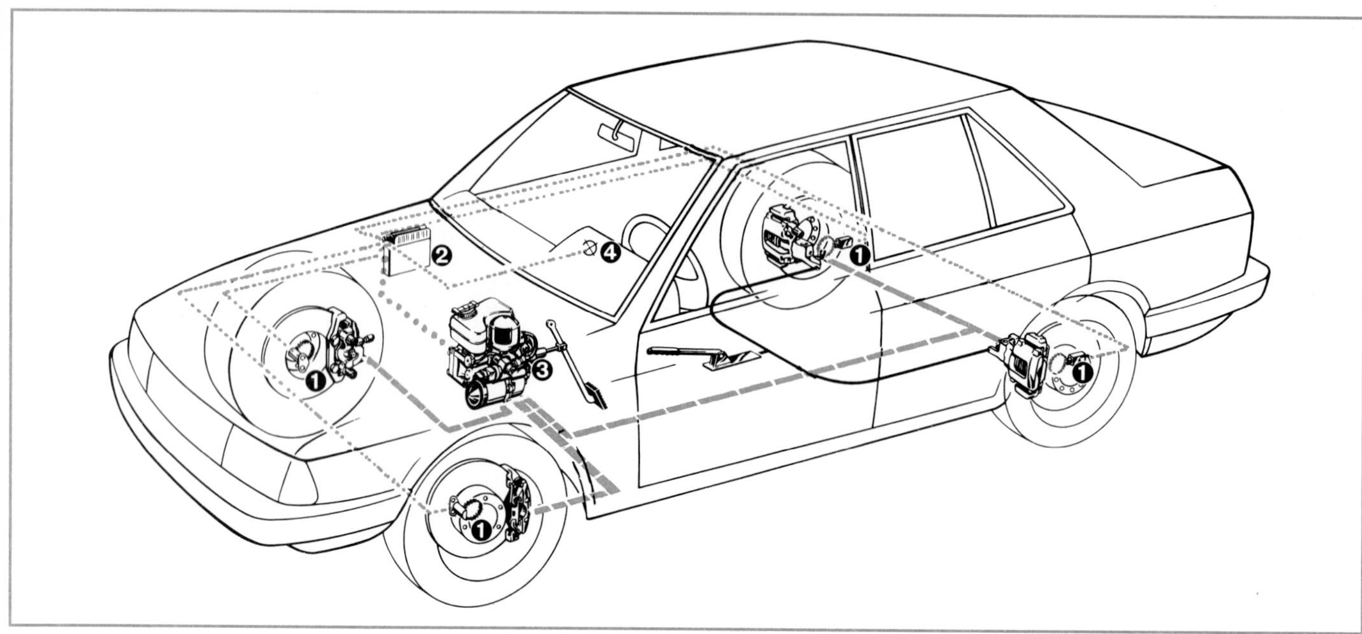

Figure 48-42. Integral anti-lock brake system. 1–Speed sensor at each wheel. 2–Electronic controller. 3–Hydraulic actuator. 4–Warning lamp. (Alfred Teves Corp.)

accumulator. In *non-integrated anti-lock brake systems,* a conventional master cylinder/booster assembly is used. See Figure 48-43.

Some General Motors vehicles are equipped with an actuator that uses electric motors instead of hydraulic valves to regulate the brake pressure. Unlike conventional ABS systems, these systems cannot increase pressure in the brake system.

The anti-lock ***control module*** is a computer that uses the signals from the wheel speed sensors to determine when

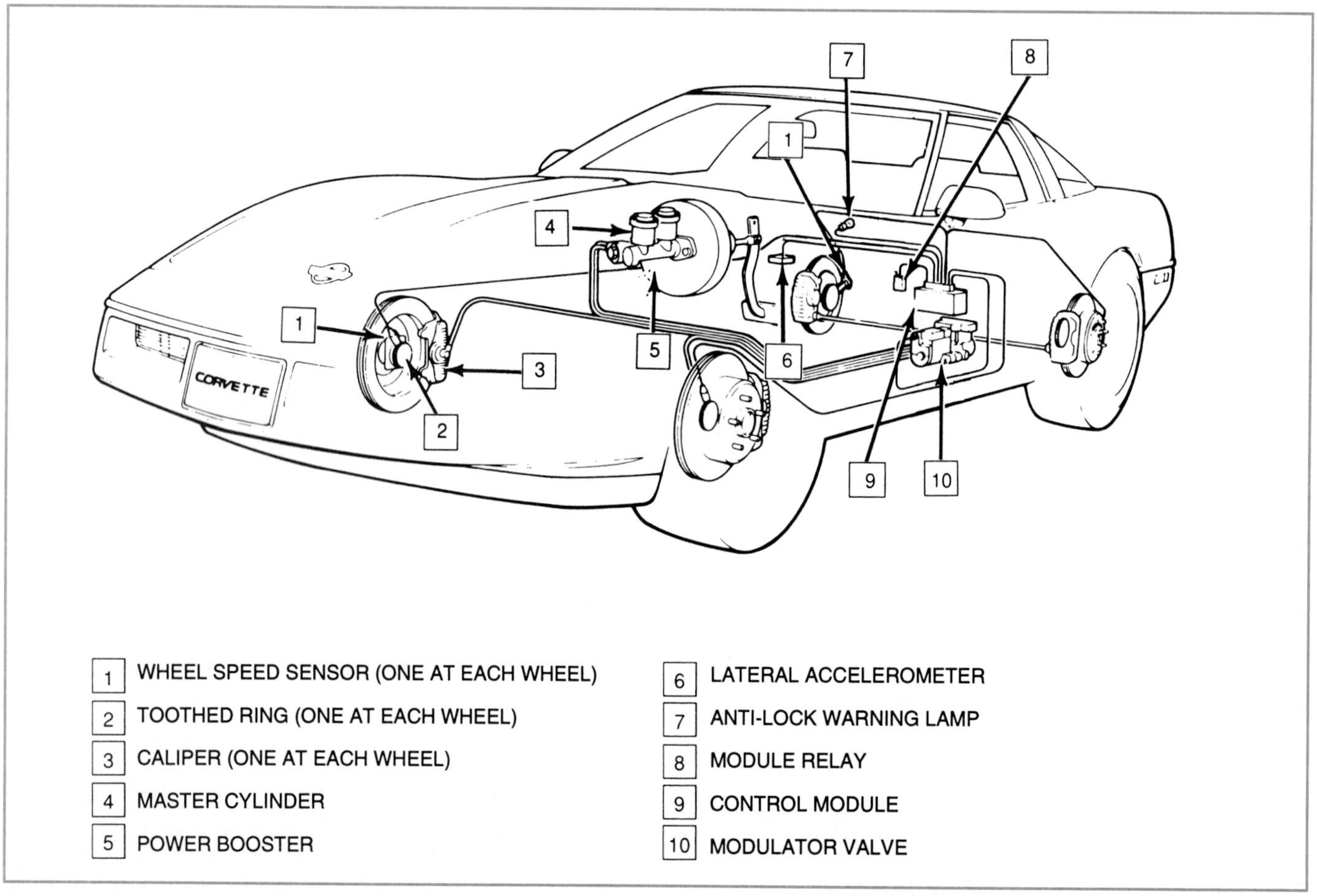

Figure 48-43. Non-integral anti-lock brake system. Note the location of the hydraulic actuator. (General Motors)

and how the anti-lock system should operate. When a wheel is nearing a lockup condition, the control module signals the hydraulic actuator to regulate fluid pressure to the affected wheel.

Anti-lock Brake System Operation

During periods of normal braking, the anti-lock portion of the brake system does not operate. Nevertheless, the sensors continuously monitor the speed of wheel rotation and send signals to the control module. When the brake pedal is pressed, brake fluid flows from the master cylinder, through the hydraulic actuator, and into the brake caliper, Figure 48-44.

When the control module detects that a wheel is nearing lockup, it signals a solenoid valve in the hydraulic actuator to block the fluid passage between the master cylinder and the wheel brake caliper. When this occurs, pressure is trapped between the caliper and the hydraulic actuator. Master cylinder fluid pressure cannot flow through the solenoid valve and the brake pressure at the affected wheel is held constant, Figure 48-45.

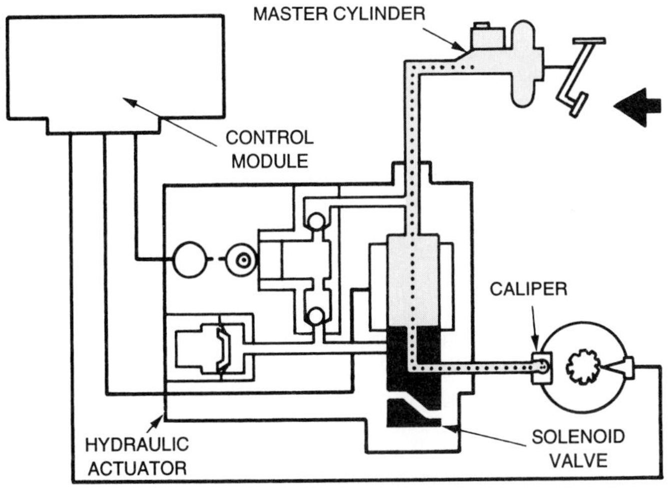

Figure 48-44. During normal braking, fluid flows directly through the solenoid into the caliper.

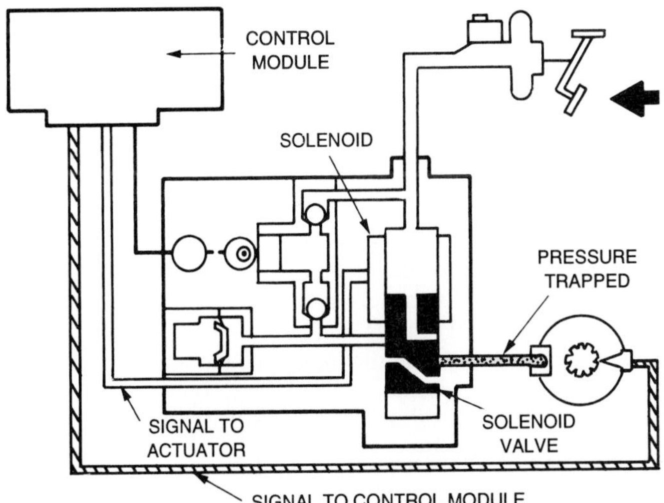

Figure 48-45. When the control unit detects potential wheel lockup, it prompts the solenoid to block fluid flow to the wheel.

When the control module detects a complete lockup, it commands the actuator to decrease pressure to the affected wheel caliper. To accomplish this, the solenoid valve in the actuator moves to cut off fluid pressure from the master cylinder and to allow brake fluid at the caliper to flow into the accumulator reservoir, Figure 48-46. At the same time, a pump inside the actuator forces the fluid in the accumulator back into the master cylinder. When this occurs, pressure at the wheel is decreased.

When all the wheels are rotating normally, the solenoid valve in the actuator returns to its original position and the conventional braking system takes over. If necessary, a typical anti-lock system can repeat this cycle up to 15 times a second.

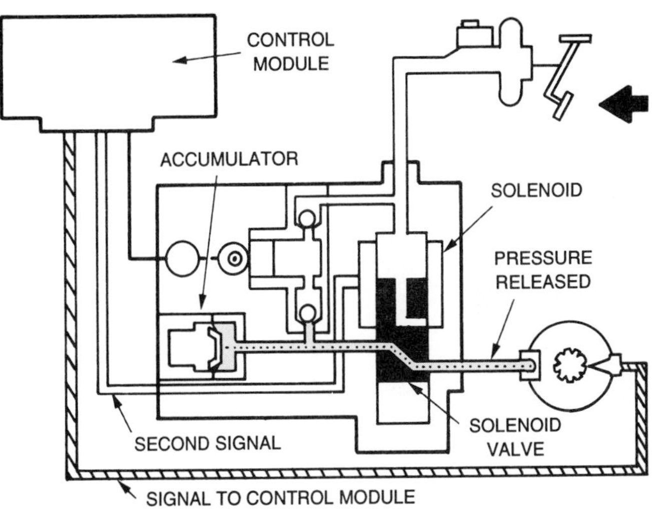

Figure 48-46. If a wheel locks up, the solenoid releases pressure at the wheel's caliper by allowing fluid to flow back into the accumulator.

Brake Service

Warning: Breathing dust containing asbestos fibers can cause serious bodily harm. Asbestos is a known carcinogen–a substance which tends to cause cancer. Since brake and clutch friction materials contain asbestos, do not create airborne dust by grinding, sanding, or by cleaning these parts with a dry brush or with compressed air. Instead, wear a mask with an approved air filter and flush brake and clutch parts with water or use a vacuum source. Special equipment is available to contain the asbestos particles, Figure 48-47 and Figure 48-48.

Hydraulic System Service

In order to operate satisfactorily, the various parts of the hydraulic brake system must be in good mechanical condition and the system full of clean brake fluid of the approved type. Mineral oil of any kind will swell and ruin the rubber cups and other parts of the system. Furthermore, mineral oil does not have the proper viscosity characteristics for use in an automobile.

Figure 48-47. An asbestos cleaning system has a large cleaning tank with a viewing window, air gun, and air and vacuum attachments. A powerful vacuum cleaner picks up dust and asbestos fibers blasted loose by the compressed air. (Nilfisk of America, Inc.)

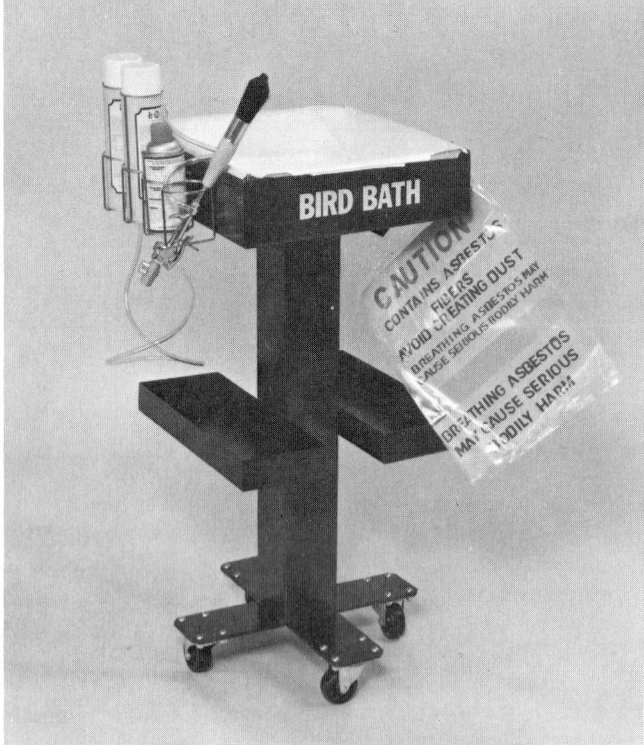

Figure 48-48. "Bird bath" type wetting treatment controls asbestos and acts as a brake cleaner and parts washer. This system uses filters and disposable bags. (U.S. Sales Co.)

The fluid must be clean. Dirt in the valves will cause them to leak. If there is any doubt about the condition of the old brake fluid, drain it out and flush the system. Flushing equipment and adapters are available. Flushing will avoid clogging of ports, sticking valves, leaking and scored cylinders, and erratic brake action. In addition, periodic flushing (once a year is usual recommendation) will remove any gum from the old fluid, condensed moisture, bits of scale and rubber, etc.

Before adding new fluid to the brake system, inspect the flexible hoses to make sure that they are not weakened, frayed, or swollen. All connections and fittings should be checked for leaks and to make sure that lines are securely fastened to the frame to avoid vibration and eventual breakage. Sometimes lines get kinked, dented, or worn thin from rubbing against sheet metal. If defective in any way, brake lines should be replaced.

If the master cylinder and wheel cylinders are known to be in good condition, fresh fluid can be added and the system "bled" to remove all air. If there is any air in the system, the pedal will have a "spongy" feel since hydraulic pressure is compressing the air.

Servicing Hydraulic Cylinders

When any work must be done on either the master cylinder, calipers, or wheel cylinders, absolute cleanliness is of utmost importance. Solvents or gasoline should NOT be used to clean the boots, cups, grommets, diaphragms, or any rubber parts. Alcohol is the proper cleaning fluid.

The cylinder bore must be free of scratches, grooves, or pits. A cast iron master cylinder or wheel cylinder can be polished with a special hone made for this purpose. (Note: do not hone aluminum master cylinders.)

Bleeding Brakes

There are two general methods used to bleed air from hydraulic brake systems. The manual method requires two people. Pressure bleeding is faster and only requires the services of one person. However, it involves the use of special pressure flushing and bleeding equipment. This equipment usually consists of a closed, airtight container of brake fluid to which air pressure is applied. See Figure 48-49. With either power or manual bleeding, a hose is attached to the bleeder valve and the other end immersed in a glass jar containing brake fluid. This enables bubbles to be seen and avoids waste of fluid, Figure 48-50.

The master cylinder fill plug opening and area around it must be thoroughly cleaned before the plug is removed. Then, the container of fluid is connected to the fill opening by suitable fittings and flexible hose. The bleeder forces fluid under pressure to each caliper and wheel cylinder. Each is bled, in turn, by opening the bleeder valve and closing it when the fluid is clear and bubbles no longer appear.

When bleeding brakes by the manual method, it is necessary to watch the level of the fluid in the master cylinder. If it gets too low, air will be drawn into the cylinder. If possible, the master cylinder is bled first. If reconditioning on the bench, it can be bled before reinstallation as shown in Figure 48-51.

To bleed the system manually at each wheel, generally start with right rear; next, left rear; then, right front; and left front. However, consult the manufacturer's service manual for the correct bleeding sequence for the particular vehicle being serviced.

Open the bleeder valve and have your helper slowly press the brake pedal to the floor. Close the bleeder and have your helper slowly release the pedal, then wait 15 sec.

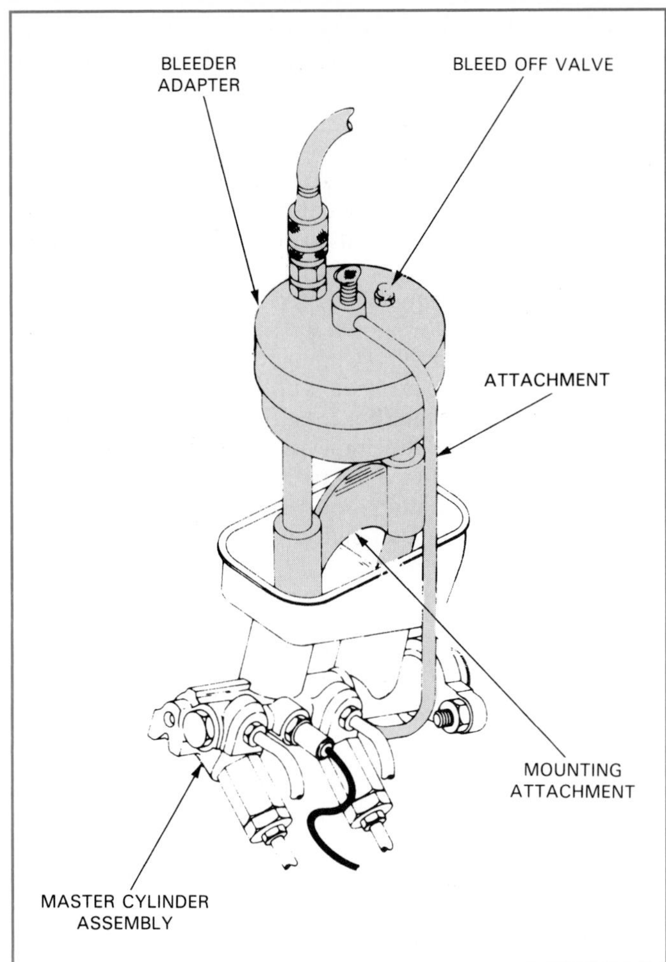

Figure 48-49. A pressurized bleeder ball and special adapters are used to flush and/or bleed a brake hydraulic system. An adapter is shown attached to the master cylinder. (Cadillac)

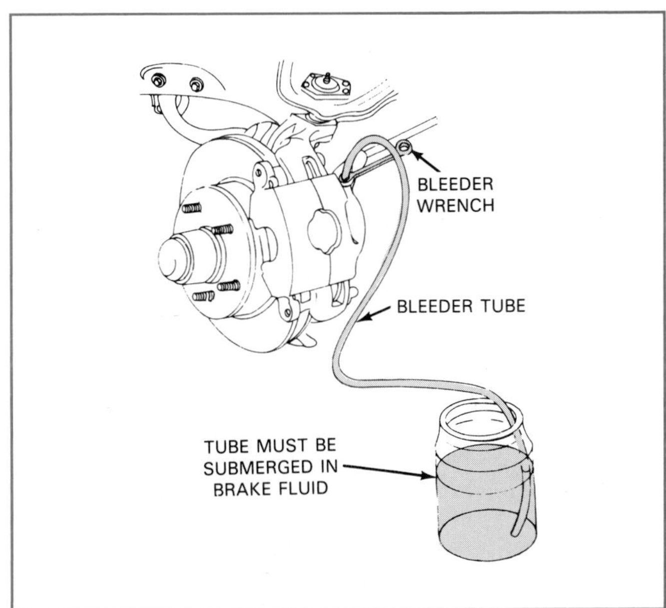

Figure 48-50. Proper brake bleeding at the calipers or wheel cylinders calls for the use of a bleeder tube and a jar filled with brake fluid. When the tube is immersed in fluid and the bleeder valve is opened, bubbles indicate the release of air from the hydraulic system. (Cadillac)

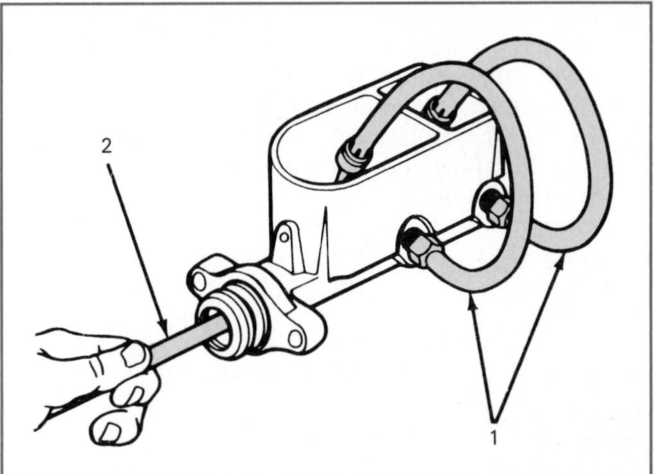

Figure 48-51. Bench bleeding of the master cylinder is done by: 1–Making two bleed tubes and installing them in the outlet ports. Place the other end of the tubes in the reservoirs. 2–With the reservoirs filled with brake fluid, the push rod is actuated until bubbles in the fluid disappear. (Chrysler)

Repeat this operation until no bubbles appear in the brake fluid in the glass jar. Then, proceed to bleed each other wheel in the recommended sequence. The 15 sec. pauses allow air to collect in large pockets that will be released more quickly and completely.

After bleeding, check the master cylinder reservoir for proper fluid level, approximately 1/4 in. from the top of the reservoir.

Disc Brake Service

All disc brake services begin with sight, sound, and stopping tests. The feel of the brake pedal adds a check on the condition of the hydraulic brake system.

Stopping the car will indicate whether the brakes pull in one direction, stop straight, or require excessive effort to stop. Listening while stopping permits fair diagnosis of braking noises such as rattles, groans, squeals, or chatter. Some models are equipped with brake wear sensors, which contact the rotor to signal when the friction pads are worn. Take a wheel off and visually inspect the outboard shoe and lining assembly at each end of the caliper. Check the inboard lining through the hole on top of the caliper, Figure 48-52.

A good rule-of-thumb guide to the need for lining replacement is to compare lining thickness to the thickness of the metal shoe. If the lining is not as thick as the metal shoe, it should be replaced. If the thickness of the lining is marginal, remove the caliper, carefully check the condition of the lining, and measure its thickness. Compare this measurement with manufacturer's specification. Note: If lining requires replacement, always replace both front wheel sets to assure equal braking action.

Caliper Removal

To remove a disc brake caliper from most General Motors cars:

1. Siphon 2/3 of the brake fluid from the master cylinder reservoir.
2. Hoist the vehicle.
3. Remove the wheel and tire assembly.
4. Reinstall two lug nuts on the hub to retain the rotor.

5. Position adjustable pliers as shown in Figure 48-53 and squeeze the pliers to force the piston to the bottom of the caliper bore.
6. Remove the bolt holding the inlet fitting.
7. Remove the boots and the two mounting bolts.
8. Lift the caliper off the mounting bracket and away from the rotor.

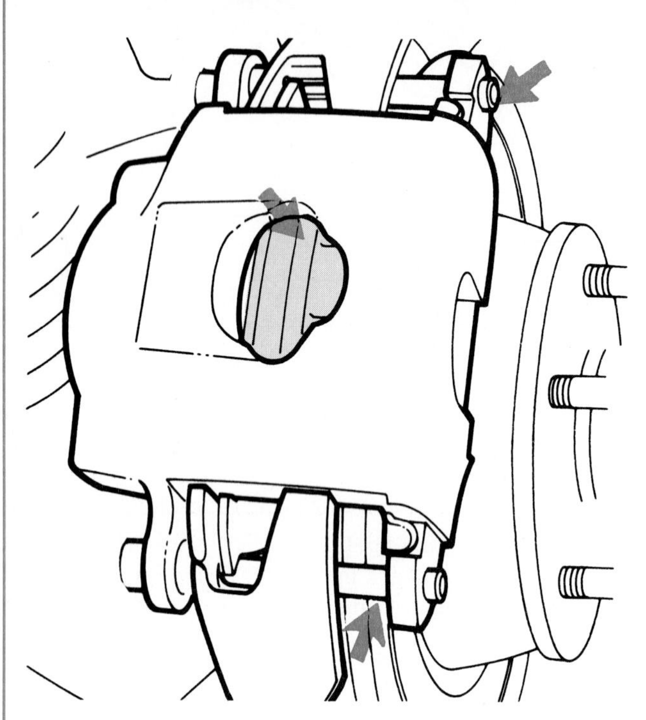

Figure 48-52. Visual inspection of the inboard brake shoe and lining assembly can be made through the hole in the top of the caliper. The outboard shoe and lining can be viewed from the end of the caliper. (Buick)

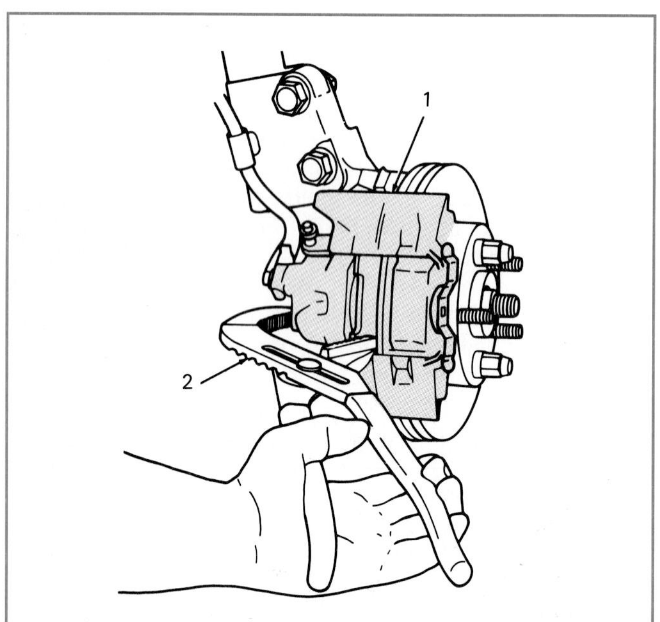

Figure 48-53. In some disc brake applications, pliers can be used to compress the piston to the bottom of the caliper bore. 1–Caliper. 2–Pliers. (Oldsmobile)

9. Remove the inboard brake shoe.
10. Use adjustable pliers to straighten the bent-over shoe tab and remove the outboard brake shoe.

Brake Shoe Installation

To install disc brake shoes (friction pads):

1. Force the piston into the caliper bore until it bottoms.
2. Remove the sleeves and bushings from the mounting bolt holes.
3. Lubricate the new sleeves and bushings with silicone grease and install them in the mounting bolt holes.
4. Install the inboard brake shoe, Figure 48-54.
5. Install the outboard shoe with the wear sensor at the leading edge of the shoe. See Figure 48-55. Use a ball peen hammer to clinch the shoe tab.
6. Install the caliper over the rotor in the mounting bracket.
7. Install the mounting bolts and torque them to the manufacturer's specifications.
8. Connect the inlet fitting and torque to specifications.
9. Install the tire and wheel assembly, lower the car, and torque the wheel lugs or nuts to specifications.
10. Refill the master cylinder reservoir with brake fluid. Test brake pedal reserve. If the pedal is spongy, bleed the system.

Caliper Overhaul

To overhaul a disc brake caliper:

1. Remove the caliper as outlined in the caliper removal procedure.
2. Place the caliper assembly on clean work bench, loosen the bleeder screw, and drain out the remaining fluid. Retighten the bleeder screw.

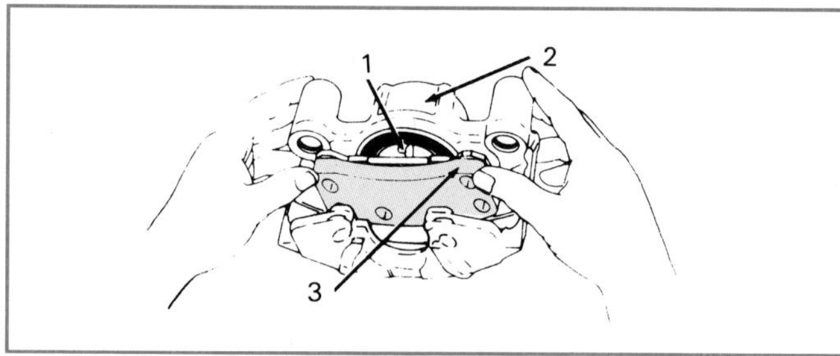

Figure 48-54. Drawing illustrates how to install an inboard brake shoe and lining assembly in a disc brake caliper. 1–Shoe retainer spring. 2–Caliper housing. 3–Inboard shoe and lining. (Oldsmobile)

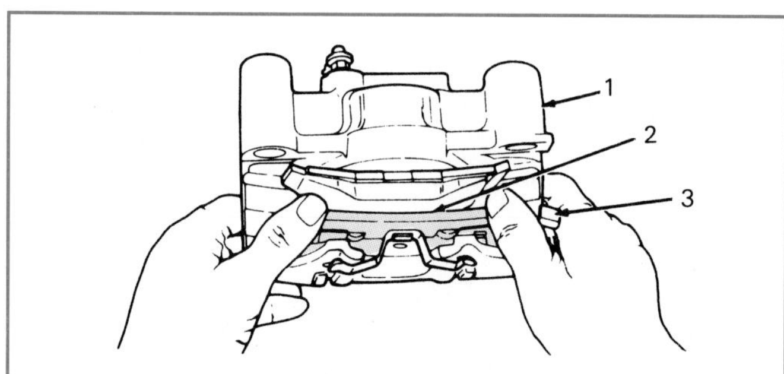

Figure 48-55. Drawing shows how to install the outboard brake shoe and lining assembly in a disc brake caliper. 1–Caliper housing. 2–Outboard shoe and lining. 3–Wear sensor. (Oldsmobile)

3. Place the caliper on a bench. Put a shop towel opposite the piston and feed compressed air through the inlet port until the piston is forced out. See Figure 48-56.
4. Remove the dust boot from the groove in the caliper.
5. Use a thin-bladed plastic or wooden tool to remove the piston seal from the bore of the caliper.
6. Clean and inspect the piston for scoring, pitting, corrosion, or worn spots in the plating.
7. Blow air through the passageways in the caliper. Inspect the caliper bore for scoring, pitting, scratches, or corrosion. Use crocus cloth to clean the bore; then wash the bore with denatured alcohol and blow it dry.
8. Use crocus cloth to clean all metal-to-metal contacts.
9. Coat the caliper bore and new piston seal with brake fluid. Place the seal in the bore groove, making sure it is not twisted.
10. Fit a new dust boot over the piston with a small screwdriver. Figure 48-57.
11. Apply even pressure downward on the piston until it bottoms in the caliper bore.
12. Install the boot in the caliper housing counterbore and seat the boot with a suitable tool.
13. Replace the sleeves and bushings, and install new brake shoes as described in steps 2-5 in the brake shoe installation procedure.
14. Before installing the caliper on the rotor, check the lateral runout of the rotor. Tighten the spindle nut to remove play from the wheel bearings. Fasten a dial indicator to the spindle, Figure 48-58, or to the steering linkage so that the point of the stylus contacts the rotor face about one inch from the rotor edge. Check rotor runout for one revolution and compare the reading with the manufacturer's specification (ranges from .002 to .005 in. or .05 to .13 mm).
Check the rotor for thickness and parallelism. Use a micrometer to measure rotor thickness and thickness variation at five equidistant points from the outer edge of the rotor. (Thickness variation calls for maximum of .0005 in. or .013 mm).
15. Service the rotor as required (clean, resurface, or replace). See Figures 48-59 and 48-60.
16. Clean the mounting bracket, especially metal-to-metal contacts.
17. Slowly slide the caliper down over the rotor until holes in the caliper line up with holes in the mounting bracket.
18. Install the mounting bolts, torquing them to specification.
19. Install the bolt holding the inlet fitting, torquing it to specification.
20. Bleed the system.

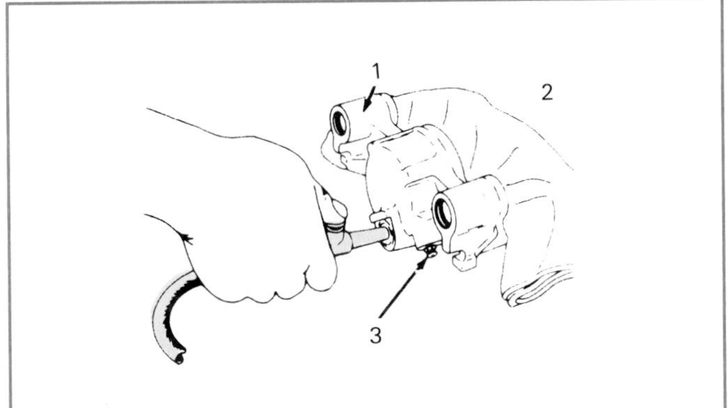

Figure 48-56. To remove the caliper piston, place a shop towel opposite the piston, and then use air pressure to blow the piston from the caliper bore. 1–Caliper housing. 2–Shop towel. 3–Bleeder valve. (Oldsmobile)

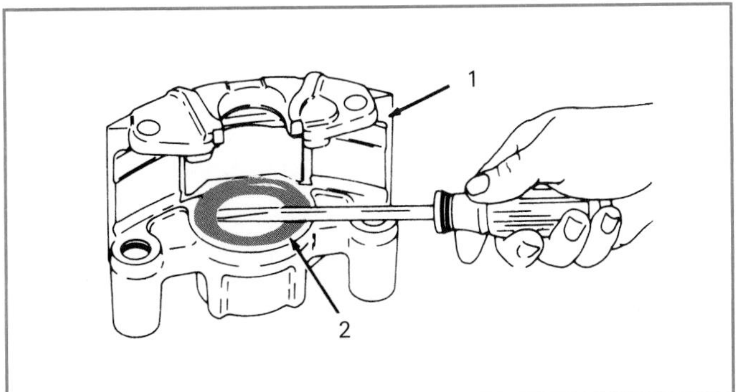

Figure 48-57. A small screwdriver is used to install the dust boot over the caliper piston. 1–Caliper housing. 2–Boot. (Oldsmobile)

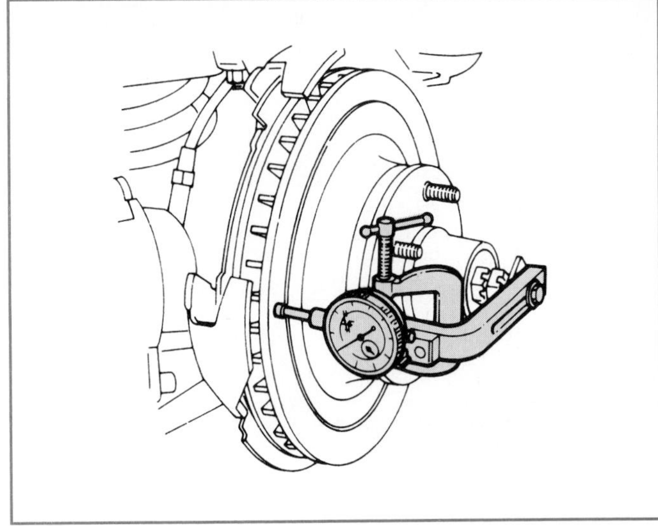
Figure 48-58. A lateral runout check with a dial indicator gives an accurate test of the flatness of the machined surface of the rotor. (Buick)

Figure 48-59. A service technician positions twin cutters independently and prepares to simultaneously cut both surfaces of a rotor. (Ammco Tools, Inc.)

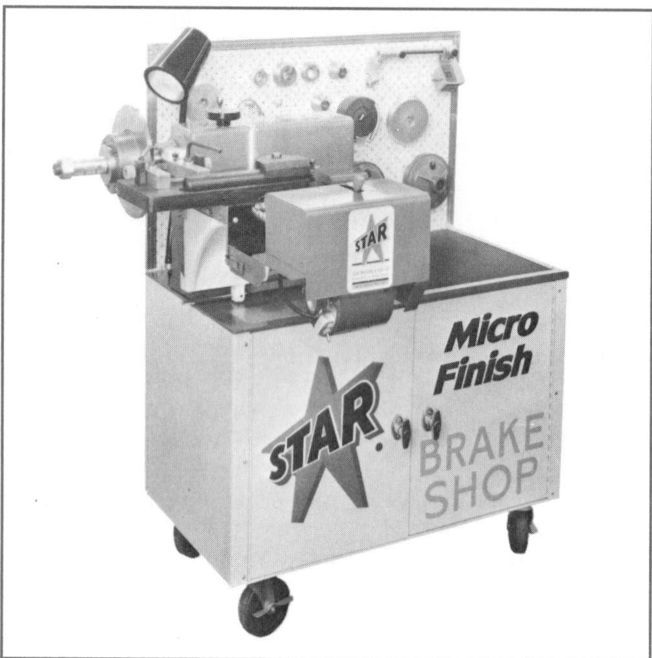

Figure 48-60. This disc/drum lathe is designed to micro-finish disc brake rotors without grinding. Cutters machine both rotor surfaces at the same time. A rotating tool plate changes the disc lathe to a drum turning lathe. (Star Machine and Tool Co.)

21. Install the tire and wheel assembly and lower the car.
22. Torque the wheel lugs or nuts to specification.

Special Procedures. Disc brake service on other-than-GM vehicles is similar to the above procedures. However, design differences and special notes and cautions are contained in the manufacturers' service manuals. Refer to an appropriate service manual for specific service procedures.

Drum Brake Service

Drum brakes utilize internal expanding brake shoe assemblies to create the friction and heat required to slow and stop the rotating drums. The brake lining is a friction material attached to the near semicircular metal shoe by rivets or by bonding.

With riveting, the rivets are countersunk about two thirds of the way through the lining and exactly the same size as the rivet head for greater strength. Also, the hole in the lining is the same size as the hole in the brake shoe.

With bonding, a cement is used between the shoe and lining, and the assembly is placed in an oven for curing. With either riveting or bonding, the lining must adhere tightly to the shoe, yet with minimum resistance to the dissipation of the heat of braking.

The surface of the brake lining of newly relined shoes may not conform accurately to the surface of the brake drum. New lining has slight high and low spots. Or, if the drum has been reconditioned, it will be slightly larger in diameter and will not conform to the arc of the brake shoes.

Brake shoes should be ground with special brake shoe-grinding equipment, not only to smooth the surface, but to conform to the curvature of the brake drum. Always wear a respirator when grinding brake lining and see that the machine's exhaust system is working properly.

If the brake shoes are used without grinding, the high spots of the lining will do all the braking, and much higher than normal temperatures will result. High heat will quickly heat check or completely ruin new lining.

Care must be exercised so that no grease, oil, or brake fluid reaches the brake lining. Any fluid contamination will affect the coefficient of friction and grabbing brakes will result. In this connection, always replace the grease seals when new brake lining is installed. Also, wheel cylinders should be examined to make sure they are not leaking fluid. When handling brake shoes, care must be taken to avoid "fingerprinting" the lining.

When lubricating the front wheel bearings, use grease specified for that purpose, and only enough to lubricate the bearing. Excess lubricant may get on the brake lining and ruin it. Or, a low melting point grease may thin out and enter the brake shoe/drum area.

Brake Drums

The surface of the brake drum must be smooth and free from galling, ridges, and heat checks. In addition, the drum must not be bell-mouthed or out-of-round. The ridges, galling, and check marks are visible, but a drum gauge should be used to check brake drum diameter, Figure 48-61. The manner in which the brake lining is worn on the shoe will also indicate the condition of the drum. A drum that is bell-mouthed, for example, will cause the lining to wear more on one side of the shoe than on the other.

Another important reason for measuring the diameter of the drum is to note whether there is enough metal to permit reconditioning. Passenger car brake drums should not be reconditioned more than 0.060 in. (1.5 mm) oversize. If more than 0.060 in. is removed (0.030 in. per side), it will severely weaken the drum. The drum will become oval when the brakes are applied, and, because of less metal, it will operate at much higher temperatures with attendant brake fade and short lining life.

Brake drums can be reconditioned either by turning on a lathe, Figure 48-62, or by grinding. Both methods are used extensively. The regrinding method is used particularly in cases where the drum has hard spots.

When preparing to turn a drum on a lathe, care must be exercised that the lathe tool is sharpened correctly. Also, tool feed must be correct. If too fast, it would produce a "screw thread" surface which would cause rapid wear of the brake lining. Follow equipment manufacturer's directions, cautions, and specifications.

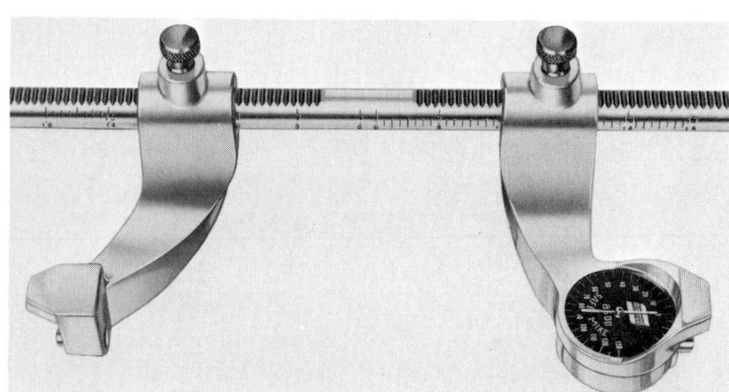

Figure 48-61. A brake drum micrometer is designed to "mike" drums on or off the lathe. This instrument checks drum diameter and out-of-roundness in .005" increments. (Ammco Tools, Inc.)

Figure 48-62. This combination disc and drum brake service center turns disc and drum at same time. The lathe automatically turns off when cuts are completed. Spindle speeds and feeds are factory set. (Hofmann Corp.)

Drum Brake Overhaul

When servicing single anchor automatic adjuster drum brake assemblies on rear-wheel drive cars, Figures 48-63 and 48-64, a typical overhaul procedure includes:

1. Raise the vehicle and remove the wheel and tire assembly.
2. Remove the drum. If necessary, back off the brake shoe adjustment. See Figure 48-65.
3. Use special equipment to remove asbestos particles from the brake assembly and the backing plate.
4. Remove the return springs, adjuster cable, and anchor plate.
5. Disengage and remove the adjusting lever.
6. Remove the spring from the pivot.
7. Pull the shoes away from the anchor and wheel cylinder and remove the star wheel assembly.
8. Remove the parking brake strut and the anti-rattle spring.
9. Remove the shoe hold-down assemblies.
10. Back off the parking brake cable adjustment, disconnect the cable, and remove the lever.
11. Remove the brake shoes.
12. Clean the backing plate thoroughly, polish all shoe contact ledges with fine emery cloth, and then coat the ledges with special lubricant. See Figure 48-64.
13. Lubricate the pivot end of the parking brake lever and insert the lever into the hole in the secondary shoe from the inner side of the shoe web.
14. Connect the parking brake cable to the inside of the lever.
15. Place the secondary shoe against the backing plate and anchor, and then slide the shoe web into the wheel cylinder or the wheel cylinder push rod.
16. Slide the parking brake strut into the lever slot and install the anti-rattle spring in the proper position on the strut.
17. Slide the primary shoe into position on the backing plate and into the wheel cylinder or wheel cylinder push rod.
18. Install the anchor plate and adjuster cable.
19. Install the primary shoe return spring.
20. Hold the cable guide in position on the secondary shoe and install the return spring through the guide from the shoe web to the anchor pin.
21. Install the star wheel assembly between the heels of the shoes with the star wheel next to the secondary shoe. NOTE: Star wheels generally are stamped L and R for the left and right wheel brake assemblies respectively. Install as indicated.

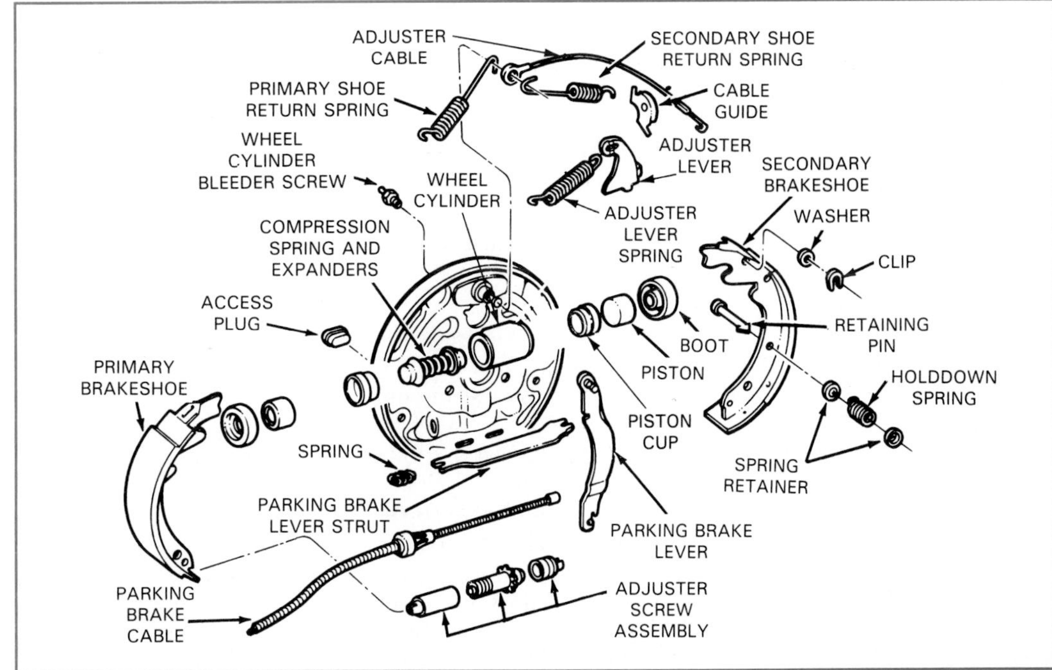

Figure 48-63. Exploded view of single anchor automatic adjuster drum brake assembly reveals the parts relationship for proper disassembly and reassembly of the rear wheel drum brake. (Chrysler)

1. BACKING PLATE
2. HOLD-DOWN PINS
3. ANCHOR PIN
4. PARKING BRAKE LEVER
5. SECONDARY SHOE
6. SHOE GUIDE
7. PARKING BRAKE STRUT
8. STRUT SPRING
9. ACTUATOR LEVER
10. ACTUATOR LINK
11. RETURN SPRING
12. HOLD-DOWN SPRING
13. LEVER PIVOT
14. LEVER RETURN SPRING
15. PAWL
16. ADJUSTING SCREW ASSEMBLY
17. ADJUSTING SCREW SPRING
18. PRIMARY SHOE

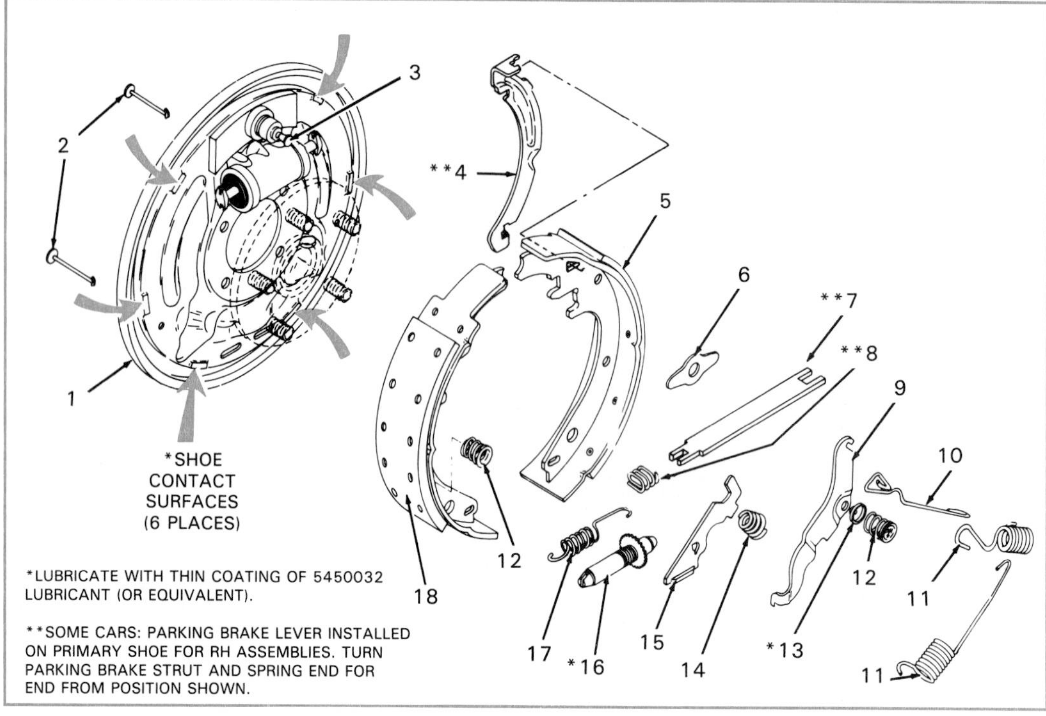

Figure 48-64. Exploded view details the makeup of a single anchor automatic adjuster drum brake. (Oldsmobile)

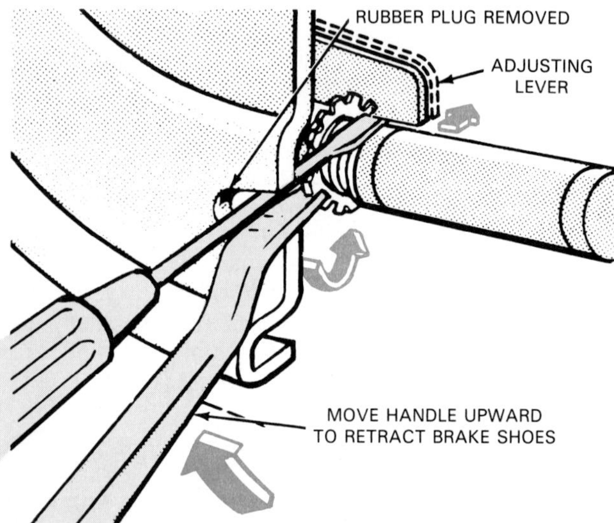

Figure 48-65. To back off brake shoe adjustment, use a screwdriver to lift the adjusting lever away from the star wheel. Then turn the star wheel with a brake adjusting tool. (Ford)

22. Install the adjusting lever and spring over the pivot pin, and then lock the lever in position.
23. Install the hold-down assemblies.
24. Place the adjuster cable over the guide and hook the end of the overload spring in the adjusting lever.
25. Inspect the friction surface of the drum for the amount of wear and the degree of scoring.
26. If necessary, resurface the drum on a brake drum lathe. See Figures 48-66 and 48-67.
27. Adjust the brake drum gauge to drum size, Figure 48-68.
28. Place the other side of the gauge across the brake shoe diameter and adjust the star wheel to expand the brake shoes to "fit" the gauge. Proper shoe-to-drum clearance is built into the gauge.
29. Install the brake drum and the wheel and tire assembly.

Figure 48-66. This computerized brake lathe has a "touch" panel to control the precise speeds and feeds on both finish and rough cuts on drums and rotors. The unit has a safety shield, cross-feed travel limiters, and an emergency stop button. (Ammco Tools, Inc.)

30. Lower the vehicle, then adjust the parking brake cables.

When servicing "leading-trailing" non-servo type rear wheel brake assemblies on front-wheel drive cars, Figure 48-69, a typical overhaul procedure includes:

1. Raise the vehicle and remove the wheel and tire assembly.

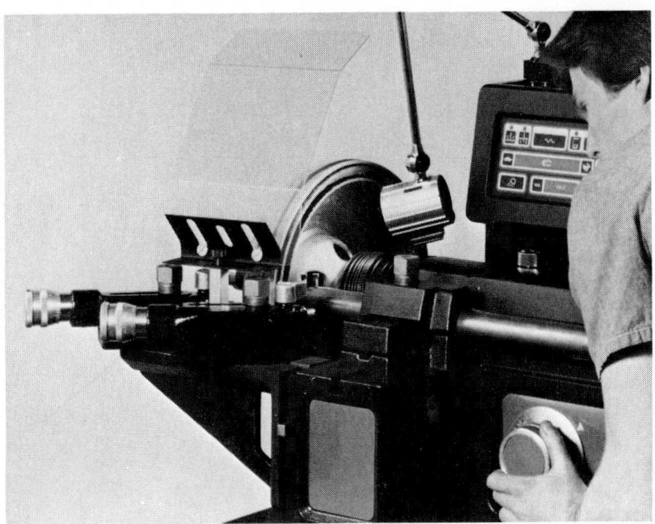

Figure 48-67. This service technician is using a computerized brake lathe to machine a brake drum. The technician positions the boring bar, and then sets the dial for the proper depth of cut. (Ammco Tools, Inc.)

2. Remove the hub and drum assembly. If necessary, back off the brake shoe adjustment.
3. Use special equipment to remove the asbestos particles from the brake assembly and backing plate.
4. Install the clamp over the wheel cylinder pistons.
5. Remove the shoe hold-down assemblies.

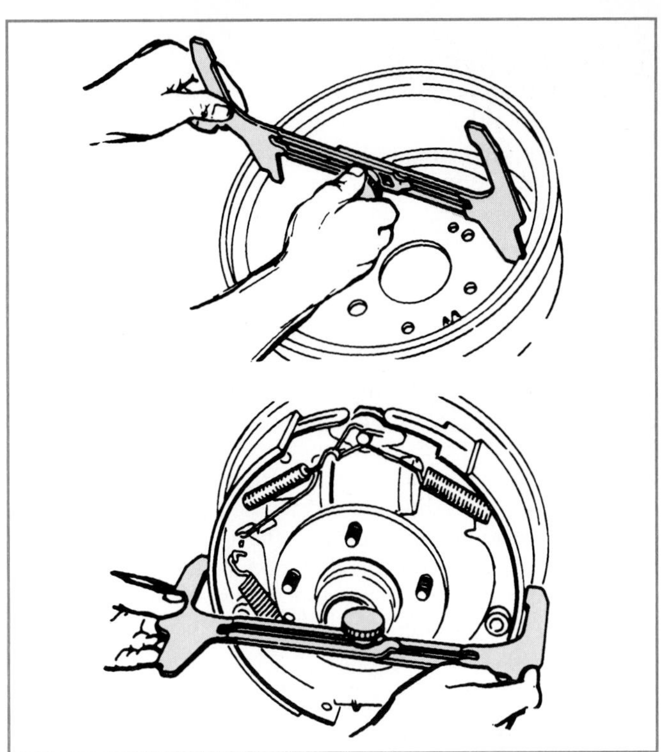

Figure 48-68. To adjust brake shoes to fit the drum: Top–Adjust the gauge to the drum diameter. Bottom–Adjust the star wheel to make the shoes fit the other side of the gauge. (Pontiac)

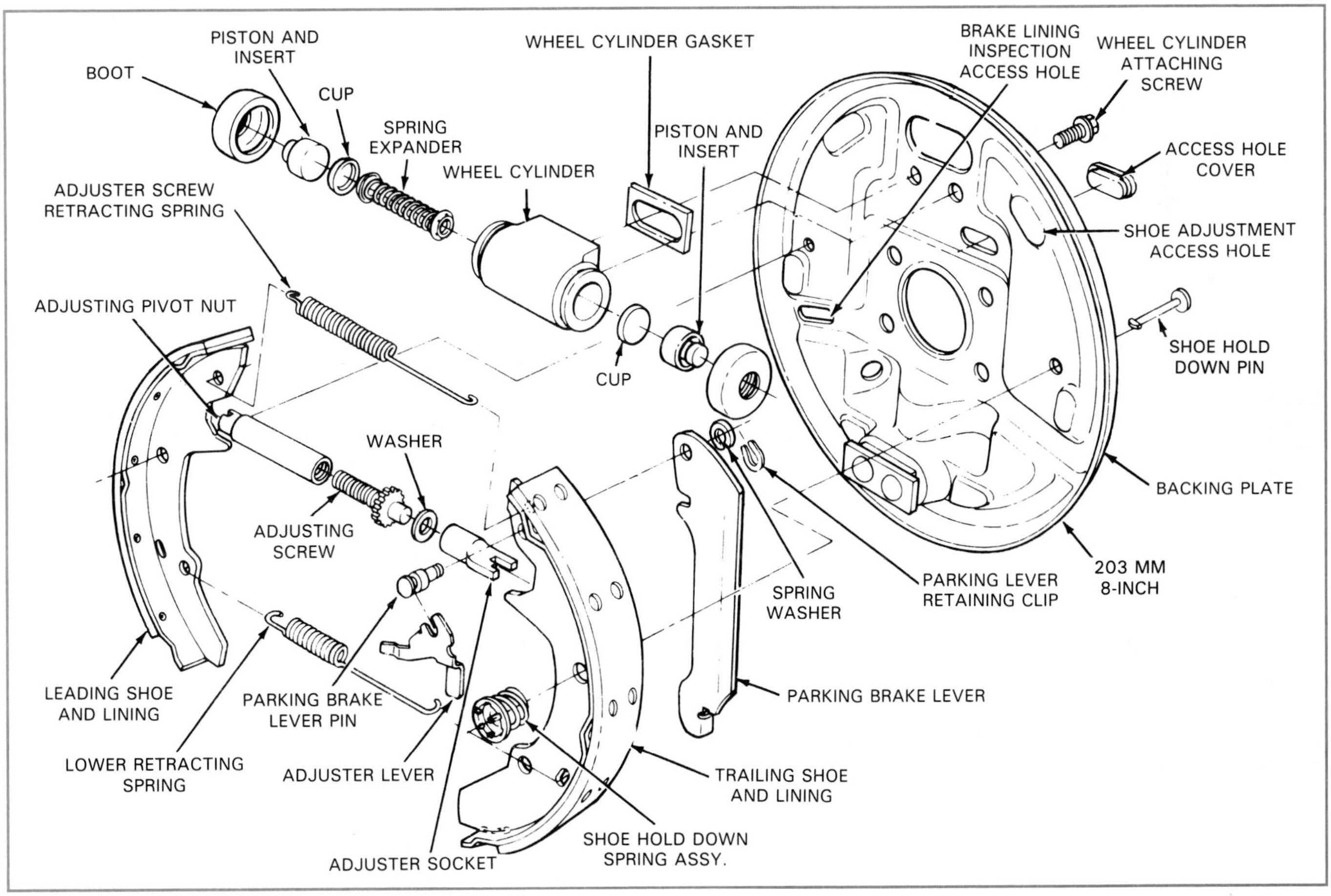

Figure 48-69. Exploded view of a leading-trailing type drum brake assembly can aid in disassembly and reassembly operations during brake overhaul procedures. (Ford)

6. Lift the entire mechanical brake assembly (shoes, springs, and adjuster) from the backing plate, Figure 48-70. Use care to avoid bending the adjusting lever.
7. Remove the parking brake cable from the parking brake lever.
8. Remove the lower and upper retracting springs, freeing the adjuster mechanism.
9. Remove the retaining clip and spring washer, and slide the lever off the parking brake lever pin on the trailing shoe.
10. Clean the backing plate thoroughly, polish all shoe contact ledges with fine emery cloth, and then coat the ledges with special, high-temperature lubricant.
11. Apply lubricant to the adjuster screw threads and the socket end of the adjusting screw.
12. Install the adjuster washer, Figure 48-69, over the socket end of adjusting screw; then install socket.
13. Turn the adjusting screw into the adjusting pivot nut to the limit of the threads, and then back it off one turn.
14. Use the spring washer and a new retaining clip to attach the parking brake lever to the trailing shoe. Crimp the clip.
15. Attach the parking brake cable to the parking brake lever.
16. Install the lower shoe retracting spring and place the assembly on the backing plate, sliding the shoes downward inside the shoe retaining plate. See Figure 48-69.
17. Install the adjuster screw assembly between the leading shoe slot and the slot in the trailing shoe and the parking brake lever, Figure 48-71.
18. Attach the upper shoe retracting spring to the leading shoe slot. Stretch the other end of the spring to engage the notch on the adjuster lever. Make sure that the lever contacts the star wheel.
19. Inspect the friction surface of the drum for the amount of wear and the degree of scoring.
20. If necessary, resurface the drum on a brake drum lathe.

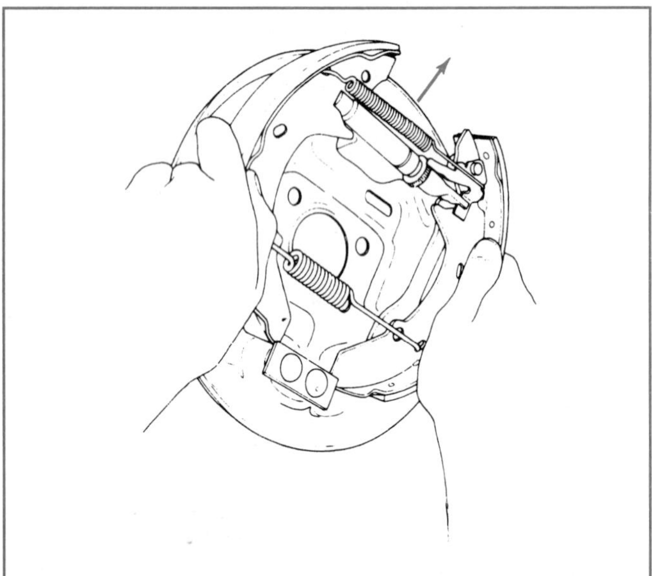
Figure 48-70. After the hold-down assemblies are removed, the entire brake assembly can be lifted up and away from the anchors and the backing plate. (Ford)

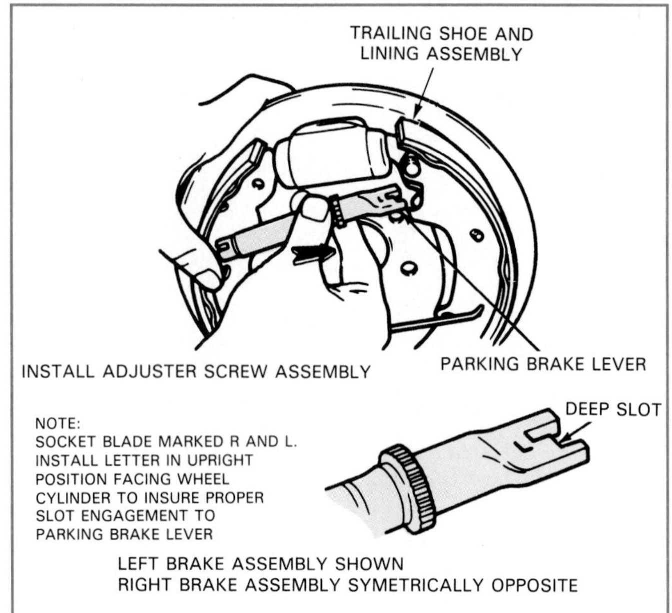

Figure 48-71. With the mechanical brake assembly in place on the backing plate, install the adjuster screw assembly as shown and noted. (Ford)

21. Adjust the brake drum gauge to the drum size. Place the other end of the gauge across the brake shoe diameter, hold the automatic adjusting lever away from the star wheel, and expand the shoes to fit the gauge.
22. Install the brake drum and the wheel and tire assembly.
23. Lubricate and adjust the wheel bearings.
24. Lower the vehicle and adjust the parking brake cables.
25. Bleed the brake system.

Troubleshooting Brakes

Excessive Pedal Travel

- Air in brake lines.
- Fluid leak.
- Faulty automatic adjusters.
- Maladjusted master cylinder push rod.
- Worn drum brake lining.
- Fluid bypassing quick take-up valve to reservoir.
- Partial brake system failure.

Excessive Pedal Effort

- Glazed or poor quality brake lining.
- Sticking wheel cylinder or caliper pistons.
- Calipers binding on mounting pins.
- Binding or damaged pedal linkage.
- Partial brake system failure.
- Excessively worn brake linings.
- Clogged quick take-up valve.
- Insufficient vacuum to power brake unit.
- Restricted or clogged lines or hoses.
- Contaminated brake fluid.
- Malfunctioning master cylinder.
- Faulty proportioning valve.

- Leaking or loose power brake unit vacuum hose.
- Defective power brake unit.

Pedal Spongy

- Air in hydraulic system.
- Bent or distorted drum brake shoes.

Pedal Pulsates

- Out-of-round drums.
- Excessive lateral runout of rotor.

Slow Pedal Return

- Clogged holes in quick take-up valve.

Brakes Grab

- Grease or fluid on linings.
- Maladjusted parking brake cables.
- Heat-spotted or scored brake drums or rotors.
- Maladjusted master cylinder push rod.
- Loose caliper attaching bolts.
- Binding brake pedal mechanism.
- Malfunctioning power brake unit.

Brakes Drag

- Contaminated brake fluid.
- Maladjusted parking brake cables.
- Faulty automatic adjusters.
- Sticking wheel cylinders or caliper pistons.
- Brake pedal binding at pivot.
- Maladjusted master cylinder push rod.
- Malfunctioning master cylinder.
- Faulty metering valve.
- Faulty proportioning valve.
- Restricted lines or hoses.

Brakes Fade

- Defective master cylinder.
- External fluid leak.
- Vapor lock in system.
- Thin brake drums.
- Crystallized brake lining.

Brakes Chatter

- Loose or missing brake assembly attaching parts.
- Bent or distorted brake shoes.
- Glazed brake lining.
- Loose caliper attaching bolts.
- Loose front suspension parts.
- Heat-spotted or scored brake drum or rotor.
- Excessive lateral runout of rotor.
- Out-of-parallel rotor.
- Loose wheel bearings.

Brakes Pull to One Side

- Unequal air pressure in front tires.
- Unmatched tires on same axle.
- Grease or fluid on brake lining.
- Loose caliper attaching bolts.
- Seized wheel cylinder or caliper.
- Restricted brake lines or hoses.
- Worn or damaged wheel bearings.
- Loose front suspension parts.
- Faulty combination valve.

Scraping Noise from Brakes

- Worn out brake lining.
- Uneven brake lining wear.
- Contaminated brake lining.
- Bent, broken, distorted brake shoes.
- Loose or missing brake assembly attaching parts.
- Incorrect wheel bearing adjustment.
- Loose front suspension parts.
- Interference between caliper and wheel or rotor.
- Scored or tapered brake drum.

Brakes Squeak

- Worn out brake lining.
- Glazed or poor quality brake lining.
- Contaminated brake lining.
- Excessive brake lining dust.
- Weak, damaged, or incorrect shoe retracting springs.
- Heat-spotted or scored brake drum or rotor.
- Burred or rusted caliper.
- Rough or dry drum brake backing plate ledges.

Brake Warning Light On

- Insufficient fluid in master cylinder reservoirs.
- Hydraulic system failure.
- Parking brake on or not fully released.
- Insufficient vacuum to power brake unit.

Power Brake System Service

Generally, the same kinds of operational problems can occur on cars with either power brakes or standard brakes. Excessive pedal effort, excessive pedal travel, dragging brakes, and grabbing brakes all could be caused by a malfunction in cars with or without power brakes.

However, note in Troubleshooting Brakes how much more prevalent the possible causes are in the mechanical and hydraulic parts of the overall brake system rather than in the power brake unit. Therefore, when brake trouble occurs, these systems should be checked out first.

GM Single Diaphragm Unit

With regard to specific power brake problems:

1. Hard pedal could be caused by a restricted air filter, vacuum failure, defective diaphragm, worn or distorted action plate or levers, cracked or broken power piston or retainer. See Figure 48-72.
2. Failure to release could be caused by a blocked passage in power piston, air valve stuck closed, broken piston return spring or air valve spring.

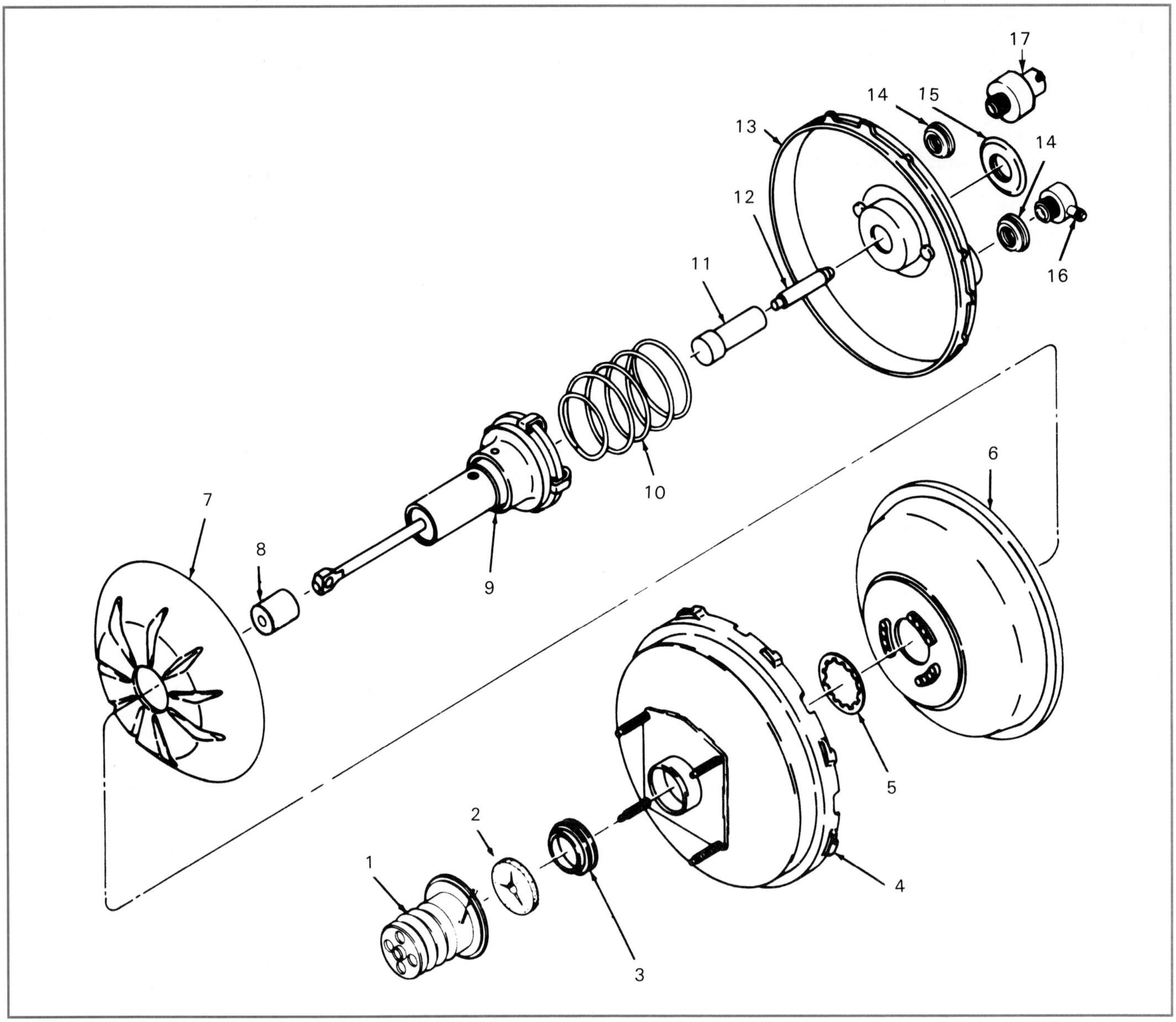

Figure 48-72. Exploded view of a General Motors single diaphragm power brake unit shows the relationship of interior and exterior parts. 1–Boot. 2–Silencer. 3–Power piston bearing. 4–Rear housing. 5–Diaphragm retainer. 6–Diaphragm. 7–Diaphragm support. 8–Filter. 9–Power piston and push rod assembly. 10–Return spring. 11–Reaction retainer. 12–Piston rod. 13–Front housing. 14–Grommet. 15–Front housing seal. 16–Vacuum check valve. 17–Vacuum switch. (Buick)

3. Dragging brakes could be caused by a piston rod (master cylinder push rod) of incorrect length. Out-of-limits push rod will cause primary cup to overlap compensating port of master cylinder.

A special disassembly and reassembly tool, Figure 48-73, is required to unlock the two housings of the typical General Motors single or tandem diaphragm power brake unit shown in Figure 48-72.

After disassembly, components may be inspected and replaced if defective. The power piston should not be disassembled. The inside diameter of the diaphragm lip should be lubricated and fit into the diaphragm support. A new diaphragm retainer must be installed, using a special driving tool.

The special disassembly and reassembly tool is used to lock the two housings together, Figure 48-73. A special gauge is used to check master cylinder push rod "height" with the power unit placed in a padded vise with front

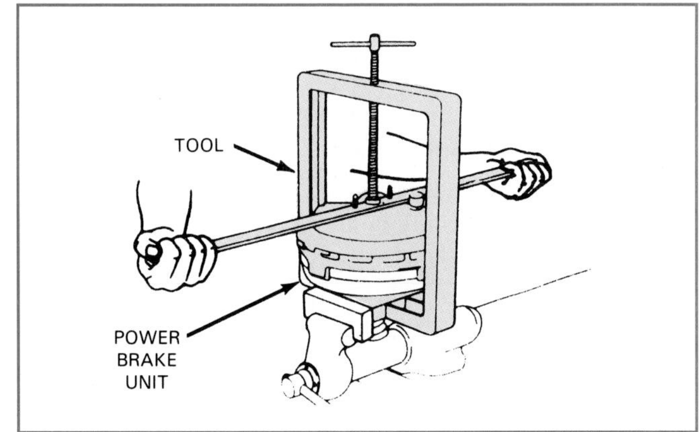

Figure 48-73. A special holding fixture is used to apply pressure to the power brake unit. Then the lever is turned counterclockwise to unlock the front and rear housings. The lever is turned clockwise to lock the housings. (Buick)

housing up. See Figure 48-74. If the push rod is out of limits, it must be replaced with an adjustable service push rod.

GM Tandem Diaphragm Unit

Service operations on the General Motors single and tandem diaphragm power brake units are similar. Again, a holding fixture is needed to unlock and lock the front and rear housings. A special assembly cone is used over the push rod end of the power piston to aid in reassembling the secondary diaphragm and related parts. A special go/no-go gauge is used to check "height" of the master cylinder push rod.

Bendix Single Diaphragm Unit

Chrysler and Ford use the Bendix single diaphragm power brake unit on many late-model cars. When servicing cars having a damaged or inoperative Bendix power brake unit, disassembly is not recommended. The unit is serviced as a complete assembly only.

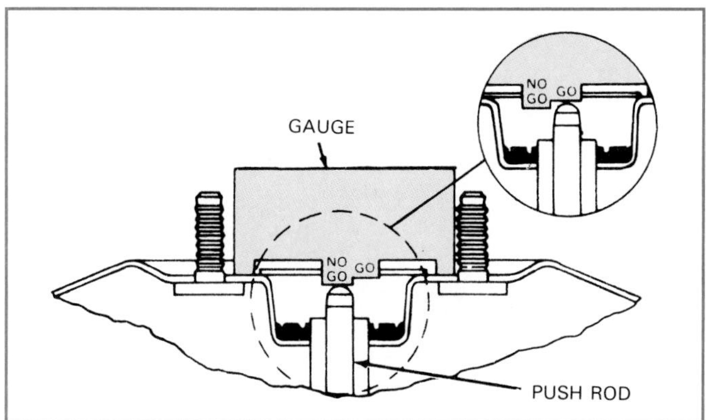

Figure 48-74. After reassembly of a General Motors single or tandem diaphragm power brake unit, a special go/no-go gauge is used to check the master cylinder push rod height. (Buick)

The Bendix unit on Chrysler and some Ford cars uses a factory adjusted or nonadjustable master cylinder push rod. No attempt should be made to adjust this type of push rod.

Hydro-Boost II

The Hydro-Boost II power brake, Figure 48-75, is also a part of the power steering system. Therefore, trouble in the steering system (low fluid level, low steering pump pressure, etc.) may affect operation of Hydro-Boost II.

When trouble occurs, certain preliminary checks should be made:

1. Check level of brake fluid in master cylinder reservoir. Fill, if low.
2. Check level of power steering fluid in pump reservoir. Fill, if low.
3. Check power steering pump belt for condition and/or damage. Replace belt or adjust belt tension.
4. Check all power steering lines, brake lines and hoses, and connections for leaks.
5. Check Hydro-Boost II assembly for leaks.
6. Check engine idle speed and adjust if necessary.
7. Check power steering pump pressure.

Fluid leaks from the Hydro-Boost II unit can be stopped by installing replacement seal kits:

1. Input assembly seal.
2. Power piston/accumulator seal.
3. Housing-to-housing cover seal.
4. Spool valve seal.
5. Return port fitting O-ring.

Seal replacement and correction of internal problems (faulty spool valve or piston/accumulator) requires disassembly of the Hydro-Boost II unit. See Figure 48-75.

GM Powermaster Brakes

The Powermaster brake assembly is a self-contained power brake system that utilizes a hydraulic booster and

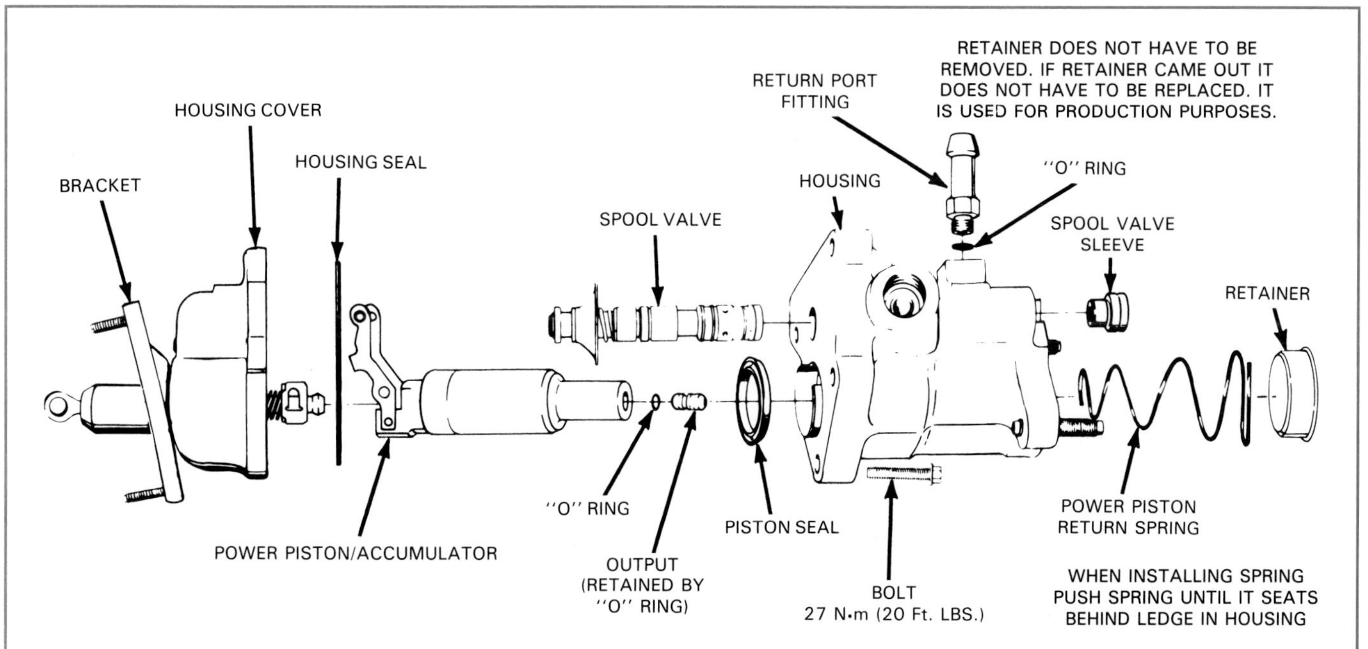

Figure 48-75. Exploded view of Hydro-Boost II power brake unit provides identification and gives the relative location of parts. Also note service cautions. (Oldsmobile)

master cylinder pressurized by a nitrogen charged accumulator to provide a power assist for braking. See Figure 48-76. A dual-pressure switch controls the fluid pressure level in the accumulator by turning an electro-hydraulic pump on and off as needed.

Brake fluid level checks are especially important with the Powermaster system. First and foremost, the accumulator must be depressurized before servicing. Otherwise, opening the hydraulic system could cause brake fluid to be sprayed out at high pressure.

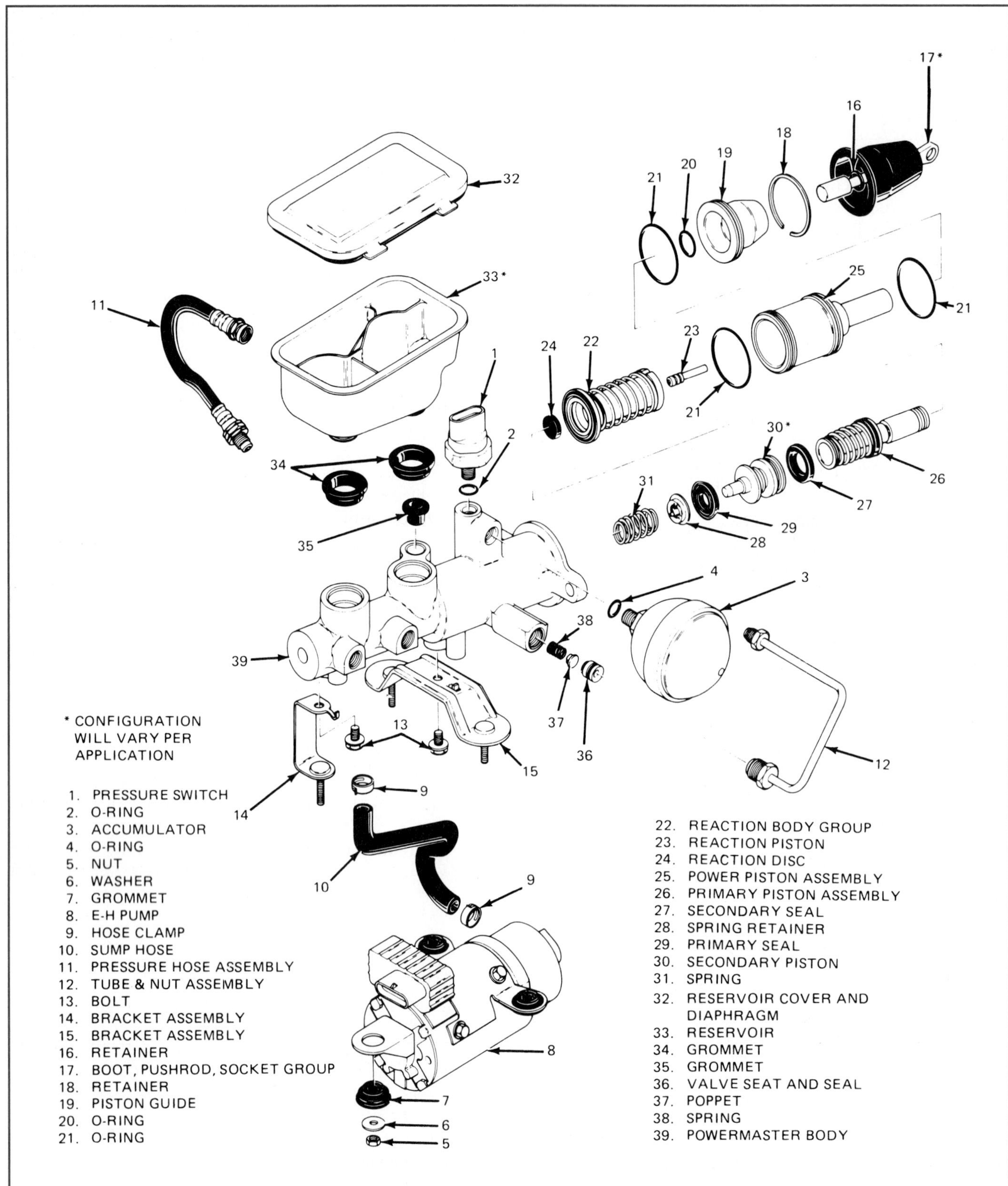

Figure 48-76. Exploded view shows the arrangement of parts of a General Motors Powermaster brake assembly. Key elements of the assembly include: 1–Dual pressure switch. 3–Accumulator. 8–Electro-hydraulic pump. 25–Power piston. (Buick)

To depressurize the accumulator, apply and release the brake pedal at about 50 lb. of force for at least 10 cycles. This will return fluid to the master cylinder reservoir so that fluid level checks can be made.

After depressurizing the accumulator, clean the master cylinder reservoir cover, remove the cover, and check the fluid levels. Markings on both sides of the reservoir indicate maximum and minimum levels.

If levels are low, fill to the marks with clean brake fluid meeting DOT-3 specifications. Replace the reservoir cover.

To bleed the booster assembly, turn on the ignition and let the pump restore pressure to the system. Turn off the ignition and pump the brakes to discharge the accumulator. Repeat this entire procedure 10 times to be sure that all air is removed from the booster.

Troubleshooting and Servicing Anti-lock Brake Systems

Warning: Many anti-lock brake systems operate at extremely high pressures. Never service an anti-lock brake system without relieving system pressure properly. Refer to the manufacturer's manual for proper procedures for safely releasing pressure. Loosening brake lines without relieving pressure can result in serious injury.

Most anti-lock brake systems are equipped with a warning lamp to inform the operator of a system malfunction. If the warning light is activated, visually inspect the system for problems. Wheel sensors should be inspected for signs of physical damage. A buildup of foreign material between the rotor's teeth can cause the control module to set a trouble code. Check all wires for damage and make sure that all connections are tight. Also, make sure that the correct size tires are installed on the vehicle. If the wrong tires are installed on a vehicle with anti-lock brakes, the sensors may send incorrect signals to the control module.

To facilitate troubleshooting procedures, most anti-lock brake systems have self-diagnostic capabilities. The first step in troubleshooting anti-lock brake systems is to retrieve trouble codes stored in the anti-lock control module's memory. In many cases, a scan tool is needed to retrieve codes from the control module. Always consult the vehicle's service manual for the appropriate method. The trouble codes should be compared to the appropriate trouble code chart to determine potential problems. After using the trouble code chart to interpret the codes, most manufacturers recommend specific pinpoint tests to verify malfunctions.

Many manufacturers recommend checking wheel speed sensors with an ohmmeter to determine their resistance. If the reading does not fall within specifications, the sensor should be replaced. Always make sure that the wiring from the sensor is routed correctly. Improper wiring can provide false information to the control module and cause a dangerous handling problem when the anti-lock system is activated.

If a faulty hydraulic actuator is suspected, it should be tested according to the manufacturer's recommendations. Manufacturers usually recommend specific ohmmeter tests to determine the condition of the solenoid valves inside of the actuator. Most hydraulic actuators cannot be serviced in the field and, therefore, must be replaced as a unit.

If a faulty anti-lock control module is suspected, check the input voltage to the unit. If the control module does not receive sufficient voltage, it will not operate properly. Check the wiring to and from the control module, and make sure all connections are clean and secure. Verify the proper operation of all related anti-lock system components before condemning the control module.

Review Questions–Chapter 48

Write your answers on a separate sheet of paper. Do not write in this book.

1. The brake system is a balanced set of mechanical and hydraulic devices used to halt the motion of the vehicle by means of _____.
2. The vehicle must be brought to a stop in a much shorter time than is required to bring it up to speed. True or False?
3. There are three basic types of brake lining in current use. Which of the following materials is NOT installed?
   (A) Asbestos.
   (B) Non-asbestos organic.
   (C) Metallic.
   (D) Semi-metallic.
4. Under extreme braking conditions, which type of brake lining is used?
5. Disc brake rotor braking surfaces are precisely machined for quality of finish, thickness, parallelism, and absence of _____.
6. The use of _____ for the braking surface of brake drums is almost universal.
   (A) steel
   (B) cast iron
   (C) aluminum
   (D) aluminum alloy
7. Disc brakes are self adjusting. True or False?
8. There are many factors that contribute to the effectiveness of drum brakes. Name four factors.
9. Hydraulic brake fluid must meet special requirements spelled out in SAE Specification J1703. Brake fluids meeting this specification are labeled:
   (A) DOT-1 or DOT-2.
   (B) DOT-3 or DOT-4.
   (C) DOT-5 or DOT-6.
   (D) DOT-7 or DOT-8.
10. Most late-model cars utilize a _____ (front-to-rear or diagonal) split hydraulic system.
11. The hydraulic brake system combination valve usually combines three individual valves. Which of the following is not part of the combination valve?
    (A) Pressure differential valve.
    (B) Quick take-up valve.
    (C) Proportioning valve.
    (D) Metering valve.
12. Why do some original brake hoses and equivalent replacement hoses have a lengthwise white stripe?

13. Most power brake applications utilize _____ units.
    (A) vacuum suspended
    (B) air suspended
    (C) hydraulic booster
    (D) electro-hydraulic booster
14. Anti-lock brake systems use _____ _____ _____ to monitor the rate of wheel rotation.
15. When servicing brake parts, breathing dust containing brake lining fibers may cause serious bodily harm. What type of lining is this?
16. A special hone can be used to polish the bore of a _____ master cylinder. Do not hone _____ master cylinder bores.
17. There are two general methods of bleeding air from hydraulic brake systems. What are they?
18. A customer complains of a pulsating brake pedal. Technician A says it could be caused by an out-of-round brake drum. Technician B says it could be caused by excessive lateral runout of disc brake rotors. Who is right?
    (A) A only.
    (B) B only.
    (C) Both A & B.
    (D) Neither A nor B.
19. A car owner complains that the brakes drag. Technician A says it could be caused by an external brake fluid leak. Technician B says it could be caused by vapor lock in the hydraulic system. Who is right?
    (A) A only.
    (B) B only.
    (C) Both A & B.
    (D) Neither A nor B.
20. With regard to specific GM single diaphragm power brake units, hard pedal has many possible causes. Name three.

Match the question number for each of the following brake assemblies with the letter designated for each correct associated term.

21. _____ Rotor.
22. _____ Drum.
23. _____ Disc brake.
24. _____ Drum brake.
25. _____ Brake lines.
26. _____ Master cylinder.
27. _____ Parking brake.
28. _____ Power brake.
29. _____ Hydro-Boost II.
30. _____ Anti-lock brake.

(A) Brake fluid.
(B) Diaphragm.
(C) Cable and lever.
(D) Wheel sensor.
(E) Friction pads.
(F) Power steering fluid.
(G) Caliper.
(H) Primary piston.
(I) Wheel cylinder.
(J) Brake shoes.

Chapter 49
Automobile Air Conditioning

After studying this chapter, you will be able to:

- Describe the fundamentals of air conditioning.
- List the major parts of an air conditioning system and the purpose of each.
- Summarize the principles of air conditioning.
- Explain why R-134A is being used in the air conditioning systems of late-model vehicles.
- Explain how the heating system works.
- Tell how an air conditioning compressor and clutch operates.
- List the different types of air conditioning systems.
- Explain how to service an air conditioning system, including proper refrigerant recovery techniques.
- Troubleshoot an air conditioning system.

Automobile Air Conditioning

The history of automotive air conditioning, in terms of cooling by refrigeration, dates back to a few buses in the late 1930s and a few thousand Packards in the early 1940s. Now, more than three-fourths of the new cars sold each year are equipped with factory installed air conditioning and over a half-million aftermarket units are installed each year.

Fundamentals of Refrigeration

Air conditioning (A/C) is the process by which surrounding air is cooled and dehumidified. In an automobile, this process is performed by a closed refrigeration system that circulates ***refrigerant*** under pressure. See Figure 49-1. While making its rounds, the refrigerant cycles from vapor to liquid, absorbing heat from the warm air inside the passenger compartment and discharging it to outside air, Figure 49-2.

Changes from a liquid to a vapor are often accomplished by means of ***heat*** and ***evaporation.*** Heat, for example, causes water to boil and sends vapor (gas) into the air.

This same vapor can be returned to liquid form (water) by ***cooling*** and ***condensation.*** If a glass of cold water is placed in a warm room, the warm air collects on the outside of the glass, becomes cooler, and condenses into water.

This transformation of liquid into vapor and vapor into liquid occurs at atmospheric pressure. Higher pressures can also be used to reduce a vapor to liquid form. It is this evaporation that has a cooling effect. For example, you jump in a pool on a hot summer day. After you get out, you feel cooler. It is the water evaporating off your body that makes you feel cooler.

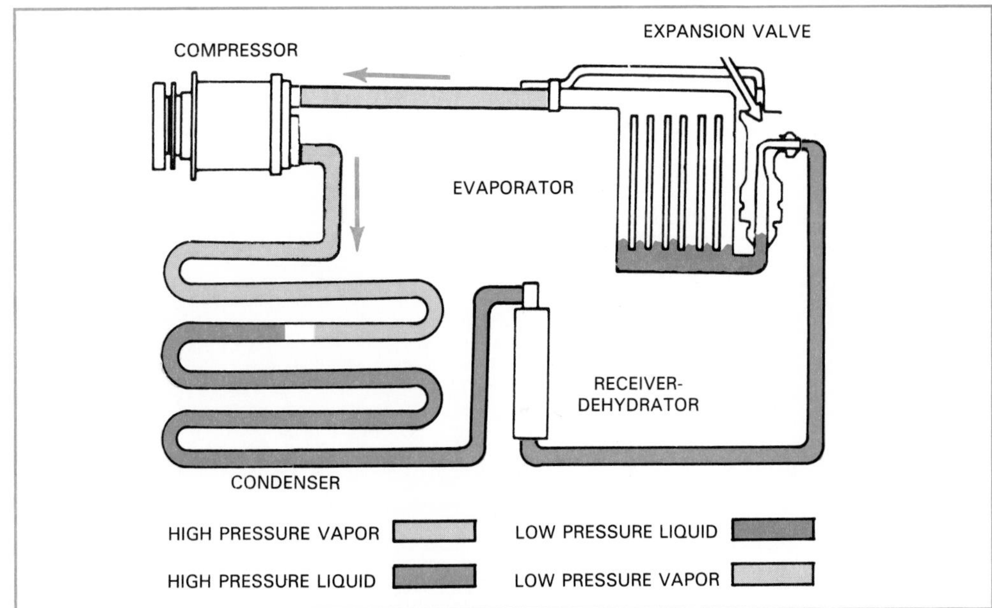

Figure 49-1. Schematic traces refrigerant flow in a basic air conditioning system. Refrigerant is a liquid in red high-pressure area. It then becomes a vapor in light-blue low-pressure area.

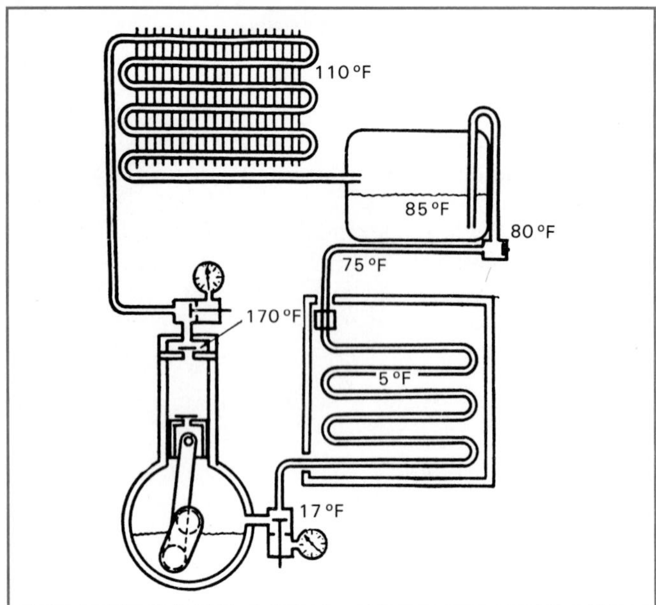

Figure 49-2. The refrigeration process is based on thermal law that fluids absorb heat while changing from a liquid to a vapor and they give up heat while changing from a vapor to a liquid.

Basically, automotive air conditioning systems operate on these principles of evaporation and condensation. In the passenger compartment end of the system, the liquid refrigerant is sprayed into an evaporator where it vaporizes. At the other end, refrigerant vapor is pumped into the condenser where it condenses into a liquid.

These two key steps directly relate to principles stated in this two-part thermal law:

- A fluid will absorb heat when it changes from a liquid to a vapor. This process occurs in the ***evaporator,*** which is placed in the passenger compartment specifically for the purpose of removing heat.
- A fluid will give off heat when it changes from a vapor to a liquid. This principle is put to use in the ***condenser,*** which generally is positioned in the airstream in front of the engine cooling system radiator.

Each of these principles is utilized in automotive air conditioning by a series of major components that are connected by tubing and hoses, and actuated by a belt-driven compressor that pressurizes the refrigerant.

Five major elements do the job of circulating, condensing, and vaporizing the refrigerant. These include compressor, condenser, receiver-drier (or accumulator-drier), thermostatic expansion valve (or orifice tube), and evaporator, Figure 49-3. See CCOT Principles.

Principles of Air Conditioning

Here is how a typical automotive air conditioning system works:

1. Hot refrigerant vapor (gas) is drawn into the compressor, where the vapor is placed under high pressure and is pumped into the condenser, Figure 49-1.
2. In the condenser, a change occurs as intake air passing through the core removes heat from the refrigerant vapor as it changes to its liquid state.
3. Refrigerant, having done its job of discharging heat, then flows into the receiver-drier, where it is filtered, demoisturized, and stored for use as required to meet cooling needs.
4. As the compressor continues to pressurize the system, liquid refrigerant under high pressure is circulated from the receiver-drier to the thermostatic expansion valve.
5. The expansion valve then meters refrigerant into the inlet side of the evaporator.

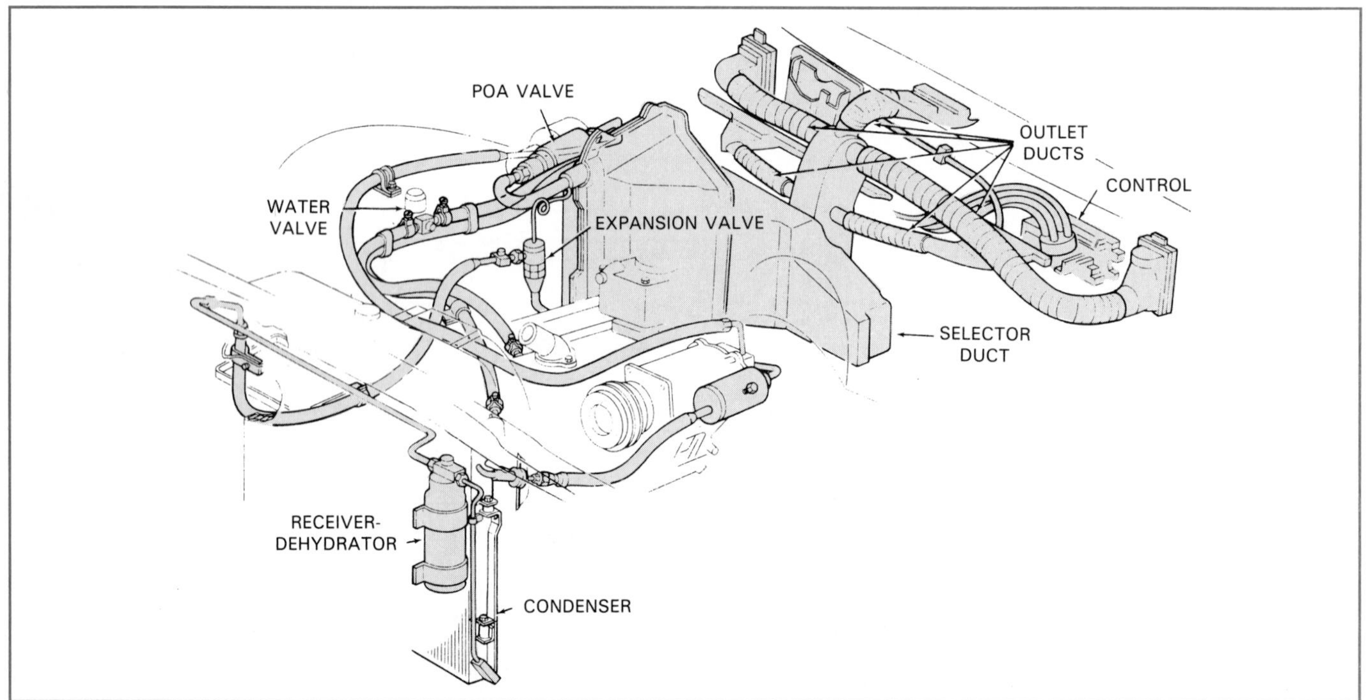

Figure 49-3. Layout of earlier Chevrolet air conditioning system includes the identification of major components, connecting hoses, metal lines, controls, ducts, and related water valve. (Chevrolet)

6. Pressure drops at this point as the refrigerant (suddenly released to the broad area of the evaporator coils) vaporizes and absorbs heat from the air in the passenger compartment.
7. This heat-laden, low-pressure refrigerant vapor is then drawn into the compressor to start another refrigeration cycle.

In operation, the refrigerant constantly recycles in the sealed system from a vapor to a liquid to a vapor. Meanwhile, heat in the passenger compartment is constantly being absorbed by the refrigerant and carried away under pressure to be given off to the atmosphere. In effect, the automotive air conditioning system is a ***heat transfer unit,*** cooling the air by removing the heat.

However, to better understand how an air conditioner works, you need to know the nature of heat, the effect of heat and pressure on the state of matter, how heat is transferred from one object to another, and how cooling action is accomplished.

Nature of Heat

Specifically, the words hot and cold are relative terms that refer to the degree of heat that is present. An object or thing is considered to be hot or cold only when it is related to something else.

If an exhaust manifold is "hot to the touch," it merely is hotter than the hand of the person touching it. If an auto shop is said to be "cold," the air within it simply contains less heat than does the air in a comfortably warm room. All these terms relate to the presence of heat. Cold refers only to the degree that heat is absent.

Actually, heat is a form of energy that has no substance. It is contained in all matter to some degree of intensity or concentration. Because of this characteristic, it is termed "sensible heat" or "temperature," which can be measured on a thermometer.

Based on the fact that heat stimulates matter, it logically follows that heat can be used to change the state of matter. Whether it is in a solid state, a liquid state, or a gaseous state, matter will change if some outside source is used to add or remove enough heat.

How fast matter will change its state, and the temperature at which it changes, depends on the makeup and movement of its molecules. Ice, for example, is matter in a solid state. It will melt at 33°F (0.6°C) and become water, a liquid state. Water will boil at 212°F (100°C) and become steam, a gaseous state.

Heat Transfer. An unusual characteristic of heat is that it always flows (transfers) from hotter to cooler objects by one or more of three methods: conduction, convection, or radiation.

Conduction of heat is the condition when a solid object gradually heats up particle-by-particle. Metal objects heat by conduction and are considered to be good thermal conductors. Copper, for example, is used in air conditioner condensers so that the heat will readily transfer from the refrigerant, to the copper coils and fins, to the air.

Convection of heat occurs in liquids and gases as heated portions rise and are displaced by cooler portions, creating a convection current. Convection of heat takes place, for example, when a furnace circulates heated air within a room.

Radiation is the transfer of heat by waves through space, such as rays of the sun. Actually, anything heated gives off radiated energy. It may be reflected (by a car painted a light color) or it may be absorbed (by a car painted a dark color).

Automobile Heating Systems

Conditioning the air in the passenger compartment of an automobile involves heating, cooling, and dehumidification. Therefore, the car heating and air conditioning systems are designed to have much in common. For example, the two systems make joint use of a ***plenum chamber*** under the dash as a means of moving conditioned air into the passenger compartment. See Figure 49-4.

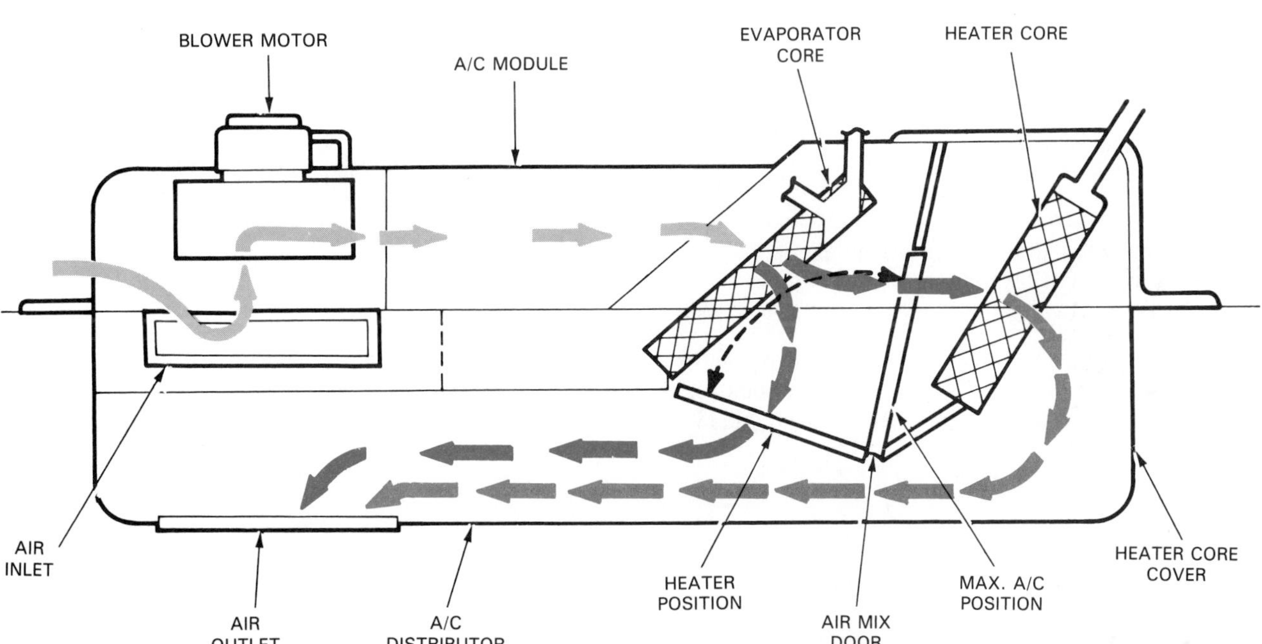

Figure 49-4. Top view shows a typical plenum chamber made up of an A/C module and a heater core cover. Note the location of the blower motor, evaporator core, and heater core. The dashed line depicts the operating range of the air mix door. (Cadillac)

The heat required under cold weather conditions usually is provided by circulating hot coolant from the water pump through heater hoses and the heater core. Then, blower action forces incoming air across the tubes and fins of the heater core, and heated air is discharged at outlets in and under the dash. See Figure 49-5.

Conditioned Air

When weather conditions become uncomfortably hot, air conditioning cools and dehumidifies the passenger compartment. When A/C controls are set, the evaporator serves to absorb heat from the air passing through it. By the process of liquid refrigerant changing into a vapor, heat from the passenger compartment is absorbed and carried away by the circulating refrigerant. See Principles of A/C covered earlier.

The "conditioned" air enters the passenger compartment by way of various ducts and louvers. Doors in the ducts are moved mechanically, electrically, or by vacuum as directed by settings on the control panel on the dash. See Figures 49-6 and 49-7.

In some systems, a control lever moves an air mix door from heater position (closed to A/C airflow) to maximum A/C position (closed to heater core airflow). See Figure 49-4. In-between settings provide a "blend" of A/C airflow and heated airflow to satisfy the driver's particular needs.

In other systems, Figure 49-3, heated airflow is controlled by the adjustment of a ***water valve*** installed at the inlet side of the heater core. The water valve is connected by a cable to the control panel on the dash. In the ***heat*** position, the water valve is wide open, allowing full flow of hot coolant through the heater core. In the ***cool*** position, the valve is closed, allowing restricted flow.

Comfort Considerations

In dealing with human comfort, other things besides actual temperature must be considered:

- Humidity control.
- Air movement and circulation.
- Air filtering, cleaning, and purification.

The amount of ***humidity*** in the air affects the rate of evaporation of perspiration. If the air contains much moisture, one may feel uncomfortable even if the air is relatively cool.

Air circulation is also important because if cool, dry air is moved past a warm body, radiation of heat from the body will increase.

Air filtering, cleaning, and ***purification*** are necessary to keep out dust, eliminate smoke and odors, and add to comfort. For these reasons, it is necessary to consider factors other than the actual temperature attained if an air conditioning system can be expected to operate efficiently and satisfactorily.

Types of Refrigerant

R-12 is a ***chlorofluorocarbon*** (CFC) that has been used as a refrigerant in automotive air conditioning systems

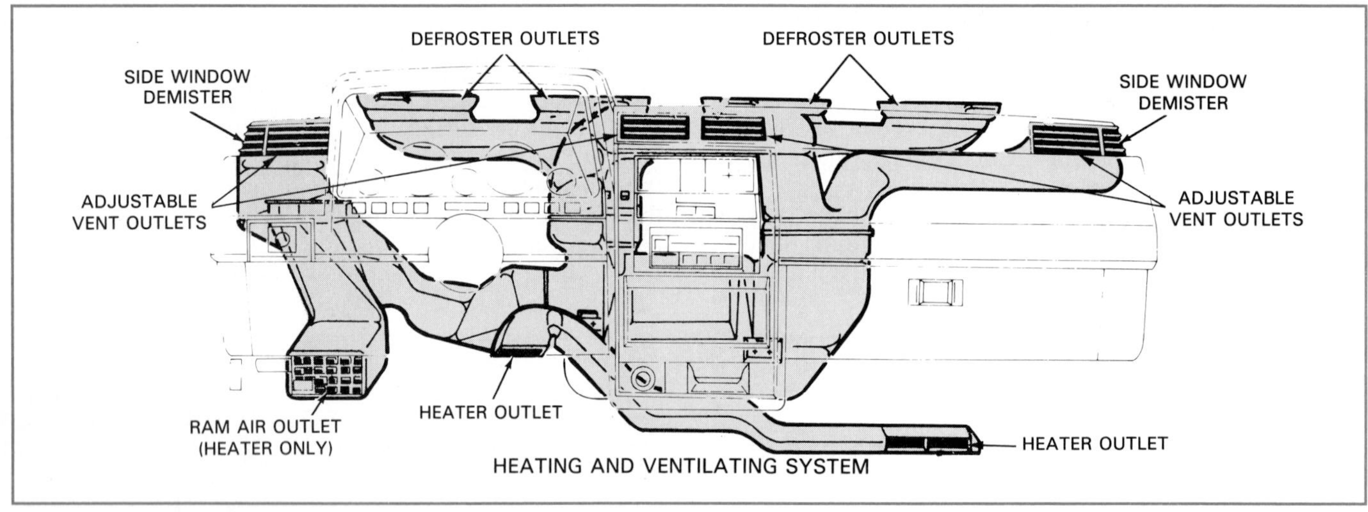

Figure 49-5. Phantom front view of a dash panel reveals the location of the airflow ducts and outlets of a typical car heating and ventilating system. (Chrysler)

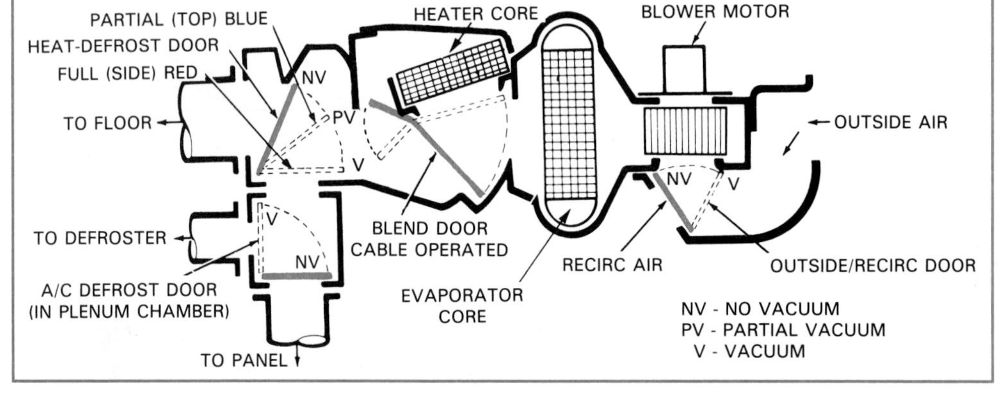

Figure 49-6. Top view pictures another arrangement of components in a plenum chamber. Vacuum-operated doors are shown in varied positions. The blend door is cable operated. (Ford)

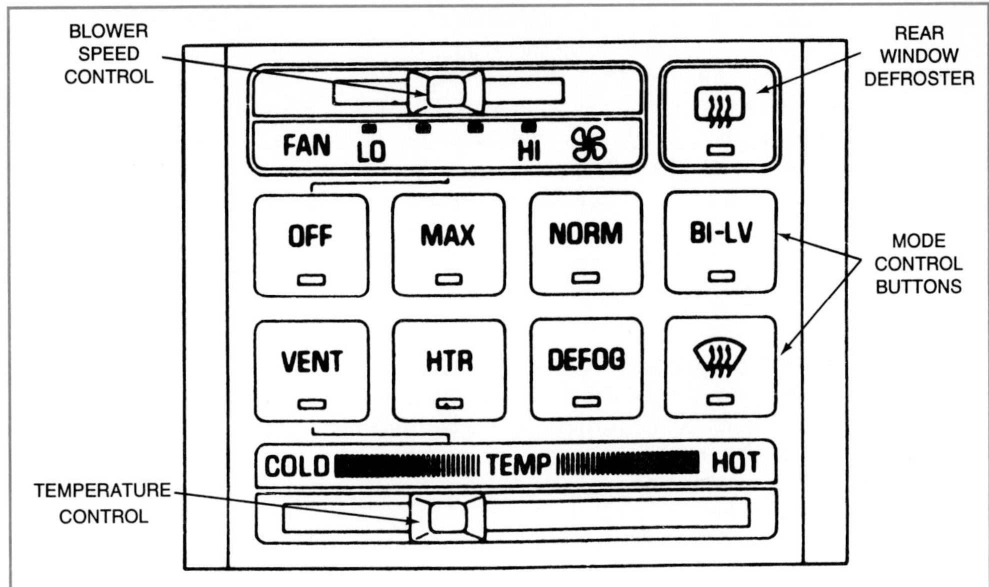

Figure 49-7. Typical control panel for A/C and heating contains control levers and clearly indicated settings for desired temperature, blower speed, and direction of airflow. (Ford)

for many years. However, scientists now believe that CFCs are harmful to the earth's ozone layer. Consequently, legislation has been passed to ban the production of CFCs by 1996. In preparation for this action, manufacturers are now using an environmentally safe refrigerant in their air conditioning systems. This refrigerant is known as ***R-134A.*** Although R-12 is still found in many systems, it must not be released into the atmosphere during routine air conditioning service. Special ***recovery/recycling equipment*** must now be used when servicing air conditioning systems.

Requirements of Refrigerant

The ability to absorb and discharge heat is the prime requirement of any refrigerant. With its high boiling point, water is not suitable for use as a refrigerant. Refrigerant-12 (R-12), on the other hand, boils at -22°F (-30°C). Similarly, R-134A boils at -15°F (-26°C). Both refrigerants absorb heat readily.

A refrigerant's ability to absorb heat can be shown in terms of how much heat is required to cause it to change from one state to another without changing its temperature. Consider that the amount of heat being applied to or being given off by any object is measured in ***British thermal units*** (Btu). As established, one Btu is the amount of heat required to raise the temperature of a pound of water one degree Fahrenheit at sea level pressure.

The basic Btu measurement can be used to illustrate how well R-12 serves as a refrigerant. In order to change water to steam at 212°F (100°C), each pound of water must absorb 970 Btu. To change R-12 to a vapor at 5°F (-15°C), only 69.5 Btu per pound are needed.

The ability to change state easily and repeatedly, yet maintain good stability in either state, is what makes R-12 and R-134A especially well suited for repeated recycling within the air conditioning system.

Another point in favor of these refrigerants is their reaction to pressure. An increase in pressure will raise the boiling point of a liquid refrigerant, while a drop in pressure will lower the boiling point. This ***pressure-temperature relationship*** works well with refrigerant in the system. By changing the pressure on the refrigerant, its temperature can be controlled. This, in turn, controls how much heat the refrigerant can absorb and how readily it rids itself of the heat when the tubing carrying the refrigerant is exposed to outside air.

The value of this pressure-temperature relationship lies in the fact that pressure tests made on the "low side" will reveal the refrigerant temperature at this point in the system. For example, if the pressure reading on the low side is 30 psi, the temperature of the evaporator coils and fins will be down near the 32°F (0°C) mark. Therefore, you immediately know that the air conditioning system is running efficiently enough to cool the passenger compartment.

The objective of automobile air conditioning, then, is to get the refrigerant temperature low enough that the evaporator will reach its coldest point without icing up.

Working Parts of Air Conditioning Systems

A typical automotive air conditioning system consists of five major components: compressor, condenser, receiver-drier, thermostatic expansion valve, and evaporator, Figure 49-3.

Other parts are used (suction throttling valve, evaporator pressure regulator, for example), but only to control and increase the efficiency of the system. High-pressure hoses and metal lines connect the various parts and form the continuous circuit for recirculation of the refrigerant.

Each of the major components is equally important to the system. A malfunction of any one of these units will interrupt the heat transfer cycle and disrupt operation of the whole system.

Compressor

The ***compressor*** is the power unit of the A/C system. It pumps out refrigerant vapor under high pressure and high heat on the discharge side (high side of system) and sucks in low pressure vapor on the intake side (low side). See Figure 49-1.

Pressure builds because of a restriction in the high side of the system in the form of the thermostatic expansion valve or an orifice tube. See CCOT Principles. The small valve or metered orifice offers resistance to the flow of pressurized refrigerant to build pressure behind it.

The heat buildup is obtained when heat molecules in the low-pressure refrigerant (returning from the evaporator) are concentrated by the pressurizing effect of compressor operation. This action serves to raise the temperature of the refrigerant vapor flowing to the condenser, stimulating rapid heat flow from the hot refrigerant to cooler outside air. Remember, heat always flows from hotter objects to cooler objects.

The basic types of air conditioning compressors are:

- Two-cylinder reciprocating piston compressors.
- Swash (wobble) plate compressors.
- Scotch yoke compressors.

Two-cylinder Compressors. Conventional ***reciprocating piston compressors*** usually have two cylinders arranged in a parallel "Vee." Some earlier original equipment A/C systems and most aftermarket (hang-on) installations use compressors of reciprocating piston design, powered by an engine-driven V-belt.

During operation of a typical two-stroke cycle reciprocating piston compressor, the piston creates a suction on the downstroke (intake). This draws the intake valve open and sucks refrigerant vapor into the cylinder. On the upstroke (compression), the piston pressurizes the refrigerant, forcing it past the exhaust valve and into the hoses and metal lines to the condenser. With an ambient temperature of 70° to 80°F (21 to 27°C), the hot refrigerant vapor leaves the compressor at 175 to 195 psi (1207 to 1345 kPa) to trigger system operation.

Swash Plate Compressors. The ***swash plate compressor*** contains a swash (wobble) plate mounted diagonally on a straight shaft. These compressors generally have five or six cylinders. The General Motors six-cylinder compressor shown in Figure 49-8 has three sets of opposing cylinders and three double-acting pistons. The pistons are connected to the swash plate by piston balls.

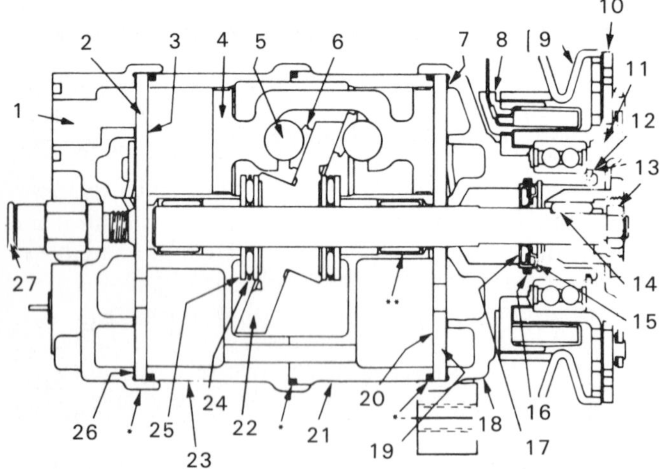

Figure 49-8. Typical GM six-cylinder swash plate compressor. 1–Suction port. 2–Rear valve plate. 3–Suction reed plate 4–Piston and ring assembly. 5–Piston ball. 6–Shoe disc. 7–Head gasket. 8–Clutch coil assembly. 9–Pulley rotor. 10–Clutch driver. 11–Pulley bearing. 12–Bearing retainer rings. 13–Shaft nut. 14–Shaft key. 15–Seal retainer. 16–Seal O-ring. 17–Shaft seal. 18–Front head. 19–Front valve plate. 20–Suction reed plate. 21–Front cylinder. 22–Shaft and swash plate assembly. 23–Rear cylinder. 24–Thrust bearing. 25–Thrust race. 26–Head gasket. 27–Pressure relief valve. 28–Rear head. *Cylinder O-ring seals. **Shaft bearing. (Cadillac)

As the compressor shaft rotates, the swash plate wobbles, causing the pistons to move back and forth in the cylinders. Each cylinder has a set of reed valves for intake and exhaust. Passages from the valves are connected to one high side port and one low side port. Piston action creates high pressure at the high side port and suction at the low side port of the compressor.

Similar six-cylinder swash plate compressors are used on some Ford A/C systems, Figure 49-9. Also, Chrysler uses a six-cylinder swash plate compressor in some of its A/C systems, Figure 49-10.

Some GM A/C systems use a five-cylinder compressor with a variable position swash plate, Figure 49-11. The swash plate is positioned by a bellows-actuated control valve that senses the demand for air conditioning under all conditions without cycling. Under high load conditions, the control valve increases the swash plate angle for greater displacement to meet the demand. During low load conditions, the valve decreases the swash plate angle to reduce displacement.

Scotch Yoke Compressors. The ***scotch yoke compressor*** is a radial unit designed to change rotary motion to reciprocating motion without the use of connecting rods or piston balls. The scotch yoke design has four pistons mounted 90° from each other. See Figure 49-12. The op-

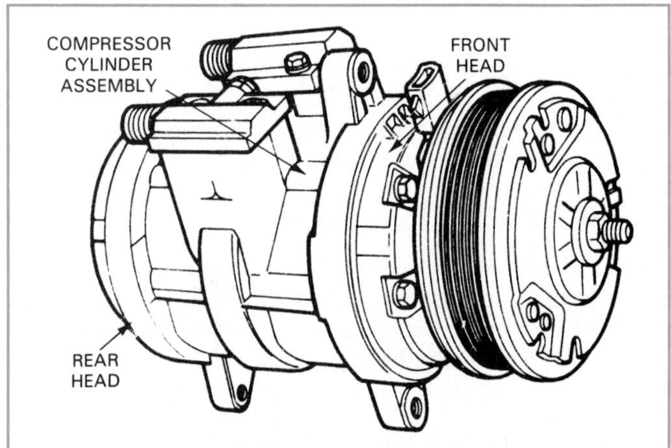

Figure 49-9. Makeup of this Ford six-cylinder compressor is similar to the GM compressor shown in Figure 49-8. The swash plate actuates three double-acting pistons in a front and rear cylinder assembly. (Ford)

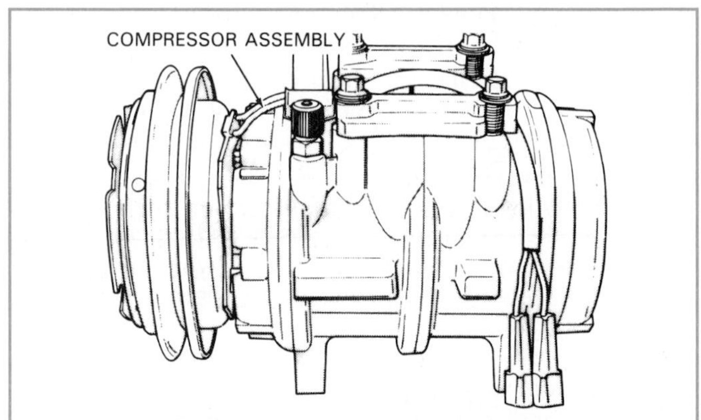

Figure 49-10. The Chrysler six-cylinder compressor also utilizes a swash plate to operate the double-acting pistons in sequence within three sets of opposing cylinders. (Chrysler)

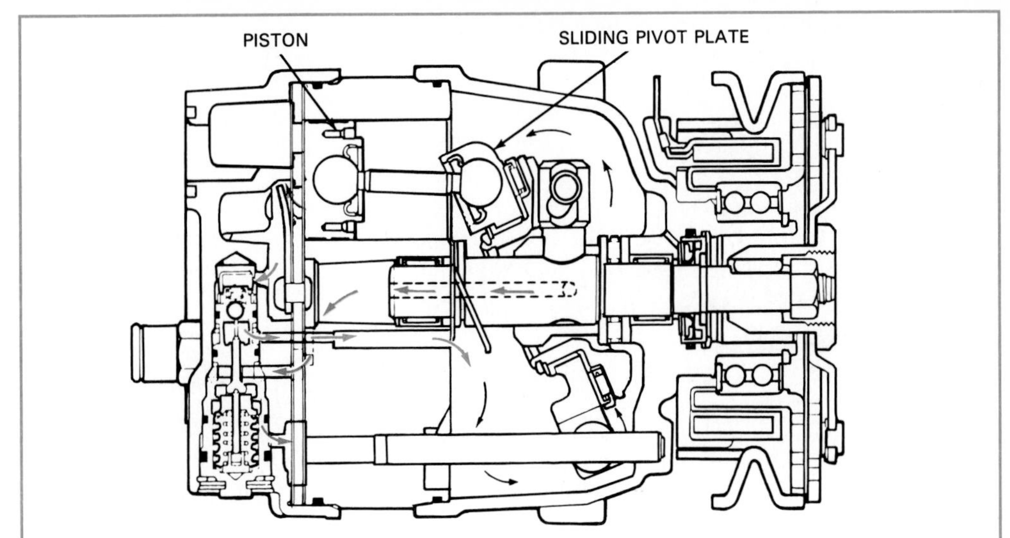

Figure 49-11. Chevrolet variable displacement compressor. Bellows-actuated valve at the lower left controls the position of the swash plate. The position of the swash plate determines compressor displacement. Arrow code is: black, crankcase refrigerant flow; red, suction pressure; blue, discharge. (Chevrolet)

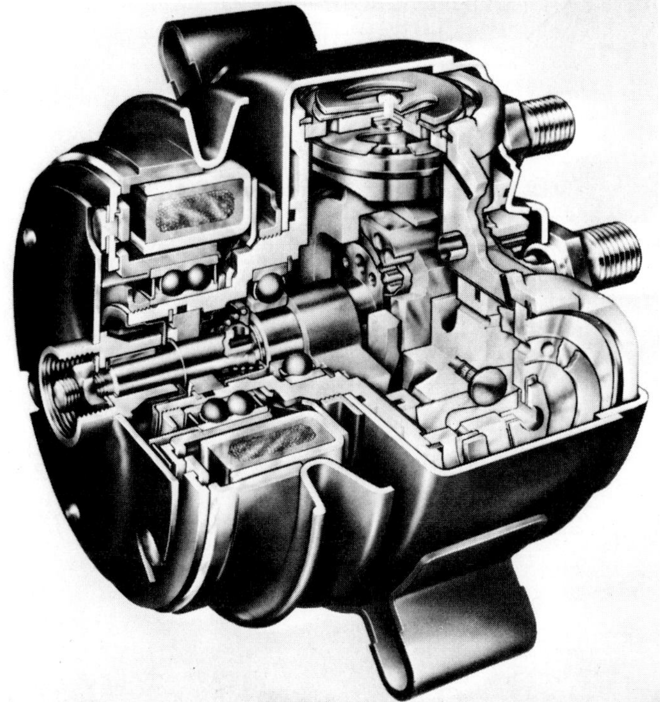

Figure 49-12. A scotch yoke compressor utilizes a yoke-type mechanism and an eccentric on the compressor shaft to change the rotary motion of shaft to the reciprocating motion of pistons. (Tecumseh Products Co.)

posed pistons are pressed into a yoke that rides on a slide block on the compressor shaft eccentric.

In operation, refrigerant enters the crankcase of the compressor from the rear. On the suction stroke, the refrigerant is drawn through reeds attached to the top of the pistons. The refrigerant is then discharged through the valve plate, and it flows out the connector block at the rear of the compressor.

Compressor Clutches

Compressors used in automobile air conditioning systems generally are equipped with an electromagnetic clutch which energizes and de-energizes to engage and disengage the compressor. Two types of clutches are in general use: the stationary field coil type, Figure 49-13, and the once popular rotating coil type.

The ***stationary clutch field coil*** is mounted on the front end of the compressor. The pulley rotates freely on the compressor body. Electrical connections are made directly to the coil leads. When the A/C system is turned ON, the clutch field coil and compressor hub are drawn to the pulley by magnetic force, and the clutch field coil and pulley are locked together as a unit. The compressor shaft then turns the field coil and pulley-and-hub assembly for compressor operation.

The ***rotating coil clutch*** has a magnetic coil mounted in the pulley, and it rotates with the pulley. It operates electrically through connections to a stationary brush assembly and rotating slip rings. When signaled by an automatic thermostatic switch, the clutch permits the compressor to engage or disengage as required for adequate air conditioning.

The clutch, in effect, is the connecting link between the compressor pulley and the compressor. The belt-driven pulley is always in rotation while the engine is running. The compressor is in rotation and operation only when the clutch engages it to the pulley.

Service Valves and Gauge Port Fittings

Compressor service valves are built into some systems. They serve as a point of attachment for test gauges or servicing hoses. The service valves are three-position controls: front-seated, mid-position, and back-seated. See Figure 49-14.

Position of this double-faced valve is controlled by rotating the valve stem with a service valve wrench. Clockwise rotation will seat the front face of the valve and shut off all refrigerant flow in the system. This position will isolate the compressor from the rest of the system.

Counterclockwise rotation will unseat the valve and open the system to refrigerant flow (mid-position).

Further counterclockwise rotation of the valve stem will seat the rear face of the valve. This position opens the system to the flow of refrigerant but shuts off refrigerant to the test connector. See Figure 49-14. The service valves are used for testing pressure, for isolating the compressor for

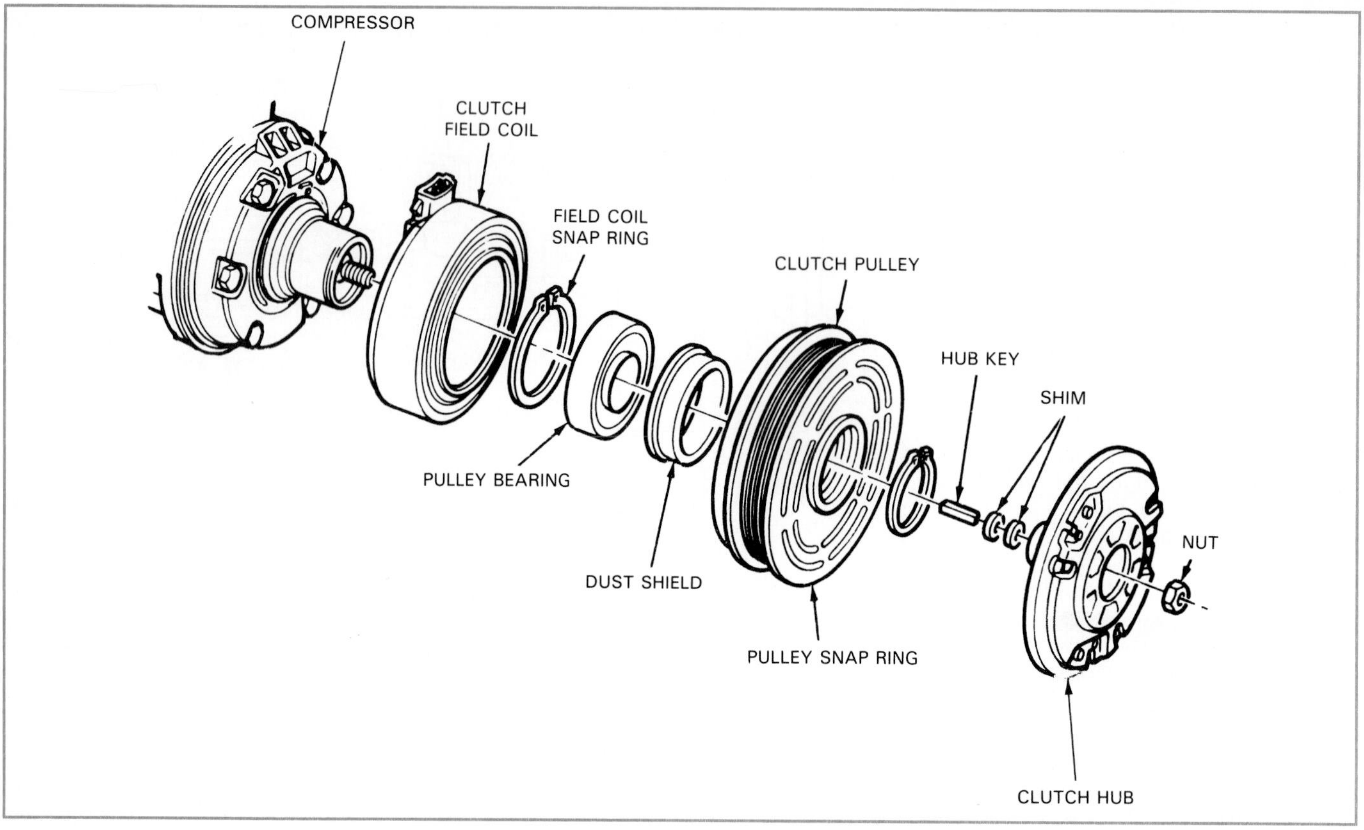

Figure 49-13. Exploded view details the parts of a typical compressor clutch assembly. With the A/C off, the pulley freewheels. With the A/C on, the field coil engages the pulley and the compressor operates. (Ford)

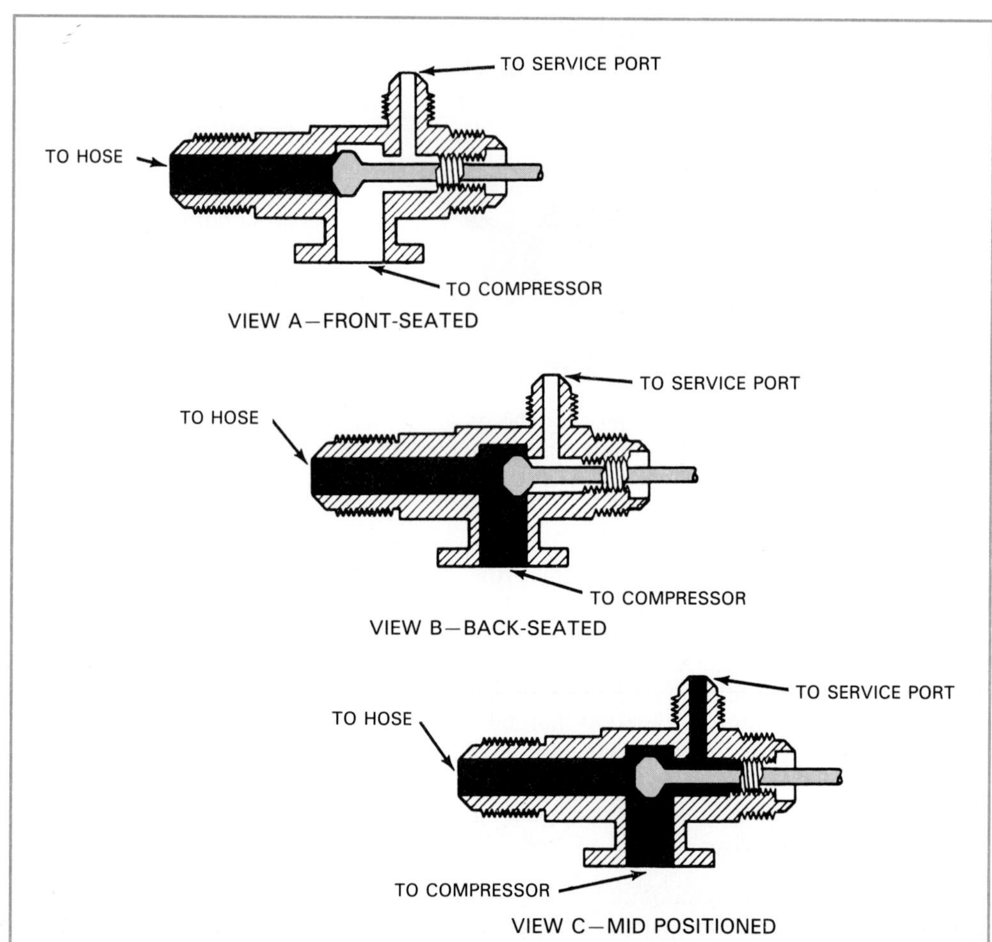

Figure 49-14. Compressor service valve operating positions. A–For isolating compressor from A/C system. B–For normal operation of system. C–For testing, evacuating, and charging system. (Ford)

repair or replacement; and for discharging, evacuating, and charging the system.

Instead of service valves, modern compressors have ***Schrader*** or ***Dill service connectors*** or ***gauge port fittings,*** Figure 49-15. Special test hoses are available to fit these connectors, or adapters can be used with standard test hoses. The refrigerant is sealed in the system until the special hose or adapter is attached. Removal of the hose or adapter closes the system. Systematic checks are performed with a manifold gauge set, Figure 49-16.

Condenser

The ***condenser*** in the air conditioning system is a device used to change high pressure refrigerant vapor to a liquid. See Figure 49-17. It does this by providing a means for emitting heat from the hot refrigerant to the cooler atmosphere.

The means by which the condenser performs its function is a design factor. The hot refrigerant is in contact with the inner walls of as many feet of A/C tubing as possible. This tubing is placed in the airstream to bring about a heat transfer situation. When the refrigerant vapor reaches the pressure and temperature that causes condensation, a large quantity of heat is given off and the hot refrigerant vapor changes to a warm liquid.

The condenser consists of tubing crisscrossed through thin, supporting, cooling fins. In construction, it resembles an engine radiator and usually is mounted directly in front of the radiator. This places it in the best position to receive the benefits of ram air flowing into the engine compartment while the vehicle is in motion.

When the vehicle is at rest or moving slowly, the belt-driven cooling fan draws outside air across the condenser coils and fins. Many late model cars are equipped with a thermostatically controlled electric fan, especially front wheel drive cars with transverse engine design. See Chapter 17, ENGINE COOLING SYSTEMS. In some engines in air conditioned cars, clutch-type cooling fans "en-

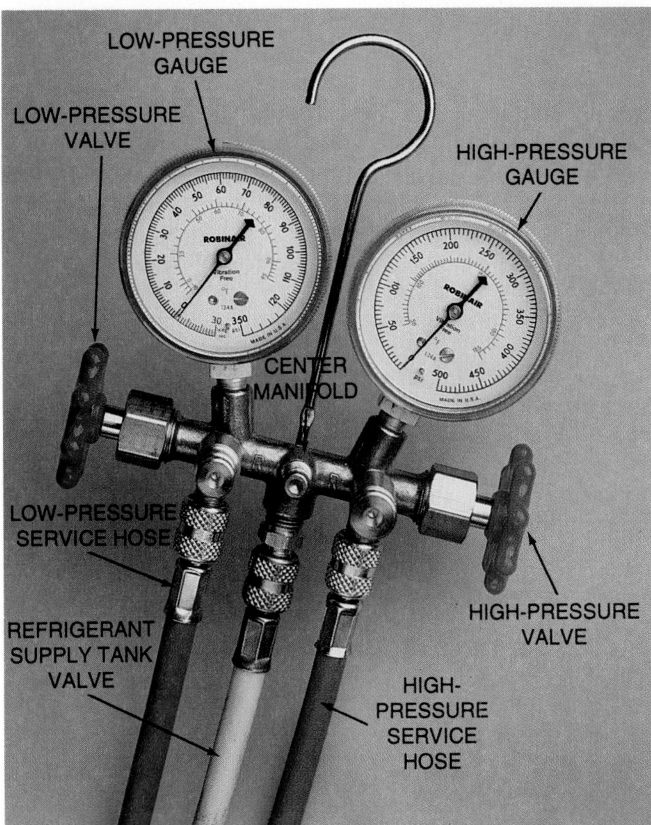

Figure 49-16. A manifold gauge set can be attached to the compressor service valves or to the service gauge port fittings to test, discharge, evacuate, and charge A/C system. (Ford)

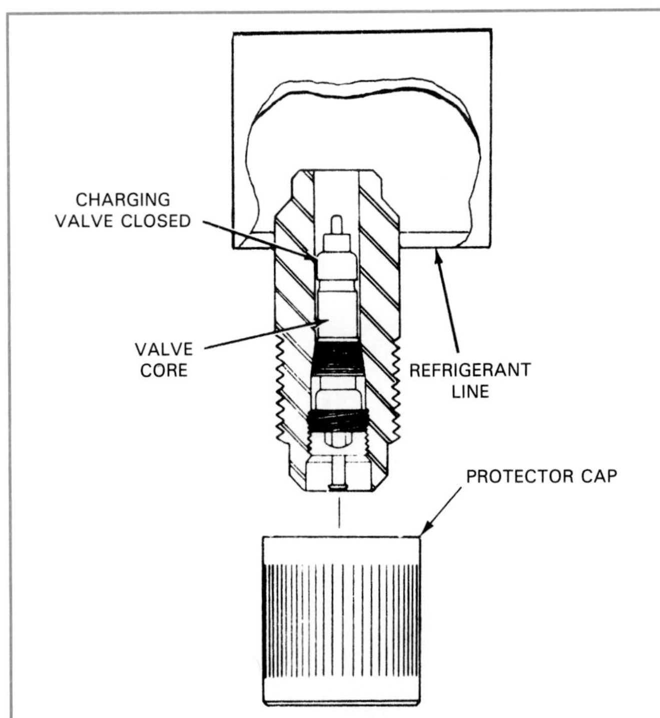

Figure 49-15. Gauge port fittings have replaced service valves on most modern compressors. Gauge port fittings use Schrader or Dill valve cores, which are similar to familiar tire valves, to simplify test hose attachment. (Ford)

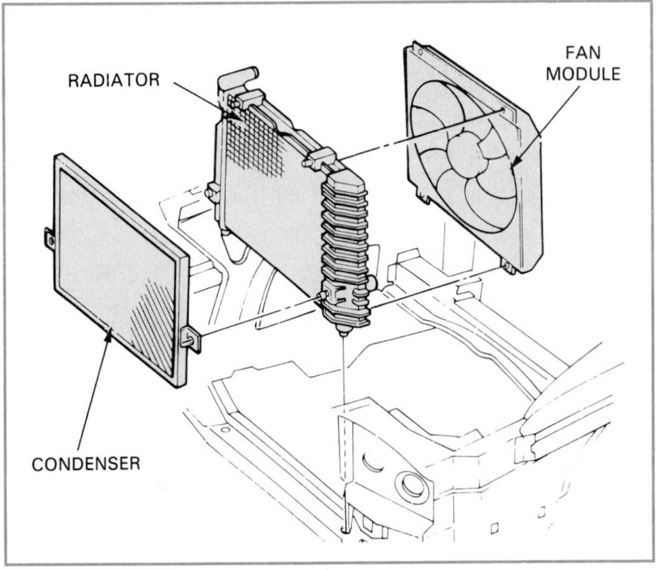

Figure 49-17. The condenser used in an A/C system is a heat exchanger. Hot refrigerant vapor enters the top of the condenser, cools as it passes through the coils, gives up heat to the surrounding air, and then condenses into a liquid. (Chrysler)

gage" to permit full rpm at low vehicle speeds and "slip" at high speed when ram air cooling takes over.

Designed to achieve a similar effect is the flexible blade fan found in some air conditioned applications. The blades of this unit have a high pitch at rest and at low rotational speeds to create a strong airflow. At high speeds, the flexible blades flatten out. As the pitch of the blades decreases, so does the airflow the fan creates. Again, ram air at high speed furnishes the necessary airflow for efficient condenser operation.

In operation, refrigerant vapor under high pressure enters the condenser through an inlet at the top. Under an average heat load, the upper 1/2 or 2/3 of the condenser coils contain hot refrigerant vapor changing into a hot liquid. The lower 1/2 or 1/3 will carry the warm liquid refrigerant. This liquid, still under high pressure, flows from an outlet at the bottom of the condenser through a refrigerant line to the receiver-drier (dehydrator).

Receiver-Drier

The ***receiver-drier*** is next in line in the series of five major components that make up an automotive air conditioning system. See Figure 49-18. The receiver-drier is the storage tank for liquid refrigerant, and it also contains a fiber and a ***desiccant*** (drying agent) to remove foreign particles and moisture from the circulating refrigerant.

It is necessary to have a place in the system to store the refrigerant because the demands of the evaporator vary under different operating conditions. The filter and drying agent are required to keep harmful contaminants from circulating through the system.

A ***sight glass*** provided for viewing the condition of the refrigerant charge usually is built in or adjacent to the top of the receiver-drier assembly, Figure 49-18. It windows the interior of the system at a point where the charge of liquid refrigerant passing it reveals whether or not the system is fully charged.

A "clear" glass indicates that the system has a full charge of refrigerant. If bubbles appear, air has entered the system. A milky white cloudiness signals that the desiccant is escaping from the receiver-drier and is circulating through the system with the refrigerant.

The receiver-drier receives the high pressure liquid refrigerant from the condenser and delivers it through tubing to the thermostatic expansion valve.

Thermostatic Expansion Valve

The ***thermostatic expansion valve,*** Figure 49-19, is a metering device that removes pressure from the liquid refrigerant so that it can expand and become refrigerant vapor in the evaporator. The metering action is performed by an orifice (restriction that permits compressor to build up pressure on high side of system) within the valve body. The refrigerant enters the expansion valve as a warm, high pressure liquid. It passes through the orifice and is released from the valve as a cold, low-pressure, atomized liquid.

Actually, the thermostatic expansion valve has three functions: metering, modulating, and controlling. Its metered orifice, Figure 49-19, releases the pressure on the liquid refrigerant to change it from high to low and provide a starting point for the "low side" of the air conditioning system.

Its thermostatically controlled valve opens and closes, usually on signal from a thermal bulb connected to the outlet of the evaporator. This creates a modulating effect as the valve varies the flow of liquid refrigerant to the orifice. If the outlet gets warm, the bulb signals the thermostatic valve to open and allow greater refrigerant flow. When the outlet cools, the bulb triggers the valve to close and restrict flow.

The control feature of the thermostatic expansion valve ties in with the modulating function. When the valve opens or closes, it must respond quickly to changes in heat load at the outlet of the evaporator. No liquid refrigerant must leave the evaporator and enter the compressor or damage to internal parts will result. Therefore, the thermostatic expansion valve must respond immediately to the signals sent by the thermal bulb to ensure that vaporization

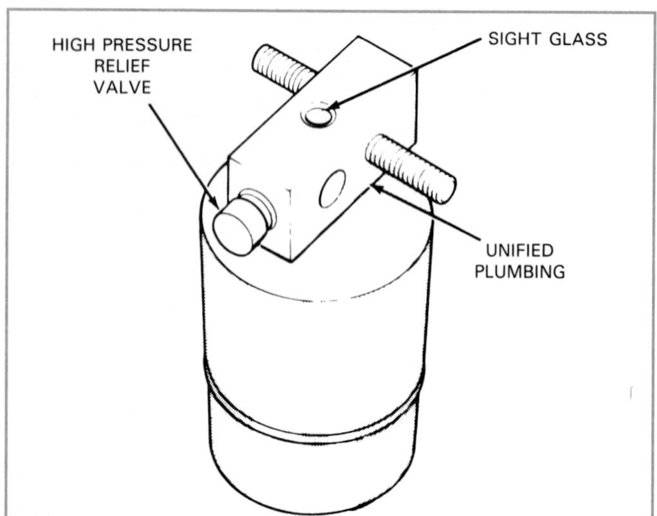

Figure 49-18. The receiver-drier stores liquid refrigerant and removes moisture that could cause freezing in the A/C system. Most units contain filters, screens, and a drying agent. (Chrysler)

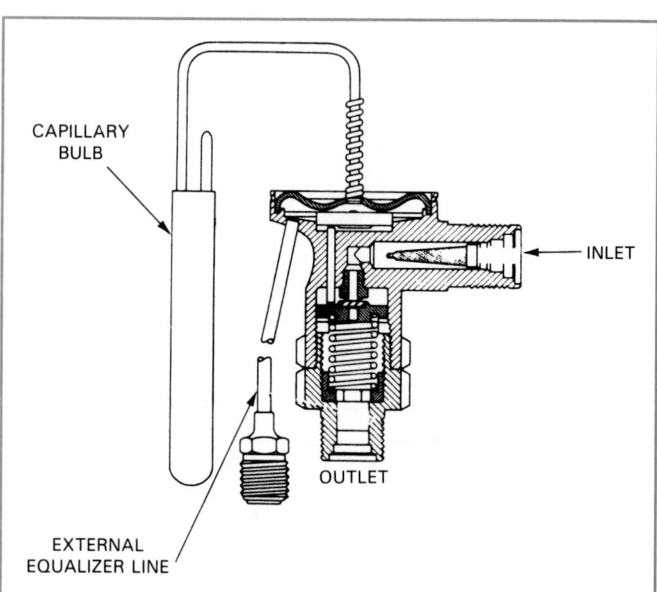

Figure 49-19. The thermostatic expansion valve meters liquid refrigerant under high pressure into the low pressure area of evaporator, as directed by a temperature-sensing bulb located at the evaporator outlet.

of the R-12 is completed by the time it reaches the outlet of the evaporator. Also see CCOT Principles.

Evaporator

The ***evaporator*** is another heat exchanger in the air conditioning system, Figure 49-20. In contrast to the condenser, however, its coils carry cold refrigerant that picks up heat from the passenger compartment to cool the interior.

The evaporator is similar to the condenser in construction. It, too, consists of coils of tubing mounted in a series of thin cooling fins. Generally, the evaporator is mounted in a housing under the cowl where warm air from the passenger compartment is blown by a fan across its coils and fins.

The evaporator receives the cold, low pressure, atomized liquid refrigerant from the thermostatic expansion valve. As this cold liquid passes through the coils of the evaporator, heat naturally moves from the warm air through the cool coils and into the cold refrigerant.

When the liquid refrigerant reaches a pressure and temperature that will cause evaporation, a large quantity of heat will move from the air into the refrigerant and the low pressure atomized liquid will change to a low pressure refrigerant vapor. This vapor returns to the inlet, or low side, of the compressor, where the whole refrigeration cycle begins again.

Valves-in-receiver Air Conditioning System

The five major elements of a basic automobile air conditioning system have been described. However, other elements are contained in related A/C systems. For example, General Motors introduced a system in which a ***valves-in-receiver*** (VIR) performs the functions of the receiver-drier, thermostatic expansion valve, sight glass, and POA (pilot operated absolute) suction throttling valve. See Figure 49-21.

The VIR assembly is mounted next to the evaporator, which eliminates the need for an external equalizer line between the thermostatic expansion valve and the outlet of the POA valve. The equalizer function is accomplished by a drilled hole (equalizer port) between the two valve cavities in the VIR housing. See Figure 49-22.

Also eliminated are the thermobulb and capillary line for the thermostatic expansion valve. The diaphragm of the VIR expansion valve is exposed to the refrigerant vapor

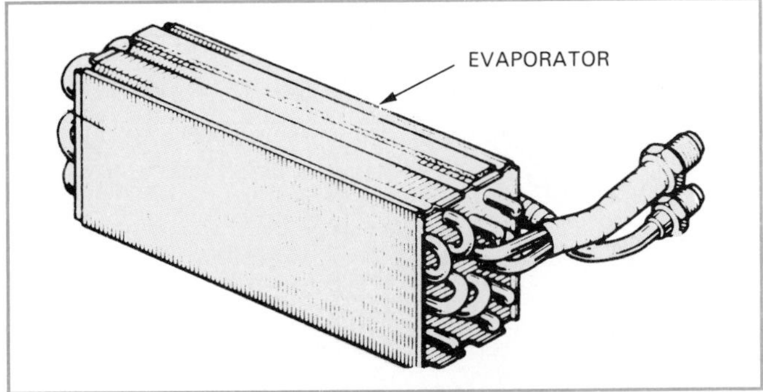

Figure 49-20. The evaporator has coils and fins like the condenser, but it functions in reverse. The evaporator receives atomized liquid refrigerant, which vaporizes and absorbs heat from the passenger compartment. (Chrysler)

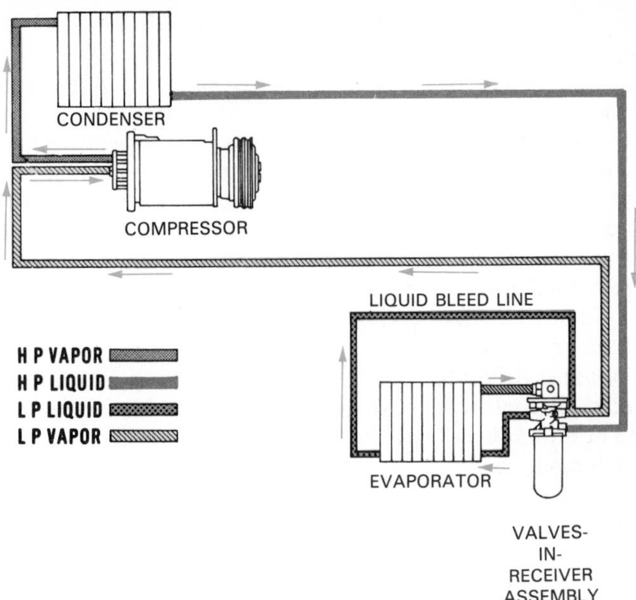

Figure 49-21. The General Motors valves-in-receiver A/C system features a VIR assembly that replaces three assemblies previously used: the thermostatic expansion valve, receiver-drier, and POA suction throttling valve.

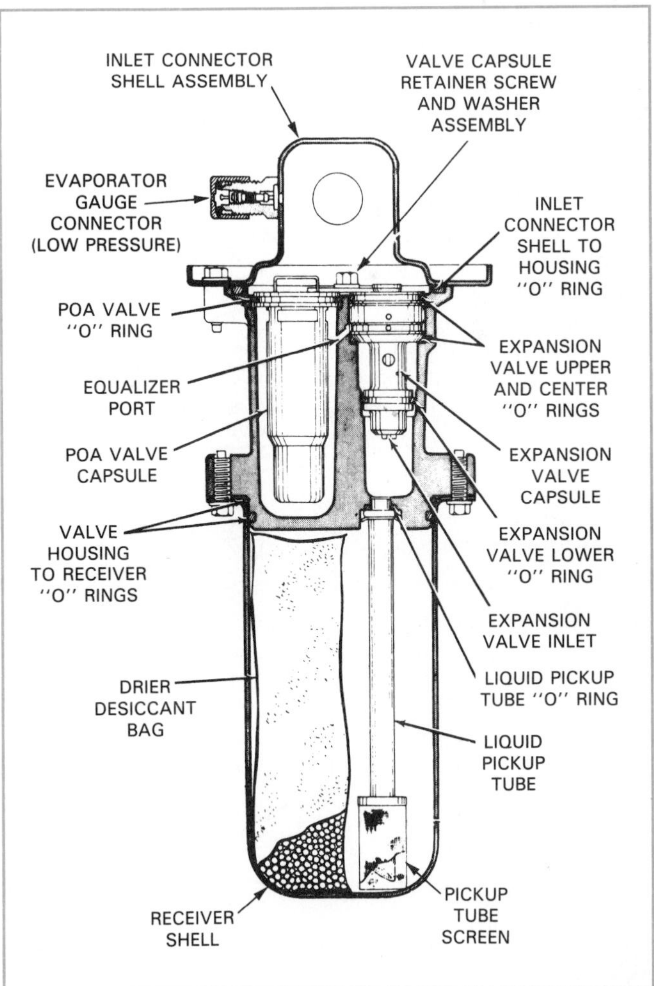

Figure 49-22. The valves-in-receiver unit combines the two major valves, the receiver-drier, and the sight glass to control evaporator pressure and to regulate the amount of refrigerant being metered into evaporator.

entering the VIR unit from the outlet of the evaporator. The sight glass is located in the valve housing at the inlet end of the thermostatic valve cavity, where it gives a liquid indication of the refrigerant level.

The VIR thermostatic expansion valve controls the flow of refrigerant to the evaporator by sensing the temperature and pressure of the refrigerant vapor as it passes through the VIR unit on its way to the compressor. The POA suction throttling valve controls the flow of refrigerant from the evaporator to maintain a constant evaporator pressure of 30 psi. These are capsule-type valves. When found to be defective, the complete valve capsule must be replaced.

The drier desiccant is contained in a bag in the receiver shell, Figure 49-22. It is replaceable by removing the shell and old bag and installing a new bag of desiccant.

CCOT Air Conditioning System

Many late model Ford and General Motors cars equipped with manual or automatic temperature control (ATC) air conditioning use a ***cycling clutch orifice tube*** (CCOT) or a ***fixed-orifice system.*** See Figure 49-23. These systems are designed to cycle the compressor on and off to maintain desired passenger compartment cooling and to prevent evaporator freeze-up.

Control of the refrigeration cycle (on and off) is done with a ***pressure cycling switch,*** Figure 49-24. This switch is the freeze-protection device in the system. It senses low side pressure as an indicator of evaporator temperature.

When the driver selects an air conditioning mode (MAX, NORM, etc.), voltage is supplied to the compressor clutch coil. Compressor operation reduces low-side pressure; the pressure cycling switch opens and de-energizes the compressor clutch coil. Then, as the system equalizes, the pressure cycling switch contacts close, re-energizing the compressor clutch coil.

This refrigeration cycle continues as a means of maintaining evaporator discharge air at 33°F (1°C), with slight variation due to outside air temperature and humidity.

The CCOT refrigeration cycle begins at the compressor:

1. Refrigerant enters the compressor as a low-pressure, low-temperature vapor, and it leaves as a high-pressure, high-temperature vapor. See Figure 49-24.
2. The vapor flows to the condenser, where it gives up heat to cooler air passing through, and the refrigerant changes to a high-pressure liquid.
3. The liquid refrigerant then passes through an orifice tube where it becomes a low-pressure, low-temperature liquid that is fed into the evaporator.
4. Warm outside (or inside) air passes through the evaporator coils, where it gives up its heat, and the refrigerant changes to a low-pressure, low-temperature vapor.
5. Refrigerant vapor flows to the accumulator-drier, Figure 49-25. If any liquid refrigerant passes through the

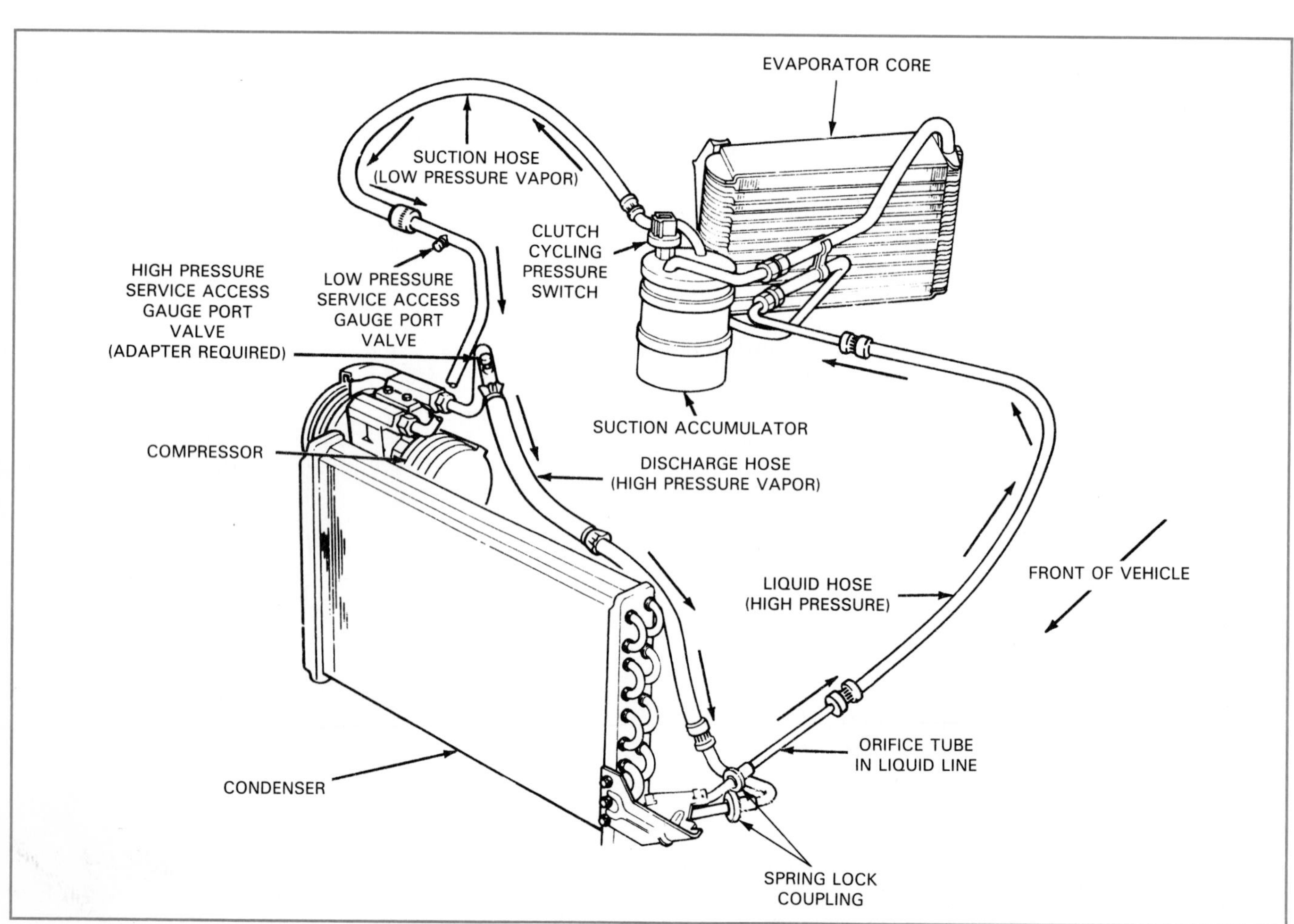

Figure 49-23. Diagram traces refrigerant flow in a Ford fixed-orifice A/C system. Also, note the relative location of the assemblies, especially the positioning of the compressor on the transverse-mounted engine. (Ford)

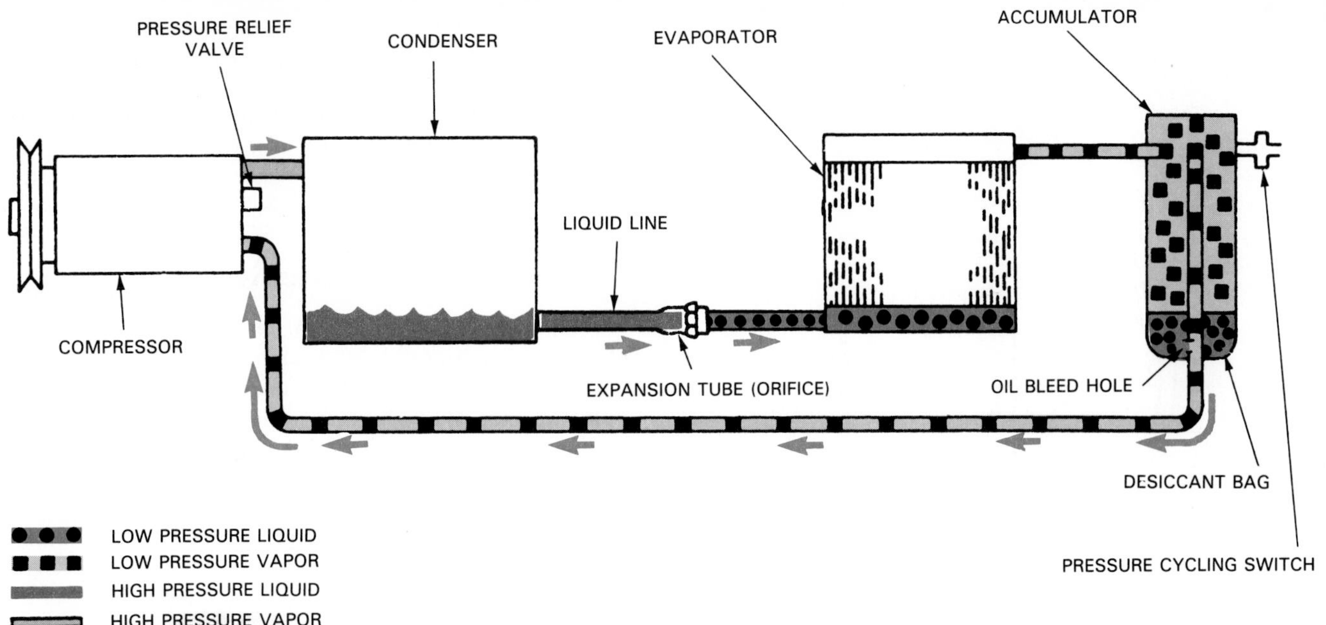

Figure 49-24. Diagram points out the components and the direction of refrigerant flow in a GM cycling clutch orifice tube A/C system. Note that an accumulator-drier replaces the receiver-drier and that it is located at the evaporator outlet rather than at the condenser outlet. (Buick)

evaporator, it is separated from the vapor in the accumulator-drier.

6. From the accumulator-drier, low-pressure, low-temperature vapor returns to the compressor, and the refrigeration cycle begins again.

VDOT Air Conditioning System

A ***variable displacement orifice tube (VDOT) A/C system*** is installed on several late model General Motors vehicles. The VDOT system employs the five-cylinder, variable displacement A/C compressor shown in Figure 49-11. This compressor is designed to vary pumping displacement to match air conditioning needs. A bellows actuated control valve in the compressor senses suction pressure and varies the swash plate angle in response to heat load. Clutch cycling is not required.

The variable displacement compressor also utilizes a low pressure cut-off switch that will disengage the compressor clutch in case of system low charge due to a refrigerant leak.

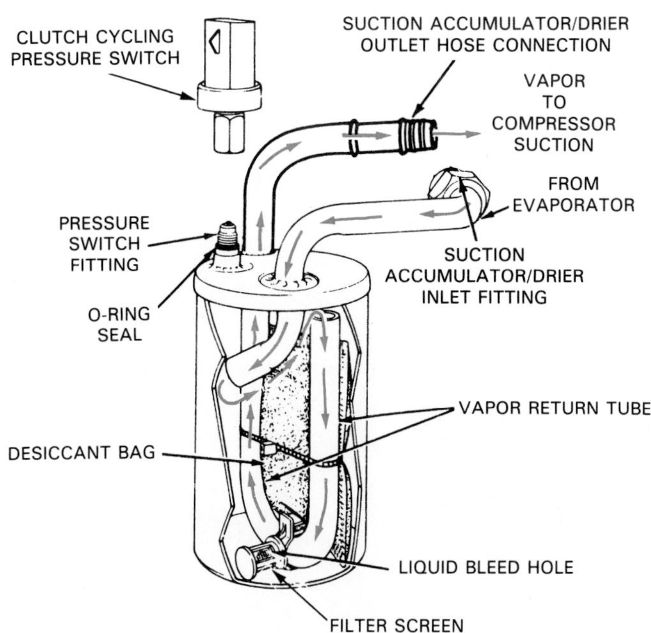

Figure 49-25. The Ford suction accumulator-drier is mounted directly to the evaporator core outlet in a fixed orifice A/C system. A desiccant bag absorbs moisture. The clutch cycling pressure switch attaches to a fitting on top of the canister. (Ford)

Safe Ways to Handle Refrigerants

Labels on refrigerant containers usually include a safe handling warning. Refrigerant is available in drums and cans. Since the refrigerant in the container is under considerable pressure at ordinary temperatures, you must observe certain precautions to prevent accidents or damage to the air conditioning system:

1. Always wear goggles when working with a refrigerant. Do not allow liquid refrigerant to strike your eyes (could cause blindness) or body (could cause frostbite). If an accident does occur, immediately wash your eyes with diluted boric acid or another suitable eyewash solution. See a doctor immediately.
2. Discharge refrigerant slowly into a recovery/recycling unit. Fast discharge could bleed refrigerant oil from system along with refrigerant.
3. Always discharge refrigerant in a well-ventilated area. Large quantities of refrigerant vapor in a small, poorly ventilated room can cause suffocation.
4. Do not have sparks or open flames in working area.
5. R-12 vapor passing over an open flame will give off a toxic phosgene gas. Therefore, leak testing with a Halide or propane torch, Figure 49-26, should be done in a well-ventilated area. Also, do not weld or steam clean A/C systems.
6. Do not use anything except pure refrigerant and refrigerant oil to air conditioning system. Anything else may

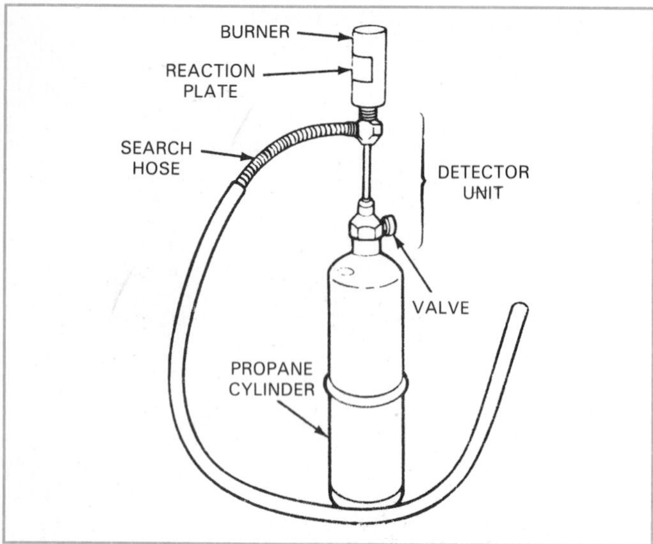

Figure 49-26. Halide-type refrigerant leak detector utilizes a small flame and a search hose to "sniff" for leaks in the A/C system. The flame changes color if a leak is detected. (Ford)

contaminate refrigerant or cause it to become chemically unstable. Also, R-12 and R-134A are incompatible and must never be mixed. Special equipment is available that can be used to identify the type of refrigerant in an air conditioning system. See Figure 49-27.

7. Handle refrigerant containers with care. Do not drop or strike containers.
8. Wear gloves when handling a damp refrigerant container; bare hands may freeze to container. If this does happen, wet the container with water to free your hand from can.
9. To warm a refrigerant container, use hot water (or rags saturated with hot water) at a temperature of not more than 125°F (52°C). Never use a direct flame or heater.
10. Store your refrigerant containers in a cool, dry place. Never store them in direct sunlight or near a heater. If a refrigerant is stored in a drum, keep drum in upright position and install a metal cap over outlet connection.
12. Use care when transporting refrigerant drums or cans. Do not carry refrigerant containers in passenger compartment of your car. If hauling containers in an open truck, use a cover to protect refrigerant from radiant heat of sun.

How Moisture Affects Refrigerant

All top quality refrigerants recommended for use in automobile air conditioning systems are formulated to high standards of chemical purity. They are sealed in suitable containers for safe shipment and delivery. However, if moisture, air, dirt, or some other contaminant enters the air conditioning system, the refrigerant will lose its effectiveness as a cooling agent.

Moisture, especially, is a serious refrigerant contaminant because it also causes damage to internal parts. The unwanted water reacts with R-12 to form hydrochloric acid. The more water in the refrigerant, the more concentrated the hydrochloric acid becomes. The strong acid eats holes in the evaporator and condenser coils, damages aluminum parts of the compressor, and corrodes valves and fittings. All the while the hydrochloric acid is reacting with metal parts, oxides are being given off to further contaminate the refrigerant and affect its ability to absorb and discharge heat.

Moisture usually enters the system through a break in a refrigerant line or by way of an improperly sealed connection. To combat this threat of contamination by moisture, all automotive air conditioning systems are fitted with a container of desiccant (receiver-drier or accumulator-drier). This drying agent will absorb all moisture in the system, up to its saturation point.

If an A/C system is contaminated by moisture, the best way to remove it is by using a ***vacuum pump,*** Figure 49-28, to evacuate all traces of refrigerant, air, and moisture. Once repairs have been made and a new receiver-drier or accu-

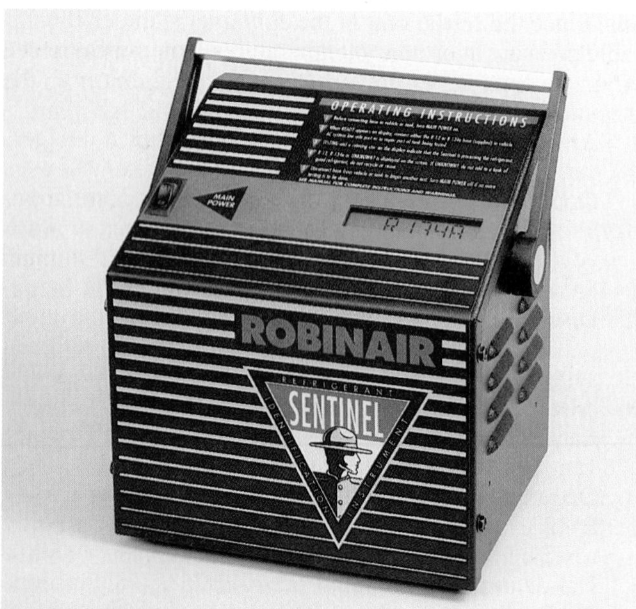

Figure 49-27. This unit can be used to identify the type of refrigerant in an air conditioning system. (Robinair Div., SPX Corp.)

Figure 49-28. A vacuum pump is mandatory equipment for servicing all A/C systems. It serves to evacuate the system of refrigerant, air, and moisture.

mulator-drier is installed, the system can be evacuated and recharged with pure R-12.

The Need for Refrigerant Oil

All automotive air conditioning systems require internal lubrication of seals, gaskets, the thermostatic expansion valve, and the moving parts of the compressor. To accomplish this, a moisture-free ***refrigerant oil*** is circulated through the system with the refrigerant.

Use non-foaming oil formulated specifically for use in each air conditioning system. In R-12 systems, mineral oil is commonly used. A polyalkylene glycol (PAG) or an ester-based oil is used in R-134A systems. This highly refined oil comes in several grades or viscosities for use in automotive air conditioning systems. Oils of 500 or 525 viscosity are most commonly used.

Reciprocating piston compressors usually have an oil sump and an oil dipstick. The oil level of this type of compressor should be checked every time the air conditioner is serviced. Most ***axial piston compressors*** must be removed from the vehicle for an oil check and refill. GM five- and six-cylinder swash plate compressors, for example, call for removal and oil drain. The drain oil is retained, measured, and discarded. Pure refrigerant oil of the same amount is then installed.

On certain ***radial compressors,*** the refrigerant oil can be charged through the compressor suction (low side) port. Check service manual for compressor being serviced.

Precautions in handling refrigerant oil include:

1. Replace used refrigerant oil if there is any doubt about its condition.
2. Discard used oil.
3. Use only approved refrigerant oil in air conditioning systems.
4. Buy refrigerant oil in smallest size containers consistent with immediate needs.
5. Do not transfer refrigerant oil from one container to another.
6. Make sure cap is tight on refrigerant oil container when not in use.
7. When installing refrigerant oil, make sure it is proper type and viscosity for system being serviced.

Refrigerant oils have been dewaxed, dried, and otherwise processed to keep pace with rapid advances in compressor design. These special oils are shipped in tightly capped containers to prevent contamination before use.

Air Conditioning Service Tools and Equipment

Various hand and specialty tools are needed to install and service automobile air conditioners. A manifold gauge set, refrigerant leak detector, vacuum pump, thermometer, tachometer, and goggles are needed to test and service these systems. Additionally, special recovery/recycling units are needed to recover refrigerants when discharging an air conditioning system. See Figure 49-29. Automatic temperature control (ATC) system analyzers are also available.

The ***manifold gauge set,*** Figure 49-16, is used to test pressure on the high and low sides of the compressor. There are usually two gauges in the set (some systems require three gauges). The gauges are mounted on a manifold assembly, complete with shutoff valves.

Figure 49-29. Typical refrigerant recovery/recycling system. This type of unit must be used whenever discharging an air conditioning system. (Robinair Div., SPX Corp.)

Connections to the compressor are made at the suction and discharge service valves, or to connectors on the compressor fitted with "Schrader" or "Dill" valves. The suction (low pressure) side of the compressor is where the hose from the evaporator attaches. The discharge (high pressure) side is where the hose to the condenser attaches.

The manifold gauge set also has a center port to which a hose can be attached to bleed excess refrigerant from the system. In addition, it can be used to discharge (purge) refrigerant from the system, evacuate air and moisture, and charge the system with refrigerant.

The ***leak detector*** may be anything from a colored dye additive for the refrigerant, a Halide detector, or a sophisticated electronic unit, Figure 49-30, that provides maximum sensitivity and accuracy when used according to the manufacturer's operating instructions.

The *colored dye leak detector* is added to the refrigerant. Then, with the air conditioning system in operation, any discoloration at a hose connection will reveal the point of leakage.

The *halide detector,* or propane torch, is a commonly used refrigerant leak detector, Figure 49-26. In operation, the unit's sampling hose is moved under all parts and connections of the air conditioning system. Throughout the test, the color of the flame is observed. A blue flame is normal; yellow indicates a slight leak; purple signals a high-quantity leak of R-12 vapor. This test should be made in a well-ventilated area, because Refrigerant-12 passing over an open flame will give off a toxic phosgene gas.

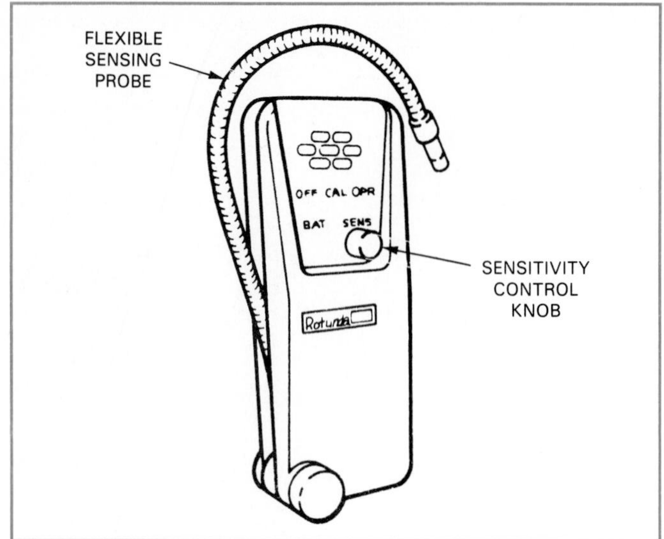

Figure 49-30. In operation, this electronic refrigerant leak detector gives off a steady, slow "ticking." The probe is moved around the system. If a leak exists, the ticking will become more rapid and shrill. (Ford)

The ***vacuum pump,*** Figure 49-28, is a device used to evacuate (remove air and moisture from) the air conditioning system. The pump hoses are connected to the suction and discharge ports of the compressor, then the unit is plugged into a 120 volt ac receptacle and turned on. In operation, the pump draws out air and moisture until a vacuum of 25 to 29 in. Hg. is created.

The ***recovery/recycling unit*** is used to remove refrigerant from the air conditioning system. This unit stores the refrigerant until it can be recycled. During the recycling process, all moisture and air is removed from the refrigerant. Some manufacturers produce a mobile ***air conditioning service center,*** which includes the recovery/recycling unit, vacuum pump, pressure gauges, automatic timers, test hoses and connectors, switches, controls, and a stock of refrigerant. See Figure 49-31.

Figure 49-31. This mobile service station contains all the equipment needed to safely discharge, evacuate, and recharge A/C systems. (Robinair Div., SPX Corp.)

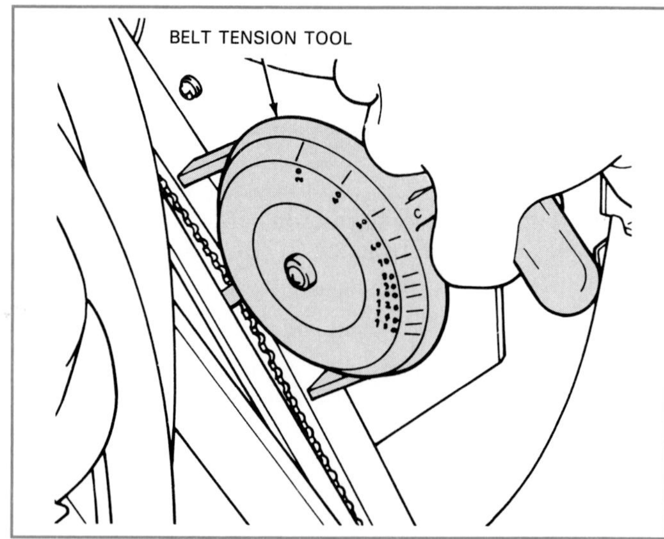

Figure 49-32. The correct tension of the compressor drive belt is required for effective A/C system operation. (Ford)

Servicing the Air Conditioning System

When an automotive air conditioner is not cooling properly, check the condition of engine cooling system components. Check the condition of the V-belts, Figure 49-32, or serpentine (V-ribbed) belt. Inspect the fan shroud, radiator, and pressure cap. Look for signs of coolant leakage and/or refrigerant leakage. Also check the air conditioning system for loose or broken compressor mounting brackets, improper hose routing, condition of the condenser (clogged with bugs, leaves, etc.), and receiver-drier or accumulator-drier (age and appearance).

Caution: When performing air conditioning diagnosis on vehicles equipped with a catalytic converter, warm engine to normal operating temperature before attempting to idle engine for periods greater than five (5) minutes. Once choke is open and fast idle speed drops to normal idle, diagnosis and adjustments can be made.

Then, clean or uncap the sight glass and run the engine at 1500 to 2000 rpm. Make an operational test of the air conditioner with the hood up and the doors open (unless otherwise specified by the manufacturer). Adjust the air conditioning controls for maximum cooling with the blower at high speed.

Place a large fan in front of the vehicle to substitute fan airflow for ram airflow through the condenser. Run the engine for approximately 15 minutes to stabilize all parts of the system.

Place a thermometer in an air conditioning discharge duct. Place another thermometer in engine compartment. Drop blower speed to "low." Close doors and hood.

Check the sight glass. A clear glass indicates that the system is fully charged (or empty if system fails to blow cold air). Bubbles in the glass point to a low refrigerant level. Check the thermometer reading at the air discharge duct; it should be 35 to 45°F (2 to 7°C). If not, shut off engine and prepare to discharge the refrigerant from the air conditioning system.

Discharging and Recovering Refrigerant

Discharging (purging) the air conditioning system is the act of releasing refrigerant from the high and low sides of the system until no pressure exists. As mentioned, the refrigerant must never be discharged into the atmosphere. Instead, it must be captured in a recovery/recycling unit.

To discharge the system:

1. Protect your eyes with goggles.
2. Remove the compressor port caps and install the manifold gauge set, Figure 49-33.
3. Attach the test hose to the center connection of the manifold assembly. Attach the other end of the hose to the recovery/recycling unit as outlined in the unit's operating instructions.
4. Turn on the power to the recovery unit.
5. Open the manifold gauge valves slightly to allow the refrigerant to slowly escape from the system.
6. Press the start button on the recovery unit to activate the recovery process.
7. After all refrigerant has been recovered, the system will go into a slight vacuum. This can be verified by observing the readings on the manifold gauges. At this point, the recovery unit should be shut off.
8. Close the manifold gauge valves and allow the system to remain closed for approximately two minutes.
9. If the vacuum level remains constant, disconnect the manifold gauge hoses from the recycling unit.
10. If the vacuum level drops, repeat steps 4-8 until the vacuum remains constant.

Evacuating the Air Conditioning System

Evacuation is the process by which all air and moisture is removed from the air conditioning system. Using a heavy-duty vacuum pump, it takes at least 60 minutes to "pull down" the system to approximately 29.5 in. Hg.

To evacuate the system:

1. Connect the manifold gauge set hoses to the compressor low- and high-pressure ports, using an adapter, if necessary.
2. Connect the manifold gauge set center hose to a heavy-duty vacuum pump.
3. Open the manifold gauge set valves.
4. Plug the vacuum pump power cord into a 120 volt ac electrical receptacle and turn on the pump.
5. Operate the pump and watch the vacuum reading on the low-side gauge. When the gauge reading reaches at least 25 in. Hg., allow the pump to run an additional 30 minutes.
6. Close both the low- and high-side manifold gauge set valves and shut off the vacuum pump.
7. Vacuum should hold at the point of shut-down for 3 to 5 minutes if the system is free of leaks.

Charging the Air Conditioning System

Before disconnecting center manifold hose from vacuum pump, have sufficient refrigerant available to charge system. Also, make use of a safety valve to prevent high pressure from causing a backflow of refrigerant into the tank.

To charge the system:

1. Install a safety valve on the tank of refrigerant.
2. Disconnect the center manifold hose from the vacuum pump and attach the hose to the tank valve. See Figure 49-33.
3. With the refrigerant tank in the upright position, open the low-side manifold gauge valve, allowing the refrigerant vapor to enter system.
4. Observe the gauges. As soon as both gauge needles stop rising, close the low-side manifold hand valve and the tank valve.
5. Start the engine and run it at fast idle. Adjust the air conditioner controls for maximum cooling with the blower at high speed.

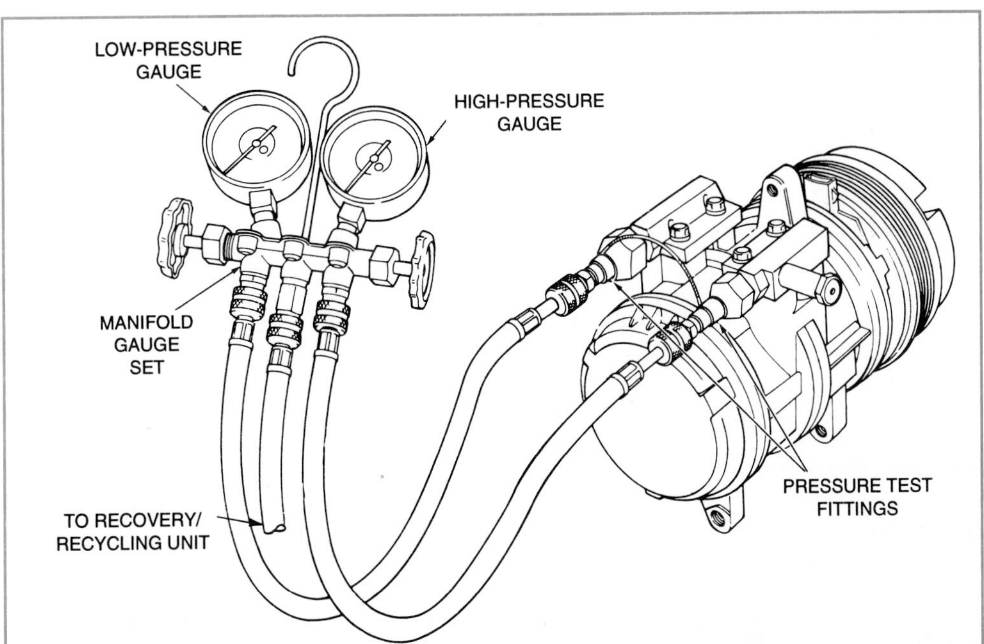

Figure 49-33. Proper installation of a manifold gauge set to the compressor ports is shown for discharging refrigerant. For charging an A/C system, the center hose is connected to refrigerant supply. (Ford)

6. Open the tank valve and the low-side manifold hand valve to draw additional refrigerant through the low side. Check the system capacity chart for the full charge amount. Note: Never open the high-side manifold hand valve when engine is running. If the system does not accept enough refrigerant, rock the tank from side to side or place the tank in a container of water heated to 125°F (52°C) to increase the flow of refrigerant.
7. Observe the high-side gauge reading to avoid overcharging the system. In most cases, the high-side pressure should not exceed 240 psi (1656 kPa). Observe the low-side gauge reading. It should not exceed 60 psi (414 kPa).
8. When the high- and low-side gauge pressures reach normal levels (15 to 30 psi [103 to 206 kPa] low side; 175 to 195 psi [1207 to 1345 kPa] high side), and bubbles disappear in the sight glass, close the low-side manifold hand valve and the tank valve.
9. Check the thermometer reading at the air discharge duct nearest the evaporator. Normal reading should be 35 to 45°F (2 to 7°C) with the blower at low speed.
10. Stop the engine. Remove the manifold gauge hoses from the compressor ports and install the service port caps.
11. Remove the refrigerant tank from the center manifold hose.

Retrofitting R-12 Air Conditioning Systems

Although R-12 refrigerant is still available for use when servicing A/C systems, it may be desirable in some cases to retrofit R-12 systems to operate on R-134A. Initially, this was thought to be a costly and time-consuming undertaking that involved the replacement of several major components. However, tests have shown that the A/C systems in most late-model vehicles can be retrofitted with relatively few changes. Refer to the manufacturer's recommendations when retrofitting an R-12 air conditioning system.

Troubleshooting Heating Systems

Insufficient or No Heat

- Low coolant level.
- Loose fan belt.
- Clogged heater core.
- Faulty engine thermostat.
- Maladjusted control cables.
- Collapsed or pinched vacuum hoses.
- Leaking vacuum hose or vacuum motor.
- Binding airflow doors.
- Maladjusted temperature door.
- Sluggish blower motor.
- Defective blower motor.
- Inoperative blower motor switch.

Troubleshooting Air Conditioning Systems

No Refrigeration Action

- Loose or broken drive belt.
- Slipping compressor clutch.
- Inoperative compressor.
- Defective expansion valve.
- Faulty fixed-orifice tube.
- Clogged screen in receiver-drier or expansion valve.
- Clogged filter in accumulator-drier.
- Plugged liquid refrigerant line.
- Open clutch cycling switch.
- Poor connection at clutch connector or clutch cycling switch.
- Inoperative blower motor.
- Blown fuse or defective circuit breaker.

Insufficient Cool Air

- Low refrigerant charge.
- Slipping compressor clutch.
- Loose drive belt.
- Clogged condenser.
- Clogged evaporator.
- Defective evaporator control valve.
- Faulty expansion valve.
- Faulty fixed-orifice tube.
- Clogged receiver-drier screen.
- Clogged accumulator-drier filter.
- Moisture or air in system.
- Refrigerant overcharge.

Insufficient or No Air Discharge

- Defective blower motor.
- Inoperative blower motor switch.
- Sluggish blower motor.
- Blown fuse or defective circuit breaker.
- Broken or disconnected blower motor wire.
- Obstructed air passages.
- Binding airflow door.
- Maladjusted control cables.

System Runs Too Cold

- Faulty thermostatic control.
- Maladjusted linkage to control panel.
- Partially plugged A/C suction line.
- Closed clutch cycling switch.

System Cools Intermittently

- Slipping compressor clutch.
- Defective circuit breaker.
- Faulty blower motor or blower motor switch.
- Loose compressor clutch coil connection or poor ground.
- Defective thermostatic control.
- Stuck evaporator control valve.
- Moisture in system, causing unit to ice up intermittently.
- Air in system.

System Noisy

- Refrigerant overcharge.
- Low refrigerant charge.
- Incorrect oil level.
- Internal damage to compressor.

- Loose compressor mounting.
- Loose blower motor.
- Loose drive belt pulley bolts.
- Moisture in system.

Automatic Temperature Control

Automatic temperature control (ATC) is the general term for the various types of automatic air conditioning systems. See Figure 49-34. ATC features completely automatic control of discharge air temperature. ATC also controls the circulation and humidity of the air inside the automobile.

The only apparent difference between manual and automatic air conditioning systems is in the control panel. With ATC, the driver selects the temperature and the ATC system functions to maintain that temperature, regardless of outside temperature changes.

Many air conditioning, heating, ventilating, and defrosting systems are controlled by a ***computer*** or ***microprocessor.*** These electronic control systems automatically adjust doors, blower speeds, and compressor cycling. See Figure 49-35. The driver sets a particular temperature on the control panel and the system automatically adjusts various devices to obtain that temperature and airflow in the passenger compartment.

The computer uses input from various ***temperature sensors*** to produce outputs for automatically controlling the ATC system. GM temperature sensors, for example, include: in-car, outside, high side, low side, and engine coolant.

Some computers also have a self-test or a self-diagnostic capability. If computer input indicates that a problem exists, the computer will send faulty information to the control panel. The panel, in turn, will display a warning light or readout when the driver or service technician touches a combination of buttons or uses a jumper wire across two test terminals. A chart in the manufacturer's service manual tells what each trouble code means so that the problem area can be isolated.

ATC Preliminary Checks

If an automatic temperature control system is not working properly, consider that these automatic systems generally use the same "basic system" as the manual control model produced by the same manufacturer. See Figures 49-24 and 49-36. Therefore, first manually inspect cooling system and A/C components to see that all are in good condition and correctly adjusted. Examine and manually check hose and line connections. Check vacuum hoses, electrical connections, fuses, control lever operation, and blower operation.

Clean debris from the condenser fins. Check the condition and tension of drive belts. Check cooling system hoses, radiator, pressure cap, cooling fan, and coolant level.

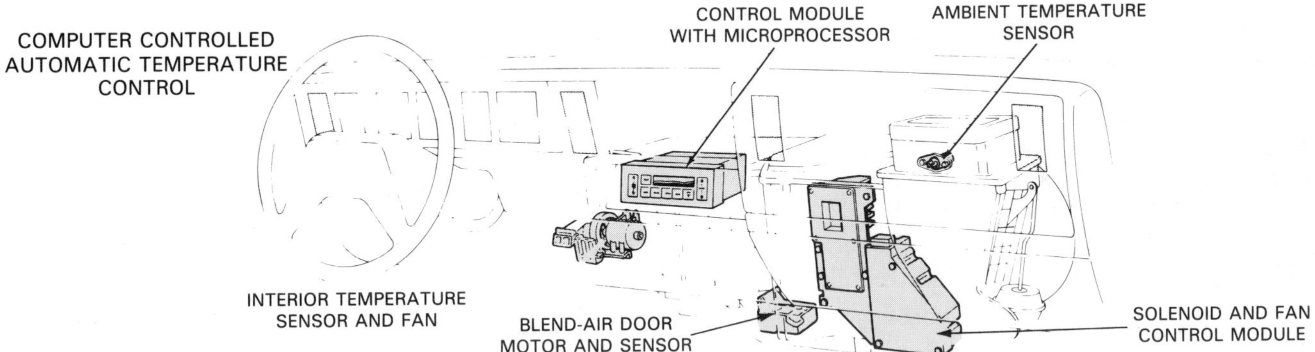

Figure 49-34. A microprocessor-controlled ATC system regulates the temperature of incoming air and makes adjustments every seven seconds to maintain the desired temperature. (Chrysler)

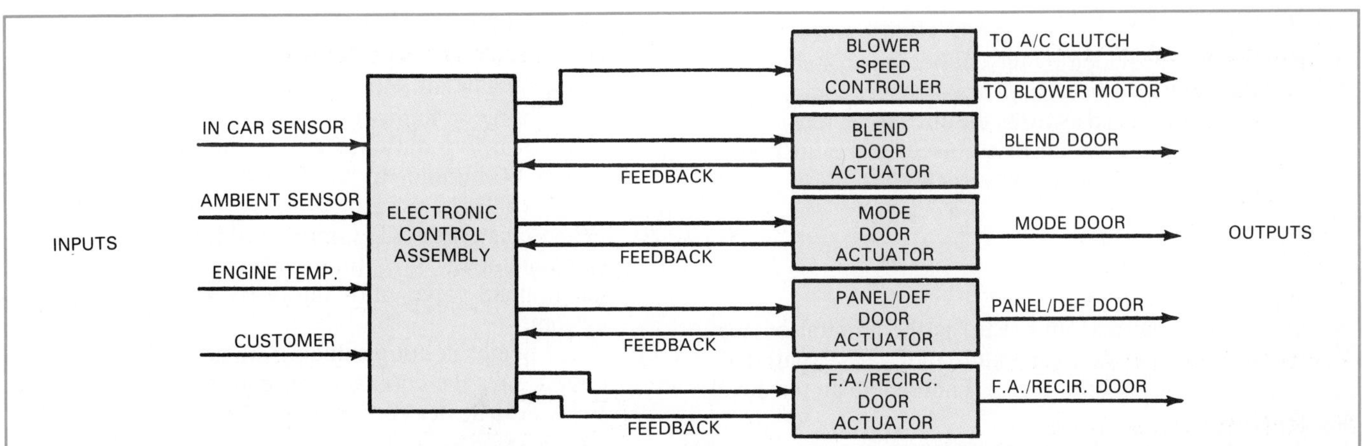

Figure 49-35. This block diagram of an electronic ATC system shows the inputs and outputs to and from the electronic control assembly. A self-test feature included in the control assembly lets the technician utilize a "trouble code" to locate the source of an A/C problem. (Ford)

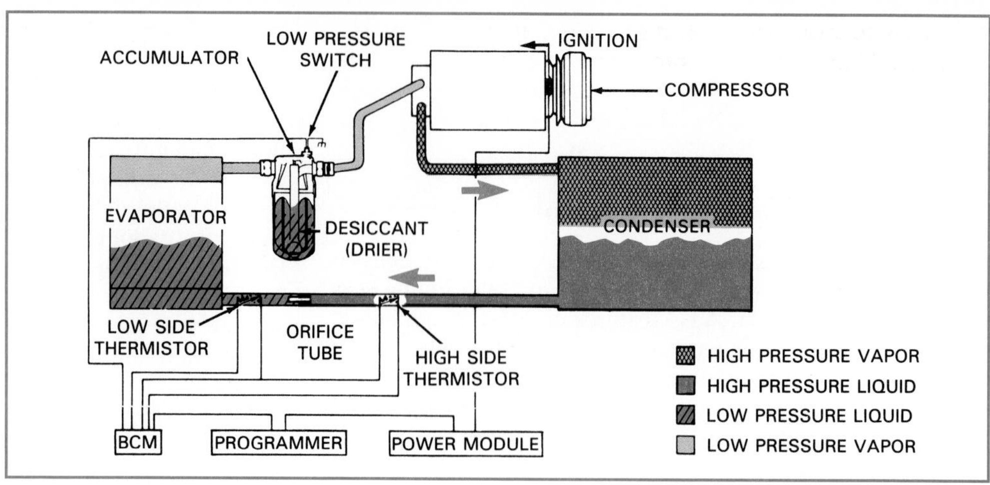

Figure 49-36. This diagram outlines the arrangement of the components and the direction of refrigerant flow in an electronic climate control system. The basic refrigeration elements are the same as in a manual A/C system. However, automatic temperature control units, including the BCM (Body Control Module), are added. (Cadillac)

Make an operational test of the ATC system. Check the sight glass for bubbles (low on refrigerant). Test high-side and low-side pressures with a manifold gauge set.

Further tests of the more complicated controls and ATC system electronics (various temperature sensors, servo assemblies, control panel devices, and computer or microprocessor) call for specialized test equipment and extensive test procedures. These procedures based on manufacturer's computer diagnostics and fault code charts are beyond the scope of this text.

Chapter 49–Review Questions

Write your answers on a separate sheet of paper. Do not write in this book.

1. Air conditioning is the process by which surrounding air is _____ and _____.
2. Fluids give up heat when changing from a vapor to a liquid. True or False?
3. Heat always flows from _____ to _____ (hotter to cooler or cooler to hotter) objects.
4. A typical air conditioning and heating plenum chamber houses all but one of the following assemblies. Which one is NOT in the plenum chamber?
   (A) Heater core.
   (B) Evaporator.
   (C) Condenser.
   (D) Blower.
5. How is heat provided by the car heating system?
6. By what process is heat from the passenger compartment absorbed and carried away by the circulating refrigerant?
7. Which refrigerant is currently used in the air conditioning system of most new vehicles?
   (A) R-12.
   (B) R-134A.
   (C) R-20.
   (D) R-500.
8. One British thermal unit (Btu) is the amount of heat required to raise the temperature of a _____ (gallon or pound) of water one degree Fahrenheit at sea level pressure.
9. Name three types of A/C compressors.
10. Which type of compressor uses a control valve to increase or decrease the swash plate angle for greater or lesser displacement?
11. The belt-driven compressor clutch pulley is always in rotation while the engine is running. True or False?
12. Compressor service valves are three-position controls: front-seated, _____, and back-seated.
13. Which of the major components of any A/C system provides a means of emitting heat from the hot refrigerant to the cooler atmosphere?
    (A) Evaporator.
    (B) Receiver-drier.
    (C) Thermostatic expansion valve.
    (D) Condenser.
14. What is indicated if bubbles appear in sight glass?
    (A) System is fully charged with refrigerant.
    (B) System is low on refrigerant.
    (C) Refrigerant is fully discharged from system.
    (D) Moisture in system.
15. Which component replaces the conventional thermostatic expansion valve in GM's CCOT A/C system?
16. Give five safety precautions to observe when working on an air conditioning system.
17. A vacuum pump is used to evaluate all traces of refrigerant, air, and _____.
18. The manifold gauge set has a center port to which a hose can be attached to perform several service operations. Which of the following is NOT a center port operation?
    (A) Test pressure in system.
    (B) Discharge refrigerant from system.
    (C) Evacuate air and moisture.
    (D) Charge system with refrigerant.
19. Using a heavy-duty vacuum pump, it takes approximately 60 minutes to "pull down" the A/C system to _____ in. Hg.
20. When charging A/C system, hold refrigerant tank upright and open _____ (high-side or low-side) manifold gauge hand valve, allowing refrigerant vapor to enter system.
21. A car heater is not producing sufficient heat. Technician A says the coolant level may be low. Technician B says the heater core may be clogged. Who is right?
    (A) A only.
    (B) B only.
    (C) Both A & B.
    (D) Neither A nor B.

22. An air conditioning system has no refrigeration action. Technician A says the compressor clutch may be slipping. Technician B says the compressor clutch may have a closed cycling switch. Who is right?
    (A) A only.
    (B) B only.
    (C) Both A & B.
    (D) Neither A nor B.
23. An air conditioning system is noisy. Technician A says it could be caused by a refrigerant overcharge. Technician B says it could be caused by a low refrigerant charge. Who is right?
    (A) A only.
    (B) B only.
    (C) Both A & B.
    (D) Neither A nor B.
24. In automatic temperature control systems, the computer uses input from various temperature sensors to produce outputs for automatically controlling the ATC systems. Name four sensors.
25. Automatic temperature control systems generally use the same "basic system" as the manual control model produced by the same manufacturer. True or False?

In some vehicles, heating and air conditioning ducts are routed to the rear passenger compartment. This particular vehicle features a five-speed blower that can be controlled by the rear passengers. (Cadillac)

Late-model vehicles are equipped with a wide variety of safety features.

Chapter 50
Safety Systems

After studying this chapter, you will be able to:

❍ List dozens of major advances in automotive safety.
❍ Describe current front seat lap/shoulder belt systems.
❍ Explain how automatic seat belt systems operate.
❍ Tell how air bags work.
❍ Compare the construction and function of the three major types of energy absorbing bumper systems.
❍ Describe the operation of a modern anti-lock braking system.

Safety Systems

Safety has always been a key word for automotive engineers. First came the lights, horns, and mechanical brakes; then the emergency brakes, rear view mirrors, windshield wipers, and pneumatic tires were introduced.

Next, the car manufacturers gave us safety wheel rims, Figure 50-1, and tubeless tires; power brakes and power steering; safety glass, windshield washers and defrosters; dual headlamps, turn signals, and seat belts; warning buzzers, chimes, and indicator lights; neutral safety switches and steering wheel locks; snow tires, radial tires, and puncture-sealing tires; split brake systems, Figure 50-2, and self-adjusting brakes; hood safety catches; coolant reserve systems; rear window wipers, defoggers, defrosters, Figure 50-3.

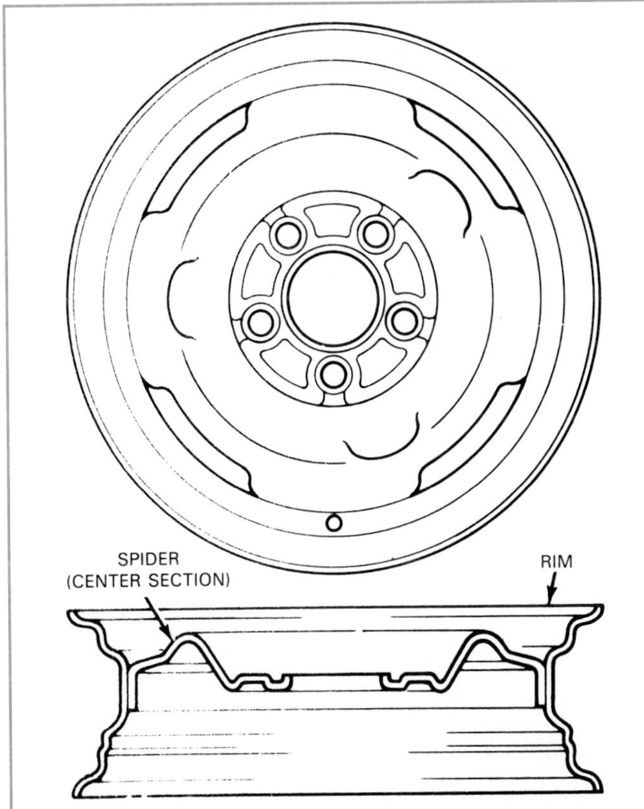

Figure 50-1. The safety wheel rim was a simple yet major advance. In case of tire failure, the raised sections around the rim help hold the beads of the tire in position on the wheel until the vehicle can be brought to a safe stop. (Chrysler)

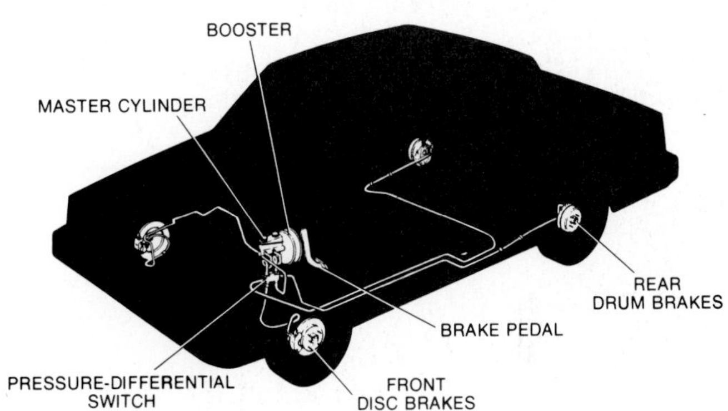

Figure 50-2. A split brake system is provided by a dual master cylinder and two separate hydraulic systems. Some have separate front and rear systems. Others have diagonally balanced systems as shown here.

Figure 50-3. Good rearward visibility is an important safety feature afforded by a rear window wiper and a window defogger/defroster system.

Then came the government safety push for collapsible steering columns; padded steering wheels and dashboards; recessed control knobs; head restraints; padded armrests and visors; positive seat anchorages; non-slip seat tracks; positive door locks; side-impact door beams; energy-absorbing bumpers; fuel system integrity; reinforced panels, pillars, and floor pans; dull finishes on reflective surfaces; and voice alert systems.

The latest safety features being developed or installed include anti-lock brake systems, automatic seat belts, air bags, high-mounted stop lamps, and anti-lacerative (plastic-layered) windshields.

Seat Belt Systems

Seat belts and ***shoulder belts*** of various types have been used in passenger cars for many years. See Figures 50-4 and 50-5. The lap belt and shoulder belt are fixed to a connector. The lap belt usually has an ***automatic locking retractor,*** while the shoulder belt and lap/shoulder belt have an ***inertial-locking retractor*** that locks only when the vehicle stops abruptly. In most seat belt systems in U.S. cars, a mechanical inertial-locking retractor is used. This type of retractor has a pendulum weight, Figure 50-6, that locks the belt during rapid deceleration of the car. A few cars, however, are equipped with an electronic unit, Figure 50-7, that senses when the car is stopping abruptly. It then triggers the locking drive for the belt tightener in a matter of milliseconds.

Front seat belts generally incorporate a "timed" reminder lamp and sound signal (buzzing). These warnings are designed to remind the driver and passengers to fasten lap and shoulder belts when the ignition key is turned to the on position. If the driver's seat belt is buckled, the buzzer will not operate but the "Fasten Seat Belt" reminder lamp will stay on for four to eight seconds. If the driver's belt is not buckled, the reminder lamp and sound signal will automatically shut off after the four to eight second interval.

Figure 50-4. This automatic safety belt system meets the U.S. government requirement for a passive restraint system.

Lap belt-to-floor pan and shoulder belt-to-roof panel or quarter panel fasteners are especially important. Failure

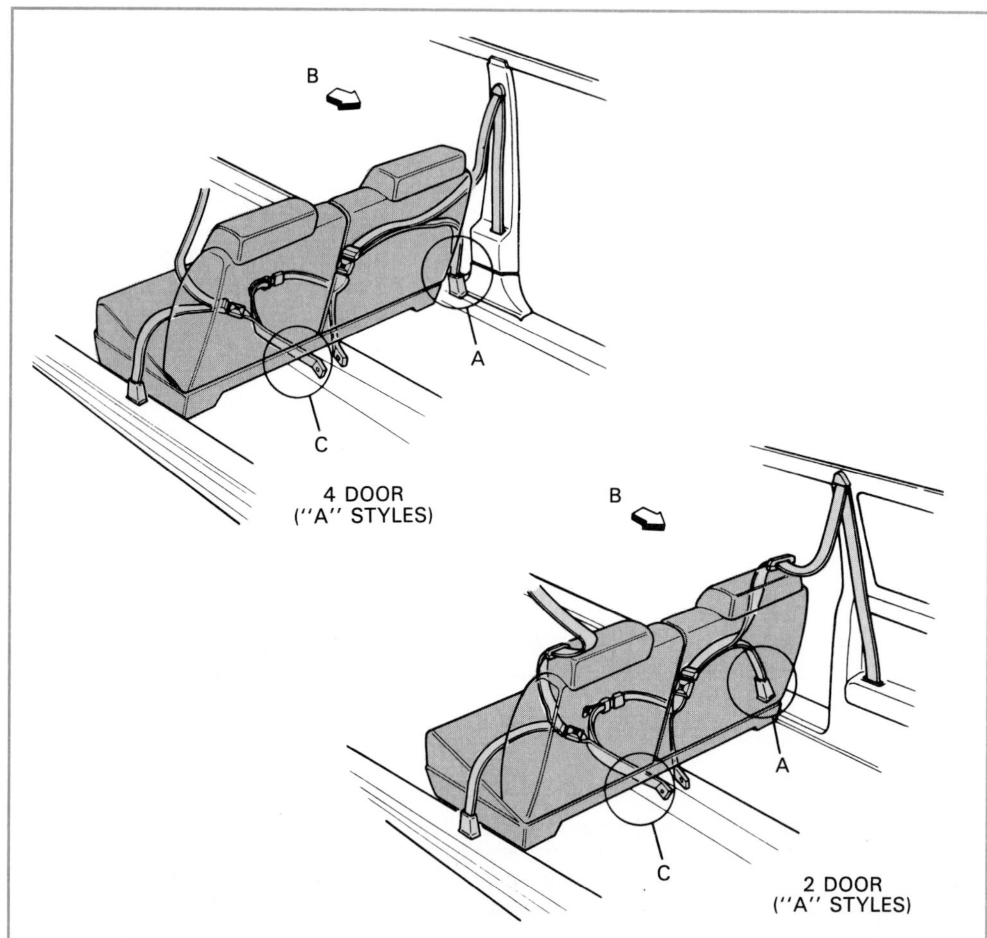

Figure 50-5. Correct location and mounting of hardware and routing of belts is vital to the convenient use and proper operation of lap/shoulder belt systems. (Fisher Body Div., General Motors Corp.)

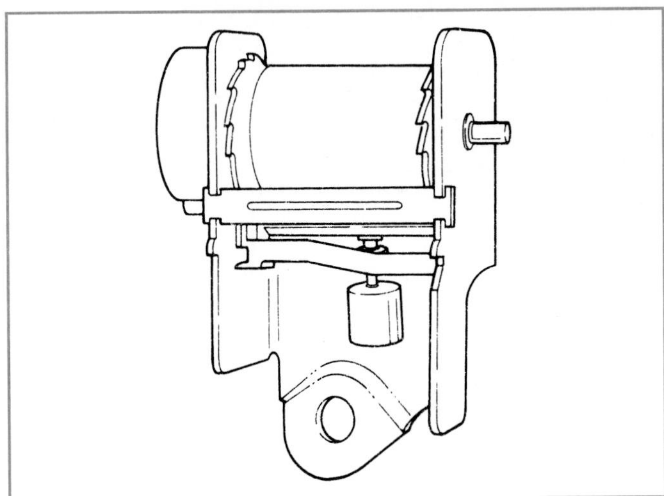

Figure 50-6. A seat belt retractor allows the belt to move in or out as wearer desires until a sudden deceleration of the vehicle occurs. Then, the retractor automatically locks the belt to restrain the forward motion of the wearer. (Ford)

Figure 50-7. At speeds above 10 mph, this electronic unit senses sudden deceleration and signals the belt tightener to restrain the belted individual. (Robert Bosch Corp.)

of these attaching parts could affect the performance of vital components and systems, and/or could result in major repair expenses. Fasteners must be replaced with a replacement part of the same part number or its equivalent. Correct torque values must be observed during reassembly.

Automatic Seat Belts

Most seat belt systems are ***active.*** That is, the user must do something manually (buckle up) to make the system operable. The law regarding air bags and/or seat belts calls for ***passive*** (automatic) systems.

The air bag system is "passive." In order to qualify under the law effective with the introduction of the 1989 models, the seat belt system must be passive or the vehicle must be equipped with an air bag. One such system is pictured in Figure 50-8.

The ***automatic seat belt system*** has shoulder belts that enclose the driver and front seat passenger as they get into the car and shut their doors. This protects the occupants during a crash by means of diagonal restraint across the chest.

The automatic seat belt system also has a ***knee restraint*** to prevent the occupant from sliding under the seat

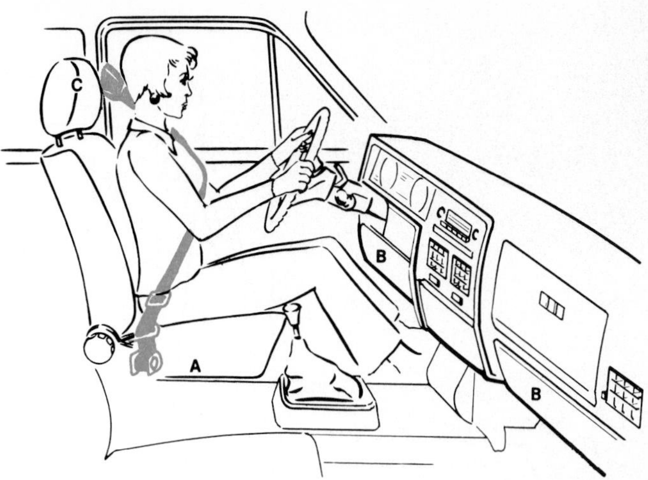

Figure 50-8. Automatic seat belt requires no buckling up or adjustment by the driver or front-seat passenger. Front seat occupants merely "get in" and close the door. (Volkswagen of America, Inc.)

belt. The shoulder belt allows reasonably free movement during ordinary driving. The belt reel mechanism has a sensor which detects sudden forward movement of the occupant or abrupt deceleration of the car (as with a frontal crash). The reel locks in position, freezing belt length and preventing further forward movement of the occupant.

For post-crash purposes (or any other reason), the shoulder belt can be unfastened at the buckle on the door. Also, some automatic seat belt systems prevent restarting of the engine once it has been shut off unless both belts are again fastened in place.

Air Bag Systems

Air bags are standard equipment on many late-model vehicles. Air bag systems are designed to deploy when a vehicle is involved in a frontal collision of adequate force. Most air bag systems consist of several common components, including:

- Impact sensors.
- Control module.
- Coil assembly.
- Air bag module.

These components work together to fully deploy the air bag within 50 milliseconds of impact. See Figures 50-9 and 50-10. After full deployment, the air bag deflates in approximately 100 milliseconds.

The ***impact sensors*** are usually located on the front section of a vehicle's frame or on each side of the radiator housing. An impact sensor is essentially an open switch that is designed to close when an impact occurs that is severe enough to warrant air bag deployment. See Figure 50-11.

The ***control module*** is a computer that performs several functions in the air bag system. The module monitors the operation of the components in the air bag system, warns the driver of system malfunctions by activating the air bag indicator light, and stores trouble codes. ***Trouble codes*** are used during air bag system troubleshooting to help pinpoint the problem source.

Most control modules provide the air bag system with an alternate source of power if battery voltage is lost during

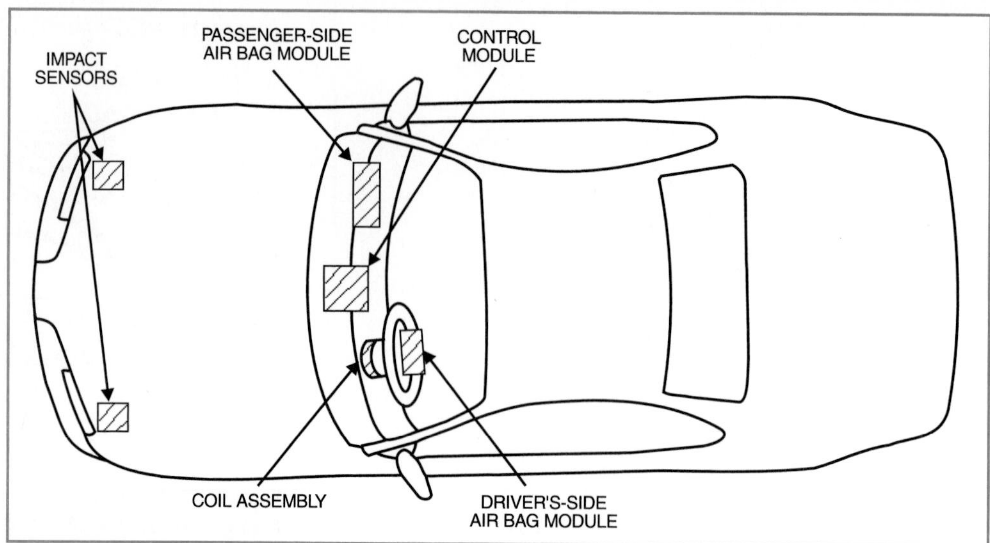

Figure 50-9. Typical air bag system components.

Figure 50-10. During a collision, air bags are deployed on both the driver's side and the passenger side in many vehicles. (BMW)

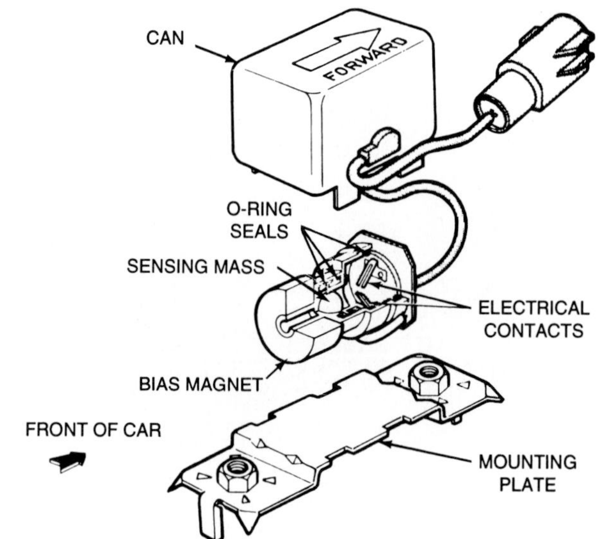

Figure 50-11. Typical impact sensor. During a collision, the sensing mass breaks away from the bias magnet and strikes the electrical contacts. This closes the contacts and triggers the air bag system.

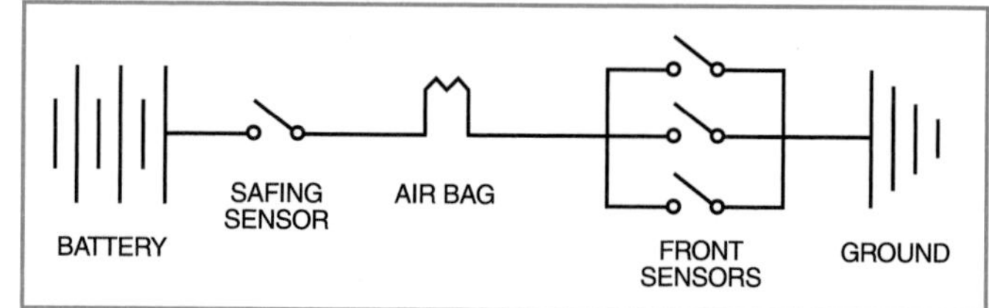

Figure 50-12. Schematic of an air bag system. Note that the safing sensor and at least one impact sensor must close before the air bag(s) can be deployed.

an accident. The control module also contains a safing sensor. This sensor is designed to prevent accidental air bag deployment and to prevent a faulty front impact sensor from activating the air bag system. In order for deployment to occur, the safing sensor must close with at least one of the impact sensors, Figure 50-12.

The ***coil assembly*** consists of two current-carrying coils that are attached to the vehicle's steering column. As the steering wheel is rotated, these coils provide a continuous electrical connection between the inflator module and control module. A typical coil assembly is illustrated in Figure 50-13.

The ***air bag module*** is located in the steering wheel in driver's-side air bag systems, Figure 50-14. Passenger-side inflator modules are usually mounted above the glove box on the passenger side of the vehicle. See Figure 50-15. The air bag module contains an *inflatable fabric air bag,* an *igniter,* and an *inflator* (gas generating material). See Figure 50-16.

Operation of Air Bag Systems

If a vehicle is involved in a severe frontal collision, the impact sensors close. If at least one impact sensor and the safing sensor in the control module close, a signal is sent to the igniter in the air bag module. When signaled, the igniter generates a heat. The heat ignites a gas generating material in the inflator. This gas generating material releases a large amount of harmless gas, which quickly fills the air bag. As mentioned, this entire sequence of events occurs in less than 50 milliseconds. The inflated air bag prevents the driver and the front passenger from striking the steering wheel, the dashboard, and the windshield.

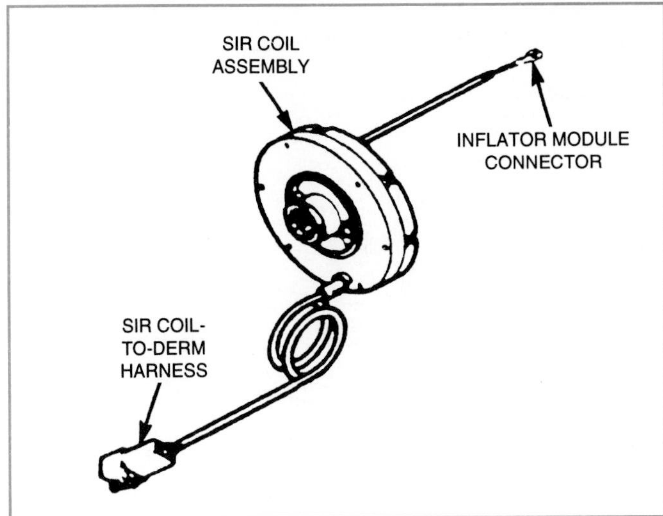

Figure 50-13. The coil assembly maintains an electrical connection between the inflator module and the control module. (General Motors)

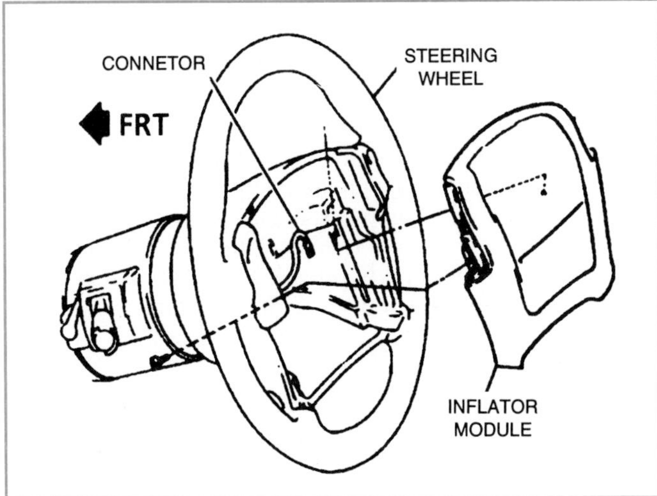

Figure 50-14. Location of the air bag module in a driver's-side air bag system. (General Motors)

Troubleshooting Air Bag Systems

Caution: Always consult an appropriate service manual before attempting to troubleshoot an air bag system. Most manufacturers require the use of special equipment when testing an air bag system. Using incorrect equipment or test procedures can activate the system.

Most air bag systems have self-diagnostic capabilities. The self-diagnostic system should be used when troubleshooting the air bag system. Procedures for accessing trouble codes vary. Consult the manufacturer's service manual before attempting to trigger the diagnostic system. Most manufacturers recommend the use of a special scan tool to retrieve codes.

Many components in an air bag system cannot be repaired. If trouble codes indicate a faulty component, it must generally be replaced. To prevent accidental air bag deployment, always disable the system before beginning service procedures. Most manufacturers recommend disconnecting the battery. In some systems, however, the igniter must be disconnected. This prevents the control module's alternate power source from triggering the system.

Servicing a Deployed Air Bag System

Most manufacturers recommend replacement of all related parts after an air bag has been deployed. Some, however, only require the replacement of the inflator module and the igniter. Always replace the items called out in the service manual. In some systems, reusing sensors or the control module may cause unprompted air bag deployment.

During air bag deployment, ***sodium hydroxide powder*** is released into the vehicle's interior. This powder can irritate the skin, eyes, nose, and throat. Wear rubber gloves and safety glasses when removing a deployed bag. After the bag has been removed, vacuum the interior thoroughly to remove residual powder. Make sure to vacuum the heater and air conditioner outlets. If residue remains, wipe down the interior with a damp cloth. Follow the manufacturer's recommendations for proper air bag disposal.

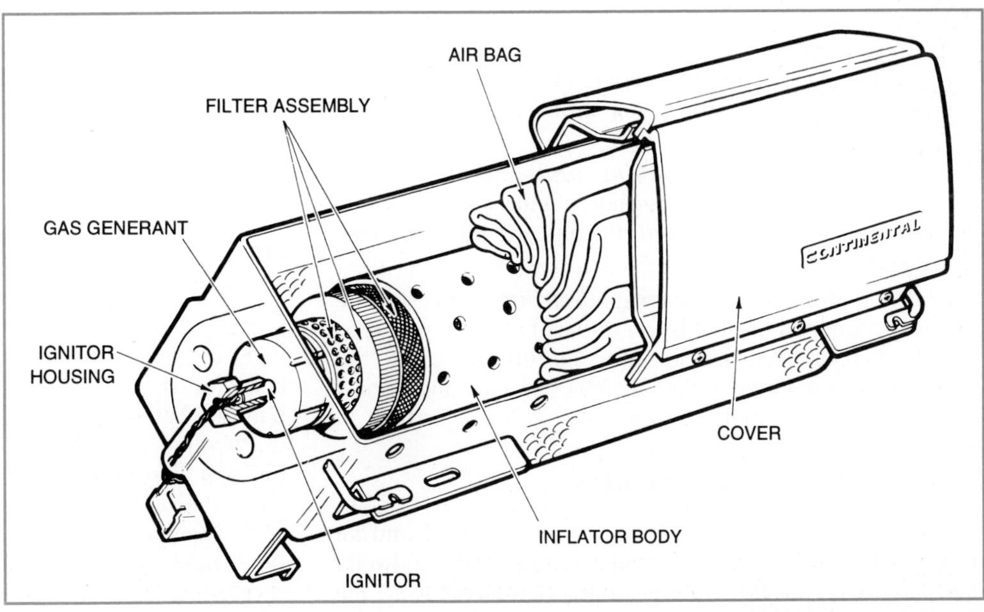

Figure 50-15. Passenger-side air bag module. (Ford)

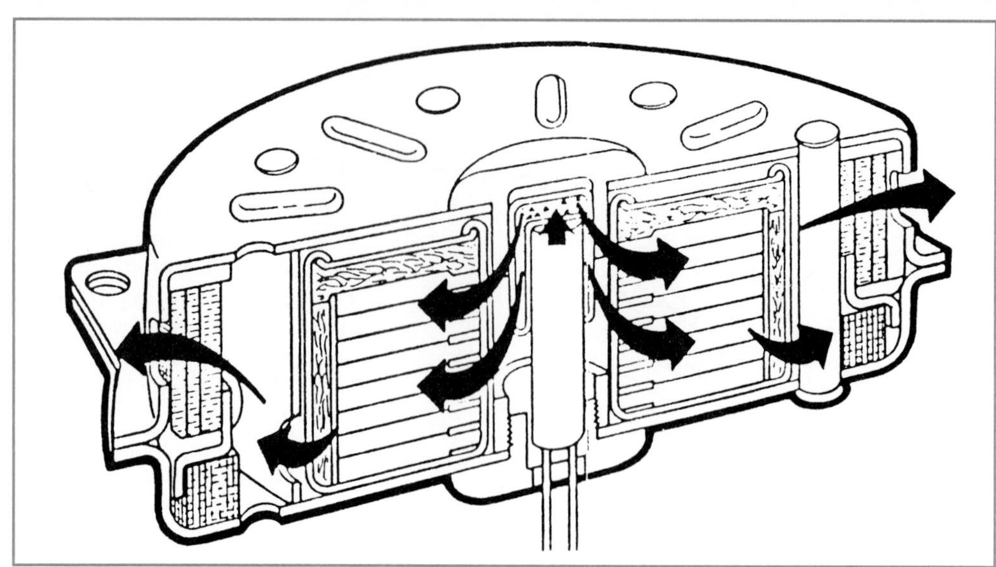

Figure 50-16. This inflator is for a driver's-side air bag. Note the location of the igniter. (Ford)

Air Bag Service Precautions

There are several precautions that should be taken when working on or near an air bag system to reduce the risk of damage to the system, including:

- Always disable the air bag system before attempting to service any component on or near the system.
- Never subject the inflator module to temperatures over 175°F (79.4°C).
- Only use the test equipment recommended by the manufacturer when servicing air bag systems.
- Use extreme care when handling a live inflator module. Accidental deployment can cause serious injury.
- If any air bag system component is accidentally dropped, it should be replaced.

Energy Absorbing Bumper Systems

By law, auto manufacturers are required to install ***bumper systems*** that will protect vehicle safety systems in a barrier impact of five miles per hour. The manufacturers have devised many different systems to absorb the energy of a low-speed impact, but all are one of three major types:

- ***Fluid/gas energy absorbing unit***–Energy absorber that is similar to a hydraulic shock absorber, but with a nitrogen gas preload that acts as a piston return after impact. See Figure 50-17.
- ***Fluid/spring energy absorbing unit***–Energy absorber that is similar to a shock absorber, but has a spring inside the hydraulic unit that returns the unit and bumper to the original position.
- ***Plastic pad/impact bar energy absorbing units***–Plastic honeycomb pad backed by an impact bar. This pad-type energy absorber, or isolator, uses no fluids or gases, but compresses on impact; then the bumper, pad, and impact bar return to original position.

How Fluid/Gas Unit Operates

The bumper system utilizing hydraulic fluid and an inert gas consists of a piston tube assembly and a cylinder tube assembly. In extended position, Figure 50-18A, the piston tube is filled with gas and the cylinder tube is filled with hydraulic fluid.

Upon impact, the energy absorber is collapsed, Figure 50-18B, and the hydraulic fluid is forced from the cylinder tube into the piston tube through an orifice. The flow of fluid is controlled by the metering pin which, in turn, controls the energy absorbing action.

The incoming fluid displaces the floating piston, which compresses the gas in the piston tube. After impact, the pressure of the compressed gas behind the floating piston forces the hydraulic fluid back into the cylinder tube. The energy absorber unit is extended to its normal position and the bumper returns to its original position.

Servicing Fluid/Gas Units

If an impact causes an energy absorber to leak or damages it so that it is inoperable, it should be replaced. Likewise, if the unit does not return to its original position after being compressed 3/8 in. or more, replace the defective unit.

Caution: Observe these precautions when handling energy absorbing devices: Do not apply heat to unit. Do not weld in area near unit. Do not work around bent sheet metal that may keep energy absorber from extending (possibility of spring-back).

If the energy absorber will not extend or if it is to be discarded, relieve the gas pressure by drilling a 1/8 in. hole in the piston tube. See Figure 50-19. Be sure to wear approved safety glasses.

How Fluid/Spring Unit Operates

The hydraulic bumper system, Figure 50-20, absorbs impact forces and dissipates impact energy. The outer cylinder of the energy absorber attaches to the frame or underbody of the car; the inner cylinder is attached to the bumper. When an impact load reaches approximately 8000 lb., a valve in the hydraulic unit opens and fluid is forced through a set of orifices (small openings). Impact energy is converted to heat, which is dissipated to the air and adjacent metal surfaces.

Once the impact force is removed, the heavy-duty spring inside the hydraulic unit returns the energy absorber

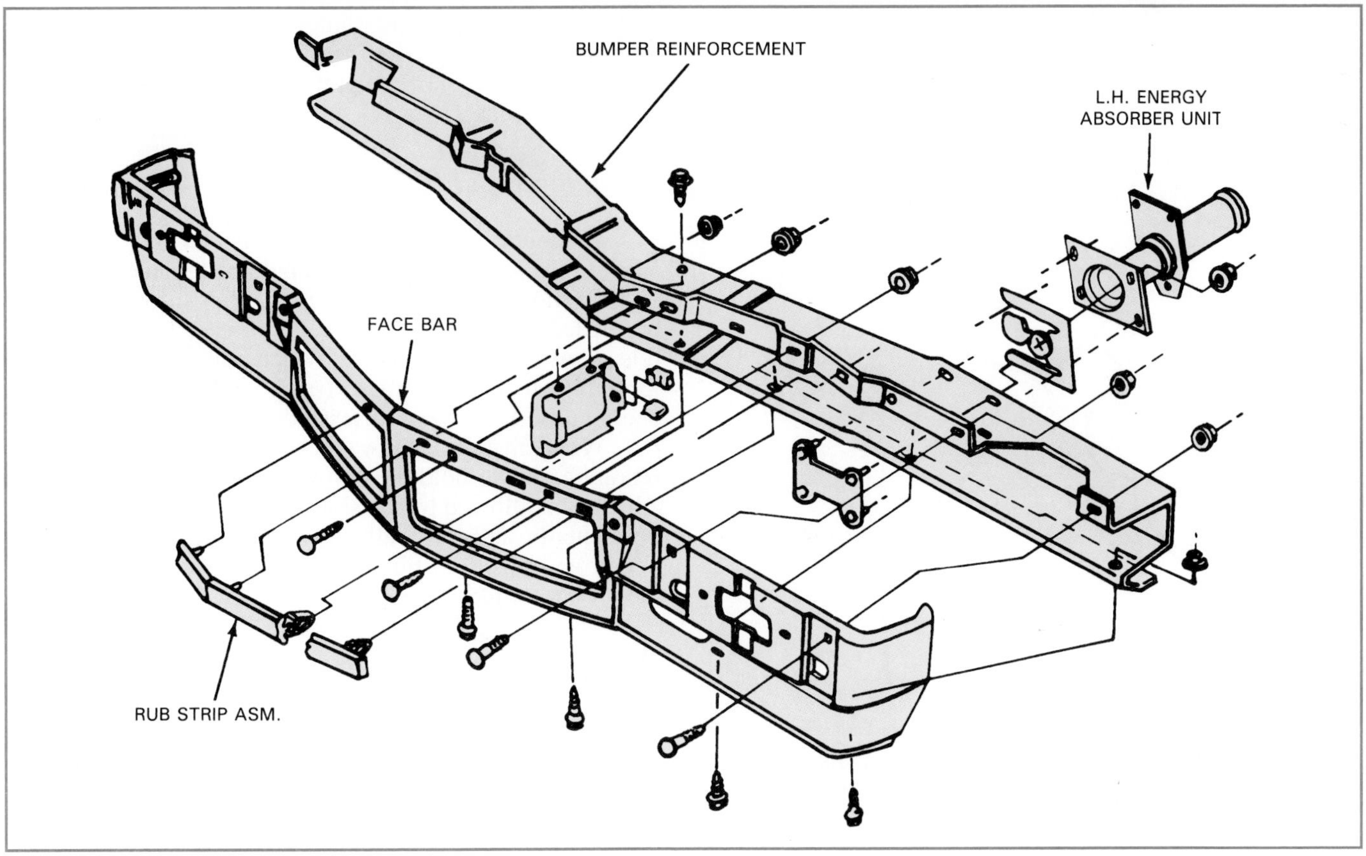

Figure 50-17. Energy absorbers used on the front and rear bumpers of certain cars use hydraulic fluid as a dampening medium during frontal impacts. Inert gas is used to maintain the unit in the extended position. (Pontiac)

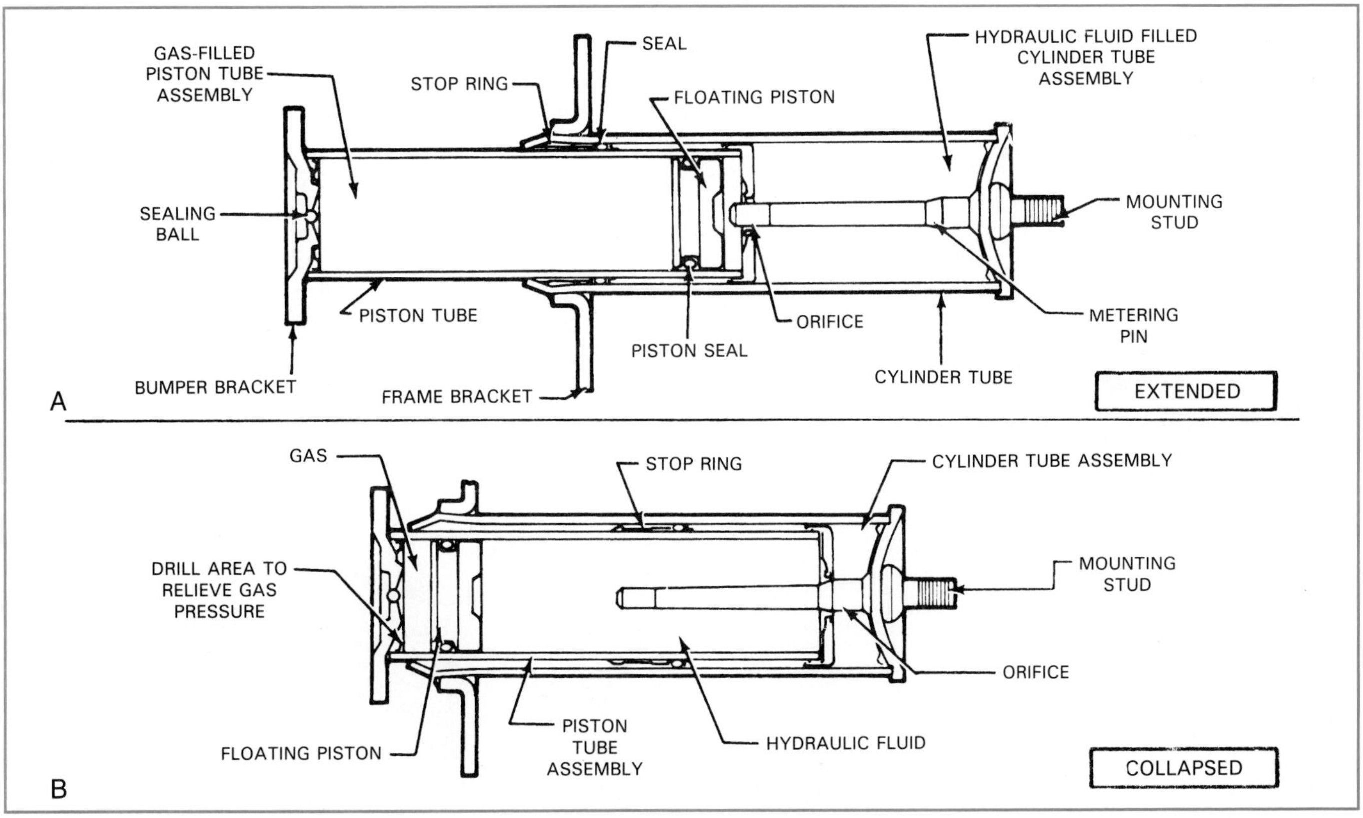

Figure 50-18. A–In the extended position, the piston tube of the energy absorber is filled with gas and the cylinder tube is filled with hydraulic fluid. B–In the collapsed position, hydraulic fluid forces the floating piston to compress the gas and the unit absorbs the impact on the bumper. (Pontiac)

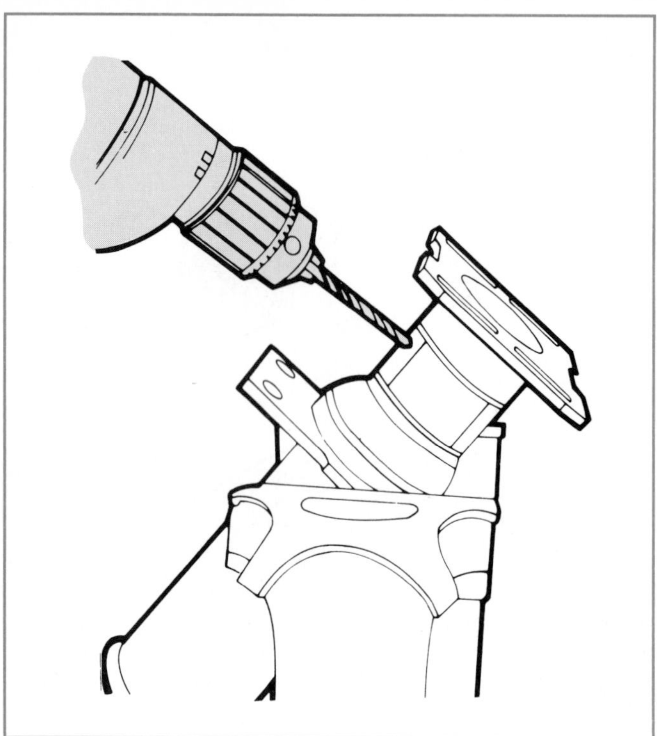

Figure 50-19. If a gas/hydraulic fluid energy absorber is damaged, it should be relieved of gas pressure before disposal. To do this, wear safety glasses and drill a 1/8 in. hole in the small cylinder. (Chevrolet)

and the bumper to their normal positions. See Figure 50-21. These units are matched to the weight of the vehicle by the length of the stroke of the unit. The larger the vehicle: the longer the stroke.

Servicing Fluid/Spring Units

Hydraulic energy absorbing units that are damaged or stuck in the retracted position should be replaced.

Caution: Units stuck in retracted position should not be drilled to relieve pressure. Drilling a hole can cause release of 8000 psi pressure, which could cause injury. If loosening attaching bolts to frame and bumper do not let energy absorber extend, discard the unit.

When installing new energy absorbers, tighten the retaining nuts to hold the bumper in place, then utilize the adjustment allowed by the slotted holes to shift the bumper horizontally and vertically to obtain the correct bumper height and position. Finally, tighten the attaching nuts to the proper torque.

Plastic Pad/Impact Bar Units

Bumper assemblies that rely on the energy absorbing characteristics of a plastic fascia and plastic honeycomb pad backed by an impact bar, Figure 50-22, have no moving parts. If damage is sustained to any of the bumper assembly elements, unit replacement is required. See Figure 50-23.

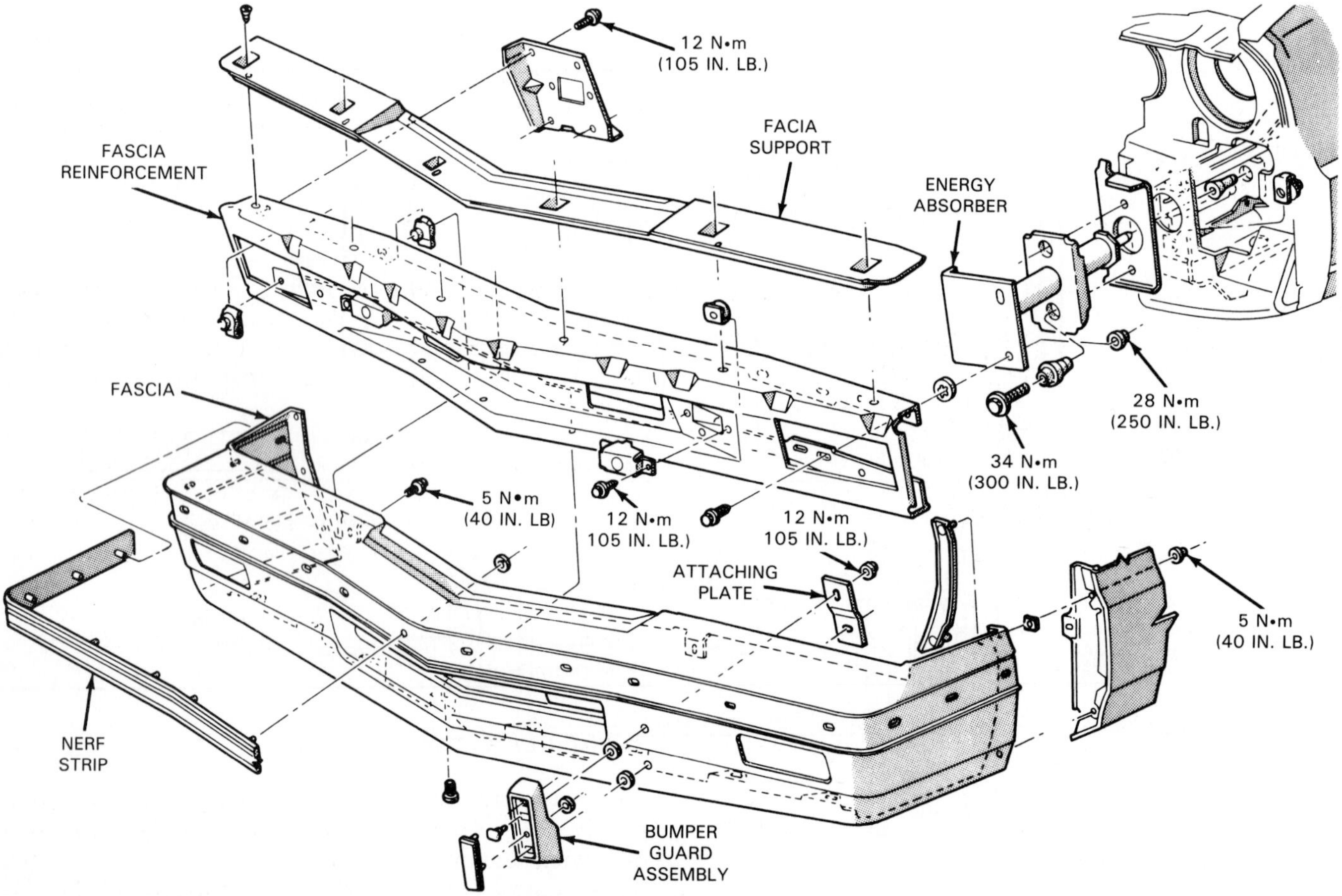

Figure 50-20. Chrysler cars use hydraulic impact energy absorbers to mount the front and rear bumpers on the body frame supports. (Chrysler)

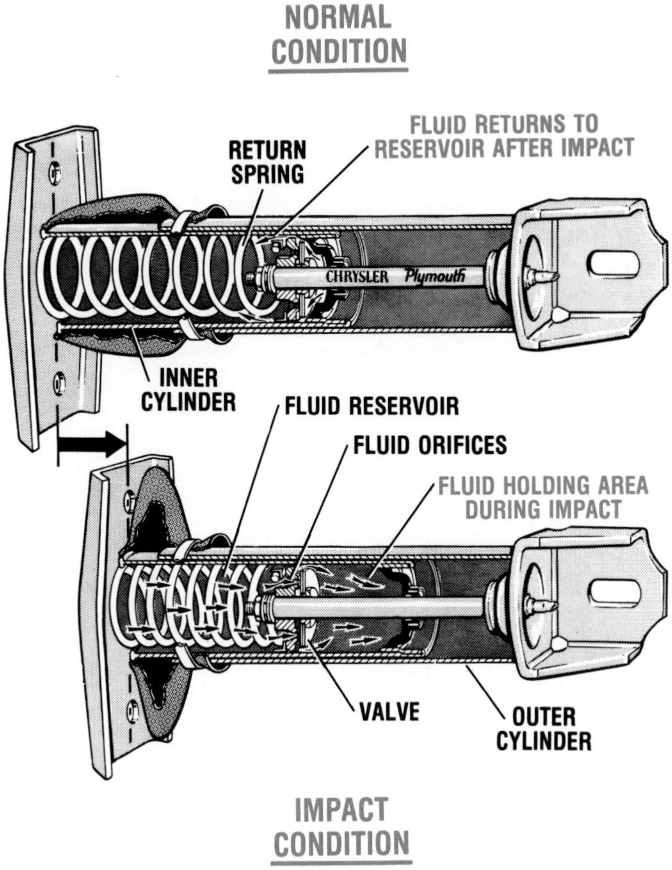

NORMAL CONDITION

RETURN SPRING

FLUID RETURNS TO RESERVOIR AFTER IMPACT

CHRYSLER Plymouth

INNER CYLINDER

FLUID RESERVOIR

FLUID ORIFICES

FLUID HOLDING AREA DURING IMPACT

VALVE

OUTER CYLINDER

IMPACT CONDITION

Figure 50-21. Energy absorbers used on the bumpers of Chrysler cars utilize hydraulic action and heat transfer to absorb impact. A spring returns the energy absorber and bumper to the normal position. (Chrysler)

Figure 50-22. Some U.S. and foreign cars use bumper face bars made of urethane. This plastic "fascia" is backed by a plastic honeycomb energy absorber and a steel impact bar.

If the honeycomb pad energy absorber must be replaced, drill out the pop rivets and install a new absorber with nuts, bolts, and lock washers.

Other Safety Features

Many innovative and reassuring types of safety features have been developed in recent years, and more of the same are being researched for incorporation in models yet to be introduced. Some of these are briefly described and pictured here.

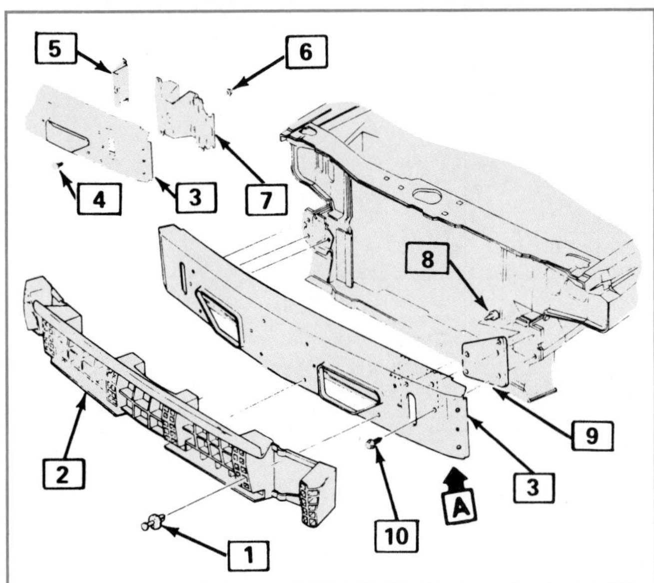

Figure 50-23. Oldsmobile front bumper assembly (less plastic face bar). 1–Retainer. 2–Energy absorber. 3–Impact bar. 4–Bolt. 5–Reinforcement. 6–Nut. 7–Bracket. 8–Retainer. 9–Reinforcement. 10–Bolt/screw. (Oldsmobile)

Anti-lock Brake System

Certain vehicles are equipped with four-wheel ***anti-lock brake systems,*** Figure 50-24. These systems are designed to prevent wheel lockup during periods of hard braking. See Chapter 48 for additional information on anti-lock brake systems.

Anti-lacerative Windshield

Certain cars feature an ***anti-lacerative windshield*** designed to virtually eliminate facial cuts from broken windshields in auto accidents. This windshield is said to have superior abrasion resistance and chemical resistant properties.

The anti-lacerative windshield generally has a two-part plastic layer applied to its inside surface. These layers are in addition to the construction of the high-penetration-resistance (HPR) windshields currently in use. The HPR windshields consist of a layer of laminated plastic between two sheets of glass.

The anti-lacerative windshield requires no special care. However, abrasive cleaning agents or metal scrapers should not be used on the inner surface.

High-mounted Stop Lamp

Government regulations now require ***high-mounted stop lamps*** on new cars to provide an additional indication of vehicle braking. The attention-getting feature of the high-mounted lamp is expected to help reduce the frequency and severity of rear collisions, especially in heavy traffic situations. See Figure 50-25.

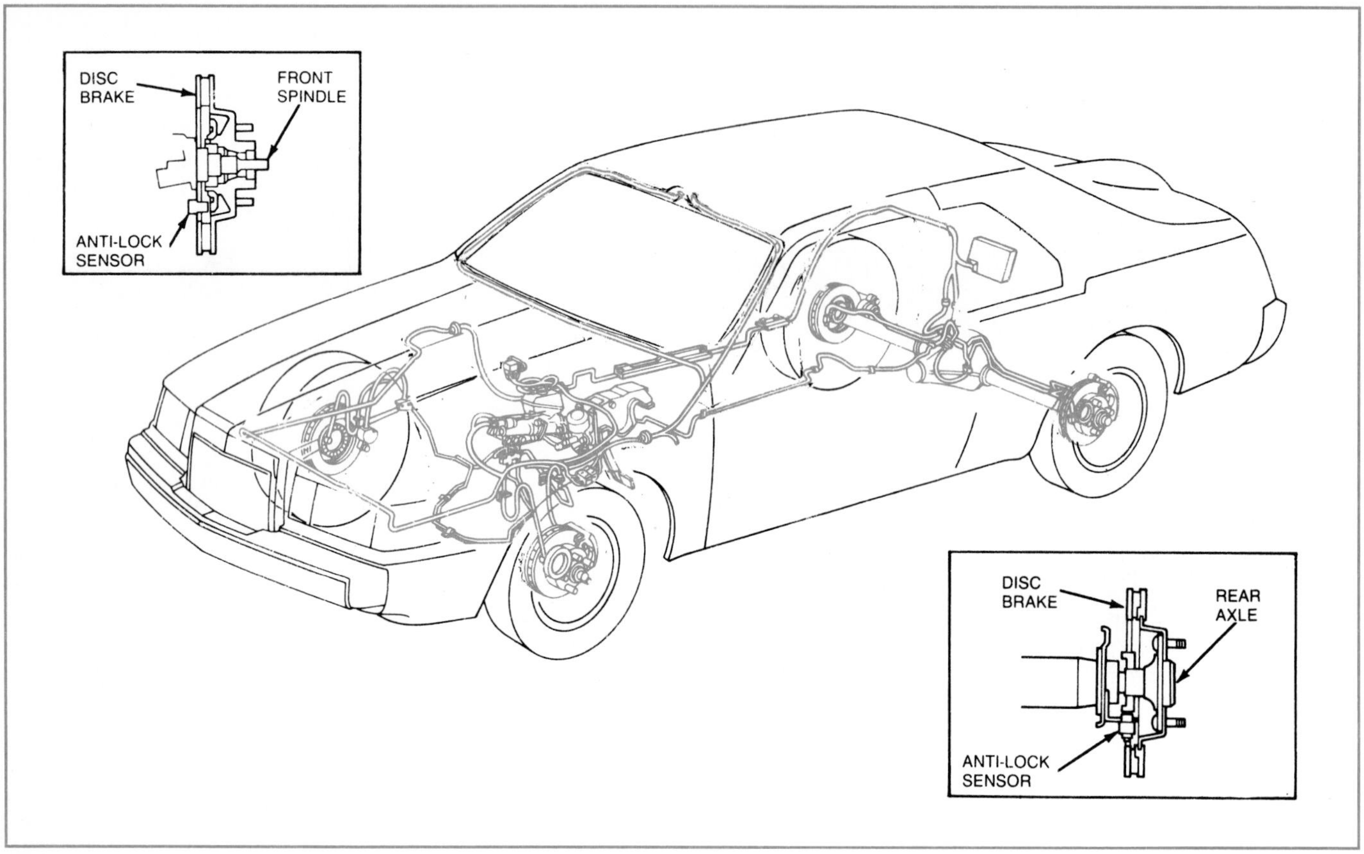

Figure 50-24. Some vehicles are equipped with a four-wheel anti-lock disc brake system. This system uses sensors (inset) at all four wheels to sense wheel lock conditions that will trigger anti-lock (pulsating) braking action. (Ford)

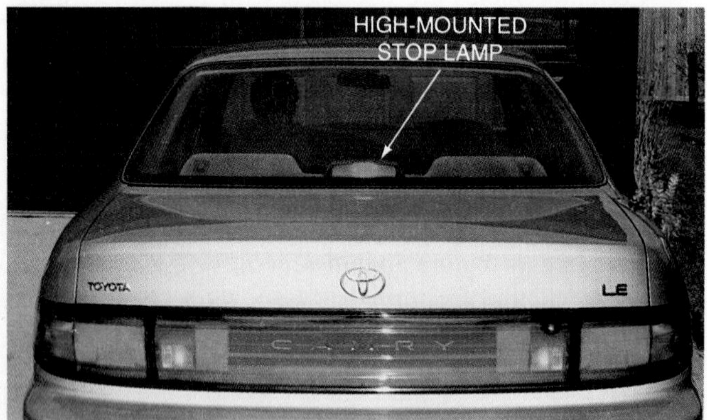

Figure 50-25. A high-mounted stop lamp is required on all new passenger cars. It is designed to provide a more positive warning to the drivers of trailing vehicles.

Voice Alert Systems

The use of electronic ***voice alert systems*** is broadening each new model year, and the messages these systems provide are likewise being expanded. The systems basically are "voice" warnings to enhance those provided by instruments, lights, and buzzers. Voice warnings, it has been found, virtually eliminate any chance of the driver overlooking a potential problem.

One manufacturer's cars so equipped provide the following functions or voice warnings:

- Your headlights are on.
- Don't forget your keys.
- Your washer fluid is low.
- Your fuel is low.
- Your electrical system is malfunctioning. Prompt service is required.
- Your parking brake is on.
- A door is ajar.
- Please fasten your seat belts.
- Your engine is overheating. Prompt service is required.
- Your engine oil pressure is low. Prompt service is required.
- All monitored systems are functioning.

Information Centers

Information centers provide visual displays of various kinds. Some consist of data panels on the dash or digital warnings that light up to alert the driver to certain vehicle conditions. See Figure 50-26.

Also in the realm of driver information systems, electronics are making possible the inclusion of *message centers* on the instrument panel. The buttons can be manipulated by the driver or passenger to request liquid crystal displays of the condition of most all vital functions of the vehicle.

In this regard, many of the requests require in-vehicle diagnostic capability. That is, a given request for information could result in the diagnosis that the system under inquiry is about to fail. Armed with this advance warning, the driver could possibly ensure his own safety by correcting the problem or having it corrected.

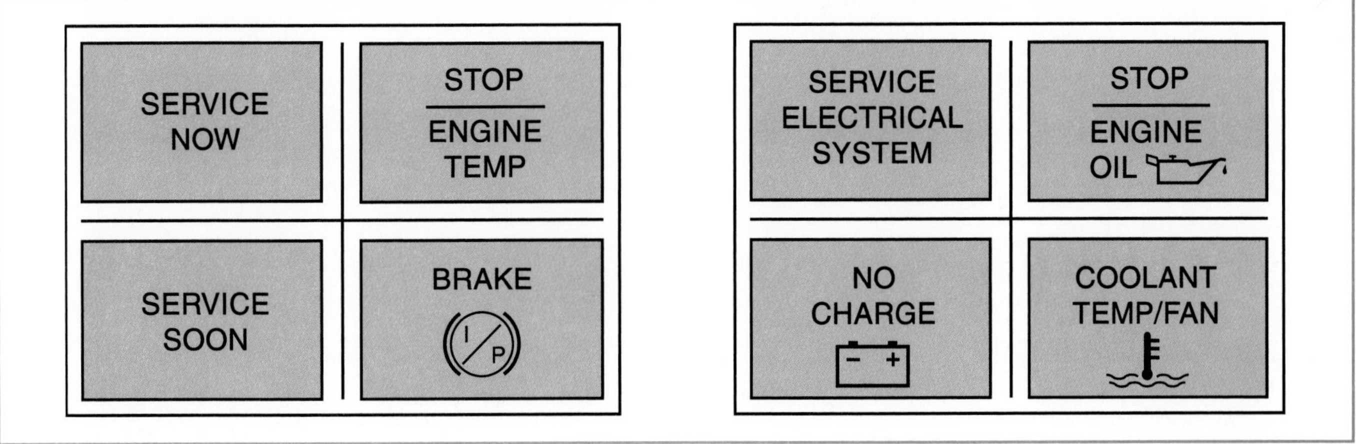

Figure 50-26. The speedometer cluster telltale warning lights on this instrument panel serve to warn driver of impending problems. (Cadillac)

Chapter 50–Review Questions

Write your answers on a separate sheet of paper. Do not write in this book.

1. What is the special safety feature of a safety wheel rim?
   (A) One piece steel wheel.
   (B) Raised sections around rim that hold tire beads in place.
   (C) Drop center construction of wheel.
   (D) Air tight construction of wheel.
2. A typical lap/shoulder seat belt has an inertial retractor. What is the function of this type of retractor?
3. Seat belt fasteners must be replaced with a replacement part of the same _____, or its _____.
4. Automatic seat belts are _____ (active or passive).
5. Air bag systems are _____ (active or passive).
6. The automatic seat belt system usually includes _____.
7. Name the main components in a typical air bag system.
8. Air bag systems are designed to deploy the air bag(s) within _____ of impact.
   (A) 2 seconds
   (B) 50 milliseconds
   (C) 1 millisecond
   (D) None of the above.
9. If battery voltage is lost during a collision, the air bag will not deploy. True or False?
10. The _____ sensor prevents a faulty impact sensor from activating the air bag system.
11. Passenger car manufacturers are required to install bumper systems that will protect vehicle safety systems in a barrier impact of _____ mph.
    (A) 5
    (B) 10
    (C) 12
    (D) 15
12. Explain the operation of a hydraulic fluid/inert gas type of energy absorber.
13. If a hydraulic fluid/inert gas energy absorber will not extend or is to be discarded, what precautions should be taken?
14. What is the function of the heavy-duty spring in a hydraulic fluid/spring type of energy absorber?
15. Hydraulic fluid/spring type of energy absorbers that are damaged or stuck in the extended position should be _____.
16. These defective units should not be drilled to relieve pressure. True or False?
17. The anti-lock brake system prevents wheel _____ during hard braking.

This vehicle is equipped with both halogen headlamps and fog lamps. (Saturn)

Chapter 51
Lamps, Lighting Circuits, Wiring, Horns, Wipers, and Washers

After studying this chapter, you will be able to:

- Explain how the complete automobile lighting circuit is divided into individual circuits and a common ground.
- State functions of electronic headlight dimming devices and headlight delay systems.
- Give service tips on headlamp and bulb replacement.
- Describe headlight aiming procedures.
- Explain wire gauge numbering system.
- Tell how the horn circuit operates and what tests and adjustments can be made.
- List the different types of wiper motor construction.
- Describe how the washer system works.

Lamps and Lighting Circuits

Modern automobiles are loaded with ***lamps.*** A typical, fully equipped, four door sedan has more than 70 interior and exterior lamps. They range from a miniature indicator lamp of .15 candle power to a backup lamp of 32 candle power.

In current draw, automobile lighting ranges from about .27 amp for a rear window defogger switch lamp to over 5 amps for a sealed beam (unit) headlamp or composite (reflector-lens-bulb) headlamp. See Figure 51-1.

The automobile ***lighting circuit*** includes the battery, frame, all the lights, and various switches that control their use. The lighting circuit is known as the ***single wire system*** since it uses the car frame for the return.

The complete lighting circuit of the modern passenger car can be broken down into individual circuits, each having one or more lights and switches. See Figure 51-2. In each separate circuit, the lights are connected in parallel, and the controlling switch is in series between the group of lights and the battery.

The parking lights, for example, are connected in parallel and controlled by a single switch. In some installations, one switch controls the connection to the battery while a selector switch determines which of two circuits is energized. The headlights, with their upper and lower beams, are an example of this type of circuit.

In some instances, such as the courtesy lights, several switches may be connected in parallel so that any switch may be used to turn on the lights.

Main Lighting Switch

The ***main lighting switch*** (headlamp switch) is the heart of the lighting system. It controls the headlights, parking lights, side marker lights, taillights, license plate light, instrument panel lights, and interior lights. See Figure 51-3. Individual switches are provided for special purpose lights,

Figure 51-1. Flush-mounted, aerodynamic composite headlamps have a clear plastic lens bonded to a molded plastic reflector with a socket and replaceable bulb.

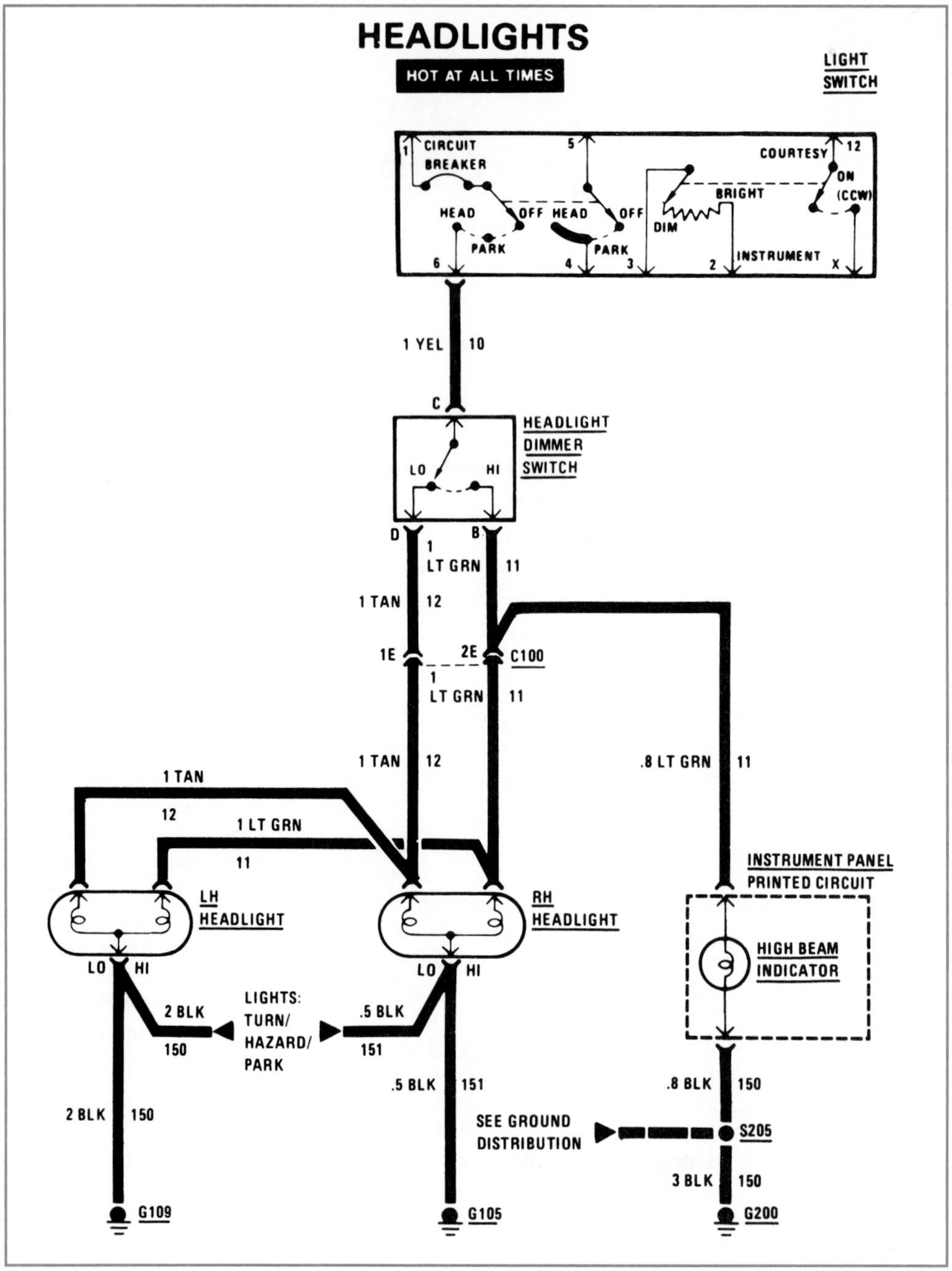

Figure 51-2. This electrical schematic provides the full details of a headlight circuit from the light switch to the headlamps. (Cadillac)

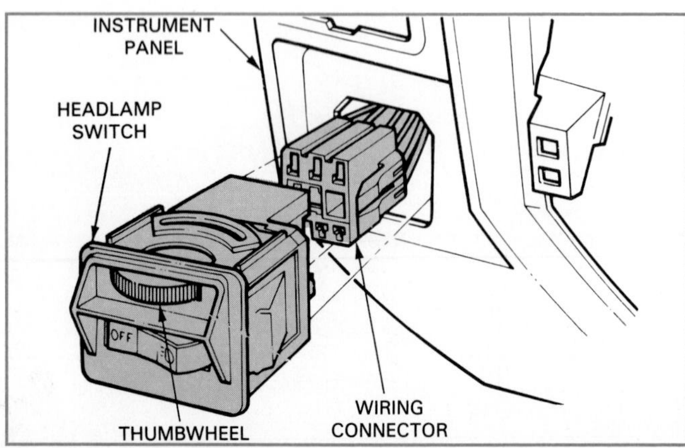

Figure 51-3. This headlamp switch has three positions, a built-in circuit breaker, and a thumb-wheel rheostat that controls the instrument panel lighting. (Ford)

such as directional signals, hazard warning flasher, backup lights, and courtesy lights. See Figure 51-4.

The main lighting switch may be of either the "push-pull" or "push-pull with rotary contact" type. A typical switch will have three positions: off, parking, and headlamps. Some switches also contain a rheostat to control the brightness of the instrument panel lights. The rheostat is operated by rotating the control knob, separating it from the push-pull action of the main lighting switch.

Fuses and Circuit Breakers

A ***fuse block,*** Figure 51-5, generally is connected between the battery and the main lighting switch. Usually, the fuse block is mounted on the driver's side of the firewall.

When a short circuit or overload occurs in a circuit, the fuse burns out, Figure 51-6, and opens that circuit so no

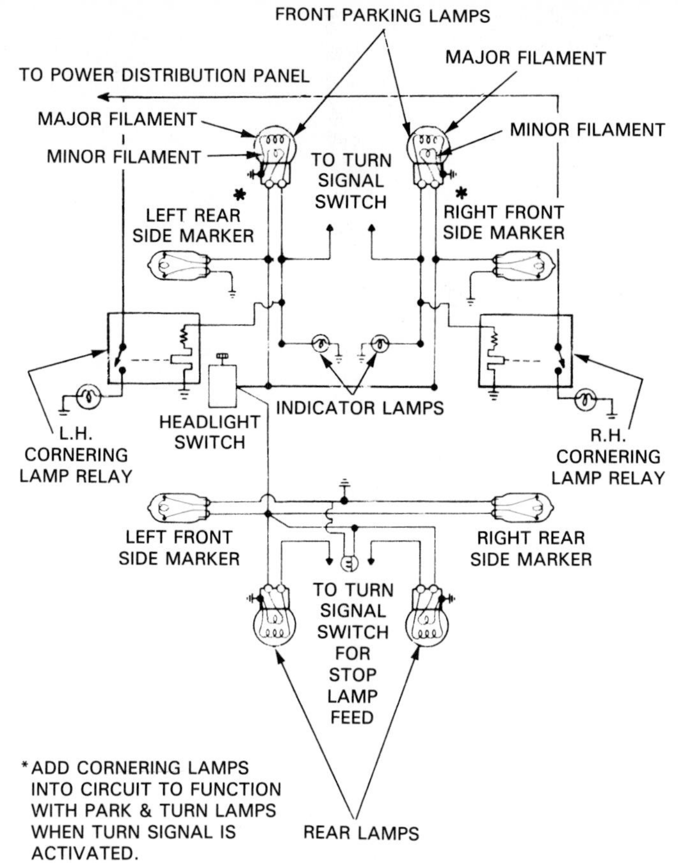

Figure 51-4. The headlight switch also controls other front, rear, and interior lighting. Turn signal lamps, indicator lamps, and cornering lamps are operated by the turn signal switch. (Ford)

further damage will result. Excess current will open a circuit breaker's terminals, indicating there is something wrong in that circuit. The circuit breaker will remain open until the trouble is corrected.

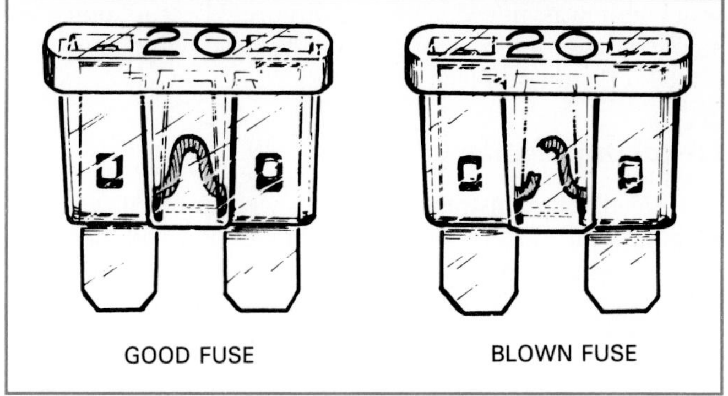

Figure 51-6. Fuse blocks on most cars contain miniaturized fuses with blade-type terminals for increased circuit protection and greater reliability. (Buick)

Headlamp Types

A conventional ***sealed beam headlamp*** incorporates one or two filaments (thread-like conductors), a reflector, and a lens in an airtight optical assembly. The filaments are correctly focused in relation to the reflector and lens at the time of manufacture.

All sealed beam headlamps are either round or rectangular. Number 1 is embossed on round sealed beam units having a single filament: 1A appears on rectangular units with a single filament. Number 2 is embossed on round units having two filaments; 2A appears on rectangular units with two filaments.

Basically, single filament sealed beam units are used in four-lamp systems to provide the principal portion of the upper beam (distant illumination). Two filament units, on the other hand, are used in four-lamp systems to provide the lower beam (road ahead illumination) and a secondary portion of the upper beam. Two type 2 or 2A double filament sealed beam units are used in two-lamp systems.

In a variation of the conventional built-in filament type of sealed beam headlamp, the ***halogen bulb*** sealed

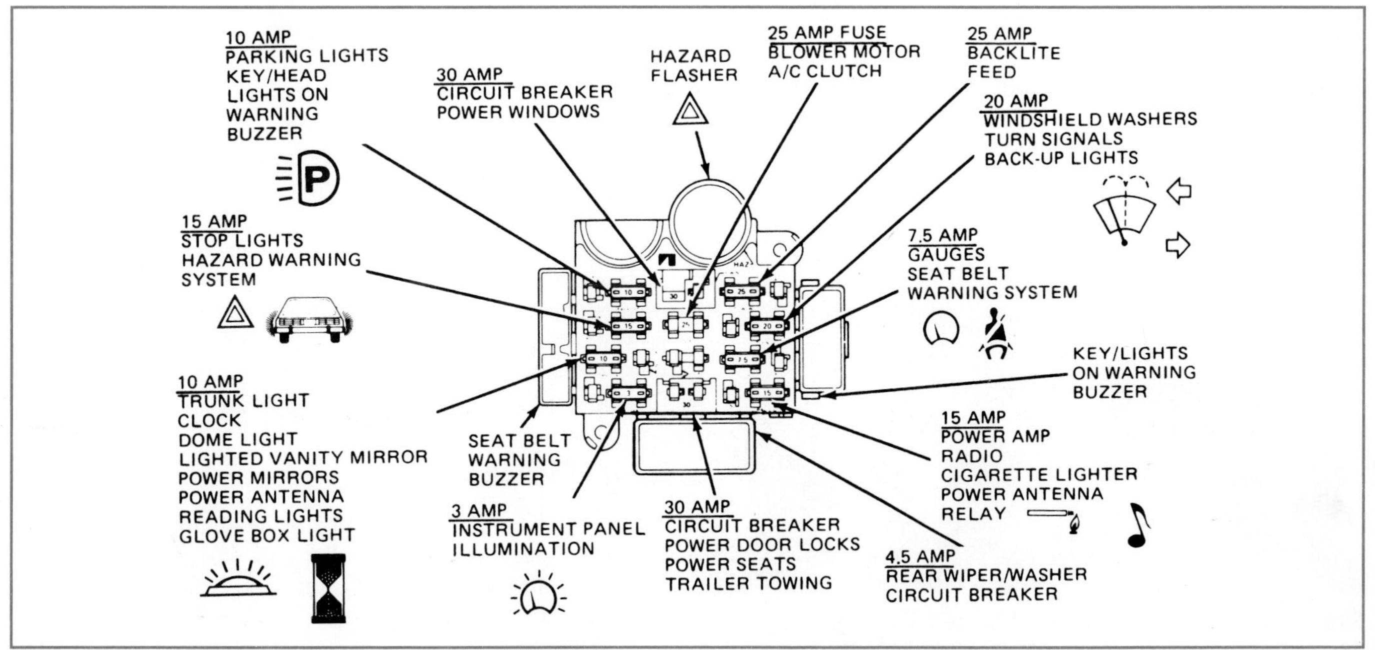

Figure 51-5. A fuse block locates fuses, circuit breakers, and flashers on a single, easily accessible panel. (Chrysler)

beam unit was introduced. See Figure 51-7. A tungsten-halogen inner bulb is supported by lead wires inside a sealed reflector and lens assembly.

Headlamp Construction

Headlamp construction has changed in recent years in keeping with modern vehicle exterior design and electrical power demands. Aerodynamic styling to reduce high speed drag requires flush-mounted headlamps of a small vertical dimension. Therefore, rectangular low-profile headlamps, Figure 51-8, became the popular choice of design engineers.

The quest for reduced aerodynamic drag also resulted in the introduction of ***composite headlamps.*** See Figure 51-9. The composite headlamp is a reflector and lens system designed for a specific vehicle model and contoured to that vehicle's requirements. Separate replaceable halogen bulbs are used in composite headlamps. See Figure 51-10.

Concealed Headlamps

A long-standing method of reducing aerodynamic drag is by means of ***concealed headlamps.*** See Figure 51-11. With this setup, the driver can operate the car at higher speeds in daylight and experience minimum drag. Movable doors that conceal the headlamps close to present flush fitting sheet metal to reduce air resistance in the headlamp area.

Most concealed headlamp doors, Figure 51-11, are electrically operated. A single motor and gear box power two drive shafts that open and close the doors.

Figure 51-7. The small, rectangular halogen headlamp on the left provides the same lighting characteristics as larger lamp on the right. The smaller unit allows a low, aerodynamic front-end design. (Chrysler)

Figure 51-8. Low-profile, flush-mounted, rectangular headlamps provide an aerodynamic design that reduces a vehicle's coefficient of drag.

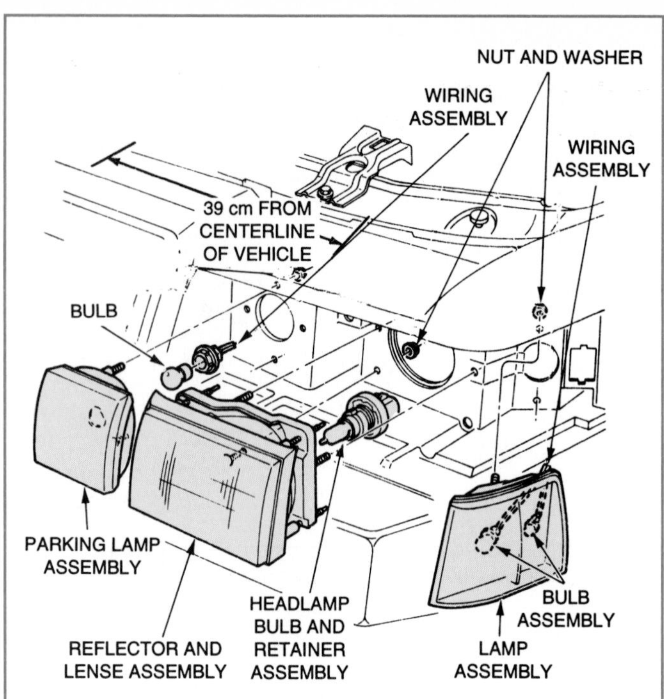

Figure 51-9. Composite headlamps utilize a reflector and lens assembly and a separate bulb. Replacing the bulb does not require re-aiming of headlamp. (Ford)

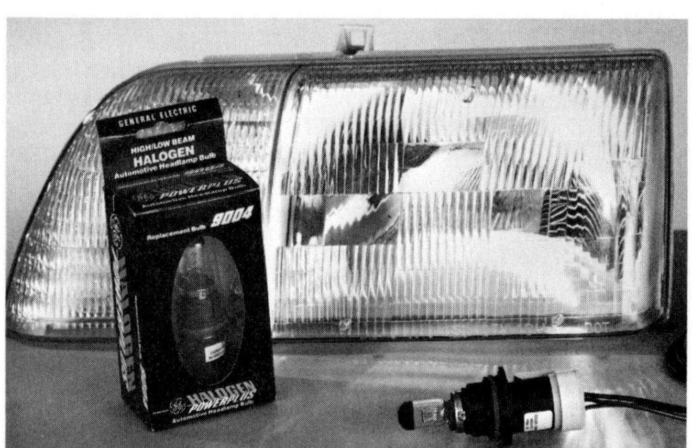

Figure 51-10. A replacement halogen bulb and retaining ring assembly is pictured with its composite reflector and lens assembly. (General Electric Co.)

Some car makers installed a concealed headlamp door system powered by intake manifold vacuum. In one such system, the headlamps were fitted in a barrel housing that pivoted into position when the linkage system was actuated by power cylinder push rods. A relay valve controlled the vacuum to the power cylinders. A manual valve was provided so the doors could be opened in emergency situations.

Lamp Switches

Sealed beam and composite headlamps provide the choice of driving with the help of ***low beams*** or ***high beams.*** A ***dimmer switch,*** Figure 51-12, permits selection of the required headlight beam.

When the main lighting switch completes the circuit to the headlamps, the low beam lights the way for city driving

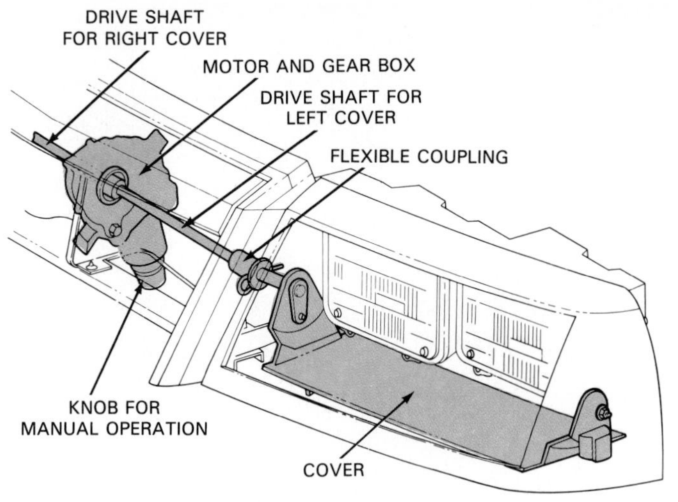

Figure 51-11. Concealed headlamps provide better aerodynamics and improved appearance. A manual override can be used to open headlamp doors in the event of an electrical failure. (Chrysler)

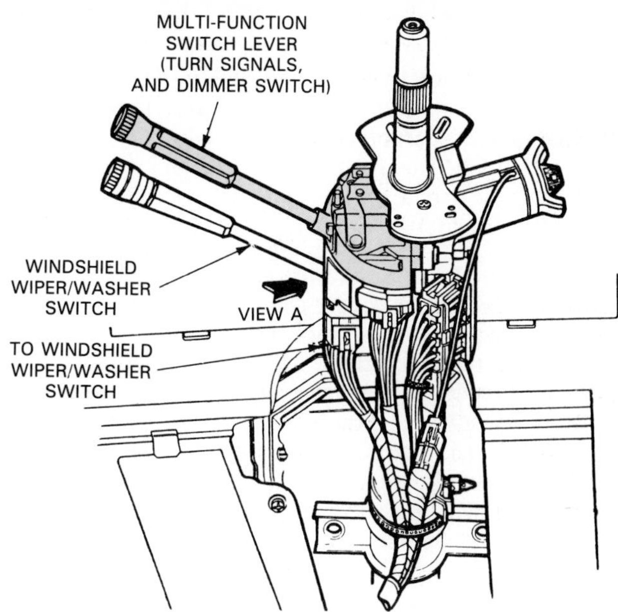

Figure 51-12. A dimmer switch for controlling headlight high or low beam selection usually is incorporated into the multi-function switch lever. (Ford)

and for use when meeting oncoming traffic on the highway. When the dimmer switch is actuated, the single filament headlamps go on, along with the high beam of the two filament headlamps. The next actuation of the dimmer switch returns the headlighting system to low beams only on the two filament lamps.

Some cars are equipped with an electronic headlight dimming device. This device automatically switches the headlights from high beam to low beam in response to light from an approaching vehicle or light from the taillight of a vehicle being overtaken.

One ***automatic headlamp dimmer*** utilizes a sensor-amplifier unit, a high-low beam relay, a dimmer switch, a driver sensitivity control, and wiring harnesses. See Figure 51-13. The sensor-amplifier is used to operate the high-low

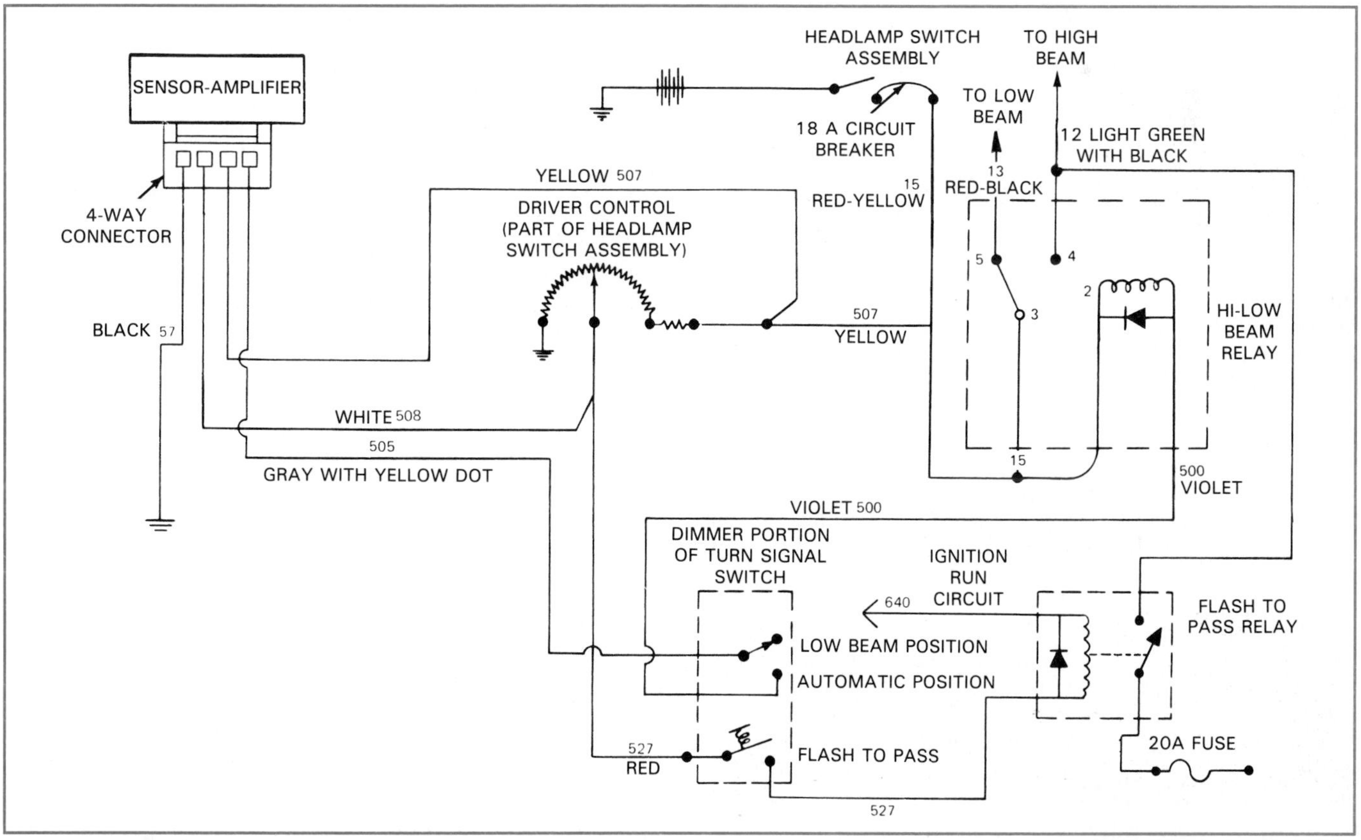

Figure 51-13. Circuit diagram of a typical automatic headlamp dimmer illustrates the system in the low beam or automatic off position. (Ford)

beam power relay for switching headlight beams. The relay has heavy-duty contacts to handle the switching actions.

The dimmer switch in the automatic headlamp dimming system is a special override type. It is located in the steering column as part of a combination dimmer, horn, and turn signal switch. The override action occurs when a slight pull toward the driver on the multi-function switch lever provides high beam headlights regardless of the amount of light on the sensor-amplifier.

Headlamp Delay Systems

Headlamp delay systems (Autolamp, Twilight Sentinel, etc.) automatically control headlamp operation after the ignition switch and main lighting switch are turned off. See Figure 51-14. The system, controlled by the driver, provides a lights-on situation on a time-delay basis so that the occupants will have the convenience of headlighting when leaving the vehicle. The system automatically delays switching off the headlamps for a period of time preselected by the driver (up to 4 1/2 min., depending on the type of system).

In addition, the system also can be "switched" to a light sensitive, automatic on-off control of the headlamps and other exterior lamps. A light sensitive photocell is mounted in an area exposed to outside light. With the main lighting switch off and the automatic control on, the system will turn on the headlamps when natural outside light diminishes.

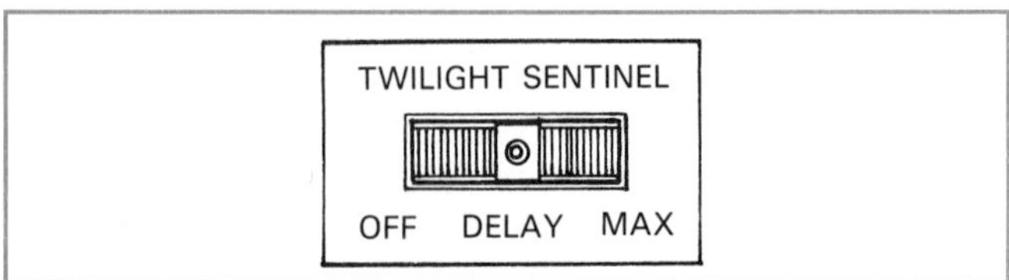

Figure 51-14. The convenience system automatically controls the operation of the exterior lights according to the amount of ambient light present. Also for convenience, the headlamp delay system will keep lights on for a set time after the ignition is turned off. (Cadillac)

Fog Lamps

Fog lamps are gaining renewed popularity, both in original equipment and aftermarket installations. See Figure 51-15. Standard equipment lamps generally are built into the front bumper or suspended below the bumper, Figure 51-16. Aftermarket fog lamps are available in kits that include lamps, halogen bulbs, impact resistant plastic covers, and a prewired harness with inline fuse holder and switch.

Direction Signal Switch

The ***direction signal switch,*** Figure 51-17, is installed just below the hub of the steering wheel. A manually controlled lever projecting from the switch permits the driver to signal the direction of the turn about to be made. Moving the switch handle down will light the "turn signal" lamps on the left front and left rear of the car, signaling a left turn. Moving the switch upward will light the turn signal lamps on the right (front and rear), signaling a right turn. With the

Figure 51-15. Fog lamps are factory installed on some cars and are either built into or suspended below the front bumper.

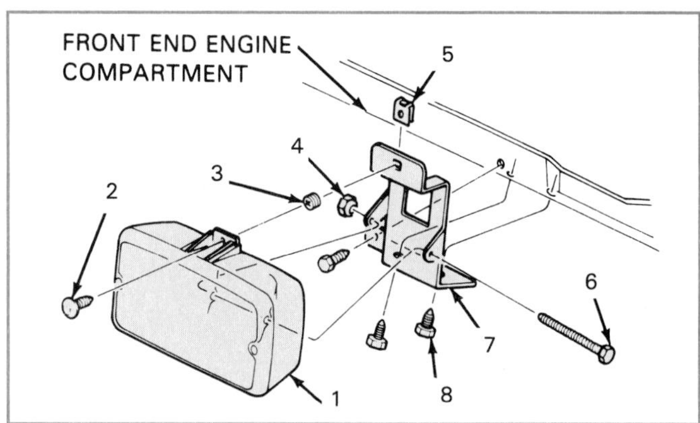

Figure 51-16. Detail of a suspended fog lamp mounting is shown. 1–Lamp assembly. 2–Screw. 3–Spring. 4/5–Nuts. 6–Screw. 7–Bracket. 8–Screw assembly. (Cadillac)

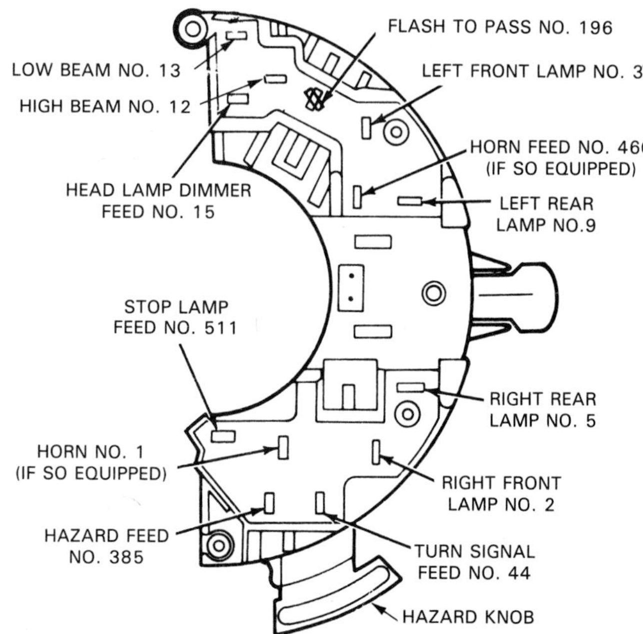

Figure 51-17. This direction signal switch is part of a multi-function switch assembly that includes the headlamp dimmer and hazard flasher switches. (Ford)

switch in a position to indicate a turn, lights are alternately turned on and off by a ***turn signal flasher,*** Figure 51-18.

Incorporated in the direction (turn) signal switch is the ***lane change switch mechanism.*** This feature provides the driver the opportunity to signal a lane change by holding the turn lever against a detent, then releasing it to cancel the signal immediately after the maneuver is completed.

The ***hazard warning flasher*** is also associated with the turn signal switch. This flasher actuates the hazard warning system. When the control knob is operated, all front and rear turn signal lamps light and flash simultaneously.

The hazard warning switch control knob generally is mounted on the upper portion of the steering column. The flasher usually is located under the instrument panel on or near the fuse block.

Stoplight Switch

In order to signal a stop, a brake-pedal operated ***stoplight switch*** is provided to operate the vehicle's stop lamps. In addition to lighting the conventional rear lamps, the switch also operates the center high-mounted stop lamp, Figure 51-19, that became mandatory on later models.

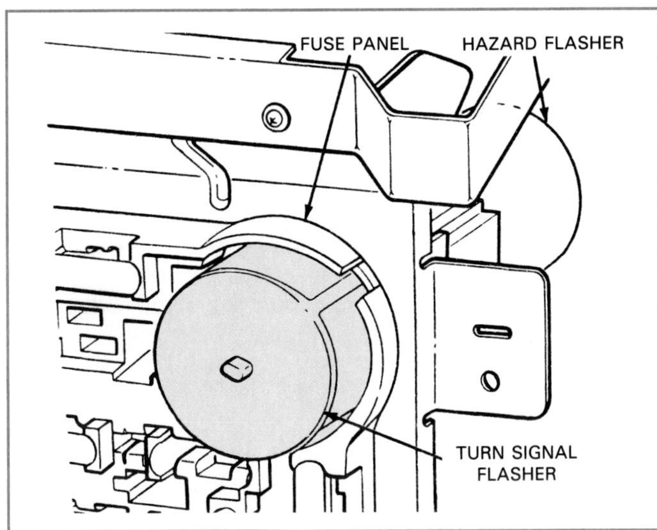

Figure 51-18. The flasher that controls on/off operation of the turn signal lamps is often located in the fuse panel. (Ford)

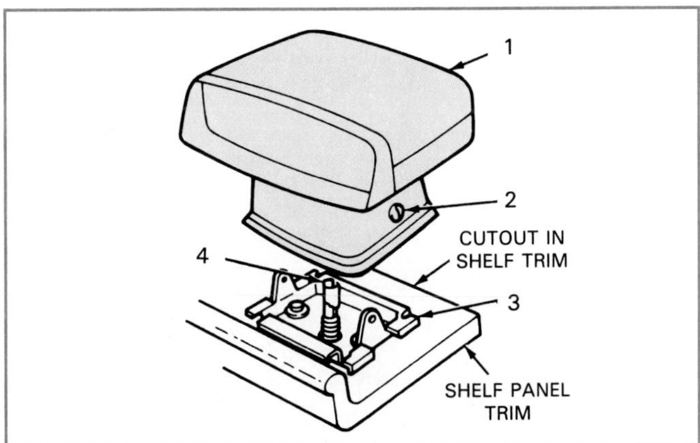

Figure 51-19. Detail drawing shows high-mounted stop lamp in the rear shelf panel trim: 1–Stop lamp assembly. 2–Attaching screw. 3–Mounting bracket. 4–Wiring harness. (Cadillac)

A typical stoplight switch and its location are shown in Figure 51-20. Note that cruise control equipped vehicles of this make also utilize a vacuum release valve. In this case, both the vacuum release valve and the stoplight switch are actuated by movement of the brake pedal.

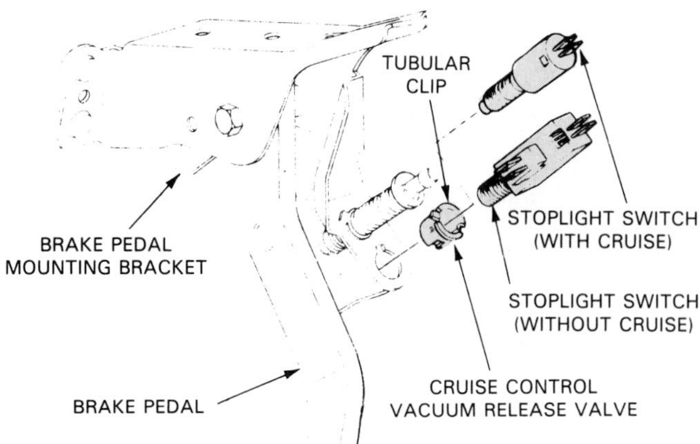

Figure 51-20. Two types of brake-pedal-actuated stop light switches are depicted. Note that in both applications, the stop light switch is installed in the lower hole in the bracket. (Cadillac)

Lamp Service

Short life and frequent burning out of lamps usually results from excessive voltage. This, in turn, may result from loose or corroded electrical connections in the battery circuit, or the charging rate may be too high.

Lighting outages in pairs (headlamps, parking lamps, tail lamps) could be caused by a defective main lighting switch. Use an ohmmeter to test the continuity of the circuit involved. Use the meter probes to check for an "open" at the switch terminals for the circuit being tested. See Figure 51-21.

Dim lights result from low voltage, which may be caused by loose or corroded terminals in the lamp circuit. Possibly, the charging rate may be too low or the battery may be defective.

The wiring in lighting circuits should be inspected periodically for loose or corroded connections, or for chafed insulation. The connections at junction blocks and plug-in connectors should be carefully checked. Switches, bulb sockets, lamp shells, reflectors, and lenses should be inspected for loose mounting and corrosion.

In order to overcome the effects of rust, it frequently is necessary to solder a lead to a lamp socket case and ground the other end of the lead on the frame.

The voltage drop between the various lamp sockets (not the holder, reflector, or shell) and ground should be measured with a low-reading voltmeter. Each light should be turned on when making this test for high resistance at ground connections. If any reading is obtained on the voltmeter, it is an indication that there is resistance present. The shell and socket must be thoroughly cleaned to obtain a good electrical connection.

Another test that should be made is checking voltage drop between the battery and each individual lamp. To make this test, connect a long positive lead of a voltmeter to the positive battery terminal. Attach a test probe to the other lead of the voltmeter. Turn on the lights and touch the

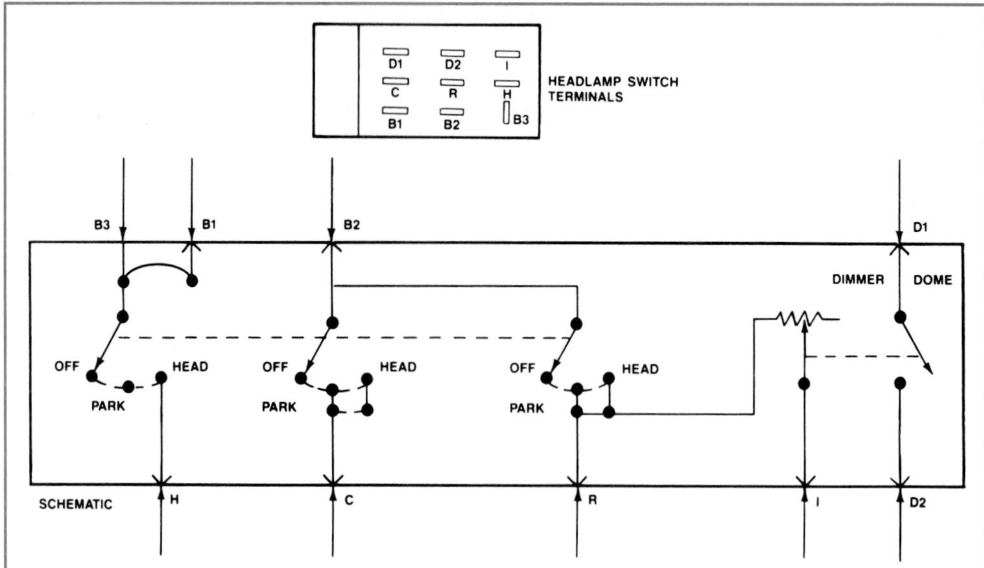

Figure 51-21. This service manual circuit drawing of a headlamp switch and terminal locations can be used as a guide for tests for open circuits. H–Headlamp. C–Chime voice alert. R–Park lamp. I–Panel lamp dimmer. D1/D2–Dome lamp dimmer. (Ford)

voltmeter probe to the insulated terminal of each lamp. The voltage drop should be less than 0.6 volt.

If voltage drop is greater than 0.6 volt, follow the circuit back through the switch to locate the part of the circuit in which the loss occurs. If the loss in voltage is due to a defective part, it should be replaced. Usually, the loss will be found at a terminal or plug-in connector. Cleaning and tightening will overcome the trouble.

Replacing Sealed Beam Units

To replace a sealed beam headlamp:

1. Remove the screws that secure the headlamp door (bezel), then remove the door. See Figure 51-22.
2. On some models, unhook the springs that hold the retaining ring in position.
3. Remove the screws that hold the retaining ring to the shell assembly (mounting ring). Do not turn the adjusting screws.
4. Remove retaining ring.
5. Pull the lamp forward and remove the electrical connector.
6. Remove the lamp.
7. Reverse this procedure to install the new headlamp.

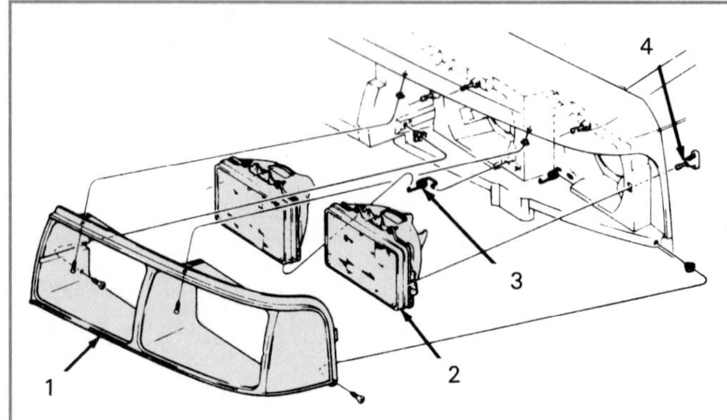

Figure 51-22. Exploded view shows sealed beam headlamp mounting details. 1–Bezel assembly. 2–Headlamp assembly. 3–Spring. 4–Adjuster assembly. (Oldsmobile)

Replacing Halogen Bulbs

When servicing composite headlamps for a halogen bulb burnout, handle the bulb by its plastic base only. Halogen bulbs contain gas under pressure and may shatter if mishandled or dropped. After removing the burned out bulb, immediately install a new bulb in the socket to keep contaminants from entering the headlamp body. Also, do not energize the halogen bulb until it is safely contained in the headlamp body.

To replace a halogen bulb:

1. Place the main lighting switch in the off position.
2. Remove the electrical connector from the bulb.
3. Unlock the bulb retaining ring and remove the ring and bulb from the socket, Figure 51-23.
4. Position a replacement halogen bulb with the flat side of the plastic base up and lock the retaining ring in place.
5. Install the electrical connector on the bulb base.
6. Turn on the main lighting switch and check headlamp operation.

Replacing Front, Side, and Rear Bulbs

Bulb replacement, other than headlamps, is a simple operation. Some lamp assemblies require removal of the bezel and lens for access to the defective bulb (fog lamps, parking lamps, backup lamps). Others are accessible from the inside rear of the particular lamp assembly (front side

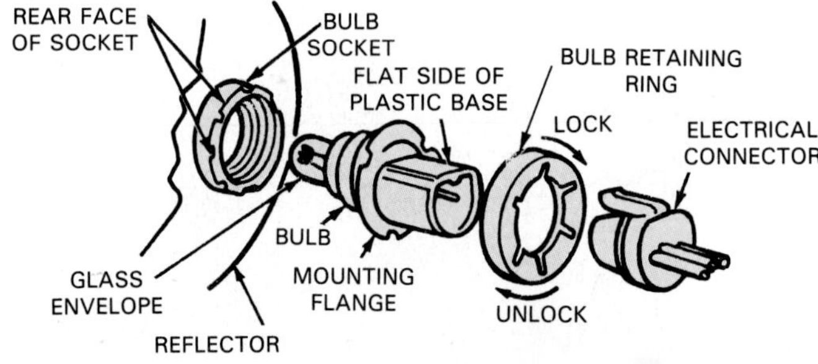

Figure 51-23. Exploded view details order of position of a composite headlamp socket, replaceable headlamp bulb, bulb retaining ring, and electrical terminal. (Ford)

marker lamps, cornering lamps, tail lamps, stop lamps). See Figure 51-24.

Many of the front, side, and rear lamp assemblies are fitted with halogen bulbs. See Figure 51-25. Therefore, the previously stated handling caution should be observed.

Aiming Headlights

To facilitate aiming the headlights, adjusting screws are provided. In most cases, the screws for vertical aiming are at the top of the headlamp, Figure 51-26. The horizontal aim adjusting screws are at the side. The aim adjusting screws should not be turned unless it is necessary to aim the headlights.

The three guide points formed in the front of the headlamp lens are used with ***mechanical aimers.*** See Figure 51-27. The equipment is provided with an accurate level, so it is not necessary for the vehicle to be on a level floor.

To check headlight aim:

1. Calibrate the aimers according to the equipment manufacturer's directions.
2. Install the proper set of adaptors on the aimers.
3. Mount the headlamps so that the steel inserts on the adaptors contact the guide points on the headlamp lens.

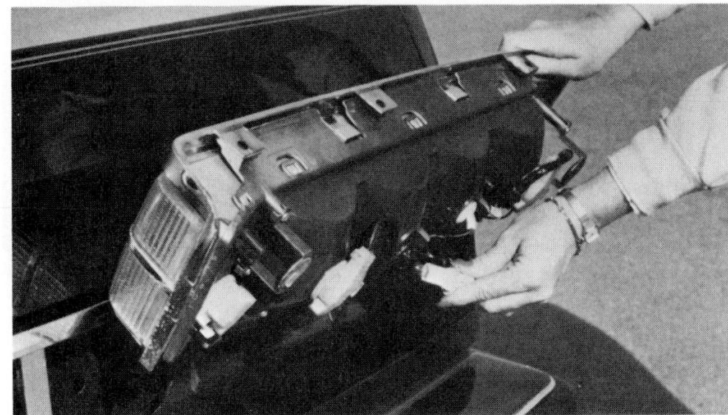

Figure 51-24. Many bulbs can generally be replaced from the rear of the lamp assembly by means of a snap-in socket arrangement. A hinged tail lamp panel is shown. (Buick)

Figure 51-25. A "family" of halogen bulbs for signal lamps, backup lamps, high-mount stop lamps, etc., is pictured. (General Electric Corp.)

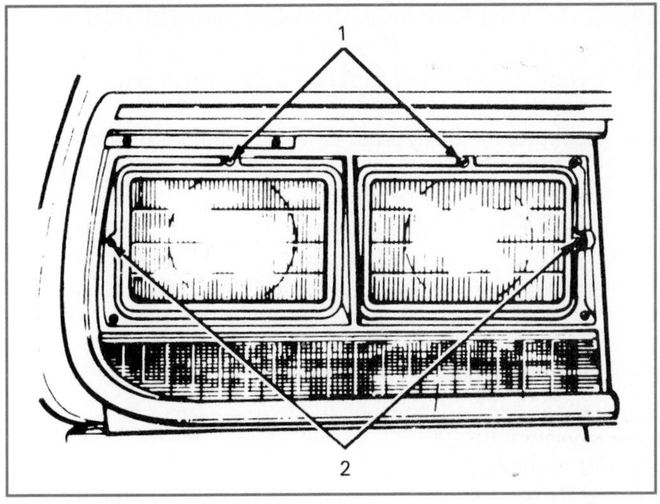

Figure 51-26. Adjust headlight aim by turning the horizontal and/or vertical adjusting screw in the lamp housing: 1–Above the sealed beam unit. 2 –At side of the sealed beam unit. (Chrysler)

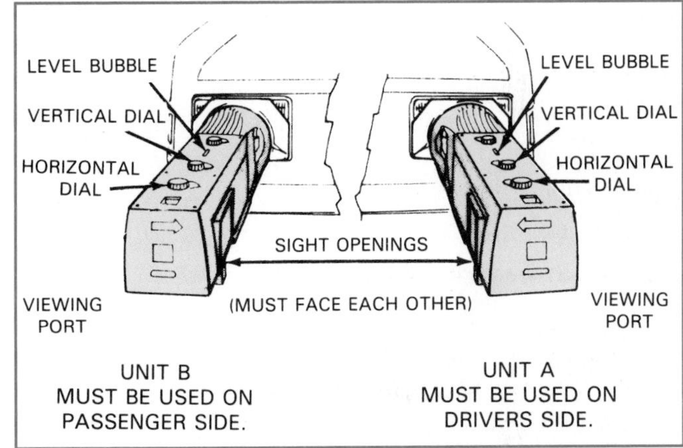

Figure 51-27. Calibrate mechanical aimers and then position them on opposite headlamps. The sight openings must face each other. Set zero on the horizontal dial. (Chrysler)

4. Set zero on the horizontal dial.
5. Check the split image and target line in the viewing port, Figure 51-28. If the image is aligned, horizontal aim is correct.
6. If the image is misaligned, turn the adjusting screw on the side of headlamp to align the image on the target line. Make the final adjustment in the clockwise direction.
7. Repeat steps 4, 5, and 6 on the opposite headlamp.
8. Set zero on the vertical dial. If the level bubble is centered, the vertical aim is correct.

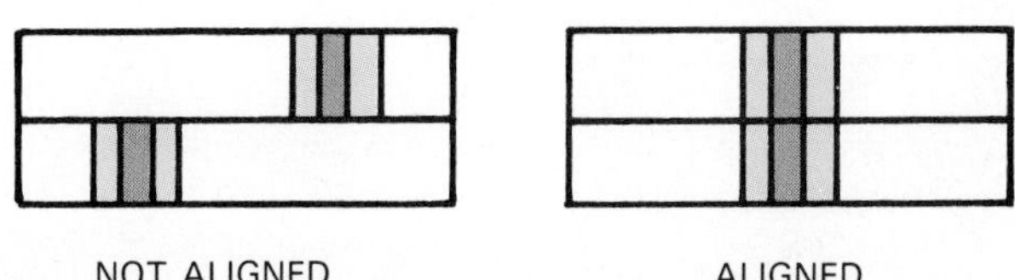

NOT ALIGNED ALIGNED

Figure 51-28. If the split image in the viewing port is not aligned, turn the horizontal adjusting screw on the headlamp until the image aligns on the target line. This will provide correct horizontal aim. (Chrysler)

9. If the level bubble is off center, turn the vertical adjusting screw at the top of the headlamp until the level bubble is centered, Figure 51-29. Finish with a clockwise turn.
10. Recheck the horizontal aim and readjust if necessary.
11. On four-headlamp systems, repeat the aiming process on the other two headlamps.

Aiming by Wall Layout. Headlights also may be aimed by using a wall layout. In using this setup, the floor must be level and tires correctly inflated. Draw a line on the floor parallel to the wall and exactly 25 ft. from it. Position the car at right angles to the wall with the headlamps right over the line marked on the floor. Then, referring to Figures 51-30 and 51-31, proceed as follows:

1. Measure the height of the center of the headlamps from the floor.
2. Transfer this measurement to the wall and draw a horizontal line.
3. Measure the width of the windshield and rear window. Find the center and mark it with tape.
4. Sight through the rear window, aligning the tapes and establishing a vertical centerline on the wall layout.
5. Add a line to the wall layout in line with the vertical centerline of the left headlamp.
6. Add a line to the wall layout in line with the vertical centerline of the right headlamp.
7. Turn on the headlights and check the high-intensity zones against those shown in Figure 51-30 (low beam) and Figure 51-31 (high beam).

Figure 51-29. With zero set on the vertical dial, turn the vertical adjusting screw on the headlamp until the level bulb is centered. This will provide correct vertical aim. (PPG Industries, Inc.)

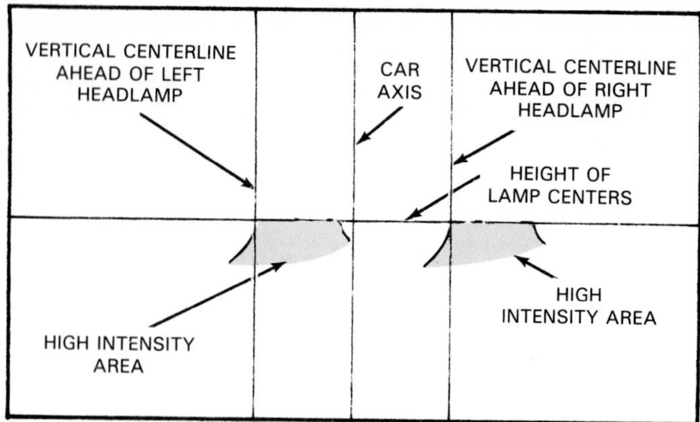

Figure 51-30. Create the wall layout as indicated. With the vehicle on a level floor 25 ft. from the wall, correct high intensity area of the low beam should appear as shown. (Chrysler)

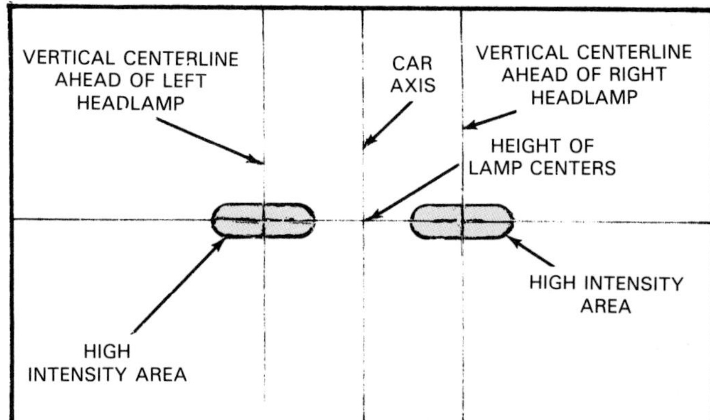

Figure 51-31. With the vehicle in place for aiming the headlights by means of a wall layout, the correct high intensity area of the high beam should appear as shown. (Chrysler)

Wires and Cables

Wires and ***cables*** are conductors of electricity. Usually made of annealed copper, they are used to carry electricity to the various electrical devices and equipment on passenger cars and trucks.

These wires and cables must be the correct size for the application and have proper insulation. If the wire or cable is too small in cross section or too long for its size, its resistance will be too great and valuable voltage will be lost. This, in turn, will result in poor operation of the electrical device in that circuit.

Lighting Wire Sizes

Wire size and ***length*** determines the resistance of the wire. Wire and cable sizes are expressed by a ***gauge number,*** which indicates the cross-sectional area of the conductor. Note in the Wire Gauge Table in Figure 51-32 that the cross-sectional area of the wires is given in metric size (mm^2) and in circular mils. The diameter is given in decimals of an inch. A ***circular mil*** is a unit of area equal to the area of a circle one mil in diameter. A ***mil*** is a unit of length equal to .001 in. Also note in the table that the larger the diameter of the wire or cable, the smaller the gauge size number.

CONDUCTORS			
SAE Wire Size (gauge)	Metric Wire Size (mm²)	Minimum Cross-sectional Area (circular mils)	Diameter (in.)
20	0.5	1072	.032
18	0.8	1537	.040
16	1.0	2336	.051
14	2.0	3702	.064
12	3.0	5833	.081
10	5.0	9343	.102
8	8.0	14810	.129
6	13.0	25910	.162
4	19.0	37360	.204
2	32.0	62450	.258
1	40.0	77790	.289
0	50.0	98980	.325

Figure 51-32. Wire and cable size is given in gauge number, metric area, circular mils, and diameter in decimals of an inch.

Cables are made up of a number of strands of wire. The cross-sectional area of a cable is equal to the circular mil area of a single strand times the number of strands. Special gauges are available for measuring the gauge size of wires and cables. See Figure 51-33. Many multi-purpose electrician's pliers feature wire size holes for stripping, cutting, and crimping operations.

Remember, the resistance of a length of wire or cable decreases as its cross section increases. Therefore, it is advisable to use wire of relatively large cross section. In general, nothing smaller than No. 16 gauge wire should be used for lights of low candle power. For headlights and back up lights, and other lights of high candle power, wire of still larger gauge is required.

When comparing cables, consider that the external diameter of the insulated wire or cable has nothing to do with its current-carrying capacity. Thick insulation will make a small gauge wire look much larger. It is important that only the size of the metal conductors are compared.

Low-tension Primary Cables

Battery Cables are ***low-tension primary cables*** that connect the battery to the rest of the starting and charging circuits. Because a starting motor cranking an engine will draw approximately 200 amps of current, the battery cables must be of sufficient size to carry such heavy current.

Battery-to-starter and battery-to-ground cables range from gauge size No. 6 through No. 4/0. See Figure 51-34. Passenger car battery cables usually are No. 1 or No. 2 gauge. The insulation may be thermoplastic, synthetic rubber, or cross-linked polyurethane.

Because the cables are close to the battery and could corrode, it is important that the cables make good electrical contact with the cable clamps. Likewise, clamps must make good electrical contact with the battery posts. Any looseness or corrosion between the cable and its clamp, or between cable clamp and battery, will result in high resistance and consequent voltage drop.

High resistance between cables and terminals can be checked easily by means of a voltmeter. With a current of approximately 20 amps flowing, connect one lead of a voltmeter to the cable. Connect the other lead to the other cable terminal. Voltage drop in the starter-to-ground circuit should not be more than 0.1 volt.

Low-tension primary cables other than battery cables range from gauge size No. 20 through No. 4. See Figure 51-32. Low-tension primary cable insulation could be thermoplastic, thermoplastic with a braided cover, synthetic rubber, or cross-linked polyurethane.

Resistor Ignition Cable

To reduce interference with radio and TV reception, automotive ignition systems are provided with resistance in the secondary circuit. ***Resistor spark plugs*** or special ***resistor ignition cable*** may be used. In order to work efficiently in modern ignition systems, it is essential that the resistor ignition cable is capable of producing a specified designed resistance. Currently, SAE (Society of Automotive Engineers) specifications for resistor ignition cable call for 3000 to 7000 ohms per foot for low resistance (LR) cable and 6000 to 12,000 ohms per foot for high resistance (HR) cable.

In addition, resistor cables must be covered with ample insulation that will withstand heat, cold, moisture, oil, grease, chafing, and corona. ***Corona*** is an electrical phenomenon not readily visible, but it rapidly deteriorates rubber. The passage of high-tension electricity through a cable builds up a surrounding electrical field. The electrical field

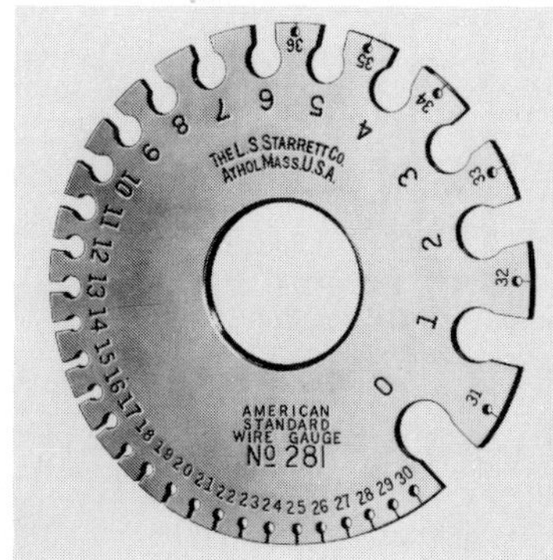

Figure 51-33. A typical wire gauge is pictured. A wire being checked is placed in various gauge openings until a "proper fit" is obtained. The openings are coded in wire gauge sizes. (L.S. Starrett Co.)

BATTERY CABLES			
SAE Wire Size (gauge)	Metric Wire Size (mm²)	Minimum Cross-sectional Area (circular mils)	Diameter (in.)
6	13.0	25910	.162
4	19.0	37360	.204
2	32.0	62450	.258
1	40.0	77790	.289
0	50.0	98980	.325
2/0	62.0	125100	.365
3/0	81.0	158600	.410
4/0	103.0	205500	.460

Figure 51-34. Battery cables are heavy gauge size. This chart covers wire gauge sizes from No. 6 through No. 4/0. Passenger cars generally use No. 1 or No. 2.

liberates oxygen in the surrounding air to form ozone, which will attack the rubber insulation if it is not properly protected. Ozone causes the rubber to deteriorate and lose its insulating qualities. Electrical losses result which, in turn, will seriously weaken the spark at the plug gap.

Service-wise, never pull on the resistor ignition cable and rubber boot when disconnecting the cable from the terminal of a spark plug. Rather grasp, twist, and lift the boot (and cable) from the plug. Also, never puncture the insulation of a resistor ignition cable when making a connection for timing an engine. The puncture probably would sever the conductor, and eventual failure would result.

When checking the condition of resistor ignition cables, carefully examine both the insulation and the terminals. Bend the cable to form a small circle, then note if any cracks appear in the insulation. Replace the set of cables if the insulation is cracked, dried out, brittle, or fails to meet resistance tests by ohmmeter. Resistor ignition cable is available in custom lengths designed for installation on specific makes and models of engines.

Before replacing resistor ignition cables, thoroughly clean each distributor cap socket. When installing the cables, be sure to push them to the bottom of the cap sockets. If not, the spark will jump the air gap and cause corrosion and burned contacts. Press the boots firmly in place over the towers of the distributor cap.

Care must be taken when replacing high-tension ignition cables to install them in their original position. Not only must they be connected to the correct spark plug, but they also must be placed in the correct slot in their respective brackets. If this is not done, cross firing will result and maximum power will not be attained.

Basically, the wires should be located in their brackets so that the cables for cylinders next in firing order are as far apart as possible. For example: if the firing order for a V-8 engine is 1-5-4-2-6-3-7-8, the cables for cylinders No. 4 and No. 2 should be separated as much as possible since cylinder No. 2 fires immediately after cylinder No. 4.

Wiring Harnesses and Connectors

The car manufacturers have made significant improvements in the durability and serviceability of engine and chassis electrical systems. They have designed and produced modular instrument panels or instrument clusters. They have installed halogen headlamps for 25 to 50 percent more light output. They made lamp sockets more durable, lamps longer lasting, and wire and cable insulation less affected by contaminants. They have made greater use of plastics to avoid rusting. They have provided multi-function switch levers for safety and convenience.

The car manufacturers have upgraded electrical wiring harnesses, harness routing systems, bulkhead connectors, and inline connectors. The harnesses and harness routing system used on many General Motors cars is shown in Figure 51-35. Typical harnesses include: engine, power distribution, air conditioning, body and chassis, front and rear lighting, instrument panel and interior lighting.

To complement the electrical wiring harnesses, the car manufacturers have devised systems of multi-pin bulkhead connectors and inline connectors that interconnect the major wiring harnesses. See Figure 51-36. Each connector can be disconnected to simplify testing and diagnosis.

Computers and Diagnostic Displays

Add to these electrical system advances increased use of ***on-board computers.*** Units such as Electronic Control Modules (ECM) accept inputs from various sensors, switches, and relays and provide outputs that control many electrical and electronic systems. Computers also supply information for instrument panel diagnostic displays. Full coverage of these complicated systems is beyond the scope of this text.

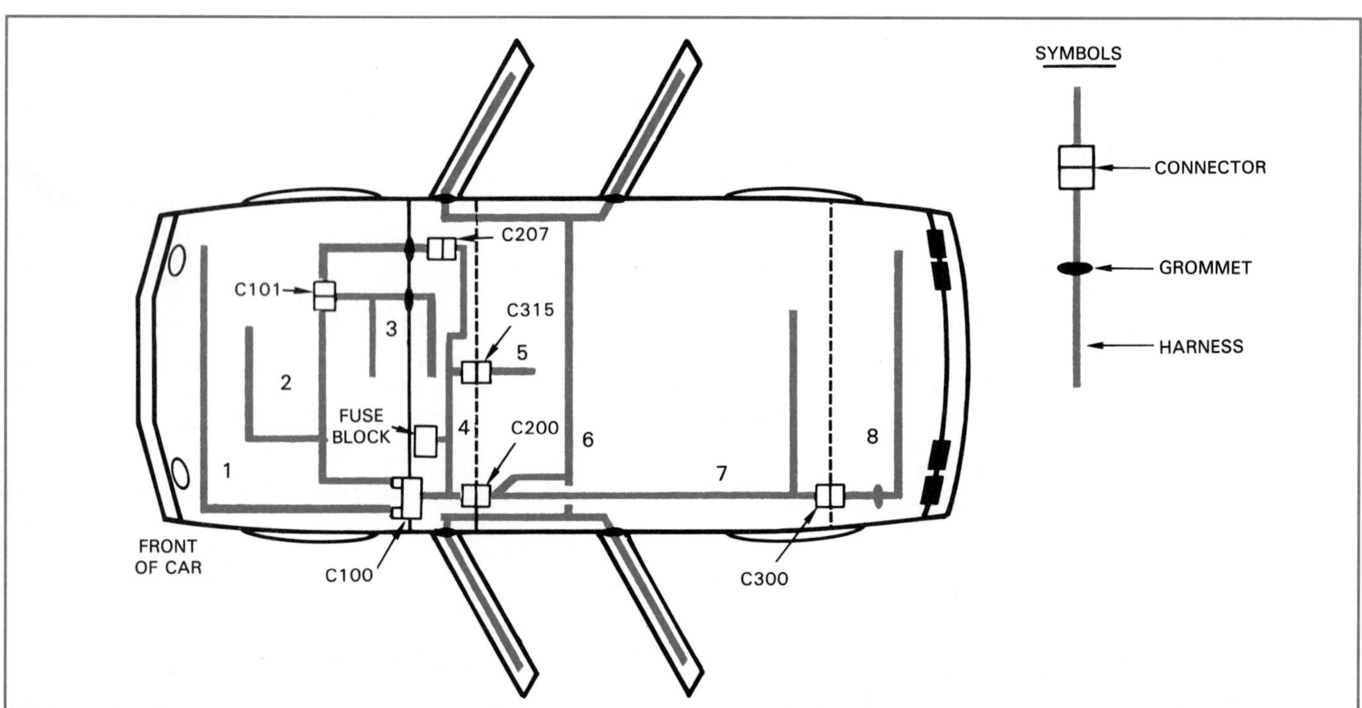

Figure 51-35. This diagram illustrates a typical electrical harness routing system and connectors. Harnesses include: 1–Forward lamp. 2–Engine. 3–Air conditioning. 4–Instrument panel. 5–Console. 6–Cross body. 7–Body front. 8–Body rear. (Cadillac)

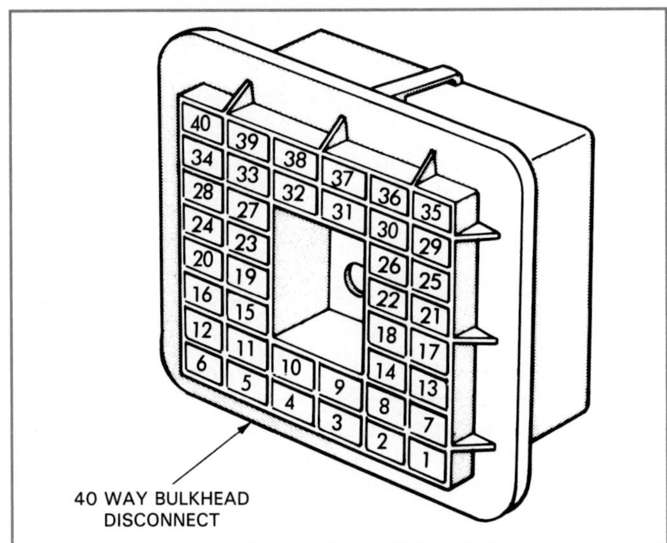

Figure 51-36. Car manufacturers' service manuals identify bulkhead connector cavities by number, circuit, and wire color codes. For example: 13–Left turn signal. 14–Right turn signal. 25–Parking lamps. 29–Headlamp low beam. 30–Headlamp high beam. (Chrysler)

To aid service personnel in understanding these systems, the car manufacturers provide hundreds of extra service manual pages of explanatory and diagnostic information, including:

- ***Electrical schematics***–Picture electrical current paths when the system is in proper operation, Figure 51-2 on page 682.
- ***Component location lists***–Give specific locations of parts of the circuit.
- ***System checks***–Tell how the circuit should be operated and what should occur when the system is in operation.
- ***Troubleshooting hints***–Provide tests and give suggested shortcuts for solving problems in a given circuit.
- ***System diagnosis***–Lists a step-by-step procedure designed to pin point the cause of a malfunction in a circuit.
- ***Circuit operation***–Describes circuit components and how the circuit works.
- ***Harness connector faces***–Show the cavity or terminal locations and wiring color codes and terminals to help locate test points.
- ***Harness routing views***–Show the routing of major wiring harnesses and the location of connectors. See Figure 51-35.

With modern technology shaping the design, construction, and operation of today's passenger cars, service technicians need to make a continuing study of latest automotive developments and service procedures. With this in mind, consider the car manufacturers' service manuals as "specialty tools" needed to meet and reach your automotive occupational goals.

Horns

Horns on passenger cars provide the driver with a means of sounding an audible warning signal. The horn electrical circuit generally includes the battery, fuse or fusible link, horn relay, horn(s), steering column wiring harness, horn switch, and body sheet metal. See Figure 51-37.

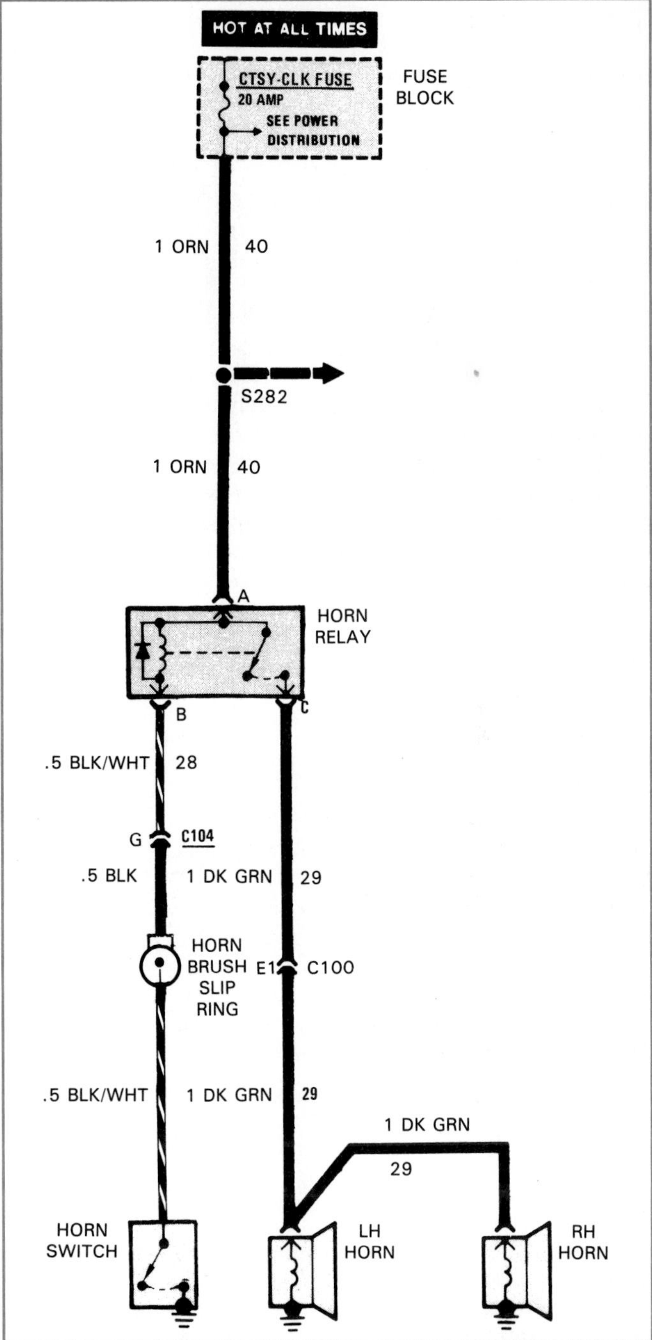

Figure 51-37. Typical horn electrical circuit is fed by a "hot" lead from the fuse block. Pressing the horn switch completes the ground circuit to the horn relay, where contacts close and current flows to the horn. (Pontiac)

Often, a cadmium plated screw is used to ground the horn to the body of the vehicle.

Horns usually are located in the forward part of the engine compartment, Figure 51-38, or in the front fender well. The horn switch is built into the steering wheel, Figure 51-39, or incorporated into the multi-function switch lever (also turn signals, dimmer switch).

Horn Relay and Fusible Link

Horns on passenger cars use an electromagnetically actuated diaphragm to produce a resonating air column (sound) in the horn projector. Horn operation requires

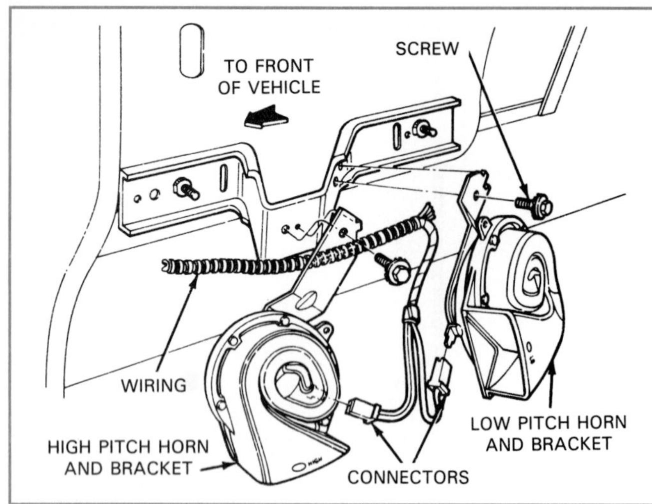

Figure 51-38. Horns are located in pairs at the front of a vehicle. They are usually grounded to the frame or body sheet metal. (Ford)

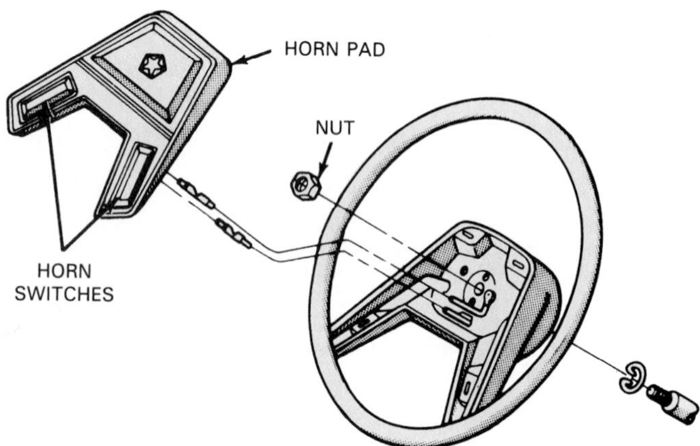

Figure 51-39. Some horn switches are built into a horn pad mounted on the steering wheel. Pressing the horn pad completes the horn circuit to ground. (Chrysler)

fairly high current (4.5 amps minimum), so a ***horn relay*** is used to make a more direct connection between the horn and battery. In that way, voltage drop is lessened and higher voltage is available for operating the horn diaphragm. Often, the horn circuit is fused.

In some cases, a ***fusible link*** is used in the main wiring harness just ahead of the horn relay. The fusible link is a protective device that consists of a smaller gauge wire that will "blow" if the horn circuit is grounded or overloaded. New links generally must be crimped or soldered in place, Figure 51-40.

Horn Troubleshooting

If a horn fails to sound when the switch is depressed, check the condition of the fuse or fusible link. Next, connect a jumper wire from the battery positive terminal to the horn terminal. If the horn still does not operate, provide a good ground for the horn. If the horn operates, the existing ground connection is at fault. Correct by removing the ground wire and establishing a good electrical connection to clean and shiny sheet metal. If necessary, replace the used screw with a cadmium plated screw.

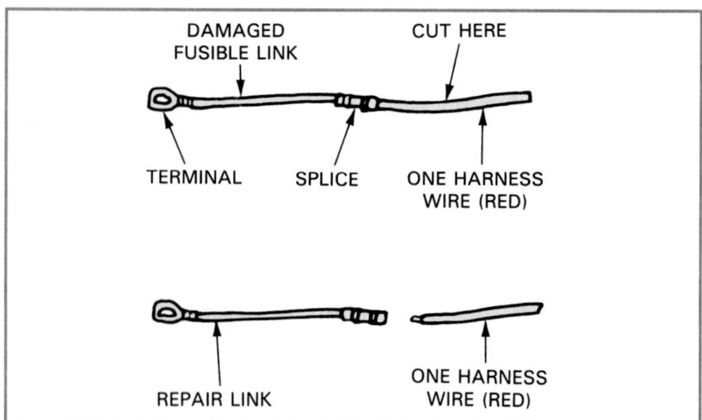

Figure 51-40. To replace a fusible link, cut off the damaged link beyond the splice, strip the wire, and install the repair link. Be sure to crimp the splice in two places. (Cadillac)

If the horn operated when the jumper wire was placed between the battery terminal and the horn terminal, perform the following procedure:

1. Connect a voltmeter and an ammeter to the horn and the battery.
2. If current reading is 20 amps or more, a short is indicated. Replace the horn.
3. If current reads zero amps, turn the horn adjusting screw, Figure 51-41, counterclockwise until the ammeter reads 4.5 to 5.5 amps at 11.5 to 12.5 volts. Note: Turn the adjusting screw only 1/10 of a turn at a time while observing changes in ammeter readings.
4. Clinch the horn housing metal against the adjusting screw to lock it in place.
5. If minimum amps adjustment cannot be reached, replace the horn.
6. If specified amps adjustment can be made, but the horn fails to operate, replace the horn.
7. Also check all mounting bolts and electrical connections to see that they are tight and inspect the condition of the horn circuit wiring.
8. If the horn fails to operate after taking preceding steps, substitute a known good horn relay for the old one and/or check the condition of the horn switch.

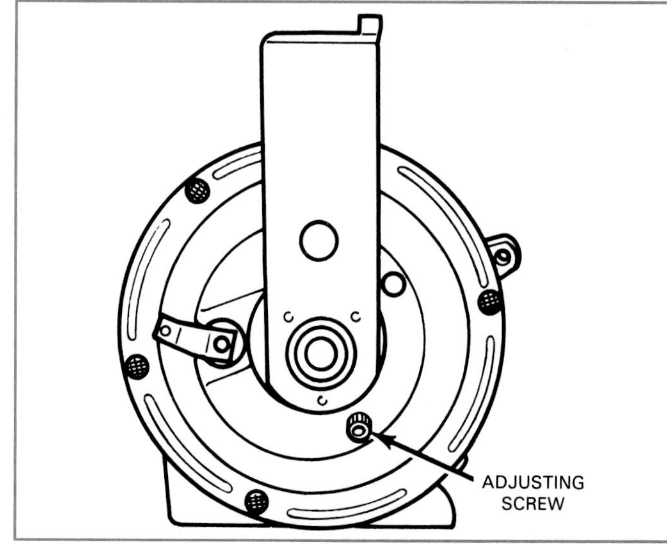

Figure 51-41. The horn adjusting screw controls horn operation in two ways: amperage draw and horn tone. (Cadillac)

If the horn sounds continuously, disconnect horn relay wire and wires from horn terminals. The usual cause for horn blowing without depressing the horn switch is a grounded wire to the horn switch or a grounded switch. Another possibility is a faulty horn relay. Use an ohmmeter to test horn relay continuity. Voltage is applied to the relay at all times. Closing the horn switch grounds the relay coil, contacts close, and current flows to the horn. Therefore, there should be no current flow through the relay until the horn switch is depressed. If the ohmmeter shows current flow through the relay at all times, replace the relay.

If the horn sounds intermittently on turns, the horn brush slip ring under the steering wheel is defective.

If the tone and character of the horn signal is weak, try turning the horn adjusting screw in short moves until the tone indicates best point of adjustment.

Principles of a Direct Current (DC) Motor

To understand how the speed of a ***wiper motor*** is controlled, there are two principles that must be understood. The first, the stronger the magnetic field or the more windings in an armature, the slower the motor turns. The second, the slower the armature turns, the more current the motor draws while increasing its torque.

Wiper Motor Construction

There are three different types of motors that can be used for windshield wipers, Figure 51-42. The ***permanent magnet motor*** does not use field windings. This design has two ceramic magnets, Figure 51-43, that are cemented to the field frame. Also, this type needs less energy than the other types of motor design. However, the switch must be wired in series. This can create many areas of resistance. The ***shunt-wound motor*** provides a consistent speed, but does not provide much torque upon starting. The ***compound motor*** has a strong starting torque and provides a consistent speed, but is the most expensive.

Most cars also have an ***intermittent wiper system,*** Figures 51-44 and 51-45. This permits the driver to select a delayed wipe that operates only every three to thirty seconds in this mode.

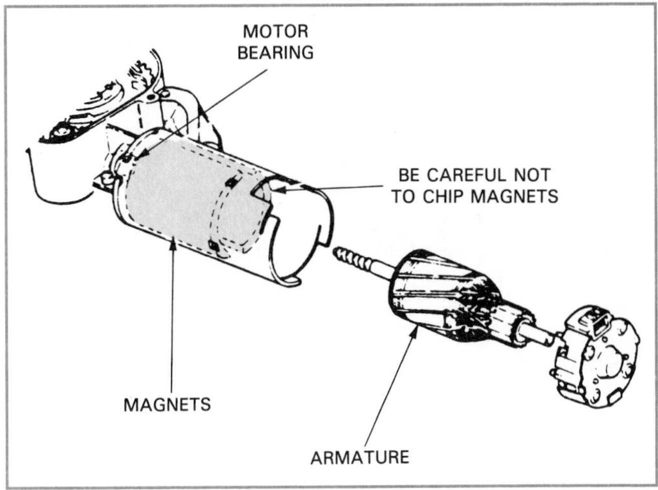

Figure 51-43. A permanent magnet motor contains no field windings. (Oldsmobile)

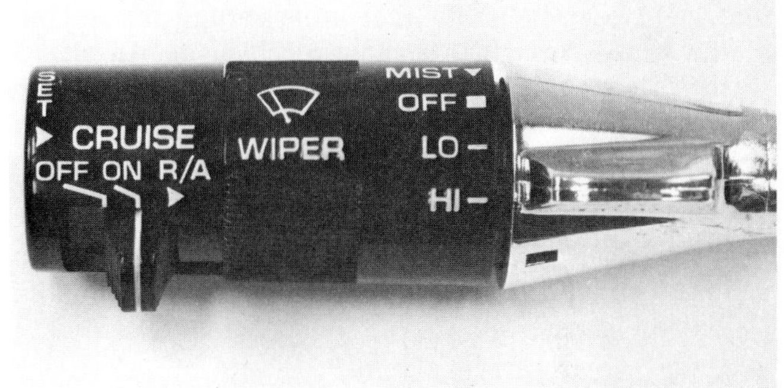

Figure 51-44. Some wiper controls are mounted at the end of the turn signal lever. Note that the cruise control selector is also located there. (Chevrolet)

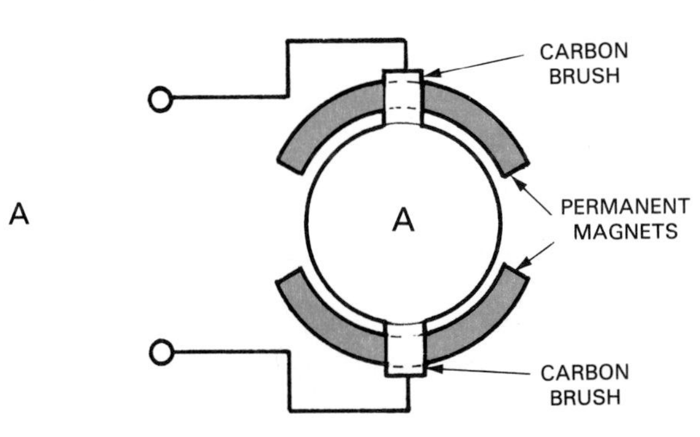

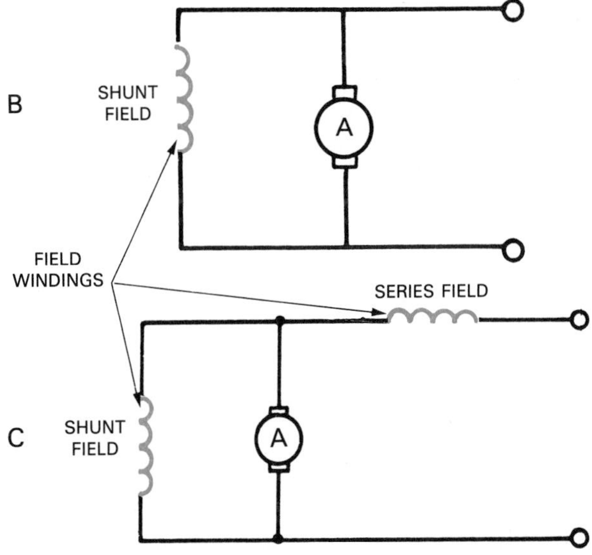

Figure 51-42. Wiper motor construction. A–Permanent magnet motor. B–Shunt-wound motor has field winding parallel with armature. C–Compound motor has field windings parallel to, and in series with, the armature.

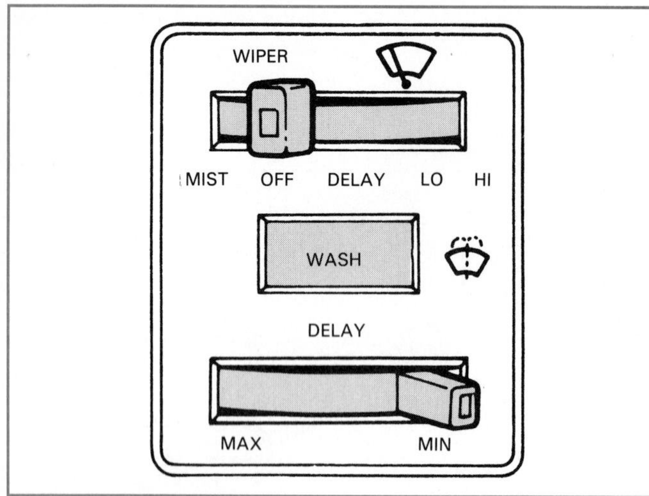

Figure 51-45. Some wiper controls are mounted on the dash.

GM Wipers

A typical wiper/washer unit is the wiper assembly shown in Figure 51-46. It incorporates a depressed park system that places the wiper blades below the hood line in the parked position.

The relay control consists of a relay coil, relay armature, and switch assembly. It controls starting and stopping of the wiper through a latching mechanism. An electric washer pump is mounted on the gear box section of the wiper. It is driven by the wiper unit gear assembly.

Ford Wipers

Two types of motors are used, the depressed park type and the non-depressed park type. A view of a motor used is shown in Figure 51-47.

Chrysler Wipers

Chrysler cars either have a two-speed or three-speed wiper system that uses an electric washer pump. On cars with the non-depressed park system, the wiper blades park in the lowest portion of the wiper pattern. On cars with the depressed park system, the blades automatically park in the depressed position.

The two-speed wiper motor has a permanent magnet field, controlled by feeding current to different brushes for low and high speeds. The low speed circuit uses a torque limiting resistor.

Chrysler's three-speed wiper motors all have the depressed park feature. It is accomplished by means of an eccentric motor shaft and by reversing the direction of motor rotation. When the switch is turned off, the inner shaft of the motor stops, while the outer shaft rotates 180°. This changes the length of the drive link/crank to park the wiper blades in the depressed position, Figure 51-48. All Chrysler windshield wiper systems use a circuit breaker with the wiper switch to protect the circuitry of the wiper system and the car.

Troubleshooting

For any electric windshield wiper to work trouble free, it is essential that the motor, linkage, and drive pivots do

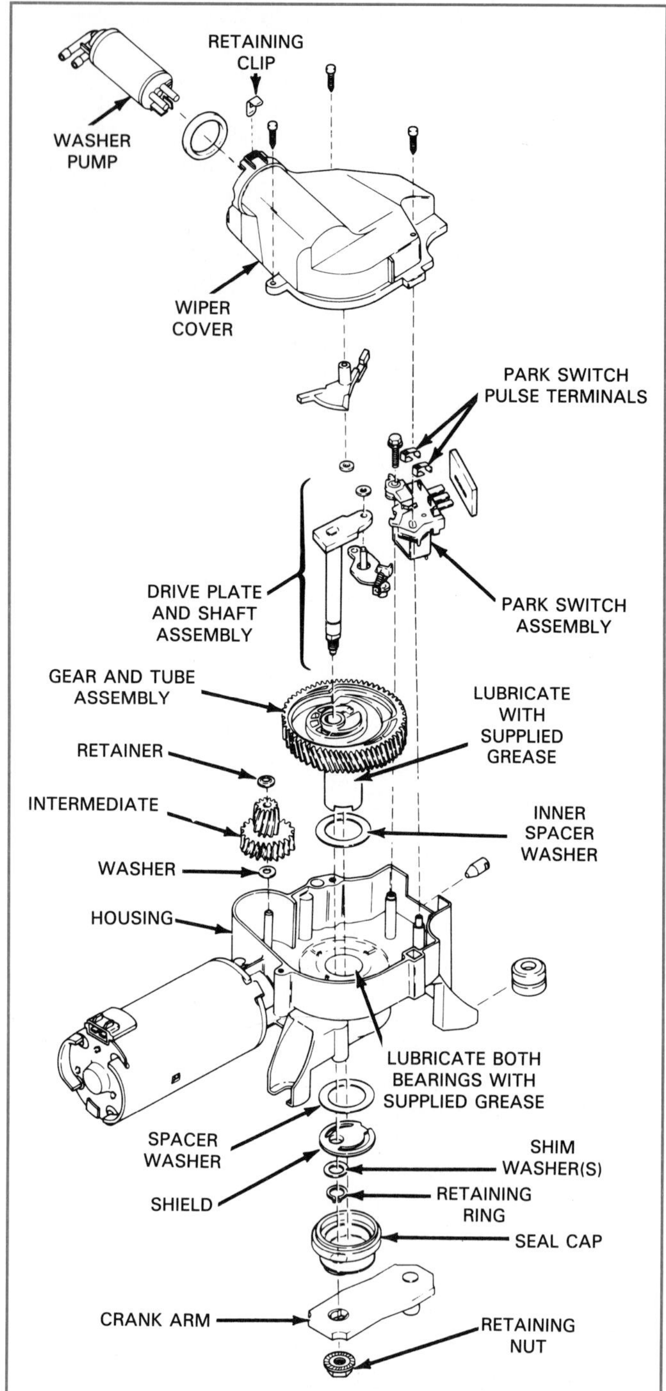

Figure 51-46. This wiper motor is combined with a washer pump. (Oldsmobile)

not bind. The wiper system may be noisy, slow, balky, or inoperative.

Noisy operation of electric wipers is sometimes caused by too much end play of the armature. The amount of end play varies with different makes. Noise will also be caused by incorrect relation between the motor and the linkage and pivot shaft assemblies. Reducing friction in the drive mechanism should reduce noise and binding.

Failure to operate can be caused by a blown fuse, open circuit, loose wiring harness connector, wiper motor not grounded, or a bad wiper switch or motor.

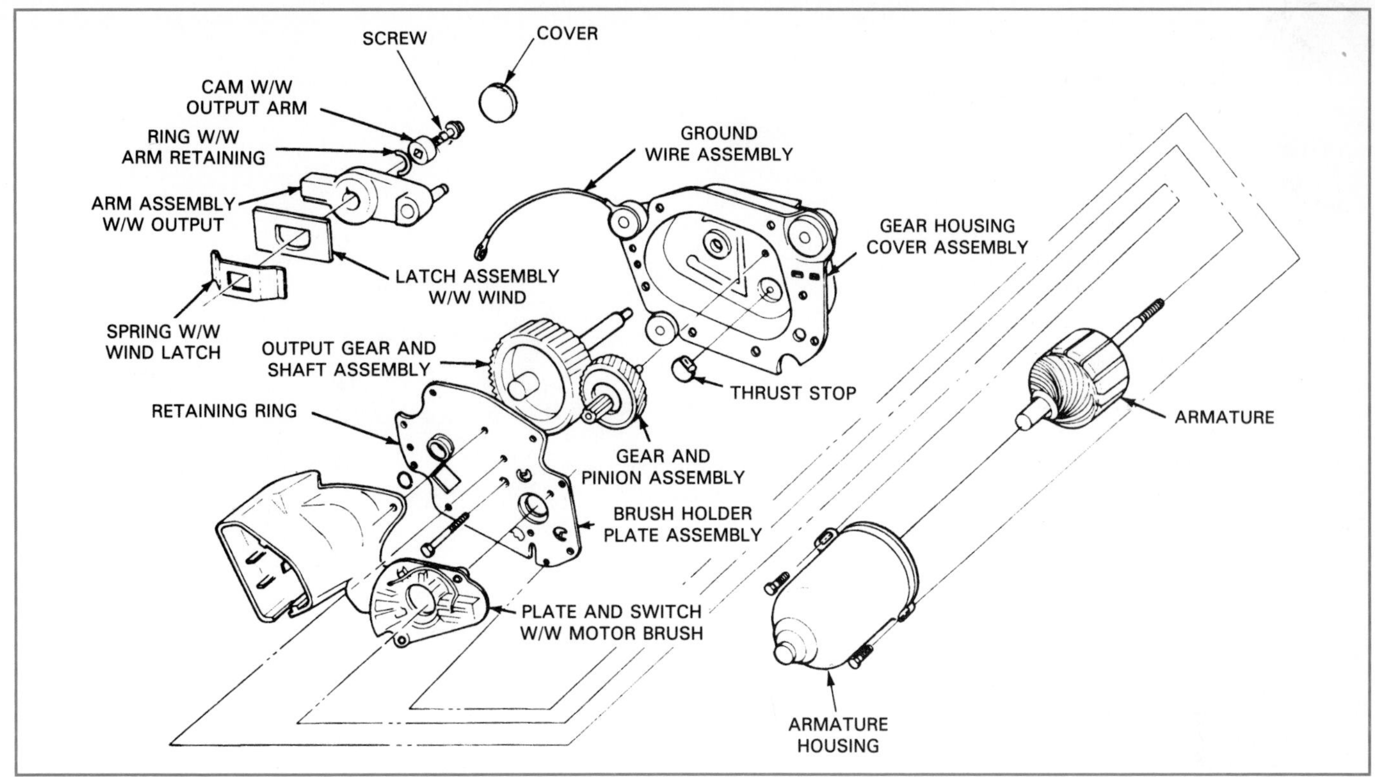

Figure 51-47. Construction of a Ford wiper motor.

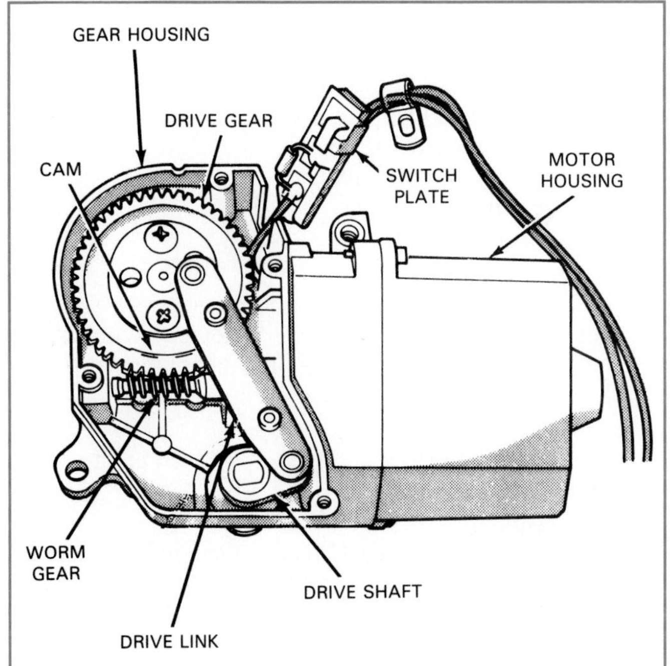

Figure 51-48. Construction of a Chrysler wiper motor.

Windshield Washers

All cars use an electric ***windshield washer.*** A positive displacement washer pump is used. On some, the motor is placed in the washer reservoir. On others, it is driven by the wiper motor, Figure 51-46.

When the pump is attached to the wiper motor, the four-lobe cam actuates a spring-loaded follower. However, the pump does not operate all the time that the wiper motor is running. This is because the pumping mechanism is locked out and no pumping action occurs.

In this design, Figure 51-49, the solenoid plunger is pulled toward the coil, allowing the ratchet pawl to engage the ratchet wheel. It then starts to rotate, one tooth at a time. Each lobe of the cam actuates the follower. The follower, in turn, moves the piston actuator plate and piston away from the valve assembly and compresses the piston spring. This creates a vacuum in the pump cylinder through the intake valve, Figure 51-50. As the high point of each cam lobe passes the follower, the piston spring expands. This forces the piston toward the valves, pressurizing the washer solution so it flows out the exhaust valves to the spray nozzles.

Intake and exhaust strokes occur four times for each revolution of the wiper motor output gear. The pumping

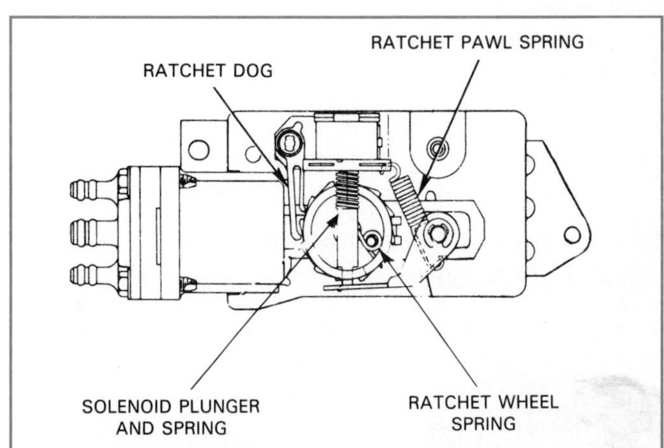

Figure 51-49. The control section of a GM washer pump is shown.

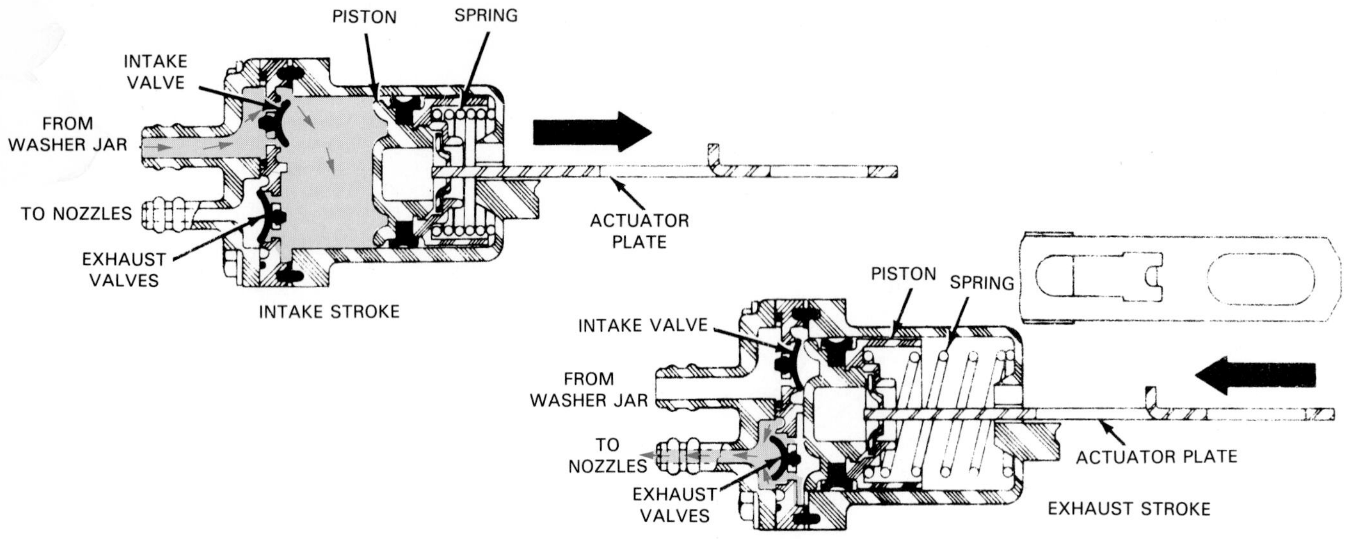

Figure 51-50. The intake and exhaust stroke of a washer pump. (Oldsmobile)

cycle is completed automatically when the ratchet wheel has been rotated through 360°, Figure 51-49. Then, the spring-loaded plunger pushes through an opening in the rim of the ratchet wheel, pushing the pawl away from the ratchet teeth. At this point, the ratchet wheel has moved to a position where it is holding the piston actuator plate in a lockout position until the washer switch is pressed again.

Troubleshooting Washers

When troubleshooting washer pumps, check the following:

Washer Inoperative

- Not enough washer solution.
- Hoses damaged, loose, or kinked.
- Plugged screen at end of reservoir hose.
- Wiper switch bad.
- Pump valve bad.
- Plugged washer nozzles.
- Loose electrical connection to washer pump or wiper switch.
- Open circuit in feed wire to pump solenoid coil.
- Pump solenoid coil bad.
- Missing ratchet wheel tooth.
- Missing ratchet pawl spring.

Washer Pumps Continuously While Wiper Is Operating

- Wiper switch is bad.
- Grounded wire from pump solenoid to switch.
- Missing ratchet wheel tooth.
- Ratchet wheel pawl or dog not contracting ratchet wheel teeth.
- Lock-out tang broken or bent on piston actuator plate.

Chapter 51–Review Questions

Write your answers on a separate sheet of paper. Do not write in this book.

1. The lighting circuit is known as the _____ because it uses the car frame for the return.
2. What is the purpose of the rheostat used on some main lighting switches?
3. For identification, number 1A appears on rectangular sealed beam units with a single filament. True or False?
4. The _____ headlamp is a reflector and lens system designed for a specific vehicle model and contoured to that vehicle's requirements.
   (A) aerodynamic
   (B) concealed
   (C) composite
   (D) halogen
5. An electronic headlamp _____ device switches the headlights from high beam to low beam in response to light from an approaching vehicle.
   (A) delay
   (B) dimming
   (C) light sensitive
   (D) sentinel
6. The lane change switch mechanism is incorporated into the _____ switch.
7. Give two causes of excessive voltage in the lighting circuit.
8. What is the permissible voltage drop between the battery positive terminal and the insulated terminal of each lamp being tested?
   (A) 0.06 volt.
   (B) 0.1 volt.
   (C) 0.3 volt.
   (D) 0.6 volt.
9. Halogen bulbs contain gas under pressure and may shatter if mishandled or dropped. True or False?
10. What provision is made in the front of a headlamp lens to assist in aiming the headlights?
11. Wire and cable sizes are expressed by a _____.

12. The resistance of a length of wire or cable decreases as its cross section _____ (increases or decreases).
13. Why are automotive ignition systems provided with resistance in the secondary circuit?
14. Bulkhead connectors and inline connectors that interconnect major wiring harnesses can be disconnected to simplify _____.

Match the question number for each of the following service manual categories with the letter designated for each correct associated phrase.

15. ___ Circuit operation.
16. ___ System diagnosis.
17. ___ Electrical schematics.
18. ___ System checks.
19. ___ Troubleshooting hints.
20. ___ Harness connector faces.
    (A) Tells how circuit should be operated and what should occur.
    (B) Provides tests and gives shortcuts for solving problems.
    (C) Show cavity or terminal locations.
    (D) Lists step-by-step procedure to pinpoint the cause of a malfunction.
    (E) Describes circuit components and how a circuit works.
    (F) Picture electrical current paths.
21. A shunt-wound motor has:
    (A) permanent magnets.
    (B) a field winding parallel with the armature.
    (C) a field winding parallel to, and in series with, the armature.
    (D) a field winding in series with the armature.
22. A compound motor has:
    (A) permanent magnets.
    (B) a field winding parallel with the armature.
    (C) a field winding parallel to, and in series with, the armature.
    (D) a field winding in series with the armature.
    (E) None of the above.
23. What is meant by a depressed park system?
24. What is meant by a non-depressed park system?
25. What are the two principles of a direct-current motor?
26. Friction in the drive system of the wipers causes:
    (A) noise.
    (B) binding.
    (C) Both A & B.
    (D) Neither A nor B.
27. Some wipers have the selector switch on the turn signal lever. True or False?
28. Some washer pumps are mounted:
    (A) on the wiper motor.
    (B) in the washer reservoir.
    (C) Both A & B.
    (D) Neither A nor B.
29. If the washer pumps all of the time while the wipers operate, the most common cause is:
    (A) a blown fuse.
    (B) an open circuit.
    (C) a wiper switch needs to be changed.
    (D) None of the above.

This vehicle is equipped with a heads-up display, which projects vehicle speed and other information onto the base of the windshield. (GM Hughes Electronics)

Chapter 52

Speedometers and Speed Control Systems

After studying this chapter, you will be able to:

- ❍ Explain how an analog speedometer operates.
- ❍ Describe how a digital speedometer operates.
- ❍ List the different types of digital display.
- ❍ Troubleshoot an analog speedometer/odometer, including the cable.
- ❍ Explain how the cruise control servo operates.
- ❍ List the components of a cruise control system.
- ❍ Describe the different cruise control systems.

Analog Speedometers

The ***analog speedometer*** used on cars indicates the speed of the car and records distance traveled, Figure 52-1.

A speedometer is driven by a flexible cable connected to the speedometer pinion within the transmission.

Speedometers are calibrated in miles per hour and/or in kilometers. When the instrument also records the distance traveled, it is recorded in miles or kilometers. That portion of the instrument is known as the ***odometer,*** Figure 52-1. Most odometers record the total distance traveled. Some also record the distance of individual trips. These can be reset to zero, Figure 52-2.

Figure 52-1. A typical analog speedometer. Note that there is a trip odometer and total mileage odometer. The trip odometer can be reset.

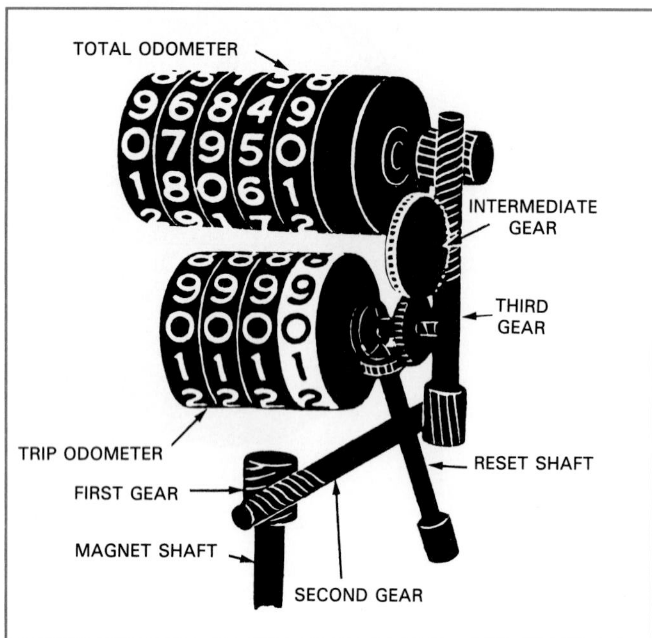

Figure 52-2. Speedometer gear train from a magnet shaft.

To measure the speed of the car and the distance traveled, many internal parts are needed.

Speedometer Operation

The speedometer and odometer are driven by a cable housed in a casing, Figure 52-3. The cable is connected to a gear at the transmission. This gear is designed for a specific model, tire size, and rear axle ratio.

In most cases, the speedometer is designed to convert 1001 revolutions of the drive cable into one mile on the odometer. In other words, 1001 cable revolutions in a minute, will result in a speed indication of 60 mph.

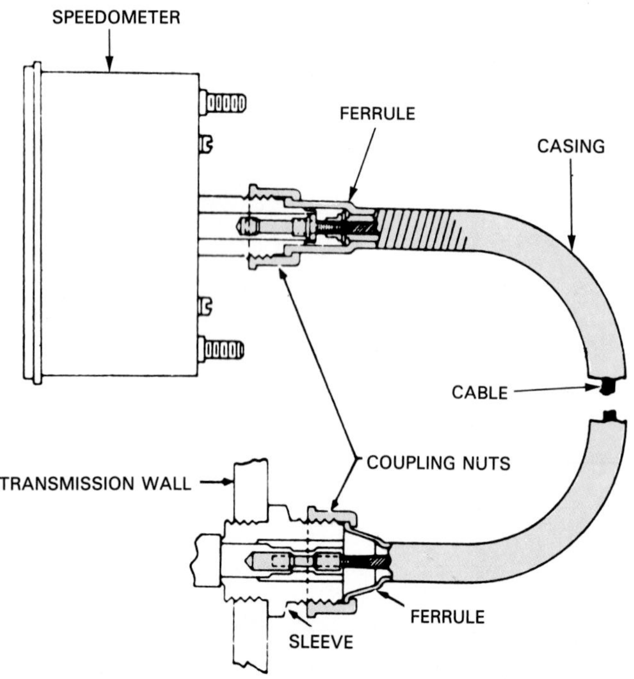

Figure 52-3. Speedometer cable from the transmission speedometer head.

Speed Indication

The ***speed indication*** of an analog speedometer works on the magnetic principle. It includes a revolving permanent magnet driven by the cable connected to the transmission. Around this permanent magnet is a stationary field plate. Between the magnet and field plate is a nonmagnetic movable speed cup on a spindle. The magnet revolves within the speed cup, Figure 52-4.

The revolving magnet sets up a rotating magnetic field which exerts a pull on the speed cup, making it revolve in the same direction. The movement of the speed cup is retarded and held steady by a hairspring attached to the speed cup spindle. The speed cup comes to rest at a point where the magnetic drag is just balanced by the retarding force created by the hairspring. An additional function of the hairspring is to pull the pointer of the instrument back to zero when the magnet stops rotating.

There is no mechanical connection between the revolving magnet and the speed cup. As the speed of the magnet increases, due to the movement of the car, the magnet drag on the speed cup also increases and pulls the speed cup further around. In that way, a faster speed is indicated by the pointer on the face of the dial.

The magnetic field is constant, and the amount of movement of the speed cup is (at all times) proportional to the speed at which the magnet is being rotated. Temperature effect on the magnet is compensated for by a special alloy attached to the magnet. This applies to all magnetically driven speedometers, including disc and indicating cylinder types.

Speedometer Accuracy

The accuracy of a speedometer and odometer is affected by the size of the tires, the rear axle ratio, and the gears used to drive the speedometer. Changing tire size or rear axle ratio alters the accuracy of the speedometer and odometer.

To provide accuracy of the instrument, car manufacturers provide many drive pinions for their speedometers. Some speedometer drive pinions may be interchanged because of the pinion adapter, Figure 52-5.

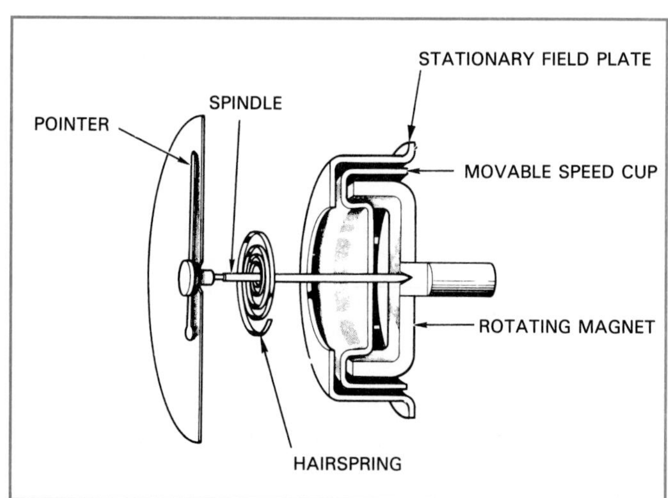

Figure 52-4. The speed cup, magnet, field plate, hairspring, and pointer of an analog speedometer.

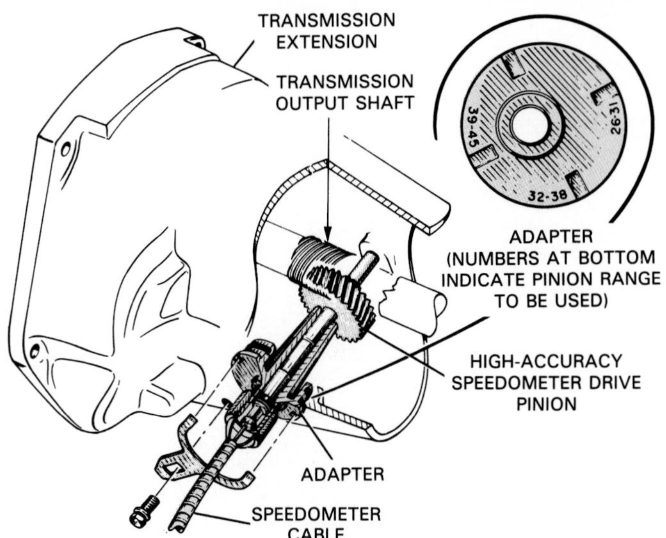

Figure 52-5. Speedometer drive pinion and adapter. The adapter must be positioned in relation to the number of teeth indicated on the pinion, or indicated speed will be incorrect. (Dodge)

Inspection and Lubrication

To test the speedometer for a tight mechanism, insert a test cable and turn. No binding or tightness should be felt. The test cable is the drive end of a short length of speedometer cable. A fast spin of the test cable should swing the pointer of the instrument from zero to about half scale. From half scale, the pointer should quickly return to zero. This indicates that the hairspring and magnet are in good working order. The same basic test also applies to the drum or indicator cylinder type of speedometer. The indicator cylinder should advance to at least 30 mph, then quickly return to zero.

To test the speedometer for calibration, place the unit in a test stand and run at various speeds. Compare readings of speedometer and test stand pointer movement.

Operate speedometer long enough to record two to three miles. All figure wheels should be lined up evenly, except those wheels which may be operating. If too much grease is present in the speedometer head, the cable and casing should be cleaned.

When lubricating a speedometer cable, the special lubricant should be applied lightly. Too much lubrication may result in the lubricant working up the cable and into the speedometer head.

Speedometer Cable

Speedometer cables break as the result of age, lack of lubrication, or because the cable casing has sharp bends. To correct the problem of sharp bends, the clamps holding the casing must be relocated to straighten the casing. When the bends have damaged the inside of the casing, it will be necessary to replace the assembly. The rough spots tend to cause binding, friction, and rapid wear of the cable.

Another cause of frequent breakage of the speedometer cable is too much friction in the speedometer head. The test for this condition has been described. Withdraw the cable, spread a thin coat of speedometer cable grease evenly over the lower two-thirds of the cable. Do not apply grease to the entire cable as that would result in the lubricant working up the cable into the speedometer head and causing damage.

After applying the lubricant to the cable, insert the cable into the upper end of the casing, lower end first. This will spread the grease evenly over the entire length of the cable.

Connect the upper end of the casing to the speedometer case, making sure that the cable tip engages in the speedometer drive member. Tighten the ferrule nut, finger tight. Then, twist the lower end of the cable with your fingers to make sure it turns freely. A sharp twist of the cable should cause the speedometer needle to register. Then, connect the lower end of the casing to the transmission fitting, making sure that the cable fits in the speedometer driven gear.

Troubleshooting

Most problems in the speedometers start in the drive cable. The cable may be broken, kinked, frayed, or in need of lubrication. If the speedometer pointer fluctuates, the problem may be caused by a kinked cable. Or, the trouble may be in the speedometer head. The kinked cable rubs in its housing and winds up, slowing down the pointer. The cable then unwinds suddenly and the pointer jumps.

To check a cable for kinks, remove it from the casing and lay it on a flat surface. Then, rotate one end of the cable with the fingers. If the cable turns smoothly, it is not kinked. But if part of the cable turns suddenly, it is kinked and should be replaced.

Another method of testing a cable for kinks is to hold each end in your hands with the cable looped down in front of you. Then rotate the ends of the cable slowly with your fingers. If the cable is kinked it will "flop" and not turn smoothly, Figure 52-6.

Cables should be inspected for fraying and wear. Cable fraying indicates sharp turns or a bad casing. If needed, replace cable and casing, then reroute assembly removing sharp turns. Visually check cable tips for straightness. A cable that lacks stiffness should be replaced.

Other speedometer troubles and possible causes include the following:

Pointer Fluctuates

- Defective cable or casing.
- Worn or dirty spindle bearings.
- Excessive end play in magnet shaft.
- Dirt or grease on magnet or speed cup.
- Speed cup assembly rusted at spindle ends.
- Worn main frame magnet shaft bearing (shaft side play should not exceed .003 in.).
- Bent speed cup spindle.
- Field plate not positioned correctly.
- Worn first, second, or third gears.

Pointer Does Not Return to Zero

- Weak, broken, or improperly adjusted hairspring.
- Pointer improperly set.
- Front jewel too tight.
- Dirt or grease in mechanism.

	CAUSE	PROCEDURE
	LOOSE FERRULE AT SPEEDO HEAD.	PUSH FERRULE AGAINST SPEEDO HEAD AND RECHECK FOR NOISE.
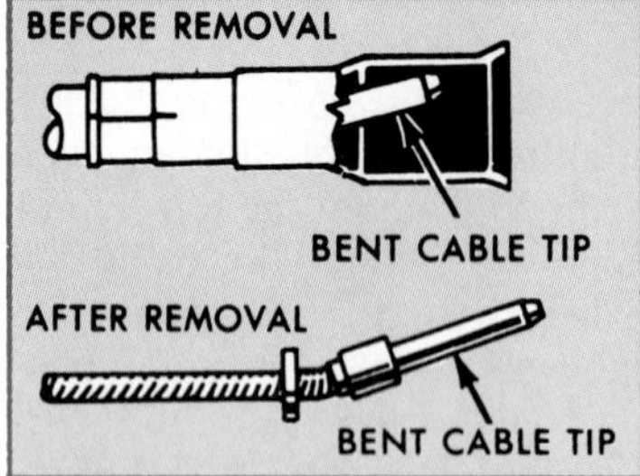 BEFORE REMOVAL BENT CABLE TIP AFTER REMOVAL BENT CABLE TIP	BEND CABLE TIP AT SPEEDO HEAD.	REPLACE (LUBRICATE ENTIRE LENGTH OF CABLE WITH A THIN COAT OF SPEEDOMETER CABLE LUBRICANT.)
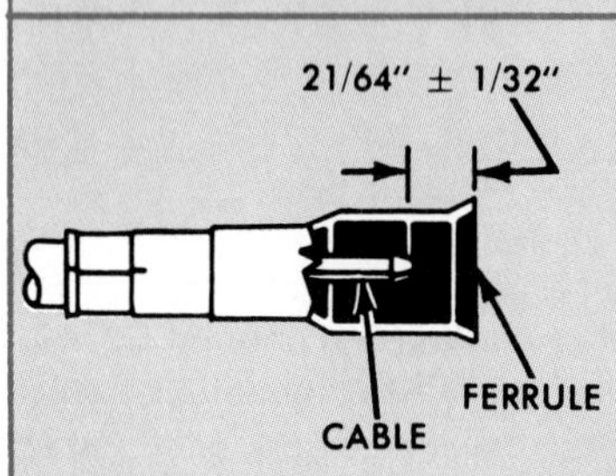 21/64" ± 1/32" FERRULE CABLE	CABLE EXTENDS TOO FAR INTO TRANSMISSION.	DISCONNECT FERRULE AT SPEEDO HEAD WITH LOWER END STILL CONNECTED. PUSH CABLE INTO SHAFT UNTIL IT BOTTOMS. THE CABLE MUST BE RECESSED 21/64" ± 1/32" FROM THE END OF THE FERRULE. IF TOO LONG OR TOO SHORT, REPLACE CABLE AND RECHECK FOR NOISE. NOTE: DO NOT CUT OFF CABLE
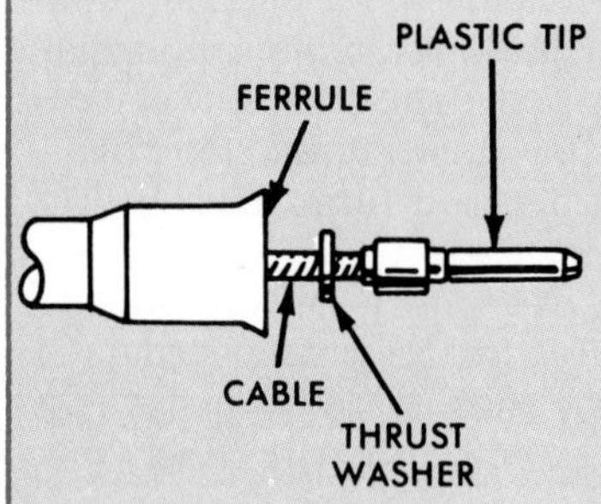 PLASTIC TIP FERRULE CABLE THRUST WASHER	DOUBLE OR MISSING THRUST WASHER ON CABLE AT SPEEDO HEAD.	ONLY ONE THRUST WASHER IF USED BEHIND THE PLASTIC TIP. IF WASHER IS MISSING (MAKE SURE IT IS NOT STUCK INSIDE THE FERRULE), REMOVE CABLE, ADD PROPER THICKNESS WASHER, INSTALL CABLE IN CASING, AND RECHECK FOR NOISE. IF TWO WASHERS ARE PRESENT (MAKE SURE ONE IS NOT STUCK INSIDE FERRULE), REMOVE ONE OF THEM, INSTALL CABLE IN CASING, AND RECHECK FOR NOISE.
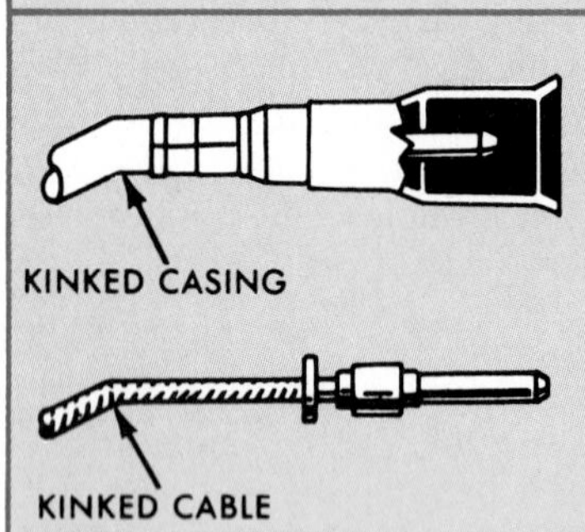 KINKED CASING KINKED CABLE	CABLE AND/OR CASING IS KINKED.	DISCONNECT FERRULE FROM SPEEDO HEAD AND PULL OUT CABLE. IF CABLE HANGS UP DURING REMOVAL, CABLE AND.CASING MAY BE KINKED. INSPECT CABLE, AND IF IT IS KINKED, REPLACE. RECHECK FOR NOISE. IF CABLE REMOVAL IS NORMAL, INSPECT IT FOR KINKING. IF IT IS KINKED, REPLACE AND RECHECK FOR NOISE. (LUBRICATE ENTIRE LENGTH OF CABLE WITH THIN COAT OF SPEEDOMETER CABLE LUBRICANT.)
	CABLE IS NOT PROPERLY LUBRICATED.	APPLY A THIN COAT OF SPEEDOMETER CABLE LUBRICANT ALONG ENTIRE LENGTH OF CABLE, INSTALL IN CASING AND RECHECK FOR NOISE.
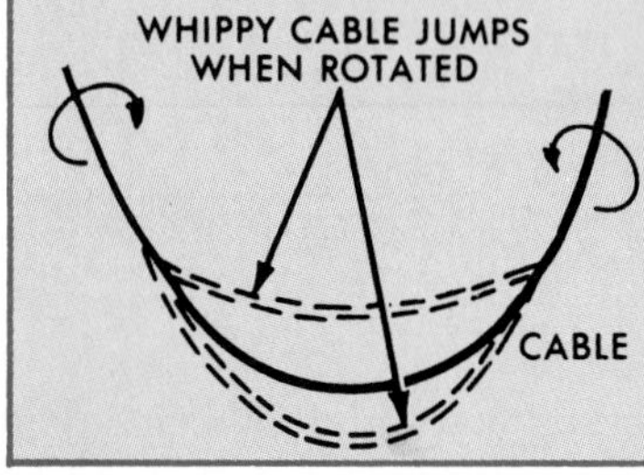 WHIPPY CABLE JUMPS WHEN ROTATED CABLE	CABLE IS "WHIPPY."	HOLD CABLE IN POSITION SHOWN AND ROTATE. A "WHIPPY" CABLE DOES NOT TURN SMOOTHLY, BUT JUMPS. IF THIS CONDITION EXISTS, REPLACE WITH A NEW PROPERLY LUBRICATED CABLE AND RECHECK FOR NOISE.

Figure 52-6. Causes and cures for noisy speedometer operation. (Cadillac)

Incorrect Speed Indication

- Dirty or grease-filled mechanism.
- Out of calibration.
- Out of balance pointer.

Note: Pointer balance may be checked by turning speedometer clockwise to different positions while it is running at a set speed. Indicated speed variation means that the pointer or speed cup is out of balance.

Incorrect Speed Over Half of Scale

- Hairspring coils touching.
- Field plate eccentric with speed cup.
- Indicator drum out of balance.

Excessive Noise

- Too much end play in magnet shaft.
- Worn frame bearings.
- Worn gears.

Inoperative Odometer

- First gear stripped.
- Excessive end play in second gear.
- Second and third gears stripped, warped, or worn.
- Damaged idler gears.

Odometer Readings Incorrect

- Worn second or third worm gears.
- Wrong transmission drive gear.
- Stripped transmission drive gear.
- Wrong tire size.
- Wrong rear axle ratio.

Digital Speedometers

Unlike an analog speedometer, the ***digital speedometer,*** Figure 52-7, is operated by a vehicle speed sensor, Figure 52-8. It produces electrical pulses that are processed by the computer. The computer, then, turns on segments of a display to form numbers, which is the speed of the car. The display types can be Light Emitting Diode (LED), Liquid Crystal Display (LCD), Vacuum Fluorescent Display (VFD), or Cathode Ray Tube (CRT).

Figure 52-7. A digital display dash is sometimes referred to as an electronic dash. (Chrysler)

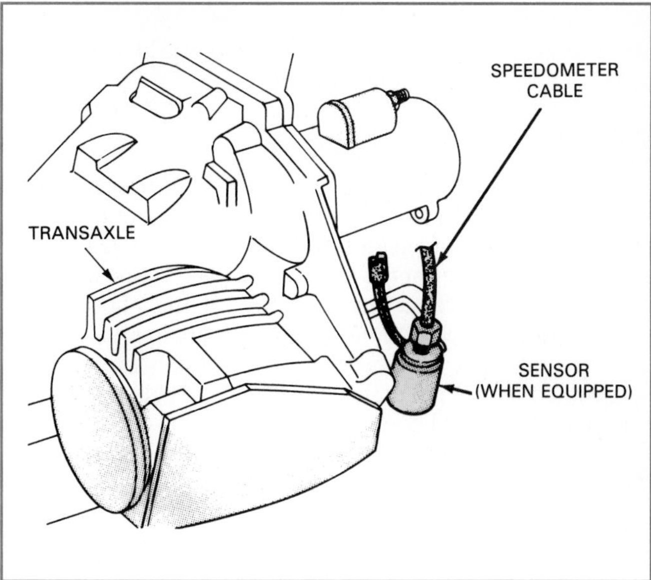

Figure 52-8. The vehicle speed sensor sends electrical pulses to the computer. (Chrysler)

Light Emitting Diode

The ***light emitting diode*** (LED) is a semiconductor diode. When light is introduced at its junction, light can be seen at the one end with the naked eye. The color of the light, most of the time, is red. This is due to the type of semiconductor that is used, which in this case is gallium arsenide. The display is composed of many segments that are turned off and on to form numbers, Figure 52-9. When a segment is turned on, light is allowed through a specific diode. The problem with the LED digital dash is that it cannot be seen in bright sunlight.

Liquid Crystal Display

The ***liquid crystal display*** (LCD) has voltage applied to its crystal. This causes the crystal's molecules to be aligned as to form a straight line. When outside light enters the section that has voltage applied to it, it turns black to form numbers, Figure 52-9. The section of crystal that has voltage applied to it is determined by the computer. The

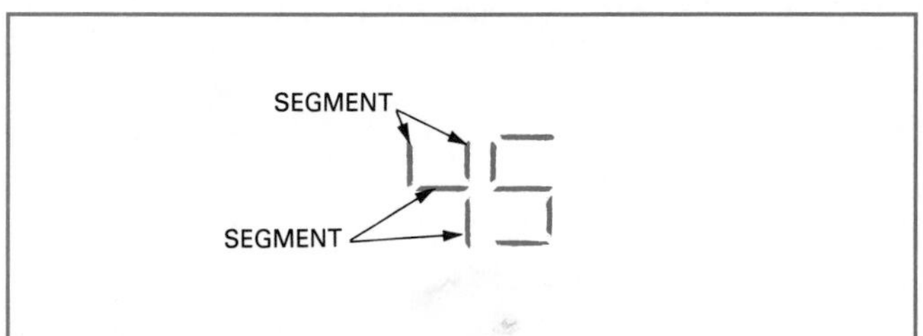

Figure 52-9. Segments are turned off and on by the computer to form numbers. These numbers indicate the speed and/or mileage of the car.

problem with the LCD digital dash is that it must be illuminated so that it can be seen at night. Also, the LCD does not work well in extreme cold weather.

Vacuum Fluorescent Display

The ***vacuum fluorescent display*** (VFD) uses a special resistance wire heated by passing current through it. A coating on the filament, when heated, produces electrons. The electrons are attracted to an anode. The anode is coated with phosphor. When the electrons hit the phosphor, it emits a bluish-green light. The electrons are applied only to the segments that are needed to form numbers, which is determined by the computer, Figure 52-9. This is the most common of the display types. However, it must be mounted and isolated from vibrations or it will fail. This is accomplished by mounting it to rubber bushings.

Cathode Ray Tube

The ***cathode ray tube*** (CRT) is the same as a television. However, numbers are displayed instead of pictures. The cathode emits electrons. The anode attracts the electrons. The electrons pass through the anode and strike a coating of phosphorus on the inside of the screen to form the numbers. The computer decides which segments will be turned on to form the numbers, Figure 52-9.

By touching the screen at certain points, a menu will appear and the driver will select the desired display, whether it is the speed of the car or the diagnostic mode. In the diagnostic mode, the powertrain, brakes, air conditioning, and electrical systems can be monitored. An "OK" will be next to the listed system if there are no problems. If there are problems with a specific system, a logical sequence of screens will appear to aid diagnosis.

Digital Odometers

The ***digital odometer chip,*** Figure 52-10, can be replaced if it is defective without replacing the entire speedometer cluster. However, a new odometer chip will register zero mileage. On the other hand, if the cluster has to be replaced, the old odometer chip can be transferred to the new cluster, Figure 52-11. With this procedure, the new

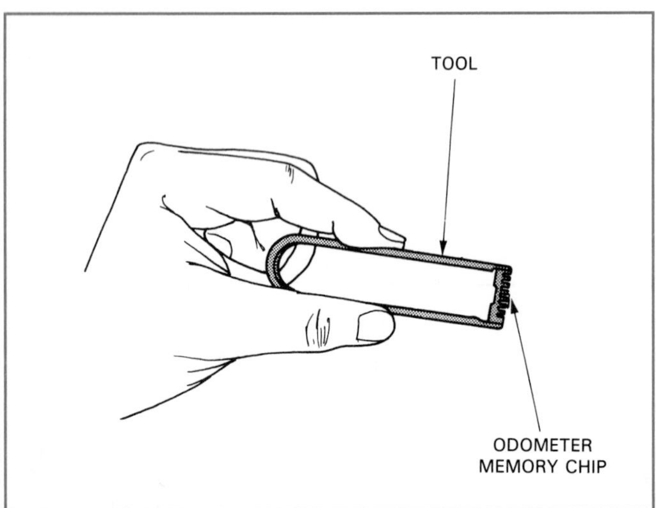

Figure 52-10. An odometer chip retains the mileage in its memory. (Chrysler)

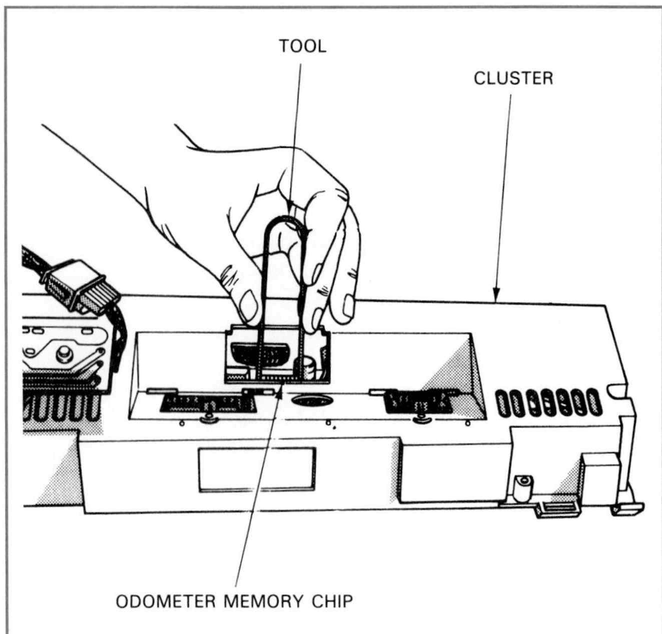

Figure 52-11. The odometer chip is serviced separately from the digital dash. (Chrysler)

cluster will display the current mileage, as the chip retains the mileage in its memory.

Troubleshooting

To verify if the speed sensor is operating properly, turn the drive wheels by hand with the ignition turned to the ON position. If no speed is indicated, replace the sensor with a known good sensor. Repeat the test. If there is still no indication of speed, the electronic dash will have to be tested. The electronic dash has self-diagnostic capabilities. Consult the individual service manuals for test procedures.

Speed Control

Speed control systems installed by the car manufacturers vary in makeup and controls, but all are designed to automatically regulate the car speed set by the driver. This speed will be maintained until a new rate of speed is set, the brake pedal is depressed, or the system is turned off by the driver.

Servo Operation

While some servos use a ***governor*** to maintain the speed setting, Figure 52-12, others use a ***variable inductance position sensor,*** Figure 52-13. Both are vented to manifold vacuum and atmospheric pressure.

Governor Type

Manifold vacuum entering the servo housing, Figure 52-14, is controlled by the control valve. The control valve position is determined by the governor, Figure 52-12, which is driven by the speedometer cable. As car speed is increased, the governor weights are thrown outward, which pushes on the follower. The follower, then, pushes on the core. When the locking coil is energized, the armature

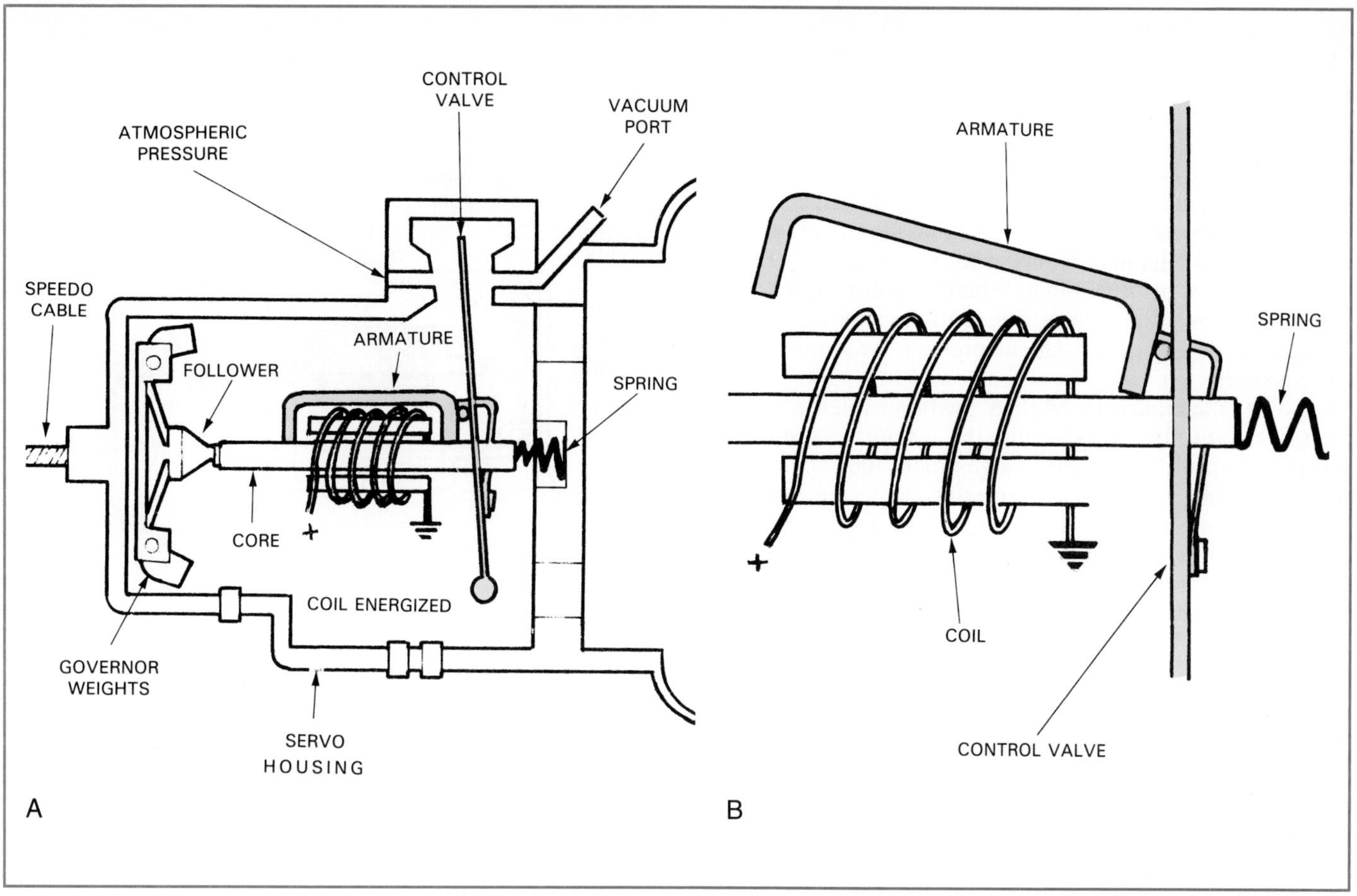

Figure 52-12. Governor-type cruise control servo. A–When the system has been engaged, the armature locks the control valve to the core. On a level road with the system engaged, the control valve will be between the vacuum port and the atmospheric pressure port. B–The armature is in a de-energized position. Note that the armature is attached to the control valve. (Chrysler)

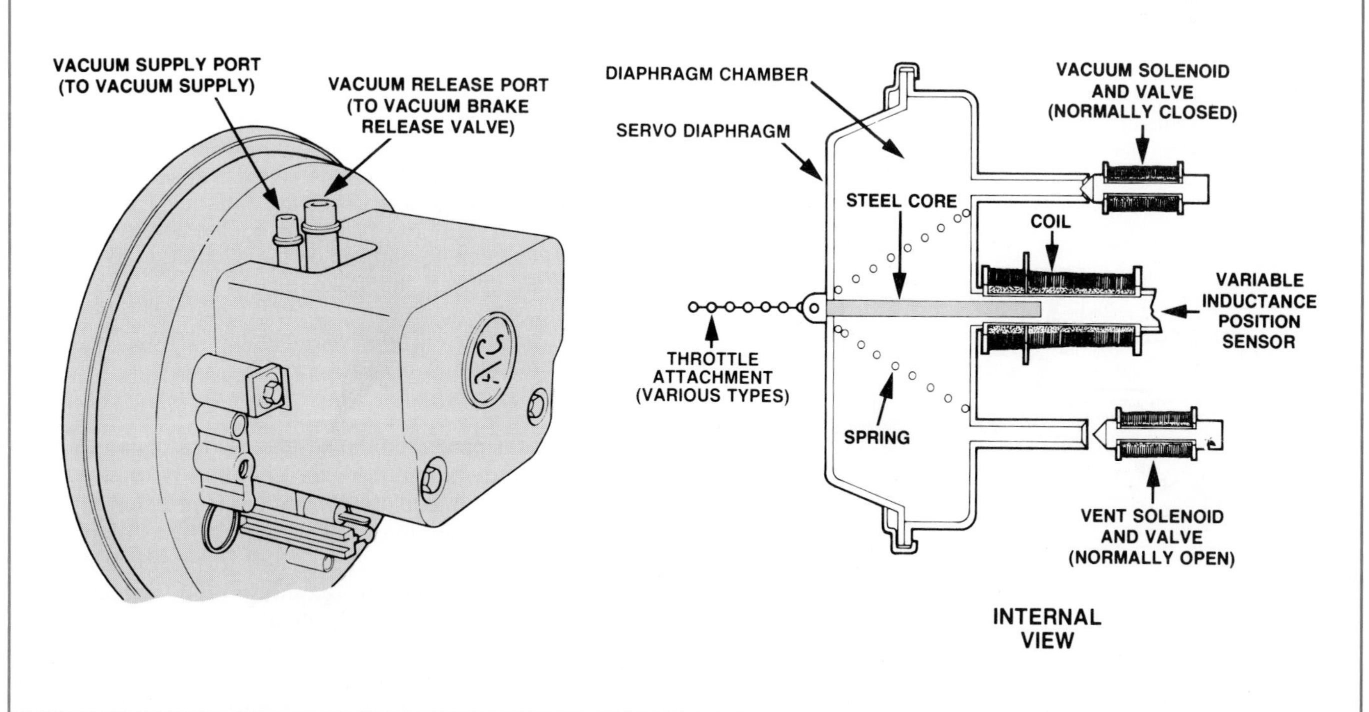

Figure 52-13. Variable inductance type cruise control servo. The vacuum solenoid is energized by an electronic module during periods of low vacuum when the cruise control is engaged. The low-vacuum condition is determined by the position of the steel core in the coil. (AC Spark Plug)

locks the core to the control valve, thereby connecting the two. So, when the armature is energized and the core moves, the control valve is adjusted.

When the car is on a level road, the desired speed is maintained when the control valve is between the air bleed and the manifold vacuum port, Figure 52-12. If the car speed is reduced by going up a steep grade, the vent to atmospheric pressure, Figure 52-14, is closed off by the control valve. This maintains the set speed, as the vacuum can then act on the diaphragm. When a car descends a steep grade, the governor pushes the control valve against the vacuum port, Figure 52-15, to prevent the engine from overspeeding.

When the brakes are applied, the brake release valve is energized, Figure 52-15, and the vacuum is dumped through the port. The control valve blocks the vacuum port to prevent any vacuum from entering while the brake release valve is energized. The cruise control system is then disengaged until the driver depresses the "resume" or "set" button. This forces the brake release valve against its seat, blocking atmospheric pressure from entering the servo housing.

Variable Inductance Type

The servo, Figure 52-13, is controlled by an electronic module. The position of the steel core in the coil creates a specific voltage signal that is sent to the module. If the steel core deviates from its original position while the cruise control is energized, a different voltage signal is sent to the module. The module then energizes or de-energizes the vacuum or vent solenoid. This closes or opens the respective valves.

During a cruise condition on a level road, with the cruise control turned on, the vent and vacuum solenoid are both de-energized. This causes each valve to be closed. Since vacuum is supplied to the diaphragm in the servo, the vacuum pulls the diaphragm against spring pressure. Since the diaphragm is attached to the throttle linkage through a bead chain, it pulls on the throttle linkage and then keeps it at a specified position.

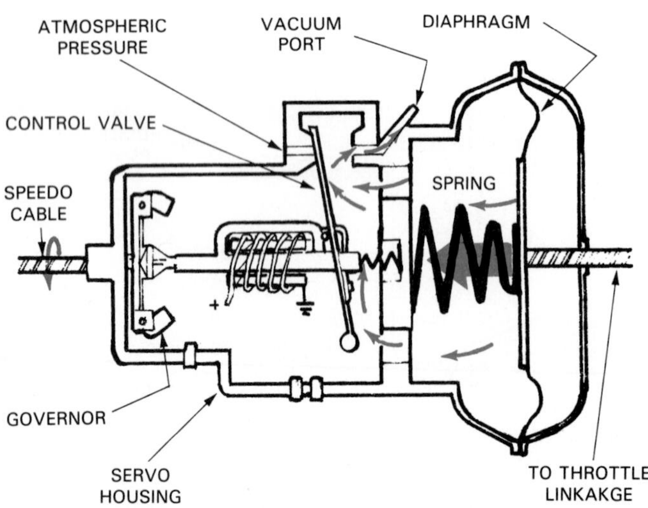

Figure 52-14. Vacuum pulls the diaphragm against spring pressure. A cable is attached to the diaphragm and moves in the same direction. This cable is also attached to the throttle linkage, and it pulls and holds the linkage. This action maintains a set speed. (Chrysler)

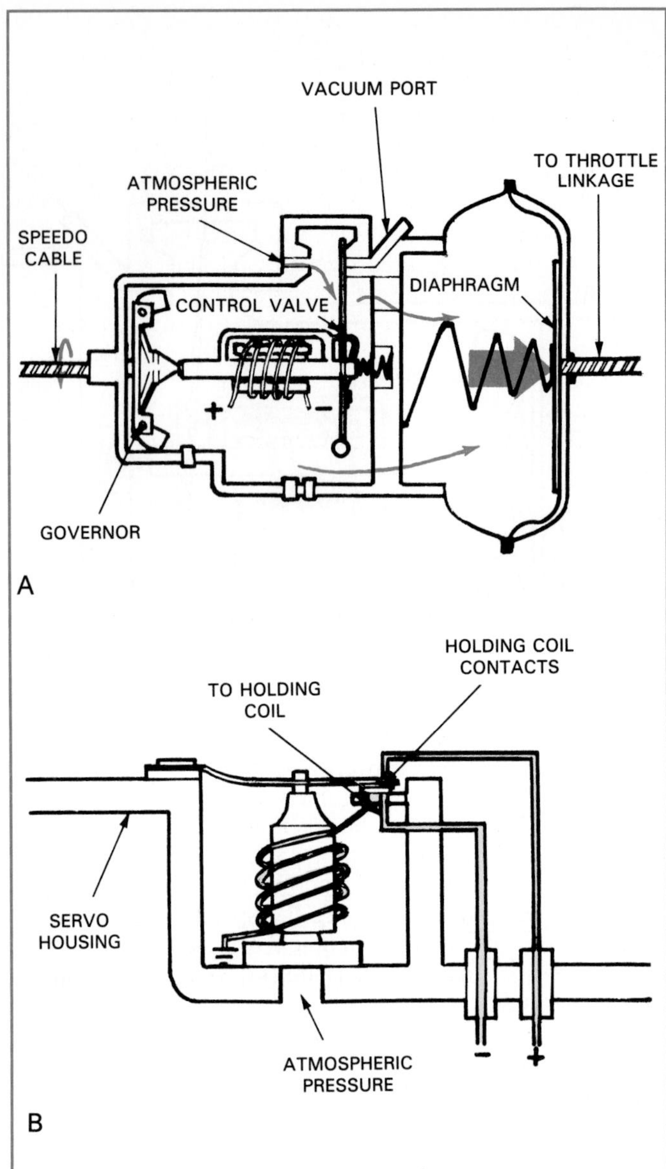

Figure 52-15. Servo operation that prevents the engine from overspeeding. A–When the vehicle is descending a steep grade, the governor pushes the control valve against the vacuum port. During vehicle braking, the control valve also blocks vacuum from acting on the diaphragm. B–When the brakes are applied, the brake release valve opens, allowing atmospheric pressure to act on the diaphragm. The brake release valve will not close until the "resume" or "set" button is depressed. (Chrysler)

If a load is placed on the engine, such as a car going up a steep grade, the vacuum in the chamber is reduced. The spring pressure, inside the chamber, is greater than the vacuum. The spring then pushes out on the diaphragm. Since the steel core is also attached to the diaphragm, it moves in the direction of the diaphragm. The voltage signal from the coil to the module is changed because of the new position of the steel core. The module, then, energizes the vacuum solenoid, and opens the valve. This exposes the diaphragm to more vacuum, which pulls the diaphragm and the steel core back to their original position. The vacuum solenoid is then de-energized. The vent solenoid remains de-energized during the process.

However, if the car is going down a steep grade, vacuum will remain high and pull on the diaphragm. This pushes the steel core further into the coil, and changes the voltage signal sent to the module. The module, then, energizes the vent solenoid. This will open the vent valve exhausting the vacuum in the chamber. The diaphragm and steel core then return to their original position. The vacuum solenoid remains de-energized during the process.

When the brake pedal is depressed, the vent solenoid is energized and the valve is opened. The vacuum solenoid and valve remain closed. Also, an extra vacuum release port is opened during this time to speed up the dumping of the vacuum from the chamber upon brake application. The cruise control system then disengages until the driver presses the "resume" or "set" button.

Chrysler Speed Control

The speed control system used on Chrysler cars is electrically actuated and vacuum operated. A slide switch mounted on the turn signal lever has three positions: "off," "on," and "resume speed," Figure 52-16. The "set speed" button is located in the end of the lever.

To engage the Chrysler system, the driver moves the slide switch to the "on" position, accelerates the car to the desired rate of speed, then presses and releases the "set speed" button. This sets the speed memory of the system and engages it to hold the car speed at that rate.

To disengage the speed control system, the driver makes a light or normal brake application. This disengages the control unit without erasing the speed memory. If the driver moves the slide switch to "off," or turns off the ignition switch, the system is disengaged and the speed memory is erased.

The "resume" position of the slide switch is used after the driver has applied the brake pedal. As mentioned, braking disengages the control unit without erasing the speed memory. Pressing the "resume" button, then, allows the car to return to the last memorized speed.

To increase the speed, the driver accelerates the car to the higher rate of speed, then depresses and releases the "speed set" button. Or, to increase the rate of speed by small degrees, tap the "speed set" button while the speed control unit is engaged and the car's speed will rise slightly.

To decrease speed, the driver taps the brake pedal slightly to disengage the speed control system. When the car decelerates to the new speed, the "speed set" button is depressed and then released.

As with other speed control systems, Chrysler's system permits the driver to accelerate at any time. When the greater speed is no longer needed, the driver releases the accelerator pedal and the speed control is resumed.

In addition to the sliding switch, Chrysler's speed control system uses a servo unit, Figure 52-17, throttle cable assembly, and stop lamp switch, which is located at the brake pedal, Figure 52-18.

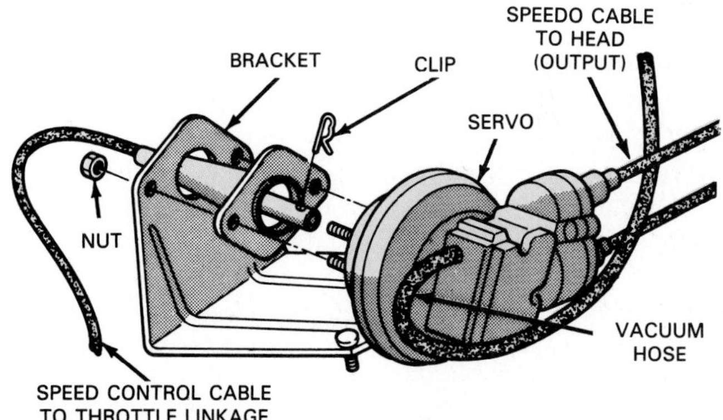

Figure 52-17. Speed control servo, control cable, and speedometer cable connections. (Chrysler)

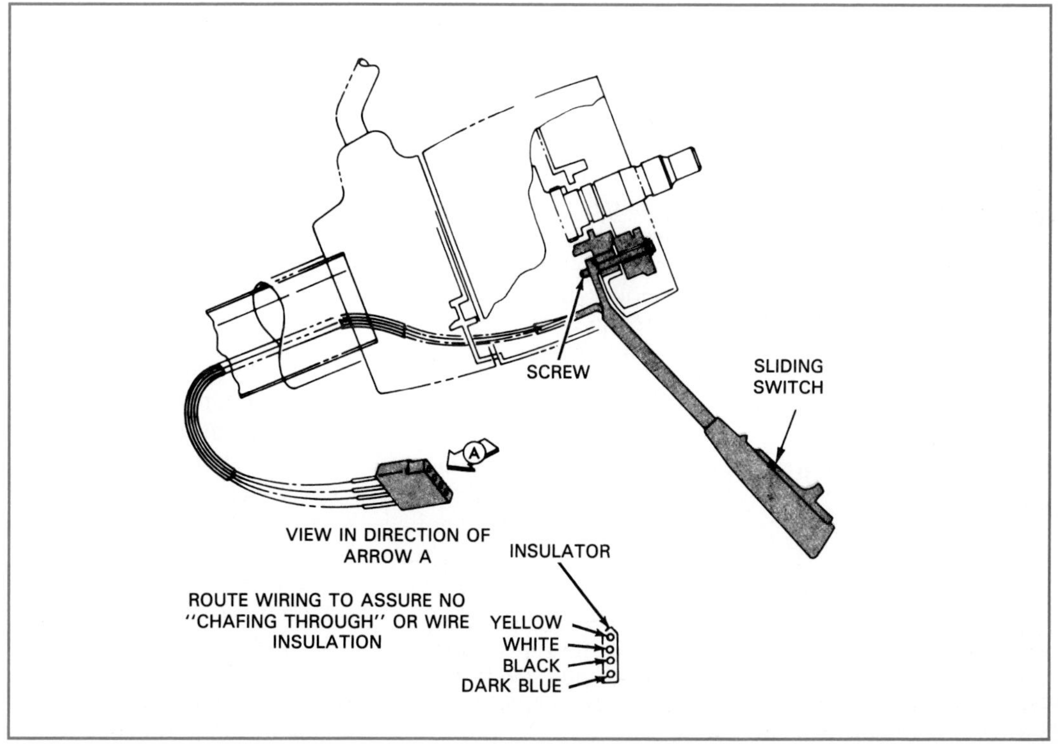

Figure 52-16. This control system uses a sliding switch in the turn signal lever.

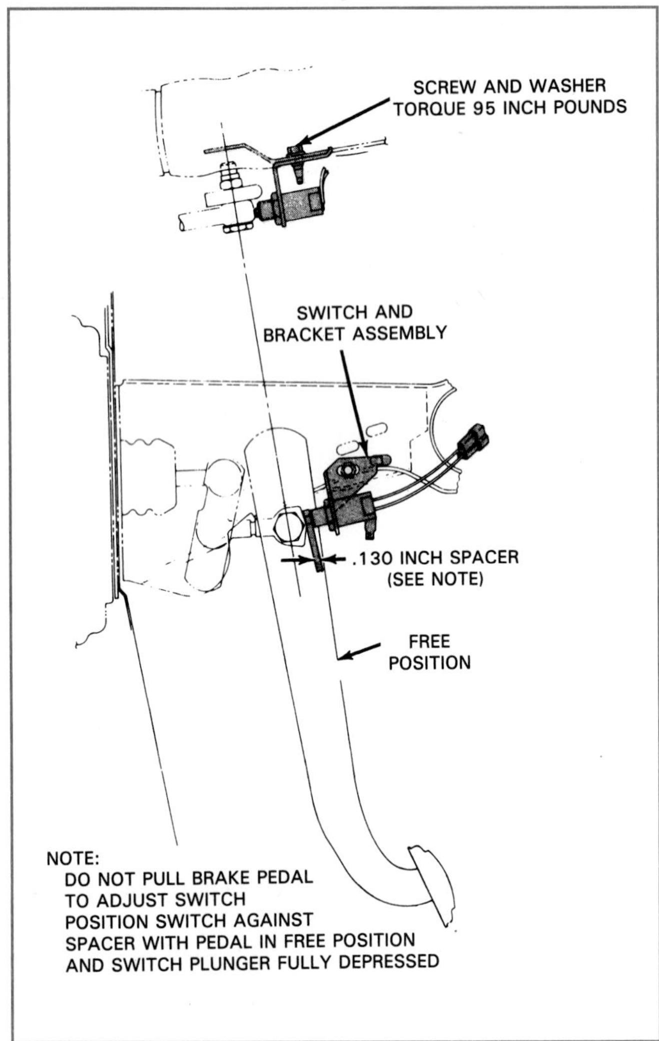

Figure 52-18. The stop lamp switch also energizes brake release valve in the servo housing.

Speed Increase/Decrease

If the speed of the car increases or decreases upon activating the speed control system, and: (1) Engine is properly tuned, (2) Engine is not pulling a load, (3) Throttle cable is properly adjusted, then the servo should be adjusted, Figure 52-19. The lock-in screw is turned counterclockwise 1/4 turn for each one mph decrease in speed. However, the lock-in screw is turned clockwise 1/4 turn for each one mph increase in speed. The lock-in screw can be turned only two turns in either direction. Any more will damage the servo.

Ford's Speed Control

The speed control system used on Ford cars includes an "off-on" switch, "set-accel" and "coast" switches, servo (throttle actuator) assembly, speed control sensor, amplifier assembly, check valve assembly, vacuum reserve tank, vacuum connections, wiring, and linkage.

The switches are located in the steering wheel spokes, Figure 52-20. To use Ford's speed control system, the engine must be running and the car traveling at from 30 to 80 mph. Then, by actuating the "on-off" switch in the steering wheel, the system is ready to accept a set speed signal.

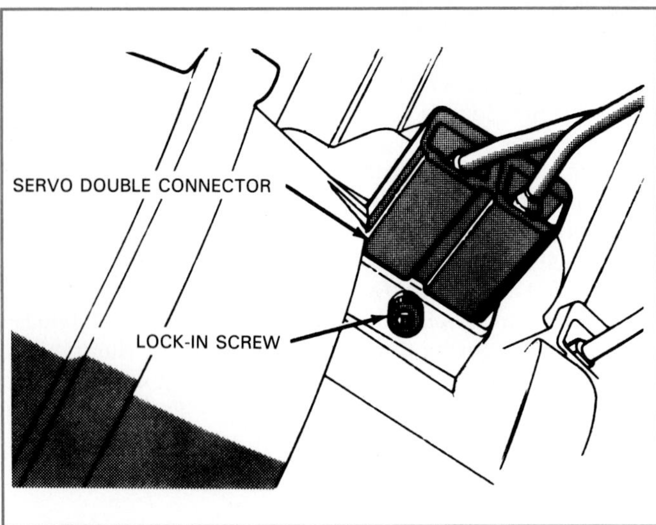

Figure 52-19. Lock-in screw can be adjusted to compensate for speed increase or decrease. Do not adjust the screw more than two turns in either direction.

Once the car is at a designated speed, the driver presses, then releases, the "set-accel" button. This speed will be maintained until a new rate of speed is set by the driver, the brake pedal is depressed, or the system is turned off by the driver.

If a reduced speed is desired, the driver can tap the brakes, and set the new speed by pressing the "set-accel" button. Or, the driver can apply the brakes, press the "coast" switch and allow the car to coast down to the new speed. Then, upon releasing the "coast" switch, the new speed is set. However, if the car speed drops below 30 mph, the driver must accelerate and reset it.

If an increased speed is desired, the driver can depress the accelerator until the higher rate of speed is reached. The "set-accel" button is depressed, then released, and the car maintains the new set speed.

GM's Cruise Control

General Motor's cruise control system allows the driver to set a desired rate of speed (over 30, 35, or 40 mph, depending on car application), which the system will automatically maintain.

GM speed control systems include:

- Engagement switch–Located on the end of the turn signal lever, Figure 52-21.
- Servo unit–Mounted on the left inner front fender and connected by a cable to the throttle linkage.
- Brake release switch–Mounted on brake pedal bracket. It energizes the brake release valve when the brake pedal is depressed.

As with other speed control systems, the driver of a GM car accelerates it to the cruising speed desired. Next, the "set" button is depressed and then released. This allows the cruise system to take over throttle control and maintain this speed in spite of changes in terrain.

The GM system automatically disengages whenever the brake pedal is depressed. To resume "cruise control," the driver presses the "resume" button. The driver can adjust the speed upward by accelerating to the new rate of

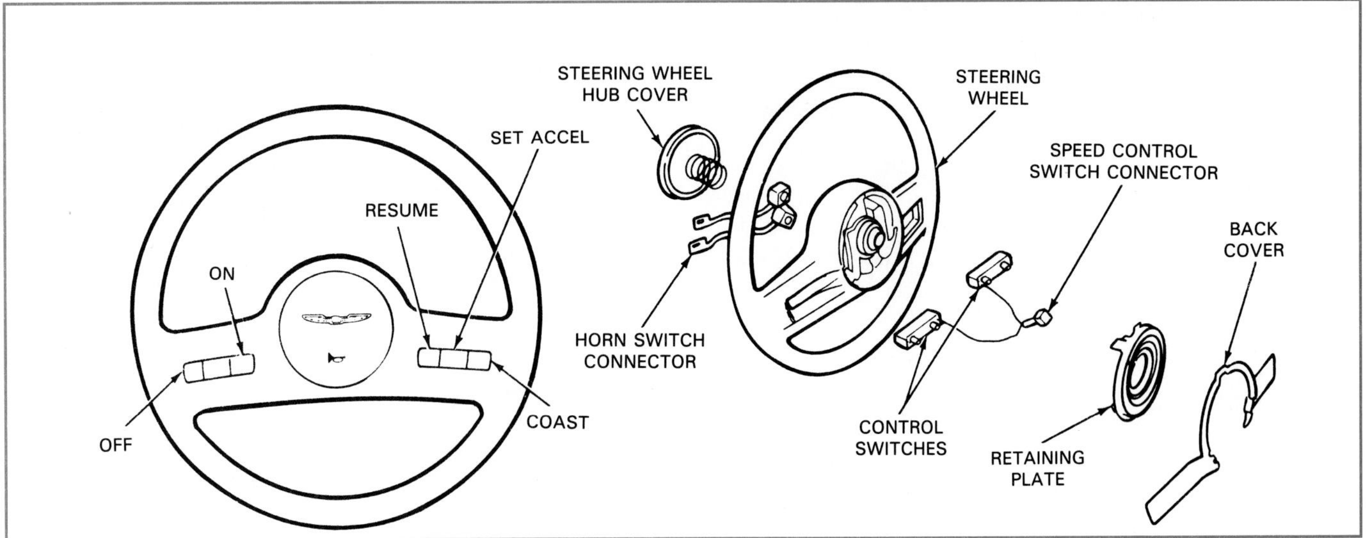

Figure 52-20. In some systems, the cruise control selector switch is located on the steering wheel. (Ford)

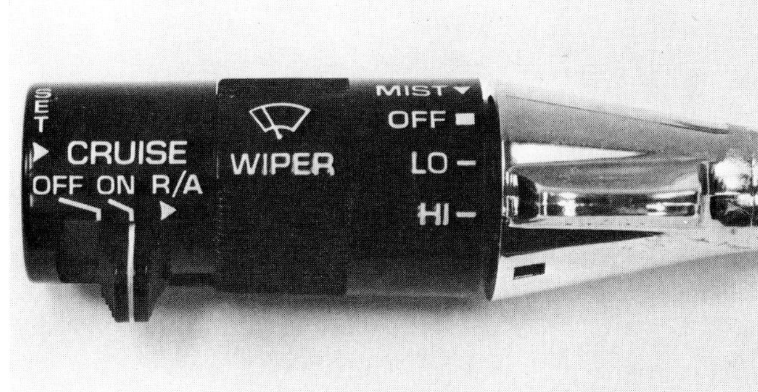

Figure 52-21. In some systems, the cruise control selector switch is combined with the windshield wiper selector in the turn signal lever. (Chevrolet)

speed, then depress the "set" button. To override the system at any time, the driver depresses the accelerator (to pass another car, for example). Release of the accelerator pedal will return the car to the previous constant cruising speed.

Chapter 52–Review Questions

Write your answers on a separate sheet of paper. Do not write in this book.

1. How is an analog speedometer driven?
2. The speedometer shows only the speed of the car. True or False?
3. On what principle does the speed indicating portion of an analog speedometer operate?
   (A) Electronic.
   (B) Mechanical.
   (C) Magnetic.
   (D) Electrical.
4. What is used to control the pull on the speed cup?
   (A) Hairspring.
   (B) Mechanical brake.
   (C) Magnetic brake.
5. Describe analog speedometer operation.
6. What does an odometer record?
7. How is an analog odometer driven?
8. How many revolutions of the drive cable will register one mile on the meter?
   (A) 101 revolutions.
   (B) 1001 revolutions.
   (C) 3.77 revolutions.
   (D) 4.01 revolutions.
9. Where do most troubles in a speedometer start?
10. Describe the procedure for checking a speedometer cable for kinks.
11. Describe a method of checking an analog speedometer to see if there is binding present.
12. What is the result of too much friction in the speed cup bearing?
    (A) Speedometer indicates higher than normal speed.
    (B) Speedometer indicates lower than normal speed.
    (C) Incorrect odometer readings.
13. Name two reasons that a speedometer cable becomes frayed.
14. Will too much end play in the magnet shaft cause the speedometer pointer to fluctuate? Yes or No?
15. A digital speedometer operates the same as an analog speedometer. True or False?
16. What is the most common type of digital speedometer display?
17. Describe how a digital speedometer operates.
18. The components of a cruise control system include the:
    (A) servo.
    (B) selection control.
    (C) brake disengagement switch.
    (D) All of the above.
    (E) None of the above.
19. Technician A states that manifold vacuum can enter the servo (either type) housing. Technician B states that atmospheric pressure can enter the servo (either type) housing.
    Who is right?
    (A) A only.
    (B) B only.
    (C) Both A & B.
    (D) Neither A nor B.

20. The core is directly connected to the control valve of the governor-type system. True or False?
21. The amount of atmospheric pressure or vacuum that enters the servo (either type) is regulated. True or False?
22. Technician A states that during a low-vacuum condition with the cruise control energized, the control valve closes or blocks off the atmospheric port in the servo (governor type) housing. Technician B states that during periods of high vacuum with the cruise control energized, the control valve blocks or closes the vacuum port in the servo (governor type) housing. Who is right?
    (A) A only.
    (B) B only.
    (C) Both A & B.
    (D) Neither A nor B.
23. With the cruise control energized (governor type), the control valve is between the atmospheric port and vacuum port when on a level road. True or False?
24. During braking, atmospheric pressure enters the servo (either type) housing. True or False?
25. Vacuum is supplied to the servo (either type) housing. True or False?
26. Explain what must be done for the cruise control to regain control of the throttle after the brakes have been applied? What must be done after accelerating to pass another car?
27. The control module energizes the vent and vacuum solenoid on the variable inductance type servo. True or False?
28. Technician A states that on a variable inductance type servo, the vacuum and vent valves are open during a cruise condition on a level road with the cruise control energized. Technician B states that on a variable inductance type servo, the vent valve is opened under low-vacuum conditions when the cruise control is energized. Who is right?
    (A) A only.
    (B) B only.
    (C) Both A & B.
    (D) Neither A nor B.
29. Technician A states that the position of the steel core in the coil (variable inductance type) determines which valve is opened. Technician B states that to prevent overspeeding of the engine when the car is going down a steep grade, the vent valve is opened (variable inductance type) while the vacuum valve remains closed. Who is right?
    (A) A only.
    (B) B only.
    (C) Both A & B.
    (D) Neither A nor B.

Chapter 53
Body Repairing and Refinishing

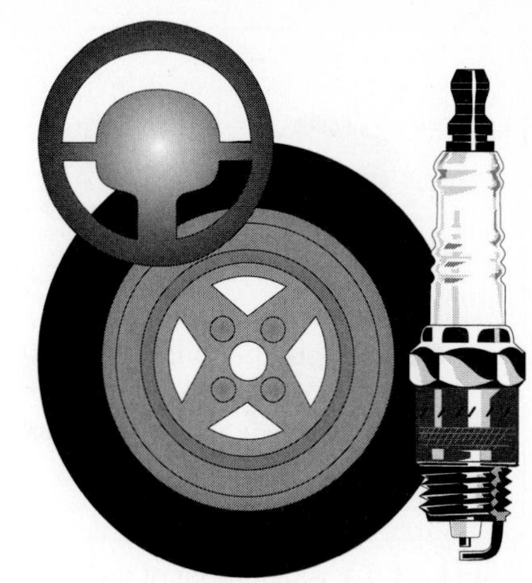

After studying this chapter, you will be able to:

- ❍ Demonstrate the procedure for straightening a damaged panel.
- ❍ Explain how to replace a damaged panel.
- ❍ Describe the welding and cutting procedures used on late-model vehicles.
- ❍ Explain why it is important to properly prepare a surface before painting.
- ❍ Describe the most common spray gun types used for auto body work.
- ❍ Describe the various types of paints available for automotive refinishing.

Body Work

No matter how badly a body panel or fender has been damaged, it can be straightened. Special tools and equipment are needed, plus skill on the technician's part. However, in cases of severe damage, it may be quicker and cheaper to replace the part than to repair it.

Straightening sheet metal is much easier than it appears to be. With modern equipment and tools, the work proceeds at a fast pace. The needed skill can be attained in a short time by practicing on junked fenders, doors, or panels.

The ease and speed with which sheet metal can be straightened is largely dependent on starting the repair work in the right way. When done correctly, the amount of ***dinging*** is reduced, Figure 53-1. Also, ***stretching*** of the sheet metal will be kept to a minimum, and the amount of hand ***filing*** and ***sanding*** will be reduced.

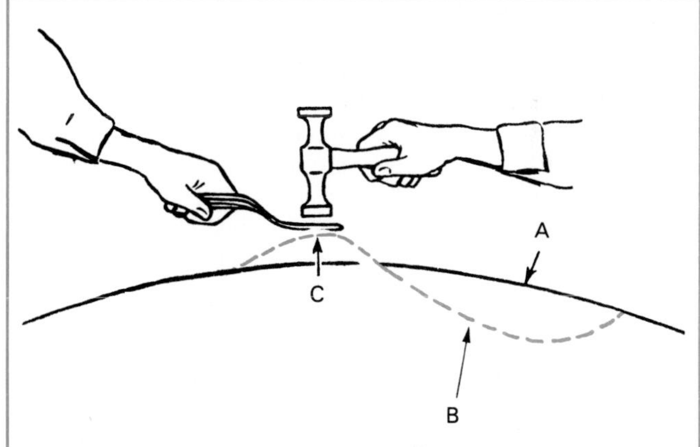

Figure 53-1. Apply pressure first at the ridge farthest from the point where the panel was struck.

When straightening a wrinkled panel, the damage should be removed in the reverse of the order in which it was made. When a collision occurs, there will be a major depression in the panel, followed by a buckled area and a series of ridges.

Without proper instruction, a technician will apply pressure at the spot where the panel was struck first and where it is depressed the most. The correct method is to apply pressure at the ridge farthest from the point where the body was struck first. When this is done, the entire damaged area will spring back into its original position.

To make the procedure clear, assume that the original form of the panel is shown at A in Figure 53-1. Point B is where it was struck, and point C is a ridge that was formed last. As indicated, start the straightening process at point C. Place a spoon, Figure 53-2, on top of the ridge and strike it with a mallet or hammer. Follow the ridge with the spoon and mallet, and you will find that as the ridge is removed, the major depression at B will also spring back and conform very closely to the original contour of the panel.

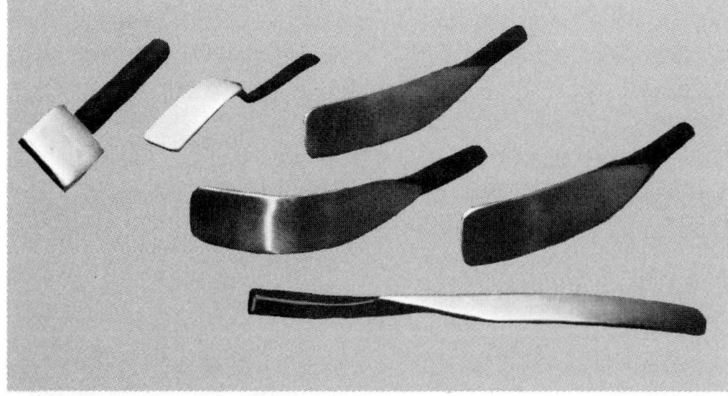

Figure 53-2. Spoons are used to restore sheet metal to its original shape. (Snap-on Tools)

The few remaining dents are then removed with a dolly block, Figure 53-3, and a hammer. Select a dolly block with a face of the same curvature as the panel. Hold it under the panel and strike the high point of the dents with a dinging hammer. In this way, the dolly block acts as an anvil. The blows tend to stretch the metal by making it thinner.

Hammers, Spoons, and Dolly Blocks

As mentioned, ***hammers, spoons,*** and ***dolly blocks*** are often used to straighten damaged panels. All that is needed of the hammer is to press the sheet metal back into position.

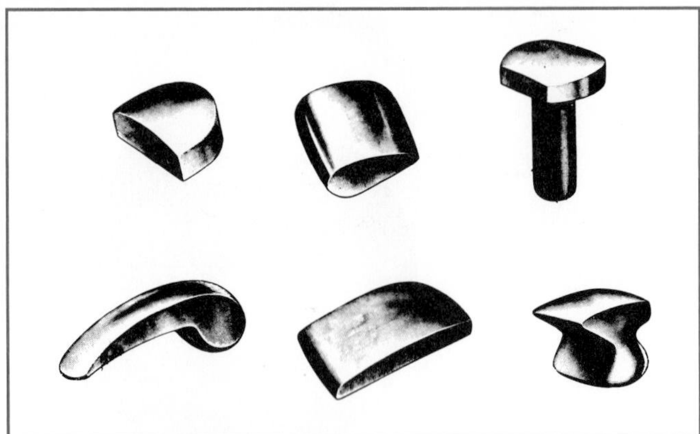

Figure 53-3. Assortment of dolly blocks. Top–Heel, utility, and mushroom dollies. Bottom–Wedge, toe, and general-purpose dollies.

Therefore, several light hammer blows should be used rather than a few heavy ones. If the metal is stretched, a large bulge will result, which will need shrinking.

The hammer blows should be at the rate of 60 per minute. Try to "pull" the hammer so it strikes the surface of the sheet metal with a sliding, or glancing, blow.

Note, too, that when the dent rises above the surface of the dolly block, the hammer should strike the center of the dent. If the dent is below the surface of the metal and toward the dolly, place the dolly against the head of the dent and direct the hammer blows against the edge of the dent. Hold the hammer loosely with the thumb along the top of the handle for better control of the bounce.

There are many types of hammers, Figure 53-4. They come in many face configurations (square faces, round faces, serrated faces) and varying shank lengths (pointed shanks, roughing hammers, etc.). Each is designed for a specific type of work. These hammers are not to be used to strike against other hardened objects. They are to be used only for striking sheet metal.

A short-shank hammer is needed where there is not much space to work. The long-shank type is needed when working in a deep contour. The serrated-face hammer is for shrinking metal; the tapered-shank type is for working on molding, etc. All should be included in a body worker's tool kit.

There are a variety of spoons, Figure 53-2, and dolly blocks, Figure 53-3. Each is shaped and sized to make certain tough jobs easy. The spoons are used on polished surfaces. That is, the spoon is placed against the finished surface of a panel and is struck with the hammer. Spoons can be used as dollies if space prevents the use of regular dollies. They are also used for prying a bulge in a door or trunk lid back into place.

Dollies vary in weight, shape, and contour so that they will conform to the curve of the panel and can be used in cramped quarters. Some provide grooves for working beads and molding. Skill in using these tools can be quickly attained by working on junk panels and fenders. The point is to have a wide selection of spoons, dollies, and hammers so that all types of body work can be handled.

As the dent in the body panel is being removed, rub your hand over the surface. This will help determine those spots that need more straightening. Then, when this method fails to show any high or low spots, use the body file, Figures 53-5 and 53-6. Only light cuts should be made. Remember that the purpose is not to remove metal, but to show the areas that need further attention with the dolly and hammer. Use a sander to locate the few irregularities. This will remove any roughness that cannot be removed with the dolly. Sometimes the hammer and dolly method cannot be used due to structural interference. When this occurs, pull rods or slide hammers must be used.

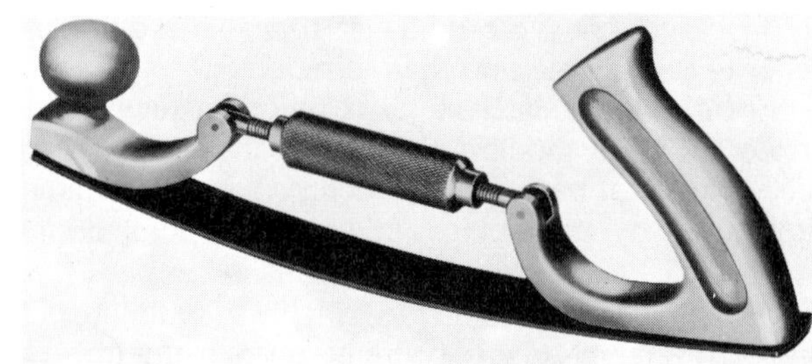

Figure 53-5. Holder for flexible mill tooth file.

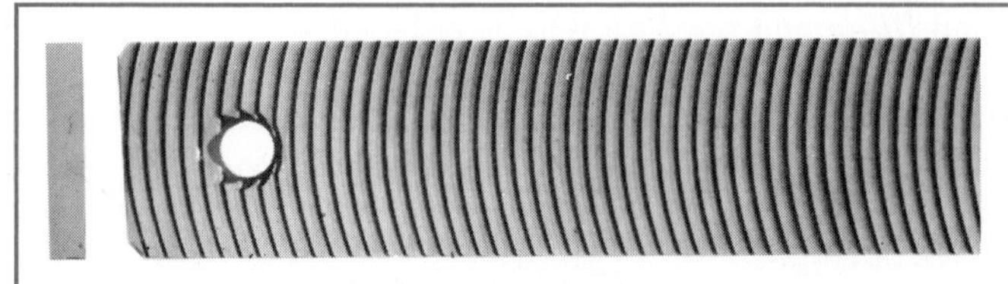

Figure 53-6. Flexible mill tooth file.

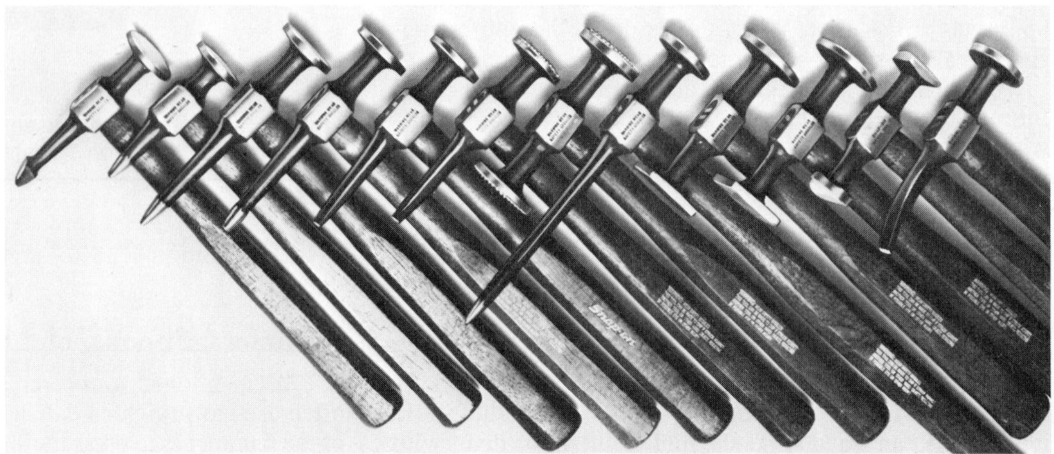

Figure 53-4. A variety of body hammers is needed for different types of body work. (Snap-on Tools)

Using Pull Rods and Slide Hammers

When removing dents and creases from body panels, a great deal of time is often needed to remove inside trim. Also, the work is complicated when the damage is located in doors and rear trunk lids. In these areas, metal braces and other structural members make it hard to use the dolly and hammer method.

On many jobs, the use of ***pull rods*** and/or ***slide hammers*** makes it unnecessary to remove inside trim since the work is done entirely from the outside of the damaged panel. The procedure is to drill a series of 9/64″ (3 mm) holes in the deepest part of the crease. These holes should be about 1/4″ (6 mm) apart. The crease is then worked by inserting the hooked ends of the pull rods in the holes and pulling on the handles, Figure 53-7A, or by screwing the slide hammer into each hole and slamming the sliding weight rearward, Figure 53-7B. Start at the front of the crease and work to the rear. Light reflection is a big help in locating high and low spots.

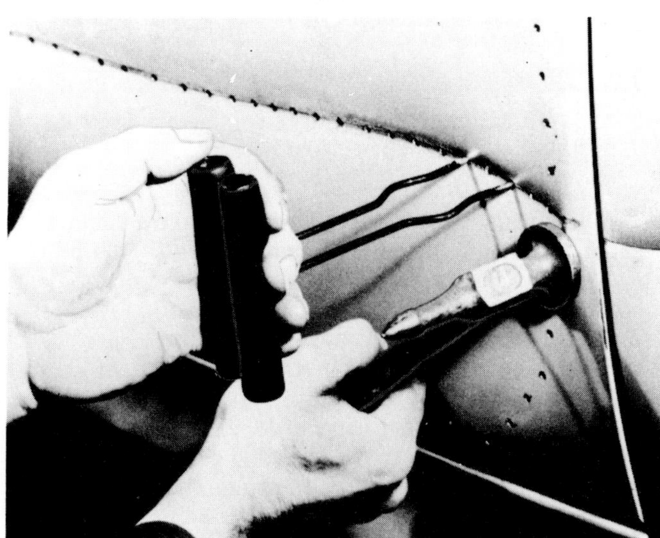

A

B

Figure 53-7. Drill a series of 9/64″ holes in the deepest part of the dent. A–Dent is then pulled out with rods. B–Dent is pulled out with a slide hammer until the damaged panel is aligned with the original contour. (Chilton's Motor/Age)

Body Filler

After a dent has been lifted to the original contour and the paint has been removed from the dent and the surrounding area, ***body filler*** is applied. First, etch the bare metal where the filler will be applied. This will remove any dirt, grease, and rust from the surface. Mix the filler with correct amount of ***hardener*** until it becomes one color, Figure 53-8. Apply the mixture to the panel using a plastic spreader, Figure 53-9. Make sure that the car has been at room temperature (70°F) for 24 hours prior to applying the filler. An infrared lamp should also be used on humid days. Direct the lamp toward the panel at a distance of three feet. After the filler has dried, shape it to the contour of the body, Figures 53-10 and 53-11.

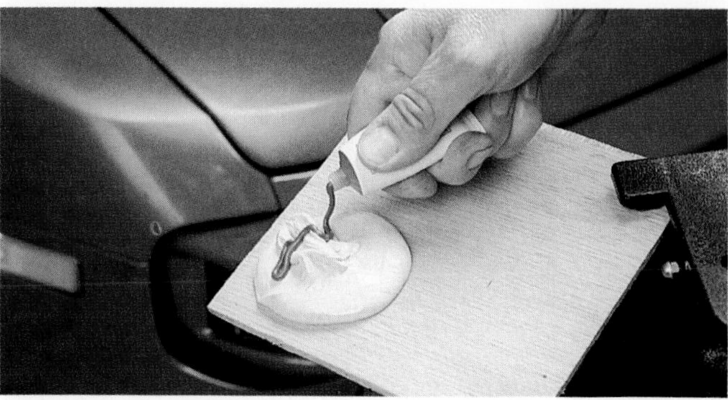

Figure 53-8. Mixing plastic body filler with hardener on a pallet. A golf ball size of filler needs about a 1″ ribbon of hardener. Mix thoroughly. (Oatey Co.)

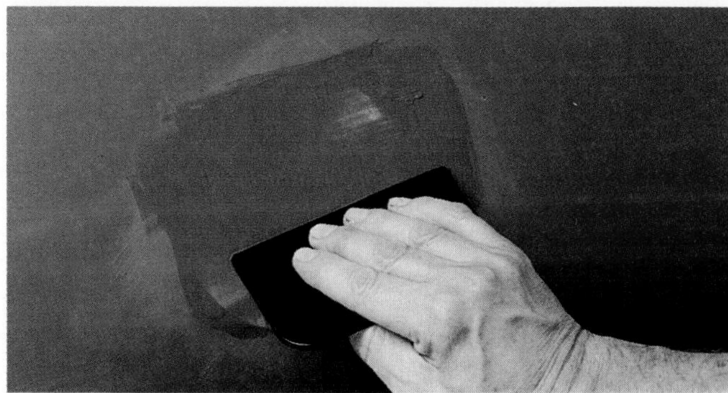

Figure 53-9. Apply filler evenly to the dented portion of the panel. The filler should not be thicker than 1/8″ or it will crack when dry. (Oatey Co.)

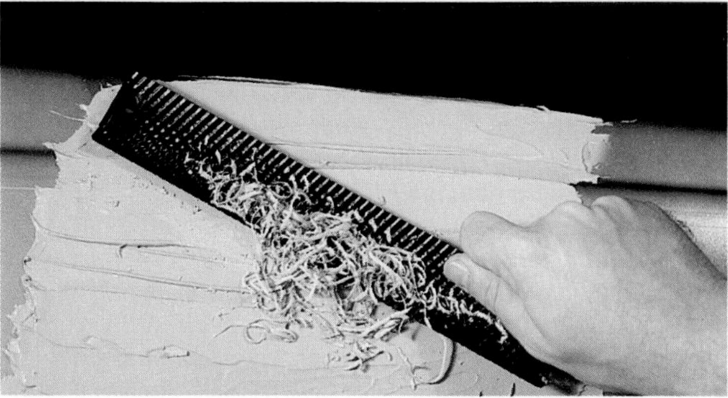

Figure 53-10. Using a special file to shape body filler after it has dried. (Oatey Co.)

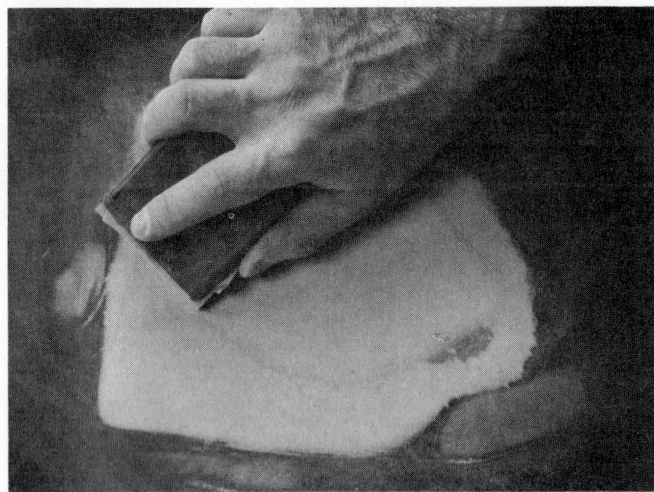

A

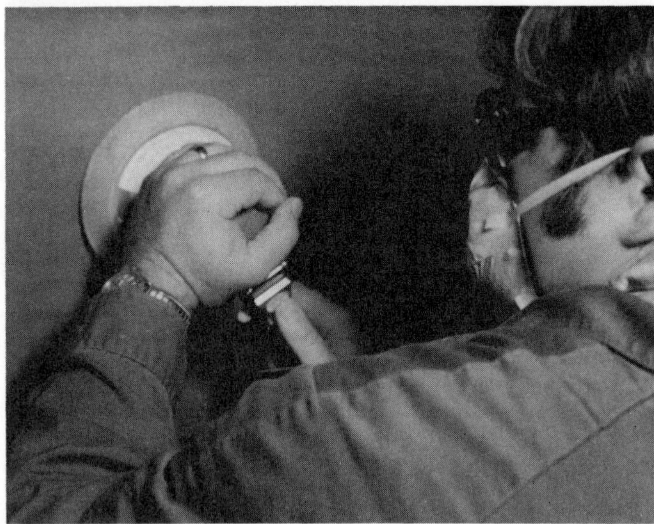

B

Figure 53-11. Sand the filler smooth after roughing it to shape. A–Hand sanding. B–Sanding with an orbital sander. (Marson Corp. and 3M Co.)

Power Straightening

While the hand dolly and dinging hammer are used most of the time, there is a trend toward the use of ***power dinging equipment.*** Electric and pneumatic power tools of this type are available from a number of manufacturers. On panels where they can be used, a lot of time can be saved. Also, power tools will not stretch the metal as much as a dolly and hammer.

It is awkward to use power dinging hammers on car tops and other large areas where damage is more than 18″-20″ from the edge of the panel. Power equipment works well where damage is close to the edge.

Another piece of equipment for straightening bodies is the ***hydraulic jack,*** or ***hydraulic ram.*** This type of repair equipment has fittings designed to remove dents and to push or pull damaged panels and parts back into position, Figure 53-12. Specific applications include straightening diamond-shaped door and window frames, squaring bodies, correcting door curvature, and repairing frames and bumpers.

Figure 53-12. Spreading an engine compartment opening with hydraulic equipment. (Hein-Werner)

When using hydraulic equipment to take a dent out of a panel, the method used with hand dollies should be followed. Apply pressure first at the outer edge of the dent, then work around the dent. Gradually work toward the center. Complete the work with a hand dolly.

Before starting to straighten a panel, clean all the dirt from both sides. Also, remove any undercoating from the fenders and panels. This can be done by scraping or by heating it lightly with a torch. Mud and grit that stick to the panels will mar the surface of the straightening tools. Undercoating will make the job harder.

Unitized Bodies

The use of heat and heavy-duty jacks must be controlled when straightening ***unitized bodies.*** Care must be taken because of the difference in the type of metal in the body. It is possible to pull damaged areas back into place and in alignment by means of lightweight jacks and hydraulic equipment without the use of heat.

However, many body shops find that repairs can be made faster if special equipment is used. With certain types of equipment, the damaged car is first secured to a ***bench*** (floor or rack type), Figure 53-13. Then, corrective pulls and/or pushes are made at several points at the same time. Dimensional drawings of the car are needed when working on a unitized body.

When checking a unitized body for misalignment, measurements are taken between reference points on the car and compared to those on the drawings. These measurements are indicated not only in the horizontal plane, but also vertically from the floor or from the bench to which the car has been secured. These dimensions are held to 1/16″ (1.6 mm) limits.

Damaged areas should be roughed out before taking any measurements for squaring up the body. In severe

Figure 53-13. Unibody repairs are often performed on a bench-type straightening unit. (VICA)

cases, reinforcement brackets and other inner construction must be removed before restoration of the outer shell and pillars. This will prevent excessive strain on the parts. Always straighten, install, and secure such parts before attempting to align the unitized body.

Filing and Sanding

After the sheet metal has been made as smooth as possible with a hammer and dolly, file or sand the surface to remove any tool marks or other small dents. Also, sand back (feather) the paint, Figure 53-14, surrounding the edges of the straightened area of sheet metal. This is important because a smooth surface is needed for the filler, primer, and other coats of refinishing material. Special files, sanding materials, and equipment designed for auto body work are available.

A ***body file*** is flexible and is made to fit a special holder, Figure 53-5. The ***holder*** can be adjusted to arch the file to conform to the curve of the body panel. The teeth of the file are curved and are designed to cut fast without loading up when used on the sheet metal of the body.

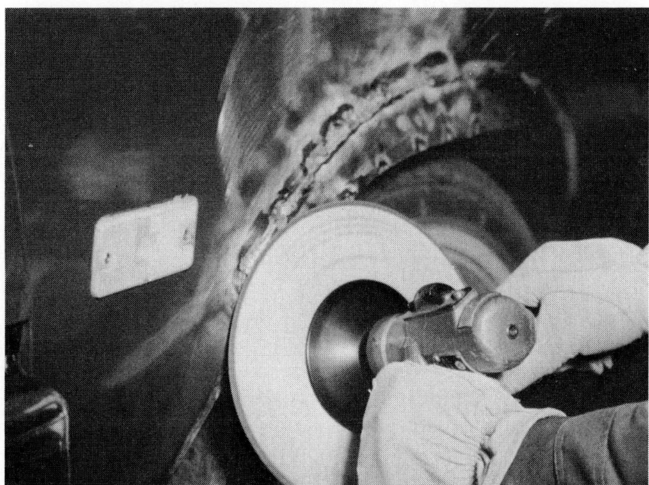

Figure 53-14. Grinding sheet metal. Note the feathered edges. (3M Co.)

The surface is filed first in one direction, and then at a right angle. On the return stroke, the file should be lifted from the surface being filed. This will not only produce a smoother surface, but it will also prolong the life of the file. Dragging the file along the surface of the metal on the return stroke will tend to dull the teeth. It is important to note that special body files can be resharpened.

Because a sanding disk is flexible, it will follow the larger indentations in a body. For that reason, a ***power sander*** is used to locate the high and low spots when the straightening process has been nearly completed. Of course, its main function is for the final finishing of the metal surface. A sander can also be used to remove paint or other refinishing material that surrounds the damaged area. This is known as ***featheredging.***

Before sanding a panel, select the disk having the correct abrasive for the surface. Many shops use three different grits to prepare the surface for repainting. They first use a #16 grit disk to remove rust and loose paint. This is followed with a #24 grit disk for surfacing the metal, restoring contours, and cutting down welds. Then, a #50 grit disk is used.

For sharply curved surfaces, which cannot be reached by normal sanders, special cone-type sanders are needed. These sanders will reach curved surfaces around headlights, fender joints, back deck panels, etc.

As mentioned, the surface of the straightened panel must be sanded. The edges surrounding the repair must also be sanded. Some body workers use a disk-type sander, Figure 53-14. In disk featheredging, a #100 grit disk is recommended. A #80 grit disk is used in the sander and for hand sanding too, with #220 grit being used for finished featheredging.

When disk sanding, hold the disk grinding machine at an angle of 20° to the work, Figure 53-15.

Apply enough pressure so that about 1″ of the disk is bent and is in contact with the surface being sanded. The

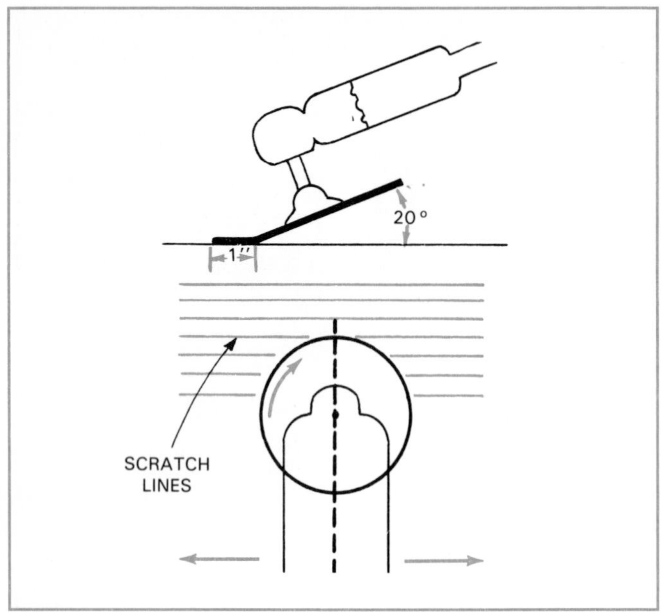

Figure 53-15. Hold the disk sander 20° to the surface of the panel.

disk sander should never be operated so the entire area of the disk is flat against the surface of the work, nor at an extreme angle.

Also, the disk sander should not be swung in an arc. It should always be moved so that it is perpendicular to the scratch lines. By sanding in this fashion, less conditioning is needed to prepare the metal for priming.

A sander should be operated so that the scratch lines will be parallel. Hand sanding should produce the same effect.

Removing Sand Scratches

Sand scratches have ruined many jobs which otherwise would have been perfect. These scratches do not show up until after the finish coat has been sprayed.

Unless the person repairing and smoothing the metal does a good job, it will be impossible for the painter to fill the scratches so that they will not show. Careless filing or bearing too hard on a coarse disk leaves scratches, gouges, and furrows that are hard to fill.

Many body workers use a coarse disk for roughing and cutting down weld spots. Then, the major part of the sanding is done with a #24 disk and final finishing of the metal with a disk of #50 or #80 grit. Even with such care, some sand scratches may occur because of small burrs or fins of torn metal along the edges of the sand scratches. It pays to follow up the heavy power sanding with a little hand sanding using #150 paper.

While primers have been improved in their ability to fill and cover a surface, they cannot be depended on to do a job with a single coat. Apply several coats of primer and allow ample time for each coat to dry. This is better than applying a single heavy coat, since it is hard to tell when the heavy coat has dried all the way through.

Use fine paper when sanding priming coats. #220 or #240 paper will produce scratches that show through the first coats. In some cases, this paper can be used for the first sanding of primers. However, body technicians suggest using #320 or #360 first and finishing with #400 paper.

When lacquer is used to finish a car, the lacquer thinner penetrates the undercoat and causes swelling where the undercoat is heaviest. The swelling will be greater if the lacquer is sanded and polished before all the thinner has evaporated. A good practice is to first spray a light fog coat of lacquer. This will reduce the possibility of sand scratch swelling, which spoils the appearance.

Scratches can also be caused in the final polishing of the finish coat if care is not used in the selection of the rubbing compound. The finer the abrasive in the rubbing coat, the less chance there is of scratches.

When doing spot painting, featheredge the spot. Give the area and edge a final sanding with #360 or #400 paper to remove any scratches. If rubbing compound is used, clean the area with a good wax-and-grease remover.

Exercise care with synthetic enamel. While it does not contain strong solvents, the high luster of the enamel will magnify any scratches that may be present.

Patching Rusted Areas

When body panels have become rusted through, Figure 53-16, many body workers repair the damage using one of the methods developed for this purpose. One popular method involves using sheets of special ***fabric,*** such as fiberglass. First, sand the surface to remove all traces of rust, paint, and other foreign material. Then, fill it with resin-soaked fiberglass patches, cutting the final patch large enough to lap over the surrounding undamaged surfaces.

After the fiberglass patches dry, grind them as smooth as possible. Then, apply body filler over the fiberglass patches, Figures 53-8 to 53-11. This allows the filler to be shaped. This is done because the fiberglass is too hard to shape to the contour of the body when it is dry.

Warning: Use special care when adding hardener (catalyst) to fiberglass resin. If one drop of hardener gets in your eye, it will progressively destroy eye tissue and result in blindness.

Figure 53-16. Rust has eaten a hole in this panel.

Replacing Panels

Instead of straightening a badly damaged area, time can be saved by installing a new panel or part. In the case of a damaged body panel, cut out the damaged area and weld in a section of a new panel. Replacement panels are available. The entire panel or a portion of the panel can be replaced, depending on the size of the damaged area.

The procedure for replacing a panel is as follows. Rough out and shape the damaged area, making sure that the undamaged portion is in correct contour and is not sprung out of alignment. Measure the piece of metal to be replaced, Figure 53-17. Take these measurements from the edge of the panel, the molding, or beading. This is important since these points are to be transferred to the replacement panel.

Next, scribe a line around the area to be cut from the service panel and cut along the scribed line. The method of cutting will vary with the type of equipment available.

Straighten the edges of this portion of new panel and position the new section over the damaged area. Scribe a line around its outer edge, and use this line as a guide in cutting out the damaged area.

After straightening the cut edge of the fender on the car, fit the new section in position and hold it by means of C-clamps, Figure 53-18. Tack weld the section in place, starting the welds at the top center. Work out to the sides, and then down the sides. Make a continuous weld, doing about 6″ at a time. To reduce distortion, stagger the welds.

With a grooved dolly, hammer the weld so it is about 1/16″ below the surface of the surrounding panel, Figure 53-19. Sand the area around the weld with a power sander or file the surface to produce the correct contour. Next, fill the groove with body filler. Then, sand the surface to prepare it for painting. If the damaged area to be replaced is at a pillar post or at a spot-welded seam, split the seam by driving a thin chisel between the two pieces.

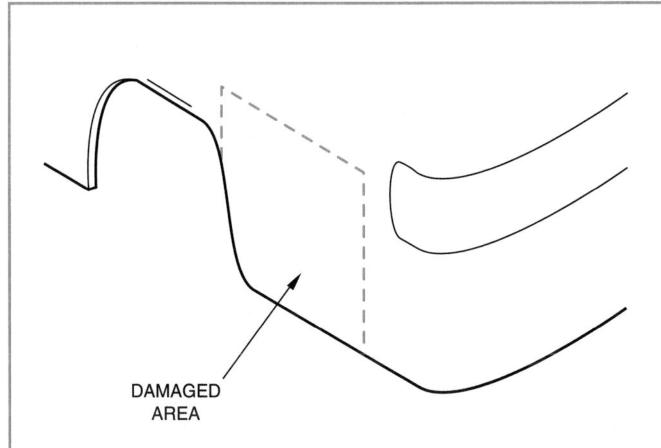

Figure 53-17. Outline the damaged area of fender as shown.

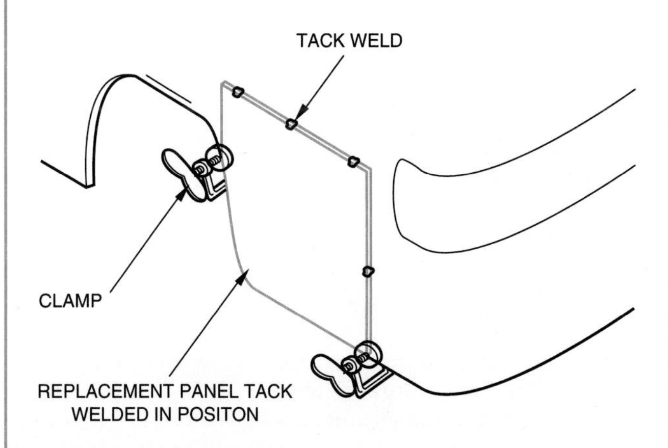

Figure 53-18. Secure the new section of fender in place with C-clamps, and then weld it in place.

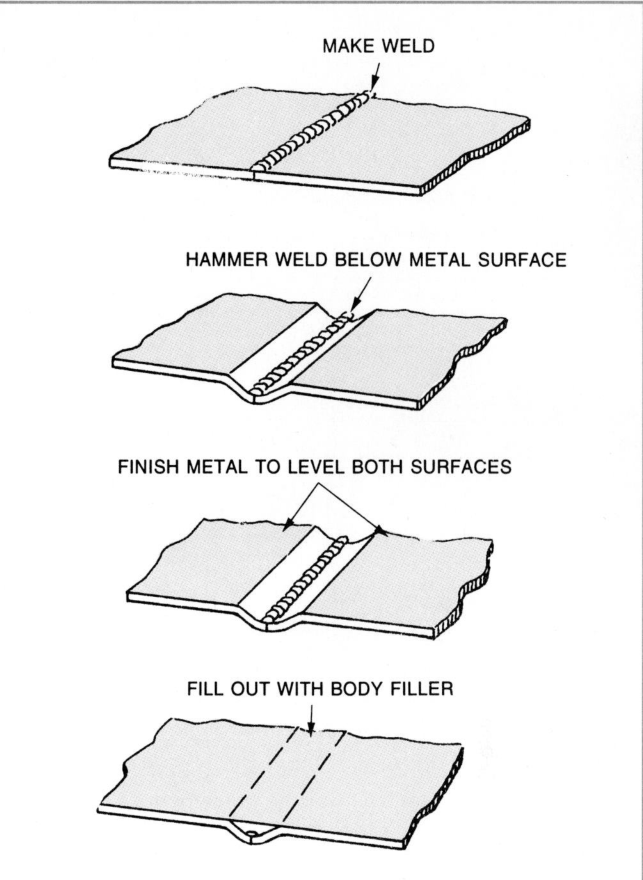

Figure 53-19. Steps in covering a welded joint with body filler.

Welding

Skill in using ***welding equipment*** is not hard to develop. In the past, oxyacetylene welding equipment was used when making auto body repairs. However, this method creates too much heat and destroys the properties of the high-strength steels used in late-model vehicles. Therefore, ***metal inert gas (MIG) welders*** are use when repairing late-model vehicles, Figure 53-20. MIG welding leaves a narrow heat-affected zone, reducing the chance of metal damage. Additionally, MIG welding techniques are easier to master than oxyacetylene techniques. Therefore, MIG welding is recommended for most auto body repairs. Most MIG welding units are self contained and utilize a continuous wire filler electrode and a cover gas, which prevents air from contacting the weld. See Figure 53-21.

The typical procedure for using a MIG welder is as follows. Before welding a body panel, clean the repair area so that both sides of the joint are free of dirt, rust, paint, etc. After cleaning the joint area, align the pieces to be welded. Hold the welding gun approximately 3/8″ (10mm) from work surface and pull the trigger. The gun should be held stationary until the electrode touches the work surface and an arc is formed.

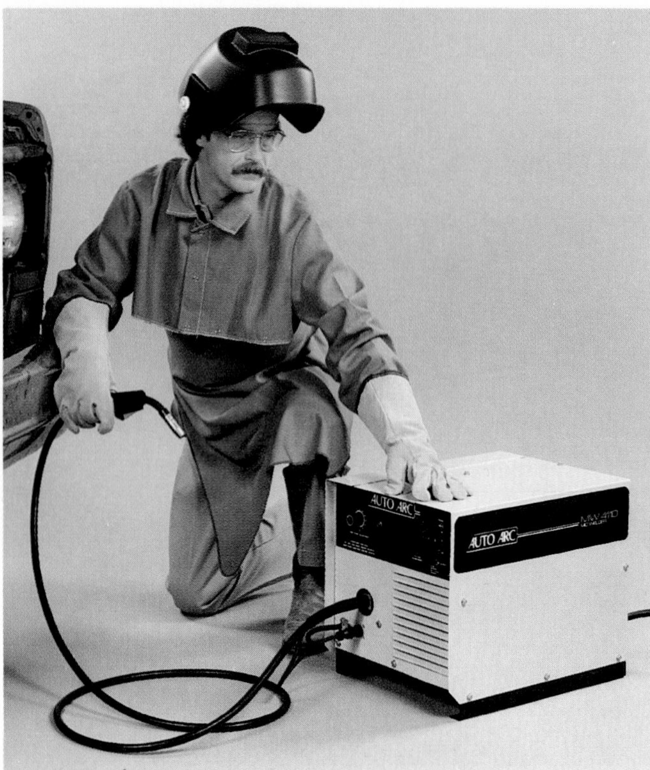

Figure 53-20. Typical MIG welding equipment.

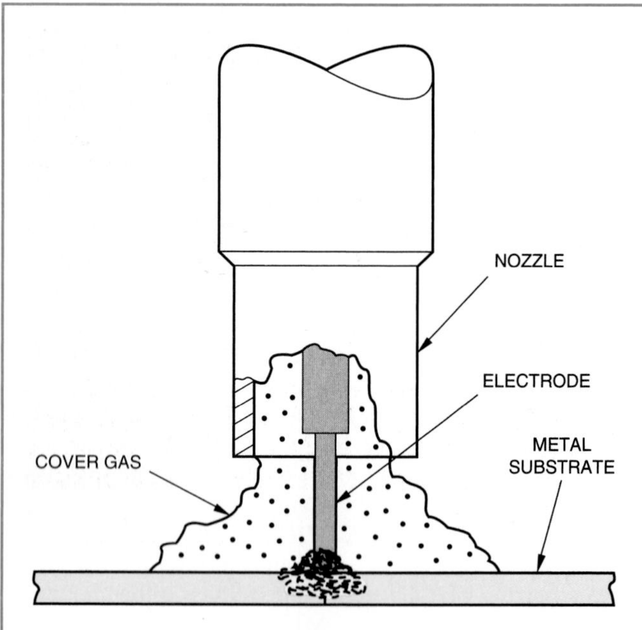

Figure 53-21. MIG welder being used to join two pieces of metal.

Once an arc has formed, move the gun along the joint to form a continuous weld bead. When the weld is complete, simply release the trigger. If necessary, the welding equipment can be adjusted to achieve the desired weld. Weld quality is controlled by adjusting the voltage setting, wire feed, and travel speed.

Another welding process frequently used when repairing late-model vehicles is ***spot welding.*** Instead of producing a continuous weld bead, spot welding equipment welds several small areas, or spots. Spot welding can be used to join high-strength steel components with sufficient strength and minimal distortion.

A compression resistance spot welder is shown in Figure 53-22. To use this piece of equipment, the joint to be welded is gripped between the welder's electrodes. When the welder is activated, a high-amperage, low-voltage current passes between the electrodes to generate heat. This heat produces a two-sided spot weld at the point of electrode contact, Figure 53-23.

As mentioned, ***oxyacetylene welding*** must be reserved for use on older vehicles. However, it is beneficial to understand oxyacetylene techniques. In oxyacetylene welding, practice, adjustment of the flame, and the selection of the correct tip are the main concerns.

Before starting any gas welding job, the oxygen and acetylene cylinders must be chained to a post or placed in a cylinder truck, Figure 53-24. This prevents them from being tipped over. Before attaching the regulators, each valve should be opened slightly to blow any dirt from the valve seat.

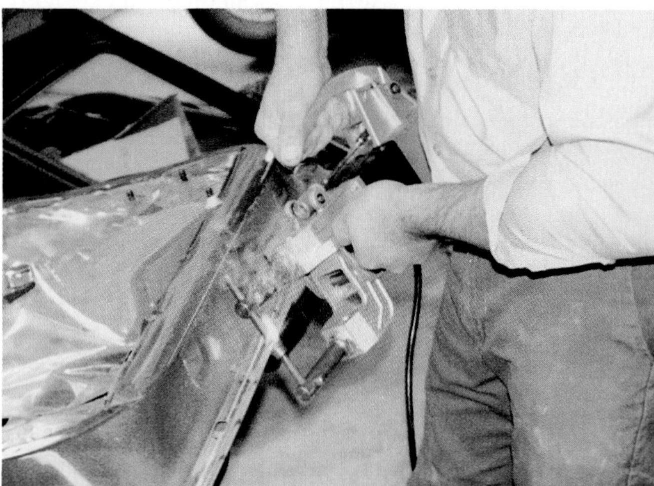

Figure 53-22. A compression resistance spot welder can be used to make many auto body repairs. (LORS Machinery, Inc.)

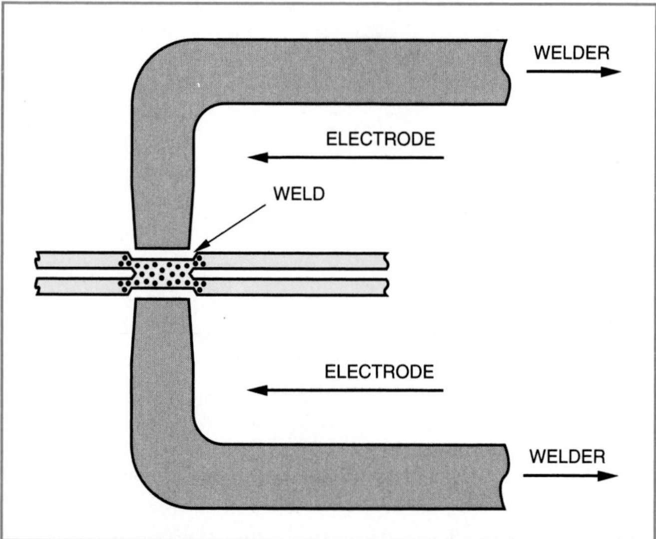

Figure 53-23. Schematic of a compression resistance spot welding operation.

Figure 53-24. Oxygen and acetylene tanks should be chained to a truck.

> Warning: To avoid danger of fire, be sure there is no flame (or spark) close to the acetylene cylinder. Always be certain that fire extinguishers are nearby. Acetylene hoses are red and have left-hand threads. Oxygen hoses are green and have right-hand threads.

Install the oxygen regulator and open the handwheel. The lower gauge will register the pressure in the tank. Attach the acetylene regulator and open the acetylene valve about 1/2 turn.

Connect the welding hoses to their regulators. Attach the welding head (tip) and torch, Figure 53-25, to the other end of the hoses. The size tip selected will depend on the type of welding to be done. The smallest tip is used when welding body sheet metal.

Different pressures are needed for welding different thicknesses of metal. For welding sheet metal, acetylene pressure should be 5 psi and oxygen pressure should be 10 psi.

To light the torch, open the oxygen valve 1/4 turn. Then open the acetylene valve one full turn and light the gas at the tip with a friction-type lighter. Never use matches. When lighting the gas, have the tip of the torch turned down and away from any person.

Adjust the flame by opening the oxygen valve slowly. The flame will change from a yellow acetylene flame to a blue flame, which is called a reducing flame. Start with an excess acetylene flame. Then, adjust to a neutral flame by closing the acetylene valve until the acetylene "feather" around the tip of the inner cone of the flame disappears, Figure 53-26.

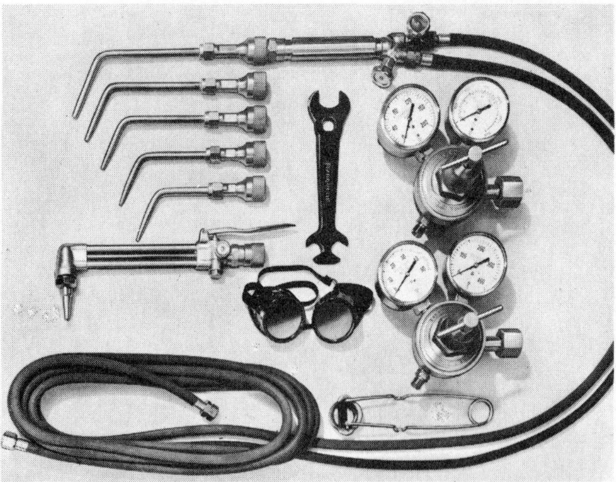
Figure 53-25. Welding tips, cutting torch, gauges, welding goggles, wrenches, and igniter.

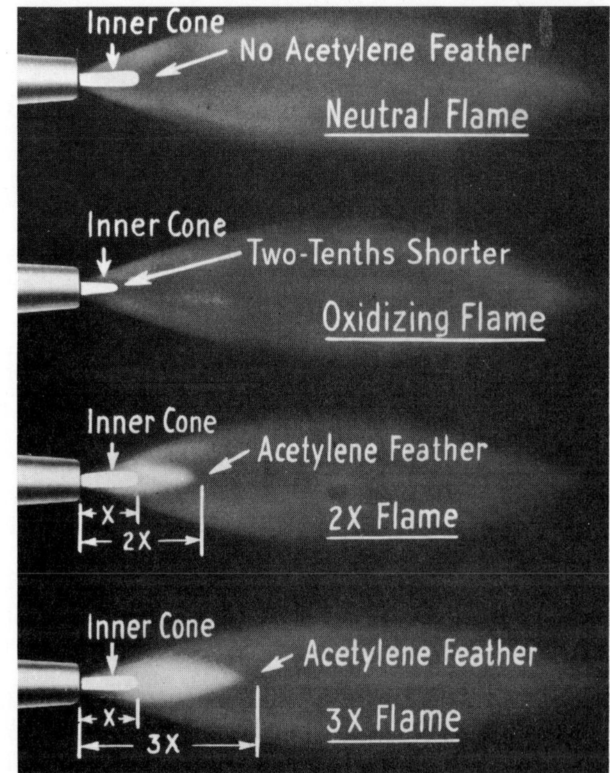

Figure 53-26. Adjust to a neutral flame by increasing acetylene or reducing oxygen until the desired acetylene feather is obtained.

To obtain an oxidizing flame, increase the oxygen or decrease the acetylene until the inner cone of the flame is about 1/5 shorter. If the flame is yellow or backfires, readjust the acetylene to 10 psi and open the torch needle valve more. If this does not correct the problem, the torch needs cleaning.

To weld sheet metal, a neutral flame should be used. Skill can be attained by practicing on strips of sheet metal. At first, do not attempt to weld two pieces of sheet steel together, but move the flame across the surface of the sheet metal, carrying the "puddle" along the surface, Figure 53-27. Do not use welding rod.

The purpose of this exercise is to obtain skill in carrying a puddle across the surface of the sheet. The torch

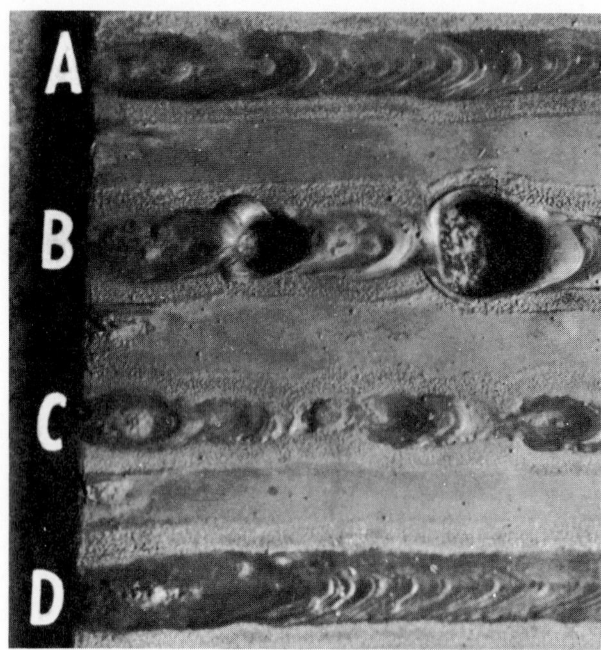

Figure 53-27. Results of a practice piece. A and D–Proper results. B–Too much heat. C–Not enough heat. (Linde Div. of Union Carbide)

should be held so that the flame points in the direction in which the weld will be made and at an angle of about 45°. The inner cone of the flame should be about 1/8″ from the surface of the sheet.

Hold the torch in this position until a pool of molten metal about 1/4″ in diameter is formed. Then, move the torch slowly to move the puddle in the desired direction to obtain an even ripple effect. Swing the torch from side to side in a small arc. If you move the torch too slowly, holes may be burned through the sheet metal. If you move it too quickly, the needed melting and overlapping of the puddles will not be obtained.

After skill is attained without using a welding rod, repeat the exercise using a welding rod, Figure 53-28. The addition of the welding rod will produce a slight ridge of metal above the surface of the sheet.

When using a welding rod, hold the rod in about the same position as the welding torch. Hold it in the left hand and at an angle of slightly more than 45°. Try to bring the spot on the sheet and the tip of the welding rod to the melting temperature at the same time. The best position for the end of the welding rod is just inside the outer end of the flame. The flame is concentrated on the spot at the start of the weld.

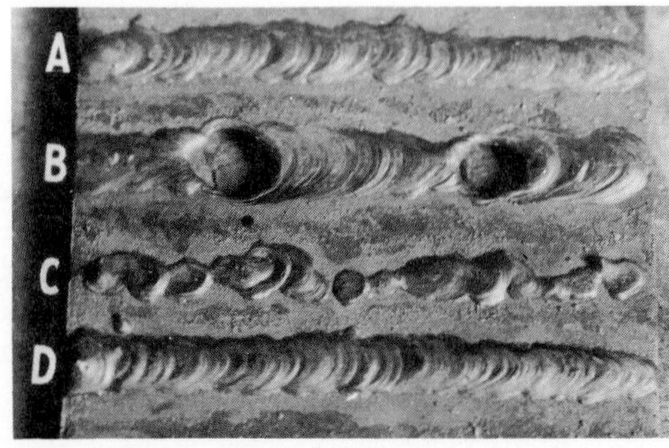

Figure 53-28. Good and poor welds. A and D–Satisfactory. B–Too much heat. C–Not enough heat. (Linde Div. of Union Carbide)

After having practiced with a welding rod, place the edges of two pieces of sheet metal 1/16″ apart and weld them together. In this case, make sure that the welding action penetrates through to the underside of the sheet so that the weld will have enough strength.

During the welding action, control the welding puddle so it will not fall through the gap. However, the metal added from the rod must be fused with the base metal on both sides of the joint. Once skill has been attained in welding small pieces of sheet metal together, try welding a fender or body panel.

Cutting Body Panels

With the type of car body used today, many shops replace sections of panels rather than straightening them. In cases of severe damage, this saves time and enables the shop to turn out more jobs per day. Replacement panels are available from car dealers and parts jobbers.

Cutting out panels for replacement is simple with modern equipment. Although an oxyacetylene torch, Figure 53-29, or an electric arc welder can be used, most manufacturers recommend the use of ***plasma arc cutters.*** Unlike oxyacetylene and electric cutting equipment, plasma arc cutters make clean, fast cuts without destroying the properties of high-strength steels.

When cutting sheet metal with a plasma cutting torch, place the nozzle directly on a conductive part of the workpiece and press the torch switch to trigger the plasma arc. Move the torch slowly across the workpiece to produce the cut. If the torch does not cut completely through the metal, reduce the speed of torch travel.

A special torch is needed to cut sheet metal with oxyacetylene, Figure 53-29. It differs from the one used for welding. A cutting torch provides a stream of pure oxygen, which does the cutting after the starting point of the cut has been heated to a cherry red by small oxyacetylene flames.

In the cutting torch, the oxyacetylene flames are produced at a series of openings in the tip. These openings surround the central opening, or jet, from which the oxygen passes. Details of construction vary with manufacturers.

Cutting is accomplished when the sheet metal is heated red hot, then exposed to the oxygen. Not only is the oxide that is formed melted, but some of the unoxidized steel is heated enough so that it, too, is melted.

When using a cutting torch, follow the same safety precautions presented for welding. Fire extinguishers should be nearby. It is unsafe to feed oxygen into a confined space, since it will cause oil, wood, clothing, or sound deadening material to burn with great intensity once it ignites.

When cutting out a body panel, mark the line with chalk where the cut is to be made. Make allowance for the width of the metal that will be melted, keeping the chalk mark 1/2″ from the line. Remove any upholstery or other material from the other side of the body panel.

Use both hands when cutting metal with a torch–one to control the flow of oxygen and the other to steady the torch. Hold the torch nozzle at a right angle to the surface of the work and in the same spot until the metal is bright red; then open the oxygen valve. As soon as the flame starts

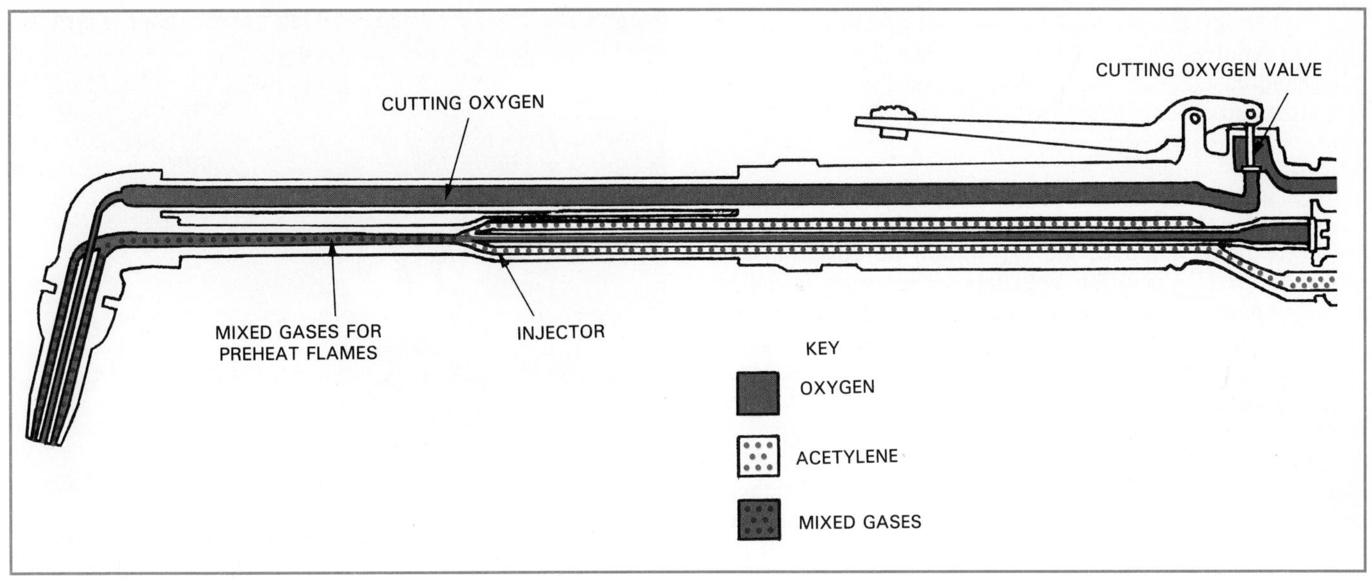

Figure 53-29. Sectional view of an oxyacetylene cutting torch.

cutting, there will be a shower of sparks from the metal. After the flame starts cutting, move the torch slowly in the desired direction.

If you move the torch too slowly, heat from the preheating flames will melt the edges of the cut and produce a ragged appearance. If you move it too fast, the cutting jet will fail to go through the metal. Should this occur, close the oxygen valve and reheat the point where the cut stopped. Then, reopen the oxygen valve to start the cut again.

As mentioned, cutting can also be done with electric arc welding equipment. While any electric arc welder can be used for cutting, the use of large, high-capacity units results in too wide a cut. Smaller, low-amperage units are preferred for cutting and welding body sheet metal.

Although hand shears can be used, various ***power-driven cutters*** are generally preferred, Figure 53-30. These cutters can cut curves with radii as small as 1″, and they will cut sheet metal up to .040″. They do not bend or stretch the metal.

Figure 53-30. A power cutter can be used on body panels.

Painting

The following procedure is for preparing a surface for touch-up and for refinishing individual panels. It is also used for the entire car if the original paint is in poor shape.

Before painting begins, it is essential that you prepare the surface for the paint by removing all traces of wax, grease, oil, and dirt. If the paint on the car or truck is of poor quality, remove it.

In this final preparation of the body before applying paint, you have many methods to choose from. The method you select depends on the condition of the existing paint and the available equipment.

If the paint on the car is in good condition (good adherence and without surface defects), it must be cleaned to remove oil and wax. In some cases, the surface must be sanded lightly with a disk sander.

If paint must be removed, an open-grained disk of #16 to #24 grit is needed. Hold the disk at a slight angle to the surface and work it forward and backward. This will remove most of the old finish. Follow with a #50 close-grained disk to remove scratches.

If the paint is being removed from only a portion of the panel, taper the sanded area into the old paint to produce a featheredge. Follow up with a #150 grit paper in a block sander, and complete the featheredge by water sanding with wet-or-dry paper of #280 or #320 grit. Some manufacturers of abrasive paper advise different grits with variations of the above procedure. Follow the instructions of the manufacturer.

For removing paint from the entire car, many shops prefer ***sandblasting, hot caustic strippers,*** or ***paint removers.*** When using paint removers, follow the manufacturer's instructions. The procedure is to apply the remover to the surface with a paintbrush or sponge. Then, after the proper time interval, scrape the paint from the surface with a putty knife. Because of fumes created by the paint remover, the room should be well ventilated.

Use the special cleaner before and after the final sanding. Directions that come with the cleaner should be followed. When wiping the surface, do not use the normal shop cloths, because they retain a certain amount of grease or other chemicals from the laundry. If air is used to blow off dust, the compressor supplying the air must be fitted with a water trap so the air is free of oil and moisture. Another point to remember is not to touch the clean surface with your hands. Natural oil from the skin will cause poor adhesion, and the finish will peel.

Apply the primer coats as soon as possible after the paint is removed. This is important when the surface has been sandblasted, because the metal surface is almost in the raw state and quickly starts rusting.

Masking

In order to protect surfaces and panels while adjacent areas are being painted, the car should be covered with paper secured in position with tape. The paper is called ***masking paper,*** and the tape is known as ***masking tape.***

Manufacturers of masking tape and paper have gone to great expense to improve their products. Their research in this field has produced special tape and paper dispensers, Figure 53-31, as well as shortcut methods of masking.

Good masking paper will not permit paint to seep through to the panel it is protecting. The tape must adhere easily to painted and unpainted surfaces, chrome, and other materials. It must have a strong texture so that it will not tear readily while being applied. The masking tape must also retain its adhering qualities when it is drenched during wet sanding operations. Flexibility is another necessary quality. This is important when applying the tape to curves.

One method has the tape applied along the edge of the masking paper so that half the width of the tape extends beyond the edge of the paper. When the masking paper is positioned on the car, the exposed area of the tape is pressed against the panel or trim to hold the paper in place. See Figure 53-32.

Figure 53-32. Before applying paint, the vehicle must be masked. This technician is applying masking paper to a windshield. (Oatey Co.)

Figure 53-31. Dispenser for masking paper and tape.

Some manufacturers warn that masking tape should never be pulled or stretched during application. The proper method is to lay it down easily as it comes from the roll. In this way, it will not pull back during painting. By not stretching the tape's backing, it is permitted to expand and contract without pulling away when the solvents are applied. For inside curves, narrow moldings and tabbing, 1/4″ or 1/2″ tapes are used. For wider moldings, 3/4″ and 1″ are more satisfactory.

Air Requirements

The first step in setting up a paint department is to make sure there is enough air to handle the spray guns and other equipment. Also, the ***air compressor*** must be in good shape and it must deliver its rated capacity. Many shops install a separate compressor for paint work. This avoids overloading the shop air compressor.

To get the best performance and long life from any air compressor, it must be serviced and inspected at regular intervals. A compressor and its water trap need proper care if clean air is to be supplied.

Follow the manufacturer's service instructions. If instructions are not available, change the oil in the compressor every 60 to 90 days. Clean the air filter each month. Drain the water trap every morning. In extremely humid weather, this should be done many times each day.

If the equipment has a separate receiver with a pop valve, check it to make sure that it is operating. Otherwise, check the pressure gauges and switches, noting the time to cut-in and cut-out. This time interval, compared to the specified time, will serve as a warning for many air supply system troubles.

Check all lines for leaks. When installing a new system, be sure to select pipe of proper size to carry the needed amount of air. Also, when installing the piping, see that it drains back to the receiver, rather than toward the air hose.

The air hose, too, must be of proper size to keep air pressure drop at a minimum. Common sizes of spray gun air hose are 1/4″, 5/16″, and 3/8″. The smaller the diameter, the greater the loss in pressure. Therefore, 3/8″ diameter hose is preferred.

Spray Guns

There are several types of ***spray guns*** available for refinishing automobiles. ***Siphon feed guns*** use compressed air to create a vacuum that draws paint into the gun, Figure 53-33. The paint is usually held in a one-quart container that is attached to the gun. ***Pressure feed guns*** use air pressure to force paint through a hose and into the gun. The paint is contained in a separate tank or pot, Figure 53-34.

Gravity feed guns rely on gravity to force paint into the gun. Paint in gravity fed guns is contained in a small cup mounted on top of the gun. Gravity feed guns are generally used for touch-up work. See Figure 53-35.

High-volume, low-pressure (HVLP) guns look similar to conventional siphon feed guns, Figure 53-36. However, these guns atomize paint into low-speed particles. HVLP guns apply more paint to the surface than other guns, and they reduce overspray by 75-80%.

The condition of the spray gun and the way in which it is used determines the quality of the paint job. It is impossible to do a good job of spray painting with a gun that has not been cleaned or is otherwise bad. Follow the manufacturer's recommendations for cleaning and maintaining the spray gun.

The compressed air used for spraying must be free of moisture, oil, and dirt. Pressures must be regulated. The compressor must be equipped with pressure regulator, Figure 53-37, which provides clean, filtered air for painting.

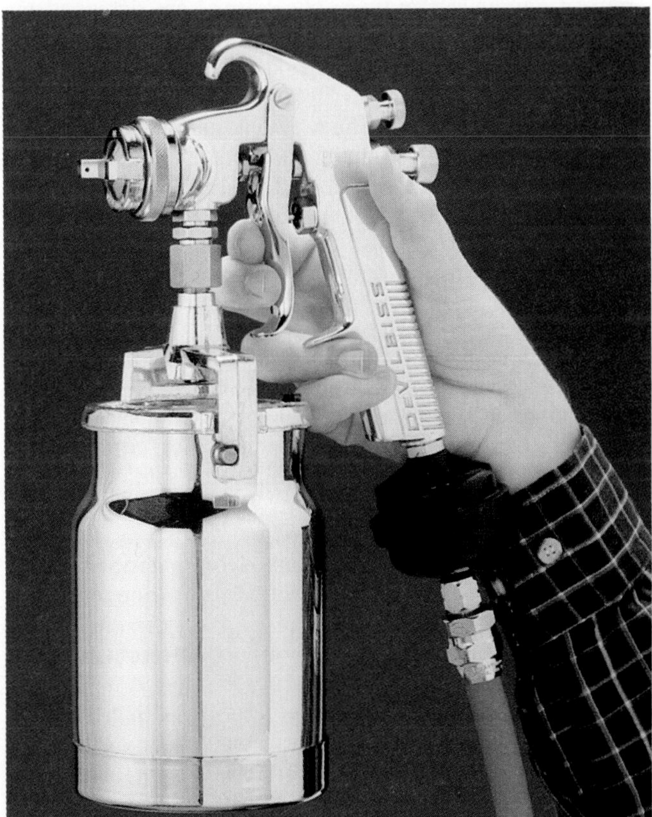

Figure 53-33. Typical siphon feed spray gun. (DeVilbiss)

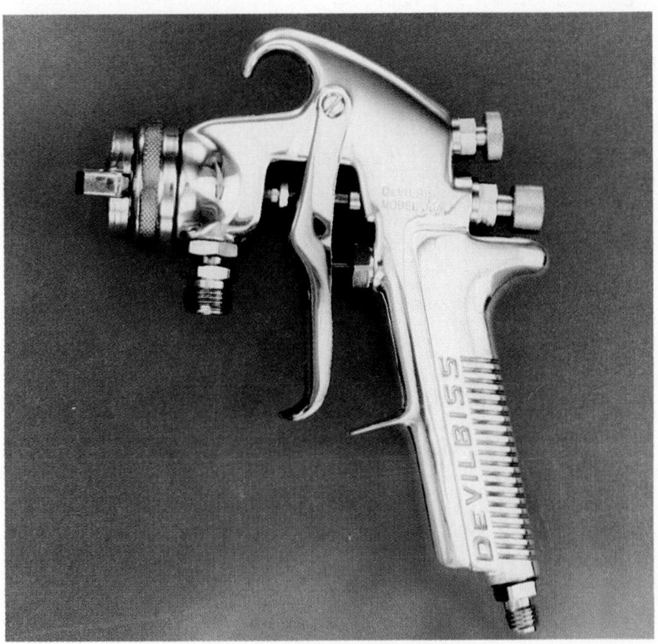

A

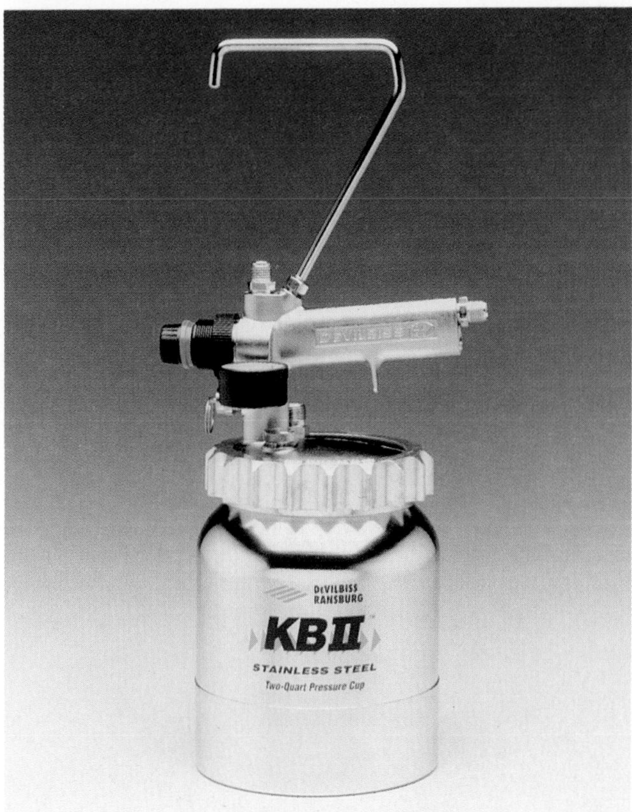

B

Figure 53-34. A–Pressure feed spray gun. B–Remote paint tank. (DeVilbiss)

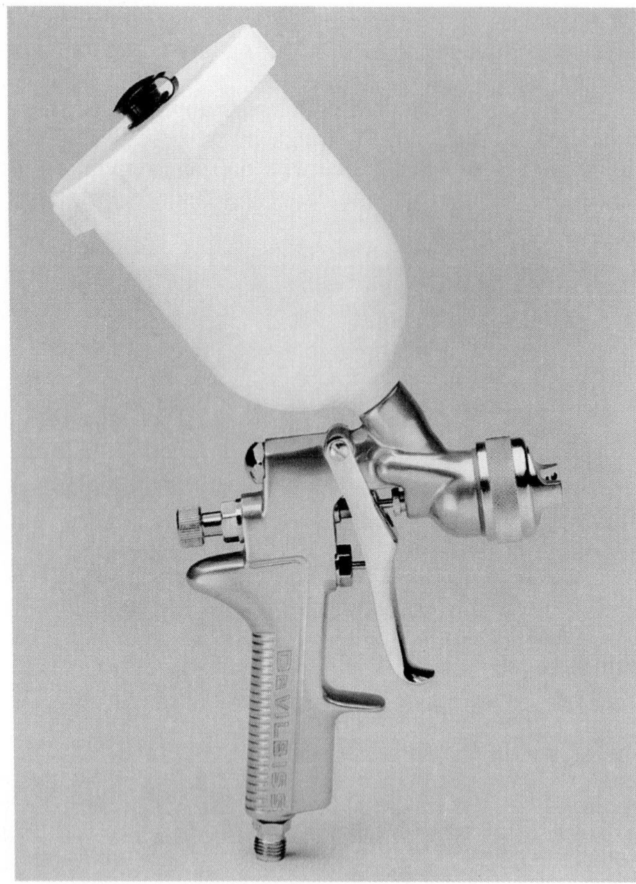

Figure 53-35. This gravity feed gun can be used to touch up small areas. (DeVilbiss)

Figure 53-36. HVLP spray guns reduce overspray. (Binks)

Figure 53-37. This pressure regulator is combined with a water trap. The water trap holds moisture that has condensed in the compressor. The water trap should be drained daily by opening a valve at bottom of trap. (DeVilbiss)

To ensure that the compressed air used for spray painting is clean and free from oil or moisture, the air compressor must have a ***water trap.*** These units are designed not only to prevent oil and water vapor from reaching the gun, but also to supply air at specified pressures for different types of spray paint.

Spray guns generally have two adjustments. One controls the amount of fluid being sprayed. The other governs spray shape, so that a round or fan-shaped spray can be obtained. The various patterns obtained from a spray gun are shown in Figure 53-38.

Tips on Spraying

Anyone can spray paint. But to do a job that will dry smooth and lustrous (no sag or ripple) takes skill that can only be attained with practice.

The gun commonly used for refinishing cars is of the siphon feed type, Figure 53-39. With this gun, the trigger controls both the air and the paint. Spray guns for professional work have many tips, needles, and spray cups that will adapt the gun for use with any type material and any size job. Most shops have several guns–one each for primer, lacquer, synthetic enamel, and acrylic enamel. In this way, there is no danger of mixing different types of paints, which results in a poor paint job.

One of the "musts" in spray painting is that the paint should have the correct ***viscosity.*** This can be determined by following the instructions on the paint can. Too many painters determine the viscosity by the rate at which the paint runs from the stirring rod. This can lead to trouble, since only a slight change in viscosity can spoil a good job.

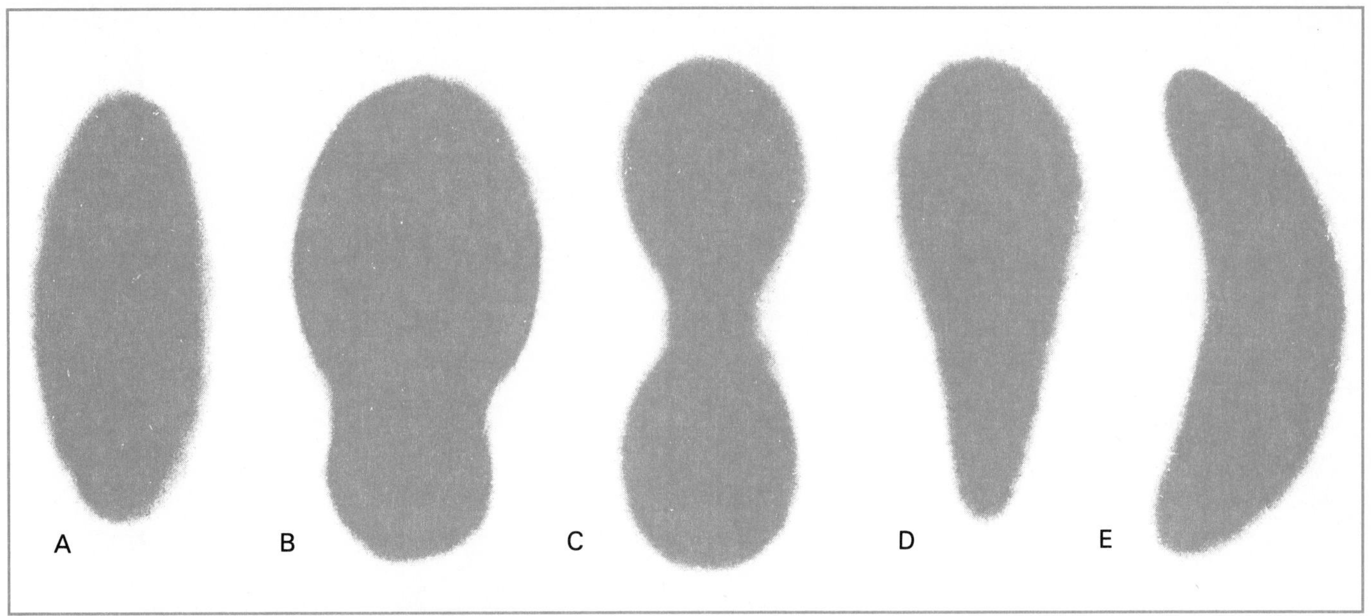

Figure 53-38. Proper and improper spray patterns. A–Correct spray pattern. B–Not enough air pressure. C–Air pressure too high. This can also be corrected by increasing the width of the spray pattern. D–Fluid has dried around the tip of the nozzle, causing this pattern. E–This pattern caused by a clogged wing port.

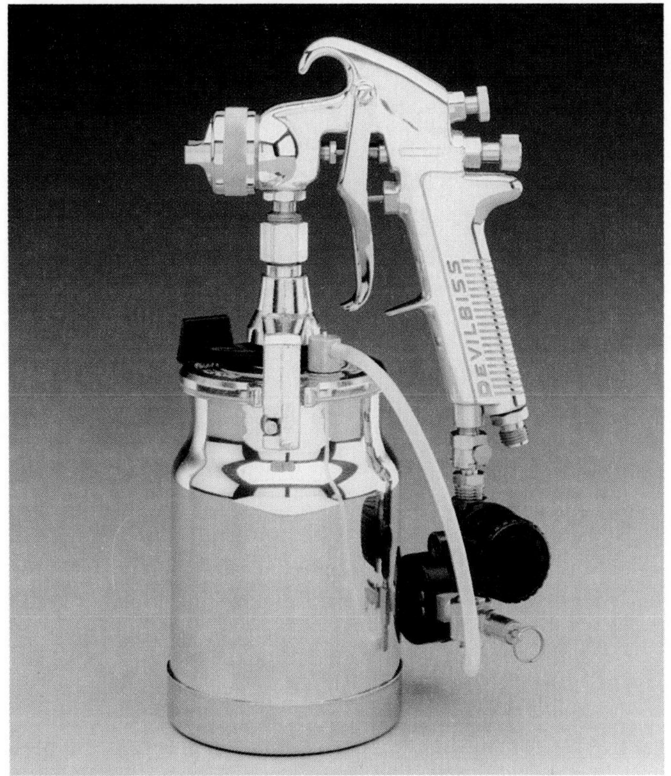

Figure 53-39. Spray guns of the siphon cup type are commonly used for automotive refinishing. (DeVilbiss)

This happens because the amount of thinner not only determines the thickness of the coat, but it also affects the evaporation rate between the time the material leaves the gun and the time it contacts the panel.

High viscosities result in sag and orange peel. Low viscosities produce improper flow-out and waste thinner. To avoid these problems, measure the thinner and paint in a graduated measuring cup.

The ***temperature*** at which the spraying is done is also a factor in turning out a good job. This applies not only to the temperature of the shop, but to the temperature of the car as well. The shop should be maintained at 70°F. Try to bring the car into the shop well in advance of spraying time so that it reaches the same temperature as the shop.

Another factor in applying a good paint job is the thickness of the paint film on the surface. A thick film takes longer to dry than a thin one. As a result, the paint will sag, ripple, or orange peel.

You should produce a coat that will remain wet long enough for proper flow-out, but no longer. The amount of material you spray on a surface with one stroke of a gun will depend on the width of the fan, the distance of the gun from the sprayed surface, the air pressure, and the amount of thinner used.

The speed of the spray stroke will also affect the thickness of the coat. The best method is to adjust the gun to obtain a wet film that will remain wet only long enough for good flow-out. Get the final finish thickness by spraying another coat after the first one has dried.

Standard spray guns are designed to give best performance when held at a distance of 8″-12″ from the work surface. When the gun is held too close, the air pressure tends to ripple the wet film if the film is too thick. If the distance is too great, a large percent of the thinner will evaporate in the spraying operation. Orange peel or a dry film will result, because the spray droplets will not have time to flow together.

Hold the spray gun at the specified distance from the work. Do not tilt it or hold it at an angle. Also, never swing the gun in an arc; move it parallel to the work. The only time it is allowable to fan the gun is when you want the paint to thin out over the edges of a small spot. The effects of incorrect handling of the spray gun are shown in Figure 53-40.

The spray gun with an attached cup is good enough for most jobs. Many bodies have undercut surfaces where it is

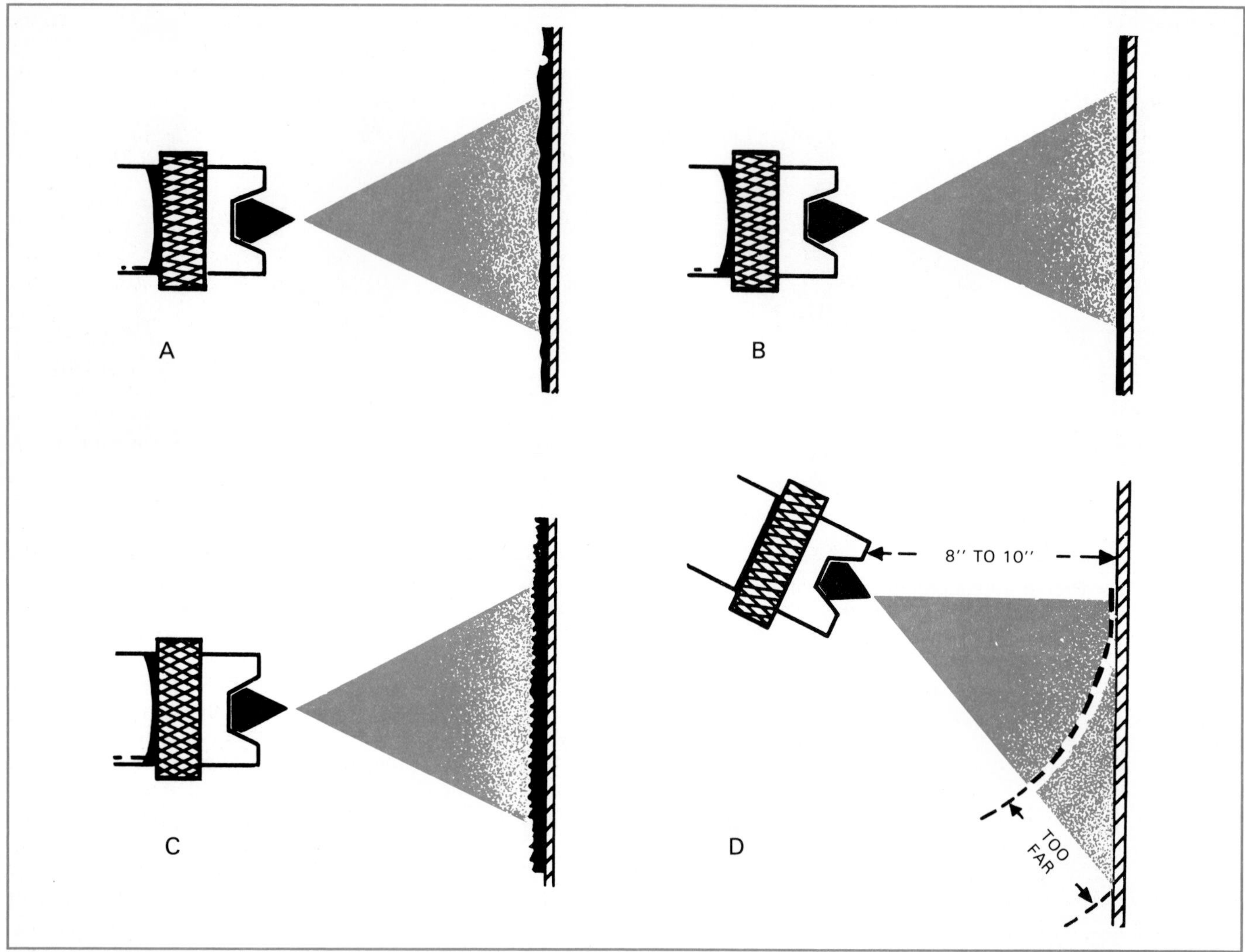

Figure 53-40. Cause and effect of proper and improper paint application. A–A heavy coat of paint produces a ripple or orange peel. This may be caused by a dirty nozzle, spraying too close to the surface, an excessively thin paint film, low air pressure, slow spray gun movement, or excessive overlap. B–Good flow-out is obtained when paint is thinned properly, air pressure is correct, speed of gun movement is correct, and overlap is approximately 50%. C–Thin paint coat is rough, dry, and lacks luster. This may be caused by using the wrong air nozzle, holding gun too far from the surface, moving gun too fast, or improper overlap. D–Thickness of paint will vary if the gun is fanned or held at an angle.

necessary to hold the gun at such an angle that a gun with attached cup cannot be used. A gun with a remote or separate cup is needed.

Guns with special spray heads have been developed to properly atomize acrylic paints. A pressure of 40 to 45 psi is enough to produce the needed shade, maximum amount of leveling, and high gloss. Higher pressure causes orange peel and a lighter shade with iridescent colors. There are many variables that affect the outcome of a paint job.

Refinishing Materials

Acrylic lacquers, acrylic enamels, urethane enamels, and synthetic enamels are now being used in refinishing. Thinners, primers, surfacers, reducers, solvents, sealers, and metal conditioners are needed as well. Descriptions of common refinishing materials are given below:

- ***Acrylic lacquer***–This material dries by evaporation of volatile solvents. Since is remains more or less soluble, the new coat of acrylic lacquer will bond with the original coat.
- ***Acrylic enamel***–A solvent blend of binder and pigment materials, acrylic enamel dries in two stages. The first stage is oxidation of the solvent. The second is oxidation of the binder. No polishing is needed.
- ***Urethane enamel***–Used in the refinishing of cars, urethane provides a hard, tile-like finish. It has high gloss, improved flow and appearance, good adhesion, and flexibility. Urethane enamel dries slower than acrylic enamel.
- ***Synthetic enamel***–Not soluble in most solvents, synthetic enamel is currently used for refinishing cars.
- ***Primer surfacers***–These are designed to improve adhesion to the metal and to fill slight surface imperfections. After drying, the primer surfacer is sanded smooth. Two types are available. One is used under acrylic enamels. Another is used under acrylic lacquers.
- ***Primers***–For adhesion to special surfaces, manufacturers provide primers. These are different from primer surfacers. Primers are widely used when painting aluminum or galvanized surfaces. If the surface also needs filling, a primer surfacer is applied over the primer.

- ***Sealers***–These are used for sealing sanding scratches made when preparing to paint over an acrylic surface. Special bleeder sealer is used over a red or maroon surface.
- ***Thinners and reducers***–These are solvents used to thin or reduce paints to the desired viscosity (thickness). Thinners are used for acrylic products. Reducers are used for synthetic base materials.
- ***Putty***–Made of the same material as the primer surfacer, putty is used for filling deep nicks and scratches.
- ***Wax and polish removers***–Traces of wax, polish, or grease must be removed from the surface before applying paint. Removers are used to do this job, or flaking will result.
- ***Metal conditioners***–These compounds are applied to metal after all paint has been removed to prevent rusting.
- ***Tack rag***–This is a specially treated cheese cloth. It has been dipped in a thin nondrying varnish. Used to wipe the surface of the car before painting, it removes all traces of dust.
- ***Rubbing compounds***–Mildly abrasive, these pastes or liquids are used to polish acrylic lacquer surfaces. They bring a higher polish to the surface.

Selecting Paint

When refinishing a car, the use of proper materials is important. Fewer troubles arise if the material used for refinishing is the same as the material originally used.

Today, most cars are refinished in acrylic enamel or acrylic lacquer. Nitrocellulose lacquer is used only when there is little drying time. This material may also be used for retouching small scratches.

Synthetic enamels are often used in repainting cars originally finished with enamel. Complete panels should be refinished when enamel is used for repair because it is hard to spot paint a small area without leaving a ring around the spot.

Some painters prefer acrylic enamel because compounding is not needed. Others will use synthetic enamel because of lower costs. When a striking appearance is wanted, many shops prefer urethane enamels.

Matching Colors

Even though ready-mixed paints for standard car colors are available, the number is so great that no jobber carries a complete line. The painter is often faced with the mixing of colors.

Matching colors is not easy. Since cars are being turned out with more shades and tones, painters are finding their work harder. The problem of fading hinders the situation. Many manufacturers provide instructions, specialized equipment, and basic colors that help solve the color matching problem. Nevertheless, the most important part in mixing colors is that the painter must have good color perception.

Clean equipment is a must when matching colors. Dust, old paint, or other material will spoil the effect. Thoroughly stir each basic color or mixture. Do your color matching in sunlight. Artificial light changes tints and tones. Tightly close cans of paint not in use to reduce evaporation of the solvents.

Since almost all shades darken on drying, wait until the color is dry before making comparisons. When matching a color on a car, remove all waxes and polish because they tend to change the color. Also, when making comparisons, the larger the surface, the lighter the color will appear because of light reflection. Always compare areas of equal size.

Preparing Old Finishes for Paint

Poorly prepared surfaces are shown in Figure 53-41. Before refinishing a vehicle, you must determine whether the original finish is lacquer or enamel. To make a quick check, moisten a finger with lacquer thinner and rub a small area. If the finish is lacquer, it will dissolve. To distinguish between nitrocellulose lacquer and acrylic lacquer, rub a small area with silicone polish remover. Acrylic lacquer will rub off, while nitrocellulose lacquer will not be affected by the polish remover.

On lacquer jobs that are to be refinished with lacquer, you have to prevent swelling of the old coat. Swelling occurs when sanding has been done, and unless you can keep the new solvents from reaching the old finish, no amount of care will prevent the old scratches from showing.

Swelling of the old coat does not occur on the unmarred or scratched surface of the lacquer, which is covered with an insoluble outer layer. It does occur when the new lacquer contacts freshly exposed surfaces in the scratches. After all the solvents have evaporated and the new finish shrinks, small furrows following the scratches will result.

Therefore, it is necessary to use a ***sealer*** on lacquer repaint jobs where much of the old refinishing material remains. Apply the sealer after sanding and treating the bare metal. Sealer has good adhesion to the old finish and will prevent penetration of the new lacquer and prevent swelling. If it is necessary to use any primer surfacer for filling rough spots, apply this first. Then after sanding, apply the sealer.

Enamel finishes must be sanded before being refinished. Make sure that the abrasive is not too coarse and sand the old finish to produce a good surface for the new finish. A surfacer is not needed if the enamel is in good condition. If the old enamel is badly worn and pitted, use a surfacer or primer for better adhesion and appearance.

Modern primers, glazing putties, fabric patches, and body filler will fill almost any rough surface. However, the surface should be as smooth as possible before any of these are applied.

After the primer and/or other surfacing material is applied, thorough sanding is needed. Many painters recommend three or four grades of paper, ranging from coarse to fine. For example, use a #16 open-grained paper first followed by #50 close-grained paper. Final sanding should be done with #150 paper.

Modern surfacing and refinishing materials have made auto painting simple. However, good appearance and long life of the finish depend on the care taken in preparing the surface for the final coats.

Applying Lacquer over Old Finishes

1. Remove old wax or silicone polish with special remover. Wet sand the old finish using a #320 paper.
2. Using clean air, blow out all cracks.

PROBLEM	CAUSES	REPAIR
BLISTERING: BUBBLY OR SWOLLEN APPEARANCE. 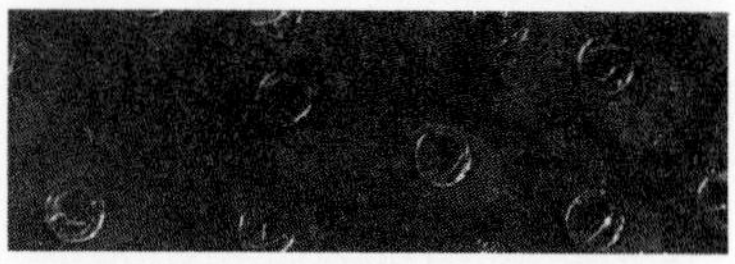	❍ TRAPPED SOLVENTS ❍ PAINTING OVER GREASE OR OIL ❍ RUST UNDER SURFACE ❍ MOISTURE IN SPRAY LINES ❍ PROLONGED EXPOSURE OF FILM TO HIGH HUMIDITY	REMOVE ALL BLISTERS BY SANDING. IF NECESSARY, SAND TO BARE METAL. AFTER SANDING, REFINISH THE SURFACE. TO PREVENT BLISTERING, CLEAN AND TREAT METAL THOROUGHLY; ALLOW AMPLE DRYING TIME BETWEEN COATS; AND DRAIN WATER FROM AIR LINES. IF TEMPERATURE AND HUMIDITY ARE HIGH, USE OVERLY FAST THINNERS.
CHALKING: DULLING AND POWDERING OF THE PAINT FILM	❍ EXCESSIVE WEATHERING AND SUNLIGHT	APPLY PASTE CLEANER, FOLLOWED BY POLISH. IN EXTREME CASES, COMPLETE REFINISHING IS NECESSARY.
CHECKING: DEEP CRACKS 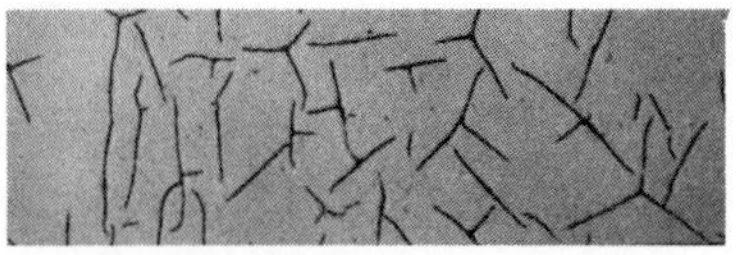	❍ SPRAYING A NEW FINISH OVER PREVIOUSLY CRACKED FINISH ❍ SPRAYING AN EXCESSIVELY THICK FINISH COAT OVER UNDERCOATS ❍ SPRAYING IMPROPERLY MIXED TOPCOATS ❍ HEAVY APPLICATION OF FINISH COAT WITH INSUFFICIENT TIME BETWEEN COATS	SAND DOWN TO SMOOTH FINISH. IF NECESSARY, SAND TO BARE METAL. AVOID EXTREME TEMPERATURES, SPRAY UNIFORM COATS, AND ALLOW PROPER DRYING TIME BETWEEN COATS.
FISH EYES: SMALL, CRATER-LIKE OPENINGS IN THE FINISH 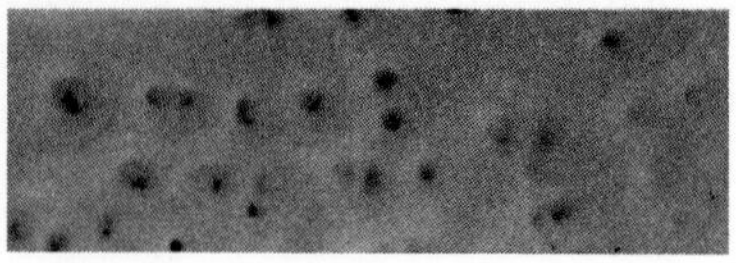	❍ SPRAYING OVER SILICONE ❍ IMPROPERLY CLEANED SUBSTRATE	IF THE FINISH IS STILL WET, WASH OFF PAINT. THOROUGHLY CLEAN SURFACES AND REFINISH.
LIFTING: A SWELLING OF WET FILM.	❍ RECOATING IMPROPERLY CURED ENAMEL ❍ IMPROPER DRYING OF PREVIOUS COAT ❍ SPRAYING OVER A SURFACE THAT HAS NOT BEEN PROPERLY CLEANED ❍ USING ACRYLIC LACQUER OVER ENAMEL OR ACRYLIC ENAMEL UNDERCOATS	MATERIAL MUST BE REMOVED AND THE SURFACE MUST BE REFINISHED.
MOTTLED SURFACE: BLOTCHY, UNEVEN APPEARANCE	❍ PAINT APPLIED ON SURFACE THAT HAS BEEN TREATED WITH SILICONE TYPE POLISH	SAND DOWN TO BARE METAL, REMOVE ALL TRACES OF POLISH, AND REFINISH.
ORANGE PEEL: FINISH THAT LOOKS LIKE THE SURFACE OF AN ORANGE	❍ EXCESSIVE AIR PRESSURE ❍ GUN FANNING BEFORE PAINT DROPLETS HAVE A CHANCE TO FLOW ❍ COLOR COATS NOT REDUCED ENOUGH TO PERMIT PROPER ATOMIZATION ❍ IMPROPER THINNING OR REDUCING ❍ SPRAY EQUIPMENT NOT PROPERLY ADJUSTED ❍ GUN HELD TOO FAR AWAY ❍ SHOP TEMPERATURES TOO HIGH	ON ENAMEL, USE A FINE COMPOUND TO RUB OUT ORANGE PEEL. ON LACQUER, SAND OR USE RUBBING COMPOUND. IF NECESSARY, REMOVE PAINT AND REFINISH.

Figure 53-41. Typical paint defects.

PROBLEM	CAUSES	REPAIR
PEELING: A FILM SEPARATION OCCURRING BETWEEN TWO LAYERS OF FINISH	❍ IMPROPER CLEANING ❍ POOR SURFACE PREPARATION ❍ INCOMPATIBILITY OF ONE COAT TO ANOTHER	REMOVE OLD FINISH FROM AN AREA LARGER THAN THE AFFECTED ZONE. PROPERLY CLEAN AND TREAT THE SURFACE, THEN REFINISH. FOR MATERIALS OTHER THAN STEEL, USE RECOMMENDED PRIMERS.
PIN POINT BLISTERING: SMALL, BROKEN BLISTERS THAT HAVE THE APPEARANCE OF PITS 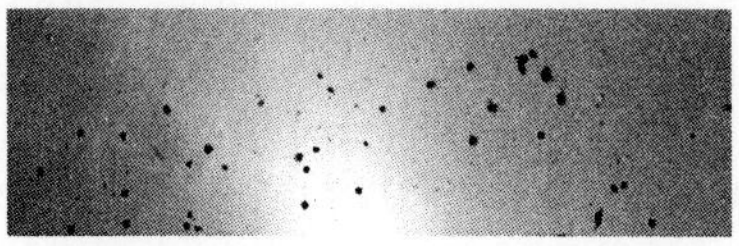	❍ TRAPPED SOLVENTS ❍ PAINTING OVER GREASE OR OIL ❍ RUST UNDER THE SURFACE ❍ MOISTURE IN THE SPRAY LINES ❍ PROLONGED EXPOSURE OF FILM TO HIGH HUMIDITY	SAND DOWN TO BARE METAL AND REFINISH.
PITTING: FINISH DISTORTIONS	❍ OIL OR MOISTURE ESCAPING THROUGH THE AIR LINES	SAND DOWN TO SMOOTH SURFACE AND REFINISH. OVERHAUL COMPRESSOR AND SEPARATOR TO CORRECT TROUBLE.
RUNS OR SAGS: FAILURE OF COATING TO ADHERE UNIFORMLY OVER THE SURFACE 	❍ SLOW THINNER OR REDUCER ❍ OVER-REDUCED COLOR COATS ❍ TOO LITTLE AIR PRESSURE WHEN APPLYING COLOR COATS ❍ COLOR COATS SPRAYED OVER WAX, OIL, OR GREASE ❍ EXCESSIVELY HEAVY FINISHING COATS ❍ REFINISHING MATERIALS OR WORK SURFACE THAT IS TOO HOT OR COLD	IF THE FINISH IS WET, USE A FINE CAMEL HAIR BRUSH TO BRUSH OUT THE SAG AND RECOAT THE SURFACE. IF THE FINISH IS COMPLETELY DRY, REMOVE EXCESS PAINT BY SANDING WITH A FINE GRIT ABRASIVE PAPER. COMPOUND, POLISH, OR REFINISH AS REQUIRED.
RUST: RAISED SECTION OF THE FINISH; BLISTERING	❍ POOR PENETRATION ❍ IMPROPER CLEANING OF SURFACE	SAND SURFACE, TREAT SURFACE WITH RUST REMOVER, AND REFINISH.
WATER SPOTTING: SPOTTY APPEARANCE AND DULLING OF GLOSS IN SPOTS 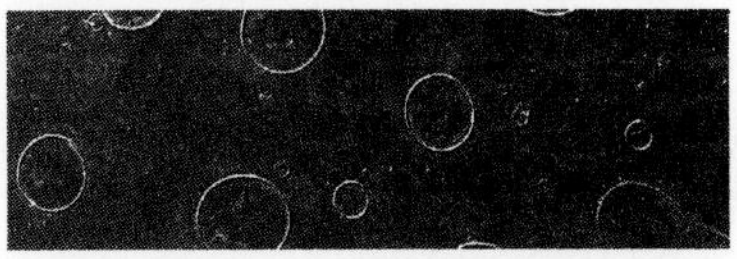	❍ FINISH IS EXPOSED TO WATER BEFORE BEING COMPLETELY DRY ❍ ALTERNATE EXPOSURE TO SUN AND RAIN	USE A FINE RUBBING COMPOUND AND RUB LIGHTLY WITH A DAMP CLOTH. IF POLISHING FAILS, REFINISH. TO PREVENT RECURRENCE, KEEP CAR OUT OF RAIN AND DO NOT WASH UNTIL PAINT IS COMPLETELY DRY.
WRINKLING: A SHRIVELING OF THE FINISH 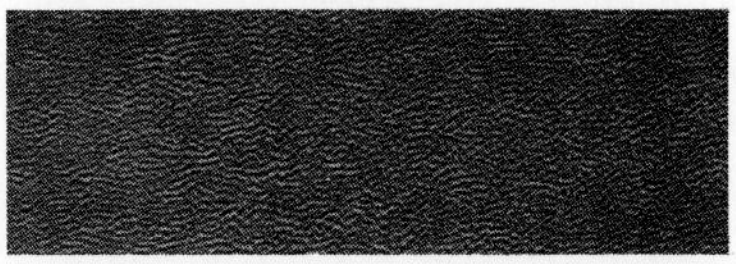	❍ EXCESSIVELY HEAVY ENAMEL COLOR COATS ❍ EXTREMELY HIGH TEMPERATURE OR HUMIDITY CONDITIONS ❍ ENAMEL SPRAYED IN HOT SUN ❍ FRESHLY PAINTED SURFACE EXPOSED TO SUNLIGHT ❍ ENAMEL FINISH COATS REDUCED WITH LACQUER OR ACRYLIC LACQUER THINNER INSTEAD OF ENAMEL REDUCER	REMOVE FINISH AND RECOAT.

Figure 53-41. Typical paint defects. (Continued)

3. Clean the surface with special grease, rust, and wax remover.
4. Spray surfacer on bare metal spots. If needed, use spot putty or equivalent.
5. Wet sand undercoats with #320 paper. If any spots are sanded through to base metal, spray them again with surfacer and wet sand.
6. Seal the scratches with a special sealer if the car was finished with lacquer.
7. Blow out cracks with clean air.
8. Again, clean the surface with the special cleaner.
9. Apply lacquer color coats. Three double coats are recommended.
10. Wet sand with #400 paper.
11. Polish.

Applying Enamel over Old Finishes

1. Remove all the wax and silicone polish with special cleaner.
2. Wet sand the old finish with #320 paper.
3. Clean the surface with a special wax, grease, and rust remover.
4. Spray on undercoats.
5. Sand the undercoats with #280 paper.
6. Respray if sanding has gone to base metal.
7. Resand the undercoat.
8. Blow out all cracks with clean air.
9. Clean the surface with special cleaner to remove any hand marks.
10. Wipe the surface with a tack rag to remove lint and dust.
11. Spray a light coat of enamel over all cracks.
12. Apply a tack coat and follow immediately with a full coat of enamel. If drying lights are not available, allow the paint to dry at least 12 hours in a dust-free room.

Soft Body Parts

Many parts on modern cars are made of ***synthetic materials.*** See Figure 53-42. These parts need special treatment when being restored after damage.

Minor tears, splits, and cracks can be repaired by first cleaning with naptha solvent. Next, apply a thin coating of special adhesive on the edges or sides to be bonded. Then, position the torn, split or cracked surfaces so they come together in their original position. Apply firm hand pressure to the bonded area for about one minute. Follow all instructions for use of the particular adhesive.

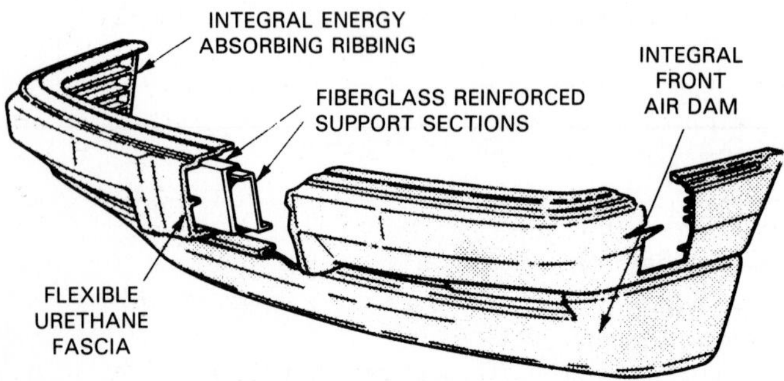

Figure 53-42. This front bumper is made of synthetic materials to reduce weight of car. (PPG Industries)

To repair minor gouges and holes in synthetic material, first roughen the damaged area with coarse sandpaper of about #36 grit. Flame treat the exposed surface with a propane torch with about a 1″ (2.5 cm) blue flame. Move the flame back and forth over the exposed surface two or three times. Be sure to keep the flame moving.

Then, apply special adhesive. Follow the instructions with the material, paying attention to the mixing process. Be sure to slightly overfill the area so that it protrudes over the surrounding area. If a hole is being filled, masking or aluminum tape should be applied to the under surface to lend support to the filler material.

If a heat curing system is being used, heat to 190°F (88°C) for 20 minutes with a heat lamp placed 4 to 5 ft. (1.2 to 1.5 m) away.

If the air dry system is being used, wait one to three hours at room temperature for curing before sanding. When the area is cured, sand with #240 fine cut paper to bring the surface to the proper contour. Then, finish sand with #400 paper. If needed, apply a second coating of filler paste. The surface can then be primed with special primer designed for synthetic surfaces.

Many thermoplastic components can be welded. Special plastic welding equipment and filler rods are used to fuse the plastic pieces together. If necessary, a backing patch can be applied before the weld is made. Always follow the manufacturer's instructions. After welding, the repair can be smoothed with #240 paper.

To repaint replacement parts and spot repairs, use color coat designed for use on synthetic materials. This special paint can be used on parts such as flexible bumpers, fender extensions, stone, or gravel shields. These parts are supplied primed and ready for installation.

Identifying Plastics

It is important to know what kind of plastic is used on the car. This is so the proper painting materials and procedures can be used. There are three different types of plastic frequently used in late-model vehicles. They are ***ABS, polypropylene,*** and ***vinyl.***

To determine which plastic is used, cut a small piece from the back side of a panel. Holding the piece of plastic with a pair of needle nose pliers, hold a lit match to the piece of plastic. If the smoke becomes black, Figure 53-43, the plastic is ABS. If there is very little smoke, the plastic is polypropylene, Figure 53-43. To determine if the plastic is vinyl, heat a piece of copper wire and touch the backside of a panel. Next, hold this piece of copper wire with the melted plastic in a flame. If the flame becomes bluish-green, the plastic is vinyl, Figure 53-43.

Painting Polypropylene

Painting polypropylene parts involves the use of a special primer. Since polypropylene is a hard plastic, it can be color coated and primed with a normal acrylic lacquer. Failure to use the needed primer will result in color coat lifting or peeling off of the panel. Allow primer to dry at least one minute, and no longer than 10 minutes. This is known as the flash time. Then, apply acrylic lacquer color

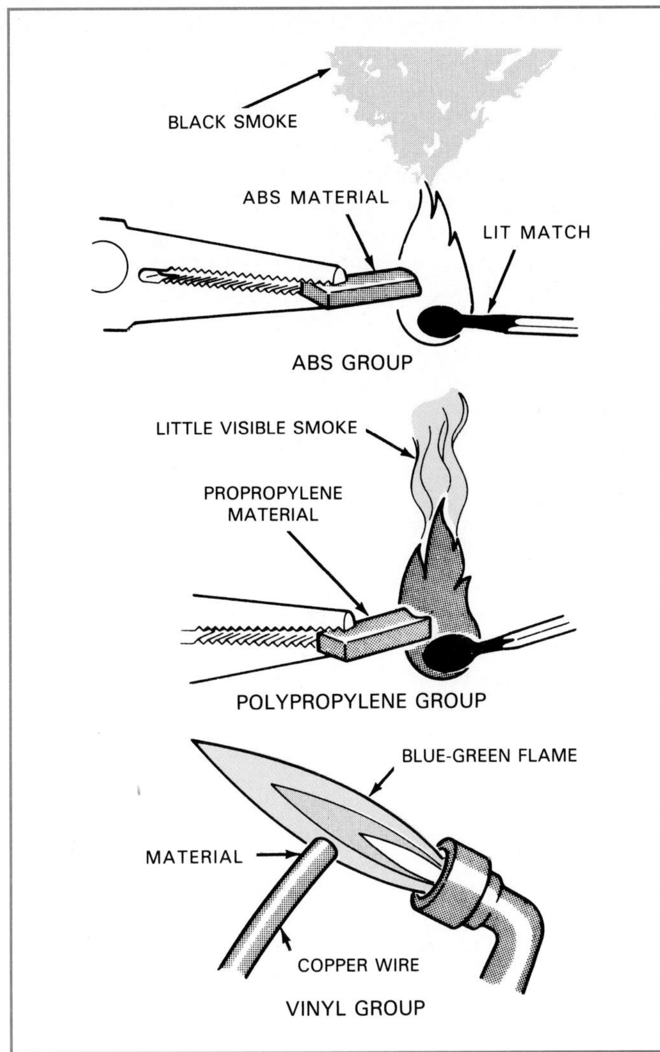

Figure 53-43. Identifying plastics. (Chrysler)

as needed. Applying the paint during this time provides the best adhesion.

Painting ABS Plastics

ABS plastic needs no primer. Prep the surface with Acrylic-Clean or the equivalent. Apply normal acrylic lacquer.

The paint for vinyl and flexible ABS plastic involves the use of an interior vinyl color and a clear vinyl top coat, Figure 53-44. No primer or primer sealer is needed. Prep the surface with a solvent and wipe dry with a lint free cloth. Apply several coats, but allow a flash time between coats. Apply one coat of vinyl clear coat with proper gloss level to match adjoining parts. The clear coat prevents the color coat from rubbing off after drying.

Repairing Water and Dust Leaks

Leaks often result from the dislocation of ***weatherstripping.*** These are easy to locate and repair. In other cases, special effort and procedures are needed to locate, then repair the problem. If the exact location of the source of a leak is not known, first inspect the area of the leak for watermarks, rust, or dust trails. Then trace these marks back to the source.

Plastic Type	Examples	Painting Procedure
Rigid Vinyl	Bumper Fillers	Flex Agent Required
RIM Urethane (Reaction Injection Moulding)	Fascias	Flex Agent Required
TPU (Thermoplastic Urethane)	End Caps Soft (Same as RIM)	Flex Agent Required
TPO (Thermoplastic Olefin)	Bumper Fillers	Flex Agent Required
FRP (Fiberglass Reinforced Polyester)	Nose Cones (Hard)	Same as Steel
Phenolic	Ash Trays	Same as Steel
Nylon	Spoliers, Louvers	Same as Steel
ABS (Acrylo-nitrile/ Butadiene/Styrene	Louvers	No Flex Agent
Polypropylene	Hard Seat Back, Garnish Moulding	No Flex Agent
Flexible ABS	Dash	No Flex Agent

Figure 53-44. When refinishing some plastics, a flex agent must be added to the paint. (Chrysler)

If there are no marks to follow, you will need to use a water hose to help find the trouble spot. Sit in the car while your partner sprays water over the outside of the suspected leak area. Watch for water trickling in, and try to locate the exact point of entry. You may have to remove head lining or other trim to locate the source of the leak.

Another method of locating leaks is to fill a syringe with powdered chalk, water, or a mixture of the two. Syinges can be purchased at any drugstore and powdered chalk is available at most hardware stores. Spray the suspected seam with the contents of the syringe. The dust formed by this operation will quickly show the point of entry of the rain and dust.

A variety of materials are used for correcting water and dust leaks, including:

- Black caulk and sealer.
- Gray caulking cord.
- Auto body sealer.
- Rubber cement.
- Metallic caulk and sealer.
- Pressure gun for applying caulk.
- Sponge rubber stripping.

Before attempting to repair any leaks around doors or deck lids, make sure that the doors and lids are correctly fitted. Poor fits always result in water and dust leaks.

The easiest method of checking the fit of doors and deck lids is to note whether the edges of the door or lid are the same distance from the surrounding body panel. When that has been corrected, slide a feeler gauge (.005″) or a dollar bill along the weatherstripping with the door or deck lid closed. If no resistance is noticed to the passage of the feeler gauge, or a dollar bill, leakage will occur at that point. Repair leaks by installing new weatherstripping, cementing it in place with sealer.

Leaks around the windshield can be repaired by means of the pressure gun filled with black caulk and sealer. Slide the nozzle of the pressure gun between the rubber and the glass, and force the compound as shown in Figure 53-45. The area in which to apply sealer, when leaks occur, is between the windshield weatherstripping and the body flange. In some cases of leaks around the windshield or rear window, you must remove the glass, then replace it, using ample sealing compound. Areas where leaks may occur are shown in Figure 53-46.

Leaks may also occur through bolt and nut holes used to attach chrome trim to the body panels. This can be overcome by applying special sealer to each of the clips and nut ends.

Figure 53-47 shows the location of the weatherstripping of a deck lid. In some cases, the weatherstripping can

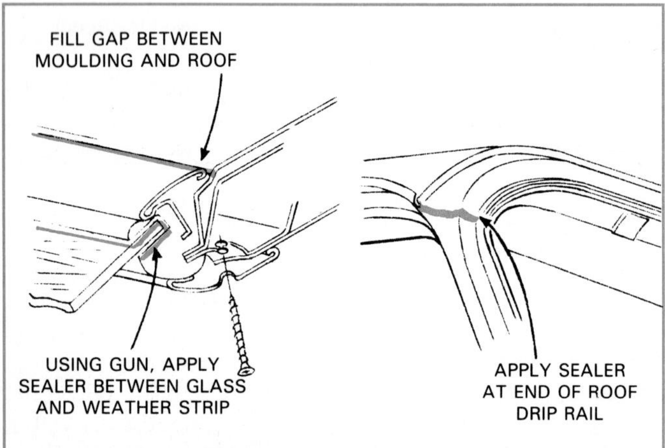

Figure 53-45. Areas of a windshield that may develop a leak.

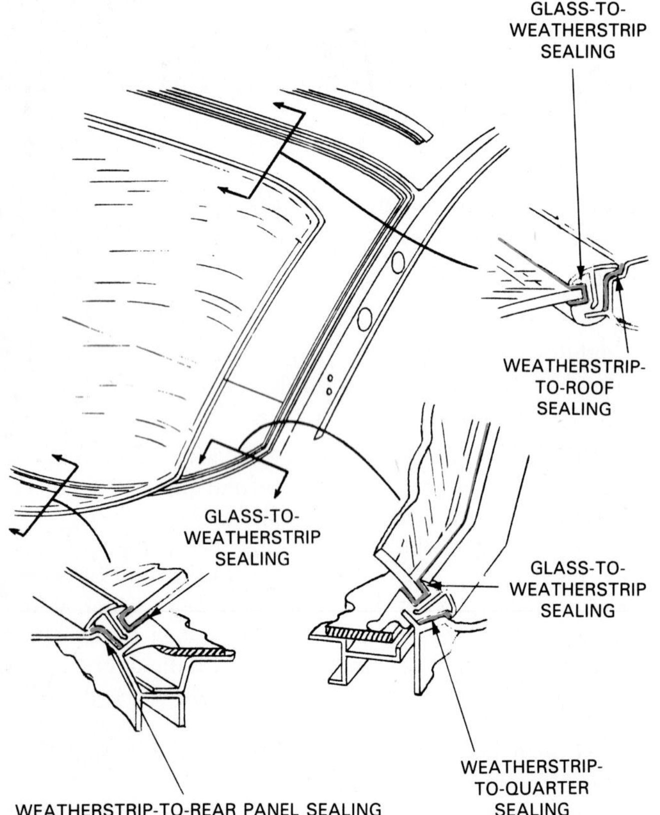

Figure 53-46. Caulking may be needed around the rear window to eliminate leaks.

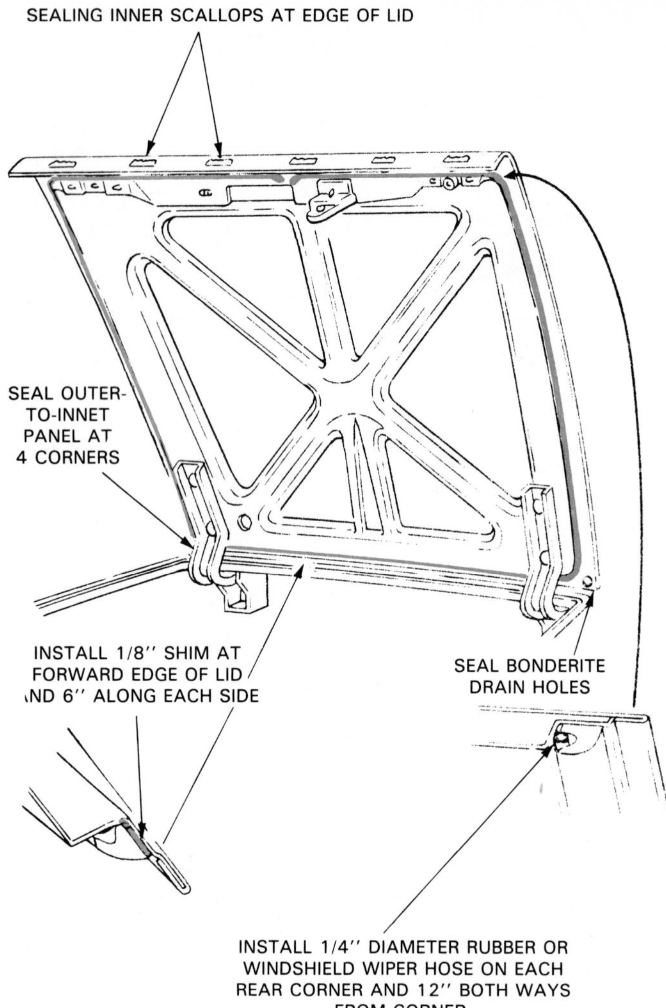

Figure 53-47. A rear deck lid may leak in these areas.

be built up by inserting a 1/8″ weatherstripping under the original weatherstripping.

When water leaks into the passenger compartment around the doors and cowl hinge pillar, make sure that all drain holes on the bottom of each door are open. Also, remove the door trim panel and inspect the bottom edge of the water shield. A good seal to the door must be maintained around the shield. Check by pouring water into the door at the belt line to make sure that none of it will splash past the shield. Leaks at the cowl hinge pillar may be corrected by installing a drain tube inside each hinge pillar.

Drain Locations

Car bodies are designed for draining water that enters certain areas. The locations of the drain holes are shown in Figure 53-48. These drain holes must be clean to ensure proper drainage. Each door has at least two drain holes. In some cases, the holes are covered by a sealing strip that prevents dust entry into the body. Deck lids have drain holes on either side to provide drainage for any moisture that may collect in the inner lid. Convertible models have a drain hole to the rear of each door. A short drain hose prevents the entrance of dust.

Figure 53-48. Drain holes prevent the body from rusting. Make sure to keep the holes open so that water can escape.

Chapter 53–Review Questions

Write your answers on a separate sheet of paper. Do not write in this book.

1. When straightening a dented panel, the damage should be removed:
   (A) from the point where the panel was struck.
   (B) from the ridge farthest from the point where the panel was struck.
2. If a dent rises above the surface of a dolly block, the hammer should strike the:
   (A) center of the dent.
   (B) edge of the dent.
3. What is the purpose of a body file?
4. Describe what is meant by the term featheredging.
5. For what purpose is body filler used?
6. Describe the procedure for replacing a portion of a body panel.
7. Why is MIG welding equipment used when repairing late-model vehicles?
8. What is the purpose of masking?
9. HVLP spray guns can reduce overspray by 75-80%. True or False?
10. Before applying any paint, what should be done to the surface of the panel?
11. Why should primer be applied immediately after the paint has been removed.
12. What is wrong if the spray pattern of a spray gun is heavy at the ends and light at the center?
13. How far should a spray gun be held from the surface of the work?
14. What material should be used when repairing the surface of a body painted with acrylic lacquer?
15. ABS plastic gives off little smoke. True or False?

This vehicle has plastic composite body panels. The front fenders and rear quarter panels are a polyphenylene-ether/polyamide blend. The door panels are a rigid blend of acrylonitrile butadiene styrene/polycarbonate. (Saturn)

The automobile industry offers a variety of career opportunities. These automotive design engineers are preparing a clay model of a prototype vehicle. (Ford)

Chapter 54
Career Opportunities and Technician Certification

After studying this chapter, you will be able to:

- ❍ Identify careers directly involved with automotive service.
- ❍ Describe duties of various levels of service technicians.
- ❍ Explain why specialty service technicians are necessary.
- ❍ Describe duties of supervisory and management level personnel in a car manufacturer's dealership.
- ❍ Name career opportunities in automotive service-related businesses.

Automotive Careers

The automotive field offers almost unlimited career opportunities. In the service area alone, typical job classifications include apprentice auto service technician, Figure 54-1; general service technician; master technician; specialty technician; truck service technician; auto body and paint technician; auto service adviser/writer; shop supervisor; service manager; service training instructor; factory service representative; vocational teacher or auto technology instructor, Figure 54-2.

Consider, too, that specialty technicians are trained in a specific phase of repair work. They spend full time servicing vehicles having problems in their area of expertise (expert skill or knowledge).

Figure 54-1. Apprentice auto service technicians receive three or four years of well-rounded instruction and on-the-job experience. (Hunter Engineering)

A Growing Field

With the ongoing and predicted advances being made by the car manufacturers' research and development engineers, service technicians are meeting new challenges each new model year. At the same time, the need is being created for new kinds of "specialists" in the areas of electronic engine control, carburetion and fuel injection, emission control, front-wheel drive/four-wheel drive, and automatic temperature control.

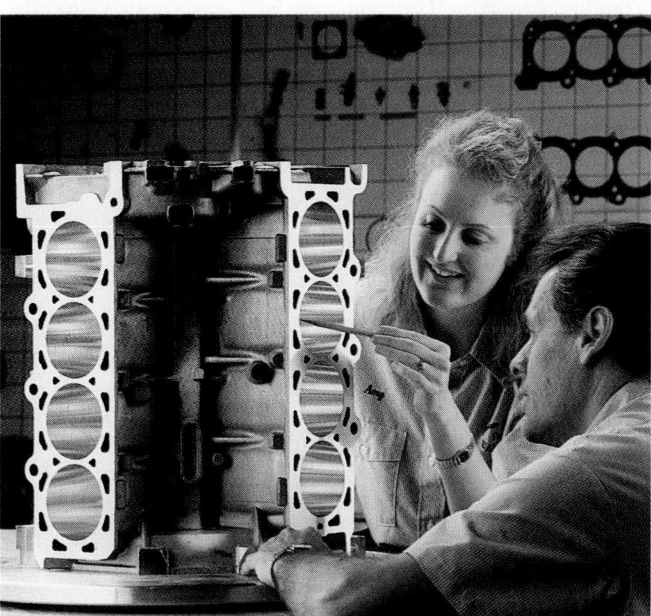

Figure 54-2. Vocational teachers not only teach auto technology, they also attend classes sponsored by parts and equipment manufacturers. This helps them keep current with the latest technological advances and service procedures. (Ford)

There is a shortage of trained auto service technicians, and the ever increasing complexity of modern vehicles only serves to worsen the shortage and heighten the need for "specialists."

To meet the need for trained service technicians, car manufacturers–both domestic (U.S.) and foreign–are expanding their training facilities. They are presenting their "Opportunities in Automotive Service" programs at high school and community college "career days." They are assisting automotive programs at these schools by donating engines, transmissions, and other major assemblies for hands-on training.

Car manufacturers' dealers also are involved in cooperative vocational education programs in the automotive field. These programs combine classroom instruction with supervised, part-time employment planned to contribute to a student's overall education and employability.

The students' schedule, basically, is balanced between academic subjects required for graduation and employment in an automotive service establishment. The cooperative vocational education program is designed to bridge the gap between school and full-time employment in the automotive service industry.

The Job Market

Mechanically inclined students and recent graduates who have had some training in automotive service and repair work should consider these facts about motor vehicles and the nation's work force.

According to the Motor Vehicle Manufacturers Association of the United States, Inc.:

- Nearly 162 million cars, trucks, and buses are registered in the United States.
- About 585,000 automotive-related businesses are in operation in the U.S.
- Over 12.4 million persons are employed in the manufacture, distribution, maintenance, and commercial use of motor vehicles. About one out of every six private, nonagriculture workers in the U.S. is employed in an automotive-related occupation. See Figures 54-3 and 54-4.

These facts and figures are a good indication of the tremendous breadth of the automotive field. With these facts in mind, those mechanically inclined job seekers may take a different view of the career opportunities available in this field.

Job Descriptions

The following brief job descriptions are designed to familiarize you with some of the many areas of opportunity that exist in the automotive industry. While the usual first step for the job seeker is to investigate the role of the trainee or apprentice, you should also view this first job opportunity as a stepping stone toward a higher position and greater earnings.

Apprentice Service Technician

Apprentice auto service technicians divide their work time between the "classroom" and the shop, Figure 54-1. They learn the trade by studying principles of operation in a structured apprenticeship training program, and by applying service techniques taught on the job by experienced technicians. During the three or four year training program, the apprentices are regularly tested and studies continue for the duration of the program.

During the course of apprenticeship training, the apprentices receive periodic raises in pay until they reach the journeyman status at the end of the program. Even as general service technicians, however, the study of new developments and latest servicing techniques goes on.

Figure 54-3. Suppliers of automotive parts and assemblies play a major role in the overall success of the wide-ranging automotive field. This subassembler is carefully installing engine components. (Nissan)

Figure 54-4. This assembly line worker is responsible for installing inner door mechanisms. (Ford)

General Service Technician

A general auto service technician's job assignments call for a broad range of both light and heavy repair, Figure 54-5. General technicians must know how to diagnose trouble and maintain all systems of automotive vehicles in good working order by applying recommended service procedures.

The technician's skill depends upon sound education in the principles of automotive service, on-the-job experience in service and repair, and constant upgrading of know-how to keep abreast of technological changes in the field. Small wonder, then, that good service technicians are well paid, and their work is always in demand.

With the current trend toward specialization in automotive service and repair, general auto service technicians are becoming more involved with troubleshooting and diagnosis. They pinpoint the problem area through a study of symptoms and the results of road tests and various tests with diagnostic equipment. Once the problem area is established, a specialty technician takes over the service and repair assignment.

Specialty Service Technicians

Speciality service technicians, or specialists, concentrate on a single phase of repair work. They choose a specialty they feel they are well qualified to perform. Then, they further improve efficiency and proficiency through daily involvement with jobs of a similar nature.

Examples of specialties from among the many areas that make up the "general" total are the following:

- Front end service technicians–align and balance wheels, repair steering mechanisms and suspension systems. With the current trend toward compact front wheel drive vehicles, the front end technician has much more complicated techniques to master.
- Brake service technicians–troubleshoot and correct brake system problems. They service disc brakes, drum brakes, brake boosters or power brake units, parking brakes, and anti-skid systems, Figure 54-6.
- Auto electrical technicians–analyze problems with starting, charging, ignition, and lighting systems. They perform tests on electrical components and circuits, and make necessary repairs or unit replacements. Auto electrical technicians trained and qualified to do so, diagnose engine electronic control systems problems by means of on-board computers or sophisticated test equipment.
- Auto radiator service technicians–clean radiators in special tanks filled with caustic solutions. They locate leaks and make repairs. They install new radiator cores, heater cores, A/C condensers, A/C evaporators, automatic transmission oil coolers and, in some specialty shops, they repair or replace fuel tanks.
- Air conditioning service technicians–install and service automotive A/C systems. They troubleshoot cooling problems and make necessary repairs that usually require evacuation of the refrigerant and recharging and retesting after the repair is made. Automatic temperature control systems require the services of trained special-

Figure 54-5. A general service technician must be able to repair a variety of systems. This technician is installing new belts and hoses on an engine. (Dayco)

Figure 54-6. Specialty service technicians master a specific area of automotive service work and devote full time to performing their specialty. This specialist is servicing a brake assembly. (Nilfisk)

ists in shops having special instrumentation to test the electronic controls involved.

- Automatic transmission service technicians–diagnose problems of slippage, shifting, and noise. They road test the vehicle, make on-car inspections, oil pressure tests, air pressure tests, and a stall test before removing the transmission, if necessary, for major internal repairs. On-car repairs involve shift linkage adjustments, band adjustments, fluid changes, seal replacement, control valve body cleaning, and parts replacements.

Truck Service Technician

A truck service technician needs service know-how, plus special skills and strength to handle heavy parts and assemblies, both manually and with the aid of various heavy duty jacks, cranes or chain hoists, wheel dollies, and hydraulic presses. See Figure 54-7. While tolerances, in general, are greater and "fits" are less critical, service techniques remain basically the same as passenger car work. However, some areas require special training such as double reduction axles, full floating axles, air brakes, etc.

In establishing certification tests for master heavy-duty truck technician, the National Institute for Automotive Service Excellence breaks down the truck service specialities into gasoline engines, diesel engines, drive train, brakes, suspension and steering, and electrical systems.

Master Service Technician

The master technician inherits the particularly troublesome service assignments–repeat comebacks, unusual symptoms, mysterious noises, etc. See Figure 54-8. The master technician also helps get work back on schedule by filling in for absent technicians, authorizes repairs when unexpected defects are found, oversees the apprenticeship training program, and generally represents the dealership at the car manufacturer's service school.

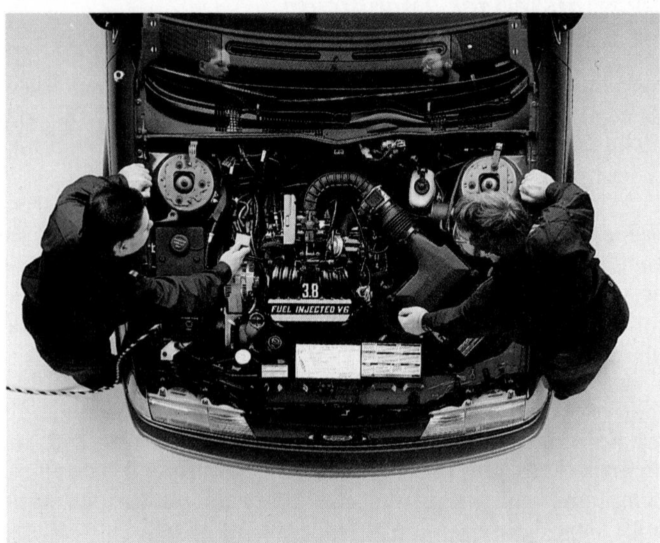

Figure 54-8. These master service technicians are connecting a diagnostic analyzer to help pinpoint a problem in the computerized engine control system. (Ford)

Auto Body and Paint Technicians

Body and paint technicians perform auto body and chassis repair and realignment, along with carefully controlled refinishing procedures. In the process, they operate various setups of pulling and straightening equipment and install replacement panels and structural parts. Their collision repair work and paint spraying requires separate facilities. New equipment operation must be mastered. Latest repair and refinishing techniques must be learned and applied. See Figure 54-9.

Auto Service Adviser/Writer

The service writer greets customers and writes repair orders based on symptoms described by the car owner,

Figure 54-7. This truck service technician is balancing a wheel on a large truck. (Hunter)

Figure 54-9. Auto body and paint technicians are also specialists, often to a point of specializing either in body repair or paint spraying. This particular technician specializes in body repair. (LORS Machinery, Inc.)

Figure 54-10. The repair orders must clearly and concisely state the problems and possible solutions service writers generally have a background in troubleshooting and diagnosis. They also must be familiar with the content of current factory service bulletins covering complaints from the field.

Shop Supervisor

The shop supervisor is directly in charge of the service technicians–directing, routing, and scheduling service and repair work. The supervisor helps hire, transfer, promote, and discharge technicians to meet the needs of the service department. The supervisor also instructs and oversees the technicians in their work procedures, inspects finished repairs, and is responsible for quality service and satisfactory shop operation.

DRIVEABILITY QUESTIONNAIRE

Please complete the form as **accurately** as possible to provide our technicians with the best opportunity to **FIX-IT-RIGHT**. Check the areas that correspond with your particular problem. Blanks have been provided in specific areas for your use, if additional comments are required.

Customer Name ____________ Vehicle Year and Type ____________

MAJOR SYMPTOM

☐ Hard Starting*
☐ Starts and Dies
☐ Idle Rough*
☐ Idle Speed too High
☐ Idle Speed too
☐ Dies at Idle*
☐ Poor
Had Problem
Problem Began After Vehicle Accumulated ________ Miles

☐ Surge*
☐ Driven 2
☐ After Driven 10 Miles
☐ Wet Weather, Rain/Snow
☐ Damp Weather, Fog
☐ On Acceleration
☐ On Deceleration
☐ At Constant Speeds
☐ During Braking
☐ While Turning Corners

☐ Engine
ccessories
☐

Fuel Tank Level During Occurrence:
☐ ¼ or Less
☐ ½
☐ ¾ or More
☐ All Levels

CUSTOMER DRIVING HABITS

DO YOU?
☐ Start Cold Engine and Drive Immediately
☐ Start Cold Engine Allow Warm-Up Period
☐ Use Mainly on Highways
☐ Use Mainly within City
Average Distance of Miles Driven Daily: ________

FUEL USED?
☐ No Lead, Regular
☐ No Lead, Premium
☐ Regular Leaded
☐ Blends of Gasohol
Brand of Fuel Used: ________

* Defined on reverse side

Figure 54-10. A good service adviser uses a check sheet like this when questioning a customer about performance problems. This eliminates or reduces diagnostic time for the technician that works on the car.

Service Manager

The service manager is the department head in charge of planning, supervising, and coordinating the activities of all shop employees. Primarily responsible for hiring, transferring, promoting, and discharging workers, the service manager oversees scheduling of appointments for service and repair work, training of apprentices, and familiarizing technicians with new service procedures. The service manager also reviews records of operation to plan cost control measures, improve shop practices, and raise work standards. Other duties include investigation of complaints, assignment of responsibility for service errors, and adjustments of bills or charges. In addition, the service manager must try to build business for the service department with advertising and sales promotion activities.

Motor Vehicle Salesperson

Motor vehicle sales is the job for you if you enjoy selling. Experience in the service department will give you an excellent background for sales work. If you know the mechanics of a vehicle, you can do a much better job of explaining the mechanical and electronic features of a car or truck to a potential customer, then demonstrating it and comparing the vehicle with competing makes.

Sales Manager

A sales manager has charge of the entire selling activity of the dealership. This is one of the top positions in the retail automotive field. It usually is held by someone who has made a success of selling over a period of years and one who has managerial ability. The sales manager must spearhead the sales and service operations, and therefore must work closely with the owners, service manager, parts manager, and shop supervisor.

Parts Manager

The parts manager for a car or truck dealership has an important job of ordering, stocking, and selling replacement parts and accessories. The parts manager supplies the dealership shop needs and sells parts and accessories at wholesale to independent garages, service stations, and specialty shops in the community. Training in service work and a vast knowledge of part numbers and part locations are necessary. Also required is the ability to maintain an adequate stock–yet not an overstock–of parts. See Figure 54-11.

Jobber Salesperson

Jobber sales is a job in the parts and accessories field that should appeal to a sales-minded young person with some automotive service training. A jobber salesperson, representing a wholesale parts house, travels over a certain territory selling the products of several manufacturers to automotive repair and supply shops.

Figure 54-11. The parts manager keeps service technicians supplied with correct replacement parts and assemblies. Other service outlets and do-it-yourselfers are also served by the parts department. (Triad)

Closely related is the counter sales specialist who not only sells replacement parts and accessories over the jobber's counter, but also offers installation advice to do-it-yourselfers.

Car Manufacturers Representatives

Employment with car manufacturers often attracts individuals with service technician's training and other customer relations-oriented qualifications. Positions include factory district manager; factory supervisor, Figure 54-12; factory service representative; factory parts manager; factory service instructor; and research laboratory technician.

Car Factory/Supplier Employees

Employees in car manufacturers' factories or with original equipment suppliers also make good use of training in jobs such as subassembly; final assembly, Figure 54-13; assembly quality control, Figure 54-14; dynamometer testing; experimental driver; driver technician; and engineering garage technician.

Figure 54-13. Final assembly worker installs seats in a vehicle. (Nissan)

Figure 54-12. Supervisor for auto manufacturer conducts employee involvement session to discuss job-related problems and how to solve them. (Ford)

Figure 54-14. Quality control technicians study a vehicle for proper body panel fit and finish. (Honda)

Vocational Teacher or Auto Technology Instructor

Teaching is an interesting and rewarding career. If you obtain experience in automotive service work, have a good knowledge of automotive construction and principles of operation, and have teaching ability, you may qualify for one of many careers in this field. You might be employed by a car manufacturer or parts/equipment supplier to train service personnel in new technological advances. Or, you might want to teach automotive service classes in a public school, trade school, or a private vocational school. Still another teaching opportunity presents itself with replacement parts manufacturers, conducting service clinics or symposiums.

Insurance Adjuster and Claim Examiner

Insurance adjuster and claim examiner are jobs that insurance companies like to fill with young people who, in addition to other academic qualifications, have automotive service training. Knowledge of auto body work, refinishing, and replacement parts pricing is vital.

Sales Representatives

Sales and service representatives work for companies that supply parts and/or equipment to the automotive industry. They frequently are aggressive, high-caliber people who began their careers in automotive service stations, independent shops, or department store automotive facilities.

Owners of Service Stations or Specialty Repair Shops

Owners and lessees of service stations usually get their start in the business as pump attendant or technician's helper in the station's service bays. Owners and franchisees of specialty repair shops (muffler shops, tire dealerships, fast oil change and lube chains, brake service centers, transmission service outlets, etc.) probably learned the business from the "bottom up."

Entrepreneurship

An ***entrepreneur*** is one who undertakes ownership of a business or enterprise. ***Entrepreneurship*** is that person's ability to organize, manage, and assume the risks of operating the business.

Owning your own business is the goal of some auto technicians. This requires a certain type of person. Not everyone is suited to owning a business. Besides your technical skills, business skills and schooling are needed. As an owner, you must have good public relation skills and be a leader at work as well as in the community. Most of all, you must be fair and honest with your customers and employees. At times this can be a real juggling act and can be a cause of great stress and pressure. There are disadvantages and advantages of having your own business.

Disadvantages of Entrepreneurship

There are more disadvantages of having your own business than advantages. First, about 80-85% of small business firms fail in the first year. If you make it past the first year, you may spend from 16 to 20 hours a day at work. You will have to work weekends to do all of the required paper work. You will not be able to take time off for a vacation for two to three years after starting the business. Most important, you must find good people that can be trusted to work for your firm.

Advantages of Entrepreneurship

The most common reason people want to own a business is to be their own boss. The only person you will have to answer to is the customer. The financial return is another reason some start their own business. Some entrepreneurs have become millionaires overnight. However, most of the time it can take from three to four years before showing a profit.

Once the business is established, you can set your own hours. On the other hand, if you spend too much time away from the business, it more than likely will fail unless you have a good manager that can be trusted.

Success

A good owner has to have many qualities. You must be aggressive and take the initiative. This is the sign of a leader. You must set good examples for your employees by being on time, dependable, fair, honest, and responsible. You must be able to get along with people.

Communication is another essential element of business management. You must be able to instruct your employees. They must be comfortable with you so that they will ask questions when they do not know the answer, Figure 54-15.

You must set high goals for yourself and the business, then see them through. You must be a good manager so that your expenses do not exceed your income. You must be innovative or creative as to how you will meet the competition. Sounds hard, but it is rewarding when things go right.

Types of Ownership

There are several types of ownership possible. You may own the business entirely yourself. This is called a ***sole proprietorship.*** It means you assume all the profits as well as the losses.

A ***partnership*** is another form of ownership. At least two people are jointly responsible for the profits and losses. However, one person may own a greater percentage of the business than the other. There may even be a silent partner. A silent partner supplies the needed funds and receives his or her share of the profits without being involved in the day-to-day operation of the business.

The business may also be turned into a ***corporation,*** which is a business association endowed by law with the rights and liabilities of an individual. There are certain advantages and disadvantages of turning a business into a corporation. The primary advantage is that if the business is sued, none of the stockholders can be sued. A stockholder "buys" a small percentage of the business, hoping that the value of the stock will increase over the original purchase price. Most of the time the person who operates the business has controlling interest–at least 51% of the available stock.

The disadvantage of incorporation is that there are government regulations that must be met and a charter created that is approved by the state. Any changes must be approved by the state. A charter must be drawn up or amended by a lawyer.

The Three A's

There are many expenses involved in running a business. Attorneys, accountants, and advertising are three big expenses in addition to paying rent for the building.

Attorneys are needed to draw up legal documents, read contracts before you sign, and represent you in the event of any legal conflicts.

Accountants are needed to keep your books and prepare your taxes. There are so many tax laws that it is not possible for the average person to know all of them and run a business.

Advertising is a must. Without advertising, people will not know you are in business. Also, they will not know your prices and services to compare to the competition. All of this takes money.

Technician Certification

The National Institute for Automotive Service Excellence (ASE) offers a series of voluntary certification tests, providing technicians with the opportunity to demonstrate their knowledge of troubleshooting and repair techniques. ASE offers eight standard certification tests in the automobile area, including:

- Engine Repair.
- Automatic Transmission/Transaxle.
- Manual Drive Train and Axles.

Figure 54-15. An entrepreneur must be able to teach as well as manage the business.

- Suspension and Steering.
- Brakes.
- Electrical/Electronics Systems.
- Heating and Air Conditioning.
- Engine Performance.

A technician who passes one or more of these tests and has at least two years of work experience in the automotive field is certified as an ASE Automobile Technician. A technician who passes all eight tests and meets the experience requirement is certified as a Master Automobile Technician.

In addition to the eight basic automobile tests, ASE offers tests in Medium/Heavy Truck, Body/Paint, Engine Machinist, and Alternate Fuels. An Advanced Engine Performance Test is also offered.

For more information on ASE certification, write to:
National Institute for Automotive Service Excellence
13505 Dulles Technology Drive
Herndon, Virginia 22071-3415

Review Questions–Chapter 54

1. The need for specialist in the automotive industry continues to grow. True or False?
2. Apprentice auto service technicians divide their time between the automotive shop and the _____.
3. The general auto service technician performs:
   (A) troubleshooting procedures.
   (B) light repairs.
   (C) heavy repairs.
   (D) None of the above.
4. Name three areas in which automotive technicians may specialize.
5. _____ _____ are often called on to solve difficult service assignments.
6. The service writer is responsible for:
   (A) transferring technicians.
   (B) ordering parts.
   (C) completing repair orders.
   (D) None of the above.
7. The service manager coordinates the activities of all shop employees. True or False?
8. A(n) _____ is a person who starts a business or an enterprise.
9. List several advantages and disadvantages of owning a business.
10. All automotive technicians must take ASE certification tests. True or False?

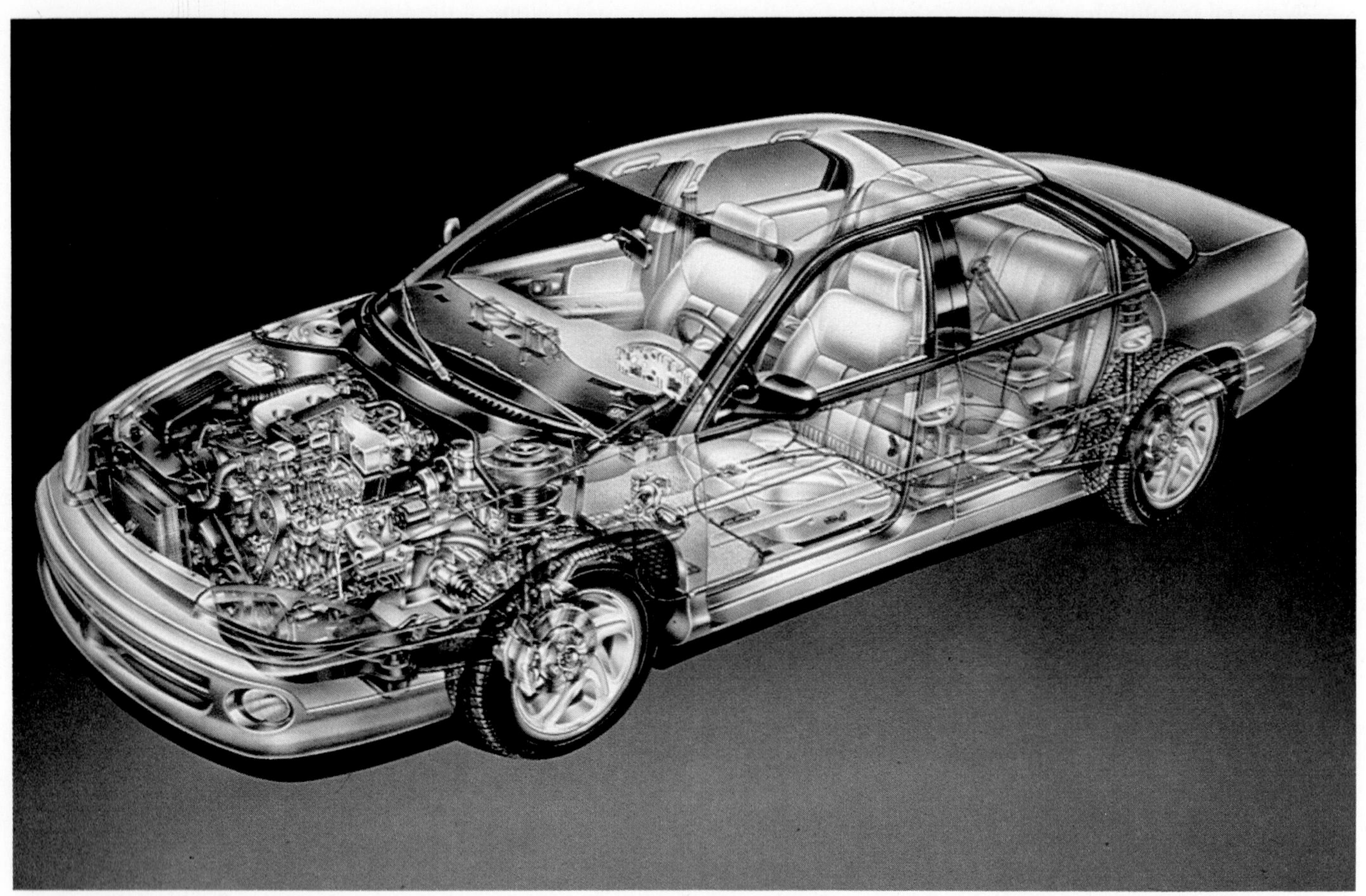

This cutaway of a late-model vehicle shows the systems and components that are commonly serviced by the automotive technician. (Chrysler)

Appendix

CONVERSION TABLES

LINEAR:				
Millimeters	×	.0394	=	Inches
Inches	×	25.400	=	Millimeters
Centimeters	×	.394	=	Inches
Inches	×	2.54	=	Centimeters
Meters	×	3.2809	=	Feet
Feet	×	.3048	=	Meters
Kilometers	×	.6214	=	Miles
Miles	×	1.6093	=	Kilometers
AREA:				
Square centimeters	×	.1550	=	Square inches
Square inches	×	6.4515	=	Square centimeters
Square meters	×	10.7641	=	Square feet
Square feet	×	.0929	=	Square meters
Square kilometers	×	247.1098	=	Acres
Acres	×	.0041	=	Square kilometers
Hectares	×	2.471	=	Acres
Acres	×	.4047	=	Hectares
VOLUME:				
Cubic centimeters	×	.0610	=	Cubic inches
Cubic inches	×	16.3866	=	Cubic centimeters
Cubic meters	×	35.3156	=	Cubic feet
Cubic feet	×	.0283	=	Cubic meters
Quarts	×	0.9465	=	Liters
Liters	×	1.0565	=	Quarts
Liters	×	61.023	=	Cubic inches
Cubic inches	×	.0164	=	Liters
Liters	×	.2652	=	U.S. Gallons
U.S. Gallons	×	3.7854	=	Liters
MASS:				
Grams	×	15.4324	=	Grains
Grains	×	.0648	=	Grams
Grams	×	.0353	=	Ounces, avoirdupois
Ounces, avoirdupois	×	28.3495	=	Grams
Kilograms	×	2.2046	=	Pounds
Pounds	×	.4536	=	Kilograms
Metric tons (1 000 kilograms)	×	1.1023	=	Tons (2000 pounds)
Tons (2000 pounds)	×	.9072	=	Metric tons

Continued.

PRESSURE:				
Kilopascals	×	.145	=	Pounds per square inch
Pounds per square inch	×	6.895	=	Kilopascals
TORQUE:				
Newton-meters	×	.7376	=	Pound feet
Pound feet	×	1.3558	=	Newton-meters
Pound-inch	×	0.11298	=	Newton-meters
POWER:				
Kilowatts	×	1.3405	=	Horsepower
Horsepower	×	.746	=	Kilowatts
FORCE:				
Pounds	×	4.45	=	Newtons
Newtons	×	.225	=	Pounds
Kilograms	×	9.8	=	Newtons
Newtons	×	.102	=	Kilograms
VELOCITY:				
Mph	×	1.6093	=	Km/h
Km/h	×	.621	=	Mph
TEMPERATURE:				
(°F − 32)	÷	1.8	=	°C
(1.8 × °C)	+	32	=	°F

DETERMINING SPEED/DISTANCE TRAVELED:

To find the distance a car travels in one foot each second, and the speed (mph) is known:

Indicated speed (mph) × 1.47 = ft./seconds.

However, if the distance (ft.) and time (seconds) is known, and the speed (mph) is unknown, then:

1. Distance (ft) ÷ time (seconds) = ft./sec.; then
2. Ft./sec. ÷ 1.47 = speed (mph)

DECIMAL AND METRIC EQUIVALENTS

FRACTIONS	DECIMAL IN.	METRIC MM.	FRACTIONS	DECIMAL IN.	METRIC MM.
1/64	.015625	.39688	33/64	.515625 . . .	13.09687
1/32	.03125	.79375	17/32	.53125	13.49375
3/64	.046875	1.19062	35/64	.546875 . . .	13.89062
1/16	.0625	1.58750	9/16	.5625	14.28750
5/64	.078125	1.98437	37/64	.578125 . . .	14.68437
3/32	.09375	2.38125	19/32	.59375	15.08125
7/64	.109375	2.77812	39/64	.609375 . . .	15.47812
1/8	.125	3.1750	5/8	.625	15.87500
9/64	.140625	3.57187	41/64	.640625 . . .	16.27187
5/32	.15625	3.96875	21/32	.65625	16.66875
11/64	.171875	4.36562	43/64	.671875 . . .	17.06562
3/16	.1875	4.76250	11/16	.6875	17.46250
13/64	.203125	5.15937	45/64	.703125 . . .	17.85937
7/32	.21875	5.55625	23/32	.71875	18.25625
15/64	.234375	5.95312	47/64	.734375 . . .	18.65312
1/4	.250	6.35000	3/4	.750	19.05000
17/64	.265625	6.74687	49/64	.765625 . . .	19.44687
9/32	.28125	7.14375	25/32	.78125	19.84375
19/64	.296875	7.54062	51/64	.796875 . . .	20.24062
5/16	.3125	7.93750	13/16	.8125	20.63750
21/64	.328125	8.33437	53/64	.828125 . . .	21.03437
11/32	.34375	8.73125	27/32	.84375	21.43125
23/64	.359375	9.12812	55/64	.859375 . . .	21.82812
3/8	.375	9.52500	7/8	.875	22.22500
25/64	.390625	9.92187	57/64	.890625 . . .	22.62187
13/32	.40625	10.31875	29/32	.90625	23.01875
27/64	.421875	10.71562	59/64	.921875 . . .	23.41562
7/16	.4375	11.11250	15/16	.9375	23.81250
29/64	.453125	11.50937	61/64	.953125 . . .	24.20937
15/32	.46875	11.90625	31/32	.96875	24.60625
31/64	.484375	12.30312	63/64	.984375 . . .	25.00312
1/2	.500	12.70000	1	1.00	25.40000

AUTOMOTIVE ABBREVIATIONS

AMP. - AMPERE(S)
A/C - AIR CONDITIONING
ACC - AUTOMATIC CLIMATE CONTROL
ADJ. - ADJUST
A/F - AIR/FUEL (AS IN AIR/FUEL RATIO)
AIR - AIR INJECTION REACTION SYSTEM
ALC - AUTOMATIC LEVEL CONTROL
ALCL - ASSEMBLY LINE COMMUNICATIONS LINK
ALT. - ALTITUDE
APT - ADJUSTABLE PART THROTTLE
AT - AUTOMATIC TRANSMISSION
ATC - AUTOMATIC TEMPERATURE CONTROL
ATDC - AFTER TOP DEAD CENTER

BARO - BAROMETRIC ABSOLUTE PRESSURE SENSOR
BAT. - BATTERY
BAT. + - POSITIVE TERMINAL
BBL. - BARREL
BHP - BRAKE HORSEPOWER
BP - BACK PRESSURE
BTDC - BEFORE TOP DEAD CENTER

CAT. CONV. - CATALYTIC CONVERTER
CB - CITIZENS BAND (RADIO)
CC - CATALYTIC CONVERTER
CUBIC CENTIMETER
CONVERTER CLUTCH
CCC - COMPUTER COMMAND CONTROL
CCDIC - CLIMATE CONTROL DRIVER INFORMATION CENTER
CCOT - CYCLING CLUTCH (ORIFICE) TUBE
CCP - CONTROLLED CANISTER PURGE
C.E. - CHECK ENGINE
CEAB - COLD ENGINE AIRBLEED
CEMF - COUNTER ELECTROMOTIVE FORCE
CID - CUBIC INCH DISPLACEMENT
CL - CLOSED LOOP
CLCC - CLOSED LOOP CARBURETOR CONTROL
CLTBI - CLOSED LOOP THROTTLE BODY INJECTION
CONV. - CONVERTER
CP - CANISTER PURGE
CU. IN. - CUBIC INCH
CV - CONSTANT VELOCITY
CYL. - CYLINDER(S)

DBB - DUAL BED BEAD
DBM - DUAL BED MONOLITH
DEFI - DIGITAL ELECTRONIC FUEL INJECTION
DFI - DIGITAL FUEL INJECTION
DIFF. - DIFFERENTIAL
DIST. - DISTRIBUTOR

EAC - ELECTRONIC AIR CONTROL VALVE
EAS - ELECTRONIC AIR SWITCHING VALVE
ECC - ELECTRONIC COMFORT CONTROL
ECM - ELECTRONIC CONTROL MODULE
ECS - EMISSION CONTROL SYSTEM
ECU - ENGINE CALIBRATION UNIT
EEC - EVAPORATIVE EMISSION CONTROL
EFE - EARLY FUEL EVAPORATION
EFI - ELECTRONIC FUEL INJECTION
EGR - EXHAUST GAS RECIRCULATION
ELC - ELECTRONIC LEVEL CONTROL
EMF - ELECTROMOTIVE FORCE
EMR - ELECTRONIC MODULE RETARD
EOS - EXHAUST OXYGEN SENSOR
ESC - ELECTRONIC SPARK CONTROL
EST - ELECTRONIC SPARK TIMING
ETC - ELECTRONIC TEMPERATURE CONTROL
ETCC - ELECTRONIC TOUCH COMFORT CONTROL
ETR - ELECTRONICALLY TUNED RECEIVER
EXH. - EXHAUST

FMVSS - FEDERAL MOTOR VEHICLE SAFETY STANDARDS
FT. LB. - FOOT POUNDS (TORQUE)
FWD - FRONT WHEEL DRIVE

HD - HEAVY DUTY
HEI - HIGH ENERGY IGNITION
HG. - MERCURY
HI. ALT. - HIGH ALTITUDE
HVAC - HEATER-VENT-AIR CONDITIONING
HVACM - HEATER-VENT-AIR CONDITIONING MODULE
HVM - HEATER-VENT-MODULE

IAC - IDLE AIR CONTROL
IC - INTEGRATED CIRCUIT
ID - IDENTIFICATION
- INSIDE DIAMETER
ILC - IDLE LOAD COMPENSATOR
IP - INSTRUMENT PANEL
ISC - IDLE SPEED CONTROL

km - KILOMETER
km/h - KILOMETER PER HOUR
KV - KILOVOLTS (THOUSANDS OF VOLTS)
km/L - KILOMETERS/LITER (mpg)
kPa - KILOPASCALS

L - LITER
LF - LEFT FRONT
LR - LEFT REAR

MAN. VAC. - MANIFOLD VACUUM
MAF - MASS AIR FLOW
MAP - MANIFOLD ABSOLUTE PRESSURE
MAT - MANIFOLD AIR TEMPERATURE SENSOR
M/C - MIXTURE CONTROL
MPG - MILES PER GALLON
MPH - MILES PER HOUR
MT - MANUAL TRANSMISSION

N·m - NEWTON METERS (TORQUE)

OD - OUTSIDE DIAMETER
OL - OPEN LOOP
OSM - OUTPUT SWITCHING MODULE
O_2 - OXYGEN

PAIR - PULSE AIR INJECTION REACTION SYSTEM
P/B - POWER BRAKES
PCV - POSITIVE CRANKCASE VENTILATION
PECV - POWER ENRICHMENT CONTROL VALVE
P/N - PARK, NEUTRAL
PROM - PROGRAMMABLE, READ ONLY MEMORY
P/S - POWER STEERING
PSI - POUNDS PER SQUARE INCH
PT. - PINT

QT. - QUART

R - RESISTANCE
R-4 - RADIAL FOUR CYL. A/C COMPRESSOR
RF - RIGHT FRONT
RPM - REVOLUTIONS PER MINUTE
RR - RIGHT REAR
RTV - ROOM TEMPERATURE VULCANIZING (SEALER)
RVR - RESPONSE VACUUM REDUCER

SAE - SOCIETY OF AUTOMOTIVE ENGINEERS
SI - SYSTEM INTERNATIONAL
SOL. - SOLENOID

TAC - THERMOSTATIC AIR CLEANER
TACH - TACHOMETER
TBI -THROTTLE BODY INJECTION
TCC - TRANSMISSION CONVERTER CLUTCH
TCS - TRANSMISSION CONTROLLED SPARK
TDC - TOP DEAD CENTER
TPS - THROTTLE POSITION SENSOR
TV - THROTTLE VALVE
TVRS - TELEVISION & RADIO SUPPRESSION
TVS - THERMAL VACUUM SWITCH

U-JOINT - UNIVERSAL JOINT

V - VOLT(S)
V-8 - EIGHT CYLINDER ENGINE - ARRANGED IN A "V"
VAC. - VACUUM
VATS - VEHICLE ANTI-THEFT SYSTEM
VIN - VEHICLE IDENTIFICATION NUMBER
VMV - VACUUM MODULATOR VALVE
VSS - VEHICLE SPEED SENSOR

W/ - WITH
W/B - WHEEL BASE
W/O - WITHOUT
WOT - WIDE OPEN THROTTLE

PHYSICAL PROPERTIES OF CERTAIN METALS

METAL	MELTING POINT (F)	BOILING POINT (F)	COMMENTS
Aluminum	1,215	4,100	1. Does not return to original shape after being overheated. 2. Oxidizes (becomes dull) with heat. 3. Good conductor of electricity and heat. 4. Resists corrosion. 5. Exists in the ore corundum and bauxite; must be separated from the ore. 6. Malleable and ductile metal. 7. Very reflective. 8. A nonferrous metal.
Antimony	1,167	2,516	1. Expands while cooling. 2. Brittle metal.
Cadmium	609	1,409	1. Poisonous. 2. Ductile and malleable metal.
Chrome	3,407	4,829	1. Hard metal and wear resistant. 2. Resists rusting. 3. Used in alloys and electroplating.
Cobalt	2,728	5,250	1. Remains hard up to 1,800 °F. 2. A ferrous metal. 3. Occurs in nature combined with iron and nickel.
Copper	1,981	4,217	1. Excellent conductor of heat and electricity. 2. Ductile and malleable metal.
Gold	1,945	4,586	1. Excellent conductor of heat and electricity. 2. Resists rust and tarnishing. 3. Ductile and malleable metal. 4. Very expensive.
Iron (steel)	2,790	5,400	1. Will return to its original shape after being overheated. 2. Heavy, but ductile and malleable metal. 3. A ferrous metal. 4. Rusts very easily.
Lead	620	2,950	1. Resists corrosion. 2. Radiation cannot penetrate through it. 3. Heavy (dense), but a very soft malleable and ductile metal.
Lithium	357	12,426	1. Lightest known metal. 2. Used in nuclear reactions.
Magnesium	1,203	2,030	1. 30% lighter than aluminum. 2. Shavings are easy to catch on fire; use sand to put out a magnesium fire. 3. Malleable and ductile metal. 4. Produces an intense white light while burning.
Manganese	2,273	3,900	1. Wear resistant. 2. Strengthens steel by removing oxides and sulfur. 3. A hard and brittle metal. 4. A nonferrous metal.
Mercury	−102	675	1. A liquid at normal temperatures. 2. A poisonous metal. 3. Used in thermometers and barometers. 4. Also referred to as quick silver.
Molybdenum	4,730	10,000	1. A hard metal, but softer than chrome. 2. When alloyed with steel, it allows steel to keep it's cutting edge when heated.
Nickel	2,651	6,110	1. Controls thermal expansion of metal. 2. Hard metal; used basically in alloys and electroplating. 3. Malleable and ductile metal. 4. Resists corrosion.
Platinum	3,220	7,770	1. Used as a catalyst. 2. Very expensive. 3. Heavy, but ductile and malleable metal. 4. Does not corrode.
Palladium	2,826	7,200	1. Used as a catalyst. 2. Malleable and ductile metal.

PHYSICAL PROPERTIES OF CERTAIN METALS			
METAL	**MELTING POINT (F)**	**BOILING POINT (F)**	**COMMENTS**
Silver	1,761	3,551	1. Excellent conductor of electricity and heat. 2. Very expensive. 3. Ductile and a very malleable metal.
Sodium	208	1,638	1. Explosive reaction when mixed with water.
Tin	450	4,118	1. A flash coating on other metals provides excellent lubrication properties. 2. A soft, malleable, and ductile metal at ordinary temperatures.
Titanium	3,035	5,900	1. Strong as steel, but 45% lighter. 2. 60% heavier than aluminum, but twice as strong.
Tungsten	6,170	10,706	1. Metal with the highest melting/boiling point. 2. Resists acids. 3. Resists abrasions. 4. Heavy, hard, and ductile metal. 5. Also called wolfram.
Vanadium	3,110	5,432	1. Adds tensile strength to steel. 2. Malleable and ductile metal.
Zinc	786	1,661	1. Prevents rust. 2. Ductile in its pure form, but brittle in its commercial form.

METAL ALLOYS	
ALLOY	**METALS INVOLVED:**
Brass	Copper and zinc
Bronze	Copper and tin
Nichrome	Nickel and chrome
Stainless steel	Chrome, steel, and nickel
Stellite	Cobalt, tungsten, and chrome
White gold	Gold and palladium

TYPES OF ELASTOMERS

NATURAL RUBBER

Provides high resilience and tensile strength. Also, its resistance to wear and flexibility is good at low temperatures. Temperature range is from −55 to +90 °C. However, it does not wear well when exposed to petroleum products, sunlight, ozone, or oxygen.

NEOPRENE

Provides good resistance to weather, petroleum products, water, and heat. Also, it provides resilience and flexibility.

NITRILE

Provides excellent resistance to petroleum products and acids. However, it is not compatible with synthetic oil. Temperature range is from −53 to +121 °C.

EPDM

Provides excellent resistance to the weather and heat. Temperature range is from −50 to +150 °C. It also provides excellent dielectric qualities and its cost is low. However, it should not be exposed to petroleum products and is not as resilient and strong as natural rubber.

HYPALON

Provides excellent resistance to the weather, ozone, acids, heat, petroleum products, and abrasions.

SILICONE

Provides excellent high and low temperature qualities. Temperature range is from −60 to +200 °C. Also, it provides good resistance to the weather, petroleum products, flexing, and fatigue.

VITON

Provides excellent resistance to petroleum products at high and low temperatures. Also, it provides good resistance to chemical action and low compression set, while providing strength and resilience. Temperature range is from −40 to +204 °C.

TEFLON

Provides a material that is inert with all chemicals. It also provides a nonstick (slippery) surface.

Dictionary of Automotive Terms

A

AAA: American Automobile Association.

Abrasion: Wearing or rubbing away.

ABS: Anti-lock brake system.

A/C: Air conditioning.

Accelerator: A pedal for regulating speed of an engine.

Accelerator pump: Small pump in carburetor, operated by accelerator pedal linkage, which supplies additional fuel needed for acceleration of vehicle.

Acetylene or oxyacetylene welding: Utilization of an acetylene flame to heat metal to fusion or melting point when uniting it.

Ackerman principle: Design having wheel spindles mounted on axle ends to permit spindles to be turned at an angle to axle for steering purposes.

Acrylic: A surface finish, made from synthetic polymers, which dries by solvent evaporation.

Active material: In a storage battery, peroxide of lead (brown) in positive plates and metallic lead (gray) in negative plates upon which sulphuric acid acts.

Actuator: An output device controlled by the computer.

Adaptor carburetor: A device attached to a gasoline carburetor which permits an internal combustion engine to run either on gasoline or liquefied petroleum gas (LP-Gas).

Additive: In automotive oils, material added to oil to give it certain properties. Example: to lessen its tendency to thicken at low temperature.

ADS: Association of Diesel Specialists.

AEA: Automotive Electronic Association.

AERA: Automotive Engine Rebuilder's Association.

Air: A gas containing approximately 4/5 nitrogen, 1/5 oxygen, and some carbonic gas. Also, abbreviation for Air Injection Reaction system.

Air bag: Protective device designed to serve as a "pillow" between front seat occupants and vehicle interior immediately following a frontal or front-angle crash.

Air cleaner: A device for filtering, cleaning, and removing dust from intake air to an engine, air compressor, etc.

Air conditioning: Process by which surrounding air is cooled and dehumidified.

Airflow meter: Measures rate at which air enters engine.

Airflow sensor: Sensor that monitors the amount of air entering a vehicle's throttle body or carburetor.

Air/fuel ratio: Ratio by weight of fuel compared to air in carburetor mixture.

Air gap: Space between spark plug electrodes, starting motor and generator armatures, field shoes, etc.

Air horn: Air inlet of carburetor to which air cleaner is ordinarily attached.

Air injection system: Means of injecting fresh air into hot gases in exhaust manifold to reduce emissions.

Air-lock: A bubble of air trapped in a fluid circuit which interferes with normal circulation of fluid.

Air spring: An air-filled bag or device that is pressurized to provide spring action.

ALDL: Assembly line diagnostic link. Diagnostic connector.

Alignment: An adjustment to bring related components into a line.

All-wheel drive: Four-wheel drive capability with automatic shifts.

Allen wrench: A hexagonal wrench, which is "L" shaped, fits into a recessed hexagonal hole.

Alloy: A mixture of different metals. Example: solder is an alloy of lead and tin.

Alternating current: An electric current alternating back and forth in direction of flow.

Alternator: Generator in which alternating current is changed to direct current by means of rectifiers (diodes).

Aluminum: A metal, noted for its lightness, often alloyed with small quantities of other metals.

Ambient: Surrounding on all sides.

Ammeter: An instrument for measuring flow of electric current.

Ampere: Unit of measurement for flow of electric current.

Ampere-hour capacity: A term used to indicate capacity of a storage battery. Example: delivery of a certain number of amperes for a certain number of hours.

Analog computer: Imitates signal it receives and adjusts actuators proportionately.

Annealing: A process of softening metal. Example: heating and slow cooling of a piece of iron.

Annular ball bearing: A ball bearing with a nonadjustable inner and outer race or races.

Annulus: In planetary gear system, an internal ring gear that operates in conjunction with a sun gear, pinion gears, and pinion carrier. See Ring gear.

Anode: A positive pole of an electric current.

Antifreeze: A material, such as ethylene glycol, added to water to lower its freezing point.

Antifriction bearing: A bearing constructed with balls or rollers between journal and bearing surface to provide rolling instead of sliding friction.

Anti-lock brake system: Provides rapid and repeated brake applications and releases to bring vehicle to a stop without brake lockup or skidding.

Antismog device: A special part or system designed to reduce or eliminate emission of noxious gases from exhaust of engine. See Exhaust emissions.

Aperture: An opening, hole, or port.

API: American Petroleum Institute.

Arc welding: A method of utilizing an electric current jumping an air gap to provide heat for welding metal.

Arcing: Electricity bridging gap between two electrodes.

Armature: Part of an electrical device which includes main, current-carrying winding.

Articulated mounting: A term used where parts are connected by links and links are anchored to provide a double hinging action.

Asbestos: A natural fibrous mineral with a great heat resisting ability.

ASE: National Institute for Automotive Service Excellence.

ASIA: Automotive Service Industry Association.

ASME: American Society of Mechanical Engineers.

Aspect ratio: Ratio of tire section height to section width.

ATA: American Trucking Association.

ATF: Automatic transmission fluid.

Atmospheric pressure: Weight of air at sea level, about 14.7 psi.

Atom: Smallest distinct chemical unit of a substance, composed of electrons, neutrons, and protons.

Automatic level control: Front and rear load leveling by means of four rubber or plastic air springs or air adjustable shock absorbers or shock struts.

Automatic ride control: Electronically operated soft or firm ride as required.

Automatic steering effect: Built-in tendency of an automobile to resume travel in a straight line when released from a turn.

Axle: Shaft or shafts of a vehicle upon which wheels are mounted.

B

B & S gauge: Brown and Sharpe gauge, which is a standard measure of wire size. Smaller the number, larger the wire.

Backfire: Ignition of fuel mixture in intake manifold or exhaust manifold.

Backlash: Clearance or "play" between the teeth of two gears.

Back pressure: A resistance to free flow, such as a restriction in the exhaust system.

Baffle or baffle plate: An obstruction for checking or deflecting flow of gases or sound.

Balk ring: A friction-regulated pawl or plunger used to facilitate engagement of gears.

Ball bearing: An antifriction bearing consisting of a hardened inner and outer race with hardened steel balls interposed between two races.

Barometric pressure sensor: Sensor that measures atmospheric pressure.

Battery: Any number of complete electrical cells assembled in one housing or case.

Battery capacity: amount of current battery will deliver.

Battery plate: Component made of special active materials contained in cast grids.

Battery ratings: Standards of power-delivering capability of batteries as established by Battery Council International.

BCI: Battery Council International.

BCM: Body computer module.

BDC: Bottom dead center.

Bead: Part of tire shaped to fit the rim.

Bearing: A part in which a journal, shaft, or pivot turns or moves.

Bell housing: Covering around flywheel and clutch or torque converter.

Belted bias tires: Carcass construction has ply cords that extend diagonally from bead to bead at alternate angles plus two or more belts of cord that circle tire under tread.

Bendix gear or bendix drive: A gear mounted on a screw shaft attached to starting motor armature, which automatically engages and disengages electric starting motor.

Benzol: A by-product of manufacture of coke. Sometimes it is used as an engine fuel.

Bezel: A grooved ring in which a transparent instrument cover is placed.

BHP: Brake horsepower is a measurement of power developed by an engine in actual operation.

Bias ply: Pneumatic tire structure in which ply cords extend diagonally from bead to bead, laid at alternate angles.

Bleed: To remove air from hydraulic brake system while fluid in system is under pressure. Also, slowly reducing pressure in an air conditioning system by releasing liquid refrigerant or vapor.

Blowby: A leakage or loss of pressure, often used with reference to leakage of compression past piston ring between piston and cylinder.

Body computer module: Key element of self-diagnostic system used to control vehicle functions based on monitored inputs.

Boiling point: Temperature at atmospheric pressure at which bubbles or vapors rise to surface and escape.

Bonded lining: Brake lining cemented to shoes or bands which eliminates need for rivets.

Booster: A mechanical or hydraulic device attached to brake or steering system to increase power or effectiveness.

Bore: Diameter of a cylinder. Also, to enlarge a hole as distinguished from making a hole with a drill.

Boring bar: A stiff bar equipped with multiple cutting bits used to machine a series of bearing bores in proper alignment with each other.

Boss: An extension or strengthened section, such as projections within a piston which support piston pin or piston pin bushings.

Bottled gas: Liquefied petroleum gas compressed and contained in portable cylinders.

Bounce: Applied to engine valves, a condition where valve is not held tightly to its seat when cam is not lifting it. Also, a condition where breaker points make and break contact when they should remain closed.

Brake: An energy conversion mechanism used to retard, stop, or hold a vehicle.

Brake anchor: Pivot pin or brake backing plate against which the brake shoe bears.

Brake band: A band within a brake drum, to which lining is attached.

Brake bleeding: Procedure for removing air from the lines of a hydraulic system.

Brake cylinder: A cylinder in which a movable piston converts pressure to mechanical force to move brake shoes against braking surface of the drum or the rotor.

Brake disc: Parallel-faced circular plate against which brake lining is forced to retard vehicle. Also Rotor.

Brake drum: A metal cylinder attached to wheel and acted upon by friction material.

Brake "fade": A condition where repeated severe applications of brakes cause expansion of brake drum or loss of frictional ability or both, which results in impaired braking efficiency.

Brake fluid: A compounded liquid for use in hydraulic brake systems, which must meet exacting conditions (impervious to heat, freezing, thickening, bubbling, etc.).

Brake flushing: A procedure for removing fluid from a brake system and washing out sediment.

Brake horsepower: Actual horsepower delivered by crankshaft. Brake horsepower is measured by means of a dynamometer or prony brake.

Brake hose: A flexible conductor for transmission of fluid under pressure in brake system.

Brake lining: A material having a suitable coefficient of friction, which is attached to brake shoe and which contacts brake drum to retard vehicle.

Brake shoe: Carrier to which brake lining is attached, used to force lining in contact with brake drum or rotor.

Brake shoe heel: Generally, end of brake shoe opposite anchor pin.

Brake shoe toe: Generally, end of brake shoe nearest anchor pin.

Braze: To join two pieces of metal with use of a comparatively high melting point material. Example: join two pieces of steel by using brass or bronze as a solder.

Breaker arm: Movable part of a pair of contact points in an ignition distributor.

Breaker points: Two separable points, usually faced with silver, platinum, or tungsten, which interrupt primary circuit in distributor for purpose of inducing a high tension current in ignition system.

Break-in: Process of wearing into a desirable fit between surfaces of two new or reconditioned parts.

Brinell hardness: A scale for designating degree of hardness possessed by a substance.

Broach: To finish surface of metal by pushing or pulling a multiple edge cutting tool over or through it.

Brushes: Bars of carbon or other conducting material which contact commutator of an electric motor or generator.

BTU (British Thermal Unit): A measurement of amount of heat required to raise temperature of 1 lb. of water 1°F.

Burnish: To smooth or polish by use of a sliding tool under pressure.

Bushing: A removable liner for a bearing.

Butane: A petroleum hydrocarbon compound which has a boiling point of about 32°F, which is used as engine fuel. Loosely referred to as Liquefied Petroleum Gas and often combined with Propane.

Bypass: An alternate path for a flowing substance.

C

Calibrate: To determine or adjust graduation or scale of any instrument giving quantitative measurements.

Calibration: A precise factory setting made to produce a given output or effect.

Caliper: Nonrotational components of disc brake that straddles disc and contains hydraulic components.

Calipers: An adjustable tool for determining inside or outside diameter by contact and retaining dimension for measurement or comparison.

Calorific value: A measure of heating value of fuel.

Calorimeter: An instrument to measure amount of heat given off by a substance when burned.

Calorie: Metric measurement of amount of heat required to raise 1 gram of water from 0° to 1° Celsius.

Cam: Multi-lobed cam rotating in ignition distributor, which serves to interrupt primary circuit to induce a high tension spark for ignition.

Cam angle: Number of degrees of rotation of distributor shaft during which contact points are closed.

Cam ground piston: A piston ground to a slightly oval shape which, under heat of operation, becomes round.

Camber: In wheel alignment, outward or inward tilt of wheel at top.

Camshaft: Shaft containing lobes or cams which operate engine valves.

Canister: Reservoir of evaporative emission control system, usually containing activated charcoal granules for absorbing fuel vapors.

Cape chisel: A metal cutting chisel shaped to cut or work in channels or grooves.

Carbon: A common, nonmetallic element that is an excellent conductor of electricity. It also forms in combustion chamber of an engine during burning of fuel and lubricating oil.

Carbon dioxide: Compressed into solid form, this material is known as "dry ice" and remains at a temperature of -109°F. It goes directly from a solid to a vapor state.

Carbon monoxide: Gas formed by incomplete combustion. Colorless, odorless, poisonous.

Carbonize: Process of carbon formation within an engine. Examples: deposits on spark plugs and within combustion chamber.

Carburetor: A device for automatically mixing fuel in proper proportion with air to produce a combustible gas.

Carburetor "icing": A term used to describe formation of ice on a carburetor throttle plate during certain atmospheric conditions.

Carcass: Tire structure except for sidewall and tread.

Cardan joint: A universal joint with corresponding yokes at right angle with each other.

CAS: Cleaner air system.

Case-harden: To harden the surface of steel.

Castellate: Formed to resemble a castle battlement. Example: a castellated nut.

Caster: In wheel alignment, backward or forward tilt of steering axis.

Catalytic converter: Emission control device in exhaust stream that chemically treats exhaust gases after combustion to oxidize noxious emissions.

Cathode: Negative pole of an electric current.

CCC: Computer command control.

CCEC: Constant current electronic circuit.

CCOT: Cycling clutch orifice tube air conditioning system.

CCS: Controlled combustion system.

CEC: Combination emission control.

Cell: Unit of a battery containing a group of positive and negative plates along with electrolyte.

Celsius: A scale of temperature measurement on which, under standard atmospheric pressure, water freezes at 0° and boils at 100°.

Center of gravity: Point of a body from which it could be suspended, or on which it could be supported, and be in balance. Example: center of gravity of a wheel is center of wheel hub.

Centigrade: See Celsius.

Centrifugal force: A force which tends to move a body away from its center of rotation. Example: a whirling weight attached to a string.

Centrifuge brake drums: To combine strength of steel with desirable friction characteristics of cast iron, a lining of cast iron is sprayed on inside of a steel drum. Both metals are handled while hot to encourage fusing of two metals.

CFI: Central fuel injection.

Chamfer: A bevel or taper at edge of a hole.

Charge (or Recharge): Passing an electrical current through a battery to restore it to activity. Also, filling and pressurizing an air conditioning system with refrigerant.

Chase: To straighten up or repair damaged threads.

Chassis: Framework of a vehicle without a body and fenders.

Chassis dynamometer: A machine for measuring amount of power delivered to drive wheels of a vehicle.

Check valve: A gate or valve which allows passage of gas or fluid in one direction only.

Chemical compound: Combination of two or more chemical elements, which can be a gas, a liquid, or a solid.

Chemical element: Gaseous, liquid, or solid matter which cannot be divided into simpler form.

Chilled iron: Cast iron with hardened surface.

Chip: To cut with a chisel.

Choke: A reduced passage. Example: valve in carburetor air inlet to cut down volume of air admitted.

Chromium steel: An alloy of steel with a small amount of chromium to produce a metal which is highly resistant to oxidation and corrosion.

Circuit: Path of electric current, fluids, or gases. Examples: for electricity, a wire; for fluids and gases, a pipe.

Circuit breaker: A device for interrupting an electrical circuit; often automatic and also known as contact breaker, interrupter, cut-out, or relay.

Circular mil: Unit of area equal to area of a circle one mil in diameter.

Clearance: Space allowed between two parts. Example: space between a journal and a bearing.

Clockwise rotation: Rotation in same direction as hands of a clock.

Clutch: Friction device used to connect and disconnect a driving force from a driven member.

CO: Carbon monoxide.

Coefficient of friction: Amount of friction developed between two surfaces pressed together and moved one on the other.

Coil: Ignition transformer designed to increase primary voltage.

Coil spring: Spiral-shaped, coiled steel or steel alloy, compression type suspension device.

"Cold" manifold: An intake manifold not heated by exhaust gas.

Combination valve: Brake system hydraulic control device includes a pressure differential valve, metering valve, and proportioning valve.

Combustion: Process of burning.

Combustion chamber: Volume of cylinder above piston with piston on top center.

Commutator: A ring of adjacent copper bars, insulated from each other, to which wires of armature or winding are attached.

Compensating port: An opening in a brake master cylinder to permit fluid return to reservoir.

Composite headlamps: Reflector and lens system designed for specific vehicle model.

Compound: A mixture of two or more ingredients.

Compound winding: Two electric windings: one in series, other in shunt or parallel with other electric units or equipment. Applied to electric motors or generators: one winding is shunted across armature; other is in series with armature.

Compression: Reduction in volume of a gas. Also, condition when coil spring is squeezed together. Opposite of tension.

Compression ratio: Volume of cylinder and combustion chamber with piston at bottom center as compared with volume of chamber at end of compression stroke.

Compressor: Engine-driven unit that circulates and pressurizes refrigerant in air conditioning system. Also, unit that pressures air in truck air brake system. Also, component of a turbocharger that pumps air into engine.

Computer controlled coil ignition: System that incorporates no distributor.

Concealed headlamps: Headlamp doors close to present flush fitting sheet metal to reduce air resistance in headlamp area.

Concentric: Two circles having same center but different diameters.

Condensation: Process of a vapor becoming a liquid. Reverse of evaporation.

Condenser: Device for turning refrigerant vapor into liquid, causing heat to be discharged from refrigerant. Also, a device for temporarily collecting and storing a surge of electrical current for later discharge.

Conductance: Current-carrying ability of a wire or electrical component.

Conductor: A material along or through which electricity will flow with slight resistance. Silver, copper, and carbon are good conductors.

Connecting rod: Rod that connects piston to crankshaft.

Constant mesh transmission: An arrangement of gearing where gears remain in mesh instead of sliding in and out of engagement.

Constant velocity: Double universal joint that cancels out vibrations caused by driving power being transmitted through an angle.

Contact points: See breaker points.

Contraction: A reduction in mass or dimension. Opposite of expansion.

Control module: Used in electronic ignition systems to switch current on and off in primary circuit.

Convection: A transfer of heat by circulating heated air.

Converter: Applied to liquefied petroleum gas: a device which converts or changes LP-Gas from liquid to vapor for use in engine.

Coolant: Liquid circulated through cooling system of a "water-cooled" engine, usually a mixture of about 50 percent ethylene glycol and 50 percent water.

Coolant temperature sensor: Sensor that monitors the temperature of the engine coolant.

Cord: Textile, steel wire strands, etc., forming plies of a tire.

Core hole plug: See freeze plug.

Corporation: Business association endowed by law with the rights and liabilities of an individual.

Corrode: To eat away gradually as if by gnawing, especially by rust.

Counterbore: To enlarge a hole to a given depth.

Counterclockwise rotation: Rotating opposite direction of hands on a clock.

Countershaft: Intermediate shaft in transmission that transfers motion from one shaft to another.

Countersink: To cut or form a depression to allow head of a screw to go below surface.

Coupling: A connecting means for transferring movement from one part to another. May be mechanical, hydraulic, or electrical.

Cowl: Portion of body between engine compartment and driver, which ordinarily contains instruments used by operator.

Crankcase: Housing within which crankshaft operates.

Crankcase dilution: Under certain conditions of operation, unburned portions of fuel get past piston rings into crankcase where they "thin" engine lubricating oil.

Cranking circuit: Battery, starting motor, ignition switch, and related electrical wiring.

Crankshaft: Main shaft of an engine which, in conjunction with connecting rods, changes reciprocating motion of pistons into rotary motion.

Crankshaft counterbalance: Series of weights attached to or forged integrally with crankshaft and placed to offset reciprocating weight of each piston and rod assembly.

Crossmember: Crosswise structural component of vehicle frame or unitized body.

CRT: Cathode ray tube.

Crude oil: Liquid oil as it comes from the ground.

C3I: Computer controlled coil ignition.

CTO: Coolant temperature override.

Cu. in.: Cubic inch.

Curb weight: Weight of a vehicle, (without driver or load), including fuel, coolant, oil, and all standard equipment items.

Current: Flow of electricity.

Cut-out: A valve used to divert exhaust gases directly to atmosphere instead of through muffler.

CVT: Continuously variable transmission.

Cycle: A series of events which are repeated. Example: intake, compression, power, and exhaust strokes of an internal combustion engine.

Cylinder: A round hole having some depth bored to receive a piston. Also referred to as "bore."

Cylinder block: Largest single part of an engine. Basic or main mass of metal in which cylinders are bored or placed.

Cylinder head: A detachable portion of an engine fastened securely to cylinder block which contains all or a portion of combustion chamber.

Cylinder head gasket: Seal between engine block and cylinder head.

Cylinder sleeve: A liner or tube interposed between piston and cylinder wall or cylinder block to provide a readily renewable wearing surface for cylinder.

D

Dash: Also known as firewall. A partition between engine and operator.

Dashpot: A device consisting of a piston and cylinder with a restricted opening used to slow down or delay operation of some moving part.

DC: Direct current.

Dead center: Extreme upper or lower position of crankshaft throw at which point piston is not moving in either direction.

Dead rear axle: A rear axle that does not turn. Example: rear axle of front wheel drive car.

Degree: Abbreviated deg. or indicated by a small ° placed alongside of a figure. May be used to designate temperature readings or angularity (one degree is 1/360 part of a circle).

Demagnetize: To remove magnetization of a pole which has previously been magnetized.

Denatured alcohol: Ethyl alcohol to which a denaturant has been added.

Density: Relative mass of matter in a given volume.

Depolarize: To remove polarity. Example: to demagnetize a permanent magnet.

Desiccant: Drying agent used in air conditioning system to remove excess moisture.

Detergent: A compound of a soap-like nature used in engine oil to remove engine deposits and hold them in suspension in oil.

Detonation: An engine sound that indicates a too rapid burning or explosion of air-fuel mixture in engine cylinders. It becomes audible through a vibration of combustion chamber walls.

Detonation sensor: Sensor that converts abnormal engine vibrations, such as knocking and pinging, into electrical signals.

Diagnosis: Refers to use of instruments to determine cause of improper function of parts or systems of a vehicle.

Diagnostic code: Code displayed on instrument panel which can be used to determine area in system where malfunction may be located.

Dial gauge: A type of test instrument which indicates precise readings on a dial.

Diaphragm: A flexible partition or wall separating two cavities.

Die: One of a pair of hardened metal blocks for forming metal into a desired shape. Also, a device for cutting external threads.

Die casting: An accurate and smooth casting made by pouring molten metal or composition into a metal mold or die under pressure.

Diesel engine: Named after its developer, Dr. Rudolph Diesel, engine ignites fuel in cylinder from heat generated by compression. Fuel is an oil rather than gasoline and no spark plug or carburetor is required.

Dieseling: Engine tends to keep running after ignition key is turned off.

Differential: Gear system which permits one drive wheel to turn faster than the other.

Digital computer: An ON-OFF computer that turns actuator on, or it remains in OFF position.

Dilution: See Crankcase dilution.

Dimmer switch: Permits selection of headlamp low beams or high beams.

Diode: An electronic device that permits current to flow through it in one direction only.

Direct current: Electric current which flows continuously in one direction. Example: current from a storage battery.

Direct drive: In automobile transmissions: refers to direct engagement between engine and drive shaft where engine crankshaft and drive shaft turn at same rpm.

Direct ignition system: Distributorless system which carries high voltage from ignition coils to spark plugs.

Direction signal switch: Permits driver to signal direction of turn.

Disc brake: Brake system utilizing rotors to which frictional forces are applied to retard motion of vehicle.

Discharge: Flow of electric current from a battery. Also, to bleed some or all refrigerant from an air conditioning system. Opposite of charge.

Displacement: See Engine displacement.

Distortion: A warpage or change in form from original shape.

Distributor rotor: Designed to rotate and distribute high tension current to towers of distributor cap.

Distributors: A valve, often rotary in design, which conducts a vapor or fluid to a number of outlets. Example: diesel engine oil distributors. See Ignition distributor.

Domains: Groups of atoms that have same magnetic polarity.

Double reduction axle: A drive axle construction in which two sets of reduction gears are used for extreme reduction of gear ratio.

Dowel pin: A pin inserted in matching holes in two parts to maintain those parts in fixed relation to each other.

Down-draft: Carburetor in which mixture flows downward to engine.

Downshift: Forcing a shift to a lower gear.

Drag link: Connecting rod or link between steering gear pitman arm and steering control linkage.

Draw: To form by a stretching process, or to soften hard metal.

Draw-filing: File is drawn across work at right angles.

Drier: A device containing a desiccant in liquid refrigerant line to absorb moisture in an air conditioning system.

Drill: A tool for making a hole, or to sink a hole with a pointed cutting tool rotated under pressure.

Drive-fit: Term used when shaft is slightly larger than hole and must be forced in place.

Driveline: Universal joints, drive shaft, and other parts connecting transmission with driving axles.

Drive shaft: Shaft connecting transmission output shaft to differential drive pinion shaft.

Drive train: All parts that generate power and transmit it to driving wheels.

Driving axles: Used to hold, align, and drive rear wheels and support weight of vehicle on rear wheel drive cars, or half shafts on front wheel drive cars that provide torque force to front wheels.

Drop forging: A piece of steel shaped between dies while hot.

Dry charged battery: A complete battery unit which does not contain liquid electrolyte.

Dry sleeve: A metal barrel or sleeve which is pressed into an oversize cylinder bore.

Dual fuel engine: An engine equipped to operate on two different fuels such as gasoline and LP-Gas.

Dual master cylinder: Primary unit consisting of two sections for displacing fluid under pressure in a split hydraulic brake system.

Dual reduction axle: A drive axle construction with two sets of pinions and gears, either of which can be used.

Duraspark system: Ford electronic ignition system.

Dwell meter: An instrument for measuring cam angle.

Dwell period: See Cam angle.

Dynamo: A generator of electricity.

Dynamometer: A machine for measuring power produced by an internal combustion engine.

E

ECC: Electronic climate control.

Eccentric: One circle within another circle not having the same center.

ECM: Electronic control module.

Economizer: A device installed in a carburetor to control amount of fuel used under certain conditions.

ECU: Electronic control unit.

EEC: Evaporative emission controls or electronic engine control.

EECS: Evaporative emissions control system.

EFE: Early fuel evaporation system.

EFI: Electronic fuel injection.

EGR: Exhaust gas recirculation.

ELC: Electronic level control.

Electric welding: Welding by using an electric current to melt both metal (work) and welding rod, or electrode.

Electrode: Refers to insulated center rod and rod attached to shell of spark plug. Also, welding rod.

Electrolyte: A mixture of sulphuric acid and distilled water used in storage batteries.

Electromagnet: A coil of insulated wire wound around an iron rod (or series of rods). The rod will be magnetized when an electric current is passed through wire. Example: a solenoid magnet.

Electromagnetic induction: Voltage is induced in a coil of wire by moving coil through a magnetic field or by keeping coil stationary and moving magnetic field.

Electron: That portion of an atom which carries a negative charge of electricity.

Electronic ignition: A system that electronically controls current flow in primary circuit.

Electronically controlled transmission: A transmission that relies on sensors, an electronic control unit (ECU), and solenoids to control torque convertor lockup and shift points.

Engine speed sensor: Sensor that sends information about engine speed (rpm) and piston position to the electronic control unit.

Element: One set of positive battery plates and one set of negative plates, complete with separators and assembled together.

Elliott steering knuckle: Type of axle in which ends of axle beam straddle spindle.

EMF: Electromotive force, or voltage.

Emissions: Harmful components of exhaust gas, fuel vapors, and crankcase fumes released to atmosphere.

Emulsion: a milk-like viscous mixture of two liquids.

Enamel: A combination of varnish and coloring pigment, sometimes heated during or after application to provide a hard surface.

En-bloc: Refers to cylinder block of an engine cast in one section.

End play: Amount of lengthwise clearance between parts.

Energy: Prime source of power generated to propel a vehicle.

Energy absorbing bumper: System designed to protect vehicle safety systems during impact at low speed.

Engine: Prime source of power generated to propel a vehicle.

Engine displacement: Sum of piston displacement of all engine cylinders. See Piston displacement.

Engine torque: Amount of twisting effort exerted by crankshaft of engine.

Engine tune-up: Service operation designed to restore engine's best level of performance while maintaining good fuel economy and minimum exhaust emissions.

Entrepreneur: One who undertakes ownership of a business or enterprise.

Entrepreneurship: A person's ability to organize, manage, and assume risks of operating a business.

EPA: Environmental Protection Agency.

ESC: Electronic spark control.

EST: Electronic spark timing.

Ethyl gasoline: Gasoline to which a compound of tetraethyl lead, ethylene dibromide, and ethylene dichloride has been added.

Ethylene glycol: Liquid chemical mixed with water to form low-freezing-point coolant.

Evacuate: To create a vacuum in an air conditioning system to remove all traces of air and moisture.

EVRV: Electronic vacuum regulator valve.

Exhaust back pressure: Pressure exerted in exhaust system in reverse direction.

Exhaust emissions: Products of combustion that are discharged through exhaust system of vehicle.

Exhaust gas analyzer: An instrument for determining efficiency with which an engine is burning fuel.

Exhaust pipe: Pipe connecting engine to muffler to conduct spent gases away from engine.

Expansion: An increase in size. Example: when a metal rod is heated, it increases in length and diameter. Opposite of contraction.

Expansion plug: See Freeze plug.

Expansion valve: See Thermostatic expansion valve.

Extreme pressure lubricants (E.P.): A lubricant to which an ingredient has been added to increase lubricant's ability to withstand high pressures between gear teeth, etc.

F

Fahrenheit (F): A scale of temperature measurement on which, under standard atmospheric pressure, water freezes at 32° and boils at 212°.

Feedback: System of air-fuel mixture control utilizing a computer controlled stepper motor.

Feeler gauge: A metal strip or blade, finished accurately with regard to thickness, used for measuring clearance between two parts.

Ferrous metal: Metals which contain iron or steel, enabling them to be magnetized.

F-head engine: An engine designed with one valve in cylinder block at side of piston and other valve in cylinder head above piston.

Field: Area in which magnetic flow occurs in a generator or starting motor.

Field coil: A coil of insulated wire surrounding field pole.

File: To finish or trim with a hardened metal tool with cutting ridges.

Fillet: A rounded filling between two parts joined at an angle.

Filter: A device designed to remove suspended impurities or particles of foreign matter from intake air, fuel system, or lubricating system.

Firewall: Insulated partition between engine and vehicle occupants.

Firing order: Sequence in which combustible mixture is ignited in cylinders of engine.

Fit: Satisfactory contact between two machined surfaces.

Flange: A projecting rim or collar on an object for keeping it in place.

Flare: A flange or a cone-shaped end applied to a piece of tubing to provide a means of sealing two similarly angled areas formed in fitting body and the nut.

Flash point: Temperature at which an oil will flash and burn.

Float: A hollow part which is lighter than fuel or fluid in which it rests, and ordinarily used to operate a valve controlling entrance of fuel or fluid.

Floating piston pin: A piston pin which is free to turn or oscillate in both connecting rod and piston.

Float level: Predetermined setting of float to control height of fuel in carburetor bowl, usually regulated by means of a suitable valve.

Flooding: Too much fuel for operating conditions. Also, too much liquid refrigerant being metered into evaporator of an air conditioning system.

Fluid: A liquid, gas, or vapor.

Fluid coupling: A hydraulic clutch used to transmit engine torque to transmission gears. See Fluid drive.

Fluid drive: A pair of vaned rotating elements held close to each other without touching. Rotation is imparted to driven member by driving member through resistance of a body of oil.

Flutter: See Bounce.

Flux: Electric or magnetic lines of force passing or flowing in a magnetic field. Also, material used to cause joining metal to adhere to both parts to be joined.

Flywheel: A heavy wheel in which energy is absorbed and stored by means of momentum.

Foot pound (or ft./lb.): A measure of amount of energy or work required to lift 1 lb. 1 ft.

Force: The amount of push or pull exerted on an object.

Force-fit: See Drive fit.

Forge: To shape metal while hot and plastic by hammering.

Forward bias: Conductive condition that exists when current flows through a diode.

Four-cycle engine: Engine in which an explosion occurs every other revolution of crankshaft. A cycle, also known as Otto cycle, is considered 1/2 revolution of crankshaft. Strokes are: suction, compression, power, exhaust.

Four-gas analyzer: Equipment for testing exhaust gas for hydrocarbons, carbon monoxide, carbon dioxide, and oxygen.

Four-wheel drive: Power transfer system that permits a vehicle to be driven by all four wheels.

Free-wheeling: A mechanical device in which driving member imparts motion to a driven member in one direction but not other.

Freeze plug: A disc- or cup-shaped metal device inserted in a hole in a casting through which core was removed when casting was formed.

Freezing point: Temperature at which coolant starts to freeze, based on mixture percentages and pressure.

Freon: A particular brand of refrigerant.

Friction: Resistance to relative motion between two bodies in contact.

Fuel: Substance that will burn and release heat.

Fuel knock: See Detonation.

Fulcrum: A support, often wedge-shaped, on which a lever pivots when it lifts an object.

Full-floating axle: Drive axle construction where axle driving shaft does not carry vehicle weight.

Fuse: A piece of wire which will carry a limited amount of current only, then melt and open electrical circuit as a safety measure to avoid damage from excessive current flow.

Fusible link: Special length of smaller gauge wire designed to "blow" if heavy current flows in circuit.

G

Galvanize: To coat with a molten alloy of lead and tin to prevent rusting.

Galvanometer: An instrument used for location, measurement, and direction of an electric current.

Gas: A substance which can be changed in volume and shape according to temperature and pressure applied to it. Example: air can be compressed into smaller volume or expanded by application of heat.

Gassing: Bubbling of battery electrolyte which occurs during process of charging a battery.

Gasket: Anything used as a packing, such as a substance placed between two metal surfaces to act as a seal.

Gear ratio: Number of revolutions made by a driving gear as compared to number of revolutions made by a driven gear of different size. Example: if one gear makes three revolutions while other gear makes one revolution, gear ratio is 3 to 1 .

Generator: A device consisting of an armature, field coils, and other parts which, when rotated, will generate electricity.

Glaze: An extremely smooth or glossy engine cylinder surface polished over a long period of time by friction of piston rings.

Glaze breaker: A tool for removing glossy surface finish in an engine cylinder.

Governor: A device to control and regulate speed. May be mechanical, hydraulic, or electrical.

Gram: A unit of measure of weight or mass equal to 0.03527 oz.

Grid: Metal framework of an individual battery plate in which active material is placed.

Grind: To finish or polish a surface by means of an abrasive wheel.

Groove: Space between two adjacent tire tread ribs.

Gross horsepower: Brake horsepower of an engine with optimum ignition setting and without allowing for power losses caused by engine's accessory units.

Gross torque: Maximum torque developed by crankshaft of engine without allowing for power absorbed by engine's accessory units.

Ground: Terminal of battery connected to frame of vehicle to serve as "return wire" to complete electrical circuit.

Group: A set of battery plates, either positive or negative, joined together but not assembled with separators.

Growler: An electrical device for testing electric motor armatures.

Gum: Oxidized petroleum products that accumulate in fuel system, carburetor, or engine parts.

H

Halogen headlamps: Tungsten-halogen bulb used in sealed beam unit or as separate bulb in composite headlamp.

Hard pedal: A loss in braking efficiency so that an excessive amount of pressure is needed to actuate brakes.

Hard solder: Uniting two pieces of metal with a material having a melting point higher than "soft" solder. Example: silver soldering.

Harmonic balancer: A device designed to reduce torsional or twisting vibration which occurs along length of crankshaft used in multiple cylinder engines.

Hazard warning flasher: Actuates warning system of flashing front and rear turn signal lamps.

Hazardous wastes: Automotive wastes that are on the EPA's list of hazardous materials or that have one or more hazardous characteristics.

HC: Hydrocarbons.

Header: Special exhaust pipes, used on high performance engines to reduce back pressure.

Headlamp delay system: Automatically controls headlamp ON-OFF operation after ignition and main lighting switch are turned OFF.

Heat exchanger: A device that utilizes exhaust system heat to aid in fuel vaporization.

Heat riser: Passage between exhaust and intake manifolds.

Heat sink: Metal bracket in end frame of alternator that contains and absorbs heat from diodes.

Heat treatment: A combination of heating and cooling operations timed and applied to a metal in a solid state in a way that will produce desired properties.

Heel: Outside or larger half of gear tooth. Also, end of brake shoe not against anchor.

HEI: High energy ignition.

Helical: Shaped like a coil of wire or a screw thread.

Helical gear: A gear design where gear teeth are cut at an angle to shaft.

HEMI: Hemispherical or dome-shaped combustion chamber in some engines.

Herringbone gear: A pair of helical gears designed to operate together in form of a V.

High tension: Secondary or induced high voltage electrical current. Circuit includes wiring from ignition distributor cap to coil and to each spark plug.

Hg: Chemical symbol for mercury.

High side: High pressure portion of an air conditioning system.

Hole theory: Assumption that movement of a free electron from atom to atom leaves a hole in the atom it left, which is filled by another free electron.

Hone: An abrasive tool for correcting small irregularities or differences in diameter in an engine cylinder, brake cylinder, etc.

Horn: Provides driver with means of sounding an audible warning signal.

Horsepower: Energy required to lift 550 lb. 1 ft. in 1 sec.

Hotchkiss drive: A driving axle design in which axle torque is absorbed by chassis springs or control arms.

HP: Horsepower: energy required to lift 550 lb. 1 ft. in 1 second is 1 hp.

Hydraulic: Pertains to fluids in motion, such as hydraulically operated brakes, hydraulic torque converters, power steering, etc.

Hydraulic actuator: Unit in an anti-lock brake system that can increase brake pressure, decrease brake pressure, or hold brake pressure steady based on signals it receives from the control module.

Hydraulic brake system: System in which brake operation and control utilizes hydraulic brake fluid.

Hydrocarbon: Any compound composed entirely of carbon and hydrogen.

Hydrometer: An instrument for determining state of charge in a battery by measuring specific gravity of electrolyte.

Hydrostatic gauge: Used in referring to gauges, such as a gasoline tank gauge, where depth of gasoline in tank controls air in connecting line to instrument which registers depth on a scale or dial.

Hypoid gears: A design of pinion and ring gear where centerline of pinion is offset from centerline of ring gear.

I

ID: Inside diameter.

Idle speed: The rpm of a spark ignition engine with closed throttle opening at manufacturer's recommended speed.

Idle speed motor: Actuator used to increase idle speed when the engine is under a heavy load.

Ignition coil: Electrical device used to step up battery voltage to a level high enough to fire spark plugs.

Ignition distributor: An electrical device usually containing circuit breaker for primary circuit and providing a means for conveying secondary or high tension current to spark plug wires as required.

Ignition system: Means for igniting fuel in cylinders. Includes spark plugs, wiring, distributor, ignition coil, and source of electrical current.

Ignition timing: Synchronization of distributor to engine so ignition takes place in each cylinder at proper time.

IHP: Indicated horsepower developed by an engine and a measure of pressure of explosion within cylinder expressed in pounds per square inch.

IMCO: Improved combustion.

Impact sensor: An impact sensor is essentially an open switch that is designed to close when an impact occurs that is severe enough to warrant air bag deployment.

Included angle: Combined angles of camber and steering axis inclination.

Independent suspension: A construction in which wheel on one side of vehicle may rise or fall independently of wheel on other side.

Induction: Influence of magnetic fields of different strength not electrically connected to one another.

Induction coil: Essentially a transformer which, through induction, creates a high tension current by means of an increase in voltage.

Induction hardening: Method of heating cast iron (valve seats, for example) to about 1700°F, which hardens it to a depth of .05 to .08 in.

Inertia: A physical law that tends to keep a motionless body at rest or keep a moving body in motion. Effort is required to start a mass moving or to retard it once it is in motion.

Information centers: Visual displays which alert driver to certain vehicle conditions.

Inhibitor: A material to restrain or hinder some unwanted action. Example: a rust inhibitor added to cooling systems to retard formation of rust.

Injector: A pump that injects a fluid or gas into a cylinder or chamber. Also, fuel injection system electrical solenoid which, when energized, allows fuel to enter combustion chamber.

Inlet valve: See Intake valve.

Input shaft: Transmission shaft which receives power from engine and transmits it to transmission gears.

Inputs: Information from various sensors that tells electronic control module how engine is performing.

Insulation: Any material, which does not conduct electricity, used to prevent leakage of current from a conductor. Also, a material which does not readily conduct heat.

Insulator: A nonconducting material or shield covering an electrical conductor.

Intake manifold or inlet pipe: Tube or housing used to conduct air/fuel mixture from carburetor to engine cylinders.

Intake valve: A valve which permits a fluid or gas to enter a chamber and seals against exit.

Integral: Formed as a unit with another part.

Intensify: To increase or concentrate. Example: increase voltage of an electrical current.

Intercell connectors: Battery element terminal posts.

Intermediate gear: Transmission gear or gears between low and high.

Intermittent: Motion or action that occurs at intervals.

Internal combustion: Burning of a fuel within an enclosed space.

J

Journal: That part of a shaft or axle in actual contact with bearing.

Jump spark: A high tension electrical current which jumps through the air from one terminal to another.

Jump start: Use of jumper cables to transfer power from a good battery to a discharged battery.

K

Key: A small block inserted between shaft and hub to prevent circumferential movement.

Keyway or keyseat: A groove or slot cut to permit insertion of a key.

Kickdown switch: An electrical switch used to cause a transmission to downshift from a higher to a lower gear ratio.

Kilometer: A metric measurement of distance which is equivalent to approximately 5/8 of a mile.

Kilowatt: A measure of electrical energy consisting of 1000 watts or 1 1/3 horsepower.

Kingpin: Shaft around which steering spindle of a truck front wheel turns.

Kingpin inclination: Angle at which kingpin is inclined inward from true vertical centerline.

Knock: Term used to describe various noises in an engine made by loose or worn mechanical parts, preignition, detonation, etc.

Knock sensor: See Detonation sensor.

Knurl: To indent or roughen a finished surface.

L

Lacquer: In automotive painting, a solution of solids in solvents that evaporate with great rapidity.

Laminate: To build up or construct out of a number of thin sheets. Example: laminated core in an electric motor or generator.

Land: Metal portion separating the grooves that rings ride against.

Lapping: Process of fitting one surface to another by rubbing them together with an abrasive material between two surfaces.

Lateral runout: Amount of side movement of a rotating wheel, tire, or rotor from the vertical.

Lathe: Machine on which a piece of solid material is spun on a horizontal axis and shaped by a fixed cutting or abrading tool.

Lb.: Pound.

Lead burning: Joining two pieces of lead by melting or fusing the metal.

Left hand rule: To determine direction of lines of force, grasp conductor with left hand thumb extended in direction of current flow. Fingers indicate direction of lines of force.

L-head engine: An engine design in which both valves are located on one side of engine cylinder.

Lift: Maximum distance valve head is raised off its seat.

Limited-slip differential: Directs power flow to axle of wheel having best traction.

Limiter: Device placed on carburetor idle mixture adjustment screw so that richness of mixture can be made only within predetermined limits.

Liner: Usually a thin section placed between two parts. Example: a replaceable cylinder liner in an engine.

Linkage: Any series of rods, yokes, and levers, etc., used to transmit motion from one unit to another.

Liquid: Neither a gas nor a solid. Any substance which assumes shape of vessel in which it is placed without changing volume.

Liquid withdrawal system: A method of piping where liquid is taken from bottom of an LP-Gas tank and converted into gas by a vaporizer.

Liter: A measure of volume equal to 61.027 cu. in.

Live: Electrical parts connected to insulated side of electrical system. Example: an insulated wire connected to battery.

Live axle: Shaft through which power travels from drive axle gears to driving wheels.

Load range: Tire designation, with a letter (A, B, C, etc.), used to identify a given size tire with its load and inflation limits. Replaces term ply rating.

Lock washer: A form of washer designed to prevent attaching nut from working loose.

Lockup torque converter: Converter with internal mechanism that locks turbine to impeller in direct drive.

Longitudinal: Lengthwise.

Lost motion: See Backlash.

Louver or louvre: Openings or vents in hood or body, usually intended for ventilation.

Low pedal: A condition where excessive clearance at some point in braking system causes full pedal movement for application of brakes.

Low side: Low pressure portion of an air conditioning system.

Low speed: Gearing provided in an automobile which causes greatest number of revolutions of engine as compared to driving wheels.

LP-Gas: Liquefied petroleum gas: Made usable as a fuel for internal combustion engines by compressing volatile petroleum gases to liquid form. LP-Gas must be kept under pressure or at low temperature in order to remain in liquid form.

Lug: Extension of battery plate grid for connecting plate to strap.

Lugging: Reduction in speed due to increased load.

M

MacPherson strut: Long, telescopic shock absorber strut surrounded by a coil spring.

Magnet (Permanent): A piece of hard steel often bent into a "U" shape to create and retain opposite poles when charged with magnetic power.

Magnetic field: Flow of magnetic force or magnetism between opposite poles of a magnet.

Magnetism: Invisible force that attracts certain materials such as steel.

Magneto: An electrical device which generates alternating current when rotated by an outside source of power. Device used to generate either low tension or high tension current.

Malfunction: Problem in system that affects normal operation.

Malleable casting: A casting which has been toughened by annealing.

Manganese bronze: An alloy of copper, zinc, and manganese.

Manifold: A pipe with multiple openings used to connect various cylinders to one inlet or outlet.

Manifold absolute pressure sensor (MAP sensor): Sensor that monitors the engine's intake manifold pressure.

Manifold air temperature sensor (MAT sensor): Sensor that monitors the temperature of the air entering the intake manifold.

Manifold gauge set: Instrument used to test pressures on high and low sides of compressor. Also, can be used to discharge refrigerant, evacuate air and moisture, and charge air conditioning system with refrigerant.

Manifold heat control valve: Thermostatically controlled valve that diverts hot exhaust gases around intake manifold during cold engine starting.

Manifold vacuum: Source of vacuum in manifold below carburetor throttle plate.

Manometer: A device for measuring a vacuum, consisting of a "U" shaped tube partially filled with fluid. One end of tube is open to air, other is connected to chamber in which vacuum is to be measured. A column of mercury 30 in. high equals 14.7 psi, which is atmospheric pressure at sea level. Readings are given in inches of mercury (Hg).

Manual: Pertaining to or done with the hands. Also, requiring or using physical skill or energy.

MAP sensor: Manifold Absolute Pressure sensor tells computer how much pressure is in the intake manifold.

Master cylinder: Single or dual primary unit for displacing hydraulic fluid under pressure in brake system.

Material safety data sheets: Sheets that contain information on the handling of hazardous wastes, the use of protective equipment, and the procedures to follow in case of an accident.

MCU: Microprocessor control unit.

MCV: Manifold control valve.

Mechanical efficiency: Ratio between indicated horsepower and brake horsepower of an engine.

Melting point: Temperature at which solid material becomes liquid.

MEMA: Motor and Equipment Manufacturers Association.

Mercury column: A reference term used in connection with a manometer.

Metal inert gas welding (MIG welding): Welding technique used when repairing late-model vehicles. MIG welding leaves a narrow heat-affected zone, reducing the chance of damage to high-strength steels. Additionally, MIG welding techniques are easier to master than oxyacetylene techniques.

Meter: A measure of length equal to 39.37 in.

Metering: Passage of liquid or gas through a fixed orifice or nozzle, diameter of which determines volume of flow.

Metering valve: Limits hydraulic pressure to front disc brakes until predetermined front input pressure is reached.

Methanol or wood alcohol: A poisonous alcohol made synthetically or from distillation of wood.

MEWA: Motor and Equipment Wholesalers Association.

Micro finish: Degree of surface roughness, measured with a profilometer.

Micrometer: A measuring instrument for either external or internal measurement in thousandths and sometimes ten thousandths of inches.

Mil: Unit of length equal to .001 in.

Mill: To cut or machine with rotating tooth cutters.

Millimeter (mm): One millimeter is metric equivalent of .039370 of an inch. One inch is equivalent to 25.4 mm.

Misfiring: Failure of an explosion to occur in one or more cylinders while engine is running. This may be a continuous or intermittent failure.

Mixture control solenoid: Actuator used on carbureted vehicles to move the carburetor's metering rod in and out of the metering jet.

Mode: A particular state of operation.

Modulator: A pressure regulating device used in automatic transmissions.

Monel metal: Corrosion resistant alloy of nickel, copper, iron, and manganese.

Monitoring: Maintaining a continuous control of an operation or function, varying control as required by specific conditions.

Mono-block: All cylinders of an engine are contained in one casting. Same as en-bloc or in-block.

Motor: Principally, a machine which converts electrical energy to mechanical energy.

Mph: Miles per hour.

Muffler: A chamber attached to exhaust pipe which allows exhaust gases to expand and cool. It is usually fitted with baffles or porous plates and serves to reduce noise created by exhaust.

Multiple disc: A clutch having a number of driving and driven discs as compared to a single plate clutch.

MVMA: Motor Vehicle Manufacturers Association.

N

NADA: National Automobile Dealers Association.

NAPA: National Automotive Parts Association.

NC: Normally closed.

Needle bearing: An antifriction bearing using many rollers of small diameter in relation to their length.

Negative pole: Point from which an electrical current flows as it passes through circuit. Designated by a minus sign (-).

Net horsepower: Brake horsepower remaining at flywheel of engine to do useful work after power required by engine accessories has been provided.

Net torque: Torque available at flywheel of engine after power required by engine accessories has been provided.

Neutral safety switch: Eliminates possibility of starting engine when transmission selector lever is in position to drive car.

Neutron: Portion of an atom which carries no electrical charge and, with protons, form central core of atom about which electrons rotate.

Newton meter (N·m): One Newton meter is the metric equivalent of .7376 pound feet.

Nickel steel: Nickel is alloyed with steel to form a heat and corrosion resistant metal.

Nitrogen oxides: See Oxides of nitrogen.

NO: Normally Open.

Noble metal: Rare or precious metals used as catalyst agent in catalytic converters.

Nonferrous metals: Metals which contain no iron or very little iron, and not subject to rusting.

North pole: Pole of a magnet from which lines of force start. Opposite of south pole.

NOx: Nitrogen oxides.

NPN: Three-element transistor made of two types of semiconductor materials.

O

Octane number: A unit of measurement on a scale intended to indicate tendency of a fuel to knock.

OD: Outside diameter.

Odometer: A device for measuring and registering number of miles traveled.

Ohm: A measurement of resistance to flow of an electrical current through a conductor.

Ohmmeter: An instrument for measuring resistance in ohms.

Ohm's law: Mathematical relationship between voltage, resistance, and amount of current in an electrical circuit. It states: $E = I \times R$; $I = E \div R$; $R = E \div I$.

Oil cooler: Device incorporated into design of radiator on automatic transmission-equipped cars to keep transmission fluid at a lower temperature.

One-way clutch: See Freewheeling.

Open circuit: An incomplete electrical circuit.

Orifice: Small opening in a tube, pipe, or valve.

Orifice tube: Tube with calibrated opening, used in place of expansion valve in some air conditioning systems.

OSAC: Orifice spark advance control.

Oscillate: To swing back and forth like a pendulum.

Oscilloscope: An electronic device used to observe and measure instantaneous voltage in an electrical circuit.

OSHA: Occupational Safety and Health Administration.

Otto cycle: Four stroke cycle named after man who adopted principle of four stroke operation in an engine cylinder. They are: suction, compression, power, and exhaust.

Out of round: Condition where engine cylinder bore has greater wear at one diameter than another.

Output: Functions controlled by electronic control unit.

Output shaft: Shaft which receives power from transmission and transmits it to vehicle drive shaft.

Overdrive: Any arrangement of gearing which produces more revolutions of driven shaft than driving shaft.

Overhead valve or valve-in-head engine (OHV): An engine design having valves located in cylinder head directly above pistons.

Overrunning clutch or coupling: See Freewheeling.

Oxides of nitrogen: Compounds of nitrous oxides and nitrogen dioxide produced by combustion process, especially at high temperatures.

Oxidize: To combine an element with oxygen or convert into its oxide. Examples: when carbon burns, it combines with oxygen to form carbon dioxide or carbon monoxide; iron combines with oxygen in air to form an oxide of iron, or rust.

Oxygen sensor: Exhaust device that detects amount of oxygen (O_2) in exhaust stream and sends information to electronic control module.

P

Pad: Disc brake friction material generally molded to metal backing, or shoe.

Pancake engine: A design where cylinders are laid horizontal to obtain a minimum of height.

Parallel circuit: An electrical circuit having more than one path.

Parking brake: Brake system used to hold one or more brakes continuously in applied position.

Particulates: Minute solid particles emitted from vehicle's exhaust.

Partnership: Business owned by at least two people.

Pawl: A pivoted bar adapted to engage with teeth of a ratchet to prevent or impart motion.

PCV: Positive crankcase ventilation.

Peak inverse voltage: Amount of voltage a diode can take in reverse direction without being damaged.

Peen: To stretch over by pounding with rounded end of a hammer.

Periphery: Circumference of a circle. Example: tread of a tire.

Petcock: A small valve placed in a fluid circuit for draining purposes.

Petroleum: A group of liquid and gaseous compounds composed of carbon and hydrogen.

Phillips screw or screwdriver: A type of screwhead having a "cross" instead of a "slot" for a corresponding type of screwdriver.

Phosphor-bronze: An alloy consisting of copper, tin, and lead sometimes used in heavy-duty bearings.

Pilot shaft: Tool used temporarily to align parts of a mechanism being assembled.

Pilot valve: A small valve used to control action of a larger valve.

Pinging: Sound produced when either preignition or detonation occurs.

Pinion: A small gear which engages a larger gear.

Pinion carrier: Mounting or bracket which retains bearings supporting a pinion shaft.

Piston: A cylindrical part, closed at one end, which is connected to the crankshaft by a connecting rod. Force of explosion in cylinder is exerted against closed end of piston causing connecting rod to move crankshaft.

Piston collapse: A condition describing a sudden reduction in diameter of piston skirt due to heat or stress.

Piston displacement: Volume of air moved or displaced by moving piston from one end of its stroke to other.

Piston head: Part of piston above the rings.

Piston lands: Parts of piston between piston rings.

Piston pin: Journal for bearing in small end of an engine connecting rod which also passes through piston walls.

Piston ring: An expanding ring placed in grooves of piston to provide a seal to prevent passage of fluid or gas past piston.

Piston ring expander: A spring placed behind piston ring in groove to increase pressure of ring against cylinder wall.

Piston ring gap: Clearance between ends of piston ring.

Piston ring groove: Slots in piston in which piston rings are placed.

Piston skirt: Part of piston below the rings.

Piston skirt expander: A spring or other device inserted in piston skirt to compensate for collapse or decrease in diameter.

Pitman arm: Lever extending from steering gear to which steering linkage is attached.

Pitot tube: An instrument for measuring fluid velocity by means of difference in pressure between tip and side openings.

Pivot: A pin or short shaft upon which another part rests or turns, or about which another part rotates or oscillates.

Planetary gears: A system of gearing which is modeled after solar system. A pinion is surrounded by an internal ring gear with planet gears in mesh between ring gear and pinion.

Planet carrier: Carrier or bracket in a planetary system which contains shafts upon which pinions or planet gears turn.

Planet gears: Gears interposed between ring gear and sun gear and meshing with both in a planetary system.

Plasma arc cutters: Cutting equipment that makes clean, fast cuts without destroying the properties of high-strength steels.

Platinum: An expensive metal having an extremely high melting point and good electrical conductivity.

Plug-in diagnosis: On-board computer provides means for special test equipment to be plugged in for making a series of programmed tests to check condition of various units and systems on car.

Ply: Layer of rubber-coated parallel cords forming tire body, or carcass.

Ply rating: See Load range.

Pneumatic: Pertaining to air. Example: a device operated by air pressure is a pneumatic device.

PNP: Three-element transistor made of two layers of semiconductor materials.

POA: Pilot operated absolute valve in some air conditioning systems.

Polarity: Refers to positive or negative terminal of a battery of an electric circuit; also north or south pole of a magnet.

Poppet valve: A valve structure consisting of a circular head with an elongated stem attached in center. It is designed to open and close a circular hole or port.

Porcelain: General term applied to material or element used for insulating center electrode of a spark plug.

Port: An opening in cylinder head or engine block for intake air-fuel mixture or exhaust gas flow. Also, to smooth and enlarge passageways to intake valves.

Ported vacuum: Source of vacuum in carburetor above closed throttle plate.

Positive crankcase ventilation: System for clearing engine crankcase of blowby gases.

Positive crankcase ventilation valve: Device that regulates amount of airflow through crankcase.

Positive pole: Point to which current returns after passing through a circuit. Designated by plus sign (+).

Post: Heavy, circular part to which a group of battery plates is attached, and which extends through cell cover to provide a means of attachment to adjacent cell or battery cable.

Potential: An indication of amount of energy available.

Potential difference: A difference of electrical pressure that sets up a flow of electric current.

Potential drop: A loss of electrical pressure due to resistance of leakage.

Power brakes: Hydraulic, vacuum, air, or electrohydraulic boost.

Power steering: Application of hydraulic or mechanical power in addition to manual power in steering of an automobile.

Power take-off: A device, usually mounted on side of transmission or transfer case, used to transmit engine power to wheels.

Power train: Group of components used to transmit power to wheels-clutch, transmission, universal joints, drive shaft, and rear axle.

PPM: Parts Per Million.

Preheating: Application of heat as a preliminary step to some further thermal or mechanical treatment.

Preignition: Ignition occurring earlier than intended. Example: explosive mixture being fired in a cylinder by a flake of incandescent carbon before electric spark occurs.

Preloading: To adjust a small amount of pressure on an antifriction bearing to eliminate any looseness.

Press-fit: See Drive fit.

Pressure: Force per unit of area.

Pressure differential valve: Senses unbalanced hydraulic pressure between two halves of the split brake system.

Pressure-vacuum cap: Fuel tank filler cap designed to prevent loss of fuel or vapor from tank.

Primary brake shoe: Brake shoe in a set which initiates the self-energizing action.

Primary circuit: A low voltage circuit energized by battery to begin ignition circuit.

Primary winding: A wire which conducts low tension current to be transformed by induction into high tension current in secondary winding of ignition coil.

Primary wires: Wiring circuit used for conducting low tension or primary current to points where it is used.

PROM (Programmable Read Only Memory): PROM contains permanent information about how components should perform under various operating conditions.

Proportioning valve: Regulates outlet pressure to rear brakes.

Proton: Portion of an atom which carries a positive charge of electricity.

Prony brake: A machine for testing power of an engine while running against a friction brake.

Propane: A petroleum hydrocarbon compound which has a boiling point about - 44°F. It is used as an engine fuel and is loosely referred to as LP-Gas. It is often combined with butane.

Propeller shaft: Drive shaft connecting transmission with rear axle.

Proportioning valve: Device used to improve braking balance during heavy brake application.

PSI: Pounds per square inch.

Pulse air system: An exhaust emission control system that uses exhaust pulse in a pipe to permit air to be drawn into exhaust system.

Purge: To remove air and moisture from an air conditioning system or component by flushing with a dry gas refrigerant.

Push rod: A connecting link in an operating mechanism. Example: rod between valve lifter and rocker arm on an overhead valve engine.

Q

Quadrant: Designates gearshift or transmission control lever selector mounting.

Quenching: A process of rapid cooling of hot metal by contact with liquids, gases, or solids.

Quick test: A functional diagnostic test of Ford's EEC system that displays test results as a series of service codes.

R

R-12: CFC refrigerant found in many automobile air conditioning systems. R-12 is believed to destroy the earth's ozone layer and, therefore, is no longer used in late-model vehicles. When servicing vehicles equipped with R-12, the refrigerant must be recovered and recycled.

R-134A: Non-CFC air conditioning refrigerant that is considered environmentally safe. R-134A is now being used in all late-model vehicles.

Race: A finished inner and outer surface in which or on which ball bearings or roller bearings operate.

Race cam: A type of camshaft for race car engines which increases lift of valve, speed of valve opening and closing, length of time valve is held open, etc. Also known as Full, Three-quarter, or Semi-race cams, depending upon design.

Radial ply: Pneumatic tire structure in which ply cords extend from bead to bead at right angles to centerline of tire.

Radial runout: Variation in diameter of a wheel, tire, or rotor from a specified amount.

Radiation: Transfer of heat by rays. Example: heat from sun.

Radius rods: Rods attached to axle and to frame to maintain correct horizontal position of axle, yet permit vertical motion.

RAM (Random Access Memory): Memory that serves as a temporary storage place for data from the sensors.

Ram air: Air forced through a condenser or radiator, or into a carburetor air cleaner snorkel, by movement of a vehicle.

Ratio: Relation or proportion that one number bears to another.

Ream: To finish a hole accurately with a rotating fluted tool.

Recap: Adding top strip of synthetic or reclaimed rubber to buffed and roughened surface of a worn tire.

Receiver-drier: Storage tank and filter for liquid refrigerant and containing a drying agent to remove moisture from circulating refrigerant. Also called "receiver-dehydrator."

Reciprocating: A back and forth movement. Example: action of a piston in a cylinder.

Recovery/recycling equipment: Equipment that must now be used when servicing air conditioning systems. This equipment captures refrigerant removed from an air conditioning system and stores or recycles it.

Rectifier: An electrical device for transforming or changing alternating current into direct current.

Refrigerant: A substance used in an air conditioning system which absorbs and gives up heat as it changes from a liquid to a vapor to a liquid.

Regulator: An automatic pressure reducing valve.

Relative humidity: Actual moisture content in air in relation to total moisture that air can hold at a given temperature.

Relay: Switching device operated by a low current circuit that controls opening and closing of another circuit of higher current capacity.

Relief: Amount one surface is set below or above another surface.

Relieving: Removal of some metal from around racing engine valves and between cylinder and valves to facilitate flow of gases.

Resistance: Opposition to flow of current in an electrical component or circuit.

Resistor: A current-consuming piece of metal wire or carbon inserted into circuit to decrease flow of electricity.

Resource Conservation and Recovery Act: Federal act that covers businesses that generate, transport, or manage hazardous wastes.

Retard: To cause spark to occur at a later time in cycle of engine operation. Opposite of spark advance.

Retread: Used tire with new rubber bonded to worn surface from shoulder to shoulder.

Reverse bias: Nonconductive condition that exists when current flow is blocked by a diode.

Reverse Elliot steering knuckle: Type of axle construction in which steering spindle straddles ends of axle beam.

Rheostat: A variable resistor. Example, the switch that dims the dash lights.

Rim: Metal support for tire on wheel.

Ring gear: Outer gear within which other gears revolve in a planetary system. Also, driven gear which mates with drive pinion in a differential assembly.

Rivet: To attach with rivets or to batter or upset end of a pin.

RMA: Rubber Manufacturers Association.

Rocker arm: A lever located on a fulcrum or shaft, one end bearing on valve stem, other on push rod.

Rockwell hardness: A scale for designating degrees of hardness possessed by a substance.

Roller bearing: An inner and outer race upon which hardened steel rollers operate.

ROM (Read Only Memory): Memory that contains the computer's operating instructions (programs). It also stores general information that tells the computer how various components should perform under specific operating conditions.

Rotary engine: Wankel type internal combustion engine causes cycle of intake, compression, expansion, and exhaust by rotation of a triangular rotor in a housing shaped roughly like a figure 8. Air-fuel mixture enters and burned gases are ejected through ports covered and uncovered by movement of rotor.

Rotary valve: A valve construction in which ported holes come into and out of register with each other to allow entrance and exit of fluids or gases.

Rotor: Parallel-faced circular plate against which brake lining is forced to retard vehicle. Also, a rotating part of an electrical or mechanical device.

Rotor runout: Lateral movement of rotor friction surface as it rotates past a fixed point.

Rpm: Revolutions per minute.

Rubber: An elastic vibration-absorbing material of natural or synthetic origin.

Running fit: Where sufficient clearance has been allowed between shaft and journal to allow free running without overheating.

Run-on: See Dieseling.

Runout: Out-of-round condition of a rotating part.

S

SAE: Society of Automotive Engineers.

SAE steels: A numerical index used to identify composition of SAE steel.

SAE thread: A table of threads set up by Society of Automotive Engineers that determines number of threads per inch. Example: a quarter inch diameter rod with an SAE thread would have 28 threads per inch.

Safety factor: Degree of strength above normal requirements which serves as insurance against failure.

Safety relief valve: A spring-loaded valve designed to open and relieve excessive pressure in a device when it exceeds a predetermined safe point.

Sandblast: To clean a surface by means of sand propelled by compressed air.

Saybolt test: A method of measuring viscosity of oil with use of a viscosimeter.

Scale: A flaky deposit occurring on steel or iron. Ordinarily used to describe accumulation of minerals and metals accumulating in an automobile cooling system.

Score: A scratch, ridge, or groove marring a finished surface.

SCR: Silicon controlled rectifier.

Sealed beam lamps: Lamp construction with reflector, lens, and filament hermetically sealed in one unit.

Seat: A surface, usually machined, upon which another part rests or seats. Example: surface upon which a valve face rests.

Seat belt: Passenger restraint system, usually consisting of a lap belt and a shoulder belt.

Secondary brake shoe: Brake shoe in a set which is energized by primary shoe and increases servo, or self-energizing, action of brake.

Secondary circuit: Electrical circuit designed to produce and deliver high voltage to spark plugs.

Secondary winding: A wire in which a secondary or high tension current is created by induction due to interruption of current in adjacent primary winding of an ignition coil.

Section height: Height of an inflated tire from bottom of the bead to the top of the tread.

Section width: Width between exteriors of sidewalls of an inflated tire at its widest point.

Sediment: Active material of battery plates that is gradually shed and accumulates below the plates.

Seize: When a surface moving upon another sticks, it is said to seize. For example: a piston seizes in a cylinder due to a lack of lubrication or overexpansion due to excessive heat.

Selective transmission: Arrangement of gearing and shifting device in which it is possible to go directly from neutral position into any desired pair of gears.

Self-energization: Placing of brake shoes so that drum tends to drag lining along with it, resulting in a wedging action between anchor and drum.

Self test: A part of functional diagnostic test procedure that verifies operation of sensors and actuators, detects hard faults, and stores information for later retrieval.

Semiconductor: Manufactured material somewhere between range of conductors and nonconductors.

Semi-diesel: A semi-diesel engine operates on comparatively high compression and utilizes solid injection of fuel. However, it does use an electrical ignition system rather than depend solely upon heat generated by compression to furnish ignition.

Semi-floating axle: A drive axle construction in which axle shafts support weight of car.

Sensor: A device which mechanically, electrically, or thermally senses a state of change and activates a mechanism to compensate for change.

Separators: Sheets of rubber or wood inserted between positive and negative battery plates of a cell to prevent contact with each other.

Series circuit: An electrical circuit having only one path.

Series parallel circuit: An electrical circuit having some devices connected in series and others in parallel.

Series winding: An electric winding or coil of wire in series with other electrical equipment.

Serpentine belt: Single belt that drives all accessories. It is a combination of a V-ribbed belt and a flat back belt.

Service codes: A series of two digit numbers that represent results of a self test.

Service port: A fitting on service valve for attachment of a gauge.

Servo: Automatic transmission hydraulic piston and cylinder assembly used to control drum bands.

Servo action: A brake construction in which a primary shoe pushes a secondary shoe to generate self-energization.

Shackle bolt: A link for connecting one end of a chassis spring to frame which allows spring end to oscillate laterally.

Shear: To cut between two blades.

Shim: Thin sheets used as spacers between two parts. Example: shims between control arm pivot shaft and frame serve to adjust caster and camber.

Shimmy: In automobile steering, a wobbling or shaking of front wheels.

Shock absorber: A device to provide hydraulic friction to control excessive deflection of automobile springs.

Short circuit: To provide a shorter electrical path. Often used to indicate an accidental ground in an electrical device or conductor.

Shrink fit: An exceptionally tight fit. Example: if shaft or part is slightly larger than hole in which it is to be inserted, outer part is heated above its normal operating temperature or inner part chilled below its normal operating temperature, or both, and assembled in this condition. Upon cooling, a shrink fit is obtained.

Shunt: To bypass or turn aside. Also, an alternate path for current in electrical apparatus.

Shunt winding: An electric winding or coil of wire which forms a bypass or alternate path for electric current. Example: in certain electric generators or motors, each end of field winding is connected to an armature brush.

Shuttle valve: A valve for diverting pressure from one channel to another.

Sidewall: Portion of tire between tread and bead.

Silencer: See Mufflers.

Silicon: A nonmetallic element, often alloyed with steel.

Silicon controlled rectifier: Semiconductor having an anode, cathode, and gate.

Silicon steel: An alloy of silicon and chromium with steel, often used for exhaust valves.

Silicone: Any of a group of semiorganic polymers, used in lubricants, adhesives, and protective coverings.

Silver soldering: See Hard solder.

Single wire system: Lighting circuit which uses car frame for return.

Sleeve valve: A reciprocating sleeve or sleeves with ported openings placed between piston and cylinders of an engine to serve as valves.

Sliding fit: Where sufficient clearance has been allowed between shaft and journal to allow free running without overheating.

Slip-in bearing: A liner, made to extremely accurate measurements, which can be used for replacement purposes without additional fitting.

Slip Rings: Insulated metal rings mounted on alternator rotor shaft on which brushes make continuous sliding contact.

Sludge: A pasty composition of oxidized petroleum products and an emulsion formed by a mixture of engine oil and water that clogs oil lines and passages.

Smog: Unburned hydrocarbons combined with oxides of nitrogen and acted upon by sunlight.

Smoke: Matter in exhaust emissions that obscures transmission of light.

Solder: An alloy of lead and tin used to unite two metal parts.

Soldering: To unite two pieces of metal with a material having a comparatively low melting point.

Sole proprietorship: Business owned entirely by one person.

Solenoid: An iron core, surrounded by a coil of wire, which moves due to magnetic attraction when electric current is fed to coil. Often used to actuate mechanisms by electrical means.

Solid injection: System used in full diesel and semi-diesel, where fuel in fluid state is injected into cylinder rather than a mixture of air and fuel drawn from a carburetor.

Solid state: Electronic device or assembly that does not have moving parts.

Solvent: A solution which dissolves some other material. Example: water is a solvent for sugar.

South pole: Pole of a magnet to which lines of force flow. Opposite of north pole.

Spacer, spacer washer: A sheet of metal or other material placed between two surfaces to reduce clearance or to provide a better thrust surface for a fastener.

Spark: An electric current possessing sufficient voltage to jump through air from one conductor to another.

Spark advance: To cause spark to occur at an earlier time in cycle of engine operation. Opposite of retard.

Spark gap: Space between electrodes of a spark plug which spark jumps.

Spark plug: A device, inserted in combustion chamber of an engine, containing a side electrode and insulated center electrode spaced to provide a gap for firing an electrical spark to ignite air-fuel mixture.

Specific gravity: Relative weight of a substance compared to water. Example: if a cubic inch of acid weighs twice as much as a cubic inch of water, specific gravity is 2.0.

Speed control: Accessory system designed to maintain rate of speed of vehicle desired by driver.

Speedometer: A device for measuring and indicating speed of a vehicle in miles per hour and/or kilometers per hour.

Spindle: Machined steel shaft that supports wheel bearings that bear a portion of weight of vehicle. Shaft upon which wheels are mounted and rotate.

Spiral bevel gear: A ring gear and pinion in which the mating teeth are curved.

Splayed spring: A design in which leaf springs are placed at other than a 90° angle to axle.

Spline: A long keyway.

Spline joint: Two mating parts that have a series of splines around their circumferences, one inner and one outer, to provide a longitudinally movable joint without any circumferential motion.

Split hydraulic brake system: Service brake system with two separate hydraulic circuits to provide braking action in one circuit if other one fails.

Spongy brake pedal: Air in hydraulic lines, distortion or stretching of connecting parts, or swelling of hydraulic hose may allow pedal to be spongy or springy instead of solid.

Spot weld: To attach in spots by localized fusion of metal parts with aid of an electric current.

Springs: Suspension devices including leaf, coil, air type, or torsion bars.

Sprung weight: A term used to describe all parts of an automobile that are supported by car springs. Example: frame, engine, body, payload, etc.

Spur gear: A gear in which teeth are cut parallel to shaft.

Spurt-hole: A hole drilled through a connecting rod and bearing that allows oil under pressure to be squirted out of bearing for additional lubrication of cylinder walls.

Sq. ft.: Square feet.

Sq. in.: Square inch.

SSI: Solid state ignition.

Starting motor: An electromagnetic device that converts electrical energy into mechanical energy.

Static electricity: Atmospheric electricity as distinguished from electricity produced by mechanical means.

Stator: A wheel having curved blades interposed between torque converter pump and turbine elements. Also, a metal frame of alternator with three stationary windings that give overlapping pulses of alternating current.

Steel casting: Cast iron to which varying amounts of scrap steel have been added.

Steering axis inclination: Angle formed by centerline of suspension ball joints and true vertical centerline.

Steering gear: Gears in steering unit. Also, assembly of parts and units required to control angularity of wheels to body of a vehicle.

Steering geometry: See Toe-out on turns.

Steering knuckle: Part about which front wheel pivots when turning.

Steering post or column: Shaft connecting steering gear unit with steering wheel.

Steering spindle: A journal or shaft upon which steerable wheels of a vehicle are mounted.

Stellite: An alloy of cobalt, chrome, and tungsten often used for exhaust valve seat inserts. It has a high melting point, good corrosion resistance, and unusual hardness when hot.

Stoplight switch: Brake pedal operated switch which completes circuit to vehicle's stop lamps.

Strap: A lead section to which battery plates of a group are joined.

Stress: Force or strain to which a material is subjected.

Stroboscope: A term applied to an ignition timing light which, when connected to distributor points, gives effect of making a mark on a rapidly rotating pulley or harmonic balancer.

Stroke: Distance traveled by a piston from BDC to TDC.

Stroking: Remachining crankshaft throws "off center" to alter stroke.

Stud: A rod that threads on both ends.

Suction: Suction exists in a vessel when pressure is lower than atmospheric pressure. See Vacuum.

Sulfated: When a battery is improperly charged, or allowed to remain in a discharged condition for some length of time, plates will be coated with an abnormal amount of lead sulfate.

Sump: Fluid reservoir.

Sun gear: Central gear around which other gears revolve.

Supercharger: A blower or pump which forces air into cylinders at higher than atmospheric pressure, enabling more gasoline to be burned and more power to be produced.

Suspension: Use of front and rear springs to suspend a vehicle's frame, body or unitized body, engine and power train above wheels.

Sweat: To join metal pieces by clamping them together with solder in between, then applying heat.

Switching sensors: Sensors that turn on and off in response to specific conditions.

Synchromesh: A device used in transmission gearing to facilitate meshing of two gears by causing speed of both gears to coincide.

Synchronize: To cause two events to occur in unison or at same time.

T

Tachometer: A device for measuring and indicating speed of an engine.

Tap: To cut threads in a hole with a tapered, fluted, threaded tool.

Taper: Condition where cylinder is worn more at top of bore than at bottom.

Tappet: Adjusting screw for varying clearance between valve stem and cam. May be built into valve lifter in L-head engine or installed in rocker arm on an overhead valve engine.

TBI: Throttle body injection.

TCS: Transmission controlled spark.

TDC: Top dead center.

Temper: To change characteristics of metal by application of heat.

Temperature: Heat intensity measured on a thermometer.

Tension: Effort that is devoted toward elongation or "stretching" of a material.

Terminal: A junction point where electrical connections are made.

TFI: Thick film ignition.

T-head engine: An engine design in which inlet valves are placed on one side of the cylinder and exhaust valves placed on other.

Thermac: GM's thermostatically controlled air cleaner system.

Thermactor: Ford air pump type exhaust emission control system.

Thermal efficiency: A gallon of fuel contains potential energy in the form of heat when burned in combustion chamber. Some heat is lost and some is converted into power. Thermal efficiency is ratio of work accomplished compared to total quantity of heat contained in fuel.

Thermal reactor: Emission control device that accepts raw exhaust gases from engine and subjects them to extremely high temperatures to oxidize noxious emissions.

Thermistor: Resistor that changes its resistance inversely with temperature.

Thermostat: A heat-controlled valve used in cooling system of engine to regulate flow of water between cylinder block and radiator. Also, a valve used in modern air cleaners in which inlet air temperature is regulated.

Thermostatic expansion valve: Metering device that removes pressure from liquid refrigerant, permitting it to expand and vaporize in evaporator.

Thermostatic vacuum switch: A temperature sensitive switch which allows spark advance when engine idles for long periods.

Thermo-syphon: A method of cooling an engine which utilizes difference in specific gravity of hot and cold water. No pump is used, but water passages are larger than in pump type circulation system.

Three way catalyst: Dual catalytic converter that controls HC, CO, and NOx.

Throttle position sensor (TPS): Sensor that monitors the position of the throttle valve and varies its resistance in relation to the position of the throttle shaft.

Throttle stop solenoid: A device that maintains engine at a speed over curb idle.

Throw: Distance from center of crankshaft main bearing to center of connecting rod journal.

Tie rod: Metal rod connecting steering spindle arms on opposite side of vehicle.

Timing chain: Chain used to drive camshaft of an engine.

Timing gears: Any group of gears driven from engine crankshaft to cause valves, ignition, and other engine-driven apparatus to operate at desired time during engine cycle.

Tire: A tubular corded carcass covered with rubber or synthetic rubber, mounted on a wheel and inflated to provide traction for moving and stopping the vehicle.

Tire valve: Air check that opens under air pressure and closes when pressure is removed.

Toe: Inside half of a gear tooth. Also, end of brake shoe against anchor.

Toe-out on turns: Related angles assumed by front wheels of vehicle when turning.

Tolerance: A permissible variation between two extremes of a specification of dimensions.

Torque: Effort devoted toward twisting or turning.

Torque converter: Assembly of rotating elements in a fluid-filled housing used to multiply engine torque to geartrain of automatic transmission.

Torque wrench: A special wrench with a built-in indicator to measure applied force.

Torsion bar: Rod with built-in twist to provide spring action.

Torus: An oil-filled member of a torque converter.

Tramp: An oscillating motion and heavy vibration when wheels are turning.

Transaxle: Transmission and differential combined in one unit.

Transducer: An electrically activated vacuum regulator.

Transfer case: Power takeoff to drive both axles on four wheel drive vehicle.

Transformer: An electrical device, such as a high tension coil, which transforms or changes characteristics of an electrical current.

Transistor: In electronics, a miniature amplifying or switching device.

Transistor ignition: Ignition system utilizing transistors, a special coil, and conventional breaker points.

Transmission: A system of trading speed for power, or vice versa, through gearing or torque conversion. It includes various devices and combinations for changing ratio between engine revolutions and driving wheel revolutions.

Transmission controlled spark advance: A system used to control ignition spark advance by means of transmission gear selection.

Transverse: Crosswise.

Tread: Portion of tire that comes in contact with road. Also, distance between center of tires at points where they contact road surface.

Tread wear indicators: Crosswise strips molded into tire to signal need for tire replacement when tread is worn.

Trouble code: Engine self diagnosis. Electronic control module questions sensor reading and stores code for which circuit trouble is located.

Troubleshooting: Process of diagnosing possible sources of trouble by observation and testing.

Tune-up: A process of accurate and careful adjustments and parts replacements to obtain utmost in engine performance.

Turbine: A series of blades on a wheel, situated at an angle to the shaft, against which fluids or gases are impelled to impart rotary motion to shaft.

Turbocharger: A device which utilizes pressure of exhaust gases to drive a supercharger which, in turn, forces more air into cylinders.

Turbulence: A disturbed, irregular motion of fluids or gases.

Turning radius: Diameter of a circle which a vehicle can be turned around.

TVS: Thermostatic vacuum switch.

TWC: Three way catalyst.

Two-cycle engine: An engine design permitting a power stroke once for each revolution of the crankshaft.

U

UIC: Universal integrated circuit.

Undercoating: Spraying insulating material on exposed undersections of an automobile to retard corrosion and deaden noise.

Unibody: Design which incorporates body and frame of vehicle in a single structure.

Universal joint: A connection for transmitting power from a driving to a driven shaft through an angle.

Unleaded gasoline: Motor fuel containing no tetraethyl lead additive.

Unsprung weight: Weight that includes wheels, axles, etc., that are not supported by car springs.

Updraft: A carburetor in which mixture flows upward to engine.

Upper-cylinder lubrication: A method of introducing a lubricant into fuel or intake manifold in order to permit lubrication of upper cylinder, valve guides, etc.

Upset: To compress at ends, causing an increase in diameter.

V

Vacuum: A pressure less than atmospheric pressure (14.7 psi at sea level).

Vacuum advance: Advancing ignition spark timing by applying or increasing vacuum to distributor vacuum unit.

Vacuum control: A diaphragm attached to ignition distributor spark advance which is controlled by changing of vacuum in intake manifold.

Vacuum gauge: An instrument designed to measure degree of vacuum existing in a chamber.

Vacuum power unit (motor): A device for use in opening doors in heating and air conditioning systems.

Vacuum pump: Used to remove air and moisture from air conditioning system.

Valve: A device for opening and sealing an aperture.

Valve clearance: Gap allowed between end of valve stem and valve lifter or rocker arm to compensate for expansion due to heat.

Valve face: Part of valve which mates with, and rests upon, a seating surface.

Valve grinding: A process of mating valve seat and valve face.

Valve head: Portion of a valve upon which valve face is machined.

Valve-in-head engine (OHV): See Overhead valve engine.

Valve key or valve lock: Key, keeper, washer, or other device which holds valve spring cup or washer in place on valve stem.

Valve lifter: Solid part or hydraulic plunger placed between cam and valve on an engine.

Valve margin: Space or rim on a poppet valve between surface of head and surface of valve face.

Valve overlap: An interval expressed in degrees where both valves of an automobile engine cylinder are open at same time.

Valve seat: Mating surface upon which valve face rests.

Valve spring: A spring attached to a valve to return it to seat after lift is released.

Valve stem: Portion of valve which rests within a guide.

Valve stem guide: A bushing or hole for valve stem.

Valve timing: Indicates relative position of valve (open or closed) to piston in its travel, in crankshaft degrees.

Valve train: Mechanism or linkage used to transmit motion of engine cam to valve stem, causing valve to open.

Vanes: Any plate or blade attached to an axis and moved by or in air or a liquid.

Vaporize: Transforming or helping to transform a liquid into a vapor.

Vapor lock: A condition in which fuel boils in fuel system, forming bubbles which retard or stop flow of fuel to carburetor.

Vapor pressure: Pressure developed over a liquid in a closed vessel, depending upon liquid and temperature.

Vapor withdrawal: A system of piping and connections to operate an engine directly on vapor taken from top of an LP-Gas tank.

V-belt: Drives accessory by wedging action in a pulley groove.

VDOT: Variable displacement orifice tube air conditioning system.

Vehicle speed sensor: Sensor that tells the computer how fast the car is traveling.

Venturi: Two tapering streamlined tubes joined at their small ends to reduce internal diameter.

Vibration damper: See Harmonic balancer.

VIN: Vehicle identification number.

VIR: Valve in receiver. Found in some air conditioning systems.

Viscosimeter: An instrument for determining viscosity of an oil by passing a certain quantity at a definite temperature through a standard size orifice or port. Time required for oil to pass through, expressed in seconds, gives viscosity.

Viscosity: Considered to be internal friction of a fluid. Also, resistance to flow, or adhesiveness characteristics, of an oil.

Voice alert system: Audible warnings to enhance those provided by instruments, lights, and buzzers.

Volatility: Tendency of fluid to evaporate rapidly. Example: gasoline is more volatile than kerosene, since it evaporates at lower temperature.

Volt: A unit of electrical force that will cause a current of one ampere to flow through a resistance of one ohm.

Voltage: Electromotive force which causes current to flow in a circuit.

Voltage drop: Decrease in voltage as current passes through a resistance.

Voltage regulator: An electrical device for regulating voltage output.

Voltmeter: An instrument for measuring voltage in an electrical circuit.

Volume: Measure of space expressed as cubic inches or cubic centimeters.

Volumetric efficiency: A combination between ideal and actual efficiency of an internal combustion engine. If engine completely filled each cylinder on each induction stroke, volumetric efficiency of engine would be 100 percent. In actual operation, however, volumetric efficiency is lowered by inertia of the gases, friction between gases and manifolds, temperature of gases, and pressure of air entering carburetor. Volumetric efficiency is ordinarily increased by use of large valves, ports, and manifolds and can be further increased with aid of a supercharger.

Vortex: A whirling movement or mass of liquid or air.

W

Wandering: A condition in which front wheels of an automobile tend to turn slowly in first one direction, then the other, interfering with directional control or stability.

Wankel engine: A rotary type internal combustion engine.

Water column: A reference term used in connection with a manometer.

Watt: A measuring unit of electrical power. It is obtained by multiplying amperes by volts.

Wedge block: Combustion chamber design in which top of piston and surface of block form an angle.

Weight transfer effect: Since center of gravity of vehicle is located above centers of wheel rotation, a sudden stoppage of vehicle tends to cause center of gravity to move forward, thus throwing more weight on front wheels and less on rear wheels.

Welding: To join two pieces of metal by heating them to their melting point.

Wet sleeve: A metal barrel or sleeve which is inserted in an engine cylinder in contact with coolant.

Wheel cylinder: Unit for converting hydraulic fluid pressure to mechanical force for actuation of brake shoes and lining against brake drum.

Wheelbase: Distance between centerlines of front and rear axles.

Wheel speed sensors: Sensors used in the anti-lock brake systems to determine the rate of wheel rotation.

White metal: An alloy of tin, lead, and antimony having a low melting point and a low coefficient of friction.

Wire harness: Wires grouped together in a sleeve and interconnecting electrical components of vehicle.

Wiring diagram: A detailed drawing of all wiring, connections, and units that are connected together in an electrical circuit.

Worm gear: A shaft having an extremely coarse thread which is designed to operate in engagement with a toothed wheel, as a pair of gears.

WOT: Wide open throttle.

Wringing-fit: A fit with less clearance than for a running or sliding fit. Shaft will enter hole by means of twisting and pushing by hand.

Wrist pin: See Piston pin.

Index

A

B

C

D

E

F

G

H

I

M

N

O

P

Q

R

S

T

U

V

W